THE McGRAW-HILL
BOOK OF DRAMA

THE McGRAW-HILL
BOOK OF DRAMA

James Howe

William A. Stephany

McGraw-Hill, Inc.
New York   St. Louis   San Francisco   Auckland   Bogotá
Caracas   Lisbon   London   Madrid   Mexico City   Milan   Montreal
New Delhi   San Juan   Singapore   Sydney   Tokyo   Toronto

THE McGRAW-HILL BOOK OF DRAMA

Acknowledgments appear on pages 1095–1098 and on this page by reference.

This book is printed on acid-free paper.

1 2 3 4 5 6 7 8 9 0   DOC/DOC   9 9 8 7 6 5

ISBN 0-07-061224-2

This book was set in Galliard by Better Graphics, Inc.
The editors were Steve Pensinger and David A. Damstra;
the designer was Carol A. Couch;
the production supervisor was Denise L. Puryear.
R. R. Donnelley & Sons Company was printer and binder.

Cover Photo: Spencer Gore. *The Balcony at the Alhambra.*
        City of York Art Gallery/Bridgeman Art Library,
        London/Superstock.

Library of Congress Cataloging-in-Publication Data

The McGraw-Hill book of drama / [compiled by] James Howe, William A.
    Stephany.
        p.   cm.
    A collection of plays by various authors, with an interpretive
essay written by the compilers included after each play, and
excerpts from theoretical essays by various authors included in the
introduction.
    ISBN 0-07-061224-2
    1. Drama—Collections.   I. Howe, James (date).   II. Stephany,
William A.   III. McGraw-Hill, inc.
PN6112.M32   1995
808.82—dc20
                                            94-37960

ABOUT THE AUTHORS

James Howe is professor emeritus of English at the University of Vermont, where he taught for 28 years before taking early retirement in order to concentrate on writing, painting, and Buddhist studies. Besides articles and papers, Professor Howe has published books on writing style, on the plays of Christopher Marlowe, and most recently on those of William Shakespeare. He and Professor Stephany have previously collaborated in co-teaching a survey of English and American Literature (for five years), and in writing and editing the drama section of an introduction to literature textbook, *Angles of Vision*. He is a graduate of Dartmouth College and earned his Ph.D. at New York University.

William A. Stephany is professor of English at the University of Vermont, where he has taught a variety of courses in medieval studies as well as courses on drama. He is a graduate of LeMoyne College and has a Ph.D. from the University of Delaware. Many of his scholarly publications, including a book on Canto I of *Inferno*, have been on Dante. He has also collaborated on various pedagogical publications, both on teaching the Middle Ages and on the relationship of writing to reading and teaching, including sections of the books, *Reading, Writing and the Study of Literature* and *Angles of Vision*.

CONTENTS

PREFACE

This anthology is meant to be useful to students and professors in a variety of courses. There are enough texts from the classical tradition—the Greeks, Shakespeare, and the seventeenth and eighteenth centuries—as well as from the development of naturalism, realism, expressionism, absurdism, and so on to underwrite a historical survey course showing how drama changed or developed over more than two millennia. In addition, the anthology includes so many twentieth-century and especially so many contemporary plays that it could also serve as the principal text in courses on modern or on contemporary drama. Many of the selections focus primarily on women as authors and as subjects; our intent is that the book could also be used in women's studies courses. And because we have selected texts which reflect America's cultural diversity, the anthology would serve as well in courses focusing on race and ethnicity in literature.

There are six plays here by women, from Aphra Behn's *The Rover*, written three centuries ago, to texts written in the past two decades by Marsha Norman, Caryl Churchill, and Elaine Jackson. Feminist and gender issues are also central concerns in works by male writers, from Aristophanes' *Lysistrata* to David Henry Hwang's *M. Butterfly*. We have included six plays by Americans of color—African-American, Asian-American, and Latino—and four plays by writers outside the Anglo-American canon that confront issues arising from imperialism and postcolonialism: plays by Derek Walcott, Wole Soyinka, Athol Fugard, and the collaborators Percy Mtwa, Mbongeni Ngema, and Barney Simon. While these texts make the anthology potentially useful for more specialized courses, our main purpose in striving to be inclusive is to enable teachers of more general drama courses to select texts from a wide cultural range.

Another of the ways in which we have tried to make this anthology useful to students is to treat them as equal partners in the learning process. As teachers, as readers, and as writers, we believe that every way of reading a play is a particular reader's choice. Each of us reads out of our own experience of life and of reading. In a sense, our way of reading is us; whatever we read, we convert into "us," into our individual way of thinking and feeling. One implication of this view is that every reading is an act of appropriation; we readers enter into the work and determine its shape; we intervene in its creation and in its generation of effects.

Consciously or unconsciously, we make it become what we want or need it to be. We can see only what we are prepared to see, not the things to which we are blind. Articulate or inarticulate, brilliant or not so brilliant, conscious or not conscious, we all read and interpret on our own terms. Perhaps the main business of education is to make us aware of this fact, aware of what we do, including what we do to the texts we read, so that we can see ourselves more clearly than before. Only then can we decide if we would like to try to change, to expand our repertory of reading strategies (several of which the anthology and the teacher might model), to learn new facts and ideas and attitudes, and to try them on, to feel how they fit.

One implication of all this should be made explicit: We believe that it is dangerous to tell other readers what they *should* think about anything, including a play, because every approach and every interpretation or way of reading has a hidden agenda. A teacher's job may be in part to expose that agenda so that it can be evaluated by the reader. But we know that the most brilliant minds of our time are likely to disagree about what is the "right" agenda. Teaching what to think is not the business of educators. Rather, we teachers are in the business of teaching others *how* to think—and to see and to articulate—clearly.

It was therefore with great tentativeness that we decided to write the interpretive essays which you will find just after each play. We are aware of the danger of this practice, that interventions of this type might prejudice a student's reading in advance, might determine which terms of discussion seem legitimate, and might even predetermine a reader's conclusions. In spite of our reservations, however, we have chosen to include these essays because we believe that they serve a useful purpose: as model readings that demonstrate a variety of interpretive possibilities, while making some of each play's background available. We hope that these essays will provoke dissent and disagreement and in this way start a dialogue within the reader's mind which, by extension, will spread into discussion in the classroom.

A related reason—both practical and pedagogical—for our including these essays in the text is that we are uncomfortable with the traditional instructor's manual, and so we offer them as an alternative. The two of us collaborated a few years ago on the drama section of *Angles of Vision*, an introduction-to-literature anthology published by McGraw-Hill, and as part of that project wrote the drama section of that book's instructor's manual. We decided that the most helpful format for such a manual would be a series of brief interpretive essays on the plays, rather than a series of questions about them. Questions can too often feel manipulative: Their form is democratic, but their reality can often be directive, pushing students toward specific ways of reading and thinking. The essays allowed us to be forthright about presenting some of our ideas as our ideas, and allowed teachers to react against or build upon them as they saw fit. For this book, we decided to include such essays within the anthology itself, furnishing students with the same information which we provide to teachers. We dislike the implication of concealing potentially helpful information from students and hope that by including the essays we will encourage teachers and students alike to displace authority with reason.

There are also several other tools in this book which we hope will be empowering for students. We have included excerpts from theoretical writings by many authors, from Aristotle to the present, whose ideas can be applied to study of the theater generally and of the plays in this collection specifically. There is not enough material in this section to make the student an expert, but there is enough to give the flavor of a variety of possible approaches to drama, from the traditions of genre and mode to postmodernist problematizing. In addition, there is a set of questions, some traditional, some more contemporary, all intended to be open-ended in order to encourage thoughtfulness rather than a particular "right" answer; you will find them immediately after our Introduction and just before the anthology of plays.

In addition to this traditional question format, we have included several more experimental writing exercises. They appear immediately after the Introduction and before the set of questions just referred to. We believe that writing not only facilitates learning but also *causes* it. To put our ideas into written language is to give them order and discipline, to force ourselves to become coherent. Frequently in the struggle to "get it right," to say coherently exactly what we think we mean, we find that we must extend our thoughts to their logical conclusion: We discover what we were "really" thinking, the "truth" that was intellectually just out of reach. We become aware not only of what we think but also of the implications of what we think. We also externalize our ideas, so that they become available to ourselves for evaluation, for experiment, and for revision.

Regardless of our apparent subject, at some level we are always writing about ourselves, always evoking our own way of perceiving and thinking. In these exercises, then, we encourage an alternative to the formal papers which we assume no teacher needs our help to formulate and for which few students will want our help. Rather, we here encourage informal and very often personal writing, the kind that might not be done for a grade, the kind that can allow writers to try out unfamiliar ideas to see where they lead or how they might be formulated; the kind that ferrets out the roots in personal history of a reaction to a line or scene or character; the kind that allows the stumbling necessary to find one's own perception and one's own idea, or that follows a perception through to its implications; the kind that involves the act of discovering where a particular idea leads, testing it for interest and importance and validity. A course-related journal is one way in which to encourage this kind of writing.

In this process, we hope that students will learn that their meaning, like everyone's, is constructed, not "natural" and not necessarily "true." To learn this about one's own work is to learn something profound about one's world as well. Instructors of writing-intensive courses have always known this fact of education; we hope this text will encourage courses which concentrate on plays to be included in campuswide writing programs.

As we mentioned earlier, the two of us originally coedited the drama section of the anthology *Angles of Vision*. That book was the product of collaboration with eight other colleagues at the University of Vermont. Those were happy intellectual times: Our ongoing dialogues about literature and pedagogy and our joint efforts in editing and revising each other's work have so helped shape our professional identities that we are aware of their presence in this book as well. For this presence, we wish to thank our colleagues.

James Howe
William A. Stephany

THE McGRAW-HILL
BOOK OF DRAMA

READING SCRIPT INTO PLAY

Drama differs in several basic ways from other literary genres. Unlike the author of a poem or story or essay, the playwright does not intend his or her words primarily to be *read* in private, but to be *heard* as they are spoken by actors on a stage. Reading a play in private will always be in some respect an unnatural act. A play's primary space is not your bedroom or the library, but the theater, where it can be staged by a group of players before a live audience. When we read a play, therefore, we should be aware of what we are missing: the infectiousness of being in the theater and sharing a communal experience, the power which comes from seeing a tangibly "real" performance by live actors, the challenge of being confronted by someone else's idea of how the play should be presented.

However, this book—and a literature course on drama for which it might be required—asks you to perform exactly this kind of unnatural act. This is because there are some compensations for reading a play rather than watching it in a theater. When we read we can stop to make marginal jottings or turn back a few pages (or a few acts) to check on the accuracy of our memory of an earlier moment—things we cannot do in the theater. As readers, we have the leisure to consider alternative interpretations of a line, a character, a scene, even of the play as a whole. As readers, we are even able to make the decisions that a director has already made for us when we go to the theater. In fact, readers are *required* to direct their own play: to imagine its actors and actresses, its costumes and setting, while at the same time responding as its audience as well. Unless we do these things, we cannot read it as a play at all.

This all makes reading a play extremely challenging. We have to make interpretive decisions, but without many of the specifically narrative clues that might help us if we were reading fiction; and we do not have the *dramatic* clues—tone of voice or facial expression or bodily gestures—which would help us if we saw the play acted in a theater. If we look at the beginning of William Shakespeare's *Hamlet,* for example, we are immediately confronted with the following stage direction and dialogue:

Elsinore. Platform of the Castle.

[*Enter Bernardo and Francisco, two Sentinels.*]

BERNARDO. Who's there?
FRANCISCO. Nay, answer me; stand, and unfold yourself.
BERNARDO. Long live the king!
FRANCISCO. Bernardo?
BERNARDO. He.
FRANCISCO. You come most carefully upon your hour.

If we were sitting in an audience watching a performance of the play, we would see a soldier standing or walking alertly and a second soldier from another part of the stage encountering him. From his costume, from his posture, and perhaps from the setting (if, for example, it were made to represent the ramparts of a castle), we might guess that the first is on guard duty. Such a guess seems confirmed by his opening line, the sentry's traditional question: "Who's there?"

However, the situation seems reversed. Francisco's response to Bernardo is the second line of the play, and it shows that he recognizes Bernardo's question as a departure from what is normal. "Nay, answer *me*," he insists, and then issues a more formal version of the sentry's challenge: "Stand, and unfold yourself," that is, stop advancing and identify yourself. Francisco is the guard on duty; he is the one who is supposed to challenge others, yet it is the newcomer, Bernardo, who first challenges *him*. (This role reversal is much easier to "get" when we see a performance than when we read these lines.) The situation is also odd in another way: Bernardo, as the soldier who will relieve Francisco, should *expect* Francisco to be at his post; he shouldn't be surprised to find him there. So why would he have to ask, "Who's there?" Who else would be there?

Bernardo responds to Francisco's challenge with what seems to be the password—"Long live the king!"—and is recognized. The little crisis passes, but we are left with questions. Why is Bernardo so nervous? Who did he expect Francisco to be? And why is Francisco so jumpy, especially since Bernardo has arrived to relieve him right on schedule?

It turns out that they are expecting a ghost who has appeared to them twice already at about this hour. (Since it is the ghost of the recently deceased king, there is also a level of irony in Bernardo's password.) Later in this scene, when the ghost arrives, they will have questions about how to deal with it; this air of mystery will intensify throughout the play. Broken or misleading ceremonies will also repeat themselves. Indeed, this is a *play* of questions and mysteries, and its first two lines put us immediately into its atmosphere.

In asking ourselves questions like these and in responding to this atmosphere, we would be reacting to the play as it is enacted before us by specific actors under the guidance of a specific director on a specific occasion. When we read the play, rather than seeing it performed, these questions are intensified. Instead of responding to a play as acted, we need to imagine for ourselves the meaning of each speech, the tone of voice of each speaker, the physical postures and gestures each might assume, ultimately the significance of what is said. We have to figure out for ourselves how every speech sounds and looks, and only then can we begin to answer that first set of questions. All this is very demanding, but unless we do it, for us this script will not become a play.

CONVENTIONS OF DRAMATIC SCRIPTS

In order to do this kind of reading, we need to be familiar with some of the conventions of dramatic writing—some of the rules of the playwright's game. By far the greatest part of any script will consist of the **dialogue** to be spoken by the actors. The brief excerpt from the beginning of *Hamlet* presents us with a typical example of the primary conventions of scriptwriting and also with the special problem we face in reading a play. Remember that a script is written for people who wish to stage the play, and it is the needs of this audience, not those of a reading audience, that determine the form of a script. The two major conventions are the following:

1. Individual actors need to know when one character's speech ends and another's begins, and so the playwright's convention is to place the new speaking character's name before each speech. This practice allows actors to scan down the page and easily locate their next speaking part.

2. Sometimes the playwright provides the player with a **stage direction.** Usually these directions to the players are printed in italics to set them off from the words to be spoken. Stage directions are the playwright's primary means (apart from dialogue) of communicating with the people who are putting on the play. They might give instructions to the players or to the music director or to the costume designer. They might even, like the lengthy stage direction that precedes Tom's first speech in *The Glass Menagerie* (see p. 589), provide elaborate instructions to the set designer about how the stage should be constructed.

HOW CONVENTIONS WORK: THE READER'S CHALLENGE

The central problem confronting every playwright is how to communicate to an audience through dialogue alone, without the luxury of a narrative voice to serve as intermediary. The writer's intellectual attitudes or thematic concerns can be expressed only indirectly, filtered through the language and actions of characters interacting on a stage.

Sometimes, however, playwrights try to find alternative ways to communicate directly to an audience. In Shakespeare's day, for example, playwrights used the aside and the soliloquy. In an **aside,** a character turns toward the audience and says something perfectly audible to them, but supposedly not to anyone on stage. Since the audience is farther from the speaker than are the characters onstage, this is clearly not "realistic." Also, the character who speaks to the audience but not to the other characters momentarily projects himself or herself beyond the boundaries of the play and into the world of the audience, momentarily destroying the comfortable distance which usually separates us from the fictional space of the stage. However, this is a "convention" which the audience then came to the theater prepared to accept. In another Shakespearean convention, the **soliloquy,** a character who is alone on stage speaks aloud about his or her emotional or psychic state for the audience to overhear. Both of these conventions are designed to provide the audience with necessary information about how characters are thinking or feeling, often about their otherwise concealed motivation. They allow the writer temporarily to exercise the power available to a fiction writer who is using a narrator to explain a character or an action. While these devices seem artificial to us, they may have been as invisibly "conventional" to audiences in an earlier age as our modern, high-tech equivalent of the voice-over is to us: An actor stares off moodily, his or her recorded voice speaks, and we accept the convention that we are able to overhear an "inner voice."

These are exceptional devices, however, and quickly seem silly if overused. Normally both dramatist and audience have to accept and cope with the limits of dramatic form, and this requires sensitivity to detail by both of them. Writers have to let detail work for them through indirection, and readers, in a complementary act, need to be alert to detail in order to understand. In fact, the hardest part of reading a play, as opposed to a novel or short story, is the absence of a narrator's voice standing between us and the dialogue. This is the drama reader's special challenge. Stage directions telling the actor how the character feels or moves or looks sometimes help, but usually we are dependent upon context to answer such questions.

Our clue may be the way another character reacts to the first character's words. As if to anger? To irony? To joking? We need to infer from such reactions how the original line might have been delivered. But then how dependable is *that* character? Do you trust his or her reactions? You will need to read the entire play to determine a character's identity.

The following dialogue occurs early in Lorraine Hansberry's play *A Raisin in the Sun*. It is set in the 1950s, in an apartment on Chicago's black South Side. Ruth is a mother, Travis her 10- or 11-year-old son. By reading this passage very carefully, we will see some of the inferences we can draw about these characters' relationship and, more specifically, about the tensions of this particular morning's pre-school conversation. After the passage, we will give you an example of one way of reading it; we will try to show how much we can learn by reading between the lines as well as by reading the lines themselves, by taking into account what is suggested as well as what is stated directly.

RUTH. Sit down and have your breakfast, Travis.
TRAVIS. Mama, this is Friday. [*Gleefully*] Check coming tomorrow, huh?
RUTH. You get your mind off money and eat your breakfast.
TRAVIS [*Eating*]. This is the morning we supposed to bring fifty cents to school.
RUTH. Well, I ain't got no fifty cents this morning.
TRAVIS. Teacher says we have to.
RUTH. I don't care what teacher say. I ain't got it. Eat your breakfast, Travis.
TRAVIS. I *am* eating.
RUTH. Hush up now and just eat!

[*The boy gives her an exasperated look for her lack of understanding, and eats grudgingly*]

TRAVIS. You think Grandmama would have it?
RUTH. No! And I want you to stop asking your grandmother for money, you hear me?
TRAVIS [*Outraged*]. Gaaaleee! I don't ask her, she just gimme it sometimes!
RUTH. Travis Willard Younger—I got too much on me this morning to be—
TRAVIS. Maybe Daddy—
RUTH. *Travis!*

[*The boy hushes abruptly. They are both quiet and tense for several seconds*]

TRAVIS [*Presently*]. Could I maybe go carry some groceries in front of the supermarket for a little while after school then?
RUTH. Just hush, I said. [*Travis jabs his spoon into his cereal bowl viciously, and rests his head in anger upon his fists*] If you through eating, you can get up over there and make up your bed.

[*The boy obeys stiffly and crosses the room, almost mechanically, to the bed and more or less carefully folds the covering. He carries the bedding into his mother's room and returns with his books and cap*]

TRAVIS [*Sulking and standing apart from her unnaturally*]. I'm gone.
RUTH [*Looking up from the stove to inspect him automatically*]. Come here. [*He crosses to her and she studies his head*] If you don't take this comb and fix this here head, you better! [*Travis puts down his books with a great sigh of oppression, and crosses to the mirror. His mother mutters under her breath about his "slubbornness"*] 'Bout to march out of here with that head looking just like chickens slept in it! I just don't know where you get your slubborn ways . . . And get your jacket, too. Looks chilly out this morning.

TRAVIS [*With conspicuously brushed hair and jacket*]. I'm gone.

RUTH. Get carfare and milk money [*Waving one finger*] — and not a single penny for no caps, you hear me?

TRAVIS [*With sullen politeness*]. Yes'm.

[*He turns in outrage to leave. His mother watches after him as in his frustration he approaches the door almost comically. When she speaks to him, her voice has become a very gentle tease.*]

RUTH [*Mocking; as she thinks he would say it*]. Oh, Mama makes me so mad sometimes, I don't know what to do! [*She waits and continues to his back as he stands stock-still in front of the door*] I wouldn't kiss that woman good-bye for nothing in this world this morning! [*The boy finally turns around and rolls his eyes at her, knowing the mood has changed and he is vindicated; he does not, however, move toward her yet*] Not for nothing in this world! [*She finally laughs aloud at him and holds out her arms to him and we see that it is a way between them, very old and practiced. He crosses to her and allows her to embrace him warmly but keeps his face fixed with masculine rigidity. She holds him back from her presently and looks at him and runs her fingers over the features of his face. With utter gentleness—*] Now—whose little old angry man are you?

TRAVIS [*The masculinity and gruffness start to fade at last*]. Aw gaalee—Mama . . .

RUTH [*Mimicking*]. Aw—gaaaaalleeeee, Mama! [*She pushes him, with rough playfulness and finality, toward the door*] Get on out of here or you going to be late.

TRAVIS [*In the face of love, new aggressiveness*]. Mama, could I *please* go carry groceries?

RUTH. Honey, it's starting to get so cold evenings.

The first thing you might notice about this dialogue is the enormous range of emotions that Travis goes through in a short period of time. His first words are spoken "gleefully," but it's downhill from there. In the ensuing dialogue, Ruth expresses unyielding hostility, and Travis's ongoing reactions are specified in the stage directions: He goes from "exasperated" to "outraged" to "sulking"; he "rests his head in anger upon his fists," utters "a great sigh of oppression," and answers "with sullen politeness." It is unusual to have so many specific stage directions about how a character should react. Maybe Hansberry felt the need to offer more guidance to a child actor than a more experienced actor would need (or want). Whatever the reason, it allows us to be unusually confident about how Travis is reacting and therefore to draw uncommonly secure inferences about his mother's actions on the basis of those reactions.

If you were to look only at Ruth's speeches, you might decide that she is a model of bad parenting. In fact, until she turns playful and loving when Travis approaches the door to leave, Ruth's speeches consist of nothing but directives and put-downs. In these few speeches, she issues seventeen separate commands; four times she directly denies or negates what Travis says; twice she throws in statements apparently calculated to make him feel guilty (about how much she's "got on her" this morning and about his "slubborness"); and twice she resorts to naked power, once calling on him by all three names—Travis Willard Younger—and then cutting him off in midsentence with the italicized and exclamation-pointed "*Travis!*" She seems wholly insensitive to his potential embarrassment in not being able to produce the fifty cents that his teacher expects. Her barrage begins with, "Sit down and have your breakfast," and it ends with "not a single penny for no caps, you hear me," and in between it never relents for a moment.

Is this her normal behavior? Is this the way they usually interact? We can never be certain, of course, but it would seem doubtful. Travis seems too spontaneous at the start of the dialogue, too resourceful in the middle (in suggesting that he hustle work at the supermarket), and too trusting and open to her affection at the end to be a habitually abused child. We wonder, then, what could have triggered this apparently abnormal hostility from a normally loving mother. If this were a transcript of a real conversation, the answer might not be significant. Everybody has bad days, and we all tolerate occasional slumps in those we love and depend upon. But this is not life; it is a play. This is not conversation; it is dialogue—and we expect dialogue to matter. After all, these words did not just happen. Someone chose for them to be here, and it is fair for us to ask why. To do this we have to draw inferences.

One approach is to try to isolate what it was that first set Ruth to the attack. Perhaps it is that both of Travis's first two speeches concern money, the mysterious check that is expected tomorrow and the fifty cents he needs in school. His apparently innocent remarks about money seem to touch some submerged anxiety in his mother, and she lashes out. We know even this early in the play that money is a problem for the Younger family. In the opening moments of the play we have seen that Travis sleeps on the living room sofa and that the family shares a common bathroom in the hall with at least one other apartment. And yet Ruth's reaction seems so extreme that something specific, something beyond everyday anxiety about poverty seems to be working on her.

Let's try a different line of questioning. Look back at those specific moments when Ruth seemed to pull rank on Travis, when she resorted to unanswerable power, cutting him off in midthought by using his name as the verbal equivalent of a slap. Those moments would be even more arresting, even more painful, if we saw them on stage. What prompted them? On each occasion, they are Ruth's responses to her son's mentioning other family members who might give him the money he wants. We need to read the rest of the play to see how this approach might begin to open up our understanding of Ruth's behavior. As it turns out, the family is in the midst of a very specific financial dilemma, one that centers on another mother--son relationship, between exactly those two absent figures, Grandmama and Daddy, who are really in the background throughout this dialogue between Ruth and Travis. We do not yet know everything that is going on, but because Hansberry has written with such care, if we are alert readers we can infer what her thematic concerns are. In a way that is not yet clear to us, but already hinted at, maternal love and the anger and frustration of children will be at the center of this play.

We might also notice that the words of Ruth and Travis in this brief exchange seem very realistic. Our first reaction is likely to be that Hansberry "got it right." More than just sounding true to life, though, these words are crafted into a remarkably concise introduction to some of the main aspects of the play's characters, plot, and thematic concerns, almost like an overture at the beginning of a piece of music. This brief episode demonstrates the way a well-crafted play has the power to reach out into our world and at the same time to reverberate within its own. It can do this for us, however, only if we play our part as readers and draw intelligent inferences from the way characters speak and interact.

EXPOSITION

To illustrate more fully how a reader can draw inferences from the dialogue of a play, we will now look at the way a particular play in this anthology, *Lysistrata*, approaches a challenge which every playwright faces—the challenge of **expositon.** This is the term that is traditionally used to refer to the problem of how to provide background information about the play's plot and character, information that an audience must have in order to understand what is going on.

To explore this issue as fully as we can, we will provide a model reading of a slightly longer passage than the one we studied from *A Raisin in the Sun;* we will study most of the first episode of *Lysistrata*. However, we want to emphasize that this model is meant to be an example of how a reading *can* be done; it is definitely *not* intended as "the correct reading." Instead, it is a model of a *method,* a *process* which you must go through for yourself, a process that will probably lead you to different answers from ours, and even to different questions from the ones we ask here.

Lysistrata is one of the best-known comedies that has survived from ancient Greece. It was written by Aristophanes, the only writer of comedies whose work has survived from the fifth century B.C., the golden age of ancient Greek drama. The play begins when the title character walks on stage. She is joined by her friend Kleonike, and the two of them converse until, at the end of our excerpt, groups of women enter from two different directions to meet them. In the rest of the scene, not included here, Lysistrata details the two parts of her plan to end the war which has been raging throughout Greece for a generation: The young women will go on a "marriage strike," denying sex until their husbands agree to stop fighting, while the older women will sieze the city treasury on the Akropolis, making it impossible for the men to go on financing the war.

Begin by reading this scene straight through for yourself to get a feel for it. As you do, notice how Aristophanes whets our curiosity, how he gets us to want to know more than we do, how he keeps us interested by refusing to satisfy our desire for knowledge too quickly.

SCENE: A street in Athens. In the background, the Akropolis; center, its gateway, the Propylaia. The time is early morning. Lysistrata is discovered alone, pacing back and forth in furious impatience.

LYSISTRATA
  Women!
  Announce a debauch in honor of Bacchos,
  a spree for Pan, some footling fertility field day,
  and traffic stops—these streets are absolutely clogged
  with frantic females banging on tambourines. No urging
  for an orgy!
        But *today*—there's not one woman here.

[*Enter Kleonike.*]

Correction: one. Here comes my next door neighbor.
—Hello, Kleonike.

KLEONIKE

Hello to *you,* Lysistrata.
—But what's the fuss? Don't look so barbarous, baby;
knitted brows just aren't your style.

LYSISTRATA

It doesn't   10
matter, Kleonike—I'm on fire right down to the bone.
I'm positively ashamed to be a woman—a member
of a sex which can't even live up to male slanders!
To hear our husbands talk, we're *sly:* deceitful,
always plotting, monsters of intrigue. . . .

KLEONIKE

[*Proudly.*]

That's us!

LYSISTRATA   15
And so we agreed to meet today and plot
an intrigue that really deserves the name of monstrous . . .
and WHERE are the women?
Slyly asleep at home—
they won't get up for anything!

KLEONIKE
Relax, honey.
They'll be here. You know a woman's way is hard—   20
mainly the way out of the house: fuss over hubby,
wake the maid up, put the baby down, bathe him,
feed him . . .

LYSISTRATA
Trivia. They have more fundamental business
To engage in.

KLEONIKE
Incidentally, Lysistrata, just why are you
calling this meeting? Nothing teeny, I trust?   25

LYSISTRATA
Immense.

KLEONIKE
Hmm. And pressing?

LYSISTRATA
Unthinkably tense.

KLEONIKE
Then where IS everybody?

LYSISTRATA
Nothing like that. If it were,
we'd already be in session. Seconding motions.
—No, *this* came to hand some time ago. I've spent
my nights kneading it, mulling it, filing it down   30

KLEONIKE
Too bad. There can't be very much left.

LYSISTRATA
                                        Only this:
the hope and salvation of Hellas lies with the WOMEN!

KLEONIKE
Lies with the women? Now *there's* a last resort.

LYSISTRATA
It lies with us to decide affairs of state
and foreign policy.
                    The Spartan Question: Peace   35
or Extirpation?

KLEONIKE
            How *fun!*
                    I cast an Aye for Extirpation!

LYSISTRATA
The Utter Annihilation of every last Boiotian?

KLEONIKE
AYE!—I mean Nay. Clemency, please, for those scrumptious
eels.

LYSISTRATA
    And as for Athens . . . I'd rather not put
the thought into words. Just fill in the blanks, if you will.   40
—To the point: If we can meet and reach agreement
here and now with the girls from Thebes and the Peloponnese,
we'll form an alliance and save the States of Greece!

KLEONIKE
Us? Be practical. Wisdom from women? There's nothing
cosmic about cosmetics—and Glamor is our only talent.   45
All we can do is *sit,* primped and painted,
made up and dressed up,

[*Getting carried away in spite of her argument.*]

                        ravishing in saffron wrappers,
peekaboo peignoirs, exquisite negligees, those chic,
expensive little slippers that come from the East . . .

LYSISTRATA
Exactly. You've hit it. I see our way to salvation   50
in just such ornamentation—in slippers and slips, rouge
and perfumes, negligees and decolletage . . . .

KLEONIKE
                            How so?

LYSISTRATA
So effectively that not one husband will take up his spear
against another . . .

KLEONIKE
            Peachy!
                    I'll have that kimono
dyed . . .

LYSISTRATA
    . . . or shoulder his shield . . .

KLEONIKE
                                        squeeze into that daring   55
negligee . . .

LYSISTRATA
    . . . or unsheathe his sword!

KLEONIKE
                                  . . . and buy those slippers!

LYSISTRATA
Well, now. Don't you think the girls should be here?

KLEONIKE
Be here? Ages ago—they should have flown!

[*She stops.*]

But no. You'll find out. These are authentic Athenians:
no matter what they do, they do it late.   60

LYSISTRATA
But what about the out-of-town delegations? There isn't
a woman here from the Shore; none from Salamis . . .

KLEONIKE
That's quite a trip. They usually get on board
at sunup. Probably riding at anchor now.

LYSISTRATA
I thought the girls from Acharnai would be here first.   65
I'm especially counting on them. And they're not here.

KLEONIKE
I think Theogenes' wife is under way.
When I went by, she was hoisting her sandals . . .

[*Looking off right.*]

                                      But look!
Some of the girls are coming!

[*Women enter from the right. Lysistrata looks off to the left where more—a ragged lot—are straggling in.*]

The first thing you might notice as the play opens is how little we know. The directions for staging are minimal: We know only that a street in Athens, in front of the Akropolis, is represented. And when Lysistrata enters, it is as though we pick her up in midthought. Why is she so upset? Why should "women" be "here" "*today*"? Yet even in these opening lines, although their main effect is to leave us in mystery, Lysistrata begins to provide the details that will enable us to understand what is happening: She complains that, although her fellow women are quick to turn out for orgies, parties, and even "field day" foot races (in honor of Bacchos or Pan or, probably, Aphrodite), there is now "not one woman here" (6). We do not learn why this is upsetting until their meeting is mentioned in line 16; the importance of this meeting waits until line 32: "The hope and salvation of Hellas [Greece] lies with the WOMEN!" However, as each increment of information is given us, we want to know more. Knowing the importance of this meeting, we still do not know the precise reason for calling it in the first place. How can Greek survival depend on this meeting? Aristophanes feeds us information slowly, keeping us in suspense.

Although Aristophanes withholds most of this information about plot at the beginning of the play, he is, however, providing something else: information about the characters. Lysistrata sums up a general prejudice against women: When something truly momentous turns up, all the women stay "slyly asleep at home" (17–18). Women are regarded as superficial, lazy, self-indulgent. At first glance, Kleonike might seem to be an exception to this view since she has shown up, and almost on time. But her first lines are, "Don't look so barbarous, baby;/knitted brows just aren't your style" (9–10). She seems more concerned with Lysistrata's attractiveness than with her friend's feeling of frustration. Both characters are women, but they seem preoccupied with putting women (including themselves) down.

Perhaps this is the place to remember that the author was a male and that his society, which was also his audience, was rigidly patriarchal. Kleonike suggests this sexism, in fact, when she makes excuses for the women who have not shown up by describing how the limited social roles available to them interfere with independent action. Women are wives and mothers and semiservants, and these obligations come first, before other activities, such as attending meetings (20–23). We might wonder whether this excuse implies social criticism or is just a statement about the inescapable realities of feminine identity in Greek society.

These two women then collaborate in a joke about the bigness of the "thing" for which Kleonike suddenly imagines Lysistrata to have called all Greek women together. Lysistrata has a big plan in mind which has kept her from sleeping, but Kleonike turns it into a sexual pun. Lysistrata herself acknowledges that all women are united in their love for "*this*" (29): All the women would be here already "if it were" anything "like that" (27). It sounds as though these women are characterizing themselves and all other women as wanting only one thing, sexual satisfaction.

As the scene goes on, however, Lysistrata seems to change. She does not deny her interest in sex, but she also claims to be interested in saving her country and asserts that its survival depends on Greek women (32). In her following lines she mentions a series of areas in Greece (Boiotia, Thebes, the Peloponnese, Salamis, Acharnai), all of whose citizens are on one side or the other in the ongoing war between her city, Athens, and its rival, Sparta. Lysistrata wants to unite women from all parts of Greece in order to end the war (41–43).

Kleonike's speeches, however, provide a constant counterpoint. Lysistrata talks nobly, but Kleonike reminds us of the view (here held by a woman!) that if Greece must depend on women, "*There's* a last resort" (33). Her response to the possible liquidation of the Boiotians is a lament for a lost sensory pleasure—the eels that come from there (38–39). Her description of typical women sitting "primped and painted," dressed to be sexually alluring (46–49), makes us wonder if women are capable of anything but servitude or exciting sexual desire in men. She and those like her seem mentally imprisoned; she is willing to be limited to her biological drives and her male-imposed social roles.

Lysistrata, though, is different. Although she acknowledges her own sexuality, she refuses to be limited by it. Like Kleonike, she knows that men too have sexual drives; unlike Kleonike, she seems to see this as an opportunity for action rather than a condemnation to subservience. She has, therefore, devised a plan, and although we do not yet know its full details, we are beginning to gather enough information to be able to speculate about it. Let us examine some of the hints we have received.

Lysistrata says that she (and the other women she has called to the meeting) will use the very symbols of their female subservience, their sexually suggestive clothing, to teach men not to fight: "Slippers and slips, rouge/and perfumes, negligees and decolletage" (51–52) will be the very things which will stop men from using their spears, shields, and swords (53–56). She will use the implements of their enslavement to set them free. Women's alleged weakness: "I'm positively ashamed to be a woman—a member/of a sex which can't even live up to male slanders!" (12–13)—the aspect of female identity which men use to demean them will be used to control men. The war between the sexes will become more than just a metaphor for sexual or romantic gamesmanship; it will become an actual confrontation of power between men and women. Using their sexual attractiveness as their weapon, they will engage in a battle designed to end fighting.

At the end of this part of the opening scene, the situation is beginning to be clarified, but we are still left with many questions. Can women, through political action, re-create themselves according to a set of ideals and achieve a self-determined identity? And even if they can, is this dramatic premise still at some level a cruel antifeminist joke? What are we to think of women who use their sexual attractiveness as a military tactic? Will the play go further and question whether women have a value beyond biological utility? Will it question whether men do? Might this play be less about the conflict of men against women and more about humanity regardless of gender? We need to read on in order to figure out the fundamental tone which colors the play's central dramatic situation.

However, we can say at this point that the play is raising questions which are still important to us today. Feminist literary analysis, for example, has as a main concern the question of gender roles in a particular society: What roles are open to a woman or to a man? Who decides what these roles are? What options are open to a man or a woman in coping with them? We should also remember that sometimes a play remains open-ended, that it might not try to give a clear answer to the questions that it raises. Instead, it might try to present the issues involved that make its question important and that we need to think about in order to find our own answer. In this case, of course, to a large degree it is up to you—up to the director—to decide how you read this script and what kind of play you make it into.

In doing so, you will, of course, do your best to determine whether the author, here Aristophanes, is implying a thematic attitude toward the characters and the social roles they are playing. If a character seems happy with a limiting social role, is the author encouraging or discouraging that attitude, or simply showing the way things are? It may be worth repeating that the question is complicated in this case by the fact that *Lysistrata* is a play written by a male dramatist in a society where only males were eligible for citizenship. Knowing this, do you think that Lysistrata and Kleonike are right about what women most want? Or are they just expressing the author's typical male fantasy? Or are there other considerations which might cause such an author in that place and time to construct such characters?

THE STRUCTURE OF A PLAY: SCENES AND ACTS

When we read whole plays rather than short episodes, we encounter more complex aspects of dramatic structure. In general, a play's dialogue is divided into units called **scenes.** A scene consists of the action that is staged for an audience as if in a single physical space and during an unbroken period of time. The specific form that this dramatic convention takes is, like others, often dictated by the physical nature of the stage for which a play is written. On the modern stage, change of scene is sometimes marked by the raising of a curtain at its beginning and the lowering of a curtain at its end, sometimes by changing the lighting, most obviously perhaps by turning all stage lights off to show that one scene has ended and back on when a new one begins.

Earlier stages, which lacked these modern devices, had others available. For example, the theaters in ancient Greece and in Shakespeare's London did not have curtains to separate actors from audience, and, since plays were staged outdoors in daylight, they had no opportunity to manipulate lighting. A scene in this type of play begins when characters walk onto an unoccupied stage, and it ends when all the characters leave (or are carried off) so that the stage is again unoccupied. During the time that a group of characters remains onstage, the setting is fixed and the amount of time that passes in the theater more or less corresponds to the amount of time depicted from the lives of the characters. According to the conventions of Shakespeare's theater, when new characters enter a previously emptied stage to start a new scene, the play has probably moved to a different imagined time and a different imagined space. (Usually, but not always. The first few lines of the new scene will generally let us know.)

The ancient Greek theater was similar, but with one difference—the presence of a chorus. This was a group of actors who moved and spoke in unison and who represented some group of people affected by the play's actions. Early in the play, they entered their area of the theater, between the audience and the main actors, and they remained there until the end. Scenes in Greek drama, therefore, are marked by the entrances and exits of the main characters, as well as by the songs and dances performed by the chorus during the intervals when the acting area is otherwise empty. Since the acting area is never totally empty in a classical Greek play, however, most plays are set in only one place and enact fictional events that span more or less the same amount of time required to enact them.

No matter how a scene may be marked off by the conventions of a particular stage, however, one essential fact about it is always true: It is the playwright's basic compositional unit. As such, it has a reason for being in the play, and it has probably been arranged very carefully to accomplish its objectives. It is always a good idea, therefore, to ask yourself when a scene is over what has just happened. What did you know at the beginning of the scene and what do you now know that is different? How do characters change in the scene? On the basis of what? Events? Words? Errors in judgment? How does the plot develop in this scene? In other words, just what has happened here?

In addition to examining what happens in individual scenes, you might ask how two or more scenes are interrelated. The way this question is phrased might seem to prejudice the case by presupposing that the parts *are* interrelated, but for most plays this will be a reasonable assumption. For example, are there ways in which one episode might help you understand another which occurs just before or just after it? **Juxtaposition,** literally "placing beside," is the term for this structural device. If you were to take the dialogue between Ruth and Travis which we excerpted earlier in this Introduction and place it in its original context within *A Raisin in the Sun,* you would find an example of juxtaposition. Immediately before the first words we quoted, Walter, Ruth's husband and Travis' father, exited from the stage (and their apartment) to go out to the bathroom in the hall; immediately after the last words we quoted, Walter reenters. The entire episode between mother and son is framed by this reminder of the family's inadequate housing and by an ongoing awareness that Walter, whose situation is in some ways similar to that of his son, will soon be returning to his own breakfast.

Scenes are also sometimes combined into larger units called **acts.** Modern plays are often divided into acts to define intermissions when the audience can stretch, get something to drink, take a bathroom break. Playwrights are likely to shape their material so the audience will reach this intermission with a sense that the play has reached a climax. In traditional plays such as those of Shakespeare, however, acts are essentially textual, not dramatic, units. As you *read* the play, you may be aware of acts, but nothing happens onstage to signal to a theater audience that one act has ended and another begun. Still, if the units are logically intended by the play-wright—and since every one of Shakespeare's plays has exactly the same number of acts, five, you can guess that he probably did think and compose in these terms—you can ask questions about acts that are similar to those we asked about scenes. What movements of plot and what developments of character occur within the act? How does the act fit into the structure of the play as a whole? Do the scenes within the same act seem to reinforce one another?

Finally, do all the events presented in a play move toward the resolution of one action, or does the play have one or more **subplots?** You will find that such subplots often illuminate the main plot, by presenting either a reinforcing parallel action or an ironically contrastive one. When there is a subplot, you might look for a close thematic relationship between it and the main plot. If there is no such relationship, you might consider why the playwright is violating this expected structure. What effect is achieved?

THE TWO MASKS: TRAGEDY AND COMEDY

When we move from scenes and acts to a consideration of complete plays, it is useful to remind ourselves of the two most common of traditional forms in Western drama, **comedy** and **tragedy.** Even when plays seem very different from one another, they are often just different variations on one or both of these two basic forms. *Lysistrata,* for example, the play we have most recently been looking at, is a comedy, so we might consider that genre first.

In comedy, perhaps it goes without saying, we expect laughter and a happy ending, but we should differentiate among at least three kinds of laughter. It is possible to laugh *with* a character whom we like or admire; if this character triumphs at the end, for example, we might laugh in celebration. On the other hand, when we laugh *at* characters, it is usually because of some incongruity in behavior: because they are not as good or as clever as they think they are or as they should be. This kind of comedy, which shows us the characters' vice or foolishness—and, if we are honest, our own as well—is **satire.** Characters are held up to some standard of social or moral behavior and found wanting. Writers of satire have usually claimed that they are motivated by a desire to reform the behavior being satirized. Their motivations can be more complex, however. Sometimes people excluded from power satirize those in power to express their moral outrage and frustration over *not* being able to accomplish reform. A third kind of laughter is not so much *with* or *at* anything; it is neither celebratory nor judgmental. Instead, it seems to come out of the sheer need to express ourselves through laughter. What happens onstage seems so crazy, so incongruous to our normal view of reality that the world seems turned upside down. It seems so exaggerated that its resemblance to our normal world is almost lost. A play that provokes this kind of laughter might be called **farce.** The laughter itself can signal our recognition of a whole *world* out of kilter, not just a character. Comedy, therefore, can be philosophical or it can be escapist. It can express a wide range of emotions. It can present a world of miracles or a world of horrors. It can make us laugh in joy or in ironic despair.

Since we know that tragedy is different, that it will be "sad," we might think that it is the opposite of comedy; but they are near cousins. They give us similar information, even though they approach that information differently. Both remind us of our human weaknesses, but comedy has us laugh at them rather than cry over them. It shows us how our weaknesses make our triumphs fragile, rather than how they can lead to catastrophe. At the end of a comedy, we often sense that the happy ending of Act 5 would fall apart into tragedy if there were an Act 6. By the end of a tragedy, we often sense that the destructive forces in the play have been spent. In a sixth act, new life could begin. Comedy may be seen as the sequel to tragedy, tragedy the sequel to comedy. They are different sides of the same coin.

They do have important differences, though. Whereas there is likely to be a group of equally important characters in classical comedy, many of whom will be common people like ourselves, in tragedy one character will be the primary focal point and, particularly in Greek and Shakespearean tragedy, this character will be heroic, larger than life. Whereas in classical comedy most characters will be reintegrated back into society, in classical tragedy the main character is isolated from society throughout (by accomplishment or status at the beginning, by suffering at the end). Usually the society is sick and can return to health only with the exile or death of the hero or heroine. Whereas comedy typically distances us from the characters so that we can laugh at them, tragedy sobers us by bringing us close to the main character in sympathy so that we, too, experience the pain.

There are other qualities of tragedy which it is also useful for us to examine. For instance, the Greek philosopher Aristotle defined this form as a unified and significant action which involves the fall of a great or representative person. However much the times and the nature of theater have changed (and however much people disagree about how to interpret aspects of Aristotle's analysis), this definition remains the essential basis for discussions of tragedy. At the start, the hero is likely to be a figure of power and authority, and at the end to be powerless, humbled, dependent, rejected—and usually dead. For Aristotle, however, although the fall may be sad, it need not be considered either good or bad, but simply the way life is. It is a reminder to us that good things do not always last; that when things look best, the worst may be coming; that most of the time we are blind to this reality; and that this blindness is one of our principal weaknesses.

Its effect on its audience, says Aristotle, is purgative. It provides us with a **katharsis,** to use the Greek word that has been adopted into English, a purgation of pity and terror. In classical tragedy, these emotions are heightened throughout a play which is likely to seem relentless in its forces, inexorable in its chain of causally interrelated actions, until finally the built-up tension is released in the play's climactic moment. According to Aristotle, typically we pity the hero or heroine for suffering an unmerited misfortune due to frailty or error; or due to inherent and inevitable human limitations; or due to askewness, to being somehow unsynchronized with the world, or with fate, or just simply with the way of things. It is not necessarily a moral issue at all; no "fatal flaw" is required. It is just that the main character intended one thing, but something else happened, and the cause of this "something else" is also the source of our terror or fear, the second of the emotions which Aristotle identifies as particularly "purged" by tragedy. The forces which act on this main character act in our lives also; this fate could just as easily happen to us. And so we are led to see what the main character did not, at least not until it was too late: our human blindness. In katharsis, then, we are purged not only of pity and terror, but also of our superficial way of seeing the world. We may be prepared to see the paradox of much tragedy: that suffering, shame, and even evil can result in good—in self-recognition, in moral reform, even in exaltation. The great person, exposed to great pain, is challenged to live up to the fullest human possibilities.

SOME MODERN VARIATIONS ON THE TRADITIONAL MASKS

Comedy and tragedy provide complementary perspectives on life and complementary dramatic forms to express them in. Yet because the form of a play helps to define (and therefore limit) what a playwright can think and feel and express, many playwrights in the twentieth century have felt the need to change these generic conventions. Recent playwrights have been influenced by philosophical uncertainty about why people and their world behave as they do, as well as by much new thinking about the importance of class, gender, and ethnic identity. The traditional generic forms were based on assumptions about these issues which are now often in question, so that modern writers have sometimes felt the need to modify the classical genres to express their new ideas, sometimes actually creating new dramatic forms by combining elements from each of the older ones.

For example, modern writers of tragedy have not been comfortable with traditional assumptions of aristocratic or upper-class superiority. Often, therefore, they have attempted to make a common or typical person into the main character, and this, in turn, requires a redefinition of what a hero or heroine is, as well as a redefinition of the notion of tragedy itself. In *The Poetics,* Aristotle presupposed that serious drama would focus on events in the life of a "great man," someone with the power to shape events in the surrounding world. The discovery of limits to this power is in fact one of the common outcomes of the plot of traditional tragedy. Many twentieth-century writers, however, are likely to begin with the assumption that society imposes inescapable restraints on human freedom, that social and economic forces powerfully influence human "personality," and therefore that there may be no such thing as a hero or heroine. In addition, in comedy as well as tragedy, the optimistic Judeo-Christian beliefs that suffering can be educative, that it can remind us of our natural virtues, even that we can know the way we ought to behave and what we ought to believe, are often viewed with suspicion. Both the pain of tragedy and the laughter of comedy now often seem to be based on disillusionment rather than on the discovery of wisdom or social harmony. Indeed, when a playwright follows traditional forms in this modern era, it is frequently to express disbelief in them and in the assumptions they seem to imply about our world. Experiments in combining such forms often portray the horrors of life that were traditionally the subject of tragedy yet at the same time provoke the laughter we used to associate with comedy. This results sometimes in a disillusioned view of a world without clear meaning; whatever happens seems to happen at random, by chance as much as by intention, and therefore without pattern or goal. Whatever happens, that is, often seems absurd; the term **theater of the absurd** has been used collectively to describe plays by some of the most influential playwrights of the 1950s and 1960s.

This widespread desire on the part of playwrights to alter or escape traditional dramatic forms has led them to a new consciousness of dramatic form itself, as well as to experiments in how to manipulate it to get audience responses which are different from the traditional ones. In an apparent tragedy, for example, a playwright might deliberately make the "hero" unsympathetic, or might create a world full of contradictions so that we cannot know what to sympathize with or what to value. In other plays, the characters might speak self-consciously about themselves as characters in a play, reminding us in the audience that they are invented things, not real people; that we are watching a pretense of reality, not a scene from real life. At the same time these plays, by breaking the boundaries between pretense and reality, encourage us to see ourselves as being somehow like these invented characters. Each of these kinds of plays is disconcerting: Our normal expectations of what happens in a theater are deliberately challenged. Instead of becoming emotionally involved with the characters, we are distanced from them. They become objects of contemplation rather than fellow humans, but they may force us to become objects of our own contemplation as well. In general, modern playwrights are less interested in portraying traditional values than in forcing us to think about ourselves and our world by presenting that world, as well as the theater in which it appears, in unfamiliar terms.

One implication of this consciousness of genres applies to all plays in all ages: Because we have more or less predictable expectations when we go to a tragedy, and different but equally predictable ones when we anticipate a comedy, a playwright can deliberately manipulate these expectations. Sometimes it is the subtle differences between what the playwright gives us and what we expected that provides a play with its particular twist of meaning. This is true even for plays from ancient Greece.

For example, if *Lysistrata* seems to get us to laugh at women, is this done so that we will see how stupid our (male) prejudices are? Might this be why *women* put themselves down at the start of that play? There are usually several possibilities, so be alert.

THE LANGUAGE OF DRAMA

At this point, let us leave the comedy *Lysistrata* 2,000 years behind and turn to the beginning of Shakespeare's tragedy *Othello*. The biggest difference we will notice at first will not be in dramatic form, but in language. At first, the language of *Othello* will seem more difficult than that of *Lysistrata* because we printed *Lysistrata* in modern English translation, while Shakespeare's play is presented here more or less in the language of its earliest performance in 1604. In fact, however, the language is not so different as it seems. It is the ancestor of our own modern English, and after you have worked with it for a short time you will see its resemblances to ours; gradually, you are likely to feel at home with it.

The advantage to reading Shakespeare's original language is that it is extremely rich. Earlier in this Introduction we compared drama to narrative fiction, but there are also ways in which it is similar to poetry. Shakespeare not only writes in poetic form (his blank verse line usually has ten syllables and five stresses) but also writes with the kind of verbal compression and intensity that we associate with lyric poetry. He offers a particularly clear example of an idea we have been discussing throughout this chapter: that there are indirect uses of language which say more, not less, and say it powerfully.

Shakespeare, then, offers us a good reason to present another model reading, this time of the opening two-thirds of the first scene of *Othello*. As you will quickly see, many of its words and phrases suggest more than one meaning, each of which may be important: Shakespeare often says two or three things at the same time. Also, he sometimes uses an image early in a scene or a play, then builds on that image later by clustering a variety of related images around it, or by using the same image again and again in different situations, so that its meaning changes or develops as the scene goes on. The following passage offers a rich opportunity to observe the power of poetic language in a play.

The play opens with the stage direction, *"Enter Roderigo and Iago."* All we have are the names of two characters, and we do not even have this much in performance, where we just see the two characters walk onstage in midconversation. Whatever else we are to learn about these characters—including their names—we will need to figure out for ourselves through the words the players speak to each other. Among the things we learn in this way is that two men are talking to each other at night in a street in the Italian city of Venice, just outside the house of a prominent citizen named Brabantio (74–78). The principal action of this part of the scene occurs when they conclude their conversation and rouse him from his sleep (78–81).

At this point, we ask you to read the first 117 lines of the play:

Act I

SCENE I

Venice. A Street.

[*Enter Roderigo and Iago.*]

RODERIGO. Tush! Never tell me. I take it much unkindly
  That thou, Iago, who hast had my purse
  As if the strings were thine, shouldst know of this.
IAGO. 'Sblood, but you will not hear me!
  If ever I did dream of such a matter,   5
  Abhor me.
RODERIGO. Thou told'st me thou didst hold him in thy hate.
IAGO. Despise me if I do not. Three great ones of the city,
  In personal suit to make me his Lieutenant,
  Off-capped to him; and, by the faith of man   10
  (I know my price), I am worth no worse a place.
  But he, as loving his own pride and purposes,
  Evades them with a bombast circumstance
  Horribly stuff'd with epithets of war;
  And, in conclusion,   15
  Nonsuits my mediators; for, "Certes," says he,
  "I have already chose my officer."
  And what was he?
  Forsooth, a great arithmetician,
  One Michael Cassio, a Florentine   20
  (A fellow almost damn'd in a fair wife),
  That never set a squadron in the field,
  Nor the division of a battle knows
  More than a spinster,—unless the bookish theoric,
  Wherein the toged consuls can propose   25
  As masterly as he. Mere prattle, without practice,
  Is all his soldiership; but he, sir, had the election,
  And I (of whom his eyes had seen the proof
  At Rhodes, at Cyprus, and on other grounds
  Christian and heathen) must be be-lee'd and calm'd   30
  By Debitor-and-Creditor. This counter-caster,
  He, in good time, must his lieutenant be,
  And I—God bless the mark!—his Moorship's Ancient.
RODERIGO. By Heaven, I rather would have been his hangman.
IAGO. Why, there's no remedy. 'Tis the curse of service.   35
  Preferment goes by letter and affection,
  And not by old graduation, where each second
  Stood heir to the first. Now, sir, be judge yourself
  Whether I in any just term am affin'd
  To love the Moor.

RODERIGO.   I would not follow him then.   40

IAGO. O sir, content you,
   I follow him to serve my turn upon him;
   We cannot all be masters, nor all masters
   Cannot be truly follow'd. You shall mark
   Many a duteous and knee-crooking knave,   45
   That (doting on his own obsequious bondage)
   Wears out his time much like his master's ass,
   For naught but provender, and when he's old,—cashiered!
   Whip me such honest knaves. Others there are
   Who, trimm'd in forms and visages of duty,   50
   Keep yet their hearts attending on themselves,
   And throwing but shows of service on their lords,
   Do well thrive by 'em, and when they have lin'd their coats
   Do themselves homage. These fellows have some soul,
   And such a one do I profess myself. For, sir,   55
   It is as sure as you are Roderigo,
   Were I the Moor, I would not be Iago.
   In following him, I follow but myself;
   Heaven is my judge, not I for love and duty,
   But seeming so for my peculiar end.   60
   For when my outward action does demonstrate
   The native act and figure of my heart
   In complement extern, 'tis not long after
   But I will wear my heart upon my sleeve
   For daws to peck at. I am not what I am.   65

RODERIGO. What a full fortune does the thick-lips owe,
   If he can carry't thus!

IAGO.   Call up her father.
   Rouse him, make after him, poison his delight,
   Proclaim him in the street, incense her kinsmen,
   And though he in a fertile climate dwell,   70
   Plague him with flies; though that his joy be joy,
   Yet throw such changes of vexation on't
   As it may lose some color.

RODERIGO. Here is her father's house. I'll call aloud.

IAGO. Do; with like timorous accent and dire yell   75
   As when (by night and negligence) the fire
   Is spied in populous cities.

RODERIGO. What, ho, Brabantio! Signior Brabantio, ho!

IAGO. Awake! what, ho, Brabantio! Thieves! Thieves! Thieves!
   Look to your house, your daughter, and your bags!   80
   Thieves! Thieves!

[Brabantio at a window, above.]

BRABANTIO. What is the reason of this terrible summons?
   What is the matter there?

RODERIGO. Signior, is all your family within?

IAGO. Are your doors lock'd?

BRABANTIO.   Why, wherefore ask you this?   85

IAGO. 'Zounds, sir, you're robb'd!—For shame, put on your gown!—
  Your heart is burst, you have lost half your soul.
  Even now, now, very now, an old black ram
  Is tupping your white ewe. Arise, arise!
  Awake the snorting citizens with the bell,   90
  Or else the devil will make a gransire of you.
  Arise, I say.
BRABANTIO. What! have you lost your wits?
RODERIGO. Most reverend signior, do you know my voice?
BRABANTIO. Not I. What are you?
RODERIGO. My name is Roderigo.
BRABANTIO.   The worser welcome.   95
  I have charg'd thee not to haunt about my doors.
  In honest plainness thou hast heard me say
  My daughter is not for thee; and now, in madness,
  Being full of supper and distempering draughts,
  Upon malicious bravery dost thou come   100
  To start my quiet.
RODERIGO. Sir, sir, sir!
BRABANTIO.   But thou must needs be sure,
  My spirit and my place have in them power
  To make this bitter to thee.
RODERIGO.   Patience, good sir.
BRABANTIO. What tell'st thou me of robbing? This is Venice.   105
  My house is not a grange.
RODERIGO.   Most grave Brabantio,
  In simple and pure soul I come to you.
IAGO. 'Zounds, sir, you are one of those that will
  not serve God if the devil bid you. Because we come
  to do you service and you think we are ruffians, you'll   110
  have your daughter covered with a Barbary horse;
  you'll have your nephews neigh to you; you'll have
  coursers for cousins, and gennets for germans.
BRABANTIO. What profane wretch art thou?
IAGO. I am one, sir, that comes to tell you, your   115
  daughter and the Moor are now making the beast
  with two backs.

    After you have read this part of the scene through, you can return to look for
the details that might help you to figure out more precisely just what has happened
and what we have learned in this brief bit of stage business—and it is an enormous
amount that Shakespeare gets done here. This is a classic example of "dramatic
compression": A great deal of telling detail is packed into the matter of a few
minutes. Let us look again at the opening lines:

RODERIGO. Tush! Never tell me! I take it much unkindly
  That thou, Iago, who hast had my purse
  As if the strings were thine, shouldst know of this.

IAGO. 'Sblood, but you will not hear me!
  If ever I did dream of such a matter,
  Abhor me.

As in *Lysistrata,* the play begins with an air of mystery; the two characters are apparently in the middle of an ongoing conversation, and we have no idea what it is that they are talking about. We would understand more if we knew what "this" refers to in line 3, presumably the same thing referred to by the other character in line 5 as "such a matter," but they are so intent in their dialogue that neither of them stops to fill us in. This is like conversation in real life, but it is hard on us as readers.

In fact, the specific matter that concerns them is not even mentioned again until lines 66–67: "What a full fortune does the thick-lips owe [own],/If he can carry't thus!" And even here we *still* do not know what would constitute this "full fortune" or what it is that he needs to carry off. Not until lines 88–89 do we begin to figure things out, when Iago cries to Brabantio, "Even now, now, very now, an old black ram/Is tupping your white ewe." The title character, the Moor, an older black man, is, at least in Iago's imaginings, at this very moment having sex with a younger white woman, Brabantio's daughter, a relationship which Iago assumes the father does not know about and would not approve of.

In the world of the play this situation is potentially explosive. No wonder it has preoccupied Iago and Roderigo from the beginning. But apparently Shakespeare does not yet want our full attention on this, the major premise of the plot. Instead, like Aristophanes, he puts our attention on the two characters who open the play. Why? What can we learn of them before the action makes its decisive shift to involve Brabantio after line 67? We need to go back to the play's beginning and see what their dialogue tells us.

Shakespeare makes us feel that we are breaking into the middle of an important conversation. Roderigo's first three lines show anger. He seems to have trusted Iago, and now he feels betrayed because of something Iago just told him a moment ago, just before the play began. It is natural for us to concentrate, to try to figure out where we are in this tense exchange between two men who seem to have been friends. Iago's first speech frustrates our hope for an explanation: He protests his innocence and teases us with a reference to what he has been talking about just before the play began. "You're just not listening to me," he says, in effect. "I never dreamed that such a thing would happen." What thing? Roderigo still seems to feel betrayed. In saying, "Thou told'st me thou didst hold him in thy hate," he suggests that Iago is a hypocrite, that Iago's alleged hatred of "him" has been called into question by "this." We are still puzzled.

Iago's response, the first lengthy speech of the play (8–33), fixes this mysterious "him" character in the center of our attention, even though he is not onstage. Iago reassures Roderigo that he does hate "him" and with good reason: Iago is evidently a soldier who wanted to be promoted to lieutenant, second in command of Othello's army (9–17). Instead, Michael Cassio, a military theoretician with no practical experience in battle, gets the promotion, and Iago is given what to him is the insultingly lower rank of "his Moorship's Ancient" or, as we would say, his ensign (18–33). Iago's anger, apparent in his derisively invented term "his Moorship" (apparent because it mocks the term "his worship"), seems to persuade Roderigo that Iago is telling the truth. His response suggests that he is sympathetic to the injustice Iago feels: "By heaven, I rather would have been his hangman" than his ancient. The tension between them has been resolved by their common reassertion of their hatred for "him," the title character.

Having successfully calmed Roderigo, Iago next generalizes about the corruption of the modern world, where "Preferment goes by letter and affection," by favoritism and whim, rather than by experience, by seniority. He concludes (38–40) by asking Roderigo to judge whether he should feel any obligation "to love the Moor." Roderigo responds, "I would not follow him then." However, although this response is what Iago expects, it also suggests a difference between the two men. At one level, Roderigo's line may suggest an upper-class insensitivity to the needs of someone who has had to work his way up the ladder of promotion rung by rung. A secondary effect of his words is to make Iago defensive. How can he keep his dignity if he serves a person he hates, one who allegedly mistreats him?

Iago's self-defense (41–65) is extremely odd. He begins, "I follow him to serve my turn upon him," and ends, "I am not what I am." He describes himself as a hypocrite, a person who pretends loyalty to his master but who actually has none. His justification is found in his previous speech: Since he is unjustly treated, he himself is justified in being unjust, or at least deceptive, in return. Surprisingly, he goes further: "Whip me such honest knaves" as those who are true and loyal servants. It would be one thing to say they are stupid, that they will be mistreated in this corrupt modern age. But whip them? For honesty? What kind of man is this Iago? It is not just that he *justifies* hypocrisy. He actually *praises* it. He seems to be as corrupt as the new world against which he just finished complaining.

What are we to think of Iago, then? If he boasts that he would lie to Othello about his loyalty, can we believe what he tells Roderigo about his hatred? Can we believe anything a character like this says? For example, about Othello's unfairness? Or about the corruption of the age? Or even about his own motives? On the other hand, this speech seems to be a completely honest statement about himself. Who would praise his own hypocrisy except a person who was telling the truth? That is clearly what Roderigo thinks, and we might, too. It is as if Iago were baring his soul both to Roderigo and to us. It is not actually a soliloquy, but in this respect the speech is like one. And, typically, we like a person who is honest with us about himself. Since we are taken into Iago's confidence, just as Roderigo is, we too might like him and even trust him. He seems somehow honest in his dishonesty, leaving us a little uncertain about how we feel. We need to delay deciding while we gather more information.

As his attention turns toward Brabantio, his words convey a new degree of venom: "Call up her father./Rouse him, make after him, poison his delight" (67–68). Is it Brabantio or Othello whose delight he would poison? To whom does "his" refer? Remember his complaint about the unfairness of the age he lives in. There may be a general ill will here, not just against Othello. And when the "poison" is joined to the image of an emergency like a city fire (76–77), we sense his urgency in wanting to spread the alarm, wanting to spread "poison" all through the aristocratic world of Venice.

When he finally tells Brabantio—and us, too, at last—what the subject of the whole scene has been so far, his terms are even more than venomous: "an old black ram/Is tupping your white ewe." He is a racist, or at least he deliberately appeals to the racist feelings of Brabantio, emphasizing the difference between Othello's black-ness and his daughter's whiteness. And he describes their mating as unnatural, as bestial (a ram and a ewe). A little later, he uses the bestial imagery in grotesquely playful ways, turning it into an extended metaphor of the Moor as an Arabian stallion and adorning the figure of speech thickly with alliteration: "You'll have your daughter covered with a Barbary horse; you'll have your nephews neigh to you; you'll have coursers for cousins, and gennets for germans" (110–113). ("Gennets" and "germans" are exotic words for horses and relatives.) In his next speech he again mentions "your daughter and the Moor" as "making the beast with two backs" (115–117). He seems obsessed with the idea that their sexuality is gross, crude, and unnatural.

By this point in the scene, we have figured out the situation that Roderigo and Iago have been talking about, and we have also discovered a number of things about Iago: that he seems appealing and honest (or at least open) to us and Roderigo, and that he claims to be angered both by general social injustice and by personal injustice. These qualities might tempt us to be sympathetic. But we also learn that he is angered by his thwarted ambition and wants revenge, that he is a self-serving hypocrite, that he is a racist; and we might begin to suspect (from his overactive imagination) that he is also obsessed with Brabantio's daughter, Desdemona, as a sexual object. He is envious not only of Othello's position in the army but also of his position with Desdemona. In general, he is envious of Othello's *power*.

IMAGERY

We know these things not only from what he says but also from the way he says them. Part of this way of speaking is his use of **imagery.** Words and phrases like "poison," "old black ram," and "the beast with two backs" do not just express an idea, but express it in a way which gives it sensory content, which makes the idea powerful to us by implicitly comparing it to something we can imagine.

At this point, let's take advantage of one of the prerogatives we have as readers of this play that would not be available to us if we were watching it in a theater. Let's backtrack and focus on some of the imagery which has already been used in the first scene. At lines 66–67, Roderigo says:

> What a full fortune does the thick-lips owe,
> If he can carry't thus!

Earlier, we saw that either Iago is a racist or that he is appealing to the racism of Brabantio. We also saw that Roderigo is an aristocrat (he seemed not to understand Iago's problem about thwarted ambition when he said, "I would not follow him then" at line 40). Roderigo now shows that he, too, like the senator Brabantio, and probably also like Iago, seems to be a racist. Indeed, this seems to be a *society* of racists.

Moreover, notice that Iago shouts up at the senator, Desdemona's father: "Awake! What, ho, Brabantio! Thieves! Thieves! Thieves!/Look to your house, your daughter, and your bags!/Thieves! Thieves!" (79–81). When Brabantio comes to the window, this imagery of theft continues: "Are your doors lock'd" (85)? And again: " 'Zounds, sir, you're robb'd!—For shame, put on your gown!" (86). On our first reading of the play, we might be confused at this point. Has Brabantio really been a victim of robbery? As we are about to learn, only one thing has been taken from him: his daughter. We might ask, then, what this implies about a father's relationship to his daughter. Under what legal circumstances can a father be "robbed" of her? Would this be true for a wife also?

We have learned from this imagery that a person who is white and male believes himself to have all the rights and power in this society. Perhaps this helps explain why the three characters in this first scene seem so bitter toward the as-yet-unnamed Othello. He is black, and he has both the power and the woman that all three of the white men want, in their different ways, to possess.

This imagery, then, opens an issue that is a tremendous problem not only for blacks and women, but also for white men, and not only in Shakespeare's era. If we pause to think about the dynamics of power, we will realize that people who have power, even such great power as to be able to possess other people, define themselves by their ability to live up to that power. As a result, they have to protect it; otherwise, they risk losing their status and maybe even their sense of identity. Status, then, can be a burden as well as an advantage. With it comes insecurity. Iago's question, "Are your doors lock'd?" goes to the heart of the white male ego: Iago's emphasis on blackness, on "an old black ram" who is also "the devil" (91), who threatens miscegenation, who not only steals Brabantio's property but pollutes the blood of his family—who steals his family's honor—completes the threat to white patriarchal society.

This portrait of a whole society, accomplished in only 117 lines, makes us curious about this black man, this white woman, and their love. Together, they seem powerful enough to threaten the entire city, yet neither of them appears in this first scene. It will be exciting to see them onstage.

A RETROSPECTIVE VIEW OF THE MODEL READINGS

We could ask many other questions about this scene. For instance, we could ask what kind of person would defy her entire society for love? We could also speculate about the immense pressure this racist and sexist society will put on a black man and a runaway white woman who have married each other, and what this might do to their relationship. But we have done enough to make the point we intended, the point that we have been making throughout this Introduction: that in reading plays, we need to be alert to the tiniest hints of information, to ask questions about them, to maintain a running dialogue with the lines, to test ideas. We need to remember that reading is an act of imagination, although a disciplined one; that if a play is worth rereading, several lines of investigation will usually be possible. We can take off with one of them for a while, and then we can check it in rereading. If we find that our first reaction no longer makes sense, we can shelve that line of thought and start another. That is the advantage we readers have over the theater audience.

At the same time, we need to imagine ourselves as directors in the theater as we read. We have to imagine what the play looks like, how it feels and sounds, as well as what its meanings are. In fact, sometimes the most important suggestion about meaning will be precisely that, the way it looks and feels and sounds as you imagine it in a theater. In this way we convert our script into a play.

DO IT YOURSELF: WRITING ABOUT DRAMA

At this point we want to help you empower yourself as a student to learn how to learn on your own—to do for yourself the kind of reading of plays that we have been encouraging throughout this Introduction. A primary way of doing this is to write about the plays you read. Nothing helps your reading more than writing. It helps you do the work of questioning, interpreting, and staging these plays. For this reason, we want to encourage you to continue to use writing as a means of discovering and clarifying your own ideas, not only for the plays you will read in this course but also for whatever you encounter after it.

We are not necessarily talking about traditional, formal, assigned papers, although writing of this sort is extremely useful and will almost certainly be involved in most literature courses. In recognition of their importance, we have included in the last section of this Introduction a long set of questions which are specifically designed to help you think about how to analyze *any* play and, from that analysis, how to discover topics and theses for precisely this formal, assigned kind of writing. Here, however, we are proposing a different, informal kind of writing. It is informal because, assigned or not, written for your professor to see or not, it is primarily undertaken for *your* sake, to help you articulate for yourself precisely what you feel and think as a result of reading a play. It is your place to work out what you think and feel, and why, and perhaps to second-guess yourself, to think again, to try on new ideas and new ways of thinking. It is your place of exploration, your place to learn by expanding what you already know. It can be valuable for professors to see this writing because they can see how much you are thinking and they can help guide you in doing it. For these reasons, they might very well assign such writing.

But writing of this sort does not *need* to be assigned in order to be valuable. Nor does it need to be graded in order to be validated. You and your friends might simply decide to do it because it is useful in your work of learning. A journal would be a good place in which to collect these writings, for then you can refer to them and build on them as it seems helpful.

In this spirit, we suggest here three basic kinds of informal writing, although sometimes two or more kinds will be combined in the same suggested assignment. One kind asks you to write about yourself, to remember or imagine yourself in situations like the ones in the plays you read. These writings are intended to help you see, through working it out in words, parallels in your own experience to that of the characters and the importance in your own life of the issues which the characters face. This kind of understanding, in turn, can help you imagine what kinds of people and situations a particular play presents. A second kind of writing is more analytic. It asks you to do for yourself the kind of inferential reading that we have exemplified in our model readings in this Introduction in order to prove to yourself that you can do it on your own and that writing it out helps you to do it—that you can generate your own ideas and questions by yourself or with your fellow students. The third kind of writing is imaginative. It asks you to learn the conventions, limitations, and potential of dramatic form by using it yourself, by writing dialogue in various forms and styles and for various purposes.

1. Think back to a specific, brief moment from your childhood in which you interacted with a member of your family, a moment no longer than the length of the exchange between Ruth and Travis quoted earlier in this Introduction. It does not need to be a painful moment, but it should be one that affected you emotionally in a powerful way. As you look back upon it now, in the light of who you have become, can you see a way in which that moment expresses something more important than you could then have recognized? Important, perhaps, for what it reveals about you or the other person or your relationship or your values or your family's values? Write a brief dialogue, perhaps no longer than 50 or 100 lines, not counting stage directions, in which you try to capture both the feeling of that moment as you experienced it and also what you now see as its significance. Write it in the dialogue/stage direction form we have been discussing.

2. Read the dialogue you have just written aloud to a friend. As you listen to it, and hear it through another's ears, does it seem that you "got it right"? Do the speeches sound the way you imagine yourself and the other person in your memory really sounded? If not, what would you need to change to make it seem "right"? Perhaps add more slang terms, for example? A more informal brand of language? Revise the passage so that it catches the *flavor* of the scene you remember (or the scene as it seems to want to be written) as truthfully as possible.

3. It is tempting to look down on the characters in *Lysistrata,* or in any play, who have accepted their limiting social roles. However, if we think about it, we might find that we are not much different. For example, you might think about who *you* are. Is there a part of you that you can separate from the roles you play? You have been given the role of student, and of your parents' child, and of woman or man, and probably many more as well. Other roles you may have chosen for yourself. If might be helpful to make a list of them all. Then focus on any one of these roles you play. Did you pick it for yourself, or was it given to you? (Being a college student is a role that comes to mind.) Now that you are playing it, how does it restrict your freedom? Is there a way in which it enhances your freedom? If you abandoned it, how would your life be changed? How would your sense of who you are be changed? How would it affect other people who are close to you?

4. Think back to the first dialogue which we suggested that you write. Is there a connection between that experience and one of the roles you have just been thinking about? If so, revise that first dialogue to make the

connection clearer. Are there other cases where a moment from an earlier time in your life seems to anticipate one of the roles you now find yourself playing?

5. Take one of the passages of dialogue you have already written and expand it into a scene. Or write a new dialogue which portrays an important moment in your past, then expand it into a scene. The goal of this expansion will be to generate movement or change toward an imagined or actually remembered conclusion, even a climax, toward a moment that clarifies the importance of the passage presented in the original dialogue. For example, a second character could react to the situation you have already presented in dialogue form: This new character might learn something about herself, or about the original character, or even about the world. Or she could do something that provokes a response which is even more powerful and revealing than the original dialogue itself. For example, she might see her situation so clearly that she actually decides to change her life. (It is not necessary, by the way, to be slavishly faithful to the details of your biography. If you change or invent the "facts" in order to be "more true" to a fictional experience, you are discovering the normal working method of writers who create imaginative literature of all kinds.)

6. Write a completely new scene which either reinforces or contrasts with an important idea in the scene you wrote or expanded for number 5. Imagine this new scene to be part of the same play, enacted in sequence with your first scene. By placing these two passages side by side you could undercut the original, or you could make it stronger; you could show that its situation applies only to one time and place, or suggest that it is always true. Try your own hand at juxtaposition.

7. Rethink one of the scenes you have written in terms of how it might fit into a comedy or a tragedy. Imagine the story line for the full play, then revise the scene so that it will perform a specific function in a specific place within your tragedy or comedy.

8. Imagine one of your scenes being acted behind footlights, with concealed overhead lighting and realistic staging. Write out some of the details which you imagine about what the sets, props, and painted background look like to achieve this realistic effect. Now imagine your scene with the lights *not* concealed, but openly visible to the audience, with a completely blank background, painted black, and a bare stage (no sets, no props). Write out some of the stage directions for this different method of staging. How do you imagine this change would affect audience reaction to your scene? Does your sense of the stage for which you are writing (and its potential effect on the audience) affect *how* you write the scene?

9. Imagine how the characters would be costumed in this scene you just worked on. Would the costumes be different if the staging did not attempt

a pretense of realism than if it did? Now imagine radically different costumes for the scene. Describe (or draw) them. How does this change affect the way you imagine the theater audience would respond to the scene? (And how does this affect your writing?)

10. Return to one of the scenes which you have written, or write a new passage of dialogue between two characters based on a crucial event in your past. Now read this scene or passage carefully, as though it were written by Shakespeare. Are there places where you find that your words speak to each other, places where your imagery or figurative language seems of a piece? Try to see ways in which you might revise the dialogue to achieve this effect more consistently. Revise it with particular emphasis on the specific words selected and the way they speak to each other, so that your main points are implied more powerfully.

11. Practice the inferential method of reading which we have modeled for *A Raisin in the Sun, Lysistrata,* and *Othello* by doing your own, similar reading of the first episode of another play in this anthology. In doing so, your first step will be to read carefully with pencil in hand, underlining key words, drawing lines connecting words and ideas that seem to speak to each other, jotting your own ideas in the margins. Once you have begun to assemble your evidence in this way, try organizing it into topics and categories. As you do so, and then as you actually write your sentences and paragraphs, be open to the possibility of discovering previously unforeseen connections and relationships in the scene. Writing is not just the process of transcribing what you know; it is also the process of *discovering* what you know.

   In this analysis, pay particular attention to images which are repeated or built on and to phrases which echo or answer other phrases. Try paraphrasing the meaning of these images and phrases into explicit statements. If some of them are difficult to paraphrase, try to explain why. How is language working to produce meaning in these phrases?

12. Several of the previous informal writings concerned your attitude toward the roles *you* play. As readers, how can we determine a *character's* attitude toward *his or her* social roles? This is a large question. To find answers, it might be useful to break it down into smaller issues. For example, what function in society do the women of *Lysistrata* seem to have? (We can ask this question about any individual character, or any group of characters, in any play.) In other words, what do they do? Does their society dictate this function, or do they choose it? In what ways, if any, does it suit them or make them happy? In what ways does it restrict them or make them unhappy? Why, then, would you accept, or choose, such a role?

13. How can we determine an *author's* attitude toward the characters and the roles they are playing? For example, although a female character might seem satisfied with a social role that limits her, a play could reinforce that attitude in women, or challenge it, or seem neutral and simply be trying to

show it as "the way things are." The submissive woman, for example, can be applauded, condemned, laughed at, or treated sympathetically, depending on the play's agenda.

14. Imagine that you are going to produce and direct a play from this anthology. Ask yourself what effect you want the play to make on the audience, and then write out the staging details which will help the play achieve that effect. You could include information about costumes, lighting, stage sets, props, backdrop painting, stage size and shape, the nature of the actors, special effects (visual or auditory)—whatever seems helpful to you. You might ask yourself if you could get the same effect with less material, if you could make more efficient use of fewer resources. In this exercise, you are being asked to think of the relationship between the things on the stage and the audience, and you are also being asked to choose one effect rather than some others as your preference for the play you are working on.

    In addition to these fairly specific writing possibilities, we suggest two more general ones which we believe can be helpful to you in exploring and expanding what you know:

15. Keep a reading journal as you work your way through a play. Write a page or so in response to each act of a play as you finish it. Here, instead of beginning with a specific traditional question, you might begin by asking yourself why you liked or did not like the act, or you might write to clarify why it is that you feel confused by a scene or by a character's role. Sometimes, if you can figure out why you are confused, you are not confused any more.

16. Create your own audience for your writing, one that does not necessarily include your teacher, at least not at every stage in the writing process. For example, exchange your writing with a friend in the class. Every writer we know of—*every* writer—shows his or her written work to friends while the writing is in process in order to get some feedback about what works and what does not. Let yourself have the fun of doing what professional writers do. Better still, get together with a *group* of students and exchange your work with one another in collaborative learning. In academic circles, we often encourage people to pursue individual, isolated learning experiences, and academic writing is often done like that. But it does not have to be, and maybe it *should not* be. Writing can be—maybe *ought* to be—a means of communication and of self-definition and self-actualization. Writers who come to love their craft are often part of a group of writers who give one another support and constructive criticism. If you formed that kind of group for yourself as you write about drama, you might be amazed at what happens.

QUESTIONS ABOUT DRAMA

In providing you with model readings of parts of several plays, we have tried to suggest by example the kinds of questions that a dramatic text might raise for you as readers, and also the kinds of responses you might make to such questions. In the immediately preceding section, we have also suggested ways of using informal writing to help you in this process. As additional help, we list below a series of questions which can be applied to nearly any play. Although some will be more useful than others for a particular script, the test of their usefulness will be the same for each: Does your answer lead you to ask still another question, so that you become engaged in an ongoing process of questioning? They are valuable only if they do this, if they stimulate your curiosity to think more and more deeply about the play, to enter into dialogue with it, to discover other issues which are not listed here because they are unique to the particular play which you are reading now and to yourself as an individual reader. For example, if you were to question the meaning of the "raisin" image in *A Raisin in the Sun,* your questions should lead you beyond raisins, possibly to other images, to other actions, and finally to possible meanings in the play as a whole. Your answer to our question should be the starting point for a series of questions of your own.

It is in this spirit that we offer the following *general* questions to help you figure out for yourself what *specific* questions you need to raise about any given play. Use them as questions to write about in your journal, as questions to bring to class for discussion, and as the basis for discovering ideas, topics, and theses to be used in longer, formal papers about the plays.

Questions About Plot and Structure

1. What is the principal *conflict* in the play? Does it involve an internal conflict in one character? Or one character against another? Or one group against another? Or an individual or a group against nature? Against some person or force larger than nature? (A clue to identifying the conflict: The characters are most interested in and perform most of their actions because of it. They fight against it; they strive for it; they escape it; in their dialogue, they are preoccupied with it.)

2. Is the play *unified*? When we have finished reading it, can we look back and see that all its episodes somehow moved in the same direction, toward the same final meaning or dramatic effect? Does each incident seem to grow logically out of some preceding incident and lead naturally to what follows? Is there a part that seems *not* to fit this formula of the well-made play? Sometimes parts fit into the whole in unexpected ways, to give it a twist of meaning that is surprising. Consider the possibility that the part which *seems* not to fit may be the most important part of the play, not the

playwright's mistake. See if you can find a way to read the play that makes this "strange" part logical. *Warning:* Sometimes the parts may fit together too easily; the problems in the plot might be solved so much more easily than would be likely in real life that you cannot believe in the plot's resolution. The play might seem forced and unnatural. Often this kind of imposed and superficial order really masks a profoundly unresolved social, psychological, or artistic problem—possibly an issue which the playwright does not know how to deal with fully. Are there places in the play where a complex problem is resolved so simplistically or so tidily that you end up questioning whether so simple or tidy a resolution is possible (or desirable)?

3. Traditionally (since Aristotle) people have spoken of moments of "reversal" in drama, when the fortunes of a tragic character take a decisively downward turn or when the fortunes of a comic character begin to rise. Is there such a moment in this play?

4. Traditionally (since Aristotle) people have spoken of moments of "discovery" or "recognition" in drama, when a main character learns the significance of a person or thing or situation previously unknown or inadequately understood. Is there such a moment in this play?

Questions About Character

5. A character whose personality seems to evolve is sometimes called a **developing character.** Is there any such character in the play you are reading? What kind of change occurs in this character? Is it a change in personality or attitude, in opinion or values or ideals, perhaps in behavior? Is it a large one or a small one? What causes this change? For example, the cause might be an event, or it could just be something another character says. How is this change presented dramatically? Does it seem natural, that is, is it consistent with the character's previous attitudes or behavior? Does it seem adequately motivated?

6. Another possibility is that an apparent change to a new mode of behavior is actually rooted in the depths of the character as previously presented. Instead of a developing character, do we have one who is really just revealing his or her true character more fully than before? A complex character, one who seems realistic, is usually either a developing or **revealed character.** In the case of these revealed characters, it is not they who change so much as our perception of them: We regard them in one way at first, but as more is revealed about them our first impression changes, and in retrospect we reconsider our earlier impressions of them. When we recognize characters in this way, they strike us as familiar because this is the way we perceive the other people with whom we

regularly interact. Think about the people in class with you right now. Has your first impression of any of them changed as the semester has progressed? If so, do you think this is because they have changed? Or because, as you have gotten to know them better, you have modified your initial perception? Characters in plays are often "revealed" in just this way, so that early episodes need to be reinterpreted later, in the light of the events that follow.

7. Does the play you are reading make use of **contrasting characters?** In particular, are minor characters ever left relatively undeveloped so that, instead of attracting attention primarily to themselves, they direct attention to some complementary or contrasting aspect of the more developed main characters? A character so used is often called a **foil** of the major character. The metaphor comes from jewelry making, where a piece of gold foil placed behind a translucent gem reflects and intensifies the light that passes through it, in this way showing off the gem with greater clarity than it has by itself. Perhaps Travis could be said to serve this function in *A Raisin in the Sun,* acting as a foil for his father, Walter.

Questions About Language and Texture

8. Is there some consistent strain of **imagery** in the play's figurative language, especially in its metaphors and similes? If so, is it merely decorative, or is it functional as well? Does it, for example, reinforce, modify, or in some other way illuminate an aspect of plot, character, or theme? Think, for example, of the racist images which both Iago and Roderigo use to refer to Othello and of the imagery of robbery and theft which is used to refer to Brabantio's daughter's elopement. What might the nature of the play's imagery reveal about the characters who use it and about the thematic concerns of the author who wrote it?

9. Are any of the objects (or characters) in the play dealt with in a way that suggests that they might be **symbols?** We need to be very careful about how we use this term. A symbol is not, for example, an abstraction. Just the opposite, it is a concrete object which gains specific conceptual or emotional value because of the way it is used or talked about. This meaning is not inherent in the object but rather grows from the way it operates in the play, and in general a symbol will reinforce or help refine the play's effect and meaning. Ordinarily, it will *not* provide some secret clue to a meaning that would be otherwise inaccessible. Think, for example, about the collection of glass animals from which *The Glass Menagerie* takes its title. They serve at a literal level to help define the interior decor of the play's domestic setting, but as the play progresses, they gradually take on a central significance which reinforces any interpretation of Laura and of the play. Even a character's name can sometimes imply thematic significance. Be careful not to push these possibilities too far, but some-

times the point seems inescapable. "Lysistrata," for example, means "dis-
bander of the armies" in Greek.

10. Irony in a play can be verbal or situational, but there is another kind of
    irony so characteristic of drama that it is called **dramatic irony.** This is the
    term used when we in the audience know details that some of the
    characters on stage do not know. By showing us a character's ignorance of
    the full truth of a situation, for example, it can be used to demonstrate
    that character's blindness. In tragedy, this blindness could lead to catastro-
    phe, as it does in *Oedipus the King* and *Othello;* in comedy, it causes us to
    laugh at the fool.

Other Questions

11. The **setting** of a play will usually be significant; be careful to avoid treating
    it superficially. It is usually easy to identify, but it is harder to analyze its
    importance. This is the only reason for considering it seriously, however.
    For example, in the case of *Lysistrata,* the play's action is set on the same
    hill where it was first produced in the theater. Its subject is in some sense
    the Athenian audience which watches the play, a fact which must some-
    how figure into our calculations about its tone and meaning.

12. **Titles** are carefully chosen by playwrights. What does the title of the play
    you are reading suggest about its meaning? For example, Lorraine Hans-
    berry's title, *A Raisin in the Sun,* is an allusion to Langston Hughes'
    poem "Dream Deferred," whose meaning can enlarge our sense of the
    play (see the headnote to the play on page 684). Playwrights will almost
    always choose titles that will imply part of what they think matters in their
    plays.

13. The final—and perhaps most difficult—questions will be about meaning,
    about significance. What are the play's **thematic concerns?** How do you
    interpret the play? What subjects does it seem to comment on? In the
    essays which follow each play we have suggested some of the directions
    your inquiry might start with but, again, only in the spirit of providing a
    springboard from which you can leap to your own ideas. Remember that a
    play usually reveals most of its significance through indirection, since the
    author cannot manipulate narrative voice for emphasis. However, some-
    times the playwright will state the play's intentions directly in a character's
    dialogue. Therefore, be especially alert to moments in the play that seem
    undramatic: lengthy speeches that seem especially "talky," that express
    generalizations about thematic concerns without furthering the action
    very much. Still, we also need to remember that even a "talky" character
    does not necessarily speak for the author. Playwrights can be tricky, and
    that is part of the fun of constructing your plays from their scripts.

SOME THEORETICAL PERSPECTIVES

Tragedy and Comedy

ARISTOTLE

Aristotle was, with Socrates and Plato, one of the three famous ancient Greek philosophers from the fourth century B.C. who have, by and large, determined the direction of western philosophy. In his work usually referred to in English by the title *The Poetics*, Aristotle turned his analytical methodology to works of literature, especially to drama, and within drama, especially to tragedy. As in other fields of philosophy, the questions Aristotle raised remain central—here to subsequent literary criticism and literary theory. Aristotle's primary model for tragedy was Sophocles' *Oedipus the King*. As this excerpt indicates, Aristotle emphasizes the effects tragedy has on its audience, and also explains how the dramatic techniques of tragedy achieve these effects.

from *The Poetics*

Translated by S. H. Butcher

From Book VI Tragedy, then, is an imitation of an action that is serious, complete, and of a certain magnitude; in language embellished with each kind of artistic ornament, the several kinds being found in separate parts of the play; in the form of action, not of narrative, through pity and fear effecting the proper purgation of these emotions. . . .

From Book VIII Unity of plot does not, as some persons think, consist in the unity of the hero. For infinitely various are the incidents in one man's life which cannot be reduced to unity; and so, too, there are many actions of one man out of which we cannot make one action. Hence the error, as it appears, of all poets who have composed a Heracleid, a Theseid, or other poems of the kind. They imagine that as Heracles was one man, the story of Heracles must also be a unity. But Homer, as in all else he is of surpassing merit, here too—whether from art or natural genius—seems to have happily discerned the truth. In composing the Odyssey he did not include all the adventures of Odysseus—such as his wound on Parnassus, or his feigned madness at the mustering of the host—incidents between which there was no necessary or probable connexion; but he made the Odyssey, and likewise the Iliad, to centre round an action that in our sense of the word is one. As therefore, in the other imitative arts, the imitation is one when the object imitated is one, so the plot, being an imitation of an action, must imitate one action and that a whole, the structural union of the parts being such that, if any one of them is displaced or removed, the whole will be disjointed and disturbed. For a thing whose presence or absence makes no visible difference, is not an organic part of the whole.

From Book IX   It is, moreover, evident from what has been said, that it is not the function of the poet to relate what has happened, but what may happen,—what is possible according to the law of probability or necessity. The poet and the historian differ not by writing in verse or in prose. The work of Herodotus might be put into verse, and it would still be a species of history, with metre no less than without it. The true difference is that one relates what has happened, the other what may happen. Poetry, therefore, is a more philosophical and a higher thing than history: for poetry tends to express the universal, history the particular. By the universal I mean how a person of a certain type will on occasion speak or act, according to the law of probability or necessity. . . .

Of all plots and actions the epeisodic are the worst. I call a plot 'epeisodic' in which the episodes or acts succeed one another without probable or necessary sequence. Bad poets compose such pieces by their own fault, good poets, to please the players; for, as they write show pieces for competition, they stretch the plot beyond its capacity, and are often forced to break the natural continuity.

But again, Tragedy is an imitation not only of a complete action, but of events inspiring fear or pity. Such an effect is best produced when the events come on us by surprise; and the effect is heightened when, at the same time, they follow as cause and effect. The tragic wonder will then be greater than if they happened of themselves or by accident; for even coincidences are most striking when they have an air of design. We may instance the statue of Mitys at Argos, which fell upon his murderer while he was a spectator at a festival, and killed him. Such events seem not to be due to mere chance. Plots, therefore, constructed on these principles are necessarily the best.

From Book X   Plots are either Simple or Complex, for the actions in real life, of which the plots are an imitation, obviously show a similar distinction. An action which is one and continuous in the sense above defined, I call Simple, when the change of fortune takes place without Reversal of the Situation and without Recognition.

A Complex action is one in which the change is accompanied by such Reversal, or by Recognition, or by both. These last should arise from the internal structure of the plot, so that what follows should be the necessary or probable result of the preceding action. It makes all the difference whether any given event is a case of *propter hoc* or *post hoc*.

From Book XI   Reversal of the Situation is a change by which the action veers round to its opposite, subject always to our rule of probability or necessity. Thus in the Oedipus, the messenger comes to cheer Oedipus and free him from his alarms about his mother, but by revealing who he is, he produces the opposite effect. . . .

Recognition, as the name indicates, is a change from ignorance to knowledge, producing love or hate between the persons destined by the poet for good or bad fortune. The best form of recognition is coincident with a Reversal of the Situation, as in the Oedipus. There are indeed other forms. Even inanimate things of the most trivial kind may in a sense be objects of recognition. Again, we may recognise or discover whether a person has done a thing or not. But the recognition which is most intimately connected with the plot and action is, as we have said, the recognition of persons. This recognition, combined with Reversal, will produce either pity or fear; and actions producing these effects are those which, by our definition, Tragedy represents. Moreover, it is upon such situations that the issues of good or bad fortune will depend. Recognition, then, being between persons, it may happen that one person only is recognised by the other—when the latter is already known—or it may be necessary that the recognition should be on both sides. . . .

From Book XIII   As the sequel to what has already been said, we must proceed to consider what the poet should aim at, and what he should avoid, in constructing his plots; and by what means the specific effect of Tragedy will be produced.

A perfect tragedy should, as we have seen, be arranged not on the simple but on the complex plan. It should, moreover, imitate actions which excite pity and fear, this being the distinctive mark of tragic imitation. It follows plainly, in the first place, that the change of fortune presented must not be the spectacle of a virtuous man brought from prosperity to adversity; for this moves neither pity nor fear; it merely shocks us. Nor, again, that of a bad man passing from adversity to prosperity; for nothing can be more alien to the spirit of Tragedy; it possesses no single tragic quality; it neither satisfies the moral sense nor calls forth pity or fear. Nor, again, should the downfall of the utter villain be exhibited. A plot of this kind would, doubtless, satisfy the moral sense, but it would inspire neither pity nor fear; for pity is aroused by unmerited misfortune, fear by the misfortune of a man like ourselves. Such an event, therefore, will be neither pitiful nor terrible. There remains, then, the character between these two extremes,—that of a man who is not eminently good and just, yet whose misfortune is brought about not by vice or depravity, but by some error or frailty. He must be one who is highly renowned and prosperous,—a personage like Oedipus, Thyestes, or other illustrious men of such families.

A well constructed plot should, therefore, be single in its issue, rather than double as some maintain. The change of fortune should not be from bad to good, but, reversely, from good to bad. It should come about as the result not of vice, but of some great error or frailty, in a character either such as we have described, or better rather than worse. The practice of the stage bears out our view. At first the poets recounted any legend that came in their way. Now, the best tragedies are founded on the story of a few houses,—on the fortunes of Alcmaeon, Oedipus, Orestes, Meleager, Thyestes, Telephus, and those others who have done or suffered something terrible. A tragedy, then, to be perfect according to the rules of art should be of this construction. . . .

NORTHROP FRYE

Northrop Frye's *The Anatomy of Criticism,* written in 1957, describes comedy, as well as tragedy and other genres; here, we have chosen to illustrate his view of comedy. This work is often described as structuralist: Frye emphasizes aspects of plot structure which repeat themselves in many works within a particular genre, so that these plot sequences come to define a reader's expectations of what a genre is and does. These sequences, in turn, are often interpreted in mythic or archetypal terms. It is presumed that there are basic patterns of human experience and identity which transcend particular historical times and that these different patterns and different aspects of human identity are more or less accurately imaged by the patterns and personages in classical (and other) myths. In this way, the patterns of literature are believed to parallel essential truths in human experience; literary genres are believed to express the different modes of human perception.

from *The Anatomy of Criticism*

What normally happens is that a young man wants a young woman, that his desire is resisted by some opposition, usually paternal, and that near the end of the play some twist in the plot enables the hero to have his will. In this simple pattern there are several complex elements. In the first place, the movement of comedy is usually a movement from one kind of society to another. At the beginning of the play the obstructing characters are in charge of the play's society, and the audience recognizes that they are usurpers. At the end of the play the device in the plot that brings hero and heroine together causes a new society to crystallize around the hero, and the moment when this crystallization occurs is the point of resolution in the action, the comic discovery, *anagnorisis* or *cognitio.*

The appearance of this new society is frequently signalized by some kind of party or festive ritual, which either appears at the end of the play or is assumed to take place immediately afterward. . . .

The obstacles to the hero's desire . . . are usually parental, hence comedy often turns on a clash between a son's and a father's will. Thus the comic dramatist as a rule writes for the younger men in his audience, and the older members of almost any society are apt to feel that comedy has something subversive about it. . . .

The tendency of comedy is to include as many people as possible in its final society: the blocking characters are more often reconciled or converted than simply repudiated. Comedy often includes a scapegoat ritual of expulsion which gets rid of some irreconcilable character, but exposure and disgrace make for pathos, or even tragedy. *The Merchant of Venice* seems almost an experiment in coming as close as possible to upsetting the comic balance. . . .

There are two ways of developing the form of comedy: one is to throw the main emphasis on the blocking characters; the other is to throw it forward on the scenes of discovery and reconciliation. One is the general tendency of comic irony, satire, realism, and studies of manners; the other is the tendency of Shakespearean and other types of romantic comedy. . . .

Comedy usually moves toward a happy ending, and the normal response of the audience to a happy ending is "this should be," which sounds like a moral judgement. So it is, except that it is not moral in the restricted sense, but social. Its opposite is not the villainous but the absurd. . . . In tragedy . . . enmity almost always includes hatred; comedy is different, and one feels that the social judgement against the absurd is closer to the comic norm than the moral judgement against the wicked.

The question then arises of what makes the blocking character absurd. Ben Jonson explained this by his theory of the "humor," the character dominated by what Pope calls a ruling passion. The humor's dramatic function is to express a state of what might be called ritual bondage. He is obsessed by his humor, and his function in the play is primarily to repeat his obsession. A sick man is not a humor, but a hypochondriac is, because, *qua* hypochondriac, he can never admit to good health, and can never do anything inconsistent with the role that he has prescribed for himself. . . .

The humor in comedy is usually someone with a good deal of social prestige and power, who is able to force much of the play's society into line with his obsession. Thus the humor is intimately connected with the theme of the absurd or irrational law that the action of comedy moves toward breaking. . . .

The society emerging at the conclusion of comedy represents, by contrast, a kind of moral norm, or pragmatically free society. Its ideals are seldom defined or formulated: definition and formulation belong to the humors, who want predictable activity. We are simply given to understand that the newly-married couple will live happily ever after, or that at any rate they will get along in a relatively unhumorous and clear-sighted manner. That is one reason why the character of the successful hero is so often left undeveloped: his real life begins at the end of the play, and we have to believe him to be potentially a more interesting character than he appears to be. . . .

Thus the movement . . . from a society controlled by habit, ritual bondage, arbitrary law and the older characters to a society controlled by youth and pragmatic freedom is fundamentally, as the Greek words suggest, a movement from illusion to reality. Illusion is whatever is fixed or definable, and reality is best understood as its negation: whatever reality is, it's not *that*. Hence the importance of the theme of creating and dispelling illusion in comedy: the illusions caused by disguise, obsession, hypocrisy, or unknown parentage. . . .

Comedy ranges from the most savage irony to the most dreamy wish-fulfilment romance, but its structural patterns and characterization are much the same throughout its range.

GEORGE MEREDITH AND HENRI BERGSON

George Meredith's "Essay on Comedy" and Henri Bergson's "Laughter" were both written in the late nineteenth century, within only a few years of each other (Meredith began his work in 1877; Bergson, in 1884). Both Meredith and Bergson locate comedy in an attitude of the perceiver, relating that attitude to comedy's function in society, rather than in the apparently objective qualities of plot and archetypal human identity which interest Frye. The two might, however, disagree about precisely what that attitude is.

from George Meredith, *"Essay on Comedy"*

The comic poet is in the narrow field, or enclosed square, of the society he depicts; and he addresses the still narrower enclosure of men's intellects, with reference to the operation of the social world upon their characters. He is not concerned with beginnings or endings or surroundings, but with what you are now weaving. To understand his work and value it, you must have a sober liking of your kind, and a sober estimate of our civilized qualities. The aim and business of the comic poet are misunderstood, his meaning is not seized nor his point of view taken, when he is accused of dishonoring our nature and being hostile to sentiment, tending to spitefulness and making an unfair use of laughter. Those who detect irony in comedy do so because they choose to see it in life. Poverty, says the satirist, 'has nothing harder in itself than that it makes men ridiculous.' But poverty is never ridiculous to comic perception until it attempts to make its rags conceal its bareness in a forlorn attempt at decency, or foolishly to rival ostentation. . . . Humorist and satirist frequently hunt together as ironists in pursuit of the grotesque, to the exclusion of the comic. That was an affecting moment in the history of the Prince Regent, when the First Gentleman of Europe burst into tears at a sarcastic remark of Beau Brummell's on the cut of his coat. Humor, satire, irony, pounce on it altogether as their common prey. The Comic Spirit eyes, but does not touch, it. Put into action, it would be farcical. It is too gross for comedy.

Incidents of a kind casting ridicule on our unfortunate nature, instead of our conventional life, provoke derisive laughter, which thwarts the comic idea. But derision is foiled by the play of the intellect. Most of doubtful causes in contest are open to comic interpretation, and any intellectual pleading of a doubtful cause contains germs of an idea of comedy.

The laughter of satire is a blow in the back or the face. The laughter of comedy is impersonal and of unrivaled politeness, nearer a smile—often no more than a smile. It laughs through the mind, for the mind directs it; and it might be called the humor of the mind.

One excellent test of the civilization of a country, as I have said, I take to be the flourishing of the comic idea and comedy; and the test of true comedy is that it shall awaken thoughtful laughter.

If you believe that our civilization is founded in common sense (and it is the first condition of sanity to believe it), you will, when contemplating men, discern a Spirit overhead; not more heavenly than the light flashed upward from glassy surfaces, but luminous and watchful; never shooting beyond them, nor lagging in the rear; so closely attached to them that it may be taken for a slavish reflex, until its features are studied. It has the sage's brows, and the sunny malice of a faun lurks at the corners of the half-closed lips drawn in an idle wariness of half-tension. That slim feasting smile, shaped like the long-bow, was once a big round satyr's laugh, that flung up the brows like a fortress lifted by gunpowder. The laugh will come again, but it will be of the order of the smile, finely-tempered, showing sunlight of the mind, mental richness rather than noisy enormity. Its common aspect is one of unsolicitous observation, as if surveying a full field and having leisure to dart on its chosen morsels, without any fluttering eagerness. Men's future upon earth does not attract it; their honesty and shapeliness in the present does; and whenever they wax out of proportion, overblown, affected, pretentious, bombastical, hypocritical, pedantic, fantastically delicate; whenever it sees them self-deceived or hoodwinked, given to run riot in idolatries, drifting into vanities, congregating in absurdities, planning short-sightedly, plotting dementedly; whenever they are at variance with their professions, and violate the unwritten but perceptible laws binding them in consideration one to another; whenever they offend sound reason, fair justice; are false in humility or mined with conceit, individually, or in the bulk; the Spirit overhead will look humanely malign, and cast an oblique light on them, followed by volleys of silvery laughter. That is the Comic Spirit.

Not to distinguish it is to be bull-blind to the spiritual, and to deny the existence of a mind of man where minds are in working conjunction.

from Henri Bergson, *"Laughter"*

Translated by Cloudesley Brereton and Fred Rothwell

The comic is that side of a person which reveals his likeness to a thing, that aspect of human events which, through its peculiar inelasticity, conveys the impression of pure mechanism, of automatism, of movement without life. Consequently it expresses an individual or collective imperfection which calls for an immediate corrective. This corrective is laughter, a social gesture that singles out and represses a special kind of absentmindedness in men and in events. . . .

Comedy can only begin at the point where our neighbor's personality ceases to affect us. It begins, in fact, with what might be called *a growing callousness to social life*. Any individual is comic who automatically goes his own way without troubling himself about getting into touch with the rest of his fellow-beings. It is the part of laughter to reprove his absentmindedness and wake him out of his dream. . . .

In laughter we always find an unavowed intention to humiliate, and consequently to correct our neighbour, if not in his will, at least in his deed. This is the reason a comedy is far more like real life than a drama is. The more sublime the drama, the more profound the analysis to which the poet has had to subject the raw materials of daily life in order to obtain the tragic element in its unadulterated form. On the contrary, it is only in its lower aspects, in light comedy and farce, that comedy is in striking contrast to reality: the higher it rises, the more it approximates to life; in fact, there are scenes in real life so closely bordering on high-class comedy that the stage might adopt them without changing a single word. . . .

It must be acknowledged, however, to the credit of mankind, that there is no essential difference between the social ideal and the moral. We may therefore admit, as a general rule, that it is the faults of others that make us laugh, provided we add that they make us laugh by reason of their *unsociability* rather than of their *immorality*. What, then, are the faults capable of becoming ludicrous, and in what circumstances do we regard them as being too serious to be laughed at?

We have already given an implicit answer to this question. The comic, we said, appeals to the intelligence pure and simple; laughter is incompatible with emotion. Depict some fault, however trifling, in such a way as to arouse sympathy, fear, or pity; the mischief is done, it is impossible for us to laugh. On the other hand, take a downright vice,—even one that is, generally speaking, of an odious nature,—you may make it ludicrous if, by some suitable contrivance, you arrange so that it leaves our emotions unaffected. Not that the vice *must* then be ludicrous, but it *may*, from that time forth, become so. *It must not arouse our feelings;* that is the sole condition really necessary, though assuredly it is not sufficient. . . .

Laughter is, above all, a corrective. Being intended to humiliate, it must make a painful impression on the person against whom it is directed. By laughter, society avenges itself for the liberties taken with it. It would fail in its object if it bore the stamp of sympathy or kindness.

The Absurd

MARTIN ESSLIN

Martin Esslin's *The Theatre of the Absurd* was first published in 1961, after a decade that began with Ionesco's opening barrage of new theater, including his *Jack,* which is anthologized here. Esslin identified this new work by Ionesco and Beckett, among others, as symptomatic of a new and disillusioned age which required a new kind of play as its expression. He thought of this new drama as a hybrid born of new uses and new combinations for traditional forms, as the following excerpts suggest.

from *The Theatre of the Absurd*

After two terrible wars, there are still many who are . . . searching for a way in which they can, with dignity, confront a universe deprived of what was once its centre and its living purpose, a world deprived of a generally accepted integrating principle, which has become disjointed, purposeless—absurd.

The Theatre of the Absurd is one of the expressions of this search. It bravely faces up to the fact that for those to whom the world has lost its central explanation and meaning, it is no longer possible to accept art forms still based on the continuation of standards and concepts that have lost their validity; that is, the possibility of knowing the laws of conduct and ultimate values, as deducible from a firm foundation of revealed certainty about the purpose of man in the universe.

In expressing the tragic sense of loss at the disappearance of ultimate certainties the Theatre of the Absurd, by a strange paradox, is also a symptom of what probably comes nearest to being a genuine religious quest in our age: an effort, however timid and tentative, to sing, to laugh, to weep—and to growl—if not in praise of God (whose name, in Adamov's phrase, has for so long been degraded by usage that it has lost its meaning), at least in search of a dimension of the Ineffable; an effort to make man aware of the ultimate realities of his condition, to instil in him again the lost sense of cosmic wonder and primeval anguish, to shock him out of an existence that has become trite, mechanical, complacent, and deprived of the dignity that comes of awareness. For God is dead, above all, to the masses who live from day to day and have lost all contact with the basic facts—and mysteries—of the human condition with which, in former times, they were kept in touch through the living ritual of their religion, which made them parts of a real community and not just atoms in an atomized society.

The Theatre of the Absurd forms part of the unceasing endeavour of the true artists of our time to breach this dead wall of complacency and automatism and to re-establish an awareness of man's situation when confronted with the ultimate reality of his condition. As such, the Theatre of the Absurd fulfils a dual purpose and presents its audience with a two-fold absurdity.

In one of its aspects it castigates, satirically, the absurdity of lives lived unaware and unconscious of ultimate reality. This is the feeling of the deadness and mechanical senselessness of half-conscious lives, the feeling of 'human beings secreting inhumanity', which Camus describes in *The Myth of Sisyphus:*

> In certain hours of lucidity, the mechanical aspect of their gestures, their senseless pantomime, makes stupid everything around them. A man speaking on the telephone behind a glass partition—one cannot hear him but observes his trivial gesturing. One asks oneself, why is he alive? This malaise in front of man's own inhumanity, this incalculable letdown when faced with the image of what we are, this 'nausea', as a contemporary writer calls it, also is the Absurd.[1]

This is the experience that Ionesco expresses in plays like *The Bald Prima Donna* or *The Chairs,* Adamov in *La Parodie,* or N. F. Simpson in *A Resounding Tinkle.* It represents the satirical, parodistic aspect of the Theatre of the Absurd, its social criticism, its pillorying of an unauthentic, petty society. This may be the most easily accessible, and therefore most widely recognized, message of the Theatre of the Absurd, but it is far from being its most essential or most significant feature.

In its second, more positive aspect, behind the satirical exposure of the absurdity of inauthentic ways of life, the Theatre of the Absurd is facing up to a deeper layer of absurdity—the absurdity of the human condition itself in a world where the decline of religious belief has deprived man of certainties. When it is no longer possible to accept complete closed systems of values and revelations of divine purpose, life must be faced in its ultimate, stark reality. That is why, in the analysis of the dramatists of the Absurd . . . , we have always seen man stripped of the accidental circumstances of social position or historical context, confronted with the basic choices, the basic situations of his existence. . . .

Concerned as it is with the ultimate realities of the human condition, the relatively few fundamental problems of life and death, isolation and communication, the Theatre of the Absurd, however grotesque, frivolous, and irreverent it may appear, represents a return to the original, religious function of the theatre—the confrontation of man with the spheres of myth and religious reality. Like ancient Greek tragedy and the medieval mystery plays and baroque allegories, the Theatre of the Absurd is intent on making its audience aware of man's precarious and mysterious position in the universe.

The difference is merely that in ancient Greek tragedy—and comedy—as well as in the medieval mystery play and the baroque *auto sacramental,* the ultimate realities concerned were generally known and universally accepted metaphysical systems, while the Theatre of the Absurd expresses the absence of any such generally accepted cosmic system of values. Hence, much more modestly, the Theatre of the Absurd makes no pretence at explaining the ways of God to man. It can merely present, in anxiety or with derision, an individual human being's intuition of the ultimate realities as he experiences them; the fruits of one man's descent into the depths of his personality, his dreams, fantasies, and nightmares.

While former attempts at confronting man with the ultimate realities of his condition projected a coherent and generally recognized version of the truth, the Theatre of the Absurd merely communicates one poet's most intimate and personal intuition of the human situation, his own *sense of being,* his individual vision of the world. This is the *subject-matter* of the Theatre of the Absurd, and it determines its *form,* which must, of necessity, represent a convention of the stage basically different from the 'realistic' theatre of our time.

1. Camus, *Le Mythe de Sisyphe* (Paris: Gallimard, 1942), p. 29.

As the Theatre of the Absurd is not concerned with conveying information or presenting the problems or destinies of characters that exist outside the author's inner world, as it does not expound a thesis or debate ideological propositions, it is not concerned with the representation of events, the narration of the fate or the adventures of characters, but instead with the presentation of one individual's basic situation. It is a theatre of situation as against a theatre of events in sequence, and therefore it uses a language based on patterns of concrete images rather than argument and discursive speech. And since it is trying to present a sense of being, it can neither investigate nor solve problems of conduct or morals.

Because the Theatre of the Absurd projects its author's personal world, it lacks objectively valid characters. It cannot show the clash of opposing temperaments or study human passions locked in conflict, and is therefore not dramatic in the accepted sense of the term. Nor is it concerned with telling a story in order to communicate some moral or social lesson. . . .

A son who tells his father that he loves and respects him is objectively bound to be, in fact, filled with the deepest Oedipal hatred of his father. He may not know it, but he means the opposite of what he says. And the subconscious has a higher content of reality than the conscious utterance.

The relativization, devaluation, and criticism of language are also the prevailing trends in contemporary philosophy. . . .

But even more significant than these tendencies in Marxist, psychological, and philosophical thinking is the trend of the times in the workaday world of the man in the street. Exposed to the incessant, and inexorably loquacious, onslaught of the mass media, the press, and advertising, the man in the street becomes more and more sceptical toward the language he is exposed to. The citizens of totalitarian countries know full well that most of what they are told is double-talk, devoid of real meaning. They become adept at reading between the lines; that is, at guessing at the reality the language conceals rather than reveals. In the West, euphemisms and circumlocutions fill the press or resound from the pulpits. And advertising, by its constant use of superlatives, has succeeded in devaluing language to a point where it is a generally accepted axiom that most of the words one sees displayed on billboards or in the coloured pages of magazine advertising are as meaningless as the jingles of television commercials. A yawning gulf has opened between language and reality.

Apart from the general devaluation of language in the flood of mass communications, the growing specialization of life has made the exchange of ideas on an increasing number of subjects impossible between members of different spheres of life which have each developed their own specialized jargons. As Ionesco says, in summarizing, and enlarging on, the views of Antonin Artaud:

> As our knowledge becomes separated from life, our culture no longer contains ourselves (or only an insignificant part of ourselves), for it forms a 'social' context into which we are not integrated. So the problem becomes that of bringing our life back into contact with our culture, making it a living culture once again. To achieve this, we shall first have to kill 'the respect for what is written down in black and white' . . . to break up our language so that it can be put together again in order to re-establish contact with 'the absolute', or, as I should prefer to say, 'with multiple reality'; it is imperative to 'push human beings again towards seeing themselves as they really are'.[2]

2. Ionesco, 'Ni un dieu, ni un démon', *Cahiers de la Compagnie Madeleine Renaud—Jean-Louis Barrault*, Paris, nos. 22–3, May 1958, p. 131.

That is why communication between human beings is so often shown in a state of breakdown in the Theatre of the Absurd. It is merely a satirical magnification of the existing state of affairs. Language has run riot in an age of mass communication. It must be reduced to its proper function—the expression of authentic content, rather than its concealment. But this will be possible only if man's reverence toward the spoken or written word as a means of communication is restored, and the ossified clichés that dominate thought (as they do in the limericks of Edward Lear or the world of Humpty Dumpty) are replaced by a living language that serves it. And this, in turn, can be achieved only if the limitations of logic and discursive language are recognized and respected, and the uses of poetic language acknowledged.

The means by which the dramatists of the Absurd express their critique—largely instinctive and unintended—of our disintegrating society are based on suddenly confronting their audiences with a grotesquely heightened and distorted picture of a world that has gone mad. This is a shock therapy that achieves . . . the inhibition of the audience's identification with the characters on the stage (which is the age-old and highly effective method of the traditional theatre) and its replacement by a detached, critical attitude.

If we identify ourselves with the main character in a play, we automatically accept his point of view, see the world in which he moves with *his* eyes, feel *his* emotions. . . .

In the Theatre of the Absurd, on the other hand, the audience is confronted with characters whose motives and actions remain largely incomprehensible. With such characters it is almost impossible to identify; the more mysterious their action and their nature, the less human the characters become, the more difficult it is to be carried away into seeing the world from their point of view. Characters with whom the audience fails to identify are inevitably comic. If we identified with the figure of farce who loses his trousers, we should feel embarrassment and shame. If, however, our tendency to identify has been inhibited by making such a character grotesque, we laugh at his predicament. We see what happens to him from the outside, rather than from his own point of view. As the incomprehensibility of the motives, and the often unexplained and mysterious nature of the characters' actions in the Theatre of the Absurd effectively prevent identification, such theatre is a comic theatre in spite of the fact that its subject-matter is sombre, violent, and bitter. That is why the Theatre of the Absurd transcends the category of comedy and tragedy and combines laughter with horror.

Metatheater

LIONEL ABEL

Lionel Abel published *Metatheatre: A New View of Dramatic Form* in 1963 as a conscious challenge to Esslin's book, published two years earlier. Abel believes that disillusionment is not new and that what is fundamentally different about the *avant garde* drama of the 1950s and 1960s is not its disillusionment, but its attitude toward dramatic form. He believes the distinguishing characteristic of much that is new on the stage is its metadramatic quality, its tendency to treat a play as an open rather than a closed form and to point out to the audience its own consciousness of itself as play—that is, as pretense, as illusion, as a made thing, *not* as an attempt to create the illusion that it is "real." In this brief excerpt, Abel contrasts the attitude toward reality implied by traditional dramatic forms (which he encloses here within the term "tragedy") and the attitude which he believes is implied by metatheater.

from *Metatheatre*

To summarize the values and disvalues of tragedy and metatheatre:

Tragedy gives by far the stronger sense of the reality of the world. Metatheatre gives by far the stronger sense that the world is a projection of human consciousness.

Tragedy glorifies the structure of the world, which it supposedly reflects in its own form. Metatheatre glorifies the unwillingness of the imagination to regard any image of the world as ultimate.

Tragedy makes human existence more vivid by showing its vulnerability to fate. Metatheatre makes human existence more dreamlike by showing that fate can be overcome.

Tragedy tries to mediate between the world and man. Tragedy wants to be on both sides. Metatheatre assumes there is no world except that created by human striving, human imagination.

Tragedy cannot operate without the assumption of an ultimate order. For metatheatre, order is something continually improvised by men.

There is no such thing as humanistic tragedy. There is no such thing as religious metatheatre. George Lukacs has said that the principal spectator of tragedy is God. I cannot imagine God present at a play of Shaw, Pirandello, or Genet. I cannot imagine Godot enjoying *Waiting for Godot*.

Tragedy, from the point of view of metatheatre, is our dream of the real. Metatheatre, from the point of view of tragedy, is as real as are our dreams.

Nicolai Hartmann distinguishes the "depth of succession" from the "breadth of simultaneity." The first is the province of tragedy. The second belongs to metatheatre.

Tragedy transcends optimism and pessimism, taking us beyond both these attitudes. Metatheatre makes us forget the opposition between optimism and pessimism by forcing us to wonder.

Shall we not stop lamenting the "death" of tragedy and value justly the dramatic form which Western civilization—and that civilization only—has been able to create and to refine?

Against Tradition

ANTONIN ARTAUD AND JOHN McGRATH

The two essays by Antonin Artaud excerpted here were published in France in 1932 and 1933, while John McGrath's *A Good Night Out* was published in England in 1981. Artaud is a visionary and McGrath, a socialist. However, although their habits of thought are very different, as are their conceptions of what the theater can be, they agree that it can be important to society and that to reach its possibilities it must change radically. McGrath's essay was originally written as a public lecture, and some of the rhetoric appropriate to oral delivery is still evident. Internal references at the start of the excerpt indicate that it was originally the third in a series of weekly lectures delivered at Cambridge University.

from Antonin Artaud, *The Theater of Cruelty*

Translated by Helen Weaver

Instead of relying on texts that are regarded as definitive and as sacred we must first of all put an end to the subjugation of the theater to the text, and rediscover the notion of a kind of unique language halfway between gesture and thought.

This language can only be defined in terms of the possibilities of dynamic expression in space as opposed to the expressive possibilities of dialogue. And what theater can still wrest from speech is its potential for expansion beyond words, for development in space, for a dissociative and vibratory effect on our sensibilities. This is the function of intonations, the particular way a word is uttered. And beyond the auditory language of sounds, this is the function of the visual language of objects, movements, attitudes, gestures, but provided their meaning, their physiognomy, their combinations, are extended until they become signs and these signs become a kind of alphabet. Once the theater has become aware of this language in space, which is a language of sounds, cries, lights, onomatopoeia, it must organize it by making the characters and the objects true hieroglyphs, and by utilizing their symbolism and their correspondences in relation to all organs and on all levels.

The question for the theater, then, is to create a metaphysics of speech, gesture, and expression, in order to rescue it from its psychological and human stagnation. But all this can be of use only if there is behind such an effort a kind of real metaphysical temptation, an appeal to certain unusual ideas which by their very nature cannot be limited, or even formally defined. These ideas, which have to do with Creation, with Becoming, with Chaos, and are all of a cosmic order, provide an elementary notion of a realm from which the theater has become totally estranged. These ideas can create a kind of passionate equation between Man, Society, Nature, and Objects.

It is not a question, however, of putting metaphysical ideas directly on the stage, but of creating various kinds of temptations, of indrafts of air around these ideas. And humor with its anarchy, poetry with its symbolism and its images, provide a kind of elementary notion of how to channel the temptation of these ideas.

We must now consider the purely material aspect of this language. That is, of all the ways and means it has of acting on the sensibility.

It would be meaningless to say that this language relies on music, dance, pantomime, or mimicry. Obviously it utilizes movements, harmonies, and rhythms, but only insofar as they can converge in a kind of central expression, without favoring any particular art. This does not mean, either, that it does not make use of ordinary events, ordinary passions, but it uses them only as a springboard, just as HUMOR-AS-DESTRUCTION, through laughter, can serve to win over to its side the habits of reason.

from Antonin Artaud, *An End to Masterpieces*

Translated by Helen Weaver

One reason for the asphyxiating atmosphere in which we live without possible escape or recourse—and for which we are all responsible, even the most revolutionary among us—is this respect for what has already been written, formulated, or painted, what has been given form, as if all expression were not finally exhausted and had not reached the point where things must fall apart if they are to begin again.

We must put an end to this idea of masterpieces reserved for a so-called elite, and which the mass of people do not understand; we must realize that the mind has no restricted districts like those set apart for clandestine sexual encounters.

The masterpieces of the past are good for the past: they are not good for us. We have a right to say what has been said and even what has not been said in a way which pertains to us, which is immediate and direct, which corresponds to present modes of feeling, and which everyone will understand.

It is idiotic to blame the masses for having no sense of the sublime, when we confuse the sublime with one of its formal manifestations, which are always dead manifestations. And if, for example, the modern mass audience no longer understands *Oedipus Rex,* I would go so far as to say that this is the fault of *Oedipus Rex* and not the fault of the audience.

In *Oedipus Rex* there is the theme of Incest and the idea that nature ridicules morality, and that there are forces at large somewhere which we would do well to beware of, whether we call these forces *destiny* or something else.

There is also the presence of an epidemic of the plague which is a physical embodiment of these forces. But all this is in costumes and in language which have lost all contact with the crude and epileptic rhythm of our time. Sophocles speaks grandly perhaps, but in a manner that is no longer relevant to the age. He speaks too subtly for this age, as if he were speaking beside the point.

However, a mass audience that trembles at train wrecks, that is familiar with earthquakes, plague, revolution, war, that is sensitive to the disorderly throes of love, is capable of reaching all these high ideas and asks only to be made aware of them, provided one speaks to them in their own language, and provided these ideas do not come to them by way of costumes and an overrefined language which belong to dead ages, ages that will never be brought to life again.

Today, as in the past, the masses are hungry for mystery: they ask only to become aware of the laws according to which destiny is revealed and perhaps to guess the secret of its manifestations.

Let us leave textual criticism to academic drudges and formal criticism to aesthetes, and recognize that what has been said need not be said again; that an expression does not work twice, does not live twice; that all words, once uttered, are dead and are effective only at the moment when they are uttered; that a form that has been used has no function but to urge us to look for another; and that the theater is the only place in the world where a gesture, once made, can never be exactly duplicated.

If the masses do not come to literary masterpieces it is because these masterpieces are literary, that is, fixed; and fixed in forms that no longer respond to the needs of the time.

Far from blaming the masses and the public, we should blame the formal screen which we interpose between ourselves and the masses, and this new form of idolatry of fixed masterpieces which is one of the aspects of bourgeois conformity.

This conformity which causes us to confuse sublimity, ideas, things with the forms they have assumed down through the ages and in ourselves—in our mentalities, the mentalities of snobs, fops, and aesthetes whom the public no longer understands.

There is no point in accusing the bad taste of a public that slakes its thirst with nonsense, as long as one has not shown the public a valid spectacle; and I defy anyone to show me *here* a valid spectacle, valid in the highest sense of theater, since the last great romantic melodramas, that is, in the past hundred years.

The public which takes the false for the true has a feeling for the true, and always responds to it when it does appear. However, it is not on the stage that one must look for truth today, but in the street; and if one offers the crowd in the streets an opportunity to show its human dignity, it will always do so.

If the masses have lost the habit of going to the theater; if we have all come to regard the theater as an inferior art, a means of vulgar distraction, and to use it as an outlet for our bad instincts—this is because we have been told too often that it was theater, that is, lies and illusion. It is because for four hundred years, that is, since the Renaissance, we have become accustomed to a purely descriptive and narrative theater, a theater that tells us about psychology.

It is because much ingenuity has been exerted to bring to life on the stage creatures that are plausible but detached, with the spectacle on one side and the audience on the other—and because the masses are no longer shown anything but the mirror image of what they are.

Shakespeare himself is responsible for this aberration and for this decay, for this disinterested idea of the theater according to which a theatrical performance leaves the audience intact, without one image thrown off that produces its vibration in the organism, leaving an impression that will never be erased.

If in Shakespeare man is sometimes preoccupied by that which transcends him, ultimately it is always a question of the consequences of this preoccupation for man, that is, of psychology.

Psychology, with its relentless effort to reduce the unknown to the known, that is, the daily and the ordinary, is the cause of this decline and this terrible loss of energy, which seems to me to have reached its lowest point. And it seems to me that both the theater and we ourselves must have done with psychology.

Indeed, I believe that on this point we are all in agreement and that there is no need to descend to the revolting level of modern French theater in order to condemn psychological theater.

Stories about money, money anxieties, social climbing, throes of love untouched by altruism, sexuality sprinkled with an eroticism lacking in mystery, may be psychology, but they are not theater. These anxieties, this lechery, these ruttings in the presence of which we are reduced to lip-smacking voyeurs, turn to revolution and to vinegar: we must become aware of this.

But this is not the most serious aspect.

If Shakespeare and his imitators have gradually instilled in us an idea of art for art's sake, with art on one side and life on the other, one could rely on this ineffectual and lazy idea as long as life outside held together. But it is now clear from too many signs that everything that once sustained our lives is coming apart, that we are all mad, desperate, and sick. And I urge *us* to react.

This idea of a detached art, of poetry as something charming that exists only to beguile our leisure time, is a decadent idea, and it demonstrates loudly our capacity for castration. . . .

We must put an end to this superstition of texts and of *written* poetry. Written poetry is valuable once, and after that it should be destroyed. Let the dead poets make way for the others. And we should be able to see that it is our veneration for what has already been done, however beautiful and valuable it may be, that petrifies us, that immobilizes us and keeps us from making contact with the underlying force, whether you call it mental energy, the life force, the determinism of exchanges, the lunar menses, or whatever you like. Beneath the poetry of texts there is poetry pure and simple, without form and without text. And just as the efficacy of those masks that are used in the magical rites of certain tribes is exhausted—and the masks are then good for nothing but to be put in museums—so the poetic efficacy of a text is exhausted; but the poetry and efficacy of the theater are exhausted least quickly, since they include the action of what is expressed in gestures and in speech, and which never occurs twice in the same way.

from John McGrath, *A Good Night Out*

The sub-title of these lectures is: 'Contemporary Theatre and the *Mediation* of Reality'. It is not the *Meditation* of Reality as announced in the Cambridge University Lecture list—a misprint entirely appropriate to this place of learning. I am trying to discuss a more active intervention by the theatre in forming contemporary life and contributing to the future of our society.

I could have called them 'Telling the Story'—because that's what theatre does. You go into a space, and some other people use certain devices to tell you a story. Because they have power over you, in a real sense, while you are there, they make a choice, with political implications, as to which story to tell—and how to tell it.

But we go in, watch their story, and come out, changed. If their work is good, and skilfully written, presented and acted, we come out feeling exhilarated: we are more alive for seeing it, more aware of the possibilities of the human race, more fully human ourselves. So far, so wonderfully universal. But this story we watch can have a meaning: a very specific meaning. What if we are black, say, and we go to see some splendidly effective, but completely racist theatre show? What if we are Jewish, and go to see a piece of anti-semitic drama such as one could easily see in Germany in the 1930s? Are we quite so exhilarated? Quite so fully human? Or would we not feel demeaned, excluded from humanity, diminished in our possibilities and a great deal more pessimistic about the future of the human race than when we went in? The meaning, and value, of theatre can clearly change from country to country, group to group, and—significantly—from class to class.

What does this mean then? That not *all* stories are so wonderfully universal? That the political and social values of the play cannot be the same for one audience as they are for another? What a terribly confusing state of affairs!

How can you know where you stand? How can you be suitably academic, objective and withdrawn? How can you make a universally valid *judgement*?

It is next to impossible to take the existence of various different audiences into account, to codify their possible reactions to a piece of theatre, to evaluate a piece of theatre from *within several frameworks*. So what do we do? Well, I'll tell you what most of us do—we take the point of view of a *normal* person—usually that of a well-fed, white, middle class, sensitive but sophisticated literary critic: and we *universalize* it as *the* response.

The effect of such a practice is to enshrine certain specific values and qualities of a play above others. For example, mystery—or mysteriousness as it so often becomes. How often has this 'all-pervading air of mystery' been praised by critic and academic alike, from Yeats's *Purgatory* down through Beckett to our own cut-price product, Harold Pinter? Mystery, the ingredient that leavens the loaf—or should I say makes the dough rise?

But many audiences don't like mystery, in that sense of playing games with knowledge, and words, and facts. They become impatient, they want to know what the story is meant to be about, what is supposed to have happened. They wish a different order of mystery. But because we have universalized the critical response to 'mystery' that proclaims it as a truly wonderful thing, we now have to dismiss those audiences as philistine, as outside true theatre culture, as—and this is the Arnold Wesker refinement—in need of education. My belief, and the basis of my practice as a writer in the theatre for the last ten years, has been that there *are* indeed different kinds of audiences, with different theatrical values and expectations, and that we have to be very careful before consigning one audience and its values to the critical dustbin. Unfortunately, almost all the current assumptions of critical thought do precisely that, by universalizing white middle-class sensitive but sophisticated taste to the status of exclusive arbiter of a true art or culture. I intend to devote the third of these lectures to a more detailed analysis of the differences of value between the two main kinds of theatre audience in this country, the 'educated' middle-class audience, and the 'philistine' working-class audience. For the time being let me just note that there is indeed a difference, and that I do not accept the following assumptions:

1. that art is universal, capable of meaning the same to all people;

2. that the more 'universal' it is, the better it is;

3. that the 'audience' for theatre is an idealized white, middle-class, etc., person and that all theatre should be dominated by the tastes and values of such a person;

4. that, therefore, an audience without such an idealized person's values is an inferior audience; and

5. that the so-called 'traditional values' of English literature are now anything other than an indirect cultural expression of the dominance over the whole of Britain of the ruling class of the south-east of England.

To be more specific, I *do* believe that there is a working-class audience for theatre in Britain which makes demands, and which has values, which are different from those enshrined in our idealized middle-class audience. That these values are not less 'valid'—whatever that means—no less rich in potential for a thriving theatre-culture, no thinner in 'traditions' and subtleties than the current dominant theatre-culture, and that these values and demands contain within them the seeds of a new basis for making theatre that could in many ways be more appropriate to the last quarter of the twentieth century than the stuff that presently goes on at the National Theatre, or at the Aldwych.

Having planted the revolutionary suggestion that middle-class theatre is not by definition the only, or even necessarily the best, kind of theatre, I would like to complicate matters further by talking a little about the 'language'—as they say—of theatre.

Why is the question of the 'language' of theatre a problem? First, let us glance at recent cinema criticism. Here we see a fairly clear consensus, whatever may be the opinions about it, on the subject of the 'language' of cinema. The 'language' of cinema includes the text, the *mise-en-scène,* the lighting, the editing, the locations, the performances, the casting, the camera angles, the use of filters, the music, the effects-track, the framing—in short, everything that is communicated by the reels of celluloid which make up the experience of cinema when adequately projected.

Theatre, however, is still discussed as if it were a book. Now I hope I don't need to say that there does exist a huge body of *dramatic literature,* which is rarely performed and whose 'language' is indeed that of words on the page—and it is far from inadequate as a source of immense literary pleasure.

And of course there is no doubt that words constitute a major element in the language of theatre. But I would remind you that words, the text, may well not be a decisive element in theatre. In fact, the sum total of what happens on the stage may not, in extreme circumstances, be decisive, as Mrs Lincoln once remarked.

I must emphasise that the language of theatre is possibly even more extensive than that normally ascribed to cinema. For not only must the text, *mise-en-scène,* lighting, performances, casting, music, effects, placing on the stage all be taken into account in order to arrive at a description of the stage event, but also the nature of the audience, the nature, social, geographical and physical, of the venue, the price of tickets, the availability of tickets, the nature and placing of the pre-publicity, where the nearest pub is, and the relationships between all these considerations themselves and of each with what is happening on stage. For when we discuss theatre, we are discussing a social event, and a very complex social event, with a long history and many elements, each element also having a long and independent history.

To complicate matters further, each occasion of theatre is different, evanescent and impossible to record. Of course this does not reduce us to silence. But what it does do all too often is to reduce the language of theatre that is studied academically to the most easily obtainable—the words. Perhaps that study will include pictures of the set or leading actors, and descriptions of the theatre building, but, above all, it will be concerned with the words said to have been uttered on the stage. You can buy them in a book, they never change, they are convenient objects of study. But words are not the 'language' of theatre, and by exclusively attending to them we reduce, impoverish the event for academic convenience. The act of *creating theatre* has nothing to do with the making of dramatic literature: dramatic literature is what is sometimes left behind when theatre has been and gone. . . .

The devices and conventions of theatre are very much part of the language, and can, at times, be decisive. They do indeed have meaning, quite apart from that they 'carry' in terms of 'content'. And in the case of bourgeois theatre, the meaning of these devices and conventions is most frequently one which supports the cultural, social, political and economic dominance of the ruling and middle classes, and is hostile to the growth to full cultural maturity of—and of course any increase in the political power of—the working class. Now this is quite a serious message to be putting across before you have even written your play. As I indicated last week, it can often be a message which cancels out the meaning of the 'content' of an apparently 'progressive' piece of writing, or at least creates enough contradictions and confusions to render it meaningless. It is a message to which I, and many others, are opposed.

Perhaps it would be valuable to clarify one or two political points. I can see no way of discussing contemporary theatre, or the way reality is mediated, without the participants in the discussion declaring, or at least being aware of, their political position. A minimal statement of my own position might be summarised as follows: ours is a class society, and, notwithstanding the welfare state, nationalisation, the TUC and the Labour Party, the class which owns, controls or manages private capital and state capital is a coherent social entity with immense power; the British state and its institutions are organized in the interests of that ruling class, which is supported in its position of power by intermediate classes dependent upon the social order it creates for their well-being and their superiority over the working class, i.e., the middle and professional classes, and the petty bourgeoisie; and all these classes combine to reproduce this system because it works in their interest, and the most effective way to reproduce the system is to create an overpowering ideology which penetrates all areas of the individual consciousness, in order to legitimate class rule and maintain it. I see the bourgeois theatre in all its forms as part of that legitimating ideology. In opposition there are sections of, or individuals within, all the above groups and classes: they are, however, powerless without the main opposition group, those who are in fact exploited,—economically, physically, medically, culturally, socially—the much maligned working class.

The interests of this class are in contradiction to those of the ruling class, who need more production for less money in order to survive in a competitive world market. The working class in Britain expresses its opposition most vociferously in terms of cash, simple economist demands which have succeeded to some extent in raising the level of material welfare of many workers and their families. But these ignore those other forms of deprivation and exploitation, which actually keep the working class in an inferior position and perpetuate the class structure of late capitalism.

MICHEL FOUCAULT

In the preceding excerpts from Antonin Artaud we have seen a demand that both the authority of a text in determining the nature of a play, and the authority of evaluations which assign greatness to a play, must be obliterated. In the excerpt from John McGrath, we have seen closely related beliefs: a denial of the universality of any play and an assertion that the manner of writing and staging any play is ideologically charged. Michel Foucault was in the forefront of contemporary efforts to understand the machinery by which particular societies work, and therefore by which individuals in a particular society are pressured, and by which the defining ideology governing (and limiting) individual lives is set. In this excerpt from an essay first published in 1969, Foucault discusses the implications of his social analysis for the concept we have traditionally called "the author," but which he calls the "author-function" at some times and the "subject" at others. Where Artaud and McGrath argue about plays and the theater, Foucault investigates their presumed creator. However, by thinking of "authors" in terms of the forces which work on them, rather than as independent creators, he attempts to undermine this basic assumption of traditional literary criticism.

from *What Is an Author?*

Translated by Donald F. Bouchard and Sherry Simon

Suspicions arise concerning the absolute nature and creative role of the subject. But the subject should not be entirely abandoned. It should be reconsidered, not to restore the theme of an originating subject, but to seize its functions, its intervention in discourse, and its system of dependencies. We should suspend the typical questions: how does a free subject penetrate the density of things and endow them with meaning; how does it accomplish its design by animating the rules of discourse from within? Rather, we should ask: under what conditions and through what forms can an entity like the subject appear in the order of discourse; what position does it occupy; what functions does it exhibit; and what rules does it follow in each type of discourse? In short, the subject (and its substitutes) must be stripped of its creative role and analysed as a complex and variable function of discourse.

The author—or what I have called the "author-function"—is undoubtedly only one of the possible specifications of the subject and, considering past historical transformations, it appears that the form, the complexity, and even the existence of this function are far from immutable. We can easily imagine a culture where discourse would circulate without any need for an author. Discourses, whatever their status, form, or value, and regardless of our manner of handling them, would unfold in a pervasive anonymity. No longer the tiresome repetitions:

"Who is the real author?"

"Have we proof of his authenticity and originality?"

"What has he revealed of his most profound self in his language?"

New questions will be heard:

"What are the modes of existence of this discourse?"

"Where does it come from; how is it circulated; who controls it?"

"What placements are determined for possible subjects?"

"Who can fulfill these diverse functions of the subject?"

Behind all these questions we would hear little more than the murmur of indifference:

"What matter who's speaking?"

AN ANTHOLOGY OF PLAYS

THE GREEK THEATER

The ancient Greek theater was communal. The one in Athens, for example, provided seats (stone benches) for all 16,000 of its citizens. Set in an open-air amphitheater, its center was a circular acting area which was nearly surrounded by the semicircular rings of audience rising above it. This central acting area was bare, with neither scenery nor artificial lighting. The modern theater's visual separation of players from audience—by footlights and spotlights, for instance—did not yet exist. Since both the stage and the audience shared the same lighting, the actors were embedded, as it were, within their community—ringed on three sides by the audience with whom they shared the same natural light. As a result, these ancient Greek actors were in a position to represent their community, its history and legends, its ideas and beliefs, even its skepticism about these beliefs. In this theater, the most important ideas of Greek society were made part of public life and public debate.

This playing area was invested with a strong sense of the sacred. Its actors were privileged to enact the intertwined religious and social heritage of their community. Indeed, as if to emphasize this point, the theater itself was always dedicated to a god. In Athens, site of the first performances of the Greek plays in this text, the god was Dionysus; his theater was on the side of the hill of rock whose smoothed top was called the Akropolis, where the major government and religious buildings were placed. Chief among these buildings was the Parthenon, the temple of the city's patron goddess, Athena. If one drew a straight line from the center of the acting area in the theater of Dionysus through the center of the audience, this line would climb up the hill behind the audience, cross the Akropolis to the Parthenon, and lead directly within to a huge statue of the goddess herself. The nature and placement of the theater were integral to the belief structure of its society.

Within a performance, this sense of community was further reinforced by the chorus, a group of actors who chanted and danced in unison and who represented either the citizens as a whole or a particular and significant segment of the citizens (the elders, the women, etc.). The dramatic style of the plays produced in this theater is more suggestive of religious ritual than of real life. The action alternates between the songs of the chorus and the scenes in which a very limited number of characters speak to one another in dialogue. Sophocles is generally credited with the innovation of adding a third actor onstage; previously only two characters at a time were represented. The leader of the chorus, acting as the group's representative, could also engage in dialogue with the main characters. When an exchange of dialogue is completed, the characters leave the stage and the chorus comes forward to comment on it. Frequently its point of view is the cue for our own reactions, since it often seems to provide something of a model response to the play's events.

Also, since the chorus never leaves its area during the play and thus is always present before the audience, the play's fictional time and place does not change, once established. If the imagined space is established as the public area outside of the palace of King Oedipus in Thebes, that is what it remains throughout the duration of the play. How could it change if the chorus remains always present outside his door? This convention is usually referred to as **unity of place**. In addition, the amount of time imagined to have elapsed during the play is identical to the amount of time it takes to enact the play. If the play lasts for two hours, it depicts two hours from the lives of the characters. This second convention is usually referred to as **unity of time**. The result of this spatial and temporal concentration is that Greek plays typically portray a single climactic moment in a hero's life. His or her whole life turns on the events of a few minutes, but those minutes imply the events of a lifetime—or more, as in the case of Oedipus, where the significant events began before his life was conceived.

A classical Greek play typically presents no violent action and uses no sets; we see only a series of scenes in which two, or sometimes three, men on a bare stone circle speak from behind face masks whose expressions are set in different extremes of human emotions. They represent types of people as much as they do individuals. What we hear them speak is poetry, not realistic speech. The plots of these plays, particularly in tragedy, are likely to be taken from traditional legends, so that suspense is not a major concern: The audience knows the ending in advance. Our interest is not so much in how the action will turn out, but in the new twist that the playwright gives the familiar material, the new nuances of meaning he teases from it. As modern readers coming to these plays for the first time, we must concentrate on *how* things happen as much as on what it is that happens.

Sophocles

OEDIPUS THE KING

Translated by Robert Bagg

About the Author   Sophocles (495?–406 B.C.) is probably the most famous of ancient Greek tragic playwrights, better known today than his two great contemporaries, the older Aeschylus and the younger Euripides. Living in Athens during the century of that city's rise to political and cultural preeminence among the Greek city-states, a century in which the city even took on the pretensions of empire for a while, he was at the center of the so-called Golden Age of Greece. After the victorious conclusion to the Persian Wars in 479 B.C., Pericles had the ruined Akropolis buildings rebuilt; the Parthenon was begun in 447 B.C. and finished fifteen years later. This was the age of the world's first democracy, whose core was a citizens' assembly. It was the age of the physician Hippocrates, whose oath medical doctors still take; of the sculptor Phidias and the poet Pindar, as well as many architects and philosophers of great skill and following. Socrates himself died only seven years after Sophocles. It was also an age in which envy and fear of Athens led in 431 B.C. to the Peloponnesian War between Athens and Sparta and their respective allies, a war which divided all Greece into two camps and raised questions about their common culture, much as all civil wars do.

During this period Sophocles served his fellow Athenians in a variety of political, military, and religious roles. He was by turns an imperial treasurer, a diplomat, a general, and a priest. At the same time he was best known as a prolific and innovative playwright. In 468 B.C., in his first drama contest with the vastly more experienced Aeschylus, he won. Overall, 123 plays are attributed to him by ancient accounts; although only seven have survived, the one reprinted here served in the next century as Aristotle's model of what a tragedy should be.

About the Play   *Oedipus the King* is probably the best known of all Greek plays. As the primary basis for Aristotle's study of tragedy in *The Poetics*, it has become central to subsequent thinking about the nature of tragedy. The legend of Oedipus was well known to the ancient Greeks. To avoid fulfillment of the prophecy that Oedipus would kill his father and marry his mother, his parents, the king and queen of Thebes, ordered that the helpless infant be left to die on the mountain that separates the territories of Thebes and Corinth. However, their well-intentioned deputy gave the child instead to a shepherd who, in turn, gave him to the king and queen of Corinth, and they raised him in the royal household. Hearing the prophecy himself, and believing his foster parents to be his true parents, Oedipus ran away from Corinth to avoid fulfilling the prophecy. When the play opens, Oedipus has become king of Thebes and—as the ancient Greek audience well knew—has already fulfilled the prophecy. While running away from his predicted fate, he had encountered and killed a stranger who turned out to be Laius, his true father. When he arrived at Thebes, he had solved the riddle of the Sphinx and thereby destroyed this monster which had haunted the city. The riddle had been, "What walks on four legs at dawn, on two legs at noon, and on three legs at sunset?" The answer to the riddle is "a person," who crawls on all fours in infancy, walks upright at maturity, and walks with the aid of a staff in old age. For ridding it of its oppressor, the grateful city offered him marriage to its widowed queen—his mother, Jocasta.

This is a play, then, about a man who was faced with a terrible prophecy about his fate, who did everything he could to avoid this fate, and who made himself a king entirely by his own abilities. It raises some of the most troubling issues of human existence: the relationship between fate (or destiny, or the circumstances to which we are born) and free will, our ability to create our own destiny; the relationship of the present to the past and the future; the difficulty of our knowing what is true of the future or of the present, of the world or even of ourselves; the difficulty and consequences of coming to terms with the truth once we discover it. We could say that these issues are universal because we all must deal with them. (The answer to the Sphinx's riddle also suggests that something universal is involved.) Part of the appeal of this play is that it faces them directly, simply, without extraneous local concerns and without pretending that they are easier to solve than they are. It is this toughness in dealing with the hard aspects of life which gives this play its realism; we feel that if anything positive is suggested by the play's end, that affirmation is fairly earned. Life is not, in this play, made to seem easier than it is.

One of the play's thematic patterns requires particular comment. The character Tiresias is a blind prophet; he cannot see, yet he knows the truth about the future and the past. Although in the present he has the identity of an old man, in the past he has also been a woman. Through him, the play seems to imply that truth is beyond sight, sex, and gender, that to see truly one must not be distracted by the superficial appearances of normal sight or by worldly desires (such as are exemplified by the desire one sex feels for the other). This becomes clearest in the unusual concentration of tragic effects; the climax of the play coincides with both its **catastrophe** (the scene in which unmerited suffering is meted out) and its **recognition scene** (in which we and, in this case, the hero recognize his true identity). In this scene, Oedipus finds a way to enact for himself the full implications of the issues which Tiresias embodies.

CHARACTERS

Speaking

OEDIPUS, King of Thebes
PRIEST of Zeus
KREON, Jocasta's brother
CHORUS of older Theban men
LEADER of the Chorus

TIRESIAS, blind prophet of Apollo
JOCASTA, Oedipus' wife
MESSENGER from Corinth
HERDSMAN, formerly of Laius' house
SERVANT, from Oedipus' house

Silent

Delegation of Thebans, mostly young
Attendants and maids

Boy to lead Tiresias
Antigone and Ismene, Oedipus' daughters

SCENE

Before the Royal Palace in Thebes. The palace has an imposing central double door. Two altars stand near it; one is to Apollo. The delegation of Thebans enters carrying olive branches wound with wool strips and gathers by the altars and stairs to the palace. The light and atmosphere are oppressive. Oedipus enters through the great doors.

OEDIPUS. My children, the newest to descend
    from ancient Kadmos into my care:
    why have you rushed *here*, to these seats,
    your wool-strung boughs begging

2 Kadmos: The legendary founder of Thebes and its first king. **4 wool-strung boughs:** Of laurel and olive, and wound with strips of wool, these branches were carried as emblems of supplication to a divinity. The branches were left on the altars, awaiting an answer to the appeal. What must have been highly unusual here is the use of suppliant boughs to seek help not from a god but from a mortal man.

for god's help? Our city is oppressed—
with incense smoke and cries of mourners
and prayers sung to the Healing God.
I thought it wrong to let messengers
speak for you, my sons, I must hear
your words myself, so I have come out, I,   10
Oedipus, the name that all men know.
Speak to me, old man. Yours
is the natural voice for the rest.
What concerns drive you to me?
Fear? Reassurance? Be certain
I will give all the help I can.
I would be hard indeed if I didn't
pity those who approach me like this.

PRIEST. You rule my country, Oedipus, and you see
who comes to your altars, how mixed   20
we are in years: children too weak
to travel far, old men worn down by age,
priests like myself, the priest of Zeus,
a picked group of our best young men.
More of us wait with wool-strung boughs
in the markets, or at Athena's two temples,
or watch the embers at Ismenus' shrine
for the glow of prophecy.

                              You can see for yourself
our city going under, too weak to lift   30
its head clear of each deadly surge.
Plague is killing our flowering farmland,
it's killing our grazing cattle. Our women
in labor give birth to nothing.

                              A burning god
rakes his fire through our city;
he hates us with fever, he empties
the House of Kadmos—but he makes

black Hades rich, with our groans and tears.
We don't believe you are the gods' equal, King,   40
but I, and these children, ask help here,
at your hearth, because we put you first, of all men,
at handling trouble—or confronting gods.
You came to Thebes, you broke us free
of the tax we paid with our lives
to the rasping Singer. No one prompted you,
you were not taught by any of us.
We tell ourselves, you had a god's help
when you pulled us back to life.
Once more, Oedipus, we need your power.   50
We beg you, each in our own pain—
find our lost strength!—by learning
what you can from a god's voice
or what some man can tell you.

                              I know this:
advice from men proven right in the past
will meet a crisis with the surest force.
Act as our greatest man! Act
as you did when you first seized fame!
Our country believes your nerve saved us then.   60
Don't let us look back on your rule, saying,
once he raised us, but later let us fall.
Lift us to safety!—so that no misstep
ever again will bring Thebes down.

Good luck came with you, a bird from god's will,
the day you rescued us. Be that same man now.
If you are going to rule us, King, it's better
to rule the living than a lifeless waste.
A walled city is nothing, a ship is nothing,
when there's no one aboard to man it.   70

---

7 **prayers . . . Healing God:** Lit. "paeans." A paean was a hymn to Apollo in his role as healer of disease. **27–28 Ismenus' shrine . . . prophecy:** The Ismenian temple was dedicated to Apollo and Melia, the source of the Ismenos, one of the two Theban rivers. The embers in the temple would be those under an animal recently burnt as a sacrifice whose remains could be read to interpret the will of a god, in this case Apollo's will. **32 Plague:** The plague that had struck Thebes was general, destroying crops, animals, and people. The fiery heat characteristic of the fever is referred to again at II. 230–31. The resemblance between the plague in *Oedipus the King* and the Athenian plague of 430: as described by Thucydides has led some scholars to suggest a date for the play shortly after 429 B.C. **35 A burning god:** The assumption is that a general and devastating plague must have been caused by a divinity, as was the plague in the first book of *The Iliad.* In I. 227 the burning god is said by the chorus to be Ares, by which they mean "violence" or "destructiveness."

39 Hades: The god who presides over the underworld. **40–43 We don't . . . confronting gods:** The Priest explains why he, a man who himself has access to divinity, comes to Oedipus, a political leader, for help in this crisis. Oedipus has proven his ability to act effectively in situations requiring direct contact with a divinity. **44–46 free . . . rasping Singer:** The Sphinx is the rasping Singer who arrived in Thebes shortly after Laius' departure. She destroyed the young Thebans (the "tax") by posing a riddle, which, if not answered correctly, resulted in the death of the unsuccessful answerer. In some versions the victims were thrown from a cliff, in others they were strangled, perhaps in some sexual embrace. The word "Sphinx" is related in Greek to the verb meaning "to strangle." Oedipus' triumph was to solve the riddle and kill the Sphinx, thus liberating Thebes from a reign of terror. **53 god's voice:** An oracle; an interpretation of a divine signal. **65 Good luck:** The first of many invocations of the Greek concept of *Tyche*, which can mean "luck" or "chance." I have generally translated "luck" when the speaker was gratified, "chance" when the outcome seems uncertain or unfortunate.

OEDIPUS. I do pity you, children. Don't think I'm
    unaware.
I know what need brings you: this sickness
harms you all. Yet, sick as you are,
not one of you suffers a sickness like mine.
Yours is a private grief, you feel
only what touches you. But my heart grieves
for you, for myself, and for our city.
You've come to wake me to all this.
There was truly no need. I haven't been asleep.
I have wept tears enough, for long enough;   80
my thoughts have raced down every twisting path.
The only cure all my thinking found
I've set in motion: I've sent Kreon,
my wife's brother, to Phoebus at Delphi,
to hear what action or what word of mine
will save this town. Already, counting what day
this is, I'm anxious: what is Kreon doing?
He takes too long, more than he needs.
But when he comes, I'd be the criminal
not to do all the god shows me to do.   90
PRIEST. Your words have just been made good: your
    men
are now signaling me that Kreon's here.
OEDIPUS. O Lord Apollo,
may the luck he brings save us! Luck so bright
we can see it—just as we see him now.

[Kreon enters from the countryside, wearing a laurel crown.]

PRIEST. Only a man whose news is sweet comes home
wearing a crown of laurel speckled with berries.
OEDIPUS. We'll soon know, he's within earshot.
    Prince!
Brother kinsman, son of Menoikeos!
What kind of answer have you brought from
    god?   100
KREON. A good one. I call nothing unbearable
if luck can straighten it, and bless the outcome.
OEDIPUS. But what did the god say? There's nothing
    in your words—
so far—to cheer me or to frighten me.
KREON. Will you hear it in front of these men?
If so, I'll speak. Otherwise we go inside.
OEDIPUS. Speak here, to all of us. I suffer more
for these men than for my own life.
KREON. Then I'll report what I heard from Apollo,
who did not hide his meaning.   110
He commands we drive out what corrupts us,
what makes our land sick. We now harbor
something incurable. He says: purge it.
OEDIPUS. Tell me the source of our trouble.
How do we cleanse ourselves?
KREON. By banishing a man—or by killing him. It's
    blood,
it's kin-murder that brings this storm on our city.
OEDIPUS. Did god name this man whose luck dooms
    him?

---

72 **I know what need:** It may seem that this speech contradicts Oedipus' earlier professed ignorance of the suppliants' purpose. Here he reveals his concern and reports specific actions he has taken. His questions in the play's opening speech search for fears and desires in the people he's not yet aware of, for new developments, and so are not in conflict with the grasp of the situation he shows here. **this sickness:** Oedipus refers to the literal "sickness" of the suppliants, all victims in some respect of the plague, and to his own metaphorical "sickness"— his mental suffering for his fellow Thebans. But a Greek audience would have understood that the "sickness" which affects Oedipus and of which he is unaware, is not metaphorical at all but a pollution of his entire being. Sophocles at other moments in the play will reveal his characters' metaphoric speech to be unexpectedly and horrifyingly literal. **88 He takes too long:** Because the Pythonness at Delphi delivered answers to questioners once a month, the shortest possible elapsed time for a trip from Thebes to Delphi and back would be about four or five days. **93 Lord Apollo:** This exclamation could be as much an impromptu prayer as an oath. The stage might contain a statue of Apollo to whom Oedipus turns or nods as he speaks these lines. **97:** A laurel crown was the customary sign that a pilgrimage to a shrine or an oracle had been a success.

99 **Menoikeos:** One of the "Sown Men" who grew up instantly and fully armed in Thebes when Kadmos seeded the earth with the dragon's teeth. Pronounced Me née kius. **101–2 I call . . . outcome:** A deliberately obscure answer. Kreon here resists, until directed by Oedipus, revealing the shocking nature of the oracle he has received. The lines also suggest another of Kreon's characteristics, his habitual use of a Sophist's quibbling idiom. **105–6 in front . . . go inside:** Kreon gives Oedipus the option of keeping Thebes in the dark concerning the disturbing accusations in the oracle. **110 did not hide:** Oracles (frequently delivered in lines of hexameter verse) were sometimes cryptic and demanded interpretation. The oracles to Oedipus are among the rare ones in Greek myth that meant exactly what they literally said. Kreon remarks on the lack of evasion or surface difficulty in this new oracle. **116 banishing . . . killing:** Apollo offers Thebes a choice of methods for purging itself of Liaus' murderer. Both modes—death or exile—were possible in such situations. This choice recurs several times in the play—when Oedipus charges Kreon with the crime and when Oedipus and Kreon debate Oedipus' ultimate fate. **116–17** The presence in a city of someone who had shed the blood of his own family was absolutely horrifying and unacceptable to a Greek. Even in the late fifth century B.C. lawyers made dramatic use of this horror when prosecuting murderers.

KREON. You know, King, that our city was ruled once
 by Laius, before you came to take the helm? 120

OEDIPUS. So I've heard. Though I never saw him.

KREON. Laius was murdered. Now, to avenge him,
 god
 wills you to strike down with your own hands
 those men whose hands struck Laius down.

OEDIPUS. Where do I find these men? How do I track
 vague footprints from a bygone crime?

KREON. The god said: look here, in our land.
 Nothing's caught that we don't chase—
 what we ignore goes free.

OEDIPUS. Was Laius killed at home? Or in the
 countryside? 130
 Or did they murder him on foreign ground?

KREON. He said when he left that his journey would
 take him
 into god's presence. But he never came home.

OEDIPUS. Did none of his troop see and report
 what happened? Is there no one
 to question whose answers might help?

KREON. All killed but a single terrified
 survivor, able to tell us but one fact.

OEDIPUS. What fact? One fact might point to many,
 if we had one small clue to raise our hopes. 140

KREON. They had the bad luck, he said, to meet
 bandits
 who struck them with a force many hands strong.
 It wasn't the violence of one man.

OEDIPUS. What bandit would risk such a huge crime
 unless somebody here hired him to do it?

KREON. That was our thought, but fresh trouble
 obsessed us. With Laius dead,
 who was to lead our revenge?

OEDIPUS. But here was your kingship murdered!
 What kind of trouble could have blocked your
 search? 150

KREON. The Sphinx's song. So wily, so baffling!—
 she forced us to forget the dark past
 to confront what lay at our feet.

OEDIPUS. I will go back, start fresh,
 and clear up all this darkness.
 Apollo was exactly right, and so were you,
 to turn our minds back to the murdered man.
 And now it's time I joined your search
 for vengeance, which our land and the god deserve.
 I don't do it to placate any distant kin, 160
 I will dispel this poison for my own sake.
 Laius' killer might one day come for me,
 exacting vengeance with that same hand.
 So to defend the dead man serves my interest.
 Rise, children, quick, up from the altar,
 raise those branches that appeal to god.
 Someone go call the people of Kadmos here.
 Tell them I'm ready to do anything.
 If god is with us, we will survive.
 If not, our ruin has already happened. 170

[Exit Oedipus, into the palace.]

PRIEST. Stand, children. The thing we came for
 the king himself has promised to do.
 Let god Apollo, who commands us to act,
 lift this plague off our lives! Apollo our savior!

[The Theban suppliants leave; the Chorus enters.]

CHORUS. What will you say to Thebes,
 Voice from Zeus? What sweet sounds
 bring your will from golden Delphi
 to our bright city?

---

123 own hands: The first of many references to hands, especially hands that shed blood. In Greek law the hands of a person who committed a crime retained the pollution inherent in that crime, regardless of motive or intent. Here Oedipus' avenging hands are paired rhetorically with the hands that murdered Laius. The two pairs of hands will be shown to be only one pair, Oedipus' own. **132–33 journey . . . into god's presence:** The Greek word *theoros* is translated by this phrase. A *theoros* was a witness or see-er of a divine rite or event. We know from sources outside the play that Laius was bound for Delphi, where he would cross Oedipus' path. But by not naming Delphi, Sophocles permits Oedipus to postpone facing the possibility that Laius and he met on the road to Delphi. **144 bandit:** Though Kreon clearly used the plural, Oedipus speaks of one singular bandit with chilling unconscious accuracy. But because his sentence is a hypothetical question, it is logically proper. **146 fresh trouble:** Kreon portrays a rapid sequence of events: Laius' departure; news of his death; attack by the Sphinx; arrival of Oedipus; death of the Sphinx. The elapsed time might have been a few days only, or at most a week or two.

150 blocked: The Greek word so translated, *empodon*, refers to stumbling, tripping, impeding the legs. **153 at our feet:** Kreon continues the foot image, which may carry a glancing reference to Oedipus' own swollen feet. **163 exacting vengeance:** Oedipus strangely imagines himself the victim of a second crime by Laius' original murderer. That this should be an act of "vengeance" is hard to explain given the state of Oedipus' knowledge, but it will indeed be an act of vengeance when the same hands that killed Laius blind Oedipus. **167 people of Kadmos:** Theban citizens. When they arrive, the Chorus will represent the "people of Kadmos." **176 Voice from Zeus:** Though Apollo was the resident deity who issued his prophecies through the Pythonness at Delphi, the Chorus here attributes the commands to Zeus, the ultimate source of knowledge and power.

We're at the breaking point,
terror ranges through our minds.   180
Our wild cries reach for you,
Healing God from Delos—
in holy dread we ask: does your will
bring a new threat, or an old doom
come back as the years wheel by?
Say it, Great Voice,
you who answer us always,
speak as Hope's golden child.

Athena, your help is the first we ask,
immortal daughter of Zeus,   190
then Artemis your sister
who protects our land, sitting throned
in the heart of our marketplace.
And Apollo, whose shots
hit from far off! Our three
defenders from death: come now!
If once you fought off destruction
by blowing away the fires of our pain,
come to us now!

The blows I suffer are past count.   200
Plague kills my friends,
thought finds no spear
to keep a man safe.
Our rich earth shrivels what it grows,
our women in labor scream
but nothing's born. One life
after another flies,
you see them go
birds driving their strong wings
faster than flash-fire   210
to the shore of the sunset god.

Our city dies as its people die
those countless deaths, her children
rot in the streets, unmourned,
spreading more death.
Young wives and gray mothers
wash to our altars, their cries
carry from all sides, sobbing
for help, each lost in her pain.

A hymn shining to the Healer   220
is darkened by a grieving voice,
a flute in a courtyard.
Help us, Goddess,
golden child of Zeus,
send us the bright face
we need: Strength.

Force that raging killer, the god Ares,
to turn his back and run from our land.
He murders without armor now
but we, the victims of his fever,   230
shout in the hot blast of his charge.
Blow Ares to the great searoom
of Amphitrité, banish him
under a booming wind
to jagged harbors in the seas
roiling off Thrace. If night
doesn't finish the god's black work,
the day will finish it.
The lightning waits
in your fiery will,   240
Zeus, Father. Send its blast
to kill the god killing us.

Apollo,
lord of the morning light, draw back
your curving bowstring
of twined gold—fire the sure arrows
that rake our attackers and keep them at bay.
Artemis, carry your radiance
into battle, on bright quick feet
down through the morning hills.   250
I call on the god whose hair
flows through its golden band,
whose name is our country's own,
Bakkhos!—the wine-flushed!—who comes
to the maenads' cries, who runs
in their midst: Bakkhos!—
come here on fire,
a pine-torch flaring,

---

182 **Delos:** The island at the center of the Cyclades, sacred birthplace of Apollo, was the navel of the sea, as Delphi was the navel of the earth. **184 new threat . . . old doom:** It is an old doom that the Voice of Zeus will invoke against the murderer of Laius. The Chorus distinguishes between a curse that has been known for some years and one that has newly emerged. **189–94 Athena, Artemis, Apollo:** The three divinities are here invoked in a military prayer to focus their powers on rescuing Thebes. The Chorus does not know which god may be the truly relevant one. **211 sunset god:** Hades

232–33 great searoom/of Amphitrité: Amphitrité was a sea nymph whose home was the Atlantic Ocean, hence her name became synonymous with that ocean. **236 off Thrace:** The Black Sea, where the Thracians lived, who, being warlike, took Ares as their primary god. **236–38 If night . . . finish it.:** Meaning obscure. Gould suggests that the phrase means something like, "if the night lets anything survive, the day moves in to finish it." **242 god killing us:** Ares. **250 morning hills:** In southwestern Asia Minor, where Artemis was worshipped, with her brother Apollo, as a fire deity. Sophocles puns on the similar words to stress the light-bearing character of the sibling gods. **253 name . . . country's own:** Bakkhos was a native Theban, the son of Zeus and Semele, Kadmos' daughter. **255 maenads:** Revelers loyal to Dionysos. Lit. "Madwomen."

to face with us the one god
all the gods hate: Ares!   260

[*Oedipus has entered while the Chorus was singing. Now he
speaks.*]

OEDIPUS. I heard your prayer. Prayer may save you
      yet—
if you will trust me and do what I say:
work with me toward the one cure
this plague demands of us.
Help will come, the plague will lift.
I now outlaw the killer myself, by these words.
I act as a stranger, not familiar
either with this crime or accounts of it.
Unless I can mesh some clue I hold
with something known of the killer,   270
I will be tracking him alone, on a cold trail.
Since I came later to join your ranks,
when the crime itself was past history,
there are some things that you,
the sons of Kadmos, must tell me.
If any of you knows how Laius,
son of Labdacus, died, he must
instantly tell me all he knows.
He must not be frightened of naming
himself the guilty one: I swear   280
he'll suffer nothing worse than exile.
Or if you know of someone else,
a foreigner who struck the blow, speak up.
I will reward you now, I will thank you always.
But if you know the killer and don't speak,
out of fear, to shield kin or yourself,
listen to what that silence will cost you.
I order everyone in my land
where I hold power and sit as king:
don't let that man under your roof,   290
don't speak with him, no matter who he is.
Don't pray or sacrifice with him,
don't pour purifying water for him.

I say this to all my people:
drive him from your houses.
He is our sickness. He poisons us.
This the Pythian god has shown me.
Believe me, I am the ally in this
both of the god and the dead king.
I pray god that the unseen killer,   300
whoever he is, and whether he killed
alone or had help, be cursed with a life
as evil as he is, a life
of utter human deprivation.
I pray this, too: if he's found at my hearth,
inside my house, and I know that he's there,
may the curses I aimed at others punish me.
I charge you all—give my words force,
for my sake and the god's, for our dead land
stripped barren of its harvests,   310
forsaken by its gods.
Even if god had not forced the issue,
this crime should not have gone uncleansed.
You should have looked to it!—the dead man
not only being noble, but your king.
But as my luck would have it,
I have his power, his bed—a wife
who shares our seed, and had she borne
the children of us both, she
might have linked us closer still. But Laius   320
had no luck fathering children, and fate
itself soon struck a blow at his head.
It's these concerns make me defend Laius
as I would my own father. There is nothing
I won't try, to trace his murder
back to the killer's hand.
I act in this for Labdacus and Polydorus,
for Kadmos and Agenor—for our whole line of kings.
I warn those who disobey me:
god make their fields harvest dust,   330
their women's bodies harvest death.
                              O you gods,

kill them with something worse
than this plague killing us now.
For all the rest of us, who are
loyal sons of Kadmos:
may Justice fight with us,
the gods be always at our side.

---

267 as a stranger: According to Athenian law a blood relative of a slain person should act to interdict his murderer. Unknowingly, Oedipus is in fact such a relative, though here he acts as a representative of the state speaking for the next of kin who is presumed to be absent. **269–70 mesh some clue:** The word translated "clue" is *symbolon*, a fragment of some larger object, typically a potsherd, which could be matched to fit its other half to establish the identity of a messenger or long-lost parent or relative. **272 came later:** Oedipus arrived in Thebes after the report of Laius' death had reached the city. **277 Labdacus:** An earlier king of Thebes. **290–93 roof . . . speak . . . pray . . . sacrifice . . . pour:** The interdiction Oedipus decrees reveals extreme sensitivity, which would be felt by a Greek of Sophocles' time, to contact with a person whose own hand had committed a defiling act.

320–21 Laius had no luck . . . children: An example of words that carry a second meaning to be grasped when the true facts of Oedipus' life are known. Oedipus means to say that Laius was childless, but the words also suggest that any child Laius fathered was the *source* of his ill fortune. **322 struck a blow:** This idiom through which Oedipus pictures Laius' death is uncannily appropriate to the manner in which he actually met death: a blow to the head, struck by Oedipus himself. **328 line of kings:** My gloss added to explain Oedipus' list.

CHORUS. King, your curse forces me to speak.
  None of us is the killer.   340
  And none of us can point to him.
  Apollo ordered us to search,
  now *he* must find the killer.
OEDIPUS. So he must. But what man could force a
  god against his will?
LEADER. Let me suggest a second course of action.
OEDIPUS. Don't stop at two if you have more.
LEADER. Tiresias is the man whose power of seeing
  shows him most nearly what Apollo sees.
  King, he might make brilliantly clear   350
  what you most want to learn.
OEDIPUS. I've acted already not to lose this chance.
  At Kreon's urging I've sent for him—twice now.
  The fact that he still hasn't come I find strange.
LEADER. There were some old rumors—too faint to
  help us now.
OEDIPUS. I'll study every word. What did those
  rumors say?
LEADER. That Laius was killed by some travelers.
OEDIPUS. That's something even I have heard. But
  the man
  who actually did it—no one sees.
LEADER. If fear means anything to him   360
  he won't linger in Thebes
  once he has heard that curse of yours.
OEDIPUS. If murder didn't frighten him, my words
  won't.
LEADER. There is the man who will convict him:
  god's prophet, led here at last.
  God gave to him what he gave no one else.
  The truth is living in his mind.

[*Enter Tiresias, led by a boy.*]

OEDIPUS. Tiresias, you are master of the hidden
  world.

You can read earth and sky, you know
what omens to expound, what to keep secret.   370
Though your eyes can't see it,
you are aware of the plague
attacking us. To fight it, we can find
no savior or defense but you, my Lord.
For we now have Apollo's answer—
you will have heard it from others:
to end this plague we must root out Laius' killers.
Find them, then kill them or banish them.
Help us do it. Don't begrudge us
what you divine from birdcries, show us   380
any escape prophecy has shown you.
Rescue Thebes! Rescue yourself, and me!
Take charge of our defilement, and stop
this poison from the murdered man
which sickens and destroys us.
We're in your hands. To help another
is the best use a man can make of his powers.
TIRESIAS. The most terrible knowledge is the kind
  it would pay no wise man to use.
  I knew this, but I forgot it.   390
  I should never have come.
OEDIPUS. What's this? You've come—but with no
  desire to help?
TIRESIAS. Let me go home. Take my advice now.
  Your   life
  will be easier to bear—so will mine.
OEDIPUS. Strange words. And hardly kind—to hold
  back
  god's crucial guidance from your own people.
TIRESIAS. I see that you've spoken out today
  when silence was called for. I'm silent now
  to spare me your mistake.
OEDIPUS. For god's sake do not turn your back   400
  if you understand any of this! We kneel and beg.
TIRESIAS. You beg out of ignorance. I'll never speak.
  If I made my griefs plain, you would see your own.
OEDIPUS. Then you know and won't help us? You
  intend
  to betray us all and destroy Thebes?

---

340 None of us . . . killer: The blunt denial is understandable, because Oedipus has addressed the Chorus as if it potentially harbored Laius' killer. 348 Tiresias: The blind Theban prophet who figures in many of the most famous myths of his native city. His association with the god Apollo, and his access to the god's knowledge, are crucial here, because Apollo is the source of the oracles that have predicted Oedipus' incest and patricide. 353 Kreon's urging: An important point. Later, when Tiresias accuses Oedipus of causing the pollution, Oedipus remembers that it was Kreon who advised consulting the seer. Kreon's involvement thus lends plausibility to Oedipus' counter-charges. 357 travelers: The Leader substitutes a word that is nearer the truth than Kreon's "bandits." Oedipus does not react to the difference. 359 who did it: Here I accept an anonymous conjecture. The manuscripts actually say "the one who saw it no one sees." The conjecture fits the context of the next three speeches, which concern not the eyewitness, but the killer, the one who did it.

397 spoken out: Tiresias refers here most probably to Oedipus' speech cursing Laius' murderer. Less probably, he might be referring to the plea with which Oedipus greets Tiresias. The manuscripts contain a possible variant of this line, which Gould translates, "I see your understanding comes to you inopportunely. So that won't happen to me. . . ." This version makes sense in the larger context of Oedipus' discovery of his true past. I have, however, translated the version that seems to make the most sense in the immediate context. 404 Then you know: Tiresias' scornful refusal to respond must seem not only inexplicable to Oedipus, but unacceptable. Tiresias must be made to tell what the city needs to know for its salvation. Oedipus' fury is fully justified as necessary to force the truth from him.

TIRESIAS. I'll cause no grief to you or me. Why ask
  futile questions? You'll learn nothing.

OEDIPUS. So the traitor won't answer.
  You would enrage a rock.

                  Still won't speak?   410
  Are you without feelings—or beyond their reach?

TIRESIAS. You blame this rage on me, do you? Rage?
  You haven't seen her yet, the kind
  that's married to your life. *You* find fault with *me*?

OEDIPUS. Who wouldn't be enraged at the words
  you're using to insult Thebes?

TIRESIAS. Truth will come. My silence can't hide it.

OEDIPUS. Must it come? Good reason to speak it now.

TIRESIAS. I prefer not to speak. Rage at that, if you
  like,
  with the most savage fury your heart knows.   420

OEDIPUS. I'm angry enough now to speak my mind.
  I think you helped plot the murder. No,
  you can't have struck the blow itself.
  Had you eyes, though, I would have said
  you alone were the killer

TIRESIAS. That's your truth? Hear mine: I say
  honor the curse your own mouth spoke.
  From today, don't you speak to me,
  or to your people here. You are the plague.
  You ruin your own land.   430

OEDIPUS. So the appalling charge has been at last
  flushed out, into the open.
  Now where will you run?

TIRESIAS. Where you can't reach. To truth, where I'm
  strong.

OEDIPUS. Who put this truth in your mouth? Not
  your prophet's trade.

TIRESIAS. You did. By forcing me to speak

OEDIPUS. Speak what? Repeat it so I understand.

TIRESIAS. I made no sense the first time?
  Are you provoking me to use the word?

OEDIPUS. You made no sense at any time. Try once
  more.   440

TIRESIAS. I say: you are the killer you would find.

OEDIPUS. The second time is even more outrageous.
  You'll wish you'd never spoken.

TIRESIAS. Shall I feed your fury with more words?

OEDIPUS. Say anything. It's all the same worthless
  noise.

TIRESIAS. I say that you are living unaware
  in the most hideous intimacy
  with your nearest and most loving kin.
  You have arrived at evil—which you cannot see.

OEDIPUS. You think you can savage me? Forever?
  Unscathed?   450

TIRESIAS. Forever. Truth lasts.

OEDIPUS. Truth lasts for some, but your "truth"
  won't—
  you have blind eyes, blind ears, and a blind brain.

TIRESIAS. And you're a wretched fool, lashing me with
  taunts
  every man here will soon aim at you.

OEDIPUS. You survive in the care of black
  unbroken night! You can't hurt me
  or any man who sees the sunlight.

TIRESIAS. It isn't I who will cause your fall.
  Apollo is enough. You're his concern.   460

OEDIPUS. Did you invent these lies? Or did Kreon?

TIRESIAS. Kreon is not your disease. You are.

OEDIPUS. Wealth, and a king's power,
  the skill that wins every time—
  how much envious malice they provoke!
  To rob me of power—power I didn't want,
  but which this city thrust into my hands—
  my oldest friend here, loyal Kreon, worked
  quietly against me—aching to steal my throne.
  He hired for the purpose this fortuneteller—   470
  conniving bogus beggar-priest!—
  who sees the main chance clearly
  but is a blind groper in his art.

  Tell us now, where did you ever
  prove your claim to a seer's power?
  Why—when the Sphinx who barked black songs
  was hounding us—why wasn't it *your* answer
  that freed the city? Her riddle wasn't the sort
  just anyone who happened by could solve:
  prophetic skill was needed then,   480
  the kind you didn't have, skill learned

431–32 charge . . . flushed out: The metaphor is from hunting and suggests first that the accusation is like an animal driven from its cover, and second that Tiresias himself has become an animal fleeing Oedipus' wrath. **435 put this truth . . . mouth:** According to other interpretations of this line, Oedipus is asking Tiresias who *taught* him the truth. A scholiast of the twelfth century suggested the interpretation I have adopted, which better fits Tiresias' response. **439 provoking me to use . . . word:** The word in question is "killer," which Tiresias is provoked to use in his next speech, although he has shied from speaking it until now.

446–47 living . . . intimacy: This phrase normally means "to live under the same roof," but it also frequently means "to have sexual intercourse with." **457 You can't hurt me:** This phrase could also mean "I shall not harm you." My translation is governed by acceptance of Brunck's emendation in the next speech. **461 Or did Kreon?:** Searching for an explanation for what he sees as false and treasonous accusations by Tiresias, Oedipus connects the fact that it was Kreon who recommended calling in Tiresias with the fact that banishing Oedipus would leave Kreon in position to assume the throne. **471 bogus beggar-priest:** A *magus* (fortuneteller) was from Persia, known to Greeks as an unreliable and corruptible breed.

from birds or from a god. Yet it was Oedipus,
who knew nothing, that silenced her,
because my wit seized the answer,
needing no help from birds.
Now it is I, this same man, for whom you plot
disgrace and exile, thinking you will
maneuver close to Kreon's throne.
But your scheme to rid Thebes of this plague
will destroy only you—and the man who
    planned it.   490
You look now so near death—otherwise I'd make
    you
the first victim of your own plot.

LEADER. He spoke in anger, Oedipus—
but so did you, if you'll hear what we think.
We don't need angry words, we need insight—
how best to manage what the god commands.

TIRESIAS. You may be king, but my right
to answer makes me your equal.
In this respect, I am as much
my own master as you are.   500
You do not own my life.
Apollo does. Nor am I Kreon's man.
Hear me out.
Since you have thrown my blindness at me
I will tell you what your eyes don't see:
the evil you are mired in.
               You don't see
where you live or who shares your house.
Do you know your parents?
              You are their enemy 510
in this life and down there with the dead.
And soon their double curse—
your father's and your mother's lash—
will whip you out of Thebes
on terrorstruck feet.
Your eyes will then see darkness
which now see life.
         Your shriek
will try to hide itself in every cave.

What mountain outcrop on Cithairon   520
won't roar your screaming back at you,
when what your marriage means strikes home,
shows you the house that took you in: you sailed
your lucky wind to a most foul harbor.
Evils you can't guess
will level you to what you are,
to what your children are.
Go on, throw muck at Kreon, and at
the warning spoken through my mouth.
But there will never be a man   530
ground into wretchedness as you shall be.

OEDIPUS. Shall I wait for him to attack me more?
May you be damned. Go. Leave my doors
now! Turn your back and go.

TIRESIAS. I'm here only because you sent for me.

OEDIPUS. Had I known the madness you would speak
I wouldn't have hurried to get you here.

TIRESIAS. I may seem crazed to you, but your natural
parents thought I had an able mind.

OEDIPUS. My parents? Wait. Who is my father? 540

TIRESIAS. Today, you will be born. Into ruin.

OEDIPUS. You always have a murky riddle in your
mouth.

TIRESIAS. Don't you excel us all at finding answers?

OEDIPUS. Sneer at my mind. But you must face the
power it won.

TIRESIAS. That very luck is what destroyed you.

OEDIPUS. If I save Thebes, I won't care what happens
to me.

TIRESIAS. I will leave you to that. Boy, guide me out.

OEDIPUS. Yes, let him take you home.
Here, you are painfully underfoot. Gone,
you'll take away a great source of grief. 550

TIRESIAS. I'll go. But first I must finish
what you brought me to do—
your face won't frighten me.
The man you have been looking for,
the one your curses threaten, the man
you had outlawed in Laius' death:
I say that man is here—
             you think him a foreigner,
but he will prove himself a Theban native,
though he'll find no joy in that news. 560
A blind man who has eyes now,
a beggar who's now rich, he'll jab
his stick, feeling the road to foreign lands.

[*Oedipus enters the palace.*]

He will soon be shown father and brother
to his own children, son and husband

---

483 who knew nothing: Oedipus himself stresses the difference between his ability to solve problems intellectually and Tiresias' failure to solve them using the arts of prophecy. Oedipus boasts of his "ignorance" but is in fact truly and desperately ignorant of the hidden facts that will ruin him. **515 terrorstruck feet:** The phrase may mean that the curse itself pursuing Oedipus is "terrible footed." But the sound of the word for "terrible footed," *deinopous*, echoes Oedipus' name so as to suggest that it is Oedipus' feet that are in some way terrible—or terrified. Because Oedipus' name means "Swollenfoot" and the marks on his feet from the bonds pinning them when he was exposed at birth gave him that name, the terror in his feet touches the significance of his name and his origin.

to the mother who bore him—she took
his father's seed and his seed,
and he took his own father's life.

You go inside. Think through what I have said.
If I have lied, say of me then   570
I am a prophet with no mind.

[*Exit Tiresias.*]

CHORUS. Who is the man
who inspires the rock voice
of Delphi to speak out?
This crime that sickens speech
is the work of his red hands.
Now he will need legs strong enough
to outrun wild horses of the storm.
Apollo is ready to strike:
armed with lightning,   580
he and the Fates close in,
grim beings who don't miss.

From snowfields
high on Parnassus
the word blazes out to us all:
track down the man no one sees.
He takes cover in thick brush,
he drives up the mountain
bull-like to its rocks and caves,
going his bleak and hunted way,   590
still struggling to escape the doom
earth from her sacred mouth has spoken:
but that doom buzzes low,
never far from his ear.

Fear is what the man who reads birds
makes us feel, fear we can't fight.
We can't accept what he says,
we have no power to challenge.
We thrash in doubt, we can't see
even the present clearly,   600
much less the future.
And we've heard of no feud
embittering the House
of Oedipus in Corinth
against the House of Laius here,

no past trouble and none now,
no proof that would make us accuse
our king's fame, as he works
to avenge this murder
done to our royal house.   610

Zeus and Apollo are infallible,
they know what happens to mankind.
But there is no way to prove
whether an earthbound prophet
ever sees more of the future
than we do, though in knowledge and skill
one man may surpass another.
But never, not till I see
the charges proved against him,
will I give my credence   620
to a man who blames Oedipus.
All of us saw his brilliance
prevail, when the wingèd virgin
Sphinx came at him: his winning
won him the people.
My heart can't find him guilty.

[*Kreon enters.*]

KREON. Citizens, I hear that King Oedipus
has made a fearful charge against me.
I'm here to prove it false.
If he thinks anything I've said or done   630
has made this crisis worse, or injured him—
then I have no more wish to live.
This is no minor charge.
It's the most deadly I could suffer,
if my city, my own people, you!—
believe I'm a traitor.
LEADER. He could have spoken in a flash
of anger with no thought behind it.
KREON. Did he say *I* persuaded the prophet to lie?
LEADER. That's what he said. What he meant wasn't
clear.   640
KREON. When he announced my guilt—tell me
how his eyes looked. Did he seem sane?
LEADER. I can't say. I don't question what my rulers
do.
Here he comes, now, out of the palace.

[*Oedipus enters.*]

581 **Fates:** The *keres*, who execute the will of Zeus and Apollo.   584
Parnassus: The mountain home of the Muses; visible from Thebes.
592 **earth . . . mouth:** Lit. "from earth's mid-navel." The navel was
a white stone at Delphi, at the spot where such oracles or "dooms" as
mentioned here were spoken. The navel or *omphalos* was an avenue of
communication to the wisdom of the earth.   595 **man who reads
birds:** Tiresias

607 **no proof:** Lit. "touchstone" (*basanos*). The chorus seeks a touchstone (which streaks black when rubbed with true gold) before it will
accept Tiresias' accusations. Such a touchstone would be some feud or
crime that set the Corinthian royal house against the Theban House of
Kadmos. But no such feud or crime is known to the Chorus.

OEDIPUS. So? You would come here? You have the nerve
  to face me in my house? When you're
  exposed as its master's murderer?
  Caught trying to steal my kingship?
  In god's name what weakness did you see
  in me—that led you to plot this?   650
  Am I a coward or a fool?
  Did you suppose I wouldn't notice
  your quiet moves? Not fight back if I did?
  Aren't you attempting something
  downright stupid—to win absolute power
  without partisans or even friends?
  For that you'll need money and a mob.
KREON. Stop!
          Give me time to answer you.
  Let me speak before you judge me.   660
OEDIPUS. You're a formidable speaker. But I listen
  badly to someone trying to destroy me.
KREON. I'll prove you are mistaken to think that.
OEDIPUS. Your malice is too blatant to deny.
KREON. Why do you prize your perversity?
  If you think it's a virtue, your mind's deranged.
OEDIPUS. *Your* mind's deranged, if you think a man
  can attack a brother kinsman and not suffer.
KREON. I'll grant that. Now: *how* have *I* attacked you?
OEDIPUS. Did you, or did you not, urge me   670
  to send for that venerated prophet?
KREON. Yes. I'd give the same advice now.
OEDIPUS. How long ago was it that King Laius . . .
KREON. Laius? Did what? Why speak of him?
OEDIPUS. . . . was lost in that murderous attack?
KREON. That was far back in the past.
OEDIPUS. Did this seer practice his craft here, then?
KREON. With the same skill and respect he has now.
OEDIPUS. Back then, did he ever mention my name?
KREON. Not in my hearing.   680
OEDIPUS. You did investigate the murder, though?
KREON. Of course we did. We found out nothing.
OEDIPUS. Why didn't your expert seer accuse me then?
KREON. I don't know. When I've no facts, I don't speak.
OEDIPUS. There's something you know well enough to explain.
KREON. What's that? I'm holding nothing back.
OEDIPUS. Just this. If that seer hadn't conspired with you,
  he would never have called me Laius' killer.
KREON. If he said that, *you heard him*, I didn't.
  I think I've a right now to some answers from you.   690

OEDIPUS. Question me. I have no blood on my hands.
KREON. Did you marry my sister?
OEDIPUS. Do you expect me to deny that?
KREON. You both have equal power in this country?
OEDIPUS. I give her all she asks.
KREON. Do I share power with you both as an equal?
OEDIPUS. You shared our power and betrayed us with it.
KREON. You're wrong. Think it through rationally, as I have.
  Who would prefer a king's anxious life
  to one that let him sleep at night—   700
  if his share of power still equaled a king's?
  Nothing in my nature lusts for sheer power.
  It's enough for me to enjoy a king's rights,
  enough for any man who values restraint.
  All I want, you give me—and it comes with no fear.
  To be king would rob my life of its ease.
  How could my share of power be more pleasant
  than this painless pre-eminence, this ready
  influence I have? I'm not yet so misguided
  that I go looking for honors that are burdens.   710
  But as things stand, I'm greeted and wished well
  on all sides. Those who want something from you
  come to me, their best hope of gaining it.
  Should I quit this good life for a worse one?
  Treason has no chance to corrupt
  a healthy mind like my own:
  I have no love for such exploits.
  Nor would I join someone who did.
  Test me. Go to Delphi yourself. Find out
  whether I brought back the oracle's exact words.   720
  Then if you find I plotted with that omen-reader,
  seize me and kill me—not on your authority
  alone, but on mine too, for I'd vote my own death.
  But don't convict me because of a wild thought
  you can't prove, which only you believe.
  And there's no justice in your reckless confusion
  of evil men with good ones, traitors with friends.
  To reject a true friend is like suicide—
  it costs us a life loved as we love our own.
  Time will instruct you in these truths, for time   730
  alone is the sure test of a just man,
  but you can know a bad man in one day.
LEADER. That's sound advice, King,
  for someone anxious not to fall.
  Too quick a mind can stumble.
OEDIPUS. When a conspirator moves
  abruptly and in secret against me,
  I must out-plot him and strike first.

If I pause and do nothing
he'll win his purpose   740
while I'm losing mine.

KREON. What is your purpose? My banishment?

OEDIPUS. No. It's your death I want.

KREON. If you will begin by defining "envy" . . .

OEDIPUS. You talk as though you refuse to believe
me.

KREON. How can I if you won't use reason?

OEDIPUS. I reason in my own interest.

KREON. You ought to reason in mine as well.

OEDIPUS. In a traitor's interest?

KREON. What if you're wrong?   750

OEDIPUS. I must still rule.

KREON. Not if it's selfish rule.

OEDIPUS. Did you hear him, Thebes!

KREON. Thebes isn't just *your* city. It's mine as well!

LEADER. My Lords, stop this. Here's Jocasta
leaving the palace—at the right time
to calm you both. She'll see that this feud ends.

[*Enter Jocasta from the palace.*]

JOCASTA. Wretched men. Why are you out here
recklessly yelling at each other?
Aren't you ashamed? With Thebes sick and
dying   760
you two fight out some personal grievance?
You go inside, Oedipus. Kreon, go home.
Don't make us all miserable over nothing.

KREON. Sister, it's worse than that. Oedipus your husband
threatens either to drive me
from my own country, or have me killed.

OEDIPUS. That's right. I've caught him plotting
against my life.
And his technique is lying prophecy.

KREON. I ask the gods to sicken and destroy me
if I did any of the things you charge me with.   770

JOCASTA. Believe what he says, Oedipus.
Accept that oath he just made to the gods.
Do it for my sake too, and for these men.

---

769 I ask the gods: Kreon makes a formal declaration of innocence which invokes the gods; his innocence is instantly respected as valid by all but Oedipus. **774 Give in:** Ll. 774–823 are a *kommos*, a sung expression of grief or strong emotion in which the chorus joins one or more of the main characters. To judge by the root meaning of *kommos*, which is *beat*, this portion must have had a more strongly accented rhythm than the rest of the dialogue. Here the strong emotion might be the realization by all present of the gravity of what is happening.

LEADER. Give in to him, Lord, we beg you.
Do what your mind and instinct tell you.

OEDIPUS. What do you want me to do?

LEADER. Believe him. This man was never a fool,
now he's given himself the force of a great oath.

OEDIPUS. Do you realize what you're asking?

LEADER. I do.   780

OEDIPUS. Then say it to me outright.

LEADER. Groundless rumor shouldn't be used by you
to dishonor a friend who swears his innocence.

OEDIPUS. Is it clear to you all
that you ask my exile or my death?

LEADER. No! We ask neither. By the god
outshining all others, the Sun—
may I die the worst of deaths, die it
godless and friendless, if I want those things.
This dying land grinds pain into my soul—   790
grinds it the more if the bitterness
you two stir up adds to our misery.

OEDIPUS. Then let him go, though it means my
death,
or my exile from here in disgrace.
What moves my pity are your words,
not his. My hate goes with him.

KREON. You are as bitter when you yield
as you are savage in your rage.
But natures like your own
punish themselves the most—   800
which is the way it should be.

OEDIPUS. Leave me alone. Go.

KREON. I'll go. You can see nothing now.
But these men see that I'm right.

[*Kreon goes off.*]

LEADER. Lady, what keeps you from taking your man
in?

JOCASTA. I will, when someone tells me what happened here.

LEADER. Loose talk made one man's suspicion flare
up,
which stung the other's sense of justice.

JOCASTA. Both sides were at fault?

LEADER. Both sides.   810

JOCASTA. What was at issue?

LEADER. Don't ask that. Our land needs no more trouble.
No more trouble! Stop it now where it stands.

OEDIPUS. I know you mean well when you try to calm
me,
but do you realize what it does to me?

LEADER. King, I have said this more than once.

I would be mad, or have lost my good sense,
if I lost faith in you: you
who wrenched our loved country
back on course when you found her   820
wandering crazed with suffering.
Steer us straight, again—now—
with all your inspired luck.

JOCASTA. In god's name, King, tell me why
you've hardened your mind in this rage.

OEDIPUS. I'll tell you, for it's you I respect, not the
men.
Kreon caused my rage by his plots against me.

JOCASTA. Go on. Explain what provoked the quarrel.

OEDIPUS. He says I murdered Laius.

JOCASTA. Does he know this himself? Or did someone
tell him?   830

OEDIPUS. Neither. He sent that vicious seer to make
the charge
so he could keep his own mouth innocent.

JOCASTA. Then you can clear yourself of all his
charges.
Listen to me, for I can make you believe
that no man, ever, has mastered prophecy.
This one incident will prove it.
A long time back, an oracle reached Laius—
I don't say that Apollo himself sent it,
but the priests who interpret him did—
which said that when Laius came to die   840
his killer would be a son born to him and me.
Yet, as we heard the story, foreign bandits
murdered Laius at a place where three roads meet.

[*Oedipus reacts with sudden intensity to her words.*]

But that son of ours was less than three days old
when Laius pierced and yoked its ankle joints,
and had it left, by someone else's hands,
on a mountain far from any roads. Apollo failed!
That time Apollo failed to make Laius die
the way he feared—at the hands of his own son.
Does that show you how much sense   850
prophetic voices make of our lives?
You can forget them. When god wants
something to happen, he makes it happen,
then he shows it to us—all with ease.

OEDIPUS. Just now, as I listened to you, Lady, my
heart raced,
something in my memory woke up terrified.

JOCASTA. What chilling thought turned you toward
me like that?

OEDIPUS. I thought you said that Laius
was struck down where three roads meet.

JOCASTA. That's what I said—it's the story
we still hear.   860

OEDIPUS. Tell me the place where it happened.

JOCASTA. It happened on a road in Phokis, at the fork
where roads come in from Delphi and from Daulis.

OEDIPUS. How much time has passed since it happened?

JOCASTA. We heard the news just before you came to
power.

OEDIPUS. O Zeus! What is this you have willed me to
do?

JOCASTA. Oedipus, you're heartstricken. What is it?

OEDIPUS. Don't ask me yet. Describe Laius to me.
Was he a young man just reaching his prime?

JOCASTA. He was tall, with some white showing
in his hair.   870
He looked then not very different from you now.

OEDIPUS. It's my ruin. I think that savage curse I
spoke
in such ignorance is mine—it damns me.

JOCASTA. What are you saying? Your face makes me
tremble, Lord.

OEDIPUS. I have a desperate fear the prophet sees.
But there is one more fact you must tell me.

JOCASTA. I'm so frightened I can hardly answer.

OEDIPUS. Did Laius go with just a few, or the large
troop
of armed men one expects of a prince?

JOCASTA. There were only five men. One was a 880
herald, there was a wagon for Laius to ride.

OEDIPUS. Ah! Now I can see it. Who told you this,
Lady?

JOCASTA. Our slave. The one man who survived and
came home.

OEDIPUS. Is he by chance on call here in our house?

JOCASTA. No. When he returned here, and saw
that you had all dead Laius' power,
he touched my hands and begged me to send him
out to our farmlands and sheepfolds,
so he'd be far away and out of sight.
I sent him. He was deserving—though a
slave—   890
of a much larger favor than he asked.

OEDIPUS. Can he be sent for immediately?

JOCASTA. Of course. But why do you insist on it?

---

872 **that savage curse:** The interdiction Oedipus declared against
Laius' murderer at ll. 290–307. 880 **a herald:** It is possible that the
presence of a herald should have indicated to Oedipus that the party
contained a prince or ruler. 887 **begged me:** A touch on the arm
was a formal supplication (like clasping a person's knees) which
appealed to piety in the hope of achieving a favorable response.

OEDIPUS. I'm so afraid, Lady, that I've said far
   too much. That's the reason I wish to see him now.
JOCASTA. I'll make him come. But I think I've a right
   to know what so deeply disturbs you, Lord.
OEDIPUS. So much of what I dreaded has happened,
   I will tell you everything I fear.
   No one has more right than you do,   900
   to know the risks to which I'm now exposed.
   Polybos of Corinth was my father.
   My mother was Merope, a Dorian.
   I was the leading citizen there
   until this chance happening   •
   challenged me. Shocking enough—
   but I took it much too hard.
   It was this: a drunk man at a feast swore
   that I was not Polybos' real son.
   Though seething, I said nothing. All that day   910
   I barely held it in. But next morning
   I put my question to mother and father.
   They were enraged at this man, and the insult
   he'd shot at me. Their words reassured me.
   Yet, the thing kept pounding in my mind.
   It stalked me. So, without telling my parents,
   I traveled to the Pythian oracle.
   But Apollo would not honor me
   with the knowledge I craved.
                      Instead,   920
   his words flashed other things—
   horror and disgust—at me:
   that I would be my mother's lover,
   that I would show a kind of children to the world
   it could not bear to look at, that I
   would murder the father whose seed I am.
   Once I had heard the god say that, I fled
   far from Corinth, measuring my distance
   from home by its place in the stars. I ran
   for someplace where I'd never see come true   930
   outrages like those predicted for me.
   But my flight carried me to just the place
   where you say that the king was killed.
   Oh, woman, here is the truth.
   As I strode toward those joining paths
   a herald, a colt-drawn wagon, and a man
   like the one you describe, met me.
   The man out front and the old man himself
   tried to crowd me off the roadway.
   The driver, who was forcing me aside,   940
   I smashed in anger.
                The old man watched me,
   he measured my approach, then leaning out
   he lunged down with his two-spiked goad
   at the center of my skull.

                 He was more than repaid:
   I hit him so fast with the staff
   this hand held, he was knocked back
   rolling off the cart, and lay face up.
   And then I killed them all.   950

   But if this stranger and Laius . . . were the same
     blood,
   whose triumph could be worse than mine?
   Is there a man born the gods hate more?
   Nobody, no Theban, no foreigner,
   can bring me into his home.
   No one can speak with me.
   They must all drive me out.
   I am the man who leveled—
   no one else!—this curse at myself.
   I love his wife with my hands   960
   repulsive from her husband's blood.
   Has not evil soaked through me
   poisoning my whole being?
   I must be banished, but I can't
   return to my parents, I can't set foot
   in my homeland, because there—
   I would marry my own mother.
   I would kill Polybos my father
   who gave me birth and brought me up.
   If someone said that things like these   970
   could only be the work of a savage god,
   he would be speaking the truth.
   O you perfect and terrifying gods! Never,
   never, let the day these things happen
   come to me. Let me be wiped from men's eyes
   before I see my body gripped
   by such shame and devastation.
LEADER. What you say terrifies us, Lord. But don't
   lose hope
   until you've heard it from the eyewitness.
OEDIPUS. That is the one hope I have left—   980
   to wait for that man to come from the fields.
JOCASTA. When he comes, what will you try to find
   out?
OEDIPUS. This: if his story matches yours,
   then I will have escaped destruction.
JOCASTA. What did you hear that was crucial in mine?
OEDIPUS. He told you Laius was killed by bandits.
   If he will still claim there were several,
   then I cannot be the killer. One man
   cannot be many. But if he says: one man,
   braving the road alone, did it,   990
   there's no more doubt.
   The evidence drags me down.
JOCASTA. Never. I told it just as he told me.

Be sure of it. He can't take back what he said—
the whole city heard him, not just me.
And even if he does change his story now
he can't show us that Laius' murder
happened as the god predicted.　　　　　Apollo
unmistakably said my son would kill Laius.　　　1000
That poor doomed child never had a chance
to kill his father because he was killed first.
I will never react to an oracle
by fearing everything in sight.

OEDIPUS. You've thought this out well. But you must
　　still send for that herdsman. Don't fail me.

JOCASTA. I'll send for him now. But come inside.
　　Would I do anything to displease you?

[Oedipus and Jocasta enter the palace.]

CHORUS. Let my speech, and all my acts,
　　prove my love for what's pure.　　　　　　　　1010
　　May my luck hold me, lifelong,
　　to the great far-reaching laws
　　who stride through the light-filled
　　skies they were born to. Olympos
　　alone was their father,
　　no human mind conceived them;
　　those laws never sleep or forget—
　　a mighty god lives in them
　　who does not age.
　　The tyrant is fathered　　　　　　　　　　　1020
　　by his violent will—
　　violent, and flushed
　　with wealth and power
　　which do him no good
　　but ruin his purpose,
　　he climbs his city to the ramparts—
　　then plunges to a sudden doom
　　where his quick feet are no help.
　　But there's another fighting will
　　I ask god never to destroy—　　　　　　　　1030
　　the will that makes our city thrive.
　　God protects us: I'll never stop
　　believing that.

　　If a man goes through life
　　speaking and showing contempt,
　　fears no Justice, feels no awe
　　for stone gods in their shrines,
　　let a harsh death punish
　　the doomed indulgence of that man.
　　For he's dishonest when he wins,　　　　　　1040
　　he can't resist disgraceful acts,
　　his hand reaches for things

too sacred to be touched.
　　When crimes like these, which god hates,
　　are not punished—but *honored*—
　　what good man will think his life safe
　　from god's arrows winging at his soul?
　　Why should I dance to *this* holy song?

　　If prophecies no longer lead
　　straight to events all men can see,　　　　　1050
　　I will honor no longer
　　the untouchable holy place,
　　Earth's navel at Delphi.
　　I will not go to Olympia
　　or the temple at Abai.
　　You, Zeus who hold power, if Zeus
　　king of all is your right name,
　　turn your mind to what's happening here:
　　prophecies made to Laius grow weak,
　　men are ignoring them,　　　　　　　　　　1060
　　Apollo is nowhere
　　glorious with praise:
　　the gods lose force.

[Jocasta enters from the palace carrying a suppliant's branch
and some smouldering incense. She approaches the altar of
Apollo near the palace door.]

JOCASTA. Lords of my country, this thought
　　came to me: to visit the gods' shrines
　　with a branch and incense in my hands.
　　For Oedipus lets alarms of every kind
　　inflame his mind. He won't let past
　　experience calm his present fears,
　　as a man of sense would.　　　　　　　　　1070
　　He's at the mercy of everybody's
　　terrifying words. Since he won't listen to me,
　　Apollo—you are the nearest god—

[Enter Messenger from the countryside.]

　　I come praying for your good will
　　as my branch shows. Cleanse us, cure our sickness.
　　When we see Oedipus distraught, we all shake,
　　like sailors catching fear from a nervous helmsman.

MESSENGER. Can you point out to me, strangers,
　　the house where King Oedipus lives? Or better,
　　can you tell me where the king is now?　　　1080

LEADER. He lives in that house, stranger. He's inside.
　　This woman is the mother of his children.

1053–55 Delphi, Olympia, Abai: All holy shrines and the goal of
religious pilgrimages.

MESSENGER. I wish her joy, and her family joy,
   that comes when a marriage bears fruit.
JOCASTA. No less to you, stranger, for those kind
    words.
   What have you to tell us or to ask us?
MESSENGER. Great news, Lady, for you and your
    mate.
JOCASTA. What is this news? Who sent you to us?
MESSENGER. I've come from Corinth. My news
   should make you very happy—though   1090
   it will sadden you some as well.
JOCASTA. What is it? How can it possibly do both?
MESSENGER. They're going to make him king. The
    people
   of the Isthmus want Oedipus to rule them.
JOCASTA. Isn't old Polybos still in power?
MESSENGER. No more. Death has put him in the
    tomb.
JOCASTA. Old man, are you saying that Polybos has
    died?
MESSENGER. Kill me if that's not the truth.

[Jocasta turns to a servant girl, who runs inside.]

JOCASTA. Girl, run to your master with this news.
   You oracles of the gods! Where are you now?   1100
   The man Oedipus feared he would kill,
   the man he ran from, that man's dead.
   Chance killed him, not Oedipus. Chance!

[Oedipus enters quickly from the palace.]

OEDIPUS. Darling Jocasta, my loving wife,
   why did you ask me to come out?
JOCASTA. Listen to what this man has to say.
   See what it does to god's proud oracle.
OEDIPUS. Where is he from? What is the news he has?
JOCASTA. From Corinth. He says Polybos your father
   is dead.
OEDIPUS. Say it, old man. I want to hear it from your
    mouth.   1110
MESSENGER. If the plain fact is what you want first,
   have no doubt he is dead and gone.
OEDIPUS. Was it treason, or did disease bring him
    down?
MESSENGER. A slight push tips an old man into still-
    ness.
OEDIPUS. Then it was some sickness that killed him?
MESSENGER. That, and the long years he had lived.
OEDIPUS. O yes, wife, why should we search Pythian
    smoke
   or be terrorized by birds screaming up there?

If signs like these had been telling the truth
I would have killed my father. But he's dead.   1120
He's safely in the ground, and I'm here,
who never raised a spear. Unless—
he died of longing for me, and that
is what my killing him means. No more than that.
This time, Polybos' death has swept
those worthless oracles with him to Hades.
JOCASTA. Didn't I promise you before they were
    worthless?
OEDIPUS. You did. But I was too worried to believe
   you.
JOCASTA. It's time to stop caring about all this.
OEDIPUS. I must care. I must not touch my
    mother's bed.   1130
JOCASTA. What should a human being fear?
   Chance is what shapes our lives.
   There's no such thing as real foreknowledge.
   The best life is one taken as it comes.
   This marriage with your mother—don't fear it.
   In their very dreams, too, many men
   have slept with their own mothers.
   A man who shrugs off such things
   as meaningless will bear his life best.
OEDIPUS. A brave speech which I would
    like to believe.   1140
   But how can I if my mother is still living?
   While she lives, I will live in fear,
   though you do your best to reason with me.
JOCASTA. Your father's tomb is a great flood of light.
OEDIPUS. Great, yes! But she's alive—she is my fear.
MESSENGER. What woman do you fear?
OEDIPUS. I dread that oracle from the god, stranger.
MESSENGER. Would it be wrong for someone else to
    know it?
OEDIPUS. No, you may hear it. Apollo told me
   I would become my mother's lover, that I   1150
   would have my father's blood on these hands.
   I haven't gone near Corinth since I heard that.
   Ever since, I have been lucky—yet,
   what happiness to see
   our parents with our own eyes!
MESSENGER. Did this oracle force you into exile?
OEDIPUS. To keep me from being my father's killer,
    old man.
MESSENGER. Then let me free you from your fear,
    King.
   I came here only with helping you in mind.
OEDIPUS. I would give anything to be
    free of fear.   1160
MESSENGER. I confess I came partly for that reason—
   to be favored by you when you've come home.

OEDIPUS. I'll never live where my parents live.

MESSENGER. My son, you can't possibly know what you're doing.

OEDIPUS. Why is that, old man? In god's name, tell me.

MESSENGER. Is it because of them you won't go home?

OEDIPUS. I am afraid Apollo told the truth.

MESSENGER. Afraid you'd do your parents unforgivable harm?

OEDIPUS. Exactly that, old man. I am in constant fear.

MESSENGER. Your fear is groundless. Do you grasp that?   1170

OEDIPUS. How can it be groundless if I'm their son?

MESSENGER. But Polybos was no relation to you.

OEDIPUS. What? Polybos was not my father?

MESSENGER. No more than I am. The same.

OEDIPUS. How the same? He fathered me and you didn't.

MESSENGER. He didn't father you any more than I did.

OEDIPUS. Why did he say, then, I was his son?

MESSENGER. He took you from my hands as a gift.

OEDIPUS. He loved me so much—knowing I came from you?

MESSENGER. His lack of children taught him to love you.   1180

OEDIPUS. And you? Did you buy me? Or find me somewhere?

MESSENGER. I found you. In the wooded hollows of Cithairon.

OEDIPUS. Why were you traveling out there?

MESSENGER. I had charge of sheep grazing those slopes.

OEDIPUS. A migrant hired to work our flocks?

MESSENGER. I saved your life that day, my son.

OEDIPUS. From what? Was something wrong with me?

MESSENGER. Your ankles might answer that question.

OEDIPUS. You know that? Why do you name my oldest wound?

MESSENGER. I cut the thongs that pierced and laced your feet.   1190

OEDIPUS. From birth I've carried the shame of those scars.

MESSENGER. That luck named you, Oedipus. That's who you are.

OEDIPUS. Did my mother or my father do this?
Speak the truth for god's sake.

MESSENGER. I don't know. The man who gave you to me will know that.

OEDIPUS. You took me from someone?
You didn't chance on me yourself?

MESSENGER. I took you from another shepherd.

OEDIPUS. Who was he? Tell me as plainly as you can.   1200

MESSENGER. He was known as someone who worked for Laius.

OEDIPUS. The same Laius who was once king *here*?

MESSENGER. The same one. This man worked as his shepherd.

OEDIPUS. Is he alive? Can I see him?

MESSENGER. A native could answer that better.

OEDIPUS. Does anyone here know what's become of this shepherd? Has someone seen him in town or in the fields? Speak up now. The time has come to make all of it known.

LEADER. I believe he means that same herdsman 1210 you've already sent for. Jocasta is the best one to ask.

OEDIPUS. Lady, do you recall the man we ordered here?
Is it that man he speaks of?

JOCASTA. Why ask about him? Don't pursue it, Oedipus,
don't waste a thought on his words. It's nothing.

OEDIPUS. I can't give up with clues like these in my hands.
How can I fail now to solve my birth?

JOCASTA. For god's sake, stop searching if you want to live.
Let my sickness be enough for us both.   1220

OEDIPUS. Accept it! My mother might be from slaves for three generations back—
would that make you lowborn?

JOCASTA. Please listen to me: do nothing more.

OEDIPUS. I cannot listen. I must have the truth.

JOCASTA. I'm thinking now only of what's best for you.

OEDIPUS. "What's best for me" exasperates me now.

JOCASTA. You poor child! Never find out who you are.

OEDIPUS. Someone bring me that herdsman. Let her glory in her precious birth.   1230

JOCASTA. Oh you poor doomed child! That is the only name
I can call you now. No other, forever!

[*Jocasta runs into the palace.*]

LEADER. Why has she gone, Oedipus,
driven out by some savage grief?
Evil is going to burst from this silence.

OEDIPUS. Let it burst! My seed may be base born,
   but I will see at last what it is.
   It may well be that my birth
   humiliates her female pride.
   But I, who have always known I am   1240
   the child of Luck, whose gifts are always good,
   will never know disgrace.
   Luck is my mother, my brothers are the months
   who measured out the low times
   in my life and the great ones.
   If these are my true kinsmen,
   how could I betray my nature
   by giving up the great search
   now that will find my birth?
CHORUS. By the gods of Olympos, if I have   1250
   a prophet's reach of eye and mind—
   tomorrow's moonlight
   will shine on you, Cithairon.
   Oedipus will honor you—
   his native mountain,
   his nurse, his mother. Nothing
   will keep us from dancing
   then, mountain joyful to our king!
   We call out to Phoebus Apollo:
   be the cause of our joy!   1260

[*Chorus turns toward Oedipus.*]

My son, who was your mother
out there? Which long-lived nymph
loved Pan in his mountain roaming?
Or did Apollo father you
on one of his swift brides
in the pleasing highlands?
Was it Hermes, Lord of Kyllene?
Or did Bakkhos of the mountain peaks
take you—a joyful find—
from the girls whose games he shares: 1270
the nymphs of Helikon?
OEDIPUS. Old men,
   if I can recognize a man I've never met,
   I think I see the herdsman we've been waiting for.
   Our fellow would be old, like the stranger coming.
   Those leading him are my own men.
   But I expect you'll know him better.
   Some of you will know him by sight.

[*Enter Herdsman, led by Oedipus' servants.*]

LEADER. I do know him. He is from Laius' house,
   a trusted shepherd if he ever had one.   1280
OEDIPUS. I ask you to speak first, Corinthian:
   is this the man you mean?
MESSENGER.   You're looking at him.
OEDIPUS. Now you, old man. Turn your eyes toward me.
   Answer every question I ask you.
   Did you once come from Laius' house?
HERDSMAN. I did. I wasn't a bought slave,
   I was born and raised in their house.
OEDIPUS. What was your work? How did you spend your time?
HERDSMAN. My life has been spent tending sheep.   1290
OEDIPUS. In what region did you normally work?
HERDSMAN. Mainly Cithairon, and the country around there.

[*Oedipus gestures toward the Messenger.*]

OEDIPUS. That man. Do you recall ever seeing him . . .
HERDSMAN. Recall him how? Doing what? Which man?

[*Oedipus goes to the Messenger and puts his hand on him.*]

OEDIPUS. This man right here. Have you ever seen him before?
HERDSMAN. Not that I recognize—not right away.
MESSENGER. It's no wonder, master. His memory's faded,
   but I'll revive it for him. I'm sure he knows me.
   We worked the pastures on Cithairon together—
   he with his two flocks, me with one—   1300
   for three whole grazing seasons, from early spring
   until Arcturus rose. When the weather turned cold
   I'd drive my flock home to its winter pens,
   he drove his away to Laius' sheepfolds.
   Do I describe what happened, old friend? Or don't I?
HERDSMAN. That's the truth, but it was so long ago.
MESSENGER. Do you remember giving me a boy
   I was to raise as my own son?
HERDSMAN. What? Why ask me that?

1263 **Pan:** A god holy to rural people, appropriate to events on Mt. Cithairon.   1267 **Hermes . . . Kyllene:** Like Pan, Hermes was a god well known to country people. Kyllene is a mountain in Arcadia, appropriate haunt of both Pan and Hermes.

1302 **Arcturus:** A star near the Big Dipper, which, when it appeared in September, signaled the end of summer in Greece.

MESSENGER. There, friend, is the man who
    was that boy.   1310

[*He nods toward Oedipus.*]

HERDSMAN. Damn you! Shut up and say nothing.

OEDIPUS. Don't you attack him for his words, old
    man.
    Your own ask to be punished far more.

HERDSMAN. Tell me, royal master, what I've done
    wrong.

OEDIPUS. You didn't answer him about the boy.

HERDSMAN. He's trying to make something out of
    nothing.

OEDIPUS. Speak willingly, or you'll speak under tor-
    ture.

HERDSMAN. Dear god! Don't hurt me, I'm an old
    man.

OEDIPUS. One of you bind his arms behind his back.

[*Servants approach the Herdsman and start to seize his
arms.*]

HERDSMAN. Why this, you doomed man? What
    else must you know?   1320

OEDIPUS. Did you give this man the child he claims
    you gave?

HERDSMAN. I did. I wish I had died that day.

OEDIPUS. You'll die yet if you don't speak the truth.

HERDSMAN. Answering you is what will get me killed.

OEDIPUS. I think this man is determined to stall.

HERDSMAN. No! I've said once that I gave him the
    boy.

OEDIPUS. Did the boy come from your house? Or
    someone else's?

HERDSMAN. Not from my house. Someone gave him
    to me.

OEDIPUS. Name the person! Name the house!

HERDSMAN. Don't ask that of me, master. For
    god's sake, don't.   1330

OEDIPUS. You will die if I ask one more time.

HERDSMAN. He was a child from the house of Laius.

OEDIPUS. A slave? Or was he born to Laius' own
    blood?

HERDSMAN. I've come to the terror—which I must
    speak.

OEDIPUS. And which I must hear. But I will hear it.

HERDSMAN. The child was said to be Laius' own son.
    Your lady in the house would know that best.

OEDIPUS. *She* gave you the child?

HERDSMAN.   She gave him, King.

OEDIPUS. To do what?   1340

HERDSMAN.   I was to let it die.

OEDIPUS. Kill her own child?

HERDSMAN.   She feared prophecies.

OEDIPUS. What prophecies?

HERDSMAN.   That this child would kill
    his father.

OEDIPUS. Why, then, did you give him to this old
    man?

HERDSMAN. I pitied him, master. The man would
    take him,
    I hoped, to a new home in another land.
    But that man saved him for this—
    the worst grief of all. If the child   1350
    he speaks of is you, master, you know,
    now, all the evil of your birth and life.

OEDIPUS. All! All! It has all happened,
    it was all true. O light! May this
    be the last time I see you.
    You see now who I am. I am
    the child who must not be born,
    I loved where I must not love,
    I killed where I must not kill.

[*Oedipus runs into the palace.*]

CHORUS. Men and women who live and die,   1360
    I set no value on your lives.
    Which one of you ever, who reaches
    for the true blessedness that lasts,
    seizes more than what seems blest?
    You live in that seeming
    a brief time, then you plunge.
    Your fate teaches me this, Oedipus,
    yours, you suffering man, the story
    god spoke through you: praise
    no human life, none, for its luck.   1370

O Zeus, no man drew a bow like this man,
    he shot his arrow home,
    winning power and pleasure and wealth,
    he killed the virgin Sphinx
    whose talons curl, who sang
    the god's black oracles.
    He fought death in our land,
    he towered against its threat.
    I've called you my king since that time,
    honoring you mightily, my Oedipus,   1380
    who wield the might of Thebes.

But now!—nobody's story
    has the sorrow of yours.
    O my Oedipus, this is your fame:
    the welcome of one harbor was enough

for you, both child and father, when your plow
drove through the room where women love.
How can the furrow your father plowed
not have screamed before now, at you, doomed
    man?

Time, who sees all, caught you   1390
living a life you never willed.
Time damns this marriage which is
no marriage, where the fathered child
fathered children himself.
O son of Laius, I wish
I'd never seen you. I fill my lungs
to cry with all my power,
to speak the truth in my heart:
you gave me once new breath,
Oedipus, but now you pour   1400
darkness through my eyes.

[Enter Servant from the palace.]

SERVANT. Masters, always the most honored men in
    our land,
    what crushing deeds you will see and hear!—
    whose sorrow you must bear, if you still feel
    a born Theban's love for the House of Labdacus.
    I don't think rivers could wash the evil
    out of this house, not the Danube or the Phasis,
    it hides so much suffering, which is now
    coming to light. But what happened inside
    was not involuntary evil, it was willed.   1410
    The griefs that hurt us worse are those
    we think we've chosen for ourselves.
LEADER. What we already knew made us suffer.
    Do you want to add more?
SERVANT. It is brief news to give or hear.
    Our royal lady Jocasta's dead.
LEADER. That pitiable woman. How did she die?
SERVANT. She killed herself. You will be spared the
    worst
    because you weren't there to see it.
    But you will hear exactly as I can   1420
    tell it, what that wretched woman suffered.
    She came raging through the courtyard
    straight for her marriage bed, the fists
    of both her hands clenched in her hair.
    Once in, she slammed the doors shut, calling out
    to Laius, so long dead, remembering
    the living seed of long ago, who killed Laius,

the mother living on to breed with her son
more ruined children.

                 She grieved for the bed   1430
where she had loved, and given birth
to all those doubled lives—
husband fathered by husband,
children sired by her child.
From here on I don't know how she died,
because Oedipus burst in shouting,
taking our eyes from her misery.
We watched him, stunned, as he plowed through us
feverishly asking each man for his spear,
demanding his wife who was not a wife,   1440
but the twice-mothering earth
out of whom he and his children came.
He was raving, but some divine hand
drove him toward his wife—none of us near him
    did.
With a savage yell, as though guided there,
he lunged at the double doors, and wrenching
hollow bolts from their sockets,
he broke through into the room. There we saw her,
the woman above us, hanging by her neck,
twisting there in a noose of tangled cords.   1450
He saw her, anguish roaring from deep inside him,
he reached and loosened the noose that held her.
When the poor lifeless woman was laid on the
    ground,
this was the terror we saw now: he pulled
the long pins of hammered gold from her gown,
these pins he raised and punched into his eyes
back through the sockets, shouting these words:
"Eyes, now you will never see
the evil I suffered and the evil I caused.
Now you will see blackness! Not those lives   1460
you should never have seen, not those yearned-for
faces you so long failed to know."
While he sang these tortured words,
not once, but many times his raised hands
struck his eyes. And the blood kept coming,
drenching his beard and cheeks, not a few wet
    drops—
a black storm of bloody hail lashed his face.

What this man and this woman did
broke so much evil loose, that evil joins
the whole of both their lives in grief.   1470
The happiness they once knew was real—
but now that happiness is ruin,
screaming, death, disgrace. Each misery
we have a name for has come here.
LEADER. Has his grief eased at all?

1407 **Phasis:** the Phasis is a river near the Russian/Iranian border, on
the edge of what was then the known world.

SERVANT. He shouts for someone to open the door-
    bolts:
  "Show this city its father-killer," he cries,
  "Show it its mother's. . . ." He spoke the word, I
    can't.
  He wants to banish himself from the land,
  not curse this house any longer   1480
  by living here under his own curse.
  He's so weak now, though, he needs to be helped.
  No one could stand up under a sickness like his.
  Look there. The doorbolts are sliding open.
  You will witness a vision of suffering
  even those it revolts must pity.

[*Oedipus emerges from the slowly opening palace doors. He
is blinded, with blood on his face and clothes, but the effect
should arouse more awe and pity than shock. He moves
with the aid of a servant.*]

LEADER. An eerie terror fills men's eyes
  at this pure and helpless anguish,
  more moving than any
  my eyes have ever touched.   1490
                          Man of pain,
  what madness has claimed you?
  Name the god who leapt
  from beyond our knowledge
  to make your naked life his enemy.

[*Moans.*]

  I cannot look at you—
  though I want so powerfully
  to speak with you, to learn from you,
  though your suffering grips my eyes—
  so strong are the shivers of awe   1500
  you send through me.
OEDIPUS. Ahhh! My whole life,
  my whole being is wretched.
  Where am I?
  Where does my misery lead?
  Is my voice
  fluttering lost out there
  like a stunned bird's?
  Where has my god thrown me down?
LEADER. In a cruel place, unbearable to see or
    hear.   1510
OEDIPUS. Darkness buries me in her hate, she
  takes me in her black hold.
  It's an unspeakable blackness,
  it can't be fought off,
  it keeps coming,

blowing evil all over me.
  Ahhh.
  Two things together strike deep in me:
  the pins plunged in my eyes,
  those crimes driving through my mind.   1520
LEADER. It is no wonder you feel
  nothing but pain now
  in both your mind and your flesh.
OEDIPUS. Ah friend, my faithful servant still,
  how gentle you are to the blind man.
  I know you are near me: your voice
  finds me in my darkness.
LEADER. What you did terrifies us. How could you
  kill your eyes? What god raised your hand?
OEDIPUS. Apollo, friends, it was Apollo   1530
  who did this. He made evil,
  perfect evil of my life.
  But the hand
  that struck these eyes
  was my hand.
  It was I in my wretchedness
  who struck, no one else.
  What good was there left for my eyes to see?
  I could see nothing in this world now
  with a glad heart.   1540
LEADER. You are right to say it.
OEDIPUS. Who could I look at? Or love?
  Whose greeting could I
  answer with fondness, friends?
  Drive me quickly from this place,
  the most ruined, most cursed,
  most god-hated man who ever lived.
LEADER. You're broken by what happened, you're
    broken
  by what's happening in your mind.
  I wish you'd never learned the truth.   1550
OEDIPUS. May the man die
  who found me in the pasture,
  who cut the thongs from my feet, . . .
  who saved me from that death for a worse life,
  a life I cannot thank him for.
  Had I died then, I would have caused
  no great grief to my people and myself.
LEADER. I wish he had let you die.
OEDIPUS. I'd not have come home to kill my father,
  no one could call me lover   1560

1530–32 **Apollo . . . did this. He made . . . perfect evil of my life:**
Lit. "It was Apollo, friends, Apollo who brought to completion these
my evils (*pathea*)." A *pathos* (sing.) is here, as often in Greek literature,
an unmerited suffering sent by a god.

of her from whose body I came.
I have no god now.
I'm son to a fouled mother,
I fathered children in the bed
where my father gave me
deadly life. If ever an evil
rules all other evils
it is my evil, it is the life
god gave to Oedipus.

LEADER. How can I say you acted wisely? You   1570
  blinded yourself. Why didn't you choose death?

OEDIPUS. There was no other way but mine.
  Don't try to persuade me now. No more advice.
  If I had eyes, how could those eyes
  bear the sight of my father among the dead?
  Or my poor wronged mother—look at her? I've
    done them
  violence hanging could not justly punish.
  Should I ache to see my children,
  children born to the life that mine must live?
  Never. Not with my eyes. Nor this city,   1580
  its towers, nor the light shining
  from our stone gods. I lost my right to these loves
  when I commanded we outlaw the vile killer—
  myself!—totally wretched, though I won power
  like no other Theban, now proven by the gods
  the defiled son of our dead king.
  Once I found out my own sickness
  how could my eyes look calmly on my people?
  They could not! If I could deafen my ears
  I would, I'd deaden my whole body,   1590
  go blind and deaf to shut those evils out.
  The silence in my mind would be sweet.
  Oh Cithairon, why did you take me in?
  Or once you had me, why didn't you
  kill me instantly? My birth would have left no trace.
  O Polybos and Corinth, I thought you
  were my ancestral strength, the house of my fathers.
  I was their glorious boy growing up,
  but my life there was a fair skin
  over a festering disease. My vile self   1600
  now shows its vile birth.
                  You,
  three roads, and you, darkest ravine,
  you, grove of oaks, you, narrow place
  where those three paths drank blood from my
    hands,
  my fathering blood pouring into you.
  Do you remember what I did while you watched?
  And when I came here, what I did then?
  O marriages! You marriages! You made us,

we sprang to life, then from the same seed   1610
you burst fathers, brothers, sons,
kinsmen shedding kinsmen's blood,
brides and mothers and wives—the most loathsome
atrocities that strike mankind.
I must not name what should never have been.
If you love the gods, hide me out there,
kill me, throw me into the sea,
anywhere I will be lost from your eyes.
Come take me. Don't shrink from touching
this ruined man. Believe me. Don't fear me.   1620
I am the only man in all the world
who can carry these sorrows.

LEADER. Kreon will help you. He's come when we
    need him.
  He can act, he can advise you.
  He is the only ruler we have left
  to protect Thebes in your place.

OEDIPUS. Do I know words that he will listen to?
  What would make him believe me?
  I wronged him so deeply.
  I proved myself so false to him.   1630

[Kreon enters.]

KREON. I don't come to mock you, Oedipus.
  I won't dwell on the wrongs you did me.
  Men, even if you are not sensitive
  to human feeling, keep some awe
  for the nurturing light flaming from the Sun.
  Don't leave this stark defilement in the open.
  The earth, the holy rain, the light, all hate it.
  Take him quickly back to the palace.
  If these sorrows are shared
  only by our bloodkin,   1640
  it will spare us impiety.

OEDIPUS. I feared worse from you. I thank god
  you show your noble kindness to me,
  who am worthless. I have one thing to ask.
  It is for your sake, not mine.

KREON. What do you want, that makes you ask it like
    that?

OEDIPUS. Expel me quickly to some place . . . no
    living person will find me.

KREON. I would have done that. But now I must first
  ask the god what I should do.   1650

OEDIPUS. He's given you his command already.
  I killed my father. I am unholy. I must die.

KREON. The god did say that. But what has happened
  to us is so desperate, we must be
  absolutely sure before we act.

OEDIPUS. What else is there to know about me? I'm
    lost.
KREON. This time, I think even you will trust the god.
OEDIPUS. I will. But there is something I charge you,
    yourself, to do. I beg it! Bury her
    who's lying inside as you think proper.   1660
    Give her the rites due your kinswoman.
    As for me, don't doom my father's city
    by having me haunt it while I live.
    Let me live out my life on the mountain,
    on Cithairon, my own famous mountain,
    which my father and mother while they lived
    had chosen as my rightful tomb. Let me die
    out there, just as my parents decreed I die.
    And yet, I know this now:
    no sickness can kill me, nothing can.   1670
    I was saved from that death
    to face an evil awesome and unknown.
    Let my fate take me now, where it will.

    My children, Kreon.
    My sons will not need help from you—they're
      grown.
    They'll find a way to live anywhere.
    But my poor wretched girls, who never
    ate anywhere but at my table—
    they've never been without me.
    I fed them with my own hands.   1680
                           Care for them.
    If you can do it, let me touch them now,
    let me give in to my grief.
    Grant it Kreon, from your great heart.
    Touching them with my hands, I would
    imagine them as my eyes once saw them.

[*The gentle sobbing of Oedipus' two daughters is heard
offstage. Soon two small girls enter.*]

    Is it?
    O gods, do I hear my children sobbing?
    Has Kreon pitied me?
    Has he given me my own dear children?   1690
    Has he?
KREON. I have. I brought them to you
    because I knew how much joy
    as always, you would take in them.
OEDIPUS. Bless this kindness of yours. Bless your luck.
    May the gods guard you better than they did me.
    Children, where are you? Come to me.
    These are your brother's hands, hands
    of the man who created you, hands that changed
    my once bright eyes to these black sockets.   1700

He, children, saw nothing, knew nothing,
he fathered you in his own place of life,
where his own seed grew. I can still weep
for you, though I can't see you.

[*Oedipus takes his daughters in his arms.*]

I imagine how bitter your lives will be.
I know how men will force you to live.
What great occasions could you join, what festivals,
without being sent home in tears,
forbidden any share in the holy joy?
When it's time for your marriage, my
    daughters,   1710
what man would risk all the revulsion,
the gods' hatred for me that will wound you,
just as that hatred destroyed my parents?
Do we lack any evil? Your father killed
his father, he started lives where his began,
he took you from the place he was sown,
the place he was born.
                    Those are the insults
you will face. Who will marry you?
No man, my children. You will grow old   1720
unmarried, living a dried-up childless life.

Kreon, you are the only father they have left,
for the parents who conceived them are both lost.
Keep them from rootless wandering,
unmarried and helpless. They are your kin.
Don't bring them down to what I am.
Pity them. They are so young, and but for you,
alone. Touch my hand, kind man,
make that touch your promise.

[*Kreon touches him.*]

Children, had you been old enough to
    comprehend,   1730
I would have taught you more.
My prayer now can be no more than this:
that you live always where people
allow you peace, to make your life
better than your father's was.
KREON. Enough grief. Go inside now.
OEDIPUS. Bitter words, which I must obey.
KREON. Time runs out on all things.
OEDIPUS. Grant my request before I go.
KREON. Tell me, I'll hear you.   1740
OEDIPUS. Banish me from my homeland.
KREON. Ask god to do that, not me.
OEDIPUS. I am the man the gods hate most.

KREON. Then you will have your wish.

OEDIPUS. Do you consent?

KREON. I never promise when I can't be sure.

OEDIPUS. Then lead me inside.

KREON. Come. Let go of your children now.

OEDIPUS. Do not take them from me.

KREON. Let go of your power, too.   1750
 You won power, but it did not
 stay with you all your life.

[*Kreon leads Oedipus into the palace.*]

CHORUS. Thebans, that man is the same Oedipus
 whose great mind solved the famous riddle.

He was a most powerful man.
Which of us, seeing his glory,
did not wish his luck could be ours?
Now, look at what wreckage the seas
of savage trouble make of his life.
To know a man's truth, wait   1760
to see his life end.
Look at him on that day.
Don't call a man god's friend
until he has come through life
and crossed over into death
never having been god's victim.   1766

[*Exit.*]

ESSAY: AN APPROACH TO THE PLAY

A central concern of this play seems to be the ambiguous status of the search for knowledge. Once Oedipus devotes himself to uncovering the truth about the murder of Laius, he is relentless, pursuing all leads, even when it seems certain that doing so ensures his own destruction. Tiresias tries to prevent the investigation; Jocasta tries to curtail it when she sees where it will lead; the shepherd who gave him away risks torture rather than cooperate. Still Oedipus refuses to abandon the search. His name, in fact, is a pun which implies this aspect of his character. His foster parents named him Oedipus, "swollen foot," presumably because of the aftereffects of his foot binding when an infant. The name also puns in other ways, however, that are more central to the plot and theme of Sophocles' play. The first half of his name, *vida*, sounds like the Greek words for "I know" and "I see," reminders both of the quest he engages in in the play and its tragic result. In the play's first scene he commits himself to uncovering the truth; by the end, when he finally sees in a figurative sense, he is literally blind—in the condition of Tiresias at the play's beginning.

In part because Aristotle seemed to regard the play as his paradigmatic tragedy in *The Poetics* (an excerpt from which appears earlier in the text), discussions of the play have generally been bound up with discussions of the nature of tragedy. The play's evocation of a sense of inevitability in plot and its raising of questions of human autonomy and responsibility, for example, have in part shaped our perception of what constitutes tragedy, as does the character of Oedipus as "tragic hero." Other characters, whether major or minor, seem to serve as foils of Oedipus, including Laius, dead before the play begins but present throughout in the plague, in people's memories, in Oedipus' story about the encounter at Phocis. What we discover in that encounter is that father and son share a similar sense of self-importance and an impetuosity that caused Laius to strike out at Oedipus and Oedipus to strike back, an impetuosity that we see in the reaction of both men to the Delphic oracle and in Oedipus' reactions during the play.

Oedipus is renowned in Thebes as the one who had used his superior intellectual cleverness to deliver the city from its previous "plague," the Sphinx, and he seems at the beginning of the play to be confident that he will save them once more. We can see this aspect of his character by reading the play's prologue carefully, comparing the moment of Kreon's arrival with the news from the Delphic oracle (beginning at line 101) to what follows this news. In the speech with which Oedipus begins the play, he reveals a good deal about himself and about his self-image. For example, his attitude toward the citizens of Thebes—he calls them his children—is decidedly paternal, and his self-confidence (or is it self-centeredness?) is evident in his repeated use of first-person pronouns and his self-characterization as "I, Oedipus, who bear the famous name." When the priest speaks to him of the concerns of his fellow Thebans, he addresses Oedipus in words that evoke the rhetoric of prayer. He seems to have been granted—and maybe to have fostered—a quasi-divine status in the community. Part of the play's startling effect is how radically changed this status is going to be in just a couple of hours.

The exact nature of the Sphinx riddle is itself connected to questions about the ambiguous status of knowledge. The answer to the riddle is "a human being," but less generically it is Oedipus himself, who began life as the hobbled child on four legs, who walks self-assuredly on stage at the beginning of the play on two legs, and who will, at its conclusion, be led off, in effect, on three. He is himself the answer to the riddle of the Sphinx. Part of the emotional effect of the play for many readers is this realization that what happens to Oedipus seems to have universal import: The answer to the riddle is both "a human being" and "Oedipus."

The same instinct that made him a hero also makes him a victim. In solving the current mystery—who killed Laius—he condemns himself, even as the focus of his questioning shifts during the course of the play from "who killed Laius?" to "who is Oedipus?" In this way the value of his curiosity, and even of his accomplishments, is called into question in what has come to be seen as the classic example of dramatic irony. Dramatic irony depends upon a difference in knowledge between what a character knows and what the audience knows. When Oedipus begins his response to the priest by assuring him that, "sick as you are,/not one of you suffers a sickness like mine" (73–74), we, who know the plot of the legend from the outset, hear more in these words than the assertion that the concerned father of the city suffers more than his sick children. Other examples of dramatic irony might also be found by a careful reading of the remainder of the prologue, after the arrival of Kreon.

We are prepared to see this irony very early, in fact, for the opening two speeches in particular, combined with our foreknowledge of the plot in general, place us in Tiresias' position almost from the beginning. We know through prior familiarity with the myth what he knows as seer. The dialogue with Tiresias therefore raises some troubling questions. Knowing what we do, would we answer Oedipus' question? Tiresias arrives committed not to speak the truth he knows, and yet Oedipus gets him to talk. If we study how Oedipus does this, and how he responds after he hears what Tiresias has to say, we learn much about how and why Oedipus plays into the prophecy so completely, even though his intentions are the reverse.

Indeed, the central role played by the prophetic knowledge of Tiresias and the Delphic oracle, both in the play itself and in the episodes from the myth that precede the play, raises questions about the degree of freedom humans have. Are the lives of the characters in this play determined by themselves or by some other force?

If controlled by some greater power, is this power benevolent, indifferent, or sadistic toward humans? Is Oedipus a noble character victimized by forces beyond his control? Was his "fate" inescapable? Such questions about individual autonomy have implications for one's view of what is moral, as well as for one's view of what history can tell us. At a literary level, the relationship of plot and character is questioned— do characters cause the events they perform, or do events form the characters? From our point of view—unlike that of the characters, but very like that of a fifth-century B.C. Athenian audience looking back at a story which alleges to have taken place in the mythic past—it is not the future but the past which is unchangeable and seems "inevitable." From a literary point of view, our act of rereading a narrative or of seeing a play for a second time puts us into the position of Tiresias or the oracle. As we have already suggested, this may be an artificial perspective which unnaturally exaggerates the power of fate. We see what *did* happen and the events leading to it; the process may look to us like inescapable causation. But can we be sure that alternatives were unavailable?

Looking backward, we see what appear to be irresistible forces at work in *Oedipus the King*, frustrating human intentions: People who do their best to avoid a hostile fate unexpectedly fulfill it. However, the oracle never commanded any character to behave in a particular way. The oracle foretold what *would* happen, and the son of Laius and Jocasta *did* kill his father and marry his mother as the oracle predicted. But the oracle did not say that he *had* to do so. Did the oracle, then, really *compel* the behavior of Laius or of Oedipus? In parallel fashion we might ask, does *our* foreknowledge of the plot compel their behavior? Had they been different people, with different personalities, would the oracle still inevitably have been fulfilled? If Laius had chosen to raise Oedipus, would his son have killed him? If Oedipus had persisted in his questioning of the oracle about his parentage (or had returned from Delphi to what he thought was his hometown of Corinth and to what he thought were his parents), would he ever have killed his father? Perhaps it is precisely human freedom and individuality that achieve the history that has been foreseen—foreseen, but not predetermined. Perhaps. And yet, however much we may rationally try to describe them away, the play continues to raise questions that demand answers about the limits of human freedom. Oedipus seems noble in the play—and even ennobled by what happens in it—but does his nobility come from accepting his "fate"? Or from accepting responsibility for his own chosen behavior?

Euripides

THE BACCHAE

Translated by Michael Cacoyannis

About the Author   Euripides (480/81–406 B.C.) was some fifteen years younger than Sophocles; both died in 406. They wrote at the same time in the same city, Athens, for the same theater, a theater dedicated to the god Dionysus. Euripides wrote at least eighty-eight plays for this theater, of which nineteen survive. However, he won only five festival prizes during his life, compared to at least seventy-two for his older rival. In general, he is considered a more experimental dramatist than Sophocles, and he seems more skeptical about traditional Athenian (and Greek) beliefs. For example, he did not write trilogies but instead developed his ideas and problems within the more limited scope of single plays. Perhaps because of this, he uses the chorus more obviously than his contemporaries as a device to develop his plays' thematic aspects.

About the Play   *The Bacchae* is one of Euripides' very last plays, probably written in the year before he died, and was presented for the first time in the year after his death. The main conflict is between the Theban ruler Pentheus and the god Dionysus, yet the title characters are the women (including those of the chorus) who give themselves up to the power of the god. Despite the lecherous reputation of Bacchus/Dionysus and the moralist's fear of the irrational and where it may lead, this devotion of the Bacchae does not generally lead to terrible or even unchaste activities. However, as this play shows, it *can* lead to such activities, for here a mother helps a mob of women tear her son the king into pieces with their bare hands and fingernails. This is an act which is not only horrible in itself, but destructive of family—a reversal of mother-love—and socially subversive from the perspective of both class and gender. With the death of Pentheus, the fabric of social order is torn completely apart.

CHARACTERS

DIONYSUS, also called Bromius and Bacchus
CHORUS OF ASIAN BACCHAE, followers of
 Dionysus
TEIRESIAS, a blind seer
CADMUS, former king of Thebes

PENTHEUS, his grandson and present king
A GUARD
A HERDSMAN
A MESSENGER
AGAVE, daughter of Cadmus and mother of Pentheus

SCENE

Before the king's palace in Thebes. Across from the gates, in the downstage area, is the tomb of Semele (Dionysus' mother), half-ruined and thickly covered with vine. Every now and then, a strand of smoke rises up out of the stones. Access to the city can be gained on all sides. Upstage left is the way to Mount Cithaeron.

There is a crash of thunder, followed by an eerie stillness, accentuated by the rustling of leaves. Out of it grows a distant drone of women's voices, and Dionysus appears.

He carries a thyrsus (a stick twined with ivy), and his scant dress, draped with animal skin, suggests the Orient. His flowing blond hair, cascading around his shoulders, and his lithe, smooth-skinned limbs complement the feline, almost feminine grace of his movements.

DIONYSUS. I, Dionysus, son of Zeus, am back in Thebes.
I was born here, of Semele, daughter of Cadmus,
blasted from her womb by a bolt of blazing thunder.
Why am I here? A god in the shape of a man,
walking by the banks of Ismenus, the waters of Dirce?
Look out there! That house in ruins,
still smoking, smoldering still with unquenchable flame,
is my mother's monument,
her thunder-dug grave,
undying evidence of spiteful Hera's rage.
Let's give some praise to Cadmus,
who turned it into consecrated ground, a living temple
that I shrouded with clustering vine.
I left behind the gold-abounding lands
of Lydia and of Phrygia,
Persia's sun-beaten plains and Bactria's giant walls,
crossing the winter-scorched earth of the Medes
and the length of happy Arabia, in short,
all Asia down to its shimmering seashores
where Greeks and barbarians freely mingle
in teeming, shapely-towered cities,
and here I am. In Greece.
This is the first of its cities I visit.
I danced my way throughout the East,
spreading my rituals far and wide— a God
made manifest to men.
Of all Greek cities, Thebes is the one I chose
to rouse into a new awareness,
dressing Greek bodies in fawnskins,
planting the thyrsus in Greek hands,
my ivied spear.
My mother's sisters—
were there ever more unsisterly sisters—
gossiped that this Dionysus was no child of Zeus,
that Semele having slept with some man
proceeded—on Cadmus' cunning advice—
to attribute her sinful conception to God.
No wonder Zeus struck her dead, they would prattle,
taking a lover and brazenly lying!
Well! These sisters, all three,
I've stung into a frenzy and steered them
from their homes into the mountains,
where I left them raving. Complete of course
with full orgiastic trappings. What is more,
all the women of Thebes, but all,
I've sent stampeding out of doors. They're up there now,
milling with Cadmus' daughters under the fresh-smelling pines
or high upon the rocks. This town must learn,
even against its will, how much it costs
to scorn God's mysteries and to be purged.
So shall I vindicate my virgin mother
and reveal myself to mortals as a God,
the son of God.
Now hear this.
King Cadmus has conferred the powers of his throne
with all attending honors on his grandson, Pentheus.
This God-fighting upstart snubs me; banishes my name
from public sacrifice and private prayer.
He'll soon find out, and every Theban with him,
whose birthright is divine and whose is not.
Once that score is settled, I'll move on
to manifest myself in other lands. But should this town,
in blind anger, take up arms to drive my Bacchae
from the hills,
I'll give them war,
leading my women's army to the charge.
To this end,
I have disguised myself as a mortal,
adopting the ways and features of a man.

[The Chorus of Asian Bacchae appears during the following lines, coming from the same direction as Dionysus. They wear fawnskins and garlands of ivy leaves and flowers twined around their necks. Apart from the thyrsus, several carry skin drums of various shapes, which they beat as the action—or their emotion—requires]

You! Women of Tmolus, Lydia's towering mountain,
my band of initiates, you,
whom I unplucked from your primitive lands
to be my road companions and my friends,
raise up your native Phrygian drums
that pulse to rhythms that are mother earth's and mine.
Surround the royal home of Pentheus with your beat
and turn the city out to see. Meanwhile,
I'll make my way to those Cithaeron slopes
that seethe with Theban Bacchae
and join their dance.

[Dionysus goes off toward Mount Cithaeron to a rising crescendo of drumbeats]

CHORUS. Out of the heart of Asia
down from the sacred heights of Tmolus
have I come. For the God—
Bromius, Bacchus, Dionysus—
fatigue is sweet to the limbs,
and effortless effort the trek
when you are shouting with joy.
Who is there in the street? Who?
Who is lurking in the house? Stand still,
stand back and hold your breath,
while I chant a prayer immemorial,
in praise of Dionysus.

Oh, happy the man who, blessed by his knowledge
  of God,
discovers purity.
Who opens his heart to togetherness.
Who joins in mountain-dancing
and sacred cleansing rituals. He,
who sanctifies the orgies of Cybele,
the mother of fertility,
waving the thyrsus high,
crowning his head with ivy,
in honor of Dionysus.

Go, Bacchae, go, go, go! Bring
God's godly son—our Bromius—
down from the Phrygian hills
out into the spacious streets of Greece—
the home of Dionysus.
Him,
whom his mother carried
to premature and painful birth
when in a crash of thunder
she was death-struck by a fiery bolt.
But quicker than death,
Zeus swept him up and plunged him
into a makeshift womb—
secure from Hera's eyes—
in the thick of his thigh,
stitched with stitches of gold.
As time ripened into fate
he delivered the bull-horned God
and crowned him with a crown of serpents.
Thus was created the custom
for thyrsus-carrying maenads
to twine snakes in their hair.

Oh, Thebes, Semele's nurse,
crest your walls with ivy.
Burst into greenness, burst
into a blaze of bryony,
take up the bacchanalian beat

with branches of oak and of fir,
cover your flesh with fawnskin
fringed with silver-white fleece
and lifting the fennel,
touch God
in a fit of sanctified frenzy.
Then all at once, the whole land will dance!
Bacchus will lead the dancing throngs to the mountain,
the mountain,
which is home to that mob of women,
who rebelled against shuttle and loom
answering the urge
of Dionysus.

Oh holy heights of Crete
cradling the caves of the Curetes
where Zeus was born.
There, the triple-crested Corybantes
traced in vibrant skin
the circle of my joy.
They married its percussive strength
to the wailing sweetness of flutes,
then put it into Rhea's hands
to draw the earth-beat out
and make it throb in Bacchic song.
In time, the frenzied Satyrs
from the Mother-Goddess stole the drum
and struck up dances for the feasts,
held every second year,
to honor and give joy to Dionysus.

How sweet to the body, when
breaking loose from the mountain revels
you collapse to the ground in a fawnskin
after hunting the goat.
How sweet the kill—
the fresh-smelling blood—
the sacramental relishing
of raw flesh . . .

Oh Asia, great mother,
my distant mountain home!
How the mind races back
to those peaks that clang in glory,
of Bromius, evoë . . .
Your ground flows with milk,
flows with wine, flows with nectar from the bees.
Like smoke from a Syrian incense,
the fragrant God arises with his torch of pine.
He runs, he dances in a whirl of flame,
he rouses the faithful
crazing their limbs with his roar,

while he races the wind,
his soft hair streaming behind.
And his call resounds like thunder:
"Go, my bacchae, go!
Let Tmolus with its golden streams
reverberate with songs of Dionysus,
and the vibrant crash of drums.
Sing out in joy
with loud Phrygian cries,
while the holy sweet-throated flute
climbs the holy scale and the scaling maenads climb
up the mountain,
the mountain."

It is then, that a girl like me
knows happiness. When she is free,
like a filly playfully prancing
around its mother,
in fields without fences.

[*The Chorus withdraws silently to one side as Teiresias
enters, ivy-crowned and with a fawnskin over his shoulders.
His festive dress seems oddly out of step with his old age
and ascetic bearing. Being blind, he carries a staff, tipped
with ivy leaves*]

TEIRESIAS. Who is at the gates? Go call Cadmus out,
  Cadmus, son of Agenor who sailed from distant
    Sidon
  to build the fortress walls of Thebes.
  Just say Teiresias wants him. He already knows
  why I am here. We made a pact, he and I
  —old me with him who is older still—
  to take up the thyrsus, put on our fawnskins
  and top them with garlands of twirling ivy.

[*Cadmus comes out of the palace, forestalling the Guard
who is about to call him. Like Teiresias, he is very old and
looks equally incongruous in his Dionysiac garb*]

CADMUS. Dear friend! I knew you were here by the
    sound of your voice,
  the voice of wisdom that makes a wise man wel-
    come.
  I come to you ready, dressed to please God,
  as indeed I should, for is not Dionysus
  my own daughter's son! Now that mankind has seen
    his light
  we must do our very best to exalt him. So!
  Where should we dance? Where do we fling a leg
  and toss our grizzly heads? It is for you
  to guide me, Teiresias, though you be as ancient as
    I.

Initiation is your job. I'll never tire night or day,
  of thumping the ground with my thyrsus. Oh, what
    bliss
  to forget how very old one is!
TEIRESIAS. You speak the way I feel. Young again
  and just as tempted to try a little dance.
CADMUS. You don't think that a carriage—for the
    mountains—
  would be more sensible?
TEIRESIAS. Indeed no.
  That would diminish our respect for the God.
CADMUS. Then let me, being older, be your nurse-
  maid, old man.
TEIRESIAS. We'll let the God lead us. No need to exert
  ourselves.
CADMUS. Are we the only men in Thebes to dance to
  Bacchus?
TEIRESIAS. The only ones with healthy minds. The
  rest   are sick.
CADMUS. We are wasting time. Here, take my hand.
TEIRESIAS. And you take mine. There, get a good
  grip.
CADMUS. After all, who am I, a mortal, to put down
  the Gods?
TEIRESIAS. Only fools play speculative games with the
    Gods.
  But we, we cling to what we learned from our
    fathers,
  beliefs that are as old as time and as immune
  to the onslaught of words, no matter how clever the
    theory,
  how complex the argument, the human mind can
    invent.
  No doubt people will say it's a disgrace—
  an old man like me, dancing, with ivy in my hair.
  Well, let them! Who ever heard of God
  segregating the young from the old,
  saying these should dance and these should not?
  He expects to be honored by one and all,
  not by degrees or in sections.
CADMUS. Teiresias, you cannot see the light
  so let my words enlighten you.
  I see Pentheus, the son of Echion, to whom
  I've handed over all powers of state,
  rushing toward the palace.
  How wild he looks! There's something in the wind.
  Let's hear.

[*Pentheus bursts onto the stage, accompanied by his military
guard. He is about the same age as Dionysus, whom he
resembles in looks but little else. Austerely dressed, he is as
angular in his masculinity as he is strident when, as now, he*

is in a rage. He does not notice Cadmus and Teiresias, who have crept out of his way.]

PENTHEUS. What an unholy mess!
　No sooner does one venture on a journey,
　than rumor plagues the town and things get out of
　　hand.
　Our women, I am told, have left their homes,
　in a religious trance—what travesty!—
　and scamper up and down the wooded mountains,
　　dancing
　in honor of this newfangled God, Dionysus,
　whoever he may be.
　In the middle of each female group
　of revelers, I hear,
　stands a jar of wine, brimming! And that taking
　　turns,
　they steal away, one here, one there, to shady nooks,
　where they satisfy the lechery of men,
　pretending to be priestesses,
　performing their religious duties. Ha!
　That performance reeks more of Aphrodite than of
　　Bacchus.
　The ones I have already caught are being guarded,
　　manacled
　and safely locked behind bars. The others, still at
　　large,
　I shall thrash out of the mountains, the lot,
　including my own mother, Agave, and her sisters
　Ino and Autonoe, I'll slap them into irons, I swear,
　I'll put a stop to this orgiastic filth!
　The other news
　is that some stranger has arrived in town,
　a sorcerer from Lydia, a conjurer of sorts,
　with golden scented hair tumbling down to his
　　shoulders,
　a skin that glows like wine, and eyes
　that promise Aphrodite's secret charms.
　He spends his nights and days with girls, I hear,
　enticing them with his Bacchic witchcraft.
　Just let me catch him hanging round these streets,
　and his thyrsus-tapping, hair-tossing days are over.
　His body will be looking for his head.
　He is the one who spreads the tale
　that Dionysus is a God,
　hatched from the thigh of Zeus,
　in which he had been sewn. As if we didn't know
　the truth about Dionysus and his liar of a mother,
　both of them burned to a cinder by a bolt of flame
　hurled by Zeus, her so-called bedmate.
　Foul-mouthed foreigner! His tongue will earn him
　the foulest punishment my power can pronounce.

Death by hanging! Let him be warned, whoever he
　may be.

[He turns to go and sees Teiresias first, then Cadmus]

　Ye Gods! What new marvel have we here? Teiresias,
　the prophet, all dolled up in spotted skins!
　And my mother's father—how grotesque—
　playing bacchant with his wand and all!
　I am ashamed, sir! How can a man so old
　be so devoid of sense!
　Take off that ivy, will you?
　And drop that thyrsus. Now! Do you hear?
　This is all *your* doing, Teiresias! Using him,
　to launch this new God to the masses.
　Convenient, isn't it? Give religion a boost
　and prophets grow fat, raking in the profits
　from reading the stars and fire-magic.
　You can thank your white hairs for being here and
　　not in prison,
　chained with those raving females; just the place for
　　frauds
　who encourage their obnoxious rituals. Take my
　　word,
　when women are allowed to feast on wine, there is
　　no telling
　to what lengths their filthy minds will go!
CHORUS. The blasphemy of the man! Who are you
　to think you can insult the Gods? Or Cadmus,
　who sowed the seed from which you sprang?
　Are you so bent on shaming your father's house?
TEIRESIAS. When a sensible man
　has a good cause to defend, to be eloquent
　is no great feat. Your tongue is so nimble
　one might think you had some sense, but your
　　words
　contain none at all. The powerful man
　who matches insolence with glibness is worse than a
　　fool.
　He is a public danger!
　This new God whom you dismiss,
　no words of mine can attain
　the greatness of his coming power in Greece. Young
　　man,
　two are the forces most precious to mankind.
　The first is Demeter, the Goddess.
　She is the Earth—or any name you wish to call
　　her—
　and she sustains humanity with solid food.
　Next came the son of the virgin, Dionysus,
　bringing the counterpart to bread, wine
　and the blessings of life's flowing juices.

His blood, the blood of the grape,
lightens the burden of our mortal misery.
When, after their daily toils, men drink their fill,
sleep comes to them, bringing release from all their
     troubles.
There is no other cure for sorrow. Though himself a
     God,
it is his blood we pour out
to offer thanks to the Gods. And through him,
we are blessed.
You mock the legend
of his being stitched inside the thigh of Zeus!
Let me teach you how legends are born.
When Zeus snatched the infant God out of the
     flames
and lifted him to Olympus, Hera, his wife,
schemed to have him thrown out of heaven. But
     Zeus,
with typical God's wit, devised his own counterplot.
He tore some pieces off the sky that envelopes the
     earth,
and presented them to nagging Hera
as the salvaged limbs of the child,
while he rushed the real Dionysus to safety.
Men, however, through retelling a story,
often wander from the truth. In time,
out of a mere play of words, grew this myth,
that the child had been salvaged *in* the limbs of
     Zeus.
This God is also a prophet. Possession by his ecstasy,
his sacred frenzy, opens the soul's prophetic eyes.
Those whom his spirit takes over completely
often with frantic tongues foretell the future.
His power even stretches to the realm of war.
You can see an army, positioned and ready for
     battle,
drop their spears and run for their lives
crazed out of their wits, by the grace of Dionysus.
A day will come when you shall see him
straddling the rocks of Delphi amid a blaze of
     torches,
leaping from peak to peak, swinging and hurling
     high
his thyrsus, the emblem of his glory
acclaimed throughout Greece. So Pentheus,
listen to me. Do not mistake the rule of force
for true power. Men are not shaped by force.
Nor should you boast of wisdom, when everyone
     but you
can see how sick your thoughts are. Instead,
welcome this God to Thebes. Exalt him with wine,
garland your head and join the Bacchic revels.

It's not for Dionysus to force women to be modest.
As in all things, moderation depends on our nature.
Remember this! No amount of Bacchic revels
can corrupt an honest woman.
Also, remember your own deep pleasure
when the crowds swarm outside your gates
and shout glory to your name.
Why should not *he*
be glad to have his name exalted?
I say he is.
So I—and Cadmus, whom you ridicule—
will wear our ivy crowns and will dance.
Old as we are, I promise you we'll dance.
And nothing you can ever say will make me
turn against the Gods. For you are sick,
possessed by madness so perverse, no drug can cure,
no madness can undo.
CHORUS. Your words, old man,
   most wisely balance
   respect for the Gods.
   Without shaming Apollo
   you honor our Bromius, as a great God.

[*Cadmus approaches Pentheus, carefully trying to humor
him*]

CADMUS. My boy, Teiresias has advised you well.
   Stay close to us! Don't step outside the rules.
   Just now you were up in the air, not thinking,
   but thinking that you were. For even if you are right
   and this God is not a God, why say it?
   Why not call him one?
   You have everything to gain from such a lie
   that makes Semele, your aunt, the mother of a God.
   Think what an honor for the whole family!
   Remember Actaeon, my Actaeon, what a miserable
        end he came to—
   my own grandson, torn limb from limb, in this very
        same valley
   by the meat-devouring hounds that he himself had
        reared,
   for the price of one boast: that he
   was a better hunter than Artemis.
   Don't risk the same fate. Here,
   let me put this ivy on your head.
   Join us in paying homage to Dionysus!

[*Pentheus swings around, knocking the thyrsus out of
Cadmus' hand. The old man staggers and falls to the ground*]

PENTHEUS. Keep your hands off me! Go! Run to your
   Bacchic revels.

I want none of your senile folly
rubbing off on me! As for him,
your tutor in idiocy, I'll deal with him.
Run, someone, straight to this man's lair,
his rock of prophecy. Dig it up with crowbars,
topple it, tear the stones from their sockets,
smash it into dust.
Throw his holy emblems to the winds, the drunken
    winds.
That will sting him to the quick. The rest of you,
scour the city, find this effeminate stranger
who afflicts our women with this new disease
and who befouls our beds. And when you catch
    him,
drag him here in chains.
He'll taste the people's justice when he's stoned to
    death,
regretting every bitter moment of his fun in Thebes.

[The Guards run off in several directions]

TEIRESIAS. Poor fool! You don't know what you are
    saying.
You were out of your mind before. Now you are
    stark mad.
Come, Cadmus. The two of us will go and pray
both for this man—undeserving monster though he
    is—
and for Thebes, that the God might spare us all
from some new calamity. Take up your thyrsus
and follow me. Try to support me and I'll support
    you.
It would be a shocking sight, two old men
sharing one fall! But never mind. Anything
so long as Dionysus, son of Zeus, is served.
Oh Cadmus, Pentheus is another name for grief.
Watch over your house, for grief is stalking in his
    steps.
This is not prophecy but blatant fact.
You can tell a dangerous fool by his own words.

[Teiresias and Cadmus exit as Pentheus strides into the
palace]

CHORUS. Holiness, power all transcending
soaring higher than the Gods
yet floating down on golden wings
to touch the earth, do you hear this man?
Do you hear the blasphemy
of Pentheus the unholy, hurled at Semele's son,
my Bromius, whom the garlanded Gods
when they feast on his bounty and his beauty
rate first among the first?

He is life's liberating force,
He is release of limbs and communion through
    dance.
He is laughter and music in flutes.
He is repose from all cares—he is sleep!
When his blood bursts from the grape
and flows across tables laid in his honor
to fuse with our blood,
he gently, gradually, wraps us in shadows
of ivy-cool sleep.

The unbridled tongue,
the arrogant frenzy of fools,
lead headlong to disaster.
But the tranquil life
of the wisely content
is anchored in rock and protects
the home from the storm.
The Gods may be far.
Yet, out of the lazy heavens,
they observe the ways of men.
Knowledge is not wisdom.
A knowing mind that ignores its own limits
has a very short span. And the man
who aims too high
never reaps what lies within his grasp.
Such is the folly—
and I know none worse—
of perversely ambitious, fanatical men.

Oh, to be in Cyprus,
the island-home of Aphrodite,
where the spirits of love
thrill the blood of men with magic breezes.
Or in that mythical land of the many-mouthed river
whose floods make deserts bloom.
Or where the muses play, Pieria,
whose peerless beauty
lovingly hugs the slopes of Olympus.
Oh, Bromius, my Bromius take me there!
Pave the way with romp and with prayer,
to the land of the Graces,
the land of Desire!
Where freedom is law
and women can revel with Bacchus.

The divine son of Zeus rejoices in festivity.
Of all his loves, the first is Peace,
the great benefactress
who cherishes the lives of young men.
He gives to the poor as he gives to the rich
the sorrow-killing drug of wine.
He hates only those who spurn
the daylight joys and the night's delights

that make life rich. How prudent
to keep one's heart and mind
away from those who think they know all.
Give me the simple wisdom and faith
of ordinary people. And I will make it mine.

[*Pentheus steps out of the palace, as several guards enter,
leading Dionysus. His hands are shackeled.*]

GUARD. Pentheus, here we are. All that you asked is
    done.
We hunted down the prey you sent us out to catch.
An easy job, I have to own. You see,
the animal was tame, sir. Made no attempt to run,
just stood there, very friendly, holding out his
    hands.
He didn't flinch or lose that flush
of wine-glow in his cheeks, but always smiling urged
    us
to tie him up and turn him in. He even stepped
    right up—
to save me from the trouble. That made me feel
    ashamed
and I mumbled: "Look, stranger, this is not my
    doing.
I'm just a soldier carrying out the orders of the
    king."
But there is more. Those raving women
that you'd clapped in chains
and locked up in your prison—
well, sir, they're gone,
they're on the loose, prancing their way into the
    glens,
laughing and calling Bacchus, their chosen God.
The chains around their feet just fell apart,
the prison doors unbarred themselves,
untouched by human hand. If you ask me,
this stranger who has come to Thebes,
is capable of many miracles.
I had my say.
The rest is up to you.
PENTHEUS. Untie his hands.
Now I have him in my net, no amount of agile tricks
can help him slip away.

[*The Guards unshackle Dionysus' hands and step aside,
clearing the stage for the confrontation*]

So! You cut a handsome figure, I'll give you that!
Quite tempting—
I mean to women—the object, I don't doubt,
of your presence here in Thebes.
Your curls are soft!

A bit too long for wrestling, but very pretty
the way they hug your cheeks, so lovingly.
And what fair skin you have, so well looked-after!
But then, you don't expose it to the sun, do you?
You like the darker places,
where you can hunt desire with your beauty.
Now then! To start with, where are you from?
DIONYSUS. That's easy to answer, though nothing to
    boast of.
You must have heard of Mount Tmolus,
famous for its flowers.
PENTHEUS. So I have. It rings the city of Sardis.
DIONYSUS. I come from there. Lydia is my country.
PENTHEUS. Where did you learn these orgiastic rituals
that you bring to Greece?
DIONYSUS. Dionysus initiated me.
He is the son of Zeus.
PENTHEUS. Which Zeus? A native of those parts,
who coins new Gods?
DIONYSUS. No. The same Zeus who married Semele
in these parts of yours.
PENTHEUS. Did he possess you in your sleep
or by appearing to your eyes?
DIONYSUS. Face to face. He shared his mysteries with
    me.
PENTHEUS. What lies behind these mysteries, accord-
    ing to you?
DIONYSUS. That only the initiated may know.
PENTHEUS. And those who *are* initiated,
what are the benefits they gain?
DIONYSUS. You may not hear. Though you would
gain by knowing.
PENTHEUS. A crafty answer, baited to sting my curi-
    osity.
DIONYSUS. Wrong. Our mysteries abhor the probing
ears of impious men.
PENTHEUS. This God you saw, or that you say you
saw, what is he like?
DIONYSUS. Like the likeness of his choice. Not mine.
PENTHEUS. Another devious answer and devoid of
sense.
DIONYSUS. What makes no sense is talking sense to a
fool.
PENTHEUS. Is this the first place to which you've
brought your God?
DIONYSUS. Throughout the Orient, people celebrate
his dance.
PENTHEUS. I believe it. Next to the Greeks,
they're all barbarians.
DIONYSUS. In this, they're more civilized.
The standards differ.
PENTHEUS. Do you perform your mysteries
during the day or by night?

DIONYSUS. Mostly by night.
  The dark is more conducive to worship.
PENTHEUS. You mean to lechery and bringing out the
  filth in women.
DIONYSUS. Those who look for filth, can find it at the
  height of noon.
PENTHEUS. You're going to pay for that rash, per-
  verted mouth of yours.
DIONYSUS. And you for being a crass and ignorant
  blasphemer.
PENTHEUS. Oho! Our Bacchus-fiend is getting bold!
  Crossing swords with words, not bad!
DIONYSUS. Do tell me how you'll punish me.
  What torture have you in mind?
PENTHEUS. First, I'll chop your dainty curls off. At
  the   roots!
DIONYSUS. My hair is holy. I grow it long for God.

[*Unable to carry out his threat, Pentheus takes another tack,
trying to reestablish his authority*]

PENTHEUS. Next, you'll hand that thyrsus over. Now!
DIONYSUS. Come and take it yourself.
  I hold it in the name of Dionysus.

[*Dionysus holds out his thyrsus, but Pentheus cannot move.
In his impotence, he flings empty threats at him*]

PENTHEUS. Last—I'll have you bodily removed.
  I'll throw you in my dungeons.
DIONYSUS. The God himself will set me free. I only
  have to ask him.
PENTHEUS. If you can get those raving bacchants to
  invoke him with you,
  perhaps he will materialize!
DIONYSUS. He's here now. He sees what is being
  done to me.
PENTHEUS. Where *is* he? To me he's quite invisible.
DIONYSUS. Where I am. Your lack of faith has blurred
  your vision.
PENTHEUS. [*to the Guards, beside himself*]
  Seize him! He's mocking me and he is mocking
  Thebes.
DIONYSUS. Let fools be warned. Place no chains on
  me.
PENTHEUS. And I say chain him. I am the only power
  here.
DIONYSUS. You do not know what your life is
  or what you do, or who you are.
PENTHEUS. I am Pentheus, son of Echion. And
  Agave.

DIONYSUS. To boast of that name is to court your
  own doom.
PENTHEUS. Away with him!
  Lock him up inside the stables, within my easy
  reach.
  Let him wallow in the murky darkness that he loves
  and dance his head off!
  As for these women,
  your fellow travelers and your accomplices in evil,
  I'll either have them sold as slaves
  or put their hands to different work. At my looms!
  That will stop them thumping those infernal drums.

[*Dionysus holds out his hands, encouraging the Guards to
manacle them*]

DIONYSUS. I shall go. But nothing fateful, that is not
    my fate,
  can come to me.
  As for you, Dionysus himself, whose Godship you
    deny,
  will call you to account for your outrageous con-
    duct.
  When you lay hands on me, it is *him* you put in
    prison.

[*The Guards lead Dionysus away. Pentheus exits*]

CHORUS. O Dirce, nymph of the sacred stream
  sprung from the mighty river, Achelöus.
  Once in your crystalline pools
  you cradled the infant God,
  snatched by Zeus, his father,
  from the mouth of the living flame.
  And the father cried: "Come, Dithyrambus,
  born to be reborn from this male womb of mine!
  I name you Bacchus. And Thebes
  will someday know you by that name."
  Why then, merciful Dirce,
  when I come to you with garlands
  and group-binding love, do you turn away?
  Why do you spurn? Hound me?
  I swear by the clustered grape,
  you will learn to care for him,
  who is Bromius, great in the East.

  What fury, what venomous fury
  rages in Pentheus,
  the earthborn and earthbound,
  spawned by the sperm of the snake!
  No man,

but a monster caged up in a man,
leaping through eyes of blood
to strike at the kill,
a vicious dwarf with giant dreams
pitting his strength against the Gods.
Soon, too soon, I fear
he will bind me with chains,
me, who am bound to Bacchus with freedom.
He has plunged my comrade,
my leader in the dance,
in the black depths of his dungeon.

Oh Dionysus, son of God,
do you see our sufferings?
Do you see your faithful
in helpless agony before the oppressor?
Oh lord, come down from Olympus.
Shake your golden thyrsus
and stifle the murderer's insolent fury.
Where are you, God?
Leading your band of revelers
through the wilds of Nysa,
haven of free-roaming beasts?
On the towering crags of Corycia?
Or in the secret glens of Olympus,
where Orpheus once, making music with his lyre,
gathered the trees around him,
gathered the spellbound beasts?

Oh happy, happy Pieria!
Bacchus honors you.
He will come to you with dances,
crossing the swirling torrents of Axios,
waving the whirling maenads on
across the mighty banks of Lydias,
bountiful father of rivers,
into that land of gushing waters,
blessed with the grace of its horses
and the fertile beauty of its pastures.

[As the Chorus falls silent, a voice is heard—that of
Dionysus—calling as if from the guts of the earth. Agitated,
the Chorus scatters around the stage]

DIONYSUS. Io! Hear me! Oh, my bacchae!
  Do you hear my cry? Io, my bacchae! Io!
CHORUS. Who calls? Where does it come from, this
      cry,
  calling in the voice of Dionysus?
DIONYSUS. Io! Io! Again I cry to you—
  I, the son of Semele and of Zeus.
CHORUS. Io, Io, lord! Our lord!

Come to us, come to your loving companions,
your group of worshipers.
Oh, Bromius, Bromius!
DIONYSUS. Earthquake almighty,
  shake the floor of the world!

[The stage grows dark. A low rumble is heard, building in
intensity, until everything seems to be reeling. The Chorus
sways and stumbles, crazed with fear]

CHORUS. Ah, look!
  The palace of Pentheus is trembling!
  It's reeling! It will collapse!
  Dionysus is within the walls! Kneel to him!
  The stones of the pillars are cracking!
  They're crashing to the ground!
  Bromius is here! Blasting the roof with his laughter!
DIONYSUS. Let the blazing bolt of lightning strike!
  Burn down the palace of Pentheus! Burn it down!

[A flash of lightning is followed by a crash of thunder, and
flames leap up from Semele's tomb]

CHORUS. Ah! Ah!
  Over there, do you see?
  Look how the fire leaps
  out of Semele's holy tomb!
  How the lurking flame
  left there once by the bolt of Zeus,
  springs to life!
  Down, trembling maenads. Fling your bodies to the
      ground.
  He rises from the ruins
  of the once-mighty house,
  that he himself has laid to dust.
  Here he comes, the son of God.

[The women fling themselves to the ground, covering their
heads. As the lights build up, Dionysus comes out of the
palace and threads his way among them, helping them rise]

DIONYSUS. Women of Asia, my barbarians!
  Why are you cowering, trembling, on the ground?
  I know! It seems you saw, as I did,
  how Bacchus shook the palace of Pentheus.
  But come! Rise to your feet.
  Shed the fear from your limbs.
CHORUS. Light of lights, oh leader of our holy dance!
  What joy to see your face!
  Without you, I was lost.
DIONYSUS. Have you so little faith as to despair
  the moment I was led to Pentheus' murky prison?

CHORUS. What else could I do?
Who would be there to protect me
if some misfortune came to you? But tell us,
how did you escape that godless man?
DIONYSUS. It was easy.
I freed myself without undue exertion!
CHORUS. But were your hands not shackled?
DIONYSUS. Ah! There I had him, made him look an
utter fool.

All the while that he was thinking he was binding
me,
me he didn't even touch! He fed on pure illusion.
You see, in the stable where he held me,
in strictest isolation, as he thought,
he came upon a bull and straightaway
tried to bind it by the hooves and knees.
He was panting with rage, sending showers of sweat
flying off his body, digging teeth into his lips,
while I sat quietly by and watched. Just then,
out of nowhere, Bacchus came and shook the
palace,
setting his mother's tomb ablaze with flames.
Seeing this and thinking that the palace was on fire,
Pentheus went rushing around in circles,
shouting to his slaves to carry water from the river.
Every hand was put to the toil—for nothing!
Then, afraid I had escaped, he stopped his labors,
drew his sinister sword and charged toward the
palace.
In that very instant, Dionysus—
I'm presuming it was he, I can but guess—
planted in his path a ghost,
uncannily resembling me.
Pentheus lunged at it, slashing the luminous air
and thinking with relish that he was killing me.
But that's not all the God had in store for him!
To demolish his pride even further,
he brought the palace crashing down onto the
stables,
burying them beneath a heap of rubble, a sight to
make
my imprisonment bitter to him.
Sheer exhaustion has now made him drop his sword.
He is prostrate—as any man should be,
who dares to wage a war with God.
As for me, I calmly walked out of the palace,
to join you here,
without another thought for Pentheus.
But wait! I think I hear his footsteps, stamping
through the court.
His lordship threatens to emerge. I wonder what
he'll say after this!

Let him stir up a storm. He shall not ruffle me.
A wise man knows restraint. His strength is his
detachment.

[*Pentheus enters furiously*]

PENTHEUS. It's an outrage! He's got away! From *me*!
That stranger,
that man I'd clapped in chains.

[*He spots Dionysus among the Chorus*]

Ha! There he is!
What is the meaning of all this?
How did you escape?
How dare you show your face outside my doors?
DIONYSUS. Get hold of yourself! Tread lightly or
you'll trip.
PENTHEUS. How did you get here? How did you
escape?
DIONYSUS. Did I not tell you—or did you not hear—
that somebody would set me free?
PENTHEUS. Who? Can you only talk in empty riddles?
DIONYSUS. He who makes the clustering vine
grow for mankind.
PENTHEUS. You mean he who drives our women from
their homes!
DIONYSUS. For that splendid insult, I'm sure Dionysus
thanks you.
PENTHEUS. Seal off the city.
Go around the towers and bolt all gates!
DIONYSUS. Whatever for?
Can't Gods jump higher than your city walls?
PENTHEUS. You're clever—very clever—
except where it counts.
DIONYSUS. It's where it counts the most that I am
clever.
However, listen first to this man,
who comes from the mountains.
He brings you news!
We shall wait here. No, we shall not run away, I
promise!

[*A Herdsman enters from the direction of Mount Cithaeron.
He is panting with fatigue and excitement*]

HERDSMAN. Pentheus, ruler of Thebes, my king,
I come straight from Cithaeron,
leaving behind its craggy slopes, where dazzling
snowdrifts
never melt!
PENTHEUS. That you've come, we know. Now get on
with your message.

HERDSMAN. I saw them. The Bacchae. Those raving women
who, stung by holy frenzy, went darting off into the wilds
in a flurry of bare feet.
I couldn't wait to tell you, King,
you and everyone in Thebes, the weird,
the awesome things they do, miraculous beyond belief.
But, first, I want to know. Can I speak freely, frankly,
of their goings on, or must I trim my tongue?
Truth is, I'm a little scared of your lordship.
You're so impatient, so fierce of temper—
just like a king, only more.

PENTHEUS. Speak on. No matter what you tell me,
it's not you that I shall blame. Besides,
to penalize a man for telling you the truth,
is wrong. But the more harrowing your tale about the Bacchae,
the more crushing the punishment that I shall inflict
upon that man who put our women up
to these vicious new tricks.

HERDSMAN. The sun's first rays had just begun
to spill their warmth upon the earth,
and I was steering my cattle up the slopes
to the pastures near the ridge, when suddenly
I see three bands of women—resting from their dance.
Autonoe at the head of one,
Ino of another,
and Agave, your mother, of the third—all fast asleep,
wherever exhaustion had dropped them;
some with heads lying back on pillowy branches,
others stretched out on beds of matted oak leaves,
but modestly, serenely, sir, not the way you think.
They were not drunk with wine,
or seduced by the music of flutes,
so they'd be in raptures,
or chasing wild erotic pleasures in the woods.
But then, your mother, alerted by the lowing
of our horned bulls, sprang up,
and with a ringing cry urged the bacchae
to rouse themselves from sleep. And they,
shedding the bloom of sleep from their eyes, nimbly rose—
a sight miraculously orderly and graceful—
women young and old, and girls as yet unmarried.
First, they let their hair fall down their shoulders
and those whose fawnskins had come loose
fastened them up, while others girdled theirs

with snakes that licked their cheeks. Some,
mothers with newborn babies left at home,
cradled young gazelles or wild wolf cubs in their arms
and fed them at their full-blown breasts
that brimmed with milk.
Then they wreathed their heads with shoots
of ivy, oak and flowering bryony.
One of them lifted a thyrsus, struck a rock
and water gushed from it as cool as mountain snow.
Another drove a stick into the ground
and at the bidding of the God,
wine came bubbling up.
Those who wanted milk
just scratched the soil lightly with their fingers
and white streams flowed, while from their ivy-crested wands
sweet honey dripped like sparkling dew.
Oh, King,
if you had been there and had seen,
you would have offered grateful prayers to the God
you now denounce.
Well, we cowherds and shepherds of those parts
get together and discussed these marvels,
these awesome things we had witnessed.
And one of our crowd, one who's always sneaking up to town,
very smooth with words, held forth to us and said:
"You people living in these holy glens,
what do you say we hunt Agave out,
drag her away from her orgies and do a service to the king, her son!"
He talked good sense, we thought, so we hid ourselves
low among the thickets, waiting in ambush.
At a given hour, all the Bacchae
shook the thyrsus for the revels to start
and their voices joined into a single cry:
"Bacchus, son of Zeus, oh Bromius, evoë."
And the whole mountain reeled,
possessed by their ecstatic dance,
and the beasts too and the trees,
suddenly everything but everything
was on the move. Then, quite by chance,
Agave came whirling past me, and I,
leaping out from my cover in the bushes,
tried to seize her. But she called out, yelling:
"Come, my fleet-footed hounds!
We're being hunted by these men! Take up your thyrsus
and follow, follow me!" At this, we fled
and barely escaped being torn to pieces

by these God-struck maenads.
But our cattle—
our herds grazing on the grassy slopes—oh!
They fell upon them with their naked hands.
You could see a woman sink her nails into a cow,
with its udders full, and lift it, bellowing, high above
   her head.
Others dragged young heifers, ripping them apart.
Everywhere you looked,
ribs and cloven hooves
were flying through the air.
And from the pine branches
dangled lumps of flesh that dripped with blood.
   Majestic bulls,
one minute aiming their horns with all their furious
   pride,
the next were stumbling to the ground,
overwhelmed by the swarming hands of girls,
their bones stripped clean of all their flesh,
faster than you could blink your royal eyes.
Then, taking off with sudden speed, like birds,
they swooped down the hillside to the flatlands—
fattened with crops by the river Asopos—
and like a rampaging army they burst into the
   villages
that nestle in Cithaeron's foothills.
They ransacked everything in sight.
They snatched young children out of homes,
carried them on their shoulders along with other
   plunder
and everything stayed put, without being tied.
   Nothing,
not even bronze or iron, fell to the somber earth.
Flames flickered in their hair and did not burn them.
The villagers, enraged, of course, by all this havoc,
took arms against the Bacchae. Then,
what a spectacle, my king, how eerie!
Their pointed spears drew no blood,
while the women, just hurling the thyrsus,
opened wounds, the women, sir, turned men to
   flight!
That could not have been without some godly
   power.
They went back then
to the haunts from which they started,
those fountains which their God had sprung for
   them.
They washed their bodies clean of blood
and from their cheeks, the serpents licked away the
   stains.
Oh, my king, this God, whoever he may be,
is powerful in many things. It was he,

so they say, who gave to us, poor mortals,
the gift of wine, that numbs all sorrows.
If wine should ever cease to be,
then so will love.
No pleasures left for men.

CHORUS. It frightens me to speak
   my free thoughts
   freely in a tyrant's presence.
   But let the truth be told:
   Among the Gods, Dionysus is second to none.

PENTHEUS. So, it has come!
   This Bacchic violence, this hysteria,
   spreading like a raging fire, is already upon us.
   We are disgraced in the eyes of all Greece.
   This is no time for apathy. You!
   Go to the Electran gate, run!
   Call every able-bodied man to arms!
   Mobilize the cavalry in full!
   Everyone who can use a sling or spring a bow,
   I want them all. We march against the bacchae.
   It will be a black day indeed
   when men sit back and endure such conduct from
      their women.

[*The Guard runs off. The Herdsman creeps out without
being noticed.*
*Dionysus turns to Pentheus and speaks to him soberly, rea-
soning with him, as if casting a spell*]

DIONYSUS. Pentheus, nothing I can say will move
   you, *that* I know.
   Yet even so!
   In spite even of the grievous wrong you've done me,
   I shall warn you again. Do not take arms against a
      God.
   Let things be. Dionysus will not let you
   drive his Bacchae from their sacred mountain
      haunts.

PENTHEUS. I need no lectures from you.
   You've escaped from prison once—relish that!
   Or do you want me to send you right back?

DIONYSUS. If I were you,
   I would offer him a sacrifice. Not angry threats,
   which, you being mortal, he a God,
   is just like kicking barefoot at a rock.

PENTHEUS. Sacrifice? Exactly what I plan to offer him.
   Women's blood—most suitably supplied by his own
      victims.
   I ll drench the glens of Cithaeron with it!

DIONYSUS. Unless you're routed. Which you will be.
   The lot of you. Just think of the disgrace!
   Your shields of bronze being beaten back by sticks
      of ivy!

PENTHEUS. This stranger's like a nightmare that you
    can't shake off.
  Whether you ignore him or kick him, he will have
    his say.
DIONYSUS. Friend, it still is possible to put things
    right.
PENTHEUS. How? By making myself a slave of my
    slaves?
DIONYSUS. I shall bring those women back to Thebes
    without the help of weapons.
PENTHEUS. Ha! This is another of your artful tricks.
DIONYSUS. A trick? Is using my power to save you a
    trick?
PENTHEUS. No. It's a conspiracy with them—those
    Bacchae—
  so that you can revel on forever.
DIONYSUS. True. Conspiracy if you like—but with a
    God.

[Pentheus, who has been steadily losing ground, wavers.
Suddenly, breaking out of the spell, he springs away, yelling]

PENTHEUS. My arms! Go fetch my arms.
  And you stop talking.
DIONYSUS. Ah!
  How would you like to *see* them
  all cooped up together in the hills,
  having their orgies?
PENTHEUS. Would I? I'd pay a fortune in gold for
    that.
DIONYSUS. Why, what gives you such a passionate
    desire?
PENTHEUS. Mind you, I would be very sorry
  to see them drunk. . . .
DIONYSUS. But for all your sorrow
  you will be delighted to see them, will you not?
PENTHEUS. Oh, yes, very. I could crouch beneath the
    pines, silently.
DIONYSUS. However well you hide, they'll find you
    out.
PENTHEUS. That makes sense. I'll go openly! Of
    course!
DIONYSUS. Well, shall we go? You'll undertake the
    journey?
PENTHEUS. The sooner the better. I'll blame you for
    delaying me.
DIONYSUS. Wait! First you must dress yourself in
    something soft and feminine.
PENTHEUS. What! I, a man, look like a woman?
DIONYSUS. If they see you as a man, they'll kill you.
PENTHEUS. You're talking sense again. Shrewd as an
    old wizard, aren't you?

DIONYSUS. Dionysus tells me what to say.
PENTHEUS. Sensible as your suggestion is, how can I
    make it work?
DIONYSUS. I will come inside and dress you myself.
PENTHEUS. Dress me? In what—a woman's dress?
  Oh no, I'd be ashamed.
DIONYSUS. I see! You're no longer keen to watch the
    maenads?
PENTHEUS. What exactly do I have to wear?
DIONYSUS. On your head, long flowing hair.
PENTHEUS. And then? What style of outfit do you
    have in mind?
DIONYSUS. Robes down to your feet and veils in your
    hair.
PENTHEUS. And to go with that? What else?
DIONYSUS. A dappled fawnskin and a thyrsus in your
    hand.
PENTHEUS. No, never!
DIONYSUS. Then fight with the bacchae.
  And be ready for a bloodbath.
PENTHEUS. You're right.
  It's good tactics to spy on them first.
DIONYSUS. Wiser and safer
  than to invite violence by using it.
PENTHEUS. But how shall I pass through the city
    without being seen?
DIONYSUS. We shall take lonely and deserted streets.
  I'll be your guide.
PENTHEUS. Anything, so long as I'm not jeered at by
    any of those Bacchae.
  I need to think it over. I'll go in . . . and decide.
DIONYSUS. As you please.
  I am prepared for all eventualities.
PENTHEUS. I leave you. I shall re-emerge,
  either to lead my army to the mountains
  or to fall in with your plans.

[Pentheus goes into the palace]

DIONYSUS. Women, there goes a man walking straight
    into the net.
  He shall visit the Bacchae
  and there find punishment and death.
  Dionysus, to your work. I know you are near.
  Be revenged on this man.
  But, first, unhinge his mind,
  make it float into madness.
  Sane, he never will accept to wear a woman's dress.
  But once his wits have broken loose, he will.
  I want the whole of Thebes to laugh
  as I parade him through the streets,
  laugh at this womanly man, this terrifying king,

whose arrogant threats still thunder in our ears.
I shall go to him. Time to deck him out
in the clothes he shall take with him to Hades,
slaughtered by his own mother's hands.
So shall Pentheus come to know Dionysus, son of
   Zeus,
a God sprung from nature, like nature most cruel,
and, yet, most gentle to mankind.

[*Dionysus follows Pentheus into the palace*]

CHORUS. When, oh when,
  in an all-night trance
  shall I dance again,
  bare feet flashing, head rushing
  through the coolness of leaves,
  like a fawn that frolics
  in the green delights of the forest,
  free from the deadly snares of the hunt.
  Oh, but till then,
  the terror of leaping
  clear of the intricate nets
  and the pouncing claws of hounds
  unleashed by the hunter's frenzied command,
  fleeing like a shuddering breeze
  over the marshlands, over the river,
  to the sheltering arms of the forest
  to exult as the thick-sprouting trees
  close their shadows around it
  in dark pools of solitude
  empty of men.

What is wisdom? Which
  of all the God-given gifts
  is more beneficial to man
  than the power to hold
  an enemy powerless at bay?
  That which is good is welcome forever.

Slowly, but implacably,
  divine power moves
  to strike at the arrogant man
  who brazenly worships
  his own image as God
  and not the Gods themselves.
  But they are there.
  Above us, in us, around us
  the Gods lie subtly in ambush.
  At a point in time they pounce
  on the impious man.
  No mortal act, no human thought
  shall trespass beyond the age-old truths,
  fortressed by tradition and custom.

Faith costs little.
  To believe in some essence supreme
  is to believe in life;
  to draw strength from whatever
  is rooted in time
  and in Nature's inscrutable logic.

What is wisdom? Which,
  of all the God-given gifts
  is more beneficial to man
  than the power to hold
  an enemy powerless at bay?
  That which is good is welcome forever.

Happy the man who escapes
  from the raging seas into port.
  Happy the man who withstands
  life's assaults.
  Somehow, in some way, some man surpasses some
    other
  in position and fortune.
  For the millions of men there are millions of hopes.
  For some, these ripen into happiness,
  for others into nothing.
  Count lucky the man who is happy on this one day.

[*Dionysus emerges from the palace. He turns and calls to Pentheus*]

DIONYSUS. You, lusting to see what you are unfit to
    see,
  thinking unthinkable thoughts,
  you, yes you, Pentheus, come out.
  Reveal yourself as a woman!
  Let's see this maenad in her Bacchic dress,
  who goes to spy on her mother and her friends.

[*Pentheus comes slowly out of the palace. He wears a woman's dress and a veil over his long golden curls, and he carries a thyrsus. He walks as if in a trance, trying to keep his balance*]

  Well! You look exactly
  like one of Cadmus' daughters.
PENTHEUS. Strange! I seem to see two suns
  and—two Thebes, yes,
  two cities, two, each with seven gates. And you—
  walking there before me—are you a bull?
  I could wager that you are one,
  with those horns
  that have sprouted from your head!
  Were you one before? An animal? I mean a bull,
  decidedly a bull!

DIONYSUS. The God is with us. Though angry before,
   now he's been placated and walks beside us gra-
     ciously.
   Now you see what you ought to see.

PENTHEUS [*posing narcissistically*].
   How do I look? Like Ino,
   or do I carry myself more like my mother, Agave?

DIONYSUS. Looking at you, I could swear I was seeing
   one of them.
   Oh dear! One of your curls is out of place!
   It should be tucked in as I arranged it.

PENTHEUS. It must have shaken loose indoors
   when I was tossing my head, getting into a Bacchic
     mood.

DIONYSUS. Let me, whose job it is to serve your grace,
   put it back in place! And hold your head still.

PENTHEUS. Come along then, fix it. I'm all yours
   now.

DIONYSUS. Your girdle too has slipped. And your
     skirt,
   how unevenly it drapes around your ankles!

PENTHEUS. Yes, now I see it. At least on the right.
   On the left, it hangs well to the heel.

DIONYSUS. You may think me your best friend yet
   when, much to your surprise, you see how docile
     the Bacchae are.

PENTHEUS. Do I hold the thyrsus in the right hand or
     the left to be like them exactly?

DIONYSUS. In the right.

   And swing it up as you swing your right foot for-
     ward.

[*He watches with wry amusement as Pentheus executes his
instructions*]

   I do applaud the change in your mind.

PENTHEUS [*incongruously showing off his masculinity*].
   Do you think I could lift the whole of Cithaeron,
   Bacchae and all, upon my shoulders?

DIONYSUS. If you wished, you could. Before, your
     mind was unsound.
   Now it works the way it should.

PENTHEUS. Shall we take up crowbars?
   Or shall I put my shoulders to the cliffs and wrench
     them loose,
   while my hands tear down the peaks?

DIONYSUS. It wouldn't do to wreck the playgrounds
     of the nymphs,
   the groves where Pan sits piping!

PENTHEUS. You are right. It's demeaning to conquer
   women by force. I shall hide among the pines.

DIONYSUS. You will hide where you must hide and
     you'll be hidden,
   as well as any spy should be, when peeping on his
     fellow maenads.

PENTHEUS. I can see them now—crouched among
     the bushes
   like mating birds, trapped in each other's loving
     arms.

DIONYSUS. Now we both know what you long to go
     and watch.
   You may even catch them—if they don't catch you
     first.

PENTHEUS. Lead me through the very heart of
     Thebes.
   Let them all see that I alone among them,
   am *man* enough to dare.

DIONYSUS. You and you alone bear the burden for the
     city.
   The struggle that awaits you is great.
   Your destiny is unique.
   Come. I shall take you safely there.
   Someone else will bring you back.

PENTHEUS. You mean my mother!

PENTHEUS. In triumph! For everyone to see.

PENTHEUS. It is for that I go.

DIONYSUS. You will be carried home—

PENTHEUS. You thrill me!

DIONYSUS. —carried in your mother's arms.

PENTHEUS. Now you're spoiling me!

DIONYSUS. The way you *should* be spoiled

PENTHEUS. No less than I deserve.

[*Pentheus exits*]

DIONYSUS. Go, terrifying man, go your terrifying way
   to the terror you'll be privileged to know,
   the glory that will hoist you to the skies.
   Stretch out your arms, Agave,
   and you, her sisters, daughters of Cadmus.
   I bring him! This man so young,
   I bring him to his ultimate struggle.
   The victory is mine. The victor Dionysus.
   The event will tell the rest.

[*Dionysus exits*]

CHORUS. Run, swift hounds of madness, run,
   run to the mountain,
   find the faithful possessed,
   the daughters of Cadmus,
   goad them, lash them, turn them loose
   on the woman-posing, woman-hating maniac

perversely spying in skirts.
His mother will spot him first,
through a crack in the rocks,
through a break in the trees.
She'll cry to the maenads:
"What creature is this, prowling on the hills,
prying on the Bacchae,
these hills, our hills, the hills of the holy revels?
Who bore him? A woman?
No woman's blood in such as him.
A gorgon's seed, whelped from a she-wolf."

Arrive,
come Justice, arise,
shining with the flash of your sword! And drive,
drive it clean through the throat
of the godless, lawless, ruthless son of Echion,
the earthborn, the earthbound.

Justice is balance.
His mind, unbalanced,
reels with sick, iniquitous passion,
profaning the mysteries of God,
lusting to violate Nature herself,
the Holy Mother.
On he goes, up he goes,
his fury outracing his madness
as he plunges toward the unassailable goal,
the matching of visible force with invincible
    strength.
He will die, as he must. It is the Law.
The invisible line drawn by the Gods
that no man can overstep.
Call it humility, acceptance, or just faith.
To know that our days are but as dust,
to be content with that and love each living particle,
is our only strength. But strength enough
to make our peace with grief.
Let others crowd their minds with scholarly wisdom.
Them I do not envy. I rejoice in keeping
my mind open to pursue the simple, attainable
    things
that are also the greatest.
Within that pursuit
lies the only known measure for happiness—
purity through loving by day and by night;
joyful acceptance of the godliness in me
which reconciles me humbly with the powers
    beyond.

Come Justice! Arise! Arrive,
shining with the flash of your sword. And drive,

drive it clean through the throat
of the godless, lawless, ruthless son of Echion,
the earthborn, the earthbound.

Come, God—
Bromius, Bacchus, Dionysus—
burst into life, burst
into being, be a mighty bull,
a hundred-headed snake,
a fire-breathing lion.
Burst into smiling life, oh Bacchus!
Smile at the hunter of the Bacchae,
smile and cast your noose.
And smiling, always smiling, watch
the maddened herd of maenads
burst upon him, bring him down,
trample him to death.

[A Messenger arrives running from the direction of Mount
Cithaeron]

MESSENGER. Oh, House, once happy throughout
    Greece!
    Oh, envied race sown by Cadmus
    in this Theban earth! I weep for you—
    poor servant though I am!
CHORUS. What is it? Is there news from the Bacchae?
MESSENGER. Pentheus is dead. The son of Echion is
    dead.
CHORUS. Oh, Bromius, God of Joy! Yours is the
    glory!
MESSENGER. What did you say? Have you no shame,
    woman?
    You rejoice at my master's misfortune?
CHORUS. I'm not one of you.
    To you Greeks, I'm a barbarian from the East.
    I speak my own language of worship.
    I'm free from the fear of your chains!
MESSENGER. If you think the state of Thebes is short
    of men—
CHORUS. Dionysus, not Thebes, rules over me.
    Dionysus is my state.
MESSENGER. Well, I suppose one should excuse you.
    But when disaster strikes
    to jubilate after the fact is not decent.
CHORUS. Tell me all. Speak. What kind of death did
    he die,
    the oppressor, the master of oppression?
MESSENGER. After leaving the city,
    we made our way through the farmlands
    to the river Asopus, and, crossing it,
    we struck into the foothills of Cithaeron—
    Pentheus and myself, for I was escorting my master,

and that stranger who was acting as our guide.
Finally, we reached a wooded glen,
and now we paused, our voices hushed,
our footsteps muffled by the grass,
as we glided through the trees—to see and not be
    seen.
And there, looking down into a gorge,
sheer between two cliffs and full of streams,
we saw them, the maenads, quietly sitting
in the thick-knit shadows of the pines,
their hands aflutter with their happy tasks.
Some were dressing up their thyrsus
replacing old ivy with fresh green shoots.
Others, playful like colts, whose mouths
had just been freed from bridles, sang out in turn,
tossing their Bacchic tunes from throat to throat.
Pentheus—unhappy man—
somehow could not see all those women.
"Stranger," he said, "from where we stand
I cannot quite detect those so-called maenads.
But if I climbed the tallest pine tree on the ridge
I'd have a proper view of their obscene activities."
Then I saw the stranger work a living miracle.
Gripping the highest branch of a sky-piercing pine
he firmly bent it down, down,
down to the dark earth, till it arched like a bow,
as perfectly curved as a rim of wood,
flexed to hug the circle of a wheel.
So did the stranger arch that tree to the ground—
a feat no mortal hand could do.
Then, setting Pentheus astride the topmost branch,
he slowly let the sturdy trunk spring up again,
letting it glide smoothly through his grip,
so as not to throw him off.
Sheer into the sheer sky it went,
with my master riding on the top,
easier for the maenads now to see than he could
    them.
But barely had he risen into view
when the stranger was nowhere to be seen.
And a voice clanged through the mountain air—
that of Dionysus, I suppose—calling out:
"Women! I deliver unto you
the man who mocks at you and me
and at our holy mysteries. Now punish him!"
And as he spoke, a dazzling shaft of light
flashed between heaven and earth, binding them
    together.
The very air stood still. Throughout the glens, the
    trees
stifled the voice of their leaves

and in the hush, no beast was heard.
The Bacchae, who had heard the voice but not the
    words,
sprang up, their eyes and ears alert.
Then came the voice again. And now they knew,
Cadmus' daughters knew, the clear command of
    Bacchus.
Bursting forth, like a flock of racing doves,
Agave and her sisters and all the bacchae with them
up the cliffside, through the torrents,
over the boulders they leapt,
their limbs charged by the rage of their God.
And when they saw my master perched upon the
    pine,
first they scampered up a wall of rock,
across from where he soared, and pelted him with
    stones
and branches, stripped and hurled like spears.
Like hail they flung their sticks of thyrsus
at their pitiful target.
But still their aim fell short of the ill-fated wretch,
suspended on his dizzy perch,
beyond their furious reach, yet trapped without
    escape.
At last, like a bolt of forest lightning,
they struck an oak tree clear of branches,
and using them as levers,
tried to pry the pine tree from its roots.
But even then, their efforts failed. Agave then cried
    out.
"Maenads come, surround the trunk
and grip it with your fists.
Shake down this climbing animal
or he'll reveal the secrets of our holy dance."
A swarm of hands now swept upon the pine
and tore it from the earth. Then, plunging from the
    heights,
reeling toward the ground,
down, down, came Pentheus, with one continuous
    yell,
aware of his impending doom.
His mother,
as priestess of the ritual killing,
was first to fall upon him.
He stripped his head, tore everything away,
hoping that Agave, wretched woman,
would know him and not kill him.
He touched her cheeks and cried:
"No Mother, no, it is I,
your child, your Pentheus, born to you in Echion's
    house!"

Have pity on me, Mother, I have wronged
but do not kill your son for my offense, not me,
    your son!''
She was foaming at the mouth.
Her eyes bulged, rolling wildly.
There was no corner of her mind
not possessed by Bacchus.
She was insane, oblivious to her son!
Seizing his left arm just above the wrist
and pushing with her foot against his chest
she wrenched his arm clean out of the shoulder.
It was not her strength that did it
but the God's power racing in her blood.
Ino, her sister, was working on the other side,
tearing off his flesh. And now Autonoe
pounced upon him, followed by the whole rabid
    pack.
The mountains boomed with shrill confusion—
Pentheus wailing while there was still a gasp left in
    him,
the women howling in their triumph.
One carried off an arm,
another a foot with the boot still on it.
They laid his ribs bare—clawed them clean.
His blood still warm on their hands,
they tossed the flesh of Pentheus back and forth
like children playing games.
Nothing is left of him. His body
lies scattered—some of it on the jagged rocks,
some buried in the forest thickets—
by no means easy to recover.
Except for his poor head. His mother has it,
proudly in her grip. She raises it high
on her thyrsus point—that head
she thinks is of some forest beast—
and carries it through the glades of Cithaeron,
leaving her sisters dancing with those raving women.
She is on her way here, inside the city,
exulting in her fearful and pathetic quarry.
She cries out to Bacchus, calling him
"fellow-hunter," "my ally in the kill,"
"the victor of our chase"! Oh, what a victory!
What a triumph of tears! But I am going.
I want no more part of this unnatural horror.
Just let me get away, far away,
before Agave comes home.
I am but a simple man, yet to me
reverence and humility before the Gods
is best for all men. It is also the only wisdom.
If only men would use it. So I think.

[*The Messenger exits, leaving the Chorus in a state of fear
and exultation*]

CHORUS. Dance for Bacchus,
    dance.
    Let voices boom
    in song
    for the doom
    of Pentheus seed of the dragon.
    Pentheus,
    dragged to his death
    by the folds of his female dress,
    pulled *down* into darkness
    by the gentle thyrsus
    he held so *high*.
    Pentheus, the profane,
    marched by a bull to his slaughter.
    Oh Thebes! Oh Theban Bacchae!
    What a victory you have won!
    What a ringing triumph
    to be drowned in wailing and tears.
    Yet—salute one must
    the horror and the glory
    of the final reckoning,
    that embrace of blood
    between a mother and her child
    that she herself has killed.
    But look! I see Agave, Pentheus' mother,
    running wild-eyed toward the palace.
    Prepare yourselves
    for the roaring voice of the God of Joy.

[*Agave enters, holding the head of Pentheus. Her dress is
torn and there is blood on her hands and arms. She comes to
a sudden stop as she sees the Chorus, clinging to her trophy
with jealous pride*]

AGAVE. Women of Asia, Bacchae—
CHORUS. Me? What do you want of *me*?
AGAVE. From the mountain, I have brought it.
    All the way, a tender branch,
    fresh-cut, with curly shoots. A beautiful catch.
CHORUS. We see. And we accept you.
    We shall cry out together.
AGAVE. Without a trap, I trapped it.
    A lion—a savage whelp of a lion.
    Look! Look at it!
CHORUS. In what wilderness, how?
AGAVE. Cithaeron . . .
CHORUS. Cithaeron?
AGAVE. Killed him. Most totally.
CHORUS. But who, whose hands?
AGAVE. Mine first! Mine is the prize for striking first!
    You know what the other women are singing?
    Agave, the best. Agave, most blest.
CHORUS. Who else? Whose hands?

AGAVE. Oh, Cadmus' . . .

CHORUS. Cadmus!

AGAVE. Cadmus' daughters. My sisters,
yes, but only after me, after *me*,
did *they* lay hands on the quarry.
Oh, what a fortunate hunting.

CHORUS. The God knows when to smile.

AGAVE. Come feast with me. Share in my success.

CHORUS. Share—unhappy woman?

AGAVE. The beast is young! See how the down
blooms upon its cheek like newborn silk,
under the rich, soft mane.

CHORUS. The hair does make it look indeed
like a beast of the woods.

AGAVE. Bacchus,
skilled hunter that he is,
most skillfully unleashed his maenads
and led them to the kill.

CHORUS. God is the king of hunters.

AGAVE. Do you praise me?

CHORUS. We do—praise you.

AGAVE. So will Cadmus soon.
So will all his people.

CHORUS. And Pentheus?
Will he also praise his mother?

AGAVE. He *will* praise her
when he sees the lion she has caught.
Is it not glorious?

CHORUS. Prodigious.

AGAVE. Prodigiously conquered.

CHORUS. You rejoice?

AGAVE. More! I exult!
My conquest is great, plain to see!
And great the acclaim it deserves.

CHORUS. Show then, poor woman, show to everyone
in Thebes
this priceless trophy you have carried proudly home.

[*Agave parades the stage, proudly exhibiting the head of
Pentheus*]

AGAVE. You, people of this high-towered city,
subjects of this mighty country, look!
Here is my trophy! *Here* is the quarry
we, your women, hunted down, yes *we*—
and not with nets or hooks or pointed spears—
but with our own bare arms, our hands, our delicate
fingers.
Now what are they worth, your manly boasts?
Where *is* the pride in power that relies
on hideous tools of war? *We* didn't need them.
With our hands we captured this beast of prey
and ripped it limb from limb.

But where is my father?
He is old, but he should come.
And Pentheus, my son,
where is he? Fetch him, someone. Tell him
his mother wants him. With a ladder.
He shall set it up against the front
of his palace. Firmly—for he mustn't slip—
and nail high upon the highest wall,
so all the town can see
his mother's triumph in the hunt,
this lion's head, my trophy, yes *mine*!

[*Cadmus enters, followed by attendants carrying a makeshift
stretcher with the covered remains of Pentheus. They remain
upstage while Cadmus speaks*]

CADMUS. Come men, follow me.
Bear your pitiful burden
of that which was Pentheus, my Pentheus,
to his home. Follow me with—
oh, those broken limbs that I painfully assembled
after a long and dismal search
up in the glens of Cithaeron, where they lay
scattered far and wide among the forest crags,
in tiny fragments, hard to find.
I had already left the mountain revels
and was entering the city with Teiresias,
when news was brought to me
of my daughters' atrocious deed.
I hurried back to the hills, to return, this time,
with this boy, dismembered by the maenads.
There on the wooded slopes I saw Autonoe,
my poor Actaeon's mother, and with her Ino,
both still possessed with frenzy. But Agave, I was
told,
was seen running, raving, on her way here.
Oh! Too true, alas, I see her now.
A sight to make eyes bleed!

AGAVE. Father!
Be proud! As proud as any mortal man can be.
For you have sired the bravest daughters ever
in the world. I mean all three of us,
but me above the rest. From now on,
no more weaving at the loom, no little chores for
me.
I'm meant for greater things—for hunting
savage beasts with my bare hands.
Oh Father, you see what I carry in my arms?
It is the prize I have won—yours,
to hang upon your walls.
Receive it, Father, in your hands. Rejoice in my
conquest,
and summon all your friends to join our royal feast.

Let them see how fortunate you are. How blest
by the splendor of my deed.
CADMUS. Oh misery, oh grief beyond all measure.
I cannot look on this, this—murder—
yes, murder, done by those pitiful hands you're so
proud of!
And you would offer such a victim to the Gods,
expecting Thebes and me to sit in at your feast?
How just—yet how unfair—the price the God
had made us pay. Dionysus, lord of joy,
born of our blood, has cruelly laid us low!
AGAVE. How disagreeable old men can be!
Why does he look so mournful?
I wish my son would emulate his mother!
Go hunting in the wilds with the young men of
Thebes
and outshine them all!
But all he knows, that boy, is how to fight the Gods.
He should be scolded, Father! Yes!
And you're the one to do it. Well?
Is no one going to fetch him,
to see me in my happiness?
CADMUS. Oh daughter, daughter!
If ever you come out of this and know what you
have done,
you'll suffer pain insufferable. And if your mind
remains forever drugged against reality,
your happiness, being all delusion, is but the great-
est misery.
AGAVE. What is there that is wrong?
Why all this talk of misery?

[*Making a decision, Cadmus approaches Agave and talks to
her with low intensity, trying to pull her out of her trance*]

CADMUS. Listen to me! Do as I say.
First, look up at the sky.
AGAVE. I'm looking. What am I supposed to see?
CADMUS. Is it the same as always?
Or does it seem changed to your eyes?
AGAVE. It is brighter than before—more luminous.
CADMUS. And inside you?
Is there still that lightness? Like floating?
AGAVE. I do not grasp your meaning.
Yet—I feel different somehow. More—awake.
As if—something has shifted in my head.
CADMUS. Do my words reach you now?
Can you answer clearly?
AGAVE. Yes, but I forget.
What were we talking of, Father?

CADMUS. When you reached womanhood,
whose house did you marry into?
AGAVE. You gave me to a man of our Theban dragon-
race.
His name was Echion.
CADMUS. In your husband's house—you bore a son.
Who was he?
AGAVE. Pentheus. Echion's son and mine.
CADMUS. And whose face is that
you're holding in your hand?
AGAVE. A lion's—so the hunting women say. . . .
CADMUS. Now look straight at it.
There's little effort in that.
AGAVE [*turning her head away*].
Ah! What is this! What am I holding?
CADMUS [*grasping her head, forcing her to look*].
Look at it! Go on looking
till you know what it is!
AGAVE. I see—oh, Gods, no, not this grief,
not this agony . . .
CADMUS. Does it seem like a lion now?
AGAVE. No. It is Pentheus—his head—
in my hands.
CADMUS. We wept for him
long before you knew.
AGAVE. Who killed him?
How did he come into my hands?
CADMUS. Oh, merciless truth—you always come too
soon.
AGAVE. Tell me! Now! My heart is leaping out
to the horror I must hear.
CADMUS. It was *you*! You and your sisters!
You killed him!
AGAVE. Where? Where did he die?
Here at home? Or where?
CADMUS. In those same glens where Actaeon
was torn to pieces by his hounds.
AGAVE. Cithaeron? Why?
What evil fate drove him there?
CADMUS. He went to mock the God
and you, his Bacchic revelers!
AGAVE. But we? How did we get there?
CADMUS. You were driven mad.
The whole town was possessed.
AGAVE. Now I see it all.
Dionysus! He destroyed us.
CADMUS. You denied his deity,
reviled his name in public.

[*A pause. The violence of their despair ebbs into a quiet but
piercing grief*]

AGAVE. Father, where is the body
  of my beloved son?

CADMUS. Here! I have brought it home,
  broken, painfully retrieved.

AGAVE. Broken? But are his limbs together,
  decently composed?

CADMUS. What humans hands could do,
  ours did. Not much.

AGAVE. Oh, if only mine could undo what they have
  done.

CADMUS. Too late. When guilty people are struck
  mad,
  their madness knows no guilt.

AGAVE. My guilt—my madness, yes!
  But what did Pentheus have to do with that?

CADMUS. He was like you, contemptuous of the God.
  And in a single devastating blow, the God
  has brought us down, your sisters, you, this boy—
  ruining my house and me. I had no son,
  no male heir of my blood but him,
  sprung from your unhappy womb! And now he's
    gone—
  abominably, shamefully cut down—
  he who was the pillar of my house.
  Oh, my child, my king, my grandson,
  our guiding light you were,
  the keeper of our future.
  This city held you in its awe. When you were near,
  no man would dare to slight this gray old head,
  for fear of you. And now I, Cadmus the great,
  who sowed the Theban race and reaped a glorious
    harvest,
  must go away, dishonored, an outcast from my
    home.
  Oh, dearest one—to me as dear in death,
  as when you were in life—
  never again will you touch my face
  and call me Grandfather and hug me in your arms
    and say:
  "Has anybody done you wrong? Has anyone upset
    you,
  made you sad? Just tell me who
  and, Grandfather, I'll punish him myself."
  And now you're gone, as miserably dead
  as I'm alive, your mother broken,
  none of us left but torn by grief.
  If there be any man who challenges or scorns
  the unseen powers,
  let him look on this boy's death and accept
  that which is God.

CHORUS. I grieve for you, Cadmus.

  Though your grandson's punishment is just.
  For you it is too cruel.

AGAVE [In a strange, almost impersonal voice].
  Father,
  you see this woman
  standing where I do.
  She is your daughter.
  Yet nothing is there left of what she was.
  In one quick stroke, her hands,
  blind and driven by the Gods,
  have split her life in two.
  Whatever was before
  has crumbled, vanished,
  behind a wall of blood.
  For her—for me—
  there's only now. An endless now,
  stretching like a dark and empty desert
  without past or future.
  My son is dead. His mother killed him.
  I am his mother. Those few words contain
  horror, shame, anguish so immense
  that no living creature should be able to endure.
  Yet I live. How or why, I do not know.
  And no longer do I ask to understand. For, if I do,
  I might sin again and be denied the one last favor
  that would be any mother's right to ask.

CADMUS. What it that, my daughter?

AGAVE. To prepare my son for his journey to the dead.
  He cannot go like this! I know my hands are cursed,
  polluted with blood of my blood,
  yet whose but mine can make whole again
  that body that they proudly reared to manhood?

CADMUS. Oh, daughter! The holy laws forbid the
    ones who kill
  to care for their victims.

AGAVE. My victim? Yes! But, Gods, I DID NOT
    KNOW!
  If my son deserved to die and I deserved to kill him,
  you've had your way! A little charity is all I ask!
  To be allowed to wash him clean of blood with tears
  and sing a dirge for every broken limb!
  Oh, Father, spare me a little of the pity
  that the Gods must feel for you.
  Just let me put my son to sleep—
  and let the Gods do what they want with me.
  Punish me with death or life, I do not care!

[Cadmus signals to the attendants, who approach slowly
with Pentheus' remains]

CHORUS. Bring forth your sorrowful burden.

Do what you can, my daughter.
But do not linger more than it is seemly.
And steel your heart against a sight
hard for any mortal eyes to bear,
but most of all a mother's.

[*The attendants stop near Agave. During the following lines, she sets Pentheus' head next to his mangled limbs, caressing them as she laments on her knees*]

AGAVE. Put him down.
Oh, my child! My son!
Your mother's here
to heal your wounds and give you back your beauty,
that she herself reduced to . . . this! Oh no!
Proud head
that not so long ago these hateful eyes reviled
and now drench with tears. Rest where you belong.
   Remember
how once you nestled in my arms?
Oh dearest face—tender cheek, so young—
sweet mouth that suckled at my breast,
now forever closed. If you could speak,
what would you say to wrench your mother's heart,
that I have not already said a thousand times!
Oh my prince!
These noble limbs that soon I should have dressed
for some young girl, your bride,
how lifeless now they lie—
unnaturally, mercilessly mangled—
Oh I cannot! Help me!
No, no—I must be strong. Go someone, bring a shroud
fit for the burial of this king, my son.
My eyes shall not betray him with weakness.

[*Cadmus takes off his cloak and approaches Agave*]

CADMUS. Here, my daughter,
  take this old man's cloak. And come away.
AGAVE. Yes, Father. A little while and I am done.

[*ceremoniously holding the cloak over Pentheus' remains*]

I wash your wounds.
With this princely shroud I cover your head.
I bind your limbs with love,
flesh of my flesh,
in life as in death,
forever.

[*Agave covers the remains with the cloak. In the hush, the Chorus sounds drained and disoriented*]

CHORUS. O Dionysus,
we feel you near,
stirring like molten lava
under the ravaged earth,
flowing from the wounds of your trees
in tears of sap,
screaming with the rage
of your hunted beasts.

How terrible your vengeance against those
who harness your forces
to their laws of unnatural order.
A free and open mind
is safe against the excesses
lurking in the secret juices of your plants.
But those who try to strangle you
in the roots of their own nature,
who oppress and are oppressed,
through you, achieve their own destruction.

[*Dionysus appears, suspended in space above the palace, as the bull-horned God*]

DIONYSUS. Hear me all! I speak to you now as Dionysus,
a God revealed to mortal eyes.
I came back to this land of my virgin birth,
to suffer the indignities that only human folly can invent.
I was mocked at, chained, thrown in prison. Men like Pentheus
who abuse their power in defiance of the Gods
shall ever rediscover the inexorable terror of divine justice.
Now you, his kin, were made to kill the tyrant that you gloried in.
You are unclean. And you shall go your separate ways,
leaving Thebes forever, to rid it from the curse of your pollution.
Had you been willing to be wise when you had all,
today, instead of losing all, you would be thriving allies
of the son of Zeus, your friend.
CADMUS. Spare us, Dionysus. We have sinned.
DIONYSUS. Too late to know me now. You did not when you should.
AGAVE. We were wrong and we confess.
But you are merciless!
DIONYSUS. I am a God.
And when insulted, Gods do not forgive.
AGAVE. The Gods should be above the passions of mere men.

DIONYSUS. [*in a distant, tired voice*]
  So it was ordained from the beginning
  by the almighty father, Zeus.
AGAVE. It is decided, old man. Give up.
  The cruelty of the Gods demands our banishment.
DIONYSUS. Then go. Why delay the inevitable.

[*Agave and Cadmus begin to cross the stage, moving in opposite directions*]

CADMUS. Oh child, what a terrible fate has overtaken
    us,
  you, your sisters, and your wretched father.
  A derelict old man, I'm doomed to live,
  despised, in foreign lands. For sufferings like mine
  there is no respite ever. Even when I sail
  down the silent river to the world of the dead
  I shall find no rest.
AGAVE. I shall live, Father. Alone, deprived of you.

[*As Agave and Cadmus pass each other, she turns and embraces him*]

CADMUS. Poor child,
  why do you fold your arms around me,
  like a swan sheltering its useless, old father?
AGAVE. Where am I to go? Cast out, unwanted,
  whom can I turn to?
CADMUS. I do not know, my daughter.
  Your father cannot help you.

AGAVE. Farewell, my home. Farewell, my city.
  I leave you for exile. My once bridal bed
  I leave you for misery.
  Father, I weep for you.
CADMUS. Strange! I still feel pity
  for you and for your sisters.
AGAVE. Brutal! Brutally ruthless the fate
  Dionysus hurled at your house.
DIONYSUS [*fading away*].
  Yes. And ruthlessly brutal the way
  you dishonored his name in Thebes.
AGAVE. Farewell, my father.
CADMUS. Poor child, farewell.
  Oh words—how futile you can be.
AGAVE. Take me, someone, to my sisters,
  my pitiful sisters, that I must lead to exile.
  I want to go far,
  out of the sight of cursed Cithaeron
  and Cithaeron out of my sight.
  To a place no thyrsus threatens—or haunts
  even in memory. Let those who wish,
  be Bacchae after me.
CHORUS. The Gods take many forms.
  They manifest themselves in unpredictable ways.
  What we most expect
  does not happen.
  And for the least expected
  God finds a way.
  This is what happened here today.

ESSAY: AN APPROACH TO THE PLAY

From one point of view, *The Bacchae* is a conventional tragedy The ruler Pentheus refuses to admit that the new god Dionysus is in fact a god. He tries to imprison all those who worship the new god, ironically fearing that the new devotion will rip the traditional social fabric apart, an effect which his own denial of Dionysus actually accomplishes. He is arrogant and blind, both to the reality of the god and to himself: He fails to see his own limits. In conventional Greek tragedy, this sin of *hybris* explains Pentheus' fall.

However, he is also mocked and humiliated. Dionysus puts him under his spell of madness, tricks him into dressing as a woman (and, thereby, into representing himself as the opposite of what he really believes about himself), lets him think he is the hunter when actually we know he is the prey (like Acteaon, to whom there are several comparisons in the play); and after going to the place where each year a sacrifice is made to this god, Pentheus himself becomes the sacrifice, and his own mother (equally blinded by her god-induced madness), the executioner. Every aspect of this sacrifice is an ironic reversal of what the characters when "sane" would believe and do. And because the victim is stripped of his dignity, tricked into becoming the plaything of the god whose power he denies, and because his end is so horrible, the play's conclusion seems to distance us, to make us see it as an ironically horrifying and demeaning spectacle, rather than to exalt us into a sympathetic response. It teaches us a lesson about the cost of arrogance and of not respecting the gods, but it may not elicit the emotion of pity which is often thought typical of tragedy.

However, if we do not sympathize with Pentheus, his antagonist may seem even less appealing. When a god uses his power so horribly, and merely because the victim would not acknowledge him to be a god, the god himself may seem petty, even egotistical, if we judge him by human standards. Yet this play was written to be performed in a theater dedicated to this very god. In such a theatrical situation, would it not have seemed blasphemous to criticize him? Perhaps it is appropriate that a god be inhuman, that he be portrayed almost as a manifestation of pure power, of the absolute right of godhead, a right which humans cannot comprehend and to which they cannot aspire. There is no sentimentality in this play, no easy solution to the human dilemma that although we are capable of limitless aspiration, we are nonetheless limited. Human life is full of pain which is inescapable: To aspire to get beyond that pain is to be torn apart.

There is also another side to the god. His province is wine, whose power allows humans temporarily to forget their pain. He is also associated with the irrational in the guises of celebration and orgy, and with creativity as well. To humans who know a god when they see one, who acknowledge their limits, Dionysus is neither destructive nor immoral. The play is tragic insofar as it shows the price of *not* knowing one's limits.

Conventionally, Dionysus is on the side of chaos and disorder both in their "good" and in their "bad" manifestations, but this does *not* mean that he is necessarily "*against*" their opposites. He does not have, or champion, rationality or discipline or order; another god, Apollo, does that. Dionysus and Apollo, though different, however, are not necessarily in conflict. From the god's (and, apparently, the play's) perspective, Pentheus' problem is not that he represents order and reason and discipline within his kingdom (all qualities the Greeks associated with maleness) but that he is arrogant about these qualities. He assumes that only they are good and that those who disagree deserve prison. He goes further, denying the legitimacy and power of the god who represents alternatives. From the social point of view, Pentheus is repressive. This is true from the psychological point of view as well: He represses a side of himself which, we all know, is as much a part of our humanity as is our reason. He is blind to his own nature, as well as to the god's (until, ironically, he is possessed and thus no longer in rational control). To be blind to oneself *is* to be blind to, or at least to misinterpret, the world. Not knowing himself, for example, he *always* misinterprets the meaning of the smile which is Dionysus' theatrical mask.

To be sure, Dionysus is inhuman and we cannot "like" him. His enigmatic smile is unchanging, however horrifying the actions he witnesses, and his "effeminacy" relates him to attitudes and behavior which Greek culture coded as "feminine"—qualities perceived as nonrational or irrational—but which in reality are human, a part of us all. Men addicted to the male stereotype of strong discipline, order, and reason feel silly when they participate in the Dionysian revels. And yet participation in them makes men more fully human.

In rejecting this full humanity and the god, Pentheus rejects himself as well. Perhaps it is fitting that he be destroyed. We must know our limits, acknowledge that we are not fully in control, accept the fact that we contain more than we know, recognize the demands of the gods and of human nature. We may no longer believe in the god Dionysus, but we must still acknowledge the power within us which he represents. To this degree we, like the Greeks, are born into a fate, a destiny, a human inheritance which is inescapable, which will work itself out in each of us, however differently from individual to individual.

Unlike the plot of the earlier play *Oedipus the King*, in which the workings of fate which have already occurred are gradually uncovered before us, this later play presents these workings in process, as they are unfolding in the present tense. If the earlier play places us in closer sympathy with the tragic hero, in this later one we are placed more directly in his shoes. His failure to bring himself into harmony with the demands of his world is one we might easily make ourselves. His shoes are very uncomfortable, but we do in fact often try to wear them.

Aristophanes

LYSISTRATA

Translated by Douglass Parker

About the Author   Two generations younger than Sophocles, Aristophanes (450?–380? B.C.) is the only ancient Greek playwright whose comedies have survived—thirteen plays produced between 425 and 388 B.C. They frequently make fun of contemporary political and intellectual figures; though often wildly obscene and farcical, they usually deal with serious and controversial subjects in Athenian society.

About the Play   *Lysistrata* was produced in the middle of the great Peloponnesian War between the city-states of Athens and Sparta, with most of the Greek world involved by alliance with one side or the other. From the Athenian point of view, it was a very bad time. Their economy had been severely weakened by their recent unsuccessful attack on Sicily, one which had also undermined confidence in Athenian civic idealism, since it seemed to many to be an unwarranted attack against a weaker group of fellow Greeks, and now they were feeling militarily threatened themselves. The play seems to attack those attitudes of Greek citizens—its males—which not only had produced this society but also made war seem to be its natural expression. Perhaps Aristophanes focused on war in order to examine the main destructive forces within Athens and, implicitly, within all Greece.

     As presented in this play, war becomes a political expression of the machismo which the men of ancient Greece also expressed in their relationships with women. By dealing with gender issues in a wartime setting, Aristophanes was able simultaneously to explore the effects of sexism and the futility of war. However, although his female characters hold men and their "heroic" nature up to ridicule, Aristophanes' full intentions are uncertain. Are women less aggressive than men in this play? Or is it mainly their weapons which are different? Are women out for peace and equality, or for taking power from men so that they can have it for themselves? Are they for peace because peace is more sane than war, or because in peace women have a better chance at power? At the end the military situation has changed, but has there been a change in the relations between men and women?

     More questions may be raised when we consider some of the qualities of the society for which this play was produced and what these qualities might imply about its members. For example, only male heads of households were eligible to be citizens and to vote in democratic Athens. Menial work, including personal and domestic service, was done not by Athenian citizens, but by women and by slaves from other states. Only men acted on the stage. There is some uncertainty still about whether women were even allowed to see comedy in the theater. In other words, we should imagine ancient Athens as an extraordinarily proud, sexist, racist, male-dominated culture. In this theater in this society at this time, when the supporters of war would be feeling unusually defensive, can we take what a male playwright says about women's potential power over men and against war at face value? Perhaps. But perhaps we can see it with equal ease as a male joke at women's expense: Since women are valuable primarily as sex objects, what would happen if they withheld services? We cannot know how Aristophanes intended his play, nor how his audience received it. What *is* clear is that through his satire Aristophanes raises issues about gender and about social organization that are still among our central concerns today.

     We remind you that the beginning of the play is analyzed in some detail in the Introduction to this book (pp. 9–14).

CHARACTERS

LYSISTRATA
KLEONIKE ⎫ Athenian women
MYRRHINE
LAMPITO, a Spartan woman
ISMENIA, a Boiotian girl
KORINTHIAN GIRL
POLICEWOMAN
KORYPHAIOS OF THE MEN
CHORUS OF OLD MEN of Athens
KORYPHAIOS OF THE WOMEN
CHORUS OF OLD WOMEN of Athens
COMMISSIONER of Public Safety

FOUR POLICEMEN
KINESIAS, Myrrhine's husband
CHILD of Kinesias and Myrrhine
SLAVE
SPARTAN HERALD
SPARTAN AMBASSADOR
FLUTE-PLAYER
ATHENIAN WOMEN
PELOPONNESIAN WOMEN
PELOPONNESIAN MEN
ATHENIAN MEN

SCENE

A street in Athens. In the background, the Akropolis; center, its gateway, the Propylaia. The time is early morning. Lysistrata is discovered alone, pacing back and forth in furious impatience.

LYSISTRATA
Women!
Announce a debauch in honor of Bacchos,
a spree for Pan, some tootling fertility fieldday,
and traffic stops—these streets are absolutely clogged
with frantic females banging on tambourines. No urg-
   ing
for an orgy!
                    But *today*—there's not one woman here.

[*Enter Kleonike.*]

Correction: one. Here comes my next door neighbor.
—Hello, Kleonike.

KLEONIKE
                    Hello to *you*, Lysistrata.
—But what's the fuss? Don't look so barbarous, baby;
knitted brows just aren't your style.

LYSISTRATA
                              It doesn't
matter, Kleonike—I'm on fire right down to the bone.
I'm positively ashamed to be a woman—a member
of a sex which can't even live up to male slanders!
To hear our husbands talk, we're *sly*: deceitful,
always plotting, monsters of intrigue. . . .

KLEONIKE

[*Proudly.*]

                              That's us!

LYSISTRATA
And so we agreed to meet today and plot
an intrigue that really deserves the name of mon-
   strous . . .
and WHERE are the women?
                              Slyly asleep at home—
they won't get up for anything!

KLEONIKE
                              Relax, honey.
They'll be here. You know a woman's way is hard—
mainly the way out of the house: fuss over hubby,
wake the maid up, put the baby down, bathe him,
feed him . . .

LYSISTRATA
              Trivia. They have more fundamental
   business
to engage in.

KLEONIKE
Incidentally, Lysistrata, just why are you
calling this meeting? Nothing teeny, I trust?

LYSISTRATA
Immense.

KLEONIKE
         Hmmm. And pressing?

LYSISTRATA
                              Unthinkably tense.

KLEONIKE
Then where IS everybody?

LYSISTRATA

Nothing like that. If it were,
we'd already be in session. Seconding motions.
—No, *this* came to hand some time ago. I've spent
my nights kneading it, mulling it, filing it down. . . .

KLEONIKE

Too bad. There can't be very much left.

LYSISTRATA

Only this:
the hope and salvation of Hellas lies with the WOMEN!

KLEONIKE

Lies with the women? Now *there's* a last resort.

LYSISTRATA

It lies with us to decide affairs of state
and foreign policy.
                    The Spartan Question: Peace
or Extirpation?

KLEONIKE

How *fun*!
                    I cast an Aye for Extirpation!

LYSISTRATA

The Utter Annihilation of every last Boiotian?

KLEONIKE

AYE!—I mean Nay. Clemency, please, for those
    scrumptious
eels.

LYSISTRATA

And as for Athens . . . I'd rather not put
the thought into words. Just fill in the blanks, if you
    will.
—To the point: If we can meet and reach agreement
here and now with the girls from Thebes and the Pel-
    oponnese,
we'll form an alliance and save the States of Greece!

KLEONIKE

Us? Be practical. Wisdom from women? There's
    nothing
cosmic about cosmetics—and Glamor is our only
    talent.
All we can do is *sit*, primped and painted,
made up and dressed up,

[*Getting carried away in spite of her argument.*]

ravishing in saffron wrappers,
peekaboo peignoirs, exquisite negligees, those chic,
expensive little slippers that come from the East . . .

LYSISTRATA

Exactly. You've hit it. I see our way to salvation
in just such ornamentation—in slippers and slips, rouge
and perfumes, negligees and decolletage. . . .

KLEONIKE

How so?

LYSISTRATA

So effectively that not one husband will take up his
    spear
against another . . .

KLEONIKE

Peachy!
                    I'll have that kimono
dyed . . .

LYSISTRATA

. . . or shoulder his shield . . .

KLEONIKE

. . . squeeze into that daring
negligee . . .

LYSISTRATA

. . . or unsheathe his sword'

KLEONIKE

. . . and buy those slippers!

LYSISTRATA

Well, now. Don't you think the girls should be here?

KLEONIKE

Be here? Ages ago—they should have flown!

[*She stops.*]

But no. You'll find out. These are authentic Athenians:
no matter what they do, they do it late.

LYSISTRATA

But what about the out-of-town delegations? There
    isn't
a woman here from the Shore; none from Salamis . . .

KLEONIKE

That's quite a trip. They usually get on board
at sunup. Probably riding at anchor now.

LYSISTRATA

I thought the girls from Acharnai would be here first.
I'm especially counting on them. And they're not
    here.

KLEONIKE

I think Theogenes' wife is under way.
When I went by, she was hoisting her sandals . . .

[*Looking off right.*]

But look!

Some of the girls are coming!

[*Women enter from the right. Lysistrata looks off to the left
where more—a ragged lot—are straggling in.*]

LYSISTRATA

And more over here!

KLEONIKE

Where did you find *that* group?

LYSISTRATA

They're from the outskirts.

KLEONIKE

Well, that's something. If you haven't done anything else,
you've really ruffled up the outskirts.

[*Myrrhine enters guiltily from the right.*]

MYRRHINE

Oh, Lysistrata,
we aren't late, are we?

Well, *are* we?

Speak to me!

LYSISTRATA

What is it, Myrrhine? Do you want a medal for tardiness?
Honestly, such behavior, with so much at stake . . .

MYRRHINE

I'm sorry. I couldn't find my girdle in the dark.
And anyway, we're here now. So tell us all about it,
whatever it is.

KLEONIKE

No, wait a minute. Don't
begin just yet. Let's wait for those girls from Thebes
and the Peloponnese.

LYSISTRATA

Now *there* speaks the proper attitude.

[*Lampito, a strapping Spartan woman, enters left, leading a pretty Boiotian girl (Ismenia) and a huge, steatopygous Korinthian.*]

And here's our lovely Spartan.

Hel*lo*, Lampito
dear.
Why, darling, you're simply ravishing! Such
a blemishless complexion—so clean, so out-of-doors!
And will you look at that figure—the pink of
perfection!

KLEONIKE

I'll bet you could strangle a bull.

LAMPITO

I calklate so.
Hit's fitness whut done it, fitness and dancin'. You
know
the step?

[*Demonstrating.*]

Foot it out back'ards an' toe yore twitchet.

[*The women crowd around Lampito.*]

KLEONIKE

What unbelievably beautiful bosoms!

LAMPITO

Shuckins,
whut fer you tweedlin' me up so? I feel like a heifer
come fair-time.

LYSISTRATA

[*Turning to Ismenia.*]

And who is this young lady here?

LAMPITO

Her kin's purt-near the bluebloodiest folk in Thebes—
the First Fam'lies of Boiotia.

LYSISTRATA

[*As they inspect Ismenia.*]

Ah, picturesque Boiotia:
her verdant meadows, her fruited plain . . .

KLEONIKE

[*Peering more closely.*]

Her sunken
garden where no grass grows. A cultivated country.

LYSISTRATA

[*Gaping at the gawking Korinthian.*]

And who is *this*—er—little thing?

LAMPITO

She hails
from over by Korinth, but her kinfolk's quality—
mighty
big back there.

KLEONIKE

[*On her tour of inspection.*]

She's mighty big back *here*.

LAMPITO

The womenfolk's all assemblied. Who-all's notion
was this-hyer confabulation?

LYSISTRATA

Mine.

LAMPITO

Git on with the give-out.
I'm hankerin' to hear.

MYRRHINE

Me, too! I can't imagine
what could be so important. Tell us about it!

LYSISTRATA

Right away.
—But first, a question. It's not
an involved one. Answer yes or no.

[*A pause.*]

MYRRHINE

Well, ASK it!

LYSISTRATA

It concerns the fathers of your children—your husbands, absent
on active service. I know you all have men
abroad.
—Wouldn't you like to have them home?

KLEONIKE

My husband's been gone for the last five months! Way
up
to Thrace, watchdogging military waste. It's horrible!

MYRRHINE

Mine's been posted to Pylos for seven whole months!

LAMPITO

My man's no sooner rotated out of the line
than he's plugged back in. Hain't no discharge in this
war!

KLEONIKE

And lovers can't be had for love or money,
not even synthetics. Why, since those beastly Milesians
revolted and cut off the leather trade, that handy
do-it-yourself kit's *vanished* from the open market!

LYSISTRATA

If I can devise a scheme for ending the war,
I gather I have your support?

KLEONIKE

You can count on me!
If you need money, I'll pawn the shift off my back—

[*Aside.*]

and drink up the cash before the sun goes down.

MYRRHINE

Me, too! I'm ready to split myself right up
the middle like a mackerel, and give you half!

LAMPITO

Me, too! I'd climb Taygetos Mountain plumb
to the top to git the leastes' peek at Peace!

LYSISTRATA

Very well, I'll tell you. No reason to keep a secret.

[*Importantly, as the women cluster around her.*]

We can force our husbands to negotiate Peace,
Ladies, by exercising steadfast Self-Control—
By Total Abstinence . . .

[*A pause.*]

KLEONIKE

From WHAT?

MYRRHINE

Yes, what?

LYSISTRATA

You'll do it?

KLEONIKE

Of course we'll do it! We'd even *die*!

LYSISTRATA

Very well,
then here's the program:
Total Abstinence
from SEX!

[*The cluster of women dissolves.*]

—Why are you turning away? Where are you going?

[*Moving among the women.*]

—What's this? Such stricken expressions! Such gloomy
gestures!
—Why so pale!
—Whence these tears?
What IS this?
Will you do it or won't you?
Cat got your tongue?

KLEONIKE

Afraid I can't make it. Sorry.
On with the War!

MYRRHINE

Me neither. Sorry.
On with the War!

LYSISTRATA

This from
my little mackerel? The girl who was ready, a minute
ago, to split herself right up the middle?

KLEONIKE

[*Breaking in between Lysistrata and Myrrhine.*]

Try something else. Try anything. If you say so,
I'm willing to walk through fire barefoot.
                                    But not
to give up SEX—there's nothing like it, Lysistrata!

LYSISTRATA

[*To Myrrhine.*]

And you?

MYRRHINE
            Me, too! I'll walk through fire.

LYSISTRATA
                                    Women!
Utter sluts, the entire sex! Will-power,
nil. We're perfect raw material for Tragedy,
the stuff of heroic lays. "Go to bed with a god
and then get rid of the baby"—that sums us up!

[*Turning to Lampito.*]

—Oh, Spartan, be a dear. If *you* stick by me,
just you, we still may have a chance to win.
Give me your vote.

LAMPITO
                Hit's right onsettlin' fer gals
to sleep all lonely-like, withouten no humpin'.
But I'm on yore side. We shore need Peace, too.

LYSISTRATA
You're a darling—the only woman here
worthy of the name!

KLEONIKE
                Well, just suppose we *did*,
as much as possible, abstain from . . . what you said,
you know—not that we *would*—could something like
  that
bring Peace any sooner?

LYSISTRATA
                    Certainly. Here's how it works:
We'll paint, powder, and pluck ourselves to the last
detail, and stay inside, wearing those filmy
tunics that set off everything we *have*—
                        and then
slink up to the men. They'll snap to attention, go
  absolutely
mad to love us—
            but we won't let them. We'll Abstain.
—I imagine they'll conclude a treaty rather quickly.

LAMPITO

[*Nodding.*]

Menelaos he tuck one squint at Helen's bubbies
all nekkid, and plumb throwed up.

[*Pause for thought.*]

                        Throwed up his sword.

KLEONIKE
Suppose the men just leave us flat?

LYSISTRATA
                            In that case,
we'll have to take things into our own hands.

KLEONIKE
There simply isn't any reasonable facsimile!
—Suppose they take us by force and drag us off
to the bedroom against our wills?

LYSISTRATA
                        Hang on to the door.

KLEONIKE
Suppose they beat us?

LYSISTRATA
                Give in—but be bad sports.
Be nasty about it—they don't enjoy these forced
affairs. So make them suffer.
                        Don't worry; they'll stop
soon enough. A married man wants harmony—
cooperation, not rape.

KLEONIKE
                    Well, I suppose so. . . .

[*Looking from Lysistrata to Lampito.*]

If *both* of you approve this, then so do we.

LAMPITO
Hain't worried over our menfolk none. We'll bring
  'em
round to makin' a fair, straightfor'ard Peace
withouten no nonsense about it. But take this rackety
passel in Athens: I misdoubt no one could make 'em
give over thet blabber of theirn.

LYSISTRATA
                        They're our concern.
Don't worry. We'll bring them around.

LAMPITO
                        Not likely.
Not long as they got ships kin still sail straight,
an' thet fountain of money up thar in Athene's temple.

LYSISTRATA
That point is quite well covered:

We're taking over
the Akropolis, including Athene's temple, today.
It's set: Our oldest women have their orders.
They're up there now, pretending to sacrifice, waiting
for us to reach an agreement. As soon as we do,
they seize the Akropolis.

LAMPITO

The way you put them
thengs,
I swear I can't see how we kin possibly lose!

LYSISTRATA
Well, now that it's settled, Lampito, let's not lose
any time. Let's take the Oath to make this binding.

LAMPITO
Just trot out thet-thar Oath. We'll swear it.

LYSISTRATA

Excellent.

—Where's a policewoman?

[A huge girl, dressed as a Skythian archer (the Athenian
police) with bow and circular shield, lumbers up and
gawks.]

—What are *you* looking
for?

[Pointing to a spot in front of the women.]

Put your shield down here.

[The girl obeys.]

No, hollow *up*!

[The girl reverses the shield. Lysistrata looks about brightly.]

—Someone give me the entrails.

[A dubious silence.]

KLEONIKE

Lysistrata, what kind
of an Oath are we supposed to swear?

LYSISTRATA

The Standard.
Aischylos used it in a play, they say—the one where
you slaughter a sheep and swear on a shield.

KLEONIKE

Lysistrata,
you *do not* swear an Oath for *Peace* on a *shield*!

LYSISTRATA
What Oath do you want?

[Exasperated.]

Something bizarre and
expensive?
A fancier victim—"Take one white horse and disem-
bowel"?

KLEONIKE
White horse? The symbolism's too obscure.

LYSISTRATA

*Then how
do we swear this oath?*

KLEONIKE
Oh, *I* can tell you
that, if you'll let me.

First, we put an enormous
black cup right here—hollow up, of course.
Next, into the cup we slaughter a jar of Thasian
wine, and swear a mighty Oath that we won't . . .
dilute it with water.

LAMPITO

[To Kleonike.]

Let me corngratulate you—
that were the beatenes' Oath I ever heerd on!

LYSISTRATA

[Calling inside.]

Bring out a cup and a jug of wine!

[Two women emerge, the first staggering under the weight of
a huge black cup, the second even more burdened with a
tremendous wine jar. Kleonike addresses them.]

KLEONIKE

You darlings!
What a tremendous display of pottery!

[Fingering the cup.]

A girl
could get a glow just *holding* a cup like this!

[She grabs it away from the first woman, who exits.]

LYSISTRATA

[Taking the wine jar from the second serving woman (who
exits), she barks at Kleonike.]

Put that down and help me butcher this boar!

[*Kleonike puts down the cup, over which she and Lysistrata together hold the jar of wine (the "boar"). Lysistrata prays.*]

> O Mistress Persuasion,
> O Cup of Devotion,
> Attend our invocation:
> Accept this oblation,
> Grant our petition,
> Favor our mission.

[*Lysistrata and Kleonike tip up the jar and pour the gurgling wine into the cup. Myrrhine, Lampito, and the others watch closely.*]

MYRRHINE
Such an attractive shade of blood. And the spurt— pure Art!

LAMPITO
        Hit shore do smell mighty purty!

[*Lysistrata and Kleonike put down the empty wine jar.*]

KLEONIKE
Girls, let me be the first

[*Launching herself at the cup.*]

                    to take the Oath!

LYSISTRATA

[*Hauling Kleonike back.*]

You'll have to wait your turn like everyone else.
—Lampito, how do we manage with this mob?
                                Cumbersome.
—Everyone place her right hand on the cup.

[*The women surround the cup and obey.*]

I need a spokeswoman. One of you to take
the Oath in behalf of the rest.

[*The women edge away from Kleonike, who reluctantly finds herself elected.*]

                    The rite will conclude
with a General Pledge of Assent by all of you, thus
confirming the Oath. Understood?

[*Nods from the women. Lysistrata addresses Kleonike.*]

                    Repeat after me:

LYSISTRATA
I will withhold all rights of access or entrance

KLEONIKE
I will withhold all rights of access or entrance

LYSISTRATA
From every husband, lover, or casual acquaintance

KLEONIKE
from every husband, lover, or casual acquaintance

LYSISTRATA
Who moves in my direction in erection.
                                —Go on.

KLEONIKE
who m-moves in my direction in erection.
                                Ohhhhh!
—Lysistrata, my knees are shaky. Maybe I'd better . . .

LYSISTRATA
I will create, imperforate in cloistered chastity,

KLEONIKE
I will create, imperforate in cloistered chastity,

LYSISTRATA
A newer, more glamorous, supremely seductive me

KLEONIKE
a newer, more glamorous, supremely seductive me

LYSISTRATA
And fire my husband's desire with my molten allure—

KLEONIKE
and fire my husband's desire with my molten allure—

LYSISTRATA
But remain, to his panting advances, icily pure.

KLEONIKE
but remain, to his panting advances, icily pure.

LYSISTRATA
If he should force me to share the connubial couch,

KLEONIKE
If he should force me to share the connubial couch,

LYSISTRATA
I refuse to return his stroke with the teeniest twitch.

KLEONIKE
I refuse to return his stroke with the teeniest twitch.

LYSISTRATA
I will not lift my slippers to touch the thatch

KLEONIKE
I will not lift my slippers to touch the thatch

LYSISTRATA
Or submit sloping prone in a hangdog crouch.

KLEONIKE
or submit sloping prone in a hangdog crouch.

LYSISTRATA

If I this oath maintain,
may I drink this glorious wine.

KLEONIKE

If I this oath maintain,
May I drink this glorious wine.

LYSISTRATA

But if I slip or falter,
let me drink water.

KLEONIKE

But if I slip or falter,
let me drink water.

LYSISTRATA

—And now the General Pledge of Assent:

WOMEN

A-MEN!

LYSISTRATA

Good. I'll dedicate the oblation.

[*She drinks deeply.*]

KLEONIKE

Not too much,
darling. You know how anxious we are to become
allies and friends.
　　　　　　　Not to mention *staying* friends.

[*She pushes Lysistrata away and drinks. As the women take
their turns at the cup, loud cries and alarums are heard
offstage.*]

LAMPITO

What-all's that bodacious ruckus?

LYSISTRATA

Just what I told you:
It means the women have taken the Akropolis.
　Athene's
Citadel is ours!
　　　　　It's time for you to go,
Lampito, and set your affairs in order in Sparta.

[*Indicating the other women in Lampito's group.*]

Leave these girls here as hostages.

[*Lampito exits left. Lysistrata turns to the others.*]

　　　　　　　　　　Let's hurry inside
the Akropolis and help the others shoot the bolts.

KLEONIKE

Don't you think the men will send reinforcements
against us as soon as they can?

LYSISTRATA

So where's the worry?
The men can't burn their way in or frighten us out.
The Gates are ours—they're proof against fire and
　fear—
and they open only on our conditions.

KLEONIKE

Yes!
That's the spirit—let's deserve our reputations:

[*As the women hurry off into the Akropolis.*]

UP THE SLUTS!
　　　WAY FOR THE OLD IMPREGNABLES!

[*The door shuts behind the women, and the stage is empty.*]

[*A pause, and the Chorus of men shuffles on from the left in
two groups, led by their Koryphaios. They are incredibly
aged Athenians; though they may acquire spryness later in
the play, at this point they are sheer decrepitude. Their
normally shaky progress is impeded by their burdens: each
man not only staggers under a load of wood across his
shoulders, but has his hands full as well—in one, an earthen
pot containing fire (which is in constant danger of going
out); in the other, a dried vinewood torch, not yet lit. Their
progress toward the Akropolis is very slow.*]

KORYPHAIOS OF MEN

[*To the right guide of the First Semichorus, who is stumbling
along in mild agony.*]

Forward, Swifty, keep 'em in step! Forget your shoul-
　der.
I know these logs are green and heavy—but duty, boy,
　duty!

SWIFTY

[*Somewhat inspired, he quavers into slow song to set a pace
for his group.*]

　　　I'm never surprised. At my age, life
　　　is just one damned thing after another.
　　　And yet, I never thought my wife
　　　was anything more than a home-grown bother.
　　　　　But now, dadblast her,
　　　　　she's a National Disaster!

FIRST SEMICHORUS OF MEN

　　　What a catastrophe—
　　　　MATRIARCHY!
They've brought Athene's statue to heel,
they've put the Akropolis under a seal,

they've copped the whole damned common-
weal . . .
What is there left for them to steal?

KORYPHAIOS OF MEN

[*To the right guide of the Second Semichorus—a slower
soul, if possible, than Swifty.*]

Now, Chipper, speed's the word. The Akropolis, on
the double!
Once we're there, we'll pile these logs around them,
and convene
a circuit court for a truncated trial. Strictly impartial:
With a show of hands, we'll light a spark of justice
under
every woman who brewed this scheme. We'll burn
them all
on the first ballot—and the first to go is Ly . . .

[*Pause for thought.*]

is Ly . . .

[*Remembering and pointing at a spot in the audience.*]

is *Lykon's wife*—and there she is, right over there!

CHIPPER

[*Taking up the song again.*]

I won't be twitted, I won't be guyed,
I'll teach these women not to trouble us!
Kleomenes the Spartan tried
expropriating our Akropolis
some time ago—
ninety-five years or so—

SECOND SEMICHORUS OF MEN
but he suffered damaging losses
when he ran across US!
He breathed defiance—and more as well:
No bath for six years—you could tell.
We fished him out of the Citadel
and quelled his spirit—but not his smell.

KORYPHAIOS OF MEN
That's how I took him. A savage siege:
Seventeen ranks
of shields were massed at that gate, with blanket infantry cover.
I slept like a baby.
So when mere women (who gall
the gods
and make Euripides sick) try the same trick, should I
sit idly by?

Then demolish the monument I won at
Marathon!

FIRST SEMICHORUS OF MEN

[*Singly.*]

—The last lap of our journey?
—I greet it with some dismay.
—The danger doesn't deter me,
—but
it's uphill
—all the way.
—Please, somebody,
—find a jackass
to drag these logs
—to the top.
—I ache to join the fracas,
—but
my shoulder's aching
—to stop.

SWIFTY
Backward there's no turning.
Upward and onward, men!
And keep those firepots burning, or
we make this trip again.

CHORUS OF MEN

[*Blowing into their firepots, which promptly send forth
clouds of smoke.*]

With a puff (pfffff). . . .
and a cough (hhhhhh). . . .
The smoke! I'll choke! Turn it off!

SECOND SEMICHORUS OF MEN

[*Singly.*]

—Damned embers.
—Should be muzzled.
—There oughta be a law.
—They jumped me
—when I whistled
—and then
they gnawed my eyeballs
—raw.
—There's lava in my lashes.
—My lids are oxidized.
—My brows are braised.
—These ashes are
volcanoes
—in disguise.

CHIPPER

> This way, men. And remember,
> the Goddess needs our aid.
> So don't be stopped by cinders. Let's
> press on to the stockade!

CHORUS OF MEN

[*Blowing again into their firepots, which erupt as before.*]

> With a huff (hfffff). . . .
> and a chuff (chffff). . . .
> Drat that smoke. Enough is enough!

KORYPHAIOS OF MEN

[*Signalling the Chorus, which has now tottered into position before the Akropolis gate, to stop, and peering into his firepot.*]

Praise be to the gods, it's awake. There's fire in the old
  fire yet.
—Now the directions. See how they strike you:
> First, we deposit
these logs at the entrance and light our torches. Next,
  we crash
the gate. When that doesn't work, we request admission. Politely.
When *that* doesn't work, we burn the damned door
  down, and smoke
these women into submission.
> That seem acceptable?
Good.
Down with the load . . . ouch, that smoke!
  Sonofabitch!

[*A horrible tangle results as the Chorus attempts to deposit the logs. The Koryphaios turns to the audience.*]

Is there a general in the house? We have a logistical
  problem. . . .

[*No answer. He shrugs.*]

Same old story. Still at loggerheads over in Samos.

[*With great confusion, the logs are placed somehow.*]

That's better. The pressure's off. I've got my backbone
  back.

[*To his firepot.*]

What, pot! You forgot your part in the plot?

> Urge that smudge
> to be hot on the dot and scorch my torch.
> > Got it, pot?

[*Praying.*]

> Queen Athene, let these strumpets
> crumple before our attack.
> Grant us victory, male supremacy . . .
> and a testimonial plaque.

[*The men plunge their torches into firepots and arrange themselves purposefully before the gate. Engaged in their preparations, they do not see the sudden entrance, from the right, of the Chorus of Women, led by their Koryphaios. These wear long cloaks and carry pitchers of water. They are very old—though not so old as the men—but quite spry. In their turn, they do not perceive the Chorus of Men.*]

KORYPHAIOS OF WOMEN

[*Stopping suddenly.*]

What's this—soot? And smoke as well? I may be all
  wet,
but this might mean fire. Things look dark, girls: we'll
  have to dash.

[*They move ahead, at a considerably faster pace than the men.*]

FIRST SEMICHORUS OF WOMEN

[*Singly.*]

> Speed! Celerity!   Save our sorority
> from arson. Combustion.   And heat exhaustion.
> Don't let our sisterhood   shrivel to blisterhood.
> > Fanned into slag by hoary typhoons.
> > By flatulent, nasty, gusty baboons.
> > > We're late! Run!
> > > The girls might be done!

[*Tutte.*]

> Filling my pitcher   was absolute torture:
> The fountains in town   are so *crowded* at dawn,
> glutted with masses   of the lower classes
> blatting and battering,   shoving, and shattering
> jugs. But I juggled   my burden, and wriggled
> away to extinguish   the igneous anguish
> > of neighbor, and sister, and daughter—
> > Here's Water!

SECOND SEMICHORUS OF WOMEN

[*Singly.*]

Get wind of the news?   The gaffers are loose.
The blowhards are off   with fuel enough
to furnish a bathhouse.   But the finish is pathos:
    They're scaling the heights with a horrid pro-
        posal.
    They're menacing women with rubbish disposal!
        How ghastly—how gauche!
        burned up with the trash!

[*Tutte.*]

Preserve me, Athene,   from gazing on any
matron or maid   auto-da-fé'd.
Cover with grace   these redeemers of
    Greece
from battles, insanity,   Man's inhumanity.
Gold-browed goddess,   hither to aid us!
Fight as our ally,   join in our sally
    against pyromaniac slaughter—
        Haul Water!

KORYPHAIOS OF WOMEN

[*Noticing for the first time the Chorus of Men, still busy at their firepots, she cuts off a member of her Chorus who seems about to continue the song.*]

Hold it. What have we here? You don't catch true-blue
    patriots
red-handed. These are authentic degenerates, male,
    taken
in flagrante.

KORYPHAIOS OF MEN
            Oops. Female troops. This could be upset-
    ting.
I didn't expect such a flood of reserves.

KORYPHAIOS OF WOMEN
                    Merely a spearhead.
If our numbers stun you, watch that yellow streak
    spread. We
represent just one percent of one percent of This
    Woman's Army.

KORYPHAIOS OF MEN
Never been confronted with such backtalk. Can't allow
    it. Somebody
pick up a log and pulverize that brass.
                    Any volunteers?

[*There are none among the male chorus.*]

KORYPHAIOS OF WOMEN
Put down the pitchers, girls. If they start waving that
    lumber,
we don't want to be encumbered.

KORYPHAIOS OF MEN
                    Look, men, a few
    sharp jabs
will stop that jawing. It never fails.
                    The poet Hipponax
swears by it.

[*Still no volunteers. The Koryphaios of Women advances.*]

KORYPHAIOS OF WOMEN
            Then step right up. Have a jab at me.
Free shot.

KORYPHAIOS OF MEN

[*Advancing reluctantly to meet her.*]

            Shut up! I'll peel your pelt. I'll pit your pod.

KORYPHAIOS OF WOMEN
The name is Stratyllis. I dare you to lay one finger on
    me.

KORYPHAIOS OF MEN
I'll lay on you with a fistful. Er—any specific threats?

KORYPHAIOS OF WOMEN

[*Earnestly.*]

I'll crop your lungs and reap your bowels, bite by bite,
and leave no balls on the body for other bitches to
    gnaw.

KORYPHAIOS OF MEN

[*Retreating hurriedly.*]

Can't beat Euripides for insight. And I quote:
                    *No creature's found
so lost to shame as Woman.*
                    Talk about realist play-
    wrights!

KORYPHAIOS OF WOMEN
Up with the water, ladies. Pitchers at the ready, place!

KORYPHAIOS OF MEN
Why the water, you sink of iniquity? More sedition?

KORYPHAIOS OF WOMEN
Why the fire, you walking boneyard? Self-cremation?

KORYPHAIOS OF MEN
I brought this fire to ignite a pyre and fricassee your
    friends.

KORYPHAIOS OF WOMEN
I brought this water to douse your pyre. Tit for tat.

KORYPHAIOS OF MEN
You'll douse my fire? Nonsense!

KORYPHAIOS OF WOMEN
                    You'll see, when the
facts soak in.

KORYPHAIOS OF MEN
I have the torch right here. Perhaps I should barbecue
you.

KORYPHAIOS OF WOMEN
If you have any soap, I could give you a bath.

KORYPHAIOS OF MEN
                    A bath from those
polluted hands?

KORYPHAIOS OF WOMEN
            Pure enough for a blushing young
bridegroom.

KORYPHAIOS OF MEN
Enough of that insolent lip.

KORYPHAIOS OF WOMEN
                It's merely freedom of
speech.

KORYPHAIOS OF MEN
I'll stop that screeching!

KORYPHAIOS OF WOMEN
                You're helpless outside of the
jury-box.

KORYPHAIOS OF MEN

[*Urging his men, torches at the ready, into a charge.*]

Burn, fire, burn!

KORYPHAIOS OF WOMEN

[*As the women empty their pitchers over the men.*]

        And cauldron bubble.

KORYPHAIOS OF MEN

[*Like his troops, soaked and routed.*]

            Arrgh!

KORYPHAIOS OF WOMEN
                Goodness.
What seems to be the trouble? Too hot?

KORYPHAIOS OF MEN
                Hot, hell!
Stop it!
What do you think you're doing?

KORYPHAIOS OF WOMEN
                If you must know,
I'm gardening.
Perhaps you'll bloom.

KORYPHAIOS OF MEN
                Perhaps I'll fall right off the
vine!
I'm withered, frozen, shaking . . .

KORYPHAIOS OF WOMEN
                Of course. But,
providentially,
you brought along your smudgepot.
                The sap should
rise eventually.

[*Shivering, the Chorus of Men retreats in utter defeat.*]

[*A Commissioner of Public Safety enters from the left, followed quite reluctantly by a squad of police—four Skythian
archers. He surveys the situation with disapproval.*]

COMMISSIONER
Fire, eh? Females again—spontaneous combustion
of lust. Suspected as much.
                Rubadubdubbing, inces-
sant
incontinent keening for wine, damnable funeral
foofaraw for Adonis resounding from roof to roof—
heard it all before . . .

[*Savagely, as the Koryphaios of Men tries to interpose a
remark.*]

                and WHERE?
                The ASSEMBLY!
Recall, if you can, the debate on the Sicilian Question:
That bullbrained demagogue Demostratos (who will
    rot, I trust)
rose to propose a naval task force.
                His wife,
writhing with religion on a handy roof, bleated
a dirge:
        'BEREFT! OH WOE OH WOE FOR
ADONIS!"
And so of course Demostratos, taking his cue,
outblatted her:
                "A DRAFT! ENROLL THE WHOLE
OF ZAKYNTHOS!"
His wife, a smidgin stewed, renewed her yowling:
"OH GNASH YOUR TEETH AND BEAT YOUR
    BREASTS
FOR ADONIS!"
And so of course Demostratos (that god-detested blot,

that foul-lunged son of an ulcer) gnashed tooth and
  nail
and voice, and bashed and rammed his program
  through.
And THERE is the Gift of Women:
                              MORAL CHAOS!

KORYPHAIOS OF MEN
Save your breath for actual felonies, Commissioner;
see what's happened to us! Insolence, insults,
these we pass over, but not lese-majesty:
                                    We're flooded
with indignity from those bitches' pitchers—like a
  bunch
of weak-bladdered brats. Our cloaks are sopped. We'll
  sue!

COMMISSIONER
Useless. Your suit won't hold water. Right's on their
  side.
For female depravity, gentlemen, WE stand guilty—
we, their teachers, preceptors of prurience, accomplices
before the fact of fornication. We sowed them in sexual
license, and now we reap rebellion.
                              The proof?
Consider. Off we trip to the goldsmith's to leave
an order:
            "That bangle you fashioned last spring for
  my wife is sprung. She was thrashing around last
  night, and the prong popped out of the bracket. I'll
  be tied up all day—I'm boarding the ferry right
  now—but my wife'll be home. If you get the time,
  please stop by the house in a bit and see if you can't
  do something—anything—to fit a new prong into
  the bracket of her bangle."
                        And bang.
Another one ups to a cobbler—young, but no apprentice,
full kit of tools, ready to give his awl—
and delivers this gem:
                    "My wife's new sandals are
  tight.
The cinch pinches her pinkie right where she's sensitive.
Drop in at noon with something to stretch her cinch
and give it a little play."
                        And a cinch it is.
Such hanky-panky we have to thank for today's
Utter Anarchy: I, a Commissioner of Public
Safety, duly invested with extraordinary powers
to protect the State in the Present Emergency, have
  secured

a source of timber to outfit our fleet and solve
the shortage of oarage. I need the money immediately . . . and WOMEN, no less, have locked me
  out of the Treasury!

[Pulling himself together.]

—Well, no profit in standing around.

[To one of the archers.]

                                    Bring
the crowbars. I'll jack these women back on their
  pedestals!
—WELL, you slack-jawed jackass? What's the attraction?
Wipe that thirst off your face. I said crowbar, not
  saloon!
—All right, men, all together. Shove those bars
underneath the gate and HEAVE!

[Grabbing up a crowbar.]

                              I'll take this side.
And now let's root them out, men, ROOT them out.
One, Two . . .

[The gates to the Akropolis burst open suddenly, disclosing
Lysistrata. She is perfectly composed and bears a large spindle. The Commissioner and the Police fall back in consternation.]

LYSISTRATA
            Why the moving equipment?
I'm quite well motivated, thank you, and here I am.
Frankly, you don't need crowbars nearly so much as
  brains.

COMMISSIONER
Brains? O name of infamy! Where's a policeman?

[He grabs wildly for the First Archer and shoves him toward
Lysistrata.]

Arrest that woman!
                    Better tie her hands behind her.

LYSISTRATA
By Artemis, goddess of the hunt, if he lays a finger
on me, he'll rue the day he joined the force!

[She jabs the spindle viciously at the First Archer, who leaps,
terrified, back to his comrades.]

COMMISSIONER
What's this—retreat? Never! Take her on the flank.

[*The First Archer hangs back. The Commissioner grabs the Second Archer.*]

—Help him.
            —Will the two of you kindly TIE HER
UP?

[*He shoves them toward Lysistrata. Kleonike, carrying a large chamber pot, springs out of the entrance and advances on the Second Archer.*]

KLEONIKE
By Artemis, goddess of the dew, if you so much
as touch her, I'll stomp the shit right out of you!

[*The two Archers run back to their group.*]

COMMISSIONER
Shit? Shameless! Where's another policeman?

[*He grabs the Third Archer and propels him toward Kleonike.*]

Handcuff *her* first. Can't stand a foul-mouthed female.

[*Myrrhine, carrying a large, blazing lamp, appears at the entrance and advances on the Third Archer.*]

MYRRHINE
By Artemis, bringer of light, if you lay a finger
on her, you won't be able to stop the swelling!

[*The Third Archer dodges her swing and runs back to the group.*]

COMMISSIONER
Now what? Where's an officer?

[*Pushing the Fourth Archer toward Myrrhine.*]

                        Apprehend that woman!
I'll see that *somebody* stays to take the blame!

[*Ismenia the Boiotian, carrying a huge pair of pincers, appears at the entrance and advances on the Fourth Archer.*]

ISMENIA
By Artemis, goddess of Tauris, if you go near
that girl, I'll rip the hair right out of your head!

[*The Fourth Archer retreats hurriedly.*]

COMMISSIONER
What a colossal mess: Athens' Finest—
finished!

[*Arranging the Archers.*]

        —Now, men, a little *esprit de corps.* Worsted
by women? Drubbed by drabs?
                        Never!
                                Regroup,
reform that thin red line.
                Ready?
                        CHARGE!

[*He pushes them ahead of him.*]

LYSISTRATA
I warn you. We have four battalions behind us—
full-armed combat infantrywomen, trained
from the cradle . . .

COMMISSIONER
Disarm them, Officers! Go for the hands!

LYSISTRATA

[*Calling inside the Akropolis.*]

MOBILIZE THE RESERVES!

[*A horde of women, armed with household articles, begins to pour from the Akropolis.*]

                        Onward, you ladies
    from hell!
Forward, you market militia, you battle-hardened
bargain hunters, old sales campaigners, grocery
grenadiers, veterans never bested by an overcharge!
You troops of the breadline, doughgirls—
                                        INTO THE
    FRAY!
Show them no mercy!
                Push!
                        Jostle!
                                Shove!
Call them nasty names!
                Don't be ladylike.

[*The women charge and rout the Archers in short order.*]

Fall back—don't strip the enemy! The day is ours!

[*The women obey, and the Archers run off left. The Commissioner, dazed, is left muttering to himself.*]

COMMISSIONER
Gross ineptitude. A sorry day for the Force.

LYSISTRATA
Of course. What did you expect? We're not slaves;

we're freeborn Women, and when we're scorned, we're full
of fury. Never Underestimate the Power of a Woman.

COMMISSIONER

Power? You mean Capacity. I should have remembered
the proverb: *The lower the tavern, the higher the dudgeon.*

KORYPHAIOS OF MEN

Why cast your pearls before swine, Commissioner? I
    know you're a civil
servant, but don't overdo it. Have you forgotten the
    bath
they gave us—in public,
                              fully dressed,
                                        totally soapless?
Keep rational discourse for *people*!

[*He aims a blow at the Koryphaios of Women, who dodges
and raises her pitcher.*]

KORYPHAIOS OF WOMEN

I might point out that lifting
one's hand against a neighbor is scarcely civilized
    behavior—
and entails, for the lifter, a black eye.
                              I'm really peaceful by nature,
compulsively inoffensive—a perfect doll. My ideal is a
    well-bred
repose that doesn't even stir up dust . . .

[*Swinging at the Koryphaios of Men with the pitcher.*]

                                        unless some
    no-good lowlife
tries to rifle my hive and gets my dander up!

[*The Koryphaios of Men backs hurriedly away, and the
Chorus of Men goes into a worried dance.*]

CHORUS OF MEN

[*Singly.*]

        O Zeus, what's the use of this constant abuse?
        How do we deal with this female zoo?
        Is there no solution to Total Immersion?
            What can a poor man DO?

[*Tutti.*]

        Query the Adversary!
        Ferret out their story!

What end did they have in view,
    to seize the city's sanctuary,
    snatch its legendary eyrie,
    snare an area so very
        terribly taboo?

KORYPHAIOS OF MEN

[*To the Commissioner.*]

Scrutinize those women! Scour their depositions—
    assess their rebuttals!
Masculine honor demands this affair be probed to the
    bottom!

COMMISSIONER

[*Turning to the women from the Akropolis.*]

All right, you. Kindly inform me, dammit, in your own
    words:
What possible object could you have had in blockading the Treasury?

LYSISTRATA

We thought we'd deposit the money in escrow and
    withdraw you men
from the war.

COMMISSIONER
                    The money's the cause of the war?

LYSISTRATA
                              And all our internal
disorders—the Body Politic's chronic bellyaches: What
    causes
Peisandros' frantic rantings, or the raucous caucuses of
    the Friends
of Oligarchy? The chance for graft.
                              But now, with the money up there,
they can't upset the City's equilibrium—or lower its
    balance.

COMMISSIONER
And what's your next step?

LYSISTRATA
                              Stupid question. We'll
    budget the money.

COMMISSIONER
You'll budget the money?

LYSISTRATA
                              Why should you find that so
    shocking?
We budget the household accounts, and you don't
    object at all.

COMMISSIONER
That's different.

LYSISTRATA

Different? How?

COMMISSIONER

The War Effort needs
this money!

LYSISTRATA

Who needs the War Effort?

COMMISSIONER

Every patriot who pulses
to save
all that Athens holds near and dear . . .

LYSISTRATA

Oh, *that*.

Don't worry.
We'll save you.

COMMISSIONER

You will save us?

LYSISTRATA

Who else?

COMMISSIONER

But this is unscrupulous!

LYSISTRATA

We'll save you. You can't deter us.

COMMISSIONER

Scurrilous!

LYSISTRATA

You seem disturbed.
This makes it difficult. But, still—we'll save you.

COMMISSIONER

Doubtless illegal!

LYSISTRATA

We deem it a duty. For friendship's sake.

COMMISSIONER

Well, forsake this friend:
I DO NOT WANT TO BE SAVED, DAMMIT!

LYSISTRATA

All the more reason.
It's not only Sparta; now we'll have to save you from
you.

COMMISSIONER

Might I ask where you women conceived this concern
about War and Peace?

LYSISTRATA

[*Loftily.*]

We shall explain.

COMMISSIONER

[*Making a fist.*]

Hurry up, and you won't
get hurt.

LYSISTRATA

Then *listen*. And do try to keep your hands to
yourself.

COMMISSIONER

[*Moving threateningly toward her.*]

I can't. Righteous anger forbids restraint, and
decrees . . .

KLEONIKE

[*Brandishing her chamber pot.*]

Multiple fractures?

COMMISSIONER

[*Retreating.*]

Keep those croaks for yourself, you old crow!

[*To Lysistrata.*]

All right, lady, I'm ready. Speak.

LYSISTRATA

I shall proceed:
When the War began, like the prudent, dutiful wives
that we are,
we tolerated you men, and endured your actions in
silence. (Small wonder—
you wouldn't let us say boo.)
You were not precisely
the answer
to a matron's prayer—we knew you too well, and
found out more.
Too many times, as we sat in the house, we'd hear that
you'd done it
again—manhandled another affair of state with your
usual
staggering incompetence. Then, masking our worry
with a nervous laugh,
we'd ask you, brightly, "How was the Assembly today,
dear? Anything
in the minutes about Peace?" And my husband would
give

his stock reply.

"What's that to you? Shut up!" and I did.

KLEONIKE

[*Proudly.*]

I never shut up!

COMMISSIONER

I trust you were shut up. Soundly.

LYSISTRATA

Regardless, *I* shut up.

And then we'd learn that you'd passed another decree, fouler

than the first, and we'd ask again: "Darling, how *did* you manage

anything so idiotic?" And my husband, with his customary glare,

would tell me to spin my thread, or else get a clout on the head.

And of course he'd quote from Homer:

Yᵉ *menne must see to*

yᵉ *warre.*

COMMISSIONER

Apt and irrefutably right.

LYSISTRATA

Right, you miserable misfit?

To keep us from giving advice while you fumbled the City away

in the Senate? Right, indeed!

But this time was really too much:

Wherever we went, we'd hear you engaged in the same conversation:

"What Athens needs is a Man."

"But there isn't a Man in the country."

"You can say that again."

There was obviously no time to lose.

We women met in immediate convention and passed a unanimous

resolution: To work in concert for safety and Peace in Greece.

We have valuable advice to impart, and if you can possibly

deign to emulate our silence, and take your turn as audience,

we'll rectify you—we'll straighten you out and set you right.

COMMISSIONER

You'll set *us* right? You go too far. I cannot permit such a statement to . . .

LYSISTRATA

Shush.

COMMISSIONER

I categorically decline to shush

for some confounded woman, who wears—as a constant reminder

of congenital inferiority, an injunction to public silence—a veil!

Death before such dishonor!

LYSISTRATA

[*Removing her veil.*]

If that's the only obstacle . . .

I feel you need a new panache,

so take the veil, my dear Commissioner, and drape it thus—

and SHUSH!

[*As she winds the veil around the startled Commissioner's head, Kleonike and Myrrhine, with carding-comb and wool-basket, rush forward and assist in transforming him into a woman.*]

KLEONIKE

Accept, I pray, this humble comb.

MYRRHINE

Receive this basket of fleece as well.

LYSISTRATA

Hike up your skirts, and card your wool,

and gnaw your beans—and stay at home!

While we write Homer:

Yᵉ *WOMEN must see to* yᵉ *warre!*

[*To the Chorus of Women, as the Commissioner struggles to remove his new outfit.*]

Women, weaker vessels, arise!

Put down your pitchers.

It's our turn, now. Let's supply our friends with some moral support.

[*The Chorus of Women dances to the same tune as the Men, but with much more confidence.*]

CHORUS OF WOMEN

[*Singly.*]

Oh, yes! I'll dance to bless their success.
Fatigue won't weaken my will. Or my
    knees.
I'm ready to join in any jeopardy,
    with girls as good as *these*!

[*Tutte.*]

A tally of their talents
convinces me they're giants
of excellence. To commence:
there's Beauty, Duty, Prudence, Sci-
    ence,
Self-Reliance, Compliance, Defiance,
and Love of Athens in balanced alliance
    with Common Sense!

KORYPHAIOS OF WOMEN

[*To the women from the Akropolis.*]

Autochthonous daughters of Attika, sprung from the
    soil that bore
your mothers, the spiniest, spikiest nettles known to
    man,
prove your mettle and attack! Now is no time to dilute
    your
anger. You're running ahead of the wind!

LYSISTRATA

                    We'll wait for the wind
from heaven. The gentle breath of Love and his
    Kyprian mother
will imbue our bodies with desire, and raise a storm to
    tense
and tauten these blasted men until they crack. And
    soon
we'll be on every tongue in Greece—the *Pacifiers*.

COMMISSIONER

                    That's quite
a mouthful. How will you win it?

LYSISTRATA

                First, we intend to
    withdraw
that crazy Army of Occupation from the downtown
    shopping section.

KLEONIKE
Aphrodite be praised!

LYSISTRATA

              The pottery shop and the groc-
    ery stall
are overstocked with soldiers, clanking around like
    those maniac Korybants,
armed to the teeth for a battle.

COMMISSIONER

              A Hero is Always Pre-
    pared!

LYSISTRATA
I suppose he is. But it does look silly to shop for
    sardines
from behind a shield.

KLEONIKE

           I'll second that. I saw
a cavalry captain buy vegetable soup on horseback. He
    carried
the whole mess home in his helmet.

                 And then that fel-
    low from Thrace,
shaking his buckler and spear—a menace straight from
    the stage.
The saleslady was stiff with fright. He was hogging her
    ripe figs—free.

COMMISSIONER
I admit, for the moment, that Hellas' affairs are in one
    hell of
a snarl. But how can you set them straight?

LYSISTRATA

                 Simplicity itself.

COMMISSIONER
Pray demonstrate.

LYSISTRATA

           It's rather like yarn. When a hank's
    in a tangle,
we lift it—*so*—and work out the snarls by winding it
    up
on spindles, now this way, now that way.

            That's how we'll wind up the War,
if allowed: We'll work out the snarls by sending Special
    Commissions—
back and forth, now this way, now that way—to ravel
    these tense
international kinks.

COMMISSIONER

           I lost your thread, but I know
    there's a hitch.
Spruce up the world's disasters with spindles—
    typically woolly
female logic.

LYSISTRATA

      If *you* had a scrap of logic, you'd adopt
our wool as a master plan for Athens.

COMMISSIONER

              What course of action
does the wool advise?

LYSISTRATA

           Consider the City as fleece,
  recently
shorn. The first step is Cleansing: Scrub it in a public
  bath,
and remove all corruption, offal, and sheepdip.
              Next, to the couch
for Scutching and Plucking: Cudgel the leeches and
  similar vermin
loose with a club, then pick the prickles and cockleburs
  out.
As for the clots—those lumps that clump and cluster
  in knots
and snarls to snag important posts—you comb these
  out,
twist off their heads, and discard.
           Next, to raise the
  City's
nap, you card the citizens together in a single basket
of common weal and general welfare. Fold in our loyal
Resident Aliens, all Foreigners of proven and tested
  friendship,
and any Disenfranchised Debtors. Combine these
  closely with the rest.
Lastly, cull the colonies settled by our own people:
these are nothing but flocks of wool from the City's
  fleece,
scattered throughout the world. So gather home these
  far-flung
flocks, amalgamate them with the others.
         Then, draw-
  ing this blend
of stable fibers into one fine staple, you spin a mighty
bobbin of yarn—and weave, without bias or seam, a
  cloak
to clothe the City of Athens!

COMMISSIONER

          This is too much! The City's
died in the wool, worsted by the distaff side—by
  women
who bore no share in the War. . . .

LYSISTRATA

           None, you hope-
  less hypocrite?

The quota we bear is double. First, we delivered our
  sons
to fill out the front lines in Sicily . . .

COMMISSIONER

            Don't   tax   me
  with that memory.

LYSISTRATA

Next, the best years of our lives were levied. Top-level
  strategy
attached our joy, and we sleep alone.
             But it's not the
  matrons
like us who matter. I mourn for the virgins, bedded in
  single
blessedness, with nothing to do but grow old.

COMMISSIONER

          Men *have* been known
to age, as well as women.

LYSISTRATA

          No, not as well as—better.
A man, an absolute antique, comes back from the war,
  and he's barely
doddered into town before he's married the veriest
  nymphet.
But a woman's season is brief; it slips, and she'll have
  no husband,
but sit out her life groping at omens—and finding no
  men.

COMMISSIONER

Lamentable state of affairs. Perhaps we can rectify
  matters:

[*To the audience*]

TO EVERY MAN JACK, A CHALLENGE:
              ARISE!
Provided you can . . .

LYSISTRATA

Instead, Commissioner, why not simply curl up and
  die?
          Just buy a coffin; here's the place.

[*Banging him on the head with her spindle.*]

          I'll knead you a cake for the wake—and
  these

[*Winding the threads from the spindle around him.*]

         make excellent wreaths. So Rest In Peace.

KLEONIKE

[*Emptying the chamber pot over him.*]

Accept these tokens of deepest grief.

MYRRHINE

[*Breaking her lamp over his head.*]

A final garland for the dear deceased.

LYSISTRATA

May I supply any last request?
Then run along. You're due at the wharf:
Charon's anxious to sail—
you're holding up the boat for Hell!

COMMISSIONER

This is monstrous—maltreatment of a public official—
maltreatment of ME!
I must repair directly
to the Board of Commissioners, and present my colleagues concrete
evidence of the sorry specifics of this shocking attack!

[*He staggers off left. Lysistrata calls after him.*]

LYSISTRATA

You won't haul us into court on a charge of neglecting
the dead, will you? (How like a man to insist
on his rights—even his last ones.) Two days between
death
and funeral, that's the rule.
Come back here early
day after tomorrow, Commissioner:
We'll lay you out.

[*Lysistrata and her women re-enter the Akropolis. The Koryphaios of Men advances to address the audience.*]

KORYPHAIOS OF MEN

Wake up, Athenians! Preserve your freedom—the time
is Now!

[*To the Chorus of Men.*]

Strip for action, men. Let's cope with the current
mess.

[*The men put off their long mantles, disclosing short tunics
underneath, and advance toward the audience.*]

CHORUS OF MEN

This trouble may be terminal; it has a loaded odor,
an ominous aroma of constitutional rot.

My nose gives a prognosis of radical disorder—
it's just the first installment of an absolutist plot!
The Spartans are behind it:
they must have masterminded
some morbid local contacts (engineered by
Kleisthenes).
Predictably infected,
these women straightway acted
to commandeer the City's cash. They're feverish to
freeze
my be-all,
my end-all . . .
my *payroll*!

KORYPHAIOS OF MEN

The symptoms are clear. Our birthright's already nib-
bled. And oh, so
daintily: WOMEN ticking off troops for improper eti-
quette.
WOMEN propounding their featherweight views on
the fashionable use
and abuse of the shield. And (if any more proof were
needed) WOMEN
nagging us to trust the Nice Laconian, and put our
heads
in his toothy maw—to make a dessert and call it
Peace.
They've woven the City a seamless shroud, bedecked
with the legend
DICTATORSHIP.
But I won't be hemmed in. I'll use
their weapon
against them, and uphold the right by sneakiness.
With knyf under cloke,
gauntlet in glove, sword in olivebranch,

[*Slipping slowly toward the Koryphaios of Women.*]

I'll take up my post
in Statuary Row, beside our honored National Heroes,
the natural foes of tyranny: Harmodios,
Aristogeiton,
and Me.

[*Next to her.*]

Striking an epic pose, so, with the full approval
of the immortal gods,
I'll bash this loathesome hag in
the jaw!

[*He does, and runs cackling back to the Men. She shakes a
fist after him.*]

KORYPHAIOS OF WOMEN
Mama won't know her little boy when he gets home!

[*To the Women, who are eager to launch a full-scale attack.*]

Let's not be hasty, fellow . . . hags. Cloaks off first.

[*The Women remove their mantles, disclosing tunics very like those of the Men, and advance toward the audience.*]

CHORUS OF WOMEN
We'll address you, citizens, in beneficial, candid,
   patriotic accents, as our breeding says we must,
since, from the age of seven, Athens graced me with a
   splendid
   string of civic triumphs to signalize her trust:
      I was Relic-Girl quite early,
      then advanced to Maid of Barley;
in Artemis' "Pageant of the Bear" I played the lead.
      To cap this proud progression,
      I led the whole procession
at Athene's Celebration, certified and pedigreed
        —that cachet
        so distingué—
        a *Lady!*

KORYPHAIOS OF WOMEN

[*To the audience.*]

I trust this establishes my qualifications. I may, I take
   it, address
the City to its profit? Thank you.
                 I admit to being a
   woman—
but don't sell my contribution short on that account.
   It's better
than the present panic. And my word is as good as my
   bond,
because I hold stock in Athens—stock I paid for in
   sons.

[*To the Chorus of Men.*]

—But you, you doddering bankrupts, where are your
   shares in the State?

[*Slipping slowly toward the Koryphaios of Men.*]

Your grandfathers willed you the Mutual Funds from
   the Persian War—
and where are they?

[*Nearer.*]

             You dipped into capital, then lost
   interest . . .
and now a pool of your assets won't fill a hole in the
   ground.
All that remains is one last potential killing—Athens.
Is there any rebuttal?

[*The Koryphaios of Men gestures menacingly. She ducks down, as if to ward off a blow, and removes a slipper.*]

              Force is a footling resort. I'll take
my very sensible shoe, and paste you in the jaw!

[*She does so, and runs back to the women.*]

CHORUS OF MEN
      Their native respect for our manhood is small,
      and keeps getting smaller. Let's bottle their
      gall.
      The man who won't battle has no balls at all!

KORYPHAIOS OF MEN
All right, men, skin out of the skivvies. Let's give them
   a whiff
of Man, full strength. No point in muffling the essential Us.

[*The men remove their tunics.*]

CHORUS OF MEN
      A century back, we soared to the Heights
        and beat down Tyranny there.
      Now's the time to shed our moults
      and fledge our wings once more,
        to rise to the skies in our reborn force,
        and beat back Tyranny here!

KORYPHAIOS OF MEN
No fancy grappling with these grannies; straightforward strength. The tiniest
toehold, and those nimble, fiddling fingers will have
   their foot
in the door, and we're done for.
              No amount of know-how can lick
a woman's knack.
           They'll want to build ships . . . next
   thing we know,
we're all at sea, fending off female boarding parties.
(Artemisia fought us at Salamis. Tell me, has anyone
   caught her
yet?)
      But we're *really* sunk if they take up horses.
   Scratch
the Cavalry:

A woman is an easy rider with a natural
seat.
Take her over the jumps bareback, and she'll never slip
her mount (That's how the Amazons nearly took
   Athens. On horseback.
Check on Mikon's mural down in the Stoa.)
                                             Anyway,
the solution is obvious. Put every woman in her
   place—stick her
in the stocks.
                   To do this, first snare your women
around the neck.

[*He attempts to demonstrate on the Koryphaios of Women.
After a brief tussle, she works loose and chases him back to
the Men.*]

CHORUS OF WOMEN
   The beast in me's eager and fit for a brawl.
   Just rile me a bit and she'll kick down the wall.
   You'll bawl to your friends that you've no balls
      at all.

KORYPHAIOS OF WOMEN
All right, ladies, strip for action. Let's give them a
   whiff
of *Femme Enragée*—piercing and pungent, but not at
   all tart.

[*The women remove their tunics.*]

CHORUS OF WOMEN
   We're angry. The brainless bird who tangles
      with *us* has gummed his last mush.
   In fact, the coot who even heckles
      is being daringly rash.
   So look to your nests, you reclaimed
      eagles—
      whatever you lay, we'll squash!

KORYPHAIOS OF WOMEN
Frankly, you don't faze me. *For* me, I have my
   friends—
Lampito from Sparta; that genteel girl from Thebes,
   Ismenia—
committed to me forever. *Against* me, *you*—
   permanently
out of commission. So do your damndest.
                                        Pass a law.
Pass seven. Continue the winning ways that have made
   your name
a short and ugly household word.
                              Like yesterday:
I was giving a little party, nothing fussy, to honor

the goddess Hekate. Simply to please my daughters,
   I'd invited
a sweet little thing from the neighborhood—flawless
   pedigree, perfect
taste, a credit to any gathering—a Boiotian eel.
But she has to decline. Couldn't pass the border.
   You'd passed a law.
Not that you care for my party. You'll overwork your
   right of passage
till your august body is overturned,
                              and   you   break
   your silly neck!

[*She deftly grabs the Koryphaios of Men by the ankle and
upsets him. He scuttles back to the Men, who retire in
confusion.*]

[*Lysistrata emerges from the citadel, obviously distraught.*]

KORYPHAIOS OF WOMEN

[*Mock-tragic.*]

Mistress, queen of this our subtle scheme,
why burst you from the hall with brangled brow?

LYSISTRATA
Oh, wickedness of woman! The female mind
does sap my soul and set my wits a-totter.

KORYPHAIOS OF WOMEN
What drear accents are these?

LYSISTRATA
The merest truth.

KORYPHAIOS OF WOMEN
Be nothing loath to tell the tale to friends.

LYSISTRATA
'Twere shame to utter, pain to hold unsaid.

KORYPHAIOS OF WOMEN
Hide not from me affliction which we share.

LYSISTRATA
In briefest compass,

[*Dropping the paratragedy.*]

                              we want to get laid.

KORYPHAIOS OF WOMEN
                                        By Zeus!

LYSISTRATA
No, no, not HIM!
                   Well, that's the way things are.
I've lost my grip on the girls—they're mad for men!
But sly—they slip out in droves.

A minute ago,
I caught one scooping out the little hole
that breaks through just below Pan's grotto.
One
had jerry-rigged some block-and-tackle business
and was wriggling away on a rope.
Another just flat
deserted.
Last night I spied one mounting a sparrow,
all set to take off for the nearest bawdyhouse. I hauled
her back by the hair.
And excuses, pretexts for overnight
passes? I've heard them all.
Here comes one. Watch.

[To the First Woman, as she runs out of the Akropolis.]

—You, there! What's your hurry?

FIRST WOMAN

I have to get home.
I've got all this lovely Milesian wool in the house,
and the moths will simply batter it to bits!

LYSISTRATA
I'll bet.
Get back inside.

FIRST WOMAN

I swear I'll hurry right back!
—Just time enough to spread it out on the couch?

LYSISTRATA
Your wool will stay unspread. And you'll stay here.

FIRST WOMAN
Do I have to let my piecework rot?

LYSISTRATA

Possibly.

[The Second Woman runs on.]

SECOND WOMAN
Oh dear, oh goodness, what shall I do—my flax!
I left and forgot to peel it!

LYSISTRATA
Another one.
She suffers from unpeeled flax.
—Get back inside!

SECOND WOMAN
I'll be right back. I just have to pluck the fibers.

LYSISTRATA
No. No plucking. You start it, and everyone else
will want to go and do their plucking, too.

[The Third Woman, swelling conspicuously, hurries on,
praying loudly.]

THIRD WOMAN
O Goddess of Childbirth, grant that I not deliver
until I get me from out this sacred precinct!

LYSISTRATA
What sort of nonsense is this?

THIRD WOMAN

I'm due—any second!

LYSISTRATA
You weren't pregnant yesterday.

THIRD WOMAN

Today I am—
a miracle!
Let me go home for a midwife, please!
I may not make it!

LYSISTRATA

[Restraining her.]

You can do better
than that.

[Tapping the woman's stomach and receiving a metallic
clang.]

What's this? It's hard.

THIRD WOMAN

I'm going to have a boy.

LYSISTRATA
Not unless he's made of bronze. Let's see.

[She throws open the Third Woman's cloak, exposing a huge
bronze helmet.]

Of all the brazen . . . You've stolen the helmet from
Athene's
statue! Pregnant, indeed!

THIRD WOMAN

I am so pregnant!

LYSISTRATA
Then why the helmet?

THIRD WOMAN
I thought my time might come
while I was still on forbidden ground. If it did,
I could climb inside Athene's helmet and have
my baby there.
The pigeons do it all the time.

LYSISTRATA
Nothing but excuses!

[Taking the helmet.]

              This is your baby. I'm afraid
you'll have to stay until we give it a name.

THIRD WOMAN
But the Akropolis is *awful*. I can't even sleep! I saw
the snake that guards the temple.

LYSISTRATA
                  That snake's a fabri-
   cation

THIRD WOMAN
I don't care *what* kind it is—I'm *scared*!

*[The other women, who have emerged from the citadel,
crowd around.]*

KLEONIKE
And those goddamned holy owls! All night long,
tu-wit, tu-wu—they're hooting me into my grave!

LYSISTRATA
Darlings, let's call a halt to this hocus-pocus.
You miss your men—now isn't that the trouble?

[Shamefaced nods from the group.]

Don't you think they miss you just as much?
I can assure you, their nights are every bit
as hard as yours. So be good girls; endure!
Persist a few days more, and Victory is ours.
It's fated: a current prophecy declares that the men
will go down to defeat before us, provided that *we*
maintain a United Front.

[Producing a scroll.]

             I happen to have
a copy of the prophecy.

KLEONIKE
             Read it!

LYSISTRATA
            Silence, *please*:

[Reading from the scroll.]

But when the swallows, in flight from the
   hoopoes, have flocked to a hole
on high, and stoutly eschew their
   accustomed perch on the pole,
yea, then shall Thunderer Zeus to

their suff'ring establish a stop,
by making the lower the upper . . .

KLEONIKE
Then *we'll* be lying on top?

LYSISTRATA
But should these swallows, indulging their
   lust for the perch, lose heart,
dissolve their flocks in winged dissension,
   and singly depart
the sacred stronghold, breaking the
   bands that bind them together—
then know them as lewd, the pervertedest
   birds that ever wore feather.

KLEONIKE
There's nothing obscure about *that* oracle. Ye gods!

LYSISTRATA
Sorely beset as we are, we must not flag
or falter. So back to the citadel!

[As the women troop inside.]

              And if we fail
that oracle, darlings, our image is absolutely *mud*!

[She follows them in. A pause, and the Choruses assemble.]

CHORUS OF MEN
            I have a simple
            tale to relate you,
            a sterling example
            of masculine virtue:

     The huntsman bold Melanion
         was once a harried quarry.
The women in town tracked him down
         and badgered him to marry.

     Melanion knew the cornered male
         eventually cohabits.
Assessing the odds, he took to the woods
         and lived by trapping rabbits.

     He stuck to the virgin stand, sustained
         by rabbit meat and hate,
and never returned, but ever remained
         an alfresco celibate.

     Melanion is our ideal;
         his loathing makes us free.
Our dearest aim is the gemlike flame
         of his misogyny.

OLD MAN
Let me kiss that wizened cheek. . . .

OLD WOMAN

[*Threatening with a fist.*]

A wish too rash for that withered flesh.

OLD MAN
and lay you low with a highflying kick.

[*He tries one and misses.*]

OLD WOMAN
Exposing an overgrown underbrush.

OLD MAN
A hair behind, historically, means
  masculine force: Myronides
harassed the foe with his mighty mane,
  and furry Phormion swept the seas
    of enemy ships, never meeting his match—
      such was the nature of his thatch.

CHORUS OF WOMEN
            I offer an anecdote
            for your opinion,
            an adequate antidote
            for your Melanion:

        Timon, the noted local grouch,
          put rusticating hermits
      out of style by building his wilds
        inside the city limits

        He shooed away society
        with natural battlements:
      his tongue was edgèd; his shoulder, frigid;
        his beard, a picket fence.

      When random contacts overtaxed him,
        he didn't stop to pack,
    but loaded curses on the male of the species,
      left town, and never came back.

        Timon, you see, was a misanthrope
        in a properly narrow sense:
      his spleen was vented only on men . . .
        we were his dearest friends.

OLD WOMAN

[*Making a fist.*]

Enjoy a chop to that juiceless chin?

OLD MAN

[*Backing away.*]

      I'm jolted already. Thank you, no.

OLD WOMAN
      Perhaps a trip from a well-turned shin?

[*She tries a kick and misses.*]

OLD MAN
      Brazenly baring the mantrap below.

OLD WOMAN
At least it's *neat*. I'm not too sorry.
  to have you see my daintiness.
My habits are still depilatory;
  age hasn't made me a bristly mess.
    Secure in my smoothness, I'm never in doubt—
      though even down is out.

[*Lysistrata mounts the platform and scans the horizon. When her gaze reaches the left, she stops suddenly.*]

LYSISTRATA
Ladies, attention! Battle stations, please!
And quickly!

[*A general rush of women to the battlements.*]

KLEONIKE
            What is it?

MYRRHINE
                  What's all the shouting for?

LYSISTRATA
A MAN!

[*Consternation.*]

      Yes, it's a man. And he's coming this way!.
Hmm. Seems to have suffered a seizure. Broken out
with a nasty attack of love.

[*Prayer, aside.*]

            O Aphrodite,
        Mistress all-victorious,
        mysterious, voluptuous,
        you who make the crooked straight . . .
        don't let this happen to US!

KLEONIKE
I don't care who he is—*where is he?*

LYSISTRATA

[*Pointing.*]

                              Down there—
just flanking that temple—Demeter the Fruitful.

KLEONIKE

                                        My.

Definitely a man.

MYRRHINE

[*Craning for a look.*]

          I wonder who it can be?

LYSISTRATA
See for yourselves—Can anyone identify him?

MYRRHINE
Oh lord, I can.
               That is my husband—Kinesias.

LYSISTRATA

[*To Myrrhine.*]

Your duty is clear.
               Pop him on the griddle, twist
the spit, braize him, baste him, stew him in his own
juice, do him to a turn. Sear him with kisses,
coyness, caresses, *everything*—
                    but stop where Our Oath
begins.

MYRRHINE
Relax. I can take care of this.

LYSISTRATA
                    Of course
you can, dear. Still, a little help can't hurt, now
can it! I'll just stay around for a bit
and—er—poke up the fire.
                    —Everyone else inside!

[*Exit all the women but Lysistrata, on the platform, and
Myrrhine, who stands near the Akropolis entrance, hidden
from her husband's view. Kinesias staggers on, in erection
and considerable pain, followed by a male slave who carries
a baby boy.*]

KINESIAS
OMIGOD OUCH!
Hypertension, twinges. . . . I can't hold out much
   more.

I'd rather be dismembered.
                    How long, ye gods, how long?

LYSISTRATA

[*Officially.*]

WHO GOES THERE?
          WHO PENETRATES OUR POSITIONS?

KINESIAS
Me.

LYSISTRATA
A Man?

KINESIAS
          Every inch.

LYSISTRATA
                    Then inch yourself out
of here. Off Limits to Men.

KINESIAS
                    This *is* the limit.
Just who are *you* to throw me out?

LYSISTRATA
                    The Lookout.

KINESIAS
Well, look here, Lookout. I'd like to see Myrrhine.
How's the outlook?

LYSISTRATA
                    Unlikely. Bring Myrrhine
to you? The idea!
                    Just by the by, who are you?

KINESIAS
A private citizen. Her husband, Kinesias.

LYSISTRATA
                              No!
Meeting you—I'm overcome!
                    Your name, you know,
is not without its fame among us girls.

[*Aside.*]

—Matter of fact, we have a name for *it.*—
I swear, you're never out of Myrrhine's mouth.
She won't even nibble a quince, or swallow an egg,
without reciting, "Here's to Kinesias!"

KINESIAS
                    For god's sake,

will you . . .

LYSISTRATA

[*Sweeping on over his agony.*]

Word of honor, it's true. Why, when
we discuss our husbands (you know how women are),
Myrrhine refuses to argue. She simply insists;
"Compared with Kinesias, the rest have *nothing*!"
    Imagine!

KINESIAS
Bring her out here!

LYSISTRATA
                        Really! And what would I
get out of this?

KINESIAS
                    You see my situation. I'll raise
whatever I can. This can all be yours.

LYSISTRATA
                            Goodness.
It's really her place. I'll go and get her.

[*She descends from the platform and moves to Myrrhine, out
of Kinesias' sight.*]

KINESIAS
                            Speed!
—Life is a husk. She left our home, and happiness
went with her. Now pain is the tenant. Oh, to enter
that wifeless house, to sense that awful emptiness,
to eat that tasteless, joyless food—it makes
it hard, I tell you.
                    Harder all the time.

MYRRHINE

[*Still out of his sight, in a voice to be overheard.*]

Oh, I *do* love him! I'm mad about him! But he
doesn't want my love. Please don't make me see him.

KINESIAS
Myrrhine darling, why do you *act* this way?
Come down here!

MYRRHINE

[*Appearing at the wall.*]

                        Down there? Certainly not!

KINESIAS
It's me, Myrrhine. I'm begging you. Please come
    down.

MYRRHINE
I don't see why you're begging me. You don't need
    me.

KINESIAS
I don't need you? I'm at the end of my rope!

MYRRHINE
I'm leaving.

[*She turns. Kinesias grabs the boy from the slave.*]

KINESIAS
                No! Wait! At least you'll have to listen
to the voice of your child.

[*To the boy, in a fierce undertone.*]

                        —(Call your mother!)

[*Silence.*]

                                    . . . to the voice
of your very own child . . .
                        —(Call your mother, brat!)

CHILD
MOMMYMOMMYMOMMY!

KINESIAS
Where's your maternal instinct? He hasn't been
    washed
or fed for a week. How can you be so pitiless?

MYRRHINE
Him I pity. Of all the pitiful excuses
for a father. . . .

KINESIAS
                Come down here, dear. For the baby's sake.

MYRRHINE
Motherhood! I'll have to come. I've got no choice.

KINESIAS

[*Soliloquizing as she descends.*]

It may be me, but I'll swear she looks years younger—
and gentler—her eyes caress me. And then they flash:
that anger, that verve, that high-and-mighty air!
She's fire, she's ice—and I'm caught right in the
    middle.

MYRRHINE

[*Taking the baby.*]

Sweet babykins with such a nasty daddy!
Here, let Mummy kissums. Mummy's little darling.

KINESIAS

[*The injured husband.*]

You should be ashamed of yourself, letting those women
lead you around. Why do you DO these things?
You only make me suffer and hurt your poor,
sweet self.

MYRRHINE
                    Keep your hands away from me!

KINESIAS
But the house, the furniture, everything we own—
    you're letting
it go to hell!

MYRRHINE
                    Frankly, I couldn't care less.

KINESIAS
But your weaving's unraveled—the loom is full of
    chickens!
You couldn't care less about *that*?

MYRRHINE
                                        I certainly couldn't.

KINESIAS
And the holy rites of Aphrodite? Think how long
that's been.
                    Come on, darling, let's go home.

MYRRHINE
I absolutely refuse!
                    Unless you agree to a truce
to stop the war!

KINESIAS
                    Well, then, if that's your decision,
we'll STOP the war!

MYRRHINE
                        Well, then, if that's your decision,
I'll come back—*after* it's done.
                            But, for the present,
I've sworn off.

KINESIAS
                    At least lie down for a minute.
We'll talk.

MYRRHINE
            I know what you're up to—NO!
—And yet. . . . I really can't say I don't love you . . .

KINESIAS
                                    You love me?
So what's the trouble? *Lie down.*

MYRRHINE
                            Don't be disgusting.
In front of the baby?

KINESIAS
                        Er . . . no. Heaven Forfend.

[*Taking the baby and pushing it at the slave.*]

—Take this home.

[*The slave obeys.*]

                —Well, darling, we're rid of the kid . . .
let's go to bed!

MYRRHINE
                Poor dear.
                        But where does one do
this sort of thing?

KINESIAS
                    Where? All we need is a little
nook. . . . We'll try Pan's grotto. Excellent spot.

MYRRHINE

[*With a nod at the Akropolis.*]

I'll have to be pure to get back in *there*. How can I
    expunge my pollution?

KINESIAS
                            Sponge off in the pool next door.

MYRRHINE
I did swear an Oath. I'm supposed to perjure myself?

KINESIAS
Bother the Oath. Forget it—I'll take the blame.

[*A pause.*]

MYRRHINE
Now I'll go get us a cot.

KINESIAS
                        No! Not a cot!
The ground's enough for us.

MYRRHINE
                            I'll get the cot.
For all your faults, I refuse to put you to bed
in the dirt.

[*She exits into the Akropolis.*]

KINESIAS
            She certainly loves me. That's nice to know.

MYRRHINE

[*Returning with a rope-tied cot.*]

Here. You hurry to bed while I undress.

[*Kinesias lies down.*]

Gracious me—I forgot. We need a mattress.

KINESIAS

Who wants a mattress? Not me!

MYRRHINE

Oh, yes, you do.
It's perfectly squalid on the ropes.

KINESIAS

Well, give me a kiss
to tide me over.

MYRRHINE

Voilà.

[She pecks at him and leaves.]

KINESIAS

OoolaLAlala!
—Make it a quick trip, dear.

MYRRHINE

[Entering with the mattress, she waves Kinesias off the cot and lays the mattress on it.]

Here we are.
Our mattress. Now hurry to bed while I undress.

[Kinesias lies down again.]

Gracious me—I forgot. You don't have a pillow.

KINESIAS

I do not need a pillow.

MYRRHINE

I know, but I do.

[She leaves.]

KINESIAS

What a lovefeast! Only the table gets laid.

MYRRHINE

[Returning with a pillow.]

Rise and shine!

[Kinesias jumps up. She places the pillow.]

And now I have everything I need.

KINESIAS

[Lying down again.]

You certainly do.
Come here, my little jewelbox!

MYRRHINE

Just taking off my bra.

Don't break your promise:
no cheating about the Peace.

KINESIAS

I swear to god,
I'll die first!

MYRRHINE

[Coming to him.]

Just look. You don't have a blanket.

KINESIAS

I didn't plan to go camping—I want to make love!

MYRRHINE

Relax. You'll get your love. I'll be right back.

[She leaves.]

KINESIAS

Relax! I'm dying a slow death by dry goods!

MYRRHINE

[Returning with the blanket.]

Get up!

KINESIAS

[Getting out of bed.]

I've been up for hours. I was up before I was up.

[Myrrhine spreads the blanket on the mattress, and he lies down again.]

MYRRHINE

I presume you want perfume?

KINESIAS

Positively NO!

MYRRHINE

Absolutely yes—whether you want it or not.

[She leaves.]

KINESIAS

Dear Zeus, I don't ask for much—but please let her spill it.

MYRRHINE

[Returning with a bottle.]

Hold out your hand like a good boy.

Now rub it in.

KINESIAS

[*Obeying and sniffing.*]

This is to quicken desire? Too strong. It grabs
your nose and bawls out: *Try again tomorrow.*

MYRRHINE
I'm *awful*! I brought you that rancid Rhodian brand.

[*She starts off with the bottle.*]

KINESIAS
This is just *lovely*. Leave it, woman!

MYRRHINE
                 Silly!

[*She leaves.*]

KINESIAS
God damn the clod who first concocted perfume!

MYRRHINE

[*Returning with another bottle.*]

Here, try this flask.

KINESIAS
           Thanks—but you try mine.
Come to bed, you witch—
               and please stop bringing
things!

MYRRHINE
     That is exactly what I'll do.
There go my shoes.
           Incidentally, darling, you *will*
remember to vote for the truce?

KINESIAS
               I'LL THINK IT
  OVER!

[*Myrrhine runs off for good.*]

That woman's laid me waste—destroyed me, root
and branch!
        I'm scuttled,
           gutted,
              up the spout!
And Myrrhine's gone!

[*In a parody of a tragic kommos.*]

Out upon't! But how? But where?
Now I have lost the fairest fair,
how stick my courage to yet another
screwing-place? Aye, there's the rub—
And yet, this wagging, wanton babe
must soon be laid to rest, or else . . .
Ho, Pandar!
        Pandar!
             I'd hire a nurse.

KORYPHAIOS OF MEN
     Grievous your bereavement, cruel
     the slow tabescence of your soul.
     I bid my liquid pity mingle.

     Oh, where the soul, and where, alack!
     the cod to stand the taut attack
     of swollen prides, the scorching tensions
     that ravine up the lumbar regions?
        His morning lay
        has gone astray.

KINESIAS

[*In agony.*]

     O Zeus, reduce the throbs, the throes!

KORYPHAIOS OF MEN
     I turn my tongue to curse the cause
     of your affliction—that jade, that slut,
     that hag, that ogress . . .

KINESIAS
                No! Slight not
     my light-o'-love, my dove, my sweet!

KORYPHAIOS OF MEN
     Sweet!
       O Zeus who rul'st the sky,
     snatch that slattern up on high,
     crack thy winds, unleash thy thunder,
     tumble her over, trundle her under,
     juggle her from hand to hand;
     twirl her ever near the ground—
     drop her in a well-aimed fall
     on our tortured comrade's tool!

[*Kinesias exits left.*
A Spartan Herald enters from the right, holding his cloak
together in a futile attempt to conceal his condition.]

HERALD
This Athens? Where-all kin I find the Council of Elders
or else the Executive Board? I brung some news.

[*The Commissioner, swathed in his cloak, enters from the left.*]

COMMISSIONER
And what are you—a man? A signpost? a joint-stock company?

HERALD
          A herald, sonny, a honest-to-Kastor herald. I come to chat 'bout thet-there truce.

COMMISSIONER
. . . carrying a concealed weapon? Pretty under-handed.

HERALD

[*Twisting to avoid the Commissioner's direct gaze.*]

Hain't done no such a thang!

COMMISSIONER
                    Very well, stand still.
Your cloak's out of crease—hernia? Are the roads that bad?

SPARTAN
I swear this feller's plumb tetched in the haid!

COMMISSIONER

[*Throwing open the Spartan's cloak, exposing the phallus.*]

                                        You
clown, you've got an erection!

SPARTAN

[*Wildly embarrassed.*]

                    Hain't got no sech a thang!
You stop this-hyer foolishment!

COMMISSIONER
                    What *have* you got there, then?

SPARTAN
Thet-thur's a Spartan epistle. In code.

COMMISSIONER
                    I have the key.

[*Throwing open his cloak.*]

Behold another Spartan epistle. In code.

[*Tiring of teasing.*]

Let's get down to cases. I know the score, so tell me the truth.

                    How are things with you in
Sparta?

HERALD
Thangs is up in the air. The whole Alliance is purt-near 'bout to explode. We'uns'll need buckets, 'stead of women.

COMMISSIONER
                    What was the cause of this outburst?
The great god Pan?

HERALD
                    Nope. I'll lay 'twere Lampito, most likely. She begun, and then they was off and runnin' at the post in a bunch, every last little gal in Sparta, drivin' their menfolk away from the winner's circle

COMMISSIONER
    How are you taking this?

HERALD
                    Painful-like.
Everyone's doubled up worse as a midget nursin' a wick in a midnight wind come moon-dark time. Cain't even tetch them little old gals on the moosey without we all agree to a Greece-wide Peace.

COMMISSIONER
Of course!
                    A universal female plot—all Hellas risen in rebellion—I should have known!
                                        Return
to Sparta with this request:
                    Have them despatch us
a Plenipotentiary Commission, fully empowered to conclude an armistice. I have full confidence that I can persuade our Senate to do the same, without extending myself. The evidence is at hand.

HERALD
I'm a-flyin', Sir! I hev never heered your equal!

[*Exeunt hurriedly, the Commissioner to the left, the Herald to the right.*]

KORYPHAIOS OF MEN
    The most unnerving work of nature,
    the pride of applied immorality,
    is the common female human.
    No fire can match, no beast can best her.
    O Unsurmountability,
    thy name—worse luck—is Woman.

KORYPHAIOS OF WOMEN

After such knowledge, why persist
in wearing out this fecklesss
war between the sexes?
When can I apply for the post
of ally, partner, and general friend?

KORYPHAIOS OF MEN

I won't be ployed to revise, re-do,
amend, extend, or bring to an end
my irreversible credo:
Misogyny Forever!
—The answer's never.

KORYPHAIOS OF WOMEN

All right. Whenever you choose.
But, for the present, I refuse
to let you look your absolute worst,
parading around like an unfrocked freak:
I'm coming over and get you dressed.

[*She dresses him in his tunic, an action (like others in this scene) imitated by the members of the Chorus of Women toward their opposite numbers in the Chorus of Men.*]

KORYPHAIOS OF MEN

This seems sincere. It's not a trick.
Recalling the rancor with which I stripped,
I'm overlaid with chagrin.

KORYPHAIOS OF WOMEN

Now you resemble a man,
not some ghastly practical joke.
And if you show me a little respect
(and promise not to kick), I'll extract
the beast in you.

KORYPHAIOS OF MEN

[*Searching himself.*]

          What beast in me?

KORYPHAIOS OF WOMEN

That insect. There. The bug that's stuck
in your eye.

KORYPHAIOS OF MEN

[*Playing along dubiously.*]

        This gnat?

KORYPHAIOS OF WOMEN

             Yes, nitwit!

KORYPHAIOS OF MEN

                Of course.

That steady, festering agony. . . .
You've put your finger on the source

of all my lousy troubles. Please
roll back the lid and scoop it out.
I'd like to see it.

KORYPHAIOS OF WOMEN

              All right, I'll do it.

[*Removing the imaginary insect.*]

Although, of all the impossible cranks. . . .
Do you sleep in a swamp! Just look at this.
I've never seen a bigger chigger.

KORYPHAIOS OF MEN

                 Thanks.

Your kindness touches me deeply. For years,
that thing's been sinking wells in my eye.
Now you've unplugged me. Here come the tears.

KORYPHAIOS OF WOMEN

I'll dry your tears, though I can't say why.

[*Wiping away the tears.*]

Of all the irresponsible boys. . . .
And I'll kiss you.

KORYPHAIOS OF MEN

         Don't you kiss me!

KORYPHAIOS OF WOMEN

What made you think you had a choice?

[*She kisses him.*]

KORYPHAIOS OF MEN

All right, damn you, that's enough of that ingrained
   palaver.
I can't dispute the truth or logic of the pithy old
   proverb:
              Life with women is hell.
              Life without women is hell, too.
And so we conclude a truce with you, on the following
   terms:
in future, a mutual moratorium on mischief in all its
   forms.
Agreed?—Let's make a single chorus and start our
   song.

[*The two Choruses unite and face the audience.*]

CHORUS OF MEN

        We're not about to introduce
        the standard personal abuse—
           the Choral Smear
        Of Present Persons (usually,
        in every well-made comedy,
           inserted here).

Instead, in deed and utterance, we
shall now indulge in philanthropy
    because we feel
that members of the audience
endure, in the course of current events,
    sufficient hell.
Therefore, friends, be rich! Be flush!
Apply to us, and borrow cash
    in large amounts.
The Treasury stands behind us—there—
and we can personally take care
    of small accounts.
Drop up today. Your credit's good.
Your loan won't have to be repaid
    in full until
the war is over. And then, your debt
is only the money you actually get—
    nothing at all.

CHORUS OF WOMEN
Just when we meant to entertain
some madcap Karystian men-about-town
    —such flawless taste!—
the present unpleasantness intervened,
and now we fear the feast we planned
    will go to waste.
The soup is waiting, rich and thick;
I've sacrificed a suckling pig
    —the pièce de résistance—
whose toothsome cracklings should amaze
the most fastidious gourmets—
    you, for instance.
To everybody here, I say
take potluck at my house today
    with me and mine.
Bathe and change as fast as you can,
bring the children, hurry down,
    and walk right in.
Don't bother to knock. No need at all.
My house is yours. Liberty Hall.
    What are friends for?
Act self-possessed when you come over;
it may help out when you discover
    I've locked the door.

[*A delegation of Spartans enters from the right, with difficulty. They have removed their cloaks, but hold them before
themselves in an effort to conceal their condition.*]

KORYPHAIOS OF MEN
What's this? Behold the Spartan ambassadors,
   dragging their beards,
pussy-footing along. It appears they've developed
   a hitch in the crotch.

[*Advancing to greet them.*]

Men of Sparta, I bid you welcome!
               And now
to the point: What predicament brings you among us?
SPARTAN
We-uns is up a stump. Hain't fit fer chatter.

[*Flipping aside his cloak.*]

Here's our predicament. Take a look for yourselfs.
KORYPHAIOS OF MEN
Well, I'll be damned—a regular disaster area.
Inflamed. I imagine the temperature's rather intense?
SPARTAN
Hit ain't the heat, hit's the tumidity.
                  But words
won't help what ails us. We-uns come after Peace.
Peace from any person, at any price.

[*Enter the Athenian delegation from the left, led by Kinesias.
They are wearing cloaks, but are obviously in as much
travail as the Spartans.*]

KORYPHAIOS OF MEN
Behold our local Sons of the Soil, stretching
their garments away from their groins, like wrestlers.
   Grappling
with their plight. Some sort of athlete's disease, no
   doubt.
An outbreak of epic proportions
                  Athlete's foot?
No. Could it be athlete's . . . . ?
KINESIAS

[*Breaking in.*]

               Who can tell us
how to get hold of Lysistrata? We've come as delegates
to the Sexual Congress.

[*Opening his cloak.*]

             Here are our credentials.
KORYPHAIOS OF MEN

[*Ever the scientist, looking from the Athenians to the Spartans and back again.*]

The words are different, but the malady seems the
   same.

[*To Kinesias.*]

Dreadful disease. When the crisis reaches its height,
what do you take for it?

KINESIAS

Whatever comes to hand.
But now we've reached the bitter end. It's Peace
or we fall back on Kleisthenes.

And he's got a waiting
list.

KORYPHAIOS OF MEN

[To the Spartans.]

Take my advice and put your clothes on. If someone
from that self-appointed Purity League comes by, you
may
be docked. That's what they did to the statues of
Hermes.

KINESIAS

[Since he has not yet noticed the Spartans, he interprets the
warning as meant for him, and hurriedly pulls his cloak
together, as do the other Athenians.]

Thank you. That's excellent advice.

SPARTAN

Hit shorely is.
Hain't nothing to argue after. Let's git dressed.

[As they put on their cloaks, the Spartans are finally noticed
by Kinesias.]

KINESIAS
Welcome, men of Sparta! This is a shameful
disgrace to masculine honor.

SPARTAN

Hit could be worser.
Ef them Herm-choppers seed us all fired up,
they'd *really* take us down a peg or two.

KINESIAS
Gentlemen, let's descend to details. Specifically,
why are you here?

SPARTAN

Ambassadors. We come to dicker
'bout thet-thur Peace.

KINESIAS

Perfect! Precisely our purpose.
Let's send for Lysistrata. Only she can reconcile
our differences. There'll be no Peace for us without
her.

SPARTAN
We-uns ain't fussy. Call Lysistratos, too, if you want.

[The gates to the Akropolis open, and Lysistrata emerges,
accompanied by her handmaid, Peace—a beautiful girl
without a stitch on. Peace remains out of sight by the gates
until summoned.]

KORYPHAIOS OF MEN
Hail, most virile of women! Summon up all your experience:
Be terrible and tender,
lofty and lowbrow,
severe and
demure.
Here stand the Leaders of Greece, enthralled by your
charm.
They yield the floor to you and submit their claims for
your arbitration.

LYSISTRATA
Really, it shouldn't be difficult, if I can catch them
all bothered, before they start to solicit each
other.
I'll find out soon enough. Where's Peace?
—Come here.

[Peace moves from her place by the gates to Lysistrata. The
delegations goggle at her.]

Now, dear, first get those Spartans and bring
them to me.
Take them by the hand, but don't be pushy about
it,
not like our husbands (no savoir-faire at all!).
Be a lady, be proper, do just what you'd do at
home:
if hands are refused, conduct them by the handle.

[Peace leads the Spartans to a position near Lysistrata.]

And now a hand to the Athenians—it doesn't matter
where; accept any offer—and bring *them* over.

[Peace conducts the Athenians to a position near Lysistrata,
opposite the Spartans.]

You Spartans move up closer—right *here*—

[To the Athenians.]

and *you*
stand over *here*.
—And now attend my speech.

[This the delegations do with some difficulty, because of the
conflicting attractions of Peace, who is standing beside her
mistress.]

I am a woman—but not without some wisdom:
my native wit is not completely negligible,
and I've listened long and hard to the discourse of my
    elders—
my education is not entirely despicable.
                                        Well,
now that I've got you, I intend to give you hell,
and I'm perfectly right. Consider your actions:
                                        At festi-
vals,
in Pan-Hellenic harmony, like true blood-brothers,
    you share
the selfsame basin of holy water, and sprinkle
altars all over Greece—Olympia, Delphoi
Thermopylai . . . (I could go on and on, if length
were my only object.)
                      But now, when the Persians sit
    by
and wait, in the very presence of your enemies, you
    fight
each other, destroy *Greek* men, destroy *Greek* cities!
—Point One of my address is now concluded.

KINESIAS

[*Gazing at Peace.*]

I'm destroyed, if this is drawn out much longer!

LYSISTRATA

[*Serenely unconscious of the interruption.*]

—Men of Sparta, I direct these remarks to you.
Have you forgotten that a Spartan suppliant once
    came
to beg assistance from Athens? Recall Perikleidas:
Fifty years ago, he clung to our altar,
his face dead-white above his crimson robe, and
    pleaded
for an army. Messene was pressing you hard in revolt,
and to this upheaval, Poseidon, the Earthshaker, added
another.
        But Kimon took four thousand troops
from Athens—an army which saved the state of Sparta.
Such treatment have you received at the hands of
    Athens,
you who devastate the country that came to your aid!

KINESIAS

[*Stoutly; the condemnation of his enemy has made him
forget the girl momentarily.*]

You're right, Lysistrata. The Spartans are clearly in the
    wrong!

SPARTAN

[*Guiltily backing away from Peace, whom he has attempted
to pat.*]

Hit's wrong, I reckon, but that's the purtiest
    behind . . .

LYSISTRATA

[*Turning to the Athenians.*]

—Men of Athens, do you think I'll let *you* off?
Have you forgotten the Tyrant's days, when you wore
the smock of slavery, when the Spartans turned to the
    spear,
cut down the pride of Thessaly, despatched the friends
of tyranny, and dispossessed your oppressors?
                                        Recall:
On that great day, your only allies were Spartans;
your liberty came at their hands, which stripped away
your servile garb and clothed you again in Freedom!

SPARTAN

[*Indicating Lysistrata.*]

Hain't never seed no higher type of woman.

KINESIAS

[*Indicating Peace.*]

Never saw one I wanted so much to top.

LYSISTRATA

[*Oblivious to the byplay, addressing both groups.*]

With such a history of mutual benefits conferred
and received, why are you fighting? Stop this wicked-
    ness!
Come to terms with each other! What prevents you?

SPARTAN

We'd a heap sight druther make Peace, if we was
    indemnified
with a plumb strategic location.

[*Pointing at Peace's rear.*]

                                We'll take thet butte.

LYSISTRATA
Butte?

SPARTAN

    The Promontory of Pylos—Sparta's Back Door.
We've missed it fer a turrible spell.

[*Reaching.*]

                                  Hev to keep our
hand in.

KINESIAS

[*Pushing him away.*]

           The price is too high—you'll never take that!

LYSISTRATA
Oh, let them have it.

KINESIAS

                 What room will we have left
for maneuvers?

LYSISTRATA

             Demand another spot in exchange.

KINESIAS

[*Surveying Peace like a map as he addresses the Spartan.*]

Then you hand over to us—uh, let me see—
let's try Thessaly—

[*Indicating the relevant portions of Peace.*]

              First of all, Easy Mountain . . .
then the Maniac Gulf behind it . . .
                      and down to
  Megara
for the legs . . .

SPARTAN

             You cain't take all of thet! Yore plumb
out of yore mind!

LYSISTRATA

[*To Kinesias.*]

          Don't argue. Let the legs go.

[*Kinesias nods. A pause. General smiles of agreement.*]

KINESIAS

[*Doffing his cloak.*]

I feel an urgent desire to plow a few furrows.

SPARTAN

[*Doffing his cloak.*]

Hit's time to work a few loads of fertilizer in.

LYSISTRATA
Conclude the treaty and the simple life is yours.
If such is your decision, convene your councils,
and then deliberate the matter with your allies.

KINESIAS
Deliberate? Allies?
                We're over-extended now!
Wouldn't every ally approve of our position—
Union Now?

SPARTAN
              I know I kin speak for ourn.

KINESIAS
And I for ours.
             Even the Karystian gigolos.

LYSISTRATA
I heartily approve.
           Now first attend to your purifica-
  tion,
then we, the women, will welcome you to the Citadel
and treat you to all the delights of a home-cooked
  banquet.
Then you'll exchange your oaths and pledge your
  faith,
and every man of you will take his wife
and depart for home.

[*Lysistrata and Peace enter the Akropolis.*]

KINESIAS
              Let's hurry!

SPARTAN
                Lead on, everwhich
  way's yore pleasure.

KINESIAS
             This way, then—and HURRY!

[*The delegations exeunt at a run.*]

CHORUS OF WOMEN
      I'd never stint on anybody.
      And now I include, in my boundless bounty,
          the younger set.
      Attention, you parents of teenage girls
      about to debut in the social whirl,
         Here's what you get:
      Embroidered linens, lush brocades,
      a huge assortment of ready-mades,
         from mantles to shifts;

plus bracelets and bangles of solid gold—
every item my wardrobe holds—
    absolute gifts!
Don't miss this offer. Come to my place,
barge right in, and make your choice.
    You can't refuse.
Everything there must go today.
Finders keepers—cart it away!
    How can you lose?
Don't spare me. Open all the locks.
Break every seal. Empty every box.
    Keep ferreting—
And your sight's considerably better than
    mine
if you should possibly chance to find
    a single thing.

CHORUS OF MEN

Troubles, friend? Too many mouths
to feed, and not a scrap in the house
    to see you through?
Faced with starvation? Don't give it a
    thought.
Pay attention; I'll tell you what
    I'm gonna do.
I overbought. I'm overstocked.
Every room in my house is clogged
    with flour (best ever),
glutted with luscious loaves whose size
you wouldn't believe. I need the space;
    do me a favor:
Bring gripsacks, knapsacks, duffle bags,
pitchers, cisterns, buckets, and kegs
    around to me.
A courteous servant will see to your needs,
he'll fill them up with A-1 wheat—
    and all for free!
—Oh. Just one final word before
you turn your steps to my front door:
    I happen to own
a dog. Tremendous animal.
Can't stand a leash. And bites like hell—
    better stay home.

[*The united Chorus flocks to the door of the Akropolis.*]

KORYPHAIOS OF MEN

[*Banging at the door.*]

Hey, open up in there!

[*The door opens, and the Commissioner appears. He wears a wreath, carries a torch, and is slightly drunk. He addresses the Koryphaios.*]

COMMISSIONER

        You know the Regulations.
Move along!

[*He sees the entire Chorus.*]

    —And why are YOU lounging around?
I'll wield my trusty torch and scorch the lot!

[*The Chorus backs away in mock horror. He stops and looks at his torch.*]

—*This* is the bottom of the barrel. A cheap burlesque
    bit.
I refuse to do it. I have my pride.

[*With a start, he looks at the audience, as though hearing a protest. He shrugs and addresses the audience.*]

        —No choice, eh?
Well, if that's the way it is, we'll take the trouble.
Anything to keep you happy.

[*The Chorus advances eagerly.*]

KORYPHAIOS OF MEN

        Don't forget us!
We're in this, too. Your trouble is ours!

COMMISSIONER

[*Resuming his character and jabbing with his torch at the Chorus.*]

        Keep moving!
Last man out of the way goes home without hair!
Don't block the exit. Give the Spartans some room.
They've dined in comfort; let them go home in peace.

[*The Chorus shrinks back from the door. Kinesias, wreathed and quite drunk, appears at the door. He speaks his first speech in Spartan.*]

KINESIAS

Hain't never seed such a spread! Hit were splen-
    diferous!

COMMISSIONER

I gather the Spartans won friends and influenced peo-
    ple?

KINESIAS

And *we've* never been so brilliant. It was the wine.

COMMISSIONER

Precisely.

> The reason? A sober Athenian is just
non compos. If I can carry a little proposal
I have in mind, our Foreign Service will flourish,
guided by this rational rule:

> *No Ambassador*
Without a Skinful.

> Reflect on our past performance:
Down to a Spartan parley we troop, in a state
of disgusting sobriety, looking for trouble. It muddles
our senses: we read between the lines; we hear,
not what the Spartans say, but what we suspect
they might have been about to be going to say.
We bring back paranoid reports—cheap fiction, the
   fruit
of temperance. Cold-water diplomacy, pah!

> Contrast
this evening's total pleasure, the free-and-easy
give-and-take of friendship: If we were singing,

> *Just Kleitagora and me,*
> *Alone in Thessaly,*

and someone missed his cue and cut in loudly,

> *Ajax, son of Telamon,*
> *He was one hell of a man—*

no one took it amiss, or started a war;
we clapped him on the back and gave three cheers.

[*During this recital, the Chorus has sidled up to the door.*]

—Dammit, are you back here again?

[*Waving his torch.*]

> Scatter!
Get out of the road! Gangway, you gallowsbait!

KINESIAS

Yes, everyone out of the way. They're coming out.

[*Through the door emerge the Spartan delegation, a flutist,
the Athenian delegation, Lysistrata, Kleonike, Myrrhine, and
the rest of the women from the citadel, both Athenian and
Peloponnesian. The Chorus splits into its male and female
components and draws to the sides to give the procession
room.*]

SPARTAN

[*To the flutist.*]

Friend and kinsman, take up them pipes a yourn.
I'd like fer to shuffle a bit and sing a right sweet
song in honor of Athens and us'uns, too.

COMMISSIONER

[*To the flutist.*]

Marvelous, marvelous—come, take up your pipes!

[*To the Spartan.*]

I certainly love to see you Spartans dance.

[*The flutist plays, and the Spartan begins a slow dance.*]

SPARTAN

> Memory,
> send me
> your Muse,
> who knows
>   our glory,
>   knows Athens'—
> Tell the story:
> At Artemision
> like gods, they stampeded
> the hulks of the Medes, and
>   beat them.

> And Leonidas
> leading us—
> the wild boars
> whetting their tusks.
> And the foam flowered,
> flowered and flowed,
> down our cheeks
> to our knees below.
> The Persians there
> like the sands of the sea—

> Hither, huntress,
> virgin, goddess,
> tracker, slayer,
> to our truce!
> Hold us ever
> fast together;
> bring our pledges
> love and increase;
> wean us from the
> fox's wiles—

> Hither, huntress!
> Virgin, hither!

LYSISTRATA

[*Surveying the assemblage with a proprietary air.*]

Well, the preliminaries are over—very nicely, too.
So, Spartans,

[*Indicating the Peloponnesian women who have been hostages.*]

take these girls back home. And *you*

[*To the Athenian delegation, indicating the women from the Akropolis.*]

take *these* girls. Each man stand by his wife, each wife
by her husband. Dance to the gods' glory, and thank
   them
for the happy ending. And, from now on, please be
   careful.
Let's not make the same mistakes again.

[*The delegations obey; the men and women of the chorus join again for a rapid ode.*]

CHORUS

Start the chorus dancing,
Summon all the Graces,
Send a shout to Artemis in invocation.
Call upon her brother,
healer, chorus master,
Call the blazing Bacchus, with his maddened
   muster.

Call the flashing, fiery Zeus, and
call his mighty, blessed spouse, and
call the gods, call all the gods,
to witness now and not forget
our gentle, blissful Peace—the gift,
   the deed of Aphrodite.
      Ai!
   Alalai! Paion!
   Leap you! Paion!
   Victory! Alalai!
Hail! Hail! Hail!

LYSISTRATA
Spartan, let's have another song from you, a new one.

SPARTAN

Leave darlin' Taygetos,
Spartan Muse! Come to us
once more, flyin'
and glorifyin'
Spartan themes:
the god at Amyklai,
bronze-house Athene,
Tyndaros' twins,
the valiant ones,
playin' still by Eurotas' streams.

Up! Advance!
Leap to the dance!

Help us hymn Sparta,
lover of dancin',
lover of foot-pats,
where girls go prancin'
like fillies along Eurotas' banks,
whirlin' the dust, twinklin' their shanks,
shakin' their hair
like Maenads playin'
and jugglin' the thyrsis,
in frenzy obeyin'
Leda's daughter, the fair, the pure
Helen, the mistress of the choir.

Here, Muse, here!
Bind up your hair!

Stamp like a deer! Pound your feet!
Clap your hands! Give us a beat!

Sing the greatest,
sing the mightiest,
sing the conqueror,
sing to honor her—

Athene of the Bronze House!
Sing Athene!

[*Exeunt omnes, dancing and singing.*]

ESSAY: AN APPROACH TO THE PLAY

One traditional approach to plays, particularly to older classics which seem to have "stood the test of time," is to explore what they have to say about "the human condition." One assumption which underlies this kind of exploration is that there are in fact qualities which are essentially human, which transcend time and place, which make us all brothers and sisters in our common human identity. Another assumption behind this approach to reading is that the old classics continue to be read because they express these enduring qualities—because they remain relevant to our common human experience. From this point of view, we ask of Aristophanes what he can teach us about ourselves.

Before examining this approach to *Lysistrata*, since the play is centrally about the relationship of men and women, we need to remind ourselves of an important distinction: that between sex and gender. "Sex" is a biological term; "gender," a cultural one. "Male" and "female" are both biological terms referring to a "fact of life," to a physical difference necessary for reproduction, but "masculine" and "feminine" are terms which a culture uses to define—and to prescribe and reproduce—the different behaviors that seem to it appropriate for males and for females. Different cultures have different perceptions of what constitutes masculinity and femininity, and these perceptions seem inescapably to become an expression not of the way people "are" (or else all cultures would have more nearly identical gender attitudes) but of a desire or hope for the way people should or could be, particularly in their relationships with each other.

Given the fertility of the human imagination, such desires or hopes should be expected to cover an immensely wide range, but in any given culture a few models—or perhaps one—will become the dominant expression of what constitutes appropriately masculine or feminine behavior. Some corollaries follow. (1) Gender definitions will frequently be an expression of power and will serve, whether this is the primary intention or not, to perpetuate the distribution of power (and historically it is men who have usually seized this power). The stakes are quite simply too high for this not to be a temptation, stakes which include who does what kind of work, who is primarily responsible for child rearing, the terms under which sexual pleasure will be available, the social structures through which we transmit our culture's values to the next generations, the social forms through which our sense of identity and self-worth is reinforced on a daily basis through inescapable social interaction—with members of both the same and the opposite sex. (2) With so much at stake, the social pressure to conform to expected gender roles is enormous. Think of how difficult life is for the man who is considered unmasculine or the women who is considered unfeminine. (3) Because of the close connection of the cultural term "gender" to the biological and therefore apparently "natural" term "sex," attitudes about gender are even more likely than other cultural forms to come to seem natural, an expression of the way things are and, therefore, inevitable, unchangeable. After all, the implicit male argument about women often seems to go: What could be more natural than sex and than giving birth to and nurturing our children? Because gender roles are frequently alleged to be "natural," people who transgress or subvert traditional gender roles are likely to be perceived not only as socially threatening but also as "unnatural."

The main premise underlying the implicit comic argument in *Lysistrata* is that the sex drive is a common human denominator affecting the behavior of both sexes; to this degree, one can assume that the play is about "human nature." It also assumes that the sex drive is stronger for men, although whether or not this assumption is in fact "true to nature" is a moot point. The assumption is that women find it difficult to live without sex, but for men it is impossible, and Lysistrata's scheme exploits this presumed difference by an act of sexual economics: If men regard sex with women as a necessity of life, women can conspire to make the commodity scarce and thereby gain leverage in subsequent negotiations which affect not only domestic policy, but foreign policy as well. Seeing this "sex strike" of the younger women as a form of economic action makes the second half of Lysistrata's plan seem more complementary than it otherwise might: The older women seize the state's treasury, located in a vault on the Akropolis, and in this way make it impossible for the men to finance the war. The two groups of women are symbolically parallel in asserting control over a "treasure" which men have previously regarded as theirs to control.

The play continues to be infectiously funny, whether staged in public or, as you have probably done, read in private. But why? Part of the play's comic effect derives from Aristophanes' skill at writing farce. As internal references in the play imply, the male characters seem to have been depicted on stage with oversized phalluses which get progressively more erect as the play—and their period of abstinence—continues, and these organs are often paralleled by matching swords, which provide a visual emblem of the play's central premise. However, if part of the play's appeal is that the social structure it parodies is so familiar, so like our own, does this mean that it satirizes "universal human nature," or is it a reminder that our culture is related to, in some ways descended from, that of classical Greece, so that the play's familiarity is our recognition of a family resemblance? To be sure, the play purports to be about sexual difference and therefore about "nature," but underlying the play are attitudes about gender specific to its culture; and in fundamental ways, however much we may have altered details of women's lives for the better, we have inherited that culture and continue to perpetuate aspects of many of its gender values.

Part of the play's appeal may be that it serves as something of a safety valve for pent-up social pressures. It is unlikely that its function in ancient Athenian society would have been revolutionary, that Aristophanes was a feminist hoping through his play to overthrow male supremacy and inaugurate an age of gender equality. He was a male playwright, writing for what was apparently an all-male audience, or perhaps for an audience segregated by sex with the men in the preferred seats, and for an all-male cast. The spirit of the play seems to be more one of social inversion than of subversion: The women's control is clearly seen as temporary, perhaps something like the late medieval custom of the Lord of Misrule, where the chief offices of church and state were taken over for a festival day by members of the lower class. When the period of celebration is over, society returns to its familiar structure, and when the play is over, and the "serious" point about pan-Hellenic unity (among Greek warriors) is made, Greek domestic society can return to what it "should" be. The fact of gender hierarchy can be acknowledged without being threatened, even while the play reinforces male attitudes about gender.

Lysistrata's scheme takes for granted male perceptions of female behavior:

Women define themselves as vain, pampered, indecisive, and addicted to sex. In particular, they are preoccupied with male sex organs; they cannot get enough, and the bigger the better. Are these actually women's main concerns? It is difficult for us to say for certain how women felt about such matters in ancient Greece, but in our world (and we are aware that we have made a point of the danger of such extrapolations from one culture to another) these attitudes would be less likely to be part of women's self-definitions than expressions of male fantasy. However, by placing these ideas into the mouths of women, particularly when they speak intimately among themselves, Aristophanes makes them seem part of human nature, attitudes shared by both men and women.

In writing about this play, we find ourselves walking a difficult line. The play is uproariously funny, and Aristophanes' craft as comic playwright is stunning and admirable. We do not want to be perceived as killjoys, nor as promoters of "political correctness." Still, we do not want to obscure the cultural values that are embedded in the play and which the play's humor may obscure. To ignore these issues is to allow the play—to use a metaphor from a different ancient Greek war—to be a Trojan Horse: We invite it into our course because it is so funny and so skillfully written, but there may be dangerous baggage concealed within. Calling attention to this danger allows us to enjoy the play on its own terms, yet at the same time to acknowledge important aspects of our own culture and to recognize the processes by which cultural values are transmitted.

SHAKESPEARE AND HIS THEATER

William Shakespeare (1564–1616), English actor and poet and the world's best-known playwright, was born in Stratford-upon-Avon twelve years before the construction of the first permanent theater building since those of the Roman Empire a thousand years earlier. By the time of his death he had written all or part of thirty-eight plays. He is represented in this book by *The Merchant of Venice* (1596), a play conventionally classified as a mature comedy, and by two tragedies, *Hamlet* (1600–1601) and *Othello* (1604). He also wrote many history plays and romances, as well as sonnets and more extended poems, and experimented widely, particularly with dramatic form.

Shakespeare's Globe Theater was built in 1599, shortly before the first production of *Hamlet* about a year later, although the theater in which *Merchant* was first produced was probably not markedly different. Our knowledge of the details of these early theaters remains less than certain, but there is a general consensus that the Globe was housed in a circular or polygonal (probably octagonal) building and that its inside walls held three tiers of roofed galleries for the more privileged part of the audience. The rest of the viewers stood or sat on the floor of the theater, in the open air. The stage thrust itself out about halfway across this theater space, so that it was ringed on three sides by its audience. There was no restriction about who could go to the theater, and it could accommodate perhaps 3,000 people. These probabilities, coupled with the facts that it was a daylight and a repertory theater (a set series of plays were enacted in rotation by the same company of actors), make it a community theater somewhat like the Greek.

However, there were also important differences. Although all actors were males (highly trained boys enacted female roles), they did not wear masks. Although the stories were often borrowed from other writers, the audience did not usually know the ending in advance. There was therefore interest in the individuality of a character and in the suspense value of a plot, at the same time that important public ideas could be discussed as they had been in the Greek theater. Because of the system of official censorship, however, it is uncertain how much freedom a playwright had in the expression of ideas. Some plays from this period surely presented attitudes toward God, gender roles, ethnicity, and monarchy which served as propaganda supporting the views of the established church, the reigning monarch, or other dominant social or political constituencies. Sometimes, however, it seems that Shakespeare presents a more critical and unsympathetic attitude toward the customs and beliefs of his age than we might expect from these conditions.

William Shakespeare

THE MERCHANT OF VENICE

Edited and with notes by A. D. Richardson III

About the Play   *The Merchant of Venice* was probably written and staged about 1596, only four years after Shakespeare's first play was produced. He had developed swiftly and was then in the middle of a period in which he was writing many successful comedies. (*A Midsummer Night's Dream* precedes it by only a year.) In *Merchant,* the role of the romantic heroine Portia takes on unusual importance and power, an importance that female roles will sustain in his later comedies. On the other hand, the character of Shylock is in many ways a stereotype of villainy and foolishness: The Jew as moneylender and hater of Christians had become a traditional attitude by this time in England. This representation may have been topical at the time of the play, for in 1594 a medical doctor to Queen Elizabeth, a Portuguese Jew, was executed for an alleged attempt to poison his royal patient. The evidence has been questioned, as have the motives of the accusers, but there was great contemporary interest in this sensational case, and it is likely that Shakespeare is capitalizing on it here, regardless of how we choose to interpret the character or the play.

Merchant has generally been called a comedy, not so much for the laughter it provokes as because it seems to have a happy ending. The Venetian citizens triumph: By the play's conclusion, the romantic lovers Bassanio and Portia are together, and the merchant Antonio has preserved his life and regained his wealth. On the other side, the villain Shylock has been thwarted in his attempt to kill Antonio, has converted to Christianity, and has been forced to leave his money to his daughter, who, against his wishes, had fallen in love with and married a Christian.

Further, this triumph is primarily the heroine's, Portia's. From this point of view, it is a feminist play in which the beautiful young woman begins as a conventional romantic object to the romantic hero but very quickly becomes much larger, a character far more powerful than he. She is clever enough to outsmart a villain who has himself been clever enough to force the entire Venetian legal system to do his bidding against its collective will, and then she controls her new husband, all the while loving and forgiving everybody. She seems to be a fully empowered woman.

CHARACTERS

THE DUKE OF VENICE
THE PRINCE OF MOROCCO, suitor to Portia
THE PRINCE OF ARRAGON, suitor to Portia
ANTONIO, a merchant of Venice
BASSANIO, his friend and suitor to Portia
GRATIANO, friend to Antonio and Bassanio
SALERIO, friend to Antonio and Bassanio
SOLANIO, friend to Antonio and Bassanio
LORENZO, in love with Jessica
SHYLOCK, a Jew
TUBAL, a Jew, friend to Shylock

LAUNCELOT GOBBO, a clown, servant to Shylock
OLD GOBBO, father to Launcelot
LEONARDO, servant to Bassanio
BALTHAZAR, servant to Portia
STEPHANO, servant to Portia
PORTIA, an heiress of Belmont
NERISSA, her waiting-woman
JESSICA, daughter to Shylock
Magnificoes of Venice, Officers of the Court of Justice, a Gaoler, Servants, and other attendants.
[SCENE: Venice, and Portia's house at Belmont]

Act I

SCENE I

[*Enter Antonio, Salerio, and Solanio.*]

ANTONIO. In sooth I know not why I am so sad,
  It wearies me, you say it wearies you;
  But how I caught it, found it, or came by it,
  What stuff 'tis made of, whereof it is born,
  I am to learn;   5
  And such a want-wit sadness makes of me,
  That I have much ado to know myself.
SALERIO. Your mind is tossing on the ocean,
  There where your argosies with portly sail
  Like signiors and rich burghers on the flood,   10
  Or as it were the pageants of the sea,
  Do overpeer the petty traffickers
  That cursy to them, do them reverence
  As they fly by them with their woven wings.   14
SOLANIO. Believe me sir, had I such venture forth,
  The better part of my affections would
  Be with my hopes abroad. I should be still
  Plucking the grass to know where sits the wind,
  Piring in maps for ports, and piers, and roads;
  And every object that might make me fear   20
  Misfortune to my ventures, out of doubt
  Would make me sad.
SALERIO.   My wind, cooling my broth,
  Would blow me to an ague, when I thought
  What harm a wind too great might do at sea.
  I should not see the sandy hour-glass run,   25
  But I should think of shallows, and of flats,
  And see my wealthy Andrew dock'd in sand,
  Vailing her high top lower than her ribs
  To kiss her burial. Should I go to church
  And see the holy edifice of stone   30

And not bethink me straight of dangerous rocks,
Which touching but my gentle vessel's side
Would scatter all her spices on the stream,
Enrobe the roaring waters with my silks,
And in a word, but even now worth this,   35
And now worth nothing? Shall I have the thought
To think on this, and shall I lack the thought
That such a thing bechanc'd would make be sad?
But tell not me, I know Antonio
Is sad to think upon his merchandize.   40
ANTONIO. Believe me no, I thank my fortune for it,
  My ventures are not in one bottom trusted,
  Nor to one place: nor is my whole estate
  Upon the fortune of this present year:
  Therefore my merchandize makes me not sad.   45
SOLANIO. Why then you are in love.
ANTONIO.   Fie, fie.
SOLANIO. Not in love neither; then let us say you are
    sad
  Because you are not merry; and 'twere as easy
  For you to laugh and leap, and say you are merry
  Because you are not sad. Now by two-headed Janus,
  Nature hath fram'd strange fellows in her time: 51
  Some that will evermore peep through their eyes,
  And laugh like parrots at a bag-piper.
  And other of such vinegar aspect,   54
  That they'll not show their teeth in way of smile,
  Though Nestor swear the jest be laughable.

[*Enter Bassanio, Lorenzo, and Gratiano.*]

SALERIO. Here comes Bassanio, your most noble
    kinsman,
  Gratiano and Lorenzo. Fare ye well,
  We leave you now with better company.
SOLANIO. I would have stayed till I had made you
    merry,   60
  If worthier friends had not prevented me.

Editor's note on the Shakespeare plays: Line numbers in the text correspond to the footnote gloss numbers; in the prose passages they are not necessarily consistent with line counts.

1. In sooth: truth. **3. caught it:** i.e. Antonio's melancholy. **9. argosies:** merchant ships from Ragusa or Venice. **portly:** stately; also corpulent. **11. pageants:** an allusion to the large decorated machines or pageant wagons drawn about the streets in pageants. **12. overpeer:** look down upon. **13. cursy:** a common variant of 'curtsey.' **15. venture:** a risky enterprise. **17. still:** continually. **19. Piring:** peering. **roads:** sheltered waters where ships might anchor safely. **26. flats:** shoals. **28–29. Vailing . . . burial:** lower her topsails so far as to kiss her own burial ground i.e. to capsize completely.

35–36. but . . . nothing: at one moment worth all this concern, at the next a total loss. **38. bechanc'd:** if it happened. **42. bottom:** the lowest part of the hull, hence a ship. **47. then . . . sad:** in reading, contracted to 'then let's say you're sad.' **50. Janus:** the two-headed Roman deity, guardian of doorways, who had one smiling and one sad countenance. **52. peep:** squint, as when laughing. **54. other:** others, an old plural. *aspect* (stressed ‿ ́), appearance. **56. Nestor:** Homeric hero, the symbol of wise old age. **61. prevented:** forestalled.

ANTONIO. Your worth is very dear in my regard.
  I take it your own business calls on you,
  And you embrace th' occasion to depart.
SALERIO. Good morrow my good Lords.   65
BASSANIO. Good signiors both, when shall we laugh?
  Say when?
  You grow exceeding strange; must it be so?
SALERIO. We'll make our leisures to attend on yours.

[*Exeunt Salerio and Solanio.*]

LORENZO. My Lord Bassanio, since you have
    found Antonio
  We two will leave you, but at dinner time   70
  I pray you have in mind where we must meet.
BASSANIO. I will not fail you.
GRATIANO. You look not well signior Antonio,
  You have too much respect upon the world;
  They lose it that do buy it with much care.   75
  Believe me you are marvellously chang'd.
ANTONIO. I hold the world but as the world Gra-
    tiano,
  A stage, where every man must play a part,
  And mine a sad one.
GRATIANO.   Let me play the fool,
  With mirth and laughter let old wrinkles come, 80
  And let my liver rather heat with wine,
  Than my heart cool with mortifying groans.
  Why should a man whose blood is warm within,
  Sit like his grandshire, cut in alablaster?   84
  Sleep when he wakes? and creep into the jaundice
  By being peevish? I tell thee what Antonio,
  I love thee, and it is my love that speaks:
  There are a sort of men, whose visages
  Do cream and mantle like a standing pond
  And do a willful stillness entertain,   90
  With purpose to be dress'd in an opinion
  Of wisdom, gravity, profound conceit,
  As who should say, I am sir Oracle,
  And when I ope my lips, let no dog bark.
  O my Antonio, I do know of these   95

That therefore only are reputed wise,
For saying nothing: when I am very sure
If they should speak, would almost dam those ears
Which hearing them would call their brothers fools,
I'll tell thee more of this another time.   100
But fish not with this melancholy bait
For this fool gudgeon, this opinion: 102
Come good Lorenzo, fare ye well a while,
I'll end my exhortation after dinner.
LORENZO. Well, we will leave you then till dinner
    time.   105
  I must be one of these same dumb wise men,
  For Gratiano never lets me speak.
GRATIANO. Well, keep me company but two years
    moe,
  Thou shalt not know the sound of thine own
    tongue.
ANTONIO. Fare you well, I'll grow a talker for this
    gear.   110
GRATIANO. Thanks i' faith, for silence is only com-
    mendable
  In a neat's tongue dried, and a maid not vendible.

[*Exeunt Gratiano and Lorenzo.*]

ANTONIO. It is that any thing now.   113
BASSANIO. Gratiano speaks an infinite deal of noth-
  ing, more than any man in all Venice, his reasons
  are two grains of wheat hid in two bushels of chaff:
  you shall seek all day ere you find them, and when
  you have them they are not worth the search.
ANTONIO. Well, tell me now, what lady is the same
  To whom you swore a secret pilgrimage   120
  That you today promis'd to tell me of?
BASSANIO. 'Tis not unknown to you Antonio
  How much I have disabled mine estate,
  By something showing a more swelling port 124
  Than my faint means would grant continuance:
  Nor do I now make moan to be abridg'd
  From such a noble rate, but my chief care
  Is to come fairly off from the great debts
  Wherein my time something too prodigal
  Hath left me gag'd: to you Antonio   130
  I owe the most in money, and in love,

---

66. **laugh:** i.e. laugh together. 67. **strange:** distant. 74. **You . . . world:** you worry too much about the world, i.e. material things. 78: **A stage:** The idea of the world as a stage was common. 82. **heart . . . groans:** groans were thought to drain blood from the heart. 84. **alablaster:** common form of 'alabaster'; a reference to monument effigies. 85. **wakes:** probably sits up for a revelry. 89. **cream and mantle:** surface over with a grave covering, as cream covers milk, or algae a stagnant pond. 91. **opinion:** reputation. 92. **conceit:** understanding. 93. **As . . . say:** as much as to say. **sir Oracle:** the very personification of an oracle.

96–97. **only . . . nothing:** cf. Proverbs 17.28 98–99. **If . . . fools:** cf. Matthew 5:22. 102. **gudgeon:** a very small fish, often used to mean a credulous fool. 108. **moe:** more in number. 110. **gear:** business. 112. **neat's . . . dried:** a beef tongue prepared to be eaten. **maid . . . vendible:** an old maid. 124. **something:** somewhat. **swelling:** inflated. **port:** style of living. 127. **rate:** style. 128. **fairly:** honorably. 129. **time:** youth. 130. **gag'd:** pledged.

And from your love I have a warranty
To unburthen all my plots and purposes,
How to get clear of all the debts I owe.   134
ANTONIO. I pray you good Bassanio let me know it,
And if it stand as you yourself still do,
Within the eye of honor, be assur'd
My purse, my person, my extremest means
Lie all unlock'd to your occasions.
BASSANIO. In my school days, when I had lost one
     shaft,   140
I shot his fellow of the selfsame flight
The selfsame way, with more advised watch
To find the other forth, and by adventuring both,
I oft found both. I urge this childhood proof,
Because what follows is pure innocence.   145
I owe you much, and like a willful youth,
That which I owe is lost, but if you please
To shoot another arrow that self way
Which you did shoot the first, I do not doubt,
As I will watch the aim, or to find both,   150
Or bring your latter hazard back again,
And thankfully rest debtor for the first.
ANTONIO. You know me well, and herein spend but
     time
To wind about my love with circumstance,
And out of doubt you do me now more wrong 155
In making question of my uttermost
Than if you had made waste of all I have.
Then do but say to me what I should do
That in your knowledge may by me be done,
And I am prest unto it; therefore speak.   160
BASSANIO. In Belmont is a lady richly left,
And she is fair, and fairer than that word,
Of wondrous virtues, sometimes from her eyes
I did receive fair speechless messages:
Her name is Portia, nothing undervalu'd   165
To Cato's daughter, Brutus' Portia,
Nor is the wide world ignorant of her worth,
For the four winds blow in from every coast
Renowned suitors, and her sunny locks
Hang on her temples like a golden fleece,   170

Which makes her seat of Belmont Colchos' strond,
And many Jasons come in quest of her.
O my Antonio, had I but the means
To hold a rival place with one of them,
I have a mind presages me such thrift,   175
That I should questionless be fortunate.
ANTONIO. Thou know'st that all my fortunes are at
     sea,
Neither have I money, nor commodity
To raise a present sum, therefore go forth
Try what my credit can in Venice do,   180
That shall be rack'd even to the uttermost,
To furnish thee to Belmont to fair Portia.
Go presently enquire, and so will I
Where money is, and I no question make
To have it of my trust, or for my sake.   185

[Exeunt.]

SCENE II

[Enter Portia with her waiting woman Nerissa.]

PORTIA. By my troth Nerissa, my little body is aweary
of this great world.
NERISSA. You would be sweet Madam, if your miseries
were in the same abundance as your good fortunes
are, and yet for aught I see, they are as sick that
surfeit with too much, as they that starve with nothing; it is no mean happiness therefore to be seated in
the mean, superfluity comes sooner by white hairs,
but competency lives longer.
PORTIA. Good sentences, and well pronounc'd.   10
NERISSA. They would be better if well followed.
PORTIA. If to do were as easy as to know what were
good to do, chapels had been churches, and poor
men's cottages princes' palaces. It is a good divine
that follows his own instructions. I can easier   15
teach twenty what were good to be done, than be
one of the twenty to follow mine own teaching. The
brain may devise laws for the blood, but a hot
temper leaps ore a cold decree, such a hare is madness the youth, to skip ore the meshes of good   20

133. **To unburthen:** (elided to 't'unburthen'), unburden. 137. **eye:**
sight, presence. 139. **occasions:** needs. 140. **shaft:** arrow. 141.
his: its. **selfsame flight:** i.e. of equal size and weight. 142.
advised: careful. 143. **forth:** out. **adventuring:** risking. 145.
innocence: guilelessness. 146–47. **and . . . lost:** and like a willful
youth, I have lost what I owe you. 148. **self:** same. 150–51.
Or . . . Or: either . . . or. 151. **hazard:** that which is risked. 152.
rest: remain. 154. **To . . . circumstance:** to 'beat about the
bush.' 156. **In . . . uttermost:** in questioning whether I would do
my utmost for you. 160. **prest:** prepared, ready. 163. **sometimes:**
formerly.

171. **strond:** strand or beach. 175. **presages:** which presages. **thrift:** success; Bassanio speaks in merchant's terms. 179.
present sum: ready cash. 181. **rack'd:** stretched. **even:** read
'e'en.' 183. **presently:** immediately. 185. **To . . . sake:** to get it
'on my credit' or 'through personal friendship.'
8. **mean:** middle. 10. **sentences:** maxims. 13. **had been:** would
have been.

counsel the cripple; but this reasoning is not in fashion to choose me a husband. O me, the word 'choose.' I may neither choose who I would, nor refuse who I dislike. So is the will of a living daughter curb'd by the will of a dead father. Is it not hard, Nerissa, that I cannot choose one, nor refuse none?

NERISSA. Your father was ever virtuous, and holy men at their death have good inspirations, therefore the lott'ry that he hath devised in these three chests of gold, silver, and lead, whereof who chooses his meaning, chooses you, will no doubt never be chosen by any rightly, but one who you shall rightly love. But what warmth is there in your affection towards any of the princely suitors that are already come?

PORTIA. I pray thee over-name them, and as thou namest them, I will describe them, and according to my description level at my affection.

NERISSA. First, there is the Neapolitan prince.

PORTIA. Ay, that's a colt indeed, for he doth nothing but talk of his horse, and he makes it a great appropriation to his own good parts that he can shoe him himself; I am much afraid my lady his mother played false with a smith.

NERISSA. Then is there the County Palentine.

PORTIA. He doth nothing but frown (as who should say, and you will not have me, choose), he hears merry tales and smiles not, I fear he will prove the weeping philosopher when he grows old, being so full of unmannerly sadness in his youth. I had rather be married to a death's head with a bone in his mouth, than to either of these. God defend me from these two.

NERISSA. How say you by the French lord, Monsieur Le Bon?

PORTIA. God made him, and therefore let him pass for a man, in truth I know it is a sin to be a mocker, but he, why he hath a horse better than the Neapolitan's, a better bad habit of frowning than the Count Palentine, he is every man in no man, if a trassell sing, he falls straight a-cap'ring, he will fence with his own shadow. If I should marry him, I should marry twenty husbands; if he would despise me, I

would forgive him, for if he love me to madness, I shall never requite him.

NERISSA. What say you than to Fauconbridge, the young baron of England?

PORTIA. You know I say nothing to him, for he understands not me, nor I him. He hath neither Latin, French, nor Italian, and you will come into the Court and swear that I have a poor pennyworth in the English; he is a proper man's picture, but alas who can converse with a dumb-show? How oddly he is suited, I think he bought his doublet in Italy, his round hose in France, his bonnet in Germany, and his behavior everywhere.

NERISSA. What think you of the Scottish lord his neighbor?

PORTIA. That he hath a neighborly charity in him, for he borrowed a box of the ear of the Englishman, and swore he would pay him again when he was able. I think the Frenchman became his surety, and seal'd under for another.

NERISSA. How like you the young German, the Duke of Saxony's nephew?

PORTIA. Very vildly in the morning when he is sober, and most vildly in the afternoon when he is drunk. When he is best, he is a little worse than a man, and when he is worst, he is little better than a beast, and the worst fall that ever fell, I hope I shall make shift to go without him.

NERISSA. If he should offer to choose, and choose the right casket, you should refuse to perform your Father's will, if you should refuse to accept him.

PORTIA. Therefore for fear of the worst, I pray thee set a deep glass of Rhenish wine on the contrary casket, for if the devil be within, and that temptation without, I know he will choose it. I will do anything, Nerissa, ere I will be married to a sponge.

NERISSA. You need not fear lady the having any of these lords, they have acquainted me with their determinations, which is indeed to return to their home, and to trouble you with no more suit, unless you may be won by some other sort than your father's imposition, depending on the caskets.

PORTIA. If I live to be as old as Sibylla, I will die as chaste as Diana, unless I be obtained by the manner

23. **may:** can. 27. **holy:** pious and righteous. 31. **his:** its. 32. **shall:** will. 36. **over-name them:** name them over. 38. **level:** guess. 40. **colt:** a young and foolish person. 45. **County:** Count. 46–7. **as . . . say:** as much as to say. 47. **and:** if. **choose:** do as you please. 49. **weeping philosopher:** Heraclitus of Ephesus, who always wept when he beheld mankind. 53. **by:** about. 58–59. **if . . . a-cap'ring:** i.e. he will dance regardless of the tune. 59. **trassell:** throstle or thrush.

71. **proper . . . picture:** i.e. he is a fine looking man. 72. **dumb-show:** pantomime. 73. **suited:** dressed. 85. **vildly:** vilely. 87–88. **best . . . beast:** a pun, since both words were pronounced alike. 89. **and the worst fall:** if the worst should happen (that ever happened). 91. **should:** would. 95. **contrary:** wrong. 103. **sort:** manner. 105. **Sibylla:** the Cumaean Sibyl, to whom Apollo promised an extraordinarily long life.

of my father's will; I am glad this parcel of wooers
are so reasonable, for there is not one among them
but I dote on his very absence: and I pray God grant
them a fair departure.   110

NERISSA. Do you not remember, lady, in your father's
time, a Venetian, a scholar and a soldier that
came hether in company of the Marquis of Mont-
ferrat?   114

PORTIA. Yes, yes, it was Bassanio, as I think, so was he
call'd.

NERISSA. True madam, he of all the men that ever my
foolish eye look'd upon, was the best deserving a fair
lady.   119

PORTIA. I remember him well, and I remember him
worthy of thy praise. How now, what news?

[Enter a Servingman.]

SERVINGMAN. The four strangers seek for you
madam, to take their leave; and there is a forerunner
come from a fifth, the Prince of Morocco, who
brings word the prince his master will be here
tonight.

PORTIA. If I could bid the fifth welcome with so good
heart as I can bid the other four farewell, I should
be glad of his approach: if he have the condition of a
saint, and the complexion of a divel, I had rather he
should shrive me than wive me.   130
Come Nerissa. Sirrah go before;
Whiles we shut the gate upon one wooer, another
knocks at the door.

[Exeunt.]

SCENE III

[Enter Bassanio with Shylock the Jew.]

SHYLOCK. Three thousand ducats, well.

BASSANIO. Ay, sir, for three months.

SHYLOCK. For three months, well.

BASSANIO. For the which, as I told you, Antonio shall
be bound.   5

SHYLOCK. Antonio shall become bound, well.

BASSANIO. May you stead me? Will you pleasure me?
Shall I know your answer?

SHYLOCK. Three thousand ducats for three months,
and Antonio bound.   10

BASSANIO. Your answer to that.

SHYLOCK. Antonio is a good man.

BASSANIO. Have you heard any imputation to the
contrary?   14

SHYLOCK. Ho no, no, no, no: my meaning in saying
he is a good man is to have you understand me that
he is sufficient, yet his means are in supposition: he
hath an argosy bound to Tripolis, another to the
Indies, I understand moreover upon the Rialto, he
hath a third at Mexico, a fourth for England, and
other ventures he hath sqand'red abroad, but ships
are but boards, sailors but men, there be land rats
and water rats, water thieves, and land thieves, I
mean pirates, and then there is the peril of waters,
winds, and rocks; the man is notwithstanding sufficient, three thousand ducats, I think I may take his
bond.   27

BASSANIO. Be assur'd you may.

SHYLOCK. I will be assur'd I may: and that I may be
assured, I will bethink me. May I speak with An-
tonio?   31

BASSANIO. If it please you to dine with us.

SHYLOCK. Yes, to smell pork, to eat of the habitation
which your prophet the Nazarite conjured the divel
into. I will buy with you, sell with you, talk with
you, walk with you, and so following; but I will not
eat with you, drink with you, nor pray with you. What
news on the Rialto? Who is he comes here?   38

[Enter Antonio.]

BASSANIO. This is signior Antonio.

SHYLOCK. [Aside.] How like a fawning publican he
looks.
I hate him for he is a Christian:
But more, for that in low simplicity
He lends out money gratis, and brings down
The rate of usance here with us in Venice.
If I can catch him once upon the hip,   45
I will feed fat the ancient grudge I bear him.
He hates our sacred nation, and he rails,
Even there where merchants most do congregate,
On me, my bargains, and my well-won thrift,
Which he calls interest. Cursed be my tribe   50
If I forgive him.

BASSANIO. Shylock, do you hear.

---

113. hether: hither. 128. condition: character.
5. bound: pledged. 7. stead: aid.

12. good: sound. 17. sufficient: well-to-do, solvent. 19. Rialto:
the exchange in Venice. 22. be: are. 33–38. Yes . . . here? Cf.
Matthew 2:23. 40. fawning publican: see Luke 18:10–14. 42.
simplicity: foolishness. 44. usance: usury. 45. catch . . . hip:
catch him at a disadvantage. 49. thrift: to Shylock a euphemism for
usury.

SHYLOCK. I am debating of my present store,
   And by the near guess of my memory
   I cannot instantly raise up the gross
   Of full three thousand ducats—what of that?   55
   Tubal, a wealthy Hebrew of my tribe
   Will furnish me. But soft! How many months
   Do you desire? [*To Antonio.*] Rest you fair, good sig-
       nior.
   Your worship was the last man in our mouths.
ANTONIO. Shylock, albeit I neither lend nor borrow
   By taking, nor by giving of excess,   61
   Yet to supply the ripe wants of my friend,
   I'll break a custom: [*To Bassanio.*] is he yet possess'd
   How much ye would?
SHYLOCK. Ay, ay, three thousand ducats.   65
ANTONIO. And for three months.
SHYLOCK. I had forgot, three months, [*To Bassanio.*]
       you told me so.
   Well then, your bond; and let me see, but hear
       you,
   Me thoughts you said, you neither lend nor borrow
   Upon advantage.
ANTONIO.   I do never use it.   70
SHYLOCK. When Jacob graz'd his uncle Laban's
       sheep,
   This Jacob from our holy Abram was
   (As his wise mother wrought in his behalf)
   The third possessor; ay, he was the third.
ANTONIO. And what of him, did he take
       interest?   75
SHYLOCK. No, not take interest, not as you would say
   Directly int'rest, mark what Jacob did,
   When Laban and himself were compromis'd
   That all the eanlings which were streak'd and pied
   Should fall as Jacob's hire. The ewes being
       rank,   80
   In end of autumn turned to the rams,
   And when the work of generation was
   Between these woolly breeders in the act,
   The skillful shepherd pil'd me certain wands,
   And in the doing of the deed of kind,   85
   He stuck them up before the fulsome ewes,
   Who then conceiving, did in eaning time
   Fall parti-color'd lambs, and those were Jacob's.

This was a way to thrive, and he was blest,
   And thrift is blessing if men steal it not.   90
ANTONIO. This was a venture sir that Jacob serv'd
       for,
   A thing not in his power to bring to pass,
   But sway'd and fashion'd by the hand of heaven.
   Was this inserted to make interest good?
   Or is your gold and silver ewes and rams?   95
SHYLOCK. I cannot tell, I make it breed as fast,
   But note me signior.
ANTONIO.   Mark you this Bassanio,
   The divel can cite Scripture for his purpose,
   An evil soul producing holy witness,
   Is like a villain with a smiling cheek,   100
   A goodly apple rotten at the heart.
   O what a goodly outside falsehood hath.
SHYLOCK. Three thousand ducats, 'tis a good round
       sum.
   Three months from twelve, then let me see the rate.
ANTONIO. Well Shylock, shall we be beholding to
       you?   105
SHYLOCK. Signior Antonio, many a time and oft
   In the Rialto you have rated me
   About my moneys and my usances;
   Still have I borne it with a patient shrug,
   (For suff'rance is the badge of all our tribe).   110
   You call me misbeliever, cut-throat dog,
   And spet upon my Jewish gabardine,
   And all for use of that which is mine own.
   Well then, it now appears you need my help;
   Go to then, you come to me, and you say,   115
   'Shylock, we would have moneys,' you say so,
   You that did void your rheum upon my beard,
   And foot me as you spurn a stranger cur
   Over your threshold. Moneys is your suit.
   What should I say to you? Should I not say,   120
   'Hath a dog money? Is it possible
   A cur can lend three thousand ducats?' or
   Shall I bend low, and in a bondman's key
   With bated breath, and whisp-'ring humbleness,
   Say this: 125
   'Fair sir, you spet on me on Wednesday last,
   You spurn'd me such a day; another time,

---

54. **gross:** total amount. 61. **excess:** usury. 63. **possess'd:** informed. 69. **Me thoughts:** it seemed (to me). 70. **advantage:** another synonym for usury. 71–90. see Genesis 30:33–43. **compromis'd:** come to terms. 79. **eanlings:** new lambs. 80. **rank:** ready for breeding. 84. **pil'd . . . wands:** stripped (for himself) certain sticks. 85. **kind:** nature. 86. **fulsome:** lustful. 88. **Fall:** let fall, gave birth to. **parti-color'd:** pied, mixed in color.

105. **beholding:** *beholden.* 107. **rated:** berated. 112. **spet:** common form either past or present of the verb 'to spit.' **gabardine:** a loose upper garment, not necessarily peculiar to Jews but possibly a traditional costume for Jewish characters on the Elizabethan stage. 117. **void . . . rheum:** spit. 118. **foot:** kick. 119. **Moneys:** a common plural form often not distinguished from the singular. 123. **bondman's key:** the tones of a slave.

You call'd me dog, and for these courtesies
I'll lend you thus much moneys'?
ANTONIO. I am as like to call thee so again,   130
  To spet on thee again, to spurn thee too.
  If thou wilt lend this money, lend it not
  As to thy friends, for when did friendship take
  A breed for barren metal of his friend?
  But lend it rather to thine enemy,   135
  Who if he break, thou may'st with better face
  Exact the penalty.
SHYLOCK.   Why look you how you storm,
  I would be friends with you, and have your
    love,
  Forget the shames that you have stain'd me with,
  Supply your present wants, and take no doit   140
  Of usance for my moneys, and you'll not hear me,
  This is kind I offer.
BASSANIO. This were kindness.
SHYLOCK. This kindness will I show,
  Go with me to a notary, seal me there   145
  Your single bond, and in a merry sport
  If you repay me not on such a day,
  In such a place, such sum or sums as are
  Express'd in the condition, let the forfeit
  Be nominated for an equal pound   150
  Of your fair flesh, to be cut off and taken
  In what part of your body pleaseth me.
ANTONIO. Content in faith, I'll seal to such a
    bond,
  And say there is much kindness in the Jew.   154
BASSANIO. You shall not seal to such a bond for me,
  I'll rather dwell in my necessity.

ANTONIO. Why fear not man, I will not forfeit it.
  Within these two months, that's a month before
  This bond expires, I do expect return
  Of thrice three times the value of this bond.   160
SHYLOCK. O father Abram, what these Christians
    are,
  Whose own hard dealings teaches them suspect
  The thoughts of others. Pray you tell me this,
  If he should break his day what should I gain
  By the exaction of the forfeiture?   165
  A pound of man's flesh taken from a man,
  Is not so estimable, profitable neither
  As flesh of muttons, beefs, or goats. I say
  To buy his favor, I extend this friendship,
  If he will take it, so, if not adieu,   170
  And for my love I pray you wrong me not.
ANTONIO. Yes Shylock, I will seal unto this bond.
SHYLOCK. Then meet me forthwith at the
    notary's,
  Give him direction for this merry bond,
  And I will go and purse the ducats straight,   175
  See to my house left in the fearful guard
  Of an unthrifty knave: and presently
  I'll be with you.
ANTONIO.   Hie thee gentle Jew.
  The Hebrew will turn Christian, he grows
    kind.   179
BASSANIO. I like not fair terms, and a villain's mind.
ANTONIO. Come on, in this there can be no dismay,
  My ships come home a month before the day.

[Exeunt]

Act II

SCENE I

[Enter Morochus, Prince of Morocco, a tawny Moor all in
white, and three or four followers accordingly with Portia,
Nerissa, and their train.]

MOROCCO. Mislike me not for my complexion,
  The shadow'd livery of the burnish'd sun,
  To whom I am a neighbor, and near bred.
  Bring me the fairest creature northward born,
  Where Phoebus' fire scarce thaws the icicles,   5

134. breed: increase, i.e. interest. 136. break: go bankrupt; break
his pledge. 140. doit: a small Dutch coin, hence a trifling sum.
142. kind: fashion, mode of action 145-46. seal . . . bond: set
your seal to a bond needing no other surety. 150. nominated for:
named as. 155-56. You . . . necessity: the two lines form a couplet. 156. I'll . . . necessity: I had rather remain in need.

175. straight: at once. 176. fearful: to be feared.
2. shadowed: dark, an heraldic term. livery: servant's uniform;
Morocco says his dark skin shows him to be a servant of the sun. 5.
Phoebus: Greco-Roman god of the sun.

And let us make incision for your love,
To prove whose blood is reddest, his or mine.
I tell thee lady this aspect of mine
Hath fear'd the valiant, (by my love I swear),
The best regarded virgins of our clime   10
Have lov'd it too; I would not change this hue,
Except to steal your thoughts my gentle queen.
PORTIA. In terms of choice I am not solely led
By nice direction of a maiden's eyes,
Besides, the lott'ry of my destiny   15
Bars me the right of voluntary choosing;
But if my father had not scanted me,
And hedg'd me by his wit to yield myself
His wife, who wins me by that means I told you,
Yourself (renowned prince) then stood as fair   20
As any comer I have look'd on yet
For my affection.
MOROCCO.   Even for that I thank you,
Therefore I pray you lead me to the caskets
To try my fortune: by this scimitar
That slew the Sophy, and a Persian prince   25
That won three fields of Sultan Solyman,
I would orestare the sternest eyes that look,
Outbrave the heart most daring on the earth,
Pluck the young sucking cubs from the she-bear,
Yea, mock the lion when a roars for prey   30
To win thee, lady. But alas the while!
If Hercules and Lichas play at dice
Which is the better man, the greater throw
May turn by fortune from the weaker hand;
So is Alcides beaten by his page,   35
And so may I, blind Fortune leading me,
Miss that which one unworthier may attain,
And die with grieving.
PORTIA.   You must take your chance,
And either not attempt to choose at all,   39
Or swear before you choose, if you choose wrong
Never to speak to lady afterward
In way of marriage; therefore he advis'd.
MOROCCO. Nor will not; come bring me unto
    my chance.

PORTIA. First forward to the temple, after dinner
Your hazard shall be made.
MOROCCO.   Good fortune then,   45
To make me bless'd or cursed'st among men.

[Exeunt.]

SCENE II

[Enter Launcelot Gobbo, the Clown alone.]

LAUNCELOT. Certainly, my conscience will serve me
to run from this Jew my master; the fiend is at mine
elbow, and tempts me, saying to me, 'Gobbo, Launcelot Gobbo, good Launcelot, or good Gobbo,' or
'good Launcelot Gobbo, use your legs, take the
start, run away.' My conscience says, 'No; take heed
honest Launcelot, take heed honest Gobbo,' or as
aforesaid 'honest Launcelot Gobbo, do not run,
scorn running with thy heels.' Well, the most courageous fiend bids me pack. 'Fia!' says the fiend,
'away!' says the fiend, 'for the heavens rouse up a
brave mind' says the fiend, 'and run.' Well, my
conscience, hanging about the neck of my heart,
says very wisely to me: 'My honest friend
Launcelot'—being an honest man's son, or rather
an honest woman's son, for indeed my father did
something smack, something grow to; he had a kind
of taste—well, my conscience says, 'Launcelot
budge not!'— 'Budge!' says the fiend.— 'Budge
not,' says my conscience. 'Conscience,' say I, 'you
counsel well,—Fiend' say I, 'you counsel well,'—to
be rul'd by my conscience, I should stay with the
Jew, my master, who (God bless the mark) is a kind
of devil: and to run away from the Jew I should be
ruled by the fiend, who (saving your reverence) is
the devil himself: certainly the Jew is the very devil
incarnation, and in my conscience, my conscience is
but a kind of hard conscience, to offer to counsel
me to stay with the Jew; the fiend gives the more

---

7. blood . . . reddest: the phrase 'red-blooded' is still in use, meaning 'courageous.' **8. aspect:** (stressed ⏑ —́) appearance. **9. fear'd:** frightened. **10. clime:** climate, i.e., country. **14. nice direction:** discriminating instruction. **17. scanted:** restricted. **20. fair:** a quibbling reference to the Moor's complexion. **24. scimitar:** a curved sword. **25. Sophy:** king (shah) of Persia. N. **26. fields:** battlefields. **Sultan Solyman:** the Turkish emperor. **27. orestare:** outstare. **30. a:** he. **32. Lichas:** the page who brought Hercules the poisoned shirt of Nessus; see Ovid, *Metamorphoses* 9; no story of a game of dice is known. **35. Alcides:** another name for Hercules. **page:** *rage*. **42. advis'd:** careful. **43. Nor will not:** i.e. speak to lady afterward.

44. to the temple: i.e. to take the oath.
1. serve: allow. **3–8. Gobbo . . . Gobbo:** Launcelot affects legal precision. **10. Fia!:** Italian *via*, go! **11. for the heavens:** for heaven's sake. **17. something smack:** taste a little. **grow to:** a phrase used of milk burned in the pan, (and therefore tasting unpleasant); probably has bawdy overtones. **23. God . . . mark:** a phrase used apologetically before a profane or indecent remark. **25. saving . . . reverence:** another apology for an indelicate remark. **27. incarnation:** malapropism for 'incarnate'; Launcelot's humor is often in his linguistic blunders.

friendly counsel; I will run fiend, my heels are at
your commandment, I will run.   30

[*Enter old Gobbo with a basket.*]

GOBBO. Master young man, you I pray you, which is
the way to Master Jew's?

LAUNCELOT. O heavens! this is my true begotten
father, who being more than sand-blind, high
gravel-blind, knows me not, I will try confusions
with him.

GOBBO. Master young gentleman, I pray you
which is the way to Master Jew's?

LAUNCELOT. Turn up on your right hand at the next
turning, but at the next turning of all on your left;
marry at the very next turning turn of no hand, but
turn down indirectly to the Jew's house.   41

GOBBO. Be God's sonties, 'twill be a hard way to hit;
can you tell me whether one Launcelot that dwells
with him, dwell with him or no?

LAUNCELOT. Talk you of young Master Launcelot?
[*Aside.*] Mark me now, now will I raise the waters.
Talk you of young Master Launcelot?

GOBBO. No master, sir, but a poor man's son, his
father though I say't is an honest exceeding poor
man, and God be thanked well to live.   50

LAUNCELOT. Well, let his father be what a will, we
talk of young Master Launcelot.

GOBBO. Your worship's friend and Launcelot sir.

LAUNCELOT. But I pray you ergo old man, ergo I
beseech you, talk you of young Master Launcelot?

GOBBO. Of Launcelot an't please your mastership.

LAUNCELOT. Ergo Master Launcelot,—talk not of
Master Launcelot father, for the young gentleman
according to fates and destinies, and such odd sayings, the sisters three, and such branches of learning,
is indeed deceased, or as you would say in plain
terms, gone to heaven.

GOBBO. Marry God forbid! the boy was the very staff
of my age, my very prop.   64

LAUNCELOT. Do I look like a cudgel or a hovel post,
a staff, or a prop? Do you know me father?

GOBBO. Alack the day! I know you not young gentleman, but I pray you tell me, is my boy—God rest
his soul—alive or dead?

LAUNCELOT. Do you not know me father?   70

GOBBO. Alack sir, I am sand-blind, I know you not.

LAUNCELOT. Nay indeed if you had your eyes you
might fail of the knowing me: it is a wise father that
knows his own child. Well, old man, I will tell you
news of your son,—give me your blessing, truth will
come to light, murder cannot be hid long, a man's
son may, but in the end truth will out.

GOBBO. Pray you sir stand up, I am sure you are not
Launcelot my boy.   79

LAUNCELOT. Pray you, let's have no more fooling
about it, but give me your blessing; I am Launcelot
your boy that was, your son that is, your child that
shall be.

GOBBO. I cannot think you are my son.   84

LAUNCELOT. I know not what I shall think of that,
but I am Launcelot the Jew's man, and I am sure
Margery your wife is my mother.

GOBBO. Her name is Margery indeed,—I'll be sworn
if thou be Launcelot, thou art mine own flesh and
blood, Lord worship'd might he be, what a beard
hast thou got; thou hast got more hair on thy chin,
than Dobbin my fill-horse has on his tail.   92

LAUNCELOT. It should seem then that Dobbin's tail
grows backward. I am sure he had more hair of his
tail than I have of my face when I last saw him.

GOBBO. Lord, how art thou chang'd; how dost thou
and thy master agree?—I have brought him a
present;—how 'gree you now?   98

LAUNCELOT. Well, well, but for mine own part, as I
have set up my rest to run away, so will I not rest till

---

31. you: Old Gobbo changes to the more familiar *thou* when he finally recognizes his son. **34. sand-blind:** (from Old English *sam-blind,* half-blind) partially blind, as opposed to stone blind; Launcelot invents an intermediate degree, 'gravel blind.' **35. confusions:** malapropism for 'conclusions'; cf. Hamlet III.4.1955–6: 'and like the famous ape,/to try conclusions . . .' **38–41. Turn . . . house:** obviously nonsense. Launcelot is clowning by using what is known today as double talk. **42. Be God's sonties:** by God's saints. **45. Master:** by assuming this title, Launcelot is putting on airs. **46. waters:** tears. **50. well to live:** well to do. **53. and Launcelot:** i.e. plain Launcelot. **54. ergo:** therefore, (from Latin) a word which had become a joke because it had been so overworked. **56. an't:** and it, i.e., if it. **58. father:** a common form of address. **60. sisters three:** the Fates of classical mythology.

73–74. it . . . child: a proverbial saying, though usually transposed. **76. truth . . . long:** two proverbs. **82–83. your . . . shall be:** Launcelot is playing, somewhat irreverently, on the liturgical phrase 'was in the beginning, is now, and ever shall be.' **90. Lord . . . he be:** *Lord* is an exclamation, and *worship'd might he be* an added phrase to escape being irreverent. **90–91. what . . . got:** the speech suggests that blind Gobbo feels the back of Launcelot's head, and mistakes his long hair for a beard. **92. fill-horse:** a cart horse. **94. backward:** i.e. shorter, with a reference also to Old Gobbo's mistake; see gloss to ll. 90–91, above. **100. set . . . rest:** determined, a phrase from a card game called Primero, where it means to hazard one's final stake. It also meant to settle into an abode, and had bawdy overtones.

I have run some ground; my master's a very Jew,—
give him his present, give him a halter, I am fam-
ish'd in his service. You may tell every finger I have
with my ribs;—father I am glad you are come, give
me your present to one Master Bassanio, who
indeed gives rare new liveries,—if I serve not him, I
will run as far as God has any ground. O rare fortune, here comes the man, to him father, for I am a
Jew if I serve the Jew any longer.   109

[Enter Bassanio with Leonardo and a follower or two.]

BASSANIO. You may do so, but let it be so hasted that
supper be ready at the farthest by five of the clock;
see these letters delivered, put the liveries to making,
and desire Gratiano to come anon to my lodging.

[Exit one of his men.]

LAUNCELOT. To him father.   115
GOBBO. God bless your worship.
BASSANIO. Gramercy, wouldst thou aught with me?
GOBBO. Here's my son sir, a poor boy.
LAUNCELOT. Not a poor boy sir, but the rich Jew's
man that would sir as my father shall specify.   120
GOBBO. He hath a great infection sir, as one would
say to serve.
LAUNCELOT. Indeed the short and the long is, I serve
the Jew, and have a desire as my father shall specify.
GOBBO. His master and he (saving your worship's rev-
erence) are scarce cater-cousins.   126
LAUNCELOT. To be brief, the very truth is, that the
Jew, having done me wrong, doth cause me as my
father—being I hope an old man—shall frutify unto
you.   130
GOBBO. I have here a dish of doves that I would
bestow upon your worship, and my suit it—
LAUNCELOT. In very brief, the suit is impertinent to
myself, as your worship shall know by this honest
old man, and though I say it, though old man, yet
poor man my father.   136
BASSANIO. One speak for both; what would you?

LAUNCELOT. Serve you sir.
GOBBO. That is the very defect of the matter sir.
BASSANIO. I know thee well, thou hast obtain'd thy
suit;   140
Shylock thy master spoke with me this day,
And hath preferr'd thee,—if it be preferment
To leave a rich Jew's service, to become
The follower of so poor a gentleman.   144
LAUNCELOT. The old proverb is very well parted
between my master Shylock and you sir, you have
'the grace of God' sir, and he hath 'enough.'
BASSANIO. Thou speak'st it well; go father with thy
son
Take leave of thy old master, and enquire
My lodging out,— [To his followers.] give him a
livery   150
More guarded than his fellows'; see it done.
LAUNCELOT. Father in; I cannot get a service, no! I
have ne'er a tongue in my head, well; if any man in
Italy have a fairer table which doth offer to swear
upon a book, I shall have good fortune; go to,
here's a simple line of life, here's a small trifle of
wives; alas, fifteen wives is nothing, eleven widows
and nine maids is a simple coming in for one man,
and then to 'scape drowning thrice, and to be in
peril of my life with the edge of a featherbed, here
are simple 'scapes. Well, if Fortune be a woman
she's a good wench for this gear; father come, I'll
take my leave of the Jew in the twinkling.

[Exit with old Gobbo.]

BASSANIO. I pray thee good Leonardo think on this,
These things being bought and orderly bestowed
Return in haste, for I do feast tonight   166
My best esteem'd acquaintance; hie thee, go!
LEONARDO. My best endeavors shall be done herein.

[Begins to leave.]

[Enter Gratiano.]

---

101. very: true. 105. me: ethical dative, untranslatable. 107. as far . . . ground: proverbial. 118–19. poor . . . poor: unfortunate . . . needy. 121. infection: malapropism for 'affection,' meaning, desire. 126. cater-cousins: intimate friends. 129. frutify: mal-apropism for 'certify.'

142. preferr'd: recommended. 145. proverb: 'He that hath the grace of God hath enough.' 151. guarded: ornamented with braid. 153–61. if any man . . . simple 'scapes: Launcelot reads his own palm; this passage is undoubtedly more of Launcelot's 'confusion.' 154. table: a term of palmistry, meaning palm of the hand. 156. simple . . . life: unremarkable life-line. 158. coming in: income, also probably has bawdy overtones linked with what follows. 160. peril . . . featherbed: a cant phrase referring to the danger of marry-ing. 162. gear: sort of thing. 165. bestowed: i.e. aboard ship.

GRATIANO. Where's your master?   169
LEONARDO. Yonder sir, he walks.

[*Exit.*]

GRATIANO. Signior Bassanio.
BASSANIO. Gratiano.
GRATIANO. I have suit to you.
BASSANIO. You have obtain'd it.
GRATIANO. You must not deny me, I must go with
     you to Belmont.   175
BASSANIO. Why then you must, but hear thee Grati-
     ano,
     Thou art too wild, too rude, and bold of voice,
     Parts that become thee happily enough,
     And in such eyes as ours appear not faults,   179
     But where thou art not known, why there they
     show
     Something too liberal;—pray thee take pain
     To allay with some cold drops of modesty
     Thy skipping spirit, lest through thy wild behavior
     I be misconst'red in the place I go to,
     and lose my hopes.
GRATIANO.   Signior Bassanio, hear me,   185
     If I do not put on a sober habit,
     Talk with respect, and swear but now and then,
     Wear prayer books in my pocket, look demurely,
     Nay more, while grace is saying hood mine eyes
     Thus with my hat, and sign and say "amen";   190
     Use all the observance of civility
     Like one well studied in a sad ostent
     To please his grandam, never trust me more.
BASSANIO. Well, we shall see your bearing.
GRATIANO. Nay but I bar tonight, you shall not
     gauge me   195
     By what we do tonight.
BASSANIO.   No, that were pity,
     I would entreat you rather to put on
     Your boldest suit of mirth, for we have friends
     That purpose merriment; but fare you well,
     I have some business.   200
GRATIANO. And I must to Lorenzo and the rest,
     But we will visit you at supper time.

[*Exeunt.*]

SCENE III

[*Enter Jessica and Launcelot the Clown.*]

JESSICA. I am sorry thou wilt leave my father so,
     Our house is hell, and thou, a merry devil,
     Didst rob it of some taste of tediousness,
     But fare thee well, there is a ducat for thee,
     And Launcelot, soon at supper shalt thou see   5
     Lorenzo, who is thy new master's guest,
     Give him this letter; do it secretly,
     And so farewell: I would not have my father
     See me in talk with thee.   9
LAUNCELOT. Adieu, tears exhibit my tongue, most
     beautiful pagan, most sweet Jew. If a Christian do
     not play the knave and get thee, I am much
     deceived, but adieu, these foolish drops do some-
     thing drown my manly spirit, adieu.
[*Exit.*]
JESSICA. Farewell good Launcelot.   15
     Alack, what heinous sin is it in me
     To be asham'd to be my father's child?
     But though I am a daughter to his blood
     I am not to his manners. Oh Lorenzo
     If thou keep promise I shall end this strife,   20
     Become a Christian and thy loving wife!
[*Exit.*]

SCENE IV

[*Enter Gratiano, Lorenzo, Salerio, and Solanio.*]

LORENZO. Nay, we will slink away in supper time,
     Disguise us at my lodging, and return all in an hour.
GRATIANO. We have not made good preparation.
SALERIO. We have not spoke us yet of torch-bearers.
SOLANIO. 'Tis vile unless it may be quaintly order'd,
     And better in my mind not undertook.   6
LORENZO. 'Tis now but four of clock, we have two
     hours
     To furnish us.

[*Enter Launcelot with a letter.*]

     Friend Launcelot, what's the news?

---

181. liberal: free, unrestrained.   182. allay: dilute; read 't'allay.'
184. misconst'red: misconstrued.   186. habit: literally garment, but
Gratiano obviously means 'appearance.'   189-90. hood . . . hat:
hats were worn at dinner.   191. the observance: read 'th' observance.'   192. sad ostent: solemn face.   194-95. bearing . . . bar: a
jingle.

10. exhibit: Launcelot's blunder for 'inhibit.'   13. something:
somewhat.
1. in: during   4. spoke us: bespoke for ourselves.   5. quaintly:
elegantly.

LAUNCELOT. And it shall please you to break up this,
  it shall seem to signify.   10
LORENZO. I know the hand; in faith 'tis a fair hand,
  And whiter than the paper it writ on
  Is the fair hand that writ.
GRATIANO.   Love news in faith.
LAUNCELOT. By your leave sir.
LORENZO. Whither goest thou?   15
LAUNCELOT. Marry sir, to bid my old master the Jew
  to sup tonight with my new master the Christian.
LORENZO. Hold, here take this. Tell gentle Jessica
  I will not fail her; speak it privately.
  Go Gentlemen, will you prepare you for this mask
    tonight?   20
  I am provided of a torch-bearer.

[Exit Launcelot the Clown.]

SALERIO. Ay, marry, I'll be gone about it straight.
SOLANIO. And so will I.
LORENZO. Meet me and Gratiano at Gratiano's lodg-
  ing
  Some hour hence.
SALERIO. 'Tis good we do so.   25

[Exeunt Salerio and Solanio.]

GRATIANO. Was not that letter from fair Jessica?
LORENZO. I must needs tell thee all. She hath
  directed
  How I shall take her from her father's house,
  What gold and jewels she is furnish'd with,
  What page's suit she hath in readiness.   30
  If ere the Jew her father come to heaven,
  It will be for his gentle daughter's sake;
  And never dare misfortune cross her foot,
  Unless she do it under this excuse,
  That she is issue to a faithless Jew.   35
  Come go with me, peruse this as thou goest.
  Fair Jessica shall be my torch-bearer.   *[Exeunt.]*

SCENE V

[Enter Shylock the Jew and his man that was the Clown.]

SHYLOCK. Well, thou shalt see, thy eyes shall be thy
  judge,

The difference of old Shylock and Bassanio;
  What Jessica!—Thou shalt not gormandize
  As thou hast done with me—what Jessica!—
  And sleep, and snore, and rend apparel out.   5
  Why Jessica I say!
LAUNCELOT. Why Jessica!
SHYLOCK. Who bids thee call? I do not bid thee call.
LAUNCELOT. Your worship was wont to tell me, I
  could do nothing without bidding.   10

[Enter Jessica.]

JESSICA. Call you? What is your will?
SHYLOCK. I am bid forth to supper, Jessica.
  There are my keys; but wherefore should I go?
  I am not bid for love; they flatter me,
  But yet I'll go in hate, to feed upon   15
  The prodigal Christian. Jessica my girl,
  Look to my house. I am right loath to go.
  There is some ill a-brewing towards my rest,
  For I did dream of money bags tonight.   19
LAUNCELOT. I beseech you sir, go. My young master
  doth expect your reproach.
SHYLOCK. So do I his.
LAUNCELOT. And they have conspired together, I will
  not say you shall see a masque, but if you do, then it
  was not for nothing that my nose fell a-'bleeding on
  black Monday last, at six o'clock i' th' morning,
  falling out that year on Ash-Wensday was four year
  in th' afternoon.
SHYLOCK. What, are there masques? Hear you me
  Jessica,
  Lock up my doors, and when you hear the
    drum   30
  And the vile squealing of the wry-neck'd fife
  Clamber not you up to the casements then,
  Nor thrust your head into the public street
  To gaze on Christian fools with varnish'd faces;
  But stop my house's ears, I mean my
    casements,   35
  Let not the sound of shallow fopp'ry enter
  My sober house. By Jacob's staff I swear
  I have no mind of feasting forth tonight:

---

9. **break up:** break the seal, or open.   **20. mask:** entertainment, with dancing, at which the guests wore masks and were attended by torch-bearers.   **31. ere:** ever.   **32. gentle:** a pun on 'Gentile.' The words were spelled and pronounced alike.   **33. her foot:** i.e. her path.   **34. she:** misfortune.   **35. she:** Jessica.

14. **bid for love:** invited because they like me.   **15. feed upon:** i.e. feed at the expense of, but also carries the unpleasant overtones of devour.   **19. tonight:** last night.   **21. reproach:** Launcelot's blunder for 'approach.'   **25. nose . . . a-bleeding:** nose bleeds were considered ominous by the superstitious.   **26. black Monday:** Easter Monday, so-called because in 1360 it was so cold and stormy that many men died on horseback.   **31. wry-neck'd fife:** so called because the player had to twist his neck in order to play.   **34. varnish'd:** painted.   **36. fopp'ry:** foolishness.

But I will go: go you before me sirrah.
Say I will come.   40
LAUNCELOT. I will go before sir.
   Mistress, look out at window for all this,
      There will come a Christian by
      Will be worth a Jewess' eye.
SHYLOCK. What says that fool of Hagar's offspring?
   ha?   45
JESSICA. His words were 'Farewell mistress,' nothing
   else.
SHYLOCK. The patch is kind enough, but a huge
   feeder,
   Snail slow in profit, and he sleeps by day
   More than a wildcat; drones hive not with me,
   Therefore I part with him, and part with him   50
   To one that I would have him help to waste
   His borrow'd purse. Well Jessica go in,
   Perhaps I will return immediately.
   Do as I bid you, shut doors after you.
   Fast bind, fast find—   55
   A proverb never stale in thrifty mind.   [Exit.]
JESSICA. Farewell, and if my fortune be not cross'd,
   I have a father, you a daughter, lost.   [Exit.]

SCENE VI

[Enter the maskers, Gratiano and Salerio.]

GRATIANO. This is the penthouse under which
   Lorenzo
   Desir'd us to make stand.
SALERIO.   His hour is almost past.
GRATIANO. And it is marvel he out-dwells his hour,
   For lovers ever run before the clock.
SALERIO. O ten times faster Venus' pigeons fly   5
   To seal love's bonds new made, than they are wont
   To keep obliged faith unforfeited.
GRATIANO. That ever holds: who riseth from a feast
   With that keen appetite that he sits down?
   Where is the horse that doth untread again   10
   His tedious measures with the unbated fire
   That he did pace them first; all things that are

Are with more spirit chased than enjoy'd.
How like a younger or a prodigal
The scarfed bark puts from her native bay,   15
Hugg'd and embraced by the strumpet wind,
How like the prodigal doth she return
With over-weather'd ribs and ragged sail—
Lean, rent, and beggar'd by the strumpet wind?

[Enter Lorenzo.]

SALERIO. Here comes Lorenzo; more of this here-
   after.   20
LORENZO. Sweet friends, your patience for my long
   abode
   Not I but my affairs have made you wait.
   When you shall please to play the thieves for wives
   I'll watch as long for you then; approach—
   Here dwells my father Jew. How, who's
   within?   25

[Enter Jessica above.]

JESSICA. Who are you? Tell me for more certainty,
   Albeit I'll swear that I do know your tongue.
LORENZO. Lorenzo, and thy love.
JESSICA. Lorenzo certain, and my love indeed,
   For who love I so much? And now who
   knows   30
   But you Lorenzo, whether I am yours?
LORENZO. Heaven and thy thoughts are witness that
   thou art.
JESSICA. Here, catch this casket, it is worth the pains.
   I am glad 'tis night, you do not look on me,
   For I am much asham'd of my exchange: 35
   But love is blind, and lovers cannot see
   The pretty follies that themselves commit,
   For if they could, Cupid himself would blush
   To see me thus transformed to a boy.   39
LORENZO. Descend, for you must be my torch-
   bearer.
JESSICA. What, must I hold a candle to my shames?
   They in themselves (goodsooth) are too too light.
   Why, 'tis an office of discovery, love,
   And I should be obscur'd.

---

45. **Hagar's offspring:** Hagar was a gentile slave belonging to Sarah, Abraham's wife. Her son was an outcast. 47. **patch:** fool. 49. **wildcat:** which sleeps all day because it prowls all night. 55. **fast . . . find:** proverbial.
1. **penthouse:** a porch. This is a suggestion of the overhang of the upper stage. 3. **out-dwells:** outstays. 5. **Venus' pigeons:** the goddess of love's chariot was drawn by doves. Here Salerio uses the phrase to mean 'lovers.' 6. **wont:** accustomed. 10. **untread:** retrace. 11. **measures:** paces.

14. **younger:** younger son. 15. **scarfed:** a method of joining timbers; also, probably, 'decorated with flags.' 16. **strumpet wind:** a reference to the harlots with whom the Prodigal wasted his substance; see Luke 15. 21. **abode:** delay. 25. **How:** an exclamation to attract attention, like 'hey!' 31. **yours:** i.e. the one you love. 35. **exchange:** of a boy's garb for her own. 42. **light:** a pun, with 'faithless' as the secondary meaning. 43. **discovery:** revealing. 44. **obscur'd:** hidden. Lorenzo puns on a further sense, 'disguised,' in the following lines.

LORENZO.   So are you sweet
  Even in the lovely garnish of a boy,   45
  But come at once,
  For the close night doth play the runaway,
  And we are stay'd for at Bassanio's feast.
JESSICA. I will make fast the doors and gild myself
  With some moe ducats, and be with you
    straight.   50
GRATIANO. Now by my hood a gentle, and no Jew.
LORENZO. Beshrow me but I love her heartily,
  For she is wise, if I can judge of her,
  And fair she is, if that mine eyes be true,
  And true she is, as she hath prov'd herself;   55
  And therefore like herself, wise, fair, and true,
  Shall she be placed in my constant soul.

[Enter Jessica.]

  What, art thou come? On gentlemen, away!
  Our masking mates by this time for us stay.

[Exit with Jessica and Salerio; Gratiano lags behind.]

[Enter Antonio.]

ANTONIO. Who's there?   60
GRATIANO. Signior Antonio?
ANTONIO. Fie, fie Gratiano, where are all the rest?
  'Tis nine o'clock. Our friends all stay for you.
  No masque tonight. The wind is come about.
  Bassanio presently will go aboard;   65
  I have sent twenty out to seek for you.
GRATIANO. I am glad on't; I desire no more delight
  Than to be under sail, and gone tonight.   [Exeunt.]

SCENE VII

[Enter Portia with Morocco and both their trains.]

PORTIA. Go, draw aside the curtains and discover
  The several caskets to this noble Prince.
  Now make your choice.
MOROCCO. This first of gold, who this inscription
    bears:
  'Who chooseth me, shall gain what many men
    desire.'   5

The second silver, which this promise carries:
'Who chooseth me, shall get as much as he
  deserves.'
This third, dull lead, with warning all as blunt,
'Who chooseth me, must give and hazard all he
  hath.'
How shall I know if I do choose the right?   10
PORTIA. The one of them contains my picture, Prince.
  If you choose that, then I am yours withal.
MOROCCO. Some God direct my judgment; let me
    see,
  I will survey th' inscriptions back again.
  What says this leaden casket?   15
  'Who chooseth me, must give and hazard all he
    hath.'
  Must give—for what? for lead, hazard for lead?
  This casket threatens—men that hazard all
  Do it in hope of fair advantages;
  A golden mind stoops not to shows of dross,   20
  I'll then nor give nor hazard aught for lead.
  What says the silver with her virgin hue?
  'Who chooseth me, shall get as much as he
    deserves.'
  As much as he deserves—pause there Morocco,
  And weigh thy value with an even hand;   25
  If thou be'st rated by thy estimation
  Thou dost deserve enough, and yet enough
  May not extend so far as to the lady:
  And yet to be afeard of my deserving
  Were but a weak disabling of my self.   30
  As much as I deserve; why that's the lady.
  I do in birth deserve her, and in fortunes,
  In graces, and in qualities of breeding:
  But more than these, in love I do deserve,
  What if I stray'd no farther, but chose here?   35
  Let's see once more this saying grav'd in gold:
  'Who chooseth me shall gain what many men desire.'
  Why that's the lady; all the world desires here.
  From the four corners of the earth they come
  To kiss this shrine, this mortal breathing saint.   40
  The Hyrcanian deserts, and the vasty wilds
  Of wide Arabia are as throughfares now
  For princes to come view fair Portia.

---

45. garnish: dress. **47. close:** secretive. **48. stay'd for:** awaited. **50. moe:** more (in number). **51. by my hood:** an asseveration dating back to Middle English; see the *OED*. **gentle:** Gentile. **65. presently:** immediately.
1. discover: reveal. **4. who:** sometimes used for 'which.'

8. dull . . . blunt: a double pun; *dull*, blunt of edge, and *blunt*, outspoken and base. **20. shows:** displays. **dross:** scum thrown off in smelting, worthless matter. **25. even:** impartial. **30. disabling:** disparagement. **40. shrine . . . saint:** the lover's attitude to his lady was often compared to the worship of a saint. **41. Hyrcanian deserts:** a notoriously wild area south of the Caspian Sea. **vasty:** vast.

The watery kingdom, whose ambitious head
Spets in the face of heaven, is no bar   45
To stop the foreign spirits, but they come
As o'er a brook to see fair Portia.
One of these three contains her heavenly picture.
Is't like the lead contains her? 'Twere damnation
To think so base a thought; it were too gross   50
To rib her cerecloth in the obscure grave—
Or shall I think in silver she's immur'd
Being ten times undervalued to tried gold?
O sinful thought! never so rich a gem   54
Was set in worse than gold. They have in England
A coin that bears the figure of an angel
Stamp'd in gold; but that's insculp'd upon:
But here an angel in a golden bed
Lies all within. Deliver me the key;
Here do I choose, and thrive I as I may.   60
PORTIA. There take it prince, and if my form lie there
   Then I am yours.
MOROCCO.   O hell! what have we here?
   A carrion death, within whose empty eye
   There is a written scroll—I'll read the writing.

[Reads.]

     All that glisters is not gold,   65
     Often have you heard that told,
     Many a man his life hath sold
     But my outside to behold,
     Gilded timber do worms infold.
     Had you been as wise as bold,   70
     Young in limbs, in judgment old,
     Your answer had not been inscroll'd,
     Fare you well, your suit is cold.

MOROCCO. Cold indeed and labor lost,
   Then farewell heat, and welcome frost.   75
   Portia adieu; I have too griev'd a heart.
   To take a tedious leave; thus losers part.   [Exit.]
PORTIA. A gentle riddance; draw the curtains, go,
   Let all of his complexion choose me so.   [Exeunt.]

SCENE VIII

[Enter Salerio and Solanio.]

SALERIO. Why man I saw Bassanio under sail,
   With him is Gratiano gone along;
   And in their ship I am sure Lorenzo is not.
SOLANIO. The villain Jew with outcries rais'd the
     duke,
   Who went with him to search Bassanio's ship.   5
SALERIO. He came too late; the ship was under sail,
   But there the duke was given to understand
   That in a gondola were seen together
   Lorenzo and his amorous Jessica.
   Besides, Antonio certified the duke   10
   They were not with Bassanio in his ship.
SOLANIO. I never heard a passion so confus'd.
   So strange, outrageous, and so variable
   As the dog Jew did utter in the streets,
   'My daughter! O my ducats! O my daughter!   15
   Fled with a Christian! O my Christian ducats!
   Justice, the law, my ducats, and my daughter!
   A sealed bag, two sealed bags of ducats
   Of double ducats, stolne from me by my daughter!
   And jewels, two stones, two rich and precious
     stones,
   Stolne by my daughter! Justice! Find the girl!   21
   She hath the stones upon her, and the ducats.'
SALERIO. Why all the boys in Venice follow him,
   Crying his stones, his daughter, and his ducats.
SOLANIO. Let good Antonio look he keep his
     day   25
   Or he shall pay for this.
SALERIO.   Marry well rememb'red,—
   I reason'd with a Frenchman yesterday,
   Who told me, in the narrow seas that part
   The French and English, there miscarried
   A vessel of our country richly fraught: 30
   I thought upon Antonio when he told me,
   And wish'd in silence that it were not his.
SOLANIO. You were best to tell Antonio what you
     hear,
   Yet do not suddenly, for it may grieve him.   34

---

44. **watery kingdom:** ocean.   45. **spets:** spits.   50. **base:** a pun, since lead is a base metal.   51. **rib:** enclose. **cerecloth:** a wax-impregnated cloth used to wrap the dead.   56–57. **coin . . . gold:** the 'angel' was a gold coin in current use, bearing the image of the archangel Michael.   57. **insculp'd:** engraved.   58. **angel . . . bed:** Portia's picture in the casket of gold.   59–60: **key . . . may:** a rhyme.   61. **form:** image.   61–62. **there . . . here:** a rhyme.   63. **death:** a death's head.   65. **All . . . gold:** a common proverb.   69. **Gilded timber:** i.e. a decorated tomb.   79. **complexion:** both 'coloring' and 'disposition.'

7–9. **given . . . Jessica:** presumably a false report.   9. **amorous:** loving or lovable.   12. **passion:** passionate outburst.   15. **My daughter . . . daughter!:** Barabas in Marlowe's *Jew of Malta*, II.1.47–48, cries 'Oh my girl,/My gold, my fortune, my felicity . . .'   19. **double ducats:** coins double the value of the ordinary ducat.   25. **keep . . . day:** i.e. the day the bond is due.   27. **reason'd:** talked.   29. **miscarried:** was lost.

SALERIO. A kinder gentleman treads not the earth,
  I saw Bassanio and Antonio part,
  Bassanio told him he would make some speed
  Of his return; he answered, 'Do not so,
  Slubber not business for my sake Bassanio,
  But stay the very riping of the time,   40
  And for the Jew's bond which he hath of me
  Let it not enter in your mind of love.
  Be merry, and employ your chiefest thoughts
  To courtship, and such fair ostents of love
  As shall conveniently become you there.'   45
  And even there his eye being big with tears,
  Turning his face, he put his hand behind him,
  And with affection wondrous sensible
  He wrung Bassanio's hand, and so they parted.
SOLANIO. I think he only loves the world for him.
  I pray thee let us go and find him out   51
  And quicken his embraced heaviness
  With some delight or other.
SALERIO.   Do we so.
[Exeunt.]

SCENE IX

[Enter Nerissa and a Servitor.]

NERISSA. Quick, quick I pray thee, draw the curtain
    straight.
  The Prince of Arragon hath tane his oath,
  And comes to his election presently.

[Enter the Prince of Arragon, his train, and Portia.]

PORTIA. Behold, there stand the caskets, noble Prince,
  If you choose that wherein I am contain'd   5
  Straight shall our nuptial rites be solemniz'd;
  But if you fail, without more speech my lord,
  You must be gone from hence immediately.
ARRAGON. I am enjoin'd by oath to observe three
    things,
  First, never to unfold to any one   10
  Which casket 'twas I chose; next, if I fail
  Of the right casket, never in my life
  To woo a maid in way of marriage;

  Lastly, if I do fail in fortune of my choice,
  Immediately to leave you and be gone.   15
PORTIA. To these injunctions every one doth swear
  That comes to hazard for my worthless self.
ARRAGON. And so have I address'd me; fortune now
  To my heart's hope: gold, silver, and base
    lead.   19
  'Who chooseth me, must give and hazard all he
    hath.'
  You shall look fairer ere I give or hazard.
  What says the golden chest? Ha; let me see:
  'Who chooseth me, shall gain what many men
    desire.'
  What many men desire—that 'many' may be meant
  By the fool multitude that choose by show,   25
  Not learning more than the fond eye doth teach,
  Which pries not to th' interior, but like the martlet
  Builds in the weather on the outward wall,
  Even in the force and road of casualty.
  I will not choose what many men desire,   30
  Because I will not jump with common spirits,
  And rank me with the barbarous multitudes.
  Why then to thee thou silver treasure house,
  Tell me once more what title thou dost bear.   34
  'Who chooseth me shall get as much as he deserves,'
  And well said too; for who shall go about
  To cozen Fortune, and be honorable
  Without the stamp of merit? Let none presume
  To wear an undeserved dignity:
  O that estates, degrees, and offices,   40
  Were not deriv'd corruptly, and that clear honor
  Were purchas'd by the merit of the wearer!
  How many then should cover that stand bare?
  How many be commanded that command?
  How much low peasantry would then be
    gleaned   45
  From the true seed of honor? and how much honor
  Pick'd from the chaff and ruin of the times,
  To be new-varnish'd; well, but to my choice.
  'Who chooseth me shall get as much as he deserves,'
  I will assume desert; give me a key for this,   50
  And instantly unlock my fortunes here.

---

39. slubber: perform carelessly. 40. stay . . . time: stay until your business is concluded. 42. mind . . . love: mind which is full of love. 44. ostents: demonstrations. 46. there: then. 48. sensible: evident or sensitive. 50. I . . . him: I think he values this world only because Bassanio is in it. 52. embraced: i.e. Antonio holds fast to his melancholy
1. straight: immediately. 2. tane: taken. 3. election: choice.

18. address'd me: prepared myself. fortune: good luck. 25. By: for. 26. fond: foolish. 27. martlet: swift, a bird. 28. in the weather: in an exposed place. 29. force and road of casualty: power and path of misfortune. 31. jump: agree. 37. cozen: deceive. 38. stamp: certifying imprint; cf. 'hallmark.' Arragon asks who shall cheat Fortune by pretending to be honorable without having any real merit. 40. degrees: rank. 41. deriv'd: obtained. 43. cover . . . bare: i.e. be masters who now are servants (hats were doffed in the presence of a superior). 45. gleaned: plucked. 47. ruin: 'desolation,' but also, perhaps, 'refuse.' 48. new-varnishe'd: repainted, i.e. with the outward appearance of nobility. 50. assume: take on.

PORTIA. Too long a pause for that which you find
     there.
ARRAGON. What's here? The portrait of a blinking
     idiot
     Presenting me a schedule, I will read it.
     How much unlike art thou to Portia!   55
     How much unlike my hopes and my deservings!
     'Who chooseth me shall have as much as he
          deserves?'
     Did I deserve no more then a fool's head?
     Is that my prize? Are my deserts no better?   59
PORTIA. To offend and judge are distinct offices,
     And of opposed natures.
ARRAGON.   What is here?

[Reads.]

     The fire seven times tried this,
     Seven times tried that judgment is
     That did never choose amiss,
     Some there be that shadows kiss,   65
     Such have but a shadow's bliss.
     There be fools alive, Iwis,
     Silver'd ore, and so was this.
     Take what wife you will to bed,
     I will ever be your head;   70
     So be gone, you are sped.

ARRAGON. Still more fool I shall appear
     By the time I linger here,
     With one fool's head I came to woo,
     But I go away with two.   75
     Sweet adieu, I'll keep my oath,
     Patiently to bear my wroth.

[Exit Arragon and his train.]

PORTIA. Thus hath the candle sing'd the moth;
     O these deliberate fools when they do choose,
     They have the wisdom by their wit to lose.   80
NERISSA. The ancient saying is no heresy,
     Hanging and wiving goes by destiny.
PORTIA. Come draw the curtain Nerissa.

[Enter Messenger.]

MESSENGER. Where is my lady?
PORTIA.   Here, what would my
     lord?
MESSENGER. Madam, there is alighted at your gate
     A young Venetian, one that comes before   86
     To signify th' approaching of his lord,
     From whom he bringeth sensible regreets;
     To wit (besides commends and courteous breath)
     Gifts of rich value; yet I have not seen   90
     So likely an ambassador of love.
     A day in April never came so sweet
     To show how costly summer was at hand,
     As this fore-spurrer comes before his lord.
PORTIA. No more I pray thee, I am half afeard   95
     Thou wilt say anon he is some kin to thee,
     Thou spend'st such high-day wit in praising him:
     Come come Nerissa, for I long to see
     Quick Cupid's post that comes so mannerly.
NERISSA. Bassanio lord, love if thy will it be.   100

[Exeunt.]

Act III

SCENE I

[Enter Solanio and Salerio.]

SOLANIO. Now what news on the Rialto?
SALERIO. Why yet it lives there uncheck'd, that An-
     tonio hath a ship of rich lading wrack'd on the nar-
     row seas; the Goodwins I think they call the place, a
very dangerous flat, and fatal, where the carcases of
many a tall ship lie buried, as they say, if my gossip
Report be an honest woman of her word.   7

54. schedule: writing. 67. Iwis: certainly. 71. sped: done
for. 77. wroth: displeasure.
3–4. narrow seas: the Dover Strait, where the dangerous shoals
known as the Goodwin Sands are located.

78. moth: pronounced to rhyme with *oath*, and *wroth*. 79. deliberate: deliberating; the choice should be dictated not by reason, but by
love. 82. Hanging . . . destiny: a proverb. 84. my lord: Portia is
probably being light-hearted in answering the messenger thus; such a
response as 'Yes, sir,' spoken with gaiety to a subordinate, is not
uncommon today. 88. sensible regreets: tangible greetings. 89.
commends: commendations. breath: words. 93. costly: rich. 97.
high-day: high-flown. 99. post: messenger. 100. Bassanio . . .
be: Nerissa evidently has a premonition that it is Bassanio.

SOLANIO. I would she were as lying a gossip in that, as ever knapp'd ginger, or made her neighbors believe she wept for the death of a third husband; but it is true, without any slips of prolixity, or crossing the plain highway of talk, that the good Antonio, the honest Antonio; O that I had a title good enough to keep his name company!—

SALERIO. Come, the full stop.   15

SOLANIO. Ha, what sayest thou? Why, the end is, he hath lost a ship.

SALERIO. Let me say 'amen' betimes, lest the devil cross my prayer, for here he comes in the likeness of a Jew.

[Enter Shylock.]

How now Shylock, what news among the merchants?   21

SHYLOCK. You knew, none so well, none so well as you, of my daughter's flight.

SALERIO. That's certain, I (for my part) knew the tailor that made the wings she flew withal.   25

SOLANIO. And Shylock (for his own part) knew the bird was fledge, and then it is the complexion of them all to leave the dam.

SHYLOCK. She is damn'd for it.   29

SALERIO. That's certain, if the devil may be her judge.

SHYLOCK. My own flesh and blood to rebel!

SOLANIO. Out upon it old carrion! Rebels it at these years?   34

SHYLOCK. I say my daughter is my flesh and my blood.

SALERIO. There is more difference between thy flesh and hers, than between jet and ivory; more between your bloods, than there is between red wine and Rhenish: but tell us, do you hear whether Antonio have had any loss at sea or no?   41

SHYLOCK. There I have another bad match, a bankrupt, a prodigal, who dare scarce show his head on the Rialto, a beggar that was us'd to come so smug upon the mart. Let him look to his bond! He was wont to lend money for a Christian cursy. Let him look to his bond!

SOLANIO. Why I am sure if he forfeit, thou wilt not take his flesh. What's that good for?   49

SHYLOCK. To bait fish withal, if it will feed nothing else, it will feed my revenge. He hath disgrac'd me, and hind'red me half a million, laugh'd at my losses, mock'd at my gains, scorned my nation, thwarted my bargains, cooled my friends, heated mine enemies, and what's his reason? I am a Jew. Hath not a Jew eyes? Hath not a Jew hands, organs, dimensions, senses, affections, passions? fed with the same food, hurt with the same weapons, subject to the same diseases, healed by the same means, warmed and cooled by the same winter and summer as a Christian is? If you prick us, do we not bleed? If you tickle us, do we not laugh? If you poison us, do we not die? And if you wrong us, shall we not revenge? If we are like you in the rest, we will resemble you in that. If a Jew wrong a Christian, what is his humility? Revenge. If a Christian wrong a Jew, what should his sufferance be by Christian example? Why revenge. The villany you teach me I will execute, and it shall go hard but I will better the instruction.   69

[Enter a man from Antonio.]

SERVANT. Gentlemen, my master Antonio is at his house, and desires to speak with you both.

SALERIO. We have been up and down to seek him.

[Enter Tubal.]

SOLANIO. Here comes another of the tribe, a third cannot be match'd, unless the devil himself turn Jew.

[Exeunt Gentlemen Solanio and Salerio with servant.]

SHYLOCK. How now Tubal? What news from Genoa? hast thou found my daughter?   76

TUBAL. I often came where I did hear of her, but cannot find her.

SHYLOCK. Why there, there, there, there! A diamond gone cost me two thousand ducats in Frankfort— the curse never fell upon our nation till now, I never felt it till now—two thousand ducats in that and

---

9. knapp'd: chewed. Ginger seems to have been associated with old women. **11. slips:** lapses. **15. full stop:** the period (punctuation mark); Salerio wants Solanio to finish his sentence. **25. wings:** the torch-bearer's suit. **27. fledge:** fledged, ready to fly. **complexion:** nature. **32. flesh and blood:** Shylock, of course, means his own child; Solanio chooses to take the phrase as meaning 'sensual desires and passion.' **33. carrion:** dead flesh, a common term of abuse. **40. Rhenish:** a white wine, considered less rich and strong than red. **42. match:** deal. **46. cursy:** courtesy.

50. bait: to use as bait for. **52. hind'red:** kept me from making. **65. what . . . humility?:** i.e. how does he show Christian charity? **66. sufferance:** patience. **74. cannot be match'd:** cannot be found to match them. **80. Frankfort:** an international fair was held there twice a year.

other precious precious jewels; I would my daughter were dead at my foot, and the jewels in her ear; would she were hears'd at my foot, and the ducats in her coffin: No news of them? Why so—and I know not what's spent in the search: why thou loss upon loss, the thief gone with so much, and so much to find the thief, and no satisfaction, no revenge, nor no ill luck stirring but what lights a my shoulders, no sighs but a my breathing, no tears but a my shedding. 91

TUBAL. Yes, other men have ill luck too—Antonio (as I heard in Genoa)—

SHYLOCK. What, what, what? ill luck, ill luck?

TUBAL. —hath an argosy cast away coming from Tripolis. 96

SHYLOCK. I thank God, thank God! is it true, is it true?

TUBAL. I spoke with some of the sailors that escaped the wrack. 100

SHYLOCK. I thank thee good Tubal, good news, good news! ha ha! heard in Genoa!

TUBAL. Your daughter spent in Genoa, as I heard, one night four-score ducats. 104

SHYLOCK. Thou stick'st a dagger in me, I shall never see my gold again, four-score ducats at a sitting? four score ducats!

TUBAL. There came divers of Antonio's creditors in my company to Venice, that swear, he cannot choose but break. 110

SHYLOCK. I am very glad of it, I'll plague him, I'll torture him; I am glad of it.

TUBAL. One of them showed me a ring that he had of your daughter for a monkey. 114

SHYLOCK. Out upon her! thou torturest me Tubal, it was my turkies; I had it of Leah when I was a bachelor; I would not have given it for a wilderness of monkeys. 119

TUBAL. But Antonio is certainly undone.

SHYLOCK. Nay, that's true, that's very true. Go Tubal fee me an officer; bespeak him a fortnight before, I will have the heart of him if he forfeit, for were he out of Venice I can make what merchandise I will. Go Tubal, and meet me at our synagogue; go good Tubal, at our synagogue Tubal. [Exeunt.]

SCENE II

[Enter Bassanio, Portia, Gratiano, Nerissa and all their trains.]

PORTIA. I pray you tarry, pause a day or two
Before you hazard, for in choosing wrong
I lose your company; therefore forbear a while.
There's something tells me (but it is not love)
I would not lose you, and you know yourself, 5
Hate counsels not in such a quality;
But lest you should not understand me well—
And yet a maiden hath no tongue, but thought—
I would detain you here some month or two
Before you venture for me. I could teach you 10
How to choose right, but then I am forsworn,
So will I never be—so may you miss me—
But if you do, you'll make me wish a sin,
That I had been forsworn. Beshrow your eyes,
They have ore-look'd me and divided me, 15
One half of me is yours, the other half yours,
Mine own I would say: but if mine then yours,
And so all yours; O these naughty times
Puts bars between the owners and their rights,
And so though yours not yours. Prove it so, 20
Let Fortune go to hell for it, not I.
I speak too long, but 'tis to peize the time,
To ech it, and to draw it out in length,
To stay you from election.
BASSANIO.   Let me choose,
For as I am, I live upon the rack. 25
PORTIA. Upon the rack Bassanio? then confess
What treason there is mingled with your love.
BASSANIO. None but that ugly treason of mistrust,
Which makes me fear th' enjoying of my love—
There may as well be amity and life 30
'Tween snow and fire, as treason and my love.
PORTIA. Ay, but I fear you speak upon the rack
Where men enforced do speak any thing.
BASSANIO. Promise me life, and I'll confess the truth.
PORTIA. Well then, confess and live.
BASSANIO.   'Confess and love'

---

85. hears'd: in her coffin. **91. a . . . shedding**: the *a*'s obviously represent *of 's*. **110. break**: become 'broke' or bankrupt. **116. turkies**: turquoise, a stone thought to have the power of reconciling man and wife. **122. fee me**: hire me. **124. make . . . merchandise**: drive what bargain.

1. day or two: note that by line 9 Portia refers to a month or two. **4. but . . . love**: Portia pays lip service to a maidenly modesty; but as the speech continues, she cannot conceal her feelings. **15. ore-look'd**: bewitched with the evil eye. **18. naughty**: wicked. **20. Prove it so**: if it prove so. **22. peize**: augment. **23. ech**: eke, increase. **29. fear**: fear for.

Had been the very sum of my confession. 36
O happy torment, when my torturer
Doth teach me answers for deliverance,
But let me to my fortune and the caskets.
PORTIA. Away then, I am lock'd in one of them,
If you do love me, you will find me out. 41
Nerissa and the rest, stand all aloof,
Let music sound while he doth make his choice,
Then if he lose, he makes a swanlike end,
Fading in music. That the comparison 45
May stand more proper, my eye shall be the stream
And wat'ry deathbed for him; he may win,
And what is music then? Then music is
Even as the flourish, when true subjects bow
To a new-crowned monarch. Such it is, 50
As are those dulcet sounds in break of day,
That creep into the dreaming bridegroom's ear,
And summon him to marriage. Now he goes
With no less presence, but with much more love
Than young Alcides, when he did redeem 55
The virgin tribute, paid by howling Troy
To the sea-monster; I stand for sacrifice,
The rest aloof are the Dardanian wives
With bleared visages come forth to view
The issue of th' exploit. Go Hercules! 60
Live thou, I live—with much much more dismay,
I view the fight, than thou that mak'st the fray.

[*A Song the whilst Bassanio comments on the caskets to himself.*]

[*Song.*]

> Tell me where is Fancy bred,
> Or in the heart, or in the head?
> How begot, how nourished? 65
> ALL. Reply, reply.
> It is engend'red in the eye,
> With gazing fed, and Fancy dies
> In the cradle where it lies
> Let us all ring Fancy's knell. 70

I'll begin it:
Ding, dong, bell.
ALL. Ding, dong, bell.

BASSANIO. So may the outward shows be least them-
selves,
The world is still deceiv'd with ornament— 75
In law, what plea so tainted and corrupt,
But being season'd with a gracious voice,
Obscures the show of evil? In religion
What damned error but some sober brow
Will bless it, and approve it with a text, 80
Hiding the grossness with fair ornament?
There is no vice so simple, but assumes
Some mark of virtue on his outward parts;
How many cowards whose hearts are all as false
As stairs of sand, wear yet upon their chins 85
The beards of Hercules and frowning Mars,
Who inward search'd, have livers white as milk?—
And these assume but valor's excrement
To render them redoubted. Look on beauty,
And you shall see 'tis purchas'd by the weight, 90
Which therein works a miracle in nature,
Making them lightest that wear most of it;
So are those crisped snaky golden locks
Which maketh such wanton gambols with the wind
Upon supposed fairness, often known 95
To be the dowry of a second head,
The skull that bred them, in the sepulcher.
Thus ornament is but the guiled shore
To a most dangerous sea, the beauteous scarf
Veiling an Indian beauty; in a word, 100
The seeming truth which cunning times put on
To entrap the wisest. Therefore then thou gaudy
gold,
Hard food for Midas, I will none of thee,
Nor none of thee thou pale and common
drudge 104
'Tween man and man; but thou, thou meager lead

44. swan . . . end: according to ancient belief the swan sang a sweet song just before its death, hence a 'swan song.' **51–53. dulcet . . . marriage:** it was the custom to play music beneath the bridegroom's window on the morning of his wedding day. **54. presence:** noble bearing. **55. Alcides:** Hercules, who rescued the daughter of the Trojan king from being sacrificed to a sea-monster, not for love but for the horses her father had promised him, see Ovid, *Metamorphoses* 11.199 ff. **58. Dardanian:** Trojan. **59. bleared:** tearful. **63. Fancy:** foolish affection or infatuation. **64. or . . . or:** either . . . or. **66. Reply, reply:** a choral refrain, like the final 'Ding, dong, bell.' **68–69. Fancy . . . lies:** i.e. infatuation is short-lived and shallow, never growing beyond the cradle stage (in the eye).

74. So . . . themselves: Bassanio's first words echo the tone of the song. **75. still:** always. **80. approve:** confirm. **87. livers . . . milk:** the liver of a coward was supposedly white, hence the expression, sometimes still used, 'lily-livered.' **88. excrement:** outgrowth, i.e. the 'beards' of l. 86, above. **93. crisped:** curled. **95. supposed:** fictitious. **96. dowry:** endowment. **97. skull . . . sepulcher:** Bassanio is speaking, of course, of the deceptive appearance of a wig, the hairs of which belonged rightfully to someone now dead. **98. guiled:** treacherous. **100. Indian beauty:** an Indian beauty would not have seemed beautiful to the Elizabethan. **103. hard . . . Midas:** all that King Midas touched, including food and drink, turned to gold; see Ovid, *Metamorphoses*, 11. **104–5. pale . . . man:** silver, the metal of common coins constantly passed between men.

Which rather threaten'st than dost promise aught,
Thy paleness moves me more than eloquence,
And here choose I—joy be the consequence!
PORTIA. How all the other passions fleet to air,   109
As doubtful thoughts, and rash embrac'd despair,
And shudd'ring fear, and green-eyed jealousy.
O love be moderate; allay thy ecstasy,
In measure rain thy joy, scant this excess!
I feel too much thy blessing, make it less
For fear I surfeit.
BASSANIO.   What find I here?   115
Fair Portia's counterfeit! What demi-god
Hath come so near creation? Move these eyes?
Or whether riding on the balls of mine
Seem they in motion? Here are sever'd lips
Parted with sugar breath, so sweet a bar   120
Should sunder such sweet friends: here in her hairs
The painter plays the spider, and hath woven
A golden mesh t' entrap the hearts of men
Faster than gnats in cobwebs; but her eyes—
How could he see to do them? Having made
    one,   125
Me thinks it should have power to steal both his
And leave itself unfurnish'd. Yet look how far
The substance of my praise doth wrong this shadow
In underprizing it—so far this shadow   129
Doth limp behind the substance. Here's the scroll,
The continent and summary of my fortune.

[Reads.]

You that choose not by the view
Chance as fair, and choose as true,
Since this fortune falls to you,
Be content, and seek no new.   135
If you be well pleas'd with this,
And hold your fortune for your bliss,
Turn you where your lady is,
And claim her with a loving kiss.

A gentle scroll. Fair lady, by your leave,   140
I come by note to give, and to receive,
Like one of two contending in a prize

That thinks he hath done well in people's eyes:
Hearing applause and universal shout,
Giddy in spirit, still gazing in a doubt   145
Whether those peals of praise be his or no,
So thrice fair lady stand I even so,
As doubtful whether what I see be true,
Until confirm'd, sign'd, ratified by you.   149
PORTIA. You see me Lord Bassanio where I stand,
Such as I am; though for my self alone
I would not be ambitious in my wish
To wish my self much better, yet for you,
I would be trebled twenty times my self,
A thousand times more fair, ten thousand
    times   155
More rich, that only to stand high in your account,
I might in virtues, beauties, livings, friends
Exceed account: but the full sum of me
Is sum of something: which to term in gross,
Is an unlesson'd girl, unschool'd, unpractis'd,   160
Happy in this, she is not yet so old
But she may learn; happier than this,
She is not bred so dull but she can learn;
Happiest of all, is that her gentle spirit
Commits itself to yours to be directed,   165
As from her lord, her governor, her king.
My self, and what is mine, to you and yours
Is now converted. But now I was the lord
Of this fair mansion, master of my servants,
Queen o'er myself, and even now, but now,   170
This house, these servants, and this same myself
Are yours, my lord's, I give them with this ring,
Which when you part from, lose, or give away,
Let it presage the ruin of your love,
And be my vantage to exclaim on you.   175
BASSANIO. Madam, you have bereft me of all words,
Only my blood speaks to you in my veins,
And there is such confusion in my powers,
As after some oration fairly spoke
By a beloved prince, there doth appear   180
Among the buzzing pleased multitude.
Where every something being blent together,
Turns to a wild of nothing, save of joy

107. paleness: lead is also pale, contrasted to 'gaudy gold,' above. 113. In . . . joy: send down thy joy in moderation; also a pun with 'rein.' Scant: diminish. 116. counterfeit: likeness. 117. Hath . . . creation: has painted such a lifelike picture. 118. Or whether: or. 127. unfurnish'd: i.e. with the other of the pair. 128. shadow: picture. 130. substance: the original 131. continent: container. 133. Chance as fair: have as fair a chance. 141. by note: by the instruction of the scroll, but also an allusion to a bill of dues. 142. prize: prize contest.

157. livings: incomes. 159. sum of something: Portia is playing on the sound of sum: she uses the vague term something, and goes on to itemize the sum in modest terms. Note the use of commercial terms again. to . . . gross: to give the full sum. 168. But now: only a moment ago. lord: i.e., the noble owner. Portia's use of such masculine terms lends greater force to ll. 170–72. 170. even now, but now: emphatic to stress the rapidity of change in the situation. 175. vantage: favorable opportunity; cf. the term 'advantage' in tennis scoring. exclaim on: reproach. 183. wild: wilderness; here used figuratively.

Express'd, and not express'd; but when this ring
Parts from this finger, then parts life from hence,
O then be bold to say Bassanio's dead.   186
NERISSA. My lord and lady, it is now our time
That have stood by and seen our wishes prosper,
To cry good joy, good joy my lord and lady!   189
GRATIANO. My Lord Bassanio, and my gentle lady,
I wish you all the joy that you can wish;
For I am sure you can wish none from me,
And when your honors mean to solemnize
The bargain of your faith I do beseech you
Even at that time I may be marri'd too.   195
BASSANIO. With all my heart, so thou canst get a wife.
GRATIANO. I thank your lordship; you have got me
   one.
My eyes my lord can look as swift as yours:
You saw the mistress, I beheld the maid;
You lov'd; I lov'd—for intermission.   200
No more pertains to me my lord than you;
Your fortune stood upon the caskets there,
And so did mine too, as the matter falls:
For wooing here until I sweat again,
And swearing till my very roof was dry   205
With oaths of love, at last (if promise last)
I got a promise of this fair one here
To have her love: provided that your fortune
Achiev'd her mistress.
PORTIA.   Is this true Nerissa?   209
NERISSA. Madam it is, so you stand pleas'd withal.
BASSANIO. And do you Gratiano mean good faith?
GRATIANO. Yes, faith my lord.
BASSANIO. Our feast shall be much honor'd in your
   marriage.
GRATIANO. We'll play with them the first boy for a
   thousand ducats.
NERISSA. What and stake down?   215
GRATIANO. No, we shall nere win at that sport and
   stake down.
  But who comes here? Lorenzo and his infidel!
What! and my old Venetian friend Salerio?

[*Enter Lorenzo, Jessica, and Salerio a messenger from
Venice.*]

BASSANIO. Lorenzo and Salerio, welcome hether,
If that the youth of my new int'rest here   220
Have power to bid you welcome. By your leave
I bid my very friends and countrymen,
Sweet Portia, welcome.
PORTIA.   So do I my lord,
They are entirely welcome.   224
LORENZO. I thank your honor; for my part, my lord,
My purpose was not to have seen you here,
But meeting with Salerio by the way
He did entreat me past all saying nay
To come with him along.
SALERIO.   I did my Lord,
And I have reason for it; Signior Antonio   230
Commends him to you. [*Gives Bassanio a letter.*]
BASSANIO.   Ere I ope this letter
I pray you tell me how my good friend doth.
SALERIO. Not sick my lord unless it be in mind,
Nor well, unless in mind; his letter there
Will show you his estate.   235

[*Bassanio opens the letter.*]

GRATIANO. Nerissa, cheer yond stranger, bid her wel-
   come.
Your hand Salerio, what's the news from Venice?
How doth that royal merchant good Antonio?
I know he will be glad of our success,
We are the Jasons, we have won the fleece.   240
SALERIO. I would you had won the fleece that he hath
   lost.
PORTIA. There are some shrowd contents in yond
   same paper.
That steals the color from Bassanio's cheek,
Some dear friend dead, else nothing in the world
Could turn so much the constitution   245
Of any constant man. What worse and worse?
With leave Bassanio, I am half your self,
And I must freely have the half of any thing
That this same paper brings you.
BASSANIO.   O sweet Portia,
Here are a few of the unpleasant'st words   250
That ever blotted paper. Gentle lady

192. you . . . me: i.e. you can wish nothing that I would not wish for
you. 196. so: provided. 200. intermission: respite, perhaps in the
sense of idling. 205. roof: i.e. of his mouth. 215. and . . . down:
a bawdy quibble. 216. nere: never.

220–21. If . . . welcome: if my new status (as Portia's betrothed)
gives me the right to welcome you (as a host would do). 222. very:
true. 234. unless in mind: unless he meets his losses philosophically. 235. estate: condition. 240. Jasons: although Antonio's
was the argosy. 241. you had: read 'you'd.' fleece: a pun on
'fleets.' 242. shrowd: shrewd, evil. 245. turn: change. constitution: five syllables here. 246. constant: steadfast.

When I did first impart my love to you,
I freely told you all the wealth I had
Ran in my veins—I was a gentleman,
And then I told you true; and yet dear lady   255
Rating my self at nothing, you shall see
How much I was a braggart. When I told you
My state was nothing, I should then have told you
That I was worse than nothing; for indeed
I have engag'd my self to a dear friend,   260
Engag'd my friend to his mere enemy
To feed my means. Here is a letter lady,
The paper as the body of my friend,
And every word in it a gaping wound
Issuing life blood. But is it true Salerio?   265
Hath all his ventures fail'd? What not one hit?
From Tripolis, from Mexico and England
From Lisbon, Barbary, and India,
And not one vessel scape the dreadful touch
of merchant-marring rocks?

SALERIO.   Not one my lord.   270
Besides, it should appear, that if he had
The present money to discharge the Jew,
He would not take it: never did I know
A creature that did bear the shape of man
So keen and greedy to confound a man.   275
He plies the duke at morning and at night,
And doth impeach the freedom of the state
If they deny him justice. Twenty merchants,
The duke himself, and the magnificoes
Of greatest port have all persuaded with him,   280
But none can drive him from the envious plea
Of forfeiture, of justice, and his bond.
JESSICA. When I was with him, I have heard him swear
To Tubal and to Chus, his countrymen,
That he would rather have Antonio's flesh   285
Than twenty times the value of the sum
That he did owe him; and I know, my lord,
If law, authority, and power deny not,
It will go hard with poor Antonio.
PORTIA. Is it your dear friend that is thus in
  trouble?   290
BASSANIO. The dearest friend to me, the kindest man,
  The best-condition'd and unweari'd spirit

In doing courtesies, and one in whom
The ancient Roman honor more appears
Than any that draws breath in Italy.   295
PORTIA. What sum owes he the Jew?
BASSANIO. For me, three thousand ducats.
PORTIA.   What, no
  more?
  Pay him six thousand, and deface the bonds.
  Double six thousand, and then treble that,
  Before a friend of this description   300
  Shall lose a hair through Bassanio's fault.
  First go with me to church, and call me wife,
  And then away to Venice to your friend:
  For never shall you lie by Portia's side
  With an unquiet soul. You shall have gold   305
  To pay the petty debt twenty times over.
  When it is paid, bring your true friend along,
  My maid Nerissa, and my self meantime
  Will live as maids and widows. Come away,
  For you shall hence upon your wedding day;   310
  Bid your friends welcome, show a merry cheer,
  Since you are dear bought, I will love you dear.
  But let me hear the letter of your friend.
BASSANIO. [Reads.] *Sweet Bassanio, my ships have all
  miscarried, my creditors grow cruel, my estate is very
  low, my bond to the Jew is forfeit, and since in paying
  it, it is impossible I should live, all debts are clear'd
  between you and I if I might but see you at my death;
  nothwithstanding, use your pleasure, if your love do
  not persuade you to come, let not my letter.*   321
PORTIA. O love! dispatch all business and be gone.
BASSANIO. Since I have your good leave to go away,
  I will make haste; but till I come again,
  No bed shall ere be guilty of my stay,   325
  Nor rest be interposer 'twixt us twain.

                                    [*Exeunt.*]

SCENE III

[*Enter Shylock the Jew, and Solanio, and Antonio, and the
Jailer.*]

SHYLOCK. Jailer, look to him, tell not me of mercy,
  This is the fool that lent out money gratis.
  Jailer, look to him.
ANTONIO.   Hear me yet good Shylock.
SHYLOCK. I'll have my bond; speak not against my
  bond,

---

260. engag'd: indebted. **261. mere:** absolute. **272. present:**
ready. **273. He:** i.e. Shylock. **275. keen:** savage, cruel. **con-**
found: ruin. **277. impeach:** call in question. **279. magnificoes:**
chief men of Venice. **280. port:** importance. **persuaded:** pleaded.
281. envious: malignant. **284. Chus:** (or *Cush*) (see Gen. 10:6–
8). **292. best-condition'd:** best-natured.

311. cheer: spirit.

I have sworn an oath, that I will have my bond: 5
Thou call'dst me dog before thou hadst a cause,
But since I am a dog, beware my fangs;
The duke shall grant me justice, I do wonder
Thou naughty jailer that thou art so fond
To come abroad with him at his request.   10
ANTONIO. I pray thee hear me speak.
SHYLOCK. I'll have my bond. I will not hear thee
        speak,
I'll have my bond, and therefore speak no more.
I'll not be made a soft and dull-ey'd fool,
To shake the head, relent, and sigh, and yield   15
To Christian intercessors. Follow not,
I'll have no speaking, I will have my bond.

[Exit Shylock the Jew.]

SOLANIO. It is the most impenetrable cur
That ever kept with men.
ANTONIO.   Let him along,
I'll follow him no more with bootless prayers,   20
He seeks my life, his reason well I know;
I oft deliver'd from his forfeitures
Many that have at times made moan to me,
Therefore he hates me.
SOLANIO. I am sure the duke will never grant   25
This forfeiture to hold.
ANTONIO. The duke cannot deny the course of law;
For the commodity that strangers have
With us in Venice, if it be denied,
Will much impeach the justice of the state,   30
Since that the trade and profit of the city
Consisteth of all nations. Therefore go,
These griefs and losses have so bated me
That I shall hardly spare a pound of flesh
Tomorrow, to my bloody creditor.   35
Well jailer on, pray God Bassanio come
To see me pay his debt, and then I care not.

[Exeunt.]

SCENE IV

[Enter Portia, Nerissa, Lorenzo, Jessica, and Balthazar, a man
of Portia's.]

9. naughty: wicked. fond: foolish. 16. intercessors: mediators.
19. kept: lived. 20. bootless: unavailing. 27. deny: prevent. 28.
commodity: convenience. 33. bated: dejected, and also reduced in
weight.

LORENZO. Madam, although I speak it in your pres-
        ence,
You have a noble and a true conceit
Of godlike amity, which appears most strongly
In bearing thus the absence of your lord.
But if you knew to whom you show this honor,   5
How true a gentleman you send relief,
How dear a lover of my lord your husband,
I know you would be prouder of the work
Than customary bounty can enforce you.
PORTIA. I never did repent for doing good,   10
Nor shall not now: for in companions
That do converse and waste the time together,
Whose souls do bear an egall yoke of love,
There must be needs a like proportion
Of lineaments, of manners, and of spirit;   15
Which makes me think that this Antonio
Being the bosom lover of my lord,
Must needs be like my lord. If it be so,
How little is the cost I have bestow'd
In purchasing the semblance of my soul,   20
From out the state of hellish cruelty;
This comes too near the praising of my self,
Therefore no more of it; hear other things.
Lorenzo I commit into your hands,
The husbandry and manage of my house,   25
Until my lord's return; for mine own part
I have toward heaven breath'd a secret vow,
To live in prayer and contemplation,
Only attended by Nerissa here,
Until her husband and my lord's return,   30
There is a monastery two miles off,
And there we will abide. I do desire you
Not to deny this imposition,
The which my love and some necessity
Now lays upon you.
LORENZO.   Madam, with all my heart,   35
I shall obey you in all fair commands.
PORTIA. My people do already know my mind,
And will acknowledge you and Jessica
In place of Lord Bassanio and my self.
So fare you well till we shall meet again.   40
LORENZO. Fair thoughts and happy hours attend on
        you.
JESSICA. I wish your ladyship all heart's content.

2. conceit: conception. 9. Than . . . you: than ordinary goodness
can incline you to be. 12. waste: spend, not necessarily waste-
ful. 13. egall: equal. 14. needs: of necessity. proportion: harmony. 17. bosom: intimate. 20. my soul: Bassanio. 25.
husbandry and manage: care and management. 33. imposition:
command.

PORTIA. I thank you for your wish, and am well
    pleas'd
    To wish it back on you: fare you well Jessica.

[Exeunt Jessica and Lorenzo.]

Now Balthazar, as I have ever found thee honest
    true,   45
    So let me find thee still. Take this same letter,
    And use thou all th' endeavor of a man,
    In speed to Mantua, see thou render this
    Into my cousin's hands, Doctor Bellario,   49
    And look what notes and garments he doth give
    thee,
    Bring them I pray thee with imagin'd speed
    Unto the traject, to the common ferry
    Which trades to Venice; waste no time in words
    But get thee gone, I shall be there before thee.   54
BALTHAZAR. Madam, I go with all convenient speed.

[Exit.]

PORTIA. Come on Nerissa, I have work in hand
    That you yet know not of; we'll see our husbands
    Before they think of us.
NERISSA.   Shall they see us?
PORTIA. They shall Nerissa, but in such a habit,
    That they shall think we are accomplished   60
    With that we lack; I'll hold thee any wager
    When we are both accouter'd like young men,
    I'll prove the prettier fellow of the two,
    And wear my dagger with the braver grace,
    And speak between the change of man and
    boy,   65
    With a reed voice, and turn two mincing steps
    Into a manly stride; and speak of frays
    Like a fine bragging youth; and tell quaint lies
    How honorable ladies sought my love,
    Which I denying, they fell sick and died.   70
    I could not do withal: then I'll repent,
    And wish for all that, that I had not kill'd them,
    And twenty of these puny lies I'll tell,
    That men shall swear I have discontinued school
    Above a twelve-month: I have within my mind   75
    A thousand raw tricks of these bragging Jacks,
    Which I will practise.

NERISSA.   Why, shall we turn to men?
PORTIA. Fie, what a question's that,
    If thou were near a lewd interpreter!
    But come, I'll tell thee all my whole device   80
    When I am in my coach, which stays for us
    At the park gate and therefore haste away,
    For we must measure twenty miles today.

              [Exeunt.]

SCENE V

[Enter Launcelot the Clown, and Jessica.]

LAUNCELOT. Yes truly, for look you, the sins of the
    father are to be laid upon the children, therefore I
    promise you, I fear you, I was always plain with you,
    and so now I speak my agitation of the matter:
    therefore be a good cheer, for truly I think you are
    damn'd; there is but one hope in it that can do you
    any good, and that is but a kind of bastard hope
    neither.
JESSICA. And what hope is that I pray thee?   9
LAUNCELOT. Marry you may partly hope that your
    father got you not, that you are not the Jew's
    daughter.
JESSICA. That were a kind of bastard hope indeed, so
    the sins of my mother should be visited upon me.
LAUNCELOT. Truly then I fear you are damn'd both
    by father and mother: thus when I shun Scylla your
    father, I fall into Charybdis your mother; well, you
    are gone both ways.
JESSICA. I shall be sav'd by my husband; he hath made
    me a Christian.   20
LAUNCELOT. Truly the more to blame he; we were
    Christians enow before, e'en as many as could well
    live one by another. This making of Christians will
    raise the price of hogs; if we grow all to be pork
    eaters, we shall not shortly have a rasher on the coals
    for money.   26

[Enter Lorenzo.]

JESSICA. I'll tell my husband Launcelot what you
    say—here he comes!

---

51. imagin'd: all imaginable. 52. traject: strait or ferry. 59. habit:
costume. 60. accomplished: equipped. 61. that: what. 65.
change: of voice. 68. quaint: ingenious. 71. I . . . withal: I could
not help it. 75. I have: read 'I've.' 76. Jacks: fellows.

3. I fear you: I fear for you. 4. agitation: malapropism for 'cogita-
tion.' 5. a: of. 16–17. Scylla . . . Charybdis: In Homer's *Odyssey*
Scylla was a monster who preyed upon seamen passing through the
Strait of Messina. Opposite her cave was the whirlpool of Charybdis. 22. enow: enough. 25. rasher: i.e. of bacon.

LORENZO. I shall grow jealous of you shortly Launcelot, if you thus get my wife into corners. 30

JESSICA. Nay, you need not fear us Lorenzo, Launcelot and I are out, he tells me flatly there's no
mercy for me in heaven, because I am a Jew's
daughter: and he says you are no good member of
the commonwealth, for in converting Jews to Christians, you raise the price of pork. 36

LORENZO. I shall answer that better to the common-
wealth than you can the getting up of the negro's
belly. The Moor is with child by you Launcelot!

LAUNCELOT. It is much that the Moor should be
more than reason; but if she be less than an honest
woman, she is indeed more than I took her for. 42

LORENZO. How every fool can play upon the word; I
think the best grace of wit will shortly turn into
silence, and discourse grow commendable in none
only but parrots. Go in sirrah, bid them prepare for
dinner. 47

LAUNCELOT. That is done sir, they have all stomachs! 49

LORENZO. Goodly Lord, what a wit-snapper are you;
then bid them prepare dinner!

LAUNCELOT. That is done too sir, only 'cover' is the
word.

LORENZO. Will you cover then sir?

LAUNCELOT. Not so sir neither, I know my duty. 55

LORENZO. Yet more quarreling with occasion! Wilt
thou show the whole wealth of thy wit in an instant?
I pray thee understand a plain man in his plain
meaning: go to thy fellows, bid them cover the
table, serve in the meat, and we will come in to
dinner. 60

LAUNCELOT. For the table sir, it shall be serv'd in; for
the meat sir, it shall be cover'd; for your coming in
to dinner sir, why let it be as humors and conceits
shall govern. [Exit Launcelot the Clown.]

LORENZO. O dear discretion, how his words are
suited! 65
The fool hath planted in his memory
An army of good words, and I do know
A many fools that stand in better place,
Garnish'd like him, that for a tricksy word
Defy the matter. How cheer'st thou Jessica? 70
And now good sweet, say thy opinion,
How dost thou like the Lord Bassanio's wife?

JESSICA. Past all expressing, it is very meet
The Lord Bassanio live an upright life
For having such a blessing in his lady, 75
He find the joys of heaven here on earth,
And if on earth he do not merit it,
In reason he should never come to heaven.
Why, if two gods should play some heavenly match,
And on the wager lay two earthly women, 80
And Portia one; there must be something else
Pawn'd with the other, for the poor rude world
Hath not her fellow.

LORENZO.   Even such a husband.
Hast thou of me, as she is for a wife.

JESSICA. Nay, but ask my opinion too of that. 85

LORENZO. I will anon, first let us go to dinner.

JESSICA. Nay, let me praise you while I have a stomach.

LORENZO. No pray thee, let it serve for table talk,
Then howsomere thou speak'st 'mong other things,
I shall digest it.

JESSICA.   Well, I'll set you forth. [Exeunt.]

Act IV

SCENE I

[Enter the Duke, the Magnificoes, Antonio, Bassanio, and
Gratiano (Salerio, and others).]

DUKE. What, is Antonio here?

ANTONIO. Ready, so please your grace.

DUKE. I am sorry for thee. Thou art come to answer

---

30. into corners: into secret places. 32. are out: have quarreled.
40–42. It . . . for: an elaborate punning on *Moor* and *more,* which
were pronounced alike. 41. reason: what is reasonable. 49. stomachs: appetites. 52. 'cover': lay the tablecloth. Launcelot puns on
cover, to cover the head. 56. quarreling . . . occasion: disputing at
every chance. 61. table: here Launcelot means the meal itself.

62. cover'd: served on a covered platter. 63. humors and conceits:
whims and fancies. 65. dear discretion: precious discrimination.
suited: adapted to the turns of conversation. 68. A many: many.
better place: better jobs. 69. Garnish'd: dressed. tricksy: smart.
70. Defy the matter: confuse the issue. how . . . thou: what
cheer? 82. Pawn'd: staked. 87. stomach: meaning (1) 'appetite,'
(2) 'inclination.' 89. howsomere: however. 90. set you forth:
praise you highly; the phrase also refers to laying out a feast.

A stony adversary, an inhuman wretch,
Uncapable of pity, void, and empty   5
From any dram of mercy.
ANTONIO.   I have heard
Your grace hath tane great pains to qualify
His rigorous course; but since he stands obdurate,
And that no lawful means can carry me
Out of his envy's reach, I do oppose   10
My patience to his fury, and am arm'd
To suffer with a quietness of spirit,
The very tyranny and rage of his.
DUKE. Go one and call the Jew into the court.   14
SALERIO. He is ready at the door, he comes my lord.

[Enter Shylock.]

DUKE. Make room, and let him stand before our face.
Shylock the world thinks, and I think so too,
That thou but lead'st this fashion of thy malice
To the last hour of act, and then 'tis thought   19
Thou'lt show thy mercy and remorse more strange,
Than is thy strange apparent cruelty;
And where thou now exactst the penalty,
Which is a pound of this poor merchant's flesh,
Thou wilt not only loose the forfeiture,
But touch'd with human gentleness and love,   25
Forgive a moity of the principal,
Glancing an eye of pity on his losses
That have of late so huddled on his back,
Enow to press a royal merchant down,
And pluck commiseration of his state   30
From brassy bosoms and rough hearts of flints,
From stubborn Turks, and Tartars never train'd
To offices of tender courtesy.
We all expect a gentle answer Jew!
SHYLOCK. I have possess'd your grace of what I pur-
    pose,   35
And by our holy Sabbath have I sworn
To have the due and forfeit of my bond.
If you deny it, let the danger light
Upon your charter and your city's freedom.
You'll ask me why I rather choose to have   40
A weight of carrion flesh, than to receive
Three thousand ducats: I'll not answer that,
But say it is my humor; is it answer'd?
What if my house be troubled with a rat,
And I be pleas'd to give ten thousand ducats   45

To have it baind? What, are you answer'd yet?
Some men there are love not a gaping pig,
Some that are mad if they behold a cat,
And others, when the bagpipe sings i' th' nose,
Cannot contain their urine; for affection,   50
Master of passion, sways it to the mood
Of what it likes or loathes—now for your answer:
As there is no firm reason to be rend'red
Why he cannot abide a gaping pig,
Why he a harmless necessary cat,   55
Why he a woolen bagpipe, but of force
Must yield to such inevitable shame,
As to offend, himself being offended;
So can I give no reason, nor I will not,
More than a lodg'd hate, and a certain loathing   60
I bear Antonio, that I follow thus
A losing suit against him. Are you answer'd?
BASSANIO. This is no answer, thou unfeeling man,
To excuse the current of thy cruelty.
SHYLOCK. I am not bound to please thee with my
    answers.   65
BASSANIO. Do all men kill the things they do not love?
SHYLOCK. Hates any man the thing he would not kill?
BASSANIO. Every offence is not a hate at first!
SHYLOCK. What, would'st thou have a serpent sting
    thee twice?
ANTONIO. I pray you think you question with the
    Jew—   70
You may as well go stand upon the beach,
And bid the main flood bate his usual height,
You may as well use question with the wolf,
Why he hath made the ewe bleak for the lamb:
You may as well forbid the mountain pines   75
To wag their high tops, and to make no noise
When they are fretten with the gusts of heaven:
You may as well do any thing most hard
As seek to soften that—than which what's harder?—
His Jewish heart. Therefore I do beseech you   80
Make no moe offers, use no farther means,
But with all brief and plain conveniency
Let me have judgment, and the Jew his will.

---

46. baind: poisoned.   47. gaping pig: the whole pig, head and all;
often served at a banquet.   50–52. for affection . . . loathes: for a
man's passion is governed by his likes and dislikes.   50. affection:
liking or disliking.   it: refers to 'my humor' l.43.   56. woolen: the
bag is commonly covered with cloth.   60. lodg'd: deep seated.   62.
losing suit: if Shylock wins his case, he will still have lost his money
and gained only a useless pound of flesh.   70. question: dispute.
72. main flood: ocean tide.   bate: lessen.   74. bleak: bleat. This
could be a misprint for 'bleat,' but 'blake' is a Somerset version of
'bleat' and had the same vowel sound.   77. fretten: fretted.   82.
conveniency: convenience.

---

7. qualify: moderate.   10. envy's: malice's.   13. tyranny: violence.   21. apparent: seeming; but also evident.   22. where:
whereas.   24. loose: release.   26. moity: moiety, portion.   33.
offices: duties.   35. possess'd: informed.   43. humor: whim.

BASSANIO. For thy three thousand ducats here is six.

SHYLOCK. If every ducat in six thousand ducats   85
  Were in six parts, and every part a ducat,
  I would not draw them, I would have my bond!

DUKE. How shalt thou hope for mercy rend'ring
  none?

SHYLOCK. What judgment shall I dread, doing no
  wrong?
  You have among you many a purchas'd slave,   90
  Which like your asses, and your dogs and mules
  You use in abject and in slavish parts,
  Because you bought them; shall I say to you,
  Let them be free, marry them to your heirs?
  Why sweat they under burthens? Let their beds   95
  Be made as soft as yours, and let their palates
  Be season'd with such viands? You will answer
  "The slaves are ours"—so do I answer you:
  The pound of flesh which I demand of him
  Is dearly bought, 'tis mine and I will have it.   100
  If you deny me, fie upon your law!
  There is no force in the decrees of Venice.
  I stand for judgment—answer, shall I have it?

DUKE. Upon my power I may dismiss this court,
  Unless Bellario, a learned doctor,   105
  Whom I have sent for to determine this,
  Come here today.

SALERIO.   My lord, here stays without
  A messenger with letters from the doctor,
  New come from Padua.

DUKE.   Bring us the letters. Call the
  messenger.

BASSANIO. Good cheer Antonio! What man, courage
  yet!   110
  The Jew shall have my flesh, blood, bones and all,
  Ere thou shalt lose for me one drop of blood!

ANTONIO. I am a tainted wether of the flock,
  Meetest for death—the weakest kind of fruit
  Drops earliest to the ground, and so let me;   115
  You cannot better be employ'd Bassanio,
  Than to live still and write mine epitaph.

[Enter Nerissa.]

DUKE. Came you from Padua from Bellario?

NERISSA. From both, my lord. Bellario greets your
  grace.

BASSANIO. Why dost thou whet thy knife so
  earnestly?   120

SHYLOCK. To cut the forfeiture from that bankrout
  there.

GRATIANO. Not on thy sole, but on thy soul, harsh
  Jew,
  Thou mak'st thy knife keen; but no metal can,
  No, not the hangman's axe bear half the keenness
  Of thy sharp envy; can no prayers pierce thee?   125

SHYLOCK. No, none that thou hast wit enough to
  make.

GRATIANO. O be thou damn'd, inexecrable dog!
  And for thy life let justice be accus'd;
  Thou almost mak'st me waver in my faith,
  To hold opinion with Pythagoras,   130
  That souls of animals infuse themselves
  Into the trunks of men: thy currish spirit
  Govern'd a wolf, who, hang'd for human slaughter,
  Even from the gallows did his fell soul fleet,
  And whilst thou lay'st in thy unhallow'd dam;   135
  Infus'd itself in thee; for thy desires
  Are wolvish, bloody, starv'd, and ravenous.

SHYLOCK. Till thou canst rail the seal from off my
  bond,
  Thou but offend'st thy lungs to speak so loud:
  Repair thy wit good youth, or it will fall   140
  To cureless ruin. I stand here for law.

DUKE. This letter from Bellario doth commend
  A young and learned doctor to our court.
  Where is he?

NERISSA.   He attendeth here hard by.   144
  To know your answer whether you'll admit him.

DUKE. With all my heart. Some three or four of you
  Go give him courteous conduct to this place,
  Meantime the court shall hear Bellario's letter.   148

[Reads.]

*Your Grace shall understand, that at the receipt of your
letter I am very sick, but in the instant that your
messenger came, in loving visitation was with me a
young doctor of Rome; his name is Balthazar. I
acquainted him with the cause in controversy between
the Jew and Antonio the merchant, we turn'd ore
many books together; he is furnished with my opinion,
which bettered with his own learning, the greatness
whereof I cannot enough commend, comes with him at
my importunity, to fill up your grace's request in my
stead. I beseech you let his lack of years be no impedi-*

---

87. **draw:** take.   92. **parts:** actions.   95. **burthens:** a common form of 'burdens.'   104. **Upon:** according to.   114. **Meetest:** best fit.

121. **bankrout:** bankrupt.   124. **hangman's:** executioner's.   127. **inexecrable:** abhorrent.   128. **And . . . accus'd:** let justice itself be accused for permitting you to live.   134. **fell:** cruel.   139. **offend'st:** injurest.   147. **conduct:** escort.

ment to let him lack a reverend estimation, for I
never knew so young a body with so old a head. I leave
him to your gracious acceptance, whose trial shall
better publish his commendation.   164

[*Enter Portia for Balthazar.*]

DUKE. You hear the learn'd Bellario what he writes,
  And here I take it, is the doctor come.
  Give me your hand, come you from old Bellario?
PORTIA. I did my lord.
DUKE.   You are welcome, take your
  place.
  Are you acquainted with the difference
  That holds this present question in the court?   170
PORTIA. I am informed throughly of the cause,—
  Which is the merchant here? and which the Jew?
DUKE. Antonio and old Shylock, both stand forth.
PORTIA. Is your name Shylock?
SHYLOCK.   Shylock is my name.
PORTIA. Of a strange nature is the suit you follow,
  Yet in such rule, that the Venetian law   176
  Cannot impugn you as you do proceed.
  You stand within his danger, do you not?
ANTONIO. Ay, so he says.
PORTIA.   Do you confess the bond?
ANTONIO. I do.
PORTIA.   Then must the Jew be merciful.   180
SHYLOCK. On what compulsion must I? Tell me that.
PORTIA. The quality of mercy is not strain'd,
  It droppeth as the gentle rain from heaven
  Upon the place beneath. It is twice blest:
  It blesseth him that gives, and him that takes,   185
  'Tis mightiest in the mightiest, it becomes
  The thronèd monarch better than his crown.
  His scepter shows the force of temporal power,
  The attribute to awe and majesty,
  Wherein doth sit the dread and fear of kings;   190
  But mercy is above this sceptred sway,
  It is enthroned in the hearts of kings,
  It is an attribute to God himself;
  And earthly power doth then show likest God's
  When mercy seasons justice. Therefore Jew,   195
  Though justice be thy plea, consider this,
  That in the course of justice, none of us
  Should see salvation. We do pray for mercy,
  And that same prayer doth teach us all to render

The deeds of mercy. I have spoke thus much   200
  To mitigate the justice of thy plea,
  Which if thou follow, this strict court of Venice
  Must needs give sentence 'gainst the merchant there.
SHYLOCK. My deeds upon my head, I crave the law,
  The penalty and forfeit of my bond.   205
PORTIA. Is he not able to discharge the money?
BASSANIO. Yes, here I tender it for him in the court,
  Yea, twice the sum; if that will not suffice,
  I will be bound to pay it ten times ore
  On forfeit of my hands, my head, my heart.   210
  If this will not suffice, it must appear
  That malice bears down truth. And I beseech you
  Wrest once the law to your authority;
  To do a great right, do a little wrong,
  And curb this cruel devil of his will.   215
PORTIA. It must not be, there is no power in Venice
  Can alter a decree established;
  'Twill be recorded for a precedent,
  And many an error by the same example
  Will rush into the state. It cannot be.   220
SHYLOCK. A Daniel come to judgment! yea a Daniel!
  O wise young judge how I do honor thee!
PORTIA. I pray you let me look upon the bond.
SHYLOCK. Here 'tis most reverend doctor, here it is.
PORTIA. Shylock, there's thrice thy money off'red
  thee.   225
SHYLOCK. An oath, an oath, I have an oath in heaven!
  Shall I lay perjury upon my soul?
  No, not for Venice.
PORTIA.   Why this bond is forfeit,
  And lawfully by this the Jew may claim
  A pound of flesh, to be by him cut off   230
  Nearest the merchant's heart. Be merciful,
  Take thrice thy money; bid me tear the bond.
SHYLOCK. When it is pay'd, according to the tenure.
  It doth appear you are a worthy judge,
  You know the law, your exposition   235
  Hath been most sound. I charge you by the law,
  Whereof you are a well-deserving pillar,
  Proceed to judgment. By my soul I swear,
  There is no power in the tongue of man
  To alter me, I stay here on my bond.   240
ANTONIO. Most heartily I do beseech the court
  To give the judgment.
PORTIA.   Why then, thus it is,
  You must prepare your bosom for his knife.

171. throughly: thoroughly. **176. rule:** order. **178. danger:** power. **184. blest:** full of blessing. **197–98. That . . . salvation:** i.e. if God's justice were not tempered by His mercy, we should all be damned.

219. error: miscarriage of justice. **221. Daniel:** from ancient times the name Daniel ('God is my judge') has been associated with righteous judgment. **233. tenure:** tenor, the actual wording of a legal document.

SHYLOCK. O noble judge! O excellent young man!

PORTIA. For the intent and purpose of the law   245
　Hath full relation to the penalty,
　Which here appeareth due upon the bond.

SHYLOCK. 'Tis very true, O wise and upright judge!
　How much more elder art thou than thy
　　looks!   249

PORTIA. Therefore lay bare your bosom.

SHYLOCK.   Ay, his breast;
　So says the bond, doth it not noble judge?
　'Nearest his heart,' those are the very words.

PORTIA. It is so; are there balance here to weigh the
　flesh?

SHYLOCK. I have them ready.

PORTIA. Have by some surgeon Shylock, on your
　charge,   255
　To stop his wounds, lest he do bleed to death.

SHYLOCK. Is it so nominated in the bond?

PORTIA. It is not so express'd, but what of that?
　'Twere good you do so much for charity.

SHYLOCK. I cannot find it, 'tis not in the bond.   260

PORTIA. You merchant, have you anything to say?

ANTONIO. But little. I am arm'd and well prepar'd,
　Give me your hand Bassanio, fare you well,
　Grieve not that I am falne to this for you;
　For herein Fortune shows herself more kind   265
　Than is her custom. It is still her use
　To let the wretched man outlive his wealth,
　To view with hollow eye and wrinkled brow
　An age of poverty; from which ling'ring penance
　Of such misery doth she cut me off.   270
　Commend me to your honorable wife;
　Tell her the process of Antonio's end;
　Say how I lov'd you, speak me fair in death;
　And when the tale is told, bid her be judge
　Whether Bassanio had not once a love.   275
　Repent but you that you shall lose your friend
　And he repents not that he pays your debt.
　For if the Jew do cut but deep enough,
　I'll pay it instantly with all my heart.

BASSANIO. Antonio, I am married to a wife   280
　Which is as dear to me as life itself,
　But life itself, my wife, and all the world,
　Are not with me esteem'd above thy life.
　I would lose all, ay sacrifice them all
　Here to this devil, to deliver you.

PORTIA. Your wife would give you little thanks for
　that

If she were by to hear you make the offer.

GRATIANO. I have a wife who I protest I love;
　I would she were in heaven, so she could
　Entreat some power to change this currish
　　Jew.   290

NERISSA. 'Tis well you offer it behind her back,
　The wish would make else an unquiet house.

SHYLOCK. These be the Christian husbands; I have a
　daughter—
　Would any of the stock of Barrabas
　Had been her husband, rather than a Christian.   295
　We trifle time, I pray thee pursue sentence.

PORTIA. A pound of that same merchant's flesh is
　thine,
　The court awards it, and the law doth give it.

SHYLOCK. Most rightful judge!

PORTIA. And you must cut this flesh from off his
　breast,   300
　The law allows it, and the court awards it.

SHYLOCK. Most learned judge! a sentence, come pre-
　pare

PORTIA. Tarry a little, there is something else;
　This bond doth give thee here no jot of blood,
　The words expressly are 'a pound of flesh'   305
　Take then thy bond, take thou thy pound of flesh,
　But in the cutting it, if thou dost shed
　One drop of Christian blood, thy lands and goods
　Are by the laws of Venice confiscate
　Unto the state of Venice.

GRATIANO.   O upright judge!   310

SHYLOCK. Is that the law?

PORTIA.   Thyself shall see the act;
　For as thou urgest justice, be assur'd
　Thou shalt have justice more than thou desir'st.

GRATIANO. O learned judge! mark Jew, a learned
　judge.   314

SHYLOCK. I take this offer then; pay the bond thrice
　And let the Christian go.

BASSANIO.   Here is the money.

PORTIA.   Soft,
　The Jew shall have all justice, soft, no haste!
　He shall have nothing but the penalty.

GRATIANO. O Jew, an upright judge, a learned
　judge!   319

PORTIA. Therefore prepare thee to cut off the flesh;
　Shed thou no blood, nor cut thou less nor more
　But just a pound of flesh; if thou tak'st more
　Or less than a just pound, be it but so much

246. Hath . . . to: is fully in accord with. 253. balance: scales, a plural form. 259. charity: from Latin *caritas;* spiritual (brotherly) love. 262. arm'd: ready. 264. falne: fallen.

288. who: whom. 293. be: are. 294. Barrabas: the name of Marlowe's Jew of Malta. 309. confiscate: confiscated (old past participle).

As makes it light or heavy in the substance,
Or the division of the twentieth part   325
Of one poor scruple, nay if the scale do turn
But in the estimation of a hair,
Thou diest, and all thy goods are confiscate.
GRATIANO. A second Daniel, a Daniel, Jew!
Now infidel, I have you on the hip.   330
PORTIA. Why doth the Jew pause? Take thy forfeiture.
SHYLOCK. Give me my principal, and let me go.
BASSANIO. I have it ready for thee, here it is.
PORTIA. He hath refus'd it in the open court,
He shall have merely justice and his bond.   335
GRATIANO. A Daniel still say I, a second Daniel!
I thank thee Jew for teaching me that word.
SHYLOCK. Shall I not have barely my principal?
PORTIA. Thou shalt have nothing but the forfeiture
To be so taken at thy peril Jew.   340
SHYLOCK. Why then the devil give him good of it.
I'll stay no longer question.
PORTIA.   Tarry Jew,
The law hath yet another hold on you.
It is enacted in the laws of Venice,
If it be prov'd against an alien,   345
That by direct, or indirect attempts
He seek the life of any citizen,
The party 'gainst the which he doth contrive,
Shall seize one half his goods, the other half
Comes to the privy coffer of the state,   350
And the offender's life lies in the mercy
Of the Duke only, 'gainst all other voice.
In which predicament I say thou stand'st:
For it appears by manifest proceeding,
That indirectly, and directly too   355
Thou hast contriv'd against the very life
Of the defendant; and thou hast incurr'd
The danger formerly by me rehears'd.
Down therefore, and beg mercy of the Duke.
GRATIANO. Beg that thou may'st have leave to hang
thyself,   360
And yet thy wealth being forfeit to the state,
Thou hast not left the value of a cord,
Therefore thou must be hang'd at the state's charge.
DUKE. That thou shalt see the difference of our spirit
I pardon thee thy life before thou ask it.   365
For half thy wealth, it is Antonio's,
The other half comes to the general state,
Which humbleness may drive unto a fine.

PORTIA. Ay, for the state, not for Antonio.
SHYLOCK. Nay, take my life and all, pardon not
that;   370
You take my house, when you do take the prop
That doth sustain my house. You take my life
When you do take the means whereby I live.
PORTIA. What mercy can you render him Antonio?
GRATIANO. A halter gratis, nothing else for God's
sake.   375
ANTONIO. So please my lord the Duke, and all the
court
To quit the fine for one-half of his goods,
I am content; so he will let me have
The other half in use, to render it
Upon his death unto the gentleman   380
That lately stole his daughter.
Two things provided more, that for this favor
He presently become a Christian:
The other, that he do record a gift
Here in the court of all he dies possess'd   385
Unto his son Lorenzo and his daughter.
DUKE. He shall do this, or else I do recant
The pardon that I late pronounced here.
PORTIA. Art thou contented Jew? What dost thou
say?   389
SHYLOCK. I am content.
PORTIA.   Clerk, draw a deed of gift.
SHYLOCK. I pray you give me leave to go from hence,
I am not well, send the deed after me,
And I will sign it.
DUKE.   Get thee gone, but do it.
GRATIANO. In christ'ning shalt thou have two god-
fathers,   394
Had I been judge, thou should'st have had ten
more,
To bring thee to the gallows, not to the font.

[Exit Shylock.]

DUKE. Sir, I entreat you home with me to dinner.
PORTIA. I humbly do desire your grace of pardon,
I must away this night toward Padua,
And it is meet I presently set forth.   400
DUKE. I am sorry that your leisure serves you not.
Antonio, gratify this gentleman,
For in my mind you are much bound to him.

[Exit Duke and his train.]

---

326. scruple: a minute portion (20 grains).   **330. on the hip:** at a disadvantage, a wrestling term, cf. I.3.45.   **342. I'll . . . question:** I'll wait no longer for questioning.   **348. contrive:** plot.   **368. which . . . fine:** i.e. which humility on your part may lead us to count as a fine (a lesser penalty than death).

377. quit: remit.   **378. so:** if.   **379. in use:** in trust.   **383. presently:** immediately.   **395. ten more:** i.e. a jury of twelve to pronounce the death sentence.   **402. gratify:** reward.

BASSANIO. Most worthy gentleman, I and my friend
  Have by your wisdom been this day acquitted   405
  Of grievous penalties, in lieu whereof,
  Three thousand ducats due unto the Jew
  We freely cope your courteous pains withal.
ANTONIO. And stand indebted over and above
  In love and service to you evermore.   410
PORTIA. He is well paid that is well satisfied,
  And I delivering you, am satisfied,
  And therein do account myself well paid,
  My mind was never yet more mercenary.
  I pray you know me when we meet again,   415
  I wish you well, and so I take my leave.
BASSANIO. Dear sir, of force I must attempt you
    further—
  Take some remembrance of us as a tribute,
  Not as fee; grant me two things I pray you—
  Not to deny me, and to pardon me.   420
PORTIA. You press me far, and therefore I will yield—
[To Antonio.] Give me your gloves, I'll wear them for
    your sake,
[To Bassanio.] And for your love I'll take this ring from
    you.
  Do not draw back your hand, I'll take no more,
  And you in love shall not deny me this!   425
BASSANIO. This ring good sir? alas it is a trifle,
  I will not shame myself to give you this!
PORTIA. I will have nothing else but only this,
  And now me thinks I have a mind to it!
BASSANIO. There's more depends on this than on the
    value.   430
  The dearest ring in Venice will I give you,
  And find it out by proclamation,
  Only for this I pray you pardon me!
PORTIA. I see sir you are liberal in offers,—
  You taught me first to beg, and now me
    thinks   435
  You teach me how a beggar should be answer'd.
BASSANIO. Good sir, this ring was given me by my
    wife,
  And when she put it on, she made me vow
  That I should neither sell, nor give, nor lose it.
PORTIA. That scuse serves many men to save their
    gifts—   440
  And if your wife be not a madwoman,

And know how well I have deserv'd this ring,
She would not hold out enemy for ever
For giving it to me. Well, peace be with you.   444

[Exeunt Portia and Nerissa.]

ANTONIO. My Lord Bassanio, let him have the ring,
  Let his deservings and my love withal
  Be valued 'gainst your wife's commandment.
BASSANIO. Go Gratiano, run and overtake him,
  Give him the ring, and bring him if thou canst
  Unto Antonio's house. Away, make haste!   450

[Exit Gratiano.]

Come, you and I will thither presently,
And in the morning early will we both
Fly toward Belmont. Come Antonio.   [Exeunt.]

SCENE II

[Enter Portia and Nerissa.]

PORTIA. Inquire the Jew's house out, give him this
    deed,
  And let him sign it, we'll away tonight,
  And be a day before our husbands home.
  This deed will be well welcome to Lorenzo!

[Enter Gratiano.]

GRATIANO. Fair sir, you are well oretane.   5
  My Lord Bassanio upon more advice,
  Hath sent you here this ring, and doth entreat
  Your company at dinner.
PORTIA.
                That cannot be;
  His ring I do accept most thankfully,
  And so I pray you tell him. Furthermore,   10
  I pray you show my youth old Shylock's house.
GRATIANO. That will I do.
NERISSA.   Sir, I would speak with you:
  [Aside.] I'll see if I can get my husband's ring
  Which I did make him swear to keep forever.
PORTIA. Thou may'st I warrant, we shall have old
    swearing   15

---

408. cope: requite.   414. My . . . mercenary: I have never been
much interested in monetary gain.   425. And . . . love: a common
polite phrase, though Portia is playing on the irony of the situation.   430. There's . . . value: i.e. more than the ring's value is at
stake.   440 scuse: a variant form of 'excuse.'

1. deed: deed of gift. There is a pun on the word in l. 4.   5. oretane:
overtaken.   6. advice: consideration.   15. old: any amount of.

That they did give the rings away to men;
But we'll outface them, and outswear them too:
Away, make haste, thou knowst where I will tarry.

NERISSA. Come good sir, will you show me to this
    house?

Act V

SCENE I

[*Enter Lorenzo and Jessica.*]

LORENZO. The moon shines bright. In such a night as
    this,
    When the sweet wind did gently kiss the trees,
    And they did make no noise, in such a night
    Troilus me thinks mounted the Trojan walls,
    And sigh'd his soul toward the Grecian tents   5
    Where Cressid lay that night.
JESSICA.   In such a night
    Did Thisbe fearfully oretrip the dew,
    And saw the lion's shadow ere himself,
    And ran dismay'd away.
LORENZO.   In such a night
    Stood Dido with a willow in her hand   10
    Upon the wild sea-banks, and waft her love
    To come again to Carthage.
JESSICA.   In such a night
    Medea gather'd the enchanted herbs
    That did renew old Aeson.
LORENZO.   In such a night
    Did Jessica steal from the wealthy Jew,   15
    And with an unthrift love did run from Venice,
    As far as Belmont.
JESSICA.
                In such a night
    Did young Lorenzo swear he lov'd her well,
    Stealing her soul with many vows of faith,
    And nere a true one.
LORENZO.   In such a night   20
    Did pretty Jessica (like a little shrow)
    Slander her love, and he forgave it her.
JESSICA. I would out-night you did no body come;
    But hark! I hear the footing of a man.

[*Enter a Messenger.*]

LORENZO. Who comes so fast in silence of the night?
MESSENGER. A friend!
LORENZO. A friend! What friend? Your name I pray
    you, friend?
MESSENGER. Stephano is my name, and I bring word
    My mistress will before the break of day
    Be here at Belmont, she doth stray about   30
    By holy crosses where she kneels and prays
    For happy wedlock hours.
LORENZO.   Who comes with her?
MESSENGER. None but a holy hermit and her maid.
    I pray you, is my master yet return'd?
LORENZO. He is not, nor we have not heard from
    him;   35
    But go we in, I pray thee, Jessica,
    And ceremoniously let us prepare
    Some welcome for the mistress of the house.

[*Enter Launcelot the Clown.*]

LAUNCELOT. Sola, sola: wo ha, ho sola, sola!
LORENZO. Who calls?   40
LAUNCELOT. Sola, did you see Master Lorenzo? Mas-
    ter Lorenzo. Sola, sola.
LORENZO. Leave hollowing man—here!
LAUNCELOT. Sola, where, where?
LORENZO. Here!   45
LAUNCELOT. Tell him there's a post come from my
    master, with his horn full of good news. My master
    will be here ere morning.   [*Exit.*]
LORENZO. Sweet soul, let's in, and there expect their
    coming
    And yet no matter; why should we go in?   50
    My friend Stephano, signify I pray you
    Within the house, your mistress is at hand,
    And bring your music forth into the air.

---

7. **oretrip:** run lightly over. 10. **willow:** the symbol of a foresaken lover. 11. **waft:** wafted. 14. **Aeson:** father of Jason. 16. **unthrift:** unthrifty. 21. **shrow:** shrew. 24. **footing:** footsteps.

31. **crosses:** wayside shrines. 39. **Sola . . . sola!:** Launcelot imitates the sound of a postboy's horn. 43. **hollowing:** yelling. 47. **horn:** Launcelot confuses (probably deliberately) the postboy's horn with a horn of plenty.

[*Exit Stephano.*]

How sweet the moonlight sleeps upon this bank,
Here will we sit, and let the sounds of music   55
Creep in our ears—soft stillness and the night
Become the touches of sweet harmony.
Sit Jessica, look how the floor of heaven
Is thick inlaid with patens of bright gold,   59
There's not the smallest orb which thou behold'st
But in his motion like an angel sings,
Still quiring to the young-ey'd cherubins;
Such harmony is in immortal souls,
But whilst this muddy vesture of decay
Doth grossly close it in, we cannot hear it: 65

[*Enter Musicians.*]

Come ho, and wake Diana with a hymn,
With sweetest touches pierce your mistress' ear,
And draw her home with music.

[*Play music.*]

JESSICA. I am never merry when I hear sweet music.
LORENZO. The reason is your spirits are attentive.
For do but note a wild and wanton herd   71
Or race of youthful and unhandled colts
Fetching mad bounds, bellowing and neighing loud,
Which is the hot condition of their blood;
If they but hear perchance a trumpet sound,   75
Or any air of music touch their ears,
You shall perceive them make a mutual stand,
Their savage eyes turn'd to a modest gaze,
By the sweet power of music. Therefore the poet
Did feign that Orpheus drew trees, stones, and
    floods,   80
Since naught so stockish hard and full of rage,
But music for the time doth change his nature.
The man that hath no music in himself,
Nor is not moved with concord of sweet sounds,
Is fit for treasons, stratagems, and spoils,   85
The motions of his spirit are dull as night,

And his affections dark as Erebus.
Let no such man be trusted. Mark the music.

[*Enter Portia and Nerissa.*]

PORTIA. That light we see is burning in my hall.
How far that little candle throws his beam!   90
So shines a good deed in a naughty world.
NERISSA. When the moon shone we did not see the
    candle.
PORTIA. So doth the greater glory dim the less,
A substitute shines brightly as a king
Until a king be by, and then his state   95
Empties itself, as doth an inland brook
Into the main of waters. Music, hark!
NERISSA. It is your music, madam, of the house.
PORTIA. Nothing is good I see without respect,—
Methinks it sounds much sweeter than by day.   100
NERISSA. Silence bestows that virtue on it, madam.
PORTIA. The crow doth sing as sweetly as the lark
When neither is attended; and I think
The nightingale if she should sing by day
When every goose is cackling, would be
    thought   105
No better a musician than the wren.
How many things by season, season'd are
To their right praise, and true perfection!
Peace!—how the moon sleeps with Endymion,
And would not be awak'd.
LORENZO.   That is the voice,   110
Or I am much deceiv'd of Portia.
PORTIA. He knows me as the blind man knows the
    cuckoo—
By the bad voice!
LORENZO.   Dear lady welcome home!
PORTIA. We have bin praying for our husbands' wel-
    fare,
Which speed we hope the better for our
    words.   115
Are they return'd?
LORENZO.   Madam, they are not yet;
But there is come a messenger before
To signify their coming.

---

57. become: befit. **59. patens:** shallow dishes or plates. **60–61. There's . . . sings:** cf. Job 38:7, "the morning stars sang together . . ." **62. Still:** always. **quiring:** choiring, singing. **64–65. But . . . it:** while the immortal soul is prisoner to the body, it cannot hear it. **70. spirits:** mental faculties. **72. race:** breed, but also perhaps a contest of speed. **77. mutual:** common. **79–80. Therefore . . . floods:** Orpheus, the musician of Thrace, about whom Ovid and others wrote, was so skilled that even inanimate objects fell under the spell of his music. **81. stockish hard:** unfeeling as a block. **85. spoils:** plunder.

87. Erebus: the term came to be synonymous with Hades. **91. naughty:** worthless, wicked. **97. main of waters:** ocean. **99. Nothing . . . respect:** nothing is absolutely good—the quality of goodness varies according to the circumstances. **103. attended:** listened to. **107. season:** appropriate occasion. **108. perfection:** four syllables here. **109. how . . . Endymion:** Diana, the chaste goddess of the moon, fell in love with the shepherd Endymion and caused him to sleep forever on Mt. Latmos. Portia refers to Lorenzo and Jessica.

PORTIA.   Go in Nerissa.
  Give order to my servants, that they take
  No note at all of our being absent hence,   120
  Nor you Lorenzo, Jessica, nor you.
LORENZO. Your husband is at hand, I hear his
  trumpet,
  We are no tell-tales, madam, fear you not.
PORTIA. This night me thinks is but the daylight sick,
  It looks a little paler, 'tis a day,   125
  Such as the day is when the sun is hid.

[Enter Bassanio, Antonio, Gratiano, and their followers.]

BASSANIO. We should hold day with the Antipodes,
  If you would walk in absence of the sun.
PORTIA. Let me give light, but let me not be light,
  For a light wife doth make a heavy husband,   130
  And never be Bassanio so for me,
  But God sort all. You are welcome home my lord.
BASSANIO. I thank you, madam—give welcome to my
  friend,
  This is the man, this is Antonio,
  To whom I am so infinitely bound.   135
PORTIA. You should in all sense be much bound to
  him,
  For as I hear he was much bound for you.
ANTONIO. No more than I am well acquitted of.
PORTIA. Sir, you are very welcome to our house:
  It must appear in other ways than words,   140
  Therefore I scant this breathing courtesy.
GRATIANO. By yonder moon I swear you do me
  wrong!
  In faith I gave it to the judge's clerk!
  Would he were gelt that had it for my part,
  Since you do take it love, so much at heart.   145
PORTIA. A quarrel ho, already, what's the matter?
GRATIANO. About a hoop of gold, a paltry ring
  That she did give to me, whose posy was
  For all the world like cutler's poetry
  Upon a knife, 'Love me and leave me not.'   150
NERISSA. What, talk you of the posy or the value?
  You swore to me when I did give it you,

That you would wear it till your hour of death,
And that it should lie with you in your grave.   154
Though not for me, yet for your vehement oaths,
You should have been respective and have kept it.
Gave it a judge's clerk! No, God's my judge,
The clerk will nere wear hair on's face that had it.
GRATIANO. He will, and if he live to be a man.
NERISSA. Ay, if a woman live to be a man.   160
GRATIANO. Now by this hand I gave it to a youth,
  A kind of boy, a little scrubbed boy,
  No higher than thyself, the judge's clerk,
  A prating boy that begg'd it as a fee—
  I could not for my heart deny it him.   165
PORTIA. You were to blame, I must be plain with you,
  To part so slightly with your wife's first gift,
  A thing stuck on with oaths upon your finger,
  And so riveted with faith unto your flesh.
  I gave my love a ring, and made him swear   170
  Never to part with it, and here he stands:
  I dare be sworn for him he would not leave it,
  Nor pluck it from his finger, for the wealth
  That the world masters. Now in faith Gratiano,
  You give your wife too unkind a cause of grief,
  And 'twere to me I should be mad at it.   176
BASSANIO. *[Aside.]* Why I were best to cut my left
  hand off,
  And swear I lost the ring defending it.
GRATIANO. My Lord Bassanio gave his ring away
  Unto the judge that begg'd it, and indeed   180
  Deserv'd it too; and then the boy his clerk
  That took some pains in writing, he begg'd mine,
  And neither man nor master would take ought
  But the two rings.
PORTIA.   What ring gave you my Lord?
  Not that, I hope, which you receiv'd of me   185
BASSANIO. If I could add a lie unto a fault,
  I would deny it; but you see my finger
  Hath not the ring upon it, it is gone.
PORTIA. Even so void is your false heart of truth.
  By heaven I will nere come in your bed   190
  Until I see the ring!
NERISSA.   Nor I in yours.
  Till I again see mine.
BASSANIO.   Sweet Portia,
  If you did know to whom I gave the ring,
  If you did know for whom I gave the ring,
  And would conceive for what I gave the ring,   195
  And how unwillingly I left the ring,

127–28. We . . . sun: if you walk in the night, it becomes day, as it now is on the other side of the earth. Bassanio has overheard Portia's last speech, and pays her a loving compliment. **129–30. Let . . . husband:** Portia quibbles on *light* as (1) 'sunshine,' (2) 'immoral' or 'faithless,' and (3) 'absence of weight,' figuratively, as in 'light-hearted' (by implication when she speaks of a 'heavy husband'). **132. sort:** arrange. **136. in all sense:** in all reason, or in every way. **141. breathing:** of mere words. **144. gelt:** gelded. **148. Posy:** engraved motto. Rings were often so engraved, and occasionally so were knives. **150. leave:** part with.

156. respective: careful. **159. and if:** if. **162. scrubbed:** scrubby. **172. leave:** cf. l. 150, above. **176. And:** if.

When naught would be accepted but the ring,
You would abate the strength of your displeasure!

PORTIA. If you had known the virtue of the ring,
  Or half her worthiness that gave the ring,   200
  Or your own honor to contain the ring,
  You would not then have parted with the ring.
  What man is there so much unreasonable
  If you had pleas'd to have defended it
  With any terms of zeal, wanted the modesty   205
  To urge the thing held as a ceremony?
  Nerissa teaches me what to believe,
  I'll die for't but some woman had the ring!

BASSANIO. No, by my honor, madam, by my soul
  No woman had it, but a civil doctor,   210
  Which did refuse three thousand ducats of me,
  And begg'd the ring, the which I did deny him,
  And suffer'd him to go displeas'd away,
  Even he that had held up the very life   214
  Of my dear friend. What should I say, sweet lady?
  I was enforc'd to send it after him,
  I was beset with shame and courtesy,
  My honor would not let ingratitude
  So much besmear it. Pardon me, good lady,
  For by these blessed candles of the night,   220
  Had you been there, I think you would have begg'd
  The ring of me to give the worthy doctor.

PORTIA. Let not that doctor ere come near my house
  Since he hath got the jewel that I lov'd,
  And that which you did swear to keep for me,   225
  I will become as liberal as you,
  I'll not deny him any thing I have,
  No, not my body, nor my husband's bed.
  Know him I shall, I am well sure of it.   229
  Lie not a night from home. Watch me like Argus,
  If you do not, if I be left alone,
  Now by mine honor which is yet mine own,
  I'll have that doctor for my bedfellow.

NERISSA. And I his clerk: therefore be well advis'd
  How you do leave me to mine own
    protection.   235

GRATIANO. Well, do you so; let not me take him then,
  For if I do, I'll mar the young clerk's pen.

ANTONIO. I am th' unhappy subject of these quarrels.

PORTIA. Sir, grieve not you—you are welcome notwithstanding.   239

BASSANIO. Portia, forgive me this enforced wrong,

And in the hearing of these many friends
I swear to thee, even by thine own fair eyes
Wherein I see myself.

PORTIA.   Mark you but that!
  In both my eyes he doubly sees himself:
  In each eye one—swear by your double self,   245
  And there's an oath of credit.

BASSANIO.   Nay, but hear me.
  Pardon this fault, and by my soul I swear
  I never more will break an oath with thee.

ANTONIO. I once did lend my body for his wealth,
  Which but for him that had your husband's
    ring   250
  Had quite miscarri'd. I dare be bound again,
  My soul upon the forfeit, that your lord
  Will never more break faith advisedly.

PORTIA. Then you shall be his surety: give him this,
  And bid him keep it better than the other.   255

ANTONIO. Here Lord Bassanio, swear to keep this
  ring.

BASSANIO. By heaven it is the same I gave the doctor.

PORTIA. I had it of him; pardon me Bassanio,
  For by this ring the doctor lay with me.

NERISSA. And pardon me my gentle Gratiano,   260
  For that same scrubbed boy, the doctor's clerk,
  In lieu of this, last night did lie with me.

GRATIANO. Why this is like the mending of highways
  In summer where the ways are fair enough!
  What, are we cuckolds ere we have deserv'd it?   265

PORTIA. Speak not so grossly—you are all amaz'd;
  Here is a letter, read it at your leisure,
  It comes from Padua from Bellario,
  There you shall find that Portia was the doctor,
  Nerissa there her clerk, Lorenzo here   270
  Shall witness I set forth as soon as you,
  And even but now return'd. I have not yet
  Enter'd my house. Antonio you are welcome,
  And I have better news in store for you
  Than you expect. Unseal this letter soon;   275
  There you shall find three of your argosies
  Are richly come to harbor suddenly.
  You shall now know by what strange accident
  I chanced on this letter.

ANTONIO.   I am dumb!

BASSANIO. Were you the doctor, and I knew you
  not?   280

---

199. **virtue:** power. **201. contain:** retain. **205–6. wanted . . . ceremony:** would have lacked the sensitivity to have urged you to keep it as a sacred symbol. **220. these . . . night:** these stars. **226. liberal:** a quibble: (1) 'generous,' (2) 'licentious.' **230. from:** away from. **Argus:** who had a hundred eyes.

249. **wealth:** welfare. **262. in lieu of:** in return for. **263–64. Why . . . enough:** i.e. Gratiano and Bassanio were made to suffer shame when they were guiltless. **266. grossly:** (1) 'stupidly,' (2) 'indelicately.'

GRATIANO. Were you the clerk that is to make me
   cuckold?

NERISSA. Ay, but the clerk that never means to do it,
   Unless he live until he be a man.

BASSANIO. Sweet doctor, you shall be my bedfellow,
   When I am absent then lie with my wife.   285

ANTONIO. Sweet lady, you have given me life and
   living;
   For here I read for certain that my ships
   Are safely come to road.

PORTIA.   How now Lorenzo?
   My clerk hath some good comforts too for you.

NERISSA. Ay, and I'll give them him without a fee.
   There do I give to you and Jessica   291
   From the rich Jew a special deed of gift
   After his death, of all he dies possess'd of.

LORENZO. Fair ladies, you drop manna in the way

Of starved people.

PORTIA.   It is almost morning,   295
   And yet I am sure you are not satisfied
   Of these events at full. Let us go in,
   And charge us there upon inter'gatories,
   And we will answer all things faithfully.

GRATIANO. Let it be so, the first inter'gatory   300
   That my Nerissa shall be sworn on, is,
   Whether till the next night she had rather stay,
   Or go to bed now being two hours to day.
   But were the day come, I should wish it dark
   Till I were couching with the doctor's clerk.   305
   Well, while I live, I'll fear no other thing
   So sore, as keeping safe Nerissa's ring.

[Exeunt.]

FINIS

---

286. living: wealth. **288. road:** anchorage.   **307. ring:** a bawdy pun, like *pen*, l. 237.

ESSAY: AN APPROACH TO THE PLAY

Despite *Merchant*'s apparently happy ending, there are several factors to consider which might make us wonder how happy the ending actually is. One is the issue of money. The villain Shylock is a Jew who is criticized by the Christian Venetians for charging interest when he lends money. They argue that the Bible says it is unnatural for something not alive (such as gold and silver) to reproduce itself. They prefer a social economy that functions through a myth of spontaneous generosity. By example, the merchant Antonio is in the middle of a cash-flow crisis (all his inventory is on the high seas), so he borrows money from Shylock to lend *without* interest to his friend Bassanio. Bassanio in turn needs this money in order to woo Portia in the style to which aristocratic young ladies are accustomed. However, if he is successful in his wooing, as her husband he will also be legal master of Portia's fortune, which he needs to pay off his prior debts to Antonio. The purity of Bassanio's love for Portia and his motive for wooing her are, therefore, inescapably compromised. And Antonio's motive for making the deal with Shylock may not be so selfless as he says it is either, since without that loan Bassanio will never be able to pay him back.

    A second problematized issue is ethnicity (this could be related to Portia's racism in the caskets plot—see her final speeches in 1.2 and 2.7, as well as Morocco's opening of 2.1). Shylock, like all Jews, is denied Venetian citizenship; he is treated badly by the Christians because he is a Jew, a point Antonio makes clear in the third scene. Shylock is therefore able to say that the revenge he tries to take on Antonio by removing a pound of flesh is actually justice, that he is merely imitating the Christians in wanting vengeance. He is, he says, just like them in all important ways; they have taught him how to behave, and they deserve whatever they get. He makes his case so memorably that we may be prepared to condemn the hypocrisy of the Christian Venetians—but then how do we read a comic ending which seems to reward them and reinforce their values? We may instead continue at the end to sympathize with Shylock, who is defeated in part by having been defined as an "alien" (4.1.345). Does the play consciously ask us to celebrate a comic triumph awarded to racists? (Or are such reservations raised only by a later, "politically correct" reading?)

A third problematic issue is Portia's triumphant feminism. At the beginning of the play, in the contest over the caskets, her authority derives from the position she is given by her dead father's will. In the trial scene in Act 4, her authority comes from her ability to impersonate a male lawyer. And in Act 5 her power comes from her ability to manipulate her husband. This Venice is sexist as well as racist. Even a very clever woman can empower herself only in relation to men and within terms established by a male-dominated power structure. Thus she says that in her disguise as a lawyer in Act 4 she will exaggerate the way young men behave in order to show how silly they are.

Because her role was played in Shakespeare's time by a boy, her high "reed voice" (3.4.66) will be heard by the audience even when she pretends to be a man. We are, therefore, constantly reminded during the trial scene that it is a woman who uses Shylock's own weapon, the letter of the law, more stringently even than he. We may be glad for this double cleverness when she defeats Shylock, for we have probably hoped that Antonio would be freed. She may seem our proxy onstage, doing what we would like to have done. However, when she continues to use Shylock's weapon against him, tightening the logic of the law into a straitjacket, forcing him on threat of death to give up everything—his daughter, his wealth, his religion—we may feel uncomfortable. She does not seem to give Shylock the mercy which earlier she had urged him to give Antonio. If her only objective is to save Antonio, she does not need to destroy Shylock so completely. Does her behavior also carry out the audience's desire to break Shylock? Portia's similarity to Shylock in both method and purpose may imply our similarity as well: How much are we like our proxy, and how uneasy is the comic celebration of the ending?

Her manipulation of her new husband in Act 5 may also be more than good fun. Perhaps Shakespeare is here reminding us about the injustices we ourselves frequently commit and our need to find some way to avoid them. The fairy tale elements of the caskets plot may seem unbelievable, but they teach a lesson whose truth becomes more complex and more palpable as the rest of the play unfolds: Things are not as they seem. This is true of subsequent events in the play—and perhaps of us and our lives as well.

William Shakespeare

HAMLET

Edited and with notes by Tucker Brooke and Jack Randall Crawford

About the Play   Hamlet seems to be an idealistic college student caught in an evil or at least mysterious world who is given a morally complex task: In Act 1, the ghost of his dead father asks him to kill his murderer. The moral complexity of this demand is intensified by the fact that the murderer is Claudius, the man who is also Hamlet's stepfather and the king. Killing, even in revenge, is against the law of the church. Seeking private vengeance violates the law of the land. Killing of a relative violates the kinship code. And killing the king in Shakespeare's age was considered an outrage, a sacrilege against God's anointed representative. The ghost has called upon Hamlet to act in a way that breaks powerful social, ecclesiastical, and political taboos.

In traversing this moral minefield, Hamlet behaves in a generally sympathetic way. Given the difficulty he faces, we might even think him heroic. And yet he treats the only women in the play brutishly, continually reprimands himself for delaying the vengeance he seems to believe in, unfeelingly kills his girlfriend's father and two old school friends, and at times seems literally out of his mind. It is often tempting to consider him too weak for his mission, misogynistic, even villainous. This uncertainty about the character of Hamlet is echoed in the play. Near the end of Act 1 he warns his friend Horatio that he will sometimes "put an antic disposition on" (1.5.171), that he will sometimes pretend to be mad. In Act 2, several characters make different guesses about why he seems so disturbed. All this may encourage us, too, to join the game of psychoanalyzing Hamlet. In addition, he is playing a deadly cat-and-mouse game with Claudius—he wants to be certain of his guilt before acting—and the heightened tension of this plot reinforces our desire to understand the character.

Yet as often as he speaks obliquely, he also speaks rationally, most obviously when talking to the players or when talking about playing. Part of his game is setting up the play within the play in 3.2, which reenacts crucial elements of what happened before *Hamlet* began and influences everything which follows. In fact there is much playing in this play, on several levels, and a great deal of espionage in which characters observe one another, in some ways acting like a theater audience. Polonius teaches his son Laertes how to seem the ideal man (1.3), then instructs Reynaldo on how to spy on him (2.1), while at the same time he himself is acting for Claudius as a spy on Hamlet. Rosencrantz and Guildenstern, and even Ophelia, are also recruited in this spy game, and in one way or another, Hamlet will be implicated in the deaths of them all.

As a result, the play keeps its focus on the problem of seeing the difference between "seeming" of various kinds and the underlying reality. At the center of this motif is Hamlet, who is the subject not only of everybody else's speculations but also of his own: He is uncertain about what to do, or even whether he wants to live. His play within the play, "The Murder of Gonzago," reminds us that the whole of *Hamlet* is itself also make-believe, even while it exercises real power in the world of the play *Hamlet*, both on the character who produces it and on many of those in its audience who watch it. This is, then, a philosophical play as well as a crime drama, one which questions the nature of reality and even questions whether we can know anything with certainty in a world of misleading appearances.

The relations of parents and children are also an important element in this play. There are three father-and-son pairs, as well as one daughter and one mother. It is interesting to contrast the ways in which the parents in three different families treat their children, and perhaps even more important to see the contrasts among the ways the children respond to their parents. The most complex of these familial situations is Hamlet's; contrasting his with the others' is likely to clarify our understanding of him and of the play.

CHARACTERS

CLAUDIUS, the new king of Denmark.

HAMLET, son to the late, and nephew to the present king. ·

FORTINBRAS, prince of Norway.

POLONIUS, a lord and high official (probably Lord Chamberlain).

LAERTES, his son.

HORATIO, the friend of Hamlet.

VOLTIMAND, courtier.

CORNELIUS, courtier.

ROSENCRANTZ, courtier.

GUILDENSTERN, courtier.

OSRIC, courtier.

MARCELLUS, a Danish officer.

FRANCISCO, soldier on sentry duty.

BERNARDO, soldier on sentry duty.

REYNALDO, servant to Polonius.

A Norwegian captain.

Players on tour.

Two clowns, gravediggers.

English ambassador, a priest, a gentleman, soldiers, sailor, messenger, and various attendants.

GERTRUDE, queen of Denmark and mother of Hamlet.

OPHELIA, daughter of Polonius.

GHOST of Hamlet's father.

[SCENE: the royal castle of Elsinore (Helsingør), Denmark, and its environs.]

Act I

SCENE I

Elsinore. Platform of the Castle

[*Enter Bernardo and Francisco, two Sentinels.*]

BERNARDO. Who's there?

FRANCISCO. Nay, answer me; stand, and unfold yourself.

BERNARDO. Long live the king!

FRANCISCO. Bernardo?   4

BERNARDO. He.

FRANCISCO. You come most carefully upon your hour.

BERNARDO. 'Tis now struck twelve; get thee to bed, Francisco.

FRANCISCO. For this relief much thanks; 'tis bitter cold,   8
And I am sick at heart.

BERNARDO. Have you had quiet guard?

FRANCISCO.   Not a mouse stirring.

BERNARDO. Well, good night.
If you do meet Horatio and Marcellus,   12
The rivals of my watch, bid them make haste.

[*Enter Horatio and Marcellus.*]

FRANCISCO. I think I hear them. Stand, ho! Who is there?

HORATIO. Friends to this ground.

MARCELLUS.   And liegemen to the Dane.

FRANCISCO. Give you good night.

MARCELLUS.   O, farewell, honest soldier.   16
Who hath reliev'd you?

FRANCISCO.   Bernardo hath my place.
Give you good night. [*Exit Francisco.*]

S. d. **Platform:** level space on castle ramparts.

13. rivals: partners.   **16. Give you:** God give you.

MARCELLUS.   Holla! Bernardo!

BERNARDO.   Say,—
  What, is Horatio there?

HORATIO.   A piece of him.

BERNARDO. Welcome, Horatio; welcome, good Mar-
    cellus.   20

MARCELLUS. What, has this thing appear'd again to-
    night?

BERNARDO. I have seen nothing.

MARCELLUS. Horatio says 'tis but our fantasy,
  And will not let belief take hold of him   24
  Touching this dreaded sight twice seen of us.
  Therefore I have entreated him along
  With us to watch the minutes of this night,
  That if again this apparition come,   28
  He may approve our eyes and speak to it.

HORATIO. Tush, tush! 'twill not appear.

BERNARDO.   Sit down
    awhile,
  And let us once again assail your ears,
  That are so fortified against our story,   32
  What we have two nights seen.

HORATIO.   Well, sit we down,
  And let us hear Bernardo speak of this.

BERNARDO. Last night of all,
  When yond same star that's westward from the
      pole   36
  Had made his course t' illume that part of heaven
  Where now it burns, Marcellus and myself,
  The bell then beating one,—

[Enter Ghost.]

MARCELLUS. Peace! break thee off; look, where it
    comes again!   40

BERNARDO. In the same figure, like the king that's
    dead.

MARCELLUS. Thou art a scholar; speak to it, Horatio.

BERNARDO. Looks 'a not like the king? mark it,
    Horatio.

HORATIO. Most like: it harrows me with fear and
    wonder.   44

BERNARDO. It would be spoke to.

MARCELLUS.   Question it,
    Horatio.

HORATIO. What art thou that usurp'st this time of
    night,

Together with that fair and warlike form
In which the majesty of buried Denmark   48
Did sometimes march? by heaven I charge thee,
    speak!

MARCELLUS. It is offended.

BERNARDO.   See! it stalks away.

HORATIO. Stay! speak, speak! I charge thee, speak!

[Exit Ghost.]

MARCELLUS. 'Tis gone, and will not answer.   52

BERNARDO. How now, Horatio! you tremble and
    look pale.
  Is not this something more than fantasy?
  What think you on 't?

HORATIO. Before my God, I might not this
      believe   56
  Without the sensible and true avouch
  Of mine own eyes.

MARCELLUS.   Is it not like the king?

HORATIO. As thou art to thyself:
  Such was the very armor he had on   60
  When he the ambitious Norway combated;
  So frown'd he once, when, in an angry parle,
  He smote the sleaded pole-axe on the ice.
  'Tis strange.   64

MARCELLUS. Thus twice before, and jump at this dead
      hour,
  With martial stalk hath he gone by our watch.

HORATIO. In what particular thought to work I know
      not;
  But in the gross and scope of my opinion,   68
  This bodes some strange eruption to our state.

MARCELLUS. Good now, sit down, and tell me, he
      that knows,
  Why this same strict and most observant watch
  So nightly toils the subject of the land;   72
  And why such daily cast of brazen cannon,
  And foreign mart for implements of war;
  Why such impress of shipwrights, whose sore task
  Does not divide the Sunday from the week;   76
  What might be toward, that this sweaty haste
  Doth make the night joint-laborer with the day:
  Who is't that can inform me?

---

23. **fantasy:** imagination. **29. approve:** confirm. **31. assail your ears:** i.e., try to tell you. **43. 'a:** dialect form of 'he' (sometimes 'it'). **mark:** observe closely.

49. **sometimes:** formerly. **57. sensible:** involving the use of one of the senses. **avouch:** assurance. **62. parle:** verbal encounter. **63. sleaded:** weighted (as a sledge-hammer). **pole-axe:** battle-ax. **65. jump:** just. **67. thought:** train of thinking. **68. gross and scope:** general drift. **72. toils:** causes to toil. **subject:** people, subjects. **73. cast:** founding. **74. mart:** traffic. **75. impress:** enforced service. **77. toward:** in preparation.

HORATIO.   That can I;
  At least, the whisper goes so. Our last king,   80
  Whose image even but now appear'd to us,
  Was, as you know, by Fortinbras of Norway,
  Thereto prick'd on by a most emulate pride,
  Dar'd to the combat; in which our valiant
    Hamlet   84
  (For so this side of our known world esteem'd him,)
  Did slay this Fortinbras; who by a seal'd compact,
  Well ratified by law and heraldry,
  Did forfeit with his life all those his lands   88
  Which he stood seiz'd of, to the conqueror;
  Against the which a moiety competent
  Was gaged by our king, which had return'd
  To the inheritance of Fortinbras,   92
  Had he been vanquisher; as, by the same cov'nant,
  And carriage of the article design'd,
  His fell to Hamlet. Now, sir, young Fortinbras,
  Of unimproved mettle hot and full,   96
  Hath in the skirts of Norway here and there
  Shark'd up a list of lawless resolutes,
  For food and diet, to some enterprise
  That hath a stomach in 't; which is no other,
  As it doth well appear unto our state,   101
  But to recover of us by strong hand
  And terms compulsatory, those foresaid lands
  So by his father lost. And this, I take it,   104
  Is the main motive of our preparations,
  The source of this our watch and the chief head
  Of this post-haste and romage in the land.
BERNARDO. I think it be no other but e'en so;   108
  Well may it sort that this portentous figure
  Comes armed through our watch, so like the king
  That was and is the question of these wars.
HORATIO. A mote it is to trouble the mind's eye.   112
  In the most high and palmy state of Rome,
  A little ere the mightiest Julius fell,
  The graves stood tenantless and the sheeted dead
  Did squeak and gibber in the Roman streets.   116
  [Astounding portents fill'd the element,]

As stars with trains of fire and dews of blood,
Disasters in the sun; and the moist star
Upon whose influence Neptune's empire stands
Was sick almost to doomsday with eclipse;   120
And even the like precurse of fear'd events,
As harbingers preceding still the fates
And prologue to the omen coming on,
Have heaven and earth together demonstrated
Unto our climatures and countrymen.   125

[*Enter Ghost again.*]

But, soft, behold! lo, where it comes again!
I'll cross it, though it blast me. Stay, illusion!
If thou hast any sound, or use of voice,   128
Speak to me!   [*It spreads his arms.*]
If there be any good thing to be done,
That may to thee do ease and grace to me,
Speak to me!   132
If thou art privy to thy country's fate,
Which happily foreknowing may avoid,
O speak!
Or if thou hast uphoarded in thy life   136
Extorted treasure in the womb of earth,
For which, they say, you spirits oft walk in death,

[*The cock crows.*]

Speak of it: stay, and speak! Stop it, Marcellus.   139
MARCELLUS. Shall I strike at it with my partisan?
HORATIO. Do, if it will not stand.
BERNARDO.   'Tis here!
HORATIO.   'Tis here!

[*Exit Ghost.*]

MARCELLUS. 'Tis gone!
  We do it wrong, being so majestical,
  To offer it the show of violence;   144
  For it is, as the air, invulnerable,
  And our vain blows malicious mockery.
BERNARDO. It was about to speak when the cock
  crew.
HORATIO. And then it started like a guilty thing
  Upon a fearful summons. I have heard,   149
  The cock, that is the trumpet to the morn,

---

83. **prick'd on:** incited. **emulate:** ambitious. **85. this side . . . world:** i.e., all Europe. **89. seiz'd of:** possessed of. **90. moiety competent:** equal amount. **91. gaged:** staked. **94. carriage:** import. **design'd:** drawn up. **96. unimproved mettle:** untested courage. **hot and full:** exceedingly ardent. **97. skirts:** outskirts. **98. Shark'd up:** picked up at haphazard. **resolutes:** desperadoes. **103. compulsatory:** involving compulsion. **106. head:** origin. **107. romage:** commotion, bustle. **109. sort:** fit. **112. mote:** minute particle of dust. **113. palmy state:** flourishing sovereignty.

118. **As:** such as. **119. Disasters:** unfavorable omens. **moist star:** moon. **121. precurse:** heralding. **122. still:** constantly. **123. prologue:** introduction. **omen:** catastrophe. **127. cross:** meet, face. **129. s.d. his:** its (the ghost's). **131. [do] grace:** do honor to. **134. happily:** haply.

Doth with his lofty and shrill-sounding throat
Awake the god of day; and at his warning,   152
Whether in sea or fire, in earth or air,
Th' extravagant and erring spirit hies
To his confine; and of the truth herein
This present object made probation.   156
MARCELLUS. It faded on the crowing of the cock.
  Some say that ever 'gainst that season comes
  Wherein our Saviour's birth is celebrated,
  This bird of dawning singeth all night long   160
  And then, they say, no spirit dare stir abroad;
  The nights are wholesome; then no planets strike,
  No fairy takes, nor witch hath power to charm,
  So hallow'd and so gracious is that time.   164
HORATIO. So have I heard and do in part believe it.
  But, look, the morn in russet mantle clad,
  Walks o'er the dew of yon high eastward hill.
  Break we our watch up; and by my advice   168
  Let us impart what we have seen to-night
  Unto young Hamlet, for, upon my life,
  This spirit, dumb to us, will speak to him.
  Do you consent we shall acquaint him with it,
  As needful in our loves, fitting our duty?   173
MARCELLUS. Let's do 't, I pray; and I this morning
      know
  Where we shall find him most conveniently. [Exeunt.]

SCENE II

The King's Council Chamber

[Flourish. Enter Claudius King of Denmark, Gertrude the
Queen, members of the Council as Polonius and his son
Laertes, Voltimand and Cornelius, Hamlet, cum aliis.]

KING. Though yet of Hamlet our dear brother's death
  The memory be green, and that it us befitted
  To bear our hearts in grief and our whole kingdom
  To be contracted in one brow of woe,   4
  Yet so far hath discretion fought with nature
  That we with wisest sorrow think on him,
  Together with remembrance of ourselves.
  Therefore our sometime sister, now our queen,   8

Th' imperial jointress of this warlike state,
Have we, as 'twere with a defeated joy,
With an auspicious and a dropping eye,
With mirth in funeral and with dirge in
    marriage,   12
In equal scale weighing delight and dole,
Taken to wife. Nor have we herein barr'd
Your better wisdoms, which have freely gone
With this affair along. For all, our thanks.   16
Now follows that you know young Fortinbras,
Holding a weak supposal of our worth,
Or thinking by our late dear brother's death
Our state to be disjoint and out of frame,   20
Colleagued with this dream of his advantage.
He hath not fail'd to pester us with message,
Importing the surrender of those lands
Lost by his father with all bands of law   24
To our most valiant brother. So much for him.
Now for ourself and for this time of meeting.
Thus much the business is: we have here writ
To Norway, uncle of young Fortinbras,   28
Who, impotent and bed-rid, scarcely hears
Of this his nephew's purpose, to suppress
His further gait herein in that the levies,
The lists and full proportions are all made   32
Out of his subject; and we here dispatch
You, good Cornelius, and you, Voltimand,
For bearers of this greeting to old Norway,
Giving to you no further personal power   36
To business with the king more than the scope
Of these delated articles allow.
Farewell and let your haste commend your duty.
CORNELIUS. ⎱ In that and all things will we show our
VOLTIMAND. ⎰ duty.   40
KING. We doubt it nothing: heartily farewell.

[Exeunt Voltimand and Cornelius.]

And now, Laertes, what's the news with you?
You told us of some suit; what is't, Laertes?
You cannot speak of reason to the Dane,   44
And lose your voice. What wouldst thou beg,
    Laertes,

154. **extravagant:** vagrant. **erring:** wandering. **hies:** hastens.
155. **confine:** place of confinement. 156. **probation:** proof.
158. **'gainst that:** by the time that. 163. **takes:** bewitches. 164.
gracious: instinct with goodness. 166. **russet:** gray or reddish-
brown (betokening dull weather)
I. ii. s.d. **Flourish:** a trumpet call. 4. **one brow of woe:** unanimity
of sorrow.

9. **jointress:** joint possessor. 10. **defeated:** dispirited. 11. **an auspicious:** one happy. **a dropping:** one tearful. 13. **dole:** grief. 17.
Now . . . know: I must next inform you. 18. **weak supposal:** low
opinion. 20. **disjoint:** at loose ends. **frame:** order. 21. **Colleagued . . . advantage:** conspired with himself to profit by this imaginary opportunity. 23. **Importing:** bearing as its purport. 24.
bands: assurances. 31. **gait:** proceeding. **in that:** because. 32.
proportions: supplies, forces. 33. **his subject:** liegemen of Norway. 38. **delated:** expressly stated. 45. **lose your voice:** speak to
no purpose.

That shall not be my offer, not thy asking?
The head is not more native to the heart,
The hand more instrumental to the mouth,   48
Than is the throne of Denmark to thy father.
What wouldst thou have, Laertes?
LAERTES.   Dread my lord,
Your leave and favor to return to France;
From whence though willingly I came to
    Denmark,   52
To show my duty in your coronation,
Yet now, I must confess, that duty done,
My thoughts and wishes bend again toward France
And bow them to your gracious leave and
    pardon.   56
KING. Have you your father's leave? What says Polo-
    nius?
POLONIUS. He hath, my lord, wrung from me my
    slow leave
By laborsome petition, and at last
Upon his will I seal'd my hard consent.   60
I do beseech you, give him leave to go.
KING. Take thy fair hour, Laertes; time be thine,
And thy best graces spend it at thy will.
But now, my cousin Hamlet, and my son,—   64
HAMLET. [Aside.] A little more than kin, and less than
    kind.
KING. How is it that the clouds hang on you?
HAMLET. Not so, my lord; I am too much i' th' sun.
QUEEN. Good Hamlet, cast thy nighted color
    off,   68
And let thine eye look like a friend on Denmark.
Do not for ever with thy vailed lids
Seek for thy noble father in the dust.
Thou know'st 'tis common; all that lives must
    die,   72
Passing through nature to eternity.
HAMLET. Ay, madam, it is common.
QUEEN.   If it be,
Why seems it so particular with thee?
HAMLET. Seems, madam! Nay, it is; I know not
    'seems.'   76
'Tis not alone my inky cloak, good mother,
Nor customary suits of solemn black,
Nor windy suspiration of forc'd breath,

No, nor the fruitful river in the eye,   80
Nor the dejected havior of the visage,
Together with all forms, moods, shapes of grief
That can denote me truly. These indeed seem,
For they are actions that a man might play: 84
But I have that within which passes show;
These but the trappings and the suits of woe.
KING. 'Tis sweet and cómmendable in your nature,
    Hamlet,
To give these mourning duties to your father.   88
But, you must know, your father lost a father;
That father lost, lost his, and the survivor bound
In filial obligation for some term
To do obsequious sorrow; but to perséver   92
In obstinate condolement is a course
Of impious stubbornness; 'tis unmanly grief.
It shows a will most incorrect to heaven,
A heart unfortified, a mind impatient,   96
An understanding simple and unschool'd:
For what we know must be and is as common
As any the most vulgar thing to sense,
Why should we in our peevish opposition   100
Take it to heart? Fie! 'tis a fault to heaven,
A fault against the dead, a fault to nature,
To reason most absurd, whose common theme
Is death of fathers, and who still hath cried,   104
From the first corse till he that died to-day,
'This must be so.' We pray you, throw to earth
This unprevailing woe, and think of us
As of a father; for let the world take note,   108
You are the most immediate to our throne,
And with no less nobility of love
Than that which dearest father bears his son
Do I impórtune you. For your intent   112
In going back to school in Wittenberg,
It is most retrograde to our desire;
And we beseech you, bend you to remain
Here in the cheer and comfort of our eye,   116
Our chiefest courtier, cousin, and our son.
QUEEN. Let not thy mother lose her prayers, Hamlet.
I pray thee, stay with us; go not to Wittenberg.
HAMLET. I shall in all my best obey you,
    madam.   120

---

47. **native:** closely and congenitally connected. **48. instrumental:** serviceable. **50. Dread my lord:** my revered lord. **51. leave and favor:** kind permission. **56. leave and pardon:** indulgence [to depart]. **60. hard:** given with difficulty. **63. graces:** virtues. **64. cousin:** nephew **70. vailed:** down-cast. **72. common:** the common lot. **75. particular:** personal. **79. windy suspiration:** tempestuous sighing. **forc'd:** against one's will.

80. **fruitful:** copious. **81. havior:** behavior. **83. denote:** portray. **90. bound:** was bound. **92. obsequious:** dutiful. **93. condolement:** sorrowing. **95. incorrect to:** unchastened toward. **99. vulgar . . . sense:** common experience. **105. corse:** corpse. **106. throw to earth:** drop (like a burden on one's back). **107. unprevailing:** unavailing. **109. most immediate:** next in succession. **114. retrograde:** contrary. **115. bend:** incline.

KING. Why, 'tis a loving and a fair reply!
  Be as ourself in Denmark.—Madam, come.
  This gentle and unforc'd accord of Hamlet
  Sits smiling to my heart; in grace whereof,   124
  No jocund health that Denmark drinks to-day,
  But the great cannon to the clouds shall tell,
  And the king's rouse the heavens shall bruit again,
  Re-speaking earthly thunder. Come away.   128

[*Flourish. Exeunt all but Hamlet.*]

HAMLET. O that this too too solid flesh would melt,
  Thaw and resolve itself into a dew!
  Or that the Everlasting had not fix'd
  His canon 'gainst self-slaughter! O God! God!   132
  How weary, stale, flat, and unprofitable
  Seem to me all the uses of this world.
  Fie on 't! ah, fie! 'tis an unweeded garden,
  That grows to seed; things rank and gross in
     nature   136
  Possess it merely. That it should come to this!
  But two months dead! nay, not so much, not two.
  So excellent a king, that was to this
  Hyperion to a satyr; so loving to my mother   140
  That he might not beteem the winds of heaven
  Visit her face too roughly. Heaven and earth!
  Must I remember? why, she would hang on him,
  As if increase of appetite had grown   144
  By what it fed on; and yet, within a month,—
  Let me not think on 't! Frailty, thy name is woman.
  A little month; or ere those shoes were old
  With which she follow'd my poor father's body,
  Like Niobe, all tears, why she,   149
  O God! a beast, that wants discourse of reason,
  Would have mourn'd longer,—married with my
     uncle,
  My father's brother, but no more like my father
  Than I to Hercules. Within a month,   153
  Ere yet the salt of most unrighteous tears
  Had left the flushing in her galled eyes,
  She married. O most wicked speed, to post
  With such dexterity to incestuous sheets.   157
  It is not, nor it cannot come to, good.—
  But break, my heart, for I must hold my tongue.

[*Enter Horatio, Marcellus and Bernardo.*]

HORATIO. Hail to your lordship!
HAMLET.   I am glad to see you
  well.
  Horatio! or I do forget myself.
HORATIO. The same, my lord, and your poor servant
  ever.
HAMLET. Sir, my good friend; I'll change that name
  with you.
  And what make you from Wittenberg, Horatio?
  Marcellus?   165
MARCELLUS. My good lord.—
HAMLET. I am very glad to see you. [*To Bernardo.*]
  Good even, sir.
  But what, in faith, make you from Wittenberg?
HORATIO. A truant disposition, good my lord.   169
HAMLET. I would not hear your enemy say so,
  Nor shall you do my ear that violence,
  To make it truster of your own report   172
  Against yourself; I know you are no truant.
  But what is your affair in Elsinore?
  We'll teach you to drink deep ere you depart.
HORATIO. My lord, I came to see your father's
  funeral.   176
HAMLET. I prithee, do not mock me, fellow-student.
  I think it was to see my mother's wedding.
HORATIO. Indeed, my lord, it follow'd hard upon.
HAMLET. Thrift, thrift, Horatio! the funeral bak'd
  meats   180
  Did coldly furnish forth the marriage tables.
  Would I had met my dearest foe in heaven
  Or ever I had seen that day, Horatio!
  My father, methinks I see my father.   184
HORATIO. Where, my lord?
HAMLET.   In my mind's eye,
  Horatio.
HORATIO. I saw him once; 'a was a goodly king.
HAMLET. 'A was a man! take him for all in all,
  I shall not look upon his like again.   188
HORATIO. My lord, I think I saw him yesternight.
HAMLET. Saw? Who?
HORATIO. My lord, the king your father.
HAMLET.   The king,
  my father?
HORATIO. Season your admiration for a while   192
  With an attent ear, till I may deliver,

---

127. **rouse:** revelry, 'carousing'. **bruit:** echo. 130. **resolve:** dissolve. 132. **canon:** divine law. 134. **uses:** usages. 137. **merely:** entirely. 141. **beteem:** allow. 150. **discourse of reason:** reasoning power. 155. **left the flushing:** ceased to produce redness. **galled:** sore with weeping. 156. **post:** hasten. 157. **dexterity:** facility.

163. **change that name:** share the name of friend. 169. **disposition:** temperament. 180. **bak'd meats:** meat pies. 181. **coldly:** when cold. 182. **dearest:** direst. 183. **Or:** before. 192. **Season:** temper, qualify. **admiration:** wonder. 193. **attent:** attentive.

Upon the witness of these gentlemen,
This marvel to you.
HAMLET.   For God's love, let me hear.
HORATIO. Two nights together had these
    gentlemen,   196
Marcellus and Bernardo, on their watch,
In the dead waste and middle of the night,
Been thus encounter'd: a figure like your father,
Armed at point exactly, cap-a-pe,   200
Appears before them, and with solemn march
Goes slow and stately by them. Thrice he walk'd
By their oppress'd and fear-surprised eyes,
Within his truncheon's length; whilst they,
    distill'd   204
Almost to jelly with the act of fear,
Stand dumb and speak not to him. This to me
In dreadful secrecy impart they did,
And I with them the third night kept the watch;
Where, as they had deliver'd, both in time,   209
Form of the thing, each word made true and good,
The apparition comes. I knew your father;
These hands are not more like.
HAMLET.   But where was this?
MARCELLUS. My lord, upon the platform where we
    watch.   213
HAMLET. Did you not speak to it?
HORATIO.   My lord, I did;
But answer made it none; yet once methought
It lifted up it head and did address   216
Itself to motion, like as it would speak;
But even then the morning cock crew loud,
And at the sound it shrunk in haste away
And vanish'd from our sight.
HAMLET.   'Tis very strange.   220
HORATIO. As I do live, my honor'd lord, 'tis true;
And we did think it writ down in our duty
To let you know of it.
HAMLET. Indeed, indeed, sirs, but this troubles
    me.   224
Hold you the watch to-night?
ALL.   We do, my lord.
HAMLET. Arm'd, say you?
ALL.   Arm'd, my lord.
HAMLET.   From top
    to toe?
ALL. My lord, from head to foot.
HAMLET. Then saw you not his face.   228

HORATIO. O yes, my lord; he wore his beaver up.
HAMLET. What! look'd he frowningly?
HORATIO. A countenance more in sorrow than in
    anger.
HAMLET. Pale or red?   232
HORATIO. Nay, very pale.
HAMLET.   And fix'd his eyes upon you?
HORATIO. Most constantly.
HAMLET.   I would I had been there.
HORATIO. It would have much amaz'd you.
HAMLET.   Very like.   236
Stay'd it long?
HORATIO.   While one with moderate haste
Might tell a hundreth.
BOTH.   Longer, longer.
HORATIO. Not when I saw 't.
HAMLET.   His beard was grizzled, no?
HORATIO. It was, as I have seen it in his life,   240
A sable silver'd.
HAMLET.   I will watch to-night;
Perchance 'twill walk again.
HORATIO.   I warr'nt it will.
HAMLET. If it assume my noble father's person,
I'll speak to it, though hell itself should gape 244
And bid me hold my peace. I pray you all,
If you have hitherto conceal'd this sight,
Let it be tenable in your silence still;
And whatsomever else shall hap to-night,   248
Give it an understanding, but no tongue.
I will requite your loves. So, fare you well.
Upon the platform, 'twixt eleven and twelve,
I'll visit you.
ALL.   Our duty to your honor.   252
HAMLET. Your loves, as mine to you. Farewell.

[*Exeunt all but Hamlet.*]

My father's spirit in arms! all is not well;
I doubt some foul play. Would the night were
    come!
Till then sit still, my soul: foul deeds will rise,   256
Though all the earth o'erwhelm them, to men's
    eyes.

[*Exit.*]

---

200. **at point:** in full readiness.   **cap-a-pe:** from head to foot.   204. **truncheon:** officer's staff.   **distill'd:** melted.   205. **act:** operation.   216. **it:** its.

229. **beaver:** face-guard of a helmet.   238. **tell:** count.   **hundreth:** hundred (a Norse form).   239. **grizzled:** grey.   241. **sable:** heraldic term for black.   247. **Let . . . tenable:** see that you keep it.   248. **whatsomever:** whatever.

SCENE III

Polonius' Apartment in the Castle

[*Enter Laertes and Ophelia, his sister.*]

LAERTES. My necessaries are embark'd; farewell:
  And, sister, as the winds give benefit
  And convoy is assistant, do not sleep,
  But let me hear from you.
OPHELIA.   Do you doubt that?   4
LAERTES. For Hamlet, and the trifling of his favor,
  Hold it a fashion and a toy in blood,
  A violet in the youth of primy nature,
  Forward, not permanent, sweet, not lasting,   8
  The perfume and suppliance of a minute;
  No more.
OPHELIA.   No more but so?
LAERTES.   Think it no more:
  For nature crescent does not grow alone
  In thews and bulk, but as this temple waxes,   12
  The inward service of the mind and soul
  Grows wide withal. Perhaps he loves you now,
  And now no soil nor cautel doth besmirch
  The virtue of his will; but you must fear.   16
  His greatness weigh'd, his will is not his own,
  For he himself is subject to his birth.
  He may not, as unvalu'd persons do,
  Carve for himself, for on his choice depends   20
  The safety and health of this whole state;
  And therefore must his choice be circumscrib'd
  Unto the voice and yielding of that body
  Whereof he is the head. Then if he says he loves
    you,   24
  It fits your wisdom so far to believe it
  As he in his particular act and place
  May give his saying deed; which is no further
  Than the main voice of Denmark goes withal.   28
  Then weigh what loss your honor may sustain,
  If with too credent ear you list his songs,

Or lose your heart, or your chaste treasure open
  To his unmaster'd importunity.   32
  Fear it, Ophelia, fear it, my dear sister;
  And keep you in the rear of your affection,
  Out of the shot and danger of desire.
  The chariest maid is prodigal enough   36
  If she unmask her beauty to the moon;
  Virtue itself 'scapes not calumnious strokes;
  The canker galls the infants of the spring
  Too oft before their buttons be disclos'd,   40
  And in the morn and liquid dew of youth
  Contagious blastments are most imminent.
  Be wary then; best safety lies in fear:
  Youth to itself rebels, though none else near.   44
OPHELIA. I shall the effect of this good lesson keep,
  As watchman to my heart. But, good my brother,
  Do not, as some ungracious pastors do,
  Show me the steep and thorny way to heaven,
  Whiles, like a puff'd and reckless libertine,   49
  Himself the primrose path of dalliance treads,
  And recks not his own rede.
LAERTES.   O fear me not.

[*Enter Polonius.*]

  I stay too long, but here my father comes.   52
  A double blessing is a double grace;
  Occasion smiles upon a second leave.
POLONIUS. Yet here, Laertes? aboard, aboard, for
    shame!
  The wind sits in the shoulder of your sail,   56
  And you are stay'd for. There, my blessing with
    thee!
  And these few precepts in thy memory
  Look thou cháracter. Give thy thoughts no tongue,
  Nor any unproportion'd thought his act.   60
  Be thou familiar, but by no means vulgar;
  Those friends thou hast, and their adoption tried,
  Grapple them unto thy soul with hoops of steel;
  But do not dull thy palm with entertainment   64
  Of each new-hatch'd, unfledg'd comráde. Beware

---

2. **give benefit:** are favorable. 3. **convoy:** means of conveyance. 6. **fashion:** mere form. **toy in blood:** passing amorous fancy. 7. **primy:** spring-like. 8. **Forward:** precocious. 9. **suppliance:** diversion. 11. **crescent:** growing. 12. **thews:** bodily strength. **temple:** body. 14. **withal:** also. 15. **soil:** blemish. **cautel:** trickery. 16. **virtue of his will:** his virtuous intentions. 19. **unvalu'd:** untitled. 23. **voice and yielding:** approval and compliance. 26. **place:** position as a prince. 27. **deed:** effect. 30. **credent:** trustful. **list:** listen to.

32. **unmaster'd:** unrestrained. 36. **chariest:** most scrupulous. 39. **canker:** caterpillar. **galls:** injures. **infants:** young plants. 40. **buttons:** buds. **disclos'd:** opened. 41. **liquid dew:** while the dew is still fresh. 42. **blastments:** blights. 47. **ungracious:** graceless. 49. **puff'd:** bloated from excess. 50. **primrose path:** path of pleasure. 51. **recks:** heeds. **rede:** counsel. **fear me not:** don't worry about me. 54. **Occasion:** opportunity. **smiles upon:** favors me with. 59. **character:** inscribe. 60. **unproportion'd:** inordinate. 61. **familiar:** friendly. 64. **dull thy palm:** make yourself less sensitive to true friendship. 65. **unfledg'd:** immature.

Of entrance to a quarrel, but, being in,
Bear 't that th' opposed may beware of thee.
Give every man thy ear, but few thy voice;   68
Take each man's censure, but reserve thy judgment.
Costly thy habit as thy purse can buy,
But not express'd in fancy; rich, not gaudy;
For the apparel oft proclaims the man,   72
And they in France of the best rank and station
Are of a most select and generous clef in that.
Neither a borrower, nor a lender be;
For loan oft loses both itself and friend,   76
And borrowing dulleth edge of husbandry.
This above all: to thine own self be true,
And it must follow, as the night the day,
Thou canst not then be false to any man.   80
Farewell; my blessing season this in thee!

LAERTES. Most humbly do I take my leave, my lord.

POLONIUS. The time invites you; go, your servants
    tend.

LAERTES. Farewell, Ophelia; and remember well
    What I have said to you.

OPHELIA.   'Tis in my memory lock'd,
    And you yourself shall keep the key of it.   86

LAERTES. Farewell.   [Exit Laertes.]

POLONIUS. What is 't, Ophelia, he hath said to you?

OPHELIA. So please you, something touching the
    Lord Hamlet.

POLONIUS. Marry, well bethought:
'Tis told me, he hath very oft of late
Given private time to you; and you yourself   92
Have of your audience been most free and boun-
    teous.
If it be so,—as so 'tis put on me,
And that in way of caution,—I must tell you,
You do not understand yourself so clearly   96
As it behoves my daughter and your honor.
What is between you? give me up the truth.

OPHELIA. He hath, my lord, of late made many
    tenders
Of his affection to me.   100

POLONIUS. Affection! pooh! you speak like a green
    girl,
Unsifted in such perilous circumstance.
Do you believe his tenders, as you call them?

OPHELIA. I do not know, my lord, what I should
    think.   104

POLONIUS. Marry, I'll teach you: think yourself a
    baby,
That you have ta'en these tenders for true pay,
Which are not sterling. Tender yourself more dearly;
Or (not to crack the wind of the poor phrase,
Running it thus) you'll tender me a fool.   109

OPHELIA. My lord, he hath impórtun'd me with love
In honorable fashion.

POLONIUS. Ay, fashion you may call it. Go to, go
    to.   112

OPHELIA. And hath given countenance to his speech,
    my lord,
With almost all the holy vows of heaven.

POLONIUS. Ay, springes to catch woodcocks. I do
    know,
When the blood burns, how prodigal the soul   116
Lends the tongue vows: these blazes, daughter,
Giving more light than heat, extinct in both,
Even in their promise, as it is a-making,
You must not take for fire. From this time   120
Be somewhat scanter of your maiden presence;
Set your entreatments at a higher rate
Than a command to parley. For Lord Hamlet,
Believe so much in him: that he is young,   124
And with a larger tether may he walk
Than may be given you. In few, Ophelia,
Do not believe his vows, for they are brokers,
Not of that dye which their investments show,
But mere implorators of unholy suits,   129
Breathing like sanctified and pious bawds,
The better to beguile. This is for all:
I would not, in plain terms, from this time forth,
Have you so slander any moment leisure,   133
As to give words or talk with the Lord Hamlet.
Look to 't, I charge you; come your ways.

OPHELIA. I shall obey, my lord.   [Exeunt.]

SCENE IV

The Platform of the Castle

[Enter Hamlet, Horatio, and Marcellus.]

---

69. **censure:** opinion.   **71. express'd in fancy:** singular in design. **74. generous:** aristocratic.   **clef:** musical key, tone.   **77. husbandry:** thrift.   **81. season this:** make my admonition palatable.   **83. tend:** are in waiting.   **92. private time:** time in private visits.   **94. put on:** impressed on.   **99. tenders:** offers.   **101. green:** inexperienced. **102. Unsifted:** untried.   **circumstance:** state of affairs.

107. **sterling:** legal currency.   **115. springes:** snares.   **122. entreatments:** interviews.   **126. In few:** briefly.   **127. brokers:** gobetweens, procurers.   **128. investments:** vestments, clothes.   **129. implorators:** solicitors.   **133. slander:** bring reproach upon.

HAMLET. The air bites shrewdly; it is very cold.

HORATIO. It is a nipping and an eager air.

HAMLET. What hour now?

HORATIO.   I think it lacks of twelve.

MARCELLUS. No, it is struck.   4

HORATIO. Indeed? I heard it not: it then draws near
    the season
    Wherein the spirit held his wont to walk.

[A flourish of trumpets, and two pieces (of ordnance) go off.]

What does this mean, my lord?

HAMLET. The king doth wake to-night and takes his
    rouse,   8
    Keeps wassail, and the swaggering up-spring reels;
    And, as he drains his draughts of Rhenish down,
    The kettle-drum and trumpet thus bray out
    The triumph of his pledge.

HORATIO.   Is it a custom?   12

HAMLET. Ay, marry, is 't:
    But to my mind, though I am native here
    And to the manner born, it is a custom
    More honor'd in the breach than the
      observance.   16
    This heavy-headed revel east and west
    Makes us traduc'd and tax'd of other nations;
    They clepe us drunkards, and with swinish phrase
    Soil our addition; and indeed it takes   20
    From our achievements, though perform'd at
      height,
    The pith and marrow of our attribute.
    So, oft it chances in particular men,
    That for some vicious mole of nature in them,   24
    As, in their birth (wherein they are not guilty,
    Since nature cannot choose his origin),
    By the o'ergrowth of some complexion,
    Oft breaking down the pales and forts of
      reason,   28
    Or by some habit that too much o'er-leavens
    The form of plausive manners; that these men,
    Carrying, I say, the stamp of one defect,
    Being nature's livery, or fortune's star,—   32

    His virtues else, be they as pure as grace,
    As infinite as man may undergo,
    Shall in the general censure take corruption
    From that particular fault. The dram of eale   36
    Doth all the noble substance oft adulter
    To his own scandal.

[Enter Ghost.]

HORATIO.   Look, my lord, it comes!

HAMLET. Angels and ministers of grace defend us!
    Be thou a spirit of health or goblin damn'd,   40
    Bring with thee airs from heaven or blasts from hell,
    Be thy intents wicked or charitable,
    Thou com'st in such a questionable shape
    That I will speak to thee. I'll call thee Hamlet,   44
    King, father, royal Dane! O answer me:
    Let me not burst in ignorance, but tell
    Why thy canóniz'd bones, hearsed in death,
    Have burst their cerements; why the sepulchre,   48
    Wherein we saw thee quietly inurn'd,
    Hath op'd his ponderous and marble jaws,
    To cast thee up again? What may this mean,
    That thou, dead corse, again in cómplete steel   52
    Revisits thus the glimpses of the moon,
    Making night hideous; and we fools of nature
    So horridly to-shake our disposition
    With thoughts beyond the reaches of our souls?   56
    Say, why is this? wherefore? what should we do?

[Ghost beckons Hamlet.]

HORATIO. It beckons you to go away with it,
    As if it some impartment did desire
    To you alone.

MARCELLUS.   Look, with what courteous
    action   60
    It waves you to a more removed ground:
    But do not go with it.

HORATIO.   No, by no means.

HAMLET. It will not speak. Then, I will follow it.

HORATIO. Do not, my lord.

---

2. **eager:** sharp.   8. **wake:** hold a revel by night.   9. **Keeps wassail:** holds a drinking-bout.   **up-spring:** wild dance of German origin. 10. **Rhenish:** Rhine wine.   12. **pledge:** toast.   18. **traduc'd and tax'd:** defamed and censured.   19. **clepe:** call.   **swinish phrase:** name of 'pigs'.   20. **Soil our addition:** blemish our good name. 21. **at height:** to the maximum.   22. **attribute:** reputation. 24. **mole:** blemish.   27. **complexion:** natural tendency, 'humor'. 28. **pales:** defensive enclosures.   29. **o'er-leavens:** makes too light. 30. **plausive:** pleasing.   32. **nature's livery:** a natural attribute. **fortune's star:** the position in which one is placed by fortune.

34. **undergo:** bear the weight of.   36. **dram:** minute quantity.   **eale:** e'il, evil.   38. **scandal:** shame.   39. **ministers of grace:** messengers of God.   40. **spirit of health:** good spirit.   **goblin:** evil spirit.   43. **questionable:** inviting question.   47. **canoniz'd:** buried according to the Church's rule.   **hearsed:** coffined.   48. **cerements:** waxen grave-clothes.   49. **inurn'd:** interred.   53. **glimpses of the moon:** the earth by night.   54. **fools of nature:** stupid in nature's presence. 55. **to-shake our disposition:** shatter our composure.   56. **reaches:** capacities.   59. **impartment:** communication.

HAMLET.   Why, what should be the
     fear?   64
I do not set my life at a pin's fee;
And for my soul, what can it do to that,
Being a thing immortal as itself?
It waves me forth again; I'll follow it.   68
HORATIO. What if it tempt you toward the flood, my
     lord,
Or to the dreadful summit of the cliff
That beetles o'er his base into the sea,
And there assume some other horrible form,   72
Which might deprive your sovereignty of reason
And draw you into madness? think of it;
The very place puts toys of desperation,
Without more motive, into every brain   76
That looks so many fadoms to the sea
And hears it roar beneath.
HAMLET. It waves me still. Go on! I'll follow thee.
MARCELLUS. You shall not go, my lord.
HAMLET.   Hold off your hands!   80
HORATIO. Be rul'd; you shall not go.
HAMLET.   My fate cries
     out,
And makes each petty arture in this body
As hardy as the Némean lion's nerve.
Still am I call'd. Unhand me, gentlemen!   84
By heaven, I'll make a ghost of him that lets me.
I say, away!—Go on! I'll follow thee.

[Exeunt Ghost and Hamlet.]

HORATIO. He waxes desperate with imagination.
MARCELLUS. Let's follow; 'tis not fit thus to obey
     him.
HORATIO. Have after. To what issue will this come?
MARCELLUS. Something is rotten in the state of Den-
     mark.
HORATIO. Heaven will direct it.
MARCELLUS.   Nay, let's follow him.

[Exeunt.]

65. at . . . fee: at even a trifling value. **69. flood:** sea. **71. beetles:**
overhangs threateningly. **73. deprive . . . reason:** dethrone reason
from its sovereignty. **75. toys of desperation:** whims involving
thoughts of self-destruction. **77. fadoms:** fathoms. **82. arture:**
artery. **83. nerve:** sinew, tendon. **85. lets:** hinders. **89. issue:**
outcome.

SCENE V

A more remote Part of the Platform

[Enter Ghost and Hamlet.]

HAMLET. Whither wilt thou lead me? speak; I'll go no
     further.
GHOST. Mark me.
HAMLET.   I will.
GHOST.   My hour is almost come,
When I to sulphurous and tormenting flames
Must render up myself.
HAMLET.   Alas, poor ghost.   4
GHOST. Pity me not, but lend thy serious hearing
To what I shall unfold.
HAMLET.   Speak; I am bound to hear.
GHOST. So art thou to revenge, when thou shalt hear.
HAMLET. What?   8
GHOST. I am thy father's spirit,
Doom'd for a certain term to walk the night,
And for the day confin'd to fast in fires,
Till the foul crimes done in my days of nature
Are burnt and purg'd away. But that I am forbid
To tell the secrets of my prison-house,
I could a tale unfold whose lightest word
Would harrow up thy soul, freeze thy young
     blood,   16
Make thy two eyes, like stars, start from their
     spheres,
Thy knotted and combined locks to part,
And each particular hair to stand an end,
Like quills upon the fretful porpentine.   20
But this eternal blazon must not be
To ears of flesh and blood. List, list, oh list!
If thou didst ever thy dear father love—
HAMLET. O God!   24
GHOST. Revenge his foul and most unnatural murther.
HAMLET. Murther!
GHOST. Murther most foul, as in the best it is;
But this most foul, strange, and unnatural.   28
HAMLET. Haste me to know't, that I, with wings as
     swift

17. spheres: orbits. **18. knotted:** neatly arranged. **combined:**
smoothly combed. **19. an:** on. **20. porpentine:** porcupine. **21.
eternal blazon:** revelation of eternity. **25. unnatural:** i.e., for one
brother to kill another.

As meditation or the thoughts of love,
May sweep to my revenge.
GHOST.   I find thee apt;
And duller shouldst thou be than the fat weed   32
That roots itself in ease on Lethe wharf,
Wouldst thou not stir in this. Now, Hamlet, hear:
'Tis given out that, sleeping in my orchard,
A serpent stung me. So the whole ear of
    Denmark   36
Is by a forged process of my death
Rankly abus'd; but know, thou noble youth,
The serpent that did sting thy father's life
Now wears his crown.
HAMLET.   O my prophetic soul!   40
My uncle?
GHOST. Ay, that incestuous, that adulterate beast,
With witchcraft of his wit, with traitorous gifts,—
O wicked wit and gifts, that have the power   44
So to seduce!—won to his shameful lust
The will of my most seeming-virtuous queen.
O Hamlet, what a falling-off was there!
From me, whose love was of that dignity   48
That it went hand in hand even with the vow
I made to her in marriage; and to decline
Upon a wretch whose natural gifts were poor
To those of mine!   52
But virtue, as it never will be mov'd,
Though lewdness court it in a shape of heaven,
So lust, though to a radiant angel link'd,
Will sate itself in a celestial bed,   56
And prey on garbage.
But, soft! methinks I scent the morning air;
Brief let me be. Sleeping within my orchard,
My custom always of the afternoon,   60
Upon my secure hour thy uncle stole,
With juice of cursed hebona in a vial,
And in the porches of my ears did pour
The leperous distilment; whose effect   64
Holds such an enmity with blood of man
That swift as quicksilver it courses through
The natural gates and alleys of the body,
And with a sudden vigor it doth posset   68
And curd, like eager droppings into milk,

The thin and wholesome blood. So did it mine;
And a most instant tetter bark'd about,
Most lazar-like, with vile and loathsome crust,
All my smooth body.   73
Thus was I, sleeping, by a brother's hand,
Of life, of crown, of queen, at once dispatch'd;
Cut off even in the blossoms of my sin,   76
Unhousel'd, disappointed, unanel'd,
No reckoning made, but sent to my account
With all my imperfections on my head.
[HAMLET]. O horrible! O horrible! most
    horrible!   80
[GHOST]. If thou hast nature in thee, bear it not;
Let not the royal bed of Denmark be
A couch for luxury and damned incest.
But, howsomever thou pursu'st this act,   84
Taint not thy mind, nor let thy soul contrive
Against thy mother aught. Leave her to heaven,
And to those thorns that in her bosom lodge,
To prick and sting her. Fare thee well at once!   88
The glow-worm shows the matin to be near,
And 'gins to pale his uneffectual fire;
Adieu, adieu, adieu! Remember me.   [Exit.]
HAMLET. O all you host of heaven! O earth! What
    else?   92
And shall I couple hell? O fie! Hold, hold, my heart!
And you, my sinews, grow not instant old,
But bear me stiffly up. Remember thee?
Ay, thou poor ghost, while memory holds a
    seat   96
In this distracted globe. Remember thee?
Yea, from the table of my memory
I'll wipe away all trivial fond records,
All saws of books, all forms, all pressures past,   100
That youth and observation copied there;
And thy commandment all alone shall live
Within the book and volume of my brain,
Unmix'd with baser matter: yes, by heaven!   104
O most pernicious woman!
O villain, villain, smiling, damned villain!

---

31. **apt:** ready to learn. 33. **wharf:** bank. 35. **orchard:** garden. 37. **process:** narrative. 38. **abus'd:** deceived. 42. **adulterate:** adulterous. 62. **hebona:** yew, notorious for its poisonous properties, but henbane and ebony are also involved. 64. **leperous:** causing leprosy. 67. **gates and alleys:** streets and lanes. 68. **posset:** curdle. 69. **eager:** sour.

71. **instant:** instantaneous. **tetter:** skin eruption. **bark'd about:** covered (as with bark). 72. **lazar-like:** leprous-like. 75. **dispatch'd:** bereft. 77. **Unhousel'd:** without having received the Holy Communion. **disappointed:** unprepared. **unanel'd:** without having received extreme unction. 78. **reckoning:** confession and absolution. 83. **luxury:** lasciviousness. 89. **matin:** morning. 90. **uneffectual:** heatless. 97. **distracted globe:** confused head. 98. **table:** writing-tablet. 99. **fond:** foolish. 100. **saws:** maxims. **pressures:** impressions—as of a seal.

My tables! Meet it is I set it down,
That one may smile, and smile, and be a
   villain;   108
At least I'm sure it may be so in Denmark.

[*Writing.*]

So; uncle, there you are. Now to my word.
It is, 'Adieu, adieu! remember me.'
I have sworn 't.   112
HORATIO AND MARCELLUS WITHIN. My lord! my
   lord!

[*Enter Horatio and Marcellus.*]

MARCELLUS.   Lord Hamlet!
HORATIO. Heaven secure him!
HAMLET.   So be it!
HORATIO. Illo, ho, ho, my lord!
HAMLET. Hillo, ho, ho, boy! come, bird, come.
MARCELLUS. How is 't, my noble lord?
HORATIO.   What news, my lord?   117
HAMLET. O wonderful!
HORATIO.   Good my lord, tell it.
HAMLET. No; you will reveal it.
HORATIO. Not I, my lord, by heaven!
MARCELLUS.   Nor I, my lord.   120
HAMLET. How say you, then? would heart of man
   once think it?
But you'll be secret?
BOTH.   Ay, by heaven, my lord.
HAMLET. There's ne'er a villain dwelling in all Den-
   mark,
But he's an arrant knave.   124
HORATIO. There needs no ghost, my lord, come from
   the grave,
To tell us this.
HAMLET.   Why, right; you are in the right;
And so, without more circumstance at all,
I hold it fit that we shake hands and part;   128
You, as your business and desire shall point you,—
For every man hath business and desire,
Such as it is,—and, for my own poor part,
I will go pray.   132
HORATIO. These are but wild and whirling words, my
   lord.

HAMLET. I am sorry they offend you, heartily;
Yes, faith, heartily.
HORATIO.   There's no offence, my lord.
HAMLET. Yes, by Saint Patrick, but there is,
   Horatio,   136
And much offence, too. Touching this vision here,
It is an honest ghost, that let me tell you.
For your desire to know what is between us,
O'ermaster 't as you may. And now, good
   friends,   140
As you are friends, scholars, and soldiers,
Give me one poor request.
HORATIO. What is 't, my lord? we will.
HAMLET. Never make known what you have seen
   tonight.   144
BOTH. My lord, we will not.
HAMLET.   Nay, but swear 't.
HORATIO.   In faith,
My lord, not I.
MARCELLUS.   Nor I, my lord, in faith.
HAMLET. Upon my sword.
MARCELLUS.   We have sworn, my lord, already.
HAMLET. Indeed, upon my sword, indeed.   148
GHOST. Swear.   [*Ghost cries under the stage.*]
HAMLET. Ha, ha, boy! sayst thou so? art thou there,
   true-penny?
Come on,—you hear this fellow in the cellarage,—
Consent to swear.
HORATIO.   Propose the oath, my lord.   152
HAMLET. Never to speak of this that you have seen.
   Swear by my sword.
GHOST. Swear.
HAMLET. *Hic et ubique?* then we'll shift our
   ground.   156
Come hither, gentlemen, and lay your hands
Again upon my sword. Swear by my sword
Never to speak of this that you have heard.
GHOST. Swear by his sword.   160
HAMLET. Well said, old mole! canst work i' th' earth
   so fast?
A worthy pioner! once more remove, good friends.
HORATIO. O day and night, but this is wondrous
   strange!
HAMLET. And therefore as a stranger give it
   welcome.   164
There are more things in heaven and earth, Horatio,
Than are dreamt of in your philosophy.
But come;

---

110. **word:** watch-word. 115. **Illo, ho, ho:** falconer's hunting
call. 116. **come, bird, come:** call which falconers use to their hawk
in the air. 124. **arrant:** thoroughgoing. 127. **circumstance:** formality. 133. **whirling:** eddying, incoherent.

140. **O'ermaster 't:** conquer it. 150. **true-penny:** honest fellow. 156. *Hic et ubique:* here and everywhere. 162. **pioner:** dig-
ger, miner.

Here, as before, never, so help you mercy,   168
How strange or odd soe'er I bear myself,—
As I perchance hereafter shall think meet
To put an antic disposition on,—
That you, at such times seeing me, never shall,   172
With arms encumber'd thus, or this head-shake,
Or by pronouncing of some doubtful phrase,
As, 'Well, well, we know,' or, 'We could, an˙if we
    would;'
Or, 'If we list to speak,' or, 'There be, an if they
    might;'   176
Or such ambiguous giving out, to note
That you know aught of me. This do swear,
So grace and mercy at your most need help you.

GHOST. Swear.   [*They swear.*]
HAMLET. Rest, rest, perturbed spirit! So, gentle-
    men,   181
With all my love I do commend me to you:
And what so poor a man as Hamlet is
May do t' express his love and friending to
    you,   184
God willing, shall not lack. Let us go in together;
And still your fingers on your lips, I pray.
The time is out of joint. O cursed spite,
That ever I was born to set it right!   188
Nay, come, let's go together.

[*Exeunt.*]

Act II

SCENE I

Polonius' Apartment in the Castle

[*Enter old Polonius with his man Reynaldo.*]

POLONIUS. Give him this money and these notes,
    Reynaldo.
REYNALDO. I will, my lord.
POLONIUS. You shall do marvel's wisely, good
    Reynaldo,
Before you visit him, to make inquire   4
Of his behavior
REYNALDO.   My lord, I did intend it.
POLONIUS. Marry, well said, very well said. Look you,
    sir,
Inquire me first what Danskers are in Paris;
And how, and who, what means, and where they
    keep,   8
What company, at what expense; and finding
By this encompassment and drift of question
That they do know my son, come you more nearer
Than your particular demands will touch it.   12

Take you, as 'twere, some distant knowledge of him;
As thus, 'I know his father, and his friends,
And in part him.' Do you mark this, Reynaldo?
REYNALDO. Ay, very well, my lord.   16
POLONIUS. 'And in part him; but,' you may say, 'not
    well:
But if 't be he I mean, he's very wild,
Addicted so and so'; and there put on him
What forgeries you please: marry, none so rank
As may dishonor him; take heed of that;   21
But, sir, such wanton, wild, and usual slips
As are companions noted and most known
To youth and liberty.
REYNALDO.   As gaming, my lord?   24
POLONIUS. Ay, or drinking, fencing, swearing,
    Quarrelling, drabbing,—you may go so far.
REYNALDO. My lord, that would dishonor him.
POLONIUS. Faith, no, as you may season it in the
    charge.   28
You must not put another scandal on him,
That he is open to incontinency.
That's not my meaning; but breathe his faults so
    quaintly
That they may seem the taints of liberty,   32

---

170. meet: proper. 171. antic: fantastic. 173. encumber'd:
folded. 174. doubtful: ambiguous. 176. an if: an intensive form
of if. 177. to note: to give a sign.
1. notes: instructions. 3. marvel's: marvelously. 4. inquire: investigation. 7. Danskers: Danes. 8. keep: live. 10. encompassment: 'talking round' a subject. question: conversation. 12.
particular demands: concrete questions.

187. spite: vexatious circumstance.
13. Take: assume. 19. put on: impute to. 20. forgeries: invented
tales. rank: excessive. 22. wanton: unrestrained. 26. drabbing:
wenching. 28. season: flavor. charge: accusation. 30. incontinency: habitual loose behavior. 31. breathe . . . quaintly: hint . . .
cleverly. 32. taints of liberty: blemishes due to high spirits.

The flash and outbreak of a fiery mind,
A savageness in unreclaimed blood,
Of general assault.
REYNALDO.   But, my good lord,—
POLONIUS. Wherefore should you do this?
REYNALDO.   Ay, my lord,   36
I would know that.
POLONIUS.   Marry, sir, here's my drift;
And I believe it is a fetch of warrant.
You laying these slight sullies on my son,
As 'twere a thing a little soil'd i' th' working,   40
Mark you,
Your party in converse, him you would sound,
Having ever seen in the prenominate crimes
The youth you breathe of guilty, be assur'd,   44
He closes with you in this consequence:
'Good sir,' or so, or 'friend,' or 'gentleman,'
According to the phrase or the addition
Of man and country—
REYNALDO.   Very good, my lord.   48
POLONIUS. And then, sir, does 'a this,—'a does,—
what was
I about to say? By the mass I was about to say
something. Where did I leave?
REYNALDO. At 'closes in the consequence,'   52
At 'friend or so,' and 'gentleman.'
POLONIUS. At 'closes in the consequence'? Ay, marry;
He closes thus: 'I know the gentleman;
I saw him yesterday, or th' other day,   56
Or then, or then, with such or such; and, as you say,
There was 'a gaming, there o'ertook in 's rouse,
There falling out at tennis'; or perchance,
'I saw him enter such a house of sale,'   60
Videlicet, a brothel, or so forth.
See you now;
Your bait of falsehood takes this carp of truth;
And thus do we of wisdom and of reach,   64
With windlasses and with assays of bias,
By indirections find directions out.
So by my former lecture and advice
Shall you my son. You have me, have you not?   68

REYNALDO. My lord, I have.
POLONIUS.   God be wi' ye; fare ye
well.
REYNALDO. Good my lord!
POLONIUS. Observe his inclination in yourself.
REYNALDO. I shall, my lord.   72
POLONIUS. And let him ply his music.
REYNALDO.   Well, my lord.
POLONIUS. Farewell!   [Exit Reynaldo.]

[Enter Ophelia.]

                    How now, Ophelia! what's the
matter?
OPHELIA. O my lord, my lord! I have been so
affrighted.
POLONIUS. With what, i' th' name of God?   76
OPHELIA. My lord, as I was sewing in my closet,
Lord Hamlet, with his doublet all unbrac'd,
No hat upon his head; his stockings foul'd,
Ungarter'd, and down-gyved to his ankle;—   80
Pale as his shirt, his knees knocking each other,
And with a look so piteous in purport
As if he had been loosed out of hell
To speak of horrors, he comes before me.   84
POLONIUS. Mad for thy love?
OPHELIA.   My lord, I do not know;
But truly I do fear it.
POLONIUS.   What said he?
OPHELIA. He took me by the wrist and held me hard,
Then goes he to the length of all his arm,   88
And, with his other hand thus o'er his brow,
He falls to such perusal of my face
As 'a would draw it. Long stay'd he so.
At last, a little shaking of mine arm,   92
And thrice his head thus waving up and down,
He rais'd a sigh so piteous and profound
As it did seem to shatter all his bulk
And end his being. That done, he lets me go,   96
And with his head over his shoulder turn'd,
He seem'd to find his way without his eyes,
For out o'doors he went without their help,
And to the last bended their light on me.   100
POLONIUS. Come, go with me. I will go seek the
king.
This is the very ecstasy of love,
Whose violent property fordoes itself

34. savageness: wildness. unreclaimed: untamed. 35. Of general
assault: to which all are liable. 38. fetch of warrant: justifiable
trick. 39. sullies: blemishes. 43. prenominate: aforesaid. 45.
closes . . . consequence: confides in you as follows. 51. leave: leave
off. 58. o'ertook in 's rouse: unable to hold his liquor. 61. Videlicet: namely. 64. reach: resourcefulness. 65. windlasses: round-
about ways. assays of bias: indirect approaches. 66. indirections:
devious courses. directions: the straight facts. 67. lecture: instruction.

71. in yourself: for yourself. 73. ply: keep up. 77. closet: sitting
room. 78. doublet: close-fitting coat. unbrac'd: unfastened. 80.
down-gyved: hanging down like gyves or fetters. 90. perusal: scru-
tiny. 95. bulk: frame. 102. ecstasy: madness. 103. property:
nature. fordoes: destroys.

And leads the will to desperate undertakings   104
As oft as any passion under heaven
That does afflict our natures. I am sorry.
What! have you given him any hard words of late?

OPHELIA. No, my good lord; but, as you did com-
mand,   108
I did repel his letters and denied
His access to me.

POLONIUS.   That hath made him mad.
I am sorry that with better heed and judgment
I had not coted him. I fear'd he did but trifle,   112
And meant to wrack thee, but beshrew my jealousy!
By heaven, it is as proper to our age
To cast beyond ourselves in our opinions
As it is common for the younger sort   116
To lack discretion. Come, go we to the king.
This must be known, which, being kept close, might
move
More grief to hide than hate to utter love.
Come.   [Exeunt.]

SCENE II

The Lobby in the Castle

[Flourish. Enter King and Queen, Rosencrantz and
Guildenstern, cum aliis.]

KING. Welcome, dear Rosencrantz and Guildenstern.
Moreover that we much did long to see you,
The need we have to use you did provoke
Our hasty sending. Something have you heard   4
Of Hamlet's transformation. So I call it,
Sith nor th' exterior nor the inward man
Resembles that it was. What it should be,
More than his father's death, that thus hath put
him   8
So much from th' understanding of himself,
I cannot dream of. I entreat you both,
That being of so young days brought up with him,
And since so neighbor'd to his youth and
havior,   12
That you vouchsafe your rest here in our court
Some little time; so by your companies

To draw him on to pleasures and to gather,
So much as from occasion you may glean,   16
Whether aught to us unknown afflicts him thus,
That, open'd, lies within our remedy.

QUEEN. Good gentlemen, he hath much talk'd of
you;
And sure I am two men there are not living   20
To whom he more adheres. If it will please you
To show us so much gentry and good will
As to expend your time with us awhile,
For the supply and profit of our hope,   24
Your visitation shall receive such thanks
As fits a king's remembrance.

ROSENCRANTZ.   Both your majesties
Might, by the sovereign power you have of us,
Put your dread pleasures more into command
Than to entreaty.

GUILDENSTERN.   But we both obey,   29
And here give up ourselves in the full bent,
To lay our service freely at your feet
To be commanded.   32

KING. Thanks, Rosencrantz and gentle Guildenstern.

QUEEN. Thanks, Guildenstern and gentle Rosen-
crantz;
And I beseech you instantly to visit
My too much changed son. Go, some of you,   36
And bring these gentlemen where Hamlet is.

GUILDENSTERN. Heavens make our presence and our
practices
Pleasant and helpful to him!

QUEEN.   Ay, amen!

[Exeunt Rosencrantz and Guildenstern (attended).]

[Enter Polonius.]

POLONIUS. Th' ambassadors from Norway, my good
lord,   40
Are joyfully return'd.

KING. Thou still hast been the father of good news.

POLONIUS. Have I, my lord? Assure you, my good
liege,
I hold my duty as I hold my soul,   44
Both to my God and to my gracious king;
And I do think—or else this brain of mine
Hunts not the trail of policy so sure

---

112. coted: observed (obsolete form of 'quote'). 113. wrack:
ruin. beshrew: curse. jealousy: suspicion, mistrust. 114. our
age: us old folk. 115. cast . . . ourselves: be over subtle.
11. of so young days: from such early youth. 12. neighbor'd . . .
havior: near in age and occupation. 13. vouchsafe your rest: please
to reside.

17. not in Folio. 18. open'd: revealed. 22. gentry: courtesy. 24.
supply and profit: aid and successful outcome. 26. as . . . remembrance: as is suitable to a king's gratitude. 30. in the full bent: to
the utmost degree (an archery term). 47. policy: conduct of public
affairs.

As it hath us'd to do—that I have found   48
The very cause of Hamlet's lunacy.
KING. O speak of that! that do I long to hear.
POLONIUS. Give first admittance to th' ambassadors;
My news shall be the fruit to that great feast.   52
KING. Thyself do grace to them, and bring them in.

[Exit Polonius.]

He tells me, my dear Gertrude, he hath found
The head and source of all your son's distemper.
QUEEN. I doubt it is no other but the main: 56
His father's death and our o'erhasty marriage.
KING. Well, we shall sift him.

[Enter Polonius, Voltimand, and Cornelius.]

                    Welcome, my good friends!
Say, Voltimand, what from our brother Norway?
VOLTIMAND. Most fair return of greetings and
     desires.   60
Upon our first, he sent out to suppress
His nephew's levies, which to him appear'd
To be a preparation 'gainst the Polack;
But, better look'd into, he truly found   64
It was against your highness: whereat griev'd
That so his sickness, age, and impotence
Was falsely borne in hand, sends out arrests
On Fortinbras; which he in brief obeys,   68
Receives rebuke from Norway, and, in fine,
Makes vow before his uncle never more
To give th' assay of arms against your majesty.
Whereon old Norway, overcome with joy,   72
Gives him three thousand crowns in annual fee,
And his commission to employ those soldiers,
So levied as before, against the Polack;
With an entreaty, herein further shown,   76

[Giving a paper.]

That it might please you to give quiet pass
Through your dominions for this enterprise,
On such regards of safety and allowance
As therein are set down.
KING.   It likes us well;   80
And at our more consider'd time we'll read,
Answer, and think upon this business.

Meantime we thank you for your well-took labor.
Go to your rest; at night we'll feast together.
Most welcome home.

[Exeunt ambassadors.]

POLONIUS.   This business is well ended.   85
My liege, and madam, to expostulate
What majesty should be, what duty is,
Why day is day, night night, and time is time,
Were nothing but to waste night, day, and time.
Therefore, since brevity is the soul of wit,
And tediousness the limbs and outward flourishes,
I will be brief. Your noble son is mad.   92
Mad call I it; for to define true madness,
What is 't but to be nothing else but mad?
But let that go.
QUEEN.   More matter, with less art.
POLONIUS. Madam, I swear I use no art at all.   96
That he is mad, 'tis true; 'tis true 'tis pity;
And pity 'tis 'tis true: a foolish figure,
But farewell it, for I will use no art.
Mad let us grant him, then; and now remains
That we find out the cause of this effect,   101
Or rather say, the cause of this defect,
For this effect defective comes by cause.
Thus it remains, and the remainder thus.
Perpend.   105
I have a daughter (have while she is mine)
Who, in her duty and obedience, mark,
Hath given me this. Now, gather and surmise.

[Reads the letter.]

"To the celestial, and my soul's idol, the most beau-
     tified Ophelia.—"   109

That's an ill phrase, a vile phrase; 'beautified' is a
vile phrase; but you shall hear. Thus:

"In her excellent white bosom, these, &c.—"   112

QUEEN. Came this from Hamlet to her?
POLONIUS. Good madam, stay awhile; I will be faith-
     ful.

"Doubt thou the stars are fire;
     Doubt that the sun doth move;   116

---

52. fruit: dessert. 56. main: chief point. 60. desires: good
wishes. 67. borne in hand: deluded. 69. in fine: in conclusion. 71. assay: trial. 80. likes: pleases. 81. consider'd: fit for
considering.

86. expostulate: set forth one's views. 90. wit: judgment, understanding. 91. flourishes: embellishments. 98. figure: figure of
rhetoric. 105. Perpend: consider. 109. beautified: beautiful, or,
accomplished.

Doubt truth to be a liar;
　　But never doubt I love.
O dear Ophelia! I am ill at these numbers: I have
not art to reckon my groans; but that I love thee
best, O most best, believe it. Adieu.
　　　Thine evermore, most dear lady, whilst this
　　　machine is to him,
　　　　　　　　　　　　　　　　Hamlet."

This in obedience hath my daughter shown me,
And more above,—hath his solicitings,
As they fell out by time, by means, and place,
All given to mine ear.
KING.　　　　　　　　But how hath she　　128
　　Receiv'd his love?
POLONIUS.　　　　　What do you think of me?
KING. As of a man faithful and honorable.
POLONIUS. I would fain prove so. But what might
　　you think,
When I had seen this hot love on the wing,—　132
As I perceiv'd it, (I must tell you that)
Before my daughter told me,—what might you,
Or my dear majesty, your queen here, think,
If I had play'd the desk or table-book,　　136
Or given my heart a winking, mute and dumb,
Or look'd upon this love with idle sight?
What might you think? No, I went round to work,
And my young mistress thus I did bespeak:　140
'Lord Hamlet is a prince, out of thy star;
This must not be:' and then I prescripts gave her,
That she should lock herself from his resort,
Admit no messengers, receive no tokens.　144
Which done, she took the fruits of my advice;
And he, repelled,—a short tale to make,—
Fell into a sadness, then into a fast,
Thence to a watch, thence into a weakness,　148
Thence to a lightness, and by this declension
Into the madness wherein now he raves,
And all we mourn for.
KING.　　　　　　　Do you think 'tis this?
QUEEN. It may be, very like.　　152
POLONIUS. Hath there been such a time,—I'd fain
　　know that,—

That I have positively said, 'Tis so,'
When it prov'd otherwise?
KING.　　　　　　　　Not that I know.
POLONIUS. Take this from this, if this be other-
　　wise.　　156

[Pointing to his head and shoulder.]

If circumstances lead me, I will find
Where truth is hid, though it were hid indeed
Within the center.
KING.　　　　　　How may we try it further?
POLONIUS. You know sometimes he walks four hours
　　together　　160
　　Here in the lobby.
QUEEN.　　　　　　So he does indeed.
POLONIUS. At such a time I'll loose my daughter to
　　him.
Be you and I behind an arras then.
Mark the encounter; if he love her not,　164
And be not from his reason fallen thereon,
Let me be no assistant for a state,
But keep a farm and carters.
KING.　　　　　　　　We will try it.

[Enter Hamlet reading on a book.]

QUEEN. But look, where sadly the poor wretch comes
　　reading.　　168
POLONIUS. Away! I do beseech you, both away.
　　I'll board him presently. O, give me leave.

[Exeunt King and Queen.]

　　How does my good Lord Hamlet?
HAMLET. Well, God-a-mercy.　　172
POLONIUS. Do you know me, my lord?
HAMLET. Excellent well. You are a fishmonger.
POLONIUS. Not I, my lord.
HAMLET. Then I would you were so honest a
　　man.　　176
POLONIUS. Honest, my lord?
HAMLET. Ay, sir; to be honest, as this world goes, is to
　　be one man picked out of ten thousand.
POLONIUS. That's very true, my lord.　　180
HAMLET. For if the sun breed maggots in a dead dog,
　　being a god kissing carrion,—Have you a daughter?
POLONIUS. I have, my lord.

---

119. **ill at:** unskilled at making. **numbers:** verses. **120. reckon:** number metrically, scan. **123. machine:** bodily frame. **126. more above:** more too. **127. fell out:** occurred. **means:** opportunities of access. **137. winking:** a short nap, i.e., allowed my heart to connive. **139. round:** straightforwardly. **140. bespeak:** address. **141. out of thy star:** above the position allotted thee by fortune. **142. prescripts:** positive orders. **148. watch:** state of sleeplessness. **149. lightness:** lightheadedness. **declension:** downward course.

159. **center:** middle point of the earth. **163. arras:** hanging tapestry. **170. board:** accost. **presently:** immediately.

HAMLET. Let her not walk i' the sun. Conception is a blessing, but as your daughter may conceive, friend, look to 't.   186

POLONIUS. [*Aside.*] How say you by that? Still harping on my daughter. Yet he knew me not at first; 'a said I was a fishmonger. 'A is far gone; and truly in my youth I suffered much extremity for love, very near this. I'll speak to him again. What do you read, my lord?   192

HAMLET. Words, words, words.

POLONIUS. What is the matter, my lord?

HAMLET. Between who?

POLONIUS. I mean the matter that you read, my lord.   196

HAMLET. Slanders, sir: for the satirical rogue says here that old men have grey beards, that their faces are wrinkled, their eyes purging thick amber and plum-tree gum, and that they have a plentiful lack of wit, together with most weak hams. All which, sir, though I most powerfully and potently believe, yet I hold it not honesty to have it thus set down; for yourself, sir, shall grow old as I am, if, like a crab, you could go backward.   205

POLONIUS. [*Aside.*] Though this be madness, yet there is method in 't. Will you walk out of the air, my lord?

HAMLET. Into my grave?   208

POLONIUS. Indeed, that's out of the air. [*Aside.*] How pregnant sometimes his replies are! a happiness that often madness hits on, which reason and sanity could not so prosperously be delivered of. I will leave him and suddenly contrive the means of meeting between him and my daughter. My honorable lord, I will most humbly take my leave of you.   215

HAMLET. You cannot take from me anything that I will more willingly part withal,—except my life, except my life, except my life.

POLONIUS. Fare you well, my lord.   [*Going.*]

HAMLET. These tedious old fools!

[*Enter Guildenstern and Rosencrantz.*]

POLONIUS. You go to seek the Lord Hamlet? There he is.

ROSENCRANTZ. [*To Polonius.*] God save you, sir!   222

[*Exit Polonius.*]

GUILDENSTERN. My honored lord!

ROSENCRANTZ. My most dear lord!

HAMLET. My excellent good friends! How dost thou, Guildenstern? Ah, Rosencrantz! Good lads, how do you both?   227

ROSENCRANTZ. As the indifferent children of the earth.

GUILDENSTERN. Happy in that we are not over happy; on Fortune's cap we are not the very button.

HAMLET. Nor the soles of her shoe?   231

ROSENCRANTZ. Neither, my lord.

HAMLET. Then you live about her waist, or in the middle of her favors?

GUILDENSTERN. Faith, her privates we.   235

HAMLET. In the secret parts of Fortune? O, most true; she is a strumpet. What news?

ROSENCRANTZ. None, my lord, but that the world's grown honest.   239

HAMLET. Then is doomsday near; but your news is not true. Let me question more in particular. What have you, my good friends, deserved at the hands of Fortune, that she sends you to prison hither?

GUILDENSTERN. Prison, my lord!   244

HAMLET. Denmark's a prison.

ROSENCRANTZ. Then is the world one.

HAMLET. A goodly one; in which there are many confines, wards, and dungeons, Denmark being one o' the worst.   249

ROSENCRANTZ. We think not so, my lord.

HAMLET. Why, then, 'tis none to you; for there is nothing either good or bad but thinking makes it so. To me it is a prison.   253

ROSENCRANTZ. Why, then your ambition makes it one; 'tis too narrow for your mind.

HAMLET. O God, I could be bounded in a nutshell, and count myself a king of infinite space, were it not that I have bad dreams.   258

GUILDENSTERN. Which dreams, indeed, are ambition, for the very substance of the ambitious is merely the shadow of a dream.   261

HAMLET. A dream itself is but a shadow.

ROSENCRANTZ. Truly, and I hold ambition of so airy and light a quality that it is but a shadow's shadow.   264

HAMLET. Then are our beggars bodies, and our monarchs and outstretched heroes the beggars' shadows. Shall we to the court? for, by my fay, I cannot reason.

---

194. **matter:** substance. 199. **purging:** discharging. 203. **honesty:** decency. 210. **pregnant:** full of meaning. **happiness:** appropriateness. 212. **prosperously:** successfully. 217. **withal:** with.

228. **indifferent:** ordinary, average. 264. **quality:** nature. 266. **outstretched:** strutting. 267. **fay:** faith. **reason:** argue.

BOTH. We'll wait upon you.   268

HAMLET. No such matter. I will not sort you with the rest of my servants, for, to speak to you like an honest man, I am most dreadfully attended.) But, in the beaten way of friendship, what make you at Elsinore?

ROSENCRANTZ. To visit you, my lord; no other occasion.   274

HAMLET. Beggar that I am, I am even poor in thanks, but I thank you: and sure, dear friends, my thanks are too dear a halfpenny. Were you not sent for? Is it your own inclining? Is it a free visitation? Come, come, deal justly with me: come, come; nay, speak.

GUILDENSTERN. What should we say, my lord?   280

HAMLET. Why anything, but to the purpose. You were sent for; and there is a kind of confession in your looks which your modesties have not craft enough to color. I know the good king and queen have sent for you.   285

ROSENCRANTZ. To what end, my lord?

HAMLET. That you must teach me. But let me conjure you, by the rights of our fellowship, by the consonancy of our youth, by the obligation of our ever-preserved love, and by what more dear a better proposer could charge you withal, be even and direct with me, whether you were sent for or no.   292

ROSENCRANTZ. [Aside to Guildenstern.] What say you?

HAMLET. Nay, then, I have an eye of you. If you love me, hold not off.

GUILDENSTERN. My lord, we were sent for.   296

HAMLET. I will tell you why; so shall my anticipation prevent your discovery, and your secrecy to the king and queen moult no feather. I have of late,—but wherefore I know not,—lost all my mirth, forgone all custom of exercises; and indeed it goes so heavily with my disposition that this goodly frame, the earth, seems to me a sterile promontory; this most excellent canopy, the air, look you, this brave o'erhanging firmament, this majestical roof fretted with golden fire, why, it appeareth nothing to me but a foul and pestilent congregation of vapors. What a piece of work is a man! How noble in reason! how infinite in faculties! in form and moving how express and admirable! in action   310 how like an angel! in apprehension how like a god! the beauty of the world, the paragon of animals. And yet to me what is this quintessense of dust? Man delights not me; no, nor woman neither, though by your smiling you seem to say so.

ROSENCRANTZ. My lord, there was no such stuff in my thoughts.   316

HAMLET. Why did ye laugh, then, when I said 'man delights not me'?

ROSENCRANTZ. To think, my lord, if you delight not in man, what lenten entertainment the players shall receive from you. We coted them on the way; and hither are they coming, to offer you service.   322

HAMLET. He that plays the king shall be welcome, his majesty shall have tribute of me; the adventurous knight shall use his foil and target; the lover shall not sigh gratis; the humorous man shall end his part in peace; the clown shall make those laugh whose lungs are tickle o' the sere; and the lady shall say her mind freely, or the blank verse shall halt for 't. What players are they?   330

ROSENCRANTZ. Even those you were wont to take delight in, the tragedians of the city.

HAMLET. How chances it they travel? Their residence, both in reputation and profit, was better both ways.

ROSENCRANTZ. I think their inhibition comes by the means of the late innovation.   336

HAMLET. Do they hold the same estimation they did when I was in the city? Are they so followed?

ROSENCRANTZ. No, indeed are they not.   339

HAMLET. How comes it? Do they grow rusty?

ROSENCRANTZ. Nay, their endeavor keeps in the wonted pace: but there is, sir, an aery of children, little eyases, that cry out on the top of question, and are most tyrannically clapped for 't. These are now the fashion, and so berattle the common stages (so they call them) that many wearing rapiers are afraid of goose-quills, and dare scarce come thither.   347

---

268. **wait upon:** attend. 269. **sort:** class. 272. **beaten:** well-worn, reliable. 278. **free:** voluntary. 284. **color:** disguise. 287. **conjure:** adjure. 288–289. **consonancy:** harmony. 290–291. **better proposer:** more skillful exhorter. 291. **even:** straightforward. 294. **have an eye of you:** have an eye upon you. 298. **prevent:** precede. **discovery:** disclosure. 304. **brave:** splendid. 305. **fretted:** adorned.

309. **faculties:** powers. 310. **express:** well-modelled. 311. **apprehension:** understanding. 315. **stuff:** matter. 320. **lenten:** meagre. 321. **coted:** passed. 325. **foil and target:** sword and shield. 326. **humorous man:** actor of whimsical characters. 328. **tickle o' the sere:** yield easily to any impulse. 329. **halt:** limp. 333. **residence:** remaining at headquarters. 335. **inhibition:** hindrance. 337. **estimation:** reputation. 342. **aery:** nest. 343. **eyases:** young hawks. **cry . . . question:** deal pungently with the latest gossip. 344. **tyrannically:** outrageously. 345. **berattle:** decry. 346. **many wearing rapiers:** many men of quality. 346–347. **afraid of goose-quills:** afraid of being satirized.

HAMLET. What, are they children? who maintains 'em? how are they escoted? Will they pursue the quality no longer than they can sing? Will they not say afterwards, if they should grow themselves to common players (as it is most like, if their means are no better) their writers do them wrong to make them exclaim against their own succession? 354

ROSENCRANTZ. Faith, there has been much to-do on both sides, and the nation holds it no sin to tarre them to controversy. There was for a while no money bid for argument, unless the poet and the player went to cuffs in the question. 359

HAMLET. Is 't possible?

GUILDENSTERN. O, there has been much throwing about of brains.

HAMLET. Do the boys carry it away?

ROSENCRANTZ. Ay, that they do, my lord—Hercules and his load too. 365

HAMLET. It is not very strange; for my uncle is king of Denmark, and those that would make mouths at him while my father lived give twenty, forty, fifty, a hundred ducats apiece for his picture in little. 'Sblood, there is something in this more than natural, if philosophy could find it out. [A flourish.]

GUILDENSTERN. There are the players. 372

HAMLET. Gentlemen, you are welcome to Elsinore. Your hands! come then; th' appurtenance of welcome is fashion and ceremony. Let me comply with you in this garb, lest my extent to the players (which, I tell you, must show fairly outwards) should more appear like entertainment than yours. You are welcome; but my uncle-father and aunt-mother are deceived.

GUILDENSTERN. In what, my dear lord? 380

HAMLET. I am but mad north-north-west. When the wind is southerly, I know a hawk from a handsaw.

[Enter Polonious.]

POLONIUS. Well be with you, gentlemen! 383

HAMLET. Hark you, Guildenstern, and you too! at each ear a hearer. That great baby you see there is not yet out of his swaddling-clouts.

ROSENCRANTZ. Happily he is the second time come to them, for they say an old man is twice a child. 388

HAMLET. I will prophesy he comes to tell me of the players; mark it.—You say right, sir; o' Monday morning. 'Twas then indeed.

POLONIUS. My lord, I have news to tell you.

HAMLET. My lord, I have news to tell you. When Roscius was an actor in Rome,— 394

POLONIUS. The actors are come hither, my lord.

HAMLET. Buzz, buzz!

POLONIUS. Upon my honor,—

HAMLET.

      Then came each actor on his ass,—

POLONIUS. The best actors in the world, either for tragedy, comedy, history, pastoral, pastoral-comical, historical-pastoral, (tragical-historical, tragical-comical-historical-pastoral), scene individable, or poem unlimited: Seneca cannot be too heavy, nor Plautus too light. For the law of writ and the liberty, these are the only men. 405

HAMLET. O Jephthah, judge of Israel, what a treasure hadst thou!

POLONIUS. What a treasure had he, my lord?

HAMLET. Why,

      One fair daughter and no more,
      The which he loved passing well.

POLONIUS. [Aside.] Still on my daughter. 412

HAMLET. Am I not i' the right, old Jephthah?

POLONIUS. If you call me Jephthah, my lord, I have a daughter that I love passing well.

HAMLET. Nay, that follows not. 416

POLONIUS. What follows, then, my lord?

HAMLET. Why,

      As by lot, God wot.

And then, you know, 420

      It came to pass, as most like it was.—

---

349. escoted: maintained. 350. quality: profession. 352. common players: professional players. 354. succession: future, inheritance. 356. tarre: incite. 358. argument: subject-matter, plot. 359. cuffs: blows. 363. carry it away: carry the day. 367. mouths: grimaces. 369. in little: in a miniature. 370. 'Sblood: God's blood. 374. appurtenance: proper accompaniment. 375. comply: observe the formalities of courtesy. 376. garb: manner. extent: showing of kindness. 378. entertainment: hospitality.

386. swaddling-clouts: bandages in which newborn children were wrapped. 396. Buzz, buzz: an exclamation of contempt. 406. Jephthah: hero of an old ballad quoted below. 421. 'as most like it was': as was most probable.

The first row of the pious chanson will show you more, for look where my abridgment comes.   423

[*Enter four or five Players.*]

You are welcome, masters; welcome, all. I am glad to see thee well. Welcome, good friends. O, my old friend? Why thy face is valanced since I saw thee last: com'st thou to beard me in Denmark? What, my young lady and mistress! By 'r lady, your ladyship is nearer to heaven than when I saw you last by the altitude of a chopine. Pray God, your voice, like a piece of uncurrent gold, be not cracked within the ring. Masters, you are all welcome. We'll e'en to 't like French falconers, fly at anything we see: we'll have a speech straight. Come, give us a taste of your quality; come, a passionate speech.   435

PLAYER. What speech, my good lord?

HAMLET. I heard thee speak me a speech once, but it was never acted; or, if it was, not above once; for the play, I remember, pleased not the million; 'twas caviary to the general: but it was (as I received it, and others, whose judgments in such matters cried in the top of mine) an excellent play, well digested in the scenes, set down with as much modesty as cunning. I remember one said there were no sallets in the lines to make the matter savory, nor no matter in the phrase that might indict the author of affection; but called it an honest method, as wholesome as sweet, and by very much more handsome than fine. One speech in 't I chiefly loved; 'twas Æneas' tale to Dido; and thereabout of it especially, where he speaks of Priam's daughter. If it live in your memory, begin at this line: let me see, let me see:—   452

"The rugged Pyrrhus, like th' Hyrcanian beast,—"

'Tis not so. It begins with Pyrrhus:—

"The rugged Pyrrhus, he, whose sable arms,
Black as his purpose, did the night resemble

When he lay couched in the ominous horse,
Hath now this dread and black complexion smear'd
With heraldry more dismal. Head to foot
Now is he total gules, horridly trick'd   460
With blood of fathers, mothers, daughters, sons,
Bak'd and impasted with the parching streets,
That lend a tyrannous and a damned light
To their lords' murther. Roasted in wrath and fire,
And thus o'er-sized with coagulate gore,
With eyes like carbuncles, the hellish Pyrrhus
Old grandsire Priam seeks."

So proceed you.   468

POLONIUS. 'Fore God, my lord, well spoken! with good accent and good discretion.

PLAYER.   "Anon, he finds him
Striking too short at Greeks; his antique sword,
Rebellious to his arm, lies where it falls,   472
Repugnant to command. Unequal match'd,
Pyrrhus at Priam drives, in rage strikes wide;
But with the whiff and wind of his fell sword
Th' unnerved father falls. Then senseless Ilium,   476
Seeming to feel this blow, with flaming top
Stoops to his base, and with a hideous crash
Takes prisoner Pyrrhus' ear: for lo, his sword,
Which was declining on the milky head   480
Of reverend Priam, seem'd i' th' air to stick.
So as a painted tyrant Pyrrhus stood,
And like a neutral to his will and matter,
Did nothing.   484
But as we often see against some storm
A silence in the heavens, the rack stand still,
The bold winds speechless and the orb below
As hush as death, anon the dreadful thunder   488
Doth rend the region; so, after Pyrrhus' pause,
A roused vengeance sets him new a-work;
And never did the Cyclops' hammers fall

---

422. row: stanza, or column of print. **chanson:** song. **423. abridgment:** something to cut short my talk. **426. valanced:** 'curtained,' with a beard. **430. chopine:** a Venetian raised shoe worn by women. **431. uncurrent:** not passable as lawful coinage. **434. straight:** immediately. **441–442. cried in the top of:** spoke with a louder voice of authority than. **442. digested:** arranged. **443. modesty:** moderation. **444. cunning:** skill in technique. **446. indict:** convict. **447. affection:** affectation. **449. fine:** elaborately fashioned.

460. total gules: red all over. **trick'd:** spotted. **462. impasted:** made into a crust. **465. o'er-sized:** covered with something like size, a kind of glue. **466. carbuncles:** glittering red stones, rubies. **473. Repugnant to:** resisting. **475. fell:** cruel. **476. senseless:** incapable of feeling. **482. painted tyrant:** picture of an oppressor. **483. a neutral:** one indifferent. **matter:** task. **485. against:** just before. **486. rack:** mass of cloud. **488. anon:** presently. **489. region:** the air. **491. Cyclops':** Vulcan's workmen's.

On Mars's armor, forg'd for proof eterne,   492
With less remorse than Pyrrhus' bleeding sword
Now falls on Priam.
Out, out, thou strumpet Fortune! All you gods,
In general synod take away her power,   496
Break all the spokes and fellies from her wheel,
And bowl the round nave down the hill of heaven
As low as to the fiends!''
POLONIUS. This is too long.   500
HAMLET. It shall to the barber's, with your beard.
   Prithee, say on: he's for a jig or a tale of bawdry, or
   he sleeps. Say on; come to Hecuba.

PLAYER. But who, O who, had seen the mobled
   queen—

HAMLET. 'The mobled queen'?   505
POLONIUS. That's good; 'mobled queen' is good.

PLAYER. Run barefoot up and down, threat'ning the
   flames   507
With bisson rheum,—a clout upon that head
Where late the diadem stood, and for a robe,
About her lank and all o'er-teemed loins,
A blanket, in the alarm of fear caught up,—   511
Who this had seen, with tongue in venom steep'd,
'Gainst Fortune's state would treason have
   pronounc'd.
But if the gods themselves did see her then,
When she saw Pyrrhus make malicious sport
In mincing with his sword her husband's limbs,
The instant burst of clamor that she made
(Unless things mortal move them not at all)
Would have made milch the burning eyes of
   heaven   519
And passion in the gods.

POLONIUS. Look! wh'er he has not turned his color
   and has tears in 's eyes. Prithee, no more.   522
HAMLET. 'Tis well. I'll have thee speak out the rest of
   this soon. Good my lord, will you see the players

well bestowed? Do you hear, let them be well used,
   for they are the abstract and brief chronicles of the
   time. After your death you were better have a bad
   epitaph than their ill report while you live.
POLONIUS. My lord, I will use them according to
   their desert.   530
HAMLET. God's bodkin, man, much better! Use every
   man after his desert, and who shall 'scape whipping?
   Use them after your own honor and dignity: the less
   they deserve, the more merit is in your bounty. Take
   them in.   535
POLONIUS. Come, sirs.
HAMLET. Follow him, friends: we'll hear a play tomor-
   row. [Exit Polonius (with all the Players but the First.]
   Dost thou hear me, old friend; can you play the
   Murther of Gonzago?   540
PLAYER. Ay, my lord.
HAMLET. We'll ha 't to-morrow night. You could, for
   a need, study a speech of some dozen or sixteen
   lines, which I would set down and insert in 't, could
   you not?
PLAYER. Ay, my lord.   546
HAMLET. Very well. Follow that lord, and look you
   mock him not. [Exit Player. To Rosencrantz and
   Guildenstern.] My good friends, I'll leave you till
   night. You are welcome to Elsinore.   550
ROSENCRANTZ. Good my lord!
HAMLET. Ay, so! Goodbye to you!

[Exeunt Rosencrantz and Guildenstern. Manet Hamlet.]

                              Now I am alone.
O what a rogue and peasant slave am I!
Is it not monstrous that this player here,   554
But in a fiction, in a dream of passion,
Could force his soul so to his own conceit
That from her working all the visage wann'd,
Tears in his eyes, distraction in 's aspect,   558
A broken voice, and his whole function suiting
With forms to his conceit? and all for nothing!
For Hecuba?
What's Hecuba to him or he to Hecuba,   562
That he should weep for her? What would he do

---

492. **proof eterne:** eternal impenetrability. 496. **synod:** assembly. 497. **fellies:** the pieces of wood of which the circumference is made. 498. **nave:** hub. 502. **jig:** lively dance, often accompanied by coarse comic verses or dialogue. 504. **mobled:** muffled. 508. **bisson rheum:** blinding tears. **clout:** piece of cloth. 510. **o'er-teemed:** exhausted by excessive child-bearing. 519. **milch:** milky, moist. 521. **turned . . . color:** grown pale.

525. **bestowed:** lodged. 526. **abstract:** summary. 542–43. **for a need:** in case of necessity. 552. **s.d. Manet:** remains on the stage. 553. **peasant:** base. 556. **conceit:** imagination. 557. **wann'd:** grew pale. 559. **function:** action of the body. **suiting:** fitting. 560. **forms:** bodily expression.

Had he the motive and the cue for passion
That I have? He would drown the stage with tears,
And cleave the general ear with horrid speech,   566
Make mad the guilty and appal the free,
Confound the ignorant, and amaze indeed
The very faculties of eyes and ears.
Yet I,   570
A dull and muddy-mettled rascal, peak,
Like John-a-dreams, unpregnant of my cause,
And can say nothing; no, not for a king,
Upon whose property and most dear life   574
A damn'd defeat was made. Am I a coward?
Who calls me villain? breaks my pate across?
Plucks off my beard and blows it in my face?   577
Tweaks me by the nose? gives me the lie i' th'
    throat,
As deep as to the lungs? Who does me this, ha?
'Swounds, I should take it, for it cannot be
But I am pigeon-liver'd, and lack gall
To make oppression bitter, or ere this   582
I should ha' fatted all the region kites
With this slave's offal. Bloody, bawdy villain!
Remorseless, treacherous, lecherous, kindless
    villain!   585
(O! vengeance!)

Why, what an ass am I! This is most brave
That I, the son of a dear murthered,
Prompted to my revenge by heaven and hell,
Must like a whore unpack my heart with words,
And fall a-cursing like a very drab,   591
A scullion! Fie upon it, foh!
About, my brains!—Hum,—. I have heard,
That guilty creatures sitting at a play   594
Have by the very cunning of the scene
Been struck so to the soul that presently
They have proclaim'd their malefactions;
For murther, though it have no tongue, will speak
With most miraculous organ. I'll have these players
Play something like the murther of my father
Before mine uncle. I'll observe his looks,
I'll tent him to the quick. If 'a do blench,   602
I know my course. The spirit that I have seen
May be a de'il, and the de'il hath power
T' assume a pleasing shape;—yea, and perhaps
Out of my weakness and my melancholy   606
(As he is very potent with such spirits)
Abuses me to damn me. I'll have grounds
More relative than this. The play's the thing   609
Wherein I'll catch the conscience of the king. [Exit.]

Act III

SCENE I

A Room in the Castle

[Enter King, Queen, Polonius, Ophelia, Rosencrantz,
Guildenstern, and Lords.]

KING. And can you by no drift of conference
    Get from him why he puts on this confusion,
    Grating so harshly all his days of quiet
    With turbulent and dangerous lunacy?   4

ROSENCRANTZ. He does confess he feels himself dis-
    tracted,
    But from what cause 'a will by no means speak.
GUILDENSTERN. Nor do we find him forward to be
    sounded,
    But with a crafty madness keeps aloof,   8
    When we would bring him on to some confession
    Of his true state.
QUEEN.   Did he receive you well?
ROSENCRANTZ. Most like a gentleman.
GUILDENSTERN. But with much forcing of his disposi-
    tion.   12

566. horrid: horrible.   567. free: free from offence, guiltless.   571.
muddy-mettled: dull-spirited.   peak: mope about.   572. John-
a-dreams: dreamy fellow.   unpregnant of: not quickened by.   575.
defeat: destruction.   580. 'Swounds: God's wounds.   581. But:
but that.   pigeon-liver'd: meek.   582. make oppression bitter:
make me feel the bitterness of oppression.   583. region kites: vul-
tures of the air.   585. kindless: unnatural.
1. drift of conference: turn of the conversation.   2. confusion:
distraction.   3. Grating: harassing.

592. scullion: the lowest household servant.   593. About, my
brains: let me think less wildly.   602. tent: probe.   blench: start
aside.   604. de'il: devil.   609. relative: relevant, to the purpose.
7. forward: ready, disposed.   12. forcing of his disposition: constraint.

ROSENCRANTZ. Niggard of question, but of our demands
 Most free in his reply.

QUEEN.   Did you assay him
 To any pastime?

ROSENCRANTZ. Madam, it so fell out that certain players   16
 We o'er-raught on the way; of these we told him,
 And there did seem in him a kind of joy
 To hear of it. They are about the court,
 And, as I think, they have already order   20
 This night to play before him.

POLONIUS.   'Tis most true;
 And he beseech'd me to entreat your majesties
 To hear and see the matter.

KING. With all my heart; and it doth much content me   24
 To hear him so inclin'd.
 Good gentlemen, give him a further edge,
 And drive his purpose into these delights.

ROSENCRANTZ. We shall, my lord.

[Exeunt Rosencrantz and Guildenstern.]

KING.   Sweet Gertrude, leave us too;
 For we have closely sent for Hamlet hither,   29
 That he, as 'twere by accident, may here
 Affront Ophelia.
 Her father and myself (lawful espials)   32
 Will so bestow ourselves that, seeing unseen,
 We may of their encounter frankly judge,
 And gather by him, as he is behav'd,
 If 't be th' affliction of his love or no   36
 That thus he suffers for.

QUEEN.   I shall obey you.
 And for your part, Ophelia, I do wish
 That your good beauties be the happy cause
 Of Hamlet's wildness; so shall I hope your virtues   40
 Will bring him to his wonted way again,
 To both your honors.

OPHELIA.   Madam, I wish it may.

[Exit Queen.]

POLONIUS. Ophelia, walk you here. Gracious, so please you,
 We will bestow ourselves. [To Ophelia.] Read on this book,   44
 That show of such an exercise may color
 Your loneliness. We are oft to blame in this;
 'Tis too much prov'd that with devotion's visage
 And pious action we do sugar o'er   48
 The devil himself.

KING. [Aside.]   O 'tis too true!
 How smart a lash that speech doth give my conscience!
 The harlot's cheek, beautied with plastering art,
 Is not more ugly to the thing that helps it   52
 Than is my deed to my most painted word.
 O heavy burthen!

POLONIUS. I hear him coming; let's withdraw, my lord.

[Exeunt King and Polonius.]

[Enter Hamlet.]

HAMLET. To be, or not to be, that is the question: 56
 Whether 'tis nobler in the mind to suffer
 The slings and arrows of outrageous fortune,
 Or to take arms against a sea of troubles
 And by opposing end them. To die: to sleep.   60
 No more; and by a sleep to say we end
 The heart-ache and the thousand natural shocks,
 That flesh is heir to: 'tis a consummation
 Devoutly to be wish'd. To die: to sleep.   64
 To sleep? perchance to dream. Ay, there's the rub;
 For in that sleep of death what dreams may come,
 When we have shuffled off this mortal coil,
 Must give us pause. There's the respect   68
 That makes calamity of so long life;
 For who would bear the whips and scorns of time,
 Th' oppressor's wrong, the proud man's contumely,
 The pangs of dispriz'd love, the law's delay,   72
 The insolence of office, and the spurns
 That patient merit of th' unworthy takes,
 When he himself might his quietus make

43. **Gracious . . . you:** if it please your Grace. 45. **exercise:** religious devotion. 47. **too much prov'd:** found by too frequent experience. 52. **to:** in comparison with. **the thing:** the beautifying cosmetic. 65. **rub:** obstacle. 67. **shuffled off:** sloughed off. **mortal coil:** turmoil of mortal life. 68. **give us pause:** cause us to hesitate. **respect:** consideration. 72. **dispriz'd:** held in contempt. 73. **office:** people holding official position. **spurns:** insults. 75. **quietus:** release from life.

13. **Niggard of question:** sparing of conversation. 14. **assay:** tempt. 17. **o'er-raught:** overtook. 26. **edge:** incitement. 29. **closely:** privately. 31. **Affront:** meet. 32. **espials:** spies. 34. **frankly:** freely. 40. **wildness:** madness.

With a bare bodkin? Who would fardels bear,   76
To grunt and sweat under a weary life,
But that the dread of something after death,
The undiscover'd country from whose bourn
No traveller returns, puzzles the will,   80
And makes us rather bear those ills we have
Than fly to others that we know not of?
Thus conscience does make cowards of us all,
And thus the native hue of resolution   84
Is sicklied o'er with the pale cast of thought,
And enterprises of great pitch and moment
With this regard their currents turn awry,
And lose the name of action.—Soft you now!   88
The fair Ophelia! Nymph, in thy orisons
Be all my sins remember'd.

OPHELIA.   Good my lord,
How does your honor for this many a day?

HAMLET. I humbly thank you; well, well, well.   92

OPHELIA. My lord, I have remembrances of yours,
That I have longed long to re-deliver;
I pray you now, receive them.

HAMLET.   No, not I.
I never gave you aught.   96

OPHELIA. My honor'd lord, you know right well you
   did;
And, with them, words of so sweet breath compos'd
As made the things more rich. Their perfume lost,
Take these again, for to the noble mind   100
Rich gifts wax poor when givers prove unkind.
There, my lord.

HAMLET. Ha, ha! are you honest?

OPHELIA. My lord!   104

HAMLET. Are you fair?

OPHELIA. What means your lordship?

HAMLET. That if you be honest and fair, your honesty
should admit no discourse to your beauty.   108

OPHELIA. Could beauty, my lord, have better commerce than with honesty?

HAMLET. Ay, truly; for the power of beauty will
sooner transform honesty from what it is to a bawd
than the force of honesty can translate beauty into
his likeness. This was sometimes a paradox, but now
the time gives it proof. I did love you once.   115

OPHELIA. Indeed, my lord, you made me believe so.

HAMLET. You should not have believed me, for virtue
cannot so inoculate our old stock but we shall relish
of it. I loved you not.

OPHELIA. I was the more deceived.   120

HAMLET. Get thee to a nunnery. Why wouldst thou
be a breeder of sinners? I am myself indifferent
honest, but yet I could accuse me of such things
that it were better my mother had not borne me. I
am very proud, revengeful, ambitious, with more
offences at my beck than I have thoughts to put
them in, imagination to give them shape, or time to
act them in. What should such fellows as I do crawling between earth and heaven? We are arrant knaves
all; believe none of us. Go thy ways to a nunnery.—
Where's your father?   131

OPHELIA. At home, my lord.

HAMLET. Let the doors be shut upon him, that he
may play the fool nowhere but in 's own house.
Farewell.

OPHELIA. O help him, you sweet heavens!   136

HAMLET. If thou dost marry, I'll give thee this plague
for thy dowry: be thou as chaste as ice, as pure as
snow, thou shalt not escape calumny. Get thee to a
nunnery. Go; farewell. Or if thou wilt needs marry,
marry a fool; for wise men know well enough what
monsters you make of them. To a nunnery, go, and
quickly too. Farewell.   143

OPHELIA. O heavenly powers, restore him!

HAMLET. I have heard of your paintings too, well
enough. God hath given you one face, and you
make yourselves another. You jig, you amble, and
you lisp. You nickname God's creatures, and make
your wantonness your ignorance. Go to, I'll no
more on 't; it hath made me mad. I say, we will have
no mo marriage. Those that are married already, all
but one, shall live; the rest shall keep as they are. To
a nunnery, go.   [Exit Hamlet.]

OPHELIA. O what a noble mind is here o'er-
thrown!   154
The courtier's, soldier's, scholar's, eye, tongue,
   sword;
Th' expectancy and rose of the fair state,
The glass of fashion and the mould of form,
Th' observ'd of all observers, quite, quite down!

---

76. **fardels:** burdens. **79. bourn:** boundary. **80. puzzles:** frustrates. **83. conscience:** the ability to think. **84. native hue:** healthy
complexion. **85. cast:** tinge. **86. pitch and moment:** elevation and
importance. **87. regard:** consideration. **currents:** courses. **89.
orisons:** prayers **91. for this many a day:** all this long time. **103.
honest:** sincere. **107. honest:** here in special sense of 'chaste'.
109--10. commerce: intercourse. **114. paradox:** absurdity. **115.
time:** present age.

118. **inoculate:** engraft. **relish:** taste. **122. indifferent:** tolerably. **126. beck:** command. **145. your paintings:** i.e., that women
paint their faces. **148. nickname:** travesty. **148--49. make your
wantonness your ignorance:** affect ignorance as a mask for wantonness. **150. on 't:** of it. **151. mo:** more. **156. expectancy and
rose:** hope and pride. **157. glass:** mirror. **mould:** model.

And I, of ladies most deject and wretched,   159
That suck'd the honey of his music vows,
Now see that noble and most sovereign reason,
Like sweet bells jangled, out of tune and harsh;
That unmatch'd form and feature of blown
    youth   163
Blasted with ecstasy. O woe is me,
T' have seen what I have seen, see what I see!

[*Enter King and Polonius.*]

KING. Love! his affections do not that way tend;
    Nor what he spake, though it lack'd form a
        little,   167
    Was not like madness. There's something in his soul
    O'er which his melancholy sits on brood,
    And I do doubt, the hatch and the disclose
    Will be some danger; which for to prevent,   171
    I have in quick determination
    Thus set it down: he shall with speed to England
    For the demand of our neglected tribute.
    Haply the seas and countries different   175
    With variable objects shall expel
    This something-settled matter in his heart,
    Whereon his brain's still-beating puts him thus
    From fashion of himself. What think you on 't?
POLONIUS. It shall do well: but yet do I believe   180
    The origin and commencement of his grief
    Sprung from neglected love. How now, Ophelia!
    You need not tell us what Lord Hamlet said;
    We heard it all. My lord, do as you please;   184
    But if you hold it fit, after the play
    Let his queen mother all alone entreat him
    To show his grief. Let her be round with him,   187
    And I'll be plac'd (so please you) in the ear
    Of all their conference. If she find him not,
    To England send him, or confine him where
    Your wisdom best shall think.
KING.   It shall be so.
    Madness in great ones must not unwatch'd go.

[*Exeunt.*]

SCENE II

A Hall in the Castle

[*Enter Hamlet and three of the Players.*]

HAMLET. Speak the speech, I pray you, as I pronounced it to you, trippingly on the tongue; but if you mouth it, as many of our players do, I had as lief the town-crier spoke my lines. Nor do not saw the air too much with your hand, thus; but use all gently, for in the very torrent, tempest, and (as I may say) whirlwind of your passion, you must acquire and beget a temperance that may give it smoothness. O it offends me to the soul to hear a robustious periwig-pated fellow tear a passion to tatters, to very rags, to split the ears of the groundlings, who for the most part are capable of nothing but inexplicable dumb-shows and noise. I would have such a fellow whipped for o'er-doing Termagant. It out-herods Herod: pray you, avoid it.   15
PLAYER. I warrant your honor.
HAMLET. Be not too tame neither, but let your own discretion be your tutor. Suit the action to the word, the word to the action, with this special observance, that you o'erstep not the modesty of nature; for anything so overdone is from the purpose of playing, whose end, both at the first and now, was and is to hold, as 'twere, the mirror up to nature, to show virtue her own feature, scorn her own image, and the very age and body of the time his form and pressure. Now this overdone, or come tardy off, though it makes the unskilful laugh, cannot but make the judicious grieve, the censure of the which one must in your allowance o'erweigh a whole theater of others. O there be players that I have seen play and heard others praise, and that highly (not to speak it profanely) that, neither having the accent of Christians nor the gait of Chris-

---

161. **sovereign:** supreme.   163. **feature:** proportion of the whole body.   **blown:** full-blown.   164. **Blasted:** withered.   170. **disclose:** opening of the shell, coming to life.   176. **variable objects:** variety of interests.   177. **something-settled:** somewhat settled.   178. **still-beating:** constant hammering.   179. **fashion of himself:** his ordinary manner.   189. **find:** see through, interpret.

2. **trippingly:** rapidly, but with neat articulation.   3. **mouth:** speak loudly with false emphasis and indistinctness.   8. **acquire and beget:** achieve yourself and inspire in your hearers.   **temperance:** moderation.   10. **robustious:** boisterous.   **periwig-pated:** wearing a wig.   12. **capable of:** able to enjoy.   21. **from:** alien to.   25–26. **very age . . . pressure:** even the contemporary and actual quality of the present time.   26. **pressure:** impressed character, stamp.   26–27. **come tardy off:** inadequately done.   29. **the which one:** one of whom.   **allowance:** estimation.

tian, pagan, nor man, have so strutted and bellowed
that I have thought some of nature's journeymen
had made men and not made them well, they imitated humanity so abominably.

PLAYER. I hope we have reformed that indifferently
with us, sir.   38

HAMLET. O reform it altogether. And let those that
play your clowns speak no more than is set down for
them; for there be of them that will themselves
laugh, to set on some quantity of barren spectators
to laugh too, though in the mean time some necessary question of the play be then to be considered.
That's villainous, and shows a most pitiful ambition
in the fool that uses it. Go, make you ready.

[*Exeunt Players.*]

[*Enter Polonius, Guildenstern, and Rosencrantz.*]

How now, my lord? will the king hear this piece of
work?

POLONIUS. And the queen too, and that
presently.   48

HAMLET. Bid the players make haste.   [*Exit Polonius.*]
Will you two help to hasten them?

ROSENCRANTZ. Ay, my lord.   51

[*Exeunt they two.*]

HAMLET. What, ho! Horatio!

[*Enter Horatio.*]

HORATIO. Here, sweet lord, at your service.

HAMLET. Horatio, thou art e'en as just a man
As e'er my conversation cop'd withal.   55

HORATIO. O, my dear lord,—

HAMLET.   Nay, do not think I
flatter;
For what advancement may I hope from thee,
That no revénue hast but thy good spirits
To feed and clothe thee? Why should the poor be
flatter'd?   59
No, let the candied tongue lick ábsurd pomp,
And crook the pregnant hinges of the knee

Where thrift may follow fawning. Dost thou hear?
Since my dear soul was mistress of her choice
And could of men distinguish, her election   64
Hath seal'd thee for herself; for thou hast been
As one, in suffering all, that suffers nothing,
A man that fortune's buffets and rewards   67
Hast ta'en with equal thanks; and bless'd are those
Whose blood and judgment are so well co-mingled
That they are not a pipe for fortune's finger
To sound what stop she please. Give me that
man   71
That is not passion's slave, and I will wear him
In my heart's core, ay, in my heart of heart,
As I do thee. Something too much of this.
There is a play to-night before the king.   75
One scene of it comes near the circumstance
Which I have told thee of my father's death.
I prithee, when thou seest that act afoot,
Even with the very comment of thy soul   79
Observe my uncle. If his occulted guilt
Do not itself unkennel in one speech,
It is a damned ghost that we have seen,
And my imaginations are as foul   83
As Vulcan's stithy. Give him heedful note,
For I mine eyes will rivet to his face,
And after we will both our judgments join
In censure of his seeming.

HORATIO.   Well, my lord.   87
If 'a steal aught the whilst this play is playing,
And 'scape detecting, I will pay the theft.

HAMLET. They are coming to the play. I must be idle.
Get you a place.   91

[*Enter King, Queen, Polonius, Ophelia, Rosencrantz,
Guildenstern, and other Lords attendant, with his Guard
carrying torches. Danish March. Sound a Flourish.*]

KING. How fares our cousin Hamlet?

HAMLET. Excellent, i' faith; of the chameleon's dish. I
eat the air, promise-crammed. You cannot feed
capons so.   95

---

35. **journeymen:** laborers not yet master of their trade. **41. there be of them:** there are some. **42. barren:** barren of wit. **54. just:** fair-minded, righteous. **55. cop'd withal:** came in contact with. **60. candied:** flattering. **lick:** pay court to (like a dog). **absurd:** silly. **61. pregnant hinges:** easily bent joints.

62. **thrift:** profit. **64. election:** choice. **65. seal'd:** registered unchangeably. **69. blood:** passions. **71. stop:** a hole in wind instruments for controlling the sound. **79. very comment:** most intense observation. **80. occulted:** hidden. **81. itself unkennel:** come to light (like a fox driven from its hole). **84. stithy:** blacksmith's shop, forge. **87. censure:** careful criticism. **seeming:** appearance. **90. be idle:** act mad.

KING. I have nothing with this answer, Hamlet. These words are not mine.

HAMLET. No, nor mine now. [*To Polonius.*] My lord, you played once i' th' university, you say? 99

POLONIUS. That did I, my lord, and was accounted a good actor.

HAMLET. What did you enact? 102

POLONIUS. I did enact Julius Caesar. I was killed i' the Capitol. Brutus killed me.

HAMLET. It was a brute part of him to kill so capital a calf there. Be the players ready? 106

ROSENCRANTZ. Ay, my lord; they stay upon your patience.

QUEEN. Come hither, my dear Hamlet, sit by me.

HAMLET. No, good mother, here's metal more attractive. 110

POLONIUS. [*To the King.*] O ho! do you mark that?

HAMLET. Lady, shall I lie in your lap?

OPHELIA. No, my lord.

HAMLET. I mean, my head upon your lap?

OPHELIA. Ay, my lord. 115

HAMLET. Do you think I meant country matters?

OPHELIA. I think nothing, my lord.

HAMLET. That's a fair thought to lie between maids' legs.

OPHELIA. What is, my lord? 120

HAMLET. Nothing.

OPHELIA. You are merry, my lord.

HAMLET. Who, I?

OPHELIA. Ay, my lord. 124

HAMLET. O God, your only jig-maker. What should a man do but be merry? for look you how cheerfully my mother looks, and my father died within's two hours. 128

OPHELIA. Nay, 'tis twice two months, my lord.

HAMLET. So long? Nay, then, let the de'il wear black, for I'll have a suit of sables. O heavens! die two months ago, and not forgotten yet? Then there's hope a great man's memory may outlive his life half a year; but, by 'r lady, 'a must build churches then, or else shall 'a suffer not thinking on with the hobby-horse, whose epitaph is, 'For, O! for, O! the hobby-horse is forgot.' 137

[*Hautboys play. The dumb-show enters.*]

[*Enter a King and a Queen very lovingly, the Queen embracing him. She kneels and makes show of protestation unto him. He takes her up and declines his head upon her neck; lays him down upon a bank of flowers. She, seeing him asleep, leaves him. Anon comes in a fellow, takes off his crown, kisses it, and pours poison in the King's ears, and exit. The Queen returns, finds the King dead, and makes passionate action. The Poisoner, with some two or three Mutes, comes in again, seeming to lament with her. The dead body is carried away. The Poisoner woos the Queen with gifts; she seems loath and unwilling awhile, but in the end accepts his love. Exeunt.*]

OPHELIA. What means this, my lord?

HAMLET. Marry, this is miching Malicho; it means mischief. 140

OPHELIA. Belike this show imports the argument of the play.

[*Enter Prologue.*]

HAMLET. We shall know by this fellow. The players cannot keep counsel; they'll tell all. 144

OPHELIA. Will 'a tell us what this show meant?

HAMLET. Ay, or any show that you will show him. Be not you ashamed to show, he'll not shame to tell you what it means. 148

OPHELIA. You are naught, you are naught. I'll mark the play.

PROLOGUE. For us and for our tragedy 151
Here stooping to your clemency,
We beg your hearing patiently.

HAMLET. Is this a prologue, or the posy of a ring?

OPHELIA. 'Tis brief, my lord.

HAMLET. As woman's love.

[*Enter (Player) King and Queen.*]

P. KING. Full thirty times hath Phoebus' cart gone round 157
Neptune's salt wash and Tellus' orbed ground,
And thirty dozen moons with borrow'd sheen
About the world have times twelve thirties been,

---

96. have nothing with: can make nothing of. **105. brute part:** stupid act. **107. stay upon:** wait for. **patience:** leisure. **116. country matters:** uncouth conduct. **125. your only jig-maker:** I am the best jig-maker there is; cf. n. on II. ii. 502. **127. within's:** within this. **131. suit of sables:** suit of rich furs. **135. suffer not thinking on:** be forgotten. **136. hobby-horse:** one of the participants in the morris dance.

S. d. Hautboys: wooden double-reed instruments of high pitch. **S. d. Mutes:** actors without speaking parts (but here all are mutes). **139. miching Malicho:** skulking mischief. **141. imports the argument:** amounts to a synopsis. **144. counsel:** secret. **149. naught:** wanton. **152. stooping:** bowing. **154. posy:** motto. **157. cart:** chariot. **158. wash:** sea. **159. borrow'd sheen:** reflected light.

Since love our hearts and Hymen did our hands
Unite commutual in most sacred bands.   162
P. QUEEN. So many journeys may the sun and moon
Make us again count o'er ere love be done!
But, woe is me! you are so sick of late,   165
So far from cheer and from your former state,
That I distrust you. Yet though I distrust,
Discomfort you, my lord, it nothing must;
For women fear too much, even as they love,
And women's fear and love hold quantity,
In neither aught, or in extremity.   171
Now what my love is, proof hath made you know;
And as my love is siz'd, my fear is so.
Where love is great, the littlest doubts are fear;
Where little fears grow great, great love grows
there.   175
P. KING. Faith, I must leave thee, love, and shortly
too.
My operant powers their functions leave to do,
And thou shalt live in this fair world behind,
Honor'd, belov'd; and haply one as kind   179
For husband shalt thou—
P. QUEEN.   O confound the rest!
Such love must needs be treason in my breast.
In second husband let me be accurst;
None wed the second but who kill'd the first.
HAMLET. [Aside.] That's wormwood, wormwood.
P. QUEEN. The instances that second marriage move
Are base respects of thrift, but none of love;
A second time I kill my husband dead,   187
When second husband kisses me in bed.
P. KING. I do believe you think what now you speak,
But what we do determine oft we break.
Purpose is but the slave to memory,   191
Of violent birth, but poor validity;
Which now, like fruit unripe, sticks on the tree,
But fall unshaken when they mellow be.
Most necessary 'tis that we forget   195
To pay ourselves what to ourselves is debt;
What to ourselves in passion we propose,
The passion ending, doth the purpose lose.
The violence of either grief or joy   199
Their own enactures with themselves destroy;
Where joy most revels grief doth most lament,
Grief joys, joy grieves, on slender accident.

This world is not for aye, nor 'tis not strange
That even our loves should with our fortunes
change,   204
For 'tis a question left us yet to prove
Whether love lead fortune or else fortune love.
The great man down, you mark his favorite
flies;   207
The poor advanc'd makes friends of enemies.
And hitherto doth love on fortune tend,
For who not needs shall never lack a friend;
And who in want a hollow friend doth try   211
Directly seasons him his enemy.
But, orderly to end where I begun,
Our wills and fates do so contrary run
That our devices still are overthrown,   215
Our thoughts are ours, their ends none of our own.
So think thou wilt no second husband wed,
But die thy thoughts when thy first lord is dead.
P. QUEEN. Nor earth to me give food, nor heaven
light!   219
Sport and repose lock from me day and night!
To desperation turn my trust and hope!
An anchor's cheer in prison be my scope!
Each opposite that blanks the face of joy   223
Meet what I would have well, and it destroy!
Both here and hence pursue me lasting strife,
If, once a widow, ever I be wife!
HAMLET. If she should break it now!   227
P. KING. 'Tis deeply sworn. Sweet, leave me here
awhile;
My spirits grow dull, and fain I would beguile
The tedious day with sleep.   [Sleeps.]
P. QUEEN.   Sleep rock thy brain;
And never come mischance between us twain! [Exit.]
HAMLET. Madam, how like you this play?   232
QUEEN. The lady doth protest too much, me-
thinks.
HAMLET. O, but she'll keep her word.   235
KING. Have you heard the argument? Is there no
offence in 't?
HAMLET. No, no, they do but jest,—poison in jest.
No offence i' th' world.
KING. What do you call the play?
HAMLET. The Mouse-trap. Marry, how? Tropically.
This play is the image of a murther done in Vienna.
Gonzago is the duke's name; his wife, Baptista. You

---

162. commutual: an intensive form of 'mutual'. 167. I distrust
you: I have misgivings on your account. 170. quantity: proportion. 171. In . . . extremity: nothing of either, or else an
excess. 177. operant: vital. 185. instances: motives, induce-
ments. move: suggest. 192. validity: strength. 200. enactures:
fulfilments.

211. hollow: insincere. 216. ends: results. 219. Nor . . . nor:
neither . . . nor. 220. Sport: pleasure. 222. anchor's: anchorite's. 223. opposite: contrary thing. blanks: blanches, makes
pale. 241. Tropically: figuratively. 242. image: representation.

shall see anon. 'Tis a knavish piece of work: but what of that? Your majesty and we that have free souls, it touches us not. Let the galled jade wince, our withers are unwrung.   247

[*Enter Player as Lucianus.*]

This is one Lucianus, nephew to the King.

OPHELIA. You are as good as a chorus, my lord.

HAMLET. I could interpret between you and your love, if I could see the puppets dallying.   251

OPHELIA. You are keen, my lord, you are keen.

HAMLET. It would cost you a groaning to take off mine edge.   254

OPHELIA. Still better, and worse.

HAMLET. So you must take your husbands. Begin, murtherer; leave thy damnable faces, and begin. Come; the croaking raven doth bellow for revenge.

LUCIANUS. Thoughts black, hands apt, drugs fit, and time agreeing;
Confederate season, else no creature seeing.
Thou mixture rank, of midnight weeds collected,
With Hecate's ban thrice blasted, thrice infected,
Thy natural magic and dire property,   263
On wholesome life usurps immediately.

[*Pours the poison in his ears.*]

HAMLET. 'A poisons him i' the garden for his estate. His name's Gonzago. The story is extant, and written in very choice Italian. You shall see anon how the murtherer gets the love of Gonzago's wife.   268

OPHELIA. The king rises.

HAMLET. What, frighted with false fire?

QUEEN. How fares my lord?

POLONIUS. Give o'er the play.   272

KING. Give me some light! Away!

POLONIUS. Lights, lights, lights!

[*Exeunt all but Hamlet and Horatio.*]

HAMLET.

Why, let the stricken deer go weep,
  The hart ungalled play,
For some must watch while some must sleep: 276
  Thus runs the world away.

Would not this, sir, and a forest of feathers (if the rest of my fortunes turn Turk with me) with two Provincial roses on my razed shoes, get me a fellowship in a cry of players?

HORATIO. Half a share.

HAMLET. A whole one, I.   284

For thou dost know, O Damon dear,
  This realm dismantled was
Of Jove himself; and now reigns here
  A very, very—pajock.   288

HORATIO. You might have rimed.

HAMLET. O good Horatio, I'll take the ghost's word for a thousand pound. Didst perceive?

HORATIO. Very well, my lord.   292

HAMLET. Upon the talk of the poisoning?

HORATIO. I did very well note him.

HAMLET. Ah, ha! Come, some music! come, the recorders!   296

For if the king like not the comedy,
  Why then, belike he likes it not, perdy.

Come, some music!

[*Enter Rosencrantz and Guildenstern.*]

GUILDENSTERN. Good my lord, vouchsafe me a word with you.   300

HAMLET. Sir, a whole history.

GUILDENSTERN. The king, sir,—

HAMLET. Ay, sir, what of him?   303

GUILDENSTERN. Is in his retirement marvellous distempered.

HAMLET. With drink, sir?

GUILDENSTERN. No, my lord, with choler.   306

HAMLET. Your wisdom should show itself more richer to signify this to the doctor; for, for me to put him to his purgation would perhaps plunge him into more choler.   310

GUILDENSTERN. Good my lord, put your discourse

---

246. **galled jade:** horse sore from chafing. **withers:** shoulders. 247. **unwrung:** not galled. 260. **Confederate season:** time conspiring to assist. 272. **Give o'er:** stop.

279. **forest of feathers:** an allusion to the plumes worn by actors. 280. **turn Turk:** play the renegade. 281. **Provincial roses:** rosettes imitating the damask rose. **razed:** slashed, i.e, with cuts or openings. 281–82. **fellowship:** partnership. **cry:** company. 283. **share:** i.e., in the profits of the company. 288. **pajock:** scarecrow. 295. **recorders:** wind instruments of the flute type. 298. **perdy:** a corruption of *par dieu.* 304. **distempered:** disordered. 306. **choler:** anger. 309. **purgation:** purging.

into some frame, and start not so wildly from my affair.

HAMLET. I am tame, sir; pronounce.

GUILDENSTERN. The queen, your mother, in most great affliction of spirit, hath sent me to you.

HAMLET. You are welcome.   316

GUILDENSTERN. Nay, good my lord, this courtesy is not of the right breed. If it shall please you to make me a wholesome answer, I will do your mother's commandment; if not, your pardon and my return shall be the end of my business.   321

HAMLET. Sir, I cannot.

ROSENCRANTZ. What, my lord?

HAMLET. Make you a wholesome answer. My wit's diseased; but, sir, such answer as I can make, you shall command; or, rather, as you say, my mother. Therefore no more, but to the matter. My mother, you say,—   328

ROSENCRANTZ. Then, thus she says: your behavior hath struck her into amazement and admiration.

HAMLET. O wonderful son, that can so 'stonish a mother! But is there no sequel at the heels of this mother's admiration? Impart.   333

ROSENCRANTZ. She desires to speak with you in her closet ere you go to bed.

HAMLET. We shall obey, were she ten times our mother. Have you any further trade with us?

ROSENCRANTZ. My lord, you once did love me.

HAMLET. And do still, by these pickers and stealers.

ROSENCRANTZ. Good my lord, what is your cause of distemper? You do surely bar the door upon your own liberty, if you deny your griefs to your friend.   342

HAMLET. Sir, I lack advancement.

ROSENCRANTZ. How can that be when you have the voice of the king himself for your succession in Denmark?

[Enter the Players, with recorders.]

HAMLET. Ay, sir, but 'While the grass grows,'—the proverb is something musty.—O, the recorders! Let me see one. To withdraw with you,—Why do you go about to recover the wind of me, as if you would drive me into a toil?   350

GUILDENSTERN. O! my lord, if my duty be too bold, my love is too unmannerly.

HAMLET. I do not well understand that. Will you play upon this pipe?

GUILDENSTERN. My lord, I cannot.   357

HAMLET. I pray you.

GUILDENSTERN. Believe me, I cannot.

HAMLET. I do beseech you.

GUILDENSTERN. I know no touch of it, my lord.

HAMLET. It is as easy as lying. Govern these ventages with your fingers and thumb, give it breath with your mouth, and it will discourse most eloquent music. Look you, these are the stops.

GUILDENSTERN. But these cannot I command to any utterance of harmony. I have not the skill.   365

HAMLET. Why, look you now, how unworthy a thing you make of me. You would play upon me; you would seem to know my stops; you would pluck out the heart of my mystery; you would sound me from my lowest note to the top of my compass. And there is much music, excellent voice, in this little organ, yet cannot you make it speak. 'Sblood, do you think I am easier to be played on than a pipe? Call me what instrument you will, though you can fret me, yet you cannot play upon me.   375

[Enter Polonius.]

God bless you, sir!

POLONIUS. My lord, the queen would speak with you, and presently.

HAMLET. Do you see yonder cloud, that's almost in shape of a camel?   380

POLONIUS. By the mass, and 'tis like a camel, indeed.

HAMLET. Methinks it is like a weasel.

POLONIUS. It is backed like a weasel.   383

HAMLET. Or like a whale?

POLONIUS. Very like a whale.

HAMLET. Then I will come to my mother by and by. [Aside.] They fool me to the top of my bent. [Aloud.] I will come by and by.   388

POLONIUS. I will say so.   [Exit.]

HAMLET. By and by is easily said. Leave me, friends.

[Exeunt all but Hamlet.]

'Tis now the very witching time of night,   391
When churchyards yawn and hell itself breathes out

---

312. frame: sensible form.   313. pronounce: speak.   318. of the right breed: pure-bred, genuine.   319. wholesome: sincere.   339. pickers and stealers: hands.   342. liberty: freedom of action.   344. voice: vote.   348. withdraw with: speak privately with.   349. recover the wind of: get advantage of.   350. toil: snare.

359. know no touch: have no skill at all.   360. ventages: holes, stops.   370. compass: range of voice.   386. by and by: at once.   387. top . . . bent: limit of my endurance.   391. witching: when spells are cast.

Contagion to this world. Now could I drink hot
  blood,
And do such bitter business as the day   394
Would quake to look on. Soft! now to my mother!
O heart, lose not thy nature; let not ever
The soul of Nero enter this firm bosom.
Let me be cruel, not unnatural;   398
I will speak daggers to her, but use none.
My tongue and soul in this be hypocrites:
How in my words somever she be shent,
To give them seals never, my soul, consent!   402

[Exit.]

SCENE III

A Room in the Castle

[Enter King, Rosencrantz, and Guildenstern.]

KING. I like him not, nor stands it safe with us
  To let his madness range. Therefore prepare you.
  I your commission will forthwith dispatch,
  And he to England shall along with you.   4
  The terms of our estate may not endure
  Hazard so near us as doth hourly grow
  Out of his braves.
GUILDENSTERN.   We will ourselves provide.
  Most holy and religious fear it is   8
  To keep those many many bodies safe
  That live and feed upon your majesty.
ROSENCRANTZ. The single and peculiar life is bound
  With all the strength and armor of the mind   12
  To keep itself from noyance; but much more
  That spirit upon whose weal depends and rests
  The lives of many. The cesse of majesty
  Dies not alone, but like a gulf doth draw   16
  What's near it with it. It is a massy wheel,
  Fix'd on the summit of the highest mount,
  To whose huge spokes ten thousand lesser things
  Are mortis'd and adjoin'd; which, when it falls, 20
  Each small annexment, petty consequence,

Attends the boisterous ruin. Never alone
  Did the king sigh, but with a general groan.   23
KING. Arm you, I pray you, to this speedy voyage;
  For we will fetters put about this fear,
  Which now goes too free-footed.
ROSENCRANTZ.   We will haste us.

[Exeunt Gentlemen.]

[Enter Polonius.[

POLONIUS. My lord, he's going to his mother's closet.
  Behind the arras I'll convey myself   28
  To hear the process. I'll warr'nt she'll tax him home;
  And, as you said, and wisely was it said,
  'Tis meet that some more audience than a mother,
  Since nature makes them partial, should o'erhear
  The speech, of vantage. Fare you well, my liege. 33
  I'll call upon you ere you go to bed
  And tell you what I know.
KING.   Thanks, dear my lord.

                              [Exit Polonius]

O my offence is rank, it smells to heaven!   36
It hath the primal eldest curse upon 't;
A brother's murther. Pray can I not.
Though inclination be as sharp as will,
My stronger guilt defeats my strong intent,   40
And, like a man to double business bound,
I stand in pause where I shall first begin,
And both neglect. What if this cursed hand
Were thicker than itself with brother's blood,   44
Is there not rain enough in the sweet heavens
To wash it white as snow? Whereto serves mercy
But to confront the visage of offence?
And what's in prayer but this twofold force,   48
To be forestalled, ere we come to fall,
Or pardon'd, being down? Then I'll look up;
My fault is past. But, O, what form of prayer
Can serve my turn? 'Forgive me my foul
  murther?'   52
That cannot be, since I am still possess'd

401. How . . . somever: c.f. I. v. 84. shent: rebuked. 402. give
them seals: confirm them by making words into deeds.
1. like him not: distrust him. 2. range: rove, roam. 3. forthwith
dispatch: prepare at once. 5. terms: condition. 7. braves: defi-
ances. 8. fear: caution. 11. single and peculiar: individual and
private. 13. noyance: harm. 14. weal: welfare. 15. cesse:
decease. 16. gulf: whirlpool. 21. annexment: appendage.

22. Attends: accompanies. 24. Arm: prepare. 29. process: interview. tax . . . home: censure effectually. 33. of vantage: in addition. 37. primal: primeval. 44. thicker than itself: made more
than double its normal thickness. 47. confront: oppose directly.
49. forestalled: prevented in anticipation.

Of those effects for which I did the murther,
My crown, mine own ambition, and my queen.
May one be pardon'd and retain th' offence?   56
In the corrupted currents of this world
Offence's gilded hand may shove by justice,
And oft 'tis seen the wicked prize itself
Buys out the law; but 'tis not so above.   60
There is no shuffling, there the action lies
In his true nature, and we ourselves compell'd
Even to the teeth and forehead of our faults
To give in evidence. What then? what rests?   64
Try what repentance can. What can it not?
Yet what can it, when one cannot repent?
O wretched state! O bosom black as death!
O limed soul, that struggling to be free   68
Art more engag'd! Help, angels! make assay!
Bow, stubborn knees; and heart with strings of steel
Be soft as sinews of the new-born babe.
All may be well.   [*He kneels.*]

[*Enter Hamlet.*]

HAMLET. Now might I do it pat, now 'a is
    praying!   73
And now I'll do 't. And so 'a goes to heaven;
And so am I reveng'd? That would be scann'd.
A villain kills my father, and for that,   76
I, his sole son, do this same villain send
To heaven.
Why, this is hire and salary, not revenge.
'A took my father grossly, full of bread,   80
With all his crimes broad blown, as flush as May;
And how his audit stands who knows save heaven?
But in our circumstance and course of thought
'Tis heavy with him. And am I then reveng'd,   84
To take him in the purging of his soul,
When he is fit and season'd for his passage?
No.
Up, sword, and know thou a more horrid hent;   88

When he is drunk asleep, or in his rage,
Or in th' incestuous pleasure of his bed,
At game a-swearing, or about some act
That has no relish of salvation in 't.   92
Then trip him, that his heels may kick at heaven,
And that his soul may be as damn'd and black
As hell, whereto it goes. My mother stays.—
This physic but prolongs thy sickly days.   [*Exit.*]
KING. [*rising.*] My words fly up, my thoughts remain
    below.   97
Words without thoughts never to heaven go. [*Exit.*]

SCENE IV

The Queen's Closet

[*Enter Queen and Polonius.*]

POLONIUS. 'A will come straight. Look you lay home
    to him. Tell him his pranks have been too broad to
      bear with,
    And that your Grace hath screen'd and stood
      between
    Much heat and him. I'll silence me e'en here.   4
    Pray you, be round with him.
HAMLET. [*within.*] Mother, mother, mother!
QUEEN.   I'll warrant you;
    Fear me not. Withdraw, I hear him coming.

[*Polonius hides behind the arras.*]

[*Enter Hamlet.*]

HAMLET. Now, mother, what's the matter?   8
QUEEN. Hamlet, thou hast thy father much offended.
HAMLET. Mother, you have my father much offended.
QUEEN. Come, come, you answer with an idle
    tongue.
HAMLET. Go, go, you question with a wicked
    tongue.   12
QUEEN. Why, how now, Hamlet!
HAMLET.   What's the matter
    now?
QUEEN. Have you forgot me?
HAMLET.   No, by the rood, not
    so.

---

54. effects: i.e., things acquired by an action. **55. ambition:** i.e., the realization of ambition (so also *offence* in 56). **58. gilded hand:** hand using bribes of gold. **59. wicked prize:** reward of wickedness. **60. Buys out:** corrupts. **61. shuffling:** trickery. **lies:** used in its legal sense. **63. teeth and forehead:** very face. **64. rests:** remains. **68. limed:** caught with bird-lime. **69. engag'd:** entangled. **73. pat:** to a nicety. **75. would:** requires to. **scann'd:** examined, considered. **79. hire and salary:** i.e., a reward. **80. full of bread:** without opportunity to fast. **81. broad blown:** in full bloom. **flush:** lusty. **82. audit:** account. **83. in . . . thought:** according to our vague ideas. **86. passage:** i.e., to the other world. **88. know . . . hent:** let me grasp you at a more horrid moment.

92. relish: flavor. **96. physic:** medicine, i.e., the postponement. **1. lay home:** talk plainly. **2. broad:** free, unrestrained. **4. heat:** anger. **silence me:** withdraw into silence. **14. rood:** cross.

You are the queen, your husband's brother's wife;
And,—would it were not so!—you are my
   mother.   16
QUEEN. Nay then, I'll set those to you that can speak.
HAMLET. Come, come, and sit you down; you shall
   not budge.
You go not till I set you up a glass
Where you may see the inmost part of you.   20
QUEEN. What wilt thou do? thou wilt not murther
   me?
Help, help, ho!
POLONIUS. What, ho! help! help! help!
HAMLET. How now! a rat? Dead, for a ducat, dead!

[*Kills Polonius through the arras*]

POLONIUS. O, I am slain!
QUEEN.   O me, what hast thou
   done?
HAMLET. Nay, I know not. Is it the king?
QUEEN. O, what a rash and bloody deed is this!
HAMLET. A bloody deed! almost as bad, good
   mother,   29
As kill a king, and marry with his brother.
QUEEN. As kill a king?
HAMLET.   Ay, lady, 'twas my word.

[*Lifts up the arras and discovers Polonius.*]

Thou wretched, rash, intruding fool, farewell!
I took thee for thy better. Take thy fortune;   33
Thou find'st to be too busy is some danger.
[*To the Queen.*] Leave wringing of your hands. Peace!
   sit you down,
And let me wring your heart; for so I shall
If it be made of penetrable stuff,   37
If damned custom have not braz'd it so
That it be proof and bulwark against sense.
QUEEN. What have I done that thou dar'st wag thy
   tongue
In noise so rude against me?
HAMLET.   Such an act   41
That blurs the grace and blush of modesty,
Calls virtue hypocrite, takes off the rose
From the fair forehead of an innocent love

And sets a blister there, makes marriage vows
As false as dicers' oaths. O, such a deed   46
As from the body of contraction plucks
The very soul, and sweet religion makes
A rhapsody of words! Heaven's face does glow,
Yea, this solidity and compound mass,   50
With tristful visage as against the doom,
Is thought-sick at the act.
QUEEN.   Ay me! what act,
That roars so loud and thunders in the index?
HAMLET. Look here, upon this picture, and on
   this,   54
The counterfeit presentment of two brothers.
See what a grace was seated on this brow:
Hyperion's curls, the front of Jove himself,   57
An eye like Mars, to threaten and command,
A station like the herald Mercury
New-lighted on a heaven-kissing hill,
A combination and a form indeed,   61
Where every god did seem to set his seal,
To give the world assurance of a man.
This was your husband. Look you, now, what fol-
   lows.
Here is your husband, like a mildew'd ear   65
Blasting his wholesome brother. Have you eyes?
Could you on this fair mountain leave to feed,
And batten on this moor? Ha! have you eyes?
You cannot call it love, for at your age   69
The heyday in the blood is tame, it's humble,
And waits upon the judgment; and what judgment
Would step from this to this? Sense sure you have,
Else could you not have motion; but sure that sense
Is apoplex'd, for madness would not err,
Nor sense to ecstasy was ne'er so thrall'd
But it reserv'd some quantity of choice   76
To serve in such a difference. What devil was't
That thus hath cozen'd you at hoodman-blind?
Eyes without feeling, feeling without sight,
Ears without hands or eyes, smelling sans all,
Or but a sickly part of one true sense   81

47. contraction: marriage contract. **49. rhapsody:** meaningless string. **glow:** blush. **50. this solidity and compound mass:** the solid and composite earth. **51. tristful:** sad. **doom:** doomsday. **53. index:** table of contents, prelude. **55. counterfeit presentment:** portrayed likeness. **57. front:** forehead. **59. station:** poise. **65. ear:** ear of wheat. **68. batten:** grow fat. **moor:** a barren upland. **70. heyday:** youthful high spirits. **72. Sense:** control of the physical senses. **74. apoplex'd:** atrophied. **75. thrall'd:** enslaved. **76. quantity of choice:** power to choose. **78. cozen'd:** cheated. **hoodman-blind:** blind man's bluff. **80. sans:** without.

24. for: i.e., I wager. **38. braz'd it:** made it brazen. **39. proof and bulwark:** an impenetrable defence. **sense:** feeling.

Could not so mope.
O shame! where is thy blush? Rebellious hell,
If thou canst mutine in a matron's bones,
To flaming youth let virtue be as wax   85
And melt in her own fire: proclaim no shame
When the compulsive ardor gives the charge,
Since frost itself as actively doth burn,
And reason panders will.

QUEEN.   O Hamlet, speak no more!
Thou turn'st mine eyes into my very soul;   90
And there I see such black and grained spots
As will not leave their tinct.

HAMLET.   Nay, but to live   92
In the rank sweat of an enseamed bed,
Stew'd in corruption, honeying and making love
Over the nasty sty,

QUEEN.   O speak to me no more!
These words like daggers enter in my ears.   96
No more, sweet Hamlet!

HAMLET.   A murtherer and a villain;
A slave that is not twentieth part the tithe
Of your precedent lord; a vice of kings;
A cutpurse of the empire and the rule,
That from a shelf the precious diadem stole,   101
And put it in his pocket!

QUEEN.   No more!

[Enter Ghost.]

HAMLET. A king of shreds and patches,—
Save me, and hover o'er me with your wings,
You heavenly guards! What would your gracious
    figure?

QUEEN. Alas! he's mad!   106

HAMLET. Do you not come your tardy son to chide,
That, laps'd in time and passion, lets go by
Th' important acting of your dread command?
O, say.

GHOST.   Do not forget. This visitation   110
Is but to whet thy almost blunted purpose.
But, look, amazement on thy mother sits.
O, step between her and her fighting soul.

Conceit in weakest bodies strongest works.
Speak to her, Hamlet.

HAMLET.   How is it with you, lady?

QUEEN. Alas, how is 't with you,
That you bend your eye on vacancy   117
And with th' incorporal air do hold discourse?
Forth at your eyes your spirits wildly peep;
And, as the sleeping soldiers in th' alarm,
Your bedded hair, like life in excrements,   121
Start up and stand an end. O gentle son,
Upon the heat and flame of thy distemper
Sprinkle cool patience. Whereon do you look?

HAMLET. On him, on him! Look you, how pale he
    glares!
His form and cause conjoin'd, preaching to
    stones,   126
Would make them capable.—Do not look upon me;
Lest with this piteous action you convert
My stern effects. Then what I have to do
Will want true color,—tears perchance for
    blood.   130

QUEEN. To whom do you speak this?

HAMLET.   Do you see nothing there?

QUEEN. Nothing at all; yet all that is I see.

HAMLET. Nor did you nothing hear?

QUEEN.   No, nothing but ourselves.

HAMLET. Why, look you there! look, how it steals
    away!
My father, in his habit as he liv'd!   135
Look, where he goes, even now, out at the portal.

[Exit Ghost.]

QUEEN. This is the very coinage of your brain: 137
This bodiless creation ecstasy
Is very cunning in.

HAMLET.   Ecstasy!
My pulse, as yours, doth temperately keep time,
And makes as healthful music. It is not
    madness   141
That I have utter'd. Bring me to the test,
And I the matter will re-word, which madness

---

82. **mope:** act aimlessly.   84. **mutine:** rise in mutiny.   87. **charge:** command.   89. **panders:** ministers to the gratifications of.   91. **grained:** ingrained.   92. **leave their tinct:** lose their color.   93. **enseamed:** greasy.   94. **honeying:** talking sweetly.   98. **tithe:** tenth part (i.e., not one two-hundreth).   99. **precedent:** former. **vice: buffoon.**   100. **cutpurse:** pickpocket.   108. **laps'd in time and passion:** frittering away time and energy.   109. **important:** urgent.

114. **Conceit:** imagination.   118. **incorporal:** incorporeal.   121. **bedded:** smooth, flatly brushed. **hair:** hairs. **life in excrements:** dead tissue come alive.   122. **an end:** on end.   126. **conjoin'd:** united.   127. **capable:** capable of feeling.   128. **convert:** translate.   129. **My stern effects:** the sternness of my deeds.   130. **want true color:** not be what it should.   135. **habit . . . liv'd:** familiar costume.   143. **re-word:** repeat word for word.

Would gambol from. Mother, for love of grace,
Lay not that flattering unction to your soul,   145
That not your trespass but my madness speaks.
It will but skin and film the ulcerous place,
Whiles rank corruption, mining all within,   148
Infects unseen. Confess yourself to heaven;
Repent what's past; avoid what is to come;
And do not spread the compost on the weeds
To make them ranker. Forgive me this my
    virtue,   152
For in the fatness of these pursy times
Virtue itself of vice must pardon beg,
Yea, curb and woo for leave to do him good.
QUEEN. O Hamlet, thou hast cleft my heart in twain.
HAMLET. O throw away the worser part of it,   157
And live the purer with the other half.
Good night; but go not to my uncle's bed;
Assume a virtue, if you have it not.   160
That monster, custom, who all sense doth eat
Of habits evil, is angel yet in this,
That to the use of actions fair and good
He likewise gives a frock or livery   164
That aptly is put on. Refrain to-night,
And that shall lend a kind of easiness
To the next abstinence: the next more easy;
For use almost can change the stamp of nature,
And either tame the devil or throw him out
With wondrous potency. Once more, good night,
And when you are desirous to be bless'd,
I'll blessing beg of you. For this same lord,   172
I do repent; but heaven hath pleas'd it so,
To punish me with this, and this with me,
That I must be their scourge and minister.
I will bestow him, and will answer well   176
The death I gave him. So, again, good night.
I must be cruel only to be kind:
Thus bad begins and worse remains behind.
One word more, good lady.
QUEEN.   What shall I do?   180
HAMLET. Not this, by no means, that I bid you do:

Let the bloat king tempt you again to bed,
Pinch wanton on your cheek, call you his mouse;
And let him, for a pair of reechy kisses,   184
Or paddling in your neck with his damn'd fingers,
Make you to ravel all this matter out,
That I essentially am not in madness,
But mad in craft. 'Twere good you let him
    know;   188
For who that's but a queen, fair, sober, wise,
Would from a paddock, from a bat, a gib,
Such dear concernings hide? who would do so?
No, in despite of sense and secrecy,   192
Unpeg the basket on the house's top,
Let the birds fly, and, like the famous ape,
To try conclusions in the basket creep,
And break your own neck down.   196
QUEEN. Be thou assur'd, if words be made of breath,
And breath of life, I have no life to breathe
What thou hast said to me.
HAMLET. I must to England; you know that?
QUEEN.   Alack!
I had forgot. 'Tis so concluded on.   201
HAMLET. There's letters seal'd, and my two school-
    fellows,
Whom I will trust as I will adders fang'd,
They bear the mandate; they must sweep my way
And marshal me to knavery. Let it work,   205
For 'tis the sport to have the enginer
Hoist with his own petar; and t' shall go hard
But I will delve one yard below their mines,   208
And blow them at the moon. O 'tis most sweet,
When in one line two crafts directly meet!
This man shall set me packing.
I'll lug the guts into the neighbor room.—   212
Mother, good night indeed.—This counsellor
Is now most still, most secret, and most grave,
Who was in life a foolish prating knave.
Come, sir, to draw toward an end with you.   216
Good night, mother.

[*Exit Hamlet tugging in Polonius.*]

---

144. gambol from: skip away from. grace: God. 145. unction: salve. 148. mining: undermining. 153. fatness: grossness. pursy: corpulent. 155. curb and woo: bow and beg. him: i.e., vice. 163. use: habitual practice. 171. be bless'd: become blessed. 176. answer: account for.

182. bloat: bloated. 183. wanton: wantonly. 184. reechy: greasy. 185. paddling: playing fondly. 187. essentially: in my essential nature. 190. paddock: toad. gib: tom-cat. 191. dear concernings: affairs dearly concerning one. 195. conclusions: experiments. 196. down: in the fall. 204. mandate: command. sweep my way: clear my path. 205. marshal: conduct. 206. enginer: maker of military engines, sapper. 207. Hoist: blown up. petar: small bomb. 207–8. 't shall . . . will: it shall not be for lack of trying if I do not.

Act IV

SCENE I

A Room in the Castle

[*Enter King and Queen, with Rosencrantz and Guildenstern.*]

KING. There's matter in these sighs, these profound
    heaves,
  You must translate. 'Tis fit we understand them.
  Where is your son?
QUEEN. Bestow this place on us a little while.   4

[*Exeunt Rosencrantz and Guildenstern.*]

  Ah, mine own lord, what have I seen to-night!
KING. What, Gertrude? How does Hamlet?
QUEEN. Mad as the sea and wind, when both contend
  Which is the mightier. In his lawless fit,   8
  Behind the arras hearing something stir,
  Whips out his rapier, cries, 'A rat! a rat!'
  And in this brainish apprehension kills
  The unseen good old man.
KING.   O heavy deed!   12
  It had been so with us had we been there.
  His liberty is full of threats to all;
  To you yourself, to us, to every one.
  Alas, how shall this bloody deed be answer'd?   16
  It will be laid to us, whose providence
  Should have kept short, restrain'd, and out of haunt,
  This mad young man. But so much was our love,
  We would not understand what was most fit,   20
  But like the owner of a foul disease,
  To keep it from divulging, let it feed
  Even on the pith of life. Where is he gone?
QUEEN. To draw apart the body he hath kill'd,   24
  O'er whom his very madness, like some ore
  Among a mineral of metals base,
  Shows itself pure. 'A weeps for what is done.
KING. O Gertrude, come away!   28
  The sun no sooner shall the mountains touch
  But we will ship him hence; and this vile deed

We must with all our majesty and skill
Both countenance and excuse. Ho, Guilden-
    stern!   32

[*Enter Rosencrantz and Guildenstern.*]

Friends both, go join you with some further aid.
Hamlet in madness hath Polonius slain,
And from his mother's closet hath he dragg'd him.
Go seek him out; speak fair, and bring the body
Into the chapel. I pray you haste in this.   37

[*Exeunt Gentlemen.*]

Come, Gertrude, we'll call up our wisest friends;
And let them know both what we mean to do
and what's untimely done. [So, haply, slander,]
Whose whisper o'er the world's diameter,   41
As level as the cannon to his blank
Transports his poison'd shot, may miss our name,
And hit the woundless air. O, come away!   44
My soul is full of discord and dismay.

                       [*Exeunt.*]

SCENE II

Another Room in the Castle

[*Enter Hamlet.*]

HAMLET. Safely stowed.
GENTLEMEN WITHIN. Hamlet! Lord Hamlet!
HAMLET. What noise? who calls on Hamlet?
  O, here they come.   4

[*Enter Rosencrantz and Guildenstern.*]

ROSENCRANTZ. What have you done, my lord, with
  the dead body?
HAMLET. Compounded it with dust, whereto 'tis kin.
ROSENCRANTZ. Tell us where 'tis, that we may take it
  thence
  And bear it to the chapel.   8

---

1. **heaves**: prolonged sighs. **11. brainish apprehension**: insane illusion. **12. heavy**: grievous. **17. providence**: foresight. **18. short**: tethered. **out of haunt**: out of company. **22. divulging**: becoming known. **26. mineral**: mine.

36. **fair**: courteously. **41. diameter**: extent from side to side. **42. level**: straight. **blank**: white spot in the centre of a target.

HAMLET. Do not believe it.

ROSENCRANTZ. Believe what?

HAMLET. That I can keep your counsel and not mine own. Besides, to be demanded of a sponge, what replication should be made by the son of a king?

ROSENCRANTZ. Take you me for a sponge, my lord?   14

HAMLET. Ay, sir, that soaks up the king's countenance, his rewards, his authorities. But such officers do the king best service in the end. He keeps them, like an ape an apple, in the corner of his jaw; first mouthed, to be last swallowed. When he needs what you have gleaned, it is but squeezing you, and, sponge, you shall be dry again.   21

ROSENCRANTZ. I understand you not, my lord.

HAMLET. I am glad of it. A knavish speech sleeps in a foolish ear.

ROSENCRANTZ. My lord, you must tell us where the body is, and go with us to the king.   26

HAMLET. The body is with the king, but the king is not with the body. The king is a thing—

GUILDENSTERN. A thing, my lord!

HAMLET. Of nothing. Bring me to him. (Hide fox, and all after.)

[Exeunt.]

SCENE III

Another Room in the Castle

[Enter King and two or three.]

KING. I have sent to seek him and to find the body.
How dangerous is it that this man goes loose!
Yet must not we put the strong law on him:
He's lov'd of the distracted multitude,   4
Who like not in their judgment but their eyes;
And where 'tis so, th' offender's scourge is weigh'd,
But never the offence. To bear all smooth and even,
This sudden sending him away must seem   8
Deliberate pause. Diseases desperate grown
By desperate appliance are reliev'd
Or not at all.

[Enter Rosencrantz.]

                    How now! what hath befall'n?

ROSENCRANTZ. Where the dead body is bestow'd, my lord,   12
We cannot get from him.

KING.   But where is he?

ROSENCRANTZ. Without, my lord, guarded, to know your pleasure.

KING. Bring him before us.

ROSENCRANTZ. Ho, Guildenstern! bring in my lord.   16

[Enter Hamlet and Guildenstern.]

KING. Now, Hamlet, where's Polonius?

HAMLET. At supper.

KING. At supper! Where?   19

HAMLET. Not where he eats, but where 'a is eaten. A certain convocation of politic worms are e'en at him. Your worm is your only emperor for diet: we fat all creatures else to fat us, and we fat ourselves for maggots. Your fat king and your lean beggar is but variable service,—two dishes, but to one table. That's the end.

KING. Alas, alas!   27

HAMLET. A man may fish with the worm that hath eat of a king, and eat of the fish that hath fed of that worm.

KING. What dost thou mean by this?   31

HAMLET. Nothing, but to show you how a king may go a progress through the guts of a beggar.

KING. Where is Polonius?   34

HAMLET. In heaven. Send thither to see. If your messenger find him not there, seek him i' th' other place yourself. But, indeed, if you find him not within this month, you shall nose him as you go up the stairs into the lobby.   39

KING. [*To some Attendants.*] Go seek him there.

HAMLET. 'A will stay till you come.

[Exeunt Attendants.]

KING. Hamlet, this deed, for thine especial safety,—
Which we do tender, as we dearly grieve   43
For that which thou hast done,—must send thee hence
With fiery quickness. Therefore prepare thyself.

---

12. to be demanded of: on being questioned by.   **13. replication:** reply.   **15-16. countenance:** favor.   **16. authorities:** offices of authority.   **30. Hide fox, and all after:** signal cry in a children's game.

6. scourge: punishment.   **7. bear:** execute.   **smooth and even:** pleasantly and equably.   **9. Deliberate pause:** judicially considered.   **10. appliance:** remedy.

21. convocation: assembly.   **politic:** crafty.   **25. variable service:** variety of courses.   **33. progress:** state journey.

The bark is ready and the wind at help,
Th' associates tend, and everything is bent   47
For England.
HAMLET.   For England?
KING.   Ay, Hamlet.
HAMLET.   Good.
KING. So is it, if thou knew'st our purposes.
HAMLET. I see a cherub that sees them. But, come;
    for England! Farewell, dear mother.   51
KING. Thy loving father, Hamlet.
HAMLET. My mother. Father and mother is man and
    wife, man and wife is one flesh, and so, my mother.
    Come, for England!   [Exit.]
KING. Follow him at foot; tempt him with speed
    aboard.
Delay it not, I'll have him hence to-night.   57
Away! for everything is seal'd and done
That else leans on th' affair. Pray you, make
    haste.   59

[Exeunt Rosencrantz and Guildenstern.]

And, England, if my love thou hold'st at aught,—
As my great power thereof may give thee sense,
Since yet thy cicatrice looks raw and red
After the Danish sword, and thy free awe   63
Pays homage to us,—thou mayst not coldly set
Our sovereign process, which imports at full,
By letters congruing to that effect,
The present death of Hamlet. Do it, England;
For like the hectic in my blood he rages,   68
And thou must cure me. Till I know 'tis done,
Howe'er my haps, my joys were ne'er begun.
          [Exit.]

SCENE IV

Open Country near the Castle

[Enter Fortinbras with his army over the stage.]

FORTINBRAS. Go, captain, from me greet the Danish
    king.
Tell him that by his licence Fortinbras

Craves the conveyance of a promis'd march
Over his kingdom. You know the rendezvous.   4
If that his majesty would aught with us,
We shall express our duty in his eye,
And let him know so.
CAPTAIN.   I will do 't, my lord.
FORTINBRAS. Go softly on.

[Exit with army, leaving Captain.]

[Enter Hamlet, Rosencrantz, & c.]

HAMLET. Good sir, whose powers are these?
CAPTAIN. They are of Norway, sir.
HAMLET. How purpos'd, sir, I pray you?
CAPTAIN. Against some part of Poland.   12
HAMLET. Who commands them, sir?
CAPTAIN. The nephew to old Norway, Fortinbras.
HAMLET. Goes it against the main of Poland, sir,
    Or for some frontier?   16
CAPTAIN. Truly to speak, and with no addition,
    We go to gain a little patch of ground
    That hath in it no profit but the name.
    To pay five ducats, five, I would not farm it;   20
    Nor will it yield to Norway or the Pole
    A ranker rate, should it be sold in fee.
HAMLET. Why, then the Polack never will defend it.
CAPTAIN. Yes, it is already garrison'd.   24
HAMLET. Two thousand souls and twenty thousand
    ducats
    Will not debate the question of this straw.
    This is th' imposthume of much wealth and peace,
    That inward breaks, and shows no cause
    without   28
    Why the man dies. I humbly thank you, sir.
CAPTAIN. God we wi' you, sir.   [Exit.]
ROSENCRANTZ.   Will 't please you go,
    my lord?
HAMLET. I'll be with you straight. Go a little before.

[Exeunt all except Hamlet.]

How all occasions do inform against me   32
And spur my dull revenge! What is a man,
If his chief good and market of his time
Be but to sleep and feed? A beast, no more.

---

47. **bent:** prepared. **56. at foot:** close behind. **59. leans on:** depends upon. **61. thereof may give thee sense:** may make you think of it. **62. cicatrice:** scar. **63. free awe:** awe still felt but no longer enforced by arms. **64. set:** esteem. **65. process:** formal command. **66. congruing:** agreeing. **68. hectic:** wasting fever. **70. haps:** fortunes.

3. **the conveyance of:** escort during the course of. **6. in his eye:** in his presence. **8. softly:** slowly. **9. power:** troops. **15. main:** chief part. **17. no addition:** without adding fine words. **22. ranker:** richer. **sold in fee:** sold absolutely. **26. debate:** bring to a settlement. **straw:** trifling matter. **27. imposthume:** abscess. **34. market of:** way to dispose of.

Sure he that made us with such large discourse,   36
Looking before and after, gave us not
That capability and godlike reason
To fust in us unus'd. Now whether it be
Bestial oblivion, or some craven scruple   40
Of thinking too precisely on th' event
(A thought, which, quarter'd, hath but one part
    wisdom,
And ever three parts coward) I do not know
Why yet I live to say 'This thing's to do,'   44
Sith I have cause and will and strength and means
To do 't. Examples gross as earth exhort me:
Witness this army of such mass and charge,
Led by a delicate and tender prince,   48
Whose spirit with divine ambition puff'd
Makes mouths at the invisible event,
Exposing what is mortal and unsure
To all that fortune, death and danger dare,   52
Even for an egg-shell. Rightly to be great
Is not to stir without great argument,
But greatly to find quarrel in a straw
When honor's at the stake. How stand I then,
That have a father kill'd, a mother stain'd,   57
Excitements of my reason and my blood,
And let all sleep, while, to my shame, I see
The imminent death of twenty thousand men,
That for a fantasy and trick of fame   61
Go to their graves like beds, fight for a plot
Whereon the numbers cannot try the cause,
Which is not tomb enough and continent   64
To hide the slain? O, from this time forth,
My thoughts be bloody, or be nothing worth!
                                                    [Exit.]

SCENE V

A Room in the Castle

[Enter Queen, Horatio, and a Gentleman.]

QUEEN. I will not speak with her.
GENTLEMAN. She is importunate, indeed distract:
    Her mood will needs be pitied.

QUEEN.   What would she
    have?
GENTLEMAN. She speaks much of her father; says she
    hears   4
There's tricks i' th' world; and hems, and beats her
    heart;
Spurns enviously at straws, speaks things in doubt
That carry but half sense. Her speech is nothing,
Yet the unshaped use of it doth move   8
The hearers to collection. They aim at it,
And botch the words up fit to their own thoughts;
Which, as her winks and nods and gestures yield
    them,
Indeed would make one think there might be
    thought,
Though nothing sure, yet much unhappily.   13
HORATIO. 'Twere good she were spoken with, for she
    may strew
Dangerous conjectures in ill-breeding minds.
QUEEN. Let her come in.   [Exit Gentleman.]
To my sick soul, as sin's true nature is,   17
Each toy seems prologue to some great amiss.
So full of artless jealousy is guilt,
It spills itself in fearing to be spilt.   20

[Enter Ophelia distracted.]

OPHELIA. Where is the beauteous majesty of Den-
    mark?
QUEEN. How now, Ophelia!   [She sings.]
OPHELIA.

        How should I your true love know
            From another one?   24
        By his cockle hat and staff,
            And his sandal shoon.

QUEEN. Alas! sweet lady, what imports this song?
OPHELIA. Say you? nay, pray you, mark.   [Song.]   28

        He is dead and gone, lady,
            He is dead and gone;
        At his head a grass-green turf;
            At his heels a stone.   32

    O, ho!

---

36. **large discourse:** latitude of comprehension. **39. fust:** become mouldy. **40. Bestial oblivion:** animal-like forgetfulness. **41. event:** outcome. **44. to do:** i.e., still undone. **46. gross:** weighty. **47. charge:** expense. **54. argument:** cause. **58. Excitements:** incentives. **61. trick:** trifle. **64. continent:** (a sufficient) receptacle. **2. importunate:** persistent.

5. **tricks:** deceptions. 6. **Spurns:** kicks. **enviously:** spitefully. **in doubt:** ambiguous. 8. **unshaped:** artless. 9. **collection:** inference. **aim:** guess. 11. **Which:** the words. **yield them:** interpret her words. 13. **nothing:** not at all. **much:** very. 15. **ill-breeding:** plotting ill. 18. **great amiss:** calamity. 19. **artless jealousy:** foolish anxiety. 20. **spills:** ruins. 25. **cockle hat:** pilgrim's hat. 26. **shoon:** shoes.

QUEEN. Nay, but Ophelia,—

OPHELIA. Pray you, mark.

White his shroud as the mountain snow,— 36

[Enter King.]

QUEEN. Alas! look here, my lord.

OPHELIA.

Larded all with sweet flowers;
Which bewept to the ground did—not—go
With true-love showers. 40

KING. How do you, pretty lady?

OPHELIA. Well, God 'ild you! They say the owl was
a baker's daughter. Lord! we know what we are,
but know not what we may be. God be at your
table! 45

KING. Conceit upon her father.

OPHELIA. Pray, let's have no words of this; but when
they ask you what it means, say you this:

To-morrow is Saint Valentine's day, 49
All in the morning betime,
And I a maid at your window,
To be your Valentine. 52
Then up he rose, and donn'd his clo'es,
And dupp'd the chamber door;
Let in the maid, that out a maid
Never departed more. 56

KING. Pretty Ophelia!

OPHELIA. Indeed, la, without an oath, I'll make an
end on 't:

By Gis and by Saint Charity,
Alack, and fie for shame! 60
Young men will do 't, if they come to 't:
By Cock they are to blame.
Quoth she, before you tumbled me,
You promis'd me to wed. 64

He answers:

So would I ha' done, by yonder sun,
An thou hadst not come to my bed.

KING. How long hath she been thus? 67

OPHELIA. I hope all will be well. We must be patient;
but I cannot choose but weep to think they would
lay him i' th' cold ground. My brother shall know of
it: and so I thank you for your good counsel. Come,
my coach! Goodnight, ladies; good night, sweet
ladies; good night, good night. [Exit.]

KING. Follow her close. Give her good watch, I pray
you. [Exit Horatio.]
O, this is the poison of deep grief; it springs 76
All from her father's death. O Gertrude, Gertrude!
When sorrows come, they come not single spies,
But in battalions. First, her father slain;
Next, your son gone, and he most violent
author 80
Of his own just remove; the people muddied,
Thick and unwholesome in their thoughts and whis-
pers
For good Polonius' death,—and we have done but
greenly,
In hugger-mugger to inter him; poor Ophelia
Divided from herself and her fair judgment, 85
Without the which we are pictures, or mere beasts.
Last, and as much containing as all these,
Her brother is in secret come from France, 88
Feeds on his wonder, keeps himself in clouds,
And wants not buzzers to infect his ear
With pestilent speeches of his father's death;
Wherein necessity, of matter beggar'd, 92
Will nothing stick our person to arraign
In ear and ear. O my dear Gertrude, this,
Like to a murdering-piece, in many places
Gives me superfluous death. [A noise within.]

QUEEN. Alack! what noise is this?

KING. Attend!

[Enter a Messenger.]

Where are my Switzers? Let them guard the
door. 97
What is the matter?

MESSENGER. Save yourself, my lord!
The ocean, overpeering of his list,
Eats not the flats with more impetuous haste

---

81. remove: removal. muddied: stirred up. 83. greenly: foolishly. 84. In hugger-mugger: secretly. 89. wonder: doubt. in
clouds: in gloom, or, invisible. 90. buzzers: tale-bearers. 92.
Wherein: i.e., in which pestilent speeches. necessity: poverty (of
argument). 93. nothing stick: not at all hesitate. 94. In ear and
ear: in many ears. 95. murdering-piece: small 'anti-personnel' cannon. 97. Switzers: Swiss guards. 99. overpeering: rising
above. list: boundary.

---

38. Larded: garnished. 42. God 'ild: God reward. 54. dupp'd:
opened. 59. by Gis: by Jesus. 62. Cock: perversion of 'God' in
oaths.

Than young Laertes, in a riotous head,   101
O'erbears your officers. The rabble call him lord,
And as the world were now but to begin,
Antiquity forgot, custom not known,   104
The ratifiers and props of every word,
They cry, 'Choose we! Laertes shall be king!'
Caps, hands, and tongues applaud it to the clouds,
'Laertes shall be king, Laertes king!'   108

[*A noise within.*]

QUEEN. How cheerfully on the false trail they cry!
  O, this is counter, you false Danish dogs!
KING. The doors are broke.

[*Enter Laertes with others.*]

LAERTES. Where is the king? Sirs, stand you all with-
  out.
ALL. No, let's come in.   113
LAERTES.   I pray you, give me leave.
ALL. We will! we will!
LAERTES. I thank you: keep the door.   [*Mob retires.*]
  O thou vile king!
  Give me my father.
QUEEN.   Calmly, good Laertes.   117
LAERTES. That drop of blood that's calm proclaims
  me bastard,
  Cries cuckold to my father, brands the harlot
  Even here, between the chaste unsmirched brows
  Of my true mother.
KING.   What is the cause, Laertes?
  That thy rebellion looks so giantlike?   122
  Let him go, Gertrude; do not fear our person.
  There's such divinity doth hedge a king
  That treason can but peep to what it would,
  Acts little of his will. Tell me, Laertes,   126
  Why thou art thus incens'd. Let him go, Gertrude.
  Speak, man.
LAERTES. Where is my father?
KING.   Dead.
QUEEN.   But not by him.
KING. Let him demand his fill.   129
LAERTES. How came he dead? I'll not be juggled
  with.
  To hell, allegiance! vows, to the blackest devil!
  Conscience and grace, to the profoundest pit!

I dare damnation. To this point I stand,   133
  That both the worlds I give to negligence.
  Let come what comes! only I'll be reveng'd
  Most throughly for my father.
KING.   Who shall stay you?
LAERTES. My will, not all the world: 137
  And for my means, I'll husband them so well,
  They shall go far with little.
KING.   Good Laertes,
  If you desire to know the certainty
  Of your dear father, is 't writ in your revenge,   141
  That, swoopstake, you will draw both friend and
    foe,
  Winner and loser?
LAERTES. None but his enemies.
KING.   Will you know them
    then?
LAERTES. To his good friends thus wide I'll ope my
  arms;   145
  And like the kind life-rendering pelican,
  Repast them with my blood.
KING.   Why, now you speak
  Like a good child and a true gentleman.
  That I am guiltless of your father's death,   149
  And am most sensibly in grief for it,
  It shall as level to your judgment peer
  As day does to your eye.
A NOISE WITHIN. [*Voices.*] Let her come in.
LAERTES. How now! what noise is that?

[*Enter Ophelia.*]

  O heat, dry up my brains! tears seven times salt,
  Burn out the sense and virtue of mine eye!
  By heaven, thy madness shall be paid with weight,
  Till our scale turn the beam. O rose of May!
  Dear maid, kind sister, sweet Ophelia!   158
  O heavens! is 't possible a young maid's wits
  Should be as mortal as an old man's life?
  (Nature is fine in love, and where 'tis fine   161
  It sends some precious instance of itself
  After the thing it loves.)
OPHELIA.

    They bore him barefac'd on the bier;   [*Song.*]
    Hey non nonny, nonny, hey nonny;   165
    And in his grave rain'd many a tear—

---

101. **head:** hostile advance.   110. **counter:** following the trail in a direction opposite to that which the game has taken.   119. **cuckold:** husband with an unfaithful wife.   125. **peep:** look from tiptoe (as over a hedge).   132. **grace:** God's grace.

134. **both the worlds:** this world and the next.   137. **My will:** as regards my will.   140. **certainty:** the real truth.   142. **swoopstake:** indiscriminately.   147. **Repast:** feed.   150. **sensibly:** feelingly.   151. **peer:** show itself.   155. **sense and virtue:** feeling and power.   156. **paid with weight:** heavily paid for.   157. **of May:** early-blooming, delicate.

Fare you well, my dove!

LAERTES. Hadst thou my wits, and didst persuade revenge,

It could not move thus.   169

OPHELIA.

> You must sing, a-down a-down,
> And you call him a-down-a.

O how the wheel becomes it! It is the false steward that stole his master's daughter.   173

LAERTES. This nothing's more than matter.

OPHELIA. There's rosemary, that's for remembrance; pray you, love, remember: and there is pansies, that's for thoughts.   177

LAERTES. A document in madness, thoughts and remembrance fitted.

OPHELIA. There's fennel for you, and columbines; there's rue for you, and here's some for me; we may call it herb of grace o' Sundays. O, you must wear your rue with a difference. There's a daisy; I would give you some violets, but they withered all when my father died. They say he made a good end.   185

> For bonny sweet Robin is all my joy.

LAERTES. Thought and affliction, passion, hell itself, She turns to favor and to prettiness.   188

OPHELIA.

> And will 'a not come again?   [Song.]
>   And will 'a not come again?
>   No, no, he is dead;
>   Go to thy deathbed,   192
>   He never will come again.
>
>   His beard was as white as snow
>   All flaxen was his poll,
>   He is gone, he is gone,   196
>   And we castaway moan:
>   God ha' mercy on his soul!

And of all Christian souls, I pray God. God be wi' you!   [Exit Ophelia.]

LAERTES. Do you see this, O God?   201

KING. Laertes, I must cómmune with your grief, Or you deny me right. Go but apart,

Make choice of whom your wisest friends you will,   204
And they shall hear and judge 'twixt you and me.
If by direct or by collateral hand
They find us touch'd, we will our kingdom give,
Our crown, our life, and all that we call ours   208
To you in satisfaction; but if not,
Be you content to lend your patience to us,
And we shall jointly labor with your soul
To give it due content.

LAERTES.   Let this be so.   212
His means of death, his óbscure burial,
No trophy, sword, nor hatchment o'er his bones,
No noble rite nor formal ostentation,
Cry,—to be heard as 'twere from heaven to earth,—
That I must call 't in question.

KING.   So you shall;   217
And where th' offence is let the great axe fall.
I pray you go with me.   [Exeunt.]

SCENE VI

Another Room in the Castle

[Enter Horatio with an Attendant.]

HORATIO. What are they that would speak with me?

ATTENDANT. Seafaring men, sir. They say they have letters for you.

HORATIO. Let them come in.   [Exit Attendant.]
I do not know from what part of the world   4
I should be greeted, if not from Lord Hamlet.

[Enter Sailor.]

SAILOR. God bless you, sir.

HORATIO. Let him bless thee too.

SAILOR. 'A shall, sir, an 't please him. There's a letter for you, sir. It came from th' ambassador that was bound for England,—if your name be Horatio, as I am let to know it is.   11

HORATIO. [reads the letter.] "Horatio, when thou shalt have overlooked this, give these fellows some means to the king: they have letters for him. Ere we were

---

178. **document:** lesson. 180. **fennel:** emblem of flattery. **columbines:** emblems of thanklessness. 181. **rue:** emblem of repentance. 183. **daisy:** emblem of dissemblers. 184. **violets:** emblems of faithfulness. 187. **passion:** suffering. 188. **favor:** charm. 195. **poll:** head ('pow' in dialect). 197. **castaway:** bereaved ones. 202. **commune:** consult. 203. **right:** equitable treatment.

204. **whom your:** whichever. 206. **collateral:** indirect. 207. **touch'd:** implicated. 213. **means:** manner. 214. **trophy:** memorial emblem. **hatchment:** tablet displaying armorial bearings. 215. **ostentation:** ceremony. 216. **Cry:** cry out, proclaim. **to be heard:** so loud as to be heard. 217. **call 't in question:** demand an explanation. 13. **overlooked:** perused.

two days old at sea, a pirate of very warlike appointment gave us chase. Finding ourselves too slow of
sail, we put on a compelled valor, and in the grapple
I boarded them. On the instant they got clear of our
ship, so I alone became their prisoner. They have
dealt with me like thieves of mercy, but they knew
what they did; I am to do a good turn for them. Let
the king have the letters I have sent, and repair thou
to me with as much speed as thou wouldst fly death.
I have words to speak in thine ear will make thee
dumb; yet are they much too light for the bore of
the matter. These good fellows will bring thee
where I am. Rosencrantz and Guildenstern hold
their course for England. Of them I have much to
tell thee. Farewell!

> He that thou knowest thine,
> Hamlet."

Come, I will give you way for these your
   letters,   32
And do 't the speedier that you may direct me
To him from whom you brought them.

                                  [*Exeunt.*]

SCENE VII

A Room in the Castle

[*Enter King and Laertes.*]

KING. Now must your conscience my acquittance seal,
  And you must put me in your heart for friend,
  Sith you have heard, and with a knowing ear,
  That he which hath your noble father slain   4
  Pursu'd my life.
LAERTES.   It well appears; but tell me
  Why you proceeded not against these feats,
  So crimeful and so capital in nature,
  As by your safety, greatness, wisdom, all things, 8
  You mainly were stirr'd up.
KING.   O, for two special
    reasons,
  Which may to you perhaps seem much unsinew'd,
  But yet to me they 're strong. The queen his mother

Lives almost by his looks, and for myself,—   12
My virtue or my plague, be it either which,—
She's so conjunctive to my life and soul
That, as the star moves not but in his sphere,
I could not but by her. The other motive   16
Why to a public count I might not go
Is the great love the general gender bear him,
Who, dipping all his faults in their affection,
Work like the spring that turneth wood to
    stone,—   20
Convert his gyves to graces; so that my arrows,
Too slightly timber'd for so loud a wind,
Would have reverted to my bow again,
And not where I had aim'd them.   24
LAERTES. And so have I a noble father lost,
  A sister driven into desperate terms,
  Whose worth, if praises may go back again,
  Stood challenger-on-mount of all the age   28
  For her perfections. But my revenge will come.
KING. Break not your sleeps for that. You must not
    think
  That we are made of stuff so flat and dull
  That we can let our beard be shook with danger
  And think it pastime. You shortly shall hear
    more.   33
  I lov'd your father, and we love ourself,
  And that, I hope, will teach you to imagine,—

[*Enter a Messenger with letters.*]

How now, what news?
MESSENGER.   Letters, my lord, from
    Hamlet.
  These to your majesty; this to the queen.   37
KING. From Hamlet? who brought them?
MESSENGER. Sailors, my lord, they say; I saw them
    not.
  They were given me by Claudio, he receiv'd
    them   40
  Of him that brought them.
KING.   Laertes, you shall hear
    them.—
  Leave us.   [*Exit Messenger.*]

15–16. appointment: equipment. **22. repair:** come. **25. bore:** literally, calibre, hence importance. **32. way:** passage.
3. knowing: convinced. **5. Pursu'd:** sought. **7. capital:** punishable by death. **8. your safety:** regard for your safety. **greatness:** position. **wisdom:** intelligence in general. **9. mainly:** strongly. **10. unsinew'd:** weak.

13. be . . . which: whichever it be. **14. conjunctive:** closely united. **16. could not but by her:** could not move except beside her, (could not live without her). **17. count:** legal indictment. **18. general gender:** common people. **21. gyves:** leg-irons, marks of shame. **22. Too slightly timber'd:** too light. **23. reverted:** returned. **28. challenger-on-mount:** mounted challenger, ready in the lists.

"High and mighty, you shall know I am set naked
on your kingdom. To-morrow shall I beg leave to
see your kingly eyes; when I shall (first asking your
pardon thereunto) recount the occasion of my sudden and more strange return."

What should this mean? Are all the rest come
 back?   48
Or is it some abuse, and no such thing?
LAERTES. Know you the hand?
KING.   'Tis Hamlet's character. 'Naked'!
And in a postscript here, he says, 'alone.' 51
Can you advise me?
LAERTES. I'm lost in it, my lord. But let him come!
It warms the very sickness in my heart
That I shall live and tell him to his teeth, 55
'Thus didest thou.'
KING.   If it be so, Laertes,—
As how should it be so? how otherwise?—
Will you be rul'd by me?
LAERTES.   Ay, my lord;
So you will not o'er-rule me to a peace. 59
KING. To thine own peace. If he be now return'd,
As checking at his voyage, and that he means
No more to undertake it, I will work him
To an exploit now ripe in my device,   63
Under the which he shall not choose but fall;
And for his death no wind of blame shall breathe,
But even his mother shall uncharge the practice
And call it accident.
LAERTES.   My lord, I will be rul'd; 67
The rather, if you could devise it so
That I might be the organ.
KING.   It falls right.
You have been talk'd of since your travel much,
And that in Hamlet's hearing, for a quality 71
Wherein, they say, you shine. Your sum of parts
Did not together pluck such envy from him
As did that one, and that, in my regard,
Of the unworthiest siege.
LAERTES.   What part is that, my lord? 75
KING. A very riband in the cap of youth,
Yet needful too, for youth no less becomes
The light and careless livery that it wears
Than settled age his sables and his weeds 79

Importing health and graveness. Two months since
Here was a gentleman of Normandy.
I've seen myself, and serv'd against, the French,
And they can well on horseback; but this gallant
Had witchcraft in 't. He grew unto his seat,
And to such wondrous doing brought his horse,
As had he been incorps'd and demi-natur'd
With the brave beast. So far he topp'd my
 thought,   87
That I, in forgery of shapes and tricks,
Come short of what he did.
LAERTES.   A Norman was 't?
KING. A Norman.
LAERTES. Upon my life, Lamound.
KING.   The very same. 91
LAERTES. I know him well. He is the brooch indeed
And gem of all the nation.
KING. He made confession of you,
And gave you such a masterly report   95
For art and exercise in your defence,
And for your rapier most especially,
That he cried out, 'twould be a sight indeed
If one could match you. The scrimers of their
 nation,
He swore, had neither motion, guard, nor
 eye,   100
If you oppos'd them. Sir, this report of his
Did Hamlet so envenom with his envy
That he could nothing do but wish and beg 103
Your sudden coming o'er, to play with you.
Now, out of this,—
LAERTES.   What out of this, my lord?
KING. Laertes, was your father dear to you?
Or are you like the painting of a sorrow, 107
A face without a heart?
LAERTES.   Why ask you this?
KING. Not that I think you did not love your father,
But that I know love is begun by time,
And that I see, in passages of proof,   111
Time qualifies the spark and fire of it.
There lives within the very flame of love
A kind of wick or snuff that will abate it,
And nothing is at a like goodness still, 115
For goodness, growing to a plurisy,
Dies in his own too-much. That we would do,

---

43. naked: without resources. 49. abuse: imposture. 50. character: handwriting 61. checking: stopping short. 66. uncharge:
acquit of guilt. practice: strategem. 69. organ: instrument. falls:
happens. 75. siege: rank. part: attribute. 76. riband: ribbon.
78. livery: garb. 79. weeds: garments.

80. health: prosperity. 83. can well: are skilled. 87. topp'd: sur-
passed. 94. confession: report. 96. art and exercise: theory and
practice. defence: science of defence. 99. scrimers: fencers. 104.
play: fence. 116. plurisy: fulness.

We should do when we would, for this 'would'
    changes,
And hath abatements and delays as many   119
As there are tongues, are hands, are accidents;
And then this 'should' is like a spendthrift's sigh,
That hurts by easing. But, to the quick o' th' ulcer:
Hamlet comes back. What would you undertake
To show yourself in deed your father's son   124
More than in words?
LAERTES.   To cut his throat i' th' church.
KING. No place, indeed, should murther sanctuarize;
    Revenge should have no bounds. But, good
        Laertes,   127
    Will you do this: keep close within your chamber?
    Hamlet return'd shall know you are come home.
    We'll put on those shall praise your excellence,
    And set a double varnish on the fame   131
    The Frenchman gave you,—bring you, in fine,
        together,
    And wager on your heads. He, being remiss,
    Most generous, and free from all contriving,
    Will not peruse the foils; so that with ease,   135
    Or with a little shuffling, you may choose
    A sword unbated, and in a pass of practice
    Requite him for your father.
LAERTES.   I will do 't;
    And for that purpose I'll anoint my sword.   139
    I bought an unction of a mountebank
    So mortal that, but dip a knife in it,
    Where it draws blood no cataplasm so rare,
    Collected from all simples that have virtue   143
    Under the moon, can save the thing from death
    That is but scratch'd withal. I'll touch my point
    With this contagion, that if I gall him slightly,
    It may be death.
KING.   Let's further think of this,   147
    Weigh what convenience both of time and means
    May fit us to our shape. If this should fail,
    And that our drift look through our bad perform-
        ance,
    'Twere better not assay'd. Therefore this
        project   151
    Should have a back or second, that might hold,
    If this should blast in proof. Soft! let me see.

We'll make a solemn wager on your cunnings.
I ha t':   155
When in your motion you are hot and dry,—
As make your bouts more violent to that end,—
And that he calls for drink, I'll have prepar'd him
A chalice for the nonce, whereon but sipping,
If he by chance escape your venom'd stuck,   160
Our purpose may hold there. But stay! what noise?

[Enter Queen.]

How, sweet queen?
QUEEN. One woe doth tread upon another's
    heel,   163
    So fast they follow. Your sister's drown'd, Laertes.
LAERTES. Drown'd! O, where?
QUEEN. There is a willow grows aslant a brook,
    That shows his hoar leaves in the glassy stream.
    There with fantastic garlands did she come   168
    Of crowflowers, nettles, daisies, and long purples,
    That liberal shepherds give a grosser name,
    But our cold maids do dead men's fingers call
        them.   171
    There, on the pendent boughs her coronet weeds
    Clambering to hang, an envious sliver broke,
    When down her weedy trophies and herself
    Fell in the weeping brook. Her clothes spread
        wide,   175
    And mermaid-like awhile they bore her up;
    Which time she chanted snatches of old tunes,
    As one incapable of her own distress,
    Or like a creature native and indu'd   179
    Unto that element; but long it could not be
    Till that her garments, heavy with their drink,
    Pull'd the poor wretch from her melodious lay
    To muddy death.
LAERTES.   Alas, then, she is drown'd?   183
QUEEN. Drown'd, drown'd.
LAERTES. Too much of water hast thou, poor Ophelia,
    And therefore I forbid my tears; but yet
    It is our trick, nature her custom holds,   187
    Let shame say what it will. When these are gone,
    The woman will be out. Adieu, my lord!

---

119. **abatements:** diminutions. **130. put on:** instigate. **those:** certain persons who. **133. remiss:** easy-going. **135. peruse:** inspect. **137. unbated:** not blunted. **pass of practice:** treacherous thrust. **139. anoint:** smear. **142. cataplasm:** poultice. **143. simples:** medicinal herbs. **149. our shape:** part we purpose to act. **153. blast in proof:** burst when tested (as of a cannon).

154. **cunnings:** skill. **156. motion:** bodily exertion. **159. for the nonce:** for the purpose. **160. stuck:** thrust. **167. hoar:** greyish-white. **169. crowflowers:** buttercups. **long purples:** early purple. **170. liberal:** free-spoken. **172. coronet:** garlanded. **178. incapable:** having no understanding. **179. indu'd:** endowed with qualities fitting her. **187. trick:** hereditary trait.

I have a speech of fire, that fain would blaze,
But that this folly douts it.   [*Exit.*]
KING.   Let's follow, Gertrude.

How much I had to do to calm his rage!   192
Now fear I this will give it start again.
Therefore let's follow.   [*Exeunt.*]

Act V

SCENE I

A Churchyard near Elsinore

[*Enter two Clowns.*]

[FIRST] CLOWN. Is she to be buried in Christian
burial when she wilfully seeks her own salvation?

OTHER. I tell thee she is. Therefore make her grave
straight. The crowner hath sat on her and finds it
Christian burial.   5

CLOWN. How can that be, unless she drowned herself
in her own defence?

OTHER. Why, 'tis found so.

CLOWN. It must be *se offendendo*; it cannot be else.
For here lies the point: if I drown myself wittingly, it
argues an act, and an act hath three branches; it is to
act, to do, to perform. Argal, she drowned herself
wittingly.

OTHER. Nay, but hear you, goodman delver,—   14

CLOWN. Give me leave. Here lies the water; good.
Here stands the man; good. If the man go to this
water and drown himself, it is, will he, nill he, he
goes; mark you that! But if the water come to him
and drown him, he drowns not himself. Argal, he
that is not guilty of his own death shortens not his
own life.   21

OTHER. But is this law?

CLOWN. Ay, marry, is 't; crowner's quest law.   23

OTHER. Will you ha' the truth on 't? If this had not
been a gentlewoman, she should have been buried
out o' Christian burial.   26

CLOWN. Why, there thou sayest; and the more pity
that great folk should have countenance in this
world to drown or hang themselves more than their
even Christen. Come, my spade! There is no ancient

gentlemen but gardeners, ditchers, and grave-
makers. They hold up Adam's profession.   32

OTHER. Was he a gentleman?

CLOWN. 'A was the first that ever bore arms.

OTHER. Why, he had none.   35

CLOWN. What! art a heathen? How dost thou understand the Scripture? The Scripture says, Adam
digged; could he dig without arms? I'll put another
question to thee. If thou answerest me not to the
purpose, confess thyself—

OTHER. Go to.   41

CLOWN. What is he that builds stronger than either
the mason, the shipwright, or the carpenter.

OTHER. The gallows-maker; for that frame outlives a
thousand tenants.   45

CLOWN. I like thy wit well. In good faith the gallows
does well, but how does it well? It does well to
those that do ill. Now thou dost ill to say the
gallows is built stronger than the church. Argal, the
gallows may do well to thee. To 't again; come!

OTHER. Who builds stronger than a mason, a shipwright, or a carpenter?   52

CLOWN. Ay, tell me that, and unyoke.

OTHER. Marry, now I can tell.

CLOWN. To 't.

OTHER. Mass, I cannot tell.   56

[*Enter Hamlet and Horatio afar off.*]

CLOWN. Cudgel thy brains no more about it, for your
dull ass will not mend his pace with beating; and
when you are asked this question next, say, 'a grave-
maker.' The houses he makes lasts till doomsday.
Go, get thee to Yaughan and fetch me a stoup of
liquor.

[*Exit other Clown.*]

[*Clown digs and sings.*]

191. douts: extinguishes.
4. straight: at once. crowner: coroner. sat on: passed on. 11.
branches: divisions. 12. Argal: corruption of ergo, therefore. 14.
goodman delver: Mr. Sexton. 23. quest: inquest. 30. even Christen: fellow Christian.

41. Go to: out with it! 61. stoup: two quart measure.

In youth, when I did love, did love,
   Methought it was very sweet.
To contract—oh—the time, for—ah—my behove,
O methought there—ah—was nothing—ah—meet.

HAMLET. Has this fellow no feeling of his business,
   that he sings at grave-making?   68
HORATIO. Custom hath made it in him a property of
   easiness.
HAMLET. 'Tis e'en so; the hand of little employment
   hath the daintier sense.   72
CLOWN.

      But age, with his stealing steps,   [*Song.*]
         Hath claw'd me in his clutch,
      And hath shipp'd me intil the land,
         As if I had never been such.   76

[*Throws up a skull.*]

HAMLET. That skull had a tongue in it and could sing
   once. How the knave jowls it to the ground, as if 't
   were Cain's jaw-bone, that did the first murther!
   This might be the pate of a politician which this ass
   now o'erreaches, one that would circumvent God,
   might it not?   82
HORATIO. It might, my lord.
HAMLET. Or of a courtier, which could say, 'Good
   morrow, sweet lord! How dost thou, good lord?'
   This might be my Lord Such-a-one, that praised my
   Lord Such-a-one's horse when 'a went to beg it,
   might it not?   88
HORATIO. Ay, my lord.
HAMLET. Why, e'en so, and now my Lady Worm's:
   chapless, and knocked about the mazzard with a
   sexton's spade. Here's fine revolution, an we had
   the trick to see 't. Did these bones cost no more the
   breeding but to play at loggats with 'em? Mine ache
   to think on 't.   95
CLOWN.

      A pick-axe and a spade, a spade,   [*Song.*]
         For and a shrouding sheet;
      O, a pit of clay for to be made
         For such a guest is meet.

[*Throws up another skull.*]

HAMLET. There's another! Why may not that be the
   skull of a lawyer? Where be his quiddities now, his
   quillets, his cases, his tenures, and his tricks? Why
   does he suffer this rude knave now to knock him
   about the sconce with a dirty shovel, and will not
   tell him of his action of battery? Hum! This fellow
   might be in 's time a great buyer of land, with his
   statutes, his recognizances, his fines, his double
   vouchers, his recoveries. (Is this the fine of his fines,
   and the recovery of his recoveries,) to have his fine
   pate full of fine dirt? Will his vouchers vouch him no
   more of his purchases, and double ones too, than
   the length and breadth of a pair of indentures? The
   very conveyances of his lands will scarcely lie in this
   box, and must th' inheritor himself have no more,
   ha?
HORATIO. Not a jot more, my lord.   115
HAMLET. Is not parchment made of sheep skins?
HORATIO. Ay, my lord, and of calves' skins too.   117
HAMLET. They are sheep and calves which seek out
   assurance in that. I will speak to this fellow. Whose
   grave 's this, sirrah?
CLOWN. Mine, sir,

      O, a pit of clay for to be made   122
         For such a guest is meet.

HAMLET. I think it be thine indeed, for thou liest
   in 't.
CLOWN. You lie out on 't, sir, and therefore 't is
   not yours. For my part, I do not lie in 't, yet it is
   mine.   128
HAMLET. Thou dost lie in 't, to be in 't and say it is
   thine. 'Tis for the dead, not for the quick. Therefore
   thou liest.
CLOWN. 'Tis a quick lie, sir. 'Twill away again from
   me to you.
HAMLET. What man dost thou dig it for?   134
CLOWN. For no man, sir.
HAMLET. What woman, then?
CLOWN. For none, neither.
HAMLET. Who is to be buried in 't?   138
CLOWN. One that was a woman, sir; but, rest her soul,
   she's dead.
HAMLET. How absolute the knave is! we must speak
   by the card, or equivocation will undo us. By the

---

65. **contract:** shorten (with pleasure). **behove:** benefit. **66. meet:**
good enough. **72. sense:** sensibility. **75. intil:** into. **78. jowls:**
dashes. **79. Cain's jaw-bone, that:** the jaw-bone of Cain, who.
87. went: went about, attempted. **91. chapless:** lacking the lower
jaw. **mazzard:** head.

101. **quiddities:** subtleties. **102. quillets:** minute distinctions.
104. sconce: head. **108. fine:** end. **112. indentures:** mutual
agreements. **119. assurance:** security. **141. absolute:** precise.
142. by the card: with precision.

Lord, Horatio, this three years I have took note of it; the age is grown so picked that the toe of the peasant comes so near the heel of the courtier he galls his kibe.—How long hast thou been grave-maker? 146

CLOWN. Of all the days i' th' year, I came to 't that day that our last King Hamlet overcame Fortinbras.

HAMLET. How long is that since? 149

CLOWN. Cannot you tell that? Every fool can tell that. It was that very day that young Hamlet was born,—he that is mad and sent into England. 152

HAMLET. Ay, marry! Why was he sent into England?

CLOWN. Why, because 'a was mad. 'A shall recover his wits there; or if 'a do not, 'tis no great matter there. 156

HAMLET. Why?

CLOWN. 'Twill not be seen in him there. There the men are as mad as he. 159

HAMLET. How came he mad?

CLOWN. Very strangely, they say.

HAMLET. How, strangely? 162

CLOWN. Faith, e'en with losing his wits.

HAMLET. Upon what ground?

CLOWN. Why, here in Denmark. I have been sexton here, man and boy, thirty years. 166

HAMLET. How long will a man lie i' th' earth ere he rot?

CLOWN. Faith, if 'a be not rotten before 'a die (as we have many pocky corses now-a-days, that will scarce hold the laying in) 'a will last you some eight year or nine year. A tanner will last you nine year.

HAMLET. Why he more than another? 173

CLOWN. Why, sir, his hide is so tanned with his trade that 'a will keep out water a great while, and your water is a sore decayer of your whoreson dead body. Here's a skull now hath lien you i' th' earth three-and-twenty years. 178

HAMLET. Whose was it?

CLOWN. A whoreson mad fellow's it was. Whose do you think it was?

HAMLET. Nay, I know not. 182

CLOWN. A pestilence on him for a mad rogue! 'a poured a flagon of Rhenish on my head once. This same skull, sir, was Sir Yorick's skull, the king's jester.

HAMLET. This!

CLOWN. E'en that. 188

HAMLET. Let me see. [Takes the skull.] Alas, poor Yorick! I knew him, Horatio; a fellow of infinite jest, of most excellent fancy. He hath bore me on his back a thousand times; and now, how abhorred in my imagination it is! my gorge rises at it. Here hung those lips that I have kissed I know not how oft. Where be your gibes now? your gambols? your songs? your flashes of merriment, that were wont to set the table on a roar? Not one now, to mock your own grinning; quite chapfallen. Now get you to my lady's chamber, and tell her, let her paint an inch thick, to this favor she must come. Make her laugh at that. Prithee, Horatio, tell me one thing.

HORATIO. What's that, my lord? 202

HAMLET. Dost thou think Alexander looked o' this fashion i' th' earth?

HORATIO. E'en so.

HAMLET. And smelt so? pah! 206

[Puts down the skull.]

HORATIO. E'en so, my lord.

HAMLET. To what base uses we may return, Horatio! Why may not imagination trace the noble dust of Alexander till 'a find it stopping a bunghole? 210

HORATIO. 'Twere to consider too curiously, to consider so.

HAMLET. No, faith, not a jot; but to follow him thither with modesty enough, and likelihood to lead it; as thus: Alexander died, Alexander was buried, Alexander returneth to dust; the dust is earth. Of earth we make loam, and why of that loam, whereto he was converted, might they not stop a beer-barrel?

Imperious Caesar, dead and turn'd to clay,
  Might stop a hole to keep the wind away. 220
O that that earth, which kept the world in awe,
  Should patch a wall t' expel the winter's flaw!

But soft! but soft awhile! Here comes the king.

[Enter King, Queen, Laertes, a Priest, and a Coffin, with Lords attendant.]

The queen, the courtiers! Who is this they
  follow? 224
And with such maimed rites? This doth betoken
The corse they follow did with desperate hand
Fordo it own life. 'Twas of some estate.
Couch we awhile, and mark. 228

200. favor: appearance. 211. curiously: minutely. 214. modesty: moderation. likelihood: probability. 222. flaw: squall of wind. 227. Fordo it: undo its. estate: rank. 228. Couch: remain concealed.

144. picked: fastidious. 146. kibe: chilblain. 176. sore: grievous. whoreson: plagued. 177. lien: lain.

[Retires with Horatio.]

LAERTES. What ceremony else?

HAMLET.   That is Laertes,
A very noble youth. Mark.

LAERTES. What ceremony else?

PRIEST. Her obsequies have been as far enlarg'd   232
As we have warranty. Her death was doubtful,
And but that great command o'ersways the order,
She should in ground unsanctified been lodg'd
Till the last trumpet; for charitable prayers,   236
Shards, flints, and pebbles should be thrown on her.
Yet here she is allow'd her virgin crants,
Her maiden strewments, and the bringing home
Of bell and burial.   240

LAERTES. Must there no more be done?

PRIEST.   No more be
done.
We should profane the service of the dead
To sing a requiem and such rest to her
As to peace-parted souls.

LAERTES.   Lay her i' th' earth,   244
And from her fair and unpolluted flesh
May violets spring! I tell thee, churlish priest,
A ministering angel shall my sister be
When thou liest howling.

HAMLET.   What! the fair Ophelia?   248

QUEEN. *[Scattering flowers.]* Sweets to the sweet! fare-
well!
I hop'd thou shouldst have been my Hamlet's wife.
I thought thy bride-bed to have deck'd, sweet maid,
And not have strew'd thy grave.

LAERTES.   O treble woe   252
Fall ten times treble on that cursed head
Whose wicked deed thy most ingenious sense
Depriv'd thee of. Hold off the earth awhile,
Till I have caught her once more in mine arms.

[Leaps in the grave.]

Now pile your dust upon the quick and dead,
Till of this flat a mountain you have made   258
T' o'er-top old Pelion or the skyish head
Of blue Olympus.

HAMLET. *[Advancing.]* What is he whose grief
Bears such emphasis? whose phrase of sorrow   261
Conjures the wandering stars, and makes them stand

Like wonder-wounded bearers? This is I,
Hamlet the Dane.   *[Hamlet leaps in after Laertes.]*

LAERTES.   The devil take thy soul!   264

[Grapples with him.]

HAMLET. Thou pray'st not well.
I prithee take thy fingers from my throat;
For though I am not splenetive and rash,
Yet have I in me something dangerous,   268
Which let thy wisdom fear. Hold off thy hand!

KING. Pluck them asunder.

QUEEN.   Hamlet! Hamlet!

ALL. Gentlemen!

HORATIO.   Good my lord, be quiet.

[The Attendants part them, and they come out of the grave.]

HAMLET. Why, I will fight with him upon this theme
Until my eyelids will no longer wag.

QUEEN. O my son, what theme?

HAMLET. I lov'd Ophelia. Forty thousand brothers
Could not with all their quantity of love   276
Make up my sum. What wilt thou do for her?

KING. O, he is mad, Laertes.

QUEEN. For love of God, forbear him.

HAMLET. 'Swounds, show me what thou't do.
Woo't weep? woo't fight? woo't fast? woo't tear
thyself?   281
Woo't drink up eisel? eat a crocodile?
I'll do 't. Dost thou come here to whine?
To outface me with leaping in her grave?   284
Be buried quick with her, and so will I.
And if thou prate of mountains, let them throw
Millions of acres on us, till our ground,
Singeing his pate against the burning zone,   288
Make Ossa like a wart! Nay, an thou'lt mouth,
I'll rant as well as thou.

QUEEN.   This is mere madness,
And thus a while the fit will work on him.
Anon, as patient as the female dove,   292
When that her golden couplets are disclos'd,
His silence will sit drooping.

HAMLET.   Hear you, sir.
What is the reason that you use me thus?
I lov'd you ever,—but it is no matter.   296

---

232. **enlarg'd:** extended.   233. **warranty:** warrant.   **doubtful:** suspicious.   235. **been:** have been.   237. **Shards:** fragments of pottery.   238. **crants:** garland.   239. **strewments:** flowers strewn on a
grave.   244. **peace-parted:** piously deceased.   254. **ingenious:** delicately sensitive.   262. **wandering stars:** planets.

267. **splenetive:** quick-tempered.   279. **forbear him:** leave him
alone.   281. **Woo't:** wilt thou.   282. **eisel:** vinegar (associated with
gall).   288. **burning zone:** 'coelum igneum,' heavenly region of fire.

Let Hercules himself do what he may,
  The cat will mew and dog will have his day.   [*Exit.*]
KING. I pray thee, good Horatio, wait upon him.

[*Exit Horatio.*]

[*To Laertes.*] Strengthen your patience in our last night's
    speech.   300
We'll put the matter to the present push.—
Good Gertrude, set some watch over your son.
This grave shall have a living monument.
An hour of quiet shortly shall we see;   304
Till then, in patience our proceeding be.   [*Exeunt.*]

SCENE II

The Hall in the Castle

[*Enter Hamlet and Horatio.*]

HAMLET. So much for this, sir; now shall you see the
    other.
  You do remember all the circumstance?
HORATIO. Remember it, my lord!
HAMLET. Sir, in my heart there was a kind of
    fighting   4
That would not let me sleep. Methought I lay
Worse than the mutines in the bilboes. Rashly,—
And prais'd be rashness for it (let us know,
Our indiscretion sometimes serves us well   8
When our deep plots do pall; and that should learn
    us
There's a divinity that shapes our ends,
Rough-hew them how we will)—
HORATIO.   That is most cer-
    tain.
HAMLET. Up from my cabin,   12
My sea gown scarf'd about me, in the dark
Grop'd I to find out them, had my desire,
Finger'd their packet, and in fine withdrew
To mine own room again; making so bold   16
(My fears forgetting manners) to unseal
Their grand commission, where I found, Horatio,
(Ah, royal knavery!) an exact command,—
Larded with many several sorts of reasons   20

Importing Denmark's health and England's too,
With, ho! such bugs and goblins in my life,—
That, on the supervise, no leisure bated,
No, not to stay the grinding of the axe,   24
My head should be struck off.
HORATIO.   Is 't possible?
HAMLET. Here's the commission: read it at more lei-
    sure.
  But wilt thou hear now how I did proceed?
HORATIO. I beseech you.   28
HAMLET. Being thus be-netted round with villainies,
Ere I could make a prologue to my brains
They had begun the play. I sat me down,
Devis'd a new commission, wrote it fair.—   32
I once did hold it, as our statists do,
A baseness to write fair and labor'd much
How to forget that learning, but, sir, now
It did me yeoman's service. Wilt thou know   36
Th' effect of what I wrote?
HORATIO.   Ay, good my lord.
HAMLET. An earnest conjuration from the king,
As England was his faithful tributary,
As love between them like the palm might
    flourish,   40
As peace should still her wheaten garland wear
And stand a comma 'tween their amities,
And many such-like 'As'es of great charge,
That, on the view and knowing of these
    contents,   44
Without debatement further, more or less,
He should those bearers put to sudden death,
Not shriving-time allow'd.
HORATIO.   How was this seal'd?
HAMLET. Why, even in that was heaven ordinant.   48
I had my father's signet in my purse,
Which was the model of that Danish seal.—
Folded the writ up in the form of th' other,
Subscrib'd it, gave 't th' impression, plac'd it
    safely,   52
The changeling never known. Now, the next day
Was our sea-fight, and what to this was sequent
Thou know'st already.
HORATIO. So Guildenstern and Rosencrantz go
    to 't.   56

---

300. **in:** in the thought of. **301. present push:** immediate trial.
303. living: lasting.
6. mutines: mutineers. **bilboes:** shackles. **9. pall:** fail. **15. Finger'd:** pilfered.

23. supervise: perusal. **bated:** deducted. **29. be-netted:**
ensnared. **33. statists:** statesmen. **36. yeoman's service:** good and
faithful service. **41. wheaten garland:** emblem of peace. **42.
comma:** bond of connection. **47. shriving-time:** time for absolution. **48. ordinant:** controlling. **50. model:** exact likeness. **52.
Subscrib'd:** signed. **impression:** i.e., of the seal. **53. changeling:**
substitute.

HAMLET. Why, man, they did make love to this
    employment;
  They are not near my conscience. Their defeat
  Does by their own insinuation grow.
  'Tis dangerous when the baser nature comes   69
  Between the pass and fell-incensed points
  Of mighty opposites.
HORATIO.   Why, what a king is this!
HAMLET. Does it not, think thee, stand me now
    upon?
  He that hath kill'd my king and whor'd my
    mother,   64
  Popp'd in between th' election and my hopes,
  Thrown out his angle for my proper life,
  And with such cozenage—is 't not perfect con-
    science
  To quit him with this arm? and is 't not to be
    damn'd
  To let this canker of our nature come   69
  In further evil?
HORATIO. It must be shortly known to him from
    England
  What is the issue of the business there.   72
HAMLET. It will be short. The interim is mine,
  And a man's life's no more than to say 'One.'
  But I am very sorry, good Horatio,
  That to Laertes I forgot myself,   76
  For by the image of my cause I see
  The portraiture of his. I'll court his favors:
  But sure the bravery of his grief did put me
  Into a towering passion.
HORATIO.   Peace! who comes here?   80

[Enter young Osric.]

OSRIC. Your lordship is right welcome back to Den-
    mark.
HAMLET. I humbly thank you, sir. [Aside to Horatio.]
  Dost know this water-fly?   84
HORATIO. [Aside to Hamlet.] No, my good lord.
HAMLET. [Aside to Horatio.] Thy state is the more gra-
    cious, for 'tis a vice to know him. He hath much
    land, and fertile. Let a beast be lord of beasts, and
    his crib shall stand at the king's mess. 'Tis a chough,
    but, as I say, spacious in the possession of dirt. 90
OSRIC. Sweet lord, if your lordship were at leisure, I
    should impart a thing to you from his majesty.

HAMLET. I will receive it, sir, with all diligence of
    spirit. Put your bonnet to his right use; 'tis for the
    head.   95
OSRIC. I thank your lordship. It is very hot.
HAMLET. No, believe me, 'tis very cold; the wind is
    northerly.   98
OSRIC. It is indifferent cold, my lord, indeed.
HAMLET. But yet methinks it is very sultry and hot for
    my complexion.   101
OSRIC. Exceedingly, my lord. It is very sultry, as
    'twere,—I cannot tell how. But, my lord, his maj-
    esty bade me signify to you that 'a has laid a great
    wager on your head. Sir, this is the matter,— 105
HAMLET. I beseech you, remember—

[Hamlet moves him to put on his hat.]

OSRIC. Nay, good my lord, for my ease, in good faith.
    Sir, here is newly come to court Laertes,—believe
    me, an absolute gentleman, full of most excellent
    differences, of very soft society and great showing.
    Indeed, to speak feelingly of him, he is the card or
    calendar of gentry, for you shall find in him the
    continent of what part a gentleman would see. 113
HAMLET. Sir, his definement suffers no perdition in
    you; though, I know, to divide him inventorially
    would dozy th' arithmetic of memory, and yet but
    yaw neither, in respect of his quick sail. But, in the
    verity of extolment, I take him to be a soul of great
    article, and his infusion of such dearth and rareness
    as, to make true diction of him, his semblable is his
    mirror, and who else would trace him his umbrage,
    nothing more.   122
OSRIC. Your lordship speaks most infallibly of him.
HAMLET. The concernancy, sir? why do we wrap the
    gentleman in our more rawer breath?
OSRIC. Sir?
HORATIO. Is 't not possible to understand in another
    tongue? You will to 't, sir, really.   128
HAMLET. What imports the nomination of this gentle-
    man?
OSRIC. Of Laertes?   131

---

59. **insinuation:** intrusion.   61. **fell-incensed:** cruelly angered.   62.
opposites: opponents.   63. **stand . . . upon:** vitally concern.   66.
angle: fishing-hook.   **proper:** own.   67. **cozenage:** cheating.   79.
bravery: ostentatious display.   89. **chough:** small chattering bird.

109. **absolute:** perfect.   110. **differences:** distinguishing features.
soft: gentle.   111. **card:** map.   114. **definement:** description.
perdition: loss.   115. **divide inventorially:** catalogue.   116. **dozy:**
make giddy.   117. **yaw:** stagger.   **neither:** too.   118–19. **great
article:** large scope.   119. **infusion:** character imparted by nature.
120. **semblable:** like.   121. **trace:** follow.   **umbrage:** shadow.
124. **concernancy:** relevance.   125. **more rawer:** too unskilled.
128. **You will to 't:** You will acquire the art.   129. **nomination:**
naming.

HORATIO. His purse is empty already. All 's golden words are spent.

HAMLET. Of him, sir.

OSRIC. I know you are not ignorant—   135

HAMLET. I would you did, sir; yet in faith, if you did, it would not much approve me. Well, sir.

OSRIC. You are not ignorant of what excellence Laertes is—

HAMLET. I dare not confess that, lest I should compare with him in excellence; but to know a man well were to know himself.   142

OSRIC. I mean, sir, for his weapon; but in the imputation laid on him by them, in his meed he's unfellowed.

HAMLET. What's his weapon?

OSRIC. Rapier and dagger.   147

HAMLET. That's two of his weapons, but,—well.

OSRIC. The king, sir, hath wagered with him six Barbary horses, against the which he has impawned, as I take it, six French rapiers and poniards, with their assigns; as girdle, hanger, and so. Three of the carriages, in faith, are very dear to fancy, very responsive to the hilts, most delicate carriages and of very liberal conceit.   155

HAMLET. What call you the carriages?

HORATIO. I knew you must be edified by the margent, ere you had done.

OSRIC. The carriages, sir, are the hangers.   159

HAMLET. The phrase would be more germane to the matter, if we could carry a cannon by our sides. I would it might be hangers till then. But, on; six Barbary horses against six French swords, their assigns, and three liberal-conceited carriages; that's the French bet against the Danish. Why is this all impawned, as you call it?

OSRIC. The king, sir, hath laid that in a dozen passes between yourself and him, he shall not exceed you three hits. He hath laid on twelve for nine, and it would come to immediate trial, if your lordship would vouchsafe the answer.   171

HAMLET. How if I answer no?

OSRIC. I mean, my lord, the opposition of your person in trial.

HAMLET. Sir, I will walk here in the hall. If it please his majesty, it is the breathing time of day with me.

Let the foils be brought, the gentleman willing, and the king hold his purpose, I will win for him an I can; if not, I will gain nothing but my shame and the odd hits.   180

OSRIC. Shall I deliver you so?

HAMLET. To this effect, sir, after what flourish your nature will.   183

OSRIC. I commend my duty to your lordship.

HAMLET. Yours, yours. [Exit Osric.] He does well to commend it himself; there are no tongues else for 's turn.   187

HORATIO. This lapwing runs away with the shell on his head.

HAMLET. 'A did comply, sir, with his dug before 'a sucked it. Thus has he—and many more of the same bevy, that I know the drossy age dotes on—only got the tune of the time and outward habit of encounter, a kind of yesty collection which carries them through and through the most fond and winnowed opinions, and do but blow them to their trial, the bubbles are out.   197

[Enter a Lord.]

LORD. My lord, his majesty commended him to you by young Osric, who brings back to him that you attend him in the hall. He sends to know if your pleasure hold to play with Laertes, or that you will take longer time.   202

HAMLET. I am constant to my purposes; they follow the king's pleasure. If his fitness speaks, mine is ready, now or whensoever, provided I be so able as now.

LORD. The king and queen and all are coming down.   206

HAMLET. In happy time.

LORD. The queen desires you to use some gentle entertainment to Laertes before you fall to play.

HAMLET. She well instructs me. [Exit Lord.]

HORATIO. You will lose this wager, my lord.

HAMLET. I do not think so. Since he went into France, I have been in continual practice. I shall win at the odds, but thou wouldst not think how ill all 's here about my heart. But it is no matter.   217

137. approve me: commend me.   140–41: compare with: vie with. 143–44: imputation: reputation.   meed: merit, worth. unfellowed: without an equal.   150. impawned: staked.   152. assigns: appurtenances.   hanger: strap from which a sword is suspended.   152–53: carriages: hangers.   153: dear to fancy: unusual in design.   154. delicate: finely wrought.   155. liberal conceit: tasteful design.   176. breathing time: exercise period.

188: lapwing: plover, a vivacious little bird.   188–89. with . . . head: almost before he is hatched.   190. comply: use fine language. 192. drossy: frivolous.   193. tune: mood.   193–94. outward . . . encounter: superficial mannerisms.   194. yesty: frothy.   209. In happy time: at an appropriate time.

HORATIO. Nay, good my lord,—

HAMLET. It is but foolery, but it is such a kind of gaingiving as would perhaps trouble a woman. 220

HORATIO. If your mind dislike anything, obey it. I will forestall their repair hither and say you are not fit. 222

HAMLET. Not a whit, we defy augury; there is special providence in the fall of a sparrow. If it be now, 'tis not to come; if it be not to come, it will be now; if it be not now, yet it will come: the readiness is all. Since no man has aught of what he leaves, what is 't to leave betimes? Let be.

[Enter King, Queen, Laertes and Lords, with other Attendants with foils and gauntlets. A table and flagons of wine on it.]

KING. Come, Hamlet, come, and take this hand from me.

[The King puts the hand of Laertes into that of Hamlet.]

HAMLET. Give me your pardon, sir. I've done you wrong;
But pardon 't, as you are a gentleman.
This presence knows, and you must needs have heard,
How I am punish'd with a sore distraction.
What I have done,   234
That might your nature, honor, and exception
Roughly awake, I here proclaim was madness.
Was 't Hamlet wrong'd Laertes? Never Hamlet.
If Hamlet from himself be ta'en away,   238
And when he's not himself does wrong Laertes,
Then Hamlet does it not; Hamlet denies it.
Who does it then? His madness. If 't be so,
Hamlet is of the faction that is wrong'd;   242
His madness is poor Hamlet's enemy.
Sir, in this audience,
Let my disclaiming from a purpos'd evil
Free me so far in your most generous thoughts,
That I have shot my arrow o'er the house,   247
And hurt my brother.

LAERTES.   I am satisfied in nature,
Whose motive in this case should stir me most
To my revenge; but in my terms of honor   250
I stand aloof, and will no reconcilement
Till by some elder masters of known honor
I have a voice and precedent of peace,
To keep my name ungor'd. But till that time,

I do receive your offer'd love like love,   255
And will not wrong it.

HAMLET.   I embrace it freely,
And will this brothers' wager frankly play.
Give us the foils. Come on.

LAERTES.   Come, one for me.

HAMLET. I'll be your foil, Laertes. In mine ignorance
Your skill shall, like a star i' th' darkest night,
Stick fiery off indeed.

LAERTES.   You mock me, sir.

HAMLET. No, by this hand.   262

KING. Give them the foils, young Osric. Cousin Hamlet,
You know the wager?

HAMLET.   Very well, my lord;
Your Grace has laid the odds o' th' weaker side.

KING. I do not fear it. I have seen you both;
But since he is better'd, we have therefore odds.

LAERTES. This is too heavy; let me see another.

HAMLET. This likes me well. These foils have all a length?

OSRIC. Ay, my good lord.   270

[Prepare to play.]

KING. Set me the stoups of wine upon that table.
If Hamlet give the first or second hit,
Or quit in answer of the third exchange,
Let all the battlements their ordnance fire.   274
The king shall drink to Hamlet's better breath;
And in the cup an union shall he throw,
Richer than that which four successive kings
In Denmark's crown have worn. Give me the cups;   278
And let the kettle to the trumpet speak,
The trumpet to the cannoneer without,
The cannons to the heavens, the heaven to earth:
'Now the king drinks to Hamlet!'
                        Come, begin![Trumpets the while.]
And you, the judges, bear a wary eye.

HAMLET. Come on, sir.

LAERTES.   Come, my lord.   [They play.]

HAMLET.   One.

LAERTES.   No.

HAMLET.   Judgment.

OSRIC. A hit, a very palpable hit.

[Drum, trumpets and shot. Flourish. A piece goes off.]

---

220. gaingiving: foreboding. 232. presence: royal assembly. 235. exception: disapproval. 253. voice: opinion. 254. ungor'd: uninjured.

261. stick . . . off: stand out in relief. 276. union: pearl. 279. kettle: kettledrum.

LAERTES.   Well; again.
KING. Stay; give me drink. Hamlet, this pearl is thine.
Here's to thy health. Give him the cup.   287

[*Trumpets sound; and shot goes off.*]

HAMLET. I'll play this bout first; set it by awhile.
Come.— [*They play.*] Another hit! What say you?
LAERTES. A touch, a touch, I do confess 't.   290
KING. Our son shall win.
QUEEN.   He's fat and scant of breath.
Here, Hamlet, take my napkin, rub thy brows.
The queen carouses to thy fortune, Hamlet.

[*Takes Hamlet's cup.*]

HAMLET. Good madam!
KING.   Gertrude, do not drink!   294
QUEEN. I will, my lord; I pray you, pardon me.
KING. [*Aside.*] It is the poison'd cup! it is too late.
HAMLET. I dare not drink yet, madam. By and by.
QUEEN. Come, let me wipe thy face.   298
LAERTES. My lord, I'll hit him now.
KING.   I do not think 't.
LAERTES. [*Aside.*] And yet it is almost against my con-
science.
HAMLET. Come, for the third! Laertes, you but dally;
I pray you, pass with your best violence   302
I am afeard you make a wanton of me.
LAERTES. Say you so? come on.   [*Play.*]
OSRIC. Nothing, neither way.
LAERTES. Have at you now.

[*In scuffling they change rapiers.*]

KING.   Part them! they are incens'd.
HAMLET. Nay, come again!   [*The Queen falls.*]
OSRIC. Look to the queen there. Ho!
HORATIO. They bleed on both sides. How is it, my
lord?
OSRIC. How is 't Laertes?
LAERTES. Why, as a woodcock to mine own springe,
Osric.   310
I am justly kill'd with mine own treachery.
HAMLET. How does the queen?
KING.   She sounds to see them bleed.
QUEEN. No, no, the drink, the drink! O my dear
Hamlet!   313
The drink, the drink! I am poison'd.   [*Dies.*]

HAMLET. O villainy! Ho! let the door be lock'd.
Treachery! seek it out.   [*Laertes falls.*]
LAERTES. It is here, Hamlet. Hamlet, thou art slain;
No medicine in the world can do thee good.   318
In thee there is not half an hour's life.
The treacherous instrument is in thy hand,
Unbated and envenom'd. The foul practice
Hath turn'd itself on me. Lo, here I lie,   322
Never to rise again. Thy mother's poison'd.
I can no more. The king, the king's to blame.
HAMLET. The point envenom'd too?
Then, venom, to thy work!   [*Hurts the King.*]
ALL.   Treason! treason!   326
KING. O yet defend me, friends; I am but hurt.
HAMLET. Here, thou incestuous, murd'rous, damned
Dane,
Drink off this potion! Is thy union here?   329
Follow my mother.   [*King dies.*]
LAERTES.   He is justly serv'd;
It is a poison temper'd by himself.
Exchange forgiveness with me, noble Hamlet:
Mine and my father's death come not upon thee,
Nor thine on me!   [*Dies.*]
HAMLET. Heaven make thee free of it! I follow
thee.   335
I am dead, Horatio. Wretched queen, adieu!
You that look pale and tremble at this chance,
That are but mutes or audience to this act,   338
Had I but time (as this fell sergeant, death,
Is strict in his arrest) O, I could tell you—
But let it be. Horatio, I am dead;   341
Thou liv'st. Report me and my cause aright
To the unsatisfied.
HORATIO.   Never believe it!
I am more an antique Roman than a Dane.
Here's yet some liquor left.
HAMLET.   As th' art a man,   345
Give me the cup! let go! by heaven, I'll have 't!
O good Horatio, what a wounded name
(Things standing thus unknown) shall live behind
me.
If thou didst ever hold me in thy heart,   349
Absent thee from felicity awhile,
And in this harsh world draw thy breath in pain,
To tell my story.

[*A march afar off and shout within.*]

What warlike noise is this?

---

291. **fat:** out of training.   292. **napkin:** handkerchief.   302. **pass:**
thrust.   303. **wanton:** pampered child.   312. **sounds:** swoons.

331. **temper'd:** compounded.   339. **sergeant:** sheriff's officer.

[*Enter Osric.*]

OSRIC. Young Fortinbras, with conquest come from
     Poland,   353
   To the ambassadors of England gives
   This warlike volley.
HAMLET.   O, I die, Horatio;
   The potent poison quite o'er-crows my spirit.
   I cannot live to hear the news from England,   357
   But I do prophesy th' election lights
   On Fortinbras. He has my dying voice.
   So tell him, with th' occurrents, more and less,
   Which have solicited—The rest is silence.   [*Dies.*]
HORATIO. Now cracks a noble heart. Good night,
     sweet prince,   362
   And flights of angels sing thee to thy rest!
   Why does the drum come hither?

[*Enter Fortinbras, and English Ambassador, with drum, colors, and Attendants.*]

FORTINBRAS. Where is this sight?
HORATIO.   What is it you would see?   365
   If aught of woe or wonder, cease your search.
FORTINBRAS. This quarry cries on havoc. O proud
     death,
   What feast is toward in thine eternal cell,
   That thou so many princes at a shot   369
   So bloodily hast struck?
AMBASSADOR.   The sight is dismal,
   And our affairs from England come too late.
   The ears are senseless that should give us hearing,
   To tell him his commandment is fulfill'd,   373
   That Rosencrantz and Guildenstern are dead.
   Where should we have our thanks?
HORATIO.   Not from his mouth,
   Had it th' ability of life to thank you.   376
   He never gave commandment for their death.

---

356. **o'er-crows:** triumphs over.   360. **occurrents:** incidents.   361.
solicited: moved.   363. **flights:** troops.   367. **quarry:** heap of
slain.   **cries on havoc:** proclaims merciless.

But since, so jump upon this bloody question,
You from the Polack wars, and you from England,
Are here arriv'd, give order that these bodies
High on a stage be placed to the view;   381
And let me speak to th' yet unknowing world
How these things came about. So shall you hear
Of carnal, bloody, and unnatural acts,
Of accidental judgments, casual slaughters,   385
Of deaths put on by cunning and forc'd cause,
And, in this upshot, purposes mistook
Fall'n on th' inventors' heads. All this can I
Truly deliver.
FORTINBRAS.   Let us haste to hear it,   389
   And call the noblest to the audience.
   For me, with sorrow I embrace my fortune.
   I have some rights of memory in this kingdom,
   Which now to claim my vantage doth invite
     me.   393
HORATIO. Of that I shall have also cause to speak,
   And from his mouth whose voice will draw on
     more.
   But let this same be presently perform'd,
   Even while men's minds are wild, lest more mis-
     chance
   On plots and errors happen.
FORTINBRAS.   Let four captains   398
   Bear Hamlet like a soldier to the stage;
   For he was likely, had he been put on,
   To have prov'd most royal. And for his passage
   The soldiers' music and the rites of war   402
   Speak loudly for him!
   Take up the bodies. Such a sight as this
   Becomes the field, but here shows much amiss.
   Go bid the soldiers shoot.   406

[*Exeunt marching, after the which a peal of ordnance are shot off.*]

---

381. **stage:** platform.   385. **casual:** unpremeditated.   386. **forc'd:**
unreal.   392. **rights of memory:** ancient claims.   395. **draw on
more:** be seconded by others.   400. **been put on:** been put to the
proof, tried.

ESSAY: AN APPROACH TO THE PLAY

This play is so complex that it has been compared to a Rorschach test; interpretations tell us as much about the values and personality of the reader as about the play. Given that we have already introduced many of the major issues which the play seems to present, however, we will here risk discussing some possible interpretations, but with great caution.

One issue that the play's language expresses explicitly is the relationship between what "seems" to be true and what "is," as Hamlet puts it in the second scene. This issue is introduced even earlier, in the opening scene, with the broken ritual of the changing of the guard, discussed in the Introduction (pages 3–4). In the following scene another ceremonial occasion—established authority's representation of its stability, wisdom, and parental concern for its subjects—is broken by Hamlet's refusal to dress gaily, by his refusal to falsify his true feelings, at bottom by his mourning for his father. Shortly, the ghost will tear open the entire fabric of this state, giving us a glimpse of the criminality behind its fair "shows."

At times, Hamlet's soliloquies and apparently "mad" speeches undercut this surface appearance of political stability, as in his "O that this too too solid flesh would melt" soliloquy (1.2.129 ff.), or in his lament that this wondrous "piece of work," man, "delights not me" (2.2.299 ff.). But more often he uses his soliloquies to berate himself for delaying his revenge. Since the early nineteenth century, one of the most common interpretations of Hamlet's character has been that he is victimized by indecision, that he knows what needs to be done but cannot bring himself to do it. However, the justice of these self-accusations is uncertain. "O what a rogue and peasant slave am I!" (2.2.553 ff.) comes in the middle of his decisively undertaken plan to catch the conscience of the king. A little later the ghost appears to Hamlet and reminds him to kill Claudius. But it appears to no one else, so the status of its "reality" is uncertain; and it comes just after Hamlet has mistakenly killed Polonius, thinking he is killing the king. If this manifestation of the ghost is a hallucination born of Hamlet's guilt because he believes he has delayed his vengeance, one wonders what Hamlet would have to do to satisfy himself. Perhaps the self-doubts he voices are normal to anybody under such extreme conditions. Perhaps he does not really delay at all. We, too, might be extremely prudent in evaluating an apparent ghost's credibility before assassinating a king at its command.

Beginning in the second act, perhaps in response to these extreme conditions, Hamlet investigates the relationships between seeming and being, between appearance and reality, and much of this investigation explores the varied aspects of playing or acting. He will pretend to be mad; he will discuss and illustrate the nature of an acting style (an imitative style of pretense) which holds "the mirror up to nature" (3.2.23); he will lament the fact that an actor playing a role seems to have stronger feelings than he, a real person suffering real adversity (2.2.553–592); he will refer directly to the competitive theater situation in which the Globe Theater is situated (2.2.348–365); and he will revise, rehearse, produce, and act as chorus for a play within the play which tells *Hamlet*'s prehistory (apparently faithfully), allegedly to corroborate the ghost's narrative by tricking Claudius into revealing his guilty conscience. However, even while Hamlet produces this little play of brother killing brother, in the role of chorus he identifies the murderer as the victim's *nephew*—his own relationship to Claudius. This fictionalized version of past truth does more than raise the curtain which hid the present administration's corruption. It also threatens Claudius. One function of "The Mousetrap" is to discover Claudius' guilt; for the self-doubting avenger, another may be to alert Claudius and prod him into counter-attack. From this perspective, we might say that Hamlet deliberately creates a situation from which there can be no escape, a situation in which the delay that seems to cause his sense of guilt becomes impossible. His antagonist has been activated. (He also creates a situation in which Claudius—acting decisively—can exile Hamlet without public backlash; after all, the apparently mad Hamlet *has* publicly threatened assassination, however indirectly.)

The play's focus on "playing" is not merely Hamlet's vehicle for revenge, however. It is also a way of questioning the nature of truth itself, for to re-present "truth" is to control how it is conceived. There are political implications to the rewriting of history. Although "The Murder of Gonzago" seems to be true (it agrees with the ghost's version of the past and succeeds in catching Claudius), its dumb show also accentuates its quality of pretense. So does the subtle insertion of the nephew as murderer. It is impossible for us to know if other details are also untrue. Moreover, in his references to the Globe Theater, Hamlet the character seems to comment on the situation in which *Hamlet* the play is "now," at this moment in 1601, being performed. And at 5.2.10, Hamlet gives himself up to the larger script of the "divinity that shapes our ends." It is suggestive that the form this script takes is another play within the main play, this time a royal entertainment, the duel with Laertes, complete with its own playing area marked off on the stage and with most of the characters as its audience. In this duel, again "real" action occurs: "people" die, real bodies accumulate that they may "High on a stage be placed to the view" (5.2.381), on a raised area on the raised Globe stage, on a stage within the stage.

If we imagine watching *Hamlet* in the spirit with which we watch most plays, assuming that its story pretends for the time of its presentation to be "true," our pleasure in the play will depend to a large degree on our ability to pretend to believe in this "truth," to care about the characters and what happens to them. Seeing the play in this spirit, these piled bodies will be imagined as illustrating the tale told by Horatio at the dying Hamlet's request (5.2.345–352). However, because the play as a whole has focused on the relationship between "playing" and "truth," we can no longer be sure what tale Horatio will tell. Will it have the same relationship to *Hamlet* that "The Murder of Gonzago" has to *Hamlet*'s prehistory? Will not Horatio revise *Hamlet* to serve his own ends? Will he not rewrite history to justify Hamlet more clearly than *Hamlet* does?

Or does this ending bring to climax the play's questioning of truth in another way? Perhaps we are to conceive of *Hamlet* itself as Horatio's Hamlet-justifying tale, to look back at the play and see it as propaganda, and therefore to repudiate our conventional pretense of belief. Is *Hamlet* then a repetition of *Hamlet*, its own play within itself? Perhaps Shakespeare insinuates himself in this way into his play, making us aware of its constructed nature, aware of the constructed nature of history, his warning that everything from theater to royal ideology is but pretense, a self-interested falsification. It may be that in this way he also reminds us that every interpretation (including this one) is a revision, a retelling of the original (if such a true thing could ever be discovered) in our own terms. In undermining his text, then, Shakespeare may also subvert his audience, on whose Horatio-like complicity the continual retelling of his tale depends.

William Shakespeare

OTHELLO

Edited and with notes by Tucker Brooke and Lawrence Mason

About the Play   *Othello* was produced about three years after *Hamlet*. Although its story seems much simpler than the earlier play, the perspectives from which it can be seen are nearly as various. It is, for example, the tragedy of a noble outsider, a princely black African who achieves great stature in an alien society entirely by his own abilities, becoming commander-in-chief of the Venetian army. It is also the story of a man not entirely sure of his position in this alien culture who tries to cement it by marrying a rich white Venetian aristocrat. It is an intense study of what happens to two lovers who depend very greatly on each other, as well as an intense exploration of the psychological implications of race and gender issues for such a couple when they have distanced themselves from their respective societies.

In addition to being the tragedy of Othello, the play is also the tragedy of Othello's wife, Desdemona, who believes as he does that she should be submissive, obedient, and faithful. But the situation is self-defeating for both. Her fidelity breeds insecurity in Othello, possibly because he doubts that his white wife and new society can fully accept him, and it creates a set of contradictions for Desdemona. She demonstrates her love for Othello by leaving her father without his permission, simultaneously rebelling against Venetian social values and creating a situation in which even her husband can be suspicious of her capacity for loyalty.

We might also question Iago's motive for misleading Othello into doubting his wife's fidelity. This action may be the play's central puzzle: Why does Othello trust his friend more than his beloved Desdemona? We can see the cleverness of Iago's hypocrisy, but somehow this in itself does not account for his success. Why is Othello so ready to believe him?

Students may also wish to read pages 20–27 of the Introduction, where the beginning of *Othello* is analyzed in some detail.

CHARACTERS

OTHELLO, the Moor.

BRABANTIO, Father to Desdemona.

CASSIO, an honorable Lieutenant.

IAGO, a villain ['ancient' or standard-bearer, and third in command to Othello].

RODERIGO, a gulled gentleman.

DUKE OF VENICE

Senators.

MONTANO, Governor of Cyprus.

Gentlemen of Cyprus.

LODOVICO and GRATIANO } two noble Venetians [kinsman and brother, respectively, to Brabantio].

Sailors.

Clown [in Othello's retinue].

DESDEMONA, wife to Othello [and daughter to Brabantio].

EMILIA, wife to Iago.

BIANCA, a courtesan.

[Messengers, Herald, Officers, Musicians, and Attendants

SCENE: Act I, at Venice; Acts II–V, at a sea-port (Famagosta) in Cyprus.]

Act I

SCENE I

Venice. A Street

[*Enter Roderigo and Iago.*]

RODERIGO. Tush! Never tell me! I take it much un-
kindly
  That thou, Iago, who hast had my purse
  As if the strings were thine, shouldst know of this.
IAGO. 'Sblood, but you will not hear me!   4
  If ever I did dream of such a matter,
  Abhor me.
RODERIGO. Thou told'st me thou didst hold him in
  thy hate.
IAGO. Despise me if I do not. Three great ones of the
  city,   8
  In personal suit to make me his lieutenant,
  Off-capp'd to him; and, by the faith of man
  (I know my price), I am worth no worse a place.
  But he, as loving his own pride and purposes,   12
  Evades them with a bombast circumstance
  Horribly stuff'd with epithets of war;
  And, in conclusion,
  Nonsuits my mediators; for, 'Certes,' says he,   16
  'I have already chose my officer.'
  And what was he?
  Forsooth, a great arithmetician,
  One Michael Cassio, a Florentine   20
  (A fellow almost damn'd in a fair wife),
  That never set a squadron in the field,
  Nor the division of a battle knows
  More than a spinster,—unless the bookish
  theoric,   24
  Wherein the toged consuls can propose
  As masterly as he. Mere prattle, without practice,
  Is all his soldiership; but he, sir, had the election,
  And I (of whom his eyes had seen the proof   28
  At Rhodes, at Cyprus, and on other grounds

Christian and heathen) must be be-lee'd and calm'd
By Debitor-and-Creditor. This counter-caster,
He, in good time, must his lieutenant be,   32
And I—God bless the mark!—his Moorship's
  ancient.
RODERIGO. By heaven, I rather would have been his
  hangman.
IAGO. Why, there's no remedy. 'Tis the curse of ser-
  vice.
  Preferment goes by letter and affection,   36
  And not by old gradation, where each second
  Stood heir to the first. Now, sir, be judge yourself,
  Whether I in any just term am affin'd
  To love the Moor.
RODERIGO.   I would not follow him then.   40
IAGO. O sir, content you.
  I follow him to serve my turn upon him;
  We cannot be all masters, nor all masters
  Cannot be truly follow'd. You shall mark   44
  Many a duteous and knee-crooking knave,
  That (doting on his own obsequious bondage)
  Wears out his time much like his master's ass,
  For nought but provender, and when he's old,—
  cashier'd!
  Whip me such honest knaves. Others there are   49
  Who, trimm'd in forms and visages of duty,
  Keep yet their hearts attending on themselves,
  And throwing but shows of service on their
  lords,   52
  Do well thrive by 'em, and when they have lin'd
  their coats
  Do themselves homage. Those fellows have some
  soul,
  And such a one do I profess myself. For, sir,
  It is as sure as you are Roderigo,   56
  Were I the Moor, I would not be Iago.
  In following him, I follow but myself;
  Heaven is my judge, not I for love and duty,
  But seeming so for my peculiar end.   60

---

5. matter: (i.e., the marriage of Othello and Desdemona 10. Off-
capp'd: doffed their caps 11. price: value 16. Nonsuits: rebuffs
Certes: positively 23. division . . . battle: disposition of a battle-
line 24. unless: except, unless you count bookish theoric: book-
taught theory 25. toged consuls: councillors in their togas or robes
of peace propose: converse, discourse 27. election: appointment

32. in good time: (phrase of contempt) forsooth 33. ancient:
ensign 36. letter: commendatory letter, influence affection: favoritism 37. old gradation: the old order of seniority 42. to serve . . .
him: to use him for my own advantage 49. Whip me, etc.: i.e., I
think they should be whipped 50. visages: outward semblances
53. lin'd their coats: filled their pockets 59. not I: I do not do
it 60. seeming so: seeming loving and dutiful peculiar: private

For when my outward action does demónstrate
The native act and figure of my heart
In complement extern, 'tis not long after
But I will wear my heart upon my sleeve   64
For daws to peck at. I am not what I am.

RODERIGO. What a full fortune does the thick-lips
  owe,
  If he can carry't thus!

IAGO.   Call up her father.
  Rouse him, make after him, poison his delight,   68
  Proclaim him in the street, incense her kinsmen,
  And though he in a fertile climate dwell,
  Plague him with flies; though that his joy be joy,
  Yet throw such chances of vexation on't   72
  As it may lose some color.

RODERIGO. Here is her father's house. I'll call aloud.

IAGO. Do; with like timorous accent and dire yell
  As when (by night and negligence) the fire   76
  Is spied in populous cities.

RODERIGO. What, ho, Brabantio! Signior Brabantio,
  ho!

IAGO. Awake! what, ho, Brabantio! thieves! thieves!
  thieves!
  Look to your house, your daughter, and your
    bags!   80
  Thieves! thieves!

[Brabantio at a window, above.]

BRABANTIO. What is the reason of this terrible summons?
  What is the matter there?

RODERIGO. Signior, is all your family within?   84

IAGO. Are your doors lock'd?

BRABANTIO   Why, wherefore ask you
  this?

IAGO. 'Zounds, sir, you're robb'd!—For shame, put
  on your gown!—
  Your heart is burst, you have lost half your soul.
  Even now, now, very now, an old black ram   88
  Is tupping your white ewe. Arise, arise!
  Awake the snorting citizens with the bell,
  Or else the devil will make a grandsire of you.
  Arise, I say.

BRABANTIO. What! have you lost your wits?

RODERIGO. Most reverend signior, do you know my
  voice?

BRABANTIO. Not I. What are you?

RODERIGO. My name is Roderigo.

BRABANTIO.   The worser welcome!
  I have charg'd thee not to haunt about my
    doors.   96
  In honest plainness thou hast heard me say
  My daughter is not for thee; and now, in madness,
  Being full of supper and distempering draughts,
  Upon malicious bravery dost thou
    come   100
  To start my quiet.

RODERIGO. Sir, sir, sir!

BRABANTIO.   But thou must needs be sure,
  My spirit and my place have in them power
  To make this bitter to thee.

RODERIGO.   Patience, good sir.   104

BRABANTIO. What tell'st thou me of robbing? This is
  Venice.
  My house is not a grange.

RODERIGO.   Most grave Brabantio,
  In simple and pure soul I come to you.   107

IAGO. 'Zounds, sir, you are one of those that will not
  serve God if the devil bid you. Because we come to
  do you service and you think we are ruffians, you'll
  have your daughter covered with a Barbary horse;
  you'll have your nephews neigh to you; you'll have
  coursers for cousins and gennets for germans.   113

BRABANTIO. What profane wretch art thou?

IAGO. I am one, sir, that come to tell you, your
  daughter and the Moor are now making the beast
  with two backs.   117

BRABANTIO. Thou art a villain.

IAGO.   You are a senator.

BRABANTIO. This thou shalt answer. I know thee,
  Roderigo.

RODERIGO. Sir, I will answer anything. But, I beseech
  you,   120
  If't be your pleasure and most wise consent
  (As partly, I find, it is) that your fair daughter,
  At this odd-even and dull watch o' th' night,
  Transported with no worse nor better guard   124
  But with a knave of common hire, a góndolier,
  To the gross clasps of a lascivious Moor—

---

62. **native act**: innate operation **figure**: configuration 63. **complement extern**: outward counterpart **'tis . . . But**: 'twill not be long
before 66. **owe**: possess 67. **carry't**: get away with it 72. **chances
of vexation**: vexatious accidents 73. **As**: that 76. **by night and
negligence**: amid nocturnal repose 90. **snorting**: snoring

100. **bravery**: bravado 101. **start**: disturb 106 **grange**: lonely
farmhouse 112. **nephews**: grandchildren 113. **coursers**: swift and
spirited horses **gennets**: small Spanish horses **germans**: near relatives

If this be known to you, and your allowance,
We then have done you bold and saucy
   wrongs.   128
But if you know not this, my manners tell me
We have your wrong rebuke. Do not believe
That, from the sense of all civility,
I thus would play and trifle with your
   reverence.   132
Your daughter (if you have not given her leave,
I say again) hath made a gross revolt,
Tying her duty, beauty, wit and fortunes
In an extravagant and wheeling stranger   136
Of here and everywhere. Straight satisfy yourself.
If she be in her chamber or your house,
Let loose on me the justice of the state
For thus deluding you.
BRABANTIO.   Strike on the tinder, ho!   140
Give me a taper! call up all my people!
This accident is not unlike my dream.
Belief of it oppresses me already.
Light, I say! light!   [Exit.]
IAGO.   Farewell, for I must leave you.   144
It seems not meet nor wholesome to my place
To be produc'd (as, if I stay, I shall)
Against the Moor; for I do know the state
(However this may gall him with some check)   148
Cannot with safety cast him; for he's embark'd
With such loud reason to the Cyprus wars,
Which even now stand in act, that, for their souls,
Another of his fathom they have not   152
To lead their business. In which regard,
Though I do hate him as I do hell's pains,
Yet for necessity of present life,
I must show out a flag and sign of love,   156
Which is indeed but sign. That you shall surely find
   him,
Lead to the Sagittary the raised search,
And there will I be with him. So, farewell.   [Exit.]

[Enter below Brabantio in his night gown, and Servants with torches.]

BRABANTIO. It is too true an evil. Gone she is,   160
And what's to come of my despised time

Is nought but bitterness. Now, Roderigo,
Where didst thou see her? O unhappy girl!
With the Moor, sayst thou? Who would be a
   father!   164
How didst thou know 'twas she? O, she deceives me
Past thought. What said she to you? Get mo tapers!
Raise all my kindred! Are they married, think you?
RODERIGO. Truly, I think they are.   168
BRABANTIO. O heaven! How got she out? O treason
   of the blood!
Fathers, from hence trust not your daughters' minds
By what you see them act. Is there not charms
By which the property of youth and maidhood   172
May be abus'd? Have you not read, Roderigo,
Of some such thing?
RODERIGO.   Yes, sir, I have indeed.
BRABANTIO. Call up my brother. O, would you had
   had her!
Some one way, some another! Do you know   176
Where we may apprehend her and the Moor?
RODERIGO. I think I can discover him, if you please
To get good guard and go along with me.
BRABANTIO. Pray, lead me on. At every house I'll
   call;   180
I may command at most. Get weapons, ho!
And raise some special officers of night.
On, good Roderigo. I'll deserve your pains. [Exeunt.]

SCENE II

Another Street. Before the Sagittary

[Enter Othello, Iago, and Attendants with torches.]

IAGO. Though in the trade of war I have slain men,
Yet do I hold it very stuff o' th' conscience
To do no contriv'd murder. I lack iniquity
Sometimes to do me service. Nine or ten times   4
I had thought t' have yerk'd him here under the
   ribs.
OTHELLO. 'Tis better as it is.

---

127. **your allowance**: what you approve of 131. **from . . . all**: deprived of all regard for 136. **extravagant and wheeling**: vagabond and itinerant 146. **produc'd**: brought forward as witness 148. **check**: rebuke 149. **cast**: dismiss **embark'd**: engaged, committed 150. **loud reason**: pressing necessity 151. **stand in act**: are actually under way 152. **fathom**: capacity 158. **Sagittary**: an inn 159. **S.d. night gown**: dressing robe 161. **what's . . . time**: the remainder of my wretched life

166. **mo**: more 172. **property**: nature 175. **brother**: i.e., Gratiano 182. **officers of night**: night watchmen
2. **stuff**: substance, essence 3. **contriv'd**: premeditated 5 **yerk'd**: struck (with dagger)

IAGO.   Nay, but he prated,
And spoke such scurvy and provoking terms
Against your Honor   8
That with the little godliness I have
I did full hard forbear him. But, I pray, sir,
Are you fast married? Be assur'd of this,
That the magnifico is much belov'd,   12
And hath in his effect a voice potential
As double as the duke's. He will divorce you,
Or put upon you what restraint and grievance
The law, with all his might to enforce it on,   16
Will give him cable.
OTHELLO.   Let him do his spite.
My services which I have done the Signory
Shall out-tongue his complaints. 'Tis yet to know
(Which when I know that boasting is an
    honor   20
I shall promulgate), I fetch my life and being
From men of royal siege, and my demerits
May speak unbonneted to as proud a fortune
As this that I have reach'd. For know, Iago,   24
But that I love the gentle Desdemona,
I would not my unhoused free condition
Put into circumscription and confine
For the sea's worth. But, look! what lights come
    yond?   28
IAGO. Those are the raised father and his friends.
You were best go in.
OTHELLO.   Not I. I must be found.
My parts, my title, and my perfect soul
Shall manifest me rightly. Is it they?   32
IAGO. By Janus, I think no.

[Enter Cassio with lights, Officers and torches.]

OTHELLO. The servants of the duke, and my lieute-
    nant.
The goodness of the night upon you, friends!
What is the news?
CASSIO.   The duke does greet you,
    general,   36
And he requires your haste-post-haste appearance,
Even on the instant.
OTHELLO.   What's the matter, think you?

CASSIO. Something from Cyprus, as I may divine.
It is a business of some heat. The galleys   40
Have sent a dozen sequent messengers
This very night at one another's heels,
And many of the consuls, rais'd and met,
Are at the duke's already. You have been hotly call'd
    for;
When being not at your lodging to be found,   45
The Senate sent above three several quests
To search you out.
OTHELLO.   'Tis well I'm found by you.
I will but spend a word here in the house,   48
And go with you.

[Enters the Sagittary.]

CASSIO.   Ancient, what makes he here?
IAGO. Faith, he to-night hath boarded a land carrack.
If it prove lawful prize, he's made for ever.
CASSIO. I do not understand.
IAGO.   He's married.
CASSIO.   To who?   52
IAGO. Marry, to—

[Re-enter Othello.]

                Come, captain, will you go?
OTHELLO.   Have with you.
CASSIO. Here comes another troop to seek for you.
IAGO. It is Brabantio. General, be advis'd;
    He comes to bad intent.

[Enter Brabantio, Roderigo, and others, with lights and
weapons.]

OTHELLO.   Holla! stand there!   56
RODERIGO. Signior, it is the Moor.
BRABANTIO.   Down with him! Thief!

[They draw on both sides.]

IAGO. You, Roderigo! Come, sir, I am for you.
OTHELLO. Keep up your bright swords, for the dew
    will rust 'em.
Good signior, you shall more command with
    years   60
Than with your weapons.

---

12. **magnifico**: title of Venetian nobles 17. **give . . . cable**: permit **his spite**: whatever spite urges 18. **Signory**: governing body of
Venice 19. **'Tis yet to know**: i.e,. the world doesn't yet know 22.
siege: rank **demerits**: deserts 27. **confine**: confinement 31.
parts: abilities **perfect**: blameless 33. **Janus**: two-faced Roman god
of beginnings

40. **heat**: urgency 41. **sequent**: successive 43. **consuls**: senators
50. **carrack**: large merchant vessel 59. **Keep up**: keep sheathed

BRABANTIO. O thou foul thief! Where hast thou
    stow'd my daughter?
  Damn'd as thou art, thou hast enchanted her;
  For I'll refer me to all things of sense,   64
  If she in chains of magic were not bound,
  Whether a maid so tender, fair, and happy,
  So opposite to marriage that she shunn'd
  The wealthy curled darlings of our nation,   68
  Would ever have ('t'incur a general mock)
  Run from her guardage to the sooty bosom
  Of such a thing as thou—to fear, not to delight.
  Judge me the world, if 'tis not gross in sense   72
  That thou hast practis'd on her with foul charms,
  Abus'd her delicate youth with drugs or minerals
  That weakens motion. I'll have't disputed on.
  'Tis probable, and palpable to thinking.   76
  I therefore apprehend and do attach thee
  For an abuser of the world, a practiser
  Of arts inhibited and out of warrant.
  Lay hold upon him. If he do resist,   80
  Subdue him at his peril.
OTHELLO.   Hold your hands,
  Both you of my inclining and the rest.
  Were it my cue to fight, I should have known it
  Without a prompter. Wh'er will you that I go 84
  To answer this your charge?
BRABANTIO.   To prison, till fit time
  Of law and course of direct session
  Call thee to answer.
OTHELLO.   What if I do obey?
  How may the duke be therewith satisfied,   88
  Whose messengers are here about my side
  Upon some present business of the state
  To bring me to him?
OFFICER.   'Tis true, most worthy signior.
  The duke's in council, and your noble self,   92
  I am sure, is sent for.
BRABANTIO.   How? The duke in council!
  In this time of the night! Bring him away.
  Mine's not an idle cause. The duke himself,
  Or any of my brothers of the state,   96
  Cannot but feel this wrong as 'twere their own;
  For if such actions may have passage free,
  Bondslaves and pagans shall our statesmen be.

[Exeunt.]

---

64. **of sense:** capable of judgment   **70. guardage:** guardian's shelter   **72. judge . . . world:** let the world judge   **gross in sense:** manifest to the reason   **75. motion:** *inward impulse (cf. I.iii.331)* **have't disputed on:** refer it to specialists   **79. out of warrant:** unwarranted   **84. Wh'er:** whither   **86. course . . . session:** due order of special procedure

SCENE III

The Doge's Palace

[*Enter Duke and Senators, set at a table with lights and Attendants.*]

DUKE. There is no composition in these news
  That gives them credit.
1. SENATOR.   Indeed, they are disproportion'd.
  My letters say a hundred and seven galleys.
DUKE. And mine, a hundred forty.
2. SENATOR.   And mine, two hundred.   4
  But though they jump not on a just account
  (As in these cases, where the aim reports,
  'Tis oft with difference), yet do they all confirm
  A Turkish fleet, and bearing up to Cyprus.   8
DUKE. Nay, it is possible enough to judgment.
  I do not so secure me in the error,
  But the main article I do approve
  In fearful sense.
SAILOR WITHIN. What, ho! what, ho! what, ho!   12
OFFICER. A messenger from the galleys.

[*Enter Sailor.*]

DUKE.   Now! The
  business?
SAILOR. The Turkish preparation makes for Rhodes.
  So was I bid report here to the state
  By Signior Angelo.   16
DUKE. How say you by this change?
1. SENATOR.   This cannot be,
  By no assay of reason. 'Tis a pageant
  To keep us in false gaze. When we consider
  Th'importancy of Cyprus to the Turk,   20
  And let ourselves again but understand
  That as it more concerns the Turk than Rhodes,
  So may he with more facile question bear it,
  For that it stands not in such warlike brace,   24
  But altogether lacks th'abilities
  That Rhodes is dress'd in—if we make thought of
    this,
  We must not think the Turk is so unskilful
  To leave that latest which concerns him first,   28

---

1. **composition:** consistency **5. jump:** agree **just:** exact **6. aim:** conjecture **9 to judgment:** when judicially considered **18. assay of reason:** reasonable test **pageant:** feigned show **19. in false gaze:** looking in the wrong direction **23. with . . . it:** carry it with less effort **24. brace:** readiness

Neglecting an attempt of ease and gain
To wake and wage a danger profitless.
DUKE. Nay, in all confidence, he's not for Rhodes.
OFFICER. Here is more news.   32

[Enter a Messenger.]

MESSENGER. The Ottomites, reverend and gracious,
Steering with due course toward the isle of Rhodes,
Have there injointed them with an after fleet.
1. SENATOR. Ay, so I thought. How many, as you
guess?
MESSENGER. Of thirty sail; and now they do re-stem
Their backward course, bearing with frank appear-
ance
Their purposes toward Cyprus. Signior Montano,
Your trusty and most valiant servitor,   40
With his free duty recommends you thus,
And prays you to believe him.
DUKE. 'Tis certain then, for Cyprus.
Marcus Luccicos is not here in town?   44
1. SENATOR. He's now in Florence.
DUKE. Write from us: wish him post-post-haste dis-
patch.
1. SENATOR. Here comes Brabantio and the valiant
Moor.

[Enter Brabantio, Othello, Cassio, Iago, Roderigo, and Officers.]

DUKE. Valiant Othello, we must straight employ
you   48
Against the general enemy Ottomon.
[To Brabantio.] I did not see you. Welcome, gentle
signior;
We lack'd your counsel and your help to-night.
BRABANTIO. So did I yours. Good your Grace, pardon
me.   52
Neither my place nor aught I heard of business
Hath rais'd me from my bed, nor doth the general
care
Take hold on me, for my particular grief
Is of so floodgate and o'erbearing nature   56
That it engluts and swallows other sorrows
And it is still itself.
DUKE.   Why, what's the matter?
BRABANTIO. My daughter! O my daughter!
ALL.   Dead?

BRABANTIO.   Ay, to me,
She is abus'd, stol'n from me, and corrupted   60
By spells and medicines bought of mountebanks;
For nature so preposterously to err
Being not deficient, blind, or lame of sense,
Sans witchcraft could not.   64
DUKE. Whoe'er he be that in this foul proceeding
Hath thus beguil'd your daughter of herself
And you of her, the bloody book of law
You shall yourself read in the bitter letter   68
After your own sense; yea, though our proper son
Stood in your action.
BRABANTIO.   Humbly I thank your Grace.
Here is the man, this Moor; whom now, it seems,
Your special mandate for the state affairs   72
Hath hither brought.
ALL.   We are very sorry for't.
DUKE. [to Othello]. What, in your own part, can you
say to this?
BRABANTIO. Nothing but 'This is so.'
OTHELLO. Most potent, grave, and reverend
signiors,   76
My very noble and approv'd good masters:
That I have ta'en away this old man's daughter,
It is most true; true, I have married her.
The very head and front of my offending   80
Hath this extent, no more. Rude am I in my speech,
And little bless'd with the soft phrase of peace,
For since these arms of mine had seven years' pith
Till now some nine moons wasted, they have
us'd   84
Their dearest action in the tented field;
And little of this great world can I speak
More than pertains to feats of broil and battle,
And therefore little shall I grace my cause   88
In speaking for myself. Yet, by your gracious
patience,
I will a round unvarnish'd tale deliver
Of my whole course of love: what drugs, what
charms,
What conjuration, and what mighty magic,   92
(For such proceedings am I charg'd withal)
I won his daughter.
BRABANTIO.   A maiden never bold;
Of spirit so still and quiet, that her motion

---

61. mountebanks: itinerant vendors of nostrums 64. Sans: without could not: would be impossible 69. proper: own 70. Stood
. . . action: were involved by your charge 74. part: behalf 77.
approv'd: esteemed 80. head and front: i.e., the most glaring
part 84. wasted: past, ago 91–94. what . . . won: with what
drugs, etc., I won 93. withal: with

30. wake and wage: start and carry through 35. after: reserve 41.
recommends: informs 56. floodgate: torrential

Blush'd at herself! And she, in spite of nature, 96
Of years, of country, credit, everything,
To call in love with what she fear'd to look on!
It is a judgment maim'd and most imperfect
That will confess perfection so could err 100
Against all rules of nature and must be driven
To find out practices of cunning hell,
Why this should be. I therefore vouch again
That with some mixtures powerful o'er the
    blood, 104
Or with some dram conjur'd to this effect,
He wrought upon her.

DUKE.   To vouch this is no proof,
Without more certain and more overt test
Than these thin habits and poor likelihoods 108
Of modern seeming to prefer against him.

1. SENATOR. But, Othello, speak.
Did you by indirect and forced courses
Subdue and poison this young maid's affec-
    tions? 112
Or came it by request and such fair question
As soul to soul affordeth?

OTHELLO.   I do beseech you,
Send for the lady to the Sagittary,
And let her speak of me before her father. 116
If you do find me foul in her report,
The trust, the office I do hold of you,
Not only take away, but let your sentence
Even fall upon my life.

DUKE.   Fetch Desdemona hither. 120

[Exit two or three.]

OTHELLO. Ancient, conduct them. You best know the
    place.

[Exit Iago.]

And till she come, as truly as to heaven
I do confess the vices of my blood,
So justly to your grave ears I'll present 124
How I did thrive in this fair lady's love,
And she in mine.

DUKE. Say it, Othello.

OTHELLO. Her father lov'd me; oft invited me, 128
Still question'd me the story of my life
From year to year, the battles, sieges, fortunes
That I have pass'd.

I ran it through, even from my boyish days 132
To th' very moment that he bade me tell it.
Wherein I spake of most disastrous chances,
Of moving accidents by flood and field,
Of hair-breadth 'scapes i' th' imminent deadly
    breach, 136
Of being taken by the insolent foe
And sold to slavery, of my redemption thence
And portance in my traveller's history.
Wherein of antres vast and deserts idle, 140
Rough quarries, rocks and hills whose heads touch
    heaven,
It was my hint to speak (such was the process),
And of the Cannibals that each other eat,
The Anthropophagi, and men whose heads 144
Do grow beneath their shoulders. This to hear
Would Desdemona seriously incline:
But still the house-affairs would draw her thence,
Which ever as she could with haste dispatch 148
She'd come again, and with a greedy ear
Devour up my discourse. Which I observing,
Took once a pliant hour and found good means
To draw from her a prayer of earnest heart 152
That I would all my pilgrimage dilate,
Whereof by parcels she had something heard,
But not intentively. I did consent;
And often did beguile her of her tears, 156
When I did speak of some distressful stroke
That my youth suffer'd. My story being done,
She gave me for my pains a world of sighs.
She swore, i' faith, 'twas strange, 'twas passing
    strange;
'Twas pitiful, 'twas wondrous pitiful.
She wish'd she had not heard it, yet she wish'd
That heaven had made her such a man. She thank'd
    me,
And bade me, if I had a friend that lov'd her, 164
I should but teach him how to tell my story,
And that would woo her. Upon this heat I spake.
She lov'd me for the dangers I had pass'd,
And I lov'd her that she did pity them. 168
This only is the witchcraft I have us'd.
Here comes the lady; let her witness it.

[Enter Desdemona, Iago, and the rest.]

DUKE. I think this tale would win my daughter too.
    Cood Brabantio, 172

---

103. vouch: assert 108. thin habits: insubstantial appearances
109. modern: mere, trivial 111. forced: violent 113. question:
conversation 128. invited me: entertained me as guest 129. Still:
constantly

139. portance: behavior 140. antres: caves 142. hint: cue
process: narrative 151. pliant: suitable 153. dilate: relate in
full 154. by parcels: piecemeal 155. intentively: with undistracted
attention 166. Upon this heat: while the iron was hot

Take up this mangled matter at the best.
Men do their broken weapons rather use
Than their bare hands.
BRABANTIO.   I pray you, hear her speak.
If she confess that she was half the wooer,   176
Destruction on my head, if my bad blame
Light on the man! Come hither, gentle mistress.
Do you perceive in all this noble company
Where most you owe obedience?
DESDEMONA.   My noble father,   180
I do perceive here a divided duty.
To you I am bound for life and education.
My life and education both do learn me
How to respect you: you are the lord of duty,   184
I am hitherto your daughter. But here's my hus-
    band;
And so much duty as my mother show'd
To you, preferring you before her father,
So much I challenge that I may profess   188
Due to the Moor my lord.
BRABANTIO.   God be with you! I have done.
Please it your Grace, on to the state affairs.
I had rather to adopt a child than get it.
Come hither, Moor: 192
I here do give thee that with all my heart
(which, but thou hast already, with all my heart)
I would keep from thee. For your sake, jewel,
I am glad at soul I have no other child,   196
For thy escape would teach me tyranny,
To hang clogs on 'em. I have done, my lord.
DUKE. Let me speak like yourself and lay a sentence,
Which, as a grise or step, may help these
    lovers   200
Into your favor.
When remedies are past, the griefs are ended
By seeing the worst, which late on hopes depended.
To mourn a mischief that is past and gone   204
Is the next way to draw more mischief on.
What cannot be preserv'd when Fortune takes,
Patience her injury a mockery makes.
The robb'd that smiles steals something from the
    thief;
He robs himself that spends a bootless grief.   209
BRABANTIO. So let the Turk of Cyprus us beguile,
We lose it not so long as we can smile.
He bears the sentence well that nothing bears   212

But the free comfort which from thence he hears;
But he bears both the sentence and the sorrow
That, to pay grief, must of poor patience borrow.
These sentences, to sugar, or to gall,   216
Being strong on both sides, are equivocal:
But words are words; I never yet did hear
That the bruis'd heart was pierced through the ear.
Beseech you, now to the affairs of state.   220
DUKE. The Turk with a most mighty preparation
makes for Cyprus. Othello, the fortitude of the place
is best known to you; and though we have there a
substitute of most allowed sufficiency, yet opinion, a
sovereign mistress of effects, throws a more safer
voice on you. You must therefore be content to
slubber the gloss of your new fortunes with this
more stubborn and boisterous expedition.   229
OTHELLO. The tyrant custom, most grave senators,
Hath made the flinty and steel couch of war
My thrice-driven bed of down. I do agnize   232
A natural and prompt alacrity
I find in hardness, and do undertake
These present wars against the Ottomites.
Most humbly therefore bending to your state,   236
I crave fit disposition for my wife,
Due reference of place and exhibition,
With such accommodation and besort
As levels with her breeding.
DUKE.   If you please,
Be't at her father's.
BRABANTIO.   I'll not have it so.
OTHELLO. Nor I.
DESDEMONA.   Nor I. I would not there reside,
To put my father in impatient thoughts
By being in his eye. Most gracious duke,   244
To my unfolding lend your prosperous ear,
And let me find a charter in your voice
T'assist my simpleness.
DUKE.   What would you? Speak.
DESDEMONA. That I did love the Moor to live with
    him,   248
My downright violence and storm of fortunes
May trumpet to the world. My heart's subdu'd
Even to the very quality of my lord.
I saw Othello's visage in his mind,   252

---

173. **at the best:** as best you may 183. **learn:** teach 191. **get:** beget 197. **escape:** escapade 200. **grise:** stair 202. **griefs:** distresses of mind, anxieties 203. **which:** (refers to 'griefs') 205. **next:** nearest 209. **bootless:** unavailing 210. **let:** i.e., suppose 212. **sentence:** adage (with pun on 'court sentence')

219. **pierced:** probed, touched 225. **opinion . . . effects:** reputation, a great producer of results 227. **slubber:** sully 232. **driven:** sifted **agnize:** acknowledge 233. **alacrity:** congeniality, hearty sympathy 234. **hardness:** austerity 238. **reference:** assignment **exhibition:** allowance 239. **besort:** suitable retinue 245. **unfolding:** explanation **prosperous:** favoring 246. **charter:** official sanction 249. **storm:** forcible seizure 251. **quality:** profession

And to his honors and his valiant parts
Did I my soul and fortunes consecrate.
So that, dear lords, if I be left behind,
A moth of peace, and he go to the war, 256
The rites for which I love him are bereft me,
And I a heavy interim shall support
By his dear absence. Let me go with him.
OTHELLO. Your voices, lords! Beseech you, let her will 260
Have a free way. I therefore beg it not
To please the palate of my appetite,
Nor to comply with heat the young affects
In my distinct and proper satisfaction, 264
But to be free and bounteous to her mind;
And heaven defend your good souls that you think
I will your serious and great business scant
For she is with me. No, when light-wing'd toys 268
Of feather'd Cupid seel with wanton dulness
My speculative and offic'd instruments,
That my disports corrupt and taint my business,
Let housewives make a skillet of my helm, 272
And all indign and base adversities
Make head against my estimation!
DUKE. Be it as you shall privately determine,
Either for her stay or going. Th' affair cries haste, 276
And speed must answer. You must hence to-night.
DESDEMONA. To-night, my lord?
DUKE.   This night.
OTHELLO.   With all my heart.
DUKE. At ten i' the morning here we'll meet again.
Othello, leave some officer behind, 280
And he shall our commission bring to you;
With such things else of quality or respect
As doth concern you.
OTHELLO.   Please your Grace, my ancient.
A man he is of honesty and trust. 284
To his conveyance I assign my wife,
With what else needful your good Grace shall think
To be sent after me.

DUKE.   Let it be so.
Good night to every one. [To Brabantio.] And, noble signior, 288
If virtue no delighted beauty lack,
Your son-in-law is far more fair than black.
1. SENATOR. Adieu, brave Moor! use Desdemona well.
BRABANTIO. Look to her, Moor, if thou hast eyes to see: 292
She has deceiv'd her father, and may thee.
OTHELLO. My life upon her faith!

[Exeunt Duke, Senators, Officers, &c.]

                    Honest Iago,
My Desdemona must I leave to thee:
I prithee, let thy wife attend on her; 296
And bring her after in the best advantage.—
Come, Desdemona; I have but an hour
Of love, of worldly matters and direction
To spend with thee. We must obey the time. 300

[Ex. Moor and Desdemona.]

RODERIGO. Iago!
IAGO. What sayst thou, noble heart?
RODERIGO. What will I do, think'st thou?
IAGO. Why, go to bed, and sleep. 304
RODERIGO. I will incontinently drown myself.
IAGO. Well, if thou dost, I shall never love thee after it. Why, thou silly gentleman? 307
RODERIGO. It is silliness to live when to live is a torment; and then have we a prescription to die when death is our physician. 310
IAGO. O, villainous! I ha' looked upon the world for four times seven years, and since I could distinguish between a benefit and an injury, I never found a man that knew how to love himself. Ere I would say I would drown myself for the love of a guinea-hen, I would change my humanity with a baboon. 316
RODERIGO. What should I do? I confess it is my shame to be so fond, but it is not in my virtue to amend it.
IAGO. Virtue! a fig! 'Tis in ourselves that we are thus or thus. Our bodies are gardens, to the which our wills are gardeners; so that if we will plant nettles or sow lettuce, set hyssop and weed up thyme, supply it with

260. voices: favorable votes **263. heat . . . affects:** lust which the young incline to **264. distinct and proper:** separate and personal **266. defend:** forbid **268. For:** because **toys:** trifles **270. speculative . . . instruments:** eyes which should see and perform duties **272. skillet:** kettle **helm:** helmet **273. indign:** unworthy **274. Make head:** take arms **estimation:** fame **282. quality or respect:** general importance or detail (almost 'genus' and 'species')

289. delighted: delighting **305. incontinently:** immediately **316. change:** exchange one gender of herbs or distract it with many, either to have it sterile with idleness or manured with industry, why, the power and corrigible authority of this lies in our wills. If the balance of our lives had not one scale of reason to poise another of sensuality, the blood and baseness of our natures would conduct us to most preposterous conclusions. But we have reason to cool our raging motions, our carnal stings, our unbitted lusts, whereof I take this that you call love to be a sect or scion.

RODERIGO. It cannot be. 334

IAGO. It is merely a lust of the blood and a permission of the will. Come, be a man. Drown thyself? Drown cats and blind puppies. I profess me thy friend, and I confess me knit to thy deserving with cables of perdúrable toughness. I could never better stead thee than now. Put money in thy purse. Follow these wars; defeat thy favor with an usurped beard. I say, put money in thy purse. It cannot be that Desdemona should long continue her love unto the Moor,—put money in thy purse,—nor he his to her. It was a violent commencement, and thou shalt see an answerable sequestration. Put but money in thy purse. These Moors are changeable in their wills. Fill thy purse with money. The food that to him now is as luscious as locusts, shall be to him shortly as acerb as the coloquintida. She must change for youth. When she is sated with his body, she will find the error of her choice. She must have change, she must. Therefore put money in thy purse. If thou wilt needs damn thyself, do it a more delicate way than drowning. Make all the money thou canst. If sanctimony and a frail vow betwixt an erring barbarian and a supersubtle Venetian be not too hard for my wits and all the tribe of hell, thou shalt enjoy her: therefore make money. A pox o' drowning! 'tis clean out of the way. Seek thou rather to be hanged in compassing thy joy than to be drowned and go without her. 362

RODERIGO. Wilt thou be fast to my hopes if I depend on the issue?

IAGO. Thou art sure of me. Go, make money. I have told thee often, and I tell thee again and again, I hate the Moor. My cause is hearted: thine hath no less reason. Let us be conjunctive in our revenge against him. If thou canst cuckold him, thou dost thyself a pleasure, me a sport. There are many events in the womb of time which will be delivered. Traverse! go! provide thy money! We will have more of this to-morrow. Adieu. 373

RODERIGO. Where shall we meet i' th' morning?

IAGO. At my lodging.

RODERIGO. I'll be with thee betimes. 376

IAGO. Go to; farewell. Do you hear, Roderigo?

RODERIGO. What say you?

IAGO. No more of drowning, do you hear?

RODERIGO. I am chang'd. (I'll sell all my
land.) 380

IAGO. Go to; farewell. Put money enough in your
purse.   [Exit Roderigo.]
Thus do I ever make my fool my purse;
For I mine own gain'd knowledge should profane,
If I would time expend with such a snipe 384
But for my sport and profit. I hate the Moor,
And it is thought abroad that 'twixt my sheets
He's done my office. I know not if't be true,
But I, for mere suspicion in that kind, 388
Will do as if for surety. He holds me well.
The better shall my purpose work on him.
Cassio's a proper man. Let me see now.—
To get his place, and to plume up my will 392
In double knavery: how? how? Let's see.—
After some time t'abuse Othello's ear
That he is too familiar with his wife.
He has a person and a smooth dispose 396
To be suspected, fram'd to make women false;
The Moor a free and open nature too,
That thinks men honest that but seem to be so,
And will as tenderly be led by th' nose 400
As asses are.
I have't! it is engender'd! Hell and night
Must bring this monstrous birth to the world's light.

[Exit.]

---

324. **gender:** kind 325. **manured:** cultivated 326. **corrigible authority:** correcting control 327. **balance:** weighing instrument 328. **poise:** offset, counterbalance 331. **motions:** impulses 332. **unbitted:** unbridled 333. **sect:** variety **scion:** off-shoot 339. **perdúrable:** most durable **stead:** aid 341. **defeat thy favor:** disguise thy face **usurped:** false 346. **answerable sequestration:** similarly hasty parting 349. **locusts:** cassia fistula, a sweet fruit 350. **acerb:** bitter **coloquintida:** an intensely bitter drug (imported from Cyprus) 356. **erring:** roving; cf. n. on I.i.136

367. **hearted:** deep-seated in the heart 368. **conjunctive:** united 369. **cuckold him:** seduce his wife 371. **Traverse:** march 377. **Go to:** come, come! 388. **in that kind:** of that sort 391. **proper:** fine, good-looking 394. **abuse:** deceive 396. **dispose:** manner

Act II

SCENE I

Famagosta, capital of Cyprus. An open place near the quay

[*Enter Montano, Governor of Cyprus, with two other Gentlemen.*]

MONTANO. What from the cape can you discern at
    sea?
1. GENTLEMEN. Nothing at all. It is a high-wrought
    flood;
  I cannot 'twixt the haven and the main
  Descry a sail.   4
MONTANO. Methinks the wind does speak aloud at
    land;
  A fuller blast ne'er shook our battlements.
  If it hath ruffian'd so upon the sea,
  What ribs of oak, when mountains melt on
    them,   8
  Can hold the mortise? What shall we hear of this?
2. GENTLEMEN. A segregation of the Turkish fleet;
  For do but stand upon the foaming shore,
  The chidden billow seems to pelt the clouds;   12
  The wind-shak'd surge, with high and monstrous
    mane,
  Seems to cast water on the burning bear
  And quench the guards of th' ever-fixed pole.
  I never did like molestation view   16
  On the enchafed flood.
MONTANO.   If that the Turkish fleet
  Be not enshelter'd and embay'd, they are drown'd.
  It is impossible they bear it out.

[*Enter a third Gentleman.*]

3. GENTLEMAN. News, lads! our wars are done.   20
  The desperate tempest hath so bang'd the Turks
  That their designment halts. A noble ship of Venice
  Hath seen a grievous wrack and sufferance
  On most part of their fleet.   24
MONTANO. How! is this true?

3. GENTLEMAN.   The ship is here put in,
  La Veronesa. Michael Cassio,
  Lieutenant to the warlike Moor Othello,
  Is come on shore; the Moor himself at sea,   28
  And is in full commission here for Cyprus.
MONTANO. I am glad on't; 'tis a worthy governor.
3. GENTLEMAN. But this same Cassio, though he
    speak of comfort
  Touching the Turkish loss, yet he looks sadly   32
  And prays the Moor be safe, for they were parted
  With foul and violent tempest.
MONTANO.   Pray heaven he be;
  For I have serv'd him, and the man commands
  Like a full soldier. Let's to the seaside, ho!   36
  As well to see the vessel that's come in
  As to throw out our eyes for brave Othello,
  (Even till we make the main and th' aerial blue
  An indistinct regard.)
3. GENTLEMAN.   Come, let's do so;   40
  For every minute is expectancy
  Of more arrivance.

[*Enter Cassio.*]

CASSIO. Thanks to the valiant of this warlike isle,
  That so approve the Moor! And let the heavens   44
  Give him defence against the elements,
  For I have lost him on a dangerous sea.
MONTANO. Is he well shipp'd?
CASSIO. His bark is stoutly timber'd, and his pilot   48
  Of very expert and approv'd allowance.
  Therefore my hopes, not surfeited to death,
  Stand in bold cure.
MESSENGER WITHIN. A sail!—a sail!—a sail!

[*Enter a Messenger.*]

CASSIO. What noise?   52
MESSENGER. The town is empty. On the brow o' th'
    sea
  Stand ranks of people, and they cry, 'A sail!'
CASSIO. My hopes do shape him for the governor.

[*A shot.*]

---

3. **main**: open ocean   **9. hold the mortise**: remain unshattered   **10. segregation**: dispersal   **15. guards**: two stars in Ursa Minor   **pole**: pole-star   **16. molestation**: disturbance   **19. bear it out**: ride it out   **22. designment**: enterprise   **23. sufferance**: disaster

26. La Veronesa: 'The Lady of Verona' (the ship's name)   **36. full**: thorough   **39, 40.** till the sea and sky become indistinguishable   **42. more arrivance**: further arrivals   **49.** Of very allowed and approved expertness

2. GENTLEMAN. They do discharge the shot of cour- 56
    tesy.
  Our friends, at least.
CASSIO.   I pray you, sir, go forth,
  And give us truth who 'tis that is arriv'd.
2. GENTLEMAN. I shall.   [Exit.]
MONTANO. But, good lieutenant, is your general
    wiv'd?   60
CASSIO. Most fortunately. He hath achiev'd a maid
  That paragons description and wild fame;
  One that excels the quirks of blazoning pens,
  And in th' essential vesture of creation   64
  Does tire the ingen-giver.

[Enter 2. Gentleman.]

               Now, who has put in?
2. GENTLEMAN. 'Tis one Iago, ancient to the general.
CASSIO. He's had most favorable and happy speed.
  Tempests themselves, high seas, and howling
    winds,   68
  The gutter'd rocks, and congregated sands,
  Traitors ensteep'd to clog the guiltless keel,
  As having sense of beauty, do omit
  Their mortal natures, letting go safely by   72
  The divine Desdemona.
MONTANO.   What is she?
CASSIO. She that I spoke of, our great captain's cap-
    tain,
  Left in the conduct of the bold Iago,
  Whose footing here anticipates our thoughts   76
  A sennight's speed. Great Jove, Othello guard,
  And swell his sail with thine own powerful breath,
  That he may bless this bay with his tall ship,
  Make love's quick pants in Desdemona's arms,   80
  Give renew'd fire to our extincted spirits,
  And bring all Cyprus comfort!

[Enter Desdemona, Iago, Emilia, and Roderigo with Attendants.]

                O! behold,
  The riches of the ship is come ashore.
  Ye men of Cyprus, let her have your knees.   84
  Hail to thee, lady! and the grace of heaven,
  Before, behind thee, and on every hand,
  Enwheel thee round!

DESDEMONA.   I thank you, valiant Cassio.
  What tidings can you tell me of my lord?   88
CASSIO. He is not yet arriv'd; nor know I aught
  But that he's well, and will be shortly here.
DESDEMONA. O, but I fear! How lost you company?

[Cry within. 'A sail!—a sail!']

CASSIO. The great contention of the sea and skies   92
  Parted our fellowship. But hark! a sail. [Guns heard.]
2. GENTLEMAN. They give their greeting to the cita-
    del:
  This likewise is a friend.
CASSIO.   So speaks this voice. See for the news!

[Exit 2. Gentleman.]

  Good ancient, you are welcome. [Kisses Emilia.] Wel-
    come, mistress.   96
  Let it not gall your patience, good Iago,
  That I extend my manners. 'Tis my breeding
  That gives me this bold show of courtesy.
IAGO. Sir, would she give you so much of her
    lips   100
  As of her tongue she oft bestows on me,
  You'd have enough.
DESDEMONA.   Alas, she has no speech.
IAGO. In faith, too much.
  I find it still when I have list to sleep.   104
  Marry, before your ladyship, I grant,
  She puts her tongue a little in her heart,
  And chides with thinking.
EMILIA. You have little cause to say so.   108
IAGO. Come on, come on! You are pictures out
    o'doors,
  Bells in your parlors, wild cats in your kitchens,
  Saints in your injuries, devils being offended,
  Players in your housewifery, and housewives in your
    beds.
DESDEMONA. O fie upon thee, slanderer!   113
IAGO. Nay, it is true, or else I am a Turk.
  You rise to play and go to bed to work.
EMILIA. You shall not write my praise.
IAGO.   No, let me not.   116
DESDEMONA. What wouldst thou write of me, if thou
    shouldst praise me?

---

62. paragons: surpasses **63. quirks:** subtleties **blazoning:** extoll-
ing **64.** in the beauties of soul with which nature has clothed
her **69. gutter'd:** jagged **70. ensteep'd:** submerged **72. mortal:**
deadly **75. conduct:** escort **77. sennight's:** week's **84. knees:**
obeisance **87. Enwheel:** encircle

98. extend: elaborate **104. list:** inclination **109. pictures:** i.e.,
paint your faces **110. Bells:** janglers **111. Saints . . . injuries:**
adopt a saintly air when saying spiteful things **112. housewifery,**
housewives

IAGO. O gentle lady, do not put me to't,
  For I am nothing if not critical.
DESDEMONA. Come on; assay. There's one gone to
  the harbor?
IAGO. Ay, madam.   121
DESDEMONA. I am not merry, but I do beguile
  The thing I am by seeming otherwise.
  Come, how wouldst thou praise me?   124
IAGO. I am about it, but indeed my invention comes
  from my pate as birdlime does from frieze. It plucks
  out brains and all. But my muse labors, and thus she
  is deliver'd.   128

  If she be fair and wise.—Fairness and wit:
  The one's for use, the other useth it.

DESDEMONA. Well prais'd! How if she be black and
  witty?
IAGO.

  If she be black, and thereto have a wit,   132
  She'll find a white that shall her blackness fit.

DESDEMONA. Worse and worse.
EMILIA. How if fair and foolish?
IAGO.

  She never yet was foolish that was fair,   136
  For even her folly help'd her to an heir.

DESDEMONA. These are old fond paradoxes to make
  fools laugh i' th' alehouse. What miserable praise
  hast thou for her that's foul and foolish?   140
IAGO.

  There's none so foul and foolish thereunto
  But does foul pranks which fair and wise ones do.

DESDEMONA. O heavy ignorance that praises the
  worst best! But what praise couldst thou bestow on
  a deserving woman indeed? one that, in the authority of her merits, did justly put on the vouch of very
  malice itself?   147

IAGO.

  She that was ever fair and never proud,
  Had tongue at will and yet was never loud;
  Never lack'd gold and yet went never gay,   150
  Fled from her wish and yet said 'Now I may';
  She that being anger'd, her revenge being nigh,
  Bade her wrong stay and her displeasure fly;
  She that in wisdom never was so frail   154
  To change the cod's head for the salmon's tail;
  She that could think and ne'er disclose her mind,
  See suitors following and not look behind:
  She was a wight, if ever such wights were,—

DESDEMONA. To do what?   159
IAGO.

  To suckle fools and chronicle small beer.

DESDEMONA. O most lame and impotent conclusion!
  Do not learn of him, Emilia, though he be thy
  husband. How say you, Cassio? Is he not a most
  profane and liberal counsellor?   164
CASSIO. He speaks home, madam. You may relish him
  more in the soldier than in the scholar.
IAGO. [aside] He takes her by the palm. Ay, well said,
  whisper! With as little a web as this will I ensnare as
  great a fly as Cassio. Ay, smile upon her, do! I will
  gyve thee in thine own courtship. [Cassio speaks to
  Desdemona in dumbshow.] You say true, 'tis so, indeed. If such tricks as these strip you out of your
  lieutenantry, it had been better you had not kissed
  your three fingers so oft, which now again you
  are most apt to play the sir in. Very good! well
  kissed! an excellent courtesy! 'tis so, indeed. Yet
  again your fingers to your lips? would they were
  clyster-pipes for your sake!

[Trumpets within.]

  The Moor! I know his trumpet.
CASSIO. 'Tis truly so.
DESDEMONA. Let's meet him and receive him.   180
CASSIO. Lo, where he comes!

[Enter Othello and Attendants.]

---

120. assay: essay, attempt 123. The . . . am: my real feeling 125.
invention: imagination 126. frieze: rough woolen cloth 131.
black: brunette 133. white: quibble on 'wight' (cf. line 158) 137.
folly: lewdness 138. fond: foolish 140. foul: ugly 146. put on:
clothe herself in vouch: favorable testimony

149. Had tongue at will: was good at talking 160. chronicle, etc.:
keep petty household accounts 164. liberal: licentious 165.
home: to the point 166. in the: in the character of 167. said:
done 170. gyve: fetter courtship: courtliness 175. apt: ready
sir: gallant 177. clyster-pipes: tubes for injections

OTHELLO. O my fair warrior!

DESDEMONA. My dear Othello!

OTHELLO. It gives me wonder great as my content
To see you here before me. O my soul's joy, 184
If after every tempest come such calms,
May the winds blow till they have waken'd death!
And let the laboring bark climb hills of seas
Olympus-high, and duck again as low 188
As hell's from heaven! If it were now to die,
'Twere now to be most happy, for I fear
My soul hath her content so absolute
That not another comfort like to this 192
Succeeds in unknown fate.

DESDEMONA. The heavens forbid
But that our loves and comforts should increase
Even as our days do grow.

OTHELLO. Amen to that, sweet powers!
I cannot speak enough of this content. 196
It stops me here. It is too much of joy;
And this, and this, the greatest discords be [*They kiss.*]
That e'er our hearts shall make!

IAGO. [*aside*]. O! you are well tun'd now, 200
But I'll set down the pegs that make this music,
As honest as I am.

OTHELLO. Come, let us to the castle.—
News, friends! Our wars are done. The Turks are
drown'd.
How does my old acquaintance of this isle?— 204
Honey, you shall be well desir'd in Cyprus;
I have found great love amongst them. O my sweet,
I prattle out of fashion, and I dote
In mine own comforts. I prithee, good Iago, 208
Go to the bay and disembark my coffers.
Bring thou the master to the citadel;
He is a good one, and his worthiness
Does challenge much respect. Come,
Desdemona! 212
Once more, well met at Cyprus!

[*Ex. Othello and Desdemona with all except Iago and
Roderigo.*]

IAGO. [*to Roderigo.*] Do thou meet me presently at the
harbor. Come hither. If thou be'st valiant (as they say
base men being in love have then a nobility in their
natures more than is native to them), list me. The
lieutenant to-night watches on the court of guard.
First, I must tell thee this: Desdemona is directly in
love with him. 220

RODERIGO. With him? Why, 'tis not possible.

IAGO. Lay thy finger thus, and let thy soul be
instructed. Mark me with what violence she first
loved the Moor but for bragging and telling her
fantastical lies. And will she love him still for prating?
Let not thy discreet heart think it. Her eye must be
fed; and what delight shall she have to look on the
devil? When the blood is made dull with the act of
sport, there should be, again to inflame it, and to give
satiety a fresh appetite, loveliness in favor, sympathy
in years, manners, and beauties; all which the Moor is
defective in. Now, for want of these required conve-
niences, her delicate tenderness will find itself
abused, begin to heave the gorge, disrelish and abhor
the Moor. Very nature will instruct her in it, and
compel her to some second choice. Now, sir, this
granted (as it is a most pregnant and unforced position), who stands so eminently in the degree of this
fortune as Cassio does? A knave very voluble, no
farder conscionable than in putting on the mere form
of civil and humane seeming for the better compassing of his salt and hidden affections? ⟨Why, none;
why, none.⟩ A subtle, slippery knave, a finder-out of
occasions, that has an eye can stamp and counterfeit
advantages, though true advantage never present
itself. ⟨A devilish knave!⟩ Besides, the knave is handsome, young, and hath all those requisites in him that
folly and green minds look after. A pestilent complete
knave! and the woman has found him already. 250

RODERIGO. I cannot believe that in her. She's full of
most bless'd condition. 252

IAGO. Bless'd fig's end! The wine she drinks is made
of grapes. If she had been bless'd, she would never
have loved the Moor. ⟨Bless'd pudding!⟩ Didst thou
not see her paddle with the palm of his hand? ⟨Didst
not mark that?⟩ 257

RODERIGO. Yes, ⟨that I did;⟩ but that was but courtesy.

IAGO. Lechery, by this hand! an index and obscure
prologue to the history of lust and foul thoughts.
They met so near with their lips that their breaths

---

182. warrior: (because he finds her among the soldiers) **183. content:** blissful happiness **197. here:** in his heart **201. set . . . pegs:**
untune the strings by loosening **205. well desir'd:** much sought
after **210. master:** ship's captain

217. list: hear **218. court:** post **222. thus:** on the lips (i.e., be
silent) **234. heave the gorge:** be nauseated **237. pregnant:**
obvious **239. voluble:** fickle **240. farder:** further **conscionable:**
conscientious **242. salt:** lewd **249. found him:** recognized his
qualities **252. condition:** quality

embraced together. ⟨Villainous thoughts, Roderigo!⟩ When these mutualities so marshal the way, hard at hand comes the ⟨master and⟩ main exercise, the incorporate conclusion. ⟨Pish!⟩ But, sir, be you ruled by me: I have brought you from Venice. Watch you to-night. For your command, I'll lay't upon you. Cassio knows you not. I'll not be far from you. Do you find some occasion to anger Cassio, either by speaking too loud, or tainting his discipline, or from what other cause you please which the time shall more favorably minister. 272

RODERIGO. Well.

IAGO. Sir, he is rash and very sudden in choler, and haply «with his truncheon» may strike at you. Provoke him that he may, for even out of that will I cause these of Cyprus to mutiny, whose qualification shall come into no true taste again but by the displanting of Cassio. So shall you have a shorter journey to your desires by the means I shall then have to prefer them, and the impediment most profitably removed without the which there were no expectation of our prosperity. 283

RODERIGO. I will do this, if you can bring it to any opportunity.

IAGO. I warrant thee. Meet me by and by at the citadel. I must fetch his necessaries ashore. Farewell.

RODERIGO. Adieu. [Exit.]

IAGO. That Cassio loves her, I do well believe't; 289
That she loves him, 'tis apt, and of great credit.
The Moor (howbeit that I endure him not)
Is of a constant, noble, loving, nature; 292
And I dare think he'll prove to Desdemona
A most dear husband. Now, I do love her too,—
Not out of absolute lust (though peradventure
I stand accountant for as great a sin), 296
But partly led to diet my revenge,
For that I do suspect the lusty Moor
Hath leap'd into my seat; the thought whereof
Doth like a poisonous mineral gnaw my
     inwards, 300
And nothing can nor shall content my soul
Till I am even'd with him, wife for wife,—
Or failing so, yet that I put the Moor
At least into a jealousy so strong 304

That judgment cannot cure. Which thing to do,
If this poor trash of Venice, whom I thrash
For his quick hunting, stand the putting-on,
I'll have our Michael Cassio on the hip, 308
Abuse him to the Moor in the rank garb
(For I fear Cassio with my night-cap too),
Make the Moor thank me, love me, and reward me
For making him egregiously an ass 312
And practising upon his peace and quiet
Even to madness. 'Tis here, but yet confus'd:
Knavery's plain face is never seen till us'd. [Exit.]

SCENE II

A Street

[Enter Othello's Herald, with a proclamation.]

HERALD. It is Othello's pleasure, our noble and valiant general, that, upon certain tidings now arrived, importing the mere perdition of the Turkish fleet, every man put himself into triumph; some to 4
dance, some to make bonfires, each man to what sport and revels his addiction leads him; for, besides these beneficial news, it is the celebration of his nuptial. So much was his pleasure should be 8
proclaimed. All offices are open, and there is full liberty of feasting from this present hour of five till the bell have tolled eleven. Heaven bless the isle of Cyprus and our noble general Othello! [Exit.]

SCENE III

The 'Court of Guard' or Guard-post

[Enter Othello, Desdemona, Cassio, and Attendants.]

OTHELLO. Good Michael, look you to the guard to-night.
     Let's teach ourselves that honorable stop,
     Not to outsport discretion.

---

263. **mutualities:** intimacies **marshal:** lead 265. **incorporate:** carnal 267. **command:** authorization 270. **tainting:** disparaging 272. **minister:** provide 274. **in choler:** when enraged 277. **qualification:** pacification 278. **true taste:** satisfactory state 281. **prefer:** promote 290. **apt . . . credit:** natural and very credible 296. **accountant:** accountable 297. **diet:** feed 300. **mineral:** drug

307. **putting-on:** urging 309. **rank garb:** grossest fashion 313. **practising upon:** using wiles against 314. **to madness:** to the point of driving him mad
3. **mere perdition:** complete destruction 4. **put . . . triumph:** give himself up to celebrating the occasion 6. **addiction:** inclination 9. **offices:** storerooms, kitchens
2. **stop:** caution (musical figure)

CASSIO. Iago hath direction what to do; 4
But, notwithstanding, with my personal eye
Will I look to't.

OTHELLO. Iago is most honest.
Michael, good night. To-morrow with your earliest
Let me have speech with you.
[*To Desdemona.*] Come, my dear love. 8
The purchase made, the fruits are to ensue;
The profit's yet to come 'twixt me and you.
Good night.

[*Ex. Othello and Desdemona and Attendants.*]

[*Enter Iago.*]

CASSIO. Welcome, Iago; we must to the watch. 12

IAGO. Not this hour, lieutenant; 'tis not yet ten
o'clock. Our general cast us thus early for the love
of his Desdemona,—who let us not therefore blame.
He hath not yet made wanton the night with her,
and she is sport for Jove. 17

CASSIO. She's a most exquisite lady.

IAGO. And, I'll warrant her, full of game.

CASSIO. Indeed, she is a most fresh and delicate creature. 21

IAGO. What an eye she has! Methinks it sounds a
parley of provocation.

CASSIO. An inviting eye, and yet methinks right modest. 25

IAGO. And when she speaks, is it not an alarum to
love?

CASSIO. She is indeed perfection. 28

IAGO. Well, happiness to their sheets! Come, lieutenant, I have a stoup of wine, and here without are a
brace of Cyprus gallants that would fain have a
measure to the health of black Othello. 32

CASSIO. Not to-night, good Iago. I have very poor
and unhappy brains for drinking. I could well wish
courtesy would invent some other custom of entertainment.

IAGO. O they are our friends. But one cup. I'll drink
for you.

CASSIO. I have drunk but one cup to-night, and that
was craftily qualified too, and, behold, what innovation it makes here. I am unfortunate in the infirmity,
and dare not task my weakness with any more. 42

IAGO. What, man! 'tis a night of revels. The gallants
desire it.

CASSIO. Where are they?

IAGO. Here at the door. I pray you, call them in. 46

CASSIO. I'll do't; but it dislikes me. [*Exit.*]

IAGO. If I can fasten but one cup upon him,
With that which he hath drunk to-night al-
ready, 49
He'll be as full of quarrel and offence
As my young mistress' dog. Now, my sick fool
Roderigo,
Whom love hath turn'd almost the wrong side
out, 52
To Desdemona hath to-night carous'd
Potations pottle-deep; and he's to watch.
Three lads of Cyprus, noble swelling spirits,
That hold their honors in a wary distance, 56
The very elements of this warlike isle,
Have I to-night fluster'd with flowing cups,
And they watch too. Now, 'mongst this flock of
drunkards,
Am I to put our Cassio in some action 60
That may offend the isle. But here they come.
If consequence do but approve my dream,
My boat sails freely, both with wind and stream.

[*Enter Cassio, Montano, and Gentlemen. Boys following
with wine.*]

CASSIO. 'Fore God, they have given me a rouse already.

MONTANO. Good faith, a little one. Not past a pint, as
I am a soldier. 66

IAGO. Some wine, ho!

[*Sings.*]

> And let me the canikin clink, clink,
> And let me the canikin clink.
> A soldier's a man; 70
> O man's life's but a span;
> Why then let a soldier drink.

Some wine, boys!

CASSIO. 'Fore God, an excellent song.

IAGO. I learned it in England, where indeed they are
most potent in potting. Your Dane, your German,
and your swag-bellied Hollander,—drink, ho!—are
nothing to your English. 78

---

47. **dislikes me:** is distasteful to me 54. **pottle-deep:** to the bottom
of the tankard 57. **elements:** typical representatives 64. **rouse:**
bumper 68. **canikin:** little can or mug (an affectionate diminutive)
76. **potent in potting:** mighty in drinking 77. **swag-bellied:** fat-
paunched

15. **who:** whom (Othello) 23. **parley:** trumpet-call 26. **alarum:**
summons 30. **stoup:** large measure (often two quarts) 40. **qualified:** diluted **innovation:** disturbance 41. **here:** in my head

CASSIO. Is your Englishman so exquisite in his drinking?   80
IAGO. Why, he drinks you with facility your Dane dead
drunk. He sweats not to overthrow your Almain. He
gives your Hollander a vomit ere the next pottle can
be filled.   84
CASSIO. To the health of our general!
MONTANO. I am for it, lieutenant; and I'll do you
justice.
IAGO. O sweet England!   88

[*Sings*]

> King Stephen was and—a worthy peer,
>   His breeches cost him but a crown.
> He held them sixpence all too dear,
>   With that he call'd the tailor lown.   92
> He was a wight of high renown,
>   And thou art but of low degree.
> 'Tis pride that pulls the country down,
>   Then take thine owd cloak about thee.   96

Some wine, ho!
CASSIO. 'Fore God, this is a more exquisite song than
the other.
IAGO. Will you hear't again?   100
CASSIO. No; for I hold him to be unworthy of his place
that does those things. Well, God's above all; and
there be souls must be saved, and there be souls must
not be saved.   104
IAGO. It's true, good lieutenant.
CASSIO. For mine own part,—no offence to the general, nor any man of quality,—I hope to be saved.
IAGO. And so do I too, lieutenant.   108
CASSIO. Ay; but, by your leave, not before me. The
lieutenant is to be saved before the ancient. Let's
have no more of this; let's to our affairs. God forgive
us our sins! Gentlemen, let's look to our business. Do
not think, gentlemen, I am drunk. This is my ancient;
this is my right hand, and this is my left hand. I am
not drunk now. I can stand well enough, and I speak
well enough.   116
GENTLEMAN. Excellent well.
CASSIO. Why, very well, then. You must not think then
that I am drunk.   [*Exit.*]
MONTANO. To the platform, masters. Come, let's set
the watch.   120

IAGO. You see this fellow that is gone before.
He is a soldier fit to stand by Caeser
And give direction; and do but see his vice.
'Tis to his virtue a just equinox,   124
The one as long as th' other. 'Tis pity of him.
I fear the trust Othello puts him in,
On some odd time of his infirmity,
Will shake this island.
MONTANO.   But is he often thus?   128
IAGO. 'Tis evermore the prologue to his sleep:
He'll watch the horologe a double set,
If drink rock not his cradle.
MONTANO.   It were well
The general were put in mind of it.   132
Perhaps he sees it not, or his good nature
Prizes the virtue that appears in Cassio,
And looks not on his evils. Is not this true?

[*Enter Roderigo.*]

IAGO. [*aside to him*]. How now, Roderigo?   136
I pray you, after the lieutenant. Go!   [*Exit Roderigo.*]
MONTANO. And 'tis great pity that the noble Moor
Should hazard such a place as his own second
With one of an ingraft infirmity.   140
It were an honest action to say
So to the Moor.
IAGO.   Not I, for this fair island:
I do love Cassio well, and would do much
                      [*Cry*] 'Help! Help!'' [*within.*]
To cure him of this evil. But hark! what noise?   144

[*Enter Cassio, driving in Roderigo.*]

CASSIO. Zounds! You rogue, you rascal!
MONTANO. What's the matter, lieutenant?
CASSIO. A knave teach me my duty! I'll beat the knave
into a twiggen bottle.   148
RODERIGO. Beat me!
CASSIO. Dost thou prate, rogue?   [*Striking Roderigo.*]
MONTANO. [*Staying him.*] Nay, good lieutenant. I pray
you, sir, hold your hand.   152
CASSIO. Let me go, sir, or I'll knock you o'er the
mazzard.
MONTANO. Come, come; you're drunk.   155
CASSIO. Drunk!   [*They fight.*]
IAGO. [*aside to Roderigo.*] Away, I say! Go out, and cry
a mutiny. [*Exit Roderigo.*]

---

82. **Almain:** German   86. **do you justice:** keep pace with you in drinking   92. **lown:** loon, lout   96. **owd:** old   120. **platform:** rampart

124. **just equinox:** exact equivalent (virtue and vice are equal in him)   140. **ingraft:** firmly rooted   154. **mazzard:** head

Nay, good lieutenant! God's will, gentlemen!
Help, ho! Lieutenant! Sir Montano! sir!   160
Help, masters! Here's a goodly watch indeed!

[A bell rung.]

Who's that that rings the bell? *Diablo*, ho!
The town will rise. God's will! lieutenant, hold!
You will be sham'd for ever.   164

[Enter Othello and Gentlemen with weapons.]

OTHELLO.   What is the matter here?
MONTANO. Zounds! I bleed still. I am hurt to the
   death.
OTHELLO. Hold, for your lives!
IAGO. Hold, hold lieutenant! Sir Montano! gentle-
   men!
Have you forgot all sense of place and duty?   168
Hold! the general speaks to you; hold for shame!
OTHELLO. Why, how now, ho! from whence arises
   this?
Are we turn'd Turks, and to ourselves do that
Which heaven has forbid the Ottomites?   172
For Christian shame put by this barbarous brawl.
He that stirs next to carve for his own rage
Holds his soul light; he dies upon his motion.
Silence that dreadful bell! it frights the isle   176
From her propriety. What's the matter, masters?
Honest Iago, that looks dead with grieving,
Speak, who began this? On thy love, I charge thee.
IAGO. I do not know. Friends all but now, even now,
In quarter and in terms like bride and groom   181
Devesting them for bed; and then, but now
(As if some planet had unwitted men)
Swords out, and tilting one at other's breast,   184
In opposition bloody. I cannot speak
Any beginning to this peevish odds,
And would in action glorious I had lost
These legs that brought me to a part of it!   188
OTHELLO. How came it, Michael, you were thus for-
   got?
CASSIO. I pray you, pardon me; I cannot speak.
OTHELLO. Worthy Montano, you were wont be civil.
The gravity and stillness of your youth   192
The world hath noted, and your name is great
In mouths of wisest censure. What's the matter,
That you unlace your reputation thus

And spend your rich opinion for the name   196
Of a night-brawler? give me answer to't.
MONTANO. Worthy Othello, I am hurt to danger.
Your officer, Iago, can inform you
(While I spare speech, which something now offends
   me)   200
Of all that I do know; nor know I aught
By me that's said or done amiss this night,
Unless self-charity be sometime a vice,
And to defend ourselves it be a sin   204
When violence assails us.
OTHELLO.   Now, by heaven,
My blood begins my safer guides to rule,
And passion, having my best judgment collied,
Assays to lead the way. Zounds! If I stir,   208
Or do but lift this arm, the best of you
Shall sink in my rebuke. Give me to know
How this foul rout began, who set it on;
And he that is approv'd in this offence,   212
Though he had twinn'd with me—both at a birth—
Shall lose me. What! in a town of war,
Yet wild, the people's hearts brimful of fear,
To manage private and domestic quarrels   216
In night, and on the court and guard of safety!
'Tis monstrous. Iago, who began't?
MONTANO. If partially affin'd, or leagu'd in office,
Thou dost deliver more or less than truth,   220
Thou art no soldier.
IAGO.   Touch me not so near.
I had rather have this tongue cut from my mouth
Than it should do offence to Michael Cassio;
Yet I persuade myself, to speak the truth   224
Shall nothing wrong him. Thus it is, general.
Montano and myself being in speech,
There comes a fellow crying out for help,
And Cassio following him with determin'd
   sword   228
To execute upon him. Sir, this gentleman
Steps in to Cassio, and entreats his pause.
Myself the crying fellow did pursue,
Lest by his clamor (as it so fell out)   232
The town might fall in fright. He, swift of foot,
Outran my purpose, and I return'd the rather
For that I heard the clink and fall of swords,
And Cassio high in oath, which till to-night   236
I ne'er might say before. When I came back

---

174. **carve for:** satisfy   177. **From her propriety:** out of her very
being   181. **In . . . terms:** on a footing   186. **odds:** quarrel   194.
Censure: judgment   195. **unlace:** undo

196. **opinion:** good name   200. **something:** somewhat   **offends:**
harms   207. **collied:** blackened (as with coal)   211. **rout:**
riot   212. **approv'd:** convicted   216. **manage:** set on foot   219.
partially affin'd: bound by partiality   234. **rather:** sooner

(For this was brief), I found them close together,
At blow and thrust, even as again they were
When you yourself did part them.   240
More of this matter can I not report,
But men are men; the best sometimes forget.
Though Cassio did some little wrong to him,
As men in rage strike those that wish them
    best,   244
Yet surely Cassio, I believe, receiv'd
From him that fled some strange indignity,
Which patience could not pass.
OTHELLO.   I know, Iago,
Thy honesty and love doth mince this matter,   248
Making it light to Cassio. Cassio, I love thee;
But never more be officer of mine—

[Enter Desdemona, with others.]

Look, if my gentle love be not rais'd up!—
[To Cassio.] I'll make thee an example.
DESDEMONA.   What's the matter?
OTHELLO. All's well now, sweeting. Come away to
    bed.—
Sir, for your hurts, myself will be your surgeon.
Lead him off.   [Montano is led off.]
Iago, look with care about the town,   256
And silence those whom this vile brawl distracted.
Come, Desdemona; 'tis the soldiers' life,
To have their balmy slumbers wak'd with strife.

[Ex. Moor, Desdemona, and Attendants.]

IAGO. What! are you hurt, lieutenant?   260
CASSIO. Ay, past all surgery.
IAGO. Marry, God forbid!
CASSIO. Reputation, reputation, ⟨reputation! O!⟩ I
    have lost my reputation. I have lost the immortal
    part «sir,» of myself, and what remains is bestial. My
    reputation, ⟨Iago, my reputation!⟩   266
IAGO. As I am an honest man, I thought you had
    received some bodily wound. There is more sense in
    that than in reputation. Reputation is an idle and
    most false imposition, oft got without merit, and
    lost without deserving. You have lost no reputation
    at all, unless you repute yourself such a loser. What,

man! there are ways to recover the general again.
You are but now cast in his mood (a punishment
more in policy than in malice), even so as one would
beat his offenceless dog to affright an imperious
lion. Sue to him again, and he is yours.   277
CASSIO. I will rather sue to be despised than to
    deceive so good a commander with so slight, so
    drunken, and so indiscreet an officer. Drunk! and
    speak parrot! and squabble, swagger, swear, and dis-
    course fustian with one's own shadow! O thou invis-
    ible spirit of wine! if thou hast no name to be known
    by, let us call thee devil!   284
IAGO. What was he that you followed with your
    sword? What had he done to you?
CASSIO. I know not.
IAGO. Is't possible?   288
CASSIO. I remember a mass of things, but nothing
    distinctly; a quarrel, but nothing wherefore. O God!
    that men should put an enemy in their mouths to
    steal away their brains; that we should, with joy,
    revel, pleasure, and applause, transform ourselves
    into beasts.
IAGO. Why, but you are now well enough. How came
    you thus recovered?   296
CASSIO. It hath pleased the devil drunkenness to give
    place to the devil wrath. One unperfectness shows
    me another, to make me frankly despise my-
    self.   299
IAGO. Come, you are too severe a moraler. As the
    time, the place, and the condition of this country
    stands, I could heartily wish this had not so befallen,
    but since it is as it is, mend it for your own
    good.   303
CASSIO. I will ask him for my place again. He shall tell
    me I am a drunkard. Had I as many mouths as
    Hydra, such an answer would stop them all. To be
    now a sensible man, by and by a fool, and presently
    a beast! ⟨O strange!⟩ Every inordinate cup is
    unblessed and the ingredience is a devil.   309
IAGO. Come, come; good wine is a good familiar crea-
    ture if it be well used. Exclaim no more against it.
    And, good lieutenant, I think you think I love you.
CASSIO. I have well approved it, sir. I drunk!   313
IAGO. You or any man living may be drunk at some

---

243. **him:** i.e., Montano   270. **imposition:** adjunct

274. **mood:** temporary feeling   280. **speak parrot:** use words irra-
tionally   281. **discourse fustian:** talk nonsense   300. **moraler:** mor-
alizer   310. **familiar:** domestic

time. I'll tell you what you shall do. Our general's wife is now the general. I may say so in this respect, for that he has devoted and given up himself to the contemplation, mark, and denotement of her parts and graces. Confess yourself freely to her; importune her help to put you in your place again. She is of so free, so kind, so apt, so blessed a disposition, that she holds it a vice in her goodness not to do more than she is requested. This broken joint between you and her husband entreat her to splinter; and my fortunes against any lay worth naming, this crack of your love shall grow stronger than it was before. 327

CASSIO. You advise me well.

IAGO. I protest, in the sincerity of love and honest kindness.

CASSIO. I think it freely; and betimes in the morning will I beseech the virtuous Desdemona to undertake for me. I am desperate of my fortunes if they check me here. 333

IAGO. You are in the right. Good night, lieutenant; I must to the watch.

CASSIO. Good night, honest Iago! [Exit Cassio.]

IAGO. And what's he, then, that says I play the villain,
When this advice is free I give and honest,
Probal to thinking and indeed the course
To win the Moor again? For 'tis most easy 340
Th' inclining Desdemona to subdue
In any honest suit; she's fram'd as fruitful
As the free elements. And then for her
To win the Moor,—were't to renounce his baptism
All seals and symbols of redeemed sin,
His soul is so enfetter'd to her love,
That she may make, unmake, do what she list,
Even as her appetite shall play the god 348
With his weak function. How am I, then, a villain
To counsel Cassio to this parallel course
Directly to his good? Divinity of hell!
When devils will their blackest sins put on, 352
They do suggest at first with heavenly shows,
As I do now; for while this honest fool
Plies Desdemona to repair his fortunes,

And she for him pleads strongly to the Moor, 356
I'll pour this pestilence into his ear
That she repeals him for her body's lust;
And, by how much she strives to do him good,
She shall undo her credit with the Moor. 360
So will I turn her virtue into pitch,
And out of her own goodness make the net
That shall enmesh them all.

[Enter Roderigo.]

How now, Roderigo? 363

RODERIGO. I do follow here in the chase, not like a hound that hunts, but one that fills up the cry. My money is almost spent; I have been to-night exceedingly well cudgelled; and I think the issue will be, I shall have so much experience for my pains; and so, with no money at all and a little more wit, return again to Venice.

IAGO. How poor are they that have not patience!
What wound did ever heal but by degrees? 372
Thou know'st we work by wit and not by witchcraft,
And wit depends on dilatory time.
Does't not go well? Cassio has beaten thee,
And thou by that small hurt hast cashiered
Cassio. 376
Though other things grow fair against the sun,
Yet fruits that blossom first will first be ripe.
Content thyself awhile. By the mass, 'tis morning;
Pleasure and action make the hours seem
short. 380
Retire thee; go where thou art billeted.
Away, I say; thou shalt know more hereafter.
Nay, get thee gone. [Exit Roderigo.]
Two things are to be done:
My wife must move for Cassio to her
mistress— 384
I'll set her on—;
Myself awhile to draw the Moor apart,
And bring him jump when he may Cassio find
Soliciting his wife. Ay, that's the way. 388
Dull not device by coldness and delay. [Exit.]

---

318. denotement: observation **324. splinter:** bind with splints **325. lay:** wager **339. Probal:** probable **342. fruitful:** bountiful **349. function:** character **350. parallel:** straight **352. put on:** instigate **353. suggest:** tempt

358. repeals: recalls to favor **365. cry:** pack of hounds (i.e., I merely go through the motions) **387. jump:** precisely

Act III

SCENE I

Before the Citadel

[Enter Cassio with Musicians.]

CASSIO. Masters, play here, I will content your pains.
  Something that's brief, and bid 'Good morrow, general.'

[They play, and enter the Clown.]

CLOWN. Why, masters, ha' your instruments been at
  Naples, that they speak i' th' nose thus?   4
MUSICIAN. How, sir? how?
CLOWN. Are these, I pray, called wind-instruments?
MUSICIAN. Ay, marry, are they, sir.
CLOWN. O! thereby hangs a tail.   8
MUSICIAN. Whereby hangs a tale, sir?
CLOWN. Marry, sir, by many a wind-instrument that I
  know. But, masters, here's money for you; and the
  general so likes your music that he desires you, of all
  loves, to make no more noise with it.
MUSICIAN. Well, sir, we will not.   14
CLOWN. If you have any music that may not be heard,
  to't again; but (as they say) to hear music the general does not greatly care.
MUSICIAN. We ha' none such, sir.   18
CLOWN. Then put up your pipes in your bag, for I'll
  away. Go; vanish into air; away!   [Exeunt Musicians.]
CASSIO. Dost thou hear, my honest friend?
CLOWN. No, I hear not your honest friend; I hear
  you.
CASSIO. Prithee, keep up thy quillets. There's a poor
  piece of gold for thee. If the gentlewoman that
  attends the general's wife be stirring, tell her there's
  one Cassio entreats her a little favor of speech. Wilt
  thou do this?   27
CLOWN. She is stirring, sir. If she will stir hither, I
  shall seem to notify unto her.
CASSIO. Do, good my friend.   [Exit Clown.]

[Enter Iago.]

             In happy time, Iago.

IAGO. You ha' not been a-bed, then?
CASSIO. Why, no. The day had broke   32
  Before we parted. I ha' made bold, Iago,
  To send in to your wife. My suit to her
  Is that she will to virtuous Desdemona
  Procure me some accéss.
IAGO.   I'll send her to you presently;   36
  And I'll devise a mean to draw the Moor
  Out of the way, that your converse and business
  May be more free.   39
CASSIO. I humbly thank you for't.   [Exit Iago.]
                  I never knew

  A Florentine more kind and honest.

[Enter Emilia.]

EMILIA. Good morrow, good lieutenant. I am sorry
  For your displeasure but all will soon be well.
  The general and his wife are talking of it,   44
  And she speaks for you stoutly. The Moor replies
  That he you hurt is of great fame in Cyprus
  And great affinity and that in wholesome wisdom
  He might not but refuse you; but he protests he
    loves you,
  And needs no other suitor but his likings   49
  To take the saf'st occasion by the front
  To bring you in again.
CASSIO.   Yet, I beseech you,
  If you think fit, or that it may be done,   52
  Give me advantage of some brief discourse
  With Desdemona alone.
EMILIA.   Pray you, come in.
  I will bestow you where you shall have time
  To speak your bosom freely.
CASSIO.   I am much bound to you.

[Exeunt.]

SCENE II

A Room in the Citadel

[Enter Othello, Iago, and other Gentlemen.]

OTHELLO. These letters give, Iago, to the pilot,
  And by him do my duties to the state.

12, 13. of all loves: for goodness' sake   23. quillets: quibbles   25. stirring: up and dressed (in the morning)   30. In happy time: well met

36. presently: immediately   43. displeasure: misfortune   47. affinity: family connection   56. bosom: private thoughts and feelings

That done, I will be walking on the works;
 Repair there to me.
IAGO.   Well, my good lord, I'll do't.   4
OTHELLO. This fortification, gentlemen, shall we see't?
GENTLEMAN. We wait upon your lordship.   [Exeunt.]

SCENE III

The garden of the Citadel

[Enter Desdemona, Cassio, and Emilia.]

DESDEMONA. Be thou assur'd, good Cassio, I will do
 All my abilities in thy behalf.
EMILIA. Good madam, do. I know it grieves my hus-
  band,
 As if the case were his.   4
DESDEMONA. O that's an honest fellow! Do not
  doubt, Cassio,
 But I will have my lord and you again
 As friendly as you were.
CASSIO.   Bounteous madam,
 Whatever shall become of Michael Cassio,   8
 He's never anything but your true servant.
DESDEMONA. O, sir, I thank you. You do love my
  lord.
 You have known him long; and be you well assur'd
 He shall in strangeness stand no farther off   12
 Than in a politic distance.
CASSIO.   Ay, but, lady,
 That policy may either last so long,
 Or feed upon such nice and waterish diet,
 Or breed itself so out of circumstances,   16
 That, I being absent and my place supplied,
 My general will forget my love and service.
DESDEMONA. Do not doubt that. Before Emilia here
 I give thee warrant of thy place. Assure thee,   20
 If I do vow a friendship, I'll perform it
 To the last article. My lord shall never rest;
 I'll watch him tame, and talk him out of patience;
 His bed shall seem a school, his board a shrift;   24
 I'll intermingle everything he does
 With Cassio's suit. Therefore be merry, Cassio;
 For thy solicitor shall rather die
 Than give thy cause away.   28

[Enter Othello and Iago at a distance.]

EMILIA. Madam, here comes my lord.
CASSIO. Madam, I'll take my leave.
DESDEMONA. Why, stay, and hear me speak.
CASSIO. Madam, not now. I am very ill at ease,   32
 Unfit for mine own purposes.
DESDEMONA. Well, do your discretion.   [Exit Cassio.]
IAGO. Ha! I like not that.
OTHELLO.   What dost thou say?
IAGO. Nothing, my lord; or if—I know not what.   36
OTHELLO. Was not that Cassio parted from my wife?
IAGO. Cassio, my lord? No, sure, I cannot think it,
 That he would steal away so guilty-like,
 Seeing you coming.
OTHELLO.   I do believe 'twas he.   40
DESDEMONA. How now, my lord!
 I have been talking with a suitor here,
 A man that languishes in your displeasure.
OTHELLO. Who is't you mean?   44
DESDEMONA. Why, your lieutenant, Cassio. Good my
  lord,
 If I have any grace or power to move you,
 His present reconciliation take;
 For if he be not one that truly loves you,   48
 That errs in ignorance and not in cunning,
 I have no judgment in an honest face.
 I prithee call him back.
OTHELLO.   Went he hence now?
DESDEMONA. Yes, faith; so humbled,   52
 That he has left part of his griefs with me.
 I suffer with him. Good love, call him back.
OTHELLO. Not now, sweet Desdemon. Some other
  time.
DESDEMONA. But shall't be shortly?
OTHELLO.   The sooner, sweet, for you. 56
DESDEMONA. Shall't be to-night at supper?
OTHELLO.   No, not to-night.
DESDEMONA. To-morrow dinner then?
OTHELLO.   I shall not dine at home.
 I meet the captains at the citadel.
DESDEMONA. Why then, to-morrow night, or Tues-
  day morn;   60
 On Tuesday noon, or night; on Wednesday morn.
 I prithee name the time, but let it not
 Exceed three days. I' faith, he's penitent;
 And yet his trespass, in our common reason   64
 (Save that they say, the wars must make examples
 Out of their best), is not almost a fault
 T' incur a private check. When shall he come?

---

12. strangeness: estrangement   **15. nice:** finical   **waterish:** watered, thin   **19. doubt:** fear   **24. shrift:** Confessional

34. do your discretion: do what seems to you discreet   **66. not almost:** almost not, scarcely

Tell me, Othello. I wonder in my soul,   68
What you could ask me that I should deny,
Or stand so mammering on. What? Michael Cassio,
That came a-wooing with you, and so many a time,
When I have spoke of you dispraisingly,   72
Hath ta'en your part; to have so much to do
To bring him in! By'r Lady, I could do much—

OTHELLO. Prithee, no more! Let him come when he
    will.
I will deny thee nothing.

DESDEMONA.   Why, this is not a boon.   76
'Tis as I should entreat you wear your gloves,
Or feed on nourishing dishes, or keep you warm,
Or sue to you to do a peculiar profit
To your own person. Nay, when I have a suit   80
Wherein I mean to touch your love indeed,
It shall be full of poise and difficúlty,
And fearful to be granted.

OTHELLO.   I will deny thee nothing.
Whereon, I do beseech thee, grant me this,   84
To leave me but a little to myself.

DESDEMONA. Shall I deny you? No. Farewell, my
    lord.

OTHELLO. Farewell, my Desdemona. I'll come to thee
    straight.

DESDEMONA. Emilia, come. Be it as your fancies teach
    you.   88
Whate'er you be, I am obedient.

[*Exeunt Desdemona and Emilia.*]

OTHELLO. Excellent wretch! Perdition catch my soul
    But I do love thee! and when I love thee not,
    Chaos is come again.   92

IAGO. My noble lord,—

OTHELLO.   What dost thou say, Iago?

IAGO. Did Michael Cassio, when you woo'd my lady,
    Know of your love?

OTHELLO. He did, from first to last. Why dost thou
    ask?   96

IAGO. But for a satisfaction of my thought.
    No further harm.

OTHELLO.   Why of thy thought, Iago?

IAGO. I did not think he had been acquainted with
    her.

OTHELLO. O yes; and went between us very oft.   100

IAGO. Indeed?

OTHELLO. Indeed? ay, indeed. Discern'st thou aught
    in that?
    Is he not honest?

IAGO.   Honest, my lord?

OTHELLO.   Honest? ay, honest.

IAGO. My lord, for aught I know.   104

OTHELLO. What dost thou think?

IAGO.   Think, my lord?

OTHELLO.   Think, my lord?
By heaven, he echoes me,
As if there were some monster in his thought
Too hideous to be shown.—Thou didst mean
    something.
I heard thee say but now, thou lik'st not that,   109
When Cassio left my wife. What didst not like?
And when I told thee he was of my counsel
In my whole course of wooing, thou criedst,
    'Indeed?'   112
And didst contract and purse thy brow together,
As if thou then hadst shut up in thy brain
Some horrible conceit. If thou dost love me,
Show me thy thought.   116

IAGO. My lord, you know I love you.

OTHELLO.   I think thou dost;
And, for I know thou'rt full of love and honesty,
And weigh'st thy words before thou give 'em
    breath,
Therefore these stops of thine fright me the
    more;   120
For such things in a false disloyal knave
Are tricks of custom, but in a man that's just
They are close delations, working from the heart
That passion cannot rule.

IAGO.   For Michael Cassio,   124
I dare be sworn I think that he is honest.

OTHELLO. I think so too.

IAGO.   Men should be what they seem;
Or those that be not, would they might seem none!

OTHELLO. Certain, men should be what they
    seem.   128

IAGO. Why then, I think Cassio's an honest man.

OTHELLO. Nay, yet there's more in this.
I pray thee, speak to me as to thy thinkings,
As thou dost ruminate, and give thy worst of
    thoughts
The worst of words.

---

70. **mammering:** hesitating   74. **in:** into favor   82. **poise:**
weight   90. **wretch:** expression of utmost fondness

111. **of my counsel:** in my confidence   115. **conceit:** idea   120.
stops: pauses, reticences   122. **tricks of custom:** habitual tricks
123. **close delations:** covert, involuntary accusations

IAGO.   Good my lord, pardon me;
  Though I am bound to every act of duty,
  I am not bound to that all slaves are free to.
  Utter my thoughts? Why, say they are vile and
    false;   136
  As where's that palace whereinto foul things
  Sometimes intrude not? who has a breast so pure
  But some uncleanly apprehensions
  Keep leets and law-days, and in session sit   140
  With meditations lawful?
OTHELLO. Thou dost conspire against thy friend,
    Iago,
  If thou but think'st him wrong'd, and mak'st his ear
  A stranger to thy thoughts.
IAGO.   I do beseech you,   144
  Though I perchance am vicious in my guess
  (As, I confess, it is my nature's plague
  To spy into abuses, and oft my jealousy
  Shapes faults that are not)—I entreat you then,
  From one that so imperfectly conjects,   149
  You'ld take no notice, nor build yourself a trouble
  Out of my scattering and unsure observance.
  It were not for your quiet nor your good,   152
  Nor for my manhood, honesty, or wisdom,
  To let you know my thoughts.
OTHELLO.   Zounds! What dost thou mean?
IAGO. Good name in man, and woman, dear my lord,
  Is the immediate jewel of our souls.   156
  Who steals my purse steals trash. 'Tis something,
    nothing;
  'Twas mine, 'tis his, and has been slave to thou-
    sands;
  But he that filches from me my good name
  Robs me of that which not enriches him,   160
  And makes me poor indeed.
OTHELLO. By heaven, I'll know thy thought.
IAGO. You cannot, if my heart were in your hand;
  Nor shall not, whilst 'tis in my custody.   164
OTHELLO. Ha!
IAGO.   O beware, my lord, of jealousy!
  It is the green-ey'd monster which doth mock
  The meat it feeds on. That cuckold lives in bliss
  Who, certain of his fate, loves not his
    wronger;   168
  But, O, what damned minutes tells he o'er
  Who dotes, yet doubts; suspects, yet strongly loves!

OTHELLO. O misery!
IAGO. Poor and content is rich, and rich
    enough,   172
  But riches fineless is as poor as winter
  To him that ever fears he shall be poor.
  Good God, the souls of all my tribe defend
  From jealousy.
OTHELLO.   Why, why is this?   176
  Think'st thou I'd make a life of jealousy,
  To follow still the changes of the moon
  With fresh suspicions? No; to be once in doubt
  Is once to be resolv'd. Exchange me for a goat 180
  When I shall turn the business of my soul
  To such exsufflicate and blown surmises,
  Matching thy inference. 'Tis not to make me jealous
  To say my wife is fair, feeds well, loves
    company,   184
  Is free of speech, sings, plays, and dances well.
  Where virtue is, these are more virtuous.
  Nor from mine own weak merits will I draw
  The smallest fear or doubt of her revolt;   188
  For she had eyes and chose me. No, Iago.
  I'll see before I doubt; when I doubt, prove;
  And, on the proof, there is no more but this:
  Away at once with love or jealousy!   192
IAGO. I am glad of this; for now I shall have reason
  To show the love and duty that I bear you
  With franker spirit. Therefore (as I am bound)
  Receive it from me—I speak not yet of proof.   196
  Look to your wife. Observe her well with Cassio.
  Wear your eye thus, not jealous nor secure.
  I would not have your free and noble nature
  Out of self-bounty be abus'd. Look to't!   200
  I know our country disposition well;
  In Venice they do let God see the pranks
  They dare not show their husbands. Their best con-
    science
  Is not to leave undone, but keep unknown.   204
OTHELLO. Dost thou say so?
IAGO. She did deceive her father, marrying you:
  And when she seem'd to shake and fear your looks,
  She lov'd them most.
OTHELLO.   And so she did.
IAGO.   Why, go to, then.   208
  She that so young could give out such a seeming,
  To seel her father's eyes up close as oak,—

---

139. **But:** but therein 140. **leets:** synonymous with 'law-days' (**keep leet:** hold court) 145. **Though:** supposing, granting that **vicious:** wrong 149. **conjects:** imagine 151. **scattering:** random 166, 167. **mock . . . feeds on:** tantalizes its victim

173. **fineless:** endless 180. **resolv'd:** freed from uncertainty 182. **exsufflicate:** puffed up, empty 195. **as I am bound:** this being my duty 200. **self-bounty:** inherent generosity 201. **country:** native

He thought 'twas witchcraft—but I am much to
  blame.
I humbly do beseech you of your pardon   212
For too much loving you.
OTHELLO.   I am bound to thee for ever.
IAGO. I see, this hath a little dash'd your spirits.
OTHELLO. Not a jot, not a jot.
IAGO.   I' faith, I fear it has.
I hope you will consider what is spoke   216
Comes from my love. But I do see you're mov'd.
I am to pray you not to strain my speech
To grosser issues nor to larger reach
Than to suspicion.   220
OTHELLO. I will not.
IAGO.   Should you do so, my lord,
My speech should fall into such vile success
As my thoughts aim not at. Cassio's my trusty
  friend—
My lord, I see you're mov'd.
OTHELLO.   No, not much mov'd.   224
I do not think but Desdemona's honest.
IAGO. Long live she so! and long live you to think so!
OTHELLO. And, yet, how nature erring from itself,—
IAGO. Ay, there's the point: as (to be bold with you)
Not to affect many proposed matches   229
Of her own clime, complexion, and degree,
Whereto, we see, in all things nature tends—
Foh! one may smell, in such a will, most rank,   232
Foul disproportion, thoughts unnatural.
But pardon me; I do not in position
Distinctly speak of her, though I may fear
Her will, recoiling to her better judgment,   236
May fall to match you with her country forms
And happily repent.
OTHELLO.   Farewell, farewell.
If more thou dost perceive, let me know more.
Set on thy wife to observe. Leave me, Iago.   240
IAGO. My lord, I take my leave.   [Going.]
OTHELLO. Why did I marry? This honest creature,
  doubtless,
Sees and knows more, much more, than he unfolds.
IAGO. [returning]. My lord, I would I might entreat
  your honor   244
To scan this thing no further; leave it to time.
Though it be fit that Cassio have his place
(For sure he fills it up with great ability),
Yet if you please to hold him off awhile,   248

You shall by that perceive him and his means.
Note if your lady strain his entertainment
With any strong or vehement importunity;
Much will be seen in that. In the mean time,   252
Let me be thought too busy in my fears,
As worthy cause I have to fear I am,
And hold her free, I do beseech your honor.
OTHELLO. Fear not my government.   256
IAGO. I once more take my leave.   [Exit.]
OTHELLO. This fellow's of exceeding honesty,
And knows all qualities, with a learned spirit
Of human dealing. If I do prove her haggard,   260
Though that her jesses were my dear heartstrings,
I'd whistle her off and let her down the wind,
To prey at fortune. Haply, for I am black,
And have not those soft parts of conversation   264
That chamberers have, or for I am declin'd
Into the vale of years (yet that's not much)—
She's gone, I am abus'd, and my relief
Must be to loathe her. O curse of marriage!   268
That we can call these delicate creatures ours,
And not their appetites. I had rather be a toad,
And live upon the vapor of a dungeon,
Than keep a corner in the thing I love   272
For others' uses. Yet, 'tis the plague of great ones;
Prerogativ'd are they less than the base.
'Tis destiny unshunnable, like death:
Even then this forked plague is fated to us   276
When we do quicken.
                 Look, where she comes!
If she be false, O then heaven mocks itself.
I'll not believe't.

[Enter Desdemona and Emilia.]

DESDEMONA. How now, my dear Othello?
Your dinner and the generous islanders   280
By you invited do attend your presence.
OTHELLO. I am to blame.
DESDEMONA.   Why is your speech so faint?
Are you not well?
OTHELLO. I have a pain upon my forehead here.
DESDEMONA. Faith, that's with watching; 'twill away
  again.

---

222. success: consequences 225. honest: virtuous 234. position: formal logical thesis 236. recoiling: adjusting itself 237. fall: chance country forms: the types she has been accustomed to 238. happily: perhaps

249. means: the methods he uses 250. strain his entertainment: urge his reinstatement 255. free: guiltless 256. government: self control 259. qualities: kinds of people 259, 260. learned . . . dealing: mind expert in human intercourse 264. soft . . . conversation: effeminate talents in social intercourse 265. chamberers: wanton courtiers 274. Prerogativ'd: privileged, protected 276. forked plague: cuckold's horns 277. When . . . quicken: in prenatal life 280. generous: noble, of gentle birth 285. watching: lack of sleep

Let me but bind your head; within this hour
  It will be well.
OTHELLO.   Your napkin is too little.

[*He puts the handkerchief from him, and it drops.*]

  Let it alone. Come, I'll go in with you.   288
DESDEMONA. I am very sorry that you are not well.

[*Exeunt Othello and Desdemona*]

EMILIA. I am glad I have found this napkin.
  This was her first remembrance from the Moor.
  My wayward husband hath a hundred times   292
  Woo'd me to steal it, but she so loves the token
  (For he conjur'd her she should ever keep it)
  That she reserves it evermore about her
  To kiss and talk to. I'll have the work ta'en
    out,   296
  And give't Iago.
  What he will do with it heaven knows, not I.
  I nothing know, but for his fantasy—

[*Enter Iago.*]

IAGO. How now! what do you here alone?   300
EMILIA. Do not you chide. I have a thing for you.
IAGO. A thing for me? It is a common thing—
EMILIA. Ha!
IAGO. To have a foolish wife.   304
EMILIA. O, is that all? What will you give me now
  For that same handkerchief?
IAGO.   What handkerchief?
EMILIA. What handkerchief?
  Why, that the Moor first gave to Desdemona;   308
  That which so often you did bid me steal.
IAGO. Hast stol'n it from her?
EMILIA. No, faith. She let it drop by negligence,
  And, to th' advantage, I, being here, took't
    up.   312
  Look, here it is.
IAGO.   A good wench! give it me.
EMILIA. What will you do with't, that you have been
  so earnest
  To have me filch it?
IAGO.   Why, what's that to you?

[*Snatches it.*]

EMILIA. If it be not for some purpose of import,   316
  Give me't again. Poor lady, she'll run mad
  When she shall lack it.
IAGO. Be not acknown on't. I have use for it.
  Go, leave me.   [*Exit Emilia.*]
  I will in Cassio's lodging lose this napkin,   321
  And let him find it. Trifles light as air
  Are to the jealous confirmations strong
  As proofs of holy writ; this may do something.   324
  The Moor already changes with my poison.
  Dangerous conceits are in their natures poisons,
  Which at the first are scarce found to distaste,
  But, with a little act upon the blood,   328
  Burn like the mines of sulphur. I did say so.
  Look, where he comes!

[*Enter Othello.*]

                 Not poppy, nor mandragora,
  Nor all the drowsy syrups of the world,
  Shall ever medicine thee to that sweet sleep   332
  Which thou ow'dst yesterday.
OTHELLO.   Ha! ha! false to me?
IAGO. Why, how now, general? No more of that.
OTHELLO. Avaunt! be gone! Thou hast set me on the
  rack.
  I swear 'tis better to be much abus'd
  Than but to know't a little.
IAGO.   How now, my lord?
OTHELLO. What sense had I of her stol'n hours of
  lust?
  I saw't not, thought it not, it harm'd not me.
  I slept the next night well, was free and merry;   340
  I found not Cassio's kisses on her lips.
  He that is robb'd, not wanting what is stol'n,
  Let him not know't and he's not robb'd at all.
IAGO. I am sorry to hear this.   344
OTHELLO. I had been happy if the general camp,
  Pióners and all, had tasted her sweet body,
  So I had nothing known. O, now for ever
  Farewell the tranquil mind! farewell content!   348
  Farewell the plumed troops and the big wars
  That make ambition virtue! O, farewell!
  Farewell the neighing steed, and the shrill trump,
  The spirit-stirring drum, th' ear-piercing fife,   352
  The royal banner, and all quality,
  Pride, pomp, and circumstance of glorious war!

---

319. **Be . . . on't**: admit no knowledge of it   328. **with . . . act**: after brief operation   329. **I did say so**: just as I was saying!   330. **mandragora**: mandrake, a narcotic   342. **wanting**: missing   346. **Pioners**: miners, military menials   354. **circumstance**: ceremony

---

287. **napkin**: handkerchief   296. **work ta'en out**: embroidery copied

And, O ye mortal engines, whose wide throats
Th' immortal Jove's great clamor counterfeit,   356
Farewell! Othello's occupation's gone!

IAGO. Is't possible, my lord?

OTHELLO. Villain, be sure thou prove my love a
     whore,
Be sure of it! Give me the ocular proof;   360
Or by the worth of man's eternal soul,
Thou hadst been better have been born a dog
Than answer my wak'd wrath.

IAGO.   Is't come to this?

OTHELLO. Make me to see't; or, at the least, so prove
     it   364
That the probation bear no hinge nor loop
To hang a doubt on, or woe upon thy life!

IAGO. My noble lord,—

OTHELLO. If thou dost slander her and torture
     me,   368
Never pray more. Abandon all remorse;
On horror's head horrors accumulate;
Do deeds to make heaven weep, all earth amaz'd;
For nothing canst thou to damnation add   372
Greater than that.

IAGO.   O grace! O heaven defend me!
Are you a man? Have you a soul or sense?
God be wi' you! Take mine office. O wretched fool!
That liv'st to make thine honesty a vice.   376
O monstrous world! Take note, take note, O world,
To be direct and honest is not safe.
I thank you for this profit, and from hence
I'll love no friend, sith love breeds such
     offence.   380

OTHELLO. Nay, stay. Thou shouldst be honest.

IAGO. I should be wise, for honesty's a fool,
And loses that it works for.

⟨OTHELLO.   By the world,
I think my wife be honest and think she is
     not;   384
I think that thou art just and think thou art not.
I'll have some proof. Her name, that was as fresh
As Dian's visage, is now begrim'd and black
As mine own face. If there be cords or knives,   388
Poison or fire or suffocating streams,
I'll not endure it. Would I were satisfied!

IAGO⟩. I see, sir, you are eaten up with passion.
I do repent me that I put it to you.   392
You would be satisfied?

OTHELLO.   Would? Nay, I will!

IAGO. And may; but how? How satisfied, my lord?
Would you, the supervisor, grossly gape on,
Behold her topp'd?

OTHELLO.   Death and damnation! O!   396

IAGO. It were a tedious difficulty, I think,
To bring them to that prospect. Damn them, then,
If ever mortal eyes do see them bolster
More than their own. What then? how then?   400
What shall I say? Where's satisfaction?
It is impossible you should see this,
Were they as prime as goats, as hot as monkeys,
As salt as wolves in pride, and fools as gross   404
As ignorance made drunk. But yet, I say,
If imputation, and strong circumstances,
Which lead directly to the door of truth,
Will give you satisfaction, you may have't.   408

OTHELLO. Give me a living reason she's disloyal.

IAGO. I do not like the office;
But sith I am enter'd in this cause so far
(Prick'd to't by foolish honesty and love),   412
I will go on. I lay with Cassio lately;
And, being troubled with a raging tooth,
I could not sleep.
There are a kind of men so loose of soul   416
That in their sleeps will mutter their affairs.
One of this kind is Cassio.
In sleep I heard him say, 'Sweet Desdemona,
Let us be wary, let us hide our loves!'   420
And then, sir, would he gripe and wring my hand,
Cry out 'Sweet creature!' and then kiss me hard,
As if he pluck'd up kisses by the roots
That grew upon my lips; then laid his leg   424
Over my thigh, and sigh'd, and kiss'd; and then
Cried, 'Cursed fate, that gave thee to the Moor!'

OTHELLO. O monstrous! monstrous!

IAGO.   Nay, this was but his dream.

OTHELLO. But this denoted a foregone
     conclusion.   428

IAGO. 'Tis a shrewd doubt, though it be but a dream;
And this may help to thicken other proofs
That do demonstrate thinly.

OTHELLO.   I'll tear her all to pieces!

IAGO. Nay, but be wise. Yet we see nothing
     done;   432

---

355. engines: cannon 356. great clamor: thunder 365. proba-tion: proof hinge nor loop: pivot nor strap 369. remorse: com-punction 370. accumulate: pile up 379. profit: profitable lesson 380. sith: since 392. put: confided

399. bolster: bed (together) 403. prime: ardent 404. in pride: in heat 406. imputation . . . circumstances: opinion based on strong circumstantial evidence 409. living: real, not sham 428. foregone conclusion: a previous experience 429. shrewd doubt: ground for dire suspicion 430. thicken: give substance to

She may be honest yet. Tell me but this:
Have you not sometimes seen a handkerchief
Spotted with strawberries in your wife's hand?
OTHELLO. I gave her such a one. 'Twas my first
    gift.   436
IAGO. I know not that; but such a handkerchief
    (I am sure it was your wife's) did I to-day
    See Cassio wipe his beard with.
OTHELLO.   If't be that,—
IAGO. If it be that, or any that was hers,   440
    It speaks against her with the other proofs.
OTHELLO. O that the slave had forty thousand lives!
    One is too poor, too weak, for my revenge.
    Now do I see 'tis true. Look here, Iago;   444
    All my fond love thus do I blow to heaven.

[Hisses contemptuously.]

    'Tis gone.
    Arise, black vengeance, from thy hollow cell!
    Yield up, O love, thy crown and hearted
        throne   448
    To tyrannous hate. Swell, bosom, with thy fraught,
    For 'tis of aspics' tongues!
IAGO.   Pray, be content.
OTHELLO. O blood! Iago, blood!   451
IAGO. Patience, I say. Your mind, perhaps, may
    change.
OTHELLO. Never Iago. Like to the Pontic sea,
    Whose icy current and compulsive course
    Ne'er feels retiring ebb, but keeps due on
    To the Propontic and the Hellespont,   456
    Even so my bloody thoughts, with violent pace,
    Shall ne'er look back, ne'er ebb to humble love,
    Till that a capable and wide revenge
    Swallow them up.   [He kneels.]
                        Now, by yond marble heaven,
    In the due reverence of a sacred vow   461
    I here engage my words.
IAGO.   Do not rise yet.   [Kneels.]
    Witness, you ever-burning lights above!
    You elements that clip us round about!   464
    Witness that here Iago doth give up
    The execution of his wit, hands, heart,
    To wrong'd Othello's service! Let him command,
    And to obey shall be in me remorse,   468
    What bloody work soever.   [They rise.]

435. Spotted: embroidered 442. the slave: Cassio 447. hollow
cell: underground prison 449. fraught: freight, burden 450.
aspics': asps', venomous snakes' content: quiet 459. capable:
comprehensive 460. marble: inflexible 464. clip: enclose 466.
execution: exercise 468. remorse: conscience

OTHELLO.   I greet thy love,
    Not with vain thanks, but with acceptance boun-
        teous,
    And will upon the instant put thee to't.
    Within these three days let me hear thee say   472
    That Cassio's not alive.
IAGO. My friend is dead; 'tis done as you request.
    But let her live.
OTHELLO.   Damn her, lewd minx! O, damn her!
    Come, go with me apart. I will withdraw   476
    To furnish me with some swift means of death
    For the fair devil. Now art thou my lieutenant.
IAGO. I am your own for ever.   [Exeunt.]

SCENE IV

Before the Citadel

[Enter Desdemona, Emilia, and the Clown.]

DESDEMONA. Do you know, sirrah, where Lieutenant
    Cassio lies?
CLOWN. I dare not say he lies anywhere.
DESDEMONA. Why, man?   4
CLOWN. He is a soldier, and for one to say a soldier
    lies is stabbing.
DESDEMONA. Go to! Where lodges he?
⟨CLOWN. To tell you where he lodges is to tell you
    where I lie.   9
DESDEMONA. Can anything be made of this?⟩
CLOWN. I know not where he lodges, and for me to
    devise a lodging, and say he lies here or he lies there,
    were to lie in mine own throat.   13
DESDEMONA. Can you inquire him out, and be edi-
    fied by report?
CLOWN. I will catechize the world for him; that is,
    make questions, and by them answer.   17
DESDEMONA. Seek him. Bid him come hither; tell
    him I have moved my lord in his behalf, and hope
    all will be well.   20
CLOWN. To do this is within the compass of man's
    wit, and therefore I will attempt the doing it.

[Exit Clown.]

DESDEMONA. Where should I lose that handkerchief,
    Emilia?

471. to't: to the test
14–15. be edified by report: make intelligent use of what you hear

EMILIA. I know not, madam.   24

DESDEMONA. Believe me, I had rather have lost my purse
  Full of cruzadoes; and but my noble Moor
  Is true of mind, and made of no such baseness
  As jealous creatures are, it were enough   28
  To put him to ill thinking.

EMILIA.   Is he not jealous?

DESDEMONA. Who, he? I think the sun where he was born
  Drew all such humors from him.

EMILIA.   Look where he comes!

DESDEMONA. I will not leave him now till Cassio   32
  Be call'd to him.

[Enter Othello.]

           How is't with you, my lord?

OTHELLO. Well, my good lady. [Aside.] O hardness to dissemble!—
  How do you, Desdemona?

DESDEMONA.   Well, my good lord.

OTHELLO. Give me your hand. This hand is moist, my lady.

DESDEMONA. It yet has felt no age nor known no sorrow.   37

OTHELLO. This argues fruitfulness and liberal heart:
  Hot, hot, and moist. This hand of yours requires
  A séquester from liberty, fasting and prayer,   40
  Much castigation, exercise devout;
  For here's a young and sweating devil here
  That commonly rebels. 'Tis a good hand,
  A frank one.

DESDEMONA. You may, indeed, say so,   44
  For 'twas that hand that gave away my heart.

OTHELLO. A liberal hand! The hearts of old gave hands,
  But our new heraldry is hands not hearts.

DESDEMONA. I cannot speak of this. Come now, your promise.

OTHELLO. What promise, chuck?   49

DESDEMONA. I have sent to bid Cassio come speak with you.

OTHELLO. I have a salt and sorry rheum offends me.
  Lend me thy handkerchief.

DESDEMONA.   Here, my lord.   52

OTHELLO. That which I gave you.

DESDEMONA.   I have it not about me.

OTHELLO. Not?

DESDEMONA.   No, 'faith, my lord.

OTHELLO.   That is a fault.
  That handkerchief
  Did an Egyptian to my mother give.   56
  She was a charmer and could almost read
  The thoughts of people. She told her, while she kept it,
  'Twould make her amiable and subdue my father
  Entirely to her love, but if she lost it   60
  Or made a gift of it, my father's eye
  Should hold her loathly, and his spirits should hunt
  After new fancies. She dying gave it me;
  And bid me, when my fate would have me wive,   64
  To give it her. I did so,—and take heed on't;
  Make it a darling like your precious eye.
  To lose or give't away were such perdition
  As nothing else could match.

DESDEMONA.   Is't possible?   68

OTHELLO. 'Tis true. There's magic in the web of it.
  A sibyl, that had number'd in the world
  The sun to course two hundred compasses,
  In her prophetic fury sew'd the work.   72
  The worms were hallow'd that did breed the silk,
  And it was dy'd in mummy which the skilful
  Conserv'd of maidens' hearts.

DESDEMONA.   I' faith? is't true?

OTHELLO. Most veritable; therefore look to't well.   76

DESDEMONA. Then would to God that I had never seen it!

OTHELLO. Ha? wherefore?

DESDEMONA. Why do you speak so startingly and rash?

OTHELLO. Is't lost? is't gone? Speak! Is't out o' the way?   80

DESDEMONA. Heaven bless us!

OTHELLO.   Say you?

DESDEMONA. It is not lost: but what an if it were?

OTHELLO. How!

DESDEMONA. I say, it is not lost.

OTHELLO.   Fetch't, let me see't.   84

DESDEMONA. Why, so I can, sir, but I will not now.
  This is a trick to put me from my suit.
  Pray you, let Cassio be receiv'd again.

---

26. **cruzadoes:** Portuguese gold coins   40. **séquester:** separation
49. **chuck:** chick (term of endearment)   51. **sorry rheum:** distressing discharge (of eye or nose)

57. **charmer:** witch   70. **sibyl:** inspired prophetess   71. **course . . . compasses:** make . . . revolutions   74. **mummy:** drug made from embalmed bodies   79. **startingly and rash:** impetuously and fast

OTHELLO. Fetch me that handkerchief. My mind mis-
    gives.
DESDEMONA. Come, come;   89
  You'll never meet a more sufficient man.
OTHELLO. The handkercher!
DESDEMONA.   I pray, talk me of Cassio.
OTHELLO. The handkerchief!
DESDEMONA.   A man that all his time   92
  Hath founded his good fortunes on your love,
  Shar'd dangers with you,—
OTHELLO. The handkerchief!
DESDEMONA.   I' faith, you are to blame.
OTHELLO. Zounds!   [Exit Othello.]
EMILIA. Is not this man jealous?   97
DESDEMONA. I ne'er saw this before.
  Sure, there's some wonder in this handkerchief.
  I am most unhappy in the loss of it.   100
EMILIA. 'Tis not a year or two shows us a man.
  They are all but stomachs, and we all but food.
  They eat us hungerly, and when they are full
  They belch us. Look you! Cassio and my
    husband.   104

[Enter Iago and Cassio.]

IAGO. There is no other way; 'tis she must do't.
  And, lo, the happiness! Go and impórtune her.
DESDEMONA. How now, good Cassio? what's the
  news with you?
CASSIO. Madam, my former suit I do beseech
  you   108
  That by your virtuous means I may again
  Exist, and be a member of his love
  Whom I with all the office of my heart
  Entirely honor. I would not be delay'd.   112
  If my offence be of such mortal kind
  That nor my service past, nor present sorrows,
  Nor purpos'd merit in futurity,
  Can ransom me into his love again,   116
  But to know so must be my benefit.
  So shall I clothe me in a forc'd content,
  And shut myself up in some other course
  To fortune's alms.
DESDEMONA.   Alas, thrice-gentle Cassio,   120
  My advocation is not now in tune.

My lord is not my lord; nor should I know him,
Were he in favor as in humor alter'd.
So help me every spirit sanctified,   124
As I have spoken for you all my best
And stood within the blank of his displeasure
For my free speech. You must awhile be patient.
What I can do I will, and more I will   128
Than for myself I dare. Let that suffice you.
IAGO. Is my lord angry?
EMILIA.   He went hence but now,
  And certainly in strange unquietness.
IAGO. Can he be angry? I have seen the cannon,   132
  When it hath blown his ranks into the air,
  And, like the devil, from his very arm
  Puff'd his own brother,—and can he be angry?
  Something of moment then. I will go meet
    him;   136
  There's matter in't indeed, if he be angry.
DESDEMONA. I prithee, do so.   [Exit Iago.]
                  Something, sure, of state,
  Either from Venice, or some unhatch'd practice
  Made démonstrable here in Cyprus to him,   140
  Hath puddled his clear spirit; and in such cases
  Men's natures wrangle with inferior things,
  Though great ones are their object. 'Tis even so;
  For let our finger ache, and it endues   144
  Our other healthful members ev'n to that sense
  Of pain. Nay, we must think men are not gods,
  Nor of them look for such observancy
  As fits the bridal. Beshrew me much, Emilia,   148
  I was (unhandsome warrior as I am)
  Arraigning his unkindness with my soul;
  But now I find I had suborn'd the witness,
  And he's indicted falsely.   152
EMILIA. Pray heaven it be state-matters, as you think,
  And no conception, nor no jealous toy
  Concerning you.
DESDEMONA. Alas the day! I never gave him
  cause.   156
EMILIA. But jealous souls will not be answer'd so.
  They are not ever jealous for the cause,
  But jealous for they are jealous. 'Tis a monster
  Begot upon itself, born on itself.   160
DESDEMONA. Heaven keep that monster from
  Othello's mind!

---

102. but . . . but: merely . . . merely 106. the happiness: what
luck! 111. office: duty 114. nor . . . nor: neither . . . nor 117.
But: merely 119. shut . . . in: confine myself to 120. To . . .
alms: in pursuit of fortune's favor

123. humor: disposition 126. blank: range (literally, target) 139.
unhatch'd practice: undeveloped plot 141. puddled: muddied, disturbed 144. endues: brings 147. observancy: tender devotion
148. Beshrew: a mild imprecation 149. unhandsome . . . am: i.e.,
failing in this test to be a 'fair warrior' (cf. II.i.182) 154. conception: fancy toy: whim

EMILIA. Lady, amen.

DESDEMONA. I will go seek him. Cassio, walk here-
  about.
  If I do find him fit, I'll move your suit   164
  And seek to effect it to my uttermost.

CASSIO. I humbly thank your ladyship.

[*Exeunt Desdemona and Emilia.*]

[*Enter Bianca.*]

BIANCA. 'Save you, friend Cassio!

CASSIO.   What make you from home?
  How is it with you, my most fair Bianca?   168
  I' faith, sweet love, I was coming to your house.

BIANCA. And I was going to your lodging, Cassio.
  What! keep a week away? seven days and nights?
  Eight score eight hours? and lovers' absent
    hours,   172
  More tedious than the dial eight score times?
  O weary reckoning!

CASSIO.   Pardon me, Bianca,
  I have this while with leaden thoughts been press'd,
  But I shall, in a more continuate time,   176
  Strike off this score of absence. Sweet Bianca,

[*giving her Desdemona's handkerchief*]

  Take me this work out.

BIANCA.   O Cassio! whence came this?

This is some token from a newer friend;
  To the felt absence now I feel a cause;   180
  Is't come to this? ⟨Well, well.⟩

CASSIO.   Go to, woman!
  Throw your vile guesses in the devil's teeth,
  From whence you have them. You are jealous now
  That this is from some mistress, some
    remembrance.   184
  No, by my faith, Bianca.

BIANCA.   Why, whose is it?

CASSIO. I know not, sweet. I found it in my chamber.
  I like the work well. Ere it be demanded
  (As like enough it will), I'd have it copied. 188
  Take it and do't; and leave me for this time.

BIANCA. Leave you? wherefore?

CASSIO. I do attend here on the general,
  And think it no addition nor my wish   192
  To have him see me woman'd.

⟨BIANCA.   Why, I pray you?

CASSIO. Not that I love you not.⟩

BIANCA.   But that you do not love me.
  I pray you, bring me on the way a little
  And say if I shall see you soon at night.   196

CASSIO. 'Tis but a little way that I can bring you,
  For I attend here; but I'll see you soon.

BIANCA. 'Tis very good. I must be circumstanc'd.

[*Exeunt.*]

Act IV

SCENE I

Before the Citadel

[*Enter Othello and Iago.*]

IAGO. Will you think so?

OTHELLO.   Think so, Iago!

IAGO.   What!
  To kiss in private?

OTHELLO.   An unauthoriz'd kiss.

IAGO. Or to be naked with her friend abed
  An hour or more, not meaning any harm?   4

OTHELLO. Naked abed, Iago, and not mean harm?
  It is hypocrisy against the devil.
  They that mean virtuously, and yet do so,
  The devil their virtue tempts, and they tempt
    heaven.   8

IAGO. So they do nothing, 'tis a venial slip.
  But if I give my wife a handkerchief,—

OTHELLO. What then?

IAGO. Why, then, 'tis hers, my lord; and, being
    hers,   12
  She may, I think, bestow't on any man.

OTHELLO. She is protectress of her honor too.
  May she give that?

---

167. **'Save:** God save, preserve in health 172. **Eight score eight:**
168 176. **continuate:** uninterrupted

192. **no . . . wish:** neither advantageous nor desirable 193.
woman'd: accompanied by a woman 199. **be circumstanc'd:** yield
to circumstances
6. **hypocrisy against:** an attempt to cheat

IAGO. Her honor is an essence that's not seen.   16
   They have it very oft that have it not;
   But for the handkerchief,—
OTHELLO. By heaven, I would most gladly have
      forgot it.
   Thou said'st (O it comes o'er my memory   20
   As doth the raven o'er the infected house,
   Boding to all) he had my handkerchief.
IAGO. Ay, what of that?
OTHELLO.   That's not so good now.
IAGO.   What
   If I had said I had seen him do you wrong?   24
   Or heard him say (as knaves be such abroad,
   Who having, by their own importunate suit
   Or voluntary dotage of some mistress,
   Convinced or supplied them, cannot choose   28
   But they must blab)—
OTHELLO.   Hath he said anything?
IAGO. He hath, my lord; but be you well assur'd,
   No more than he'll unswear.
OTHELLO.   What hath he said?
IAGO. Faith, that he did—I know not what he
      did.   32
OTHELLO. What? what?
IAGO. Lie—
OTHELLO.   With her?
IAGO.   With her, on her—what you will.
OTHELLO. Lie with her! lie on her! We say, lie on her,
   when they belie her. Lie with her? Zounds, that's
   fulsome!   Handkerchief!—confessions!—handker-
   chief! (To confess, and be hanged for his labor.
   First, to be hanged, and then to confess: I tremble
   at it. Nature would not invest herself in such shad-
   owing passion without some instruction. It is not
   words that shake me thus. Pish! Noses, ears, and
   lips. Is't possible?—Confess!—Handkerchief!—O
   devil!)   [Falls in a trance.]
IAGO. Work on,   45
   My medicine, work! Thus credulous fools are
      caught;
   And many worthy and chaste dames even thus,
   All guiltless, meet reproach. What, ho! my
      lord!   48
   My lord, I say! Othello!

[Enter Cassio.]

How now, Cassio!

CASSIO. What's the matter?
IAGO. My lord is fallen into an epilepsy.
   This is his second fit; he had one yesterday.   52
CASSIO. Rub him about the temples.
IAGO.   No, forbear.
   The lethargy must have his quiet course.
   If not he foams at mouth, and by and by
   Breaks out to savage madness. Look! he stirs.   56
   Do you withdraw yourself a little while,
   He will recover straight. When he is gone,
   I would on great occasion speak with you.

[Exit Cassio.]

   How is it, general? Have you not hurt your
      head?   60
OTHELLO. Dost thou mock me?
IAGO.   I mock you! no, by heaven.
   Would you would bear your fortunes like a man!
OTHELLO. A horned man's a monster and a beast.
IAGO. There's many a beast then, in a populous
      city,   64
   And many a civil monster.
OTHELLO. Did he confess?
IAGO.   Good sir, be a man.
   Think every bearded fellow that's but yok'd
   May draw with you. There's millions now alive   68
   That nightly lie in those unproper beds
   Which they dare swear peculiar. Your case is better.
   O, 'tis the spite of hell, the fiend's arch-mock,
   To lip a wanton in a secure couch,   72
   And to suppose her chaste. No, let me know;
   And knowing what I am, I know what she shall be.
OTHELLO. O, thou art wise, 'tis certain.
IAGO.   Stand you awhile apart;
   Confine yourself but in a patient list.   76
   Whilst you were here o'erwhelmed with your grief
   (A passion most unsuiting such a man),
   Cassio came hither. I shifted him away,
   And laid good 'scuse upon your ecstasy;   80
   Bade him anon return and here speak with me,
   The which he promis'd. Do but encave yourself,
   And mark the fleers, the gibes, and notable scorns
   That dwell in every region of his face;   84
   For I will make him tell the tale anew,

28. **Convinced:** overcome (those who needed importuning) **supplied:** satisfied (those who doted voluntarily)

54. **his:** its 63. **horned man:** a deceived husband 65. **civil;** civilian 67. **yok'd:** yoked in matrimony 68. **draw:** draw the same cart, endure the same ignominy 69. **unproper:** not their own 70. **peculiar:** their own 72. **lip:** kiss **secure:** care-free 74. **what she shall be:** i.e., what I am to call her 76. **patient list:** the bounds of patience 80. **ecstasy:** fit 82. **encave:** conceal

Where, how, how oft, how long ago, and when
He has, and is again to cope your wife.
I say, but mark his gesture. Marry, patience;   88
Or I shall say you're all in all in spleen,
And nothing of a man.

OTHELLO.   Dost thou hear, Iago?
I will be found most cunning in my patience,
But—dost thou hear?—most bloody.

IAGO.   That's not amiss;   92
But yet keep time in all. Will you withdraw?

[Othello goes apart.]

Now will I question Cassio of Bianca,
A housewife that by selling her desires
Buys herself bread and clothes. It is a creature   96
That dotes on Cassio (as 'tis the strumpet's plague
To beguile many and be beguil'd by one).
He, when he hears of her, cannot refrain
From the excess of laughter. Here he comes.   100

[Enter Cassio.]

As he shall smile, Othello shall go mad;
And his unbookish jealousy must cónstrue
Poor Cassio's smiles, gestures, and light behavior
Quite in the wrong. [Aloud.] How do you now,
     lieutenant?   104

CASSIO. The worser that you give me the addition
Whose want even kills me.

IAGO. Ply Desdemona well, and you are sure on't.
[Speaking lower.] Now, if this suit lay in Bianca's
     power,
How quickly should you speed!

CASSIO.   Alas! poor caitiff!   109

OTHELLO. Look how he laughs already!

IAGO. I never knew a woman love man so.

CASSIO. Alas! poor rogue! I think, i' faith, she loves
me.   112

OTHELLO. Now he denies it faintly, and laughs it out.

IAGO. Do you hear, Cassio?

OTHELLO.   Now he impórtunes him
To tell it o'er. Go to! well said, well said.

IAGO. She gives it out that you shall marry her.   116
Do you intend it?

CASSIO. Ha, ha, ha!

OTHELLO. Do you triumph, Roman? do you
     triumph?   119

CASSIO. I marry her! ⟨what? a customer?⟩ I prithee,
bear some charity to my wit; do not think it so
unwholesome. Ha, ha, ha!

OTHELLO. So, so, so, so. Laugh that wins!

IAGO. Faith, the cry goes you shall marry her.   124

CASSIO. Prithee, say true.

IAGO. I am a very villain else.

OTHELLO. Have you scored me? Well!   127

CASSIO. This is the monkey's own giving out. She is
persuaded I will marry her, out of her own love and
flattery, not out of my promise.

OTHELLO. Iago beckons me. Now he begins the
story.

CASSIO. She was here even now; she haunts me in
every place. I was t'other day talking on the sea
bank with certain Venetians, and thither comes the
bauble, and falls me thus about my neck—   135

OTHELLO. Crying, 'O dear Cassio!' as it were. His
gesture imports it.

CASSIO. So hangs and lolls and weeps upon me; so
hales and pulls me. Ha, ha, ha!   139

OTHELLO. Now he tells how she plucked him to my
chamber. O, I see that nose of yours, but not that
dog I shall throw it to.

CASSIO. Well, I must leave her company.

IAGO. Before me! look where she comes!   144

CASSIO. 'Tis such another fitchew! marry, a perfumed
one!
What do you mean by this haunting of me?   147

BIANCA. Let the devil and his dam haunt you! What
did you mean by that same handkerchief you gave
me even now? I was a fine fool to take it. I must
take out the work? A likely piece of work, that you
should find it in your chamber and not know who
left it there! This is some minx's token, and I must
take out the work! There, give it your hobby-horse,
wheresoever you had it. I'll take out no work on't.

CASSIO. How now, my sweet Bianca? how now? how
now?   157

OTHELLO. By heaven, that should be my handkerchief!

BIANCA. An you'll come to supper to-night, you may.
An you will not, come when you are next prepared
for.   [Exit.]

87. cope: encounter 93. keep time: proceed fittingly 102.
unbookish: unskilled 105. addition: title 109. speed: prosper
caitiff: wretch (used pityingly) 119. Roman: used metaphorically, in
association with 'triumph'

120. customer: prostitute 121. wit: intelligence 122. unwholesome: unsound 123. Laugh: let him laugh 127. scored: notched
130. flattery: self-flattery, delusion 135. bauble: plaything 145.
such another: a patronizingly fond intensive, like modern 'such a'
fitchew: amorous creature (literally, polecat) 154. hobby-horse:
harlot 159. An: if 160. next: (implying 'never')

IAGO. After her! after her!

CASSIO. Faith, I must. She'll rail i' the street else.

IAGO. Will you sup there?   164

CASSIO. Faith, I intend so.

IAGO. Well, I may chance to see you, for I would very
fain speak with you.

CASSIO. Prithee, come; will you?   168

IAGO. Go to! Say no more.   [Exit Cassio.]

OTHELLO. [advancing]. How shall I murder him, Iago?

IAGO. Did you perceive how he laughed at his vice?

OTHELLO. O Iago!   172

IAGO. And did you see the handkerchief?

OTHELLO. Was that mine?

IAGO. Yours, by this hand. And to see how he prizes
the foolish woman your wife! She gave it him, and
he hath given it his whore.   177

OTHELLO. I would have him nine years a-killing. A
fine woman! a fair woman! a sweet woman!

IAGO. Nay, you must forget that.   180

OTHELLO. Ay, let her rot and perish, and be damned
to-night, for she shall not live. No, my heart is
turned to stone. I strike it, and it hurts my hand. O,
the world has not a sweeter creature. She might lie
by an emperor's side and command him tasks.

IAGO. Nay, that's not your way.   186

OTHELLO. Hang her! I do but say what she is. So
delicate with her needle! An admirable musician! O,
she will sing the savageness out of a bear. Of so high
and plenteous wit and invention!   190

IAGO. She's the worse for all this.

OTHELLO. O, a thousand, a thousand times. And
then, of so gentle a condition!

IAGO. Ay, too gentle.   194

OTHELLO. Nay, that's certain. But yet the pity of it,
Iago! ⟨O, Iago, ⟨the pity⟩ of it, Iago!⟩

IAGO. If you be so fond over her iniquity, give her
patent to offend; for, if it touches not you, it comes
near nobody.

OTHELLO. I will chop her into messes. Cuckold
me—   200

IAGO. O, 'tis foul in her.

OTHELLO. With mine officer!

IAGO. That's fouler.   203

OTHELLO. Get me some poison, Iago, this night. I'll
not expostulate with her, lest her body and beauty
unprovide my mind again. This night, Iago.

IAGO. Do it not with poison. Strangle her in her bed,
even the bed she hath contaminated.   208

OTHELLO. Good, good. The justice of it pleases. Very
good.

IAGO. And for Cassio, let me be his undertaker.
You shall hear more by midnight.   212

OTHELLO. Excellent good.   [A trumpet.]
                    What trumpet is that same?

IAGO. Something from Venice, sure. 'Tis Lodovico,
Come from the duke; and see, your wife is with him.

[Enter Lodovico, Desdemona, and Attendants.]

LODOVICO. God save you, worthy general!

OTHELLO.   With all my heart, sir.   216

LODOVICO. The duke and senators of Venice greet
you.

[Gives him a letter.]

OTHELLO. I kiss the instrument of their pleasures.

[Opens the letter and reads.]

DESDEMONA. And what's the news, good cousin
Lodovico?

IAGO. I am very glad to see you, signior.   220
Welcome to Cyprus.

LODOVICO. I thank you. How does Lieutenant Cassio?

IAGO. Lives, sir.

DESDEMONA. Cousin, there's fall'n between him and
my lord
An unkind breach, but you shall make all well.   225

OTHELLO. Are you sure of that?

DESDEMONA. My lord?

OTHELLO. [reads]. 'This fail you not to do, as you
will'—   228

LODOVICO. He did not call. He's busy in the paper.
Is there division 'twixt thy lord and Cassio?

DESDEMONA. A most unhappy one. I would do much.
T'atone them for the love I bear to Cassio.   232

OTHELLO. Fire and brimstone!

DESDEMONA.   My lord?

OTHELLO.   Are you wise?

DESDEMONA. What! is he angry?

LODOVICO.   May be the letter mov'd him;
For, as I think, they do command him home,
Deputing Cassio in his government.   236

---

186. **your way:** the way for you (to think of her) 198. **patent:**
license 206. **unprovide:** unfit, weaken

211. **undertaker:** caretaker (i.e., settle him) 232. **atone:** reconcile 233. **Are you wise:** sardonic; Have you no wisdom? 236.
government: office

DESDEMONA. By my truth, I am glad on't.

OTHELLO.   Indeed?

DESDEMONA.   My lord?

OTHELLO. I am glad to see you mad.

DESDEMONA.   How, sweet Othello?

OTHELLO. Devil!   [Strikes her.]

DESDEMONA.   I have not deserved this.

LODOVICO. My lord, this would not be believ'd in Venice,   240

Though I should swear I saw't. 'Tis very much.

Make her amends, she weeps.

OTHELLO.   O devil, devil!

If that the earth could teem with women's tears,

Each drop she falls would prove a crocodile.   244

Out of my sight!

DESDEMONA. [going]. I will not stay to offend you.

LODOVICO. Truly, an obedient lady!

I do beseech your lordship, call her back.

OTHELLO. Mistress!

DESDEMONA.   My lord?

OTHELLO.   What would you with her, sir?

LODOVICO. Who, I, my lord?   249

OTHELLO. Ay, you did wish that I would make her turn.

Sir, she can turn, and turn, and yet go on,

And turn again. And she can weep, sir, weep;   252

And she's obedient, as you say, obedient,

Very obedient.—Proceed you in your tears.—

Concerning this, sir,—o well painted passion!—

I am commanded here—Get you away;   256

I'll send for you anon.—Sir, I obey the mandate,

And will return to Venice.—Hence! avaunt!

[Exit Desdemona.]

Cassio shall have my place. And, sir, to-night,

I do entreat that we may sup together.   260

You are welcome, sir, to Cyprus.—Goats and monkeys!

[Exit.]

LODOVICO. Is this the noble Moor whom our full senate

Call all-in-all sufficient? Is this the nature

Whom passion could not shake, whose solid virtue   264

The shot of accident nor dart of chance

Could neither graze nor pierce?

IAGO.   He is much chang'd.

LODOVICO. Are his wits safe? is he not light of brain?

IAGO. He's that he is. I may not breathe my censure.

What he might be (if what he might he is not)   269

I would to heaven he were!

LODOVICO.   What! strike his wife!

IAGO. Faith, that was not so well; yet would I knew

That stroke would prove the worst!

LODOVICO.   Is it his use?   272

Or did the letters work upon his blood,

And new-create this fault?

IAGO.   Alas, alas!

It is not honesty in me to speak

What I have seen and known. You shall observe him,   276

And his own courses will denote him so

That I may save my speech. Do but go after

And mark how he continues.

LODOVICO. I am sorry that I am deceiv'd in him.

[Exeunt.]

SCENE II

A Room in the Citadel

[Enter Othello and Emilia.]

OTHELLO. You have seen nothing, then?

EMILIA. Nor ever heard, nor ever did suspect.

OTHELLO. Yes, you have seen Cassio and she together.

EMILIA. But then I saw no harm, and then I heard   4

Each syllable that breath made up between 'em.

OTHELLO. What! did they never whisper?

EMILIA. Never, my lord.

OTHELLO.   Nor send you out o' the way?

EMILIA.   Never.

OTHELLO. To fetch her fan, her gloves, her mask, nor nothing?   8

EMILIA. Never, my lord.

OTHELLO. That's strange.

EMILIA. I durst, my lord, to wager she is honest,

Lay down my soul at stake. If you think other,   12

Remove your thought. It doth abuse your bosom.

If any wretch have put this in your head,

Let heaven requite it with the serpent's curse!

For if she be not honest, chaste, and true,   16

---

243. teem with: be impregnated by **244. falls:** lets fall **255. painted passion:** simulated emotion

272. use: custom **273. blood:** temper

11. to wager: in pledge that ('durst' goes with 'Lay down') **12. other:** otherwise **15. serpent's curse:** cf. Genesis 3. 14

There's no man happy; the purest of their wives
Is foul as slander.
OTHELLO.   Bid her come hither. Go.

[*Exit Emilia.*]

She says enough; yet she's a simple bawd
That cannot say as much. This is a subtle
    whore,   20
A closet lock and key of villainous secrets;
And yet she'll kneel and pray. I have seen her do't.

[*Enter Desdemona and Emilia.*]

DESDEMONA. My lord, what is your will?
OTHELLO.   Pray, chuck, come hither.
DESDEMONA. What is your pleasure?
OTHELLO.   Let me see your
    eyes;
    Look in my face.
DESDEMONA.   What horrible fancy's this?   25
OTHELLO. [*to Emilia*]. Some of your function, mistress.
    Leave procreants alone and shut the door;
    Cough or cry 'hem' if anybody come.   28
    Your mystery, your mystery. Nay, dispatch.
                                              [*Exit Emilia.*]
DESDEMONA. Upon my knees, what does your speech
    import?
    I understand a fury in your words
    But not the words.   32
OTHELLO. Why, what art thou?
DESDEMONA.   Your wife, my lord; your true
    And loyal wife.
OTHELLO.   Come, swear it, damn thyself;
    Lest being like one of heaven, the devils themselves
    Should fear to seize thee. Therefore be double
        damn'd.
    Swear thou art honest.
DESDEMONA.   Heaven doth truly know it.
OTHELLO. Heaven truly knows that thou art false as
    hell.
DESDEMONA. To whom, my lord? with whom? how
    am I false?
OTHELLO. Ah! Desdemon! Away, away, away!   40
DESDEMONA. Alas, the heavy day! Why do you weep?
    Am I the motive of these tears, my lord?
    If haply you my father do suspect
    An instrument of this your calling back,   44

Lay not your blame on me. If you have lost him,
    Why I have lost him too.
OTHELLO.   Had it pleas'd heaven
    To try me with affliction, had they rain'd
    All kinds of sores and shames on my bare
        head,   48
    Steep'd me in poverty to the very lips,
    Given to captivity me and my utmost hopes,
    I should have found in some part of my soul
    A drop of patience. But, alas! to make me   52
    A fixed figure for the time of scorn
    To point his slow unmoving fingers at!
    Yet could I bear that too. Well! very well!
    But there, where I have garner'd up my heart,   56
    Where either I must live or bear no life;
    The fountain from the which my current runs
    Or else dries up: to be discarded thence,
    Or keep it as a cistern for foul toads   60
    To knot and gender in! Turn thy complexion there,
    Patience, thou young and rose-lipp'd cherubin.
    I here look grim as hell!
DESDEMONA. I hope my noble lord esteems me hon-
    est.   64
OTHELLO. O, ay. As summer flies are in the shambles,
    That quicken even with blowing.
    O thou black weed, why art so lovely fair?
    Thou smell'st so sweet that the sense aches at
        thee.   68
    Would thou hadst ne'er been born!
DESDEMONA. Alas, what ignorant sin have I commit-
    ted?
OTHELLO. Was this fair paper, this most goodly book,
    Made to write 'whore' on? What committed?   72
    (Committed! O thou public commoner!
    I should make very forges of my cheeks,
    That would to cinders burn up modesty,
    Did I but speak thy deeds. What committed?)   76
    Heaven stops the nose at it and the moon winks,
    The bawdy wind that kisses all it meets
    Is hush'd within the hollow mine of earth,
    And will not hear't. What committed?   80
    Impudent strumpet!
DESDEMONA.   By heaven, you do me wrong.
OTHELLO. Are not you a strumpet?
DESDEMONA.   No, as I am a Christian.
    If to preserve this vessel for my lord
    From any other foul unlawful touch   84
    Be not to be a strumpet, I am none.
OTHELLO. What! not a whore?

---

20. This: Emilia **21. closet lock and key:** instrument of conceal
ment **26. function:** profession (i.e., of procuress) **29. mystery:**
trade **42. motive:** cause

49. Steep'd: submerged (cf. 'ensteep'd,' II.i.70) **61. gender:**
engender, multiply

DESDEMONA.   No, as I shall be sav'd.

OTHELLO. Is't possible?

DESDEMONA. O heaven, forgiveness!

OTHELLO.   I cry you mercy, then.   88
   I took you for that cunning whore of Venice
   That married with Othello. You, mistress,
   That have the office opposite to Saint Peter,
   And keep the gate of hell!

[Enter Emilia.]

                         You, you, ay, you!   92
   We have done our course. There's money for your
      pains.
   I pray you, turn the key and keep our counsel.

                                           [Exit.]

EMILIA. Alas! what does this gentleman conceive?
   How do you, madam? how do you, my good
      lady?   96

DESDEMONA. Faith, half asleep.

EMILIA. Good madam, what's the matter with my
   lord?

DESDEMONA. With who?

EMILIA.   Why, with my lord, madam.

DESDEMONA. Who is thy lord?

EMILIA.   He that is yours, sweet lady.

DESDEMONA. I have none; do not talk to me, Emilia;
   I cannot weep, nor answer have I none,
   But what should go by water. Prithee, to-night
   Lay on my bed our wedding sheets.
      Remember;   104
   And call thy husband hither.

EMILIA.   Here is a change indeed!

[Exit.]

DESDEMONA. 'Tis meet I should be us'd so, very
   meet.
   How have I been behav'd, that he might stick
   The small'st opinion on my greatest abuse?   108

[Enter Iago and Emilia.]

IAGO. What is your pleasure, madam? How is't with
   you?

DESDEMONA. I cannot tell. Those that do teach
   young babes

Do it with gentle means and easy tasks.   112
He might have chid me so, for, in good faith,
I am a child to chiding.

IAGO. What is the matter, lady?

EMILIA. Alas! Iago, my lord hath so bewhor'd
   her,   116
   Thrown such despite and heavy terms upon her,
   As true hearts cannot bear.

DESDEMONA. Am I that name, Iago?

IAGO.   What name, fair lady?

DESDEMONA. Such as she says my lord did say I
   was.   120

EMILIA. He call'd her whore. A beggar in his drink
   Could not have laid such terms upon his callet.

IAGO. Why did he so?

DESDEMONA. I do not know. I am sure I am none
   such.   124

IAGO. Do not weep, do not weep. Alas the day!

EMILIA. Has she forsook so many noble matches,
   Her father, and her country, and her friends,
   To be call'd whore? Would it not make one
      weep?   128

DESDEMONA. It is my wretched fortune.

IAGO.   Beshrew him for't!
   How comes this trick upon him?

DESDEMONA.   Nay, heaven doth know.

EMILIA. I will be hang'd if some eternal villain,
   Some busy and insinuating rogue,   132
   Some cogging, cozening slave, to get some office
   Have not devis'd this slander. I'll be hang'd else.

IAGO. Fie! there is no such man. It is impossible.

DESDEMONA. If any such there be, heaven pardon
   him!   136

EMILIA. A halter pardon him, and hell gnaw his bones!
   Why should he call her whore? who keeps her com-
      pany?
   What place? what time? what form? what likelihood?
   The Moor's abus'd by some outrageous
      knave,   140
   Some base notorious knave, some scurvy fellow.
   O heaven! that such companions thou'dst unfold,
   And put in every honest hand a whip
   To lash the rascal naked through the world,   144
   Even from the east to the west!

IAGO.   Speak within doors.

---

88. **forgiveness:** grant me power to forgive this! **cry you mercy:** ask your pardon ("I cry" to be read: Cry) 89. **whore of Venice:** a variety with an international fame 94. **turn the key:** open the door 103. **go by water:** express itself in tears 107, 108. **stick . . . abuse:** even slightly regard my worst offence as an offence

122. **callet:** basest of low women 130. **trick:** vagary 133. **cogging, cozening:** deceiving, cheating 141. **notorious:** egregious, preëminent 142. **companions:** base fellows **unfold:** expose 145. **within doors:** quietly, not from the house-tops

EMILIA. O, fie upon him! Some such squire he was
   That turn'd your wit the seamy side without,
   And made you to suspect me with the Moor.   148
IAGO. You are a fool. Go to!
DESDEMONA.   O good Iago,
   What shall I do to win my lord again?
   Good friend, go to him; for, by this light of heaven,
   I know not how I lost him. Here I kneel.   152
   If e'er my will did trespass 'gainst his love,
   Either in discourse of thought or actual deed,
   Or that mine eyes, mine ears, or any sense
   Delighted them in any other form;   156
   Or that I do not yet, and ever did,
   And ever will (though he do shake me off
   To beggarly divorcement) love him dearly,
   Comfort forswear me! Unkindness may do
      much;   160
   And his unkindness may defeat my life,
   But never taint my love. I cannot say 'whore.'
   It does abhor me now I speak the word;
   To do the act that might th' addition earn   164
   Not the world's mass of vanity could make me.
IAGO. I pray you be content. 'Tis but his humor.
   The business of the state does him offence
   And he does chide with you.   168
DESDEMONA. If 'twere no other,—   [Trumpets within.]
IAGO.   'Tis but so, I warr'nt you.
   Hark how these instruments summon you to
      supper,
   And the great messengers of Venice stay.
   Go in, and weep not. All things shall be well.   172

[Ex. women.]

[Enter Roderigo.]

   How now, Roderigo?
RODERIGO. I do not find that thou deal'st justly with
   me.
IAGO. What in the contrary?   175
RODERIGO. Every day thou daffest me with some
   device, Iago; and rather, as it seems to me, thou
   keepest from me all conveniency, than suppliest me
   with the least advantage of hope. I will indeed no

longer endure it, nor am I yet persuaded to put up
   in peace what already I have foolishly suffered.   181
IAGO. Will you hear me, Roderigo?
RODERIGO. Faith, I have heard too much, for your
   words and performance are no kin together.   184
IAGO. You charge me most unjustly.
RODERIGO. ⟨With nought but truth.⟩ I have wasted
   myself out of my means. The jewels you have had
   from me to deliver to Desdemona would half have
   corrupted a votarist. You have told me she has
   received them, and returned me expectations and
   comforts of sudden respect and acquittance, but I
   find none.
IAGO. Well, go to! Very well.   192
RODERIGO. Very well? go to? I cannot go to, man;
   nor 'tis not very well. By this hand, I say 'tis very
   scurvy, and begin to find myself fopped in it.
IAGO. Very well.   196
RODERIGO. I tell you 'tis not very well. I will make
   myself known to Desdemona. If she will return me
   my jewels, I will give over my suit and repent my
   unlawful solicitation. If not, assure yourself I will
   seek satisfaction of you.   201
IAGO. You have said now?
RODERIGO. Ay, and said nothing but what I protest
   intendment of doing.   204
IAGO. Why, now I see there's mettle in thee, and even
   from this instant do build on thee a better opinion
   than ever before. Give me thy hand, Roderigo.
   Thou hast taken against me a most just exception;
   but yet, I protest, I have dealt most directly in thy
   affair.   210
RODERIGO. It hath not appeared.
IAGO. I grant indeed it hath not appeared, and your
   suspicion is not without wit and judgment. But,
   Roderigo, if thou hast that within thee indeed,
   which I have greater reason to believe now than ever
   (I mean purpose, courage, and valor), this night
   show it. If thou the next night following enjoyest
   not Desdemona, take me from this world with
   treachery and devise engines for my life.   219
RODERIGO. Well, ⟨what is it?⟩ is it within reason and
   compass?
IAGO. Sir, there is especial commission come from
   Venice to depute Cassio in Othello's place.   223
RODERIGO. Is that true? Why, then Othello and
   Desdemona return again to Venice.

---

154. **discourse of thought:** day-dreaming 155. **that:** if 160.
Comfort . . . me: may happiness forsake me 161. **defeat:**
destroy 163. **It does abhor me:** I feel abhorrence 165. **vanity:**
vain treasure 168. **chide with:** quarrel with, 'take it out on' 171.
stay: are waiting 175. What evidence have you against me? 176.
daffest me: puttest me off 178. **conveniency:** opportunity 179.
advantage: increase, furthering

---

180. **put up:** accept 189. **votarist:** religious devotee, nun 191.
sudden respect: immediate notice 195. **fopped:** swindled 202.
said: finished your speech 209. **directly:** straightforwardly 219.
engines for: plots against

IAGO. O, no! he goes into Mauritania, and takes away with him the fair Desdemona, unless his abode be lingered here by some accident; wherein none can be so determinate as the removing of Cassio.

RODERIGO. How do you mean, removing of him?   230

IAGO. Why, by making him uncapable of Othello's place. Knocking out his brains.

RODERIGO. And that you would have me to do!   233

IAGO. Ay; if you dare do yourself a profit and right. He sups to-night with a harlotry, and thither will I go to him. He knows not yet of his honorable fortune. If you will watch his going thence (which I will fashion to fall out between twelve and one), you may take him at your pleasure. I will be near to second your attempt, and he shall fall between us. Come, stand not amazed at it, but go along with me. I will show you such a necessity in his death that you shall think yourself bound to put it on him. It is now high supper-time, and the night grows to waste. About it.   245

RODERIGO. I will hear further reason for this.

IAGO. And you shall be satisfied.   [Exeunt.]

SCENE III

State Bedroom in the Citadel

[Enter Othello, Lodovico, Desdemona, Emilia, and Attendants.]

LODOVICO. I do beseech you, sir, trouble yourself no further.

OTHELLO. O pardon me; 'twill do me good to walk.

LODOVICO. Madam, good night. I humbly thank your ladyship.

DESDEMONA. Your honor is most welcome.

OTHELLO.   Will you walk, sir?—
O! Desdemona.   5

DESDEMONA. My lord?

OTHELLO. Get you to bed o' the instand. I will be returned forthwith. Dispatch your attendant there. Look it be done.   9

DESDEMONA. I will, my lord.

[Exit Othello, with Lodovico and Attendants.]

EMILIA. How goes it now? He looks gentler than he did.

DESDEMONA. He says he will return incontinent.   12
He hath commanded me to go to bed,
And bade me to dismiss you.

EMILIA.   Dismiss me!

DESDEMONA. It was his bidding. Therefore, good Emilia,
Give me my nightly wearing, and adieu.   16
We must not now displease him.

EMILIA. I would you had never seen him.

DESDEMONA. So would not I. My love doth so approve him,
That even his stubbornness, his checks and frowns,—   20
Prithee, unpin me,—have grace and favor in them.

EMILIA. I have laid those sheets you bade me on the bed.

DESDEMONA. All's one. Good faith! how foolish are our minds!
If I do die before thee, prithee, shroud me   24
In one of those same sheets.

EMILIA.   Come, come, you talk!

DESDEMONA. My mother had a maid call'd Barbary:
She was in love, and he she lov'd prov'd mad
And did forsake her. She had a song of 'willow';   28
An old thing 'twas, but it express'd her fortune,
And she died singing it. That song to-night
Will not go from my mind. I have much to do
But to go hang my head all at one side,   32
And sing it like poor Barbary. Prithee, dispatch.

EMILIA. Shall I go fetch your night-gown?

DESDEMONA.   No, unpin me here.
This Lodovico is a proper man.

EMILIA. A very handsome man.   36

DESDEMONA. He speaks well.

EMILIA. I know a lady in Venice would have walked barefoot to Palestine for a touch of his nether lip.

[Desdemona sings.]

The poor soul sat sighing by a sycamore tree,—   40
    Sing all a green willow.
Her hand on her bosom, her head on her knee,—
    Sing willow, willow, willow.

---

226. **Mauritania:** supposed land of the Moors   228. **lingered:** prolonged   229. **determinate:** decisive   244. **grows to waste:** is wasting away

2. **pardon me:** don't mention it   4. **Will you walk:** shall we start?

12. **incontinent:** immediately   23. **All's one:** no matter   25. **talk:** talk idly   27. **mad:** inconstant, wild   32. **But to:** not to

The fresh streams ran by her, and murmur'd her moans.
  Sing willow, &c.
Her salt tears fell from her, and soften'd the stones.
  Sing willow, &c.

Lay by these.—   48

              Willow, willow.

Prithee, hie thee; he'll come anon.

  Sing all a green willow must be my garland.
  Let nobody blame him, his scorn I approve,—

Nay, that's not next.) Hark! who is it that knocks?
EMILIA. It is the wind.   54
DESDEMONA.

  I call'd my love false love; but what said he then?
    Sing willow, &c.
  If I court mo women, you'll couch with mo men.

Now get thee gone. Good night. Mine eyes do itch;
Does that bode weeping?

EMILIA.   'Tis neither here nor there.
DESDEMONA. I have heard it said so. O these men,
  these men!
Dost thou in conscience think (tell me, Emilia)   61
That there be women do abuse their husbands
In such gross kind?
EMILIA.   There be some such, no question.
DESDEMONA. Wouldst thou do such a deed for all the
  world?   64
EMILIA. Why, would not you?
DESDEMONA.   No, by this heavenly light!
EMILIA. Nor I neither by this heavenly light. I might
do't as well i' th' dark.   67
DESDEMONA. Wouldst thou do such a deed for all the
  world?
EMILIA. The world is a huge thing. It is a great price
for a small vice.
DESDEMONA. Good troth, I think thou wouldst
  not.   71

EMILIA. By my troth, I think I should, and undo't
when I had done it. Marry, I would not do such a
thing for a joint-ring, nor for measures of lawn, nor
for gowns, petticoats, nor caps, nor any petty exhibition. But for the whole world? Ud's pity! who
would not make her husband a cuckold to make him
a monarch? I should venture purgatory for't.   78
DESDEMONA. Beshrew me, if I would do such a
  wrong
For the whole world.
EMILIA. Why, the wrong is but a wrong i' the world;
and having the world for your labor, 'tis a wrong in
your own world, and you might quickly make it
right.
DESDEMONA. I do not think there is any such
  woman.   84
EMILIA. Yes, a dozen; and as many to the vantage,
as would store the world they played for.
⟨But I do think it is their husbands' faults
If wives do fall. Say that they slack their duties,   88
And pour our treasures into foreign laps,
Or else break out in peevish jealousies,
Throwing restraint upon us; or say they strike us,
Or scant our former having in despite;   92
Why, we have galls, and though we have some
  grace,
Yet have we some revenge. Let husbands know
Their wives have sense like them. They see and
  smell,
And have their palates both for sweet and
  sour,   96
As husbands have. What is it that they do
When they change us for others? Is it sport?
I think it is. And doth affection breed it?
I think it doth. Is't frailty that thus errs?   100
It is so too. And have not we affections,
Desires for sport, and frailty as men have?
Then, let them use us well; else let them know,
The ills we do, their ills instruct us so.⟩   104
DESDEMONA. Good night, good night! God me such
  usage send,
Not to pick bad from bad, but by bad mend!

[*Exeunt.*]

72–73. undo't . . . done: see lines 81–83   **74. joint-ring:** ring made
in interlocking halves   **85. to the vantage:** to boot, in addition   **92.
having:** allowance, pin-money   **despite:** spite   **93. galls:** spirit to
resent injury   **95. sense:** sensations, feelings   **99. affection:** inclination   **105. usage:** code of conduct

50. hie thee: make haste

Act V

SCENE I

A Street near Bianca's lodging

[*Enter Iago and Roderigo.*]

IAGO. Here, stand behind this bulk. Straight will he come.
  Wear thy good rapier bare, and put it home.
  Quick, quick. Fear nothing; I'll be at thy elbow.
  It makes us, or it mars us. Think of that,   4
  And fix most firm thy resolution.
RODERIGO. Be near at hand. I may miscarry in't.
IAGO. Here, at thy hand. Be bold, and take thy stand.

[*Retires.*]

RODERIGO. I have no great devotion to the deed;   8
  And yet he has given me satisfying reasons.
  'Tis but a man gone. Forth, my sword! he dies.
IAGO. I have rubb'd this young quat almost to the sense,
  And he grows angry. Now, whether he kill
  Cassio,   12
  Or Cassio him, or each do kill the other,
  Every way makes me gain. Live Roderigo,
  He calls me to a restitution large
  Of gold and jewels that I bobb'd from him,   16
  As gifts to Desdemona.
  It must not be. If Cassio do remain,
  He has a daily beauty in his life
  That makes me ugly; and, besides, the Moor   20
  May unfold me to him. There stand I in peril.
  No, he must die. Be it so! I hear him coming.

[*Enter Cassio.*]

RODERIGO. I know his gait; 'tis he. Villain, thou diest!

[*Makes a pass at Cassio.*]

CASSIO. That thrust had been my enemy indeed   24
  But that my coat is better than thou think'st.
  I will make proof of thine.

[*Draws, and wounds Roderigo.*]

RODERIGO.   O! I am slain!

[*Iago from behind wounds Cassio in the leg, and exit.*]

CASSIO. I am maim'd for ever! Light, ho! murder! murder!   [*Falls.*]

[*Enter Othello at a distance.*]

OTHELLO. The voice of Cassio. Iago keeps his word.
RODERIGO. O villain that I am!
OTHELLO.   Hark! 'Tis even so.   29
CASSIO. O, help, ho! light! a surgeon!
OTHELLO. 'Tis he. O brave Iago, honest and just,
  That hast such noble sense of thy friend's wrong!   32
  Thou teachest me. Minion, your dear lies dead,
  And your fate hies apace. Strumpet, I come!
  Forth of my heart those charms, thine eyes, are blotted.
  Thy bed, lust-stain'd, shall with lust's blood be spotted.   [*Exit Othello.*]   36

[*Enter Lodovico and Gratiano at a distance.*]

CASSIO. What ho! no watch? no passage? murder! murder!
GRATIANO. 'Tis some mischance. The cry is very direful.
CASSIO. O, help!
LODOVICO. Hark!   40
RODERIGO. O wretched villain!
LODOVICO. Two or three groan. It is a heavy night;
  These may be counterfeits. Let's think't unsafe
  To come in to the cry without more help.   44
RODERIGO. Nobody come? then shall I bleed to death.
LODOVICO. Hark!

[*Enter Iago, with a light.*]

GRATIANO. Here's one comes in his shirt, with light and weapons.
IAGO. Who's there? Whose noise is this that cries on murder?   48

---

1. **bulk:** projecting shelter 11. **quat:** pimple (cf. modern 'scab') **sense:** quick 14. **Live Roderigo:** if Roderigo live 16. **bobb'd from him:** cheated him out of 25. **coat:** i.e., he wore defensive armor under his outer garments

33. **Minion:** hussy 37. **passage:** passers-by 42. **heavy:** doleful (cf. V.ii.98) 48. **cries on:** shouts

LODOVICO. We do not know.

IAGO.   Did not you hear a cry?

CASSIO. Here, here! For heaven's sake, help me.

IAGO.   What's the matter?

GRATIANO. This is Othello's ancient, as I take it.

LODOVICO. The same indeed. A very valiant fellow.

IAGO. What are you here that cry so grievously?   53

CASSIO. Iago? O, I am spoil'd, undone by villains!
    Give me some help.

IAGO. O my lieutenant! what villains have done
    this?   56

CASSIO. I think that one of them is hereabout,
    And cannot make away.

IAGO.   O treacherous villains!
    [To Lodovico and Gratiano.] What are you there?
    Come in, and give some help.

RODERIGO. O help me here!   60

CASSIO. That's one of them.

IAGO.   O murderous slave! O
    villain!

[Stabs Roderigo.]

RODERIGO. O damn'd Iago! O inhuman dog!

IAGO. Kill men i' the dark! Where be those bloody
    thieves?
    How silent is this town! Ho! murder! murder!
    What may you be? are you of good or evil?   65

LODOVICO. As you shall prove us, praise us.

IAGO. Signior Lodovico?

LODOVICO. He, sir.   68

IAGO. I cry you mercy. Here's Cassio hurt by villains.

GRATIANO. Cassio?

IAGO. How is it, brother?

CASSIO. My leg is cut in two.

IAGO.   Marry, heaven
    forbid!   72
    Light, gentlemen. I'll bind it with my shirt.

[Enter Bianca.]

BIANCA. What is the matter, ho? who is't that cried?

IAGO. Who is't that cried!

BIANCA. O my dear Cassio! O my sweet Cassio!   76
    Cassio! Cassio!

IAGO. O notable strumpet! Cassio, may you suspect
    Who they should be that thus have mangled you?

CASSIO. No.   80

GRATIANO. I am sorry to find you thus. I have been to
    seek you.

IAGO. Lend me a garter. So. O for a chair,
    To bear him easily hence!

BIANCA. Alas! he faints! O Cassio, Cassio, Cassio!   84

IAGO. Gentlemen all, I do suspect this trash
    To bear a part in this.
    Patience awhile, good Cassio. ⟨Come, come.⟩
    Lend me a light. Know we this face, or no?   88
    Alas! my friend and my dear countryman,
    Roderigo? no: yes, sure. O heaven! Roderigo.

GRATIANO. What? of Venice?

IAGO. Even he, sir. Did you know him?

GRATIANO.   Know him? ay.   92

IAGO. Signior Gratiano? I cry you gentle pardon.
    These bloody accidents must excuse my manners,
    That so neglected you.

GRATIANO.   I am glad to see you.

IAGO. How do you, Cassio? O, a chair, a chair!

GRATIANO. Roderigo!   [A chair brought in.]

IAGO. He. 'Tis he.—O! that's well said; the chair.
    Some good man bear him carefully from hence.
    I'll fetch the general's surgeon. [To Bianca.] For you,
    mistress,   100
    Save you your labor. He that lies slain here, Cassio,
    Was my dear friend. What malice was betwixt you?

CASSIO. None in the world; nor do I know the man.

IAGO. [To Bianca.] What! look you pale? O, bear him
    out o' the air.

[Cassio borne off.]

Stay you, good gentlemen. Look you pale,
    mistress?—   105
    Do you perceive the gastness of her eye?—
    Nay, if you stare, we shall hear more anon.—
    Behold her well, I pray you, look upon her.   108
    Do you see, gentlemen? nay, guiltiness
    Will speak though tongues were out of use.

[Enter Emilia.]

EMILIA. 'Las! what's the matter? what's the matter,
    husband?

IAGO. Cassio has here been set on in the dark   112
    By Roderigo and fellows that are 'scap'd.
    He's almost slain, and Roderigo dead.

EMILIA. Alas, good gentleman! alas, good Cassio!

IAGO. This is the fruit of whoring. Pray, Emilia,   116
    Go know of Cassio where he supp'd to-night—
    What! do you shake at that?

---

59. What: who   **66. praise:** appraise, estimate

82. chair: a plain chair, probably
106. gastness: ghastliness   **117. know:** learn

BIANCA. He supp'd at my house, but I therefore shake
  not.

IAGO. O, did he so? I charge you, go with me.

EMILIA. Fie, fie upon thee, strumpet!   121

BIANCA. I am no strumpet, but of life as honest
  As you that thus abuse me.

EMILIA.   As I! foh! fie upon thee!

IAGO. Kind gentlemen, let's go see poor Cassio
  dress'd.
  Come, mistress, you must tell's another tale.   125
  Emilia, run you to the citadel,
  And tell my lord and lady what has happ'd.
  Will you go on afore? [*Aside.*] This is the night
  That either makes me or fordoes me quite.   129

[*Exeunt.*]

SCENE II

State Bedroom in the Citadel

[*Enter Othello with a light, and Desdemona in her bed.*]

OTHELLO. It is the cause, it is the cause, my soul.
  Let me not name it to you, you chaste stars!
  It is the cause. Yet I'll not shed her blood,
  Nor scar that whiter skin of hers than snow,   4
  And smooth as monumental alabaster.
  Yet she must die, else she'll betray more men.
  Put out the light, and then put out the light.
  If I quench thee, thou flaming minister,   8
  I can again thy former light restore,
  Should I repent me; but once put out thy light,
  Thou cunning'st pattern of excelling nature,
  I know not where is that Promethean heat   12
  That can thy light relume. When I have pluck'd thy
    rose,
  I cannot give it vital growth again.
  It needs must wither. I'll smell it on the tree.

[*He kisses her.*]

  O balmy breath, that doth almost persuade   16
  Justice to break her sword! One more, one more.
  Be thus when thou art dead, and I will kill thee
  And love thee after. Once more, and this the last!

So sweet was ne'er so fatal. I must weep,   20
  But they are cruel tears. This sorrow's heavenly,
  It strikes where it doth love. She wakes.

DESDEMONA. Who's there? Othello?

OTHELLO.   Ay, Desdemona.

DESDEMONA. Will you come to bed, my lord?   24

OTHELLO. Have you pray'd to-night, Desdemon?

DESDEMONA.   Ay, my lord.

OTHELLO. If you bethink yourself of any crime
  Unreconcil'd as yet to heaven and grace,
  Solicit for it straight.   28

DESDEMONA. Alas, my lord, what may you mean by
    that?

OTHELLO. Well, do it, and be brief. I will walk by.
  I would not kill thy unprepared spirit.
  No (heaven forfend!), I would not kill thy soul.   32

DESDEMONA. Talk you of killing?

OTHELLO.   Ay, I do.

DESDEMONA.   Then heaven
  Have mercy on me!

OTHELLO.   Amen! with all my heart.

DESDEMONA. If you say so, I hope you will not kill
    me.

OTHELLO. Humh!   36

DESDEMONA. And yet I fear you; for you are fatal
    then
  When your eyes roll so. Why I should fear I know
    not,
  Since guiltiness I know not; but yet I feel I fear.

OTHELLO. Think on thy sins.

DESDEMONA.   They are loves I bear to you.   40

OTHELLO. Ay, and for that thou diest.

DESDEMONA. That death's unnatural that kills for lov-
    ing.
  Alas, why gnaw you so your nether lip?
  Some bloody passion shakes your very frame.   44
  These are porténts, but yet, I hope, I hope,
  They do not point on me.

OTHELLO.   Peace, and be still!

DESDEMONA. I will so. What's the matter?

OTHELLO. That handkerchief which I so lov'd and
    gave thee
  Thou gav'st to Cassio.

DESDEMONA.   No, by my life and soul!   49
  Send for the man and ask him.

OTHELLO.   Sweet soul, take heed,
  Take heed of perjury. Thou'rt on thy death-bed.

DESDEMONA. Ay, but not yet to die.

---

129. fordoes: unmakes, destroys
12. Promethean heat: divine fire   **13. relume:** rekindle

27. grace: God's mercy   **28. Solicit:** pray   **30. by:** apart   **32. forfend:** forbid

OTHELLO.   Yes, presently.   52
Therefore confess thee freely of thy sin;
For to deny each article with oath
Cannot remove nor choke the strong conception
That I do groan withal. Thou art to die.   56
DESDEMONA. Then Lord have mercy on me!
OTHELLO.   I say, amen.
DESDEMONA. And have you mercy too! I never did
Offend you in my life; never lov'd Cassio
But with such general warranty of heaven   60
As I might love. I never gave him token.
OTHELLO. By heaven, I saw my handkerchief in his
hand.
O perjur'd woman! thou dost stone my heart,
And mak'st me call what I intend to do   64
A murder, which I thought a sacrifice.
I saw the handkerchief.
DESDEMONA.   He found it then.
I never gave it him. Send for him hither;
Let him confess a truth.
OTHELLO.   He has confess'd.   68
DESDEMONA. What, my lord?
OTHELLO. That he hath—uds death!
DESDEMONA.   How? unlawfully?
OTHELLO. Ay.
DESDEMONA. He will not say so.
OTHELLO.   No; his mouth is
stopp'd.
Honest Iago hath ta'en order for't.   72
DESDEMONA. O! my fear interprets. What! is he dead?
OTHELLO. Had all his hairs been lives, my great
revenge
Had stomach for them all.
DESDEMONA. Alas, he is betray'd and I undone!   76
OTHELLO. O strumpet! Weep'st thou for him to my
face?
DESDEMONA. O, banish me, my lord, but kill me not!
OTHELLO. Down, strumpet!
DESDEMONA. Kill me to-morrow; let me live to-
night!   80
OTHELLO. Nay, an you strive,—
DESDEMONA. But half an hour!
OTHELLO.   Being done, there is no pause.
DESDEMONA. But while I say one prayer!
OTHELLO.   It is too late. [He stifles her.]
DESDEMONA. O Lord, Lord, Lord!   84

[Emilia calls within.] My lord, my lord! what, ho! my
lord, my lord!
OTHELLO. What noise is this? Not dead? not yet quite
dead?
I that am cruel am yet merciful;
I would not have thee linger in thy pain.   88
So, so.
EMILIA. [within]. What, ho! my lord, my lord!
OTHELLO.   Who's there?
EMILIA. [within]. O! good my lord, I'ld speak a word
with you.
OTHELLO. Yes; 'tis Emilia.—By and by.—She's dead.
'Tis like she comes to speak of Cassio's death.   92
The noise was high. Ha! no more moving?
Still as the grave. Shall she come in? Were't good?
I think she stirs again: no. What's the best?
If she come in, she'll sure speak to my wife: 96
My wife! my wife! what wife? I have no wife:
O, insupportable! O heavy hour!
Methinks it should be now a huge eclipse
Of sun and moon, and that the affrighted
globe   100
Should yawn at alteration.
EMILIA. [within].   I do beseech you
That I may speak with you, O good my lord.
OTHELLO. I had forgot thee. O, come in, Emilia!—
Soft, by and by.—Let me the curtains
draw.—   104
Where art thou?   [Unlocks the door.]

[Enter Emilia.]

                            What's the matter with thee now?
EMILIA. O! my good lord, yonder's foul murders
done.
OTHELLO. What! how?
EMILIA.   But now, my lord.
OTHELLO. It is the very error of the moon.   108
She comes more near the earth than she was wont,
And makes men mad.
EMILIA. Cassio, my lord, has kill'd a young Venetian
Call'd Roderigo.
OTHELLO.   Roderigo kill'd!   112
And Cassio kill'd!
EMILIA.   No, Cassio is not kill'd.
OTHELLO. Not Cassio kill'd! then murder's out of
tune,
And sweet revenge grows harsh.
DESDEMONA. O falsely, falsely murder'd.

---

60. general . . . heaven: permission granted by heaven to all **63. stone:** make stony **72. order:** measures **75. stomach:** appetite

95. What's the best: 'what's best to do?' **104. Soft:** stop, wait **107. But:** just **108. error:** aberration

EMILIA.   O Lord! what cry is that?   116
OTHELLO. That? what?
EMILIA. Out and alas! it is my lady's voice.
   Help! Help, ho! help! O lady, speak again!
   Sweet Desdemona! O sweet mistress, speak!   120
DESDEMONA. A guiltless death I die.
EMILIA. O! who has done this deed?
DESDEMONA. Nobody. I myself. Farewell!
   Commend me to my kind lord. O farewell!
   [She dies.]
OTHELLO. Why, how should she be murder'd?
EMILIA.   Alas, who knows?   125
OTHELLO. You heard her say herself it was not I.
EMILIA. She said so. I must needs report a truth.
OTHELLO. She's like a liar gone to burning hell.   128
   'Twas I that kill'd her.
EMILIA.   O the more angel she,
   And you the blacker devil.
OTHELLO. She turn'd to folly, and she was a whore.
EMILIA. Thou dost belie her, and thou art a
   devil.   132
OTHELLO. She was false as water.
EMILIA.   Thou art rash as fire to say
   That she was false. O she was heavenly true.
OTHELLO. Cassio did top her. Ask thy husband else.
   O I were damn'd beneath all depth in hell   136
   But that I did proceed upon just grounds
   To this extremity. Thy husband knew it all.
EMILIA. My husband?
OTHELLO. Thy husband.   140
EMILIA. That she was false to wedlock?
OTHELLO. Ay, with Cassio. Nay, had she been true,
   If heaven would make me such another world
   Of one entire and perfect chrysolite,   144
   I'd not have sold her for it.
EMILIA. My husband?
OTHELLO.   Ay, 'twas he that told me first.
   An honest man he is, and hates the slime
   That sticks on filthy deeds.
EMILIA.   My husband?   148
OTHELLO. What needs this iterance, woman? I say thy
   husband.
EMILIA. O mistress! villainy hath made mocks with
   love.
   My husband say that she was false?
OTHELLO.   He, woman.
   I say, thy husband; dost understand the word?   152
   My friend, thy husband, honest, honest Iago.

EMILIA. If he say so, may his pernicious soul
   Rot half a grain a day! He lies to the heart.
   She was too fond of her most filthy bargain.   156
OTHELLO. Ha!
EMILIA. Do thy worst.
   This deed of thine is no more worthy heaven
   Than thou wast worthy her.
OTHELLO.   Peace! you were best.   160
EMILIA. Thou hast not half the power to do me harm
   As I have to be hurt. O gull! O dolt!
   As ignorant as dirt! Thou hast done a deed,—
   I care not for thy sword. I'll make thee
   known,   164
   Though I lost twenty lives. Help! help, ho! help!
   The Moor has kill'd my mistress! Murder! murder!

[Enter Montano, Gratiano, Iago, and others.]

MONTANO. What is the matter? How now, general?
EMILIA. O, are you come, Iago? You have done
   well,   168
   That men must lay their murders on your neck.
GRATIANO. What is the matter?
EMILIA. Disprove this villain if thou be'st a man:
   He says thou told'st him that his wife was
   false.   172
   I know thou didst not. Thou'rt not such a villain.
   Speak, for my heart is full.
IAGO. I told him what I thought, and told no more
   Than what he found himself was apt and true.   176
EMILIA. But did you ever tell him she was false?
IAGO. I did.
EMILIA. You told a lie, an odious damned lie;
   Upon my soul, a lie, a wicked lie.   180
   She false with Cassio! Did you say with Cassio?
IAGO. With Cassio, mistress. Go to, charm your
   tongue.
EMILIA. I will not charm my tongue; I am bound to
   speak.
   My mistress here lies murder'd in her bed.   184
ALL. O heavens forfend!
EMILIA. And your reports have set the murder on.
OTHELLO. Nay, stare not, masters. It is true indeed.
GRATIANO. 'Tis a strange truth.   188
MONTANO. O monstrous act!
EMILIA.   Villainy! villainy!
   villainy!
   I think upon't, I think, I smell't. O villainy!
   I thought so then. I'll kill myself for grief.
   O villainy, villainy!

---

131. folly: unchastity **143. such another:** another such (as large as this one) **144. chrysolite:** a precious stone, green in color **149. iterance:** repetition **150. made mocks with:** made a dupe of

162. gull: fool **182. charm:** silence, as if by a magic spell

IAGO. What! are you mad? I charge you, get you
    home.

EMILIA. Good gentlemen, let me have leave to speak.
    'Tis proper I obey him, but not now.
    Perchance, Iago, I will ne'er go home.   196

OTHELLO. Oh! Oh! Oh!   [*Othello falls on the bed.*]

EMILIA.   Nay, lay thee down and roar,
    For thou hast kill'd the sweetest innocent
    That e'er did lift up eye.

OTHELLO.   O! she was foul.
    I scarce did know you, uncle. There lies your
    niece,   200
    Whose breath, indeed, these hands have newly
    stopp'd.
    I know this act shows terrible and grim.

GRATIANO. Poor Desdemon, I am glad thy father's
    dead.
    Thy match was mortal to him, and pure grief   204
    Shore his old thread a-twain. Did he live now,
    This sight would make him do a desperate turn,
    Yea, curse his better angel from his side,
    And fall to reprobation.   208

OTHELLO. 'Tis pitiful; but yet Iago knows
    That she with Cassio hath the act of shame
    A thousand times committed. Cassio confess'd it;
    And she did gratify his amorous works   212
    With the recognizance and pledge of love
    Which I first gave her. I saw it in his hand.
    It was a handkerchief, an antique token
    My father gave my mother.   216

EMILIA. O God! O heavenly God!

IAGO.   Zounds! hold your peace.

EMILIA. 'Twill out, 'twill out! I hold my peace, sir?
    No!
    No, I will speak as liberal as the north.
    Let heaven and men and devils, let them all,   220
    All, all, cry shame against me, yet I'll speak.

IAGO. Be wise, and get you home.

EMILIA.   I will not.

[*Iago threatens Emilia.*]

GRATIANO.   Fie!
    Your sword upon a woman?

EMILIA. O thou dull Moor! that handkerchief thou
    speak'st of   224
    I found by fortune and did give my husband,
    For often with a solemn earnestness

(More than, indeed, belong'd to such a trifle)
    He begg'd of me to steal it.

IAGO.   Villainous whore!   228

EMILIA. She give it Cassio? No, alas! I found it,
    And I did give't my husband.

IAGO.   Filth, thou liest!

EMILIA. By heaven, I do not. I do not, gentlemen.
    O murderous coxcomb! what should such a
    fool   232
    Do with so good a wife?

OTHELLO.   Are there no stones in heaven
    But what serves for the thunder? Precious villain!

[*The Moor runs at Iago. Iago kills his wife.*]

GRATIANO. The woman falls. Sure, he has kill'd his
    wife.   [*Exit Iago.*]

EMILIA. Ay, ay. O lay me by my mistress' side.   236

GRATIANO. He's gone, but his wife's kill'd.

MONTANO. 'Tis a notorious villain. [*To Gratiano.*] Take
    you this weapon,
    Which I have here recover'd from the Moor.
    Come, guard the door without. Let him not
    pass,   240
    But kill him rather. I'll after that same villain,
    For 'tis a damned slave.   [*Ex. Montano and Gratiano.*]

OTHELLO.   I am not valiant neither,
    But every puny whipster gets my sword.
    But why should honor outlive honesty?   244
    Let it go all.

EMILIA.   What did thy song bode, lady?
    Hark, canst thou hear me? I will play the swan,
    And die in music.   [*Sings.*]

         Willow, willow, willow.   248

Moor, she was chaste. She lov'd thee, cruel Moor.
    So come my soul to bliss as I speak true.
    So speaking as I think, I die, I die.   [*She dies.*]

OTHELLO. I have another weapon in this
    chamber.   252
    It is a sword of Spain, the ice brook's temper.
    O here it is.—Uncle, I must come forth.

GRATIANO [*within*]. If thou attempt it, it will cost thee
    dear.
    Thou hast no weapon, and perforce must
    suffer.   256

---

205. **Shore:** cut   206. **do . . . turn:** commit some desperate deed
208. **reprobation:** damnation   213. **recognizance:** token   219. **as . . . north:** as freely and strongly as the north wind

239. **recover'd:** taken   243. **whipster:** (cf. modern whipper-snapper) stripling   244. **honor:** mere dignity   **honesty:** fundamental righteousness   253. **ice brook's temper:** tempered in icy water

OTHELLO. Look in upon me then, and speak to me,
　Or, naked as I am, I will assault thee.

[*Enter Gratiano.*]

GRATIANO. What is the matter?
OTHELLO.　　　　　　　　Behold! I have a weapon.
　A better never did itself sustain　　　　　　260
　Upon a soldier's thigh. I have seen the day
　That with this little arm and this good sword
　I have made my way through more impediments
　Than twenty times your stop. But O vain
　　boast!　　　　　　　　　　　　　　　264
　Who can control his fate? 'Tis not so now.
　⟨Be not afraid, though you do see me weapon'd.
　Here is my journey's end, here is my butt
　And very sea-mark of my utmost sail.　　　268
　Do you go back dismay'd? 'Tis a lost fear.
　Man but a rush against Othello's breast,
　And he retires. Where should Othello go?—
　Now, how dost thou look now? O ill-starr'd
　　wench!⟩　　　　　　　　　　　　　　272
　Pale as thy smock! When we shall meet at compt,
　This look of thine will hurl my soul from heaven,
　And fiends will snatch at it. Cold, cold, my girl,
　Even like thy chastity.　　　　　　　　276
　O cursed, cursed slave! Whip me, ye devils,
　From the possession of this heavenly sight!
　Blow me about in winds! roast me in sulphur!
　Wash me in steep-down gulfs of liquid fire!　280
　O Desdemona! Desdemona! dead!
　O! O! O!

[*Enter Lodovico, Montano, Iago (prisoner), and Officers, Cassio in a chair.*]

LODOVICO. Where is this rash and most unfortunate
　man?
OTHELLO. That's he that was Othello. Here I
　am.　　　　　　　　　　　　　　　　284
LODOVICO. Where is that viper? bring the villain
　forth.
OTHELLO. I look down towards his feet, but that's a
　fable.
　If that thou be'st a devil, I cannot kill thee.

[*Wounds Iago.*]

258. naked: unarmed (as Gratiano supposed)　**264. stop:** power of prevention　**267. butt:** goal (literally, target)　**268. sea-mark:** beacon, limit　**269. lost:** wasted, unnecessary　**270. Man:** wield　**rush:** bulrush, reed　**273. compt:** reckoning, on the Judgment Day　**278. possession:** haunting obsession　**286. I look for the devil's outward sign, a cloven hoof**

LODOVICO. Wring his sword from him.
IAGO.　　　　　　　I bleed, sir, but not kill'd.　288
OTHELLO. I am not sorry neither. I'd have thee live,
　For in my sense 'tis happiness to die.
LODOVICO. O thou Othello that wert once so good,
　Fall'n in the practice of a damned slave,　292
　What shall be said to thee?
OTHELLO.　　　　　　　　Why, anything:
　An honorable murderer, if you will;
　For nought did I in hate, but all in honor.
LODOVICO. This wretch hath part confess'd his villainy.　　　　　　　　　　　　　296
　Did you and he consent in Cassio's death?
OTHELLO. Ay.
CASSIO. Dear general, I did never give you cause.
OTHELLO. I do believe it, and I ask you pardon.　300
　Will you, I pray, demand that demi-devil
　Why he hath thus ensnar'd my soul and body.
IAGO. Demand me nothing. What you know, you
　know:
　From this time forth I never will speak word.　304
LODOVICO. What! not to pray?
GRATIANO.　　　　　　　Torments will ope your lips.
OTHELLO. Well, thou dost best.
LODOVICO. Sir, you shall understand what hath
　befall'n,
　Which, as I think, you know not. Here is a
　　letter　　　　　　　　　　　　　　308
　Found in the pocket of the slain Roderigo,
　And here another. The one of them imports
　The death of Cassio to be undertook
　By Roderigo.　　　　　　　　　　312
OTHELLO. O villain!
CASSIO.　　　　　　Most heathenish and most gross!
LODOVICO. Now here's another discontented paper,
　Found in his pocket too; and this, it seems,
　Roderigo mean t' have sent this damned
　　villain,　　　　　　　　　　　　316
　But that, belike, Iago in the nick
　Came in and satisfied him.
OTHELLO. O the pernicious caitiff!
　How came you, Cassio, by that handkerchief
　That was my wife's?
CASSIO.　　　　　　I found it in my chamber;　320
　And he himself confess'd it even now
　That there he drop'd it for a special purpose
　Which wrought to his desire.
OTHELLO.　　　　　　　　O fool! fool! fool!

292. practice: sinister scheme　**317. nick:** nick of time

CASSIO. There is besides in Roderigo's letter   324
    How he upbraids Iago that he made him
    Brave me upon the watch, whereon it came
    That I was cast: and even but now he spake
    (After long seeming dead): Iago hurt him,   328
    Iago set him on.
LODOVICO. You must forsake this room and go with
    us.
    Your power and your command is taken off,
    And Cassio rules in Cyprus. For this slave,   332
    If there be any cunning cruelty
    That can torment him much and hold him long,
    It shall be his. You shall close prisoner rest,
    Till that the nature of your fault be known   336
    To the Venetian state. Come, bring him away.
OTHELLO. Soft you! A word or two before you go.
    I have done the state some service, and they know't;
    No more of that. I pray you, in your letters,   340
    When you shall these unlucky deeds relate,
    Speak of them as they are. Nothing extenuate,
    Nor set down aught in malice. Then must you speak
    Of one that lov'd not wisely but too well;   344
    Of one not easily jealous, but, being wrought,
    Perplex'd in the extreme; of one whose hand
    (Like the base Indian) threw a pearl away
    Richer than all his tribe; of one whose súbdu'd
    eyes,   348
    Albeit unused to the melting mood,

    Drops tears as fast as the Arabian trees
    Their méd'cinable gum. Set you down this;
    And say besides, that in Aleppo once,   352
    Where a malignant and a turban'd Turk
    Beat a Venetian and traduc'd the state,
    I took by the throat the circumcised dog,
    And smote him thus.   [He stabs himself.]
LODOVICO. O bloody period!
GRATIANO.   All that's spoke is marr'd.   357
OTHELLO. I kiss'd thee ere I kill'd thee. No way but
    this,
    Killing myself to die upon a kiss.   [He dies.]
CASSIO. This did I fear, but thought he had no
    weapon;
    For he was great of heart.
LODOVICO.   [To Iago.] O Spartan dog,   361
    More fell than anguish, hunger, or the sea,
    Look on the tragic loading of this bed!
    This is thy work. The object poisons sight;   364
    Let it be hid, Gratiano, keep the house,
    And seize upon the fortunes of the Moor,
    For they succeed to you. To you, lord governor,
    Remains the censure of this hellish villain,   368
    The time, the place, the torture. O, enforce it!
    Myself will straight aboard, and to the state
    This heavy act with heavy heart relate.

[Exeunt omnes.]

---

357. **period:** ending, close   361. **Spartan:** for fierceness and taciturnity   362. **fell:** deadly   366. **seize upon:** take legal possession of   367. **succeed:** descend in succession (as nearest relative of Desdemona)   369. **enforce it:** make it severe.

331. **taken off:** revoked   345. **wrought:** wrought upon, worked up   346. **Perplex'd:** desperately troubled

ESSAY: AN APPROACH TO THE PLAY

In our Introduction we encouraged you to see texts as open rather than closed—open to many different ways of reading—and we also encouraged you to see yourselves as readers who complete the cycle of communication which the author opens. We would like to go further and suggest that each way of interpreting involves a choice not only to read in one way instead of another, but to accept one set of assumptions about life in the world rather than another, to see that our assumptions about ourselves, about society, and about the act of reading itself govern the way we read. *Othello* provides an excellent example. It has become a truism that Shakespeare, as the primary cultural icon of our language, is the writer whose work every new critical position seeks to capture as its exemplar. As a result, his work is under continual critical revision, and in recent years this seems to be particularly true of *Othello*. The play's dominant readings over the years have been based on the assumption that Othello and Desdemona are both noble and virtuous characters who are destroyed by the evil manipulations of Iago. In this traditional view, Iago is a self-confessed villain quite different and separate from his Venetian society (note his praise of self-serving hypocrisy at 1.1.41–65), and it is his devilish skill (see 5.2.286–288 for a suggestion of Iago's devilish qualities) which acts *upon* his essentially passive and unsuspecting victims. In recent years, however, this view of the play has been called into question from several social (and therefore critical) perspectives. This reading assumes that the play presents Venetian society as essentially fair-minded (rather like us, of course) and that Iago's villainy is therefore aberrant. However, such readings mystify that society (and ours) by making it seem benign or even enlightened in that it seems to sanction a black man's nobility and an interracial marriage. By defining Iago as alienated from "normal" Venetian values of fairness, the larger society can remain guiltless in the tragedy. By concentrating on Desdemona's moral virtue and integrity, the limitations of her gender role and the fact of her acceptance of it can be ignored. By concentrating on Othello's nobility, the fact of his blackness in a white society is rendered unemphatic. To a very large degree, this traditional reading obscures the degree to which our sense of identity is constructed for us by our society, and yet awareness of this issue may be the essential condition of a free mind.

Earlier in this century, under the influence of a pervasive interest in psychology, chinks began to be seen in Othello's nobility. For instance, to the crucial question, "Why does Othello trust Iago instead of Desdemona if he loves her so?" the answer posed was that he is somehow inwardly blind and that their love may not be so ideal as it seems. His summary of their courtship and love (see especially 1.3.167–168) makes it seem that the relationship's primary appeal is that it strengthens his ego while feeding the previously sheltered rich girl's desire for vicarious adventure. In this view, Othello's famous final speech (particularly 5.2.342–346) seems not a noble perception of the truth but the continuation of a tragic blindness he has displayed throughout the play, now reduced to the level of being self-serving. Although this reading puts some of the responsibility for the tragedy on Othello's own inner nature, it continues to consider Iago an alienated villain, both Desdemona and her society unproblematical, and Othello's blackness still a non-issue.

By contrast, many contemporary readings have considered Venetian society to be culpable: It has created the circumstances in which the destruction of black Othello and female Desdemona seem nearly inevitable and in which Iago is a conscious enactor of the very values which Venetian society itself subconsciously holds. We will present here one such reading which incorporates many aspects of the play confronted by contemporary critics. We will do so by focusing on one character at a time, trying in this way to compromise neither the complexity nor the clarity of these issues.

Othello   He is an outsider who has succeeded by his own abilities in an alien society. A black African, presumably a Muslim by birth and perhaps still so, he does the work of white European Christians by leading their army against people more like himself (the Turks) than the Venetians are. In his desire to succeed and be accepted in Venice, he has been mentally "colonized": He has come to adopt the values of, and has come to think like, members of the Venetian ruling class. He even marries a Venetian aristocrat, a match which seems to solidify the social status he has earned. And yet, for all his success and for all his power, he remains insecure. This insecurity may be suggested initially by the ego-gratifying nature of his relationship with Desdemona; its potential for tragedy seems inherent in the nature of their love and in the values of the culture in which they live. Love breeds insecurity by its very nature, insofar as we allow ourselves to be vulnerable to our beloved; this insecurity is heightened in the degree to which (1) one depends on the relationship and (2) one is different from the beloved. Othello's relationship seems likely to maximize this insecurity. Presumably he realizes that the republic he serves is racist; in the first scene the speeches of Roderigo, Iago, and Brabantio make such an attitude seem extremely deep-seated. Othello, having internalized Venetian values so fundamentally, may have come to see himself, at some level of consciousness, as an alien, as a potential threat, perhaps even as a beast (to adopt Iago's characterization), and yet he must act counter to this set of perceptions whenever he is to act in his own self-interest. He can marry Desdemona only by eloping, and Brabantio and Iago never entirely let him forget this contradiction—that he has "stolen" his wife.

In business-minded Venice (Iago in particular is full of references to money, some literal and some metaphoric, but notice Lodovico, the Venetian spokesman, at the end—5.2.365–367—and Brabantio's "theft" references in 1.1), there is great emphasis on the importance of possession and on the power which derives from it. This emphasis highlights an aspect of love as well, one which, though true to experience, is often obscured by what we normally believe. It is usual to associate love with desire, and desire with romantic fulfillment as well as with lust. However, in some relationships desire may be less a function of love than of the need to possess, of the need to be in relationship rather than alone, and of the need to cement that relationship by controlling the partner. This form of desire is felt particularly by the insecure, and it virtually guarantees feelings of jealousy. A male-dominant society which requires mastery of one's wife as a sign of masculine identity intensifies the male need to control; when this pressure is applied to a man who is unsure of his place in that society, feelings of insecurity which lead to jealousy and which are self-threatening are doubly intensified. In this assessment of love, we might decide that Othello believes Iago because Iago tells him that what he is already prepared to fear is true. These fears, then, become a self-fulfilling prophecy: With Iago's help, he believes they are already enacted, that they are history, not prophecy. And he fulfills Iago's prejudices about himself: In his language, beginning in Act 3, he actually does become bestial, just as he will later in deed as well. He himself makes his own worst nightmare into truth.

Desdemona   The key question to ask of her may be why she remains loyal to Othello. Perhaps she, too, is colonized by her society, has come to accept as "true" or "natural" the values of a society that defines her as inferior and that limits her freedom. Her culture asks her to be a wife who is erotic, obedient, and loyal. Because she accommodates herself to this role so well, both her society *and she herself* believe this role to be natural, the way woman is, rather than constructed. However, because eroticism and obedience are seen as natural, this perfect woman cannot be mastered by her husband. For if Desdemona's eroticism and obedience are not seen as induced by Othello, but rather as natural aspects of what it is to be a woman, then Othello can never feel confident that he "controls" her, even though he must if he is to think himself a true Venetian. Desdemona is all too eager to try to fulfill the roles expected of her. She is willing to serve as a token, a medium of exchange transferred from Brabantio to Othello and conferring value on its owner. She is compliant and deferential to her husband; indeed, it is because she maintains virtuous silence about the injustice done to her that Iago can manipulate her. However, the more Desdemona tries to be perfect in a world of such contradictory values, the more she defeats herself. The only way to be perfect in such a world, it seems, is to be dead, a beautiful but changeless thing (see 5.2.18–19).

The Other Women   Emilia is no revolutionary, and like Desdemona she is marginalized in her society. However, there are moments when she provides a female consciousness which is an alternative to that of Desdemona. Particularly in one speech in Act 4 (3.85–104), she asserts the equality of women, and when at last she learns the truth about her husband, she speaks out in accusation. Bianca, the only woman whom Shakespeare allows to live throughout the play, is submissive and erotic without expecting marriage, or (a variation on Iago's view) she is a prostitute, an independent businesswoman who fits in with, or at least does not threaten, Venetian values. Both of these characters suggest a larger view of women than the rest of the characters provide, and this view offers the reader an opening within the text itself for alternative readings of these other characters.

Iago   There are two key questions to ask about him: What is the source of his power? And why does he do what he does? He is the embodiment of Venetian values but, unlike Venice, he is completely aware of his hypocrisy, and his racism is consciously self-serving rather than believed to be natural. This self-awareness is certainly an important source of his power, as it allows him to bring unspoken Venetian values to the surface, where they can be actively used. However, although his ambition (including vengeance) is conscious, the sexism with which it is allied (as it is with Othello) may not be. The fact that it is he who supplies the images of carnal infidelity so graphically, first to Brabantio and then to Othello, may therefore suggest that he, too, is obsessed with Desdemona. From this perspective, we could think of Iago as Othello's psychic twin. In activating the imagining of Desdemona's infidelity to Othello, he gratifies himself not only by destroying his master and his lady, but by enjoying her in his own imagination—this may be the decisive aspect of Iago's otherwise enigmatic motivation. For Othello's receptive imagination, Iago enacts his own fantasy. In a sexist society, it may seem natural that male Othello would believe male Iago before female Desdemona (and that she be denied a voice in her own defense). Their ways of seeing and feeling are so similar that their male bonding may well seem inevitable, and this, too, is a source of Iago's power. Indeed, his Venetian qualities may provide him with both his motive for victimizing Othello and his ability to succeed in it.

Metadrama and Its Construction of Character and Plot   Othello wins Desdemona, he *tells* the Senate (and incidentally us in the play's audience) in Act 1, by telling her stories. His self-presentation in both cases is an enactment, a role geared toward a specific audience to achieve a desired emotional effect. In Act 5, just before killing himself, Othello again tries to direct how people will tell his story, the interpretive angle from which it will be seen (5.2.340–356). In a different way, Iago, too, invents a fiction (that Desdemona is sleeping with Cassio) and gets everyone in the cast to participate in enacting some role in that fiction. In this sense, *Othello* is doubly Iago's play: It is about him as much as about Othello, and he is the one who creates its plot and directs its presentation. He himself, moreover, is the actor personified, the person who can take on any role because he *seems* to have no core identity ("I am not what I am"—1.1.65), *even though he does* (see above: the idea that his fiction enacts his own obsession with Desdemona, as well as Othello's). Finally, in the play's last couplet, Lodovico, the state's spokesman, says that he will indeed tell the story "to the state." Is our play, then, a reenactment of Lodovico's story? If so, is it the version Othello had in mind? Is it a version that is crafted so that the state will not be offended? Perhaps even so that it will be reaffirmed? As usual, Shakespeare, who himself had to submit his plays to a censor before they were performed, reminds us that his play is a re-presentation, a constructed work, possibly constructed to achieve some purpose. As he thus deconstructs his work, he insinuates himself within it, reminding us that it is not "true," but his fiction. We might then ask: Does Shakespeare here affirm or expose Venetian values? Is Iago (and Lodovico) Shakespeare's substitute or device? Either could be "true"; an answer is likely to be based on what one chooses to believe about Shakespeare.

THE SEVENTEENTH AND EIGHTEENTH CENTURIES

Molière

TARTUFFE

Translated by Curtis Hidden Page

About the Author   Molière, the stage name by which we know Jean Baptiste Poqueline (1622–1673), defied family and church for a theatrical career. Born in Paris, he spent a dozen years in a touring company of professional actors in the provinces before returning to his birthplace in 1658. As a result of these diverse theatrical experiences, his work after this date often combines elements of popular dramatic forms (such as the stereotypically exaggerated characters of the *commedia dell'arte* tradition) with the more restrained neoclassical comedy of manners, a convention admired by his aristocratic Parisian audience. As actor and playwright in his own theater, and working under royal patronage, he and his plays were continuously successful for the remaining fifteen years of his life.

He is important to the history of English, as well as French, theater because he became the model of taste for the seventeenth-century English royalists, many of whom, after they lost the civil war to Oliver Cromwell, lived within the French aristocratic circle in Paris. When the English monarchy was restored in 1660, these aristocrats returned to England and carried with them to the London stage a familiarity with the conventions of French comedy which he helped shape. (The subject of English royalist exiles in another country, Spain, is the partial subject of Aphra Behn's play *The Rover,* also printed in this volume; her play exemplifies both the modifications that the English tended to make in Molière's version of the comedy of manners and their indebtedness to him.)

Molière's death brought together his love of the theater and his defiance of convention in a cruelly ironic way: He died as a result of a hemorrhage in his lungs which occurred while he was on stage, acting the last scene of one of his own plays, a play titled *The Imaginary Invalid*.

About the Play   The playwright first produced *Tartuffe* in 1664 in three acts, then revised it for five years before presenting it again, this time in its full five-act form. Its success was immediate and, over the centuries, it has continued to be presented more frequently than any of Molière's other plays. Like many of these other plays, it is essentially a drawing room comedy of manners: Its main scenes occur indoors, within a stage designed to make these scenes seem realistic. Much of the humor in this genre comes from the ways in which characters are governed—often, we might say enslaved—by social custom, including their sometimes rigid attempts to live up to customs that will gain them the acceptance of fashionable society.

Typically in Molière, then, it is the characters who make a play memorable. He is able to enlarge the dimensions of his mannered contemporary subjects so that they retain their significance for us still. This is especially the case with this play's title character, the religious hypocrite Tartuffe. In contemporary terms, we might find similar examples not only in the more charismatic kind of religious leaders but also in many politicians who claim to stand for reform and, therefore, in some way "for the people."

CHARACTERS

MADAME PERNELLE, mother of Orgon
ORGON, husband of Elmire
ELMIRE, wife of Orgon
DAMIS, son of Orgon
MARIANE, daughter of Orgon, in love with Valère
VALÈRE, in love with Mariane
CLÉANTE, brother-in-law of Orgon

TARTUFFE, a hypocrite
DORINE, Mariane's maid
MR. LOYAL, a bailiff
A Police Officer
FLIPOTTE, Madame Pernelle's servant

SCENE: Paris

Act I

SCENE I

[*Madame Pernelle and Flipotte, her servant; Elmire, Mariane, Cléante, Damis, Dorine*]

MADAME PERNELLE. Come, come, Flipotte, and let
   me get away.
ELMIRE. You hurry so, I hardly can attend you.
MADAME PERNELLE. Then don't, my daughter-in-
   law. Stay where you are.
   I can dispense with your polite attentions.
ELMIRE. We're only paying what is due you, mother.
   Why must you go away in such a hurry?
MADAME PERNELLE. Because I can't endure your
   carryings-on,
   And no one takes the slightest pains to please me.
   I leave your house, I tell you, quite disgusted;
   You do the opposite of my instructions;
   You've no respect for anything; each one
   Must have his say; it's perfect pandemonium.
DORINE. If . .
MADAME PERNELLE. You're a servant wench, my girl,
   and much
   Too full of gab, and too impertinent
   And free with your advice on all occasions.
DAMIS. But . . .
MADAME PERNELLE. You're a fool, my boy—f, o, o, l
   Just spells your name. Let grandma tell you that
   I've said a hundred times to my poor son,
   Your father, that you'd never come to good
   Or give him anything but plague and torment.
MARIANE. I think . . .
MADAME PERNELLE. O dearie me, his little sister!
   You're all demureness, butter wouldn't melt
   In *your* mouth, one would think to look at you.
   Still waters, though, they say . . . you know the
   proverb;

And I don't like your doings on the sly.
ELMIRE. But, mother . . .
MADAME PERNELLE. Daughter, by your leave, your
   conduct
   In everything is altogether wrong;
   You ought to set a good example for 'em;
   Their dear departed mother did much better.
   You are extravagant; and it offends me,
   To see you always decked out like a princess.
   A woman who would please her husband's eye
   Alone, wants no such wealth of fineries.
CLÉANTE. But, madam, after all . . .
MADAME PERNELLE.   Sir, as for you,
   The lady's brother, I esteem you highly,
   Love and respect you. But, sir, all the same,
   If I were in my son's, her husband's, place,
   I'd urgently entreat you not to come
   Within our doors. You preach a way of living
   That decent people cannot tolerate.
   I'm rather frank with you; but that's my way—
   I don't mince matters, when I mean a thing.
DAMIS. Mr. Tartuffe, your friend, is mighty lucky . . .
MADAME PERNELLE. He is a holy man, and must be
   heeded;
   I can't endure, with any show of patience,
   To hear a scatterbrains like you attack him.
DAMIS. What! Shall I let a bigot criticaster
   Come and usurp a tyrant's power here?
   And shall we never dare amuse ourselves
   Till this fine gentleman deigns to consent?
DORINE. If we must hark to him, and heed his
   maxims,
   There's not a thing we do but what's a crime;
   He censures everything, this zealous carper.
MADAME PERNELLE. And all he censures is well
   censured, too.
   He wants to guide you on the way to heaven;
   My son should train you all to love him well.

DAMIS. No, madam, look you, nothing—not my
    father
  Nor anything—can make me tolerate him.
  I should belie my feelings not to say so.
  His actions rouse my wrath at every turn;
  And I foresee that there must come of it
  An open rupture with this sneaking scoundrel.
DORINE. Besides, 'tis downright scandalous to see
  This unknown upstart master of the house—
  This vagabond, who hadn't, when he came,
  Shoes to his feet, or clothing worth six farthings,
  And who so far forgets his place, as now
  To censure everything, and rule the roost!
MADAME PERNELLE. Eh! Mercy sakes alive! Things
    would go better
  If all were governed by his pious orders.
DORINE. He passes for a saint in your opinion.
  In fact, he's nothing but a hypocrite.
MADAME PERNELLE. Just listen to her tongue!
DORINE. I wouldn't trust him,
  Nor yet his Lawrence, without bonds and surety.
MADAME PERNELLE. I don't know what the servant's
    character
  May be; but I can guarantee the master
  A holy man. You hate him and reject him
  Because he tells home truths to all of you.
  'Tis sin alone that moves his heart to anger,
  And heaven's interest is his only motive.
DORINE. Of course. But why, especially of late,
  Can he let nobody come near the house?
  Is heaven offended at a civil call
  That he should make so great a fuss about it?
  I'll tell you, if you like, just what I think;

[Pointing to Elmire]

  Upon my word, he's jealous of our mistress.
MADAME PERNELLE. You hold your tongue, and
    think what you are saying.
  He's not alone in censuring these visits;
  The turmoil that attends your sort of people,
  Their carriages forever at the door,
  And all their noisy footmen, flocked together,
  Annoy the neighbourhood, and raise a scandal.
  I'd gladly think there's nothing really wrong;
  But it makes talk; and that's not as it should be.
CLÉANTE. Eh! madam, can you hope to keep folk's
    tongues
  From wagging? It would be a grievous thing
  If, for the fear of idle talk about us,
  We had to sacrifice our friends. No, no;
  Even if we could bring ourselves to do it,
  Think you that everyone would then be silenced?

  Against backbiting there is no defence
  So let us try to live in innocence,
  To silly tattle pay no heed at all,
  And leave the gossips free to vent their gall.
DORINE. Our neighbour Daphne, and her little
    husband,
  Must be the ones who slander us, I'm thinking.
  Those whose own conduct's most ridiculous,
  Are always quickest to speak ill of others;
  They never fail to seize at once upon
  The slightest hint of any love affair,
  And spread the news of it with glee, and give it
  The character they'd have the world believe in.
  By others' actions, painted in their colors,
  They hope to justify their own; they think,
  In the false hope of some resemblance, either
  To make their own intrigues seem innocent,
  Or else to make their neighbours share the blame
  Which they are loaded with by everybody.
MADAME PERNELLE. These arguments are nothing to
    the purpose.
  Orante, we all know, lives a perfect life;
  Her thoughts are all of heaven; and I have heard
  That she condemns the company you keep.
DORINE. O admirable pattern! Virtuous dame!
  She lives the model of austerity;
  But age has brought this piety upon her,
  And she's a prude, now she can't help herself.
  As long as she could capture men's attentions
  She made the most of her advantages;
  But, now she sees her beauty vanishing,
  She wants to leave the world, that's leaving her,
  And in the specious veil of haughty virtue
  She'd hide the weakness of her worn-out charms.
  That is the way with all your old coquettes;
  They find it hard to see their lovers leave 'em;
  And thus abandoned, their forlorn estate
  Can find no occupation but a prude's.
  These pious dames, in their austerity,
  Must carp at everything, and pardon nothing.
  They loudly blame their neighbours' way of living,
  Not for religion's sake, but out of envy,
  Because they can't endure to see another
  Enjoy the pleasures age has weaned them from.
MADAME PERNELLE. [to Elmire] There! That's the kind
    of rigmarole to please you,
  Daughter-in-law. One never has a chance
  To get a word in edgewise, at your house,
  Because this lady holds the floor all day;
  But none the less, I mean to have my say, too.
  I tell you that my son did nothing wiser
  In all his life, than take this godly man
  Into his household; heaven sent him here,

In your great need, to make you all repent;
For your salvation, you must hearken to him;
He censures nothing but deserves his censure.
These visits, these assemblies, and these balls,
Are all inventions of the evil spirit.
You never hear a word of godliness
At them—but idle cackle, nonsense, flimflam.
Our neighbour often comes in for a share,
The talk flies fast, and scandal fills the air;
It makes a sober person's head go round,
At these assemblies, just to hear the sound
Of so much gab, with not a word to say;
And as a learned man remarked one day
Most aptly, 'tis the Tower of Babylon,
Where all, beyond all limit, babble on.
And just to tell you how this point came in . . .

[*To Cléante*]

So! Now the gentleman must snicker, must he?
Go find fools like yourself to make you laugh
And don't . . .

[*To Elmire*]

              Daughter, good-bye; not one word more.
As for this house, I leave the half unsaid;
But I shan't soon set foot in it again.

[*Cuffing Flipotte*]

Come, you! What makes you dream and stand
   agape,
Hussy! I'll warm your ears in proper shape!
March, trollop, march!

SCENE II

[*Cléante, Dorine*]

CLÉANTE. I won't escort her down,
  For fear she might fall foul of me again;
  The good old lady . . .
DORINE.   Bless us! What a pity
  She shouldn't hear the way you speak of her!
  She'd surely tell you you're too "good" by half,
  And that she's not so "old" as all that, neither!
CLÉANTE. How she got angry with us all for nothing!
  And how she seems possessed with her Tartuffe!
DORINE. Her case is nothing, though, beside her
   son's!
  To see him, you would say he's ten times worse!

His conduct in our late unpleasantness[1]
Had won him much esteem, and proved his courage
In service of his king; but now he's like
A man besotted, since he's been so taken
With this Tartuffe. He calls him brother, loves him
A hundred times as much as mother, son,
Daughter, and wife. He tells him all his secrets
And lets him guide his acts, and rule his conscience.
He fondles and embraces him; a sweetheart
Could not, I think, be loved more tenderly;
At table he must have the seat of honour,
While with delight our master sees him eat
As much as six men could; we must give up
The choicest tidbits to him; if he belches,
      (*'tis a servant speaking*)[2]
Master exclaims: "God bless you!"—Oh, he dotes
Upon him! he's his universe, his hero;
He's lost in constant admiration, quotes him
On all occasions, takes his trifling acts
For wonders, and his words for oracles.
The fellow knows his dupe, and makes the most
  on't,
He fools him with a hundred marks of virtue,
Gets money from him all the time by canting,
And takes upon himself to carp at us.
Even his silly coxcomb of a lackey
Makes it his business to instruct us too;
He comes with rolling eyes to preach at us,
And throws away our ribbons, rouge, and patches.
The wretch, the other day, tore up a kerchief
That he had found, pressed in the *Golden Legend*,
Calling it a horrid crime for us to mingle
The devil's finery with holy things.

SCENE III

[*Elmire, Mariane, Damis, Cléante, Dorine*]

ELMIRE. [*to Cléante*] You're very lucky to have missed
  the speech
  She gave us at the door. I see my husband
  Is home again. He hasn't seen me yet,
  So I'll go up and wait till he comes in.
CLÉANTE. And I, to save time, will await him here;
  I'll merely say good-morning, and be gone.

[1] Referring to the rebellion called La Fronde, during the minority of
Louis XIV.

[2] Molière's note, inserted in the text of all the old editions. It is a
curious illustration of the desire for uniformity and dignity of style in
dramatic verse of the seventeenth century that Molière feels called on to
apologize for a touch of realism like this. Indeed, these lines were even
omitted when the play was given.

SCENE IV

[*Cléante, Damis, Dorine*]

DAMIS. I wish you'd say a word to him about
My sister's marriage; I suspect Tartuffe
Opposes it, and puts my father up
To all these wretched shifts. You know, besides,
How nearly I'm concerned in it myself;
If love unites my sister and Valère,
I love his sister too; and if this marriage
Were to . . .
DORINE.   He's coming.

SCENE V

[*Orgon, Cléante, Dorine*]

ORGON. Ah! Good morning, brother.
CLÉANTE. I was just going, but am glad to greet you.
Things are not far advanced yet, in the country?
ORGON. Dorine . . .

[*To Cléante*]

                    Just wait a bit, please, brother-in-law.
Let me allay my first anxiety
By asking news about the family.

[*To Dorine*]

Has everything gone well these last two days?
What's happening? And how is everybody?
DORINE. Madam had fever, and a splitting headache
Day before yesterday, all day and evening.
ORGON. And how about Tartuffe?
DORINE.   Tartuffe? He's well;
He's mightly well; stout, fat, fair, rosy-lipped.
ORGON. Poor man!
DORINE.   At evening she had nausea
And could't touch a single thing for supper,
Her headache still was so severe.
ORGON.   And how
About Tartuffe?
DORINE.   He supped alone, before her,
And unctuously ate up two partridges,
As well as half a leg o' mutton, deviled.
ORGON. Poor man!
DORINE.   All night she couldn't get a wink
Of sleep, the fever racked her so; and we
Had to sit up with her till daylight.

ORGON.   How
About Tartuffe?
DORINE.   Gently inclined to slumber,
He left the table, went into his room,
Got himself straight into a good warm bed,
And slept quite undisturbed until next morning.
ORGON. Poor man!
DORINE.   At last she let us all persuade her,
And got up courage to be bled; and then
She was relieved at once.
ORGON.   And how about
Tartuffe?
DORINE.   He plucked up courage properly,
Bravely entrenched his soul against all evils.
And, to replace the blood that she had lost,
He drank at breakfast four huge draughts of wine.
ORGON. Poor man!
DORINE.   So now they both are doing well;
And I'll go straightway and inform my mistress
How pleased you are at her recovery.

SCENE VI

[*Orgon, Cléante*]

CLÉANTE. Brother, she ridicules you to your face;
And I, though I don't want to make you angry,
Must tell you candidly that she's quite right.
Was such infatuation ever heard of?
And can a man to-day have charms to make you
Forget all else, relieve his poverty,
Give him a home, and then . . . ?
ORGON.   Stop there,
good brother,
You do not know the man you're speaking of.
CLÉANTE. Since you will have it so, I do not know
him;
But after all, to tell what sort of man
He is . . .
ORGON.   Dear brother, you'd be charmed to
know him;
Your raptures over him would have no end.
He is a man . . . who . . . ah! . . . in fact . . . a man
Whoever does his will, knows perfect peace,
And counts the whole world else, as so much dung.
His converse has transformed me quite; he weans
My heart from every friendship, teaches me
To have no love for anything on earth;
And I could see my brother, children, mother,
And wife, all die, and never care—a snap.
CLÉANTE. Your feelings are humane, I must say,
brother!

ORGON. Ah! If you'd seen him, as I saw him first,
　　You would have loved him just as much as I.
　　He came to church each day, with contrite mien,
　　Kneeled, on both knees, right opposite my place,
　　And drew the eyes of all the congregation,
　　To watch the fervour of his prayers to heaven;
　　With deep-drawn sighs and great ejaculations,
　　He humbly kissed the earth at every moment;
　　And when I left the church, he ran before me
　　To give me holy water at the door.
　　I learned his poverty, and who he was,
　　By questioning his servant, who is like him,
　　And gave him gifts; but in his modesty
　　He always wanted to return a part.
　　"It is too much," he'd say, "too much by half;
　　I am not worthy of your pity." Then,
　　When I refused to take it back, he'd go,
　　Before my eyes, and give it to the poor.
　　At length heaven bade me take him to my home,
　　And since that day, all seems to prosper here.
　　He censures everything, and for my sake
　　He even takes great interest in my wife;
　　He lets me know who ogles her, and seems
　　Six times as jealous as I am myself.
　　You'd not believe how far his zeal can go:
　　He calls himself a sinner just for trifles;
　　The merest nothing is enough to shock him;
　　So much so, that the other day I heard him
　　Accuse himself for having, while at prayer,
　　In too much anger caught and killed a flea.
CLÉANTE. Zounds, brother, you are mad, I think! Or else
　　You're making sport of me, with such a speech.
　　What are you driving at with all this nonsense . . . ?
ORGON. Brother, your language smacks of atheism;
　　And I suspect your soul's a little tainted
　　Therewith. I've preached to you a score of times
　　That you'll draw down some judgment on your head.
CLÉANTE. That is the usual strain of all your kind;
　　They must have every one as blind as they.
　　They call you atheist if you have good eyes;
　　And if you don't adore their vain grimaces,
　　You've neither faith nor care for sacred things.
　　No, no; such talk can't frighten me; I know
　　What I am saying; heaven sees my heart.
　　We're not the dupes of all your canting mummers;
　　There are false heroes—and false devotees;
　　And as true heroes never are the ones
　　Who make much noise about their deeds of honour,
　　Just so true devotees, whom we should follow,
　　Are not the ones who make so much vain show.
　　What! Will you find no difference between

Hypocrisy and genuine devoutness?
　　And will you treat them both alike, and pay
　　The self-same honour both to masks and faces
　　Set artifice beside sincerity,
　　Confuse the semblance with reality,
　　Esteem a phantom like a living person,
　　And counterfeit as good as honest coin?
　　Men, for the most part, are strange creatures, truly!
　　You never find them keep the golden mean;
　　The limits of good sense, too narrow for them,
　　Must always be passed by, in each direction;
　　They often spoil the noblest things, because
　　They go too far, and push them to extremes.
　　I merely say this by the way, good brother.
ORGON. You are the sole expounder of the doctrine;
　　Wisdom shall die with you, no doubt, good brother,
　　You are the only wise, the sole enlightened,
　　The oracle, the Cato, of our age.
　　All men, compared to you, are downright fools.
CLÉANTE. I'm not the sole expounder of the doctrine,
　　And wisdom shall not die with me, good brother.
　　But this I know, though it be all my knowledge,
　　That there's a difference 'twixt false and true.
　　And as I find no kind of hero more
　　To be admired than men of true religion,
　　Nothing more noble or more beautiful
　　Than is the holy zeal of true devoutness;
　　Just so I think there's naught more odious
　　Than whited sepulchres of outward unction,
　　Those barefaced charlatans, those hireling zealots,
　　Whose sacrilegious, treacherous pretence
　　Deceives at will, and with impunity
　　Makes mockery of all that men hold sacred;
　　Men who, enslaved to selfish interests,
　　Make trade and merchandise of godliness,
　　And try to purchase influence and office
　　With false eye-rollings and affected raptures;
　　Those men, I say, who with uncommon zeal
　　Seek their own fortunes on the road to heaven;
　　Who, skilled in prayer, have always much to ask,
　　And live at court to preach retirement;
　　Who reconcile religion with their vices,
　　Are quick to anger, vengeful, faithless, tricky,
　　And, to destroy a man, will have the boldness
　　To call their private grudge the cause of heaven;
　　All the more dangerous, since in their anger
　　They use against us weapons men revere,
　　And since they make the world applaud their passion,
　　And seek to stab us with a sacred sword.
　　There are too many of this canting kind.
　　Still, the sincere are easy to distinguish;
　　And many splendid patterns may be found,

In our own time, before our very eyes
Look at Ariston, Périandre, Oronte,
Alcidamas, Clitandre, and Polydore;
No one denies their claim to true religion;
Yet they're no braggadocios of virtue,
They do not make insufferable display,
And their religion's human, tractable;
They are not always judging all our actions,
They'd think such judgment savoured of
    presumption;
And, leaving pride of words to other men,
'Tis by their deeds alone they censure ours.
Evil appearances find little credit
With them; they even incline to think the best
Of others. No caballers, no intriguers,
They mind the business of their own right living.
They don't attack a sinner tooth and nail,
For sin's the only object of their hatred;
Nor are they over-zealous to attempt
Far more in heaven's behalf than heaven would have
    'em.
That is my kind of man, that is true living,
That is the pattern we should set ourselves.
Your fellow was not fashioned on this model;
You're quite sincere in boasting of his zeal;
But you're deceived, I think, by false pretences.

ORGON. My dear good brother-in-law, have you quite
    done?

CLÉANTE. Yes.

ORGON.   I'm your humble servant.

    [Starts to go.]

CLÉANTE.   Just a word.
    We'll drop that other subject. But you know
    Valère has had the promise of your daughter.

ORGON. Yes.

CLÉANTE.   You had named the happy day.

ORGON.   'Tis true.

CLÉNTE. Then why put off the celebration of it?

ORGON. I can't say.

CLÉANTE.   Can you have some other plan
    In mind?

ORGON.   Perhaps.

CLÉANTE.   You mean to break your word?

ORGON. I don't say that.

CLÉANTE.   I hope no obstacle
    Can keep you from performing what you've
        promised.

ORGON. Well, that depends.

CLÉANTE.   Why must you beat about?
    Valère has sent me here to settle matters.

ORGON. Heaven be praised!

CLÉANTE.   What answer shall I take
    him?

ORGON. Why, anything you please.

CLÉANTE.   But we must know
    Your plans. What are they?

ORGON.   I shall do the will
    Of Heaven.

CLÉANTE.   Come, be serious. You've given
    Your promise to Valère. Now will you keep it?

ORGON. Good-bye.

CLÉANTE. [alone] His love, methinks, has much to
    fear;
    I must go let him know what's happening here.

Act II

SCENE I

[Orgon, Mariane]

ORGON. Now, Mariane.

MARIANE.   Yes, father?

ORGON.   Come; I'll tell you
    A secret.

MARIANE.   Yes . . . What are you looking for?

ORGON. [looking into a small closet-room] To see there's
    no one there to spy upon us;
    That little closet's mighty fit to hide in.

There! We're all right now. Mariane, in you
I've always found a daughter dutiful
And gentle. So I've always loved you dearly.

MARIANE. I'm grateful for your fatherly affection.

ORGON. Well spoken, daughter. Now, prove you
    deserve it
    By doing as I wish in all respects.

MARIANE. To do so is the height of my ambition.

ORGON. Excellent well. What say you of—Tartuffe?

MARIANE. Who? I?

ORGON.   Yes, you. Look to it how you
    answer.

MARIANE. Why! I'll say of him—anything you please.

SCENE II

[*Orgon, Mariane; Dorine (coming in quietly and standing behind Orgon, so that he does not see her)*]

ORGON. Well spoken. A good girl. Say then, my
    daughter,
That all his person shines with noble merit,
That he has won your heart, and you would like
To have him, by my choice, become your husband.
    Eh?
MARIANE. Eh?
ORGON.   What say you?
MARIANE.   Please, what did you say?
ORGON. What?
MARIANE.   Surely I mistook you, sir?
ORGON.   How now?
MARIANE. Who is it, father, you would have me say
Has won my heart, and I would like to have
Become my husband, by your choice?
ORGON.   Tartuffe.
MARIANE. But, father, I protest it isn't true!
Why should you make me tell this dreadful lie?
ORGON. Because I mean to have it be the truth.
Let this suffice for you: I've settled it.
MARIANE. What, father, you would . . . ?
ORGON.   Yes, child,
    I'm resolved
To graft Tartuffe into my family.
So he must be your husband. That I've settled.
And since your duty . . .

[*Seeing Dorine*]

                  What are you doing there?
Your curiosity is keen, my girl,
To make you come eavesdropping on us so.
DORINE. Upon my word, I don't know how the
    rumour
Got started—if 'twas guess-work or mere chance—
But I had heard already of this match,
And treated it as utter stuff and nonsense.
ORGON. What! Is the thing incredible?
DORINE.   So much so
I don't believe it even from yourself, sir.
ORGON. I know a way to make you credit it.
DORINE. No, no, you're telling us a fairy tale!
ORGON. I'm telling you just what will happen shortly.
DORINE. Stuff!
ORGON.   Daughter, what I say is in good
    earnest.

DORINE. There, there, don't take your father seri-
    ously;
He's fooling.
ORGON.   But I tell you . . .
DORINE.   No. No use.
They won't believe you.
ORGON.   If I let my anger . . .
DORINE. Well, then, we do believe you; and the worse
For you it is. What! Can a grown-up man
With that expanse of beard across his face
Be mad enough to want . . . ?
ORGON.   You hark to me:
You've taken on yourself here in this house
A sort of free familiarity
That I don't like, I tell you frankly, girl.
DORINE. There, there, let's not get angry, sir, I beg
    you.
But are you making game of everybody?
Your daughter's not cut out for bigot's meat;
And he has more important things to think of.
Besides, what can you gain by such a match?
How can a man of wealth, like you, go choose
A wretched vagabond for son-in-law?
ORGON. You hold your tongue. And know, the less he
    has,
The better cause have we to honour him.
His poverty is honest poverty;
It should exalt him more than worldly grandeur,
For he has let himself be robbed of all,
Through careless disregard of temporal things
And fixed attachment to the things eternal.
My help may set him on his feet again,
Win back his property—a fair estate
He has at home, so I'm informed—and prove him
For what he is, a true-born gentleman.
DORINE. Yes, so he says himself. Such vanity
But ill accords with pious living, sir.
The man who cares for holiness alone
Should not so loudly boast his name and birth;
The humble ways of genuine devoutness
Brook not so much display of earthly pride.
Why should he be so vain? . . . But I offend you:
Let's leave his rank, then,—take the man himself:
Can you without compunction give a man
Like him possession of a girl like her?
Think what a scandal's sure to come of it!
Virtue is at the mercy of the fates,
When a girl's married to a man she hates;
The best intent to live an honest woman
Depends upon the husband's being human,
And men whose brows are pointed at afar
May thank themselves their wives are what they are.

For to be true is more than woman can,
With husbands built upon a certain plan;
And he who weds his child against her will
Owes heaven account for it, if she do ill.
Think then what perils wait on your design.

ORGON. [to Mariane] So! I must learn what's what
    from her, you see!

DORINE. You might do worse than follow my advice.

ORGON. Daughter, we can't waste time upon this
    nonsense;
  I know what's good for you, and I'm your father.
  True, I had promised you to young Valère;
  But, first, they tell me he's inclined to gamble,
  And then, I fear his faith is not quite sound.
  I haven't noticed that he's regular
  At church.

DORINE.   You'd have him run there just when you
    do.
  Like those who go on purpose to be seen?

ORGON. I don't ask your opinion on the matter.
  In short, the other is in Heaven's best graces,
  And that is richer quite beyond compare.
  This match will bring you every joy you long for;
  'Twill be all steeped in sweetness and delight.
  You'll live together, in your faithful loves,
  Like two sweet children, like two turtle-doves;
  You'll never fail to quarrel, scold, or tease,
  And you may do with him whate'er you please.

DORINE. With him? Do naught but give him horns,
    I'll warrant.

ORGON. Out on thee, wench!

DORINE.   I tell you he's cut out
    for't;
  However great your daughter's virtue, sir,
  His destiny is sure to prove the stronger.

ORGON. Have done with interrupting. Hold your
    tongue.
  Don't poke your nose in other people's business.

DORINE. [She keeps interrupting him, just as he turns and
    starts to speak to his daughter.] If I make bold, sir, 'tis
    for your own good.

ORGON. You're too officious; pray you, hold your
    tongue.

DORINE. 'Tis love of you . . .

ORGON.   I want none of your
    love.

DORINE. Then I will love you in your own despite.

ORGON. You will, eh?

DORINE.   Yes, your honour's dear to me;
  I can't endure to see you made the butt
  Of all men's ridicule.

ORGON.   Won't you be still?

DORINE. 'Twould be a sin to let us make this match.

ORGON. Won't you be still, I say, you impudent viper!

DORINE. What! you are pious, and you lose your
    temper?

ORGON. I'm all wrought up, with your confounded
    nonsense;
  Now, once for all, I tell you hold your tongue.

DORINE. Then mum's the word; I'll take it out in
    thinking.

ORGON. Think all you please; but not a syllable
  To me about it, or . . . you understand!

[Turning to his daughter.]

  As a wise father, I've considered all
  With due deliberation.

DORINE.   I'll go mad
  If I can't speak.

[She stops the instant he turns his head.]

ORGON.   Though he's no lady's man,
  Tartuffe is well enough . . .

DORINE.   A pretty phiz!

ORGON. So that, although you may not care at all
  For his best qualities . . .

DORINE.   A handsome dowry!

[Orgon turns and stands in front of her, with arms folded,
eyeing her.]

  Were I in her place, any man should rue it
  Who married me by force, that's mighty certain;
  I'd let him know, and that within a week,
  A woman's vengeance isn't far to seek.

ORGON. [to Dorine] So—nothing that I say has any
    weight?

DORINE. Eh? What's wrong now? I didn't speak to
    you.

ORGON. What were you doing?

DORINE.   Talking to myself.

ORGON. Oh! Very well. [Aside.] Her monstrous impu-
    dence
  Must be chastised with one good slap in the face.

[He stands ready to strike her, and, each time he speaks to
his daughter, he glances toward her; but she stands still and
says not a word.]

ORGON. Daughter, you must approve of my
    design. . . .
  Think of this husband . . . I have chosen for you. . . .

[*To Dorine*]

    Why don't you talk to yourself? DORINE.   Nothing to say.
DORINE.
ORGON. One little word more.
DORINE.   Oh, no, thanks. Not
    now.
ORGON. Sure, I'd have caught you.
DORINE.   Faith, I'm no such
    fool.
ORGON. So, daughter, now obedience is the word;
    You must accept my choice with reverence.
DORINE. [*running away*] You'd never catch me
    marrying such a creature.
ORGON. [*swinging his hand at her and missing her*]
    Daughter, you've such a pestilent hussy there
    I can't live with her longer, without sin.
    I can't discuss things in the state I'm in.
    My mind's so flustered by her insolent talk,
    To calm myself, I must go take a walk.

SCENE III

[*Mariane, Dorine*]

DORINE. Say, have you lost the tongue from out your
    head?
    And must I speak your rôle from A to Zed?
    You let them broach a project that's absurd,
    And don't oppose it with a single word!
MARIANE. What can I do? My father is the master.
DORINE. Do? Everything, to ward off such disaster.
MARIANE. But what?
DORINE.   Tell him one doesn't love by
    proxy;
    Tell him you'll marry for yourself, not him;
    Since you're the one for whom the thing is done,
    You are the one, not he, the man must please;
    If his Tartuffe has charmed him so, why let him
    Just marry him himself—no one will hinder.
MARIANE. A father's rights are such, it seems to me,
    That I could never dare to say a word.
DORINE. Come, talk it out. Valère has asked your
    hand:
    Now do you love him, pray, or do you not?
MARIANE. Dorine! How can you wrong my love so
    much,
    And ask me such a question? Have I not
    A hundred times laid bare my heart to you?
    Do you not know how ardently I love him?

DORINE. How do I know if heart and words agree,
    And if in honest truth you really love him?
MARIANE. Dorine, you wrong me greatly if you doubt
    it;
    I've shown my inmost feelings, all too plainly.
DORINE. So then, you love him?
MARIANE.   Yes, devotedly.
DORINE. And he returns your love, apparently?
MARIANE. I think so.
DORINE.   And you both alike are eager
    To be well married to each other?
MARIANE.   Surely.
DORINE. Then what's your plan about this other
    match?
MARIANE. To kill myself, if it is forced upon me.
DORINE. Good! That's a remedy I hadn't thought of.
    Just die, and everything will be all right.
    This medicine is marvellous, indeed!
    It drives me mad to hear folk talk such nonsense.
MARIANE. Oh, dear, Dorine, you get in such a
    temper!
    You have no sympathy for people's troubles.
DORINE. I have no sympathy when folk talk nonsense,
    And flatten out as you do, at a pinch.
MARIANE. But what can you expect?—if one is
    timid?—
DORINE. But what is love worth, if it has no courage?
MARIANE. Am I not constant in my love for him?
    Is't not his place to win me from my father?
DORINE. But if your father is a crazy fool,
    And quite bewitched with his Tartuffe? And breaks
    His bounden word? Is that your lover's fault?
MARIANE. But shall I publicly refuse and scorn
    This match, and make it plain that I'm in love?
    Shall I cast off for him, whate'er he be,
    Womanly modesty and filial duty?
    You ask me to display my love in public . . . ?
DORINE. No, no, I ask you nothing. You shall be
    Mister Tartuffe's; why, now I think of it,
    I should be wrong to turn you from this marriage.
    What cause can I have to oppose your wishes?
    So fine a match! An excellent good match!
    Mister Tartuffe! Oh ho! No mean proposal!
    Mister Tartuffe, sure, take it all in all,
    Is not a man to sneeze at—oh, by no means!
    'Tis no small luck to be his happy spouse.
    The whole world joins to sing his praise already;
    He's noble—in his parish; handsome too;
    Red ears and high complexion—oh, my lud!
    You'll be too happy, sure, with him for husband.
MARIANE. Oh dear! . . .

DORINE.   What joy and pride will fill
   your heart
  To be the bride of such a handsome fellow!
MARIANE. Oh, stop, I beg you; try to find some way
  To help break off the match. I quite give in,
  I'm ready to do anything you say.
DORINE. No, no, a daughter must obey her father,
  Though he should want to make her wed a monkey.
  Besides, your fate is fine. What could be better!
  You'll take the stage-coach to his little village,
  And find it full of uncles and cousins,
  Whose conversation will delight you. Then
  You'll be presented in their best society.
  You'll even go to call, by way of welcome,
  On Mrs. Bailiff, Mrs. Tax-Collector,
  Who'll patronise you with a folding-stool.
  There, once a year, at carnival, you'll have—
  Perhaps—a ball; with orchestra—two bag-pipes;
  And sometimes a trained ape, and Punch and Judy;
  Though if your husband . . .
MARIANE.   Oh, you'll kill me.
  Please
  Contrive to help me out with your advice.
DORINE. I thank you kindly.
MARIANE.   Oh! Dorine, I beg
  you . . .
DORINE. To serve you right, this marriage must go
  through.
MARIANE. Dear girl!
DORINE.   No.
MARIANE.   If I say I love Valère . . .
DORINE. No, no. Tartuffe's your man, and you shall
  taste him.
MARIANE. You know I've always trusted you; now
  help me . . .
DORINE. No, you shall be, my faith! Tartuffified.
MARIANE. Well, then, since you've no pity for my fate
  Let me take counsel only of despair;
  It will advise and help and give me courage;
  There's one sure cure, I know, for all my troubles.

[She starts to go.]

DORINE. There, there! Come back. I can't be angry
  long.
  I must take pity on you, after all.
MARIANE. Oh, don't you see, Dorine, if I must bear
  This martyrdom, I certainly shall die.
DORINE. Now don't you fret. We'll surely find some
  way.
  To hinder this . . . But here's Valère, your lover.

SCENE IV

[Valère, Mariane, Dorine]

VALÈRE. Madam, a piece of news—quite new to me—
  Has just come out, and very fine it is.
MARIANE. What piece of news?
VALÈRE.   Your marriage with
  Tartuffe.
MARIANE. 'Tis true my father has this plan in mind.
VALÈRE. Your father, madam . . .
MARIANE.   Yes, he's changed
  his plans,
  And did but now propose it to me.
VALÈRE.   What!
  Seriously?
MARIANE. Yes, he was serious,
  And openly insisted on the match.
VALÈRE. And what's your resolution in the matter,
  Madam?
MARIANE. I don't know.
VALÈRE.   That's a pretty answer.
  You don't know?
MARIANE.   No.
VALÈRE.   No?
MARIANE.   What do you advise?
VALÈRE. I? My advice is, marry him, by all means.
MARIANE. That's your advice?
VALÈRE.   Yes.
MARIANE.   Do you mean it?
VALÈRE.   Surely.
  A splendid choice, and worthy your acceptance.
MARIANE. Oh, very well, sir! I shall take your counsel
VALÈRE. You'll find no trouble taking it, I warrant.
MARIANE. No more than you did giving it, be sure.
VALÈRE. I gave it, truly, to oblige you, madam.
MARIANE. And I shall take it to oblige you, sir.
DORINE. [withdrawing to the back of the stage] Let's see
  what this affair will come to.
VALÈRE.   So,
  That is your love? And it was all deceit
  When you . . .
MARIANE.   I beg you, say no more of that.
  You told me, squarely, sir, I should accept
  The husband that is offered me; and I
  Will tell you squarely that I mean to do so,
  Since you have given me this good advice.
VALÈRE. Don't shield yourself with talk of my advice.
  You had your mind made up, that's evident;

And now you're snatching at a trifling pretext
To justify the breaking of your word.

MARIANE. Exactly so.

VALÈRE. Of course it is; your heart
Has never known true love for me.

MARIANE. Alas!
You're free to think so, if you please.

VALÈRE. Yes, yes,
I'm free to think so; and my outraged love
May yet forestall you in your perfidy,
And offer elsewhere both my heart and hand.

MARIANE. No doubt of it; the love your high deserts
May win . . .

VALÈRE. Good Lord, have done with my
deserts!
I know I have but few, and you have proved it.
But I may find more kindness in another;
I know of someone, who'll not be ashamed
To take your leavings, and make up my loss.

MARIANE. The loss is not so great; you'll easily
Console yourself completely for this change.

VALÈRE. I'll try my best, that you may well believe.
When we're forgotten by a woman's heart,
Our pride is challenged; we, too, must forget;
Or if we cannot, must at least pretend to.
No other way can man such baseness prove,
As be a lover scorned, and still in love.

MARIANE. In faith, a high and noble sentiment.

VALÈRE. Yes; and it's one that all men must approve.
What! Would you have me keep my love alive,
And see you fly into another's arms
Before my very eyes; and never offer
To someone else the heart that you had scorned?

MARIANE. Oh, no, indeed! For my part, I could wish
That it were done already.

VALÈRE. What! You wish it?

MARIANE. Yes.

VALÈRE. This is insult heaped on injury;
I'll go at once and do as you desire.

[He takes a step or two as if to go away.]

MARIANE. Oh, very well then.

VALÈRE. [turning back] But remember this.
'Twas you that drove me to this desperate pass.

MARIANE. Of course.

VALÈRE. [turning back again] And in the plan that I
have formed
I only follow your example.

MARIANE. Yes.

VALÈRE. [at the door] Enough; you shall be punctually
obeyed.

MARIANE. So much the better.

VALÈRE. [coming back again] This is once for all.

MARIANE. So be it, then.

VALÈRE. [He goes toward the door, but just as he reaches
it, turns around] Eh?

MARIANE. What?

VALÈRE. You didn't call me?

MARIANE. I? You are dreaming.

VALÈRE. Very well, I'm gone.
Madam, farewell.

[He walks slowly away.]

MARIANE. Farewell, sir.

DORINE. I must say
You've lost your senses and both gone clean daft!
I've let you fight it out to the end o' the chapter
To see how far the thing could go. Oho, there,
Mister Valère!

[She goes and seizes him by the arm, to stop him. He makes
a great show of resistance.]

VALÈRE. What do you want, Dorine?

DORINE. Come here.

VALÈRE. No, no, I'm quite beside myself.
Don't hinder me from doing as she wishes.

DORINE. Stop!

VALÈRE. No. You see, I'm fixed, resolved, determined.

DORINE. So!

MARIANE. [aside] Since my presence pains him, makes
him go,
I'd better go myself, and leave him free.

DORINE. [leaving Valère, and running after Mariane] Now
t'other! Where are you going?

MARIANE. Let me be.

DORINE. Come back.

MARIANE. No, no, it isn't any use.

VALÈRE. [aside] 'Tis clear the sight of me is torture to
her;
No doubt, t'were better I should free her from it.

DORINE. [leaving Mariane and running after Valère] Same
thing again! Deuce take you both, I say.
Now stop your fooling; come here, you; and you.

[She pulls first one, then the other, toward the middle of the
stage.]

VALÈRE. [to Dorine] What's your idea?

MARIANE. [to Dorine]   What can you
    mean to do?
DORINE. Set you to rights, and pull you out o' the
    scrape.

[To Valère]

   Are you quite mad, to quarrel with her now?
VALÈRE. Didn't you hear the things she said to me?
DORINE. [to Mariane] Are you quite mad, to get in
    such a passion?
MARIANE. Didn't you see the way he treated me?
DORINE. Fools, both of you.

[To Valère]

            She thinks of nothing
  else
But to keep faith with you, I vouch for it.

[To Mariane]

   And he loves none but you, and longs for nothing
   But just to marry you, I stake my life on't.
MARIANE. [to Valère] Why did you give me such advice
    then, pray?
VALÈRE. [to Mariane] Why ask for my advice on such a
    matter?
DORINE. You both are daft, I tell you. Here, your
    hands.

[To Valère]

  Come, yours.
VALÈRE. [giving Dorine his hand] What for?
DORINE. [to Mariane]   Now,
    yours.
MARIANE. [giving Dorine her hand]   But
    what's the use?
DORINE. Oh, quick now, come along. There, both of
    you—
    You love each other better than you think.

[Valère and Mariane hold each other's hands some time
without looking at each other.]

VALÈRE. [at last turning toward Mariane] Come, don't be
    so ungracious now about it;
    Look at a man as if you didn't hate him.

[Mariane looks sideways toward Valère, with just a bit of a
smile.]

DORINE. My faith and troth, what fools these lovers
    be!
VALÈRE. [to Mariane] But come now, have I not a just
    complaint?
    And truly, are you not a wicked creature
    To take delight in saying what would pain me?
MARIANE. And are you not yourself the most
    ungrateful . . . ?
DORINE. Leave this discussion till another time;
    Now, think how you'll stave off this plaguey
    marriage.
MARIANE. Then tell us how to go about it.
DORINE.   Well,
    We'll try all sorts of ways.

[To Mariane]

            Your father's daft;

[To Valère]

   This plan is nonsense.

[To Mariane]

            You had better humour
   His notions by a semblance of consent,
   So that in case of danger, you can still
   Find means to block the marriage by delay.
   If you gain time, the rest is easy, trust me.
   One day you'll fool them with a sudden illness,
   Causing delay; another day, ill omens:
   You've met a funeral, or broke a mirror,
   Or dreamed of muddy water. Best of all,
   They cannot marry you to anyone
   Without your saying yes. But now, methinks,
   They mustn't find you chattering together.

[To Valère]

   You, go at once and set your friends at work
   To make him keep his word to you; while we
   Will bring the brother's influence to bear,
   And get the step-mother on our side, too.
   Good-bye.
VALÈRE. [to Mariane] Whatever efforts we may make,
    My greatest hope, be sure, must rest on you.
MARIANE. [to Valère] I cannot answer for my father's
    whims;
    But no one save Valère shall ever have me.
VALÈRE. You thrill me through with joy! Whatever
    comes . . .

DORINE. Oho! These lovers! Never done with
    prattling!
  Now go.
VALÈRE. [*starting to go, and coming back again*] One last
  word . . .

Act III

SCENE I

[*Damis, Dorine*]

DAMIS. May lightning strike me dead this very instant,
    May I be everywhere proclaimed a scoundrel,
    If any reverence or power shall stop me,
    And if I don't do straightway something desperate!
DORINE. I beg you, moderate this towering passion;
    Your father did but merely mention it.
    Not all things that are talked of turn to facts;
    The road is long, sometimes, from plans to acts.
DAMIS. No, I must end this paltry fellow's plots,
    And he shall hear from me a truth or two.
DORINE. So ho! Go slow now. Just you leave the
    fellow—
    Your father too—in your step-mother's hands.
    She has some influence with this Tartuffe,
    He makes a point of heeding all she says,
    And I suspect that he is fond of her.
    Would God 'twere true!—'Twould be the height of
    humour
    Now, she has sent for him, in your behalf,
    To sound him on this marriage, to find out
    What his ideas are, and to show him plainly
    What troubles he may cause, if he persists
    In giving countenance to this design.
    His man says, he's at prayers, I mustn't see him,
    But likewise says, he'll presently be down.
    So off with you, and let me wait for him.
DAMIS. I may be present at this interview.
DORINE. No, no! They must be left alone.
DAMIS.   I won't
  So much as speak to him.
DORINE.   Go on! We know you
  And your high tantrums. Just the way to spoil
    things!
  Be off.
DAMIS. No, I must see—I'll keep my temper.

DORINE.   What a gabble and pother!
  Be off! By this door, you. And you, by t'other.

[*She pushes them off, by the shoulders, in opposite
directions.*]

DORINE. Out on you, what a plague! He's coming.
  Hide!

[*Damis goes and hides in the closet at the back of the stage.*]

SCENE II

[*Tartuffe, Dorine*]

TARTUFFE. [*speaking to his valet, off the stage, as soon as
  he sees Dorine is there*] Lawrence, put up my hair-
  cloth shirt and scourge,
    And pray that Heaven may shed its light upon you.
    If any come to see me, say I'm gone
    To share my alms among the prisoners.
DORINE. [*aside*] What affectation and what showing
  off!
TARTUFFE. What do you want with me?
DORINE.   To tell
  you . . .
TARTUFFE. [*taking a handkerchief from his pocket*] Ah!
  Before you speak, pray take this handkerchief.
DORINE. What?
TARTUFFE.   Cover up that bosom, which I can't
  Endure to look on. Things like that offend
  Our souls, and fill our minds with sinful thoughts.
DORINE. Are you so tender to temptation, then,
    And has the flesh such power upon your senses?
    I don't know how you get in such a heat;
    For my part, I am not so prone to lust,
    And I could see you stripped from head to foot,
    And all your hide not tempt me in the least.
TARTUFFE. Show in your speech some little modesty,
    Or I must instantly take leave of you.
DORINE. No, no, I'll leave you to yourself; I've only
    One thing to say: Madam will soon be down,
    And begs the favour of a word with you.
TARTUFFE. Ah! Willingly.
DORINE. [*aside*]   How gentle all at once!
  My faith, I still believe I've hit upon it.

TARTUFFE. Will she come soon?

DORINE.   I think I hear her
    now.
    Yes, here she is herself; I'll leave you with her.

SCENE III

[Elmire, Tartuffe]

TARTUFFE. May Heaven's overflowing kindness ever
    Give you good health of body and of soul,
    And bless your days according to the wishes
    And prayers of its most humble votary!

ELMIRE. I'm very grateful for your pious wishes.
    But let's sit down, so we may talk at ease.

TARTUFFE. *[after sitting down]* And how are you
        recovered from your illness?

ELMIRE. *[sitting down also]* Quite well; the fever soon
        let go its hold.

TARTUFFE. My prayers, I fear, have not sufficient
        merit
    To have drawn down this favour from on high;
    But each entreaty that I made to Heaven
    Had for its object your recovery.

ELMIRE. You're too solicitous on my behalf.

TARTUFFE. We could not cherish your dear health too
        much;
    I would have given mine, to help restore it.

ELMIRE. That's pushing Christian charity too far;
    I owe you many thanks for so much kindness.

TARTUFFE. I do far less for you than you deserve.

ELMIRE. There is a matter that I wished to speak of
    In private; I am glad there's no one here
    To listen.

TARTUFFE. Madam, I am overjoyed.
    'Tis sweet to find myself alone with you.
    This is an opportunity I've asked
    Of Heaven, many a time; till now, in vain.

ELMIRE. All that I wish, is just a word from you,
    Quite frank and open, hiding nothing from me.

*[Damis, without their seeing him, opens the closet door
halfway.]*

TARTUFFE. I too could wish, as Heaven's especial
        favour,
    To lay my soul quite open to your eyes,
    And swear to you, the trouble that I made
    About those visits which your charms attract,
    Does not result from any hatred toward you,
    But rather from a passionate devotion,
    And purest motives . . .

ELMIRE.   That is how I take it,
    I think 'tis my salvation that concerns you.

TARTUFFE. *[pressing her finger tips]* Madam, 'tis so; and
        such is my devotion . . .

ELMIRE. Ouch! but you squeeze too hard.

TARTUFFE.   Excess
    of zeal.
    In no way could I ever mean to hurt you,
    And I'd as soon . . .

[He puts his hand on her knee.]

ELMIRE.   What's your hand doing there?

TARTUFFE. Feeling your gown; the stuff is very soft.

ELMIRE. Let be, I beg you; I am very ticklish.

[She moves her chair away, and Tartuffe brings his nearer.]

TARTUFFE. *[handling the lace yoke of Elmire's dress]* Dear
        me how wonderful in workmanship
    This lace is! They do marvels, nowadays;
    Things of all kinds were never better made.

ELMIRE. Yes, very true. But let us come to business.
    They say my husband means to break his word.
    And marry Mariane to you. Is't so?

TARTUFFE. He did hint some such thing; but truly,
        madam,
    That's not the happiness I'm yearning after;
    I see elsewhere the sweet compelling charms
    Of such a joy as fills my every wish.

ELMIRE. You mean you cannot love terrestrial things.

TARTUFFE. The heart within my bosom is not stone.

ELMIRE. I well believe your sighs all tend to Heaven,
    And nothing here below can stay your thoughts.

TARTUFFE. Love for the beauty of eternal things
    Cannot destroy our love for earthly beauty;
    Our mortal senses well may be entranced
    By perfect works that Heaven has fashioned here.
    Its charms reflected shine in such as you,
    And in yourself, its rarest miracles;
    It has displayed such marvels in your face,
    That eyes are dazed, and hearts are rapt away;
    I could not look on you, the perfect creature,
    Without admiring Nature's great Creator,
    And feeling all my heart inflamed with love
    For you, His fairest image of Himself.
    At first I trembled lest this secret love
    Might be the Evil Spirit's artful snare;
    I even schooled my heart to flee your beauty,
    Thinking it was a bar to my salvation.
    But soon, enlightened, O all lovely one,
    I saw how this my passion may be blameless,

How I may make it fit with modesty,
And thus completely yield my heart to it.
'Tis, I must own, a great presumption in me
To dare make you the offer of my heart;
My love hopes all things from your perfect
    goodness,
And nothing from my own poor weak endeavour.
You are my hope, my stay, my peace of heart;
On you depends my torment or my bliss;
And by your doom of judgment, I shall be
Blest, if you will; or damned, by your decree.

ELMIRE. Your declaration's turned most gallantly;
But truly, it is just a bit surprising.
You should have better armed your heart, methinks,
And taken thought somewhat on such a matter.
A pious man like you, known everywhere . . .

TARTUFFE. Though pious, I am none the less a man;
And when a man beholds your heavenly charms,
The heart surrenders, and can think no more.
I know such words seem strange, coming from me;
But, madam, I'm no angel, after all;
If you condemn my frankly made avowal
You only have your charming self to blame.
Soon as I saw your more than human beauty,
You were thenceforth the sovereign of my soul;
Sweetness ineffable was in your eyes,
That took by storm my still resisting heart,
And conquered everything, fasts, prayers, and tears,
And turned my worship wholly to yourself.
My looks, my sighs, have spoke a thousand times;
Now, to express it all, my voice must speak.
If but you will look down with gracious favour
Upon the sorrows of your worthless slave,
If in your goodness you will give me comfort
And condescend unto my nothingness,
I'll ever pay you, O sweet miracle,
An unexampled worship and devotion.
Then too, with me your honour runs no risk;
With me you need not fear a public scandal.
These court gallants, that women are so fond of,
Are boastful of their acts, and vain in speech;
They always brag in public of their progress;
Soon as a favour's granted, they'll divulge it;
Their tattling tongues, if you but trust to them,
Will foul the altar where their hearts have
    worshipped.
But men like me are so discreet in love,
That you may trust their lasting secrecy.
The care we take to guard our own good name
May fully guarantee the one we love;
So you may find, with hearts like ours sincere,
Love without scandal, pleasure without fear.

ELMIRE. I've heard you through—your speech is
    clear, at least.
But don't you fear that I may take a fancy
To tell my husband of your gallant passion,
And that a prompt report of this affair
May somewhat change the friendship which he
    bears you?

TARTUFFE. I know that you're too good and
    generous,
That you will pardon my temerity,
Excuse, upon the score of human frailty,
The violence of passion that offends you,
And not forget, when you consult your mirror,
That I'm not blind, and man is made of flesh.

ELMIRE. Some women might do otherwise, perhaps,
But I am willing to employ discretion,
And not repeat the matter to my husband;
But in return, I'll ask one thing of you:
That you urge forward, frankly and sincerely,
The marriage of Valère to Mariane;
That you give up the unjust influence
By which you hope to win another's rights;
And . . .

SCENE IV

[Elmire, Damis, Tartuffe]

DAMIS. [coming out of the closet-room where he had been
    hiding] No, I say! This thing must be made public.
I was just there, and overheard it all;
And Heaven's goodness must have brought me
    there
On purpose to confound this scoundrel's pride
And grant me means to take a signal vengeance
On his hypocrisy and arrogance,
And undeceive my father, showing up
The rascal caught at making love to you.

ELMIRE. No, no; it is enough if he reforms,
Endeavouring to deserve the favour shown him.
And since I've promised, do not you belie me.
'Tis not my way to make a public scandal;
An honest wife will scorn to heed such follies,
And never fret her husband's ears with them.

DAMIS. You've reasons of your own for acting thus;
And I have mine for doing otherwise.
To spare him now would be a mockery;
His bigot's pride has triumphed all too long
Over my righteous anger, and has caused
Far too much trouble in our family.

The rascal all too long has ruled my father,
And crossed my sister's love, and mine as well.
The traitor now must be unmasked before him:
And Providence has given me means to do it.
To Heaven I owe the opportunity,
And if I did not use it now I have it,
I should deserve to lose it once for all.

ELMIRE. Damis . . .

DAMIS.   No, by your leave; I'll not be
   counselled.
I'm overjoyed. You needn't try to tell me
I must give up the pleasure of revenge.
I'll make an end of this affair at once;
And, to content me, here's my father now.

SCENE V

[Orgon, Elmire, Damis, Tartuffe]

DAMIS. Father, we've news to welcome your arrival,
   That's altogether novel, and surprising.
   You are well paid for your caressing care,
   And this fine gentleman rewards your love
   Most handsomely, with zeal that seeks no less
   Than your dishonour, as has now been proven.
   I've just surprised him making to your wife
   The shameful offer of a guilty love.
   She, somewhat over gentle and discreet,
   Insisted that the thing should be concealed;
   But I will not condone such shamelessness,
   Nor so far wrong you as to keep it secret.

ELMIRE. Yes, I believe a wife should never trouble
   Her husband's peace of mind with such vain gossip;
   A woman's honour does not hang on telling;
   It is enough if she defend herself;
   Or so I think; Damis, you'd not have spoken,
   If you would but have heeded my advice.

SCENE VI

[Orgon, Damis, Tartuffe]

ORGON. Just Heaven! Can what I hear be credited?

TARTUFFE. Yes, brother, I am wicked, I am guilty,
   A miserable sinner, steeped in evil,
   The greatest criminal that ever lived.
   Each moment of my life is stained with soilures;
   And all is but a mass of crime and filth;
   Heaven, for my punishment, I see it plainly,
Would mortify me now. Whatever wrong
They find to charge me with, I'll not deny it
But guard against the pride of self-defence.
Believe their stories, arm your wrath against me,
And drive me like a villain from your house;
I cannot have so great a share of shame
But what I have deserved a greater still.

ORGON. [to his son] You miscreant, can you dare, with
   such a falsehood,
   To try to stain the whiteness of his virtue?

DAMIS. What! The feigned meekness of this hypocrite
   Makes you discredit . . .

ORGON.   Silence, cursèd plague!

TARTUFFE. Ah! Let him speak; you chide him
   wrongfully;
   You'd do far better to believe his tales.
   Why favour me so much in such a matter?
   How can you know of what I'm capable?
   And should you trust my outward semblance,
      brother,
   Or judge therefrom that I'm the better man?
   No, no; you let appearances deceive you;
   I'm anything but what I'm thought to be,
   Alas! and though all men believe me godly,
   The simple truth is, I'm a worthless creature.

[To Damis]

   Yes, my dear son, say on, and call me traitor,
   Abandoned scoundrel, thief, and murderer;
   Heap on me names yet more detestable,
   And I shall not gainsay you; I've deserved them;
   I'll bear this ignominy on my knees,
   To expiate in shame the crimes I've done.

ORGON. [to Tartuffe] Ah, brother, 'tis too much!

[To his son]

                                        You'll
      not relent,
   You blackguard?

DAMIS.   What! His talk can so
      deceive you . . .

ORGON. Silence, you scoundrel!

[To Tartuffe]

                          Brother, rise, I
      beg you.

[To his son]

   Infamous villain!

DAMIS.　　　　　　　Can he . . .
ORGON.　　　　　　　　　　Silence!
DAMIS.　　　　　　　　　　　　What . . .
ORGON. Another word, I'll break your every bone.
TARTUFFE. Brother, in God's name, don't be angry
　　with him!
　　I'd rather bear myself the bitterest torture
　　Than have him get a scratch on my account.
ORGON. [to his son] Ungrateful monster!
TARTUFFE.　　　　　　　　　　Stop. Upon
　　my knees
　　I beg you pardon him . . .
ORGON. [throwing himself on his knees too, and embrac-
　　ing Tartuffe]　　　　　Alas! How can you?

[To his son]

　　Villain! Behold his goodness!
DAMIS.　　　　　　　　So . . .
ORGON.　　　　　　　　　　Be still.
DAMIS. What! I . . .
ORGON.　　　　　　Be still, I say. I know your motives
　　For this attack. You hate him, all of you;
　　Wife, children, servants, all let loose upon him,
　　You have recourse to every shameful trick
　　To drive this godly man out of my house;
　　The more you strive to rid yourselves of him,
　　The more I'll strive to make him stay with me;
　　I'll have him straightway married to my daughter,
　　Just to confound the pride of all of you.
DAMIS. What! Will you force her to accept his hand?
ORGON. Yes, and this very evening, to enrage you,
　　Young rascal! Ah! I'll brave you all, and show you
　　That I'm the master, and must be obeyed.
　　Now, down upon your knees this instant, rogue,
　　And take back what you said, and ask his pardon.
DAMIS. Who? I? Ask pardon of that cheating
　　scoundrel . . . ?
ORGON. Do you resist, you beggar, and insult him?
　　A cudgel, here! a cudgel!

[To Tartuffe]

　　　　　　　　　Don't restrain me.

[To his son]

　　Off with you! Leave my house this instant, sirrah,
　　And never dare set foot in it again.
DAMIS. Yes, I will leave your house, but . . .
ORGON.　　　　　　　　　　　　Leave it
　　quickly,

You reprobate, I disinherit you,
And give you, too, my curse into the bargain.

SCENE VII

[Orgon, Tartuffe]

ORGON. What! So insult a saintly man of God!
TARTUFFE. Heaven, forgive him all the pain he gives
　　me![3]

[To Orgon]

　　Could you but know with what distress I see
　　Them try to vilify me to my brother!
ORGON. Ah!
TARTUFFE. The mere thought of such ingratitude
　　Makes my soul suffer torture, bitterly . . .
　　My horror at it . . . Ah! my heart's so full
　　I cannot speak . . . I think I'll die of it.
ORGON. [in tears, running to the door through which he
　　drove away his son] Scoundrel! I wish I'd never let
　　you go,
　　But slain you on the spot with my own hand.

[To Tartuffe]

　　Brother, compose yourself, and don't be angry.
TARTUFFE. Nay, brother, let us end these painful
　　quarrels.
　　I see what troublous times I bring upon you,
　　And think 'tis needful that I leave this house.
ORGON. What! You can't mean it?
TARTUFFE.　　　　　　　　Yes, they hate me
　　here,
　　And try, I find, to make you doubt my faith.
ORGON. What of it? Do you find I listen to them?
TARTUFFE. No doubt they won't stop there. These
　　same reports
　　You now reject, may some day win a hearing.
ORGON. No, brother, never.

---

[3] Some modern editions have adopted the reading, preserved by tradition as that of the earliest stage version:

　　　　Heaven, forgive him even as I forgive him!

Voltaire gives still another reading:

　　　　Heaven, forgive me even as I forgive him!

Whichever was the original version, it appears in none of the early
editions, and Molière probably felt forced to change it on account of
its too close resemblance to the Biblical phrase.

TARTUFFE.   Ah! my friend, a woman
  May easily mislead her husband's mind.
ORGON. No, no.
TARTUFFE.   So let me quickly go away
  And thus remove all cause for such attacks.
ORGON. No, you shall stay; my life depends upon it.
TARTUFFE. Then I must mortify myself. And yet,
  If you should wish . . .
ORGON.   No, never!
TARTUFFE.   Very well, then;
  No more of that. But I shall rule my conduct
  To fit the case. Honour is delicate,
  And friendship binds me to forestall suspicion,
  Prevent all scandal, and avoid your wife.
ORGON. No, you shall haunt her, just to spite them
  all.

'Tis my delight to set them in a rage;
You shall be seen together at all hours
And what is more, the better to defy them,
I'll have no other heir but you; and straightway
I'll go and make a deed of gift to you,
Drawn in due form, of all my property.
A good true friend, my son-in-law to be,
Is more to me than son, and wife, and kindred.
You will accept my offer, will you not?
TARTUFFE. Heaven's will be done in everything!
ORGON.   Poor
  man!
We'll go make haste to draw the deed aright,
And then let envy burst itself with spite!

Act IV

SCENE I

[*Cléante, Tartuffe*]

CLÉANTE. Yes, it's become the talk of all the town,
  And makes a stir that's scarcely to your credit;
  And I have met you, sir, most opportunely,
  To tell you in a word my frank opinion.
  Not to sift out this scandal to the bottom,
  Suppose the worst for us—suppose Damis
  Acted the traitor, and accused you falsely;
  Should not a Christian pardon this offence,
  And stifle in his heart all wish for vengeance?
  Should you permit that, for your petty quarrel,
  A son be driven from his father's house?
  I tell you yet again, and tell you frankly,
  Everyone, high or low, is scandalised;
  If you'll take my advice, you'll make it up,
  And not push matters to extremities.
  Make sacrifice to God of your resentment;
  Restore the son to favour with his father.
TARTUFFE. Alas! So far as I'm concerned, how gladly
  Would I do so! I bear him no ill will;
  I pardon all, lay nothing to his charge,
  And wish with all my heart that I might serve him;
  But Heaven's interests cannot allow it;
  If he returns, then I must leave the house.
  After his conduct, quite unparalleled,
  All intercourse between us would bring scandal;
  God knows what everyone's first thought would be!

They would attribute it to merest scheming
On my part—say that conscious of my guilt
I feigned a Christian love for my accuser,
But feared him in my heart, and hoped to win him
And underhandedly secure his silence.
CLÉANTE. You try to put us off with specious phrases;
  But all your arguments are too far-fetched.
  Why take upon yourself the cause of Heaven?
  Does Heaven need our help to punish sinners?
  Leave to itself the care of its own vengeance,
  And keep in mind the pardon it commands us;
  Besides, think somewhat less of men's opinions,
  When you are following the will of Heaven.
  Shall petty fear of what the world may think
  Prevent the doing of a noble deed?
  No!—let us always do as Heaven commands,
  And not perplex our brains with further questions.
TARTUFFE. Already I have told you I forgive him;
  And that is doing, sir, as Heaven commands.
  But after this day's scandal and affront
  Heaven does not order me to live with him.
CLÉANTE. And does it order you to lend your ear
  To what mere whim suggested to his father,
  And to accept the gift of his estates,
  On which, in justice, you can make no claim?
TARTUFFE. No one who knows me, sir, can have the
  thought
That I am acting from a selfish motive.
The goods of this world have no charms for me;
I am not dazzled by their treacherous glamour;
And if I bring myself to take the gift

Which he insists on giving me, I do so,
To tell the truth, only because I fear
This whole estate may fall into bad hands,
And those to whom it comes may use it ill
And not employ it, as is my design,
For Heaven's glory and my neighbours' good.

CLÉANTE. Eh, sir, give up these conscientious scruples
That well may cause a rightful heir's complaints.
Don't take so much upon yourself, but let him
Possess what's his, at his own risk and peril;
Consider, it were better he misused it,
Than you should be accused of robbing him.
I am astounded that unblushingly
You could allow such offers to be made!
Tell me—has true religion any maxim
That teaches us to rob the lawful heir?
If Heaven has made it quite impossible
Damis and you should live together here,
Were it not better you should quietly
And honourably withdraw, than let the son
Be driven out for your sake, dead against
All reason? 'Twould be giving, sir, believe me,
Such an example of your probity . . .

TARTUFFE. Sir, it is half-past three; certain devotions
Recall me to my closet; you'll forgive me
For leaving you so soon.

CLÉANTE. [alone]   Ah!

SCENE II

[*Elmire, Mariane, Cléante, Dorine*]

DORINE. [*to Cléante*] Sir, we beg you
To help us all you can in her behalf;
She's suffering almost more than heart can bear;
This match her father means to make to-night
Drives her each moment to despair. He's coming.
Let us unite our efforts now, we beg you,
And try by strength or skill to change his purpose.

SCENE III

[*Orgon, Elmire, Mariane, Cléante, Dorine*]

ORGON. So ho! I'm glad to find you all together.

[*To Mariane*]

Here is the contract that shall make you happy,
My dear. You know already what it means.

MARIANE. (*on her knees before Orgon*)
Father, I beg you, in the name of Heaven
That knows my grief, and by whate'er can move
   you,
Relax a little your paternal rights,
And free my love from this obedience!
Oh, do not make me, by your harsh command,
Complain to Heaven you ever were my father;
Do not make wretched this poor life you gave me.
If, crossing that fond hope which I had formed,
You'll not permit me to belong to one
Whom I have dared to love, at least, I beg you
Upon my knees, oh, save me from the torment
Of being possessed by one whom I abhor!
And do not drive me to some desperate act
By exercising all your rights upon me.

ORGON. [*a little touched*] Come, come, my heart, be
   firm! no human weakness!

MARIANE. I am not jealous of your love for him;
Display it freely; give him your estate,
And if that's not enough, add all of mine;
I willingly agree, and give it up,
If only you'll not give him me, your daughter;
Oh, rather let a convent's rigid rule
Wear out the wretched days that Heaven allots me.

ORGON. These girls are ninnies!—always turning nuns
When fathers thwart their silly love-affairs.
Get on your feet! The more you hate to have him,
The more 'twill help you earn your soul's salvation.
So, mortify your senses by this marriage,
And don't vex me about it any more.

DORINE. But what . . . ?

ORGON.   You hold your tongue, before
   your betters.
Don't dare to say a single word, I tell you.

CLÉANTE. If you will let me answer, and advise . . .

ORGON. Brother, I value your advice most highly;
'Tis well thought out; no better can be had;
But you'll allow me—not to follow it.

ELMIRE. [*to her husband*] I can't find words to cope
   with such a case;
Your blindness makes me quite astounded at you.
You are bewitched with him, to disbelieve
The things we tell you happened here to-day.

ORGON. I am your humble servant, and can see
Things, when they're plain as noses on folks' faces,
I know you're partial to my rascal son,
And didn't dare to disavow the trick
He tried to play on this poor man; besides,
You were too calm, to be believed; if that
Had happened, you'd have been far more disturbed.

ELMIRE. And must our honour always rush to arms

At the mere mention of illicit love?
Or can we answer no attack upon it
Except with blazing eyes and lips of scorn?
For my part, I just laugh away such nonsense;
I've no desire to make a loud to-do.
Our virtue should, I think, be gentle-natured;
Nor can I quite approve those savage prudes
Whose honour arms itself with teeth and claws
To tear men's eyes out at the slightest word.
Heaven preserve me from that kind of honour!
I like my virtue not to be a vixen,
And I believe a quiet cold rebuff
No less effective to repulse a lover.

ORGON. I know . . . and you can't throw me off the
    scent.
ELMIRE. Once more, I am astounded at your
    weakness;
    I wonder what your unbelief would answer,
    If I should let you see we've told the truth?
ORGON. See it?
ELMIRE.   Yes.
ORGON.   Nonsense.
ELMIRE.   Come! If I should find
    A way to make you see it clear as day?
ORGON. All rubbish.
ELMIRE.   What a man! But answer me.
    I'm not proposing now that you believe us;
    But let's suppose that here, from proper hiding,
    You should be made to see and hear all plainly;
    What would you say then, to your man of virtue?
ORGON. Why, then, I'd say   say nothing. It can't
    be.
ELMIRE. Your error has endured too long already,
    And quite too long you've branded me a liar.
    I must at once, for my own satisfaction,
    Make you a witness of the things we've told you.
ORGON. Amen! I take you at your word. We'll see
    What tricks you have, and how you'll keep your
      promise.
ELMIRE. [to Dorine] Send him to me.
DORINE. [to Elmire]   The man's a
    crafty codger,
    Perhaps you'll find it difficult to catch him.
ELMIRE. [to Dorine] Oh no! A lover's never hard to
    cheat,
    And self-conceit leads straight to self-deceit.
    Bid him come down to me.

[To Cléante and Mariane]

             And you, withdraw.

SCENE IV

[Elmire, Orgon]

ELMIRE. Bring up this table, and get under it.
ORGON. What?
ELMIRE.   One essential is to hide you well.
ORGON. Why under there?
ELMIRE.   Oh, dear! Do as I say;
    I know what I'm about, as you shall see.
    Get under, now, I tell you; and once there
    Be careful no one either sees or hears you.
ORGON. I'm going a long way to humour you,
    I must say; but I'll see you through your scheme.
ELMIRE. And then you'll have, I think, no more to
    say.

[To her husband, who is now under the table.]

    But mind, I'm going to meddle with strange
      matters;
    Prepare yourself to be in no wise shocked.
    Whatever I may say must pass, because
    'Tis only to convince you, as I promised.
    By wheedling speeches, since I'm forced to do it,
    I'll make this hypocrite put off his mask,
    Flatter the longings of his shameless passion,
    And give free play to all his impudence.
    But, since 'tis for your sake, to prove to you
    His guilt, that I shall feign to share his love,
    I can leave off as soon as you're convinced,
    And things shall go no farther than you choose.
    So, when you think they've gone quite far enough,
    It is for you to stop his mad pursuit,
    To spare your wife, and not expose me farther
    Than you shall need, yourself, to undeceive you.
    It is your own affair, and you must end it
    When . . . Here he comes. Keep still, don't show
      yourself.

SCENE V

[Tartuffe, Elmire; Orgon (under the table)]

TARTUFFE. They told me that you wished to see me
    here.
ELMIRE. Yes. I have secrets for your ear alone.
    But shut the door first, and look everywhere
    For fear of spies.

[Tartuffe goes and closes the door, and comes back.]

We surely can't afford
Another scene like that we had just now;
Was ever anyone so caught before!
Damis did frighten me most terribly
On your account; you saw I did my best
To baffle his design, and calm his anger.
But I was so confused, I never thought
To contradict his story; still, thank Heaven,
Things turned out all the better, as it happened,
And now we're on an even safer footing.
The high esteem you're held in, laid the storm;
My husband can have no suspicion of you,
And even insists, to spite the scandal-mongers,
That we shall be together constantly;
So that is how, without the risk of blame,
I can be here locked up with you alone,
And can reveal to you my heart, perhaps
Only too ready to allow your passion.

TARTUFFE. Your words are somewhat hard to
    understand,
Madam; just now you used a different style.

ELMIRE. If that refusal has offended you,
How little do you know a woman's heart!
How ill you guess what it would have you know,
When it presents so feeble a defence!
Always, at first, our modesty resists
The tender feelings you inspire us with.
Whatever cause we find to justify
The love that masters us, we still must feel
Some little shame in owning it; and strive
To make as though we would not, when we would.
But from the very way we go about it
We let a lover know our heart surrenders,
The while our lips, for honour's sake, oppose
Our heart's desire, and in refusing promise.
I'm telling you my secret all too freely
And with too little heed to modesty.
But—now that I've made bold to speak—pray tell
    me.
Should I have tried to keep Damis from speaking,
Should I have heard the offer of your heart
So quietly, and suffered all your pleading,
And taken it just as I did—remember—
If such a declaration had not pleased me,
And, when I tried my utmost to persuade you
Not to accept the marriage that was talked of,
What should my earnestness have hinted to you
If not the interest that you've inspired,
And my chagrin, should such a match compel me
To share a heart I want all to myself?

TARTUFFE. 'Tis, past a doubt, the height of happiness,
  To hear such words from lips we dote upon;

Their honeyed sweetness pours through all my
    senses
Long draughts of suavity ineffable.
My heart employs its utmost zeal to please you,
And counts your love its one beatitude;
And yet that heart must beg that you allow it
To doubt a little its felicity.
I well might think these words an honest trick
To make me break off this approaching marriage;
And if I may express myself quite plainly,
I cannot trust these too enchanting words
Until the granting of some little favour
I sigh for, shall assure me of their truth
And build within my soul, on firm foundations,
A lasting faith in your sweet charity.

ELMIRE. [coughing to draw her husband's attention] What!
Must you go so fast?—and all at once
Exhaust the whole love of a woman's heart?
She does herself the violence to make
This dear confession of her love, and you
Are not yet satisfied, and will not be
Without the granting of her utmost favours?

TARTUFFE. The less a blessing is deserved, the less
We dare to hope for it; and words alone
Can ill assuage our love's desires. A fate
Too full of happiness, seems doubtful still;
We must enjoy it ere we can believe it.
And I, who know how little I deserve
Your goodness, doubt the fortunes of my daring;
So I shall trust to nothing, madam, till
You have convinced my love by something real.

ELMIRE. Ah! How our love enacts the tyrant's rôle,
And throws my mind into a strange confusion!
With what fierce sway it rules a conquered heart,
And violently will have its wishes granted!
What! Is there no escape from your pursuit?
No respite even?—not a breathing space?
Nay, is it decent to be so exacting,
And so abuse by urgency the weakness
You may discover in a woman's heart?

TARTUFFE. But if my worship wins your gracious
    favour,
Then why refuse me some sure proof thereof?

ELMIRE. But how can I consent to what you wish,
Without offending Heaven you talk so much of?

TARTUFFE. If Heaven is all that stands now in my way,
I'll easily remove that little hindrance;
Your heart need not hold back for such a trifle.

ELMIRE. But they affright us so with Heaven's
    commands!

TARTUFFE. I can dispel these foolish fears, dear
    madam;

I know the art of pacifying scruples.
Heaven forbids, 'tis true, some satisfactions;
But we find means to make things right with
   Heaven.

[*'Tis a scoundrel speaking.*]⁴

There is a science, madam, that instructs us
How to enlarge the limits of our conscience
According to our various occasions,
And rectify the evil of the deed
According to our purity of motive.
I'll duly teach you all these secrets, madam;
You only need to let yourself be guided.
Content my wishes, have no fear at all;
I answer for't, and take the sin upon me.

[*Elmire coughs still louder.*]

Your cough is very bad.
ELMIRE.   Yes, I'm in torture.
TARTUFFE. Would you accept this bit of licorice?
ELMIRE. The case is obstinate, I find; and all
   The licorice in the world will do no good.
TARTUFFE. 'Tis very trying.
ELMIRE.   More than words can say.
TARTUFFE. In any case, your scruple's easily
   Removed. With me you're sure of secrecy,
   And there's no harm unless a thing is known.
   The public scandal is what brings offence,
   And secret sinning is not sin at all.
ELMIRE. [*after coughing again*] So then, I see I must
   resolve to yield;
   I must consent to grant you everything,
   And cannot hope to give full satisfaction
   Or win full confidence, at lesser cost.
   No doubt 'tis very hard to come to this;
   'Tis quite against my will I go so far;
   But since I must be forced to it, since nothing
   That can be said suffices for belief,
   Since more convincing proof is still demanded,
   I must make up my mind to humour people.
   If my consent give reason for offence,
   So much the worse for him who forced me to it;
   The fault can surely not be counted mine.
TARTUFFE. It need not, madam; and the thing
   itself . . .
ELMIRE. Open the door, I pray you, and just see
   Whether my husband's not there, in the hall.

⁴ Molière's note, in the original edition.

TARTUFFE. Why take such care for him? Between
   ourselves,
   He is a man to lead round by the nose.
   He's capable of glorying in our meetings;
   I've fooled him so, he'd see all, and deny it.
ELMIRE. No matter; go, I beg you, look about,
   And carefully examine every corner.

SCENE VI

[*Orgon, Elmire*]

ORGON. [*crawling out from under the table*] That is, I
   own, a man . . . abominable!
   I can't get over it; the whole thing floors me.
ELMIRE. What? You come out so soon? You cannot
   mean it!
   Get back under the table; 'tis not time yet;
   Wait till the end, to see, and make quite certain,
   And don't believe a thing on mere conjecture.
ORGON. Nothing more wicked e'er came out of Hell.
ELMIRE. Dear me! Don't go and credit things too
   lightly.
   No, let yourself be thoroughly convinced;
   Don't yield too soon, for fear you'll be mistaken.

[*As Tartuffe enters, she makes her husband stand behind
her.*]

SCENE VII

[*Tartuffe, Elmire, Orgon*]

TARTUFFE. [*not seeing Orgon*] All things conspire
   toward my satisfaction,
   Madam, I've searched the whole apartment
   through.
   There's no one here; and now my ravished soul . . .
ORGON. [*stopping him*] Softly! You are too eager in
   your amours;
   You needn't be so passionate. Ah ha!
   My holy man! You want to put it on me!
   How is your soul abandoned to temptation!
   Marry my daughter, eh?—and want my wife, too?
   I doubted long enough if this was earnest,
   Expecting all the time the tone would change;
   But now the proof's been carried far enough;
   I'm satisfied, and ask no more, for my part.

ELMIRE. [*to Tartuffe*] 'Twas quite against my character
  to play
This part; but I was forced to treat you so.
TARTUFFE. What? You believe . . . ?
ORGON.   Come, now, no
  protestations.
Get out from here, and make no fuss about it.
TARTUFFE. But my intent . . .
ORGON.   That talk is out of
  season.
You leave my house this instant.
TARTUFFE.   You're the one
  To leave it, you who play the master here!
  This house belongs to me, I'll have you know,
  And show you plainly it's no use to turn
  To these low tricks, to pick a quarrel with me,
  And that you can't insult me at your pleasure,
  For I have wherewith to confound your lies,
  Avenge offended Heaven, and compel
  Those to repent who talk to me of leaving.

SCENE VIII

[*Elmire, Orgon*]

ELMIRE. What sort of speech is this? What can it
  mean?
ORGON. My faith, I'm dazed. This is no laughing
  matter.
ELMIRE. What?
ORGON.   From his words I see my great mistake;
  The deed of gift is one thing troubles me.
ELMIRE. The deed of gift . . .
ORGON.   Yes, that is past recall.
  But I've another thing to make me anxious.
ELMIRE. What's that?
ORGON.   You shall know all. Let's see at
  once
  Whether a certain box is still upstairs.

Act V

SCENE I

[*Orgon, Cléante*]

CLÉANTE. Whither away so fast?
ORGON.   How should I know?
CLÉANTE. Methinks we should begin by taking
  counsel
  To see what can be done to meet the case.
ORGON. I'm all worked up about that wretched box.
  More than all else it drives me to despair.
CLÉANT. That box must hide some mighty mystery?
ORGON. Argas, my friend who is in trouble, brought it
  Himself, most secretly, and left it with me.
  He chose me, in his exile, for this trust;
  And on these documents, from what he said,
  I judge his life and property depend.
CLÉANTE. How could you trust them to another's
  hands?
ORGON. By reason of a conscientious scruple.
  I went straight to my traitor, to confide
  In him; his sophistry made me believe
  That I must give the box to him to keep,
  So that, in case of search, I might deny

My having it at all, and still, by favour
  Of this evasion, keep my conscience clear
  Even in taking oath against the truth.
CLÉANTE. Your case is bad, so far as I can see;
  This deed of gift, this trusting of the secret
  To him, were both—to state my frank opinion—
  Steps that you took too lightly; he can lead you
  To any length, with these for hostages;
  And since he holds you at such disadvantage,
  You'd be still more imprudent, to provoke him;
  So you must go some gentler way about.
ORGON. What! Can a soul so base, a heart so false,
  Hide neath the semblance of such touching fervour?
  I took him in, a vagabond, a beggar! . . .
  'Tis too much! No more pious folk for me!
  I shall abhor them utterly forever,
  And henceforth treat them worse than any devil.
CLÉANTE. So! There you go again, quite off the
  handle!
  In nothing do you keep an even temper.
  You never know what reason is, but always
  Jump first to one extreme, and then the other.
  You see your error, and you recognise
  That you've been cozened by a feigned zeal;
  But to make up for't, in the name of reason,

Why should you plunge into a worse mistake,
And find no difference in character
Between a worthless scamp, and all good people?
What! Just because a rascal boldly duped you
With pompous show of false austerity,
Must you needs have it everybody's like him,
And no one's truly pious nowadays?
Leave such conclusions to mere infidels;
Distinguish virtue from its counterfeit,
Don't give esteem too quickly, at a venture,
But try to keep, in this, the golden mean.
If you can help it, don't uphold imposture;
But do not rail at true devoutness, either;
And if you must fall into one extreme,
Then rather err again the other way.

SCENE II

[*Damis, Orgon, Cléante*]

DAMIS. What! father, can the scoundrel threaten you,
  Forget the many benefits received,
  And in his base abominable pride
  Make of your very favours arms against you?
ORGON. Too true, my son. It tortures me to think
  on't.
DAMIS. Let me alone, I'll chop his ears off for him.
  We must deal roundly with his insolence;
  'Tis I must free you from him at a blow;
  'Tis I, to set things right, must strike him down.
CLÉANTE. Spoke like a true young man. Now just
  calm down,
  And moderate your towering tantrums, will you?
  We live in such an age, with such a king,
  That violence can not advance our cause.

SCENE III

[*Madame Pernelle, Orgon, Elmire, Cléante, Mariane, Damis, Dorine*]

MADAME PERNELLE. What's this? I hear of fearful
  mysteries!
ORGON. Strange things indeed, for my own eyes to
  witness;
  You see how I'm requited for my kindness,
  I zealously receive a wretched beggar,
  I lodge him, entertain him like my brother,
  Load him with benefactions every day,

Give him my daughter, give him all my fortune:
And he meanwhile, the villain, rascal, wretch,
Tries with black treason to suborn my wife,
And not content with such a foul design,
He dares to menace me with my own favours,
And would make use of those advantages
Which my too foolish kindness armed him with,
To ruin me, to take my fortune from me,
And leave me in the state I saved him from.
DORINE. Poor man!
MADAME PERNELLE. My son, I cannot possibly
  Believe he could intend so black a deed.
ORGON. What?
MADAME PERNELLE. Worthy men are still the sport of
  envy.
ORGON. Mother, what do you mean by such a speech?
MADAME PERNELLE. There are strange goings-on
  about your house,
  And everybody knows your people hate him.
ORGON. What's that to do with what I tell you now?
MADAME PERNELLE. I always said, my son, when you
  were little:
  That virtue here below is hated ever;
  The envious may die, but envy never.
ORGON. What's that fine speech to do with present
  facts?
MADAME PERNELLE. Be sure, they've forged a
  hundred silly lies . . .
ORGON. I've told you once, I saw it all myself.
MADAME PERNELLE. For slanderers abound in
  calumnies . . .
ORGON. Mother, you'd make me damn my soul. I tell
  you
  I saw with my own eyes his shamelessness.
MADAME PERNELLE. Their tongues for spitting
  venom never lack,
  There's nothing here below they'll not attack.
ORGON. Your speech has not a single grain of sense.
  I saw it, harkee, saw it, with these eyes
  I saw—d'ye know what *saw* means?—must I say it
  A hundred times, and din it in your ears?
MADAME PERNELLE. My dear, appearances are oft
  deceiving,
  And seeing shouldn't always be believing.
ORGON. I'll go mad.
MADAME PERNELLE. False suspicions may delude,
  And good to evil oft is misconstrued.
ORGON. Must I construe as Christian charity
  The wish to kiss my wife!
MADAME PERNELLE.   You must, at least,
  Have just foundation for accusing people,
  And wait until you see a thing for sure.

ORGON. The devil! How could I see any surer?
  Should I have waited till, before my eyes,
  He . . . No, you'll make me say things quite
    improper.
MADAME PERNELLE. In short, 'tis known too pure a
    zeal inflames him;
  And so, I cannot possibly conceive
  That he should try to do what's charged against
    him.
ORGON. If you were not my mother, I should say
  Such things! . . . I know not what, I'm so enraged!
DORINE. [*to Orgon*] Fortune has paid you fair, to be so
    doubted;
  You flouted our report, now yours is flouted.
CLÉANTE. We're wasting time here in the merest
    trifling,
  Which we should rather use in taking measures
  To guard ourselves against the scoundrel's threats.
DAMIS. You think his impudence could go so far?
ELMIRE. For one, I can't believe it possible;
  Why, his ingratitude would be too patent.
CLÉANTE. Don't trust to that; he'll find abundant
    warrant
  To give good colour to his acts against you;
  And for less cause than this, a strong cabal
  Can make one's life a labyrinth of troubles.
  I tell you once again: armed as he is
  You never should have pushed him quite so far.
ORGON. True; yet what could I do? The rascal's pride
  Made me lose all control of my resentment.
CLÉANTE. I wish with all my heart that some pretence
  Of peace could be patched up between you two.
ELMIRE. If I had known what weapons he was armed
    with,
  I never should have raised such an alarm,
  And my . . .
ORGON. [*to Dorine, seeing Mr. Loyal come in*] Who's
    coming now? Go quick, find out.
  I'm in a fine state to receive a visit!

SCENE IV

[*Orgon, Madame Pernelle, Elmire, Mariane, Cléante, Damis,
Dorine, Mr. Loyal*]

MR. LOYAL. [*to Dorine, at the back of the stage*] Good
    day, good sister. Pray you, let me see
  The master of the house.

DORINE.   He's occupied;
  I think he can see nobody at present.
MR. LOYAL. I'm not by way of being unwelcome here.
  My coming can, I think, nowise displease him;
  My errand will be found to his advantage.
DORINE. Your name, then?
MR. LOYAL.   Tell him simply that his
    friend
  Mr. Tartuffe has sent me, for his goods . . .
DORINE. [*to Orgon*] It is a man who comes, with civil
    manners,
  Sent by Tartuffe, he says, upon an errand
  That you'll be pleased with.
CLÉANTE. [*to Orgon*]   Surely you must see
    him,
  And find out who he is, and what he wants.
ORGON. [*to Cléante*] Perhaps he's come to make it up
    between us:
  How shall I treat him?
CLÉANTE.   You must not get angry;
  And if he talks of reconciliation
  Accept it.
MR. LOYAL. [*to Orgon*] Sir, good-day. And Heaven
    send
  Harm to your enemies, favour to you.
ORGON. [*aside to Cléante*] This mild beginning suits
    with my conjectures
  And promises some compromise already.
MR. LOYAL. All of your house has long been dear to
    me;
  I had the honour, sir, to serve your father.
ORGON. Sir, I am much ashamed, and ask your
    pardon
  For not recalling now your face or name.
MR. LOYAL. My name is Loyal. I'm from Normandy.
  My office is court-bailiff, in despite
  Of envy; and for forty years, thank Heaven,
  It's been my fortune to perform that office
  With honour. So I've come, sir, by your leave
  To render service of a certain writ . . .
ORGON. What, you are here to . . .
MR. LOYAL.   Pray, sir, don't be
    angry.
  'Tis nothing, sir, but just a little summons:—
  Order to vacate, you and yours, this house,
  Move out your furniture, make room for others,
  And that without delay or putting off,
  As needs must be . . .
ORGON.   I? Leave this house?
MR. LOYAL.   Yes,
    please, sir.
  The house is now, as you well know, of course,

Mr. Tartuffe's. And he, beyond dispute,
Of all your goods is henceforth lord and master
By virtue of a contract here attached,
Drawn in due form, and unassailable.

DAMIS. [to Mr. Loyal] Your insolence is monstrous, and
    astounding!

MR. LOYAL. [to Damis] I have no business, sir, that
    touches you;

[Pointing to Orgon]

This is the gentleman. He's fair and courteous,
And knows too well a gentleman's behaviour
To wish in any wise to question justice.

ORGON. But . . .

MR. LOYAL.   Sir, I know you would not for a
    million
Wish to rebel; like a good citizen
You'll let me put in force the court's decree.

DAMIS. Your long black gown may well, before you
    know it,
Mister Court-bailiff, get a thorough beating.

MR. LOYAL. [to Orgon] Sir, make your son be silent or
    withdraw.
I should be loath to have to set things down,
And see your names inscribed in my report.

DORINE. [aside] This Mr. Loyal's looks are most
    disloyal.

MR. LOYAL. I have much feeling for respectable
And honest folk like you, sir, and consented
To serve these papers, only to oblige you,
And thus prevent the choice of any other
Who, less possessed of zeal for you than I am
Might order matters in less gentle fashion.

ORGON. And how could one do worse than order
    people
Out of their house?

MR. LOYAL.   Why, we allow you time;
And even will suspend until to-morrow
The execution of the order, sir.
I'll merely, without scandal, quietly,
Come here and spend the night, with half a score
Of officers; and just for form's sake, please,
You'll bring your keys to me, before retiring.
I will take care not to disturb your rest,
And see there's no unseemly conduct here.
But by to-morrow, and at early morning,
You must make haste to move your least belongings;
My men will help you—I have chosen strong ones
To serve you, sir, in clearing out the house.
No one could act more generously, I fancy,
And, since I'm treating you with great indulgence,

I beg you'll do as well by me, and see
I'm not disturbed in my discharge of duty.

ORGON. I'd give this very minute, and not grudge it,
The hundred best gold louis I have left,
If I could just indulge myself, and land
My fist, for one good square one, on his snout.

CLÉANTE. [aside to Orgon] Careful!—don't make
    things worse.

DAMIS.   Such insolence!
I hardly can restrain myself. My hands
Are itching to be at him.

DORINE.   By my faith,
With such a fine broad back, good Mr. Loyal,
A little beating would become you well.

MR. LOYAL. My girl, such infamous words are
    actionable.
And warrants can be issues against women.

CLÉANTE. [to Mr. Loyal] Enough of this discussion, sir;
    have done.
Give us the paper, and then leave us, pray.

MR. LOYAL. Then au revoir. Heaven keep you from
    disaster!

ORGON. May Heaven confound you both, you and
    your master!

SCENE V

[Orgon, Madame Pernelle, Elmire, Cléante, Mariane, Damis,
Dorine]

ORGON. Well, mother, am I right or am I not?
This writ may help you now to judge the matter.
Or don't you see his treason even yet?

MADAME PERNELLE. I'm all amazed, befuddled, and
    beflustered!

DORINE. [to Orgon] You are quite wrong, you have no
    right to blame him;
This action only proves his good intentions.
Love for his neighbour makes his virtue perfect;
And knowing money is a root of evil,
In Christian charity, he'd take away
Whatever things may hinder your salvation.

ORGON. Be still. You always need to have that told
    you.

CLÉANTE. [to Orgon] Come, let us see what course you
    are to follow.

ELMIRE. Go and expose his bold ingratitude.
Such action must invalidate the contract;
His perfidy must now appear too black
To bring him the success that he expects.

SCENE VI

[*Valère, Orgon, Madame Pernelle, Elmire, Cléante, Mariane, Damis, Dorine*]

VALÈRE. 'Tis with regret, sir, that I bring bad news;
But urgent danger forces me to do so.
A close and intimate friend of mine, who knows
The interest I take in what concerns you,
Has gone so far, for my sake, as to break
The secrecy that's due to state affairs,
And sent me word but now, that leaves you only
The one expedient of sudden flight.
The villain who so long imposed upon you,
Found means, an hour ago, to see the prince,
And to accuse you (among other things)
By putting in his hands the private strong-box
Of a state-criminal, whose guilty secret,
You, failing in your duty as a subject,
(He says) have kept. I know no more of it
Save that a warrant's drawn against you, sir,
And for the great surety, that same rascal
Comes with the officer who must arrest you.
CLÉANTE. His rights are armed; and this is how the scoundrel
Seeks to secure the property he claims.
ORGON. Man is a wicked animal, I'll own it!
VALÈRE. The least delay may still be fatal, sir.
I have my carriage, and a thousand louis,
Provided for your journey, at the door.
Let's lose no time; the bolt is swift to strike,
And such as only flight can save you from.
I'll be your guide to seek a place of safety,
And stay with you until you reach it, sir.
ORGON. How much I owe to your obliging care!
Another time must serve to thank you fitly;
And I pray Heaven to grant me so much favour
That I may some day recompense your service.
Good-bye; see to it, all of you . . .
CLÉANTE.   Come hurry;
We'll see to everything that's needful, brother.

SCENE VII

[*Tartuffe, An Officer, Madame Pernelle, Orgon, Elmire, Cléante, Mariane, Valère, Damis, Dorine*]

TARTUFFE. [*stopping Orgon*] Softly, sir, softly; do not run so fast;

You haven't far to go to find your lodging;
By order of the prince, we here arrest you.
ORGON. Traitor! You saved this worst stroke for the last;
This crowns your perfidies, and ruins me.
TARTUFFE. I shall not be embittered by your insults,
For Heaven has taught me to endure all things.
CLÉANTE. Your moderation, I must own, is great.
DAMIS. How shamelessly the wretch makes bold with Heaven!
TARTUFFE. Your ravings cannot move me; all my thought
Is but to do my duty.
MARIANE.   You must claim
Great glory from this honourable act.
TARTUFFE. The act cannot be aught but honourable,
Coming from that high power which sends me here.
ORGON. Ungrateful wretch, do you forget 'twas I
That rescued you from utter misery?
TARTUFFE. I've not forgot some help you may have given;
But my first duty now is toward my prince.
The higher power of that most sacred claim
Must stifle in my heart all gratitude;
And to such puissant ties I'd sacrifice
My friend, my wife, my kindred, and myself.
ELMIRE. The hypocrite!
DORINE.   How well he knows the trick
Of cloaking him with what we most revere!
CLÉANTE. But if the motive that you make parade of
Is perfect as you say, why should it wait
To show itself, until the day he caught you
Soliciting his wife? How happens it
You have not thought to go inform against him
Until his honour forces him to drive you
Out of his house? And though I need not mention
That he'd just given you his whole estate,
Still, if you meant to treat him now as guilty,
How could you then consent to take his gift?
TARTUFFE. [*to the Officer*] Pray, sir, deliver me from all this clamour;
Be good enough to carry out your order.
THE OFFICER. Yes, I've too long delayed its execution;
'Tis very fitting you should urge me to it;
So therefore, you must follow me at once
To prison, where you'll find your lodging ready.
TARTUFFE. Who? I, sir?
THE OFFICER.   You.
TARTUFFE.   Buy why to prison?
THE OFFICER.   You
Are not the one to whom I owe account.

You, sir [*to Orgon*], recover from your hot alarm.
Our prince is not a friend to double dealing,
His eyes can read men's inmost hearts, and all
The art of hypocrites cannot deceive him.
His sharp discernment sees things clear and true;
His mind cannot too easily be swayed,
For reason always holds the balance even.
He honours and exalts true piety
But knows the false, and views it with disgust.
This fellow was by no means apt to fool him;
Far subtler snares have failed against his wisdom,
And his quick insight pierced immediately
The hidden baseness of this tortuous heart.
Accusing you, the knave betrayed himself,
And by true recompense of Heaven's justice
He stood revealed before our monarch's eyes
A scoundrel known before by other names,
Whose horrid crimes, detailed at length, might fill
A long-drawn history of many volumes.
Our monarch—to resolve you in a word—
Detesting his ingratitude and baseness,
Added his horror to his other crimes,
And sent me hither under his direction
To see his insolence out-top itself,
And force him then to give you satisfaction.
Your papers, which the traitor says are his,
I am to take from him, and give you back;
The deed of gift transferring your estate
Our monarch's sovereign will makes null and void;
And for the secret personal offence
Your friend involved you in, he pardons you:
Thus he rewards your recent zeal, displayed
In helping to maintain his rights, and shows
How well his heart, when it is least expected,
Knows how to recompense a noble deed,

And will not let true merit miss its due,
Remembering always rather good than evil.
DORINE. Now, Heaven be praised!
MADAME PERNELLE.   At last I breathe
   again.
ELMIRE. A happy outcome!
MARIANE.   Who'd have dared to hope
   it?
ORGON. [*to Tartuffe, who is being led off by the officer*]
   There, traitor! Now you're . . .

SCENE VIII

[*Madame Pernelle, Orgon, Elmire, Mariane, Cléante, Valère, Damis, Dorine*]

CLÉANTE.   Brother, hold!—and
   don't
   Descend to such indignities, I beg you.
   Leave the poor wretch to his unhappy fate,
   And let remorse oppress him, but not you.
   Hope rather that his heart may now return
   To virtue, hate his vice, reform his ways,
   And win the pardon of our glorious prince;
   While you must straightway go, and on your knees
   Repay with thanks his noble generous kindness.
ORGON. Well said! We'll go, and at his feet kneel
   down
   With joy to thank him for his goodness shown;
   And his first duty done, with honours due,
   We'll then attend upon another, too.
   With wedded happiness reward Valère,
   And crown a lover noble and sincere.

ESSAY: AN APPROACH TO THE PLAY

Part of the interest in the title character is his ambiguity. It is clear that he is very much interested in the pleasures of the flesh, in spite of his protestations to the contrary, and that he is interested in wealth, even if it means not only dispossessing a son but even displacing a male head of a household. And yet he himself very rarely shows his own hypocrisy until near the play's end, although he does continually quote the Bible about not valuing the flesh and about the value of humility. Instead, it is principally those who surround Tartuffe's main disciple, Orgon, who call him a hypocrite. And although we see that they may be right, most of them stand to lose something if Orgon persists in his belief. The judgments against Tartuffe are suspect, then, because they usually come from characters who are not objective. In addition, with the exception of the rather ineffectual Cléante, during most of the play it is hard to be confident of a positive example to counteract Tartuffe's apparently negative behavior. It is hard to be sure what standards the play upholds.

There is also some ambiguity about the title character's relationship to the social world which Molière's play describes. His language is the language of the Bible and of the teachings of the church. At the time of the play, opinion was divided about whether Molière's intention was to expose a religious hypocrite, which would threaten no one except other religious hypocrites, or to expose the church itself, which always used the very language used by Tartuffe and was always getting richer—frequently at the expense of other, often deserving and sometimes devout, people. An example of the self-serving use of language and ideas associated with the church occurs in Act 3, during Tartuffe's attempt to seduce Elmire. Here he combines Biblical paraphrase with a spiritual argument common to Christian neo-Platonism, an argument in which the appreciation of a "miracle" of physical beauty is believed to inspire one's soul to the contemplation of Higher Things. Nonetheless, it remains unclear whether the author intended this play to be a direct criticism of the normal political workings of the church, however suggestive of this idea it may be.

The character of Orgon is similarly ambiguous. As head of his household, he is responsible for the well-being of many people, including his daughter Mariane, his son Damis, and his wife Elmire (although she knows how to take care of herself). He is an autocratic father, willing to require his daughter to marry Tartuffe instead of the man she loves, willing to disinherit his son, and truly concerned only when he discovers that he has also signed away his own rights. He seems both sexist and narrow-mindedly selfish, an authoritarian patriarch who seems typical of this aspect of his society, and Molière exposes it to criticism in a way which lays bare its potentially threatening nature.

At the same time, however, Orgon is a typically devout Christian. He is generous; he believes Tartuffe because Tartuffe says what Orgon has been taught to believe is true; and therefore he seems to be more than the conventional gullible fool of satire. In this case, what we recognize as the character's weakness is also a desirable trait: Faith is a defining quality for a religious person. Where to draw the line between faith and foolishness is always difficult: To be religious at all is to be at least somewhat foolish by secular standards. But Orgon's situation seems again to pose this fundamental question: Is Molière presenting him just as an extreme example of gullible devotion, or as an example of exactly what the church seems to want—and to create—and therefore as an implicit satire of the institutional church?

From the point of view of Molière's society, there may be a second way in which his religious zeal is ambiguous: in its effect on his family life. A patriarch who ignores his daughter's wishes might not seem so foolish, but one who uses his paternal power to disinherit his son would seem outrageous. Even more outrageous is a husband whose proprietory view of marriage allows him to push his wife to the brink of adultery in order to prove not her virtue, which is unquestioned, but Tartuffe's credibility, as if this were a more important issue.

However, this play is also ambivalent about even more basic issues of social power than those of religion and male dominance. It penetrates to the very foundation of the state by its implications about the use of law, about the politics in which law is grounded, and even about the state's political head and symbol, the king. Tartuffe has manipulated the law so that he actually has the power to dispossess Orgon and his dependents from his own house. In this he resembles Shylock in Shakespeare's *The Merchant of Venice*, who has learned how to manipulate the law so that he can force his will upon the state, even against its own desires. This is the ultimate political power. Indeed, from the point of view of the status quo, as articulated in Act 5 by Mr. Loyal, the primary function of politics is to uphold the law. In a monarchy, of course, the status quo is always seen by the ruler as desirable; the alternative is to invite a change in rulers. As long as religion and the law are consistent with one another, then, it is the job of the state to support them both, for these three together present a united front in defense of established authority and power—in defense, ultimately, of the king. Put in such terms, the helplessness of Orgon, the credulous follower of apparent virtue, the very kind of person the state says it values, is exposed. He is, thanks to his obedient loyalty, on the brink of destruction. Great drama of character can present a figure whose situation and characteristics are so extreme as to be laughable, yet whose similarities to what is officially sanctioned or fashionable are so clear that to ridicule him, as satire encourages us in the audience to do, is to risk exposing not only the *dangers* of his behavior but also its self-contradictions.

Orgon is saved at the very end, and Tartuffe vanquished, by the king, who is said to see behind appearances, to see Tartuffe's hypocrisy and Orgon's virtue, and to reward each as morality requires. But the king does so without appearing onstage, enacting his justice through deputies, and only at the last moment. For these reasons, his decrees to straighten things out at the end have been called the play's *deus ex machina*, literally its "god from the machine," a reference to a convention in late classical drama in which a god is lowered to the stage to impose an apparently arbitrary resolution which does not develop naturally from the characters or the plot, or even from values clearly espoused by the play.

If the plot had been resolved according to the principles on which it had so far unfolded, Tartuffe would take over Orgon's house, disinherit Orgon's son, marry his daughter, and presumably beget his own heirs, all in the name of the joint authority of law and religion. That the king is said to see Tartuffe's religious insincerity does not invalidate Tartuffe's legal position. In order to right wrongs, the authority of the state is forced to invalidate the very law on which it is founded. The illogical conclusion of the plot actually puts the authority of the monarch in question and places religion in a position of ambiguity. Molière has written a profoundly unsettling play, and this may be why it continues to interest us.

The extreme positions taken by the key characters (Orgon's docility and Tartuffe's combination of intellectual acuity and lack of humanity) are suggestive of farce more than sophisticated comedy of manners. This form of drama is traditionally associated more with the common people than with the court. Thus it is the commonsense wisdom of the maid Dorine that turns Mariane against her forced marriage to Tartuffe. In spite of the court's approval of this and other plays by Molière, these dramatic elements from the common discourse of popular drama may suggest the larger thematic predicament in which this play places authority and its relation to law and religion. The three supposed props of the social hierarchy of power which culminated in the monarch himself are put seriously into question.

Aphra Behn

THE ROVER

About the Author   Although Aphra Behn (1640–1689) was the first professional woman of letters in our language—the first woman to support herself entirely by writing—we do not know where in England she was born, nor even what her maiden name was. Her last name as we have it was her husband's, but he was a mere blip in her life, a foreign (probably Dutch) businessman who married her in 1664 and died the following year. He seems to have left her little else than a name, certainly no financial security: In the year after his death, she worked in Belgium as a spy for the English government, and two years after that she was imprisoned for debt. She continued writing for the rest of her life, having over twenty of her plays produced and publishing short novels, stories, and two volumes of poetry as well. Her plays were successful in her own lifetime, and their popularity continued until fashions in drama decisively changed in the middle of the eighteenth century.

About the Play   Behn's most famous work, *The Rover* was first produced in 1667 as one of three or four of her plays produced in the 1676–77 season. King Charles II came to see it, along with most of high-society London. It is an example of Restoration comedy, a genre extremely popular between 1660 and 1700, an adaptation of the comedy of manners which Molière had made popular in France in the previous generation, but a variant with a distinctively English twist.

In general, Restoration comedy makes fun of characters who fail to live up to an aristocratic code of conduct because they lack both wit and the self-knowledge which wit may imply. Characters who try too obviously to imitate aristocratic manners and customs, and therefore fail, are called "fops," and they are satirized, as are characters who are too dull even to try to imitate them. The plays presuppose that their failure at manners is symptomatic of their limitations as human beings, of their lacking not only wit and cleverness but also self-awareness and even civilized taste.

From a modern point of view, such plays may seem intolerant, unnecessarily and even casually cruel. They consistently criticize the old, the ugly, and the provincial, as the cheating of the naive country-bred Blunt by Lucetta shows in *The Rover*. By contrast, the plays consistently praise the young, the beautiful, and the urban aristocracy, those who set the standard of taste for this courtly society. This standard, then, is aesthetic rather than moral, and in this play, Willmore and Hellena are the characters who best live up to it. The hero and heroine who know themselves well enough to be in control of any situation, never to be at a loss in society, to be witty in word and deed because they see through the inadequacies of others and can exploit them, while recognizing and adapting their own weaknesses—this is the social ideal, the person of grace and self-possession, the "truewit."

The main activity by which a character's excellence is measured in the leisured society of these plays is the one which is its primary concern, the sexual chase. Yet in this chase, it often seems that ego—winning—is more important than love, more important even than the gratification of sexual desire, as Blunt illustrates when he tells Florinda that he will "have" her "not that I care for the enjoyment, but to let thee see I have ta'en deliberated malice to thee" (4.5.54–56).

A word about vocabulary and staging before you begin the play: A "friend" is often a lover of either sex, and a "Mrs." is not necessarily married but *is* an adult female. The convention of love at first sight was still current and often referred to. In imagining this play onstage, you need to know that actresses played female roles for the first time in this age. It is probably a good idea to read the play once before trying to digest some other ideas which are related to these facts.

PROLOGUE

Written by a Person of Quality

Wits, like Physicians, never can agree,
When of a different Society;
And Rabel's Drops were never more cry'd down
By all the Learned Doctors of the Town,
Than a new Play, whose Author is unknown:
Nor can those Doctors with more Malice sue
(And powerful Purses) the dissenting Few,
Than those with an insulting Pride, do rail
At all who are not of their own Cabal.
If a Young Poet hit your Humour right,
You judge him then out of Revenge and Spite;
So amongst Men there are ridiculous Elves,
Who Monkeys hate for being too like themselves:
So that the Reason of the Grand Debate,
Why Wit so oft is damn'd, when good Plays take,
Is, that you censure as you love or hate.
Thus, like a learned Conclave, Poets sit,
Catholick Judges both of Sense and Wit,
And damn or save, as they themselves think fit.
Yet those who to others Faults are so severe,
Are not so perfect, but themselves may err.
Some write correct indeed, but then the whole

(Bating their own dull Stuff i' th' Play) is stole:
As Bees do suck from Flowers their Honey-dew,
So they rob others, striving to please you.
Some write their Characters genteel and fine,
But then they do so toil for every Line,
That what to you does easy seem, and plain,
Is the hard issue of their labouring Brain.
And some th' Effects of all their Pains we see,
Is but to mimick good Extempore.
Others by long Converse about the Town,
Have Wit enough to write a lewd Lampoon,
But their chief Skill lies in a Bawdy Song.
In short, the only Wit that's now in Fashion
Is but the Gleanings of good Conversation.
As for the Author of this coming Play,
I ask'd him what he thought fit I should say,
In thanks for your good Company to day:
He call'd me Fool, and said it was well known,
You came not here for our sakes, but your own.
New Plays are stuff'd with Wits, and with Debauches,
That crowd and sweat like Cits in May-day Coaches.

CHARACTERS

Men

DON ANTONIO, the Vice-Roy's Son,
DON PEDRO, a Noble Spaniard, his Friend,
BELVILE, an English Colonel, in love with Florinda,
WILLMORE, the ROVER,
FREDERICK, an English Gentleman, and Friend to
    Belvile and Blunt,
BLUNT, an English Country Gentleman,

STEPHANO, Servant to Don Pedro,
PHILIPPO, Lucetta's Gallant,
SANCHO, Pimp to Lucetta,
BISKY and SEBASTIAN, two Bravoes to Angelica.
Officers and Soldiers.
Page to Don Antonio.

Women

FLORINDA, Sister to Don Pedro,
HELLENA, a gay young Woman design'd for a Nun,
    and Sister to Florinda,
VALERIA, a Kinswoman to Florinda,
ANGELICA BIANCA, a famous Courtezan,
MORETTA, her Woman,

CALLIS, Governess to Florinda and Hellena
LUCETTA, a jilting Wench,

Servants, other Masqueraders, Men and Women.

SCENE: Naples, in Carnival-time.

Act I

SCENE I

A Chamber.

[*Enter Florinda and Hellena.*]

FLORINDA. What an impertinent thing is a young Girl bred in a Nunnery! How full of Questions! Prithee no more Hellena; I have told thee more than thou understand'st already.

HELLENA. The more's my Grief; I wou'd fain know as much as you, which makes me so inquisitive; nor is't enough to know you're a Lover, unless you tell me too, who 'tis you sigh for.

FLORINDA. When you are a Lover, I'll think you fit for a Secret of that nature.

HELLENA. 'Tis true, I was never a Lover yet—but I begin to have a shrewd Guess, what 'tis to be so, and fancy it very pretty to sigh, and sing, and blush and wish, and dream and wish, and long and wish to see the Man; and when I do, look pale and tremble; just as you did when my Brother brought home the fine English Colonel to see you—what do you call him? Don Belvile.

FLORINDA. Fie Hellena.

HELLENA. That Blush betrays you—I am sure 'tis so—or is it Don Antonio the Vice-Roy's Son?—or perhaps the rich old Don Vincentio, whom my Father designs for your Husband?—Why do you blush again?

FLORINDA. With Indignation; and how near soever my Father thinks I am to marrying that hated Object, I shall let him see I understand better what's due to my Beauty, Birth and Fortune, and more to my Soul, than to obey those unjust Commands.

HELLENA. Now hang me, if I don't love thee for that dear Disobedience. I love Mischief strangely, as most of our Sex do, who are come to love nothing else—But tell me, dear Florinda, don't you love that fine Anglese?—for I vow next to loving him my self, 'twill please me most that you do so, for he is so gay and so handsom.

FLORINDA. Hellena, a Maid design'd for a Nun ought not to be so curious in a Discourse of Love.

HELLENA. And dost thou think that ever I'll be a Nun? Or at least till I'm so old, I'm fit for nothing else. Faith no, Sister; and that which makes me long to know whether you love Belvile, is because I hope he has some mad Companion or other, that will spoil my devotion; nay I'm resolved to provide my self this Carnival, if there be e'er a handsom Fellow of my Humour above Ground, tho I ask first.

FLORINDA. Prithee be not so wild.

HELLENA. Now you have provided your self with a Man, you take no Care for poor me—Prithee tell me, what dost thou see about me that is unfit for Love—have not I a world of Youth? a Humour gay? a Beauty passable? a Vigour desirable? well shap'd? clean limb'd? sweet breath'd? and Sense enough to know how all these ought to be employ'd to the best Advantage: yes, I do and will. Therefore lay aside your Hopes of my Fortune, by my being a Devotee, and tell me how you came acquainted with this Belvile; for I perceive you knew him before he came to Naples.

FLORINDA. Yes, I knew him at the Siege of Pampelona, he was then a Colonel of French Horse, who when the Town was ransack'd, nobly treated my Brother and my self, preserving us from all Insolencies; and I must own (besides great Obligations) I have I know not what, that pleads kindly for him about my Heart, and will suffer no other to enter—But see my Brother.

[*Enter Don Pedro, Stephano, with a Masquing Habit, and Callis.*]

DON PEDRO. Good morrow Sister. Pray when saw you your Lover Don Vincentio?

FLORINDA. I know not, Sir—Callis, when was he here? for I consider it so little, I know not when it was.

DON PEDRO. I have a Command from my Father here to tell you, you ought not to despise him, a Man of so vast a Fortune, and such a Passion for you—Stephano methinks—[*Puts on his Masquing Habit.*]

FLORINDA. A Passion for me! 'tis more than e'er I saw, or had a desire should be known—I hate Vincentio, and I would not have a Man so dear to me as my Brother follow the ill Customs of our Country, and make a Slave of his Sister—And Sir, my Father's Will, I'm sure, you may divert.

DON PEDRO. I know not how dear I am to you, but I wish only to be rank'd in your Esteem, equal with the English Colonel Belvile—Why do you frown and blush? Is there any Guilt belong to the Name of that Cavalier?

FLORINDA. I'll not deny I value Belvile, when I was expos'd to such Dangers as the licens'd Lust of common Soldiers threatned, when Rage and Conquest flew thro the City—then Belvile, this Criminal for my sake, threw himself into all Dangers to save my Honour, and will you now allow him my Esteem?

DON PEDRO. Yes, pay him what you will in Honour—but you must consider Don Vincentio's Fortune, and the Jointure he'll make you.

FLORINDA. Let him consider my Youth, Beauty and Fortune; which ought not to be thrown away on his Age and Jointure.

DON PEDRO. 'Tis true, he's not so young and fine a Gentleman as that Belvile—but what Jewels will that Cavalier present you with? those of his Eyes and Heart?

HELLENA. And are not those better than any Don Vincentio has brought from the Indies?

DON PEDRO. Why how now! Has your Nunnery-breeding taught you to understand the Value of Hearts and Eyes?

HELLENA. Better than to believe Vincentio deserves Value from any Woman—He may perhaps encrease her Bags, but not her Family.

DON PEDRO. This is fine—Go up to your Devotion, you are not design'd for the Conversation of Lovers.

HELLENA. Nor Saints yet a while I hope. [Aside.] Is't not enough you make a Nun of me, but you must cast my Sister away too, exposing her to a worse confinement than a religious Life?

DON PEDRO. The Girl's mad—Is it a Confinement to be carry'd into the Country, to an ancient Villa belonging to the Family of the Vincentio's these five hundred Years, and have no other Prospect than that pleasing one of seeing all her own that meets her Eyes—a fine Air, large Fields and Gardens, where she may walk and gather Flowers?

HELLENA. When? By Moon-Light? For I'm sure she dares not encounter with the heat of the Sun; that were a Task only for Don Vincentio and his Indian Breeding, who loves it in the Dog-days—And if these be her daily Divertisements, what are those of the Night, to lie in a wide Moth-eaten Bed-Chamber with Furniture in Fashion in the Reign of King Sancho the First; the Bed that which his Fore-fathers liv'd and dy'd in.

DON PEDRO. Very well.

HELLENA. This Apartment (new furbisht and fitted out for the young Wife) he (out of Freedom) makes his Dressing-room; and being a frugal and a jealous Coxcomb, instead of a Valet to uncase his feeble Carcase, he desires you to do that Office—Signs of Favour, I'll assure you, and such as you must not hope for, unless your Woman be out of the way.

DON PEDRO. Have you done yet?

HELLENA. That Honour being past, the Giant stretches it self, yawns and sighs a Belch or two as loud as a Musket, throws himself into Bed, and expects you in his foul Sheets, and e'er you can get your self undrest, calls you with a Snore or two—And are not these fine Blessings to a young Lady?

DON PEDRO. Have you done yet?

HELLENA. And this Man you must kiss, nay, you must kiss none but him too—and nuzzle thro his Beard to find his Lips—and this you must submit to for threescore Years, and all for a Jointure.

DON PEDRO. For all your Character of Don Vincentio, she is as like to marry him as she was before.

HELLENA. Marry Don Vincentio! hang me, such a Wedlock would be worse than Adultery with another Man: I had rather see her in the Hostel de Dieu, to waste her Youth there in Vows, and be a Handmaid to Lazers and Cripples, than to lose it in such a Marriage.

DON PEDRO. You have consider'd, Sister, that Belvile has no Fortune to bring you to, is banisht his Country, despis'd at home, and pity'd abroad.

HELLENA. What then? the Vice-Roy's Son is better than that Old Sir Fifty. Don Vincentio! Don Indian! he thinks he's trading to Gambo still, and wou'd barter himself (that Bell and Bauble) for your Youth and Fortune.

DON PEDRO. Callis, take her hence, and lock her up all this Carnival, and at Lent she shall begin her everlasting Penance in a Monastery.

HELLENA. I care not, I had rather be a Nun, than be oblig'd to marry as you wou'd have me, if I were design'd for't.

DON PEDRO. Do not fear the Blessing of that Choice—you shall be a Nun.

HELLENA. [Aside.] Shall I so? you may chance to be mistaken in my way of Devotion—A Nun! yes I am like to make a fine Nun! I have an excellent Humour for a Grate: No, I'll have a Saint of my own to pray to shortly, if I like any that dares venture on me.

DON PEDRO. Callis, make it your Business to watch this wild Cat. As for you Florinda, I've only try'd you all this while, and urg'd my Father's Will; but mine is, that you would love Antonio, he is brave and young, and all that can complete the Happiness of a gallant Maid—This Absence of my Father will give us opportunity to free you from Vincentio, by marrying here, which you must do tomorrow.

FLORINDA. Tomorrow!

DON PEDRO. Tomorrow, or 'twill be too late—'tis not my Friendship to Antonio, which makes me urge this, but Love to thee, and Hatred to Vincentio—therefore resolve upon't tomorrow.

FLORINDA. Sir, I shall strive to do, as shall become your Sister.

DON PEDRO. I'll both believe and trust you—Adieu.

[Ex. Don Pedro and Stephano]

HELLENA. As become his Sister!—That is, to be as resolved your way, as he is his—[Hellena goes to Callis.]

FLORINDA. I ne'er till now perceiv'd my Ruin near,
I've no Defence against Antonio's Love,
For he has all the Advantages of Nature,
The moving Arguments of Youth and Fortune.

HELLENA. But hark you, Callis, you will not be so cruel to lock me up indeed: will you?

CALLIS. I must obey the Commands I hate—besides, do you consider what a Life you are going to lead?

HELLENA. Yes, Callis, that of a Nun: and till then I'll be indebted a World of Prayers to you, if you let me now see, what I never did, the Divertisements of a Carnival.

CALLIS. What, go in Masquerade? 'twill be a fine fare-well to the World I take it—pray what wou'd you do there?

HELLENA. That which all the World does, as I am told, be as mad as the rest, and take all innocent Freedom—Sister, you'll go too, will you not? come prithee be not sad—We'll out-wit twenty Brothers, if you'll be ruled by me—Come put off this dull Humour with your Clothes, and assume one as gay, and as fantastick as the Dress my Cousin Valeria and I have provided, and let's ramble.

FLORINDA. Callis, will you give us leave to go?

CALLIS. I have a youthful Itch of going my self. [Aside.] —Madame, if I thought your Brother might not know it, and I might wait on you, for by my troth I'll not trust young Girls alone.

FLORINDA. Thou see'st my Brother's gone already, and thou shalt attend and watch us.

[Enter Stephano.]

STEPHANO. Madam, the Habits are come, and your Cousin Valeria is drest, and stays for you.

FLORINDA. 'Tis well—I'll write a Note, and if I chance to see Belvile, and want an opportunity to speak to him, that shall let him know what I've resolv'd in favour of him.

HELLENA. Come, let's in and dress us. [Exeunt.]

SCENE II

A long Street.

[Enter Belvile melancholy, Blunt and Frederick.]

FREDERICK. Why, what the Devil ails the Colonel, in a time when all the World is gay, to look like mere Lent thus? Hadst thou been long enough in Naples to have been in love, I should have sworn some such Judgment had befall'n thee.

BELVILE. No, I have made no new Amours since I came to Naples.

FREDERICK. You have left none behind you in Paris.

BELVILE. Neither.

FREDERICK. I can't divine the Cause then; unless the old Cause, the want of Money.

BLUNT. And another old Cause, the want of a Wench—Wou'd not that revive you?

BELVILE. You're mistaken, Ned.

BLUNT. Nay, 'Sheartlikins, then thou art past Cure.

FREDERICK. I have found it out; thou hast renew'd thy Acquaintance with the Lady that cost thee so many Sighs at the Siege of Pampelona—pox on't, what d'ye call her—her Brother's a noble Span-iard—Nephew to the dead General—Florinda—ay, Florinda—And will nothing serve thy turn but that damn'd virtuous Woman, whom on my Conscience thou lov'st in spite too, because thou seest little or no possibility of gaining her?

BELVILE. Thou art mistaken, I have Interest enough in that lovely Virgin's Heart, to make me proud and vain, were it not abated by the Severity of a Brother, who perceiving my Happiness—

FREDERICK. Has civilly forbid thee the House?

BELVILE. 'Tis so, to make way for a powerful Rival, the Vice-Roy's Son, who has the advantage of me, in being a Man of Fortune, a Spaniard, and her Brother's Friend; which gives him liberty to make his Court, whilst I have recourse only to Letters, and distant Looks from her Window, which are so soft and kind as those which Heav'n sends down on Penitents.

BLUNT. Hey dey! 'Sheartlikins, Simile! by this Light

the Man is quite spoil'd—Frederick, what the Devil are we made of, that we cannot be thus concern'd for a Wench?—'Sheartlikens, our Cupids are like the Cooks of the Camp, they can roast or boil a Woman, but they have none of the fine Tricks to set 'em off, no Hogoes to make the Sauce pleasant, and the Stomach sharp.

FREDERICK. I dare swear I have had a hundred as young, kind and handsom as this Florinda; and Dogs eat me, if they were not as troublesome to me i'th' Morning as they were welcome o'er night.

BLUNT. And yet, I warrant, he wou'd not touch another Woman, if he might have her for nothing.

BELVILE. That's thy Joy, a cheap Whore.

BLUNT. Why, 'dsheartlikins, I love a frank Soul— When did you ever hear of an honest Woman that took a Man's Money? I warrant 'em good ones— But, Gentlemen, you may be free, you have been kept so poor with Parliaments and Protectors, that the little Stock you have is not worth preserving— but I thank my Stars, I had more Grace than to forfeit my Estate by Cavaliering.

BELVILE. Methinks only following the Court should be sufficient to entitle 'em to that.

BLUNT. 'Sheartlikins, they know I follow it to do it no good, unless they pick a hole in my Coat for lending you Money now and then; which is a greater Crime to my Conscience, Gentlemen, than to the Common-wealth.

[Enter Willmore.]

WILLMORE. Ha! dear Belvile! noble Colonel!

BELVILE. Willmore! welcome ashore, my dear Rover!—what happy Wind blew us this good Fortune?

WILLMORE. Let me salute you my dear Frederick and then command me—How is't honest Lad?

FREDERICK. Faith, Sir, the old Complement, infinitely the better to see my dear mad Willmore again— Prithee why camest thou ashore? and where's the Prince?

WILLMORE. He's well, and reigns still Lord of the watery Element—I must aboard again within a Day or two, and my Business ashore was only to enjoy my self a little this Carnival.

BELVILE. Pray know our new Friend, Sir, he's but bashful, a raw Traveller, but honest, stout, and one of us.

[Embraces Blunt.]

WILLMORE. That you esteem him, gives him an Interest here.

BLUNT. Your Servant, Sir.

WILLMORE. But well—Faith I'm glad to meet you again in a warm Climate, where the kind Sun has its god-like Power still over the Wine and Women.— Love and Mirth are my Business in Naples; and if I mistake not the Place, here's an excellent Market for Chapmen of my Humour.

BELVILE. See here be those kind Merchants of Love you look for.

[Enter several Men in masquing Habits, some playing on Musick, others dancing after; Women drest like Courtesans, with Papers pinn'd to their Breasts, and Baskets of Flowers in their Hands.]

BLUNT. 'Sheartlikins, what have we here?

FREDERICK. Now the Game begins.

WILLMORE. Fine pretty Creatures! may a Stranger have leave to look and love?—What's here—*Roses for every Month*! [Reads the Paper.]

BLUNT. Roses for every Month! what means that?

BELVILE. They are, or wou'd have you think they're Courtesans, who here in Naples are to be hir'd by the Month.

WILLMORE. Kind and obliging to inform us—Pray where do these Roses grow? I would fain plant some of 'em in a Bed of mine.

WOMAN. Beware such Roses, Sir.

WILLMORE. A Pox of Fear: I'll be bak'd with thee between a pair of Sheets, and that's thy proper Still, so I might but strew such Roses over me and under me—Fair one, wou'd you wou'd give me leave to gather at your Bush this idle Month, I wou'd go near to make some Body smell of it all the Year after.

BELVILE. And thou hast need of such a Remedy, for thou stinkest of Tar and Rope-ends, like a Dock or Pesthouse.

[The Woman puts her self into the Hands of a Man, and Exit.]

WILLMORE. Nay, nay, you shall not leave me so.

BELVILE. By all means use no Violence here.

WILLMORE. Death! just as I was going to be damnably in love, to have her led off! I could pluck that Rose out of his Hand, and even kiss the Bed, the Bush it grew in.

FREDERICK. No Friend to Love like a long Voyage at Sea.

BLUNT. Except a Nunnery, Frederick.

WILLMORE. Death! but will they not be kind, quickly be kind? Thou know'st I'm no tame Sigher, but a rampant Lion of the Forest.

[*Two Men drest all over with Horns of several sorts, making Grimaces at one another, with Papers pinn'd on their Backs, advance from the farther end of the Scene.*]

BELVILE. Oh the fantastical Rogues, how they are dress'd! 'tis a Satire against the whole Sex.

WILLMORE. Is this a Fruit that grows in this warm Country?

BELVILE. Yes: 'Tis pretty to see these Italians start, swell, and stab at the Word Cuckold, and yet stumble at Horns on every Threshold.

WILLMORE. See what's on their Back—*Flowers for every Night*. [*Reads.*]
—Ah Rogue! And more sweet than Roses of ev'ry Month! This is a Gardiner of Adam's own breeding.

[*They dance.*]

BELVILE. What think you of those grave People?—is a Wake in Essex half so mad or extravagant?

WILLMORE. I like their sober grave way, 'tis a kind of legal authoriz'd Fornication, where the Men are not chid for't, nor the Women despis'd, as amongst our dull English; even the Monsieurs want that part of good Manners.

BELVILE. But here in Italy a Monsieur is the humblest best-bred Gentleman—Duels are so baffled by Bravo's, that an Age shows not one, but between a Frenchman and a Hang-man, who is as much too hard for him on the Piazza, as they are for a Dutchman on the new Bridge—But see another Crew.

[*Enter Florinda, Hellena, and Valeria, drest like Gipsies; Callis and Stephano, Lucetta, Philippo and Sancho in Masquerade.*]

HELLENA. Sister, there's your Englishman, and with him a handsome proper Fellow—I'll to him, and instead of telling him his Fortune, try my own.

WILLMORE. Gipsies, on my Life—Sure these will prattle if a Man cross their Hands. [*Goes to Hellena*]— Dear pretty (and I hope) young Devil, will you tell an amorous Stranger what Luck he's like to have?

HELLENA. Have a care how you venture with me, Sir, lest I pick your Pocket, which will more vex your English Humour, than an Italian Fortune will please you.

WILLMORE. How the Devil cam'st thou to know my Country and Humour?

HELLENA. The first I guess by a certain forward Impudence, which does not displease me at this time; and the Loss of your Money will vex you, because I hope you have but very little to lose.

WILLMORE. Egad Child, thou'rt i'th' right; it is so little, I dare not offer it thee for a Kindness—But cannot you divine what other things of more value I have about me, that I would more willingly part with?

HELLENA. Indeed no, that's the Business of a Witch, and I am but a Gipsy yet—Yet, without looking in your Hand, I have a parlous Guess,'tis some foolish Heart you mean, an inconstant English Heart, as little worth stealing as your Purse.

WILLMORE. Nay, then thou dost deal with the Devil, that's certain—Thou hast guess'd as right as if thou hadst been one of that Number it has languisht for—I find you'll be better acquainted with it; nor can you take it in a better time, for I am come from Sea, Child; and Venus not being propitious to me in her own Element, I have a world of Love in store— Wou'd you would be good-natur'd, and take some on't off my Hands.

HELLENA. Why—I could be inclin'd that way—but for a foolish Vow I am going to make—to die a Maid.

WILLMORE. Then thou art damn'd without Redemption; and as I am a good Christian, I ought in charity to divert so wicked a Design—therefore prithee dear Creature, let me know quickly when and where I shall begin to set a helping hand to so good a Work.

HELLENA. If you should prevail with my tender Heart (as I begin to fear you will, for you have horrible loving Eyes) there will be difficulty in't that you'll hardly undergo for my sake.

WILLMORE. Faith Child, I have been bred in Dangers, and wear a Sword that has been employ'd in a worse Cause, than for a handsome kind Woman—Name the Danger—let it be any thing but a long Siege, and I'll undertake it.

HELLENA. Can you storm?

WILLMORE. Oh, most furiously.

HELLENA. What think you of a Nunnery-wall? for he that wins me, must gain that first.

WILLMORE. A Nun! Oh how I love thee for't! there's no Sinner like a young Saint—Nay, now there's no denying me: the old Law had no Curse (to a Woman) like dying a Maid; witness Jephtha's Daughter.

HELLENA. A very good Text this, if well handled; and I perceive, Father Captain, you would impose no severe Penance on her who was inclin'd to console herself before she took Orders.

WILLMORE. If she be young and handsome.

HELLENA. Ay, there's it—but if she be not—

WILLMORE. By this Hand, Child, I have an implicit Faith, and dare venture on thee with all Faults— besides, 'tis more meritorious to leave the World when thou hast lasted and prov'd the Pleasure on't, than 'twill be a Virtue in thee, which now will be pure Ignorance.

HELLENA. I perceive, good Father Captain, you design only to make me fit for Heaven—but if on the contrary you should quite divert me from it, and bring me back to the World again, I should have a new Man to seek I find; and what a Grief that will be—for when I begin, I fancy I shall love like any thing: I never try'd yet.

WILLMORE. Egad, and that's kind—Prithee, dear Creature, give me Credit for a Heart, for faith I'm a very honest Fellow—Oh, I long to come first to the Banquet of Love; and such a swinging Appetite I bring—Oh, I'm impatient. Thy Lodging, Sweetheart, thy Lodging, or I'm a dead Man!

HELLENA. Why must we be either guilty of Fornication or Murder, if we converse with you Men?— And is there no difference between leave to love me, and leave to lie with me?

WILLMORE. Faith, Child, they were made to go together.

LUCETTA. Are you sure this is the man? [Pointing to Blunt.]

SANCHO. When did I mistake your Game?

LUCETTA. This is a stranger, I know by his gazing; if he be brisk he'll venture to follow me; and then, if I understand my Trade, he's mine; he's English too, and they say that's a sort of good-natur'd loving People, and have generally so kind an Opinion of themselves, that a Woman with any Wit may flatter 'em into any sort of Fool she pleases.

BLUNT. 'Tis so—she is taken—I have Beauties which my false Glass at home did not discover.

[She often passes by Blunt, and gazes on him; he struts, and cocks, and walks, and gazes on her.]

FLORINDA. This Woman watches me so, I shall get no Opportunity to discover myself to him, and so miss the intent of my coming—But as I was saying, Sir— by this Line you should be a Lover. [Looking in his Hand.]

BELVILE. I thought how right you guess'd, all Men are in love, or pretend to be so—Come, let me go, I'm weary of this fooling. [Walks away.]

FLORINDA. I will not, till you have confess'd whether the Passion that you have vow'd Florinda be true of false.

[She holds him, he strives to get from her.]

BELVILE. Florinda! [Turns quick towards her.]

FLORINDA. Softly.

BELVILE. Thou hast nam'd one will fix me here for ever.

FLORINDA. She'll be disappointed then, who expects you this Night at the Garden-gate, and if you'll fail not—as let me see the other Hand—you will go near to do—she vows to die or make you happy. [Looks on Callis, who observes 'em.]

BELVILE. What canst thou mean?

FLORINDA. That which I say—Farewel. [Offers to go.]

BELVILE. Oh charming Sybil stay, complete that Joy, which, as it is, will turn into Distraction!—Where must I be? at the Garden-gate? I know it—at night, you say—I'll sooner forfeit Heaven than disobey.

[Enter Don Pedro and other Masquers, and pass over the Stage.]

CALLIS. Madam, your Brother's here.

FLORINDA. Take this to instruct you farther.

[Gives him a Letter, and goes off.]

FREDERICK. Have a care, Sir, what you promise; this may be a Trap laid by her Brother to ruin you.

BELVILE. Do not disturb my Happiness with Doubts.

[Opens the Letter.]

WILLMORE. My pretty Creature, a Thousand Blessings on thee; still in this Habit, you say, and after Dinner at this Place.

HELLENA. Yes, if you will swear to keep your Heart, and not bestow it between this time and that.

WILLMORE. By all the little Gods of Love I swear, I'll leave it with you; and if you run away with it, those Deities of Justice will revenge me. [Ex. all the Women.]

FREDERICK. Do you know the Hand?

BELVILE. 'Tis Florinda's.

All Blessings fall upon the virtuous Maid.

FREDERICK. Nay, no Idolatry, a sober Sacrifice I'll allow you.

BELVILE. Oh Friends! the welcom'st News, the softest Letter!—nay, you shall see it; and could you now be serious, I might be made the happiest Man the Sun shines on.

WILLMORE. The Reason of this mighty Joy?

BELVILE. See how kindly she invites me to deliver her from the threatned Violence of her Brother—will you not assist me?

WILLMORE. I know not what thou mean'st, but I'll make one at any Mischief where a Woman's concern'd—but she'll be grateful to us for the Favour, will she not?

BELVILE. How mean you?

WILLMORE. How should I mean? Thou know'st there's but one way for a Woman to oblige me.

BELVILE. Don't prophane—the Maid is nicely virtuous.

WILLMORE. Who pox, then she's fit for nothing but a Husband; let her e'en go, Colonel.

FREDERICK. Peace, she's the Colonel's Mistress, Sir.

WILLMORE. Let her be the Devil; if she be thy Mistress, I'll serve her—name the way.

BELVILE. Read here this Postscript. [Gives him a Letter.]

WILLMORE. [Reads.] At Ten at night—at the Garden-Gate—of which, if I cannot get the Key, I will contrive a way over the Wall—come attended with a Friend or two.—Kind heart, if we three cannot weave a String to let her down a Garden-Wall, 'twere pity but the Hangman wove one for us all.

FREDERICK. Let her alone for that: your Woman's Wit, your fair kind Woman, will out-trick a Brother or a Jew, and contrive like a Jesuit in Chains—but see, Ned Blunt is stoln out after the Lure of a Damsel. [Ex. Blunt and Lucetta.]

BELVILE. So he'll scarce find his way home again, unless we get him cry'd by the Bell-man in the Market-place, and 'twou'd sound prettily—a lost English Boy of Thirty.

FREDERICK. I hope 'tis some common crafty Sinner, one that will fit him; it may be she'll sell him for Peru, the Rogue's sturdy and would work well in a Mine; at least I hope she'll dress him for our Mirth; cheat him of all, then have him well-favour'dly bang'd, and turn'd out naked at Midnight.

WILLMORE. Prithee what Humour is he of, that you wish him so well?

BELVILE. Why, of an English Elder Brother's Humour, educated in a Nursery, with a Maid to tend him till Fifteen, and lies with his Grand-mother till he's of Age; one that knows no pleasure beyond riding to the next Fair, or going up to London with his right Worshipful Father in Parliament-time; wearing gay Clothes, or making honourable Love to his Lady Mother's Laundry-Maid: gets drunk at a Hunting-Match, and ten to one then gives some Proofs of his Prowess—A pox upon him, he's our Banker, and has all our Cash about him, and if he fail we are all broke.

FREDERICK. Oh let him alone for that matter, he's of a damn'd stingy Quality, that will secure our Stock; I know not in what Danger it were indeed, if the Jilt should pretend she's in love with him, for 'tis a kind believing Coxcomb; otherwise if he part with more than a Piece of Eight—geld him: for which offer he may chance to be beaten, if she be a Whore of the first Rank.

BELVILE. Nay the Rogue will not be easily beaten, he's stout enough; perhaps if they talk beyond his Capacity, he may chance to exercise his Courage upon some of them; else I'am sure they'll find it as difficult to beat as to please him.

WILLMORE. 'Tis a lucky Devil to light upon so kind a Wench!

FREDERICK. Thou hadst a great deal of talk with thy little Gipsy, coud'st thou do no good upon her? for mine was hard-hearted.

WILLMORE. Hang her, she was some damn'd honest Person of Quality, I'm sure, she was so very free and witty. If her Face be but answerable to her Wit and Humour, I wou'd be bound to Constancy this Month to gain her. In the mean time, have you made no kind Acquaintance since you came to Town?—you do not use to be honest so long, Gentlemen.

FREDERICK. Faith Love has kept us honest, we have been all fir'd with a Beauty newly come to Town, the famous Paduana Angelica Bianca.

WILLMORE. What, the Mistress of the dead Spanish General?

BELVILE. Yes, she's now the only ador'd Beauty of all the Youth in Naples, who put on all their Charms to appear lovely in her sight, their Coaches, Liveries, and themselves, all gay, as on a Monarch's Birth-Day, to attract the Eyes of this fair Charmer, while she has the Pleasure to behold all languish for her that see her.

FREDERICK. 'Tis pretty to see with how much Love the Men regard her, and how much Envy the Women.

WILLMORE. What Gallant has she?

BELVILE. None, she's expos'd to Sale, and four Days in the Week she's yours—for so much a Month.

WILLMORE. The very Thought of it quenches all manner of Fire in me—yet prithee let's see her.

BELVILE. Let's first to Dinner, and after that we'll pass the Day as you please—but at Night ye must all be at my Devotion.

WILLMORE. I will not fail you. [*Exeunt.*]

Act II

SCENE I

The Long Street.

[*Enter Belvile and Frederick in Masquing-Habits, and Willmore in his own Clothes, with a Vizard in his Hand.*]

WILLMORE. But why thus disguis'd and muzzl'd?

BELVILE. Because whatever Extravagances we commit in these Faces, our own may not be oblig'd to answer 'em.

WILLMORE. I shou'd have chang'd my Eternal Buss too; but no matter, my little Gipsy wou'd not have found me out then: for if she shou'd change hers, it is impossible I should know her, unless I should hear her prattle—A Pox on't, I cannot get her out of my Head: Pray Heaven, if ever I do see her again, she prove damnable ugly, that I may fortify myself against her Tongue.

BELVILE. Have a care of Love, for o' my conscience she was not of a Quality to give thee any hopes.

WILLMORE. Pox on 'em, why do they draw a Man in then? She has play'd with my Heart so, that 'twill never lie still, till I have met with some kind Wench, that will play the Game out with me—Oh for my Arms full of soft, white, kind—Woman! such as I fancy Angelica.

BELVILE. This is her House, if you were but in stock to get admittance; they have not din'd yet; I perceive the Picture is not out.

[*Enter Blunt.*]

WILLMORE. I long to see the Shadow of the fair Substance, a Man may gaze on that for nothing.

BLUNT. Colonel, thy Hand—and thine Frederick. I have been an Ass, a deluded Fool, a very Coxcomb from my Birth till this Hour, and heartily repent my little Faith.

BELVILE. What the Devil's the matter with thee Ned?

BLUNT. Oh such a Mistress, Frederick. such a Girl!

WILLMORE. Ha! where?

FREDERICK. Ay where!

BLUNT. So fond, so amorous, so toying and fine! and all for sheer Love, ye Rogue! Oh how she lookt and kiss'd! and sooth'd my Heart from my Bosom. I cannot think I was awake, and yet methinks I see and feel her Charms still—Frederick.—Try if she have not left the Taste of her balmy Kisses upon my Lips—

[*Kisses him.*]

BELVILE. Ha, ha, ha!

WILLMORE. Death Man, where is she?

BLUNT. What a Dog was I to stay in dull England so long—How have I laught at the Colonel when he sigh'd for Love! but now the little Archer has reveng'd him, and by his own Dart, I can guess at all his Joys, which then I took for Fancies, mere Dreams and Fables—Well, I'm resolv'd to sell all in Essex, and plant here for ever.

BELVILE. What a Blessing 'tis, thou hast a Mistress thou dar'st boast of; for I know thy Humour is rather to have a proclaim'd Clap, than a secret Amour.

WILLMORE. Dost know her Name?

BLUNT. Her Name? No, 'sheartlikins: what care I for Names?—

She's fair, young, brisk and kind, even to ravishment: and what a Pox care I for knowing her by another Title.

WILLMORE. Didst give her any thing?

BLUNT. Give her!—Ha, ha, ha! why, she's a Person of Quality—That's a good one, give her! 'sheartlikins dost think such Creatures are to be bought? Or are we provided for such a Purchase? Give her quoth ye? Why she presented me with this Bracelet, for the

Toy of a Diamond I us'd to wear: No, Gentlemen, Ned Blunt is not every Body—She expects me again tonight.

WILLMORE. Egad that's well; we'll all go.

BLUNT. Not a Soul: No, Gentlemen, you are Wits; I am a dull Country Rogue, I.

FREDERICK. Well, Sir, for all your Person of Quality, I shall be very glad to understand your Purse be secure; 'tis our whole Estate at present, which we are loth to hazard in one Bottom: come, Sir, unload.

BLUNT. Take the necessary Trifle, useless now to me, that am belov'd by such a Gentlewoman— 'sheartlikins Money! Here take mine too.

FREDERICK. No, keep that to be cozen'd, that we may laugh.

WILLMORE. Cozen'd!—Death! wou'd I cou'd meet with one, that wou'd cozen me of all the Love I cou'd spare tonight.

FREDERICK. Pox 'tis some common Whore upon my Life.

BLUNT. A Whore! yes with such Clothes! such Jewels! such a House! such Furniture, and so attended! a Whore!

BELVILE. Why yes, Sir, they are Whores, tho they'll neither entertain you with Drinking, Swearing, or Bawdy; are Whores in all those gay Clothes, and right Jewels; are Whores with great Houses richly furnisht with Velvet Beds, Store of Plate, handsome Attendance, and fine Coaches, are Whores and errant ones.

WILLMORE. Pox on't, where do these fine Whores live?

BELVILE. Where no Rogue in Office yclep'd Constables dare give 'em Laws, nor the Wine-inspir'd Bullies of the Town break their Windows; yet they are Whores, tho this Essex Calf believe them Persons of Quality.

BLUNT. 'Sheartlikins, y'are all Fools, there are things about this Essex Calf, that shall take with the Ladies, beyond all your Wit and parts—This Shape and Size, Gentlemen, are not to be despis'd; my Waist tolerably long, with other inviting Signs that shall be nameless.

WILLMORE. Egad I believe he may have met with some Person of Quality that may be kind to him.

BELVILE. Dost thou perceive any such tempting things about him, shou'd make a fine Woman, and of Quality, pick him out from all Mankind, to throw away her Youth and Beauty upon, nay, and her dear Heart too?—no, no, Angelica has rais'd the price too high.

WILLMORE. May she languish for mankind till she die, and be damn'd for that one Sin alone.

[Enter two Bravoes, and hang up a great Picture of Angelica's, against the Balcony, and two little ones at each side of the Door.]

BELVILE. See there the fair Sign to the Inn, where a Man may lodge that's Fool enough to give her Price.

[Willmore gazes on the Picture.]

BLUNT. 'Sheartlikins, Gentlemen, what's this?

BELVILE. A famous Courtesan that's to be sold.

BLUNT. How! to be sold! nay then I have nothing to say to her—sold! what Impudence is practis'd in this Country?—with Order and Decency Whoring's establish'd here by virtue of the Inquisition—Come let's be gone, I'm sure we're no Chapman for this Commodity.

FREDERICK. Thou art none, I'm sure, unless thou coud'st have her in thy Bed at the price of a Coach in the Street.

WILLMORE. How wondrous fair she is—a Thousand Crowns a Month—by Heaven as many Kingdoms were too little. A plague of this Poverty—of which I ne'er complain, but when it hinders my Approach to Beauty, which Virtue ne'er cou'd purchase.

[Turns from the Picture.]

BLUNT. What's this?—*[Reads]* *A Thousand Crowns a Month*!
—'Sheartlikins, here's a Sum! sure 'tis a mistake.
—Hark you Friend, does she take or give so much by the Month!

FREDERICK. A Thousand Crowns! Why, 'tis a Portion for the Infanta.

BLUNT. Hark ye Friends, won't she trust?

BRAVO. This is a Trade, Sir, that cannot live by Credit.

[Enter Don Pedro in Masquerade, follow'd by Stephano.]

BELVILE. See, here's more Company, let's walk off a while.

[Don Pedro Reads. Exeunt English.]

[Enter Angelica and Moretta in the Balcony, and draw a Silk Curtain.]

DON PEDRO. Fetch me a Thousand Crowns, I never wisht to buy this Beauty at an easier Rate. *[Passes off.]*

ANGELICA. Prithee what said those Fellows to thee?

BRAVO. Madam, the first were Admirers of Beauty

only; but no purchasers; they were merry with your Price and Picture, laught at the Sum, and so past off.

ANGELICA. No matter, I'm not displeas'd with their rallying; their Wonder feeds my Vanity, and he that wishes to buy, gives me more Pride, than he that gives my Price can make me Pleasure.

BRAVO. Madam, the last I knew thro all his Disguises to be Don Pedro, Nephew to the General, and who was with him in Pampelona.

ANGELICA. Don Pedro! my old Gallant's Nephew! When his Uncle dy'd, he left him a vast Sum of Money; it is he who was so in love with me at Padua, and who us'd to make the General so jealous.

MORETTA. Is this he that us'd to prance before our Window, and take such care to show himself an amorous Ass? if I am not mistaken, he is the likeliest man to give your Price.

ANGELICA. The Man is brave and generous, but of an Humour so uneasy and inconstant, that the Victory over his Heart is as soon lost as won; a Slave that can add little to the Triumph of the Conqueror: but Inconstancy's the Sin of all Mankind, therefore I'm resolv'd that nothing but God shall charm my heart.

MORETTA. I'm glad on't; 'tis only Interest that Women of our Profession ought to consider: tho I wonder what has kept you from that general Disease of our Sex so long, I mean that of being in love.

ANGELICA. A kind, but sullen Star, under which I had the Happiness to be born; yet I have had no time for Love; the bravest and noblest of Mankind have purchas'd my Favours at so dear a Rate, as if no Coin but gold were current with our Trade—But here's Don Pedro again, fetch me my Lute—for 'tis for him or Don Antonio the Vice-Roy's Son, that I have spread my Nets.

[Enter at One Door Don Pedro, and Stephano; Don Antonio and Diego at the other Door, with People following him in Masquerade, antickly attir'd, some with Musick: they both go up to the Picture.]

ANTONIO. A thousand Crowns! had not the Painter flatter'd her, I shou'd not think it dear.

DON PEDRO. Flatter'd her! by Heaven he cannot. I have seen the Original, nor is there one Charm here more than adorns her Face and Eyes; all this soft and sweet, with a certain languishing Air, that no Artist can represent.

ANTONIO. What I heard of her Beauty before had fir'd my Soul, but this confirmation of it has blown it into a flame.

PAGE. Sir, I have known you throw away a thousand Crowns on a worse Face, and tho y' are near your Marriage, you may venture a little Love here; Florinda—will not miss it.

DON PEDRO. Ha! Florinda! Sure 'tis Antonio.

ANTONIO. Florinda! name not that those distant Joys, there's not one thought of her will check my Passion here.

DON PEDRO. Florinda scorn'd! and all my hopes defeated of the possession of Angelica! [A Noise of a Lute above. Antonio gazes up.] Her Injuries by Heaven he shall not boast of.

[Song to a Lute above.]

SONG.

When Damon first began to love,
He languisht in a soft Desire,
And knew not how the Gods to move,
To lessen or increase his Fire.
For Cælia in her charming Eyes
Wore all Love's Sweet, and all his Cruelties.
                    II.
But as beneath a Shade he lay,
Weaving of Flow'rs for Cælia's Hair,
She chanc'd to lead her Flock that way,
And saw the am'rous Shepherd there.
She gaz'd around upon the Place,
And saw the Grove (resembling Night)
To all the Joys of Love invite,
Whilst guilty Smiles and Blushes drest her Face.
At this the bashful Youth all Transport grew,
And with kind Force he taught the Virgin how
To yield what all his Sighs cou'd never do.

ANTONIO. By Heav'n she's charming fair!

[Angelica throws open the Curtains, and bows to Antonio, who pulls off his Vizard, and bows and blows up Kisses. Pedro unseen looks in his Face.]

DON PEDRO. 'Tis he, the false Antonio?

ANTONIO. Friend, where must I pay my offering of Love?

[To the Bravo.]

My Thousand Crowns I mean.

DON PEDRO. That Offering I have design'd to make, And yours will come too late.

ANTONIO. Prithee be gone, I shall grow angry else, And then thou art not safe.

DON PEDRO. My Anger may be fatal, Sir, as yours;
  And he that enters here may prove his Truth.
ANTONIO. I know not who thou art, but I am sure
  thou're worth my killing, and aiming at Angelica.

[They draw and fight.]

[Enter Willmore and Blunt, who draw and part'em.]

BLUNT. 'Sheartlikins, here's fine doings.
WILLMORE. Tilting for the Wench I'm sure—nay gad,
  if that wou'd win her, I have as good a Sword as the
  best of ye—Put up—put up, and take another time
  and place, for this is design'd for Lovers only.

[They all put up.]

DON PEDRO. We are prevented; dare you meet me to
  morrow on the Molo?
  For I've a Title to a better quarrel,
  That of Florinda, in whose credulous Heart
  Thou'st made an Int'rest and destroy'd my Hopes.
ANTONIO. Dare?
  I'll meet thee there as early as the Day.
DON PEDRO. We will come thus disguis'd, that who-
  soever chance to get the better, he may escape
  unknown.
ANTONIO. It shall be so. [Ex. Don Pedro and Stephano.]
  Who shou'd this Rival be? unless the English Colo-
  nel, of whom I've often heard Don Pedro speak; it
  must be he, and time he were removed, who lays a
  Claim to all my Happiness.

[Willmore having gaz'd all this while on the Picture, pulls
down a little one.]

WILLMORE. This Posture's loose and negligent,
  The Sight on't wou'd beget a warm desire
  In Souls, whom Impotence and Age had chill'd.
  —This must along with me.
BRAVO. What means this rudeness, Sir?—restore the
  Picture.
ANTONIO. Ha! Rudeness committed to the fair
  Angelica!—Restore the Picture, Sir.
WILLMORE. Indeed I will not, Sir.
ANTONIO. By Heav'n but you shall.
WILLMORE. Nay, do not show your Sword; if you do,
  by this dear Beauty—I will show mine too.
ANTONIO. What right can you pretend to't?
WILLMORE. That of Possession which I will
  maintain—you perhaps have 1000 Crowns to give
  for the Original.
ANTONIO. No matter, Sir, you shall restore the Pic-
  ture.

ANGELICA. Oh Moretta! what's the matter?

[Angelia and Moretta above.]

ANTONIO. Or leave your Life behind.
WILLMORE. Death! you lye—I will do neither.
ANGELICA. Hold I command you, if for me you fight.

[They fight, the Spaniards join with Antonio, Blunt laying on
like mad. They leave off and bow.]

WILLMORE. How heavenly fair she is!—ah Plague of
  her Price.
ANGELICA. You Sir in Buff, you that appear a Soldier,
  that first began this Insolence.
WILLMORE. 'Tis true, I did so, if you call it Insolence
  for a Man to preserve himself; I saw your charming
  Picture, and was wounded: quite thro my Soul each
  pointed Beauty ran; and wanting a Thousand
  Crowns to procure my Remedy, I laid this little
  Picture to my Bosom—which if you cannot allow
  me, I'll resign.
ANGELICA. No, you may keep the Trifle.
ANTONIO. You shall first ask me leave, and this.

[Fight again as before.]

[Enter Belvile and Frederick who join with the English.]

ANGELICA. Hold; will you ruin me?—Biskey, Sebastian, part them. [The Spaniards are beaten off.]
MORETTA. Oh Madam, we're undone, a pox upon
  that rude Fellow, he's set on to ruin us: we shall
  never see good days, till all these fighting poor
  Rogues are sent to the Gallies.

[Enter Belvile, Blunt and Willmore, with their Shirts bloody.]

BLUNT. 'Sheartlikins, beat me at this Sport, and I'll
  ne'er wear Sword more.
BELVILE. The Devil's in thee for a mad Fellow, thou
  art always one at an unlucky Adventure.—Come
  let's be gone whilst we're safe, and remember these
  are Spaniards, a sort of People that know how to
  revenge an Affront.

[To Willmore]

FREDERICK. You bleed; I hope you are not wounded.
WILLMORE. Not much:—a plague upon your Dons, if
  they fight no better they'll ne'er recover Flanders.—
  What the Devil was't to them that I took down the
  Picture?

BLUNT. Took it! 'Sheartlikins, we'll have the great one too; 'tis ours by Conquest.—Prithee help me up, and I'll pull it down.—

ANGELICA. Stay Sir, and e'er you affront me further, let me know how you durst commit this Outrage— To you I speak Sir, for you appear like a Gentleman.

WILLMORE. To me, Madam?—Gentlemen, your Servant.

[Belvile stays him.]

BELVILE. Is the Devil in thee? Do'st know the danger of entring the House of an incens'd Courtesan?

WILLMORE. I thank you for your care—but there are other matters in hand, there are, tho we have no great Temptation.—Death! let me go.

FREDERICK. Yes, to your Lodging, if you will, but not in here.—Damn these gay Harlots—by this Hand I'll have as sound and handsome a Whore for a Patacoone.—Death, Man, she'll murder thee.

WILLMORE. Oh! fear me not, shall I not venture where a Beauty calls? a lovely charming Beauty? for fear of danger! when by Heaven there's none so great as to long for her, whilst I want Money to purchase her.

FREDERICK. Therefore 'tis loss of time, unless you had the thousand Crowns to pay.

WILLMORE. It may be she may give a Favour, at least I shall have the pleasure of saluting her when I enter, and when I depart.

BELVILE. Pox, she'll as soon lie with thee, as kiss thee, and sooner stab than do either—you shall not go.

ANGELICA. Fear not, Sir, all I have to wound with is my Eyes.

BLUNT. Let him go, 'Sheartlikins, I believe the Gentlewoman means well.

BELVILE. Well, take thy Fortune, we'll expect you in the next Street.—Farewell Fool,—farewell—

WILLMORE. B'ye Colonel—   [Goes in.]

FREDERICK. The Rogue's stark mad for a Wench.
        [Exeunt.]

SCENE II

A fine Chamber.

[Enter Willmore, Angelica, and Moretta.]

ANGELICA. Insolent Sir, how durst you pull down my Picture?

WILLMORE. Rather, how durst you set it up, to tempt poor amorous Mortals with so much Excellence? which I find you have but too well consulted by the unmerciful price you set upon't.—Is all this Heaven of Beauty shown to move Despair in those that cannot buy? and can you think the effects of that Despair shou'd be less extravagant than I have shown?

ANGELICA. I sent for you to ask my Pardon, Sir, not to aggravate your Crime.—I thought I should have seen you at my Feet imploring it.

WILLMORE. You are deceived, I came to rail at you, and talk such Truths too, as shall let you see the Vanity of that Pride, which taught you how to set such a Price on Sin. For such it is, whilst that which is Love's due is meanly barter'd for.

ANGELICA. Ha, ha, ha, alas good Captain, what pity 'tis your edifying Doctrine will do no good upon me—Moretta, fetch the Gentleman a Glass, and let him survey himself, to see what Charms he has,— and guess my Business. [Aside in a soft Tone.]

MORETTA. He knows himself of old, I believe those Breeches and he have been acquainted ever since he was beaten at Worcester.

ANGELICA. Nay, do not abuse the poor Creature.—

MORETTA. Good Weather-beaten Corporal, will you march off? we have no need of your Doctrine, tho you have of our Charity; but at present we have no Scraps, we can afford no kindness for God's sake; in fine, Sirrah, the Price is too high i'th' Month for you, therefore troop, I say.

WILLMORE. Here, good Fore-Woman of the Shop, serve me, and I'll be gone.

MORETTA. Keep it to pay your Laundress, your Linen stinks of the Gun-Room; for here's no selling by Retail.

WILLMORE. Thou hast sold plenty of thy stale Ware at a cheap Rate.

MORETTA. Ay, the more silly kind Heart I, but this is an Age wherein Beauty is at higher Rates.—In fine, you know the price of this.

WILLMORE. I grant you 'tis here set down a thousand Crowns a Month—Bawd, take your black Lead and sum it up, that I may have a Pistole-worth of these vain gay things, and I'll trouble you no more.

MORETTA. Pox on him, he'll fret me to Death:— abominable Fellow, I tell thee, we only sell by the whole Piece.

WILLMORE. 'Tis very hard, the whole Cargo or nothing—Faith, Madam, my Stock will not reach it, I cannot be your Chapman.—Yet I have Countrymen in Town, Merchants of Love, like me; I'll see if they'l put for a share, we cannot lose much by it, and what we have no use for, we'll sell upon the Friday's Mart, at—Who gives more? I am studying, Madam, how to purchase you, tho at present I am unprovided of Money.

ANGELICA. Sure this from any other Man would anger me—nor shall he know the Conquest he has made—Poor angry Man, how I despise this railing.

WILLMORE. Yes, I am poor—but I'am a Gentleman,
And one that scorns this Baseness which you practise.
Poor as I am, I would not sell myself,
No, not to gain your charming high-priz'd Person.
Tho I admire you strangely for your Beauty,
Yet I contemn your Mind.
—And yet I wou'd at any rate enjoy you;
At your own rate—but cannot—See here
The only Sum I can command on Earth;
I know not where to eat when this is gone:
Yet such a Slave I am to Love and Beauty.
This last I'll sacrifice to enjoy you.
—Nay, do not frown, I know you are to be bought,
And wou'd be bought by me
For a mean trifling Sum, if I could pay it down.
Which happy knowledge I will still repeat,
And lay it to my Heart, it has a Virtue in't,
And soon will curse those Wounds your Eyes have made.
—And yet—there's something so divinely powerful there—
Nay, I will gaze—to let you see my Strength.

[*Holds her, looks on her, and pauses and sighs.*]

By Heaven, bright Creature—I would not for the World thy Fame were half so fair as is thy Face.

[*Turns her away from him.*]

ANGELICA. [*Aside.*] His words go thro me to the very Soul.—If you have nothing else to say to me.

WILLMORE. Yes, you shall hear how infamous you are—
For which I do not hate thee:
But that secures my Heart, and all the Flames it feels
Are but so many Lusts,
I know it by their sudden bold intrusion.
The Fire's impatient and betrays, 'tis false—
For had it been the purer Flame of Love,
I should have pin'd and languish'd at your Feet,
E'er found the Impudence to have discover'd it.
I now dare stand your Scorn, and your Denial.

MORETTA. Sure, she's bewitcht, that she can stand thus tamely, and hear his saucy railing.—Sirrah, will you be gone?

ANGELICA. How dare you take this liberty? Withdraw.

[*To Moretta.*]

—Pray tell me, Sir, are you not guilty of the same mercenary Crime? When a Lady is proposed to you for a Wife, you never ask, how fair, discreet, or virtuous she is; but what's her Fortune—which if but small, you cry—She will not do my business—and basely leave her, tho she languish for you.—Say, is not this as poor?

WILLMORE. It is a barbarous Custom, which I will scorn to defend in our Sex, and do despise in yours.

ANGELICA. Thou art a brave Fellow! put up thy Gold, and know that were thy Fortune large, as is thy Soul, thou shouldst not buy my Love, couldst thou forget those mean effects of Vanity, which set me out to sale; and as a Lover, prize my yielding Joys.
Canst thou believe they'l be entirely thine,
Without considering they were mercenary?

WILLMORE. I cannot tell, I must bethink me first—
[*Aside.*] ha, Death, I'm going to believe her.

ANGELICA. Prithee confirm that Faith—or if thou canst not—flatter me a little, 'twill please me from thy Mouth.

WILLMORE. [*Aside.*] Curse on thy charming Tongue! dost thou return My feign'd Contempt with so much subtilty?
Thou'st found the easiest way into my Heart,
Tho I yet know that all thou say'st is false.

[*Turning from her in a Rage.*]

ANGELICA. By all that's good 'tis real,
I never lov'd before, tho oft a Mistress.
—Shall my first Vows be slighted?

WILLMORE. [*Aside.*] What can she mean?

ANGELICA. I find you cannot credit me. [*In an angry tone.*]

WILLMORE. I know you take me for an errant Ass,
An Ass that may be sooth'd into Belief,
And then be us'd at pleasure.
    But, Madam, I have been so often cheated
By perjur'd, soft, deluding Hypocrites,
That I've no Faith left for the cozening Sex,
Especially for Women of your Trade.

ANGELICA. The low esteem you have of me, perhaps
May bring my Heart again:
For I have Pride that yet surmounts my Love.

[*She turns with Pride, he holds her.*]

WILLMORE. Throw off this pride, this Enemy to Bliss,
   And show the Power of Love: 'tis with those Arms
   I can be only vanquisht, made a Slave.
ANGELICA. Is all my mighty Expectation vanisht?
   —No, I will not hear thee talk,—thou hast a Charm
   In every word, that draws my Heart away.
   And all the thousand Trophies I design'd,
   Thou hast undone—Why art thou soft?
   Thy Looks are bravely rough, and meant for War.
   Could thou not storm on still?
   I then perhaps had been as free as thou.
WILLMORE. [Aside.] Death! how she throws her Fire
   about my Soul!
   —Take heed, fair Creature, how you raise my
     Hopes,
   Which once assum'd pretend to all Dominion.
   There's not a joy thou hast in store
   I shall not then command:
   For which I'll pay thee back my Soul, my Life.
   Come, let's begin th' account this happy minute.
ANGELICA. And will you pay me then the Price I ask?
WILLMORE. Oh, why dost thou draw me from an
   awful Worship,
   By showing thou art no Divinity?
   Conceal the Fiend, and shew me all the Angel;
   Keep me but ignorant, and I'll be devout,
   And pay my Vows for ever at this Shrine.

[Kneels, and kisses her Hand.]

ANGELICA. The Pay I mean is but thy Love for mine.
   —Can you give that?
WILLMORE. Intirely—come, let's withdraw: where I'll
   renew my Vows,—and breathe 'em with such
   Ardour, thou shalt not doubt my Zeal.
ANGELICA. Thou hast a Power too strong to be
   resisted.

[Ex. Willmore and Angelica.]

MORETTA. Now my Curse go with you—Is all our
   Project fallen to this? to love the only Enemy to our
   Trade? Nay, to love such a Shameroon, a very Beggar; nay, a Pirate-Beggar, whose Business is to rifle
   and be gone, a No-Purchase, No-Pay Tatter-
   demalion, an English Piccaroon; a Rogue that fights
   for daily Drink, and takes a Pride in being loyally
   lousy—Oh, I could curse now, if I durst—This is
   the Fate of most Whores.

   Trophies, which from believing Fops we win,
   Are Spoils to those who cozen us again.

Act III

SCENE I

A Street.

[Enter Florinda, Valeria, Hellena, in Antick different Dresses
from what they were in before, Callis attending.]

FLORINDA. I Wonder what should make my Brother
   in so ill a Humour: I hope he has not found out our
   Ramble this Morning.
HELLENA. No, if he had, we should have heard on't at
   both Ears, and have been mew'd up this Afternoon;
   which I would not for the World should have
   happen'd—Hey ho! I'm sad as a Lover's Lute.
VALERIA. Well, methinks we have learnt this Trade of
   Gipsies as readily as if we had been bred upon the
   Road to Loretto; and yet I did so fumble, when I
   told the Stranger his Fortune, that I was afraid I

should have told my own and yours by mistake—
   But methinks Hellena has been very serious ever
   since.
FLORINDA. I would give my Garters she were in love,
   to be reveng'd upon her, for abusing me—How is't
   Hellena?
HELLENA. Ah!—would I had never seen my mad
   Monsieur—and yet for all your laughing I am not in
   love—and yet this small Acquaintance, o'my Conscience, will never out of my Head.
VALERIA. Ha, ha, ha.—I laugh to think how thou art
   fitted with a Lover, a Fellow that, I warrant, loves
   every new Face he sees.
HELLENA. Hum—he has not kept his Word with me
   here—and may be taken up—that Thought is not
   very pleasant to me—what the Deuce should this be
   now that I feel?
VALERIA. What is't like?

HELLENA. Nay, the Lord knows—but if I should be hanged, I cannot choose but be angry and afraid, when I think that mad Fellow should be in love with any Body but me—What to think of my self I know not—Would I could meet with some true damn'd Gipsy, that I might know my Fortune.

VALERIA. Know it! why there's nothing so easy: thou wilt love this wandring Inconstant till thou find'st thy self hanged about his Neck, and then be as mad to get free again.

FLORINDA. Yes, Valeria; we shall see her bestride his Baggage-horse, and follow him to the Campaign.

HELLENA. So, so; now you are provided for, there's no care taken of poor me—But since you have set my Heart a wishing, I am resolv'd to know for what. I will not die of the Pip, so I will not.

FLORINDA. Art thou mad to talk so? Who will like thee well enough to have thee, that hears what a mad Wench thou art?

HELLENA. Like me! I don't intend every he that likes me shall have me, but he that I like: I shou'd have staid in the Nunnery still, if I had lik'd my Lady Abbess as well as she lik'd me. No, I came thence, not (as my wife Brother imagines) to take an eternal Farewell of the World, but to love and to be belov'd; and I will be belov'd, or I'll get one of your Men, so I will.

VALERIA. Am I put into the Number of Lovers?

HELLENA. You! my Couz, I know thou art too good-natur'd to leave us in any Design: Thou won't venture a Cast, tho thou comest off a Loser, especially with such a Gamester—I observ'd your Man, and your willing Ears incline that way; and if you are not a Lover, 'tis an Art soon learnt—that I find. [Sighs.]

FLORINDA. I wonder how you learnt to love so easily, I had a thousand Charms to meet my Eyes and Ears, e'er I cou'd yield; and 'twas the knowledge of Belvile's Merit, not the surprizing Person, took my Soul—Thou art too rash to give a Heart at first sight.

HELLENA. Hang your considering Lover; I ne'er thought beyond the Fancy, that 'twas a very pretty, idle, silly kind of Pleasure to pass ones time with, to write little, soft, nonsensical Billets, and with great difficulty and danger receive Answers; in which I shall have my Beauty prais'd, my Wit admir'd (tho little or none) and have the Vanity and Power to know I am desirable; then I have the more Inclination that way, because I am to be a Nun, and so shall not be suspected to have any such earthly Thoughts about me—But when I walk Thus—and sigh thus—they'll think my Mind's upon my Mon-astery, and cry, how happy 'tis she's so resolv'd!—But not a Word of Man.

FLORINDA. What a mad Creature's this!

HELLENA. I'll warrant, if my Brother hears either of you sigh, he cries (gravely)—I fear you have the Indiscretion to be in love, but take heed of the Honour of our House, and your own unspotted Fame; and so he conjures on till he has laid the soft-wing'd God in your Hearts, or broke the Birds-nest—But see here comes your Lover: but where's my inconstant? let's step aside, and we may learn something. [Go aside.]

[Enter Belvile, Frederick and Blunt.]

BELVILE. What means this? the Picture's taken in.

BLUNT. It may be the Wench is good-natur'd, and will be kind *gratis*. Your Friend's a proper handsome Fellow.

BELVILE. I rather think she has cut his Throat and is fled: I am mad he should throw himself into Dangers—Pox on't, I shall want him tonight—let's knock and ask for him.

HELLENA. My Heart goes a-pit-a-pat, for fear 'tis my Man they talk of. [Knock, Moretta above.]

MORETTA. What would you have?

BELVILE. Tell the Stranger that enter'd here about two Hours ago, that his Friends stay here for him.

MORETTA. A Curse upon him for Moretta, would he were at the Devil—but he's coming to you. [Enter Willmore.]

HELLENA. I, I, 'tis he. Oh how this vexes me.

BELVILE. And how, and how, dear Lad, has Fortune smil'd? Are we to break her Windows, or raise up Altars to her? hah!

WILLMORE. Does not my Fortune sit triumphant on my Brow? dost not see the little wanton God there all gay and smiling? have I not an Air about my Face and Eyes, that distinguish me from the Crowd of common Lovers? By Heav'n, Cupid's Quiver has not half so many Darts as her Eyes—Oh such a *Bona Roba*, to sleep in her Arms is lying in Fresco, all perfum'd Air about me.

HELLENA. Here's fine encouragement for me to fool on. [Aside.]

WILLMORE. Hark ye, where didst thou purchase that rich Canary we drank today? Tell me, that I may adore the Spigot, and sacrifice to the Butt: the Juice was divine, into which I must dip my Rosary, and then bless all things that I would have bold or fortunate.

BELVILE. Well, Sir, let's go take a Bottle, and hear the Story of your Success.

FREDERICK. Would not French Wine do better?

WILLMORE. Damn the hungry Balderdash; cheerful Sack has a generous Virtue in't, inspiring a successful Confidence, give Eloquence to the Tongue, and Vigour to the Soul; and has in a few Hours completed all my Hopes and Wishes. There's nothing left to raise a new Desire in me—Come let's be gay and wanton—and Gentlemen, study, study what you want, for here are Friends—that will supply, Gentlemen,—hark! what a charming sound they make—'tis he and the Gold whilst here, shall beget new Pleasures every moment.

BLUNT. But hark ye Sir, you are not married, are you?

WILLMORE. All the Honey of Matrimony, but none of the Sting, Friend.

BLUNT. 'Sheartlikins, thou'rt a fortunate Rogue.

WILLMORE. I am so Sir, let these inform you.—Ha, how sweetly they chime! Pox of Poverty, it makes a Man a Slave, makes Wit and Honour sneak, my Soul grew lean and rusty for want of Credit.

BLUNT. 'Sheartlikins, this I like well, it looks like my lucky Bargain! Oh how I long for the Approach of my Squire, that is to conduct me to her House again. Why! here's two provided for.

FREDERICK. By this Light y're happy Men.

BLUNT. Fortune is pleased to smile on us, Gentlemen,—to smile on us.

[*Enter Sancho, and pulls Blunt by the Sleeve. They go aside.*]

SANCHO. Sir, my Lady expects you—she has remov'd all that might oppose your Will and Pleasure—and is impatient till you come.

BLUNT. Sir, I'll attend you—Oh the happiest Rogue! I'll take no leave, lest they either dog me, or stay me.

[*Exit with Sancho.*]

BELVILE. But then the little Gipsy is forgot?

WILLMORE. A Mischief on thee for putting her into my thoughts; I had quite forgot her else, and this Night's Debauch had drunk her quite down.

HELLENA. Had it so, good Captain? [*Claps him on the Back.*]

WILLMORE. Ha! I hope she did not hear.

HELLENA. What afraid of such a Champion!

WILLMORE. Oh! you're a fine Lady of your word, are you not? to make a Man languish a whole day—

HELLENA. In tedious search of me.

WILLMORE. Egad Child thou're in the right, hadst thou seen what a melancholy Dog I have been ever since I was a Lover, how I have walkt the Streets like a Capuchin, with my Hands in my Sleeves—Faith Sweatheart, thou wouldst pity me.

HELLENA. Now, if I should be hang'd, I can't be angry with him, he dissembles so heartily—Alas good Captain, what pains you have taken—Now were I ungrateful not to reward so true a Servant.

WILLMORE. Poor Soul! that's kindly said, I see thou bearest a Conscience—come then for a beginning show me thy dear Face.

HELLENA. I'm afraid, my small Acquaintance, you have been staying that swinging stomach you boasted of this morning; I remember then my little Collation would have gone down with you, without the Sauce of a handsome Face—Is your Stomach so queasy now?

WILLMORE. Faithlong fasting, Child, spoils a Man's Appetite—yet if you durst treat, I could so lay about me still.

HELLENA. And would you fall to, before a Priest says Grace?

WILLMORE. Oh fie, fie, what an old out-of-fashion'd thing hast thou nam'd? Thou cou'dst not dash me more out of Countenance, shouldst thou show me an ugly Face.

[*Whilst he is seemingly courting Hellena, enter Angelica, Moretta, Biskey, and Sebastian, all in Masquerade: Angelica sees Willmore and starts.*]

ANGELICA. Heavens, is't he? and passionately fond to see another Woman?

MORETTA. What cou'd you expect less from such a Swaggerer?

ANGELICA. Expect! as much as I paid him, a Heart intire, which I had Pride enough to think when e'er I gave, it would have rais'd the Man above the Vulgar, made him all Soul, and that all soft and constant.

HELLENA. You see, Captain, how willing I am to be Friends with you, till Time and Ill-luck make us Lovers; and ask you the Question first, rather than put your Modesty to the blush, by asking me: for alas, I know you Captains are such strict Men, severe Observers of your Vows to Chastity, that 'twill be hard to prevail with your tender Conscience to marry a young willing Maid.

WILLMORE. Do not abuse me, for fear I should take thee at they Word, and marry thee indeed, which I'm sure will be Revenge sufficient.

HELLENA. O' my Conscience, that will be our Destiny, because we are both of one humour; I am as inconstant as you, for I have considered, Captain, that a handsome Woman has a great deal to do whilst her Face is good, for then is our Harvest-time to gather Friends; and should I in these days of my Youth, catch a fit of foolish Constancy, I were undone; 'tis loitering by day-light in our great Journey: therefore declare, I'll allow but one year for Love, one year for Indifference, and one year for Hate—and then—go hang you self—for I profess my self the gay, the kind, and the inconstant—the Devil's in't if this won't please you.

WILLMORE. Oh most damnably!—I have a Heart with a hole quite thro it too, no Prison like mine to keep a Mistress in.

ANGELICA. Perjur'd Man! how I believe thee now!
                               [*Aside.*]

HELLENA. Well, I see our Business as well as Humours are alike, yours to cozen as many maids as will trust you, and I as many Men as have Faith—See if I have not as desperate a lying look, as you can have for the heart of you. [*Pulls off her Vizard; he starts.*]
—How do you like it Captain?

WILLMORE. Like it! by Heav'n, I never saw so much Beauty. Oh the Charms of those sprightly black Eyes, that strangely fair Face, full of Smiles and Dimples! those soft round melting cherry Lips! and small even white Teeth! not to be exprest, but silently adored!—Oh one Look more, and strike me dumb, or I shall repeat nothing else till I am mad.

[*He seems to court her to pull off her Vizard; she refuses.*]

ANGELICA. I can endure no more—nor is it fit to interrupt him; for if I do, my Jealousy has so destroy'd my Reason,—I shall undo him—Therefore I'll retire. And you Sebastian [*To one of her Bravoes*] follow that Woman, and learn who 'tis; while you tell the Fugitive, I would speak to him instantly. [*To the other Bravo.*]

[*Exit.*]

[*This while Florinda is talking to Belvile, who stands sullenly. Frederick courting Valeria.*]

VALERIA. Prithee dear Stranger, be not so sullen; for tho you have lost your Love, you see my Friend frankly offers you hers, to play with in the mean time.

BELVILE. Faith Madam, I'm sorry I can't play at her Game.

FREDERICK. Pray leave your Intercession, and mind your own Affair, they'll better agree apart; he's a modest Sigher in Company, but alone no Woman escapes him.

FLORINDA. Sure he does but rally—yet if it should be true—I'll tempt him farther—Believe me noble Stranger, I'm no common Mistress—and for a little proof on't—wear this Jewel—nay, take it, Sir, 'tis right, and Bills of Exchange may sometimes miscarry.

BELVILE. Madam, why am I chose out of all Mankind to be the Object of your Bounty?

VALERIA. There's another civil Question askt.

FREDERICK. Pox of's Modesty, it spoils his own Markets, and hinders mine.

FLORINDA. Sir, from my Window I have often seen you; and Women of Quality have so few opportunities for Love, that we ought to lose none.

FREDERICK. Ay, this is something! here's a Woman!— When shall I be blest with so much kindness from your fair Mouth?—[*Aside to Belvile.*] Take the Jewel, Fool.

BELVILE. You tempt me strangely, Madam, every way.

FLORINDA. So, if I find him false, my whole Repose is gone. [*Aside.*]

BELVILE. And but for a Vow I've made to a very fine lady, this Goodness had subdu'd me.

FREDERICK. Pox on't, be kind, in pity to me be kind, for I am to thrive here but as you treat her Friend.

HELLENA. Tell me what did you in yonder House, and I'll unmasque.

WILLMORE. Yonder House—oh—I went to—a—to—why there's a Friend of mine lives there.

HELLENA. What a she, or a he Friend?

WILLMORE. A Man upon my Honour! a Man—A She Friend! no, no, Madam, you have done my Business, I thank you.

HELLENA. And was't your Man Friend, that had more Darts in's Eyes than Cupid carries in's whole Budget of Arrows?

WILLMORE. So—

HELLENA. Ah such a *Bona Roba*: to be in her Arms is lying in Fresco, all perfumed Air about me—Was this your Man Friend too?

WILLMORE. So—

HELLENA. That gave you the He, and the She—Gold, that begets young Pleasures.

WILLMORE. Well, well, Madam, then you see there are Ladies in the World, that will not be cruel—there are Madam, there are—

HELLENA. And there be Men too as fine, wild, inconstant Fellows as your self, there be Captain, there be, if you go to that now—therefore I'm resolv'd—

WILLMORE. Oh!

HELLENA. To see your Face no more—

WILLMORE. Oh!

HELLENA. Till tomorrow.

WILLMORE. Egad you frightened me.

HELLENA. Nor then neither, unless you'l swear never to see that Lady more.

WILLMORE. See her!—why! never to think of Womankind again?

HELLENA. Kneel, and swear. [*Kneels, she gives him her hand.*]

WILLMORE. I do, never to think—to see—to love— nor lie with any but thy self.

HELLENA. Kiss the Book.

WILLMORE. Oh, most religiously. [*Kisses her Hand.*]

HELLENA. Now what a wicked Creature am I, to damn a proper Fellow.

CALLIS. Madam, I'll stay no longer, 'tis e'en dark. [*To Florinda.*]

FLORINDA. However, Sir, I'll leave this with you— that when I'm gone, you may repent the opportunity you have lost by your Modesty. [*Gives him the Jewel, which is her Picture, and Exit. He gazes after her.*]

WILLMORE. 'Twill be an Age till tomorrow,—and till then I will most impatiently expect you—Adieu, my dear pretty Angel. [*Exeunt all the Women.*]

BELVILE. Ha! Florinda's Picture! 'twas she her self— what a dull Dog was I? I would have given the World for one minute's discourse with her.—

FREDERICK. This comes of your Modesty,—ah, pox on your Vow, 'twas ten to one but we had lost the Jewel by't.

BELVILE. Willmore! the blessed'st Opportunity lost!— Florinda, Friends, Florinda!

WILLMORE. Ah Rogue! such black Eyes, such a Face, such a Mouth, such Teeth,—and so much Wit!

BELVILE. All, all, and a thousand Charms besides.

WILLMORE. Why dost thou know her?

BELVILE. Know her! ay, ay, and a Pox take me with all my Heart for being modest.

WILLMORE. But hark ye, Friend of mine, are you my Rival? and have I been only beating the Bush all this while?

BELVILE. I understand thee not—I'm mad—see here—

[*Shows the Picture.*]

WILLMORE. Ha! whose Picture is this?—'tis a fine Wench.

FREDERICK. The Colonel's Mistress, Sir.

WILLMORE. Oh, oh, here—I thought it had been

another Prize—come, come, a Bottle will set thee right again. [*Gives the Picture back.*]

BELVILE. I am content to try, and by that time 'twill be late enough for our Design.

WILLMORE. Agreed.

Love does all day the Soul's great Empire keep,
But Wine at night lulls the soft God asleep.

SCENE II

Lucetta's House.

[*Enter Blunt and Lucetta with a Light.*]

LUCETTA. Now we are safe and free, no fears of the coming home of my old jealous Husband, which made me a little thoughtful when you came in first—but now Love is all the business of my Soul.

BLUNT. I am transported—[*Aside.*] Pox on't, that I had but some fine things to say to her, such as Lovers use—I was a Fool not to learn of Frederick a little by Heart before I came—something I must say.—'Sheartlikins, sweet Soul, I am not us'd to complement, but I'm an honest Gentleman, and thy humble Servant.

LUCETTA. I have nothing to pay for so great a Favour, but such a Love as cannot but be great, since at first sight of that sweet Face and Shape it made me your absolute Captive.

BLUNT. [*Aside.*] Kind heart, how prettily she talks! Egad I'll show her Husband a Spanish Trick; send him out of the World, and marry her: she's damnably in love with me, and will ne'er mind Settlements, and so there's that saved.

LUCETTA. Well, Sir, I'll go and undress me, and be with you instantly.

BLUNT. Make haste then, for 'dsheartlikins, dear Soul, thou canst not guess at the pain of a longing Lover, when his Joys are drawn within the compass of a few minutes.

LUCETTA. You speak my Sense, and I'll make haste to provide it. [*Aside.*]

BLUNT. 'Tis a rare Girl, and this one night's enjoyment with her will be worth all the days I ever past in Essex—Would she'd go with me into England, tho to say truth, there's plenty of Whores there already. But a pox on 'em they are such mercenary prodigal Whores, that they want such a one as this, that's free and generous, to give 'em good Examples:—Why, what a House she has! how rich and fine!

SANCHO. Sir, my Lady has sent me to conduct you to her Chamber. [*Ex. Sancho.*]

BLUNT. Sir, I shall be proud to follow—Here's one of her Servants too: 'dsheartlikins, by his Garb and Gravity he might be a Justice of Peace in Essex, and is but a Pimp here. [*Exit.*]

[*The Scene changes to a Chamber with an Alcove-Bed in it, a Table, &c. Lucetta in Bed. Enter Sancho and Blunt, who takes the Candle of Sancho at the Door.*]

SANCHO. Sir, my Commission reaches no farther.

BLUNT. Sir, I'll excuse your Complement:—what, in Bed my sweet Mistress?

LUCETTA. You see, I still out-do you in kindness.

BLUNT. And thou shalt see what haste I'll make to quit scores—oh the luckiest Rogue! [*Undresses himself.*]

LUCETTA. Shou'd you be false or cruel now!

BLUNT. False, 'Sheartlikins, what dost thou take me for a Jew? an insensible Heathen,—A Pox of thy old jealous Husband: and he were dead, egad, sweet Soul, it shou'd be none of my fault, if I did not marry thee.

LUCETTA. It never shou'd be mine.

BLUNT. Good Soul, I'm the fortunatest Dog!

LUCETTA. Are you not undrest yet?

BLUNT. As much as my Impatience will permit.

[*Goes towards the Bed in his Shirt and Drawers.*]

LUCETTA. Hold, Sir, put out the Light, it may betray us else.

BLUNT. Any thing, I need no other Light but that of thine Eyes! [*Aside.*] —'dsheartlikins, there I think I had it.

[*Puts out the Candle, the Bed descends, he gropes about to find it.*]

—Why—why—where am I got? what not yet?—where are you sweetest?—ah, the Rogue's silent now—a pretty Love-trick this—how she'll laugh at me anon!—you need not, my dear Rogue! you need not! I'm all on a fire already—come, come, now call me in for pity—Sure I'm enchanted! I have been round the Chamber, and can find neither Woman, nor Bed—I lockt the Door, I'm sure she cannot go that way; or if she cou'd, the Bed cou'd not—Enough, enough, my pretty Wanton, do not carry the Jest to far—Ha, betray'd? Dogs! Rogues! Imps! help! help!

[*Lights on a Trap, and is let down.*]

[*Enter Lucetta, Philippo, and Sancho with a light.*]

PHILIPPO. Ha, ha, ha, he's dispatcht finely.

LUCETTA. Now, Sir, had I been coy, we had mist of this Booty.

PHILIPPO. Nay when I saw 'twas a substantial Fool, I was mollified; but when you dote upon a Serenading Coxcomb, upon a Face, fine Clothes, and a Lute, it makes me rage.

LUCETTA. You know I never was guilty of that Folly, my dear Philippo, but with your self—But come let's see what we have got by this.

PHILIPPO. A rich Coat!—Sword and Hat!—these Breeches too—are well lin'd!—see here a Gold Watch!—a Purse! ha! Gold!—at least two hundred Pistoles! a bunch of Diamond Rings; and one with the Family Arms!—a Gold Box!—with a Medal of his King! and his Lady Mother's Picture!—these were sacred Reliques, believe me!—see, the Wasteband of his Breeches have a Mine of Gold!—Old Queen Bess's. We have a Quarrel to her ever since Eighty Eight, and may therefore justify the Theft, the Inquisition might have committed it.

LUCETTA. See, a Bracelet of bow'd Gold, these his Sister ty'd about his Arm at parting—but well—for all this, I fear his being a Stranger may make a noise, and hinder our Trade with them hereafter.

PHILIPPO. That's our security; he is not only a Stranger to us, but to the Country too—the Common-Shore into which he is descended, thou know'st conducts him into another Street, which this Light will hinder him from ever finding again—he knows neither your Name, nor the Street where your House is, nay, nor the way to his own Lodgings.

LUCETTA. And art not thou an unmerciful Rogue, not to afford him one Night for all this?—I should not have been such a Jew.

PHILIPPO. Blame me not Lucetta, to keep as much of thee as I can to my self—come, that thought makes me wanton,—let's to Bed,—Sancho, lock up these.

This is the Fleece which Fools do bear,
Design'd for witty Men to share. [*Exeunt.*]

[*The Scene changes, and discovers Blunt, creeping out of a Common Shore, his Face, etc. all dirty.*]

BLUNT. Oh Lord! [*Climbing up.*]

I am got out at last, and (which is a Miracle) without a Clue—and now to Damning and Cursing,—but if that would ease me, where shall I begin? with my Fortune, my self, or the Quean that cozen'd me—What a Dog was I to believe in Women! Oh Coxcomb—ignorant conceited Coxcomb! to fancy she cou'd be enamour'd with my Person, at the first sight enamour'd—Oh, I'm a cursed Puppy, 'tis plain, Fool was writ upon my Forehead, she perceiv'd it,—saw the Essex Calf there—for what Allurements could there be in this Countenance? which I can indure, because I'm acquainted with it—Oh, dull, silly Dog! to be thus sooth'd into a Cozening! Had I been drunk, I might fondly have credited the young Quean!—but as I was in my right Wits, to be thus cheated, confirms I am a dull believing English Country Fop.—But my Comrades! Death and the Devil, there's the worst of all—then a Ballad will be sung to Morrow on the Prado, to a lousy Tune of the enchanted Squire, and the annihilated Damsel—But Frederick that Rogue, and the Colonel, will abuse me beyond all Christian patience—had she left me my Clothes, I have a Bill of Exchange at home wou'd have sav'd my Credit—but now all hope is taken from me—Well, I'll home (if I can find the way) with this Consolation, that I am not the first kind of believing Coxcomb; but there are, Gallants, many such good Natures amongst ye.

And tho you've better Arts to hide your Follies,
Adsheartlikins y'are all as errant Cullies.

SCENE III

The Garden, in the Night.

[*Enter Florinda undress'd, with a Key, and a little Box.*]

FLORINDA. Well, thus far I'm in my way to Happiness; I have got myself free from Callis; my Brother too, I find by yonder light is got into his Cabinet, and thinks not of me: I have by good Fortune got the Key of the Garden Back-door,—I'll open it, to prevent Belvile's knocking,—a little noise will now alarm my Brother. Now am I as fearful as a young Thief. [*Unlocks the Door.*]
Hark,—what noise is that?—Oh, 'twas the Wind that plaid amongst the Boughs.—Belvile stays long, methinks—it's time—stay—for fear of a surprize, I'll hide these Jewels in yonder Jessamin.

[*She goes to lay down the Box.*]

[*Enter Willmore drunk.*]

WILLMORE. What the Devil is become of these Fellows, Belvile and Frederick? They promis'd to stay at the next corner for me, but who the Devil knows the corner of a full Moon?—Now—whereabouts am I—hah—what have we here? a Garden!—a very convenient place to sleep in—hah—what has God sent us here?—a Female—by this light, a Woman; I'm a Dog if it be not a very Wench.—

FLORINDA. He's come!—hah—who's there?

WILLMORE. Sweet Soul, let me salute thy Shoe-string.

FLORINDA. 'Tis not my Belvile—good Heavens, I know him not.—Who are you, and from whence come you?

WILLMORE. Prithee—prithee Child—not so many hard Questions—let it suffice I am here, Child—Come, come kiss me.

FLORINDA. Good Gods! what luck is mine?

WILLMORE. Only good luck Child, parlous good luck.—Come hither,—'tis a delicate shining Wench,—by this Hand she's perfum'd, and smells like any Nosegay.—Prithee dear Soul, let's not play the Fool, and lose time,—precious time—for as Gad shall save me, I'm as honest a Fellow as breathes, tho I am a little disguis'd at present.—Come, I say,—why, thou may'st be free with me, I'll be very secret. I'll not boast who 'twas oblig'd me, not I—for hang me if I know thy Name.

FLORINDA. Heavens! what a filthy Beast is this!

WILLMORE. I am so, and thou oughtst the sooner to lie with me for that reason,—for look you Child, there will be no Sin in't, because 'twas neither design'd nor premeditated; 'tis pure Accident on both sides—that's a certain thing now—Indeed should I make love to you, and you vow Fidelity—and swear and lye till you believ'd and yielded—Thou art therefore (as thou art a good Christian) oblig'd in Conscience to deny me nothing. Now—come, be kind, without any more idle prating.

FLORINDA. Oh, I am ruin'd—wicked man, unhand me.

WILLMORE. Wicked! Egad Child, a Judge, were he young and vigorous, and saw those Eyes of thine, would know 'twas they gave the first blow—the first provocation.—Come, prithee let's lose no time, I say—this is a fine convenient place.

FLORINDA. Sir, let me go, I conjure you, or I'll call out.

WILLMORE. Ay, ay, you were best to call Witness, to see how finely you treat me—do.—

FLORINDA. I'll cry Murder, Rape, or any thing, if you do not instantly let me go.

WILLMORE. A Rape! Come, come, you lye you Baggage, you lye: What, I'll warrant you would fain have the World believe now that you are not so forward as I. No, not you,—why at this time of Night was your Cobwebdoor set open, dear Spider,—but to catch Flies?—Hah come—or I shall be damnably angry.—Why what a Coil is here.—

FLORINDA. Sir, can you think—

WILLMORE. That you'd do it for nothing? oh, oh, I find what you'd be at—look here, here's a Pistole for you—here's a work indeed—here—take it, I say.—

FLORINDA. For Heaven's sake, Sir, as you're a Gentleman.

WILLMORE. So—now—she would be wheedling me for more—what you will not take it then—you're resolv'd you will not.—Come, come, take it, or I'll put it up again; for, look ye, I never give more.—Why, how now Mistress, are you so high i'th' Mouth, a Pistole won't down with you?—hah—why, what a work's here—in good time—come, no struggling, be gone—But an y'are good at a dumb Wrestle, I'm for ye,—look ye,—I'm for ye.— [She struggles with him.]

[Enter Belvile and Frederick.]

BELVILE. The Door is open, a Pox of this mad Fellow, I'm angry that we've lost him, I durst have sworn he had follow'd us.

FREDERICK. But you were so hasty, Colonel, to be gone.

FLORINDA. Help, help,—Murder!—help—oh, I'm ruin'd.

BELVILE. Ha, sure that's Florinda's Voice.

[Comes up to them.]

—A Man! Villain, let go that lady.

[Willmore turns and draws, Frederick interposes.]

FLORINDA. Belvile! Heavens! my Brother too is coming and 'twill be impossible to escape.—Belvile, I conjure you to walk under my Chamber-window, from whence I'll give you some instructions what to do—This rude Man has undone us. [Exit.]

WILLMORE. Belvile!

[Enter Don Pedro, Stephano, and other Servants with Lights.]

DON PEDRO. I'm betray'd; run Stephano, and see if Florinda be safe. [Exit Stephano.]
So whoe'er they be, all is not well, I'll to Florinda's Chamber. [They fight, and Don Pedro's party beats 'em out; going out, meets Stephano.]

STEPHANO. You need not, Sir, the poor Lady's fast asleep, and thinks no harm: I wou'd not awake her Sir, for fear of frightning her with your danger.

DON PEDRO. I'm glad she's there—Rascals, how came the Garden-Door open?

STEPHANO. That Question comes too late, Sir, some of my Fellow-Servants Masquerading I'll warrant.

DON PEDRO. Masquerading! a lewd Custom to debauch our Youth—there's something more in this than I imagine.

[Exeunt.]

SCENE IV

The Street.

[Enter Belvile in Rage, Frederick holding him, and Willmore, melancholy.]

WILLMORE. Why, how the Devil shou'd I know Florinda?

BELVILE. Ah plague of your ignorance! if it had not been Florinda, must you be a Beast?—a Brute, a senseless Swine?

WILLMORE. Well, Sir, you see I am endu'd with Patience—I can bear—tho egad y're very free with me methinks.—I was in good hopes the Quarrel wou'd have been on my side, for so uncivilly interrupting me.

BELVILE. Peace Brute, whilst thou're safe—oh, I'm distracted.

WILLMORE. Nay, nay, I'm an unlucky Dog, that's certain.

BELVILE. Ah curse upon the Star that rul'd my Birth! or whatsoever other Influence that makes me still so wretched.

WILLMORE. Thou break'st my Heart with these Complaints; there is no Star in fault, no Influence but Sack, the cursed Sack I drank.

FREDERICK. Why, how the Devil came you so drunk?

WILLMORE. Why, how the Devil came you so sober?

BELVILE. A curse upon his thin Skull, he was always before-hand that way.

FREDERICK. Prithee, dear Colonel, forgive him, he's sorry for his fault.

BELVILE. He's always so after he has done a mischief—a plague on all such Brutes.

WILLMORE. By this Light I took her for an errant Harlot.

BELVILE. Damn your debaucht Opinion: tell me Sot, hadst thou so much sense and light about thee to distinguish her to be a Woman, and coud'st not see something about her Face and Person, to strike an awful Reverence into thy Soul?

WILLMORE. Faith no, I considered her as mere a Woman as I cou'd wish.

BELVILE. 'Sdeath I have no patience—draw, or I'll kill you.

WILLMORE. Let that alone till tomorrow, and if I set not all right again, use your Pleasure.

BELVILE. Tomorrow, damn it.
The spiteful Light will lead me to no happiness.
Tomorrow is Antonio's, and perhaps
Guides him to my undoing;—oh that I could meet
This Rival, this powerful Fortunate.

WILLMORE. What then?

BELVILE. Let thy own Reason, or my Rage instruct thee.

WILLMORE. I shall be finely inform'd then, no doubt; hear me Colonel—hear me—show me the Man and I'll do his Business.

BELVILE. I know him no more than thou, or if I did, I should not need thy aid

WILLMORE. This you say is Angelica's House, I promis'd the kind Baggage to lie with her tonight.

[Offers to go in. Enter Antonio and his Page. Antonio knocks on the Hilt of his Sword.]

ANTONIO. You paid the thousand Crowns I directed?

PAGE. To the Lady's old Woman, Sir, I did.

WILLMORE. Who the Devil have we here?

BELVILE. I'll now plant my self under Florinda's Window, and if I find no comfort there, I'll die.

[Ex. Belvile and Frederick]

[Enter Moretta.]

MORETTA. Page!

PAGE. Here's my Lord.

WILLMORE. How is this, a Piccaroon going to board my Frigate! here's one Chafe-Gun for you.

[Drawing his Sword, justles Antonio who turns and draws. They fight, Antonio falls.]

MORETTA. Oh, bless us, we are all undone!

[Runs in, and shuts the Door.]

PAGE. Help, Murder!

[Belvile returns at the noise of fighting.]

BELVILE. Ha, the mad Rogue's engag'd in some unlucky Adventure again.

[Enter two or three Masqueraders.]

MASQUERADER. Ha, a Man kill'd!

WILLMORE. How! a Man kill'd! then I'll go home to sleep.

[Puts up, and reels out. Exit Masquers another way.]

BELVILE. Who shou'd it be! pray Heaven the Rogue is safe, for all my Quarrel to him. [As Belvile is groping about, enter an Officer and six Soldiers.]

SOLDIER. Who's there?

OFFICER. So, here's one dispatcht—secure the Murderer.

BELVILE. Do not mistake my Charity for Murder: I came to his Assistance. [Soldiers seize on Belvile.]

OFFICER. That shall be tried, Sir.—St. Iago, Swords drawn in the Carnival time! [Goes to Antonio.]

ANTONIO. Thy Hand prithee.

OFFICER. Ha, Don Antonio! look well to the Villain there.—How is't, Sir?

ANTONIO. I'm hurt.

BELVILE. Has my Humanity made me a Criminal?

OFFICER. Away with him.

BELVILE. What a curst Chance is this!

[Ex. Soldiers with Belvile]

ANTONIO. This is the Man that has set upon me twice—carry him to my Apartment till you have further Orders from me. [To the Officer. Ex. Antonio led.]

Act IV

SCENE I

A fine Room.

[*Discovers Belvile, as by Dark alone.*]

BELVILE. When shall I be weary of railing on Fortune,
who is resolv'd never to turn with Smiles upon
me?—Two such Defeats in one Night—none but
the Devil and that mad Rogue could have contri'vd
to have plagued me with—I am here a Prisoner—
but where?—Heaven knows—and if there be Murder done, I can soon decide the Fate of a Stranger in
a Nation without Mercy—Yet this is nothing to the
Torture my Soul bows with, when I think of losing
my fair, my dear Florinda.—Hark—my Door
opens—a Light—a Man—and seems of Quality—
arm'd too.—Now shall I die like a Dog without
defence.

[*Enter Antonio in a Night-Gown, with a Light; his Arm in a
Scarf, and a Sword under his Arm: He sets the Candle on the
Table.*]

ANTONIO. Sir, I come to know what Injuries I have
done you, that could provoke you to so mean an
Action, as to attack me basely, without allowing
time for my Defence.

BELVILE. Sir, for a Man in my Circumstances to plead
Innocence, would look like Fear—but view me well,
and you will find no marks of a Coward on me, nor
any thing that betrays that Brutality you accuse me
of.

ANTONIO. In vain, Sir, you impose upon my Sense,
You are not only he who drew on me last Night,
But yesterday before the same House, that of
Angelica.
Yet there is something in your Face and Mein—

BELVILE. I own I fought to day in the defence of a
Friend of mine, with whom you (if you're the same)
and your Party were first engag'd.
Perhaps you think this Crime enough to kill me,
But if you do, I cannot fear you'll do it basely.

ANTONIO. No, Sir, I'll make you fit for a Defence
with this. [*Gives him the Sword.*]

BELVILE. This Gallantry surprizes me—nor know I
how to use this Present, Sir, against a Man so brave.

ANTONIO. You shall not need;
For know, I come to snatch you from a Danger

That is decreed against you;
Perhaps your Life, or long Imprisonment:
And 'twas with so much Courage you offended,
I cannot see you punisht.

BELVILE. How shall I pay this Generosity?

ANTONIO. It had been safer to have killed another,
Than have attempted me:
To shew your danger, Sir, I'll let you know my
Quality;
And 'tis the Vice-Roy's Son whom you have
wounded.

BELVILE. The Vice-Roy's son!
Death and Confusion! was this Plague reserved
To complete all the rest?—[*Aside.*] oblig'd by him!
The Man of all the World, I wou'd destroy.

ANTONIO. You seem disorder'd, Sir.

BELVILE. Yes, trust me, Sir, I am, and 'tis with pain
That Man receives such Bounties,
Who wants the pow'r to pay 'em back again.

ANTONIO. To gallant Spirits 'tis indeed uneasy;
—But you may quickly over-pay me, Sir.

BELVILE. Then I am well—[*Aside.*] kind Heaven! but
set us even, That I may fight with him, and keep my
Honour safe.
—Oh, I'm impatient, Sir, to be discounting
The mighty Debt I owe you; command me
quickly—

ANTONIO. I have a Quarrel with a Rival, Sir,
About the Maid we love.

BELVILE. [*Aside.*] Death, 'tis Florinda he means—
That Thought destroys my Reason, and I shall kill
him—

ANTONIO. My Rival, Sir,
Is one has all the Virtues Man can boast of.

BELVILE. Death! who shou'd this be? [*Aside.*]

ANTONIO. He challeng'd me to meet him on the
Molo,
As soon as Day appear'd; but last Night's quarrel
Has made my Arm unfit to guide a Sword.

BELVILE. I apprehend you, Sir, you'd have me kill the
Man
That lays a claim to the Maid you speak of.
—I'll do't—I'll fly to do it.

ANTONIO. Sir, do you know her?

BELVILE. —No, Sir, but 'tis enough she is admired by
you.

ANTONIO. Sir, I shall rob you of the Glory on't,
For you must fight under my Name and Dress.

BELVILE. That Opinion must be strangely obliging

that makes you think I can personate the brave
Antonio, whom I can but strive to imitate.
ANTONIO. You say too much to my Advantage.
Come, Sir, the Day appears that calls you forth.
Within, Sir, is the Habit. [*Exit Antonio.*]
BELVILE. Fantastick Fortune, thou deceitful Light,
That cheats the wearied Traveller by Night,
Tho on a Precipice each step you tread,
I am resolv'd to follow where you lead. [*Exit.*]

SCENE II

The Molo.

[*Enter Florinda and Callis in Masques, with Stephano.*]

FLORINDA. [*Aside.*] I'm dying with my fears; Belvile's
not coming,
As I expected, underneath my Window, Makes me
believe that all those Fears are true. —Canst thou
not tell with whom my Brother fights?
STEPHANO. No Madam, they were both in Masquerade, I was by when they challeng'd one another, and
they had decided the Quarrel then, but were prevented by some Cavaliers; which made 'em put it off
till now—but I am sure 'tis about you they fight.
FLORINDA. Nay then 'tis with Belvile, for what other
Lover have I that dares fight for me, except Antonio? and he is too much in favour with my
Brother—If it be he, for whom shall I direct my
Prayers to Heaven?
STEPHANO. Madam, I must leave you; for if my Master see me, I shall be hang'd for being your
Conductor.—I escap' narrowly for the Excuse I
made for you last night i'th' Garden.
FLORINDA. And I'll reward thee for't—prithee no
more.

[*Exit Stephano.*]

[*Enter Don Pedro in his masque Habit.*]

DON PEDRO. Antonio's late today, the place will fill,
and we may be prevented. [*Walks about.*]
FLORINDA. Antonio! sure I heard amiss. [*Aside.*]
DON PEDRO. But who would not excuse a happy
Lover,
When soft fair Arms confine the yielding Neck;
And the kind Whisper languishingly breathes,

Must you be gone so soon?
Sure I had dwelt for ever on her Bosom.
—But stay, he's here.

[*Enter Belvile drest in Antonio's Clothes.*]

FLORINDA. 'Tis not Belvile, half my Fears are vanisht.
DON PEDRO. Antonio!—
BELVILE. This must be he. [*Aside.*]
You're early, Sir,—I do not use to be out out-done
this way.
DON PEDRO. The wretched, Sir, are watchful, and 'tis
enough You have the advantage of me in Angelica.
BELVILE. [*Aside.*] Angelica! or I've mistook my Man!
Or else Antonio,
Can he forget his Interest in Florinda,
And fight for common Prize?
DON PEDRO. Come, Sir, you know our terms—
BELVILE. By Heaven, not I. [*Aside.*]
—No talking, I am ready, Sir.

[*Offers to fight, Florinda runs in.*]

FLORINDA. Oh, hold! whoe'er you be, I do conjure
you hold. [*To Belvile.*]
DON PEDRO. Florinda!
BELVILE. Florinda imploring for my Rival!
DON PEDRO. Away, this Kindness is unseasonable.

[*Puts her by, they fight; she runs in just as Belvile disarms
Don Pedro.*]

FLORINDA. Who are you, Sir, that dare deny my
Prayers?
BELVILE. Thy Prayers destroy him; if thou wouldst
preserve him,
Do that thou'rt unacquainted with, and curse him.

[*She holds him.*]

FLORINDA. By all you hold most dear, by her you
love,
I do conjure you, touch him not.
BELVILE. By her I love!
See—I obey—and at your Feet resign
The useless Trophy of my Victory.

[*Lays his Sword at her Feet.*]

DON PEDRO. Antonio, you've done enough to prove
you love Florinda.
BELVILE. Love Florinda!

Does Heaven love Adoration, Pray'r, or Penitence?
Love her! here Sir,—your Sword again.

[*Snatches up the Sword, and gives it him.*]

Upon this Truth I'll fight my Life away.
DON PEDRO. No, you've redeem'd my Sister, and my
Friendship!
BELVILE. Don Pedro!

[*He gives him Florinda and pulls off his Vizard to show his
Face, and puts it on again.*]

DON PEDRO. Can you resign your Claims to other
Women,
And give your Heart intirely to Florinda?
BELVILE. Intire, as dying Saints Confessions are.
I can delay my happiness no longer.
This minute let me make Florinda mine:
DON PEDRO. This minute let it be—no time so
proper,
This Night my Father will arrive from Rome,
And possibly may hinder what we propose.
FLORINDA. Oh Heavens! this Minute!

[*Enter Masqueraders, and pass over.*]

BELVILE. Oh, do not ruin me!
DON PEDRO. The place begins to fill; and that we may
not be observ'd, do you walk off to St. Peter's
Church, where I will meet you, and conclude your
Happiness.
BELVILE. I'll meet you there—if there be no more
Saints Churches in Naples. [*Aside.*]
FLORINDA. Oh stay, Sir, and recall your hasty Doom:
Alas I have not yet prepar'd my Heart
To entertain so strange a Guest.
DON PEDRO. Away, this silly Modesty is assum'd too
late.
BELVILE. Heaven, madam! what do you do?
FLORINDA. Do! despise the Man that lays a Tyrant's
Claim
To what he ought to conquer by Submission.
BELVILE. You do not know me—move a little this
way.

[*Draws her aside.*]

FLORINDA. Yes, you may even force me to the Altar,
But not the holy Man that offers there
Shall force me to be thine.

[*Don Pedro talks to Callis this while.*]

BELVILE. Oh do not lose so blest an opportunity!
See—'tis your Belvile—not Antonio,
Whom your mistaken Scorn and Anger ruins.

[*Pulls off his Vizard.*]

FLORINDA. Belvile!
Where was my Soul it cou'd not meet thy Voice,
And take this knowledge in?

[*As they are talking, enter Willmore finely drest, and Frederick.*]

WILLMORE. No Intelligence! no News of Belvile yet—
well I am the most unlucky Rascal in Nature—
ha!—am I deceiv'd—or is it he—look.
FREDERICK. —'Tis he—my dear Belvile.

[*Vizard falls out on's hand, runs and embraces him.*]

BELVILE. Hell and Confusion seize thee!
DON PEDRO. Ha! Belvile! I beg your Pardon, Sir.

[*Takes Florinda from him.*]

BELVILE. Nay, touch her not, she's mine by Conquest,
Sir. I won her by my Sword.
WILLMORE. Did'st thou so—and egad Child we'll
keep her by the Sword. [*Draws on Don Pedro, Belvile
goes between.*]
BELVILE. Stand off.
Thou'rt so profanely lewd, so curst by Heaven,
All Quarrels thou espousest must be fatal.
WILLMORE. Nay, an you be so hot, my Valour's coy,
and shall be courted when you want it next.

[*Puts up his Sword.*]

BELVILE. You know I ought to claim a Victor's right.

[*To Don Pedro.*]

But you're the Brother to divine Florinda,
To whom I'm such a Slave—to purchase her,
I durst not hurt the Man she holds so dear.
DON PEDRO. 'Twas by Antonio's, not by Belvile's
Sword,
This Question should have been decided, Sir:
I must confess much to your Bravery's due,
Both now, and when I met you last in Arms.
But I am nicely punctual in my word,
As Men of Honour ought, and beg your Pardon.
—For this Mistake another Time shall clear.

[Aside to Florinda as they are going out.]

—This was some Plot between you and Belvile:
But I'll prevent you.

[Belvile looks after her, and begins to walk up and down in a Rage.]

WILLMORE. Do not be modest now, and lose the Woman: but if we shall fetch her back, so—
BELVILE. Do not speak to me.
WILLMORE. Not speak to you!—Egad I'll speak to you, and will be answered too.
BELVILE. Will you, Sir?
WILLMORE. I know I've done some mischief, but I'm so dull a Puppy, that I am the Son of a Whore, if I know how, or where—prithee inform my Understanding.—
BELVILE. Leave me I say, and leave me instantly.
WILLMORE. I will not leave you in this humour, nor till I know my Crime.
BELVILE. Death, I'll tell you, Sir—

[Draws and runs at Willmore, he runs out; Belvile after him, Frederick interposes.]

[Enter Angelica, Moretta, and Sebastian.]

ANGELICA. Ha—Sebastian—Is not that Willmore? haste, haste, and bring him back.
FREDERICK. The Colonel's mad—I never saw him thus before; I'll after 'em, lest he do some mischief, for I am sure Willmore will not draw on him. *[Exit.]*
ANGELICA. I am all Rage! my first desires defeated for one, for ought he knows, that has no other Merit than her Quality,—her being Don Pedro's Sister—He loves her: I know 'tis so—dull, dull, insensible—He will not see me now tho oft invited;
And broke his Word last night—false perjur'd Man!
—He that but yesterday fought for my Favours,
And would have made his Life a Sacrifice
To've gain'd one Night with me,
Must now be hired and courted to my Arms.
MORETTA. I told you what wou'd come on't, but Moretta's an old doting Fool—Why did you give him five hundred Crowns, but to set himself out for other Lovers? You shou'd have kept him poor, if you had meant to have had any good from him.
ANGELICA. Oh, name not such mean Trifles.—Had I given him all my Youth has earn'd from Sin,
I had not lost a Thought nor Sigh upon't.
But I have given him my eternal Rest.

My whole Repose, my future Joys, my Heart;
My Virgin Heart. Moretta! oh 'tis gone!
MORETTA. Curse on him, here he comes;
How fine she has made him too!

[Enter Willmore and Sebastastian. Angelica turns and walks away.]

WILLMORE. How now, turn'd Shadow?
Fly when I pursue, and follow when I fly!

> Stay gentle Shadow of my Dove, *[Sings.]*
>   And tell me e'er I go,
>   Whether the Substance may not prove
>   A fleeting Thing like you.

There's a soft kind Look remaining yet.

[As she turns she looks on him.]

ANGELICA. Well, Sir, you may be gay; all Happiness, all Joys pursue you still, Fortune's your Slave, and gives you every hour choice of new Hearts and Beauties, till you are cloy'd with the repeated Bliss, which others vainly languish for—But know, false man, that I shall be reveng'd. *[Turns away in a Rage.]*
WILLMORE. So, 'gad, there are of those faint-hearted Lovers, whom such a sharp Lesson next their Hearts would make as impotent as Fourscore pox o' this whining—my Bus'ness is to laugh and love—a pox on't; I hate your sullen Lover, a Man shall lose as much time to put you in Humour now, as would serve to gain a new Woman.
ANGELICA. I scorn to cool that Fire I cannot raise,
Or do the Drudgery of your virtuous Mistress.
WILLMORE. A virtuous Mistress! Death, what a thing thou hast found out for me! why what the Devil should I do with a virtuous Woman?—a sort of ill-natur'd Creatures, that take a Pride to torment a Lover. Virtue is but an infirmity in Women, a Disease that renders even the handsome ungrateful; whilst the ill-favour'd for want of Sollicitations and Address, only fancy themselves so.—I have lain with a Woman of Quality, who has all the while been railing at Whores.
ANGELICA. I will not answer for your Mistress's Virtue,
Tho she be young enough to know no Guilt:
And I could wish you would persuade my Heart,
'Twas the two hundred thousand Crowns you courted.

WILLMORE. Two hundred thousand Crowns! what Story's this?—what Trick?—what Woman?—ha.

ANGELICA. How strange you make it! have you forgot the Creature you entertain'd on the Piazza last night?

WILLMORE. Ha, my Gipsy worth two hundred thousand Crowns!—[*Aside.*] oh how I long to be with her—pox, I knew she was of Quality.

ANGELICA. False Man, I see my Ruin in thy Face. How many Vows you breath'd upon my Bosom, Never to be unjust—have you forgot so soon?

WILLMORE. Faith no, I was just coming to repeat 'em—[*Aside.*] but here's a Humour indeed—would make a man a Saint—Wou'd she'd be angry enough to leave me, and command me not to wait on her.

[*Enter Hellena, drest in Man's Clothes.*]

HELLENA. This must be Angelica, I know it by her mumping Matron here—Ay, ay, 'tis she: my mad Captain's with her too, for all this swearing—how this inconstant Humour makes me love him:—pray, good grave Gentlewoman, is not this Angelica?

MORETTA. My too young Sir, it is—I hope 'tis one from Don Antonio. [*Goes to Angelica.*]

HELLENA. Well, something I'll to do vex him for this. [*Aside.*]

ANGELICA. I will not speak with him; am I in humour to receive a Lover?

WILLMORE. Not speak with him! why, I'll be gone—and wait your idler minutes—Can I shew less Obedience to the thing I love so fondly [*Offers to go.*]

ANGELICA. A fine Excuse this—stay—

WILLMORE. And hinder your Advantage: should I repay your Bounties so ungratefully?

ANGELICA. Come hither, Boy,—that I may let you see How much above the Advantages you name I prize one Minute's Joy with you.

WILLMORE. Oh, you destroy me with this Endearment.

[*Impatient to be gone.*]

—Death, how shall I get away?—Madam, 'twill not be fit I should be seen with you—besides, it will not be convenient—and I've a Friend—that's dangerously sick.

ANGELICA. I see you're impatient—yet you shall stay.

WILLMORE. And miss my Assignation with my Gipsy.

[*Aside, and walks about impatiently.*]

HELLENA. Madam, [*Moretta brings Hellena, who addresses herself to Angelica.*] You'l hardly pardon my intrusion,
When you shall know my Business;
And I'm too young to tell my Tale with Art:
But there must be a wondrous store of Goodness
Where so much Beauty dwells.

ANGELICA. A pretty Advocate, whoever sent thee,—Prithee proceed—Nay, Sir, you shall not go.

[*To Willmore who is stealing off.*]

WILLMORE. Then shall I lose my dear Gipsy for ever.—Pox on't, she stays me out of spite. [*Aside.*]

HELLENA. I am related to a Lady, Madam,
Young, rich, and nobly born, but has the fate
To be in love with a young English Gentleman.
Strangely she loves him, at first sight she lov'd him,
But did adore him when she heard him speak;
For he, she said, had Charms in every word,
That fail'd not to surprize, to wound, and conquer—

WILLMORE. Ha, Egad I hope this concerns me. [*Aside.*]

ANGELICA. 'Tis my false Man, he means,—would he were gone. This Praise will raise his Pride and ruin me.—[*To Willmore.*] Well, since you are so impatient to be gone, I will release you, Sir.

WILLMORE. [*Aside.*] Nay, then I'm sure 'twas me he spoke of, this cannot be the Effects of Kindness in her.
—No, Madam, I've consider'd better on't,
And will not give you cause of Jealousy.

ANGELICA. But, Sir, I've—business, that—

WILLMORE. This shall not do, I know 'tis but to try me.

ANGELICA. Well, to your Story, Boy,—tho 'twill undo me. [*Aside.*]

HELLENA. With this Addition to his other Beauties,
He won her unresisting tender Heart,
He vow'd and sigh'd, and swore he lov'd her dearly;
And she believ'd the cunning Flatterer,
And thought her self the happiest Maid alive:
Today was the appointed time by both,
To consummate their bliss;
The Virgin, Altar, and the Priest were drest,
And whilst she languisht for the expected Bridegroom,
She heard, he paid his broken Vows to you.

WILLMORE. So, this is some dear Rogue that's in love with me, and this way lets me know it; or if it be not

me, she means some one whose place I may supply.
[*Aside.*]

ANGELICA. Now I perceive the cause of thy impatience to be gone, and all the business of this glorious Dress.

WILLMORE. Damn the young Prater, I know not what he means.

HELLENA. Madam,
In your fair Eyes I read too much concern
To tell my farther Business.

ANGELICA. Prithee sweet Youth talk on, thou may'st perhaps Raise here a Storm that may undo my Passion,
And then I'll grant thee anything.

HELLENA. Madam, 'tis to intreat you, (oh unreasonable!)
You wou'd not see this Stranger;
For if you do, she vows you are undone,
Tho Nature never made a Man so excellent;
And sure he'ad been a God, but for Inconstancy.

WILLMORE. Ah, Rogue, how finely he's instructed!
[*Aside.*]
—'Tis plain some Woman that has seen me *en passant.*

ANGELICA. Oh, I shall burst with Jealousy! do you know the Man you speak of?—

HELLENA. Yes, Madam, he us'd to be in Buff and Scarlet.

ANGELICA. [*To Willmore.*] Thou, false as Hell, what canst thou say to this?

WILLMORE. By Heaven—

ANGELICA. Hold, do not damn thy self—

HELLENA. Nor hope to be believ'd.

[*He walks about, they follow.*]

ANGELICA. Oh, perjur'd Man!
Is't thus you pay my generous Passion back?

HELLENA. Why wou'd you, Sir, abuse my Lady's Faith?

ANGELICA. And use me so inhumanely?

HELLENA. A Maid so young, so innocent—

WILLMORE. Ah, young Devil!

ANGELICA. Dost thou not know thy Life is in my Power?

HELLENA. Or think my Lady cannot be reveng'd?

WILLMORE. So, so, the Storm comes finely on. [*Aside.*]

ANGELICA. Now thou art silent, Guilt has struck thee dumb. Oh, hadst thou still been so, I'd liv'd in safety.

[*She turns away and weeps.*]

WILLMORE. Sweetheart, the Lady's Name and House—quickly: I'm impatient to be with her.—

[*Aside to Hellena, looks towards Angelica to watch her turning; and as she comes towards them, he meets her.*]

HELLENA. So now is he for another Woman. [*Aside.*]

WILLMORE. The impudent'st young thing in Nature!
I cannot persuade him out of his Error, Madam.

ANGELICA. I know he's in the right,—yet thou'st a Tongue
That wou'd persuade him to deny his Faith. [*In Rage walks away.*]

WILLMORE. Her Name, her Name, dear Boy—[*Said softly to Hellena*]

HELLENA. Have you forgot it, Sir?

WILLMORE. [*Aside.*] Oh, I perceive he's not to know I am a Stranger to his Lady.
—Yes, yes, I do know—but—I have forgot the—

[*Angelica turns.*]

—By Heaven, such early Confidence I never saw.

ANGELICA. Did I not charge you with this Mistress, Sir?
Which you denied, tho I beheld your Perjury.
This little Generosity of thine has render'd back my Heart.

[*Walks away.*]

WILLMORE. So, you have made sweet work here, my little Mischief, Look your Lady be kind and good-natur'd now, or I shall have but a cursed Bargain on't.

[*Angelica turns towards them.*]

—The Rogue's bred up to Mischief,
Art thou so great a Fool to credit him?

ANGELICA. Yes, I do; and you in vain impose upon me.—Come hither, Boy—Is not this he you speak of?

HELLENA. I think—it is; I cannot swear, but I vow he has just such another lying Lover's look.

[*Hellena looks in his Face, he gazes on her.*]

WILLMORE. Hah! do not I know that Face?—
By Heaven, my little Gipsy! what a dull Dog was I?

Had I but lookt that way, I'd known her.
Are all my hopes of a new Woman banisht? [*Aside.*]
—Egad, if I don't fit thee for this, hang me.
—Madam, I have found out the Plot.

HELLENA. Oh, Lord, what does he say? am I discover'd now?

WILLMORE. Do you see this young Spark here?

HELLENA. He'll tell her who I am.

WILLMORE. Who do you think this is?

HELLENA. Ay, ay, he does know me.—Nay, dear Captain, I'm undone if you discover me.

WILLMORE. Nay, nay, no cogging; she shall know what a precious Mistress I have.

HELLENA. Will you be such a Devil?

WILLMORE. Nay, nay, I'll teach you to spoil sport you will not make.—This small Ambassador comes not from a Person of Quality, as you imagine, and he says; but from a very errant Gipsy, the talkingst, pratingst, cantingst little Animal thou ever saw'st.

ANGELICA. What news you tell me! that's the thing I mean.

HELLENA. Wou'd I were well off the place.—If ever I go a Captain-hunting again.— [*Aside.*]

WILLMORE. Mean that thing? that Gipsy thing? thou mayst as well be jealous of thy Monkey, or Parrot, as her: a German Motion were worth a dozen of her, and a Dream were a better Enjoyment, a Creature of a Constitution fitter for Heaven than Man.

HELLENA. Tho I'm sure he lyes, yet this vexes me. [*Aside.*]

ANGELICA. You are mistaken, she's a Spanish Woman made up of no such dull Materials.

WILLMORE. Materials! Egad, an she be made of any that will either dispense, or admit of Love, I'll be bound to continuance.

HELLENA. Unreasonable Man, do you think so? [*Aside to him.*]

WILLMORE. You may return, my little Brazen Head, and tell your lady, that till she be handsome enough to be belov'd, or I dull enough to be religious, there will be small hopes of me.

ANGELICA. Did you not promise then to marry her?

WILLMORE. Not I by Heaven.

ANGELICA. You cannot undeceive my fears and torments, till you have vow'd you will not marry her.

HELLENA. If he swears that, he'll be reveng'd on me indeed for all my Rogueries.

ANGELICA. I know what Arguments you'll bring against me, Fortune and Honour.

WILLMORE. Honour! I tell you, I hate it in your Sex; and those that fancy themselves possest of that Foppery, are the most impertinently troublesome of all Woman-kind, and will transgress nine Commandments to keep one: and to satisfy your Jealousy I swear—

HELLENA. Oh, no swearing, dear Captain— [*Aside to him.*]

WILLMORE. If it were possible, I should ever be inclin'd to marry, it shou'd be some kind young Sinner, one that has Generosity enough to give a favour handsomely to one that can ask it discreetly, one that has Wit enough to manage an Intrigue of Love—oh, how civil such a Wench is, to a Man that does her the Honour to marry her.

ANGELICA. By Heaven, there's no Faith in any thing he says.

[*Enter Sebastian.*]

SEBASTIAN. Madam, Don Antonio—

ANGELICA. Come hither.

HELLENA. Ha, Antonio! he may be coming hither, and he'll certainly discover me, I'll therefore retire without a Ceremony. [*Exit Hellena.*]

ANGELICA. I'll see him, get my Coach ready.

SEBASTIAN. It waits you, Madam.

WILLMORE. This is lucky: what, Madam, now I may be gone and leave you to the enjoyment of my Rival?

ANGELICA. Dull Man, that canst not see how ill, how poor
That false dissimulation looks—Be gone,
And never let me see thy cozening Face again,
Lest I relapse and kill thee.

WILLMORE. Yes, you can spare me now,—farewell till you are in better Humour—I'm glad of this release—
Now for my Gipsy:
For tho to worse we change, yet still we find
New Joys, new Charms, in a new Miss that's kind.

[*Ex. Willmore.*]

ANGELICA. He's gone, and in this Ague of my Soul
The shivering Fit returns;
Oh with what willing haste he took his leave,
As if the long'd for Minute were arriv'd,
Of some blest Assignation.
In vain I have consulted all my Charms,
In vain this Beauty priz'd, in vain believ'd
My Eyes cou'd kindle any lasting Fires.
I had forgot my Name, my Infamy,
And the Reproach that Honour lays on those

That dare pretend a sober passion here.
Nice Reputation, tho it leave behind
More Virtues than inhabit where that dwells,
Yet that once gone, those Virtues shine no more.
—Then since I am not fit to be belov'd,
I am resolv'd to think on a Revenge
On him that sooth'd me thus to my undoing.

[*Exeunt.*]

SCENE III

A Street.

[*Enter Florinda and Valeria in Habits different from what they have been seen in.*]

FLORINDA. We're happily escap'd, yet I tremble still.

VALERIA. A Lover and fear! why, I am but half a one, and yet I have Courage for any Attempt. Would Hellena were here. I wou'd fain have had her as deep in this Mischief as we, she'll fare but ill else I doubt.

FLORINDA. She pretended a Visit to the Augustine Nuns, but I believe some other design carried her out, pray Heavens we light on her.
—Prithee what didst do with Callis?

VALERIA. When I saw no Reason wou'd do good on her, I follow'd her into the Wardrobe, and as she was looking for something in a great Chest, I tumbled her in by the Heels, snatcht the Key of the Apartment where you were confin'd, lockt her in, and left her bawling for help.

FLORINDA. 'Tis well you resolve to follow my Fortunes, for thou darest never appear at home again after such an Action.

VALERIA. That's according as the young Stranger and I shall agree.—But to our Business—I deliver'd your Letter, your Note to Belvile, when I got out under pretence of going to Mass, I found him at his Lodging, and believe me it came reasonably; for never was Man in so desperate a Condition. I told him of your Resolution of making your escape to-day, if your Brother would be absent long enough to permit you; if not, die rather than be Antonio's.

FLORINDA. Thou shou'dst have told him I was confin'd to my Chamber upon my Brother's suspicion, that the Business on the Molo was a Plot laid between him and I.

VALERIA. I said all this, and told him your Brother was now gone to his Devotion, and he resolves to visit every Church till he find him; and not only undeceive him in that, but caress him so as shall delay his return home.

FLORINDA. Oh Heavens! he's here, and Belvile with him too. [*They put on their Vizards.*]

[*Enter Don Pedro, Belvile, Willmore; Belvile and Don Pedro seeming in serious Discourse.*]

VALERIA. Walk boldly by them, I'll come at a distance, lest he suspect us.

[*She walks by them, and looks back on them.*]

WILLMORE. Ha! Woman! and of an excellent Mien!

DON PEDRO. She throws a kind look back on you.

WILLMORE. Death, 'tis a likely Wench, and that kind look shall not be cast away—I'll follow her.

BELVILE. Prithee do not.

WILLMORE. Do not! By Heavens to the Antipodes, with such an Invitation. [*She goes out, and Willmore follows her.*]

BELVILE. 'Tis a mad Fellow for a Wench.

[*Enter Frederick.*]

FREDERICK. Oh Colonel, such News!

BELVILE. Prithee what?

FREDERICK. News that will make you laugh in spite of Fortune.

BELVILE. What, Blunt has had some damn'd Trick put upon him, cheated, bang'd, or clapt?

FREDERICK. Cheated, Sir, rarely cheated of all but his Shirt and Drawers; the unconscionable Whore too turn'd him out before Consummation, so that traversing the Streets at Midnight, the Watch found him in this Fresco, and conducted him home: By Heaven 'tis such a flight, and yet I durst as well have been hang'd as laugh at him, or pity him; he beats all that do but ask him a Question, and is in such an Humour—

DON PEDRO. Who is't has met with this ill usage, Sir?

BELVILE. A Friend of ours, whom you must see for Mirth's sake. [*Aside.*] I'll imploy him to give Florinda time for an escape.

DON PEDRO. What is he?

BELVILE. A young Countryman of ours, one that has been educated at so plentiful a rate, he yet ne'er knew the want of Money, and 'twill be a great Jest to see how simply he'll look without it. For my part I'll lend him none, and Rogue knows not how to put on a borrowing Face, and ask first. I'll let him see how good 'tis to play our parts whilst I play his—Prithee Frederick do you go home and keep him in that posture till we come. [*Exeunt.*]

[*Enter Florinda from the farther end of the Scene, looking behind her.*]

FLORINDA. I am followed still—hah—my Brother too advancing this way, good Heavens defend me from being seen by him. [*She goes off.*]

[*Enter Willmore, and after him Valeria, at a little distance.*]

WILLMORE. Ah! There she sails, she looks back as she were willing to be boarded, I'll warrant her Prize.

[*He goes out, Valeria following.*]

[*Enter Hellena, just as he goes out, with a Page.*]

HELLENA. Hah, is not that my Captain that has a Woman in chase?—'tis not Angelica. Boy, follow those People at a distance, and bring me an Account where they go in.—I'll find his Haunts, and plague him everywhere.—ha—my Brother! [*Exit Page.*]

[*Belvile, Willmore, Don Pedro cross the Stage: Hellena runs off. Scene changes to another Street. Enter Florinda.*]

FLORINDA. What shall I do, my Brother now pursues me. Will no kind Power protect me from his Tyranny?—Hah, here's a Door open, I'll venture in, since nothing can be worse than to fall into his Hands, my Life and Honour are at stake, and my Necessity has no choice.

[*She goes in.*]

[*Enter Valeria, and Hellena's Page peeping after Florinda.*]

PAGE. Here she went in, I shall remember this House.

[*Exit Boy.*]

VALERIA. This is Belvile's Lodgings; she's gone in as readily as if she knew it—hah—here's that mad Fellow again, I dare not venture in—I'll watch my Opportunity. [*Goes aside.*]

[*Enter Willmore, gazing about him.*]

WILLMORE. I have lost her hereabouts—Pox on't she must not see me so.

[*Goes out. Scene changes to Blunt's Chamber, discovers him sitting on a Couch in his Shirt and Drawers, reading.*]

BLUNT. So, now my Mind's a little at Peace, since I have resolv'd Revenge—a Pox on this Taylor tho, for not bringing home the Clothes I bespoke; and a Pox of all poor Cavaliers, a Man can never keep a spare Suit for 'en; and I shall have these Rogues come in and find me naked; and then I'm undone; but I'm resolv'd to arm myself—the Rascals shall not insult over me too much.

[*Puts on an old rusty Sword and Buss-Belt.*]

—Now, how like a Morrice-Dancer I am equipt—a fine Lady-like Whore to cheat me thus, without affording me a Kindness for my Money, a Pox light on her, I shall never be reconciled to the Sex more, she has made me as faithless as a Physician, as uncharitable as a Churchman, and as ill-natur'd as a Poet. O how I'll use all Womenkind hereafter! what wou'd I give to have one of 'em within my reach now! any Mortal thing in Petticoats, kind Fortune, send me; and I'll forgive thy last Night's Malice—Here's a cursed Book too, (a Warning to all young Travellers) that can instruct me how to prevent such Mischiefs now 'tis too late. Well, 'tis a rare convenient thing to read a little now and then, as well as hawk and hunt. [*Sits down again and reads.*]

[*Enter to him Florinda.*]

FLORINDA. This House is haunted sure, 'tis well furnisht and no living thing inhabits it—hah—a Man! Heavens how he's attir'd! Sure 'tis some Ropedancer, or Fencing-Master; I tremble now for fear, and yet I must venture now to speak to him—Sir, if I may not interrupt your Meditations— [*He starts up and gazes.*]

BLUNT. Hah—what's here? Are my wishes granted? and is not that a she Creature? Adsheartlikins 'tis what wretched thing art thou—hah!

FLORINDA. Charitable Sir, you've told yourself already what I am; a very wretched Maid, forc'd by a strange unlucky Accident, to seek a safety here, and must be ruin'd, if you do not grant it.

BLUNT. Ruin'd! Is there any Ruin so inevitable as that which now threatens thee? Dost thou know, miserable Woman, into what Den of Mischiefs thou art fall'n? what a Bliss of Confusion?—hah—dost not see something in my looks that frights thy guilty Soul, and makes thee wish to change that Shape of Woman for any humble Animal, or Devil? for those were safer for thee, and less mischievous.

FLORINDA. Alas, what mean you, Sir? I must confess your Looks have something in 'em makes me fear; but I beseech you, as you seem a Gentleman, pity a harmless Virgin, that takes your House for Sanctuary.

BLUNT. Talk on, talk on, and weep too, till my faith return. Do, flatter me out of my Senses again—a harmless Virgin with a Pox, as much one as t'other, adsheartlikins. Why, what the Devil can I not be safe in my House for you? not in my Chamber? nay, even being naked too cannot secure me. This is an Impudence greater than has invaded me yet.— Come no Resistance.

[Pulls her rudely.]

FLORINDA. Dare you be so cruel?

BLUNT. Cruel, adsheartlikins as a Gally-slave, or a Spanish Whore: Cruel, yes, I will kiss and beat thee all over; kiss and see thee all over; thou shalt lie with me too, not that I care for the Injoyment, but to let you see I have ta'en deliberated Malice to thee, and will be revenged on one Whore for the Sins of another; I will smile and deceive thee, flatter thee, and beat thee, kiss and swear, and lye to thee, imbrace thee and rob thee, as she did me, fawn on thee, imbrace thee and rob the, as she did me, fawn on thee, and strip thee stark naked, then hang thee out of my Window by the Heels, with a Paper of scurvey Verses fasten'd to thy Breast, in praise of damnable Women—Come, come along.

FLORINDA. Alas, Sir, must I be sacrific'd for the Crimes of the most infamous of my Sex? I never understood the Sins you name.

BLUNT. Do, persuade the Fool you love him, or that one of you can be just or honest; tell me I was not an easy Coxcomb, or any strange impossible Tale: it will be believ'd sooner than thy false Showers or Protestations. A Generation of damn'd Hypocrites, to flatter my very Clothes from my back! dissembling Witches! are these the Returns you make an honest Gentleman that trusts, believes, and loves you?—But if I be not even with you—Come along, or I shall—

[Pulls her again.]

[Enter Frederick.]

FREDERICK. Hah, what's here to do?

BLUNT. Adsheartlikins, Frederick. I am glad thou art come, to be a Witness of my dire Revenge.

FREDERICK. What's this, a Person of Quality too, who is upon the Ramble to supply the Defects of some grave impotent Husband.

BLUNT. No, this has another Pretence, some very unfortunate Accident brought her hither, to save a Life pursued by I know not who, or why, and forc'd to take sanctuary here at Fools Haven. Adsheartlikins to me of all Mankind for Protection? Is the Ass to be cajol'd again, think ye? No, young one, no Prayers or Tears shall mitigate my Rage; therefore prepare for both my Pleasure of Enjoyment and Revenge, for I am resolved to make up my Loss here on thy Body, I'll take it out in kindness and in beating.

FREDERICK. Now Mistress of mine, what do you think of this?

FLORINDA. I think he will not—dares not be so barbarous.

FREDERICK. Have a care, Blunt, she fetch'd a deep Sigh, she is inamour'd with thy Shirt and Drawers, she'll strip thee even of that. There are of her Calling such unconscionable Baggages, and such dexterous Thieves, they'll flay a Man, and he shall ne'er miss his Skin, till he feels the Cold. There was a Country-man of ours robb'd of a Row of Teeth whilst he was sleeping, which the Jilt made him buy again when he wak'd—You see, Lady, how little Reason we have to trust you.

BLUNT. 'Dsheartlikins, why, this is most abominable.

FLORINDA. Some such Devils there may be, but by all that's holy I am none such, I entered here to save a Life in danger.

BLUNT. For no goodness I'll warrant her.

FREDERICK. Faith, Damsel, you had e'en confess the plain Truth, for we are Fellows not to be caught twice in the same Trap: Look on that Wreck, a tight Vessel when he set out of Haven, well trim'd and laden, and see how a Female Piccaroon of this Island of Rogues has shatter'd him, and canst thou hope for any Mercy?

BLUNT. No, no, Gentlewoman, come along, adsheartlikins we must be better acquainted—we'll both lie with her, and then let me alone to bang her.

FREDERICK. I am ready to serve you in matters of Revenge, that has a double Pleasure in't.

BLUNT. Well said. You hear, little one, how you are condemn'd by publick Vote to the Bed within, there's no resisting your Destiny, Sweetheart. [*Pulls her.*]

FLORINDA. Stay, Sir, I have seen you with Belvile, an English Cavalier, for his sake use me kindly; you know how, Sir.

BLUNT. Belvile! why, yes, Sweeting, we do know Belvile, and wish he were with us now, he's a Cormorant at Whore and Bacon, he'd have a Limb or two of thee, my Virgin Pullet: but 'tis no matter, we'll leave him the Bones to pick.

FLORINDA. Sir, if you have any Esteem for that Belvile, I conjure you to treat me with more Gentleness; he'll thank you for the Justice.

FREDERICK. Hark ye, Blunt, I doubt we are mistaken in this matter.

FLORINDA. Sir, if you find me not worth Belvile's Care, use me as you please; and that you may think I merit better treatment than you threaten—pray take this Present—

[*Gives him a Ring: He looks on it.*]

BLUNT. Hum—A Diamond! why, 'tis a wonderful Virtue now that lies in this Ring, a mollifying Virtue; adsheartlikins there's more persuasive Rhetorick in't, than all her Sex can utter.

FREDERICK. I begin to suspect something; and 'twou'd anger us vilely to be truss'd up for a Rape upon a Maid of Quality, when we only believe we ruffle a Harlot.

BLUNT. Thou art a credulous Fellow, but adsheartlikins I have no Faith yet; why, my Saint prattled as parlously as this does, she gave me a Bracelet too, a Devil on her: but I sent my Man to sell it today for Necessaries, and it prov'd as counterfeit as her Vows of Love.

FREDERICK. However let it reprieve her till we see Belvile.

BLUNT. That's hard, yet I will grant it.

[*Enter a Servant.*]

SERVANT. Oh, Sir, the Colonel is just come with his new Friend and a Spaniard of Quality, and talks of having you to Dinner with 'em.

BLUNT. 'Dsheartlikins, I'm undone!—I would not see 'em for the World: Harkye, Frederick. lock up the Wench in your Chamber.

FREDERICK. Fear nothing, Madam, whate'er he threatens, you're safe whilst in my Hands. [*Ex. Frederick and Florinda.*]

BLUNT. And Sirrah—upon your Life, say—I am not at home—or that I am asleep—or—or any thing—away—I'll prevent their coming this way. [*Locks the Door and Exit.*]

Act V

SCENE I

Blunt's Room.

[*After a great knocking at his Chamber-door, enter Blunt softly, crossing the Stage in his Shirt and Drawers, as before.*]

Ned, Ned Blunt, Ned Blunt. [*Call within.*]

BLUNT. The Rogues are up in Arms, 'dsheartlikins, this villainous Frederick has betray'd me, they have heard of my blessed Fortune.

Ned Blunt, Ned Ned—[*and knocking within.*]

BELVILE. Why, he's dead, Sir, without dispute dead, he has not been seen to day; let's break open the Door—here—Boy—

BLUNT. Ha, break open the Door! 'dsheartlikins that mad Fellow will be as good as his word.

BELVILE. Boy, bring something to force the Door.

[*A great noise within at the Door again.*]

BLUNT. So, now must I speak in my own Defence, I'll try what Rhetorick will do—hold—hold, what do you mean Gentlemen, what do you mean?

BELVILE. Oh Rogue, art alive? prithee open the Door, and convince us.

BLUNT. Yes, I am alive Gentlemen—but at present a little busy.

BELVILE. How! Blunt! grown a man of Business! come, come, open, and let's see this Miracle. [*within.*]

BLUNT. No, no, no, no Gentlemen, 'tis no great Business—but—I am—at—my Devotion,— 'dsheartlikins, will you not allow a man time to pray?

BELVILE. Turn'd religious! a greater Wonder than the first, therefore open quickly, or we shall unhinge, we shall. [*within.*]

BLUNT. This won't do—Why, hark ye, Colonel; to tell you the plain Truth, I am about a necessary Affair of Life.—I have a Wench with me—you apprehend me? the Devil's in't if they be so uncivil as to disturb me now.

WILLMORE. How, a Wench! Nay, then we must enter and partake; no Resistance,—unless it be your Lady of Quality, and then we'll keep our distance.

BLUNT. So, the Business is out.

WILLMORE. Come, come, lend more hands to the Door,—now heave altogether—so, well done, my Boys—

[*Breaks open the Door.*]

[*Enter Belvile, Willmore, Frederick and Don Pedro: Blunt looks simply, they all laugh at him, he lays his hand on his Sword, and comes up to Willmore.*]

BLUNT. Hark ye, Sir, laugh out your laugh quickly, d'ye hear, and be gone, I shall spoil your sport else; 'dsheartlikins, Sir, I shall—the Jest has been carried on too long,—[*Aside.*] a Plague upon my Taylor—

WILLMORE. 'Sdeath, how the Whore has drest him! Faith, Sir, I'm sorry.

BLUNT. Are you so, Sir? keep't to your self then Sir, I advise you, d'ye hear? for I can as little endure your Pity as his Mirth. [*Lays his Hand on's Sword.*]

BELVILE. Indeed, Willmore, thou wert a little too rough with Ned Blunt's Mistress; call a Person of Quality Whore, and one so young, so handsome, and so eloquent!—ha, ha, ha.

BLUNT. Hark ye, Sir, you know me, and know I can be angry; have a care—for 'dsheartlikins I can fight too—I can Sir,—do you mark me—no more.

BELVILE. Why so peevish, good Ned? some Disappointments, I'll warrant—What! did the jealous Count her Husband return just in the nick?

BLUNT. Or the Devil, Sir,—d'ye laugh? [*They laugh.*]

Look ye, settle me a good sober Countenance, and that quickly to, or you shall know Ned Blunt is not—

BELVILE. Not everybody, we know that.

BLUNT. Not an Ass, to be laught at, Sir.

WILLMORE. Unconscionable Sinner, to bring a Lover so near his Happiness, a vigorous passionate Lover, and then not only cheat him of his Moveables, but his Desires too.

BELVILE. Ah, Sir, a Mistress is a Trifle with Blunt, he'll have a dozen the next time he looks abroad; his Eyes have Charms not to be resisted: there needs no more than to expose that taking Person to the view of the Fair, and he leads 'em all in Triumph.

DON PEDRO. Sir, tho I'm a stranger to you, I'm asham'd at the rudeness of my Nation, and could you learn who did it, would assist you to make an Example of 'em.

BLUNT. Why, ay, there's one speaks sense now, and handsomly; and let me tell you Gentlemen, I should not have shew'd my self like a Jack-Pudding, thus to have made you Mirth, but that I have revenge within my power; for know, I have got into my possession a Female, who had better have fallen under any Curse, than the Ruin I design her; 'dsheartlikins, she assaulted me here in my own Lodgings, and had doubtless committed a Rape upon me, had not this Sword defended me.

FREDERICK. I knew not that, but o' my Conscience thou hadst ravisht her, had she not redeem'd herself with a Ring—let's see't Blunt. [*Blunt shows the Ring.*]

BELVILE. Hah!—the Ring I gave Florinda when we exchang'd our Vows!—hark ye Blunt—

[*Goes to whisper to him.*]

WILLMORE. No whispering, good Colonel, there's a Woman in the case, no whispering.

BELVILE. Hark ye, Fool, be advis'd, and conceal both the Ring and the Story, for your Reputation's sake; don't let People know what despis'd Cullies we English are: to be cheated and abus'd by one Whore, and another rather bribe thee than be kind to thee, is an Infamy to our Nation.

WILLMORE. Come, come, where's the Wench? we'll see her, let her be what she will, we'll see her.

DON PEDRO. Ay, ay, let us see her, I can soon discover whether she be of Quality, or for your Diversion.

BLUNT. She's in Frederick's Custody.

WILLMORE. Come, come, the Key.

[To Frederick, who gives him the Key, they are going.]

BELVILE. Death! what shall I do?—stay Gentlemen—
yet if I hinder 'em, I shall discover all—hold, let's
go one at once—give me the Key.

WILLMORE. Nay, hold there, Colonel, I'll go first.

FREDERICK. Nay, no Dispute, Ned and I have the
property of her.

WILLMORE. Damn Property—then we'll draw Cuts.

[Belvile goes to whisper Willmore.]

Nay, no Corruption, good Colonel: come, the longest Sword carries her.— *[They all draw, forgetting Don
Pedro, being a Spaniard, had the longest.]*

BLUNT. I yield up my Interest to you Gentlemen, and
that will be Revenge sufficient.

WILLMORE. The Wench is yours—*[To Don Pedro.]* Pox
of his Toledo, I had forgot that.

FREDERICK. Come, Sir, I'll conduct you to the Lady.

[Ex. Frederick and Don Pedro.]

BELVILE. *[Aside.]* To hinder him will certainly
discover—Dost know, dull Beast, what Mischief
thou hast done?

[Willmore walking up and down out of Humour.]

WILLMORE. Ay, ay, to trust our Fortune to Lots, a
Devil on't, 'twas madness, that's the Truth on't.

BELVILE. Oh intolerable Sot!

*[Enter Florinda, running masqu'd, Don Pedro after her, Will-
more gazing round her.]*

FLORINDA. Good Heaven, defend me from discovery.

[Aside.]

DON PEDRO. 'Tis but in vain to fly me, you are fallen
to my Lot.

BELVILE. Sure she is undiscover'd yet, but now I fear
there is no way to bring her off.

WILLMORE. Why, what a Pox is not this my Woman,
the same I follow'd but now?

[Don Pedro talking to Florinda, who walks up and down.]

DON PEDRO. As if I did not know ye, and your Business here.

FLORINDA. Good Heaven! I fear he does indeed—

[Aside.]

DON PEDRO. Come, pray be kind, I know you meant
to be so when you enter'd here, for these are proper
Gentlemen.

WILLMORE. But, Sir—perhaps the Lady will not be
impos'd upon, she'll choose her Man.

DON PEDRO. I am better bred, than not to leave her
Choice free.

[Enter Valeria, and is surpriz'd at the sight of Don Pedro.]

VALERIA. Don Pedro here! there's no avoiding him.

[Aside.]

FLORINDA. Valeria! then I'm undone— *[Aside.]*

VALERIA. Oh! have I found you, Sir—

[To Don Pedro, running to him.]

—The strangest Accident—if I had breath—to tell
it.

DON PEDRO. Speak—is Florinda safe? Hellena well?

VALERIA. Ay, ay Sir—Florinda—is safe—from any
fears of you.

DON PEDRO. Why, where's Florinda?—speak.

VALERIA. Ay, where indeed, Sir? I wish I could inform
you,—But to hold you no longer in doubt—

FLORINDA. Oh, what will she say? *[Aside.]*

VALERIA. She's fled away in the Habit of one of her
Pages, Sir—but Callis thinks you may retrieve her
yet, if you make haste away; she'll tell you, Sir, the
rest—if you can find her.

DON PEDRO. Dishonourable Girl, she has undone my
Aim—Sir—you see my necessity of leaving you, and
I hope you'll pardon it: my Sister, I know, will make
her flight to you; and if she do, I shall expect she
should be render'd back.

BELVILE. I shall consult my Love and Honour, Sir.

[Ex. Don Pedro.]

FLORINDA. My dear Preserver, let me imbrace thee.

[To Valleria.]

WILLMORE. What the Devil's all this?

BLUNT. Mystery by this Light.

VALERIA. Come, come, make haste and get your selves married quickly, for your Brother will return again.

BELVILE. I am so surpriz'd with Fears and Joys, so amaz'd to find you here in safety, I can scarce persuade my Heart into a Faith of that I see—

WILLMORE. Harkye, Colonel, is this that Mistress who has cost you so many Sighs, and me so many Quarrels with you?

BELVILE. It is—Pray give him the Honour of your Hand. [To Florinda.]

WILLMORE. Thus it must be receiv'd then.

[Kneels and kisses her Hand.]

And with it give your Pardon too.

FLORINDA. The Friend to Belvile may command me any thing.

WILLMORE. Death, wou'd I might, 'tis a surprizing Beauty. [Aside.]

BELVILE. Boy, run and fetch a Father instantly. [Ex. Boy.]

FREDERICK. So, now do I stand like a Dog, and have not a Syllable to plead my own Cause with: by this Hand, Madam, I was never thorowly confounded before, nor shall I ever more dare look up with Confidence, till you are pleased to pardon me.

FLORINDA. Sir, I'll be reconcil'd to you on one Condition, that you'll follow the Example of your Friend, in marrying a Maid that does not hate you, and whose Fortune (I believe) will not be unwelcome to you.

FREDERICK. Madam, had I no inclinations that way, I shou'd obey your kind Commands.

BELVILE. Who, Frederick marry; he has so few Inclinations for Womankind, that had he been possest of Paradise, he might have continu'd there to this Day, if no Crime but Love cou'd have disinherited him.

FREDERICK. Oh, I do not use to boast of my Intrigues.

BELVILE. Boast! why thou do'st nothing but boast; and I dare swear, wer't thou as Innocent from the Sin of the Grape, as thou art from the Apple, thou might'st yet claim that right in Eden which our first Parents lost by too much loving.

FREDERICK. I wish this Lady would think me so modest a Man.

VALERIA. She shou'd be sorry then, and not like you half so well, and I shou'd be loth to break my Word with you; which was, That if your Friend and mine are agreed, it shou'd be a Match between you and I.

[She gives him her Hand.]

FREDERICK. Bear witness, Colonel, 'tis a Bargain.

[Kisses her Hand.]

BLUNT. I have a Pardon to beg too; but adsheartlikins I am so out of Countenance, that I am a Dog if I can say any thing to purpose.

FLORINDA. Sir, I heartily forgive you all.

BLUNT. That's nobly said, sweet Lady—Belvile, prithee present her her Ring again, for I find I have not Courage to approach her myself.

[Gives him the Ring, he gives it to Florinda.]

[Enter Boy.]

BOY. Sir, I have brought the Father that you sent for.

BELVILE. 'Tis well, and now my dear Florinda, let's fly to complete that mighty Joy we have so long wish'd and sigh'd for.—Come Frederick. you'll follow.

FREDERICK. Your Example, Sir, 'twas ever my Ambition in War, and must be so in Love.

WILLMORE. And must not I see this juggling Knot ty'd?

BELVILE. No, thou shalt do us better Service, and be our Guard, lest Don Pedro's sudden Return interrupt the Ceremony.

WILLMORE. Content; I'll secure this Pass.

[Ex. Belvile, Florinda, Frederick, and Valeria.]

[Enter Boy.]

BOY. Sir, there's a Lady without wou'd speak to you.

[To Willmore.]

WILLMORE. Conduct her in, I dare not quit my Post.

BOY. And Sir, your Taylor waits you in your Chamber.

BLUNT. Some comfort yet, I shall not dance naked at the Wedding. [Ex. Blunt and Boy.]

[Enter again the Boy, conducting in Angelica in a masquing Habit and a Vizard. Willmore runs to her.]

WILLMORE. This can be none but my pretty Gipsy—
Oh, I see you can follow as well as fly—Come,
confess thyself the most malicious Devil in Nature,
you think you have done my Bus'ness with
Angelica—

ANGELICA. Stand off, base Villain— [*She draws a Pistol
and holds to his Breast.*]

WILLMORE. Hah, 'tis not she: who art thou? and
what's thy Business?

ANGELICA. One thou hast injur'd, and who comes to
kill thee for't.

WILLMORE. What the Devil canst thou mean?

ANGELICA. By all my Hopes to kill thee—

[*Holds still the Pistol to his Breast, he going back, she
following still.*]

WILLMORE. Prithee on what Acquaintance? for I
know thee not.

ANGELICA. Behold this Face!—so lost to thy Remembrance! And then call all thy Sins about thy Soul,
[*Pulls off her Vizard.*] And let them die with thee.

WILLMORE. Angelica!

ANGELICA. Yes, Traitor.
Does not thy guilty Blood run shivering thro thy
Veins?
Hast thou no Horrour at this Sight, that tells thee,
Thou hast not long to boast thy shameful Con-
quest?

WILLMORE. Faith, no Child, my Blood keeps its old
Ebbs and Flows still, and that usual Heat too, that
cou'd oblige thee with a Kindness, had I but opportunity.

ANGELICA. Devil! dost wanton with my Pain—have at
thy Heart.

WILLMORE. Hold, dear Virago! hold thy Hand a little,
I am not now at leisure to be kill'd—hold and hear
me—[*Aside.*] Death, I think she's in earnest.

ANGELICA. Oh if I take not heed,
My coward Heart will leave me to his Mercy.

[*Aside, turning from him.*]

—What have you, Sir, to say?—but should I hear thee,
Thoud'st talk away all that is brave about me:

[*Follows him with the Pistol to his Breast.*]

And I have vow'd thy Death, by all that's sacred.

WILLMORE. Why, then there's an end of a proper
handsome Fellow, that might have liv'd to have
done good Service yet:—That's all I can say to't.

ANGELICA. Yet—I wou'd give thee—time for Penitence.

[*Pausingly.*]

WILLMORE. Faith, Child, I thank God, I have ever
took care to lead a good, sober, hopeful Life, and
am of a Religion that teaches me to believe, I shall
depart in Peace.

ANGELICA. So will the Devil: tell me.
How many poor believing Fools thou hast undone;
How many Hearts thou hast betray'd to ruin!
—Yet these are little Mischiefs to the Ills
Thoust taught mine to commit: thou'st taught it
Love.

WILLMORE. Egad 'twas shrewdly hurt the while.

ANGELICA. —Love, that has robb'd it of its Uncon-
cern,
Of all that Pride that taught me how to value it,
And in its room a mean submissive Passion was
convey'd,
That made me humbly bow, which I ne'er did
To anything but Heaven.
—Thou, perjur'd Man, didst this, and with thy
Oaths,
Which on thy Knees thou didst devoutly make,
Soften'd my yielding Heart—And then, I was a
Slave—
Yet still had been content to've worn my Chains,
Worn 'em with Vanity and Joy for ever,
Hadst thou not broke those Vows that put them on.
—'Twas then I was undone.

[*All this while follows him with a Pistol to his Breast.*]

WILLMORE. Broke my Vows! why, where hast thou
lived?
Amongst the Gods! For I never heard of mortal
Man,
That has not broke a thousand Vows.

ANGELICA. Oh, Impudence!

WILLMORE. Angelica! that Beauty has been too long
tempting,
Not to have made a thousand Lovers languish,
Who in the amorous Favour, no doubt have sworn
Like me; did they all die in that Faith? still adoring?
I do not think they did.

ANGELICA. No, faithless Man: had I repaid their Vows, as I did thine, I wou'd have kill'd the ungrateful that had abandon'd me.

WILLMORE. This old General has quite spoil'd thee, nothing makes a Woman so vain, as being flatter'd; your old Lover ever supplies the Defects of Age, with intolerable Dotage, vast Charge, and that which you call Constancy; and attributing all this to your own Merits, you domineer, and throw your Favours in's Teeth, upbraiding him still with the Defects of Age, and cuckold him as often as he deceives your Expectations. But the gay, young, brisk, Lover, that brings his equal Fires, and can give you Dart for Dart, he'll be as nice as you sometimes.

ANGELICA. All this thou'st made me know, for which I hate thee.

Had I remain'd in innocent Security,
I shou'd have thought all Men were born my Slaves;
And worn my Pow'r like Lightning in my Eyes,
To have destroy'd at Pleasure when offended.
—But when Love held the Mirror, the undeceiving Glass,
Reflected all the weakness of my Soul, and made me know,
My richest Treasure being lost, my Honour,
All the remaining Spoil cou'd not be worth
The Conqueror's Care or Value.
—Oh how I fell like a long worship'd Idol,
Discovering all the Cheat!
Wou'd not the Incense and rich Sacrifice,
Which blind Devotion offer'd at my Altars,
Have fall'n to thee?
Why woud'st thou then destroy my fancy'd Power?

WILLMORE. By Heaven thou art brave, and I admire thee strangely.

I wish I were that dull, that constant thing,
Which thou woudst have, and Nature never meant me:
I must, like chearful Birds, sing in all Groves,
And perch on every Bough,
Billing the next kind She that flies to meet me;
Yet after all cou'd build my Nest with thee,
Thither repairing when I'd lov'd my round,
And still reserve a tributary Flame.
—To gain your Credit, I'll pay you back your Charity,
And be oblig'd for nothing but for Love.

[Offers her a Purse of Gold.]

ANGELICA. Oh that thou wert in earnest!

So mean a Thought of me,
Wou'd turn my Rage to Scorn, and I shou'd pity thee,
And give thee leave to live;
Which for the publick Safety of our Sex,
And my own private Injuries, I dare not do.
Prepare— [Follows, still, as before.]
—I will no more be tempted with Replies.

WILLMORE. Sure—

ANGELICA. Another Word will damn thee! I've heard thee talk too long. [She follows him with a Pistol ready to shoot: he retires still amaz'd.

[Enter Don Antonio, his Arm in a Scarf, and lays hold on the Pistols.]

ANTONIO. Hah! Angelica!

ANGELICA. Antonio! What the Devil brought thee hither?

ANTONIO. Love and Curiosity, seeing your Coach at Door. Let me disarm you of this unbecoming Instrument of Death.— [Takes away the Pistol.] Amongst the Number of your Slaves, was there not one worthy the Honour to have fought your Quarrel?
—Who are you Sir, that are so very wretched To merit Death from her?

WILLMORE. One, Sir, that cou'd have made a better End of an amorous Quarrel without you, than with you.

ANTONIO. Sure 'tis some Rival—hah—the very Man took down her Picture yesterday—the very same that set on me last night—Blest opportunity— [Offers to shoot him.]

ANGELICA. Hold, you're mistaken Sir,

ANTONIO. By Heaven the very same!
—Sir, what pretentions have you to this Lady?

WILLMORE. Sir, I don't use to be examin'd, and am ill at all Disputes but this— [Draws, Antonio offers to shoot.]

ANGELICA. Oh, hold! you see he's arm'd with certain Death:

[To Willmore.]

—And you, Antonio, I command you hold,
By all the Passion you've so lately vow'd me.

[Enter Don Pedro, sees Antonio, and stays.]

DON PEDRO. Hah, Antonio! and Angelica! [*Aside.*]

ANTONIO. When I refuse Obedience to your Will,
May you destroy me with your mortal Hate.
By all that's Holy I adore you so,
That even my Rival, who has Charms enough
To make him fall a Victim to my Jealousy,
Shall live, nay, and have leave to love on still.

DON PEDRO. What's this I hear? [*Aside.*]

ANGELICA. Ah, thus, 'twas thus he talk'd, and I believ'd.

[*Pointing to Willmore.*]

—Antonio, yesterday,
I'd not have sold my Interest in his heart,
For all the Sword has won and lost in Battle,
—But now to show my utmost of Contempt,
I give thee Life—which if thou would'st preserve,
Live where my Eyes may never see thee more,
Live to undo someone, whose Soul may prove
So bravely constant to revenge my Love.

[*Goes out, Antonio follows, but Don Pedro pulls him back.*]

DON PEDRO. Antonio—stay.

ANTONIO. Don Pedro—

DON PEDRO. What Coward Fear was that prevented thee
From meeting me this Morning on the Molo?

ANTONIO. Meet thee?

DON PEDRO. Yes me; I was the Man that dar'd thee to't.

ANTONIO. Hast thou so often seen me fight in War,
To find no better Cause to excuse my Absence?
—I sent my Sword and one to do thee Right,
Finding my self uncapable to use a Sword.

DON PEDRO. But 'twas Florinda's Quarrel that we fought,
And you, to show how little you esteem'd her,
Sent me your Rival, giving him your Interest.
—But I have found the Cause of this Affront,
And when I meet you fit for the Dispute,
—I'll tell you my Resentment.

ANTONIO. I shall be ready, Sir, e'er long to do you Reason.

[*Exit Antonio.*]

DON PEDRO. If I cou'd find Florinda, now whilst my

Anger's high, I think I shou'd be kind, and give her to Belvile in Revenge.

WILLMORE. Faith, Sir, I know not what you wou'd do, but I believe the Priest within has been so kind.

DON PEDRO. How! my Sister married?

WILLMORE. I hope by this time she is, and bedded too, or he has not my longings about him.

DON PEDRO. Dares he do thus? Does he not fear my Pow'r?

WILLMORE. Faith not all all. If you will go in, and thank him for the Favour he has done your Sister, so; if not, Sir, my Power's greater in this House than yours; I have a damn'd surly Crew here, that will keep you till the next Tide, and then clap you on board my Prize; my Ship lies but a League off the Molo, and we shall show your Donship a damn'd Tramontana Rover's Trick.

[*Enter Belvile.*]

BELVILE. This Rogue's in some new Mischief—hah, Don Pedro return'd!

DON PEDRO. Colonel Belvile!, I hear you have married my Sister.

BELVILE. You have heard truth then, Sir.

DON PEDRO. Have I so? then, Sir, I wish you Joy.

BELVILE. How!

DON PEDRO. By this Embrace I do, and I am glad on't.

BELVILE. Are you in earnest?

DON PEDRO. By our long Friendship and my Obligations to thee, I am. The sudden Change I'll give you Reasons for anon. Come lead me to my Sister, that she may know I now approve her Choice. [*Exit Belvile with Don Pedro.*]

[*Willmore goes to follow them. Enter Hellena as before in Boy's Clothes, and pulls him back.*]

WILLMORE. Ha! my Gipsy—Now a thousand Blessings on thee for this Kindness. Egad Child I was e'en in despair of ever seeing thee again; my Friends are all provided for within, each Man his kind Woman.

HELLENA. Hah! I though they had serv'd me some such Trick.

WILLMORE. And I was e'en resolv'd to go aboard, condemn myself to my lone Cabin, and the Thoughts of thee.

HELLENA. And cou'd you have left me behind? wou'd you have been so ill-natur'd?

WILLMORE. Why, 'twou'd have broke my Heart Child—but since we are met again, I defy foul Weather to part us.

HELLENA. And wou'd you be a faithful Friend now, if a Maid shou'd trust you.

WILLMORE. For a Friend I cannot promise, thou art of a Form so excellent, a Face and Humour too good for cold dull Friendship; I am parlously afraid of being in love Child, and you have not forgot how severely you have us'd me.

HELLENA. That's all one, such Usage you must still look for, to find out all your Haunts, to rail at you to all that love you, till I have made you love only me in your own Defence, because nobody else will love.

WILLMORE. But hast thou no better Quality to recommend thyself by?

HELLENA. Faith none Captain—Why, 'twill be the greater Charity to take me for thy Mistress, I am a lone Child, a kind of Orphan Lover; and why I shou'd die a Maid, and in a Captain's Hands too, I do not understand.

WILL. Egad, I was never claw'd away with Broad Sides from any Female before, thou hast one Virtue I adore, good-Nature; I hate a coy demure Mistress, she's as troublesome as a Colt, I'll break none; no give me a mad Mistress when mew'd, and in flying on I dare trust upon the Wing, that whilst she's kind will come to the Lure.

HELLENA. Nay as kind as you will good Captain, whilst it lasts, but let's lose no time.

WILLMORE. My time's as precious to me, as thine can be; therefore dear Creature, since we are so well agreed, let's retire to my Chamber, and if ever thou wert treated with such savory Love—Come—My Bed's prepar'd for such a Guest, all clean and sweet as they fair self; I love to steal a Dish and a Bottle with a Friend, and hate long Graces—Come let's retire and fall to.

HELLENA. 'Tis but getting my Consent, and the Business is soon done; let but old Gaffer Hymen and his Priest say Amen to't; and I dare lay my Mother's Daughter by as proper a Fellow as your Father's Son, without fear or blushing.

WILLMORE. Hold, hold, no Bugg Words Child, Priest and Hymen: prithee add Hangman to 'em to make up the Consort—No, no, we'll have no Vows but Love, Child, nor Witness but the Lover; the kind Deity injoins naught but love and enjoy. Hymen and Priest wait still upon Portion, and Joynture; Love and Beauty have their own Ceremonies. Marriage is as certain a Bane to Love, as lending Money is to Friendship: I'll neither ask nor give a Vow, tho I could be content to turn Gipsy, and become a Left-hand Bridegroom, to have the Pleasure of working that great Miracle of making a Maid a Mother, if you durst venture; 'tis pure Gipsy that, and if I miss I'll lose my Labour.

HELLENA. And if you do not lose, what shall I get? A Cradle full of Noise and Mischief, with a Pack of Repentance at my Back? Can you teach me to weave Incle to pass my time with? 'Tis pure Gipsy that too.

WILLMORE. I can teach thee to weave a true Love's Knot better.

HELLENA. So can my Dog.

WILLMORE. Well, I see we are both upon our Guard, and I see there's no way to conquer good Nature, but by yielding—here—give me thy Hand—one Kiss and I am thine—

HELLENA. One Kiss! How like my Page he speaks; I am resolv'd you shall have none, for asking such a sneaking Sum—He that will be satisfied with one Kiss will never die of that Longing; good Friend single-Kiss, is all your talking come to this?—A Kiss, a Caudle! farewel Captain single-Kiss. [*Going out he stays her.*]

WILLMORE. Nay if we part so, let me die like a Bird upon a Bough, at the Sheriff's Charge. By Heaven, both the Indies shall not buy thee from me. I adore thy Humour and will marry thee, and we are so of one Humour, it must be a Bargain—give me thy Hand—

[*Kisses her Hand.*]

And now let the blind ones (Love and Fortune) do their worst.

HELLENA. Why, God-a-mercy, Captain!

WILLMORE. But harkye—The Bargain is now made; but is it not fit we shou'd know each other's Names? That when we have Reason to curse one another hereafter, and People ask me who 'tis I give to the Devil, I may be least be able to tell what Family you came of.

HELLENA. Good reason, Captain; and where I have cause, (as I doubt not but I shall have plentiful) that I may know at whom to throw my—Blessings—I beseech ye your Name.

WILLMORE. I am call'd Robert the Constant.

HELLENA. A very fine Name! pray was it your Faulkner or Butler that christen'd you? Do they not use to whistle when they call you?

WILLMORE. I hope you have a better, that a Man may name without crossing himself, you are so merry with mine.

HELLENA. I am call'd Hellena the Inconstant.

[Enter Don Pedro, Belvile, Florinda, Frederick, Valeria.]

DON PEDRO. Ha! Hellena!

FLORINDA. Hellena!

HELLENA. The very same—hah my Brother! now Captain shew your Love and Courage; stand to your Arms, and defend me bravely, or I am lost for ever.

DON PEDRO. What's this I hear? false Girl, how came you hither, and what's your Business? Speak.

[Goes roughly to her.]

WILLMORE. Hold off, Sir, you have leave to parly only.

[Puts himself between.]

HELLENA. I had e'en as good tell it, as you guess it. Faith Brother, my Business is the same with all living Creatures of my Age, to love, and be loved, and here's the Man.

DON PEDRO. Perfidious Maid, hast thou deceiv'd me too, deceiv'd thy self and Heaven?

HELLENA. 'Tis time enough to make my Peace with that: Be you but kind, let me alone with Heaven.

DON PEDRO. Belvile!, I did not expect this false Play from you; was't not enough you'd gain Florinda (which I pardon'd) but your lewd Friends too must be inrich'd with the Spoils of a noble Family?

BELVILE. Faith Sir, I am as much surpriz'd at this as you can be: Yet, Sir, my Friends are Gentlemen, and ought to be esteem'd for their Misfortunes, since they have the Glory to suffer with the best of Men and Kings; 'tis true, he's a Rover of Fortune, yet a Prince aboard his little wooden World.

DON PEDRO. What's this to the maintenance of a Woman of her Birth and Quality?

WILLMORE. Faith Sir, I can boast of nothing but a Sword which does me Right where-e'er I come, and has defended a worse Cause than a Woman's: and

since I lov'd her before I either knew her Birth or Name, I must pursue my Resolution and marry her.

DON PEDRO. And is all your holy Intent of becoming a Nun debauch'd into a Desire of Man?

HELLENA. Why—I have consider'd the matter Brother, and find the Three hundred thousand Crowns my Uncle left me (and you cannot keep from me) will be better laid out in Love than in Religion, and turn to as good an Account—let most Voices carry it, for Heaven or the Captain?

ALL CRY. A Captain, a Captain.

HELLENA. Look ye Sir, 'tis a clear Case.

DON PEDRO. Oh I am mad—if I refuse, my Life's in Danger—[Aside.]
—Come—There's one motive induces me—take her—I shall now be free from the fear of her Honour; guard it you now, if you can, I have been a Slave to't long enough. [Gives her to him.]

WILLMORE. Faith Sir, I am of a Nation, that are of opinion a Woman's Honour is not worth guarding, when she has a mind to part with it.

HELLENA. Well said, Captain.

DON PEDRO. This was your Plot Mistress, but I hope you have married one that will revenge my Quarrel to you—

[To Valeria.]

VALERIA. There's no altering Destiny, Sir.

DON PEDRO. Sooner than a Woman's Will, therefore I forgive you all—and wish you may get my Father's Pardon as easily; which I fear.

[Enter Blunt drest in a Spanish Habit, looking very ridiculously; his Man adjusting his Band.]

MAN. 'Tis very well, Sir.

BLUNT. Well Sir, 'dsheartlikins I tell you 'tis damnable ill Sir—A Spanish Habit, good Lord! Cou'd the Devil and my Taylor devise no other Punishment for me, but the Mode of a Nation I abominate?

BELVILE. What the matter, Ned?

BLUNT. Pray view me round, and judge—[Turns round.]

BELVILE. I must confess thou art a kind of an odd Figure.

BLUNT. In a Spanish Habit with a Vengeance! I had rather be in the Inquisition for Judaism, than in this

Doublet and Breeches; a Pillory were an easy Collar to this, three Handfuls high; and these Shoes too are worse than the Stocks, with the Sole an inch shorter than my Foot: In fine, Gentlemen, methinks I look altogether like a Bag of Bays stuff'd full of Fools flesh.

BELVILE. Methinks 'tis well, and makes thee look *en Cavalier.*

Come, Sir, settle your Face, and salute our Friends, Lady—

BLUNT. Hah! Say'st thou so, my little Rover?

[*To Hellena.*]

Lady—(if you be one) give me leave to kiss your Hand, and tell you, adsheartlikins, for all I look so, I am your humble Servant—A Pox of my Spanish Habit.

WILLMORE. Hark—what's this? [*Musick is heard to Play.*]

[*Enter Boy.*]

BOY. Sir as the custom is, the gay People in Masquer-ade, who make every Man's House their own, are coming up.

[*Enter several Men and Women in masquing Habits, with Musick, they put themselves in order and dance.*]

BLUNT. Adsheartlikins, wou'd 'twere lawful to pull off their false Faces, that I might see if my Doxy were not amongst 'em.

BELVILE. Ladies and Gentlemen, since you are come so *a propos,* you must take a small Collation with us.

[*To the Masquers.*]

WILLMORE. Whilst we'll to the Good Man within, who stays to give us a Cast of his Office. [*To Hellena.*]
—Have you no trembling at the near approach?

HELLENA. No more than you have in an Engagement or a Tempest.

WILLMORE. Egad thou'rt a grave Girl, and I admire thy Love and Courage.

Lead on, no other Dangers they can dread,
Who venture in the Storms o'th'Marriage-Bed.

[*Exeunt.*]

EPILOGUE

The banisht Cavaliers! a Roving Blade!
A popish Carnival! a Masquerade!
The Devil's in't if this will please the Nation,
  In these our blessed Times of Reformation,
When Conventicling is so much in Fashion,
And yet—
That mutinous Tribe less Factions do beget,
Than your continual differing in Wit;
Your Judgment's (as your Passions) a Disease;
Nor Muse nor Miss your Appetite can please;
You're grown as nice as queasy Consciences,
Whose each Convulsion, when the Spirit moves,
Damns every thing that Maggot disapproves.
With canting Rule you wou'd the Stage refine,
And to dull Method all our Sense confine.
With th' Insolence of Common-wealths you rule,
Where each gay Fop, and politick brave Fool

On Monarch Wit impose without controul.
As for the last who seldom sees a Play,
Unless it be the old Black-Fryers way,
Shaking his empty Noddle o'er Bamboo,
He crys—Good Faith, these Plays will never do.
—Ah, Sir, in my young days what lofty Wit,
What high-strain'd Scenes of Fighting were there writ;
These are slight airy Toys. But tell me, pray,
What has the House of Commons done to day?
Then shews his Politicks, to let you see
Of State Affairs he'll judge as notably,
As he can do of Wit and Poetry.
The younger Sparks, who hither do resort,
Cry—
Pox o' your gentle things, give us more Sport;
—Damn me, I'm sure twill never please the Court.
Such Fops are never pleas'd, unless the Play

Be stuff'd with Fools, as brisk and dull as they:
Such might the Half-Crown spare, and in a Glass
At home behold a more accomplisht Ass,
Where they may set their Cravats, Wigs, and Faces,
And practice all their Buffoonry Grimaces;

See how this—Huff becomes—this Dammy—stare—
Which they at home may act, because they dare,
But—must with prudent Caution do elsewhere.
Oh that our Nokes, or Tony Lee cou'd show
A Fop but half so much to th' Life as you.

ESSAY: AN APPROACH TO THE PLAY

In 1642 a bloody civil war began in England between the Puritans, supporters of the powers of Parliament, the rising urban middle class, and radical Protestantism, and the cavaliers, supporters of the monarchy, the traditional rural aristocracy, and the established Church of England. When the Puritans won, supporters of the king fled into exile, many to France, where they discovered French patterns of courtship and manners, as well as the rather restrained version of the comedy of manners typified by the plays of Molière. In 1660 the Commonwealth which the Puritans had established to replace the traditional monarchy failed, no provision for succession of power could be worked out, and the English king and aristocrats returned to England from continental Europe in a spirit of triumph, determined to transform English society along the lines they had seen in France. *The Rover*, written after the restoration of the monarchy, is set in Spain during the period when the Puritans ruled England and the aristocratic characters in exile were dispossessed of their property. Because the characters have no estate to return to, as well as because of their sexual inconstancy, they are "rovers." The title of the play is a pun, in which the economic meaning reinforces the erotic one.

In Restoration comedies, the plot is typically a complex set of romantic intrigues; the play's "hero" or "heroine" will be the winner of these intrigues and will be judged the epitome of social excellence and elegance. Winning and losing, getting and not getting, are at the heart of this society. Heroes and heroines outsmart the others, including their own sexual partners, without losing self-possession; The sexual "game" is about not losing one's equanimity, about not showing love or jealousy—at least not in public.

It is therefore a social as well as an emotional risk for characters to allow the chase to become more than a game, to become a pursuit in which the emotions are seriously engaged. Thus when Angelica threatens Willmore with a gun near the end of the play, she has lost the social game by showing that she is jealous, that she feels betrayed, that in fact she loves. If the code seems callous, at least there is no double standard: Women and men behave similarly and are judged similarly for their cleverness, self-awareness, and self-discipline. When at the beginning of the play Hellena, who is about to become a nun, confesses that she would prefer to have a lover, the fundamental similarity between men and women is immediately established.

There are at least two ways of looking at such a play's relationship to social "reality." One is that its plot is an accurate reflection of the dominant pursuit of the leisured class not only at home but also in the theater itself, which was a primary site for social activity. Young men and women who wished to show themselves off to potential lovers sat in the middle of the theater on ground level, in what was called "the pit." Those who wished to observe them sat in boxes overlooking the pit. Glances and notes were exchanged and assignations made, even as the play, which was portraying this same sexual game, was being performed. In a very direct way, the play was about the behavior of its audience in the theater, as well as about its pursuits outside the theater. Indeed, in scenery and in costume as well as in sexuality, the stage on which these plays were produced was realistic, and this, too, was new in England. (The Shakespearean theater, by contrast, had no represented scenes and depended on language to suggest changes of locale.) Scenery was painted in perspective to look like the scene described in the play, and these scenes in turn resembled ones which were familiar to the audience in real life (although in the case of *The Rover*, of course, the setting was Spanish rather than English).

Restoration comedy's focus on sexual intrigue in large part reflects the larger society's customs and marriage laws. Aristocratic men and women were expected to marry a person chosen by their parents (usually by the father). Marriage was essentially a business deal of social and economic benefit to the two families. Within this context, a woman had no legal control over money, even if she was rich. In general, her father had that authority and passed it on to her husband, as Florinda concedes in Act 5. (Typically, only a widow could be financially independent.) In such a situation, marriage and love were unrelated, and it was generally accepted in the leisured classes that both men and women would find love and romance outside of matrimony. The twin assumptions that adulterous sexual pursuits are "natural" and that marriage is essentially a financial arrangement (one which perpetuates the financial bondage of women) are reflected in the play's startling attitudes toward the buying and selling of daughters, the frank sexual pursuit of beauty, and the casual view of adultery. Of all the women in the play, only one can afford to exalt personal affection above financial interests: Angelica, the successful independent business-woman who falls in love with the (relatively) poor Willmore.

An additional reason for the sexual frankness of the Restoration stage is that for the first time actresses, not boy actors, played female roles on the English stage. This frankness was further emphasized by the desire of some actresses to exaggerate their physical assets onstage not only to enhance their *roles* as sexual objects, but also to attract the personal patronage of a wealthy man in the audience. The best-known success story in this vein is that of the actress Nell Gwynn, who became the king's mistress for seventeen years, bore him two children, and lived in great comfort. In this sexist society, the stage provided many dimensions in which women could engage in the sexual politics necessary to survival. The stage did not merely mirror its society and audience in the theater; it also interacted with it.

Viewed in this way, it may be more than incidental to observe that the playwright Behn herself could easily have been the heroine "truewit" of her own, or anybody else's, Restoration comedy. Although she had a continuing relationship with the lawyer and rake John Hoyle, she kept her own independence by remaining unmarried. Indeed, to support herself in a man's field, writing, was in itself an assertion of independence. Although her plays in many respects are very similar to those written by men, she puts far greater emphasis on the social fact of female repression by law and custom than they do.

In *The Rover*, she also presents a more romantic image of the relations between the sexes than is conventional in this genre. The agreement struck by Willmore and Hellena is fully self-aware. She gives herself up to him in the conscious judgment that getting love in a marriage between equals is good value received for giving up control of her money. It is the basis for a romantic love that was shortly to become more fashionable than it was in Behn's time, perhaps her hope for something better for women than marriages arranged as part of men's business deals.

Richard Brinsley Sheridan

THE RIVALS

About the Author   Richard Brinsley Sheridan (1751–1816) was born in Ireland of an actor father and a playwright mother, and his family settled in the fashionable spa city of Bath, England, when he was twenty. Within three years he had taken Elizabeth Linley, the most desired young woman of this highly social town, to Europe to protect her from another's unwelcome advances, then returned to England, fought two duels in her defense, and, finally overcoming her father's objections, married her. *The Rivals* was produced in London two years later, and two other plays by Sheridan followed at the Covent Garden Theater. When David Garrick retired from a long and brilliant career managing the rival Drury Lane Theater in 1776, Sheridan and a group of partners bought it, and he became its principal manager. His play *A School for Scandal* opened there the next year and was an immediate sensation. He is credited with being a shrewd theater manager as well as a distinguished politician—elected to the House of Commons in 1780, he served there for more than thirty years, a period in which his personal prestige grew greatly. However, his political office left him little energy to devote to his literary career. Then, in the last years of his life, his fortunes suffered a reversal. When he had to rebuild the Drury Lane after a fire in the 1790s and then again in 1809, he was financially ruined, and in 1812 he failed to win reelection to Parliament.

About the Play   *The Rivals* (1775) was Sheridan's first play and, after revisions, his first "hit," a change from the sentimental "weeping comedy" of the middle 1800s. His contemporaries reacted with delight. Its emphasis on wit and intrigue bears more resemblance to the work of writers such as Molière and Behn a century before than it does to the majority of the writers of his own time. It is dominated by the schemes of lovers, by the satire of particular and recognizable (though exaggerated) social types, and by a witty style of commentary on the contemporary scene. It is different from Molière and Behn, however, in the nature of the affections which its lovers feel for each other.

In the intervening century, both the nature of the stage hero and heroine, and the nature of their love, had changed. By 1775 society was dominated by an urban middle class, and it was Parliament, rather than the king, who held the main political power. Reflecting the values of this new society, the lead dramatic character was no longer an aristocratic rake whose major claim to admiration was his or her ability to seduce as many as possible of the opposite sex. Nor was it still considered dramatically desirable to have people fall in love with the seducer while he or she remained emotionally unaffected. Instead, the idea of love had become firmly attached to marriage and to reciprocated feelings. Words such as "delicacy" and "sentiment," suggesting affection for one's beloved, had become popular. Indeed, the idea of love at the time of Sheridan is recognizably similar to the "romantic" expectations which remain in our century an ideal for human relationships. Sheridan, then, is writing for an audience and a society in which the fundamental realities of power, and therefore of belief, have changed. And even though some of the dialect of eighteenth-century London may occasionally make the wit difficult to follow, and even though some customs are different from ours, his world is one we begin to recognize as like our own.

The central premise of the plot is that Lydia Languish and Captain Anthony Absolute love one another, but that in order for her to marry him he must pretend to be the (relatively) impoverished Ensign Beverley. There are no important social obstacles to this union; Sir Anthony, the father of the male romantic lead, thinks their marriage an excellent idea, as does Lydia's influential aunt, Mrs. Malaprop. Although there is a rival, Bob Acres, he is not a serious threat. What makes the plot move is not an external obstacle, then, but an internal one: Lydia's desire for adventure. She wants to escape the stultifying conventions of the older generation in favor of the romantic self-abandonment of elopement. This desire represents a problem because the main part of her fortune, which would allow her to lead a genteel and comfortable life, depends on Mrs. Malaprop's approval, and Mrs. Malaprop expects for her a good (that is, wealthy) marriage with Captain Absolute. On the other side, Captain Absolute must pretend not to have a well-to-do family in order to satisfy Lydia's desire for adventure, so he must woo his beloved on her terms, pretending the relative poverty of an ensign's lower rank and lesser family. However, he is less indifferent than she about giving up her—or his own—fortune. Love is important to him, but he would like comfort as well, and to get comfort it is necessary to allow parents to domineer—or at least to seem to be in control.

CHARACTERS

CAPTAIN ABSOLUTE

LYDIA LANGUISH

SIR ANTHONY ABSOLUTE, father of Captain
  Absolute

MRS. MALAPROP, aunt of Lydia Languish

FAULKLAND

JULIA MELVILLE, cousin of Lydia Languish

BOB ACRES

SIR LUCIUS O'TRIGGER

FAG, valet of Captain Absolute

LUCY, lady's maid of Lydia Languish

DAVID, valet of Bob Acres

COACHMAN

MAID

BOY

SERVANTS

SCENE. Bath.

TIME OF ACTION: Within one day.

Act I

SCENE I

A street in Bath.

[*Coachman crosses the stage.—Enter Fag, looking after him.*]

FAG. What!—Thomas! Sure, 'tis he?—What!—Thomas!—Thomas!

COACHMAN. Hey! Odd's life!—Mr. Fag!—give us your hand, my old fellow-servant.

FAG. Excuse my glove, Thomas:—I'm dev'lish glad to see you, my lad: why, my prince of charioteers, you look as hearty!—but who the deuce thought of seeing you in Bath!

COACHMAN. Sure, Master, Madam Julia, Harry, Mrs. Kate, and the postilion be all come!

FAG. Indeed!

COACHMAN. Aye! Master thought another fit of the gout was coming to make him a visit: so he'd a mind to gi't the slip, and whip! we were all off at an hour's warning.

FAG. Aye, aye! hasty in everything, or it would not be Sir Anthony Absolute!

COACHMAN. But tell us, Mr. Fag, how does young master? Odd! Sir Anthony will stare to see the Captain here!

FAG. I do not serve Captain Absolute now.

COACHMAN. Why sure!

FAG. At present I am employed by Ensign Beverley.

COACHMAN. I doubt, Mr. Fag, you ha'n't changed for the better.

FAG. I have not changed, Thomas.

COACHMAN. No! why, didn't you say you had left young master?

FAG. No.—Well, honest Thomas, I must puzzle you no farther: briefly then—Captain Absolute and Ensign Beverley are one and the same person.

COACHMAN. The devil they are!

FAG. So it is indeed, Thomas; and the *Ensign*-half of my master being on guard at present—the *Captain* has nothing to do with me.

COACHMAN. So, so!—What, this is some freak, I warrant!—Do tell us, Mr. Fag, the meaning o't—you know I ha' trusted you.

FAG. You'll be secret, Thomas?

COACHMAN. As a coach-horse.

FAG. Why then the cause of all this is—Love—Love,

Thomas, who (as you may get read to you) has been a masquerader ever since the days of Jupiter.

COACHMAN. Aye, aye;—I guessed there was a lady in the case: but pray, why does your master pass only for *Ensign*? Now if he had shammed *General*, indeed—

FAG. Ah! Thomas, there lies the mystery o' the matter. Hark'ee, Thomas, my master is in love with a lady of a very singular taste: a lady who likes him better as a *half-pay Ensign* than if she knew he was son and heir to Sir Anthony Absolute, a baronet of three thousand a year!

COACHMAN. That is an odd taste indeed!—but has she got the stuff, Mr. Fag? is she rich, hey?

FAG. Rich!—why, I believe she owns half the stocks—Z—ds! Thomas, she could pay the national debt as easily as I could my washerwoman! She has a lap-dog that eats out of gold—she feeds her parrot with small pearls—and all her thread-papers are made of bank-notes!

COACHMAN. Bravo!—Faith!—Odd! I warrant she has a set of thousands at least. But does she draw kindly with the Captain?

FAG. As fond as pigeons.

COACHMAN. May one hear her name?

FAG. Miss Lydia Languish. But there is an old tough aunt in the way; though, by the bye, she has never seen my master, for he got acquainted with Miss while on a visit in Gloucestershire.

COACHMAN. Well—I wish they were once harnessed together in matrimony.—But pray, Mr. Fag, what kind of a place is this Bath? I ha' heard a deal of it—here's a mort o' merrymaking, hey?

FAG. Pretty well, Thomas, pretty well—'tis a good lounge. In the morning we go to the Pump-room (though neither my master nor I drink the waters); after breakfast we saunter on the Parades, or play a game at billiards; at night we dance: but d—n the place, I'm tired of it: their regular hours stupefy me—not a fiddle nor a card after eleven! However, Mr. Faulkland's gentleman and I keep it up a little in private parties—I'll introduce you there, Thomas; you'll like him much.

COACHMAN. Sure I know Mr. Du-Peigne—you know his master is to marry Madam Julia.

FAG. I had forgot.—But Thomas, you must polish a little—indeed you must. Here now—this wig! what the devil do you do with a *wig*, Thomas?—none of the London whips of any degree of *ton* wear *wigs* now.

COACHMAN. More's the pity! more's the pity, I say—Odd's life! when I heard how the lawyers and doctors had took to their own hair, I thought how 'twould go next:—Odd rabbit it! when the fashion had got foot on the Bar, I guessed 'twould mount to the Box! But 'tis all out of character, believe me, Mr. Fag: and look'ee, I'll never gi' up mine—the lawyers and doctors may do as they will.

FAG. Well, Thomas, we'll not quarrel about that.

COACHMAN. Why, bless you, the gentlemen of the professions ben't all of a mind—for in our village now, tho'ff *Jack Gauge*, the *exciseman*, has ta'en to his carrots, there's little Dick, the farrier, swears he'll never forsake his *bob*, tho' all the college should appear with their own heads!

FAG. Indeed! well said, Dick! But hold—mark! mark! Thomas.

COACHMAN. Zooks! 'tis the Captain—Is that the lady with him?

FAG. No! no! that is Madam Lucy—my master's mistress's maid. They lodge at that house—but I must after him to tell him the news.

COACHMAN. Odd! he's giving her money!—Well, Mr. Fag—

FAG. Good-bye, Thomas.—I have an appointment in Gyde's Porch this evening at eight; meet me there, and we'll make a little party.

[*Exeunt severally.*]

SCENE II

A dressing-room in Mrs. Malaprop's lodgings.

[*Lydia sitting on a sofa, with a book in her hand. Lucy, as just returned from a message.*]

LUCY. Indeed, Ma'am, I traversed half the town in search of it: I don't believe there's a circulating library in Bath I ha'n't been at.

LYDIA. And could not you get *The Reward of Constancy*?

LUCY. No, indeed, Ma'am.

LYDIA. Nor *The Fatal Connection*?

LUCY. No, indeed, Ma'am.

LYDIA. Nor *The Mistakes of the Heart*?

LUCY. Ma'am, as ill-luck would have it, Mr. Bull said Miss Sukey Saunter had just fetched it away.

LYDIA. Heigh-ho! Did you inquire for *The Delicate Distress*?

LUCY. Or *The Memoirs of Lady Woodford*? Yes, indeed, M'am. I asked everywhere for it; and I might have brought it from Mr. Frederick's, but Lady Slattern Lounger, who had just sent it home, had so soiled and dog's-eared it, it wa'nt fit for a Christian to read.

LYDIA. Heigh-ho!—Yes, I always know when Lady Slattern has been before me. She has a most observing thumb; and I believe cherishes her nails for the convenience of making marginal notes.—Well, child, what *have* you brought me?

LUCY. Oh! here, Ma'am. [*Taking books from under her cloak, and from her pockets.*] This is *The Gordian Knot*, and this *Peregrine Pickle*. Here are *The Tears of Sensibility* and *Humphry Clinker*. This is *The Memoirs of a Lady of Quality, written by herself*, and here the second volume of *The Sentimental Journey*.

LYDIA. Heigh-ho!—What are those books by the glass?

LUCY. The great one is only *The Whole Duty of Man*—where I press a few blonds, Ma'am.

LYDIA. Very well—give me the *sal volatile*.

LUCY. Is it in a blue cover, Ma'am?

LYDIA. My smelling bottle, you simpleton!

LUCY. Oh, the drops!—Here, Ma'am.

LYDIA. Hold!—here's some one coming—quick! see who it is.

[*Exit Lucy.*]

Surely I heard my cousin Julia's voice!

[*Re-enter Lucy.*]

LUCY. Lud! Ma'am, here is Miss Melville.

LYDIA. Is it possible!—

[*Enter Julia.*]

My dearest Julia, how delighted am I!—[*Embrace.*] How unexpected was this happiness!

JULIA. True, Lydia—and our pleasure is the greater; but what has been the matter?—you were denied to me at first!

LYDIA. Ah! Julia, I have a thousand things to tell you! But first inform me what has conjured you to Bath? Is Sir Anthony here?

JULIA. He is—we are arrived within this hour, and I suppose he will be here to wait on Mrs. Malaprop as soon as he is dressed.

LYDIA. Then, before we are interrupted, let me impart to you some of my distress! I know your gentle nature will sympathize with me, though your prudence may condemn me! My letters have informed you of my whole connexion with Beverley—but I have lost him, Julia! My aunt has discovered our intercourse by a note she intercepted, and has con-

fined me ever since! Yet, would you believe it? she has fallen absolutely in love with a tall Irish baronet she met one night since we have been here, at Lady Macshuffle's rout.

JULIA. You jest, Lydia!

LYDIA. No, upon my word. She really carries on a kind of correspondence with him, under a feigned name though, till she chooses to be known to him; but it is a *Delia* or a *Celia*, I assure you.

JULIA. Then surely she is now more indulgent to her niece.

LYDIA. Quite the contrary. Since she has discovered her own frailty she is become more suspicious of mine. Then I must inform you of another plague! That odious Acres is to be in Bath to-day; so that I protest I shall be teased out of all spirits!

JULIA. Come, come, Lydia, hope the best. Sir Anthony shall use his interest with Mrs. Malaprop.

LYDIA. But you have not heard the worst. Unfortunately I had quarreled with my poor Beverley just before my aunt made the discovery, and I have not seen him since to make it up.

JULIA. What was his offence?

LYDIA. Nothing at all! But, I don't know how it was, as often as we had been together we had never had a quarrel! And, somehow, I was afraid he would never give me an opportunity. So last Thursday I wrote a letter to myself to inform myself that Beverley was at that time paying his addresses to another woman. I signed it *your friend unknown*, showed it to Beverley, charged him with his falsehood, put myself in a violent passion, and vowed I'd never see him more.

JULIA. And you let him depart so, and have not seen him since?

LYDIA. 'Twas the next day my aunt found the matter out. I intended only to have teased him three days and a half, and now I've lost him forever!

JULIA. If he is as deserving and sincere as you have represented him to me, he will never give you up so. Yet consider, Lydia, you tell me he is but an ensign, and you have thirty thousand pounds!

LYDIA. But you know I lose most of my fortune if I marry without my aunt's consent, till of age; and that is what I have determined to do ever since I knew the penalty. Nor would I love the man who would wish to wait a day for the alternative.

JULIA. Nay, this is caprice!

LYDIA. What, does Julia tax me with caprice? I thought her lover Faulkland had enured her to it.

JULIA. I do not love even *his* faults.

LYDIA. But a-propos—you have sent to him, I suppose?

JULIA. Not yet, upon my word, nor has he the least idea of my being in Bath. Sir Anthony's resolution was so sudden I could not inform him of it.

LYDIA. Well, Julia, you are your own mistress (though under the protection of Sir Anthony), yet have you for this long year been a slave to the caprice, the whim, the jealousy of this ungrateful Faulkland, who will ever delay assuming the right of a husband, while you suffer him to be equally imperious as a lover.

JULIA. Nay, you are wrong entirely. We were contracted before my father's death. That, and some consequent embarrassments, have delayed what I know to be my Faulkland's most ardent wish. He is too generous to trifle on such a point. And for his character, you wrong him there too. No, Lydia, he is too proud, too noble to be jealous: if he is captious, 'tis without dissembling; if fretful, without rudeness. Unused to the fopperies of love, he is negligent of the little duties expected from a lover— but being unhackneyed in the passion, his affection is ardent and sincere; and as it engrosses his whole soul, he expects every thought and emotion of his mistress to move in unison with his. Yet, though his pride calls for this full return, his humility makes him undervalue those qualities in him which would entitle him to it; and not feeling why he should be loved to the degree he wishes, he still suspects that he is not loved enough. This temper, I must own, has cost me many unhappy hours; but I have learned to think myself his debtor for those imperfections which arise from the ardour of his attachment.

LYDIA. Well, I cannot blame you for defending him. But tell me candidly, Julia, had he never saved your life, do you think you should have been attached to him as you are? Believe me, the rude blast that overset your boat was a prosperous gale of love to him.

JULIA. Gratitude may have strengthened my attachment to Mr. Faulkland, but I loved him before he had preserved me; yet surely that alone were an obligation sufficient—

LYDIA. Obligation! Why, a water-spaniel would have done as much! Well, I should never think of giving my heart to a man because he could swim!

JULIA. Come, Lydia, you are too inconsiderate.

LYDIA. Nay, I do but jest.—What's here?

[Enter Lucy in a hurry.]

LUCY. O Ma'am, here is Sir Anthony Absolute just come home with your aunt.

LYDIA. They'll not come here.—Lucy, do you watch.

[Exit Lucy]

JULIA. Yet I must go. Sir Anthony does not know I am here, and if we meet, he'll detain me, to show me the town. I'll take another opportunity of paying my respects to Mrs. Malaprop, when she shall treat me, as long as she chooses, with her select words so ingeniously *misapplied*, without being *mispronounced*.

[Re-enter Lucy.]

LUCY. O lud! Ma'am, they are both coming upstairs.

LYDIA. Well, I'll not detain you, coz. Adieu, my dear Julia. I'm sure you are in haste to send to Faulkland. There—through my room you'll find another staircase.

JULIA. Adieu.—[Embrace.]

[Exit Julia.]

LYDIA. Here, my dear Lucy, hide these books. Quick, quick! Fling *Peregrine Pickle* under the toilet— throw *Roderick Random* into the closet—put *The Innocent Adultery* into *The Whole Duty of Man*— thrust *Lord Aimworth* under the sofa—cram *Ovid* behind the bolster—there—put *The Man of Feeling* into your pocket—so, so,—now lay *Mrs. Chapone* in sight, and leave *Fordyce's Sermons* open on the table.

LUCY. Oh burn it, Ma'am! the hair-dresser has torn away as far as *Proper Pride*.

LYDIA. Never mind—open at *Sobriety*.—Fling me *Lord Chesterfield's Letters*.—Now for 'em.

[Enter Mrs. Malaprop, and Sir Anthony Absolute.]

MRS. MALAPROP. There, Sir Anthony, there sits the deliberate simpleton who wants to disgrace her family, and lavish herself on a fellow not worth a shilling!

LYDIA. Madam, I thought you once—

MRS. MALAPROP. You thought, Miss! I don't know any business you have to think at all. Thought does not become a young woman. But the point we would request of you is, that you will promise to forget this fellow—to illiterate him, I say, quite from your memory.

LYDIA. Ah! Madam! our memories are independent of our wills. It is not so easy to forget.

MRS. MALAPROP. But I say it is, Miss; there is nothing on earth so easy as to *forget*, if a person chooses to set about it. I'm sure I have so much forgot your poor dear uncle as if he had never existed—and I thought it my duty so to do; and let me tell you, Lydia, these violent memories don't become a young woman.

SIR ANTHONY. Why sure she won't pretend to remember what she's ordered not!—aye, this comes of her reading!

LYDIA. What crime, Madam, have I committed to be treated thus?

MRS. MALAPROP. Now don't attempt to extirpate yourself from the matter; you know I have proof controvertible of it. But tell me, will you promise to do as you're bid? Will you take a husband of your friend's choosing?

LYDIA. Madam, I must tell you plainly, that had I no preference for anyone else, the choice you have made would be my aversion.

MRS. MALAPROP. What business have you, Miss, with *preference* and *aversion*? They don't become a young woman; and you ought to know, that as both always wear off, 'tis safest in matrimony to begin with a little *aversion*. I am sure I hated your poor dear uncle before marriage as if he'd been a blackamoor—and yet, Miss, you are sensible what a wife I made!—and when it pleased heaven to release me from him, 'tis unknown what tears I shed! But suppose we were going to give you another choice, will you promise us to give up this Beverley?

LYDIA. Could I belie my thoughts so far as to give that promise, my actions would certainly as far belie my words.

MRS. MALAPROP. Take yourself to your room. You are fit company for nothing but your own ill-humours.

LYDIA. Willingly, Ma'am—I cannot change for the worse.

[*Exit Lydia.*]

MRS. MALAPROP. There's a little intricate hussy for you!

SIR ANTHONY. It is not to be wondered at, Ma'am—all this is the natural consequence of teaching girls to read. Had I a thousand daughters, by heaven! I'd as soon have them taught the black art as their alphabet!

MRS. MALAPROP. Nay, nay, Sir Anthony, you are an absolute misanthropy.

SIR ANTHONY. In my way hither, Mrs. Malaprop, I observed your niece's maid coming forth form a circulating library! She had a book in each hand—they were half-bound volumes, with marble covers! From that moment I guessed how full of duty I should see her mistress!

MRS. MALAPROP. Those are vile places, indeed!

SIR ANTHONY. Madam, a circulating library in a town is an evergreen tree of diabolical knowledge! It blossoms through the year! And depend on it, Mrs. Malaprop, that they who are so fond of handling the leaves, will long for the fruit at last.

MRS. MALAPROP. Fie, fie, Sir Anthony, you surely speak laconically!

SIR ANTHONY. Why, Mrs. Malaprop, in moderation, now, what would you have a woman know?

MRS. MALAPROP. Observe me, Sir Anthony. I would by no means wish a daughter of mine to be a progeny of learning; I don't think so much learning becomes a young woman; for instance—I would never let her meddle with Greek, or Hebrew, or Algebra, or Simony, or Fluxions, or Paradoxes, or such inflammatory branches of learning—neither would it be necessary for her to handle any of your mathematical, astronomical, diabolical instruments;—but, Sir Anthony, I would send her, at nine years old, to a boarding-school, in order to learn a little ingenuity and artifice. Then, Sir, she should have a supercilious knowledge in accounts—and as she grew up, I would have her instructed in geometry, that she might know something of the contagious countries—but above all, Sir Anthony, she should be mistress of orthodoxy, that she might not misspell, and mispronounce words so shamefully as girls usually do; and likewise that she might reprehend the true meaning of what she is saying. This, Sir Anthony, is what I would have a woman know—and I don't think there is a superstitious article in it.

SIR ANTHONY. Well, well, Mrs. Malaprop, I will dispute the point no further with you; though I must confess that you are a truly moderate and polite arguer, for almost every third word you say is on my side of the question. But, Mrs. Malaprop, to the more important point in debate—you say you have no objection to my proposal.

MRS. MALAPROP. None, I assure you. I am under no positive engagement with Mr. Acres, and as Lydia is so obstinate against him, perhaps your son may have better success.

SIR ANTHONY. Well, Madam, I will write for the boy directly. He knows not a syllable of this yet, though I have for some time had the proposal in my head. He is at present with his regiment.

MRS. MALAPROP. We have never seen your son, Sir Anthony; but I hope no objection on his side.

SIR ANTHONY. Objection!—let him object if he dare! No, No, Mrs. Malaprop, Jack knows that the least demur puts me in a frenzy directly. My process was always very simple—in their young days, 'twas "Jack do this";—if he demurred—I knocked him down—and if he grumbled at that—I always sent him out of the room.

MRS. MALAPROP. Aye, and the properest way, o' my conscience!—nothing is so conciliating to young people as severity. Well, Sir Anthony, I shall give Mr. Acres his discharge, and prepare Lydia to receive your son's invocations; and I hope you will represent *her* to the Captain as an object not altogether illegible.

SIR ANTHONY. Madam, I will handle the subject prudently. Well, I must leave you—and let me beg you, Mrs. Malaprop, to enforce this matter roundly to the girl; take my advice—keep a tight hand; if she rejects this proposal—clap her under lock and key—and if you were just to let the servants forget to bring her dinner for three or four days, you can't conceive how she'd come about!

[Exit Sir Anthony.]

MRS. MALAPROP. Well, at any rate I shall be glad to get her from under my intuition. She has somehow discovered my partiality for Sir Lucius O'Trigger—sure, Lucy can't have betrayed me! No, the girl is such a simpleton, I should have made her confess it.—[Calls.] Lucy!—Lucy—Had she been one of your artificial ones, I should never have trusted her.

[Enter Lucy]

LUCY. Did you call, Ma'am?

MRS. MALAPROP. Yes, girl. Did you see Sir Lucius while you was out?

LUCY. No, indeed, Ma'am, not a glimpse of him.

MRS. MALAPROP. You are sure, Lucy, that you never mentioned—

LUCY. O Gemini! I'd sooner cut my tongue out.

MRS. MALAPROP. Well, don't let your simplicity be imposed on.

LUCY. No, Ma'am.

MRS. MALAPROP. So, come to me presently, and I'll give you another letter to Sir Lucius; but mind, Lucy—if ever you betray what you are intrusted with (unless it be other people's secret to me) you forfeit my malevolence forever, and your being a simpleton shall be no excuse for your locality.

[Exit Mrs. Malaprop.]

LUCY. Ha! ha! ha!—So, my dear *simplicity*, let me give you a little respite—[*altering her manner*]—let girls in my station be as fond as they please of appearing expert, and knowing in their trusts—commend me to a mask of *silliness*, and a pair of sharp eyes for my own interest under it! Let me see to what account have I turned my *simplicity* lately—[*looks at a paper.*] For *abetting Miss Lydia Languish in a design of running away with an Ensign!—in money—sundry times—twelve pound twelve—gowns, five—hats, ruffles, caps, &c., &c.—numberless! From the said Ensign, within this last month, six guineas and a half.*—About a quarter's pay!—Item, *from Mrs. Malaprop, for betraying the young people to her*—when I found matters were likely to be discovered—*two guineas, and a black paduasoy.*—Item, *from Mr. Acres, for carrying divers letters*—which I never delivered—*two guineas, and a pair of buckles.*—Item, *from Sir Lucius O'Trigger—three crowns—two gold pocket-pieces—and a silver snuffbox!*—Well done, *simplicity!*—Yet I was forced to make my Hibernian believe that he was corresponding, not with the *aunt!*, but with the *niece*: for, though not overrich, I found he had too much pride and delicacy to sacrifice the feelings of a gentleman to the necessities of his fortune.

[Exit.]

Act II

SCENE I

Captain Absolute's lodgings.

[Captain Absolute and Fag.]

FAG. Sir, while I was there Sir Anthony came in; I told him you had sent me to inquire after his health, and to know if he was at leisure to see you.

ABSOLUTE. And what did he say on hearing I was at Bath?

FAG. Sir, in my life I never saw an elderly gentleman

more astonished! He started back two or three paces, rapped out a dozen interjectoral oaths, and asked what the devil had brought you here!

ABSOLUTE. Well, Sir, and what did you say?

FAG. Oh, I lied, Sir—I forget the precise lie; but you may depend on't, he got no truth from me. Yet, with submission, for fear of blunders in future, I should be glad to fix what *has* brought us to Bath, in order that we may lie a little consistently. Sir Anthony's servants were curious, Sir, very curious indeed.

ABSOLUTE. You have said nothing to them?

FAG. Oh, not a word, Sir—not a word. Mr. Thomas, indeed, the coachman (whom I take to be the discreetest of whips)—

ABSOLUTE. 'Sdeath!—you rascal! you have not trusted him!

FAG. Oh, *no*, Sir!—no—no—not a syllable, upon my veracity! He was, indeed, a little inquisitive; but I was sly, Sir—devilish sly!—My master (said I), honest Thomas (you know, Sir, one says *honest* to one's inferiors), is come to Bath to *recruit*—yes, Sir—I said, *to recruit*—and whether for men, money, or constitution, you know, Sir, is nothing to him, nor anyone else.

ABSOLUTE. Well—*recruit* will do—let it be so—

FAG. Oh, Sir, recruit will do surprisingly—indeed, to give the thing an air, I told Thomas that your Honour had already enlisted five disbanded chairmen, seven minority waiters, and thirteen billiard markers.

ABSOLUTE. You blockhead, never say more than is necessary.

FAG. I beg pardon, Sir—I beg pardon—But with submission, a lie is nothing unless one supports it. Sir, whenever I draw on my invention for a good current lie, I always forge indorsements, as well as the bill.

ABSOLUTE. Well, take care you don't hurt your credit by offering too much security. Is Mr. Faulkland returned?

FAG. He is above, Sir, changing his dress.

ABSOLUTE. Can you tell whether he has been informed of Sir Anthony's and Miss Melville's arrival?

FAG. I fancy not, Sir; he has seen no one since he came in but his gentleman, who was with him at Bristol.—I think, Sir, I hear Mr. Faulkland coming down—

ABSOLUTE. Go tell him I am here.

FAG. Yes, Sir [*going*]. I beg pardon, Sir, but should Sir Anthony call, you will do me the favor to remember that we are *recruiting*, if you please.

ABSOLUTE. Well, well.

FAG. And in tenderness to my character, if your Honour could bring in the chairmen and waiters, I shall esteem it as an obligation; for though I never scruple a lie to serve my master, yet it hurts one's conscience to be found out.

[*Exit.*]

ABSOLUTE. Now for my whimsical friend—if he does not know that his mistress is here, I'll tease him a little before I tell him—

[*Enter Faulkland.*]

Faulkland, you're welcome to Bath again; you are punctual in your return.

FAULKLAND. Yes; I had nothing to detain me when I had finished the business I went on. Well, what news since I left you? How stand matters between you and Lydia?

ABSOLUTE. Faith, much as they were; I have not seen her since our quarrel; however, I expect to be recalled every hour.

FAULKLAND. Why don't you persuade her to go off with you at once?

ABSOLUTE. What, and lose two-thirds of her fortune? You forget that, my friend. No, no, I could have brought her to that long ago.

FAULKLAND. Nay then, you trifle too long—if you are sure of *her*, propose to the aunt *in your own character*, and write to Sir Anthony for his consent.

ABSOLUTE. Softly, softly, for though I am convinced my little Lydia would elope with me as Ensign Beverley, yet am I by no means certain that she would take me with the impediment of our friend's consent, a regular humdrum wedding, and the reversion of a good fortune on my side; no, no, I must prepare her gradually for the discovery, and make myself necessary to her, before I risk it.—Well, Faulkland, you'll dine with us to-day at the hotel?

FAULKLAND. Indeed, I cannot: I am not in spirits to be of such a party.

ABSOLUTE. By heavens! I shall forswear your company. You are the most teasing, captious, incorrigible lover! Do love like a man!

FAULKLAND. I own I am unfit for company.

ABSOLUTE. Am not *I* a lover; aye, and a romantic one too? Yet do I carry everywhere with me such a confounded farrago of doubts, fears, hopes, wishes, and all the flimsy furniture of a country miss's brain!

FAULKLAND. Ah! Jack, your heart and soul are not, like mine, fixed immutably on one only object. You throw for a large stake, but losing—you would stake, and throw again. But I have set my sum of happiness on this cast, and not to succeed were to be stripped of all.

ABSOLUTE. But, for heaven's sake! what grounds for apprehension can your whimsical brain conjure up at present?

FAULKLAND. What grounds for apprehension did you say? Heavens! are there not a thousand! I fear for her spirits—her health—her life. My absence may fret her; her anxiety for my return, her fears for me, may oppress her gentle temper. And for her health—does not every hour bring me cause to be alarmed? If it rains, some shower may even then have chilled her delicate frame! If the wind be keen, some rude blast may have affected her! The heat of noon, the dews of the evening, may endanger the life of her, for whom only I value mine. O! Jack, when delicate and feeling souls are separated, there is not a feature in the sky, not a movement of the elements, not an aspiration of the breeze, but hints some cause for a lover's apprehension!

ABSOLUTE. Aye, but we may choose whether we will take the hint or not. So then, Faulkland, if you were convinced that Julia were well and in spirits, you would be entirely content?

FAULKLAND. I should be happy beyond measure—I am anxious only for that.

ABSOLUTE. Then to cure your anxiety at once—Miss Melville is in perfect health, and is at this moment in Bath!

FAULKLAND. Nay, Jack—don't trifle with me.

ABSOLUTE. She is arrived here with my father within this hour.

FAULKLAND. Can you be serious?

ABSOLUTE. I thought you knew Sir Anthony better than to be surprised at a sudden whim of this kind. Seriously then, it is as I tell you—upon my honour.

FAULKLAND. My dear friend!—Hollo, DuPeigne! my hat—my dear Jack—now nothing on earth can give me a moment's uneasiness.

[Enter Fag.]

FAG. Sir, Mr. Acres just arrived is below.

ABSOLUTE. Stay, Faulkland, this Acres lives within a mile of Sir Anthony, and he shall tell you how your mistress has been ever since you left her.—Fag, show the gentleman up.

[Exit Fag.]

FAULKLAND. What, is he much acquainted in the family?

ABSOLUTE. Oh, very intimate. I insist on your not going: besides, his character will divert you.

FAULKLAND. Well, I should like to ask him a few questions.

ABSOLUTE. He is likewise a rival of mine—that is of my *other self's*, for he does not think his friend Captain Absolute ever saw the lady in question; and it is ridiculous enough to hear him complain to me of *one Beverley*, a concealed skulking rival, who—

FAULKLAND. Hush! He's here.

[Enter Acres.]

ACRES. Hah! my dear friend, noble captain, and honest Jack, how dost thou? Just arrived, faith, as you see. Sir, your humble servant. Warm work on the roads, Jack!—Odds whips and wheels! I've travelled like a comet, with a tail of dust all the way as long as the Mall.

ABSOLUTE. Ah! Bob, you are indeed an eccentric planet, but we know your attraction hither. Give me leave to introduce Mr. Faulkland to you; Mr. Faulkland, Mr. Acres.

ACRES. Sir, I am most heartily glad to see you: Sir, I solicit your connexions.—Hey, Jack—what—this is Mr. Faulkland, who—?

ABSOLUTE. Aye, Bob, Miss Melville's Mr. Faulkland.

ACRES. Odd so! she and your father can be but just arrived before me—I suppose you have seen them Ah! Mr. Faulkland, you are indeed a happy man.

FAULKLAND. I have not seen Miss Melville yet, Sir. I hope she enjoyed full health and spirits in Devonshire?

ACRES. Never knew her better in my life, Sir—never better. Odds blushes and blooms! she has been as healthy as the German Spa.

FAULKLAND. Indeed! I did hear that she had been a little indisposed.

ACRES. False, false, Sir—only said to vex you: quite the reverse, I assure you.

FAULKLAND. There, Jack, you see she has the advantage of me; I had almost fretted myself ill.

ABSOLUTE. Now are you angry with your mistress for not having been sick.

FAULKLAND. No, no, you misunderstood me: yet surely a little trifling indisposition is not an unnatural consequence of absence from those we love. Now confess—isn't there something unkind in this violent, robust, unfeeling health?

ABSOLUTE. Oh, it was very unkind of her to be well in your absence, to be sure!

ACRES. Good apartments, Jack.

FAULKLAND. Well, Sir, but you were saying that Miss Melville has been so *exceedingly* well—what, then she has been merry and gay, I suppose? Always in spirits—hey?

ACRES. Merry! Odds crickets! she has been the belle and spirit of the company wherever she has been—so lively and entertaining! so full of wit and humour!

FAULKLAND. There, Jack, there! Oh, by my soul! there is an innate levity in woman, that nothing can overcome. What! happy, and I away!

ABSOLUTE. Have done—how foolish this is! Just now you were only apprehensive for your mistress's *spirits*.

FAULKLAND. Why, Jack, have I been the joy and spirit of the company?

ABSOLUTE. No, indeed, you have not.

FAULKLAND. Have I been lively and entertaining?

ABSOLUTE. Oh, upon my word, I acquit you.

FAULKLAND. Have I been full of wit and humour?

ABSOLUTE. No, faith; to do you justice, you have been confoundedly stupid indeed.

ACRES. What's the matter with the gentleman?

ABSOLUTE. He is only expressing his great satisfaction at hearing that Julia has been so well and happy—that's all—hey, Faulkland?

FAULKLAND. Oh! I am rejoiced to hear it—yes, yes, she has a *happy* disposition!

ACRES. That she has indeed. Then she is so accomplished—so sweet a voice—so expert at her harpsichord—such a mistress of flat and sharp, squallante, rumblante, and quiverante! There was this time month—Odds minims and crotchets! how she did chirrup at Mrs. Piano's concert!

FAULKLAND. There again, what say you to this? You see she has been all mirth and song—not a thought of me!

ABSOLUTE. Pho! man, is not music the food of love?

FAULKLAND. Well, well, it may be so.—Pray, Mr.— what's his d—d name? Do you remember what songs Miss Melville sung?

ACRES. Not I, indeed.

ABSOLUTE. Stay now, they were some pretty, melancholy, purling-stream airs, I warrant; perhaps you may recollect; did she sing *"When absent from my soul's delight"*?

ACRES. No, that wa'nt it.

ABSOLUTE. Or *"Go, gentle gales"*?—*"Go, gentle gales!"* [*Sings.*]

ACRES. Oh no! nothing like it. Odds! now I recollect one of them—*"My heart's my own, my will is free."*

[*Sings.*]

FAULKLAND. Fool! fool that I am! to fix all my happiness on such a trifler! 'Sdeath! to make herself the pipe and ballad-monger of a circle! to soothe her light heart with catches and glees! What can you say to this, Sir?

ABSOLUTE. Why, that I should be glad to hear my mistress had been so merry, *Sir*.

FAULKLAND. Nay, nay, nay—I am not sorry that she has been happy—no, no, I am glad of that—I would not have had her sad or sick—yet surely a sympathetic heart would have shown itself even in the choice of a song: she might have been temperately healthy, and, somehow, plaintively gay; but she has been dancing too, I doubt not!

ACRES. What does the gentleman say about dancing?

ABSOLUTE. He says the lady we speak of dances as well as she sings.

ACRES. Aye, truly, does she—there was at our last race-ball—

FAULKLAND. Hell and the devil! There! there!—I told you so! I told you so! Oh! she thrives in my absence! Dancing! But her whole feelings have been in opposition with mine! I have been anxious, silent, pensive, sedentary—my days have been hours of care, my nights of watchfulness. She has been all Health! Spirit! Laugh! Song! Dance! Oh! d—n'd, d—n'd levity!

ABSOLUTE. For heaven's sake! Faulkland, don't expose yourself so. Suppose she has danced, what then? Does not the ceremony of society often oblige—

FAULKLAND. Well, well, I'll contain myself. Perhaps, as you say, for form sake. What, Mr. Acres, you were praising Miss Melville's manner of dancing a *minuet*—hey?

ACRES. Oh I dare insure her for that—but what I was going to speak of was her *country dancing*. Odds swimmings! she has such an air with her!

FAULKLAND. Now disappointment on her! Defend this, Absolute, why don't you defend this? Country-dances! jigs, and reels! Am I to blame now? A minuet I could have forgiven—I should not have minded that—I say I should not have regarded a minuet—but *country-dances*! Z—ds! had she made one in a cotillion—I believe I could have forgiven even that—but to be monkey-led for a night! to run the gauntlet through a string of amorous palming puppies! to show paces like a managed filly! O Jack, there never can be but *one* man in the world whom a truly modest and delicate woman ought to pair with in a *country-dance*; and even then, the rest of the couples should be her great uncles and aunts!

ABSOLUTE. Aye, to be sure!—grandfathers and grandmothers!

FAULKLAND. If there be but one vicious mind in the Set, 'twill spread like a contagion—the action of their pulse beats to the lascivious movement of the jig—their quivering, warm-breathed sighs impregnate the very air—the atmosphere becomes electrical to love, and each amorous spark darts through every link of the chain! I must leave you—I own I am somewhat flurried—and that confounded looby has perceived it. [*Going.*]

ABSOLUTE. Nay, but stay, Faulkland, and thank Mr. Acres for his good news.

FAULKLAND. D—n his news!

[*Exit Faulkland.*]

ABSOLUTE. Ha! ha! ha! Poor Faulkland! Five minutes since—"nothing on earth could give him a moment's uneasiness!"

ACRES. The gentleman wa'n't angry at my praising his mistress, was he?

ABSOLUTE. A little jealous, I believe, Bob.

ACRES. You don't say so? Ha! ha! jealous of me?—that's a good joke.

ABSOLUTE. There's nothing strange in that, Bob: let me tell you, that sprightly grace and insinuating manner of yours will do some mischief among the girls here.

ACRES. Ah! you joke—ha! ha!—mischief—ha! ha! But you know I am not my own property; my dear Lydia has forestalled me. She could never abide me in the country, because I used to dress so badly—but odds frogs and tambours! I shan't take matters so here—now ancient madam has no voice in it. I'll make my old clothes know who's master. I shall straightway cashier the hunting-frock, and render my leather breeches incapable. My hair has been in training some time.

ABSOLUTE. Indeed!

ACRES. Aye—and tho'ff the side curls are a little restive, my hindpart takes to it very kindly.

ABSOLUTE. O, you'll polish, I doubt not.

ACRES. Absolutely, I propose so. Then if I find out this Ensign Beverley, odds triggers and flints! I'll make him know the difference o't.

ABSOLUTE. Spoke like a man—but pray, Bob, I observe you have got an odd kind of a new method of swearing—

ACRES. Ha! ha! you've taken notice of it? 'Tis genteel, isn't it? I didn't invent it myself, though; but a commander in our militia—a great scholar, I assure you—says that there is no meaning in the common oaths, and that nothing but their antiquity makes them respectable, because, he says, the ancients would never stick to an oath or two, but would say, by Jove! or by Bacchus! or by Mars! or by Venus! or by Pallas! according to the sentiment; so that to swear with propriety, says my little major, the "oath should be an echo to the sense"; and this we call the *oath referential*, or *sentimental swearing*—ha! ha! ha! 'tis genteel, isn't it?

ABSOLUTE. Very genteel, and very new, indeed—and I dare say will supplant all other figures of imprecation.

ACRES. Aye, aye, the best terms will grow obsolete. Damns have had their day.

[*Enter Fag.*]

FAG. Sir, there is a gentleman below desires to see you. Shall I show him into the parlour?

ABSOLUTE. Aye—you may.

ACRES. Well, I must be gone—

ABSOLUTE. Stay; who is it, Fag?

FAG. Your father, Sir.

ABSOLUTE. You puppy, why didn't you show him up directly?

[*Exit Fag.*]

ACRES. You have business with Sir Anthony. I expect a message from Mrs. Malaprop at my lodgings. I have sent also to my dear friend, Sir Lucius O'Trigger. Adieu, Jack! We must meet at night, when you shall give me a dozen bumpers to little Lydia.

ABSOLUTE. That I will, with all my heart.

[*Exit Acres.*]

Now for a parental lecture. I hope he has heard nothing of the business that has brought me here. I wish the gout had held him fast in Devonshire, with all my soul!

[*Enter Sir Anthony.*]

Sir, I am delighted to see you here; and looking so well! Your sudden arrival at Bath made me apprehensive for your health.

SIR ANTHONY. Very apprehensive, I dare say, Jack. What, you are recruiting here, hey?

ABSOLUTE. Yes, Sir, I am on duty.

SIR ANTHONY. Well, Jack, I am glad to see you, though I did not expect it, for I was going to write to you on a little matter of business. Jack, I have been considering that I grow old and infirm, and shall probably not trouble you long.

ABSOLUTE. Pardon me, Sir, I never saw you look more strong and hearty; and I pray frequently that you may continue so.

SIR ANTHONY. I hope your prayers may be heard with all my heart. Well then, Jack, I have been considering that I am so strong and hearty, I may continue to plague you a long time. Now, Jack, I am sensible that the income of your commission, and what I have hitherto allowed you, is but a small pittance for a lad of your spirit.

ABSOLUTE. Sir, you are very good.

SIR ANTHONY. And it is my wish, while yet I live, to have my boy make some figure in the world. I have resolved, therefore, to fix you at once in a noble independence.

ABSOLUTE. Sir, your kindness overpowers me—such generosity makes the gratitude of reason more lively than the sensations even of filial affection.

SIR ANTHONY. I am glad you are so sensible of my attention—and you shall be master of a large estate in a few weeks.

ABSOLUTE. Let my future life, Sir, speak my gratitude: I cannot express the sense I have of your munificence. Yet, Sir, I presume you would not wish me to quit the army?

SIR ANTHONY. Oh, that shall be as your wife chooses.

ABSOLUTE. My wife, Sir!

SIR ANTHONY. Aye, aye—settle that between you— settle that between you.

ABSOLUTE. A *wife*, Sir, did you say?

SIR ANTHONY. Aye, a wife—why; did not I mention her before?

ABSOLUTE. Not a word of her, Sir.

SIR ANTHONY. Odd so!—I mus'n't forget *her*, though. Yes, Jack, the independence I was talking of is by a marriage—the fortune is saddled with a wife—but I suppose that makes no difference.

ABSOLUTE. Sir! Sir!—you amaze me!

SIR ANTHONY. Why, what the devil's the matter with the fool? Just now you were all gratitude and duty.

ABSOLUTE. I was, Sir—you talked to me of independence and a fortune, but not a word of a wife.

SIR ANTHONY. Why—what difference does that make? Odd's life, Sir! if you have the estate, you must take it with the live stock on it, as it stands.

ABSOLUTE. If my happiness is to be the price, I must beg leave to decline the purchase. Pray, Sir, who is the lady?

SIR ANTHONY. What's that to you, Sir? Come, give me your promise to love, and to marry her directly.

ABSOLUTE. Sure, Sir, this is not very reasonable, to summon my affections for a lady I know nothing of!

SIR ANTHONY. I am sure, Sir,'tis more unreasonable in you to *object* to a lady you know nothing if.

ABSOLUTE. Then, Sir, I must tell you plainly that my inclinations are fixed on another—my heart is engaged to an angel.

SIR ANTHONY. Then pray let it send an excuse. It is very sorry—but *business* prevents its waiting on her.

ABSOLUTE. But my vows are pledged to her.

SIR ANTHONY. Let her foreclose, Jack; let her foreclose; they are not worth redeeming: besides, you have the angel's vows in exchange, I suppose; so there can be no loss there.

ABSOLUTE. You must excuse me, Sir, if I tell you, once for all, that in this point I cannot obey you.

SIR ANTHONY. Hark'ee, Jack: I have heard you for some time with patience—I have been cool—quite cool; but take care—you know I am compliance itself when I am not thwarted—no one more easily led when I have my own way; but don't put me in a frenzy.

ABSOLUTE. Sir, I must repeat it—in this I cannot obey you.

SIR ANTHONY. Now, d—n me! if ever I call you *Jack* again while I live!

ABSOLUTE. Nay, Sir, but hear me.

SIR ANTHONY. Sir, I won't hear a word—not a word! not one word! so give me your promise by a nod— and I'll tell you what, Jack—I mean, you dog—if you don't, by—

ABSOLUTE. What, Sir, promise to link myself to some mass of ugliness! to—

SIR ANTHONY. Z—ds! Sirrah! the lady shall be as ugly as I choose: she shall have a hump on each shoulder; she shall be as crooked as the Crescent; her one eye shall roll like the Bull's in Cox's Museum—she shall have a skin like a mummy, and the beard of a Jew— she shall be all this, Sirrah!—yet I'll make you ogle her all day, and sit up all night to write sonnets on her beauty.

ABSOLUTE. This is reason and moderation indeed!

SIR ANTHONY. None of your sneering, puppy! no grinning, jackanapes!

ABSOLUTE. Indeed, Sir, I never was in a worse humour for mirth in my life.

SIR ANTHONY. 'Tis false, Sir! I know you are laughing in your sleeve; I know you'll grin when I am gone, Sirrah!

ABSOLUTE. Sir, I hope I know my duty better.

SIR ANTHONY. None of your passion, Sir! none of your violence! if you please. It won't do with me, I promise you.

ABSOLUTE. Indeed, Sir, I never was cooler in my life.

SIR ANTHONY. 'Tis a confounded lie!—I know you are in a passion in your heart; I know you are, you hypocritical young dog! But it won't do.

ABSOLUTE. Nay, Sir, upon my word.

SIR ANTHONY. So you will fly out! Can't you be cool, like me? What the devil good can *passion* do! *Passion* is of no service, you impudent, insolent, overbearing reprobate!—There you sneer again! don't provoke me! But you rely upon the mildness of my temper—you do, you dog! you play upon the meekness of my disposition! Yet take care—the patience of a saint may be overcome at last!—but mark! I give you six hours and a half to consider of this: if you then agree, without any condition, to do everything on earth that I choose, why—confound you! I may in time forgive you. If not, z—ds! don't enter the same hemisphere with me! don't dare to breathe the same air, or use the same light with me; but get an atmosphere and a sun of your own! I'll strip you of your commission; I'll lodge a five-and-threepence in the hands of trustees, and you shall live on the interest. I'll disown you, I'll disinherit you, I'll unget you! and—d—n me, if ever I call you Jack again!

[*Exit Sir Anthony.*]

[*Absolute solus.*]

ABSOLUTE. Mild, gentle, considerate Father—I kiss your hands. What a tender method of giving his opinion in these matters Sir Anthony has! I dare not trust him with the truth. I wonder what old wealthy hag it is that he wants to bestow on me! Yet he married himself for love! and was in his youth a bold intriguer, and a gay companion!

[*Enter Fag.*]

FAG. Assuredly, Sir, our father is wrath to a degree; he comes downstairs eight or ten steps at a time—

muttering, growling, and thumping the bannisters all the way: I, and the cook's dog, stand bowing at the door—rap! he gives me a stroke on the head with his cane; bids me carry that to my master; then kicking the poor turnspit into the area, d—ns us all for a puppy triumvirate! Upon my credit, Sir, were I in your place, and found my father such very bad company, I should certainly drop his acquaintance.

ABSOLUTE. Cease your impertinence, Sir, at present. Did you come in for nothing more? Stand out of the way!

[*Pushes him aside, and exit.*]

[*Fag solus.*]

FAG. Soh! Sir Anthony trims my master. He is afraid to reply to his father—then vents his spleen on poor Fag! When one is vexed by one person, to revenge one's self on another who happens to come in the way is the vilest injustice. Ah! it shows the worst temper—the basest—

[*Enter Errand Boy.*]

BOY. Mr. Fag! Mr. Fag! your master calls you.

FAG. Well, you little dirty puppy, you need not bawl so!—The meanest disposition! the—

BOY. Quick, quick, Mr. Fag.

FAG. *Quick, quick!*, you impudent jackanapes! am I to be commanded by you too? you little, impertinent, insolent, kitchen-bred—

[*Exit, kicking and beating him.*]

SCENE II

The North Parade.

[*Enter Lucy.*]

LUCY. So—I shall have another rival to add to my mistress's list—Captain Absolute. However, I shall not enter his name till my purse has received notice in form. Poor Acres is dismissed! Well, I have done him a last friendly office in letting him know that Beverley was here before him. Sir Lucius is generally more punctual when he expects to hear from his *dear Dalia*, as he calls her: I wonder he's not here! I have a little scruple of conscience from this deceit;

though I should not be paid so well, if my hero knew that *Delia* was near fifty, and her own mistress.

[*Enter Sir Lucius O'Trigger.*]

SIR LUCIUS. Hah! my little embassadress—upon my conscience, I have been looking for you; I have been on the South Parade this half-hour.

LUCY. [*speaking simply.*] O Gemini! and I have been waiting for your worship here on the North.

SIR LUCIUS. Faith—maybe that was the reason we did not meet; and it is very comical, too, how you could go out and I not see you—for I was only taking a nap at the Parade Coffee-house, and I chose the *window* on purpose that I might not miss you.

LUCY. My stars! Now I'd wager a sixpence I went by while you were asleep.

SIR LUCIUS. Sure enough it must have been so—and I never dreamt it was so late, till I waked. Well, but my little girl, have you got nothing for me?

LUCY. Yes, but I have: I've got a letter for you in my pocket.

SIR LUCIUS. Oh faith! I guessed you weren't come empty-handed—well—let me see what the dear creature says.

LUCY. There, Sir Lucius. [*Gives him a letter.*]

SIR LUCIUS. [*reads.*] *Sir—there is often a sudden incentive impulse in love, that has a greater induction than years of domestic combination: such was the commotion I felt at the first superfluous view of Sir Lucius O'Trigger.*—Very pretty, upon my word.—*Female punctuation forbids me to say more; yet let me add, that it will give me joy infallible to find Sir Lucius worthy the last criterion of my affections.* DELIA. Upon my conscience! Lucy, your lady is a great mistress of language. Faith, she's quite the queen of the dictionary!—for the devil a word dare refuse coming at her call—though one would think it was quite out of hearing.

LUCY. Aye, Sir, a lady of her experience—

SIR LUCIUS. Experience! what, at seventeen?

LUCY. O true, Sir—but then she reads so—my stars! how she will read off-hand!

SIR LUCIUS. Faith, she must be very deep read to write this way—though she is rather an arbitrary writer too—for here are a great many poor words pressed into the service of this note, that would get their *habeas corpus* from any court in Christendom.

LUCY. Ah! Sir Lucius, if you were to hear how she talks of you!

SIR LUCIUS. Oh tell her I'll make her the best husband in the world, and Lady O'Trigger into the bargain! But we must get the old gentlewoman's consent—and do everything fairly.

LUCY. Nay, Sir Lucius, I thought you wa'n't rich enough to be so nice!

SIR LUCIUS. Upon my word, young woman, you have hit it: I am so poor that I can't afford to do a dirty action. If I did not want money I'd steal your mistress and her fortune with a great deal of pleasure. However, my pretty girl [*gives her money*] , here's a little something to buy you a ribband; and meet me in the evening, and I'll give you an answer to this. So, hussy, take a kiss beforehand to put you in mind.

[*Kisses her.*]

LUCY. O lud! Sir Lucius—I never seed such a gemman! My lady won't like you if you're so impudent.

SIR LUCIUS. Faith she will, Lucy—That same—pho! what's the name of it?—*Modesty!*—is a quality in a lover more praised by the women than liked; so, if your mistress asks you whether Sir Lucius ever gave you a kiss, tell her *fifty*—my dear.

LUCY. What, would you have me tell her a lie?

SIR LUCIUS. Ah, then, you baggage! I'll make it a truth presently.

LUCY. For shame now; here is someone coming.

SIR LUCIUS. Oh faith, I'll quiet your conscience.

[*Sees Fag.—Exit, humming a tune.*]

[*Enter Fag.*]

FAG. So, so, Ma'am. I humbly beg pardon.

LUCY. O lud!—now, Mr. Fag, you flurry one so.

FAG. Come, come, Lucy, here's no one by—so a little less simplicity, with a grain or two more sincerity, if you please. You play false with us, Madam. I saw you give the baronet a letter. My master shall know this, and if he don't call him out—I will.

LUCY. Ha! ha! ha! you gentlemen's gentlemen are so hasty. That letter was from Mrs. Malaprop, simpleton. She is taken with Sir Lucius's address.

FAG. How! what tastes some people have! Why, I suppose I have walked by her window an hundred times. But what says our young lady? Any message to my master?

LUCY. Sad news, Mr. Fag! A worse rival than Acres! Sir Anthony Absolute has proposed his son.

FAG. What, Captain Absolute?

LUCY. Even so. I overheard it all.

FAG. Ha! ha! ha!—very good, faith. Good-bye, Lucy, I must away with this news.

LUCY. Well—you may laugh, but it is true, I assure you. [*Going.*] But—Mr. Fag—tell your master not to be cast down by this.

FAG. Oh, he'll be so disconsolate!

LUCY. And charge him not to think of quarrelling with young Absolute.

FAG. Never fear!—never fear!

LUCY. Be sure—bid him keep up his spirits.

FAG. We will—we will.

[*Exeunt severally.*]

Act III

SCENE I

The North Parade.

[*Enter Absolute.*]

ABSOLUTE. 'Tis just as Fag told me, indeed. Whimsical enough, faith! My father wants to *force* me to marry the very girl I am plotting to run away with! He must not know of my connexion with her yet awhile. He has too summary a method of proceeding in these matters. However, I'll read my recantation instantly. My conversion is something sudden, indeed, but I can assure him it is very *sincere.*—So, so—here he comes. He looks plaguy gruff. [*Steps aside.*]

[*Enter Sir Anthony.*]

SIR ANTHONY. No—I'll die sooner than forgive him. *Die,* did I say? I'll live these fifty years to plague him. At our last meeting, his impudence had almost put me out of temper. An obstinate, passionate, self-willed boy! Who can he take after? This is my return for getting him before all his brothers and sisters!—for putting him, at twelve years old, into a marching regiment, and allowing him fifty pounds a year, beside his pay ever since! But I have done with him; he's anybody's son for me. I never will see him more—never—never—never—never!

ABSOLUTE. Now for a penitential face.

SIR ANTHONY. Fellow, get out of my way.

ABSOLUTE. Sir, you see a penitent before you.

SIR ANTHONY. I see an impudent scoundrel before me.

ABSOLUTE. A sincere penitent. I am come, Sir, to acknowledge my error, and to submit entirely to your will.

SIR ANTHONY. What's that?

ABSOLUTE. I have been revolving, and reflecting, and considering on your past goodness, and kindness, and condescension to me.

SIR ANTHONY. Well, Sir?

ABSOLUTE. I have been likewise weighing and balancing what you were pleased to mention concerning duty, and obedience, and authority.

SIR ANTHONY. Well, puppy?

ABSOLUTE. Why, then, Sir, the result of my reflections is—a resolution to sacrifice every inclination of my own to your satisfaction.

SIR ANTHONY. Why, now you talk sense—absolute sense—I never heard anything more sensible in my life. Confound you, you shall be *Jack* again!

ABSOLUTE. I am happy in the appellation.

SIR ANTHONY. Why then, Jack, my dear Jack, I will now inform you who the lady really is. Nothing but your passion and violence, you silly fellow, prevented my telling you at first. Prepare, Jack, for wonder and rapture! prepare! What think you of Miss Lydia Languish?

ABSOLUTE. Languish! What, the Languishes of Worcestershire?

SIR ANTHONY. Worcestershire! No. Did you never meet Mrs. Malaprop and her niece, Miss Languish, who came into our country just before you were last ordered to your regiment?

ABSOLUTE. Malaprop! Languish! I don't remember ever to have heard the names before. Yet, stay—I think I do recollect something.—*Languish! Languish!* She squints, don't she? A little, red-haired girl?

SIR ANTHONY. Squints? A red-haired girl! Z—ds, no!

ABSOLUTE. Then I must have forgot; it can't be the same person.

SIR ANTHONY. Jack! Jack! what think you of blooming, love-breathing seventeen?

ABSOLUTE. As to that, Sir, I am quite indifferent. If I can please you in the matter, 'tis all I desire.

SIR ANTHONY. Nay, but Jack, such eyes! such eyes! so innocently wild! so bashfully irresolute! Not a glance but speaks and kindles some thought of love! Then, Jack, her cheeks! her cheeks, Jack! so deeply blushing at the insinuations of her tell-tale eyes! Then, Jack, her lips!—O Jack, lips smiling at their own discretion; and if not smiling, more sweetly pouting, more lovely in sullenness!

ABSOLUTE. [aside.] That's she, indeed. Well done, old gentleman!

SIR ANTHONY. Then, Jack, her neck!—O Jack! Jack!

ABSOLUTE. And which is to be mine, Sir, the niece of the aunt?

SIR ANTHONY. Why, you unfeeling, insensible puppy, I despise you! When I was of your age, such a description would have made me fly like a rocket! The *aunt*, indeed! Odd's life! when I ran away with your mother, I would not have touched anything old or ugly to gain an empire.

ABSOLUTE. Not to please your father, Sir?

SIR ANTHONY. To please my father! Z—ds! not to please—Oh, my father!—Odd so!—yes—yes!—if my father, indeed, had desired—that's quite another matter. Though he wa'n't the indulgent father that I am, Jack.

ABSOLUTE. I dare say not, Sir.

SIR ANTHONY. But, Jack, you are not sorry to find your mistress is so beautiful?

ABSOLUTE. Sir, I repeat it; if I please you in this affair, 'tis all I desire. Not that I think a woman the worse for being handsome; but, Sir, if you please to recollect, you before hinted something about a hump or two, one eye, and a few more graces of that kind. Now, without being very nice, I own I should rather choose a wife of mine to have the usual number of limbs, and a limited quantity of back: and though *one* eye may be very agreeable, yet as the prejudice has always run in favor of *two*, I would not wish to affect a singularity in that article.

SIR ANTHONY. What a phlegmatic sot it is! Why, Sirrah, you're an anchorite! a vile, insensible stock. You a soldier! you're a walking block, fit only to dust the company's regimentals on! Odd's life! I've a great mind to marry the girl myself!

ABSOLUTE. I am entire at your disposal, Sir; if you should think of addressing Miss Languish yourself, I suppose you would have me marry the *aunt*, or if you should change your mind, and take the old lady—'tis the same to me—I'll marry the *niece*.

SIR ANTHONY. Upon my word, Jack, thou'rt either a very great hypocrite, or—But come, I know your indifference on such a subject must be all a lie—I'm sure it must—come, now—damn your demure face!—come, confess, Jack—you have been lying—ha'n't you? you have been playing the hypocrite, hey?—I'll never forgive you if you ha'n't been lying and playing the hypocrite.

ABSOLUTE. I'm sorry, Sir, that the respect and duty which I bear to you should be so mistaken.

SIR ANTHONY. Hang your respect and duty! But come along with me, I'll write a note to Mrs. Malaprop, and you shall visit the lady directly. Her eyes shall be the Promethean torch to you—come along. I'll never forgive you if you don't come back stark mad with rapture and impatience. If you don't, egad, I'll marry the girl myself!

[*Exeunt.*]

SCENE II

Julia's dressing-room.

[*Faulkland solus.*]

FAULKLAND. They told me Julia would return directly; I wonder she is not yet come! How mean does this captious, unsatisfied temper of mine appear to my cooler judgment! Yet I know not that I indulge it in any other point: but on this one subject, and to this one subject, whom I think I love beyond my life, I am ever ungenerously fretful, and madly capricious! I am conscious of it—yet I cannot correct myself! What tender, honest joy sparkled in her eyes when we met! How delicate was the warmth of her expressions! I was ashamed to appear less happy, though I had come resolved to wear a face of coolness and upbraiding. Sir Anthony's presence prevented my proposed expostulations, yet I must be satisfied that she has not been so *very* happy in my absence. She is coming! Yes! I know the nimbleness of her tread when she thinks her impatient Faulkland counts the moments of her stay.

[*Enter Julia.*]

JULIA. I had not hoped to see you again so soon.

FAULKLAND. Could I, Julia, be contented with my first welcome—restrained as we were by the presence of a third person?

JULIA. O Faulkland, when your kindness can make me

thus happy, let me not think that I discovered something of coldness in your first salutation.

FAULKLAND. 'Twas but your fancy, Julia. I *was* rejoiced to see you—to see you in such health. Sure I had no cause for coldness?

JULIA. Nay then, I see you have taken something ill. You must not conceal from me what it is.

FAULKLAND. Well then—shall I own to you—that my joy at hearing of your health and arrival here, by your neighbour Acres, was somewhat damped by his dwelling much on the high spirits you had enjoyed in Devonshire—on your mirth, your singing, dancing, and I know not what! For such is my temper, Julia, that I should regard every mirthful moment in your absence as a treason to constancy. The mutual tear that steals down the cheek of parting lovers is a compact that no smile shall live there till they meet again.

JULIA. Must I never cease to tax my Faulkland with this teasing minute caprice? Can the idle reports of a silly boor weigh in your breast against my tried affection?

FAULKLAND. They have no weight with me, Julia: no, no—I am happy if you have been so—yet only say that you did not sing with *mirth*—say that you *thought* of Faulkland in the dance.

JULIA. I never can be happy in your absence. If I wear a countenance of content, it is to show that my mind holds no doubt of my Faulkland's truth. If I seemed sad, it were to make malice triumph, and say that I had fixed my heart on one who left me to lament his roving, and my own credulity. Believe me, Faulkland, I mean not to upbraid you when I say that I have often dressed sorrow in smiles, lest my friends should guess whose unkindness had caused my tears.

FAULKLAND. You were ever all goodness to me. Oh, I am a brute when I but admit a doubt of your true constancy!

JULIA. If ever, without such cause from you, as I will not suppose possible, you find my affections veering but a point, may I become a proverbial scoff for levity and base ingratitude.

FAULKLAND. Ah! Julia, that last word is grating to me. I would I had no title to your *gratitude*! Search your heart, Julia; perhaps what you have mistaken for love, is but the warm effusion of a too thankful heart!

JULIA. For what quality must I love you?

FAULKLAND. For no quality! To regard me for any quality of mind or understanding were only to *esteem* me. And for person—I have often wished myself deformed, to be convinced that I owed no obligation *there* for any part of your affection.

JULIA. Where Nature has bestowed a show of nice attention in the features of a man, he should laugh at it as misplaced. I have seen men who in *this* vain article perhaps might rank above you; but my heart has never asked my eyes if it were so or not.

FAULKLAND. Now this is not well from *you*, Julia. I despise person in a man. Yet if you loved me as I wish, though I were an Æthiop, you'd think none so fair.

JULIA. I see you are determined to be unkind. The *contract* which my poor father bound us in gives you more than a lover's privilege.

FAULKLAND. Again, Julia, you raise ideas that feed and justify my doubts. I would not have been more free—no—I am proud of my restraint. Yet—yet—perhaps your high respect alone for this solemn compact has fettered your inclinations, which else had made a worthier choice. How shall I be sure, had you remained unbound in thought and promise, that I should still have been the object of your persevering love?

JULIA. Then try me now. Let us be free as strangers as to what is past: *my* heart will not feel more liberty!

FAULKLAND. There now! so hasty, Julia! so anxious to be free! If your love for me were fixed and ardent, you would not loose your hold, even though I wished it!

JULIA. Oh, you torture me to the heart! I cannot bear it.

FAULKLAND. I do not mean to distress you. If I loved you less I should never give you an uneasy moment. But hear me. All my fretful doubts arise from this: women are not used to weigh, and separate the motives of their affections; the cold dictates of prudence, gratitude, of filial duty, may sometimes be mistaken for the pleadings of the heart. I would not boast—yet let me say that I have neither age, person, or character to found dislike on; my fortune such as few ladies could be charged with *indiscretion* in the match. O Julia! when *Love* receives such countenance from *Prudence*, nice minds will be suspicious of its birth.

JULIA. I know not whither your insinuations would tend, but as they seem pressing to insult me, I will spare you the regret of having done so. I have given you no cause for this!

[*Exit in tears.*]

FAULKLAND. In tears! Stay, Julia: stay but for a

moment.—The door is fastened! Julia—my soul—but for one moment. I hear her sobbing! 'Sdeath! what a brute am I to use her thus! Yet stay!—Aye she is coming now. How little resolution there is in woman! How a few soft words can turn them!—No, faith!—she is *not* coming either! Why, Julia—my love—say but that you forgive me—come but to tell me that. Now, this is being *too* resentful.—Stay! she *is* coming too—I thought she would—no *steadiness* in anything! her going away must have been a mere trick then. She sha'n't see that I was hurt by it. I'll affect indifference. [*Hums a tune: then listens.*] —No—Z—ds! she's *not* coming!—nor don't intend it, I suppose. This is not *steadiness*, but *obstinacy*! Yet I deserve it. What, after so long an absence to quarrel with her tenderness!—'twas barbarous and unmanly! I should be ashamed to see her now. I'll wait till her just resentment is abated—and when I distress her so again, may I lose her forever, and be linked instead to some antique virago, whose gnawing passions, and long hoarded spleen shall make me curse my folly half the day, and all the night!

[*Exit.*]

SCENE III

Mrs. Malaprop's lodgings.

[*Mrs. Malaprop, with a letter in her hand, and Captain Absolute.*]

MRS. MALAPROP. Your being Sir Anthony's son, Captain, would itself be a sufficient accommodation; but from the ingenuity of your appearance, I am convinced you deserve the character here given of you.

ABSOLUTE. Permit me to say, Madam, that as I never yet have had the pleasure of seeing Miss Languish, my principal inducement in this affair at present is the honour of being allied to Mrs. Malaprop; of whose intellectual accomplishments, elegant manners, and unaffected learning, no tongue is silent.

MRS. MALAPROP. Sir, you do me infinite honour! I beg, Captain, you'll be seated. [*Sit.*] Ah! few gentlemen now-a-days know how to value the ineffectual qualities in a woman! few think how a little knowledge becomes a gentlewoman! Men have no sense now but for the worthless flower of beauty!

ABSOLUTE. It is but too true, indeed, Ma'am. Yet I fear our ladies should share the blame—they think

our admiration of *beauty* so great, that *knowledge* in *them* would be superfluous. Thus, like garden-trees, they seldom show fruit till time has robbed them of the more specious blossom. Few, like Mrs. Malaprop and the orange-tree, are rich in both at once!

MRS. MALAPROP. Sir—you overpower me with good-breeding. [*Aside.*] He is the very pineapple of politeness!—You are not ignorant, Captain, that this giddy girl has somehow contrived to fix her affections on a beggarly, strolling, eaves-dropping Ensign, whom none of us have seen, and nobody knows anything of.

ABSOLUTE. Oh, I have heard the silly affair before. I'm not at all prejudiced against her on *that* account.

MRS. MALAPROP. You are very good, and very considerate, Captain. I am sure I have done everything in my power since I exploded the affair! Long ago I laid my positive conjunctions on her never to think on the fellow again; I have since laid Sir Anthony's preposition before her; but, I'm sorry to say, she seems resolved to decline every particle that I enjoin her.

ABSOLUTE. It must be very distressing, indeed, Ma'am.

MRS. MALAPROP. Oh! it gives me the hydrostatics to such a degree! I thought she had persisted from corresponding with him; but behold this very day I have interceded another letter from the fellow! I believe I have it in my pocket.

ABSOLUTE. [*aside.*] Oh the devil! my last note.

MRS. MALAPROP. Aye, here it is.

ABSOLUTE. [*aside.*] Aye, my note, indeed! Oh the little traitress Lucy!

MRS. MALAPROP. There, perhaps you may know the writing. [*Gives him the letter.*]

ABSOLUTE. I think I have seen the hand before—yes, I certainly must have seen this hand before—

MRS. MALAPROP. Nay, but read it, Captain.

ABSOLUTE. [*reads*]. *"My soul's idol, my adored Lydia!"*—Very tender, indeed!

MRS. MALAPROP. Tender! aye, and profane, too, o' my conscience!

ABSOLUTE. *"I am excessively alarmed at the intelligence you send me, the more so as my new rival"*—

MRS. MALAPROP. That's *you*, Sir.

ABSOLUTE. *"Has universally the character of being an accomplished gentleman, and a man of honour."*—Well, that's handsome enough.

MRS. MALAPROP. Oh, the fellow had some design in writing so.

ABSOLUTE. That he had, I'll answer for him, Ma'am.

MRS. MALAPROP. But go on, Sir—you'll see presently.

ABSOLUTE. *"As for the old weather-beaten she-dragon who guards you"*—Who can he mean by that?

MRS. MALAPROP. Me! Sir—*me!*—he means *me!* There—what do you think now? But go on a little further.

ABSOLUTE. Impudent scoundrel!—*"it shall go hard but I will elude her vigilance, as I am told that the same ridiculous vanity which makes her dress up her coarse features, and deck her dull chat with hard words which she don't understand"*—

MRS. MALAPROP. There, Sir! an attack upon my language! What do you think of that?—an aspersion upon my parts of speech! Was ever such a brute? Sure if I reprehend anything in this world, it is the use of my oracular tongue, and a nice derangement of epitaphs!

ABSOLUTE. He deserves to be hanged and quartered! Let me see— *"same ridiculous vanity"*—

MRS. MALAPROP. You need not read it again, Sir.

ABSOLUTE. I beg pardon, Ma'am— *"does also lay her open to the grossest deceptions from flattery and pretended admiration"*—an impudent coxcomb!— *"so that I have a scheme to see you shortly with the old harridan's consent, and even to make her a go-between in our interviews."*—Was ever such assurance!

MRS. MALAPROP. Did you ever hear anything like it? He'll elude my vigilance, will he? Yes, yes! ha! ha! He's very likely to enter these doors! We'll try who can plot best!

ABSOLUTE. So we will, Ma'am—so we will. Ha! ha! ha! A conceited puppy, ha! ha! ha! Well, but Mrs. Malaprop, as the girl seems so infatuated by this fellow, suppose you were to wink at her corresponding with him for a little time—let her even plot an elopement with him—then do you connive at her escape—while *I*, just in the nick, will have the fellow laid by the heels, and fairly contrive to carry her off in his stead.

MRS. MALAPROP. I am delighted with the scheme; never was anything better perpetrated!

ABSOLUTE. But, pray, could not I see the lady for a few minutes now? I should like to try her temper a little.

MRS. MALAPROP. Why, I don't know—I doubt she is not prepared for a visit of this kind. There is a decorum in these matters.

ABSOLUTE. O Lord! she won't mind *me*—only tell her Beverley—

MRS. MALAPROP. Sir!—

ABSOLUTE. [*aside*]. Gently, good tongue.

MRS. MALAPROP. What did you say of Beverley?

ABSOLUTE. Oh, I was going to propose that you should tell her, by way of jest, that it was Beverley who was below—she'd come down fast enough then—ha! ha! ha!

MRS. MALAPROP. 'Twould be a trick she well deserves. Besides, you know the fellow tells her he'll get my consent to see her—ha! ha! Let him if he can, I say again. [*Calling.*] Lydia, come down here!—He'll make me a *go-between in their interviews!*—ha! ha! ha!—Come down, I say, Lydia!—I don't wonder at your laughing, ha! ha! ha!—his impudence is truly ridiculous.

ABSOLUTE. 'Tis very ridiculous, upon my soul, Ma'am, ha! ha! ha!

MRS. MALAPROP. The little hussy won't hear. Well, I'll go and tell her at once who it is. She shall know that Captain Absolute is come to wait on her. And I'll make her behave as becomes a young woman.

ABSOLUTE. As you please, Ma'am.

MRS. MALAPROP. For the present, Captain, your servant. Ah! you've not done laughing yet, I see— *elude my vigilance!*—yes, yes, ha! ha! ha!

[*Exit.*]

ABSOLUTE. Ha! ha! ha! one would think now that I might throw off all disguise at once, and seize my prize with security—but such is Lydia's caprice that to undeceive were probably to lose her. I'll see whether she knows me. [*Walks aside, and seems engaged in looking at the pictures.*]

[*Enter Lydia.*]

LYDIA. What a scene am I now to go through! Surely nothing can be more dreadful than to be obliged to listen to the loathsome addresses of a stranger to one's heart. I have heard of girls persecuted as I am, who have appealed in behalf of their favoured lover to the generosity of his rival: suppose I were to try it. There stands the hated rival—an officer, too!—but oh, how unlike my Beverley! I wonder he don't begin. Truly he seems a very negligent wooer! Quite at his ease, upon my word! I'll speak first. [*Aloud.*] Mr. Absolute.

ABSOLUTE. Madam. [*Turns around.*]

LYDIA. O heavens! Beverley!

ABSOLUTE. Hush!—hush, my life! Softly! Be not surprised.

LYDIA. I am so astonished! and so terrified! and so overjoyed! For heaven's sake! how came you here?

ABSOLUTE. Briefly—I have deceived your aunt. I was informed that my new rival was to visit here this evening, and contriving to have him kept away, have passed myself on *her* for Captain Absolute.

LYDIA. Oh, charming! And she really takes you for young Absolute?

ABSOLUTE. Oh, she's convinced of it.

LYDIA. Ha! ha! ha! I can't forbear laughing to think how her sagacity is overreached!

ABSOLUTE. But we trifle with our precious moments. Such another opportunity may not occur. Then let me now conjure my kind, my condescending angel, to fix the time when I may rescue her from undeserved persecution, and with a licensed warmth plead for my reward.

LYDIA. Will you then, Beverley, consent to forfeit that portion of my paltry wealth? that burden on the wings of love?

ABSOLUTE. Oh, come to me—rich only thus—in loveliness. Bring no portion to me but thy love— 'twill be generous in you, Lydia—for well you know, it is the only dower your poor Beverley can repay.

LYDIA. How persuasive are his words! How charming will poverty be with him!

ABSOLUTE. Ah! my soul, what a life will we then live! Love shall be our idol and support! We will worship him with a monastic strictness; abjuring all worldly toys, to center every thought and action there. Proud of calamity, we will enjoy the wreck of wealth; while the surrounding gloom of adversity shall make the flame of our pure love show doubly bright. By heavens! I would fling all goods of fortune from me with a prodigal hand to enjoy the scene where I might clasp my Lydia to my bosom, and say, the world affords no smile to me—but here. [*Embracing her.*] —[*Aside.*] If she hold out now the devil is in it!

LYDIA. [*aside*]. Now could I fly with him to the Antipodes! but my persecution is not yet come to a crisis.

[*Enter Mrs. Malaprop, listening.*]

MRS. MALAPROP. [*aside*]. I am impatient to know how the little hussy deports herself.

ABSOLUTE. So pensive, Lydia!—is then your warmth abated?

MRS. MALAPROP. [*aside*]. *Warmth abated!* So! she has been in a passion, I suppose.

LYDIA. No—nor ever can while I have life.

MRS. MALAPROP. [*aside*]. An ill-tempered little devil! She'll be *in a passion all her life*—will she?

LYDIA. Think not the idle threats of my ridiculous aunt can ever have any weight with me.

MRS. MALAPROP. [*aside*]. Very dutiful, upon my word!

LYDIA. Let her choice be Captain Absolute, but Beverley is mine.

MRS. MALAPROP. [*aside*]. I am astonished at her assurance!—to his face—this is to his face!

ABSOLUTE. Thus then let me enforce my suit. [*Kneeling.*]

MRS. MALAPROP. [*aside*]. Aye—poor young man! down on his knees entreating for pity! I can contain no longer.—[*Aloud.*] Why, thou vixen! I have overheard you.

ABSOLUTE. [*aside*]. Oh, confound her vigilance!

MRS. MALAPROP. Captain Absolute—I know not how to apologize for her shocking rudeness.

ABSOLUTE. [*aside*]. So—all's safe, I find.—[*Aloud.*] I have hopes, Madam, that time will bring the young lady—

MRS. MALAPROP. Oh, there's nothing to be hoped for from her! She's as headstrong as an allegory on the banks of Nile.

LYDIA. Nay, Madam, what do you charge me with now?

MRS. MALAPROP. Why, thou unblushing rebel— didn't you tell this gentleman to his face that you loved another better?—didn't you say you never would be his?

LYDIA. No, Madam—I did not.

MRS. MALAPROP. Good heavens! what assurance! Lydia, Lydia, you ought to know that lying don't become a young woman! Didn't you boast that Beverley—that stroller Beverley—possessed your heart? Tell me that, I say.

LYDIA. 'Tis true, Ma'am, and none but Beverley—

MRS. MALAPROP. Hold—hold, Assurance! you shall not be so rude.

ABSOLUTE. Nay, pray Mrs. Malaprop, don't stop the young lady's speech: she's very welcome to talk thus—it does not hurt *me* in the least, I assure you.

MRS. MALAPROP. You are *too* good, Captain—*too* amiably patient—but come with me, Miss. Let us see you again soon, Captain. Remember what we have fixed.

ABSOLUTE. I shall, Ma'am.

MRS. MALAPROP. Come, take a graceful leave of the gentleman.

LYDIA. May every blessing wait on my Beverley, my loved Bev—

MRS. MALAPROP. Hussy! I'll choke the word in your throat!—come along—come along.

[*Exeunt severally, Absolute kissing his hand to Lydia—Mrs. Malaprop stopping her from speaking.*]

SCENE IV

Acres's lodgings.

[*Acres and David, Acres as just dressed.*]

ACRES. Indeed, David—do you think I become it so?

DAVID. You are quite another creature, believe me, master, by the Mass! an' we've any luck we shall see the Devon monkeyrony in all the print-shops in Bath!

ACRES. Dress *does* make a difference, David.

DAVID. 'Tis all in all, I think. Difference! why, an' you were to go now to Clod-Hall, I am certain the old lady wouldn't know you: Master Butler wouldn't believe his own eyes, and Mrs. Pickle would cry, "Lard presarve me!"—our dairy-maid would come giggling to the door, and I warrant Dolly Tester, your Honour's favourite, would blush like my waistcoat. Oons! I'll hold a gallon, there a'n't a dog in the house but would bark, and I question whether *Phillis* would wage a hair of her tail!

ACRES. Aye, David, there's nothing like polishing.

DAVID. So I says of your Honour's boots; but the boy never heeds me!

ACRES. But, David, has Mr. De-la-Grace been here? I must rub up my balancing, and chasing, and boring.

DAVID. I'll call again, Sir.

ACRES. Do—and see if there are any letters for me at the post office.

DAVID. I will. By the Mass, I can't help looking at your head! If I hadn't been by at the cooking, I wish I may die if I should have known the dish again myself!

[*Exit.*]

[*Acres comes forward, practising a dancing step.*]

ACRES. Sink, slide—coupee! Confound the first inventor of cotillions! say I—they are as bad as algebra to us country gentlemen. I can walk a minuet easy enough when I'm forced! and I have been accounted a good stick in a country-dance. Odds jigs and tabours! I never valued your cross-over to couple—figure in—right and left—and I'd foot it with e'er a captain in the county! But these outlandish heathen allemandes and cotillions are quite beyond me! I shall never prosper at 'em, that's sure. Mine are true-born English legs—they don't understand their curst French lingo! their *pas* this, and *pas* that, and *pas* t'other! D—n me! my feet dont' like to be call paws! No, 'tis certain I have most anti-Gallican toes!

[*Enter servant.*]

SERVANT. Here is Sir Lucius O'Trigger to wait on you, Sir.

ACRES. Show him in.

[*Enter Sir Lucius.*]

SIR LUCIUS. Mr. Acres, I am delighted to embrace you.

ACRES. My dear Sir Lucius, I kiss your hands.

SIR LUCIUS. Pray, my friend, what has brought you so suddenly to Bath?

ACRES. Faith! I have followed Cupid's Jack-a-Lantern, and find myself in a quagmire at last. In short, I have been very ill-used, Sir Lucius. I don't choose to mention names, but look on me as on a very ill-used gentleman.

SIR LUCIUS. Pray, what is the case? I ask no names.

ACRES. Mark me, Sir Lucius, I fall as deep as need be in love with a young lady—her friends take my part—I follow her to Bath—send word of my arrival, and receive answer that the lady is to be otherwise disposed of. This, Sir Lucius, I call being ill-used.

SIR LUCIUS. Very ill, upon my conscience. Pray, can you divine the cause of it?

ACRES. Why, there's the matter: she has another lover, one Beverley, who, I am told, is now in Bath. Odds slanders and lies! he must be at the bottom of it.

SIR LUCIUS. A rival in the case, is there? And you think he has supplanted you unfairly?

ACRES. Unfairly!—to be sure he has. He never could have done it fairly.

SIR LUCIUS. Then sure you know what is to be done!

ACRES. Not I, upon my soul!

SIR LUCIUS. We wear no swords here, but you understand me.

ACRES. What! fight him?

SIR LUCIUS. Aye, to be sure: what can I mean else?

ACRES. But he has given me no provocation.

SIR LUCIUS. Now, I think he has given you the greatest provocation in the world. Can a man commit a more heinous offence against another than to fall in love with the same woman? Oh, by my soul, it is the most unpardonable breach of friendship!

ACRES. Breach of friendship! Aye, aye; but I have no acquaintance with this man. I never saw him in my life.

SIR LUCIUS. That's no argument at all—he has the less right then to take such a liberty.

ACRES. 'Gad, that's true. I grow full of anger, Sir Lucius! I fire apace! Odds hilts and blades! I find a man may have a deal of valour in him and not know it! But couldn't I contrive to have a little right of my side?

SIR LUCIUS. What the devil signifies *right* when your *honour* is concerned? Do you think Achilles, or my little Alexander the Great ever inquired where the right lay? No, by my soul, they drew their broadswords, and left the lazy sons of peace to settle the justice of it.

ACRES. Your words are a grenadier's march to my heart! I believe courage must be catching! I certainly do feel a kind of valour rising, as it were—a kind of courage as I may say. Odds flints, pans, and triggers! I'll challenge him directly.

SIR LUCIUS. Ah, my little friend! if we had Blunderbuss-Hall here—I could show you a range of ancestry, in the O'Trigger line, that would furnish the New Room, every one of whom had killed his man! For though the mansion-house and dirty acres have slipped through my fingers, I thank heaven our honour, and the family-pictures, are as fresh as ever.

ACRES. O Sir Lucius! I have had ancestors too! every man of 'em colonel or captain in the militia! Odds balls and barrels! say no more—I'm braced for it. The thunder of your words has soured the milk of human kindness in my breast! Z—ds! as the man in the play says, "I could do such deeds!"

SIR LUCIUS. Come, come, there must be no passion at all in the case—these things should always be done civilly.

ACRES. I must be in a passion, Sir Lucius—I must be in a rage. Dear Sir Lucius, let me be in a rage, if you love me. Come, here's pen and paper. [*Sits down to write.*] I would the ink were red! Indite, I say, indite! How shall I begin? Odds bullets and blades! I'll write a good bold hand, however.

SIR LUCIUS. Pray compose yourself.

ACRES. Come now, shall I begin with an oath? Do, Sir Lucius, let me begin with a damme.

SIR LUCIUS. Pho! pho! do the thing decently and like a Christian. Begin now— "*Sir*"—

ACRES. That's too civil by half.

SIR LUCIUS. "*To prevent the confusion that might arise*"—

ACRES. Well—

SIR LUCIUS. "*From our both addressing the same lady*"—

ACRES. Aye—there's the reason—"*same lady*"—Well—

SIR LUCIUS. "*I shall expect the honour of your company*"—

ACRES. Z—ds! I'm not asking him to dinner.

SIR LUCIUS. Pray be easy.

ACRES. Well then— "*honour of your company*"—

SIR LUCIUS. "*To settle our pretensions*"—

ACRES. Well—

SIR LUCIUS. Let me see—aye, King's-Mead-Fields will do— "*In King's-Mead-Fields.*"

ACRES. So that's done.—Well, I'll fold it up presently; my own crest—a hand and dagger shall be the seal.

SIR LUCIUS. You see now, this little explanation will put a stop at once to all confusion or misunderstanding that might arise between you.

ACRES. Aye, we fight to prevent any misunderstanding.

SIR LUCIUS. Now, I'll leave you to fix your own time. Take my advice, and you'll decide it this evening if you can; then let the worst come of it, 'twill be off your mind to-morrow.

ACRES. Very true.

SIR LUCIUS. So I shall see nothing more of you, unless it be by letter, till the evening. I would do myself the honour to carry your message; but, to tell you a secret, I believe I shall have just another affair on my own hands. There is a gay captain here who put a jest on me lately at the expense of my country, and I only want to fall in with the gentleman to call him out.

ACRES. By my valour, I should like to see you fight first! Odd's life! I should like to see you kill him, if it was only to get a little lesson.

SIR LUCIUS. I shall be very proud of instructing you. Well for the present—but remember now, when you meet your antagonist, do everything in a mild and agreeable manner. Let your courage be as keen, but at the same time as polished, as your sword.

[*Exeunt severally.*]

Act IV

SCENE I

Acres's lodgings.

[*Acres and David.*]

DAVID. Then, by the Mass, Sir! I would do no such thing—ne'er a Sir Lucius O'Trigger in the kingdom should make me fight, when I wa'n't so minded. Oons! what will the old lady say when she hears o't!

ACRES. Ah! David, if you had heard Sir Lucius! Odds sparks and flames! he would have roused your valour

DAVID. Not he, indeed. I hates such blood-thirsty cormorants. Look'ee, master, if you'd wanted a bout at boxing, quarterstaff, or shortstaff, I should never be the man to bid you cry off: but for your curst sharps and snaps, I never knew any good come of 'em.

ACRES. But my honour, David, my honour! I must be very careful of my honour.

DAVID. Aye, by the Mass! and I would be very careful of it; and I think in return my *honour* couldn't do less than to be very careful of me.

ACRES. Odds blades! David, no gentleman will ever risk the loss of his honour!

DAVID. I say then, it would be but civil in *honour* never to risk the loss of a *gentleman*. Look'ee, master, this *honour* seems to me to be a marvellous false friend; aye, truly, a very courtier-like servant. Put the case, I was a gentleman (which, thank God, no one can say of me); well—my honour makes me quarrel with another gentleman of my acquaintance. So—we fight. (Pleasant enough that.) Boh!—I kill him (the more's my luck). Now, pray who gets the profit of it? Why, my *honour*. But put the case that he kills me!—by the Mass! I go to the worms, and my honour whips over to my enemy!

ACRES. No, David—in that case, odds crowns and laurels!—your honour follows you to the grave.

DAVID. Now, that's just the place where I could make a shift to do without it.

ACRES. Z—ds, David, you're a coward! It doesn't become my valour to listen to you. What, shall I disgrace my ancestors? Think of that, David—think what it would be to disgrace my ancestors!

DAVID. Under favour, the surest way of not disgracing them is to keep as long as you can out of their company. Look'ee now, master, to go to them in such haste—with an ounce of lead in your brains—I should think might as well be let alone. Our ancestors are very good kind of folks; but they are the last people I should choose to have a visiting acquaintance with.

ACRES. But David, now, you don't think there is such very, very, *very* great danger, hey? Odds life! people often fight without any mischief done!

DAVID. By the Mass, I think 'tis ten to one against you! Oons! here to meet some lion-headed fellow, I warrant, with his d—n'd double-barrelled swords, and cut-and-thrust pistols! Lord bless us! it makes me tremble to think o't. Those be such desperate bloody-minded weapons! Well, I never could abide 'em! from a child I never could fancy 'em! I suppose there a'n't so merciless a beast in the world as your loaded pistol!

ACRES. Z—ds! I *won't* be afraid! Odds fire and fury! you sha'n't make me afraid! Here is the challenge, and I have sent for my dear friend Jack Absolute to carry it for me.

DAVID. Aye, i' the name of mischief, let *him* be the messenger. For my part, I wouldn't lend a hand to it for the best horse in your stable. By the Mass! it don't look like another letter! It is, as I may say, a designing and malicious-looking letter! and I warrant smells of gunpowder, like a soldier's pouch! Oons! I wouldn't swear it mayn't go off!

ACRES. Out, you poltroon! You ha'n't the valour of a grasshopper.

DAVID. Well, I say no more—'twill be sad news, to be sure, at Clod-Hall!—but I ha' done. How Phillis will howl when she hears of it! Aye, poor bitch, she little thinks what shooting her master's going after! And I warrant old Crop, who has carried your Honour, field and road, these ten years, will curse the hour he was born. [*Whimpering.*]

ACRES. It won't do, David—I am determined to fight—so get along, you coward, while I'm in the mind.

[*Enter Servant.*]

SERVANT. Captain Absolute, Sir.

ACRES. Oh! show him up.

[*Exit Servant.*]

DAVID. Well, heaven send we be all alive this time to-morrow.

ACRES. What's that! Don't provoke me, David!

DAVID. Good-bye, master. [*Whimpering.*]

ACRES. Get along, you cowardly, dastardly, croaking raven.

[*Exit David.*]

[*Enter Absolute.*]

ABSOLUTE. What's the matter, Bob?

ACRES. A vile, sheep-hearted blockhead! If I hadn't the valour of St. George and the dragon to boot—

ABSOLUTE. But what did you want with me, Bob?

ACRES. Oh! There—[*gives him the challenge*].

ABSOLUTE. "*To Ensign Beverley.*" [*Aside.*] So—what's going on now? [*Aloud.*] Well, what's this?

ACRES. A challenge!

ABSOLUTE. Indeed! Why, you won't fight him, will you, Bob?

ACRES. 'Egad, but I will, Jack. Sir Lucius has wrought me to it. He has left me full of rage, and I'll fight this evening, that so much good passion mayn't be wasted.

ABSOLUTE. But what have I to do with this?

ACRES. Why, as I think you know something of this fellow, I want you to find him out for me, and give him this mortal defiance.

ABSOLUTE. Well, give it to me, and trust me he gets it.

ACRES. Thank you, my dear friend, my dear Jack; but it is giving you a great deal of trouble.

ABSOLUTE. Not in the least—I beg you won't mention it. No trouble in the world, I assure you.

ACRES. You are very kind. What it is to have a friend! You couldn't be my second—could you Jack?

ABSOLUTE. Why no, Bob—not in *this* affair. It would not be quite so proper.

ACRES. Well then, I must get my friend Sir Lucius. I shall have your good wishes, however, Jack.

ABSOLUTE. Whenever he meets you, believe me.

[*Enter Servant.*]

SERVANT. Sir Anthony Absolute is below, inquiring for the Captain.

ABSOLUTE. I'll come instantly. Well, my little hero, success attend you. [*Going.*]

ACRES. Stay—stay, Jack. If Beverley should ask you what kind of a man your friend Acres is, do tell him I am a devil of a fellow—will you, Jack?

ABSOLUTE. To be sure I shall. I'll say you are a determined dog—hey, Bob?

ACRES. Aye, do, do—and if that frightens him, 'egad, perhaps he mayn't come. So tell him I generally kill a man a week—will you, Jack?

ABSOLUTE. I will, I will; I'll say you are called in the country "*Fighting Bob!*"

ACRES. Right, right—'tis all to prevent mischief; for I don't want to take his life if I clear my honour.

ABSOLUTE. No!—that's very kind of you.

ACRES. Why, you don't wish me to kill him—do you, Jack?

ABSOLUTE. No, upon my soul, I do not. But a devil of a fellow, hey? [*Going.*]

ACRES. True, true—but stay—stay, Jack. You may add that you never saw me in such a rage before—a most devouring rage!

ABSOLUTE. I will, I will.

ACRES. Remember, Jack—a determined dog!

ABSOLUTE. Aye, aye, "*Fighting Bob!*"

[*Exeunt severally.*]

SCENE II

Mrs. Malaprop's lodgings.

[*Mrs. Malaprop and Lydia.*]

MRS. MALAPROP. Why, thou perverse one! tell me what you can object to him? Isn't he a handsome man? tell me that. A genteel man? a pretty figure of a man?

LYDIA. [*aside*]. She little thinks whom she is praising!—[*Aloud.*] So is Beverley, Ma'am.

MRS. MALAPROP. No caparisons, Miss, if you please! Caparisons don't become a young woman. No! Captain Absolute is indeed a fine gentleman!

LYDIA. [*aside*]. Aye, the Captain Absolute *you* have seen.

MRS. MALAPROP. Then he's *so* well bred; *so* full of alacrity, and adulation! and has *so much* to say for himself—in such good language, too! His physiognomy so grammatical! Then his presence is so noble! I protest, when I saw him, I thought of what Hamlet says in the play: "Hesperian curls!—the front of *Job* himself! An eye, like *March*, to threaten at command—a station, like Harry Mercury, new"—something about kissing on a hill—however, the similitude struck me directly.

LYDIA. [aside]. How enraged she'll be presently when she discovers her mistake!

[Enter Servant.]

SERVANT. Sir Anthony and Captain Absolute are below, Ma'am.

MRS. MALAPROP. Show them up here.

[Exit Servant.]

Now, Lydia, I insist on your behaving as becomes a young woman. Show your good breeding at least, though you have forgot your duty.

LYDIA. Madam, I have told you my resolution; I shall not only give him no encouragement, but I won't even speak to, or look at him. [Flings herself into a chair with her face from the door.]

[Enter Sir Anthony and Absolute.]

SIR ANTHONY. Here we are, Mrs. Malaprop, come to mitigate the frowns of unrelenting beauty—and difficulty enough I had to bring this fellow. I don't know what's the matter; but if I hadn't held him by force, he'd have given me the slip.

MRS. MALAPROP. You have infinite trouble, Sir Anthony, in the affair. I am ashamed for the cause!—[Aside to her.] Lydia, Lydia, rise, I beseech you!—pay your respects!

SIR ANTHONY. I hope, Madam, that Miss Languish has reflected on the worth of this gentleman, and the regard due to her aunt's choice, and my alliance.—[Aside to him.] Now, Jack, speak to her!

ABSOLUTE. [aside]. What the devil shall I do!—[Aloud.] You see, Sir, she won't even look at me whilst you are here. I knew she wouldn't! I told you so. Let me entreat you, Sir, to leave us together!

[Absolute seems to expostulate with his father.]

LYDIA. [aside]. I wonder I ha'n't heard my aunt exclaim yet! Sure she can't have looked at him! Perhaps their regimentals are alike, and she is something blind.

SIR ANTHONY. I say, Sir, I won't stir a foot yet!

MRS. MALAPROP. I am sorry to say, Sir Anthony, that my affluence over my niece is very small.—[Aside to her.] Turn round, Lydia; I blush for you!

SIR ANTHONY. May I not flatter myself that Miss Languish will assign what cause of dislike she can have to my son! Why don't you begin, Jack?—[Aside to him.] Speak, you puppy—speak!

MRS. MALAPROP. It is impossible, Sir Anthony, she can have any. She will not say she has.—[Aside to her.] Answer, hussy! why don't you answer?

SIR ANTHONY. Then, madam, I trust that a childish and hasty predilection will be no bar to Jack's happiness.—[Aside to him.] Z—ds! Sirrah! why don't you speak?

LYDIA. [aside]. I think my lover seems as little inclined to conversation as myself. How strangely blind my aunt must be!

ABSOLUTE. Hem! hem!—Madam—hem!—[Absolute attempts to speak, then returns to Sir Anthony.] —Faith! Sir, I am so confounded! and so—so—confused! I told you I should be so, Sir, I knew it. The—the—tremor of my passion entirely takes away my presence of mind.

SIR ANTHONY. But it don't take away your voice, fool, does it? Go up, and speak to her directly!

[Absolute makes signs to Mrs. Malaprop to leave them together.

MRS. MALAPROP. Sir Anthony, shall we leave them together?—[Aside to her.] Ah! you stubborn little vixen!

SIR ANTHONY. Not yet, Ma'am, not yet!—[Aside to him.] What the devil are you at? Unlock your jaws, Sirrah, or—

[Absolute draws near Lydia.]

ABSOLUTE. [aside]. Now heaven send she may be too sullen to look round! I must disguise my voice.—[Speaks in a low hoarse tone.] Will not Miss Languish lend an ear to the mild accents of true love? Will not—

SIR ANTHONY. What the devil ails the fellow? Why don't you speak out?—not stand croaking like a frog in a quinsy!

ABSOLUTE. The—the—excess of my awe, and my—my—my modesty quite choke me!

SIR ANTHONY. Ah! your modesty again! I'll tell you what, Jack, if you don't speak out directly, and glibly, too, I shall be in such a rage! Mrs. Malaprop, I wish the lady would favour us with something more than a side-front!

[Mrs. Malaprop seems to chide Lydia.]

ABSOLUTE. So! All will out I see! [Goes up to Lydia, speaks softly.] Be not surprised, my Lydia; suppress all surprise at present.

LYDIA. [aside]. Heavens! 'tis Beverley's voice! Sure he can't have imposed on Sir Anthony, too!—[Looks round by degrees, then starts up.] Is this possible—my Beverley!—how can this be?—my Beverley?

ABSOLUTE. [aside]. Ah! 'tis all over.

SIR ANTHONY. Beverley!—the devil!—Beverley! What can the girl mean? This is my son, Jack Absolute!

MRS. MALAPROP. For shame, hussy! for shame! your head runs so on that fellow that you have him always in your eyes! Beg Captain Absolute's pardon directly.

LYDIA. I see no Captain Absolute, but my loved Beverley!

SIR ANTHONY. Z—ds! the girl's mad!—her brain's turned by reading!

MRS. MALAPROP. O' my conscience, I believe so! What do you mean by Beverley, hussy? You saw Captain Absolute before to-day; there he is—your husband that shall be.

LYDIA. With all my soul, Ma'am. When I refuse my Beverley—

SIR ANTHONY. Oh! she's as mad as Bedlam! Or has this fellow been playing us a rogue's trick! Come here, Sirrah!—who the devil are you?

ABSOLUTE. Faith, Sir, I am not quite clear myself, but I'll endeavour to recollect.

SIR ANTHONY. Are you my son, or not? Answer for your mother, you dog, if you won't for me.

MRS. MALAPROP. Aye, Sir, who are you? Oh mercy! I begin to suspect!—

ABSOLUTE. [aside]. Ye Powers of Impudence befriend me!—[Aloud.] Sir Anthony, most assuredly I am your wife's son; and that I sincerely believe myself to be yours also, I hope my duty has always shown.—Mrs. Malaprop, I am your most respectful admirer—and shall be proud to add affectionate nephew.—I need not tell my Lydia, that she sees her faithful Beverley, who, knowing the singular generosity of her temper, assumed that name, and a station which has proved a test of the most disinterested love, which he now hopes to enjoy in a more elevated character.

LYDIA. [sullenly]. So!—there will be no elopement after all!

SIR ANTHONY. Upon my soul, Jack, thou art a very impudent fellow! to do you justice, I think I never saw a piece of more consummate assurance!

ABSOLUTE. Oh you flatter me, Sir—you compliment—'tis my modesty you know, Sir—my modesty that has stood in my way.

SIR ANTHONY. Well, I am glad you are not the dull, insensible varlet you pretended to be, however! I'm glad you have made a fool of your father, you dog—I am. So this was your penitence, your duty, and obedience! I thought it was d—d sudden! You never heard their names before, not you! What! The Languishes of Worcestershire, hey?—if you could please me in the affair, 'twas all you desired!—Ah! you dissembling villain! What!—[pointing to Lydia] she squints, don't she?—a little red-haired girl!—hey? Why you hypocritical young rascal! I wonder you a'n't ashamed to hold up your head!

ABSOLUTE. 'Tis with difficulty, Sir. I am confused—very much confused, as you must perceive.

MRS. MALAPROP. O lud! Sir Anthony!—a new light breaks in upon me! Hey! how! what! Captain, did you write the letters then? What!—am I to thank you for the elegant compilation of "an old weather-beaten she-dragon"—hey? O mercy! was it you that reflected on my parts of speech?

ABSOLUTE. Dear Sir! my modesty will be overpowered at last, if you don't assist me. I shall certainly not be able to stand it!

SIR ANTHONY. Come, come, Mrs. Malaprop, we must forget and forgive. Odd's life! matters have taken so clever a turn all of sudden, that I could find in my heart to be so good-humoured! and so gallant!—hey! Mrs. Malaprop!

MRS. MALAPROP. Well, Sir Anthony, since you desire it, we will not anticipate the past; so mind, young people: our retrospection will now be all to the future.

SIR ANTHONY. Come, we must leave them together; Mrs. Malaprop, they long to fly into each other's arms. I warrant!—[Aside.] Jack—isn't the cheek as I said, hey?—and the eye, you rogue!—and the lip—hey? Come, Mrs. Malaprop, we'll not disturb their tenderness—theirs is the time of life for happiness!—[Sings.] "Youth's the season made for joy"—hey! Odd's life! I'm in such spirits, I don't know what I couldn't do! Permit me, Ma'am.—[Gives his hand to Mrs. Malaprop. Sings.] Tol-de-rol!—'gad, I should like a little fooling myself. Tol-de-rol! [Exit singing, and handing Mrs. Malaprop.]

[Lydia sits sullenly in her chair.]

ABSOLUTE. [aside]. So much thought bodes me no good.—[Aloud.] So grave, Lydia!

LYDIA. Sir!

ABSOLUTE. [aside]. So!—egad! I thought as much! That d—d monosyllable has froze me!—[Aloud.] What, Lydia, now that we are as happy in our friends' consent, as in our mutual vows—

LYDIA. [*peevishly*]. *Friends' consent*, indeed!

ABSOLUTE. Come, come, we must lay aside some of our romance—a little *wealth* and *comfort* may be endured after all. And for your fortune, the lawyers shall make such settlements as—

LYDIA. *Lawyers*! I *hate* lawyers!

ABSOLUTE. Nay then, we will not wait for their lingering forms but instantly procure the licence, and—

LYDIA. The *licence*! I *hate* license!

ABSOLUTE. O my love! be not so unkind! Thus let me intreat—[*kneeling*].

LYDIA. Pshaw! what signifies kneeling when you know I *must* have you?

ABSOLUTE. [*rising*]. Nay, Madam, there shall be no constraint upon your inclinations, I promise you. If I have lost your heart, I resign the rest.—[*Aside.*] 'Gad, I must try what a little *spirit* will do.

LYDIA. [*rising*]. Then, Sir, let me tell you, the interest you had there was acquired by a mean, unmanly imposition, and deserved the punishment of fraud. What, you have been treating *me* like a child!—humouring my romance! and laughing, I suppose, at your success!

ABSOLUTE. You wrong me, Lydia, you wrong me. Only hear—

LYDIA. So, while *I* fondly imagined we were deceiving my relations, and flattered myself that I should outwit and incense them all—behold! my hopes are to be crushed at once, by my aunt's consent and approbation!—and *I* am myself the only dupe at last! [*Walking about in heat.*] But here, Sir, here is the picture—Beverley's picture! [*taking a miniature from her bosom*] which I have worn, night and day, in spite of threats and entreaties! There, Sir [*flings it at him*]—and be assured I throw the original from my heart as easily.

ABSOLUTE. Nay, nay, Ma'am, we will not differ as to that. Here [*taking out a picture*], here is Miss Lydia Languish. What a difference! Aye, *there* is the heavenly assenting smile that first gave soul and spirit to my hopes!—those are the lips which sealed a vow, as yet scarce dry in Cupid's calendar!—and *there*, the half resentful blush that *would* have checked the ardour of my thanks. Well, all that's past—all over indeed! There, Madam, in beauty, that copy is not equal to you, but in my mind its merit over the original, in being still the same, is such—that—I cannot find in my heart to part with it. [*Puts it up again.*]

LYDIA. [*softening*]. 'Tis *your own* doing, Sir. I—I—I suppose you are perfectly satisfied.

ABSOLUTE. Oh, most certainly. Sure now this is much better than being in love! Ha! ha! ha!—there's some spirit in *this*! What signifies breaking some scores of solemn promises, half an hundred vows, under one's hand, with the marks of a dozen or two angels to witness!—all that's of no consequence, you know. To be sure, people will say that Miss didn't know her own mind—but never mind that: or perhaps they may be ill-natured enough to hint that the gentleman grew tired of the lady and forsook her—but don't let that fret you.

LYDIA. There's no bearing his insolence. [*Bursts into tears.*]

[*Enter Mrs. Malaprop and Sir Anthony.*]

MRS. MALAPROP. [*entering*]. Come, we must interrupt your billing and cooing a while.

LYDIA. This is worse than your treachery and deceit, you base ingrate! [*Sobbing.*]

SIR ANTHONY. What the devil's the matter now! Z—ds! Mrs. Malaprop, this is the *oddest billing* and *cooing* I ever heard! But what the deuce is the meaning of it? I'm quite astonished!

ABSOLUTE. Ask the lady, Sir.

MRS. MALAPROP. Oh mercy! I'm quite analysed, for my part! Why, Lydia, what is the reason of this?

LYDIA. Ask the *gentleman*, Ma'am.

SIR ANTHONY. Z—ds! I shall be in a frenzy!—Why, Jack, you are not come out to be anyone else, are you?

MRS. MALAPROP. Aye, Sir, there's no more *trick*, is there? You are not like Cerberus, *three* gentlemen at once, are you?

ABSOLUTE. You'll not let me speak. I say the lady can account for this much better than I can.

LYDIA. Ma'am, you once commanded me never to think of Beverley again. There is the man— I now obey you:—for, from this moment I renounce him forever.

[*Exit Lydia.*]

MRS. MALAPROP. Oh mercy! and miracles! what a turn here is! Why, sure, Captain, you haven't behaved disrespectfully to my niece?

SIR ANTHONY. Ha! ha! ha!—ha! ha! ha!—now I see it—ha! ha! ha!—now I see it—you have been too lively, Jack.

ABSOLUTE. Nay, Sir, upon my word—

SIR ANTHONY. Come, no lying, Jack—I'm sure 'twas so.

MRS. MALAPROP. O lud! Sir Anthony! Oh fie, Captain!

ABSOLUTE. Upon my soul, Ma'am—

SIR ANTHONY. Come, no excuses; Jack; why, your father, you rogue, was so before you: the blood of the Absolutes was always impatient. Ha! ha! ha! poor little Lydia!—why, you've frightened her, you dog, you have.

ABSOLUTE. By all that's good, Sir—

SIR ANTHONY. Z—ds! say no more, I tell you. Mrs. Malaprop shall make your peace.—You must make his peace, Mrs. Malaprop; you must tell her 'tis Jack's way—tell her 'tis all our ways—it runs in the blood of our family! Come, away, Jack—ha! ha! ha! Mrs. Malaprop—a young villain! [*Pushes him out.*]

MRS. MALAPROP. Oh, Sir Anthony! Oh fie, Captain!

[*Exeunt severally.*]

SCENE III

The North Parade.

[*Enter Sir Lucius O'Trigger.*]

SIR LUCIUS. I wonder where this Captain Absolute hides himself. Upon my conscience! these officers are always in one's way in love-affairs. I remember I might have married Lady Dorothy Carmine, if it had not been for a little rogue of a major, who ran away with her before she could get a sight of me! And I wonder too what it is the ladies can see in them to be so fond of them—unless it be a touch of the old serpent in 'em, that makes the little creatures be caught, like vipers, with a bit of red cloth.—Hah!— isn't this the Captain coming?—faith it is! There is a probability of succeeding about that fellow that is mighty provoking! Who the devil is he talking to?

[*Steps aside.*]

[*Enter Captain Absolute.*]

ABSOLUTE. To what fine purpose I have been plotting! A noble reward for all my schemes, upon my soul! A little gypsy! I did not think her romance could have made her so d—d absurd either. 'Sdeath, I never was in a worse humour in my life! I could cut my own throat, or any other person's, with the greatest pleasure in the world!

SIR LUCIUS. Oh, faith! I'm in the luck of it—I never could have found him in a sweeter temper for my purpose—to be sure I'm just come in the nick! Now to enter into conversation with him, and so quarrel genteelly. [*Sir Lucius goes up to Absolute.*] —With regard to that matter, Captain, I must beg leave to differ in opinion with you.

ABSOLUTE. Upon my word then, you must be a very subtle disputant, because, Sir, I happened just then to be giving no opinion at all.

SIR LUCIUS. That's no reason. For give me leave to tell you, a man may *think* an untruth as well as *speak* one.

ABSOLUTE. Very true, Sir, but if a man never utters his thoughts I should think they might stand a chance of escaping controversy.

SIR LUCIUS. Then, Sir, you differ in opinion with me, which amounts to the same thing.

ABSOLUTE. Hark'ee, Sir Lucius—if I had not before known you to be a gentleman, upon my soul, I should not have discovered it at this interview, for what you can drive at, unless you mean to quarrel with me, I cannot conceive!

SIR LUCIUS. I humbly thank you, Sir, for the quickness of your apprehension. [*Bowing.*] You have named the very thing I would be at.

ABSOLUTE. Very well, Sir—I shall certainly not balk your inclinations—but I should be glad you would please to explain your motives.

SIR LUCIUS. Pray, Sir, be easy: the quarrel is a very pretty quarrel as it stands—we should only spoil it by trying to explain it. However, your memory is very short or you could not have forgot an affront you passed on me within this week. So no more, but name your time and place.

ABSOLUTE. Well, Sir, since you are so bent on it, the sooner the better; let it be this evening—here, by the Spring-Gardens. We shall scarcely be interrupted.

SIR LUCIUS. Faith! that same interruption in affairs of this nature shows very great ill-breeding. I don't know what's the reason, but in England, if a thing of this kind gets wind, people make such a pother that a gentleman can never fight in peace and quietness. However, if it's the same to you, Captain, I should take it as a particular kindness if you'd let us meet in King's-Mead-Fields, as a little business will call me there about six o'clock, and I may dispatch both matters at once.

ABSOLUTE. 'Tis the same to me exactly. A little after six, then, we will discuss this matter more seriously.

SIR LUCIUS. If you please, Sir, there will be very pretty small-sword light, though it won't do for a long shot. So that matter's settled! and my mind's at ease!

[*Exit Sir Lucius.*]

[*Enter Faulkland, meeting Absolute.*]

ABSOLUTE. Well met. I was going to look for you. O Faulkland! all the daemons of spite and disappointment have conspired against me! I'm so vexed that if I had not the prospect of a resource in being knocked o' the head by the by, I should scarce have spirits to tell you the cause.

FAULKLAND. What can you mean? Has Lydia changed her mind? I should have thought her duty and inclination would now have pointed to the same object.

ABSOLUTE. Aye, just as the eyes do of a person who squints: when her love-eye was fixed on me—t'other—her eye of duty, was finely obliqued:—but when duty bid her point that the same way—off t'other turned on a swivel, and secured its retreat with a frown!

FAULKLAND. But what's the resource you—

ABSOLUTE. Oh, to wind up the whole, a good-natured Irishman here has [*mimicking Sir Lucius*] begged leave to have the pleasure of cutting my throat, and I mean to indulge him—that's all.

FAULKLAND. Prithee, be serious.

ABSOLUTE. 'Tis fact, upon my soul. Sir Lucius O'Trigger—you know him by sight—for some affront, which I am sure I never intended, has obliged me to meet him this evening at six o'clock: 'tis on that account I wished to see you—you must go with me.

FAULKLAND. Nay, there must be some mistake, sure. Sir Lucius shall explain himself—and I dare say matters may be accommodated. But this evening, did you say? I wish it had been any other time.

ABSOLUTE. Why? there will be light enough. There will (as Sir Lucius says) "be very pretty small-sword light, though it won't do for a long shot." Confound his long shots!

FAULKLAND. But I am myself a good deal ruffled by a difference I have had with Julia. My vile tormenting temper has made me treat her so cruelly that I shall not be myself till we are reconciled.

ABSOLUTE. By heavens, Faulkland, you don't deserve her.

[*Enter Servant, gives Faulkland a letter.*]

FAULKLAND. O Jack! this is from Julia. I dread to open it. I fear it may be to take a last leave—perhaps to bid me return her letters and restore—Oh! how I suffer for my folly!

ABSOLUTE. Here—let me see. [*Takes the letter and opens it.*] Aye, a final sentence indeed!—'tis all over with you, faith!

FAULKLAND. Nay, Jack—don't keep me in suspense.

ABSOLUTE. Hear then.—"*As I am convinced that my dear* FAULKLAND'*s own reflections have already upbraided him for his last unkindness to me, I will not add a word on the subject. I wish to speak with you as soon as possible.—Yours ever and truly,* JULIA."—There's stubbornness and resentment for you! [*Gives him the letter.*] Why, man, you don't seem one whit happier at this.

FAULKLAND. Oh, yes, I am—but—but—

ABSOLUTE. Confound your *buts*. You never hear anything that would make another man bless himself, but you immediately d—n it with a *but*.

FAULKLAND. Now, Jack, as you are my friend, own honestly—don't you think there is something forward, something indelicate, in this haste to forgive? Women should never sue for reconciliation: that should always come from us. They should retain their coldness till *wooed* to kindness—and their *pardon*, like their *love*, should "not unsought be won."

ABSOLUTE. I have not patience to listen to you—thou'rt incorrigible!—so say no more on the subject. I must go to settle a few matters. Let me see you before six—remember—at my lodgings. A poor industrious devil like me, who have toiled, and drudged, and plotted to gain my ends, and am at last disappointed by other people's folly, may in pity be allowed to swear and grumble a little; but a captious sceptic in love, a slave to fretfulness and whim, who has no difficulties but of his own creating, is a subject more fit for ridicule than compassion!

[*Exit Absolute.*]

FAULKLAND. I feel his reproaches, yet I would not change this too exquisite nicety for the gross content with which *he* tramples on the thorns of love. His engaging me in this duel has started an idea in my head, which I will instantly pursue. I'll use it as the touchstone of Julia's sincerity and disinterestedness. If her love prove pure and sterling ore, my name will rest on it with honour!—and once I've stamped it there, I lay aside my doubts forever—; but if the dross of selfishness, the alloy of pride predominate, 'twill be best to leave her as a toy for some less cautious fool to sigh for.

[*Exit Faulkland.*]

Act V

SCENE I

Julia's dressing-room.

[*Julia sola.*]

JULIA. How this message has alarmed me! What dreadful accident can he mean? why such charge to be alone? O Faulkland! how many unhappy moments, how many tears, have you cost me!

[*Enter Faulkland.*]

JULIA. What means this?—why this caution, Faulkland?

FAULKLAND. Alas! Julia, I am come to take a long farewell.

JULIA. Heavens! what do you mean?

FAULKLAND. You see before you a wretch whose life is forfeited. Nay, start not! the infirmity of my temper has drawn all this misery on me. I left you fretful and passionate—an untoward accident drew me into a quarrel—the event is that I must fly this kingdom instantly. O Julia, had I been so fortunate as to have called you mine entirely before this mischance had fallen on me, I should not so deeply dread my banishment!

JULIA. My soul is oppressed with sorrow at the nature of your misfortune: had these adverse circumstances arisen from a less fatal cause, I should have felt strong comfort in the thought that I could not chase from your bosom every doubt of the warm sincerity of my love. My heart has long known no other guardian. I now entrust my person to your honour—we will fly together. When safe from pursuit, my father's will may be fulfilled, and I receive a legal claim to be the partner of your sorrows, and tenderest comforter. Then on the bosom of your wedded Julia, you may lull your keen regret to slumbering; while virtuous love, with a cherub's hand, shall smooth the brow of upbraiding thought, and pluck the thorn from compunction.

FAULKLAND. O Julia! I am bankrupt in gratitude! But the time is so pressing, it calls on you for so hasty a resolution—would you not wish some hours to weigh the advantages you forego, and what little compensation poor Faulkland can make you beside his solitary love?

JULIA. I ask not a moment. No, Faulkland, I have loved you for yourself: and if I now, more than ever, prize the solemn engagement which so long has pledged us to each other, it is because it leaves no room for hard aspersions on my fame, and puts the seal of duty to an act of love.—But let us not linger. Perhaps this delay—

FAULKLAND. 'Twill be better I should not venture out again till dark. Yet am I grieved to think what numberless distresses will press heavy on your gentle disposition!

JULIA. Perhaps your fortune may be forfeited by this unhappy act. I know not whether 'tis so, but sure that alone can never make us unhappy. The little I have will be sufficient to support us; and exile never should be splendid.

FAULKLAND. Aye, but in such an abject state of life, my wounded pride perhaps may increase the natural fretfulness of my temper, till I become a rude, morose companion, beyond your patience to endure. Perhaps the recollection of a deed my conscience cannot justify may haunt me in such gloomy and unsocial fits that I shall hate the tenderness that would relieve me, break from your arms, and quarrel with your fondness!

JULIA. If your thoughts should assume so unhappy a bent, you will the more want some mild and affectionate spirit to watch over and console you, one who, by bearing *your* infirmities with gentleness and resignation, may teach you *so* to bear the evils of your fortune.

FAULKLAND. Julia, I have proved you to the quick! and with this useless device I throw away all my doubts. How shall I plead to be forgiven this last unworthy effect of my restless, unsatisfied disposition?

JULIA. Has no such disaster happened as you related?

FAULKLAND. I am ashamed to own that it was all pretended; yet in pity, Julia, do not kill me with resenting a fault which never can be repeated, but sealing, this once, my pardon, let me to-morrow, in the face of heaven, receive my future guide and monitress, and expiate my past folly by years of tender adoration.

JULIA. Hold, Faulkland! That you are free from a crime which I before feared to name, heaven knows how sincerely I rejoice! These are tears of thankfulness for that! But that your cruel doubts should have urged you to an imposition that has wrung my heart, gives me now a pang more keen than I can express!

FAULKLAND. By heavens! Julia—

JULIA. Yet hear me. My father loved you, Faulkland! and you preserved the life that tender parent gave me; in his presence I pledged my hand—joyfully pledged it—where before I had given my heart. When, soon after, I lost that parent, it seemed to me that Providence had, in Faulkland, shown me whither to transfer without a pause my grateful duty, as well as my affection: hence I have been content to bear from you what pride and delicacy would have forbid me from another. I will not upbraid you by repeating how you have trifled with my sincerity.

FAULKLAND. I confess it all! yet hear—

JULIA. After such a year of trial, I might have flattered myself that I should not have been insulted with a new probation of my sincerity, as cruel as unnecessary! I now see it is not in your nature to be content or confident in love. With this conviction, I never will be yours. While I had hopes that my persevering attention and unreproaching kindness might in time reform your temper, I should have been happy to have gained a dearer influence over you; but I will not furnish you with a licensed power to keep alive an incorrigible fault, at the expense of one who never would contend with you.

FAULKLAND. Nay, but Julia, by my soul and honour, if after this—

JULIA. But one word more. As my faith has once been given to you, I never will barter it with another. I shall pray for your happiness with the truest sincerity; and the dearest blessing I can ask of heaven to send you will be to charm you from that unhappy temper which alone has prevented the performance of our solemn engagement. All I request of *you* is that you will yourself reflect upon this infirmity, and when you number up the many true delights it has deprived you of, let it not be your *least* regret that it lost you the love of one, who would have followed you in beggary through the world!

[*Exit.*]

FAULKLAND. She's gone!—forever! There was an awful resolution in her manner, that riveted me to my place. O fool!—dolt!—barbarian! Curst as I am with more imperfections than my fellow-wretches, kind Fortune sent a heaven-gifted cherub to my aid, and, like a ruffian, I have driven her from my side! I must now haste to my appointment. Well, my mind is tuned for such a scene. I shall wish only to become a principal in it, and reverse the tale my cursed folly put me upon forging here. O love!—tormentor—fiend! whose influence, like the moon's, acting on men of dull souls, makes idiots of them, but meeting subtler spirits, betrays their course, and urges sensibility to madness!

[*Exit.*]

[*Enter Maid and Lydia.*]

MAID. My mistress, Ma'am, I know, was here just now—perhaps she is only in the next room.

[*Exit Maid.*]

LYDIA. Heigh-ho! Though he has used me so, this fellow runs strangely in my head. I believe one lecture from my grave cousin will make me recall him.

[*Enter Julia.*]

LYDIA. O Julia, I am come to you with such an appetite for consolation.—Lud! child, what's the matter with you? You have been crying! I'll be hanged if that Faulkland has not been tormenting you!

JULIA. You mistake the cause of my uneasiness. Something *has* flurried me a little. Nothing that you can guess at.— [*Aside.*] I would not accuse Faulkland to a sister!

LYDIA. Ah! whatever vexations you may have, I can assure you mine surpass them.—You know who Beverley proves to be?

JULIA. I will now own to you, Lydia, that Mr. Faulkland had before informed me of the whole affair. Had young Absolute been the person you took him for, I should not have accepted your confidence on the subject without a serious endeavour to counteract your caprice.

LYDIA. So, then, I see I have been deceived by everyone! But I don't care—I'll never have him.

JULIA. Nay, Lydia—

LYDIA. Why, is it not provoking? when I thought we were coming to the prettiest distress imaginable, to find myself made a mere Smithfield bargain of at last! There had I projected one of the most sentimental elopements! so becoming a disguise! so amiable a ladder of ropes! Conscious moon—four horses—Scotch parson—with such surprise to Mrs. Malaprop, and such paragraphs in the newspapers! Oh, I shall die with disappointment!

JULIA. I don't wonder at it!

LYDIA. Now—sad reverse!—what have I to expect, but, after a deal of flimsy preparation, with a bishop's licence, and my aunt's blessing, to go simpering up to the altar; or perhaps be cried three times in a country-church, and have an unmannerly fat clerk ask the consent of every butcher in the parish to join John Absolute and Lydia Languish, Spinster! Oh, that I should live to hear myself called Spinster!

JULIA. Melancholy, indeed!

LYDIA. How mortifying to remember the dear delicious shifts I used to be put to, to gain half a minute's conversation with this fellow! How often have I stole forth in the coldest night in January, and found him in the garden, stuck like a dripping statue! There would he kneel to me in the snow, and sneeze and cough so pathetically! he shivering with cold, and I with apprehension! and while the freezing blast numbed our joints, how warmly would he press me to pity his flame, and glow with mutual ardour! Ah, Julia, that was something like being in love!

JULIA. If I were in spirits, Lydia, I should chide you only by laughing heartily at you: but it suits more the situation of my mind, at present, earnestly to entreat you not to let a man, who loves you with sincerity, suffer that unhappiness from your caprice, which I know too well caprice can inflict.

LYDIA. O lud! what has brought my aunt here?

[Enter Mrs. Malaprop, Fag, and David.]

MRS. MALAPROP. So! so! here's fine work!—here's fine suicide, parricide, and simulation going on in the fields! and Sir Anthony not to be found to prevent the antistrophe!

JULIA. For heaven's sake, madam, what's the meaning of this?

MRS. MALAPROP. That gentleman can tell you—'twas he enveloped the affair to me.

LYDIA. [to Fag]. Do Sir, will you, inform us.

FAG. Ma'am, I should hold myself very deficient in every requisite that forms the man of breeding if I delayed a moment to give all the information in my power to a lady so deeply interested in the affair as you are.

LYDIA. But quick! quick, Sir!

FAG. True, Ma'am, as you say, one should be quick in divulging matters of this nature; for should we be tedious, perhaps while we are flourishing on the subject, two or three lives may be lost!

LYDIA. O patience! Do, Ma'am, for heaven's sake! tell us what is the matter!

MRS. MALAPROP. Why, murder's the matter! slaughter's the matter! killing's the matter! But he can tell you the perpendiculars.

LYDIA. Then, prithee, Sir, be brief.

FAG. Why then, Ma'am—as to murder, I cannot take upon me to say—and as to slaughter, or manslaughter, that will be as the jury finds it.

LYDIA. But who, Sir—who are engaged in this?

FAG. Faith, Ma'am, one is a young gentleman whom I should be very sorry anything was to happen to—a very pretty behaved gentleman! We have lived much together, and always on terms.

LYDIA. But who is this? who! who! who!

FAG. My master, Ma'am, my master—I speak of my master.

LYDIA. Heavens! What, Captain Absolute!

MRS. MALAPROP. Oh, to be sure, you are frightened now!

JULIA. But who are with him, Sir?

FAG. As to the rest, Ma'am, this gentleman can inform you better than I.

JULIA. [to David]. Do speak, friend.

DAVID. Look'ee, my lady—by the Mass! there's mischief going on. Folks don't use to meet for amusement with fire-arms, fire-locks, fire-engines, fire-screens, fire-office, and the devil knows what other crackers beside! This, my lady, I say, has an angry favour.

JULIA. But who is there beside Captain Absolute, friend?

DAVID. My poor master—under favour, for mentioning him first. You know me, my lady—I am David, and my master, of course, is, or *was*, Squire Acres. Then comes Squire Faulkland.

JULIA. Do, Ma'am, let us instantly endeavour to prevent mischief.

MRS. MALAPROP. Oh fie—it would be very inelegant in us: we should only participate things.

DAVID. Ah! do, Mrs. Aunt, save a few lives. They are desperately given, believe me. Above all, there is tnat bloodthirsty Philistine, Sir Lucius O'Trigger.

MRS. MALAPROP. Sir Lucius O'Trigger! O mercy! have they drawn poor little dear Sir Lucius into the scrape? Why, how you stand, girl! you have no more feeling than one of the Derbyshire putrefactions!

LYDIA. What are we to do, Madam?

MRS. MALAPROP. Why, fly with the utmost felicity, to be sure, to prevent mischief. Here, friend—you can show us the place?

FAG. If you please, Ma'am, I will conduct you.—David, do you look for Sir Anthony.

[Exit David.]

MRS. MALAPROP. Come, girls!—this gentleman will exhort us.—Come, Sir, you're our envoy—lead the way, and we'll precede.

FAG. Not a step before the ladies for the world!

MRS. MALAPROP. You're sure you know the spot?

FAG. I think I can find it, Ma'am; and one good thing is we shall hear the report of the pistols as we draw near, so we can't well miss them; never fear, Ma'am, never fear.

[Exeunt, he talking.]

SCENE II

South Parade.

[Enter Absolute, putting his sword under his greatcoat.]

ABSOLUTE. A sword seen in the streets of Bath would raise as great an alarm as a mad dog. How provoking this is in Faulkland! never punctual! I shall be obliged to go without him at last. Oh, the devil! here's Sir Anthony! How shall I escape him? [Muffles up his face, and takes a circle to go off.]

[Enter Sir Anthony.]

SIR ANTHONY. How one may be deceived at a little distance! Only that I see he don't know me, I could have sworn that was Jack!—Hey! 'Gad's life! it is. Why, Jack!—what are you afraid of, hey!—Sure, I'm right.—Why, Jack!—Jack Absolute! [Goes up to him.]

ABSOLUTE. Really, Sir, you have the advantage of me: I don't remember ever to have had the honour. My name is Saunderson, at your service.

SIR ANTHONY. Sir, I beg your pardon—I took you—hey!—why, z—ds! it is—stay—[looks up to his face]. So, so—your humble servant, Mr. Saunderson! Why, you scoundrel, what tricks are you after now?

ABSOLUTE. Oh! a joke, Sir, a joke! I came here on purpose to look for you, Sir.

SIR ANTHONY. You did! Well, I am glad you were so lucky. But what are you muffled up so for? What's this for?—hey?

ABSOLUTE. 'Tis cool, Sir; isn't it?—rather chilly, somehow. But I shall be late—I have a particular engagement.

SIR ANTHONY. Stay. Why, I thought you were looking for me? Pray, Jack, where is't you are going?

ABSOLUTE. Going, Sir!

SIR ANTHONY. Aye—where are you going?

ABSOLUTE. Where am I going?

SIR ANTHONY. You unmannerly puppy!

ABSOLUTE. I was going, Sir, to—to—to—to Lydia—Sir, to Lydia, to make matters up if I could; and I was looking for you, Sir, to—to—

SIR ANTHONY. To go with you, I suppose. Well, come along.

ABSOLUTE. Oh! z—ds! no, Sir, not for the world! I wished to meet with you, Sir—to—to—to—. You find it cool, I'm sure, Sir—you'd better not stay out.

SIR ANTHONY. Cool!—not at all. Well, Jack—and what will you say to Lydia?

ABSOLUTE. O, Sir, beg her pardon, humour her, promise and vow. But I detain you, Sir—consider the cold air on your gout.

SIR ANTHONY. Oh, not at all!—not at all! I'm in no hurry. Ah! Jack, you youngsters, when once you are wounded here—[putting his hand to Absolute's breast] Hey! what the deuce have you got there?

ABSOLUTE. Nothing, Sir—nothing.

SIR ANTHONY. What's this? here's something d—d hard!

ABSOLUTE. Oh, trinkets, Sir! trinkets—a bauble for Lydia!

SIR ANTHONY. Nay, let me see your taste. [Pulls his coat open, the sword falls.] Trinkets!—a bauble for Lydia! Z—ds! Sirrah, you are not going to cut her throat, are you?

ABSOLUTE. Ha! ha! ha! I thought it would divert you, Sir; though I didn't mean to tell you till afterwards.

SIR ANTHONY. You didn't? Yes, this is a very diverting trinket, truly!

ABSOLUTE. Sir, I'll explain to you. You know, Sir,

Lydia is romantic, dev'lish romantic, and very absurd of course. Now, Sir, I intend, if she refuses to forgive me, to unsheathe this sword and swear I'll fall upon its point, and expire at her feet!

SIR ANTHONY. Fall upon a fiddle-stick's end! Why, I suppose it is the very thing that would please her. Get along, you fool.

ABSOLUTE. Well, Sir, you shall hear of my success— you shall hear. "O Lydia!—forgive me, or this pointed steel"—says I.

SIR ANTHONY. "O, booby! stab away and welcome" —says she. Get along!—and d—n your trinkets!

[Exit Absolute.]

[Enter David, running.]

DAVID. Stop him! Stop him! Murder! Thief! Fire! Stop fire! Stop fire! O! Sir Anthony—call! call! bid 'em stop! Murder! Fire!

SIR ANTHONY. Fire! Murder! Where?

DAVID. Oons! he's out of sight! and I'm out of breath, for my part! O, Sir Anthony, why didn't you stop him? why didn't you stop him?

SIR ANTHONY. Z—ds! the fellow's mad! Stop whom? Stop Jack?

DAVID. Aye, the Captain, Sir! there's murder and slaughter—

SIR ANTHONY. Murder!

DAVID. Aye, please you, Sir Anthony, there's all kinds of murder, all sorts of slaughter to be seen in the fields: there's fighting going on, Sir—bloody sword-and-gun fighting!

SIR ANTHONY. Who are going to fight, dunce?

DAVID. Everybody that I know of, Sir Anthony— everybody is going to fight; my poor master, Sir Lucius O'Trigger, your son, the Captain—

SIR ANTHONY. Oh, the dog! I see his tricks.—Do you know the place?

DAVID. King's-Mead-Fields.

SIR ANTHONY. You know the way?

DAVID. Not an inch; but I'll call the mayor— aldermen—constables—church-wardens—and beadles—we can't be too many to part them.

SIR ANTHONY. Come along—give me your shoulder! we'll get assistance as we go. The lying villain! Well, I shall be in such a frenzy! So—this was the history of his trinkets! I'll bauble him!

[Exeunt.]

SCENE III

King's-Mead-Fields

[Sir Lucius and Acres, with pistols.]

ACRES. By my valour! then, Sir Lucius, forty yards is a good distance. Odds levels and aims! I say it is a good distance.

SIR LUCIUS. Is it for muskets or small fieldpieces? Upon my conscience, Mr. Acres, you must leave those things to me. Stay now—I'll show you. [Measures paces along the stage.] There now, that is a very pretty distance—a pretty gentleman's distance.

ACRES. Z—ds! we might as well fight in a sentry-box! I tell you, Sir Lucius, the farther he is off, the cooler I shall take my aim.

SIR LUCIUS. Faith! then I suppose you would aim at him best of all if he was out of sight!

ACRES. No, Sir Lucius, but I should think forty, or eight and thirty yards—

SIR LUCIUS. Pho! pho! nonsense! Three or four feet between the mouths of your pistols is as good as a mile.

ACRES. Odds bullets, no! By my valour! there is no merit in killing him so near: do, my dear Sir Lucius, let me bring him down at a long shot—a long shot, Sir Lucius, if you love me!

SIR LUCIUS. Well—the gentleman's friend and I must settle that. But tell me now, Mr. Acres, in case of an accident, is there any little will or commission I could execute for you?

ACRES. I am much obliged to you, Sir Lucius, but I don't understand—

SIR LUCIUS. Why, you may think there's no being shot at without a little risk, and if an unlucky bullet should carry a *quietus* with it—I say it will be no time then to be bothering you about family matters.

ACRES. A *quietus*!

SIR LUCIUS. For instance, now—if that should be the case—would you choose to be pickled and sent home? or would it be the same to you to lie here in the Abbey? I'm told there is very snug lying in the Abbey.

ACRES. Pickled! Snug lying in the Abbey! Odds tremors! Sir Lucius, don't talk so!

SIR LUCIUS. I suppose, Mr. Acres, you never were engaged in an affair of this kind before?

ACRES. No, Sir Lucius, never before.

SIR LUCIUS. Ah! that's a pity! there's nothing like being used to a thing. Pray now, how would you receive the gentleman's shot?

ACRES. Odds files! I've practiced that. There, Sir Lucius—there [*puts himself in an attitude*] —a side-front, hey? Odd! I'll make myself small enough: I'll stand edge-ways.

SIR LUCIUS. Now—you're quite out, for if you stand so when I take my aim—[*levelling at him*].

ACRES. Z—ds! Sir Lucius—are you sure it is not cocked?

SIR LUCIUS. Never fear.

ACRES. But—but—you don't know—it may go off of its own head!

SIR LUCIUS. Pho! be easy. Well, now if I hit you in the body, my bullet has a double chance, for if it is misses a vital part on your right side, 'twill be very hard if it don't succeed on the left!

ACRES. A vital part!

SIR LUCIUS. But, there—fix yourself so. [*Placing him.*] Let him see the broad side of your full front—there—now a ball or two may pass clean through your body, and never do any harm at all.

ACRES. Clean through me! a ball or two clean through me!

SIR LUCIUS. Aye, may they; and it is much the genteelest attitude into the bargain.

ACRES. Look'ee! Sir Lucius—I'd just as lieve be shot in an awkward posture as a genteel one—so, by my valour! I will stand edge-ways.

SIR LUCIUS. [*looking at his watch*]. Sure they don't mean to disappoint us. Hah? No, faith—I think I see them coming.

ACRES. Hey! what! coming—

SIR LUCIUS. Aye. Who are those yonder getting over the stile?

ACRES. There are two of them indeed! Well—let them come—hey, Sir Lucius? We—we—we—we—won't run.

SIR LUCIUS. Run!

ACRES. No—I say—we *won't* run, by my valour!

SIR LUCIUS. What the devil's the matter with you?

ACRES. Nothing—nothing—my dear friend—my dear Sir Lucius—but—I—I—I don't feel quite so bold, somehow—as I did.

SIR LUCIUS. Oh fie! consider your honour.

ACRES. Aye—true—my honour. Do, Sir Lucius, edge in a word or two every now and then about my honour.

SIR LUCIUS. [*looking*]. Well, here they're coming.

ACRES. Sir Lucius—if I wa'n't with you, I should almost think I was afraid. If my valour should leave me! Valour will come and go.

SIR LUCIUS. Then, pray, keep it fast while you have it.

ACRES. Sir Lucius—I doubt it is going—yes—my valour is certainly going! it is sneaking off! I feel it oozing out as it were at the palms of my hands!

SIR LUCIUS. Your honour—your honour. Here they are.

ACRES. Oh mercy! now that I were safe at Clod-Hall! or could be shot before I was aware!

[*Enter Faulkland and Absolute.*]

SIR LUCIUS. Gentlemen, your most obedient—hah!—what—Captain Absolute! So, I suppose, Sir, you are come here, just like myself—to do a kind office, first for your friend—then to proceed to business on your own account.

ACRES. What, Jack! my dear Jack! my dear friend!

ABSOLUTE. Hark'ee, Bob, Beverley's at hand.

SIR LUCIUS. Well, Mr. Acres, I don't blame your saluting the gentleman civilly. So, Mr. Beverley [*to Faulkland*], if you'll choose your weapons, the Captain and I will measure the ground.

FAULKLAND. *My* weapons, Sir!

ACRES. Odd's life! Sir Lucius, I'm not going to fight Mr. Faulkland; these are my particular friends.

SIR LUCIUS. What, Sir, did not you come here to fight Mr. Acres?

FAULKLAND. Not I, upon my word, Sir.

SIR LUCIUS. Well, now, that's mighty provoking! But I hope, Mr. Faulkland, as there are three of us come on purpose for the game, you won't be so cantankerous as to spoil the party by sitting out.

ABSOLUTE. Oh pray, Faulkland, fight to oblige Sir Lucius.

FAULKLAND. Nay, if Mr. Acres is so bent on the matter—

ACRES. No, no, Mr. Faulkland—I'll bear my disappointment like a Christian. Look'ee, Sir Lucius, there's no occasion at all for me to fight; and if it is the same to you, I'd as lieve let it alone.

SIR LUCIUS. Observe me, Mr. Acres—I must not be trifled with. You have certainly challenged somebody, and you came here to fight him. Now, if that gentleman is willing to represent him, I can't see, for my soul, why it isn't just the same thing.

ACRES. Why no, Sir Lucius—I tell you, 'tis one Beverley I've challenged—a fellow you see, that dare not show his face! If *he* were here, I'd make him give up his pretensions directly!

ABSOLUTE. Hold, Bob—let me set you right. There is no such man as Beverley in the case. The person who assumed that name is before you; and as his pretensions are the same in both characters, he is ready to support them in whatever way you please.

SIR LUCIUS. Well, this is lucky! Now you have an opportunity—

ACRES. What, quarrel with my dear friend Jack Absolute? Not if he were fifty Beverley! Z—ds! Sir Lucius, you would not have me be so unnatural.

SIR LUCIUS. Upon my conscience, Mr. Acres, your valour has *oozed* away with a vengeance!

ACRES. Not in the least! Odds backs and abettors! I'll be your second with all my heart, and if you should get a *quietus!,* you may command me entirely. I'll get you *snug lying* in the *Abbey here;* or *pickle* you, and send you over to Blunderbuss-Hall, or anything of the kind, with the greatest pleasure.

SIR LUCIUS. Pho! pho! you are little better than a coward.

ACRES. Mind, gentlemen he calls me a *coward;* coward was the word, by my valour!

SIR LUCIUS. Well, Sir?

ACRES. Look'ee, Sir Lucius, 'tisn't that I mind the word coward—*coward* may be said in joke. But if you had called me a *poltroon,* odds daggers and balls!—

SIR LUCIUS. Well, Sir?

ACRES. —I should have thought you a very ill-bred man.

SIR LUCIUS. Pho! you are beneath my notice.

ABSOLUTE. Nay, Sir Lucius, you can't have a better second than my friend Acres. He is a most *determined dog,* called in the country, *Fighting Bob.* He generally *kills a man a week;* don't you, Bob?

ACRES. Aye—at home!

SIR LUCIUS. Well then, Captain, 'tis we must begin. So come out, my little counsellor [*draws his sword*], and ask the gentleman whether he will resign the lady without forcing you to proceed against him.

ABSOLUTE. Come on then, Sir [*draws*]; since you won't let it be an amicable suit, here's my reply.

[*Enter Sir Anthony, David, and the Women.*]

DAVID. Knock 'em all down, sweet Sir Anthony; knock down my master in particular, and bind his hands over to their good behavior!

SIR ANTHONY. Put up, Jack, put up, or I shall be in a frenzy. How came you in a duel, Sir?

ABSOLUTE. Faith, Sir, that gentleman can tell you better than I; 'twas he called on me, and you know, Sir, I serve his Majesty.

SIR ANTHONY. Here's a pretty fellow! I catch him going to cut a man's throat, and he tells me to serve his Majesty! Z—ds! Sirrah, then how durst you draw the King's sword against one of his subjects?

ABSOLUTE. Sir, I tell you! That gentleman called me out, without explaining his reasons.

SIR ANTHONY. Gad! Sir, how came you to call my son out, without explaining your reasons?

SIR LUCIUS. Your son, Sir, insulted me in a manner which my honour could not brook.

SIR ANTHONY. Z—ds! Jack, how durst you insult the gentleman in a manner which his honour could not brook?

MRS. MALAPROP. Come, come, let's have no honour before ladies. Captain Absolute, come here. How could you intimidate us so? Here's Lydia has been terrified to death for you.

ABSOLUTE. For fear I should be killed, or escape, Ma'am?

MRS. MALAPROP. Nay, no delusions to the past. Lydia is convinced; speak, child.

SIR LUCIUS. With your leave, Ma'am, I must put in a word here. I believe I could interpret the young lady's silence. Now mark—

LYDIA. What is it you mean, Sir?

SIR LUCIUS. Come, come, Delia, we must be serious now—this is no time for trifling.

LYDIA. 'Tis true, Sir; and your reproof bids me offer this gentleman my hand, and solicit the return of his affections.

ABSOLUTE. O! my little angel, say you so? Sir Lucius, I perceive there must be some mistake here. With regard to the affront which you affirm I have given you, I can only say that it could not have been intentional. And as you must be convinced that I should not fear to support a real injury, you shall now see that I am not ashamed to atone for an inadvertency. I ask your pardon. But for this lady, while honoured with her approbation, I will support my claim against any man whatever.

SIR ANTHONY. Well said, Jack! and I'll stand by you, my boy.

ACRES. Mind, I give up all my claim—I make no pretensions to anything in the world—and if I can't get a wife without fighting for her, by my valour! I'll live a bachelor.

SIR LUCIUS. Captain, give me your hand—an affront handsomely acknowledged becomes an obligation—and as for the lady, if she chooses to deny her own handwriting here—[*takes out letters*].

MRS. MALAPROP. Oh, he will dissolve my mystery! Sir Lucius, perhaps there's some mistake—perhaps, I can illuminate—

SIR LUCIUS. Pray, old gentlewoman, don't interfere where you have no business. Miss Languish, are you my Delia, or not?

LYDIA. Indeed, Sir Lucius, I am not.

[Lydia and Absolute walk aside.]

MRS. MALAPROP. Sir Lucius O'Trigger, ungrateful as you are, I own the soft impeachment—pardon my blushes, I am Delia.

SIR LUCIUS. You Delia!—pho! pho! be easy.

MRS. MALAPROP. Why, thou barbarous Vandyke!— those letters are mine. When you are more sensible of my benignity, perhaps I may be brought to encourage your addresses.

SIR LUCIUS. Mrs. Malaprop, I am extremely sensible of your condescension; and whether you or Lucy have put this trick upon me, I am equally beholden to you. And to show you I'm not ungrateful— Captain Absolute! since you have taken that lady from me, I'll give you my Delia into the bargain.

ABSOLUTE. I am much obliged to you, Sir Lucius; but here's our friend, Fighting Bob, unprovided for.

SIR LUCIUS. Hah! little Valour—here, will you make your fortune?

ACRES. Odds wrinkles! No. But give me your hand, Sir Lucius; forget and forgive; but if ever I give you a chance of *pickling* me again, say Bob Acres is a dunce, that's all.

SIR ANTHONY. Come, Mrs. Malaprop, don't be cast down—you are in your bloom yet.

MRS. MALAPROP. O Sir Anthony!—men are all barbarians—

[All retire but Julia and Faulkland.]

JULIA. [aside]. He seems dejected and unhappy—not sullen. There was some foundation, however, for the tale he told me. O woman! how true should be your judgment, when your resolution is so weak!

FAULKLAND. Julia! how can I sue for what I so little deserve? I dare not presume—yet Hope is the child of Penitence.

JULIA. Oh! Faulkland, you have not been more faulty in your unkind treatment of me than I am now in wanting inclination to resent it. As my heart honestly bids me place my weakness to the account of love, I should be ungenerous not to admit the same plea for yours.

FAULKLAND. Now I shall be blest indeed!

[Sir Anthony comes forward.]

SIR ANTHONY. What's going on here? So you have been quarrelling too, I warrant. Come, Julia, I never interfered before; but let me have a hand in the matter at last. All the faults I have ever seen in my friend Faulkland seemed to proceed from what he calls the *delicacy* and *warmth* of his affection for you. There, marry him directly, Julia; you'll find he'll mend surprisingly!

[The rest come forward.]

SIR LUCIUS. Come now, I hope there is no dissatisfied person but what is content; for as I have been disappointed myself, it will be very hard if I have not the satisfaction of seeing other people succeed better—

ACRES. You are right, Sir Lucius. So, Jack, I wish you joy—Mr. Faulkland the same.—Ladies,—come now, to show you I'm neither vexed nor angry, odds tabours and pipes! I'll order the fiddles in half an hour to the New Rooms, and I insist on your all meeting me there.

SIR ANTHONY. Gad! Sir, I like your spirit; and at night we single lads will drink a health to the young couples, and a husband to Mrs. Malaprop.

FAULKLAND. Our partners are stolen from us, Jack—I hope to be congratulated by each other—yours for having checked in time the errors of an ill-directed imagination which might have betrayed an innocent heart; and *mine,* for having, by her gentleness and candour, reformed the unhappy temper of one who by it made wretched whom he loved most, and tortured the heart he ought to have adored.

ABSOLUTE. Well, Faulkland, we have both tasted the bitters, as well as the sweets, of love—with this difference only, that *you* always prepared the bitter cup for yourself, while *I*—

LYDIA. Was always obliged to *me* for it, hey! Mr. Modesty?—But come, no more of that: our happiness is now as unalloyed as general.

JULIA. Then let us study to preserve it so; and while Hope pictures to us a flattering scene of future Bliss, let us deny its pencil those colors which are too bright to be lasting. When Hearts deserving Happiness would unite their fortunes, Virtue would crown them with an unfading garland of modest, hurtless flowers; but ill-judging Passion will force the gaudier Rose into the wreath, whose thorn offends them, when its leaves are dropt!

[Exeunt omnes.]

ESSAY: AN APPROACH TO THE PLAY

For Lydia the plot is simple: Elope and live in a love that will make poverty irrelevant. However, she has no idea of what even so-called genteel poverty might be like. She seems never to have missed a meal, for example, let alone been without servants or a private house. While she is the force which makes the plot move, she is also therefore the object of a gentle satire of the unrealistic, sentimentalized attitudes of the middle classes, or perhaps of the attitudes of the protected young women of this class whose education consisted mainly of reading sentimental novels. Mrs. Malaprop's unique combination of pretensions to knowledge and misuse of words makes a similar point about women, though in a more openly satiric way.

Analyzing Captain Absolute is more complicated, for he is more realistic, though equally loving: He wants Lydia's love, but without sacrificing her fortune or his own. These desires seem incompatible. To win Lydia's affection, he must pretend to be the ensign and seem to sacrifice comfort for love; yet to retain their fortunes, he must be seen by Lydia's aunt, Mrs. Malaprop, as well as by his own father, to be Captain Absolute, son of Sir Anthony.

This problem which he faces reflects the contradictory view of the age toward love: that it is both a practical affair in which parents have the final choice, and at the same time a reciprocal romantic relationship between equals. Patriarchal values are particularly emphasized by Sir Anthony's tyrannical insistence on his son's obedience. Although both female romantic leads, Julia as well as Lydia, are willing to give up everything for love, the young men are caught in different versions of this impasse between love and obedience and seem both less single-minded and less admirable than the women. This portrayal of men by a male playwright may also reveal the inherent contradictions within this society between its professions of patriarchy and the realities of its sexual politics, particularly in the new "age of feeling."

Women, too, are satirized, however. Lydia's reading taste runs to novels—the most popular books of the time, books whose popularity was based on their support of this new ideology of "feeling." These novels reinforced aspects of human experience which women were stereotypically thought to represent, and their mainly female readers were often trivialized by male critics for displaying those impractical sympathetic affections which the novels sought to elicit. When her aunt comes to visit, however, Lydia prominently displays copies of *Fordyce's Sermons* and *Lord Chesterfield's Letters*, suggesting that her taste runs toward matters of reason and morality, rather than toward romance. Her society teaches her to falsify herself, and if she is not aware of that fact, she is at least aware of the pressure that this contradiction causes in her life. (There seems to be some ambivalence about these satiric portraits, perhaps because the male playwright feels analogous, though different, pressure himself.)

Faulkland, on the other hand, gives us a full-length satiric portrait of the new stereotypical male hero, the man of feeling. Sheridan's relatively straightforward ridicule of this character may suggest the conservative side of his generally ambivalent sensibility. Faulkland is so worried by Julia's emotions, and by everyone else's, that he cannot ever decide on his own about a course of action. He is so full of feeling that he seems to lack all conviction. Why Julia loves him seems something of a puzzle, and at one point she almost decides that he is too uncommitted for her to give herself to him in marriage. This satire of "feeling" has a light touch, however. It is not worse than the old patriarchal rigidities, and both Lydia and Faulkland manage to "get" their beloveds. It is a principle which the age felt important, even if it was ambivalent about it.

Bob Acres is a type from the older school, from the generation of Aphra Behn in the previous century. He is a combination of the fop and braggart coward: He pretends to be fashionable, even to having invented a new way to swear, and he actually begins to enter into a duel, although of course with great reluctance. In each of these situations, he is comically exposed as an imposter. His social pretensions are mocked, and his fear during the dueling scene demonstrates the hollowness of his courage.

By the end of the play, both Lydia and Julia have finally given themselves up. This is necessary for the happy ending, but one wonders if it is convincing. Will Faulkland ever have enough force of character to satisfy Julia? Will Lydia ever stop pouting about her failure to elope? Both have succumbed to the compromised conventions of a contradictory middle-class society. Perhaps this "happy" conclusion is a final revelation of the continuing powerlessness of middle-class women and a critique of the society which seems to nurture and require this powerlessness in spite of the high value it claims to place on "feeling."

MODERN DRAMA

Henrik Ibsen

THE WILD DUCK

Translated by Frances E. Archer

About the Author　　Henrik Ibsen (1828–1906) lived in Germany and Italy from 1864 to 1891, and it was from abroad that he wrote most of his best-known works, but his major plays are always set in his native Norway. Because of his exploration of controversial social issues and universal mythic themes, he is often considered one of the founders of a uniquely "modern" drama, and his plays remain influential and regularly produced a century and more after their composition. His early works (1850 to 1873) were largely poetic dramas, often set in the historical past or in some mythic realm, but beginning in 1877 he shifted to the "photographic realism" that is usually associated with his mature style, and between 1877 and 1896 he wrote the eleven prose plays upon which his reputation rests as one of the founders of modern drama.

　　The most common setting for these plays—the interior of a home in his contemporary Norway—provides a classic example of what is often called a "fourth-wall" stage: the stage is arranged to look like a room, with its furnishings, three of its walls, and its windows and doors all visible, but with the fourth wall—the one through which the audience looks in upon the action—removed. It used to be common, even in Ibsen's own lifetime, to dismiss him as a writer whose primary interest in these plays was in this faithful reproduction of the details of everyday middle-class life and as a writer of so-called problem plays, plays which dramatize some specific, currently controversial social issue. The three plays written immediately before _The Wild Duck_ have seemed to many to give credence to this view: _A Doll's House_ (1879), in which women's rights is a central issue; _Ghosts_ (1881), which deals with the medical and social effects of venereal disease; and _An Enemy of the People_ (1883), in which a scientist's sense of social responsibility (he has discovered that the water in a local health spa is polluted) risks undermining his town's financial well-being.

About the Play　　To treat Ibsen's plays as mere exercises in dramatic journalism, however, is to trivialize some of the most powerful plays ever written, and perhaps the fact that some people did perceive them in this way helps explain some aspects of _The Wild Duck_ (1884). The play's main characters are a photographer (who is ineffectual) and a social reformer (who causes social harm), and in the play perceiving the truth about oneself and one's social situation seems potentially devastating. Moreover, while the stage represents a combination photographer's studio and family sitting room and is filled with details from modern bourgeois life, it is dominated by the mysterious attic space behind it which is never seen by the audience, but where Hialmar Ekdal and his father have created a pretend wilderness, stocked with felled trees, rabbits to hunt, and, most prominently, the wild duck.

　　The result is that this is a play where seemingly petty domestic issues become intertwined with and expressions of aspects of momentous historical change, played out against a background of mythic significance. The modern industrialism that has created Hialmar's tawdry, overcrowded urban life was built on the pillaging of state parkland. In the play, the imagination and the world of nature have both been wounded. Do they reassert themselves as indestructible, or do they remain only as maimed grotesques which serve to remind us of what has been lost? What does the play suggest about the possibility for heroic behavior in this world? These are questions that can be addressed only through attention to the texture of the play's language.

A good place to start may be with the wild duck itself, perhaps one of the most famous symbols in all of dramatic literature. It is clear to anyone who sees or reads the play that the duck means more than herself. She is spoken of so often and in ways that attribute to her a significance beyond the ornithological that there can be no mistaking that she has some larger meaning. Just what that significance is, however, is a matter for discussion. Such an exploration might begin by asking: Is her situation analogous to that of one of the characters? If it is, to whose? This exploration might then progress to other questions: If the wild duck's situation is analogous to the situation of one character, perhaps it is analogous to that of more than one? Perhaps it suggests something about issues of larger dimension than an individual character seems able to represent? Is there a way in which the duck brings the thematic concerns of the whole play into focus? Whatever she may mean, there is a way in which this creature, never seen on stage, dominates the play.

Two final points about Ibsen's dramatic practice. Unlike most dramatists, he presents his stage directions from the audience's, rather than the players', point of view. As you try to imagine the setting of his play, therefore, remember that if he says there is a door off to the right, he means to the right as we would look in through the fourth wall. (Most playwrights would mean to the right as an actor would look out at the audience through that wall.) The second point has to do with *exposition*. Typically in an Ibsen play, the exposition is deferred. Whereas someone like Shakespeare usually tries to make clear to the audience whatever it needs to know to understand the action by the end of Act 1, Ibsen often withholds necessary facts until the final act. Perhaps he was influenced by the then new genre of the mystery story, since this practice does add an element of the "whodunit" to many of Ibsen's plays. They are in this respect the opposite of a play such as *Oedipus the King*, where the audience knew the plot in advance. If you want to respond fully to a play like *The Wild Duck*, and to catch the full effect of its dramatic irony, therefore, it may be even more necessary than with other plays for you to reread it.

CHARACTERS

WERLE, a merchant, manufacturer, etc.
GREGERS WERLE, his son.
OLD EKDAL.
HIALMAR EKDAL, his son, a photographer.
GINA EKDAL, Hialmar's wife.
HEDVIG, their daughter, a girl of fourteen.
MRS. SÖRBY, Werle's housekeeper.
RELLING, a doctor.
MOLVIK, ex-student of theology.
GRÅBERG, Werle's bookkeeper.
PETTERSEN, Werle's servant.
JENSEN, a hired waiter.

A FLABBY GENTLEMAN.
A THIN-HAIRED GENTLEMAN.
A SHORT-SIGHTED GENTLEMAN.
Six other gentlemen, guests at Werle's dinner-party.
Several hired waiters.

The first act passes in Werle's house, the remaining acts at Hialmar Ekdal's.

Pronunciation of Names: Gregers Werle = Grayghers Verlë; Hialmar Ekdal = Yalmar Aykdal; Gina = Gheena; Gråberg = Groberg; Jensen = Yensen.

Act I

At Werle's house. A richly and comfortably furnished study; bookcases and upholstered furniture; a writing-table, with papers and documents, in the centre of the room; lighted lamps with green shades, giving a sub-dued light. At the back, open folding-doors with cur-tains drawn back. Within is seen a large and handsome room, brilliantly lighted with lamps and branching candlesticks. In front, on the right (in the study), a small baize door leads into Werle's office. On the left, in front, a fireplace with a glowing coal fire, and farther back a double door leading into the dining-room.

Werle's servant, Pettersen, in livery, and Jensen, the hired waiter, in black, are putting the study in order. In the large room, two or three other hired waiters are moving about, arranging things and light-ing more candles. From the dining room, the hum of conversation and laughter of many voices are heard; a glass is tapped with a knife; silence follows, and a toast is proposed; shouts of "Bravo!" and then again a buzz of conversation.

PETTERSEN. [*Lights a lamp on the chimney-place and places a shade over it.*] Hark to them, Jensen! now the old man's on his legs holding a long palaver about Mrs. Sörby.

JENSEN. [*Pushing forward an arm-chair.*] Is it true, what folks say, that they're—very good friends, eh?

PETTERSEN. Lord knows.

JENSEN. I've heard tell as he's been a lively customer in his day.

PETTERSEN. May be.

JENSEN. And he's giving this spread in honour of his son, they say.

PETTERSEN. Yes. His son came home yesterday.

JENSEN. This is the first time I ever heard as Mr. Werle had a son.

PETTERSEN. Oh yes, he has a son, right enough. But he's a fixture, as you might say, up at the Höidal works. He's never once come to town all the years I've been in service here.

A WAITER. [*In the doorway of the other room.*] Pettersen, here's an old fellow wanting—

PETTERSEN. [*Mutters.*] The devil—who's this now?

[*Old Ekdal appears from the right, in the inner room. He is dressed in a threadbare overcoat with a high collar; he wears*

woollen mittens, and carries in his hand a stick and a fur cap. Under his arm, a brown paper parcel. Dirty red-brown wig and small grey moustache.]

PETTERSEN. [*Goes towards him.*] Good Lord—what do you want here?

EKDAL. [*In the doorway.*] Must get into the office, Pet-tersen.

PETTERSEN. The office was closed an hour ago, and—

EKDAL. So they told me at the front door. But Grå-berg's in there still. Let me slip in this way, Pet-tersen; there's a good fellow. [*Points towards the baize door.*] It's not the first time I've come this way.

PETTERSEN. Well, you may pass. [*Opens the door.*] But mind you go out again the proper way, for we've got company.

EKDAL. I know, I know—h'm! Thanks, Pettersen, good old friend! Thanks! [*Mutters softly.*] Ass!

[*He goes into the office; Petterson shuts the door after him.*]

JENSEN. Is he one of the office people?

PETTERSEN. No, he's only an outside hand that does odd jobs of copying. But he's been a tip-topper in his day, has old Ekdal.

JENSEN. You can see he's been through a lot.

PETTERSEN. Yes; he was an army officer, you know.

JENSEN. You don't say so?

PETTERSEN. No mistake about it. But then he went into the timber trade or something of the sort. They say he once played Mr. Werle a very nasty trick. They were partners in the Höidal works at the time. Oh, I know old Ekdal well, I do. Many a nip of bitters and bottle of ale we two have drunk at Madam Eriksen's.

JENSEN. He don't look as if he'd much to stand treat with.

PETTERSEN. Why, bless you, Jensen, it's me that stands treat. I always think there's no harm in being a bit civil to folks that have seen better days.

JENSEN. Did he go bankrupt then?

PETTERSEN. Worse than that. He went to prison.

JENSEN. To prison!

PETTERSEN. Or perhaps it was the Penitentiary. [*Lis-tens.*] Sh! They're leaving the table.

[*The dining-room door is thrown open from within, by a couple of waiters. Mrs. Sörby comes out conversing with two gentlemen. Gradually the whole company follows, amongst them Werle. Last come Hialmar Ekdal and Gregers Werle.*]

MRS. SÖRBY. [*In passing, to the servant.*] Tell them to serve the coffee in the music-room, Pettersen.

PETTERSEN. Very well, Madam.

[*She goes with the two Gentlemen into the inner room, and thence out to the right. Pettersen and Jensen go out the same way.*]

A FLABBY GENTLEMAN. [*To a Thin-haired Gentleman.*] Whew! What a dinner!—It was no joke to do it justice!

THE THIN-HAIRED GENTLEMAN. Oh, with a little good-will one can get through a lot in three hours.

THE FLABBY GENTLEMAN. Yes, but afterwards, afterwards, my dear Chamberlain!

A THIRD GENTLEMAN. I hear the coffee and maraschino are to be served in the music-room.

THE FLABBY GENTLEMAN. Bravo! Then perhaps Mrs. Sörby will play us something.

THE THIN-HAIRED GENTLEMAN. [*In a low voice.*] I hope Mrs. Sörby mayn't play us a tune we don't like, one of these days!

THE FLABBY GENTLEMAN. Oh no, not she! Bertha will never turn against her old friends.

[*They laugh and pass into the inner room.*]

WERLE. [*In a low voice, dejectedly.*] I don't think anybody noticed it, Gregers.

GREGERS. [*Looks at him.*] Noticed what?

WERLE. Did you not notice it either?

GREGERS. What do you mean?

WERLE. We were thirteen at table.

GREGERS. Indeed? Were there thirteen of us?

WERLE. [*Glances towards Hialmar Ekdal.*] Our usual party is twelve. [*To the others.*] This way, gentlemen!

[*Werle and the others, all except Hialmar and Gregers, go out by the back, to the right.*]

HIALMAR. [*Who has overheard the conversation.*] You ought not to have invited me, Gregers.

GREGERS. What! Not ask my best and only friend to a party supposed to be in my honour—?

HIALMAR. But I don't think your father likes it. You see I am quite outside his circle.

GREGERS. So I hear. But I wanted to see you and have a talk with you, and I certainly shan't be staying long. Ah, we two old schoolfellows have drifted far apart from each other. It must be sixteen or seventeen years since we met.

HIALMAR. Is it so long?

GREGERS. It is indeed. Well, how goes it with you? You look well. You have put on flesh, and grown almost stout.

HIALMAR. Well, "stout" is scarcely the word; but I daresay I look a little more of a man than I used to.

GREGERS. Yes, you do; your outer man is in first-rate condition.

HIALMAR. [*In a tone of gloom.*] Ah, but the inner man! That is a very different matter, I can tell you! Of course you know of the terrible catastrophe that has befallen me and mine since last we met.

GREGERS. [*More softly.*] How are things going with your father now?

HIALMAR. Don't let us talk of it, old fellow. Of course my poor unhappy father lives with me. He hasn't another soul in the world to care for him. But you can understand that this is a miserable subject for me.—Tell me, rather, how you have been getting on up at the works.

GREGERS. I have had a delightfully lonely time of it— plenty of leisure to think and think about things. Come over here; we may as well make ourselves comfortable.

[*He seats himself in an arm-chair by the fire and draws Hialmar down into another alongside of it.*]

HIALMAR. [*Sentimentally.*] After all, Gregers, I thank you for inviting me to your father's table; for I take it as a sign that you have got over your feeling against me.

GREGERS. [*Surprised.*] How could you imagine I had any feeling against you?

HIALMAR. You had at first, you know.

GREGERS. How at first?

HIALMAR. After the great misfortune. It was natural enough that you should. Your father was within an ace of being drawn into that—well, that terrible business.

GREGERS. Why should that give me any feeling against you? Who can have put that into your head?

HIALMAR. I know it did, Gregers; your father told me so himself.

GREGERS. [*Starts.*] My father! Oh indeed. H'm.—Was that why you never let me hear from you?—not a single word.

HIALMAR. Yes.

GREGERS. Not even when you made up your mind to become a photographer?

HIALMAR. Your father said I had better not write to you at all, about anything.

GREGERS. [*Looking straight before him.*] Well well, perhaps he was right.—But tell me now, Hialmar: are you pretty well satisfied with your present position?

HIALMAR. [*With a little sigh.*] Oh yes, I am; I have really no cause to complain. At first, as you may guess, I felt it a little strange. It was such a totally new state of things for me. But of course my whole circumstances were totally changed. Father's utter, irretrievable ruin,—the shame and disgrace of it, Gregers—

GREGERS. [*Affected.*] Yes, yes; I understand.

HIALMAR. I couldn't think of remaining at college; there wasn't a shilling to spare; on the contrary, there were debts—mainly to your father I believe—

GREGERS. H'm—

HIALMAR. In short, I thought it best to break, once for all, with my old surroundings and associations. It was your father that specially urged me to it; and since he interested himself so much in me—

GREGERS. My father did?

HIALMAR. Yes, you surely knew that, didn't you? Where do you suppose I found the money to learn photography, and to furnish a studio and make a start? All that costs a pretty penny, I can tell you.

GREGERS. And my father provided the money?

HIALMAR. Yes, my dear fellow, didn't you know? I understood him to say he had written to you about it.

GREGERS. Not a word about his part in the business. He must have forgotten it. Our correspondence has always been purely a business one. So it was my father that—!

HIALMAR. Yes, certainly. He didn't wish it to be generally known; but he it was. And of course it was he, too, that put me in a position to marry. Don't you—don't you know about that either?

GREGERS. No, I haven't heard a word of it. [*Shakes him by the arm.*] But, my dear Hialmar, I can't tell you what pleasure all this gives me—pleasure, and self-reproach. I have perhaps done my father injustice after all—in some things. This proves that he has a heart. It shows a sort of compunction—

HIALMAR. Compunction—?

GREGERS. Yes, yes—whatever you like to call it. Oh, I can't tell how glad I am to hear this of father.—So you are a married man, Hialmar! That is further than I shall ever get. Well, I hope you are happy in your married life?

HIALMAR. Yes, thoroughly happy. She is as good and

capable a wife as any man could wish for. And she is by no means without culture.

GREGERS. [*Rather surprised.*] No, of course not.

HIALMAR. You see, life is itself an education. Her daily intercourse with me—And then we know one or two rather remarkable men, who come a good deal about us. I assure you, you would hardly know Gina again.

GREGERS. Gina?

HIALMAR. Yes; had you forgotten that her name was Gina?

GREGERS. Whose name? I haven't the slightest idea—

HIALMAR. Don't you remember that she used to be in service here?

GREGERS. [*Looks at him.*] Is it Gina Hansen—?

HIALMAR. Yes, of course it is Gina Hansen.

GREGERS. —who kept house for us during the last year of my mother's illness?

HIALMAR. Yes, exactly. But, my dear friend, I'm quite sure your father told you that I was married.

GREGERS. [*Who has risen.*] Oh yes, he mentioned it; but not that— [*Walking about the room.*] Stay—perhaps he did—now that I think of it. My father always writes such short letters. [*Half seats himself on the arm of the chair.*] Now, tell me, Hialmar—this is interesting—how did you come to know Gina—your wife?

HIALMAR. The simplest thing in the world. You know Gina did not stay here long; everything was so much upset at that time, owing to your mother's illness and so forth, that Gina was not equal to it all; so she gave notice and left. That was the year before your mother died—or it may have been the same year.

GREGERS. It was the same year. I was up at the works then. But afterwards—?

HIALMAR. Well, Gina lived at home with her mother, Madam Hansen, an excellent hard-working woman, who kept a little eating-house. She had a room to let too; a very nice comfortable room.

GREGERS. And I suppose you were lucky enough to secure it?

HIALMAR. Yes; in fact, it was your father that recommended it to me. So it was there, you see, that I really came to know Gina.

GREGERS. And then you got engaged?

HIALMAR. Yes. It doesn't take young people long to fall in love—; h'm—

GREGERS. [*Rises and moves about a little.*] Tell me: was it after your engagement—was it then that my father—I mean was it then that you began to take up photography?

HIALMAR. Yes, precisely. I wanted to make a start, and

to set up house as soon as possible; and your father and I agreed that this photography business was the readiest way. Gina thought so too. Oh, and there was another thing in its favour, by-the-bye: it happened, luckily, that Gina had learnt to retouch.

GREGERS. That chimed in marvellously.

HIALMAR. [*Pleased, rises.*] Yes, didn't it? Don't you think it was a marvellous piece of luck?

GREGERS. Oh, unquestionably. My father seems to have been almost a kind of providence for you.

HIALMAR. [*With emotion.*] He did not forsake his old friend's son in the hour of his need. For he has a heart, you see.

MRS. SÖRBY. [*Enters, arm-in-arm with Werle.*] Nonsense, my dear Mr. Werle; you mustn't stop there any longer staring at all the lights. It's very bad for you.

WERLE. [*Lets go her arm and passes his hand over his eyes.*] I daresay you are right.

[*Pettersen and Jensen carry round refreshment trays.*]

MRS. SÖRBY. [*To the Guests in the other room.*] This way, if you please, gentlemen. Whoever wants a glass of punch must be so good as to come in here.

THE FLABBY GENTLEMAN. [*Comes up to Mrs. Sörby.*] Surely, it isn't possible that you have suspended our cherished right to smoke?

MRS. SÖRBY. Yes. No smoking here, in Mr. Werle's sanctum, Chamberlain.

THE THIN-HAIRED GENTLEMAN. When did you enact these stringent amendments on the cigar law, Mrs. Sörby?

MRS. SÖRBY. After the last dinner, Chamberlain, when certain persons permitted themselves to overstep the mark.

THE THIN-HAIRED GENTLEMAN. And may one never overstep the mark a little bit, Madame Bertha? Not the least little bit?

MRS. SÖRBY. Not in any respect whatsoever, Mr. Balle.

[*Most of the Guests have assembled in the study; servants hand round glasses of punch.*]

WERLE. [*To Hialmar, who is standing beside a table.*] What are you studying so intently, Ekdal?

HIALMAR. Only an album, Mr. Werle.

THE THIN-HAIRED GENTLEMAN. [*Who is wandering about.*] Ah, photographs! They are quite in your line of course.

THE FLABBY GENTLEMAN. [*In an arm-chair.*] Haven't you brought any of your own with you?

HIALMAR. No, I haven't.

THE FLABBY GENTLEMAN. You ought to have; it's very good for the digestion to sit and look at pictures.

THE THIN-HAIRED GENTLEMAN. And it contributes to the entertainment, you know.

THE SHORT-SIGHTED GENTLEMAN. And all contributions are thankfully received.

MRS. SÖRBY. The Chamberlains think that when one is invited out to dinner, one ought to exert oneself a little in return, Mr. Ekdal.

THE FLABBY GENTLEMAN. Where one dines so well, that duty becomes a pleasure.

THE THIN-HAIRED GENTLEMAN. And when it's a case of the struggle for existence, you know—

MRS. SÖRBY. I quite agree with you!

[*They continue the conversation, with laughter and joking.*]

GREGERS. [*Softly.*] You must join in, Hialmar.

HIALMAR. [*Writhing.*] What am I to talk about?

THE FLABBY GENTLEMAN. Don't you think, Mr. Werle, that Tokay may be considered one of the more wholesome sorts of wine?

WERLE. [*By the fire.*] I can answer for the Tokay you had to-day, at any rate; it's of one of the very finest seasons. Of course you would notice that.

THE FLABBY GENTLEMAN. Yes, it had a remarkably delicate flavour.

HIALMAR. [*Shyly.*] Is there any difference between the seasons?

THE FLABBY GENTLEMAN. [*Laughs.*] Come! That's good!

WERLE. [*Smiles.*] It really doesn't pay to set fine wine before you.

THE THIN-HAIRED GENTLEMAN. Tokay is like photographs, Mr. Ekdal: they both need sunshine. Am I not right?

HIALMAR. Yes, light is important no doubt.

MRS. SÖRBY. And it's exactly the same with Chamberlains—they, too, depend very much on sunshine,[1] as the saying is.

THE THIN-HAIRED GENTLEMAN. Oh fie! That's a very threadbare sarcasm!

THE SHORT-SIGHTED GENTLEMAN. Mrs. Sörby is coming out—

THE FLABBY GENTLEMAN. —and at our expense, too. [*Holds up his finger reprovingly.*] Oh, Madame Bertha, Madame Bertha!

[1] The "sunshine" of Court favour.

MRS. SÖRBY. Yes, and there's not the least doubt that the seasons differ greatly. The old vintages are the finest.

THE SHORT-SIGHTED GENTLEMAN. Do you reckon me among the old vintages?

MRS. SÖRBY. Oh, far from it.

THE THIN-HAIRED GENTLEMAN. There now! But me, dear Mrs. Sörby—?

THE FLABBY GENTLEMAN. Yes, and me? What vintage should you say that we belong to?

MRS. SÖRBY. Why, to the sweet vintages, gentlemen.

[She sips a glass of punch. The gentlemen laugh and flirt with her.]

WERLE. Mrs. Sörby can always find a loop-hole—when she wants to. Fill your glasses, gentlemen! Pettersen, will you see to it—! Gregers, suppose we have a glass together. [Gregers does not move.] Won't you join us, Ekdal? I found no opportunity of drinking with you at table.

[Gråberg, the Bookkeeper, looks in at the baize door.]

GRÅBERG. Excuse me, sir, but I can't get out.

WERLE. Have you been locked in again?

GRÅBERG. Yes, and Flakstad has carried off the keys.

WERLE. Well, you can pass out this way.

GRÅBERG. But there's some one else—

WERLE. All right; come through, both of you. Don't be afraid.

[Gråberg and Old Ekdal come out of the office.]

WERLE. [Involuntarily.] Ugh!

[The laughter and talk among the Guests cease. Hialmar starts at the sight of his father, puts down his glass, and turns towards the fireplace.]

EKDAL. [Does not look up, but makes little bows to both sides as he passes, murmuring.] Beg pardon, come the wrong way. Door locked—door locked. Beg pardon.

[He and Gråberg go out by the back, to the right.]

WERLE. [Between his teeth.] That idiot Gråberg!

GREGERS. [Open-mouthed and staring, to Hialmar.] Why surely that wasn't—!

THE FLABBY GENTLEMAN. What's the matter? Who was it?

GREGERS. Oh, nobody, only the bookkeeper and some one with him.

THE SHORT-SIGHTED GENTLEMAN. [To Hialmar.] Did you know that man?

HIALMAR. I don't know—I didn't notice—

THE FLABBY GENTLEMAN. What the deuce has come over every one?

[He joins another group who are talking softly.]

MRS. SÖRBY. [Whispers to the Servant.] Give him something to take with him;—something good, mind

PETTERSEN. [Nods.] I'll see to it. [Goes out.]

GREGERS. [Softly and with emotion, to Hialmar.] So that was really he!

HIALMAR. Yes.

GREGERS. And you could stand there and deny that you knew him!

HIALMAR. [Whispers vehemently.] But how could I—!

GREGERS. —acknowledge your own father?

HIALMAR. [With pain.] Oh, if you were in my place—

[The conversation amongst the Guests, which has been carried on in a low tone, now swells into constrained joviality.]

THE THIN-HAIRED GENTLEMAN. [Approaching Hialmar and Gregers in a friendly manner.] Aha! Reviving old college memories, eh? Don't you smoke, Mr. Ekdal? May I give you a light? Oh, by-the-bye, we mustn't—

HIALMAR. No, thank you, I won't—

THE FLABBY GENTLEMAN. Haven't you a nice little poem you could recite to us, Mr. Ekdal? You used to recite so charmingly.

HIALMAR. I am sorry I can't remember anything.

THE FLABBY GENTLEMAN. Oh, that's a pity. Well, what shall we do, Balle?

[Both Gentlemen move away and pass into the other room.]

HIALMAR. [Gloomily.] Gregers—I am going! When a man has felt the crushing hand of Fate, you see—Say good-bye to your father for me.

GREGERS. Yes, yes. Are you going straight home?

HIALMAR. Yes. Why?

GREGERS. Oh, because I may perhaps look in on you later.

HIALMAR. No, you mustn't do that. You must not come to my home. Mine is a melancholy abode, Gregers; especially after a splendid banquet like this. We can always arrange to meet somewhere in the town.

MRS. SÖRBY. [Who has quietly approached.] Are you going, Ekdal?

HIALMAR. Yes.

MRS. SÖRBY. Remember me to Gina.

HIALMAR. Thanks.

MRS. SÖRBY. And say I am coming up to see her one of these days.

HIALMAR. Yes, thank you. [*To Gregers.*] Stay here; I will slip out unobserved.

[*He saunters away, then into the other room, and so out to the right.*]

MRS. SÖRBY. [*Softly to the Servant, who has come back.*] Well, did you give the old man something?

PETTERSEN. Yes; I sent him off with a bottle of cognac.

MRS. SÖRBY. Oh, you might have thought of something better than that.

PETTERSEN. Oh no, Mrs. Sörby; cognac is what he likes best in the world.

THE FLABBY GENTLEMAN. [*In the doorway with a sheet of music in his hand.*] Shall we play a duet, Mrs. Sörby?

MRS. SÖRBY. Yes, suppose we do.

THE GUESTS. Bravo, bravo!

[*She goes with all the Guests through the back room, out to the right. Gregers remains standing by the fire. Werle is looking for something on the writing-table, and appears to wish that Gregers would go; as Gregers does not move, Werle goes towards the door.*]

GREGERS. Father, won't you stay a moment?

WERLE. [*Stops.*] What is it?

GREGERS. I must have a word with you.

WERLE. Can it not wait till we are alone?

GREGERS. No, it cannot, for perhaps we shall never be alone together.

WERLE. [*Drawing nearer.*] What do you mean by that?

[*During what follows, the pianoforte is faintly heard from the distant music-room.*]

GREGERS. How has that family been allowed to go so miserably to the wall?

WERLE. You mean the Ekdals, I suppose.

GREGERS. Yes, I mean the Ekdals. Lieutenant Ekdal was once so closely associated with you.

WERLE. Much too closely; I have felt that to my cost for many a year. It is thanks to him that I—yes I— have had a kind of slur cast upon my reputation.

GREGERS. [*Softly.*] Are you sure that he alone was to blame?

WERLE. Who else do you suppose—?

GREGERS. You and he acted together in that affair of the forests—

WERLE. But was it not Ekdal that drew the map of the tracts we had bought—that fraudulent map! It was he who felled all that timber illegally on Government ground. In fact, the whole management was in his hands. I was quite in the dark as to what Lieutenant Ekdal was doing.

GREGERS. Lieutenant Ekdal himself seems to have been very much in the dark as to what he was doing.

WERLE. That may be. But the fact remains that he was found guilty and I acquitted.

GREGERS. Yes, I know that nothing was proved against you.

WERLE. Acquittal is acquittal. Why do you rake up these old miseries that turned my hair grey before its time? Is that the sort of thing you have been brooding over up there, all these years? I can assure you, Gregers, here in the town the whole story has been forgotten long ago—so far as *I* am concerned.

GREGERS. But that unhappy Ekdal family.

WERLE. What would you have had me do for the people? When Ekdal came out of prison he was a broken-down being, past all help. There are people in the world who dive to the bottom the moment they get a couple of slugs in their body, and never come to the surface again. You may take my word for it, Gregers, I have done all I could without positively laying myself open to all sorts of suspicion and gossip—

GREGERS. Suspicion—? Oh, I see.

WERLE. I have given Ekdal copying to do for the office, and I pay him far, far more for it than his work is worth—

GREGERS. [*Without looking at him.*] H'm; that I don't doubt.

WERLE. You laugh? Do you think I am not telling you the truth? Well, I certainly can't refer you to my books, for I never enter payments of that sort.

GREGERS. [*Smiles coldly.*] No, there are certain payments it is best to keep no account of.

WERLE. [*Taken aback.*] What do you mean by that?

GREGERS. [*Mustering up courage.*] Have you entered what it cost you to have Hialmar Ekdal taught photography?

WERLE. I? How "entered" it?

GREGERS. I have learnt that it was you who paid for his training. And I have learnt, too, that it was you who enabled him to set up house so comfortably.

WERLE. Well, and yet you talk as though I had done nothing for the Ekdals! I can assure you these people have cost me enough in all conscience.

GREGERS. Have you entered any of these expenses in your books?

WERLE. Why do you ask?

GREGERS. Oh, I have my reasons. Now tell me: when you interested yourself so warmly in your old friend's son—it was just before his marriage, was it not?

WERLE. Why, deuce take it—after all these years, how can I—?

GREGERS. You wrote a letter about that time—a business letter, of course; and in a postscript you mentioned—quite briefly—that Hialmar Ekdal had married a Miss Hansen.

WERLE. Yes, that was quite right. That was her name.

GREGERS. But you did not mention that this Miss Hansen was Gina Hansen—our former housekeeper.

WERLE. [With a forced laugh of derision.] No; to tell the truth, it didn't occur to me that you were so particularly interested in our former housekeeper.

GREGERS. No more I was. But [lowers his voice] there were others in this house who were particularly interested in her.

WERLE. What do you mean by that? [Flaring up.] You are not alluding to me, I hope?

GREGERS. [Softly but firmly.] Yes, I am alluding to you.

WERLE. And you dare—You presume to—How can that ungrateful hound—that photographer fellow—how dare he go making such insinuations!

GREGERS. Hialmar has never breathed a word about this. I don't believe he has the faintest suspicion of such a thing.

WERLE. Then where have you got it from? Who can have put such notions in your head?

GREGERS. My poor unhappy mother told me; and that the very last time I saw her.

WERLE. Your mother! I might have known as much! You and she—you always held together. It was she who turned you against me, from the first.

GREGERS. No, it was all that she had to suffer and submit to, until she broke down and came to such a pitiful end.

WERLE. Oh, she had nothing to suffer or submit to; not more than most people, at all events. But there's no getting on with morbid, overstrained creatures—that I have learnt to my cost.—And you could go on nursing such a suspicion—burrowing into all sorts of old rumours and slanders against your own father! I must say, Gregers, I really think that at your age you might find something more useful to do.

GREGERS. Yes, it is high time.

WERLE. Then perhaps your mind would be easier than it seems to be now. What can your object in remaining up at the works, year out and year in, drudging away like a common clerk, and not drawing a farthing more than the ordinary monthly wage? It is downright folly.

GREGERS. Ah, if I were only sure of that.

WERLE. I understand you well enough. You want to be independent; you won't be beholden to me for anything. Well, now there happens to be an opportunity for you to become independent, your own master in everything.

GREGERS. Indeed? In what way—?

WERLE. When I wrote you insisting on your coming to town at once—h'm—

GREGERS. Yes, what is it you really want of me? I have been waiting all day to know.

WERLE. I want to propose that you should enter the firm, as partner.

GREGERS. I? Join your firm? As partner?

WERLE. Yes. It would not involve our being constantly together. You could take over the business here in town, and I should move up to the works.

GREGERS. You would?

WERLE. The fact is, I am not so fit for work as I once was. I am obliged to spare my eyes, Gregers; they have begun to trouble me.

GREGERS. They have always been weak.

WERLE. Not as they are now. And besides, circumstances might possibly make it desirable for me to live up there—for a time, at any rate.

GREGERS. That is certainly quite a new idea to me.

WERLE. Listen, Gregers: there are many things that stand between us; but we are father and son after all. We ought surely to be able to come to some sort of understanding with each other.

GREGERS. Outwardly, you mean, of course?

WERLE. Well, even that would be something. Think it over, Gregers. Don't you think it ought to be possible? Eh?

GREGERS. [Looking at him coldly.] There is something behind all this.

WERLE. How so?

GREGERS. You want to make use of me in some way.

WERLE. In such a close relationship as ours, the one can always be useful to the other.

GREGERS. Yes, so people say.

WERLE. I want very much to have you at home with me for a time. I am a lonely man Gregers; I have always felt lonely, all my life through; but most of all now that I am getting up in years. I feel the need of some one about me—

GREGERS. You have Mrs. Sörby.

WERLE. Yes, I have her; and she has become, I may say, almost indispensable to me. She is lively and even-tempered; she brightens up the house; and that is a very great thing for me.

GREGERS. Well then, you have everything just as you wish it.

WERLE. Yes, but I am afraid it can't last. A woman so situated may easily find herself in a false position, in the eyes of the world. For that matter it does a man no good, either.

GREGERS. Oh, when a man gives such dinners as you give, he can risk a great deal.

WERLE. Yes, but how about the woman, Gregers? I fear she won't accept the situation much longer; and even if she did—even if, out of attachment to me, she were to take her chance of gossip and scandal and all that—? Do you think, Gregers—you with your strong sense of justice—

GREGERS. [Interrupts him.] Tell me in one word: are you thinking of marrying her?

WERLE. Suppose I were thinking of it? What then?

GREGERS. That's what I say: what then?

WERLE. Should you be inflexibly opposed to it!

GREGERS. Not at all. Not by any means.

WERLE. I was not sure whether your devotion to your mother's memory—

GREGERS. I am not overstrained.

WERLE. Well, whatever you may or may not be, at all events you have lifted a great weight from my mind. I am extremely pleased that I can reckon on your concurrence in this matter.

GREGERS. [Looking intently at him.] Now I see the use you want to put me to.

WERLE. Use to put you to? What an expression!

GREGERS. Oh, don't let us be nice in our choice of words—not when we are alone together, at any rate. [With a short laugh.] Well well! So this is what made it absolutely essential that I should come to town in person. For the sake of Mrs. Sörby, we are to get up a pretence at family life in the house—a tableau of filial affection! That will be something new indeed.

WERLE. How dare you speak in that tone!

GREGERS. Was there ever any family life here? Never since I can remember. But now, forsooth, your plans demand something of the sort. No doubt it will have an excellent effect when it is reported that the son has hastened home, on the wings of filial piety, to the grey-haired father's wedding-feast. What will then remain of all the rumours as to the wrongs the poor dead mother had to submit to? Not a vestige. Her son annihilates them at one stroke.

WERLE. Gregers—I believe there is no one in the world you detest as you do me.

GREGERS. [Softly.] I have seen you at too close quarters.

WERLE. You have seen me with your mother's eyes. [Lowers his voice a little.] But you should remember that her eyes were—clouded now and then.

GREGERS. [Quivering.] I see what you are hinting at. But who was to blame for mother's unfortunate weakness? Why you, and all those—! The last of them was this woman that you palmed off upon Hialmar Ekdal, when you were— Ugh!

WERLE. [Shrugs his shoulders.] Word for word as if it were your mother speaking!

GREGERS. [Without heeding.] And there he is now, with his great, confiding, childlike mind, compassed about with all this treachery—living under the same roof with such a creature, and never dreaming that what he calls his home is built upon a lie! [Comes a step nearer.] When I look back upon your past, I seem to see a battle-field with shattered lives on every hand.

WERLE. I begin to think the chasm that divides us is too wide.

GREGERS. [Bowing, with self-command.] So I have observed; and therefore I take my hat and go.

WERLE. You are going! Out of the house?

GREGERS. Yes. For at last I see my mission in life.

WERLE. What mission?

GREGERS. You would only laugh if I told you.

WERLE. A lonely man doesn't laugh so easily, Gregers.

GREGERS. [Pointing towards the background.] Look, father,—the Chamberlains are playing blind-man's-buff with Mrs. Sörby.—Good-night and good-bye.

[He goes out by the back to the right. Sounds of laughter and merriment from the Company, who are now visible in the outer room.]

WERLE. [Muttering contemptuously after Gregers.] Ha—! Poor wretch—and he says he is not overstrained!

Act II

Hialmar Ekdal's studio, a good-sized room, evidently in the top storey of the building. On the right, a sloping roof of large panes of glass, half-covered by a blue curtain. In the right-hand corner, at the back, the entrance door; farther forward, on the same side, a door leading to the sitting room. Two doors on the opposite side, and between them an iron stove. At the back, a wide double sliding-door. The studio is plainly but comfortably fitted up and furnished. Between the doors on the right, standing out a little from the wall, a sofa with a table and some chairs; on the table a lighted lamp with a shade; beside the stove an old arm-chair. Photographic instruments and apparatus of different kinds lying about the room. Against the back wall, to the left of the double door, stands a bookcase containing a few books, boxes, and bottles of chemicals, instruments, tools, and other objects. Photographs and small articles, such as camel's-hair pencils, paper, and so forth, lie on the table.

Gina Ekdal sits on a chair by the table, sewing. Hedvig is sitting on the sofa, with her hands shading her eyes and her thumbs in her ears, reading a book.

GINA. [*Glances once or twice at Hedvig, as if with secret anxiety; then says:*] Hedvig.

HEDVIG. [*Does not hear.*]

GINA. [*Repeats more loudly.*] Hedvig!

HEDVIG. [*Takes away her hands and looks up.*] Yes, mother?

GINA. Hedvig dear, you mustn't sit reading any longer now.

HEDVIG. Oh mother, mayn't I read a little more? Just a little bit?

GINA. No no, you must put away your book now. Father doesn't like it; he never reads hisself in the evening.

HEDVIG. [*Shuts the book.*] No, father doesn't care much about reading.

GINA. [*Puts aside her sewing and takes up a lead pencil and a little account-book from the table.*] Can you remember how much we paid for the butter to-day?

HEDVIG. It was one crown sixty-five.

GINA. That's right. [*Puts it down.*] It's terrible what a lot of butter we get through in this house. Then there was the smoked sausage, and the cheese—let me see—[*Writes*] —and the ham—[*Adds up.*] Yes, that makes just—

HEDVIG. And then the beer.

GINA. Yes, to be sure. [*Writes.*] How it do mount up! But we can't manage with no less.

HEDVIG. And then you and I didn't need anything hot for dinner, as father was out.

GINA. No; that was so much to the good. And then I took eight crowns fifty for the photographs.

HEDVIG. Really! So much as that?

GINA. Exactly eight crowns fifty.

[*Silence. Gina takes up her sewing again, Hedvig takes paper and pencil and begins to draw, shading her eyes with her left hand.*]

HEDVIG. Isn't it jolly to think that father is at Mr. Werle's big dinner-party?

GINA. You know he's not really Mr. Werle's guest. It was the son invited him. [*After a pause.*] We have nothing to do with that Mr. Werle.

HEDVIG. I'm longing for father to come home. He promised to ask Mrs. Sörby for something nice for me.

GINA. Yes, there's plenty of good things going in that house, I can tell you.

HEDVIG. [*Goes on drawing.*] And I believe I'm a little hungry too.

[*Old Ekdal, with the paper and parcel under his arm and another parcel in his coat pocket, comes in by the entrance door.*]

GINA. How late you are to-day, grandfather!

EKDAL. They had locked the office door. Had to wait in Gråberg's room. And then they let me through—h'm.

HEDVIG. Did you get some more copying to do, grandfather?

EKDAL. This whole packet. Just look.

GINA. That's capital.

HEDVIG. And you have another parcel in your pocket.

EKDAL. Eh? Oh never mind, that's nothing. [*Puts his stick away in a corner.*] This work will keep me going a long time, Gina. [*Opens one of the sliding-doors in the back wall a little.*] Hush! [*Peeps into the room for a moment, then pushes the door carefully to again.*] Hee-hee! They're fast asleep, all the lot of them. And she's gone into the basket herself. Hee-hee!

HEDVIG. Are you sure she isn't cold in that basket, grandfather?

EKDAL. Not a bit of it! Cold? With all that straw? [*Goes towards the farther door on the left.*] There are matches in here, I suppose.

GINA. The matches is on the drawers.

[*Ekdal goes into his room.*]

HEDVIG. It's nice that grandfather has got all that copying.

GINA. Yes, poor old father; it means a bit of pocket-money for him.

HEDVIG. And he won't be able to sit the whole fore-noon down at that horrid Madam Eriksen's.

GINA. No more he won't. [*Short silence.*]

HEDVIG. Do you suppose they are still at the dinner-table?

GINA. Goodness knows; as like as not.

HEDVIG. Think of all the delicious things father is having to eat! I'm certain he'll be in splendid spirits when he comes. Don't you think so, mother?

GINA. Yes; and if only we could tell him that we'd got the room let—

HEDVIG. But we don't need that this evening.

GINA. Oh, we'd be none the worse of it, I can tell you. It's no use to us as it is.

HEDVIG. I mean we don't need it this evening, for father will be in a good humour at any rate. It is best to keep the letting of the room for another time.

GINA. [*Looks across at her.*] You like having some good news to tell father when he comes home in the evening?

HEDVIG. Yes; for then things are pleasanter somehow.

GINA. [*Thinking to herself.*] Yes, yes, there's something in that.

[*Old Ekdal comes in again and is going out by the foremost door to the left.*]

GINA. [*Half turning in her chair.*] Do you want something out of the kitchen, grandfather?

EKDAL. Yes, yes, I do. Don't you trouble. [*Goes out.*]

GINA. He's not poking away at the fire, is he? [*Waits a moment.*] Hedvig, go and see what he's about.

[*Ekdal comes in again with a small jug of steaming hot water.*]

HEDVIG. Have you been getting some hot water, grandfather?

EKDAL. Yes, hot water. Want it for something. Want to write, and the ink has got as thick as porridge.— h'm.

GINA. But you'd best have your supper, first, grand-father. It's laid in there.

EKDAL. Can't be bothered with supper, Gina. Very busy, I tell you. No one's to come to my room. No one—h'm.

[*He goes into his room; Gina and Hedvig look at each other.*]

GINA. [*Softly.*] Can you imagine where he's got money from?

HEDVIG. From Gråberg, perhaps.

GINA. Not a bit of it. Gråberg always sends the money to me.

HEDVIG. Then he must have got a bottle on credit somewhere.

GINA. Poor grandfather, who'd give him credit?

[*Hialmar Ekdal, in an overcoat and grey felt hat, comes in from the right.*]

GINA. [*Throws down her sewing and rises.*] Why, Ekdal. Is that you already?

HEDVIG. [*At the same time jumping up.*] Fancy your coming so soon, father!

HIALMAR. [*Taking off his hat.*] Yes, most of the people were coming away.

HEDVIG. So early?

HIALMAR. Yes, it was a dinner-party, you know.

[*Is taking off his overcoat.*]

GINA. Let me help you.

HEDVIG. Me too.

[*They draw off his coat; Gina hangs it up on the back wall.*]

HEDVIG. Were there many people there, father?

HIALMAR. Oh no, not many. We were about twelve or fourteen at table.

GINA. And you had some talk with them all?

HIALMAR. Oh yes, a little; but Gregers took me up most of the time.

GINA. Is Gregers as ugly as ever?

HIALMAR. Well, he's not very much to look at. Hasn't the old man come home?

HEDVIG. Yes, grandfather is in his room, writing.

HIALMAR. Did he say anything?

GINA. No, what should he say?

HIALMAR. Didn't he say anything about—? I heard something about his having been with Gråberg. I'll go in and see him for a moment.

GINA. No, no, better not.

HIALMAR. Why not? Did he say he didn't want me to go in?

GINA. I don't think he wants to see nobody this evening—

HEDVIG. [*Making signs.*] H'm—h'm!

GINA. [*Not noticing.*] —he has been in to fetch hot water—

HIALMAR. Aha! Then he's—

GINA. Yes, I suppose so.

HIALMAR. Oh God! my poor old white-haired father!—Well, well; there let him sit and get all the enjoyment he can.

[*Old Ekdal, in an indoor coat and with a lighted pipe, comes from his room.*]

EKDAL. Got home? Thought it was you I heard talking.

HIALMAR. Yes, I have just come.

EKDAL. You didn't see me, did you?

HIALMAR. No; but they told me you had passed through—so I thought I would follow you.

EKDAL. H'm, good of you, Hialmar.—Who were they, all those fellows?

HIALMAR. Oh, all sorts of people. There was Chamberlain Flor, and Chamberlain Balle, and Chamberlain Kaspersen, and Chamberlain—this, that, and the other—I don't know who all—

EKDAL. [*Nodding.*] Hear that, Gina! Chamberlains every one of them!

GINA. Yes, I hear as they're terrible genteel in that house nowadays.

HEDVIG. Did the Chamberlains sing, father? Or did they read aloud?

HIALMAR. No, they only talked nonsense. They wanted me to recite something for them; but I knew better than that.

EKDAL. You weren't to be persuaded, eh?

GINA. Oh, you might have done it.

HIALMAR. No; one mustn't be at everybody's beck and call. [*Walks about the room.*] That's not my way, at any rate.

EKDAL. No no; Hialmar's not to be had for the asking, he isn't.

HIALMAR. I don't see why I should bother myself to entertain people on the rare occasions when I go into society. Let the others exert themselves. These fellows go from one great dinner-table to the next and gorge and guzzle day out and day in. It's for them to bestir themselves and do something in return for all the good feeding they get.

GINA. But you didn't say that?

HIALMAR. [*Humming.*] Ho-ho-ho—; faith, I gave them a bit of my mind.

EKDAL. Not the Chamberlains?

HIALMAR. Oh, why not? [*Lightly.*] After that, we had a little discussion about Tokay.

EKDAL. Tokay! There's a fine wine for you!

HIALMAR. [*Comes to a standstill.*] It may be a fine wine. But of course you know the vintages differ; it all depends on how much sunshine the grapes have had.

GINA. Why, you know everything, Ekdal.

EKDAL. And did they dispute that?

HIALMAR. They tried to; but they were requested to observe that it was just the same with Chamberlains—that with them, too, different batches were of different qualities.

GINA. What things you do think of!

EKDAL. Hee-hee! So they got that in their pipes too?

HIALMAR. Right in their teeth.

EKDAL. Do you hear that, Gina? He said it right in the very teeth of all the Chamberlains.

GINA. Fancy—! Right in their teeth!

HIALMAR. Yes, but I don't want it talked about. One doesn't speak of such things. The whole affair passed off quite amicably of course. They were nice, genial fellows; I didn't want to wound them—not I!

EKDAL. Right in their teeth, though—!

HEDVIG. [*Caressingly.*] How nice it is to see you in a dress-coat! It suits you so well, father.

HIALMAR. Yes, don't you think so? And this one really sits to perfection. It fits almost as if it had been made for me;—a little tight in the arm-holes perhaps;—help me, Hedvig. [*Takes off the coat.*] I think I'll put on my jacket. Where is my jacket, Gina?

GINA. Here it is. [*Brings the jacket and helps him.*]

HIALMAR. That's it! Don't forget to send the coat back to Molvik first thing to-morrow morning.

GINA. [*Laying it away.*] I'll be sure and see to it.

HIALMAR. [*Stretching himself.*] After all, there's a more homely feeling about this. A free-and-easy indoor costume suits my whole personality better. Don't you think so, Hedvig?

HEDVIG. Yes, father.

HIALMAR. When I loosen my necktie into a pair of flowing ends—like this—eh?

HEDVIG. Yes, that goes so well with your mustache and the sweep of your curls.

HIALMAR. I should not call them curls exactly; I should rather say locks.

HEDVIG. Yes, they are two big for curls.

HIALMAR. Locks describes them better.

HEDVIG. [*After a pause, twitching his jacket.*] Father.

HIALMAR. Well, what is it?

HEDVIG. Oh, you know very well.

HIALMAR. No, really I don't—

HEDVIG. [*Half laughing, half whimpering.*] Oh yes, father; now don't tease me any longer!

HIALMAR. Why, what do you mean?

HEDVIG. [*Shaking him.*] Oh what nonsense; come, where are they, father? All the good things you promised me, you know?

HIALMAR. Oh—if I haven't forgotten all about them!

HEDVIG. Now you're only teasing me, father! Oh, it's too bad of you! Where have you put them?

HIALMAR. No, I positively forgot to get anything. But wait a little! I have something else for you, Hedvig.

[*Goes and searches in the pockets of the coat.*]

HEDVIG. [*Skipping and clapping her hands.*] Oh mother, mother!

GINA. There, you see; if you only give him time—

HIALMAR. [*With a paper.*] Look, here it is.

HEDVIG. That? Why, that's only a paper.

HIALMAR. That is the bill of fare, my dear; the whole bill of fare. Here you see: "Menu"—that means bill of fare.

HEDVIG. Haven't you anything else?

HIALMAR. I forgot the other things, I tell you. But you may take my word for it, these dainties are very unsatisfying. Sit down at the table and read the bill of fare, and then I'll describe to you how the dishes taste. Here you are, Hedvig.

HEDVIG. [*Gulping down her tears.*] Thank you.

[*She seats herself, but does not read; Gina makes signs to her; Hialmar notices it.*]

HIALMAR. [*Pacing up and down the room.*] It's monstrous what absurd things the father of a family is expected to think of; and if he forgets the smallest trifle, he is treated to sour faces at once. Well, well, one gets used to that too. [*Stops near the stove, by the old man's chair.*] Have you peeped in there this evening, father?

EKDAL. Yes, to be sure I have. She's gone into the basket.

HIALMAR. Ah, she has gone into the basket. Then she's beginning to get used to it.

EKDAL. Yes; just as I prophesied. But you know there are still a few little things—

HIALMAR. A few improvements, yes.

EKDAL. They've got to be made, you know.

HIALMAR. Yes, let us have a talk about the improvements, father. Come, let us sit on the sofa.

EKDAL. All right. H'm—think I'll just fill my pipe first. Must clean it out, too. H'm.

[*He goes into his room.*]

GINA. [*Smiling to Hialmar.*] His pipe!

HIALMAR. Oh yes yes, Gina; let him alone—the poor shipwrecked old man.—Yes, these improvements—we had better get them out of hand to-morrow.

GINA. You'll hardly have time to-morrow, Ekdal.

HEDVIG. [*Interposing.*] Oh yes he will, mother!

GINA. —for remember them prints that has to be retouched; they've sent for them time after time.

HIALMAR. There now! those prints again! I shall get them finished all right! Have any new orders come in?

GINA. No, worse luck; to-morrow I have nothing but those two sittings, you know.

HIALMAR. Nothing else? Oh no, if people won't set about things with a will—

GINA. But what more can I do? Don't I advertise in the papers as much as we can afford?

HIALMAR. Yes, the papers, the papers; you see how much good they do. And I suppose no one has been to look at the room either?

GINA. No, not yet.

HIALMAR. That was only to be expected. If people won't keep their eyes open—. Nothing can be done without a real effort, Gina!

HEDVIG. [*Going towards him.*] Shall I fetch you the flute, father?

HIALMAR. No; no flute for me; *I* want no pleasures in this world. [*Pacing about.*] Yes, indeed I will work to-morrow; you shall see if I don't. You may be sure I shall work as long as my strength holds out.

GINA. But my dear good Ekdal, I didn't mean it in that way.

HEDVIG. Father, mayn't I bring in a bottle of beer?

HIALMAR. No, certainly not. I require nothing, nothing— [*Comes to a standstill.*] Beer? Was it beer you were talking about?

HEDVIG. [*Cheerfully.*] Yes, father; beautiful fresh beer.

HIALMAR. Well—since you insist upon it, you may bring in a bottle.

GINA. Yes, do; and we'll be nice and cosy.

[*Hedvig runs towards the kitchen door.*]

HIALMAR. [*By the stove, stops her, looks at her, puts his*

arm round her neck and presses her to him.] Hedvig, Hedvig!

HEDVIG. [*With tears of joy.*] My dear, kind father!

HIALMAR. No, don't call me that. Here have I been feasting at the rich man's table,—battening at the groaning board—! And I couldn't even—!

GINA. [*Sitting at the table.*] Oh nonsense, nonsense, Ekdal.

HIALMAR. It's not nonsense! And yet you mustn't be too hard upon me. You know that I love you for all that.

HEDVIG. [*Throwing her arms round him.*] And we love you, oh so dearly, father!

HIALMAR. And if I am unreasonable once in a while,—why then—you must remember that I am a man beset by a host of cares. There, there! [*Dries his eyes.*] No beer at such a moment as this. Give me the flute.

[*Hedvig runs to the bookcase and fetches it.*]

HIALMAR. Thanks! That's right. With my flute in my hand and you two at my side—ah—!

[*Hedvig seats herself at the table near Gina; Hialmar paces backwards and forwards, pipes up vigorously, and plays a Bohemian peasant dance, but in a slow plaintive tempo, and with sentimental expression.*]

HIALMAR. [*Breaking off the melody, holds out his left hand to Gina, and says with emotion:*] Our roof may be poor and humble, Gina; but it is home. And with all my heart I say: here dwells my happiness.

[*He begins to play again; almost immediately after, a knocking is heard at the entrance door.*]

GINA. [*Rising.*] Hush, Ekdal,—I think there's some one at the door.

HIALMAR. [*Laying the flute on the bookcase.*] There! Again! [*Gina goes and opens the door.*]

GREGERS WERLE. [*In the passage.*] Excuse me—

GINA. [*Starting back slightly.*] Oh!

GREGERS. —does not Mr. Ekdal, the photographer, live here?

GINA. Yes, he does.

HIALMAR. [*Going towards the door.*] Gregers! You here after all? Well, come in then.

GREGERS. [*Coming in.*] I told you I would come and look you up.

HIALMAR. But this evening—? Have you left the party?

GREGERS. I have left both the party and my father's house.—Good evening, Mrs. Ekdal. I don't know whether you recognise me?

GINA. Oh yes; it's not difficult to know young Mr. Werle again.

GREGERS. No, I am like my mother; and no doubt you remember her.

HIALMAR. Left your father's house, did you say?

GREGERS. Yes, I have gone to a hotel.

HIALMAR. Indeed. Well, since you're here, take off your coat and sit down.

GREGERS. Thanks.

[*He takes off his overcoat. He is now dressed in a plain grey suit of a countrified cut.*]

HIALMAR. Here, on the sofa. Make yourself comfortable.

[*Gregers seats himself on the sofa; Hialmar takes a chair at the table.*]

GREGERS. [*Looking around him.*] So these are your quarters, Hialmar—this is your home.

HIALMAR. This is the studio, as you see—

GINA. But it's the largest of our rooms, so we generally sit here.

HIALMAR. We used to live in a better place; but this flat has one great advantage: there are such capital outer rooms—

GINA. And we have a room on the other side of the passage that we can let.

GREGERS. [*To Hialmar.*] Ah—so you have lodgers too?

HIALMAR. No, not yet. They're not so easy to find, you see; you have to keep your eyes open. [*To Hedvig.*] What about that beer, eh?

[*Hedvig nods and goes out into the kitchen.*]

GREGERS. So that is your daughter?

HIALMAR. Yes, that is Hedvig.

GREGERS. And she is your only child?

HIALMAR. Yes, the only one. She is the joy of our lives, and—[*lowering his voice*] —at the same time our deepest sorrow, Gregers.

GREGERS. What do you mean?

HIALMAR. She is in serious danger of losing her eyesight.

GREGERS. Becoming blind?

HIALMAR. Yes. Only the first symptoms have appeared as yet, and she may not feel it much for some time. But the doctor has warned us. It is coming, inexorably.

GREGERS. What a terrible misfortune! How do you account for it?

HIALMAR. [*Sighs.*] Hereditary, no doubt.

GREGERS. [*Starting.*] Hereditary?

GINA. Ekdal's mother had weak eyes.

HIALMAR. Yes, so my father says; I can't remember her.

GREGERS. Poor child! And how does she take it?

HIALMAR. Oh, you can imagine we haven't the heart to tell her of it. She dreams of no danger. Gay and careless and chirping like a little bird, she flutters onward into a life of endless night. [*Overcome.*] Oh, it is cruelly hard on me, Gregers.

[*Hedvig brings a tray with beer and glasses, which she sets upon the table.*]

HIALMAR. [*Stroking her hair.*] Thanks, thanks, Hedvig.

[*Hedvig puts her arm round his neck and whispers in his ear.*]

HIALMAR. No, no bread and butter just now. [*Looks up.*] But perhaps you would like some, Gregers.

GREGERS. [*With a gesture of refusal.*] No, no thank you.

HIALMAR. [*Still melancholy.*] Well, you can bring in a little all the same. If you have a crust, that is all I want. And plenty of butter on it, mind.

[*Hedvig nods gaily and goes out into the kitchen again.*]

GREGERS. [*Who has been following her with his eyes.*] She seems quite strong and healthy otherwise.

GINA. Yes. In other ways there's nothing amiss with her, thank goodness.

GREGERS. She promises to be very like you, Mrs. Ekdal. How old is she now?

GINA. Hedvig is close on fourteen; her birthday is the day after to-morrow.

GREGERS. She is pretty tall for her age, then.

GINA. Yes, she's shot up wonderful this last year.

GREGERS. It makes one realise one's own age to see these young people growing up.—How long is it now since you were married?

GINA. We've been married—let me see—just on fifteen years.

GREGERS. Is it so long as that?

GINA. [*Becomes attentive; looks at him.*] Yes, it is indeed.

HIALMAR. Yes, so it is. Fifteen years all but a few months. [*Changing his tone.*] They must have been long years for you, up at the works, Gregers.

GREGERS. They seemed long while I was living them; now they are over, I hardly know how the time has gone.

[*Old Ekdal comes from his room without his pipe, but with his old-fashioned uniform cap on his head; his gait is somewhat unsteady.*]

EKDAL. Come now, Hialmar, let's sit down and have a good talk about this—h'm—what was it again?

HIALMAR. [*Going towards him.*] Father, we have a visitor here—Gregers Werle.—I don't know if you remember him.

EKDAL. [*Looking at Gregers, who has risen.*] Werle? Is that the son? What does he want with me?

HIALMAR. Nothing; it's me he has come to see.

EKDAL. Oh! Then there's nothing wrong?

HIALMAR. No, no, of course not.

EKDAL. [*With a large gesture.*] Not that I'm afraid, you know; but—

GREGERS. [*Goes over to him.*] I bring you a greeting from your old hunting-grounds, Lieutenant Ekdal.

EKDAL. Hunting-grounds?

GREGERS. Yes, up in Höidal, about the works, you know.

EKDAL. Oh, up there. Yes, I knew all those places well in the old days.

GREGERS. You were a great sportsman then.

EKDAL. So I was, I don't deny it. You're looking at my uniform cap. I don't ask anybody's leave to wear it in the house. So long as I don't go out in the streets with it—

[*Hedvig brings a plate of bread and butter, which she puts upon the table.*]

HIALMAR. Sit down, father, and have a glass of beer. Help yourself, Gregers.

[*Ekdal mutters and stumbles over to the sofa. Gregers seats himself on the chair nearest to him, Hialmar on the other side of Gregers. Gina sits a little way from the table, sewing; Hedvig stands beside her father.*]

GREGERS. Can you remember, Lieutenant Ekdal, how Hialmar and I used to come up and visit you in the summer and at Christmas?

EKDAL. Did you? No, no, no; I don't remember it. But sure enough I've been a tidy bit of a sportsman in my day. I've shot bears too. I've shot nine of 'em, no less.

GREGERS. [*Looking sympathetically at him.*] And now you never get any shooting?

EKDAL. Can't just say that, sir. Get a shot now and

then perhaps. Of course not in the old way. For the woods you see—the woods, the woods—! [*Drinks.*] Are the woods fine up there now?

GREGERS. Not so fine as in your time. They have been thinned a good deal.

EKDAL. Thinned? [*More softly, and as if afraid.*] It's dangerous work that. Bad things come of it. The woods revenge themselves.

HIALMAR. [*Filling up his glass.*] Come—a little more, father.

GREGERS. How can a man like you—such a man for the open air—live in the midst of a stuffy town, boxed within four walls?

EKDAL. [*Laughs quietly and glances at Hialmar.*] Oh, it's not so bad here. Not at all so bad.

GREGERS. But don't you miss all the things that used to be a part of your very being—the cool sweeping breezes, the free life in the woods and on the uplands, among beasts and birds—?

EKDAL. [*Smiling.*] Hialmar, shall we let him see it?

HIALMAR. [*Hastily and a little embarrassed.*] Oh no no, father; not this evening.

GREGERS. What does he want to show me?

HIALMAR. Oh, its only something—you can see it another time.

GREGERS. [*Continues, to the old man.*] You see I have been thinking, Lieutenant Ekdal, that you should come up with me to the works; I am sure to be going back soon. No doubt you could get some copying there too. And here, you have nothing on earth to interest you—nothing to liven you up.

EKDAL. [*Stares in astonishment at him.*] Have *I* nothing on earth to—!

GREGERS. Of course you have Hialmar; but then he has his own family. And a man like you, who has always had such a passion for what is free and wild—

EKDAL. [*Thumps the table.*] Hialmar, he shall see it!

HIALMAR. Oh, do you think it's worth while, father? It's all dark.

EKDAL. Nonsense; it's moonlight. [*Rises.*] He shall see it, I tell you. Let me pass! Come and help me, Hialmar.

HEDVIG. Oh yes, do, father!

HIALMAR. [*Rising.*] Very well then.

GREGERS. [*To Gina.*] What is it?

GINA. Oh, nothing so very wonderful, after all.

[*Ekdal and Hialmar have gone to the back wall and are each pushing back a side of the sliding door; Hedvig helps the old man; Gregers remains standing by the sofa; Gina sits still and sews. Through the open doorway a large, deep irregular garret is seen with odd nooks and corners; a couple of stove-pipes running through it, from rooms below. There are sky-lights through which clear moonbeams shine in on some parts of the great room; others lie in deep shadow.*]

EKDAL. [*To Gregers.*] You may come close up if you like.

GREGERS. [*Going over to them.*] Why, what is it?

EKDAL. Look for yourself. H'm.

HIALMAR. [*Somewhat embarrassed.*] This belongs to father, you understand.

GREGERS. [*At the door, looks into the garret.*] Why, you keep poultry, Lieutenant Ekdal.

EKDAL. Should think we did keep poultry. They've gone to roost now. But you should just see our fowls by daylight, sir!

HEDVIG. And there's a—

EKDAL. Sh—sh! don't say anything about it yet.

GREGERS. And you have pigeons too, I see.

EKDAL. Oh yes, haven't we just got pigeons! They have their nest-boxes up there under the roof-tree; for pigeons like to roost high, you see.

HIALMAR. They aren't all common pigeons.

EKDAL. Common! Should think not indeed! We have tumblers, and a pair of pouters, too. But come here! Can you see that hutch down there by the wall?

GREGERS. Yes; what do you use it for?

EKDAL. That's where the rabbits sleep, sir.

GREGERS. Dear me; so you have rabbits too?

EKDAL. Yes, you may take my word for it, we have rabbits! He wants to know if we have rabbits, Hialmar! H'm! But now comes the thing, let me tell you! Here we have it! Move away, Hedvig. Stand here; that's right,—and now look down there.—Don't you see a basket with straw in it?

GREGERS. Yes. And I can see a fowl lying in the basket.

EKDAL. H'm—"a fowl"—

GREGERS. Isn't it a duck?

EKDAL. [*Hurt.*] Why, of course it's a duck.

HIALMAR. But what kind of duck, do you think?

HEDVIG. It's not just a common duck—

EKDAL. Sh!

GREGERS. And it's not a Muscovy duck either.

EKDAL. No, Mr.—Werle; it's not a Muscovy duck; for it's a wild duck!

GREGERS. Is it really? A wild duck?

EKDAL. Yes, that's what it is. That "fowl" as you call it—is the wild duck. It's our wild duck, sir.

HEDVIG. My wild duck. It belongs to me.

GREGERS. And can it live up here in the garret? Does it thrive?

EKDAL. Of course it has a trough of water to splash about in, you know.

HIALMAR. Fresh water every other day.

GINA. [*Turning towards Hialmar.*] But my dear Ekdal, it's getting icy cold here.

EKDAL. H'm, we had better shut up then. It's as well not to disturb their night's rest, too. Close up, Hedvig.

[*Hialmar and Hedvig push the garret doors together.*]

EKDAL. Another time you shall see her properly. [*Seats himself in the arm-chair by the stove.*] Oh, they're curious things, these wild ducks, I can tell you.

GREGERS. How did you manage to catch it, Lieutenant Ekdal?

EKDAL. *I* didn't catch it. There's a certain man in this town whom we have to thank for it.

GREGERS. [*Starts slightly.*] That man was not my father, was he?

EKDAL. You've hit it. Your father and no one else. H'm.

HIALMAR. Strange that you should guess that, Gregers.

GREGERS. You were telling me that you owed so many things to my father; and so I thought perhaps—

GINA. But we didn't get the duck from Mr. Werle himself—

EKDAL. It's Håkon Werle we have to thank for her, all the same, Gina. [*To Gregers.*] He was shooting from a boat, you see, and he brought her down. But your father's sight is not very good now. H'm; she was only wounded.

GREGERS. Ah! She got a couple of slugs in her body, I suppose.

HIALMAR. Yes, two or three.

HEDVIG. She was hit under the wing, so that she couldn't fly.

GREGERS. And I suppose she dived to the bottom, eh?

EKDAL. [*Sleepily, in a thick voice.*] Of course. Always do that, wild ducks do. They shoot to the bottom as deep as they can get, sir—and bite themselves fast in the tangle and seaweed—and all the devil's own mess that grows down there. And they never come up again.

GREGERS. But your wild duck came up again, Lieutenant Ekdal.

EKDAL. He had such an amazingly clever dog, your father had. And that dog—he dived in after the duck and fetched her up again.

GREGERS. [*Who has turned to Hialmar.*] And then she was sent to you here?

HIALMAR. Not at once; at first your father took her home. But she wouldn't thrive there; so Pettersen was told to put an end to her—

EKDAL. [*Half asleep.*] H'm—yes—Pettersen—that ass—

HIALMAR. [*Speaking more softly.*] That was how we got her, you see; for father knows Pettersen a little; and when he heard about the wild duck he got him to hand her over to us.

GREGERS. And now she thrives as well as possible in the garret there?

HIALMAR. Yes, wonderfully well. She has got fat. You see, she has lived in there so long now that she has forgotten her natural wild life; and it all depends on that.

GREGERS. You are right there, Hialmar. Be sure you never let her get a glimpse of the sky and the sea—. But I mustn't stay any longer; I think your father is asleep.

HIALMAR. Oh, as for that—

GREGERS. By, by-the-bye—you said you had a room to let—a spare room?

HIALMAR. Yes; what then? Do you know of anybody—?

GREGERS. Can *I* have that room?

HIALMAR. You?

GINA. Oh no, Mr. Werle, you—

GREGERS. May I have the room? If so, I'll take possession first thing to-morrow morning.

HIALMAR. Yes, with the greatest pleasure—

GINA. But, Mr. Werle, I'm sure it's not at all the sort of room for you.

HIALMAR. Why, Gina! how can you say that?

GINA. Why, because the room's neither large enough nor light enough, and—

GREGERS. That really doesn't matter, Mrs. Ekdal.

HIALMAR. I call it quite a nice room, and not at all badly furnished either.

GINA. But remember the pair of them underneath.

GREGERS. What pair?

GINA. Well, there's one as has been a tutor—

HIALMAR. That's Molvik—Mr. Molvik, B.A.

GINA. And then there's a doctor, by the name of Relling.

GREGERS. Relling? I know him a little; he practised for a time up in Höidal.

GINA. They're a regular rackety pair, they are. As often as not, they're out on the loose in the evenings; and then they come home at all hours, and they're not always just—

GREGERS. One soon gets used to that sort of thing. I daresay I shall be like the wild duck—

GINA. H'm; I think you ought to sleep upon it first, anyway.

GREGERS. You seem very unwilling to have me in the house, Mrs. Ekdal.

GINA. Oh no! What makes you think that?

HIALMAR. Well, you really behave strangely about it, Gina. [To Gregers.] Then I suppose you intend to remain in the town for the present?

GREGERS. [Putting on his overcoat.] Yes, now I intend to remain here.

HIALMAR. And yet not at your father's? What do you propose to do, then?

GREGERS. Ah, if I only knew that, Hialmar, I shouldn't be so badly off! But when one has the misfortune to be called Gregers—! "Gregers"—and then "Werle" after it; did you ever hear anything so hideous?

HIALMAR. Oh, I don't think so at all.

GREGERS. Ugh! Bah! I feel I should like to spit upon the fellow that answers to such a name. But when a man is once for all doomed to be Gregers—Werle in this world, as I am—

HIALMAR. [Laughs.] Ha ha! If you weren't Gregers Werle, what would you like to be?

GREGERS. If I could choose, I should like best to be a clever dog.

GINA. A dog!

HEDVIG. [Involuntarily.] Oh no!

GREGERS. Yes, an amazingly clever dog; one that goes to the bottom after wild ducks when they dive and bite themselves fast in tangle and sea-weed, down among the ooze.

HIALMAR. Upon my word now, Gregers—I don't in the least know what you're driving at.

GREGERS. Oh well, you might not be much the wiser if you did. It's understood, then, that I move in early to-morrow morning. [To Gina.] I won't give you any trouble; I do everything for myself. [To Hialmar.] We can talk about the rest to-morrow.— Good-night, Mrs. Ekdal. [Nods to Hedvig.] Good-night.

GINA. Good-night, Mr. Werle.

HEDVIG. Good-night.

HIALMAR. [Who has lighted a candle.] Wait a moment; I must show you a light; the stairs are sure to be dark.

[Gregers and Hialmar go out by the passage door.]

GINA. [Looking straight before her, with her sewing in her lap.] Wasn't that queer-like talk about wanting to be a dog?

HEDVIG. Do you know, mother—I believe he meant something quite different by that.

GINA. Why, what should he mean?

HEDVIG. Oh, I don't know; but it seemed to me he meant something different from what he said—all the time.

GINA. Do you think so? Yes, it was sort of queer.

HIALMAR. [Comes back.] The lamp was still burning. [Puts out the candle and sets it down.] Ah, now one can get a mouthful of food at last. [Begins to eat the bread and butter.] Well, you see, Gina—if only you keep your eyes open—

GINA. How, keep your eyes open—?

HIALMAR. Why, haven't we at last had the luck to get the room let? And just think—to a person like Gregers—a good old friend.

GINA. Well, I don't know what to say about it.

HEDVIG. Oh mother, you'll see; it'll be such fun!

HIALMAR. You're very strange. You were so bent upon getting the room let before; and now you don't like it.

GINA. Yes I do, Ekdal; if it had only been to some one else— But what do you suppose Mr. Werle will say?

HIALMAR. Old Werle? It doesn't concern him.

GINA. But surely you can see that there's something amiss between them again, or the young man wouldn't be leaving home. You know very well those two can't get on with each other.

HIALMAR. Very likely not, but—

GINA. And now Mr. Werle may fancy it's you that has egged him on.

HIALMAR. Let him fancy so, then! Mr. Werle has done a great deal for me; far be it from me to deny it. But that doesn't make me everlastingly dependent upon him.

GINA. But, my dear Ekdal, maybe grandfather 'll suffer for it. He may lose the little bit of work he gets from Gråberg.

HIALMAR. I could almost say: so much the better! Is it not humiliating for a man like me to see his grey-haired father treated as a pariah? But now I believe the fulness of time is at hand. [Takes a fresh piece of bread and butter.] As sure as I have a mission in life, I mean to fulfil it now!

HEDVIG. Oh yes, father, do!

GINA. Hush! Don't wake him!

HIALMAR. [More softly.] I will fulfil it, I say. The day shall come when— And that is why I say it's a good thing we have let the room; for that makes me more independent. The man who has a mission in life must be independent. [By the arm-chair, with emotion.]

Poor old white-haired father! Rely on your Hialmar. He has broad shoulders—strong shoulders, at any rate. You shall yet wake up some fine day and— [*To Gina.*] Do you not believe it?

GINA. [*Rising.*] Yes, of course I do; but in the mean-

time suppose we see about getting him to bed.

HIALMAR. Yes, come.

[*They take hold of the old man carefully.*]

Act III

Hialmar Ekdal's studio. It is morning: the daylight shines through the large window in the slanting roof; the curtain is drawn back.

Hialmar is sitting at the table, busy retouching a photograph; several others lie before him. Presently Gina, wearing her hat and cloak, enters by the passage door; she has a covered basket on her arm.

HIALMAR. Back already, Gina?

GINA. Oh yes, one can't let the grass grow under one's feet.

[*Sets her basket on a chair, and takes off her things.*]

HIALMAR. Did you look in at Gregers' room?

GINA. Yes, that I did. It's a rare sight, I can tell you; he's made a pretty mess to start off with.

HIALMAR. How so?

GINA. He was determined to do everything for himself, he said; so he sets to work to light the stove, and what must he do but screw down the damper till the whole room is full of smoke. Ugh! There was a smell fit to—

HIALMAR. Well, really!

GINA. But that's not the worst of it; for then he thinks he'll put out the fire, and goes and empties his water-jug into the stove, and so makes the whole floor one filthy puddle.

HIALMAR. How annoying!

GINA. I've got the porter's wife to clear up after him, pig that he is! But the room won't be fit to live in till the afternoon.

HIALMAR. What's he doing with himself in the meantime?

GINA. He said he was going out for a little while.

HIALMAR. I looked in upon him too, for a moment— after you had gone.

GINA. So I heard. You've asked him to lunch.

HIALMAR. Just to a little bit of early lunch, you know. It's his first day—we can hardly do less. You've got something in the house, I suppose?

GINA. I shall have to find something or other.

HIALMAR. And don't cut it too fine, for I fancy Relling and Molvik are coming up too. I just happened to meet Relling on the stairs, you see; so I had to—

GINA. Oh, are we to have those two as well?

HIALMAR. Good Lord—a couple more or less can't make any difference.

OLD EKDAL. [*Opens his door and looks in.*] I say, Hialmar— [*Sees Gina.*] Oh!

GINA. Do you want anything, grandfather?

EKDAL. Oh no, it doesn't matter. H'm!

[*Retires again.*]

GINA. [*Takes up the basket.*] Be sure you see that he doesn't go out.

HIALMAR. All right, all right. And, Gina, a little herring-salad wouldn't be a bad idea; Relling and Molvik were out on the loose again last night.

GINA. If only they don't come before I'm ready for them—

HIALMAR. No, of course they won't; take your own time.

GINA. Very well; and meanwhile you can be working a bit.

HIALMAR. Well, I am working! I am working as hard as I can!

GINA. Then you'll have that job off your hands, you see.

[*She goes out to the kitchen with her basket. Hialmar sits for a time pencilling away at the photograph, in an indolent and listless manner.*]

EKDAL. [*Peeps in, looks round the studio, and says softly:*] Are you busy?

HIALMAR. Yes I'm toiling at these wretched pictures—

EKDAL. Well well, never mind,—since you're so busy—h'm! [*He goes out again; the door stands open.*]

HIALMAR. [*Continues for some time in silence; then he lays down his brush and goes over to the door.*] Are you busy, father?

EKDAL. [*In a grumbling tone, within.*] If you're busy, I'm busy too. H'm!

HIALMAR. Oh, very well, then. [*Goes to his work again.*]

EKDAL. [*Presently, coming to the door again.*] H'm; I say, Hialmar, I'm not so very busy, you know.

HIALMAR. I thought you were writing.

EKDAL. Oh, devil take it! can't Gråberg wait a day or two? After all, it's not a matter of life and death.

HIALMAR. No; and you're not his slave either.

EKDAL. And about that other business in there—

HIALMAR. Just what I was thinking of. Do you want to go in. Shall I open the door for you?

EKDAL. Well, it wouldn't be a bad notion.

HIALMAR. [*Rises.*] Then we'd have that off our hands.

EKDAL. Yes, exactly. It's got to be ready first thing to-morrow. It is to-morrow, isn't it? H'm?

HIALMAR. Yes, of course it's to-morrow.

[*Hialmar and Ekdal push aside each his half of the sliding door. The morning sun is shining in through the skylights; some doves are flying about; others sit cooing, upon the perches; the hens are heard clucking now and then, further back in the garret.*]

HIALMAR. There; now you can get to work, father.

EKDAL. [*Goes in.*] Aren't you coming too?

HIALMAR. Well really, do you know—; I almost think— [*Sees Gina at the kitchen door.*] I? No; I haven't time; I must work.—But now for our new contrivance—

[*He pulls a cord, a curtain slips down inside, the lower part consisting of a piece of old sailcloth, the upper part of a stretched fishing net. The floor of the garret is thus no longer visible.*]

HIALMAR. [*Goes to the table.*] So! Now, perhaps I can sit in peace for a little while.

GINA. Is he rampaging in there again?

HIALMAR. Would you rather have had him slip down to Madam Eriksen's. [*Seats himself.*] Do you want anything? You know you said—

GINA. I only wanted to ask if you think we can lay the table for lunch here?

HIALMAR. Yes; we have no early appointment, I suppose?

GINA. No, I expect no one to-day except those two sweethearts that are to be taken together.

HIALMAR. Why the deuce couldn't they be taken together another day!

GINA. Don't you know, I told them to come in the afternoon, when you are having your nap.

HIALMAR. Oh, that's capital. Very well, let us have lunch here then.

GINA. All right; but there's no hurry about laying the cloth; you can have the table for a good while yet.

HIALMAR. Do you think I am not sticking at my work? I'm at it as hard as I can!

GINA. Then you'll be free later on, you know.

[*Goes out into the kitchen again. Short pause.*]

EKDAL. [*In the garret doorway, behind the net.*] Hialmar!

HIALMAR. Well?

EKDAL. Afraid we shall have to move the water-trough, after all.

HIALMAR. What else have I been saying all along?

EKDAL. H'm—h'm—h'm.

[*Goes away from the door again. Hialmar goes on working a little; glances towards the garret and half rises. Hedvig comes in from the kitchen.*]

HIALMAR. [*Sits down again hurriedly.*] What do you want?

HEDVIG. I only wanted to come in beside you, father.

HIALMAR. [*After a pause.*] What makes you go prying around like that? Perhaps you are told off to watch me?

HEDVIG. No, no.

HIALMAR. What is your mother doing out there?

HEDVIG. Oh, mother's in the middle of making the herring-salad. [*Goes to the table.*] Isn't there any little thing I could help you with, father?

HIALMAR. Oh no. It is right that I should bear the whole burden—so long as my strength holds out. Set your mind at rest, Hedvig; if only your father keeps his health—

HEDVIG. Oh no, father! You mustn't talk in that horrid way.

[*She wanders about a little, stops by the doorway and looks into the garret.*]

HIALMAR. Tell me, what is he doing?

HEDVIG. I think he's making a new path to the water-trough.

HIALMAR. He can never manage that by himself! And here am I doomed to sit—!

HEDVIG. [*Goes to him.*] Let me take the brush, father; I can do it, quite well.

HIALMAR. Oh nonsense; you will only hurt your eyes.

HEDVIG. Not a bit. Give me the brush.

HIALMAR. [*Rising.*] Well, it won't take more than a minute or two.

HEDVIG. Pooh, what harm can it do then? [*Takes the brush.*] There! [*Seats herself.*] I can begin upon this one.

HIALMAR. But mind you don't hurt your eyes! Do you hear? *I* won't be answerable; you do it on your own responsibility—understand that.

HEDVIG. [*Retouching.*] Yes yes, I understand.

HIALMAR. You are quite clever at it, Hedvig. Only a minute or two, you know.

[*He slips through by the edge of the curtain into the garret. Hedvig sits at her work. Hialmar and Ekdal are heard disputing inside.*]

HIALMAR. [*Appears behind the net.*] I say, Hedvig—give me those pincers that are lying on the shelf. And the chisel. [*Turns away inside.*] Now you shall see, father. Just let me show you first what I mean!

[*Hedvig has fetched the required tools from the shelf, and hands them to him through the net.*]

HIALMAR. Ah, thanks. I didn't come a moment too soon.

[*Goes back from the curtain again; they are heard carpentering and talking inside. Hedvig stands looking in at them. A moment later there is a knock at the passage door; she does not notice it.*]

GREGERS WERLE. [*Bareheaded, in indoor dress, enters and stops near the door.*] H'm—!

HEDVIG. [*Turns and goes towards him.*] Good morning. Please come in.

GREGERS. Thank you. [*Looking towards the garret.*] You seem to have workpeople in the house.

HEDVIG. No, it is only father and grandfather. I'll tell them you are here.

GREGERS. No no, don't do that; I would rather wait a little. [*Seats himself on the sofa.*]

HEDVIG. It looks so untidy here—

[*Begins to clear away the photographs.*]

GREGERS. Oh, don't take them away. Are those prints that have to be finished off?

HEDVIG. Yes, they are a few I was helping father with.

GREGERS. Please don't let me disturb you.

HEDVIG. Oh no.

[*She gathers the things to her and sits down to work; Gregers looks at her, meanwhile, in silence.*]

GREGERS. Did the wild duck sleep well last night?

HEDVIG. Yes, I think so, thanks.

GREGERS. [*Turning towards the garret.*] It looks quite different by day from what it did last night in the moonlight.

HEDVIG. Yes, it changes ever so much. It looks different in the morning and in the afternoon; and it's different on rainy days from what it is in fine weather.

GREGERS. Have you noticed that?

HEDVIG. Yes, how could I help it?

GREGERS. Are you, too, fond of being in there with the wild duck?

HEDVIG. Yes, when I can manage it—

GREGERS. But I suppose you haven't much spare time; you go to school, no doubt.

HEDVIG. No, not now; father is afraid of my hurting my eyes.

GREGERS. Oh; then he reads with you himself?

HEDVIG. Father has promised to read with me; but he has never had time yet.

GREGERS. Then is there nobody else to give you a little help?

HEDVIG. Yes, there is Mr. Molvik; but he is not always exactly— quite—

GREGERS. Sober?

HEDVIG. Yes, I suppose that's it!

GREGERS. Why, then you must have any amount of time on your hands. And in there I suppose it is a sort of world by itself?

HEDVIG. Oh yes, quite. And there are such lots of wonderful things.

GREGERS. Indeed?

HEDVIG. Yes, there are big cupboards full of books; and a great many of the books have pictures in them.

GREGERS. Aha!

HEDVIG. And there's an old bureau with drawers and flaps, and a big clock with figures that go out and in. But the clock isn't going now.

GREGERS. So time has come to a standstill in there— in the wild duck's domain.

HEDVIG. Yes. And then there's an old paint-box and things of that sort; and all the books.

GREGERS. And you read the books, I suppose?

HEDVIG. Oh yes, when I get the chance. Most of

them are English though, and I don't understand English. But then I look at the pictures.—There is one great big book called "Harrison's History of London."[2] It must be a hundred years old; and there are such heaps of pictures in it. At the beginning there is Death with an hour-glass and a woman. I think that is horrid. But then there are all the other pictures of churches, and castles, and streets, and great ships sailing on the sea.

GREGERS. But tell me, where did all those wonderful things come from?

HEDVIG. Oh, an old sea captain once lived here, and he brought them home with him. They used to call him "The Flying Dutchman." That was curious, because he wasn't a Dutchman at all.

GREGERS. Was he not?

HEDVIG. No. But at last he was drowned at sea; and so he left all those things behind him.

GREGERS. Tell me now—when you are sitting in there looking at the pictures, don't you wish you could travel and see the real world for yourself?

HEDVIG. Oh no! I mean always to stay at home and help father and mother.

GREGERS. To retouch photographs?

HEDVIG. No, not only that. I should love above everything to learn to engrave pictures like those in the English books.

GREGERS. H'm. What does your father say to that?

HEDVIG. I don't think father likes it; father is strange about such things. Only think, he talks of my learning basket-making, and straw-plaiting! But I don't think that would be much good.

GREGERS. Oh no, I don't think so either.

HEDVIG. But father was right in saying that if I had learnt basket-making I could have made the new basket for the wild duck.

GREGERS. So you could; and it was you that ought to have done it, wasn't it?

HEDVIG. Yes, for it's my wild duck.

GREGERS. Of course it is.

HEDVIG. Yes, it belongs to me. But I lend it to father and grandfather as often as they please.

GREGERS. Indeed? What do they do with it?

HEDVIG. Oh, they look after it, and build places for it, and so on.

GREGERS. I see; for no doubt the wild duck is by far the most distinguished inhabitant of the garret?

HEDVIG. Yes, indeed she is; for she is a real wild fowl,

you know. And then she is so much to be pitied; she has no one to care for, poor thing.

GREGERS. She has no family, as the rabbits have—

HEDVIG. No. The hens too, many of them, were chickens together; but she has been taken right away from all her friends. And then there is so much that is strange about the wild duck. Nobody knows her, and nobody knows where she came from either.

GREGERS. And she has been down in the depths of the sea.

HEDVIG. [With a quick glance at him, represses a smile and asks:] Why do you say "the depths of the sea"?

GREGERS. What else should I say?

HEDVIG. You could say "the bottom of the sea."[3]

GREGERS. Oh, mayn't I just as well say the depths of the sea?

HEDVIG. Yes; but it sounds so strange to me when other people speak of the depths of the sea.

GREGERS. Why so? Tell me why?

HEDVIG. No, I won't; it's so stupid.

GREGERS. Oh no, I am sure it's not. Do tell me why you smiled.

HEDVIG. Well, this is the reason: whenever I come to realise suddenly—in a flash—what is in there, it always seems to me that the whole room and everything in it should be called "the depths of the sea."—But that is so stupid.

GREGERS. You mustn't say that.

HEDVIG. Oh yes, for you know it is only a garret.

GREGERS. [Looks fixedly at her.] Are you so sure of that?

HEDVIG. [Astonished.] That it's a garret?

GREGERS. Are you quite certain of it?

[Hedvig is silent, and looks at him open-mouthed. Gina comes in from the kitchen with the table things.]

GREGERS. [Rising.] I have come in upon you too early.

GINA. Oh, you must be somewhere; and we're nearly ready now, any way. Clear the table, Hedvig.

[Hedvig clears away her things; she and Gina lay the cloth during what follows. Gregers seats himself in the arm-chair and turns over an album.]

GREGERS. I hear you can retouch, Mrs. Ekdal.

GINA. [With a side glance.] Yes, I can.

GREGERS. That was exceedingly lucky.

GINA. How—lucky?

GREGERS. Since Ekdal took to photography, I mean.

---

[2] *A New and Universal History of the Cities of London and Westminster*, by Walter Harrison. London, 1775, folio.

[3] Gregers here uses the old-fashioned expression "havsens bund," while Hedvig would have him use the more commonplace "havets bund" or "havbunden."

HEDVIG. Mother can take photographs too.

GINA. Oh, yes; I was bound to learn that.

GREGERS. So it is really you that carry on the business, I suppose?

GINA. Yes, when Ekdal hasn't time himself—

GREGERS. He is a great deal taken up with his old father, I daresay.

GINA. Yes; and then you can't expect a man like Ekdal to do nothing but take car-de-visits of Dick, Tom and Harry.

GREGERS. I quite agree with you; but having once gone in for the thing—

GINA. You can surely understand, Mr. Werle, that Ekdal's not like one of your common photographers.

GREGERS. Of course not; but still—

[A shot is fired within the garret.]

GREGERS. [Starting up.] What's that?

GINA. Ugh! now they're firing again!

GREGERS. Have they firearms in there?

HEDVIG. They are out shooting.

GREGERS. What! [At the door of the garret.] Are you shooting, Hialmar?

HIALMAR. [Inside the net.] Are you there? I didn't know; I was so taken up— [To Hedvig.] Why did you not let us know?

[Comes into the studio.]

GREGERS. Do you go shooting in the garret?

HIALMAR. [Showing a double-barrelled pistol.] Oh, only with this thing.

GINA. Yes, you and grandfather will do yourselves a mischief some day with that there pigstol.

HIALMAR. [With irritation.] I believe I have told you that this kind of firearm is called a pistol.

GINA. Oh, that doesn't make it much better, that I can see.

GREGERS. So you have become a sportsman too, Hialmar?

HIALMAR. Only a little rabbit-shooting now and then. Mostly to please father, you understand.

GINA. Men are strange beings; they must always have something to pervert theirselves with.

HIALMAR. [Snappishly.] Just so; we must always have something to divert ourselves with.

GINA. Yes, that's just what I say.

HIALMAR. H'm. [To Gregers.] You see the garret is fortunately so situated that no one can hear us shooting. [Lays the pistol on the top shelf of the book-case.] Don't touch the pistol, Hedvig! One of the barrels is loaded; remember that.

GREGERS. [Looking through the net.] You have a fowling-piece too, I see.

HIALMAR. That is father's old gun. It's of no use now; something has gone wrong with the lock. But it's fun to have it all the same; for we can take it to pieces now and then, and clean and grease it, and screw it together again.—Of course, it's mostly father that fiddle-faddles with all that sort of thing.

HEDVIG. [Beside Gregers.] Now you can see the wild duck properly.

GREGERS. I was just looking at her. One of her wings seems to me to droop a bit.

HEDVIG. Well, no wonder; her wing was broken, you know.

GREGERS. And she trails one foot a little. Isn't that so?

HIALMAR. Perhaps a very little bit.

HEDVIG. Yes, it was by that foot the dog took hold of her.

HIALMAR. But otherwise she hasn't the least thing the matter with her; and that is simply marvellous for a creature that has a charge of shot in her body, and has been between a dog's teeth—

GREGERS. [With a glance at Hedvig.] —and that has lain in the depths of the sea—so long.

HEDVIG. [Smiling.] Yes.

GINA. [Laying the table.] That blessëd wild duck! What a lot of fuss you do make over her.

HIALMAR. H'm;—will lunch soon be ready?

GINA. Yes, directly. Hedvig, you must come and help me now.

[Gina and Hedvig go out into the kitchen.]

HIALMAR. [In a low voice.] I think you had better not stand there looking in at father; he doesn't like it. [Gregers moves away from the garret door.] Besides I may as well shut up before the others come. [Claps his hands to drive the fowls back.] Shh—shh, in with you! [Draws up the curtain and pulls the doors together.] All the contrivances are my own invention. It's really quite amusing to have things of this sort to potter with, and to put to rights when they get out of order. And it's absolutely necessary, too; for Gina objects to having rabbits and fowls in the studio.

GREGERS. To be sure; and I suppose the studio is your wife's special department?

HIALMAR. As a rule, I leave the everyday details of business to her; for then I can take refuge in the parlour and give my mind to more important things.

GREGERS. What things may they be, Hialmar?

HIALMAR. I wonder you have not asked that question sooner. But perhaps you haven't heard of the invention?

GREGERS. The invention? No.

HIALMAR. Really? Have you not? Oh no, out there in the wilds—

GREGERS. So you have invented something, have you?

HIALMAR. It is not quite completed yet; but I am working at it. You can easily imagine that when I resolved to devote myself to photography, it wasn't simply with the idea of taking likenesses of all sorts of commonplace people.

GREGERS. No; your wife was saying the same thing just now.

HIALMAR. I swore that if I consecrated my powers to this handicraft, I would so exalt it that it should become both an art and a science. And to that end I determined to make this great invention.

GREGERS. And what is the nature of the invention? What purpose does it serve?

HIALMAR. Oh, my dear fellow, you mustn't ask for details yet. It takes time, you see. And you must not think that my motive is vanity. It is not for my own sake that I am working. Oh no; it is my life's mission that stands before me night and day.

GREGERS. What is your life's mission?

HIALMAR. Do you forget the old man with the silver hair?

GREGERS. Your poor father? Well, but what can you do for him?

HIALMAR. I can raise up his self-respect from the dead, by restoring the name of Ekdal to honour and dignity.

GREGERS. Then that is your life's mission?

HIALMAR. Yes. I will rescue the shipwrecked man. For shipwrecked he was, by the very first blast of the storm. Even while those terrible investigations were going on, he was no longer himself. That pistol there—the one we use to shoot rabbits with—has played its part in the tragedy of the house of Ekdal.

GREGERS. The pistol? Indeed?

HIALMAR. When the sentence of imprisonment was passed—he had the pistol in his hand—

GREGERS. Had he—?

HIALMAR. Yes; but he dared not use it. His courage failed him. So broken, so demoralised was he even then! Oh, can you understand it? He, a soldier; he, who had shot nine bears, and who was descended from two lieutenant-colonels—one after the other of course. Can you understand it, Gregers?

GREGERS. Yes, I understand it well enough.

HIALMAR. I cannot. And once more the pistol played a part in the history of our house. When he had put on the grey clothes and was under lock and key— oh, that was a terrible time for me, I can tell you. I kept the blinds drawn down over both my windows. When I peeped out, I saw the sun shining as if nothing had happened. I could not understand it. I saw people going along the street, laughing and talking about indifferent things. I could not understand it. It seemed to me that the whole of existence must be at a standstill—as if under an eclipse.

GREGERS. I felt like that too, when my mother died.

HIALMAR. It was in such an hour that Hialmar Ekdal pointed the pistol at his own breast.

GREGERS. You too thought of—!

HIALMAR. Yes.

GREGERS. But you did not fire?

HIALMAR. No. At the decisive moment I won the victory over myself. I remained in life. But I can assure you it takes some courage to choose life under circumstances like those.

GREGERS. Well, that depends on how you look at it.

HIALMAR. Yes, indeed, it takes courage. But I am glad I was firm: for now I shall soon perfect my invention; and Dr. Relling thinks, as I do myself, that father may be allowed to wear his uniform again. I will demand that as my sole reward.

GREGERS. So that is what he meant about his uniform—?

HIALMAR. Yes, that is what he most yearns for. You can't think how my heart bleeds for him. Every time we celebrate any little family festival—Gina's and my wedding day, or whatever it may be—in comes the old man in the lieutenant's uniform of happier days. But if he only hears a knock at the door—for he daren't show himself to strangers, you know—he hurries back to his room again as fast as his old legs can carry him. Oh, it's heartrending for a son to see such things!

GREGERS. How long do you think it will take you to finish your invention?

HIALMAR. Come now, you mustn't expect me to enter into particulars like that. An invention is not a thing completely under one's own control. It depends largely on inspiration—on intuition—and it is almost impossible to predict when the inspiration may come.

GREGERS. But it's advancing?

HIALMAR. Yes, certainly, it is advancing. I turn it over in my mind every day; I am full of it. Every afternoon, when I have had my dinner, I shut myself up in the parlour, where I can ponder undisturbed. But I can't be goaded to it; it's not a bit of good; Relling says so too.

GREGERS. And you don't think that all that business in the garret draws you off and distracts you too much?

HIALMAR. No no no; quite the contrary. You mustn't say that. I cannot be everlastingly absorbed in the same laborious train of thought. I must have something alongside of it to fill up the time of waiting. The inspiration, the intuition, you see—when it comes, it comes, and there's an end of it.

GREGERS. My dear Hialmar, I almost think you have something of the wild duck in you.

HIALMAR. Something of the wild duck? How do you mean?

GREGERS. You have dived down and bitten yourself fast in the undergrowth.

HIALMAR. Are you alluding to the well-nigh fatal shot that has broken my father's wing—and mine too?

GREGERS. Not exactly to that. I don't say that your wing has been broken; but you have strayed into a poisonous marsh, Hialmar; an insidious disease has taken hold of you, and you have sunk down to die in the dark.

HIALMAR. I? To die in the dark? Look here, Gregers, you must really leave off talking such nonsense.

GREGERS. Don't be afraid; I shall find a way to help you up again. I too have a mission in life now; I found it yesterday.

HIALMAR. That's all very well; but you will please leave me out of It. I can assure you that—apart from my very natural melancholy, of course—I am as contented as any one can wish to be.

GREGERS. Your contentment is an effect of the marsh poison.

HIALMAR. Now, my dear Gregers, pray do not go on about disease and poison; I am not used to that sort of talk. In my house nobody ever speaks to me about unpleasant things.

GREGERS. Ah, that I can easily believe.

HIALMAR. It's not good for me you see. And there are no marsh poisons here, as you express it. The poor photographer's roof is lowly, I know—and my circumstances are narrow. But I am an inventor, and I am the breadwinner of a family. That exalts me above my mean surroundings.—Ah, here comes lunch!

[Gina and Hedvig bring bottles of ale, a decanter of brandy, glasses, etc. At the same time, Relling and Molvik enter from the passage; they are both without hat or overcoat. Molvik is dressed in black.]

GINA. [Placing the things upon the table.] Ah, you two have come in the nick of time.

RELLING. Molvik got it into his head that he could smell herring-salad, and then there was no holding him.—Good morning again, Ekdal.

HIALMAR. Gregers, let me introduce you to Mr. Molvik. Doctor— Oh, you know Relling, don't you?

GREGERS. Yes, slightly.

RELLING. Oh, Mr. Werle, junior! Yes, we two have had one or two little skirmishes up at the Höidal works. You've just moved in?

GREGERS. I moved in this morning.

RELLING. Molvik and I live right under you; so you haven't far to go for the doctor and the clergyman, if you should need anything in that line.

GREGERS. Thanks, it's not quite unlikely; for yesterday we were thirteen at table.

HIALMAR. Oh, come now, don't let us get upon unpleasant subjects again!

RELLING. You may make your mind easy, Ekdal; I'll be hanged if the finger of fate points to you.

HIALMAR. I should hope not, for the sake of my family. But let us sit down now, and eat and drink and be merry.

GREGERS. Shall we not wait for your father?

HIALMAR. No, his lunch will be taken in to him later. Come along!

[The men seat themselves at table, and eat and drink. Gina and Hedvig go in and out and wait upon them.]

RELLING. Molvik was frightfully screwed yesterday, Mrs. Ekdal.

GINA. Really? Yesterday again?

RELLING. Didn't you hear him when I brought him home last night.

GINA. No, I can't say I did.

RELLING. That was a good thing, for Molvik was disgusting last night.

GINA. Is that true, Molvik?

MOLVIK. Let us draw a veil over last night's proceedings. That sort of thing is totally foreign to my better self.

RELLING. [To Gregers.] It comes over him like a sort of possession, and then I have to go out on the loose with him. Mr. Molvik is dæmonic, you see.

GREGERS. Dæmonic?

RELLING. Molvik is dæmonic, yes.

GREGERS. H'm.

RELLING. And dæmonic natures are not made to walk straight through the world; they must meander a little now and then.—Well, so you still stick up there at those horrible grimy works?

GREGERS. I have stuck there until now.

RELLING. And did you ever manage to collect that claim you went about presenting?

GREGERS. Claim? [*Understands him.*] Ah, I see.

HIALMAR. Have you been presenting claims, Gregers?

GREGERS. Oh, nonsense.

RELLING. Faith, but he has, though! He went round to all the cottars' cabins presenting something he called "the claim of the ideal."

GREGERS. I was young then.

RELLING. You're right; you were very young. And as for the claim of the ideal—you never got it honoured while *I* was up there.

GREGERS. Nor since either.

RELLING. Ah, then you've learnt to knock a little discount off, I expect.

GREGERS. Never, when I have a true man to deal with.

HIALMAR. No, I should think not, indeed. A little butter, Gina.

RELLING. And a slice of bacon for Molvik.

MOLVIK. Ugh! not bacon! [*A knock at the garret door.*]

HIALMAR. Open the door, Hedvig; father wants to come out.

[*Hedvig goes over and opens the door a little way; Ekdal enters with a fresh rabbit-skin; she closes the door after him.*]

EKDAL. Good morning, gentlemen! Good sport to-day. Shot a big one.

HIALMAR. And you've gone and skinned it without waiting for me—!

EKDAL. Salted it too. It's good tender meat, is rabbit; it's sweet; it tastes like sugar. Good appetite to you, gentlemen! [*Goes into his room.*]

MOLVIK. [*Rising.*] Excuse me—; I can't—; I must get downstairs immediately—

RELLING. Drink some soda water, man!

MOLVIK. [*Hurrying away.*] Ugh—ugh!

[*Goes out by the passage door.*]

RELLING. [*To Hialmar.*] Let us drain a glass to the old hunter.

HIALMAR. [*Clinks glasses with him.*] To the undaunted sportsman who has looked death in the face!

RELLING. To the grey-haired—[*Drinks.*] By-the-bye, is his hair grey or white?

HIALMAR. Something between the two, I fancy; for that matter, he has very few hairs left of any colour.

RELLING. Well well, one can get through the world with a wig. After all, you are a happy man, Ekdal; you have your noble mission to labour for—

HIALMAR. And I do labour, I can tell you.

RELLING. And then you have your excellent wife, shuffling quietly in and out in her felt slippers, with that see-saw walk of hers, and making everything cosy and comfortable about you.

HIALMAR. Yes, Gina—[*Nods to her.*] —you are a good helpmate on the path of life.

GINA. Oh, don't sit there cricketizing me.

RELLING. And your Hedvig too, Ekdal!

HIALMAR. [*Affected.*] The child, yes! The child before everything! Hedvig, come here to me. [*Strokes her hair.*] What day is to-morrow, eh?

HEDVIG. [*Shaking him.*] Oh no, you're not to say anything, father.

HIALMAR. It cuts me to the heart when I think what a poor affair it will be; only a little festivity in the garret—

HEDVIG. Oh, but that's just what I like!

RELLING. Just you wait till the wonderful invention sees the light, Hedvig!

HIALMAR. Yes indeed—then you shall see—! Hedvig, I have resolved to make your future secure. You shall live in comfort all your days. I will demand—something or other—on your behalf. That shall be the poor inventor's sole reward.

HEDVIG. [*Whispering, with her arms round his neck.*] Oh you dear, kind father!

RELLING. [*To Gregers.*] Come now, don't you find it pleasant, for once in a way, to sit at a well-spread table in a happy family circle?

HIALMAR. Ah yes, I really prize these social hours.

GREGERS. For my part, I don't thrive in marsh vapours.

RELLING. Marsh vapours?

HIALMAR. Oh, don't begin with that stuff again!

GINA. Goodness knows there's no vapours in this house, Mr. Werle; I give the place a good airing every blessed day.

GREGERS. [*Leaves the table.*] No airing you can give will drive out the taint I mean.

HIALMAR. Taint!

GINA. Yes, what do you say to that, Ekdal!

RELLING. Excuse me—may it not be you yourself that have brought the taint from those mines up there?

GREGERS. It is like you to call what I bring into this house a taint.

RELLING. [*Goes up to him.*] Look here, Mr. Werle, junior: I have a strong suspicion that you are still carrying about that "claim of the ideal" large as life, in your coat-tail pocket.

GREGERS. I carry it in my breast.

RELLING. Well, wherever you carry it, I advise you not to come dunning us with it here, so long as *I* am on the premises.

GREGERS. And if I do so none the less?

RELLING. Then you'll go head-foremost down the stairs; now I've warned you.

HIALMAR. [*Rising.*] Oh, but Relling—!

GREGERS. Yes, you may turn me out—

GINA. [*Interposing between them.*] We can't have that, Relling. But I must say, Mr. Werle, it ill becomes you to talk about vapours and taints, after all the mess you made with your stove.

[*A knock at the passage door.*]

HEDVIG. Mother, there's somebody knocking.

HIALMAR. There now, we're going to have a whole lot of people!

GINA. I'll go—[*Goes over and opens the door, starts, and draws back.*] Oh—oh dear!

[*Werle, in a fur coat, advances one step into the room.*]

WERLE. Excuse me; but I think my son is staying here.

GINA. [*With a gulp.*] Yes.

HIALMAR. [*Approaching him.*] Won't you do us the honour to—?

WERLE. Thank you, I merely wish to speak to my son.

GREGERS. What is it? Here I am.

WERLE. I want a few words with you, in your room.

GREGERS. In my room? Very well— [*About to go.*]

GINA. No, no, your room's not in a fit state—

WERLE. Well then, out in the passage here; I want to have a few words with you alone.

HIALMAR. You can have them here, sir. Come into the parlour, Relling.

[*Hialmar and Relling go off to the right. Gina takes Hedvig with her into the kitchen.*]

GREGERS. [*After a short pause.*] Well, now we are alone.

WERLE. From something you let fall last evening, and from your coming to lodge with the Ekdals, I can't help inferring that you intend to make yourself unpleasant to me, in one way or another.

GREGERS. I intend to open Hialmar Ekdal's eyes. He shall see his position as it really is—that is all.

WERLE. Is that the mission in life you spoke of yesterday?

GREGERS. Yes. You have left me no other.

WERLE. Is it I, then, that have crippled your mind, Gregers?

GREGERS. You have crippled my whole life. I am not thinking of all that about mother— But it's thanks to you that I am continually haunted and harassed by a guilty conscience.

WERLE. Indeed! It is your conscience that troubles you, is it?

GREGERS. I ought to have taken a stand against you when the trap was set for Lieutenant Ekdal. I ought to have cautioned him; for I had a misgiving as to what was in the wind.

WERLE. Yes, that was the time to have spoken.

GREGERS. I did not dare to, I was so cowed and spiritless. I was mortally afraid of you—not only then, but long afterwards.

WERLE. You have got over that fear now, it appears.

GREGERS. Yes, fortunately. The wrong done to old Ekdal, both by me and by—others, can never be undone; but Hialmar I can rescue from all the falsehood and deception that are bringing him to ruin.

WERLE. Do you think that will be doing him a kindness?

GREGERS. I have not the least doubt of it.

WERLE. You think our worthy photographer is the sort of man to appreciate such friendly offices?

GREGERS. Yes, I do.

WERLE. H'm—we shall see.

GREGERS. Besides, if I am to go on living, I must try to find some cure for my sick conscience.

WERLE. It will never be sound. Your conscience has been sickly from childhood. That is a legacy from your mother, Gregers—the only one she left you.

GREGERS. [*With a scornful half-smile.*] Have you not yet forgiven her for the mistake you made in supposing she would bring you a fortune?

WERLE. Don't let us wander from the point.—Then you hold to your purpose of setting young Ekdal upon what you imagine to be the right scent?

GREGERS. Yes, that is my fixed resolve.

WERLE. Well, in that case I might have spared myself this visit; for of course it is useless to ask whether you will return home with me?

GREGERS. Quite useless.

WERLE. And I suppose you won't enter the firm either?

GREGERS. No.

WERLE. Very good. But as I am thinking of marrying again, your share in the property will fall to you at once.[4]

GREGERS. [Quickly.] No, I do not want that.

WERLE. You don't want it?

GREGERS. No, I dare not take it, for conscience' sake.

WERLE. [After a pause.] Are you going up to the works again?

GREGERS. No; I consider myself released from your service.

WERLE. But what are you going to do?

GREGERS. Only to fulfil my mission; nothing more.

WERLE. Well, but afterwards? What are you going to live upon?

GREGERS. I have laid by a little out of my salary.

WERLE. How long will that last?

GREGERS. I think it will last my time.

WERLE. What do you mean?

GREGERS. I shall answer no more questions.

WERLE. Good-bye then, Gregers.

GREGERS. Good-bye. [Werle goes.]

HIALMAR. [Peeping in.] He's gone, isn't he?

GREGERS. Yes.

[Hialmar and Relling enter; also Gina and Hedvig from the kitchen.]

RELLING. That luncheon-party was a failure.

GREGERS. Put on your coat, Hialmar; I want you to come for a long walk with me.

HIALMAR. With pleasure. What was it your father wanted? Had it anything to do with me?

GREGERS. Come along. We must have a talk. I'll go and put on my overcoat.

[Goes out by the passage door.]

GINA. You shouldn't go out with him, Ekdal.

RELLING. No, don't you do it. Stay where you are.

HIALMAR. [Gets his hat and overcoat.] Oh, nonsense! When a friend of my youth feels impelled to open his mind to me in private—

RELLING. But devil take it—don't you see that the fellow's mad, cracked, demented!

GINA. There, what did I tell you! His mother before him had crazy fits like that sometimes.

HIALMAR. The more need for a friend's watchful eye. [To Gina.] Be sure you have dinner ready in good time. Good-bye for the present.

[Goes out by the passage door.]

RELLING. It's a thousand pities the fellow didn't go to hell through one of the Höidal mines.

GINA. Good Lord! what makes you say that?

RELLING. [Muttering.] Oh, I have my own reasons.

GINA. Do you think young Werle is really mad?

RELLING. No, worse luck; he's no madder than most other people. But one disease he has certainly got in his system.

GINA. What is it that's the matter with him?

RELLING. Well, I'll tell you, Mrs. Ekdal. He is suffering from an acute attack of integrity.

GINA. Integrity?

HEDVIG. Is that a kind of disease?

RELLING. Yes, it's a national disease; but it only appears sporadically. [Nods to Gina.] Thanks for your hospitality.

[He goes out by the passage door.]

GINA. [Moving restlessly to and fro.] Ugh, that Gregers Werle—he was always a wretched creature.

HEDVIG. [Standing by the table, and looking searchingly at her.] I think all this is very strange.

Act IV

Hialmar Ekdal's studio. A photograph has just been taken; a camera with a cloth over it, a pedestal, two chairs, a folding table, etc., are standing out in the room. Afternoon light; the sun is going down; a little later it begins to grow dusk.

Gina stands in the passage doorway, with a little box and a wet glass plate in her hand, and is speaking to somebody outside.

---

[4] By Norwegian law, before a widower can marry again, a certain proportion of his property must be settled on his children by his former marriage.

GINA. Yes, certainly. When I make a promise I keep it. The first dozen shall be ready on Monday. Good afternoon.

[*Some one is heard going downstairs. Gina shuts the door, slips the plate into the box, and puts it into the covered camera.*]

HEDVIG. [*Comes in from the kitchen.*] Are they gone?

GINA. [*Tidying up.*] Yes, thank goodness, I've got rid of them at last.

HEDVIG. But can you imagine why father hasn't come home yet?

GINA. Are you sure he's not down in Relling's room?

HEDVIG. No, he's not; I ran down the kitchen stair just now and asked.

GINA. And his dinner standing and getting cold, too.

HEDVIG. Yes, I can't understand it. Father's always so careful to be home to dinner!

GINA. Oh, he'll be here directly, you'll see.

HEDVIG. I wish he would come; everything seems so queer to-day.

GINA. [*Calls out.*] There he is!

[*Hialmar Ekdal comes in at the passage door.*]

HEDVIG. [*Going to him.*] Father! Oh what a time we've been waiting for you!

GINA. [*Glancing sidelong at him.*] You've been out a long time, Ekdal.

HIALMAR. [*Without looking at her.*] Rather long, yes.

[*He takes off his overcoat; Gina and Hedvig go to help him; he motions them away.*]

GINA. Perhaps you've had dinner with Werle?

HIALMAR. [*Hanging up his coat.*] No.

GINA. [*Going towards the kitchen door.*] Then I'll bring some in for you.

HIALMAR. No; let the dinner alone. I want nothing to eat.

HEDVIG. [*Going nearer to him.*] Are you not well, father?

HIALMAR. Well? Oh yes, well enough. We have had a tiring walk, Gregers and I.

GINA. You didn't ought to have gone so far, Ekdal, you're not used to it.

HIALMAR. H'm; there's many a thing a man must get used to in this world. [*Wanders about the room.*] Has any one been here whilst I was out?

GINA. Nobody but the two sweethearts.

HIALMAR. No new orders?

GINA. No, not to-day.

HEDVIG. There will be some to-morrow, father, you'll see.

HIALMAR. I hope there will; for to-morrow I am going to set to work in real earnest.

HEDVIG. To-morrow! Don't you remember what day it is to-morrow?

HIALMAR. Oh yes, by-the-bye—. Well, the day after, then. Henceforth I mean to do everything myself; I shall take all the work into my own hands.

GINA. Why, what can be the good of that, Ekdal? It'll only make your life a burden to you. I can manage the photography all right; and you can go on working at your invention.

HEDVIG. And think of the wild duck, father,—and all the hens and rabbits and—!

HIALMAR. Don't talk to me of all that trash! From to-morrow I will never set foot in the garret again.

HEDVIG. Oh but, father, you promised that we should have a little party—

HIALMAR. H'm, true. Well then, from the day after to-morrow. I should almost like to wring that cursèd wild duck's neck!

HEDVIG. [*Shrieks.*] The wild duck!

GINA. Well I never!

HEDVIG. [*Shaking him.*] Oh no, father; you know it's my wild duck!

HIALMAR. That is why I don't do it. I haven't the heart to—for your sake, Hedvig. But in my inmost soul I feel that I ought to do it. I ought not to tolerate under my roof a creature that has been through those hands.

GINA. Why, good gracious, even if grandfather did get it from that poor creature, Pettersen—

HIALMAR. [*Wandering about.*] There are certain claims—what shall I call them?—let me say claims of the ideal—certain obligations, which a man cannot disregard without injury to his soul.

HEDVIG. [*Going after him.*] But think of the wild duck,—the poor wild duck!

HIALMAR. [*Stops.*] I tell you I will spare it—for your sake. Not a hair of its head shall be—I mean, it shall be spared. There are greater problems than that to be dealt with. But you should go out a little now, Hedvig, as usual; it is getting dusk enough for you now.

HEDVIG. No, I don't care about going out now.

HIALMAR. Yes do; it seems to me your eyes are blinking a great deal; all these vapours in here are bad for you. The air is heavy under this roof.

HEDVIG. Very well then, I'll run down the kitchen stair and go for a little walk. My cloak and hat?—oh, they're in my own room. Father—be sure you don't do the wild duck any harm whilst I'm out.

HIALMAR. Not a feather of its head shall be touched. [*Draws her to him.*] You and I, Hedvig—we two—! Well, go along.

[*Hedvig nods to her parents and goes out through the kitchen.*]

HIALMAR. [*Walks about without looking up.*] Gina.

GINA. Yes?

HIALMAR. From to-morrow—or, say, from the day after to-morrow—I should like to keep the household account-book myself.

GINA. Do you want to keep the accounts too, now?

HIALMAR. Yes; or to check the receipts at any rate.

GINA. Lord help us! that's soon done.

HIALMAR. One would hardly think so; at any rate you seem to make the money go a very long way. [*Stops and looks at her.*] How do you manage it?

GINA. It's because me and Hedvig, we need so little.

HIALMAR. Is it the case that father is very liberally paid for the copying he does for Mr. Werle?

GINA. I don't know as he gets anything out of the way. I don't know the rates for that sort of work.

HIALMAR. Well, what does he get, about? Let me hear!

GINA. Oh, it varies; I daresay it'll come to about as much as he costs us, with a little pocket-money over.

HIALMAR. As much as he costs us! And you have never told me this before!

GINA. No, how could I tell you? It pleased you so much to think he got everything from you.

HIALMAR. And he gets it from Mr. Werle.

GINA. Oh well, he has plenty and to spare, he has.

HIALMAR. Light the lamp for me, please!

GINA. [*Lighting the lamp.*] And of course we don't know as it's Mr. Werle himself; it may be Gråberg—

HIALMAR. Why attempt such an evasion?

GINA. I don't know; I only thought—

HIALMAR. H'm!

GINA. It wasn't me that got grandfather that copying. It was Bertha, when she used to come about us.

HIALMAR. It seems to me your voice is trembling.

GINA. [*Putting the lamp-shade on.*] Is it?

HIALMAR. And your hands are shaking, are they not?

GINA. [*Firmly.*] Come right out with it, Ekdal. What has he been saying about me?

HIALMAR. Is it true—can it be true that—that there was an—an understanding between you and Mr. Werle, while you were in service there?

GINA. That's not true. Not at that time. Mr. Werle did

come after me, that's a fact. And his wife thought there was something in it, and then she made such a hocus-pocus and hurly-burly, and she hustled me and bustled me about so, that I left her service.

HIALMAR. But afterwards, then?

GINA. Well, then I went home. And mother—well, she wasn't the woman you took her for, Ekdal; she kept on worrying and worrying at me about one thing and another—for Mr. Werle was a widower by that time.

HIALMAR. Well, and then?

GINA. I suppose you've got to know it. He gave me no peace until he'd had his way.

HIALMAR. [*Striking his hands together.*] And this is the mother of my child! How could you hide this from me?

GINA. Yes, it was wrong of me; I ought certainly to have told you long ago.

HIALMAR. You should have told me at the very first;—then I should have known the sort of woman you were.

GINA. But would you have married me all the same?

HIALMAR. How can you dream that I would?

GINA. That's just why I didn't dare tell you anything, then. For I'd come to care for you so much, you see; and I couldn't go and make myself utterly miserable—

HIALMAR. [*Walks about.*] And this is my Hedvig's mother. And to know that all I see before me—[*Kicks at a chair*]—all that I call my home—I owe to a favoured predecessor! Oh that scoundrel Werle!

GINA. Do you repent of the fourteen—the fifteen years as we've lived together?

HIALMAR. [*Placing himself in front of her.*] Have you not every day, every hour, repented of the spider's-web of deceit you have spun around me? Answer me that! How could you help writhing with penitence and remorse?

GINA. Oh, my dear Ekdal, I've had all I could do to look after the house and get through the day's work—

HIALMAR. Then you never think of reviewing your past?

GINA. No; Heaven knows I'd almost forgotten those old stories.

HIALMAR. Oh, this dull, callous contentment! To me there is something revolting about it. Think of it—never so much as a twinge of remorse!

GINA. But tell me, Ekdal—what would have become of you if you hadn't had a wife like me?

HIALMAR. Like you—!

GINA. Yes; for you know I've always been a bit more practical and wide-awake than you. Of course I'm a year or two older.

HIALMAR. What would have become of me!

GINA. You'd got into all sorts of bad ways when first you met me; that you can't deny.

HIALMAR. "Bad ways" do you call them? Little do you know what a man goes through when he is in grief and despair—especially a man of my fiery temperament.

GINA. Well, well, that may be so. And I've no reason to crow over you, neither; for you turned a moral of a husband, that you did, as soon as ever you had a house and home of your own.—And now we'd got everything so nice and cosy about us; and me and Hedvig was just thinking we'd soon be able to let ourselves go a bit, in the way of both food and clothes.

HIALMAR. In the swamp of deceit, yes.

GINA. I wish to goodness that detestable being had never set his foot inside our doors!

HIALMAR. And I, too, thought my home such a pleasant one. That was a delusion. Where shall I now find the elasticity of spirit to bring my invention into the world of reality? Perhaps it will die with me; and then it will be your past, Gina, that will have killed it.

GINA. [Nearly crying.] You mustn't say such things, Ekdal. Me, that has only wanted to do the best I could for you, all my days!

HIALMAR. I ask you, what becomes of the breadwinner's dream? When I used to lie in there on the sofa and brood over my invention, I had a clear enough presentiment that it would sap my vitality to the last drop. I felt even then that the day when I held the patent in my hand—that day—would bring my—release. And then it was my dream that you should live on after me, the dead inventor's well-to-do widow.

GINA. [Drying her tears.] No, you mustn't talk like that, Ekdal. May the Lord never let me see the day I am left a widow!

HIALMAR. Oh, the whole dream has vanished. It is all over now. All over!

[Gregers Werle opens the passage door cautiously and looks in.]

GREGERS. May I come in?

HIALMAR. Yes, come in.

GREGERS. [Comes forward, his face beaming with satisfaction, and holds out both his hands to them.] Well, dear friends—! [Looks from one to the other, and whispers to Hialmar.] Have you not done it yet?

HIALMAR. [Aloud.] It is done.

GREGERS. It is?

HIALMAR. I have passed through the bitterest moments of my life.

GREGERS. But also, I trust, the most ennobling.

HIALMAR. Well, at any rate, we have got through it for the present.

GINA. God forgive you, Mr. Werle.

GREGERS. [In great surprise.] But I don't understand this.

HIALMAR. What don't you understand?

GREGERS. After so great a crisis—a crisis that is to be the starting-point of an entirely new life—of a communion founded on truth, and free from all taint of deception—

HIALMAR. Yes yes, I know; I know that quite well.

GREGERS. I confidently expected, when I entered the room, to find the light of transfiguration shining upon me from both husband and wife. And now I see nothing but dullness, oppression, gloom—

GINA. Oh, is that it? [Takes off the lamp-shade.]

GREGERS. You will not understand me, Mrs. Ekdal. Ah well, you, I suppose, need time to—. But you, Hialmar? Surely you feel a new consecration after the great crisis.

HIALMAR. Yes, of course I do. That is—in a sort of way.

GREGERS. For surely nothing in the world can compare with the joy of forgiving one who has erred, and raising her up to oneself in love.

HIALMAR. Do you think a man can so easily throw off the effects of the bitter cup I have drained?

GREGERS. No, not a common man, perhaps. But a man like you—!

HIALMAR. Good God! I know that well enough. But you must keep me up to it, Gregers. It takes time, you know.

GREGERS. You have much of the wild duck in you, Hialmar.

[Relling has come in at the passage door.]

RELLING. Oho! is the wild duck to the fore again?

HIALMAR. Yes; Mr. Werle's wing-broken victim.

RELLING. Mr. Werle's—? So it's him you are talking about?

HIALMAR. Him and—ourselves.

RELLING. [*In an undertone to Gregers.*] May the devil fly away with you!

HIALMAR. What is that you are saying?

RELLING. Only uttering a heartfelt wish that this quack-salver would take himself off. If he stays here, he is quite equal to making an utter mess of life, for both of you.

GREGERS. These two will not make a mess of life, Mr. Relling. Of course, I won't speak of Hialmar—him we know. But she, too, in her innermost heart, has certainly something loyal and sincere—

GINA. [*Almost crying.*] You might have let me alone for what I was, then.

RELLING. [*To Gregers.*] Is it rude to ask what you really want in this house?

GREGERS. To lay the foundations of a true marriage.

RELLING. So you don't think Ekdal's marriage is good enough as it is?

GREGERS. No doubt it is as good a marriage as most others, worse luck. But a true marriage it has yet to become.

HIALMAR. You have never had eyes for the claims of the ideal, Relling.

RELLING. Rubbish, my boy!—But excuse me, Mr. Werle: how many—in round numbers—how many true marriages have you seen in the course of your life?

GREGERS. Scarcely a single one.

RELLING. Nor I either.

GREGERS. But I have seen innumerable marriages of the opposite kind. And it has been my fate to see at close quarters what ruin such a marriage can work in two human souls.

HIALMAR. A man's whole moral basis may give away beneath his feet; that is the terrible part of it.

RELLING. Well, I can't say I've ever been exactly married, so I don't pretend to speak with authority. But this I know, that the child enters into the marriage problem. And you must leave the child in peace.

HIALMAR. Oh—Hedvig! my poor Hedvig!

RELLING. Yes, you must be good enough to keep Hedvig outside of all this. You two are grown-up people; you are free, in God's name, to make what mess and muddle you please of your life. But you must deal cautiously with Hedvig, I tell you; else you may do her a great injury.

HIALMAR. An injury!

RELLING. Yes, or she may do herself an injury—and perhaps others too.

GINA. How can you know that, Relling?

HIALMAR. Her sight is in no immediate danger, is it?

RELLING. I am not talking about her sight. Hedvig is at a critical age. She may be getting all sorts of mischief into her head.

GINA. That's true—I've noticed it already! She's taken to carrying on with the fire, out in the kitchen. She calls it playing at house-on-fire. I'm often scared for fear she really sets fire to the house.

RELLING. You see; I thought as much.

GREGERS. [*To Relling.*] But how do you account for that?

RELLING. [*Sullenly.*] Her constitution's changing, sir.

HIALMAR. So long as the child has me—! So long as I am above ground—! [*A knock at the door.*]

GINA. Hush, Ekdal; there's some one in the passage. [*Calls out.*] Come in!

[*Mrs. Sörby, in walking dress, comes in.*]

MRS SÖRBY. Good evening.

GINA. [*Going towards her.*] Is it really you, Bertha?

MRS. SÖRBY. Yes, of course it is. But I'm disturbing you, I'm afraid?

HIALMAR. No, not at all; an emissary from that house—

MRS. SÖRBY. [*To Gina.*] To tell the truth, I hoped your men-folk would be out at this time. I just ran up to have a little chat with you, and to say good-bye.

GINA. Good-bye? Are you going away, then?

MRS. SÖRBY. Yes, to-morrow morning,—up to Höi-dal. Mr. Werle started this afternoon. [*Lightly to Gregers.*] He asked me to say good-bye for him.

GINA. Only fancy—!

HIALMAR. So Mr. Werle has gone? And now you are going after him?

MRS. SÖRBY. Yes, what do you say to that, Ekdal?

HIALMAR. I say: beware!

GREGERS. I must explain the situation. My father and Mrs. Sörby are going to be married.

HIALMAR. Going to be married!

GINA. Oh Bertha! So it's come to that at last!

RELLING. [*His voice quivering a little.*] This is surely not true?

MRS. SÖRBY. Yes, my dear Relling, it's true enough.

RELLING. You are going to marry again?

MRS. SÖRBY. Yes, it looks like it. Werle has got a special license, and we are going to be married quite quietly, up at the works.

GREGERS. Then I must wish you all happiness, like a dutiful stepson.

MRS. SÖRBY. Thank you very much—if you mean what you say. I certainly hope it will lead to happiness, both for Werle and for me.

RELLING. You have every reason to hope that. Mr.

Werle never gets drunk—so far as I know; and I don't suppose he's in the habit of thrashing his wives, like the late lamented horse-doctor.

MRS. SÖRBY. Come now, let Sörby rest in peace. He had his good points, too.

RELLING. Mr. Werle has better ones, I have no doubt.

MRS. SÖRBY. He hasn't frittered away all that was good in him, at any rate. The man who does that must take the consequences.

RELLING. I shall go out with Molvik this evening.

MRS. SÖRBY. You mustn't do that, Relling. Don't do it—for my sake.

RELLING. There's nothing else for it. [*To Hialmar.*] If you're going with us, come along.

GINA. No, thank you. Ekdal doesn't go in for that sort of dissertation.

HIALMAR. [*Half aloud, in vexation.*] Oh, do hold your tongue!

RELLING. Good-bye, Mrs.—Werle.

[*Goes out through the passage door.*]

GREGERS. [*To Mrs. Sörby.*] You seem to know Dr. Relling pretty intimately.

MRS. SÖRBY. Yes, we have known each other for many years. At one time it seemed as if things might have gone further between us.

GREGERS. It was surely lucky for you that they did not.

MRS. SÖRBY. You may well say that. But I have always been wary of acting on impulse. A woman can't afford absolutely to throw herself away.

GREGERS. Are you not in the least afraid that I may let my father know about this old friendship?

MRS. SÖRBY. Why, of course I have told him all about it myself.

GREGERS. Indeed?

MRS. SÖRBY. Your father knows every single thing that can, with any truth, be said about me. I have told him all; it was the first thing I did when I saw what was in his mind.

GREGERS. Then you have been franker than most people, I think.

MRS. SÖRBY. I have always been frank. We women find that the best policy.

HIALMAR. What do you say to that, Gina?

GINA. Oh, we're not all alike, us women aren't. Some are made one way, some another.

MRS. SÖRBY. Well, for my part, Gina, I believe it's wisest to do as I've done. And Werle has no secrets either, on his side. That's really the great bond between us, you see. Now he can talk to me as openly as a child. He has never had the chance to do that before. Fancy a man like him, full of health and vigour, passing his whole youth and the best years of his life in listening to nothing but penitential sermons! And very often the sermons had for their text the most imaginary offences—at least so I understand.

GINA. That's true enough.

GREGERS. If you ladies are going to follow up this topic, I had better withdraw.

MRS. SÖRBY. You can stay so far as that's concerned. I shan't say a word more. But I wanted you to know that I had done nothing secretly or in an underhand way. I may seem to have come in for a great piece of luck; and so I have, in a sense. But after all, I don't think I am getting any more than I am giving. I shall stand by him always, and I can tend and care for him as no one else can, now that he is getting helpless.

HIALMAR. Getting helpless?

GREGERS. [*To Mrs. Sörby.*] Hush, don't speak of that here.

MRS. SÖRBY. There is no disguising it any longer, however much he would like to. He is going blind.

HIALMAR. [*Starts.*] Going blind? That's strange. He too going blind!

GINA. Lots of people do.

MRS. SÖRBY. And you can imagine what that means to a business man. Well, I shall try as well as I can to make my eyes take the place of his. But I mustn't stay any longer; I have such heaps of things to do.— Oh, by-the-bye, Ekdal, I was to tell you that if there is anything Werle can do for you, you must apply to Gråberg.

GREGERS. That offer I am sure Hialmar Ekdal will decline with thanks.

MRS. SÖRBY. Indeed? I don't think he used to be so—

GINA. No, Bertha, Ekdal doesn't need anything from Mr. Werle now.

HIALMAR. [*Slowly, and with emphasis.*] Will you present my compliments to your future husband, and say that I intend very shortly to call upon Mr. Gråberg—

GREGERS. What! You don't really mean that?

HIALMAR. To call upon Mr. Gråberg, I say, and obtain an account of the sum I owe his principal. I will pay that debt of honour—ha ha ha! a debt of honour, let us call it! In any case, I will pay the whole, with five percent interest.

GINA. But, my dear Ekdal, God knows we haven't got the money to do it.

HIALMAR. Be good enough to tell your future husband that I am working assiduously at my invention.

Please tell him that what sustains me in this laborious task is the wish to free myself from a torturing burden of debt. That is my reason for proceeding with the invention. The entire profits shall be devoted to releasing me from my pecuniary obligations to your future husband.

MRS. SÖRBY. Something has happened here.

HIALMAR. Yes, you are right.

MRS. SÖRBY. Well, good-bye. I had something else to speak to you about, Gina; but it must keep till another time. Good-bye.

[*Hialmar and Gregers bow silently. Gina follows Mrs. Sörby to the door.*]

HIALMAR. Not beyond the threshold, Gina!

[*Mrs. Sörby goes; Gina shuts the door after her.*]

HIALMAR. There now, Gregers; I have got that burden of debt off my mind.

GREGERS. You soon will, at all events.

HIALMAR. I think my attitude may be called correct.

GREGERS. You are the man I have always taken you for.

HIALMAR. In certain cases, it is impossible to disregard the claim of the ideal. Yet, as the breadwinner of a family, I cannot but writhe and groan under it. I can tell you it is no joke for a man without capital to attempt the repayment of a long-standing obligation, over which, so to speak, the dust of oblivion had gathered. But it cannot be helped: the Man in me demands his rights.

GREGERS. [*Laying his hand on Hialmar's shoulder.*] My dear Hialmar—was it not a good thing I came?

HIALMAR. Yes.

GREGERS. Are you not glad to have had your true position made clear to you?

HIALMAR. [*Somewhat impatiently.*] Yes, of course I am. But there is one thing that is revolting to my sense of justice.

GREGERS. And what is that?

HIALMAR. It is that—but I don't know whether I ought to express myself so unreservedly about your father.

GREGERS. Say what you please, so far as I am concerned.

HIALMAR. Well then, is it not exasperating to think that it is not I, but he, who will realise the true marriage?

GREGERS. How can you say such a thing?

HIALMAR. Because it is clearly the case. Isn't the marriage between your father and Mrs. Sörby founded upon complete confidence, upon entire and unreserved candour on both sides? They hide nothing from each other, they keep no secrets in the background; their relation is based, if I may put it so, on mutual confession and absolution.

GREGERS. Well, what then?

HIALMAR. Well, is not that the whole thing? Did you not yourself say that this was precisely the difficulty that had to be overcome in order to found a true marriage?

GREGERS. But this is a totally different matter, Hialmar. You surely don't compare either yourself or your wife with those two—? Oh, you understand me well enough.

HIALMAR. Say what you like, there is something in all this that hurts and offends my sense of justice. It really looks as if there were no just providence to rule the world.

GINA. Oh no, Ekdal; for God's sake don't say such things.

GREGERS. H'm; don't let us get upon those questions.

HIALMAR. And yet, after all, I cannot but recognise the guiding finger of fate. He is going blind.

GINA. Oh, you can't be sure of that.

HIALMAR. There is no doubt about it. At all events there ought not to be; for in that very fact lies the righteous retribution. He has hoodwinked a confiding fellow creature in days gone by—

GREGERS. I fear he has hoodwinked many.

HIALMAR. And now comes inexorable, mysterious Fate, and demands Werle's own eyes.

GINA. Oh, how dare you say such dreadful things! You make me quite scared.

HIALMAR. It is profitable, now and then, to plunge deep into the night side of existence.

[*Hedvig, in her hat and cloak, comes in by the passage door. She is pleasurably excited, and out of breath.*]

GINA. Are you back already?

HEDVIG. Yes, I didn't care to go any farther. It was a good thing, too; for I've just met some one at the door.

HIALMAR. It must have been that Mrs. Sörby.

HEDVIG. Yes.

HIALMAR. [*Walks up and down.*] I hope you have seen her for the last time.

[*Silence. Hedvig, discouraged, looks first at one and then at the other, trying to divine their frame of mind.*]

HEDVIG. [*Approaching, coaxingly.*] Father.

HIALMAR. Well—what is it, Hedvig?

HEDVIG. Mrs. Sörby had something with her for me.

HIALMAR. [*Stops.*] For you?

HEDVIG. Yes. Something for to-morrow.

GINA. Bertha has always given you some little thing on your birthday.

HIALMAR. What is it?

HEDVIG. Oh, you mustn't see it now. Mother is to give it to me to-morrow morning before I'm up.

HIALMAR. What is all this hocus-pocus that I am to be kept in the dark about!

HEDVIG. [*Quickly.*] Oh no, you may see if it you like. It's a big letter.

[*Takes the letter out of her cloak pocket.*]

HIALMAR. A letter too?

HEDVIG. Yes, it is only a letter. The rest will come afterwards, I suppose. But fancy—a letter! I've never had a letter before. And there's "Miss" written upon it. [*Reads.*] "Miss Hedvig Ekdal." Only fancy—that's me!

HIALMAR. Let me see that letter.

HEDVIG. [*Hands it to him.*] There it is.

HIALMAR. That is Mr. Werle's hand.

GINA. Are you sure of that, Ekdal?

HIALMAR. Look for yourself.

GINA. Oh, what do *I* know about such-like things?

HIALMAR. Hedvig, may I open the letter—and read it?

HEDVIG. Yes, of course you may, if you want to.

GINA. No, not to-night, Ekdal; it's to be kept till to-morrow.

HEDVIG. [*Softly.*] Oh, can't you let him read it! It's sure to be something good; and then father will be glad, and everything will be nice again.

HIALMAR. I may open it then?

HEDVIG. Yes do, father. I'm so anxious to know what it is.

HIALMAR. Well and good. [*Opens the letter, takes out a paper, reads it through, and appears bewildered.*] What is this—!

GINA. What does it say?

HEDVIG. Oh yes, father—tell us!

HIALMAR. Be quiet. [*Reads it through again; he has turned pale, but says with self-control:*] It is a deed of gift, Hedvig.

HEDVIG. Is it? What sort of gift am I to have?

HIALMAR. Read for yourself.

[*Hedvig goes over and reads for a time by the lamp.*]

HIALMAR. [*Half-aloud, clenching his hands.*] The eyes! The eyes—and then that letter!

HEDVIG. [*Leaves off reading.*] Yes, but it seems to me that it's grandfather that's to have it.

HIALMAR. [*Takes the letter from her.*] Gina—can you understand this?

GINA. I know nothing whatever about it; tell me what's the matter.

HIALMAR. Mr. Werle writes to Hedvig that her old grandfather need not trouble himself any longer with the copying, but that he can henceforth draw on the office for a hundred crowns a month—

GREGERS. Aha!

HEDVIG. A hundred crowns, mother! I read that.

GINA. What a good thing for grandfather!

HIALMAR. —a hundred crowns a month so long as he needs it—that means, of course, so long as he lives.

GINA. Well, so he's provided for, poor dear.

HIALMAR. But there is more to come. You didn't read that, Hedvig. Afterwards this gift is to pass on to you.

HEDVIG. To me! The whole of it?

HIALMAR. He says that the same amount is assured to you for the whole of your life. Do you hear that, Gina?

GINA. Yes, I hear.

HEDVIG. Fancy—all that money for me! [*Shakes him.*] Father, father, aren't you glad—?

HIALMAR. [*Eluding her.*] Glad! [*Walks about.*] Oh what vistas—what perspectives open up before me! It is Hedvig, Hedvig that he showers these benefactions upon!

GINA. Yes, because it's Hedvig's birthday—

HEDVIG. And you'll get it all the same, father! You know quite well I shall give all the money to you and mother.

HIALMAR. To mother, yes! There we have it.

GREGERS. Hialmar, this is a trap he is setting for you.

HIALMAR. Do you think it's another trap?

GREGERS. When he was here this morning he said: Hialmar Ekdal is not the man you imagine him to be.

HIALMAR. Not the man—!

GREGERS. That you shall see, he said.

HIALMAR. He meant you should see that I would let myself be bought off—!

HEDVIG. Oh mother, what does all this mean?

GINA. Go and take off your things.

[Hedvig goes out by the kitchen door, half-crying.]

GREGERS. Yes, Hialmar—now is the time to show who was right, he or I.

HIALMAR. [Slowly tears the paper across, lays both pieces on the table, and says:] Here is my answer.

GREGERS. Just what I expected.

HIALMAR. [Goes over to Gina, who stands by the stove, and says in a low voice:] Now please make a clean breast of it. If the connection between you and him was quite over when you—came to care for me, as you call it—why did he place us in a position to marry?

GINA. I suppose he thought as he could come and go in our house.

HIALMAR. Only that? Was not he afraid of a possible contingency?

GINA. I don't know what you mean.

HIALMAR. I want to know whether—your child has the right to live under my roof.

GINA. [Draws herself up; her eyes flash.] You ask that!

HIALMAR. You shall answer me this one question: Does Hedvig belong to me—or—? Well!

GINA. [Looking at him with cold defiance.] I don't know.

HIALMAR. [Quivering a little.] You don't know!

GINA. How should I know? A creature like me—

HIALMAR. [Quietly turning away from her.] Then I have nothing more to do in this house.

GREGERS. Take care, Hialmar! Think what you are doing!

HIALMAR. [Puts on his overcoat.] In this case, there is nothing for a man like me to think twice about.

GREGERS. Yes indeed, there are endless things to be considered. You three must be together if you are to attain the true frame of mind for self-sacrifice and forgiveness.

HIALMAR. I don't want to attain it. Never, never! My

hat! [Takes his hat.] My home has fallen in ruins about me. [Bursts into tears.] Gregers, I have no child!

HEDVIG. [Who has opened the kitchen door.] What is that you're saying? [Coming to him.] Father, father!

GINA. There, you see!

HIALMAR. Don't come near me, Hedvig! Keep far away. I cannot bear to see you. Oh! those eyes—! Good-bye.

[Makes for the door.]

HEDVIG. [Clinging close to him and screaming loudly.] No! no! Don't leave me!

GINA. [Cries out.] Look at the child, Ekdal! Look at the child!

HIALMAR. I will not! I cannot! I must get out—away from all this!

[He tears himself away from Hedvig, and goes out by the passage door.]

HEDVIG. [With despairing eyes.] He is going away from us, mother! He is going away from us! He will never come back again!

GINA. Don't cry, Hedvig. Father's sure to come back again.

HEDVIG. [Throws herself sobbing on the sofa.] No, no, he'll never come home to us any more.

GREGERS. Do you believe I meant all for the best, Mrs. Ekdal?

GINA. Yes, I daresay you did; but God forgive you, all the same.

HEDVIG. [Lying on the sofa.] Oh, this will kill me! What have I done to him? Mother, you must fetch him home again!

GINA. Yes yes yes; only be quiet, and I'll go out and look for him. [Puts on her outdoor things.] Perhaps he's gone in to Relling's. But you mustn't lie there and cry. Promise me!

HEDVIG. [Weeping convulsively.] Yes, I'll stop, I'll stop; if only father comes back!

GREGERS. [To Gina, who is going.] After all, had you not better leave him to fight out his bitter fight to the end?

GINA. Oh, he can do that afterwards. First of all, we must get the child quieted.

[Goes out by the passage door.]

HEDVIG. [Sits up and dries her tears.] Now you must tell

me what all this means. Why doesn't father want me any more?

GREGERS. You mustn't ask that till you are a big girl—quite grown-up.

HEDVIG. [Sobs.] But I can't go on being as miserable as this till I'm grown-up.—I think I know what it is.—Perhaps I'm not really father's child.

GREGERS. [Uneasily.] How could that be?

HEDVIG. Mother might have found me. And perhaps father has just got to know it; I've read of such things.

GREGERS. Well, but if it were so—

HEDVIG. I think he might be just as fond of me for all that. Yes, fonder almost. We got the wild duck in a present, you know, and I love it so dearly all the same.

GREGERS. [Turning the conversation.] Ah, the wild duck, by-the-bye! Let us talk about the wild duck a little, Hedvig.

HEDVIG. The poor wild duck! He doesn't want to see it any more either. Only think, he wanted to wring its neck!

GREGERS. Oh, he won't do that.

HEDVIG. No; but he said he would like to. And I think it was horrid of father to say it; for I pray for the wild duck every night, and ask that it may be preserved from death and all that is evil.

GREGERS. [Looking at her.] Do you say your prayers every night?

HEDVIG. Yes.

GREGERS. Who taught you to do that?

HEDVIG. I myself; one time when father was very ill, and had leeches on his neck, and said that death was staring him in the face.

GREGERS. Well?

HEDVIG. Then I prayed for him as I lay in bed; and since than I have always kept it up.

GREGERS. And now you pray for the wild duck too?

HEDVIG. I thought it was best to bring in the wild duck; for she was so weakly at first.

GREGERS. Do you pray in the morning, too?

HEDVIG. No, of course not.

GREGERS. Why not in the morning as well?

HEDVIG. In the morning it's light, you know, and there's nothing in particular to be afraid of.

GREGERS. And your father was going to wring the neck of the wild duck that you love so dearly?

HEDVIG. No; he said he ought to wring its neck, but he would spare it for my sake; and that was kind of father.

GREGERS. [Coming a little nearer.] But suppose you were to sacrifice the wild duck of your own free will for his sake.

HEDVIG. [Rising.] The wild duck!

GREGERS. Suppose you were to make a free-will offering, for his sake, of the dearest treasure you have in the world!

HEDVIG. Do you think that would do any good?

GREGERS. Try it, Hedvig.

HEDVIG. [Softly, with flashing eyes.] Yes, I will try it.

GREGERS. Have you really the courage for it, do you think?

HEDVIG. I'll ask grandfather to shoot the wild duck for me.

GREGERS. Yes, do. But not a word to your mother about it.

HEDVIG. Why not?

GREGERS. She doesn't understand us.

HEDVIG. The wild duck! I'll try it to-morrow morning.

[Gina comes in by the passage door.]

HEDVIG. [Going towards her.] Did you find him, mother?

GINA. No, but I heard as he had called and taken Relling with him.

GREGERS. Are you sure of that?

GINA. Yes, the porter's wife said so. Molvik went with them too, she said.

GREGERS. This evening, when his mind so sorely needs to wrestle in solitude—!

GINA. [Takes off her things.] Yes, men are strange creatures, so they are. The Lord only knows where Relling has dragged him to! I ran over to Madam Eriksen's, but they weren't there.

HEDVIG. [Struggling to keep back her tears.] Oh, if he should never come home any more!

GREGERS. He will come home again. I shall have news to give him to-morrow; and then you shall see how he comes home. You may rely upon that, Hedvig, and sleep in peace. Good-night.

[He goes out by the passage door.]

HEDVIG. [Throws herself sobbing on Gina's neck.] Mother, mother!

GINA. [Pats her shoulder and sighs.] Ah yes; Relling was right, he was. That's what comes of it when crazy creatures go about presenting the claims of the—what-you-may-call-it.

Act V

Hialmar Ekdal's studio. Cold, grey, morning light. Wet snow lies upon the large panes of the sloping roof-window.

　　Gina comes from the kitchen with an apron and bib on, and carrying a dusting-brush and a duster; she goes towards the sitting-room door. At the same moment Hedvig comes hurriedly in from the passage.

GINA. [*Stops.*] Well?

HEDVIG. Oh, mother, I almost think he's down at Relling's.

GINA. There, you see!

HEDVIG. —because the porter's wife says she could hear that Relling had two people with him when he came home last night.

GINA. That's just what I thought.

HEDVIG. But it's no use his being there, if he won't come up to us.

GINA. I'll go down and speak to him at all events.

[*Old Ekdal, in dressing gown and slippers, and with a lighted pipe, appears at the door of his room.*]

EKDAL. Hialmar— Isn't Hialmar at home?

GINA. No, he's gone out.

EKDAL. So early? And in such a tearing snowstorm? Well well; just as he pleases; I can take my morning walk alone.

[*He slides the garret door aside; Hedvig helps him; he goes in; she closes it after him.*]

HEDVIG. [*In an undertone.*] Only think, mother, when poor grandfather hears that father is going to leave us.

GINA. Oh, nonsense; grandfather mustn't hear anything about it. It was a heaven's mercy he wasn't at home yesterday in all that hurly-burly.

HEDVIG. Yes, but—

[*Gregers comes in by the passage door.*]

GREGERS. Well, have you any news of him?

GINA. They say he's down at Relling's.

GREGERS. At Relling's! Has he really been out with those creatures?

GINA. Yes, like enough.

GREGERS. When he ought to have been yearning for solitude, to collect and clear his thoughts—

GINA. Yes, you may well say so.

[*Relling enters from the passage.*]

HEDVIG. [*Going to him.*] Is father in your room?

GINA. [*At the same time.*] Is he there?

RELLING. Yes, to be sure he is.

HEDVIG. And you never let us know!

RELLING. Yes; I'm a brute. But in the first place I had to look after the other brute; I mean our dæmonic friend, of course; and then I fell so dead asleep that—

GINA. What does Ekdal say to-day?

RELLING. He says nothing whatever.

HEDVIG. Doesn't he speak?

RELLING. Not a blessed word.

GREGERS. No no; I can understand that very well.

GINA. But what's he doing then?

RELLING. He's lying on the sofa, snoring.

GINA. Oh is he? Yes, Ekdal's a rare one to snore.

HEDVIG. Asleep? Can he sleep?

RELLING. Well, it certainly looks like it.

GREGERS. No wonder, after the spiritual conflict that has rent him—

GINA. And then he's never been used to gadding about out of doors at night.

HEDVIG. Perhaps it's a good thing that he's getting sleep, mother.

GINA. Of course it is; and we must take care we don't wake him up too early. Thank you, Relling. I must get the house cleaned up a bit now, and then— Come and help me, Hedvig.

[*Gina and Hedvig go into the sitting-room.*]

GREGERS. [*Turning to Relling.*] What is your explanation of the spiritual tumult that is now going on in Hialmar Ekdal?

RELLING. Devil a bit of a spiritual tumult have *I* noticed in him.

GREGERS. What! Not at such a crisis, when his whole life has been placed on a new foundation—? How can you think that such an individuality as Hialmar's—?

RELLING. Oh, individuality—he! If he ever had any tendency to the abnormal developments you call individuality, I can assure you it was rooted out of him while he was still in his teens.

GREGERS. That would be strange indeed,—considering the loving care with which he was brought up.

RELLING. By those two high-flown, hysterical maiden aunts, you mean?

GREGERS. Let me tell you that they were women who never forgot the claim of the ideal—but of course you will only jeer at me again.

RELLING. No, I'm in no humour for that. I know all about those ladies; for he has ladled out no end of rhetoric on the subject of his "two soul-mothers." But I don't think he has much to thank them for. Ekdal's misfortune is that in his own circle he has always been looked upon as a shining light—

GREGERS. Not without reason, surely. Look at the depth of his mind!

RELLING. *I* have never discovered it. That his father believed in it I don't so much wonder; the old lieutenant has been an ass all his days.

GREGERS. He has had a child-like mind all his days; that is what you cannot understand.

RELLING. Well, so be it. But then, when our dear, sweet Hialmar went to college, he at once passed for the great light of the future amongst his comrades too! He was handsome, the rascal—red and white—a shop-girl's dream of manly beauty; and with his superficially emotional temperament, and his sympathetic voice, and his talent for declaiming other people's verses and other people's thoughts—

GREGERS. [*Indignantly.*] Is it Hialmar Ekdal you are talking about in this strain?

RELLING. Yes, with your permission; I am simply giving you an inside view of the idol you are grovelling before.

GREGERS. I should hardly have thought I was quite stone blind.

RELLING. Yes you are—or not far from it. You are a sick man, too, you see.

GREGERS. You are right there.

RELLING. Yes. Yours is a complicated case. First of all there is that plaguy integrity-fever; and then—what's worse—you are always in a delirium of hero-worship; you must always have something to adore, outside yourself.

GREGERS. Yes, I must certainly seek it outside myself.

RELLING. But you make such shocking mistakes about every new phoenix you think you have discovered. Here again you have come to a cotter's cabin with your claim of the ideal; and the people of the house are insolvent.

GREGERS. If you don't think better than that of Hialmar Ekdal, what pleasure can you find in being everlastingly with him?

RELLING. Well, you see, I'm supposed to be a sort of a doctor—save the mark! I can't but give a hand to the poor sick folk who live under the same roof with me.

GREGERS. Oh, indeed! Hialmar Ekdal is sick too, is he!

RELLING. Most people are, worse luck.

GREGERS. And what remedy are you applying in Hialmar's case?

RELLING. My usual one. I am cultivating the life-illusion[5] in him.

GREGERS. Life—illusion? I didn't catch what you said.

RELLING. Yes, I said illusion. For illusion, you know, is the stimulating principle.

GREGERS. May I ask with what illusion Hialmar is inoculated?

RELLING. No, thank you; I don't betray professional secrets to quacksalvers. You would probably go and muddle his case still more than you have already. But my method is infallible. I have applied it to Molvik as well. I have made him "dæmonic." That's the blister I have to put on his neck.

GREGERS. Is he not really dæmonic then?

RELLING. What the devil do you mean by dæmonic! It's only a piece of gibberish I've invented to keep up a spark of life in him. But for that, the poor harmless creature would have succumbed to self-contempt and despair many a long year ago. And then the old lieutenant! But he has hit upon his own cure, you see.

GREGERS. Lieutenant Ekdal? What of him?

RELLING. Just think of the old bear-hunter shutting himself up in that dark garret to shoot rabbits! I tell you there is not a happier sportsman in the world than that old man pottering about in there among all that rubbish. The four or five withered Christmas trees he has saved up are the same to him as the whole great fresh Höidal forest; the cock and the hens are big game-birds in the fir-tops; and the rabbits that flop about the garret floor are the bears he has to battle with—the mighty hunter of the mountains!

GREGERS. Poor unfortunate old man! Yes; he has indeed had to narrow the ideals of his youth.

RELLING. While I think of it, Mr. Werle, junior—

---

5 "Livslögnen," literally "the life-lie."

don't use that foreign word: ideals. We have the excellent native word: lies.

GREGERS. Do you think the two things are related?

RELLING. Yes, just about as closely as typhus and putrid fever.

GREGERS. Dr. Relling, I shall not give up the struggle until I have rescued Hialmar from your clutches!

RELLING. So much the worse for him. Rob the average man of his life-illusion, and you rob him of his happiness at the same stroke. [*To Hedvig, who comes in from the sitting-room.*] Well, little wild-duck-mother, I'm just going down to see whether papa is still lying meditating upon that wonderful invention of his. [*Goes out by the passage door.*]

GREGERS. [*Approaches Hedvig.*] I can see by your face that you have not yet done it.

HEDVIG. What? Oh, that about the wild duck! No.

GREGERS. I suppose your courage failed when the time came.

HEDVIG. No, that wasn't it. But when I awoke this morning and remembered what we had been talking about, it seemed so strange.

GREGERS. Strange?

HEDVIG. Yes, I don't know—. Yesterday evening, at the moment, I though there was something so delightful about it; but since I have slept and thought of it again, it somehow doesn't seem worth while.

GREGERS. Ah, I thought you could not have grown up quite unharmed in this house.

HEDVIG. I don't care about that, if only father would come up—

GREGERS. Oh, if only your eyes had been opened to that which gives life its value—if you possessed the true, joyous, fearless spirit of sacrifice, you would soon see how he would come up to you.—But I believe in you still, Hedvig.

[*He goes out by the passage door.*]

[*Hedvig wanders about the room for a time; she is on the point of going into the kitchen when a knock is heard at the garret door. Hedvig goes over and opens it a little; old Ekdal comes out; she pushes the door to again.*]

EKDAL. H'm, it's not much fun to take one's morning walk alone

HEDVIG. Wouldn't you like to go shooting, grandfather?

EKDAL. It's not the weather for it to-day. It's so dark there, you can scarcely see where you're going.

HEDVIG. Do you never want to shoot anything besides the rabbits?

EKDAL. Do you think the rabbits aren't good enough?

HEDVIG. Yes, but what about the wild duck?

EKDAL. Ho-ho! are you afraid I shall shoot your wild duck? Never in the world. Never.

HEDVIG. No, I suppose you couldn't; they say it's very difficult to shoot wild ducks.

EKDAL. Couldn't! Should rather think I could.

HEDVIG. How would you set about it, grandfather?— I don't mean with my wild duck, but with others?

EKDAL. I should take care to shoot them in the breast, you know; that's the surest place. And then you must shoot against the feathers, you see—not the way of the feathers.

HEDVIG. Do they die then, grandfather?

EKDAL. Yes, they die right enough—when you shoot properly. Well, I must go and brush up a bit. H'm—understand—h'm. [*Goes into his room.*]

[*Hedvig waits a little, glances towards the sitting-room door, goes over to the bookcase, stands on tip-toe, takes the double-barrelled pistol down from the shelf, and looks at it. Gina, with brush and duster, comes from the sitting-room. Hedvig hastily lays down the pistol, unobserved.*]

GINA. Don't stand raking amongst father's things, Hedvig.

HEDVIG. [*Goes away from the bookcase.*] I was only going to tidy up a little.

GINA. You'd better go into the kitchen, and see if the coffee's keeping hot; I'll take his breakfast on a tray, when I go down to him.

[*Hedvig goes out. Gina begins to sweep and clean up the studio. Presently the passage door is opened with hesitation, and Hialmar Ekdal looks in. He has on his overcoat, but not his hat; he is unwashed, and his hair is dishevelled and unkempt. His eyes are dull and heavy.*]

GINA. [*Standing with the brush in her hand, and looking at him.*] Oh, there now, Ekdal—so you've come after all?

HIALMAR. [*Comes in and answers in a toneless voice.*] I come—only to depart again immediately.

GINA. Yes, yes, I suppose so. But, Lord help us! what a sight you are!

HIALMAR. A sight?

GINA. And your nice winter coat too! Well, that's done for.

HEDVIG. [*At the kitchen door.*] Mother, hadn't I better—? [*Sees Hialmar, gives a loud scream of joy, and runs to him.*] Oh, father, father!

HIALMAR. [*Turns away and makes a gesture of repulsion.*] Away, away, away! [*To Gina.*] Keep her away from me, I say!

GINA. [*In a low tone.*] Go into the sitting-room, Hedvig. [*Hedvig does so without a word.*]

HIALMAR. [*Fussily pulls out the table-drawer.*] I must have my books with me. Where are my books?

GINA. Which books?

HIALMAR. My scientific books, of course; the technical magazines I require for my invention.

GINA. [*Searches in the bookcase.*] Is it these here paper-covered ones?

HIALMAR. Yes, of course.

GINA. [*Lays a heap of magazines on the table.*] Shan't I get Hedvig to cut them for you?

HIALMAR. I don't require to have them cut for me.

[*Short silence.*]

GINA. Then you're still set on leaving us, Ekdal?

HIALMAR. [*Rummaging amongst the books.*] Yes, that is a matter of course, I should think.

GINA. Well, well.

HIALMAR. [*Vehemently.*] How can I live here, to be stabbed to the heart every hour of the day?

GINA. God forgive you for thinking such vile things of me.

HIALMAR. Prove—!

GINA. I think it's you as has got to prove.

HIALMAR. After a past like yours? There are certain claims—I may almost call them claims of the ideal—

GINA. But what about grandfather? What's to become of him, poor dear?

HIALMAR. I know my duty; my helpless father will come with me. I am going out into the town to make arrangements—. H'm—[*hesitatingly*] has any one found my hat on the stairs?

GINA. No. Have you lost your hat?

HIALMAR. Of course I had it on when I came in last night; there's no doubt about that; but I couldn't find it this morning.

GINA. Lord help us! where have you been to with those two ne'er-do-wells?

HIALMAR. Oh, don't bother me about trifles. Do you suppose I am in the mood to remember details?

GINA. If only you haven't caught cold, Ekdal.

[*Goes out into the kitchen.*]

HIALMAR. [*Talks to himself in a low tone of irritation, whilst he empties the table-drawer.*] You're a scoundrel, Relling!—You're a low fellow!—Ah, you shameless tempter!—I wish I could get some one to stick a knife into you!

[*He lays some old letters on one side, finds the torn document of yesterday, takes it up and looks at the pieces; puts it down hurriedly as Gina enters.*]

GINA. [*Sets a tray with coffee, etc., on the table.*] Here's a drop of something hot, if you'd fancy it. And there's some bread and butter and a snack of salt meat.

HIALMAR. [*Glancing at the tray.*] Salt meat? Never under this roof! It's true I have not had a mouthful of solid food for nearly twenty-four hours; but no matter.— My memoranda! The commencement of my autobiography! What has become of my diary, and all my important papers? [*Opens the sitting-room door but draws back.*] She is there too!

GINA. Good Lord! the child must be somewhere!

HIALMAR. Come out.

[*He makes room, Hedvig comes, scared, into the studio.*]

HIALMAR. [*With his hand upon the door-handle, says to Gina:*] In these, the last moments I spend in my former home, I wish to be spared from interlopers— [*Goes into the room.*]

HEDVIG. [*With a bound towards her mother, asks softly, trembling.*] Does that mean me?

GINA. Stay out in the kitchen, Hedvig; or, no—you'd best go into your own room. [*Speaks to Hialmar as she goes in to him.*] Wait a bit, Ekdal; don't rummage so in the drawers; *I* know where everything is.

HEDVIG. [*Stands a moment immovable, in terror and perplexity, biting her lips to keep back the tears; then she clenches her hands convulsively, and says softly:*] The wild duck.

[*She steals over and takes the pistol from the shelf, opens the garret door a little way, creeps in, and draws the door to after her.*]

[*Hialmar and Gina can be heard disputing in the sitting-room.*]

HIALMAR. [*Comes in with some manuscript books and old loose papers, which he lays upon the table.*] That portmanteau is of no use! There are a thousand and one things I must drag with me.

GINA. [*Following with the portmanteau.*] Why not leave all the rest for the present, and only take a shirt and a pair of woollen drawers with you?

HIALMAR. Whew!—all these exhausting preparations—!

[*Pulls off his overcoat and throws it upon the sofa.*]

GINA. And there's the coffee getting cold.

HIALMAR. H'm.

[*Drinks a mouthful without thinking of it, and then another.*]

GINA. [*Dusting the backs of the chairs.*] A nice job you'll have to find such another big garret for the rabbits.

HIALMAR. What! Am I to drag all those rabbits with me too?

GINA. You don't suppose grandfather can get on without his rabbits.

HIALMAR. He must just get used to doing without them. Have not *I* to sacrifice very much greater things than rabbits!

GINA. [*Dusting the bookcase.*] Shall I put the flute in the portmanteau for you?

HIALMAR. No. No flute for me. But give me the pistol!

GINA. Do you want to take the pigstol with you?

HIALMAR. Yes. My loaded pistol.

GINA. [*Searching for it.*] It's gone. He must have taken it in with him.

HIALMAR. Is he in the garret?

GINA. Yes, of course he's in the garret.

HIALMAR. H'm—poor lonely old man.

[*He takes a piece of bread and butter, eats it, and finishes his cup of coffee.*]

GINA. If we hadn't have let that room, you could have moved in there.

HIALMAR. And continued to live under the same roof with—! Never,—never!

GINA. But couldn't you put up with the sitting-room for a day or two? You could have it all to yourself.

HIALMAR. Never within these walls!

GINA. Well then, down with Relling and Molvik.

HIALMAR. Don't mention those wretches' names to me! The very thought of them almost takes away my appetite.—Oh no, I must go out into the storm and the snow-drift,—go from house to house and seek shelter for my father and myself.

GINA. But you've got no hat, Ekdal! You've been and lost your hat, you know.

HIALMAR. Oh those two brutes, those slaves of all the vices! A hat must be procured. [*Takes another piece of bread and butter.*] Some arrangement must be made. For I have no mind to throw away my life, either. [*Looks for something on the tray.*]

GINA. What are you looking for?

HIALMAR. Butter.

GINA. I'll get some at once. [*Goes into the kitchen.*]

HIALMAR. [*Calls after her.*] Oh it doesn't matter; dry bread is good enough for me.

GINA. [*Brings a dish of butter.*] Look here; this is fresh churned.

[*She pours out another cup of coffee for him; he seats himself on the sofa, spreads more butter on the already buttered bread, and eats and drinks awhile in silence.*]

HIALMAR. Could I, without being subject to intrusion—intrusion of any sort—could I live in the sitting-room there for a day or two?

GINA. Yes, to be sure you could, if you only would.

HIALMAR. For I see no possibility of getting all father's things out in such a hurry.

GINA. And besides, you've surely got to tell him first as you don't mean to live with us others no more.

HIALMAR. [*Pushes away his coffee cup.*] Yes, there is that too; I shall have to lay bare the whole tangled story to him—. I must turn matters over; I must have breathing-time; I cannot take all these burdens on my shoulders in a single day.

GINA. No, especially in such horrible weather as it is outside.

HIALMAR. [*Touching Werle's letter.*] I see that paper is still lying about here.

GINA. Yes, *I* haven't touched it.

HIALMAR. So far as I am concerned it is mere waste paper—

GINA. Well, *I* have certainly no notion of making any use of it.

HIALMAR. —but we had better not let it get lost all the same;—in all the upset when I move, it might easily—

GINA. I'll take good care of it, Ekdal.

HIALMAR. The donation is in the first instance made to father, and it rests with him to accept or decline it.

GINA. [*Sighs.*] Yes, poor old father—

HIALMAR. To make quite safe— Where shall I find some gum?

GINA. [*Goes to the bookcase.*] Here's the gum-pot.

HIALMAR. And a brush?

GINA. The brush is here too. [*Brings him the things.*]

HIALMAR. [*Takes a pair of scissors.*] Just a strip of paper at the back—[*Clips and gums.*] Far be it from me to lay hands upon what is not my own—and least of all upon what belongs to a destitute old man—and to—the other as well.—There now. Let it lie there for a time; and when it is dry, take it away. I wish never to see that document again. Never!

[*Gregers Werle enters from the passage.*]

GREGERS. [*Somewhat surprised.*] What,—are you sitting here, Hialmar?

HIALMAR. [*Rises hurriedly.*] I had sunk down from fatigue.

GREGERS. You have been having breakfast, I see.

HIALMAR. The body sometimes makes its claims felt too.

GREGERS. What have you decided to do?

HIALMAR. For a man like me, there is only one course possible. I am just putting my most important things together. But it takes time, you know.

GINA. [*With a touch of impatience.*] Am I to get the room ready for you, or am I to pack your portmanteau?

HIALMAR. [*After a glance of annoyance at Gregers.*] Pack—and get the room ready!

GINA. [*Takes the portmanteau.*] Very well; then I'll put in the shirt and the other things.

[*Goes into the sitting-room and draws the door to after her.*]

GREGERS. [*After a short silence.*] I never dreamed that this would be the end of it. Do you really feel it a necessity to leave house and home?

HIALMAR. [*Wanders about restlessly.*] What would you have me do?—I am not fitted to bear unhappiness, Gregers. I must feel secure and at peace in my surroundings.

GREGERS. But can you not feel that here? Just try it. I should have thought you had firm ground to build upon now—if only you start afresh. And remember, you have your invention to live for.

HIALMAR. Oh don't talk about my invention. It's perhaps still in the dim distance.

GREGERS. Indeed!

HIALMAR. Why, great heavens, what would you have me invent? Other people have invented almost everything already. It becomes more and more difficult every day—

GREGERS. And you have devoted so much labour to it.

HIALMAR. It was that blackguard Relling that urged me to it.

GREGERS. Relling?

HIALMAR. Yes, it was he that first made me realise my aptitude for making some notable discovery in photography.

GREGERS. Aha—it was Relling!

HIALMAR. Oh, I have been so truly happy over it! Not so much for the sake of the invention itself, as

because Hedvig believed in it—believed in it with a child's whole eagerness of faith.—At least, I have been fool enough to go and imagine that she believed in it.

GREGERS. Can you really think that Hedvig has been false towards you?

HIALMAR. I can think anything now. It is Hedvig that stands in my way. She will blot out the sunlight from my whole life.

GREGERS. Hedvig! Is it Hedvig you are talking of? How should she blot out your sunlight?

HIALMAR. [*Without answering.*] How unutterably I have loved that child! How unutterably happy I have felt every time I came home to my humble room, and she flew to meet me, with her sweet little blinking eyes. Oh, confiding fool that I have been! I loved her unutterably;—and I yielded myself up to the dream, the delusion, that she loved me unutterably in return.

GREGERS. Do you call that a delusion?

HIALMAR. How should I know? I can get nothing out of Gina; and besides, she is totally blind to the ideal side of these complications. But to you I feel impelled to open my mind, Gregers. I cannot shake off this frightful doubt—perhaps Hedvig has never really and honestly loved me.

GREGERS. What would you say if she were to give you a proof of her love? [*Listens.*] What's that? I thought I heard the wild duck—?

HIALMAR. It's the wild duck quacking. Father's in the garret.

GREGERS. Is he? [*His face lights up with joy.*] I say you may yet have proof that your poor misunderstood Hedvig loves you!

HIALMAR. Oh, what proof can she give me? I dare not believe in any assurances from that quarter.

GREGERS. Hedvig does not know what deceit means.

HIALMAR. Oh Gregers, that is just what I cannot be sure of. Who knows what Gina and that Mrs. Sörby may many a time have sat here whispering and tattling about? And Hedvig usually has her ears open, I can tell you. Perhaps the deed of gift was not such a surprise to her, after all. In fact, I'm not sure but that I noticed something of the sort.

GREGERS. What spirit is this that has taken possession of you?

HIALMAR. I have had my eyes opened. Just you notice;—you'll see, the deed of gift is only a beginning. Mrs. Sörby has always been a good deal taken up with Hedvig; and now she has the power to do whatever she likes for the child. They can take her from me whenever they please.

GREGERS. Hedvig will never, never leave you.

HIALMAR. Don't be so sure of that. If only they beckon to her and throw out a golden bait—! And oh! I have loved her so unspeakably! I would have counted it my highest happiness to take her tenderly by the hand and lead her, as one leads a timid child through a great dark empty room!—I am cruelly certain now that the poor photographer in his humble attic has never really and truly been anything to her. She has only cunningly contrived to keep on a good footing with him until the time came.

GREGERS. You don't believe that yourself, Hialmar.

HIALMAR. That is just the terrible part of it—I don't know what to believe,—I never can know it. But can you really doubt that it must be as I say? Ho-ho, you have far too much faith in the claim of the ideal, my good Gregers! If those others came, with the glamour of wealth about them, and called to the child:—"Leave him: come to us: here life awaits you—'"

GREGERS. [Quickly.] Well, what then?

HIALMAR. If I then asked her: Hedvig, are you willing to renounce that life for me? [Laughs scornfully.] No thank you! You would soon hear what answer I should get.

[A pistol shot is heard from within the garret.]

GREGERS. [Loudly and joyfully.] Hialmar!

HIALMAR. There now; he must needs go shooting too.

GINA. [Comes in.] Oh Ekdal, I can hear grandfather blazing away in the garret by hisself.

HIALMAR. I'll look in—

GREGERS. [Eagerly, with emotion.] Wait a moment! Do you know what that was?

HIALMAR. Yes, of course I know.

GREGERS. No you don't know. But I do. That was the proof!

HIALMAR. What proof?

GREGERS. It was a child's free-will offering. She has got your father to shoot the wild duck.

HIALMAR. To shoot the wild duck!

GINA. Oh, think of that—!

HIALMAR. What was that for?

GREGERS. She wanted to sacrifice to you her most cherished possession; for then she thought you would surely come to love her again.

HIALMAR. [Tenderly, with emotion.] Oh, poor child!

GINA. What things she does think of!

GREGERS. She only wanted your love again, Hialmar. She could not live without it.

GINA. [Struggling with her tears.] There, you can see for yourself, Ekdal.

HIALMAR. Gina, where is she?

GINA. [Sniffs.] Poor dear, she's sitting out in the kitchen, I dare say.

HIALMAR. [Goes over, tears open the kitchen door, and says:] Hedvig, come, come in to me! [Looks round.] No, she's not here.

GINA. Then she must be in her own little room.

HIALMAR. [Without.] No, she's not here either. [Comes in.] She must have gone out.

GINA. Yes, you wouldn't have her anywheres in the house.

HIALMAR. Oh, if she would only come home quickly, so that I can tell her— Everything will come right now, Gregers; now I believe we can begin life afresh.

GREGERS. [Quietly.] I knew it; I knew the child would make amends.

[Old Ekdal appears at the door of his room; he is in full uniform, and is busy buckling on his sword.]

HIALMAR. [Astonished.] Father! Are you there?

GINA. Have you been firing in your room?

EKDAL. [Resentfully, approaching.] So you go shooting alone, do you, Hialmar?

HIALMAR. [Excited and confused.] Then it wasn't you that fired that shot in the garret?

EKDAL. Me that fired? H'm.

GREGERS. [Calls out to Hialmar.] She has shot the wild duck herself!

HIALMAR. What can it mean? [Hastens to the garret door, tears it aside, looks in and calls loudly:] Hedvig!

GINA. [Runs to the door.] Good God, what's that!

HIALMAR. [Goes in.] She's lying on the floor!

GREGERS. Hedvig! lying on the floor!

[Goes in to Hialmar.]

GINA. [At the same time.] Hedvig! [Inside the garret.] No, no, no!

EKDAL. Ho-ho! does she go shooting too, now?

[Hialmar, Gina, and Gregers carry Hedvig into the studio; in her dangling right hand she holds the pistol fast clasped in her fingers.]

HIALMAR. [Distracted.] The pistol has gone off. She has wounded herself. Call for help! Help!

GINA. [Runs into the passage and calls down.] Relling! Relling! Doctor Relling; come up as quick as you can!

[*Hialmar and Gregers lay Hedvig down on the sofa.*]

EKDAL. [*Quietly.*] The woods avenge themselves.

HIALMAR. [*On his knees beside Hedvig.*] She'll soon come to now. She's coming to—; yes, yes, yes.

GINA. [*Who has come in again.*] Where has she hurt herself? I can't see anything—

[*Relling comes hurriedly, and immediately after him Molvik; the latter without his waistcoat and necktie, and with his coat open.*]

RELLING. What's the matter here?

GINA. They say Hedvig has shot herself.

HIALMAR. Come and help us!

RELLING. Shot herself!

[*He pushes the table aside and begins to examine her.*]

HIALMAR. [*Kneeling and looking anxiously up at him.*] It can't be dangerous? Speak, Relling! She is scarcely bleeding at all. It can't be dangerous?

RELLING. How did it happen?

HIALMAR. Oh, we don't know—!

GINA. She wanted to shoot the wild duck.

RELLING. The wild duck?

HIALMAR. The pistol must have gone off.

RELLING. H'm. Indeed.

EKDAL. The woods avenge themselves. But I'm not afraid, all the same.

[*Goes into the garret and closes the door after him.*]

HIALMAR. Well, Relling,—why don't you say something?

RELLING. The ball has entered the breast.

HIALMAR. Yes, but she's coming to!

RELLING. Surely you can see that Hedvig is dead.

GINA. [*Bursts into tears.*] Oh my child, my child.

GREGERS. [*Huskily.*] In the depths of the sea—

HIALMAR. [*Jumps up.*] No, no, she must live! Oh, for God's sake, Relling—only a moment—only just till I can tell her how unspeakably I loved her all the time!

RELLING. The bullet has gone through her heart. Internal hemorrhage. Death must have been instantaneous.

HIALMAR. And I! I hunted her from me like an animal! And she crept terrified into the garret and died for love of me! [*Sobbing.*] I can never atone to her! I can never tell her—! [*Clenches his hands and cries, upwards.*] O thou above—! If thou be indeed! Why hast thou done this thing to me?

GINA. Hush, hush, you mustn't go on that awful way. We had no right to keep her, I suppose.

MOLVIK. The child is not dead, but sleepeth.

RELLING. Bosh!

HIALMAR. [*Becomes calm, goes over to the sofa, folds his arms, and looks at Hedvig.*] There she lies so stiff and still.

RELLING. [*Tries to loosen the pistol.*] She's holding it so tight, so tight.

GINA. No, no, Relling, don't break her fingers; let the pistol be.

HIALMAR. She shall take it with her.

GINA. Yes, let her. But the child mustn't lie here for a show. She shall go to her own room, so she shall. Help me, Ekdal.

[*Hialmar and Gina take Hedvig between them.*]

HIALMAR. [*As they are carrying her.*] Oh Gina, Gina, can you survive this!

GINA. We must help each other to bear it. For now at least she belongs to both of us.

MOLVIK. [*Stretches out his arms and mumbles.*] Blessed be the Lord; to earth thou shalt return; to earth thou shalt return—

RELLING. [*Whispers.*] Hold your tongue, you fool; you're drunk.

[*Hialmar and Gina carry the body out through the kitchen door. Relling shuts it after them. Molvik slinks out into the passage.*]

RELLING. [*Goes over to Gregers and says:*] No one shall ever convince me that the pistol went off by accident.

GREGERS. [*Who has stood terrified, with convulsive twitchings.*] Who can say how the dreadful thing happened?

RELLING. The powder has burnt the body of her dress. She must have pressed the pistol right against her breast and fired.

GREGERS. Hedvig has not died in vain. Did you not see how sorrow set free what is noble in him?

RELLING. Most people are ennobled by the actual presence of death. But how long do you suppose this nobility will last in him?

GREGERS. Why should it not endure and increase throughout his life?

RELLING. Before a year is over, little Hedvig will be nothing to him but a pretty theme for declamation.

GREGERS. How dare you say that of Hialmar Ekdal?

RELLING. We will talk of this again, when the grass has first withered on her grave. Then you'll hear him spouting about "the child too early torn from her father's heart;" then you'll see him steep himself in a syrup of sentiment and self-admiration and self-pity. Just you wait!

GREGERS. If you are right and i am wrong, then life is not worth living.

RELLING. Oh, life would be quite tolerable, after all, if only we could be rid of the confounded duns that keep on pestering us, in our poverty, with the claim of the ideal.

GREGERS. [*Looking straight before him.*] In that case, I am glad that my destiny is what it is.

RELLING. May I inquire,—what is your destiny?

GREGERS. [*Going.*] To be the thirteenth at table.

RELLING. The devil it is.

THE END

ESSAY: AN APPROACH TO THE PLAY

When Henrik Ibsen wrote *The Wild Duck* in 1884, most of his contemporaries were unsure of what to make of it, and it continues to the present to seem experimental and exploratory. The play mixes genres and styles. In the first act, for example, it brings the drunk, bumbling, and impoverished Old Ekdal through the study of the prosperous Mr. Werle in the midst of a dinner party being thrown for the social elite of Christiana (the former name of Oslo). In subsequent acts, set in the apartment of the extended Ekdal family, the old man prowls around wearing an impromptu military uniform, and he keeps slipping into an offstage back attic to hunt rabbits. The play raises questions that might be dealt with in heroic or tragic fashion, but it seems to insist on undercutting this seriousness with comic moments or on deflating it by calling attention to the insipidity of its main character. Little wonder if some students still have trouble catching its spirit.

The play is written in prose and at times seems almost to be documentary in its concentration on the details of social life, both lower class and upper class, in a modern industrial city. It might seem at times to be a snapshot from Ekdal's photography studio (and at times the characters are said to strike tableau poses, like parodies of Victorian family portraits). And yet, prose though it is, the play is in many ways similar to the poetic drama of Sophocles or of Shakespeare, and this, too, is a source of some of its difficulty. Ibsen's earliest plays were experiments in poetic drama, and his movement away from verse seems not entirely to have altered his conception of language in the theater. Figurative language combines into patterns: phrases and themes recur throughout the play, taking on new meanings in new contexts, in the process often redefining previous meanings and sometimes acquiring symbolic value. As in *Oedipus the King*, for example, motifs of blindness and vision recur throughout the play. Both Hedvig and the elder Werle are literally losing their vision, and the implication is that Hialmar, who might be expected to be perceptive, given his profession as photographer, has never properly "seen" his own situation. Gregers' self-appointed mission is to open his friend's eyes. And yet, unlike the Greek tragedy, this is a play that seems to deny heroic possibilities, one in which no one grows in wisdom or in stature from newfound knowledge. The play's closing pages seem to affirm that Hialmar—and Gregers, as well—are as blind as they ever were and that the only character who seems able to see the truth is the cynical Dr. Relling, who thinks nothing can be done but to create a lie for people to live for.

While the play is not so focused temporally as, say, *Oedipus the King,* the action is nonetheless highly compressed. Although the events which the play concerns have taken place over the past fifteen years or more in the lives of its main characters, these events all come to a head in the day and a half enacted on stage: Acts 1 and 2 take place on the same night; Act 3, on the next morning; Act 4, later that day, near sunset; and Act 5, on the following morning. The play also approximates classical tragedy's unity of place, in that Acts 2 through 5 all take place in the photographic studio in the Ekdal house, while Act 1 takes place in the study of the Werle house. Adjacent rooms are in analogous positions, and the large room in back, the wild duck's attic in the Ekdal house, is the drawing room in the Werle's. The parallels seem designed to underscore the importance of social class in the play's setting; the studio, for example, is a reminder that Hialmar needs to devote a major part of his living space to his work, while the luxury of maintaining a study is as much a monument to Werle's upper-class privilege as the liveried servants who crisscross through it. Little wonder that Hialmar feels out of place there.

These balanced stage settings are part of a pattern of structured oppositions that seem to be part of *The Wild Duck*'s conception: the contrasting diagnoses and prescriptions represented by Relling's vital lie and Gregers' summons of the ideal; the northern woods which made Werle and broke Ekdal versus the southern city where Werle lives out his success and Ekdal, his degradation; the woods where Ekdal hunted bear versus the attic where he hunts rabbits among the cut-down pine trees he has set up. Clearest of all, perhaps, is the balancing of characters: Hialmar and Gregers, Relling and Gregers, Hedvig and Gregers (the two children of Werle), Old Ekdal and the elder Werle, Mrs. Sörby and Gina, Mrs. Sörby and the first Mrs. Werle. The contrast of characters—and of concepts—seems to be one of the primary ways in which the play releases meaning.

Another way, although a tantalizingly indirect one, is through the wild duck itself, a symbol of remarkable complexity. According to legend, a wild duck when wounded dives below the water and clings to the submerged grasses, preferring to die rather than face the consequences of its injury. Through the various contexts in which it is discussed, the duck seems symbolically associated with Hedvig, with Hialmar, with Old Ekdal, and, despite his claim to be the dog whose function is to retrieve the duck, perhaps with Gregers as well. (This is trickier. His wound was different; his dive to the bottom was different; his withdrawl from life is different. But, perhaps.) The duck, wounded by the elder Werle and now nurtured in reduced circumstances by the Ekdal family, may also more broadly symbolize aspects of modern, Western, urbanized life: perhaps it suggests something of the limited possibilities for heroic behavior in general in a world which remains all too familiar to our own.

The play is maddeningly unresolved at the end. One doubts that either Gregers or Hialmar will ever be aware of their shared responsibility for Hedvig's suicide. Gregers' attempt to impose a romanticized sense of "higher morality" on Hialmar is as painful as Hialmar's ineffectual posturing, and one assumes that Relling is correct in predicting that "before a year is over, little Hedvig will be nothing to him but a pretty theme for declamation." If the play holds out any hope, it may come through the character of the elder Werle, although it is hard to see him straight, since we see him so often through the twisted glasses of Gregers and later of Hialmar. He seems in retrospect to have made peace with his past. He has been supporting the Ekdal family in secret ever since Old Ekdal bore their apparently mutual guilt alone (there may be some nobility in this support, even though it does seem partly motivated by guilt), and by the end of the play he has made provision to support their child, Hedvig. Most hopeful of all, he seems to have established a loving relationship with Mrs. Sörby, one based on total trust and honesty about the past, exactly the kind of relationship Gregers foolishly imagines that he is making possible for Hialmar and Gina.

Bernard Shaw

PYGMALION

About the Author   Bernard Shaw (1856–1950) was born in Dublin, where he worked as office boy and cashier for his family's company before relocating to London at the age of 26. In this literary and cultural center of the English-speaking world, Shaw was indefatigable, pouring out a steady stream of plays and novels, art, literary, and music criticism, and various kinds of social criticism throughout his long life. He became a socialist in 1882, and for nearly half a century was a mainstay of this movement's Fabian Society. He founded *The New Statesman*, a well-known periodical, in 1913, the same year in which he helped to establish the London School of Economics. A man of many sides and strong social convictions, he accepted the Nobel Prize for Literature in 1925 and a medal from the Irish Academy of Letters in 1934; however, his socialist beliefs and his experience as an Irishman led him to refuse the offer of an English peerage, as well as the Order of Merit.

He was a rationalist and satirist who thought his society and his fellow human beings generally were insufficiently scientific, insufficiently willing to trust their rational power in spite of the lip service paid to science in his day. Social problems in particular seemed to him to be addressed more from the dictates of prejudice and tradition than by the application of reason. As a result, he spent his life poking fun at conventional customs and beliefs, proposing more reasonable solutions than were currently in use, and considering the needs of all humans, including women and the lower classes. The interest in language which the Preface to *Pygmalion* makes explicit, and which the play itself dramatizes, was also one of Shaw's enduring concerns; he believed that if we could all use a common language and thereby communicate better with one another, many of our problems might be solved or avoided, and one of his many crusades was in behalf of such a common language.

About the Play   In classical myth, Pygmalion was a sculptor who made such a lifelike statue of a beautiful woman that he fell in love with it. Because of his great passion Venus, the goddess of love, caused the statue to come to life so that the artist and his creation could marry. Shaw places this myth firmly in the foreground of his play: Higgins takes the flower girl Liza and molds her into a new person. Like the statue in the myth, Liza takes on an unexpected will of her own. Also as in the myth, Higgins, proud of his success and impressed by her beauty and cleverness, seems to fall in love with her. In both play and myth, we can be delighted at the power of romantic love to accomplish the unexpected. We can also interpret the artist's love for his creation as pride: to love one's creation is in some measure to love one's own talent, to love oneself rather than the one who seems to be beloved. From such a point of view, this particular version of romantic love is a delusion which merely enriches the lover's ego.

It is a measure of Shaw's greatness that he presents all these sides of the story, while adding to them a sympathy for the person who is transformed.

PREFACE

A Professor of Phonetics

As will be seen later on, Pygmalion needs, not a preface, but a sequel, which I have supplied in its due place.

The English have no respect for their language, and will not teach their children to speak it. They cannot spell it because they have nothing to spell it with but an old foreign alphabet of which only the consonants—and not all of them—have any agreed speech value. Consequently no man can teach himself what it should sound like from reading it; and it is impossible for an Englishman to open his mouth without making some other Englishman despise him. Most European languages are now accessible in black and white to foreigners: English and French are not thus accessible even to Englishmen and Frenchmen. The reformer we need most today is an energetic phonetic enthusiast: that is why I have made such a one the hero of a popular play.

There have been heroes of that kind crying in the wilderness for many years past. When I became interested in the subject towards the end of the eighteen-seventies, the illustrious Alexander Melville Bell, the inventor of Visible Speech, had emigrated to Canada, where his son invented the telephone: but Alexander J. Ellis was still a London patriarch, with an impressive head always covered by a velvet skull cap, for which he would apologize to public meetings in a very courtly manner. He and Tito Pagliardini, another phonetic veteran, were men whom it was impossible to dislike. Henry Sweet, then a young man, lacked their sweetness of character: he was about as conciliatory to conventional mortals as Ibsen or Samuel Butler. His great ability as a phonetician (he was, I think, the best of them all at his job) would have entitled him to high official recognition, and perhaps enabled him to popularize his subject, but for his Satanic contempt for all academic dignitaries and persons in general who thought more of Greek than of phonetics. Once, in the days when the Imperial Institute rose in South Kensington, and Joseph Chamberlain was booming the Empire, I induced the editor of a leading monthly review to commission an article from Sweet on the imperial importance of his subject. When it arrived, it contained nothing but a savagely derisive attack on a professor of language and literature whose chair Sweet regarded as proper to a phonetic expert only. The article, being libellous, had to be returned as impossible: and I had to renounce my dream of dragging its author into the limelight. When I met him afterwards, for the first time for many years, I found to my astonishment that he, who had been a quite tolerably presentable young man, had actually managed by sheer scorn to alter his personal appearance until he had become a sort of walking repudiation of Oxford and all its traditions. It must have been largely in his own despite that he was squeezed into something called a Readership of phonetics there. The future of phonetics rests probably with his pupils, who all swore by him; but nothing could bring the man himself into any sort of compliance with the university to which he nevertheless clung by divine right in an intensely Oxonian way. I daresay his papers, if he has left any, include some satires that may be published without too destructive results fifty years hence. He was, I believe, not in the least an ill-natured man: very much the opposite, I should say; but he would not suffer fools gladly; and to him all scholars who were not rabid phoneticians were fools.

Those who knew him will recognize in my third act the allusion to the Current Shorthand in which he used to write postcards. It may be acquired from a four and sixpenny manual published by the Clarendon Press. The postcards which Mrs. Higgins describes are such as I have received from Sweet. I would decipher a sound which a cockney would represent by *zerr*, and a Frenchman by *seu*, and then write demanding with some heat what on earth it meant. Sweet, with boundless contempt for my stupidity, would reply that it not only meant but obviously was the word Result, as no other word containing that sound, and capable of making sense with the context, existed in any language spoken on earth. That less expert mortals should require fuller indications was beyond Sweet's patience. Therefore, though the whole point of his Current Shorthand is that it can express every sound in the language perfectly, vowels as well as consonants, and that your hand has to make no stroke except the easy and current ones with which you write m, n, and u, l, p, and q, scribbling them at whatever angle comes easiest to you, his unfortunate determination to make this remarkable and quite legible script serve also as a shorthand reduced it in his own practice to the most inscrutable of cryptograms. His true objective was the provision of a full, accurate, legible script for our language; but he was led past that by his contempt for the popular Pitman system of shorthand, which he called the Pitfall system. The triumph of Pitman was a triumph of business organization: there was a weekly paper to persuade you to learn Pitman: there were cheap textbooks and exercise books and transcripts of speeches for you to copy, and schools where experienced teachers coached you up to the necessary proficiency. Sweet could not organize his market in that fashion. He might as well have been the Sybil who tore up the leaves of prophecy that nobody would attend to. The four and sixpenny manual, mostly in his lithographed handwriting, that was never vulgarly advertized, may perhaps some day be taken up by a syndicate and pushed upon the public as The Times pushed the Encyclopaedia Britannica; but until then it will certainly not prevail against Pitman. I have bought three copies of it during my lifetime; and I am informed by the publishers that its cloistered existence is still a steady and healthy one. I actually learned the system several times; and yet the shorthand in which I am writing these lines is Pitman's. And the reason is, that my secretary cannot transcribe Sweet, having been perforce taught in the schools of Pitman. In America I could use the commercially organized Gregg shorthand, which has taken a hint from Sweet by making its letters writable (current, Sweet would have called them) instead of having to be geometrically drawn like Pitman's; but all these systems, including Sweet's, are spoilt by making them available for verbatim reporting, in which complete and exact spelling and word division are impossible. A complete and exact phonetic script is neither practicable nor necessary for ordinary use; but if we enlarge our alphabet to the Russian size, and make our spelling as phonetic as Spanish, the advance will be prodigious.

Pygmalion Higgins is not a portrait of Sweet, to whom the adventure of Eliza Doolittle would have been impossible; still, as will be seen, there are touches of Sweet in the play. With Higgins's physique and temperament Sweet might have set the Thames on fire. As it was, he impressed himself professionally on Europe to an extent that made his comparative personal obscurity, and the failure of Oxford to do justice to his eminence, a puzzle to foreign specialists in his subject. I do not blame Oxford, because I think Oxford is quite right in demanding a certain social amenity from its nurslings (heaven knows it is not exorbitant in its requirements!); for although I well know how hard it is for a man of genius with a seriously underrated subject to maintain serene and kindly relations with the men who underrate it, and who keep all the best places for less important subjects which they profess without originality and sometimes without much capacity for them, still, if he overwhelms them with wrath and disdain, he cannot expect them to heap honors on him.

Of the later generations of phoneticians I know little. Among them towered Robert Bridges, to whom perhaps Higgins may owe his Miltonic sympathies, though here again I must disclaim all portraiture. But if the play makes the public aware that there are such people as phoneticians, and that they are among the most important people in England at present, it will serve its turn.

I wish to boast that Pygmalion has been an extremely successful play, both on stage and screen, all over Europe and North America as well as at home. It is so intensely and deliberately didactic, and its subject is esteemed so dry, that I delight in throwing it at the heads of the wiseacres who repeat the parrot cry that art should never be didactic. It goes to prove my contention that great art can never be anything else.

Finally, and for the encouragement of people troubled with accents that cut them off from all high employment, I may add that the change wrought by Professor Higgins in the flower-girl is neither impossible nor uncommon. The modern concierge's daughter who fulfils her ambition by playing the Queen of Spain in Ruy Blas at the Théâtre Français is only one of many thousands of men and women who have sloughed off their native dialects and acquired a new tongue. Our West End shop assistants and domestic servants are bi-lingual. But the thing has to be done scientifically, or the last state of the aspirant may be worse then the first. An honest slum dialect is more tolerable than the attempts of phonetically untaught persons to imitate the plutocracy. Ambitious flower-girls who read this play must not imagine that they can pass themselves off as fine ladies by untutored imitation. They must learn their alphabet over again, and different, from a phonetic expert. Imitation will only make them ridiculous.

Act I

London at 11.15 p.m. Torrents of heavy summer rain. Cab whistles blowing frantically in all directions. Pedestrians running for shelter into the portico of St Paul's church (not Wren's cathedral but Inigo Jones's church in Covent Garden vegetable market), among them a lady and her daughter in evening dress. All are peering out gloomily at the rain, except one man with his back turned to the rest, wholly preoccupied with a notebook in which he is writing.

The church clock strikes the first quarter.

THE DAUGHTER. [in the space between the central pillars, close to the one on her left] I'm getting chilled to the bone. What can Freddy be doing all this time? He's been gone twenty minutes.

THE MOTHER. [on her daughter's right] Not so long. But he ought to have got us a cab by this.

A BYSTANDER. [on the lady's right] He wont get no cab not until half-past eleven, missus, when they come back after dropping their theatre fares.

THE MOTHER. But we must have a cab. We cant stand here until half-past eleven. It's too bad.

THE BYSTANDER. Well it aint my fault, missus.

THE DAUGHTER. If Freddy had a bit of gumption, he would have got one at the theatre door.

THE MOTHER. What could he have done, poor boy?

THE DAUGHTER. Other people get cabs. Why couldnt he?

[Freddy rushes in out of the rain from the Southampton Street side, and comes between them closing a dripping umbrella. He is a young man of twenty, in evening dress, very wet round the ankles.]

THE DAUGHTER. Well, havnt you got a cab?

FREDDY. Theres not one to be had for love or money.

THE MOTHER. Oh, Freddy, there must be one. You cant have tried.

THE DAUGHTER. It's too tiresome. Do you expect us to go and get one ourselves?

FREDDY. I tell you theyre all engaged. The rain was so sudden: nobody was prepared; and everybody had to take a cab. Ive been to Charing Cross one way and nearly to Ludgate Circus the other; and they were all engaged.

THE MOTHER. Did you try Trafalgar Square?

FREDDY. There wasnt one at Trafalgar Square.

THE DAUGHTER. Did you try?

FREDDY. I tried as far as Charing Cross Station. Did you expect me to walk to Hammersmith?

THE DAUGHTER. You havnt tried at all.

THE MOTHER. You really are very helpless, Freddy. Go again: and dont come back until you have found a cab.

FREDDY. I shall simply get soaked for nothing.

THE DAUGHTER. And what about us? Are we to stay here all night in this draught, with next to nothing on? You selfish pig—

FREDDY. Oh, very well: I'll go. I'll go. [*He opens his umbrella and dashes off Strandwards, but comes into collision with a flower girl who is hurrying in for shelter, knocking her basket out of her hands. A blinding flash of lightning, followed instantly by a rattling peal of thunder, orchestrates the incident.*]

THE FLOWER GIRL. Nah then, Freddy: look wh' y' gowin, deah.

FREDDY. Sorry [*he rushes off*].

THE FLOWER GIRL. [*picking up her scattered flowers and replacing them in the basket*] Theres menners f' yer! tə-oo banches o voylets trod into the mad. [*She sits down on the plinth of the column, sorting her flowers, on the lady's right. She is not at all a romantic figure. She is perhaps eighteen, perhaps twenty, hardly older. She wears a little sailor hat of black straw that has long been exposed to the dust and soot of London and has seldom if ever been brushed. Her hair needs washing rather badly; its mousy color can hardly be natural. She wears a shoddy black coat that reaches nearly to her knees and is shaped to her waist. She has a brown skirt with a coarse apron. Her boots are much the worse for wear. She is no doubt as clean as she can afford to be; but compared to the ladies she is very dirty. Her features are no worse than theirs; but their condition leaves something to be desired; and she needs the services of a dentist.*]

THE MOTHER. How do you know that my son's name is Freddy, pray?

THE FLOWER GIRL. Ow, eez, yə-ooa san, is e? Wal, fewd dan y' d-ooty bawmz a mather should, eed now bettern to spawl a pore gel's flahrzn than ran awy athaht pyin. Will ye-oo py me f'them? [*Here, with apologies, this desperate attempt to represent her dialect without a phonetic alphabet must be abandoned as unintelligible outside London.*]

THE DAUGHTER. Do nothing of the sort, mother. The idea!

THE MOTHER. Please allow me, Clara. Have you any pennies?

THE DAUGHTER. No. Ive nothing smaller than sixpence.

THE FLOWER GIRL. [*hopefully*] I can give you change for a tanner, kind lady.

THE MOTHER. [*to Clara*] Give it to me. [*Clara parts reluctantly*]. Now [*to the girl*] This is for your flowers.

THE FLOWER GIRL. Thank you kindly, lady.

THE DAUGHTER. Make her give you the change. These things are only a penny a bunch.

THE MOTHER. Do hold your tongue, Clara. [*To the girl*] You can keep the change.

THE FLOWER GIRL. Oh, thank you, lady.

THE MOTHER. Now tell me how you know that young gentleman's name.

THE FLOWER GIRL. I didnt.

THE MOTHER. I heard you call him by it. Dont try to deceive me.

THE FLOWER GIRL. [*protesting*] Who's trying to deceive you? I called him Freddy or Charlie same as you might yourself if you was talking to a stranger and wished to be pleasant.

THE DAUGHTER. Sixpence thrown away! Really, mamma, you might have spared Freddy that. [*She retreats in disgust behind the pillar.*]

[*An elderly gentleman of the amiable military type rushes into the shelter, and closes a dripping umbrella. He is in the same plight as Freddy, very wet about the ankles. He is in evening dress, with a light overcoat. He takes the place left vacant by the daughter.*]

THE GENTLEMAN. Phew!

THE MOTHER. [*to the gentleman*] Oh, sir, is there any sign of its stopping?

THE GENTLEMAN. I'm afraid not. It started worse than ever about two minutes ago. [*he goes to the plinth beside the flower girl; puts up his foot on it; and stoops to turn down his trouser ends*].

THE MOTHER. Oh dear! [*She retires sadly and joins her daughter*].

THE FLOWER GIRL. [*taking advantage of the military gentleman's proximity to establish friendly relations with him*] If it's worse, it's a sign it's nearly over. So cheer up, Captain: and buy a flower off a poor girl.

THE GENTLEMAN. I'm sorry. I havnt any change.

THE FLOWER GIRL. I can give you change, Captain.

THE GENTLEMAN. For a sovereign? Ive nothing less.

THE FLOWER GIRL. Garn! Oh do buy a flower off me, Captain. I can change half-a-crown. Take this for tuppence.

THE GENTLEMAN. Now dont be troublesome: theres a good girl. [*Trying his pockets*] I really havnt any change—Stop: heres three hapence, if thats any use to you [*he retreats to the other pillar*].

THE FLOWER GIRL. [*Disappointed, but thinking three halfpence better than nothing*] Thank you, sir.

THE BYSTANDER. [*to the girl*] You be careful: give him a flower for it. Theres a bloke here behind taking down every blessed word youre saying. [*All turn to the man who is taking notes*].

THE FLOWER GIRL. [*springing up terrified*] I aint done nothing wrong by speaking to the gentleman. Ive a right to sell flowers if I keep off the kerb. [*Hysterically*] I'm a respectable girl: so help me. I never spoke to him except to ask him to buy a flower off me.

[*General hubbub, mostly sympathetic to the flower girl, but deprecating her excessive sensibility. Cries of*] Dont start hollerin. Who's hurting you? Nobody's going to touch you. Whats the good of fussing? Steady on. Easy easy, etc., [*come from the elderly staid spectators, who pat her comfortingly. Less patient ones bid her shut her head, or ask her roughly what is wrong with her. A remoter group, now knowing what the matter is, crowd in and increase the noise with question and answer:*] Whats the row? What-she-do? Where is he? A tec taking her down. What! him? Yes: him over there: Took money off the gentleman, etc.

THE FLOWER GIRL. [*breaking through them to the gentleman, crying wildly*] Oh, sir, dont let him charge me. You dunno what it means to me. Theyll take away my character and drive me on the streets for speaking to gentlemen. They—

THE NOTE TAKER. [*coming forward on her right, the rest crowding after him*] There! there! there! there! who's hurting you, you silly girl? What do you take me for?

THE BYSTANDER. It's aw rawt: e's a genleman: look at his bə-oots. [*Explaining to the note taker*] She thought you was a copper's nark, sir.

THE NOTE TAKER. [*with quick interest*] Whats a copper's nark?

THE BYSTANDER. [*inapt at definition*] It's a—well, it's a copper's nark, as you might say. What else would you call it? A sort of informer.

THE FLOWER GIRL. [*still hysterical*] I take my Bible oath I never said a word—

THE NOTE TAKER. [*overbearing but good-humored*] Oh, shut up, shut up. Do I look like a policeman?

THE FLOWER GIRL. [*far from reassured*] Then what did you take down my words for? How do I know whether you took me down right? You just shew me what youve wrote about me. [*The note taker opens his book and holds it steadily under her nose, though the pressure of the mob trying to read it over his shoulders would upset a weaker man*]. Whats that? That aint proper writing. I cant read that.

THE NOTE TAKER. I can. [*Reads, reproducing her pronunciation exactly*] 'Cheer ap, Keptin: n' baw ya flahr orf a pore gel.'

THE FLOWER GIRL. [*much distressed*] It's because I called him Captain. I meant no harm. [*To the gentleman*] Oh, sir, dont let him lay a charge agen me for a word like that. You—

THE GENTLEMAN. Charge! I make no charge. [*To the note taker*] Really, sir, if you are a detective, you need not begin protecting me against molestation by young women until I ask you. Anybody could see that the girl meant no harm.

THE BYSTANDERS GENERALLY. [*demonstrating against police espionage*] Course they could. What business is it of yours? You mind your own affairs. He wants promotion, he does. Taking down people's words! Girl never said a word to him. What harm if she did? Nice thing a girl cant shelter from the rain without being insulted, etc., etc., etc. [*She is conducted by the more sympathetic demonstrators back to her plinth, where she resumes her seat and struggles with her emotion*].

THE BYSTANDER. He aint a tec. He's a blooming busy-body: thats what he is. I tell you, look at his bə-oots.

THE NOTETAKER. [*turning on him genially*] And how are all your people down at Selsey?

THE BYSTANDER. [*suspiciously*] Who told you my people come from Selsey?

THE NOTE TAKER. Never you mind. They did. [*To the girl*] How do you come to be up so far east? You were born in Lisson Grove.

THE FLOWER GIRL. [*appalled*] Oh, what harm is there in my leaving Lisson Grove? It wasnt fit for a pig to live in; and I had to pay four-and-six a week. [*In tears*] Oh, boo—hoo—oo—

THE NOTE TAKER. Live where you like; but stop that noise.

THE GENTLEMAN. [*to the girl*] Come, come! he cant touch you: you have a right to live where you please.

A SARCASTIC BYSTANDER. [*thrusting himself between the note taker and the gentleman*] Park Lane, for instance. I'd like to go into the Housing Question with you, I would.

THE FLOWER GIRL. [*subsiding into a brooding melan-*

choly over her basket, and talking very low-spiritedly to herself] I'm a good girl, I am.

THE SARCASTIC BYSTANDER. [not attending to her] Do you know where I come from?

THE NOTE TAKER. [promptly] Hoxton.

[Titterings. Popular interest in the note taker's performance increases.]

THE SARCASTIC ONE. [amazed] Well, who said I didnt? Bly me! you know everything, you do.

THE FLOWER GIRL. [still nursing her sense of injury] Aint no call to meddle with me, he aint.

THE BYSTANDER. [to her] Of course he aint. Dont you stand it from him. [To the note taker] See here: what call have you to know about people what never offered to meddle with you?

THE FLOWER GIRL. Let him say what he likes. I dont want to have no truck with him.

THE BYSTANDER. You take us for dirt under your feet, dont you? Catch you taking liberties with a gentleman!

THE SARCASTIC BYSTANDER. Yes: tell him where he come from if you want to go fortune-telling.

THE NOTE TAKER. Cheltenham, Harrow, Cambridge, and India.

THE GENTLEMAN. Quite right.

[Great laughter. Reaction in the note taker's favor. Exclamations of] He knows all about it. Told him proper. Hear him tell the toff where he come from? etc.

THE GENTLEMAN. May I ask, sir, do you do this for your living at a music hall?

THE NOTE TAKER. I've thought of that. Perhaps I shall some day.

[The rain has stopped; and the persons on the outside of the crowd begin to drop off.]

THE FLOWER GIRL. [resenting the reaction] He's no gentleman, he aint, to interfere with a poor girl.

THE DAUGHTER. [out of patience, pushing her way rudely to the front and displacing the gentleman, who politely retires to the other side of the pillar] What on earth is Freddy doing? I shall get pneumownia if I stay in this draught any longer.

THE NOTE TAKER. [to himself, hastily making a note of her pronunciation of 'monia'] Earlscourt.

THE DAUGHTER. [violently] Will you please keep your impertinent remarks to yourself.

THE NOTE TAKER. Did I say that out loud? I didnt

mean to. I beg your pardon. Your mother's Epsom, unmistakably.

THE MOTHER. [advancing between the daughter and the note taker] How very curious! I was brought up in Largelady Park, near Epsom.

THE NOTE TAKER. [uproariously amused] Ha! ha! what a devil of a name! Excuse me. [To the daughter] You want a cab, do you?

THE DAUGHTER. Dont dare speak to me.

THE MOTHER. Oh, please, please, Clara. [Her daughter repudiates her with an angry shrug and retires haughtily]. We should be so grateful to you, sir, if you found us a cab. [The note taker produces a whistle.] Oh, thank you. [She joins her daughter. The note taker blows a piercing blast.]

THE SARCASTIC BYSTANDER. There! I knowed he was a plain-clothes copper.

THE BYSTANDER. That aint a police whistle: thats a sporting whistle.

THE FLOWER GIRL. [still preoccupied with her wounded feelings] He's no right to take away my character. My character is the same to me as any lady's.

THE NOTE TAKER. I dont know whether youve noticed it; but the rain stopped about two minutes ago.

THE BYSTANDER. So it has. Why didnt you say so before? and us losing our time listening to your silliness! [He walks off towards the Strand].

THE SARCASTIC BYSTANDER. I can tell where you come from. You come from Anwell. Go back there.

THE NOTE TAKER. [helpfully] Hanwell.

THE SARCASTIC BYSTANDER. [affecting great distinction of speech] Thenk you, teacher. Haw haw! So long [he touches his hat with mock respect and strolls off].

THE FLOWER GIRL. Frightening people like that! How would he like it himself?

THE MOTHER. It's quite fine now, Clara. We can walk to a motor bus. Come. [She gathers her skirts above her ankles and hurries off towards the Strand].

THE DAUGHTER. But the cab—[her mother is out of hearing]. Oh, how tiresome! [She follows angrily].

[All the rest have gone except the note taker, the gentleman, and the flower girl, who sits arranging her basket, and still pitying herself in murmurs.]

THE FLOWER GIRL. Poor girl! Hard enough for her to live without being worried and chivied.

THE GENTLEMAN. [returning to his former place on the note taker's left] How do you do it, if I may ask?

THE NOTE TAKER. Simply phonetics. The science of speech. Thats my profession: also my hobby. Happy is the man who can make a living by his hobby! You can spot an Irishman or a Yorkshireman by his brogue. I can place any man within six miles. I can place him within two miles in London. Sometimes within two streets.

THE FLOWER GIRL. Ought to be ashamed of himself, unmanly coward!

THE GENTLEMAN. But is there a living in that?

THE NOTE TAKER. Oh, yes. Quite a fat one. This is an age of upstarts. Men begin in Kentish Town with £80 a year, and end in Park Lane with a hundred thousand. They want to drop Kentish Town; but they give themselves away every time they open their mouths. Now I can teach them—

THE FLOWER GIRL. Let him mind his own business and leave a poor girl—

THE NOTE TAKER. [*explosively*] Woman: cease this detestable boohooing instantly; or else seek the shelter of some other place of worship.

THE FLOWER GIRL. [*with feeble defiance*] Ive a right to be here if I like, same as you.

THE NOTE TAKER. A woman who utters such depressing and disgusting sounds has no right to be anywhere—no right to live. Remember that you are a human being with a soul and the divine gift of articulate speech: that your native language is the language of Shakespear and Milton and The Bible; and dont sit there crooning like a bilious pigeon.

THE FLOWER GIRL. [*quite overwhelmed, looking up at him in mingled wonder and deprecation without daring to raise her head*] Ah-ah-ah-ow-ow-ow-oo!

THE NOTE TAKER. [*whipping out his book*] Heavens! what a sound! [*He writes; then holds out the book and reads, reproducing her vowels exactly*] Ah-ah-ah-ow-ow-ow-oo!

THE FLOWER GIRL. [*tickled by the performance, and laughing in spite of herself*] Garn!

THE NOTE TAKER. You see this creature with her kerbstone English: the English that will keep her in the gutter to the end of her days. Well, sir, in three months I could pass that girl off as a duchess at an ambassador's garden party. I could even get her a place as lady's maid or shop assistant, which requires better English.

THE FLOWER GIRL. What's that you say?

THE NOTE TAKER. Yes, you squashed cabbage leaf, you disgrace to the noble architecture of these columns, you incarnate insult to the English language: I could pass you off as the Queen of Sheba. [*To the Gentleman*] Can you believe that?

THE GENTLEMAN. Of course I can, I am myself a student of Indian dialects; and—

THE NOTE TAKER. [*eagerly*] Are you? Do you know Colonel Pickering, the author of Spoken Sanscrit?

THE GENTLEMAN. I am Colonel Pickering. Who are you?

THE NOTE TAKER. Henry Higgins, author of Higgins's Universal Alphabet.

PICKERING. [*with enthusiasm*] I came from India to meet you.

HIGGINS. I was going to India to meet you.

PICKERING. Where do you live?

HIGGINS. 27A Wimpole Street. Come and see me tomorrow.

PICKERING. I'm at the Carlton. Come with me now and lets have a jaw over some supper.

HIGGINS. Right you are.

THE FLOWER GIRL. [*to Pickering, as he passes her*] Buy a flower, kind gentleman. I'm short for my lodging.

PICKERING. I really havnt any change. I'm sorry [*he backs away*].

HIGGINS. [*shocked at the girl's mendacity*] Liar. You said you could change half-a-crown.

THE FLOWER GIRL. [*rising in desperation*] You ought to be stuffed with nails, you ought. [*Flinging the basket at his feet*] Take the whole blooming basket for sixpence.

[*The church clock strikes the second quarter.*]

HIGGINS. [*hearing in it the voice of God, rebuking him for his Pharisaic want of charity to the poor girl*] A reminder. [*He raises his hat solemnly; then throws a handful of money into the basket and follows Pickering*].

THE FLOWER GIRL. [*picking up a half-crown*] Ah-ow-ooh! [*Picking up a couple of florins*] Aaah-ow-ooh! [*Picking up several coins*] Aaaaaah-ow-ooh! [*Picking up a half-sovereign*] Aaaaaaaaaaaah-ow-ooh!!!

FREDDY. [*springing out of a taxicab*] Got one at last. Hallo! [*To the girl*] Where are the two ladies that were here?

THE FLOWER GIRL. They walked to the bus when the rain stopped.

FREDDY. And left me with a cab on my hands! Damnation!

THE FLOWER GIRL. [*with grandeur*] Never mind, young man. I'm going home in a taxi. [*She sails off to the cab. The driver puts his hand behind him and holds the door firmly shut against her. Quite understanding his mistrust, she shews him her handful of money*]. A taxi fare aint no object to me, Charlie. [*He grins and opens the door*]. Here. What about the basket?

THE TAXIMAN. Give it here. Tuppence extra.

LIZA. No: I dont want nobody to see it. [*She crushes it*

into the cab and gets in, continuing the conversation through the window] Goodbye, Freddy.

FREDDY. *[dazedly raising his hat]* Goodbye.

TAXIMAN. Where to?

LIZA. Bucknam Pellis [Buckingham Palace].

TAXIMAN. What d'ye mean—Bucknam Pellis?

LIZA. Dont you know where it is? In the Green Park, where the King lives. Goodbye, Freddy. Dont let me keep you standing there. Goodbye.

FREDDY. Goodbye. *[He goes.]*

TAXIMAN. Here? Whats this about Bucknam Pellis? What business have you at Bucknam Pellis?

LIZA. Of course I havnt none. But I wasnt going to let him know that. You drive me home.

TAXIMAN. And wheres home?

LIZA. Angel Court, Drury Lane, next Meiklejohn's oil shop.

TAXIMAN. That sounds more like it, Judy. *[He drives off]*.

Let us follow the taxi to the entrance to Angel Court, a narrow little archway between two shops, one of them Meiklejohn's oil shop. When it stops there, Eliza gets out, dragging her basket with her.

LIZA. How much?

TAXIMAN. *[indicating the taximeter]* Cant you read? A shilling.

LIZA. A shilling for two minutes!!

TAXIMAN. Two minutes or ten: it's all the same.

LIZA. Well, I dont call it right.

TAXIMAN. Ever been in a taxi before?

LIZA. *[with dignity]* Hundreds and thousands of times, young man.

TAXIMAN. *[laughing at her]* Good for you, Judy. Keep the shilling, darling, with best love from all at home. Good luck! *[He drives off]*.

LIZA. *[humiliated]* Impidence!

[She picks up the basket and trudges up the alley with it to her lodging; a small room with very old wall paper hanging loose in the damp places. A broken pane in the window is mended with paper. A portrait of a popular actor and a fashion plate of ladies' dresses, all wildly beyond poor Eliza's means, both torn from newspapers, are pinned up on the wall. A birdcage hangs in the window; but its tenant died long ago: it remains as a memorial only.

These are the only visible luxuries: the rest is the irreducible minimum of poverty's needs: a wretched bed heaped with all sorts of coverings that have any warmth in them, a draped packing case with a basin and jug on it and a little looking glass over it, a chair and table, the refuse of some suburban kitchen, and an American alarum clock on the shelf above the unused fireplace: the whole lighted with a gas lamp with a penny in the slot meter. Rent: four shillings a week.]

Here Eliza, chronically weary, but too excited to go to bed, sits, counting her new riches and dreaming and planning what to do with them, until the gas goes out, when she enjoys for the first time the sensation of being able to put in another penny without grudging it. This prodigal mood does not extinguish her gnawing sense of the need for economy sufficiently to prevent her from calculating that she can dream and plan in bed more cheaply and warmly than sitting up without a fire. So she takes off her shawl and skirt and adds them to the miscellaneous bedclothes. Then she kicks off her shoes and gets into bed without any further change.

Act II

Next day at 11 a.m. Higgins's laboratory in Wimpole Street. It is a room on the first floor, looking on the street, and was meant for the drawing room. The double doors are in the middle of the back wall; and persons entering find in the corner to their right two tall file cabinets at right angles to one another against the wall. In this corner stands a flat writing-table, on which are a phonograph, a laryngoscope, a row of tiny organ pipes with a bellows, a set of lamp chimneys for singing flames with burners attached to a gas plug in the wall by an indiarubber tube, several tuning-forks of different sizes, a life-size image of half a human head, shewing in section the vocal organs, and a box containing a supply of wax cylinders for the phonograph.

Further down the room, on the same side, is a fireplace, with a comfortable leather-covered easy-chair at the side of the hearth nearest the door, and a coal-scuttle. There is a clock on the mantelpiece. Between the fireplace and the phonograph table is a stand for newspapers.

On the other side of the central door, to the left of the visitor, is a cabinet of shallow drawers. On it is a telephone and the telephone directory. The corner beyond, and most of the side wall, is occupied by a grand piano, with the keyboard at the end furthest from the door, and a bench for the player extending the full length of the keyboard. On the piano is a dessert dish heaped with fruit and sweets, mostly chocolates.

The middle of the room is clear. Besides the easy-chair, the piano bench, and two chairs at the phono-graph table, there is one stray chair. It stands near the fireplace. On the walls, engravings: mostly Piranesi and mezzotint portraits. No paintings.

Pickering is seated at the table, putting down some cards and a tuning-fork which he has been using. Higgins is standing up near him, closing two or three file drawers which are hanging out. He appears in the morning light as a robust, vital, appetizing sort of man of forty or thereabouts, dressed in a professional-looking black frock-coat with a white linen collar and black silk tie. He is of the energetic scientific type, heartily, even violently interested in everything that can be studied as a scientific subject, and careless about himself and other people, includ-ing their feelings. He is, in fact, but for his years and size, rather like a very impetuous baby 'taking notice' eagerly and loudly, and requiring almost as much watching to keep him out of unintended mischief. His manner varies from genial bullying when he is in a good humor to stormy petulance when anything goes wrong; but he is so entirely frank and void of malice that he remains likeable even in his least reasonable moments.

HIGGINS. [as he shuts the last drawer] Well, I think thats the whole show.

PICKERING. It's really amazing. I havnt taken half of it in, you know.

HIGGINS. Would you like to go over any of it again?

PICKERING. [rising and coming to the fireplace, where he plants himself with his back to the fire] No, thank you: not now. I'm quite done up for this morning.

HIGGINS. [following him, and standing beside him on his left] Tired of listening to sounds?

PICKERING. Yes. It's a fearful strain. I rather fancied myself because I can pronounce twenty-four distinct

vowel sounds; but your hundred and thirty beat me. I cant hear a bit of difference between most of them.

HIGGINS. [chuckling, and going over to the piano to eat sweets] Oh, that comes with practice. You hear no difference at first; but you keep on listening, and presently you find theyre all as different as A from B. [Mrs Pearce looks in: she is Higgins' housekeeper]. Whats the matter?

MRS PEARCE. [hesitating, evidently perplexed] A young woman asks to see you, sir.

HIGGINS. A young woman! What does she want?

MRS PEARCE. Well, sir, she says youll be glad to see her when you know what she's come about. She's quite a common girl, sir. Very common indeed. I should have sent her away, only I thought perhaps you wanted her to talk into your machines. I hope Ive not done wrong; but really you see such queer people sometimes—youll excuse me, I'm sure, sir—

HIGGINS. Oh, thats all right, Mrs Pearce. Has she an interesting accent?

MRS PEARCE. Oh, something dreadful, sir, really. I dont know how you can take an interest in it.

HIGGINS. [to Pickering] Lets have her up. Shew her up, Mrs Pearce [he rushes across to his working table and picks out a cylinder to use on the phonograph].

MRS PEARCE. [only half resigned to it] Very well, sir. It's for you to say. [She goes downstairs.]

HIGGINS. This is rather a bit of luck. I'll shew you how I make records. We'll set her talking; and I'll take it down first in Bell's Visible Speech; then in broad Romic; and then we'll get her on the phono-graph so that you can turn her on as often as you like with the written transcript before you.

MRS PEARCE. [returning] This is the young woman, sir.

[The flower girl enters in state. She has a hat with three ostrich feathers, orange, sky-blue, and red. She has a nearly clean apron and the shoddy coat has been tidied a little. The pathos of this deplorable figure, with its innocent vanity and consequential air, touches Pickering, who has already straightened himself in the presence of Mrs Pearce. But as to Higgins, the only distinction he makes between men and women is that when he is neither bullying nor exclaiming to the heavens against some featherweight cross, he coaxes women as a child coaxes its nurse when it wants to get anything out of her.]

HIGGINS. [brusquely, recognizing her with unconcealed disappointment, and at once, babylike, making an intoler-able grievance of it] Why, this is the girl I jotted down last night. She's no uses: Ive got all the records I want of the Lisson Grove lingo; and I'm not going to waste another cylinder on it. [*To the girl*] Be off with you: I dont want you.

THE FLOWER GIRL. Dont you be so saucy. You aint heard what I come for yet. [*To Mrs Pearce, who is waiting at the door for further instructions*] Did you tell him I come in a taxi?

MRS PEARCE. Nonsense, girl! what do you think a gentleman like Mr. Higgins cares what you came in?

THE FLOWER GIRL. Oh, we are proud! He aint above giving lessons, not him: I heard him say so. Well, I aint come here to ask for any compliment; and if my money's not good enough I can go elsewhere.

HIGGINS. Good enough for what?

THE FLOWER GIRL. Good enough for yə-oo. Now you know, dont you? I'm coming to have lessons, I am. And to pay for em tə-oo: make no mistake.

HIGGINS. [*stupent*] Well!!! [*Recovering his breath with a gasp*] What do you expect me to say to you?

THE FLOWER GIRL. Well, if you was a gentleman, you might ask me to sit down, I think. Dont I tell you I'm bringing you business?

HIGGINS. Pickering: shall we ask this baggage to sit down, or shall we throw her out of the window?

THE FLOWER GIRL. [*running away in terror to the piano, where she turns at bay*] Ah-ah-oh-ow-ow-ow-oo! [*Wounded and whimpering*] I wont be called a baggage when Ive offered to pay like any lady.

[*Motionless, the two men stare at her from the other side of the room, amazed.*]

PICKERING. [*gently*] But what is it you want?

THE FLOWER GIRL. I want to be a lady in a flower shop stead of sellin at the corner of Tottenham Court Road. But they wont take me unless I can talk more genteel. He said he could teach me. Well, here I am ready to pay him—not asking any favor—and he treats me zif I was dirt.

MRS PEARCE. How can you be such a foolish ignorant girl as to think you could afford to pay Mr. Higgins?

THE FLOWER GIRL. Why shouldnt I? I know what lessons cost as well as you do; and I'm ready to pay.

HIGGINS. How much?

THE FLOWER GIRL. [*coming back to him, triumphant*] Now youre talking! I thought youd come off it when you saw a chance of getting back a bit of what you chucked at me last night. [*Confidentially*] Youd had a drop in, hadnt you?

HIGGINS. [*peremptorily*] Sit down.

THE FLOWER GIRL. Oh, if youre going to make a compliment of it—

HIGGINS. [*thundering at her*] Sit down.

MRS PEARCE. [*severely*] Sit down, girl. Do as youre told.

THE FLOWER GIRL. Ah-ah-ah-ow-ow-oo! [*She stands, half rebellious, half-bewildered*].

PICKERING. [*very courteous*] Wont you sit down? [*He places the stray chair near the hearthrug between himself and Higgins*].

LIZA. [*coyly*] Dont mind if I do. [*She sits down. Pickering returns to the hearthrug*].

HIGGINS. Whats your name?

THE FLOWER GIRL. Liza Doolittle.

HIGGINS. [*declaiming gravely*]

> Eliza, Elizabeth, Betsy and Bess,
> They went to the woods to get a bird's nes':

PICKERING. They found a nest with four eggs in it:

HIGGINS. They took one apiece, and left three in it.

[*They laugh heartily at their own fun.*]

LIZA. Oh, dont be silly.

MRS PEARCE. [*placing herself behind Eliza's chair*] You mustnt speak to the gentleman like that.

LIZA. Well, why wont he speak sensible to me?

HIGGINS. Come back to business. How much do you propose to pay me for the lessons?

LIZA. Oh, I know whats right. A lady friend of mine gets French lessons for eighteenpence an hour from a real French gentleman. Well, you wouldnt have the face to ask me the same for teaching me my own language as you would for French; so I wont give more than a shilling. Take it or leave it.

HIGGINS. [*walking up and down the room, rattling the keys and his cash in his pockets*] You know, Pickering, if you consider a shilling, not as a simple shilling, but as a percentage of this girl's income, it works out as fully equivalent to sixty or seventy guineas from a millionaire.

PICKERING. How so?

HIGGINS. Figure it out. A millionaire has about £150 a day. She earns about half-a-crown.

LIZA. [*haughtily*] Who told you I only—

HIGGINS. [*continuing*] She offers me two-fifths of her day's income for a lesson. Two-fifths of a millionaire's income for a day would be somewhere about £60. It's handsome. By George, it's enormous! it's the biggest offer I ever had.

LIZA. [*rising, terrified*] Sixty pounds! What are you talking about? I never offered you sixty pounds. Where would I get—

HIGGINS. Hold your tongue.

LIZA. [weeping] But I aint got sixty pounds. Oh—

MRS PEARCE. Dont cry, you silly girl. Sit down. Nobody is going to touch your money.

HIGGINS. Somebody is going to touch you, with a broomstick, if you dont stop snivelling. Sit down.

LIZA. [obeying slowly] Ah-ah-ah-ow-oo-o! One would think you was my father.

HIGGINS. If I decide to teach you, I'll be worse than two fathers to you. Here [he offers her his silk handkerchief]!

LIZA. Whats this for?

HIGGINS. To wipe your eyes. To wipe any part of your face that feels moist. Remember: thats your handkerchief; and thats your sleeve. Dont mistake the one for the other if you wish to become a lady in a shop.

[Liza, utterly bewildered, stares helplessly at him.]

MRS PEARCE. It's no use talking to her like that, Mr Higgins: she doesnt understand you. Besides, youre quite wrong: she doesnt do it that way at all [she takes the handkerchief].

LIZA. [snatching it] Here! You give me that handkerchief. He gev it to me, not to you.

PICKERING. [laughing] He did. I think it must be regarded as her property, Mrs Pearce.

MRS PEARCE. [resigning herself] Serve you right, Mr Higgins.

PICKERING. Higgins: I'm interested. What about the ambassador's garden party? I'll say youre the greatest teacher alive if you make that good. I'll bet you all the expenses of the experiment you cant do it. And I'll pay for the lessons.

LIZA. Oh, you are real good. Thank you, Captain.

HIGGINS. [tempted, looking at her] It's almost irresistible. She's so deliciously low—so horribly dirty—

LIZA. [protesting extremely] Ah-ah-ah-ah-ow-ow-oo-oo!! I aint dirty: I washed my face and hands afore I come, I did.

PICKERING. Youre certainly not going to turn her head with flattery, Higgins.

MRS PEARCE. [uneasy] Oh, dont say that, sir: theres more ways than one of turning a girl's head; and nobody can do it better than Mr Higgins, though he may not always mean it. I do hope, sir, you wont encourage him to do anything foolish.

HIGGINS. [becoming excited as the idea grows on him] What is life but a series of inspired follies? The difficulty is to find them to do. Never lose a chance:

it doesnt come every day. I shall make a duchess of this draggletailed guttersnipe.

LIZA. [strongly deprecating this view of her] Ah-ah-ah-ow-ow-oo!

HIGGINS. [carried away] Yes: in six months—in three if she has a good ear and a quick tongue—I'll take her anywhere and pass her off as anything. We'll start today: now! this moment! Take her away and clean her, Mrs Pearce. Monkey Brand, if it wont come off any other way. Is there a good fire in the kitchen?

MRS PEARCE. [protesting] Yes; but—

HIGGINS. [storming on] Take all her clothes off and burn them. Ring up Whitely or somebody for new ones. Wrap her up in brown paper til they come.

LIZA. Youre no gentleman, youre not, to talk of such things. I'm a good girl, I am; and I know what the like of you are, I do.

HIGGINS. We want none of your Lisson Grove prudery here, young woman. Youve got to learn to behave like a duchess. Take her away, Mrs Pearce. If she gives you any trouble, wallop her.

LIZA. [springing up and running between Pickering and Mrs Pearce for protection] No! I'll call the police, I will.

MRS PEARCE. But Ive no place to put her.

HIGGINS. Put her in the dustbin.

LIZA. Ah-ah-ah-ow-ow-oo!

PICKERING. Oh come, Higgins! be reasonable.

MRS PEARCE. [resolutely] You must be reasonable, Mr. Higgins: really you must. You cant walk over everybody like this.

[Higgins, thus scolded, subsides. The hurricane is succeeded by a zephyr of amiable surprise.]

HIGGINS. [with professional exquisiteness of modulation] I walk over everybody! My dear Mrs Pearce, my dear Pickering, I never had the slightest intention of walking over anyone. All I propose is that we should be kind to this poor girl. We must help her to prepare and fit herself for her new station in life. If I did not express myself clearly it was because I did not wish to hurt her delicacy, or yours.

[Liza, reassured, steals back to her chair.]

MRS PEARCE. [to Pickering] Well, did you ever hear anything like that, sir?

PICKERING. [laughing heartily] Never, Mrs Pearce: never.

HIGGINS. [patiently] Whats the matter?

MRS PEARCE. Well, the matter is, sir, that you cant take a girl up like that as if you were picking up a pebble on the beach.

HIGGINS. Why not?

MRS PEARCE. Why not! But you dont know anything about her. What about her parents? She may be married.

LIZA. Garn!

HIGGINS. There! As the girl very properly says, Garn! Married indeed! Dont you know that a woman of that class looks a worn out drudge of fifty a year after she's married?

LIZA. Whood marry me?

HIGGINS. [suddenly resorting to the most thrillingly beautiful low tones in his best elocutionary style] By George, Eliza, the streets will be strewn with the bodies of men shooting themselves for your sake before Ive done with you.

MRS PEARCE. Nonsense, sir. You mustnt talk like that to her.

LIZA. [rising and squaring herself determinedly] I'm going away. He's off his chump, he is. I dont want no balmies teaching me.

HIGGINS. [wounded in his tenderest point by her insensibility to his elocution] Oh, indeed! I'm mad, am I? Very well, Mrs Pearce: you neednt order the new clothes for her. Throw her out.

LIZA. [whimpering] Nah-ow. You got no right to touch me.

MRS PEARCE. You see now what comes of being saucy. [Indicating the door] This way, please.

LIZA. [almost in tears] I didnt want no clothes. I wouldnt have taken them [she throws away the handkerchief]. I can buy my own clothes.

HIGGINS. [deftly retrieving the handkerchief and intercepting her on her reluctant way to the door] Youre an ungrateful wicked girl. This is my return for offering to take you out of the gutter and dress you beautifully and make a lady of you.

MRS PEARCE. Stop, Mr Higgins. I wont allow it. It's you that are wicked. Go home to your parents, girl; and tell them to take better care of you.

LIZA. I aint got no parents. They told me I was big enough to earn my own living and turned me out.

MRS PEARCE. Wheres your mother?

LIZA. I ain't got no mother. Her that turned me out was my sixth stepmother. But I done without them. And I'm a good girl, I am.

HIGGINS. Very well, then, what on earth is all this fuss about? The girl doesnt belong to anybody—is no use to anybody but me. [He goes to Mrs Pearce and begins coaxing] You can adopt her, Mrs. Pearce: I'm sure a daughter would be a great amusement to you. Now dont make any more fuss. Take her downstairs; and—

MRS PEARCE. But whats to become of her? Is she to be paid anything? Do be sensible, sir.

HIGGINS. Oh, pay her whatever is necessary: put it down in the housekeeping book. [Impatiently] What on earth will she want with money? She'll have her food and her clothes. She'll only drink if you give her money.

LIZA. [turning on him] Oh you are a brute. It's a lie: nobody ever saw the sign of liquor on me. [To Pickering] Oh, sir: youre a gentleman: dont let him speak to me like that.

PICKERING. [in good-humored remonstrance] Does it occur to you, Higgins, that the girl has some feelings?

HIGGINS. [looking critically at her] Oh no, I dont think so. Not any feelings that we need bother about. [Cheerily] Have you, Eliza?

LIZA. I got my feelings same as anyone else.

HIGGINS. [to Pickering, reflectively] You see the difficulty?

PICKERING. Eh? What difficulty?

HIGGINS. To get her to talk grammar. The mere pronunciation is easy enough.

LIZA. I dont want to talk grammar. I want to talk like a lady in a flower shop.

MRS PEARCE. Will you please keep to the point, Mr Higgins. I want to know on what terms the girl is to be here. Is she to have any wages? And what is to become of her when youve finished your teaching? You must look ahead a little.

HIGGINS. [impatiently] Whats to become of her if I leave her in the gutter? Tell me that, Mrs Pearce.

MRS PEARCE. Thats her own business, not yours, Mr Higgins.

HIGGINS. Well, when Ive done with her, we can throw her back into the gutter; and then it will be her own business again; so thats all right.

LIZA. Oh, youve no feeling heart in you: you dont care for nothing but yourself. [She rises and takes the floor resolutely]. Here! Ive had enough of this. I'm going [making for the door]. You ought to be ashamed of yourself, you ought.

HIGGINS. [snatching a chocolate cream from the piano, his eyes suddenly beginning to twinkle with mischief] Have some chocolates, Eliza.

LIZA. [*halting, tempted*] How do I know what might be in them? Ive heard of girls being drugged by the like of you.

[*Higgins whips out his penknife; cuts a chocolate in two; puts one half into his mouth and bolts it; and offers her the other half.*]

HIGGINS. Pledge of good faith, Eliza. I eat one half: you eat the other. [*Liza opens her mouth to retort: he pops the half chocolate into it*]. You shall have boxes of them, barrels of them, every day. You shall live on them. Eh?

LIZA. [*who has disposed of the chocolate after being nearly choked by it*] I wouldnt have ate it, only I'm too ladylike to take it out of my mouth.

HIGGINS. Listen, Eliza. I think you said you came in a taxi.

LIZA. Well, what if I did? Ive as good a right to take a taxi as anyone else.

HIGGINS. You have, Eliza; and in future you shall have as many taxis as you want. You shall go up and down and round the town in a taxi every day. Think of that, Eliza.

MRS PEARCE. Mr Higgins: youre tempting the girl. It's not right. She should think of the future.

HIGGINS. At her age! Nonsense! Time enough to think of the future when you havnt any future to think of. No, Eliza: do as this lady does: think of other people's futures; but never think of your own. Think of chocolates, and taxis, and gold, and diamonds.

LIZA. No: I dont want no gold and no diamonds. I'm a good girl, I am. [*She sits down again, with an attempt at dignity.*]

HIGGINS. You shall remain so, Eliza, under the care of Mrs Pearce. And you shall marry an officer in the Guards, with a beautiful mustache: the son of a marquis, who will disinherit him for marrying you, but will relent when he sees your beauty and goodness—

PICKERING. Excuse me, Higgins; but I really must interfere. Mrs Pearce is quite right. If this girl is to put herself in your hands for six months for an experiment in teaching, she must understand thoroughly what she's doing.

HIGGINS. How can she? She's incapable of understanding anything. Besides, do any of us understand what we are doing? If we did, would we ever do it?

PICKERING. Very clever, Higgins; but not to the present point. [*To Eliza*] Miss Doolittle—

LIZA. [*overwhelmed*] Ah-ah-ow-oo!

HIGGINS. There! Thats all youll get out of Eliza. Ah-ah-ow-oo! No use explaining. As a military man you ought to know that. Give her her orders: thats enough for her. Eliza: you are to live here for the next six months, learning how to speak beautifully, like a lady in a florist's shop. If youre good and do whatever youre told, you shall sleep in a proper bedroom, and have lots to eat, and money to buy chocolates and take rides in taxies. If youre naughty and idle you will sleep in the back kitchen among the black beetles, and be walloped by Mrs Pearce with a broomstick. At the end of six months you shall go to Buckingham Palace in a carriage, beautifully dressed. If the King finds out youre not a lady, you will be taken by the police to the Tower of London, where your head will be cut off as a warning to other presumptuous flower girls. If you are not found out, you shall have a present of seven-and-sixpence to start life with as a lady in a shop. If you refuse this offer you will be a most ungrateful wicked girl; and the angels will weep for you. [*To Pickering*] Now are you satisfied, Pickering? [*To Mrs Pearce*] Can I put it more plainly and fairly, Mrs Pearce?

MRS PEARCE. [*patiently*] I think youd better let me speak to the girl properly in private. I dont know that I can take charge of her or consent to the arrangement at all. Of course I know you dont mean her any harm; but when you get what you call interested in people's accents, you never think or care what may happen to them or you. Come with me, Eliza.

HIGGINS. Thats all right. Thank you. Mrs Pearce. Bundle her off to the bathroom.

LIZA. [*rising reluctantly and suspiciously*] Youre a great bully, you are. I wont stay here if I dont like. I wont let nobody wallop me. I never asked to go to Bucknam Palace. I didn't. I was never in trouble with the police, not me. I'm a good girl—

MRS PEARCE. Dont answer back, girl. You dont understand the gentleman. Come with me. [*She leads the way to the door, and holds it open for Eliza.*]

LIZA. [*as she goes out*] Well, what I say is right. I wont go near the King, not if I'm going to have my head cut off. If I'd known what I was letting myself in for, I wouldn't have come here. I always been a good girl; and I never offered to say a word to him; and I dont owe him nothing; and I dont care; and I wont be put upon; and I have my feelings the same as anyone else—

[*Mrs Pearce shuts the door; and Eliza's plaints are no longer audible.*]

Eliza is taken upstairs to the third floor greatly to her surprise; for she expected to be taken down to the scullery. There Mrs Pearce opens a door and takes her into a spare bedroom.

MRS PEARCE. I will have to put you here. This will be your bedroom.

LIZA. O-h, I couldnt sleep here, missus. It's too good for the likes of me. I should be afraid to touch anything. I aint a duchess yet, you know.

MRS PEARCE. You have got to make yourself as clean as the room: then you wont be afraid of it. And you must call me Mrs Pearce, not missus. [*She throws open the door of the dressing-room, now modernized as a bathroom*].

LIZA. Gawd! whats this? Is this where you wash clothes? Funny sort of copper I call it.

MRS PEARCE. It is not a copper. This is where we wash ourselves, Eliza, and where I am going to wash you.

LIZA. You expect me to get into that and wet myself all over! Not me. I should catch my death. I knew a woman did it every Saturday night; and she died of it.

MRS PEARCE. Mr Higgins has the gentlemen's bathroom downstairs; and he has a bath every morning, in cold water.

LIZA. Ugh! He's made of iron, that man.

MRS PEARCE. If you are to sit with him and the Colonel and be taught you will have to do the same. They wont like the smell of you if you dont. But you can have the water as hot as you like. There are two taps: hot and cold.

LIZA. [*weeping*] I couldnt. I dursnt. Its not natural: it would kill me. Ive never had a bath in my life: not what youd call a proper one.

MRS PEARCE. Well, dont you want to be clean and sweet and decent, like a lady? You know you cant be a nice girl inside if youre a dirty slut outside.

LIZA. Boohoo!!!

MRS PEARCE. Now stop crying and go back into your room and take off all your clothes. Then wrap yourself in this [*taking down a gown from its peg and handing it to her*] and come back to me. I will get the bath ready.

LIZA. [*all tears*] I cant. I wont. I'm not used to it. Ive never took off all my clothes before. It's not right: it's not decent.

MRS PEARCE. Nonsense, child. Dont you take off all your clothes every night when you go to bed?

LIZA. [*amazed*] No. Why should I? I should catch my death. Of course I take off my skirt.

MRS PEARCE. Do you mean that you sleep in the underclothes you wear in the daytime?

LIZA. What else have I to sleep in?

MRS PEARCE. You will never do that again as long as you live here. I will get you a proper nightdress.

LIZA. Do you mean change into cold things and lie awake shivering half the night? You want to kill me, you do.

MRS PEARCE. I want to change you from a frowzy slut to a clean respectable girl fit to sit with the gentlemen in the study. Are you going to trust me and do what I tell you or be thrown out and sent back to your flower basket?

LIZA. But you dont know what the cold is to me. You dont know how I dread it.

MRS PEARCE. Your bed wont be cold here: I will put a hot water bottle in it. [*Pushing her into the bedroom*] Off with you and undress.

LIZA. Oh, if only I'd a known what a dreadful thing it is to be clean I'd never have come. I didn't know when I was well off. I— [*Mrs Pearce pushes her through the door, but leaves it partly open lest her prisoner should take to flight*].

[*Mrs Pearce puts on a pair of white rubber sleeves, and fills the bath, mixing hot and cold, and testing the result with the bath thermometer. She perfumes it with a handful of bath salts and adds a palmful of mustard. She then takes a formidable looking long handled scrubbing brush and soaps it profusely with a ball of scented soap.*

Eliza comes back with nothing on but the bath gown huddled tightly round her, a piteous spectacle of abject terror.]

MRS PEARCE. Now come along. Take that thing off.

LIZA. Oh I couldnt, Mrs Pearce: I reely couldnt. I never done such a thing.

MRS PEARCE. Nonsense. Here: step in and tell me whether it's hot enough for you.

LIZA. Ah-oo! Ah-oo! It's too hot.

MRS PEARCE. [*deftly snatching the gown away and throwing Eliza down on her back*] It wont hurt you. [*She sets to work with the scrubbing brush*].

[*Eliza's screams are heartrending.*

Meanwhile the Colonel has been having it out with Higgins about Eliza. Pickering has come from the hearth to the chair and seated himself astride of it with his arms on the back to cross-examine him.]

PICKERING. Excuse the straight question, Higgins. Are you a man of good character where women are concerned?

HIGGINS. [*moodily*] Have you ever met a man of good character where women are concerned?

PICKERING. Yes: very frequently.

HIGGINS. [*dogmatically, lifting himself on his hands to the level of the piano, and sitting on it with a bounce*] Well, I havnt. I find that the moment I let a woman make friends with me, she becomes jealous, exacting, suspicious, and a damned nuisance. I find that the moment I let myself make friends with a woman, I become selfish and tyrranical. Women upset everything. When you let them into your life, you find that the woman is driving at one thing and youre driving at another.

PICKERING. At what, for example?

HIGGINS. [*coming off the piano restlessly*] Oh, Lord knows! I suppose the woman wants to live her own life; and the man wants to live his; and each tries to drag the other on to the wrong track. One wants to go north and the other south; and the result is that both have to go east, though they both hate the east wind. [*He sits down on the bench at the keyboard*]. So here I am, a confirmed old bachelor, and likely to remain so.

PICKERING. [*rising and standing over him gravely*] Come, Higgins! You know what I mean. If I'm to be in this business I shall feel responsible for that girl. I hope it's understood that no advantage is to be taken of her position.

HIGGINS. What! That thing! Sacred, I assure you. [*Rising to explain*] You see, she'll be a pupil; and teaching would be impossible unless pupils were sacred. Ive taught scores of American millionairesses how to speak English: the best looking women in the world. I'm seasoned. They might as well be blocks of wood. *I* might as well be a block of wood. It's—

[*Mrs Pearce opens the door. She has Eliza's hat in her hand. Pickering retires to the easy-chair at the hearth and sits down.*]

HIGGINS. [*eagerly*] Well, Mrs Pearce: is it all right?

MRS PEARCE. [*at the door*] I just wish to trouble you with a word, if I may, Mr. Higgins.

HIGGINS. Yes, certainly. Come in. [*She comes forward*] Don't burn that, Mrs. Pearce. I'll keep it as a curiosity. [*He takes the hat*].

MRS PEARCE. Handle it carefully, sir, please. I had to promise her not to burn it; but I had better put it in the oven for a while

HIGGINS. [*putting it down hastily on the piano*] Oh! thank you. Well, what have you to say to me?

PICKERING. Am I in the way?

MRS PEARCE. Not at all, sir. Mr Higgins: will you please be very particular what you say before the girl?

HIGGINS. [*sternly*] Of course. I'm always particular about what I say. Why do you say this to me?

MRS PEARCE. [*unmoved*] No sir: youre not at all particular when youve mislaid anything or when you get a little impatient. Now it doesnt matter before me: I'm used to it. But you really must not swear before the girl.

HIGGINS. [*indignantly*] *I* swear! [*Most emphatically*] I never swear. I detest the habit. What the devil do you mean?

MRS PEARCE. [*stolidly*] Thats what I mean, sir. You swear a great deal too much. I dont mind your damning and blasting, and what the devil and where the devil and who the devil—

HIGGINS. Mrs Pearce: this language from your lips! Really!

MRS PEARCE. [*not to be put off*] —but there is a certain word I must ask you not to use. The girl used it herself when she began to enjoy the bath. It begins with the same letter as bath. She knows no better; she learnt it at her mother's knee. But she must not hear it from your lips.

HIGGINS. [*loftily*] I cannot change myself with having ever uttered it, Mrs Pearce. [*She looks at him steadfastly. He adds, hiding an uneasy conscience with a judicial air*] Except perhaps in a moment of extreme and justifiable excitement.

MRS PEARCE. Only this morning, sir, you applied it to your boots, to the butter, and to the brown bread.

HIGGINS. Oh, that! Mere alliteration, Mrs Pearce, natural to a poet.

MRS PEARCE. Well, sir, whatever you choose to call it, I beg you not to let the girl hear you repeat it.

HIGGINS. Oh, very well, very well. Is that all?

MRS PEARCE. No, sir. We shall have to be very particular with this girl as to personal cleanliness.

HIGGINS. Certainly. Quite right. Most important.

MRS PEARCE. I mean not to be slovenly about her dress or untidy in leaving things about.

HIGGINS. [*going to her solemnly*] Just so. I intended to call your attention to that. [*He passes on to Pickering, who is enjoying the conversation immensely*]. It is these little things that matter, Pickering. Take care of the pence and the pounds will take care of themselves is as true of personal habits as of money. [*He comes to anchor on the hearthrug, with the air of a man in an unassailable position*].

MRS PEARCE. Yes, sir. Then might I ask you not to come down to breakfast in your dressing-gown, or at any rate not to use it as a napkin to the extent you do, sir. And if you would be so good as not to eat everything off the same plate, and to remember not to put the porridge saucepan out of your hand on the clean tablecloth, it would be a better example to the girl. You know you nearly choked yourself with a fishbone in the jam only last week.

HIGGINS. [routed from the hearthrug and drifting back to the piano] I may do these things sometimes in absence of mind; but surely I dont do them habitually. [Angrily] By the way: my dressing-gown smells most damnably of benzine.

MRS PEARCE. No doubt it does, Mr Higgins. But if you will wipe your fingers—

HIGGINS. [yelling] Oh very well, very well: I'll wipe them in my hair in future.

MRS PEARCE. I hope youre not offended, Mr Higgins.

HIGGINS. [shocked at finding himself thought capable of an unamiable sentiment] Not at all, not at all. Youre quite right, Mrs. Pearce: I shall be particularly careful before the girl. Is that all?

MRS PEARCE. No, sir. Might she use some of those Japanese dresses you brought from abroad? I really cant put her back into her old things.

HIGGINS. Certainly. Anything you like. Is that all?

MRS PEARCE. Thank you, sir. Thats all. [She goes out].

HIGGINS. You know, Pickering, that woman has the most extraordinary ideas about me. Here I am, a shy, diffident sort of man. Ive never been able to feel really grown-up and tremendous, like other chaps. And yet she's firmly persuaded that I'm an arbitrary overbearing bossing kind of person. I cant account for it.

[Mrs Pearce returns.]

MRS PEARCE. If you please, sir, the trouble's beginning already. Theres a dustman downstairs, Alfred Doolittle, wants to see you. He says you have his daughter here.

PICKERING. [rising] Phew! I say!

HIGGINS. [promptly] Send the blackguard up.

MRS PEARCE. Oh, very well, sir. [She goes out].

PICKERING. He may not be a blackguard, Higgins.

HIGGINS. Nonsense. Of course he's a blackguard.

PICKERING. Whether he is or not, I'm afraid we shall have some trouble with him.

HIGGINS. [confidently] Oh no: I think not. If theres any trouble he shall have it with me, not I with him. And we are sure to get something interesting out of him.

PICKERING. About the girl?

HIGGINS. No. I mean his dialect.

PICKERING. Oh!

MRS PEARCE. [at the door] Doolittle, sir. [She admits Doolittle and retires.]

[Alfred Doolittle is an elderly but vigorous dustman, clad in the costume of his profession, including a hat with a back brim covering his neck and shoulders. He has well marked and rather interesting features, and seems equally free from fear and conscience. He has a remarkably expressive voice, the result of a habit of giving vent to his feelings without reserve. His present pose is that of wounded honor and stern resolution.]

DOOLITTLE. [at the door, uncertain which of the two gentlemen is his man] Professor Iggins?

HIGGINS. Here. Good morning. Sit down.

DOOLITTLE. Morning, Governor. [He sits down magisterially] I come about a very serious matter, Governor.

HIGGINS. [to Pickering] Brought up in Hounslow. Mother Welsh, I should think. [Doolittle opens his mouth, amazed. Higgins continues] What do you want, Doolittle?

DOOLITTLE. [menacingly] I want my daughter: thats what I want. See?

HIGGINS. Of course you do. Youre her father, arnt you? You dont suppose anyone else wants her, do you? I'm glad to see you have some spark of family feeling left. She's upstairs. Take her away at once.

DOOLITTLE. [rising, fearfully taken aback] What!

HIGGINS. Take her away. Do you suppose I'm going to keep your daughter for you?

DOOLITTLE. [remonstrating] Now, now, look here, Governor. Is this reasonable? Is it fairity to take advantage of a man like this? The girl belongs to me. You got her. Where do I come in? [He sits down again.]

HIGGINS. Your daughter had the audacity to come to my house and ask me to teach her how to speak properly so that she could get a place in a flowershop. This gentleman and my housekeeper have been here all the time. [Bullying him] How dare you come here and attempt to blackmail me? You sent her here on purpose.

DOOLITTLE. [protesting] No, Governor.

HIGGINS. You must have. How else could you possibly know that she is here?

DOOLITTLE. Dont take a man up like that, Governor.

HIGGINS. The police shall take you up. This is a plant—a plot to extort money by threats. I shall telephone for the police [he goes resolutely to the telephone and opens the directory].

DOOLITTLE. Have I asked you for a brass farthing? I leave it to the gentleman here: have I said a word about money?

HIGGINS. [throwing the book aside and marching down on Doolittle with a poser] What else did you come for?

DOOLITTLE. [sweetly] Well, what would a man come for? Be human, Governor.

HIGGINS. [disarmed] Alfred: did you put her up to it?

DOOLITTLE. So help me, Governor, I never did. I take my Bible oath I aint seen the girl these two months past.

HIGGINS. Then how did you know she was here?

DOOLITTLE. ['most musical, most melancholy'] I'll tell you, Governor, if you'll only let me get a word in. I'm willing to tell you. I'm wanting to tell you. I'm waiting to tell you.

HIGGINS. Pickering: this chap has a certain natural gift of rhetoric. Observe the rhythm of his native woodnotes wild. 'I'm willing to tell you: I'm wanting to tell you: I'm waiting to tell you.' Sentimental rhetoric! thats the Welsh strain in him. It also accounts for his mendacity and dishonesty.

PICKERING. Oh, please, Higgins: I'm west country myself. [To Doolittle.] How did you know the girl was here if you didnt send her?

DOOLITTLE. It was like this, Governor. The girl took a boy in the taxi to give him a jaunt. Son of her landlady, he is. He hung about on the chance of her giving him another ride home. Well, she sent him back for her luggage when she heard you was willing for her to stop here. I met the boy at the corner of Long Acre and Endell Street.

HIGGINS. Public house. Yes?

DOOLITTLE. The poor man's club, Governor: why shouldnt I?

PICKERING. Do let him tell his story, Higgins.

DOOLITTLE. He told me what was up. And I ask you, what was my feelings and my duty as a father? I says to the boy, 'You bring me the luggage,' I says—

PICKERING. Why didn't you go for it yourself?

DOOLITTLE. Landlady wouldnt have trusted me with it, Governor. She's that kind of woman: you know. I had to give the boy a penny afore he trusted me with it, the little swine. I brought it to her just to oblige you like, and make myself agreeable. Thats all.

HIGGINS. How much luggage?

DOOLITTLE. Musical instrument, Governor. A few pictures, a trifle of jewelry, and a bird-cage. She said she didn't want no clothes. What was I to think from that, Governor? I ask you as a parent what was I to think?

HIGGINS. So you came to rescue her from worse than death eh?

DOOLITTLE. [appreciatively; relieved at being so well understood] Just so, Governor. Thats right.

PICKERING. But why did you bring her luggage if you intended to take her away?

DOOLITTLE. Have I said a word about taking her away? Have I now?

HIGGINS. [determinedly] Youre going to take her away, double quick. [He crosses to the hearth and rings the bell].

DOOLITTLE. [rising] No, Governor. Dont say that. I'm not the man to stand in my girl's light. Heres a career opening for her as you might say; and—

[Mrs Pearce opens the door and awaits orders.]

HIGGINS. Mrs Pearce: this is Eliza's father. He has come to take her away. Give her to him. [He goes back to the piano, with an air of washing his hands of the whole affair.]

DOOLITTLE. No. This is a misunderstanding. Listen here—

MRS PEARCE. He cant take her away, Mr Higgins: how can he? You told me to burn her clothes.

DOOLITTLE. Thats right. I cant carry the girl through the streets like a blooming monkey, can I? I put it to you.

HIGGINS. You have put it to me that you want your daughter. Take your daughter. If she has no clothes go out and buy her some.

DOOLITTLE. [desperate] Wheres the clothes she come in? Did I burn them or did your missus here?

MRS PEARCE. I am the housekeeper, if you please. I have sent for some clothes for the girl. When they come you can take her away. You can wait in the kitchen. This way, please.

[Doolittle, much troubled, accompanies her to the door; then hesitates: finally turns confidentially to Higgins.]

DOOLITTLE. Listen here, Governor. You and me is men of the world, aint we?

HIGGINS. Oh! Men of the world, are we? Youd better go, Mrs Pearce.

MRS PEARCE. I think so, indeed, sir. [She goes, with dignity].

PICKERING. The floor is yours, Mr Doolittle.

DOOLITTLE. [to Pickering] I thank you, Governor. [To Higgins, who takes refuge on the piano bench, a little overwhelmed by the proximity of his visitor; for Doolittle has a professional flavor of dust about him]. Well, the truth is, Ive taken a sort of fancy to you, Governor; and if you want the girl, I'm not so set on having her back home again but what I might be open to an arrangement. Regarded in the light of a young woman, she's a fine handsome girl. As a daughter she's not worth her keep; and so I tell you straight. All I ask is my rights as a father; and youre the last man alive to expect me to let her go for nothing: for I can see youre one of the straight sort, Governor. Well, whats a five-pound note to you? and whats Eliza to me? [*He turns to his chair and sits down judicially*].

PICKERING. I think you ought to know, Doolittle, that Mr Higgins's intentions are entirely honorable.

DOOLITTLE. Course they are, Governor. If I thought they wasn't, I'd ask fifty.

HIGGINS. [*revolted*] Do you mean to say that you would sell your daughter for £50?

DOOLITTLE. Not in a general way I wouldnt; but to oblige a gentleman like you I'd do a good deal, I do assure you.

PICKERING. Have you no morals, man?

DOOLITTLE. [*unabashed*] Cant afford them, Governor. Neither could you if you was as poor as me. Not that I mean any harm, you know. But if Liza is going to have a bit out of this, why not me too?

HIGGINS. [*troubled*] I dont know what to do, Pickering. There can be no question that as a matter of morals it's a positive crime to give this chap a farthing. And yet I feel a sort of rough justice in his claim.

DOOLITTLE. Thats it, Governor. Thats all I say. A father's heart, as it were.

PICKERING. Well, I know the feeling; but really it seems hardly right—

DOOLITTLE. Dont say that, Governor. Dont look at it that way. What am I, Governors both? I ask you, what am I? I'm one of the undeserving poor: thats what I am. Think of what that means to a man. It means that he's up agen middle class morality all the time. If theres anything going, and I put in for a bit of it, it's always the same story: 'Youre undeserving: so you cant have it.' But my needs is as great as the most deserving widow's that ever got money out of six different charities in one week for the death of the same husband. I dont need less than a deserving man: I need more. I dont eat less hearty than him; and I drink a lot more. I want a bit of amusement, cause I'm a thinking man. I want cheerfulness and a song and a band when I feel low. Well, they charge me just the same for everything as they charge the deserving. What is middle class morality? Just an excuse for never giving me anything. Therefore, I ask you, as two gentlemen, not to play that game on me. I'm playing straight with you. I aint pretending to be deserving. I'm undeserving: and I mean to go on being undeserving. I like it; and thats the truth. Will you take advantage of a man's nature to do him out of the price of his own daughter what he's brought up and fed and clothed by the sweat of his brow until she's growed big enough to be interesting to you two gentlemen? Is five pounds unreasonable? I put it to you; and I leave it to you.

HIGGINS. [*rising, and going over to Pickering*] Pickering: if we were to take this man in hand for three months, he could choose between a seat in the Cabinet and a popular pulpit in Wales.

PICKERING. What do you say to that, Doolittle?

DOOLITTLE. Not me, Governor, thank you kindly. Ive heard all the preachers and all the prime ministers— for I'm a thinking man and game for politics or religion or social reform same as all the other amusements—and I tell you it's a dog's life any way you look at it. Undeserving poverty is my line. Taking one station in society with another, it's—it's— well, it's the only one that has any ginger in it, to my taste.

HIGGINS. I suppose we must give him a fiver.

PICKERING. He'll make a bad use of it, I'm afraid.

DOOLITTLE. Not me, Governor, so help me I wont. Dont you be afraid that I'll save it and spare it and live idle on it. There wont be a penny of it left by Monday: I'll have to go to work same as if I'd never had it. It wont pauperize me, you bet. Just one good spree for myself and the missus, giving pleasure to ourselves and employment to others, and satisfaction to you to think it's not been throwed away. You couldnt spend it better.

HIGGINS. [*taking out his pocket book and coming between Doolittle and the piano*] This is irresistible. Lets give him ten. [*He offers two notes to the dustman*].

DOOLITTLE. No, Governor. She wouldn't have the heart to spend ten; and perhaps I shouldnt neither. Ten pounds is a lot of money: it makes a man feel prudent like; and then good-bye to happiness. You give me what I ask you, Governor: not a penny more, and not a penny less.

PICKERING. Why dont you marry that missus of yours? I rather draw the line at encouraging that sort of immorality.

DOOLITTLE. Tell her so, Governor: tell her so. *I'm* willing. It's me that suffers by it. Ive no hold on her. I got to be agreeable to her. I got to give her presents. I got to buy her clothes something sinful.

I'm a slave to that woman, Governor, just because I'm not her lawful husband. And she knows it too. Catch her marrying me! Take my advice, Governor—marry Eliza while she's young and dont know no better. If you dont youll be sorry for it after. If you do, she'll be sorry for it after; but better her than you, because youre a man, and she's only a woman and dont know how to be happy anyhow.

HIGGINS. Pickering: If we listen to this man another minute, we shall have no convictions left. [*To Doolittle*] Five pounds I think you said.

DOOLITTLE. Thank you kindly, Governor.

HIGGINS. Youre sure you wont take ten?

DOOLITTLE. Not now. Another time, Governor.

HIGGINS. [*handing him a five-pound note*] Here you are.

DOOLITTLE. Thank you, Governor. Good morning. [*He hurries to the door, anxious to get away with his booty. When he opens it he is confronted with a dainty and exquisitely clean young Japanese lady in a simple blue cotton kimono printed cunningly with small white jasmine blossoms. Mrs Pearce is with her. He gets out of her way deferentially and apologizes*]. Beg pardon, miss.

THE JAPANESE LADY. Garn! Dont you know your own daughter?

DOOLITTLE. { *exclaiming* } Bly me! it's Eliza!
HIGGINS. { *simul-* } Whats that? This!
PICKERING. { *taneously* } By Jove!

LIZA. Dont I look silly?

HIGGINS. Silly?

MRS PEARCE. [*at the door*] Now, Mr Higgins, please dont say anything to make the girl conceited about herself.

HIGGINS. [*conscientiously*] Oh! Quite right, Mrs Pearce. [*To Eliza*] Yes: damned silly.

MRS PEARCE. Please, sir.

HIGGINS. [*correcting himself*] I mean extremely silly.

LIZA. I should look all right with my hat on. [*She takes up her hat; puts it on; and walks across the room to the fireplace with a fashionable air*].

HIGGINS. A new fashion, by George! And it ought to look horrible!

DOOLITTLE. [*with fatherly pride*] Well, I never thought she'd clean up as good looking as that, Governor. She's a credit to me, aint she?

LIZA. I tell you, it's easy to clean up here. Hot and cold water on tap, just as much as you like, there is. Woolly towels, there is; and a towel horse so hot, it burns your fingers. Soft brushes to scrub yourself, and a wooden bowl of soap smelling like primroses. Now I know why ladies is so clean. Washing's a treat for them. Wish they could see what it is for the like of me!

HIGGINS. I'm glad the bathroom met with your approval.

LIZA. It didnt: not all of it; and I dont care who hears me say it. Mrs Pearce knows.

HIGGINS. What was wrong, Mrs Pearce?

MRS PEARCE. [*blandly*] Oh, nothing, sir. I doesnt matter.

LIZA. I had a good mind to break it. I didn't know which way to look. But I hung a towel over it, I did.

HIGGINS. Over what?

MRS PEARCE. Over the looking-glass sir.

HIGGINS. Doolittle: you have brought your daughter up too strictly.

DOOLITTLE. Me! I never brought her up at all, except to give her a lick of a strap now and again. Dont put it on me, Governor. She aint accustomed to it, you see: thats all. But she'll soon pick up your free-and-easy ways.

LIZA. I'm a good girl, I am; and I wont pick up no free-and-easy ways.

HIGGINS. Eliza: if you say again that youre a good girl, your father shall take you home.

LIZA. Not him. You dont know my father. All he come here for was to touch you for some money to get drunk on.

DOOLITTLE. Well, what else would I want money for? To put into the plate in church, I suppose. [*She puts out her tongue at him. He is so incensed by this that Pickering presently finds it necessary to step between them*]. Dont you give me none of your lip; and dont let me hear you giving this gentleman any of it neither, or youll hear from me about it. See?

HIGGINS. Have you any further advice to give her before you go, Doolittle? Your blessing, for instance.

DOOLITTLE. No, Governor. I aint such a mug as to put up my children to all I know myself. Hard enough to hold them in without that. If you want Eliza's mind improved, Governor, you do it yourself with a strap. So long, gentlemen. [*He turns to go*].

HIGGINS. [*impressively*] Stop. Youll come regularly to see your daughter. It's your duty, you know. My brother is a clergyman; and he could help you in your talks with her.

DOOLITTLE. [*evasively*] Certainly, I'll come, Governor. Not just this week, because I have a job at a distance. But later on you may depend on me. Afternoon, gentlemen. Afternoon, maam. [*He touches his hat to Mrs Pearce, who disdains the salutation and goes out. He winks at Higgins, thinking him probably a fellow-sufferer from Mrs Pearce's difficult disposition, and follows her].*

LIZA. Dont you believe the old liar. He'd as soon you set a bulldog on him as a clergyman. You wont see him again in a hurry.

HIGGINS. I dont want to, Eliza. Do you?

LIZA. Not me. I dont want never to see him again, I dont. He's a disgrace to me, he is, collecting dust, instead of working at his trade.

PICKERING. What is his trade, Eliza?

LIZA. Talking money out of other people's pockets into his own. His proper trade's a navvy; and he works at it sometimes too—for exercise—and earns good money at it. Aint you going to call me Miss Doolittle any more?

PICKERING. I beg your pardon, Miss Doolittle. It was a slip of the tongue.

LIZA. Oh, I dont mind; only it sounded so genteel. I should just like to take a taxi to the corner of Tottenham Court Road and get out there and tell it to wait for me, just to put the girls in their place a bit. I wouldnt speak to them, you know.

PICKERING. Better wait til we get you something really fashionable.

HIGGINS. Besides, you shouldnt cut your old friends now that you have risen in the world. Thats what we call snobbery.

LIZA. You dont call the like of them my friends now, I should hope. Theyve took it out of me often enough with their ridicule when they had the chance; and now I mean to get a bit of my own back. But if I'm to have fashionable clothes, I'll wait. I should like to have some. Mrs Pearce says youre going to give me some to wear in bed at night different to what I wear in the daytime; but it do seem a waste of money when you could get something to shew. Besides, I never could fancy changing into cold things on a winter night.

MRS PEARCE. [*coming back*] Now, Eliza. The new things have come for you to try on.

LIZA. Ah-ow-oo-ooh! [*She rushes out*].

MRS PEARCE. [*following her*] Oh, dont rush about like that, girl. [*She shuts the door behind her*].

HIGGINS. Pickering: we have taken on a stiff job.

PICKERING. [*with conviction*] Higgins: we have.

There seems to be some curiosity as to what Higgins's lessons to Eliza were like. Well, here is a sample: the first one.

Picture Eliza, in her new clothes, and feeling her inside put out of step by a lunch, dinner, and breakfast of a kind to which it is unaccustomed, seated with Higgins and the Colonel in the study, feeling like a hospital out-patient at a first encounter with the doctors.

Higgins, constitutionally unable to sit still, discomposes her still more by striding restlessly about. But for the reassuring presence and quietude of her friend the Colonel she would run for her life, even back to Drury Lane.

HIGGINS. Say your alphabet.

LIZA. I know my alphabet. Do you think I know nothing? I dont need to be taught like a child.

HIGGINS. [*thundering*] Say your alphabet.

PICKERING. Say it, Miss Doolittle. You will understand presently. Do what he tells you; and let him teach you in his own way.

LIZA. Oh well, if you put it like that—Ahyee, bəyee, cəyee, dəyee—

HIGGINS. [*with the roar of a wounded lion*] Stop. Listen to this, Pickering. This is what we pay for as elementary education. This unfortunate animal has been locked up for nine years in school at our expense to teach her to speak and read the language of Shakespear and Milton. And the result is Ahyee, Bə-yee, Cə-yee, Də-yee. [*To Eliza*] Say A, B, C, D.

LIZA. [*almost in tears*] But I'm saying it. Ahyee, Bəyee, Cə-yee—

HIGGINS. Stop. Say a cup of tea.

LIZA. A cappətə-ee.

HIGGINS. Put your tongue forward until it squeezes against the top of your lower teeth. Now say cup.

LIZA. C-c-c- I cant. C-Cup.

PICKERING. Good. Splendid, Miss Doolittle.

HIGGINS. By Jupiter, she's done it at the first shot. Pickering: we shall make a duchess of her. [*To Eliza*] Now do you think you could possibly say tea? Not tə-yee, mind: if you ever say bə-yee cə-yee də-yee again you shall be dragged round the room three times by the hair of your head. [*Fortissimo*] T.T.T.T.

LIZA. [*weeping*] I cant hear no difference cep that it sounds more genteel-like when you say it.

HIGGINS. Well, if you can hear that difference, what the devil are you crying for? Pickering: give her a chocolate.

PICKERING. No, no. Never mind crying a little, Miss Doolittle: you are doing very well; and the lessons wont hurt. I promise you I wont let him drag you round the room by your hair.

HIGGINS. Be off with you to Mrs Pearce and tell her

about it. Think about it. Try to do it by yourself: and keep your tongue well forward in your mouth instead of trying to roll it up and swallow it. Another lesson at half-past four this afternoon. Away with you.

[*Eliza, still sobbing, rushes from the room.*]

Act III

It is Mrs Higgins's at-home day. Nobody has yet arrived. Her drawing room, in a flat on Chelsea Embankment, has three windows looking on the river; and the ceiling is not so lofty as it would be in an older house of the same pretension. The windows are open, giving access to a balcony with flowers in pots. If you stand with your face to the windows, you have the fireplace on your left and the door in the right-hand wall close to the corner nearest the windows.

Mrs Higgins was brought up on Morris and Burne Jones; and her room, which is very unlike her son's room in Wimpole Street, is not crowded with furniture and little tables and nicknacks. In the middle of the room there is a big ottoman; and this, with the carpet, the Morris wallpapers, and the Morris chintz window curtains and brocade covers of the ottoman and its cushions, supply all the ornament, and are much too handsome to be hidden by odds and ends of useless things. A few good oil-paintings from the exhibitions in the Grosvenor Gallery thirty years ago (the Burne Jones, not the Whistler side of them) are on the walls. The only landscape is a Cecil Lawson on the scale of a Rubens. There is a portrait of Mrs Higgins as she was when she defied the fashion in her youth in one of the beautiful Rossettian costumes which, when caricatured by people who did not understand, led to the absurdities of popular estheticism in the eighteen-seventies.

In the corner diagonally opposite the door Mrs Higgins, now over sixty and long past taking the trouble to dress out of the fashion, sits writing at an elegantly simple writing-table with a bell button within reach of her hand. There is a Chippendale chair further back in the room between her and the window nearest her side. At the other side of the room, further forward, is an Elizabethan chair roughly carved in the taste of Inigo Jones. On the same side a piano in a decorated case. The corner between the fireplace and the window is occupied by a divan cushioned in Morris chintz.

It is between four and five in the afternoon.

The door is opened violently; and Higgins enters with his hat on.

MRS HIGGINS. [*dismayed*] Henry! [*Scolding him*] What are you doing here today? It is my at-home day: you promised not to come. [*As he bends to kiss her, she takes his hat off, and presents it to him*].

HIGGINS. Oh bother! [*He throws the hat down on the table*].

MRS HIGGINS. Go home at once.

HIGGINS. [*kissing her*] I know, mother. I came on purpose.

MRS HIGGINS. But you mustn't. I'm serious, Henry. You offend all my friends: they stop coming whenever they meet you.

HIGGINS. Nonsense! I know I have no small talk; but people dont mind. [*He sits on the settee*].

MRS HIGGINS. Oh! dont they? Small talk indeed! What about your large talk? Really, dear, you mustnt stay.

HIGGINS. I must. Ive a job for you. A phonetic job.

MRS HIGGINS. No use, dear. I'm sorry; but I cant get round your vowels; and though I like to get pretty postcards in your patent shorthand, I always have to read the copies in ordinary writing you so thoughtfully send me.

HIGGINS. Well, this isnt a phonetic job.

MRS HIGGINS. You said it was.

HIGGINS. Not your part of it. Ive picked up a girl.

MRS HIGGINS. Does that mean that some girl has picked you up?

HIGGINS. Not at all. I dont mean a love affair.

MRS HIGGINS. What a pity!

HIGGINS. Why?

And that is the sort of ordeal poor Eliza has to go through for months before we meet her again on her first appearance in London society of the professional class.

MRS HIGGINS. Well, you never fall in love with anyone under forty-five. When will you discover that there are some rather nice-looking young women about?

HIGGINS. Oh, I cant be bothered with young women. My idea of a lovable woman is somebody as like you as possible. I shall never get into the way of seriously liking young women: some habits lie too deep to be changed. [*Rising abruptly and walking about, jingling his money and his keys in his trouser pockets*] Besides, theyre all idiots.

MRS HIGGINS. Do you know what you would do if you really loved me, Henry?

HIGGINS. Oh bother! What? Marry, I suppose.

MRS HIGGINS. No. Stop fidgeting and take your hands out of your pockets. [*With a gesture of despair, he obeys and sits down again*]. Thats a good boy. Now tell me about the girl.

HIGGINS. She's coming to see you.

MRS HIGGINS. I dont remember asking her.

HIGGINS. You didnt. *I* asked her. If youd known her you wouldnt have asked her.

MRS HIGGINS. Indeed! Why?

HIGGINS. Well, it's like this. She's a common flower girl. I picked her off the kerbstone.

MRS HIGGINS. And invited her to my at-home!

HIGGINS. [*rising and coming to her to coax her*] Oh, thatll be all right. I've taught her to speak properly: and she has strict orders as to her behavior. She's to keep to two subjects: the weather and everybody's health—Fine day and How do you do, you know— and not to let herself go on things in general. That will be safe.

MRS HIGGINS. Safe! To talk about our health! about our insides! perhaps about our outsides! How could you be so silly, Henry?

HIGGINS. [*impatiently*] Well, she must talk about something. [*He controls himself and sits down again*]. Oh, she'll be all right: dont you fuss. Pickering is in it with me. Ive a sort of bet on that I'll pass her off as a duchess in six months. I started on her some months ago; and she's getting on like a house on fire. I shall win my bet. She has a quick ear; and she's been easier to teach than my middle-class pupils because she's had to learn a complete new language. She talks English almost as you talk French.

MRS HIGGINS. Thats satisfactory, at all events.

HIGGINS. Well, it is and it isnt.

MRS HIGGINS. What does that mean?

HIGGINS. You see, Ive got her pronunciation all right; but you have to consider not only how a girl pronounces, but what she pronounces; and thats where—

[*They are interrupted by the parlormaid, announcing guests.*]

THE PARLORMAID. Mrs and Miss Eynsford Hill. [*She withdraws.*]

HIGGINS. Oh Lord! [*He rises: snatches his hat from the table; and makes for the door; but before he reaches it his mother introduces him.*

Mrs and Miss Eynsford Hill are the mother and daughter who sheltered from the rain in Covent Garden. The mother is well bred, quiet, and has the habitual anxiety of straitened means. The daughter has acquired a gay air of being very much at home in society: the bravado of genteel poverty.]

MRS EYNSFORD HILL. [*to Mrs Higgins*] How do you do? [*They shake hands*].

MISS EYNSFORD HILL. How d'you do? [*She shakes*].

MRS HIGGINS. [*introducing*] My son Henry.

MRS EYNSFORD HILL. Your celebrated son! I have so longed to meet you, Professor Higgins.

HIGGINS. [*glumly, making no movement in her direction*] Delighted. [*He backs against the piano and bows brusquely*].

MISS EYNSFORD HILL. [*going to him with confident familiarity*] How do you do?

HIGGINS. [*staring at her*] Ive seen you before somewhere. I havent the ghost of a notion where; but Ive heard your voice. [*Drearily*] It doesnt matter. Youd better sit down.

MRS HIGGINS. I'm sorry to say that my celebrated son has no manners. You mustnt mind him.

MISS EYNSFORD HILL. [*gaily*] I dont. [*She sits in the Elizabethan chair*].

MRS EYNSFORD HILL. [*a little bewildered*] Not at all. [*She sits on the ottoman between her daughter and Mrs Higgins, who has turned her chair away from the writing-table*].

HIGGINS. Oh, have I been rude? I didnt mean to be.

[*He goes to the central window, through which, with his back to the company, he contemplates the river and the flowers in Battersea Park on the opposite bank as if they were a frozen desert.*

The parlormaid returns, ushering in Pickering.]

THE PARLORMAID. Colonel Pickering. [*She withdraws*].

PICKERING. How do you do, Mrs Higgins?

MRS HIGGINS. So glad youve come. Do you know Mrs Eynsford Hill—Miss Eynsford Hill? [*Exchange of bows. The Colonel brings the Chippendale chair a little forward between Mrs Hill and Mrs Higgins, and sits down*].

PICKERING. Has Henry told you what weve come for?

HIGGINS. [*over his shoulder*] We were interrupted: damn it!

MRS HIGGINS. Oh Henry, Henry, really!

MRS EYNSFORD HILL. [*half rising*] Are we in the way?

MRS HIGGINS. [*rising and making her sit down again*] No, no. You couldnt have come more fortunately: we want you to meet a friend of ours.

HIGGINS. [*turning hopefully*] Yes, by George! We want two or three people. Youll do as well as anybody else.

[*The parlormaid returns, ushering Freddy.*]

THE PARLORMAID. Mr Eynsford Hill.

HIGGINS. [*almost audibly, past endurance*] God of Heaven! another of then.

FREDDY. [*shaking hands with Mrs Higgins*] Ahdedo?

MRS HIGGINS. Very good of you to come. [*Introducing*] Colonel Pickering.

FREDDY. [*bowing*] Ahdedo?

MRS HIGGINS. I dont think you know my son, Professor Higgins.

FREDDY. [*going to Higgins*] Ahdedo?

HIGGINS. [*looking at him much as if he were a pickpocket*] I'll take my oath Ive met you before somewhere. Where was it?

FREDDY. I dont think so.

HIGGINS. [*resignedly*] It dont matter, anyhow. Sit down.

[*He shakes Freddy's hand and almost slings him on to the ottoman with his face to the window; then comes round to the other side of it.*]

HIGGINS. Well, here we are, anyhow! [*He sits down on the ottoman next Mrs Eynsford Hill, on her left*]. And now, what the devil are we going to talk about until Eliza comes?

MRS HIGGINS. Henry: you are the life and soul of the Royal Society's soirées; but really youre rather trying on more commonplace occasions.

HIGGINS. Am I? Very sorry. [*Beaming suddenly*] I suppose I am, you know. [*Uproariously*] Ha, ha!

MISS EYNSFORD HILL. [*who considers Higgins quite eligible matrimonially*] I sympathize. *I* havnt any small talk. If people would only be frank and say what they really think!

HIGGINS. [*relapsing into gloom*] Lord forbid!

MRS EYNSFORD HILL. [*taking up her daughter's cue*] But why?

HIGGINS. What they think they ought to think is bad enough, Lord knows; but what they really think

would break up the whole show. Do you suppose it would be really agreeable if I were to come out now with what *I* really think?

MISS EYNSFORD HILL. [*gaily*] Is it so very cynical?

HIGGINS. Cynical! Who the dickens said it was cynical? I mean it wouldnt be decent.

MRS EYNSFORD HILL. [*seriously*] Oh! I'm sure you dont mean that, Mr Higgins.

HIGGINS. You see, we're all savages, more or less. We're supposed to be civilized and cultured—to know all about poetry and philosophy and art and science, and so on; but how many of us know even the meanings of these names? [*To Miss Hill*] What do you know of poetry? [*To Mrs Hill*] What do you know of science? [*Indicating Freddy*] What does he know of art or science or anything else? What the devil do you imagine I know of philosophy?

MRS HIGGINS. [*warningly*] Or of manners, Henry?

THE PARLORMAID. [*opening the door*] Miss Doolittle. [*She withdraws*].

HIGGINS. [*rising hastily and running to Mrs Higgins*] Here she is, mother. [*He stands on tiptoe and makes signs over his mother's head to Eliza to indicate to her which lady is her hostess*].

[*Eliza, who is exquisitely dressed, produces an impression of such remarkable distinction and beauty as she enters that they all rise, quite fluttered. Guided by Higgins's signals, she comes to Mrs Higgins with studied grace.*]

LIZA. [*speaking with pedantic correctness of pronunciation and great beauty of tone*] How do you do, Mrs Higgins? [*She gasps slightly in making sure of the H in Higgins, but is quite successful*]. Mr. Higgins told me I might come.

MRS HIGGINS. [*cordially*] Quite right: I'm very glad indeed to see you.

PICKERING. How do you do, Miss Doolittle?

LIZA. [*shaking hands with him*] Colonel Pickering, is it not?

MRS EYNSFORD HILL. I feel sure we have met before, Miss Doolittle. I remember your eyes.

LIZA. How do you do? [*She sits down on the ottoman gracefully in the place just left vacant by Higgins*].

MRS EYNSFORD HILL. [*introducing*] My daughter Clara.

LIZA. How do you do?

CLARA. [*impulsively*] How do you do? [*She sits down on the ottoman beside Eliza, devouring her with her eyes*].

FREDDY. [*coming to their side of the ottoman*] Ive certainly not had the pleasure.

MRS EYNSFORD HILL. [*introducing*] My son Freddy.

LIZA. How do you do?

[*Freddy bows and sits down in the Elizabethan chair, infatuated.*]

HIGGINS. [*suddenly*] By George, yes: it all comes back to me! [*They stare at him*]. Covent Garden! [*Lamentably*] What a damned thing!

MRS HIGGINS. Henry, please! [*He is about to sit on the edge of the table*] Dont sit on my writing-table: youll break it.

HIGGINS. [*sulkily*] Sorry.

[*He goes to the divan, stumbling into the fender and over the fire-irons on his way; extricating himself with muttered imprecations; and finishing his disastrous journey by throwing himself so impatiently on the divan that he almost breaks it. Mrs Higgins looks at him, but controls herself and says nothing.*
    A long and painful pause ensues.]

MRS HIGGINS. [*at last, conversationally*] Will it rain, do you think?

LIZA. The shallow depression in the west of these islands is likely to move slowly in an easterly direction. There are no indications of any great change in the barometrical situation.

FREDDY. Ha! ha! how awfully funny!

LIZA. What is wrong with that, young man? I bet I got it right.

FREDDY. Killing!

MRS EYNSFORD HILL. I'm sure I hope it wont turn cold. Theres so much influenza about. It runs right through our whole family regularly every spring.

LIZA. [*darkly*] My aunt died of influenza: so they said.

MRS EYNSFORD HILL. [*clicks her tongue sympathetically*]!!!

LIZA. [*in the same tragic tone*] But it's my belief they done the old woman in.

MRS HIGGINS. [*puzzled*] Done her in?

LIZA. Y-e-e-e-es, Lord love you! Why should she die of influenza? She come through diphtheria right enough the year before. I saw her with my own eyes. Fairly blue with it, she was. They all thought she was dead; but my father he kept ladling gin down her throat til she came to so sudden that she bit the bowl off the spoon.

MRS EYNSFORD HILL. [*startled*] Dear me!

LIZA. [*piling up the indictment*] What call would a woman with that strength in her have to die of influenza? What become of her new straw hat that should have come to me? Somebody pinched it; and what I say is, them as pinched it done her in.

MRS EYNSFORD HILL. What does doing her in mean?

HIGGINS. [*hastily*] Oh, thats the new small talk. To do a person in means to kill them.

MRS EYNSFORD HILL. [*to Eliza, horrified*] You surely dont believe that your aunt was killed?

LIZA. Do I not! Them she lived with would have killed her for a hat-pin, let alone a hat.

MRS EYNSFORD HILL. But it cant have been right for your father to pour spirits down her throat like that. It might have killed her.

LIZA. Not her. Gin was mother's milk to her. Besides, he'd poured so much down his own throat that he knew the good of it.

MRS EYNSFORD HILL. Do you mean that he drank?

LIZA. Drank! My word! Something chronic.

MRS EYNSFORD HILL. How dreadful for you!

LIZA. Not a bit. It never did him no harm what I could see. But then he did not keep it up regular. [*Cheerfully*] On the burst, as you might say, from time to time. And always more agreeable when he had a drop in. When he was out of work, my mother used to give him fourpence and tell him to go out and not come back until he'd drunk himself cheerful and loving-like. Theres lots of women has to make their husbands drunk to make them fit to live with. [*Now quite at her ease*] You see, it's like this. If a man has a bit of a conscience, it always takes him when he's sober; and then it makes him low-spirited. A drop of booze just takes that off and makes him happy. [*To Freddy, who is in convulsions of suppressed laughter*]. Here! what are you sniggering at?

FREDDY. The new small talk. You do it so awfully well.

LIZA. If I was doing it proper, what was you laughing at? [*To Higgins*] Have I said anything I oughtnt?

MRS HIGGINS. [*interposing*] Not at all, Miss Doolittle.

LIZA. Well, thats a mercy, anyhow. [*Expansively*] What I always say is—

HIGGINS. [*rising and looking at his watch*] Ahem!

LIZA. [*looking round at him; taking the hint; and rising*] Well: I must go. [*They all rise. Freddy goes to the door*]. So pleased to have met you. Goodbye. [*She shakes hands with Mrs Higgins*].

MRS HIGGINS. Goodbye.

LIZA. Goodbye, Colonel Pickering.

PICKERING. Goodbye, Miss Doolittle. [*They shake hands*].

LIZA. [*nodding to the others*] Goodbye, all.

FREDDY. [*opening the door for her*] Are you walking across the Park, Miss Doolittle? If so—

LIZA. [*perfectly elegant diction*] Walk! Not bloody likely. [*Sensation*]. I am going in a taxi. [*She goes out*].

[*Pickering gasps and sits down. Freddy goes out on the balcony to catch another glimpse of Eliza.*]

MRS EYNSFORD HILL. [*suffering from shock*] Well, I really cant get used to the new ways.

CLARA. [*throwing herself discontentedly into the Elizabethan chair*] Oh, it's all right, mamma, quite right. People will think we never go anywhere or see anybody if you are so old-fashioned.

MRS EYNSFORD HILL. I daresay I am very old-fashioned; but I do hope you wont begin using that expression, Clara. I have got accustomed to hear you talking about men as rotters, and calling everything filthy and beastly; though I do think it horrible and unladylike. But this last is really too much. Dont you think so, Colonel Pickering?

PICKERING. Dont ask me. Ive been away in India for several years; and manners have changed so much that I sometimes dont know whether I'm at a respectable dinner-table or in a ship's forecastle.

CLARA. It's all a matter of habit. Theres no right or wrong in it. Nobody means anything by it. And it's so quaint, and gives such a smart emphasis to things that are not in themselves very witty. I find the new small talk delightful and quite innocent.

MRS EYNSFORD HILL. [*rising*] Well, after that, I think it's time for us to go.

[*Pickering and Higgins rise*].

CLARA. [*rising*] Oh yes: we have three at-homes to go to still. Goodbye, Mrs Higgins. Goodbye, Colonel Pickering. Goodbye, Professor Higgins.

HIGGINS. [*coming grimly at her from the divan, and accompanying her to the door*] Goodbye. Be sure you try on that small talk at the three at-homes. Dont be nervous about it. Pitch it in strong.

CLARA. [*all smiles*] I will. Goodbye. Such nonsense, all this early Victorian prudery!

HIGGINS. [*tempting her*] Such damned nonsense!

CLARA. Such bloody nonsense!

MRS EYNSFORD HILL. [*convulsively*] Clara!

CLARA. Ha! ha! [*She goes out radiant, conscious of being thoroughly up to date, and is heard descending the stairs in a stream of silvery laughter*].

FREDDY. [*to the heavens at large*] Well, I ask you—[*He gives it up, and comes to Mrs Higgins*]. Goodbye.

MRS HIGGINS. [*shaking hands*] Goodbye. Would you like to meet Miss Doolittle again?

FREDDY. [*eagerly*] Yes, I should, most awfully.

MRS HIGGINS. Well, you know my days.

FREDDY. Yes. Thanks awfully. Goodbye. [*He goes out*].

MRS EYNSFORD HILL. Goodbye, Mr Higgins.

HIGGINS. Goodbye. Goodbye.

MRS EYNSFORD HILL. [*to Pickering*] It's no use. I shall never be able to bring myself to use that word.

PICKERING. Dont. It's not compulsory, you know. Youll get on quite well without it.

MRS EYNSFORD HILL. Only, Clara is so down on me if I am not positively reeking with the latest slang. Goodbye.

PICKERING. Goodbye.

[*They shake hands*].

MRS EYNSFORD HILL. [*to Mrs Higgins*] You mustnt mind Clara. [*Pickering, catching from her lowered tone that this is not meant for him to hear, discreetly joins Higgins at the window*]. We're so poor! And she gets so few parties, poor child! She doesnt quite know. [*Mrs Higgins, seeing that her eyes are moist, takes her hand sympathetically and goes with her to the door*]. But the boy is nice. Dont you think so?

MRS HIGGINS. Oh, quite nice. I shall always be delighted to see him.

MRS EYNSFORD HILL. Thank you, dear. Goodbye. [*She goes out*].

HIGGINS. [*eagerly*] Well? Is Eliza presentable [*He swoops on his mother and drags her to the ottoman, where she sits down in Eliza's place with her son on her left*]?

[*Pickering returns to his chair on her right.*]

MRS HIGGINS. You silly boy, of course she's not presentable. She's a triumph of your art and of her dressmaker's; but if you suppose for a moment that she doesn't give herself away in every sentence she utters, you must be perfectly cracked about her.

PICKERING. But dont you think something might be done? I mean something to eliminate the sanguinary element from her conversation.

MRS HIGGINS. Not as long as she is in Henry's hands.

HIGGINS. [*aggrieved*] Do you mean that my language is improper?

MRS HIGGINS. No, dearest: it would be quite proper—say on a canal barge; but it would not be proper for her at a garden party.

HIGGINS. [*deeply injured*] Well I must say—

PICKERING. [*interrupting him*] Come, Higgins: you must learn to know yourself. I havnt heard such language as yours since we used to review the volunteers in Hyde Park twenty years ago.

HIGGINS. [*sulkily*] Oh, well, if you say so. I suppose I dont always talk like a bishop.

MRS HIGGINS. [*quieting Henry with a touch*] Colonel

Pickering: will you tell me what is the exact state of things in Wimpole Street?

PICKERING. [*cheerfully: as if this completely changed the subject*] Well, I have come to live there with Henry. We work together at my Indian Dialects; and we think it more convenient—

MRS HIGGINS. Quite so. I know all about that: it's an excellent arrangement. But where does this girl live?

HIGGINS. With us, of course. Where should she live?

MRS HIGGINS. But on what terms? Is she a servant? If not, what is she?

PICKERING. [*slowly*] I think I know what you mean, Mrs Higgins.

HIGGINS. Well, dash me if *I* do! Ive had to work at the girl every day for months to get her to her present pitch. Besides, she's useful. She knows where my things are, and remembers my appointments and so forth.

MRS HIGGINS. How does your housekeeper get on with her?

HIGGINS. Mrs Pearce? Oh, she's jolly glad to get so much taken off her hands; for before Eliza came, she used to have to find things and remind me of my appointments. But she's got some silly bee in her bonnet about Eliza. She keeps saying 'You dont think, sir': doesnt she, Pick?

PICKERING. Yes: that the formula. 'You dont think, sir.' Thats the end of every conversation about Eliza.

HIGGINS. As if I ever stop thinking about the girl and her confounded vowels and consonants. I'm worn out, thinking about her, and watching her lips and her teeth and her tongue, not to mention her soul, which is the quaintest of the lot.

MRS HIGGINS. You certainly are a pretty pair of babies, playing with your live doll.

HIGGINS. Playing! The hardest job I ever tackled: make no mistake about that, mother. But you have no idea how frightfully interesting it is to take a human being and change her into a quite different human being by creating a new speech for her. It's filling up the deepest gulf that separates class from class and soul from soul.

PICKERING. [*drawing his chair closer to Mrs Higgins and bending over to her eagerly*] Yes: it's enormously interesting. I assure you, Mrs Higgins, we take Eliza very seriously. Every week—every day almost—there is some new change. [*Closer again*] We keep records of every stage—dozens of gramophone disks and photographs—

HIGGINS. [*assailing her at the other ear*] Yes, by George: it's the most absorbing experiment I ever tackled. She regularly fills our lives up: doesnt she, Pick?

PICKERING. We're always talking Eliza.

HIGGINS. Teaching Eliza.

PICKERING. Dressing Eliza.

MRS HIGGINS. What!

HIGGINS. Inventing new Elizas.

[*speaking together*]

HIGGINS. You know, she has the most extraordinary quickness of ear:

PICKERING. I assure you, my dear Mrs Higgins, that girl

HIGGINS. just like a parrot. Ive tried her with every

PICKERING. is a genius. She can play the piano quite beautifully.

HIGGINS. possible sort of sound that a human being can make—

PICKERING. We have taken her to classical concerts and to music

HIGGINS. Continental dialects, African dialects, Hottentot

PICKERING. halls; and it's all the same to her: she plays everything

HIGGINS. clicks, things it took me years to get hold of; and

PICKERING. she hears right off when she comes home, whether it's

HIGGINS. she picks them up like a shot, right away, as if she had

PICKERING. Beethoven and Brahms or Lehar and Lionel Monckton:

HIGGINS. been at it all her life.

PICKERING. though six months ago, she'd never as much as touched a piano—

MRS HIGGINS. [*putting her fingers in her ears, as they are by this time shouting one another down with an intolerable noise*] Sh-sh-sh-sh!

[*They stop*].

PICKERING. I beg your pardon. [*He draws his chair back apologetically*].

HIGGINS. Sorry. When Pickering starts shouting nobody can get a word in edgeways.

MRS HIGGINS. Be quiet, Henry. Colonel Pickering: dont you realize that when Eliza walked into Wimpole Street, something walked in with her?

PICKERING. Her father did. But Henry soon got rid of him.

MRS HIGGINS. It would have been more to the point

if her mother had. But as her mother didnt something else did.

PICKERING. But what?

MRS HIGGINS. [*unconsciously dating herself by the word*] A problem.

PICKERING. Oh I see. The problem of how to pass her off as a lady.

HIGGINS. I'll solve that problem. Ive half solved it already.

MRS HIGGINS. No, you two infinitely stupid male creatures: the problem of what is to be done with her afterwards.

HIGGINS. I dont see anything in that. She can go her own way, with all the advantages I have given her.

MRS HIGGINS. The advantages of that poor woman who was here just now! The manners and habits that disqualify a fine lady from earning her own living without giving her a fine lady's income! Is that what you mean?

PICKERING. [*indulgently, being rather bored*] Oh, that will be all right, Mrs Higgins. [*He rises to go*].

HIGGINS. [*rising also*] We'll find her some light employment.

PICKERING. She's happy enough. Dont you worry about her. Goodbye. [*He shakes hands as if he were consoling a frightened child, and makes for the door*].

HIGGINS. Anyhow, theres no good bothering now. The thing's done. Goodbye, mother. [*He kisses her, and follows Pickering*].

PICKERING. [*turning for a final consolation*] There are plenty of openings. We'll do whats right. Goodbye.

HIGGINS. [*to Pickering as they go out together*] Lets take her to the Shakespear exhibition at Earls Court.

PICKERING. Yes: lets. Her remarks will be delicious.

HIGGINS. She'll mimic all the people for us when we get home.

PICKERING. Ripping. [*Both are heard laughing as they go downstairs*].

MRS HIGGINS. [*rises with an impatient bounce, and returns to her work at the writing-table. She sweeps a litter of disarranged papers out of the way; snatches a sheet of paper from her stationery case; and tries resolutely to write. At the third time she gives it up; flings down her pen; grips the table angrily and exclaims*] Oh, men! men! men!!!

Clearly Eliza will not pass as a duchess yet; and Higgins's bet remains unwon. But the six months are not yet exhausted; and just in time Eliza does actually pass as a princess. For a glimpse of how she did it imagine an Embassy in London one summer evening after dark. The hall door has an awning and a carpet across the sidewalk to the kerb, because a grand reception is in progress. A small crowd is lined up to see the guests arrive.

A Rolls-Royce car drives up. Pickering in evening dress, with medals and orders, alights, and hands out Eliza, in opera cloak, evening dress, diamonds, fan, flowers and all accessories. Higgins follows. The car drives off; and the three go up the steps and into the house, the door opening for them as they approach.

Inside the house they find themselves in a spacious hall from which the grand staircase rises. On the left are the arrangements for the gentlemen's cloaks. The male guests are depositing their hats and wraps there.

On the right is a door leading to the ladies' cloakroom. Ladies are going in cloaked and coming out in splendor. Pickering whispers to Eliza and points out the ladies' room. She goes into it. Higgins and Pickering take off their overcoats and take tickets for them from the attendant.

One of the guests, occupied in the same way, has his back turned. Having taken his ticket, he turns round and reveals himself as in important looking young man with an astonishingly hairy face. He has an enormous moustache, flowing out into luxuriant whiskers. Waves of hair cluster on his brow. His hair is cropped closely at the back, and glows with oil. Otherwise he is very smart. He wears several worthless orders. He is evidently a foreigner, guessable as a whiskered Pandour from Hungary; but in spite of the ferocity of his moustache he is amiable and genially voluble.

Recognizing Higgins, he flings his arms wide apart and approaches him enthusiastically.

WHISKERS. Maestro, maestro [*he embraces Higgins and kisses him on both cheeks*]. You remember me?

HIGGINS. No I dont. Who the devil are you?

WHISKERS. I am your pupil: your first pupil, your best and greatest pupil. I am little Nepommuck, the marvellous boy. I have made your name famous throughout Europe. You teach me phonetic. You cannot forget ME.

HIGGINS. Why dont you shave?

NEPOMMUCK. I have not your imposing appearance, your chin, your brow. Nobody notices me when I shave. Now I am famous: they call me Hairy Faced Dick.

HIGGINS. And what are you doing here among all these swells?

NEPOMMUCK. I am interpreter. I speak 32 languages. I am indispensable at these international parties. You

are great cockney specialist: you place a man anywhere in London the moment he open his mouth. I
place any man in Europe.

[*A footman hurries down the grand staircase and comes to
Nepommuck.*]

FOOTMAN. You are wanted upstairs. Her Excellency
cannot understand the Greek gentleman.

NEPOMMUCK. Thank you, yes, immediately. [*The footman goes and is lost in the crowd.*]

NEPOMMUCK. [*To Higgins*] This Greek diplomatist pretends he cannot speak nor understand English. He
cannot deceive me. He is the son of a Clerkenwell
watchmaker. He speaks English so villainously that
he dare not utter a word of it without betraying his
origin. I help him to pretend; but I make him pay
through the nose. I make them all pay. Ha ha! [*He
hurries upstairs*].

PICKERING. Is this fellow really an expert? Can he find
out Eliza and blackmail her?

HIGGINS. We shall see. If he finds her out I lose my
bet.

[*Eliza comes from the cloakroom and joins them.*]

PICKERING. Well, Eliza, now for it. Are you ready?

LIZA. Are you nervous, Colonel?

PICKERING. Frightfully. I feel exactly as I felt before
my first battle. It's the first time that frightens.

LIZA. It is not the first time for me, Colonel. I have
done this fifty times—hundreds of times—in my
little piggery in Angel Court in my day-dreams. I am
in a dream now. Promise me not to let Professor
Higgins wake me; for if he does I shall forget every
thing and talk as I used to in Drury Lane.

PICKERING. Not a word, Higgins. [*To Eliza*] Now
ready?

LIZA. Ready.

PICKERING. Go.

[*They mount the stairs, Higgins last. Pickering whispers to
the footman on the first landing.*]

FIRST LANDING FOOTMAN. Miss Doolittle, Colonel
Pickering, Professor Higgins.

SECOND LANDING FOOTMAN. Miss Doolittle, Colonel Pickering, Professor Higgins.

[*At the top of the staircase the Ambassador and his wife,
with Nepommuck at her elbow, are receiving.*]

HOSTESS. [*taking Eliza's hand*] How d'ye do?

HOST. [*same play*] How d'ye do? How d'ye do, Pickering.

LIZA. [*with a beautiful gravity that awes her hostess*] How
do you do? [*She passes on to the drawing room*].

HOSTESS. Is that your adopted daughter, Colonel
Pickering? She will make a sensation.

PICKERING. Most kind of you to invite her for me. [*He
passes on*].

HOSTESS. [*to Nepommuck*] Find out all about her.

NEPOMMUCK. [*bowing*] Excellency—[*he goes into the
crowd*].

HOST. How d'ye do, Higgins? You have a rival here
tonight. He introduced himself as your pupil. Is he
any good?

HIGGINS. He can learn a language in a fortnight—
knows dozens of them. A sure mark of a fool. As a
phonetician, no good whatever.

HOSTESS. How d'ye do, Professor?

HIGGINS. How do you do? Fearful bore for you this
sort of thing. Forgive my part in it. [*He passes on*].

In the drawing room and its suite of salons the reception is in full swing. Eliza passes through. She is so
intent on her ordeal that she walks like a somnambul-
ist in a desert instead of a débutante in a fashionable
crowd. They stop talking to look at her, admiring her
dress, her jewels, and her strangely attractive self.
Some of the younger ones at the back stand on their
chairs to see.

The Host and Hostess come in from the staircase
and mingle with their guests. Higgins, gloomy and
contemptuous of the whole business, comes into the
group where they are chatting.

HOSTESS. Ah, here is Professor Higgins: he will tell us
Tell us all about the wonderful young lady, Professor.

HIGGINS. [*almost morosely*] What wonderful young
lady?

HOSTESS. You know very well. They tell me there has
been nothing like her in London since people stood
on their chairs to look at Mrs Langtry.

[*Nepommuck joins the group, full of news*].

HOSTESS. Ah, here you are at last, Nepommuck. Have
you found out all about the Doolittle lady?

NEPOMMUCK. I have found out all about here. She is
a fraud.

HOSTESS. A fraud! Oh no.

NEPOMMUCK. YES, yes, She cannot deceive me. Her
name cannot be Doolittle.

HIGGINS. Why?

NEPOMMUCK. Because Doolittle is an English name. And she is not English.

HOSTESS. Oh, nonsense! She speaks English perfectly.

NEPOMMUCK. Too perfectly. Can you shew me any English woman who speaks English as it should be spoken? Only foreigners who have been taught to speak it speak it well.

HOSTESS. Certainly she terrified me by the way she said How d'ye do. I had a schoolmistress who talked like that; and I was mortally afraid of her. But if she is not English what is she?

NEPOMMUCK. Hungarian.

ALL THE REST. Hungarian!

NEPOMMUCK. Hungarian. And of royal blood. I am Hungarian. My blood is royal.

HIGGINS. Did you speak to her in Hungarian?

NEPOMMUCK. I did. She was very clever. She said 'Please speak to me in English: I do not understand French.' French! She pretends not to know the difference between Hungarian and French. Impossible: she knows both.

HIGGINS. And the blood royal? How did you find that out?

NEPOMMUCK. Instinct, maestro, instinct. Only the Magyar races can produce that air of the divine right, those resolute eyes. She is a princess.

HOST. What do you say, Professor?

HIGGINS. I say an ordinary London girl out of the gutter and taught to speak by an expert. I place her in Drury Lane.

NEPOMMUCK. Ha ha ha! Oh, maestro, maestro, you are mad on the subject of cockney dialects. The London gutter is the whole world for you.

HIGGINS. [to the Hostess] What does your Excellency say?

HOSTESS. Oh, of course I agree with Nepommuck. She must be a princess at least.

HOST. Not necessarily legitimate, of course. Morganatic perhaps. But that is undoubtedly her class.

HIGGINS. I stick to my opinion.

HOSTESS. Oh, you are incorrigible.

[*The groups breaks up, leaving Higgins isolated. Pickering joins him.*]

PICKERING. Where is Eliza? We must keep an eye on her.

[*Eliza joins them.*]

LIZA. I dont think I can bear much more. The people all stare so at me. An old lady has just told me that I speak exactly like Queen Victoria. I am sorry if I have lost your bet. I have done my best; but nothing can make me the same as these people.

PICKERING. You have not lost it, dear. You have won it ten times over.

HIGGINS. Let us get out of this. I have had enough of chattering to these fools.

PICKERING. Eliza is tired; and I am hungry. Let us clear out and have supper somewhere.

Act IV

The Wimpole Street laboratory. Midnight. Nobody in the room. The clock on the mantelpiece strikes twelve. The fire is not alight: it is a summer night.

Presently Higgins and Pickering are heard on the stairs.

HIGGINS. [*calling down to Pickering*] I say, Pick: lock up, will you? I shant be going out again.

PICKERING. Right. Can Mrs Pearce go to bed? We dont want anything more, do we?

HIGGINS. Lord, no!

[*Eliza opens the door and is seen on the lighted landing in all the finery in which she has just won Higgins's bet for him. She comes to the hearth, and switches on the electric lights there. She is tired: her pallor contrasts strongly with her dark eyes and hair; and her expression is almost tragic. She takes off her cloak; puts her fan and gloves on the piano; and sits down on the bench, brooding and silent. Higgins, in evening dress, with overcoat and hat, comes in, carrying a smoking jacket which he has picked up downstairs. He takes off the hat and overcoat; throws them carelessly on the newspaper stand; disposes of his coat in the same way; puts on the smoking jacket; and throws himself wearily into the easy-chair at the hearth. Pickering, similarly attired, comes*] *in. He also takes off his hat and overcoat, and is about to throw them on Higgins's when he hesitates.]*

PICKERING. I say: Mrs Pearce will row if we leave these things lying about in the drawing room.

HIGGINS. Oh, chuck them over the bannisters into the hall. She'll find them there in the morning and put them away all right. She'll think we were drunk.

PICKERING. We are, slightly. Are there any letters?

HIGGINS. I didnt look. *[Pickering takes the overcoats and hats and goes downstairs. Higgins begins half singing half yawning an air from La Fanciulla del Golden West. Suddenly he stops and exclaims]* I wonder where the devil my slippers are!

[Eliza looks at him darkly; then rises suddenly and leaves the room.

Higgins yawns again, and resumes his song.

Pickering returns, with the contents of the letterbox in his hand.]

PICKERING. Only circulars, and this coroneted billet-doux for you. *[He throws the circulars into the fender, and posts himself on the hearthrug, with his back to the grate].*

HIGGINS. *[glancing at the billet-doux]* Money-lender. *[He throws the letter after the circulars].*

[Eliza returns with a pair of large down-at-heel slippers. She places them on the carpet before Higgins, and sits as before without a word.]

HIGGINS. *[yawning again]* Oh Lord! What an evening! What a crew! What a silly tomfoolery! *[He raises his shoe to unlace it, and catches sight of the slippers. He stops unlacing and looks at them as if they had appeared there of their own accord].* Oh! theyre there, are they?

PICKERING. *[stretching himself]* Well, I feel a bit tired. it's been a long day. The garden party, a dinner party, and the reception! Rather too much of a good thing. But youve won your bet, Higgins. Eliza did the trick, and something to spare, eh?

HIGGINS. *[fervently]* Thank God it's over!

[Eliza flinches violently; but they take no notice of her; and she recovers herself and sits stonily as before.]

PICKERING. Were you nervous at the garden party? *I* was. Eliza didnt seem a bit nervous.

HIGGINS. Oh, she wasnt nervous. I knew she'd be all right. No: it's the strain of putting the job through all these months that has told on me. It was interest-

ing enough at first, while we were at the phonetics; but after that I got deadly sick of it. If I hadnt backed myself to do it I should have chucked the whole thing up two months ago. It was a silly notion: the whole thing has been a bore.

PICKERING. Oh come! the garden party was frightfully exciting. My heart began beating like anything.

HIGGINS. Yes, for the first three minutes. But when I saw we were going to win hands down, I felt like a bear in a cage, hanging about doing nothing. The dinner was worse: sitting gorging there for over an hour, with nobody but a damned fool of a fashionable woman to talk to! I tell you, Pickering, never again for me. No more artificial duchesses. The whole thing has been simple purgatory.

PICKERING. Youve never been broken in properly to the social routine. *[Strolling over to the piano]* I rather enjoy dipping into it occasionally myself: it makes me feel young again. Anyhow, it was a great success: an immense success. I was quite frightened once or twice because Eliza was doing it so well. You see, lots of the real people cant do it at all: theyre such fools that they think style comes by nature to people in their position; and so they never learn. Theres always something professional about doing a thing superlatively well.

HIGGINS. Yes: thats what drives me mad: the silly people dont know their own silly business. *[Rising]* However, it's over and done with; and now I can go to bed at last without dreading tomorrow.

[Eliza's beauty becomes murderous].

PICKERING. I think I shall turn in. Still, it's been a great occasion: a triumph for you. Goodnight. *[He goes].*

HIGGINS. *[following him]* Goodnight. *[Over his shoulder, at the door]* Put out the lights, Eliza; and tell Mrs Pearce not to make coffee for me in the morning: I'll take tea. *[He goes out].*

[Eliza tries to control herself and feel indifferent as she rises and walks across to the hearth to switch off the lights. By the time she gets there she is on the point of screaming. She sits down in Higgins's chair and holds on hard to the arms. Finally she gives way and flings herself furiously on the floor, raging].

HIGGINS. *[in despairing wrath outside]* What the devil have I done with my slippers? *[He appears at the door].*

LIZA. *[snatching up the slippers, and hurling them at him*

one after the other with all her force] There are your
slippers. And there. Take your slippers; and may you
never have a day's luck with them!

HIGGINS. [*astounded*] What on earth—! [*He comes to
her*]. Whats the matter? Get up. [*He pulls her up*].
Anything wrong?

LIZA. [*breathless*] Nothing wrong—with you. Ive won
your bet for you, havnt I? Thats enough for you. *I*
dont matter, I suppose.

HIGGINS. You won my bet! You! Presumptuous
insect! *I* won it. What did you throw those slippers
at me for?

LIZA. Because I wanted to smash your face. I'd like to
kill you, you selfish brute. Why didnt you leave me
where you picked me out of—in the gutter? You
thank God it's all over, and that now you can throw
me back again there, do you? [*She crisps her fingers
frantically*].

HIGGINS. [*looking at her in cool wonder*] The creature is
nervous, after all.

LIZA. [*gives a suffocated scream of fury, and instinctively
darts her nails at his face*]!!

HIGGINS. [*catching her wrists*] Ah! would you? Claws in,
you cat. How dare you shew your temper to me? Sit
down and be quiet. [*He throws her roughly into the
easy-chair*].

LIZA. [*crushed by superior strength and weight*] Whats to
become of me? Whats to become of me?

HIGGINS. How the devil do I know whats to become
of you? What does it matter what becomes of you?

LIZA. You dont care. I know you dont care. You
wouldnt care if I was dead. I'm nothing to you—
not so much as them slippers.

HIGGINS. [*thundering*] Those slippers.

LIZA. [*with bitter submission*] Those slippers. I didnt
think it made any difference now.

[*A pause. Eliza hopeless and crushed. Higgins a little
uneasy.*]

HIGGINS. [*in his loftiest manner*] Why have you begun
going on like this? May I ask whether you complain
of your treatment here?

LIZA. No.

HIGGINS. Has anybody behaved badly to you? Colonel Pickering? Mrs Pearce? Any of the servants?

LIZA. No.

HIGGINS. I presume you dont pretend that *I* have
treated you badly?

LIZA. No.

HIGGINS. I am glad to hear of it. [*He moderates his
tone*]. Perhaps youre tired after the strain of the day.
Will you have a glass of champagne? [*He moves
towards the door*].

LIZA. No. [*Recollecting her manner*] Thank you.

HIGGINS. [*good-humored again*] This has been coming
on you for some days. I suppose it was natural for
you to be anxious about the garden party. But thats
all over now. [*He pats her kindly on the shoulder. She
writhes*]. Theres nothing more to worry about.

LIZA. No. Nothing more for you to worry about. [*She
suddenly rises and gets away from him by going to the
piano bench, where she sits and hides her face*]. Oh
God! I wish I was dead.

HIGGINS. [*staring after her in sincere surprise*] Why? In
heaven's name, why? [*Reasonably, going to her*] Listen
to me, Eliza. All this irritation is purely subjective.

LIZA. I dont understand. I'm too ignorant.

HIGGINS. It's only imagination. Low spirits and nothing else. Nobody's hurting you. Nothing's wrong.
You go to bed like a good girl and sleep it off. Have
a little cry and say your prayers: that will make you
comfortable.

LIZA. I heard your prayers. 'Thank God it's all over!'

HIGGINS. [*impatiently*] Well, dont you thank God it's
all over? Now you are free and can do what you like.

LIZA. [*pulling herself together in desperation*] What am I
fit for? What have you left me fit for? Where am I to
go? What am I to do? Whats to become of me?

HIGGINS. [*enlightened, but not at all impressed*] Oh, thats
what worrying you, is it? [*He thrusts his hands into his
pockets, and walks about in his usual manner, rattling the
contents of his pockets, as if condescending to a trivial
subject out of pure kindness*]. I shouldnt bother about
it if I were you. I should imagine you wont have
much difficulty in settling yourself somewhere or
other, though I hadnt quite realized that you were
going away. [*She looks quickly at him: he does not look
at her, but examines the dessert stand on the piano and
decides that he will eat an apple*]. You might marry,
you know. [*He bites a large piece out of the apple and
munches it noisily*]. You see, Eliza, all men are not
confirmed old bachelors like me and the Colonel.
Most men are the marrying sort (poor devils!); and
youre not bad-looking: it's quite a pleasure to look
at you sometimes—not now, of course, because
youre crying and looking as ugly as the very devil;
but when youre all right and quite yourself, youre
what I should call attractive. That is, to the people
in the marrying line, you understand. You go to bed

and have a good nice rest; and then get up and look at yourself in the glass; and you wont feel so cheap.

[*Eliza again looks at him, speechless, and does not stir.*
The look is quite lost on him: he eats his apple with a dreamy expression of happiness, as it is quite a good one.]

HIGGINS. [*a genial afterthought occurring to him*] I daresay my mother could find some chap or other who would do very well.

LIZA. We were above that at the corner of Tottenham Court Road.

HIGGINS. [*waking up*] What do you mean?

LIZA. I sold flowers. I didnt sell myself. Now youve made a lady of me I'm not fit to sell anything else. I wish youd left me where you found me.

HIGGINS. [*slinging the core of the apple decisively into the grate*] Tosh, Eliza. Dont you insult human relations by dragging all this cant about buying and selling into it. You neednt marry the fellow if you dont like him.

LIZA. What else am I to do?

HIGGINS. Oh, lots of things. What about your old idea of a florist's shop? Pickering could set you up in one: he has lots of money. [*Chuckling*] He'll have to pay for all those togs you have been wearing today; and that, with the hire of the jewellery, will make a big hole in two hundred pounds. Why, six months ago you would have thought it the millennium to have a flower shop of your own. Come! youll be all right. I must clear off to bed: I'm devilish sleepy. By the way, I came down for something: I forget what it was.

LIZA. Your slippers.

HIGGINS. Oh yes, of course. You shied them at me. [*He picks them up, and is going out when she rises and speaks to him*].

LIZA. Before you go, sir—

HIGGINS. [*dropping the slippers in his surprise at her calling him Sir*] Eh?

LIZA. Do my clothes belong to me or to Colonel Pickering?

HIGGINS. [*coming back into the room as if her question were the very climax of unreason*] What the devil use would they be to Pickering?

LIZA. He might want them for the next girl you pick up to experiment on.

HIGGINS. [*shocked and hurt*] Is that the way you feel towards us?

LIZA. I dont want to hear anything more about that.

All I want to know is whether anything belongs to me. My own clothes were burnt.

HIGGINS. But what does it matter? Why need you start bothering about that in the middle of the night?

LIZA. I want to know what I may take away with me. I dont want to be accused of stealing.

HIGGINS. [*now deeply wounded*] Stealing! You shouldnt have said that, Eliza. That shews a want of feeling.

LIZA. I'm sorry. I'm only a common ignorant girl; and in my station I have to be careful. There cant be any feelings between the like of you and the like of me. Please will you tell me what belongs to me and what doesnt?

HIGGINS. [*very sulky*] You may take the whole damned houseful if you like. Except the jewels. Theyre hired. Will that satisfy you? [*He turns on his heel and is about to go in extreme dudgeon*].

LIZA. [*drinking in his emotion like nectar, and nagging him to provoke a further supply*] Stop, please. [*She takes off her jewels*]. Will you take these to your room and keep them safe? I dont want to run the risk of their being missing.

HIGGINS. [*furious*] Hand them over. [*She puts them into his hands*]. If these belonged to me instead of to the jeweller, I'd ram them down your ungrateful throat. [*He perfunctorily thrusts them into his pockets, unconsciously decorating himself with the protruding ends of the chains*].

LIZA. [*taking a ring off*] This ring isnt the jeweller's: it's the one you bought me in Brighton. I dont want it now. [*Higgins dashes the ring violently into the fireplace, and turns on her so threateningly that she crouches over the piano with her hands over her face, and exclaims*] Dont you hit me.

HIGGINS. Hit you! You infamous creature, how dare you accuse me of such a thing? It is you who have hit me. You have wounded me to the heart.

LIZA. [*thrilling with hidden joy*] I'm glad. I've got a little of my own back, anyhow.

HIGGINS. [*with dignity, in his finest professional style*] You have caused me to lose my temper: a thing that has hardly ever happened to me before. I prefer to say nothing more tonight. I am going to bed.

LIZA. [*pertly*] Youd better leave a note for Mrs Pearce about the coffee; for she wont be told by me.

HIGGINS. [*formally*] Damn Mrs Pearce; and damn the coffee; and damn you; and [*wildly*] damn my own folly in having lavished my hard-earned knowledge and the treasure of my regard and intimacy on a heartless guttersnipe. [*He goes out with impressive decorum, and spoils it by slamming the door savagely*].

[*Eliza goes down on her knees on the hearthrug to look for the ring. When she finds it she considers for a moment what to do with it. Finally she flings it down on the dessert stand and goes upstairs in a tearing rage*].

[*The furniture of Eliza's room has been increased by a big wardrobe and a sumptuous dressing-table. She comes in and switches on the electric light. She goes to the wardrobe; opens it; and pulls out a walking dress, a hat, and a pair of shoes, which she throws on the bed. She takes off her evening dress and shoes: then takes a padded hanger from the wardrobe; adjusts it carefully in the evening dress; and hangs it in the wardrobe, which she shuts with a slam. She puts on her walking shoes, her walking dress, and hat. She takes her wrist watch from the dressing-table and fastens it on. She pulls on her gloves; takes her vanity bag; and looks into it to see that her purse is there before hanging it on her wrist. She makes for the door. Every movement expresses her furious resolution.*

She takes a last look at herself in the glass.

She suddenly puts out her tongue at herself; then leaves the room, switching off the electric light at the door.

Meanwhile, in the street outside, Freddy Eynsford Hill, lovelorn, is gazing up at the second floor, in which one of the windows is still lighted.

The lights goes out.]

FREDDY. Goodnight, darling, darling, darling.

[*Eliza comes out, giving the door a considerable bang behind her*].

LIZA. Whatever are you doing here?

FREDDY. Nothing. I spend most of my nights here. It's the only place where I'm happy. Dont laugh at me, Miss Doolittle.

LIZA. Dont you call me Miss Doolittle, do you hear? Liza's good enough for me. [*She breaks down and grabs him by the shoulders*] Freddy: you dont think I'm a heartless guttersnipe, do you?

FREDDY. Oh no, no, darling: how can you imagine such a thing? You are the loveliest, dearest—

[*He loses all self-control and smothers her with kisses. She, hungry for comfort, responds. They stand there in one another's arms.*

An elderly police constable arrives].

CONSTABLE. [*scandalized*] Now then! Now then!! Now then!!!

[*They release one another hastily*].

FREDDY. Sorry, constable. Weve only just become engaged.

[*They run away*].

The constable shakes his head, reflecting on his own courtship and on the vanity of human hopes. He moves off in the opposite direction with slow professional steps.

The flight of the lovers takes them to Cavendish Square. There they halt to consider their next move.

LIZA. [*out of breath*] He didnt half give me a fright, that copper. But you answered him proper.

FREDDY. I hope I havnt taken you out of your way. Where were you going?

LIZA. To the river.

FREDDY. What for?

LIZA. To make a hole in it.

FREDDY. [*horrified*] Eliza, darling. What do you mean? What's the matter?

LIZA. Never mind. It doesnt matter now. Theres nobody in the world now but you and me, is there?

FREDDY. Not a soul.

[*They indulge in another embrace, and are again surprised by a much younger constable*].

SECOND CONSTABLE. Now then, you two! What's this? Where do you think you are? Move along here, double quick.

FREDDY. As you say, sir, double quick.

They run away again, and are in Hanover Square before they stop for another conference.

FREDDY. I had no idea the police were so devilishly prudish.

LIZA. It's their business to hunt girls off the streets.

FREDDY. We must go somewhere. We cant wander about the streets all night.

LIZA. Cant we? I think it'd be lovely to wander about forever.

FREDDY. Oh, darling.

[*They embrace again, oblivious of the arrival of a crawling taxi. It stops*].

TAXIMAN. Can I drive you and the lady anywhere, sir?

[*They start asunder*].

LIZA. Oh, Freddy, a taxi. The very thing.

FREDDY. But, damn it, Ive no money.

LIZA. I have plenty. The Colonel thinks you should never go out without ten pounds in your pocket. Listen. We'll drive about all night; and in the morning I'll call on old Mrs Higgins and ask her what I ought to do. I'll tell you all about it in the cab. And the police wont touch us there.

FREDDY. Righto!   Ripping.   [To the Taximan] Wimbledon Common. [They drive off].

Act V

Mrs Higgins's drawing room. She is at her writing-table as before. The parlormaid comes in.

THE PARLORMAID. [at the door] Mr Henry, maam, is downstairs with Colonel Pickering.

MRS HIGGINS. Well, shew them up.

THE PARLORMAID. Theyre using the telephone, maam. Telephoning to the police, I think.

MRS HIGGINS. What!

THE PARLORMAID. [coming further in and lowering her voice] Mr Henry is in a state, maam. I thought I'd better tell you.

MRS HIGGINS. If you had told me that Mr Henry was not in a state it would have been more surprising. Tell them to come up when theyve finished with the police. I suppose he's lost something.

THE PARLORMAID. Yes, maam [going].

MRS HIGGINS. Go upstairs and tell Miss Doolittle that Mr Henry and the Colonel are here. Ask her not to come down til I send for her.

THE PARLORMAID. Yes, maam.

[Higgins bursts in. He is, as the parlormaid has said, in a state].

HIGGINS. Look here, mother: heres a confounded thing!

MRS HIGGINS. Yes, dear. Good morning. [He checks his impatience and kisses her, whilst the parlormaid goes out]. What is it?

HIGGINS. Eliza's bolted.

MRS HIGGINS. [calmly continuing her writing] You must have frightened her.

HIGGINS. Frightened her! nonsense! She was left last night, as usual, to turn out the lights and all that; and instead of going to bed she changed her clothes and went right off: her bed wasnt slept in. She came in a cab for her things before seven this morning; and that fool Mrs Pearce let her have them without telling me a word about it. What am I to do?

MRS HIGGINS. Do without, I'm afraid, Henry. The girl has a perfect right to leave if she chooses.

HIGGINS. [wandering distractedly across the room] But I cant find anything. I dont know what appointments Ive got. I'm— [Pickering comes in. Mrs Higgins puts down her pen and turns away from the writing-table].

PICKERING. [shaking hands] Good morning, Mrs Higgins. Has Henry told you? [He sits down on the ottoman].

HIGGINS. What does that ass of an inspector say? Have you offered a reward?

MRS HIGGINS. [rising in indignant amazement] You dont mean to say you have set the police after Eliza?

HIGGINS. Of course. What are the police for? What else could we do? [He sits in the Elizabethan chair].

PICKERING. The inspector made a lot of difficulties. I really think he suspected us of some improper purpose.

MRS HIGGINS. Well, of course he did. What right have you to go to the police and give the girl's name as if she were a thief, or a lost umbrella, or something? Really! [She sits down again, deeply vexed].

HIGGINS. But we want to find her.

PICKERING. We cant let her go like this, you know, Mrs Higgins. What were we to do?

MRS HIGGINS. You have no more sense, either of you, than two children. Why—

[The parlormaid comes in and breaks off the conversation].

THE PARLORMAID. Mr Henry: a gentleman wants to see you very particular. He's been sent on from Wimpole Street.

HIGGINS. Oh, bother! I cant see anyone now. Who is it?

THE PARLORMAID. A Mr Doolittle, sir.

PICKERING. Doolittle! Do you mean the dustman?

THE PARLORMAID. Dustman! Oh no, sir: a gentleman.

HIGGINS. [*springing up excitedly*] By George, Pick, it's some relative of hers that she's gone to. Somebody we know nothing about. [*To the parlormaid*] Send him up, quick.

THE PARLORMAID. Yes, sir. [*She goes*].

HIGGINS. [*eagerly, going to his mother*] Genteel relatives! now we shall hear something. [*He sits down in the Chippendale chair*].

MRS HIGGINS. Do you know any of her people?

PICKERING. Only her father: the fellow we told you about.

THE PARLORMAID. [*announcing*] Mr Doolittle. [*She withdraws*].

[*Doolittle enters. He is resplendently dressed as for a fashionable wedding, and might, in fact, be the bridegroom. A flower in his buttonhole, a dazzling silk hat, and patent leather shoes complete the effect. He is too concerned with the business he has come on to notice Mrs Higgins. He walks straight to Higgins, and accosts him with vehement reproach*].

DOOLITTLE. [*indicating his own person*] See here! Do you see this? You done this.

HIGGINS. Done what, man?

DOOLITTLE. This, I tell you. Look at it. Look at this hat. Look at this coat.

PICKERING. Has Eliza been buying you clothes?

DOOLITTLE. Eliza! not she. Why would she buy me clothes?

MRS HIGGINS. Good morning, Mr Doolittle. Wont you sit down?

DOOLITTLE. [*taken aback as he becomes conscious that he has forgotten his hostess*] Asking your pardon, maam. [*He approaches her and shakes her proffered hand*]. Thank you. [*He sits down on the ottoman, on Pickering's right*]. I am that full of what has happened to me that I cant think of anything else.

HIGGINS. What the dickens has happened to you?

DOOLITTLE. I shouldnt mind if it had only happened to me: anything might happen to anybody and nobody to blame but Providence, as you might say. But this is something that you done to me: yes, you, Enry Iggins.

HIGGINS. Have you found Eliza?

DOOLITTLE. Have you lost her?

HIGGINS. Yes.

DOOLITTLE. You have all the luck, you have. I aint found her; but she'll find me quick enough now after what you done to me.

MRS HIGGINS. But what has my son done to you, Mr Doolittle?

DOOLITTLE. Done to me! Ruined me. Destroyed my happiness. Tied me up and delivered me into the hands of middle class morality.

HIGGINS. [*rising intolerantly and standing over Doolittle*] Youre raving. Youre drunk. Youre mad. I gave you five pounds. After that I had two conversations with you, at half-a-crown an hour. I've never seen you since.

DOOLITTLE. Oh! Drunk am I? Mad am I? Tell me this. Did you or did you not write a letter to an old blighter in America that was giving five millions to found Moral Reform Societies all over the world, and that wanted you to invent a universal language for him?

HIGGINS. What! Ezra D. Wannafeller! He's dead. [*He sits down again carelessly*].

DOOLITTLE. Yes: he's dead; and I'm done for. Now did you or did you not write a letter to him to say that the most original moralist at present in England, to the best of your knowledge, was Alfred Doolittle, a common dustman?

HIGGINS. Oh, after your first visit I remember making some silly joke of the kind.

DOOLITTLE. Ah! You may well call it a silly joke. It put the lid on me right enough. Just give him the chance he wanted to shew that Americans is not like us: that they reckonize and respect merit in every class of life, however humble. Them words is in his blooming will, in which, Henry Higgins, thanks to your silly joking, he leaves me a share in his Pre-digested Cheese Trust worth three thousand a year on condition that I lecture for his Wannafeller Moral Reform World League as often as they ask me up to six times a year.

HIGGINS. The devil he does! Whew! [*Brightening suddenly*] What a lark!

PICKERING. A safe thing for you, Doolittle. They wont ask you twice.

DOOLITTLE. It aint the lecturing I mind. I'll lecture them blue in the face, I will, and not turn a hair. It's making a gentleman of me that I object to. Who asked him to make a gentleman of me? I was happy. I was free. I touched pretty nigh everybody for money when I wanted it, same as I touched you, Enry Iggins. Now I am worrited; tied neck and heels; and everybody touches me for money. It's a fine thing for you, says my solicitor. Is it? says I. You mean it's a good thing for you, I says. When I was a poor man and had a solicitor once when they found a pram in the dust cart, he got me off, and got shut of me and got me shut of him as quick as he could. Same with the doctors: used to shove me out of the hospital before I could hardly stand on my legs, and nothing to pay. Now they finds out that I'm not a healthy man and cant live unless they looks after me twice a day. In the house I'm not let do a hand's turn for myself: somebody else must do it and touch me for it. A year ago I hadnt a relative in the world except two or three that wouldnt speak to me. Now Ive fifty, and not a decent week's wages among the lot of them. I have to live for others and not for myself: thats middle class morality. You talk of losing Eliza. Dont you be anxious: I bet she's on my doorstep by this: she that could support herself easy be selling flowers if I wasnt respectable. And the next one to touch me will be you, Enry Iggins. I'll have to learn to speak middle class language from you, instead of speaking proper English. Thats where youll come in; and I daresay thats what you done it for.

MRS HIGGINS. But, my dear Mr Doolittle, you need not suffer all this if you are really in earnest. Nobody can force you to accept this bequest. You can repudiate it. Isnt that so, Colonel Pickering?

PICKERING. I believe so.

DOOLITTLE. [*softening his manner in deference to her sex*] Thats the tragedy of it, maam. It's easy to say chuck it; but I havnt the nerve. Which of us has? We're all intimidated. Intimidated, maam; thats what we are. What is there for me if I chuck it but the workhouse in my old age? I have to dye my hair already to keep my job as a dustman. If I was one of the deserving poor, and had put by a bit, I could chuck it; but then why should I, acause the deserving poor might as well be millionaires for all the happiness they ever has. They dont know what happiness is. But I, as one of the undeserving poor, have nothing between me and the pauper's uniform but this here blasted three thousand a year that shoves me into the middle class. (Excuse the expression, maam; youd use it yourself if you had my provocation.) Theyve got you every way you turn: it's a choice between the Skilly of the workhouse and the Char Bydis of the middle class; and I havnt the nerve for the workhouse. Intimidated: thats what I am. Broke. Bought up. Happier men than me will call for my dust, and touch me for their tip; and I'll look on helpless, and envy them. And thats what your son has brought me to. [*He is overcome by emotion*].

MRS HIGGINS. Well, I'm very glad youre not going to do anything foolish, Mr Doolittle. For this solves the problem of Eliza's future. You can provide for her now.

DOOLITTLE. [*with melancholy resignation*] Yes, maam: I'm expected to provide for everyone now, out of three thousand a year.

HIGGINS. [*jumping up*] Nonsense! he cant provide for her. He shant provide for her. She doesnt belong to him. I paid him five pounds for her. Doolittle: either youre an honest man or a rogue.

DOOLITTLE. [*tolerantly*] A little of both, Henry, like the rest of us: a little of both.

HIGGINS. Well, you took that money for the girl; and you have no right to take her as well.

MRS HIGGINS. Henry: dont be absurd. If you want to know where Eliza is, she is upstairs.

HIGGINS. [*amazed*] Upstairs!!! Then I shall jolly soon fetch her downstairs. [*He makes resolutely for the door*].

MRS HIGGINS. [*rising and following him*] Be quiet, Henry. Sit down.

HIGGINS. I—

MRS HIGGINS. Sit down, dear; and listen to me.

HIGGINS. Oh very well, very well, very well. [*He throws himself ungraciously on the ottoman, with his face towards the windows*]. But I think you might have told us this half an hour ago.

MRS HIGGINS. Eliza came to me this morning. She told me of the brutal way you two treated her.

HIGGINS. [*bouncing up again*] What!

PICKERING. [*rising also*] My dear Mrs Higgins, she's been telling you stories. We didnt treat her brutally. We hardly said a word to her; and we parted on particularly good terms. [*Turning on Higgins*] Higgins: did you bully her after I went to bed?

HIGGINS. Just the other way about. She threw my slippers in my face. She behaved in the most outrageous way. I never gave her the slightest provocation. The slippers came bang into my face the moment I entered the room—before I had uttered a word. And used perfectly awful language.

PICKERING. [*astonished*] But why? What did we do to her?

MRS HIGGINS. I think I know pretty well what you did. The girl is naturally rather affectionate, I think. Isnt she, Mr Doolittle?

DOOLITTLE. Very tender-hearted, maam. Takes after me.

MRS HIGGINS. Just so. She had become attached to you both. She worked very hard for you, Henry. I dont think you quite realize what anything in the nature of brain work means to a girl of her class. Well, it seems that when the great day of trial came, and she did this wonderful thing for you without making a single mistake, you two sat there and never said a word to her, but talked together of how glad you were that it was all over and how you had been bored with the whole thing. And then you were surprised because she threw your slippers at you! *I* should have thrown the fire-irons at you.

HIGGINS. We said nothing except that we were tired and wanted to go to bed. Did we, Pick?

PICKERING. [*shrugging his shoulders*] That was all.

MRS HIGGINS. [*ironically*] Quite sure?

PICKERING. Absolutely. Really, that was all.

MRS HIGGINS. You didnt thank her, or pet her, or admire her, or tell her how splendid she'd been.

HIGGINS. [*impatiently*] But she knew all about that. We didnt make speeches for her, if thats what you mean.

PICKERING. [*conscience stricken*] Perhaps we were a little inconsiderate. Is she very angry?

MRS HIGGINS. [*returning to her place at the writing-table*] Well, I'm afraid she wont go back to Wimpole Street, especially now that Mr Doolittle is able to keep up the position you have thrust on her; but she says she is quite willing to meet you on friendly terms and to let bygones be bygones.

HIGGINS. [*furious*] Is she, by George? Ho!

MRS HIGGINS. If you promise to behave yourself, Henry. I'll ask her to come down. If not, go home; for you have taken up quite enough of my time.

HIGGINS. Oh, all right. Very well. Pick: you behave yourself. Let us put on our best Sunday manners for this creature that we picked out of the mud. [*He flings himself sulkily into the Elizabethan chair*].

DOOLITTLE. [*remonstrating*] Now, now, Enry Iggins! Have some consideration for my feelings as a middle class man.

MRS HIGGINS. Remember your promise, Henry. [*She presses the bell-button on the writing-table*]. Mr Doolittle: will you be so good as to step out on the balcony for a moment. I dont want Eliza to have the shock of your news until she has made it up with these two gentlemen. Would you mind?

DOOLITTLE. As you wish, lady. Anything to help Henry to keep her off my hands. [*He disappears through the window*].

[*The parlormaid answers the bell. Pickering sits down in Doolittle's place*].

MRS HIGGINS. Ask Miss Doolittle to come down, please.

THE PARLORMAID. Yes, maam. [*She goes out*].

MRS HIGGINS. Now, Henry: be good.

HIGGINS. I am behaving myself perfectly.

PICKERING. He is doing his best, Mrs Higgins.

[*A pause. Higgins throws back his head; stretches out his legs; and begins to whistle*].

MRS HIGGINS. Henry, dearest, you dont look at all nice in that attitude.

HIGGINS. [*pulling himself together*] I was not trying to look nice, mother.

MRS HIGGINS. It doesnt matter, dear. I only wanted to make you speak.

HIGGINS. Why?

MRS HIGGINS. Because you cant speak and whistle at the same time.

[*Higgins groans. Another very trying pause*].

HIGGINS. [*springing up, out of patience*] Where the devil is that girl? Are we to wait here all day?

[*Eliza enters, sunny, self-possessed, and giving a staggeringly convincing exhibition of ease of manner. She carries a little work-basket, and is very much at home. Pickering is too much taken aback to rise*].

LIZA. How do you do, Professor Higgins? Are you quite well?

HIGGINS. [*choking*] Am I— [*He can say no more*].

LIZA. But of course you are: you are never ill. So glad to see you again, Colonel Pickering. [*He rises hastily; and they shake hands*]. Quite chilly this morning, isnt it? [*She sits down on his left. He sits beside her*].

HIGGINS. Dont you dare try this game on me. I taught it to you; and it doesnt take me in. Get up and come home; and dont be a fool.

[*Eliza takes a piece of needlework from her basket, and begins to stitch at it, without taking the least notice of this outburst*].

MRS HIGGINS. Very nicely put, indeed, Henry. No woman could resist such an invitation.

HIGGINS. You let her alone, mother. Let her speak for herself. You will jolly soon see whether she has an idea that I havnt put into her head or a word that I havnt put into her mouth. I tell you I have created this thing out of the squashed cabbage leaves of Covent Garden; and now she pretends to play the fine lady with me.

MRS HIGGINS. [*placidly*] Yes, dear; but youll sit down, wont you?

[*Higgins sits down again, savagely*].

LIZA. [*to Pickering, taking no apparent notice of Higgins, and working away deftly*] Will you drop me altogether now that the experiment is over, Colonel Pickering?

PICKERING. Oh dont. You mustnt think of it as an experiment. It shocks me, somehow.

LIZA. Oh, I'm only a squashed cabbage leaf—

PICKING. [*impulsively*] No.

LIZA. [*continuing quietly*] —but I owe so much to you that I should be very unhappy if you forgot me.

PICKERING. It's very kind of you to say so, Miss Doolittle.

LIZA. It's not because you paid for my dresses. I know you are generous to everybody with money. But it was from you that I learnt really nice manners; and that is what makes one a lady, isnt it? You see it was so very difficult for me with the example of Professor Higgins always before me. I was brought up to be just like him, unable to control myself, and using bad language on the slightest provocation. And I should never have known that ladies and gentlemen didnt behave like that if you hadnt been there.

HIGGINS. Well!!

PICKERING. Oh, thats only his way, you know. He doesn't mean it.

LIZA. Oh, *I* didnt mean it either, when I was a flower girl. It was only my way. But you see I did it; and thats what makes the difference after all.

PICKERING. No doubt. Still, he taught you to speak; and I couldnt have done that, you know.

LIZA. [*trivially*] Of course: that is his profession.

HIGGINS. Damnation!

LIZA. [*continuing*] It was just like learning to dance in the fashionable way: there was nothing more than that in it. But do you know what began my real education?

PICKERING. What?

LIZA. [*stopping her work for a moment*] Your calling me Miss Doolittle that day when I first came to Wimpole Street. That was the beginning of self-respect for me. [*She resumes her stitching*]. And there were a hundred little things you never noticed, because they came naturally to you. Things about standing up and taking off your hat and opening doors—

PICKERING. Oh, that was nothing.

LIZA. Yes: things that shewed you thought and felt about me as if I were something better than a scullery-maid: though of course I know you would have been just the same to a scullery-maid if she had been let into the drawing room. You never took off your boots in the dining room when I was there.

PICKERING. You mustnt mind that. Higgins takes off his boots all over the place.

LIZA. I know. I am not blaming him. It is his way, isnt it? But it made such a difference to me that you didnt do it. You see, really and truly, apart from the things anyone can pick up (the dressing and the proper way of speaking, and so on), the difference between a lady and a flower girl is not how she behaves, but how she's treated. I shall always be a flower girl to Professor Higgins, because he always treats me as a flower girl, and always will; but I know I can be a lady to you, because you always treat me as a lady, and always will.

MRS HIGGINS. Please dont grind your teeth, Henry.

PICKERING. Well, this is really very nice of you, Miss Doolittle.

LIZA. I should like you to call me Eliza, now, if you would.

PICKERING. Thank you, Eliza, of course.

LIZA. And I should like Professor Higgins to call me Miss Doolittle.

HIGGINS. I'll see you damned first.

MRS HIGGINS. Henry! Henry!

PICKERING. [*laughing*] Why dont you slang back at him? Dont stand it. It would do him a lot of good.

LIZA. I cant. I could have done it once but now I cant go back to it. You told me, you know, that when a child is brought to a foreign country, it picks up the language in a few weeks, and forgets its own. Well, I am a child in your country. I have forgotten my own language, and can speak nothing but yours. Thats the real break-off with the corner of Tottenham Court Road. Leaving Wimpole Street finishes it.

PICKERING. [*much alarmed*] Oh! but youre coming back to Wimpole Street, arnt you? Youll forgive Higgins?

HIGGINS. [*rising*] Forgive! Will she, by George! Let her go. Let her find out how she can get on without us. She will relapse into the gutter in three weeks without me at her elbow.

[*Doolittle appears at the centre window. With a look of dignified reproach at Higgins, he comes slowly and silently to his daughter, who, with her back to the window, is unconscious of his approach.*]

PICKERING. He's incorrigible, Eliza. You wont relapse, will you?

LIZA. No: not now. Never again. I have learnt my lesson. I dont believe I could utter one of the old sounds if I tried. [*Doolittle touches her on her left shoulder. She drops her work, losing her self-possession utterly at the spectacle of her father's splendor*] A-a-a-a-a-ah-ow-ooh!

HIGGINS. [*with a crow of triumph*] Aha! Just so. A-a-a-a-ahowooh! A-a-a-a-ahowooh! A-a-a-a-ahowooh! Victory! Victory! [*He throws himself on the divan, folding his arms, and spraddling arrogantly*].

DOOLITTLE. Can you blame the girl? Dont look at me like that, Eliza. It aint my fault. Ive come into some money.

LIZA. You must have touched a millionaire this time, dad.

DOOLITTLE. I have. But I'm dressed something special today. I'm going to St George's, Hanover Square. Your stepmother is going to marry me.

LIZA. [*angrily*] Youre going to let yourself down to marry that low common woman!

PICKERING. [*quietly*] He ought to, Eliza. [*To Doolittle*] Why has she changed her mind?

DOOLITTLE. [*sadly*] Intimidated, Governor. Intimidated. Middle class morality claims its victim. Wont you put on your hat, Liza, and come and see me turned off?

LIZA. If the Colonel says I must, I—I'll [*almost sobbing*] I'll demean myself. And get insulted for my pains, like enough.

DOOLITTLE. Dont be afraid: she never comes to words with anyone now, poor woman! respectability has broke all the spirit out of her.

PICKERING. [*squeezing Eliza's elbow gently*] Be kind to them, Eliza. Make the best of it.

LIZA. [*forcing a little smile for him through her vexation*] Oh well, just to shew theres no ill feeling. I'll be back in a moment. [*She goes out*].

DOOLITTLE. [*sitting down beside Pickering*] I feel uncommon nervous about the ceremony, Colonel. I wish youd come and see me through it.

PICKERING. But youve been through it before, man. You were married to Eliza's mother.

DOOLITTLE. Who told you that, Colonel?

PICKERING. Well, nobody told me. But I concluded—naturally—

DOOLITTLE. No: that aint the natural way, Colonel: it's only the middle class way. My way was always the undeserving way. But dont say nothing to Eliza. She dont know: I always had a delicacy about telling her.

PICKERING. Quite right. We'll leave it so, if you dont mind.

DOOLITTLE. And youll come to the church, Colonel, and put me through straight?

PICKERING. With pleasure. As far as a bachelor can.

MRS HIGGINS. May I come, Mr Doolittle? I should be very sorry to miss your wedding.

DOOLITTLE. I should indeed be honored by your condescension, maam; and my poor old woman would take it as a tremenjous compliment. She's been very low, thinking of the happy days that are no more.

MRS HIGGINS. [*rising*] I'll order the carriage and get ready. [*The men rise, except Higgins*]. I shant be more than fifteen minutes. [*As she goes to the door Eliza comes in, hatted and buttoning her gloves*]. I'm going to the church to see your father married, Eliza. You had better come in the brougham with me. Colonel Pickering can go on with the bridegroom.

[*Mrs Higgins goes out. Eliza comes to the middle of the room between the centre window and the ottoman. Pickering joins her*].

DOOLITTLE. Bridegroom! What a word! It makes a man realize his position, somehow. [*He takes up his hat and goes towards the door*].

PICKERING. Before I go, Eliza, do forgive Higgins and come back to us.

LIZA. I dont think dad would allow me. Would you, dad?

DOOLITTLE. [*sad but magnanimous*] They played you off very cunning, Eliza, them two sportsmen. If it had been only one of them, you could have nailed him. But you see, there was two; and one of them chaperoned the other, as you might say. [*To Pickering*] It was artful of you, Colonel: but I bear no malice: I should have done the same myself. I been the victim of one woman after another all my life, and I dont grudge you two getting the better of Liza. I shant interfere. It's time for us to go, Colonel. So long, Henry. See you in St George's, Eliza.[*He goes out*].

PICKERING. [*coaxing*] Do stay with us, Eliza. [*He follows Doolittle*].

[*Eliza goes out on the balcony to avoid being alone with Higgins. He rises and joins her there. She immediately comes back into the room and makes for the door; but he goes along the balcony quickly and gets his back to the door before she reaches it*].

HIGGINS. Well, Eliza, youve had a bit of your own back, as you call it. Have you had enough? and are you going to be reasonable? Or do you want any more?

LIZA. You want me back only to pick up your slippers and put up with your tempers and fetch and carry for you.

HIGGINS. I havnt said I wanted you back at all.

LIZA. Oh, indeed. Then what are we talking about?

HIGGINS. About you, not about me. If you come back I shall treat you just as I have always treated you. I cant change my nature; and I dont intend to change my manners. My manners are exactly the same as Colonel Pickering's.

LIZA. Thats not true. He treats a flower girl as if she was a duchess.

HIGGINS. And I treat a duchess as if she was a flower girl.

LIZA. I see. [*She turns away composedly, and sits on the ottoman, facing the window*]. The same to everybody.

HIGGINS. Just so.

LIZA. Like father.

HIGGINS. [*grinning, a little taken down*] Without accepting the comparison at all points, Eliza, it's quite true that your father is not a snob, and that he will be quite at home in any station of life to which his eccentric destiny may call him. [*Seriously*] The great secret, Eliza, is not having bad manners or good manners or any other particular sort of manners, but having the same manner for all human souls: in short, behaving as if you were in Heaven, where there are no third-class carriages, and one soul is as good as another.

LIZA. Amen. You are a born preacher.

HIGGINS. [*irritated*] The question is not whether I treat you rudely, but whether you ever heard me treat anyone else better.

LIZA. [*with sudden sincerity*] I dont care how you treat me. I dont mind your swearing at me. I shouldnt mind a black eye: Ive had one before this. But [*standing up and facing him*] I wont be passed over.

HIGGINS. Then get out of my way: for I wont stop for you. You talk about me as if I were a motor bus.

LIZA. So you are a motor bus: all bounce and go, and no consideration for anyone. But I can do without you: dont think I cant.

HIGGINS. I know you can. I told you you could.

LIZA. [*wounded, getting away from him to the other side of the ottoman with her face to the hearth*] I know you did, you brute. You wanted to get rid of me.

HIGGINS. Liar.

LIZA. Thank you. [*She sits down with dignity*].

HIGGINS. You never asked yourself, I suppose, whether *I* could do without you.

LIZA. [*earnestly*] Dont you try to get round me. Youll have to do without me.

HIGGINS. [*arrogant*] I can do without anybody. I have my own soul: my own spark of divine fire. But [*with sudden humility*] I shall miss you, Eliza. [*He sits down near her on the ottoman*]. I have learnt something from your idiotic notions: I confess that humbly and gratefully. And I have grown accustomed to your voice and appearance. I like them, rather.

LIZA. Well, you have both of them on your gramophone and in your book of photographs. When you feel lonely without me, you can turn the machine on. It's got no feelings to hurt.

HIGGINS. I cant turn your soul on. Leave me those feelings; and you can take away the voice and the face. They are not you.

LIZA. Oh, you are a devil. You can twist the heart in a girl as easy as some could twist her arms to hurt her. Mrs Pearce warned me. Time and again she has wanted to leave you; and you always got round her at the last minute. And you dont care a bit for her. And you dont care a bit for me.

HIGGINS. I care for life, for humanity; and you are a part of it that has come my way and been built into my house. What more can you or anyone ask?

LIZA. I wont care for anybody that doesnt care for me.

HIGGINS. Commercial principles, Eliza. Like [*reproducing her Covent Garden pronunciation with professional exactness*] s'yollin voylets [*selling violets*], isnt it?

LIZA. Dont sneer at me. It's mean to sneer at me.

HIGGINS. I have never sneered in my life. Sneering doesnt become either the human face or the human soul. I am expressing my righteous contempt for Commercialism. I dont and wont trade in affection. You call me a brute because you couldnt buy a claim on me by fetching my slippers and finding my spectacles. You were a fool: I think a woman fetching a man's slippers is a disgusting sight: did I ever fetch your slippers? I think a good deal more of you for throwing them in my face. No use slaving for me and then saying you want to be cared for: who cares for a slave? If you come back, come back for the sake of good fellowship; for youll get nothing else. Youve had a thousand times as much out of me as I have out of you; and if you dare to set up your little dog's tricks of fetching and carrying slippers against my creation of a Duchess Eliza, I'll slam the door in your silly face.

LIZA. What did you do it for if you didnt care for me?

HIGGINS. [*heartily*] Why, because it was my job.

LIZA. You never thought of the trouble it would make for me.

HIGGINS. Would the world ever have been made if its

maker had been afraid of making trouble? Making life means making trouble. Theres only one way of escaping trouble; and thats killing things. Cowards, you notice, are always shrieking to have troublesome people killed.

LIZA. I'm no preacher: I dont notice things like that. I notice that you dont notice me.

HIGGINS. [*jumping up and walking about intolerantly*] Eliza: youre an idiot. I waste the treasures of my Miltonic mind by spreading them before you. Once for all, understand that I go my way and do my work without caring twopence what happens to either of us. I am not intimidated, like your father and your stepmother. So you can come back or go to the devil: which you please.

LIZA. What am I to come back for?

HIGGINS. [*bouncing up on his knees on the ottoman and leaning over it to her*] For the fun of it. Thats why I took you on.

LIZA. [*with averted face*] And you may throw me out tomorrow if I dont do everything you want me to?

HIGGINS. Yes; and you may walk out tomorrow if I dont do everything you want me to.

LIZA. And live with my stepmother?

HIGGINS. Yes, or sell flowers.

LIZA. Oh! If I only could go back to my flower basket! I should be independent of both you and father and all the world! Why did you take my independence from me? Why did I give up? I'm a slave now, for all my fine clothes.

HIGGINS. Not a bit. I'll adopt you as my daughter and settle money on you if you like. Or would you rather marry Pickering?

LIZA. [*looking fiercely round at him*] I wouldnt marry you if you asked me; and youre nearer my age than what he is.

HIGGINS. [*gently*] Than he is: not 'than what he is'.

LIZA. [*losing her temper and rising*] I'll talk as I like. Youre not my teacher now.

HIGGINS. [*reflectively*] I dont suppose Pickering would, though. He's as confirmed an old bachelor as I am.

LIZA. Thats not what I want; and dont you think it. Ive always had chaps enough wanting me that way. Freddy Hill writes to me twice and three times a day, sheets and sheets.

HIGGINS. [*disagreeably surprised*] Damn his impudence! [*He recoils and find himself sitting on his heels*].

LIZA. He has a right to if he likes, poor lad. And he does love me.

HIGGINS. [*getting off the ottoman*] You have no right to encourage him.

LIZA. Every girl has a right to be loved.

HIGGINS. What! By fools like that?

LIZA. Freddy's not a fool. And if he's weak and poor and wants me, may be he'd make me happier than my betters that bully me and dont want me.

HIGGINS. Can he make anything of you? Thats the point.

LIZA. Perhaps I could make something of him. But I never thought of us making anything of one another; and you never think of anything else. I only want to be natural.

HIGGINS. In short, you want me to be as infatuated about you as Freddy? Is that it?

LIZA. No I dont. Thats not the sort of feeling I want from you. And dont you be too sure of yourself or of me. I could have been a bad girl if I'd liked. Ive seen more of some things than you, for all your learning. Girls like me can drag gentlemen down to make love to them easy enough. And they wish each other dead the next minute.

HIGGINS. Of course they do. Then what in thunder are we quarrelling about?

LIZA. [*much troubled*] I want a little kindness. I know I'm a common ignorant girl, and you a book-learned gentleman; but I'm not dirt under your feet. What I done [*correcting herself*] what I did was not for the dresses and the taxis: I did it because we were pleasant together and I come—came—to care for you; not to want you to make love to me, and not forgetting the difference between us, but more friendly like.

HIGGINS. Well, of course. Thats just how I feel. And how Pickering feels. Eliza: youre a fool.

LIZA. Thats not a proper answer to give me [*she sinks on the chair at the writing-table in tears*].

HIGGINS. It's all youll get until you stop being a common idiot. If youre going to be a lady, youll have to give up feeling neglected if the men you know dont spend half their time snivelling over you and the other half giving you black eyes. If you cant stand the coldness of my sort of life, and the strain of it, go back to the gutter. Work til youre more a brute than a human being; and then cuddle and squabble and drink til you fall asleep. Oh, it's a fine life, the life of the gutter. It's real: it's warm: it's violent: you can feel it through the thickest skin: you can taste it and smell it without any training or any work. Not like Science and Literature and Classical Music and Philosophy and Art. You find me cold, unfeeling, selfish, dont you? Very well: be off with you to the sort of people you like. Marry some sentimental hog or other with lots of money, and a thick pair of lips to kiss you with and a thick pair of boots to kick you with. If you cant appreciate what youve got, youd better get what you can appreciate.

LIZA. [*desperate*] Oh, you are a cruel tyrant. I cant talk to you: you turn everything against me: I'm always in the wrong. But you know very well all the time that youre nothing but a bully. You know I cant go back to the gutter, as you call it, and that I have no real friends in the world but you and the Colonel. You know well I couldnt bear to live with a low common man after you two; and it's wicked and cruel of you to insult me by pretending I could. You think I must go back to Wimpole Street because I have nowhere else to go but father's. But dont you be too sure that you have me under your feet to be trampled on and talked down. I'll marry Freddy, I will, as soon as I'm able to support him.

HIGGINS. [*thunderstruck*] Freddy!!! that young fool! That poor devil who couldnt get a job as an errand boy even if he had the guts to try for it! Woman: do you not understand that I have made you a consort for a king?

LIZA. Freddy loves me: that makes him king enough for me. I dont want him to work: he wasnt brought up to it as I was. I'll go and be a teacher.

HIGGINS. Whatll you teach, in heaven's name?

LIZA. What you taught me. I'll teach phonetics.

HIGGINS. Ha! ha! ha!

LIZA. I'll offer myself as an assistant to that hairyfaced Hungarian.

HIGGINS. [*rising in a fury*] What! That impostor! that humbug! that toadying ignoramus! Teach him my methods! my discoveries! You take one step in his direction and I'll wring your neck. [*He lays hands on her*]. Do you hear?

LIZA. [*defiantly non-resistant*] Wring away. What do I care? I knew youd strike me some day. [*He lets go, stamping with rage at having forgotten himself, and recoils so hastily that he stumbles back into his seat on the ottoman*]. Aha! Now I know how to deal with you. What a fool I was not to think of it before! You cant take away the knowledge you gave me. You said I had a finer ear than you. And I can be civil and kind to people, which is more than you can. Aha! [*Purposely dropping her aitches to annoy him*] Thats done you, Enry Iggins, it az. Now I dont care that [*snapping her fingers*] for your bullying and your big talk. I'll advertize it in the papers that your duchess is only a flower girl that you taught, and that she'll teach anybody to be a duchess just the same in six months for a thousand guineas. Oh, when I think of myself crawling under your feet and being trampled on and called names, when all the time I had only to

life up my finger to be as good as you, I could just kick myself.

HIGGINS. [*wondering at her*] You damned impudent slut, you! But it's better than snivelling: better than fetching slippers and finding spectacles, isnt it? [*Rising*] By George, Eliza, I said I'd make a woman of you; and I have. I like you like this.

LIZA. Yes: you can turn round and make up to me now that I'm not afraid of you, and can do without out.

HIGGINS. Of course I do, you little fool. Five minutes ago you were like a millstone round my neck. Now youre a tower of strength: a consort battleship. You and I and Pickering will be three old bachelors instead of only two men and a silly girl.

[*Mrs Higgins returns, dressed for the wedding. Eliza instantly becomes cool and elegant*].

MRS HIGGINS. The carriage is waiting, Eliza. Are you ready?

LIZA. Quite. Is the Professor coming?

MRS HIGGINS. Certainly not. He cant behave himself in church. He makes remarks out loud all the time on the clergyman's pronunciation.

LIZA. Then I shall not see you again, Professor. Goodbye. [*She goes to the door*].

MRS HIGGINS. [*coming to Higgins*] Goodbye, dear.

HIGGINS. Goodbye, mother. [*He is about to kiss her, when he recollects something*]. Oh, by the way, Eliza, order a ham and a Stilton cheese, will you? And buy me a pair of reindeer gloves, number eights, and a tie to match that new suit of mine. You can choose the color. [*His cheerful, careless, vigorous voice shews that he is incorrigible*].

LIZA. [*disdainfully*] Number eights are too small for you if you want them lined with lamb's wool. You have three new ties that you have forgotten in the drawer of your washstand. Colonel Pickering prefers double Gloucester to Stilton; and you dont notice the difference. I telephoned Mrs Pearce this morning not to forget the ham. What you are to do without me I cannot imagine. [*She sweeps out*].

MRS HIGGINS. I'm afraid youve spoilt that girl, Henry. I should be uneasy about you and her if she were less fond of Colonel Pickering.

HIGGINS. Pickering! Nonsense: she's going to marry Freddy. Ha ha! Freddy! Freddy!! Ha ha ha ha ha!!!!!

[*He roars with laughter as the play ends*].

ESSAY: AN APPROACH TO THE PLAY

One of this play's main concerns is the problem of social class. Liza, the lower-class working girl who is suddenly snatched up into a world of new middle-class possibility, is also taken from everything with which she is familiar. She is literally at the mercy of her so-called benefactor. She demonstrates the fact that what most lower- and middle-class people think they want, a change upward in social status, requires such a complete change in manners, taste, language, and custom that it is disorienting. The change is not comfortable, as one expects, but frightening and painful.

Further, by defining Liza's upward mobility primarily in terms of speech patterns and secondarily in terms of manners and dress, Shaw exposes social-class distinctions, particularly those of the aristocratic class, as merely the product of codes which can be learned. There is, in this view, nothing sacred or "right" about the person who is accidentally born into an aristocratic family, nor is there any fairness or justice in a social hierarchy based on inherited wealth and position— whose foundation is the family into which one is born. Liza's transformation exemplifies a bourgeois upward mobility which we on this side of the Atlantic associate with the traditional American Dream; *Pygmalion* implies criticism of this "dream" as well, for it reinforces both an unfortunate sense of social-class hierarchy and a superficial sense of how happiness is achieved.

The way in which Shaw undermined the conventional social assumptions of 1912 is also related to several other ideas which have strong resonance today. The relationship between speech patterns and class status has become particularly important to students of literature in the last decade or so. We have come to understand that groups of people maintain their exclusive status at the top of their hierarchies in large part by controlling the style of language which is deemed appropriate to that hierarchy. English professors typically require students to learn to speak and write about literature in a particular style, using a particular vocabulary, and showing mastery of a particular set of assumptions about what literature is and does. The same is true within their respective professions for lawyers, doctors, economists, and, of course, politicians. People (including students) are judged on the basis of what language they speak. You belong to a group or you do not based as much on the way you talk as on whether you are energetic, intelligent, and interested. Mastery of the *discourse* of a profession is what makes you seem to belong in it; knowledge and intelligence, if expressed in "unacceptable" ways, often do not achieve this status of belonging.

Shaw could not anticipate this contemporary interest in levels of discourse, but he himself had a special interest in language which allowed him to anticipate some of its main lines. Analogously, by having Higgins insist on his status as a scientist, and by having his scientific experiment cause Liza some distress, he raises another contemporary issue, this one about the role of experts, and especially scientific experts, in making decisions which involve human values and feelings. Higgins often seems insensitive to the effects of his experiment on his laboratory specimen, Liza, and his enthusiasm for his experiment is in itself inconsistent with the ideal of disinterested scientific objectivity. Experts get carried away, just as the rest of us, and when they do, they are not being "scientific." Indeed, the problem of "human error" is one of the things we most fear about the power of science. And as with

Higgins, the expert's claim to superior knowledge mystifies this problem. Such attitudes might even be considered analogous to those exhibited by members of one social class to members of another which the first considers "lower" in status.

If Shaw's criticism of middle-class and aristocratic values seems plausible, however, it is partly because he does not portray the depths of degradation and pain to which extreme poverty can bring a person. The alternative to being conventional seems, rather, to be portrayed by Liza's father, represented as a person who *prefers* poverty to becoming middle class and respectable. He delights in being one of the "undeserving poor," turning a conventional middle-class and aristocratic assumption to his own advantage. Instead of arguing what we might expect, that he is *not* undeserving, Mr. Doolittle asserts that he has vices—and enjoys them. In fact, to try to be "deserving" (respectable) would ruin the fun. He therefore insists on being amoral and undeserving so that he will owe no one anything. He asks for a handout, but he is not greedy (he fears that he might be corrupted into being sensible if he had enough money to save some), and he warns his potential benefactor in advance of how he will use it. One of the ironies of the ending, of course, is that he does get enough money and so laments what we might otherwise expect to be his happy ending. In this way, Shaw may be subtly subverting comedy's conventionally happy resolution.

Mr. Doolittle also points out that marriage—contrary to the prevailing notion of the time—is to the man's advantage, not the woman's. Liza's stepmother has been with him for a very long time, but she will not marry him because he would then no longer need to court her. Similarly, at the end of the play, Liza wants not marriage but independence. She carries on her family's traditions in her new class status, and she has learned far more than her creator anticipated. Higgins has indeed undermined the aristocracy to which he belongs. And if Liza comes close to embodying the wisdom of the play by its end, what of its title character, the artist Higgins? What does *he* want? Is he as emancipated as he thinks?

Anton Chekhov

THE CHERRY ORCHARD

Translated by Constance Garnett

About the Author   Anton Chekhov (1860–1904) lived in Russia during the time of the czars, before the Communist revolution ended their reign. Like the character Lopahin in *The Cherry Orchard*, Chekhov was the grandson of a serf, and also like that character, he demonstrated the possibility of social mobility after the freeing of the serfs in 1863, taking a degree in medicine in 1884. However, his medical practice was in continual competition with his writing, a competition which writing won in his later life. Although he wrote short stories and plays continuously during his adulthood, his first major success in the theater came just six years before his death, with *The Seagull* in 1898. Two more successes quickly followed (*Uncle Vanya* and *The Three Sisters*) before the great final play, *The Cherry Orchard*, appeared in the year he died. All four of these later plays were produced at the new Moscow Art Theater by Konstantin Stanislavski, the famous champion of a natural-seeming acting style which remains influential today.

About the Play   Writing for this naturalistic theater, Chekhov imitated ordinary life, and in this sense he was a realist. The details of life seem more important to him than a firm plot line or a clear generic or thematic purpose. Chekhov offers us a more complex world than can be neatly fit into categories or theories, a picture of society in miniature which exemplifies the complex ambiguity of the whole. Quite often, particular characters or speeches seem irrelevant to the main plot line; often, an apparently tragic character will seem funny, or even silly, and a silly character may say profoundly important things. Thus *The Cherry Orchard* is both comic and tragic, neither a comedy nor a tragedy but something larger, less controlled, and more full than either. His plays are unlike conventional plays which simplify life to suggest that the depths of a particular situation or issue or character can be quickly penetrated, or so that a profound insight can be presented. Truthfulness counts for more in Chekhov than theory or interpretation or "profundity."

CHARACTERS

MADAME RANEVSKY (LYUBOV ANDREYEV-NA), the owner of the Cherry Orchard

ANYA, her daughter, aged 17

VARYA, her adopted daughter, aged 24

GAEV (LEONID ANDREYEVITCH), brother of Madame Ravensky

LOPAHIN (YERMOLAY ALEXEYEVITCH), a Merchant

TROFIMOV (PYOTR SERGEYEVITCH), a Student

SEMYONOV-PISHTCHIK, a Landowner

CHARLOTTA IVANOVNA, a Governess

EPIHODOV (SEMYON PANTALEYEVITCH), a Clerk

DUNYASHA, a Maid

FIRS, an old Valet, aged 87

YASHA, a young Valet

A VAGRANT

THE STATION MASTER

A POST-OFFICE CLERK

VISITORS, SERVANTS

The action takes place on the estate of Madame Ranevsky.

Act I

A room, which has always been called the nursery. One of the doors leads into Anya's room. Dawn, sun rises during the scene. May, the cherry trees in flower, but it is cold in the garden with the frost of early morning. Windows closed.

[*Enter Dunyasha with a candle and Lopahin with a book in his hand.*]

LOPAHIN. The train's in, thank God. What time is it?

DUNYASHA. Nearly two o'clock [*puts out the candle*]. It's daylight already.

LOPAHIN. The train's late! Two hours, at least [*yawns and stretches*]. I'm a pretty one; what a fool I've been. Came here on purpose to meet them at the station and dropped asleep . . . . Dozed off as I sat in the chair. It's annoying . . . . You might have waked me.

DUNYASHA. I thought you had gone [*listens*]. There, I do believe they're coming!

LOPAHIN. [*listens*]. No, what with the luggage and one thing and another [*a pause*]. Lyubov Andreyevna has been abroad five years; I don't know what she is like now . . . . She's a splendid woman. A good-natured, kind-hearted woman. I remember when I was a lad of fifteen, my poor father—he used to keep a little shop here in the village in those days—gave me a punch in the face with his fist and made my nose bleed. We were in the yard here, I forget what we'd come about—he had had a drop. Lyubov Andreyevna—I can see her now—she was a slim young girl then—took me to wash my face, and then brought me into this very room, into the nursery. "Don't cry, little peasant," says she, "it will be well in time for your wedding day" . . . [*a pause*]. Little peasant. . . . My father was a peasant, it's true, but here am I in a white waistcoat and brown shoes, like a pig in a bun shop. Yes, I'm a rich man, but for all my money, come to think, a peasant I was, and a peasant I am [*turns over the pages of the book*]. I've been reading this book and I can't make head or tail of it. I feel asleep over it [*a pause*].

DUNYASHA. The dogs have been awake all night, they feel that the mistress is coming.

LOPAHIN. Why, what's the matter with you, Dunyasha?

DUNYASHA. My hands are all of a tremble. I feel as though I should faint.

LOPAHIN. You're a spoilt soft creature, Dunyasha. And dressed like a lady too, and your hair done up. That's not the thing. One must know one's place.

[*Enter Epihodov with a nosegay; he wears a pea-jacket and highly polished creaking topboots; he drops the nosegay as he comes in.*]

EPIHODOV. [*picking up the nosegay*]. Here! the gardener's sent this, says you're to put it in the dining-room [*gives Dunyasha the nosegay*].

LOPAHIN. And bring me some kvass.

DUNYASHA. I will [*goes out*].

EPIHODOV. It's chilly this morning, three degrees of frost, though the cherries are all in flower. I can't say much for our climate [*sighs*]. I can't. Our climate is not often propitious to the occasion. Yermolay Alexeyevitch, permit me to call your attention to the fact that I purchased myself a pair of boots the day before yesterday, and they creak, I venture to assure you, so that there's no tolerating them. What ought I to grease them with?

LOPAHIN. Oh, shut up! Don't bother me.

EPIHODOV. Every day some misfortune befalls me. I don't complain, I'm used to it, and I wear a smiling face.

[*Dunyasha comes in, hands Lopahin the kvass.*]

EPIHODOV. I am going [*stumbles against a chair, which falls over*]. There! [*as though triumphant*]. There you see now, excuse the expression, an accident like that among others . . . It's positively remarkable [*goes out*].

DUNYASHA. Do you know, Yermolay Alexeyevitch, I must confess, Epihodov has made me a proposal.

LOPAHIN. Ah!

DUNYASHA. I'm sure I don't know. . . . He's a harmless fellow, but sometimes when he begins talking, there's no making anything of it. It's all very fine and expressive, only there's no understanding it. I've a sort of liking for him too. He loves me to distraction. He's an unfortunate man; every day there's something. They tease him about it—two and twenty misfortunes they call him.

LOPAHIN. [*listening*]. There! I do believe they're coming.

DUNYASHA. They are coming! What's the matter with me? . . . I'm cold all over.

LOPAHIN. They really are coming. Let's go and meet them. Will she know me? It's five years since I saw her.

DUNYASHA. [*in a flutter*]. I shall drop this very minute . . . . Ah, I shall drop.

[*There is a sound of two carriages driving up to the house. Lopahin and Dunyasha go out quickly. The stage is left empty. A noise is heard in the adjoining rooms. Firs, who has driven to meet Madame Ranevsky, crosses the stage hurriedly leaning on a stick. He is wearing old-fashioned livery and a high hat. He says something to himself, but not a word can be distinguished. The noise behind the scenes goes on increasing. A voice: "Come, let's go in here." Enter Lyubov Andreyevna, Anya, and Charlotta Ivanovna with a pet dog on a chain, all in travelling dresses. Varya in an outdoor coat with a kerchief over her head, Gaev, Semyonov-Pishtchik, Lopahin, Dunyasha with bag and parasol, servants with other articles. All walk across the room.*]

ANYA. Let's come in here. Do you remember what room this is, mamma?

LYUBOV. [*joyfully, through her tears*]. The nursery!

VARYA. How cold it is, my hands are numb. [*To Lyubov Andreyevna*] Your rooms, the white room and the lavender one, are just the same as ever, mamma.

LYUBOV. My nursery, dear delightful room. . . . I used to sleep here when I was little . . . [*cries*]. And here I am, like a little child . . . [*kisses her brother and Varya, and then her brother again*]. Varya's just the same as ever, like a nun. And I knew Dunyasha [*kisses Dunyasha*].

GAEV. The train was two hours late. What do you think of that? Is that the way to do things?

CHARLOTTA. [*to Pishtchik*]. My dog eats nuts, too.

PISHTCHIK. [*wonderingly*]. Fancy that!

[*They all go out except Anya and Dunyasha.*]

DUNYASHA. We've been expecting you so long [*takes Anya's hat and coat*].

ANYA. I haven't slept for four nights on the journey. I feel dreadfully cold.

DUNYASHA. You set out in Lent, there was snow and frost, and now? My darling! [*laughs and kisses her*]. I *have* missed you, my precious, my joy. I must tell you . . . I can't put it off a minute. . . .

ANYA. [*wearily*] What now?

DUNYASHA. Epihodov, the clerk, made me a proposal just after Easter.

ANYA. It's always the same thing with you . . . [*straightening her hair*]. I've lost all my hairpins . . . [*she is staggering from exhaustion*].

DUNYASHA. I don't know what to think, really. He does love me, he does love me so!

ANYA. [*looking towards her door, tenderly*]. My own room, my windows just as though I had never gone away. I'm home! To-morrow morning I shall get up and run into the garden. . . . Oh, if I could get to sleep! I haven't slept all the journey, I was so anxious and worried.

DUNYASHA. Pyotr Sergeyevitch came the day before yesterday.

ANYA. [*joyfully*]. Petya!

DUNYASHA. He's asleep in the bath house, he has settled in there. I'm afraid of being in their way, says he. [*Glancing at her watch*] I was to have waked him, but Varvara Mihalovna told me not to. Don't you wake him, says she.

[*Enter Varya with a bunch of keys at her waist.*]

VARYA. Dunyasha, coffee and make haste. . . . Mamma's asking for coffee.

DUNYASHA. This very minute [*goes out*].

VARYA. Well, thank God, you've come. You're home again [*petting her*]. My little darling has come back! My precious beauty has come back again!

ANYA. I have had a time of it!

VARYA. I can fancy.

ANYA. We set off in Holy Week—it was so cold then, and all the way Charlotta would talk and show off her tricks. What did you want to burden me with Charlotta for?

VARYA. You couldn't have travelled all alone, darling. At seventeen!

ANYA. We got to Paris at last, it was cold there—snow. I speak French shockingly. Mamma lives on the fifth floor, I went up to her and there were a lot of French people, ladies, an old priest with a book. The place smelt of tobacco and so comfortless. I felt sorry, oh! so sorry for mamma all at once, I put my arms round her neck, and hugged her and wouldn't let her go. Mamma was as kind as she could be, and she cried. . . .

VARYA. [*through her tears*]. Don't speak of it, don't speak of it!

ANYA. She had sold her villa at Mentone, she had nothing left, nothing. I hadn't a farthing left either, we only just had enough to get here. And mamma doesn't understand! When we had dinner at the stations, she always ordered the most expensive things and gave the waiters a whole rouble. Charlotta's just the same. Yasha too must have the same as we do; it's simply awful. You know Yasha is mamma's valet now, we brought him here with us.

VARYA. Yes, I've seen the young rascal.

ANYA. Well, tell me—have you paid the arrears on the mortgage?

VARYA. How could we get the money?

ANYA. Oh, dear! Oh, dear!

VARYA. In August the place will be sold.

ANYA. My goodness!

LOPAHIN. [peeps in at the door and moo's like a cow]. Moo! [disappears].

VARYA. [weeping]. There, that's what I could do to him [shakes her fist].

ANYA. [embracing Varya, softly]. Varya, has he made you an offer? [Varya shakes her head.] Why, but he loves you. Why is it you don't come to an understanding? What are you waiting for?

VARYA. I believe that there never will be anything between us. He has a lot to do, he has no time for me . . . and takes no notice of me. Bless the man, it makes me miserable to see him. . . . Everyone's talking of our being married, everyone's congratulating me, and all the while there's really nothing in it; it's all like a dream. [In another tone] You have a new brooch like a bee.

ANYA. [mournfully]. Mamma bought it. [Goes into her own room and in a light-hearted childish tone] And you know, in Paris I went up in a balloon!

VARYA. My darling's home again! My pretty is home again!

[Dunyasha returns with the coffee-pot and is making the coffee.]

VARYA. [standing at the door]. All day long, darling, as I go about looking after the house, I keep dreaming all the time. If only we could marry you to a rich man, then I should feel more at rest. Then I would go off by myself on a pilgrimage to Kiev, to Moscow . . . and so I would spend my life going from one holy place to another. . . . I would go on and on. . . . What bliss!

ANYA. The birds are singing in the garden. What time is it?

VARYA. It must be nearly three. It's time you were asleep, darling [going into Anya's room]. What bliss!

[Yasha enters with a rug and a travelling bag.]

YASHA. [crosses the stage, mincingly]. May one come in here, pray?

DUNYASHA. I shouldn't have known you, Yasha. How you have changed abroad.

YASHA. H'm! . . . And who are you?

DUNYASHA. When you went away, I was that high

[shows distance from floor]. Dunyasha, Fyodor's daughter. . . . You don't remember me!

YASHA. H'm! . . . You're a peach! [Looks round and embraces her: she shrieks and drops a saucer. Yasha goes out hastily.]

VARYA. [in the doorway, in a tone of vexation]. What now?

DUNYASHA. [through her tears]. I have broken a saucer.

VARYA. Well, that brings good luck.

ANYA. [coming out of her room]. We ought to prepare mamma: Petya is here.

VARYA. I told them not to wake him.

ANYA. [dreamily]. It's six years since father died. Then only a month later little brother Grisha was drowned in the river, such a pretty boy he was, only seven. It was more than mamma could bear, so she went away, went away without looking back [shuddering]. . . . How well I understand her, if only she knew! [a pause!] And Petya Trofimov was Grisha's tutor, he may remind her.

[Enter Firs: he is wearing a pea-jacket and a white waistcoat.]

FIRS. [goes up to the coffee-pot, anxiously]. The mistress will be served here [puts on white gloves]. Is the coffee ready? [Sternly to Dunyasha] Girl! Where's the cream?

DUNYASHA. Ah, mercy on us! [goes out quickly].

FIRS. [fussing round the coffee-pot]. Ech! you good-for-nothing! [Muttering to himself] Come back from Paris. And the old master used to go to Paris too . . . horses all the way [laughs].

VARYA. What is it, Firs?

FIRS. What is your pleasure? [Gleefully] My lady has come home! I have lived to see her again! Now I can die [weeps with joy!].

[Enter Lyubov Andreyevna, Gaev and Semyonov-Pishtchik; the latter is in a short-waisted full coat of fine cloth, and full trousers. Gaev, as he comes in, makes a gesture with his arms and his whole body, as though he were playing billiards.]

LYUBOV. How does it go? Let me remember. Cannon off the red!

GAEV. That's it—in off the white! Why, once, sister, we used to sleep together in this very room, and now I'm fifty-one, strange as it seems.

LOPAHIN. Yes, time flies.

GAEV. What do you say?

LOPAHIN. Time, I say, flies.

GAEV. What a smell of patchouli!

ANYA. I'm going to bed. Good-night, mamma [kisses her mother].

LYUBOV. My precious darling [*kisses her hands*]. Are you glad to be home? I can't believe it.

ANYA. Good-night, uncle.

GAEV. [*kissing her face and hands*]. God bless you! How like you are to your mother! [*To his sister*] At her age you were just the same, Lyuba.

[*Anya shakes hands with Lopahin and Pishtchik, then goes out, shutting the door after her.*]

LYUBOV. She's quite worn out.

PISHTCHIK. Aye, it's a long journey, to be sure.

VARYA. [*to Lopahin and Pishtchik*]. Well, gentlemen? It's three o'clock and time to say good-bye.

LYUBOV. [*laughs*]. You're just the same as ever, Varya [*draws her to her and kisses her*]. I'll just drink my coffee and then we will all go and rest. [*Firs puts a cushion under her feet.*] Thanks, friend. I am so fond of coffee, I drink it day and night. Thanks, dear old man [*kisses Firs*].

VARYA. I'll just see whether all the things have been brought in [*goes out*].

LYUBOV. Can it really be me sitting here? [*laughs*]. I want to dance about and clap my hands. [*Covers her face with her hands*] And I could drop asleep in a moment! God knows I love my country, I love it tenderly; I couldn't look out of the window in the train, I kept crying so. [*Through her tears*] But I must drink my coffee, though. Thank you, Firs, thanks, dear old man. I'm so glad to find you still alive.

FIRS. The day before yesterday.

GAEV. He's rather deaf.

LOPAHIN. I have to set off for Harkov directly, at five o'clock. . . . It is annoying! I wanted to have a look at you, and a little talk. . . . You are just as splendid as ever.

PISHTCHIK. [*breathing heavily*]. Handsomer, indeed. . . . Dressed in Parisian style . . . completely bowled me over.

LOPAHIN. Your brother, Leonid Andreyevitch here, is always saying that I'm a low-born knave, that I'm a money-grubber, but I don't care one straw for that. Let him talk. Only I do want you to believe in me as you used to. I do want your wonderful tender eyes to look at me as they used to in the old days. Merciful God! My father was a serf of your father and of your grandfather, but you—you—did so much for me once, that I've forgotten all that; I love you as though you were my kin . . . more than my kin.

LYUBOV. I can't sit still, I simply can't . . . [*jumps up and walks about in violent agitation*]. This happiness is too much for me. . . . You may laugh at me, I know I'm silly. . . . My own bookcase [*kisses the bookcase*]. My little table.

GAEV. Nurse died while you were away.

LYUBOV. [*sits down and drinks coffee*]. Yes, the Kingdom of Heaven be hers! You wrote me of her death.

GAEV. And Anastasy is dead. Squinting Petruchka has left me and is in service now with the police captain in the town [*takes a box of caramels out of his pocket and sucks one*].

PISHTCHIK. My daughter, Dashenka, wishes to be remembered to you.

LOPAHIN. I want to tell you something very pleasant and cheering [*glancing at his watch*]. I'm going directly . . . there's no time to say much . . . well, I can say it in a couple of words. I needn't tell you your cherry orchard is to be sold to pay your debts; the 22nd of August is the date fixed for the sale; but don't you worry, dearest lady, you may sleep in peace, there is a way of saving it. . . . This is what I propose. I beg your attention! Your estate is not twenty miles from the town, the railway runs close by it, and if the cherry orchard and the land along the river bank were cut up into building plots and then let on lease for summer villas, you would make an income of at least 25,000 roubles a year out of it.

GAEV. That's all rot, if you'll excuse me.

LYUBOV. I don't quite understand you, Yermolay Alexeyevitch.

LOPAHIN. You will get a rent of at least 25 roubles a year for a three-acre plot from summer visitors, and if you say the word now, I'll bet you what you like there won't be one square foot of ground vacant by the autumn, all the plots will be taken up. I congratulate you; in fact, you are saved. It's a perfect situation with that deep river. Only, of course, it must be cleared—all the old buildings, for example, must be removed, this house too, which is really good for nothing and the old cherry orchard must be cut down.

LYUBOV. Cut down? My dear fellow, forgive me, but you don't know what you are talking about. If there is one thing interesting—remarkable indeed—in the whole province, it's just our cherry orchard.

LOPAHIN. The only thing remarkable about the orchard is that it's a very large one. There's a crop of cherries every alternate year, and then there's nothing to be done with them, no one buys them.

GAEV. This orchard is mentioned in the 'Encyclopædia.'

LOPAHIN. [*glancing at his watch*]. If we don't decide on something and don't take some steps, on the 22nd of August the cherry orchard and the whole estate too will be sold by auction. Make up your minds! There is no other way of saving it, I'll take my oath on that. No, No!

FIRS. In old days, forty or fifty years ago, they used to dry the cherries, soak them, pickle them, make jam too, and they used—

GAEV. Be quiet, Firs.

FIRS. And they used to send the preserved cherries to Moscow and to Harkov by the waggon-load. That brought the money in! And the preserved cherries in those days were soft and juicy, sweet and fragrant. . . . They knew the way to do them then. . . .

LYUBOV. And where is the recipe now?

FIRS. It's forgotten. Nobody remembers it.

PISHTCHIK. [to Lyubov Andreyevna]. What's it like in Paris? Did you eat frogs there?

LYUBOV. Oh, I ate crocodiles.

PISHTCHIK. Fancy that now!

LOPAHIN. There used to be only the gentlefolks and the peasants in the country, but now there are these summer visitors. All the towns, even the small ones, are surrounded nowadays by these summer villas. And one may say for sure, that in another twenty years there'll be many more of these people and that they'll be everywhere. At present the summer visitor only drinks tea in his verandah, but maybe he'll take to working his bit of land too, and then your cherry orchard would become happy, rich and prosperous. . . .

GAEV. [indignant]. What rot!

[Enter Varya and Yasha]

VARYA. There are two telegrams for you, mamma [takes out keys and opens an old fashioned bookcase with a loud crack]. Here they are.

LYUBOV. From Paris [tears the telegrams, without reading them]. I have done with Paris.

GAEV. Do you know, Lyuba, how old that bookcase is? Last week I pulled out the bottom drawer and there I found the date branded on it. The bookcase was made just a hundred years ago. What do you say to that? We might have celebrated its jubilee. Though it's an inanimate object, still it is a *book* case.

PISHTCHIK. [amazed]. A hundred years! Fancy that now.

GAEV. Yes. . . . It is a thing . . . [feeling the bookcase]. Dear, honoured, bookcase! Hail to thee who for more than a hundred years hast served the pure ideals of good and justice; thy silent call to fruitful

labour has never flagged in those hundreds years, maintaining [in tears] in the generations of man, courage and faith in a brighter future and fostering in us ideals of good and social consciousness [a pause].

LOPAHIN. Yes. . . .

LYUBOV. You are just the same as ever, Leonid.

GAEV. [a little embarrassed]. Cannon off the right into the pocket!

LOPAHIN. [looking at his watch]. Well, it's time I was off.

YASHA. [handing Lyubov Andreyevna medicine]. Perhaps you will take your pills now.

PISHTCHIK. You shouldn't take medicines, my dear madam . . . they do no harm and no good. Give them here . . . honoured lady [takes the pill-box, pours the pills into the hollow of his hand, blows on them, puts them in his mouth and drinks off some kvass]. There!

LYUBOV. [in alarm]. Why, you must be out of your mind!

PISHTCHIK. I have taken all the pills.

LOPAHIN. What a glutton! [All laugh.]

FIRS. His honour stayed with us in Easter week, ate a gallon and a half of cucumbers . . . [mutters].

LYUBOV. What is he saying?

VARYA. He has taken to muttering like that for the last three years. We are used to it.

YASHA. His declining years!

[Charlotta Ivanovna, a very thin, lanky figure in a white dress with a lorgnette in her belt, walks across the stage.]

LOPAHIN. I beg your pardon, Charlotta Ivanovna, I have not had time to greet you [tries to kiss her hand].

CHARLOTTA. [pulling away her hand]. If I let you kiss my hand, you'll be wanting to kiss my elbow, and then my shoulder.

LOPAHIN. I've no luck to-day! [all laugh.]. Charlotta Ivanovna, show us some tricks!

LYUBOV. Charlotta, do show us some tricks!

CHARLOTTA. I don't want to. I'm sleepy [goes out].

LOPAHIN. In three weeks' time we shall meet again [kisses Lyubov Andreyevna's hand]. Good-bye till then—I must go. [To Gaev] Good-bye. [Kisses Pishtchik] Good-bye. [Gives his hand to Varya, then to Firs and Yasha] I don't want to go. [To Lyubov Andreyevna] If you think over my plan for the villas and make up your mind, then let me know; I will lend you 50,000 roubles. Think of it seriously.

VARYA. [angrily]. Well, do go, for goodness sake.

LOPAHIN. I'm going, I'm going [goes out].

GAEV. Low-born knave! I beg pardon, though . . . Varya is going to marry him, he's Varya's fiancé.

VARYA. Don't talk nonsense, uncle.

LYUBOV. Well, Varya, I shall be delighted. He's a good man.

PISHTCHIK. He is, one must acknowledge, a most worthy man. And my Dashenka . . . says too that . . . she says . . . various things [snores, but at once wakes up]. But all the same, honoured lady, would you oblige me . . . with a loan of 240 roubles . . . to pay the interest on my mortgage tomorrow?

VARYA. [dismayed]. No, no.

LYUBOV. I really haven't any money.

PISHTCHIK. It will turn up [laughs]. I never lose hope. I thought everything was over, I was a ruined man, and lo and behold—the railway passed through my land and . . . they paid me for it. And something else will turn up again, if not to-day, then to-morrow . . . Dashenka'll win two hundred thousand . . . she's got a lottery ticket.

LYUBOV. Well, we've finished our coffee, we can go to bed.

FIRS. [brushes Gaev, reprovingly]. You have got on the wrong trousers again! What am I do to with you?

VARYA. [softly]. Anya's asleep. [Softly opens the window] Now the sun's risen, it's not a bit cold. Look, mamma, what exquisite trees! My goodness! And the air! The starlings are singing!

GAEV. [opens another window]. The orchard is all white. You've not forgotten it, Lyuba? That long avenue that runs straight, straight as an arrow, how it shines on a moonlight night. You remember? You've not forgotten?

LYUBOV. [looking out of the window into the garden]. Oh, my childhood, my innocence! It was in this nursery I used to sleep, from here I looked out into the orchard, happiness waked with me every morning and in those days the orchard was just the same, nothing has changed [laughs with delight]. All, all white! Oh, my orchard! After the dark gloomy autumn, and the cold winter; you are young again, and full of happiness, the heavenly angels have never left you. . . . If I could cast off the burden that weighs on my heart, if I could forget the past!

GAEV. H'm! and the orchard will be sold to pay our debts; it seems strange. . . .

LYUBOV. See, our mother walking . . . all in white, down the avenue! [Laughs with delight.] It is she!

GAEV. Where?

VARYA. Oh, don't, mamma!

LYUBOV. There is no one. It was my fancy. On the right there, by the path to the arbour, there is a white tree bending like a woman. . . .

[Enter Trofimov wearing a shabby student's uniform and spectacles.]

LYUBOV. What a ravishing orchard! White masses of blossom, blue sky. . . .

TROFIMOV. Lyubov Andreyevna! [She looks round at him.] I will just pay my respects to you and then leave you at once [kisses her hand warmly]. I was told to wait until morning, but I hadn't the patience to wait any longer. . . .

[Lyubov Andreyevna looks at him in perplexity.]

VARYA. [through her tears]. This is Petya Trofimov.

TROFIMOV. Petya Trofimov, who was your Grisha's tutor. . . . Can I have changed so much?

[Lyubov Andreyevna embraces him and weeps quietly.]

GAEV. [in confusion]. There, there, Lyuba.

VARYA. [crying]. I told you, Petya, to wait till to-morrow.

LYUBOV. My Grisha . . . my boy . . . Grisha . . . my son!

VARYA. We can't help it, mamma, it is God's will.

TROFIMOV. [softly through his tears]. There . . . there.

LYUBOV. [weeping quietly]. My boy was lost . . . drowned. Why? Oh, why, dear Petya? [More quietly] Anya is asleep in there, and I'm talking loudly . . . making this noise. . . . But, Petya? Why have you grown so ugly? Why do you look so old?

TROFIMOV. A peasant-woman in the train called me a mangy-looking gentleman.

LYUBOV. You were quite a boy then, a pretty little student, and now your hair's thin—and spectacles. Are you really a student still? [Goes towards the door.]

TROFIMOV. I seem likely to be a perpetual student.

LYUBOV. [kisses her brother, then Varya.] Well, go to bed. . . . You are older too, Leonid.

PISHTCHIK. [follows her]. I suppose it's time we were asleep. . . . Ugh! my gout. I'm staying the night! Lyubov Andreyevna, my dear soul, if you could . . . to-morrow morning . . . 240 roubles.

GAEV. That's always his story.

PISHTCHIK. 240 roubles . . . to pay the interest on my mortgage.

LYUBOV. My dear man, I have no money.

PISHTCHIK. I'll pay it back, my dear . . . a trifling sum.

LYUBOV. Oh, well, Leonid will give it you. . . . You give him the money, Leonid.

GAEV. Me give it him! Let him wait till he gets it!

LYUBOV. It can't be helped, give it him. He needs it. He'll pay it back.

[*Lyubov Andreyevna, Trofimov, Pishtchik and Firs go out. Gaev, Varya and Yasha remain.*]

GAEV. Sister hasn't got out of the habit of flinging away her money. [*To Yasha*] Get away, my good fellow, you smell of the hen-house.

YASHA. [*with a grin*] And you, Leonid Andreyevitch, are just the same as ever.

GAEV. What's that? [*To Varya*] what did he say?

VARYA. [*to Yasha*]. Your mother has come from the village; she has been sitting in the servants' room since yesterday, waiting to see you.

YASHA. Oh, bother her!

VARYA. For shame!

YASHA. What's the hurry? She might just as well have come to-morrow [*goes out*].

VARYA. Mamma's just the same as ever, she hasn't changed a bit. If she had her own way, she'd give away everything.

GAEV. Yes [*a pause*]. If a great many remedies are suggested for some disease, it means that the disease is incurable. I keep thinking and racking my brains; I have many schemes, a great many, and that really means none. If we could only come in for a legacy from somebody, or marry our Anya to a very rich man, or we might go to Yaroslavl and try our luck with your old aunt, the Countess. She's very, very rich, you know.

VARYA. [*weeps*]. If God would help us.

GAEV. Don't blubber. Aunt's very rich, but she doesn't like us. First, sister married a lawyer instead of a nobleman. . . .

[*Anya appears in the doorway.*]

GAEV. And then her conduct, one can't call it virtuous. She is good, and kind, and nice, and I love her, but, however one allows for extenuating circumstances, there's no denying that she's an immoral woman. One feels it in her slightest gesture.

VARYA. [*in a whisper*]. Anya's in the doorway.

GAEV. What do you say? [*a pause*]. It's queer, there seems to be something wrong with my right eye. I don't see as well as I did. And on Thursday when I was in the district Court . . .

[*Enter Anya.*]

VARYA. Why aren't you asleep, Anya?

ANYA. I can't get to sleep.

GAEV. My pet [*kisses Anya's face and hands*]. My child [*weeps*]. You are not my niece, you are my angel, you are everything to me. Believe me, believe . . .

ANYA. I believe you, uncle. Everyone loves you and respects you . . . but, uncle dear, you must be silent . . . simply be silent. What were you saying just now about my mother, about your own sister? What made you say that?

GAEV. Yes, yes . . . [*puts his hand over his face*]. Really, that was awful! My God, save me! And to-day I made a speech to the bookcase . . . so stupid! And only when I had finished, I saw how stupid it was.

VARYA. It's true, uncle, you ought to keep quiet. Don't talk, that's all.

ANYA. If you could keep from talking, it would make things easier for you, too.

GAEV. I won't speak [*kisses Anya's and Varya's hands*]. I'll be silent. Only this is about business. On Thursday I was in the district Court; well, there was a large party of us there and we began talking of one thing and another, and this and that, and do you know, I believe that it will be possible to raise a loan on an I.O.U. to pay the arrears on the mortgage.

VARYA. If the Lord would help us!

GAEV. I'm going on Tuesday; I'll talk of it again. [*To Varya*] Don't blubber. [*To Anya*] Your mamma will talk to Lopahin; of course, he won't refuse her. And as soon as you're rested you shall go to Yaroslavl to the Countess, your great-aunt. So we shall all set to work in three directions at once, and the business is done. We shall pay off arrears, I'm convinced of it [*puts a caramel in his mouth*]. I swear on my honour, I swear by anything you like, the estate shan't be sold [*excitedly*]. By my own happiness, I swear it! Here's my hand on it, call me the basest, vilest of men, if I let it come to an auction! Upon my soul I swear it!

ANYA. [*her equanimity has returned, she is quite happy*]. How good you are, uncle, and how clever! [*Embraces her uncle.*] I'm at peace now! Quite at peace! I'm happy!

[*Enter Firs.*]

FIRS. [*reproachfully*]. Leonid Andreyevitch, have you no fear of God? When are you going to bed?

GAEV. Directly, directly. You can go, Firs. I'll . . . yes, I will undress myself. Come, children, bye-bye. We'll go into details to-morrow, but now go to bed [kisses Anya and Varya]. I'm a man of the eighties. They run down that period, but still I can say I have had to suffer not a little for my convictions in my life. It's not for nothing that the peasant loves me. One must know the peasant! One must know how . . .

ANYA. At it again, uncle!

VARYA. Uncle dear, you'd better be quiet.

FIRS. [angrily]. Leonid Andreyevitch!

GAEV. I'm coming. I'm coming. Go to bed. Potted the shot—there's a shot for you! A beauty! [Goes out, Firs hobbling after him.]

ANYA. My mind's at rest now. I don't want to go to Yaroslavl, I don't like my great-aunt, but still my mind's at rest. Thanks to uncle [sits down].

VARYA. We must go to bed. I'm going. Something unpleasant happened while you were away. In the old servants' quarters there are only the old servants, as you know—Efimyushka, Polya and Yevstigney— and Karp too. They began letting stray people in to spend the night—I said nothing. But all at once I heard they had been spreading a report that I gave them nothing but pease pudding to eat. Out of stinginess, you know. . . . And it was all Yevstigney's doing. . . . Very well, I said to myself. . . . If that's how it is, I thought, wait a bit. I sent for Yevstigney . . . [yawns]. He comes. . . . "How's this, Yevstigney," I said, "you could be such a fool as to? . . ." [Looking at Anya] Anitchka! [a pause]. She's asleep [puts her arm round Anya]. Come to bed . . . come along! [leads her!]. My darling has fallen asleep! Come . . . [They go.]

[Far away beyond the orchard a shepherd plays on a pipe. Trofimov crosses the stage and, seeing Varya and Anya, stands still.]

VARYA. 'Sh! asleep, asleep. Come, my own.

ANYA. [softly, half asleep]. I'm so tired. Still those bells. Uncle . . . dear . . . mamma and uncle. . . .

VARYA. Come, my own, come along.

[They go into Anya's room.]

TROFIMOV. [tenderly]. My sunshine! My spring!

CURTAIN

Act II

The open country. An old shrine, long abandoned and fallen out of the perpendicular; near it a well, large stones that have apparently once been tomb-stones, and an old garden seat. The road to Gaev's house is seen. On one side rise dark poplars; and there the cherry orchard begins. In the distance a row of telegraph poles and far, far away on the horizon there is faintly outlined a great town, only visible in very fine clear weather. It is near sunset. Charlotta, Yasha and Dunyasha are sitting on the seat. Epihodov is standing near, playing something mournful on a guitar. All sit plunged in thought. Charlotta wears an old forage cap; she has taken a gun from her shoulder and is tightening the buckle on the strap.

CHARLOTTA. [musingly]. I haven't a real passport of my own, and I don't know how old I am, and I always feel that I'm a young thing. When I was a little girl, my father and mother used to travel about to fairs and give performances—very good ones. And I used to dance salto-mortale and all sorts of things. And when papa and mamma died, a German lady took me and had me educated. And so I grew up and become a governess. But where I came from, and who I am, I don't know. . . . Who my parents were, very likely they weren't married . . . I don't know [takes a cucumber out of her pocket and eats]. I know nothing at all [a pause]. One wants to talk and has no one to talk to . . . I have nobody.

EPIHODOV. [plays on the guitar and sings]. "What care I for the noisy world! What care I for friends or foes!" How agreeable it is to play on the mandoline!

DUNYASHA. That's a guitar, not a mandoline [looks in a hand-mirror and powders herself].

EPIHODOV. To a man mad with love, it's a mandoline. [Sings] "Were her heart but aglow with love's mutual flame." [Yasha joins in.]

CHARLOTTA. How shockingly these people sing! Foo! Like jackals!

DUNYASHA. [to Yasha]. What happiness, though, to visit foreign lands.

YASHA. Ah, yes! I rather agree with you there [yawns, then lights a cigar].

EPIHODOV. That's comprehensible. In foreign lands everything has long since reached full complexion.

YASHA. That's so, of course.

EPIHODOV. I'm a cultivated man, I read remarkable books of all sorts, but I can never make out the tendency I am myself precisely inclined for, whether to live or to shoot myself, speaking precisely, but nevertheless I always carry a revolver. Here it is . . . [shows revolver].

CHARLOTTA. I've had enough, and now I'm going [puts on the gun]. Epihodov, you're a very clever fellow, and a very terrible one too, all the women must be wild about you. Br-r-r! [goes] These clever fellows are all so stupid; there's not a creature for me to speak to. . . . Always alone, alone, nobody belonging to me . . . and who I am, and why I'm on earth, I don't know [walks away slowly].

EPIHODOV. Speaking precisely, not touching upon other subjects, I'm bound to admit about myself, that destiny behaves mercilessly to me, as a storm to a little boat. If, let us suppose, I am mistaken, then why did I wake up this morning, to quote an example, and look round, and there on my chest was a spider of fearful magnitude . . . like this [shows with both hands]. And then I take up a jug of kvass, to quench my thirst, and in it there is something in the highest degree unseemly of the nature of a cockroach [a pause]. Have you read Buckle? [a pause]. I am desirous of troubling you, Dunyasha, with a couple of words.

DUNYASHA. Well, speak.

EPIHODOV. I should be desirous to speak with you alone [sighs].

DUNYASHA. [embarrassed]. Well—only bring me my mantle first. It's by the cupboard. It's rather damp here.

EPIHODOV. Certainly. I will fetch it. Now I know what I must do with my revolver [takes guitar and goes off playing on it].

YASHA. Two and twenty misfortunes! Between ourselves, he's a fool [yawns].

DUNYASHA. God grant he doesn't shoot himself! [a pause] I am so nervous, I'm always in a flutter. I was a little girl when I was taken into our lady's house, and now I have quite grown out of peasant ways, and my hands are white, as white as a lady's. I'm such a delicate, sensitive creature, I'm afraid of everything. I'm so frightened. And if you deceive me, Yasha, I don't know what will become of my nerves.

YASHA. [kisses her]. You're a peach! Of course a girl must never forget herself; what I dislike more than anything is a girl being flighty in her behavior.

DUNYASHA. I'm passionately in love with you, Yasha; you are a man of culture—you can give your opinion about anything [a pause].

YASHA. [yawns]. Yes, that's so. My opinion is this: if a girl loves anyone, that means that she has no principles [a pause]. It's pleasant smoking a cigar in the open air [listens]. Someone's coming this way . . . it's the gentlefolk [Dunyasha embraces him impulsively]. Go home, as though you had been to the river to bathe; go by that path, or else they'll meet you and suppose I have made an appointment with you here. That I can't endure.

DUNYASHA. [coughing softly]. The cigar has made my head ache . . . [goes off].

[Yasha remains sitting near the shrine. Enter Lyubov Andreyevna, Gaev and Lopahin.]

LOPAHIN. You must make up your mind once for all—there's no time to lose. It's quite a simple question, you know. Will you consent to letting the land for building or not? One word in answer: Yes or no? Only one word!

LYUBOV. Who is smoking such horrible cigars? [sits down].

GAEV. Now the railway line has been brought near, it's made things very convenient [sits down]. Here we have been over and lunched in town. Cannon off the white! I should like to go home and have a game.

LYUBOV. You have plenty of time.

LOPAHIN. Only one word! [Beseechingly]. Give me an answer!

GAEV. [yawning]. What do you say?

LYUBOV. [looks in her purse]. I had quite a lot of money here yesterday, and there's scarcely any left to-day. My poor Varya feeds us all on milk soup for the sake of economy; the old folks in the kitchen get nothing but pease pudding, while I waste my money in a senseless way [drops purse, scattering gold pieces]. There, they have all fallen out! [annoyed]

YASHA. Allow me, I'll soon pick them up [collects the coins].

LYUBOV. Pray do, Yasha. And what did I go off to the town to lunch for? Your restaurant's a wretched place with its music and the tablecloth smelling of soap. . . . Why drink so much, Leonid? And eat so much? And talk so much? To-day you talked a great deal again in the restaurant, and all so inappropriately. About the era of the 'seventies, about the decadents. And to whom? Talking to waiters about decadents!

LOPAHIN. Yes.

GAEV. [waving his hand]. I'm incorrigible; that's evident. [Irritably to Yasha] Why is it you keep fidgeting about in front of us!

YASHA. [laughs]. I can't help laughing when I hear your voice.

GAEV. [to his sister]. Either I or he . . .

LYUBOV. Get along! Go away, Yasha.

YASHA. [gives Lyubov Andreyevna her purse]. Directly [hardly able to suppress his laughter]. This minute . . . [goes off].

LOPAHIN. Deriganov, the millionaire, means to buy your estate. They say he is coming to the sale himself.

LYUBOV. Where did you hear that?

LOPAHIN. That's what they say in town.

GAEV. Our aunt in Yaroslavl has promised to send help; but when, and how much she will send, we don't know.

LOPAHIN. How much will she send? A hundred thousand? Two hundred?

LYUBOV. Oh, well! . . . Ten or fifteen thousand, and we must be thankful to get that.

LOPAHIN. Forgive me, but such reckless people as you are—such queer, unbusiness-like people—I never met in my life. One tells you in plain Russian your estate is going to be sold, and you seem not to understand it.

LYUBOV. What are we to do? Tell us what to do.

LOPAHIN. I do tell you every day. Every day I say the same thing. You absolutely must let the cherry orchard and the land on building leases; and do it at once, as quick as may be—the auction's close upon us! Do understand! Once make up your mind to build villas, and you can raise as much money as you like, and then you are saved.

LYUBOV. Villas and summer visitors—forgive me saying so—it's so vulgar.

GAEV. There I perfectly agree with you.

LOPAHIN. I shall sob, or scream, or fall into a fit. I can't stand it! You drive me mad! [To Gaev] You're an old woman!

GAEV. What do you say?

LOPAHIN. An old woman! [Gets up to go.]

LYUBOV. [in dismay]. No, don't go! Do stay, my dear friend! Perhaps we shall think of something.

LOPAHIN. What is there to think of?

LYUBOV. Don't go, I entreat you! With you here it's more cheerful, anyway [a pause]. I keep expecting something, as though the house were going to fall about our ears.

GAEV. [in profound dejection]. Potted the white! It fails—a kiss.

LYUBOV. We have been great sinners. . . .

LOPAHIN. You have no sins to repent of.

GAEV. [puts a caramel in his mouth]. They say I've eaten up my property in caramels [laughs].

LYUBOV. Oh, my sins! I've always thrown my money away recklessly like a lunatic. I married a man who made nothing but debts. My husband died of champagne—he drank dreadfully. To my misery I loved another man, and immediately—it was my first punishment—the blow fell upon me, here, in the river . . . my boy was drowned and I went abroad—went away for ever, never to return, not to see that river again . . . I shut my eyes, and fled, distracted, and he after me . . . pitilessly, brutally. I bought a villa at Mentone, for he fell ill there, and for three years I had no rest day or night. His illness wore me out, my soul was dried up. And last year, when my villa was sold to pay my debts, I went to Paris and there he robbed me of everything and abandoned me for another woman; and I tried to poison myself. . . . So stupid, so shameful! . . . And suddenly I felt a yearning for Russia, for my country, for my little girls . . . [dries her tears]. Lord, Lord, be merciful! Forgive my sins! Do not chastise me more! [Takes a telegram out of her pocket] I got this to-day from Paris. He implores forgiveness, entreats me to return [tears up the telegram]. I fancy there is music somewhere [listens].

GAEV. That's our famous Jewish orchestra. You remember, four violins, a flute and a double bass.

LYUBOV. That still in existence? We ought to send for them one evening, and give a dance.

LOPAHIN. [listens]. I can't hear. . . . [Hums softly] "For money the Germans will turn a Russian into a Frenchman." [Laughs] I did see such a piece at the theatre yesterday! It was funny!

LYUBOV. And most likely there was nothing funny in it. You shouldn't look at plays, you should look at yourselves a little oftener. How grey your lives are! How much nonsense you talk.

LOPAHIN. That's true. One may say honestly, we live a fool's life [pause]. My father was a peasant, an idiot; he knew nothing and taught me nothing, only beat me when he was drunk, and always with his stick. In reality I am just such another blockhead and idiot. I've learnt nothing properly. I write a wretched hand. I write so that I feel ashamed before folks, like a pig.

LYUBOV. You ought to get married, my dear fellow.

LOPAHIN. Yes . . . that's true.

LYUBOV. You should marry our Varya, she's a good girl.

LOPAHIN. Yes.

LYUBOV. She's a good-natured girl, she's busy all day long, and what's more, she loves you. And you have liked her for ever so long.

LOPAHIN. Well? I'm not against it. . . . She's a good girl [pause].

GAEV. I've been offered a place in the bank: 6,000 roubles a year. Did you know?

LYUBOV. You would never do for that! You must stay as you are.

[Enter Firs with overcoat.]

FIRS. Put it on, sir, it's damp.

GAEV. [putting it on]. You bother me, old fellow.

FIRS. You can't go on like this. You went away in the morning without leaving word [looks him over].

LYUBOV. You look older, Firs!

FIRS. What is your pleasure?

LOPAHIN. You look older, she said.

FIRS. I've had a long life. They were arranging my wedding before your papa was born . . . [laughs]. I was the head footman before the emancipation came. I wouldn't consent to be set free then; I stayed on with the old master . . . [a pause]. I remember what rejoicings they made and didn't know themselves what they were rejoicing over.

LOPAHIN. Those were fine old times. There was flogging anyway.

FIRS. [not hearing]. To be sure! The peasants knew their place, and the masters knew theirs; but now they're all at sixes and sevens, there's no making it out.

GAEV. Hold your tongue, Firs. I must go to town tomorrow. I have been promised an introduction to a general, who might let us have a loan.

LOPAHIN. You won't bring that off. And you won't pay your arrears, you may rest assured of that.

LYUBOV. That's all his nonsense. There is no such general.

[Enter Trofimov, Anya and Varya.]

GAEV. Here come our girls.

ANYA. There's mamma on the seat.

LYUBOV. [tenderly]. Come here, come along. My darlings! [Embraces Anya and Varya.] If you only knew how I love you both. Sit beside me, there, like that. [All sit down.]

LOPAHIN. Our perpetual student is always with the young ladies.

TROFIMOV. That's not your business.

LOPAHIN. He'll soon be fifty, and he's still a student.

TROFIMOV. Drop your idiotic jokes.

LOPAHIN. Why are you so cross, you queer fish?

TROFIMOV. Oh, don't persist!

LOPAHIN. [laughs]. Allow me to ask you what's your idea of me?

TROFIMOV. I'll tell you my idea of you, Yermolay Alexeyevitch: you are a rich man, you'll soon be a millionaire. Well, just as in the economy of nature a wild beast if of use, who devours everything that comes in his way, so you too have your use.

[All laugh.]

VARYA. Better tell us something about the planets, Petya.

LYUBOV. No, let us go on with the conversation we had yesterday.

TROFIMOV. What was it about?

GAEV. About pride.

TROFIMOV. We had a long conversation yesterday, but we came to no conclusion. In pride, in your sense of it, there is something mystical. Perhaps you are right from your point of view; but if one looks at it simply, without subtlety, what sort of pride can there be, what sense is there in it, if man in his physiological formation is very imperfect, if in the immense majority of cases he is coarse, dull-witted, profoundly unhappy? One must give up glorification of self. One should work, and nothing else.

GAEV. One must die in any case.

TROFIMOV. Who knows? And what does it mean—dying? Perhaps man has a hundred senses, and only the five we know are lost at death, while the other ninety-five remain alive.

LYUBOV. How clever you are, Petya!

LOPAHIN. [ironically]. Fearfully clever!

TROFIMOV. Humanity progresses, perfecting its powers. Everything that is beyond its ken now will one day become familiar and comprehensible; only we must work, we must with all our powers aid the seeker after truth. Here among us in Russia the workers are few in number as yet. The vast majority of the intellectual people I know, seek nothing, do nothing, are not fit as yet for work of any kind. They call themselves intellectual, but they treat their servants as inferiors, behave to the peasants as though they were animals, learn little, read nothing seriously, do practically nothing, only talk about science and know very little about art. They are all serious people, they all have severe faces, they all talk of weighty matters and air their theories, and yet the vast majority of us—ninety-nine per cent—live like savages, at the least thing fly to blows and abuse, eat piggishly, sleep in filth and stuffiness, bugs everywhere, stench and damp and moral impurity. And it's clear all our fine talk is only to divert our attention and other people's. Show me where to find the crèches there's so much talk about, and the reading-rooms? They only exist in novels: in real life there are none of them. There is nothing but filth and vulgarity and Asiatic apathy. I fear and dislike very serious faces. I'm afraid of serious conversations. We should do better to be silent.

LOPAHIN. You know, I get up at five o'clock in the morning, and I work from morning to night; and I've money, my own and other people's, always passing through my hands, and I see what people are made of all round me. One has only to begin to do anything to see how few honest, decent people there are. Sometimes when I lie awake at night, I think: "Oh! Lord, thou hast given us immense forests, boundless plains, the widest horizons, and living here we ourselves ought really to be giants."

LYUBOV. You ask for giants! They are no good except in story-books; in real life they frighten us.

[*Epihodov advances in the background, playing on the guitar.*]

LYUBOV. [*dreamily*]. There goes Epihodov.

ANYA. [*dreamily*]. There goes Epihodov.

GAEV. The sun has set, my friends.

TROFIMOV. Yes.

GAEV. [*not loudly, but, as it were, declaiming*]. O nature, divine nature, thou art bright with eternal lustre, beautiful and indifferent! Thou, whom we call mother, thou dost unite within thee life and death! Thou dost give life and dost destroy!

VARYA. [*in a tone of supplication*]. Uncle!

ANYA. Uncle, you are at it again!

TROFIMOV. You'd much better be cannoning off the red!

GAEV. I'll hold my tongue, I will.

[*All sit plunged in thought. Perfect stillness. The only thing audible is the muttering of Firs. Suddenly there is a sound in the distance, as it were from the sky—the sound of a breaking harp-string, mournfully dying away.*]

LYUBOV. What is that?

LOPAHIN. I don't know. Somewhere far away a bucket fallen and broken in the pits. But somewhere very far away.

GAEV. It might be a bird of some sort—such as a heron.

TROFIMOV. Or an owl.

LYUBOV. [*shudders*]. I don't know why, but it's horrid [*a pause*].

FIRS. It was the same before the calamity—the owl hooted and the samovar hissed all the time.

GAEV. Before what calamity?

FIRS. Before the emancipation [*a pause*].

LYUBOV. Come, my friends, let us be going; evening is falling. [*To Anya*] There are tears in your eyes. What is it, darling? [*Embraces her.*]

ANYA. Nothing, mamma; it's nothing.

TROFIMOV. There is somebody coming.

[*The wayfarer appears in a shabby white forage cap and an overcoat; he is slightly drunk.*]

WAYFARER. Allow me to inquire, can I get to the station this way?

GAEV. Yes. Go along that road.

WAYFARER. I thank you most feelingly [*coughing*]. The weather is superb. [*Declaims*] My brother, my suffering brother! . . . Come out to the Volga! Whose groan do you hear? . . . [*To Varya*] Mademoiselle, vouchsafe a hungry Russian thirty kopeks.

[*Varya utters a shriek of alarm.*]

LOPAHIN. [*angrily*]. There's a right and a wrong way of doing everything!

LYUBOV. [*hurriedly*]. Here, take this [*looks in her purse*]. I've no silver. No matter—here's gold for you.

WAYFARER. I thank you most feelingly! [*goes off*].

[*Laughter.*]

VARYA. [*frightened*]. I'm going home—I'm going . . . Oh, mamma, the servants have nothing to eat, and you gave him gold!

LYUBOV. There's no doing anything with me. I'm so silly! When we get home, I'll give you all I possess. Yermolay Alexeyevitch, you will lend me some more . . . !

LOPAHIN. I will.

LYUBOV. Come, friends, it's time to be going. And Varya, we have made a match of it for you. I congratulate you.

VARYA. [*through her tears*]. Mamma, that's not a joking matter.

LOPAHIN. "Ophelia, get thee to a nunnery!"

GAEV. My hands are trembling; it's a long while since I had a game of billiards.

LOPAHIN. "Ophelia! Nymph, in thy orisons be all my sins remember'd.'"

LYUBOV. Come, it will soon be supper-time.

VARYA. How he frightened me! My heart's simply throbbing.

LOPAHIN. Let me remind you, ladies and gentlemen: on the 22nd of August the cherry orchard will be sold. Think about that! Think about it!

[All go off, except Trofimov and Anya.]

ANYA. [laughing]. I'm grateful to the wayfarer! He frightened Varya and we are left alone.

TROFIMOV. Varya's afraid we shall fall in love with each other, and for days together she won't leave us. With her narrow brain she can't grasp that we are above love. To eliminate the petty and transitory which hinders us from being free and happy—that is the aim and meaning of our life. Forward! We go forward irresistibly towards the bright star that shines yonder in the distance. Forward! Do not lag behind, friends.

ANYA. [claps her hands]. How well you speak! [a pause]. It is divine here to-day.

TROFIMOV. Yes, it's glorious weather.

ANYA. Somehow, Petya, you've made me so that I don't love the cherry orchard as I used to. I used to love it so dearly. I used to think that there was no spot on earth like our garden.

TROFIMOV. All Russia is our garden. The earth is great and beautiful—there are many beautiful places in it [a pause]. Think only, Anya, your grandfather, and great-grandfather, and all your ancestors were slave-owners—the owners of living souls—and from every cherry in the orchard, from every leaf, from every trunk there are human creatures looking at you. Cannot you hear their voices? Oh, it is awful! Your orchard is a fearful thing, and when in the evening or at night one walks about the orchard, the old bark on the trees glimmers dimly in the dusk, and the old cherry trees seem to be dreaming of centuries gone by and tortured by fearful visions. Yes! We are at least two hundreds years behind, we have really gained nothing yet, we have no definite attitude to the past, we do nothing but theorise or complain of depression or drink vodka. It is clear that to begin to live in the present we must first expiate our past, we must break with it; and we can expiate it only by suffering, by extraordinary unceasing labour. Understand that, Anya.

ANYA. The house we live in has long ceased to be our own, and I shall leave it, I give you my word.

TROFIMOV. If you have the house keys, fling them into the well and go away. Be free as the wind.

ANYA. [in ecstasy]. How beautifully you said that!

TROFIMOV. Believe me, Anya, believe me! I am not thirty yet, I am young, I am still a student, but I have gone through so much already! As soon as winter comes I am hungry, sick, careworn, poor as a beggar, and what ups and downs of fortune have I not known! And my soul was always, every minute, day and night, full of inexplicable forebodings. I have a foreboding of happiness, Anya. I see glimpses of it already.

ANYA. [pensively]. The moon is rising.

[Epihodov is heard playing still the same mournful song on the guitar. The moon rises. Somewhere near the poplars Varya is looking for Anya and calling "Anya! where are you?"]

TROFIMOV. Yes, the moon is rising [a pause]. Here is happiness—here it comes! It is coming nearer and nearer; already I can hear its footsteps. And if we never see it—if we may never know it—what does it matter? Others will see it after us.

VARYA'S VOICE. Anya! Where are you?

TROFIMOV. That Varya again! [Angrily] It's revolting!

ANYA. Well, let's go down to the river. It's lovely there.

TROFIMOV. Yes, let's go. [They go.]

VARYA'S VOICE. Anya! Anya!

CURTAIN

Act III

A drawing-room divided by an arch from a larger drawing-room. A chandelier burning. The Jewish orchestra, the same that was mentioned in Act II, is heard playing in the ante-room. It is evening. In the larger drawing-room they are dancing the grand chain. The voice of Semyonov-Pishtchik: "Promenade à une paire!" Then enter the drawing-room in couples first Pishtchik and Charlotta Ivanova, then Trofimov and Lyubov Andreyevna, thirdly Anya with the Post-Office Clerk, fourthly Varya with the Station Master, and other guests. Varya is quietly weeping and wiping away her tears as she dances. In the last couple is Dunyasha. They move across the drawing-room. Pishtchik shouts: "Grand rond, balancez!" and "Les Cavaliers à genou et remerciez vos dames."

[*Firs in a swallow-tail coat brings in seltzer water on a tray. Pishtchik and Trofimov enter the drawing-room.*]

PISHTCHIK. I am a full-blooded man; I have already had two strokes. Dancing's hard work for me, but as they say, if you're in the pack, you must bark with the rest. I'm as strong, I may say, as a horse. My parent, who would have his joke—may the King-dom of Heaven be his!—used to say about our origin that the ancient stock of the Semyonov-Pishtchiks was derived from the very horse that Cal-igula made a member of the senate [*sits down*]. But I've no money, that's where the mischief is. A hun-gry dog believes in nothing but meat . . . [*snores, but at once wakes up*]. That's like me . . . I can think of nothing but money.

TROFIMOV. There really is something horsy about your appearance.

PISHTCHIK. Well . . . a horse is a fine beast . . . a horse can be sold.

[*There is a sound of billiards being played in an adjoining room. Varya appears in the arch leading to the larger drawing-room.*]

TROFIMOV. [*teasing*]. Madame Lopahin! Madame Lopahin!

VARYA. [*angrily*]. Mangy-looking gentleman!

TROFIMOV. Yes, I am a mangy-looking gentleman, and I'm proud of it!

VARYA. [*pondering bitterly*]. Here we have hired musi-cians and nothing to pay them! [*Goes out.*]

TROFIMOV. [*to Pishtchik*]. If the energy you have wasted during your lifetime in trying to find the money to pay your interest, had gone to something else, you might in the end have turned the world upside down.

PISHTCHIK. Nietzsche, the philosopher, a very great and celebrated man . . . of enormous intellect . . . says in his works that one can make forged bank-notes.

TROFIMOV. Why, have you read Nietzsche?

PISHTCHIK. What next . . . Dashenka told me. . . . And now I am in such a position, I might just as well forge banknotes. The day after to-morrow I must pay 310 roubles—130 I have procured [*feels in his pockets, in alarm*]. The money's gone! I have lost my money! [*Through his tears*] Where's the money? [*Gleefully*] Why, here it is behind the lining. . . . It has made me hot all over.

[*Enter Lyubov Andreyevna and Charlotta Ivanovna.*]

LYUBOV. [*hums the Lezginka*]. Why is Leonid so long? What can he be doing in town? [*To Dunyasha*] Offer the musicians some tea.

TROFIMOV. The sale hasn't take place, most likely.

LYUBOV. It's the wrong time to have the orchestra, and the wrong time to give a dance. Well, never mind [*sits down and hums softly*].

CHARLOTTA. [*gives Pishtchik a pack of cards*]. Here's a pack of cards. Think of any card you like.

PISHTCHIK. I've thought of one.

CHARLOTTA. Shuffle the pack now. That's right. Give it here, my dear Mr. Pishtchik. Ein, zwei, drei—now look, it's in your breast pocket.

PISHTCHIK. [*taking a card out of his breast pocket*]. The eight of spades! Perfectly right! [*Wonderingly*] Fancy that now!

CHARLOTTA. [*holding pack of cards in her hands, to Trofimov*]. Tell me quickly which is the top card.

TROFIMOV. Well, the queen of spades.

CHARLOTTA. It is! [*To Pishtchik*] Well, which card is uppermost?

PISHTCHIK. The ace of hearts.

CHARLOTTA. It is! [*claps her hands, pack of cards disap-pear*]. Ah! what lovely weather it is to-day!

[*A mysterious feminine voice which seems coming out of the floor answers her. "Oh, yes, it's magnificent weather, madam."*]

CHARLOTTA. You are my perfect ideal.

VOICE. And I greatly admire you too, madam.

STATION MASTER. [*applauding*]. The lady ventriloquist —bravo!

PISHTCHIK. [*wonderingly*]. Fancy that now! Most enchanting Charlotta Ivanovna. I'm simply in love with you.

CHARLOTTA. In love? [*Shrugging shoulders*] What do you know of love, guter Mensch, aber schlechter Musikant.

TROFIMOV. [*pats Pishtchik on the shoulder*]. You dear old horse. . . .

CHARLOTTA. Attention, please! Another trick! [*takes a travelling rug from a chair*]. Here's a very good rug; I want to sell it [*shaking it out*]. Doesn't anyone want to buy it?

PISHTCHIK. [*wonderingly*]. Fancy that!

CHARLOTTA. Ein, zwei, drei! [*quickly picks up rug she has dropped; behind the rug stands Anya; she makes a curtsey, runs to her mother, embraces her and runs back into the larger drawing-room amidst general enthusiasm.*]

LYUBOV. [*applauds*]. Bravo! Bravo!

CHARLOTTA. Now again! Ein, zwei, drei! [*lifts up the rug; behind the rug stands Varya, bowing*].

PISHTCHIK. [*wonderingly*]. Fancy that now!

CHARLOTTA. That's the end [*throws the rug at Pishtchik, makes a curtsey, runs into the larger drawing-room*].

PISHTCHIK. [*hurries after her*]. Mischievous creature! Fancy! [*Goes out.*]

LYUBOV. And still Leonid doesn't come. I can't understand what he's doing in the town so long! Why, everything must be over by now. The estate is sold, or the sale has not taken place. Why keep us so long is suspense?

VARYA. [*trying to console her*]. Uncle's bought it. I feel sure of that.

TROFIMOV. [*ironically*]. Oh, yes!

VARYA. Great-aunt sent him an authorisation to buy it in her name, and transfer the debt. She's doing it for Anya's sake, and I'm sure God will be merciful. Uncle will buy it.

LYUBOV. My aunt in Yaroslavl sent fifteen thousand to buy the estate in her name, she doesn't trust us— but that's not enough even to pay the arrears [*hides her face in her hands*]. My fate is being sealed to-day, my fate. . . .

TROFIMOV. [*teasing Varya*]. Madame Lopahin.

VARYA. [*angrily*]. Perpetual student! Twice already you've been sent down from the University.

LYUBOV. Why are you angry, Varya? He's teasing you about Lopahin. Well, what of that? Marry Lopahin if you like, he's a good man, and interesting; if you don't want to, don't! Nobody compels you, darling.

VARYA. I must tell you plainly, mamma, I look at the matter seriously; he's a good man, I like him.

LYUBOV. Well, marry him. I can't see what you're waiting for.

VARYA. Mamma. I can't make him an offer myself. For the last two years, everyone's been talking to me about him. Everyone talks; but he says nothing or else makes a joke. I see what it means. He's growing rich, he's absorbed in business, he has no thoughts for me. If I had money, were it ever so little, if I had only a hundred roubles, I'd throw everything up and go far away. I would go into a nunnery.

TROFIMOV. What bliss!

VARYA. [*to Trofimov*]. A student ought to have sense! [*In a soft tone with tears*] How ugly you've grown, Petya! How old you look! [*To Lyubov Andreyevna, no longer crying*] But I can't do without work, mamma; I must have something to do every minute.

[*Enter Yasha.*]

YASHA. [*hardly restraining his laughter*]. Epihodov has broken a billiard cue! [*Goes out.*]

VARYA. What is Epihodov doing here? Who gave him leave to play billiards? I can't make these people out [*goes out*].

LYUBOV. Don't tease her, Petya. You see she has grief enough without that.

TROFIMOV. She is so very officious, meddling in what's not her business. All the summer she's given Anya and me no peace. She's afraid of a love affair between us. What's it to do with her? Besides, I have given no grounds for it. Such triviality is not in my line. We are above love!

LYUBOV. And I suppose I am beneath love. [*Very uneasily*] Why is it Leonid's not here? If only I could know whether the estate is sold or not! It seems such an incredible calamity that I really don't know what to think. I am distracted . . . I shall scream in a minute . . . I shall do something stupid. Save me, Petya, tell me something, talk to me!

TROFIMOV. What does it matter whether the estate is sold to-day or not? That's all done with long ago. There's no turning back, the path is overgrown. Don't worry yourself, dear Lyubov Andreyevna. You mustn't deceive yourself; for once in your life you must face the truth!

LYUBOV. What truth? You see where the truth lies, but I seem to have lost my sight, I see nothing. You settle every great problem so boldly, but tell me, my dear boy, isn't it because you're young—because you haven't yet understood one of your problems through suffering? You look forward boldly, and isn't it that you don't see and don't expect anything dreadful because life is still hidden from your young eyes? You're bolder, more honest, deeper than we are, but think, be just a little magnanimous, have pity on me. I was born here, you know, my father and mother lived here, my grandfather lived here, I love this house. I can't conceive of life without the cherry orchard, and if it really must be sold, then sell me with the orchard [*embraces Trofimov, kisses him on the forehead*]. My boy was drowned here [*weeps*]. Pity me, my dear kind fellow.

TROFIMOV. You know I feel for you with all my heart.

LYUBOV. But that should have been said differently, so differently [*takes out her handkerchief, telegram falls on the floor*]. My heart is so heavy to-day. It's so noisy here, my soul is quivering at every sound, I'm shuddering all over, but I can't go away; I'm afraid to be quiet and alone. Don't be hard on me, Petya . . . I love you as though you were one of ourselves. I would gladly let you marry Anya—I swear I would—only, my dear boy, you must take your degree, you do nothing—you're simply tossed by fate from place to place. That's so strange. It is, isn't it? And you must do something with your beard to make it grow somehow [*laughs*]. You look so funny!

TROFIMOV. [*picks up the telegram*]. I've no wish to be a beauty.

LYUBOV. That's a telegram from Paris. I get one every day. One yesterday and one to-day. That savage creature is ill again, he's in trouble again. He begs forgiveness, beseeches me to go, and really I ought to go to Paris to see him. You look shocked, Petya. What am I to do, my dear boy, what am I to do? He is ill, he is alone and unhappy, and who'll look after him, who'll keep him from doing the wrong thing, who'll give him his medicine at the right time? And why hide it or be silent? I love him, that's clear. I love him! I love him! He's a millstone about my neck, I'm going to the bottom with him, but I love that stone and can't live without it [*presses Trofimov's hand*]. Don't think ill of me, Petya, don't tell me anything, don't tell me . . .

TROFIMOV. [*through his tears*]. For God's sake forgive my frankness: why, he robbed you!

LYUBOV. No! No! No! You mustn't speak like that [*covers her ears*].

TROFIMOV. He is a wretch! You're the only person that doesn't know it! He's a worthless creature! A despicable wretch!

LYUBOV. [*getting angry, but speaking with restraint*]. You're twenty-six or twenty-seven years old, but you're still a schoolboy.

TROFIMOV. Possibly.

LYUBOV. You should be a man at your age! You should understand what love means! And you ought to be in love yourself. You ought to fall in love! [*Angrily*] Yes, yes, and it's not purity in you, you're simply a prude, a comic fool, a freak.

TROFIMOV. [*in horror*]. The things she's saying!

LYUBOV. I am above love! You're not above love, but simply as our Firs here says, "You are a good-for-nothing." At your age not to have a mistress!

TROFIMOV. [*in horror*]. This is awful! The things she is saying! [*goes rapidly into the larger drawing-room clutching his head*]. This is awful! I can't stand it! I'm

going. [*Goes off, but at once returns.*] All is over between us! [*Goes off into the ante-room.*]

LYUBOV. [*shouts after him*]. Petya! Wait a minute! You funny creature! I was joking! Petya! [*There is a sound of somebody running quickly downstairs and suddenly falling with a crash. Anya and Varya scream, but there is a sound of laughter at once.*]

LYUBOV. What has happened?

[*Anya runs in.*]

ANYA. [*laughing*]. Petya's fallen downstairs! [*Runs out.*]

LYUBOV. What a queer fellow that Petya is!

[*The Station Master stands in the middle of the larger room and reads "The Magdalene," by Alexey Tolstoy. They listen to him, but before he has recited many lines strains of a waltz are heard from the ante-room and the reading is broken off. All dance. Trofimov, Anya, Varya, and Lyubov Andreyevna come in from the ante-room.*]

LYUBOV. Come, Petya—come, pure heart! I beg your pardon. Let's have a dance! [*dances with Petya*].

[*Anya and Varya dance. Firs comes in, puts his stick down near the side door. Yasha also comes into the drawing room and looks on at the dancing.*]

YASHA. What is it, old man?

FIRS. I don't feel well. In old days we used to have generals, barons and admirals dancing at our balls, and now we send for the post-office clerk and the station master and even they're not overanxious to come. I am getting feeble. The old master, the grandfather, used to give sealing-wax for all complaints. I have been taking sealing-wax for twenty years or more. Perhaps that's what's kept me alive.

YASHA. You bore me, old man! [*yawns*] It's time you were done with.

FIRS. Ach, you're a good-for-nothing! [*mutters*]

[*Trofimov and Lyubov Andreyevna dance in larger room and then on to the stage*].

LYUBOV. *Merci.* I'll sit down a little [*sits down*]. I'm tired.

[*Enter Anya.*]

ANYA. [*excitedly*]. There's a man in the kitchen has been saying that the cherry orchard's been sold to-day.

LYUBOV. Sold to whom?

ANYA. He didn't say to whom. He's gone away.

[*She dances with Trofimov, and they go off into the larger room.*]

YASHA. There was an old man gossiping there, a stranger.

FIRS. Leonid Andreyevitch isn't here yet, he hasn't come back. He has his light overcoat on, *demi-saison*, he'll catch cold for sure. Ach! Foolish young things!!

LYUBOV. I feel as though I should die. Go, Yasha, find out to whom it has been sold.

YASHA. But he went away long ago, the old chap [*laughs*].

LYUBOV. [*with slight vexation*]. What are you laughing at? What are you pleased at?

YASHA. Epihodov is so funny. He's a silly fellow, two and twenty misfortunes.

LYUBOV. Firs, if the estate is sold, where will you go?

FIRS. Where you bid me, there I'll go.

LYUBOV. Why do you look like that? Are you ill? You ought to be in bed.

FIRS. Yes [*ironically*]. Me go to bed and who's to wait here? Who's to see to things without me? I'm the only one in all the house.

YASHA. [*to Lyubov Andreyevna*]. Lyubov Andreyevna, permit me to make a request of you; if you go back to Paris again, be so kind as to take me with you. It's positively impossible for me to stay here [*looking about him, in an undertone*]. There's no need to say it, you see for yourself—an uncivilised country, the people have no morals, and then the dullness! The food in the kitchen's abominable, and then Firs runs after one muttering all sorts of unsuitable words. Take me with you, please do!

[*Enter Pishtchik.*]

PISHTCHIK. Allow me to ask you for a waltz, my dear lady. [*Lyubov Andreyevna goes with him.*] Enchanting lady, I really must borrow of you just 180 roubles [*dances*] only 180 roubles. [*They pass into the larger room.*]

YASHA. [*hums softly*]. "Knowest thou my soul's emotion."

[*In the larger drawing-room, a figure in a gray top hat and in check trousers is gesticulating and jumping about.* Shouts of "Bravo, Charlotta Ivanovna."]

DUNYASHA. [*she has stopped to powder herself*]. My young lady tells me to dance. There are plenty of **gentlemen**, and too few ladies, but dancing makes **me giddy** and makes my heart beat. Firs, the post-office clerk said something to me just now that quite took my breath away.

[*Music becomes more subdued.*]

FIRS. What did he say to you?

DUNYASHA. He said I was like a flower.

YASHA. [*yawns*]. What ignorance! [*Goes out.*]

DUNYASHA. Like a flower. I am a girl of such delicate feelings, I am awfully fond of soft speeches.

FIRS. Your head's being turned.

[*Enter Epihodov.*]

EPIHODOV. You have no desire to see me, Dunyasha. I might be an insect [*sighs*]. Ah! life!

DUNYASHA. What is it you want?

EPIHODOV. Undoubtedly you may be right [*sighs*]. But of course, if one looks at it from that point of view, if I may so express myself, you have, excuse my plain speaking, reduced me to a complete state of mind. I know my destiny. Every day some misfortune befalls me and I have long ago grown accustomed to it, so that I look upon my fate with a smile. You gave me your word, and though I—

DUNYASHA. Let us have a talk later, I entreat you, but now leave me in peace, for I am lost in reverie [*plays with her fan*].

EPIHODOV. I have a misfortune every day, and if I may venture to express myself, I merely smile at it, I even laugh.

[*Varya enters from the larger drawing-room.*]

VARYA. You still have not gone, Epihodov. What a disrespectful creature you are, really! [*To Dunyasha*] Go along, Dunyasha! [*To Epihodov*] First you play billiards and break the cue, then you go wandering about the drawing-room like a visitor!

EPIHODOV. You really cannot, if I may so express myself, call me to account like this.

VARYA. I'm not calling you to account, I'm speaking to you. You do nothing but wander from place to place and don't do your work. We keep you as a counting-house clerk, but what use you are I can't say.

EPIHODOV. [*offended*]. Whether I work or whether I talk, whether I eat or whether I play billiards, is a matter to be judged by persons of understanding and my elders.

VARYA. You dare to tell me that! [*Firing up*] You dare! You mean to say I've no understanding. Begone from here! This minute!

EPIHODOV. [*intimidated*]. I beg you to express yourself with delicacy.

VARYA. [*beside herself with anger*]. This moment! get out! away! [*He goes towards the door, she following him.*] Two and twenty misfortunes! Take yourself off! Don't let me set eyes on you! [*Epihodov has gone out, behind the door his voice, "I shall lodge a complaint against you.".*] What! You're coming back? [*Snatches up the stick Firs has put down near the door.*] Come! Come! Come! I'll show you! What! you're coming? Then take that! [*She swings the stick, at the very moment that Lopahin comes in.*]

LOPAHIN. Very much obliged to you!

VARYA. [*angrily and ironically*]. I beg your pardon!

LOPAHIN. Not at all! I humbly thank you for your kind reception!

VARYA. No need of thanks for it. [*Moves away, then looks round and asks softly*] I haven't hurt you?

LOPAHIN. Oh, no! Not at all! There's an immense bump coming up, though!

VOICES FROM LARGER ROOM. Lopahin has come! Yermolay Alexeyevitch!

PISHTCHIK. What do I see and hear? [*Kisses Lopahin.*] There's a whiff of cognac about you, my dear soul, and we're making merry here too!

[*Enter Lyubov Andreyevna.*]

LYUBOV. Is it you, Yermolay Alexeyevitch? Why have you been so long? Where's Leonid?

LOPAHIN. Leonid Andreyevitch arrived with me. He is coming.

LYUBOV. [*in agitation*]. Well! Well! Was there a sale? Speak!

LOPAHIN. [*embarrassed, afraid of betraying his joy*]. The sale was over at four o'clock. We missed our train—had to wait till half-past nine. [*Sighing heavily*] Ugh! I feel a little giddy.

[*Enter Gaev. In his right hand he has purchases, with his left hand he is wiping away his tears.*]

LYUBOV. Well, Leonid? What news? [*Impatiently, with tears*] Make haste, for God's sake!

GAEV. [*makes her no answer, simply waves his hand. To Firs, weeping*] Here, take them; there's anchovies, Kertch herrings. I have eaten nothing all day. What I have been through! [*Door into the billiard room is open. There is heard a knocking of balls and the voice of Yasha saying "Eighty-seven." Gaev's expression changes, he leaves off weeping*]. I am fearfully tired. Firs, come and help me change my things [*goes to his own room across the larger drawing-room*].

PISHTCHIK. How about the sale? Tell us, do!

LYUBOV. Is the cherry orchard sold?

LOPAHIN. It is sold.

LYUBOV. Who has bought it?

LOPAHIN. I have bought it. [*A pause. Lyubov is crushed; she would fall down if she were not standing near a chair and table.*]

[*Varya takes keys from her waist-band, flings them on the floor in middle of drawing-room and goes out.*]

LOPAHIN. I have bought it! Wait a bit, ladies and gentlemen, pray. My head's a bit muddled, I can't speak [*laughs*]. We came to the auction. Deriganov was there already. Leonid Andreyevitch only had 15,000 and Deriganov bid 30,000, besides the arrears, straight off. I saw how the land lay. I bid against him. I bid 40,000, he bid 45,000, I said 55, and so he went on, adding 5 thousands and I adding 10. Well . . . So it ended. I bid 90, and it was knocked down to me. Now the cherry orchard's mine! Mine! [*chuckles*] My God, the cherry orchard's mine! Tell me that I'm drunk, that I'm out of my mind, that it's all a dream [*stamps with his feet*]. Don't laugh at me! If my father and my grandfather could rise from their graves and see all that has happened! How their Yermolay, ignorant, beaten Yermolay, who used to run about barefoot in winter, how that very Yermolay has bought the finest estate in the world! I have bought the estate where my father and grandfather were slaves, where they weren't even admitted into the kitchen. I am asleep, I am dreaming! It is all fancy, it is the work of your imagination plunged in the darkness of ignorance [*picks up keys, smiling fondly*]. She threw away the keys; she means to show she's not the housewife now [*jingles the keys*]. Well, no matter. [*The orchestra is heard tuning up.*] Hey, musicians! Play! I want to hear you. Come, all of you, and look how Yermolay Lopahin will take the axe to the cherry orchard, how the trees will fall to the ground! We will build houses on it and our grandsons and great-grandsons will see a new life springing up there. Music! Play up!

[*Music begins to play. Lyubov Andreyevna has sunk into a chair and is weeping bitterly.*]

LOPAHIN. [*reproachfully*]. Why, why didn't you listen to me? My poor friend! Dear lady, there's no turning back now. [*With tears*] Oh, if all this could be over, oh, if our miserable disjointed life could somehow soon be changed!

PISHTCHIK. [*takes him by the arm, in an undertone*]. She's weeping, let us go and leave her alone. Come [*takes him by the arm and leads him into the larger drawing-room*].

LOPAHIN. What's that? Musicians, play up! All must be as I wish it. [*With irony*] Here comes the new master, the owner of the cherry orchard! [*Accidentally tips over a little table, almost upsetting the candelabra.*] I can pay for everything! [*Goes out with Pishtchik. No one remains on the stage or in the larger drawing-room except Lyubov, who sits huddled up, weeping bitterly. The music plays softly. Anya and Trofimov come in quickly. Anya goes up to her mother and falls on her knees before her. Trofimov stands at the entrance to the larger drawing-room*].

ANYA. Mamma! Mamma, you're crying, dear, kind, good mamma! My precious! I love you! I bless you! The cherry orchard is sold, it is gone, that's true, that's true! But don't weep, mamma! Life is still before you, you have still your good, pure heart! Let us go, let us go, darling, away from here! We will make a new garden, more splendid than this one; you will see it, you will understand. And joy, quiet, deep joy, will sink into your soul like the sun at evening! And you will smile, mamma! Come, darling, let us go!

CURTAIN

Act IV

SCENE: Same as in First Act. There are neither curtains on the windows nor pictures on the walls: only a little furniture remains piled up in a corner as if for sale. There is a sense of desolation; near the outer door and in the background of the scene are packed trunks, travelling bags, etc. On the left the door is open, and from here the voices of Varya and Anya are audible. Lopahin is standing waiting. Yasha is holding a tray with glasses full of champagne. In front of the stage Epihodov is tying up a box. In the background behind the scene a hum of talk from the peasants who have come to say good-bye. The voice of Gaev: "Thanks, brothers, thanks!"

YASHA. The peasants have come to say good-bye. In my opinion, Yermolay Alexeyevitch, the peasants are good-natured, but they don't know much about things.

[*The hum of talk dies away. Enter across front of stage Lyubov Andreyevna and Gaev. She is not weeping, but is pale; her face is quivering—she cannot speak.*]

GAEV. You gave them your purse, Lyuba. That won't do—that won't do!

LYUBOV. I couldn't help it! I couldn't help it!

[*Both go out.*]

LOPAHIN. [*in the doorway, calls after them*]. You will take a glass at parting? Please do. I didn't think to bring any from the town, and at the station I could only get one bottle. Please take a glass [*a pause*] What? You don't care for any? [*Comes away from the door*] If I'd known, I wouldn't have bought it. Well, and I'm not going to drink it. [*Yasha carefully sets the tray down on a chair.*] You have a glass, Yasha, anyway.

YASHA. Good luck to the travellers, and luck to those that stay behind! [*drinks*] This champagne isn't the real thing, I can assure you.

LOPAHIN. It cost eight roubles the bottle [*a pause*]. It's devilish cold here.

YASHA. They haven't heated the stove to-day—it's all the same since we're going [*laughs*].

LOPAHIN. What are you laughing for?

YASHA. For pleasure.

LOPAHIN. Though it's October, it's as still and sunny as though it were summer. It's just right for building! [*Looks at his watch; says in doorway*] Take note, ladies and gentlemen, the train goes in forty-seven minutes; so you ought to start for the station in twenty minutes. You must hurry up!

[*Trofimov comes in from out of doors wearing a greatcoat.*]

TROFIMOV. I think it must be time to start, the horses are ready. The devil only knows what's become of my goloshes; they're lost. [*In the doorway*] Anya! My goloshes aren't here. I can't find them.

LOPAHIN. And I'm getting off to Harkov. I am going

in the same train with you. I'm spending all the winter at Harkov. I've been wasting all my time gossiping with you and fretting with no work to do. I can't get on without work. I don't know what to do with my hands, they flap about so queerly, as if they didn't belong to me.

TROFIMOV. Well, we're just going away, and you will take up your profitable labours again.

LOPAHIN. Do take a glass.

TROFIMOV. No, thanks.

LOPAHIN. Then you're going to Moscow now?

TROFIMOV. Yes. I shall see them as far as the town, and to-morrow I shall go on to Moscow.

LOPAHIN. Yes, I daresay, the professors aren't giving any lectures, they're waiting for your arrival.

TROFIMOV. That's not your business.

LOPAHIN. How many years have you been at the University?

TROFIMOV. Do think of something newer than that— that's stale and flat [*hunts for goloshes*]. You know we shall most likely never see each other again, so let me give you one piece of advice at parting: don't wave your arms about—get out of the habit. And another thing, building villas, reckoning up that the summer visitors will in time become independent farmers—reckoning like that, that's not the thing to do either. After all, I am fond of you: you have fine delicate fingers like an artist, you've a fine delicate soul.

LOPAHIN. [*embraces him*]. Good-bye, my dear fellow. Thanks for everything. Let me give you money for the journey, if you need it.

TROFIMOV. What for? I don't need it.

LOPAHIN. Why, you haven't got a halfpenny.

TROFIMOV. Yes, I have, thank you. I got some money for a translation. Here it is in my pocket, [*anxiously*] but where can my goloshes be!

VARYA. [*from the next room*]. Take the nasty things! [*Flings a pair of goloshes on to the stage.*]

TROFIMOV. Why are you so cross, Varya? h'm! . . . but those aren't my goloshes.

LOPAHIN. I sowed three thousand acres with poppies in the spring, and now I have cleared forty thousand profit. And when my poppies were in flower, wasn't it a picture! So here, as I say, I made forty thousand, and I'm offering you a loan because I can afford to. Why turn up your nose? I am a peasant—I speak bluntly.

TROFIMOV. Your father was a peasant, mine was a chemist—and that proves absolutely nothing whatever. [*Lopahin takes out his pocket-book.*] Stop that— stop that. If you were to offer me two hundred

thousand I wouldn't take it. I am an independent man, and everything that all of you, rich and poor alike, prize so highly and hold so dear, hasn't the slightest power over me—it's like so much fluff fluttering in the air. I can get on without you. I can pass by you. I am strong and proud. Humanity is advancing towards the highest truth, the highest happiness, which is possible on earth, and I am in the front ranks.

LOPAHIN. Will you get there?

TROFIMOV. I shall get there [*a pause*]. I shall get there, or I shall show others the way to get there.

[*In the distance is heard the stroke of an axe on a tree.*]

LOPAHIN. Good-bye, my dear fellow; it's time to be off. We turn up our noses at one another, but life is passing all the while. When I am working hard without resting, then my mind is more at ease, and it seems to me as though I too know what I exist for; but how many people there are in Russia, my dear boy, who exist, one doesn't know what for. Well, it doesn't matter. That's not what keeps thing spinning. They tell me Leonid Andreyevitch has taken a situation. He is going to be a clerk at the bank—6,000 roubles a year. Only, of course, he won't stick to it—he's too lazy.

ANYA. [*in the doorway*]. Mamma begs you not to let them chop down the orchard until she's gone.

TROFIMOV. Yes, really, you might have the tact [*walks out across the front of the stage*].

LOPAHIN. I'll see to it! I'll see to it! Stupid fellows! [*Goes out after him.*]

ANYA. Has Firs been taken to the hospital?

YASHA. I told them this morning. No doubt they have taken him.

ANYA. [*to Epihodov, who passes across the drawing-room*]. Semyon Pantaleyevitch, inquire, please, if Firs has been taken to the hospital.

YASHA. [*in a tone of offence*]. I told Yegor this morning—why ask a dozen times?

EPIHODOV. Firs is advanced in years. It's my conclusive opinion no treatment would do him good; it's time he was gathered to his fathers. And I can only envy him [*puts a trunk down on a cardboard hat-box and crushes it*]. There now, of course—I knew it would be so.

YASHA. [*jeeringly*]. Two and twenty misfortunes!

VARYA. [*through the door*]. Has Firs been taken to the hospital?

ANYA. Yes.

VARYA. Why wasn't the note for the doctor taken too?

ANYA. Oh, then, we must send it after them [goes out].

VARYA. [from the adjoining room]. Where's Yasha? Tell him his mother's come to say good-bye to him.

YASHA. [waves his hand]. They put me out of all patience! [Dunyasha has all this time been busy about the luggage. Now, when Yasha is left alone, she goes up to him].

DUNYASHA. You might just give me one look, Yasha. You're going away. You're leaving me [weeps and throws herself on his neck].

YASHA. What are you crying for? [drinks the champagne]. In six days I shall be in Paris again. To-morrow we shall get into the express train and roll away in a flash. I can scarcely believe it! *Vive la France!* It doesn't suit me here—it's not the life for me; there's no doing anything. I have seen enough of the ignorance here. I have had enough of it [drinks champagne]. What are you crying for? Behave yourself properly, and then you won't cry.

DUNYASHA. [powders her face, looking in a pocket-mirror]. Do send me a letter from Paris. You know how I loved you, Yasha—how I loved you! I am a tender creature, Yasha.

YASHA. Here they are coming!

[Busies himself about the trunks, humming softly. Enter Lyubov Andreyevna, Gaev, Anya and Charlotta Ivanovna.]

GAEV. We ought to be off. There's not much time now [looking at Yasha]. What a smell of herrings!

LYUBOV. In ten minutes we must get into the carriage [casts a look about the room]. Farewell, dear house, dear old home of our fathers! Winter will pass and spring will come, and then you will be no more; they will tear you down! How much those walls have seen! [Kisses her daughter passionately.] My treasure, how bright you look! Your eyes are sparkling like diamonds! Are you glad? Very glad?

ANYA. Very glad! A new life is beginning, mamma.

GAEV. Yes, really, everything is all right now. Before the cherry orchard was sold, we were all worried and wretched, but afterwards, when once the question was settled conclusively, irrevocably, we all felt calm and even cheerful. I am a bank clerk now—I am a financier—cannon off the red. And you, Lyuba, after all, you are looking better; there's no question of that.

LYUBOV. Yes. My nerves are better, that's true. [Her hat and coat are handed to her.] I'm sleeping well. Carry out my things, Yasha. It's time. [To Anya] My darling, we shall soon see each other again. I am going to Paris. I can live there on the money your

Yaroslavl auntie sent us to buy the estate with—hurrah for auntie!—but that money won't last long.

ANYA. You'll come back soon, mamma, won't you? I'll be working up for my examination in the high school, and when I have passed that, I shall set to work and be a help to you. We will read all sorts of things together, mamma, won't we? [Kisses her mother's hands.] We will read in the autumn evenings. We'll read lots of books, and a new wonderful world will open out before us [dreamily]. Mamma, come soon.

LYUBOV. I shall come, my precious treasure [embraces her].

[Enter Lopahin. Charlotta softly hums a song.]

GAEV. Charlotta's happy; she's singing!

CHARLOTTA. [picks up a bundle like a swaddled baby]. Bye, bye, my baby. [A baby is heard crying: "Ooah! ooah!"] Hush, hush, my pretty boy! [Ooah! ooah!] Poor little thing! [Throws the bundle back.] You must please find me a situation. I can't go on like this.

LOPAHIN. We'll find you one, Charlotta Ivanovna. Don't you worry yourself.

GAEV. Everyone's leaving us. Varya's going away. We have become of no use all at once.

CHARLOTTA. There's nowhere for me to be in the town. I must go away. [Hums] What care I . . .

[Enter Pishtchik.]

LOPAHIN. The freak of nature!

PISHTCHIK. [gasping]. Oh! . . . let me get my breath. . . . I'm worn out . . . my most honoured . . . Give me some water.

GAEV. Want some money, I suppose? Your humble servant! I'll go out of the way of temptation [goes out].

PISHTCHIK. It's a long while since I have been to see you . . . dearest lady. [To Lopahin] You are here . . . glad to see you . . . a man of immense intellect . . . take . . . here [gives Lopahin] 400 roubles. That leaves me owing 840.

LOPAHIN. [shrugging his shoulders in amazement]. It's like a dream. Where did you get it?

PISHTCHIK. Wait a bit . . . I'm hot . . . a most extraordinary occurrence! Some Englishmen came along and found in my land some sort of white clay. [To Lyubov Andreyevna] And 400 for you . . . most lovely . . . wonderful [gives money]. The rest later [sips water]. A young man in the train was telling me just now that a great philosopher advises jumping off a house-top. "Jump!" says he; "the whole gist of the problem lies in that." [*Wonderingly*] Fancy that, now! Water, please!

LOPAHIN. What Englishmen?

PISHTCHIK. I have made over to them the rights to dig the clay for twenty-four years . . . and now, excuse me . . . I can't stay . . . I must be trotting on. I'm going to Znoikovo . . . to Kardamanovo . . . I'm in debt all round [*sips*] . . . To your very good health! . . . I'll come in on Thursday.

LYUBOV. We are just off to the town, and to-morrow I start for abroad.

PISHTCHIK. What! [*In agitation*] Why to the town? Oh, I see the furniture . . . the boxes. No matter . . . [*through his tears*] . . . no matter . . . men of enormous intellect . . . these Englishmen. . . . Never mind . . . be happy. God will succour you . . . no matter . . . everything in this world must have an end [*kisses Lyubov Andreyevna's hand*]. If the rumour reaches you that my end has come, think of this . . . old horse, and say: "There once was such a man in the world . . . Semyonov-Pishtchik . . . the Kingdom of Heaven be his!" . . . most extraordinary weather . . . yes. [*Goes out in violent agitation, but at once returns and says in the doorway*] Dashenka wishes to be remembered to you [*goes out*].

LYUBOV. Now we can start. I leave with two cares in my heart. The first is leaving Firs ill. [*Looking at her watch*] We have still five minutes.

ANYA. Mamma, Firs has been taken to the hospital. Yasha sent him off this morning.

LYUBOV. My other anxiety is Varya. She is used to getting up early and working; and now, without work, she's like a fish out of water. She is thin and pale, and she's crying, poor dear! [*a pause*] You are well aware, Yermolay Alexeyevitch, I dreamed of marrying her to you, and everything seemed to show that you would get married [*whispers to Anya and motions to Charlotta and both go out*]. She loves you—she suits you. And I don't know—I don't know why it is you seem, as it were, to avoid each other. I can't understand it!

LOPAHIN. I don't understand it myself, I confess. It's queer somehow, altogether. If there's still time, I'm ready now at once. Let's settle it straight off, and go ahead; but without you, I feel I shan't make her an offer.

LYUBOV. That's excellent. Why, a single moment's all that's necessary. I'll call her at once.

LOPAHIN. And there's champagne all ready too [*looking into the glasses*]. Empty! Someone's emptied them already. [*Yasha coughs.*] I call that greedy.

LYUBOV. [*eagerly*]. Capital! We will go out. Yasha, *allez*! I'll call her in. [*At the door*] Varya, leave all that; come here. Come along! [*goes out with Yasha*].

LOPAHIN. [*looking at his watch*]. Yes.

[*A pause. Behind the door, smothered laughter and whispering, and, at last, enter Varya.*]

VARYA. [*looking a long while over the things*]. It is strange, I can't find it anywhere.

LOPAHIN. What are you looking for?

VARYA. I packed it myself, and I can't remember [*a pause*].

LOPAHIN. Where are you going now, Varvara Mihailova?

VARYA. I? To the Ragulins. I have arranged to go to them to look after the house—as a housekeeper.

LOPAHIN. That's in Yashnovo? It'll be seventy miles away [*a pause*]. So this is the end of life in this house!

VARYA. [*looking among the things*]. Where is it? Perhaps I put it in the trunk. Yes, life in this house is over—there will be no more of it.

LOPAHIN. And I'm just off to Harkov—by this next train. I've a lot of business there. I'm leaving Epihodov here, and I've taken him on.

VARYA. Really!

LOPAHIN. This time last year we had snow already, if you remember; but now it's so fine and sunny. Though it's cold, to be sure—three degrees of frost.

VARYA. I haven't looked [*a pause*]. And besides, our thermometer's broken [*a pause*].

[*Voice at the door from the yard: "Yermolay Alexeyevitch!"*]

LOPAHIN. [*as though he had long been expecting this summons*]. This minute!

[*Lopahin goes out quickly. Varya sitting on the floor and laying her head on a bag full of clothes, sobs quietly. The door opens. Lyubov Andreyevna comes in cautiously.*]

LYUBOV. Well? [*a pause*] We must be going.

VARYA. [*has wiped her eyes and is no longer crying*]. Yes, mamma, it's time to start. I shall have time to get to the Ragulins to-day, if only you're not late for the train.

LYUBOV. [*in the doorway*]. Anya, put your things on.

[*Enter Anya, then Gaev and Charlotta Ivanovna. Gaev has on a warm coat with a hood. Servants and cabmen come in. Epihodov bustles about the luggage.*]

LYUBOV. Now we can start on our travels.

ANYA. [*joyfully*]. On our travels!

GAEV. My friends—my dear, my precious friends! Leaving this house for ever, can I be silent? Can I refrain from giving utterance at leave-taking to those emotions which now flood all my being?

ANYA. [*supplicatingly*]. Uncle!

VARYA. Uncle, you mustn't!

GAEV. [*dejectedly*]. Cannon and into the pocket . . . I'll be quiet. . . .

[*Enter Trofimov and afterwards Lopahin.*]

TROFIMOV. Well, ladies and gentlemen, we must start.

LOPAHIN. Epihodov, my coat!

LYUBOV. I'll stay just one minute. It seems as though I have never seen before what the walls, what the ceilings in this house were like, and now I look at them with greediness, with such tender love.

GAEV. I remember when I was six years old sitting in that window on Trinity Day watching my father going to church.

LYUBOV. Have all the things been taken?

LOPAHIN. I think all. [*Putting on overcoat, to Epihodov*] You, Epihodov, mind you see everything is right.

EPIHODOV. [*in a husky voice*]. Don't you trouble, Yermolay Alexeyevitch.

LOPAHIN. Why, what's wrong with your voice?

EPIHODOV. I've just had a drink of water, and I choked over something.

YASHA. [*contemptuously*]. The ignorance!

LYUBOV. We are going—and not a soul will be left here.

LOPAHIN. Not till the spring.

VARYA. [*pulls a parasol out of a bundle, as though about to hit someone with it. Lopahin makes a gesture as though alarmed*]. What is it? I didn't mean anything.

TROFIMOV. Ladies and gentlemen, let us get into the carriage. It's time. The train will be in directly.

VARYA. Petya, here they are, your goloshes, by that box. [*With tears*] And what dirty old things they are!

TROFIMOV. [*putting on his goloshes*]. Let us go, friends!

GAEV. [*greatly agitated, afraid of weeping*]. The train—the station! Double baulk, ah!

LYUBOV. Let us go!

LOPAHIN. Are we all here? [*Locks the side-door on left.*] The things are all here. We must lock up. Let us go!

ANYA. Good-bye, home! Good-bye to the old life!

TROFIMOV. Welcome to the new life!

[*Trofimov goes out with Anya. Varya looks round the room and goes out slowly. Yasha and Charlotta Ivanovna, with her dog, go out.*]

LOPAHIN. Till the spring, then! Come, friends, till we meet! [*Goes out.*]

[*Lyubov Andreyevna and Gaev remain alone. As though they had been waiting for this, they throw themselves on each other's necks, and break into subdued smothered sobbing, afraid of being overheard.*]

GAEV. [*in despair*]. Sister, my sister!

LYUBOV. Oh, my orchard!—my sweet, beautiful orchard! My life, my youth, my happiness, good-bye! good-bye!

VOICE OF ANYA. [*calling gaily*]. Mamma!

VOICE OF TROFIMOV. [*gaily, excitedly*]. Aa—oo!

LYUBOV. One last look at the walls, at the windows. My dear mother loved to walk about this room.

GAEV. Sister, sister!

VOICE OF ANYA. Mamma!

VOICE OF TROFIMOV. Aa—oo!

LYUBOV. We are coming. [*They go out.*]

[*The stage is empty. There is the sound of the doors being locked up, then of the carriages driving away. There is silence. In the stillness there is the dull stroke of an axe in a tree, clanging with a mournful lonely sound. Footsteps are heard. Firs appears in the doorway on the right. He is dressed as always—in a pea-jacket and white waistcoat, with slippers on his feet. He is ill.*]

FIRS. [*goes up to the doors, and tries the handles*]. Locked! They have gone . . . [*sits down on sofa*]. They have forgotten me. . . . Never mind . . . I'll sit here a bit. . . . I'll be bound Leonid Andreyevitch hasn't put his fur coat on and has gone off in his thin overcoat [*sighs anxiously*]. I didn't see after him. . . . These young people . . . [*mutters something that can't be distinguished*]. Life has slipped by as though I hadn't lived. [*Lies down*] I'll lie down a bit. . . . There's no strength in you, nothing left you—all gone! Ech! I'm good for nothing [*lies motionless*].

[*A sound is heard that seems to come from the sky, like a breaking harp-string, dying away mournfully. All is still again, and there is heard nothing but the strokes of the axe far away in the orchard.*]

CURTAIN

ESSAY: AN APPROACH TO THE PLAY

The Cherry Orchard presents an aristocratic family associated with an older agrarian social and economic system, one which was relatively static. Chekhov here emphasizes the privileges of the aristocratic class under the czars, where wealth depended on ownership of inherited land; aristocrats had only to have children to sustain their power. To most of them, even the benevolent ones, social mobility was neither desirable nor encouraged; for those below them, such movement was very difficult. The aristocrats assumed that peasants, those who lived on and worked their lands, would stay peasants. Socially enlightened aristocrats wanted peasants to be fairly fed, clothed, and housed, partly for humanitarian reasons, but also so that peasants would be content to remain peasants. They held a similar attitude toward all working-class people. The old and loyal valet Firs, although as opposed to change as his mistress, is their servant, not one of them. He is left behind at the end, discarded after a lifetime of service, and not out of hostility, but negligence. In a time of family crisis, the old family retainer is simply overlooked.

Chekhov is portraying this ancient social system in the process of breaking down, a breakdown due in part to the self-indulgence and insulation of the aristocrats themselves. They have been privileged for so long that most of them cannot imagine that anything will really change. Pishtchik tries to borrow money from Madam Ranevsky when she herself is seriously in debt, while she herself believes until nearly the end that some miracle will preserve her privilege. The servant, Firs, is often similarly unrealistic. Since nothing has ever changed before, they are inattentive to threat. This is the society that the revolution will overthrow, but the picture is, as this prerevolutionary (and precommunist) play shows, more complex than that: the aristocrats were ripe to fall.

The character Lopahin represents a different threat to the old economic order: capitalism. Instead of just living on (and off of) the land, the capitalist sees it as an investment opportunity whose purpose is to make a profit. Lopahin's father and grandfather had been serfs—peasant slaves—on this same land. His purchase of Madam Ranevsky's estate, including the cherished cherry orchard, is a sign not only of capitalism's triumph, but also of the social mobility which the new system allows, for the capitalist is tied neither to tradition nor to the land as the old aristocracy was, but instead to money. The land is not valuable in itself, but because it can be made to produce a profit, and because in itself it is convertible into cash; and as cash displaces privilege, the old landed aristocrat is also displaced. The symbol of this changing social and economic order is the sound of the ax in the orchard at the end. (It is interesting that Marx believed capitalism to be a precondition for communism. Chekhov is not attempting prophecy here, but he *is* showing a social process which Marx would have well understood.)

There are other forms of this general social breakdown as well. The two potential couples fail to get together; despite ample opportunities, the crisis of values seems to prevent all decisions from being made. Trofimov, the idealistic twice-expelled student, sees both economic sides as disgusting (as would the revolutionaries in a few years), but he is also "above" both love and money, as unrealistic as Gaev in his musings on billiards. Varya, the aristocratic young woman who is adopted, will end up as a kind of housekeeper, a semiservant. The lower stratum of society is in disorder as well: near the end of the first act, there is a reference to disturbances in the old servants' quarters, and Firs refers to the recent emancipation of serfs as a disaster, presumably because it will facilitate just such changes as Chekhov represents in Lopahin.

Expected dramatic conventions seem to be as undependable and frustrated as social institutions in the play. For example, the clerk Epihodov, a minor figure in the play, says near the start of Act 2 that he cannot figure out whether or not he wants to kill himself but always has a pistol with him in case he *should* decide. This life-and-death dilemma is given to someone of no consequence to the major characters and of no relevance to the plot; the dilemma itself seems unrelated even to the circumstances of the speaker's own life in the play. It also seems dramatically incongruous in the clerk's mouth; his dilemma seems "larger" than his role in the play, a dilemma more appropriate to a play's hero. Then at the end of the play, in the middle of deeply felt emotions, when several of the characters believe that they *are* in a tragedy, this same unheroic clerk speaks hoarsely and is asked what is wrong. In a traditional drama, we would expect a significant statement at such a potentially tragic moment: instead, Epihodov explains that he drank some water and swallowed it wrong.

Chekhov was a formative influence on writers of the theater of the absurd several decades later. He portrayed the incongruities in characters and in society, both in individual speeches and in the range of actions he included in his plots. With him, we do not look for economy of means, nor for one clear unifying idea. The end of *The Cherry Orchard* sustains the play's overall dramatic uncertainty. The stage direction says it is meant to be sad; Chekhov seems to want us to lament the loss of the old agrarian system. But his play also indicts this system for its aristocrats' lack of realism about life, their sentimentality, their inability to see beyond their own concerns to the needs of others and to the changing face of the world around them. It is a realistic portrait in miniature of the complexity of an actual social situation, one whose instability led at last to Stalin and government by terror.

Susan Glaspell

TRIFLES

About the Author   Susan Glaspell (1882–1948) is one of the central figures in twentieth-century American drama. Born in Davenport, Iowa, she remained in Iowa after graduating from Drake University in Des Moines to work as a journalist and to write fiction. She then moved to New York City, where she became part of the literary and intellectual avant garde. Shortly after her marriage in 1913, she and her husband, George Cram Cook, co-founded the seminal experimental theater, the Provincetown Players. In doing so, she was instrumental in helping to define the early twentieth-century reaction against the then-dominant American stage tradition of melodrama, as well as against the "star system" which reigned on Broadway. The Players—which operated in the summer from a theater in Provincetown, Massachusetts, at the tip of Cape Cod, and in the winter from a theater in Greenwich Village in New York City—attracted works by, among others, the novelists Djuna Barnes and Edna Ferber, the poet Edna St. Vincent Millay, and especially America's most influential early twentieth-century playwright, Eugene O'Neill. In 1915, *Suppressed Desires*, her satire of then-fashionable Freudian psychoanalysis (written with Cook) was the first play produced at their Wharf Theater in Provincetown. In the following summer she and Cook met Eugene O'Neill, and thus began his long association with this playhouse. The first of O'Neill's plays ever produced, *Bound East for Cardiff*, was presented there in 1916; because it seemed too short for a full evening's presentation, Glaspell wrote the one-act play *Trifles* to complete the bill.

For much of this century, Glaspell's contributions were forgotten, her importance by and large omitted from histories of drama. During her seven-year association with Provincetown, she contributed eleven plays (only O'Neill, with fourteen, wrote more for this group), many of them experimental in form as well as content. She and O'Neill together introduced "expressionism" to the American stage, a technique whereby other characters are presented dramatically as if seen through the eyes of the main character. Many of her plays were critical successes, perhaps most notably *The Verge* (1921), a study of a woman driven to neurosis, and *Alison's House* (1930), a play loosely based on events from the life of the poet Emily Dickinson, for which she earned a Pulitzer Prize. During the latter part of her life she turned her talents to fiction, and it was only in the early days of the women's movement of the 1970s that her work and cultural importance were "rediscovered."

About the Play   The story told in *Trifles* exists in two forms, as the 1916 play and, in a somewhat expanded version, as the short story "A Jury of Her Peers," published in the following year. Each title provides a somewhat different angle from which to examine the action. The short story title implies the question of whether Minnie Foster Wright could have been judged fairly by an all-male jury. (The Nineteenth Amendment, giving women full rights of citizenship, was still a few years in the future when Glaspell wrote.) Given the patronizing attitudes of the representatives of the legal establishment—the sheriff and the county attorney—it seems unlikely that Minnie's side of the story would have been fully told if she had gone through the legal process. *Trifles*, the title of the play, raises an even broader issue: who is empowered to determine what is trivial (and, by extension, what is important)? When the men overhear Mrs. Peters tell Mrs. Hale that the murder suspect was worried about whether her preserves had burst overnight in the cold, the men are amused and Mr. Hale says, "Well, women are used to worrying over trifles." The moment gives the play its title, and is typical of a play in which gender roles are rigidly defined and separated. The play's setting—the kitchen—was radical in its day: the men search the house and grounds for clues, passing quickly through the stage area because, as the sheriff says, "Nothing here but kitchen things." Typically drama, not unlike the legal system, focused on what went on in areas less associated with women's concerns.

CHARACTERS

GEORGE HENDERSON, county attorney
HENRY PETERS, sheriff
LEWIS HALE, a neighboring farmer

MRS. PETERS
MRS. HALE

SCENE

The kitchen in the now abandoned farmhouse of John Wright, a gloomy kitchen, and left without having been put in order—unwashed pans under the sink, a loaf of bread outside the breadbox, a dish towel on the table—other signs of incompleted work. At the rear the outer door opens and the Sheriff comes in followed by the County Attorney and Hale. The Sheriff and Hale are men in middle life, the County Attorney is a young man; all are much bundled up and go at once to the stove. They are followed by two women—the Sheriff's wife first; she is a slight wiry woman, a thin nervous face. Mrs. Hale is larger and would ordinarily be called more comfortable looking, but she is disturbed now and looks fearfully about as she enters. The women have come in slowly, and stand close together near the door.

COUNTY ATTORNEY [*rubbing his hands*]. This feels good. Come up to the fire, ladies.

MRS. PETERS [*after taking a step forward*]. I'm not—cold.

SHERIFF [*unbuttoning his overcoat and stepping away from the stove as if to mark the beginning of official business*]. Now, Mr. Hale, before we move things about, you explain to Mr. Henderson just what you saw when you came here yesterday morning.

COUNTY ATTORNEY. By the way, has anything been moved? Are things just as you left them yesterday?

SHERIFF [*looking about*]. It's just the same. When it dropped below zero last night I thought I'd better send Frank out this morning to make a fire for us—no use getting pneumonia with a big case on, but I told him not to touch anything except the stove—and you know Frank.

COUNTY ATTORNEY. Somebody should have been left here yesterday.

SHERIFF. Oh—yesterday. When I had to send Frank to Morris Center for that man who went crazy—I want you to know I had my hands full yesterday, I knew you could get back from Omaha by today and as long as I went over everything here myself—

COUNTY ATTORNEY. Well, Mr. Hale, tell just what happened when you came here yesterday morning.

HALE. Harry and I had started to town with a load of potatoes. We came along the road from my place and as I got here I said, "I'm going to see if I can't get John Wright to go in with me on a party telephone." I spoke to Wright about it once before and he put me off, saying folks talked too much anyway, and all he asked was peace and quiet—I guess you know about how much he talked himself; but I thought maybe if I went to the house and talked about it before his wife, though I said to Harry that I didn't know as what his wife wanted made much difference to John—

COUNTY ATTORNEY. Let's talk about that later, Mr. Hale. I do want to talk about that, but tell now just what happened when you got to the house.

HALE. I didn't hear or see anything; I knocked at the door, and still it was all quiet inside. I knew they must be up, it was past eight o'clock. So I knocked again, and I thought I heard somebody say, "Come in." I wasn't sure, I'm not sure yet, but I opened the door—this door [*Indicating the door by which the two women are still standing*] and there in that rocker—[*Pointing to it.*] sat Mrs. Wright.

[*They all look at the rocker.*]

COUNTY ATTORNEY. What—was she doing?

HALE. She was rockin' back and forth. She had her apron in her hand and was kind of—pleating it.

COUNTY ATTORNEY. And how did she—look?

HALE. Well, she look queer.

COUNTY ATTORNEY. How do you mean—queer?

HALE. Well, as if she didn't know what she was going to do next. And kind of done up.

COUNTY ATTORNEY. How did she seem to feel about your coming?

HALE. Why, I don't think she minded—one way or other. She didn't pay much attention. I said, "How do, Mrs. Wright, it's cold, ain't it?" And she said, "Is it?"—and went on kind of pleating at her apron. Well, I was surprised; she didn't ask me to come up to the stove, or to set down, but just sat there, not even looking at me, so I said, "I want to see John." And then she—laughed. I guess you would call it a laugh. I thought of Harry and the team outside, so I said a little sharp: "Can't I see John?" "No," she says, kind o' dull like. "Ain't he home?" says I. "Yes," says she, "he's home." "Then why can't I see him?" I asked her, out of patience. "'Cause he's dead," says she. "*Dead?*" says I. She just nodded her head, not getting a bit excited, but rockin' back and forth. "Why—where is he?" says I, not knowing what to say. She just pointed upstairs—like that [*Himself pointing to the room above*]. I got up, with the idea of going up there. I walked from there to here—then I says, "Why, what did he die of?" "He died of a rope round his neck," says she, and just went on pleatin' at her apron. Well, I went out and called Harry. I thought I might—need help. We went upstairs and there he was lyin'—

COUNTY ATTORNEY. I think I'd rather have you go into that upstairs, where you can point it all out. Just go on now with the rest of the story.

HALE. Well, my first thought was to get that rope off. It looked . . . [*Stops, his face twitches.*] . . . but Harry, he went up to him, and he said, "No, he's dead all right, and we'd better not touch anything." So we went back down stairs. She was still sitting that same way. "Has anybody been notified?" I asked. "No," says she, unconcerned. "Who did this, Mrs. Wright?" said Harry. He said it businesslike—and she stopped pleatin' of her apron. "I don't know," she says. "You don't *know?*" says Harry. "No," says she. "Weren't you sleepin' in the bed with him?" says Harry. "Yes," says she, "but I was on the inside." "Somebody slipped a rope round his neck and strangled him and you didn't wake up?" says Harry. "I didn't wake up," she said after him. We must 'a looked as if we didn't see how that could be, for after a minute she said, "I sleep sound." Harry was going to ask her more questions but I said maybe we ought to let her tell her story first to the coroner, or to the sheriff, so Harry went fast as he could to Rivers' place, where there's a telephone.

COUNTY ATTORNEY. And what did Mrs. Wright do when she knew that you had gone for the coroner?

HALE. She moved from that chair to this one over here [*Pointing to a small chair in the corner*] and just sat there with her hands held together and looking down. I got a feeling that I ought to make some conversation, so I said I had come in to see if John wanted to put in a telephone, and at that she started to laugh, and then she stopped and looked at me— scared. [*The County Attorney, who has had his notebook out, makes a note.*] I dunno, maybe it wasn't scared. I wouldn't like to say it was. Soon Harry got back, and then Dr. Lloyd came, and you, Mr. Peters, and so I guess that's all I know that you don't.

COUNTY ATTORNEY [*looking around*]. I guess we'll go upstairs first—and then out to the barn and around there. [*To the Sheriff*] You're convinced that there was nothing important here—nothing that would point to any motive.

SHERIFF. Nothing here but kitchen things.

[*The County Attorney, after again looking around the kitchen, opens the door of a cupboard closet. He gets up on a chair and looks on a shelf. Pulls his hand away, sticky.*]

COUNTY ATTORNEY. Here's a nice mess.

[*The women draw nearer.*]

MRS. PETERS [*to the other woman*]. Oh, her fruit; it did freeze. [*To the County Attorney*] She worried about that when it turned so cold. She said the fire'd go out and her jars would break.

SHERIFF. Well, can you beat the women! Held for murder and worryin' about her preserves.

COUNTY ATTORNEY. I guess before we're through she may have something more serious than preserves to worry about.

HALE. Well, women are used to worrying over trifles.

[*The two women move a little closer together.*]

COUNTY ATTORNEY [*with the gallantry of a young politician*]. And yet, for all their worries, what would we do without the ladies? [*The women do not unbend. He goes to the sink, takes a dipperful of water from the pail and pouring it into a basin, washes his hands. Starts to wipe them on the roller towel, turns it for a cleaner piece.*] Dirty towels! [*Kicks his foot against the pans under the sink.*] Not much of a housekeeper, would you say, ladies?

MRS. HALE [*stiffly*]. There's a great deal of work to be done on a farm.

COUNTY ATTORNEY. To be sure. And yet [*With a little bow to her*] I know there are some Dickson county farmhouses which do not have such roller towels.

[*He gives it a pull to expose its full length again.*]

MRS. HALE. Those towels get dirty awful quick. Men's hands aren't always as clean as they might be.

COUNTY ATTORNEY. Ah, loyal to your sex, I see. But you and Mrs. Wright were neighbors. I suppose you were friends, too.

MRS. HALE [*shaking her head*]. I've not seen much of her of late years. I've not been in this house—it's more than a year.

COUNTY ATTORNEY. And why was that? You didn't like her?

MRS. HALE. I liked her well enough. Farmers' wives have their hands full, Mr. Henderson. And then—

COUNTY ATTORNEY. Yes—?

MRS. HALE [*looking about*]. It never seemed a very cheerful place.

COUNTY ATTORNEY. No—it's not cheerful. I shouldn't say she had the homemaking instinct.

MRS. HALE. Well, I don't know as Wright had, either.

COUNTY ATTORNEY. You mean that they didn't get on very well?

MRS. HALE. No, I don't mean anything. But I don't think a place'd be any cheerfuller for John Wright's being in it.

COUNTY ATTORNEY. I'd like to talk more of that a little later. I want to get the lay of things upstairs now.

[*He goes to the left, where three steps lead to a stair door.*]

SHERIFF. I suppose anything Mrs. Peters does'll be all right. She was to take in some clothes for her, you know, and a few little things. We left in such a hurry yesterday.

COUNTY ATTORNEY. Yes, but I would like to see what you take, Mrs. Peters, and keep an eye out for anything that might be of use to us.

MRS. PETERS. Yes, Mr. Henderson.

[*The women listen to the men's steps on the stairs, then look about the kitchen.*]

MRS. HALE. I'd hate to have men coming into my kitchen, snooping around and criticising.

[*She arranges the pans under the sink which the County Attorney had shoved out of place.*]

MRS. PETERS. Of course it's no more than their duty.

MRS. HALE. Duty's all right, but I guess that deputy sheriff that came out to make the fire might have got a little of this on. [*Gives the roller towel a pull.*] Wish I'd thought of that sooner. Seems mean to talk about her for not having things slicked up when she had to come away in such a hurry.

MRS. PETERS [*Who has gone to a small table in the left rear corner of the room, and lifted one end of a towel that covers a pan*]. She had bread set.

[*Stands still.*]

MRS. HALE [*eyes fixed on a loaf of bread beside the breadbox, which is on a low shelf at the other side of the room. Moves slowly toward it*]. She was going to put this in there. [*Picks up loaf, then abruptly drops it. In a manner of returning to familiar things.*] It's a shame about her fruit. I wonder if it's all gone. [*Gets up on the chair and looks.*] I think there's some here that's all right, Mrs. Peters. Yes—here; [*Holding it toward the window.*] this is cherries, too. [*Looking again.*] I declare I believe that's the only one. [*Gets down, bottle in her hand. Goes to the sink and wipes it off on the outside.*] She'll feel awful bad after all her hard work in the hot weather. I remember the afternoon I put up my cherries last summer.

[*She puts the bottle on the big kitchen table, center of the room. With a sigh, is about to sit down in the rocking-chair. Before she is seated realizes what chair it is; with a slow look at it, steps back. The chair which she has touched rocks back and forth.*]

MRS. PETERS. Well, I must get those things from the front room closet, [*She goes to the door at the right, but after looking into the other room, steps back.*] You coming with me, Mrs. Hale? You could help me carry them.

[*They go in the other room; reappear, Mrs. Peters carrying a dress and skirt, Mrs. Hale following with a pair of shoes.*]

MRS. PETERS. My, it's cold in there.

[*She puts the clothes on the big table, and hurries to the stove.*]

MRS. HALE [*examining her skirt*]. Wright was close. I think maybe that's why she kept so much to herself. She didn't even belong to the Ladies Aid. I suppose she felt she couldn't do her part, and then you don't enjoy things when you feel shabby. She used to wear pretty clothes and be lively, when she was Minnie Foster, one of the town girls singing in the choir. But that—oh, that was thirty years ago. This all you was to take in?

MRS. PETERS. She said she wanted an apron. Funny thing to want, for there isn't much to get you dirty in jail, goodness knows. But I suppose just to make her feel more natural. She said they was in the top drawer in this cupboard. Yes, here. And then her little shawl that always hung behind the door. [*Opens stair door and looks.*] Yes, here it is.

[*Quickly shuts door leading upstairs.*]

MRS. HALE [*abruptly moving toward her*]. Mrs. Peters?

MRS. PETERS. Yes, Mrs. Hale?

MRS. HALE. Do you think she did it?

MRS. PETERS [*in a frightened voice*]. Oh, I don't know.

MRS. HALE. Well, I don't think she did. Asking for an apron and her little shawl. Worrying about her fruit.

MRS. PETERS [*starts to speak, glances up, where footsteps are heard in the room above. In a low voice*]. Mr. Peters says it looks bad for her. Mr. Henderson is awful sarcastic in a speech and he'll make fun of her sayin' she didn't wake up.

MRS. HALE. Well, I guess John Wright didn't wake when they was slipping that rope under his neck.

MRS. PETERS. No, it's strange. It must have been done awful crafty and still. They say it was such a— funny way to kill a man, rigging it all up like that.

MRS. HALE. That's just what Mr. Hale said. There was a gun in the house. He says that's what he can't understand.

MRS. PETERS. Mr. Henderson said coming out that what was needed for the case was a motive; something to show anger, or—sudden feeling.

MRS. HALE [*who is standing by the table*]. Well, I don't see any signs of anger around here. [*She puts her hand on the dish towel which lies on the table, stands looking down at table, one half of which is clean, the other half messy.*] It's wiped to here. [*Makes a move as if to finish work, then turns and looks at loaf of bread outside the breadbox. Drops towel. In that voice of coming back to familiar things.*] Wonder how they are finding things upstairs. I hope she had it a little more red-up up there. You know, it seems kind of *sneaking.* Locking her up in town and then coming out here and trying to get her own house to turn against her!

MRS. PETERS. But Mrs. Hale, the law is the law.

MRS. HALE. I s'pose 'tis. [*Unbuttoning her coat.*] Better loosen up your things, Mrs. Peters. You won't feel them when you go out.

[*Mrs. Peters takes off her fur tippet, goes to hang it on hook at back of room, stands looking at the under part of the small corner table.*]

MRS. PETERS. She was piecing a quilt.

[*She brings the large sewing basket and they look at the bright pieces.*]

MRS. HALE. It's log cabin pattern. Pretty, isn't it? I wonder if she was goin' to quilt it or just knot it?

[*Footsteps have been heard coming down the stairs. The Sheriff enters followed by Hale and the County Attorney.*]

SHERIFF. They wonder if she was going to quilt it or just knot it!

[*The men laugh; the women look abashed.*]

COUNTY ATTORNEY [*rubbing his hands over the stove*]. Frank's fire didn't do much up there, did it? Well, let's go out to the barn and get that cleared up.

[*The men go outside.*]

MRS. HALE [*resentfully*]. I don't know as there's anything so strange, our takin' up our time with little things while we're waiting for them to get the evidence. [*She sits down at the big table smoothing out a block with decision.*] I don't see as it's anything to laugh about.

MRS. PETERS [*apologetically*]. Of course they've got awful important things on their minds.

[*Pulls up a chair and joins Mrs. Hale at the table.*]

MRS. HALE [*examining another block*]. Mrs. Peters, look at this one. Here, this is the one she was working on, and look at the sewing! All the rest of it has been so nice and even. And look at this! It's all over the place! Why, it looks as if she didn't know what she was about!

[*After she has said this they look at each other, then start to glance back at the door. After an instant Mrs. Hale has pulled at a knot and ripped the sewing.*]

MRS. PETERS. Oh, what are you doing, Mrs. Hale?

MRS. HALE [*mildly*]. Just pulling out a stitch or two that's not sewed very good. [*Threading a needle.*] Bad sewing always made me fidgety.

MRS. PETERS [*nervously*]. I don't think we ought to touch things.

MRS. HALE. I'll just finish up this end. [*Suddenly stopping and leaning forward.*] Mrs. Peters?

MRS. PETERS. Yes, Mrs. Hale?

MRS. HALE. What do you suppose she was so nervous about?

MRS. PETERS. Oh—I don't know. I don't know as she was nervous. I sometimes sew awful queer when I'm just tired. [*Mrs. Hale starts to say something, looks at Mrs. Peters, then goes on sewing.*] Well, I must get these things wrapped up. They may be through sooner than we think. [*Putting apron and other things together.*] I wonder where I can find a piece of paper, and string.

MRS. HALE. In that cupboard, maybe.

MRS. PETERS [*looking in cupboard*]. Why, here's a birdcage. [*Holds it up.*] Did she have a bird, Mrs. Hale?

MRS. HALE. Why, I don't know whether she did or not—I've not been here for so long. There was a man around last year selling canaries cheap, but I don't know as she took one; maybe she did. She used to sing real pretty herself.

MRS. PETERS [*glancing around*]. Seems funny to think of a bird here. But she must have had one, or why would she have a cage? I wonder what happened to it.

MRS. HALE. I s'pose maybe the cat got it.

MRS. PETERS. No, she didn't have a cat. She's got that feeling some people have about cats—being afraid of them. My cat got in her room and she was real upset and asked me to take it out.

MRS. HALE. My sister Bessie was like that. Queer, ain't it?

MRS. PETERS [*examining the cage*]. Why, look at this door. It's broke. One hinge is pulled apart.

MRS. HALE. [*looking too*]. Looks as if someone must have been rough with it.

MRS. PETERS. Why, yes.

[*She brings the cage forward and puts it on the table.*]

MRS. HALE. I wish if they're going to find any evidence they'd be about it. I don't like this place.

MRS. PETERS. But I'm awful glad you came with me, Mrs. Hale. It would be lonesome for me sitting here alone.

MRS. HALE. It would, wouldn't it? [*Dropping her sewing.*] But I tell you what I do wish, Mrs. Peters. I wish I had come over sometimes when *she* was here. I—[*Looking around the room.*] —wish I had.

MRS. PETERS. But of course you were awful busy, Mrs. Hale—your house and your children.

MRS. HALE. I could've come. I stayed away because it weren't cheerful—and that's why I ought to have

come. I—I've never liked this place. Maybe because it's down in a hollow and you don't see the road. I dunno what it is but it's a lonesome place and always was. I wish I had come over to see Minnie Foster sometimes. I can see now—

[*She shakes her head.*]

MRS. PETERS. Well, you mustn't reproach yourself, Mrs. Hale. Somehow we just don't see how it is with other folks until—something comes up.

MRS. HALE. Not having children makes less work—but it makes a quiet house, and Wright out to work all day, and no company when he did come in. Did you know John Wright, Mrs. Peters?

MRS. PETERS. Not to know him; I've seen him in town. They say he was a good man.

MRS. HALE. Yes—good; he didn't drink, and kept his word as well as most, I guess, and paid his debts. But he was a hard man, Mrs. Peters. Just to pass the time of day with him—[*Shivers.*] Like a raw wind that gets to the bone. [*Pauses, her eye falling on the cage.*] I should think she would 'a wanted a bird. But what do you suppose went with it?

MRS. PETERS. I don't know, unless it got sick and died.

[*She reaches over and swings the broken door, swings it again. Both women watch it.*]

MRS. HALE. You weren't raised round here, were you? [*Mrs. Peters shakes her head.*] You didn't know—her?

MRS. PETERS. Not till they brought her yesterday.

MRS. HALE. She—come to think of it, she was kind of like a bird herself—real sweet and pretty, but kind of timid and—fluttery. How—she—did—change. [*Silence; then as if struck by a happy thought and relieved to get back to everyday things.*] Tell you what, Mrs. Peters, why don't you take the quilt in with you? It might take up her mind.

MRS. PETERS. Why, I think that's a real nice idea, Mrs. Hale. There couldn't possibly be any objection to it, could there? Now, just what would I take? I wonder if her patches are in here—and her things.

[*They look in the sewing basket.*]

MRS. HALE. Here's some red. I expect this has got sewing things in it. [*Brings out a fancy box.*] What a pretty box. Looks like something somebody would give you. Maybe her scissors are in here. [*Opens box. Suddenly puts her hand to her nose.*] Why—[*Mrs. Peters bends nearer, then turns her face away.*] There's something wrapped up in this piece of silk.

MRS. PETERS. Why, this isn't her scissors.

MRS. HALE [*lifting the silk*]. Oh, Mrs. Peters—it's—

[*Mrs. Peters bends closer.*]

MRS. PETERS. It's the bird.

MRS. HALE [*jumping up*]. But, Mrs. Peters—look at it! Its neck! Look at its neck! It's all—other side *to*.

MRS. PETERS. Somebody—wrung—its—neck.

[*Their eyes meet. A look of growing comprehension, of horror. Steps are heard outside. Mrs. Hale slips box under quilt pieces, and sinks into her chair. Enter Sheriff and County Attorney. Mrs. Peters rises.*]

COUNTY ATTORNEY [*as one turning from serious things to little pleasantries*]. Well, ladies have you decided whether she was going to quilt it or knot it?

MRS. PETERS. We think she was going to—knot it.

COUNTY ATTORNEY. Well, that's interesting, I'm sure. [*Seeing the birdcage.*] Has the bird flown?

MRS. HALE. [*putting more quilt pieces over the box*]. We think the—cat got it.

COUNTY ATTORNEY [*Preoccupied*]. Is there a cat?

[*Mrs. Hale glances in a quick covert way at Mrs. Peters.*]

MRS. PETERS. Well, not *now*. They're superstitious, you know. They leave.

COUNTY ATTORNEY [*to Sheriff Peters, continuing an interrupted conversation*]. No sign at all of anyone having come from the outside. Their own rope. Now let's go up again and go over it piece by piece. [*They start upstairs.*] It would have to have been someone who knew just the—

[*Mrs. Peters sits down. The two women sit there not looking at one another, but as if peering into something and at the same time holding back. When they talk now it is in the manner of feeling their way over strange ground, as if afraid of what they are saying, but as if they can not help saying it.*]

MRS. HALE. She liked the bird. She was going to bury it in that pretty box.

MRS. PETERS [*in a whisper*]. When I was a girl—my kitten—there was a boy took a hatchet, and before my eyes—and before I could get there—[*Covers her face an instant.*] If they hadn't held me back I would have—[*Catches herself, looks upstairs where steps are heard, falters weakly.*] —hurt him.

MRS. HALE [*with a slow look around her*]. I wonder how it would seem never to have had any children around. [*Pause.*] No, Wright wouldn't like the bird—a thing that sang. She used to sing. He killed that, too.

MRS. PETERS [*moving uneasily*]. We don't know who killed the bird.

MRS. HALE. I knew John Wright.

MRS. PETERS. It was an awful thing was done in this house that night, Mrs. Hale. Killing a man while he slept, slipping a rope around his neck that choked the life out of him.

MRS. HALE. His neck. Choked the life out of him.

[*Her hand goes out and rests on the birdcage.*]

MRS. PETERS [*with rising voice*]. We don't know who killed him. We don't *know*.

MRS. HALE [*her own feelings not interrupted*]. If there'd been years and years of nothing, then a bird to sing to you, it would be awful—still, after the bird was still.

MRS. PETERS [*something within her speaking*]. I know what stillness is. When we homesteaded in Dakota, and my first baby died—after he was two years old, and me with no other then—

MRS. HALE [*moving*]. How soon do you suppose they'll be through, looking for the evidence?

MRS. PETERS. I know what stillness is. [*Pulling herself back.*] The law has got to punish crime, Mrs. Hale.

MRS. HALE [*not as if answering that*]. I wish you'd seen Minnie Foster when she wore a white dress with blue ribbons and stood up there in the choir and sang. [*A look around the room.*] Oh, I *wish* I'd come over here once in a while! That was a crime! That was a crime! Who's going to punish that?

MRS. PETERS [*looking upstairs*]. We mustn't—take on.

MRS. HALE. I might have known she needed help! I know how things can be—for women. I tell you, it's queer, Mrs. Peters. We live close together and we live far apart. We all go through the same things— it's all just a different kind of the same thing. [*Brushes her eyes; noticing the bottle of fruit, reaches out for it.*] If I was you I wouldn't tell her her fruit was gone. Tell her it *ain't*. Tell her it's all right. Take this in to prove it to her. She—she may never know whether it was broke or not.

MRS. PETERS [*takes the bottle, looks about for something to wrap it in; takes petticoat from the clothes brought from the other room, very nervously begins winding this around the bottle. In a false voice*]. My, it's a good thing the men couldn't hear us. Wouldn't they just laugh! Getting all stirred up over a little thing like a—dead canary. As if that could have anything to do with—with—wouldn't they *laugh*!

[*The men are heard coming down stairs.*]

MRS. HALE [*under her breath*]. Maybe they would—maybe they wouldn't.

COUNTY ATTORNEY. No, Peters, it's all perfectly clear except a reason for doing it. But you know juries when it comes to women. If there was some definite thing. Something to show—something to make a story about—a thing that would connect up with this strange way of doing it—

[*The women's eyes meet for an instant. Enter Hale from outer door.*]

HALE. Well, I've got the team around. Pretty cold out there.

COUNTY ATTORNEY. I'm going to stay here a while by myself. [*To the Sheriff.*] You can send Frank out for me, can't you? I want to go over everything. I'm not satisfied that we can't do better.

SHERIFF. Do you want to see what Mrs. Peters is going to take in?

[*The County Attorney goes to the table, picks up the apron, laughs.*]

COUNTY ATTORNEY. Oh, I guess they're not very dangerous things the ladies have picked out. [*Moves a few things about, disturbing the quilt pieces which cover the box. Steps back.*] No, Mrs. Peters doesn't

need supervising. For that matter, a sheriff's wife is married to the law. Ever think of it that way, Mrs. Peters?

MRS. PETERS. Not—just that way.

SHERIFF [*Chuckling*]. Married to the law. [*Moves toward the other room.*] I just want you to come in here a minute, George. We ought to take a look at these windows.

COUNTY ATTORNEY [*scoffingly*]. Oh, windows!

SHERIFF. We'll be right out, Mr. Hale.

[*Hale goes outside. The Sheriff follows the County Attorney into the other room. Then Mrs. Hale rises, hands tight together, looking intensely at Mrs. Peters, whose eyes make a slow turn, finally meeting Mrs. Hale's. A moment Mrs. Hale holds her, then her own eyes point the way to where the box is concealed. Suddenly Mrs. Peters throws back quilt pieces and tries to put the box in the bag she is bearing. It is too big. She opens box, starts to take bird out, cannot touch it, goes to pieces, stands there helpless. Sound of a knob turning in the other room. Mrs. Hale snatches the box and puts it in the pocket of her big coat. Enter County Attorney and Sheriff.*]

COUNTY ATTORNEY [*facetiously*]. Well, Henry, at least we found out that she was not going to quilt it. She was going to—what is it you call it, ladies?

MRS. HALE [*her hand against her pocket*]. We call it—knot it, Mr. Henderson.

CURTAIN

ESSAY: AN APPROACH TO THE PLAY

Trifles presents a detective story with a difference; the sheriff and the prosecutor, the characters who might be expected traditionally to be the heroes, are offstage, while the focus remains on normally minor characters who, despite their lack of experience and training, solve the mystery. Interpreted through their eyes, many of the play's apparently unimportant props (unimportant from the official, conventionally male viewpoint) turn out to be the most significant clues. In traditional literary jargon, they are symbolic: the bird, the birdcage, the half-completed piece of quilting, the stove, the burst preserves—all seem to symbolize the relationship between the Wrights and help to explain what happened. As Judith Fetterley has suggested in her essay on "Jury of Her Peers," the short story highlights fundamental differences between male and female ways of reading: not only can men not interpret the clues that turn out to be decisive, they are not even able to acknowledge that they *are* clues.[1] The play undercuts the traditional dominant social status of the men,

[1] "Reading about Reading: 'A Jury of Her Peers,' 'The Murders in the Rue Morgue,' and 'The Yellow Wallpaper,'" in *Gender and Reading: Essays on Readers, Texts, and Contexts* (Baltimore and London: The Johns Hopkins University Press, 1986): 147–164.

displacing their authority with the intelligence of the women. The very basis of authority in society is implicitly redefined.

The heavily ironic resonance of the play's final line reinforces this perspective, particularly if we know something about the quilting process. Quilts are bed coverings made by stitching a layer of insulating material such as cotton or wool between two layers of fabric. In frontier America, quilting became a common form of women's folk art, several of whose characteristics may matter in Glaspell's play. The top layer of cloth usually consisted of a series of blocks made with the remnants of materials left over from making clothes; these blocks were then stitched together into geometric patterns. These patterns, in turn, would sometimes have narrative content, for example, as stylized representations of moments in the artist's life or of more generalized human experience. (Of all the possible patterns which Minnie Foster Wright might have been working on at the time of her arrest, she was stitching a block in "log cabin" design.) Eventually the completed blocks would themselves be stitched together into the quilt's decorative top piece and then the three parts combined, using either the more time-consuming and highly prized process of quilting (stitching the three layers together with thousands of tiny decorative stitches) or the quicker and less prized process of knotting. This involved combining the three layers with a series of knots spaced across the quilt, made of a relatively thick and durable thread which was run down through the three layers and back up again through an adjacent hole, where the thread would be tied off; the resulting knots and ends of thread were left visible to form a part of the decorative pattern of the whole.

Quilting was so time-consuming a process that it was difficult for one woman to complete such a project alone. Group efforts resulted—quilting bees—in which groups of women would collaborate to complete a project, combining social interaction with completion of a communal work of art. (It has become common for some contemporary scholars interested in women's issues to reclaim quilting as a metaphor for the frequently collaborative nature of much scholarship on women.) The concluding line of *Trifles* seems not only to acknowledge Minnie's exclusion from a community of women, but perhaps also to suggest something about the way Mrs. Hale and Mrs. Peters "stitch together" the pieces of her life, doing what the men could not do. As the county attorney says: "If there was some definite thing. Something to show—something to make a story about . . ." But of course he cannot "read" the quilt.

Eugene O'Neill

THE HAIRY APE

About the Author   Eugene O'Neill (1888–1953), generally considered to have been the leading force in modernizing American drama, wrote plays that were experimental in a variety of ways and that address issues which continue to concern us today. Two kinds of plays had become conventional in American theater by the 1920s: the naturalistic, which tried to imitate the observed "real world" faithfully, and the melodramatic, which tended to emphasize extreme situations, often to evoke predictable emotional responses (plays focusing on pathos, blood and thunder, hearts and flowers). The most serious thematic issues of both types involved the relations between society and its citizens. O'Neill's plays, by contrast, although they often share elements of both realism and melodrama, and although they are certainly interested in social questions, reveal a strong influence from German expressionism (where the focus is shifted from "realism" to "symbolism"), a concern for the psychological bases of modern existence, and a concern for a society dominated by fundamentally materialistic values. His plays often focus on the power of humans to transform themselves into nobler beings than their social circumstances would seem to allow, a power he also found expressed as a central concern of ancient Greek tragedy.

O'Neill's father was a star actor; the young O'Neill and his mother usually accompanied him on his acting tours, so that O'Neill's youth, until about the age of 26, when he seriously decided to become a playwright, is often described as that of a vagabond. This life took its toll on him and his family: his mother took drugs; his oldest child was a suicide; O'Neill himself had tuberculosis at one time; his misfortune continued in the last several years of his life, when he was unable to write because he had contracted Parkinson's disease. For all of the difficulties of his personal life, however, he was one of the most honored of American playwrights. Having written over thirty plays, he won a gold medal for drama from the National Institute of the Arts, no fewer than *four* Pulitzers, and in 1936 the Nobel Prize for Literature.

About the Play   *The Hairy Ape* was first presented on March 9, 1922, by the Provincetown Players, which O'Neill and Susan Glaspell had helped make famous, at their Greenwich Village winter theater in New York City (their summer playhouse on Cape Cod continues to this day). The play was an immediate success and is often revived. Several aspects of this play are typical of O'Neill. For one thing, his description of "the fireman's forecastle" at the beginning of the first scene makes it clear that the setting is meant to be symbolic rather than realistic, to suggest the *quality* of the place and its denizens rather than the way it "really" would be. The description of Yank is similar; he is not conventionally realistic. We know no one who believes himself brother to a gorilla, nor who really seems like a highly developed kind of ape. Yet Yank resembles us all in his longing to "belong" and to define himself, to have his place in the world and know what it is, to believe himself important. There may be a Darwinian theme here, a reminder not only about where we as a species come from in the evolutionary chain, but a reminder also that our sophisticated social pretensions are artificial and, perhaps, at the same time so primitive that they may be inescapable. We may all be doomed by our basic drives and by the conflicts they create with our "higher" desires.

The opening "voices," like many other speeches in this play, also indicate that O'Neill is trying to write *poetic* drama in which the characters often speak a kind of verse, yet a kind of verse expressed within the vernacular of lower-class, uneducated people. O'Neill's desire to write poetic plays may come in part from his admiration for Greek tragedy. Although this poetry denies the play an aura of verisimilitude, it suggests the inherent dignity of even the lowest classes of our society. From this perspective, too, O'Neill's emphasis seems to be on symbol and meaning rather than realism.

CHARACTERS

ROBERT SMITH, "YANK"
PADDY
LONG
MILDRED DOUGLAS
HER AUNT

SECOND ENGINEER
A GUARD
A SECRETARY OF AN ORGANIZATION
STOKERS, LADIES, GENTLEMEN, ETC.

SCENES

SCENE 1—The Firemen's forecastle of an ocean liner—an hour after sailing from New York.
SCENE II—Section of promenade deck, two days out—morning.
SCENE III—The stokehole. A few minutes later.
SCENE IV—Same as Scene I. Half an hour later.
SCENE V—Fifth Avenue, New York. Three weeks later.
SCENE VI—An island near the city. The next night.
SCENE VII—In the city. About a month later.
SCENE VIII—In the city. Twilight of the next day.

SCENE I

SCENE—The firemen's forecastle of a transatlantic liner an hour after sailing from New York for the voyage across. Tiers of narrow, steel bunks, three deep, on all sides. An entrance in rear. Benches on the floor before the bunks. The room is crowded with men, shouting, cursing, laughing, singing—a confused, inchoate uproar swelling into a sort of unity, a meaning—the bewildered, furious, baffled defiance of a beast in a cage. Nearly all the men are drunk. Many bottles are passed from hand to hand. All are dressed in dungaree pants, heavy ugly shoes. Some wear singlets, but the majority are stripped to the waist.

The treatment of this scene, or of any other scene in the play, should by no means be naturalistic. The effect sought after is a cramped space in the bowels of a ship, imprisoned by white steel. The lines of bunks, the uprights supporting them, cross each other like the steel framework of a cage. The ceiling crushes down upon the men's heads. They cannot stand upright. This accentuates the natural stooping posture which shoveling coal and the resultant overdevelopment of back and shoulder muscles have given them. The men themselves should resemble those pictures in which the appearance of Neanderthal Man is guessed at. All are hairy-chested, with long arms of tremendous power, and low, receding brows above their small, fierce, resentful eyes. All the civilized white races are represented, but except for the slight differentiation in color of hair, skin, eyes, all these men are alike.

The curtain rises on a tumult of sound. Yank is seated in the foreground. He seems broader, fiercer, more truculent, more powerful, more sure of himself than the rest. They respect his superior strength—the grudging respect of fear. Then, too, he represents to them a self-expression, the very last word in what they are, their most highly developed individual.

VOICES. Gif me trink dere, you!
  'Ave a wet!
  Salute!
  Gesundheit!
  Skoal!
  Drunk as a lord, God stiffen you!
  Here's how!
  Luck!
  Pass back that bottle, damn you!
  Pourin' it down his neck!
  Ho, Froggy! Where the devil have you been?
  La Touraine.
  I hit him smash in yaw, py Gott!
  Jenkins—the First—he's a rotten swine—
  And the coppers nabbed him—and I run—
  I like peer better. It don't pig head gif you.
  A slut, I'm sayin'! She robbed me aslape—
  To hell with 'em all!
  You're a bloody liar!
  Say dot again! [*Commotion. Two men about to fight are pulled apart.*]
  No scrappin' now!
  Tonight—
  See who's the best man!
  Bloody Dutchman!
  Tonight on the for'ard square.
  I'll bet on Dutchy.
  He packa da wallop, I tella you!
  Shut up, Wop!
  No fightin', maties. We're all chums, ain't we? [*A voice starts bawling a song*]

"Beer, beer, glorious beer!
Fill yourselves right up to here."
YANK [*for the first time seeming to take notice of the uproar about him, turns around threateningly—in a tone of contemptuous authority*]. Choke off dat noise! Where d'yuh get dat beer stuff? Beer, hell! Beer's for goils—and Dutchmen. Me for somep'n wit a kick to it! Gimme a drink, one of youse guys. [*Several bottles are eagerly offered. He takes a tremendous gulp at one of them; then, keeping the bottle in his hand, glares belligerently at the owner, who hastens to acquiesce in this robbery by saying:*] All righto, Yank. Keep it and have another. [*Yank contemptuously turns his back on the crowd again. For a second there is an embarrassed silence. Then—*]
VOICES. We must be passing the Hook.
She's beginning to roll to it.
Six days in hell—and then Southampton.
Py Yesus, I vish somepody take my first vatch for me!
Gittin' seasick, Square-head?
Drink up and forget it!
What's in your bottle?
Gin.
Dot's nigger trink.
Absinthe? It's doped. You'll go off your chump, Froggy!
Cochon![1]
Whiskey, that's the ticket!
Where's Paddy?
Going asleep.
Sing us that whisky song, Paddy. [*They all turn to an old, wizened Irishman who is dozing, very drunk, on the benches forward. His face is extremely monkey-like with all the sad, patient pathos of that animal in his small eyes.*]
Singa da song, Caruso Pat!
He's gettin' old. The drink is too much for him.
He's too drunk.
PADDY [*blinking about him, starts to his feet resentfully, swaying, holding on to the edge of a bunk*]: I'm never too drunk to sing. 'Tis only when I'm dead to the world I'd be wishful to sing at all. [*With a sort of sad contempt*] "Whisky Johnny," ye want? A chanty, ye want? Now that's a queer wish from the ugly like of you, God help you. But no mather. [*He starts to sing in a thin, nasal, doleful tone*]:
Oh, whisky is the life of man!
Whisky! O Johnny! [*They all join in on this*]
Oh, whisky is the life of man!
Whiskey for my Johnny! [*Again chorus*]

Oh, whisky drove my old man mad!
Whisky! O Johnny!
Oh, whisky drove my old man
mad!
Whisky for my Johnny!
YANK [*again turning around scornfully*]. Aw hell! Nix on dat old sailing ship stuff! All dat bull's dead, see? And you're dead, too, yuh damned old Harp, on'y yuh don't know it. Take it easy, see. Give us a rest. Nix on de loud noise. [*With a cynical grin*] Can't youse see I'm tryin' to t'ink?
ALL [*repeating the word after him as one with the same cynical amused mockery*]. Think! [*The chorused word has a brazen metallic quality as if their throats were phonograph horns. It is followed by a general uproar of hard, barking laughter.*]
VOICES. Don't be cracking your head wit ut, Yank.
You gat headache, py yingo!
One thing about it—it rhymes with drink!
Ha, ha, ha!
Drink, don't think!
Drink, don't think!
Drink, don't think! [*A whole chorus of voices has taken up this refrain, stamping on the floor, pounding on the benches with fists*]
YANK [*taking a gulp from his bottle—good naturedly*]. Aw right. Can de noise. I got yuh de foist time. [*The uproar subsides. A very drunken sentimental tenor begins to sing.*]
"Far away in Canada,
Far across the sea,
There's a lass who fondly waits
Making a home for me—"
YANK [*fiercely contemptuous*]. Shut up, yuh lousy boob! Where d'yuh get dat tripe? Home? Home, hell! I'll make a home for yuh! I'll knock yuh dead. Home! T'hell wit home! Where d'yuh get dat tripe? Dis is home, see? What d'yuh want wit home? [*Proudly*] I runned away from mine when I was a kid. On'y too glad to beat it, dat was me. Home was lickings for me, dat's all. But yuh can bet your shoit no one ain't never licked me since! Wanter try it, any of youse? Huh! I guess not. [*In a more placated but still contemptuous tone*] Goils waitin' for yuh, huh? Aw, hell! Dat's all tripe. Dey don't wait for no one. Dey double-cross yuh for a nickel. Dey're all tarts, get me? Treat 'em rough, dat's me. To hell with 'em. Tarts, dat's what, de whole bunch of 'em.
LONG [*very drunk, jumps on a bench excitedly, gesticulating with a bottle in his hand*]. Listen 'ere, Comrades. Yank 'ere is right. 'E says this 'ere stinkin' ship is our 'ome. And 'e says as 'ome is 'ell. And 'e's right! This is 'ell. We lives in 'ell, Comrades—and right enough

[1] Pig.

we'll die in it. [*Raging*] And who's ter blame, I arsks yer? We ain't. We wasn't born this rotten way. All men is born free and ekal. That's in the bleedin' Bible, maties. But what d'they care for the Bible— them lazy, bloated swine what travels first cabin? Them's the ones. They dragged us down 'til we're on'y wage slaves in the bowels of a bloody ship, sweatin', burnin' up, eatin' coal dust! Hit's them's ter blame—the damned Capitalist clarss! [*There had been a gradual murmur of contemptuous resentment rising among the men until now he is interrupted by a storm of catcalls, hisses, boos, hard laughter*]

VOICES. Turn it off!

Shut up!

Sit down!

Closa da face!

Tamn fool! [*etc.*]

YANK [*standing up and glaring at Long*]. Sit down before I knock yuh down! [*Long makes haste to efface himself. Yank goes on contemptuously*] De Bible, huh? De Cap'tlist class, huh? Aw nix on dat Salvation Army-Socialist bull. Git a soapbox! Hire a hall! Come and be saved, huh? Jerk us to Jesus, huh? Aw g'wan! I've listened to lots of guys like you, see. Yuh're all wrong. Wanter know what I t'ink? Yuh ain't no good for no one. Yuh're de bunk. Yuh ain't got no noive, get me? Yuh're yellow, dat's what. Yellow, dat's you. Say! What's dem slobs in de foist cabin got to do wit us? We're better men dan dey are, ain't we? Sure! One of us guys could clean up de whole mob wit one mit. Put one of 'em down here for one watch in de stokehole, what'd happen? Dey'd carry him off on a stretcher. Dem boids don't amount to nothin'. Dey're just baggage. Who makes dis old tub run? Ain't it us guys? Well den, we belong, don't we? We belong and dey don't. Dat's all. [*A loud chorus of approval. Yank goes on.*] As for dis bein' hell—aw, nuts! Yuh lost your noive, dat's what. Dis is a man's job, get me? It belongs. It runs dis tub. No stiffs need apply. But yuh're a stiff, see? Yuh're yellow, dat's you.

VOICES [*with a great hard pride in them*].

Righto!

A man's job!

Talk is cheap, Long.

He never could hold up his end.

Divil take him!

Yank's right. We make it go.

Py Gott, Yank say right ting!

We don't need no one cryin' over us.

Makin' speeches.

Throw him out!

Yellow!

Chuck him overboard!

I'll break his jaw for him! [*They crowd around Long threateningly*]

YANK [*half good-natured again—contemptuously*]. Aw, take it easy. Leave him alone. He ain't woith a punch. Drink up. Here's how, whoever owns dis. [*He takes a long swallow from his bottle. All drink with him. In a flash all is hilarious amiability again, back-slapping, loud talk, etc.*]

PADDY [*who has been sitting in a blinking, melancholy daze—suddenly cries out in a voice full of old sorrow*]. We belong to this, you're saying? We make the ship to go, you're saying? Yerra then, that Almighty God have pity on us! [*His voice runs into the wail of a keen, he rocks back and forth on his bench. The men stare at him, startled and impressed in spite of themselves.*] Oh, to be back in the fine days of my youth, ochone! Oh, there was fine beautiful ships them days— clippers wid tall masts touching the sky—fine strong men in them—men that was sons of the sea as if 'twas the mother that bore them. Oh, the clean skins of them, and the clear eyes, the straight backs and full chests of them! Brave men they was, and bold men surely! We'd be sailing out, bound down round the Horn maybe. We'd be making sail in the dawn, with a fair breeze, singing a chanty song wid no care to it. And astern the land would be sinking low and dying out, but we'd give it no heed but a laugh, and never a look behind. For the day that was, was enough, for we was free men—and I'm thinking 'tis only slaves do be giving heed to the day that's gone or the day to come—until they're old like me. [*With a sort of religious exaltation*] Oh, to be scudding south again wid the power of the Trade Wind driving her on steady through the nights and the days! Full sail on her! Nights and days! Nights when the foam of the wake would be flaming wid fire, when the sky'd be blazing and winking wid stars. Or the full of the moon maybe. Then you'd see her driving through the gray night, her sails stretching aloft all silver and white, not a sound on the deck, the lot of us dreaming dreams, till you'd believe 'twas no real ship at all you was on but a ghost ship like the *Flying Dutchman* they say does be roaming the seas forevermore widout touching a port. And there was the days, too. A warm sun on the clean decks. Sun warming the blood of you, and wind over the miles of shiny green ocean like strong drink to your lungs. Work—aye, hard work—but who'd mind that at all? Sure, you worked under the sky and 'twas work wid skill and daring to it. And wid the day alone, in the dog watch, smoking me pipe at ease, the lookout would be raising land maybe, and we'd see the mountains of South Americy wid the red fire of the setting sun painting their white tops and the clouds floating by them! [*His tone of exaltation ceases. He goes on mournfully.*] Yerra, what's the use of talking? 'Tis a dead man's whisper. [*To Yank resentfully*] 'Twas them days men belonged to ships, not now. 'Twas them days a ship was part of the sea, and a man was part of a ship, and the sea joined all together and made it one. [*Scornfully*] Is it one wid this you'd be, Yank—black smoke from the funnels smudging the sea, smudging the decks—the bloody engines pounding and throbbing and shaking—wid divil a sight of sun or a breath of clean air—choking our lungs wid coal dust—breaking our backs and hearts in the hell of the stokehole—feeding the bloody furnace—feeding our lives along wid the coal, I'm thinking—caged in by steel from a sight of the sky like bloody apes in the Zoo! [*With a harsh laugh*] Ho-ho, divil mend you! Is it to belong to that you're wishing? Is it a flesh and blood wheel of the engines you'd be?

YANK [*who has been listening with a contemptuous sneer, barks out the answer*]. Sure ting! Dat's me. What about it?

PADDY [*as if to himself—with great sorrow*]. Me time is past due. That a great wave wid sun in the heart of it may sweep me over the side sometime I'd be dreaming of the days that's gone!

YANK. Aw, yuh crazy Mick! [*He springs to his feet and advances on Paddy threateningly—then stops, fighting some queer struggle within himself—lets his hands fall to his sides—contemptuously*] Aw, take it easy. Yuh're aw right, at dat. Yuh're bugs, dat's all—nutty as a cuckoo. All dat tripe yuh been pullin'—Aw, dat's all right. On'y it's dead, get me? Yuh don't belong no more, see. Yuh don't get de stuff. Yuh're too old. [*Disgustedly*] But aw say, come up for air onct in a while, can't yuh? See what's happened since yuh croaked. [*He suddenly bursts forth vehemently, growing more and more excited*] Say! Sure! Sure I meant it! What de hell—Say, lemme talk! Hey! Hey, you old Harp! Hey, youse guys! Say, listen to me—wait a moment—I gotta talk, see. I belong and he don't. He's dead but I'm livin'. Listen to me! Sure I'm part of de engines! Why de hell not? Dey move, don't dey? Dey're speed, ain't dey? Dey smash trou, don't dey? Twenty-five knots a hour! Dat's goin' some! Dat's new stuff! Dat belongs! But him, he's too old. He gets dizzy. Say, listen. All dat crazy tripe about nights and days; all dat crazy tripe about stars and moons; all dat crazy tripe about suns and winds, fresh air and de rest of it—Aw hell, dat's all a dope dream! Hittin' de pipe of de past, dat's what he's doin'. He's old and don't belong no more. But me, I'm young! I'm in de pink! I move wit it! It, get me! I mean de ting dat's de guts of all dis. It ploughs trou all de tripe he's been sayin'. It blows dat up! It knocks dat dead! It slams dat offen de face of de oith! It, get me! De engines and de coal and de smoke and all de rest of it! He can't breathe and swallow coal dust, but I kin, see? Dat's fresh air for me! Dat's food for me! I'm new, get me? Hell in de stokehole? Sure! It takes a man to work in hell. Hell, sure, dat's my fav'rite climate. I eat it up! I git fat on it! It's me makes it hot! It's me makes it roar! It's me makes it move! Sure, on'y for me everyting stops. It all goes dead, get me? De noise and smoke and all de engines movin' de woild, dey stop. Dere ain't nothin' no more! Dat's what I'm sayin'. Everyting else dat makes de woild move, somep'n makes it move. It can't move witout somep'n else, see? Den yuh get down to me. I'm at de bottom, get me! Dere ain't nothin' foither. I'm de end! I'm de start! I start somep'n and de woild moves! It—dat's me!—de new dat's moiderin' de old! I'm de ting in coal dat makes it boin; I'm steam and oil for de engines; I'm de ting in noise dat makes yuh hear it; I'm smoke and express trains and steamers and factory whistles; I'm de ting in gold dat makes money! And I'm what makes iron into steel! Steel, dat stands for de whole ting! And I'm steel—steel—steel! I'm de muscles in steel, de punch behind it. [*As he says this he pounds with his fist against the steel bunks. All the men, roused to a pitch of frenzied self-glorification by his speech, do likewise. There is a deafening metallic roar, through which Yank's voice can be heard bellowing.*] Slaves, hell! We run de whole woiks. All de rich guys dat tink dey're somep'n, dey ain't nothin'! Dey don't belong. But us guys, we're in de move, we're at de bottom, de whole ting is us! [*Paddy from the start of Yank's speech has been taking one gulp after another from his bottle, at first frightenedly, as if he were afraid to listen, then desperately, as if to drown his senses, but finally has achieved complete indifferent, even amused, drunkenness. Yank sees his lips moving. He quells the uproar with a shout.*] Hey, youse guys, take it easy! Wait a moment! De nutty Harp is sayin' somep'n.

PADDY [*is heard now—throws his head back with a mocking burst of laughter*]. Ho-ho-ho-ho-ho—

YANK [*drawing back his fist, with a snarl*]. Aw! Look out who yuh're givin' the bark!

PADDY [*begins to sing the "Miller of Dee" with enormous good nature*].

> "I care for nobody, no, not I,
> And nobody cares for me."

YANK [*good-natured himself in a flash, interrupts Paddy with a slap on the bare back like a report*]. Dat's de stuff! Now yuh're gettin' wise to somep'n. Care for nobody, dat's de dope! To hell wit 'em all! And nix on nobody else carin'. I kin care for myself, get me! [*Eight bells sound, muffled, vibrating through the steel walls as if some enormous brazen gong were imbedded in the heart of the ship. All the men jump up mechanically, file through the door silently close upon each other's heels in what is very like a prisoners' lockstep. Yank slaps Paddy on the back.*] Our watch, yuh old Harp! [*Mockingly*] Come on down in hell. Eat up de coal dust. Drink in de heat. It's it, see! Act like yuh liked it, yuh better—or croak yuhself.

PADDY [*with jovial defiance*]. To the divil wid it! I'll not report this watch. Let thim log me and be damned. I'm no slave the like of you. I'll be sittin' here at me ease, and drinking, and thinking, and dreaming dreams.

YANK [*contemptuously*]. Tinkin' and dreamin', what'll that get yuh? What's tinkin' got to do wit it? We move, don't we? Speed, ain't it? Fog, dat's all you stand for. But we drive trou dat, don't we? We split dat up and smash trou—twenty-five knots a hour! [*Turns his back on Paddy scornfully*] Aw, yuh make me sick! Yuh don't belong! [*He strides out the door in rear. Paddy hums to himself, blinking drowsily.*]

CURTAIN

SCENE II

SCENE—Two days out. A section of the promenade deck. Mildred Douglas and her aunt are discovered reclining in deck chairs. The former is a girl of twenty, slender, delicate, with a pale, pretty face marred by a self-conscious expression of disdainful superiority. She looks fretful, nervous and discontented, bored by her own anemia. Her aunt is a pompous and proud—and fat—old lady. She is a type even to the point of a double chin and lorgnettes. She is dressed pretentiously, as if afraid her face alone would never indicate her position in life. Mildred is dressed all in white.

The impression to be conveyed by this scene is one of the beautiful, vivid life of the sea all about—sunshine on the deck in a great flood, the fresh sea wind blowing across it. In the midst of this, these two incongruous, artificial figures, inert and disharmonious, the elder like a gray lump of dough touched up with rouge, the younger looking as if the vitality of her stock had been sapped before she was conceived, so that she is the expression not of its life energy but merely of the artificialities that energy had won for itself in the spending.

MILDRED [*looking up with affected dreaminess*]. How the black smoke swirls back against the sky! Is it not beautiful?

AUNT [*without looking up*]. I dislike smoke of any kind.

MILDRED. My great-grandmother smoked a pipe—a clay pipe.

AUNT [*ruffling*]. Vulgar!

MILDRED. She was too distant a relative to be vulgar. Time mellows pipes.

AUNT [*pretending boredom but irritated*]. Did the sociology you took up at college teach you that—to play the ghoul on every possible occasion, excavating old bones? Why not let your great-grandmother rest in her grave?

MILDRED [*dreamily*]. With her pipe beside her—puffing in Paradise.

AUNT [*with spite*]. Yes, you are a natural born ghoul. You are even getting to look like one, my dear.

MILDRED [*in a passionless tone*]. I detest you, Aunt. [*Looking at her critically*] Do you know what you remind me of? Of a cold pork pudding against a background of linoleum tablecloth in the kitchen of a—but the possibilities are wearisome. [*She closes her eyes*]

AUNT [*with a bitter laugh*]. Merci for your candor. But since I am and must be your chaperon—in appearance—at least—let us patch up some sort of armed truce. For my part you are quite free to indulge any pose of eccentricity that beguiles you—as long as you observe the amenities—

MILDRED [*drawling*]. The inanities?

AUNT [*going on as if she hadn't heard*]. After exhausting the morbid thrills of social service work on New York's East Side—how they must have hated you, by the way, the poor that you made so much poorer in their own eyes!—you are now bent on making your slumming international. Well, I hope Whitechapel will provide the needed nerve tonic. Do not ask me to chaperon you there, however. I told your father I would not. I loathe deformity. We will hire an army of detectives and you may investigate everything—they allow you to see.

MILDRED [*protesting with a trace of genuine earnestness*]. Please do not mock at my attempts to discover how the other half lives. Give me credit for some sort of groping sincerity in that at least. I would like to help them. I would like to be of some use in the world. Is it my fault I don't know how? I would like to be sincere, to touch life somewhere. [*With weary bitterness*] But I'm afraid I have neither the vitality nor integrity. All that was burnt out in our stock before I was born. Grandfather's blast furnaces, flaming to the sky, melting steel, making millions—then father keeping those home fires burning, making more millions—and little me at the tail-end of it all. I'm a waste product in the Bessemer process—like the millions. Or rather, I inherit the acquired trait of the by-product, wealth, but none of the energy, none of the strength of the steel that made it. I am sired by gold and damned by it, as they say at the race track—damned in more ways than one. [*She laughs mirthlessly*]

AUNT [*unimpressed—superciliously*]. You seem to be going in for sincerity today. It isn't becoming to you, really—except as an obvious pose. Be as artificial as you are, I advise. There's a sort of sincerity in that, you know. And, after all, you must confess you like that better.

MILDRED [*again affected and bored*]. Yes, I suppose I do. Pardon me for my outburst. When a leopard complains of its spots, it must sound rather grotesque. [*In a mocking tone*] Purr, little leopard. Purr, scratch, tear, kill, gorge yourself and be happy—only stay in the jungle where your spots are camouflage. In a cage they make you conspicuous.

AUNT. I don't know what you are talking about.

MILDRED. It would be rude to talk about anything to you. Let's just talk. [*She looks at her wrist watch*] Well, thank goodness, it's about time for them to come for me. That ought to give me a new thrill, Aunt.

AUNT [*affectedly troubled*]. You don't mean to say you're really going? The dirt—the heat must be frightful—

MILDRED. Grandfather started as a puddler. I should have inherited an immunity to heat that would make a salamander shiver. It will be fun to put it to the test.

AUNT. But don't you have to have the captain's—or someone's—permission to visit the stokehole?

MILDRED [*with a triumphant smile*]. I have it—both his and the chief engineer's. Oh, they didn't want to at first, in spite of my social service credentials. They didn't seem a bit anxious that I should investigate how the other half lives and works on a ship. So I had to tell them that my father, the president of Nazareth Steel, chairman of the board of directors of this line, had told me it would be all right.

AUNT. He didn't.

MILDRED. How naïve age makes one! But I said he did, Aunt. I even said he had given me a letter to them—which I had lost. And they were afraid to take the chance that I might be lying. [*Excitedly*] So it's ho! for the stokehole. The second engineer is to escort me. [*Looking at her watch again*] It's time. And here he comes, I think. [*The Second Engineer enters. He is a husky, fine-looking man of thirty-five or so. He stops before the two and tips his cap, visibly embarrassed and ill-at-ease.*]

SECOND ENGINEER. Miss Douglas?

MILDRED. Yes. [*Throwing off her rugs and getting to her feet*] Are we all ready to start?

SECOND ENGINEER. In just a second, ma'am. I'm waiting for the Fourth. He's coming along.

MILDRED [*with a scornful smile*]. You don't care to shoulder this responsibility alone, is that it?

SECOND ENGINEER [*forcing a smile*]. Two are better than one. [*Disturbed by her eyes, glances out to sea—blurts out*] A fine day we're having.

MILDRED. Is it?

SECOND ENGINEER. A nice warm breeze—

MILDRED. It feels cold to me.

SECOND ENGINEER. But it's hot enough in the sun—

MILDRED. Not hot enough for me. I don't like Nature. I was never athletic.

SECOND ENGINEER [*forcing a smile*]. Well, you'll find it hot enough where you're going.

MILDRED. Do you mean hell?

SECOND ENGINEER [*flabbergasted, decides to laugh*]. Ho-ho! No, I mean the stokehole.

MILDRED. My grandfather was a puddler. He played with boiling steel.

SECOND ENGINEER [*all at sea—uneasily*]. Is that so? Hum, you'll excuse me, ma'am, but are you intending to wear that dress?

MILDRED. Why not?

SECOND ENGINEER. You'll likely rub against oil and dirt. It can't be helped.

MILDRED. It doesn't matter. I have lots of white dresses.

SECOND ENGINEER. I have an old coat you might throw over —

MILDRED. I have fifty dresses like this. I will throw this one into the sea when I come back. That ought to wash it clean, don't you think?

SECOND ENGINEER [*doggedly*]. There's ladders to climb down that are none too clean— and dark alleyways—

MILDRED. I will wear this very dress and none other.

SECOND ENGINEER. No offense meant. It's none of my business. I was only warning you—

MILDRED. Warning? That sounds thrilling.

SECOND ENGINEER [*looking down the deck—with a sigh of relief*]. There's the Fourth now. He's waiting for us. If you'll come—

MILDRED. Go on. I'll follow you. [*He goes. Mildred turns a mocking smile on her aunt.*] An oaf—but a handsome, virile oaf.

AUNT [*scornfully*]. Poser!

MILDRED. Take care. He said there were dark alleyways—

AUNT [*in the same tone*]. Poser!

MILDRED [*biting her lips angrily*]. You are right. But would that my millions were not so anemically chaste!

AUNT. Yes, for a fresh pose I have no doubt you would drag the name of Douglas in the gutter!

MILDRED. From which it sprang. Goody-by, Aunt. Don't pray too hard that I may fall into the fiery furnace.

AUNT. Poser!

MILDRED [*viciously*]. Old hag! [*She slaps her aunt insultingly across the face and walks off, laughing gaily*]

AUNT [*screams after her*]. I said poser!

CURTAIN

SCENE III

SCENE—The stokehole. In the rear, the dimly-outlined bulks of the furnaces and boilers. High overhead one hanging electric bulb sheds just enough light through the murky air laden with coal dust to pile up masses of shadows everywhere. A line of men, stripped to the waist, is before the furnace doors. They bend over, looking neither to right nor left, handling their shovels as if they were part of their bodies, with a strange, awkward, swinging rhythm. They use the shovels to throw open the furnace doors. Then from these fiery round holes in the black a flood of terrific light and heat pours full upon the men who are outlined in silhouette in the crouching, inhuman attitudes of chained gorillas. The men shovel with a rhythmic motion, swinging as on a pivot from the coal which lies in heaps on the floor behind to hurl it into the flaming mouths before them. There is a tumult of noise—the brazen clang of the furnace doors as they are flung open or slammed shut, the grating, teeth-gritting grind of steel against steel, of crunching coal. This clash of sounds stuns one's ears with its rending

dissonance. But there is order in it, rhythm, a mechanical regulated recurrence, a tempo. And rising above all, making the air hum with the quiver of liberated energy, the roar of leaping flames in the furnaces, the monotonous throbbing beat of the engines.

As the curtain rises, the furnace doors are shut. The men are taking a breathing spell. One or two are arranging the coal behind them, pulling it into more accessible heaps. The others can be dimly made out leaning on their shovels in relaxed attitudes of exhaustion.

PADDY [*from somewhere in the line—plaintively*]. Yerra, will this divil's own watch nivir end? Me back is broke. I'm destroyed entirely.

YANK [*from the center of the line—with exuberant scorn*]. Aw, yuh make me sick! Lie down and croak, why don't yuh? Always beefin', dat's you! Say, dis is a cinch! Dis was made for me! It's my meat, get me! [*A whistle is blown—a thin, shrill note from somewhere overhead in the darkness. Yank curses without resentment.*] Dere's de damn engineer crackin' de whip. He tinks we're loafin'.

PADDY [*vindictively*]. God stiffen him!

YANK [*in an exultant tone of command*]. Come on, youse guys! Git into de game! She's gittin' hungry! Pile some grub in her. Trow it into her belly! Come on now, all of youse! Open her up! [*At this last all the men, who have followed his movements of getting into position, throw open their furnace doors with a deafening clang. The fiery light floods over their shoulders as they bend round for the coal. Rivulets of sooty sweat have traced maps on their backs. The enlarged muscles form bunches of high light and shadow.*]

YANK [*chanting a count as he shovels without seeming effort.*] One—two—tree— [*His voice rising exultantly in the joy of battle*] Dat's de stuff! Let her have it! All togedder now! Sling it into her! Let her ride! Shoot de piece now! Call de toin on her! Drive her into it! Feel her move! Watch her smoke! Speed, dat's her middle name! Give her coal, youse guys! Coal, dat's her booze! Drink it up, baby! Let's see yuh sprint! Dig in and gain a lap! Dere she go-o-es. [*This last in the chanting formula of the gallery gods at the six-day bike race. He slams his furnace door shut. The others do likewise with as much unison as their wearied bodies will permit. The effect is of one fiery eye after another being blotted out with a series of accompanying bangs.*]

PADDY [*groaning*]. Me back is broke. I'm bate out—bate— [*There is a pause. Then the inexorable whistle sounds again from the dim regions above the electric light. There is a growl of cursing rage from all sides.*]

YANK [*shaking his fist upward—contemptuously*]. Take it easy dere, you! Who d'yuh tinks runnin' dis game, me or you? When I git ready, we move. Not before! When I git ready, get me!

VOICES [*approvingly*]. That's the stuff!

Yank tal him, py golly!

Yank ain't afeerd.

Goot poy, Yank!

Give him hell!

Tell 'im 'e's a bloody swine!

Bloody slave-driver!

YANK [*contemptuously*]. He ain't got no noive. He's yellow, get me? All de engineers is yellow. Dey got streaks a mile wide. Aw, to hell with him! Let's move, youse guys. We had a rest. Come on, she needs it! Give her pep! It ain't for him. Him and his whistle, dey don't belong. But we belong, see! We gotter feed de baby! Come on! [*He turns and flings his furnace door open. They all follow his lead. At this instant the Second and Fourth Engineers enter from the darkness on the left with Mildred between them. She starts, turns paler, her pose is crumbling, she shivers with fright in spite of the blazing heat, but forces herself to wave the engineers and take a few steps near the men. She is right behind Yank. All this happens quickly while the men have their backs turned.*]

YANK. Come on, youse guys! [*He is turning to get coal when the whistle sounds again in a peremptory, irritating note. This drives Yank into a sudden fury. While the other men have turned full around and stopped dumbfounded by the spectacle of Mildred standing there in her white dress, Yank does not turn far enough to see her. Besides, his head is thrown back, he blinks upward through the murk trying to find the owner of the whistle, he brandishes his shovel murderously over his head in one hand, pounding on his chest, gorilla-like, with the other, shouting.*] Toin off dat whistle! Come down outa dere, yuh yellow, brass-buttoned, Belfast bum, yuh! Come down and I'll knock yer brains out! Yuh lousy, stinkin', yellow mut of a Catholic-moiderin' bastard! Come down and I'll moider yuh! Pullin' dat whistle on me, huh? I'll show yuh! I'll crash yer skull in! I'll drive yer teet' down yer troat! I'll slam yer nose trou de back of yer head! I'll cut ycr guts out for a nickel, yuh lousy boob, yuh dirty, crummy, muck-eatin' son of a— [*Suddenly he becomes conscious of all the other men staring at something directly behind his back. He whirls defensively with a snarling, murderous growl, crouching to spring, his lips drawn back over his teeth, his small eyes gleaming ferociously. He*

sees Mildred, like a white apparition in the full light from the open furnace doors. He glares into her eyes, turned to stone. As for her, during his speech she has listened, paralyzed with horror, terror, her whole personality crushed, beaten in, collapsed, by the terrific impact of this unknown, abysmal brutality, naked and shameless. As she looks at his gorilla face, as his eyes bore into hers, she utters a low, choking cry and shrinks away from him, putting both hands up before her eyes to shut out the sight of his face, to protect her own. This startles Yank to a reaction. His mouth falls open, his eyes grow bewildered.]

MILDRED [*about to faint—to the Engineers, who now have her one by each arm—whimperingly*]. Take me away! Oh, the filthy beast! [*She faints. They carry her quickly back, disappearing in the darkness at the left, rear. An iron door clangs shut. Rage and bewildered fury rush back on Yank. He feels himself insulted in some unknown fashion in the very heart of his pride. He roars.*] God damn yuh! [*And hurls his shovel after them at the door which has just closed. It hits the steel bulkhead with a clang and falls clattering on the steel floor. From overhead the whistle sounds again in a long, angry, insistent command.*]

CURTAIN

SCENE IV

SCENE—The firemen's forecastle. Yank's watch has just come off duty and had dinner. Their faces and bodies shine from a soap and water scrubbing but around their eyes, where a hasty dousing does not touch, the coal dust sticks like black make-up, giving them a queer, sinister expression. Yank has not washed either face or body. He stands out in contrast to them, a blackened, brooding figure. He is seated forward on a bench in the exact attitude of Rodin's "The Thinker." The others, most of them smoking pipes, are staring at Yank half-apprehensively, as if fearing an outburst; half-amusedly, as if they saw a joke somewhere that tickled them.

VOICES. He ain't ate nothin'.

Py golly, a fallar gat to gat grub in him.

Divil a lie.

Yank feeda da fire, no feeda da face.

Ha-ha.

He ain't even washed hisself.

He's forgot.

Hey, Yank, you forgot to wash.

YANK [*sullenly*]. Forgot nothin'! To hell wit washin'.

VOICES. It'll stick to you.

It'll get under your skin.

Give yer the bleedin' itch, that's wot.

It makes spots on you—like a leopard.

Like a piebald nigger, you mean.

Better wash up, Yank.

You sleep better.

Wash up, Yank.

Wash up! Wash up!

YANK [*resentfully*]. Aw say, youse guys. Lemme alone. Can't youse see I'm tryin' to tink?

ALL [*repeating the word after him as one with cynical mockery*]. Think! [*The word has a brazen, metallic quality as if their throats were phonograph horns. It is followed by a chorus of hard, barking laughter.*]

YANK [*springing to his feet and glaring at them belligerently*]. Yes, tink! Tink, dat's what I said! What about it? [*They are silent, puzzled by his sudden resentment at what used to be one of his jokes. Yank sits down again in the same attitude of "The Thinker."*]

VOICES. Leave him alone.

He's got a grouch on.

Why wouldn't he?

PADDY [*with a wink at the others*]. Sure I know what's the mather. 'Tis aisy to see. He's fallen in love, I'm telling you.

ALL [*repeating the word after him as one with cynical mockery*]. Love! [*The word has a brazen metallic quality as if their throats were phonograph horns. It is followed by a chorus of hard, barking laughter.*]

YANK [*with a contemptuous snort*]. Love, hell! Hate, dat's what. I've fallen in hate, get me?

PADDY [*philosophically*]. 'Twould take a wise man to tell one from the other. [*With a bitter, ironical scorn, increasing as he goes on*] But I'm telling you it's love that's in it. Sure what else but love for us poor bastes in the stokehole would be bringing a fine lady, dressed like a white quane, down a mile of ladders and steps to be havin' a look at us? [*A growl of anger goes up from all sides*]

LONG [*jumping on a bench—hecticly*]. Hinsultin' us! Hinsultin' us, the bloody cow! And them bloody engineers! What right 'as they got to be exhibitin' us 's if we was bleedin' monkeys in a menagerie? Did we sign for hinsults to our dignity as 'onest workers? Is that in the ship's articles? You kin bloody well bet it ain't! But I knows why they done it. I arsked a deck steward 'o she was and 'e told me. 'Er old man's a bleedin' millionaire, a bloody Capitalist! 'E's got enuf bloody gold to sink this bleedin' ship! 'E makes arf the bloody steel in the world! 'E owns this bloody boat! And you and me, Comrades, we're 'is slaves! And the skipper and mates and engineers, they're 'is slaves! And she's 'is bloody daughter and we're all 'er slaves, too! And she gives 'er orders as 'ow she wants to see the bloody animals below decks and down they takes 'er! [*There is a roar of rage from all sides*]

YANK [*blinking at him bewilderedly*]. Say! Wait a moment! Is all dat straight goods?

LONG. Straight as string! The bleedin' steward as waits on 'em, 'e told me about 'er. And what're we goin' ter do, I arsks yer? 'Ave we got ter swaller 'er hinsults like dogs? It ain't in the ship's articles. I tell yer we got a case. We kin go to law—

YANK [*with abysmal contempt*]. Hell! Law!

ALL [*repeating the word after him as one with cynical mockery*]. Law! [*The word has a brazen metallic quality as if their throats were phonograph horns. It is followed by a chorus of hard, barking laughter.*]

LONG [*feeling the ground slipping from under his feet—desperately*]. As voters and citizens we kin force the bloody governments—

YANK [*with abysmal contempt*]. Hell! Governments!

ALL [*repeating the word after him as one with cynical mockery*]. Governments! [*The word has a brazen metallic quality as if their throats were phonograph horns. It is followed by a chorus of hard, barking laughter.*]

LONG [*hysterically*]. We're free and equal in the sight of God—

YANK [*with abysmal contempt*]. Hell! God!

ALL [*repeating the word after him as one with cynical mockery*]. God! [*The word has a brazen metallic quality as if their throats were phonograph horns. It is followed by a chorus of hard, barking laughter.*]

YANK [*witheringly*]. Aw, join de Salvation Army!

ALL. Sit down! Shut up! Damn fool! Sea-lawyer! [*Long slinks back out of sight*]

PADDY [*continuing the trend of his thoughts as if he had never been interrupted—bitterly*]. And there she was standing behind us, and the Second pointing at us like a man you'd hear in a circus would be saying: In this cage is a queerer kind of baboon than ever you'd find in darkest Africy. We roast them in their own sweat—and be damned if you won't hear some of thim saying they like it! [*He glances scornfully at Yank*]

YANK [*with a bewildered uncertain growl*]. Aw!

PADDY. And there was Yank roarin' curses and turning round wid his shovel to brain her—and she looked at him, and him at her—

YANK [*slowly*]. She was all white. I tought she was a ghost. Sure.

PADDY [*with heavy, biting sarcasm*]. 'Twas love at first sight, divil a doubt of it! If you'd seen the endearin' look on her pale mug when she shriveled away with her hands over her eyes to shut out the sight of him! Sure, 'twas as if she'd seen a great hairy ape escaped from the Zoo!

YANK [stung—with a growl of rage]. Aw!

PADDY. And the loving way Yank heaved his shovel at the skull of her, only she was out the door! [A grin breaking over his face] 'Twas touching, I'm telling you! It put the touch of home, swate home in the stokehole. [There is a roar of laughter from all]

YANK [glaring at Paddy menacingly]. Aw, choke dat off, see!

PADDY [not heeding him—to the others]. And her grabbin' at the Second's arm for protection. [With a grotesque imitation of a woman's voice] Kiss me, Engineer dear, for it's dark down here and me old man's in Wall Street making money! Hug me tight, darlin', for I'm afeerd in the dark and me mother's on deck makin' eyes at the skipper! [Another roar of laughter]

YANK [threateningly]. Say! What yuh tryin' to do, kid me, yuh old Harp?

PADDY. Divil a bit! Ain't I wishin' myself you'd brained her?

YANK [fiercely]. I'll brain her! I'll brain her yet, wait 'n' see! [Coming over to Paddy slowly] Say, is dat what she called me—a hairy ape?

PADDY. She looked it at you if she didn't say the word itself.

YANK [grinning horribly]. Hairy ape, huh? Sure! Dat's de way she looked at me, aw right. Hairy ape! So dat's me, huh? [Bursting into rage—as if she were still in front of him] Yuh skinny tart! Yuh white-faced bum, yuh! I'll show yuh who's a ape! [Turning to the others, bewilderment seizing him again] Say, youse guys. I was bawlin' him out for pullin' de whistle on us. You heard me. And den I seen youse lookin' at somep'n and I tought he'd sneaked down to come up in back of me, and I hopped round to knock him dead wit de shovel. And dere she was wit de light on her! Christ, yuh coulda pushed me over with a finger! I was scared, get me? Sure! I tought she was a ghost, see? She was all in white like dey wrap around stiffs. You seen her. Kin yuh blame me? She didn't belong, dat's what. And den when I come to and seen it was a real skoit and seen de way she was lookin' at me—like Paddy said—Christ, I was sore, get me? I don't stand for dat stuff from nobody. And I flung de shovel—on'y she'd beat it. [Furiously] I wished it'd banged her! I wished it'd knocked her block off!

LONG. And be 'anged for murder or 'lectrocuted? She ain't bleedin' well worth it.

YANK. I don't give a damn what! I'd be square wit her, wouldn't I? Tink I wanter let her put somep'n over on me? Tink I'm goin' to let her git away wit dat stuff? Yuh don't know me! No one ain't never put nothin' over on me and got away wit it, see!—not dat kind of stuff—no guy and no skoit neither! I'll fix her! Maybe she'll come down again—

VOICE. No chance, Yank. You scared her out of a year's growth.

YANK. I scared her? Why de hell should I scare her? Who de hell is she? Ain't she de same as me? Hairy ape, huh? [With his old confident bravado] I'll show her I'm better'n her, if she on'y knew it. I belong and she don't, see! I move and she's dead! Twenty-five knots a hour, dat's me! Dat carries her but I make dat. She's on'y baggage. Sure! [Again bewilderedly] But, Christ, she was funny lookin'! Did yuh pipe her hands? White and skinny. Yuh could see de bones through 'em. And her mush, dat was dead white, too. And her eyes, dey was like dey'd seen a ghost. Me, dat was! Sure! Hairy ape! Ghost, huh? Look at dat arm! [He extends his right arm, swelling out the great muscles] I coulda took her wit dat, wit' just my little finger even, and broke her in two. [Again bewilderedly] Say, who is dat skoit, huh? What is she? What's she come from? Who made her? Who give her de noive to look at me like dat? Dis ting's got my goat right. I don't get her. She's new to me. What does a skoit like her mean, huh? She don't belong, get me! I can't see her. [With growing anger] But one ting I'm wise to, aw right, aw right! Youse all kin bet your shoits I'll git even wit her. I'll show her if she tinks she—She grinds de organ and I'm on de string, huh? I'll fix her! Let her come down again and I'll thing her in de furnace! She'll move den! She won't shiver at nothin', den! Speed, dat'll be her! She'll belong den! [He grins horribly]

PADDY. She'll never come. She's had her belly-full, I'm telling you. She'll be in bed now, I'm thinking, wid ten doctors and nurses feedin' her salts to clean the fear out of her.

YANK [enraged]. Yuh tink I made her sick, too, do yuh? Just lookin' at me, huh? Hairy ape, huh? [In a frenzy of rage] I'll fix her! I'll tell her where to git off! She'll git down on her knees and take it back or I'll bust de face offen her! [Shaking one fist upward and beating on his chest with the other] I'll find yuh! I'm comin', d'yuh hear? I'll fix yuh, God damn yuh! [He makes a rush for the door]

VOICES. Stop him!
He'll get shot!
He'll murder her!
Trip him up!
Hold him!
He's gone crazy!

Gott, he's strong!
Hold him down!
Look out for a kick!
Pin his arms! [*They have all piled on him and, after a fierce struggle, by sheer weight of numbers have borne him to the floor just inside the door*]

PADDY [*who has remained detached*]. Kape him down till he's cooled off. [*Scornfully*] Yerra, Yank, you're a great fool. Is it payin' attention at all you are to the like of that skinny sow widout one drop of rale blood in her?

YANK [*frenziedly, from the bottom of the heap*]. She done me doit! She done me doit, didn't she? I'll git square wit her! I'll get her some way! Git offen me, youse guys! Lemme up! I'll show her who's a ape!

CURTAIN

SCENE V

SCENE—Three weeks later. A corner of Fifth Avenue in the Fifties on a fine Sunday morning. A general atmosphere of clean, well-tidied, wide street; a flood of mellow, tempered sunshine; gentle, genteel breezes. In the rear, the show windows of two shops, a jewelry establishment on the corner, a furrier's next to it. Here the adornments of extreme wealth are tantalizingly displayed. The jeweler's window is gaudy with glittering diamonds, emeralds, rubies, pearls, etc., fashioned in ornate tiaras, crowns, necklaces, collars, etc. From each piece hangs an enormous tag from which a dollar sign and numerals in intermittent electric lights wink out the incredible prices. The same in the furrier's. Rich furs of all varieties hang there bathed in a downpour of artificial light. The general effect is of a background of magnificence cheapened and made grotesque by commercialism, a background in tawdry disharmony with the clear light and sunshine on the street itself. Up the side street Yank and Long come swaggering. Long is dressed in shore clothes, wears a black Windsor tie, cloth cap. Yank is in his dirty dungarees. A fireman's cap with black peak is cocked defiantly on the side of his head. He has not shaved for days and around his fierce, resentful eyes—as around those of Long to a lesser degree—the black smudge of coal dust still sticks like make-up. They hesitate and stand together at the corner, swaggering, looking about them with a forced, defiant contempt.

LONG [*indicating it all with an oratorical gesture*]. Well, 'ere we are. Fif' Avenoo. This 'ere's their bleedin' private lane, as yer might say. [*Bitterly*] We're trespassers 'ere. Proletarians keep orf the grass!

YANK [*dully*]. I don't see no grass, yuh boob. [*Staring at the sidewalk*] Clean, ain't it? Yuh could eat a fried egg offen it. The white wings got some job sweepin' dis up. [*Looking up and down the avenue—surlily*] Where's all de white-collar stiffs yuh said was here—and de skoits—*her* kind?

LONG. In church, blarst 'em! Arskin Jesus to give 'em more money.

YANK. Choich, huh? I useter go to choich onct—sure—when I was a kid. Me old man and woman, dey made me. Dey never went demselves, dough. Always got too big a head on Sunday mornin', dat was dem. [*With a grin*] Dey was scrappers for fair, bot' of dem. On Satiday nights when dey bot' got a skinful dey could put up a bout oughter been staged at de Garden. When dey got trough dere wasn't a chair or table wit a leg under it. Or else dey bot' jumped on me for somep'n. Dat was where I loined to take punishment. [*With a grin and a swagger*] I'm a chip offen de old block, get me?

LONG. Did yer old man follow the sea?

YANK. Naw. Worked along shore. I runned away when me old lady croaked wit de tremens. I helped at truckin' and in de market. Den I shipped in de stokehole. Sure. Dat belongs. De rest was nothin'. [*Looking around him*] I ain't never seen dis before. De Brooklyn waterfront, dat was where I was dragged up. [*Taking a deep breath*] Dis ain't so bad at dat, huh?

LONG. Not bad? Well, we pays for it wiv our bloody sweat, if yer wants to know!

YANK [*with sudden angry disgust*]. Aw, hell! I don't see no one, see—like her. All dis gives me a pain. It don't belong. Say, ain't dere a back room around dis dump? Let's go shoot a ball. All dis is too clean and quiet and dolled-up, get me? It gives me a pain.

LONG. Wait and yer'll bloody well see—

YANK. I don't wait for no one. I keep on de move. Say, what yuh drag me up here for, anyway? Tryin' to kid me, yuh simp, yuh?

LONG. Yer wants to get back at 'er, don't yer? That's what yer been sayin' every bloomin' hour since she hinsulted yer.

YANK [*vehemently*]. Sure ting I do! Didn't I try to get even wit her in Southampton? Didn't I sneak on de dock and wait for her by de gangplank? I was goin' to spit in her pale mug, see! Sure, right in her popeyes! Dat woulda made me even, see? But no chanct. Dere was a whole army of plainclothes bulls around. Dey spotted me and gimme de bum's rush. I never seen her. But I'll git square wit her yet, you watch! [*Furiously*] De lousy tart! She tinks she kin get away with moider—but not wid me! I'll fix her! I'll tink of a way!

LONG [*as disgusted as he dares to be*]. Ain't that why I brought yer up 'ere—to show yer? Yer been lookin' at this 'ere 'ole affair wrong. Yer been actin' an' talkin' 's if it was all a bleedin' personal matter between yer and that bloody cow. I wants to convince yer she was on'y a representative of 'er clarss. I wants to awaken yer bloody clarss consciousness. Then yer'll see it's 'er clarss yer've got to fight, not 'er alone. There's a 'ole mob of 'em like 'er, Gawd blind 'em!

YANK [*spitting on his hands—belligerently*]. De more de merrier when I gits started. Bring on de gang!

LONG. Yer'll see 'em in arf a mo', when that church lets out. [*He turns and sees the window display in the two stores for the first time*] Blimey! Look at that, will yer? [*They both walk back and stand looking in the jeweler's. Long flies into a fury.*]. Just look at this 'ere bloomin' mess! Just look at it! Look at the bleedin' prices on 'em—more'n our 'ole bloody stokehole makes in ten voyages sweatin' in 'ell! And they—'er and 'er bloody clarss—buys 'em for toys to dangle on 'em! One of these 'ere would buy scoff for a starvin' family for a year!

YANK. Aw, cut de sob stuff! T' hell wit de starvin' family! Yuh'll be passin' de hat to me next. [*With naïve admiration*] Say, dem tings is pretty, huh? Bet yuh dey'd hock for a piece of change aw right. [*Then turning away, bored*] But, aw hell, what good are dey? Let 'er have 'em. Dey don't belong no more'n she does. [*With a gesture of sweeping the jewelers into oblivion*] All dat don't count, get me?

LONG [*who has moved to the furrier's—indignantly*]. And I s'pose this 'ere don't count neither—skins of poor, 'armless animals slaughtered so as 'er and 'ers can keep their bleedin' noses warm!

YANK [*who has been staring at something inside—with queer excitement*]. Take a slant at dat! Give it de once-over! Monkey fur—two t'ousand bucks! [*Bewilderedly*] Is dat straight goods— monkey fur? What de hell—?

LONG [*bitterly*]. It's straight enuf. [*With grim humor*] They wouldn't bloody well pay that for a 'airy ape's skin—no, nor for the 'ole livin' ape with all 'is 'ead, and body, and soul thrown in!

YANK [*clenching his fists, his face growing pale with rage as if the skin in the window were a personal insult*]. Trowin' it up in my face! Christ! I'll fix her!

LONG [*excitedly*]. Church is out. 'Ere they come, the bleedin' swine. [*After a glance at Yank's lowering face— uneasily*] Easy goes, Comrade. Keep yer bloomin' temper. Remember force defeats itself. It ain't our weapon. We must impress our demands through peaceful means—the votes of the on-marching proletarians of the bloody world!

YANK [*with abysmal contempt*]. Votes, hell! Votes is a joke, see. Votes for women! Let dem do it!

LONG [*still more uneasily*]. Calm, now. Treat 'em wiv the proper contempt. Observe the bleedin' parasites but 'old yer 'orses.

YANK [*angrily*]. Git away from me! Yuh're yellow, dat's what. Force, dat's me! De punch, dat's me every time, see! [*The crowd from church enter from the right, sauntering slowly and affectedly, their heads held stiffly up, looking neither to right nor left, talking in toneless, simpering voices. The women are rouged, calcimined, dyed, overdressed to the nth degree. The men are in Prince Alberts, high hats, spats, canes, etc. A procession of gaudy marionettes, yet with something of the relentless horror of Frankenstein monsters in their detached, mechanical unawareness.*]

VOICES. Dear Doctor Caiaphas! He is so sincere!

What was the sermon? I dozed off.

About the radicals, my dear—and the false doctrines that are being preached.

We must organize a hundred per cent American bazaar.

And let everyone contribute one one-hundredth per cent of their income tax.

What an original idea!

We can devote the proceeds to rehabilitating the veil of the temple.

But that has been done so many times.

YANK [*glaring from one to the other of them—with an insulting snort of scorn*]. Huh! Huh! [*Without seeming to see him, they make wide detours to avoid the spot where he stands in the middle of the sidewalk*]

LONG [*frightenedly*]. Keep yer bloomin' mouth shut, I tells yer.

YANK [*viciously*]. G'wan! Tell it to Sweeney! [*He swaggers away and deliberately lurches into a top-hatted gentleman, then glares at him pugnaciously*] Say, who d'yuh tink yuh're bumpin'? Tink yuh own de oith?

GENTLEMAN [*coldly and affectedly*]. I beg your pardon. [*He has not looked at Yank and passes on without a glance, leaving him bewildered*]

LONG [*rushing up and grabbing Yank's arm*]. 'Ere! Come away! This wasn't what I meant. Yer'll 'ave the bloody coppers down on us.

YANK [*savagely—giving him a push that sends him sprawling*]. G'wan!

LONG [*picks himself up—hysterically*]. I'll pop orf then. This ain't what I meant. And whatever 'appens, yer can't blame me. [*He slinks off left*]

YANK. T' hell wit youse! [*He approaches a lady—with a vicious grin and a smirking wink*] Hello, Kiddo. How's every little ting? Got anyting on for tonight? I know an old boiler down to de docks we kin crawl into. [*The lady stalks by without a look, without a change of pace. Yank turns to others—insultingly.*] Holy smokes, what a mug! Go hide yuhself before de horses shy at yuh. Gee, pipe de heine on dat one! Say, youse, yuh look like de stoin of a ferryboat. Paint and powder! All dolled up to kill! Yuh look like stiffs laid out for de boneyard! Aw, g'wan, de lot of youse! Yuh give me de eye-ache. Yuh don't belong, get me! Look at me, why don't youse dare? I belong, dat's me! [*Pointing to a skyscraper across the street which is in process of construction—with bravado*] See dat building goin' up dere? See de steel work? Steel, dat's me! Youse guys live on it and tink yuh're somep'n. But I'm *in* it, see! I'm de hoistin' engine dat makes it go up! I'm it—de inside and bottom of it! Sure! I'm steel and steam and smoke and de rest of it! It moves—speed—twenty-five stories up—and me at de top and bottom—movin'! Youse simps don't move. Yuh're on'y dolls I winds up to see 'm spin. Yuh're de garbage, get me—de leavins—de ashes we dump over de side! Now, what 'a' yuh gotta say? [*But as they seem neither to see nor hear him, he flies into a fury*] Bums! Pigs! Tarts! Bitches! [*He turns in a rage on the men, bumping viciously into them but not jarring them the least bit. Rather it is he who recoils after each collision. He keeps growling.*] Git off de oith! G'wan, yuh bum! Look where yuh're goin', can't yuh? Git outa here! Fight, why don't yuh? Put up yer mits! Don't be a dog! Fight or I'll knock yuh dead! [*But, without seeming to see him, they all answer with mechanical affected politeness*] I beg your pardon. [*Then at a cry from one of the women, they all scurry to the furrier's window*]

THE WOMAN [*ecstatically, with a gasp of delight*]. Monkey fur! [*The whole crowd of men and women chorus after her in the same tone of affected delight*] Monkey fur!

YANK [*with a jerk of his head back on his shoulders, as if he had received a punch full in the face—raging*]. I see yuh, all in white! I see yuh, yuh white-faced tart, yuh! Hairy ape, huh? I'll hairy ape yuh! [*He bends down and grips at the street curbing as if to pluck it out and hurl it. Foiled in this, snarling with passion, he leaps to the lamppost on the corner and tries to pull it up for a club. Just at that moment a bus is heard rumbling up. A fat, high-hatted, spatted gentleman runs out from the side street. He calls out plaintively.*] Bus! Bus! Stop there! [*And runs full tilt into the bending, straining Yank, who is bowled off his balance*]

YANK [*seeing a fight—with a roar of joy as he springs to his feet*]. At last! Bus, huh! I'll bust yuh! [*He lets drive a terrific swing, his fist landing full on the fat gentleman's face. But the gentleman stands unmoved as if nothing had happened.*]

GENTLEMAN. I beg your pardon. [*Then irritably*] You have made me lose my bus. [*He claps his hands and begins to scream*] Officer! Officer! [*Many police whistles shrill out on the instant and a whole platoon of policemen rush in on Yank from all sides. He tries to fight but is clubbed to the pavement and fallen upon. The crowd at the window have not moved or noticed this disturbance. The clanging gong of the patrol wagon approaches with a clamoring din.*]

CURTAIN

SCENE VI

SCENE—Night of the following day. A row of cells in the prison on Blackwell's Island. The cells extend back diagonally form right front to left rear. They do not stop, but disappear in the dark background as if they ran on, numberless, into infinity. One electric bulb from the low ceiling of the narrow corridor sheds its light through the heavy steel bars of the cell at the extreme front and reveals part of the interior. Yank can be seen within, crouched on the edge of his cot in the attitude of Rodin's "The Thinker." His face is spotted with black and blue bruises. A blood-stained bandage is wrapped around his head.

YANK [*suddenly starting as if awakening from a dream, reaches out and shakes the bars—aloud to himself, wonderingly*]. Steel. Dis is de Zoo, huh? [*A burst of hard, barking laughter comes from the unseen occupants of the cells, runs back down the tier, and abruptly ceases*]

VOICES [*mockingly*]. The Zoo? That's a new name for this coop—a damn good name!

Steel, eh? You said a mouthful. This is the old iron house.

Who is that boob talkin'?

He's the bloke they brung in out of his head. The bulls had beat him up fierce.

YANK [*dully*]. I musta been dreamin'. I tought I was in a cage at de Zoo—but de apes don't talk, do dey?

VOICES [*with mocking laughter*]. You're in a cage aw right.

A coop!

A pen!

A sty!

A kennel! [*Hard laughter—a pause*]

Say, guy! Who are you? No, never mind lying. What are you?

Yes, tell us your sad story. What's your game?

What did they jug yuh for?

YANK [*dully*]. I was a fireman—stokin' on de liners. [*Then with sudden rage, rattling his cell bars*] I'm a hairy ape, get me? And I'll bust youse all in de jaw if yuh don't lay off kiddin' me.

VOICES. Huh! You're a hard boiled duck, ain't you!

When you spit, it bounces! [*Laughter*]

Aw, can it. He's a regular guy. Ain't you?

What did he say he was—a ape?

YANK [*defiantly*]. Sure ting! Ain't dat what youse all are—apes? [*A silence. Then a furious rattling of bars from down the corridor.*]

A VOICE [*thick with rage*]. I'll show yuh who's a ape, yuh bum!

VOICES. Ssshh! Nix!

Can de noise!

Piano!

You'll have the guard down on us!

YANK [*scornfully*]. De guard? Yuh mean de keeper, don't yuh? [*Angry exclamations from all the cells*]

VOICE [*placatingly*]. Aw, don't pay no attention to him. He's off his nut from the beatin'-up he got. Say, you guy! We're waitin' to hear what they landed you for—or ain't yuh tellin'?

YANK. Sure, I'll tell youse. Sure! Why de hell not? On'y—youse won't get me. Nobody gets me but me, see? I started to tell de Judge and all he says was: "Toity days to tink it over." Tink it over! Christ, dat's all I been doin' for weeks! [*After a pause*] I was tryin' to git even wit someone, see?—someone dat done me doit.

VOICES [*cynically*]. De old stuff, I bet. Your goil, huh?

Give yuh the double-cross, huh?

That's them every time!

Did yuh beat up de odder guy?

YANK [*disgustedly*]. Aw, yuh're all wrong! Sure dere was a skoit in it—but not what youse mean, not dat old tripe. Dis was a new kind of skoit. She was dolled up all in white—in de stokehole. I tought she was a ghost. Sure. [*A pause*]

VOICES [*whispering*]. Gee, he's still nutty.

Let him rave. It's fun listenin'.

YANK [*unheeding—groping in his thoughts*]. Her hands—dey was skinny and white like dey wasn't real but painted on somep'n. Dere was a million miles from me to her—twenty-five knots a hour. She was like some dead ting de cat brung in. Sure, dat's what. She didn't belong. She belonged in de window of a toy store, or on de top of a garbage can, see! Sure! [*He breaks out angrily*] But would yuh believe it, she had de noive to do me doit. She lamped me like she was seein' somep'n broke loose from de menagerie. Christ, yuh'd oughter seen her eyes! [*He rattles the bars of his cell furiously*] But I'll get back at her yet, you watch! And if I can't find her I'll take it out on de gang she runs wit. I'm wise to where dey hangs out now. I'll show her who belongs! I'll show her who's in de move and who ain't. You watch my smoke!

VOICES [*serious and joking*]. Dat's de talkin'!

Take her for all she's got!

What was this dame, anyway? Who was she, eh?

YANK. I dunno. First cabin stiff. Her old man's a millionaire, dey says—name of Douglas.

VOICES. Douglas? That's the president of the Steel Trust. I bet.

Sure. I seen his mug in de papers.

He's filthy with dough.

VOICE. Hey, feller, take a tip from me. If you want to get back at that dame, you better join the Wobblies. You'll get some action then.

YANK. Wobblies? What de hell's dat?

VOICE. Ain't you ever heard of the I. W. W.?

YANK. Naw. What is it?

VOICE. A gang of blokes—a tough gang. I been readin' about 'em today in the paper. The guard give me the *Sunday Times*. There's a long spiel about 'em. It's from a speech made in the Senate by a guy named Senator Queen. [*He is in the cell next to Yank's. There is a rustling of paper.*] Wait'll I see if I got light enough and I'll read you. Listen. [*He reads*] "There is a menace existing in this country today which threatens the vitals of our fair Republic—as foul a menace against the very life-blood of the American Eagle as was the foul conspiracy of Cataline against the eagles of ancient Rome!"

VOICE [*disgustedly*]. Aw, hell! Tell him to salt de tail of dat eagle!

VOICE [*reading*]. "I refer to that devil's brew of rascals, jailbirds, murderers and cutthroats who libel all honest working men by calling themselves the Industrial Workers of the World; but in the light of their nefarious plots, I call them the Industrial *Wreckers* of the World!"

YANK [*with vengeful satisfaction*]. Wreckers, dat's de right dope! Dat belongs! Me for dem!

VOICE. Ssshh! [*Reading*] "This fiendish organization is a foul ulcer on the fair body of our Democracy—"

VOICE. Democracy, hell! Give him the boid, fellers— the raspberry! [*They do*]

VOICE. Ssshh! [*Reading*] "Like Cato I say to this Senate, the I. W. W. must be destroyed! For they represent an ever-present dagger pointed at the heart of the greatest nation the world has ever known, where all men are born free and equal, with equal opportunities to all, where the Founding Fathers have guaranteed to each one happiness, where Truth, Honor, Liberty, Justice, and the Brotherhood of Man are a religion absorbed with one's mother's milk, taught at our father's knee, sealed, signed, and stamped upon in the glorious Constitution of these United States!" [*A perfect storm of hisses, catcalls, boos, and hard laughter*]

VOICES [*scornfully*]. Hurrah for de Fort' of July!

Pass de hat!

Liberty!

Justice!

Honor!

Opportunity!

Brotherhood!

All [*with abysmal scorn*]. Aw, hell!

VOICE. Give that Queen Senator guy the bark! All togedder now—one—two—tree— [*A terrific chorus of barking and yapping*]

GUARD [*from a distance*]. Quiet there, youse—or I'll git the hose. [*The noise subsides*]

YANK [*with growling rage*]. I'd like to catch dat senator guy alone for a second. I'd loin him some trute!

VOICE. Ssshh! Here's where he gits down to cases on the Wobblies. [*Reads*] "They plot with fire in one hand and dynamite in the other. They stop not before murder to gain their ends, nor at the outraging of defenseless womanhood. They would tear down society, put the lowest scum in the seats of the mighty, turn Almighty God's revealed plan for the world topsy-turvey, and make of our sweet and lovely civilization a shambles, a desolation where

man, God's masterpiece, would soon degenerate back to the ape!"

VOICE [*to Yank*]. Hey, you guy. There's your ape stuff again.

YANK [*with a growl of fun*]. I got him. So dey blow up tings, do dey? Dey turn tings round, do dey? Hey, lend me dat paper, will yuh?

VOICE. Sure. Give it to him. On'y keep it to yourself, see. We don't wanter listen to no more of that slop.

VOICE. Here you are. Hide it under your mattress.

YANK [*reaching out*]. Tanks. I can't read much bit I kin manage. [*He sits, the paper in the hand at his side, in the attitude of Rodin's "The Thinker." A pause. Several snores from down the corridor. Suddenly Yank jumps to his feet with a furious groan as if some appalling thought had crashed on him—bewilderedly.*] Sure—her old man— president of de Steel Trust—makes half de steel in de world—steel—where I tought I belonged— drivin' trou—movin'—in dat—to make *her*—and cage me in for her to spit on! Christ! [*He shakes the bars of his cell door till the whole tier trembles. Irritated, protesting exclamations from those awakened or trying to get to sleep.*] He made dis—dis cage! Steel! *It* don't belong, dat's what! Cages, cells, locks, bolts, bars— dat's what it means!—holdin' me down wit him at de top! But I'll drive trou! Fire, dat melts it! I'll be fire—under de heap—fire dat never goes out—hot as hell—breakin' out in de night— [*While he has been saying this last he has shaken his cell door to a clanging accompaniment. As he comes to the "breakin' out" he seizes one bar with both hands and, putting his two feet up against the others so that his position is parallel to the floor like a monkey's, he gives a great wrench backwards. The bar bends like a licorice stick under his tremendous strength. Just at this moment the Prison Guard rushes in, dragging a hose behind him.*]

GUARD [*angrily*]. I'll loin youse bums to wake me up! [*Sees Yank*] Hello, it's you, huh? Got the D. Ts., hey? Well, I'll cure 'em. I'll drown your snakes for yuh! [*Noticing the bar*] Hell, look at dat bar bended! On'y a bug is strong enough for dat!

YANK [*glaring at him*]. Or a hairy ape, yuh big yellow bum! Look out! Here I come! [*He grabs another bar*]

GUARD [*scared now—yelling off left*]. Toin de hose on, Ben!—full pressure! And call de others—and a straitjacket! [*The curtain is falling. As it hides Yank from view, there is a splattering smash as the stream of water hits the steel of Yank's cell.*]

CURTAIN

SCENE VII

SCENE—Nearly a month later. An I. W. W. local near the waterfront, showing the interior of a front room on the ground floor, and the street outside. Moonlight on the narrow street, buildings massed in black shadow. The interior of the room, which is general assembly room, office, and reading room, resembles some dingy settlement boys' club. A desk and high stool are in one corner. A table with papers, stacks of pamphlets, chairs about it, is at center. The whole is decidedly cheap, banal, commonplace and unmysterious as a room could well be. The Secretary is perched on the stool making entries in a large ledger. An eye shade casts his face into shadows. Eight or ten men, longshoremen, iron workers, and the like are grouped about the table. Two are playing checkers. One is writing a letter. Most of them are smoking pipes. A big signboard is on the wall at the rear, "Industrial Workers of the World—Local No. 57."

YANK [*comes down the street outside. He is dressed as in Scene V. He moves cautiously, mysteriously. He comes to a point opposite the door; tiptoes softly up to it, listens, is impressed by the silence within, knocks carefully, as if he were guessing at the password to some secret rite. Listens. No answer. Knocks again a bit louder. No answer. Knocks impatiently, much louder.*]

SECRETARY [*turning around on his stool*]. What the hell is that someone knocking? [*Shouts*] Come in, why don't you? [*All the men in the room look up. Yank opens the door slowly, gingerly, as if afraid of an ambush. He looks around for secret doors, mystery, is taken aback by the commonplaceness of the room and the men in it, thinks he may have gotten in the wrong place, then sees the signboard on the wall and is reassured.*]

YANK [*blurts out*]. Hello.

MEN [*reservedly*]. Hello.

YANK [*more easily*]. I tought I'd bumped into de wrong dump.

SECRETARY [*scrutinizing him carefully*]. Maybe you have. Are you a member?

YANK. Naw, not yet. Dat's what I come for—to join.

SECRETARY. That's easy. What's your job—longshore?

YANK. Naw. Fireman—stoker on de liners.

SECRETARY [*with satisfaction*]. Welcome to our city. Glad to know you people are waking up at last. We haven't got many members in your line.

YANK. Naw. Dey're all dead to de woild.

SECRETARY. Well, you can help to wake 'em. What's your name? I'll make out your card.

YANK [*confused*]. Name? Lemme tink.

SECRETARY [*sharply*]. Don't you know your own name?

YANK. Sure; but I been just Yank for so long—Bob, dat's it—Bob Smith.

SECRETARY [*writing*]. Robert Smith. [*Fills out the rest of card*] Here you are. Cost you half a dollar.

YANK. Is dat all—four bits? Dat's easy. [*Gives the Secretary the money*]

SECRETARY [*throwing it in drawer*]. Thanks. Well, make yourself at home. No introductions needed. There's literature on the table. Take some of those pamphlets with you to distribute aboard ship. They may bring results. Sow the seed, only go about it right. Don't get caught and fired. We got plenty out of work. What we need is men who can hold their jobs—and work for us at the same time.

YANK. Sure. [*But he still stands, embarrassed and uneasy*]

SECRETARY [*looking at him—curiously*]. What did you knock for? Think we had a coon in uniform to open doors?

YANK. Naw. I tought it was locked—and dat yuh'd wanter give me the once-over trou a peephole or somep'n to see if I was right.

SECRETARY [*alert and suspicious but with an easy laugh*]. Think we were running a crap game? That door is never locked. What put that in your nut?

YANK [*with a knowing grin, convinced that this is all camouflage, a part of the secrecy*]. Dis burg is full of bulls, ain't it?

SECRETARY [*sharply*]. What have the cops got to do with us? We're breaking no laws.

YANK [*with a knowing wink*]. Sure. Youse wouldn't for woilds. Sure. I'm wise to dat.

SECRETARY. You seem to be wise to a lot of stuff none of us knows about.

YANK [*with another wink*]. Aw, dat's aw right, see. [*Then made a bit resentful by the suspicious glances from all sides*] Aw, can it! Youse needn't put me trou de toid degree. Can't youse see I belong? Sure! I'm reg'lar. I'll stick, get me? I'll shoot de woiks for youse. Dat's why I wanted to join in.

SECRETARY [*breezily, feeling him out*]. That's the right spirit. Only are you sure you understand what you've joined? It's all plain and aboveboard; still, some guys get a wrong slant on us. [*Sharply*] What's your notion of the purpose of the I. W. W.?

YANK. Aw, I know all about it.

SECRETARY [*sarcastically*]. Well, give us some of your valuable information.

YANK [*cunningly*]. I know enough not to speak outa my toin. [*Then resentfully again*] Aw, say! I'm reg'lar. I'm wise to de game. I know yuh got to watch your step wit a stranger. For all youse know, I might be a plain-clothes dick, or somep'n, dat's what yuh're tinkin', huh? Aw, forget it! I belong, see? Ask any guy down to de docks if I don't.

SECRETARY. Who said you didn't?

YANK. After I'm 'nitiated, I'll show yuh.

SECRETARY [*astounded*]. Initiated? There's no initiation.

YANK [*disappointed*]. Ain't there no password—no grip nor nothin'?

SECRETARY. What'd you think this is—the Elks—or the Black Hand?

YANK. De Elks, hell! De Black Hand, dey're a lot of yellow back-stickin' Ginees.[2] Naw. Dis is a man's gang, ain't it?

SECRETARY. You said it! That's why we stand on our two feet in the open. We got no secrets.

YANK [*surprised but admiringly*]. Yuh mean to say yuh always run wide open—like dis?

SECRETARY. Exactly.

YANK. Den yuh sure got your noive wit youse!

SECRETARY [*sharply*]. Just what was it made you want to join us? Come out with that straight.

YANK. Yuh call me? Well, I got noive, too! Here's my hand. Yuh wanter blow tings up, don't yuh? Well, dat's me! I belong!

SECRETARY [*with pretended carelessness*]. You mean change the unequal conditions of society by legitimate direct action—or with dynamite?

YANK. Dynamite! Blow it offen de oith—steel—all de cages—all de factories, steamers, buildings, jails—de Steel Trust and all dat makes it go.

SECRETARY. So—that's your idea, eh? And did you have any special job in that line you wanted to propose to us? [*He makes a sign to the men, who get up cautiously one by one and group behind Yank*]

YANK [*boldly*]. Sure, I'll come out wit it. I'll show youse I'm one of de gang. Dere's dat millionaire guy, Douglas—

SECRETARY. President of the Steel Trust, you mean? Do you want to assassinate him?

YANK. Naw, dat don't get yuh nothin'. I mean blow up de factory, de woiks, where he makes de steel. Dat's what I'm after—to blow up de steel, knock all

de steel in de woild up to de moon. Dat'll fix tings! [*Eagerly, with a touch of bravado*] I'll do it by me lonesome! I'll show yuh! Tell me where his woiks is, how to git there, all de dope. Gimme de stuff, de old butter—and watch me do de rest! Watch de smoke and see it move! I don't give a damn if dey nab me—long as it's done! I'll soive life for it—and give 'em de laugh! [*Half to himself*] And I'll write her a letter and tell her de hairy ape done it. Dat'll square tings.

SECRETARY [*stepping away from Yank*]. Very interesting. [*He gives a signal. The men, huskies all, throw themselves on Yank and before he knows it they have his legs and arms pinioned. But he is too flabbergasted to make a struggle, anyway. They feel him over for weapons.*]

MAN. No gat, no knife. Shall we give him what's what and put the boots to him?

SECRETARY. No. He isn't worth the trouble we'd get into. He's too stupid. [*He comes closer and laughs mockingly in Yank's face*] Ho-ho! By God, this is the biggest joke they've put up on us yet. Hey, you Joke! Who sent you—Burns or Pinkerton?[3] No, by God, you're such a bonehead I'll bet you're in the Secret Service! Well, you dirty spy, you rotten agent provocator, you can go back and tell whatever skunk is paying you blood-money for betraying your brothers that he's wasting his coin. You couldn't catch a cold. And tell him that all he'll ever get on us, or ever has got, is just his own sneaking plots that he's framed up to put us in jail. We are what our manifesto says we are, neither more nor less—and we'll give him a copy of that any time he calls. And as for you— [*He glares scornfully at Yank, who is sunk in an oblivious stupor*] Oh, hell, what's the use of talking? You're a brainless ape.

YANK [*aroused by the word to fierce but futile struggles*]. What's dat, yuh Sheeny bum, yuh!

SECRETARY. Throw him out, boys. [*In spite of his struggles, this is done with gusto and éclat. Propelled by several parting kicks, Yank lands sprawling in the middle of the narrow cobbled street. With a growl he starts to get up and storm the closed door, but stops bewildered by the confusion in his brain, pathetically impotent. He sits there, brooding, in as near to the attitude of Rodin's "Thinker" as he can get in his position.*]

YANK [*bitterly*]. So dem boids don't tink I belong, neider. Aw, to hell wit 'em! Dey're in de wrong pew—de same old bull—soapboxes and Salvation Army—no guts! Cut out an hour offen de job a day

---

[2] **Guinees:** slang for Italians.

[3] Private investigators.

and make me happy! Gimme a dollar more a day and make me happy! Tree square a day, and cauliflowers in de front yard—ekal rights—a woman and kids—a lousy vote—and I'm all fixed for Jesus, huh? Aw, hell! What does dat get yuh? Dis ting's in your inside, but it ain't your belly. Feedin' your face—sinkers and coffee—dat don't touch it. It's way down—at de bottom. Yuh can't grab it, and yuh can't stop it. It moves, and everything moves. It stops and de whole woild stops. Dat's me now—I don't tick, see?—I'm a busted Ingersoll,[4] dat's what. Steel was me, and I owned de woild. Now I ain't steel, and de woild owns me. Aw, hell! I can't see—it's all dark, get me? It's all wrong! [*He turns a bitter mocking face up like an ape gibbering at the moon*] Say, youse up dere, Man in de Moon, yuh look so wise, gimme de answer, huh? Slip me de inside dope, de information right from de stable—where do I get off at, huh?

A POLICEMAN [*who has come up the street in time to hear this last—with grim humor*]. You'll get off at the station, you boob, if you don't get up out of that and keep movin'.

YANK [*looking up at him—with a hard, bitter laugh*]. Sure! Lock me up! Put me in a cage! Dat's de on'y answer yuh know. G'wan, lock me up!

POLICEMAN. What you been doin'?

YANK. Enuf to gimme life for! I was born, see? Sure, dat's de charge. Write it in de blotter. I was born, get me!

POLICEMAN [*jocosely*]. God pity your old woman! [*Then matter-of-fact*] But I've no time for kidding. You're soused. I'd run you in but it's too long a walk to the station. Come on now, get up, or I'll fan your ears with this club. Beat it now! [*He hauls Yank to his feet*]

YANK [*in a vague mocking tone*]. Say, where do I go from here?

POLICEMAN [*giving him a push—with a grin, indifferently*]. Go to hell.

CURTAIN

SCENE VIII

SCENE— Twilight of the next day. The monkey house at the Zoo. One spot of clear gray light falls on the front of one cage so that the interior can be seen. The other cages are vague, shrouded in shadow from which chatterings pitched in a conversational tone can be heard. On the one cage a sign from which the word "gorilla" stands out. The gigantic animal himself on a bench in much the same attitude as Rodin's "Thinker." Yank enters from the left. Immediately a chorus of angry chattering and screeching breaks out. The gorilla turns his eyes but makes no sound or move.

YANK [*with a hard, bitter laugh*]. Welcome to our city, huh? Hail, hail, de gang's all here! [*At the sound of his voice the chattering dies away into an attentive silence. Yank walks up to the gorilla's cage and, leaning over the railing, stares in at its occupant, who stares back at him, silent and motionless. There is a pause of dead stillness. Then Yank begins to talk in a friendly confidential tone, half-mockingly, but with a deep undercurrent of sympathy.*] Say, yuh're some hard-lookin' guy, ain't yuh? I seen lots of tough nuts dat de gang called gorillas, but yuh're de foist real one I ever seen. Some chest yuh got, and shoulders, and dem arms and mits! I bet yuh got a punch in eider fist dat'd knock 'em all silly! [*This with genuine admiration. The gorilla, as if he understood, stands upright, swelling out his chest and pounding on it with his fist. Yank grins sympathetically.*] Sure, I get yuh. Yuh challenge de whole woild, huh? Yuh got what I was sayin' even if yuh muffed de woids. [*Then bitterness creeping in.*] And why wouldn't yuh get me? Ain't we both members of de same club—de Hairy Apes? [*They stare at each other—a pause—then Yank goes on slowly and bitterly*] So yuh're what she seen when she looked at me, de white-faced tart! I was you to her, get me? On'y outa de cage—broke out—free to moider her, see? Sure! Dat's what she tought. She wasn't wise dat I was in a cage, too—worser'n yours—sure—a damn sight—'cause you got some chanct to bust loose—but me— [*He grows confused*] Aw, hell! It's all wrong, ain't it? [*A pause*] I s'pose yuh wanter know what I'm doin' here, huh? I been warmin' a bench down to de Battery[5]—ever since last night. Sure, I seen de sun come up. Dat was pretty, too—all red and pink and green. I was lookin' at de skyscrapers—steel—and all de ships comin' in, sailin' out, all over de oith—and dey was steel, too. De sun was warm, dey wasn't no clouds, and dere was a breeze blowin'. Sure, it was great stuff. I got it aw

---

[4] Cheap watch.

[5] Park in New York City, southern tip of Manhattan.

right—what Paddy said about dat bein' de right dope—on'y I couldn't get *in* it, see? I couldn't belong in dat. It was over my head. And I kept tinkin'—and den I beat it up here to see what youse was like. And I waited till dey was all gone to git yuh alone. Say, how d'yuh feel sittin' in dat pen all de time, havin' to stand for 'em comin' and starin' at yuh—de white-faced, skinny tarts and de boobs what marry 'em—makin' fun of yuh, laughin' at yuh, gittin' scared of yuh—damn 'em! [*He pounds on the rail with his fist. The gorilla rattles the bars of his cage and snarls. All the other monkeys set up an angry chattering in the darkness. Yank goes on excitedly.*] Sure! Dat's de way it hits me, too. On'y yuh're lucky, see? Yuh don't belong wit 'em and yuh know it. But me, I belong wit 'em—but I don't, see? Dey don't belong wit me, dat's what. Get me? Tinkin' is hard— [*He passes one hand across his forehead with a painful gesture. The gorilla growls impatiently. Yank goes on gropingly.*] It's dis way, what I'm drivin' at. Youse can sit and dope dream in de past, green woods, de jungle and de rest of it. Den yuh belong and dey don't. Den yuh kin laugh at 'em, see? Yuh're de champ of de woild. But me—I ain't got no past to tink in, nor nothin' dat's comin', on'y what's now—and dat don't belong. Sure, you're de best off! Yuh can't tink, can yuh? Yuh can't talk neider. But I kin make a bluff at talkin' and tinkin'—a'most git away with it—a'most!—and dat's where de joker comes in. [*He laughs*] I ain't on oith and I ain't in heaven, get me? I'm in de middle tryin' to separate 'em, takin' all de woist punches from bot' of 'em. Maybe dat's what dey call hell, huh? But you, yuh're at de bottom. You belong? Sure! Yuh're de on'y one in de woild dat does, yuh lucky stiff! [*The gorilla growls proudly*] And dat's why dey gotter put yuh in a cage, see? [*The gorilla roars angrily*] Sure! Yuh get me. It beats it when you try to tink it or talk it—it's way down—deep—behind—you 'n' me we feel it. Sure! Bot' members of dis club! [*He laughs—then in a savage tone*] What de hell! T' hell wit it! A little action, dat's our meat! Dat belongs! Knock 'em down and keep bustin' 'em till dey croaks yuh wit a gat—wit steel! Sure! Are yuh game? Dey've looked at youse, ain't dey—in a cage? Wanter get even? Wanter wind up like a sport 'stead of croakin' slow in dere? [*The gorilla roars an emphatic affirmative. Yank goes on with a sort of furious exaltation.*] Sure! Yuh're reg'lar! Yuh'll stick to de finish! Me 'n' you—huh?—bot' mem-

bers of this club! We'll put up one last star bout dat'll knock 'em offen deir seats! Dey'll have to make de cages stronger after we're trou! [*The gorilla is straining at his bars, growling, hopping from one foot to the other. Yank takes a jimmy from under his coat and forces the lock on the cage door. He throws this open.*] Pardon from de governor! Step out and shake hands! I'll take yuh for a walk down Fif' Avenoo. We'll knock 'em offen de oith and croak wit de band playin'. Come on, Brother. [*The gorilla scrambles gingerly out of his cage. Goes to Yank and stands looking at him. Yank keeps his mocking tone—holds out his hand.*] Shake—de secret grip of our order. [*Something, the tone of mockery, perhaps, suddenly enrages the animal. With a spring he wraps his huge arms around Yank in a murderous hug. There is a crackling snap of crushed ribs—a gasping cry, still mocking, from Yank.*] Hey, I didn't say kiss me! [*The gorilla lets the crushed body slip to the floor; stands over it uncertainly, considering; then picks it up, throws it in the cage, shuts the door, and shuffles off menacingly into the darkness at left. A great uproar of frightened chattering and whimpering comes from the other cages. Then Yank moves, groaning, opening his eyes, and there is silence. He mutters painfully.*] Say—dey oughter match him—wit Zybszko.[6] He got me, aw right. I'm trou. Even him didn't tink I belonged. [*Then, with sudden passionate despair*] Christ, where do I get off at? Where do I fit in? [*Checking himself as suddenly*] Aw, what de hell! No squawkin', see! No quittin', get me! Croak wit your boots on! [*He grabs hold of the bars of the cage and hauls himself painfully to his feet—looks around him bewilderedly—forces a mocking laugh*] In de cage, huh? [*In the strident tones of a circus barker*] Ladies and gents, step forward and take a slant at de one and only—[*His voice weakening*] —one and original— Hairy Ape from de wilds of—[*He slips in a heap on the floor and dies. The monkeys set up a chattering, whimpering wail. And, perhaps, the Hairy Ape at last belongs.*]

CURTAIN

---

[6] Contemporary wrestling champion.

ESSAY: AN APPROACH TO THE PLAY

The "meaning" of *The Hairy Ape* seems no more conventional now than it did seven decades ago. The play is not primarily an analysis of class antagonisms, although these concerns are certainly touched upon: "They dragged us down 'til we're on'y wage slaves," says Long, the spokesman for this point of view, and his analysis often shows the intelligence of this anti-"society" perspective. But O'Neill's analysis of "society" expands beyond its conventional sense as the dominant social class to consider questions essential to the meaning of human existence. Yank (a suggestive name, surely) wants to know his use in the world. At an early optimistic point he says, "I'm part of de engines! . . . I start somep'n and de woild moves." He identifies himself with the new and the mechanized, with materialism almost as a kind of mystical force in the world.

His energy is contrasted with the bored emptiness of the privileged Mildred Douglas, who, unlike her grandfather, has lost touch with machinery and steel. In Scene 3, Yank, who feels an elemental connection to this machinery, considers himself superior to Mildred, who seems to him "new" but also "like some dead ting." She is presented as a parasite, unconscious of the "reality" that lies below the comfortable surface of the world and makes it turn. When in the same scene she is confronted with the ship's version of this "reality," confronted with how the ship on which she is a passenger moves and with the raw power of the man who identifies himself with its machinery, she simply faints.

Yet despite her powerlessness, she belongs to a social class so powerful (as Scene 5 shows in symbolic form) that for her someone like Yank literally does not exist, at least not as a person. The play's ending suggests, in fact, that Yank himself may believe in the propaganda of this society. At any rate, in Scene 5 Yank's punch has no effect at all on a "gentleman," and the women with their delight in the new fashion of "monkey fur" ignore him (whereas as a dead ape he would have been valued for his pelt). Aside from his ability to keep the engines of society running (out of sight, of course), he is useful to conventional society only as an object for the police to club (and possibly as a justification for their existence in the first place). Of course, no one in "society" notices their brutality. The similarity between the jail in Scene 6 and the ship's forecastle reinforces this class issue, but the play does not attempt to solve such problems. Unionism, for example, seems specifically to be rejected as a solution: the political machinations of the IWW, which Yank (and we) might expect to be helpful to him, turn out to be threatened by the direct force which Yank wishes to apply.

The question the play asks more centrally is, "Where do I fit in?" Rejected equally by conventional society and its union opponents, Yank actually comes to think of himself as an ape; he tries to rediscover his identify by returning to his Darwinian ancestry. As poetic drama often does, here a common figure of speech is rendered literally and is in this way shown to be not only prejudicial, but fatal. And because it is unanswered, Yank's question remains as our own. Must we be caged by society in order to avoid becoming like them, one of the living dead who inhabit the streets of this materialistic city? Or do we want to be like the union man, Long, the ineffectual intellectual opponent of society? Or again, do we want to be domesticated human gorillas, shoveling coal better than anyone else? What options does this play present?

Seventy years later, it may seem that O'Neill poses these issues in naive terms, and possibly even that his dramatic representation of them is also naive—that the issues are not so simple, and the symbolism is too obvious. But he has taken the issue of our human place in the world and in society, an issue over which we continue to puzzle, and by his symbolic approach has been able to simplify it into its essence—and implicitly into a question for which few of us have yet found clear answers. Beyond the social questions and the suggestions of their primitive and inescapable origin, we are left with questions of choice that we still need to deal with. Has our materially comfortable culture divided us into a limited number of classes, all of them fragmentary, none of them spiritually satisfying? Would we rather be comfortable parasites or energized though puzzled gorillas? How does it happen that some people gain material comfort: is life just a matter of luck, of carefully selecting your parents? By extension, what *should* we do with our lives if we are fortunate? Or if we are not? What is the relation of an individual's role and status in society to human value? This is especially a problem for a country that proudly asserts its foundation on democratic principles: *is* a common laborer the equal of anyone in our culture? Swiftly, and perhaps simply, O'Neill cuts to the core of such issues.

Samuel Beckett

ROUGH FOR THEATRE I

About the Author   Samuel Beckett (1906–1989) was born in Foxrock, County Dublin, and took both a B.A. and M.A. in French and Italian at Dublin's Trinity College. After teaching English at the École Normale in Paris, then teaching French back at Trinity College, he worked in the Irish Red Cross Hospital in France at the end of World War II and married a Frenchwoman in 1948. During much of the time before this war he lived in Paris and was often associated there with his fellow literary Irishman James Joyce. After the war he settled permanently in Paris, writing novels and stories in French, then translating them himself into English. His plays were usually written in English first, however, because Beckett believed that language to be more closely connected to concrete things, which he believed to be the essential stuff of theater, while he thought of French as more closely connected to abstractions. *Rough for Theatre I* is an exception, though: He wrote it first in French.

Beckett wrote over twenty plays of various lengths for various media (including six for radio, three for television, and one for film), as well as novels, stories, and five books of verse. Like Ionesco, in the 1950s he was associated with the theater of the absurd, but his voice is too individual and too varied for any category or movement to contain him. Among the many ways in which his genius has been recognized is his reception in 1969 of the Nobel Prize for literature.

About the Play   *Rough for Theatre I* was written in French in the late 1950s and first translated into English in 1976. It is not a complete play, but an idea for one, roughed out in sufficient detail for the playwright (or, in this case, the reader) to be able to fill in enough of the blanks to make it into a complete work. We have chosen this "rough" not only to emphasize the reader's role in completing a play, but also because it is typical of the kind of play Beckett writes in longer form: with spare stage setting, simple action, and unadorned language. He strips the basic elements of his plays to their minimum necessities and then elevates these minimal situations so that they raise fundamental philosophical issues. In this case, the characters are not even given the identity of names. They are simply A and B, the minimum designations necessary to differentiate one from the other.

The play's two characters are, as is often the case in Beckett, not merely unusual—they are bizarre: we have a blind, possibly incompetent, fiddler who begs and a person in a wheel chair who cannot walk but who can see. Their abilities (we cannot call them skills) are to some degree complementary. With the wheelchair person's sight, A could have direction. With A's ability to walk, B would no longer need to push himself along.

In such a circumscribed world, everything counts; the smallest detail is significant. But this creates a problem for the reader: in Beckett's plays much must be inferred from minimal gestures and words. In A's first speech, for example, less is said than is done, and what *is* done must be carefully observed. The many pauses to listen and the fact that the fiddle is "scraped" suggest that music has little value in itself to this man who supposedly earns his livelihood by fiddling. B's first speech acknowledges A's importance to him, but this is not the importance one would expect. His first words, "So it is not a dream," suggest a philosophical concern: Is our feeling and thinking real or imagined? Are we perhaps merely minds which imagine worlds of things, noises, and activities in order to relieve boredom or for some other equally undignified reason? But "Billy"'s scraped fiddle has given B a sensory experience that he can attach to a particular person and act. "It," he asserts, is not a dream: "the mystery is over." Having made this discovery, B considers a further possibility, a kind of marriage partnership;

they might "live together, till death ensue"—a rough paraphrase of a crucial part of a marriage ceremony. Such relationships, it is implied, although perhaps a source of comfort, may take the mystery from things.

In a very few pages and words, Beckett uses the simplest of human situations to imply large philosophical questions, and you will need to read attentively to figure out what seems to be at stake in this play. The relationship of A and B introduces considerations not only about something like marriage but also about a form of religious morality, while presenting human beings who are unable to sustain the ideals which these institutions imply. Human life is reduced in a bizarre simplicity to its elemental uncertainty and misery, in a play which may even question whether the attainment of certainty would reduce that misery.

Street corner. Ruins.

[*A, blind, sitting on a folding-stool, scrapes his fiddle. Beside him the case, half open, upended, surmounted by alms bowl. He stops playing, turns his head audience right, listens. Pause.*]

A. A penny for a poor man, a penny for a poor old man. [*Silence. He resumes playing, stops again, turns his head right, listens. Enter B right, in a wheelchair which he propels by means of a pole. He halts. Irritated.*] A penny for a poor old man!

[*Pause.*]

B. Music! [*Pause.*] So it is not a dream. At last! Nor a vision, they are mute and I am mute before them. [*He advances, halts, looks into bowl. Without emotion.*] Poor wretch. [*Pause.*] Now I may go back, the mystery is over. [*He pushes himself backwards, halts.*] Unless we join together, and live together, till death ensue. [*Pause.*] What would you say to that, Billy, may I call you Billy, like my son? [*Pause.*] Do you like company, Billy? [*Pause.*] Do you like tinned food, Billy?

A. What tinned food?

B. Corned beef, Billy, just corned beef. Enough to keep body and soul together, till summer, with care. [*Pause.*] No? [*Pause.*] A few potatoes too, a few pounds of potatoes too. [*Pause.*] Do you like potatoes, Billy? [*Pause.*] We might even let them sprout and then, when the time came, put them in the ground, we might even try that. [*Pause.*] I would choose the place and you would put them in the ground. [*Pause.*] No? [*Pause.*]

A. How are the trees doing?

B. Hard to say. It's winter, you know.

[*Pause.*]

A. Is it day or night?

B. Oh . . . [*he looks at the sky*] . . . day, if you like. No sun of course, otherwise you wouldn't have asked. [*Pause.*] Do you follow my reasoning? [*Pause.*] Have you your wits about you, Billy, have you still some of your wits about you?

A. But light?

B. Yes. [*Looks at sky.*] Yes, light, there is no other word for it. [*Pause.*] Shall I describe it to you? [*Pause.*] Shall I try to give you an idea of this light?

A. It seems to me sometimes I spend the night here, playing and listening. I used to feel twilight gather and make myself ready. I put away fiddle and bowl and had only to get to my feet, when she took me by the hand.

[*Pause.*]

B. She?

A. My woman. [*Pause.*] A woman. [*Pause.*] But now . . .

[*Pause.*]

B. Now?

A. When I set out I don't know, and when I get here I don't know, and while I am here I don't know, whether it is day or night.

B. You were not always as you are. What befell you? Women? Gambling? God?

A. I was always as I am.

B. Come!

A. [*Violently.*] I was always as I am, crouched in the dark, scratching an old jangle to the four winds!

B. [*Violently.*] We had our women, hadn't we? You yours to lead you by the hand and mine to get me out of the chair in the evening and back into it again in the morning and to push me as far as the corner when I went out of my mind.

A. Cripple? [*Without emotion.*] Poor wretch.

B. Only one problem: the about-turn. I often felt, as I struggled, that it would be quicker to go on, right round the world. Till the day I realized I could go home backwards. [*Pause.*] For example, I am at A. [*He pushes himself forward a little, halts.*] I push on to B. [*He pushes himself back a little, halts.*] And I return to A. [*With élan.*] The straight line! The vacant space! [*Pause.*] Do I begin to move you?

A. Sometimes I hear steps. Voices. I say to myself, They are coming back, some are coming back, to try and settle again, or to look for something they had left behind, or to look for someone they had left behind.

B. Come back! [*Pause.*] Who would want to come back here? [*Pause.*] And you never called out? [*Pause.*] Cried out? [*Pause.*] No?

A. Have you observed nothing?

B. Oh me you know, observe . . . I sit there, in my lair, in my chair, in the dark, twenty-three hours out of the twenty-four. [*Violently.*] What would you have me observe? [*Pause.*] Do you think we would make a match, now you are getting to know me?

A. Corned beef, did you say?

B. Apropos, what have you been living on, all this time? You must be famished.

A. There are things lying around.

B. Edible?

A. Sometimes.

B. Why don't you let yourself die?

A. On the whole I have been lucky. The other day I tripped over a sack of nuts.

B. No!

A. A little sack, full of nuts, in the middle of the road.

B. Yes, all right, but why don't you let yourself die?

A. I have thought of it.

B. [*Irritated.*] But you don't do it!

A. I'm not unhappy enough. [*Pause.*] That was always my unhap, unhappy, but not unhappy enough.

B. But you must be every day a little more so.

A. [*Violently.*] I am not unhappy enough!

[*Pause.*]

B. If you ask me we were made for each other.

A. [*Comprehensive gesture.*] What does it all look like now?

B. Oh me you know . . . I never go far, just a little up and down before my door. I never yet pushed on to here till now.

A. But you look about you?

B. No no.

A. After all those hours of darkness you don't—

B. [*Violently.*] No! [*Pause.*] Of course if you wish me to look about me I shall. And if you care to push me about I shall try to describe the scene, as we go along.

A. You mean you would guide me? I wouldn't get lost any more?

B. Exactly. I would say, Easy, Billy, we're heading for a great muckheap, turn back and wheel left when I give you the word.

A. You'd do that!

B. [*Pressing his advantage.*] Easy, Billy, easy, I see a round tin over there in the gutter, perhaps it's soup, or baked beans.

A. Baked beans!

[*Pause.*]

B. Are you beginning to like me? [*Pause.*] Or is it only my imagination?

A. Baked beans! [*He gets up, puts down fiddle and bowl on the stool and gropes towards B.*] Where are you?

B. Here, dear fellow. [*A lays hold of the chair and starts pushing it blindly.*] Stop!

A. [*Pushing the chair.*] It's a gift! A gift!

B. Stop! [*He strikes behind him with the pole. A lets go the chair, recoils. Pause. A gropes towards his stool, halts, lost.*] Forgive me! [*Pause.*] Forgive me, Billy!

A. Where am I? [*Pause.*] Where was I?

B. Now I've lost him. He was beginning to like me and I struck him. He'll leave me and I'll never see him again. I'll never see anyone again. We'll never hear the human voice again.

A. Have you not heard it enough? The same old moans and groans from the cradle to the grave.

B. [*Groaning.*] Do something for me, before you go!

A. There! Do you hear it? [*Pause. Groaning.*] I can't go! [*Pause.*] Do you hear it?

B. You can't go?

A. I can't go without my things.

B. What good are they to you?

A. None.

B. And you can't go without them?

A. No. [*He starts groping again, halts.*] I'll find them in the end. [*Pause.*] Or leave them for ever behind me.

[*He starts groping again.*]

B. Straighten my rug, I feel the cold air on my foot. [*A halts.*] I'd do it myself, but it would take too long. [*Pause.*] Do that for me, Billy. Then I may go back, settle in the old nook again and say, I have seen man for the last time, I struck him and he succored me. [*Pause.*] Find a few rags of love in my heart and die reconciled, with my species. [*Pause.*] What has you gaping at me like that? [*Pause.*] Have I said something I shouldn't have? [*Pause.*] What does my soul look like?

[*A gropes towards him.*]

A. Make a sound.

[*B makes one. A gropes towards it, halts.*]

B. Have you no sense of smell either?
A. It's the same stink everywhere. [*He stretches out his hand.*] Am I within reach of your hand?

[*He stands motionless with outstretched hand.*]

B. Wait, you're not going to do me a service for nothing? [*Pause.*] I mean unconditionally? [*Pause.*] Good God! [*Pause. He takes A's hand and draws it towards him.*]
A. Your foot.
B. What?
A. You said your foot.
B. Had I but known! [*Pause.*] Yes, my foot, tuck it in. [*A stoops, groping.*] On your knees, on your knees, you'll be more at your ease. [*He helps him to kneel at the right place.*] There.
A. [*Irritated.*] Let go my hand! You want me to help you and you hold my hand! [*B lets go his hand. A fumbles in the rug.*] Have you only one leg?
B. Just the one.
A. And the other?
B. It went bad and was removed.

[*A tucks in the foot.*]

A. Will that do?
B. A little tighter. [*A tucks in tighter.*] What hands you have! [*Pause.*]
A. [*Groping towards B's torso.*] Is all the rest there?
B. You may stand up now and ask me a favour.
A. Is all the rest there?
B. Nothing else has been removed, if that is what you mean. [*A's hand, groping higher, reaches the face, stays.*]
A. Is that your face?
B. I confess it is. [*Pause.*] What else could it be? [*A's fingers stray, stay.*] That? My wen.
A. Red?

B. Purple. [*A withdraws his hand, remains kneeling.*] What hands you have!

[*Pause.*]

A. Is it still day?
B. Day? [*Looks at sky.*] If you like. [*Looks.*] There is no other word for it.
A. Will it not soon be evening?

[*B stoops to A, shakes him.*]

B. Come, Billy, get up, you're beginning to incommode me.
A. Will it not soon be night?

[*B looks at sky.*]

B. Day . . . night . . . [*Looks.*] It seems to me sometimes the earth must have got stuck, one sunless day, in the heart of winter, in the grey of evening. [*Stoops to A, shakes him.*] Come on, Billy, up, you're beginning to embarrass me.
A. Is there grass anywhere?
B. I see none.
A. [*Vehement.*] Is there no green anywhere?
B. There's a little moss. [*Pause. A clasps his hands on the rug and rests his head on them.*] Good God! Don't tell me you're going to pray!
A. No.
B. Or weep?
A. No. [*Pause.*] I could stay like that for ever, with my head on an old man's knees.
B. Knee. [*Shaking him roughly.*] Get up, can't you!
A. [*Settling himself more comfortably.*] What peace! [*B pushes him roughly away, A falls to his hands and knees.*] Dora used to say, the days I hadn't earned enough, You and your harp! You'd do better crawling on all fours, with your father's medals pinned to your arse and a money box round your neck. You and your harp! Who do you think you are? And she made me sleep on the floor. [*Pause.*] Who I thought I was . . . [*Pause.*] Ah that . . . I never could . . . [*Pause. He gets up.*] Never could . . . [*He starts groping again for his stool, halts, listens.*] If I listened long enough I'd hear it, a string would give.
B. Your harp? [*Pause.*] What's all this about a harp?
A. I once had a little harp. Be still and let me listen.

[*Pause.*]

B. How long are you going to stay like that?

A. I can stay for hours listening to all the sounds.

[*They listen.*]

B. What sounds?
A. I don't know what they are.

[*They listen.*]

B. I can see it. [*Pause.*] I can—
A. [*Imploringly.*] Will you not be still?
B. No! [*A takes his head in his hands.*] I can see it clearly, over there on the stool. [*Pause.*] What if I took it,

Billy, and made off with it? [*Pause.*] Eh Billy, what would you say to that? [*Pause.*] There might be another old man, some day, would come out of his hole and find you playing the mouth-organ. And you'd tell him of the little fiddle you once had. [*Pause.*] Eh Billy? [*Pause.*] Or singing. [*Pause.*] Eh Billy, what would you say to that? [*Pause.*] There croaking to the winter wind [*rime with unkind*], having lost his little mouth-organ. [*He pokes him in the back with the pole.*] Eh Billy? [*A whirls round, seizes the end of the pole and wrenches it from B's grasp.*]

ESSAY: AN APPROACH TO THE PLAY

We are accustomed in both fiction and in drama to plots and characters that "make sense," to plots where events are causally related to one another and build up to a moment of some significance, and to characters whose behavior seems comprehensible and consistent. Little wonder that *Rough for Theater I* is such a disorienting experience for us. The motivation of the characters seems strained at best. For example, B assigns a name to A, but this has nothing to do with A; rather, it has to do with the namer himself, B, who once had a son of the same name. A's new name will be useful to B in helping B to remember a more fruitful time in his own life. When B asks "Billy" to join him in partnership, he offers as material reward tinned food. The arbitrariness of the behavior, its apparent insistence on lack of meaning, is so unsettling that it forces us to speculate about its meaning.

In such a bleak environment, with characters who are both "poor wretches" and in which nothing seems to matter, the limited details with which we *are* provided seem abnormally significant: details of light and dark, time of day and season of year, directions backward and forward in space, sound. Discontinuities of plot make portentous-sounding dialogue seem, at best, ironic, or perhaps simply empty. A character says "we were made for each other"; a character is an explorer who has "pushed on to here"; finding B is at first for A like finding eyes: "It's a gift!" But the two abuse each other physically and emotionally and seem motivated at times by self-interest only. Their reciprocity, instead of resulting in complementary and communal activity, seems often purposeless or even hostile. Why, for example, does the blind man take away the wheelchair person's means of mobility when it does himself no good?

In *Rough for Theater I*, Beckett presents a remarkably complex vision of ourselves with minimal stage materials. He disorients us with a stage world that seems to be unfamiliar, or "abnormal," but gradually it reveals appalling similarities to our everyday lives. By drawing these parallels in such unfamiliar terms, Beckett forces us to question the nature of our world and of ourselves. He offers no sure answers, but presents our questions in extremely concrete form. Their simplicity forces us to face them, and their disorienting quality allows us to face them because at first they seem not to be ours.

Moreover, the disorienting form of Beckett's presentation gives us the sense that his choice of detail is arbitrary rather than "natural." If there is comedy or tragedy, order or chaos, fate or nothing at all behind the mask of this stage, it seems to be because we, rather than the playwright, choose to give its "reality" these values. In fact, nothing is certain in this play. It does not encourage a particular view of the human condition or of the world in which humans find themselves; rather it encourages us to wonder who and what we are, what—if anything—we can understand, let alone make, of ourselves.

Consider the ending, for example. Even in the world of this play where, according to A, the only thing one ever heard from the human voice was "the same old moans and groans from the cradle to the grave," there has been kindness and curiosity, as well as self-assertion and cruelty. But all have been short-lived and futile. At last, in using his power to abuse A, B ends up by defeating himself. Yet in this ending, A responds in a way that is equally self-defeating for himself. He deprives B not only of his ability to hit but also of his ability to move his chair. Now, only A can move the chair, or hit, but he is blind. He has helped himself no more than B has. They seem to have become impotent enemies, each helpless either to attack the other or to sustain himself. Why does this happen? Is it that we cause our own misery, and that it is innate in us to do so—that we ourselves cause our "natural" condition and may very well never choose better? Or will A and B, or at least one of them, at last relent? And yet, if they do, so what?

Because of its refusal to assert a meaning for our lives, the theater which Beckett represents is sometimes called the theater of the absurd—"absurd" in that in its world no meaning is certain. Absurd, too, in that without clear meaning, without a defining context for our lives, everything—even those acts which we usually think most noble or heroic or even tragic—becomes incongruous, even perhaps ridiculous. What is normally serious or wonderful or sad is, in this absence of context, also funny. The comic and the tragic merge in this new genre, so that at times we may find ourselves laughing uncomfortably at the portrayal of a fellow creature's misery. This discomfort may in turn force us to reexamine our own assumptions about ourselves. We may ask: How can we laugh at this wretchedness? What within us allows such behavior?

From a slightly different perspective, this theater of Beckett's is metatheatrical: the situation and the characters are so arbitrarily atypical that we are continuously aware that they are the playwright's invention and that this theater is not concerned with verisimilitude, with imitating "normal" characters or human situations. Yet insofar as we see similarities between our lives and those onstage, one implication may be that the world *is* like the theater in being arbitrary; if so, and if nevertheless the world *does* seem to us to have meaning, then perhaps it is because we have created this meaning and imposed it. The emphasis on artificial or constructed meanings in the theater can suggest the artificiality of the meanings we construct both about ourselves and about our world. This is a theater that attempts to break down conventional forms and conventional beliefs in as many ways as it can, working to force us to rethink our assumptions about them.

In this respect, whether we call it the theater of the absurd or metatheater, Beckett's theater is unlike both comedy and tragedy, each of which *does* make assumptions about the nature of the world and how we might intelligently (and sometimes even happily) live within it. Comedy and tragedy both presuppose a world order into which we might fit ourselves, but theater of the absurd and metatheater deliberately choose *not* to do so.

Tennessee Williams

THE GLASS MENAGERIE

About the Author   Thomas Lanier "Tennessee" Williams (1911–1983) was born in Columbus, Mississippi; he attended the University of Missouri and Washington University in St. Louis before completing his bachelor's degree in 1938 at the University of Iowa. Beginning in 1935, he wrote over three dozen plays, and he won virtually all the major awards a playwright can be given in the United States, including the Pulitzer Prize twice (in 1948 for *A Streetcar Named Desire* and in 1955 for *Cat on a Hot Tin Roof*) and the New York Drama Critics Circle Award four times (the first in 1945 for *The Glass Menagerie*).

About the Play   The beginning of *The Glass Menagerie* introduces several of its central thematic concerns. The first paragraph of Williams' lengthy introductory stage direction expresses a strong attitude toward lower-middle-class society. Set in difficult economic times (the Great Depression) and featuring a character obsessed with her family's former status, the play seems to emphasize this issue of economic and social class. The first speech of the play itself, however, presents other issues. We are confronted by a narrator, Tom, who tells us that his play is about "truth in the pleasant guise of illusion." At least one of the characters, the one who is "most realistic," is also to be used "as a symbol." It would seem to be of the nature of drama that there can be no narrator: the plot is presented by characters interacting on a stage, not by a narrative voice; but Williams seems here to insist on blurring this distinction. This "narrator," in turn, emphasizes a relationship between illusion and reality as well as a symbolic dimension to reality. These ideas (among others) continue to interact in this complex play. For example, Laura and Amanda are both crippled in their relations with the outside world by their respective illusions, and this whole question of illusion seems somehow connected with questions of social and economic class.

    The form of the play itself forces us to focus on the nature of illusion: this is a play with a narrator who fills in information for us. Like an author, he is telling us his story—is having it enacted for us onstage. (Incidentally, some of the details of his story are like those in the author's life: Williams was a shoe salesman in St. Louis in this kind of neighborhood during the Depression, and his real first name was Thomas.) Yet at the same time that he "tells" his story, Tom is a character inside the story. This story seems as "real" as any other story can when enacted on a stage, but it is, as Tom says in his opening speech, "a memory play": it is all happening inside the mind of the narrator, Tom, as he looks back and relives the experiences of the character Tom, himself at an earlier age. The play becomes a way for him to explain himself and for him to discover himself—to learn why he is as he is. From this perspective, the narrator is perhaps less a narrator than the only "real" character in the play. Laura and Amanda suffered under different versions of blindness from which Tom, the narrator in the present tense, seems to believe he has escaped.

    One important question for us to ask is: is he right? If he has escaped their influence, why does he feel compelled to stage this play? And is this play, from the point of view of its own fiction, the "truth," or is it, like any memory, only one version of "reality"?

CHARACTERS

AMANDA WINGFIELD, the mother
LAURA WINGFIELD, her daughter

TOM WINGFIELD, her son
JIM O'CONNOR, the gentleman caller

SCENE—An alley in St. Louis.

PART I—Preparation for a Gentleman Caller.
PART II—The Gentleman Calls.

TIME—Now and the Past.

SCENE I

The Wingfield apartment is in the rear of the building, one of those vast hive-like conglomerations of cellular living-units that flower as warty growths in overcrowded urban centers of lower middle-class population and are symptomatic of the impulse of this largest and fundamentally enslaved section of American society to avoid fluidity and differentiation and to exist and function as one interfused mass of automatism.

The apartment faces an alley and is entered by a fire-escape, a structure whose name is a touch of accidental poetic truth, for all of these huge buildings are always burning with the slow and implacable fires of human desperation. The fire-escape is included in the set—that is, the landing of it and steps descending from it.

The scene is memory and is therefore nonrealistic. Memory takes a lot of poetic license. It omits some details; others are exaggerated, according to the emotional value of the articles it touches, for memory is seated predominantly in the heart. The interior is therefore rather dim and poetic.

At the rise of the curtain, the audience is faced with the dark, grim rear wall of the Wingfield tenement. This building, which runs parallel to the footlights, is flanked on both sides by dark, narrow alleys which run into murky canyons of tangled clotheslines, garbage cans and the sinister latticework of neighboring fire-escapes. It is up and down these side alleys that exterior entrances and exits are made, during the play. At the end of Tom's opening commentary, the dark tenement wall slowly reveals (by means of a transparency) the interior of the ground floor Wingfield apartment.

Downstage is the living room, which also serves as a sleeping room for Laura, the sofa unfolding to make her bed. Upstage, center, and divided by a wide arch or second proscenium with transparent faded portieres (or second curtain), is the dining room. In an old-fashioned what-not in the living room are seen scores of transparent glass animals. A blown-up photograph of the father hangs on the wall of the living room, facing the audience, to the left of the archway. It is the face of a very handsome young man in a doughboy's First World War cap. He is gallantly smiling, ineluctably smiling, as if to say, "I will be smiling forever."

The audience hears and sees the opening scene in the dining room through both the transparent fourth wall of the building and the transparent gauze portieres of the dining-room arch. It is during this revealing scene that the fourth wall slowly ascends, out of sight. This transparent exterior wall is not brought down again until the very end of the play, during Tom's final speech.

The narrator is an undisguised convention of the play. He takes whatever license with dramatic convention as is convenient to his purposes.

[*Tom enters dressed as a merchant sailor from alley, stage left, and strolls across the front of the stage to the fire-escape. There he stops and lights a cigarette. He addresses the audience.*]

TOM. Yes, I have tricks in my pocket, I have things up my sleeve. But I am the opposite of a stage magician. He gives you illusion that has the appearance of truth. I give you truth in the pleasant disguise of illusion. To begin with, I turn back time. I reverse it to that quaint period, the thirties, when the huge middle class of America was matriculating in a school for the blind. Their eyes had failed them, or they had failed their eyes, and so they were having their fingers pressed forcibly down on the fiery Braille alphabet of a dissolving economy. In Spain there was revolution. Here there was only shouting and confusion. In Spain there was Guernica. Here there were disturbances of labor, sometimes pretty violent, in otherwise peaceful cities such as Chicago, Cleveland, Saint Louis. . . . This is the social background of the play.

[Music.]

The play is memory. Being a memory play, it is dimly lighted, it is sentimental, it is not realistic. In memory everything seems to happen to music. That explains the fiddle in the wings. I am the narrator of the play, and also a character in it. The other characters are my mother, Amanda, my sister, Laura, and a gentleman caller who appears in the final scenes. He is the most realistic character in the play, being an emissary from a world of reality that we were somehow set apart from. But since I have a poet's weakness for symbols, I am using this character also as a symbol; he is the long delayed but always expected something that we live for. There is a fifth character in the play who doesn't appear except in this larger-than-life photograph over the mantel. This is our father who left us a long time ago. He was a telephone man who fell in love with long distances; he gave up his job with the telephone company and skipped the light fantastic out of town . . . The last we heard of him was a picture post-card from Mazatlan, on the Pacific coast of Mexico, containing a message of two words—"Hello—Good-bye!" and no address. I think the rest of the play will explain itself. . . .

[Amanda's voice becomes audible through the portieres.]

[Legend on screen: "Où sont les neiges."]

[He divides the portieres and enters the upstage areas.]

[Amanda and Laura are seated at a drop-leaf table. Eating is indicated by gestures without food or utensils. Amanda faces the audience. Tom and Laura are seated in profile.]

[The interior has lit up softly and through the scrim we see Amanda and Laura seated at the table in the upstage area.]

AMANDA [calling]. Tom?
TOM. Yes, Mother.

AMANDA. We can't say grace until you come to the table!
TOM. Coming, Mother. [He bows slightly and withdraws, reappearing a few moments later in his place at the table.]
AMANDA [to her son]. Honey, don't push with your fingers. If you have to push with something, the thing to push with is a crust of bread. And chew—chew! Animals have sections in their stomachs which enable them to digest food without mastication, but human beings are supposed to chew their food before they swallow it down. Eat food leisurely, son, and really enjoy it. A well-cooked meal has lots of delicate flavors that have to be held in the mouth for appreciation. So chew your food and give your salivary glands a chance to function!

[Tom deliberately lays his imaginary fork down and pushes his chair back from the table.]

TOM. I haven't enjoyed one bite of this dinner because of your constant directions on how to eat it. It's you that makes me rush through meals with your hawk-like attention to every bite I take. Sickening—spoils my appetite—all this discussion of animals' secretion—salivary glands—mastication!
AMANDA [lightly]. Temperament like a Metropolitan star! [He rises and crosses downstage.] You're not excused from the table.
TOM. I'm getting a cigarette.
AMANDA. You smoke too much.

[Laura rises.]

LAURA. I'll bring in the blanc mange.

[He remains standing with his cigarette by the portieres during the following.]

AMANDA [rising]. No, sister, no, sister—you be the lady this time and I'll be the darky.
LAURA. I'm already up.
AMANDA. Resume your seat, little sister—I want you to stay fresh and pretty—for gentlemen callers!
LAURA. I'm not expecting any gentlemen callers.
AMANDA [crossing out to kitchenette. Airily]. Sometimes they come when they are least expected! Why, I remember one Sunday afternoon in Blue Mountain—[Enters kitchenette.]
TOM. I know what's coming!
LAURA. Yes. But let her tell it.
TOM. Again?
LAURA. She loves to tell it.

[*Amanda returns with bowl of dessert.*]

AMANDA. One Sunday afternoon in Blue Mountain—your mother received—*seventeen!*—gentlemen callers! Why, sometimes there weren't chairs enough to accommodate them all. We had to send the nigger over to bring in folding chairs from the parish house.

TOM [*remaining at portieres*]. How did you entertain those gentlemen callers?

AMANDA. I understood the art of conversation!

TOM. I bet you could talk.

AMANDA. Girls in those days *knew* how to talk, I can tell you.

TOM. Yes?

[*Image: Amanda as a girl on a porch, greeting callers.*]

AMANDA. They knew how to entertain their gentlemen callers. It wasn't enough for a girl to be possessed of a pretty face and a graceful figure—although I wasn't slighted in either respect. She also needed to have a nimble wit and a tongue to meet all occasions.

TOM. What did you talk about?

AMANDA. Things of importance going on in the world! Never anything coarse or common or vulgar. [*She addresses Tom as though he were seated in the vacant chair at the table though he remains by portieres. He plays this scene as though he held the book.*] My callers were gentlemen—all! Among my callers were some of the most prominent young planters of the Mississippi Delta—planters and sons of planters!

[*Tom motions for music and a spot of light on Amanda.*]

[*Her eyes lift, her face glows, her voice becomes rich and elegiac.*]

[*Screen legend: "Où sont les neiges."*]

There was young Champ Laughlin who later became vice-president of the Delta Planters Bank. Hadley Stevenson who was drowned in Moon Lake and left his widow one hundred and fifty thousand in Government bonds. There were the Cutrere brothers, Wesley and Bates. Bates was one of my bright particular beaux! He got in a quarrel with that wild Wainright boy. They shot it out on the floor of Moon Lake Casino. Bates was shot through the stomach. Died in the ambulance on his way to Memphis. His widow was also well-provided for, came into eight or ten thousand acres, that's all. She

married him on the rebound—never loved her—carried my picture on him the night he died! And there was that boy that every girl in the Delta had set her cap for! That beautiful, brilliant young Fitzhugh boy from Greene County!

TOM. What did he leave his widow?

AMANDA. He never married! Gracious, you talk as though all of my old admirers had turned up their toes to the daisies!

TOM. Isn't this the first you've mentioned that still survives?

AMANDA. That Fitzhugh boy went North and made a fortune—came to be known as the Wolf of Wall Street! He had the Midas touch, whatever he touched turned to gold! And I could have been Mrs. Duncan J. Fitzhugh, mind you! But—I picked your *father*!

LAURA [*rising*]. Mother, let me clear the table.

AMANDA. No, dear, you go in front and study your typewriter chart. Or practice your shorthand a little. Stay fresh and pretty!—It's almost time for our gentlemen callers to start arriving. [*She flounces girlishly toward the kitchenette.*] How many do you suppose we're going to entertain this afternoon?

[*Tom throws down the paper and jumps up with a groan.*]

LAURA [*alone in the dining room*]. I don't believe we're going to receive any, Mother.

AMANDA [*reappearing, airily*]. What? No one—not one? You must be joking! [*Laura nervously echoes her laugh. She slips in a fugitive manner through the half-open portieres and draws them gently behind her. A shaft of very clear light is thrown on her face against the faded tapestry of the curtains. Music: "The Glass Menagerie" under faintly. Lightly.*] Not one gentleman caller? It can't be true! There must be a flood, there must have been a tornado!

LAURA. It isn't a flood, it's not a tornado, Mother. I'm just not popular like you were in Blue Mountain. . . . [*Tom utters another groan. Laura glances at him with a faint, apologetic smile. Her voice catching a little.*] Mother's afraid I'm going to be an old maid.

[*The scene dims out with "Glass Menagerie" Music.*]

SCENE II

["*Laura, Haven't You Ever Liked Some Boy?*"

On the dark stage the screen is lighted with the image of blue roses.

Gradually Laura's figure becomes apparent and the screen goes out.

The music subsides.

Laura is seated in the delicate ivory chair at the small clawfoot table.

She wears a dress of soft violet material for a kimono—her hair tied back from her forehead with a ribbon.

She is washing and polishing her collection of glass.

Amanda appears on the fire-escape steps. At the sound of her ascent, Laura catches her breath, thrusts the bowl of ornaments away and seats herself stiffly before the diagram of the typewriter keyboard as though it held her spellbound. Something has happened to Amanda. It is written in her face as she climbs to the landing: a look that is grim and hopeless and a little absurd.

She has on one of those cheap or imitation velvety-looking cloth coats with imitation fur collar. Her hat is five or six years old, one of those dreadful cloche hats that were worn in the late twenties and she is clasping an enormous black patent-leather pocketbook with nickel clasp and initials. This is her full-dress outfit, the one she usually wears to the D.A.R.

Before entering she looks through the door.

She purses her lips, opens her eyes wide, rolls them upward and shakes her head.

Then she slowly lets herself in the door. Seeing her mother's expression Laura touches her lips with a nervous gesture.

LAURA. Hello, Mother, I was— [*She makes a nervous gesture toward the chart on the wall. Amanda leans against the shut door and stares at Laura with a martyred look.*]

AMANDA. Deception? Deception? [*She slowly removes her hat and gloves, continuing the swift suffering stare. She lets the hat and gloves fall on the floor—a bit of acting.*]

LAURA [*Shakily*]. How was the D.A.R. meeting? [*Amanda slowly opens her purse and removes a dainty white handkerchief which she shakes out delicately and delicately touches to her lips and nostrils.*] Didn't you go to the D.A.R. meeting, Mother?

AMANDA [*faintly, almost inaudibly*]. —No.—No. [*Then more forcibly.*] I did not have the strength—to go to the D.A.R. In fact, I did not have the courage! I wanted to find a hole in the ground and hide myself in it forever! [*She crosses slowly to the wall and removes the diagram of the typewriter keyboard. She holds it in front of her for a second, staring at it sweetly and sorrowfully—then bites her lips and tears it in two pieces.*]

LAURA [*faintly*]. Why did you do that, Mother? [*Amanda repeats the same procedure with the chart of the Gregg Alphabet.*] Why are you—

AMANDA. Why? Why? How old are you, Laura?

LAURA. Mother, you know my age.

AMANDA. I thought that you were an adult; it seems that I was mistaken. [*She crosses slowly to the sofa and sinks down and stares at Laura.*]

LAURA. Please don't stare at me, Mother.

[*Amanda closes her eyes and lowers her head. Count ten.*]

AMANDA. What are we going to do, what is going to become of us, what is the future?

[*Count ten.*]

LAURA. Has something happened, Mother? [*Amanda draws a long breath and takes out the handkerchief again. Dabbing process.*] Mother, has—something happened?

AMANDA. I'll be all right in a minute. I'm just bewildered— [*Count five.*] —by life. . . .

LAURA. Mother, I wish that you would tell me what's happened!

AMANDA. As you know, I was supposed to be inducted into my office at the D.A.R. this afternoon. [*Image: a swarm of typewriters.*] But I stopped off at Rubicam's Business College to speak to your teachers about your having a cold and ask them what progress they thought you were making down there.

LAURA. Oh. . . .

AMANDA. I went to the typing instructor and introduced myself as your mother. She didn't know who you were. Wingfield, she said. We don't have any such student enrolled at the school! I assured her she did, that you had been going to classes since early in January. "I wonder," she said, "if you could be talking about that terribly shy little girl who dropped out of school after only a few days' attendance?" "No," I said, "Laura, my daughter, has been going to school every day for the past six weeks!" "Excuse me," she said. She took the attendance book out and there was your name, unmistakably printed, and all the dates you were absent until they decided that you had dropped out of school. I still said, "No, there must have been some mistake! There must have been some mix-up in the records!" And she said, "No—I remember her perfectly now. Her hands shook so that she couldn't hit the right keys! The first time we gave a speed-test, she broke down completely—was sick at the stomach and almost had to be carried into the washroom! After that morning she never showed up any more. We phoned the house but never got any answer—while I was working at Famous and Barr, I suppose, demonstrating those—Oh!" I felt so weak I could barely keep on my feet! I had to sit down while they got me a glass of water! Fifty dollars' tuition, all of our plans—my hopes and ambitions for you—just gone up the spout, just gone up the spout like that. [*Laura draws a long breath and gets awkwardly to her feet. She crosses to the victrola and winds it up.*] What are you doing?

LAURA. Oh! [*She releases the handle and returns to her seat.*]

AMANDA. Laura, where have you been going when you've gone out pretending that you were going to business college?

LAURA. I've just been going out walking.

AMANDA. That's not true.

LAURA. It is. I just went walking.

AMANDA. Walking? Walking? In winter? Deliberately courting pneumonia in that light coat? Where did you walk to, Laura?

LAURA. All sorts of places—mostly in the park.

AMANDA. Even after you'd started catching that cold?

LAURA. It was the lesser of two evils, Mother. [*Image: Winter scene in park.*] I couldn't go back up. I—threw up—on the floor!

AMANDA. From half past seven till after five every day you mean to tell me you walked around in the park, because you wanted to make me think that you were still going to Rubicam's Business College?

LAURA. It wasn't as bad as it sounds. I went inside places to get warmed up.

AMANDA. Inside where?

LAURA. I went in the art museum and the bird-houses at the Zoo. I visited the penguins every day! Sometimes I did without lunch and went to the movies. Lately I've been spending most of my afternoons in the Jewel-box, that big glass house where they raise the tropical flowers.

AMANDA. You did all this to deceive me, just for the deception? [*Laura looks down.*] Why?

LAURA. Mother, when you're disappointed, you get

that awful suffering look on your face, like the picture of Jesus' mother in the museum!

AMANDA. Hush!

LAURA. I couldn't face it.

[*Pause. A whisper of strings.*]

[*Legend: "The crust of humility."*]

AMANDA. [*hopelessly fingering the huge pocketbook*]. So what are we going to do the rest of our lives? Stay home and watch the parades go by? Amuse ourselves with the glass menagerie, darling? Eternally play those worn-out phonograph records your father left as a painful reminder of him? We won't have a business career—we've given that up because it gave us nervous indigestion! [*Laughs wearily.*] What is there left but dependency all our lives? I know so well what becomes of unmarried women who aren't prepared to occupy a position. I've seen such pitiful cases in the South—barely tolerated spinsters living upon the grudging patronage of sister's husband or brother's wife!—stuck away in some little mousetrap of a room—encouraged by one in-law to visit another—little birdlike women without any nest—eating the crust of humility all their life! Is that the future that we've mapped out for ourselves? I swear it's the only alternative I can think of! It isn't a very pleasant alternative, is it? Of course—some girls *do* marry. [*Laura twists her hands nervously.*] Haven't you ever liked some boy?

LAURA. Yes. I liked one once. [*Rises.*] I came across his picture a while ago.

AMANDA [*with some interest*]. He gave you his picture?

LAURA. No, it's in the year-book.

AMANDA [*disappointed*]. Oh—a high-school boy.

[*Screen image: Jim as high-school hero bearing a silver cup.*]

LAURA. Yes. His name was Jim. [*Laura lifts the heavy annual from the claw-foot table.*] Here he is in *The Pirates of Penzance*.

AMANDA [*absently*]. The what?

LAURA. The operetta the senior class put on. He had a wonderful voice and we sat across the aisle from each other Mondays, Wednesdays and Fridays in the Aud. Here he is with the silver cup for debating! See his grin?

AMANDA [*absently*]. He must have had a jolly disposition.

LAURA. He used to call me—Blue Roses.

[*Image: Blue roses.*]

AMANDA. Why did he call you such a name as that?

LAURA. When I had that attack of pleurosis—he asked me what was the matter when I came back. I said pleurosis—he thought that I said Blue Roses! So that's what he always called me after that. Whenever he saw me, he'd holler, "Hello, Blue Roses!" I didn't care for the girl that he went out with. Emily Meisenbach. Emily was the best-dressed girl at Soldan. She never struck me, though, as being sincere . . . It says in the Personal Section—they're engaged. That's—six years ago! They must be married by now.

AMANDA. Girls that aren't cut out for business careers usually wind up married to some nice man. [*Gets up with a spark of revival.*] Sister, that's what you'll do!

[*Laura utters a startled, doubtful laugh. She reaches quickly for a piece of glass.*]

LAURA. But, Mother—
AMANDA. Yes? [*Crossing to photograph.*]
LAURA [*in a tone of frightened apology*]. I'm—crippled!

[*Image: Screen.*]

AMANDA. Nonsense! Laura, I've told you never, never to use that word. Why, you're not crippled, you just have a little defect—hardly noticeable, even! When people have some slight disadvantage like that, they cultivate other things to make up for it—develop charm—and vivacity—and—*charm*! That's all you have to do! [*She turns again to the photograph.*] One thing your father had *plenty of*—was *charm*!

[*Tom motions to the fiddle in the wings.*]

[*The scene fades out with music.*]

SCENE III

[*Legend on screen: "After the fiasco—"*]

[*Tom speaks from the fire-escape landing.*]

TOM. After the fiasco at Rubicam's Business College, the idea of getting a gentleman caller for Laura began to play a more important part in Mother's calculations. It became an obsession. Like some archetype of the universal unconscious, the image of the gentleman caller haunted our small apartment. . . . [*Image: Young man at door with flowers.*] An evening at home rarely passed without some allusion to this image, this spectre, this hope. . . . Even when he wasn't mentioned, his presence hung in Mother's preoccupied look and in my sister's frightened, apologetic manner—hung like a sentence passed upon the Wingfields! Mother was a woman of action as well as words. She began to take logical steps in the planned direction. Late that winter and in the early spring—realizing that extra money would be needed to properly feather the nest and plume the bird—she conducted a vigorous campaign on the telephone, roping in subscribers to one of those magazines for matrons called *The Home-maker's Companion*, the type of journal that features the serialized sublimations of ladies of letters who think in terms of delicate cup-like breasts, slim, tapering waists, rich, creamy thighs, eyes like wood-smoke in autumn, fingers that soothe and caress like strains of music, bodies as powerful as Etruscan sculpture.

[*Screen image: Glamor magazine cover.*]

[*Amanda enters with phone on long extension cord. She is spotted in the dim stage.*]

AMANDA. Ida Scott? This is Amanda Wingfield! We *missed* you at the D.A.R. last Monday! I said to myself: She's probably suffering with that sinus condition! How is that sinus condition? Horrors! Heaven have mercy!—You're a Christian martyr, yes, that's what you are, a Christian martyr! Well, I just now happened to notice that your subscription to the *Companion's* about to expire! Yes, it expires with the next issue, honey!—just when that wonderful new serial by Bessie Mae Hopper is getting off to such an exciting start. Oh, honey, it's something that you can't miss! You remember how *Gone With the Wind* took everybody by storm? You simply couldn't go out if you hadn't read it. All everybody *talked* was Scarlett O'Hara. Well, this is a book that critics already compare to *Gone With the Wind*. It's the *Gone With the Wind* of the post-World War generation!—What?—Burning?—Oh, honey, don't let them burn, go take a look in the oven and I'll hold the wire! Heavens—I think she's hung up!

[*Dim out.*]

[*Legend on screen: "You think I'm in love with Continental Shoemakers?"*]

[*Before the stage is lighted, the violent voices of Tom and Amanda are heard.*]

[*They are quarreling behind the portieres. In front of them stands Laura with clenched hands and panicky expression.*]

[*A clear pool of light on her figure throughout this scene.*]

TOM. What in Christ's name am I—

AMANDA [*shrilly*]. Don't you use that—

TOM. Supposed to do!

AMANDA. Expression! Not in my—

TOM. Ohhh!

AMANDA. Presence! Have you gone out of your senses?

TOM. I have, that's true, *driven* out!

AMANDA. What is the matter with you, you—big—big—IDIOT!

TOM. Look—I've got *no thing*, no single thing—

AMANDA. Lower your voice!

TOM. In my life here that I can call my own! Everything is—

AMANDA. Stop that shouting!

TOM. Yesterday you confiscated my books! You had the nerve to—

AMANDA. I took that horrible novel back to the library—yes! That hideous book by that insane Mr. Lawrence. [*Tom laughs wildly.*] I cannot control the output of diseased minds or people who cater to them— [*Tom laughs still more wildly.*] BUT I WON'T ALLOW SUCH FILTH BROUGHT INTO MY HOUSE! No, no, no, no, no!

TOM. House, house! Who pays rent on it, who makes a slave of himself to —

AMANDA [*fairly screeching*]. Don't you DARE to—

TOM. No, no, *I* mustn't say things! *I've got to just*—

AMANDA. Let me tell you—

TOM. I don't want to hear any more! [*He tears the portieres open. The upstage area is lit with a turgid smoky red glow.*]

[*Amanda's hair is in metal curlers and she wears a very old bathrobe, much too large for her slight figure, a relic of the faithless Mr. Wingfield.*]

[*An upright typewriter and a wild disarray of manuscripts is on the drop-leaf table. The quarrel was probably precipitated by Amanda's interruption of his creative labor. A chair lying overthrown on the floor.*]

[*Their gesticulating shadows are cast on the ceiling by the fiery glow.*]

AMANDA. You *will* hear more, you—

TOM. No, I won't hear more, I'm going out!

AMANDA. You come right back in—

TOM. Out, out out! Because I'm—

AMANDA. Come back here, Tom Wingfield! I'm not through talking to you!

TOM. Oh, go—

LAURA [*desperately*]. —Tom!

AMANDA. You're going to listen, and no more insolence from you! I'm at the end of my patience! [*He comes back toward her.*]

TOM. What do you think I'm at? Aren't I supposed to have any patience to reach the end of, Mother? I know, I know. It seems unimportant to you, what I'm *doing*—what I *want* to do—having a little *difference* between them! You don't think that—

AMANDA. I think you've been doing things that you're ashamed of. That's why you act like this. I don't believe that you go every night to the movies. Nobody goes to the movies night after night. Nobody in their right minds goes to the movies as often as you pretend to. People don't go to the movies at nearly midnight, and movies don't let out at two A.M. Come in stumbling. Muttering to yourself like a maniac! You get three hours sleep and then go to work. Oh, I can picture the way you're doing down there. Moping, doping, because you're in no condition.

TOM [*wildly*]. No, I'm in no condition!

AMANDA. What right have you got to jeopardize your job? Jeopardize the security of us all? How do you think we'd manage if you were—

TOM. Listen! You think I'm crazy *about* the *warehouse*? [*He bends fiercely toward her slight figure.*] You think I'm in love with the Continental Shoemakers? You think I want to spend fifty-five *years* down there in that—*celotex interior*! with—*fluorescent*—*tubes*! Look! I'd rather somebody picked up a crowbar and battered out my brains—than go back mornings! I *go*! Every time you come in yelling that God damn "*Rise and Shine*!" "*Rise and Shine*!" I say to myself, "How *lucky dead* people are!" But I get up. I *go*! For sixty-five dollars a month I give up all that I dream of doing and being *ever*! And you say self—*self's* all I ever think of. Why, listen, if self is what I thought of, Mother, I'd be where he is—GONE! [*Pointing to father's picture.*] As far as the system of transportation reaches! [*He starts past her. She grabs his arm.*] Don't grab at me, Mother!

AMANDA. Where are you going?

TOM. I'm going to the *movies*!

AMANDA. I don't believe that lie!

TOM [*crouching toward her, overtowering her tiny figure.*

She backs away, gasping]. I'm going to opium dens! Yes, opium dens, dens of vice and criminals' hang-outs, Mother. I've joined the Hogan gang, I'm a hired assassin, I carry a tommy-gun in a violin case! I run a string of cat-houses in the Valley! They call me Killer, Killer Wingfield, I'm leading a double-life, a simple, honest warehouse worker by day, by night, a dynamic *czar* of the *underworld, Mother*. I go to gambling casinos, I spin away fortunes on the roulette table! I wear a patch over one eye and false mustache, sometimes I put on green whiskers. On those occasions they call me—*El Diablo*! Oh, I could tell you things to make you sleepless! My enemies plan to dynamite this place. They're going to blow us all sky-high some night! I'll be glad, very happy, and so will you! You'll go up, up on a broomstick, over Blue Mountain with seventeen gentlemen callers! You ugly—babbling old— *witch*. . . . [*He goes through a series of violent, clumsy movements, seizing his overcoat, lunging to the door, pulling it fiercely open. The women watch him, aghast. His arm catches in the sleeve of the coat as he struggles to pull it on. For a moment he is pinioned by the bulky garment. With an outraged groan he tears the coat off again, splitting the shoulder of it, and hurls it across the room. It strikes against the shelf of Laura's glass collection, there is a tinkle of shattering glass. Laura cries out as if wounded.*

[*Music legend: "The Glass Menagerie."*]

LAURA [*shrilly*]. *My glass!*—menagerie. . . . [*She covers her face and turns away.*] [*But Amanda is still stunned and stupefied by the "ugly witch" so that she barely notices this occurrence. Now she recovers her speech.*]
AMANDA [*in an awful voice*]. I won't speak to you— until you apologize! [*She crosses through portieres and draws them together behind her. Tom is left with Laura. Laura clings weakly to the mantel with her face averted. Tom stares at her stupidly for a moment. Then he crosses to shelf. Drops awkwardly to his knees to collect the fallen glass, glancing at Laura as if he would speak but couldn't.*]

[*"The Glass Menagerie" steals in as*

The scene dims out.]

SCENE IV

The interior is dark. Faint light in the alley.

A deep-voiced bell in a church is tolling the hour of five as the scene commences.

Tom appears at the top of the alley. After each solemn boom of the bell in the tower he shakes a little noise-maker or rattle as if to express the tiny spasm of man in contrast to the sustained power and dignity of the Almighty. This and the unsteadiness of his advance make it evident that he has been drinking.

As he climbs the few steps to the fire-escape landing light steals up inside. Laura appears in night-dress, observing Tom's empty bed in the front room.

Tom fishes in his pockets for the door-key, removing a motley assortment of articles in the search, including a perfect shower of movie-ticket stubs and an empty bottle. At last he finds the key, but just as he is about to insert it, it slips from his fingers. He strikes a match and crouches below the door.

TOM [*bitterly*]. One crack—and it falls through!

[*Laura opens the door.*]

LAURA. Tom! Tom, what are you doing?
TOM. Looking for a door-key.
LAURA. Where have you been all this time?
TOM. I have been to the movies.
LAURA. All this time at the movies?
TOM. There was a very long program. There was a Garbo picture and a Mickey Mouse and a travelogue and a newsreel and a preview of coming attractions. And there was an organ solo and a collection for the milk-fund—simultaneously—which ended up in a terrible fight between a fat lady and an usher!
LAURA [*innocently*]. Did you have to stay through everything?
TOM. Of course! And, oh, I forgot! There was a big stage show! The headliner on this stage show was Malvolio the Magician. He performed wonderful tricks, many of them, such as pouring water back and forth between pitchers. First it turned to wine and then it turned to beer and then it turned to whiskey. I know it was whiskey it finally turned into because he needed somebody to come up out of the audience to help him, and I came up—both shows! It was Kentucky Straight Bourbon. A very generous fellow, he gave souvenirs. [*He pulls from his back pocket a shimmering rainbow-colored scarf.*] He gave me this. This is his magic scarf. You can have it, Laura. You wave it over a canary cage and you get a bowl of gold-fish. You wave it over the gold-fish bowl and they fly away canaries. . . . But the won-

derfullest trick of all was the coffin trick. We nailed him into a coffin and he got out of the coffin without removing one nail. [*He has come inside.*] There is a trick that would come in handy for me— get me out of this 2 by 4 situation! [*Flops onto bed and starts removing shoes.*]

LAURA. Tom—Shhh!

TOM. What you shushing me for?

LAURA. You'll wake up Mother.

TOM. Goody, goody! Pay 'er back for all those "Rise an' Shines." [*Lies down, groaning.*] You know it don't take much intelligence to get yourself into a nailed-up coffin, Laura. But who in hell ever got himself out of one without removing one nail?

[*As if in answer, the father's grinning photograph lights up.*]

[*Scene dims out.*]

[*Immediately following: The church bell is heard striking six. At the sixth stroke the alarm clock goes off in Amanda's room, and after a few moments we hear her calling: "Rise and Shine! Rise and Shine! Laura, go tell your brother to rise and shine!"*]

TOM [*sitting up slowly*]. I'll rise—but I won't shine.

[*The light increases.*]

AMANDA. Laura, tell your brother his coffee is ready.

[*Laura slips into front room.*]

LAURA. Tom! It's nearly seven. Don't make Mother nervous. [*He stares at her stupidly. Beseechingly.*] Tom, speak to Mother this morning. Make up with her, apologize, speak to her!

TOM. She won't to me. It's her that started not speaking.

LAURA. If you just say you're sorry she'll start speaking.

TOM. Her not speaking—is that such a tragedy?

LAURA. Please—please!

AMANDA [*calling from kitchenette*]. Laura, are you going to do what I asked you to do, or do I have to get dressed and go out myself?

LAURA. Going, going—soon as I get on my coat! [*She pulls on a shapeless felt hat with nervous, jerky movement, pleadingly glancing at Tom. Rushes awkwardly for coat. The coat is one of Amanda's, inaccurately made-over, the sleeves too short for Laura.*] Butter and what else?

AMANDA [*entering upstage*]. Just butter. Tell them to charge it.

LAURA. Mother, they make such faces when I do that.

AMANDA. Stick and stones may break our bones, but the expression on Mr. Garfinkel's face won't harm us! Tell your brother his coffee is getting cold.

LAURA [*at door*]. Do what I asked you, will you, will you, Tom?

[*He looks sullenly away.*]

AMANDA. Laura, go now or just don't go at all!

LAURA [*rushing out*]. Going—going! [*A second later she cries out. Tom springs up and crosses to the door. Amanda rushes anxiously in. Tom opens the door.*]

TOM. Laura?

LAURA. I'm all right. I slipped, but I'm all right.

AMANDA [*peering anxiously after her*]. If anyone breaks a leg on those fire-escape steps, the landlord ought to be sued for every cent he possesses! [*She shuts door. Remembers she isn't speaking and returns to other room.*]

[*As Tom enters listlessly for his coffee, she turns her back to him and stands rigidly facing the window on the gloomy gray vault of the areaway. Its light on her face with its aged but childish features is cruelly sharp, satirical as a Daumier print.*]

[*Music under: "Ave Maria."*]

[*Tom glances sheepishly but sullenly at her averted figure and slumps at the table. The coffee is scalding hot; he sips it and gasps and spits it back in the cup. At his gasp, Amanda catches her breath and half turns. Then catches herself and turns back to window.*]

[*Tom blows on his coffee, glancing sidewise at his mother. She clears her throat. Tom clears his. He starts to rise. Sinks back down again, scratches his head, clears his throat again. Amanda coughs. Tom raises his cup in both hands to blow on it, his eyes staring over the rim of it at his mother for several moments. Then he slowly sets the cup down and awkwardly and hesitantly rises from the chair.*]

TOM [*hoarsely*]. Mother. I—I apologize. Mother. [*Amanda draws a quick, shuddering breath. Her face works grotesquely. She breaks into childlike tears.*] I'm sorry for what I said, for everything that I said, I didn't mean it.

AMANDA [*sobbingly*]. My devotion has made me a witch and so I make myself hateful to my children!

TOM. *No*, you *don't*.

AMANDA. I worry so much, don't sleep, it makes me nervous!

TOM [*gently*]. I understand that.

AMANDA. I've had to put up a solitary battle all these

years. But you're my right-hand bower! Don't fall down, don't fail!

TOM [*gently*]. I try, Mother.

AMANDA [*with great enthusiasm*]. Try and you will SUC-CEED! [*The notion makes her breathless.*] Why, you—you're just *full* of natural endowments! Both of my children—they're *unusual* children! Don't you think I know it? I'm so—*proud*! Happy and—feel I've—so much to be thankful for but—Promise me one thing, son!

TOM. What, Mother?

AMANDA. Promise, son, you'll—never be a drunkard!

TOM [*turns to her grinning*]. I will never be a drunkard, Mother.

AMANDA. That's what frightened me so, that you'd be drinking! Eat a bowl of Purina!

TOM. Just coffee, Mother.

AMANDA. Shredded wheat biscuit?

TOM. No. No, Mother, just coffee.

AMANDA. You can't put in a day's work on an empty stomach. You've got ten minutes—don't gulp! Drinking too-hot liquids makes cancer of the stomach. . . . Put cream in.

TOM. No, thank you.

AMANDA. To cool it.

TOM. No! No, thank you, I want it black.

AMANDA. I know, but it's not good for you. We have to do all that we can to build ourselves up. In these trying times we live in, all that we have to cling to is—each other. . . . That's why it's so important to—Tom, I—I sent out your sister so I could discuss something with you. If you hadn't spoken I would have spoken to you. [*Sits down.*]

TOM [*gently*]. What is it, Mother, that you want to discuss?

AMANDA. *Laura*!

[*Tom puts his cup down slowly.*]

[*Legend on screen: "Laura."*]

[*Music: "The Glass Menagerie."*]

TOM. —Oh.—Laura . . .

AMANDA [*touching his sleeve*]. You know how Laura is. So quiet but—still water runs deep! She notices things and I think she—broods about them. [*Tom looks up*]. A few days ago I came in and she was crying.

TOM. What about?

AMANDA. You.

TOM. Me?

AMANDA. She has an idea that you're not happy here.

TOM. What gave her that idea?

AMANDA. What gives her any idea? However, you do act strangely. I—I'm not criticizing, understand *that*! I know your ambitions do not lie in the warehouse, that like everybody in the whole wide world—you've had to—make sacrifices, but—Tom—Tom—life's not easy, it calls for—Spartan endurance! There's so many things in my heart that I cannot describe to you! I've never told you but I—*loved* your father. . . .

TOM [*gently*]. I know that, Mother.

AMANDA. And you—when I see you taking after his ways! Staying out late—and—well, you *had* been drinking the night you were in that—terrifying condition! Laura says that you hate the apartment and that you go out nights to get away from it! Is that true, Tom?

TOM. No. You say there's so much in your heart that you can't describe to me. That's true of me, too. There's so much in my heart that I can't describe to *you*! So let's respect each other's—

AMANDA. But, why—*why*, Tom—are you always so *restless*? Where do you go to, nights?

TOM. I—go to the movies.

AMANDA. Why do you go to the movies so much, Tom?

TOM. I go to the movies because—I like adventure. Adventure is something I don't have much of at work, so I go to the movies.

AMANDA. But, Tom, you go to the movies *entirely* too *much*!

TOM. I like a lot of adventure.

[*Amanda looks baffled, then hurt. As the familiar inquisition resumes he becomes hard and impatient again. Amanda slips back into her querulous attitude toward him.*]

[*Image on screen: Sailing vessel with Jolly Roger.*]

AMANDA. Most young men find adventure in their careers.

TOM. Then most young men are not employed in a warehouse.

AMANDA. The world is full of young men employed in warehouses and offices and factories.

TOM. Do all of them find adventure in their careers?

AMANDA. They do or they do without it! Not everybody has a craze for adventure.

TOM. Man is by instinct a lover, a hunter, a fighter, and none of those instincts are given much play at the warehouse!

AMANDA. Man is by instinct! Don't quote instinct to me! Instinct is something that people have got away from! It belongs to animals! Christian adults don't want it!

TOM. What do Christian adults want, then, Mother?

AMANDA. Superior things! Things of the mind and the spirit! Only animals have to satisfy instincts! Surely your aims are somewhat higher than theirs! Than monkeys—pigs—

TOM. I reckon they're not.

AMANDA. You're joking. However, that isn't what I wanted to discuss.

TOM [rising]. I haven't much time.

AMANDA [pushing his shoulders]. Sit down.

TOM. You want me to punch in red at the warehouse, Mother?

AMANDA. You have five minutes. I want to talk about Laura.

[Legend: "Plans and Provisions."]

TOM. All right! What about Laura?

AMANDA. We have to be making plans and provisions for her. She's older than you, two years, and nothing has happened. She just drifts along doing nothing. It frightens me terribly how she just drifts along.

TOM. I guess she's the type that people call home girls.

AMANDA. There's no such type, and if there is, it's a pity! That is unless the home is hers, with a husband!

TOM. What?

AMANDA. Oh, I can see the handwriting on the wall as plain as I see the nose in front of my face! It's terrifying! More and more you remind me of your father! He was out all hours without explanation—Then left! Good-bye! And me with a bag to hold. I saw that letter you got from the Merchant Marine. I know what you're dreaming of. I'm not standing here blindfolded. Very well, then. Then do it! But not till there's somebody to take your place.

TOM. What do you mean?

AMANDA. I mean that as soon as Laura has got somebody to take care of her, married, a home of her own, independent—why, then you'll be free to go wherever you please, on land, on sea, whichever way the wind blows you! But until that time you've got to look out for your sister. I don't say me because I'm old and don't matter! I say for your sister because she's young and dependent. I put her in

business college—a dismal failure! Frightened her so it made her sick to her stomach. I took her over to the Young People's League at the church. Another fiasco. She spoke to nobody, nobody spoke to her. Now all she does is fool with those pieces of glass and play those worn-out records. What kind of a life is that for a girl to lead?

TOM. What can I do about it?

AMANDA. Overcome selfishness! Self, self, self is all that you ever think of! [Tom springs up and crosses to get his coat. It is ugly and bulky. He pulls on a cap with earmuffs.] Where is your muffler? Put your wool muffler on! [He snatches it angrily from the closet and tosses it around his neck and pulls both ends tight.] Tom! I haven't said what I had in mind to ask you.

TOM. I'm too late to—

AMANDA [catching his arm—very importunately. Then shyly]. Down at the warehouse, aren't there some—nice young men?

TOM. No!

AMANDA. There must be—some . . .

TOM. Mother—

[Gesture.]

AMANDA. Find out one that's clean-living—doesn't drink and—ask him out for sister!

TOM. What?

AMANDA. For sister! To meet! Get acquainted!

TOM [stamping to door]. Oh, my go-osh!

AMANDA. Will you? [He opens door. Imploringly.] Will you? [He starts down.] Will you? Will you, dear?

TOM [calling back]. Yes!

[Amanda closes the door hesitantly and with a troubled but faintly hopeful expression.]

[Screen image: Glamor magazine cover.]

[Spot Amanda at phone.]

AMANDA. Ella Cartwright? This is Amanda Wingfield! How are you, honey? How is that kidney condition? [Count five.] Horrors! [Count five.] You're a Christian martyr, yes, honey, that's what you are, a Christian martyr! Well, I just happened to notice in my little red book that your subscription to the Companion has just run out! I knew that you wouldn't want to miss out on the wonderful serial starting in this new issue. It's by Bessie Mae Hopper, the first thing she's written since Honeymoon for Three. Wasn't that a strange and interesting story? Well, this one is even lovelier, I believe. It has a sophisticated society background. It's all about the horsey set on Long Island!

[*Fade out.*]

SCENE V

[*Legend on screen: "Annunciation." Fade with music.*]

It is early dusk of a spring evening. Supper has just been finished in the Wingfield apartment. Amanda and Laura in light colored dresses are removing dishes from the table, in the upstage area, which is shadowy, their movements formalized almost as a dance or ritual, their moving forms as pale and silent as moths.

Tom, in white shirt and trousers, rises from the table and crosses toward the fire-escape.

AMANDA [*as he passes her*]. Son, will you do me a favor?

TOM. What?

AMANDA. Comb your hair! You look so pretty when your hair is combed! [*Tom slouches on sofa with evening paper. Enormous caption "Franco Triumphs".*] There is only one respect in which I would like you to emulate your father.

TOM. What respect is that?

AMANDA. The care he always took of his appearance. He never allowed himself to look untidy. [*He throws down the paper and crosses to fire-escape.*] Where are you going?

TOM. I'm going out to smoke.

AMANDA. You smoke too much. A pack a day at fifteen cents a pack. How much would that amount to in a month? Thirty times fifteen is how much, Tom? Figure it out and you will be astounded at what you could save. Enough to give you a night-school course in accounting at Washington U! Just think what a wonderful thing that would be for you, son!

[*Tom is unmoved by the thought.*]

TOM. I'd rather smoke. [*He steps out on landing, letting the screen door slam.*]

AMANDA [*sharply*]. I know! That's the tragedy of it. . . .[*Alone, she turns to look at her husband's picture.*]

[*Dance music: "All the World is Waiting for the Sunrise!"*]

TOM [*to the audience*]. Across the alley from us was the Paradise Dance Hall. On evenings in spring the windows and doors were open and the music came outdoors. Sometimes the lights were turned out except for a large glass sphere that hung from the ceiling. It would turn slowly about and filter the dusk with delicate rainbow colors. Then the orchestra played a waltz or a tango, something that had a slow and sensuous rhythm. Couples would come outside, to the relative privacy of the alley. You could see them kissing behind ash-pits and telephone poles. This was the compensation for lives that passed like mine, without any change or adventure. Adventure and change were imminent in this year. They were waiting around the corner for all these kids. Suspended in the mist over Berchtesgaden, caught in the folds of Chamberlain's umbrella—In Spain there was Guernica! But here there was only hot swing music and liquor, dance halls, bars, and movies, and sex that hung in the gloom like a chandelier and flooded the world with brief, deceptive rainbows. . . . All the world was waiting for bombardments!

[*Amanda turns from the picture and comes outside.*]

AMANDA [*Sighing*]. A fire-escape landing's a poor excuse for a porch. [*She spreads a newspaper on a step and sits down, gracefully and demurely as if she were settling into a swing on a Mississippi veranda.*] What are you looking at?

TOM. The moon.

AMANDA. Is there a moon this evening?

TOM. It's rising over Garfinkel's Delicatessen.

AMANDA. So it is! A little silver slipper of a moon. Have you made a wish on it yet?

TOM. Um-hum.

AMANDA. What did you wish for?

TOM. That's a secret.

AMANDA. A secret, huh? Well, I won't tell mine either. I will be just as mysterious as you.

TOM. I bet I can guess what yours is.

AMANDA. Is my head so transparent?

TOM. You're not a sphinx.

AMANDA. No, I don't have secrets. I'll tell you what I wished for on the moon. Success and happiness for my precious children! I wish for that whenever there's a moon, and when there isn't a moon, I wish for it, too.

TOM. I thought perhaps you wished for a gentleman caller.

AMANDA. Why do you say that?

TOM. Don't you remember asking me to fetch one?

AMANDA. I remember suggesting that it would be nice for your sister if you brought home some nice young man from the warehouse. I think I've made that suggestion more than once.

TOM. Yes, you have made it repeatedly.

AMANDA. Well?

TOM. We are going to have one.

AMANDA. *What?*

TOM. A gentleman caller!

[*The annunciation is celebrated with music.*]

[*Amanda rises.*]

[*Image on screen: Caller with bouquet.*]

AMANDA. You mean you have asked some nice young man to come over?

TOM. Yep. I've asked him to dinner.

AMANDA. You really did?

TOM. I did!

AMANDA. You did, and did he—*accept?*

TOM. He did!

AMANDA. Well, well—well, well! That's—lovely!

TOM. I thought that you would be pleased.

AMANDA. It's definite, then?

TOM. Very definite.

AMANDA. Soon?

TOM. Very soon.

AMANDA. For heaven's sake, stop putting on and tell me some things, will you?

TOM. What things do you want me to tell you?

AMANDA. *Naturally* I would like to know when he's *coming!*

TOM. He's coming tomorrow.

AMANDA. *Tomorrow?*

TOM. Yep. Tomorrow.

AMANDA. But, Tom!

TOM. Yes, Mother?

AMANDA. Tomorrow gives me no time!

TOM. Time for what?

AMANDA. Preparations! Why didn't you phone me at once, as soon as you asked him, the minute that he accepted? Then, don't you see, I could have been getting ready!

TOM. You don't have to make any fuss.

AMANDA. Oh, Tom, Tom, Tom, of course I have to make a fuss! I want things nice, not sloppy! Not thrown together. I'll certainly have to do some fast thinking, won't I?

TOM. I don't see why you have to think at all.

AMANDA. You just don't know. We can't have a gen-tleman caller in a pig-sty! All my wedding silver has to be polished, the monogrammed table linen ought to be laundered! The windows have to be washed and fresh curtains put up. And how about clothes? We have to *wear* something, don't we?

TOM. Mother, this boy is no one to make a fuss over!

AMANDA. Do you realize he's the first young man we've introduced to your sister? It's terrible, dread-ful, disgraceful that poor little sister has never received a single gentleman caller! Tom, come inside! [*She opens the screen door.*]

TOM. What for?

AMANDA. I want to ask you some things.

TOM. If you're going to make such a fuss, I'll call it off, I'll tell him not to come.

AMANDA. You certainly won't do anything of the kind. Nothing offends people worse than broken engagements. It simply means I'll have to work like a Turk! We won't be brilliant, but we'll pass inspec-tion. Come on inside. [*Tom follows, groaning.*] Sit down.

TOM. Any particular place you would like me to sit?

AMANDA. Thank heavens I've got that new sofa! I'm also making payments on a floor lamp I'll have sent out! And put the chintz covers on, they'll brighten things up! Of course I'd hoped to have these walls re-papered. . . . What is the young man's name?

TOM. His name is O'Connor.

AMANDA. That, of course, means fish—tomorrow is Friday! I'll have that salmon loaf—with Durkee's dressing! What does he do? He works at the ware-house?

TOM. Of course! How else would I—

AMANDA. Tom, he—doesn't drink?

TOM. Why do you ask me that?

AMANDA. Your father *did!*

TOM. Don't get started on that!

AMANDA. He *does* drink, then?

TOM. Not that I know of!

AMANDA. Make sure, be certain! The last thing I want for my daughter's a boy who drinks!

TOM. Aren't you being a little premature? Mr. O'Con-nor has not yet appeared on the scene!

AMANDA. But will tomorrow. To meet your sister, and what do I know about his character? Nothing! Old maids are better off than wives of drunkards!

TOM. Oh, my God!

AMANDA. Be still!

TOM [*leaning forward to whisper*]. Lots of fellows meet girls whom they don't marry!

AMANDA. Oh, talk sensibly, Tom—and don't be sar-castic! [*She has gotten a hairbrush.*]

TOM. What are you doing?

AMANDA. I'm brushing that cow-lick down! What is this young man's position at the warehouse?

TOM [*submitting grimly to the brush and the interrogation*]. This young man's position is that of a shipping clerk, Mother.

AMANDA. Sounds to me like a fairly responsible job, the sort of a job *you* would be in if you just had more *get-up*. What is his salary? Have you got any idea?

TOM. I would judge it to be approximately eighty-five dollars a month.

AMANDA. Well—not princely, but—

TOM. Twenty more than I make.

AMANDA. Yes, how well I know! But for a family man, eighty-five dollars a month is not much more than you can just get by on. . . .

TOM. Yes, but Mr. O'Connor is not a family man.

AMANDA. He might be, mightn't he? Some time in the future?

TOM. I see. Plans and provisions.

AMANDA. You are the only young man that I know of who ignores the fact that the future becomes the present, the present the past, and the past turns into everlasting regret if you don't plan for it!

TOM. I will think that over and see what I can make of it.

AMANDA. Don't be supercilious with your mother! Tell me some more about this—what do you call him?

TOM. James D. O'Connor. The D. is for Delaney.

AMANDA. Irish on *both* sides! *Gracious*! And doesn't drink?

TOM. Shall I call him up and ask him right this minute?

AMANDA. The only way to find out about those things is to make discreet inquiries at the proper moment. When I was a girl in Blue Mountain and it was suspected that a young man drank, the girl whose attentions he had been receiving, if any girl *was*, would sometimes speak to the minister of his church, or rather her father would if her father was living, and sort of feel him out on the young man's character. That is the way such things are discreetly handled to keep a young woman from making a tragic mistake!

TOM. Then how did you happen to make a tragic mistake?

AMANDA. That innocent look of your father's had everyone fooled! He *smiled*—the world was *enchanted*! No girl can do worse than put herself at the mercy of a handsome appearance! I hope that Mr. O'Connor is not too good-looking.

TOM. No, he's not too good-looking. He's covered with freckles and hasn't too much of a nose.

AMANDA. He's not right-down homely, though?

TOM. Not right-down homely. Just medium homely, I'd say.

AMANDA. Character's what to look for in a man.

TOM. That's what I've always said, Mother.

AMANDA. You've never said anything of the kind and I suspect you would never give it a thought.

TOM. Don't be suspicious of me.

AMANDA. At least I hope he's the type that's up and coming.

TOM. I think he really goes in for self-improvement.

AMANDA. What reason have you to think so?

TOM. He goes to night school.

AMANDA [*beaming*]. Splendid! What does he do, I mean study?

TOM. Radio engineering and public speaking!

AMANDA. Then he has visions of being advanced in the world! Any young man who studies public speaking is aiming to have an executive job some day! And radio engineering? A thing for the future! Both of these facts are very illuminating. Those are the sort of things that a mother should know concerning any young man who comes to call on her daughter. Seriously or—not.

TOM. One little warning. He doesn't know about Laura. I didn't let on that we had dark ulterior motives. I just said, why don't you come have dinner with us? He said okay and that was the whole conversation.

AMANDA. I bet it was! You're eloquent as an oyster. However, he'll know about Laura when he gets here. When he sees how lovely and sweet and pretty she is, he'll thank his lucky stars he was asked to dinner.

TOM. Mother, you mustn't expect too much of Laura.

AMANDA. What do you mean?

TOM. Laura seems all those things to you and me because she's ours and we love her. We don't even notice she's crippled any more.

AMANDA. Don't say crippled! You know that I never allow that word to be used!

TOM. But face facts, Mother. She is and—that's not all—

AMANDA. What do you mean "not all"?

TOM. Laura is very different from other girls.

AMANDA. I think the difference is all to her advantage.

TOM. Not quite all—in the eyes of others—

strangers—she's terribly shy and lives in a world of her own and those things make her seem a little peculiar to people outside the house.

AMANDA. Don't say peculiar.

TOM. Face the facts. She is.

[*The dance-hall music changes to a tango that has a minor and somewhat ominous tone.*]

AMANDA. In what way is she peculiar—may I ask?

TOM [*gently*]. She lives in a world of her own—a world of—little glass ornaments, Mother. . . . [*Gets up. Amanda remains holding brush, looking at him, troubled.*] She plays old phonograph records and—that's about all— [*He glances at himself in the mirror and crosses to door.*]

AMANDA [*sharply*]. Where are you going?

TOM. I'm going to the movies. [*Out screen door.*]

AMANDA. Not to the movies, every night to the movies! [*Follows quickly to screen door.*] I don't believe you always go to the movies! [*He is gone. Amanda looks worriedly after him for a moment. Then vitality and optimism return and she turns from the door. Crossing to portieres.*] Laura! Laura! [*Laura answers from kitchenette.*]

LAURA. Yes, Mother.

AMANDA. Let those dishes go and come in front! [*Laura appears with dish towel. Gaily.*] Laura, come here and make a wish on the moon!

LAURA [*entering*]. Moon—moon?

AMANDA. A little silver slipper of a moon. Look over your left shoulder, Laura, and make a wish! [*Laura looks faintly puzzled as if called out of sleep. Amanda seizes her shoulders and turns her at an angle by the door.*] No! Now, darling, *wish*!

LAURA. What shall I wish for, Mother?

AMANDA [*her voice trembling and her eyes suddenly filling with tears*]. Happiness! Good Fortune!

[*The violin rises and the stage dims out.*]

SCENE VI

[*Image: High school hero.*]

TOM. And so the following evening I brought Jim home to dinner. I had known Jim slightly in high school. In high school Jim was a hero. He had tremendous Irish good nature and vitality with the scrubbed and polished look of white chinaware. He seemed to move in a continual spotlight. He was a star in basketball, captain of the debating club, president of the senior class and the glee club and he sang the male lead in the annual light operas. He was always running or bounding, never just walking. He seemed always at the point of defeating the law of gravity. He was shooting with such velocity through his adolescence that you would logically expect him to arrive at nothing short of the White House by the time he was thirty. But Jim apparently ran into more interference after his graduation from Soldan. His speed had definitely slowed. Six years after he left high school he was holding a job that wasn't much better than mine.

[*Image: Clerk.*]

He was the only one at the warehouse with whom I was on friendly terms. I was valuable to him as someone who could remember his former glory, who had seen him win basketball games and the silver cup in debating. He knew of my secret practice of retiring to a cabinet of the washroom to work on poems when business was slack in the warehouse. He called me Shakespeare. And while the other boys in the warehouse regarded me with suspicious hostility, Jim took a humorous attitude toward me. Gradually his attitude affected the others, their hostility wore off and they also began to smile at me as people smile at an oddly fashioned dog who trots across their path at some distance.

I knew that Jim and Laura had known each other at Soldan, and I had heard Laura speak admiringly of his voice. I didn't know if Jim remembered her or not. In high school Laura had been as unobtrusive as Jim had been astonishing. If he did remember Laura, it was not as my sister, for when I asked him to dinner, he grinned and said, "You know, Shakespeare, I never thought of you as having folks!"

He was about to discover that I did. . . .

[*Light up stage.*]

[*Legend on screen: "The Accent of a Coming Foot."*]

[*Friday evening. It is about five o'clock of a late spring evening which comes "scattering poems in the sky."*]

[*A delicate lemony light is in the Wingfield apartment.*]

[*Amanda has worked like a Turk in preparation for the*

gentleman caller. The results are astonishing. The new floor lamp with its rose-silk shade is in place, a colored paper lantern conceals the broken light fixture in the ceiling, new billowing white curtains are at the windows, chintz covers are on chairs and sofa, a pair of new sofa pillows make their initial appearance.]

[Open boxes and tissue paper are scattered on the floor.]

[Laura stands in the middle with lifted arms while Amanda crouches before her, adjusting the hem of the new dress, devout and ritualistic. The dress is colored and designed by memory. The arrangement of Laura's hair is changed; it is softer and more becoming. A fragile, unearthly prettiness has come out in Laura; she is like a piece of translucent glass touched by light, given a momentary radiance, not actual, not lasting.]

AMANDA [impatiently]. Why are you trembling?
LAURA. Mother, you've made me so nervous!
AMANDA. How have I made you nervous?
LAURA. By all this fuss! You make it seem so important!
AMANDA. I don't understand you, Laura. You couldn't be satisfied with just sitting home, and yet whenever I try to arrange something for you, you seem to resist it. [She gets up.] Now take a look at yourself. No, wait! Wait just a moment—I have an idea!
LAURA. What is it now?

[Amanda produces two powder puffs which she wraps in handkerchiefs and stuffs in Laura's bosom.]

LAURA. Mother, what are you doing?
AMANDA. They call them "Gay Deceivers"!
LAURA. I won't wear them!
AMANDA. You will!
LAURA. Why should I?
AMANDA. Because, to be painfully honest, your chest is flat.
LAURA. You make it seem like we were setting a trap.
AMANDA. All pretty girls are a trap, a pretty trap, and men expect them to be. [Legend: "A Pretty Trap".] Now look at yourself, young lady. This is the prettiest you will ever be! I've got to fix myself now! You're going to be surprised by your mother's appearance! [She crosses through portieres, humming gaily.]

[Laura moves slowly to the long mirror and stares solemnly at herself.]

[A wind blows the white curtains inward in a slow, graceful motion and with a faint, sorrowful sighing.]

AMANDA [off stage]. It isn't dark enough yet. [She turns slowly before the mirror with a troubled look.]

[Legend on screens: "This Is My Sister: Celebrate Her with Strings!" Music.]

AMANDA [laughing, off]. I'm going to show you something. I'm going to make a spectacular appearance!
LAURA. What is it, Mother?
AMANDA. Possess your soul in patience—you will see! Something I've resurrected from that old trunk! Styles haven't changed so terribly much after all. . . . [She parts the portieres.] Now just look at your mother! [She wears a girlish frock of yellowed voile with a blue silk sash. She carries a bunch of jonquils—the legend of her youth is nearly revived. Feverishly] This is the dress in which I led the cotillion. Won the cakewalk twice at Sunset Hill, wore one spring to the Governor's ball in Jackson! See how I sashayed around the ballroom, Laura? [She raises her skirt and does a mincing step around the room.] I wore it on Sundays for my gentlemen callers! I had it on the day I met your father—I had malaria fever all that spring. The change of climate from East Tennessee to the Delta—weakened resistance—I had a little temperature all the time—not enough to be serious—just enough to make me restless and giddy! Invitations poured in—parties all over the Delta!—"Stay in bed," said Mother, "you have fever!"—but I just wouldn't.—I took quinine but kept on going, going!—Evenings, dances!—Afternoons, long, long rides! Picnics—lovely!—So lovely, that country in May.—All lacy with dogwood, literally flooded with jonquils!—That was the spring I had the craze for jonquils. Jonquils became an absolute obsession. Mother said, "Honey, there's no more room for jonquils." And still I kept on bringing in more jonquils. Whenever, wherever I saw them, I'd say, "Stop! Stop! I see jonquils!" I made the young men help me gather the jonquils! It was a joke, Amanda and her jonquils! Finally there were no more vases to hold them, every available space was filled with jonquils. No vases to hold them? All right, I'll hold them myself! And then I— [She stops in front of the picture. Music.] met your father! Malaria fever and jonquils and then—this—boy. . . . [She switches on the rose-colored lamp.] I hope they get here before it starts to rain. [She crosses upstage and places the jon-

quils in bowl on table.] I gave your brother a little extra change so he and Mr. O'Connor could take the service car home.

LAURA [*with altered look*]. What did you say his name was?

AMANDA. O'Connor.

LAURA. What is his first name?

AMANDA. I don't remember. Oh, yes, I do. It was— Jim!

[*Laura sways slightly and catches hold of a chair.*]

[*Legend on screen: "Not Jim!"*]

LAURA [*faintly*]. Not—Jim!

AMANDA. Yes, that was it, it was Jim! I've never known a Jim that wasn't nice!

[*Music: Ominous.*]

LAURA. Are you sure his name is Jim O'Connor?

AMANDA. Yes. Why?

LAURA. Is he the one that Tom used to know in high school?

AMANDA. He didn't say so. I think he just got to know him at the warehouse.

LAURA. There was a Jim O'Connor we both knew in high school— [*Then, with effort.*] If that is the one that Tom is bringing to dinner—you'll have to excuse me, I won't come to the table.

AMANDA. What sort of nonsense is this?

LAURA. You asked me once if I'd ever liked a boy. Don't you remember I showed you this boy's picture?

AMANDA. You mean the boy you showed me in the year book?

LAURA. Yes, that boy.

AMANDA. Laura, Laura, were you in love with that boy?

LAURA. I don't know, Mother. All I know is I couldn't sit at the table if it was him!

AMANDA. It won't be him! It isn't the least bit likely. But whether it is or not, you will come to the table. You will not be excused.

LAURA. I'll have to be, Mother.

AMANDA. I don't intend to humor your silliness, Laura. I've had too much from you and your brother, both! So just sit down and compose yourself till they come. Tom has forgotten his key so you'll have to let them in, when they arrive.

LAURA [*panicky*]. Oh, Mother—*you* answer the door!

AMANDA [*lightly*]. I'll be in the kitchen—busy!

LAURA. Oh, Mother, please answer the door, don't make me do it!

AMANDA [*crossing into kitchenette*]. I've got to fix the dressing for the salmon. Fuss, fuss—silliness!—over a gentleman caller!

[*Door swings shut. Laura is left alone.*]

[*Legend: "Terror!"*]

[*She utters a low moan and turns off the lamp—sits stiffly on the edge of the sofa, knotting her fingers together.*]

[*Legend on screen: "The Opening of a Door!"*]

[*Tom and Jim appear on the fire-escape steps and climb to landing. Hearing their approach, Laura rises with a panicky gesture. She retreats to the portieres.*]

[*The doorbell. Laura catches her breath and touches her throat. Low drums.*]

AMANDA [*calling*]. Laura, sweetheart! The door!

[*Laura stares at it without moving.*]

JIM. I think we just beat the rain.

TOM. Uh-huh. [*He rings again, nervously. Jim whistles and fishes for a cigarette.*]

AMANDA [*very, very gaily*]. Laura, that is your brother and Mr. O'Connor! Will you let them in, darling?

[*Laura crosses toward kitchenette door.*]

LAURA [*breathlessly*]. Mother—you go to the door!

[*Amanda steps out of kitchenette and stares furiously at Laura. She points imperiously at the door.*]

LAURA. Please, please!

AMANDA [*in a fierce whisper*]. What is the matter with you, you silly thing?

LAURA [*desperately*]. Please, you answer it, *please*!

AMANDA. I told you I wasn't going to humor you, Laura. Why have you chosen this moment to lose your mind?

LAURA. Please, please, please, you go!

AMANDA. You'll have to go to the door because I can't!

LAURA [*despairingly*]. I can't either!

AMANDA. *Why*?

LAURA. I'm *sick*!

AMANDA. I'm sick, too—of your nonsense! Why can't you and your brother be normal people? Fantastic whims and behavior! [*Tom gives a long ring.*] Preposterous goings on! Can you give me one reason— [*Calls out lyrically.*] COMING? JUST ONE SECOND!—why should you be afraid to open a door? Now you answer it, Laura!

LAURA. Oh, oh, oh . . . [*She returns through the portieres. Darts to the victrola and winds it frantically and turns it on.*]

AMANDA. Laura Wingfield, you march right to that door!

LAURA. Yes—yes, Mother!

[*A faraway, scratchy rendition of "Dardanella" softens the air and gives her strength to move through it. She slips to the door and draws it cautiously open.*]

[*Tom enters with the caller, Jim O'Connor.*]

TOM. Laura, this is Jim. Jim, this is my sister, Laura.

JIM [*stepping inside*]. I didn't know that Shakespeare had a sister!

LAURA [*retreating stiff and trembling from the door*]. How—how do you do?

JIM [*heartily extending his hands*]. Okay!

[*Laura touches it hesitantly with hers.*]

JIM. Your hand's *cold*, Laura!

LAURA. Yes, well—I've been playing the victrola. . . .

JIM. Must have been playing classical music on it! You ought to play a little hot swing music to warm you up!

LAURA. Excuse me—I haven't finished playing the victrola. . . .

[*She turns awkwardly and hurries into the front room. She pauses a second by the victrola. Then catches her breath and darts through the portieres like a frightened deer.*]

JIM [*grinning*]. What was the matter?

TOM. Oh—with Laura? Laura is—terribly shy.

JIM. Shy, huh? It's unusual to meet a shy girl nowadays. I don't believe you ever mentioned you had a sister.

TOM. Well, now you know. I have one. Here is the *Post Dispatch*. You want a piece of it?

JIM. Uh-huh.

TOM. What piece? The comics?

JIM. Sports! [*Glances at it.*] Ole Dizzy Dean is on his bad behavior.

TOM [*disinterest*]. Yeah? [*Lights cigarette and crosses back to fire-escape door.*]

JIM. Where are *you* going?

TOM. I'm going out on the terrace.

JIM [*goes after him*]. You know, Shakespeare—I'm going to sell you a bill of goods!

TOM. What goods?

JIM. A course I'm taking.

TOM. Huh?

JIM. In public speaking! You and me, we're not the warehouse type.

TOM. Thanks—that's good news. But what has public speaking got to do with it?

JIM. It fits you for—executive positions!

TOM. Awww.

JIM. I tell you it's done a helluva lot for me.

[*Image: Executive at desk.*]

TOM. In what respect?

JIM. In every! Ask yourself what is the difference between you an' me and men in the office down front? Brains?—No!—Ability?—No! Then what? Just one little thing—

TOM. What is that one little thing?

JIM. Primarily it amounts to—social poise! Being able to square up to people and hold your own on any social level!

AMANDA [*off stage*]. Tom?

TOM. Yes, Mother?

AMANDA. Is that you and Mr. O'Connor?

TOM. Yes, Mother.

AMANDA. Well, you just make yourselves comfortable in there.

TOM. Yes, Mother.

AMANDA. Ask Mr. O'Connor if he would like to wash his hands.

JIM. Aw, no—no—thank you—I took care of that at the warehouse. Tom—

TOM. Yes?

JIM. Mr. Mendoza was speaking to me about you.

TOM. Favorably?

JIM. What do you think?

TOM. Well—

JIM. You're going to be out of a job if you don't wake up.

TOM. I am waking up—

JIM. You show no signs.

TOM. The signs are interior.

[*Image on screen: The Sailing Vessel with Jolly Roger Again.*]

TOM. I'm planning to change. [*He leans over the rail speaking with quiet exhilaration. The incandescent marquees and signs of the first-run movie houses light his face from across the alley. He looks like a voyager.*] I'm right at the point of committing myself to a future that doesn't include the warehouse and Mr. Mendoza or even a night-school course in public speaking.

JIM. What are you gassing about?

TOM. I'm tired of the movies.

JIM. Movies!

TOM. Yes, movies! Look at them— [*A wave toward the marvels of Grand Avenue.*] All of those glamorous people—having adventures—hogging it all, gobbling the whole thing up! You know what happens? People go to the *movies* instead of *moving*! Hollywood characters are supposed to have all the adventures for everybody in America, while everybody in America sits in a dark room and watches them have them! Yes, until there's a war. That's when adventure becomes available to the masses! *Everyone's* dish, not only Gable's! Then the people in the dark room come out of the dark room to have some adventures themselves—Goody, goody!—It's our turn now, to go to the South Sea Island—to make a safari—to be exotic, far-off!—But I'm not patient. I don't want to wait till then. I'm tired of the *movies* and I am *about* to move!

JIM [*incredulously*]. Move?

TOM. Yes.

JIM. When?

TOM. Soon!

JIM. Where? Where?

[*Theme Three music seems to answer the question, while Tom thinks it over. He searches among his pockets.*]

TOM. I'm starting to boil inside. I know I seem dreamy, but inside—well, I'm boiling! Whenever I pick up a shoe, I shudder a little thinking how short life is and what I am doing!—Whatever that means. I know it doesn't mean shoes—except as something to wear on a traveler's feet! [*Finds paper.*] Look—

JIM. What?

TOM. I'm a member.

JIM [*reading*]. The Union of Merchant Seamen.

TOM. I paid my dues this month, instead of the light bill.

JIM. You will regret it when they turn the lights off.

TOM. I won't be here.

JIM. How about your mother?

TOM. I'm like my father. The bastard son of a bastard!

See how he grins? And he's been absent going on sixteen years!

JIM. You're just talking, you drip. How does your mother feel about it?

TOM. Shhh!—Here comes Mother! Mother is not acquainted with my plans!

AMANDA [*enters portieres*]. Where are you all?

TOM. On the terrace, Mother.

[*They start inside. She advances to them. Tom is distinctly shocked at her appearance. Even Jim blinks a little. He is making his first contact with girlish Southern vivacity and in spite of the night-school course in public speaking is somewhat thrown off the beam by the unexpected outlay of social charm.*]

[*Certain responses are attempted by Jim but are swept aside by Amanda's gay laughter and chatter. Tom is embarrassed but after the first shock Jim reacts very warmly. Grins and chuckles, is altogether won over.*]

[*Image: Amanda as a girl*].

AMANDA [*coyly smiling, shaking her girlish ringlets*]. Well, well, well, so this is Mr. O'Connor. Introductions entirely unnecessary. I've heard so much about you from my boy. I finally said to him, Tom—good gracious!—why don't you bring this paragon to supper? I'd like to meet this nice young man at the warehouse!—Instead of just hearing him sing your praises so much! I don't know why my son is so stand-offish—that's not Southern behavior! Let's sit down and—I think we could stand a little more air in here! Tom, leave the door open. I felt a nice fresh breeze a moment ago. Where has it gone to? Mmm, so warm already! And not quite summer, even. We're going to burn up when summer really gets started. However, we're having—we're having a very light supper. I think light things are better fo' this time of year. The same as light clothes are. Light clothes an' light food are what warm weather calls fo'. You know our blood gets so thick during th' winter—it takes a while fo' us to *adjust* ou'selves!—when the season changes . . . It's come so quick this year. I wasn't prepared. All of a sudden—heavens! Already summer!—I ran to the trunk an' pulled out this light dress—Terribly old! Historical almost! But feels so good—so good an' co-ol, y'know. . . .

TOM. Mother—

AMANDA. Yes, honey?

TOM. How about—supper?

AMANDA. Honey, you go ask Sister if supper is ready! You know that Sister is in full charge of supper! Tell her you hungry boys are waiting for it. [*To Jim.*] Have you met Laura?

JIM. She—

AMANDA. Let you in? Oh, good, you've met already! It's rare for a girl as sweet an' pretty as Laura to be domestic! But Laura is, thank heavens, not only pretty but also very domestic. I'm not at all. I never was a bit. I never could make a thing but angel-food cake. Well, in the South we had so many servants. Gone, gone, gone. All vestige of gracious living! Gone completely! I wasn't prepared for what the future brought me. All of my gentlemen callers were sons of planters and so of course I assumed that I would be married to one and raise my family on a large piece of land with plenty of servants. But man proposes—and woman accepts the proposal!—To vary that old, old saying a little bit—I married no planter! I married a man who worked for the telephone company!—That gallantly smiling gentleman over there! [*Points to the picture.*] A telephone man who—fell in love with long-distance!—Now he travels and I don't even know where!—But what am I going on for about my—tribulations? Tell me yours—I hope you don't have any! Tom?

TOM [*returning*]. Yes, Mother?

AMANDA. Is supper nearly ready?

TOM. It looks to me like supper is on the table.

AMANDA. Let me look— [*She rises prettily and looks through portieres.*] Oh, lovely!—But where is Sister?

TOM. Laura is not feeling well and she says that she thinks she'd better not come to the table.

AMANDA. What?—Nonsense!—Laura? Oh, Laura!

LAURA [*Off stage, faintly*]. Yes, Mother.

AMANDA. You really must come to the table. We won't be seated until you come to the table! Come in, Mr. O'Connor. You sit over there, and I'll— Laura? Laura Wingfield! You're keeping us waiting, honey! We can't say grace until you come to the table!

[*The back door is pushed weakly open and Laura comes in. She is obviously quite faint, her lips trembling, her eyes wide and staring. She moves unsteadily toward the table.*]

[*Legend: "Terror!"*]

[*Outside a summer storm is coming abruptly. The white curtains billow inward at the windows and there is a sorrowful murmur and deep blue dusk.*]

[*Laura suddenly stumbles—she catches at a chair with a faint moan.*]

TOM. Laura!

AMANDA. Laura! [*There is a clap of thunder.*] [*Legend "Ah!"*] [*Despairingly.*] Why, Laura, you *are* sick, darling! Tom, help your sister into the living room, dear! Sit in the living room, Laura— rest on the sofa. Well! [*To the gentleman caller.*] Standing over the hot stove made her ill!—I told her that it was just too warm this evening, but— [*Tom comes back in. Laura is on the sofa.*] Is Laura all right now?

TOM. Yes.

AMANDA. What *is* that? Rain? A nice cool rain has come up! [*She gives the gentleman caller a frightened look.*] I think we may—have grace—now . . . [*Tom looks at her stupidly.*] Tom, honey—you say grace!

TOM. Oh . . . "For these and all thy mercies—" [*They bow their heads, Amanda stealing a nervous glance at Jim. In the living room Laura, stretched on the sofa, clenches her hand to her lips, to hold back a shuddering sob.*] God's Holy Name be praised—

[*The scene dims out.*]

SCENE VII

[*A Souvenir.*]

Half an hour later. Dinner is just being finished in the upstage area which is concealed by the drawn portieres.

As the curtain rises Laura is still huddled upon the sofa, her feet drawn under her, her head resting on a pale blue pillow, her eyes wide and mysteriously watchful. The new floor lamp with its shade of rose-colored silk gives a soft, becoming light to her face, bringing out the fragile, unearthly prettiness which usually escapes attention. There is a steady murmur of rain, but it is slackening and stops soon after the scene begins; the air outside becomes pale and luminous as the moon breaks out.

A moment after the curtain rises, the lights in both rooms flicker and go out.

JIM. Hey, there, Mr. Light Bulb!

[*Amanda laughs nervously.*]

[*Legend: "Suspension of a public service."*]

AMANDA. Where was Moses when the lights went out? Ha-ha. Do you know the answer to that one, Mr. O'Connor?

JIM. No, Ma'am, what's the answer?

AMANDA. In the dark! [*Jim laughs appreciably.*] Everybody sit still. I'll light the candles. Isn't it lucky we have them on the table? Where's a match? Which of you gentlemen can provide a match?

JIM. Here.

AMANDA. Thank you, sir.

JIM. Not at all, Ma'am!

AMANDA. I guess the fuse has burnt out. Mr. O'Connor, can you tell a burnt-out fuse? I know I can't and Tom is a total loss when it comes to mechanics. [*Sound: Getting Up: Voices Recede a Little to kitchenette.*] Oh, be careful you don't bump into something. We don't want our gentleman caller to break his neck. Now wouldn't that be a fine howdy-do?

JIM. Ha-ha! Where is the fuse-box?

AMANDA. Right here next to the stove. Can you see anything?

JIM. Just a minute.

AMANDA. Isn't electricity a mysterious thing? Wasn't it Benjamin Franklin who tied a key to a kite? We live in such a mysterious universe, don't we? Some people say that science clears up all the mysteries for us. In my opinion it only creates more! Have you found it yet?

JIM. No, Ma'am. All these fuses look okay to me.

AMANDA. Tom!

TOM. Yes, Mother?

AMANDA. That light bill I gave you several days ago. The one I told you we got the notices about?

TOM. Oh.—Yeah.

[*Legend: "Ha!"*]

AMANDA. You didn't neglect to pay it by any chance?

TOM. Why, I—

AMANDA. Didn't! I might have known it!

JIM. Shakespeare probably wrote a poem on that light bill, Mrs. Wingfield.

AMANDA. I might have known better than to trust him with it! There's such a high price for negligence in this world!

JIM. Maybe the poem will win a ten-dollar prize.

AMANDA. We'll just have to spend the remainder of the evening in the nineteenth century, before Mr. Edison made the Mazda lamp!

JIM. Candlelight is my favorite kind of light.

AMANDA. That shows you're romantic! But that's no excuse for Tom. Well, we got through dinner. Very considerate of them to let us get through dinner before they plunged us into everlasting darkness, wasn't it, Mr. O'Connor?

JIM. Ha-ha!

AMANDA. Tom, as a penalty for your carelessness you can help me with the dishes.

JIM. Let me give you a hand.

AMANDA. Indeed you will not!

JIM. I ought to be good for something.

AMANDA. Good for something? [*Her tone is rhapsodic.*] *You?* Why, Mr. O'Connor, nobody, *nobody's* given me this much entertainment in years—as you have!

JIM. Aw, now, Mrs. Wingfield!

AMANDA. I'm not exaggerating, not one bit! But Sister is all by her lonesome. You go keep her company in the parlor! I'll give you this lovely old candelabrum that used to be on the altar at the church of the Heavenly Rest. It was melted a little out of shape when the church burnt down. Lightning struck it one spring. Gypsy Jones was holding a revival at the time and he intimated that the church was destroyed because the Episcopalians gave card parties.

JIM. Ha-ha.

AMANDA. And how about coaxing Sister to drink a little wine? I think it would be good for her! Can you carry both at once?

JIM. Sure. I'm Superman!

AMANDA. Now, Thomas, get into this apron!

[*The door of kitchenette swings closed on Amanda's gay laughter; the flickering light approaches the portieres.*]

[*Laura sits up nervously as he enters. Her speech at first is low and breathless from the almost intolerable strain of being alone with a stranger.*]

[*The legend: "I don't suppose you remember me at all!"*]

[*In her first speeches in this scene, before Jim's warmth overcomes her paralyzing shyness, Laura's voice is thin and breathless as though she has just run up a steep flight of stairs.*]

[Jim's attitude is gently humorous. In playing this scene it should be stressed that while the incident is apparently unimportant, it is to Laura the climax of her secret life.]

JIM. Hello, there, Laura.

LAURA [*faintly*]. Hello. [*She clears her throat.*]

JIM. How are you feeling now? Better?

LAURA. Yes. Yes, thank you.

JIM. This is for you. A little dandelion wine. [*He extends it toward her with extravagant gallantry.*]

LAURA. Thank you.

JIM. Drink it—but don't get drunk! [*He laughs heartily. Laura takes the glass uncertainly; laughs shyly.*] Where shall I set the candles?

LAURA. Oh—oh, anywhere . . .

JIM. How about here on the floor? Any objections?

LAURA. No.

JIM. I'll spread a newspaper under to catch the drippings. I like to sit on the floor. Mind if I do?

LAURA. Oh, no.

JIM. Give me a pillow?

LAURA. What?

JIM. A pillow!

LAURA. Oh . . . [*Hands him one quickly.*]

JIM. How about you? Don't you like to sit on the floor?

LAURA. Oh—yes.

JIM. Why don't you, then?

LAURA. I—will.

JIM. Take a pillow! [*Laura does. Sits on the other side of the candelabrum. Jim crosses his legs and smiles engagingly at her.*] I can't hardly see you sitting way over there.

LAURA. I can—see you.

JIM. I know, but that's not fair, I'm in the limelight. [*Laura moves her pillow closer.*] Good! Now I can see you! Comfortable?

LAURA. Yes.

JIM. So am I. Comfortable as a cow. Will you have some gum?

LAURA. No, thank you.

JIM. I think that I will indulge, with your permission. [*Musingly unwraps it and holds it up.*] Think of the fortune made by the guy that invented the first piece of chewing gum. Amazing, huh? The Wrigley Building is one of the sights of Chicago—I saw it summer before last when I went up to the Century of Progress. Did you take in the Century of Progress?

LAURA. No, I didn't.

JIM. Well, it was quite a wonderful exposition. What impressed me most was the Hall of Science. Gives you an idea of what the future will be in America, even more wonderful than the present time is! [*Pause. Smiling at her.*] Your brother tells me you're shy. Is that right, Laura?

LAURA. I—I don't know.

JIM. I judge you to be an old-fashioned type of girl. Well, I think that's a pretty good type to be. Hope you don't think I'm being too personal—do you?

LAURA [*hastily, out of embarrassment*]. I believe I *will* take a piece of gum, if you—don't mind. [*Clearing her throat.*] Mr. O'Connor, have you—kept up with your singing?

JIM. Singing? Me?

LAURA. Yes. I remember what a beautiful voice you had.

JIM. When did you hear me sing?

[*Voice off stage in the pause.*]

VOICE [*off stage*].

> O blow, ye winds, heigh-ho,
> A-roving I will go!
>   I'm off to my love
>   With a boxing glove—
>   Ten thousand miles away!

JIM. You say you've heard me sing?

LAURA. Oh, yes! Yes, very often . . . I—don't suppose you remember me—at all?

JIM [*smiling doubtfully*]. You know I have an idea I've seen you before. I had that idea soon as you opened the door. It seemed almost like I was about to remember your name. But the name that I started to call you—wasn't a name! And so I stopped myself before I said it.

LAURA. Wasn't it—Blue Roses?

JIM [*springs up. Grinning.*] Blue Roses! My gosh, yes— Blue Roses! That's what I had on my tongue when you opened the door! Isn't it funny what tricks your memory plays? I didn't connect you with the high school somehow or other. But that's where it was; it was high school. I didn't even know you were Shakespeare's sister! Gosh, I'm sorry.

LAURA. I didn't expect you to. You—barely knew me!

JIM. But we did have a speaking acquaintance, huh?

LAURA. Yes, we—spoke to each other.

JIM. When did you recognize me?

LAURA. Oh, right away!

JIM. Soon as I came in the door?

LAURA. When I heard your name I thought it was

probably you. I knew that Tom used to know you a little in high school. So when you came in the door—Well, then I was—sure.

JIM. Why didn't you *say* something, then?

LAURA [*breathlessly*]. I didn't know what to say, I was—too surprised!

JIM. For goodness' sakes! You know, this sure is funny!

LAURA. Yes! Yes, isn't it, though . . .

JIM. Didn't we have a class in something together?

LAURA. Yes, we did.

JIM. What class was that?

LAURA. It was—singing—Chorus!

JIM. Aw!

LAURA. I sat across the aisle from you in the Aud.

JIM. Aw.

LAURA. Mondays, Wednesdays and Fridays.

JIM. Now I remember—you always came in late.

LAURA. Yes, it was so hard for me, getting upstairs. I had that brace on my leg—it clumped so loud!

JIM. I never heard any clumping.

LAURA [*wincing at the recollection*]. To me it sounded like—thunder!

JIM. Well, well, well, I never even noticed.

LAURA. And everybody was seated before I came in. I had to walk in front of all those people. My seat was in the back row. I had to go clumping all the way up the aisle with everyone watching!

JIM. You shouldn't have been self-conscious.

LAURA. I know, but I was. It was always such a relief when the singing started.

JIM. Aw, yes, I've placed you now! I used to call you Blue Roses. How was it that I got started calling you that?

LAURA. I was out of school a little while with pleurosis. When I came back you asked me what was the matter. I said I had pleurosis—you thought I said Blue Roses. That's what you always called me after that!

JIM. I hope you didn't mind.

LAURA. Oh, no—I liked it. You see, I wasn't acquainted with many—people. . . .

JIM. As I remember you sort of stuck by yourself.

LAURA. I—I—never had much luck at—making friends.

JIM. I don't see why you wouldn't.

LAURA. Well, I—started out badly.

JIM. You mean being—

LAURA. Yes, it sort of—stood between me—

JIM. You shouldn't have let it!

LAURA. I know, but it did, and—

JIM. You were shy with people!

LAURA. I tried not to be but never could—

JIM. Overcome it?

LAURA. No, I—I never could!

JIM. I guess being shy is something you have to work out of kind of gradually.

LAURA [*sorrowfully*]. Yes—I guess it—

JIM. Takes time!

LAURA. Yes—

JIM. People are not so dreadful when you know them. That's what you have to remember! And everybody has problems, not just you, but practically everybody has got some problems. You think of yourself as having the only problems, as being the only one who is disappointed. But just look around you and you will see lots of people as disappointed as you are. For instance, I hoped when I was going to high school that I would be further along at this time, six years later, than I am now—You remember that wonderful write-up I had in *The Torch*?

LAURA. Yes! [*She rises and crosses to table.*]

JIM. It said I was bound to succeed in anything I went into! [*Laura returns with the annual.*] Holy Jeez! *The Torch*! [*He accepts it reverently. They smile across it with mutual wonder. Laura crouches beside him and they begin to turn through it. Laura's shyness is dissolving in his warmth.*]

LAURA. Here you are in *Pirates of Penzance*!

JIM [*wistfully*]. I sang the baritone lead in that operetta.

LAURA [*rapidly*]. So—*beautifully*!

JIM [*protesting*]. Aw—

LAURA. Yes, yes—beautifully—beautifully!

JIM. You heard me?

LAURA. All three times!

JIM. No!

LAURA. Yes!

JIM. All three performances?

LAURA [*Looking down*]. Yes.

JIM. Why?

LAURA. I—wanted to ask you to—autograph my program.

JIM. Why didn't you ask me to?

LAURA. You were always surrounded by your own friends so much that I never had a chance to.

JIM. You should have just—

LAURA. Well, I—thought you might think I was—

JIM. Thought I might think you was—what?

LAURA. Oh—

JIM [*with reflective relish*]. I was beleaguered by females in those days.

LAURA. You were terribly popular!

JIM. Yeah—

LAURA. You had such a—friendly way—

JIM. I was spoiled in high school.

LAURA. Everybody—liked you!

JIM. Including you?

LAURA. I—yes, I—I did, too— [*She gently closes the book in her lap.*]

JIM. Well, well, well!—Give me that program, Laura. [*She hands it to him. He signs it with a flourish.*] There you are—better late than never!

LAURA. Oh, I—what a—surprise!

JIM. My signature isn't worth very much right now. But some day—maybe—it will increase in value! Being disappointed is one thing and being discouraged is something else. I am disappointed but I am not discouraged. I'm twenty-three years old. How old are you?

LAURA. I'll be twenty-four in June.

JIM. That's not old age!

LAURA. No, but—

JIM. You finished high school?

LAURA [*with difficulty*]. I didn't go back.

JIM. You mean you dropped out?

LAURA. I made bad grades in my final examinations. [*She rises and replaces the book and the program. Her voice strained.*] How is—Emily Meisenbach getting along?

JIM. Oh, that kraut-head!

LAURA. Why do you call her that?

JIM. That's what she was.

LAURA. You're not still—going with her?

JIM. I never see her.

LAURA. It said in the Personal Section that you were—engaged!

JIM. I know, but I wasn't impressed by that—propaganda!

LAURA. It wasn't—the truth?

JIM. Only in Emily's optimistic opinion!

LAURA. Oh—

[*Legend: "What have you done since high school?"*]

[*Jim lights a cigarette and leans indolently back on his elbows smiling at Laura with a warmth and charm which lights her inwardly with altar candles. She remains by the table and turns in her hands a piece of glass to cover her tumult.*]

JIM [*after several reflective puffs on a cigarette*]. What have you done since high school? [*She seems not to hear him.*] Huh? [*Laura looks up.*] I said what have you done since high school, Laura?

LAURA. Nothing much.

JIM. You must have been doing something these six long years.

LAURA. Yes.

JIM. Well, then, such as what?

LAURA. I took a business course at business college—

JIM. How did that work out?

LAURA. Well, not very—well—I had to drop out, it gave me—indigestion—

[*Jim laughs gently.*]

JIM. What are you doing now?

LAURA. I don't do anything—much. Oh, please don't think I sit around doing nothing! My glass collection takes up a good deal of my time. Glass is something you have to take good care of.

JIM. What did you say—about glass?

LAURA. Collection I said—I have one— [*She clears her throat and turns away again, acutely shy.*]

JIM [*abruptly*]. You know what I judge to be the trouble with you? Inferiority complex! Know what that is? That's what they call it when someone low-rates himself! I understand it because I had it, too. Although my case was not so aggravated as yours seems to be. I had it until I took up public speaking, developed my voice, and learned that I had an aptitude for science. Before that time I never thought of myself as being outstanding in any way whatsoever! Now I've never made a regular study of it, but I have a friend who says I can analyze people better than doctors that make a profession of it. I don't claim that to be necessarily true, but I can sure guess a person's psychology, Laura! [*Takes out his gum.*] Excuse me, Laura. I always take it out when the flavor is gone. I'll use this scrap of paper to wrap it in. I know how it is to get it stuck on a shoe. Yep—that's what I judge to be your principal trouble. A lack of confidence in yourself as a person. You don't have the proper amount of faith in yourself. I'm basing that fact on a number of your remarks and also on certain observations I've made. For instance that clumping you thought was so awful in high school. You say that you even dreaded to walk into class. You see what you did? You dropped out of school, you gave up an education because of a clump, which as far as I know was practically non-existent! A little physical defect is what you have. Hardly noticeable even! Magnified thousands of times by imagination! You know what my strong advice to you is? Think of yourself as *superior* in some way!

LAURA. In what way would I think?

JIM. Why, man alive, Laura! Just look about you a little. What do you see? A world full of common people! All of 'em born and all of 'em going to die! Which of them has one-tenth of your good points! Or mine! Or anyone else's, as far as that goes— Gosh! Everybody excels in some one thing. Some in many! [*Unconsciously glances at himself in the mirror.*] All you've got to do is discover in *what*! Take me, for instance. [*He adjusts his tie at the mirror.*] My interest happens to lie in electro-dynamics. I'm taking a course in radio engineering at night school, Laura, on top of a fairly responsible job at the warehouse. I'm taking that course and studying public speaking.

LAURA. Ohhhh.

JIM. Because I believe in the future of television! [*Turning back to her.*] I wish to be ready to go up right along with it. Therefore I'm planning to get in on the ground floor. In fact, I've already made the right connections and all that remains is for the industry itself to get under way! Full steam— [*His eyes are starry.*] *Knowledge—Zzzzzp! Money—Zzzzzzp— Power*! That's the cycle democracy is built on! [*His attitude is convincingly dynamic. Laura stares at him, even her shyness eclipsed in her absolute wonder. He suddenly grins.*] I guess you think I think a lot of myself!

LAURA. No—o-o-o, I—

JIM. Now how about you? Isn't there something you take more interest in than anything else?

LAURA. Well, I do—as I said—have my—glass collections—

[*A peal of girlish laughter from the kitchen.*]

JIM. I'm not right sure I know what you're talking about. What kind of glass is it?

LAURA. Little articles of it, they're ornaments mostly! Most of them are little animals made out of glass, the tiniest little animals in the world. Mother calls them a glass menagerie! Here's an example of one, if you'd like to see it! This one is one of the oldest. It's nearly thirteen. [*He stretches out his hand.*] [*Music: "The Glass Menagerie."*] Oh, be careful—if you breathe, it breaks!

JIM. I'd better not take it. I'm pretty clumsy with things.

LAURA. Go on, I trust you with him! [*Places it in his palm.*] There now—you're holding him gently! Hold him over the light, he loves the light! You see how the light shines through him?

JIM. It sure does shine!

LAURA. I shouldn't be partial, but he is my favorite one.

JIM. What kind of a thing is this one supposed to be?

LAURA. Haven't you noticed the single horn on his forehead?

JIM. A unicorn, huh?

LAURA. Mmm-hmmm!

JIM. Unicorns, aren't they extinct in the modern world?

LAURA. I know!

JIM. Poor little fellow, he must feel sort of lonesome.

LAURA [*smiling*]. Well, if he does he doesn't complain about it. He stays on a shelf with some horses that don't have horns and all of them seem to get along nicely together.

JIM. How do you know?

LAURA [*lightly*]. I haven't heard any arguments among them!

JIM [*grinning*]. No arguments, huh? Well, that's a pretty good sign! Where shall I set him?

LAURA. Put him on the table. They all like a change of scenery once in a while!

JIM [*stretching*]. Well, well, well, well—Look how big my shadow is when I stretch!

LAURA. Oh, oh, yes—it stretches across the ceiling!

JIM [*crossing to door*]. I think it's stopped raining. [*Opens fire-escape door.*] Where does the music come from?

LAURA. From the Paradise Dance Hall across the alley.

JIM. How about cutting the rug a little, Miss Wingfield?

LAURA. Oh, I—

JIM. Or is your program filled up? Let me have a look at it. [*Grasps imaginary card.*] Why, every dance is taken! I'll just have to scratch some out. [*Waltz music: "La Golondrina"*] Ahhh, a waltz! [*He executes some sweeping turns by himself then holds his arms toward Laura.*]

LAURA [*breathlessly*]. I—can't dance!

JIM. There you go, that inferiority stuff!

LAURA. I've never danced in my life!

JIM. Come on, try!

LAURA. Oh, but I'd step on you!

JIM. I'm not made out of glass.

LAURA. How—how—how do we start?

JIM. Just leave it to me. You hold your arms out a little.

LAURA. Like this?

JIM. A little bit higher. Right. Now don't tighten up, that's the main thing about it—relax.

LAURA [*laughing breathlessly*]. It's hard not to.

JIM. Okay.

LAURA. I'm afraid you can't budge me.

JIM. What do you bet I can't? [*He swings her into motion.*]

LAURA. Goodness, yes, you can!

JIM. Let yourself go, now, Laura, just let yourself go.

LAURA. I'm—

JIM. Come on!

LAURA. Trying!

JIM. Not so stiff—Easy does it!

LAURA. I know but I'm—

JIM. Loosen th' backbone! There now, that's a lot better.

LAURA. Am I?

JIM. Lots, lots better! [*He moves her about the room in a clumsy waltz.*]

LAURA. Oh, my!

JIM. Ha-ha!

LAURA. Oh, my goodness!

JIM. Ha-ha-ha! [*They suddenly bump into the table. Jim stops.*] What did we hit on?

LAURA. Table.

JIM. Did something fall off it? I think—

LAURA. Yes.

JIM. I hope that it wasn't the little glass horse with the horn!

LAURA. Yes.

JIM. Aw, aw, aw. Is it broken?

LAURA. Now it is just like all the other horses.

JIM. It's lost its—

LAURA. Horn! It doesn't matter. Maybe it's a blessing in disguise.

JIM. You'll never forgive me. I bet that that was your favorite piece of glass.

LAURA. I don't have favorites much. It's no tragedy, Freckles. Glass breaks so easily. No matter how careful you are. The traffic jars the shelves and things fall off them.

JIM. Still I'm awfully sorry that I was the cause.

LAURA [*smiling*]. I'll just imagine he had an operation. The horn was removed to make him feel less—freakish! [*They both laugh.*] Now he will feel more at home with the other horses, the ones that don't have horns . . .

JIM. Ha-ha, that's very funny! [*Suddenly serious.*] I'm glad to see that you have a sense of humor. You know—you're—well—very different! Surprisingly different from anyone else I know! [*His voice becomes soft and hesitant with a genuine feeling.*] Do you mind me telling you that? [*Laura is abashed beyond speech.*] I mean it in a nice way . . . [*Laura nods shyly, looking away.*] You make me feel sort of—I don't know how to put it! I'm usually pretty good at expressing things, but—This is something that I don't know how to say! [*Laura touches her throat and clears it—turns the broken unicorn in her hands.*] [*Even softer.*] Has anyone ever told you that you were pretty? [*Pause: music.*] [*Laura looks up slowly, with wonder, and shakes her head.*] Well, you are! In a very different way from anyone else. And all the nicer because of the difference, too. [*His voice becomes low and husky. Laura turns away, nearly faint with the novelty of her emotions.*] I wish that you were my sister. I'd teach you to have some confidence in yourself. The different people are not like other people, but being different is nothing to be ashamed of. Because other people are not such wonderful people. They're one hundred times one thousand. You're one times one! They walk all over the earth. You just stay here. They're common as—weeds, but—you—well, you're—*Blue Roses*!

[*Image on screen: Blue roses.*]

[*Music changes.*]

LAURA. But blue is wrong for—roses . . .

JIM. It's right for you—You're—pretty!

LAURA. In what respect am I pretty?

JIM. In all respects—believe me! Your eyes—your hair—are pretty! Your hands are pretty! [*He catches hold of her hand.*] You think I'm making this up because I'm invited to dinner and have to be nice. Oh, I could do that! I could put on an act for you, Laura, and say lots of things without being very sincere. But this time I am. I'm talking to you sincerely. I happened to notice you had this inferiority complex that keeps you from feeling comfortable with people. Somebody needs to build your confidence up and make you proud instead of shy and turning away and—blushing—Somebody ought to—Ought to—*kiss* you, Laura! [*His hand slips slowly up her arm to her shoulder.*] [*Music swells tumultuously.*] [*He suddenly turns her about and kisses her on the lips. When he releases her Laura sinks on the sofa with a bright, dazed look. Jim backs away and fishes in his pocket for a cigarette.*] [*Legend on screen: "Souvenir."*] Stumble-john! [*He lights the cigarette, avoiding her look. There is a peal of girlish laughter from Amanda in the kitchen. Laura slowly raises and opens her hand. It still contains the little broken glass animal. She looks at it with a tender, bewildered expression.*] Stumble-john! I shouldn't have done that—That was way off the beam. You don't smoke, do you? [*She looks up, smiling, not hearing the question. He sits beside her a little gingerly. She looks at him speechlessly—waiting. He coughs decorously and moves a little farther aside as he considers the situation and senses her feelings, dimly, with perturbation. Gently.]* Would you—care for a—mint? [*She doesn't seem to hear him but her look grows brighter even.*] Peppermint—Life Saver? My pocket's a regular drug store—wherever I go . . . [*He pops a mint in his mouth. Then gulps and decides to make a clean breast of it. He speaks slowly and gingerly.*] Laura, you know, if I had a sister like you, I'd do the same thing as Tom. I'd bring out fellows and—introduce her to them. The right type of boys of a type to—appreciate her. Only—well—he made a mistake about me. Maybe I've got no call to be saying this. That may not have been the idea in having me over. But what if it was? There's nothing wrong about that. The only trouble is that in my case—I'm not in a situation to—do the right thing. I can't take down your number and say I'll phone. I can't call up next week and—ask for a date. I thought I had better explain the situation in case you misunderstood it and—hurt your feelings. . . . [*Pause. Slowly, very slowly, Laura's look changes, her eyes returning slowly from his to the ornament in her palm.*]

[*Amanda utters another gay laugh in the kitchen.*]

LAURA [*faintly*]. You—won't—call again?

JIM. No, Laura, I can't. [*He rises from the sofa.*] As I was just explaining, I've—got strings on me, Laura, I've—been going steady! I go out all the time with a girl named Betty. She's a home-girl like you, and Catholic, and Irish, and in a great many ways we—get along fine. I met her last summer on a moonlight boat trip up the river to Alton, on the *Majestic*. Well—right away from the start it was—love! [*Legend: Love!*] [*Laura sways slightly forward and grips the arm of the sofa. He fails to notice, now enrapt in his own comfortable being.*] Being in love has made a new man of me! [*Leaning stiffly forward, clutching the arm of the sofa, Laura struggles visibly with her storm. But Jim is oblivious, she is a long way off.*] The power of love is really pretty tremendous! Love is something that—changes the whole world, Laura! [*The storm abates a little and Laura leans back. He notices her again.*] It happened that Betty's aunt took sick, she got a wire and had to go to Centralia. So Tom—when he asked me to dinner—I naturally just accepted the invitation, not knowing that you—that he—that I— [*He stops awkwardly.*] Huh—I'm a stumble-john! [*He flops back on the sofa. The holy candles in the altar of Laura's face have been snuffed out. There is a look of*

almost infinite desolation. Jim glances at her uneasily.*] I wish that you would—say something. [*She bites her lip which was trembling and then bravely smiles. She opens her hand again on the broken glass ornament. Then she gently takes his hand and raises it level with her own. She carefully places the unicorn in the palm of his hand, then pushes his fingers closed upon it.*] What are you—doing that for? You want me to have him?—Laura? [*She nods.*] What for?

LAURA. A—souvenir . . .

[*She rises unsteadily and crouches beside the victrola to wind it up.*]

[*Legend on screen: "Things have a way of turning out so badly!"*]

[*Or image: "Gentleman caller waving goodbye!—Gaily."*]

[*At this moment Amanda rushes brightly back in the front room. She bears a pitcher of fruit punch in an old-fashioned cut-glass pitcher and a plate of macaroons. The plate has a gold border and poppies painted on it.*]

AMANDA. Well, well, well! Isn't the air delightful after the shower! I've made you children a little liquid refreshment. [*Turns gaily to the gentleman caller.*] Jim, do you know that song about lemonade?

"Lemonade, lemonade
  Made in the shade and stirred with a spade—
  Good enough for any old maid!"

JIM [*uneasily*]. Ha-ha! No—I never heard it.

AMANDA. Why, Laura! You look so serious!

JIM. We were having a serious conversation.

AMANDA. Good! Now you're better acquainted?

JIM [*uncertainly*]. Ha-ha! Yes.

AMANDA. You modern young people are much more serious-minded than my generation. I was so gay as a girl!

JIM. You haven't changed, Mrs. Wingfield.

AMANDA. Tonight I'm rejuvenated! The gaiety of the occasion, Mr. O'Connor! [*She tosses her head with a peal of laughter. Spills lemonade.*] Oooo! I'm baptizing myself!

JIM. Here—let me—

AMANDA [*setting the pitcher down*]. There now. I discovered we had some maraschino cherries. I dumped them in, juice and all!

JIM. You shouldn't have gone to that trouble, Mrs. Wingfield.

AMANDA. Trouble, trouble? Why it was loads of fun!

Didn't you hear me cutting up in the kitchen? I bet your ears were burning! I told Tom how outdone with him I was for keeping you to himself so long a time! He should have brought you over much, much sooner! Well, now that you've found your way, I want you to be a very frequent caller! Not just occasional but all the time. Oh, we're going to have a lot of gay times together! I see them coming! Mmm, just breathe that air! So fresh, and the moon's so pretty! I'll skip back out—I know where my place is when young folks are having a —serious conversation!

JIM. Oh, don't go out, Mrs. Wingfield. The fact of the matter is I've got to be going.

AMANDA. Going, now? You're joking! Why, it's only the shank of the evening, Mr. O'Connor!

JIM. Well, you know how it is.

AMANDA. You mean you're a young workingman and have to keep workingmen's hours. We'll let you off early tonight. But only on the condition that next time you stay later. What's the best night for you? Isn't Saturday night the best night for you workingmen?

JIM. I have a couple of time-clocks to punch, Mrs. Wingfield. One at morning, another one at night!

AMANDA. My, but you *are* ambitious! You work at night, too?

JIM. No, Ma'am, not work but—Betty! [*He crosses deliberately to pick up his hat. The band at the Paradise Dance Hall goes into a tender waltz.*]

AMANDA. Betty? Betty? Who's—Betty! [*There is an ominous cracking sound in the sky.*]

JIM. Oh, just a girl. The girl I go steady with! [*He smiles charmingly. The sky falls.*]

[*Legend: "The sky falls."*]

AMANDA [*a long-drawn exhalation*]. Ohhhh . . . Is it a serious romance, Mr. O'Connor?

JIM. We're going to be married the second Sunday in June.

AMANDA. Ohhh—how nice! Tom didn't mention that you were engaged to be married.

JIM. The cat's not out of the bag at the warehouse yet. You know how they are. They call you Romeo and stuff like that. [*He stops at the oval mirror to put on his hat. He carefully shapes the brim and the crown to give a discreetly dashing effect.*] It's been a wonderful evening, Mrs. Wingfield. I guess this is what they mean by Southern hospitality.

AMANDA. It really wasn't anything at all.

JIM. I hope it don't seem like I'm rushing off. But I promised Betty I'd pick her up at the Wabash depot, an' by the time I get my jalopy down there her train'll be in. Some women are pretty upset if you keep 'em waiting.

AMANDA. Yes, I know—The tyranny of women! [*Extends her hand.*] Good-bye, Mr. O'Connor. I wish you luck—and happiness—and success! All three of them, and so does Laura!—Don't you, Laura?

LAURA. Yes!

JIM [*taking her hand*]. Good-bye, Laura. I'm certainly going to treasure that souvenir. And don't you forget the good advice I gave you. [*Raises his voice to a cheery shout.*] So long, Shakespeare! Thanks again, ladies—Good night!

[*He grins and ducks jauntily out.*]

[*Still bravely grimacing, Amanda closes the door on the gentleman caller. Then she turns back to the room with a puzzled expression. She and Laura don't dare to face each other. Laura crouches beside the victrola to wind it.*]

AMANDA [*faintly*]. Things have a way of turning out so badly. I don't believe that I would play the victrola. Well, well—well—Our gentleman caller was engaged to be married! Tom!

TOM [*from back*]. Yes, Mother!

AMANDA. Come in here a minute. I want to tell you something awfully funny.

TOM [*enters with macaroon and a glass of the lemonade*]. Has the gentleman caller gotten away already?

AMANDA. The gentleman caller has made an early departure. What a wonderful joke you played on us!

TOM. How do you mean?

AMANDA. You didn't mention that he was engaged to be married.

TOM. Jim? Engaged?

AMANDA. That's what he just informed us.

TOM. I'll be jiggered! I didn't know about that.

AMANDA. That seems very peculiar.

TOM. What's peculiar about it?

AMANDA. Didn't you call him your best friend down at the warehouse?

TOM. He is, but how did I know?

AMANDA. It seems extremely peculiar that you wouldn't know your best friend was going to be married!

TOM. The warehouse is where I work, not where I know things about people!

AMANDA. You don't know things anywhere! You live

in a dream; you manufacture illusions! [*He crosses to door.*] Where are you going?

TOM. I'm going to the movies.

AMANDA. That's right, now that you've had us make such fools of ourselves. The effort, the preparations, all the expense! The new floor lamp, the rug, the clothes for Laura! All for what? To entertain some other girl's fiancé! Go to the movies, go! Don't think about us, a mother deserted, an unmarried sister who's crippled and has no job! Don't let anything interfere with your selfish pleasure! Just go, go, go—to the movies!

TOM. All right, I will! The more you shout about my selfishness to me the quicker I'll go, and I won't go to the movies!

AMANDA. Go, then! Then go to the moon—you selfish dreamer!

[*Tom smashes his glass on the floor. He plunges out on the fire-escape, slamming the door. Laura screams—cut by door.*]

[*Dance-hall music up. Tom goes to the rail and grips it desperately, lifting his face in the chill white moonlight penetrating the narrow abyss of the alley.*]

[*Legend on screen: "And so good-bye . . ."*]

[*Tom's closing speech is timed with the interior pantomime. The interior scene is played as though viewed through soundproof glass. Amanda appears to be making a comforting speech to Laura who is huddled upon the sofa. Now that we cannot hear the mother's speech, her silliness is gone and she has dignity and tragic beauty. Laura's dark hair hides her face until at the end of the speech she lifts it to smile at her mother. Amanda's gestures are slow and graceful, almost dancelike, as she comforts the daughter. At the end of her speech she glances a moment at the father's picture—then withdraws through the portieres. At close of Tom's speech, Laura blows out the candles, ending the play.*]

TOM. I didn't go to the moon, I went much further—for time is the longest distance between two places—Not long after that I was fired for writing a poem on the lid of a shoe-box. I left Saint Louis. I descended the steps of this fire-escape for a last time and followed, from them on, in my father's footsteps, attempting to find in motion what was lost in space—I traveled around a great deal. The cities swept about me like dead leaves, leaves that were brightly colored but torn away from the branches. I would have stopped, but I was pursued by something. It always came upon me unawares, taking me altogether by surprise. Perhaps it was a familiar bit of music. Perhaps it was only a piece of transparent glass—Perhaps I am walking along a street at night, in some strange city, before I have found companions. I pass the lighted window of a shop where perfume is sold. The window is filled with pieces of colored glass, tiny transparent bottles in delicate colors, like bits of a shattered rainbow. Then all at once my sister touches my shoulder. I turn around and look into her eyes . . . Oh, Laura, Laura, I tried to leave you behind me, but I am more faithful than I intended to be! I reach for a cigarette, I cross the street, I run into the movies or a bar, I buy a drink, I speak to the nearest stranger—anything that can blow your candles out! [*Laura bends over the candles.*] —for nowadays the world is lit by lightning! Blow out your candles, Laura—and so good-bye. . . .

[*She blows the candles out.*]

[*The scene dissolves.*]

ESSAY: AN APPROACH TO THE PLAY

As Tennessee Williams writes in his production notes, *The Glass Menagerie* is an expressionist play and, as such, takes unusual liberties with the conventions of theater and with the normal surface texture of reality in order to portray the psychic reality which underlies them. Most of the play's stage elements—its use of music, of the fourth wall, of the progressive unfolding of a room beyond a room—are used to emphasize the internal worlds of the characters. Even the main action itself occurs within the memory of the narrator, Tom. Within this memory, Amanda is dominated by her own memory of a youth filled with gentlemen callers, a vision which, in turn, forms the code of manners and values which she tries to enforce on her children as present reality. Her memory also blinds her to crucial elements of this present: to Laura's almost literal social paralysis, the reverse of her mother's apparent social confidence, and to the legitimate discontent of her son, Tom. Amanda's blindness crushes her children so that Laura lies huddled on a sofa and Tom replicates his father by running away.

Amanda has taught Laura that her function as a woman is to be in business or to be married, but neither are roles she can fulfill because she has also been taught to believe that she is too fragile. Like the glass figures which she treasures and protects, she is too delicate for normal life, too fragile not to be protected. The glass unicorn in particular becomes an expressionist symbol, one which represents her inner sense of herself. When she gives Jim the broken unicorn, it is herself she gives, but not as her mother would have hoped: she seems to reduce herself to a souvenir.

The character Tom, as he remembers himself in this scene from his own past, also lives in a dream, as Amanda points out, but his is of the future, of adventure. His outlets for this dream in the remembered story are his frequent visits to the movies and his poems, but like his mother's dreams, his threaten the story's present: his movies threaten his mother's dream of the sufficiency of her household; his poetry threatens his warehouse job; his decision to become a merchant seaman has meant letting the electricity be turned off; his desire for adventure threatens Amanda's idea of the American Dream in which men find adventure in their careers.

It is not this desire for adventure, however, that drives the narrator Tom's need to revisit this moment of his past. He is on his adventure already in the present tense of the play as a merchant seaman. Rather, this sequence of events presumably crystallizes something for him; perhaps Williams' stage directions give us a clue as to what that is. They refer to this lower-middle-class society in which the narrator Tom remembers being entrapped, as being "fundamentally enslaved," functioning "as one interfused mass of automatism," full of "desperation." The narrator himself refers to people of this social class as "blind." Perhaps this play represents a memory of the particular style of blindness Tom knew and needed to get out of. Amanda and Laura represent a kind of enslavement born of the blindness of illusion, and it may be that he too feels threatened—or haunted—by these illusions which, though different, condemn each of them to what he sees as their lower-middle-class oblivion.

Jim comes from the outside world. If, as Tom says, he symbolizes "the long delayed but always expected something that we live for," this is ironic for Tom as well as for Laura and Amanda. For Jim is not only the inappropriate gentleman caller; he also undermines the middle-class American Dream in which the high school star believes that hard work and the development of "social poise" lead inevitably to success. After six years, he is a warehouse shipping clerk making $85 a month. If Tom wants to escape the claustrophobic world of his family and class, Jim does not offer a model. It may even be that Jim's belief in the American Dream is what will keep him from climbing out of the middle class. He cannot think beyond being a wage slave in "a dissolving economy."

Tom can. And yet at the end of the play, when the narrator returns us to the present, Tom tells us that although he has run away, he has not escaped the past. His glass menagerie is always with him. This may be another reason for his remembering this episode: it encapsulates what he left, yet what still haunts him. Will he ever be free? At the end of the narrator's final speech, when Laura blows out the candles, are we to understand that she is blowing herself out of his memory? Will this play's particular act of remembering be the final one Tom needs in order to purge his demons? And, we might also ask, what are these demons? Do they represent guilt? Regret at a precious past necessarily left behind? Recognition of his continued enslavement? He sees beyond the illusions of the others, the characters in his memory, but is this enough? Does he know what he wants? How *does* one find a replacement dream? Would the Tom we see in this play be satisfied by a change to a higher social or financial class, or is this belief, too, an illusion?

In the short run, escape may be enough. However, even if Tom's running away is satisfying, we are left with our earlier question unanswered: Why does he need to revisit this series of events? Is it that he cannot run away, no matter how hard he tries, because his "reality" is rooted in his mind? In this view, the dream of escape would be just another illusion.

Eugène Ionesco

JACK OR THE SUBMISSION

Translated by Donald M. Allen

About the Author   Eugène Ionesco (1912–1994) was born in Romania, where he became a teacher of French until 1938 when, under the threat of fascism, he moved to Paris. There, after World War II, he became a leader of the avant garde theater; in 1950 his first series of plays, including the one reprinted here, opened a decade of absurdist theater. As applied to his fifteen plays, as well as to those of Samuel Beckett and others, the word "absurd" is not given its conventional meaning. Rather, these plays take an unusual form in order to adopt an *un*conventional philosophical and dramatic perspective toward the world, often parodying conventional plays in the process. In Ionesco's hands particularly, the "absurd" became a new genre. Indeed, he might be said to be the quintessential absurdist playwright, and in *Jack or the Submission* (1950) the qualities of this genre are apparent.

About the Play   *Jack* is simultaneously a parody of and a deliberate criticism of conventional drama. It is a play without characters and events with which the audience can identify: it is impossible to get caught up in the story, in "what happens"; not only do we not much care what happens, we also cannot *understand* what happens. And yet Ionesco subtitles this play "a naturalistic comedy," knowing full well that the term "naturalistic" normally implies an imitation of real life. Perhaps he is suggesting that the characters and action are "true to life" below the surface, at a subterranean level: mothers really do sometimes love their sons in more than maternal ways, and the forms of this love can be sadistic as well as tender. Fathers really do sometimes see their sons as continuers of their male line of descendants, a line which stretches to ancestors in time past, and they do bestow honor on their sons for signs of their fitting into that line, even though these signs may be incomprehensible to the sons themselves. In this way, "reality" often contradicts itself: people speak and act in ways that are conventionally approved but have feelings, fantasies, aspirations which may be quite different, even contradictory to what one is allowed to say. Much of the apparently nonsensical and unrealistic dialogue of this play may be seen as giving expression to all these levels, the normally unspoken as well as the normally spoken, the conscious as well as the unconscious, as if they were all equally on the surface. Thus Mother Jack says to son Jack in her opening speech, "you don't love your parents any more," nor "your clothes, your sister, your grandparents!!!" as if all these items were of equal importance.

By presenting a fuller version of "reality" than is normal, and by putting all its levels on the surface, Ionesco forces us to focus on and think about the elemental issues which underlie our normal version of both reality and theater. He deliberately frustrates our expectation that in the theater we will identify with a character and get caught up in the story. His purpose— to get us to rethink our basic beliefs—is not served by the conventions of normal theater, the concept of drama as an imitation of life. For regardless of how revolutionary an author's ideas, if they are expressed in conventional terms, they will encourage us to believe that we can understand life, that it can be interpreted within our familiar forms of expression. Our normal beliefs about the nature of human life will remain unshaken. Ionesco writes elsewhere that he wants to cut through the conventional "thinking" issues of the theater and to make us realize that if all these issues were solved—poverty, for example, or class or gender relations—we would still be left with the more elemental (and disturbing) questions: Why are we here? What is our function in this life we lead? What is the essential nature of this life? Of ourselves?

His theater therefore defamiliarizes everything about the stage, as well as about "normal" life, that we might usually cling to as comfortably familiar. The lack of coherence in plot and characer, the play's deliberate self-contradictions, inconsistencies, and apparently meaningless occurrences—all are designed to raise our anxiety. He creates a conventional social situation in which many small sequences of conversation seem recognizably typical. Yet they are so wrenched out of their normal context that they make no sense. The familiar is defamiliarized, and the intensity of this defamiliarization gradually increases into an absurdity which retains alarming similarities to the familiar. We are displaced into a reevaluation of the "normal."

CHARACTERS

JACK
JACQUELINE, his sister
FATHER JACK
MOTHER JACK
GRANDFATHER JACK

GRANDMOTHER JACK
ROBERTA I ⎫ These two roles must be
ROBERTA II ⎭ played by the same actress
FATHER ROBERT
MOTHER ROBERT

SCENE

Somber decor, in gray monochrome. A messy room. There is a narrow door, not very high, upstage right. Upstage center, a window with soiled curtains, through which comes a pale, colorless light. On the wall hangs a picture that doesn't represent anything; a dirty, old, worn armchair is at stage center with a bedside table; and there are some indefinite objects, strange yet banal, such as old slippers; in a corner perhaps there is a collapsed sofa; and there are some rickety chairs.

When the curtain rises we see Jack sprawled on the equally sprawled armchair, wearing a cap, and clothes that are too small for him; he wears a sullen, ill-natured expression. Around him his parents are standing, or perhaps they are seated too. Their clothes are shabby.

The somber decor of the beginning becomes transformed by the lighting during the seduction scene, when it grows greenish, aquatic, towards the end of that scene; then it darkens again at the end of the play.

All of the characters, except Jack, could wear masks.

MOTHER JACK [weeping]. My son, my child, after all that we have done for you. After all our sacrifices! Never would I have believed you capable of this.

You were my greatest hope . . . You still are, for I cannot believe, no I cannot believe, by Jove, that you will go on being so stubborn! Then, you don't love your parents any more, you don't love your clothes, your sister, your grandparents!!! But remember, my son, remember that I gave you suck at the bottle, I let your diapers dry on you, like your sister too . . . [To Jacqueline.] Isn't that right, my daughter?

JACQUELINE. Yes, mom, that's true. Oh, after so many sacrifices, and so much finagling!

MOTHER JACK. You see . . . you see? It was I, my son, who gave you your first spankings, not your father, standing here, who could have done it better than I, for he is stronger, no, it was I, for I loved you too much. And it was I, too, who sent you from table without dessert, who kissed you, cared for you, housebroke you, taught you to progress, to transgress, to roll your r's, who left goodies for you in your socks. I taught you to climb stairs, when there were any, to rub your knees with nettles, when you wanted to be stung. I have been more than a mother to you, I've been a true sweetheart, a husband, a sailor, a buddy, a goose. I've never been deterred by any obstacle, any barricade, from satisfying all your childish whims. Oh, ungrateful son, you do not even remember how I held you on my knees and pulled out your cute little baby teeth, and tore off your toe nails so as to make you bawl like an adorable little calf.

JACQUELINE. Oh! Calves are so sweet! Moo! Moo! Moo!

MOTHER JACK. And to think you won't say a word, stubborn boy! You refuse to listen to a word I say.

JACQUELINE. He's plugged up his ears, he's wearing a disgusting look.

MOTHER JACK. I am a wretched mother. I've brought a mononster into the world; a mononster, that's what you are! Here is your grandmother, who wants to speak to you. She's tottering. She is octogeneric. Perhaps you'll be swayed by her, by her age, her past, her future.

GRANDMOTHER JACK [octogeneric voice]. Listen, listen well to me, I've had experience, there's a lot of it behind me. I, too, like you, had a great-uncle who had three addresses: he gave out the address and telephone number of two of them but never that of the third where he sometimes hid out, for he was in the secret service. [Jack obstinately remains silent.] No, I've not been able to convince him. Oh! poor us!

JACQUELINE. And here is your grandfather who would like to speak to you. Alas, he cannot. He is much too old. He is centagenet!

MOTHER JACK [weeping]. Like the Plantagenets!

FATHER JACK. He's deaf and dumb. He is tottering.

JACQUELINE. He can only toot.

GRANDFATHER JACK [in the voice of a centagenet]. Hum! Hum! Heu! Heu! Hum! [Hoarse but loud.]

> A char-ar-ming tipster
> Sang plain-ain-tive-ly-ie . . .
> I'm only eigh-eigh-tee-een
> And mor-ore's the pi-i-ty-y.

[Jack remains obstinately silent.]

FATHER JACK. It's all useless, he won't budge.

JACQUELINE. My dear brother . . . you're a naughty boyble. In spite of all the immense love I have for you, which swells my heart to the breaking point, I detest you, I exceecrate you. You're making our mamma weep, you're unstringing our father with his big ugly police inspector's mustaches, and his sweet big hairy foot full of horns. As for your grandparents, look at what you've done to them. You've not been well brought up. I'm going to punish you. Never again will I bring over my little playmates so that you can watch them make peepee. I thought you had better manners than that. Comes on, don't make our mamma weep, don't make our papa angry. Don't make grandmother and grandfather blush with shame.

FATHER JACK. You are no son of mine. I disown you. You're not worthy of my ancestors. You resemble your mother and the idiots and imbeciles in her family. This doesn't matter to her for she's only a woman, and what a woman! In short, I needn't elegize her here. I have only this to say to you: impeccably brought up, like an aristocrant, in a family of veritable leeches, of authentic torpedoes, with all the regard due to your rank, to your sex, to the talent that you possess, to the hot blood that can express—if you only wanted it to, all this that your blood itself could but suggest with imperfect words—you, in spite of all this, you show yourself unworthy, at one and the same time of your ancestors, of my ancestors, who disown you for the same reason that I do, and of your descendants who certainly will never see the light of day for they'll prefer to let themselves be killed before they ever come into being. Murderer! Patricide! You have nothing more to envy me for. When I think that I had the unfortunate idea of wishing for a son and not a red poppy! [To Mother Jack.] This is all your fault!

MOTHER JACK. Alas! My husband! I believed I was doing the right thing! I'm completely half desperate.

JACQUELINE. Ploor mamma!

FATHER JACK. This boy or this toy that you see there, who has come into the world in order to be our shame, this son or this hun, is another one of your stupid female tricks.

MOTHER JACK. Alack and alas! [To her son.] You see, because of you I suffer all this from your father who no longer minces his feelings and now abuses me.

JACQUELINE [to her brother]. Go on, tell it to the turkies.

FATHER JACK. Useless to linger longer crying over a destiny irrevocably spilt. I'll remain here no more. I want to remain worthy of my bearfors. The whole tradition, all of it, remains with me. I'm blowing this joint. Frew it!

MOTHER JACK. Oh! Oh! Oh! don't go away. [To her son.] You see, because of you, your father is leaving us.

JACQUELINE [sighing]. Kangareen!

GRANDFATHER JACK [singing]. A . . . charm . . . ing . . . tip . . . ster . . . sang . . . mur-mur . . . ing.

GRANDMOTHER JACK [to the old man]. Be quiet. Be quiet or I'll smack you.

[She hits him on the head with her fist, and smashes in his cap.]

FATHER JACK. Once and for all, I'm leaving this room to its own destiny. There's nothing else to do, anyway. I'm going to my bedroom next door. I'll pack my bags and you'll never see me again except at mealtimes and sometimes during the day and in the night to get a bite to eat. [*To Jack.*] And you'll pay me back for your nastiness. And to think it was all to make Jupiter jubilate!

JACQUELINE. Oh, Father, this is the obnubilation of puberty.

FATHER JACK. That's enough! Useless. [*He goes to the door.*] Farewell, Son of a pig in a poke, farewell, Wife, farewell, Brother, farewell, Sister of your brother.

[*He exits with a violently resolute step.*]

JACQUELINE [*bitterly*]. Of a pig in a poke! [*To her brother.*] How can you tolerate that? He's insulting her and insulting himself. And vice versa.

MOTHER JACK [*to her son*]. You see, you see, you are disowned, wretch. He'll will you the whole inheritance, but he can't, thank heaven!

JACQUELINE [*to her brother*]. It's the first time, if not the last, that he has made such a scene with mamma, and I have no idea how we're going to get out of it.

MOTHER JACK. Son! Son! Listen to me. I beg you, do not reply to my brave mother's heart, but speak to me, without reflecting on what you say. It is the best way to think correctly, as an intellectual and as a good son. [*She waits in vain for a reply; Jack obstinately remains silent.*] But you are not a good son. Come, Jacqueline, you alone have sense enough to come in out of the rain.

JACQUELINE. Oh! Mother, all roads lead to Rome.

MOTHER JACK. Let's leave your brother to his slow consumption.

JACQUELINE. Or rather to his consumbrition!

MOTHER JACK [*She starts to go, weeping, pulling her daughter by the hand, who goes unwillingly, turning her head back towards her brother. At the door Mother Jack pronounces this henceforth historic sentence*]. We'll hear about you in the newspapers, actograph!

JACQUELINE. Pawnbroker!

[*They exit together, followed by the Grandfather and the Grandmother, but they go no further than the embrasure of the door where they remain to spy, visible to the audience.*]

GRANDMOTHER JACK. Keep a watch . . . on his telephone, that's all I can tell you.

GRANDFATHER JACK [*singing waveringly*].

> Fi-i-il-thy but honest . . .
> The tip-ip-ster sang . . . [*He exits.*]

JACK [*alone, he remains silent a long moment, absorbed in

his thoughts, then gravely*]. Let's pretend that I've said nothing, and anyway, what do they want of me?

[*Silence. At the end of a long moment, Jacqueline re-enters. She goes towards her brother with an air of profound conviction; she goes up to him, stares him straight in the eye, and says.*]

JACQUELINE. Listen to me, my dear brother, dear colleague, and dear compatriot, I am going to speak to you as between the two candid eyes of brother and sister. I come to you one last time, which will certainly not be the last, but what'll you have, so much the worse. You do not understand that I have been sent to you, like a letter through the mails, stamped, stamped, by my aerial voices, bloody bad.

[*Jack remains somber.*]

JACK. Alas, blood will tell!

JACQUELINE [*she's got it*]. Ah, at last! There you've blurted out the key word!

JACK [*desperate, with a most woebegone expression*]. Show me that you are a sister worthy of a brother such as I.

JACQUELINE. Far be it from me to be guilty of such a fault. I'm going to teach you one thing. I'm not an abracante, he's not an abracante, she is not an abracante, nor are you an abracante.

JACK. So?

JACQUELINE. You don't understand me because you don't follow me. It's very simple.

JACK. That's what you think! For sisters like you hours don't count, but what a waste of time!

JACQUELINE. That's not the point. None of that has anything to do with me. But History has her eyes on us.

JACK. Oh words, what crimes are committed in your name!

JACQUELINE. I'm going to tell you the whole thing in twenty-seven words. Here it is, and try to remember it: You are chronometrable.

JACK. And the rest?

JACQUELINE. That's all. The twenty-seven words are contained in those three words, according to their gender.

JACK. Chro-no-me-trable! [*Frightened, an anguished cry.*] But, it's not possible! It's not possible!

[*He gets up, walks feverishly from one end of the stage to the other.*]

JACQUELINE. Oh yes, it is. You've got to figure it out.

JACK. Chronometrable! Chronometrable! Me? [*He calms down little by little, sits down, reflects at length, sprawled out in the armchair.*] This is not possible and if it is possible, it's frightful. But, then, I must. Cruel indecision! There's no legal protection. Hideous, frightful! All law becomes self-destroying when it's not defended.

[*Jacqueline, smiling with a triumphant air, leaves him to his agitation; she exits on tiptoe.*]

MOTHER JACK [*at the door, in a low voice*]. Did the system work?

JACQUELINE [*a finger to her lips*]. Shh! My dear mamma! We must wait, wait for the result of the operation.

[*They exit. Jack is agitated, he is about to make a decision.*]

JACK. Let's abide by the circumstances, the conclusions oblige me. It's tough, but it's the game of the rule. It applies in such cases. [*Mute debate with his conscience. Occasionally, from time to time, he mutters: "Chro-nome-trable, chr-no-me-trable?" Then, finally, worn out, in a loud voice.*] Oh well, yes, yes, na, I adore hashed brown potatoes!

[*Mother Jack and Jacqueline, who have been spying on him and only waiting for this, enter quickly, exultantly, followed by the Grandparents.*]

MOTHER JACK. Oh, my son, you are truly my son!

JACQUELINE [*to her mother*]. I told you that my idea would get him on his feet again.

GRANDMOTHER JACK. I certainly told you that to make carrots boil you have to . . .

MOTHER JACK [*to her daughter*]. Go on, little vixen. [*She embraces her son, who lets her do so without showing any sign of pleasure.*] My boy! It's really true, you really love hashed brown potatoes? You make me so happy.

JACK [*without conviction*]. Yes, I like them, I adore them!

MOTHER JACK. I'm happy, I'm proud of you! Say it again, my little Jack, say it again, let me hear it.

JACK [*like an automaton*]. I adore hashed brown potatoes! I adore hashed brown potatoes! I adore hashed brown potatoes!

JACQUELINE [*to her mother*]. Oh, you're the clever one! Don't abuse your child if you'd be a truly motherly mother. Oh, that's making Grandfather sing.

GRANDFATHER JACK [*singing*].

A char-mar-mink tip-ip-ster
was singing a song
melan-cho-li-ly and so-o-omber
full of joy and li-i-ight . . .
Let . . . the . . little . . . children
amu-mu-se themselves without gi-i-iggling
They'll . . . have plenty of time
to ru . . . ru . . . run
after the girls-girls-irls!

MOTHER JACK [*towards the door*]. Gaston, come here! Your son, your son adores hashed brown potatoes!

JACQUELINE [*same*]. Come, Papa, he's just said that he adores hashed brown potatoes!

FATHER JACK [*entering, severe*]. Is this really true?

MOTHER JACK [*to her son*]. Tell your father, my little Jackie, what you just told your sister, and what you told your darling mother all overcome with motherly feelings that shake her with delight.

JACK. I love hashed brown potatoes!

JACQUELINE. You adore them!

FATHER JACK. What?

MOTHER JACK. Speak, my darling.

JACK. Hashed brown potatoes. I adore hashed brown potatoes.

FATHER JACK [*aside*]. Can it be that all is not lost? That would be too wonderful, but not a moment too soon. [*To his wife and daughter.*] The whole she-bang?

JACQUELINE. Oh, yes, Papa, didn't you hear?

MOTHER JACK. Have confidence in your son . . . your son of sons.

GRANDMOTHER JACK. The son of my son is my son . . . and my son is your son. There is no other son.

FATHER JACK [*to his son*]. My son, solemnly, come to my arms. [*He does not embrace him.*] That's enough. I take back my renunciation. I am happy that you adore hashed brown potatoes. I reintegrate you with your ancestors. With tradition. With hashing. With everything. [*To Jacqueline.*] But he must still believe in regional aspirations.

GRANDMOTHER JACK. That's important too!

JACQUELINE. That will come, Papa, have patience, don't worry, Papa!

GRANDFATHER JACK. The char-ar-arming tip-ip-ster!

GRANDMOTHER JACK [*hitting the old man on the head*]. Crap!!!

FATHER JACK. I pardon you then. I overlook, and involuntarily moreover, all your youthful faults as well as mine, and naturally I am going to let you in on the profits of our familial and national endeavors.

MOTHER JACK. How good you are.

JACQUELINE. Oh, indigent Father!

FATHER JACK. Listen, I'm thinking it over. [*To his son.*] You will percuss. So keep at it.

JACK [*in a smothered voice*]. I adore potatoes!

JACQUELINE. Let's not waste time.

MOTHER JACK [*to her husband*]. Gaston, if that's the case, if things are that way, we could marry him off. We were only waiting for him to make honorable amends, and two would have been better than one, and he has done it. Jack, all is under control, the plan foreseen at the beginning is already realized, the engagement is completely prepared, your fiancée is here. And her parents, too. Jack, you may remain seated. Your resigned air satisfies me. But be polished to your fingernails . .

JACK. Ouf! Yes.

FATHER JACK [*striking his hands together*]. Let the fiancée enter then!

JACK. Oh! That's the agreed-on signal!

[*Enter Roberta, the fiancée, Father Robert, and Mother Robert. Father Robert enters first, big, fat, majestic, then Mother Robert, a round ball, very heavy; then the parents separate in order to let Roberta herself enter, advancing between her father and mother. She is wearing a wedding gown; her white veil conceals her face; her entrance must make a sensation. Mother Jack joyously crosses her hands on her breast; in ecstasy, she lifts her hands to heaven, then goes up to Roberta, looks at her up close, touches her, at first timidly, then paws her vigorously and finally sniffs her. Roberta's parents encourage her with friendly and eager gestures; the Grandmother also must smell the fiancée, and the Grandfather should too, while singing, "Too-oo old! . . . Char-ar-mi-ing tip-in-ipster " Father Jack does the same. Jacqueline, at the entrance of Roberta, gaily claps her hands and shouts out.*]

JACQUELINE. The future is ours!

[*Then, approaching Roberta, she lifts up her dress, screams in her ear, and, finally, smells her. The behavior of Father Jack is more dignified and restrained; he continues to exchange naughty glances and gestures with Father Robert. As for Mother Robert, at the end of the scene she finds herself immobile downstage to the left, a large smug smile on her face. The old Grandfather makes ribald, indecent gestures, wanting to do more but prevented by the old Grandmother, who says.*]

GRANDMOTHER JACK. Come . . . on . . . no . . . but . . . come . . . on . . . you're making me . . . jea . . . lous!

[*While the others are sniffing Roberta, Jack alone seems to be unimpressed; he remains seated, impassive; he snaps out a single word of scorn, aside.*]

JACK. Hill billy!

[*Mother Robert, during this appreciation, appears to be slightly intrigued, but this is only a very fugitive restlessness, and she goes back to smiling again. She makes a sign to Roberta that she should approach Jack, but Roberta is timid, and advances downstage only when led, almost dragged, by Father Robert and pushed by Mother Jack and Jacqueline. Jack makes no movement, his face remains blank.*]

FATHER JACK [*noticing that something isn't right, he remains in the background for a moment, hands on hips, murmuring*]. At least I won't be caught with my pants down.

[*Near to Jack, Father Robert catalogs his daughter, assisted by Jacqueline, Mother Jack, Mother Robert, and the Grandparents.*]

FATHER JACK. She's got feet. They're truffled.

[*Jacqueline lifts up the fiancée's dress to convince Jack.*]

JACK [*lightly raising his shoulder*]. That's natural!

JACQUELINE. And they're for walking.

MOTHER JACK. For walking!

GRANDMOTHER JACK. Why yes, the better to twickle you.

MOTHER ROBERT [*to her daughter*]. Let's see, prove it.

[*Roberta walks with her feet.*]

FATHER ROBERT. And she's got a hand!

MOTHER ROBERT. Show it.

[*Roberta shows a hand to Jack, almost sticking her fingers into his eyes.*]

GRANDMOTHER JACK [*nobody listens to her*]. Do you want a piece of advice?

JACQUELINE. For scouring pots and pans . . .

JACK. Sure enough! Sure enough! But I suspected as much.

FATHER ROBERT. And toes.

JACQUELINE. To stub! . . .

MOTHER JACK. But yes, my child!

FATHER ROBERT. And she's got armpits!

JACQUELINE. For turnspits.

GRANDMOTHER JACK [*nobody listens to her*]. Do you want a piece of advice?

MOTHER ROBERT. And what calves! true calves!

GRANDMOTHER JACK. Ah yes, like in my time!

JACK [*uninterested*]. Melanchton did better!

GRANDFATHER JACK [*singing*]. A char . . . ar . . . ming tip-ip . . . ip . . . ster . . .

GRANDMOTHER JACK [*to the old man*]. Come on, make love to me, you're my husband!

FATHER JACK. Listen carefully to me, my son. I hope that you have understood.

JACK [*resigned, acquiescent*]. Oh yes, of course . . . I was forgetting . . .

FATHER ROBERT. She's got hips . . .

MOTHER JACK. All the better to eat you, my child!

FATHER ROBERT. And then she's got green pimples on her beige skin, red breasts on a mauve background, an illuminated navel, a tongue the color of tomato sauce, pan-browned square shoulders, and all the meat needed to merit the highest commendation. What more do you need?

GRANDFATHER JACK [*singing*]. A char . . . ar . . . ming tip . . . ip . . . ster!

JACQUELINE [*shaking her head, lifting her arms, and letting them fall*]. Ah, what a brother I'm stuck with!

MOTHER JACK. He's always been difficult. I had a hard time bringing him up. All he liked was hahaha.

MOTHER ROBERT. But my dear, that's incomprehensible, it's incredible! I'd never have thought that! If I'd known this in time, I'd have taken precautions . . .

FATHER ROBERT [*proud, a little wounded*]. She's our only daughter.

GRANDFATHER JACK [*singing*]. A char . . . ar . . .ming . . . tip . . . ip . . . ster!

MOTHER JACK. This distresses me!

FATHER JACK. Jack, this is my last warning!

GRANDMOTHER JACK. Do you want a piece of advice?

JACK. Good. Then we agree! That'll go with the potatoes. [*General relief, effervescence, congratulations.*]

JACQUELINE. His honorable sentiments always end up by getting the upper hand. [*She smiles at Jack.*]

FATHER JACK. Now it's my turn to ask a simple question. Don't take it badly.

FATHER ROBERT. Oh no, it's different. Go ahead.

FATHER JACK. One single uncertainty: are there trunks?

GRANDFATHER JACK [*ribaldly*]. Hi . . . hii . . .

MOTHER ROBERT. Ah that . . .

MOTHER JACK. Perhaps that's asking too much.

FATHER ROBERT. I believe . . . heu . . . yes . . . they must be there . . . but I wouldn't know how to tell you . . .

FATHER JACK. And where then?

JACQUELINE. But Papa, don't you see, in the trunks, Papa, really!

FATHER JACK. Perfect. That's perfect. Completely satisfied. Agreed.

GRANDMOTHER JACK. Would you like a piece of advice?

MOTHER ROBERT. Ah . . . happily!

FATHER ROBERT. I knew that everything would be all right!

GRANDFATHER JACK [*singing*].

A . . . char . . . arming . . . tipster . . .
In the streets of Paris . . . [*He waltzes.*]

MOTHER JACK. In short, you'll have nothing to fear, the fit's in the fire.

FATHER JACK [*to his son*]. Good! It's a bargain. Your heart has chosen in spite of yourself!

MOTHER JACK. The word "heart" always makes me weep.

MOTHER ROBERT. Me too, it melts me.

FATHER ROBERT. It melts me in one eye, it makes me cry in the other two.

FATHER JACK. That's the truth!

JACQUELINE. Oh, there's no need to be astonished. All parents feel that way. It's a sort of sensitivity, in the true sense of the word.

FATHER JACK. That's our business!

JACQUELINE. Don't be angry, Papa. I said it without thinking. But knowingly.

GRANDMOTHER JACK. Do you want a piece of advice?

FATHER JACK. Oh, my daughter always knows how to arrange things! Besides, that's her specialty.

MOTHER ROBERT. What is her specialty?

MOTHER JACK. She doesn't have one, dear!

FATHER ROBERT. That's very natural.

FATHER JACK. Oh, it's not so natural as all that. But she's passing through a phase. [*Changing his tone.*] Finally, in short. Let's place the fiancés face to face. And let's see the face of the young bride. [*To Father and Mother Robert.*] This is only a simple formality.

FATHER ROBERT. Of course, it's normal, go ahead.

MOTHER ROBERT. We were going to suggest it to you.

GRANDMOTHER JACK [*annoyed*]. Do you want a piece of advice! . . . Well, crap!

JACQUELINE. Come on, then, the face of the bride!

[*Father Robert lifts up the white veil which hides Roberta's face. She is revealed all smiles and with two noses; murmurs of admiration, except from Jack.*]

JACQUELINE. Oh! Ravishing!

MOTHER ROBERT. What do you have to say?

FATHER JACK. Ah, if I were twenty years younger!

GRANDFATHER JACK. And me . . . ah . . . euh . . . and me!

FATHER ROBERT. Ha, ah, twenty years to the day! . . . To the window fastener!

FATHER JACK. As much as possible!

MOTHER JACK. You must be proud of her. You really are lucky. My daughter has only one!

JACQUELINE. Don't get upset, Mamma.

FATHER JACK [to Jacqueline]. It's your mother's fault.

MOTHER JACK. Oh, Gaston, you're always nagging.

JACQUELINE. This is not the time, Papa, on such a red-letter day!

FATHER ROBERT [to Jack]. You've got nothing to say? Kiss her!

GRANDMOTHER JACK. Ah, my little children . . . Would you like a piece of advice? . . . oh . . . crap!

MOTHER ROBERT. This is going to be charming! Oh, my children!

MOTHER JACK [to Jack]. You are happy, aren't you?

FATHER JACK [to Jack]. Well, then, you are a man. My expenses will be reimbursed.

MOTHER ROBERT. Come on, my son-in-law.

JACQUELINE. Come on, my brother, my sister.

FATHER ROBERT. You will get along well together, the two of you.

MOTHER JACK [to Gaston]. Oh, they are truly made for each other, and all the rest that people say on such occasions!

FATHER ROBERT, MOTHER ROBERT, FATHER AND MOTHER JACK, AND JACQUELINE. Oh! My children!

[They applaud enthusiastically.]

GRANDFATHER JACK. A char . . . ar . . . ming . . . tipipster!

JACK. No! no! She hasn't got enough! What I want is one with three noses. I tell you: three noses, at least!

[General stupefaction, consternation.]

MOTHER JACK. Oh! Isn't he naughty!

JACQUELINE [she consoles her mother, all the time speaking to her brother.] Aren't you forgetting all the handkerchiefs she'd need in the winter?

JACK. That's the least of my worries. Moreover, they would be included in the dowry.

[During this scene, Roberta doesn't understand what's going on. The Grandparents remain outside the action. From time to time, the old man wants to sing; the old lady wants to give her advice. Between times, they dance, vaguely miming the action.]

FATHER JACK. I'm going to pack my bag! I'm going to pack my bag! [To his son.] Your finer feelings are not getting the upper hand! Insensate! Listen carefully to me: truth has only two sides, but it's the third side that's best! You can take my word for it! On the other hand, I expected this.

MOTHER ROBERT. It's annoying . . . it's annoying . . . but not terribly . . . if it's only that, everything can still be arranged!

FATHER ROBERT [jovial]. This is nothing, there's nothing wrong, ladies and gentlemen. [He slaps Jack on the shoulder; Jack still sits stiffly.] We've foreseen this incident. We have at your disposal a second only daughter. And she, she's completely equipped with three noses.

MOTHER ROBERT. She's trinary. In everything, moreover. And for everything.

MOTHER JACK. Oh! What a relief! . . . The important thing is the children's future . . . Hurrah, do you hear, Jack?

JACQUELINE. Do you hear, sweetheart?

FATHER JACK. Let's try again. But I don't have much faith in it anymore. However, if you insist on it . . .

[He throws angry looks at his son.]

MOTHER JACK. Oh, Gaston, don't say that. I'm full of hope. Everything will work out.

FATHER ROBERT. Don't be afraid. You'll see. [He takes Roberta by the hand, turns her head, and leads her to the door.] You'll see.

ROBERTA I. Goodbye, everybody. [She curtsies.]

[Father Jack is dissatisfied; Mother Jack is disturbed but hopeful, she looks towards her son; Jacqueline is severe and looks at her brother with a disapproving air. Mother Robert is smiling.]

MOTHER JACK. How sweet she is, nevertheless!

MOTHER ROBERT. That doesn't matter, I tell you. You're going to see the other one now, and you won't have anything to complain about either.

JACK. One with three noses! At least one with three noses! Anyway, it's not so hard as all that.

JACQUELINE. A lily is not a tiger . . . that says it all.

[Father Robert re-enters, holding by the hand Roberta II, who *is dressed the same—after all the role is being played by the same actress; her face with three noses is revealed.*]

JACQUELINE. Thrilling! Oh, Brother, this time you can't hold out for any more.

MOTHER JACK. Oh, my child! my children! [*To Mother Robert.*] You must be darned proud of her!

MOTHER ROBERT. Somewhat, a lot, quite a bit . . . you bet!

FATHER ROBERT [*approaching Jack, holding his daughter by the hand*]. Now, my friend, you're in luck. To the bottle! Your desire has been specifically gratified. Here she is, here she is, your three-nosed fiancée!

MOTHER ROBERT. Here she is, your three-nosed fiancée.

JACQUELINE. So here she is, here she is then . . .

MOTHER JACK. My darling, you see her, she is yours, your little three-nosed bride, just as you wanted her!

FATHER JACK. What's that? You don't speak? You don't see her then? Here she is, here's the three-nosed girl for your special tastes.

JACK. No, I don't want her. She's not homely enough! She's even passable. There are others that are homelier. I want a much homelier one.

JACQUELINE. Well, now, what do you want!

FATHER ROBERT. This is too much. This is intolerable. It's inadmissible.

MOTHER ROBERT [*to Father Robert*]. You're not going to let people ridicule your daughter, your wife and yourself. Yes, we've been lured into this trap only to be ridiculed!

MOTHER JACK [*sobbing*]. Ah! ah! my God! Jack, Gaston, Jack, wicked son! If I had known I'd have strangled you in your last cradle, yes, with my maternal hands. Or I'd have aborted you! Or not have conceived you! I, I, who was so happy when I was pregnant with you . . . with a boy . . . I showed your photo to everybody, to the neighbors, to the cops! . . . Ah! ah! I am an unfortunate mother . . .

JACQUELINE. Mamma! Mamma!

[*The Grandmother gives her bit of advice, the Grandfather begins a song.*]

FATHER ROBERT. You can't get out of it that way. Ah, this can't go on like this!

MOTHER ROBERT. Don't do anything rash!

FATHER ROBERT. I demand reparations, excuses, explanations, and a total cleansing of this stain on our honor which, however, will never be completely erased! . . . at least concurrently . . .

MOTHER JACK. Ah! ah! ah! That word "concurrently" has always made me groan for it evokes concurrence!

JACQUELINE. Mamma, Mamma, don't task your brain! It isn't worth the bubble!

FATHER JACK. What do you expect me to do! Destiny has willed it. [*To his son.*] There's no word for your attitude; henceforth, you will have no need for respect. Don't count on it anymore!

MOTHER JACK. Ah! ah! ah!

JACQUELINE. Mamma, Mamma, my sweet potato Mamma!

JACK. She's not homely enough!

MOTHER ROBERT. What an insolent boy! [*To Mother Jack.*] It's shameful, madam.

JACQUELINE [*to Mother Robert*]. Leave her be! She's going to be sick.

FATHER ROBERT [*to Jack*]. Well then, my dear fellow, what do you want! My daughter, my daughter's not homely enough?

MOTHER ROBERT [*to Jacqueline*]. I don't give a damn if she is sick, your mammery! So much the butter.

FATHER ROBERT [*to Jack*]. Not homely enough! Not ugly enough! Have you really looked at her, have you eyes?

JACK. But I tell you that I don't find her ugly enough.

FATHER JACK [*to his son*]. You don't even know what you're saying!

MOTHER JACK. Ah! ah! ah!

FATHER ROBERT. Not homely enough. My daughter, my daughter to whom I have given so complicated an education? I can't get over it! It's too much!

JACQUELINE [*to her mother*]. Don't faint just yet! Wait for the end of the scene!

MOTHER ROBERT. We must assert our rights! You must demand reparations!

MOTHER JACK [*to Jacqueline*]. The end of the scream?

JACQUELINE [*to Mother Jack*]. No . . . the scene, of this scene . . .

FATHER JACK. That's all right! It's no one's fault! Nobody's to blame.

MOTHER ROBERT. It's the fault of all of you! You pack of hounds! Low scoundrels! Devils! Huns!

MOTHER JACK. Oh! Oh! Is this going to last much longer?

JACQUELINE. I don't think so.

MOTHER JACK. Oh! Oh! Oh!

JACK. But what do you want me to do, she's not homely enough. That's the way it is and that's all there is to it.

MOTHER JACK. He goes on insulting us, this puppy!

FATHER JACK. He doesn't know a thing about women!

FATHER ROBERT [to Jack]. There's no point in putting on that photogenic little pose. You're not any smarter than we are.

JACK. She's not ugly! She's not ugly! She wouldn't even sour milk . . . she's almost pretty . . .

MOTHER ROBERT. Have you any milk here so that we can see?

FATHER ROBERT. He doesn't want to, he's bluffing He knows that milk would sour. This just doesn't suit his convenience, the little prick! It's not going to work that way. I'm going to . . .

[Intervention of the Grandparents: advice, song.]

MOTHER ROBERT [to her husband]. No, I beg of you, Robert-Cornelius, none of that here, no blood between your hands, don't be so assassinous, we'll appeal directly to the law . . . in the palace of justice! . . . with all our plates.

FATHER JACK [in a terrifying voice]. I wash my hands of this! [To Jack.] I dishonor you forever, just like when you were two years old! [To everyone.] And you too, I dishonor you all!

JACK. Good. So much the better. This will be over all the faster.

[Father Jack moves towards his son. A very charged moment of silence, interrupted by:]

MOTHER JACK. Oh! Oh! Oh! . . . Poo-poo-poo-poo! [She faints.]

JACQUELINE. Mamma! Mamma! [Again a tense silence.]

FATHER JACK [to his son]. Then you've lied to us. I suspected it. I'm nobody's fool. Do you want me to tell you the truth?

JACK. Yes, for it comes from the mouths of little children.

FATHER JACK [to his son]. You've lied to us just now . . .

JACQUELINE [near her mother]. Mamma . . . Ma . . .

[She stops and turns her head, like all the other actors, towards the two Jacks. Mother Jack returns to consciousness in order to hear the grave words which Father Jack utters.]

FATHER JACK [to his son]. . . . When you declared to us, on your honor, that you adored hashed brown potatoes. Yes, you ignobly lied, lied, lied! Like alkali! This was nothing but a mean trick unworthy

of the respect that we all have borne you in this house with its noble traditions, since your infancy. The reality is really this: You don't love hashed brown potatoes, you've never loved them. You will never love them!!!

[Stupefaction, awed horror, silent contemplation. Advice from the Grandmother, song from the Grandfather.]

JACK. I exceecrate them.

FATHER ROBERT. What cynicism!

JACQUELINE. Alas! So far gone. My big brother!

MOTHER ROBERT. The unnatural son of an unfortunate mother and father!

MOTHER JACK. Ooooooh!

FATHER JACK. Let this serve as a revelation to us.

JACK. Whether this serves you as a revelation or not . . . and if it could serve you as a revelation: so much the better for you. There's nothing I can do about it, I was born like this . . . I've done all that was in my power! [Pause.] I am what I am.

MOTHER ROBERT [whispering]. What an unfeeling heart! Not a nerve twitches in his face . . .

FATHER ROBERT [whispering]. He's an intransigent stranger. Worse than that.

[The characters, except Jack, look at each other. They also look at Jack, who sits mute in his armchair, then they look again at each other in silence. Jack's last speech has created an atmosphere of restrained horror. Jack is truly a monster. They all move away on tiptoe. Roberta II has not uttered a word during this last scene, but by rather distressed gestures and a discouraged attitude of dejection has shown that she was responding to the development of the action, and now she seems lost. She appears to want to follow her parents. She takes a step towards the exit, but a gesture of her father stops her where she is.]

FATHER ROBERT [to his daughter]. You . . . chin up and do your duty!

MOTHER ROBERT [melodramatically]. Remain, unhappy girl, with your lover, since you are his presumed spouse.

[Roberta II makes a gesture of despair, but she obeys. Father Jack, Mother Jack, Jacqueline, Father Robert, Mother Robert exit on tiptoe, horrified, throwing back occasional glances, stopping often and murmuring.]

"He doesn't like hashed brown potatoes!"
"No! He doesn't like them!"
"He exceecrates them!"
"Oh, they're two of a kind."

"They're well matched."

"The young people nowadays . . ."

"Better not count on their gratitude."

"They don't like hashed brown potatoes."

[*They exit. The Grandparents exit too, more smiling than ever, strangers to the action. They all stay to spy from behind the door, frequently showing one, two, or three heads at a time. We don't see more than their grotesque heads. Roberta II, timidly, humbly, with some difficulty, decides to go sit down facing Jack, who still wears his cap on his head and remains scowling. Silence.*]

ROBERTA II [*attempting to win his interest, then, little by little, to seduce him*]. I am by nature very gay. [*She has a macabre voice.*] You could see it if you wanted to . . . I am eccentric . . . I am the gaiety in sorrow . . . in travail . . . in ruin . . . in desolation . . . Ah! Ah! Ah! . . . bread, peace, liberty, mourning and gaiety . . . [*Sobbing.*] They used to call me the gaiety ready to hand . . . the gay distress . . . [*He remains silent.*] Are you reflecting? Me too, at times. But in a mirror. [*At a given moment, she dares to rise, walk, approach Jack, to touch him, more and more sure of herself.*] I am the gaiety of death in life . . . the joy of living, of dying. [*Jack remains obstinately silent.*] They used to call me also gaiety the elder . . .

JACK. Because of your noses?

ROBERTA II. Oh no. It's because I'm taller than my sister . . . sir,

> In all the world there's not another like me.
> I'm light, frivolous, I'm very serious.
> I'm not so serious, nor very frivolous,
> I know all about making hay,
> And there are other kinds of work I can do
> Less well, as well, or even better
> I'm just the tonic for you.
> I'm honest, but don't trust me,
> With me your life will be a ball.
> I can play the piano,
> I can arch my back,
> I've been properly housebroke.
> I've had a solid bringing up . . .

JACK. Let's talk about something else!

ROBERTA II. Ah! I understand you, you're not like the others. You're a superior being. Everything I told you was false, yes. Here is something that will interest you.

JACK. It will interest me if it is the truth.

ROBERTA II. Once, I felt like taking a bath. In the bathtub, which was full almost to the brim, I saw a white guinea-pig who had made himself at home there. He was breathing under water. I leaned over in order to see him close up: I saw his snout quiver a little. He was very still. I wanted to plunge my arm into the water in order to seize him, but I was too afraid that he would bite me. They say that these little animals don't bite, but one can never be sure! He clearly saw me, he was watching me, he was on the alert. He had half-opened a tiny eye, and was looking at me, motionless. He didn't appear to be living, but he was though. I saw him in profile. I wanted to see him full face. He lifted his little head with his very tiny eyes toward me, without moving his body. Since the water was very clear, I was able to see on his forehead two dark spots, chestnut colored, perhaps. When I had a good look at them, I saw that they were swelling gently, two excrescences . . . two very tiny guinea pigs, wet and soft, his little ones that were coming out there . . .

JACK [*coldly*]. This little animal in the water, why it's cancer! Actually it was cancer that you saw in your dream. Exactly that.

ROBERTA II. I know it.

JACK. Oh! listen, I feel I can trust you.

ROBERTA II. Speak then.

JACK. When I was born, I was almost fourteen years old. That's why I was able to understand more easily than most what it was all about. Yes, I understood it quickly. I hadn't wanted to accept the situation. I said as much without mincing words. I refused to accept it. But it wasn't to these people you know, who were here a little while ago, that I said this. It was to the others. Those people you know, they don't understand very well . . . no . . . no . . . but they felt it . . . they assured me that someone would devise a remedy. They promised me some decorations, some derogations, some decors, some new flowers, some new wallpaper, new profundities. What else? I insisted. They swore that they would give me satisfaction. They swore it, reswore it, promised formally, officially, presidentially. Registered . . . I made other criticisms in order finally to declare to them that I preferred to withdraw, do you understand? They replied that they would find it hard to do without me. In short, I stipulated my absolute conditions! The situation would surely change, they said. They would take useful measures. They implored me to hope, they appealed to my understanding, to all my feelings, to my love, to my pity. This couldn't go on for long, not for too long a time, they assured me. As for me personally, I would enjoy the highest regard! . . . In order to coax me, they showed me assorted prairies, assorted mountains, assorted oceans . . . maritime, naturally . . . one star, two cathedrals chosen from among the most successful. The prairies were not at all bad . . . I fell for it! But everything was fake . . . Ah, they had lied to me. Centuries and centuries have passed! People . . . they all had the word goodness in their mouths, a bloody knife between their teeth . . . Do you understand me? I was patient, patient, patient. Someone would surely come to look for me. I had wanted to protest: there was no longer anyone . . . except those people there that you know, who do not count. They deceived me . . . And how to escape? They've boarded up the doors, the windows with nothing, they've taken away the stairs . . . One can't get out through the attic anymore, there's no way out up there . . . nevertheless, according to what I was told, they've left a few trapdoors all over the place . . . If I should find them . . . I absolutely want to go away. If one can't exit through the attic, there's always the cellar, yes, the cellar. It would be better to go out down there than to be here. Anything is preferable to my present situation. Even a new one.

ROBERTA II. Oh yes, the cellar . . . I know all the trapdoors.

JACK. We can understand each other.

ROBERTA II. Listen, I have some horses, some stallions, some brood mares, I have only those, would you like them?

JACK. Yes, tell me about your horses.

ROBERTA II. In my place, I have a neighbor who's a miller. He had a mare who dropped two sweet little foals. Very sweet, very cute. The bitch also dropped two little puppies, in the stable. The miller is old, his eyesight isn't very good. The miller took the foals to drown them in the pond, in place of the little puppies . . .

JACK. Ah! Ah!

ROBERTA II. When he realized his error, it was too late. He wasn't able to save them.

JACK [a little amused, he smiles]. Yes? Hm.

[As Roberta tells her story, Jack's smile becomes a full laugh, but he's still calm. During the following scene both Roberta and Jack develop—very slowly at first—a declamatory style; the rhythm intensifies progressively, then slows down toward the end.]

ROBERTA II. No, he wasn't able to save them. But it wasn't really the foals either that he drowned. In fact, when he returned to the stable, the miller saw that the foals were there with their mamma; the little puppies were there too with their mamma,

who was barking. But his own child, his baby who had just been born, was no longer beside his mother, the milleress. It was really the baby that he'd thrown into the water. He ran quickly to the pond. The child held out his arms and cried: "Papa, Papa" . . . It was heart-rending. Only his tiny arm could be seen which said: "Papa, Papa! Mamma, Mamma." And then he sank, and that was all. And that was all. He didn't see him again. The miller went mad. Killed his wife. Destroyed everything. Set fire to it. Hung himself.

JACK [very satisfied with this story]. What a tragic error. A sublime error!

ROBERTA II. But the foals frolic in the meadow. The little puppies have grown big.

JACK. I love your horses. They're intoxicating. Tell me another about a dog, or a horse.

ROBERTA II. The one who was engulfed in the marsh, buried alive, so that you could hear him leaping, howling, and rolling in his grave before he died?

JACK. That one or another.

ROBERTA II. Would you like the one about a horse of the desert, of a city in the Sahara?

JACK [interested, as though in spite of himself, and louder and louder]. The metropolis of the desert! . . .

ROBERTA II. All of bricks, all the houses there are made of bricks, the streets are burning . . . the fire runs through underneath . . . the dry air, the very red dust.

JACK. And the fiery dust.

ROBERTA II. The natives there have been dead for a long time, their cadavers are dessicating in the houses,

JACK. Behind the closed shutters. Behind the red iron grills.

ROBERTA II. Not a man in the empty streets. Not a beast. Not a bird. Not a blade of grass, not even a withered one. Not a rat, not a fly . . .

JACK. Metropolis of my future!

ROBERTA II. Suddenly, in the distance, a horse whinnies . . . han! han! Approaches, han! han! han! han!

JACK [suddenly happy]. Oh yes, that's it, han! han! han!

ROBERTA II. Galloping at full speed, galloping at full speed . . .

JACK. Haan! haan! haan!

ROBERTA II. There he is on the great empty square, there he is . . . He whinnies, runs around, galloping, runs around, galloping . . . runs around, galloping, runs around, galloping.

JACK. Han! han! haan! at full speed, galloping, at full speed, galloping . . . Oh yes, han! han! han! galloping, galloping, galloping as hard as he can.

ROBERTA II. His hooves: click clack click clack, galloping, striking sparks. Click . . . clack . . . clack . . . clack . . . vrr . . .

JACK. [*laughing*]. Oh yes, yes, bravo, I know, I know what's going to happen. But quickly . . . quickly . . . go on . . . hurrah . . .

ROBERTA II. He trembles, he's afraid . . . the stallion . . .

JACK. Yes, hurrah . . . He whinnies, he cries with fear, han! . . . Han! . . . He cries out his fear, han! han! let's hurry . . . let's hurry . . .

[*A blazing horse's mane crosses from one end of the stage to the other.*]

ROBERTA II. Oh! he won't escape . . . never fear . . . He turns around and around, gallops in a circle . . .

JACK. Bravo, that's it! I see . . . I see . . . a spark in his mane . . . He shakes his head . . . Ah! ah! ah! it burns him! it hurts him!

ROBERTA II. He's afraid! he gallops. In a circle. He rears! . . .

JACK. His mane is blazing! His beautiful mane . . . He cries, he whinnies. Han! han! The flame flashes up . . . His mane is blazing. His mane is burning. Han! han! burn! burn! han! han!

ROBERTA II. The more he gallops, the more the flame spreads. He is mad, he's terrified, he's in pain, he's sick, he's afraid, he's in pain . . . it flames up, it spreads all over his body! . . .

JACK. Han! han! he leaps. Oh, what flaming leaps, flaming flaming! He cries, he rears up. Stop, stop, Roberta. It's too fast . . . not so fast . . .

ROBERTA II [*aside*]. Oh . . . he called me by my given name . . . He's going to love me!

JACK. He's burning too fast . . . It's going to end! Make the fire last . . .

ROBERTA II. It's the fire that goes so fast—the flames are coming out of his ears and his nostrils, and thick smoke . . .

JACK. He screams with fear, he screams with pain. He leaps so high. He has wings of flame!

ROBERTA II. How beautiful he is, he's turning all pink, like an enormous lampshade. He wants to fly. He stops, he doesn't know what to do . . . His horseshoes smoke and redden. Haan! Through his transparent hide, we see the fire burning inside him. Han! he flames! He's a living torch . . . He's only a handful of cinders . . . He's no more, but we hear still in the distance the echo of his cries reverberating, and weakening . . . like the whinnyings of another horse in the empty streets.

JACK. My throat is parched, this has made me thirsty . . . Water, water, Ah! how he flamed, the stallion . . . how beautiful it was . . . what a flame . . . ah! [*Exhausted.*] I'm thirsty . . .

ROBERTA II. Come on . . . don't be afraid . . . I'm moist . . . My necklace is made of mud, my breasts are dissolving, my pelvis is wet, I've got water in my crevasses, I'm sinking down. My true name is Liza. In my belly, there are pools, swamps . . . I've got a house of clay. I'm always cool . . . There's moss . . . big flies, cockroaches, sowbugs, toads. Under the wet covers they make love . . . they're swollen with happiness! I wrap my arms around you like snakes; with my soft thighs . . . you plunge down and you dissolve . . . in my locks which drizzle, drizzle, rain, rain. My mouth trickles down, my legs trickle, my naked shoulders trickle, my hair trickles, everything trickles down, runs, everything trickles, the sky trickles down, the stars run, trickle down, trickle . . .

JACK [*in ecstasy*]. Cha-a-arming!

ROBERTA II. Make yourself comfortable. Why don't you take off this thing that you're wearing? What is it? Or who is it?

JACK [*still in ecstasy*]. Cha-a-arming!

ROBERTA II. What is this, on your head?

JACK. Guess! It's a kind of cat. I put it on at dawn.

ROBERTA II. Is it a castle?

JACK. I keep it on my head all day. At table, in the parlor, I never take it off. I don't tip it to people.

ROBERTA II. Is it a camel? A capricorn?

JACK. It'll strike with its paws, but it can till the soil.

ROBERTA II. Is it a catapult?

JACK. It weeps sometimes.

ROBERTA II. Is it a catarrh?

JACK. It can live under water.

ROBERTA II. Is it a catfish?

JACK. It can also float on the waves.

ROBERTA II. Is it a catamaran?

JACK. You're warm.

ROBERTA II. Is it a caterpillar?

JACK. Sometimes it likes to hide in the mountain. It's not pretty.

ROBERTA II. Is it a catamount?

JACK. It makes me laugh.

ROBERTA II. Is it a cataclysm, or a catalog?

JACK. It screams, it splits my ears.

ROBERTA II. Is it a caterwaul?

JACK. It loves ornaments.

ROBERTA II. Is it a catacomb?

JACK. No!

ROBERTA II. The cat's got my tongue.

JACK. It's a cap.

ROBERTA II. Oh, take it off. Take if off, Jack. My Jack. With me, you'll be in your element. I have some, I have as many as you want, quantities!

JACK. . . . Of caps?

ROBERTA II. No . . . of cats . . . skinless ones!

JACK. Oh, my cat . . .

[He takes off his cap, he has green hair].

ROBERTA II. Oh, my cat . . .

JACK. My cat, my catawampous.

ROBERTA II. . . . In the cellar of my castle, everything is cat . . .

JACK. Everything is cat.

ROBERTA II. All we need to designate things is one single word: cat. Cats are called cat, food: cat, insects: cat, chairs: cat, you: cat, me: cat, the roof: cat, the number one: cat, number two: cat, three: cat, twenty: cat, thirty: cat, all the adverbs: cat, all the prepositions: cat. It's easier to talk that way . . .

JACK. In order to say: I'm terribly sleepy, let's go to sleep, let's go to sleep . . .

ROBERTA II. Cat, cat, cat, cat.

JACK. In order to say: bring me some cold noodles, some warm lemonade, and no coffee . . .

ROBERTA II. Cat, cat, cat, cat, cat, cat, cat, cat.

JACK. And Jack, and Roberta?

ROBERTA II. Cat, cat.

[She takes out her hand with nine fingers that she has kept hidden under her gown.]

JACK. Oh yes! It's easy to talk now . . . In fact it's scarcely worth the bother . . . [He sees her hand with nine fingers.] Oh! You've got nine fingers on your left hand? You're rich, I'll marry you . . .

[They put their arms around each other very awkwardly. Jack kisses the noses of Roberta II, one after the other, while Father Jack, Mother Jack, Jacqueline, the Grandparents, Father Robert, and Mother Robert enter without saying a word, one after the other, waddling along, in a sort of ridiculous dance, embarrassing, in a vague circle, around Jack and Roberta II who remain at stage center, awkwardly enlaced. Father Robert silently and slowly strikes his hands together. Mother Robert, her arms clasped behind her neck, makes pirouettes, smiling stupidly. Mother Jack, with an expressionless face, shakes her shoulders in a grotesque fashion. Father Jack pulls up his pants and walks on his heels. Jacqueline nods her head, then they continue to dance, squatting down, while Jack and Roberta II squat down too, and remain motionless. The Grandparents turn around, idiotically, looking at each other, and smiling; then they squat down in their turn. All this must produce in the audience a feeling of embarrassment, awkwardness, and shame. The darkness increases. On stage, the actors utter vague miaows while turning around, bizarre moans, croakings. The darkness increases. We can still see the Jacks and Roberts crawling on the stage. We hear their animal noises, then we don't see them any more. We hear only their moans, their sighs, then all fades away, all is extinguished. Again, a gray light comes on. All the characters have disappeared, except Roberta, who is lying down, or rather squatting down, buried beneath her gown. We see only her pale face, with its three noses quivering, and her nine fingers moving like snakes.]

ESSAY: AN APPROACH TO THE PLAY

Language is used in unusual ways in this play. Phrases that are conventional and phrases that are trite, phrases that are nonsensical and phrases that are intellectual—all are brought together, sometimes in the same sentence. In a caricature of the self-righteous father, Father Jack says, "You are no son of mine. I disown you. You're not worthy of my ancestors. You resemble your mother and the idiots and imbeciles in her family. This doesn't matter to her for she's only a woman, and what a woman!" He moves from pompous posturing to the colloquial, from an idea of family heritage to a conventional put-down of women and in-laws, and then to a sexual appreciation of the very woman he has just put down. A little later he says, "I'm blowing this joint." As there is little logical relationship between one sentence or even phrase and another, there is also an uncertain relationship between what is said and what is happening onstage, and equally between what is happening onstage and what we might believe is "realistic." Words are not used to convey clear meaning. They are garbled, inconsistent, often non sequiturs. And yet each one suggests a recognizable perception in "reality."

Because much of what we do in the world is to play conventional social roles, our activities—including our words—often belie many of our true feelings. Neither actions nor words can be trusted. In fundamental ways, we are not the individual selves we believe ourselves to be; often we act as functionaries playing out conventional patterns—son, sister, father, mother, for example, with our language and behavior by and large predetermined by the roles into which we are cast. It is for this reason that the stage direction at the play's opening will (indifferently) allow the characters to wear masks: they represent universal types, not individuals. Similarly, the characters' names refer to their social functions, not to their individuality—the two fiancées are simply numbered I and II and are played by the same actress. In his emphasis on types, Ionesco's theater is conceived in terms similar to that of ancient Greece. But he then complicates these social types by insisting on a far fuller range of feeling and perception than "types" can accommodate. It is in this sense that the language of the play is at once "naturalistic" and new.

The plot, too, is "new." A son is disinherited because he will not speak, more specifically because he will not speak his love of hashed brown potatoes. His fiancée is not only evaluated visually and verbally by his family, but she is sniffed as well! The familiar male objectification of women into body parts as a way of dehumanizing them into a sexual object is here exaggerated by the *choice* of body parts: she has feet to walk with, for example! Father Robert's completely unfeeling catalogue of his daughter—"She's got green pimples on her beige skin, red breasts on a mauve background, an illuminated navel," and so on—has nothing of the sexual about it. It is a display of naming, a display of male power. And if body parts are what a woman is worth, from this point of view, the idea that three noses are better in a woman than two is quite logical. And if power, not sexual desire, is the cause of men's objectification of women, then male worship of female beauty simply reflects male lack of self-knowledge. When Jack prefers homeliness to beauty, he shows his ability to see beneath conventional belief. And when Roberta's father says that she has "all the meat needed to merit the highest commendation," he sums up this all-too-common male attitude in an uncommonly revealing way.

In this play, then, conventional or "normal" ideas are taken to their logical extremes and then acted out or given voice, so that we can see where the ideas lead, can see their absurdity. And if language, action, and characterization all lack meaning, or fail to make their meaning clear, this leads to our sense as an audience that we should cease looking for meaning in this play and give up the conventional theatrical idea of being sympathetic with a character, and hence of seeing from a particular character's point of view. We are forced to see the world of the play objectively, as if it were entirely separate from ourselves and the version of reality we believe ourselves to inhabit. The texture of this play, that is, is very close to surreal. In Roberta II's dream, near the end of the play, for example, a child's arm is said to have spoken. We must give up our desire for plausibility if we are to grant the play's expressivity, its quality of poetry, of metaphor, of a life which includes dreams and is beyond language and meaning.

At the end of the play, in the dialogue between the no longer just talking but now *declaiming* Jack and his truelove—the equally declaiming Roberta II of the three noses—there is an increasing contrast between their emphatic speaking style and their reduction of all language to the single syllable "cat." Perhaps this suggests that language has no meaning in itself, that only the concrete reality of the particular things to which language refers have existence, that we cannot know anything for certain beyond particular moments of experience, that the complexity of language and even of words is therefore superfluous. It may also suggest that conventional dramatic form, a narrative that leads, as a sentence does, from beginning to middle to end and at last to meaning—to a meaning clustered around a particular character with whom we sympathize and whose behavior relates to our own—that these dramatic conventions, too, are superfluous, empty of significance.

The final event of the play (described in the final stage direction) is a kind of physical enactment of this view. The families dance around the happy couple. We seem to have reached the conventional happy ending of comedy in which the two lovers get together and their families reintegrate them into society by celebrating their coming marriage. However, the surreal discussion between the two lovers which precedes this conclusion, as well as the dancing parents' failure to understand the situation which they are celebrating, undermines whatever might seem secure or "happy" about this ending. And as the lights fade and "miaows" are heard from characters now "crawling" in darkness, we see humans apparently reduced to animals—to cats. Perhaps this conclusion is logically necessary, an absurd version of dramatic inevitability, given what we have seen of language and of humanity.

The play's title is *Jack or the Submission*. To what does Jack submit? To his father's desire for him to marry and enter the family's lineage? Or to feign to adore hashed brown potatoes (only to his beloved can he admit he abhors them)? Or is his submission to the female, or the feminine, the earth and its wet fecundity (see Roberta II's speech just before they deconstruct language into "cat")? Or we might reconsider: Need the submission be Jack's? Could it be Roberta II's instead? Or the families'? And if we do not identify with any of the characters, perhaps they (or Jack, or Roberta II) simply represent the submission of all of us into conventional roles that are always different in fact from the verbal constructions of them that we admit to, a submission that this play renders more visible than usual. To reconsider further: Is our only alternative to such submission the silence in which Jack began? Perhaps, in the final analysis, this is a play which means to raise our awareness of this fact so that we can begin again, unimprisoned by old assumptions, to construct more honest meanings, meanings more true to the fullness of our experience, meanings which do not pretend to be uttered by language, meanings which require for their fullness both silence and darkness, a lack of falsification and reductionism.

This perception may also help us to reconsider what the word "absurd" means when we say that Ionesco is an absurdist playwright. The traditional genres of comedy and tragedy both imply value systems: they each lead us to see certain human characteristics as heroic and certain others as ridiculous. They each represent a world in which one kind of thinking is wise and another, foolish. However, Ionesco portrays a world in which nothing is so clear, in which happiness and sadness are intertwined, and it is this complex uncertainty which we call "absurd." Whatever we do is funny in the sense of having no clear point, possibly of being merely a way of killing the time we have been assigned in this version of "reality." However, whatever we do is also very sad, and for precisely the same reason. Perhaps, at last, this play forces us to face the responsibility of making our own meaning for our lives. Or of living with none. Freeing us in this way, the play and its absurdism can be profoundly liberating, sobering, and even frightening, all at the same time.

James Baldwin

BLUES FOR MISTER CHARLIE

About the Author   The fame of James Baldwin (1925–1987) rests primarily on his accomplishments as a writer of fiction and prose essays. Born in New York City into a religious family, he served briefly in his youth as a minister before devoting himself to his literary career. He lived in Paris from 1948 to 1956, in Istanbul during the 1970s, and in the final years of his life in southern France, where he died of esophageal cancer. During his expatriot years in Paris, he established his reputation as one of the world's most influential writers and lecturers on civil rights through works such as *Go Tell It on the Mountain* (1953) and the essay collection *Notes of a Native Son* (1955). His return to the United States seems to have been prompted specifically by his desire to play a more direct role in his own country's social struggles. Once here, he wrote two plays which ran on Broadway in successive years (no African-American writer had previously accomplished this): *Blues for Mr. Charlie* in 1964 and *The Amen Corner* in 1965.

About the Play   *Blues for Mr. Charlie*, as Baldwin wrote in his essay "Notes for *Blues*," is patterned broadly after the 1955 murder of Emmett Till, and the play is dedicated "to the memory of Medgar Evers, and his widow and children, and the memory of the dead children of Birmingham." These references to martyrs of the civil rights struggle of the 1950s and 1960s are reminders of the historical moment in which the play was written. (It opened on Broadway on April 23, 1964.) Emmett Till was a fourteen-year-old Chicago boy murdered in an especially brutal fashion in 1955 during a visit to an uncle in rural Mississippi. His murderer, who was acquitted by an all-white jury, subsequently admitted to the crime in a newspaper interview which he sold for $4000. Baldwin said in "Notes for *Blues*" that the murder continued to haunt him, and in this he was not alone: it is an event which seems to have been prominent in reaffirming the commitment of a generation of people working in the civil rights movement.

Medgar Evers, a personal friend of Baldwin, was appointed in 1954 as the state of Mississippi's first field secretary for the NAACP, and in the early 1960s he was a leading organizer in that state of voter registration drives and of boycotts of segregated businesses. In June of 1963, he was killed by a sniper while he stood in front of his home; the man charged with his murder was tried twice, both trials ending in hung juries. Earlier in that year, in April and May, nonviolent protesters conducting a sit-in in Birmingham, Alabama, were victims of police brutality—harassed by police dogs, beaten, swept off their feet by fire hoses, arrested— all conducted in front of the world press and on nightly television news. On September 15, four young girls were killed in Birmingham when a black church was bombed. In June of 1964, shortly after *Blues* opened on Broadway, three student civil rights workers were killed, apparently by the Ku Klux Klan, in Philadelphia, Mississippi. These were all widely publicized acts of violence that built up broad national sympathy for civil rights legislation. In that same summer, riots erupted in major cities in New Jersey, in Harlem, in Rochester, New York, and in Philadelphia. Against this backdrop of hope and fear, on July 2, Congress passed the Civil Rights Act of 1964.

Blues for Mr. Charlie was not a "hit"; reviewers in mainstream publications were generally hostile, and much of the typical (predominantly white) Broadway audience avoided it. Some thought it irresponsible, with the potential to stir up violence in an already incendiary environment. At least, it seemed to some to stir up hatred at a time when mutual acceptance seemed to be the goal of people of goodwill. Baldwin insisted that the top ticket price be

$4.80 so as to make the play available to as wide an economic group as possible, and the result is that (although the play kept losing money) performances were well attended, particularly by people who were not part of the normal "theater crowd." Estimates are that some 80 percent of the audience was black, and many whites in the audience felt threatened by the enthusiasm of the black response. In the words of the *Time* magazine reviewer, it was "a hard play for a white man to take." Perhaps a reason for resistance to the play is that it bucked the then-dominant progressive sentiment that America's racial problems could be solved through reform of our legal institutions. The problem, in this view, was one of "civil rights," a constitutional matter that could be solved by passing legislation, and a play by a major black intellectual should help build a constituency for political consensus in that direction, not reinforce divisions.

The community Baldwin presents in this play is one which is radically divided, a division continuously emphasized by the segregated stage set. As the opening stage direction specifies, Whitetown is on one side of a central aisle, Blacktown on the other. The murder takes place in what the stage direction calls an enormous gulf between the two sides. All of the acting by black characters and white characters takes place on their respective sides. Separate churches are on each side; the courtroom is segregated. During the trial scene, while the dialogue comes to sound increasingly like that of Sophocles, the citizens of Whitetown and Blacktown function like separate but equal choruses from Greek tragedy, presenting the two communities' responses to the dialogue and action in ways that accentuate their different values, perceptions, and interpretations.

Divisions run deep in the world of the play: between black and white, but also between parent and child, between men and women, between violent and nonviolent approaches to social change (symbolized by the gun and the Bible), between different notions of Christianity, between different attitudes toward sexuality, between different relationships toward the institutions of justice. The name of the minister who ends up keeping both gun and Bible in the pulpit may itself evoke these divisions: a meridian is a line with which we artificially divide the world into segments. Instead of a sentimental, reassuring vision of universal brotherhood, Baldwin provided his audience with an unfashionable presentation of tribalism. The divisions are fundamental, inherent even in each group's conceptions of and interpretations of the other's bodies: "they" are perceived as sexually different from "us." As Baldwin said to reporters about the reactions of his audience: "I haven't got the carriage trade. They think it's a play about civil rights. The play is about the state of mind and the relationship of people to each other helplessly corrupted and destroyed by this insanity you call color."

CHARACTERS

(in order of appearance)

MERIDIAN HENRY, a Negro minister

TOM
KEN
ARTHUR } Negro students
JUANITA
LORENZO
PETE

MOTHER HENRY, Meridian Henry's mother
LYLE BRITTEN, a white store-owner
JO BRITTEN, Lyle's wife
PARNELL JAMES, editor of the local newspaper
RICHARD, Meridian Henry's son
PAPA D., owner of a juke joint

HAZEL
LILLIAN
SUSAN
RALPH   } white townspeople
ELLIS
REV. PHELPS
GEORGE

THE STATE
COUNSEL FOR THE BEREAVED
Congregation of Rev. Henry's church, Pallbearers,
Blacktown, Whitetown

Act I

Multiple set, the skeleton of which, in the first two acts, is the Negro church, and, in the third act, the courthouse. The church and the courthouse are on opposite sides of a southern street; the audience should always be aware, during the first two acts, of the dome of the courthouse and the American flag. During the final act, the audience should always be aware of the steeple of the church, and the cross.

The church is divided by an aisle. The street door upstage faces the audience. The pulpit is downstage, at an angle, so that the minister is simultaneously addressing the congregation and the audience. In the third act, the pulpit is replaced by the witness stand.

This aisle also functions as the division between Whitetown and Blacktown. The action among the blacks takes place on one side of the stage, the action among the whites on the opposite side of the stage—which is to be remembered during the third act, which takes place, of course, in a segregated courtroom.

This means that Richard's room, Lyle's store, Papa D.'s joint, Jo's kitchen, etc., are to exist principally by suggestion, for these shouldn't be allowed to obliterate the skeleton, or, more accurately, perhaps, the framework, suggested above.

For the murder scene, the aisle functions as a gulf. The stage should be built out, so that the audience reacts to the enormity of this gulf, and so that Richard, when he falls, falls out of sight of the audience, like a stone, into the pit.

In the darkness we hear a shot.

Lights up slowly on Lyle, staring down at the ground. He looks around him, bends slowly and picks up Richard's body as though it were a sack. He carries him upstage, drops him.

LYLE. And may every nigger like this nigger end like this nigger—face down in the weeds!

[*Exits. Blacktown: The church. A sound of mourning begins. Meridian, Tom, Ken and Arthur.*]

MERIDIAN. No, no, no! You have to say it like you mean it—the way they really say it: nigger, nigger, nigger! *Nigger*! Tom, the way *you* saying it, it sounds like you just *might* want to make friends. And that's not the way they sound out there. Remember all that's happened. Remember we having a funeral here—tomorrow night. Remember why. Go on, hit it again.

TOM. You dirty nigger, you no-good black bastard, what you doing down here, anyway?

MERIDIAN. That's much better. Much, much better. Go on.

TOM. Hey, boy, where's your mother? I bet she's lying up in bed, just a-pumping away, ain't she, boy?

MERIDIAN. *That's* the way they sound!

TOM. Hey, boy, how much does your mother charge? How much does your sister charge?

KEN. How much does your *wife* charge?

MERIDIAN. Now you got it. You really got it now. That's them. Keep walking, Arthur. *Keep walking*!

TOM. You get your ass off these streets from around here, boy, or we going to do us some cutting—we're going to cut that big, black thing off of you, you hear?

MERIDIAN. Why you all standing around there like that? Go on and get you a nigger. Go on!

[*A scuffle.*]

MERIDIAN. All right. All right! Come on, now. Come on.

[*Ken steps forward and spits in Arthur's face.*]

ARTHUR. You black s.o.b., what the hell do you think you're doing? You mother—!

MERIDIAN. Hey, hold it! Hold it! Hold it!

[*Meridian wipes the boy's face. They are all trembling.*]

[*Mother Henry enters.*]

MOTHER HENRY. Here they come. And it looks like they had a time.

[*Juanita, Lorenzo, Pete, Jimmy, all Negro, carry placards, enter, exhausted and dishevelled, wounded; Pete is weeping. The placards bear such legends as* Freedom Now, We Want The Murderer, One Man, One Vote, *etc.*]

JUANITA. We shall overcome!

LORENZO. We shall not be moved! [*Laughs*] We were moved tonight, though. Some of us has been moved to *tears.*

MERIDIAN. Juanita, what happened?

JUANITA. Oh, just another hometown Saturday night.

MERIDIAN. Come on, Pete, come on, old buddy. Stop it. Stop it.

LORENZO. I don't blame him. I do not blame the cat. You feel like a damn fool standing up there, letting them white mothers beat on your ass—shoot, if I had my way, just once—stop crying, Pete, goddammit!

JUANITA. Lorenzo, you're in church.

LORENZO. Yeah. Well, I wish to God I was in an arsenal. I'm sorry, Meridian, Mother Henry—I don't mean that for you. I don't understand you. I don't understand Meridian here. It was his son, it was your grandson, Mother Henry, that got killed, butchered! Just last week, and yet, here you sit—in this—this—the house of this damn almighty God who don't care what happens to nobody, unless, of course, they're white. Mother Henry, I got a lot of respect for you and all that, and for Meridian, too, but that white man's God is *white.* It's that damn white God that's been lynching us and burning us and castrating us and raping our women and robbing us of everything that makes a man a man for all these hundreds of years. Now, why we sitting around here, in *His* house? If I could get my hands on Him, I'd pull Him out of heaven and drag Him through this town at the end of a rope.

MERIDIAN. No, you wouldn't.

LORENZO. I wouldn't? Yes, I would. Oh, yes, I would.

JUANITA. And then you wouldn't be any better than they are.

LORENZO. I don't want to be better than they are, why should I be better than they are? And better at what? Better at being a doormat, better at being a corpse? Sometimes I just don't know. We've been demonstrating—*non-violently*—for more than a year now and all that's happened is that now they'll let us into that crummy library downtown which was obsolete in 1897 and where nobody goes anyway; who in this town reads books? For that we paid I don't know how many thousands of dollars in fines, Jerome is still in the hospital, and we all know that Ruthie is never again going to be the swinging little chick she used to be. Big deal. Now we're picketing that great movie palace downtown where I wouldn't go on a bet; I can live without Yul Brynner and Doris Day, thank you very much. And we *still* can't get licensed to be electricians or plumbers, we still can't walk through the park, our kids still can't use the swimming pool in town. We still can't vote, we can't even get registered. Is it worth it? And these people trying to kill us, too? And we ain't even got no guns. The cops ain't going to protect us. They call up the people and tell them where we are and say, "Go get them! They ain't going to do nothing to you—they just dumb niggers!"

MERIDIAN. Did they arrest anybody tonight?

PETE. No, they got their hands full now, trying to explain what Richard's body was doing in them weeds.

LORENZO. It was wild. You know, all the time we was ducking them bricks and praying to *God* we'd get home before somebody got killed— [*Laughs*] I had a jingle going through my mind, like if I was a white man, dig? and I had to wake up every morning singing to myself, "Look at the happy nigger, he doesn't give a damn, thank God I'm not a nigger—"

TOGETHER. "—*Good Lord, perhaps I am!*"

JUANITA. You've gone crazy, Lorenzo. They've done it. You have been unfitted for the struggle.

MERIDIAN. I cannot rest until they bring my son's murderer to trial. That man who killed my son.

LORENZO. But he killed a nigger before, as I know all of you know. Nothing never happened. Sheriff just shovelled the body into the ground and forgot about it.

MERIDIAN. Parnell will help me.

PETE. Meridian, you know that *Mister* Parnell ain't going to let them arrest his ass-hole buddy. I'm sorry, Mother Henry!

MOTHER HENRY. That's all right, son.

MERIDIAN. But I think that Parnell has proven to be a pretty good friend to all of us. He's the only white man in this town who's ever *really* stuck his neck out in order to do—to do right. He's *fought* to bring about this trial—I can't tell you how hard he's fought. If it weren't for him, there'd be much less hope.

LORENZO. I guess I'm just not as nice as you are. I don't trust as many people as you trust.

MERIDIAN. We can't afford to become too distrustful, Lorenzo.

LORENZO. We can't afford to be too trusting, either. See, when a white man's a *good* white man, he's good because he wants *you* to be good. Well, sometimes I just might want to be *bad*. I got as much right to be bad as anybody else.

MERIDIAN. No, you don't.

LORENZO. Why not?

MERIDIAN. Because you know better.

[*Parnell enters.*]

PARNELL. Hello, my friends. I bring glad tidings of great joy. Is that the way the phrase goes, Meridian?

JUANITA. Parnell!

PARNELL. I can't stay. I just came to tell you that a warrant's being issued for Lyle's arrest.

JUANITA. They're going to arrest him? Big Lyle Britten? I'd love to know how you managed *that*.

PARNELL. Well, Juanita, I am not a *good* man, but I have my little ways.

JUANITA. And a whole lot of folks in this town, baby, are not going to be talking to you no more, for days and days and *days*.

PARNELL. I hope that you all will. I may have no other company. I think I should go to Lyle's house to warn him. After all, I brought it about and he *is* a friend of mine—and then I have to get the announcement into my paper.

JUANITA. So it *is* true.

PARNELL. Oh, yes. It's true.

MERIDIAN. When is he being arrested?

PARNELL. Monday morning. Will you be up later, Meridian? I'll drop by if you are—if I may.

MERIDIAN. Yes. I'll be up.

PARNELL. All right, then. I'll trundle by. Good night all. I'm sorry I've got to run.

MERIDIAN. Good night.

JUANITA. Thank you, Parnell.

PARNELL. Don't thank me, dear Juanita. I only acted—as I believed I had to act. See you later, Meridian.

[*Parnell exits.*]

MERIDIAN. I wonder if they'll convict him.

JUANITA. Convict him. Convict him. You're asking for heaven on earth. After all, they haven't even *arrested* him yet. And, anyway—why *should* they convict him? Why him? He's no worse than all the others. He's an honorable tribesman and he's defended, with blood, the honor and purity of his tribe!

[*Whitetown: Lyle holds his infant son up above his head.*]

LYLE. Hey old pisser. You hear me, sir? I expect you to control your bladder like a *gentleman* whenever your Papa's got you on his knee.

[*Jo enters.*]

He got a mighty big bladder, too, for such a little fellow.

JO. I'll tell the world he didn't steal it.

LYLE. You mighty sassy tonight.

[*Hands her the child.*]

Ain't that right, old pisser? Don't you reckon your Mama's getting kind of sassy? And what do you reckon I should do about it?

[*Jo is changing the child's diapers.*]

JO. You tell your Daddy he can start sleeping in his own bed nights instead of coming grunting in here in the wee small hours of the morning.

LYLE. And you tell your Mama if she was getting her sleep like she should be, so she can be alert every instant to your needs, little fellow, she wouldn't *know* what time I come—*grunting* in.

JO. I got to be alert to *your* needs, too, I think.

LYLE. Don't you go starting to imagine things. I just been over to the store. That's all.

JO. Til three and four o'clock in the morning?

LYLE. Well, I got plans for the store, I think I'm going to try to start branching out, you know, and I been—making plans.

JO. You thinking of branching out *now*? Why, Lyle, you know we ain't *hardly* doing no business *now*.

Weren't for the country folks come to town every Saturday, I don't know *where* we'd be. This ain't no time to be branching *out*. We barely holding *on*.

LYLE. Shoot, the niggers'll be coming back, don't you worry. They'll get over this foolishness presently. They already weary of having to drive forty-fifty miles across the state line to get their groceries—a lot of them ain't even got cars.

JO. Those that don't have cars have *friends* with cars.

LYLE. Well, friends get weary, too. Joel come in the store a couple of days ago—

JO. Papa D.? He don't count. You can always wrap him around your little finger.

LYLE. Listen, will you? He come in the store a couple of days ago to buy a sack of flour and he *told* me, he say, The niggers is *tired* running all over creation to put some food on the table. Ain't nobody going to keep on driving no forty-fifty miles to buy no sack of flour—what you mean when you say Joel don't count?

JO. I don't mean nothing. But there's something wrong with anybody when his own people don't think much of him.

LYLE. Joel's got good sense, is all. I think more of him than I think of a lot of white men, that's a fact. And he knows what's right for his people, too.

JO [*Puts son in crib*]. Well. Selling a sack of flour once a week ain't going to send this little one through college, neither. [*A pause*] In what direction were you planning to branch out?

LYLE. I was thinking of trying to make the store more—well, more colorful. Folks like color—

JO. You mean, niggers like color.

LYLE. Dammit, Jo, I ain't in business just to sell to niggers! Listen to me, can't you? I thought I'd dress it up, get a new front, put some neon signs in—and, you know, we got more space in there than we use. Well, why don't we open up a line of ladies' clothes? Nothing too fancy, but I bet you it would bring in a lot more business.

JO. I don't know. Most of the ladies I know buy their clothes at Benton's, on Decatur Street.

LYLE. The niggers don't—anyway, we could sell them the same thing. The white ladies, I mean—

JO. No. It wouldn't be the same.

LYLE. Why not? A dress is a dress.

JO. But it sounds better if you say you got it on Decatur Street! At Benton's. Anyway—where would you get the money for this branching out?

LYLE. I can get a loan from the bank. I'll get old Parnell to co-sign with me, or have him get one of his rich friends to co-sign with me.

JO. Parnell called earlier—you weren't at the store today.

LYLE. What do you mean, I wasn't at the store?

JO. Because Parnell called earlier and said he tried to get you at the store and that there wasn't any answer.

LYLE. There wasn't any business. I took a walk.

JO. He said he's got bad news for you.

LYLE. What kind of bad news?

JO. He didn't say. He's coming by here this evening to give it to you himself.

LYLE. What do you think it is?

JO. I guess they're going to arrest you?

LYLE. No, they ain't. They ain't gone crazy.

JO. I think they might. We had so much trouble in this town lately and it's been in all the northern newspapers—and now, this—this dead boy—

LYLE. They ain't got no case.

JO. No. But you was the last person to see that crazy boy—alive. And now everybody's got to thinking again—about that other time.

LYLE. That was self defense. The Sheriff said so himself. Hell, I ain't no murderer. They're just some things I don't believe is right.

JO. Nobody never heard no more about the poor little girl—his wife.

LYLE. No. She just disappeared.

JO. You never heard no more about her at all?

LYLE. How would I hear about her more than anybody else? No, she just took off—I believe she had people in Detroit somewhere. I reckon that's where she went.

JO. I felt sorry for her. She looked so lost those last few times I saw her, wandering around town—and she was so young. She was a pretty little thing.

LYLE. She looked like a pickaninny to me. Like she was too young to be married. I reckon she *was* too young for him.

JO. It happened in the store.

LYLE. Yes.

JO. How people talked! That's what scares me now.

LYLE. Talk don't matter. I hope you didn't believe what you heard.

JO. A lot of people did. I reckon a lot of people still do.

LYLE. *You* don't believe it?

JO. No. [*A pause*] You know—Monday morning—we'll be married one whole year!

LYLE. Well, can't nobody talk about *us*. That little one there ain't but two months old.

[*The door bell rings.*]

JO. That's Parnell.

[*Exits.*]

[*Lyle walks up and down, looks into the crib. Jo and Parnell enter.*]

LYLE. It's about time you showed your face in here, you old rascal! You been so busy over there with the niggers, you ain't got time for white folks no more. You sure you ain't got some nigger wench over there on the other side of town? Because, I declare—!

PARNELL. I apologize for your husband, Mrs. Britten, I really do. In fact, I'm afraid I must deplore your taste in men. If I had only seen you first, dear lady, and if you had found me charming, how much suffering I might have prevented! You got anything in this house to drink? Don't tell me you haven't, we'll both need one. Sit down.

LYLE. Bring on the booze, old lady.

[*Jo brings ice, glasses, etc.; pours drinks.*]

What you been doing with yourself?

PARNELL. Well, I seem to have switched territories. I haven't been defending colored people this week, I've been defending you. I've just left the Chief of Police.

LYLE. How is the old bastard?

PARNELL. He seems fine. But he really *is* an old bastard. Lyle—he's issuing a warrant for your arrest.

LYLE. He's going to arrest *me*? You mean, he believes I killed that boy?

PARNELL. The question of what he believes doesn't enter into it. This case presents several very particular circumstances and these circumstances force him to arrest you. I think we can take it for granted that he wouldn't arrest you if he could think of some way not to. He wouldn't arrest anybody except blind beggars and old colored women if he could think of some way not to—he's bird-brained and chicken-hearted and big-assed. The charge is murder.

JO. Murder!

LYLE. Murder?

PARNELL. Murder.

LYLE. I ain't no murderer. You know that.

PARNELL. I also know that somebody killed the boy. Somebody put two slugs in his belly and dumped his body in the weeds beside the railroad track just outside of town. Somebody did all that. We pay several eminent, bird-brained, chicken-hearted, big-assed people quite a lot of money to discourage such activity. They never do, in fact, discourage it, but, still—we must find the somebody who killed that boy. And you, my friend, according to the testimony of Joel Davis, otherwise known as Papa D., were the last person to see the boy alive. It is also known that you didn't like him—to say the least.

LYLE. Nobody liked him.

PARNELL. Ah. But it isn't nobody that killed him. *Somebody* killed him. We must find the somebody. And since you were the last person to see him alive, we must arrest you in order to clear you—or convict you.

LYLE. They'll never convict me.

PARNELL. As to that, you may be right. But you *are* going to be arrested.

LYLE. When?

PARNELL. Monday morning. Of course, you can always flee to Mexico.

LYLE. Why should I run away?

PARNELL. I wasn't suggesting that you should run away. If you did, I should urge your wife to divorce you at once, and marry me.

JO. Ah, if that don't get him out of town in a hurry, I don't know what will! The man's giving you your chance, honey. You going to take it?

LYLE. Stop talking foolishness. It looks bad for me, I guess. I swear, I don't know what's come over the folks in this town!

PARNELL. It doesn't look good. In fact, if the boy had been white, it would look very, *very* bad, and your behind would be in the jail house now. What do you mean, you don't understand what's come over the people in this town?

LYLE. Raising so much fuss about a nigger—and a northern nigger at that.

PARNELL. He was born here. He's Reverend Meridian Henry's son.

LYLE. Well, he'd been gone so long, he might as well have been a northern nigger. Went North and got ruined and come back here to make trouble—and they tell me he was a dope fiend, too. What's all this fuss about! He probably got killed by some other nigger—they do it all the time—but ain't nobody even thought about arresting one of *them*. Has niggers suddenly got to be *holy* in this town?

PARNELL. Oh, Lyle, I'm not here to discuss the sanctity of niggers. I just came to tell you that a warrant's being issued for your arrest. *You* may think that a colored boy who gets ruined in the North and then comes home to try to pull himself together deserves to die—*I* don't.

LYLE. You sound like you think I got something against colored folks—but I don't. I never have, not in all my life. But I'll be damned if I'll mix with them. That's all. I don't believe in it, and that's *all*. I don't want no big buck nigger lying up next to Josephine and that's where all this will lead to and you know it as well as I do! I'm against it and I'll do anything I have to do to stop it, yes, I will!

PARNELL. Suppose *he*—my godson there—decides to marry a Chinese girl. You know, there are an awful lot of Chinese girls in the world—I bet you didn't know that. Well, there are. Let's just say that he grows up and looks around at all the pure white women, and—saving your presence, ma'am—they make him want to puke and he decides to marry a pure Chinese girl instead. What would you do? Shoot him in order to prevent it? Or would you shoot her?

LYLE. Parnell, you're my buddy. You've *always* been my buddy. You know more about me than anybody else in the world. What's come over you? You—you ain't going to turn against me, are you?

PARNELL. No. No, I'll never turn against you. I'm just trying to make you think.

LYLE. I notice you didn't marry no Chinese girl. You just never got married at all. Women been trying to saddle old Parnell for I don't know how long—I don't know what you got, old buddy, but I'll be damned if you don't know how to use it! What about this present one—Loretta—you reckon you going to marry her?

PARNELL. I doubt it.

JO. Parnell, you're just awful. Awful!

PARNELL. I think I'm doing her a favor. She can do much better than me. I'm just a broken-down newspaper editor—the editor of a newspaper which *nobody* reads—in a dim, grim backwater.

LYLE. I thought you liked it here.

PARNELL. I don't like it here. But I love it here. Or maybe I don't. I don't know. I must go.

LYLE. What's your hurry? Why don't you stay and have pot-luck with us?

PARNELL. Loretta is waiting. I must have pot-luck with *her*. And then I have errands on the other side of town.

LYLE. What they saying over there? I reckon they praying day and night for my ass to be put in a sling, ain't they? Shoot, I don't care.

PARNELL. Don't. Life's much simpler that way. Anyway, Papa D.'s the only one doing a whole lot of talking.

JO. I told you he wasn't no good, Lyle, I told you!

LYLE. I don't know what's got into him! And we been knowing each other all these years! He must be getting old. You go back and tell him I said he's got it all *confused*—about me and that boy. Tell him you talked to me and that *I* said he must have made some mistake.

PARNELL. I'll drop in tomorrow, if I may. Good night, Jo, and thank you. Good night, Lyle.

LYLE. Good night, old buddy.

JO. I'll see you to the door.

[*Jo and Parnell exit. Lyle walks up and down.*]

LYLE. Well! *Ain't* that something! But they'll never convict me. Never in this world. [*Looks into crib*] Ain't that right, old pisser?

[*Blacktown: The church, as before.*]

LORENZO. And when they bring him to trial, I'm going to be there every day—right across the street in that courthouse—where they been dealing death out to us for all these years.

MOTHER HENRY. I used to hate them, too, son. But I don't hate them no more. They too pitiful.

MERIDIAN. No witnesses.

JUANITA. Meridian. Ah, Meridian.

MOTHER HENRY. You remember that song he used to like so much?

MERIDIAN. I sing because I'm happy.

JUANITA. I sing because I'm free.

PETE. For his eye is on the sparrow—

LORENZO. And I know he watches—me.

[*Music, very faint*]

JUANITA. There was another song he liked—a song about a prison and the light from a train that shone on the prisoners every night at midnight. I can hear him now: Lord, you wake up in the morning. You hear the ding-dong ring—

MOTHER HENRY. He had a beautiful voice.

LORENZO. Well, he was pretty tough up there in New York—till he got busted.

MERIDIAN. And came running home.

MOTHER HENRY. Don't blame yourself, honey. Don't blame yourself!

JUANITA. You go a-marching to the table, you see the same old thing—

JIMMY. All I'm going to tell you: knife, a fork, and a pan—

[*Music stronger*].

PETE. And if you say a thing about it—

LORENZO. You are in trouble with the man.

[*Lights dim in the church. We discover Richard, standing in his room, singing. This number is meant to make vivid the Richard who was much loved on the Apollo Theatre stage in Harlem, the Richard who was a rising New York star.*]

MERIDIAN. No witnesses!

[*Near the end of the song, Mother Henry enters, carrying a tray with milk, sandwiches, and cake.*]

RICHARD. You treating me like royalty, old lady—I ain't royalty. I'm just a raggedy-assed, out-of-work, busted musician. But I sure can sing, can't I?

MOTHER HENRY. You better learn some respect, you know that neither me nor your father wants that kind of language in this house. Sit down and eat, you got to get your strength back.

RICHARD. What for? What am I supposed to do with it?

MOTHER HENRY. You stop that kind of talk.

RICHARD. Stop that kind of talk, we don't want that kind of talk! Nobody cares what people feel or what they think or what they do—but stop that kind of talk!

MOTHER HENRY. Richard!

RICHARD. All right. All right. [*Throws himself on the bed, begins eating in a kind of fury.*] What I can't get over is—what in the world am I doing *here*? Way down here in the ass-hole of the world, the deep, black, funky South.

MOTHER HENRY. You were born here. You got folks here. And you ain't got no manners and you *won't* learn no sense and so you naturally got yourself in trouble and had to come to your folks. You lucky it wasn't no worse, the way you go on. You want some more milk?

RICHARD. No, old lady. Sit down.

MOTHER HENRY. I ain't got time to be fooling with you. [*But she sits down.*] What you got on your mind?

RICHARD. I don't know. How do you stand it?

MOTHER HENRY. Stand what? You?

RICHARD. Living down here with all these nowhere people.

MOTHER HENRY. From what I'm told and from what I see, the people you've been among don't seem to be any better.

RICHARD. You mean old Aunt Edna? She's all right, she just ain't very bright, is all.

MOTHER HENRY. I am not talking about Edna. I'm talking about all them other folks you got messed up with. Look like you'd have had better sense. You hear me?

RICHARD. I hear you.

MOTHER HENRY. That all you got to say?

RICHARD. It's easy for you to talk, Grandmama, you don't know nothing about New York City, or what can happen to you up there!

MOTHER HENRY. I know what can happen to you anywhere in this world. And I know right from wrong. We tried to raise you so you'd know right from wrong, too.

RICHARD. We don't see things the same way, Grandmama. I don't know if I really *know* right from wrong—I'd like to, I always dig people the most who know *anything*, especially right from wrong!

MOTHER HENRY. You've had yourself a little trouble, Richard, like we all do, and you a little tired, like we all get. You'll be all right. You a young man. Only, just try not to *go* so much, try to calm down a little. Your Daddy loves you. You his only son.

RICHARD. That's a good reason, Grandmama. Let me tell you about New York. You ain't never been North, have you?

MOTHER HENRY. Your Daddy used to tell me a little about it every time he come back from visiting you all up there.

RICHARD. Daddy don't know nothing about New York. He just come up for a few days and went right on back. That ain't the way to get to know New York. No ma'am. He *never* saw New York. Finally, I realized he wasn't never *going* to see it—you know, there's a whole lot of things Daddy's never seen? I've seen more than he has.

MOTHER HENRY. All young folks thinks that.

RICHARD. Did *you*? When you were young? Did you think you knew more than your mother and father? But I bet you really did, you a pretty shrewd old lady, quiet as it's kept.

MOTHER HENRY. No, I didn't think that. But I thought I could find *out* more, because *they* were born in slavery, but *I* was born free.

RICHARD. *Did* you find out more?

MOTHER HENRY. I found out what I had to find out—to take care of my husband and raise my children in the fear of God.

RICHARD. You know I don't believe in God, Grand-mama.

MOTHER HENRY. You don't know what you talking about. Ain't no way possible for you not to believe in God. It ain't up to you.

RICHARD. Who's it up to, then?

MOTHER HENRY. It's up to the life in you—the life in you. *That* knows where it comes from, *that* believes in God. You doubt me, you just try holding your breath long enough to die.

RICHARD. You pretty smart, ain't you? [*A pause*] I convinced Daddy that I'd be better off in New York—and Edna, she convinced him too, she said it wasn't as tight for a black man up there as it is down here. Well, that's a crock, Grandmama, believe me when I tell you. At first I thought it was true, hell, I was just a green country boy and they ain't got no signs up, dig, saying you can't go here or you can't go there. No, you got to find that out all by your lonesome. But—for awhile—I thought everything was swinging and Edna, she's so dizzy she thinks everything is *always* swinging, so there we were— like *swinging*.

MOTHER HENRY. I know Edna got lost somewhere. But, Richard—why didn't *you* come back? You knew your Daddy wanted you back, your Daddy and me both.

RICHARD. I didn't want to come back here like a whipped dog. One whipped dog running to another whipped dog. No, I didn't want that. I wanted to make my Daddy proud of me—because, the day I left here, I sure as hell wasn't proud of *him*.

MOTHER HENRY. Be careful, son. Be careful. Your Daddy's a fine man. Your Daddy loves you.

RICHARD. I know, Grandmama. But I just wish, that day that Mama died, he'd took a pistol and gone through that damn white man's hotel and shot every son of a bitch in the place. That's right. I wish he'd shot them dead. I been dreaming of that day ever since I left here. I been dreaming of my Mama falling down the steps of that hotel. *My* Mama. I never believed she fell. I *always* believed that some white man pushed her down those steps. And I know that Daddy thought so, too. But he wasn't there, he didn't know, he couldn't say nothing, he couldn't *do* nothing. I'll never forget the way he looked—whipped, whipped, whipped, whipped!

MOTHER HENRY. She fell, Richard, she *fell*. The stairs were wet and slippery and she *fell*.

RICHARD. My mother *fell* down the steps of that damn white hotel? My mother was *pushed*—you remember yourself how them white bastards was always sniffing around my mother, *always* around her—because she was pretty and *black*!

MOTHER HENRY. Richard, you can't start walking around believing that all the suffering in the world is caused by white folks!

RICHARD. I can't? Don't tell me I can't. I'm going to treat everyone of them as though they were responsible for all the crimes that ever happened in the history of the world—oh, yes! They're responsible for all the misery *I've* ever seen, and that's good enough for me. It's because my Daddy's got no power that my Mama's dead. And he ain't got no power because he's *black*. And the only way the black man's going to *get* any power is to drive all the white men into the sea.

MOTHER HENRY. You're going to make yourself sick. You're going to make yourself sick with hatred.

RICHARD. No, I'm not. I'm going to make myself well. I'm going to make myself *well* with hatred— what do you think of that?

MOTHER HENRY. It can't be done. It can never be done. Hatred is a poison, Richard.

RICHARD. Not for me. I'm going to learn how to drink it—a little every day in the morning, and then a booster shot late at night. I'm going to remember everything. I'm going to keep it right here, at the very top of my mind. I'm going to remember Mama, and Daddy's face that day, and Aunt Edna and all her sad little deals and all those boys and girls in Harlem and all them pimps and whores and gang-sters and all them cops. And I'm going to remember all the dope that's flowed through my veins. I'm going to remember everything—the jails I been in and the cops that beat me and how long a time I spent screaming and stinking in my own dirt, trying to break my habit. I'm going to remember all that, and I'll get well. I'll get well.

MOTHER HENRY. Oh, Richard. Richard. Richard.

RICHARD. Don't Richard *me*. I tell you, I'm going to get *well*.

[*He takes a small, sawed-off pistol from his pocket.*]

MOTHER HENRY. Richard, what are you doing with that gun?

RICHARD. I'm carrying it around with me, that's what I'm doing with it. This gun goes everywhere I go.

MOTHER HENRY. How long have you had it?

RICHARD. I've had it a long, long time.

MOTHER HENRY. Richard—you never—?

RICHARD. No. Not yet. But I will when I have to. I'll sure as hell take one of the bastards with me.

MOTHER HENRY. Hand me that gun. Please.

RICHARD. I can't. This is all that the man understands. He don't understand nothing else. *Nothing else!*

MOTHER HENRY. Richard—your father—think of your father—

RICHARD. Don't tell him! You hear me? [*A pause*] Don't tell him!

MOTHER HENRY. Richard. Please.

RICHARD. Take the tray away, old lady. I ain't hungry no more.

[*After a moment, Mother Henry takes the tray and exits. Richard stretches out on the bed.*]

JUANITA. [*Off*]. Meridian? Mother Henry? Anybody home in this house? [*Enters*] Oh! Excuse me.

RICHARD. I think they might be over at the church. I reckon Grandmama went over there to pray for my soul.

JUANITA. Grandmama?

RICHARD. Who are you? Don't I know you?

JUANITA. Yes. I think you might.

RICHARD. Is your name Juanita?

JUANITA. If your name is Richard.

RICHARD. I'll be damned.

JUANITA. Ain't you a mess? So you finally decided to come back here—come here, let me hug you! Why, you ain't hardly changed at all—you just a little taller but you sure didn't gain much weight.

RICHARD. And I bet you the same old tomboy. You sure got the same loud voice—used to be able to hear you clear across this town.

JUANITA. Well, it's a mighty small town, Richard, that's what you always said—and the reason my voice got so loud so early, was that I started screaming for help right quick.

[*Peter enters.*]

Do you know Pete Spivey? He's someone come on the scene since you been gone. He's going to school down here, you should pardon the expression.

RICHARD. How do you do, man? Where you from?

PETE. I'm from a little place just outside Mobile.

RICHARD. Why didn't you go North, man? If you was going to make a *move*. *That's* the place. You get lost up there and I guarantee you some swinging little chick is sure to find you.

JUANITA. We'll let that pass. Are you together? Are you ready to meet the day?

RICHARD. I am *always* together, little sister. Tell me what you got on your mind.

PETE. We thought we'd just walk around town a little and maybe stop and have a couple of drinks somewhere. Or we can drive. I got a car.

RICHARD. I didn't think I'd never see you no more, Juanita. You been here all this time.

JUANITA. I sure have, sugar. Just waiting for you to come home.

RICHARD. Don't let this chick upset you, Pete. All we ever did was climb trees together.

PETE. She's had me climbing a few trees too. But we weren't doing it together.

[*Papa D.'s juke joint: Juke box music, loud. Less frantic than Richard's song. Couples dancing, all very young, doing very lively variations of the "Twist," the "Wobble," etc. Papa D. at the counter. It is now early evening. Juanita, Pete and Richard enter.*]

JUANITA. How you making it, Papa D.? We brought someone to see you—you recognize him?

PAPA D. It seems to me I know your face, young man. Yes, I'm *sure* I know your face. Now, wait a minute, don't tell me—you ain't Shirelee Anderson's boy, are you?

RICHARD. No. I remember Shirelee Anderson, but we ain't no kin.

PETE. Try again, Papa D.

PAPA D. You your father's boy. I just recognized that smile—you Reverend Henry's son. Well, how you doing? It's nice to have you back with us. You going to stay awhile?

RICHARD. Yes sir. I think I'll be around for awhile.

PAPA D. Yeah, I remember you little old string bean of a boy, full of the devil. How long you been gone from here?

RICHARD. Almost eight years now. I left in September—it'll be eight years next month.

PAPA D. Yeah—how's your Daddy? And your Grandmother? I ain't seen them for awhile.

PETE. Ain't you been going to church, Papa D.?

PAPA D. Well, you know how it is. I try, God *knows* I try!

RICHARD. They fine, Papa D.

PAPA D. You all don't want nothing to eat?

RICHARD. We'll think about it.

[*They sit down.*]

PETE. Old Papa D. got something on everybody, don't he?

JUANITA. You better believe it.

RICHARD. He's kind of a Tom, ain't he?

PETE. Yeah. He *talks* about Mister Charlie, and he *says* he's with us—us kids—but he ain't going to do nothing to offend him. You know, he's still trading with Lyle Britten.

RICHARD. Who's Lyle Britten?

PETE. Peckerwood, owns a store nearby. And, man, you ain't *seen* a peckerwood until you've seen Lyle Britten. Niggers been trading in his store for years, man, I wouldn't be surprised but if the cat was rich—but that man still expects you to step off the sidewalk when he comes along. So we been getting people to stop buying there.

JUANITA. He shot a colored man a few years back, shot him dead, and wasn't nothing never said, much less done, about it.

PETE. Lyle had been carrying on with this man's wife, dig, and naturally, Old Bill—his name was Bill Walker, everybody called him Old Bill—wanted to put a stop to it.

JUANITA. She was a pretty little thing—real little and real black.

RICHARD. She still around here?

PETE. No. She disappeared. She went North somewhere.

RICHARD. Jive mothers. They can rape and kill our women and we can't do nothing. But if we touch one of their dried-up, pale-assed women, we get our nuts cut off. You remember that chick I was telling you about earlier, lives in Greenwich Village in New York?

PETE. What about her?

RICHARD. She's *white*, man. I got a whole *gang* of white chicks in New York. That's *right*. And they can't get enough of what little Richard's got—and I give it to them, too, baby, believe me. You say black people ain't got no dignity? Man, you ought to watch a white woman when she wants you to give her a little bit. They will do anything, baby *any*-thing! Wait—I got some pictures. That's the one lives in the Village. *Ain't* she fine? I'd hate to tell you where I've had that long yellow hair. And, dig this one, this is Sandy, her old man works on Wall Street—

PETE. We're making Juanita nervous.

JUANITA. Don't worry about *me*. I've been a big girl for a *long* time. Besides, I'm studying abnormal psychology. So please feel free. Which one is this? What does *her* father do?

RICHARD. That's Sylvia. I don't know what her father does. She's a model. She's loaded with loot.

PETE. You take money from her?

RICHARD. I take their money and they love it. Any-way, they ain't got nothing else to do with it. Every one of them's got some piss-assed, faggoty white boy on a string somewhere. They go home and marry him, dig, when they can't make it with me no more—but when they want some *loving*, funky, down-home, bring-it-on-here-and-put-it-on-the-table style—

JUANITA. They sound very sad. It must be very sad for you, too.

RICHARD. Well, I want *them* to be sad, baby, I want to screw up *their* minds *forever*. But why should *I* be so sad? Hell, I was swinging, I just about had it made. I had me some fine chicks and a fine pad and my car, and, hell, I was on my way! But then—then I screwed up.

JUANITA. We heard you were sick.

RICHARD. Who told you I was sick?

JUANITA. Your father. Your grandmother. They didn't say what the sickness was.

[*Papa D. passes their table.*]

RICHARD. Hey, Papa D., come on over here. I want to show you something.

[*Papa D. comes over.*]

Hey, look at these, man, look! Ain't they some fine chicks? And you know who *each one* of them calls: *Baby! Oh, baby?* That's right. You looking at the man.

PAPA D. Where'd you steal those pictures, boy?

RICHARD. [*Laughs*]. *Steal* them! Man, I ain't got to steal girls' pictures. I'm telling you the truth!

PAPA D. Put them pictures away. I thought you had good sense. [*He goes back to the counter.*]

RICHARD. Ain't that a bitch. He's scared because I'm carrying around pictures of white girls. That's the trouble with niggers. They all scared of the man.

JUANITA. Well, I'm *not* scared of the man. But there's just no point in running around, asking—

PETE. —to be lynched.

RICHARD. Well, okay, I'll put my pictures away, then. I sure don't want to upset nobody.

PETE. Excuse me. I'll be back.

[*Exits.*]

RICHARD. You want to dance?

JUANITA. No. Not now.

RICHARD. You want something to eat?

JUANITA. No. Richard?

RICHARD. Yeah?

JUANITA. Were you *very* sick?

RICHARD. What d'you want to know for?

JUANITA. Like that. Because I used to be your girl friend.

RICHARD. You was more like a boy than a girl, though. I couldn't go nowhere without you. You were determined to get your neck broken.

JUANITA. Well, I've changed. I'm now much more like a girl than I am like a boy.

RICHARD. You didn't turn out too bad, considering what you had to start with.

JUANITA. Thank you. I guess.

RICHARD. How come you ain't married by now? Pete, now, he seems real fond of you.

JUANITA. He *is* fond of me, we're friends. But I'm not in any hurry to get married—not now. And not here. I'm not sure I'm going to stay here. I've been working very hard, but next year I think I'll leave.

RICHARD. Where would you go?

JUANITA. I don't know. I had always intended to go North to law school and then come back down here to practice law—God knows this town could stand it. But, now, I don't know.

RICHARD. It's rough, huh?

JUANITA. It's not that so much. It *is* rough—are you all right? Do you want to go?

RICHARD. No, no. I'm all right. Go on. [*A pause*] I'm all *right*. Go *on*.

JUANITA. It's rough because you can't help being scared. I don't want to die—what was the matter with you, Richard, what were you sick with?

RICHARD. It wasn't serious. And I'm better now.

JUANITA. Well, no, that's just it. You're not really better.

RICHARD. How do you mean?

JUANITA. I watch you—

RICHARD. *Why* do you watch me?

JUANITA. I care about you.

RICHARD. You care about me! I thought you could hold your liquor better than that, girl.

JUANITA. It's not liquor. Don't you believe that anyone can care about you?

RICHARD. Care about me! Do you know how many times chicks have told me that? That they *cared* about me?

JUANITA. Well. This isn't one of those times.

RICHARD. I was a junkie.

JUANITA. A what?

RICHARD. A junkie, a dope addict, a hop-head, a mainliner—a dope fiend! My arms and my legs, too, are full of holes!

JUANITA. I asked you tell *me*, not the world.

RICHARD. Where'd Pete go?

JUANITA. He's dancing.

RICHARD. You want to dance?

JUANITA. In a minute.

RICHARD. I got hooked about five years ago. See, I couldn't stand these chicks I was making it with, and I was working real hard at my music, and, man, I was lonely. You come off a gig, you be tired, and you'd already taken as much shit as you could stand from the managers and the people in the room you were working and you'd be off to make some down scene with some patsy white-faced bitch. And so you'd make the scene and somehow you'd wake up in the morning and the chick would be beside you, alive and well, and dying to make the scene again and somehow you'd managed not to strangle her, you hadn't beaten her to death. Like you wanted to. And you get out of there and you carry this pain around inside all day and all night long. No way to beat it—no *way*. But when I started getting high, I was cool, and it didn't bother me. And I wasn't lonely then, it was all right. And the chicks—I could handle them, they couldn't reach me. And I didn't know I was hooked—until I was *hooked*. Then I started getting into trouble and I lost a lot of gigs and I had to sell my car and I lost my pad and most of the chicks, they split, naturally—but not all of them—and then I got busted and I made that trip down to Lexington and—here I am. Way *down* upon the Swanee River. But I'm going to be all right. You can bet on it.

JUANITA. I'd like to do better than that. I'd like to see to it.

RICHARD. How?

JUANITA. Well, like I used to. I won't let you go anywhere without me.

RICHARD. You *still* determined to break your neck.

JUANITA. Well, it's a neck-breaking time. I wouldn't like to appear to be above the battle.

RICHARD. Do you have any idea of what you might be letting yourself in for?

JUANITA. No. But you said you were lonely. And I'm lonely, too.

[*Lyle enters, goes to the counter. His appearance causes a change in the atmosphere, but no one appears to stop whatever they are doing.*]

LYLE. Joel, how about letting me have some change for cigarettes? I got a kind of long drive ahead of me, and I'm out.

PAPA D. Howdy, Mister Lyle, how you been? Folks ain't been seeing much of you lately.

LYLE. [*Laughs*]. That's the truth. But I reckon old friends just stays old friends. Ain't that right?

PAPA D. That's right, Mister Lyle.

JUANITA. That's Lyle Britten. The one we were talking about before.

RICHARD. I wonder what he'd do if I walked into a white place.

JUANITA. Don't worry about it. Just stay out of white places—believe me!

RICHARD. [*Laughs*]. Let's TCB—that means taking care of business. Let's see if I can dance.

[*They rise, dance. Perhaps she is teaching him the "Fight," or he is teaching her the "Pony"; they are enjoying each other. Lyle gets his change, gets cigarettes out of the machine, crosses to the counter, pauses there to watch the dancers.*]

LYLE. Joel, you know I ain't never going to be able to dance like that.

PAPA D. Ain't nothing to it. You just got to be supple, that's all. I can *yet* do it.

[*Does a grotesque sketch of the "Twist."*]

LYLE. Okay, Joel, you got it. Be seeing you now.

PAPA D. Good night, Mister Lyle.

[*On Lyle's way out, he jostles Juanita. Richard stops, holding Juanita at the waist. Richard and Lyle stare at each other.*]

LYLE. Pardon me.

RICHARD. Consider yourself pardoned.

LYLE. You new around here?

PAPA D. He just come to town a couple of days ago, Mister Lyle.

RICHARD. Yeah. I just come to town a couple of days ago, Mister Lyle.

LYLE. Well. I sure hope your stay'll be a pleasant one.

[*Exits.*]

PETE. Man, are you *anxious* to leave this world? Because he wouldn't think nothing of helping you out of it.

RICHARD. Yeah. Well, I wouldn't think nothing of helping him out of it, neither. Come on, baby, record's going to waste—let's TCB.

[*They dance.*]

So you care about me, do you? Ain't that a bitch?

[*The church: Pete and Juanita, a little apart from the others.*]

PETE. Why have you been avoiding me? Don't answer that. You started going away from me as soon as Richard came to this town. Now listen, Richard's dead but you still won't turn to me. I don't want to ask you for more than you can give, but why have you locked me out? I *know*—you liked me. We had nice times together.

JUANITA. We did. I *do* like you. Pete, I don't know. I wish you wouldn't ask me now. I wish *nobody* would ask me for anything now!

PETE. Is it because of Richard? Because if that's what it is, I'll wait—I'll wait until you know inside you that Richard's dead, but you're alive, and you're *supposed* to live, and I love you.

JUANITA. When Richard came, he—*hit*—me in some place where I'd never been touched before. I don't mean—just physically. He took all my attention—the deepest attention, maybe, that one person can give another. He needed me and he made a difference for me in this terrible world—do you see what I mean? And—it's funny—when I was with him, I didn't think of the future, I didn't dare. I didn't know if I could be strong enough to give him what he needed for as long as he would need it. It only lasted four or five days, Pete—four or five days, like a storm, like lightning! And what I saw during that storm I'll always see. Before that—I thought I knew who I was. But now I know that there are more things in me than I'll ever understand—and if I can't be faithful to myself, I'm afraid to promise I'll be faithful to one man!

PETE. I need you. I'll be faithful. That helps. You'll see.

JUANITA. So many people need so much!

PETE. So do you. So do I, Juanita. You take all my attention. My deepest attention.

JUANITA. You probably see things that I think are hidden. You probably think I'm a fool—or worse.

PETE. No. I think there's a lot of love in you, Juanita. If you'll let me help you, we can give it to the world. You can't give it to the world until you find a person who can help you—love the world.

JUANITA. I've discovered that. The world is a loveless place.

PETE. Not yet—

[*The lights of a car flash in their faces. Silence. They all listen tensely as the lights of another car approach, then pass; they watch the lights disappear. The telephone rings in the office. Mother Henry goes off to answer it. They listen to the murmur of Mother Henry's voice. Mother Henry enters.*]

MOTHER HENRY. That was Freddy Roberts. He say about two-thirty his dog started to barking and woke him up and he let the dog out on the porch and the dog run under the porch and there was two white men *under* Freddy's porch, fooling around with his gas pipes. Freddy thinks the dog bit one of them. He ran inside to get him his rifle but the rifle jammed and the men got away. He wanted to warn us, maybe they might come prowling around here.

LORENZO. Only we ain't got no rifles.

JUANITA. It was the dog that woke him up? I'll bet they come back and kill that dog!

JIMMY. What was they doing under the man's house, messing around with his gas pipes, at that hour of the morning?

PETE. They was fixing to blow up his house. They *might* be under your house, or *this* house, right now.

LORENZO. The real question is why two white men feel safe enough to come to a black neighborhood after dark in the first place. If a couple of them get their heads blown off, they don't feel so goddamn courageous!

JUANITA. I better call home.

[*Exits into office.*]

PETE. Will you have your mother call my house?

LORENZO. And have *his* mother call *my* house?

JIMMY. And tell all the people that don't have rifles or dogs to stay off their porches!

LORENZO. Tell them to fall on their knees and use their Bibles as breast-plates! Because I know that each and every one of them got *Bibles*! [*Meridian has walked to the church door, stands looking off*]

LORENZO. Don't they, Meridian?

MOTHER HENRY. Hush.

[*We hear Juanita's voice, off. Then silence falls. Lights dim on the students until they are in silhouette. Lights up on Meridian. We hear Richard's guitar, very lonely, far away.*]

[*A car door slams. The voices of young people saying good night. Richard appears, dressed as we last saw him.*]

RICHARD. Hello, Daddy. You still up?

MERIDIAN. Yeah. Couldn't sleep. How was your day?

RICHARD. It was all right. I'd forgotten what nights down here were like. You never see the stars in the city—and all these funny country sounds—

MERIDIAN. Crickets. And all kinds of bugs and worms, running around, busy, shaking all the bushes.

RICHARD. Lord, if I'd stayed here, I guess I might have married old Juanita by now, and we'd have a couple of kids and I'd be sitting around like this *every* night. What a wild thought.

MERIDIAN. You can still marry Juanita. Maybe she's been waiting for you.

RICHARD. Have you ever thought of marrying again?

MERIDIAN. I've thought of it.

RICHARD. Did you ever think of marrying Juanita?

MERIDIAN. Why do you ask me that?

RICHARD. Because I'd like to know.

MERIDIAN. *Why* would you like to know?

RICHARD. Why would you like to hide it? I'd like to know because I'm a man now, Daddy, and I can ask you to tell me the truth. I'm making up for lost time. Maybe you should try to make up for lost time too.

MERIDIAN. Yes. I've thought of marrying Juanita. But I've never spoken of it to her.

RICHARD. That's the truth?

MERIDIAN. Yes.

RICHARD. Why didn't you tell me the truth way back there? Why didn't you tell me my mother was murdered? She was pushed down them steps.

MERIDIAN. Richard, your mother's dead. People die in all kinds of ways. They die when their times comes to die. Your mother loved you and she was gone—there was nothing more I could do for her. I had to think of you. I didn't want you to be—poisoned—by useless and terrible suspicions. I didn't want to wreck your life. I knew your life was going to be hard enough. So, I let you go. I thought it might be easier for you—if I let you go. I didn't want you to grow up in this town.

RICHARD. But there was something else in it, too, Daddy. You didn't want me to look at you and be ashamed of you. And you didn't know what was in my eyes, you couldn't stand it, I could tell from the way you looked at me sometimes. That was it, wasn't it?

MERIDIAN. I thought it was better. I suppose I thought it was all over for me, anyway. And I thought I owed it to your mother and to girls like your mother, to try—try to change, to purify this town, where she was born, and where we'd been so happy, and which she loved so much. I was wrong, I guess. I was wrong.

RICHARD. You've just been a public man, Daddy, haven't you? Since that day? You haven't been a private man at all.

MERIDIAN. No. I haven't. Try to forgive me.

RICHARD. There's nothing to forgive. I've been down the road a little bit. I know what happened. I'm going to try again, Daddy.

[*A pause. Richard take out the gun.*]

Here. Grandmama saw this this morning and she got all upset. So I'll let you hold it for me. You keep it till I ask you for it, okay? But when I ask you for it, you got to give it to me. Okay?

MERIDIAN [*Takes the gun*]. Okay. I'm proud of how you've come through—all you've had to bear.

RICHARD. I'm going to get some sleep. You coming over to the house now?

MERIDIAN. Not yet.

RICHARD. Good night. Say, Daddy?

MERIDIAN. Yeah?

RICHARD. You kind of like the idea of me and Juanita getting together?

MERIDIAN. Yeah. I think it's a fine idea.

RICHARD. Well, I'm going to sleep on it, then. Good night.

MERIDIAN. Good night.

[*Richard exits.*]

[*After Richard's exit, the lights come up on the students.*]

JUANITA. Lord it's gone and started raining.

PETE. And you worried about your hair.

JUANITA. I am *not* worried about my hair. I'm thinking of wearing it the way God arranged it in the first place.

LORENZO. Now, now, Mau-Mau.

PETE. This chick is going through some weird changes.

MERIDIAN. That's understandable. We all are.

JIMMY. Well, we'll see you sometime tomorrow. It promises to be a kind of *active* day.

MERIDIAN. Yes, we've got some active days ahead of us. You all better get some sleep.

JUANITA. How're you getting home, Jimmy?

JIMMY. Pete's driving us all home.

JUANITA. And then—are you going to drive all the way to your house alone, Pete?

PETE. You're jumpy tonight. I'll stay at Lorenzo's house.

LORENZO. You can call your house from there.

MOTHER HENRY. You get some sleep, too, Meridian, it's past three o'clock in the morning. Don't you stay over here much longer.

MERIDIAN. No, I won't. Good night, all.

MOTHER HENRY. Good night, children. See you in the morning., God willing.

[*They exit. Meridian walks to the pulpit, puts his hand on the Bible. Parnell enters.*]

PARNELL. I hear it was real bad tonight.

MERIDIAN. Not as bad as it's going to get. Maybe I was wrong not to let the people arm.

PARNELL. If the Negroes were armed, it's the Negroes who'd be slaughtered. You know that.

MERIDIAN. They're slaughtered anyway. And I don't know that. I thought I knew it—but now I'm not so sure.

PARNELL. What's come over you? What's going to happen to the people in this town, this church—if you go to pieces?

MERIDIAN. Maybe they'll find a leader who can lead them someplace.

PARNELL. Somebody with a gun?

[*Meridian is silent.*]

Is that what you mean?

MERIDIAN. I'm a Christian. I've been a Christian all my life, like my Mama and Daddy before me and like their Mama and Daddy before them. Of course, if you go back far enough, you get to a point *before* Christ, if you see what I mean, B.C.—and at that point, I've been thinking, black people weren't raised to turn the other cheek, and in the hope of heaven. No, then they didn't have to take low. Before Christ. They walked around just as good as anybody else, and when they died, they didn't go to heaven, they went to join their ancestors. My son's dead, but he's not gone to join his ancestors. He was a sinner, so he must have gone to hell—if we're going to believe what the Bible says. Is that such an improvement, such a mighty advance over B.C.? I've been thinking, I've had to think—would I have *been* such a Christian if I hadn't been born black? Maybe I *had* to become a Christian in order to have any dignity at all. Since I wasn't a man in men's eyes, then I could be a man in the eyes of God. But that didn't protect my wife. She's dead, too soon, we don't really know how. That didn't protect my son—he's dead, we know how too well. That hasn't changed this town—this town, where you couldn't find a white Christian at high noon on Sunday! The eyes of God—maybe those eyes are blind—I never let myself think of that before.

PARNELL. Meridian, you can't be the man who gives the signal for the holocaust.

MERIDIAN. Must I be the man who watches while his people are beaten, chained, starved, clubbed, butchered?

PARNELL. You used to say that your people were all the people in the world—all the people God ever made, or would make. You said your race was the human race.

MERIDIAN. The human race!

PARNELL. I've never seen you like this before. There's something in your tone I've never heard before—rage—maybe hatred—

MERIDIAN. You've heard it before. You just never recognized it before. You've heard it in all those blues and spirituals and gospel songs you claim to love so much.

PARNELL. I was talking about *you*—not your history. I have a history, too. And don't be so sure I've never heard that sound. Maybe I've never heard anything else. Perhaps my life is also hard to bear.

MERIDIAN. I watched you all this week up at the Police Chief's office with me. And you know how to handle him because you're sure you're better than he is. But you both have more in common with each other than either of you have with me. And, for both of you—I watched this, I never watched it before—it was just a black boy that was dead, and that was a problem. He saw the problem one way, you saw it another way. But it wasn't a *man* that was dead, not my *son*—you held yourselves away from *that!*

PARNELL. I may have sounded—cold. It was not because I felt cold. There was no other way to sound, Meridian. I took the only tone which—it seemed to me—could accomplish what we wanted. And I *do* know the Chief of Police better than you—because I'm white. And I can make him listen to me—because I'm white. I don't know if I think I'm so much better than he is. I know what we have done—and do. But you must have mercy on us. We have no other hope.

MERIDIAN. You have never shown us any mercy at all.

PARNELL. Meridian, give me credit for knowing you're in pain. We are two men, two friends—in spite of all that could divide us. We have come too far together, there is too much at stake, for you to become black now, for me to become white. Don't accuse me. Don't accuse me. *I* didn't do it.

MERIDIAN. So was my son—innocent.

PARNELL. Meridian—when I asked for mercy a moment ago—I meant—please—please try to understand that it is not so easy to leap over fences, to give things up—all right, to surrender privilege! But if you were among the privileged you would know what I mean. It's not a matter of trying to hold *on*; the things, the privilege—are part of you, are *who* you are. It's in the *gut*.

MERIDIAN. Then where's the point of this struggle, where's the hope? If Mister Charlie can't change—

PARNELL. Who's Mister Charlie?

MERIDIAN. You're Mister Charlie. *All* white men are Mister Charlie!

PARNELL. You sound more and more like your son, do you know that? A lot of the colored people here didn't approve of him, but he said things they longed to say—said right out loud, for all the world to hear, how much he despised white people!

MERIDIAN. He didn't say things I longed to say. Maybe it was because he was my son. I didn't care *what* he felt about white people. I just wanted him to live, to have his own life. There's something you don't understand about being black, Parnell. If you're a black man, with a black son, you have to forget all about white people and concentrate on trying to save your child. That's why I let him stay up North. I was wrong, I failed, I failed. Lyle walked him up the road and killed him.

PARNELL. We don't *know* Lyle killed him. And Lyle denies it.

MERIDIAN. Of course, he denies it—what do you mean, we don't *know* Lyle killed him?

PARNELL. We *don't* know—all we can say is that it looks that way. And circumstantial evidence is a tricky thing.

MERIDIAN. *When* it involves a white man killing a black man—if Lyle didn't kill him, Parnell, who did?

PARNELL. I don't *know*. But we don't know that Lyle did it.

MERIDIAN. Lyle doesn't deny that he killed Old Bill.

PARNELL. No.

MERIDIAN. And we know how Lyle feels about colored people.

PARNELL. Well, yes. From your point of view. But—from another point of view—Lyle hasn't got anything *against* colored people. He just—

MERIDIAN. He just doesn't think they're human.

PARNELL. Well, even *that's* not true. He doesn't think they're *not* human—after all, I know him, he's hot-tempered and he's far from being the brightest man in the world—but he's not mean, he's not cruel. He's a poor white man. The poor whites have been just as victimized in this part of the world as the blacks have ever been!

MERIDIAN. For God's sake spare me the historical view! Lyle's responsible for Richard's death.

PARNELL. But, Meridian, we can't, even in our own minds, *decide* that he's guilty. We have to operate the way justice *always* has to operate and give him the benefit of the doubt.

MERIDIAN. *What* doubt?

PARNELL. Don't you see, Meridian, that now you're operating the way white people in this town operate whenever a colored man's on trial?

MERIDIAN. When was the last time one of us was on *trial* here, Parnell?

PARNELL. That *can't* have anything to do with it, it *can't*. We must forget about all—*all* the past injustice. We have to start from scratch, or do our best to start from scratch. It isn't vengeance we're after. Is it?

MERIDIAN. I don't want vengeance. I don't want to be paid back—anyway, I couldn't be. I just want Lyle to be made to know that what he did was evil. I just want this town to be forced to face the evil that it countenances and to turn from evil and do good. That's why I've stayed in this town so long!

PARNELL. But if Lyle didn't do it? Lyle is a friend of mine—a strange friend, but a friend. I love him. I know how he suffers.

MERIDIAN. *How* does he suffer?

PARNELL. He suffers—from being in the dark—from having things inside him that he can't name and can't face and can't control. He's not a wicked man. I know he's not, I've known him almost all his life! The face he turns to you, Meridian, isn't the face he turns to me.

MERIDIAN. Is the face he turns to you more real than the face he turns to me? *You* go ask him if he killed my son.

PARNELL. They're going to ask him that in court. That's why I fought to bring about this trial. And he'll say no.

MERIDIAN. I don't care what he says in court. You go ask him. If he's your friend, he'll tell you the truth.

PARNELL. No. No, he may not. He's—he's maybe a little afraid of me.

MERIDIAN. If you're *his* friend, you'll know whether he's telling you the truth or not. Go ask him.

PARNELL. I can't do it. I'm his friend. I can't betray him.

MERIDIAN. But you can betray *me*? You *are* a white man, aren't you? Just another white man—after all.

PARNELL. Even if he says yes, it won't make any difference. The jury will never convict him.

MERIDIAN. Is that why you fought to bring about the trial? I don't care what the jury does. I know he won't say yes to them. He won't say yes to me. But he might say yes to you. You say we don't know. Well, I've got a right to know. And I've got the right to ask you to find out—since you're the only man who *can* find out. And *I've* got to find out—whether we've been friends all these years, or whether I've just been your favorite Uncle Tom.

PARNELL. You know better than that.

MERIDIAN. I don't know, Parnell, any longer—any of the things I used to know. Maybe I never knew them. I'm tired. Go home.

PARNELL. You don't trust me anymore, do you, Meridian?

MERIDIAN. Maybe I never trusted you. I don't know. Maybe I never trusted myself. Go home. Leave me alone. I must look back at my record.

PARNELL. Meridian—what you ask—I don't know if I can do it for you.

MERIDIAN. I don't want you to do it for me! I want you to do it for you. Good night.

PARNELL. Good night.

[*Parnell exits. Meridian comes downstage. It is dawn.*]

MERIDIAN. My record! Would God—would *God*—would God I had died for thee—my son, my son!

CURTAIN

END OF ACT I

Act II

Whitetown: The kitchen of Lyle's house. Sunday morning. Church bells. A group of white people, all ages, men and women.

    Jo and an older woman, Hazel, have just taken a cake out of the oven. Hazel sets it out to cool.

HAZEL. It's a shame—having to rush everything this way. But it can't be helped.

JO. Yes. I'm just so upset. I can't help it. I know it's silly. I know they can't do nothing to Lyle.

HAZEL. Girl, you just put all those negative thoughts right out of your mind. We're going to have your little anniversary celebration *tonight* instead of *tomorrow* night because we have reason to believe that *tomorrow* night your husband might be called away on business. Now, you think about it that way. Don't you go around here with a great long face, trying to demoralize your guests. I won't have it. You too young and pretty for that.

LILLIAN. Hallelujah! I *do* believe that I have finally mastered this recipe.

SUSAN. Oh, good! Let me see.

LILLIAN. I've only tried it once before, and it's real hard. You've got to time it just right.

SUSAN. I have tried it and tried it and it never comes out! But yours is wonderful! We're going to eat tonight, folks!

RALPH. You supposed to be cooking something, too, ain't you?

SUSAN. I'm cooking our contribution later, at our own house. We got enough women here already, messing up Jo's kitchen.

JO. I'm just so glad you all come by I don't know what to do. Just go ahead and mess up that kitchen, I got lots of time to clean it.

ELLIS. Susan's done learned how to cook, huh?

RALPH. Oh, yeah, she's a right fine cook. All you got to do is look at me. I never weighed this much in my life.

ELLIS. Old Lyle's done gained weight in this year, too. Nothing like steady home cooking, I guess, ha-ha! It really don't seem like it was a year ago you two got married. Declare, I never thought Lyle was going to jump up and do that thing. But old Jo, here, she hooked him.

REVEREND PHELPS. Well, I said the words over them, and if I ever saw a happy man in my life, it was Big Lyle Britten that day. Both of them—there was just a light shining out of them.

GEORGE. I'd propose a toast to them, if it wasn't so early on a Sunday, and if the Reverend wasn't here.

REVEREND PHELPS. Ain't nothing wrong with toasting happy people, no matter what the day or hour.

ELLIS. You heard the Reverend! You got anything in this house we can drink to your happiness in, Mrs. Britten?

JO. I'm pretty sure we do. It's a pity Lyle ain't up yet. He ain't never slept through this much racket before.

ELLIS. No ma'am, he ain't never been what you'd call a heavy sleeper. Not before he passed out, ha-ha! We used to have us some times together, him and me, before he got him some sense and got married.

GEORGE. Let him sleep easy. He ain't got no reason not to.

JO. Lyle's always got his eye on the ball, you know— and he's just been at that store, night after night after night, drawing up plans and taking inventory and I don't know what all—because, come fall, he's planning to branch out and have a brand new store, just about. You all won't recognize the place, I guarantee you!

ELLIS. Lyle's just like his Daddy. You can't beat him. The harder a thing is, well, the surer you can be that old Lyle Britten will do it. Why, Lyle's Daddy never got old—*never*! He was drinking and running after women—and getting them, too!—until just before they put him in his grave. I could tell you stories about the old man, boy—of course, I can't tell them now, on a Sunday morning, in front of all these women!

JO. Here you are, gentlemen. I hope you all drink bourbon.

RALPH. Listen to her!

GEORGE. Ladies! Would you all like to join us in a morning toast to the happy and beloved and loving couple, Mr. and Mrs. Lyle Britten, on the day immediately preceding their first wedding anniversary?

ELLIS. The bridegroom ain't here because he's weary from all his duties, both public and private. Ha-ha! But he's a good man, and he's done a lot for us, and I know you all know what I'm talking about, and I just feel like we should honor him and his lovely young wife. Ladies! Come on, Reverend Phelps says it's all right.

SUSAN. Not too much for me, Ralph.

LILLIAN. I don't think I've ever had a drink at this hour of a Sunday morning, and in the presence of my pastor!

[*They pour, drink, and sing "For He's a Jolly Good Fellow."*]

HAZEL. Now you've started her to crying, naturally. Here, honey, you better have a little drink yourself.

JO. You all have been *so* wonderful. I can't imagine how Lyle can go on sleeping. Thank you, Hazel. Here's to all of you! [*Drinks*] Listen. They're singing over there now.

[*They listen.*]

HAZEL. Sometimes they can sound so nice. Used to take my breath away when I was a girl.

ELLIS. What's happened to this town? It was peaceful here, we all got along, we didn't have no trouble.

GEORGE. Oh, we had a little trouble from time to time, but it didn't amount to a hill of beans. Niggers was all right then, you could always get you a nigger to help you catch a nigger.

LILLIAN. That's right. They had their ways, we had ours, and everything went along the way God intended.

JO. I've never been scared in this town before—never. They was all like my own people. I never knew of anyone to mistreat a colored person—have you? And they certainly didn't *act* mistreated. But now, when I walk through this town—I'm scared—like don't know what's going to happen next. How come the colored people to hate us so much, all of a sudden? We *give* them everything they've got!

REVEREND PHELPS. Their minds have been turned. They have turned away from God. They're a simple people—warm-hearted and good-natured. But they are very easily led, and now they are harkening to the counsel of these degenerate Communist race-mixers. And they don't know what terrible harm they can bring on themselves—and on us all.

JO. You can't tell what they're thinking. Why, colored folks you been knowing all your life—you're almost afraid to hire them, almost afraid to *talk* to them—you don't know what they're thinking.

ELLIS. *I* know what they're thinking.

SUSAN. We're not much better off than the Communist countries—that's what Ralph says. *They* live in fear. They don't want us to teach God in our schools—you send your child to school and you don't know *what* kind of Godless atheist is going to be filling the little one's mind with all *kinds* of filth.

And he's going to believe it, of course, kids don't know no better. And now they tell us we got to send our kids to *school* with niggers—why, everybody *knows* that ain't going to work, won't nobody get no education, white *or* black. Niggers can't learn like white folks, they ain't got the same *interests*.

ELLIS. They got one interest. And it's just below the belly button.

GEORGE. [*Laughs*]. You know them yellow niggers? Boy, ain't they the worst kind? There own folks don't want them, don't nobody want them, and you *can't* do nothing with them—you might be able to scare a black nigger, but you can't do nothing with a yellow nigger.

REVEREND PHELPS. That's because he's a mongrel. And a mongrel is the lowest creation in the animal kingdom.

ELLIS. Mrs. Britten, you're married and all the women in this room are married and I know you've seen your husband without no clothes on—but have you seen a nigger without no clothes on? No, I guess you haven't. Well, he ain't like a white man, Mrs. Britten.

GEORGE. That's right.

ELLIS. Mrs. Britten, if you was to be raped by an orang-outang out of the jungle or a *stallion*, couldn't do you no worse than a nigger. You wouldn't be no more good for nobody. I've *seen* it.

GEORGE. That's *right*.

RALPH. That's why we men have got to be so vigilant. I tell you, I have to be away a lot nights, you know—and I bought Susan a gun and I taught her how to use it, too.

SUSAN. And I'm a pretty good shot now, too. Ralph says he's real proud of me.

RALPH. She's just like a pioneer woman.

HAZEL. I'm so glad Esther's not here to see this. She'd die of shame. She was the sweetest colored woman—you remember her. She just about raised us, used to sing us to sleep at night, and she could tell just the most beautiful stories—the kind of stories that could scare you and make you laugh and make you cry, you know? Oh, she was wonderful. I don't remember a cross word or an evil expression all the time she was with us. She was always the same. And I believe she knew more about me than my own mother and father knew. I just told her everything. Then, one of her sons got killed—he went bad, just like this boy they having a funeral for here tonight—and she got sick. I nursed her, I bathed that woman's body with my own hands. And she told me once, she said, "Miss Hazel, you are just like an angel of light." She said, "My own couldn't have done more for me than you have done." She was a wonderful old woman.

JO. I believe I hear Lyle stirring.

SUSAN. Mrs. Britten, somebody else is coming to call on you. My! It's that Parnell James! I wonder if he's sober this morning. He never *looks* sober.

ELLIS. He never acts it, either.

[*Parnell enters.*]

PARNELL. Good morning, good people! Good morning, Reverend Phelps! How good it is to see brethren—and sistren—walking together. Or, in this case, standing together—something like that, anyway; my Bible's a little rusty. Is church over already? Or are you having it here? Good morning, Jo.

JO. Good morning, Parnell. Sit down, I'll pour you a cup of coffee.

GEORGE. You look like you could use it.

REVEREND PHELPS. We were all just leaving.

PARNELL. Please don't leave on my account, Reverend Phelps. Just go on as you were, praying or singing, just as the spirit may move you. I *would* love that cup of coffee, Jo.

ELLIS. You been up all night?

PARNELL. Is that the way I look? Yes, I *have* been up all night.

ELLIS. Tom-catting around, I'll bet. Getting drunk and fooling with all the women.

PARNELL. Ah, you flatter me. And in games of chance, my friend, you have no future at all. I'm sure you always lose at poker. So *stop betting*. I was not tom-catting, I was at home, working.

GEORGE. You been over the way this morning? You been at the nigger funeral?

PARNELL. The funeral takes place this evening. And, yes, I will be there. Would you care to come along? Leaving your baseball bat at home, of course.

JO. We heard the singing—

PARNELL. Darkies are always singing. You people know that. What made you think it was a funeral?

JO. Parnell! You are the limit! Would anybody else like a little more coffee? It's still good and hot.

ELLIS. We heard that a nigger got killed. That's why we thought it was a funeral.

GEORGE. They bury their dead over the way, don't they?

PARNELL. They do when the dogs leave enough to bury, yes.

[*A pause*]

ELLIS. Dogs?

PARNELL. Yes—you know. Teeth. Barking. Lots of noise.

ELLIS. A lot of people in this town, Parnell, would like to know exactly where you stand, on a lot of things.

PARNELL. That's exactly where I stand. On a lot of things. Why don't you read my paper?

LILLIAN. I wouldn't filthy my hands with that Communist sheet!

PARNELL. Ah? But the father of your faith, the cornerstone of that church of which you are so precious an adornment, was a communist, possibly the first. He may have done some tom-catting. We *know* he did some drinking. And he knew a lot of—loose ladies and drunkards. It's all in the Bible, isn't it, Reverend Phelps?

REVEREND PHELPS. I won't be drawn into your blasphemous banter. Ellis is only asking what many of us want to know—are you with us or against us? And he's telling you what we all feel. We've put up with your irresponsibility long enough. We won't tolerate it any longer. Do I make myself clear?

PARNELL. Not at all. If you're threatening me, be specific. First of all, what's this irresponsibility that you won't tolerate? And if you aren't going to tolerate it, what *are* you going to do? Dip me in tar and feathers? Boil me in oil? Castrate me? Burn me? Cover yourselves in white sheets and come and burn crosses in front of my house? Come on, Reverend Phelps, don't stand there with your mouth open, it makes you even more repulsive than you are with it closed, and all your foul, graveyard breath comes rushing out, and it makes me want to vomit. Out with it, boy! What's on your mind?

ELLIS. You got away with a lot of things in this town, Parnell, for a long time, because your father was a big man here.

PARNELL. One at a time. I was addressing your spiritual leader.

SUSAN. He's *worse* than a nigger.

PARNELL. I take that as a compliment. I'm sure no man will ever say as much for you. Reverend Phelps?

REVEREND PHELPS. I think I speak for us all—for *myself* and for us all, when I say that our situation down here has become much too serious for flippancy and cynicism. When things were more in order here, we didn't really mind your attitude, and your paper didn't matter to us, we never read it, anyway.

ELLIS. We knew you were just a spoiled rich boy, with too much time on his hands that he didn't know what to do with.

REVEREND PHELPS. And so you started this paper and tried to make yourself interesting with all these subversive attitudes. I honestly thought that you would grow out of it.

GEORGE. Or go North.

REVEREND PHELPS. I know these attitudes were not your father's attitudes, or your mother's. I was very often invited to your home when they were alive—

PARNELL. How well I remember! What attitudes are you speaking of?

HAZEL. Race-mixing!

PARNELL. *Race-mixing*! Ladies and gentlemen, do you think anybody gives a good goddamn who you sleep with? You can go down to the swamps and couple with the snakes, for all I care, or for all anybody else cares. You may find that the snakes don't want you, but that's a problem for you and the snakes to work out, and it might prove astonishingly simple—the working out of the problem, I mean. I've never said a word about race-mixing. I've talked about social justice.

LILLIAN. That sounds Communistic to me!

PARNELL. It means that if I have a hundred dollars, and I'm black, and you have a hundred dollars, and you're white, I should be able to get as much value for *my* hundred dollars—my black hundred dollars—as you get for your *white* hundred dollars. It also means that I should have an equal opportunity to *earn* that hundred dollars—

ELLIS. Niggers can get work just as well as a white man can. Hell, *some* niggers make *more* money than me.

PARNELL. Some niggers are smarter than you, Ellis. Much smarter. And much nicer. And niggers *can't* get work just as well as a white man can, and you know it.

ELLIS. What's stopping them? They got hands.

PARNELL. Ellis, you don't really work with your *hands*—you're a salesman in a shoe store. And your boss wouldn't give that job to a nigger.

GEORGE. Well, goddammit, white men come before niggers! They *got* to!

PARNELL. Why?

[Lyle enters.]

LYLE. What's all this commotion going on in my house?

JO. Oh, Lyle, good morning! Some folks just dropped in to see you.

LYLE. It sounded like they was about to come to

blows. Good morning, Reverend Phelps, I'm glad to see you here. I'm sorry I wasn't up, but I guess my wife might have told you, I've not been sleeping well nights. When I *do* go to sleep, she just lets me sleep on.

REVEREND PHELPS. Don't you apologize, son—we understand. We only came by to let you know that we're with you and every white person in this town is with you.

JO. Isn't that nice of them, Lyle? They've been here quite a spell, and we've had *such* a nice time.

LYLE. Well, that *is* mighty nice of you, Reverend, and all of you—hey there, Ellis! Old George! And Ralph and Susan—how's married life suit you? Guess it suits you all right, ain't nobody seen you in months, ha-ha! Mrs. Proctor, Mrs. Barker, how you all? Hey! Old Parnell! What you doing up so early?

PARNELL. I was on my way to church, but they seemed to be having the meeting here. So I joined the worshippers.

LYLE. On your way to church, that's a good one. Bet you ain't been to bed yet.

PARNELL. No, I haven't.

LYLE. You folks don't mind if I have a little breakfast? Jo, bring me something to eat! Susan, you look mighty plump and rosy, you ain't keeping no secrets from us, are you?

SUSAN. I don't think so, Lyle.

LYLE. I don't know, you got that look—like a real ripe peach, just right for eating. You ain't been slack in your duty, have you, Ralph? Look at the way she's blushing! I guess you all right, boy.

ELLIS. You know what time they coming for you tomorrow?

LYLE. Sometime in the morning, I reckon. I don't know.

REVEREND PHELPS. I saw the Chief of Police the other day. He really doesn't want to do it, but his hands are tied. It's orders from higher up, from the North.

LYLE. Shoot, I know old Frank don't want to arrest me. I understand. I ain't worried. I know the people in this town is with me. I got nothing to worry about.

ELLIS. They trying to force us to put niggers on the jury—that's what I hear. Claim it won't be a fair trial if we don't.

HAZEL. Did you *ever* hear anything like that in your *life*?

LYLE. Where they going to find the niggers?

ELLIS. Oh, I bet your buddy, Parnell, has got that all figured out.

LYLE. How about it, Parnell? You going to find some niggers for them to put on that jury?

PARNELL. It's not up to me. But I might recommend a couple.

GEORGE. And how they going to get to court? You going to protect them?

PARNELL. The police will protect them. Or the State troopers—

GEORGE. That's a good one!

PARNELL. Or Federal marshals.

GEORGE. Look here, you really think there should be niggers on that jury?

PARNELL. Of course I do, and so would you, if you had any sense. For one thing, they're forty-four percent of the population of this town.

ELLIS. But they don't vote. Not most of them.

PARNELL. Well. That's also a matter of interest to the Federal government. Why *don't* they vote? They got hands.

ELLIS. You claim Lyle's your buddy—

PARNELL. Lyle *is* my buddy. That's why I want him to have a fair trial.

HAZEL. I can't listen to no more of this, I'm sorry, I just can't. Honey, I'll see you all tonight, you hear?

REVEREND PHELPS. We're all going to go now. We just wanted to see how you were, and let you know that you could count on us.

LYLE. I sure appreciate it, Reverend, believe me, I do. You make me feel much better. Even if a man knows he ain't done no wrong, still, it's a kind of troublesome spot to be in. Wasn't for my good Jo, here, I don't know what I'd do. Good morning, Mrs. Barker. Mrs. Proctor. So long, George, it's been good to see you. Ralph, you take good care of Susan, you hear? And name the first one after me— you might have to bring it on up to the jail house so I can see it.

SUSAN. Don't think like that. Everything's going to be all right.

LYLE. You're sure?

SUSAN. I guarantee it. Why they couldn't—*couldn't*— do anything to you!

LYLE. Then I believe it. I believe *you.*

SUSAN. You keep right on believing.

ELLIS. Remember what we said, Parnell.

PARNELL. So long, Ellis. See you next Halloween.

LYLE. Let's get together, boy, soon as this mess is over.

ELLIS. You bet. This mess is just about over now—we ain't going to let them prolong it. And I know just the thing'll knock all this clear out of your mind,

this, and everything else, ha-ha! Bye-bye, Mrs. Britten.

JO. Goodbye. And thanks for coming!

[*Hazel, Lillian, Susan, Ralph, Ellis, Reverend Phelps and George exit.*]

LYLE. They're nice people.

JO. Yes. They are.

PARNELL. They certainly think a lot of you.

LYLE. You ain't jealous, are you, boy? No. We've all had the same kind of trouble—it's the kind of troubles you wouldn't know about, Parnell, because you've never had to worry about making your living. But me! I been doing hard work from the time I was a puppy. Like my Mama and Daddy before me, God rest their souls, and their Mama and Daddy before them. They wore themselves out on the land—the land never give them nothing. Nothing but an empty belly and some skinny kids. I'm the only one growed up to be a man. That's because I take after my Daddy—he was skinny as a piece of wire, but he was hard as any rock. And stubborn! Lord, you ain't never seen nobody so stubborn. He should have been born sooner. Had he been born sooner, when this was still a free country, and a man could really *make* some money, I'd have been born rich as you, Parnell, maybe even richer. I tell you— the old man struggled. He worked harder than any nigger. But he left me this store.

JO. You reckon we going to be able to leave it to the little one?

LYLE. We're going to leave him more than that. That little one ain't going to have nothing to worry about. I'm going to leave him as rich as old Parnell here, and he's going to be educated, too, better than his Daddy; better, even, than Parnell!

PARNELL. You going to send him to school in Switzerland?

LYLE. *You* went there for a while, didn't you?

JO. That's where Parnell picked up all his wild ideas.

PARNELL. Yes. Be careful. There were a couple of African princes studying in the school I went to— they did a lot more studying than I did, I must say.

LYLE. African princes, huh? What were they like? Big and black, I bet, elephant tusks hanging around their necks.

PARNELL. Some of them wore a little ivory, on a chain—silver chain. They were like everybody else. Maybe they thought they were a little *better* than most of us—the Swiss girls certainly thought so.

LYLE. The *Swiss* girls? You mean they didn't have no women of their own?

PARNELL. Lots of them. Swiss women, Danish women, English women, French women, Finns, Russians, even a couple of Americans.

JO. I don't believe you. Or else they was just trying to act like foreigners. I can't stand people who try to act like something they're not.

PARNELL. They were just trying to act like women— poor things. And the Africans were men, no one had ever told them that they weren't.

LYLE. You mean there weren't no African women around at *all*? Weren't the Swiss people kind of upset at having all these niggers around with no women?

PARNELL. They didn't seem to be upset. They seemed delighted. The niggers had an awful lot of money. And there weren't many African girls around because African girls aren't educated the way American girls are.

JO. The American girls didn't *mind* going out with the Africans?

PARNELL. Not at all. It appears that the Africans were excellent dancers.

LYLE. I won't never send no daughter of mine to Switzerland.

PARNELL. Well, what about your son? *He* might grow fond of some little African princess.

LYLE. Well, that's different. I don't care about that, long as he leaves her over there.

JO. It's *not* different—how can you say that? White men ain't got no more business fooling around with black women than—

LYLE. Girl, will you stop getting yourself into an uproar? Men is different from women—they ain't as delicate. Man can do a lot of things a woman can't do, you know that.

PARNELL. You've heard the expression, sowing wild oats? Well, all the men we know sowed a lot of wild oats before they finally settled down and got married.

LYLE. That's right. Men *have* to do it. They ain't like women. Parnell is *still* sowing his wild oats—I sowed mine.

JO. And a woman that wants to be a decent woman just has to— *wait*—until the men get tired of going to bed with—harlots!—and decide to settle down!

PARNELL. Well, it sounds very unjust, I know, but that's the way it's always been. I *suppose* the decent women were waiting—though nobody seems to know *exactly* how they spent the time.

JO. Parnell!

PARNELL. Well, there *are* some who waited too long.

JO. Men ought to be ashamed. How can you blame a woman if she—goes wrong? If a decent woman can't find a decent man—why—it must happen all the time—they get tired of waiting.

LYLE. Not if they been raised right, no sir, that's what my Daddy said, and I've never known it to fail. And look at you—*you* didn't get tired of waiting. Ain't nobody in this town ever been able to say a word against you. Man, I was so scared when I finally asked this girl to marry me. I was afraid she'd turn me out of the house. Because I had been pretty wild. Parnell can tell you.

JO. I had heard.

LYLE. But she didn't. I looked at her, it seemed almost like it was the first time—you know, the first time you really *look* at a woman—and I thought, I'll be damned if I don't believe I can make it with her. I believe I can. And she looked at me like she loved me. It was in her eyes. And it was just like somebody had lifted a great big load off my heart.

JO. You shouldn't be saying these things in front of Parnell.

LYLE. Why not? I ain't got no secrets from Parnell— he knows about men and women. Look at her blush! Like I told you. Women is more delicate than men.

[He touches her face lightly.]

I know you kind of upset, sugar. But don't you be nervous. Everything's going to be all right, and we're going to be happy again, you'll see.

JO. I hope so, Lyle.

LYLE. I'm going to take me a bath and put some clothes on. Parnell, you sit right there, you hear? I won't be but a minute.

[Exits.]

JO. What a funny man he is! It don't do no good at all to get mad at him, you might as well get mad at that baby in there. Parnell? Can I ask you something?

PARNELL. Certainly.

JO. Is it true that Lyle has no secrets from you?

PARNELL. He said that *neither* of you had any secrets from me.

JO. Oh, don't play. Lyle don't know a thing about women—what they're really like, to themselves.

Men don't know. But I want to ask you a serious question. Will you answer it?

PARNELL. If I can.

JO. That means you won't answer it. But I'll ask it, anyway. Parnell—was Lyle—is it true what people said? That he was having an affair with Old Bill's wife and that's why he shot Old Bill?

PARNELL. Why are you asking me that?

JO. Because I have to know! It's true, isn't it? He had an affair with Old Bill's wife—and he had affairs with lots of colored women in this town. It's *true*. Isn't it?

PARNELL. What does it matter who he slept with before he married you, Jo? I know he had a—lot of prostitutes. Maybe some of them were colored. When he was drunk, he wouldn't have been particular.

JO. He's never talked to you about it?

PARNELL. Why would he?

JO. Men talk about things like that.

PARNELL. Men often joke about things like that. But, Jo—what one man tells another man, his friend—can't be told to women.

JO. Men certainly stick together. I wish women did. All right. You can't talk about Lyle. But tell me this. Have *you* ever had an affair with a colored girl? I don't mean a—a *night*. I mean, did she mean something to you, did you like her, did you—love her? Could you have married her—I mean, just like you would marry a white woman?

PARNELL. Jo—

JO. Oh! Tell me the truth, Parnell!

PARNELL. I loved a colored girl, yes. I think I loved her. But I was only eighteen and she was only seventeen. I was still a virgin. I don't know if she was, but I think she was. A lot of the other kids in school used to drive over to niggertown at night to try and find black women. Sometimes they bought them, sometimes they frightened them, sometimes they raped them. And they were proud of it, they talked about it all the time. I couldn't do that. Those kids made me ashamed of my own body, ashamed of everything I felt, ashamed of being white—

JO. Ashamed of being white.

PARNELL. Yes.

JO. How did you meet—this colored girl?

PARNELL. Her mother worked for us. She used to come, sometimes, to pick up her mother. Sometimes she had to wait. I came in once and found her in the library, she was reading Stendhal. *The Red and The Black*. I had just read it and we talked

about it. She was funny—very bright and solemn and very proud—and she was *scared*, scared of me, but much too proud to show it. Oh, she was funny. But she was bright.

JO. What did she look like?

PARNELL. She was the color of gingerbread when it's just come out of the oven. I used to call her Ginger—later. Her name was really Pearl. She had black hair, very black, kind of short, and she dressed it very carefully. Later, I used to tease her about the way she took care of her hair. There's a girl in this town now who reminds me of her. Oh, I loved her!

JO. What happened?

PARNELL. I used to look at her, the way she moved, so beautiful and free, and I'd wonder if at night, when she might be on her way home from someplace, any of those boys at school had said ugly things to her. And then I thought that I wasn't any better than they were, because I thought my own thoughts were pretty awful. And I wondered what she thought of me. But I didn't dare to ask. I got so I could hardly think of anyone but her. I got sick wanting to take her in my arms, to take her in my arms and love her and protect her from all those other people who wanted to destroy her. She wrote a little poetry, sometimes she'd show it to me, but she really wanted to be a painter.

JO. What happened?

PARNELL. Nothing happened. We got so we told each other everything. She was going to be a painter, I was going to be a writer. It was our secret. Nobody in the world knew about her *inside*, what she was like, and how she dreamed, but me. And nobody in the world knew about *me* inside, what I wanted, and how I dreamed, but her. But we couldn't look ahead, we didn't dare. We talked about going North, but I was still in school, and she was still in school. We couldn't be seen anywhere together—it would have given her too bad a name. I used to see her sometimes in the movies, with various colored boys. She didn't seem to have any special one. They'd be sitting in the balcony, in the colored section, and I'd be sitting downstairs in the white section. She couldn't come down to me, I couldn't go up to her. We'd meet some nights, late, out in the country, but—I didn't want to take her in the bushes, and I couldn't take her anywhere else. One day we were sitting in the library, we were kissing, and her mother came in. That was the day I found out how much black people can hate white people.

JO. What did her mother do?

PARNELL. She didn't say a word. She just looked at me. She just looked at me. I could see what was happening in her mind. She knew that there wasn't any point in complaining to my mother or my father. It would just make her daughter look bad. She didn't dare tell her husband. If he tried to do anything, he'd be killed. There wasn't anything she could do about me. I was just another horny white kid trying to get into a black girl's pants. She looked at me as though she were wishing with all her heart that she could raise her hand and wipe me off the face of the earth. I'll never forget that look. I still see it. She walked over to Pearl and I thought she was going to slap her. But she didn't. She took her by the hand, very sadly, and all she said was, "I'm ready to go now. Come on." And she took Pearl out of the room.

JO. Did you ever see her again?

PARNELL. No. Her mother sent her away.

JO. But you forgot her? You must have had lots of other girls right quick, right after that.

PARNELL. I never forgot her.

JO. Do you think of her—even when you're with Loretta?

PARNELL. Not all of the time, Jo. But some of the time—yes.

JO. And if you found her again?

PARNELL. If I found her again—yes, I'd marry her. I'd give her the children I've always wanted to have.

JO. Oh, Parnell! If you felt that way about her, if you've felt it all this time!

PARNELL. Yes. I know. I'm a renegade white man.

JO. Then Lyle could have felt that way about Old Bill's wife—about Willa Mae. I know that's not the way he feels about me. And if he felt that way—he could have shot Old Bill—to keep him quiet!

PARNELL. Jo!

JO. Yes! And if he could have shot Old Bill to keep him quiet—he could have killed that boy. He could have killed that boy. And if he did—well—that *is* murder, isn't it? It's just nothing but murder, even if the boy *was* black. Oh, Parnell! Parnell!

PARNELL. Jo, please. Please, Jo. Be quiet.

LYLE. [*Off*]. What's all that racket in there?

PARNELL. I'm telling your wife the story of my life.

LYLE. [*Off*]. Sounds pretty goddamn active.

PARNELL. You've never asked him, have you, Jo?

JO. No. No. No.

PARNELL. Well, *I* asked him—

JO. When?

PARNELL. Well, I didn't really *ask* him. But he said he didn't do it, that it wasn't true. You heard him. He wouldn't lie to me.

JO. No. He wouldn't lie to you. They say some of the niggers have guns—did you hear that?

PARNELL. Yes. I've heard it. But it's not true.

JO. *They* wouldn't lie to you, either? I've just had too much time to worry, I guess—brood and worry. Lyle's away so often nights—he spends so much time at that store. I don't know what he does there. And when he comes home, he's just dead—and he drops right off to sleep.

[*Lyle enters, carrying the child.*]

Hi, honey. What a transformation. You look like you used to look when you come courting.

LYLE. I sure didn't come courting carrying no baby. He was awake, just singing away, and carrying on with his toes. He acts like he thinks he's got a whole lot of candy attached to the end of his legs. Here. It's about time for him to eat, ain't it? How come you looking at me like that? Why you being so nice to me, all of a sudden?

PARNELL. I've been lecturing her on the duties of a wife.

LYLE. That so? Well, come on, boy, let's you and me walk down the road a piece. Believe I'll buy you a drink. You ain't ashamed to be seen with me, I hope?

PARNELL. No, I'm not ashamed to be seen with you.

JO. You going to be home for supper?

LYLE. Yeah, sugar. Come on, Parnell.

JO. You come, too, Parnell, you and Loretta, if you're free. We'd love to have you.

PARNELL. We'll try to make it. So long, Jo.

JO. So long.

[*They exit. Jo walks to the window. Turns back into the room, smiles down at the baby. Sings.*]

Hush, little baby, don't say a word,
Mama's going to buy you a mocking bird—

But you don't want no mocking bird right now, do you? I know what you want. You want something to eat. All right, Mama's going to feed you.

[*Sits, slowly begins to unbutton her blouse. Sings.*]

If that mocking bird don't sing,
Mama's going to buy you a diamond ring.

[*Lyle's Store: Early evening. Both Lyle and Parnell are a little drunk.*]

LYLE. Didn't you ever get like that? Sure, you must have got like that sometimes—just restless! You got everything you need and you can't complain about nothing—and yet, look like, you just can't be satisfied. Didn't you ever get like that? I swear, men is mighty strange! I'm kind of restless now.

PARNELL. What's the matter with you? You worried about the trial?

LYLE. No, I ain't worried about the trial. I ain't even mad at you, Parnell. Some folks think I should be, but I ain't mad at you. They don't know you like I know you. I ain't fooled by all your wild ideas. We both white and we both from around here, and we been buddies all our lives. That's all that counts. I know you ain't going to let nothing happen to me.

PARNELL. That's good to hear.

LYLE. After all the trouble started in this town—but before that crazy boy got himself killed, soon after he got here and started raising all that hell—I started thinking about her, about Willa Mae, more and more and more. She was too young for him. Old Bill, he was sixty if he was a day, he wasn't doing her no good. Yet and still, the first time I took Willa Mae, I had to fight her. I swear I did. Maybe she was frightened. But I never had to fight her again. No. It was good, boy, let me tell you, and she liked it as much as me. Hey! You still with me?

PARNELL. I'm still with you. Go on.

LYLE. What's the last thing I said?

PARNELL. That she liked it as much as you—which I find hard to believe.

LYLE. Ha-ha! I'm telling you. I never had it for nobody bad as I had it for her.

PARNELL. When did Old Bill find out?

LYLE. Old Bill? He wouldn't never have thought nothing if people hadn't started poisoning his mind. People started talking just because my Daddy wasn't well and she was up at the house so much because somebody had to look after him. First they said she was carrying on with *him*. Hell, my Daddy would sure have been willing, but he was far from able. He was really wore out by that time and he just wanted rest. Then people started to saying that it was me.

PARNELL. Old Bill ever talk to you about it?

LYLE. How was he going to talk to me about it? Hell, we was right good friends. Many's the time I helped Old Bill out when his cash was low. I used to load Willa Mae up with things from the kitchen just to make sure they didn't go hungry.

PARNELL. Old Bill never mentioned it to you? Never? He never gave you any reason to think he knew about it?

LYLE. Well, I don't know what was going on in his *mind*, Parnell. You can't never see what's in anybody's else's *mind*—you know that. He didn't *act* no different. Hell, like I say, she was young enough to be his granddaughter damn near, so I figured he thought it might be a pretty good arrangement—me doing *his* work, ha-ha! because *he* damn sure couldn't do it no more, and helping him to stay alive.

PARNELL. Then why was he so mad at you the last time you saw him?

LYLE. Like I said, he accused me of cheating him. And I ain't never cheated a black man in my life. I hate to say it, because we've always been good friends, but sometimes I think it might have been Joel—Papa D.—who told him that. Old Bill wasn't too good at figuring.

PARNELL. Why would Papa D. tell him a thing like that?

LYLE. I think he might have been a little jealous.

PARNELL. Jealous! You mean, of you and Willa Mae?

LYLE. Yeah. He ain't really an old man, you know. But I'm sure he didn't mean—for things to turn out like they did. [*A pause*] I can still see him—the way he looked when he come into this store.

PARNELL. The way *who* looked when he came into this store?

LYLE. Why—Old Bill. He looked crazy. Like he wanted to kill me. He *did* want to kill me. Crazy nigger.

PARNELL. I thought you meant the other one. But the other one didn't die in the store.

LYLE. Old Bill didn't die in the store. He died over yonder, in the road.

PARNELL. I thought you were talking about Richard Henry.

LYLE. That crazy boy. Yeah, he come in here. I don't know what was the matter with him, he hadn't seen me but one time in his life before. And I treated him like—like I would have treated *any* man.

PARNELL. I heard about it. It was in Papa D.'s joint. He was surrounded by niggers—or *you* were—

LYLE. He was dancing with one of them crazy young ones—the real pretty nigger girl—what's her name?

PARNELL. Juanita.

LYLE. That's the one. [*Juke box music, soft. Voices. Laughter*] Yeah. He looked at me like he wanted to kill me. And he insulted my wife. And I hadn't never done him no harm. [*As above, a little stronger*] But I been thinking about it. And you know what I think? Hey! You gone to sleep?

PARNELL. No. I'm thinking.

LYLE. What you thinking about?

PARNELL. Us. You and me.

LYLE. And what do you think about us—you and me? What's the point of thinking about us, anyway? We've been buddies all our lives—we can't stop being buddies now.

PARNELL. That's right, buddy. What were you about to say?

LYLE. Oh. I think a lot of the niggers in this town, especially the young ones, is turned bad. And I believe they was egging him on.

[A pause. The music stops.]

He come in here one Monday afternoon. Everybody heard about it, it was all over this town quicker'n a jack-rabbit gets his nuts off. You just missed it. You'd just walked out of here.

[Lyle rises, walks to the doors and opens them. Sunlight fills the room. He slams the screen doors shut; we see the road.]

JO. [Off]. Lyle, you want to help me bring this baby carriage inside? It's getting kind of hot out here now.

PARNELL. Let me.

[Lyle and Parnell bring in the baby carriage. Jo enters.]

JO. My, it's hot! Wish we'd gone for a ride or something. Declare to goodness, we ain't got no reason to be sitting around this store. Ain't nobody coming in here—not to buy anything, anyway.

PARNELL. I'll buy some bubble gum.

JO. You know you don't chew bubble gum.

PARNELL. Well, then, I'll buy some cigarettes.

JO. Two cartons, or three? It's all right, Parnell, the Britten family's going to make it somehow.

LYLE. Couple of niggers coming down the road. Maybe they'll drop in for a Coke.

[Exits, into back of store.]

JO. Why, no, they won't. Our Cokes is poisoned. I get up every morning before daybreak and drop the arsenic in myself.

PARNELL. Well, then, I won't have a Coke. See you, Jo. So long, Lyle!

LYLE [Off]. Be seeing you!

[Parnell exits. Silence for a few seconds. Then we hear Lyle hammering in the back. Jo picks up a magazine, begins to read. Voices. Richard and Lorenzo appear in the road.]

RICHARD. Hey, you want a Coke? I'm thirsty.

LORENZO. Let's go on a little further.

RICHARD. Man, we been walking for days, my mouth is as dry as that damn dusty road. Come on, have a Coke with me, won't take but a minute.

LORENZO. We don't trade in there. Come on—

RICHARD. Oh! Is this the place? Hell, I'd like to get another look at the peckerwood, ain't going to give him but a dime. I want to get his face fixed in my mind, so there won't be no time wasted when the time comes, you dig? [Enters the store] Hey, Mrs. Ofay Ednolbay Ydalay! you got any Coca Cola for sale?

JO. What?

RICHARD. Coke! Me and my man been toting barges and lifting bales, that's right, we been slaving, and we need a little cool. Liquid. Refreshment. Yeah, and you can take that hammer, too.

JO. Boy, what do you want?

RICHARD. A Coca Cola, ma'am. Please ma'am.

JO. They right in the box there.

RICHARD. Thank you kindly. [Takes two Cokes, opens them] Oh, this is fine, fine. Did you put them in this box with your own little dainty dish-pan hands? Sure makes them taste sweet.

JO. Are you talking to me?

RICHARD. No ma'am, just feel like talking to myself from time to time, makes the time pass faster. [At screen door] Hey, Lorenz, I got you a Coke.

LORENZO. I don't want it. Come on out of there.

JO. That will be twenty cents.

RICHARD. Twenty cents? All right. Don't you know how to say please? All the women I know say please—of course, they ain't as pretty as you. I ain't got twenty cents, ma'am. All I got is—twenty dollars!

JO. You ain't got nothing smaller?

RICHARD. No ma'am. You see, I don't never carry on me more cash than I can afford to lose.

JO. Lyle! [Lyle enters, carrying the hammer] You got any change?

LYLE. Change for a twenty? No, you know I ain't got it.

RICHARD. You all got this big, fine store and all—and you ain't got change for twenty dollars?

LYLE. It's early in the day, boy.

RICHARD. It ain't that early. I thought white folks was rich at every hour of the day.

LYLE. Now, if you looking for trouble, you just might get it. That boy outside—ain't he got twenty cents?

RICHARD. That boy outside is about twenty-four years old, and he ain't got twenty cents. Ain't no need to ask him.

LYLE. [At the door]. Boy! You got twenty cents?

LORENZO. Come on out of there, Richard! I'm tired of hanging around here!

LYLE. Boy, didn't you hear what I asked you?

LORENZO. Mister Britten, I ain't *in* the store, and I ain't *bought* nothing in the store, and so I ain't *got* to tell you whether or not I got twenty cents!

RICHARD. Maybe your wife could run home and get some change. You *got* some change at home, I know. Don't you?

LYLE. I don't stand for nobody to talk about my wife.

RICHARD. I only said you was a lucky man to have so fine a *wife*. I said maybe she could run *home* and look and see if there was any change—in the *home*.

LYLE. I seen you before some place. You that crazy nigger. You ain't from around here.

RICHARD. You *know* you seen me. And you remember where. And when. I was born right here, in this town. I'm Reverend Meridian Henry's son.

LYLE. You say that like you thought your Daddy's name was some kind of protection. He ain't no protection against *me*—him, nor that boy outside, neither.

RICHARD. I don't need no protection, do I? Not in my own home town, in the good old USA. I just dropped by to sip on a Coke in a simple country store—and come to find out the joker ain't got enough bread to change twenty dollars. Stud ain't got *nothing*—you people been spoofing the public, man.

LYLE. You put them Cokes down and get out of here.

RICHARD. I ain't finished yet. And I ain't changed my bill yet.

LYLE. Well, I ain't going to change that bill, and you ain't going to finish them Cokes. You get your black ass out of here—go on! If you got any sense, you'll get your black ass out of this town.

RICHARD. You don't own this town, you white mother-fucker. You don't *even* own twenty dollars. Don't you raise that hammer. I'll take it and beat your skull to jelly.

JO. Lyle! Don't you fight that boy! He's crazy! I'm going to call the Sheriff! [Starts toward the back, returns to counter] The baby! Lyle! Watch out for the baby!

RICHARD. A baby, huh? How many times did you have to try for it, you no-good, ball-less pecker-

wood? I'm surprised you could even get it up—look at the way you sweating now.

[Lyle raises the hammer. Richard grabs his arm, forcing it back. They struggle.]

JO. Lyle! The baby!
LORENZO. Richard!

[He comes into the store.]

JO. Please get that boy out of here, get that boy out of here—he's going to get himself killed.

[Richard knocks the hammer from Lyle's hand, and knocks Lyle down. The hammer spins across the room. Lorenzo picks it up.]

LORENZO. I don't think your husband's going to kill no more black men. Not today, Mrs. Britten. Come on, Richard. Let's go.

[Lyle looks up at them.]

LYLE. It took two of you. Remember that.
LORENZO. I didn't lay a hand on you, Mister Britten. You just ain't no match for—a *boy*. Not without your gun you ain't. Come on, Richard.
JO. You'll go to jail for this! You'll go to jail! For years!
LORENZO. We've been in jail for years. I'll leave your hammer over at Papa D.'s joint—don't look like you're going to be doing no more work today.
RICHARD [Laughs]. Look at the mighty peckerwood! On his *ass*, baby—and his woman watching! Now, who you think is the better man? Ha-ha! The master race! You let me in that tired white chick's drawers, she'll know who's the master! Ha-ha-ha!

[Exits. Richard's laughter continues in the dark. Lyle and Parnell as before.]

LYLE. Niggers was laughing at me for days. Everywhere I went.
PARNELL. You never did call the Sheriff.
LYLE. No.

[Parnell fills their glasses. We hear singing.]

PARNELL. It's almost time for his funeral.
LYLE. And may every nigger like that nigger end like that nigger—face down in the weeds!

[A pause.]

PARNELL. Was he lying face down?

LYLE. Hell, yeah, he was face down. Said so in the papers.

PARNELL. Is that what the papers said? I don't remember.

LYLE. Yeah, that's what the papers said.

PARNELL. I guess they had to turn him over—to make sure it was him.

LYLE. I reckon. [Laughs] Yeah. I reckon.

PARNELL. You and me are buddies, huh?

LYLE. *Yeah*, we're buddies—to the end!

PARNELL. I always wondered why you wanted to be my buddy. A lot of poor guys hate rich guys. I always wondered why you weren't like that.

LYLE. I ain't like that. Hell, Parnell, you're smarter than me. I know it. I used to wonder what made you smarter than me. I got to be your buddy so I could find out. Because, hell, you didn't seem so different in *other* ways—in spite of all your *ideas*. Two things we always had in common—liquor and poon-tang. We couldn't get enough of neither one. Of course, your liquor might have been a little better. But I doubt if the other could have been any better!

PARNELL. Did you find out what made me smarter?

LYLE. Yeah. You richer!

PARNELL. I'm richer! That's all you got to tell me—about Richard Henry?

LYLE. Ain't nothing more to tell. Wait till after the trial. You won't have to ask me no more questions then!

PARNELL. I've got to get to the funeral.

LYLE. Don't run off. Don't leave me here alone.

PARNELL. You're supposed to be home for supper.

LYLE. Supper can wait. Have another drink with me—be my buddy. Don't leave me here alone. Listen to them! Singing and praying! Singing and praying and laughing behind a man's back!

[*The singing continues in the dark. Blacktown: The church, packed. Meridian in the pulpit, the bier just below him.*]

MERIDIAN. My heart is heavier tonight than it has ever been before. I raise my voice to you tonight out of a sorrow and a wonder I have never felt before. Not only I, my Lord, am in this case. Everyone under the sound of my voice, and many more souls than that, feel as I feel, and tremble as I tremble, and bleed as I bleed. It is not that the days are dark—we have known dark days. It is not only that the blood runs down and no man helps us; it is not only that our children are destroyed before our eyes.

It is not only that our lives, from day to day and every hour of each day, are menaced by the people among whom you have set us down. We have borne all these things, my Lord, and we have done what the prophets of old could not do, we have sung the Lord's song in a strange land. In a strange land! What was the sin committed by our forefathers in the time that has vanished on the other side of the flood, which has had to be expiated by chains, by the lash, by hunger and thirst, by slaughter, by fire, by the rope, by the knife, and for so many generations, on these wild shores, in this strange land? Our offense must have been mighty, our crime immeasurable. But it is not the past which makes our hearts so heavy. It is the present. Lord, where is our hope? Who, or what, shall touch the hearts of the headlong and unthinking people and turn them back from destruction? When will they hear the words of John? *I know thy works, that thou art neither cold nor hot: I would that thou wert cold or hot. So, then because thou art lukewarm and neither cold nor hot, I will spew thee out of my mouth. Because thou sayest, I am rich and increased with goods, and have need of nothing; and knowest not that thou art wretched and miserable and poor and blind and naked.* Now, when the children come, my Lord, and ask which road to follow, my tongue stammers and my heart fails. I will not abandon the land—this strange land, which is my home. But can I ask the children forever to sustain the cruelty inflicted on them by those who have been their masters, and who are now, in very truth, their kinfolk, their brothers and their sisters and their parents? What hope is there for a people who deny their deeds and disown their kinsmen and who do so in the name of purity and love, in the name of Jesus Christ? What a light, my Lord, is needed to conquer so mighty a darkness! This darkness rules in us, and grows, in black and white alike. I have set my face against the darkness, I will not let it conquer me, even though it will, I know, one day, destroy this body. But, my Lord, what of the children? What shall I tell the children? I must be with you, Lord, like Jacob, and wrestle with you until the light appears—I will not let you go until you give me a sign! A sign that in the terrible Sahara of our time a fountain may spring, the fountain of a true morality, and bring us closer, oh, my Lord, to that peace on earth desired by so few throughout so many ages. Let not our suffering endure forever. Teach us to trust the great gift of life and learn to love one another and dare to walk the earth like men. Amen.

MOTHER HENRY. Let's file up, children, and say goodbye.

[*Song: "Great Getting-Up Morning." Meridian steps down from the pulpit. Meridian, Lorenzo, Jimmy and Pete shoulder the bier. A dishevelled Parnell enters. The Congregation and the Pallbearers file past him. Juanita stops.*]

JUANITA. What's the matter, Parnell? You look sick.

PARNELL. I tried to come sooner. I couldn't get away. Lyle wouldn't let me go.

JUANITA. Were you trying to beat a confession out of him? But you look as though he's been trying to beat a confession out of you. Poor Parnell!

PARNELL. Poor Lyle! He'll never confess. Never. Poor devil!

JUANITA. Poor devil! You weep for Lyle. You're luckier than I am. I can't weep in front of others. I can't say goodbye in front of others. Others don't know what it is you're saying goodbye to.

PARNELL. You loved him.

JUANITA. Yes.

PARNELL. I didn't know.

JUANITA. Ah, you're so lucky, Parnell. I know you didn't know. Tell me, where do you live, Parnell? How can you not know all of the things you do not know?

PARNELL. Why are you hitting out at me? I never thought you cared that much about me. But—oh, Juanita! There are so many things I've never been able to say!

JUANITA. There are so many things you've never been able to hear.

PARNELL. And—you've tried to tell me some of those things?

JUANITA. I used to watch you roaring through this town like a St. George thirsty for dragons. And I wanted to let you know you haven't got to do all that; dragons aren't hard to find, they're everywhere. And nobody wants you to be St. George. We just want you to be Parnell. But, of course, that's much harder.

PARNELL. Are we friends, Juanita? Please say that we're friends.

JUANITA. Friends is not exactly what you mean, Parnell. Tell the truth.

PARNELL. Yes. I've always wanted more than that, from you. But I was afraid you would misunderstand me. That you would feel that I was only trying to exploit you. In another way.

JUANITA. You've been a grown man for a long time now, Parnell. You ought to trust yourself more than that.

PARNELL. I've been a grown man far too long—ever to have dared to dream of offering myself to you.

JUANITA. Your age was never the question, Parnell.

PARNELL. Was there ever any questions at all?

JUANITA. Yes. Yes. Yes, once there was.

PARNELL. And there isn't—there can't be—anymore?

JUANITA. No. That train has gone. One day, I'll recover. I'm sure that I'll recover. And I'll see the world again—the marvelous world. And I'll have learned from Richard—how to love. I must. I can't let him die for nothing.

[*Juke box music, loud. The lights change, spot on Parnell's face. Juanita steps across the aisle. Richard appears. They dance. Parnell watches.*]

CURTAIN

END OF ACT II

Act III

Two months later. The courtroom.

The courtroom is extremely high, domed, a blinding white emphasized by a dull, somehow ominous gold. The judge's stand is center stage, and at a height. Sloping down from this place on either side, are the black and white Townspeople: the Jury; Photographers and Journalists from all over the world; microphones and TV cameras. All windows open: one should be aware of masses of people outside and one should sometimes hear their voices—their roar—as well as singing from the church. The church is directly across the street from the courthouse, and the steeple and the cross are visible throughout the act.

Each witness, when called, is revealed behind scrim and passes through two or three tableaux before moving down the aisle to the witness stand. The witness stand is downstage, in the same place, and at the same angle as the pulpit in Acts I and II.

Before the curtain rises song: "I Said I Wasn't Going To Tell Nobody, But I Couldn't Keep It To Myself."

The Judge's gavel breaks across the singing, and the curtain rises.

CLERK. [*Calling*]. Mrs. Josephine Gladys Britten!

[*Jo, serving coffee at a church social. She passes out coffee to invisible guests.*]

JO. Am I going to spend the rest of my life serving coffee to strangers in church basements? Am I?— Yes! Reverend Phelps was truly noble! As *usual*!— Reverend Phelps has been married for more than twenty years. Don't let those thoughts into your citadel! You just remember that the mind is a citadel and you can keep out all troubling thoughts!—My! Mrs. Evans! you are certainly a sight for sore eyes! I don't know how you manage to look so unruffled and *cool* and *young*! With all those *children*. And Mr. Evans. How are you tonight?—She has a baby just about every year. I don't know how she stands it. Mr. Evans don't look like that kind of man. You sure can't tell a book by its cover. Lord! I wish I was in my own home and these were *my* guests and my husband was somewhere in the room. I'm getting old! Old! Old maid! *Maid*!—Oh! Mr. Arpino! You taken time out from your engineering to come visit here with us? It sure is a pleasure to have you!—My! He is big! and dark! Like a Greek! or a Spaniard! Some people say he might have a touch of nigger blood. I don't believe that. He's just—*foreign*. That's all. He needs a hair cut. I wonder if he's got hair like that all *over* his body? Remember that your mind is a citadel. A citadel. Oh, Lord, I'm tired of serving coffee in church basements! I want, I want—Why, good evening, Ellis! and Mr. Lyle Britten! We sure don't see either of you very often! Why, Mr. Britten! You know you don't mean that! You come over here just to see little old *me*? Why, you just go right ahead and drink that coffee, I do believe you need to be sobered up

[*The light changes.*]

REVEREND PHELPS. [*Voice*]. Do you, Josephine Gladys Miles, take this man, Lyle Britten, Jr., as your lawfully wedded husband, to have and to hold, to love and to cherish, in sickness and in health, till death do you part?

JO. I do. I *do*! Oh, Lyle. I'll make you the best wife any man ever had. I *will*. Love me. Please love me. Look at me! *Look* at me! He *wanted* me. He wanted *me*! I am—Mrs. Josephine Gladys Britten!

[*The light changes again, and Jo takes the stand. We hear the baby crying.*]

BLACKTOWN. Man, that's the southern white lady you supposed to be willing to risk death for!

WHITETOWN. You know, this is a kind of hanging in reverse? Niggers out here to watch us being hanged!

THE STATE. What is your relationship to the accused?

JO. I am his wife.

THE STATE. Will you please tell us, in your own words, of your first meeting with the deceased, Richard Henry?

WHITETOWN. Don't be afraid. Just tell the truth.

BLACKTOWN. Here we go—down the river!

JO. Well, I was in the store, sitting at the counter, and pretty soon this colored boy come in, loud, and talking in just the most awful way. I didn't recognize him, I just knew he wasn't one of *our* colored people. His language was something awful, awful!

THE STATE. He was insulting? Was he insulting, Mrs. Britten?

JO. He said all kinds of things, dirty things, like— well—just like I might have been a colored girl, that's what it sounded like to me. Just like some little colored girl he might have met on a street corner and wanted—wanted to—for a night! And I was scared. I hadn't seen a colored boy act like him before. He acted like he was drunk or crazy or maybe he was under the influence of that dope. I never knew nobody to be *drunk* and act like him. His eyes was just going and he acted like he had a fire in his belly. But I tried to be calm because I didn't want to upset Lyle, you know—Lyle's mighty quick-tempered—and he was working in the back of the store, he was hammering—

THE STATE. Go on, Mrs. Britten. What happened then?

JO. Well, he—that boy—wanted to buy him two Cokes because he had a friend outside—

THE STATE. He brought a friend? He did not come there alone? Did this other boy enter the store?

JO. No, not then he didn't—I—

BLACKTOWN. Come on, bitch. We *know* what you going to say. Get it over with.

JO. I—I give him the two Cokes, and he—tried to grab my hands and pull me to him, and—I—I—he pushed himself up against me, real close and hard—

and, oh, he was just like an animal, I could—smell him! And he tried to kiss me, he kept whispering these awful, filthy things and I got scared, I yelled for Lyle! Then Lyle come running out of the back—and when the boy seen I wasn't alone in the store, he yelled for this other boy outside and this other boy come rushing in and they both jumped on Lyle and knocked him down.

THE STATE. What made you decide not to report this incident—this unproved assault—to the proper authorities, Mrs. Britten?

JO. We've had so much trouble in this town!

THE STATE. What sort of trouble, Mrs. Britten?

JO. Why, with the colored people! We've got all these northern agitators coming through here all the time, and stirring them up so that you can't hardly sleep nights!

THE STATE. Then you, as a responsible citizen of this town, were doing your best to keep down trouble? Even though you had been so brutally assaulted by a deranged northern Negro dope addict?

JO. Yes. I didn't want to stir up no more trouble. I *made* Lyle keep quiet about it. I thought it would all blow over. I knew the boy's Daddy was a preacher and that he would talk to the boy about the way he was behaving. It was all over town in a second, anyway! And look like all the colored people was on the side of that crazy boy. And Lyle's always been real good to colored people!

[*Laughter from Blacktown.*]

THE STATE. On the evening that the alleged crime was committed—or, rather, the morning—very early on the morning of the 24th of August—where were you and your husband, Mrs. Britten?

JO. We were home. The next day we heard that the boy was missing.

COUNSEL FOR THE BEREAVED. Doesn't an attempt at sexual assault seem a rather strange thing to do, considering that your store is a public place, with people continually going in and out; that, furthermore, it is located on a public road which people use, on foot and in automobiles, all of the time; and considering that your husband, who has the reputation of being a violent man, and who is, in your own words, "mighty quick tempered," was working in the back room?

JO. He didn't know Lyle was back there.

COUNSEL FOR THE BEREAVED. But he knew that someone was back there, for, according to your testimony, "He was hammering."

JO. Well, I told you the boy was crazy. He had to be crazy. Or he was on that dope.

BLACKTOWN. You ever hear of a junkie trying to rape anybody?

JO. *I didn't say rape!*

COUNSEL FOR THE BEREAVED. Were you struggling in Mr. Henry's arms when your husband came out of the back room, carrying his hammer in his hand?

JO. No. I was free then.

COUNSEL FOR THE BEREAVED. Therefore, your husband had only *your* word for the alleged attempted assault! *You* told him that Richard Henry had attempted to assault you? Had made sexual advances to you? Please answer, Mrs. Britten!

JO. Yes. I had—I had to—tell him. I'm his wife!

COUNSEL FOR THE BEREAVED. And a most loyal one. You told your husband that Richard Henry had attempted to assault you and then begged him to do nothing about it?

JO. That's right.

COUNSEL FOR THE BEREAVED. And though he was under the impression that his wife had been nearly raped by a Negro, he agreed to forgive and forget and do nothing about it? He agreed neither to call the law, nor to take the law into his own hands?

JO. Yes.

COUNSEL FOR THE BEREAVED. Extraordinary. Mrs. Britten, you are aware that Richard Henry met his death sometime between the hours of two and five o'clock on the morning of Monday, August 24th?

JO. Yes.

COUNSEL FOR THE BEREAVED. In an earlier statement, several months ago, you stated that your husband had spent that night at the store. You now state that he came in before one o'clock and went to sleep at once. What accounts for this discrepancy?

JO. It's natural. I made a mistake about the time. I got it mixed up with another night. He spent so many nights at that store!

JUDGE. The witness may step down.

[*Jo leaves the stand.*]

CLERK. [*Calls*]. Mr. Joel Davis!

[*We hear a shot. Papa D. is facing Lyle.*]

LYLE. Why'd you run down there this morning, shooting your mouth off about me and Willa Mae? Why? You been bringing her up here and taking her back all this time, what got into you this morning? Huh? You jealous, old man? Why you come running back here to tell me everything he said? To tell me how he cursed me out? Have you lost your mind? And we been knowing each other all this time. I don't understand you. She ain't the only girl you done brought here for me. Nigger, do you hear me talking to you?

PAPA D. I didn't think you'd shoot him, Mr. Lyle.

LYLE. I'll shoot any nigger talks to me like that. It was self defense, you hear me? He come in here and tried to kill me. You hear me?

PAPA D. Yes. Yes sir. I hear you, Mr. Lyle.

LYLE. That's right. You don't say the right thing, nigger, I'll blow your brains out, too.

PAPA D. Yes sir, Mr. Lyle.

[Juke box music. Papa D. takes the stand.]

WHITETOWN. He's worked hard and saved his money and ain't never had no trouble—why can't they all be like that?

BLACKTOWN. Hey, Papa D.! You can't be walking around here without no handkerchief! You might catch cold—after all *these* years!

PAPA D. Mr. Lyle Britten—he is an *oppressor*. That is the only word for that man. He ain't never give the colored man no kind of chance. I have tried to reason with that man for *years*. I say, Mr. Lyle, look around you. Don't you see that most white folks have changed their way of thinking about us colored folks? I say, Mr. Lyle, we ain't slaves no more and white folks is ready to let us have our chance. Now, why don't you just come on up to where *most* of your people are? and we can make the South a fine place for all of us to live in. That's what I say—and I tried to keep him from being so *hard* on the colored—because I sure do love my people. And I was the closest thing to Mr. Lyle, couldn't nobody else reason with him. But he was *hard*—hard and stubborn. He say, "My folks lived and died this way, and this is the way I'm going to live and die." When he was like that couldn't do nothing with him. I know. I've known him since he was born.

WHITETOWN. He's always been real good to you. You were friends!

BLACKTOWN. You loved him! Tell the truth, mother—tell the truth!

PAPA D. Yes, we were friends. And, yes, I loved him—in my way. Just like he loved me—in his way.

BLACKTOWN. You knew he was going to kill that boy—didn't you? If you knew it, why didn't you stop him?

PAPA D. Oh. Ain't none of this easy. What it was, both Mr. Lyle Britten and me, we both love money. And I did a whole lot of things for him, for a long while. Once I had to help him cover up a killing—colored man—I was in too deep myself by that time—you understand? I know you all understand.

BLACKTOWN. Did he kill that boy?

PAPA D. He come into my joint the night that boy died. The boy was alone, standing at the juke box. We'd been talking— [Richard, in the juke box light] If you think you've found all that, Richard—if you think you going to be well now, and you found you somebody who loves you—well, then, I would make tracks out of here. I would—

RICHARD. It's funny, Papa D. I feel like I'm beginning to understand my life—for the first time. I can look back—and it doesn't hurt me like it used to. I want to get Juanita out of here. This is no place for her. They're going to kill her—if she stays here!

PAPA D. You talk to Juanita about this yet?

RICHARD. No. I haven't talked to nobody about it yet. I just decided it. I guess I'm deciding it now. That's why I'm talking about it now—to you—to see if you'll laugh at me. Do you think she'll laugh at me?

PAPA D. No. She won't laugh.

RICHARD. I know I can do it. I know I can do it!

PAPA D. That boy had good sense. He was wild, but he had good sense. And I couldn't blame him too much for being so wild, it seemed to me I knew how he felt.

RICHARD. Papa D., I been in pain and darkness all my life. All my life. And this is the first time in my life I've ever felt—maybe it isn't all like that. Maybe there's more to it than that.

PAPA D. Lyle Britten come to the door— [Lyle enters] He come to the door and he say—

LYLE. You ready for me now, boy? Howdy, Papa D.

PAPA D. Howdy, Mr. Lyle, how's the world been treating you?

LYLE. I can't complain. You ready, boy?

RICHARD. No. I ain't ready. I got a record to play and a drink to finish.

LYLE. You about ready to close, ain't you, Joel?

PAPA D. Just about, Mr. Lyle.

RICHARD. I got a record to play. [Drops coin; juke box music; loud] And a drink to finish.

PAPA D. He played his record. Lyle Britten never moved from the door. And they just stood there, the two of them, looking at each other. When the record was just about over, the boy come to the bar—he swallowed down the last of his drink.

RICHARD. What do I owe you, Papa D.?

PAPA D. Oh, you pay me tomorrow. I'm closed now.

RICHARD. What do I owe you, Papa D.? I'm not sure I can pay you tomorrow.

PAPA D. Give me two dollars.

RICHARD. Here you go. Good night, Papa D. I'm ready, Charlie.

[Exits.]

PAPA D. Good night, Richard. Go on home now. Good night, Mr. Lyle. Mr. Lyle!

LYLE. Good night, Joel. You get some sleep, you hear?

[Exits]

PAPA D. Mr. Lyle! Richard! And I never saw that boy again. Lyle killed him. He killed him. I know it, just like I know I'm sitting in this chair. Just like he shot Old Bill and wasn't nothing never, never, never done about it!

JUDGE. The witness may step down.

[Papa D. leaves the stand.]

CLERK. [Calls]. Mr. Lorenzo Shannon!

[We hear a long, loud, animal cry, lonely and terrified: it is Pete, screaming. We discover Lorenzo and Pete, in jail. Night. From far away, we hear Students humming, moaning, singing: "I Woke Up This Morning With My Mind Stayed On Freedom."]

PETE. [Stammering]. Lorenzo? Lorenzo. I was dreaming—dreaming—dreaming. I was back in that courtyard and Big Jim Byrd's boys was beating us and beating us and beating us—and Big Jim Byrd was laughing. And Anna Mae Taylor was on her knees, she was trying to pray. She say, "Oh, Lord, Lord, Lord, come and help us," and they kept beating on her and beating on her and I saw the blood coming down her neck and they put the prods to her, and, oh, Lorenzo! people was just running around, just crying and moaning and you look to the right and you see somebody go down and you look to the left and you see somebody go down and they was kicking that woman, and I say, "That woman's going to have a baby, don't you kick that woman!" and they say, "No, she ain't going to have no baby," and they knocked me down and they got that prod up between my legs and they say, "You ain't going to be having no babies, neither, nigger!" And then they put that prod to my head—ah! ah!— to my *head*! Lorenzo! I can't see right! What have they done to my head? Lorenzo! Lorenzo, am I going to die! Lorenzo—they going to kill us all, ain't they? They mean to kill us all—

LORENZO. Be quiet. Be quiet. They going to come and beat us some more if you don't be quiet.

PETE. Where's Juanita? Did they get Juanita?

LORENZO. I believe Juanita's all right. Go to sleep, Pete. Go to sleep. I won't let you dream. I'll hold you.

[Lorenzo takes the stand.]

THE STATE. Did you accompany your late and great friend, Richard Henry, on the morning of August 17, to the store which is owned and run by Mr. and Mrs. Lyle Britten?

LORENZO. We hadn't planned to go there—but we got to walking and talking and we found ourselves there. And it didn't happen like she said. He picked the Cokes out of the box himself, he came to the door with the Cokes in his hand, she hadn't even moved, she was still behind the counter, he never touched that dried out little peckerwood!

WHITETOWN. Get that nigger! Who does that nigger think he is!

BLACKTOWN. Speak, Lorenzo! Go, my man!

THE STATE. You cannot expect this courtroom to believe that so serious a battle was precipitated by the question of twenty cents! There was some other reason. What was this reason? Had he—and you— been drinking?

LORENZO. It was early in the day, Cap'n. We ain't rich enough to drink in the daytime.

THE STATE. Or *smoking*, perhaps? Perhaps your friend had just had his quota of heroin for the day, and was feeling jolly—in a mood to *prove* to you what he had already suggested with those filthy photographs of himself and naked white women!

LORENZO. I never saw no photographs. White women are a problem for white men. We had not been drinking. All we was smoking was that same god- damn tobacco that made *you* rich because we picked it for you for nothing, and carried it to market for you for nothing. And I *know* ain't no heroin in this town because none of you mothers need it. You was *born* frozen. Richard was better than that. I'd rather die than be like you, Cap'n, but I'd be *proud* to be like Richard. That's all I can tell you, Mr. Boss-Man. But I know he wasn't trying to rape nobody. Rape!

THE STATE. Your Honor, will you instruct the witness that he is under oath, that this is a court of law, and that it is a serious matter to be held in contempt of court!

LORENZO. More serious than the chain gang! *I* know

I'm under oath. If there was any reason, it was just that Richard couldn't stand white people. *Couldn't stand white people*! And, now, do you want me to tell you all that I know about *that*? Do you think you could stand it? You'd cut my tongue out before you'd let me tell you all that I know about *that*!

COUNSEL FOR THE BEREAVED. You are a student here?

LORENZO. In my spare time. I just come off the chain gang a couple of days ago. I was trespassing in the white waiting room of the bus station.

COUNSEL FOR THE BEREAVED. What are you studying—in your spare time—Mr. Shannon?

LORENZO. History.

COUNSEL FOR THE BEREAVED. To your knowledge—during his stay in this town—was the late Mr. Richard Henry still addicted to narcotics?

LORENZO. No. He'd kicked his habit. He'd paid his dues. He was just trying to live. And he almost made it.

COUNSEL FOR THE BEREAVED. You were very close to him?

LORENZO. Yes.

COUNSEL FOR THE BEREAVED. To your knowledge—was he carrying about obscene photographs of himself and naked white women?

LORENZO. To my knowledge—and I would know—no. The only times he ever opened a popular magazine was to look at the Jazz Poll. No. They been asking me about photographs they say he was carrying and they been asking me about a gun I never saw. No. It wasn't like that. He was a beautiful cat, and they killed him. That's all. That's *all*.

JUDGE. The witness may step down.

LORENZO. Well! I thank you kindly, *Suh*!

[*Lorenzo leaves the stand.*]

CLERK. [*Calls*]. Miss Juanita Harmon!

[*Juanita rises from bed; early Sunday morning.*]

JUANITA. He lay beside me on that bed like a rock. As heavy as a rock—like he'd fallen—fallen from a high place—fallen so far and landed so heavy, he seemed almost to be sinking out of sight—with one knee pointing to heaven. My God. He covered me like that. He wasn't at all like I thought he was. He fell on—fell on me—like life and death. My God. His chest, his belly, the rising and the falling, the moans. How he clung, how he struggled—life and death! Life and death! Why did it all seem to me like tears? That he came to me, clung to me, plunged into me,

sobbing, howling, bleeding, somewhere inside his chest, his belly, and it all came out, came pouring out, like tears! My God, the smell, the touch, the taste, the sound, of anguish! Richard! Why couldn't I have held you closer? Held you, held you, borne you, given you life again! Have made you be born again! Oh, Richard. The teeth that gleamed, oh! when you smiled, the spit flying when you cursed, the teeth stinging when you bit—your breath, your hands, your weight, my God, when you moved in me! Where shall I go now, what shall I do? Oh. Oh. Oh. Mama was frightened. Frightened because little Juanita brought her first real lover to this house. I suppose God does for Mama what Richard did for me. Juanita! I don't care! I don't care! Yes, I want a lover made of flesh and blood, of flesh and blood, like me, I don't want to be God's mother! He can *have* His icy, snow-white heaven! If He is somewhere around this fearful planet, if I ever see Him, I will spit in His face! In God's face! How *dare* He presume to judge a living soul! A living soul. Mama is afraid I'm pregnant. Mama is afraid of so much. I'm not afraid. I hope I'm pregnant. I *hope* I am! One more illegitimate black baby—that's right, you jive mothers! And I am going to raise my baby to be a man. A *man*, you dig? Oh, let me be pregnant, let me be pregnant, don't let it all be gone! A man. Juanita. A man. Oh, my God, there are no more. For me. Did this happen to Mama sometime? Did she have a man sometime who vanished like smoke? And left her to get through this world as best she could? Is that why she married my father? Did this happen to Mother Henry? Is this how we all get to be mothers—so soon? of helpless men—because all the other men perish? No. No. No. No. What is this world like? I will end up taking care of some man, some day. Help me do it with love. Pete. Meridian. Parnell. We have been the mothers for them all. It must be dreadful to be Parnell. There is no flesh he can touch. All of it is bloody. Incest everywhere. Ha-ha! You're going crazy, Juanita. Oh, Lord, don't let me go mad. Let me be pregnant! Let me be pregnant!

[*Juanita takes the stand. One arm is in a sling.*]

BLACKTOWN. Look! You should have seen her when she *first* come out of jail! Why we always got to love *them*? How come it's *us* always got to do the loving? Because you *black*, mother! Everybody knows we *strong* on loving! Except when it comes to our women.

WHITETOWN. Black slut! What happened to her arm? Somebody had to twist it, I reckon. She looks like she might be a right pretty little girl—why is she messing up her life this way?

THE STATE. Miss Harmon, you have testified that you were friendly with the mother of the deceased. How old were you when she died?

JUANITA. I was sixteen.

THE STATE. Sixteen! You are older than the deceased?

JUANITA. By two years.

THE STATE. At the time of his mother's death, were you and Richard Henry considering marriage?

JUANITA. No. Of course not.

THE STATE. The question of marriage did not come up until just before he died?

JUANITA. Yes.

THE STATE. But between the time that Richard Henry left this town and returned, you had naturally attracted other boy friends?

BLACKTOWN. Why don't you come right out and ask her if she's a virgin, man? Save you time.

WHITETOWN. She probably pregnant right now—and don't know who the father is. That's the way they are.

THE STATE. The departure of the boy and the death of the mother must have left all of you extremely lonely?

JUANITA. It can't be said to have made us any happier.

THE STATE. Reverend Henry missed his wife, you missed your playmate. His grief and your common concern for the boy must have drawn you closer together?

BLACKTOWN. Oh, man! Get to *that*!

WHITETOWN. That's right. What about that liver-lipped preacher?

THE STATE. Miss Harmon, you describe yourself as a student. Where have you spent the last few weeks?

JUANITA. In jail! I was arrested for—

THE STATE. I am not concerned with the reasons for your arrest. How much time, all told, have you spent in jail?

JUANITA. It would be hard to say—a long time.

THE STATE. Excellent preparation for your future! Is it not true, Miss Harmon, that before the late Richard Henry returned to this town, you were considering marriage with another so-called student, Pete Spivey? Can you seriously expect this court to believe anything you now say concerning Richard Henry? Would you not say the same thing, and for the same reason, concerning the father? Concerning Pete Spivey? And how many others!

WHITETOWN. That's the way they are. It's not their fault. That's what they want us to integrate with.

BLACKTOWN. These people are sick. Sick. Sick people's been known to be made well by a little shedding of blood.

JUANITA. I am not responsible for your imagination.

THE STATE. What do you know of the fight which took place between Richard Henry and Lyle Britten, at Mr. Britten's store?

JUANITA. I was not a witness to that fight.

THE STATE. But you had seen Richard Henry before the fight? Was he sober?

JUANITA. Yes.

THE STATE. You can swear to that?

JUANITA. Yes. I can swear to it.

THE STATE. And you saw him after the fight? Was he sober then?

JUANITA. Yes. He was sober then. [*Courtroom in silhouette*] I heard about the fight at the end of the day—when I got home. And I went running to Reverend Henry's house. And I met him on the porch—just sitting there.

THE STATE. You met whom?

JUANITA. I met—Richard.

[*We discover Meridian.*]

MERIDIAN. Hello, Juanita. Don't look like that.

JUANITA. Meridian, what happened today? Where's Richard?

MERIDIAN. He's all right now. He's sleeping. We better send him away. Lyle's dangerous. You know that. [*Takes Juanita in his arms; then holds her at arm's length*] You'll go with him. Won't you?

JUANITA. Meridian—oh, my God.

MERIDIAN. Juanita, tell me something I have to know. I'll never ask it again.

JUANITA. Yes, Meridian—

MERIDIAN. Before he came—I wasn't just making it all up, was I? There was something at least—beginning—something dimly possible—wasn't there? I thought about you so much—and it was so wonderful each time I saw you—and I started hoping as I haven't let myself hope, oh, for a long time. I knew you were much younger, and I'd known you since you were a child. But I thought that maybe that didn't matter, after all—we got on so well together. I wasn't making it all up, was I?

JUANITA. No. You weren't making it up—not all of it, anyway, there was something there. We were lonely. You were hoping. I was hoping, too—oh, Meridian!

Of all the people on God's earth I would rather die than hurt!

MERIDIAN. Hush, Juanita. I know that. I just wanted to be told that I hadn't lost my mind. I've lost so much. I think there's something wrong in being—what I've become—something really wrong. I mean, I think there's something wrong with allowing oneself to become so lonely. I think that I was proud that I could bear it. Each day became a kind of test—to see if I could bear it. And there were many days when I couldn't bear it—when I walked up and down and howled and lusted and cursed and prayed—just like any man. And I've been—I haven't been as celibate as I've seemed. But my confidence—my confidence—was destroyed back there when I pulled back that rug they had her covered with and I saw that little face on that broken neck. There wasn't any blood—just water. She was soaked. Oh, my God. My God. And I haven't trusted myself with a woman since. I keep seeing her the last time I saw her, whether I'm awake or asleep. That's why I let you get away from me. It wasn't my son that did it. It was me. And so much the better for you. And him. And I've held it all in since then—what fearful choices we must make! In order not to commit murder, in order not to become too monstrous, in order to be some kind of example to my only son. Come. Let me be an example now. And kiss you on the forehead and wish you well.

JUANITA. Meridian. Meridian. Will it always be like this? Will life always be like this? Must we always suffer so?

MERIDIAN. I don't know, Juanita. I know that we must bear what we must bear. Don't cry, Juanita. Don't cry. Let's go on on.

[Exits.]

JUANITA. By and by Richard woke up and I was there. And we tried to make plans to go, but he said he wasn't going to run no more from white folks—never no more!—but was going to stay and be a man—a man!—right here. And I couldn't make him see differently. I knew what he meant, I knew how he felt, but I didn't want him to die! And by the time I persuaded him to take me away, to take me away from this terrible place, it was too late. Lyle killed him. Lyle killed him! Like they been killing all our men, for years, for generations! Our husbands, our fathers, our brothers, our sons!

JUDGE. The witness may step down.

[Juanita leaves the stand. Mother Henry helps her to her seat.]

This court is adjourned until ten o'clock tomorrow morning.

[Chaos and cacophony. The courtroom begins to empty. Reporters rush to phone booths and to witnesses. Light bulbs flash. We hear snatches of the Journalists' reports, in their various languages. Singing from the church. Blackout. The next and last day of the trial. Even more crowded and tense.]

CLERK. [Calls]. Mrs. Wilhelmina Henry!

[Mother Henry, in street clothes, walks down the aisle, takes the stand.]

THE STATE. You are Mrs. Wilhelmina Henry?
MOTHER HENRY. Yes.
THE STATE. Mrs. Henry, you—and your husband, until he died—lived in this town all your lives and never had any trouble. We've always gotten on well down here.
MOTHER HENRY. No white man never called my husband Mister, neither, not as long as he lived. Ain't no white man never called me Mrs. Henry before today. I had to get a grandson killed for that.
THE STATE. Mrs. Henry, your grief elicits my entire sympathy, and the sympathy of every white man in this town. But is it not true, Mrs. Henry, that your grandson arrived in this town armed? He was carrying a gun and, apparently, had carried a gun for years.
MOTHER HENRY. I don't know where you got that story, or why you keep harping on it. I never saw no gun.
THE STATE. You are under oath, Mrs. Henry.
MOTHER HENRY. I don't need you to tell me I'm under oath. I been under oath all my life. And I tell you, I never saw no gun.
THE STATE. Mrs. Henry, did you ever see your grandson behaving strangely—as though he were under the influence of strong drugs?
MOTHER HENRY. No. Not since he was six and they pulled out his tonsils. They gave him ether. He didn't act as strange as his Mama and Daddy. He just went on to sleep. But they like to had a fit. [Richard's song] I remember the day he was born. His mother had a hard time holding him and a hard time getting him here. But here he come, in the wintertime, late and big and loud. And my boy looked down into his little son's face and he said,

"God give us a son. God's give us a son. Lord, help us to raise him to be a good strong man."

JUDGE. The witness may step down.

CLERK. [*Calls*]. Reverend Meridian Henry!

[*Blackout. Meridian, in Sunday School. The class itself, predominately adolescent girls, is in silhouette.*]

MERIDIAN. —And here is the prophet, Solomon, the son of David, looking down through the ages, and speaking of Christ's love for His church. [*Reads*] How fair is thy love, my sister, my spouse! How much better is thy love than wine! and the smell of thine ointments than all spices! [*Pause. The silhouette of girls vanishes*] Oh, that it were one man, speaking to one woman!

[*Blackout. Meridian takes the stand.*]

BLACKTOWN. I wonder how he feels now about all that turn-the-other-cheek jazz. His son sure didn't go for it.

WHITETOWN. That's the father. Claims to be a preacher. He brought this on himself. He's been raising trouble in this town for a long time.

THE STATE. You are Reverend Meridian Henry?

MERIDIAN. That is correct.

THE STATE. And you are the father of the late Richard Henry?

MERIDIAN. Yes.

THE STATE. You are a minister?

MERIDIAN. A Christian minister—yes.

THE STATE. And you raised your son according to the precepts of the Christian church?

MERIDIAN. I tried. But both my son and I had profound reservations concerning the behavior of Christians. He wondered why they treated black people as they do. And I was unable to give him—a satisfactory answer.

THE STATE. But certainly you—as a Christian minister—did not encourage your son to go armed?

MERIDIAN. The question never came up. He was not armed.

THE STATE. He was not armed?

MERIDIAN. No.

THE STATE. You never saw him with a gun? Or with any other weapon?

MERIDIAN. No.

THE STATE. Reverend Henry—are you in a position to swear that your son never carried arms?

MERIDIAN. Yes. I can swear to it. The only time the subject was ever mentioned he told me that he was

stronger than white people and he could live without a gun.

BLACKTOWN. I bet he didn't say how.

WHITETOWN. That liver-lipped nigger is lying. He's lying!

THE STATE. Perhaps the difficulties your son had in accepting the Christian faith is due to your use of the pulpit as a forum for irresponsible notions concerning social equality, Reverend Henry. Perhaps the failure of the son is due to the failure of the father.

MERIDIAN. I am afraid that the gentleman flatters himself. I do not wish to see Negroes become the equal of their murderers. I wish us to become equal to ourselves. To become a people so free in themselves that they will have no need to—fear—others—and have no need to murder others.

THE STATE. You are not in the pulpit now. I am suggesting that you are responsible—directly responsible!—for your son's tragic fate.

MERIDIAN. I know more about that than you do. But you cannot consider my son's death to have been tragic. For you, it would have been tragic if he had lived.

THE STATE. With such a father, it is remarkable that the son lived as long as he did.

MERIDIAN. Remarkable, too, that the father lived!

THE STATE. Reverend Henry—you have been a widower for how many years?

MERIDIAN. I have been a widower for nearly eight years.

THE STATE. You are a young man still?

MERIDIAN. Are you asking me my age? I am not young.

THE STATE. You are not old. It must have demanded great discipline—

MERIDIAN. To live among you? Yes.

THE STATE. What is your relationship to the young, so-called student, Miss Juanita Harmon?

MERIDIAN. I am her old friend. I had hoped to become her father-in-law.

THE STATE. You are nothing more than old friends?

WHITETOWN. That's right. Get it out of him. Get the truth out of him.

BLACKTOWN. Leave the man *something*. Leave him something!

THE STATE. You have been celibate since the death of your wife?

BLACKTOWN. He never said he was a monk, you jive mother!

WHITETOWN. Make him tell us all about it. *All* about it.

MERIDIAN. Celibate? How does my celibacy concern you?

THE STATE. Your Honor, will you instruct the witness that he is on the witness stand, not I, and that he must answer the questions put to him

MERIDIAN. *The questions put to him*! All right. Do you accept this answer? I am a man. *A man*! I tried to help my son become a man. But manhood is a dangerous pursuit, here. And that pursuit undid him because of *your* guns, *your* hoses, *your* dogs, *your* judges, *your* law-makers, *your* folly, *your* pride, *your* cruelty, *your* cowardice, *your* money, *your* chain gangs, and *your* churches! Did you think it would endure forever? that we would pay for *your* ease forever?

BLACKTOWN. Speak, my man! Amen! Amen! Amen! Amen!

WHITETOWN. Stirring up hate! Stirring up hate! A *preacher*—stirring up hate!

MERIDIAN. Yes! I *am* responsible for the death of my son. I—hoped—I prayed—I struggled—so that the world would be different by the time he was a man than it had been when he was born. And I thought that—then—when he looked at me—he would think that I—his father—had helped to change it.

THE STATE. What about those photographs your son carried about with him? Those photographs of himself and naked white women?

BLACKTOWN. Man! Would I love to look in *your* wallet!

WHITETOWN. Make him tell us about it, make him tell us *all* about it!

MERIDIAN. Photographs? My son and naked white women? He never mentioned them to me.

THE STATE. You were closer than most fathers and sons?

MERIDIAN. I never took a poll on most fathers and sons.

THE STATE. You never discussed women?

MERIDIAN. We talked about his mother. She was a woman. We talked about Miss Harmon. *She* is a woman. But we never talked about dirty pictures. We didn't need that.

THE STATE. Reverend Henry, you have made us all aware that your love for your son transcends your respect for the truth or your devotion to the church. But—luckily for the truth—it is a matter of public record that your son was so dangerously deranged that it was found necessary, for his own sake, to incarcerate him. It was at the end of that incarceration that he returned to this town. We know that his life in the North was riotous—he brought that riot

into this town. The evidence is overwhelming. And yet, you, a Christian minister, dare to bring us this tissue of lies in defense of a known pimp, dope addict, and rapist! You are yourself so eaten up by race hatred that no word of yours can be believed.

MERIDIAN. Your judgment of myself and my motives cannot concern me at all. I have lived with that judgment far too long. The truth cannot be heard in this dreadful place. But I will tell you again what I know. I know why my son became a dope addict. I know better than you will ever know, even if I should explain it to you for all eternity, how I am responsible for that. But I know my son was not a pimp. He respected women far too much for that. And I know he was not a rapist. Rape is hard work—and, frankly, I don't think that the alleged object was my son's type at all!

THE STATE. And you are a minister?

MERIDIAN. I think I may be beginning to become one.

JUDGE. The witness may step down.

[*Meridian leaves the stand.*]

CLERK. [*Calls*]. Mr. Parnell James!

[*Parnell in his bedroom, dressed in a bathrobe. Night.*]

PARNELL. She says I called somebody else's name. What name could I have called? And she won't repeat the name. Well. That's enough to freeze the blood and arrest the holy, the liberating orgasm! Christ, how weary I am of this dull calisthenic called love—with no love in it! What name could I have called? I hope it was—a *white* girl's name, anyway! Ha-ha! How still she became! And I hardly realized it, I was too far away—and then it was too late. And she was just looking at me. Jesus! To have somebody just looking at you—just looking at you—like that—at such a moment! It makes you feel—like you woke up and found yourself in bed with your mother! I tried to find out what was wrong—poor girl! But there's nothing you can say at a moment like that—really nothing. You're caught. Well, haven't I kept telling her that there's no future for her with me? There's no future for me with anybody! But that's all right. What name could I have called? I haven't been with anybody else for a long time, a long time. She says I haven't been with her, either. I guess she's right. I've just been using her. Using her as an anchor—to hold me here, in this house, this bed—so I won't find myself on the other side of town, ruining my reputation. *What* reputation? They all know. I swear they all *know*. Know what? What's there to know? So you get drunk and you fool around a little. Come on, Parnell. There's more to it than that. That's the reason you draw blanks whenever you get drunk. Everything comes out. Everything. They see what you don't dare to see. What name could I have called? Richard would say that you've got—black fever! Yeah, and he'd be wrong—that long, loud, black mother. I wonder if she's asleep yet—or just lying there, looking at the walls. Poor girl! All your life you've been made sick, stunned, dizzy, oh, Lord! driven half mad by blackness. Blackness in front of your eyes. Boys and girls, men and women—you've bowed down in front of them all! And then hated yourself. Hated yourself for debasing yourself? Out with it, Parnell! The nigger-lover! Black boys and girls! I've wanted my hands full of them, wanted to drown them, laughing and dancing and making love—making love—wow!—and be transformed, formed, liberated out of this grey-white envelope. Jesus! I've always been afraid. Afraid of what I saw in their eyes? They don't love me, certainly. You don't love them, either! Sick with a disease only white men catch. Blackness. What is it like to be black? To look out on the world from *that* place? I give nothing! How dare she say that! My girl, if you knew what I've given! Ah. Come off it, Parnell. To *whom* have you given? What name did I call? What name did I call?

[*Blackout. Parnell and Lyle. Hunting on parnell's land.*]

LYLE. You think it's a good idea, then? You think she won't say no?

PARNELL. Well, you're the one who's got to go through it. *You've* got to ask for Miss Josephine's hand in marriage. And then you've got to live with her—for the rest of your life. Watch that gun. I've never seen you so jumpy. I might say it was a good idea if I thought she'd say no. But I think she'll say yes.

LYLE. Why would she say yes to me?

PARNELL. I think she's drawn to you. It isn't hard to be—drawn to you. Don't you know that?

LYLE. No. When I was young, I used to come here sometimes—with my Daddy. He didn't like *your* Daddy a-*tall*! We used to steal your game, Parnell—you didn't know that, did you?

PARNELL. I think I knew it.

LYLE. We shot at the game and your Daddy's overseers shot at us. But we *got* what *we* came after. *They* never got *us*!

PARNELL. You're talking an awful lot today. You nervous about Miss Josephine?

LYLE. Wait a minute. You think I ought to marry Jo?

PARNELL. I don't know who anybody should marry. Do you want to marry Jo?

LYLE. Well—I got to marry somebody. I got to have some kids. And Jo is—*clean*!

[*Parnell sights, shoots.*]

PARNELL. Goddamn!

LYLE. Missed it. Ha-ha!

PARNELL. Its probably somebody's mother.

LYLE. Watch. [*Sights, shoots*] *Ha-ha*!

PARNELL. Bravo!

LYLE. I knew it! Had my name written on it, just as pretty as you please! [*Exits, returns with his bird*] See? My Daddy taught me well. It was sport for you. It was life for us.

PARNELL. I reckon you shot somebody's baby.

LYLE. I tell you—I can't go on like this. There comes a time in a man's life when he's got to have him a little—peace.

PARNELL. You mean calm. Tranquillity.

LYLE. Yeah. I didn't mean it like it sounded. You thought I meant—no. I'm tired of—

PARNELL. Poon-tang.

LYLE. How'd you know? You tired of it, too? Hell. Yeah. I want kids.

PARNELL. Well, then—marry the girl.

LYLE. She ain't a girl no more. It might be her last chance, too. But, I swear, Parnell, she might be the only virgin left in this town. The only *white* virgin. I can vouch for the fact ain't many black ones.

PARNELL. You've been active, I know. Any kids?

LYLE. None that I know of. Ha-ha!

PARNELL. Do you think Jo might be upset—by the talk about you and Old Bill? She's real respectable, you know. She's a *librarian*.

LYLE. No. Them things happen every day. You think I ought to marry her? You really think she'll say yes?

PARNELL. She'll say yes. She'd better. I wish you luck. Name the first one after me.

LYLE. No. You be the godfather. And my best man. I'm going to name the first one after my Daddy—because he taught me more about hunting on your land than *you* know. I'll give him your middle name. I'll call him Lyle Parnell Britten, Jr.!

PARNELL. If the girl says yes.

LYLE. Well, if she says no, ain't no problem, is there? We know where to go when the going get rough, don't we, old buddy?

PARNELL. Do we? Look! Mine?

LYLE. What'll you bet?

PARNELL. The price of your wedding rings.

LYLE. You're on. Mine? *Mine*!

[*Blackout. Parnell walks down the aisle, takes the stand.*]

WHITETOWN.

Here comes the nigger-lover!

But I bet you one thing—he knows more about the truth in this case than anybody else.

He ought to—he's with them all the time.

It's sad when a man turns against his own people!

BLACKTOWN.

Let's see how the Negro's friend comes through!

They been waiting for *him*—they going to tear his behind *up*!

I don't trust him. I *never* trusted him!

Why? Because he's *white*, that's why!

THE STATE. You were acquainted with the late Richard Henry?

PARNELL. Of course. His father and I have been friends all our lives.

THE STATE. Close friends?

PARNELL. Yes. Very close.

THE STATE. And what is your relationship to the alleged murderer, Mr. Lyle Britten?

PARNELL. We, also, have been friends all our lives.

THE STATE. Close friends?

PARNELL. Yes.

THE STATE. As close as the friendship between yourself and the dead boy's father?

PARNELL. I would say so—it was a very different relationship.

THE STATE. Different in what respect, Mr. James?

PARNELL. Well, we had different things to talk about. We did different things together.

THE STATE. What sort of different things?

PARNELL. Well—hunting, for example—things like that.

THE STATE. You never went hunting with Reverend Henry?

PARNELL. No. He didn't like to hunt.

THE STATE. He told you so? He told you that he didn't like to hunt?

PARNELL. The question never came up. We led very different lives.

THE STATE. I am gratified to hear it. Is it not true, Mr. James, that it is impossible for any two people to go on a hunting trip together if either of them has any reason at all to distrust the other?

PARNELL. Well, of course that would have to be true. But it's never talked about—it's just understood.

THE STATE. We can conclude, then, that you were willing to trust Lyle Britten with your life but did not feel the same trust in Reverend Henry?

PARNELL. Sir, you may not draw any such conclusion! I have told you that Reverend Henry and I led very different lives!

THE STATE. But you have been friends all your lives. Reverend Henry is also a southern boy —he, also, I am sure, knows and loves this land, has gone swimming and fishing in her streams and rivers, and stalked game in her forests. And yet, close as you are, you have never allowed yourself to be alone with Reverend Henry when Reverend henry had a gun. Doesn't this suggest some *lack*—in your vaunted friendship?

PARNELL. Your suggestion is unwarranted and unworthy. As a soldier, I have often been alone with Negroes with guns, and it certainly never caused me any uneasiness.

THE STATE. But you were fighting a common enemy then. What was your impression of the late Richard Henry?

PARNELL. I liked him. He was very outspoken and perhaps tactless, but a very valuable person.

THE STATE. How would you describe his effect on this town? Among his own people? Among the whites?

PARNELL. His effect? He was pretty well liked.

THE STATE. That does not answer my question.

PARNELL. His effect was—kind of unsettling, I suppose. After all, he had lived in the North a long time, he wasn't used to—the way we do things down here.

THE STATE. He was accustomed to the way things are done in the North—where he learned to carry arms, to take dope, and to couple with white women!

PARNELL. I cannot testify to any of that, sir. I can only repeat that he reacted with great intensity to the racial situation in this town, and his effect on the town was, to that extent, unsettling.

THE STATE. Did he not encourage the Negroes of this town to arm?

PARNELL. Not to my knowledge, sir, no. And, in any case, they are not armed.

THE STATE. You are in a position to reassure us on this point?

PARNELL. My friends do not lie.

THE STATE. You are remarkably fortunate. You are aware of the attitude of the late Richard Henry toward white women? You saw the photographs he carried about with him?

PARNELL. We never discussed women. I never saw the photographs.

THE STATE. But you knew of their existence?

PARNELL. They were not obscene. They were simply snapshots of people he had known in the North.

THE STATE. Snapshots of white women?

PARNELL. Yes.

THE STATE. You are the first witness to admit the existence of these photographs, Mr. James.

PARNELL. It is very likely that the other witnesses never saw them. The boy had been discouraged, very early on, from mentioning them or showing them about.

THE STATE. Discouraged by whom?

PARNELL. Why—by—me.

THE STATE. But you never saw the photographs—

PARNELL. I told him I didn't want to see them and that it would be dangerous to carry them about.

THE STATE. He showed these photographs to you, but to no one else?

PARNELL. That would seem to be the case, yes.

THE STATE. What was his motive in taking you into his confidence?

PARNELL. Bravado. He wanted me to know that he had white friends in the North, that—he had been happy—in the North.

THE STATE. You did not tell his father? You did not warn your close friend?

PARNELL. I am sure that Richard never mentioned these photographs to his father. He would have been too ashamed. Those women were beneath him.

THE STATE. A white woman who surrenders to a colored man is beneath all human consideration. She has wantonly and deliberately defiled the temple of the Holy Ghost. It is clear to me that the effect of such a boy on this town was irresponsible and incendiary to the greatest degree. Did you not find your close friendship with Reverend Henry somewhat strained by the son's attempt to rape the wife of your other close friend, Lyle Britten?

PARNELL. This attempt was never mentioned before—before today.

THE STATE. You are as close as you claim to the Britten family and knew nothing of this attempted rape? How do you explain that?

PARNELL. I cannot explain it.

THE STATE. This is a court of law, Mr. James, and we will have the truth!

WHITETOWN. Make him tell the truth!

BLACKTOWN. Make him tell the truth!

THE STATE. How can you be the close friend you claim to be of the Britten family and not have known of so grave an event?

PARNELL. I—I knew of a fight. It was understood that the boy had gone to Mr. Britten's store looking for a fight. I—I cannot explain *that*, either.

THE STATE. Who told you of the fight?

PARNELL. Why—Mr. Britten.

THE STATE. And did not tell you that Richard Henry had attempted to assault his wife? Come, Mr. James!

PARNELL. We were all very much upset. Perhaps he was not so coherent as he might have been— perhaps I failed to listen closely. It was my assumption that Mrs. Britten had misconstrued the boy's actions—he had been in the North a long time, his manner was very free and bold.

THE STATE. Mrs. Britten has testified that Richard Henry grabbed her and pulled her to him and tried to kiss her. How can those actions be misconstrued?

PARNELL. Those actions are—quite explicit.

THE STATE. Thank you, Mr. James. That is all.

JUDGE. The witness may step down.

[*Parnell leaves the stand.*]

BLACKTOWN. What do you think of our fine friend *now*? He didn't do it to us rough and hard. No, he was real gentle. I hardly felt a thing. Did you? You can't never go against the word of a white lady, man, not even if you're white. Can't be done. He was sad. *Sad!*

WHITETOWN. It took him long enough! He did his best not to say it—can you imagine! So her story was true—after all! I hope he's learned his lesson. We been trying to tell him—for years!

CLERK. [*Calls*]. Mr. Lyle Britten!

[*Lyle, in the woods*]

LYLE. I wonder what he'll grow up to look like. Of course, it might be a girl. I reckon I wouldn't mind—just keep on trying till I get me a boy, ha-ha! Old Miss Josephine is something, ain't she? I really struck oil when I come across her. She's a nice woman. And she's *my* woman—I ain't got to worry about *that* a-tall! You're making big changes in your life, Lyle, and you got to be ready to take on this extra responsibility. Shoot, I'm ready. I know what I'm doing. And I'm going to work harder than I've ever worked before in my life to make Jo happy— and keep her happy—and raise our children to be fine men and women. Lord, you know I'm not a praying man. I've done a lot of wrong things in my life and I ain't never going to be perfect. I know You know that. I know You understand that. But, Lord, hear me today and help me to do what I'm supposed to do. I want to be as strong as my Mama and Daddy and raise my children like they raised me. That's what I want, oh Lord. In a few years I'll be walking here, showing my son these trees and this water and this sky. He'll have his hand in my hand, and I'll show him the world. Isn't that a funny thing! He don't even exist yet—he's just an egg in his mother's belly, and I bet you couldn't even find him with a microscope—and I put him there—and he's coming out soon—with fingers and toes and eyes—and by and by, he'll learn to walk and talk— and I reckon I'll have to spank him sometime—if he's anything like me, I know I will. Isn't that something! My son! Hurry up and get here, so I can hug you in my arms and give you a good start on your long journey!

[*Blackout. Lyle, with Papa D. Drunk. Music and dancing*]

LYLE. You remember them days when Willa Mae was around? My mind's been going back to them days. You remember? She was a hot little piece, I just had to have some of that, I just *had* to. Half the time she didn't wear no stockings, just had them brown, round legs just moving. I couldn't keep my eyes off her legs when she didn't wear no stockings. And you know what she told me? You know what she told me? She said there wasn't a nigger alive could be as good to her as me. That's right. She said she'd like to *see* the nigger could do her like I done her. You hear me, boy? That's something, ain't it? Boy— she'd just come into a room sometimes and my old pecker would stand up at attention. You ain't jealous, are you, Joel? Ha-ha! You never did hear from her no more, did you? No, I reckon you didn't. Shoot, I got to get on home. I'm a family man now, I got—great responsibilities! Yeah. Be seeing you, Joel. You don't want to close up and walk a-ways with me, do you? No, I reckon you better not. They having fun. Sure wish I could be more like you all. Bye-bye!

[*Blackout. As Lyle approaches the witness stand, the lights in the courtroom dim. We hear voices from the church, singing a lament. The lights come up.*]

JUDGE. Gentlemen of the jury, have you reached a verdict?
FOREMAN. We have, Your Honor.
JUDGE. Will the prisoner please rise?

[*Lyle rises.*]

Do you find the defendant, Mr. Lyle Britten, guilty or not guilty?
FOREMAN. Not guilty, Your Honor.

[*Cheering in Whitetown. Silence in Blacktown. The stage is taken over by Reporters, Photographers, Witnesses, Townspeople. Lyle is congratulated and embraced. Blacktown files out silently, not looking back. Whitetown files out jubilantly, and yet with a certain reluctance. Presently, the stage is empty, except for Lyle, Jo, Mother Henry, Meridian, Parnell, Juanita, and Lorenzo.*]

JO. Let's get out of here and go home. We've been here just for days. I wouldn't care if I *never* saw the insides of a courtroom again! Let's go home, sugar. We got something to celebrate!
JUANITA. We, too, must go—to another celebration. We're having a prayer meeting on the City Hall steps.
LORENZO. Prayer meeting!
LYLE. Well, it was touch and go there for awhile, Parnell, but you sure come through. I knew you would.
JO. Let's go, Lyle. The baby's hungry.
MERIDIAN. Perhaps now you can ask him to tell you the truth. He's got nothing to lose now. They can't try him again.
LYLE. Wasn't much sense in trying me now, this time, was there, Reverend? These people have been knowing me and my good Jo here all our lives, they ain't going to doubt us. And you people—you people— ought to have better sense and more things to do than running around stirring up all this hate and trouble. *That's* how your son got himself killed. He listened to crazy niggers like you!
MERIDIAN. Did you kill him?
LYLE. They just asked me that in court, didn't they? And they just decided I didn't, didn't they? Well, that's good enough for me and all those white people and so it damn sure better be good enough for you!
PARNELL. That's no answer. It's not good enough for me.
LYLE. What do you mean, that's no answer? Why isn't it an answer? Why isn't it good enough for you? You know, when you were up on the stand right now, you acted like you doubted my Jo's word. You got no right to doubt Jo's word. You ain't no better than she is! You ain't no better than me!
PARNELL. I am aware of that. God knows I have been made aware of that—for the first time in my life. But, as you and I will never be the same again— since our comedy is finished, since I have failed you

so badly—let me say this. I did not doubt Jo's word. I knew that she was lying and that you had made her lie. That was a terrible thing to do to her. It was a terrible thing that I just did to you. I really don't know if what I did to Meridian was as awful as what I did to you. I don't expect forgiveness, Meridian. I only hope that all of us will suffer past this agony and horror.

LYLE. What's the matter with you? Have you forgotten you a white man? A white man! My Daddy told me not to *never* forget I was a white man! Here I been knowing you all my life—and now I'm ashamed of you. Ashamed of you! Get on over to niggertown! I'm going home with my good wife.

MERIDIAN. What was the last thing my son said to you—before you shot him down—like a dog?

LYLE. Like a dog! You a smart nigger, ain't you?

MERIDIAN. What was the last thing he said? Did he beg you for his life?

LYLE. *That* nigger! He was too smart for that! He was too full of himself for that! He must have thought he was white. And I gave him every chance—every chance—to live!

MERIDIAN. And he refused them all.

LYLE. Do you know what that nigger said to me?

[*The light changes, so that everyone but Lyle is in silhouette. Richard appears, dressed as we last saw him, on the road outside Papa D.'s joint.*]

RICHARD. I'm ready. Here I am. You asked me if I was ready, didn't you? What's on your mind, white man?

LYLE. Boy, I always treated you with respect. I don't know what's the matter with you, or what makes you act the way you do—but you owe me an apology and I come out here tonight to get it. I mean, I ain't going away without it.

RICHARD. *I* owe *you* an apology! That's a wild idea. What am I apologizing for?

LYLE. You know, you mighty lucky to still be walking around.

RICHARD. So are you. White man.

LYLE. I'd like you to apologize for your behavior in my store that day. Now, I think I'm being pretty reasonable, ain't I?

RICHARD. You got anything to write on? I'll write you an IOU.

LYLE. Keep it up. You going to be laughing out of the other side of your mouth pretty soon.

RICHARD. Why don't you go home? And let me go home? Do we need all this shit? Can't we live without it?

LYLE. Boy, are you drunk?

RICHARD. No, I ain't drunk. I'm just tired. Tired of all this fighting. What are you trying to prove? What am *I* trying to prove?

LYLE. I'm trying to give you a break. You too dumb to take it.

RICHARD. I'm hip. You been trying to give me a break for a great, long time. But there's only one break I want. And you won't give me that.

LYLE. What kind of break do you want, boy?

RICHARD. For you to go home. And let me go home. I got things to do. I got—lots of things to do!

LYLE. I got things to do, too. I'd like to get home, too.

RICHARD. Then why are we standing here? Can't we walk? Let me walk, white man! Let me walk!

LYLE. We can walk, just as soon as we get our business settled.

RICHARD. It's settled. You a man and I'm a man. Let's walk.

LYLE. Nigger, you was born down here. Ain't you never said sir to a white man?

RICHARD. No. The only person I ever said sir to was my Daddy.

LYLE. Are you going to apologize to me?

RICHARD. No.

LYLE. Do you want to live?

RICHARD. Yes.

LYLE. Then you know what to do, then, don't you?

RICHARD. Go home. Go home.

LYLE. You facing my gun. [*Produces it*] Now, in just a minute, we can both go home.

RICHARD. You sick mother! Why can't you leave me alone? White man! I don't want nothing from you. You ain't got nothing to give me. You can't eat because none of your sad-assed chicks can cook. You can't talk because won't nobody talk to you. You can't dance because you've got nobody to dance with—don't you know I've watched you all my life? *All my life!* And *I* know your women, don't you think I don't—better than you!

[*Lyle shoots once.*]

Why have you spent so much time trying to kill me? Why are you always trying to cut off *my* cock? You worried about it? Why?

[*Lyle shoots again.*]

Okay. Okay. Okay. Keep your old lady home, you hear? Don't let her near no nigger. She might get to like it. You might get to like it, too. Wow!

[*Richard falls.*]

Juanita! Daddy! *Mama*!

[*Singing from the church. Spot on Lyle*]

LYLE. I had to kill him then. I'm a white man! Can't nobody talk that way to *me*! I had to go and get my pick-up truck and load him in it—I had to carry him on my back—and carry him out to the high weeds. And I dumped him in the weeds, face down. And then I come on home, to my good Jo here.

JO. Come on, Lyle. We got to get on home. We got to get the little one home now.

LYLE. And I ain't sorry. I want you to know that I ain't sorry!

JO. Come on, Lyle. Come on. He's hungry. I got to feed him.

[*Jo and Lyle exit.*]

MOTHER HENRY. We got to go now, children. The children is already started to march.

LORENZO. Prayer!

MERIDIAN. You know, for us, it all began with the Bible and the gun. Maybe it will end with the Bible and the gun.

JUANITA. What did you do with the gun, Meridian?

PARNELL. You have the gun—Richard's gun?

MERIDIAN. Yes. In the pulpit. Under the Bible. Like the pilgrims of old.

[*Exits.*]

MOTHER HENRY. Come on, children.

[*Singing*]

[*Pete enters.*]

PETE. [*Stammers*] Are you ready, Juanita? Shall we go now?

JUANITA. Yes.

LORENZO. Come here, Pete. Stay close to me.

[*They go to the church door. The singing swells.*]

PARNELL. Well.

JUANITA. Well. Yes, Lord!

PARNELL. Can I join you on the march, Juanita? Can I walk with you?

JUANITA. Well, we can walk in the same direction, Parnell. Come. Don't look like that Let's go on.

[*Exits*]

[*After a moment, Parnell follows.*]

CURTAIN

THE END

ESSAY: AN APPROACH TO THE PLAY

A powerful presentation of "the state of mind and the relationship of people to each other helplessly corrupted and destroyed by this insanity you call color" occurs in the dialogue at the end of Act 1 between Parnell and Meridian, two old friends who might seem to be, in the ideological spectrum of the play, "moderates." Here the minister whose son has been murdered questions the value of the nonviolence he has advocated as a strategy for his people, and Parnell, the liberal journalist, reminds him that he has always considered all the people of the world to be his people. Apparently, the men's interaction with the chief of police during the previous week has demonstrated for Meridian that the two white men understand each other on the basis of unexpressed cultural assumptions from which he is excluded. It seems to him that these shared white male cultural assumptions have converted the tragedy of his son's death into a mere intellectual problem for Parnell, a matter less of emotion than of tactics about how best to secure Lyle's arrest. The friends start to see each other less as individuals than as representatives of their races. "You're Mr. Charlie,"

Meridian says. "*All* white men are Mister Charlie." And Parnell tells Meridian, "You sound more and more like your son, do you know that?" Parnell tries to explain what it feels like to be white, and Meridian, what it feels like to be black. In seeking understanding, Parnell says that white privilege is not something you have; it is something you are, a function of identity: "It's not a matter of trying to hold *on*; the things, the privilege—are part of you, are *who* you are. It's in the *gut*."

Baldwin says that one of his objectives in writing the play was to try to understand and present the humanity of someone who could behave in such an inhuman way as Lyle, and in some ways he seems to have accomplished this. Lyle's sexual insecurities, the notion that a man of such debased sexuality could perceive himself as the chivalric defender of white womanhood (and believe that such an abstraction as this needs defending), his profound sense of social and personal inferiority in a culture that insists on white supremacy, his myth that his father's life, which seems to have been so pathetically circumscribed, is a heritage that he holds in sacred trust for his son—all these make him understandably human, however unattractive, however hateful. What makes Parnell tick may be a harder question, since he seems to be someone who should know better, a cerebral person of privileged education, perceived by at least some blacks (and by himself) as an enlightened champion of human rights. He seems to embody yet another division in the play, a white liberal who knows intellectually what is wrong with his culture but who, at the moment of truth, remains constrained emotionally by white ideology. In giving witness, he cannot bring himself to testify that a white woman lied, and so he finds ways to "tell the truth" in answering the questions asked of him without contradicting the case for the defense and without expressing his suspicions about Lyle's guilt. Etymologically, a "verdict" is a "truth-speaking," a formal declaration of the truth as determined on the basis of evidence presented. Parnell is not alone in frustrating this process (many of the witnesses fail to tell the truth), but his testimony was decisive and contrary to his own convictions.

Perhaps he finds it easier to see blacks as oppressed, long-suffering victims, objects of pity in need of rescue, than as people who are strong, free, independent, equal. At the end of Act 2, Juanita says to him: "I used to watch you roaring through this town like a St. George thirsty for dragons. And I wanted to let you know you haven't got to do all that; dragons aren't hard to find, they're everywhere. And nobody wants you to be St. George. We just wanted you to be Parnell. But, of course, that's much harder." He has a great deal of self-image invested in being perceived by Blacktown as the hero who used his skills on their behalf to finesse the system into arresting Lyle. What he actually does is to demonstrate why many blacks distrust whites, for Parnell is the most sensitive and well-intentioned portrait of his race in the play.

Whether or not a peaceful and at the same time beneficial resolution of racial tension is possible, then, remains a major issue. Baldwin said that the setting of the play is "Plaguetown, U.S.A. now. The plague is race, the plague is our concept of Christianity: and this raging plague has the power to destroy every human relationship." The imagery of the play explores the complex relationship of hatred to this disease: Is it the cause of the disease, or might it actually be part of the cure? Mother Henry tells Richard that he will make himself sick with hatred, and Richard replies that he will make himself well with it. She says hatred is a poison; he says he will drink it in small doses, to build up an immunity. The citizens of Whitetown sentimentalize about the peaceful good old days before outside agitators stirred up black anger, when, as Jo says: "I never knew of anyone to mistreat a colored person—have you? And they certainly didn't *act* mistreated." What Richard articulates is that a good deal of anger has been swallowed down over the years and has remained invisible to people like Jo.

Yet it may be that in spite of the cultural divide which the play dramatizes and even Parnell's moral failure, the play ends with a suggestion of hope: when Parnell asks Juanita if he can walk with the blacks on their picket line, she says, "Well, we can walk in the same direction. . . . Let's go on." He has forfeited too much of his former trust to be said to walk "with" them, but he *is* invited to walk in the same metaphorical direction—a direction, it is important to recognize, already selected by the citizens of Blacktown. If this is the beginning of a resolution, then, it is happening on black terms, not white, and this fact may be crucial.

It is surprising that a play which seems now to have been so prescient as was *Blues for Mr. Charlie* seemed offensive to so many whites thirty years ago. Perhaps it suffered as bearers of unwanted messages often do: more than any of the characters in the third act, the play as a whole seems to tell an uncomfortable truth without flinching and may present its own "verdict," its own proclamation of the truth. Baldwin, who said that he was trying to understand Lyle as a brother-human, also said that "while we probably cannot hope to liberate him," we can "begin working toward the liberation of his children." Lyle's and Juanita's children would both be old enough to have children by now. If telling the truth of one's convictions with directness and honesty is useful, perhaps Baldwin's play can still help liberate that next generation.

Lorraine Hansberry

A RAISIN IN THE SUN

About the Author   Lorraine Hansberry (1930–1965) came from a prominent Chicago family. Her father was a real-estate broker who founded one of the first black banks in that city and who, in the face of opposition from white neighbors, successfully carried a case to the U.S. Supreme Court against "restrictive covenants" that would limit access to housing on the basis of race. Her mother was ward commissioner for the Republican party. Her uncle Leo, Professor of African History at Howard University, had a university named after him in Nigeria. During her adolescence, major black intellectual and artistic leaders were guests in her family home, most importantly perhaps the philosopher W. E. B. DuBois, the poet Langston Hughes, and the singer–actor–political activist Paul Robeson.

Hansberry attended the University of Wisconsin for two years before deciding to study painting at the Art Institute of Chicago. From 1951 to 1955 she wrote for, and for a time edited, *Freedom*, a magazine founded by Robeson to which DuBois was a regular contributor. She turned subsequently to the theater; her first play, *A Raisin in the Sun*, was produced in New York in 1954. Then, shortly after the opening of her second play on Broadway, *The Sign in Sidney Brustein's Window*, Lorraine Hansberry died of cancer at age 34.

About the Play   *Raisin* was spectacularly successful on stage and shortly thereafter was made into a motion picture. The play won the New York Drama Critics Circle Award for 1959, making Hansberry the youngest playwright, as well as the first black writer, to win that award.

Its title is an allusion to a poem by Langston Hughes whose first line asks the question, "What happens to a dream deferred?" While writing the play, Hansberry's working title was "The Crystal Stair," the title of another Hughes poem, one celebrating black mothers who performed menial labor—specifically washing other people's stairs—so their children could climb metaphorical stairs, becoming educated and successful. Hansberry's change of title shifts the spotlight from Lena alone to all the characters, all of whom have had, or face the prospect of having, their dreams deferred. The play presents a family at a moment of crisis, when a personal loss paradoxically presents a possibility for material advancement. Hansberry uses this family crisis to imply a whole society's crisis of values, a crisis in which both sexism and racism play significant roles; however, these ideas are expressed simply, and the values invoked are ones on which large segments of black audiences and white audiences seemed able to agree. The humanity and dignity of the characters, the intensity of the plot, and the complexity of the themes combine to make this play a classic of American theater.

CHARACTERS

(In order of appearance)

RUTH YOUNGER

TRAVIS YOUNGER

WALTER LEE YOUNGER (BROTHER)

BENEATHA YOUNGER

LENA YOUNGER (MAMA)

JOSEPH ASAGAI

GEORGE MURCHISON

KARL LINDNER

BOBO

MOVING MEN

The action of the play is set in Chicago's Southside, sometime between World War II and the present.

Act I
Scene I: *Friday morning.*
Scene II: *The following morning.*

Act I

SCENE I

The Younger living room would be a comfortable and well-ordered room if it were not for a number of indestructible contradictions to this state of being. Its furnishings are typical and undistinguished and their primary feature now is that they have clearly had to accommodate the living of too many people for too many years—and they are tired. Still, we can see that at some time, a time probably no longer remembered by the family (except perhaps for Mama), the furnishings of this room were actually selected with care and love and even hope—and brought to this apartment and arranged with taste and pride.

That was a long time ago. Now the once loved pattern of the couch upholstery has to fight to show itself from under acres of crocheted doilies and couch covers which have themselves finally come to be more important than the upholstery. And here a table or a chair has been moved to disguise the worn places in the carpet; but the carpet has fought back by showing its weariness, with depressing uniformity, elsewhere on its surface.

Weariness has, in fact, won in this room. Everything has been polished, washed, sat on, used, scrubbed too often. All pretenses but living itself have long since vanished from the very atmosphere of this room.

Moreover, a section of this room, for it is not really a room unto itself, though the landlord's lease would make it seem so, slopes backward to provide a small kitchen area, where the family prepares the meals that are eaten in the living room proper, which must also serve as dining room. The single window that has been provided for these "two" rooms is located in this kitchen area. The sole natural light the family may enjoy in the course of a day is only that which fights its way through this little window.

At left, a door leads to a bedroom which is shared by Mama and her daughter, Beneatha. At right, opposite, is a second room (which in the beginning of the life of this apartment was probably a breakfast room) which serves as a bedroom for Walter and his wife, Ruth.

Time: Sometime between World War II and the present.

Place: Chicago's Southside.

At Rise. It is morning dark in the living room. Travis is asleep on the make-down bed at center. An alarm clock sounds from within the bedroom at right, and presently Ruth enters from that room and closes the door behind her. She crosses sleepily toward the window. As she passes her sleeping son she reaches down and shakes him a little. At the window she raises the shade and a dusky Southside morning light comes in feebly. She fills a pot with water and puts it on to boil. She calls to the boy, between yawns, in a slightly muffled voice.

Ruth is about thirty. We can see that she was a pretty girl, even exceptionally so, but now it is apparent that life has been little that she expected, and disappointment has already begun to hang in her face. In a few years, before thirty-five even, she will be known among her people as a "settled woman."

She crosses to her son and gives him a good, final, rousing shake.

RUTH. Come on now, boy, it's seven thirty! [*Her son sits up at last, in a stupor of sleepiness*] I say hurry up, Travis! You ain't the only person in the world got to use a bathroom! [*The child, a sturdy, handsome little boy of ten or eleven, drags himself out of the bed and almost blindly takes his towels and "today's clothes" from drawers and a closet and goes out to the bathroom, which is in an outside hall and which is shared by another family or families on the same floor. Ruth crosses to the bedroom door at right and opens it and calls in to her husband*]

Walter Lee! . . . It's after seven thirty! Lemme see you do some waking up in there now! [*She waits*] You better get up from there, man! It's after seven thirty I tell you. [*She waits again*] All right, you just go ahead and lay there and next thing you know Travis be finished and Mr. Johnson'll be in there and you'll be fussing and cussing round here like a madman! And be late too! [*She waits, at the end of patience*] Walter Lee—it's time for you to GET UP!

[*She waits another second and then starts to go into the bedroom, but is apparently satisfied that her husband has begun to get up. She stops, pulls the door to, and returns to the kitchen area. She wipes her face with a moist cloth and runs her fingers through her sleep-disheveled hair in a vain effort and ties an apron around her housecoat. The bedroom door at right opens and her husband stands in the doorway in his pajamas, which are rumpled and mismated. He is a lean, intense young man in his middle thirties, inclined to quick nervous movements and erratic speech habits—and always in his voice there is a quality of indictment*]

WALTER. Is he out yet?

RUTH. What you mean *out*? He ain't hardly got in there good yet.

WALTER [*wandering in, still more oriented to sleep than to a new day*]. Well, what was you doing all that yelling for if I can't even get in there yet? [*Stopping and thinking*] Check coming today?

RUTH. They *said* Saturday and this is just Friday and I hopes to God you ain't going to get up here first thing this morning and start talking to me 'bout no money—'cause I 'bout don't want to hear it.

WALTER. Something the matter with you this morning?

RUTH. No—I'm just sleepy as the devil. What kind of eggs you want?

WALTER. Not scrambled. [*Ruth starts to scramble eggs*] Paper come? [*Ruth points impatiently to the rolled up* Tribune *on the table, and he gets it and spreads it out and vaguely reads the front page*] Set off another bomb yesterday.

RUTH [*maximum indifference*]. Did they?

WALTER [*looking up*]. What's the matter with you?

RUTH. Ain't nothing the matter with me. And don't keep asking me that this morning.

WALTER. Ain't nobody bothering you. [*Reading the news of the day absently again*] Say Colonel McCormick is sick.

RUTH [*affecting tea-party interest*]. Is he now? Poor thing.

WALTER [*sighing and looking at his watch*]. Oh, me. [*He waits*] Now what is that boy doing in that bathroom all this time? He just going to have to start getting up earlier. I can't be being late to work on account of him fooling around in there.

RUTH [*turning on him*]. Oh, no he ain't going to be getting up no earlier no such thing! It ain't his fault that he can't get to bed no earlier nights 'cause he got a bunch of crazy good-for-nothing clowns sitting up running their mouths in what is supposed to be his bedroom after ten o'clock at night . . .

WALTER. That's what you mad about, ain't it? The things I want to talk about with my friends just couldn't be important in your mind, could they?

[*He rises and finds a cigarette in her handbag on the table and crosses to the little window and looks out, smoking and deeply enjoying this first one*]

RUTH [*almost matter of factly, a complaint too automatic to deserve emphasis*]. Why you always got to smoke before you eat in the morning?

WALTER [*at the window*]. Just look at 'em down there . . . Running and racing to work . . . [*He turns and faces his wife and watches her a moment at the stove, and then, suddenly*] You look young this morning, baby.

RUTH [*indifferently*]. Yeah?

WALTER. Just for a second—stirring them eggs. Just for a second it was—you looked real young again. [*He reaches for her; she crosses away. Then, drily*] It's gone now—you look like yourself again!

RUTH. Man, if you don't shut up and leave me alone.

WALTER [*looking out to the street again*]. First thing a man ought to learn in life is not to make love to no colored woman first thing in the morning. You all some eeeevil people at eight o'clock in the morning.

[*Travis appears in the hall doorway, almost fully dressed and quite wide awake now, his towels and pajamas across his shoulders. He opens the door and signals for his father to make the bathroom in a hurry*]

TRAVIS [*watching the bathroom*]. Daddy, come on!

[*Walter gets his bathroom utensils and flies out to the bathroom*]

RUTH. Sit down and have your breakfast, Travis.

TRAVIS. Mama, this is Friday. [*Gleefully*] Check coming tomorrow, huh?

RUTH. You get your mind off money and eat your breakfast.

TRAVIS [*eating*]. This is the morning we supposed to bring the fifty cents to school.

RUTH. Well, I ain't got no fifty cents this morning.

TRAVIS. Teacher say we have to.

RUTH. I don't care what teacher say. I ain't got it. Eat your breakfast, Travis.

TRAVIS. I *am* eating.

RUTH. Hush up now and just eat!

[*The boy gives her an exasperated look for her lack of understanding, and eats grudgingly*]

TRAVIS. You think Grandmama would have it?

RUTH. No! And I want you to stop asking your grandmother for money, you hear me?

TRAVIS [*outraged*]. Gaaaleee! I don't ask her, she just gimme it sometimes!

RUTH. Travis Willard Younger—I got too much on me this morning to be—

TRAVIS. Maybe Daddy—

RUTH. *Travis*!

[*The boy hushes abruptly. They are both quiet and tense for several seconds*]

TRAVIS [*presently*]. Could I maybe go carry some groceries in front of the supermarket for a little while after school then?

RUTH. Just hush, I said. [*Travis jabs his spoon into his cereal bowl viciously, and rests his head in anger upon his fists*] If you through eating, you can get over there and make up your bed.

[*The boy obeys stiffly and crosses the room, almost mechanically, to the bed and more or less folds the bedding into a heap, then angrily gets his books and cap*]

TRAVIS [*sulking and standing apart from her unnaturally*]. I'm gone.

RUTH [*looking up from the stove to inspect him automatically*]. Come here. [*He crosses to her and she studies his head*] If you don't take this comb and fix this here head, you better! [*Travis puts down his books with a great sigh of oppression, and crosses to the mirror. His mother mutters under her breath about his "slubbornness"*] 'Bout to march out of here with that head looking just like chickens slept in it! I just don't know where you get your slubborn ways . . . And get your jacket, too. Looks chilly out this morning.

TRAVIS [*with conspiciously brushed hair and jacket*]. I'm gone.

RUTH. Get carfare and milk money— [*Waving one finger*] —and not a single penny for no caps, you hear me?

TRAVIS [*with sullen politeness*]. Yes'm.

[*He turns in outrage to leave. His mother watches after him as in his frustration he approaches the door almost comically. When she speaks to him, her voice has become a very gentle tease*]

RUTH [*mocking; as she thinks he would say it*]. Oh, Mama makes me so mad sometimes, I don't know what to do! [*She waits and continues to his back as he stands stock-still in front of the door*] I wouldn't kiss that woman good-bye for nothing in this world this morning! [*The boy finally turns around and rolls his eyes at her, knowing the mood has changed and he is vindicated; he does not, however, move toward her yet*] Not for nothing in this world! [*She finally laughs aloud at him and holds out her arms to him and we see that it is a way between them, very old and practiced. He crosses to her and allows her to embrace him warmly but keeps his face fixed with masculine rigidity. She holds him back from her presently and looks at him and runs her fingers over the features of his face. With utter gentleness—*] Now—whose little old angry man are you?

TRAVIS [*the masculinity and gruffness start to fade at last*]. Aw gaalee—Mama . . .

RUTH [*Mimicking*]. Aw—gaaaaalleeeee, Mama! [*She pushes him, with rough playfulness and finality, toward the door*] Get on out of here or you going to be late.

TRAVIS [*in the face of love, new aggressiveness*]. Mama, could I *please* go carry groceries?

RUTH. Honey, it's starting to get so cold evenings.

WALTER [*coming in from the bathroom and drawing a make-believe gun from a make-believe holster and shooting at his son*]. What is it he wants to do?

RUTH. Go carry groceries after school at the supermarket.

WALTER. Well, let him go . . .

TRAVIS [*quickly, to the ally*]. I *have* to—she won't gimme the fifty cents . . .

WALTER [*to his wife only*]. Why not?

RUTH [*simply, and with flavor*]. 'Cause we don't have it.

WALTER [*To Ruth only*]. What you tell the boy things like that for? [*Reaching down into his pants with a rather important gesture*] Here, son—

[*He hands the boy the coin, but his eyes are directed to his wife's. Travis takes the money happily*]

TRAVIS. Thanks, Daddy.

[*He starts out. Ruth watches both of them with murder in her eyes. Walter stands and stares back at her with defiance, and suddenly reaches into his pocket again on an afterthought*]

WALTER [*without even looking at his son, still staring hard *at his wife*]. In fact, here's another fifty cents . . . Buy yourself some fruit today—or take a taxicab to school or something!

TRAVIS. Whoopee—

[*He leaps up and clasps his father around the middle with his legs, and they face each other in mutual appreciation; slowly Walter Lee peeks around the boy to catch the violent rays from his wife's eyes and draws his head back as if shot*]

WALTER. You better get down now—and get to school, man.

TRAVIS [*at the door*]. O.K. Good-bye.

[*He exits*]

WALTER [*after him, pointing with pride*]. That's *my* boy. [*She looks at him in disgust and turns back to her work*] You know what I was thinking 'bout in the bathroom this morning?

RUTH. No.

WALTER. How come you always try to be so pleasant!

RUTH. What is there to be pleasant 'bout!

WALTER. You want to know what I was thinking 'bout in the bathroom or not!

RUTH. I know what you thinking 'bout.

WALTER [*ignoring her*]. 'Bout what me and Willy Harris was talking about last night.

RUTH [*immediately—a refrain*]. Willy Harris is a good-for-nothing loudmouth.

WALTER. Anybody who talks to me has got to be a good-for-nothing loudmouth, ain't he? And what you know about who is just a good-for-nothing loudmouth? Charlie Atkins was just a "good-for-nothing loudmouth" too, wasn't he! When he wanted me to go in the dry-cleaning business with him. And now—he's grossing a hundred thousand a year. A hundred thousand dollars a year! You still call *him* a loudmouth!

RUTH [*bitterly*]. Oh, Walter Lee . . .

[*She folds her head on her arms over the table*]

WALTER [*rising and coming to her and standing over her*]. You tired, ain't you? Tired of everything. Me, the boy, the way we live—this beat-up hole—everything. Ain't you? [*She doesn't look up, doesn't answer*] So tired—moaning and groaning all the time, but you wouldn't do nothing to help, would you? You couldn't be on my side that long for nothing, could you?

RUTH. Walter, please leave me alone.

WALTER. A man needs for a woman to back him up . . .

RUTH. Walter—

WALTER. Mama would listen to you. You know she listen to you more than she do me and Bennie. She think more of you. All you have to do is just sit down with her when you drinking your coffee one morning and talking 'bout things like you do and—[*He sits down beside her and demonstrates graphically what he thinks her methods and tone should be*] —you just sip your coffee, see, and say easy like that you been thinking 'bout that deal Walter Lee is so interested in, 'bout the store and all, and sip some more coffee, like what you saying ain't really that important to you—And the next thing you know, she be listening good and asking you questions and when I come home—I can tell her the details. This ain't no fly-by-night proposition, baby. I mean we figured it out, me and Willy and Bobo.

RUTH [*with a frown*]. Bobo?

WALTER. Yeah. You see, this little liquor store we got in mind cost seventy-five thousand and we figured the initial investment on the place be 'bout thirty thousand, see. That be ten thousand each. Course, there's a couple of hundred you got to pay so's you don't spend your life just waiting for them clowns to let your license get approved—

RUTH. You mean graft?

WALTER [*frowning impatiently*]. Don't call it that. See there, that just goes to show you what women understand about the world. Baby, don't *nothing* happen for you in this world 'less you pay *somebody* off!

RUTH. Walter, leave me alone! [*She raises her head and stares at him vigorously—then says, more quietly*] Eat your eggs, they gonna be cold.

WALTER [*straightening up from her and looking off*]. That's it. There you are. Man say to his woman: I got me a dream. His woman say: Eat your eggs. [*Sadly, but gaining in power*] Man say: I got to take hold of this here world, baby! And a woman will say: Eat your eggs and go to work. [*Passionately now*] Man say: I got to change my life, I'm choking to death, baby! And his woman say—[*In utter anguish as he brings his fists down on his thighs*] —Your eggs is getting cold!

RUTH [*softly*]. Walter, that ain't none of our money.

WALTER [*not listening at all or even looking at her*]. This morning, I was lookin' in the mirror and thinking about it . . . I'm thirty-five years old; I been married eleven years and I got a boy who sleeps in the living room—[*Very, very quietly*] —and all I got to give him is stories about how rich white people live . . .

RUTH. Eat your eggs, Walter.

WALTER [*slams the table and jumps up*]. —DAMN MY

EGGS—DAMN ALL THE EGGS THAT EVER WAS!

RUTH. Then go to work.

WALTER [*looking up at her*]. See—I'm trying to talk to you 'bout myself—[*Shaking his head with the repetition*] —and all you can say is eat them eggs and go to work.

RUTH [*wearily*]. Honey, you never say nothing new. I listen to you every day, every night and every morning, and you never say nothing new. [*Shrugging*] So you would rather *be* Mr. Arnold than be his chauffeur. So—I would *rather* be living in Buckingham Palace.

WALTER. That is just what is wrong with the colored woman in this world . . . Don't understand about building their men up and making 'em feel like they somebody. Like they can do something.

RUTH [*drily, but to hurt*]. There *are* colored men who do things.

WALTER. No thanks to the colored woman.

RUTH. Well, being a colored woman, I guess I can't help myself none.

[*She rises and gets the ironing board and sets it up and attacks a huge pile of rough-dried clothes, sprinkling them in preparation for the ironing and then rolling them into tight fat balls*]

WALTER [*mumbling*]. We one group of men tied to a race of women with small minds!

[*His sister Beneatha enters. She is about twenty, as slim and intense as her brother. She is not as pretty as her sister-in-law, but her lean, almost intellectual face has a handsomeness of its own. She wears a bright-red flannel nightie, and her thick hair stands wildly about her head. Her speech is a mixture of many things; it is different from the rest of the family's insofar as education has permeated her sense of English—and perhaps the Midwest rather than the South has finally—at last—won out in her inflection; but not altogether, because over all of it is a soft slurring and transformed use of vowels which is the decided influence of the Southside. She passes through the room without looking at either Ruth or Walter and goes to the outside door and looks, a little blindly, out to the bathroom. She sees that it has been lost to the Johnsons. She closes the door with a sleepy vengeance and crosses to the table and sits down a little defeated*]

BENEATHA. I am going to start timing those people.

WALTER. You should get up earlier.

BENEATHA [*her face in her hands. She is still fighting the urge to go back to bed*]. Really—would you suggest dawn? Where's the paper?

WALTER [*pushing the paper across the table to her as he studies her almost clinically, as though he has never seen her before*]. You a horrible-looking chick at this hour.

BENEATHA [*drily*]. Good morning, everybody.

WALTER [*senselessly*]. How is school coming?

BENEATHA [*in the same spirit*]. Lovely. Lovely. And you know, biology is the greatest. [*Looking up at him*] I dissected something that looked just like you yesterday.

WALTER. I just wondered if you've made up your mind and everything.

BENEATHA [*gaining in sharpness and impatience*]. And what did I answer yesterday morning—and the day before that?

RUTH [*from the ironing board, like someone disinterested and old*]. Don't be so nasty, Bennie.

BENEATHA [*still to her brother*]. And the day before that and the day before that!

WALTER [*defensively*]. I'm interested in you. Something wrong with that? Ain't many girls who decide—

WALTER and BENEATHA [*in unison*]. —"to be a doctor."

[*Silence*]

WALTER. Have we figured out yet just exactly how much medical school is going to cost?

RUTH. Walter Lee, why don't you leave that girl alone and get out of here to work?

BENEATHA [*exits to the bathroom and bangs on the door*]. Come on out of there, please!

[*She comes back into the room*]

WALTER [*looking at his sister intently*]. You know the check is coming tomorrow.

BENEATHA [*turning on him with a sharpness all her own*]. That money belongs to Mama, Walter, and it's for her to decide how she wants to use it. I don't care if she wants to buy a house or a rocket ship or just nail it up somewhere and look at it. It's hers. Not ours—*hers*.

WALTER [*bitterly*]. Now ain't that fine! You just got your mother's interest at heart, ain't you, girl? You such a nice girl—but if Mama got that money she can always take a few thousand and help you through school too—can't she?

BENEATHA. I have never asked anyone around here to do anything for me!

WALTER. No! And the line between asking and just accepting when the time comes is big and wide—ain't it!

BENEATHA [*with fury*]. What do you want from me,

Brother—that I quit school or just drop dead, which!

WALTER. I don't want nothing but for you to stop acting holy 'round here. Me and Ruth done made some sacrifices for you—why can't you do something for the family?

RUTH. Walter, don't be dragging me in it.

WALTER. You are in it—Don't you get up and go work in somebody's kitchen for the last three years to help put clothes on her back?

RUTH. Oh, Walter—that's not fair . . .

WALTER. It ain't that nobody expects you to get on your knees and say thank you, Brother; thank you, Ruth; thank you, Mama—and thank you, Travis, for wearing the same pair of shoes for two semesters—

BENEATHA [dropping to her knees]. Well—I do—all right?—thank everybody! And forgive me for ever wanting to be anything at all! [Pursuing him on her knees across the floor] FORGIVE ME, FORGIVE ME, FORGIVE ME!

RUTH. Please stop it! Your mama'll hear you.

WALTER. Who the hell told you you had to be a doctor? If you so crazy 'bout messing 'round with sick people—then go be a nurse like other women—or just get married and be quiet . . .

BENEATHA. Well—you finally got it said . . . It took you three years but you finally got it said. Walter, give up; leave me alone—it's Mama's money.

WALTER. *He was my father, too!*

BENEATHA. So what? He was mine, too—and Travis's grandfather—but the insurance money belongs to Mama. Picking on me is not going to make her give it to you to invest in any liquor stores— [Underbreath, dropping into a chair] —and I for one say, God bless Mama for that!

WALTER [to Ruth]. See—did you hear? Did you hear!

RUTH. Honey, please go to work.

WALTER. Nobody in this house is ever going to understand me.

BENEATHA. Because you're a nut.

WALTER. Who's a nut?

BENEATHA. You—you are a nut. Thee is mad, boy.

WALTER [looking at his wife and his sister from the door, very sadly]. The world's most backward race of people, and that's a fact.

BENEATHA [turning slowly in her chair]. And then there are all those prophets who would lead us out of the wilderness—[Walter slams out of the house] —into the swamps!

RUTH. Bennie, why you always gotta be pickin' on your brother? Can't you be a little sweeter sometimes? [Door opens. Walter walks in. He fumbles with his

cap, starts to speak, clears throat, looks everywhere but at Ruth. Finally.]

WALTER [to Ruth]. I need some money for carfare.

RUTH [looks at him, then warms; teasing, but tenderly]. Fifty cents? [She goes to her bag and gets money] Here—take a taxi!

[Walter exits. Mama enters. She is a woman in her early sixties, full-bodied and strong. She is one of those women of a certain grace and beauty who wear it so unobtrusively that it takes a while to notice. Her dark-brown face is surrounded by the total whiteness of her hair, and being a woman who has adjusted to many things in life and overcome many more, her face is full of strength. She has, we can see, wit and faith of a kind that keep her eyes lit and full of interest and expectancy. She is, in a word, a beautiful woman. Her bearing is perhaps most like the noble bearing of the women of the Hereros of Southwest Africa—rather as if she imagines that as she walks she still bears a basket or a vessel upon her head. Her speech, on the other hand, is as careless as her carriage is precise—she is inclined to slur everything—but her voice is perhaps not so much quiet as simply soft]

MAMA. Who that 'round here slamming doors at this hour?

[She crosses through the room, goes to the window, opens it, and brings in a feeble little plant growing doggedly in a small pot on the window sill. She feels the dirt and puts it back out]

RUTH. That was Walter Lee. He and Bennie was at it again.

MAMA. My children and they tempers. Lord, if this little old plant don't get more sun than it's been getting it ain't never going to see spring again. [She turns from the window] —What's the matter with you this morning, Ruth? You looks right peaked. You aiming to iron all them things? Leave some for me. I'll get to 'em this afternoon. Bennie honey, it's too drafty for you to be sitting 'round half dressed. Where's your robe?

BENEATHA. In the cleaners.

MAMA. Well, go get mine and put it on.

BENEATHA. I'm not cold, Mama, honest.

MAMA. I know—but you so thin . . .

BENEATHA [irritably]. Mama, I'm not cold.

MAMA [seeing the make-down bed as Travis has left it]. Lord have mercy, look at that poor bed. Bless his heart—he tries, don't he?

[She moves to the bed Travis has sloppily made up]

RUTH. No—he don't half try at all 'cause he knows

you going to come along behind him and fix every-thing. That's just how come he don't know how to do nothing right now—you done spoiled that boy so.

MAMA [*folding bedding*]. Well—he's a little boy. Ain't supposed to know 'bout housekeeping. My baby, that's what he is. What you fix for his breakfast this morning?

RUTH [*angrily*]. I feed my son, Lena!

MAMA. I ain't meddling—[*Underbreath; busy-bodyish*] I just noticed all last week he had cold cereal, and when it starts getting this chilly in the fall a child ought to have some hot grits or something when he goes out in the cold—

RUTH [*furious*]. I gave him hot oats—is that all right!

MAMA. I ain't meddling. [*Pause*] Put a lot of nice but-ter on it? [*Ruth shoots her an angry look and does not reply*] He likes lots of butter.

RUTH [*exasperated*]. Lena—

MAMA [*to Beneatha. Mama is inclined to wander conversa-tionally sometimes*]. What was you and your brother fussing 'bout this morning?

BENEATHA. It's not important, Mama.

[*She gets up and goes to look out at the bathroom, which is apparently free, and she picks up her towels and rushes out*]

MAMA. What was they fighting about?

RUTH. Now you know as well as I do.

MAMA [*shaking her head*]. Brother still worrying hisself sick about that money?

RUTH. You know he is.

MAMA. You had breakfast?

RUTH. Some coffee.

MAMA. Girl, you better start eating and looking after yourself better. You almost thin as Travis.

RUTH. Lena—

MAMA. Uh-hunh?

RUTH. What are you going to do with it?

MAMA. Now don't you start, child. It's too early in the morning to be talking about money. It ain't Chris-tian.

RUTH. It's just that he got his heart set on that store—

MAMA. You mean that liquor store that Willy Harris want him to invest in?

RUTH. Yes—

MAMA. We ain't no business people, Ruth. We just plain working folks.

RUTH. Ain't nobody business people till they go into business. Walter Lee say colored people ain't never going to start getting ahead till they start gambling

on some different kinds of things in the world—investments and things.

MAMA. What done got into you, girl? Walter Lee done finally sold you on investing.

RUTH. No. Mama, something is happening between Walter and me. I don't know what it is—but he needs something—something I can't give him any more. He needs this chance, Lena.

MAMA [*frowning deeply*]. But liquor, honey—

RUTH. Well—like Walter say—I spec people going to always be drinking themselves some liquor.

RUTH. Well—whether they drinks it or not ain't none of my business. But whether I go into business selling it to 'em *is*, and I don't want that on my ledger this late in life. [*Stopping suddenly and studying her daughter-in-law*] Ruth Younger, what's the matter with you today? You look like you could fall over right there.

RUTH. I'm tired.

MAMA. Then you better stay home from work today.

RUTH. I can't stay home. She'd be calling up the agency and screaming at them, "My girl didn't come in today—send me somebody! My girl didn't come in!" Oh, she just have a fit . . .

MAMA. Well, let her have it. I'll just call her up and say you got the flu—

RUTH [*laughing*]. Why the flu?

MAMA. 'Cause it sounds respectable to 'em. Some-thing white people get, too. They know 'bout the flu. Otherwise they think you been cut up or some-thing when you tell 'em you sick.

RUTH. I got to go in. We need the money.

MAMA. Somebody would of thought my children done all but starved to death the way they talk about money here of late. Child, we got a great big old check coming tomorrow.

RUTH [*sincerely, but also self-righteously*]. Now that's your money. It ain't got nothing to do with me. We all feel like that—Walter and Bennie and me—even Travis.

MAMA [*thoughtfully, and suddenly very far away*]. Ten thousand dollars—

RUTH. Sure is wonderful.

MAMA. Ten thousand dollars.

RUTH. You know what you should do, Miss Lena? You should take yourself a trip somewhere. To Europe or South America or someplace—

MAMA [*throwing up her hands at the thought*]. Oh, child!

RUTH. I'm serious. Just pack up and leave! Go on away and enjoy yourself some. Forget about the family and have yourself a ball for once in your life—

MAMA [*drily*]. You sound like I'm just about ready to die. Who'd go with me? What I look like wandering 'round Europe by myself.

RUTH. Shoot—these here rich white women do it all the time. They don't think nothing of packing up they suitcases and piling on one of them big steamships and—swoosh!—they gone, child.

MAMA. Something always told me I wasn't no rich white woman.

RUTH. Well—what are you going to do with it then?

MAMA. I ain't rightly decided. [*Thinking. She speaks now with emphasis*] Some of it got to be put away for Beneatha and her schoolin'—and ain't nothing going to touch that part of it. Nothing. [*She waits several seconds, trying to make up her mind about something, and looks at Ruth a little tentatively before going on*] Been thinking that we maybe could meet the notes on a little old two-story somewhere, with a yard where Travis could play in the summertime, if we use part of the insurance for a down payment and everybody kind of pitch in. I could maybe take on a little day work again, few days a week—

RUTH [*studying her mother-in-law furtively and concentrating on her ironing, anxious to encourage without seeming to*]. Well, Lord knows, we've put enough rent into this here rat trap to pay for four houses by now . . .

MAMA [*looking up at the words "rat trap" and then looking around and leaning back and sighing—in a suddenly reflective mood—*]. "Rat trap"—yes, that's all it is. [*Smiling*] I remember just as well the day me and Big Walter moved in here. Hadn't been married but two weeks and wasn't planning on living here no more than a year. [*She shakes her head at the dissolved dream*] We was going to set away, little by little, don't you know, and buy a little place out in Morgan Park. We had even picked out the house. [*Chuckling a little*] Looks right dumpy today. But Lord, child, you should know all the dreams I had 'bout buying that house and fixing it up and making me a little garden in the back—[*She waits and stops smiling*] And didn't none of it happen.

[*Dropping her hands in a futile gesture*]

RUTH [*keeps her head down, ironing*]. Yes, life can be a barrel of disappointments, sometimes.

MAMA. Honey, Big Walter would come in here some nights back then and slump down on that couch there and just look at the rug, and look at me and look at the rug and then back at me—and I'd know he was down then . . . really down. [*After a second very long and thoughtful pause; she is seeing back to times that only she can see*] And then, Lord, when I lost that baby—little Claude—I almost thought I was going to lose Big Walter too. Oh, that man grieved hisself! He was one man to love his children.

RUTH. Ain't nothin' can tear at you like losin' your baby. .

MAMA. I guess that's how come that man finally worked hisself to death like he done. Like he was fighting his own war with this here world that took his baby from him.

RUTH. He sure was a fine man, all right. I always liked Mr. Younger.

MAMA. Crazy 'bout his children! God knows there was plenty wrong with Walter Younger—hard-headed, mean, kind of wild with women—plenty wrong with him. But he sure loved his children. Always wanted them to have something—be something. That's where Brother gets all these notions, I reckon. Big Walter used to say, he'd get right wet in the eyes sometimes, lean his head back with the water standing in his eyes and say, "Seem like God didn't see fit to give the black man nothing but dreams—but He did give us children to make them dreams seem worth while." [*She smiles*] He could talk like that, don't you know.

RUTH. Yes, he sure could. He was a good man, Mr. Younger.

MAMA. Yes, a fine man—just couldn't never catch up with his dreams, that's all.

[*Beneatha comes in, brushing her hair and looking up to the ceiling, where the sound of a vacuum cleaner has started up*]

BENEATHA. What could be so dirty on that woman's rugs that she has to vacuum them every single day?

RUTH. I wish certain young women 'round here who I could name would take inspiration about certain rugs in a certain apartment I could also mention.

BENEATHA [*shrugging*]. How much cleaning can a house need, for Christ's sakes.

MAMA [*not liking the Lord's name used thus*]. Bennie!

RUTH. Just listen to her—just listen!

BENEATHA. Oh, God!

MAMA. If you use the Lord's name just one more time—

BENEATHA [*a bit of a whine*]. Oh, Mama—

RUTH. Fresh—just fresh as salt, this girl!

BENEATHA [*drily*]. Well—if the salt loses its savor—

MAMA. Now that will do. I just ain't going to have you 'round here reciting the scriptures in vain—you hear me?

BENEATHA. How did I manage to get on everybody's wrong side by just walking into a room?

RUTH. If you weren't so fresh—

BENEATHA. Ruth, I'm twenty years old.

MAMA. What time you be home from school today?

BENEATHA. Kind of late. [*With enthusiasm*] Madeline is going to start my guitar lessons today.

[*Mama and Ruth look up with the same expression*]

MAMA. Your *what* kind of lessons?

BENEATHA. Guitar.

RUTH. Oh, Father!

MAMA. How come you done taken it in your mind to learn to play the guitar?

BENEATHA. I just want to, that's all.

MAMA [*smiling*]. Lord, child, don't you know what to do with yourself? How long it going to be before you get tired of this now—like you got tired of that little play-acting group you joined last year? [*Looking at Ruth*] And what was it the year before that?

RUTH. The horseback-riding club for which she bought that fifty-five-dollar riding habit that's been hanging in the closet ever since!

MAMA [*to Beneatha*]. Why you got to flit so from one thing to another, baby?

BENEATHA [*sharply*]. I just want to learn to play the guitar. Is there anything wrong with that?

MAMA. Ain't nobody trying to stop you. I just wonders sometimes why you has to flit so from one thing to another all the time. You ain't never done nothing with all that camera equipment you brought home—

BENEATHA. I don't flit! I—I experiment with different forms of expression—

RUTH. Like riding a horse!

BENEATHA. —People have to express themselves one way or another.

MAMA. What is it you want to express?

BENEATHA [*angrily*]. Me! [*Mama and Ruth look at each other and burst into raucous laughter*] Don't worry—I don't expect you to understand.

MAMA [*to change the subject*]. Who you going out with tomorrow night?

BENEATHA [*with displeasure*]. George Murchison again.

MAMA [*pleased*]. Oh—you getting a little sweet on him?

RUTH. You ask me, this child ain't sweet on nobody but herself—[*Underbreath*] Express herself!

[*They laugh*]

BENEATHA. Oh—I like George all right, Mama. I mean I like him enough to go out with him and stuff, but—

RUTH [*for devilment*]. What does *and stuff* mean?

BENEATHA. Mind your own business.

MAMA. Stop picking at her now, Ruth. [*She chuckles—then a suspicious sudden look at her daughter as she turns in her chair for emphasis*] What DOES it mean?

BENEATHA [*wearily*]. Oh, I just mean I couldn't ever really be serious about George. He's—he's so shallow.

RUTH. Shallow—what do you mean he's shallow? He's *Rich*!

MAMA. Hush, Ruth.

BENEATHA. I know he's rich. He knows he's rich, too.

RUTH. Well—what other qualities a man got to have to satisfy you, little girl?

BENEATHA. You wouldn't even begin to understand. Anybody who married Walter could not possibly understand.

MAMA [*outraged*]. What kind of way is that to talk about your brother?

BENEATHA. Brother is a flip—let's face it.

MAMA [*to Ruth, helplessly*]. What's a flip?

RUTH [*glad to add kindling*]. She's saying he's crazy.

BENEATHA. Not crazy. Brother isn't really crazy yet—he—he's an elaborate neurotic.

MAMA. Hush your mouth!

BENEATHA. As for George. Well. George looks good—he's got a beautiful car and he takes me to nice places and, as my sister-in-law says, he is probably the richest boy I will ever get to know and I even like him sometimes—but if the Youngers are sitting around waiting to see if their little Bennie is going to tie up the family with the Murchisons, they are wasting their time.

RUTH. You mean you wouldn't marry George Murchison if he asked you someday? That pretty, rich thing? Honey, I knew you was odd—

BENEATHA. No I would not marry him if all I felt for him was what I feel now. Besides, George's family wouldn't really like it.

MAMA. Why not?

BENEATHA. Oh, Mama—The Murchisons are honest-to-God-*live*-rich colored people, and the only people in the world who are more snobbish than rich white people are rich colored people. I thought everybody knew that. I've met Mrs. Murchison. She's a scene!

MAMA. You must not dislike people 'cause they well off, honey.

BENEATHA. Why not? It makes just as much sense as disliking people 'cause they are poor, and lots of people do that.

RUTH [*a wisdom-of-the-ages manner. To Mama*]. Well, she'll get over some of this—

BENEATHA. Get over it? What are you talking about,

Ruth? Listen, I'm going to be a doctor. I'm not worried about who I'm going to marry yet—if I ever get married.

MAMA *and* RUTH. If?

MAMA. Now, Bennie—

BENEATHA. Oh, I probably will . . . but first I'm going to be a doctor, and George, for one, still thinks that's pretty funny. I couldn't be bothered with that. I am going to be a doctor and everybody around here better understand that!

MAMA [*kindly*]. 'Course you going to be a doctor, honey, God willing.

BENEATHA [*drily*]. God hasn't got a thing to do with it.

MAMA. Beneatha—that just wasn't necessary.

BENEATHA. Well—neither is God. I get sick of hearing about God.

MAMA. Beneatha!

BENEATHA. I mean it! I'm just tired of hearing about God all the time. What has He got to do with anything? Does he pay tuition?

MAMA. You 'bout to get your fresh little jaw slapped!

RUTH. That's just what she needs, all right!

BENEATHA. Why? Why can't I say what I want to around here, like everybody else?

MAMA. It don't sound nice for a young girl to say things like that—you wasn't brought up that way. Me and your father went to trouble to get you and Brother to church every Sunday.

BENEATHA. Mama, you don't understand. It's all a matter of ideas, and God is just one idea I don't accept. It's not important. I am not going out and be immoral or commit crimes because I don't believe in God. I don't even think about it. It's just that I get tired of Him getting credit for all the things the human race achieves through its own stubborn effort. There simply is no blasted God— there is only man and it is *he* who makes miracles!

[*Mama absorbs this speech, studies her daughter and rises slowly and crosses to Beneatha and slaps her powerfully across the face. After, there is only silence and the daughter drops her eyes from her mother's face, and Mama is very tall before her*]

MAMA. Now—you say after me, in my mother's house there is still God. [*There is a long pause and Beneatha stares at the floor wordlessly. Mama repeats the phrase with precision and cool emotion*] In my mother's house there is still God.

BENEATHA. In my mother's house there is still God.

[*A long pause*]

MAMA [*walking away from Beneatha, too disturbed for triumphant posture. Stopping and turning back to her daughter*]. There are some ideas we ain't going to have in this house. Not long as I am at the head of this family.

BENEATHA. Yes, ma'am.

[*Mama walks out of the room*]

RUTH. [*almost gently, with profound understanding*]. You think you a woman, Bennie—but you still a little girl. What you did was childish—so you got treated like a child.

BENEATHA. I see. [*Quietly*] I also see that everybody thinks it's all right for Mama to be a tyrant. But all the tyranny in the world will never put a God in the heavens!

[*She picks up her books and goes out. Pause*]

RUTH [*goes to Mama's door*]. She said she was sorry.

MAMA [*coming out, going to her plant*]. They frightens me, Ruth. My children.

RUTH. You got good children, Lena. They just a little off sometimes—but they're good.

MAMA. No—there's something come down between me and them that don't let us understand each other and I don't know what it is. One done almost lost his mind thinking 'bout money all the time and the other done commence to talk about things I can't seem to understand in no form or fashion. What is it that's changing, Ruth.

RUTH [*soothingly, older than her years*]. Now . . . you taking it all too seriously. You just got strong-willed children and it takes a strong woman like you to keep 'em in hand.

MAMA [*looking at her plant and sprinkling a little water on it*]. They spirited all right, my children. Got to admit they got spirit—Bennie and Walter. Like this little old plant that ain't never had enough sunshine or nothing—and look at it . . .

[*She has her back to Ruth, who has had to stop ironing and lean against something and put the back of her hand to her forehead*]

RUTH [*trying to keep Mama from noticing*]. You . . . sure . . . loves that little old thing, don't you? . . .

MAMA. Well, I always wanted me a garden like I used to see sometimes at the back of the houses down home. This plant is close as I ever got to having one. [*She looks out of the window as she replaces the plant*] Lord, ain't nothing as dreary as the view from this window on a dreary day, is there? Why ain't you singing this morning, Ruth? Sing that "No Ways Tired." That song always lifts me up so—[*She turns at last to see that Ruth has slipped quietly to the floor, in a state of semiconsciousness*] Ruth! Ruth honey—what's the matter with you . . . Ruth!

CURTAIN

SCENE II

It is the following morning; a Saturday morning, and house cleaning is in progress at the Youngers. Furniture has been shoved hither and yon and Mama is giving the kitchen-area walls a washing down. Beneatha, in dungarees, with a handkerchief tied around her face, is spraying insecticide into the cracks in the walls. As they work, the radio is on and a Southside disk-jockey program is inappropriately filling the house with a rather exotic saxophone blues. Travis, the sole idle one, is leaning on his arms, looking out of the window.

TRAVIS. Grandmama, that stuff Bennie is using smells awful. Can I go downstairs, please?

MAMA. Did you get all them chores done already? I ain't seen you doing much.

TRAVIS. Yes'm—finished early. Where did Mama go this morning?

MAMA [*looking at Beneatha*]. She had to go on a little errand.

[*The phone rings. Beneatha runs to answer it and reaches it before Walter, who has entered from bedroom*]

TRAVIS. Where?

MAMA. To tend to her business.

BENEATHA. Haylo . . . [*Disappointed*] Yes, he is. [*She tosses the phone to Walter, who barely catches it*] It's Willie Harris again.

WALTER [*as privately as possible under Mama's gaze*]. Hello, Willie. Did you get the papers from the lawyer? . . . No, not yet. I told you the mailman doesn't get here till ten-thirty . . . No, I'll come there . . . Yeah! Right away. [*He hangs up and goes for his coat*]

BENEATHA. Brother, where did Ruth go?

WALTER [*as he exits*]. How should I know!

TRAVIS. Aw come on, Grandma. Can I go outside?

MAMA. Oh, I guess so. You stay right in front of the house, though, and keep a good lookout for the postman.

TRAVIS. Yes'm. [*He darts into bedroom for stickball and bat, reenters, and sees Beneatha on her knees spraying under the sofa with behind upraised. He edges closer to the target, takes aim, and lets her have it. She screams*] Leave them poor little cockroaches alone, they ain't bothering you none! [*He runs as she swings the spray-gun at him viciously and playfully*] —Grandma! Grandma!

MAMA. Look out there, girl, before you be spilling some of that stuff on that child!

TRAVIS [*safely behind the bastion of Mama*]. That's right—look out, now! [*He exits*]

BENEATHA [*drily*]. I can't imagine that it would hurt him—it has never hurt the roaches.

MAMA. Well, little boys' hides ain't as tough as Southside roaches. You better get over there behind the bureau. I seen one marching out of there like Napoleon yesterday.

BENEATHA. There's really only one way to get rid of them, Mama—

MAMA. How?

BENEATHA. Set fire to this building! Mama, where did Ruth go?

MAMA [*looking at her with meaning*]. To the doctor, I think.

BENEATHA. The doctor? What's the matter? [*They exchange glances*] You don't think—

MAMA [*with her sense of drama*]. Now I ain't saying what I think. But I ain't never been wrong 'bout a woman neither.

[*The phone rings*]

BENEATHA [*at the phone*]. Hay-lo . . . [*Pause, and a moment of recognition*] Well—when did you get back! . . . And how was it? . . . Of course I've missed you—in my way . . . This morning? No . . . house cleaning and all that and Mama hates it if I let people come over when the house is like this . . . You *have*? Well, that's different . . . What is it—Oh, what the hell, come on over . . . Right, see you then. *Arrividerci.*

[*She hangs up*]

MAMA [*who has listened vigorously, as is her habit*]. Who is that you inviting over here with this house looking like this? You ain't got the pride you was born with!

BENEATHA. Asagai doesn't care how houses look, Mama—he's an intellectual.

MAMA. *Who*?

BENEATHA. Asagai—Joseph Asagai. He's an African boy I met on campus. He's been studying in Canada all summer.

MAMA. What's his name?

BENEATHA. Asagai, Joseph. Ah-sah-guy . . . He's from Nigeria.

MAMA. Oh, that's the little country that was founded by slaves way back . . .

BENEATHA. No, Mama—that's Liberia.

MAMA. I don't think I never met no African before.

BENEATHA. Well, do me a favor and don't ask him a whole lot of ignorant questions about Africans. I mean, do they wear clothes and all that—

MAMA. Well, now, I guess if you think we so ignorant 'round here maybe you shouldn't bring your friends here—

BENEATHA. It's just that people ask such crazy things. All anyone seems to know about when it comes to Africa is Tarzan—

MAMA [*indignantly*]. Why should I know anything about Africa?

BENEATHA. Why do you give money at church for the missionary work?

MAMA. Well, that's to help save people.

BENEATHA. You mean save them from *heathenism*—

MAMA [*innocently*]. Yes.

BENEATHA. I'm afraid they need more salvation from the British and the French.

[*Ruth comes in forlornly and pulls off her coat with dejection. They both turn to look at her*]

RUTH [*dispiritedly*]. Well, I guess from all the happy faces—everybody knows.

BENEATHA. You pregnant?

MAMA. Lord have mercy, I sure hope it's a little old girl. Travis ought to have a sister.

[*Beneatha and Ruth give her a hopeless look for this grandmotherly enthusiasm*]

BENEATHA. How far along are you?

RUTH. Two months.

BENEATHA. Did you mean to? I mean did you plan it or was it an accident?

MAMA. What do you know about planning or not planning?

BENEATHA. Oh, Mama.

RUTH [*wearily*]. She's twenty years old, Lena.

BENEATHA. Did you plan it, Ruth?

RUTH. Mind your own business.

BENEATHA. It is my business—where is he going to live, on the *roof*? [*There is silence following the remark as the three women react to the sense of it*] Gee—I didn't mean that, Ruth, honest. Gee, I don't feel like that at all. I—I think it is wonderful.

RUTH [*dully*]. Wonderful.

BENEATHA. Yes—really.

MAMA [*looking at Ruth, worried*]. Doctor say everything going to be all right?

RUTH [*Far away*]. Yes—she says everything is going to be fine . . .

MAMA [*immediately suspicious*]. "She"—What doctor you went to?

[*Ruth folds over, near hysteria*]

MAMA [*worriedly hovering over Ruth*]. Ruth honey—what's the matter with you—you sick?

[*Ruth has her fists clenched on her thighs and is fighting hard to suppress a scream that seems to be rising in her*]

BENEATHA. What's the matter with her, Mama?

MAMA [*working her fingers in Ruth's shoulders to relax her*]. She be all right. Women gets right depressed sometimes when they get her way. [*Speaking softly, expertly, rapidly*] Now you just relax. That's right . . . just lean back, don't think 'bout nothing at all . . . nothing at all—

RUTH. I'm all right . . .

[*The glassy-eyed look melts and then she collapses into a fit of heavy sobbing. The bell rings*]

BENEATHA. Oh, my God—that must be Asagai.

MAMA [*to Ruth*]. Come on now, honey. You need to lie down and rest awhile—then have some nice hot food.

[*They exit. Ruth's weight on her mother-in-law. Beneatha, herself profoundly disturbed, opens the door to admit a rather dramatic-looking young man with a large package*]

ASAGAI. Hello, Alaiyo—

BENEATHA [*holding the door open and regarding him with pleasure*]. Hello . . . [*Long pause*] —Well—come in. And please excuse everything. My mother was very upset about my letting anyone come here with the place like this.

ASAGAI [*coming into the room*]. You look disturbed too . . . Is something wrong?

BENEATHA [*still at the door, absently*]. Yes . . . we've all got acute ghetto-itus. [*She smiles and comes toward him, finding a cigarette and sitting]* So—sit down! No! Wait! *[She whips the spraygun off sofa where she had left it and puts the cushions back. At last perches on arm of sofa. He sits]* So, how was Canada?

ASAGAI *[a sophisticate]*. Canadian.

BENEATHA *[looking at him]*. Asagai, I'm very glad you are back.

ASAGAI *[looking back at her in turn]*. Are you really?

BENEATHA. Yes—very.

ASAGAI. Why?—you were quite glad when I went away. What happened?

BENEATHA. You went away.

ASAGAI. Ahhhhhhh.

BENEATHA. Before—you wanted to be so serious before there was time.

ASAGAI. How much time must there be before one knows what one feels?

BENEATHA *[stalling this particular conversation. Her hands pressed together, in a deliberately childish gesture]*. What did you bring me?

ASAGAI *[handing her the package]*. Open it and see.

BENEATHA *[eagerly opening the package and drawing out some records and the colorful robes of a Nigerian woman]*. Oh, Asagai! . . . You got them for me! . . . How beautiful . . . and the records too!*[She lifts out the robes and runs to the mirror with them and holds the drapery up in front of herself]*

ASAGAI *[coming to her at the mirror]*. I shall have to teach you how to drape it properly. *[He flings the material about her for the moment and stands back to look at her]* Ah—*Oh-pay-gay-day, oh-ghah-mu-shay.* *[A Yoruba exclamation for admiration]* You wear it well . . . very well . . . mutilated hair and all.

BENEATHA *[turning suddenly]*. My hair—what's wrong with my hair?

ASAGAI *[shrugging]*. Were you born with it like that?

BENEATHA *[reaching up to touch it]*. No . . . of course not.

[She looks back to the mirror, disturbed]

ASAGAI *[smiling]*. How then?

BENEATHA. You know perfectly well how . . . as crinkly as yours . . . that's how.

ASAGAI. And it is ugly to you that way?

BENEATHA *[quickly]*. Oh, no—not ugly . . . *[More slowly, apologetically]* But it's so hard to manage when it's, well—raw.

ASAGAI. And so to accommodate that—you mutilate it every week?

BENEATHA. It's not mutilation!

ASAGAI *[laughing aloud at her seriousness]*. Oh . . .

please! I am only teasing you because you are so very serious about these things. *[He stands back from her and folds his arms across his chest as he watches her pulling at her hair and frowning in the mirror]* Do you remember the first time you met me at school? . . . *[He laughs]* You came up to me and you said—and I thought you were the most serious little thing I had ever seen—you said: *[He imitates her]* "Mr. Asagai—I want very much to talk with you. About Africa. You see, Mr. Asagai, I am looking for my *identity*!"

[He laughs]

BENEATHA *[turning to him, not laughing]*. Yes—

[Her face is quizzical, profoundly disturbed]

ASAGAI *[still teasing and reaching out and taking her face in his hands and turning her profile to him]*. Well . . . it is true that this is not so much a profile of a Hollywood queen as perhaps a queen of the Nile—*[A mock dismissal of the importance of the question]* But what does it matter? Assimilationism is so popular in your country.

BENEATHA *[wheeling, passionately, sharply]*. I am not an assimilationist!

ASAGAI *[the protest hangs in the room for a moment and Asagai studies her, his laughter fading]*. Such a serious one. *[There is a pause]* So—you like the robes? You must take excellent care of them—they are from my sister's personal wardrobe.

BENEATHA *[with incredulity]*. You—you sent all the way home—for me?

ASAGAI *[with charm]*. For you—I would do much more . . . Well, that is what I came for. I must go.

BENEATHA. Will you call me Monday?

ASAGAI. Yes . . . We have a great deal to talk about. I mean about identity and time and all that.

BENEATHA. Time?

ASAGAI. Yes. About how much time one needs to know what one feels.

BENEATHA. You see! You never understood that there is more than one kind of feeling which can exist between a man and a woman—or, at least, there should be.

ASAGAI *[shaking his head negatively but gently]*. No. Between a man and a woman there need be only one kind of feeling. I have that for you . . . Now even . . . right this moment . . .

BENEATHA. I know—and by itself—it won't do. I can find that anywhere.

ASAGAI. For a woman it should be enough.

BENEATHA. I know—because that's what it says in all the novels that men write. But it isn't. Go ahead and laugh—but I'm not interested in being someone's little episode in America or—[*With feminine vengeance*]. —one of them! [*Asagai has burst into laughter again*] That's funny as hell, huh!

ASAGAI. It's just that every American girl I have known has said that to me. White—black—in this you are all the same. And the same speech, too!

BENEATHA [*angrily*]. Yuk, yuk, yuk!

ASAGAI. It's how you can be sure that the world's most liberated women are not liberated at all. You all talk about it too much!

[*Mama enters and is immediately all social charm because of the presence of a guest*]

BENEATHA. Oh—Mama—this is Mr. Asagai.

MAMA. How do you do?

ASAGAI [*total politeness to an elder*]. How do you do, Mrs. Younger. Please forgive me for coming at such an outrageous hour on a Saturday.

MAMA. Well, you are quite welcome. I just hope you understand that our house don't always look like this. [*Chatterish*] You must come again. I would love to hear all about—[*Not sure of the name*] —your country. I think it's so sad the way our American Negroes don't know nothing about Africa 'cept Tarzan and all that. And all that money they pour into these churches when they ought to be helping you people over there drive out them French and Englishmen done taken away your land.

[*The mother flashes a slightly superior look at her daughter upon completion of the recitation*]

ASAGAI [*taken aback by this sudden and acutely unrelated expression of sympathy*]. Yes . . . yes . . .

MAMA [*smiling at him suddenly and relaxing and looking him over*]. How many miles is it from here to where you come from?

ASAGAI. Many thousands.

MAMA [*looking at him as she would Walter*]. I bet you don't half look after yourself, being away from your mama either. I spec you better come 'round here from time to time to get yourself some decent home-cooked meals . . .

ASAGAI [*moved*]. Thank you. Thank you very much. [*They are all quiet, then—*] Well . . . I must go. I will call you Monday, Alaiyo.

MAMA. What's that he call you?

ASAGAI. Oh—"Alaiyo." I hope you don't mind. It is what you would call a nickname, I think. It is a Yoruba word. I am a Yoruba.

MAMA [*looking at Beneatha*]. I—I thought he was from—[*Uncertain*]

ASAGAI [*understanding*]. Nigeria is my country. Yoruba is my tribal origin—

BENEATHA. You didn't tell us what Alaiyo means . . . for all I know, you might be calling me Little Idiot or something . . .

ASAGAI. Well . . . let me see . . . I do not know how just to explain it . . . The sense of a thing can be so different when it changes languages.

BENEATHA. You're evading.

ASAGAI. No—really it is difficult . . . [*Thinking*] It means . . . it means One for Whom Bread—Food—Is Not Enough. [*He looks at her*] Is that all right?

BENEATHA [*understanding, softly*]. Thank you.

MAMA [*looking from one to the other and not understanding any of it*]. Well . . . that's nice . . . You must come see us again—Mr.—

ASAGAI. Ah-sah-guy . . .

MAMA. Yes . . . Do come again.

ASAGAI. Good-bye.

[*He exits*]

MAMA [*after him*]. Lord, that's a pretty thing just went out here! [*Insinuatingly, to her daughter*] Yes, I guess I see why we done commence to get so interested in Africa 'round here. Missionaries my aunt Jenny!

[*She exits*]

BENEATHA. Oh, Mama! . . .

[*She picks up the Nigerian dress and holds it up to her in front of the mirror again. She sets the headdress on haphazardly and then notices her hair again and clutches at it and then replaces the headdress and frowns at herself. Then she starts to wriggle in front of the mirror as she thinks a Nigerian woman might. Travis enters and stands regarding her*]

TRAVIS. What's the matter, girl, you cracking up?

BENEATHA. Shut up.

[*She pulls the headdress off and looks at herself in the mirror and clutches at her hair again and squinches her eyes as if trying to imagine something. Then, suddenly, she gets her raincoat and kerchief and hurriedly prepares for going out*]

MAMA [*coming back into the room*]. She's resting now. Travis, baby, run next door and ask Miss Johnson to please let me have a little kitchen cleanser. This here can is empty as Jacob's kettle.

TRAVIS. I just came in.

MAMA. Do as you told. [*He exits and she looks at her daughter*] Where you going?

BENEATHA [*halting at the door*]. To become a queen of the Nile!

[*She exits in a breathless blaze of glory. Ruth appears in the bedroom doorway*]

MAMA. Who told you to get up?

RUTH. Ain't nothing wrong with me to be lying in no bed for. Where did Bennie go?

MAMA [*drumming her fingers*]. Far as I could make out—to Egypt. [*Ruth just looks at her*] What time is it getting to?

RUTH. Ten twenty. And the mailman going to ring that bell this morning just like he done every morning for the last umpteen years.

[*Travis comes in with the cleanser can*]

TRAVIS. She say to tell you that she don't have much.

MAMA [*angrily*]. Lord, some people I could name sure is tight-fisted! [*Directing her grandson*] —Mark two cans of cleanser down on the list there. If she that hard up for kitchen cleanser, I sure don't want to forget to get her none!

RUTH. Lena—maybe the woman is just short on cleanser—

MAMA [*not listening*]. —Much baking powder as she done borrowed from me all these years, she could of done gone into the baking business!

[*The bell sounds suddenly and sharply and all three are stunned—serious and silent—mid-speech. In spite of all the other conversations and distractions of the morning, this is what they have been waiting for, even Travis, who looks helplessly from his mother to his grandmother. Ruth is the first to come to life again*]

RUTH [*to Travis*]. *Get down them steps, boy!*

[*Travis snaps to life and flies out to get the mail*]

MAMA [*her eyes wide, her hand to her breast*]. You mean it done really come?

RUTH [*excited*]. Oh, Miss Lena!

MAMA [*collecting herself*]. Well . . . I don't know what we all so excited about 'round here for. We known it was coming for months.

RUTH. That's a whole lot different from having it come and being able to hold it in your hands . . . a piece of paper worth ten thousand dollars . . . [*Travis bursts back into the room. He holds the envelope high above his head, like a little dancer, his face is radiant and he is breathless. He moves to his grandmother with sudden slow ceremony and puts the envelope into her hands. She accepts it, and then merely holds it and looks at it*] Come on! Open it . . . Lord have mercy, I wish Walter Lee was here!

TRAVIS. Open it, Grandmama!

MAMA [*staring at it*]. Now you all be quiet. It's just a check.

RUTH. Open it . . .

MAMA [*still staring at it*]. Now don't act silly . . . We ain't never been no people to act silly 'bout no money—

RUTH [*swiftly*]. We ain't never had none before— OPEN IT!

[*Mama finally makes a good strong tear and pulls out the thin blue slice of paper and inspects it closely. The boy and his mother study it raptly over Mama's shoulders*]

MAMA. *Travis!* [*She is counting off with doubt*] Is that the right number of zeros.

TRAVIS. Yes'm . . . ten thousand dollars. Gaalee, Grandmama, you rich.

MAMA [*she holds the check away from her, still looking at it. Slowly her face sobers into a mask of unhappiness*]. Ten thousand dollars. [*She hands it to Ruth*] Put it away somewhere, Ruth. [*She does not look at Ruth; her eyes seem to be seeing something somewhere very far off*] Ten thousand dollars they give you. Ten thousand dollars.

TRAVIS [*to his mother, sincerely*]. What's the matter with Grandmama—don't she want to be rich?

RUTH [*distractedly*]. You go on out and play now, baby. [*Travis exits. Mama starts wiping dishes absently, humming intently to herself. Ruth turns to her, with kind exasperation*] You've gone and got yourself upset.

MAMA [*not looking at her*]. I spec if it wasn't for you all . . . I would just put that money away or give it to the church or something.

RUTH. Now what kind of talk is that. Mr. Younger would just be plain mad if he could hear you talking foolish like that.

MAMA [*stopping and staring off*]. Yes . . . he sure would. [*Sighing*] We got enough to do with that money, all right. [*She halts then, and turns and looks at her daughter-in-law hard; Ruth avoids her eyes and Mama wipes her hands with finality and starts to speak firmly to Ruth*] Where did you go today, girl?

RUTH. To the doctor.

MAMA [*impatiently*]. Now, Ruth . . . you know better than that. Old Doctor Jones is strange enough in his way but there ain't nothing 'bout him make somebody slip and call him "she"—like you done this morning.

RUTH. Well, that's what happened—my tongue slipped.

MAMA. You went to see that woman, didn't you?

RUTH [*defensively, giving herself away*]. What woman you talking about?

MAMA [*angrily*]. That woman who—

[*Walter enters in great excitement*]

WALTER. Did it come?

MAMA [*quietly*]. Can't you give people a Christian greeting before you start asking about money?

WALTER [*to Ruth*]. Did it come? [*Ruth unfolds the check and lays it quietly before him, watching him intently with thoughts of her own. Walter sits down and grasps it close and counts off the zeros*] Ten thousand dollars— [*He turns suddenly, frantically to his mother and draws some papers out of his breast pocket*] Mama—look. Old Willy Harris put everything on paper—

MAMA. Son—I think you ought to talk to your wife . . . I'll go on out and leave you alone if you want—

WALTER. I can talk to her later—Mama, look—

MAMA. Son—

WALTER. WILL SOMEBODY PLEASE LISTEN TO ME TODAY!

MAMA [*quietly*]. I don't 'low no yellin' in this house, Walter Lee, and you know it— [*Walter stares at them in frustration and starts to speak several times*] And there ain't going to be no investing in no liquor stores.

WALTER. But, Mama, you ain't even looked at it.

MAMA. I don't aim to have to speak on that again.

[*A long pause*]

WALTER. You ain't looked at it and you don't aim to have to speak on that again? You ain't even looked at it and *you* have decided— [*Crumpling his papers*] Well, *you* tell that to my boy tonight when you put him to sleep on the living-room couch . . . [*Turning to Mama and speaking directly to her*] Yeah—and tell it to my wife, Mama, tomorrow when she has to go

out of here to look after somebody else's kids. And tell it to *me*, Mama, every time we need a new pair of curtains and I have to watch *you* go out and work in somebody's kitchen. Yeah, you tell me then!

[*Walter starts out*]

RUTH. Where you going?

WALTER. I'm going out!

RUTH. Where?

WALTER. Just out of this house somewhere—

RUTH [*getting her coat*]. I'll come too.

WALTER. I don't want you to come!

RUTH. I got something to talk to you about, Walter.

WALTER. That's too bad.

MAMA [*still quietly*]. Walter Lee— [*She waits and he finally turns and looks at her*] Sit down.

WALTER. I'm a grown man, Mama.

MAMA. Ain't nobody said you wasn't grown. But you still in my house and my presence. And as long as you are—you'll talk to your wife civil. Now sit down.

RUTH [*suddenly*]. Oh, let him go on out and drink himself to death! He makes me sick to my stomach! [*She flings her coat against him and exits to bedroom*]

WALTER [*violently flinging the coat after her*]. And you turn mine too, baby! [*The door slams behind her*] That was my biggest mistake—

MAMA [*still quietly*]. Walter, what is the matter with you?

WALTER. Matter with me? Aint' nothing the matter with *me*!

MAMA. Yes there is. Something eating you up like a crazy man. Something more than me not giving you this money. The past few years I been watching it happen to you. You get all nervous acting and kind of wild in the eyes— [*Walter jumps up impatiently at her words*] I said sit there now, I'm talking to you!

WALTER. Mama—I don't need no nagging at me today.

MAMA. Seem like you getting to a place where you always tied up in some kind of knot about something. But if anybody ask you 'bout it you just yell at 'em and bust out the house and go out and drink somewheres. Walter Lee, people can't live with that. Ruth's a good, patient girl in her way—but you getting to be too much. Boy, don't make the mistake of driving that girl away from you.

WALTER. Why—what she do for me?

MAMA. She loves you.

WALTER. Mama—I'm going out. I want to go off somewhere and be by myself for a while.

MAMA. I'm sorry 'bout your liquor store, son. It just wasn't the thing for us to do. That's what I want to tell you about—

WALTER. I got to go out, Mama—

[*He rises*]

MAMA. It's dangerous, son.

WALTER. What's dangerous?

MAMA. When a man goes outside his home to look for peace.

WALTER [*beseechingly*]. Then why can't there never be no peace in this house then?

MAMA. You done found it in some other house?

WALTER. No—there ain't no woman! Why do women always think there's a woman somewhere when a man gets restless. [*Picks up the check*] Do you know what this money means to me? Do you know what this money can do for us? [*Puts it back*] Mama—Mama—I want so many things . . .

MAMA. Yes, son—

WALTER. I want so many things that they are driving me kind of crazy . . . Mama—look at me.

MAMA. I'm looking at you. You a good-looking boy. You got a job, a nice wife, a fine boy and—

WALTER. A job. [*Looks at her*] Mama, a job? I open and close car doors all day long. I drive a man around in his limousine and I say, "Yes, sir; no, sir; very good, sir; shall I take the Drive, sir?" Mama, that ain't no kind of job . . . that ain't nothing at all. [*Very quietly*] Mama, I don't know if I can make you understand.

MAMA. Understand what, baby?

WALTER [*quietly*]. Sometimes it's like I can see the future stretched out in front of me—just plain as day. The future, Mama. Hanging over there at the edge of my days. Just waiting for me—a big, looming blank space—full of *nothing*. Just waiting for *me*. But it don't have to be. [*Pause. Kneeling beside her chair*] Mama—sometimes when I'm downtown and I pass them cool, quiet-looking restaurants where them white boys are sitting back and talking 'bout things . . . sitting there turning deals worth millions of dollars . . . sometimes I see guys don't look much older than me—

MAMA. Son—how come you talk so much 'bout money?

WALTER [*with immense passion*]. Because it is life, Mama!

MAMA [*quietly*]. Oh— [*Very quietly*] So now it's life. Money is life. Once upon a time freedom used to be life—now it's money. I guess the world really do change . . .

WALTER. No—it was always money, Mama. We just didn't know about it.

MAMA. No . . . something has changed. [*She looks at him*] You something new, boy. In my time we was worried about not being lynched and getting to the North if we could and how to stay alive and still have a pinch of dignity too . . . Now here come you and Beneatha—talking 'bout things we ain't never even thought about hardly, me and your daddy. You ain't satisfied or proud of nothing we done. I mean that you had a home; that we kept you out of trouble till you was grown; that you don't have to ride to work on the back of nobody's streetcar— You my children—but how different we done become.

WALTER [*a long beat. He pats her hand and gets up*]. You just don't understand, Mama, you just don't understand.

MAMA. Son—do you know your wife is expecting another baby? [*Walter stands, stunned, and absorbs what his mother has said*] That's what she wanted to talk to you about. [*Walter sinks down into a chair*] This ain't for me to be telling—but you ought to know. [*She waits*] I think Ruth is thinking 'bout getting rid of that child.

WALTER [*slowly understanding*]. —No—no—Ruth wouldn't do that.

MAMA. When the world gets ugly enough—a woman will do anything for her family. *The part that's already living.*

WALTER. You don't know Ruth, Mama, if you think she would do that.

[*Ruth opens the bedroom door and stands there a little limp*]

RUTH [*beaten*]. Yes I would too, Walter. [*Pause*] I gave her a five-dollar down payment.

[*There is total silence as the man stares at his wife and the mother stares at her son*]

MAMA [*presently*]. Well— [*Tightly*]. Well—son, I'm waiting to hear you say something . . . [*She waits*] I'm waiting to hear how you be your father's son. Be the man he was . . . [*Pause. The silence shouts*] Your wife say she going to destroy your child. And I'm waiting to hear you talk like him and say we a people who give children life, not who destroys them— [*She rises*] I'm waiting to see you stand up and look like your daddy and say we done give up one baby to poverty and that we ain't going to give up nary another one . . . I'm waiting.

WALTER. Ruth— [*He can say nothing*]

MAMA. If you a son of mine, tell her! [*Walter picks up his keys and his coat and walks out. She continues, bitterly*] You . . . you are a disgrace to your father's memory. Somebody get me my hat!

CURTAIN

Act II

SCENE I

TIME: Later the same day.

AT RISE: Ruth is ironing again. She has the radio going. Presently Beneatha's bedroom door opens and Ruth's mouth falls and she puts down the iron in fascination.

RUTH. What have we got on tonight?

BENEATHA [*emerging grandly from the doorway so that we can see her thoroughly robed in the costume Asagai brought*]. You are looking at what a well-dressed Nigerian woman wears— [*She parades for Ruth, her hair completely hidden by the headdress; she is coquettishly fanning herself and with an ornate oriental fan, mistakenly more like Butterfly than any Nigerian that ever was*] Isn't it beautiful? [*She promenades to the radio and, with an arrogant flourish, turns off the good loud blues that is playing*] Enough of this assimilationist junk! [*Ruth follows her with her eyes as she goes to the phonograph and puts on a record and turns and waits ceremoniously for the music to come up. Then, with a shout—*] OCOMOGOSIAY!

[*Ruth jumps. The music comes up, a lovely Nigerian melody. Beneatha listens, enraptured, her eyes far away—"back to the past." She begins to dance. Ruth is dumbfounded*]

RUTH. What kind of dance is that?

BENEATHA. A folk dance.

RUTH [*Pearl Bailey*]. What kind of folks do that, honey?

BENEATHA. It's from Nigeria. It's a dance of welcome.

RUTH. Who you welcoming?

BENEATHA. The men back to the village.

RUTH. Where they been?

BENEATHA. How should I know—out hunting or something. Anyway, they are coming back now . . .

RUTH. Well, that's good.

BENEATHA [*with the record*].

> Alundi, alundi
> Alundi alunya
> Jop pu à jeepua
> Ang gu soooooooooo
>
> Ai yai yae . . .
> Ayehaye—alundi . . .

[*Walter comes in during this performance; he has obviously been drinking. He leans against the door heavily and watches his sister, at first with distaste. Then his eyes look off—"back to the past"—as he lifts both his fists to the roof, screaming*]

WALTER. YEAH . . . AND ETHIOPIA STRETCH FORTH HER HANDS AGAIN! . . .

RUTH [*drily, looking at him*]. Yes—and Africa sure is claiming her own tonight. [*She gives them both up and starts ironing again*].

WALTER [*all in a drunken, dramatic shout*]. Shut up! . . . I'm digging them drums . . . them drums move me! . . . [*He makes his weaving way to his wife's face and leans in close to her*] In my *heart of hearts*— [*He thumps his chest*] —I am much warrior!

RUTH [*without even looking up*]. In your heart of hearts you are much drunkard.

WALTER [*coming away from her and starting to wander around the room, shouting*]. Me and Jomo . . . [*Intently, in his sister's face. She has stopped dancing to watch him in this unknown mood*] That's my man, Kenyatta. [*Shouting and thumping his chest*] FLAMING SPEAR! HOT DAMN! [*He is suddenly in possession of an imaginary spear and actively spearing enemies all over the room*] OCOMOGOSIAY . . .

BENEATHA [*to encourage Walter, thoroughly caught up with this side of him*]. OCOMOGOSIAY, FLAMING SPEAR!

WALTER. THE LION IS WAKING . . . OWIMOWEH!

[*He pulls his shirt open and leaps up on the table and gestures with his spear*]

BENEATHA. OWIMOWEH!

WALTER [*on the table, very far gone, his eyes pure glass sheets. He sees what we cannot, that he is a leader of his people, a great chief, a descendant of Chaka, and that the hour to march has come*]. Listen, my black brothers—

BENEATHA. OCOMOGOSIAY!

WALTER. —Do you hear the waters rushing against the shores of the coastlands—

BENEATHA. OCOMOGOSIAY!

WALTER. —Do you hear the screeching of the cocks in yonder hills beyond where the chiefs meet in council for the coming of the mighty war—

BENEATHA. OCOMOGOSIAY!

[*And now the lighting shifts subtly to suggest the world of Walter's imagination, and the mood shifts from pure comedy. It is the inner Walter speaking: the Southside chauffeur has assumed an unexpected majesty*]

WALTER. —Do you hear the beating of the wings of the birds flying low over the mountains and the low places of our land—

BENEATHA. OCOMOGOSIAY!

WALTER. —Do you hear the singing of the women, singing the war songs of our fathers to the babies in the great houses? Singing the sweet war songs! [*The doorbell rings*] OH, DO YOU HEAR, MY *BLACK* BROTHERS!

BENEATHA [*completely gone*]. We hear you, Flaming Spear—

[*Ruth shuts off the phonograph and opens the door. George Murchison enters*]

WALTER. Telling us to prepare for the GREATNESS OF THE TIME! [*Lights back to normal. He turns and sees George*] Black Brother!

[*He extends his hand for the fraternal clasp*]

GEORGE. Black Brother, hell!

RUTH [*having had enough, and embarrassed for the family*]. Beneatha, you got company—what's the matter with you? Walter Lee Younger, get down off that table and stop acting like a fool . . .

[*Walter comes down off the table suddenly and makes a quick exit to the bathroom*]

RUTH. He's had a little to drink . . . I don't know what her excuse is.

GEORGE [*to Beneatha*]. Look honey, we're going *to* the theater—we're not going to be *in* it . . . so go change, huh?

[*Beneatha looks at him and slowly, ceremoniously, lifts her hands and pulls off the headdress. Her hair is close-cropped and unstraightened. George freezes mid-sentence and Ruth's eyes all but fall out of her head*]

GEORGE. What in the name of—

RUTH [*touching Beneatha's hair*]. Girl, you done lost your natural mind? Look at your head!

GEORGE. What have you done to your head—I mean your hair!

BENEATHA. Nothing—except cut it off.

RUTH. Now that's the truth—it's what ain't been done to it! You expect this boy to go out with you with your head all nappy like that?

BENEATHA [*looking at George*]. That's up to George. If he's ashamed of his heritage—

GEORGE. Oh, don't be so proud of yourself, Bennie—just because you look eccentric.

BENEATHA. How can something that's natural be eccentric?

GEORGE. That's what being eccentric means—being natural. Get dressed.

BENEATHA. I don't like that, George.

RUTH. Why must you and your brother make an argument out of everything people say?

BENEATHA. Because I hate assimilationist Negroes!

RUTH. Will somebody please tell me what assimila-who-ever means!

GEORGE. Oh, it's just a college girl's way of calling people Uncle Toms—but that isn't what it means at all.

RUTH. Well, what does it mean?

BENEATHA [*cutting George off and staring at him as she replies to Ruth*]. It means someone who is willing to give up his own culture and submerge himself completely in the dominant, and in this case *oppressive* culture!

GEORGE. Oh, dear, dear, dear! Here we go! A lecture on the African past! On our Great West African Heritage! In one second we will hear all about the great Ashanti empires; the great Songhay civilizations; and the great sculpture of Bénin—and then some poetry in the Bantu—and the whole monologue will end with the word *heritage*! [*Nastily*] Let's face it, baby, your heritage is nothing but a bunch of raggedy-assed spirituals and some grass huts!

BENEATHA. GRASS HUTS! [*Ruth crosses to her and forcibly pushes her toward the bedroom*] —See there . . . you are standing there in your splendid ignorance talking about people who were the first to smelt iron on the face of the earth! [*Ruth is pushing her through the door*] The Ashanti were performing surgical operations when the English—[*Ruth pulls the door to, with Beneatha on the other side, and smiles graciously at George. Beneatha opens the door and shouts the end of the sentence defiantly at George*] —were still tatooing themselves with blue dragons! [*She goes back inside*]

RUTH. Have a seat, George. [*They both sit. Ruth folds her hands rather primly on her lap, determined to demonstrate the civilization of the family*] Warm, ain't it? I mean for September. [*Pause*] Just like they always say about Chicago weather: If it's too hot or cold for you, just wait a minute and it'll change. [*She smiles happily at this cliché of clichés*] Everybody say it's got to do with them bombs and things they keep setting off. [*Pause*] Would you like a nice cold beer?

GEORGE. No, thank you. I don't care for beer. [*He looks at his watch*] I hope she hurries up.

RUTH. What time is the show?

GEORGE. It's an eighty-thirty curtain. That's just Chicago, though. In New York standard curtain time is eight forty.

[*He is rather proud of this knowledge*]

RUTH [*properly appreciating it*]. You get to New York a lot?

GEORGE [*offhand*]. Few times a year.

RUTH. Oh—that's nice. I've never been to New York.

[*Walter enters. We feel he has relieved himself, but the edge of unreality is still with him*]

WALTER. New York ain't got nothing Chicago ain't. Just a bunch of hustling people all squeezed up together—being "Eastern."

[*He turns his face into a screw of displeasure*]

GEORGE. Oh—you've been?

WALTER. *Plenty* of times.

RUTH [*shocked at the lie*]. Walter Lee Younger!

WALTER [*staring her down*]. Plenty! [*Pause*] What we got to drink in this house? Why don't you offer this man some refreshment. [*To George*] They don't know how to entertain people in this house, man.

GEORGE. Thank you—I don't really care for anything.

WALTER [*feeling his head; sobriety coming*]. Where's Mama?

RUTH. She ain't come back yet.

WALTER [*looking Murchison over from head to toe, scrutinizing his carefully casual tweed sports jacket over cashmere V-neck sweater over soft eyelet shirt and tie, and soft slacks, finished off with white buckskin shoes*]. Why all you college boys wear them faggoty-looking white shoes?

RUTH. Walter Lee!

[*George Murchison ignores the remark*]

WALTER [*to Ruth*]. Well, they look crazy as hell—white shoes, cold as it is.

RUTH [*crushed*]. You have to excuse him—

WALTER. No he don't! Excuse me for what? What you always excusing me for! I'll excuse myself when I needs to be excused! [*A pause*] They look as funny as them black knee socks Beneatha wears out of here all the time.

RUTH. It's the college *style*, Walter.

WALTER. Style, hell. She looks like she got burnt legs or something!

RUTH. Oh, Walter—

WALTER [*an irritable mimic*]. Oh, Walter! Oh, Walter! [*To Murchison*] How's your old man making out? I understand you all going to buy that big hotel on the Drive? [*He finds a beer in the refrigerator, wanders over to Murchison, sipping and wiping his lips with the back of his hand, and straddling a chair backwards to talk to the other man*] Shrewd move. Your old man is all right, man. [*Tapping his head and half winking for emphasis*] I mean he knows how to operate. I mean he thinks *big*, you know what I mean, I mean for a *home*, you know? But I think he's kind of running out of ideas now. I'd like to talk to him. Listen, man, I got some plans that could turn this city upside down. I mean think like he does. *Big*. Invest big, gamble big, hell, lose *big* if you have to, you know what I mean. It's hard to find a man on this whole Southside who understands my kind of thinking—you dig? [*He scrutinizes Murchison again, drinks his beer, squints his eyes and leans in close, confidential, man to man*] Me and you ought to sit down and talk sometimes, man. Man, I got me some ideas . . .

MURCHISON [*with boredom*]. Yeah—sometimes we'll have to do that, Walter.

WALTER [*understanding the indifference, and offended*].

Yeah—well, when you get the time, man. I know you a busy little boy.

RUTH. Walter, please—

WALTER [*bitterly, hurt*]. I know ain't nothing in this world as busy as you colored boys with your fraternity pins and white shoes—

RUTH [*covering her face with humiliation*]. Oh, Walter Lee—

WALTER. I see you all all the time—with the books tucked under your arms—going to your [*British A—a mimic*] "clahsses." And for what! What the hell you learning over there? Filling up your heads [*Counting off on his fingers*] —with the sociology and the psychology—but they teaching you how to be a man? How to take over and run the world? They teaching you how to run a rubber plantation or a steel mill? Naw—just to talk proper and read books and wear them faggoty-looking white shoes . . .

GEORGE [*looking at him with distaste, a little above it all*]. You're all wacked up with bitterness, man.

WALTER [*intently, almost quietly, between the teeth, glaring at the boy*]. And you—ain't you bitter, man? Ain't you just about had it yet? Don't you see no stars gleaming that you can't reach out and grab? You happy?—You contended son-of-a-bitch—you happy? You got it made? Bitter? Man, I'm a volcano. Bitter? Here I am a giant—surrounded by ants! Ants who can't even understand what it is the giant is talking about.

RUTH [*passionately and suddenly*]. Oh, Walter—ain't you with nobody!

WALTER [*violently*]. No! 'Cause ain't nobody with me! Not even my own mother!

RUTH. Walter, that's a terrible thing to say!

[*Beneatha enters, dressed for the evening in a cocktail dress and earrings, hair natural*]

GEORGE. Well—hey—[*Crosses to Beneatha; thoughtful, with emphasis, since this is a reversal*] You look great!

WALTER [*seeing his sister's hair for the first time*]. What's the matter with your head?

BENEATHA [*tired of the jokes now*]. I cut it off, Brother.

WALTER [*coming close to inspect it and walking around her*]. Well, I'll be damned. So that's what they mean by the African bush . . .

BENEATHA. Ha ha. Let's go, George.

GEORGE [*looking at her*]. You know something? I like it. It's sharp. I mean it really is. [*Helps her into her wrap*]

RUTH. Yes—I think so, too. [*She goes to the mirror and starts to clutch at her hair*]

WALTER. Oh no! You leave yours alone, baby. You might turn out to have a pin-shaped head or something!

BENEATHA. See you all later.

RUTH. Have a nice time.

GEORGE. Thanks. Good night. [*Half out the door, he reopens it. To Walter*] Good night, Prometheus!

[*Beneatha and George exit*]

WALTER [*to Ruth*]. Who is Prometheus?

RUTH. I don't know. Don't worry about it.

WALTER [*in fury, pointing after George*]. See there—they get to a point where they can't insult you man to man—they got to go talk about something ain't nobody never heard of!

RUTH. How do you know it was an insult? [*To humor him*] Maybe Prometheus is a nice fellow.

WALTER. Prometheus! I bet there ain't even no such thing! I bet that simple-minded clown—

RUTH. Walter

[*She stops what she is doing and looks at him*]

WALTER [*yelling*]. Don't start!

RUTH. Start what?

WALTER. Your nagging! Where was I? Who was I with? How much money did I spend?

RUTH [*plaintively*]. Walter Lee—why don't we just try to talk about it . . .

WALTER [*not listening*]. I been out talking with people who understand me. People who care about the things I got on my mind.

RUTH [*wearily*]. I guess that means people like Willy Harris.

WALTER. Yes, people like Willy Harris.

RUTH [*with a sudden flash of impatience*]. Why don't you all just hurry up and go into the banking business and stop talking about it!

WALTER. Why? You want to know why? 'Cause we all tied up in a race of people that don't know how to do nothing but moan, pray and have babies!

[*The line is too bitter even for him and he looks at her and sits down*]

RUTH. Oh, Walter . . . [*Softly*] Honey, why can't you stop fighting me?

WALTER [*without thinking*]. Who's fighting you? Who even cares about you?

[*This line begins the retardation of his mood*]

RUTH. Well— [*She waits a long time, and then with resignation starts to put away her things*] I guess I might as well go on to bed . . . [*More or less to herself*] I don't know where we lost it . . . but we have . . . [*Then, to him*] I—I'm sorry about this new baby, Walter. I guess maybe I better go on and do what I started . . . I guess I just didn't realize how bad things was with us . . . I guess I just didn't really realize— [*She starts out to the bedroom and stops*] You want some hot milk?

WALTER. Hot milk?

RUTH. Yes—hot milk.

WALTER. Why hot milk?

RUTH. 'Cause after all that liquor you come home with you ought to have something hot in your stomach.

WALTER. I don't want no milk.

RUTH. You want some coffee then?

WALTER. No, I don't want no coffee. I don't want nothing hot to drink. [*Almost plaintively*] Why you always trying to give me something to eat?

RUTH [*standing and looking at him helplessly*]. What *else* can I give you, Walter Lee Younger?

[*She stands and looks at him and presently turns to go out again. He lifts his head and watches her going away from him in a new mood which began to emerge when he asked her "Who cares about you?"*]

WALTER. It's been rough, ain't it, baby? [*She hears and stops but does not turn around and he continues to her back*] I guess between two people there ain't never as much understood as folks generally thinks there is. I mean like between me and you— [*She turns to face him*] How we gets to the place where we scared to talk softness to each other. [*He waits, thinking hard himself*] Why you think it got to be like that? [*He is thoughtful, almost as a child would be*] Ruth, what is it gets into people ought to be close?

RUTH. I don't know, honey. I think about it a lot.

WALTER. On account of you and me, you mean? The way things are with us. The way something done come down between us.

RUTH. There ain't so much between us, Walter . . . Not when you come to me and try to talk to me. Try to be with me . . . a little even.

WALTER [*total honestly*]. Sometimes . . . sometimes . . . I don't even know how to try.

RUTH. Walter—

WALTER. Yes?

RUTH [*coming to him, gently and with misgiving, but coming to him*]. Honey . . . life don't have to be like this. I mean sometimes people can do things so that things are better . . . You remember how we used to talk when Travis was born . . . about the way we were going to live . . . the kind of house . . . [*She is stroking his head*] Well, it's all starting to slip away from us . . .

[*He turns her to him and they look at each other and kiss, tenderly and hungrily. The door opens and Mama enters— Walter breaks away and jumps up. A beat*]

WALTER. Mama, where have you been?

MAMA. My—them steps is longer than they used to be. Whew! [*She sits down and ignores him*] How you feeling this evening, Ruth?

[*Ruth shrugs, disturbed at having been interrupted and watching her husband knowingly*]

WALTER. Mama, where have you been all day?

MAMA [*still ignoring him and leaning on the table and changing to more comfortable shoes*]. —Where's Travis?

RUTH. I let him go out earlier and he ain't come back yet. Boy, is he going to get it!

WALTER. Mama!

MAMA [*as if she has heard him for the first time*]. Yes, son?

WALTER. Where did you go this afternoon?

MAMA. I went downtown to tend to some business that I had to tend to.

WALTER. What kind of business?

MAMA. You know better than to question me like a child, Brother.

WALTER [*rising and bending over the table*]. Where were you, Mama? [*Bringing his fists down and shouting*] Mama, you didn't go do something with that insurance money, something crazy?

[*The front door opens slowly, interrupting him, and Travis peeks his head in, less than hopefully*]

TRAVIS [*to his mother*]. Mama, I—

RUTH. "Mama I" nothing! You're going to get it, boy! Get on in that bedroom and get yourself ready!

TRAVIS. But I—

MAMA. Why don't you all never let the child explain hisself.

RUTH. Keep out of it now, Lena.

[*Mama clamps her lips together, and Ruth advances toward her son menacingly*]

RUTH. A thousand times I have told you not to go off like that—

MAMA [*holding out her arms to her grandson*]. Well—at least let me tell him something. I want him to be the first one to hear . . . Come here, Travis. [*The boy obeys, gladly*] Travis— [*She takes him by the shoulder and looks into his face*] —you know that money we got in the mail this morning?

TRAVIS. Yes'm—

MAMA. Well—what you think your grandmama gone and done with that money?

TRAVIS. I don't know, Grandmama.

MAMA [*putting her finger on his nose for emphasis*]. She went out and she bought you a house! [*The explosion comes from Walter at the end of the revelation and he jumps up and turns away from all of them in a fury. Mama continues, to Travis*] You glad about the house? It's going to be yours when you get to be a man.

TRAVIS. Yeah—I always wanted to live in a house.

MAMA. All right, gimme some sugar then—[*Travis puts his arms around her neck as she watches her son over the boy's shoulder. Then, to Travis, after the embrace*] Now when you say your prayers tonight, you thank God and your grandfather—'cause it was him who give you the house—in his way.

RUTH [*taking the boy from Mama and pushing him toward the bedroom*]. Now you get out of here and get ready for your beating.

TRAVIS. Aw, Mama—

RUTH. Get on in there— [*Closing the door behind him and turning radiantly to her mother-in-law*] So you went and did it!

MAMA [*quietly, looking at her son with pain*]. Yes, I did.

RUTH [*raising both arms classically*]. PRAISE GOD! [*Looks at Walter a moment, who says nothing. She crosses rapidly to her husband*] Please, honey—let me be glad . . . you be glad too. [*She has laid her hands on his shoulders, but he shakes himself free of her roughly, without turning to face her*] Oh, Walter . . . home . . . *a home*. [*She comes back to Mama*] Well—where is it? How big is it? How much it going to cost?

MAMA. Well—

RUTH. When we moving?

MAMA [*smiling at her*]. First of the month.

RUTH [*throwing back her head with jubilance*]. Praise God!

MAMA [*tentatively, still looking at her son's back turned against her and Ruth*]. It's—it's a nice house too . . . [*She cannot help speaking directly to him. An imploring quality in her voice, her manner, makes her almost like a girl now*] Three bedrooms—nice big one for you and Ruth . . . Me and Beneatha still have to share our room, but Travis have one of his own—and [*With difficulty*] I figure if the—new baby—is a boy, we could get one of them double-decker outfits . . . And there's a yard with a little patch of dirt where I could maybe get to grow me a few flowers . . . And a nice big basement . . .

RUTH. Walter honey, be glad—

MAMA [*still to his back, fingering things on the table*]. 'Course I don't want to make it sound fancier than it is . . . It's just a plain little old house—but it's made good and solid—and it will be *ours*. Walter Lee—it makes a difference in a man when he can walk on floors that belong to *him* . . .

RUTH. Where is it?

MAMA [*frightened at this telling*]. Well—well—it's out there in Clybourne Park—

[*Ruth's radiance fades abruptly, and Walter finally turns slowly to face his mother with incredulity and hostility*]

RUTH. Where?

MAMA [*matter-of-factly*]. Four o six Clybourne Street, Clybourne Park.

RUTH. Clybourne Park? Mama, there ain't no colored people living in Clybourne Park.

MAMA [*almost idiotically*]. Well, I guess there's going to be some now.

WALTER [*bitterly*]. So that's the peace and comfort you went out and bought for us today!

MAMA [*raising her eyes to meet his finally*]. Son—I just tried to find the nicest place for the least amount of money for my family.

RUTH [*trying to recover from the shock*]. Well—well— 'course I ain't one never been 'fraid of no crackers, mind you—but—well, wasn't there no other houses nowhere?

MAMA. Them houses they put up for colored in them areas way out all seem to cost twice as much as other houses. I did the best I could.

RUTH [*struck senseless with the news, in its various degrees of goodness and trouble, she sits a moment, her fists propping her chin in thought, and then she starts to rise, bringing her fists down with vigor, the radiance spreading from cheek to cheek again*]. Well—well!—All I can say is—if this is my time in life—MY TIME—to say good-bye— [*And she builds with momentum as she starts to circle the room with an exuberant, almost tearfully happy release*] —to these Goddamned cracking walls!— [*She pounds the walls*] —and these marching roaches!— [*She wipes at an imaginary army of marching* roaches] —and this cramped little closet which ain't now or never was no kitchen! . . . then I say it loud and good, HALLELUJAH! AND GOOD-BYE MISERY . . . I DON'T NEVER WANT TO SEE YOUR UGLY FACE AGAIN! [*She laughs joyously, having practically destroyed the apartment, and flings her arms up and lets them come down happily, slowly, reflectively, over her abdomen, aware for the first time perhaps that the life therein pulses with happiness and not despair*] Lena?

MAMA [*moved, watching her happiness*]. Yes, honey?

RUTH [*looking off*]. Is there—is there a whole lot of sunlight?

MAMA [*understanding*]. Yes, child, there's a whole lot of sunlight.

[*Long pause*]

RUTH [*collecting herself and going to the door of the room Travis in*]. Well—I guess I better see 'bout Travis. [*To Mama*] Lord, I sure don't feel like whipping nobody today!

[*She exits*]

MAMA [*the mother and son are left alone now and the mother waits a long time, considering deeply, before she speaks*]. Son—you—you understand what I done, don't you? [*Walter is silent and sullen*] I—I just seen my family falling apart today—just falling to pieces in front of my eyes . . . We couldn't of gone on like we was today. We was going backwards 'stead of forwards—talking 'bout killing babies and wishing each other was dead . . . When it gets like that in life—you just got to do something different, push on out and do something bigger . . . [*She waits*] I wish you say something, son . . . I wish you'd say how deep inside you think I done the right thing—

WALTER [*crossing slowly to his bedroom door and finally turning there and speaking measuredly*]. —What you need me to say you done right for? *You* the head of this family. You run our lives like you want to. It was your money and you did what you wanted with it. So what you need for me to say it was all right for? [*Bitterly, to hurt her as deeply as he knows is possible*] So you butchered up a dream of mine—you—who always talking 'bout your children's dreams . . .

MAMA. Walter Lee—

[*He just closes the door behind him. Mama sits alone, thinking heavily*]

CURTAIN

SCENE II

Time: Friday night. A few weeks later.

At rise: Packing crates mark the intention of the family to move. Beneatha and George come in, presumably from an evening out again.

GEORGE. O.K. . . . O.K., whatever you say . . . [*They both sit on the couch. He tries to kiss her. She moves away*] Look, we've had a nice evening; let's not spoil it, huh! . . .

[*He again turns her head and tries to nuzzle in and she turns away from him, not with distaste but with momentary lack of interest; in a mood to pursue what they were talking about*]

BENEATHA. I'm *trying* to talk to you.

GEORGE. We always talk.

BENEATHA. Yes—and I love to talk.

GEORGE [*exasperated; rising*]. I know it and I don't mind it sometimes . . . I want you to cut it out, see—The moody stuff, I mean. I don't like it. You're a nice-looking girl . . . all over. That's all you need, honey, forget the atmosphere. Guys aren't going to go for the atmosphere—they're going to go for what they see. Be glad for that. Drop the Garbo routine. It doesn't go with you. As for myself, I want a nice— [*Groping*] —simple [*Thoughtfully*] —sophisticated girl . . . not a poet—O.K.?

[*He starts to kiss her, she rebuffs him again and he jumps up*]

BENEATHA. Why are you angry, George?

GEORGE. Because this is stupid! I don't go out with you to discuss the nature of "quiet desperation" or to hear all about your thoughts—because the world will go on thinking what it thinks regardless—

BENEATHA. Then why read books? Why go to school?

GEORGE [*with artificial patience, counting on his fingers*]. It's simple. You read books—to learn facts—to get grades—to pass the course—to get a degree. That's all—it has nothing to do with thoughts.

[*A long pause*]

BENEATHA. I see. [*He starts to sit*] Good night, George.

[*George looks at her a little oddly, and starts to exit. He meets Mama coming in*]

GEORGE. Oh—hello, Mrs. Younger.

MAMA. Hello, George, how you feeling?

GEORGE. Fine—fine, how are you?

MAMA. Oh, a little tired. You know them steps can get you after a day's work. You all have a nice time tonight?

GEORGE. Yes—a fine time. A fine time.

MAMA. Well, good night.

GEORGE. Good night. [*He exits. Mama closes the door behind her*] Hello, honey. What you sitting like that for?

BENEATHA. I'm just sitting.

MAMA. Didn't you have a nice time?

BENEATHA. No.

MAMA. No! What's the matter?

BENEATHA. Mama, George is a fool—honest. [*She rises*]

MAMA [*hustling around unloading the packages she has entered with. She stops*]. Is he, baby?

BENEATHA. Yes.

[*Beneatha makes up Travis' bed as she talks*]

MAMA. You sure?

BENEATHA. Yes.

MAMA. Well—I guess you better not waste your time with no fools.

[*Beneatha looks up at her mother, watching her put groceries in the refrigerator. Finally she gathers up her things and starts into the bedroom. At the door she stops and looks back at her mother*]

BENEATHA. Mama—

MAMA. Yes, baby—

BENEATHA. Thank you.

MAMA. For what?

BENEATHA. For understanding me this time.

[*She exits quickly and the mother stands, smiling a little, looking at the place where Beneatha just stood. Ruth enters*]

RUTH. Now don't you fool with any of this stuff, Lena—

MAMA. Oh, I just thought I'd sort a few things out. Is Brother here?

RUTH. Yes.

MAMA [*with concern*]. Is he—

RUTH [*reading her eyes*]. Yes.

[*Mama is silent and someone knocks on the door. Mama and Ruth exchange weary and knowing glances and Ruth*

opens it to admit the neighbor, Mrs. Johnson.[1] who is a rather squeaky wide-eyed lady of no particular age, with a newspaper under her arm*]

MAMA [*changing her expression to acute delight and a ringing cheerful greeting*]. Oh—hello there, Johnson

MRS. JOHNSON [*This is a woman who decided long ago to be enthusiastic about EVERYTHING in life and she is inclined to wave her wrist vigorously at the height of her exclamatory comments*]. Hello there, yourself! H'you this evening, Ruth?

RUTH [*not much of a deceptive type*]. Fine, Mis' Johnson, h'you?

MRS. JOHNSON. Fine. [*Reaching out quickly, playfully, and patting Ruth's stomach*] Ain't you starting to poke out none yet! [*She mugs with delight at the over-familiar remark and her eyes dart around looking at the crates and packing preparation; Mama's face is a cold sheet of endurance*] Oh, ain't we getting ready round here, though! Yessir! Lookathere! I'm telling you the Youngers is really getting ready to "move on up a little higher!"—Bless God!

MAMA [*a little drily, doubting the total sincerity of the Blesser*]. Bless God.

MRS. JOHNSON. He's good, ain't He?

MAMA. Oh yes, He's good.

MRS. JOHNSON. I mean sometimes He works in mysterious ways . . . but He works, don't He!

MAMA [*the same*]. Yes, he does.

MRS. JOHNSON. I'm just sooooo happy for y'all. And this here child— [*About Ruth*] looks like she could just pop open with happiness, don't she. Where's all the rest of the family?

MAMA. Bennie's gone to bed—

MRS. JOHNSON. Ain't no . . . [*The implication is pregnancy*] sickness done hit you—I hope . . . ?

MAMA. No—she just tired. She was out this evening.

MRS. JOHNSON [*all is a coo, an emphatic coo*]. Aw— aint' that lovely. She still going out with the little Murchison boy?

MAMA [*drily*]. Ummmm huh.

MRS. JOHNSON. That's lovely. You sure got lovely children, Younger. Me and Isaiah talks all the time 'bout what fine children you was blessed with. We sure do.

MAMA. Ruth, give Mis' Johnson a piece of sweet potato pie and some milk.

---

[1] This character and the scene of her visit were cut from the original production and early editions of the play.

MRS. JOHNSON. Oh honey, I can't stay hardly a minute—I just dropped in to see if there was anything I could do. [Accepting the food easily] I guess y'll seen the news what's all over the colored paper this week . . .

MAMA. No—didn't get mine yet this week.

MRS. JOHNSON [lifting her head and blinking with the spirit of catastrophe]. You mean you ain't read 'bout them colored people that was bombed out their place out there?

[Ruth straightens with concern and takes the paper and reads it. Johnson notices her and feeds commentary]

MRS. JOHNSON. Ain't it something how bad these here white folks is getting here in Chicago! Lord, getting so you think you right down in Mississippi! [With a tremendous and rather insincere sense of melodrama]. 'Course I thinks it's wonderful how our folks keeps on pushing out. You hear some of these Negroes round here talking 'bout how they don't go where they ain't wanted and all that—but not me, honey! [This is a lie] Wilhemenia Othella Johnson goes anywhere, any time she feels like it! [With head movement for emphasis] Yes I do! Why if we left it up to these here crackers, the poor niggers wouldn't have nothing— [She claps her hand over her mouth] Oh, I always forgets you don't 'low that word in your house.

MAMA [quietly, looking at her]. No—I don't 'low it.

MRS. JOHNSON [vigorously again]. Me neither! I was just telling Isaiah yesterday when he come using it in front of me—I said, "Isaiah, it's just like Mis' Younger says all the time—"

MAMA. Don't you want some more pie?

MRS. JOHNSON. No—no thank you; this was lovely. I got to get on over home and have my midnight coffee. I hear some people say it don't let them sleep but I finds I can't close my eyes right lessen I done had that laaaast cup of coffee . . . [She waits. A beat. Undaunted] My Goodnight coffee, I calls it!

MAMA [with much eye-rolling and communication between herself and Ruth]. Ruth, why don't you give Mis' Johnson some coffee.

[Ruth gives Mama an unpleasant look for her kindness]

MRS. JOHNSON [accepting the coffee]. Where's Brother tonight?

MAMA. He's lying down.

MRS. JOHNSON. MMmmmmm, he sure gets his beauty rest, don't he? Good-looking man. Sure is a good-looking man! [Reaching out to pat Ruth's stomach again] I guess that's how come we keep on having babies around here. [She winks at Mama] One thing 'bout Brother, he always know how to have a good time. And soooooo ambitious! I bet it was his idea y'all moving out to Clybourne Park. Lord—I bet this time next month y'all's names will have been in the papers plenty— [Holding up her hands to mark off each word of the headline she can see in front of her] "NEGROES INVADE CLYBOURNE PARK— BOMBED!"

MAMA [she and Ruth look at the woman in amazement]. We ain't exactly moving out there to get bombed.

MRS. JOHNSON. Oh, honey—you know I'm praying to God every day that don't nothing like that happen! But you have to think of life like it is—and these here Chicago peckerwoods is some baaaad peckerwoods.

MAMA [wearily]. We done thought about all that Mis' Johnson.

[Beneatha comes out of the bedroom in her robe and passes through to the bathroom. Mrs. Johnson turns]

MRS. JOHNSON. Hello there, Bennie!

BENEATHA [crisply]. Hello, Mrs. Johnson

MRS. JOHNSON. How is school?

BENEATHA [crisply]. Fine, thank you. [She goes out.]

MRS. JOHNSON [insulted]. Getting so she don't have much to say to nobody.

MAMA. The child was on her way to the bathroom.

MRS. JOHNSON. I know—but sometimes she act like ain't got time to pass the time of day with nobody ain't been to college. Oh—I ain't criticizing her none. It's just—you know how some of our young people gets when they get a little education. [Mama and Ruth say nothing, just look at her] Yes—well. Well, I guess I better get on home. [Unmoving] 'Course I can understand how she must be proud and everything—being the only one in the family to make something of herself. I know just being a chauffeur ain't never satisfied Brother none. He shouldn't feel like that, though. Ain't nothing wrong with being a chauffeur.

MAMA. There's plenty wrong with it.

MRS. JOHNSON. What?

MAMA. Plenty. My husband always said being any kind of a servant wasn't a fit thing for a man to have to be. He always said a man's hands was made to make things, or to turn the earth with—not to drive nobody's car for 'em—or— [*She looks at her own hands*] —carry they slop jars. And my boy is just like him—he wasn't meant to wait on nobody.

MRS. JOHNSON [*rising, somewhat offended*]. Mmmmmmmmm. The Youngers is too much for me! [*She looks around*] You sure one proud-acting bunch of colored folks. Well—I always thinks like Booker T. Washington said that time—"Education has spoiled many a good plow hand"—

MAMA. Is that what old Booker T. said?

MRS. JOHNSON. He sure did.

MAMA. Well, it sounds just like him. The fool.

MRS. JOHNSON [*indignantly*]. Well—he was one of our great men.

MAMA. Who said so?

MRS. JOHNSON [*nonplussed*]. You know, me and you ain't never agreed about some things, Lena Younger. I guess I better be going—

RUTH [*quickly*]. Good night.

MRS. JOHNSON. Good night. Oh— [*Thrusting it at her*] You can keep the paper! [*With a trill*] 'Night.

MAMA. Good night, Mis' Johnson.

[*Mrs. Johnson exits*]

RUTH. If ignorance was gold . . .

MAMA. Shush. Don't talk about folks behind their backs.

RUTH. You do.

MAMA. I'm old and corrupted. [*Beneatha enters*] You was rude to Mis' Johnson, Beneatha, and I don't like it at all.

BENEATHA [*at her door*]. Mama, if there are two things we, as a people, have got to overcome, one is the Klu Klux Klan—and the other is Mrs. Johnson [*She exits*]

MAMA. Smart aleck.

[*The phone rings*]

RUTH. I'll get it.

MAMA. Lord, ain't this a popular place tonight.

RUTH [*at the phone*]. Hello—Just a minute. [*Goes to door*] Walter, it's Mrs. Arnold. [*Waits. Goes back to the phone. Tense*] Hello. Yes, this is his wife speaking . . . He's lying down now. Yes . . . well, he'll be in tomorrow. He's been very sick. Yes—I know we should have called, but we were so sure he'd be able to come in today. Yes—yes, I'm very sorry. Yes . . . Thank you very much. [*She hangs up. Walter is stand-*

ing in the doorway of the bedroom behind her] That was Mrs. Arnold.

WALTER [*indifferently*]. Was it?

RUTH. She said if you don't come in tomorrow that they are getting a new man . . .

WALTER. Ain't that sad—ain't that crying sad.

RUTH. She said Mr. Arnold has had to take a cab for three days . . . Walter, you ain't been to work for three days! [*This is a revelation to her*] Where you been, Walter Lee Younger? [*Walter looks at her and starts to laugh*] You're going to lose your job.

WALTER. That's right . . . [*He turns on the radio*]

RUTH. Oh, Walter, and with your mother working like a dog every day—

[*A steamy, deep blues pours into the room*]

WALTER. That's sad too—Everything is sad.

MAMA. What you been doing for these three days, son?

WALTER. Mama—you don't know all the things a man what got leisure can find to do in this city . . . What's this—Friday night? Well—Wednesday I borrowed Willy Harris' car and I went for a drive . . . just me and myself and I drove and drove . . . Way out . . . way past South Chicago, and I parked the car and I sat and looked at the steel mills all day long. I just sat in the car and looked at them big black chimneys for hours. Then I drove back and I went to the Green Hat. [*Pause*] And Thursday—Thursday I borrowed the car again and I got in it and I pointed it the other way and I drove the other way—for hours—way, way up to Wisconsin, and I looked at the farms. I just drove and looked at the farms. Then I drove back and I went to the Green Hat. [*Pause*] And today—today I didn't get the car. Today I just walked. All over the Southside. And I looked at the Negroes and they looked at me and finally I just sat down on the curb at Thirty-ninth and South Parkway and I just sat there and watched the Negroes go by. And then I went to the Green Hat. You all sad? You all depressed? And you know where I am going right now—

[*Ruth goes out quietly*]

MAMA. Oh, Big Walter, is this the harvest of our days?

WALTER. You know what I like about the Green Hat? I like this little cat they got there who blows a sax . . . He blows. He talks to me. He ain't but 'bout five feet tall and he's got a conked head and his eyes is always closed and he's all music—

MAMA [*rising and getting some papers out of her handbag*]. Walter—

WALTER. And there's this other guy who plays the piano . . . and they got a sound. I mean they can work on some music . . . They got the best little combo in the world in the Green Hat . . . You can just sit there and drink and listen to them three men play and you realize that don't nothing matter worth a damn, but just being there—

MAMA. I've helped do it to you, haven't I, son? Walter I been wrong.

WALTER. Naw—you ain't never been wrong about nothing, Mama.

MAMA. Listen to me, now. I say I been wrong, son. That I been doing to you what the rest of the world been doing to you. [*She turns off the radio*] Walter— [*She stops and he looks up slowly at her and she meets his eyes pleadingly*] What you ain't never understood is that I ain't got nothing, don't own nothing, ain't never really wanted nothing that wasn't for you. There ain't nothing as precious to me . . . There ain't nothing worth holding on to, money, dreams, nothing else—if it means—if it means it's going to destroy my boy. [*She takes an envelope out of her handbag and puts it in front of him and he watches her without speaking or moving*] I paid the man thirty-five hundred dollars down on the house. That leaves sixty-five hundred dollars. Monday morning I want you to take this money and take three thousand dollars and put it in a savings account for Beneatha's medical schooling. The rest you put in a checking account—with your name on it. And from now on any penny that come out of it or that go in it is for you to look after. For you to decide. [*She drops her hands a little helplessly*] It ain't much, but it's all I got in the world and I'm putting it in your hands. I'm telling you to be the head of this family from now on like you supposed to be.

WALTER [*stares at the money*]. You trust me like that, Mama?

MAMA. I ain't never stop trusting you. Like I ain't never stop loving you.

[*She goes out, and Walter sits looking at the money on the table. Finally, in a decisive gesture, he gets up, and, in mingled joy and desperation, picks up the money. At the same moment, Travis enters for bed*]

TRAVIS. What's the matter, Daddy? You drunk?

WALTER [*sweetly, more sweetly than we have ever known him*]. No, Daddy ain't drunk. Daddy ain't going to never be drunk again. . . .

TRAVIS. Well, good night, Daddy.

[*The Father has come from behind the couch and leans over, embracing his son*]

WALTER. Son, I feel like talking to you tonight.

TRAVIS. About what?

WALTER. Oh, about a lot of things. About you and what kind of man you going to be when you grow up. . . . Son—son, what do you want to be when you grow up?

TRAVIS. A bus driver.

WALTER [*laughing a little*]. A what? Man, that ain't nothing to want to be!

TRAVIS. Why not?

WALTER. 'Cause, man—it ain't big enough—you know what I mean.

TRAVIS. I don't know then. I can't make up my mind. Sometimes Mama asks me that too. And sometimes when I tell her I just want to be like you—she says she don't want me to be like that and sometimes she says she does. . . .

WALTER [*gathering him up in his arms*]. You know what, Travis? In seven years you going to be seventeen years old. And things is going to be very different with us in seven years, Travis. . . . One day when you are seventeen I'll come home—home from my office downtown somewhere—

TRAVIS. You don't work in no office, Daddy.

WALTER. No—but after tonight. After what your daddy gonna do tonight, there's going to be offices—a whole lot of offices. . . .

TRAVIS. What you gonna do tonight, Daddy?

WALTER. You wouldn't understand yet, son, but your daddy's gonna make a transaction . . . a business transaction that's going to change our lives. . . . That's how come one day when you 'bout seventeen years old I'll come home and I'll be pretty tired, you know what I mean, after a day of conferences and secretaries getting things wrong the way they do . . . 'cause an executive's life is hell, man— [*The more he talks the farther away he gets*] And I'll pull the car up on the driveway . . . just a plain black Chrysler, I think, with white walls—no—black tires. More elegant. Rich people don't have to be flashy . . . though I'll have to get something a little sportier for Ruth—maybe a Cadillac convertible to do her shopping in. . . . And I'll come up the steps to the house and the gardener will be clipping away at the hedges and he'll say, "Good evening, Mr. Younger." And I'll say, "Hello, Jefferson, how are you this evening?" And I'll go inside and Ruth will come downstairs and meet me at the door and we'll kiss each other and she'll take my arm and we'll go up to your room to see you sitting on the floor with the catalogues of all the great schools in America around you. . . . All the great schools in the world! And—and I'll say, all right son—it's your seventeenth birthday, what is it you've decided? . . . Just tell me where you want to go to school and you'll *go*. Just tell me, what it is you want to be—and you'll *be* it. . . . Whatever you want to be—Yessir! [*He holds his arms open for Travis*] You just name it, son . . . [*Travis leaps into them*] and I hand you the world!

[*Walter's voice has risen in pitch and hysterical promise and on the last line he lifts Travis high*]

[*Blackout*]

SCENE III

Time: Saturday, moving day, one week later.

Before the curtain rises, Ruth's voice, a strident, dramatic church alto, cuts through the silence.

    It is, in the darkness, a triumphant surge, a penetrating statement of expectation: "Oh, Lord, I don't feel no ways tired! Children, oh, glory hallelujah!"

    As the curtain rises we see that Ruth is alone in the living room, finishing up the family's packing. It is moving day. She is nailing crates and tying cartons. Beneatha enters, carrying a guitar case, and watches her exuberant sister-in-law.

RUTH. Hey!
BENEATHA [*putting away the case*]. Hi.
RUTH [*pointing at a package*]. Honey—look in that package there and see what I found on sale this morning at the South Center. [*Ruth gets up and moves to the package and draws out some curtains*] Lookahere—hand-turned hems!
BENEATHA. How do you know the window size out there?
RUTH [*who hadn't thought of that*]. Oh—Well, they bound to fit something in the whole house. Any-

how, they was too good a bargain to pass up. [*Ruth slaps her head, suddenly remembering something*] Oh, Bennie—I meant to put a special note on that carton over there. That's your mama's good china and she wants 'em to be very careful with it.
BENEATHA. I'll do it.

[*Beneatha finds a piece of paper and starts to draw large letters on it*]

RUTH. You know what I'm going to do soon as I get in that new house?
BENEATHA. What?
RUTH. Honey—I'm going to run me a tub of water up to here . . . [*With her fingers practically up to her nostrils*] And I'm going to get in it—and I am going to sit . . . and sit . . . and sit in that hot water and the first person who knocks to tell *me* to hurry up and come out—
BENEATHA. Gets shot at sunrise.
RUTH [*laughing happily*]. You said it, sister! [*Noticing how large Beneatha is absent-mindedly making the note*] Honey, they ain't going to read that from no airplane.
BENEATHA [*laughing herself*]. I guess I always think things have more emphasis if they are big, somehow.
RUTH [*looking up at her and smiling*]. You and your brother seem to have that as a philosophy of life. Lord, that man—done changed so 'round here. You know—you know what we did last night? Me and Walter Lee?
BENEATHA. What?
RUTH [*smiling to herself*]. We went to the movies. [*Looking at Beneatha to see if she understands*] We went to the movies. You know the last time me and Walter went to the movies together?
BENEATHA. No.
RUTH. Me neither. That's how long it been. [*Smiling again*] But we went last night. The picture wasn't much good, but that didn't seem to matter. We went—and we held hands.
BENEATHA. Oh, Lord!
RUTH. We held hands—and you know what?
BENEATHA. What?
RUTH. When we come out of the show it was late and dark and all the stores and things was closed up . . . and it was kind of chilly and there wasn't many people on the streets . . . and we was still holding hands, me and Walter.
BENEATHA. You're killing me.

[*Walter enters with a large package. His happiness is deep in him; he cannot keep still with his new-found exuberance. He is singing and wiggling and snapping his fingers. He puts his package in a corner and puts a phonograph record, which he has brought in with him, on the record player. As the music, soulful and sensuous, comes up he dances over to Ruth and tries to get her to dance with him. She gives in at last to his raunchiness and in a fit of giggling allows herself to be drawn into his mood. They dip and she melts into his arms in a classic, body-melding "slow drag"*].

BENEATHA [*regarding them a long time as they dance, then drawing in her breath for a deeply exaggerated comment which she does not particularly mean*]. Talk about —olddddddddddd-fashioneddddddddd—Negroes!

WALTER [*stopping momentarily*]. What kind of Negroes? [*He says this in fun. He is not angry with her today, nor with anyone. He starts to dance with his wife again*]

BENEATHA. Old-fashioned.

WALTER [*as he dances with Ruth*]. You know, when these *New Negroes* have their convention— [*Pointing at his sister*] —that is going to be the chairman of the Committee on Unending Agitation. [*He goes on dancing, then stops*] Race, race, race! . . . Girl, I do believe you are the first person in the history of the entire human race to successfully brainwash yourself. [*Beneatha breaks up and he goes on dancing. He stops again, enjoying his tease*] Damn, even the N double A C P takes a holiday sometimes! [*Beneatha and Ruth laugh. He dances with Ruth some more and starts to laugh and stops and pantomimes someone over an operating table*] I can just see that chick someday looking down at some poor cat on an operating table and before she starts to slice him, she says . . . [*Pulling his sleeves back maliciously*] "By the way, what are your views on civil rights down there? . . ."

[*He laughs at her again and starts to dance happily. The bell sounds*]

BENEATHA. Sticks and stones may break my bones . . . words will never hurt me!

[*Beneatha goes to the door and opens it as Walter and Ruth go on with the clowning. Beneatha is somewhat surprised to see a quiet-looking middle-aged white man in a business suit holding his hat and a briefcase in his hand and consulting a small piece of paper*]

MAN. Uh—how do you do, miss. I am looking for a Mrs.— [*He looks at the slip of paper*] Mrs. Lena Younger? [*He stops short, struck dumb at the sight of the oblivious Walter and Ruth*]

BENEATHA [*smoothing her hair with slight embarrassment*]. Oh—yes, that's my mother. Excuse me [*She closes the door and turns to quiet the other two*] Ruth! Brother! [*Enunciating precisely but soundlessly: "There's a white man at the door!" They stop dancing, Ruth cuts off the phonograph, Beneatha opens the door. The man casts a curious quick glance at all of them*] Uh—come in please.

MAN [*coming in*]. Thank you.

BENEATHA. My mother isn't here just now. Is it business?

MAN. Yes . . . well, of a sort.

WALTER [*freely, the Man of the House*]. Have a seat. I'm Mrs. Younger's son. I look after most of her business matters.

[*Ruth and Beneatha exchange amused glances*]

MAN [*regarding Walter, and sitting*]. Well—My name is Karl Lindner . . .

WALTER [*stretching out his hand*]. Walter Younger. This is my wife— [*Ruth nods politely*] —and my sister.

LINDNER. How do you do.

WALTER [*amiably, as he sits himself easily on a chair, leaning forward on his knees with interest and looking expectantly into the newcomer's face*]. What can we do for you, Mr. Lindner!

LINDNER [*some minor shuffling of the hat and briefcase on his knees*]. Well—I am a representative of the Clybourne Park Improvement Association—

WALTER [*pointing*]. Why don't you sit your things on the floor?

LINDNER. Oh—yes. Thank you. [*He slides the briefcase and hat under the chair*] And as I was saying—I am from the Clybourne Park Improvement Association and we have had it brought to our attention at the last meeting that you people—or at least your mother—has bought a piece of residential property at— [*He digs for the slip of paper again*] —four o six Clybourne Street . . .

WALTER. That's right. Care for something to drink? Ruth, get Mr. Lindner a beer.

LINDNER [*upset for some reason*]. Oh—no, really. I mean thank you very much, but no thank you.

RUTH [*innocently*]. Some coffee?

LINDNER. Thank you, nothing at all.

[*Beneatha is watching the man carefully*]

LINDNER. Well, I don't know how much you folks know about our organization. [*He is a gentle man; thoughtful and somewhat labored in his manner*] It is one of these community organizations set up to look after—oh, you know, things like block upkeep and special projects and we also have what we call our New Neighbors Orientation Committee . . .

BENEATHA [*drily*]. Yes—and what do they do?

LINDNER [*turning a little to her and then returning the main force to Walter*]. Well—it's what you might call a sort of welcoming committee, I guess. I mean they, we—I'm the chairman of the committee—go around and see the new people who move into the neighborhood and sort of give them the lowdown on the way we do things in Clybourne Park.

BENEATHA [*with appreciation of the two meanings, which escape Ruth and Walter*]. Uh-huh.

LINDNER. And we also have the category of what the association calls— [*He looks elsewhere*] —uh—special community problems . . .

BENEATHA. Yes—and what are some of those?

WALTER. Girl, let the man talk.

LINDNER [*with understated relief*]. Thank you. I would sort of like to explain this thing in my own way. I mean I want to explain to you in a certain way.

WALTER. Go ahead.

LINDNER. Yes. Well. I'm going to try to get right to the point. I'm sure we'll all appreciate that in the long run.

BENEATHA. Yes.

WALTER. Be still now!

LINDNER. Well—

RUTH [*still innocently*]. Would you like another chair—you don't look comfortable.

LINDNER [*more frustrated than annoyed*]. No, thank you very much. Please. Well—to get right to the point I— [*A great breath, and he is off at last*] I am sure you people must be aware of some of the incidents which have happened in various parts of the city when colored people have moved into certain areas— [*Beneatha exhales heavily and starts tossing a piece of fruit up and down in the air*] Well—because we have what I think is going to be a unique type of organization in American community life—not only do we deplore that kind of thing—but we are trying to do something about it. [*Beneatha stops tossing and turns with a new and quizzical interest to the man*] We feel— [*gaining confidence in his mission because of the interest in the faces of the people he is talking to*] —we feel that most of the trouble in this world, when you come right down to it— [*He hits his knee for emphasis*] —most of the trouble exists because people just don't sit down and talk to each other.

RUTH [*nodding as she might in church, pleased with the remark*]. You can say that again, mister.

LINDNER [*more encouraged by such affirmation*]. That we don't try hard enough in this world to understand the other fellow's problem. The other guy's point of view.

RUTH. Now that's right.

[*Beneatha and Walter merely watch and listen with genuine interest*]

LINDNER. Yes—that's the way we feel out in Clybourne Park. And that's why I was elected to come here this afternoon and talk to you people. Friendly like, you know, the way people should talk to each other and see if we couldn't find some way to work this thing out. As I say, the whole business is a matter of *caring* about the other fellow. Anybody can see that you are a nice family of folks, hard working and honest I'm sure. [*Beneatha frowns slightly, quizzically, her head tilted regarding him*] Today everybody knows what it means to be on the outside of *something*. And of course, there is always somebody who is out to take advantage of people who don't always understand.

WALTER. What do you mean?

LINDNER. Well—you see our community is made up of people who've worked hard as the dickens for years to build up that little community. They're not rich and fancy people; just hard-working, honest people who don't really have much but those little homes and a dream of the kind of community they want to raise their children in. Now, I don't say we are perfect and there is a lot wrong in some of the things they want. But you've got to admit that a man, right or wrong, has the right to want to have the neighborhood he lives in a certain kind of way. And at the moment the overwhelming majority of our people out there feel that people get along better, take more of a common interest in the life of the community, when they share a common background. I want you to believe me when I tell you that race prejudice simply doesn't enter into it. It is a matter of the people of Clybourne Park believing, rightly or wrongly, as I say, that for the happiness of all concerned that our Negro families are happier when they live in their *own* communities.

BENEATHA [*with a grand and bitter gesture*]. This, friends, is the Welcoming Committee!

WALTER [*dumbfounded, looking at Lindner*]. Is this what you came marching all the way over here to tell us?

LINDNER. Well, now we've been having a fine conversation. I hope you'll hear me all the way through.

WALTER [*tightly*]. Go ahead, man.

LINDNER. You see—in the face of all the things I have said, we are prepared to make your family a very generous offer . . .

BENEATHA. Thirty pieces and not a coin less!

WALTER. Yeah?

LINDNER [*putting on his glasses and drawing a form out of the briefcase*]. Our association is prepared, through the collective effort of our people, to buy the house from you at a financial gain to your family.

RUTH. Lord have mercy, ain't this the living gall!

WALTER. All right, you through?

LINDNER. Well, I want to give you the exact terms of the financial arrangement—

WALTER. We don't want to hear no exact terms of no arrangements. I want to know if you got any more to tell us 'bout getting together?

LINDNER [*taking off his glasses*]. Well—I don't suppose that you feel . . .

WALTER. Never mind how I feel—you got any more to say 'bout how people ought to sit down and talk to each other? . . . Get out of my house, man.

[*He turns his back and walks to the door*]

LINDNER [*Looking around at the hostile faces and reaching and assembling his hat and briefcase*] —Well—I don't understand why you people are reacting this way. What do you think you are going to gain by moving into a neighborhood where you just aren't wanted and where some elements—well—people can get awful worked up when they feel that their whole way of life and everything they've ever worked for is threatened.

WALTER. Get out.

LINDNER [*at the door, holding a small card*]. Well—I'm sorry it went like this.

WALTER. Get out.

LINDNER [*almost sadly regarding Walter*]. You just can't force people to change their hearts, son.

[*He turns and puts his card on a table and exits. Walter pushes the door to with stinging hatred, and stands looking at it. Ruth just sits and Beneatha just stands. They say nothing. Mama and Travis enter*]

MAMA. Well—this all the packing got done since I left out of here this morning. I testify before God that my children got all the energy of the *dead*! What time the moving men due?

BENEATHA. Four o'clock. You had a caller, Mama.

[*She is smiling, teasingly*]

MAMA. Sure enough—who?

BENEATHA [*her arms folded saucily*]. The Welcoming Committee.

[*Walter and Ruth giggle*]

MAMA [*innocently*]. Who?

BENEATHA. The Welcoming Committee. They said they're sure going to be glad to see you when you get there.

WALTER [*devilishly*]. Yeah, they said they can't hardly wait to see your face.

[*Laughter*]

MAMA [*sensing their facetiousness*]. What's the matter with you all?

WALTER. Ain't nothing the matter with us. We just telling you 'bout the gentleman who came to see you this afternoon. From the Clybourne Park Improvement Association.

MAMA. What he want?

RUTH [*in the same mood as Beneatha and Walter*]. To welcome you, honey.

WALTER. He said they can't hardly wait. He said the one thing they don't have, that they just *dying* to have out there is a fine family of fine colored people! [*To Ruth and Beneatha*] Ain't that right!

RUTH [*mockingly*]. Yeah! He left his card—

BENEATHA [*handing card to Mama*]. In case.

[*Mama reads and throws it on the floor—understanding and looking off as she draws her chair up to the table on which she has put her plant and some sticks and some cord*]

MAMA. Father, give us strength. [*knowingly—and without fun*] Did he threaten us?

BENEATHA. Oh—Mama—they don't do it like that any more. He talked Brotherhood. He said everybody ought to learn how to sit down and hate each other with good Christian fellowship.

[*She and Walter shake hands to ridicule the remark*]

MAMA [*sadly*]. Lord, protect us . . .

RUTH. You should hear the money those folks raised to buy the house from us. All we paid and then some.

BENEATHA. What they think we going to do—eat 'em?

RUTH. No, honey, marry 'em.

MAMA [*shaking her head*]. Lord, Lord, Lord . . .

RUTH. Well—that's the way the crackers crumble. [*A beat*]. Joke.

BENEATHA [*laughingly noticing what her mother is doing*]. Mama, what are you doing?

MAMA. Fixing my plant so it won't get hurt none on the way . . .

BENEATHA. Mama, you going to take *that* to the new house?

MAMA. Un-huh—

BENEATHA. That raggedy-looking old thing?

MAMA [*stopping and looking at her*]. It expresses ME!

RUTH [*with delight, to Beneatha*]. So there, Miss Thing!

[*Walter comes to Mama suddenly and bends down behind her and squeezes her in his arms with all his strength. She is overwhelmed by the suddenness of it and, though delighted, her manner is like that of Ruth and Travis*]

MAMA. Look out now, boy! You make me mess up my thing here!

WALTER [*his face lit, he slips down on his knees beside her, his arms still about her*]. Mama . . . you know what it means to climb up in the chariot?

MAMA [*gruffly, very happy*]. Get on away from me now . . .

RUTH [*near the gift-wrapped package, trying to catch Walter's eye*]. Psst—

WALTER. What the old song say, Mama . . .

RUTH. Walter—Now?

[*She is pointing at the package*]

WALTER [*speaking the lines, sweetly, playfully, in his mother's face*]. I got wings . . . you got wings . . . All God's Children got wings . . .

MAMA. Boy—get out of my face and do some work . . .

WALTER. When I get to heaven gonna put on my wings, Gonna fly all over God's heaven . . .

BENEATHA [*teasingly, from across the room*]. Everybody talking 'bout heaven ain't going there!

WALTER [*to Ruth, who is carrying the box across to them*]. I don't know, you think we ought to give her that . . . Seems to me she ain't been very appreciative around here.

MAMA [*eyeing the box, which is obviously a gift*]. What is that?

WALTER [*taking it from Ruth and putting it on the table in front of Mama*]. Well—what you all think? Should we give it to her?

RUTH. Oh—she was pretty good today.

MAMA. I'll good you—

[*She turns her eyes to the box again*]

BENEATHA. Open it, Mama.

[*She stands up, looks at it, turns and looks at all of them, and then presses her hands together and does not open the package*]

WALTER [*sweetly*]. Open it, Mama. It's for you. [*Mama looks in his eyes. It is the first present in her life without its being Christmas. Slowly she opens her package and lifts out, one by one, a brand-new sparkling set of gardening tools. Walter continues, prodding*] Ruth made up the note—read it . . .

MAMA [*picking up the card and adjusting her glasses*]. "To our own Mrs. Miniver—Love from Brother, Ruth and Beneatha." Ain't that lovely . . .

TRAVIS [*tugging at his father's sleeve*]. Daddy, can I give her mine now?

WALTER. All right, son. [*Travis flies to get his gift*]

MAMA. Now I don't have to use my knives and forks no more . . .

WALTER. Travis didn't want to go in with the rest of us, Mama. He got his own. [*Somewhat amused*] We don't know what it is . . .

TRAVIS [*racing back in the room with a large hatbox and putting it in front of his grandmother*]. Here!

MAMA. Lord have mercy, baby. You done gone and bought your grandmother a hat?

TRAVIS [*very proud*]. Open it!

[*She does and lifts out an elaborate, but very elaborate, wide gardening hat, and all the adults break up at the sight of it*]

RUTH. Travis, honey, what is that?

TRAVIS [*who thinks it is beautiful and appropriate*]. It's a gardening hat! Like the ladies always have on in the magazines when they work in their gardens.

BENEATHA [*giggling fiercely*]. Travis—we were trying to make Mama Mrs. Miniver—not Scarlett O'Hara!

MAMA [*indignantly*]. What's the matter with you all! This here is a beautiful hat! [*Absurdly*] I always wanted me one just like it!

[*She pops it on her head to prove it to her grandson, and the hat is ludicrous and considerably oversized*]

RUTH. Hot dog! Go, Mama!

WALTER [*doubled over with laughter*]. I'm sorry, Mama—but you look like you ready to go out and chop you some cotton sure enough!

[*They all laugh except Mama, out of deference to Travis' feelings*]

MAMA [*gathering the boy up to her*]. Bless your heart—this is the prettiest hat I ever owned— [*Walter,Ruth and Beneatha chime in—noisily, festively and insincerely congratulating Travis on his gift*] What are we all standing around here for? We ain't finished packin' yet. Bennie, you ain't packed one book.

[*The bell rings*]

BENEATHA. That couldn't be the movers . . . it's not hardly two good yet—

[*Beneatha goes into her room. Mama starts for door*]

WALTER [*turning, stiffening*]. Wait—wait—I'll get it.

[*He stands and looks at the door*]

MAMA. You expecting company, son?
WALTER [*just looking at the door*]. Yeah—yeah . . .

[*Mama looks at Ruth, and they exchange innocent and unfrightened glances*]

MAMA [*not understanding*]. Well, let them in, son.
BENEATHA [*from her room*]. We need some more string.
MAMA. Travis—you run to the hardware and get me some string cord.

[*Mama goes out and Walter turns and looks at Ruth. Travis goes to a dish for money*]

RUTH. Why don't you answer the door, man?
WALTER [*suddenly bounding across the floor to embrace her*]. 'Cause sometimes it hard to let the future begin!

[*Stooping down in her face*]

I got wings! You got wings!
All God's children got wings!

[*He crosses to the door and throws it open. Standing there is a very slight little man in a not too prosperous business suit and with haunted frightened eyes and a hat pulled down tightly, brim up, around his forehead. Travis passes between the men and exits. Walter leans deep in the man's face, still in his jubilance*]

When I get to heaven gonna put on my wings,
Gonna fly all over God's heaven . . .

[*The little man just stares at him*]

Heaven—

[*Suddenly he stops and looks past the little man into the empty hallway*]

Where's Willy, man?
BOBO. He ain't with me.
WALTER [*not disturbed*]. Oh—come on in. You know my wife.
BOBO [*dumbly, taking off his hat*]. Yes—h'you, Miss Ruth.
RUTH [*quietly, a mood apart from her husband already, seeing Bobo*]. Hello, Bobo.
WALTER. You right on time today . . . Right on time. That's the way! [*He slaps Bobo on his back*] Sit down . . . lemme hear.

[*Ruth stands stiffly and quietly in the back of them, as though somehow she senses death, her eyes fixed on her husband*]

BOBO [*his frightened eyes on the floor, his hat in his hands*]. Could I please get a drink of water, before I tell you about it, Walter Lee?

[*Walter does not take his eyes off the man. Ruth goes blindly to the tap and gets a glass of water and brings it to Bobo*]

WALTER. There ain't nothing wrong, is there?
BOBO. Lemme tell you—
WALTER. Man—didn't nothing go wrong?
BOBO. Lemme tell you—Walter Lee. [*Looking at Ruth and talking to her more than to Walter*] You know how it was. I got to tell you how it was. I mean first I got to tell you how it was all the way . . . I mean about the money I put in, Walter Lee . . .
WALTER [*with taut agitation now*]. What about the money you put in?
BOBO. Well—it wasn't much as we told you—me and Willy— [*He stops*] I'm sorry, Walter. I got a bad feeling about it. I got a real bad feeling about it . . .
WALTER. Man, what you telling me about all this for? . . . Tell me what happened in Springfield . . .
BOBO. Springfield.
RUTH [*like a dead woman*]. What was supposed to happen in Springfield?

BOBO [to her]. This deal that me and Walter went into with Willy—Me and Willy was going to go down to Springfield and spread some money 'round so's we wouldn't have to wait so long for the liquor license . . . That's what we were going to do. Everybody said that was the way you had to do, you understand, Miss Ruth?

WALTER. Man—what happened down there?

BOBO [a pitiful man, near tears]. I'm trying to tell you, Walter.

WALTER [screaming at him suddenly]. THEN TELL ME, GODDAMMIT . . . WHAT'S THE MATTER WITH YOU?

BOBO. Man . . . I didn't go to no Springfield, yesterday.

WALTER [halted, life hanging in the moment]. Why not?

BOBO [the long way, the hard way to tell]. 'Cause I didn't have no reasons to . . .

WALTER. Man, what are you talking about!

BOBO. I'm talking about the fact that when I got to the train station yesterday morning—eight o'clock like we planned . . . Man—*Willy didn't never show up.*

WALTER. Why . . . where was he . . . where is he?

BOBO. That's what I'm trying to tell you . . . I don't know . . . I waited six hours . . . I called his house . . . and I waited . . . six hours . . . I waited in that train station six hours . . . [Breaking into tears] That was all the extra money I had in the world . . . [Looking up at Walter with the tears running down his face] Man, *Willy is gone.*

WALTER. Gone, what you mean Willy is gone? Gone where? You mean he went by himself. You mean he went off to Springfield by himself—to take care of getting the license— [Turns and looks anxiously at Ruth] You mean maybe he didn't want too many people in on the business down there? [Looks to Ruth again, as before] You know Willy got his own ways. [Looks back to Bobo] Maybe you was late yesterday and he just went on down there without you. Maybe—maybe—he's been callin' you at home tryin' to tell you what happened or something. Maybe—maybe—he just got sick. He's somewhere—he's got to be somewhere. We just got to find him—me and you got to find him. [Grabs Bobo senselessly by the collar and starts to shake him] We got to!

BOBO [in sudden angry, frightened agony]. What's the matter with you, Walter! *When a cat take off with your money he don't leave you no road maps!*

WALTER [turning madly, as though he is looking for Willy in the very room]. Willy! . . . Willy . . . don't do it . . . Please don't do it . . . Man, not with that money . . . Man, please, not with that money . . . Oh, God . . . Don't let it be true . . . [He is wandering around, crying out for Willy and looking for him or perhaps for help from God] Man . . . I trusted you . . . Man, I put my life in your hands . . . [He starts to crumble down on the floor as Ruth just covers her face in horror. Mama opens the door and comes into the room, with Beneatha behind her] Man . . . [He starts to pound the floor with his fists, sobbing wildly] —THAT MONEY IS MADE OUT OF MY FATHER'S FLESH—

BOBO [standing over him helplessly]. I'm sorry, Walter . . . [Only Walter's sobs reply. Bobo puts on his hat] I had my life staked on this deal, too . . .

[He exits]

MAMA [to Walter]. Son— [She goes to him, bends down to him, talks to his bent head] Son . . . Is it gone? Son, I gave you sixty-five hundred dollars. Is it gone? All of it? Beneatha's money too?

WALTER [lifting his head slowly]. Mama . . . I never . . . went to the bank at all . . .

MAMA [not wanting to believe him]. You mean . . . your sister's school money . . . you used that too . . . Walter? . . .

WALTER. Yessss! All of it . . . It's all gone . . .

[There is total silence. Ruth stands with her face covered with her hands; Beneatha leans forlornly against a wall, fingering a piece of red ribbon from the mother's gift. Mama stops and looks at her son without recognition and then, quite without thinking about it, starts to beat him senselessly in the face. Beneatha goes to them and stops it]

BENEATHA. Mama!

[Mama stops and looks at both of her children and rises slowly and wanders vaguely, aimlessly away from them]

MAMA. I seen . . . him . . . night after night . . . come in . . . and look at that rug . . . and then look at me . . . the red showing in his eyes . . . the veins moving in his head . . . I seen him grow thin and old before he was forty . . . working and working and working like somebody's old horse . . . killing himself . . . and you—you give it all away in a day— [She raises her arms to strike him again]

BENEATHA. Mama—

MAMA. Oh, God . . . [She looks up to Him] Look down here—and show me the strength.

BENEATHA. Mama—

MAMA [folding over]. Strength . . .

BENEATHA [plaintively]. Mama . . .

MAMA. Strength!

CURTAIN

Act III

An hour later.

At curtain, there is a sullen light of gloom in the living room, gray light not unlike that which began the first scene of Act I. At left we can see Walter within his room, alone with himself. He is stretched out on the bed, his shirt out and open, his arms under his head. He does not smoke, he does not cry out, he merely lies there, looking up at the ceiling, much as if he were alone in the world.

In the living room Beneatha sits at the table, still surrounded by the now almost ominous packing crates. She sits looking off. We feel that this is a mood struck perhaps an hour before, and it lingers now, full of the empty sound of profound disappointment. We see on a line from her brother's bedroom the sameness of their attitudes. Presently the bell rings and Beneatha rises without ambition or interest in answering. It is Asagai, smiling broadly, striding into the room with energy and happy expectation and conversation.

ASAGAI. I came over . . . I had some free time. I thought I might help with the packing. Ah, I like the look of packing crates! A household in preparation for a journey! It depresses some people . . . but for me . . . it is another feeling. Something full of the flow of life, do you understand? Movement, progress . . . It makes me think of Africa.

BENEATHA. Africa!

ASAGAI. What kind of mood is this? Have I told you how deeply you move me?

BENEATHA. He gave away the money, Asagai . . .

ASAGAI. Who gave away what money?

BENEATHA. The insurance money. My brother gave it away.

ASAGAI. Gave it away?

BENEATHA. He made an investment! With a man even Travis wouldn't have trusted with his most worn-out marbles.

ASAGAI. And it's gone?

BENEATHA. Gone!

ASAGAI. I'm very sorry . . . And you, now?

BENEATHA. Me? . . . Me? . . . Me, I'm nothing . . . Me. When I was very small . . . we used to take our sleds out in the wintertime and the only hills we had were the ice-covered stone steps of some houses down the street. And we used to fill them in with snow and make them smooth and slide down them all day . . . and it was very dangerous, you know . . . far too steep . . . and sure enough one day a kid named Rufus came down too fast and hit the sidewalk and we saw his face just split open right there in front of us . . . And I remember standing there looking at his bloody open face thinking that was the end of Rufus. But the ambulance came and they took him to the hospital and they fixed the broken bones and they sewed it all up . . . and the next time I saw Rufus he just had a little line down the middle of his face . . . I never got over that . . .

ASAGAI. What?

BENEATHA. That that was what one person could do for another, fix him up—sew up the problem, make him all right again. That was the most marvelous thing in the world . . . I wanted to do that. I always thought it was the one concrete thing in the world that a human being could do. Fix up the sick, you know—and make them whole again. This was truly being God . . .

ASAGAI. You wanted to be God?

BENEATHA. No—I wanted to cure. It used to be so important to me. I wanted to cure. It used to matter. I used to care. I mean about people and how their bodies hurt . . .

ASAGAI. And you've stopped caring?

BENEATHA. Yes—I think so.

ASAGAI. Why?

BENEATHA [bitterly]. Because it doesn't seem deep enough, close enough to what ails mankind! It was a child's way of seeing things—or an idealist's.

ASAGAI. Children see things very well sometimes—and idealists even better.

BENEATHA. I know that's what you think. Because you are still where I left off. You with all your talk and dreams about Africa! You still think you can patch up the world. Cure the Great Sore of Colonialism— [Loftily, mocking it] with the Penicillin of Independence—!

ASAGAI. Yes!

BENEATHA. Independence and then what? What about all the crooks and thieves and just plain idiots who will come into power and steal and plunder the same as before—only now they will be black and do it in the name of the new Independence—WHAT ABOUT THEM?!

ASAGAI. That will be the problem for another time. First we must get there.

BENEATHA. And where does it end?

ASAGAI. End? Who even spoke of an end? To life? To living?

BENEATHA. An end to misery! To stupidity! Don't you see there isn't any real progress, Asagai, there is only one large circle that we march in, around and around, each of us with our own little picture in front of us—our own little mirage that we think is the future.

ASAGAI. That is the mistake.

BENEATHA. What?

ASAGAI. What you just said—about the circle. It isn't a circle—it is simply a long line—as in geometry, you know, one that reaches into infinity. And because we cannot see the end—we also cannot see how it changes. And it is very odd but those who see the changes—who dream, who will not give up—are called idealists . . . and those who see only the circle—we call them the "realists"!

BENEATHA. Asagai, while I was sleeping in that bed in there, people went out and took the future right out of my hands! And nobody asked me, nobody consulted me—they just went out and changed my life!

ASAGAI. Was it your money?

BENEATHA. What?

ASAGAI. Was it your money he gave away?

BENEATHA. It belonged to all of us.

ASAGAI. But did you earn it? Would you have had it at all if your father had not died?

BENEATHA. No.

ASAGAI. Then isn't there something wrong in a house—in a world—where all dreams, good or bad, must depend on the death of a man? I never thought to see you like this, Alaiyo. You! Your brother made a mistake and you are grateful to him so that now you can give up the ailing human race on account of it! You talk about what good is struggle, what good is anything! Where are we all going and why are we bothering!

BENEATHA. AND YOU CANNOT ANSWER IT!

ASAGAI [shouting over her]. I LIVE THE ANSWER! [Pause] In my village at home it is the exceptional man who can even read a newspaper . . . or who ever sees a book at all. I will go home and much of what I will have to say will seem strange to the people of my village. But I will teach and work and things will happen, slowly and swiftly. At times it will seem that nothing changes at all . . . and then again the sudden dramatic events which make history leap into the future. And then quiet again. Retrogression even. Guns, murder, revolution. And I even will have moments when I wonder if the quiet was not better than all that death and hatred. But I will look about my village at the illiteracy and disease and ignorance and I will not wonder long. And perhaps . . . perhaps I will be a great man . . . I mean perhaps I will hold on to the substance of truth and find my way always with the right course . . . and perhaps for it I will be butchered in my bed some night by the servants of empire . . .

BENEATHA. The martyr!

ASAGAI [he smiles]. . . . or perhaps I shall live to be a very old man, respected and esteemed in my new nation . . . And perhaps I shall hold office and this is what I'm trying to tell you, Alaiyo: Perhaps the things I believe now for my country will be wrong and outmoded, and I will not understand and do terrible things to have things my way or merely to keep my power. Don't you see that there will be young men and women—not British soldiers then, but my own black countrymen—to step out of the shadows some evening and slit my then useless throat? Don't you see they have always been there . . . that they always will be. And that such a thing as my own death will be an advance? They who might kill me even . . . actually replenish all that I was.

BENEATHA. Oh, Asagai, I know all that.

ASAGAI. Good! Then stop moaning and groaning and tell me what you plan to do.

BENEATHA. Do?

ASAGAI. I have a bit of a suggestion.

BENEATHA. What?

ASAGAI [*rather quietly for him*]. That when it is all over—that you come home with me—

BENEATHA [*staring at him and crossing away with exasperation*]. Oh—Asagai—at this moment you decide to be romantic!

ASAGAI [*quickly understanding the misunderstanding*]. My dear, young creature of the New World—I do not mean across the city—I mean across the ocean: home—to Africa.

BENEATHA [*slowly understanding and turning to him with murmured amazement*]. To Africa?

ASAGAI. Yes! . . . [*Smiling and lifting his arms playfully*] Three hundred years later the African prince rose up out of the seas and swept the maiden back across the middle passage over which her ancestors had come—

BENEATHA [*unable to play*]. To—to Nigeria?

ASAGAI. Nigeria. Home. [*Coming to her with genuine romantic flippancy*] I will show you our mountains and our stars; and give you cool drinks from gourds and teach you the old songs and the ways of our people—and, in time, we will pretend that— [*Very softly*] —you have only been away for a day. Say that you'll come— [*He swings her around and takes her full in his arms in a kiss which proceeds to passion*]

BENEATHA [*pulling away suddenly*]. You're getting me all mixed up—

ASAGAI. Why?

BENEATHA. Too many things—too many things have happened today. I must sit down and think. I don't know what I feel about anything right this minute.

[*She promptly sits down and props her chin on her fist*]

ASAGAI [*charmed*]. All right, I shall leave you. No—don't get up. [*Touching her, gently, sweetly*] Just sit awhile and think . . . Never be afraid to sit awhile and think. [*He goes to door and looks at her*] How often I have looked at you and said, "Ah—so this is what the New World hath finally wrought . . ."

[*He exits. Beneatha sits on alone. Presently Walter enters from his room and starts to rummage through things, feverishly looking for something. She looks up and turns in her seat*]

BENEATHA [*hissingly*]. Yes—just look at what the New World hath wrought! . . . Just look! [*She gestures with bitter disgust*] There he is! *Monsieur le petit bour-*

geois noir—himself! There he is—Symbol of a Rising Class! Entrepreneur! Titan of the system! [*Walter ignores her completely and continues frantically and destructively looking for something and hurling things to floor and tearing things out of their place in his search. Beneatha ignores the eccentricity of his actions and goes on with the monologue of insult*] Did you dream of yachts on Lake Michigan, Brother? Did you see yourself on that Great Day sitting down at the Conference Table, surrounded by all the mighty baldheaded men in America? All halted, waiting, breathless, waiting for your pronouncements on industry? Waiting for you—Chairman of the Board! [*Walter finds what he is looking for—a small piece of white paper—and pushes it in his pocket and puts on his coat and rushes out without ever having looked at her. She shouts after him*] I look at you and I see the final triumph of stupidity in the world!

[*The door slams and she returns to just sitting again. Ruth comes quickly out of Mama's room*]

RUTH. Who was that?

BENEATHA. Your husband.

RUTH. Where did he go?

BENEATHA. Who knows—maybe he has an appointment at U.S. Steel.

RUTH [*anxiously, with frightened eyes*]. You didn't say nothing bad to him, did you?

BENEATHA. Bad? Say anything bad to him? No—I told him he was a sweet boy and full of dreams and everything is strictly peachy keen, as the ofay kids say!

[*Mama enters from her bedroom. She is lost, vague, trying to catch hold, to make some sense of her former command of the world, but it still eludes her. A sense of waste overwhelms her gait; a measure of apology rides on her shoulders. She goes to her plant, which has remained on the table, looks at it, picks it up and takes it to the window sill and sits it outside, and she stands and looks at it a long moment. Then she closes the window, straightens her body with effort and turns around to her children*]

MAMA. Well—ain't it a mess in here, though? [*A false cheerfulness, a beginning of something*] I guess we all better stop moping around and get some work done. All this unpacking and everything we got to do. [*Ruth raises her head slowly in response to the sense of the line; and Beneatha in similar manner turns very slowly to look at her mother*] One of you all better call the moving people and tell 'em not to come.

RUTH. Tell 'em not to come?

MAMA. Of course, baby. Ain't no need in 'em coming all the way here and having to go back. They charges for that too. [*She sits down, fingers to her brow, thinking*] Lord, ever since I was a little girl, I always remembers people saying, "Lena—Lena Eggleston, you aims too high all the time. You needs to slow down and see life a little more like it is. Just slow down some." That's what they always used to say down home—"Lord, that Lena Eggleston is a high-minded thing. She'll get her due one day!"

RUTH. No, Lena . . .

MAMA. Me and Big Walter just didn't never learn right.

RUTH. Lena, no! We gotta go. Bennie—tell her . . . [*She rises and crosses to Beneatha with her arms outstretched. Beneatha doesn't respond*] Tell her we can still move . . . the notes ain't but a hundred and twenty-five a month. We got four grown people in this house—we can work . . .

MAMA [*to herself*]. Just aimed too high all the time—

RUTH [*turning and going to Mama fast—the words pouring out with urgency and desperation*]. Lena—I'll work . . . I'll work twenty hours a day in all the kitchens in Chicago . . . I'll strap my baby on my back if I have to and scrub all the floors in America and wash all the sheets in America if I have to—but we got to MOVE! We got to get OUT OF HERE!!

[*Mama reaches out absently and pats Ruth's hand*]

MAMA. No—I sees things differently now. Been thinking 'bout some of the things we could do to fix this place up some. I seen a second-hand bureau over on Maxwell Street just the other day that could fit right there. [*She points to where the new furniture might go. Ruth wanders away from her*]. Would need some new handles on it and then a little varnish and it look like something brand-new. And—we can put up them new curtains in the kitchen . . . Why this place be looking fine. Cheer us all up so that we forget trouble ever come . . . [*To Ruth*] And you could get some nice screens to put up in your room round the baby's bassinet . . . [*She looks at both of them, pleadingly*] Sometimes you just got to know when to give up some things . . . and hold on to what you got . . .

[*Walter enters from the outside, looking spent and leaning against the door, his coat hanging from him*]

MAMA. Where you been, son?

WALTER [*breathing hard*]. Made a call.

MAMA. To who, son?

WALTER. To The Man. [*He heads for his room*]

MAMA. What man, baby?

WALTER [*stops in the door*]. The Man, Mama. Don't you know who The Man is?

RUTH. Walter Lee?

WALTER *The Man*. Like the guys in the streets say—The Man. Captain Boss—Mistuh Charley . . . Old Cap'n Please Mr. Bossman . . .

BENEATHA [*suddenly*]. Lindner!

WALTER. That's right! That's good. I told him to come right over.

BENEATHA [*fiercely, understanding*]. For what? What do you want to see him for!

WALTER [*looking at his sister*]. We going to do business with him.

MAMA. What you talking 'bout son?

WALTER. Talking 'bout life, Mama. You all always telling me to see life like it is. Well—I laid in there on my back today . . . and I figured it out. Life just like it is. Who gets and who don't get. [*He sits down with his coat on and laughs*] Mama, you know it's all divided up. Life is. Sure enough. Between the takers and the "tooken." [*He laughs*] I've figured it out finally. [*He looks around at them.*] Yeah. Some of us always getting "tooken." [*He laughs*] People like Willy Harris, they don't never get "tooken." And you know why the rest of us do? 'Cause we all mixed up. Mixed up bad. We get to looking 'round for the right and the wrong; and we worry about it and cry about it and stay up nights trying to figure out 'bout the wrong and the right of things all the time . . . And all the time, man, them takers is out there operating, just taking and taking. Willy Harris? Shoot—Willy Harris don't even count. He don't even count in the big scheme of things. But I'll say one thing for old Willy Harris . . . he's taught me something. He's taught me to keep my eye on what counts in this world. Yeah— [*Shouting out a little*] Thanks, Willy!

RUTH. What did you call that man for, Walter Lee?

WALTER. Called him to tell him to come over to the show. Gonna put on a show for the man. Just what he wants to see. You see, Mama, the man came here today and he told us that them people out there where you want us to move—well they so upset they willing to pay us *not* to move! [*Ha laughs again*] And—and oh, Mama—you would of been proud of the way me and Ruth and Bennie acted. We told him to get out . . . Lord have mercy! We told the man to get out! Oh, we was some proud folks this afternoon, yeah. [*He lights a cigarette*] We were still full of that old-time stuff . . .

RUTH [*coming toward him slowly*]. You talking 'bout taking them people's money to keep us from moving in that house?

WALTER. I ain't just talking 'bout it, baby—I'm telling you that's what's going to happen!

BENEATHA. Oh, God! Where is the bottom! Where is the real honest-to-God bottom so he can't go any farther!

WALTER. See—that's the old stuff. You and that boy that was here today. You all want everybody to carry a flag and a spear and sing some marching songs, huh? You wanna spend your life looking into things and trying to find the right and the wrong part, huh? Yeah. You know what's going to happen to that boy someday—he'll find himself sitting in a dungeon, locked in forever—and the takers will have the key! Forget it, baby! There ain't no causes—there ain't nothing but taking in this world, and he who takes most is smartest—and it don't make a damn bit of difference *how*.

MAMA. You making something inside me cry, son. Some awful pain inside me.

WALTER. Don't cry, Mama. Understand. That white man is going to walk in that door able to write checks for more money than we ever had. It's important to him and I'm going to help him . . . I'm going to put on the show, Mama.

MAMA. Son—I come from five generations of people who was slaves and sharecroppers—but ain't nobody in my family never let nobody pay 'em no money that was a way of telling us we wasn't fit to walk the earth. We ain't never been that poor. [*Raising her eyes and looking at him*] We ain't never been that—dead inside.

BENEATHA. Well—we are dead now. All the talk about dreams and sunlight that goes on in this house. It's all dead now.

WALTER. What's the matter with you all! I didn't make this world! It was give to me this way! Hell, yes, I want me some yachts someday! Yes, I want to hang some real pearls 'round my wife's neck. Ain't she supposed to wear no pearls? Somebody tell me—tell me, who decides which women is suppose to wear pearls in this world. I tell you I am a *man*—and I think my wife should wear some pearls in this world!

[*This last line hangs a good while and Walter begins to move about the room. The word "Man" has penetrated his consciousness; he mumbles it to himself repeatedly between strange agitated pauses as he moves about*]

MAMA. Baby, how you going to feel on the inside?

WALTER. Fine! . . . Going to feel fine . . . a man . . .

MAMA. You won't have nothing left then, Walter Lee.

WALTER [*coming to her*]. I'm going to feel fine, Mama. I'm going to look that son-of-a-bitch in the eyes and say— [*He falters*] —and say, "All right, Mr. Lindner— [*He falters even more*] —that's *your* neighborhood out there! You got the right to keep it like you want! You got the right to have it like you want! Just write the check and—the house is yours." And—and I am going to say— [*His voice almost breaks*] "And you—you people just put the money in my hand and you won't have to live next to this bunch of stinking niggers! . . ." [*He straightens up and moves away from his mother, walking around the room*] And maybe—maybe I'll just get down on my black knees . . . [*He does so; Ruth and Bennie and Mama watch him in frozen horror*] "Captain, Mistuh, Bossman— [*Groveling and grinning and wringing his hands in profoundly anguished imitation of the slow-witted movie stereotype*] A-hee-hee-hee! Oh, yassuh boss! Yasssssuh! Great white— [*Voice breaking, he forces himself to go on*] —Father, just gi' ussen de money, fo' God's sake, and we's—we's ain't gwine come out deh and dirty up yo' white folks neighborhood . . ." [*He breaks down completely*] And I'll feel fine! Fine! FINE! [*He gets up and goes into the bedroom*]

BENEATHA. That is not a man. That is nothing but a toothless rat.

MAMA. Yes—death done come in this here house. [*She is nodding, slowly, reflectively*] Done come walking in my house on the lips of my children. You what supposed to be my beginning again. You—what supposed to be my harvest. [*To Beneatha*] You—you mourning your brother?

BENEATHA. He's no brother of mine.

MAMA. What you say?

BENEATHA. I said that that individual in that room is no brother of mine.

MAMA. That's what I thought you said. You feeling like you better than he is today? [*Beneatha does not answer*] Yes? What you tell him a minute ago? That he wasn't a man? Yes? You give him up for me? You done wrote his epitaph too—like the rest of the world? Well, who give you the privilege?

BENEATHA. Be on my side for once! You saw what he just did, Mama! You saw him—down on his knees. Wasn't it you who taught me to despise any man who would do that? Do what he's going to do?

MAMA. Yes—I taught you that. Me and your daddy. But I thought I taught you something else too . . . I thought I taught you to love him.

BENEATHA. Love him? There is nothing left to love.

MAMA. There is *always* something left to love. And if you ain't learned that, you ain't learned nothing. [*Looking at her*] Have you cried for that boy today? I don't mean for yourself and for the family 'cause we lost the money. I mean for him: what he been through and what it done to him. Child, when do you think is the time to love somebody the most? When they done good and made things easy for everybody? Well then, you ain't through learning—because that ain't the time at all. It's when he's at his lowest and can't believe in hisself 'cause the world done whipped him so! When you starts measuring somebody, measure him right, child, measure him right. Make sure you done taken into account what hills and valleys he come through before he got to wherever he is.

[*Travis bursts into the room at the end of the speech, leaving the door open*]

TRAVIS. Grandmama—the moving men are downstairs! The truck just pulled up.

MAMA [*turning and looking at him*]. Are they, baby? They downstairs?

[*She sighs and sits. Lindner appears in the doorway. He peers in and knocks lightly, to gain attention, and comes in. All turn to look at him*]

LINDNER [*hat and briefcase in hand*]. Uh—hello . . .

[*Ruth crosses mechanically to the bedroom door and opens it and lets it swing open freely and slowly as the lights come up on Walter within, still in his coat, sitting at the far corner of the room. He looks up and out through the room to Lindner*]

RUTH. He's here.

[*A long minute passes and Walter slowly gets up*]

LINDNER [*coming to the table with efficiency, putting his briefcase on the table and starting to unfold papers and unscrew fountain pens*]. Well, I certainly was glad to hear from you people. [*Walter has begun the trek out of the room, slowly and awkwardly, rather like a small boy, passing the back of his sleeve across his mouth from time to time*] Life can really be so much simpler than people let it be most of the time. Well—with whom do I negotiate? You, Mrs. Younger, or your son here? [*Mama sits with her hands folded on her lap and her eyes closed as Walter advances. Travis goes closer to Lindner and looks at the papers curiously*] Just some official papers, sonny.

RUTH. Travis, you go downstairs—

MAMA [*opening her eyes and looking into Walter's*]. No. Travis, you stay right here. And you make him understand what you doing, Walter Lee. You teach him good. Like Willy Harris taught you. You show where our five generations done come to. [*Walter looks from her to the boy, who grins at him innocently*] Go ahead, son— [*She folds her hands and closes her eyes*] Go ahead.

WALTER [*at last crosses to Lindner, who is reviewing the contract*]. Well, Mr. Lindner. [*Beneatha turns away*] We called you— [*There is a profound, simple groping quality in his speech*] —because, well, me and my family [*He looks around and shifts from one foot to the other*] Well—we are very plain people . . .

LINDNER. Yes—

WALTER. I mean—I have worked as a chauffeur most of my life—and my wife here, she does domestic work in people's kitchens. So does my mother. I mean—we are plain people . . .

LINDNER. Yes, Mr. Younger—

WALTER [*really like a small boy, looking down at his shoes and then up at the man*]. And—uh—well, my father, well, he was a laborer most of his life. . . .

LINDNER [*absolutely confused*]. Uh, yes—yes, I understand. [*He turns back to the contract*].

WALTER [*a beat; staring at him*]. And my father— [*With sudden intensity*] My father almost *beat a man to death* once because this man called him a bad name or something, you know what I mean?

LINDNER [*looking up, frozen*]. No, no, I'm afraid I don't—

WALTER [*a beat. The tension hangs; then Walter steps back from it*]. Yeah. Well—what I mean is that we come from people who had a lot of *pride*. I mean—we are very proud people. And that's my sister over there and she's going to be a doctor—and we are very proud—

LINDNER. Well—I am sure that is very nice, but—

WALTER. What I am telling you is that we called you over here to tell you that we are very proud and that this— [*Signaling to Travis*]. Travis, come here. [*Travis crosses and Walter draws him before him facing the man*] This is my son, and he makes the sixth generation our family in this country. And we have all thought about your offer—

LINDNER. Well, good . . . good—

WALTER. And we have decided to move into our house because my father—my father—he earned it for us brick by brick. [*Mama has her eyes closed and is rocking back and forth as though she were in church, with* her head nodding the Amen yes] We don't want to make no trouble for nobody or fight no causes, and we will try to be good neighbors. And that's *all* we got to say about that. [*He looks the man absolutely in the eyes*] We don't want your money. [*He turns and walks away*]

LINDNER [*looking around at all of them*]. I take it then— that you have decided to occupy . . .

BENEATHA. That's what the man said.

LINDNER [*to Mama in her reverie*]. Then I would like to appeal to you, Mrs. Younger. You are older and wiser and understand things better, I am sure . . .

MAMA. I am afraid you don't understand. My son said we was going to move and there ain't nothing left for me to say. [*Briskly*] You know how these young folks is nowadays, mister. Can't do a thing with 'em! [*As he opens his mouth, she rises*] Good-bye.

LINDNER [*folding up his materials*]. Well—if you are that final about it . . . there is nothing left for me to say. [*He finishes, almost ignored by the family, who are concentrating on Walter Lee. At the door Lindner halts and looks around*] I sure hope you people know what you're getting into.

[*He shakes his head and exits*]

RUTH [*looking around and coming to life*]. Well, for God's sake—if the moving men are here—LET'S GET THE HELL OUT OF HERE!

MAMA [*into action*]. Ain't it the truth! Look at all this here mess. Ruth, put Travis' good jacket on him . . . Walter Lee, fix your tie and tuck your shirt in, you look like somebody's hoodlum! Lord have mercy, where is my plant? [*She flies to get it amid the general bustling of the family, who are deliberately trying to ignore the nobility of the past moment*] You all start on down . . . Travis child, don't go empty-handed . . . Ruth, where did I put that box with my skillets in it? I want to be in charge of it myself . . . I'm going to make us the biggest dinner we ever ate tonight . . . Beneatha, what's the matter with them stockings? Pull them things up, girl . . .

[*The family starts to file out as two moving men appear and begin to carry out the heavier pieces of furniture, bumping into the family as they move about*]

BENEATHA. Mama, Asagai asked me to marry him today and go to Africa—

MAMA [*in the middle of her getting-ready activity*]. He did? You ain't old enough to marry nobody— [*Seeing the moving men lifting one of her chairs precariously*] Darling, that ain't no bale of cotton, please handle it

so we can sit in it again! I had that chair twenty-five years . . .

[*The movers sigh with exasperation and go on with their work*]

BENEATHA [*girlishly and unreasonably trying to pursue the conversation*]. To go to Africa, Mama—be a doctor in Africa . . .

MAMA [*distracted*]. Yes, baby—

WALTER. *Africa!* What he want you to go to Africa for?

BENEATHA. To practice there . . .

WALTER. Girl, if you don't get all them silly ideas out your head! You better marry yourself a man with some loot . . .

BENEATHA [*angrily, precisely as in the first scene of the play*]. What have you got to do with who I marry!

WALTER. Plenty. Now I think George Murchison—

BENEATHA. *George Murchison!* I wouldn't marry him if he was Adam and I was Eve!

[*Walter and Beneatha go out yelling at each other vigorously and the anger is loud and real till their voices diminish. Ruth stands at the door and turns to Mama and smiles knowingly*]

MAMA [*fixing her hat at last*]. Yeah—they something all right, my children . . .

RUTH. Yeah—they're something. Let's go, Lena.

MAMA [*stalling, starting to look around at the house*]. Yes—I'm coming. Ruth—

RUTH. Yes?

MAMA [*quietly, woman to woman*]. He finally come into his manhood today, didn't he? Kind of like a rainbow after the rain . . .

RUTH [*biting her lip lest her own pride explode in front of Mama*]. Yes, Lena.

[*Walter's voice calls for them raucously*]

WALTER [*off stage*]. Y'all come on! These people charges by the hour, you know!

MAMA [*waving Ruth out vaguely*]. All right, honey—go on down. I be down directly.

[*Ruth hesitates, then exits. Mama stands, at last alone in the living room, her plant on the table before her as the lights start to come down. She looks around at all the walls and ceilings and suddenly, despite herself, while the children call below, a great heaving thing rises in her and she puts her fist to her mouth to stifle it, takes a final desperate look, pulls her coat about her, pats her hat and goes out. The lights dim down. The door opens and she comes back in, grabs her plant, and goes out for the last time*]

CURTAIN

ESSAY: AN APPROACH TO THE PLAY

In our Introduction, we provided an extended analysis of the exchange between Travis and Ruth at breakfast, an episode which provides something of an overture to many of the themes taken up in the rest of the play. This discussion about money between a mother and son anticipates the disagreement between Mama and Walter Lee—the two main characters in the play—over how to spend Big Walter's insurance money. Travis can think only of avoiding the embarrassment of showing up without the expected money, perhaps the embarrassment of seeming poor, while Ruth can think only of the limitations imposed by their economic condition, a condition that will be worsened further by the arrival of the child that only she knows she is bearing. The disagreement over money implies a difference of values.

The symbolic aspect of money, its ability to represent values, is front and center in *A Raisin in the Sun*. Money is a token of the value of human labor and of the value of goods, and it is also the means by which we exchange one for the other. In this play, because the money comes from an insurance policy, what is traded is, in a sense, a life. What is the family going to exchange Big Walter's life for? What value will it have had? His widow and his son have differing ideas about this, although their central instinct is probably similar: both want to trade it for dignity. For Lena this means security: an escape for the family from its inadequate housing and the chance for Lena finally to have a garden. For Walter it means respect: having power, prestige, admiration. Each of them sees his or her idea of this exchange as what Big Walter would have wanted his money—his life—to buy for his family.

Mama is a character who is simultaneously domineering yet loving and supportive. She intrudes into the life of her children more than seems welcome, and when she decides to use the insurance money to make a down payment on a house, her distraught son says: "*You* the head of the family. You run our lives like you want to. . . . So you butchered up a dream of mine—you—who always taking 'bout your children's dreams." And yet, throughout the play, she is associated with, indeed associates herself with, the plant, which, she says, expresses her. It substitutes for the garden that she has always wished for and implies her need to maintain roots, as well as her desire to nourish her family and help it grow

If Lena is rooted in the past and its traditions, her children seem to hold out hopes for a radically different future. Walter is filled with a restlessness that needs definition, a desire for success that seems to seek a shortcut around education and talent. Putting aside these personal limitations, however, his goals seem to be "normal" in our culture, a version of the American Dream, and he has moments of nobility, symbolically when he adopts the spirit of the African warrior and climactically when he "comes into his manhood" at the end of the play. Beneatha, on the other hand, is filled with idealism, a desire for an interesting and fulfilling life, and she rejects many of her mother's traditional values. She has decided to delay marriage in her commitment to becoming a doctor, and she has entertained a variety of avenues to what she calls self-expression, such as horseback riding, acting, and guitar playing. Her testing out of the possibilities of atheism, however, pushes her mother beyond limits and leads to the imposition by force of respect for Lena's traditional Christianity, as she compels Beneatha to affirm that "There is a God in my mother's house."

In addition, Beneatha functions particularly to probe areas of social concern such as women's rights, and she seeks her identity by exploring the West African origins of the African-American experience. The two men who show a romantic interest in Bennie, the Nigerian Asagai and George Murchison, seem to be thematically opposed: African roots versus the bourgeois assimilation of dominant American cultural values. Asagai translates Alaiyo, his Yoruba name for Beneatha, as "one for whom Bread—Food—Is not Enough," a name which implies the rejection of simple, unthinking materialistic values of the type that George seems to represent and wants her to represent. Through Asagai, Africa is presented as a place of nobility and vision, a place, like a family packing up to move, "full of the flow of life, do you understand? Movement, progress."

And yet, would Beneatha be happy married to either of these men? George seems both threatened and bored by her intelligence. He wants "a nice—simple—sophisticated girl . . . not a poet." Beneatha is attractive, and he seems primarily interested in her as a personal adornment, telling her: "I don't go out with you to discuss the nature of 'quiet desperation' or to hear all about your thoughts." One also wonders, however, whether she could ever be happy as Mrs. Asagai, given his occasionally patronizing attitude toward "the most serious little thing I ever saw." When she suggests that there are alternative possibilities in male–female relationships beyond the sexual, he responds, "For a woman it should be enough," and he dismisses American women's talk of liberation as evidence that they are not liberated at all.

One final point that should be confronted is what might be termed the comic trajectory of its plot. The general movement of the plot of *A Raisin in the Sun* is toward apparent disaster and then back up to a happy resolution. In the play's closing scenes, Lena learns to give up some of her control, especially to Walter Lee in calling on him to act as head of the family; Ruth decides against having an abortion; she and Walter begin to reestablish tenderness and gentleness in their marriage and to "talk softness to each other"; Beneatha seems to come to peace with living as part of her family; and Walter stands up for principle, refuses to be bought out by the white property owners of Clybourne Park, and so regains the dignity he had earlier lost (or perhaps gains the dignity he had never had).

Some readers, however, are troubled by the suddenness of what seems to be a mass conversion. (Some have called it a black soap opera.) Walter's behavior in particular seems to raise questions about consistency of characterization. Entrusted with the money that symbolizes his father's life, Walter gives it all, including the amount that was earmarked to send his sister to medical school, to an unscrupulous acquaintance with whom he had hoped to buy a liquor store. Even if he had not been duped by his "business" partner, he seems at best an insensitive boor for being willing to violate his mother's traditional morality by spending money which she regarded as sacred on a store that would, from her point of view, exploit the weakness of others—and to speed up the licensing process by using part of the money for bribery. In doing so, in giving away Beneatha's portion of the money, and in then deciding to accept the offer of the Clybourne Park Improvement Association to buy the house at a profit, he sacrifices all dignity, all self-esteem. His sudden change of character in the play's final scene raises dramatic questions: Is it adequately prepared for? Is it consistent with the way his character has been presented previously? Can we believe that this moment marks a permanent change in his behavior?

There may be another way of thinking about this change, however. When Walter stands up to the representative of the white community and speaks of his family's six generations in America, it may be that he becomes an important black role model. In him we see the emergence of pride in the black community's distinctive heritage in the world and in its distinctive experience in America—what it has suffered, endured, and overcome. It has been argued that such pride is a primary, if not the only, foundation on which the black community can build its future. It is provoked by the white community's failure, or inability, to understand the profundity or even the distinctiveness of this experience. Although Walter's turning point may seem sudden, from this point of view it is clearly prepared for in the scene. When Mama insists that Travis witness his exchange with Lindner, so that Walter can "teach him good," Walter begins slowly, as we might expect of this character. Shifting from one foot to the other, he is, as the stage direction says, "like a small boy, looking down at his shoes and then up at the man." But when he tries to explain about his father's life of labor—about an important part of the heritage of his family—Lindner is confused. He just wants the contract signed and seems embarrassed by the discussion. "Uh, yes—yes, I understand," he says in a way that suggests that he absolutely does not, and it is at this point, at the point of the white representative's failure, that Walter emerges into an assertion of his pride in his heritage. He changes from acting like a boy to acting like a father, and in this role he begins to teach his son, his family's next—its sixth— generation, "good."

This is a play that has been loved by white audiences, for whom the Younger family's ideals often seem comfortable and familiar: professional education or business success for the children and home ownership in a white neighborhood for the family. Its apparent underlying reassurance that all people are the same under the skin, that all want—and can achieve—what the dominant culture wants, may provide a comforting alternative to the reality of social injustice. But when we consider the nature of Walter's pride, we may be asked to recognize that even where his and his family's goals are like those of the white community, the two groups are coming from very different places in their attempts to "get there."

If, in addition, we recall the specific historical moment in which *A Raisin in the Sun* was written, our sense of this crucial difference and of the need for such role models may be reinforced. This play was written on the eve of the 1960s, when dramatic changes were occurring in the legal rights of America's racial minorities. From this point of view, perhaps the most interesting aspect of the play is its title. It is more than thirty years since the play was written, and housing in our nation's cities is still by and large segregated by race. Poverty continues to be greater and opportunities for challenging work less for nonwhites than for whites. If anything, hope for positive change seems to have been higher in 1959 than it is today. Perhaps this play now forces us to ask Langston Hughes' question with renewed urgency: What *does* happen to a dream deferred?

THE LATER TWENTIETH CENTURY

Derek Walcott

PANTOMIME

About the Author   Derek Walcott (1932–   ) received the Nobel Prize for literature in 1993, particularly for his poetic evocations of the richness of Caribbean cultural traditions and their relationship to contemporary life. His book-length epic poem *Omeros* has been especially praised.

Born in Castries on the Caribbean island of St. Lucia, Walcott took his university degree at the University of the West Indies in Jamaica in 1959; later in the same year he moved to the island of Trinidad and founded the Trinidad Theater Workshop, in which he served as director. Among his many other awards are a 1972 Obie for the play *Dream on Monkey Mountain* and a 1981 MacArthur Foundation "Genius Award." In the United States his plays have been produced by the Negro Ensemble Company, the New York Shakespeare Festival, and the Yale Repertory Theater. Having taught at Columbia, Rutgers, and New York University, Walcott is now a professor at Boston University.

About the Play   First produced in Port of Spain, Trinidad, in 1978, *Pantomime* is, like many of the plays of the ancient Greek tragedian Aeschylus and the modern South African Athol Fugard, simplified to two characters. This focus allows the play to explore an unusually rich and complex variety of perceptions from many different vantage points. Uniting several of these perceptions is the play's insistence that things are not what they seem, that we cannot trust appearances. As part of this presentation, the color of a character's skin does not reveal to us the character's thoughts, feelings, ways of coping with experience, or even social status. Differences between appearance and reality are revealed often and unexpectedly—even through a corrupted pre-colonial parrot.

Much of *Pantomime's* complexity also comes from its metadramatic qualities. The plot of this play concerns the making of another play, one adapted from Daniel DeFoe's novel *Robinson Crusoe*. There, as told from the colonialist point of view, the white master finds and befriends (and names and enslaves) the black man Friday, while the two characters who make this play-within-the-play are a white foreign owner/boss and a black native servant. These two men, however, are equals in sophistication and they are equals professionally, both having been actors in their earlier days. As the play is staged, important inversions occur. The servant Jackson appropriates the power to name when he becomes Robinson Crusoe, changing Friday's name to Thursday. In various ways, he reflects the need of any independent person to make his life for himself, on his own terms, but he also reveals the special problem faced by the postcolonial black person who needs to be independent and self-governing, but who is so steeped in the tradition of the old imperialist culture that his new identity must play against the old, rather than being entirely separate from and independent of it. He is new and not-new at the same time. Indeed, as the characters make clear late in the play, they are both aware that their enactment of *Robinson Crusoe* is also their *re*enactment of the history of race relations in the islands, and possibly in the world, even while it explores the possibility for change.

The play's metadramatic complexity begins immediately: as *Pantomime* opens the white boss Harry is rehearsing an improvised script which he himself has invented, and the black servant Jackson enters with Harry's breakfast. Even in this simple and "normal" act, however, he, too, seems to be an actor, speaking first in an English accent, then in a Creole accent, directing these two first lines to his one-man audience. When Harry does not answer, Jackson speaks to himself in yet another dialect. We do not know which of these voices, if any, is truly Jackson's, and throughout the play it is difficult to know what is pretense with Jackson Phillip and what is "true." This is also the case with Harry "Trewe." Both of these characters seem to do a lot of acting—both in *Robinson Crusoe* and in "real life" with each other—trying on pose after pose, improvising their lives just as they do the little entertainment they plan for the tourists. Very early on, indeed, Harry begins to call Jackson by his entertainment name, Friday. It is hard to separate the characters from the roles they assume in their little entertainment. *Robinson Crusoe* becomes a commentary on the larger play *Pantomime* which contains it, and on our world outside the theater as well. For where *can* we look for that which is *not* pretense? Where shall we look for that which is true? In a world full of pretense and slogans and "photo-ops," who or what can we trust?

CHARACTERS

HARRY TREWE, English, mid-forties, owner of the Castaways Guest House, retired actor

JACKSON PHILLIP, Trinidadian, forty, his factotum, retired calypsonian

The action takes place in a gazebo on the edge of a cliff, part of a guest house on the island of Tobago, West Indies.

Act I

A small summerhouse or gazebo, painted white, with a few plants and a table set for breakfast. Harry Trewe enters—in white, carrying a tape recorder which he rests on the table. He starts the machine.
HARRY. [*Sings and dances*].

It's our Christmas panto,
it's called: Robinson Crusoe.
We're awfully glad that you've shown up,
it's for kiddies as well as for grown-ups.
Our purpose is to please:
so now with our magic wand . . .

[*Dissatisfied with the routine, he switches off the machine. Rehearses his dance. Then presses the machine again*]

Just picture a lonely island
and a beach with its golden sand.
There walks a single man
in the beautiful West Indies!

[*He turns off the machine. Stands, staring out to sea. Then exits with the tape recorder. Stage empty for a few beats, then Jackson, in an open, white waiter's jacket and black trousers, but barefoot, enters with a breakfast tray. He puts the tray down, looks around*]

JACKSON. Mr. Trewe? [*English accent*] Mr. Trewe, your scramble eggs is here! *are* here! [*Creole accent*] You hear, Mr. Trewe? I here wid your eggs! [*English accent*] Are you in there? [*To himself*] And when his eggs get cold, is I to catch. [*He fans the eggs with one hand*]. What the hell I doing? That ain't go heat them. It go make them more cold. Well, he must be leap off the ledge. At long last. Well, if he ain't dead, he could call.

[*He exits with tray. Stage bare. Harry returns, carrying a hat made of goatskin and a goatskin parasol. He puts on the hat, shoulders the parasol, and circles the table. Then he recoils, looking down at the floor*]

HARRY. [*Sings and dances*]

Is this the footprint of a naked man,
or is it the naked footprint of a man,
that startles me this morning on this bright and golden
  sand.

[*To audience*]

There's no one here but I,
  just the sea and lonely sky . . .

[*Pauses*]

Yes . . . and how the hell did it go on?

[*Jackson enters, without the tray. Studies Harry*]

JACKSON. Morning, Mr. Trewe. Your breakfast ready
HARRY. So how're you this morning, Jackson?
JACKSON. Oh, fair to fine, with seas moderate, with
  waves three to four feet in open water, and you, sir?
HARRY. Overcast with sunny periods, with the possi-
  bility of heavy showers by mid-afternoon, I'd say,
  Jackson.
JACKSON. Heavy showers, Mr. Trewe?
HARRY. Heavy showers. I'm so bloody bored I could
  burst into tears.
JACKSON. I bringing in breakfast.
HARRY. You do that, Friday.
JACKSON. Friday? It ain't go keep.
HARRY. [*Gesturing*] Friday, you, bring Crusoe, me,
  breakfast now. Crusoe hungry.
JACKSON. Mr. Trewe, you come back with that same
  rake again? I tell you, I ain't no actor, and I ain't
  walking in front a set of tourists naked playing can-
  nibal. Carnival, but not cannibal.
HARRY. What tourists? We're closed for repairs. We're
  the only ones in the guest house. Apart from the
  carpenter, if he ever shows up.
JACKSON. Well, you ain't seeing him today, because
  he was out on a heavy lime last night . . . Saturday,
  you know? And with the peanuts you does pay him
  for overtime.
HARRY. All right, then. It's goodbye!

[*He climbs onto the ledge between the uprights, teetering,
walking slowly*]

JACKSON. Get off that ledge, Mr. Trewe! Is a straight
  drop to them rocks!

[*Harry kneels, arms extended, Jolson-style*]

HARRY. Hold on below there, sonny boooy! Daddy's
  a-coming. Your papa's a coming, Sonnnnneee
  Boooooooy! [*To Jackson*] You're watching the great
  Harry Trewe and his high-wire act.
JACKSON. You watching Jackson Phillip and his disap-
  pearing act.

[*Turning to leave*]

HARRY. [*Jumping down*] I'm not a suicide, Jackson. It's
  a good act, but you never read the reviews. It would
  be too exasperating, anyway.
JACKSON. What, sir?
HARRY. Attempted suicide in a Third World country.
  You can't leave a note because the pencils break,
  you can't cut your wrist with the local blades . . .
JACKSON. We trying we best, sir, since all you gone.
HARRY. Doesn't matter if we're a minority group. Sui-
  cides are taxpayers, too, you know. Jackson.
JACKSON. Except it ain't going be suicide. They go
  say I push you. So, now the fun and dance done, sir,
  breakfast now?
HARRY. I'm rotting from insomnia, Jackson. I've been
  up since three, hearing imaginary guests arriving in
  the rooms, and I haven't slept since. I nearly came
  around the back to have a little talk. I started thinking about the same bloody problem, which is, What
  entertainment can we give the guests?
JACKSON. They ain't guests, Mr. Trewe. They's casu-
  alties.
HARRY. How do you mean?
JACKSON. This hotel like a hospital. The toilet catch
  asthma, the air-condition got ague, the front-
  balcony rail missing four teet', and every minute the
  fridge like it dancing the Shango . . . brrgudup . . .
  jukjuk . . . brrugudup. Is no wonder that the carpenter collapse. Termites jumping like steel band in
  the foundations.
HARRY. For fifty dollars a day they want Acapulco?
JACKSON. Try giving them the basics: Food. Water.
  Shelter. They ain't shipwrecked, they pay in advance
  for their vacation.
HARRY. Very funny. But the ad says, "Tours" and
  "Nightly Entertainment." Well, Christ, after they've
  seen the molting parrot in the lobby and the faded
  sea fans, they'll be pretty livid if there's no "nightly
  entertainment," and so would you, right? So, Mr.
  Jackson, it's your neck and mine. We open next
  Friday.
JACKSON. Breakfast, sir. Or else is overtime.

HARRY. I kept thinking about this panto I co-authored, man. *Robinson Crusoe*, and I picked up this old script. I can bring it all down to your level, with just two characters. Crusoe, Man Friday, maybe even the parrot, if that horny old bugger will remember his lines . . .

JACKSON. Since we on the subject, Mr. Trewe, I am compelled to report that parrot again.

HARRY. No, not again, Jackson?

JACKSON. Yes.

HARRY. [*Imitating parrot*] Heinegger, Heinegger. [*In his own voice*] Correct?

JACKSON. Wait, wait! I know your explanation: that a old German called Herr Heinegger used to own this place, and that when that maquereau of a macaw keep cracking: "Heinegger, Heinegger," he remembering the Nazi and not heckling me, but it playing a little havoc with me nerves. This is my fifth report. I am marking them down. Language is ideas, Mr. Trewe. And I think that this pre-colonial parrot have the wrong idea.

HARRY. It's his accent, Jackson. He's a Creole parrot. What can I do?

JACKSON. Well, I am not saying not to give the bird a fair trial, but I see nothing wrong in taking him out the cage at dawn, blindfolding the bitch, giving him a last cigarette if he want it, lining him up against the garden wall, and perforating his arse by firing squad.

HARRY. The war's over, Jackson! And how can a bloody parrot be prejudiced?

JACKSON. The same damn way they corrupt a child. By their upbringing. That parrot survive from a pre-colonial epoch, Mr. Trewe, and if it want to last in Trinidad and Tobago, then it go have to adjust.

[*Long pause*]

HARRY. [*Leaping up*] Do you think we could work him into the panto? Give him something to do? Crusoe had a parrot, didn't he? You're right, Jackson, let's drop him from the show.

JACKSON. Mr. Trewe, you are a truly, truly stubborn man. I am *not* putting that old goatskin hat on my head and making an ass of myself for a million dollars, and I have said so already.

HARRY. You got it wrong. I put the hat on, I'm . . . Wait, wait a minute. *Cut! Cut!* You know what would be a heavy twist, heavy with irony?

JACKSON. What, Mr. Trewe?

HARRY. We reverse it.

[*Pause*]

JACKSON. You mean you prepared to walk round naked as your mother make you, in your jockstrap, playing a white cannibal in front of your own people? You're a real actor! And you got balls, too, excuse me, Mr. Trewe, to even consider doing a thing like that! Good. Joke finish. Breakfast now, eh? Because I ha' to fix the sun deck since the carpenter ain't reach.

HARRY. All right, breakfast. Just heat it a little.

JACKSON. Right, sir. The coffee must be warm still. But I best do some brand-new scramble eggs.

HARRY. Never mind the eggs, then. Slip in some toast, butter, and jam.

JACKSON. How long you in this hotel business, sir? No butter. Marge. No sugar. Big strike. Island-wide shortage. We down to half a bag.

HARRY. Don't forget I've heard you sing calypsos, Jackson. Right back there in the kitchen.

JACKSON. Mr. Trewe, every day I keep begging you to stop trying to make a entertainer out of me. I finish with show business. I finish with Trinidad. I come to Tobago for peace and quiet. I quite satisfy. If you ain't want me to resign, best drop the topic.

[*Exits. Harry sits at the table, staring out to sea. He is reciting softly to himself, then more audibly*]

HARRY.

> "Alone, alone, all all alone,
> Alone on a wide wide sea . . .
> I bit my arm, I sucked the blood,
> And cried, A sail! a sail!"

[*He removes the hat, then his shirt, rolls up his trousers, removes them, puts them back on, removes them again*]

Mastah . . . Mastah . . . Friday sorry. Friday never do it again. Master.

[*Jackson enters with breakfast tray, groans, turns to leave. Returns*].

JACKSON. Mr. Trewe, what it is going on on this blessed Sunday morning, if I may ask?

HARRY. I was feeling what it was like to be Friday.

JACKSON. Well, Mr. Trewe, you ain't mind putting back on your pants?

HARRY. Why can't I eat breakfast like this?

JACKSON. Because I am here. I happen to be here. I am the one serving you, Mr. Trewe.

HARRY. There's nobody here.

JACKSON. Mr. Harry, you putting on back your pants?

HARRY. You're frightened of something?

JACKSON. You putting on back your pants?

HARRY. What're you afraid of? Think I'm bent? That's such a corny interpretation of the Crusoe-Friday relationship, boy. My son's been dead three years, Jackson, and I'vn't had much interest in women since, but I haven't gone queer, either. And to be a flasher, you need an audience.

JACKSON. Mr. Trewe, I am trying to explain that I myself feel like a ass holding this tray in my hand while you standing up there naked, and that if anybody should happen to pass, my name is immediately mud. So, when you put back on your pants, I will serve your breakfast.

HARRY. Actors do this sort of thing. I'm getting into a part.

JACKSON. Don't bother getting into the part, get into the pants. Please.

HARRY. Why? You've got me worried now, Jackson.

JACKSON. [Exploding] *Put on your blasted pants, man! You like a blasted child, you know!*

[Silence, Harry puts on his pants]

HARRY. Shirt, too? [*Jackson sucks his teeth*] There. [*Harry puts on his shirt*] You people are such prudes, you know that? What's it in you, Jackson, that gets so Victorian about a man in his own hotel deciding to have breakfast in his own underwear, on a totally deserted Sunday morning?

JACKSON. Manners, sir. Manners.

[*He puts down the tray*]

HARRY. Sit.

JACKSON. Sit? Sit where? How you mean, sit?

HARRY. Sit, and I'll serve breakfast. You can teach me manners. There's more manners in serving than in being served.

JACKSON. I ain't know what it is eating you this Sunday morning, you hear, Mr. Trewe, but I don't feel you have any right to mama-guy me, because I is a big man with three children, all outside. Now, being served by a white man ain't no big deal for me. It happen to me every day in New York, so it's not going to be any particularly thrilling experience. I would like to get breakfast finish with, wash up, finish my work, and go for my sea bath. Now I have worked here six months and never lost my temper, but it wouldn't take much more for me to fling this whole fucking tray out in that sea and get somebody more to your sexual taste.

HARRY. [*Laughs*] Aha!

JACKSON. Not aha, oho!

HARRY. [*drawing out a chair*] Mr. Phillips . . .

JACKSON. Phillip. What?

HARRY. Your reservation.

JACKSON. You want me play this game, eh? [*He walks around, goes to a corner of the gazebo*] I'll tell you something, you hear, Mr. Trewe? And listen to me good, good. Once and for all. My sense of humor can stretch so far. Then it does snap. You see that sea out there? You know where I born? I born over there. Trinidad. I was a very serious steel-band man, too. And where I come from is a very serious place. I used to get into some serious trouble. A man keep bugging my arse once. A bad john called Boysie. Indian fellow, want to play nigger. Every day in that panyard he would come making joke with nigger boy this, and so on, and I used to just laugh and tell him stop, but he keep laughing and I keep laughing and he going on and I begging him to stop and two of us laughing, until . . . [*He turns, goes to the tray, and picks up a fork*] one day, just out of the blue, I pick up a ice pick and walk over to where he and two fellers was playing card, and I nail that ice pick through his hand to the table, and I laugh, and I walk away.

HARRY. Your table, Mr. Phillip.

[*Silence. Jackson shrugs, sits at the table*]

JACKSON. Okay, then. Until.

HARRY. You know, if you want to exchange war experiences, lad, I could bore you with a couple of mine. Want to hear?

JACKSON. My shift is seven-thirty to one. [*He folds his arms. Harry offers him a cigarette*] I don't smoke on duty.

HARRY. We put on a show in the army once. Ground crew. RAF. In what used to be Palestine. A Christmas panto. Another one. And yours truly here was the dame. The dame in a panto is played by a man. Well, I got the part. Wrote the music, the book, everything, whatever original music there was. *Aladdin and His Wonderful Vamp.* Very obscene, of course. I was the Wonderful Vamp. Terrific reaction all around. Thanks to me music-hall background. Went down great. Well, there was a party afterward. Then a big sergeant in charge of maintenance started this very boring business of confusing my genius with my life. Kept pinching my arse and so on. It got kind of boring after a while Well, he was the size of a truck, mate. And there wasn't much I could do but keep blushing and pretending to be liking it. But the Wonderful Vamp was waiting outside for him, the Wonderful Vamp and a wrench this big, and after that, laddie, it took all of maintenance to put him back again.

JACKSON. That is white-man fighting. Anyway, Mr. Trewe, I feel the fun finish; I would like, with your permission, to get up now and fix up the sun deck. 'Cause when rain fall . . .

HARRY. Forget the sun deck. I'd say, Jackson, that we've come closer to a mutual respect, and that things need not get that hostile. Sit, and let me explain what I had in mind.

JACKSON. I take it that's an order?

HARRY. You want it to be an order? Okay, it's an order.

JACKSON. It didn't sound like no order.

HARRY. Look, I'm a liberal, Jackson. I've done the whole routine. Aldermaston, Suez, Ban the Bomb, Burn the Bra, Pity the Poor Pakis, et cetera. I've even tried jumping up to the steel band at Notting Hill Gate, and I'd no idea I'd wind up in this ironic position of giving orders, but if the new script I've been given says: HARRY TREWE, HOTEL MANAGER, then I'm going to play Harry Trewe, Hotel Manager, to the hilt, damnit. So *sit* down! Please. Oh, goddamnit, *sit . . . down* . . . [*Jackson sits. Nods*] Good. Relax. Smoke. Have a cup of tepid coffee. I sat up from about three this morning, working out this whole skit in my head. [*Pause*] Mind putting that hat on for a second, it will help my point. Come on. It'll make things clearer.

[*He gives Jackson the goatskin hat. Jackson, after a pause, puts it on*]

JACKSON. I'll take that cigarette.

[*Harry hands over a cigarette*]

HARRY. They've seen that stuff, time after time. Limbo, dancing girls, fire-eating . . .

JACKSON. Light.

HARRY. Oh, sorry.

[*He lights Jackson's cigarette*]

JACKSON. I listening.

HARRY. We could turn this little place right here into a little cabaret, with some very witty acts. Build up the right audience. Get an edge on the others. So, I thought, Suppose I get this material down to two people. Me and . . . well, me and somebody else. Robinson Crusoe and Man Friday. We could work up a good satire, you know, on the master-servant— no offense—relationship. Labor-management, white-black, and so on . . . Making some trenchant points about topical things, you know. Add that show to the special dinner for the price of one ticket . . .

JACKSON. You have to have music.

HARRY. Pardon?

JACKSON. A show like that should have music. Just a lot of talk is very boring.

HARRY. Right. But I'd have to have somebody help me, and that's where I thought . . . Want to take the hat off?

JACKSON. It ain't bothering me. When you going make your point?

HARRY. We had that little Carnival contest with the staff and you knocked them out improvising, remember that? You had the bloody guests in stitches . . .

JACKSON. You ain't start to talk money yet, Mr. Harry.

HARRY. Just improvising with the quatro. And not the usual welcome to Port of Spain, I am glad to see you again, but I'll tell you, artist to artist, I recognized a real pro, and this is the point of the hat. I want to make a point about the hotel industry, about manners, conduct, to generally improve relations all around. So, whoever it is, you or whoever, plays Crusoe, and I, or whoever it is, get to play Friday, and imagine first of all the humor and then the impact of that. What you think?

JACKSON. You want my honest, professional opinion?

HARRY. Fire away.

JACKSON. I think is shit.

HARRY. I've never been in shit in my life, my boy.

JACKSON. It sound like shit to me, but I could be wrong.

HARRY. You could say things in fun about this place, about the whole Caribbean, that would hurt while people laughed. You get half the gate.

JACKSON. Half?

HARRY. What do you want?

JACKSON. I want you to come to your senses, let me fix the sun deck and get down to the beach for my sea bath. So, I put on this hat, I pick up this parasol, and I walk like a mama-poule up and down this stage and you have a black man playing Robinson

Crusoe and then a half-naked, white, fish-belly man playing Friday, and you want to tell me it ain't shit?

HARRY. It could be hilarious!

JACKSON. Hilarious, Mr. Trewe? Supposing I wasn't a waiter, and instead of breakfast I was serving you communion, this Sunday morning on this tropical island, and I turn to you, Friday, to teach you my faith, and I tell you, kneel down and eat this man. Well, kneel, nuh! What you think you would say, eh? [*Pause*] You, this white savage?

HARRY. No, that's cannibalism.

JACKSON. Is no more cannibalism than to eat a god. Suppose I make you tell me: For three hundred years I have made you my servant. For three hundred years . . .

HARRY. It's pantomime, Jackson, just keep it light . . . Make them laugh.

JACKSON. Okay. [*Giggling*] For three hundred years I served you. Three hundred years I served you breakfast in . . . in my white jacket on a white veranda, boss, bwana, effendi, bacra, sahib . . . in that sun that never set on your empire I was your shadow, I did what you did, boss, bwana, effendi, bacra, sahib . . . that was my pantomime. Every movement you made, your shadow copied . . . [*Stops giggling*] and you smiled at me as a child does smile at his shadow's helpless obedience, boss, bwana, effendi, bacra, sahib, Mr. Crusoe. Now . . .

HARRY. Now?

[*Jackson's speech is enacted in a trance-like drone, a zombie*]

JACKSON. But after a while the child does get frighten of the shadow he make. He say to himself, That is too much obedience, I better hads stop. But the shadow don't stop, no matter if the child stop playing that pantomime, and the shadow does follow the child everywhere; when he praying, the shadow pray too, when he turn round frighten, the shadow turn round too, when he hide under the sheet, the shadow hiding too. He cannot get rid of it, no matter what, and that is the power and black magic of the shadow, boss, bwana, effendi, bacra, sahib, until it is the shadow that start dominating the child, it is the servant that start dominating the master . . . [*Laughs maniacally, like The Shadow*] and that is the victory of the shadow, boss. [*Normally*] And that is why all them Pakistani and West Indians in England, all them immigrant Fridays driving all you so crazy. And they go keep driving you crazy till you go mad. In that sun that never set, they's your shadow, you can't shake them off.

HARRY. Got really carried away that time, didn't you? It's pantomime, Jackson, keep it light. Improvise!

JACKSON. You mean we making it up as we go along?

HARRY. Right!

JACKSON. Right! I in dat! [*He assumes a stern stance and points stiffly*] Robinson obey Thursday now. Speak Thursday language. Obey Thursday gods.

HARRY. Jesus Christ!

JACKSON. [*Inventing language*] Amaka nobo sakamaka khaki pants kamaluma Jesus Christ! Jesus Christ kamalogo! [*Pause. Then with a violent gesture*] Kamalongo kaba!

[*Meaning: Jesus is dead!*]

HARRY. Sure. [*Pause. Peers forward. Then speaks to an imaginary projectionist, while Jackson stands, feet apart, arms folded, frowning, in the usual stance of the Noble Savage*] Now, could you run it with the subtitles, please? [*He walks over to Jackson, who remains rigid. Like a movie director*] Let's have another take, Big Chief. [*To imaginary camera*] Roll it. Sound!

[*Jackson shoves Harry aside and strides to the table. He bangs the heel of his palm on the tabletop*]

JACKSON. Patamba! Patamba! Yes?

HARRY. You want us to strike the prop? The patamba? [*To cameraman*] Cut!

JACKSON. [*To cameraman*] Rogoongo! Rogoongo!

[*Meaning: Keep it rolling*]

HARRY. *Cut!*

JACKSON. Rogoongo, damnit! [*Defiantly, furiously, Jackson moves around, first signaling the camera to follow him, then pointing out the objects which he rechristens, shaking or hitting them violently. Slams table*] Patamba! [*Rattles beach chair*] *Backaraka! Backaraka!* [*Holds up cup, points with other hand*] *Banda!* [*Drops cup*] *Banda karan!* [*Puts his arm around Harry; points at him*] *Subu!* [*Faster, pointing*] *Masz!* [*Stamping the floor*] Zohgoooor! [*Rests his snoring head on his closed palms*] *Oma! Omaaaa!* [*Kneels, looking skyward. Pauses; eyes closed*] *Booora! Booora!* [*Meaning the world. Silence. He rises*] *Cut!*

And dat is what it was like, before you come here with your table this and cup that.

HARRY. All right. Good audition. You get twenty dollars a day without dialogue.

JACKSON. But why?

HARRY. You never called anything by the same name twice. What's a table?

JACKSON. I forget.

HARRY. I remember: patamba!

JACKSON. Patamba?

HARRY. Right. You fake.

JACKSON. That's a breakfast table. *Ogushi.* That's a dressing table. *Amanga ogushi.* I remember now.

HARRY. I'll tell you one thing, friend. If you want me to learn your language, you'd better have a gun.

JACKSON. You best play Crusoe, chief. I surrender. All you win. [*Points wearily*] Table. Chair. Cup. Man. Jesus. I accept. I accept. All you win. Long time.

[*Smiles*]

HARRY. All right, then. Improvise, then. Sing us a song. In your new language, mate. In English. Go ahead. I challenge you.

JACKSON. You what?

[*Rises, takes up parasol, handling it like a guitar, and strolls around the front row of the audience*]

[*Sings*]

> I want to tell you 'bout Robinson Crusoe.
> He tell Friday, when I do so, do so.
> Whatever I do, you must do like me.
> He make Friday a Good Friday Bohbolee;[1]
> That was the first example of slavery,
> 'Cause I am still Friday and you ain't me.
> Now Crusoe he was this Christian and all,
> And Friday, his slave, was a cannibal,
> But one day things bound to go in reverse,
> With Crusoe the slave and Friday the boss.

HARRY. Then comes this part where Crusoe sings to the goat. Little hint of animal husbandry:

[*Kneels, embraces an imaginary goat, to the melody of "Swanee"*]

[*Sings*]

> Nanny, how I love you,
> How I love you,
> My dear old nanny . . .

JACKSON. Is a li'l obscene.

HARRY. [*Music-hall style*] Me wife thought so. Know what I used to tell her? Obscene? Well, better to be obscene than not heard. How's that? Harry Trewe, I'm telling you again, the music hall's loss is calypso's gain.

[*Stops*]

[*Jackson pauses. Stares upward, muttering to himself. Harry turns. Jackson is signaling in the air with a self-congratulatory smile*]

HARRY. What is it? What've we stopped for? [*Jackson hisses for silence from Harry, then returns to his reverie. Miming*] Are you feeling all right, Jackson?

[*Jackson walks some distance away from Harry. An imaginary guitar suddenly appears in his hand. Harry circles him. Lifts one eyelid, listens to his heartbeat. Jackson revolves, Harry revolves with him. Jackson's whole body is now silently rocking in rhythm. He is laughing to himself. We hear, very loud, a calypso rhythm*]

Two can play this game, Jackson.

[*He strides around in imaginary straw hat, twirling a cane. We hear, very loud, music hall. It stops. Harry peers at Jackson*]

JACKSON. You see what you start?

[*Sings*]

> Well, a Limey name Trewe came to Tobago.
> He was in show business but he had no show,
> so in desperation he turn to me
> and said: "Mister Phillip" is the two o'we,
> one classical actor, and one Creole . . .

HARRY. Wait! Hold it, hold it, man! Don't waste that. Try and remember it. I'll be right back.

JACKSON. Where you going?

HARRY. Tape. Repeat it, and try and keep it. That's what I meant, you see?

JACKSON. You start to exploit me already?

HARRY. That's right. Memorize it.

[*Exits quickly. Jackson removes his shirt and jacket, rolls up his pants above the knee, clears the breakfast tray to one side of the floor, overturns the table, and sits in it, as if it were a boat, as Harry returns with the machine*]

What's all this? I'm ready to tape. What're you up to?

[*Jackson sits in the upturned table, rowing calmly, and from time to time surveying the horizon. He looks up toward the sky, shielding his face from the glare with one hand; then he gestures to Harry*]

[1] A Judas effigy beaten at Easter in Trinidad and Tobago.

What?

[Jackson flaps his arms around leisurely, like a large sea bird, indicating that Harry should do the same]

What? What about the song? You'll forget the bloody song. It was a fluke.

JACKSON. *[Steps out from the table, crosses to Harry, irritated]* If I suppose to help you with this stupidness, we will have to cool it and collaborate a little bit. Now, I was in that boat, rowing, and I was looking up to the sky to see a storm gathering, and I wanted a big white sea bird beating inland from a storm. So what's the trouble, Mr. Trewe?

HARRY. Sea bird? What sea bird? I'm not going to play a fekking sea bird.

JACKSON. Mr. Trewe, I'm only asking you to play a white sea bird because I am supposed to play a black explorer.

HARRY. Well, I don't want to do it. Anyway, that's the silliest acting I've seen in a long time. And Robinson Crusoe wasn't *rowing* when he got shipwrecked; he was on a huge boat. I didn't come here to play a sea bird, I came to tape the song.

JACKSON. Well, then, is either the sea bird or the song. And I don't see any reason why you have to call my acting silly. We suppose to improvise.

HARRY. All right, Jackson, all right. After I do this part, I hope you can remember the song. Now you just tell me, before we keep stopping, what I am supposed to do, how many animals I'm supposed to play, and . . . you know, and so on, and so on, and then when we get all that part fixed up, we'll tape the song, all right?

JACKSON. That suits me. Now, the way I see it here: whether Robinson Crusoe was on a big boat or not, the idea is that he got . . . *[Pause]* shipwrecked. So I . . . if I am supposed to play Robinson Crusoe my way, then I will choose the way in which I will get shipwrecked. Now, as Robinson Crusoe is rowing, he looks up and sees this huge white sea bird, which is making loud sea-bird noises, because a storm is coming. And Robinson Crusoe looks up toward the sky and sees that there is this storm. Then, there is a large wave, and Robinson Crusoe finds himself on the beach.

HARRY. Am I supposed to play the beach? Because that's white . . .

JACKSON. Hilarious! Mr. Trewe. Now look, you know, I am doing *you* a favor. On this beach, right? Then he sees a lot of goats. And, because he is naked and he needs clothes, he kills a goat, he takes off the skin, and he makes this parasol here and this hat, so he doesn't go around naked for everybody to see. Now I *know* that there is nobody there, but there is an audience, so the sooner Robinson Crusoe puts on his clothes, then the better and happier we will all be. I am going to go back in the boat. I am going to look up toward the sky. You will, *please*, make the sea-bird noises. I will do the wave, I will crash onto the sand, you will come down like a goat, I will kill you, take off your skin, make a parasol *and* a hat, and after that, then I promise you that I will remember the song. And I will sing it to the best of my ability. *[Pause]* However shitty that is.

HARRY. I said "silly." Now listen . . .

JACKSON. Yes, Mr. Trewe?

HARRY. Okay, if you're a black explorer . . . Wait a minute . . . wait a minute. If you're really a white explorer but you're black, shouldn't I play a black sea bird because I'm white?

JACKSON. Are you . . . going to extend . . . the limits of prejudice to include . . . the flora and fauna of this island? I am entering the boat.

[He is stepping into the upturned table or boat, as Harry halfheartedly imitates a bird, waving his arms]

HARRY. Kekkkk, kekkkk,
kekkk, kekkkk!

[Stops]

What's wrong?

JACKSON. What's wrong? Mr. Trewe, that is not a sea gull . . . that is some kind of . . . well, I don't know what it is . . . some kind of *jumbie* bird or something. *[Pause]* I am returning to the boat.

[He carefully enters the boat, expecting an interrupting bird cry from Harry, but there is none, so he begins to row]

HARRY. Kekk! Kekkk.

[He hangs his arms down. Pause]

Er, Jackson, wait a minute. Hold it a second. Come here a minute.

[Jackson patiently gets out of the boat, elaborately pantomiming lowering his body into shallow water, releasing his hold on the boat, swimming a little distance toward shore, getting up from the shallows, shaking out his hair and hands, wiping his hands on his trousers, jumping up and down on one foot to unplug water from his clogged ear, seeing Harry,

then walking wearily, like a man who has swum a tremendous distance, and collapsing at Harry's feet]

Er, Jackson. This is too humiliating. Now, let's just forget it and please don't continue, or you're fired.

[Jackson leisurely wipes his face with his hands]

JACKSON. It don't go so, Mr. Trewe. You know me to be a meticulous man. I didn't want to do this job. I didn't even want to work here. You convinced me to work here. I have worked as meticulously as I can, until I have been promoted. This morning I had no intention of doing what I am doing now; you have always admired the fact that whatever I begin, I finish. Now, I will accept my resignation, if you want me to, *after* we have finished this thing. But I am not leaving in the middle of a job, that has never been my policy. So you can sit down, as usual, and watch me work, but until I have finished this whole business of Robinson Crusoe being in the boat *[He rises and repeats the pantomime]* looking at an imaginary sea bird, being shipwrecked, killing a goat, making this hat *and* this parasol, walking up the beach and finding a naked footprint, which should take me into about another ten or twelve minutes, at the most, I will pack my things and I will leave, and you can play *Robinson Crusoe* all by yourself. My plans were, after this, to take the table like this . . . *[He goes to the table, puts it upright]* Let me show you: take the table, turn it all around, go under the table . . . *[He goes under the table]* and this would now have become Robinson Crusoe's hut. *[Emerges from under the table and, without looking at Harry, continues to talk]* Now, you just tell me if you think I am overdoing it, or if you think it's more or less what we agreed on? *[Pause]* Okay? But I am not resigning. *[Turns to Harry slowly]* You see, it's your people who introduced us to this culture: Shakespeare, *Robinson Crusoe*, the classics, and so on, and when we start getting as good as them, you can't leave halfway. So, I will continue? Please?

HARRY. No, Jackson. You will *not* continue. You will straighten this table, put back the tablecloth, take away the breakfast things, give me back the hat, put your jacket back on, and we will continue as normal and forget the whole matter. Now, I'm very serious, I've had enough of this farce. I would like to stop.

JACKSON. May I say what I think, Mr. Trewe? I think it's a matter of prejudice. I think that you cannot believe: one: that I can act, and two: that any black man should play Robinson Crusoe. A little while

aback, I came out here quite calmly and normally with the breakfast things and find you almost stark naked, kneeling down, and you told me you were getting into your part. Here am I getting into *my* part and you object. This is the story . . . this is history. This moment that we are now acting here is the history of imperialism; it's nothing less than that. And I don't think that I can—should—concede my getting into a part halfway and abandoning things, just because you, as my superior, give me orders. People become independent. Now, I could go down to that beach by myself with this hat, and I could play Robinson Crusoe, I could play Columbus, I could play Sir Francis Drake, I could play anybody discovering anywhere, but I don't want you to tell me when and where to draw the line! *[Pause]* Or what to discover and when to discover it. All right?

HARRY. Look, I'm sorry to interrupt you again, Jackson, but as I—you know—was watching you, I realized it's much more profound than that; that it could get offensive. We're trying to do something light, just a little pantomime, a little satire, a little picong. But if you take this thing seriously, we might commit Art, which is a kind of crime in this society . . . I mean, there'd be a lot of things there that people . . . well, it would make them think too much, and well, we don't want that . . . we just want a little . . . entertainment.

JACKSON. How do you mean, Mr. Trewe?

HARRY. Well, I mean if you . . . well, I mean. If you did the whole thing in reverse . . . I mean, okay, well, all right . . . you've got this black man . . . no, no . . . all right. You've got this man who is black, Robinson Crusoe, and he discovers this island on which there is this white cannibal, all right?

JACKSON. Yes. That is, after he has killed the goat . . .

HARRY. Yes, I know, I know. After he has killed the goat and made a . . . the hat, the parasol, and all of that . . . and, anyway, he comes across this man called Friday.

JACKSON. How do you know I mightn't choose to call him Thursday? Do I have to copy every . . . I mean, are we improvising?

HARRY. All right, so it's Thursday. He comes across this naked white cannibal called Thursday, you know. And then look at what would happen. He would have to start to . . . well, he'd have to, sorry . . . This cannibal, who is a Christian, would have to start unlearning his Christianity. He would have to be taught . . . I mean . . . he'd have to be taught by this—African . . . that everything was wrong, that what he was doing . . . I mean, for nearly two thousand years . . . was wrong. That his civilization, his culture, his whatever, was . . . *horr-ible*. Was all . . . wrong. Barbarous, I mean, you know. And Crusoe would then have to teach him things like, you know, about . . . Africa, his gods, patamba, and so on . . . and it would get very, very complicated, and I suppose ultimately it would be very boring, and what we'd have on our hands would be . . . would be a play and not a little panto-mime . . .

JACKSON. I'm too ambitious?

HARRY. No, no, the whole thing would have to be reversed; white would become black, you know . . .

JACKSON. [*Smiling*] You see, Mr. Trewe, I don't see anything wrong with that, up to now.

HARRY. Well, I do. It's not the sort of thing I want, and I think you'd better clean up, and I'm going inside, and when I come back I'd like this whole place just as it was. I mean, just before everything started.

JACKSON. You mean you'd like it returned to its pri-mal state? Natural? Before Crusoe finds Thursday? But, you see, that is not history. That is not the world.

HARRY. No, no, I don't give an Eskimo's fart about the world, Jackson. I just want this little place here *cleaned up*, and I'd like you to get back to fixing the sun deck. Let's forget the whole matter. Righto. Excuse me.

[*He is leaving. Jackson's tone will stop him*]

JACKSON. Very well. So I take it you don't want to hear the song, neither?

HARRY. No, no. I'm afraid not. I think really it was a silly idea, it's all my fault, and I'd like things to return to where they were.

JACKSON. The story of the British Empire, Mr. Trewe.

However, it is too late. The history of the British Empire.

HARRY. Now, how do you get that?

JACKSON. Well, you come to a place, you find that place as God make it; like Robinson Crusoe, you civilize the natives; they try to do something, you turn around and you say to them: "You are not good enough, let's call the whole thing off, return things to normal, you go back to your position as slave or servant, I will keep mine as master, and we'll forget the whole thing ever happened." Correct? You would like me to accept this.

HARRY. You're really making this very difficult, Jack-son. Are you hurt? Have I offended you?

JACKSON. Hurt? No, no, no. I didn't expect any less. I am not hurt. [*Pause*] I am just . . . [*Pause*]

HARRY. You're just what?

JACKSON. I am just ashamed . . . of making such a fool of myself. [*Pause*] I expected . . . a little respect. That is all.

HARRY. I respect you . . . I just, I . . .

JACKSON. No. It's perfectly all right. [*Harry goes to the table, straightens it*] I . . . no . . . I'll fix the table myself. [*He doesn't move*] I am all right, thank you. Sir. [*Harry stops fixing the table*] [*With the hint of a British accent*] Thank you very much.

HARRY. [*Sighs*] I . . . am sorry . . . er . . .

[*Jackson moves toward the table*]

JACKSON. It's perfectly all right, sir. It's perfectly all . . . right. [*Almost inaudibly*] Thank you. [*Harry begins to straighten the table again*] No, thank you very much, don't touch anything. [*Jackson is up against the table. Harry continues to straighten the table*] Don't touch anything . . . Mr. Trewe. Please. [*Jackson rests one arm on the table, fist closed. They watch each other for three beats*] Now that . . . is MY order . . .

[*They watch each other for several beats as the lights fade.*]

Act II

Noon. White glare. Harry, with shirt unbuttoned, in a deck chair reading a paperback thriller. Sound of intermittent hammering from stage left, where Jackson is repairing the sun-deck slats. Harry rises, decides he should talk to Jackson about the noise, decides against

it, and leans back in the deck chair, eyes closed. Hammering has stopped for a long while. Harry opens his eyes, senses Jackson's presence, turns suddenly, to see him standing quite close, shirtless, holding a ham-mer. Harry bolts from his chair.

JACKSON. You know something, sir? While I was up there nailing the sun deck, I just stay so and start giggling all by myself.

HARRY. Oh, yes? Why?

JACKSON. No, I was remembering a feller, you know . . . ahhh, he went for audition once for a play, you know, and the way he, you know, the way he prop . . . present himself to the people, said . . . ahmm, "You know, I am an actor, you know. I do all kind of acting, classical acting, *Creole* acting." That's when I laugh, you know? [*Pause*] I going back and fix the deck, then. [*Moves off. Stops, turns*] The . . . the hammering not disturbing you?

HARRY. No, no, it's fine. You have to do it, right? I mean, you volunteered, the carpenter didn't come, right?

JACKSON. Yes. Creole acting. I wonder what kind o' acting dat is. [*Spins the hammer in the air and does or does not catch it*] Yul Brynner. *Magnificent Seven.* Picture, papa! A kind of Western Creole acting. It ain't have no English cowboys, eh, Mr. Harry? Something wrong, boy, something wrong.

[*He exits. Harry lies back in the deck chair, the book on his chest, arms locked behind his head. Silence. Hammering violently resumes*]

[*Off*]

Kekkk, kekkkekk, kekk!
Kekkekk, kekkkekk, ekkek!

[*Harry rises, moves from the deck chair toward the sun deck*]

HARRY. *Jackson!* What the hell are you doing? What's that noise?

JACKSON. [*Off; loud*] I doing like a black sea gull, suh!

HARRY. Well, it's very distracting.

JACKSON. [*Off*] Sorry, sir.

[*Harry returns. Sits down on the deck chair. Waits for the hammering. Hammering resumes. Then stops. Silence. Then we hear*]

[*Singing loudly*]

I want to tell you 'bout Robinson Crusoe.
He tell Friday, when I do so, do so.
Whatever I do, you must do like me,
He make Friday a Good Friday Bohbolee

[*Spoken*]

And the chorus:

[*Sings*]

Laide-die
Laidie, lay-day, de-day-de-die,
Laidee-doo-day-dee-day-dee-die
Laidee-day-doh-dee-day-dee-die

Now that was the first example of slavery,
'Cause I am still Friday and you ain't me,
Now Crusoe he was this Christian and all,
Friday, his slave, was a cannibal,
But one day things bound to go in reverse,
With Crusoe the slave and Friday the boss . . .
Caiso, boy! Caiso!

[*Harry rises, goes toward the sun deck*]

HARRY. Jackson, man! Jesus!

[*He returns to the deck chair, is about to sit*]

JACKSON. [*Off*] Two more lash and the sun deck finish, sir! [*Harry waits*] Stand by . . . here they come . . . First lash . . .

[*Sound*]

Pow!
Second lash:

[*Two sounds*]

Pataow! Job complete! Lunch, Mr. Trewe? You want your lunch now? Couple sandwich or what?

HARRY. [*Shouts without turning*] Just bring a couple beers from the icebox, Jackson. And the Scotch. [*To himself*] What the hell, let's all get drunk. [*To Jackson*] Bring some beer for yourself, too, Jackson!

JACKSON. [*Off*] Thank you, Mr. Robinson . . . Thank you, Mr. Trewe, sir! *Cru-soe, Trewe-so!* [*Faster*] Crusoe-Trusoe, Robinson Trewe-so!

HARRY. Jesus, Jackson; cut that out and just bring the bloody beer!

JACKSON. [*Off*] Right! A beer for you and a beer for me! Now, what else is it going to be? A sandwich for you, but none for me.

[*Harry picks up the paperback and opens it, removing a folded sheet of paper. He opens it and is reading it carefully, sometimes lifting his head, closing his eyes, as if remembering its contents, then reading again. He puts it into a pocket quickly as Jackson returns, carrying a tray with two beers, a bottle of Scotch, a pitcher of water, and two glasses. Jackson sets them down on the table]*

I'm here, sir. At your command.

HARRY. Sit down. Forget the sandwiches, I don't want to eat. Let's sit down, man to man, and have a drink. That was the most sarcastic hammering I've ever heard, and I know you were trying to get back at me with all those noises and that Uncle Tom crap. So let's have a drink, man to man, and try and work out what happened this morning, all right?

JACKSON. I've forgotten about this morning, sir.

HARRY. No, no, no, I mean, the rest of the day it's going to bother me, you know?

JACKSON. Well, I'm leaving at half-past one.

HARRY. No, but still . . . Let's . . . Okay. Scotch?

JACKSON. I'll stick to beer, sir, thank you.

[Harry pours a Scotch and water, Jackson serves himself a beer. Both are still standing]

HARRY. Sit over there, please, Mr. Phillip. On the deck chair. *[Jackson sits on the deck chair, facing Harry]* Cheers?

JACKSON. Cheers. Cheers. Deck chair and all.

[They toast and drink]

HARRY. All right. Look, I think you misunderstood me this morning.

JACKSON. Why don't we forget the whole thing, sir? Let me finish this beer and go for my sea bath, and you can spend the rest of the day all by yourself. *[Pause]* Well. What's wrong? What happen, sir? I said something wrong just now?

HARRY. This place isn't going to drive me crazy, Jackson. Not if I have to go mad preventing it. Not physically crazy; but you just start to think crazy thoughts, you know? At the beginning it's fine; there's the sea, the palm trees, monarch of all I survey and so on, all that postcard stuff. And then it just becomes another back yard. God, is there anything deadlier than Sunday afternoons in the tropics when you can't sleep? The horror and stillness of the heat, the shining, godforsaken sea, the bored and boring clouds? Especially in an empty boarding house. You sit by the stagnant pool counting the dead leaves drifting to the edge. I daresay the terror of emptiness made me want to act. I wasn't trying to humiliate you. I meant nothing by it. Now, I don't usually apologize to people. I don't do things

to apologize for. When I do them, I mean them, but, in your case, I'd like to apologize.

JACKSON. Well, if you find here boring, go back home. Do something else, nuh?

HARRY. It's not that simple. It's a little more complicated than that. I mean, everything I own is sunk here, you see? There's a little matter of a brilliant actress who drank too much, and a car crash at Brighton after a panto . . . Well. That's neither here nor there now. Right? But I'm determined to make this place work. I gave up the theater for it.

JACKSON. Why?

HARRY. Why? I wanted to be the best. Well, among other things; oh, well, that's neither here nor there. Flopped at too many things, though. Including classical and Creole acting. I just want to make this place work, you know. And a desperate man'll try anything. Even at the cost of his sanity, maybe. I mean, I'd hate to believe that under everything else I was also prejudiced, as well. I wouldn't have any right here, right?

JACKSON. 'Tain't prejudice that bothering you, Mr. Trewe; you ain't no parrot to repeat opinion. No, is loneliness that sucking your soul as dry as the sun suck a crab shell. On a Sunday like this, I does watch you. The whole staff does study you. Walking round restless, staring at the sea. You remembering your wife and your son, not right? You ain't get over that yet?

HARRY. Jackson . . .

JACKSON. Is none of my business. But it really lonely here out of season. Is summer, and your own people gone, but come winter they go flock like sandpipers all down that beach. So you lonely, but I could make you forget all o' that. I could make H. Trewe, Esquire, a brand-new man. You come like a challenge.

HARRY. Think I keep to myself too much?

JACKSON. If! You would get your hair cut by phone. You drive so careful you make your car nervous. If you was in charge of the British Empire, you wouldn'ta lose it, you'da misplace it.

HARRY. I see, Jackson.

JACKSON. But all that could change if you do what I tell you.

HARRY. I don't want a new life, thanks.

JACKSON. Same life. Different man. But that stiff upper lip goin' have to quiver a little.

HARRY. What's all this? Obeah? "That old black magic"?

JACKSON. Nothing. I could have the next beer?

HARRY. Go ahead. I'm drinking Scotch.

[*Jackson takes the other beer, swallows deep, smacks his lips, grins at Harry*]

JACKSON. Nothing. We will have to continue from where we stop this morning. You will have to be Thursday.

HARRY. Aha, you bastard! It's a thrill giving orders, hey? But I'm not going through all that rubbish again.

JACKSON. All right. Stay as you want. But if you say yes, it go have to be man to man, and none of this boss-and-Jackson business, you see, Trewe . . . I mean, I just call you plain Trewe, for example, and I notice that give you a slight shock. Just a little twitch of the lip, but a shock all the same, eh, Trewe? You see? You twitch again. It would be just me and you, all right? You see, two of we both acting a role here we ain't really really believe in, you know. I ent think you strong enough to give people orders, and I *know* I ain't the kind who like taking *them*. So both of we doesn't have to *improvise* so much as *exaggerate*. We faking, faking all the time. But, man to man, I mean . . . [*Pause*] that could be something else. Right, Mr. Trewe?

HARRY. Aren't we man to man now?

JACKSON. No, no. We having one of them "playing man-to-man" talks, where a feller does look a next feller in the eye and say, "Le' we settle this thing, man to man," and this time the feller who smiling and saying it, his whole honest intention is to take that feller by the crotch and rip out he stones, and dig out he eye and leave him for corbeaux to pick.

[*Silence*]

HARRY. You know, that thing this morning had an effect on me, man to man now. I didn't think so much about the comedy of *Robinson Crusoe*, I thought what we were getting into was a little sad. So, when I went back to the room, I tried to rest before lunch, before you began all that vindictive hammering . . .

JACKSON. Vindictive?

HARRY. Man to man: that vindictive hammering and singing, and I thought, Well, maybe we could do it straight. Make a real straight thing out of it.

JACKSON. You mean like a tradegy. With one joke?

HARRY. Or a codemy, with none. You mispronounce words on purpose, don't you, Jackson? [*Jackson smiles*] Don't think for one second that I'm not up on your game, Jackson. You're playing the stage nigger with me. I'm an actor, you know. It's a smile in front and a dagger behind your back, right? Or the smile itself is the bloody dagger. I'm aware, chum. I'm aware.

JACKSON. The smile kinda rusty, sir, but it goes with the job. Just like the water in this hotel: [*Demonstrates*] I turn it on at seven and lock it off at one.

HARRY. Didn't hire you for the smile; I hired you for your voice. We've the same background. Old-time calypso, old-fashioned music hall:

[*Sings*]

Oh, me wife can't cook and she looks like a horse
And the way she makes coffee is grounds for divorce . . .

[*Does a few steps*]

But when love is at stake she's my Worcester sauce . . .

[*Stops*]

Used to wow them with that. All me own work. Ah, the lost glories of the old music hall, the old provincials, grimy brocade, the old stars faded one by one. The brassy pantomimes! Come from an old music-hall family, you know, Jackson. Me mum had this place she ran for broken-down actors. Had tea with the greats as a tot.

[*Sings softly, hums*]

Oh, me wife can't cook . . .

[*Silence*]

You married, Jackson?

JACKSON. I not too sure, sir.

HARRY. You're not sure?

JACKSON. That's what I said.

HARRY. I know what you mean. I wasn't sure I was when I was. My wife's remarried.

JACKSON. You showed me her photo. And the little boy own.

HARRY. But I'm not. Married. So there's absolutely no hearth for Crusoe to go home to. While you were up there, I rehearsed this thing. [*Presents a folded piece of paper*] Want to read it?

JACKSON. What . . . er . . . what is it . . . a poetry?

HARRY. No, no, not a poetry. A thing I wrote. Just a speech in the play . . . that if . . .

JACKSON. Oho, we back in the play again?

HARRY. Almost. You want to read it?

[*He offers the paper*]

JACKSON. All right.

HARRY. I thought—no offense, now. Man to man. If you were doing Robinson Crusoe, this is what you'd read.

JACKSON. You want me to read this, right?

HARRY. Yeah.

JACKSON. [*Reads slowly*] "O silent sea, O wondrous sunset that I've gazed on ten thousand times, who will rescue me from this complete desolation? . . ." [*Breaking*] All o' this?

HARRY. If you don't mind. Don't act it. Just read it. [*Jackson looks at him*] No offense.

JACKSON. [*Reads*] "Yes, this is paradise, I know. For I see around me the splendors of nature . . ."

HARRY. Don't act it . . .

JACKSON. [*Pauses; then continues*] "How I'd like to fuflee this desolate rock." [*Pauses*] Fuflee? Pardon, but what is a fuflee, Mr. Trewe?

HARRY. A fuflee? I've got "fuflee" written there?

JACKSON. [*Extends paper, points at word*] So, how you does fuflee, Mr. Harry? Is Anglo-Saxon English?

[*Harry kneels down and peers at the word. He rises*]

HARRY. It's F . . . then F-L-E-E—flee to express his hesitation. It's my own note as an actor. He quivers, he hesitates . . .

JACKSON. He quivers, he hesitates, but he still can't fuflee?

HARRY. Just leave that line out, Jackson.

JACKSON. I like it.

HARRY. *Leave it out*!

JACKSON. No fuflee?

HARRY. I said no.

JACKSON. Just because I read it wrong. I know the word "flee," you know. Like to take off. Flee. Faster than run. Is the extra *F* you put in there so close to flee that had me saying fuflee like a damn ass, but le' we leave it in, nuh? One fuflee ain't go kill anybody. Much less bite them. [*Silence*] Get it?

HARRY. Don't take this personally . . .

JACKSON. No fuflees on old Crusoe, boy . . .

HARRY. But, if you're going to do professional theater, Jackson, don't take this personally, more discipline is required. All right?

JACKSON. You write it. Why you don't read it?

HARRY. I wanted to hear it. Okay, give it back . . .

JACKSON. [*Loudly, defiantly*] "The ferns, the palms like silent sentinels, the wide and silent lagoons that briefly hold my passing, solitary reflection. The volcano . . ." [*Stops*] "The volcano." What?

HARRY. . . . "wreathed" . . .

JACKSON. Oho, oho . . . like a wreath? "The volcano *wreathed* in mist. But what is paradise without a woman? Adam in paradise!"

HARRY. Go ahead.

JACKSON. [*Restrained*] "Adam in paradise had his woman to share his loneliness, but I miss the voice of even one consoling creature, the touch of a hand, the look of kind eyes. Where is the wife from whom I vowed never to be sundered? How old is my little son? If he could see his father like this, mad with memories of them . . . Even Job had his family. But I am alone, alone, I am all alone." [*Pause*] Oho. You write this?

HARRY. Yeah.

JACKSON. Is good. Very good.

HARRY. Thank you.

JACKSON. Touching. Very sad. But something missing.

HARRY. What?

JACKSON. Goats. You leave out the goats.

HARRY. The goats. So what? What've you got with goats, anyway?

JACKSON. Very funny. Very funny, sir.

HARRY. Try calling me Trewe.

JACKSON. Not yet. That will come. Stick to the point. You ask for my opinion and I *gave* you my opinion. No doubt I don't have the brains. But *my* point is that this man ain't facing reality. *There are goats* all around him.

HARRY. You're full of shit.

JACKSON. The man is not facing reality. He is not a practical man *shipwrecked*.

HARRY. I suppose that's the difference between classical and Creole acting?

[*He pours a drink and downs it furiously*]

JACKSON. If he is not practical, he is not Robinson Crusoe. And yes, is Creole acting, yes. Because years afterward his little son could look at the parasol and the hat and look at a picture of Daddy and boast: "My daddy smart, boy. He get shipwreck and first thing he do is he build a hut, then he kill a goat or two and make clothes, a parasol and a hat." That way Crusoe *achieve* something, and his son could boast . . .

HARRY. Only his son is dead.

JACKSON. Whose son dead?

HARRY. Crusoe's.

JACKSON. No, pardner. *Your* son dead. Crusoe wife and child waiting for him, and he is a practical man and he know somebody go come and save him . . .

HARRY. [*Almost inaudibly*]

"I bit my arm, I sucked the blood,
And cried, 'A sail! a sail!'"

How the hell does he know "somebody go come and save him"? That's shit. That's not in his character at that moment. How the hell can he know? You're a cruel bastard . . .

JACKSON. [*Enraged*] *Because, you fucking ass, he has faith*!

HARRY. [*Laughing*] Faith? What faith?

JACKSON. He not sitting on his shipwrecked arse bawling out . . . what it is you have here? [*Reads*] "O . . ." Where is it? [*Reads*] "O silent sea, O wondrous sunset," and all that shit. No. He shipwrecked. He desperate, he hungry. He look up and he see this fucking goat with its fucking beard watching him and smiling, this goat with its forked fucking beard and square yellow eye just like the fucking devil, standing up there . . . [*Pantomimes the goat and Crusoe in turn*] smiling at him, and putting out its tongue and letting go one fucking *bleeeeeh*! And Robbie ent thinking 'bout his wife and son and O silent sea and O wondrous sunset; no, Robbie is the First True Creole, so he watching the goat with his eyes narrow, narrow, and he say: *blehhh*, eh? You muther-fucker, I go show you *blehhh* in your goat-ass, and vam, vam, next thing is Robbie and the goat, *mano a mano*, man to man, man to goat, goat to man, wrestling on the sand, and next thing we know we hearing one last faint, feeble *bleeeeeehhhhhhhhhhhhhh*, and Robbie is next seen walking up the beach with a goatskin hat and a goatskin umbrella, feeling like a million dollars because *he have faith*!

HARRY. [*Applauds*] Bravo! You're the Christian. I am the cannibal. Bravo!

JACKSON. If I does hammer sarcastic, you does clap sarcastic. Now I want to pee.

HARRY. I think I'll join you.

JACKSON. So because I go and pee, you must pee, too?

HARRY. Subliminal suggestion.

JACKSON. Monkey see, monkey do.

HARRY. You're the bloody ape, mate. You people just came down from the trees.

JACKSON. Say that again, please.

HARRY. I'm going to keep that line.

JACKSON. Oho! Rehearse you rehearsing? I thought you was serious.

HARRY. You go have your pee. I'll run over my monologue.

JACKSON. No, you best do it now, sir. Or it going to be on my mind while we rehearsing that what you really want to do is take a break and pee. We best go together, then.

HARRY. We'll call it the pee break. Off we go, then. How long will you be, then? You people take forever.

JACKSON. Maybe you should hold up a sign, sir, or give some sort of signal when you serious or when you joking, so I can know not to react. I would say five minutes.

HARRY. Five minutes? What is this, my friend, Niagara Falls?

JACKSON. It will take me . . . look, you want me to time it? I treat it like a ritual, I don't just pee for peeing's sake. It will take me about forty to fifty seconds to walk to the servants' toilets . . .

HARRY. Wait a second . . .

JACKSON. No, you wait, please, sir. That's almost one minute, take another fifty seconds to walk back, or even more, because after a good pee a man does be in a mood, both ruminative and grateful that the earth has received his libation, so that makes . . .

HARRY. Hold on, please.

JACKSON. [*Voice rising*] Jesus, sir, give me a break, nuh? That is almost two minutes, and in between those two minutes it have such solemn and ruminative behavior as opening the fly, looking upward or downward, the ease and relief, the tender shaking, the solemn tucking in, like you putting a little baby back to sleep, the reverse zipping or buttoning, depending on the pants, then, with the self-congratulating washing of the hands, looking at yourself for at least half a minute in the mirror, then the drying of hands as if you were a master surgeon just finish a major operation, and the walk back . . .

HARRY. You said that. Any way you look at it, it's under five minutes, and I interrupted you because . . .

JACKSON. I could go and you could time me, to see if I on a go-slow, or wasting up my employer's precious time, but I know it will take at least five, unless, like most white people, you either don't flush it, a part I forgot, or just wipe your hands fast fast or not at all . . .

HARRY. Which white people, Jackson?

JACKSON. I was bathroom attendant at the Hilton, and I know men and races from their urinary habits, and most Englishmen . . .

HARRY. Most Englishmen . . . Look, I was trying to tell you, instead of going all the way round to the servants' lavatories, pop into my place, have a quick one, and that'll be under five bloody minutes in any circumstances and regardless of the capacity. Go on. I'm all right.

JACKSON. Use your bathroom, Mr. Harry?

HARRY. Go on, will you?

JACKSON. I want to get this. You giving me permission to go through your living room, with all your valuables lying about, with the picture of your wife watching me in case I should leave the bathroom open, and you are granting me the privilege of taking out my thing, doing my thing right there among all those lotions and expensive soaps, and . . . after I finish, wiping my hands on a clean towel?

HARRY. Since you make it so vividly horrible, why don't you just walk around to the servants' quarters and take as much time as you like? Five minutes won't kill me.

JACKSON. I mean, equality is equality and art is art, Mr. Harry, but to use those clean, rough Cannon towels . . . You mustn't rush things, people have to slide into independence. They give these islands independence so fast that people still ain't recover from the shock, so they pissing and wiping their hands indiscriminately. You don't want that to happen in this guest house, Mr. Harry. Let me take my little five minutes, as usual, and if you have to go, you go to your place, and I'll go mine, and let's keep things that way until I can feel I can use your towels without a profound sense of gratitude, and you could, if you wanted, a little later maybe, walk round the guest house in the dark, put your foot in the squelch of those who missed the pit by the outhouse, that charming old-fashioned outhouse so many tourists take Polaroids of, without feeling degraded, and we can then respect each other as artists. So, I appreciate the offer, but I'll be back in five. Kindly excuse me.

[He exits]

HARRY. You've got logorrheah, Jackson. You've been running your mouth like a parrot's arse. But don't get sarcastic with me, boy!

[Jackson returns]

JACKSON. You don't understand, Mr. Harry. My problem is, I really mean what I say.

HARRY. You've been pretending indifference to this game, Jackson, but you've manipulated it your way, haven't you? Now you can spew out all that bitterness in fun, can't you? Well, we'd better get things straight around here, friend. You're still on duty. And if you stay out there too long, your job is at stake. It's . . . [Consulting his watch] five minutes to one now. You've got exactly three minutes to get in there and back, and two minutes left to finish straightening this place. It's a bloody mess.

[Silence]

JACKSON. Bloody mess, eh?

HARRY. That's correct.

JACKSON. [In exaggerated British accent] I go try and make it back in five, bwana. If I don't, the mess could be bloodier. I saw a sign once in a lavatory in Mobile, Alabama. COLORED But it didn't have no time limit. Funny, eh?

HARRY. Ape! Mimic! Three bloody minutes!

[Jackson exits, shaking his head. Harry recovers the sheet of paper from the floor and puts it back in his pants pocket. He pours a large drink, swallows it all in two large gulps, then puts the glass down. He looks around the gazebo, wipes his hands briskly. He removes the drinks tray with Scotch, the two beer bottles, glasses, water pitcher, and sets them in a corner of the gazebo. He lifts up the deck chair and sets it, sideways, in another corner. He turns the table carefully over on its side; then, when it is on its back, he looks at it. he changes his mind and carefully tilts the table back upright. He removes his shirt and folds it and places it in another corner of the gazebo. He rolls up his trouser cuffs almost to the knee. He is now half-naked. He goes over to the drinks tray and pours the bowl of melted ice, now tepid water, over his head. He ruffles his hair, his face dripping; then he sees an ice pick. He picks it up]

JACKSON'S VOICE. "One day, just out of the blue, I pick up a ice pick and walk over to where he and two fellers was playing cards, and I nail that ice pick through his hand to the table, and I laugh . . ."

[Harry drives the ice pick hard into the tabletop, steps back, looking at it. Then he moves up to it, wrenches it out, and gets under the table, the ice pick at his feet. A few beats, then Jackson enters, pauses]

JACKSON. [Laughs] What you doing under the table, Mr. Trewe? [Silence. Jackson steps nearer the table] Trewe? You all right? [Silence. Jackson crouches close to Harry] Harry, boy, you cool? [Jackson rises. Moves away some distance. He takes in the space. An arena. Then he crouches again] Ice-pick time, then?

Okay, "fee fi fo fum,

I smell the blood of an Englishman . . ."

[Jackson exits quickly. Harry waits a while, then crawls from under the table, straightens up, and places the ice pick gently on the tabletop. He goes to the drinks tray and has a *sip from the Scotch; then replaces the bottle and takes up a position behind the table. Jackson returns dressed as Crusoe—goatskin hat, open umbrella, the hammer stuck in the waistband of his rolled-up trousers. He throws something across the room to Harry's feet. The dead parrot, in a carry-away box. Harry opens it]*

One parrot, to go! Or you eating it here?

HARRY. You son of a bitch.

JACKSON. Sure. *[Harry picks up the parrot and hurls it into the sea]* First bath in five years.

[Jackson moves toward the table, very calmly]

HARRY. You're a bloody savage. Why'd you strangle him?

JACKSON. *[As Friday]* Me na strangle him, bwana. Him choke from prejudice.

HARRY. Prejudice? A bloody parrot. The bloody thing can't reason. *[Pause. They stare at each other. Harry crouches, tilts his head, shifts on his perch, flutters his wings like the parrot, squawks]* Heinegger. Heinegger. *[Jackson stands over the table and folds the umbrella]* You people create nothing. You imitate everything. It's all been done before, you see, Jackson. The parrot. Think that's something? It's from The Sea-gull. It's from Miss Julie. You can't ever be original, boy. That's the trouble with shadows, right? They can't think for themselves. *[Jackson shrugs, looking away from him]* So you take it out on a parrot. Is that one of your African sacrifices, eh?

JACKSON. Run your mouth, Harry, run your mouth.

HARRY. *[Squawks]* Heinegger . . . Heinegger . . . *[Jackson folds the parasol and moves to enter the upturned table]* I wouldn't go under there if I were you, Jackson.

[Jackson reaches into the back of his waistband and removes a hammer]

JACKSON. The first English cowboy.

[He turns and faces Harry]

HARRY. It's my property. Don't get in there.

JACKSON. The hut. That was my idea.

HARRY. The table's mine.

JACKSON. What else is yours, Harry? *[Gestures]* This whole fucking island? Dem days gone, boy.

HARRY. The costume's mine, too. *[He crosses over, almost nudging Jackson, and picks up the ice pick]* I'd like them back.

JACKSON. Suit yourself.

[Harry crosses to the other side, sits on the edge of the wall or leans against a post. Jackson removes the hat and throws it into the arena, then the parasol]

HARRY. The hammer's mine.

JACKSON. I feel I go need it.

HARRY. If you keep it, you're a bloody thief.

[Jackson suddenly drops to the floor on his knees, letting go of the hammer, weeping and cringing, and advancing on his knees toward Harry]

JACKSON. Pardon, master, pardon! Friday bad boy! Friday wicked nigger Sorry. Friday nah t'ief again. Mercy, master. Mercy. *[He rolls around on the floor, laughing]* Oh, Jesus, I go dead! I go dead. Ay-ay.

[Silence. Jackson on the floor, gasping, lying on his back. Harry crosses over, picks up the parasol, opens it, after a little difficulty, then puts on the goatskin hat. Jackson lies on the floor, silent].

HARRY. I never hit any goddamned maintenance ser-geant on the head in the service. I've never hit anybody in my life. Violence makes me sick. I don't believe in ownership. If I'd been more possessive, more authoritative, I don't think she'd have left me. I don't think you ever drove an ice pick through anybody's hand, either. That was just the two of us acting.

JACKSON. Creole acting? *[He is still lying on the floor]* Don't be too sure about the ice pick.

HARRY. I'm sure. You're a fake. You're a kind man and you think you have to hide it. A lot of other people could have used that to their own advantage. That's the difference between master and servant.

JACKSON. That master-and-servant shit finish. Bring a beer for me.

[He is still on his back]

HARRY. There's no more beer. You want a sip of Scotch?

JACKSON. Anything.

[Harry goes to the Scotch, brings over the bottle, stands over Jackson]

HARRY. Here. To me bloody wife! *[Jackson sits up, begins to move off]* What's wrong, you forget to flush it?

JACKSON. I don't think you should bad-talk her behind her back.

Derek Walcott

[He exits]

HARRY. Behind her back? She's in England. She's a star. Star? She's a bloody planet.

[Jackson returns, holding the photograph of Harry's wife]

JACKSON. If you going bad-talk, I think she should hear what you going to say, you don't think so, darling? *[Addressing the photograph, which he puts down]* If you have to tell somebody something, tell them to their face. *[Addressing the photograph]* Now, you know all you women, eh? Let the man talk his talk and don't interrupt.

HARRY. You're fucking bonkers, you know that? Before I hired you, I should have asked for a medical report.

JACKSON. Please tell your ex-wife good afternoon or something. The dame in the pantomime is always played by a man, right?

HARRY. Bullshit.

[Jackson sits close to the photograph, wiggling as he ventriloquizes]

JACKSON. *[In an Englishwoman's voice]* Is not bullshit at all, Harold. Everything I say you always saying bullshit, bullshit. How can we conduct a civilized conversation if you don't give me a chance? What have I done, Harold, oh, Harold, for you to treat me so?

HARRY. Because you're a silly selfish bitch and you **killed our son**!

JACKSON. *[Crying]* There, there, you see . . .? *[He wipes the eyes of the photograph]* You're calling me names, it wasn't my fault, and you're calling me names. Can't you ever forgive me for that, Harold?

HARRY. Ha! You never told him that, did you? You neglected to mention that little matter, didn't you, love?

JACKSON. *[Weeping]* I love you, Harold. I love you, and I loved him, too. Forgive me, O God, please, please forgive me . . . *[As himself]* So how it happen? Murder? A accident?

HARRY. *[To the photograph]* Love me? You loved me so much you get drunk and you . . . ah, ah, what's the use? What's the bloody use?

[Wipes his eye. Pause]

JACKSON. *[As wife]* I'm crying too, Harold. Let bygones be bygones . . . *[Harry lunges for the photograph, but Jackson whips it away]* *[As himself]* You miss, Harold. *[Pause; as wife]* Harold . . . *[Silence]*

Harold . . . speak to me . . . please. *[Silence]* What do you plan to do next? *[Sniffs]* What'll you do now?

HARRY. What difference does it make? . . . All right. I'll tell you what I'm going to do next, Ellen: you're such a big star, you're such a luminary, I'm going to leave you to shine by yourself. I'm giving up this bloody rat race and I'm going to take up Mike's offer. I'm leaving "the theatuh," which destroyed my confidence, screwed up my marriage, and made you a star. I'm going somewhere where I can get pissed every day and watch the sun set, like Robinson bloody Crusoe. That's what I'm going to bloody do. You always said it's the only part I could play.

JACKSON. *[As wife]* Take me with you, then. Let's get away together. I always wanted to see the tropics, the palm trees, the lagoons . . .

[Harry grabs the photograph from Jackson; he picks up the ice pick and puts the photograph on the table, pressing it down with one palm]

HARRY. All right, Ellen, I'm going to . . . You can scream all you like, but I'm going to . . .

[He raises the ice pick]

JACKSON. *[As wife]* My face is my fortune.

[He sneaks up behind Harry, whips the photograph away while Harry is poised with the ice pick]

HARRY. Your face is your fortune, eh? I'll kill her Jackson, I'll maim that smirking bitch . . .

[He lunges toward Jackson, who leaps away, holding the photograph before his face, and runs around the gazebo, shrieking]

JACKSON. *[As wife]* Help! Help! British police! My husband trying to kill me! Help, somebody, help! *[Harry chases Jackson with the ice pick, but Jackson nimbly avoids him]* *[As wife]* **Harry! Have you gone mad?**

[He scrambles onto the ledge of the gazebo. He no longer holds the photograph to his face, but his voice is the wife's].

HARRY. Get down off there, you melodramatic bitch. You're too bloody conceited to kill yourself. Get down from there, Ellen! Ellen, it's a straight drop to the sea!

JACKSON. *[As wife]* Push me, then! Push me, Harry! You hate me so much, why you don't come and push me?

HARRY. Push yourself, then. You never needed my help. Jump!

JACKSON. [*As wife*] Will you forgive me now, or after I jump?

HARRY. Forgive you? . . .

JACKSON. [*As wife*] All right, then. Goodbye!

[*He turns, teetering, about to jump*]

HARRY. [*Shouts*] *Ellen! Stop! I forgive you!* [*Jackson turns on the ledge. Silence. Harry is now sitting on the floor*] That's the real reason I wanted to do the panto. To do it better than you ever did. You played Crusoe in the panto, Ellen. I was Friday. Black bloody grease-paint that made you howl. You wiped the stage with me . . . Ellen . . . well. Why not? I was no bloody good.

JACKSON. [*As himself*] Come back to the play, Mr. Trewe. Is Jackson. We was playing Robinson Crusoe, remember?

[*Silence*] Master, Friday here . . . [*Silence*] You finish with the play? The panto? Crusoe must get up, he must make himself get up. He have to face a next day again. [*Shouts*] *I tell you: man must live!* Then, after many years, he see this naked footprint that is the mark of his salvation . . .

HARRY. [*Recites*]

"The self-same moment I could pray;
and . . . tata tee-tum-tum
The Albatross fell off and sank
Like lead into the sea."

God, my memory . . .

JACKSON. That ain't Crusoe, that is "The Rime of the Ancient Mariner."

[*He pronounces it "Marina"*]

HARRY. Mariner.

JACKSON. Marina.

HARRY. Mariner.

JACKSON. "The Rime of the Ancient Marina." So I learn it in Fourth Standard.

HARRY. It's your country, mate.

JACKSON. Is your language, pardner. I stand corrected. Now, you ain't see English crazy? I could sit down right next to you and tell you I *stand* corrected.

HARRY. Sorry. Where were we, Mr. Phillip?

JACKSON. Tobago. Where are you? It was your cue, Mr. Trewe.

HARRY. Where was I, then?

JACKSON. Ahhhm . . . That speech you was reading . . . that speech . . .

HARRY. Speech?

JACKSON. "O silent sea and so on . . . wreathed in mist . . ." Shall we take it from there, then? The paper.

HARRY. I should know it. After all, I wrote it. But prompt . . . [*Harry gives Jackson his copy of the paper, rises, walks around, looks toward the sea*] Creole or classical?

JACKSON. Don't make joke.

[*Silence. Sea-gull cries*]

HARRY. Then Crusoe, in his desolation, looks out to the sea, for the ten thousandth time, and remembers England, his wife, his little son, and speaks to himself: [*As Crusoe*] "O silent sea, O wondrous sunset that I've gazed on ten thousand times, who will rescue me from this complete desolation? Yes, this is paradise, I know. For I see around me the splendors of nature. The ferns, the palms like silent sentinels, the wide and silent lagoons that briefly hold my passing, solitary reflection. The volcano wreathed in mist. But what is paradise without a woman? Adam in paradise had his woman to share his loneli-ness . . . loneliness . . .

JACKSON. [*Prompts*] . . . but I miss the voice . . .

HARRY. [*Remembering*] "But I miss the voice . . . [*Weeping, but speaking clearly*] of even one consoling creature, the touch . . . of a hand . . . the look of kind eyes . . . Where is the wife from whom I vowed . . . never to be sundered? How old is my little son? If he could see his father like this . . . dressed in goatskins and mad with memories of them?"

[*He breaks down, quietly sobbing. A long pause*]

JACKSON. You crying or you acting?

HARRY. Acting.

JACKSON. I think you crying. Nobody could act that good.

HARRY. How would you know? You an actor?

JACKSON. Maybe not. But I cry a'ready.

HARRY. Okay, I was crying.

JACKSON. For what?

HARRY. [*Laughs*] For what? I got carried away. I'm okay now.

JACKSON. But you laughing now.

HARRY. It's the same sound. You can't tell the difference if I turn my back.

JACKSON. Don't make joke.

HARRY. It's an old actor's trick. I'm going to cry now, all right?

[*He turns, then sobs with laughter, covering and uncovering his face with his hands. Jackson stalks around, peers at him, then begins to giggle. They are now both laughing*]

JACKSON. [*Through laughter*] So . . . so . . . next Friday . . . when the tourists come . . . Crusoe . . . Crusoe go be ready for them . . . Goat race . . .

HARRY. [*Laughing*] Goat-roti!

JACKSON. [*Laughing*] Gambling.

HARRY. [*Baffled*] Gambling?

JACKSON. Goat-to-pack. Every night . . .

HARRY. [*Laughing*] Before they goat-to-bed!

JACKSON. [*Laughing*] So he striding up the beach with his little goat-ee . . .

HARRY. [*Laughing*] E-goat-istical, again.

[*Pause*]

JACKSON. You get the idea. So, you okay, Mr. Trewe?

HARRY. I'm fine, Mr. Phillip. You know . . . [*He wipes his eyes*] An angel passes through a house and leaves no imprint of his shadow on its wall. A man's life slowly changes and he does not understand the change. Things like this have happened before, and they can happen again. You understand, Jackson? You see what it is I'm saying?

JACKSON. You making a mole hill out of a mountain, sir. But I think I follow you. You know what all this make me decide, pardner?

HARRY. What?

[*Jackson picks up the umbrella, puts on the goatskin hat*]

JACKSON. I going back to the gift that's my God-given calling. I benignly resign, you fire me. With inspiration. Caiso is my true work, caiso is my true life.

[*Sings*]

Well, a Limey name Trewe come to Tobago.
He was in show business but he had no show,
so in desperation he turn to me
and said: "Mr. Phillip" is the two o' we,
one classical actor and one Creole,
let we act together with we heart and soul.
It go be man to man, and we go do it fine,
and we go give it the title of pantomime.
La da dee da da da
dee da da da da da . . .

[*He is singing as if in a spotlight. Music, audience applause. Harry joins in*]

Wait! Wait! Hold it!

[*Silence: walks over to Harry*]

Starting from Friday, Robinson, we could talk 'bout a raise?

[FADEOUT]

ESSAY: AN APPROACH TO THE PLAY

Jackson often uses such words as "pre-colonial" and "imperialst" when speaking with Harry. Not only is he a black salaried worker in white Harry's hotel, his language implies that race relations are inseparable from economic and power relations. Harry and Jackson cannot be equals while Harry pays his salary. To understand Jackson's perspective, it is important to realize that black slavery had a somewhat different history in the United States and in the Caribbean. In the United States the slaveowner typically lived on the land which his slaves worked, knew many of his slaves individually, and came to associate his power in possessing the land with his power over the slaves who worked that land. Quite apart from his thinking about his economic situation, the white slaveowner in this country typically felt that his personal power over particular individual slaves was a function of his position in the world. There was nothing a slave could do that did not require the command or permission of the master. If a slave escaped, the slaveowner felt personally diminished, felt a personal loss of power.

The experience of slavery in the islands, while at least as terrible, was different in that typically the slaveowner lived far away in Europe. Because these owners were absentees, their sense of the importance of their slaves was less personal and more purely economic than that of their counterparts in the States. Plantations existed to make money to be sent back to the owner, not as land for the master to live on. Slaves were valuable, not so much in themselves, but insofar as they could produce profits. They could be viewed objectively, like a machine, like a laboring commodity, like a capitalist investment. The relationship was far less personal: like a machine or any other item in an inventory, if they became unprofitable for any reason they could be sold and the owner's capital reinvested in some other commodity. Although the slaves had no more power in one place than another, and no less suffering, the Caribbean slave was likely to have had no personal experience of the root of white power, the owner. When independence was finally conferred, these ex-slaves were the majority population of their islands and had less of the problem of integrating themselves into an alien but dominant white culture.

What they had instead was the problem of self-governance. The problem was and remains that they had no tradition of self-governance, nor had the previous white ruling class provided them with much training or preparation for such responsibilities. One "natural" response for this postcolonial population was to copy the only tradition of government they did have experience of, even if it *was* white and European, but another equally "natural" though conflicting response was to repudiate those traditions as part of the enslaving experience, even without clear alternatives. Better the uncertainties of freedom than the same old political structures which had enslaved them. Better still, perhaps, to rediscover the other traditions of pre-colonial Africa, but they were difficult to identify: like the parrot, Africans, too, have been corrupted by their experience as the colonized.

Pantomime represents such uncertainties in the character of a sophisticated postcolonial black actor, set against a liberal white actor who means well (while living in his native England, he had demonstrated on behalf of all the politically correct causes), but who, being white, does not fully understand the implications of what it takes to *do* well, let alone the implications of being white and an owner on an island whose population has known white overseers and white capitalist owners for generations. By way of improvising and rehearsing the play within the play, Jackson teaches Harry and their audience (and we are audience both of their play and of Walcott's) about these complexities.

The complexities are not resolved. They remain elusive, just as the past of the characters, along with what they really think and feel, remains elusive. When Jackson becomes a black Robinson Crusoe, he seems in control and gives a native's twist to the discoverer/conqueror/imperialist/Columbus character, but this reversal of the old story is again reversed. In play and in "reality," the white Robinson Crusoe resumes his mastery, but now in a play and a reality which are sanctioned by the old–new Friday–Jackson. Jackson, who has better manners and self-discipline than Harry, seems almost more English than the white Englishman. He is Harry's "shadow," a mimic who can, he says, drive the Englishman mad by showing him the truth of England and Europe. Harry resumes mastery only because he is allowed to do so and only on condition that his postcolonial shadow can both copy and attack him, forcing him into self-knowledge, the relationship raising the question of who is "truly" master.

The play also leads us to wonder about Jackson: by killing the parrot, is he sublimating his desire to kill the white owner? Or is he trying to kill the colonial corruptions in himself? Or both? He, no less than Harry, has a dilemma, and the dilemma is no more resolved for him than for Harry or for us. It is implied in the issue of tourism which the play also raises. Harry caters to the tourists: his own and Jackson's financial independence both depend on them, and all the action of their play is directed toward them. Are they manipulating and exploiting the tourists? Or are the tourists their new absentee masters? The honesty with which Walcott raises such questions accounts for a large part of the play's powerful appeal.

Athol Fugard

THE ROAD TO MECCA

About the Author   Athol Fugard (1932–   ) was born in a tiny hamlet in the Karoo, the semi-arid interior of South Africa's Cape Province in which *The Road to Mecca* is set. He is descended from both the European colonial powers that until very recently had politically dominated South Africa: his father was Anglo-Irish and his mother, Afrikaans. Fugard first gained international attention as a white South African whose work revealed the oppression and social injustice inherent in his country's social policy of apartheid. Many of his early works deal with life in the townships, the settlements on the outskirts of South Africa's major cities where the black work force was required to live. Two of his best-known works from the early 1970s, *Sizwe Bansi Is Dead* (1972) and *The Island* (1973), were actually ensemble pieces, exercises in what he called play making, rather than play writing. The plays were worked out in rehearsals with his collaborators, the black actors John Kani and Winston Ntshona, two men with whom Fugard had acted as early as 1968. The actors were encouraged to improvise for each performance, so that the "text" consists of a transcription of one performance among many, made about a year after the plays' openings. Fugard's best-known play, the broadly autobiographical *"Master Harold" . . . and the Boys* (1982), deals with the complex relationship between a white adolescent and a middle-aged black man who works in the café owned by the boy's family.

In recent years, Fugard's professional career has been identified with New Haven, Connecticut, as well as with South Africa. Both *Sizwe Bansi* and *The Island* had their American premiers at the Long Wharf Theatre in New Haven, and *A Lesson from Aloes* (1978) was first staged at the Yale Repertory Theatre. *"Master Harold"* and *The Road to Mecca* (1984) also had their world premieres at the Yale Repertory, with Fugard serving as director. *The Blood Knot* (1961), the first of his plays to attract international attention, was revived at the Yale Repertory in 1985 before moving to Broadway, with Fugard again serving as director and with Fugard and the black actor Zakes Mokae re-creating the roles they had played a quarter of a century earlier in the original Johannesburg production.

About the Play   *The Road to Mecca*, written immediately after *"Master Harold,"* seems to be something of a departure from Fugard's earlier works: an introspective play that does not deal directly with his country's racial problems. According to the author, one of the origins of the play was the offhand comment of an actress friend that although he had written wonderful roles for women, he had never put two women on stage together. *The Road to Mecca* is similar to many of Fugard's plays in another way, however: it has a very limited cast, in this case three characters; he sometimes limits himself to two. In fact, there are only the two female characters on stage until the closing moment of Act 1; they are then joined by the local minister, Marius Byleveld, who remains on stage through most of Act 2, after which the original two characters are again alone on stage until the end of the play. Samuel Beckett's spare theatrical style seems to have been an important formative influence.

The play's main character is based on a real person. In the town of New Bethesda, some fifteen miles from his birthplace, Fugard owns a weekend home. In the town there lived a local recluse named Helen Martins who, after her husband's death, began making the kind of statues described in the play. She worked at them obsessively for more than fifteen years and then, after about two years of artistic inactivity, killed herself. In her later years Helen Martins developed a close friendship with a young woman social worker from Cape Town, paralleled in the play by Helen's friendship with Elsa, a liberal white teacher in a school for coloreds. Although this outline of Helen Martins' life served Fugard as the basis for his play, he reconfigured it to serve his own ends. There seems to be an autobiographical, as well as a mythic and symbolic, dimension to this reconfiguration. Helen Martins becomes Helen "Niemand," an Afrikaans word meaning "nobody," and she seems to become a figure of the artist—perhaps of the South African artist, in particular—pursuing a spiritually liberating vision which distances her from the spiritually repressive community in which she finds herself. In an interview in the journal *Theater*, Fugard said, "At one level, I almost feel that I should play the role of Helen, because Helen is me. I certainly know one thing: the little I know about whatever creative energy I've got I have invested in my writing and portrayal of Helen" [*Theater*, 16 (1), 1984:35].

CHARACTERS

MISS HELEN
ELSA
MARIUS BYLEVELD

TIME: AUTUMN 1974

PLACE: NEW BETHESDA, SOUTH AFRICA

Act I

The living room and, leading off it, the bedroom alcove of a house in the small Karoo village of New Bethesda. An extraordinary room by virtue of the attempt to use as much light and color as is humanly possible. The walls—mirrors on all of them—are all of different colors, while on the ceiling and floor are solid, multicolored geometric patterns. Yet the final effect is not bizarre but rather one of light and extravagant fantasy. Just what the room is really about will be revealed later when its candles and lamps—again, a multitude of them of every size, shape and color—are lit. The late afternoon light does, however, give some hint of the magic to come.

Miss Helen is in the bedroom alcove. A frail, birdlike little woman in her late sixties. A suggestion of personal neglect, particularly in her clothes, which are shabby and were put on with obvious indifference to the final effect. She is nervously fussing around an old-fashioned washstand, laying out towels, soap, etc., etc., and from time to time directs her attention to the living room and a door leading from it to the rest of the house. In the course of moving around she sees an overnight bag and a briefcase on the floor near the living-room entrance. She fetches these and carries them into the alcove.

Elsa enters, a strong young woman in her late twenties dressed in a track suit or something else suitable for a long motorcar ride.

ELSA. Not cold enough yet for the car to freeze up, is it?
HELEN. No. No danger of that. We haven't had any frost yet.
ELSA. I'm too exhausted to put it away. [*Collapses on the bed*] Whew! Thank God that's over. Another hour and I would have been wiped out. That road gets longer and longer every time.
HELEN. Your hot water is nearly ready.
ELSA. Good. [*Starts to unpack her overnight bag*]
HELEN. Nice clean towels . . . and I've opened that box of scented soaps you brought me last time.
ELSA. What? Oh, those. Haven't you used them yet?
HELEN. Of course not! I was keeping them for a special occasion.
ELSA. And this is it?
HELEN. Yes. An unexpected visit from you is a *very* special occasion. Is that all your luggage?
ELSA. When I said a short visit I really meant it.
HELEN. Such a long way to drive for just one night.
ELSA. I know.
HELEN. You don't think you could . . . ?
ELSA. Stay longer?
HELEN. Even just two nights?
ELSA. Impossible. We're right in the middle of exams. I've got to be in that classroom at eight-thirty on Monday morning. As it is I should be sitting at home right now marking papers. I've even brought

a pile of them with me just in case I get a chance up here. [*Starts to undress—track-suit top, sneakers and socks.*]

HELEN. Put anything you want washed on one side and I'll get a message to Katrina first thing in the morning.

ELSA. Don't bother her with that. I can do it myself.

HELEN. You can't leave without seeing Katrina! She'll never forgive me if I don't let her know you're here. Please . . . even if it's only for a few minutes.

ELSA. I won't leave without seeing Katrina, Miss Helen! But I don't need her to wash a pair of pants and a bra for me. I do my own washing.

HELEN. I'm sorry . . . I just thought you might. . . . There's an empty drawer here if you want to pack anything away.

ELSA [*An edge to her voice*]. Please stop fussing, Miss Helen! I know my way around by now.

HELEN. It's just that if I'd known you were coming, I would have had everything ready for you.

ELSA. Everything is fine just the way it is.

HELEN. No, it isn't! I don't even know that I've got enough in the kitchen for a decent supper tonight. I did buy bread yesterday, but for the rest . . .

ELSA. Please, Miss Helen! If we need anything, I'll get old Retief to open his shop for us. In any case, I'm not hungry. All I need at this moment is a good wash and a chance to unwind so that I can forget I've been sitting in a motorcar for twelve hours.

HELEN. Be patient with me, Elsie. Remember the little saying: "Patience is a virtue, virtue is a grace, and—"

ELSA [*Unexpectedly sharp*]. For God's sake, Helen! Just leave me alone for a few minutes!

[*Pause.*]

HELEN [*Timidly*]. I'll get your hot water.

[*Miss Helen exits. Elsa slumps down on the bed, her head in her hands. Miss Helen returns a few seconds later with a large kettle of hot water. She handles it with difficulty.*]

I've got the small one on for tea.

ELSA. Let me do that!

[*She jumps up and takes the kettle away from Miss Helen. The two women stand staring at each other for a few seconds. Elsa puts down the kettle and then puts her hands on Miss Helen's shoulders.*]

My turn to say sorry.

HELEN. You don't need to do that.

ELSA. Please! It will help. Sorry, Miss Helen. I also need to hear you say you forgive me.

HELEN. To tell you the truth, I was getting on my own nerves.

ELSA [*Now smiling*]. Come on.

HELEN. Oh, all right. . . . But I promise you it isn't necessary. You're forgiven.

ELSA [*Leading Miss Helen over to a chair*]. Now sit down and stop worrying about me. We're both going to close our eyes, take a deep breath and start again. Ready?

HELEN. Ready.

ELSA. One, two, three . . .

[*Closed eyes and deep breaths.*]

And now?

HELEN [*With the sly, tongue-in-cheek humor we will come to recognize as characteristic of the relaxed woman*]. Well, if you really mean it, I think the best thing is for you to get back into your car, drive around the block and arrive again. And this time I want you, please, to hoot three times the way you usually do, so that I don't think a ghost has walked in through the front door when you appear.

ELSA [*Calling Miss Helen's bluff*]. Right. Where are the car keys? [*Finds them and heads for the front door.*]

HELEN. Where are you going?

ELSA. To do what you said. Drive around the block and arrive again.

HELEN. Like that?

ELSA. Why, what's wrong?

HELEN. Elsie! Sterling Retief will have a heart attack if he sees you like that.

ELSA. But I wear less than this when I go to the beach. Oh, all right then, you old spoilsport, let's pretend.

[*Elsa runs into the other room, revs up her motorcar, grinds through all its gears and "arrives." Three blasts on the horn. The two women play the "arrival game" (specifics to be determined in rehearsal). At the end of it they come together in a good laugh.*]

If my friends in Cape Town were to have seen that! You must understand, Miss Helen, Elsa Barlow is known as a "serious young woman." Bit of a bluestocking, in fact. Not much fun there! I don't know how you did it, Helen, but you caught me with those stockings down from the first day we met. You have the rare distinction of being the only person who can make me make a fool of myself . . . and enjoy it.

HELEN. You weren't making a fool of yourself. And anyway what about me? Nearly seventy and behaving as if I were seven!

ELSA. Let's face it, we've both still got a little girl hidden away in us somewhere.

HELEN. And they like to play together.

ELSA. Mine hasn't done that for a long time.

HELEN. And I didn't even know that mine was still alive.

ELSA. *That* she most certainly is. She's the one who comes running out to play first. Feeling better?

HELEN. Much better.

[*For the moment all tensions are gone. Elsa cleans herself as thoroughly as a basin of water, a facecloth and a bar of scented soap will allow.*]

ELSA. God, this Karoo dust gets right into your pores. I can even taste it. That first mouthful of tea is going to be mud. I'll fill up all the kettles tomorrow and have a really good scrub. When did you last have one? [*Miss Helen has to think about that*] Right, settled. Your name is down for one as well. [*A few seconds of industrious scrubbing. Miss Helen watches her*] What are you thinking?

HELEN. So many things! About the way you *did* arrive. I wasn't joking. For a few seconds I did think I was seeing a ghost. I heard the front door open . . . I thought it was little Katrina, she also never knocks . . . but instead there you were. [*She wants to say more but stops herself.*]

ELSA. Go on.

HELEN. It was so strange. Almost as if you didn't really see me or anything else at first . . . didn't want to. And so cross! I've never seen you like that before.

ELSA. This isn't quite like the other times, Miss Helen.

HELEN. That's a pity. They were all good times. [*Pause*] So what sort of time is this going to be? A bad one?

ELSA [*Evenly*]. I hope not. Doesn't have to be. It depends on you.

[*Miss Helen avoids Elsa's eyes. The young woman looks around the room.*]

But you're right. I hadn't really arrived until now.

HELEN. Where were you, Elsie?

ELSA [*She thinks about the question before answering*]. Way back at the turnoff to the village from the National Road . . . or maybe a few miles further along it now . . . walking to Cradock.

HELEN. I don't understand.

ELSA. I gave a lift to a woman outside Graaff-Reinet. That's most probably where she is now. I dropped her at the turnoff to the village.

HELEN. Who was she?

ELSA [*Shrugging with apparent indifference*]. An African woman.

HELEN. Cradock! That's a long walk.

ELSA. I know.

HELEN. It's about another eighty miles from the turnoff. [*She waits for Elsa to say more.*]

ELSA. I nearly didn't stop for her. She didn't signal that she wanted a lift or anything like that. Didn't even look up when I passed . . . I was watching her in the rearview mirror. Maybe that's what told me there was a long walk ahead of her . . . the way she had her head down and just kept on walking. And then the baby on her back. It was hot out there, Miss Helen, hot and dry and a lot of empty space. . . . There wasn't a farmhouse in sight. She looked very small and unimportant in the middle of all that. Anyway, I stopped and reversed and offered her a lift. Not very graciously. I'd already been driving for ten hours and all I wanted was to get here as fast as I could. She got in and after a few miles we started talking. Her English wasn't very good, but when I finally got around to understanding what she was trying to tell me it added up to a good old South African story. Her husband, a farm laborer, had died recently, and no sooner had they buried him when the *baas* told her to pack up and leave the farm. So there she was . . . on her way to the Cradock district, where she hoped to find a few distant relatives and a place to live. [*Trying to remember the woman as clearly as possible.*] About my age. The baby couldn't have been more than a few months old. All she had with her was one of those plastic shopping bags they put your groceries in at supermarkets. I saw a pair of old slippers. She was barefoot.

HELEN. Poor woman.

ELSA. So I dropped her at the turnoff. Gave her what was left of my food and some money. She carried on walking and I drove here.

[*Pause.*]

HELEN. Is there something else?

ELSA. No. That's all.

HELEN. I'm sure somebody else will give her a lift.

ELSA [*Too easily*]. Hope so. If not, she and her baby are in for a night beside the road. There's eighty miles of the Karoo ahead of her. Shadows were already stretching out across the veld when she got out of the car. The Great Karoo! And just when I thought I was getting used to it, beginning to like it, in fact. Down in Cape Town I've actually caught myself talking rubbish about its vast space and emptiness, its awesome stillness and silence! Just like old Getruida down the road. It's that all right, but only because everything else has been all but damned out of existence. It's so obvious where you Afrikaners get your ideas of God from. Beats me how you've put up with it so long, Miss Helen. Nearly seventy years? My God, you deserve a medal. I would have packed up and left it at the first opportunity . . . and let's face it, you've had plenty of those.

HELEN. I was born here, Elsa.

ELSA. I sympathize, Miss Helen. Believe me, I truly sympathize.

HELEN. It's not really as bad as you make it sound. The few times I've been away, I've always ended up missing it and longing to be back.

ELSA. Because you wanted to get back to your work.

HELEN [*Shaking her head*]. No. Even before all that started. It grows on you, Elsa.

ELSA. Which is just about the only growing it seems to allow. For the rest, it's as merciless as the religion they preach around here. Looking out of the car window this afternoon I think I finally understood a few things about you Afrikaners . . . and it left me feeling just a little uneasy.

HELEN. You include me in all you're saying.

ELSA. Yes. You might not go to church anymore, but you're still an Afrikaner, Miss Helen. You were in there with them, singing hymns every Sunday, for a long, long time. Bit of a renegade now, I admit, but you're still one at heart.

HELEN. And that heart is merciless?

[*Pause.*]

ELSA. No. That you aren't. A lot of other things maybe, but certainly not that. Sorry, sorry, sorry . . .

HELEN. You're still very cross, aren't you? And something else as well. There's a new sound in your voice. One I haven't heard before.

ELSA. What do you mean?

HELEN. Like the way you talked about that woman on the road. Almost as if you didn't care, which I know isn't true.

ELSA. Of course I cared. I cared enough to stop and pick her up, to give her money and food. But I also don't want to fool myself. That was a sop to my conscience and nothing more. It wasn't a real contribution to her life and what she is up against. Anyway, what's the point in talking about her? She's most probably curling up in a stormwater drain at this moment—that's where she said she'd sleep if she didn't get a lift—and I feel better for a good wash.

HELEN. There it is again.

ELSA. Well, it's the truth.

HELEN. It was the way you said it.

ELSA. You're imagining things, Miss Helen. Come on, let's talk about something else. It's too soon to get serious. We've got enough time, and reasons, for that later on. What's been happening in the village? Give me the news. Your last letter didn't have much of that in it.

[*Elsa gets into clean clothes. Miss Helen starts to fold the discarded track suit. Elsa stops her.*]

I can do that.

HELEN. I just wanted to help.

ELSA. And you can do that by making a nice pot of tea and giving me the village gossip.

[*Miss Helen goes into the living room. She takes cups and saucers, etc., from a sideboard and places them on the table.*]

HELEN. I haven't got any gossip. Little Katrina is the only one who really visits me anymore, and all she wants to talk about these days is her baby. There's also Marius, of course, but he never gossips.

ELSA. He still comes snooping around, does he?

HELEN. Don't put it like that, Elsa. He's a very old friend.

ELSA. Good luck to him. I hope the friendship continues. It's just that *I* wouldn't want him for one. Sorry, Miss Helen, but I don't trust your old friend, and I have a strong feeling that Pastor Marius Byleveld feels the same way about me. So let's change the subject. Tell me about Katrina. What has she been up to?

HELEN. She's fine. And so is the baby. As prettily dressed these days as any white baby, thanks to the clothes you sent her. She's been very good to me, Elsa. Never passes my front door without dropping in for a little chat. Is always asking about you. I don't know what I would do without her. But I'm afraid Koos has started drinking again. And making all sorts of terrible threats about her and the baby. He still doesn't believe it's his child.

ELSA. Is he beating her?

HELEN. No. The warning you gave him last time seems to have put a stop to that.

ELSA. God, it makes me sick! Why doesn't she leave him?

HELEN. And then do what?

ELSA. Find somebody else! Somebody who will value her as a human being and take care of her and the child.

HELEN. She can't do that, Elsie. They're married.

ELSA. Oh, for God's sake, Helen. There's the Afrikaner in you speaking. There is nothing sacred about a marriage that abuses the woman! I'll have a talk to her tomorrow. Let's make sure we get a message to her to come around.

HELEN. Don't make things more difficult for her, Elsa.

ELSA. How much more difficult can "things" be than being married to a drunken bully? She *has* got a few rights, Miss Helen, and I just want to make sure she knows what they are. How old is she now?

HELEN. Seventeen, I think.

ELSA. At that age I was still at school dreaming about my future, and here she is with a baby and bruises. Quick, tell me something else.

HELEN. Let me see . . . . Good gracious me! Of course, yes! I have got important news. Old Getruida has got the whole village up in arms. Brace yourself, Elsa. She's applied for a license to open a liquor store.

ELSA. A what?

HELEN. A liquor store. Alcoholic beverages.

ELSA. Booze in New Bethesda?

HELEN. If you want to put it that bluntly . . . yes.

ELSA. Now that *is* headline material. Good for old Gerty. I always knew she liked her sundowner, but I never thought she'd have the spunk to go that far.

HELEN. Don't joke about it, Elsie. It's a very serious matter. The village is very upset.

ELSA. Headed, no doubt, by your old friend Pastor Marius Byleveld.

HELEN. That's right. I understand that his last sermon was all about the evils of alcohol and how it's ruining the health and lives of our Coloured folk. Getruida says he's taking unfair advantage of the pulpit and that the Coloureds get it anyway from Graaff-Reinet.

ELSA. Then tell her to demand a turn.

HELEN. At what?

ELSA. The pulpit. Tell her to demand her right to get up there and put her case . . . and remind her before she does that the first miracle was water into wine.

HELEN [*Trying not to laugh*]. You're terrible, Elsie! Old Getruida in the pulpit!

ELSA. And you're an old hypocrite, Miss Helen. You love it when I make fun of the Church.

HELEN. No, I don't. I was laughing at Gerty, not the Church. And you have no right to make me laugh. It's a very serious matter.

ELSA. Of course it is! Which is why I want to know who you think is worse: the dominee deciding what is right and wrong for the Coloured folk or old Getruida exploiting their misery?

HELEN. I'm afraid it's even more complicated than that, Elsa. Marius *is* only thinking about what's best for them, but on the other hand, Getruida has offered to donate part of her profits to their school building fund. And what about Koos? Wouldn't it make things even worse for Katrina if he had a local supply?

ELSA. They are two separate issues, Miss Helen. You don't punish a whole community because one man can't control his drinking. Which raises yet another point: has anybody bothered to ask the Coloured people what they think about it all?

HELEN. Are we going to have that argument again?

ELSA. I'm not trying to start an argument. But it does seem to me right and proper that if you're going to make decisions which affect other people, you should find out what those people think.

HELEN. It is the same argument. You know they don't do that here.

ELSA. Well, it's about time they started. I don't make decisions affecting the pupils at school without giving them a chance to say something. And they're children! We're talking about adult men and women in the year 1974.

HELEN. Those attitudes might be all right in Cape Town, Elsa, but you should know by now that the valley has got its own way of doing things.

ELSA. Well, it can't cut itself off from the twentieth century forever. Honestly, coming here is like stepping into the middle of a Chekhov play. While the rest of the world is hoping the bomb won't drop today, you people are arguing about who owns the cherry orchard. Your little world is not as safe as you would like to believe, Helen. If you think it's going to be left alone to stagnate in the nineteenth century while the rest of us hold our breath hoping we'll reach the end of the twentieth, you're in for one hell of a surprise. And it will start with your Coloured folk. They're not fools. They also read newspapers, you know. And if you don't believe me, try talking about something other than the weather and her baby next time Katrina comes around. You'll be surprised at what's going on inside that little head. As for you Helen! Sometimes the contradictions in you make me want to scream. Why do you always stand up and defend this bunch of bigots? Look at the way they've treated you.

HELEN [*Getting nervous*]. They leave me alone now.

ELSA. That is not what you said in your last letter!

HELEN. My last letter?

ELSA. Yes.

[*Pause. Helen has tensed.*]

Are you saying you don't remember it, Helen?

HELEN. No . . . I remember it.

ELSA. And what you said in it?

HELEN [*Trying to escape*]. Please, little Elsie! Not now. Let's talk about it later. I'm still all flustered with you arriving so unexpectedly. Give me a chance to collect my wits together. Please? And while I'm doing that, I'll make that pot of tea you asked for.

[*Miss Helen exits into the kitchen. Elsa takes stock of the room. Not an idle examination; rather, she is trying to see it objectively, trying to understand something. She spends a few seconds at the window, staring out at the statues in the yard. She sees a cardboard box in a corner and opens it— handfuls of colored ceramic chips. She also discovers a not very successful attempt to hide an ugly burn mark on one of the walls. Miss Helen returns with tea and biscuits.*]

ELSA. What happened here?

HELEN. Oh, don't worry about that. I'll get Koos or somebody to put a coat of paint over it.

ELSA. But what happened?

HELEN. One of the lamps started smoking badly when I was out of the room.

ELSA. And new curtains.

HELEN. Yes. I got tired of the old ones. I found a few Marie biscuits in the pantry. Will you be mother?

[*Light is starting to fade in the room. Elsa pours the tea, dividing her attention between that and studying the older woman. Miss Helen tries to hide her unease.*]

Do I get a turn now to ask for news?

ELSA. No.

HELEN. Why not?

ELSA. I haven't come up here to talk about myself.

HELEN. That's not fair!

ELSA. It's boring.

HELEN. Not to me. Come on Elsie, fair is fair. You asked me for the village gossip and I did my best. Now it's your turn.

ELSA. What do you want to know?

HELEN. Everything you would have told me about in your letters if you had kept your promise and written them.

ELSA. Good and bad news?

HELEN. I said everything . . . but try to make the good a little bit more than the bad.

ELSA. Right. The *Elsa Barlow Advertiser!* Hot off the presses! What do you want to start with? Financial, crime or sports page?

HELEN. The front-page headline.

ELSA. How's this? "Barlow to appear before School Board for possible disciplinary action."

HELEN. Not again!

ELSA. Yep.

HELEN. Oh dear! What was it this time?

ELSA. Wait for the story. "Elsa Barlow, a twenty-eight-year-old English-language teacher, is to appear before a Board of Enquiry of the Cape Town School Board. She faces the possibility of strict disciplinary action. The enquiry follows a number of complaints from the parents of pupils in Miss Barlow's Standard Nine class. It is alleged that in April this year Miss Barlow asked the class, as a homework exercise, to write a five-hundred-word letter to the State President on the subject of racial inequality. Miss Barlow teaches at a Coloured School."

HELEN. Is that true?

ELSA. Are you doubting the accuracy and veracity of the *Advertiser*?

HELEN. Elsie! Elsie! Sometimes I think you deliberately look for trouble.

ELSA. All I "deliberately look for," Miss Helen, are opportunities to make those young people in my classroom think for themselves.

HELEN. So what is going to happen?

ELSA. Depends on me, I suppose. If I appear before them contrite and apologetic, a stern reprimand. But if I behave the way I feel, I suppose I could lose my job.

HELEN. Do you want my advice?

ELSA. No.

HELEN. Well, I'm going to give it to you all the same. Say you're sorry and that you won't do it again.

ELSA. Both of those are lies, Miss Helen.

HELEN. Only little white ones.

ELSA. God, I'd give anything to be able to walk in and

tell that School Board exactly what I think of them and their educational system. But you're right, there are the pupils as well, and for as long as I'm in the classroom a little subversion is possible. Rebellion starts, Miss Helen, with just one man or woman standing up and saying, "No. Enough!" Albert Camus. French writer.

HELEN. You make me nervous when you talk like that.

ELSA. And you sound just like one of those parents. You know something? I think you're history's first reactionary-revolutionary. You're a double agent, Helen!

HELEN. Haven't you got any good news?

ELSA. Lots. I still don't smoke. I drink very moderately. I try to jog a few miles every morning.

HELEN. You're not saying anything about David.

ELSA. Turn to the lonely hearts column. There's a sad little paragraph: "Young lady seeks friendship with young man, etc., etc."

HELEN. You're talking in riddles. I was asking you about David.

ELSA. And I'm answering you. I've said nothing about him because there's nothing to say. It's over.

HELEN. You mean . . . you and David . . . ?

ELSA. Yes, that is exactly what I mean. It's finished. We don't see each other anymore.

HELEN. I knew there was something wrong from the moment you walked in.

ELSA. If you think this is me with something wrong, you should have been around two months ago. Your little Elsie was in a bad way. You were in line for an unexpected visit a lot earlier than this, Helen.

HELEN. You should have come.

ELSA. I nearly did. But your letters suggested that you weren't having such a good time either. If we'd got together at that point, we might have come up with a suicide pact.

HELEN. I don't think so.

ELSA. Joke, Miss Helen.

HELEN. Then don't joke about those things. Weren't you going to tell me?

ELSA. I'm trying to forget it, Helen! There's another reason why I didn't come up. It has left me with a profound sense of shame.

HELEN. Of what?

ELSA. Myself. The whole stupid mess.

HELEN. Mess?

ELSA. Yes, mess! Have you got a better word to describe a situation so rotten with lies and deceit that your only sense of yourself is one of disgust?

HELEN. And you were so happy when you told me about him on your last visit.

ELSA. God, that was more than just happiness, Miss Helen. It was like discovering the reason for being the person, the woman, I am for the first time in my life. And a little bit scary . . . realizing that another person could do so much to your life, to your sense of yourself. Even before it all went wrong, there were a couple of times when I wasn't so sure I liked it.

HELEN. But what happened? Was there a row about something?

ELSA [Bitter little laugh]. Row? Oh, Helen! Yes, there were plenty of those. But they were incidental. There had to be some sort of noise, so we shouted at each other. We also cried. We did everything you're supposed to.

HELEN. All I know about him is what you told me. He sounded like such a sensitive and good man, well-read and intelligent. So right for you.

ELSA. He was all of that. [A moment's hesitation. She is not certain about saying something. She decides to take the chance.] There's also something about him I didn't tell you. He's married. He has a devoted, loving wife—quite pretty in fact—and a child. A little girl. Shocked you?

HELEN. Yes. You should have told me, Elsie. I would have warned you.

ELSA. That's exactly why I didn't. I knew you would, but I was going to prove you wrong. Anyway, I didn't need any warnings. Anything you could have said to me, Helen, I'd said to myself from the very beginning . . . but I was going to prove myself wrong as well. What it all came down to finally was that there were two very different ideas about what was happening, and we discovered it too late. You see, I was in it for keeps, Helen. I knew that we were all going to get hurt, that somehow we would all end up being victims of the situation . . . but I also believed that when the time came to choose I would be the lucky winner, that he would leave his wife and child and go with me. Boy, was I wrong! Ding-dong, wrong-wrong, tolls Elsa's bell at the close of the day!

HELEN. Don't do that.

ELSA. Defense mechanism. It still hurts. I'm getting impatient for the time when I'll be able to laugh at it all. I mustn't make him sound like a complete bastard. He wasn't without a conscience. Far from it. If anything, it was too big. The end would have been a lot less messy if he'd known how to just walk away and close the door behind him. When finally the time for that did come, he sat around in pain and torment, crying—God, that was awful!—

waiting for me to tell him to go back to his wife and child. Should have seen him, Helen. He came up with postures of despair that would have made Michelangelo jealous. I know it's all wrong to find another person's pain disgusting, but that is what eventually happened. The last time he crucified himself on the sofa in my living room I felt like vomiting. He told me just once too often how much he hated himself for hurting me.

HELEN. Elsie, my poor darling. Come here.

ELSA [Taut]. I'm all right now. [Pause] Do you know what the really big word is, Helen? I had it all wrong. Like most people, I suppose I used to think it was "love." That's the big one all right, and it's quite an event when it comes along. But there's an even bigger one. Trust. And more dangerous. Because that's when you drop your defenses, lay yourself wide open, and if you've made a mistake, you're in big, big trouble. And it hurts like hell. Ever heard the story about the father giving his son his first lesson in business? [Miss Helen shakes her head] I think it's meant to be a joke, so remember to laugh. He puts his little boy high up on something or other and says to him, "Jump. Don't worry, I'll catch you." The child is nervous, of course, but Daddy keeps reassuring him: "I'll catch you." Eventually the little boy works up enough courage and does jump, and Daddy, of course, doesn't make a move to catch him. When the child has stopped crying because he has hurt himself—the father says: "Your first lesson in business, my son. Don't trust anybody." [Pause] If you tell it with a Jewish accent, it's even funnier.

HELEN. I don't think it's funny.

ELSA. I think it's ugly. That little boy is going to think twice about jumping again, and at this moment the same goes for Elsa Barlow.

HELEN. Don't speak too soon, Elsie. Life has surprised me once or twice.

ELSA. I'm talking about trust, Miss Helen. I can see myself loving somebody else again. Not all that interested in it right at the moment, but there's an even chance that it will happen again. Doesn't seem as if we've got much choice in the matter anyway. But trusting?

HELEN. You can have the one without the other?

ELSA. Oh yes. That much I've learned. I went on loving David long after I realized I couldn't trust him anymore. That is why life is just a bit complicated at the moment. A little of that love is still hanging around.

HELEN. I've never really thought about it.

ELSA. Neither had I. It needs a betrayal to get you going.

HELEN. Then I suppose I've been lucky. I never had any important trusts to betray . . . until I met you. My marriage might have looked like that, but it was habit that kept Stefanus and me together. I was never . . . open? . . . to him. Was that the phrase you used?

ELSA. Wide open.

HELEN. That's it! It's a good one. I was never "wide open" to anyone. But with you all of that changed. So it's as simple as that. Trust. I've always tried to understand what made you, and being with you, so different from anything else in my life. But, of course, that's it. I trust you. That's why my little girl can come out and play. All the doors are wide open!

ELSA [Breaking the mood]. So there, Miss Helen. You asked for the news . . .

HELEN. I almost wish I hadn't.

[Light has now faded. Miss Helen fetches a box of matches and lights the candles on the table. The room floats up gently out of the gloom, the mirrors and glitter on the walls reflecting the candlelight. Elsa picks up one of the candles and walks around the room with it, and we see something of the magic to come.]

ELSA. Still works, Miss Helen. In the car driving up I was wondering if the novelty would have worn off a little. But here it is again. You're a little wizard, you know. You make magic with your mirrors and glitter. "Never light a candle carelessly, and be sure you know what you're doing when you blow one out!" Remember saying that?

HELEN. To myself, yes. Many times.

ELSA. And to me . . . after you had stopped laughing at the expression on my face when you lit them for the first time. "Light is a miracle, Miss Barlow, which even the most ordinary human being can make happen." We had just had our first pot of tea together. Maybe I do take it all just a little for granted now. But that first time . . . I wish I could make you realize what it's like to be walking down a dusty, deserted little street in a God-forsaken village in the middle of the Karoo, bored to death by the heat and flies and silence, and then to be stopped in your tracks—and I mean stopped!—by all of that out there. And then, having barely recovered from that, to come inside and find this! Believe me, Helen, when I saw your "Mecca" for the first time, I just stood there and gaped. "What in God's name am I looking at? Camels and pyramids? Not three, but dozens of Wise Men? Owls with old motorcar headlights for eyes? Peacocks with more color and glitter than the real birds? Heat stroke? Am I hallucinating?" And then you! Standing next to a mosque made out of beer bottles and staring back at me like one of your owls! [*A good laugh at the memory*] She's mad. No question about it. Everything they've told me about her is true. A genuine Karoo nutcase. [*Walking carefully around Miss Helen in a mock attitude of wary and suspicious examination*] Doesn't look dangerous, though. Wait . . . she's smiling! Be careful, Barlow! Could be a trick. They didn't say she was violent, though. Just mad. Mad as a hatter. Go on. Take a chance. Say hello and see what happens. "Hello!"

[*Both women laugh.*]

HELEN. You're exaggerating. It wasn't like that at all.

ELSA. Yes, it was.

HELEN. And I'm saying it wasn't. To start with, it wasn't the mosque. I was repairing a mermaid.

ELSA. I forgot the mermaids!

HELEN [*Serenely certain*]. And I was the one who spoke first. I asked you to point out the direction to Mecca. You made a mistake, and so I corrected you. Then I invited you into the yard, showed you around, after which we came into the house for that pot of tea.

ELSA. That is precisely what I mean! Who would ever believe it? That you found yourself being asked to point out the direction to Mecca—not London, or New York, or Paris, but Mecca—in the middle of the Karoo by a little lady no bigger than a bird, surrounded by camels and owls . . . and mermaids! . . . made of cement? Who in their right mind is going to believe that? And then this [*The room*], your little miracle of light and color. [*Miss Helen is smiling with suppressed pride and pleasure*] You were proud of yourself, weren't you? Come on, admit it.

HELEN [*Trying hard to contain her emotion*]. Yes, I admit I was a little proud.

ELSA. Miss Helen, just a little?

HELEN [*She can't hold back any longer*]. All right, then, no! Not just a little. Oh, most definitely not. I was prouder of myself that day than I had ever been in my life. Nobody before you, or since, has done that to me. I was tingling all over with excitement as we walked around the yard looking at the statues. All those years of working on my Mecca had at last been vindicated. I've got a silly little confession to

make about that first meeting. When we came inside and were sitting in here talking and drinking tea and the light started to fade and it became time to light a candle . . . I suddenly realized I was beginning to feel shy, more shy than I had even been with Stefanus on my wedding night. It got so bad I was half-wishing you would stand up and say it was time to go! You see, when I lit the candles you were finally going to see all of me. I don't mean my face, or the clothes I was wearing—you had already seen all of that out in the yard—I mean the *real* me, because that is what this room is . . . and I desperately, oh so desperately, wanted you to like what you saw. By the time we met I had got used to rude eyes staring at me and my work, dismissing both of them as ugly. I'd lived with those eyes for fifteen years, and they didn't bother me anymore. Yours were different. In just the little time we had already been together I had ended up feeling. . . . No, more than that: I *knew* I could trust them. There's our big word again, Elsie! I was so nervous I didn't know what we were talking about anymore while I sat here trying to find enough courage to get a box of matches and light the candles. But eventually I did and you . . . you looked around the room and laughed with delight! You liked what you saw! This is the best of me, Elsa. This is what I really am. Forget everything else. Nothing, not even my name or my face, is me as much as those Wise Men and their camels traveling to the East, or the light and glitter in this room. The mermaids, the wise old owls, the gorgeous peacocks . . . all of them are *me*. And I had delighted you!

Dear God. If you only knew what you did for my life that day. How much courage, how much faith in it you gave me. Because all those years of being laughed at and thought a mad old woman had taken their toll, Elsie. When you walked into my life that afternoon I hadn't been able to work or make anything for nearly a year . . . and I was beginning to think I wouldn't ever again, that I had reached the end. The only reason I've got for being alive is my Mecca. Without that I'm . . . nothing . . . a useless old woman getting on everybody's nerves . . . and that is exactly what I had started to feel like. You revived my life.

I didn't sleep that night after you left. My Mecca was a long way from being finished! All the things I still had to do, all the statues I still had to make, came crowding in on me when I went to bed. I thought my head was going to burst! I've never been so impatient with darkness all my life. I sat up in bed all night waiting for the dawn to come so that I could start working again, and then just go on working and working.

ELSA. And you certainly did that, Miss Helen. On my next trip you proudly introduced me to a very stern Buddha, remember? The cement was still wet.

HELEN. That's quite right. That was my next one.

ELSA. Then came the Easter Island head, the one with the topknot.

HELEN. Correct.

ELSA. And you still haven't explained to me what it's doing in Mecca—and, for that matter, wise old owls and mermaids as well.

HELEN. My Mecca has got a logic of its own, Elsa. Even I don't properly understand it.

ELSA. And then my favorite! That strange creature, half-cock, half-man, on the point of dropping his trousers. Really Helen!

HELEN. That one is pure imagination. I don't know where it comes from. And I've told you before, he's not dropping his trousers, he's pulling them up.

ELSA. And I remain unconvinced. Take another good look at the expression on his face. That's anticipation, not satisfaction. Any surprises this time?

[*Pause.*]

HELEN. This time?

ELSA. Yes.

HELEN. No. There aren't any surprises this time.

ELSA. Work in progress?

HELEN. Not at the moment. I haven't managed to get started on anything since you were last here.

ELSA. What happened to the moon mosaic? Remember? Against the back wall! You were going to use those ceramic chips I brought you.

HELEN. They're safe. There in the corner.

ELSA. Yes, I saw them . . . in exactly the same spot where I left them three months ago. It sounded such a wonderful idea, Helen. You were so excited when you told me about it.

HELEN. And I still am. I've still got it.

ELSA. So what are you waiting for? Roll up your sleeves and get on with it.

HELEN. It's not as simple as that, Elsie. You see . . . that's the trouble. It's still only just an *idea* I'm *thinking* about. I can't see it clearly enough yet to start work on it. I've told you before, Elsie, I have to *see* them very clearly first. They've got to come to me inside like pictures. And if they don't, well, all I can do is wait . . . and hope that they will. I wish I knew how to make it happen, but I don't. I

don't know where the pictures come from. I can't force myself to see something that isn't there. I've tried to do that once or twice in the past when I was desperate, but the work always ended up a lifeless, shapeless mess. If they don't come, all I can do is wait . . . which is what I'm doing. [*She is revealing a lot of inner agitation.*]

ELSA [*Carefully*]. I'm listening, Miss Helen. Go on.

HELEN. I try to be patient with myself, but it's hard. There isn't all that much time left . . . and then my eyes . . . and my hands . . . they're not what they used to be. But the worst thing of all is . . . suppose that I'm waiting for nothing, that there won't be any more pictures inside ever again, that this time I *have* reached the end? Oh God, no! Please no. Anything but that. You do understand, don't you, Elsie?

ELSA. I think I do. [*She speaks quietly. It is not going to be easy.*] Come and sit down here with me, Helen. [*Miss Helen does so, but apprehensively.*] It's time to talk about your last letter, Helen.

HELEN. Do we have to do that now? Can't it wait?

ELSA. No.

HELEN. Please.

ELSA. Sorry, Helen, but we've only got tonight.

HELEN. Then don't spoil it!

ELSA. Helen . . . that letter is the reason for me being here. You do realize that, don't you?

HELEN. Yes. I guessed that was the reason for your visit. But you must make allowances, little Elsie. I wasn't feeling very well when I wrote it.

ELSA. That much is obvious.

HELEN. But I've cheered up ever so much since then. Truly. And now with your visit . . . I just know everything is going to be all right again. I was very depressed you see. I wrote it in a bad depression. But I regretted posting it the moment after I had dropped it into the letter box. I even thought about asking the postmaster if I could have it back.

ELSA. Why didn't you? [*Pause*] Or send me a telegram: "Ignore last letter. Feeling much better." Six words. That would have done it.

HELEN. I didn't think of that.

ELSA. We're wasting precious time. You wrote it, posted it, and I received it.

HELEN. So can't we now, please, just forget it?

ELSA [*Disbelief*]. Miss Helen, do you remember what you said in it?

HELEN. Vaguely.

ELSA. That's not good enough. [*She goes to the bedroom alcove and fetches the letter from her briefcase.*]

HELEN. What are you going to do?

ELSA. Read it.

HELEN. No! I don't want to hear it.

ELSA. You already have, Miss Helen. You wrote it.

HELEN. But I don't want to talk about it.

ELSA. Yes, you must.

HELEN. Don't bully me, Elsa! You know I don't know how to fight back. Please . . . not tonight. Can't we—

ELSA. No, we can't. For God's sake, Helen! We've only got tonight and maybe a little of tomorrow to talk.

HELEN. But you mustn't take it seriously.

ELSA. Too late, Helen. I already have. I've driven eight hundred miles without a break because of this. And don't lie to me. You meant every word of it. [*Pause*] I'm not trying to punish you for writing it. I've come because I want to try and help. [*She sits down at the table, pulls the candle closer and reads. She struggles a little to decipher words. The handwriting is obviously bad.*]

My very own and dearest little Elsie,

Have you finally also deserted me? This is my fourth letter to you and still no reply. Have I done something wrong? This must surely be the darkest night of my soul. I thought I had lived through that fifteen years ago, but I was wrong. This is worse. Infinitely worse. I had nothing to lose that night. Nothing in my life was precious or worth holding on to. Now there is so much and I am losing it all . . . you, the house, my work, my Mecca. I can't fight them alone, little Elsie. I need you. Don't you care about me anymore? It is only through your eyes that I now see my Mecca. I need you, Elsie. My eyesight is so bad that I can barely see the words I am writing. And my hands can hardly hold the pen. Help me, little Elsie. Everything is ending and I am alone in the dark. There is no light left. I would rather do away with myself than carry on like this.

Your ever-loving and anguished
Helen.

[*She carefully folds up the letter and puts it back in the envelope*] What's all that about losing your house. Who's trying to get you out?

HELEN. I exaggerated a little. They're not really being nasty about it.

ELSA. Who?

HELEN. The Church Council. They say it's for my own good. And I do understand what they mean, it's just that—

ELSA. Slowly, Miss Helen, slowly. I still don't know what you're talking about. Start from the beginning.

What has the Church Council got to do with you and the house? I thought it was yours.

HELEN. It is.

ELSA. So?

HELEN. It's not the house, Elsa. It's me. They discussed me . . . my situation . . . at one of their meetings.

ELSA [*Disbelief and anger*]. They *what*?

HELEN. That's how Marius put it. He . . . he said they were worried about me living here alone.

ELSA. *They* are worried about *you*?

HELEN. Yes. It's my health they are worried about.

ELSA [*Shaking her head*]. When it comes to hypocrisy—and blatant hypocrisy at that—you Afrikaners are in a class by yourselves. So tell me, did they also discuss Getruida's situation? And what about Mrs. van Heerden down at the other end of the village? They're about the same age as you and they also live alone.

HELEN. That's what I said. But Marius said it's different with them.

ELSA. In what way?

HELEN. Well, you see, because of my hands and everything else, they don't believe I can look after myself so well anymore.

ELSA. Are they right?

HELEN. No! I'm quite capable of looking after myself.

ELSA. And where are you supposed to go if you leave the village? To a niece, four times removed, in Durban, whom you've only seen a couple of times in your life?

[*Miss Helen goes to a little table at the back and fetches a form which she hands to Elsa*].

[*Reading*] "Sunshine Home for the Aged." I see. So it's like that, is it? That's the lovely old house on the left when you come into Graaff-Reinet, next to the church. In fact, it's run by the church, isn't it?

HELEN. Yes.

ELSA. That figures. It's got a beautiful garden, Miss Helen. Whenever I drive past on my way up here there are always a few old folk in their "twilight years" sitting around enjoying the sunshine. It's well named. It all looks very restful. So that's what they want to do with you. This is not your handwriting.

HELEN. No. Marius filled it in for me.

ELSA. Very considerate of him.

HELEN. He's coming to fetch it tonight.

ELSA. For an old friend he sounds a little overeager to have you on your way, Miss Helen.

HELEN. It's just that they've got a vacancy at the moment. They're usually completely full. There's a long waiting list. But I haven't signed it yet!

[*Elsa studies Miss Helen in silence for a few moments.*]

ELSA. How bad are your hands? Be honest with me.

HELEN. They're not *that* bad. I exaggerated a little in my letter.

ELSA. You could still work with them if you wanted to?

HELEN. Yes.

ELSA. Is there anything you can't do?

HELEN. I can do anything I want to, Elsie . . . if I make the effort.

ELSA. Let me see them.

HELEN. Please don't. I'm ashamed of them.

ELSA. Come on.

[*Miss Helen holds out her hands. Elsa examines them.*]

And these scabs?

HELEN. They're nothing. A little accident at the stove. I was making prickly-pear syrup for you.

ELSA. There seem to have been a lot of little accidents lately. Better be more careful.

HELEN. I will. I definitely will.

ELSA. Pain?

HELEN. Just a little. [*While Elsa studies her hands*] Just that one letter after your last visit, saying you had arrived back safely and would be writing again soon, and then nothing. Three months.

ELSA. I did write, Helen. Two very long letters.

HELEN. I never got them.

ELSA. Because I never posted them.

HELEN. Elsie! Why? They would have made all the difference in the world.

ELSA [*Shaking her head*]. No. Muddled, confused, full of self-pity. Knowing now what you were trying to deal with here, they were hardly what you needed in your life.

HELEN. You're very wrong. Anything would have been better than nothing.

ELSA. No, Helen. Believe me nothing was better than those two letters. I've still got them at home. I read them now whenever I need to count my blessings. They remind me of the mess I was in.

HELEN. That's why I feel so bad now about the letter I wrote you. My problems seem so insignificant compared with yours.

ELSA. Don't let's start that, Helen. Sorting our prob-lem priorities isn't going to get us anywhere. In any case, mine are over and done with . . . which leaves us with you. So what are you going to do?

[*Miss Helen doesn't answer. Elsa is beginning to lose patience.*]

Come *on*, Helen! If I hadn't turned up tonight, what were you going to say to Dominee Marius Byleveld when he came around?

HELEN. I was going to ask him to give me a little more time to think about it.

ELSA. You were going to *ask* him for it, not *tell* him you *wanted* it? And *do* you need more time to think about it? I thought you knew what you wanted?

HELEN. Of course I do.

ELSA. Then tell me again. And say it simply. I need to hear it.

HELEN. You know I can't leave here, Elsa!

ELSA. For a moment I was not so sure. So then what's the problem? When he comes around tonight hand this back to him . . . unsigned . . . and say no. Thank him for his trouble but tell him you are perfectly happy where you are and quite capable of looking after yourself. [*Miss Helen hesitates. A sense of increasing emotional confusion and uncertainty*] Helen, you have just said that is what you want.

HELEN. I know. It's just that Marius is such a persua-sive talker.

ELSA. Then talk back!

HELEN. I'm not very good at that. Won't you help me, little Elsie, please, and speak to him as well? You are so much better at arguing than me.

ELSA. No, I won't! And for God's sake stop behaving like a naughty child who's been called to the princi-pal's office. I'm sorry, but the more I hear about your Marius, the worse it gets. If you want my advice, you'll keep the two of us well away from each other. I *won't* argue with him on your behalf because there is nothing to argue about. This is not his house, and it most certainly is not his life that is being discussed at Church Council meetings. Who the hell do they think they are? Sitting around a table deciding what is going to happen to you!

HELEN. Marius did say that they were trying to think of what was best for me.

ELSA. No, they're not! God knows what they're think-ing about, but it's certainly not that. Dumping you with a lot of old people who've hung on for too long and nobody wants around anymore? You're still living your life, Helen, not drooling it away.

The only legal way they can get you out of this house is by having you certified. [*Awkward silence*] We all know you're as mad as a hatter, but it's not quite that bad. [*Another pause*] One little question though, Miss Helen. You haven't been going around talking about doing away with yourself to anyone have you?

HELEN. I told you, Katrina is the only person I really see anymore.

ELSA. And Marius. Don't forget him. Anyway it doesn't matter who it is. All it needs is one person to be able to stand up and testify that they heard you say it.

HELEN. Well, I haven't.

ELSA. Because it would make life a lot easier for them if they ever did try to do something. So no more of that. Okay? Did you hear me, Helen?

HELEN. Yes, I heard you.

ELSA. And while you're about it, add me to your list. I don't want to hear or read any more about it either.

HELEN. I heard you, Elsie! Why do you keep on about it?

ELSA. Because talk like that could be grounds for forcibly committing someone to a "Sunshine Home for the Aged"! I'm sorry, Helen, but what do you expect me to do? Pretend you never said it? Is that what you would have done if our situations had been reversed? If in the middle of my mess I had threatened to do that? God knows, I came near to feeling like it a couple of times. I had a small taste of how bloody pointless everything can seem to be. But if I can hang on, then you most certainly can't throw in the towel—not after all the rounds you've already won against them. So when the dominee comes around, you're going to put on a brave front. Let's get him and his stupid ideas about an old-age home right out of your life. Because you're going to say no, remember? Be as polite and civil as you like—we'll offer him tea and biscuits and discuss the weather and the evils of alcohol—but when the time comes, you're going to thank him for all his trouble and consideration and then hand this back to him with a firm "No, thank you." [*Another idea*] And just to make quite sure he gets the message, you can also mention your trip into Graaff-Reinet next week to see a doctor and an optician.

HELEN. What do you mean?

ELSA. Exactly what I said: appointments with a doctor and an optician.

HELEN. But I haven't got any.

ELSA. You will on Monday. Before I leave tomorrow I'm going to ask Getruida to take you into Graaff-Reinet next week. And this time you're going to go. There must be something they can do about your hands, even if it's just to ease the pain. And a little "regmaker" for your depressions. [*Miss Helen wants to say something*] No arguments! And to hell with your vanity as well. We all know you think you're the prettiest thing in the village, but if you need glasses, you're going to wear them. I'll make the appointments myself and phone through after you've been in to find out what the verdict is. I'm not trying to be funny, Helen. You've got to prove to the village that you are quite capable of looking after yourself. It's the only way to shut them up.

HELEN. You're going too fast for me, Elsa. You're not allowing me to say anything.

ELSA. That's quite right. How many times in the past have we sat down and tried to talk about all of this? And every time the same story: "I'll think about it, Elsa." Your thinking has got us nowhere, Helen. This time you're just going to agree . . . and that includes letting Katrina come in a couple of times each week to do the house.

HELEN. There's nothing for her to do. I can manage by myself.

ELSA. No, you can't. [*She runs her finger over a piece of furniture and holds it up for Miss Helen to see the dust.*]

HELEN. Everything would have been spotless if I had known you were coming.

ELSA. It's got to be spotless all the time! To hell with *my* visits and holidays. I don't live here. You do. I'm concerned with *your* life, Helen. And I'm also not blind, you know. I saw you struggling with that large kettle. Yes, let's talk about that. When did you last boil up enough water for a decent bath? Come on, Helen. Can't you remember? Some time ago, right? Is it because of personal neglect that you've stopped caring about yourself or because you aren't able to? Answer me.

HELEN. I can't listen to you anymore, Elsa. [*She makes a move to leave the room.*]

ELSA. Don't do that to me Helen! If you leave this room I'm getting into my car and driving back to Cape Town. You wrote that letter. I haven't made it up. All I'm trying to do is deal with it.

HELEN. No, you're not.

ELSA. Then I give up. What in God's name have we been talking about?

HELEN. A pair of spectacles and medicine for my arthritis and Katrina dusting the house—

ELSA. Do you want me to read it again?

HELEN [*Ignoring the interruption*]. You're treating that letter like a shopping list. That isn't what I was writing about.

ELSA. Then what was it?

HELEN. Darkness, Elsa! Darkness! [*She speaks with an emotional intensity and authority which forces Elsa to listen in silence.*] The Darkness that nearly smothered my life in here one night fifteen years ago. The same Darkness that used to come pouring down the chimney and into the room at night when I was a little girl and frighten me. If you still don't know what I'm talking about, blow out the candles!

But those were easy Darknesses to deal with. The one I'm talking about now is much worse. It's inside me, Else . . . it's got inside me at last and I can't light candles there. [*Pause*]

I never knew that could happen. I thought I was safe. I had grown up and I had all the candles I wanted. That is all that little girl could think about when she lay there in bed, trying to make her prayers last as long as she could because she was terrified of the moment when her mother would bend down and kiss her and take away the candle. One day she would have her very own! That was the promise: that one day when I was big enough, she would leave one at my bedside for me to light as often as I wanted. That's all that "getting big" ever meant to me—my very own candle at my bedside.

Such brave little lights! And they taught the little girl how to be that. When she saw one burning in the middle of the night, she knew what courage was. All my life they have helped me to find courage . . . until now.

I'm frightened, Elsie, more frightened than that little girl ever was. There's no "getting big" left to wait for, no prayers to say until that happens . . . and the candles don't help anymore. That is what I was trying to tell you. I'm frightened. And Marius can see it. He's no fool, Elsa. He knows that his moment has finally come.

ELSA. What moment?

HELEN. He's been waiting a long time for me to reach the end of my Mecca. I thought I had cheated him out of it, that that moment would never come.

All those years when I was working away, when it was slowly taking shape, he was there as well . . . standing in the distance, watching and waiting.

I used to peep at him through the curtains. He'd come walking past, then stop, stand there at the gate with his hands behind his back and stare at my Wise Men. And even though he didn't show anything, I know he didn't like what he saw. I used to sing when I was working. He heard me one day and came up and asked: "Are you really that happy, Helen?"

I laughed. Not at *him*, believe me not at him, but because I had a secret he would never understand. [*Pause*]

It's his turn to laugh now. But he won't, of course. He's not that sort of man. He'll be very gentle again . . . pull the curtains and close the shutters the way he did that night fifteen years ago . . . because nobody must stare into a house where there's been a death.

If my Mecca is finished, Elsa, then so is my life.

[*Elsa is overwhelmed by a sense of helplessness and defeat.*]

ELSA. I think I've had it. It's too much for one day. That woman on the road and now you. I honestly don't know how to handle it. In fact, at this moment, I don't think I know anything. I don't know what it means to be walking eighty miles to Cradock with your baby on your back. I don't know whether your Mecca is finished or not. And all I know about Darkness is that that is when you put on the lights. Jesus! I wouldn't mind somebody coming along and telling me what it does all mean.

So where does all of that leave us, Miss Helen? I'm lost. What are you going to do when he comes? [*No answer*] Ask him please—for more time? One thing I can tell you right now is that there's no point to that. If you don't say no tonight, you won't ever, in which case you might as well sign that form and get it over and done with. [*A cruel, relentless tone in her voice*] There's no point in talking about anything until that's settled. So you better think about it, Helen. While you do that, I'll see what I can organize for supper.

[*She exits into the kitchen. A man's voice off: "Anybody at home?" Marius appears in the doorway.*]

MARIUS. Miss Helen! Alone in the dark? I didn't think anybody was home.

[*Elsa appears from the kitchen.*]

Ah, Miss Barlow!

END OF ACT I

Act II

The same a few minutes later. Marius and Elsa are now at the table with Miss Helen, the center of attraction being a basket of vegetables which Marius has brought with him. He is about the same age as Miss Helen and is neatly but casually dressed. He speaks with simple sincerity and charm.

MARIUS [*Holding up a potato*]. Feast your eyes on this, Miss Barlow! A genuine Sneeuberg potato! A pinch of salt and you've got a meal, and if you want to be extravagant, add a little butter and you have indeed got a feast. We had a farmer from the Gamtoos Valley up here last week, trying to sell potatoes to us! Can you believe it? Did you see him, Helen? He had his lorry parked in front of the Post Office. What's the English expression, Miss Barlow? Coals to—where?

ELSA. Coals to Newcastle.

MARIUS. That's it! Well in this case it was very near to being an insult as well. We pride ourselves in these parts on knowing what a potato really is. And here you have it. The "apple of the earth," as the French would say. But I don't imagine that poor man will come again. Shame! I ended up feeling very sorry for him. "Don't you people like potatoes?" he asked me. What could I say? I didn't have the heart to tell him he'd wasted his time driving all this distance, that *nobody* comes to Sneeuberg to sell potatoes! And then, to make me feel really bad, he insisted on giving me a small sack of them before he drove off. I don't think he sold enough to cover the cost of his petrol back home.

I also brought you a few beets and tomatoes. The beets have passed their best now, but if you pickle and bottle them, they'll be more than all right. Have you ever treated our young friend to a taste of that, Miss Helen? [*To Elsa*] It's one of our local specialties. One thing I can assure you ladies is that these vegetables are as fresh as you are ever likely to get. I dug them up myself this afternoon.

HELEN. It's very kind of you, Marius, but you really shouldn't have bothered.

MARIUS. It wasn't any bother at all. I've got more than enough for myself stored away in the pantry. Would have been a sin to leave them to rot in the ground when somebody else could use them. And at our age we need fresh vegetables, Helen. [*Wagging a finger at her*] Marie biscuits and tea are not a balanced diet. [*To Elsa*] In the old days Helen used to have a very fine vegetable garden of her own out there. But as you can see, the humble potato has been crowded out by other things. I don't think there's enough room left out there now to grow a radish. [*He turns back to the basket.*] Yes, the Good Lord was very generous to us this past year. I don't really know that we deserve it, but our rains came just when we needed them. Not too much or too little. Believe me, young lady, we are well experienced in both those possibilities. Not so, Helen?

ELSA. The Karoo looked very dry and desolate to me as I drove through it this afternoon.

MARIUS. Dry it certainly is, but not desolate. It might appear that to a townsman's eye—as indeed it did to mine when I first came here!—but that is because we are already deep into our autumn. It will be a good few months before we see rain again.

ELSA. I've never thought of this world as having seasons . . . certainly not the soft ones. To me it has always been a landscape of extremes, too hot or too cold, too dry or else Miss Helen is writing to me about floods that have cut off the village from the outside world. It reminds me of something I once read where the desert was described as "God without mankind."

MARIUS. What an interesting thought. "God without mankind." I can't decide whether that's Catholic or Protestant. Would you know?

ELSA [*Shaking her head*]. No.

MARIUS. Who wrote it?

ELSA. A French writer. Balzac. It sums up the way I feel about the Karoo. The Almighty hasn't exactly made mankind overwelcome here, has he? In fact, it almost looks as if he resented our presence. Sorry, Dominee, I don't mean to be blasphemous or ungenerous to your world, it's just that I'm used to a gentler one.

MARIUS. You judge it too harshly, Miss Barlow. It has got its gentle moments and moods as well . . . all the more precious because there are so few of them. We can't afford to take them for granted. As you can see, it feeds us. Can any man or woman ask for more than that from the little bit of earth he lives on?

ELSA. Do you think your Coloured folk feel the same way about things?

MARIUS. Why should it be any different for them?

ELSA. I was just wondering whether they had as many reasons to be as contented as you?

MARIUS. I was talking about simple gratitude, Miss Barlow. Wouldn't you say contentment is a more complicated state of mind? One that can very easily be disturbed. But grateful? Yes! Our Coloured folk also have every reason to be. Ask them. Ask little Katrina, who visits Miss Helen so faithfully, if she or her baby have ever wanted for food . . . even when Koos has spent all his wages on liquor. There are no hungry people, white or Coloured, in this village, Miss Barlow. Those of us who are more fortunate than others are well aware of the responsibilities that go with that good fortune. But I don't want to get into an argument. It is my world—and Helen's— and we can't expect an outsider to love or understand it as we do.

ELSA. I'll put these [The vegetables] away for you, Miss Helen.

MARIUS. Don't bother to unpack them now. I'll collect the basket tomorrow after church. [Calling after Elsa as she leaves the room] And there's no need to wash them. I've already done that. Just put them straight into the pot.

[Exit Elsa.]

I've got a feeling that, given half a chance, your young friend and myself *could* very easily find ourselves in an argument. I think Miss Barlow gets a little impatient with our old-fashioned ways and attitudes. But it's too late for us to change now. Right, Helen?

HELEN. Elsa and I have already had those arguments, Marius.

MARIUS. I hope you put up a good defense on our behalf.

HELEN. I tried my best.

MARIUS. And yet the two of you still remain good friends.

HELEN. Oh yes!

MARIUS. And so it should be. A true friendship should be able to accommodate a difference of opinion. You didn't mention anything about her coming up for a visit last time we talked.

HELEN. Because I didn't know. It's an unexpected visit.

MARIUS. Will she be staying long?

HELEN. Just tonight. She goes back tomorrow.

MARIUS. Good heavens! All this way for only one night. I hope nothing is wrong.

HELEN. No. She just decided on the spur of the moment to visit me. But she's got to go back because they're very busy at school. They're right in the middle of exams.

MARIUS. I see. May I sit down for a moment, Helen?

HELEN. Of course, Marius. Forgive me, I'm forgetting my manners.

MARIUS. I won't stay long. I must put down a few thoughts for tomorrow's sermon. And, thanks to you, I know what I want to say.

HELEN. Me?

MARIUS. Yes, you. [Teasing her] You are responsible . . .

HELEN. Oh dear!

MARIUS [A little laugh]. Relax, Helen. I only said "thanks to you" because it came to me this afternoon while I was digging up your vegetables. I spent a lot of time, while I was out in the garden doing that, just leaning on my spade. My back is giving me a bit of trouble again and, to tell you the truth, I also felt lazy.

I wasn't thinking about anything in particular . . . just looking, you know, the way an old man does, looking around, recognizing once again and saying the names. Spitskop in the distance! Aasvoelkrans down at the other end of the valley. The poplars with their autumn foliage standing around as yellow and still as that candle flame!

And a lot of remembering.

As you know, Helen, I had deep and very painful wounds in my soul when I first came here. Wounds I thought would never heal. This was going to be where I finally escaped from life, turned my back on it and justified what was left of my existence by ministering to you people's simple needs. I was very wrong. I didn't escape life here, I discovered it, what it really means, the fullness and goodness of it. It's a deep and lasting regret that Aletta wasn't alive to share that discovery with me. Anyway, all of this was going on in my head when I realized I was hearing a small little voice, and the small little voice was saying, "Thank you." With every spadeful of earth that I turned when I went down on my knees to lift the potatoes out of the soil, there it was: "Thank you." It was mine! I was muttering away to myself the way we old folks are inclined to do when nobody is around. It was me saying, "Thank you."

That is what I want to do tomorrow, Helen. Give thanks, but in a way that I've never done before.

I know I've stood there in the pulpit many times telling all of you to do exactly that, but oh dear me, the cleverness and conceit in the soul of Marius Byleveld when he was doing that! I had an actor's vanity up there, Helen. I'm not saying I was a total hypocrite but, believe me, in those thanksgivings I was listening to my dominee's voice and its hoped-for eloquence every bit as much as to the true little voice inside my heart . . . the voice I heard so clearly this afternoon.

That's the voice that must speak tomorrow! And to do that I must find words as simple as the sky I was standing under this afternoon or the earth I was turning over with my spade. They have got no vanities and conceits. They are just "there." If the Almighty takes pity on us, the one gives us rain so that the other can in turn . . . give us this day our daily potato. [*A smile at this gentle little joke*] Am I making sense, Helen? Answer me truthfully.

HELEN. Yes, you are, Marius. And if all you do tomorrow is say what you have just said to me, it will be very moving and beautiful.

MARIUS [*Sincerely*]. Truly, Helen? Do you really mean that?

HELEN. Every word of it.

MARIUS. Then I will try.

My twentieth anniversary comes up next month. Yes, that is how long I've been here. Twenty-one years ago, on May the sixteenth, the Good Lord called my Aletta to his side, and just over a year later, on June the eleventh, I gave my first sermon in New Bethesda. [*A little laugh at the memory*] What an occasion that was!

I don't know if I showed it, Helen, but let me confess now that I was more than just a little nervous when I went up into the pulpit and looked down at that stern and formidable array of faces. A very different proposition from the town and city congregations I had been preaching to up until then. When Miss de Klerk played the first bars of the hymn at the end of it, I heaved a very deep sigh of relief. None of you had fallen asleep! [*Helen is shaking her head.*] What's the matter?

HELEN. Young Miss de Klerk came later. Mrs. Niewoudt was still our organist when you gave your first service.

MARIUS. Are you sure?

HELEN. Yes. Mrs. Niewoudt also played at the reception we gave you afterwards in Mr. van Heerden's house. She played the piano and Sterling Retief sang.

MARIUS. You know something, I do believe you're right! Good heavens, Helen, your memory is better than mine.

HELEN. And you had no cause to be nervous. You were very impressive.

MARIUS [*A small pause as he remembers something else*]. Yes, of course. You were in that congregation. Stefanus was at your side, as he was going to be every Sunday after that for . . . what? Another five years?

HELEN. Five years.

MARIUS. That was all a long time ago.

HELEN. More than a long time, Marius. It feels like another life.

[*Elsa returns with a tray of tea and sandwiches.*]

MARIUS. Ah, here comes your supper. I must be running along.

ELSA. Just a sandwich, Dominee. Neither of us is very hungry.

MARIUS. I'll drop by tomorrow night if that is all right with you, Helen.

ELSA. Won't you have a cup of tea with us? It's the least we can offer in return for all those lovely vegetables.

MARIUS. I don't want to intrude. Helen tells me you're here for the night, Miss Barlow. I'm sure you ladies have got things to talk about in private.

ELSA. We've already done quite a lot of that, haven't we, Helen? Please don't go because of me. I have some school work I must see to. I'll take my tea through to the other room.

HELEN. Don't go, Elsa!

ELSA. I told you I had papers to mark, Miss Helen. I'll just get on with that quietly while the two of you have a little chat.

HELEN. Please!

ELSA. All right then, if it will make you happier, I'll bring my work through and do it in here.

MARIUS. No. I've obviously come at an inconvenient time.

ELSA. Not at all, Dominee. Miss Helen was expecting you.

[*Elsa fetches the application form for the old-age home and puts it down on the table. A moment between Elsa and Marius. He turns to Helen for confirmation.*]

HELEN. Yes. I was.

ELSA. How do you like your tea?

MARIUS. Very well, if you insist. Milk but no sugar, please.

[*Elsa pours tea, then collects her briefcase from the bedroom alcove and settles down to work at a small table at the back of the room.*]

You're quite certain you want to discuss this now, Helen?

HELEN. Yes, Marius.

MARIUS. It can wait until tomorrow.

HELEN. No, I'm ready.

MARIUS. Right. Just before we start talking, Helen, the good news is that I've spoken to Dominee Gericke in Graaff-Reinet again, and the room is definitely yours—that is, if you want it, of course. But they obviously can't have it standing empty indefinitely. As it is, he's already broken the rules by putting you at the top of the waiting list, but as a personal favor. He understands the circumstances. So the sooner we decide, one way or the other, the better. But I want you to know that I do realize how big a move it is for you. I want you to be quite certain and happy in your mind that you're doing the right thing. So don't think we've got to rush into it, start packing up immediately or anything like that. A decision must be made, one way or the other, but once you've done that, you can relax and take all the time you need.

[*Marius takes spectacles, a little notebook, pen and pencil from a jacket pocket. The way he handles everything, carefully and precisely, reveals a meticulous and orderly mind. He opens the application form. Miss Helen gives Elsa the first of many desperate and appealing looks. Elsa, engrossed in her work, apparently does not notice it. Marius puts his spectacles on.*]

I know we went over this the last time, but there still are just a few questions. Yes . . . we put Stefanus's father's name down as Petrus Johannes Martins, but in the church registry it's down as Petrus *Jacobus*. [*He takes his spectacles off.*] Which one is correct, Helen? Can you remember? You were so certain of Petrus Johannes last time.

HELEN. I still am. But what did you say the other one was?

MARIUS. Petrus Jacobus.

HELEN. Jacobus . . . Johannes. . . . No, maybe I'm not.

MARIUS. In that case what I think I will do is enter it as Petrus *J.* Martins. Just as well I checked. [*He puts his spectacles on again and turns back to the form.*] And next . . . yes, the date of your confirmation. Have you been able to find the certificate?

HELEN. No, I haven't. I'm sorry, Marius. I did look, but I'm afraid my papers are all in a mess.

MARIUS [*Taking his spectacles off*]. I've been through the church records, but I can't find anything that sheds any light on it. It's not all that important, of course, but it would have been nice to have had that date as well. [*He replaces his spectacles.*] Let's see . . . what shall we do? You think you were about twelve?

HELEN. Something like that.

MARIUS. What I'll do is just pencil in 1920 and have one more look. I hate giving up on *that* one. But you surprise me, Helen—of all the dates to have forgotten.

That takes care of the form now. [*He consults his notebook.*] Yes. Two little points from Dominee Gericke, after which you can relax and enjoy your supper. He asked me—and do believe me, Helen, he was just trying to be practical and helpful, nothing else—whether you had taken care of everything by way of a last will and testament, and obviously I said I didn't know.

HELEN. What do you mean, Marius?

MARIUS. That in the event of something happening, your house and possessions will be disposed of in the way that you want them to be. Have you done that?

HELEN. I've still got a copy of Stefanus's will. He left everything to me.

MARIUS. We're talking about you, Helen. Have you seen a lawyer?

HELEN. No, I . . . I've never thought of it.

MARIUS. Then it is just as well Gericke asked. Believe me, Helen, in my time as a minister I have seen so many bitterly unhappy situations because somebody neglected to look after that side of things. Families not talking to each other! Lawsuits over a few pieces of furniture! I really do think it is something you should see to. We're at an age now when anything can happen. I had mine revised only a few months ago. [*He glances at the notebook again.*] And finally, he made the obvious suggestion that we arrange for you to visit the home as soon as possible. Just to meet the matron and other people there and to see your room. He's particularly anxious for you to see it so that you know what you need to bring on your side. He had a dreadful to-do a few months ago with a lady who tried to move a whole houseful of furniture into her little room. Don't get worried, though. There's plenty of space for personal possessions and a few of your . . . ornaments. That covers everything, I think. All that's left now is for you to sign it . . . provided you want to do that, of course.

[*He places his fountain pen, in readiness, on the form.*]

HELEN. Marius . . . please . . . please can I talk for a little bit now?

MARIUS. But of course, Helen.

HELEN. I've done a lot of thinking since we last spoke—

MARIUS. Good! We both agreed that was necessary. This is not a step to be taken lightly.

HELEN. Yes, I've done a lot of thinking, and I've worked out a plan.

MARIUS. For what, Helen?

HELEN. A plan to take care of everything.

MARIUS. Excellent!

HELEN. I'm going in to Graaff-Reinet next week, Marius, to see a doctor. I'm going to make the appointment on Monday, and I'll ask Getruida to drive me in.

MARIUS. You make it sound serious, Helen.

HELEN. No, it's just my arthritis. I'm going to get some medicine for it.

MARIUS. For a moment you had me worried. I thought the burns were possibly more serious than we had realized. But why not save yourself a few pennies and see Dr. Lubbe at the home? He looks after everybody there free of charge.

HELEN [Hanging on]. And spectacles. I'm also going to make arrangements to see an optician and get a pair of spectacles.

MARIUS. Splendid, Helen! You certainly have been making plans.

HELEN. And, finally, I've decided to get Katrina to come in two or three times a week to help me with the house.

MARIUS. Katrina?

HELEN. Little Katrina. Koos Malgas's wife.

MARIUS. I know who you're talking about, Helen. It's just . . . oh dear! I'm sorry to be the one to tell you this, Helen, but I think you are going to lose your little Katrina.

HELEN. What do you mean, Marius?

MARIUS. Koos has asked the Divisional Council for a transfer to their Aberdeen depot, and I think he will get it.

HELEN. So?

MARIUS. I imagine Katrina and the baby will go with him.

HELEN. Katrina . . . ?

MARIUS. Will be leaving the village.

HELEN. No, it can't be.

MARIUS. It's the truth, Helen.

HELEN. But she's said nothing to me about it. She was in here just a few days ago and she didn't mention anything about leaving.

MARIUS. She most probably didn't think it important.

HELEN. How can you say that Marius? Of course it is! She knows how much I depend on her. If Katrina goes, I'll be completely alone here except for you and the times when Elsa is visiting. [She is becoming increasingly distressed.]

MARIUS. Come now, Helen! It's not as bad as that. I know Katrina is a sweet little soul and that you are very fond of her, as we all are, but don't exaggerate things. There are plenty of good women in the location who can come and give you a hand in here and help you pack up . . . if you decide to move. Tell you what I'll do; if you're worried about a stranger being in here with all your personal things, I'll lend you my faithful old Nonna. She's been looking after me for ten years now, and in that time I haven't missed a single thing. You could trust her with your life.

HELEN. I'm not talking about a servant, Marius.

MARIUS. I thought we were.

HELEN. Katrina is the only friend I've got left in the village.

MARIUS. That's a hard thing you're saying, Helen. All of us still like to think of ourselves as your friends.

HELEN. I wasn't including you, Marius. You're different. But as for the others . . . no. They've all become strangers to me. I might just as well not know their names. And they treat me as if I were a stranger to them as well.

MARIUS. You're being very unfair, Helen. They behave towards you in the way you apparently want them to, which is to leave you completely alone. Really, Helen! Strangers? Old Getruida, Sterling, Jerry, Boet, Mrs. van Heerden? You grew up in this village with all of them.

To be very frank, Helen, it's your manner which now keeps them at a distance. I don't think you realize how much you've changed over the years. You're not easily recognizable to others anymore as the person they knew fifteen years ago. And then your hobby, if I can call it that, hasn't really helped matters. This is not exactly the sort of room the village ladies are used to or would feel comfortable in having afternoon tea. As for all of that out there . . . the less said about it, the better.

HELEN. I don't harm or bother anyone, Marius!

MARIUS. And does anyone harm or bother you?

HELEN. Yes! Everybody is trying to force me to leave my home.

MARIUS. Nobody is *forcing* you, Helen! In Heaven's name, where do you get that idea from? If you sign this form, it must be of your own free will.

You're very agitated tonight, Helen. Has something happened to upset you? You were so reasonable about everything the last time we talked.

You seemed to understand that the only motive on our side is to try and do what is best for you. And even then it's only in the way of advice. We can't *tell* you what to do. But if you want us to stop caring about what happens to you, we can try . . . though I don't know how our Christian consciences would allow us to do that.

HELEN. I don't believe the others care about me, Marius. All they want is to get rid of me. This village has also changed over the past fifteen years. I am not alone in that. I don't recognize it anymore as the simple, innocent world I grew up in.

MARIUS. If it's as bad as that, Helen, if you are now really that unhappy and lonely here, then I don't know why you have any doubts about leaving.

[*Miss Helen's emotional state has deteriorated steadily. Marius's fountain pen has ended up in her hand. She looks down at the application form. A few seconds' pause and then a desperate cry.*]

HELEN. Why don't you stop me, Elsa! I'm going to sign it!

ELSA [*Abandoning all pretense of being absorbed in her work*]. Then go ahead and do it! Sign that fucking form. If that's what you want to do to your life, just get it over and done with, for God's sake!

MARIUS. Miss Barlow!

ELSA [*Ignoring him*]. What are you waiting for, Helen? You're wasting our time. It's late and we want to go to bed.

HELEN. But you said I mustn't sign it.

ELSA [*Brutally*]. I've changed my mind. Do it. Hurry up and dispose of your life so that we can get on with ours.

HELEN. Stop it, Elsa. Help me. Please help me.

ELSA. Sorry, Helen. I've had more woman-battering today than I can cope with. You can at least say no. That woman on the road couldn't. But if you haven't got the guts to do that, then too bad. I'm not going to do it for you.

HELEN. I tried.

ELSA. You call that trying? All it required was one word—no.

HELEN. Please believe me, Elsa . . . I was trying!

ELSA. No good, Helen. If that's your best, then maybe you will be better off in an old-age home.

MARIUS. Gently, Miss Barlow! In Heaven's name, gently! What's got into you?

ELSA. Exhaustion, Dominee. Very near total mental and emotional exhaustion, to the point where I want to scream. I've already done that once today, and right now I wouldn't mind doing it a second time. Yes, Helen, I've had it. Why were you "crying out to me in the dark"? To be an audience when you signed away your life? Is that why I'm here? Twelve hours of driving like a lunatic for that? God. What a farce! I might just as well have stayed in Cape Town.

MARIUS. Maybe it's a pity you didn't. I think I understand now why Helen is so agitated tonight. But unfortunately you are here, and if you've got anything to say to her, in Heaven's name be considerate of the state she is in. She needs help, not to be confused and terrified even more.

ELSA. Helen understands the way I feel. We *did* do a lot of talking before you came, Dominee.

MARIUS. I'm concerned with *her* feelings, Miss Barlow, not yours. And if by any chance you are as well, then try to show some respect for her age. Helen is a much older woman than you. You were shouting at her as if she were a child.

ELSA. Me, treating her like a child? Oh my God! You can stand there and accuse me of that after what I've just seen and heard from you?

MARIUS. I don't know what you're talking about.

ELSA. Then I'll tell you. You were doing everything in your power to bully and blackmail her into signing that. You were taking the grossest advantage of what you call her confusion and helplessness. I've been trying to tell her she's neither confused nor helpless.

MARIUS. So you know what is best for her.

ELSA. No, no, no! Wrong again, Dominee. I think *she* does. And if you had given her half a chance, she would have told you that that is not being dumped in an old-age home full of old people who have reached the end of their lives. She hasn't. You forget one thing: I didn't stop her signing that form. She stopped herself.

MARIUS. It was a moment of confusion.

ELSA. There you go again! Can't you leave that word alone? She is not confused!

MARIUS. When Helen and I discussed the matter a few days ago—

ELSA. Don't talk about her as if she were not here. She's right next to you, Dominee. Ask her, for God's sake . . . but this time give her a chance to answer.

MARIUS. Don't try to goad me with blasphemy, Miss Barlow. I'm beginning to think Helen needs as much protection from you as she does from herself.

ELSA. You still haven't asked her.

MARIUS. Because I have some sympathy for her condition. Look at her! She is in no condition now, thanks to you, to think clearly about anything.

ELSA. She was an emotional mess, thanks to you, before I opened my mouth. Don't expect me to believe you really care about her.

MARIUS [*Trying hard to control himself*]. Miss Barlow, for the last time, what you do or don't believe is not of the remotest concern to me. Helen is, and my concern is that she gets a chance to live out what is left of her life as safely and happily as is humanly possible. I don't think that should include the danger of her being trapped in here when this house goes up in flames.

ELSA. What are you talking about?

MARIUS. Her accident. The night she knocked over the candle. [*Elsa is obviously at a loss*] You don't know about that? When was it, Helen? Four weeks ago? [*Pause. Miss Helen doesn't respond.*] I see. You didn't tell your friend about your narrow escape. I think I owe you an apology, Miss Barlow. I assumed you knew all about it.

ELSA. You owe me nothing. Just tell me what happened.

MARIUS. Yes, it was about four weeks ago. Helen knocked over a candle one night and set fire to the curtains. I try not to think about what would have happened if Sterling hadn't been looking out of his window at that moment and seen the flames. He rushed over, and just in time. She had stopped trying to put out the flames herself and was just standing staring at them. Even so she picked up a few bad burns on her hands. We had to get Sister Lategan out of bed to treat them. But it could have been a lot worse. [*Elsa is staring at Miss Helen.*] We don't want that on our consciences. So you see, Miss Barlow, our actions are not quite as pointless or as uncaring as they must have seemed to you.

ELSA. One of the lamps started smoking badly, and there was a little accident at the stove while you were making prickly-pear syrup for me! Oh boy! You certainly can do it, Helen. Don't let us ever again talk about trust between the two of us. Anyway, that settles it. I leave the two of you to fight it out . . . and may the best man win! I'm going to bed.

HELEN. Give me a chance to explain.

ELSA [*Ignoring the plea*]. Good night. See you in the morning. I'll be making an early start, Helen.

HELEN. Don't abandon me, Elsa!

ELSA. You've abandoned yourself, Helen! Don't accuse me of that! You were the first to jump over-board. You haven't got enough faith in your life and your work to defend them against him. You lied to me . . . and such stupid bloody lies! What was the point? For that matter, what is the point of anything? Why *did* you make me come up? And then all our talk about trust! God, what a joke. You've certainly made me make a fool of myself again, but this time I don't think it's funny. In fact, I fucking well resent it.

HELEN. I didn't tell you because I was frightened you would agree with them.

ELSA. Don't say anything, Helen. You're making it worse. [*She studies Miss Helen with cruel detachment.*] But you might have a point there. Now that I've heard about your "little accident," I'm beginning to think they might be right. [*She indicates the room.*] Corrugated iron and wooden walls? Give it half a chance and this would go up like a bonfire. [*She is hating herself, hurting herself every bit as much as she is hurting Miss Helen, but is unable to stop.*] And he says you were just standing and staring at it. What was that all about? Couldn't you make a run for it? They say that about terror—it makes you either run like hell or stand quite still. Sort of paralysis. Because it was just an accident, wasn't it, Helen? I mean, you weren't trying anything else, were you? Spite everybody by taking the house with you in a final blaze of glory! Dramatic! But it's a hell of a way to go. There are easier methods.

[*Miss Helen goes up to Elsa and stares at her*].

HELEN. Who are you?

[*The question devastates Elsa*].

MARIUS. Ladies, ladies, enough! Stop now! I don't know what's going on between the two of you, but in Heaven's name stop it. I think Helen is aware of the dangers involved, Miss Barlow. And now that you do as well, can't we appeal to you to add your weight to ours and help persuade her to do the right thing? As I am sure you now realize, our only concern has been her well-being.

ELSA. You want my help.

MARIUS. Yes. If now at last you understand why we were trying to persuade Helen to move to the home, then on her behalf I am indeed appealing to you. We don't persecute harmless old ladies, Miss Barlow.

ELSA. And one that isn't so harmless?

MARIUS. Now what are you trying to say?

ELSA. That Helen isn't harmless, Dominee. Anything but that. That's why you people can't leave her alone.

MARIUS. For fifteen years we have done exactly that.

ELSA. Stoning her house and statues at night is not leaving her alone. That is not the way you treat a harmless old lady.

MARIUS. In Heaven's name! Are you going to drag that up? Those were children, Miss Barlow, and it was a long, long time ago. It has not happened again. Do you really mean to be that unfair? Can't you bring as much understanding as you claim to have of Helen's situation to a few other things as well? You've seen what is out there . . . [He gestures at the window and Miss Helen's "Mecca".] How else do you expect the simple children of the village to react to all that? It frightens them, Miss Barlow. I'm not joking! Think back to your impressionable years as a little girl. I know for a fact that all the children in the village believe this house is haunted and that ghosts walk around out there at night. Don't scoff at them. I'm sure there were monsters and evil spirits in your childhood as well. But as I said, that was all a long, long time ago. The moment we discovered what they were doing, we in turn did everything we could to put a stop to it. Mr. Lategan, the school principal, and I both lectured them in the sternest possible manner. Come now, Miss Barlow, have you learned nothing about us in the course of the few years that you've been visiting the village?

ELSA. A lot more than I would have liked to. Those children didn't arrive at their attitude to Helen on their own. I've also heard about the parents who frighten naughty children with stories about Miss Helen's "monsters." They got the courage to start throwing stones because of what they had heard their mothers and fathers saying. And as far as *they* are concerned, Helen is anything but a harmless old lady. God, what an irony. We spend our time talking about "poor, frightened Miss Helen," whereas it's all of you who are really frightened.

MARIUS. I can only repeat what I've already said to Helen: the people you are talking about grew up with her and have known her a lot longer than you.

ELSA. Not anymore. You also said that, remember? That stopped fifteen years ago when she didn't resign herself to being the meek, churchgoing little widow you all expected her to be. Instead she did something which small minds and small souls can never forgive . . . she dared to be different! Which does make you right about one thing, Dominee. Those statues out there *are* monsters. And they are that for the simple reason that they express Helen's freedom. Yes, I never thought it was a word you would like. I'm sure it ranks as a cardinal sin in these parts. A free woman! God forgive us!

Have you ever wondered why I come up here? It's a hell of a long drive, you know, if the only reason is sympathy for a lonely old lady whom nobody is talking to anymore. And it's also not for the scenery.

She challenges me, Dominee. She challenges me into an awareness of myself and my life, of my responsibilities to both that I never had until I met her. There's a hell of a lot of talk about freedom, and all sorts of it, in the world where I come from. But it's mostly talk, Dominee, easy talk and nothing else. Not with Helen. She's lived it. One dusty afternoon five years ago, when I came walking down that road hoping for nothing more than to get away from the flies that were driving me mad, I met the first truly free spirit I have ever known. [She looks at Miss Helen.] It is her betrayal of all of that tonight that has made me behave the way I have.

[A pause. Marius has been confronted with something he has never had to deal with before.]

MARIUS. You call that . . . that nightmare out there an expression of freedom?

ELSA. Yes. Scary, isn't it? What did you call it earlier? Her hobby? [She laughs.] Oh no, Dominee. It's much more dangerous than that . . . and I think you know it.

MARIUS. In another age and time it might have been called idolatry.

ELSA. Did you hear that, Helen? [To Marius] You know what you've just said, don't you?

MARIUS [Total conviction]. Oh yes . . . yes, indeed I do. I am also choosing my words very carefully, Miss Barlow.

When I first realized that it was my duty as a friend and a Christian to raise the question with Helen of a move to an old-age home, I decided I would do so on the basis of her physical well-being and safety and nothing else. Helen will tell you that that is all we have ever talked about. I came here tonight meaning once again to do only that. But you have raised other issues, chosen to talk about more than that . . . which forces me now to do so as well. Because there is a lot more than Helen's physical well-being that has worried me, Miss Barlow—and gravely so! Those "expressions of freedom" have crowded out more than just a few fresh vegetables. I do not take them lightly anymore.

I remember the first one very clearly, Helen. I made the mistake of smiling at it, dismissing it as an idle whim coming out of your loneliness. In fact, I think that is how you yourself described it to me, as something to pass away the time. I was very wrong, wasn't I? And very slow in realizing what was really happening. I only began to feel uneasy about it all that first Sunday you weren't in church.

The moment I stood up there in front of the congregation, I knew your place was empty. But even then, you see, I thought you were sick. After the service I hurried around here, but instead of being in bed there you were outside in the yard making yet another . . . [At a loss for words] I don't really know what to call them.

HELEN [A small but calm voice. She is very still]. It was an owl, Marius. My first owl.

MARIUS. It couldn't have waited until after the service, Helen?

HELEN. Oh no! [Quietly emphatic] The picture had come to me in here the night before. I just had to go to work immediately while it was still fresh in my mind. They don't last long, Marius. After a little while it becomes very hard to remember clearly what you saw. I tried explaining to Elsa how it all works . . . but I don't suppose any of you will ever understand.

But don't ever think that missing church that Sunday was something I did lightly, Marius. You don't break the habit of a lifetime without realizing that that life will never quite be the same again. I was already dressed and ready! I had my Bible and hymnbook, I was on the point of leaving this room as I had done every Sunday for as long as I could remember . . . but I knew that if I did, I would never make that owl. . . . I think I also knew that if I didn't, that if I put aside my Bible and hymnbook, took off my hat and changed my dress and went to work . . . Yes! That was my very first owl!

MARIUS. Helen, Helen! I grieve for you! You turned your back on your church, on your faith and then on us for that? Do you realize that that is why you are now in trouble and so helplessly alone? Those statues out there can't give you love or take care of you the way we wanted to. And, God knows, we were ready to do that. But you spurned us, Helen.

You turned your back on our love and left us for the company of those cement monstrosities.

[Elsa, who has been listening and watching quietly, begins to understand.]

ELSA. Helen, listen to me. Listen to me carefully because if you understand what I'm going to say, I think everything will be all right.

They're not only frightened of you, Helen; they're also jealous. It's not just the statues that have frightened them. They were throwing stones at something much bigger than that—you. Your life, your beautiful, light-filled, glittering life. And they can't leave it alone, Helen, because they are so, so jealous of it.

HELEN [Calmly]. Is that true, Marius?

MARIUS. Helen, has your trust in me been eroded away to the extent that you can ask me that? Does she have so much power over you that you will now believe anything she says?

HELEN. Then . . . it isn't true?

MARIUS. Dear God, what is there left for me to say or do that will make you listen to me the way you do to her?

HELEN. But I have been listening to you, Marius.

MARIUS. No, you haven't! If that were so, you wouldn't be asking me to defend myself against the accusations of someone who knows nothing, nothing, about my true feelings for you. I feel as if I were on trial, Helen. For what? For caring about you? [He confronts Miss Helen.] That I am frightened of what you have done to yourself and your life, yes, that is true! When I find that the twenty years we have known each other, all that we have shared in that time, are outweighed by a handful of visits from her, then yes again. That leaves me bewildered and jealous. Don't you realize that you are being used, Helen—she as much as admitted to that—to prove some lunatic notion about freedom? And since we're talking about it, yes yet again, I do hate that word. You aren't free, Helen. If anything, exactly the opposite. Don't let her deceive you. If there is one last thing you will let me do for you, then let it be this: see yourself as I do and tell me if that is what you call being "free." A life I care about as deeply as any I have known, trapped now finally in the nightmare this house has become . . . with an illiterate little Coloured girl and a stranger from a different world as your only visitors and friends! I know I'm not welcome in here anymore. I can feel it the moment I walk in. It's unnatural, Helen. Your life has become as grotesque as those creations of yours out there.

Why, Helen? Why? I will take that question with me to my grave. What possessed you to abandon the life you had, your faith?

HELEN. What life, Marius? What faith? The one that brought me to church every Sunday? [Shaking her head] No. You were much too late if you only started worrying about that on the first Sunday I wasn't there in my place. The worst had happened long, long before that. Yes. All those years when, as Elsa said, I sat there so obediently next to Stefanus, it was all a terrible, terrible lie. I tried hard, Marius, but your sermons, the prayers, the hymns, they had all become just words. And there came a time when even they lost their meaning.

Do you know what the word "God" looks like when you've lost your faith? It looks like a little stone, a cold, round, little stone. "Heaven" is another one, but it's got an awkward, useless shape, while "Hell" is flat and smooth. All of them—damnation, grace, salvation—a handful of stones.

MARIUS. Why didn't you come to me, Helen? If only you had trusted me enough to tell me, and we had faced it together, I would have broken my soul to help you win back that faith.

HELEN. It felt too late. I'd accepted it. Nothing more was going to happen to me except time and the emptiness inside and I had got used to that . . . until the night in here after Stefanus's funeral. [Pause. She makes a decision.]

I've never told you about that night, Marius. I've told no one, not even Elsa, because it was a secret, you see, a very special one, and it had to stay that way while I was working on my Mecca. But so much has happened here tonight, it feels right to do so now. [Pause]

You brought me home from the cemetery, remember, and when we had got inside the house and you had helped me off with my coat, you put on the kettle for a pot of tea and then . . . ever so thoughtfully . . . pulled the curtains and closed the shutters. Such a small little thing, and I know that you meant well by it, that you didn't want people to stare in at me and my grief . . . but in doing that it felt as if you were putting away my life as surely as the undertaker had done to Stefanus a little earlier when he closed the coffin lid. There was even an odor of death in here with us, wasn't there, sitting in the gloom and talking, both of us in black, our

Bibles in our laps? Your words of comfort didn't help. But that wasn't your fault. You didn't know I wasn't mourning Stefanus's death. He was a good man, and it was very sad that he had died so young, but I never loved him. My black widowhood was really for my own life, Marius. While Stefanus was alive there had at least been some pretense at it . . . of a life I hadn't lived. But with him gone . . . ! You had a little girl in here with you, Marius, who had used up all the prayers she knew and was dreading the moment when her mother would bend down, blow out the candle and leave her in the dark. You lit one for me before you left—there was a lot of darkness in this room—and after you had gone I sat here with it. Such a sad little light, with its little tears of wax running down the side! I had none. Neither for Stefanus nor for myself. You see, nothing hurt anymore. That little candle did all the crying in here that night, and it burned down very low while doing that. I don't know how much time had passed, but I was just sitting here staring into its flame. I had surrendered myself to what was going to happen when it went out . . . but then instead of doing the same, allowing the darkness to defeat it, that small, uncertain little light seemed to find its courage again. It started to get brighter and brighter. I didn't know whether I was awake any longer or dreaming because a strange feeling came over me . . . that it was leading me . . . leading me far away to a place I had never been to before. [She looks around the room and speaks with authority.] Light the candles, Elsa. That one first.

[She indicates a candelabra that has been set up very prominently on a little table. Elsa lights it.]

And you know why, Marius? That is the East. Go out there into the yard and you'll see that all my Wise Men and their camels are traveling in that direction. Follow that candle on and one day you'll come to Mecca. Oh yes, Marius, it's true! I've done it. That is where I went that night and it was the candle you lit that led me there.

[She is radiantly alive with her vision.] A city, Marius! A city of light and color more splendid than anything I had ever imagined. There were palaces and beautiful buildings everywhere, with dazzling white walls and glittering minarets. Strange statues filled the courtyards. The streets were crowded with camels and turbaned men speaking a language I didn't understand, but that didn't matter because I knew, oh I just knew, it was Mecca! And I was on my way to the grand temple.

In the center of Mecca there is a temple, Marius, and in the center of the temple is a vast room with hundreds of mirrors on the walls and hanging lamps, and that is where the Wise Men of the East study the celestial geometry of light and color. I became an apprentice that night.

Light them all, Elsa, so that I can show Marius what I've learned!

[*Elsa moves around the room lighting all the candles, and as she does so its full magic and splendor is revealed. Miss Helen laughs ecstatically.*]

Look, Marius! Look! Light. Don't be nervous. It's harmless. It only wants to play. That is what I do in here. We play with it like children with a magical toy that never ceases to delight and amuse. Light just one little candle in here, let in the light from just one little star, and the dancing starts. I've even taught it how to skip around corners. Yes, I have! When I lie in bed and look in *that* mirror I can see *that* mirror, and in *that* one the full moon when it rises over the Sneeuberg *behind* my back! This is my world and I have banished darkness from it.

It is not madness, Marius. They say mad people can't tell the difference between what is real and what is not. I can. I know my little Mecca out there, and this room, for what they really are. I had to learn how to bend rusty wire into the right shape and mix sand cement to make my Wise Men and their camels, how to grind down beer bottles in a coffee mill to put glitter on my walls. My hands will never let me forget. They'll keep me sane. It's the best I could do, as near as I could get to the real Mecca. The journey is over now. This is as far as I can go.

I won't be using this [*The application form*]. I can't reduce my world to a few ornaments in a small room in an old-age home.

[*Marius takes the form. When he speaks again we sense a defeated man, an acceptance of the inevitable behind the quiet attempt to maintain his dignity.*]

MARIUS. Mecca! So that's where you went. I'll look for it on my atlas of the world when I get home tonight. That's a long way away, Helen! I didn't realize you had traveled that far from me. So to find

you I must light a candle and follow it to the East! [*He makes a helpless gesture*] No. I think I'm too old now for that journey . . . and I have a feeling that you will never come back.

HELEN. I'm also too old for another journey, Marius. It's taken me my whole life to get here.

I know I've disappointed you—most probably, bitterly so—but, whatever you do, please believe me that it wasn't intentional. I had as little choice over all that has happened as I did over the day I was born.

MARIUS. No, I think I do believe you, Helen . . . which only makes it all the harder to accept. All these years it has always felt as if I could reach you. It seemed so inevitable that I would, so right that we should find each other again and be together for what time was left to us in the same world. It seems wrong . . . terribly wrong . . . that we won't. Aletta's death was wrong in the same way.

[*Pause.*]

HELEN. What's the matter, Marius?

MARIUS. I am trying to go. It's not easy . . . trying to find the first moment of a life that must be lived out in the shadow of something that is terribly wrong.

HELEN. We're trying to say goodbye to each other, aren't we, Marius?

MARIUS. Yes, I suppose it had come to that. I never thought that was going to happen tonight, but I suppose there *is* nothing else left to say. [*He starts to go. He sees Elsa, hesitates for a few seconds, but there is nothing to say to her either.*] Be sure all the candles are out when you go to bed, Helen. [*He pauses at the door.*] I've never seen you as happy as this! There is more light in you than in all your candles put together.

[*He leaves. A silence follows his departure. Elsa eventually makes a move to start blowing out the candles.*]

HELEN. No, don't. I must do that. [*From this point on she goes around the room putting out the candles, a quiet but deliberate and grave punctuation to what follows.*]

ELSA. Tell me about his wife.

HELEN. Her name was Aletta. Aletta Byleveld. I've only seen pictures of her. She must have been a very beautiful woman.

ELSA. What happened?

HELEN. Her death?

ELSA. Yes.

HELEN. All I know is that there was a long illness. And a very painful one. They never had any children. Marius was a bitter and lonely man when he first came to the valley. Why do you ask?

ELSA. Because he was, and most probably still is, in love with you.

HELEN. Elsa . . .

ELSA. Yes. I don't suppose I would have ever guessed it if it hadn't been for tonight. Like all good Afrikaners, he does a good job of hiding his feelings. But it is very obvious now.

HELEN [Agitated]. No, Elsie. When he used the word "love" he meant it in the way—

ELSA. No, Helen. I'm not talking about the good shepherd's feelings for one of his flock. Marius Byleveld, the man, loves you Helen, the woman.

HELEN. What are you talking about? Look at me, Elsa. Look at my hands—

ELSA. You fool! Do you think that is what we see when we look at you? You heard him: "There is more light in you than in all your candles put together." And he's right. You are radiant. You can't be that naive and innocent, Helen!

[Miss Helen wants to deny it, but the validity, the possible truth, of what Elsa has said is very strong.]

It's a very moving story. Twenty years of loving you in the disguise of friendship and professional concern for your soul. [There is an unnatural and forced tone to her voice.] Anyway, that's his problem, right, Helen? You did what you had to. In fact, you deserve a few bravos for your performance tonight. I'm proud of you. I told you that you never needed me. And you did more than just say no to him. You affirmed your right, as a woman . . . [Pause] Do you love him? The way he loves you?

[Miss Helen thinks before speaking. When she does so there is no doubt about her answer.]

HELEN. No, I don't.

ELSA. Just asking. You're also an Afrikaner. You could also be hiding your real feelings the way he did. That would make it an even better story! The two of you in this Godforsaken little village, each loving the other in secret!

HELEN. Are you all right, Elsa?

ELSA. No.

HELEN. What's wrong?

ELSA. It's my turn to be jealous.

HELEN. Of what?

ELSA [With a helpless gesture]. Everything. You and him . . . and, stupid as it may sound, I feel fucking lonely as well.

HELEN. You are jealous? Of us . . . Marius and me? With your whole life still ahead of you?

ELSA. Even that woman on the road has at least got a baby in her arms at this moment. She's got something, for Christ's sake! Mind you, it's cold out there now. It could be on her back again. She might have crawled out of her stormwater drain and started walking to keep warm.

HELEN. Leave that poor woman alone now, Elsa!

ELSA. She won't leave me alone, Helen!

HELEN. For all you know, she might have got a lift.

ELSA [Another unexpected flash of cruelty]. I hope not.

HELEN [Appalled]. Elsa! That is not you talking. You don't mean that.

ELSA. Yes, I do! A lift to where, for God's sake? There's no Mecca waiting for her at the end of that road, Helen. Just the rest of her life, and there won't be any glitter on that. The sooner she knows what the score really is, the better.

HELEN. Then think about the baby, Elsa.

ELSA. What the hell do you think I've been doing? Do you think I don't care? That baby could have been mine, Helen! [Pause. Then a decision] I may as well vomit it all out tonight. Two weeks after David left me I discovered I was pregnant. I had an abortion. [Pause] Do you understand what I'm saying, Helen?

HELEN. I understand you, Elsa.

ELSA. I put an abrupt and violent end to the first real consequence my life has ever had.

HELEN. I understand, Elsa.

[Pause.]

ELSA. There is a little sequel to my story about giving that woman a lift. When I stopped at the turnoff and she got out of the car, after I had given her what was left of my food and the money in my purse, after she had stopped thanking me and telling me over and over again that God would bless me, after all of that I asked her who she was. She said: "My English name is Patience." She hitched up the baby, tightened her *doek*, picked up her little plastic shopping bag and started walking. As I watched her walk away, measuring out the next eighty miles of her life in small steps, I wanted to scream. And about a mile further on, in the *kloof*, I did exactly that. I stopped the car, switched off the engine, closed my eyes and started to scream.

I think I lost control of myself. I screamed louder and longer than I have ever done in my life. I can't describe it, Helen. I hated her, I hated the baby, I hated you for dragging me all the way up here . . . and most of all I hated myself. That baby is mine, Helen. Patience is my sister, you are our mother . . . and I still feel fucking lonely.

HELEN. Then don't be so cruel to us. There were times tonight when I hardly recognized you. Why were you doing it?

ELSA. I wanted to punish us.

HELEN. For what? What have we done to deserve that?

ELSA. I've already told you. For being old, for being black, for being born . . . for being twenty-eight years old and trusting enough to jump. For our stupid helplessness.

HELEN. You don't punish people for that, Elsa. I only felt helpless tonight when I thought I had lost you.

ELSA. So what do you want me to do, Helen?

HELEN. Stop screaming.

ELSA. And cry instead?

HELEN. What is wrong with that? Is it something to be ashamed of? I wish I still could . . . not for myself . . . for you, Patience, her little baby. Was it a boy or a girl?

ELSA. I don't know. I'll never know.

[Her moment of emotional release has finally come. She cries. Miss Helen comforts her.]

I'll be all right.

HELEN. I never doubted that for a moment.

ELSA [Total exhaustion]. God Almighty, what a day! I'm dead, Helen, dead, dead, dead . . .

HELEN. No, you're not. You're tired . . . and you've got every right and reason to be. [She fetches a blanket and puts it over Elsa's shoulders.]

ELSA. I wasn't much of a help tonight, was I?

HELEN. You were more than that. You were a "challenge." I like that word.

ELSA. But we didn't solve very much.

HELEN. Nonsense! Of course we did. Certainly as much as we could. I am going to see a doctor and an optician, and Katrina . . . [She remembers] or somebody else, will come in here a few times a week and help me with the house.

ELSA. My shopping list!

HELEN. It is as much as "we" could do, Elsa. The rest is up to myself and, who knows, maybe it will be a little easier after tonight. I won't lie to you. I can't say that I'm not frightened anymore. But at the same time I think I can say that I understand something now.

The road to my Mecca was one I had to travel alone. It was a journey on which no one could keep me company, and because of that, now that it is over, there is only me there at the end of it. It couldn't have been any other way.

You see, I meant what I said to Marius. This is as far as I can go. My Mecca is finished and with it—[Pause] I must try to say it, mustn't I?—the only real purpose my life has ever had.

[She blows out a candle.] I was wrong to think I could banish darkness, Elsa. Just as I taught myself how to light candles, and what that means, I must teach myself now how to blow them out . . . and what that means.

[She attempts a brave smile.] The last phase of my apprenticeship . . . and if I can get through it, I'll be a master!

ELSA. I'm cold.

HELEN. Cup of tea to warm you up and then bed. I'll put on the kettle.

ELSA. And I've got just the thing to go with it. [She goes into the bedroom alcove and returns with her toilet bag, from which she takes a small bottle of pills.] Valiums. They're delicious. I think you should also have one.

HELEN [All innocence]. So tiny! What are they? Artificial sweeteners?

[The unintended and gentle irony of her question is not lost on Elsa. A little chuckle becomes a good laugh.]

ELSA. That is perfect, Helen. Yes, they're artificial sweeteners.

HELEN. I don't know how I did it, but that laugh makes me as proud of myself as of any one of those statues out there.

[She exits to put on the kettle. Elsa goes to the window and looks out at Mecca. Miss Helen returns.]

ELSA. Helen, I've just thought of something. You know what the real cause of all your trouble is? You've never made an angel.

HELEN. Good Heavens, no. Why should I?

ELSA. Because I think they would leave you alone if you did.

HELEN. The village doesn't need more of those. The cemetery is full of them . . . all wings and halos, but no glitter. [*Tongue-in-cheek humor*] But if I did make one, it wouldn't be pointing up to heaven like the rest.

ELSA. No? What would it be doing?

HELEN. Come on, Elsa, you know! I'd have it pointing to the East. Where else? I'd misdirect all the good Christian souls around here and put them on the road to Mecca.

[*Both have a good laugh.*]

ELSA. God, I love you! I love you so much it hurts.

HELEN. What about trust?

[*Pause. The two women look at each other.*]

ELSA. Open your arms and catch me! I'm going to jump!

END OF PLAY

ESSAY: AN APPROACH TO THE PLAY

The spiritual dimensions of *The Road to Mecca* are complex. Helen's art is clearly intended to contrast with the repressive, orthodox, institutional Christianity which Marius serves, and both he and his parishioners come to regard her work as a reproach. (Adults shun her; little children throw stones at her.) For them her art is a form of idolatry, but for her it is an expression of spiritual freedom. The subject matter of much of her art is figures associated with wisdom in various religious traditions: the owl sacred to Athena, the Greek goddess of wisdom; the Magi, the wise men who seek the new-born king in the beginning of the Gospel of Matthew; the monumental statues of Easter Island; the Buddha. (A sidenote: Fugard himself is a Buddhist.) The most important religious aspect of the play, however, is surely implied in the title. Mecca, the birthplace of the prophet Mohammed, serves at least two functions in Islam: the place to which all able-bodied Muslims should make a pilgrimage during their lifetime and the place in whose direction Muslims should bow during the five times a day they are required to pray. As a place of pilgrimage, it serves as a physical externalization of the common metaphor of life as a spiritual journey, and the title's emphasis on the road makes this comparison inevitable. The reclusive Miss Helen never leaves home, but she has been making a spiritual journey for years, one that has placed an enormous distance between her and her neighbors. As the place toward which one bows in prayer, on the other hand, Mecca serves the devout as a daily reminder to remain centered in their spiritiual values, a quality which she seems to have achieved more fully than either the Christian Marius or the secular Elsa.

Perhaps Fugard saw in the town's name, New Bethesda, another religious echo. Bethesda is a place name that occurs in one place only in the Bible, in Chapter 5 of the Gospel of John where Jesus offended the local religious authorities by healing a man on the Sabbath. The authorities were outraged by what they perceived as a violation of religious formalities, and, according to John, this was one of the reasons for which they began to persecute Jesus. Miss Helen began her artistic/religious campaign on a Sunday, when she chose to sculpt instead of going to church, and her art has served her from then on as an alternative to organized worship and has served also to outrage the Pharasaical elements in her community.

Symbolically, Helen's art is associated with light—with the candles that she lights throughout her house and with the walls, covered with mirrors and plastered with imbedded mirror fragments so that the lights flicker and reflect crazily from all surfaces. Her fantasy world, which began as a reaction to her husband's death, is a hedge against the darkness of the grave, but also against the life-crushing ideology of her reactionary, pious Christian neighbors. There is clearly irony in the name of the retirement home Marius has in mind as her destiny: "The Sunshine Home for the Aged." However, Marius (perhaps along with the values he represents) is no easy villain as it turns out, and the symbolic candles may themselves suggest some aspects of the play's complexity. Candles are a source of heat as well as of light, and as such they are dangerous: fire is the specific danger against which Marius wishes to protect her. Marius loves Helen and has for years, and his concern is motivated by reasonable fear for her physical security as well as spiritual concern for her "lost soul." Even while Marius seems to represent the repressiveness and the masked, perhaps unconscious prejudice of his community, he seems to mean well and seems sincere, even if in an unreflective and dull-witted way. If he seems incapable of imagining an alternative social structure for his country, he also shows a sympathy for his fellow humans that embraces white and black and that makes it difficult to hate him, however despicable the social structure he helps prop up. (The Dutch Reformed Church, the established church in South Africa, still officially supported apartheid in 1984, when this play was written.)

The two female characters, meanwhile, contrast with each other in various ways. Elsa is a social activist; Helen is reclusive. Elsa has driven hundreds of miles to see Helen; Helen's journeys are all spiritual. Elsa seems indecisive; Helen is doggedly committed to her artistic vision. Elsa is young and urban and liberal; Helen is old and rural and conservative, though a "reactionary-revolutionary," as Elsa calls her. (Fugard might wish for the term to describe his own art as well, suggesting that art can be socially transformative even when it is not openly activist.)

Perhaps the women are united by the frequent references to the black woman hitchhiker—never on stage—whom Elsa picked up on the road. Fugard's working title as he wrote the play was the woman's self-identification—*My English Name Is Patience*. As Elsa tells Helen, "Patience is my sister, you are our mother." The three women seem to reflect one another. All three are lonely women "on the road" in various ways, all three are mourning lost men, and all three have been involved in very different ways in acts of creation: Helen through her art; Patience, carrying her child, persisting despite her hardships; and Elsa, who has recently aborted her pregnancy. All Elsa can offer her is a ride and a handout—some money and food to help her get through the next few hours. Patience seems to offer silent instruction to the other two on how to live in the semi-arid region of the Karoo, with all its symbolic significance for human life in general, "measuring out the next eighty miles of her life in small steps." A mile farther on, Elsa stopped the car and screamed; Helen teaches her rather to cry. The play's ending emphasizes the importance to the women of love and trust, and Helen, whose life's work has been to teach herself to light candles, must now learn how to blow them out. The example of her life has offered guidance and inspiration to the well-intentioned but somewhat ineffectual Elsa, and now presumably her death will do the same. Elsa is the schoolteacher, but it is Helen, the artist, who seems to have the most to teach in this play, both to Elsa and to her community.

Wole Soyinka

THE LION AND THE JEWEL

About the Author   Wole Soyinka (Akinwande Oluwole Soyinka) (1934–) was born in Abeokuta, in western Nigeria; he went to the University College of Ibadan and then to the University of Leeds in England, where he graduated with honors in English in 1957 and received the Doctor of Literature in 1973. A distinguished actor and director as well as playwright, he has taught in and chaired the Theater Arts Departments at Ibadan and at the University of Ife; he has also taught at the University of Lagos. He founded the Masks Theatre in Lagos in 1960, the Orison Repertory Company and the Guerilla Theatre in Ife in 1964, as well as a film company, Calpenny-Nigeria Ltd. He was recognized very quickly as a cultural leader, receiving a Rockefeller Fellowship in 1960–61 among many other awards before his Nobel Prize for literature in 1986. His fourteen plays, two works of fiction, four books of poetry, many works of nonfiction, as well as editions and translations of others have made him a cultural force not only in his own country but throughout the world. Perhaps because of this visibility, he became a political prisoner in Kaduna Prison from 1967 to 1969, much of that time in solitary confinement. The experience did nothing to diminish his social and literary zeal.

About the Play   One of the dangers in a white-dominated society's adoption of multi-culturalism is its temptation to use ideas and traditions from, for example, Africa simply to enrich or revitalize its own culture. The problem is not that such a practice is wrong in itself. Rather, the problem is that this perspective encourages the white culture to see African traditions primarily as a repository of "new" impulses, impulses which are judged valuable only to the degree that they enrich the Euro-American culture. This approach obscures the fact that Africa's traditions are at least as ancient—and equally deserving of interest on their own terms for their own sakes—as is the society which studies them. Partly for these reasons, Wole Soyinka prefers not to have his plays interpreted as portrayals of a "clash of cultures." Instead, he wants us to see the Nigerian society he portrays on its own terms; to the degree that he portrays Euro-western influences, it seems to be to show how they create stress within traditional African society rather than to emphasize the external influences in and of themselves. *The Lion and the Jewel*, for example, concentrates on some of the divisions within a particular postcolonial African society. Although its internal stresses come from reactions to western cultural values and institutions, the play has no western characters. The conflict, which occurs among members of the same society, exemplifies the problem which all once-colonized nations face as they re-create themselves after the colonial country's departure.

It is the nature of colonial powers to impose their own social institutions on the colonized—their values, their religion, their social organization—thereby depriving the colonized of their indigenous traditions and beliefs. Inevitably, the colonized are alienated from their own traditional society and from their very land: they are made to feel that they are aliens because they are forced or (at best) encouraged to adopt alien beliefs and customs and to discard or (again, at best) to adapt their more traditional ones. They often come to feel rootless, that they do not belong; this occurs even when they "succeed" in the terms approved by the colonizers. In addition, of course, they are exploited. Their most approved function is to serve not their own self-interest but that of their master. Indeed, their own self-interest is officially identified with that of the colonial country, so that, after "liberation," their crisis of values and customs often becomes more, rather than less, acute. The conflicts in *The Lion and the Jewel* dramatize part of this process.

CHARACTERS

SIDI, the Village Belle
LAKUNLE, School teacher
BAROKA, The 'Bale' of Ilujinle
SADIKU, His head wife
THE FAVOURITE
VILLAGE GIRLS

A WRESTLER
A SURVEYOR
SCHOOLBOYS
ATTENDANTS ON THE 'BALE'
Musicians, Dancers, Mummers,
Prisoners, Traders, The Village

Morning

A clearing on the edge of the market, dominated by an immense 'odan' tree. It is the village centre. The wall of the bush school flanks the stage on the right, and a rude window opens on to the stage from the wall. There is a chant of the 'Arithmetic Times' issuing from this window. It is heard a short while before the action begins. Sidi enters from left, carrying a small pail of water on her head. She is a slim girl with plaited hair. A true village belle. She balances the pail on her head with accustomed ease. Around her is wrapped the familiar broad cloth which is folded just above her breasts, leaving the shoulders bare.

Almost as soon as she appears on the stage, the schoolmaster's face also appears at the window. (The chanting continues—'Three times two are six', 'Three times three are nine', etc.) The teacher Lakunle, disappears. He is replaced by two of his pupils, aged roughly eleven, who make a buzzing noise at Sidi, repeatedly clapping their hands across the mouth. Lakunle now re-appears below the window and makes for Sidi, stopping only to give the boys admonitory whacks on the head before they can duck. They vanish with a howl and he shuts the window on them. The chanting dies away. The schoolmaster is nearly twenty-three. He is dressed in an old-style English suit, threadbare but not ragged, clean but not ironed, obviously a size or two too small. His tie is done in a very small knot, disappearing beneath a shiny black waistcoat. He wears twenty-three-inch-bottom trousers, and blanco-white tennis shoes.

LAKUNLE. Let me take it.
SIDI. No.
LAKUNLE. Let me. [*Seizes the pail. Some water spills on him.*]
SIDI [*delighted*].
  There. Wet for your pains.
  Have you no shame?

LAKUNLE. That is what the stewpot said to the fire.
  Have you no shame—at your age
  Licking my bottom? But she was tickled
  Just the same.
SIDI. The school teacher is full of stories
  This morning. And now, if the lesson
  Is over, may I have the pail?
LAKUNLE. No. I have told you not to carry loads
  On your head. But you are as stubborn
  As an illiterate goat. It is bad for the spine.
  And it shortens your neck, so that very soon
  You will have no neck at all. Do you wish to look
  Squashed like my pupils' drawings?
SIDI. Why should that worry me? Haven't you sworn
  That my looks do not affect your love?
  Yesterday, dragging your knees in the dust
  You said, Sidi, if you were crooked or fat,
  And your skin was scaly like a . . .
LAKUNLE. Stop!
SIDI. I only repeat what you said.
LAKUNLE. Yes, and I will stand by every word I spoke.
  But must you throw away your neck on that
    account?
  Sidi, it is so unwomanly. Only spiders
  Carry loads the way you do.
SIDI [*huffily, exposing the neck to advantage*].
  Well, it is my neck, not your spider.
LAKUNLE [*looks, and gets suddenly agitated*].
  And look at that! Look, look at that!

[*Makes a general sweep in the direction of her breasts.*]

Who was it talked of shame just now?
How often must I tell you, Sidi, that
A grown-up girl must cover up her . . .
Her . . . shoulders? I can see quite . . . quite
A good portion of—that! And so I imagine
Can every man in the village. Idlers
All of them, good-for-nothing shameless men

Casting their lustful eyes where
They have no business . . .

SIDI. Are you at that again? Why, I've done the fold
So high and so tight, I can hardly breathe.
And all because you keep at me so much.
I have to leave my arms so I can use them . . .
Or don't you know that?

LAKUNLE. You could wear something.
Most modest women do. But you, no.
You must run about naked in the streets.
Does it not worry you . . . the bad names,
The lewd jokes, the tongue-licking noises
Which girls, uncovered like you,
Draw after them?

SIDI. This is too much. Is it you, Lakunle,
Telling me that I make myself common talk
When the whole world knows of the madman
Of Ilujinle, who calls himself a teacher!
Is it Sidi who makes the men choke
In their cups, or you, with your big loud words
And no meaning? You and your ragged books
Dragging your feet to every threshold
And rushing them out again as curses
Greet you instead of welcome. Is it Sidi
They call a fool—even the children—
Or you with your fine airs and little sense!

LAKUNLE [first indignant, then recovers composure].
For that, what is a jewel to pigs?
If now I am misunderstood by you
And your race of savages, I rise above taunts
And remain unruffled.

SIDI [furious, shakes both fists at him].
O . . . oh, you make me want to pulp your brain.

LAKUNLE [retreats a little, but puts her aside with a very
lofty gesture].
A natural feeling, arising out of envy;
For, as a woman, you have a smaller brain
Than mine.

SIDI [madder still].
Again! I'd like to know
Just what gives you these thoughts
Of manly conceit.

LAKUNLE [very, very patronizing].
No, no. I have fallen for that trick before.
You can no longer draw me into arguments
Which go above your head.

SIDI [can't find the right words, chokes back].
Give me the pail now. And if you ever dare
To stop me in the streets again . . .

LAKUNLE. Now, now, Sidi . . .

SIDI. Give it or I'll . . .

LAKUNLE [holds on to her].
Please, don't be angry with me.

I didn't mean you in particular.
And anyway, it isn't what I say.
The scientists have proved it. It's in my books.
Women have a smaller brain than men.
That's why they are called the weaker sex.

SIDI [throws him off].
The weaker sex, is it?
Is it a weaker breed who pounds the yam
Or bends all day to plant the millet
With a child strapped to her back?

LAKUNLE. That is all part of what I say.
But don't you worry. In a year or two
You will have machines which will do
Your pounding, which will grind your pepper
Without it getting in your eyes.

SIDI. O-oh. You really mean to turn
The whole world upside down.

LAKUNLE. The world? Oh, that. Well, maybe later.
Charity, they say, begins at home.
For now, it is this village I shall turn
Inside out. Beginning with that crafty rogue,
Your past master of self-indulgence—Baroka.

SIDI. Are you still on about the Bale?
What has he done to you?

LAKUNLE. He'll find out. Soon enough, I'll let him
know.

SIDI. These thoughts of future wonders—do you buy
them
Or merely go mad and dream of them?

LAKUNLE. A prophet has honour except
In his own home. Wise men have been called mad
Before me, and after, many more shall be
So abused. But to answer you, the measure
Is not entirely of my own coinage.
What I boast is known in Lagos, that city
Of magic, in Badagry where Saro women bathe
In gold, even in smaller towns less than
Twelve miles from here . . .

SIDI. Well go there. Go to these places where
Women would understand you
If you told them of your plans with which
You oppress me daily. Do you not know
What name they give you here?
Have you lost your shame completely that jeers
Pass you over.

LAKUNLE. No. I have told you no. Shame belongs
Only to the ignorant.

SIDI. Well, I am going.
Shall I take the pail or not?

LAKUNLE. Not till you swear to marry me.

[Takes her hand, instantly soulful.]

Sidi, a man must prepare to fight alone.
But it helps if he has a woman
To stand by him, a woman who . . .
Can understand . . . like you.

SIDI. I do?

LAKUNLE. Sidi, my love will open your mind
Like the chaste leaf in the morning, when
The sun first touches it.

SIDI. If you start that I will run away.
I had enough of that nonsense yesterday.

LAKUNLE. Nonsense? Nonsense? Do you hear?
Does anybody listen? Can the stones
Bear to listen to this? Do you call it
Nonsense that I poured the waters of my soul
To wash your feet?

SIDI. You did what!

LAKUNLE. Wasted! Wasted! Sidi, my heart
Bursts into flowers with my love
But you, you and the dead of this village
Trample it with feet of ignorance.

SIDI [shakes her head in bafflement].
If the snail finds splinters in his shell
He changes house. Why do you stay?

LAKUNLE. Faith. Because I have faith.
Oh Sidi, vow to me your own undying love
And I will scorn the jibes of these bush minds
Who know no better. Swear, Sidi,
Swear you will be my wife and I will
Stand against earth, heaven, and the nine
Hells . . .

SIDI. Now there you go again.
One little thing
And you must chirrup like a cockatoo.
You talk and talk and deafen me
With words which always sound the same
And make no meaning.
I've told you, and I say it again
I shall marry you today, next week
Or any day you name.
But my bride-price must first be paid.
Aha, now you turn away.
But I tell you, Lakunle, I must have
The full bride-price. Will you make me
A laughing-stock? Well, do as you please.
But Sidi will not make herself
A cheap bowl for the village spit.

LAKUNLE. On my head let fall their scorn.

SIDI. They will say I was no virgin
That I was forced to sell my shame
And marry you without a price.

LAKUNLE. A savage custom, barbaric, out-dated,
Rejected, denounced, accursed,

Excommunicated, archaic, degrading,
Humiliating, unspeakable, redundant.
Retrogressive, remarkable, unpalatable.

SIDI. Is the bag empty? Why did you stop?

LAKUNLE. I own only the Shorter Companion
Dictionary, but I have ordered
The Longer One—you wait!

SIDI. Just pay the price.

LAKUNLE [with a sudden shout].
An ignoble custom, infamous, ignominious
Shaming our heritage before the world.
Sidi, I do not seek a wife
To fetch and carry,
To cook and scrub,
To bring forth children by the gross . . .

SIDI. Heaven forgive you! Do you now scorn
Child-bearing in a wife?

LAKUNLE. Of course I do not. I only mean . . .
Oh Sidi, I want to wed
Because I love,
I seek a life-companion . . .

[pulpit-declamatory.]

'And the man shall take the woman
And the two shall be together
As one flesh.'
Sidi, I seek a friend in need.
An equal partner in my race of life.

SIDI [attentive no more. Deeply engrossed in counting the
beads on her neck].
Then pay the price.

LAKUNLE. Ignorant girl, can you not understand?
To pay the price would be
To buy a heifer off the market stall.
You'd be my chattel, my mere property.
No, Sidi! [very tenderly.]
When we are wed, you shall not walk or sit
Tethered, as it were, to my dirtied heels.
Together we shall sit at table
—Not on the floor—and eat,
Not with fingers, but with knives
And forks, and breakable plates
Like civilized beings.
I will not have you wait on me
Till I have dined my fill.
No wife of mine, no lawful wedded wife
Shall eat the leavings off my plate—
That is for the children.
I want to walk beside you in the street.
Side by side and arm in arm
Just like the Lagos couples I have seen

High-heeled shoes for the lady, red paint
On her lips. And her hair stretched
Like a magazine photo. I will teach you
The waltz and we'll both learn the foxtrot
And we'll spend the week-end in night-clubs at
   Ibadan.
Oh I must show you the grandeur of towns
We'll live there if you like or merely pay visits.
So choose. Be a modern wife, look me in the eye
And give me a little kiss—like this.

[Kisses her.]

SIDI [backs away].
   No, don't! I tell you I dislike
   This strange unhealthy mouthing you perform.
   Every time, your gesture deceives me
   Making me think that you merely wish
   To whisper something in my ear.
   Then comes this licking of my lips with yours.
   It's so unclean. And then,
   The sound you make—'Pyout!'
   Are you being rude to me?
LAKUNLE [wearily]. It's never any use.
   Bush-girl you are, bush-girl you'll always be;
   Uncivilized and primitive—bush-girl!
   I kissed you as all educated men—
   And Christians—kiss their wives
   It is the way of civilized romance.
SIDI [lightly]. A way you mean, to avoid
   Payment of lawful bride-price
   A cheating way, mean and miserly.
LAKUNLE [violently]. It is not.

[Sidi bursts out laughing. Lakunle changes his tone to a soulful one, both eyes dreamily shut.]

Romance is the sweetening of the soul
With fragrance offered by the stricken heart.
SIDI [looks at him in wonder for a while].
   Away with you. The village says you're mad,
   And I begin to understand.
   I wonder that they let you run the school.
   You and your talk. You'll ruin your pupils too
   And then they'll utter madness just like you.

[Noise off-stage.]

There are people coming.
Give me the bucket or they'll jeer.

[Enter a crowd of youths and drummers, the girls in various stages of excitement.]

FIRST GIRL. Sidi, he has returned. He came back just
   as he said he would.
SIDI. Who has?
FIRST GIRL. The stranger. The man from the outside
   world.
   The clown who fell in the river for you.

[They all burst out laughing.]

SIDI. The one who rode on the devil's own horse?
SECOND GIRL. Yes, the same. The stranger with the
   one-eyed box.

[She demonstrates the action of a camera amidst admiring titters.]

THIRD GIRL. And he brought his new horse right into
   the village square this time. This one has only two
   feet. You should have seen him. B-r-r-rr.

[Runs around the platform driving an imaginary motor-bike.]

SIDI. And has he brought . . . ?
FIRST GIRL. The images? He brought them all. There
   was hardly any part of the village which does not
   show in the book.

[Clicks the imaginary shutter.]

SIDI. The book? Did you see the book?
   Had he the precious book
   That would bestow upon me
   Beauty beyond the dreams of a goddess?
   For so he said.
   The book which would announce
   This beauty to the world—
   Have you seen it?
THIRD GIRL. Yes, yes, he did. But the Bale is still
   feasting his eyes on the images. Oh, Sidi, he was
   right. You *are* beautiful. On the cover of the book is
   an image of you from here [touches the top of her
   head] to here [her stomach]. And in the middle leaves,
   from the beginning of one leaf right across to the
   end of another, is one of you from head to toe. Do
   you remember it? It was the one for which he made
   you stretch your arms towards the sun. [Rapturously.]
   Oh, Sidi, you looked as if, at that moment, the sun
   himself had been your lover. [They all gasp with pretended shock at this blasphemy and one slaps her playfully on the buttocks.]
FIRST GIRL. The Bale is jealous, but he pretends to be
   proud of you. And when this man tells him how

famous you are in the capital, he pretends to be
pleased, saying how much honour and fame you
have brought to the village.

SIDI [*with amazement*]. Is not Baroka's image in the
book at all?

SECOND GIRL [*contemptuous*]. Oh yes, it is. But it
would have been much better for the Bale if the
stranger had omitted him altogether. His image is in
a little corner somewhere in the book, and even that
corner he shares with one of the village latrines.

SIDI. Is that the truth? Swear! Ask Ogun to
Strike you dead.

GIRL. Ogun strike me dead if I lie.

SIDI:. If that is true, than I am more esteemed
Than Bale Baroka,
The Lion of Ilujinle.
This means that I am greater than
The Fox of the Undergrowth,
The living god among men . . .

LAKUNLE [*peevishly*]. And devil among women.

SIDI. Be silent, you.
You are merely filled with spite.

LAKUNLE. I know him what he is. This is
Divine justice that a mere woman
Should outstrip him in the end.

SIDI. Be quiet;
Or I swear I'll never speak to you again.

[*Affects sudden coyness.*]

In fact, I am not sure I'll want to wed you now.

LAKUNLE. Sidi!

SIDI. Well, why should I?
Known as I am to the whole wide world,
I would demean my worth to wed
A mere village school teacher.

LAKUNLE [*in agony*]. Sidi!

SIDI. And one who is too mean
To pay the bride-price like a man.

LAKUNLE. Oh, Sidi, don't!

SIDI [*plunging into an enjoyment of Lakunle's misery*].
Well, don't you know?
Sidi is more important even than the Bale.
More famous than that panther of the trees.
He is beneath me now—
Your fearless rake, the scourge of womanhood!
But now,
He shares the corner of the leaf
With the lowest of the low—
With the dug-out village latrine!
While I—How many leaves did my own image take?

FIRST GIRL. Two in the middle and . . .

SIDI. No, no. Let the school teacher count!
How many were there, teacher-man?

LAKUNLE. Three *pages*.

SIDI [*threateningly*]. One leaf for every heart that I shall
break.
Beware!

[*Leaps suddenly into the air.*]

Hurray! I'm beautiful!
Hurray for the wandering stranger!

CROWD. Hurray for the Lagos man!

SIDI [*wildly excited*]. I know. Let us dance the dance of
the lost
Traveller.

SHOUTS. Yes, let's.

SIDI. Who will dance the devil-horse?
You, you, you and you.

[*The four girls fall out.*]

A python. Who will dance the snake?
Ha ha! Your eyes are shifty and your ways are sly.

[*The selected youth is pushed out amidst jeers.*]

The stranger. We've got to have the being
From the mad outer world . . . You there,
No, you have never felt the surge
Of burning liquor in your milky veins.
Who can we pick that knows the walk of drunks?
You? . . . No, the thought itself
Would knock you out as sure as wine . . . Ah!

[*Turns round slowly to where Lakunle is standing with a
kindly, fatherly smile for the children at play.*]

Come on book-worm, you'll play his part.

LAKUNLE. No, no. I've never been drunk in all my
life.

SIDI. We know. But your father drank so much,
He must have drunk your share, and that
Of his great grandsons.

LAKUNLE [*tries to escape*]. I won't take part.

SIDI. You must.

LAKUNLE. I cannot stay. It's nearly time to take
Primary four in Geography.

SIDI [*goes over to the window and throws it open*].
Did you think your pupils would remain in school
Now that the stranger has returned?
The village is on holiday, you fool.

LAKUNLE [*as they drag him towards the platform*].

No, no. I won't. This foolery bores me.
It is a game of idiots. I have work of more impor-
    tance.
SIDI [*bending down over Lakunle who has been seated
    forcibly on the platform*].
You are dressed like him
You look like him
You speak his tongue
You think like him
You're just as clumsy
In your Lagos ways—
You'll do for him!

[*This chant is taken up by all and they begin to dance round
Lakunle, speaking the words in a fast rhythm. The drummers
join in after the first time, keeping up a steady beat as the
others whirl round their victim. They go faster and faster and
chant faster and faster with each round. By the sixth or
seventh, Lakunle has obviously had enough.*]

LAKUNLE [*raising his voice above the din*]. All right! I'll
    do it.
Come now, let's get it over with.

[*A terrific shout and a clap of drums. Lakunle enters into the
spirit of the dance with enthusiasm. He takes over from Sidi,
stations his cast all over the stage as the jungle, leaves the
right top-stage clear for the four girls who are to dance the
motor-car. A mime follows of the visitor's entry into Ilujinle,
and his short stay among the villagers. The four girls crouch
on the floor, as four wheels of a car. Lakunle directs their
spacing, then takes his place in the middle, and sits on air.
He alone does not dance. He does realistic miming. Soft
throbbing drums, gradually swelling in volume, and the four
'wheels' begin to rotate the upper halves of their bodies in
perpendicular circles. Lakunle clowning the driving motions,
obviously enjoying this fully. The drums gain tempo, faster,
faster, faster. A sudden crash of drums and the girls quiver
and dance the stall. Another effort at rhythm fails, and the
'stalling wheels' give a corresponding shudder, finally, and
let their faces fall on to their laps. Lakunle tampers with a
number of controls, climbs out of the car and looks underneath it. His lips indicate that he is swearing violently.
Examines the wheels, pressing them to test the pressure,
betrays the devil in him by seizing his chance to pinch the
girls' bottoms. One yells and bites him on the ankle. He
climbs hurriedly back into the car, makes a final attempt to
re-start it, gives it up and decides to abandon it. Picks up his
camera and his helmet, pockets a flask of whisky from which
he takes a swig, before beginning the trek. The drums
resume beating, a different, darker tone and rhythm, varying
with the journey. Full use of 'gangan' and 'iya ilu'. The
'trees' perform a subdued and unobtrusive dance on the
same spot. Details as a snake slithering out of the branches
and poising over Lakunle's head when he leans against a
tree for a rest. He flees, restoring his nerves shortly after by a*

*swig. A monkey drops suddenly in his path and gibbers at
him before scampering off. A roar comes from somewhere,
etc. His nerves go rapidly and he recuperates himself by
copious draughts. He is soon tipsy, battles violently with the
undergrowth and curses silently as he swats the flies off his
tortured body.*

*Suddenly, from somewhere in the bush comes the
sound of a girl singing. The Traveller shakes his head but the
sound persists. Convinced he is suffering from sun-stroke, he
drinks again. His last drop, so he tosses the bottle in the
direction of the sound, only to be rewarded by a splash, a
scream and a torrent of abuse, and finally, silence again. He
tip-toes, clears away the obstructing growth, blinks hard and
rubs his eyes. Whatever he has seen still remains. He whistles softly, unhitches his camera and begins to jockey himself
into a good position for a take. Backwards and forwards, and
his eyes are so closely glued to the lens that he puts forward
a careless foot and disappears completely. There is a loud
splash and the invisible singer alters her next tone to a
sustained scream. Quickened rhythm and shortly afterwards,
amidst sounds of splashes, Sidi appears on the stage, with a
piece of cloth only partially covering her. Lakunle follows a
little later, more slowly, trying to wring out the water from
his clothes. He has lost all his appendages except the camera. Sidi has run right across the stage, and returns a short
while later, accompanied by the Villagers. The same cast has
disappeared and re-forms behind Sidi as the Villagers. They
are in an ugly mood, and in spite of his protests, haul him off
to the town centre, in front of the 'Odan' tree.*

*Everything comes to a sudden stop as Baroka the Bale,
wiry, goateed, tougher than his sixty-two years, himself
emerges at this point from behind the tree. All go down,
prostrate or kneeling with the greetings of 'Kabiyesi' 'Baba'
etc. All except Lakunle who begins to sneak off.*]

BAROKA. Akowe. Teacher wa. Misita Lakunle.

[*As the others take up the cry 'Misita Lakunle' he is forced to
stop. He returns and bows deeply from the waist.*]

LAKUNLE. A good morning to you sir.
BAROKA. Guru morin guru morin, ngh-hn! That is
    All we get from 'alakowe'. You call at his house
    Hoping he sends for beer, but all you get is
    Guru morin. Will guru morin wet my throat?
    Well, well our man of knowledge, I hope you have
    no
    Query for an old man today.
LAKUNLE. No complaints.
BAROKA. And we are not feuding in something
    I have forgotten.
LAKUNLE. Feuding sir? I see no cause at all.
BAROKA. Well, the play was much alive until I came.
    And now everything stops, and you were leaving
    Us. After all, I knew the story and I came in

Right on cue. It makes me feel as if I was
Chief Baseje.
LAKUNLE. One hardly thinks the Bale would have the time
For such childish nonsense.
BAROKA. A-ah Mister Lakunle. Without these things you call
Nonsense, a Bale's life would be pretty dull.
Well, now that you say I am welcome, shall we
Resume your play?

[*Turns suddenly to his attendants.*]

Seize him!
LAKUNLE [*momentarily baffled*]. What for? What have I done?
BAROKA. You tried to steal our village maidenhead
Have you forgotten? If he has, serve him a slap
To wake his brain.

[*An uplifted arm being proffered, Lakunle quickly recollects and nods his head vigorously. So the play is back in performance. The Villagers gather round threatening, clamouring for his blood. Lakunle tries bluff, indignation, appeasement in turn. At a sudden signal from the Bale, they throw him down prostrate on his face. Only then does the Chief begin to show him sympathy, appear to understand the Stranger's plight, and pacify the villagers on his behalf. He orders dry clothes for him, seats him on his right and orders a feast in his honour. The Stranger springs up every second to take photographs of the party, but most of the time his attention is fixed on Sidi dancing with abandon. Eventually he whispers to the Chief, who nods in consent, and Sidi is sent for. The Stranger arranges Sidi in all sorts of magazine postures and takes innumerable photographs of her. Drinks are pressed upon him; he refuses at first, eventually tries the local brew with scepticism, appears to relish it, and drinks profusely. Before long, however, he leaves the party to be*]

sick. *They clap him on the back as he goes out, and two drummers who insist on dancing round him nearly cause the calamity to happen on the spot. However, he rushes out with his hand held to the mouth. Lakunle's exit seems to signify the end of the mime. He returns almost at once and the others discard their roles.*]

SIDI [*delightedly*]. What did I say? You played him to the bone,
A court jester would have been the life for you,
Instead of school.

[*Points contemptuously to the school.*]

BAROKA. And where would the village be, robbed of
Such wisdom as Mister Lakunle dispenses
Daily? Who would tell us where we go wrong?
Eh, Mister Lakunle?
SIDI [*hardly listening, still in the full grip of her excitement*].
Who comes with me to find the man?
But Lakunle, you'll have to come and find sense
In his clipping tongue. You see book-man
We cannot really do
Without your head.

[*Lakunle begins to protest, but they crowd him and try to bear him down. Suddenly he breaks free and takes to his heels with all the women in full pursuit. Baroka is left sitting by himself—his wrestler, who accompanied him on his entry, stands a respectful distance away—staring at the flock of women in flight. From the folds of his agbada he brings out his copy of the magazine and admires the heroine of the publication. Nods slowly to himself.*]

BAROKA. Yes, yes . . . it is five full months since last
I took a wife . . . five full months. . .

Noon

A road by the market. Enter Sidi, happily engrossed in the pictures of herself in the magazine. Lakunle follows one or two paces behind carrying a bundle of firewood which Sidi has set out to obtain. They are met in the centre by Sadiku, who has entered from the opposite side. Sadiku is an old woman, with a shawl over her head.

SADIKU. Fortune is with me. I was going to your house to see you.

SIDI [*startled out of her occupation*]. What! Oh, it is you, Sadiku.
SADIKU. The Lion sent me. He wishes you well.
SIDI. Thank him for me.

[*Then excitedly.*]

Have you seen these?
Have you seen these images of me
Wrought by the man from the capital city?

Have you felt the gloss? [*Caresses the page.*]
Smoother by far then the parrot's breast.

SADIKU. I have. I have. I saw them as soon as the city
man came . . . Sidi, I bring a message from my lord.
[*Jerks her head at Lakunle.*] Shall we draw aside a little?

SIDI. Him? Pay no more heed to that
Than you would a eunuch

SADIKU. Then, in as few words as it takes to tell,
Baroka wants you for a wife.

LAKUNLE [*bounds forward, dropping the wood*].
What! The greedy dog!
Insatiate camel of a foolish, doting race;
Is he at his tricks again?

SIDI. Be quiet, 'Kunle. You get so tiresome.
The message is for me, not you.

LAKUNLE [*down on his knees at once. Covers Sidi's hands
with kisses*].
My Ruth, my Rachel, Esther, Bathsheba
Thou sum of fabled perfections
From Genesis to the Revelations
Listen not to the voice of this infidel . . .

SIDI [*snatches her hand away*].
Now that's your other game;
Giving me funny names you pick up
In your wretched books.
My name is Sidi. And now, let me be.
My name is Sidi, and I am beautiful.
The stranger took my beauty
And placed it in my hands.
Here, here it is. I need no funny names
To tell me of my fame,
Loveliness beyond the jewels of a throne—
That is what he said.

SADIKU [*gleefully*]. Well, will you be Baroka's own
jewel?
Will you be his sweetest princess, soothing him on
weary
nights? What answer shall I give my lord?

SIDI [*wags her finger playfully at the woman*].
Ha ha. Sadiku of the honey tongue.
Sadiku, head of the Lion's wives.
You'll make no prey of Sidi with your wooing
tongue
Not this Sidi whose fame has spread to Lagos
And beyond the seas.

[*Lakunle beams with satisfaction and rises.*]

SADIKU. Sidi, have you considered what a life of bliss
awaits you? Baroke swears to take no other wife after
you. Do you know what it is to be the Bale's last
wife? I'll tell you. When he dies—and that should

not be long; even the Lion has to die sometime—
well, when he does, it means that you will have the
honour of being the senior wife of the new Bale.
And just think, until Baroka dies, you shall be his
favourite. No living in the outhouses for you, my
girl. Your place will always be in the palace: first as
the latest bride, and afterwards, as the head of the
new harem . . . It is a rich life, Sidi. I know. I have
been in that position for forty-one years.

SIDI. You waste your breath.
Why did Baroka not request my hand
Before the stranger
Brought his book of images?
Why did the Lion not bestow his gift
Before my face was lauded to the world?
Can you not see? Because he sees my worth
Increased and multiplied above his own;
Because he can already hear
The ballad-makers and their songs
In praise of Sidi, the incomparable,
While the Lion is forgotten.
He seeks to have me as his property
Where I must fade beneath his jealous hold.
Ah, Sadiku,
The school-man here has taught me certain things
And my images have taught me all the rest.
Baroka merely seeks to raise his manhood
Above my beauty
He seeks new fame
As the one man who has possessed
The jewel of Ilujinle!

SADIKU [*shocked, bewildered, incapable of making any
sense of Sidi's words*]. But Sidi, are you well? Such
nonsense never passed your lips before. Did you not
sound strange, even in your own hearing? [*Rushes
suddenly at Lakunle.*] Is this your doing, you popinjay?
Have you driven the poor girl mad at last? Such
rubbish . . . I will beat your head for this!

LAKUNLE [*retreating in panic*]. Keep away from me, old
hag.

SIDI. Sadiku, let him be.
Tell your lord that I can read his mind,
That I will none of him.
Look—judge for yourself.

[*Opens the magazine and points out the pictures.*]

He's old. I never knew till now,
He was that old . . .

[*During the rest of her speech, Sidi runs her hand over the
surface of the relevant part of the photographs, tracing the
contours with her fingers.*]

. . . To think I took
No notice of my velvet skin.
How smooth it is!
And no man ever thought
To praise the fulness of my breasts . . .

LAKUNLE [*laden with guilt and full of apology*].
Well, Sidi, I did think . . .
But somehow it was not the proper thing.

SIDI [*ignores the interruption*].
See I hold them to the warm caress

[*unconsciously pushes out her chest.*]

Of a desire-filled sun.

[*Smiles mischievously.*]

There's a deceitful message in my eyes
Beckoning insatiate men to certain doom.
And teeth that flash the sign of happiness,
Strong and evenly, beaming full of life.
Be just, Sadiku,
Compare my image and your lord's—
An age of difference!
See how the water glistens on my face
Like the dew-moistened leaves on a Harmattan
    morning
But he—his face is like a leather piece
Torn rudely from the saddle of his horse,

[*Sadiku gasps.*]

Sprinkled with the musty ashes
From a pipe that is long over-smoked.
And this goat-like tuft
Which I once thought was manly;
It is like scattered twists of grass—
Not even green—
But charred and lifeless, as after a forest fire!
Sadiku, I am young and brimming; he is spent.
I am the twinkle of a jewel
But he is the hind-quarters of a lion!

SADIKU [*recovering at last from helpless amazement*]. May
Sango restore your wits. For most surely some angry
god has taken possession of you. [*Turns around and
walks away. Stops again as she remembers something
else.*] Your ranting put this clean out of my head. My
lord says that if you would not be his wife, would
you at least come to supper at his house tonight.
There is a small feast in your honour. He wishes to
tell you how happy he is that the great capital city
has done so much honour to a daughter of Ilujinle.
You have brought great fame to your people.

SIDI. Ho ho! Do you think that I was only born
    Yesterday?
The tales of Baroka's little suppers,
I know all.
Tell your lord that Sidi does not sup with
Married men.

SADIKU. They are lies, lies. You must not believe
everything you hear. Sidi, would I deceive you? I
swear to you . . .

SIDI. Can you deny that
Every woman who has supped with him one night,
Becomes his wife or concubine the next.

LAKUNLE. Is it for nothing he is called the Fox?

SADIKU [*advancing on him*]. You keep out of this, or so
Sango be my witness. . .

LAKUNLE [*retreats just a little, but continues to talk*].
His wiliness is known even in the larger towns.
Did you never hear
Of how he foiled the Public Works attempt
To build the railway through Ilujinle.

SADIKU. Nobody knows the truth of that. It is all
    hearsay.

SIDI. I love hearsays. Lakunle, tell me all.

LAKUNLE. Did you not know it? Well sit down and
    listen.
My father told me, before he died. And few men
Know of this trick—oh he's a die-hard rogue
Sworn against our progress . . . yes . . . it was . . .
    somewhere here
The track should have been laid just along
The outskirts. Well, the workers came, in fact
It was prisoners who were brought to do
The harder part . . . to break the jungle's back . . .

[*Enter the prisoners, guarded by two warders. A white surveyor examines his map (khaki helmet, spats, etc.) The foreman runs up with his camp stool, table, etc., erects the
umbrella over him and unpacks the usual box of bush
comforts—soda siphon, whisky bottle and geometric sandwiches. His map consulted, he directs the sweat team where
to work. They begin felling, machet swinging, log dragging,
all to the rhythm of the work gang's metal percussion (rod on
gong or rude triangle, etc.) The two performers are also the
song leaders and the others fill the chorus. 'N'ijo itoro',
'Amuda el' ebe l'aiya' 'Gbe je on'ipa' etc.*]

LAKUNLE. They marked the route with stakes, ate
Through the jungle and began the tracks. Trade,
Progress, adventure, success, civilization,
Fame, international conspicuousity . . . it was
All within the grasp of Ilujinle . . .

[*The wrestler enters, stands horrified at the sight and flees.
Returns later with the Bale himself who soon assesses the*

situation. They disappear. The work continues, the surveyor occupies himself with the fly-whisk and whisky. Shortly after, a bull-roarer is heard. The prisoners falter a little, pick up again. The bull-roarer continues on its way, nearer and farther, moving in circles, so that it appears to come from all round them. The foreman is the first to break and then the rest is chaos. Sole survivor of the rout is the surveyor who is too surprised to move.

Baroka enters a few minutes later accompanied by some attendants and preceded by a young girl bearing a calabash bowl. The surveyor, angry and threatening, is prevailed upon to open his gift. From it he reveals a wad of pound notes and kola nuts. Mutual understanding is established. The surveyor frowns heavily, rubs his chin and consults his map. Re-examines the contents of the bowl, shakes his head. Baroka adds more money, and a coop of hens. A goat follows, and more money. This time 'truth' dawns on him at last, he has made a mistake. The track really should go the other way. What an unfortunate error, discovered just in time! No, no, no possibility of a mistake this time, the track should be much further away. In fact (scooping up the soil) the earth is most unsuitable, couldn't possibly support the weight of a railway engine. A gourd of palm wine is brought to seal the agreement and a kola nut is broken. Baroka's men help the surveyor pack and they leave with their arms round each other followed by the surveyor's booty.]

LAKUNLE [*as the last of the procession disappears, shakes his fist at them, stamping on the ground*].

Voluptuous beast! He loves this life too well
To bear to part from it. And motor roads
And railways would do just that, forcing
Civilization at his door. He foresaw it
And he barred the gates, securing fast
His dogs and horses, his wives and all his
Concubines . . . ah, yes . . . all those concubines
Baroka has such a selective eye, none suits him
But the best . . .

[*His eyes truly light up. Sidi and Sadiku snigger, tip-toe off stage.*]

    . . . Yes, one must grant him that.
Ah, I sometimes wish I led his kind of life.
Such luscious bosoms make his nightly pillow.
I am sure he keeps a time-table just as
I do at school. Only way to ensure fair play.
He must be healthy to keep going as he does.
I don't know what the women see in him. His eyes
Are small and always red with wine. He must
Possess some secret . . . No! I do not envy him!
Just the one woman for me. Alone I stand
For progress, with Sidi my chosen soul-mate, the
  one
Woman of my life . . . Sidi! Sidi where are you?

[*Rushes out after them, returns to fetch the discarded firewood and runs out again.*]

[*Baroka in bed, naked except for baggy trousers, calf-length. It is a rich bedroom covered in animal skins and rugs. Weapons round the wall. Also a strange machine, a most peculiar contraption with a long lever. Kneeling beside the bed is Baroka's current Favourite, engaged in plucking the hairs from his armpit. She does this by first massaging the spot around the selected hair very gently with her forefinger. Then, with hardly a break, she pulls out the hair between her finger and the thumb with a sudden sharp movement. Baroka twitches slightly with each pull. Then an aspirated 'A-ah', and a look of complete beatitude spreads all over his face.*]

FAVOURITE. Do I improve my lord?
BAROKA. You are still somewhat over-gentle with the
  pull
  As if you feared to hurt the panther of the trees.
  Be sharp and sweet
  Like the swift sting of a vicious wasp
  For there the pleasure lies—the cooling aftermath.
FAVOURITE. I'll learn, my lord.
BAROKA. You have not time, my dear.
  Tonight I hope to take another wife.
  And the honour of this task, you know,
  Belongs by right to my latest choice.
  But—A-ah—Now that was sharp.
  It had in it the scorpion's sudden sting
  Without its poison.
  It was an angry pull; you tried to hurt
  For I had made you wrathful with my boast.
  But now your anger flows in my blood-stream:
  How sweet it is! A-ah! That was sweeter still.
  I think perhaps that I shall let you stay,
  The sole out-puller of my sweat-bathed hairs.
  Ach!

[*Sits up suddenly and rubs the sore point angrily.*]

  Now that had far more pain than pleasure
  Vengeful creature, you did not caress
  The area of extraction long enough!

[*Enter Sadiku. She goes down on her knees at once and bows her head into her lap.*]

  Aha! Here comes Sadiku.
  Do you bring some balm
  To soothe the smart of my misused armpit?
  Away, you enemy!

[*Exit the Favourite.*]

SADIKU. My lord . . .

BAROKA. You have my leave to speak.
  What did she say?

SADIKU. She will not, my lord. I did my best, but she
  will have none of you.

BAROKA. It follows the pattern—a firm refusal
  At the start. Why will she not?

SADIKU. That is the strange part of it. She say's you're
  much too old. If you ask me, I think that she is
  really off her head. All this excitement of the books
  has been too much for her.

BAROKA [springs to his feet].
  She says·. . . That I am old
  That I am much too old? Did a slight
  Unripened girl say this of me?

SADIKU. My lord, I heard the incredible words with
  my ears, and I thought the world was mad.

BAROKA. But is it possible, Sadiku? Is this right?
  Did I not, at the festival of Rain,
  Defeat the men in the log-tossing match?
  Do I not still with the most fearless ones,
  Hunt the leopard and the boa at night
  And save the farmers' goats from further harm?
  And does she say I'm old?
  Did I not, to announce the Harmattan,
  Climb to the top of the silk-cotton tree,
  Break the first pod, and scatter tasselled seeds
  To the four winds—and this but yesterday?
  Do any of my wives report
  A failing in my manliness?
  The strongest of them all
  Still wearies long before the Lion does!
  And so would she, had I the briefest chance
  To teach this unfledged birdling
  That lacks the wisdom to embrace
  The rich mustiness of age . . . if I could once . . .
  Come hither, soothe me, Sadiku
  For I am wroth at heart.

[Lies back on the bed, staring up as before. Sadiku takes her
place at the foot of the bed and begins to tickle the soles of
his feet. Baroka turns to the left suddenly, reaches down the
side, and comes up with a copy of the magazine. Opens it
and begins to study the pictures. He heaves a long sigh.]

  That is good, Sadiku, very good.

[He begins to compare some pictures in the book, obviously
his own and Sidi's. Flings the book away suddenly and stares
at the ceiling for a second or two. Then, unsmiling:]

  Perhaps it is as well, Sadiku.

SADIKU. My lord, what did you say?

BAROKA. Yes, faithful one, I say it is as well.
  The scorn, the laughter and the jeers
  Would have been bitter.
  Had she consented and my purpose failed,
  I would have sunk with shame.

SADIKU. My lord, I do not understand.

BAROKA. The time has come when I can fool myself
  No more. I am no man, Sadiku. My manhood
  Ended near a week ago.

SADIKU. The gods forbid.

BAROKA. I wanted Sidi because I still hoped—
  A foolish thought I know, but still—I hoped
  That, with a virgin young and hot within,
  My failing strength would rise and save my pride.

[Sadiku begins to moan.]

  A waste of hope. I knew it even then.
  But it's a human failing never to accept
  The worst; and so I pandered to my vanity.
  When manhood must, it ends.
  The well of living, tapped beyond its depth,
  Dries up, and mocks the wastrel in the end.
  I am withered and unsapped, the joy
  Of ballad-mongers, the aged butt
  Of youth's ribaldry.

SADIKU [tearfully]. The Gods must have mercy yet.

BAROKA [as if suddenly aware of her presence, starts up].
  I have told this to no one but you,
  Who are my eldest, my most faithful wife.
  But if you dare parade my shame before the world . . .

[Sadiku shakes her head in protest and begins to stroke the
soles of his feet with renewed tenderness. Baroka sighs and
falls back slowly.]

  How irritable I have grown of late
  Such doubts to harbour of your loyalty . . .
  But this disaster is too much for one
  Checked thus as I upon the prime of youth.
  The rains that blessed me from my birth
  Number a meagre sixty-two;
  While my grandfather, that man of teak,
  Fathered two sons, late on sixty-five.
  But Okiki, my father beat them all
  Producing female twins at sixty-seven.
  Why then must I, descendant of these lions
  Forswear my wives at a youthful sixty-two
  My veins of life run dry, my manhood gone!

[His voice goes drowsy; Sadiku sighs and moans and
caresses his feet. His face lights up suddenly with rapture.]

Sango bear witness! These weary feet
Have felt the loving hands of much design
In women.
My soles have felt the scratch of harsh,
Gravelled hands.
They have borne the heaviness of clumsy,
Gorilla paws.
And I have known the tease of tiny,
Dainty hands,
Toy-like hands that tantalized
My eager senses,
Promised of thrills to come, thrills

Remaining
Unfulfilled because the fingers
Were too frail
The touch too light and faint to pierce
The incredible thickness of my soles.
But thou Sadiku, thy plain unadorned hands
Encase a sweet sensuality which age
Will not destroy. A-ah, O yayi po.
O yayi! Beyond a doubt Sadiku,
Thou art the queen of them all.

[*Falls asleep.*]

Night

The village centre. Sidi stands by the Schoolroom window, admiring her photos as before. Enter Sadiku with a longish bundle. She is very furtive. Unveils the object which turns out to be a carved figure of the Bale, naked and in full detail. She takes a good look at it, bursts suddenly into derisive laughter, sets the figure standing in front of the tree. Sidi stares in utter amazement.

SADIKU. So we did for you too did we? We did for you in the end. Oh high and mighty lion, have we really scotched you? A—ya-ya-ya . . . we women undid you in the end. I was there when it happened to your father, the great Okiki. I did for him, I, the youngest and freshest of the wives. I killed him with my strength. I called him and he came at me, but no, for him, this was not like other times. I, Sadiku, was I not flame itself and he the flax on old women's spindles? I ate him up! Race of mighty lions, we always consume you, at our pleasure we spin you, at our whim we make you dance; like the foolish top you think the world revolves around you . . . fools! fools! . . . it is you who run giddy while we stand still and watch, and draw your frail thread from you, slowly, till nothing is left but a runty old stick. I scotched Okiki, Sadiku's unopened treasure-house demanded sacrifice, and Okiki came with his rusted key. Like a snake he came at me, like a rag he went back, a limp rag, smeared in shame. . . . [*Her ghoulish laugh re-possesses her.*] Ah, take warning my masters, we'll scotch you in the end . . . [*With a yell she leaps up, begins to dance round the tree, chanting.*]

Take warning, my masters
We'll scotch you in the end.

[*Sidi shuts the window gently, comes out. Sadiku, as she comes round again, gasps and is checked in mid-song.*]

SADIKU. Oh it is you my daughter. You should have chosen a better time to scare me to death. The hour of victory is no time for any woman to die.
SIDI. Why? What battle have you won?
SADIKU. Not me alone girl. You too. Every woman. Oh my daughter, that I have lived to see this day . . . To see him fizzle with the drabbest puff of a mis-primed 'sakabula.'

[*Resumes her dance.*]

Take warning, my masters
We'll scotch you in the end.
SIDI. Wait Sadiku. I cannot understand.
SADIKU. You will my girl. You will.
Take warning my masters . . .
SIDI. Sadiku, are you well?
SADIKU. Ask no questions my girl. Just join my victory dance. Oh Sango my lord, who of us possessed your lightning and ran like fire through that lion's tale . . .
SIDI [*holds her firmly as she is about to go off again*].
Stop your loose ranting. You will not
Move from here until you make some sense.
SADIKU. Oh you are troublesome. Do you promise to tell no one?
SIDI. I swear it. Now tell me quickly.

[*As Sadiku whispers, her eyes widen.*]

O-ho-o-o-o-!
But Sadiku, if he knew the truth, why
Did he ask me to . . .

[*Again Sadiku whispers.*]

Ha ha! Some hope indeed. Oh Sadiku
I suddenly am glad to be a woman.

[*Leaps in the air.*]

We won! We won! Hurray for womankind!

[*Falls in behind Sadiku.*]

Take warning, my masters
We'll scotch you in the end. [*Lakunle enters unobserved.*]
LAKUNLE. The full moon is not yet, but
The women cannot wait.
They must go mad without it.

[*The dancing stops. Sadiku frowns.*]

SADIKU. The scarecrow is here. Begone fop! This is
the world of women. At this moment our star sits in
the centre of the sky. We are supreme. What is
more, we are about to perform a ritual. If you
remain, we will chop you up, we will make you the
sacrifice.
LAKUNLE. What is the hag gibbering?
SADIKU [*advances menacingly*]. You less than man, you
less than the littlest woman, I say begone!
LAKUNLE [*nettled*]. I will have you know that I am a
man
As you will find out if you dare
To lay a hand on me.
SADIKU [*throws back her head in laughter*]. You a man? Is
Baroka not more of a man than you? And if he is no
longer a man, then what are you? [*Lakunle, under-
standing the meaning, stands rooted, shocked.*] Come
on, dear girl, let him look on if he will. After all,
only *men* are barred from watching this ceremony.
Take warning, my masters
We'll . . .
SIDI. Stop. Sadiku stop. Oh such an idea
Is running in my head. Let me to the palace for
This supper he promised me. Sadiku, what a way
To mock the devil. I shall ask forgiveness
For my hasty words . . . No need to change
My answer and consent to be his bride—he might
Suspect you've told me. But I shall ask a month
To think on it.

SADIKU [*somewhat doubtful*]. Baroka is no child you
know, he will know I have betrayed him.
SIDI. No, he will not. Oh Sadiku let me go.
I long to see him thwarted, to watch his longing
His twitching hands which this time cannot
Rush to loosen his trouser cords.
SADIKU. You will have to match the Fox's cunning.
Use your bashful looks and be truly repentant. Goad
him my child, torment him until he weeps for
shame.
SIDI. Leave it to me. He will never suspect you of
deceit.
SADIKU [*with another of her energetic leaps*]. Yo-rooo o!
Yo-rororo o!
Shall I come with you?
SIDI. Will that be wise? You forget
We have not seen each other.
SADIKU. Away then. Away woman. I shall bide here.
Haste back and tell Sadiku how the no-man is.
Away, my lovely child.
LAKUNLE [*he has listened with increasing horror*].
No, Sidi, don't. If you care
One little bit for what I feel,
Do not go to torment the man.
Suppose he knows that you have come to jeer—
And he will know, if he is not a fool—
He is a savage thing, degenerate
He would beat a helpless woman if he could . . .
SIDI [*running off gleefully*]. Ta-raa school teacher. Wait
here for me.
LAKUNLE [*stamps his foot helplessly*].
Foolish girl! . . . And this is all your work.
Could you not keep a secret?
Must every word leak out of you
As surely as the final drops
Of mother's milk
Oozed from your flattened breast
Generations ago?
SADIKU. Watch your wagging tongue, unformed crea-
ture!
LAKUNLE. If any harm befalls her . . .
SADIKU. Woman though she is, she can take better
care of herself than you can of her. Fancy a thing
like you actually wanting a girl like that, all to your
little self. [*Walks round him and looks him up and
down.*] Ah! Oba Ala is an accommodating god. What
a poor figure you cut!
LAKUNLE. I would demean myself to bandy words
With a woman of the bush.
SADIKU. At this moment, your betrothed is supping
with the Lion.
LAKUNLE [*pleased at the use of the word 'betrothed'*].
Well, we are not really betrothed as yet,

I mean, she is not promised yet
But it will come in time, I'm sure.
SADIKU [*bursts into her cackling laughter*]. The bride-
price, is that paid?
LAKUNLE. Mind your own business.
SADIKU. Why don't you do what other men have
done. Take a farm for a season. One harvest will be
enough to pay the price, even for a girl like Sidi. Or
will the smell of the wet soil be too much for your
delicate nostrils?
LAKUNLE. I said mind your own business.
SADIKU. A—a—ah. It is true what they say then. You
are going to convert the whole village so that no
one will ever pay the bride-price again. Ah, you're a
clever man. I must admit that it is a good way for
getting out of it, but don't you think you'd use
more time and energy that way than you would
if . . .
LAKUNLE [*with conviction*]. Within a year or two, I
swear,
This town shall see a transformation
Bride-price will be a thing forgotten
And wives shall take their place by men.
A motor road will pass this spot
And bring the city ways to us.
We'll buy aluminum for all the women
Clay pots are crude and unhygienic
No man shall take more wives than one
That's why they're impotent too soon.
The ruler shall ride cars, not horses
Or a bicycle at the very least
We'll burn the forest, cut the trees
Then plant a modern park for lovers
We'll print newspapers every day
With pictures of seductive girls.
The world will judge our progress by
The girls that win beauty contests.
While Lagos builds new factories daily
We only play 'ayo' and gossip.
Where is our school of Ballroom dancing?
Who here can throw a cocktail party?
We must be modern with the rest
Or live forgotten by the world
We must reject the palm wine habit.
And take to tea, with milk and sugar.

[*Turns on Sadiku who has been staring at him in terror. She
retreats, and he continues to talk down at her as they go
round, then down and off-stage, Lakunle's hectoring voice
trailing away in the distance.*]

This is my plan, you withered face
And I shall start by teaching you.

From now you shall attend my school
And take your place with twelve-year olds.
For though you're nearly seventy,
Your mind is simple and unformed.
Have you no shame that at your age,
You neither read nor write nor think?
You spend your days as senior wife,
Collecting brides for Baroka.
And now because you've sucked him dry,
You send my Sidi to his shame. . . .

[*The scene changes to Baroka's bedroom. On the left in a
one-knee-on-floor posture, two men are engaged in a kind of
wrestling, their arms clasped round each other's waist, testing the right moment to leave. One is Baroka, the other a
short squat figure of apparent muscular power. The contest is
still in the balanced stage. In some distant part of the house,
Sidi's voice is heard lifted in the familiar general greeting,
addressed to no one in particular.*]

SIDI. A good day to the head and people
Of this house.

[*Baroka lifts his head, frowns as if he is trying to place the
voice.*]

A good day to the head and people
Of this house.

[*Baroka now decides to ignore it and to concentrate on the
contest. Sidi's voice draws progressively nearer. She enters
nearly backwards, as she is still busy admiring the room
through which she has just passed. Gasps on turning round
to see the two men.*]

BAROKA [*without looking up*]. Is Sadiku not at home
then?
SIDI [*absent-mindedly*]. Hm?
BAROKA. I asked, is Sadiku not at home?
SIDI [*recollecting herself, she curtsys quickly*]. I saw no
one, Baroka.
BAROKA. No one? Do you mean there was no one
To bar unwanted strangers from my privacy?
SIDI [*retreating*]. The house . . . seemed . . . empty.
BAROKA. Ah, I forget. This is the price I pay
Once every week, for being progressive.
Prompted by the school teacher, my servants
Were prevailed upon to form something they call
The Palace Workers' Union. And in keeping
With the habits—I am told—of modern towns,
This is their day off.
SIDI [*seeing that Baroka seems to be in a better mood, she
becomes somewhat bolder. Moves forward—saucily*].
Is this also a day off
For Baroka's wives?

BAROKA [*looks up sharply, relaxes and speaks with a casual voice*].

No, the madness has not gripped them—yet.
Did you not meet with one of them?

SIDI. No, Baroka. There was no one about.

BAROKA. Not even Ailatu, my favourite?
Was she not at her usual place,
Beside my door?

SIDI [*absently. She is deeply engrossed in watching the contest*].

Her stool is there. And I saw
The slippers she was embroidering.

BAROKA. Hm. Hm. I think I know
Where she'll be found. In a dark corner
Sulking like a slighted cockroach.
By the way, look and tell me
If she left her shawl behind.

[*So as not to miss any part of the tussle, she moves backwards, darts a quick look round the door and back again.*]

SIDI. There is a black shawl on the stool.

BAROKA [*a regretful sigh*].

Then she'll be back tonight. I had hoped
My words were harsh enough
To free me from her spite for a week or more.

SIDI. Did Ailatu offend her husband?

BAROKA. Offend? My armpit still weeps blood
For the gross abuse I suffered from one
I called my favourite.

SIDI [*in a disappointed voice*].

Oh. Is that all?

BAROKA. Is that not enough? Why child?
What more could the woman do?

SIDI. Nothing. Nothing, Baroka. I thought perhaps—
Well—young wives are known to be—
Forward—sometimes—to their husbands.

BAROKA. In an ill-kept household perhaps. But not
Under Baroka's roof. And yet,
Such are the sudden spites of women
That even I cannot foresee them all.
And child—if I lose this little match
Remember that my armpit
Burns and itches turn by turn.

[*Sidi continues watching for some time, then clasps her hand over her mouth as she remembers what she should have done to begin with. Doubtful how to proceed, she hesitates for some moments, then comes to a decision and kneels.*]

SIDI. I have come, Bale, as a repentant child.

BAROKA. What?

SIDI [*very hesitantly, eyes to the floor, but she darts a quick look up when she thinks the Bale isn't looking*].

The answer which I sent to the Bale
Was given in a thoughtless moment . . .

BAROKA. Answer, child? To what?

SIDI. A message brought by . . .

BAROKA [*groans and strains in a muscular effort*].

Will you say that again? It is true that for supper
I did require your company. But up till now
Sadiku has brought no reply.

SIDI [*amazed*]. But the other matter! Did not the Bale
Send . . . did Baroka not send . . . ?

BAROKA [*with sinister encouragement*].

What did Baroka not, my child?

SIDI [*cowed, but angry, rises*].

It is nothing, Bale. I only hope
That I am here at the Bale's invitation.

BAROKA [*as if trying to understand, he frowns as he looks at her*].

A-ah, at last I understand. You think
I took offence because you entered
Unannounced?

SIDI. I remember that the Bale called me
An unwanted stranger.

BAROKA. That could be expected. Is a man's bedroom
To be made naked to any flea
That chances to wander through?

[*Sidi turns away, very hurt.*]

Come, come, my child. You are too quick
To feel aggrieved. Of course you are
More than welcome. But I expected Ailatu
To tell me you were here.

[*Sidi curtsys briefly with her back to Baroka. After a while, she turns round. The mischief returns to her face. Baroka's attitude of denial has been a set-back but she is now ready to pursue her mission.*]

SIDI. I hope the Bale will not think me
Forward. But, like everyone, I had thought
The Favourite was a gentle woman.

BAROKA. And so had I.

SIDI [*shyly*]. One would hardly think that *she*
Would give offence without a cause.
Was the Favourite . . . in some way . . .
Dissatisfied . . . with her lord and husband?

[*With a mock curtsy, quickly executed as Baroka begins to look up.*]

BAROKA [*slowly turns towards her*].

                                 Now that
Is a question which I never thought to hear
Except from a school teacher. Do you think
The Lion has such leisure that he asks
The whys and wherefores of a woman's
Squint?

[*Sidi steps back and curtsys. As before, and throughout this
scene, she is easily cowed by Baroka's change of mood, all
the more easily as she is, in any case, frightened by her own
boldness.*]

SIDI. I meant no disrespect . . .
BAROKA [*gently*]. I know. [*Breaks off.*] Christians on my
  Father's shrines, child!
  Do you think I took offence? A—aw
  Come in and seat yourself. Since you broke in
  Unawares, and appear resolved to stay,
  Try, if you can, not to make me feel
  A humourless old ram. I allow no one
  To watch my daily exercise, but as we say,
  The woman gets lost in the woods one day
  And every wood deity dies the next.

[*Sidi curtsys, watches and moves forward warily, as if
expecting the two men to spring apart too suddenly.*]

SIDI. I think he will win.
BAROKA. Is that a wish, my daughter?
SIDI. No, but— [*Hesitates, but boldness wins.*]
                      If the tortoise cannot tumble
  It does not mean that he can stand.

[*Baroka looks at her, seemingly puzzled. Sidi turns away,
humming.*]

BAROKA. When the child is full of riddles, the mother
  Has one water-pot the less.

[*Sidi tiptoes to Baroka's back and pulls asses' ears at him.*]

SIDI. I think he will win.
BAROKA. He knows he must. Would it profit me
  To pit my strength against a weakling?
  Only yesterday, this son of—I suspect—
  A python for a mother, and fathered beyond doubt
  By a blubber-bottomed baboon,

[*The complimented man grins.*]

  Only yesterday, he nearly
  Ploughed my tongue with my front teeth
  In a friendly wrestling bout.

WRESTLER [*encouraged, makes an effort*]. Ugh. Ugh.
SIDI [*bent almost over them. Genuinely worried*].
  Oh! Does it hurt?
BAROKA. Not yet . . . but, as I was saying
  I change my wrestlers when I have learnt
  To throw them. I also change my wives
  When I have learnt to tire them.
SIDI. And is this another . . . changing time
  For the Bale?
BAROKA. Who knows? Until the finger nails
  Have scraped the dust, no one can tell
  Which insect released his bowels.

[*Sidi grimaces in disgust and walks away. Returns as she
thinks up a new idea.*]

SIDI. A woman spoke to me this afternoon.
BAROKA. Indeed. And does Sidi find this unusual—
  That a woman speak with her in the afternoon?
SIDI [*stamping*]. No. She had the message of a go-
  between.
BAROKA. Did she? Then I rejoice with you.

[*Sidi stands biting her lips. Baroka looks at her, this time
with deliberate appreciation.*]

  And now I think of it, why not?
  There must be many men who
  Build their loft to fit your height.
SIDI [*unmoving, pointedly*]. Her message came from
    one
  With many lofts.
BAROKA. Ah! Such is the greed of men.
SIDI. If Baroka were my father
    [*aside*] —which many would take him to be—

[*Makes a rude sign.*]

  Would he pay my dowry to this man
  And give his blessings?
BAROKA. Well, I must know his character.
  For instance, is the man rich?
SIDI. Rumour has it so.
BAROKA. Is he repulsive?
SIDI. He is old. [*Baroka winces.*]
BAROKA. Is he mean and miserly?
SIDI. To strangers—no. There are tales
  Of his open-handedness, which are never
  Quite without a motive. But his wives report
  —To take one little story—
  How he grew the taste for ground corn
  And pepper—because he would not pay
  The price of snuff!

[With a sudden burst of angry energy, Baroka lifts his opponent and throws him over his shoulder.]

BAROKA. A lie! The price of snuff
  Had nothing to do with it.
SIDI [*too excited to listen*]. You won!
BAROKA. By the years on my beard, I swear
  They slander me!
SIDI [*excitedly*]. You won. You won!

[She breaks into a kind of shoulder dance and sings.]

  Yokolu Yokolu. Ko ha tan bi
  Iyawo gb'oko san'le
  Oko yo 'ke . . .

[She repeats this throughout Baroka's protests. Baroka is pacing angrily up and down. The defeated man, nursing a hip, goes to the corner of the room and lifts out a low 'ako' bench. He sits on the floor, and soon, Baroka joins him; using only their arms now, they place their elbows on the bench and grip hands. Baroka takes his off again, replaces it, takes it off again and so on during the rest of his outburst.]

BAROKA. This means nothing to me of course. Nothing!
  But I know the ways of women, and I know
  Their ruinous tongues.
  Suppose that, as a child—only suppose—
  Suppose then, that as a child, I—
  And remember, I only use myself
  To illustrate the plight of many men . . .
  So, once again, suppose that as a child
  I grew to love 'tanfiri'—with a good dose of pepper
  And growing old, I found that—
  Sooner than die away, my passion only
  Bred itself upon each mouthful of
  Ground corn and pepper I consumed.
  Now, think child, would it be seemly
  At my age, and the father of children,
  To be discovered, in public
  Thrusting fistfuls of corn and pepper
  In my mouth? Is it not wise to indulge
  In the little masquerade of a dignified
  Snuff-box?—But remember, I only make
  A pleading for this prey of women's
  Malice. I feel his own injustice,
  Being myself, a daily fellow-sufferer!

[Baroka seems to realize for the first time that Sidi has paid no attention to his explanation. She is, in fact, still humming and shaking her shoulders. He stares questioningly at her.

Sidi stops, somewhat confused and embarrassed, points sheepishly to the wrestler.]

SIDI. I think this time he will win.

[Baroka's grumbling subsides slowly. He is now attentive to the present bout.]

BAROKA. Now let us once again take up
  The questioning. [*Almost timidly.*] Is this man
  Good and kindly.
SIDI. They say he uses well
  His dogs and horses.
BAROKA [*desperately*].
  Well is he fierce then? Reckless!
  Does the bush cow run to hole
  When he hears his beaters' Hei-ei-wo-rah!
SIDI. There are heads and skins of leopards
  Hung around his council room.
  But the market is also
  Full of them.
BAROKA. Is he not wise? Is he not sagely?
  Do the young and old not seek
  His counsel?
SIDI. The Fox is said to be wise
  So cunning that he stalks and dines on
  New-hatched chickens.
BAROKA [*more and more desperate*].
  Does he not beget strength on wombs?
  Are his children not tall and stout-limbed?
SIDI. Once upon a time.
BAROKA. Once upon a time?
  What do you mean, girl?
SIDI. Just once upon a time.
  Perhaps his children have of late
  Been plagued with shyness and refuse
  To come into the world. Or else
  He is so tired with the day's affairs
  That at night, he turns his buttocks
  To his wives. But there have been
  No new reeds cut by his servants,
  No new cots woven.
  And his household gods are starved
  For want of child-naming festivities
  Since the last two rains went by.
BAROKA. Perhaps he is a frugal man.
  Mindful of years to come,
  Planning for a final burst of life, he
  Husbands his strength.
SIDI [*giggling. She is actually stopped, half-way, by giggling at the cleverness of her remark*].

To husband his wives surely ought to be
A man's first duties—at all times.
BAROKA. My beard tells me you've been a pupil,
A most diligent pupil of Sadiku.
Among all shameless women,
The sharpest tongues grow from that one
Peeling bark—Sadiku, my faithful lizard!

[*Growing steadily warmer during this speech, he again slaps down his opponent's arm as he shouts 'Sadiku'.*]

SIDI [*backing away, aware that she has perhaps gone too far and betrayed knowledge of the 'secret'*].
I have learnt nothing of anyone.
BAROKA. No more. No more.
Already I have lost a wrestler
On your account. This town-bred daring
Of little girls, awakes in me
A seven-horned devil of strength.
Let one woman speak a careless word
And I can pin a wriggling—Bah!

[*Lets go the man's arm. He has risen during the last speech but held on to the man's arm, who is forced to rise with him.*]

The tappers should have called by now.
See if we have a fresh gourd by the door.

[*The wrestler goes out. Baroka goes to sit on the bed, Sidi eyeing him doubtfully.*]

What an ill-tempered man I daily grow
Towards. Soon my voice will be
The sand between two grinding stones.
But I have my scattered kindliness
Though few occasions serve to herald it.
And Sidi, my daughter, you do not know
The thoughts which prompted me
To ask the pleasure that I be your host
This evening, I would not tell Sadiku,
Meaning to give delight
With the surprise of it. Now, tell me, child
Can you guess a little at this thing?
SIDI. Sadiku told me nothing.
BAROKA. You are hasty with denial. For how indeed
Could Sadiku, since I told her
Nothing of my mind, But, my daughter,
Did she not, perhaps . . . invent some tale?
For I know Sadiku loves to be
All-knowing.

SIDI. She said no more, except the Bale
Begged my presence.
BAROKA [*rises quickly to the bait*].
Begged? Bale Baroka begged?

[*Wrestler enters with gourd and calabash-cups. Baroka relapses.*]

Ah! I see you love to bait your elders.
One way the world remains the same,
The child still thinks she is wiser than
The cotton head of age.
Do you think Baroka deaf or blind
To little signs? But let that pass.
Only, lest you fall victim to the schemes
Of busy women, I will tell you this—
I know Sadiku plays the match-maker
Without the prompting. If I look
On any maid, or call her name
Even in the course of harmless, neighbourly
Well-wishing—How fares your daughter?
—Is your sister now recovered from her
Whooping cough?—How fast your ward
Approaches womanhood! Have the village lads
Begun to gather at your door?—
Or any word at all which shows I am
The thoughtful guardian of the village health,
If it concerns a woman, Sadiku straightway
Flings herself into the role of go-between
And before I even don a cap, I find
Yet another stranger in my bed!
SIDI. It seems a Bale's life
Is full of great unhappiness.
BAROKA. I do not complain. No, my child
I accept the sweet and sour with
A ruler's grace. I lose my patience
Only when I meet with
The new immodesty with women.
Now, my Sidi, you have not caught
This new and strange disease, I hope.
SIDI [*curtsying*]. The threading of my smock—
Does Baroka not know the marking
Of the village loom?
BAROKA. But will Sidi, the pride of mothers,
Will she always wear it?
SIDI. Will Sidi, the proud daughter of Baroka,
Will she step out naked?

[*A pause. Baroka surveys Sidi in an almost fatherly manner and she bashfully drops her eyes.*]

BAROKA. To think that once I thought,
  Sidi is the eye's delight, but
  She is vain, and her head
  Is feather-light, and always giddy
  With a trivial thought. And now
  I find her deep and wise beyond her years.

[*Reaches under his pillow, brings out the now familiar magazine, and also an addressed envelope. Retains the former and gives her the envelope.*]

  Do you know what this means?
  The trim red piece of paper
  In the corner?
SIDI. I know it. A stamp. Lakunle receives
  Letters from Lagos marked with it.
BAROKA [*obviously disappointed*].
  Hm. Lakunle. But more about him
  Later. Do you know what it means—
  This little frippery?
SIDI [*very proudly*].
  Yes. I know that too. Is it not a tax on
  The habit of talking with paper?
BAROKA. Oh. Oh. I see you dip your hand
  Into the pockets of the school teacher
  And retrieve it bulging with knowledge.

[*Goes up to the strange machine, and pulls the lever up and down.*]

  Now this, not even the school teacher can tell
  What magic this performs. Come nearer,
  It will not bite.
SIDI. I have never seen the like.
BAROKA. The work dear child, of the palace black-
    smiths
  Built in full secrecy. All is not well with it—
  But I will find the cause and then Ilujinle
  Will boast its own tax on paper, made with
  Stamps like this. For long I dreamt it
  And here it stands, child of my thoughts.
SIDI [*wonder-struck*]. You mean . . . this will work some
    day?
BAROKA. Ogun has said the word. And now my girl
  What think you of that image on the stamp
  This spiderwork of iron, wood and mortar?
SIDI. Is it not a bridge?
BAROKA. It is a bridge. The longest—so they say
  In the whole country. When not a bridge,
  You'll find a print of groundnuts
  Stacked like pyramids,
  Or palm trees, or cocoa-trees, and farmers

Hacking pods, and workmen
Felling trees and tying skinned logs
Into rafts. A thousand thousand letters
By road, by rail, by air,
From one end of the world to another.
And not one human head among them;
Not one head of beauty on the stamp?
SIDI. But I once saw Lakunle's letter
  With a head of bronze.
BAROKA. A figurehead, my child, a lifeless work
  Of craft, with holes for eyes, and coldness
  For the warmth of life and love
  In youthful cheeks like yours,
  My daughter . . .

[*Pauses to watch the effect on Sidi.*]

                . . . Can you see it, Sidi?
  Tens of thousands of these dainty prints
  And each one with this legend of Sidi—

[*Flourishes the magazine, open in the middle.*]

  The village goddess, reaching out
  Towards the sun, her lover.
  Can you see it, my daughter!

[*Sidi drowns herself totally in the contemplation, takes the magazine but does not even look at it. Sits on the bed.*]

BAROKA [*very gently*].
  I hope you will not think it too great
  A burden, to carry the country's mail
  All on your comeliness.

[*Walks away, an almost business-like tone.*]

                Our beginnings will
  Of course be modest. We shall begin
  By cutting stamps for our own village alone.
  As the schoolmaster himself would say—
  Charity begins at home.

[*Pause. Faces Sidi from nearly the distance of the room.*]

                For a long time now,
  The town-dwellers have made up tales
  Of the backwardness of Ilujinle
  Until it hurts Baroka, who holds
  The welfare of his people deep at heart.
  Now, if we do this thing, it will prove more
  Than any single town has done!

[*The wrestler, who has been listening open-mouthed, drops his cup in admiration. Baroka, annoyed, realizing only now in fact that he is still in the room, waves him impatiently out.*]

I do not hate progress, only its nature
Which makes all roofs and faces look the same.
And the wish of one old man is
That here and there,

[*Goes progressively towards Sidi, until he bends over her, then sits beside her on the bed.*]

Among the bridges and the murderous roads,
Below the humming birds which
Smoke the face of Sango, dispenser of
The snake-tongue lightning; between this moment
And the reckless broom that will be wielded
In these years to come, we must leave
Virgin plots of lives, rich decay
And the tang of vapour rising from
Forgotten heaps of compost, lying
Undisturbed . . . But the skin of progress
Masks, unknown, the spotted wolf of sameness . . .
Does sameness not revolt your being,
My daughter?

[*Sidi is capable only of a bewildered nod, slowly.*]

BAROKA [*sighs, hands folded piously on his lap*].
I find my soul is sensitive, like yours,
Indeed, although there is one—no more think I—
One generation between yours and mine,
Our thoughts fly crisply through the air
And meet, purified, as one.
And our union
Is the making of this stamp.
The one redeeming grace on any paper-tax
Shall be your face. And mine,
The soul behind it all, worshipful
Of Nature for her gift of youth
And beauty to our earth. Does this
Please you, my daughter?
SIDI. I can no longer see the meaning, Baroka.
Now that you speak
Almost like the school teacher, except
Your words fly on a different path,
I find . . .
BAROKA. It is a bad thing, then, to sound
Like your school teacher?
SIDI. No Bale, but words are like beetles
Boring at my ears, and my head

Becomes a jumping bean. Perhaps after all,
As the school teacher tells me often,

[*Very miserably.*]

I have a simple mind.
BAROKA [*pats her kindly on the head*].
No, Sidi, not simple, only straight and truthful
Like a fresh-water reed. But I do find
Your school teacher and I are much alike.
The proof of wisdom is the wish to learn
Even from children. And the haste of youth
Must learn its temper from the gloss
Of ancient leather, from a strength
Knit close along the grain. The school teacher
And I, must learn one from the other.
Is this not right?

[*A tearful nod.*]

BAROKA. The old must flow into the new, Sidi,
Not blind itself or stand foolishly
Apart. A girl like you must inherit
Miracles which age alone reveals.
Is this not so?
SIDI. Everything you say, Bale,
Seems wise to me.
BAROKA. Yesterday's wine alone is strong and
blooded, child,
And though the Christians' holy book denies
The truth of this, old wine thrives best
Within a new bottle. The coarseness
Is mellowed down, and the rugged wine
Acquires a full and rounded body . . .
Is this not so—my child?

[*Quite overcome, Sidi nods.*]

BAROKA. Those who know little of Baroka think
His life one pleasure-living course.
But the monkey sweats, my child,
The monkey sweats,
It is only the hair upon his back
Which still deceives the world . . .

[*Sidi's head falls slowly on the Bale's shoulder. The Bale remains in his final body weighed-down-by-burdens-of-State attitude.
Even before the scene is completely shut off a crowd of dancers burst in at the front and dance off at the opposite side without slackening pace. In their brief appearance it should be apparent that they comprise a group of female dancers pursuing a masked male. Drumming and shouts*

continue quite audibly and shortly afterwards. They enter and re-cross the stage in the same manner.

    The shouts fade away and they next appear at the market clearing. It is now full evening. Lakunle and Sadiku are still waiting for Sidi's return. The traders are beginning to assemble one by one, ready for the evening market. Hawkers pass through with oil-lamps beside their ware. Food sellers enter with cooking-pots and foodstuffs, set up their 'adogon' or stone hearth and build a fire.

    All this while, Lakunle is pacing wretchedly, Sadiku looks on placidly.]

LAKUNLE [*he is pacing furiously*].
  He's killed her.
  I warned you. You know him,
  And I warned you.

[*Goes up all the approaches to look.*]

  She's been gone half the day. It will soon
  Be daylight. And still no news.
  Women have disappeared before.
  No trace. Vanished. Now we know how.

[*Checks, turns round.*]

  And why!
  Mock an old man, will you? So?
  You can laugh? Ha ha! You wait.
  I'll come and see you
  Whipped like a dog. Baroka's head wife
  Driven out of the house for plotting
  With a girl.

[*Each approaching footstep brings Lakunle to attention, but it is only a hawker or a passer-by. The wrestler passes. Sadiku greets him familiarly. Then, after he has passed, some significance of this breaks on Sadiku and she begins to look a little puzzled.*]

LAKUNLE. I know he has dungeons. Secret holes
  Where a helpless girl will lie
  And rot for ever. But not for nothing
  Was I born a man. I'll find my way
  To rescue her. She little deserves it, but
  I shall risk my life for her.

[*The mummers can now be heard again, distantly. Sadiku and Lakunle become attentive as the noise approaches, Lakunle increasingly uneasy. A little, but not too much notice is paid by the market people.*]

  What is that?
SADIKU. If my guess is right, it will be mummers.

[*Adds slyly.*]

  Somebody must have told them the news.
LAKUNLE. What news?

[*Sadiku chuckles darkly and comprehension breaks on the School teacher.*]

  Baroka! You dared . . . ?
  Woman, is there no mercy in your veins?
  He gave you children, and he stood
  Faithfully by you and them.
  He risked his life that you may boast
  A warrior-hunter for your lord . . . But you—
  You sell him to the rhyming rabble
  Gloating in your disloyalty.
SADIKU [*calmly dips her hand in his pocket*].
  Have you any money?
LAKUNLE [*snatching out her hand*].
  Why? What? . . . Keep away, witch! Have you
  Turned pickpocket in your dotage?
SADIKU. Don't be a miser. Will you let them go without giving you a special performance?
LAKUNLE. If you think I care for their obscenity . . .
SADIKU [*wheedling*]. Come on, school teacher. They'll expect it of you . . . The man of learning . . . the young sprig of foreign wisdom . . . You must not demean yourself in their eyes . . . you must give them money to perform for your lordship . . .

[*Re-enter the mummers, dancing straight through (more centrally this time) as before. Male dancer enters first, pursued by a number of young women and other choral idlers. The man dances in tortured movements. He and about half of his pursuers have already danced off-stage on the opposite side when Sadiku dips her hand briskly in Lakunle's pocket, this time with greater success. Before Lakunle can stop her, she has darted to the drummers and pressed a coin apiece on their foreheads, waving them to possession of the floor. Tilting their heads backwards, they drum their praises. Sadiku denies the credit, points to Lakunle as the generous benefactor. They transfer their attention to him where he stands biting his lips at the trick. The other dancers have now been brought back and the drummers resume the beat of the interrupted dance. The treasurer removes the coins from their foreheads and places them in a pouch. Now begins the dance of virility which is of course none other than the Baroka story. Very athletic movements. Even in his prime, 'Baroka' is made a comic figure, held in a kind of tolerant respect by his women. At his decline and final downfall, they are most unsparing in their taunts and tantalizing motions. Sadiku has never stopped bouncing on her toes through the dance, now she is done the honour of being invited to join at the kill. A dumb show of bashful refusals, then she joins them, reveals surprising agility for her age, to*] *the wild enthusiasm of the rest who surround and spur her on.*

With 'Baroka' finally scotched, the crowd dances away to their incoming movement, leaving Sadiku to dance on oblivious of their departure. The drumming becomes more distant and she unwraps her eyelids. Sighs, looks around her and walks contentedly towards Lakunle. As usual he has enjoyed the spectacle in spite of himself, showing especial relish where 'Baroka' gets the worst of it from his women. Sadiku looks at him for a moment while he tries to replace his obvious enjoyment with disdain. She shouts 'Boo' at him, and breaks into a dance movement, shakes a sudden leg at Lakunle.]

SADIKU. Sadiku of the duiker's feet . . . that's what
    the men used to call me. I could twist and untwist
    my waist with the smoothness of a water snake . . .
LAKUNLE. No doubt. And you are still just as slippery.
    I hope Baroka kills you for this.
    When he finds out what your wagging tongue
    Has done to him, I hope he beats you
    Till you choke on your own breath . . .

[Sidi bursts in, she has been running all the way. She throws herself on the ground against the tree and sobs violently, beating herself on the ground.]

SADIKU *[on her knees beside her]*. Why, child. What is
    the matter?
SIDI *[pushes her off]*.
    Get away from me. Do not touch me.
LAKUNLE *[with a triumphant smile, he pulls Sadiku away
    and takes her place]*.
    Oh, Sidi, let me kiss your tears . . .
SIDI *[pushes him so hard that he sits down abruptly]*.
    Don't touch me.
LAKUNLE *[dusting himself]*.
    He must have beaten her.
    Did I not warn you both?
    Baroka is a creature of the wilds,
    Untutored, mannerless, devoid of grace.

[Sidi only cries all the more, beats on the ground with clenched fists and stubs her toes in the ground.]

    Chief though he is,
    I shall kill him for this . . .
    No. Better still, I shall demand
    Redress from the central courts.
    I shall make him spend
    The remainder of his wretched life
    In prison—with hard labour.
    I'll teach him
    To beat defenceless women . . .

SIDI *[lifting her head]*.
    Fool! You little fools! It was a lie!
    The frog. The cunning frog!
    He lied to you, Sadiku.
SADIKU. Sango forbid!
SIDI. He told me . . . afterwards, crowing.
    It was a trick.
    He knew Sadiku would not keep it to herself,
    That I, or maybe other maids would hear of it
    And go to mock his plight.
    And how he laughed!
    How his frog-face croaked and croaked
    And called me little fool!
    Oh how I hate him! How I loathe
    And long to kill the man!
LAKUNLE. *[retreating.]* But Sidi, did he . . . ? I mean . . .
    Did you escape?

[Louder sobs from Sidi.]

    Speak, Sidi, this is agony.
    Tell me the worst; I'll take it like a man.
    Is it the fright which affects you so,
    Or did he . . . ? Sidi, I cannot bear the thought.
    The words refuse to form.
    Do not unman me, Sidi. Speak
    Before I burst in tears.
SADIKU *[raises Sidi's chin in her hand]*.
    Sidi, are you a maid or not?

[Sidi shakes her head violently and bursts afresh in tears.]

LAKUNLE. The Lord forbid!
SADIKU. Too late for prayers. Cheer up. It happens to
    the best of us.
LAKUNLE. Oh heavens, strike me dead!
    Earth, open up and swallow Lakunle.
    For he no longer has the wish to live.
    Let the lightning fall and shrivel me
    To dust and ashes . . .

[Recoils.]

    No, that wish is cowardly. This trial is my own.
    Let Sango and his lightning keep out of this. It
    Is my cross, and let it not be spoken that
    In the hour of need, Lakunle stood
    Upon the scales and was proved wanting.
    My love is selfless—the love of spirit
    Not of flesh.

[Stands over Sidi.]

Dear Sidi, we shall forget the past.
This great misfortune touches not
The treasury of my love.
But you will agree, it is only fair
That we forget the bride-price totally
Since you no longer can be called a maid.
Here is my hand; if on these terms,
You'll be my cherished wife.
We'll take an oath, between us three
That this shall stay
A secret to our dying days . . .

[*Takes a look at Sadiku and adds quickly.*]

Oh no, a secret even after we're dead and gone.
And if Baroka dares to boast of it,
I'll swear he is a liar—and swear by Sango too!

[*Sidi raises herself slowly, staring at Lakunle with unbeliev-
ing eyes. She is unsmiling, her face a puzzle.*]

SIDI. You would? You would marry me?
LAKUNLE [*puffs out his chest*]. Yes.

[*Without a change of expression, Sidi dashes suddenly off
the stage.*]

SADIKU. What on earth has got into her?
LAKUNLE. I wish I knew
    She took off suddenly
    Like a hunted buck.

[*Looks off-stage.*]

    I think—yes, she is,
    She is going home.
    Sadiku, will you go?
    Find out if you can
    What she plans to do.

[*Sadiku nods and goes. Lakunle walks up and down.*]

    And now I know I am the biggest fool
    That ever walked this earth.
    There are women to be found
    In every town or village in these parts,
    And every one a virgin.
    But I obey my books.

[*Distant music. Light drums, flutes, box-guitars, 'sekere'.*]

    'Man takes the fallen woman by the hand'
    And ever after they live happily.

Moreover, I will admit,
It solves the problem of her bride-price too.
A man must live or fall by his true
Principles. That, I had sworn,
Never to pay.

[*Enter Sadiku.*]

SADIKU. She is packing her things. She is gathering
    her clothes and trinkets together, and oiling herself
    as a bride does before her wedding.
LAKUNLE. Heaven help us! I am not impatient.
    Surely she can wait a day or two at least.
    There is the asking to be done,
    And then I have to hire a praise-singer,
    And such a number of ceremonies
    Must firstly be performed.
SADIKU. Just what I said but she only laughed at me
    and called me a . . . a . . . what was it now . . . a
    bra . . . braba . . . brabararian. It serves you right. It
    all comes of your teaching. I said what about the
    asking and the other ceremonies. And she looked at
    me and said, leave all that nonsense to savages and
    brabararians.
LAKUNLE. But I must prepare myself.
    I cannot be
    A single man one day and a married one the next.
    It must come gradually.
    I will not wed in haste.
    A man must have time to prepare,
    To learn to like the thought.
    I must think of my pupils too:
    Would they be pleased if I were married
    Not asking their consent . . . ?

[*The singing group is now audible even to him.*]

    What is that? The musicians?
    Could they have learnt so soon?
SADIKU. The news of a festivity travels fast. You ought
    to know that.
LAKUNLE. The goddess of malicious gossip
    Herself must have a hand in my undoing.
    The very spirits of the partial air
    Have all conspired to blow me, willy-nilly
    Down the slippery slope of grim matrimony.
    What evil have I done . . . ? Ah, here they come!

[*Enter crowd and musicians.*]

    Go back. You are not needed yet. Nor ever.
    Hence parasites, you've made a big mistake.
    There is no one getting wedded; get you home.

[*Sidi now enters. In one hand she holds a bundle, done up in a richly embroidered cloth: in the other the magazine. She is radiant; jewelled, lightly clothed, and wears light leather-thong sandals. They all go suddenly silent except for the long-drawn O-Ohs of admiration. She goes up to Lakunle and hands him the book.*]

SIDI. A present from Sidi.
  I tried to tear it up
  But my fingers were too frail.

[*To the crowd.*]

  Let us go.

[*To Lakunle.*]

  You may come too if you wish,
  You are invited.
LAKUNLE [*lost in the miracle of transformation*].
  Well I should hope so indeed
  Since I am to marry you.
SIDI [*turns round in surprise*].
  Marry who . . . ? You thought . . .
  Did you really think that you, and I . . .
  Why, did you think that after him,
  I could endure the touch of another man?
  I who have felt the strength,
  The perpetual youthful zest
  Of the panther of the trees?
  And would I choose a watered-down,
  A beardless version of unripened man?
LAKUNLE [*bars her way*].
  I shall not let you.
  I shall protect you from yourself.
SIDI [*gives him a shove that sits him down again, hard against the tree base*].
  Out of my way, book-nourished shrimp.
  Do you see what strength he has given me?
  That was not bad. For a man of sixty,
  It was the secret of God's own draught
  A deed for drums and ballads.

But you, at sixty, you'll be ten years dead!
  In fact, you'll not survive your honeymoon . . .
  Come to my wedding if you will. If not . . .

[*She shrugs her shoulders. Kneels down at Sadiku's feet.*]

  Mother of brides, your blessing . . .
SADIKU [*lays her hand on Sidi's head*]. I invoke the fertile gods. They will stay with you. May the time come soon when you shall be as round-bellied as a full moon in a low sky.
SIDI [*hands her the bundle*].
  Now bless my worldly goods.

[*Turns to the musicians.*]

  Come, sing to me of seeds
  Of children, sired of the lion stock.

[*The Musicians resume their tune. Sidi sings and dances.*]

  Mo te'ni. Mo te'ni.
  Mo te'ni. Mo te'ni.
  Sun mo mi, we mo mi
  Sun mo mi, fa mo mi
  Yarabi lo m'eyi t'o le d'omo . . .

[*Festive air, fully pervasive. Oil lamps from the market multiply as traders desert their stalls to join them. A young girl flaunts her dancing buttocks at Lakunle and he rises to the bait. Sadiku gets in his way as he gives chase. Tries to make him dance with her. Lakunle last seen, having freed himself of Sadiku, clearing a space in the crowd for the young girl. The crowd repeat the song after Sidi.*]

  Tolani Tolani
  T'emi ni T'emi ni
  Sun mo mi, we mo mi
  Sun mo mi, fa mo mi
  Yarabi lo m'eyi t'o le d'omo.

  THE END

ESSAY: AN APPROACH TO THE PLAY

The characters in *The Lion and the Jewel* seem to embody the conflicts in a postcolonial world. The schoolteacher, Lakunle, is in many ways a recognizable figure, with affinities to a stock comic character from western comedies: the pedantic scholar, so focused on one version of knowledge that he is blind to his own ignorance. Lakunle presents a particularly postcolonial version of this type, however, for he is presented as mentally colonized in a variety of ways: he not only teaches western-style subjects, but also dresses and thinks in English style. He wants Sidi to submit to western ideas of modesty and decorum; he worships books, railroads, and motorways. He is cut off from all that is traditionally African, tribal, or natural, in favor of a western idea of "progress." He is a "prophet" of the future but is completely unrealistic about the present, a fact which the young woman Sidi clearly sees; she feels restricted with him, even as she finds him appealing, and even though she, too, is corruptible. Her photographic image has been published and widely admired, and her reaction is pride and vanity.

Baroka is, by contrast, a village chief, deeply rooted in his people's traditions, the indigenous beliefs which the sophisticates of the capital city, Lagos, believe themselves to have transcended. He is resolutely antiprogress: *his* photo is not admirable; he opposes the railroad; he resolves conflict on a personal level, through charm and bribery rather than by force. In competing with the schoolteacher for Sidi, he puts her in the position of having to choose between one whose mind has been colonized and one who is master of her people's older ways. In this sense, she epitomizes the position of stress in which this and any other postcolonial society is placed.

Sadiku claims the real feminine power behind the traditional precolonial village, but she directs her power into a combat with her husband which consists in devouring his male energy, a combat she believes she has won and about which she, too, seems inappropriately vain. Baroka encourages and then manipulates these two vanities, of beauty and feminine power, in order to seduce Sidi. His power comes through trickery and sustained virility; Baroka understands people, including himself. He is able both to know and to do, to combine a kind of natural wisdom, which is different from the colonized schoolteacher's formal education, with a kind of personal power which does not rely on machines and does not threaten individuality. He is metaphorically related to clever but vulnerable animals from the folk tradition— fox, spider, tortoise—as well as to the trickster and the "lion." The relationships emphasize his ties to indigenous Nigerian culture and his heroic stature within it at the same time that they help define its traditional values, values which prize survival and gentleness more than dominance or greed. Baroka's recognition and manipulation of aging emphasizes these values in a different way: life is seen as a process, a series of transitions, with death as part of a continuum which also includes life. Lakunle and, by extension, all of urban Nigeria have been alienated from such views, which seem based on a traditional and rejected relationship to nature and which seem oppressively pessimistic to those who have adopted the new view of "progress."

There seems to be an element of sexism in the culture presented in the play. Both Sidi and Sadiku are portrayed as vain, and the play seems to presuppose that this behavior is particularly typical of women. (Baroka's success depends on the predictability of the women's reactions.) Both men, Lakunle and Baroka, view Sidi as a beautiful object, available for them to control—first to manipulate and then to buy and possess in marriage. Baroka "wins" her because he plays this game more cleverly and more powerfully: he not only seduces Sidi but also manipulates his senior wife, Sadiku, into helping him do it. Certain aspects of traditional rural Nigerian society are presented in their own terms in this play, and they are not idealized.

Arthur Kopit

INDIANS

About the Author   Arthur Kopit (1937–) was born in New York City and attended Harvard University, where in the year 1957 alone four of his plays were produced. By the time of his graduation in 1959, he had presented three more and had published the first act of an eighth. Granted a Shaw Traveling Scholarship, he then studied theater in much of western Europe. While doing so, he wrote *Oh Dad, Poor Dad, Mamma's Hung You in the Closet and I'm Feelin' So Sad*, a play which was produced first at Harvard in 1960, then in Cambridge, and finally off Broadway at the Phoenix Theater, where it enjoyed a run of 454 performances, won the Vernon Rice and the Outer Circle Awards, and brought him recognition throughout western Europe as well as in his own country. Four more plays followed before *Indians* was produced in London in 1968 by the Royal Shakespeare Company. It then played in Washington and finally, the next year, in New York. Since this play, Kopit's *Wings* has appeared on Broadway; among his many awards have been several grants from the Rockefeller Foundation, from the Gugenheim Foundation, and from the National Endowment for the Arts.

About the Play   Kopit has said that he wrote *Indians* as a response to the Vietnam War and, even more specifically, to General William Westmoreland's expression of regret about the killing of Vietnamese civilians during an American military operation in 1966. In the play's final scene, he puts Westmoreland's words into the mouth of Colonel Forsyth as he supervises the aftermath of the Wounded Knee massacre. On Christmas Day, 1890, American cavalry had attacked and destroyed a village consisting of women, children, the elderly, and the wounded in an action which effectively ended the resistance of the Dakota Sioux—the last of the native peoples of the West still in armed conflict with the U.S. government.

The playwright's reading of the general's statement provided the occasion but not the subject for the play. Kopit was searching deeper, for the origin and cause of what he regarded as the unconsciously self-serving attitude behind General Westmoreland's statement, an attitude which allows the person responsible for ordering an attack against civilians to take a stance of moral superiority and to express sadness at the result of his own orders without taking on blame or guilt. Kopit dramatizes events from the government's treatment of American Indians from 1866 to 1890, as well as the way in which our cultural institutions have shaped perceptions of those events, in his exploration of the roots of that human blindness which fuels prejudice and legitimates genocide.

The title of this play, *Indians*, seems not to be its subject: Buffalo Bill is. William Cody is the first and last character onstage, he appears in every scene, and even when he is not onstage, the action involves him in some way. Indians exist as dramatized incidents in Cody's memory, as almost everything else in the play does. "Buffalo Bill's Wild West Show," by contrast, is the play's only present-tense "reality." Beginning in 1884 and on into the twentieth century, Cody was co-producer and star of this most famous of Wild West shows. Part circus, part rodeo, part vaudeville, part theater, "The Wild West" was a huge national and international success (even playing a command performance for Queen Victoria) in part because of Cody's instinct to get figures from the American West's recent past to "impersonate" themselves. Thus not only Buffalo Bill, but figures such as Wild Bill Hickock, Calamity Jane, Annie Oakley, and a band of Native Americans (including, for different time periods, Chief Joseph and Sitting Bull) all toured with the show, staging Cody's version of "The Wild West." Interspersed with exhibitions of roping and riding and shooting that celebrated cowboy skills were crowd-pleasing scenarios enacted at every performance: Bill and other white men rescuing a stagecoach from marauding Indians, and the same group of heroes arriving in the nick of time to prevent a nighttime Indian raid on the home of unsuspecting settlers. The effect of these performances on subsequent motion pictures about the American West and indirectly on the formation of our national sense of identity was immense. "The Wild West" opens and closes the play, *Indians*, and is referred to often in the remembered sequences, for example through the interruptions of the offstage voice.

If *Indians* is about Indians, it is only because of the part they play in Buffalo Bill's memories. There they speak of what happened and give voice to the nobility of a people and to a way of life now lost; they function, too, as the image of Cody's guilt, for they make plain his role in their demise. They also show that his desire for greatness within white society led to his betrayal of his friends and suggest that white society's worship of success led, perhaps inevitably, to this betrayal. At last, Cody has to decide between two incompatible systems, both of which he seems to understand (see his explanation of Indian values in Scene 11). Not a bad man, indeed a man who is sympathetic toward Indians, perhaps even a heroic man, he nevertheless chose to act against his friends the Indians—perhaps without meaning to, perhaps even thinking he could do them some good, certainly not understanding what we are shown by watching his visions of Indians, that he *must* choose a side and that this choice for one dooms the other.

Indians is also a play about shows, about theater and image. If "reality" in this play is "The Wild West"—if the entire substance of this play is a play within the play, one which often impinges on Cody's guilt-filled and pride-filled memories—those memories themselves become smaller plays within the play within the play. They are dramatizations of Buffalo Bill's mind as he struggles to maintain his hold on his private identity as William Cody. In these memories, as in the "Show" itself, the artifice, the fact that the memories are enacted pretense, is emphasized by the way they are staged. Indians play buffaloes in scene 3; in the same scene, the Grand Duke pretends that he is Buffalo Bill and kills the Indian Spotted Tail, who nonetheless comes back later to speak; Scenes 2, 4, 6, 8, and 11 dramatize the Senate committee's political charade with the Indians; at the center of the play is Buntline's play, staged at the White House, and this presidential motif continues with the president's imper-sonation of Buffalo Bill in Scene 10. At the heart of these impersonations, of course, is William Cody as Buffalo Bill, friend of the Indian, hero of the white man, the creation of novel and stage, a creation which he comes to believe, which he becomes, and whose guilt (as the man behind his mask) dramatizes the self-destructive qualities of the role.

CHARACTERS

BUFFALO BILL	WILD BILL HICKOK
SITTING BULL	TESKANJAVILA
SENATOR LOGAN	UNCAS
SENATOR DAWES	VALETS
SENATOR MORGAN	ANNIE OAKLEY
TRIAL SOLDIERS	CHIEF JOSEPH
JOHN GRASS	JESSE JAMES
SPOTTED TAIL	BILLY THE KID
GRAND DUKE ALEXIS	PONCHO
INTERPRETER	COLONEL FORSYTH
NED BUNTLINE	LIEUTENANT
GERONIMO	REPORTERS
WHITE HOUSE USHER	SOLDIERS
OL' TIME PRESIDENT	VARIOUS INDIANS
FIRST LADY	

CHRONOLOGY FOR
A DREAMER

1846   William F. Cody born in Le Claire, Iowa, on February 26.

1866   Geronimo surrenders.

1868   William Cody accepts employment to provide food for railroad workers; kills 4,280 buffaloes. Receives nickname "Buffalo Bill."

1869   *Buffalo Bill, the King of the Border Men*, a dime novel by Ned Buntline, makes Buffalo Bill a national hero.

1872   Expedition west in honor of Grand Duke Alexis of Russia, Buffalo Bill as guide.

1876   Battle at the Little Big Horn; Custer killed.

1877   Chief Joseph surrenders.

1878   Buffalo Bill plays himself in *Scouts of the Plains*, a play by Ned Buntline.

1879   Wild Bill Hickok joins Buffalo Bill on the stage.

1883   Sitting Bull surrenders, is sent to Standing Rock Reservation.

1883   "Buffalo Bill's Wild West Show" gives first performance, is great success.

1885   Sitting Bull allowed to join Wild West Show, tours with company for a year.

1886   United States Commission visits Standing Rock Reservation to investigate Indian grievances.

1890   Sitting Bull assassinated, December 15.

1890   Wounded Knee Massacre, December 25.

The play derives, in part, from this chronology but does not strictly adhere to it.—A.K.

SCENE I

[*Audience enters to stage with no curtain. House lights dim.*

On stage: three large glass cases, one holding a larger-than-life-size effigy of Buffalo Bill in fancy embroidered buckskin. One, an effigy of Sitting Bull dressed in simple buckskin or cloth, no headdress, little if any ornamentation. The last case contains some artifacts: a buffalo skull, a bloodstained Indian shirt, and an old rifle. The surrounding stage is dark. The cases are lit by spotlights from above.

Strange music coming from all about. Sense of dislocation.

The house lights fade to dark.

Music up.

Lights on the cases slowly dim.

Sound of wind, soft at first.

The cases glide into the shadowy distance and disappear.

Eerie light now on stage; dim spotlights sweep the floor as if trying to locate something in space.

Brief, distorted strains of Western American music.

A voice reverberates from all about the theatre.]

VOICE. Cody . . . Cody . . . Cody! . . . CODY!

[*One of the spotlights passes something; a man on a horse. The spotlight slowly retraces itself, picks up the horse and rider. They are in a far corner of the stage; they move in slow motion.*

The other spotlights now move toward them, until all converge. At first, the light is dim. As they come toward us, it gets brighter.

The man is Buffalo Bill, dressed as in the museum cases. The horse is a glorious white artificial stallion with wild, glowing eyes.

They approach slowly; their slow motion gradually becoming normal speed.

Vague sound of cheering heard. Music becoming rodeolike. More identifiable.

Then, slowly, from the floor, an open-framed oval fence rises and encloses them.

The horse shies.

Tiny lights, strung beneath the top bar of the fence, glitter faintly. The spotlights—multi-colored—begin to criss-cross about the oval.

Ghostly-pale Wild West Show banners slowly descend.

Then! It's a WILD WEST SHOW!

Loud, brassy music!

Lights blazing everywhere!

The horse rears. His rider whispers a few words, calms him.

Then, a great smile on his face, Buffalo Bill begins to tour the ring, one hand slightly gripping the reins, the other proudly waving his big Stetson to the unseen surrounding crowd. Surely it is a great sight; the horse prances, struts, canters, dances to the music, leaps softly through the light, Buffalo Bill effortlessly in control of the whole world, the universe; eternity.]

BUFFALO BILL. Yessir, BACK AGAIN! That triumphant brassy music, those familiar savage drums! Should o' known I couldn't stay away! Should o' known here's where I belong! The heat o' that ol' spotlight on my face. Yessir . . . Should o' known here's where I belong. . . .

[*He takes a deep breath, closes his eyes, savors the air. A pause.*]

Reminded o' somethin' tol' me once by General Custer. You remember him—one o' the great dumb-ass men in history. Not fer nothin' that he graduated last in his class at West Point! Anyways, we was out on the plains one day, when he turned t' me, with a kind o' far-off look in his eye, an' said, "Bill! If there is one thing a man must never fear, it's makin' a personal comeback."

[He chuckles.]

Naturally, I—
VOICE [softly]. And now, to start . . .
BUFFALO BILL [startled]. Hm?
VOICE. And now to start.
BUFFALO BILL. But I . . . just . . . got up here.
VOICE. I'm sorry; it's time to start.
BUFFALO BILL. Can't you wait a second? WHAT'S THE RUSH? WAIT A SECOND!

[Silence. He takes a deep breath; quiets his horse down].

I'm sorry. But if I seem a trifle edgy to you, it's only 'cause I've just come from a truly harrowing engagement; seems my . . . manager, a . . . rather ancient gentleman, made a terrible mistake an' booked me int' what turned out t' be a ghost town! Well! I dunno what you folks know 'bout show business, but le' me tell, there is nothin' more depressin' than playin' two-a-day in a goddam ghost town!

[He chuckles. Indians appear around the outside of the ring. The horse senses their presence and shies; Buffalo Bill, as if realizing what it means, turns in terror.]

VOICE. Bill.
BUFFALO BILL. But—
VOICE. It's time.

[Pause.]

BUFFALO BILL. Be—before we start, I'd . . . just like to say—
VOICE. Bill!

[The Indians slowly approach.].

BUFFALO BILL. —to say that . . . I am a fine man. And anyone who says otherwise is WRONG!
VOICE [softly]. Bill, it's time.
BUFFALO BILL. My life is an open book; I'm not ashamed of its bein' looked at!

VOICE [coaxing tone]. Bill . . .
BUFFALO BILL. I'm sorry, this is very . . . hard . . .for me t' say. But I believe I . . . am a . . . hero . . . A GODDAM HERO!

[Indian music. His horse rears wildly. Lights change for next scene.]

SCENE II

[Light up on Sitting Bull. He is dressed simply—no feathered headdress. It is winter.]

SITTING BULL. I am Sitting Bull! . . . In the moon of the first snow-falling, in the year half my people died from hunger, the Great Father sent three wise men . . . to investigate the conditions of our reservation, though we'd been promised he would come himself.

[Lights up on Senators Logan, Morgan, and Dawes; they are flanked by armed soldiers. Opposite them, in a semicircle, are Sitting Bull's people, all huddling in tattered blankets from the cold.]

SENATOR LOGAN. Indians! Please be assured that this committee has not come to punish you or take away any of your land but only to hear your grievances, determine if they are just. And if so, remedy them. For we, like the Great Father, wish only the best for our Indian children.

[The Senators spread out various legal documents.]

SITTING BULL. They were accompanied by . . . my friend, William Cody—

[Enter Buffalo Bill, collar of his overcoat turned up for the wind.]

in whose Wild West Show I'd once appeared . . .

[Buffalo Bill greets a number of the Indians.]

in exchange for some food, a little clothing. And a beautiful horse that could do tricks.
SENATOR LOGAN. Colonel Cody has asked if he might say a few words before testimony begins.
SENATOR LOGAN. We would be honored.
BUFFALO BILL [to the Indians]. My . . . brothers.

[Pause.]

I know how disappointed you all must be that the Great Father isn't here; I apologize for having said I thought I . . . could bring him.

[*Pause.*]

However! The three men I *have* brought are by far his most trusted personal representatives. And I promise that talking to them will be the same as . . .

[*Pause. Softly.*]

. . . talking to him.

[*Long pause; he rubs his eyes as if to soothe a headache.*]

To . . . Sitting Bull, then . . .

[*He stares at Sitting Bull.*]

. . . I would like to say that I hope you can overlook your . . . disappointment. And remember what is at *stake* here. And not get angry . . . or too impatient.

[*Pause.*]

Also, I hope you will ask your people to speak with open hearts when talking to these men. And treat them with the same great respect I have always . . . shown , , , to you, for these men have come to *help* you and your people. And I am afraid they may be the only ones left, now, who can.

SITTING BULL. And though there were many among us who wanted to speak first: men like Red Cloud! And Little Hawk! And He-Who-Hears-Thunder! And Crazy Horse! Men who were great warriors, and had counted many coups! And been with us at the Little Big Horn when we *KILLED CUSTER!* . . .

[*Pause.*]

I would not let them speak. . . . For they were like me, and tended to get angry, easily.

[*Pause.*]

Instead, I asked the *young* man, John Grass, who had never fought at all, but had been to the white man's school at Carlisle. And *thought* he understood . . . something . . . of their ways.

BUFFALO BILL. Sitting Bull would like John Grass to speak first.

LOGAN. Call John Grass.

BUFFALO BILL. John Grass! Come forward.

[*Enter John Grass in a black cutaway many sizes too small for him. He wears an Indian shirt. Around his neck is a medal.*]

JOHN GRASS. *Brothers*! I am going to talk about what the Great Father told us a long time ago. He told us to give up hunting and start farming. So we did as he said, and our people grew hungry. For the land was suited to grazing not farming, and even if we'd been farmers, nothing could have grown. So the Great Father said he would send us food and clothing, but nothing came of it. So we asked him for the money he had promised us when we sold him the Black Hills, thinking, with this money we could *buy* food and clothing. But nothing came of it. So we grew ill and sad. . . . So to help us from this sadness, he sent Bishop Marty, to teach us to be Christians. But when we told him we did not wish to be Christians but wished to be like our fathers, and dance the sundance, and fight bravely against the Shawnee and the Crow! And pray to the Great Spirits who made the four winds, and the earth, and made man from the dust of this earth, Bishop Marty hit us! . . . So we said to the Great Father that we thought we would like to go *back* to hunting, because to live, we needed food. But we found that while we had been learning to farm, the buffalo had gone away. And the plains were filled now only with their bones. . . . Before we give you any more of our land, or move from here where the people we loved are growing white in their coffins, we want you to tell the Great Father to give us, who still live, what he promised he would! *No more than that.*

SITTING BULL. I prayed for the return of the buffalo!

[*Lights fade to black on everyone but Buffalo Bill.*]

[*Distant gunshot heard offstage.*]

[*Pause.*]

[*Two more gunshots.*]

[*Lights to black on Buffalo Bill.*]

SCENE III

[*Light up on Spotted Tail, standing on a ledge above the plains.*]

It is night, and he is lit by a pale moon.
The air is hot. No wind.
*A rifle shot is heard offstage, of much greater presence
than the previous shots.*
Spotted Tail peers in its direction.
Sound offstage, of wounded bulls.
*Enter an Indian dressed as a buffalo, wounded in the
eye and bellowing with pain.*
He circles the stage.
Enter two more buffaloes, also wounded in the eyes.
The first buffalo dies.
*The two other buffaloes stagger over to his side and die
beside him; another buffalo [missing an eye] enters, staggers
in a circle, senses the location of the dead buffaloes and
heads dizzily toward them—dying en route, halfway there.
Spotted Tail crouches and gazes down at them. Then he
stares up at the sky.*
Night creatures screech in the dark.
A pause.]

BUFFALO BILL [*offstage but coming closer*]. Ninety-
three, ninety-four, ninety-five . . . ninety-*six! I DID
IT!*

[*Enter, running a much younger Buffalo Bill, rifle in hand,
followed shortly by members of the U.S. Cavalry bearing
torches, and the Grand Duke's interpreter.*]

I did it, I did it! No one believed I could, but I *did
it!* One hundred buffalo—one hundred shots! "You
jus' gimme some torches," I said. "I *know* there's
buffalo around us. *Here*. Put yer ear t' the ground.
Feel it tremblin? Well. You wanna see somethin'
fantastic, you get me some torches. I'll shoot the
reflections in their eyes. I'll shoot 'em like they was
so many shiny nickels!"
INTERPRETER. I'll tell the Grand Duke you did what
you said. I know he'll be pleased.
BUFFALO BILL. Well he oughta be! I don' give exhibitions like this fer just anybody!

[*Exit the interpreter.*]

'Specially as these critters're gettin' so damn
hard t' find.

[*To the Soldiers.*]

Not like the ol' days when I was huntin' 'em fer the
railroads.

[*He laughs, gazes down at one of the buffaloes. Pause. He
looks away; squints as if in pain.*]

A SOLDIER. Are you all right, sir?
BUFFALO BILL. Uh . . . yes. Fine.

[*Exit the Soldiers.*
Buffalo Bill rubs his head.
*Spotted Tail hops down from his perch and walks up behind
Cody unnoticed; stares at him.*
Pause.
*Buffalo Bill senses the Indian's presence and turns, cocking
his rifle. The Indian makes no move.*
Buffalo Bill stares at the Indian.
Pause.]

BUFFALO BILL. *Spotted Tail!* My God. I haven't seen
you in years. How . . . ya been?

[*Slight laugh.*]

SPOTTED TAIL. *What are you doing here?*

[*Pause.*]

BUFFALO BILL. Well, well, what . . . are *you* doing
here? This isn't Sioux territory!
SPOTTED TAIL. It isn't *your* territory either.

[*Pause.*]

BUFFALO BILL. Well I'm with . . . these *people*. I'm
scoutin' for 'em.
SPOTTED TAIL. *These people* . . . must be very hungry.
BUFFALO BILL. Hm?
SPOTTED TAIL. To need so many buffalo.
BUFFALO BILL. Ah! Of course! You were following
the buffalo *also*! . . . Well listen, I'm sure my friends
won't mind you takin' some. 'Tween us, my friends
don't 'specially care for the *taste* o' buffalo meat.

[*He laughs.*]

My God, but it's good t' see you again!
SPOTTED TAIL. *Your friends*. I have been studying
them from the hills. They are very strange. They
seem neither men, nor women.
BUFFALO BILL. Well! Actually, they're sort of a new
breed o' people. Called dudes.

[*He chuckles.*]

SPOTTED TAIL. You *like* them?
BUFFALO BILL. Well . . . sure. Why not?

[*Pause.*]

I mean, obviously, they ain't the sort I've been used to. But then, things're changin' out here. An' these men are the ones who're changin' 'em. So, if you wanna be *part* o' these things, an' not left behind somewhere, you jus' plain hafta get *used* to 'em. You—uh—follow . . . what I mean?

[*Silence.*]

I mean . . . you've got to *adjust*. To the times. Make a *plan* fer yerself. I have one. You should have one, too. Fer yer own good. Believe me.

[*Long pause.*]

SPOTTED TAIL. *What is your plan?*

BUFFALO BILL. Well, my plan is t' help people. Like you, ferinstance. Or these people I'm with. More . . . even . . . than that, maybe. And, and, whatever . . . it is I *do* t' help, for it, these people may someday jus' possibly name streets after me. Cities. Counties. States! I'll . . . be as famous as Dan'l Boone! . . . An' somewhere, on top of a beautiful mountain that overlooks more plains 'n rivers than any other mountain, there might even be a statue of me sittin' on a great white horse, a-wavin' my hat t' everyone down below, thankin' 'em, fer thankin' me, fer havin' done . . . whatever . . . it is I'm gonna . . . *do* fer 'em all. How . . . come you got such a weird look on yer face?

BUNTLINE [*offstage*]. HEY, CODY! *STAY WHERE YA ARE!*

BUFFALO BILL. DON' WORRY! I AIN'T BUDGIN'!

[*To Spotted Tail.*]

That's Mister Ned Buntline, the well-known newspaper reporter. I think he's gonna do an *article* on me! General Custer, who's in charge, an' I think is pushin' fer an article on *himself*, says this may well be the most important western expedition since Lewis 'n Clark.

BUNTLINE [*offstage*]. BY THE WAY, *WHERE* ARE YA?

BUFFALO BILL. I . . . AIN'T SURE! JUST HEAD FOR THE LIGHTS!

[*He laughs to himself.*]

SPOTTED TAIL. Tell me. Who is the man everyone always bows to?

BUFFALO BILL. Oh! The Gran' Duke! He's from a place called Russia. This whole shindig's in his honor. I'm sure he'd love t' meet you. He's never seen a real Indian.

SPOTTED TAIL. There are no Indians in Russia?

[*Buffalo Bill shakes his head.*]

Then I will study him even more carefully than the others. Maybe if he takes me back to Russia with him, I will not end like my people will . . . end.

BUFFALO BILL [*startled*]. *What?*

SPOTTED TAIL. I mean, like these fools here, on the ground.

[*He stares at the buffalo.*]

BUFFALO BILL. *Ah* . . . Well, if ya don' mind my sayin', I think you're bein' a bit pessimistic. But you do what ya like. Jus' remember: these people you're studying'—some folk think *they're* the fools.

SPOTTED TAIL. Oh, no! They are not fools! *No one who is a white man can be a fool.*

[*He smiles coldly at Buffalo Bill; heraldic Russian fanfare offstage.*
Enter Russian torchbearers and trumpeters.
Buffalo Bill and Spotted Tail, in awe, back away.
Enter with much pomp and ceremony Grand Duke Alexis on a splendid litter carved like a horse. He is accompanied by his interpreter, who points out the four buffaloes to the Grand Duke as he majestically circles the clearing. He is followed by Ned Buntline, who carries a camera and tripod.]

BUFFALO BILL. My God, but that is a beautiful sight!

[*The Grand Duke comes to a halt. Majestic sweep of his arms to those around him.*]

GRAND DUKE [*Makes a regal Russian speech*].

INTERPRETER. His Excellency the Grand Duke wishes to express his heartfelt admiration of Buffalo Bill . . .

[*Music up.*]

. . . for having done what he has done tonight.

[*The Grand Duke gestures majestically. The Interpreter opens a small velvet box. Airy music. The Interpreter walks toward Buffalo Bill.*]

GRAND DUKE [*gesturing for Buffalo Bill to come forward*]. Boofilo Beel!

[*Buffalo Bill walks solemnly forward. The Interpreter takes out a medal. Buffalo Bill, deeply moved, looks around, embarrassed.*
    The Interpreter smiles and holds up the medal, gestures warmly for Buffalo Bill to kneel. He does so.
    The Interpreter places the medal, which is on a bright ribbon, around his neck.
    Flashgun goes off.]

BUNTLINE. Great picture, Cody! FRONT PAGE! My God, what a night! *What a story*! Uh . . . sorry, yer Highness. Didn't mean t' distoib ya.

[*He backs meekly away. Sets up his camera for another shot. The Grand Duke regains his composure.*]

GRAND DUKE. [*Russian speech.*]
INTERPRETER. His Excellency wonders how Buffalo Bill became such a deadly shot.
BUFFALO BILL. Oh, well, you know, just . . . practice.

[*Embarrassed laugh.*]

GRAND DUKE. [*Russian speech.*]
INTERPRETER. His Excellency says he wishes that his stupid army knew how to practice.
GRAND DUKE. [*Russian speech.*]
INTERPRETER. Better yet, he wishes you would come back with him to his palace and protect himself.
BUFFALO BILL. Oh.

[*Slight laugh.*]

Well, I'm sure the Grand Duke's in excellent hands.

[*The Interpreter whispers what Buffalo Bill has just said.*]

GRAND DUKE. Da! *Hands.*

[*He holds out his hands, then turns them and puts them around his throat.*]

BUFFALO BILL. I think His Majesty's exaggeratin'. I can't believe he's not *surrounded* by friends.
GRAND DUKE. FRIENDS!

[*He cackles and draws his sword, slashes the air.*]

Friends! Friends! . . . *Friends*!

[*He fights them off.*]

BUFFALO BILL [*to Buntline*]. I think he's worried 'bout somethin'.
BUNTLINE. Very strange behavior.
GRAND DUKE. [*Nervous Russian speech.*]
INTERPRETER. His Excellency wonders if Buffalo Bill has ever been afraid.
BUFFALO BILL. . . . Afraid?
GRAND DUKE. [*Russian word.*]
INTERPRETER. Outnumbered.
BUFFALO BILL. Ah.

[*Slight laugh.*]

Well, uh—
BUNTLINE. Go on, tell 'm. It'll help what I'm plannin' t' write.
BUFFALO BILL [*delighted*]. It *will*?
BUNTLINE. Absolutely. Look: de West is changin'—right? Well, people wanna know about it. Wanna feel . . . *part* o' things. I think *you're* what dey need. Someone t' listen to, observe, *identify* wid. No, no, really! I been studyin' you.
BUFFALO BILL. . . . You have?
BUNTLINE. I think you could be de inspiration o' dis land.
BUFFALO BILL. Now I *know* you're foolin'!
BUNTLINE. Not at all . . . Well go on. Tell 'm what he wants t' hear. T'rough my magic pen, others will hear also. . . . Donmentionit. De nation needs men like me, too.

[*He pats Cody on the shoulder and shoves him off toward the Grand Duke; Cody gathers his courage.*]

BUFFALO BILL [*to the Grand Duke*]. Well, uh . . . where can I begin? Certainly it's true that I've been outnumbered. And—uh—many times. Yes.
BUNTLINE. That's the way.
BUFFALO BILL. More times, in fact, than I can count.
BUNTLINE. Terrific.
BUFFALO BILL [*warming to the occasion*]. An' believe me, I can count pretty high!
BUNTLINE. SENSATIONAL!
BUFFALO BILL. Mind you, 'gainst *me*, twelve's normally an even battle—long's I got my two six-shooters that is.
BUNTLINE. Keep it up, keep it up!
BUFFALO BILL. THIRTEEN! If one of 'em's thin enough for a bullet t' go clean through. Fourteen if

I got a huntin' knife. Fifteen if there's a hard surface off o' which I can ricochet a few shots.

BUNTLINE. *Go on!*

BUFFALO BILL. Um twenty . . . if I got a stick o' dynamite. HUNDRED! IF THERE'S ROCKS T' START A AVALANCHE!

[*Buntline applauds.*]

What I mean is, with *me* it's never say die! Why . . . I remember once I was ridin' for the Pony Express 'tween Laramie 'n Tombstone. Suddenly, jus' past the Pecos, fifty drunk Comanches attack. Noise like a barroom whoop-di-do, arrows fallin' like hailstones! I mean, they come on me so fast they don' have time t' see my face, notice who I am, realize I'm in fact a very good *friend* o' theirs!

GRAND DUKE. FRIEND! FRIEND!

BUNTLINE [*sotto voce*]. Get off de subject!

BUFFALO BILL. Well, there was no alternative but t'fire back. Well I'd knocked off 'bout thirty o' their number when I realized I was *out* o' bullets. Just at that moment, a arrow whizzed past my head. Thinkin' fast, I reached out an' caught it. Then, usin' it like a fly swatter, I knocked away the other nineteen arrows that were headin' fer my heart. Whereupon, I stood up in the stirrups, hurled the arrow sixty yard. . . . An' killed their chief.

[*Pause.*]

Which . . . *depressed* . . . the remainin' Indians.

[*Pause.*]

And sent 'em scurryin' home. Well! That's sort o' what ya might call a typical day!

[*Bravos from everyone except the Grand Duke.*]

GRAND DUKE. [*Russian speech, quite angry.*]

INTERPRETER. His Excellency says he would like to kill a Comanche also.

BUFFALO BILL. Hm?

GRAND DUKE [*with obvious jealousy*]. Like Boofilo Beel!

INTERPRETER. Like Buffalo Bill!

GRAND DUKE. [*Excited Russian speech.*]

INTERPRETER. He will *prove* he cannot be intimidated!

GRAND DUKE. Rifle, rifle, rifle!

BUFFALO BILL [*to Buntline*]. I think my story may've worked a bit too well.

BUNTLINE. Nonsense! This is *terrific*!

[*They duck as the Grand Duke, cackling madly, scans the surrounding darkness over his rifle sight.*]

Shows you've won the Grand Duke's heart.

GRAND DUKE [*pounding his chest*]. Boofilo Beel! . . . *I am BOOFILO BEEL!*

[*He laughs demonically.*]

BUNTLINE. I think you'd better find 'm a Comanche.

BUFFALO BILL. Right! *Well.* Um . . .

[*Slight laugh.*]

That *could* be a . . . problem.

GRAND DUKE. Comanche! *Comanche!*

BUFFALO BILL. Ya see, fer one thing, the Comanches live in Texas. And we're in Missouri.

GRAND DUKE. COMANCHE! *COMANCHE!*

BUFFALO BILL. Fer another, I ain't 'xactly sure what they look like.

GRAND DUKE. Ah!

[*He fires into the darkness.*
Spotted Tail stumbles out, collapses and dies. The Grand Duke and his Interpreter delirious with joy. Buntline dumbfounded. Buffalo Bill stunned, but for vastly different reasons.]

BUNTLINE [*approaching the body cautiously*]. My God, will you look at that? Fate must be smiling!

[*He laughs weakly, stares up at the heavens in awe.*
Buffalo Bill, almost in a trance, walks over to the body; stares down at it.
Weird music heard.
The lights change color, grow vague.
All movement arrested.
Spotted Tail rises slowly and moves just as slowly toward the Grand Duke; stops.]

SPOTTED TAIL. My name is Spotted Tail. My father was a Sioux; my mother, part Cherokee, part Crow. No matter how you look at it, I'm just not a Comanche.

[*He sinks back to the ground.*
Lights return to normal, the music ends.]

GRAND DUKE. [*Baffled Russian speech.*]

INTERPRETER. His Excellency would like to know what the man he just shot has said.

[*Long pause. Buffalo Bill looks around, as if for help; all eyes upon him.*]

BUFFALO BILL [*softly*]. He said . . .

[*Pause.*]

"I . . .

[*Pause.*]

should have . . .

[*He looks at Buntline, takes a deep breath.*]

stayed at home in . . . Texas with the rest of my . . . Comanche tribe."
BUNTLINE. Fabulous!

[*He takes Spotted Tail's picture; the night sky glows from the flash.*]

Absolutely fabulous!

[*The scene fades around Buffalo Bill, who stands in the center, dizzily gripping his head.*]

SCENE IV

[*Dimly we see the Senators and Sitting Bull's Indians glide back into view.*]

BUFFALO BILL. If it *please* the honorable senators . . . there is something I would like to say to *them*, as well.

[*Pause.*]

I wish to say . . . that there is far more at stake here, today, than the discovery of Indian grievances.

[*Pause.*]

At stake are these people's lives.

[*Pause.*]

In *some* ways, more than even that. For these are not just *any* Indians. These are *Sitting Bull's* Indians. . . . The last to surrender.

[*Pause.*]

The last of a kind.

[*Long pause.*]

So, in that way, you see, they are . . . perhaps more *important* for us than . . . any others.

[*Pause.*]

For it is we, alone, who have put them on this strip of arid land. And what becomes of them is . . . our responsibility.

[*Buffalo Bill stares helplessly as the scene about him fades to black.*]

VOICE. And now, for your *pleasure*, BUFFALO BILL'S WILD WEST SHOW *PROUDLY* PRESENTS . . .

[*Lights to black.
Drum roll.*]

SCENE V

[*Stage dark; drum roll continues. Weirdly colored spotlights begin to crisscross on the empty stage.*]

VOICE. THE MOST FEROCIOUS INDIAN ALIVE! . . .

[*The bars of a large round cage slowly emerge from the floor of the stage; then, around the bars, the Wild West Show fence seen earlier.*]

THE FORMER SCOURGE OF THE SOUTHWEST! . . .

[*The lights on the fence begin to glow; eerie, fantastical atmosphere.
A tunnel-cage rolls out from the wings and connects with the large central cage.
Sound of an iron grate opening offstage.
Rodeo music up.*]

The one'n only . . . GERONIMO!

[*Enter Geronimo, crawling through the tunnel; as soon as he is in sight, he stops, lifts his head, takes in his surroundings.
Enter two Cowboy Roustabouts with prods. They are enormous men—much larger than life-size. Their muscles*

bulge against their gaudy clothes. Their faces seem frozen in a sneer. Even their gun belts are oversized.

They prod Geronimo along, raise the gate to the center cage and coax him in, closing it behind him. Then they move away.

Geronimo paces about, testing the bars with his hands.]

GERONIMO. I AM GERONIMO! WAR CHIEF OF THE GREAT CHIRICAHUA APACHES!

[He stalks about.]

Around my neck is a string of white men's genitals! MEN I HAVE KILLED! . . . Around my waist, the scalplocks of white women's genitals! WOMEN I RAPED AND KILLED! . . . *No Indian has ever killed or raped more than I.* Even the Great Spirits cannot count the number! . . . My body is painted with blood! I am red from white men's BLOOD! . . . NO ONE LIVES WHO HAS KILLED MORE WHITE MEN THAN I!

[Buffalo Bill, in his fancy buckskin, enters unnoticed by Geronimo; drum roll. He opens the cage door and walks inside.

Once inside, he closes the door and stands still.

Geronimo senses his presence and stops moving. Lifts up his head as if to hear better. Sniffs. Turns. Stares at Buffalo Bill.

Slowly, Buffalo Bill walks toward him. He stops just short of the Indian. Then defiantly turns his back.

Geronimo practically frothing.

Long pause. Geronimo does nothing.

Buffalo Bill walks calmly away, opens the cage door, and exits. Disappears into the shadows.

Geronimo stands trembling with frenzy.

Lights fade to black.]

SCENE VI

[Lights up on the Senate Committee, Sitting Bull's Indians, and Buffalo Bill.]

SENATOR LOGAN. Mister Grass, I wonder if you could be a bit more *specific* and tell us *exactly* what you think the Great Father has promised which he has not given.

JOHN GRASS. He promised to give us *as much as we would need, for as long as we would need it!*

SENATOR DAWES. Where did he promise you *that?*

JOHN GRASS. In a treaty.

SENATOR LOGAN. *What* treaty?

JOHN GRASS. A treaty signed some years ago, maybe five or six.

SENATOR LOGAN. Mister Grass, many treaties were signed five or six years ago. But frankly, I've never heard of an arrangement quite like that one.

JOHN GRASS. You took the Black Hills from us in this treaty!

SENATOR DAWES. You mean we *bought* the Black Hill in it!

[Logan glares at Dawes.]

JOHN GRASS. I have nothing else to say.

[He turns and starts to walk away.]

SENATOR LOGAN. Mister Grass! The . . . Senator . . . *apologizes* for his . . . tone.

[Pause. John Grass returns.]

JOHN GRASS. If you *bought* the Black Hills from us, where is our money?

SENATOR LOGAN. The money is in trust.

JOHN GRASS. *Trust?*

SENATOR MORGAN. He means, it's in a bank. Being *held* for you in a . . . bank. In *Washington!* Very . . . fine bank.

JOHN GRASS. Well, we would rather hold it ourselves.

SENATOR DAWES. The Great Father is worried that you've not been educated enough to spend it *wisely.* When he feels you have, you will receive every last penny of it. *Plus interest.*

[John Grass turns in fury; Logan totally exasperated with Dawes.]

BUFFALO BILL. Mister Grass, *please!* These men have come to *help* you! But their ways are *different* from yours; you must be *patient* with them.

JOHN GRASS. You said you would bring us the Great Father.

BUFFALO BILL. I *tried!* I told you! But he wouldn't come; *what else could I do?*

JOHN GRASS. You told us he was your *friend.*

BUFFALO BILL. HE *IS MY FRIEND! Look, don't you understand?* These men are your *only hope.* If you turn away from them, it's like . . . *committing suicide.*

[Pause.]

JOHN GRASS [to the Senators]. At Fort Laramie, Fort Lyon, and Fort Rice we signed treaties, parts of which have never been fulfilled.

SENATOR DAWES. *Which* parts have never been fulfilled?

JOHN GRASS. At Fort Rice the Government advised us to be at *peace*, and said that *if we did so*, we would receive a span of horses, five bulls, ten chickens, and a wagon!

SENATOR LOGAN. You . . . really believe . . . these things were in the treaty?

JOHN GRASS. We were told they were.

SENATOR LOGAN. You . . . saw them written?

JOHN GRASS. We cannot read very well, but we were *told* they were!

[*The Senators glance sadly at one another. John Grass grows confused. Pause.*]

We were also . . . promised a STEAMBOAT!

SENATOR MORGAN. A *steamboat*?

SENATOR DAWES. What in God's name were you supposed to do with a steamboat in the middle of the plains?

[*He laughs.*]

JOHN GRASS. I don't know.

[*He turns in confusion and stares at Buffalo Bill; Buffalo Bill turns helplessly to the Senators. As—*
    Lights begin to fade.]

SITTING BULL. Where is the Great Father, Cody? . . . The one you said would help us. . . . The one you said you knew *so well*.

[*As lights go to black, a Mozart minuet is heard.*]

SCENE VII

[*Lights up on White House Ballroom, in the center of which is a makeshift stage. The front drop of this stage is a melodramatic western-heroic poster with "Scouts of the Plains, by NED BUNTLINE" painted over it.*
    The Mozart stops as—
    A Negro usher enters.]

USHER. This way, Mister President.

OL' TIME PRESIDENT [*offstage*]. Thank you, George.

[*Enter the Ol' Time President in white tie and tails, cigar in mouth, brandy glass in hand.*]

This way, dear. They're about to start.

[*Enter the First Lady in a formal gown.*]

FIRST LADY. Oh, this *is* exciting! Our *first real cowboys*!

[*The Usher leads them towards a pair of Louis XIV chairs set facing the stage. Drum roll.*]

OL' TIME PRESIDENT. Sssh. Here we go.

[*They sit.*
    Enter, from behind the canvas drop, Ned Buntline. He wears an exaggerated version of plainsman's outfit.]

NED BUNTLINE. Mister President, hon'rable First Lady.
    Before you stands a character most shady,
    A knave whose presence darkens this bright earth,
    More than does the moon's eclipsing girth.
    What's that you say, I'm rude to filth espouse
    When I'm the guest of such a clean, white house?
    Fear not, there's somethin' I didn't mention:
    Recently, I found redemption.
    Ah, forgive me, I'm sorry, Ned Buntline's the name,
    It's me who's brought Bill Cody fame.
    Wrote twenty-seven books with him the hero.
    Made 'm better known than Nero.
    And though we sold 'em cheap, one for a dime,
    The two of us was rich in no time.
    As for my soul's redemption, it came thus:
    I saw the nation profit more than us.
    For with each one o' my excitin' stories,
    Cody grew t' represent its glories.
    Also helped relieve its conscience,
    By showing pessimism's nonsense.
    Later, when people asked t' *see* 'm,
    I wrote a play for him to be in;
    A scene of which we now perform for you,
    As you've so graciously implored us to.
    Cody, of course, impersonates himself,
    As does Yours Truly.
    The Crow Maiden is Italian actress
    Paula Monduli,
    Our evil Pawnee Chief, the great German actor
    Gunther Hookman.
    Our other Indians, I'm afraid,
    Come from Brooklyn.
    However, as a special treat tonight,
    A visitor is here,
    And I've added some new dialogue,
    So he might appear.
    Realize though, this man's come as Cody's friend,

He's not an actor.
Though of course in *my* play, who men *are*
Is the real factor.
So get set then for anything,
May the script be damned,
An' let's give Cody an' Wild Bill Hickok
A ROUSING HAND!

[*The First Lady and the Ol' Time President applaud enthusiastically. Buntline exits.*

The canvas drop is rolled up to reveal another canvas drop—a painted forest of the worst melodramatic order.

On stage, wooden as only the worst amateur actors can be, stand Cody and Hickok, the latter with long, glorious hair, fancy buckskin leggings, two large guns and a knife in his belt.]

BUFFALO BILL. God pray we're in time. Those Pawnee devils will do anything.

[*Silence.*]

BUNTLINE [*prompting from offstage*]. Especially . . .

[*Silence.*]

BUFFALO BILL. Think that's your line, Bill.
WILD BILL HICKOK. Oh, hell's thunder.

[*To Buntline.*]

Better give It-a-me again.
BUNTLINE. Especially . . .
HICKOK. Especially.
BUNTLINE. . . . . at their . . .
HICKOK. At their.
BUFFALO BILL [*soto voce*]. . . . dreadful annual . . .
HICKOK. Dreadful. Annual.
BUNTLINE. . . . . Festival of the Moon.
HICKOK. Festival of the Moon. Which is . . . 'bout t' happen. As it does every . . .

[*Silence.*]

BUFFALO BILL. . . .year.
HICKOK. Year.
BUNTLINE. Very good.
HICKOK. Very good.
BUNTLINE. No!
HICKOK. Whose line's that?
BUFFALO BILL. No one's. He was jus' congratulatin' you.
HICKOK. Oh, Will, fer pity's sake, le' me out o' this.
BUNTLINE. *Ad lib*!

BUFFALO BILL. Yes! Pray God we're in time to stop the Pawnee's dreadful Festival of the Moon so that I, the great Buffalo Bill, can once again—
HICKOK. Will, stop it! A man may need money, but no man needs it this bad.

[*Enter Buntline, tap-dancing the sound of horses's hooves.*]

BUFFALO BILL. Hark! Ned Buntline approaches! One o' the finest sharpshooters o' the West!
HICKOK [*under his breath*]. Couldn't hit a cow in the ass from two paces.
BUFFALO BILL. Who knows? Maybe *he* can help us in our dire strait.
HICKOK. Mister and Missus President, if you're still out there, believe me, I'm as plumb embarrassed by this dude-written sissyshit as you.
BUNTLINE. HAIL, BUFFALO BILL! Hail—uh—Wild Bill Hickok. What brings you to this unlikely place?
HICKOK. Good fuckin' question.
BUNTLINE. Could it be that you seek, as I do, the camp of Uncas, evil Pawnee Chief?
BUFFALO BILL. Yes, verily. We seek his camp so that I, the great Buffalo Bill, can, once again, save someone in distress.

[*Hickok groans.*]

This time, specifically, a virgin maiden—
HICKOK. You gotta be jokin'.
BUFFALO BILL. *Will you shut up*! Named Teskanjavila! Who, 'less I save her, faces torture, sacrifice, and certain violations.
BUNTLINE. This bein' so, *let us join forces*!
HICKOK. Boy, where's your *self-respect*?
BUNTLINE [*weakly*]. And save this virgin together.
BUFFALO BILL [*to Hickok*]. Will you leave me alone!
HICKOK. This ain't a *proper place* for a man t' be!
BUFFALO BILL. Well, I THINK IT *IS*! I think I'm doin' a lot o' good up here! Entertainin' people! Makin' 'em *happy*! Showin 'em the West! Givin' 'em somethin' t' be *proud* of! *You* go spend your life in Dodge City if you want! I got *bigger* things in mind!

[*Stunned pause.*]

BUNTLINE [*very sheepishly*]. To repeat: let us join forces and save this virgin together.
HICKOK. Buntline, if these guns were loaded, I'd—
BUNTLINE [*cueing the actors offstage*]. HARK! The maiden's name is called!
NUMEROUS VOICES [*offstage*]. Teskanjavila!

BUNTLINE. We must be near the camp of Uncas.

BUFFALO BILL. Evil Pawnee chief.

HICKOK. I'm gettin' sick.

BUNTLINE. Let us, therefore, approach with caution.

BUFFALO BILL. Guns ready.

BUNTLINE. Ears open.

BUFFALO BILL [to Hickok]. Mouths shut!

BUNTLINE. Eyes alert.

BUFFALO BILL. So that I, Buffalo Bill, may once aga—

[Hickok has walked over and is staring into his face.]

Just *what are you doin'*?

HICKOK. What're *you* doin'?

BUFFALO BILL. I'm doin' what I'm doin', *that's* what I'm doin'!

HICKOK [to Buntline]. Always was intelligent.

BUFFALO BILL. I am doin' what my country *wants*! WHAT MY BELOVED COUNTRY *WANTS*!

HICKOK [to the first family]. *This* . . . is . . . what you want?

FIRST LADY. Absolutely!

OL' TIME PRESIDENT. Best play I've seen in years!

[Hickok, staggered, sits down on the stage.]

BUFFALO BILL. When a man has a talent, a *God*-given talent, I think it's his godly duty t' make the most of it.

[Applause from the First Family. Buffalo Bill nods acknowledgement. To Hickok.]

Ya see, Bill, what you fail to understand is that I'm not being false to what I *was*. I'm simply *drawin'* on what I was . . . and raisin' it to a higher level.

[He takes a conscious pause.]

Now. On with the show!

[He points to Buntline, cueing him to give the next line.]

BUNTLINE. AVAST, AHOY! Above yon trees see the pale moon rising!

[A cardboard moon is pulled upwards.]

Feel the black night envelope us like a dark dream.

[Buntline and Cody shiver.]

Sounds of the savage forest and heard. . . . We approach on tiptoes.

BUFFALO BILL [to the First Family]. God pray we're in time.

[They drop to their bellies as the canvas drop is raised to reveal the camp of Uncas. Tied to a totem pole is Teskanjavila, writhing sensually.

Clearly phony Indians dance around her to the beat of drums. The heroes crawl slowly forward. Hickok, eyeing the girl lustfully, joins in.]

FIRST LADY. That Hickok's rather handsome, isn't he?

OL' TIME PRESIDENT. I'm watching the girl. Note her legs. How white they are. For an Indian. One can almost see the soft inner flesh of her thighs.

FIRST LADY. *This play excites me!*

OL' TIME PRESIDENT. We really should have more things like this at the White House.

[The drums grow wilder. The Indians scream; Buntline, Cody, and Hickok invade the Indian camp site. Gunshots. Indians fall dead.]

TESKANJAVILA [Italian accent]. Saved! A maiden's prayers are answered! And may I say, not a bit too soon! Already, my soft thighs had been pried open; my budding breasts pricked by the hot tip of an Indian spear. Yet, through it all, my maidenhead stayed secure. Here. In this pouch. Kept in this secret pocket. Where no one thought to look. Thus is innocence preserved! May Nazuma, God of Thunder, grant me happiness!

[Thunder heard.]

HICKOK. Buntline write that speech?

BUFFALO BILL. I think she changed it a little.

[Uncas rises from the dead.]

UNCAS [German accent]. I am Uncas, Chief of the Pawnee Indians, recently killed for my lustful ways. Yet, before the white men came and did me in, I had this vision: the white man is great, the red man nothing. So, if a white man kills a red man, we must forgive him, for God intended man to be as great as possible, and by eliminating the inferior, the great man carries on God's work. Thus, the Indian is in no way wronged by being murdered. Indeed, quite the opposite: being murdered is his purpose in life. This was my recent vision. Which has brought light to the darkness of my otherwise useless soul. . . . And now, I die again.

[*He collapses.*]

HICKOK. Buntline write that?

BUFFALO BILL. Think Hookman changed it also. They all do it. It's our style. I dunno, people seem to like it.

HICKOK. Yeah? Well then, guess it mus' be my turn!

[*He pulls out his bowie knife.*]

BUFFALO BILL. HEY!

HICKOK. Make one false move an' I'll rip you 'part, friend or no.

BUNTLINE. Bill, look—

HICKOK. As for you, Buntline, you fangless lizard, you harmless bull, you ball of—

BUNTLINE. BRING DOWN THE CURTAIN!

HICKOK. First one touches that curtain, I cuts int' mincemeat an' eats fer dinner, *raw*!

FIRST LADY. I'm trembling all over.

HICKOK. Okay, Buntline. Now we're gonna settle up the score.

BUNTLINE. Score?

HICKOK. Men jus' don' humiliate Wil' Bill Hickok.

BUNTLINE. *Hu—humiliate?*

HICKOK. Or leastways don' do it twice, bein' dead shortly after the first occasion.

BUNTLINE. Wh—what . . . 're you talkin' about?

HICKOK. 'Bout havin' to impersonate myself. 'Bout the humiliation o' havin' to impersonate my *own personal self*!

BUNTLINE. Oh.

FIRST LADY. *Fantastic!*

BUNTLINE. Well, I dunno what t' say.

HICKOK. It weren't in the deal!

BUNTLINE. Deal?

HICKOK. You said if I came here, I could play Bat Masterson!

BUNTLINE. Ah, *that*!

[*He chuckles.*]

Well, . . . if you recall, I said *maybe* you could play Bat Masterson. First, we had t' see how good you did as Hickok.

HICKOK. As *Hickok?* Chrissake, I AM Hickok!

BUNTLINE. Right.

HICKOK. Well, why in hell should I play *him* then?

BUNTLINE. Well, there's audience appeal.

FIRST LADY. There sure is!

BUNTLINE. BILL! Now—now, wait-a-second! Let's talk this over. Like gentlemen.

BUFFALO BILL. Yeah. Right. Let's . . . not get too . . . carried away. After all—

HICKOK. If you don' stay out o' this, I'm gonna slit yer stuffin' gizzard an' extract, inch by inch, what's guts in most folks, but in you is thorou' garbage.

BUFFALO BILL. Now wait-a-minute! Hold on! You— you think I'm jus' gonna stand here an'—

HICKOK. Oh, shut up! Dumb, dudelickin' FRAUD!

BUFFALO BILL. *What?*

HICKOK. If I gotta play Hickok, I'm gonna play Hickok the way Hickok should be *played*!

BUNTLINE. *Put that knife away, please!* . . . For god-sakes. Cody, *HELP ME! Cody!*

[*Buntline falls, a knife in his back. He crawls off the front of the stage; collapses.*]

FIRST LADY. He looks kind o' dead.

[*Buffalo Bill heads for the body, stunned.*]

HICKOK. Sorry, Will. Guess I just ain't used to show business yet.

[*He chuckles and turns his attention to Teskanjavila. Buffalo Bill is feeling for Buntline's pulse.*]

TESKANJAVILA. O, *Sancta Maria*, I don't like this gleam in his eye.

HICKOK [*striking a pose*].
   Hail, sweet cookie, tart of tempting flavors,
   Why've I been denied your spicy favors?

TESKANJAVILA. AH! *What're you doing?* HELP!

[*Hickok unties her from the pole, at the same time unhooking his gun belt. He works rapidly.*
Buffalo Bill lets Buntline's limp arm drop. He stares back at the stage stunned.]

FIRST LADY. Ooooh, look what he's doing now!

[*The First Family climb on the stage, the Negro Ushers bringing their chairs for them so they can have a more comfortable view.*]

   Really, we must invite this theatre crowd more often.

[*Hickok is now standing above Teskanjavila, who lies help-less at his feet. Buffalo Bill watches from off-stage, outside the ring. Also helpless.*]

HICKOK. Hickok, fastest shooter in the West, 'cept for Billy the Kid, who ain't as accurate; Hickok, deadliest shooter in the West, 'cept for Doc Holliday, who wields a sawed-off shotgun, which ain't fair; Hickok, shootinest shooter in the West, 'cept for Jesse James, who's absolutely indiscriminate; this Hickok, strong as an eagle, tall as a mountain, swift as the wind, fierce as a rattlesnake—a legend in his own time, or any other—this Hickok stands now above an Indian maiden—

TESKANJAVILA. I'm not an Indian and I'm not a maiden!

HICKOK. Who's not an Indian and not a maiden, but looks pretty good anyhow—an' asks those o' you watchin' t' note carefully the basic goodness of his very generous intentions, since otherwise . . .

[He starts to finger her clothing.]

. . . they might be mistaken for . . .

[He rips open her buckskin dress.]

. . . *LUST*!

[She is left in a frilly Merry Widow corset.]

TESKANJAVILA. Eh, bambino. If you don' mind, I'd like a little privacy.

[To the First Family.]

After all, I've not rehearsed this.

[Hickok pulls the cord, lowering the curtain.]

OL' TIME PRESIDENT. Good show, Cody! *Good show*!

[Buffalo Bill, in a daze, walks to the stage and opens the curtain.
   "Scouts of the Plains" drop seen. He stares at it. Pulls it down.
   NO ONE THERE.
   Mozart minuet heard.
   He looks around in total confusion.
   The stage and all the White House furniture begin to disappear.
   Lights fade to black, Buffalo Bill spinning dizzily in the middle.
   Music fades.]

SCENE VIII

[Lights up again on the Senate Committee.]

SENATOR LOGAN. Mister Grass. Let's leave aside the question of the steamboat. You mentioned the treaty at Fort Lyon and said that parts of that treaty had never been fulfilled. Well, I happen to be quite familiar with that particular treaty and happen to know that it is the Indians who did not fulfill its terms, not us.

JOHN GRASS. We did not *want* the cows you sent!

SENATOR LOGAN. You signed the treaty.

JOHN GRASS. We did not understand that we were to give up part of our reservation in exchange for these cows.

SENATOR DAWES. Why'd you think we were giving your twenty-five thousand cows?

JOHN GRASS. We were hungry. We thought it was for food.

SENATOR LOGAN. It wasn't explained that *only* if you gave us part of your reservation would you receive these cows?

JOHN GRASS. Yes. That was explained.

SENATOR LOGAN. And yet, you thought it was a gift.

JOHN GRASS. Yes.

SENATOR LOGAN. In other words, you thought you could have both the cows and the land?

JOHN GRASS. Yes.

SENATOR DAWES. Even though it was explained that you couldn't.

JOHN GRASS. Yes.

SENATOR MORGAN. This is quite hard to follow.

SENATOR LOGAN. Mister Grass, tell me, which would you prefer, cows or land?

JOHN GRASS. We prefer them both.

SENATOR LOGAN. Well, what if you can't have them both?

JOHN GRASS. We prefer the land.

SENATOR LOGAN. Well then, if you knew you had to give up some land to get these cows, why did you sign the treaty?

JOHN GRASS. The white men made our heads dizzy, and the signing was an accident.

SENATOR LOGAN. An accident?

JOHN GRASS. They talked in a threatening way, and whenever we asked questions, shouted and said we were stupid. Suddenly, the Indians around me rushed up and signed the paper. They were like men stumbling in the dark. I could not catch them.

SENATOR LOGAN. But you signed it, too.

[Long pause.]

SENATOR DAWES. Mister Grass. Tell me. Do the Indians really expect to keep all this land and yet do nothing toward supporting themselves?

JOHN GRASS. We do not have to support ourselves.

The Great Father promised to give us everything we ever needed; for that, we gave him the Black Hills.

SENATOR LOGAN. Mister Grass. Which do you prefer —to be self-sufficient or to be given things?

JOHN GRASS. We prefer them both.

SENATOR DAWES. Well, you can't *have* them both!

BUFFALO BILL. *Please!*

JOHN GRASS. I only know what we were promised.

SENATOR DAWES. That's *not* what you were promised!

JOHN GRASS. We believe it is.

BUFFALO BILL. *What's going on here?*

SENATOR MORGAN. Mister Grass. Wouldn't you and your people like to live like the white man?

JOHN GRASS. We are happy like the Indian!

SENATOR LOGAN. He means, you wouldn't like to see your people made *greater*, let's say?

JOHN GRASS. That is not possible! The Cheyenne and the Sioux are as great as people can be, already.

SENATOR MORGAN. Extraordinary, really.

BUFFALO BILL. Mister Grass. Surely . . . *surely* . . . your people would like to *improve their condition!*

JOHN GRASS. We would like what is owed us! If the white men want to give us more, that is fine also.

SENATOR LOGAN. Well, we'll see what we can do.

SENATOR MORGAN. Let's call the next. This is getting us nowhere.

JOHN GRASS. We would especially like the money the Great Father says he is holding for us!

SENATOR DAWES. I'm afraid that may be difficult, since, in the past, we've found that when an Indian's been given money, he's spent it all on liquor.

JOHN GRASS. When he's been given money, it's been so little there's been little else he could buy.

SENATOR MORGAN. Whatever, the Great Father does not like his Indian children getting drunk!

JOHN GRASS. Then tell the Great Father, who says he wishes us to live like white men, that when an Indian gets drunk, he is merely imitating the white men he's observed!

[*Laughter from the Indians. Logan raps his gavel.*]

SENATOR DAWES. STOP IT!

[*No effect. Logan raps more.*]

What in God's name do they think we're doing here? STOP IT!

[*Over the Indian's noise, the noise of a Wild West Show is heard; lights fade to black.*]

SCENE IX

[*Wild West Show music and crisscrossing multicolored spotlights. The rodeo ring rises from the stage, its lights glittering. Wild West Show banners descend above the ring.*]

VOICE. And now, ladies and gentlemen, let's hear it for Buffalo Bill's fantastic company of authentic western heroes . . . the fabulous ROUGHRIDERS OF THE WORLD!

[*Enter, on heroically artificial horses, the Roughriders— themselves heroically over-sized.*
    They gallop about the ring in majestic, intricate formation, whoopin' and shootin' as they do.]

With the ever-lovely . . . ANNIE OAKLEY!

[*Annie Oakley performs some startling trick shots as the others ride in circles about her.*]

And now, once again, here he is—the star of our show, the Ol' Scout himself; I mean the indestructible and ever-popular—

[*Drum roll.*]

—BUFFALO BILL!

[*Enter, on horseback, Buffalo Bill. He is in his Wild West Finery.*
    He tours the ring in triumph while his Roughriders ride after him, finally exiting to leave him in the center, alone.]

BUFFALO BILL. THANK YOU, THANK YOU! A *GREAT* show lined up tonight! With all-time favorite Johnny Baker, Texas Jack and his twelve-string guitar, the Dancin' Cavanaughs, Sheriff Brad and the Deadwood Mail Coach, Harry Philamee's Trained Prairie Dogs, the Abilene County Girls' School Trick Roping and Lasso Society, Pecos Pete and the—

VOICE. *Bill.*

BUFFALO BILL [*startled*]. Hm?

VOICE. Bring on the Indians.

BUFFALO BILL. What?

VOICE. The *Indians.*

BUFFALO BILL. Ah.

[*Buffalo Bill looks uneasily toward the wings as his company of Indians enters solemnly and in ceremonial warpaint; they carry the Sun Dance pole. At its summit is a buffalo skull.*]

And now, while my fabulous company of authentic . . . American Indians go through the ceremonial preparations of the Sun Dance, which they will re-create in all its death-defying goriness—let's give a warm welcome back to a courageous warrior, the magnificent Chief Joseph—

[*Some Cowboy Roustabouts set up an inverted tub; music for Chief Joseph's entrance.*]

—who will recite his . . . celebrated speech. CHIEF JOSEPH!

[*Enter Chief Joseph, old and hardly able to walk.*]

CHIEF JOSEPH. In the moon of the cherries blossoming, in the year of our surrender, I, Chief Joseph, and what remained of my people, the Nez Perces, were sent to a prison in Oklahoma, though General Howard had promised we could return to Idaho, where we'd always lived. In the moon of the leaves falling, still in the year of our surrender, William Cody came to see me. He was a nice man. With eyes that seemed . . . frightened; I . . . don't know why. He told me I was courageous and said he admired me. Then he explained all about his Wild West Show, in which the great Sitting Bull appeared, and said if I agreed to join, he would have me released from prison, and see that my people received food. I asked what I could do, as I was not a very good rider or marksman. And he looked away and said, "Just repeat, twice a day, three times on Sundays, what you said that afternoon when our army caught you at the Canadian border, where you'd been heading, and where you and your people would have all been safe." So I agreed. For the benefit of my people . . . And for the next year, twice a day, three times on Sundays, said this to those sitting around me in the dark, where I could not see them, a light shining so brightly in my eyes!

[*Pause.*
   He climbs up on the tub.
   Accompanied by exaggerated and inappropriate gestures.]

"Tell General Howard I know his heart. I am tired of fighting. Our chiefs have been killed. Looking Glass is dead. The old men are all dead. It is cold and we have no blankets. The children are freezing. My people, some of them, have fled to the hills and have no food or warm clothing. No one knows where they are—perhaps frozen. I want to have time to look for my children and see how many of them I can find. Maybe I shall find them among the dead. Hear me, my chiefs. I am tired. My heart is sick and sad. From where the sun now stands, I will fight no more forever. . . ."

[*He climbs down from the tub.*]

After which, the audience always applauded me.

[*Exit Chief Joseph. Pause.*]

BUFFALO BILL. The Sun Dance . . . was the one religious ceremony common to all the tribes of the plains. The Sioux, the Crow, the Blackfeet, the Kiowa, the Blood, the Cree, the Chippewa, the Arapaho, the Pawnee, the Cheyenne. It was *their* way of proving they were . . . real Indians.

[*Pause.*]

The bravest would take the ends of long leather thongs and hook them through their chest muscles, then, pull till they'd ripped them out. The greater the pain they could endure, the greater they felt the Spirits would favor them. Give them what they needed. . . . Grant them . . . salvation.

[*Pause.*]

Since the Government has officially outlawed this ritual, we will merely imitate it.

[*Pause.*]

And no one . . . will be hurt.

[*He steps back.*
   The dance begins. The Indians take the barbed ends of long leather thongs that dangle from the top of the Sun Dance pole and hook them through plainly visible chest harnesses. Then they pull back against the center and dance about it, flailing their arms and moaning as if in great pain.
   Suddenly John Grass enters. A Roustabout tries to stop him.
   The Indians are astonished to see this intruder; Buffalo Bill stunned.
   John Grass pulls the Indians out of their harnesses, rips open his shirt, and sticks the barbs through his chest muscles.
   He chants and dances. The other Indians, realizing what he's doing, blow on reed whistles, urge him on. Finally he collapses, blood pouring from his chest.

The Indians gather around him in awe.
Buffalo Bill walks slowly toward John Grass; stares down at him.
The Indians remove the Sun Dance pole and trappings.
Buffalo Bill crouches and cradles John Grass in his arms.
As lights fade to black.]

SCENE X

[Light up on White House Usher.]

USHER. The President is exercising in the gym, sir. This way.

[Enter Buffalo Bill.]

BUFFALO BILL. You're sure it's all right?
USHER. Yes, sir. He said to show you right in. Very pleased you're here.

[The Usher gestures for Cody to pass. When he does, the usher bows, turns, and leaves.
Buffalo Bill stops.
Gym noise heard.
Lights up on the Ol' Time President, dressed like Hickok and astride a mechanical horse pushed by another Usher. Near him sits an old Victrola; "On the Old Chisholm Trail" is playing.
The Ol' Time President spurs his horse onwards.
Nearby hangs a punching bag.
Buffalo Bill stares at the scene, stupefied; walks cautiously forward.]

BUFFALO BILL. Uh—
OL' TIME PRESIDENT. *Cody!* My ol' buddy! Welcome back! Long time no see!
BUFFALO BILL. Yes, sir. Long time . . . no see.
OL' TIME PRESIDENT. Wha'd'ya think o' this thing? Latest in athletic equipment. Just got it yesterday.
BUFFALO BILL. It's a . . . nice imitation.
OL' TIME PRESIDENT. More power.
USHER. Pardon?
OL' TIME PRESIDENT. *Little more power.*

[The Usher nods; the mechanical horse bounces faster.]

Good for the figure, this bronco riding. GIDDYAP! You orn'ry sonofabitch.

[He laughs; whips his horse furiously.]

BUFFALO BILL. Sir. What I've come t' talk t' you about is very important.
OL' TIME PRESIDENT. Can't hear ya. Speak up!
BUFFALO BILL *[pointing to the phonograph]*. May I turn this down?
OL' TIME PRESIDENT. Tell me. You think I look a little bit like Hickok?
BUFFALO BILL. Mr. President, would you *please stop this?*
OL' TIME PRESIDENT. What?
BUFFALO BILL. *STOP THIS!!!*
OL' TIME PRESIDENT. Whoa, Nellie.
USHER. Pardon?
OL' TIME PRESIDENT. WHOA, NELLIE!

[The usher stops the horse; shuts off the phonograph. Cold tone.]

All right. What is it?
BUFFALO BILL. Well sir, I'm here t' ask if you'd come with me t' Sitting Bull's reservation.
OL' TIME PRESIDENT. *Whose* reservation?
BUFFALO BILL. Sitting Bull's. He was in my Wild West Show for a time. And naturally, I feel a sort o' . . . obligation.

[Pause.]

Personal . . . obligation.
OL' TIME PRESIDENT. I see.
BUFFALO BILL. *I* figure you're just about the only one left now who can really help him. His people are in a desperate way.
OL' TIME PRESIDENT. Tell me; this—uh—Sitting Bull. Isn't he the one who wiped out Custer?
BUFFALO BILL. Uh, well, yes, he . . . is, but it was, ya know, nothin—uh—personal.

[Weak laugh.]

OL' TIME PRESIDENT. Can't help.
BUFFALO BILL. What?
OL' TIME PRESIDENT. I'm sorry, but I can't help.
BUFFALO BILL. *You don't understand the situation!*
OL' TIME PRESIDENT. I *don't?* All right, let's say I *want* to help. *What do I do for 'em?* Do I give 'em back their land? Do I resurrect the buffalo?
BUFFALO BILL. You can do *other* things!
OL' TIME PRESIDENT. No, Cody. *Other* people can do other things, *I* . . . must do magic. Well, I can't *do* magic for *them;* it's too late.
BUFFALO BILL. I promised Sitting Bull you'd come.

OL' TIME PRESIDENT. Then you're a fool.

BUFFALO BILL. They're going to *die*.

[*Long pause.*]

OL' TIME PRESIDENT. Tell ya what. 'Cause I'm so *grateful* to you . . . For your Wild West Show. For what it's *done*. For this country's *pride*, its *glory*.

[*Pause.*]

I'll do you a favor; I'll send a committee in my place.

BUFFALO BILL. A committee *won't be able to help!*

OL' TIME PRESIDENT. Oh, I think the gesture will mean something.

BUFFALO BILL. *To WHOM?*

[*Silence.*]

OL' TIME PRESIDENT. Being a great President, Cody, is like being a great eagle. A great . . . *hunted* eagle. I mean, you've got to know . . . *when t' stay put.*

[*He smiles.*]

On your way out, Bill, tell the guards, no more visitors today, hm?

[*He nods to the Usher, who starts to rock him again.
    As Buffalo Bill slowly leaves.
    Music back up.
    Lights fade to black.*]

SCENE XI

[*Lights up on reservation, as when last seen.
    The Indians are laughing; the Senators, rapping for silence.*]

SENATOR DAWES. *What in God's name do they think we're doing here?*

BUFFALO BILL [*to Sitting Bull*]. Please! You must tell them to stop this *noise!*

SITTING BULL. You told us you would bring the Great Father.

BUFFALO BILL. I told you! He couldn't come! It's not my fault! Besides, these men are the Great Father's representatives! Talking to them is like talking to him!

SITTING BULL. If the Great Father wants us to believe he is wise, why does he send us men who are *stupid?*

BUFFALO BILL. They're *not* stupid! They just don't see things they way *you* do!

SITTING BULL. Yes. Because they are stupid.

BUFFALO BILL. They're *not stupid!*

SITTING BULL. Then they must be blind. It is the only other explanation.

BUFFALO BILL. All right. Tell me. Do *you* understand them?

SITTING BULL. Why should I want to understand men who are stupid?

BUFFALO BILL. Because if you *don't*, your people will *starve to death.*

[*Long pause.*]

All right . . . Now. Let me try to explain some . . . *basics.*

[*To the Senators.*]

Well, as you've just seen, the Indian can be hard t' figure. What's one thing t' us is another t' him. For example, farmin'. Now the *real* problem here is not poor soil. The real problem's plowin'. Ya see, the Indian believes the earth is sacred and sees plowin' as a sacrilegious act. Well, if ya can't get 'em t' plow, how can ya teach 'em farmin'? Impossible. Fertile land's another problem. There just ain't much of it, an' what there is, the Indians prefer to use for pony racin'. Naturally, it's been explained to 'em how people can race ponies anywhere, but they *prefer* the fertile land. They say, if their ancestors raced ponies there, that's where *they* must race. . . . Another difficult problem is land itself. The majority of 'em, ya see, don't understand how land can be owned, since they believe the land was made by the Great Spirits for the benefit of everyone. So, when we do buy land from 'em, they think it's just some kind o' temporary loan, an' figure we're kind o' foolish fer payin' good money for it, much as someone 'ud seem downright foolish t' us who paid money fer the sky, say, or the ocean. Which . . . causes problems.

[*Pause.*]

Well, what I'm gettin' at is *this*: if *their* way o' seein' is hard fer *us* t' follow, ours is just as hard fer *them*. . . . There's an Old Indian legend that when the first white man arrived, he asked some Indians for enough land t' put his blanket down onto fer the night. So they said yes. An' next thing they knew, he'd unraveled this blanket till it was one long piece o' thread. Then he laid out the thread, an' when he was done, he'd roped off a couple o' square miles. Well, the Indian finds that sort o' behavior hard t' understand. That's all I have t' say. Maybe, if you think about it, some good'll finally come from all this. I dunno.

SENATOR MORGAN. Thank you. We *shall* think about it. And hope the Indians think about it, too. And cause no more disturbances like the one just now. . . . Ask Sitting Bull if he has anything to say.

BUFFALO BILL. Sitting Bull.

SITTING BULL. Of course I will speak if they desire me to. I suppose it is only such men as they desire who may say anything.

SENATOR MORGAN. Anyone here may speak. If you have something to say, we will listen. Otherwise, sit down.

SITTING BULL. Tell me, do you know who I am, that you talk as you do?

BUFFALO BILL. SITTING BULL, PLEASE!

[*Long pause.*]

SITTING BULL. I wish to say that I fear I spoke hastily just now. In calling you . . . stupid. For my friend William Cody tells me you are here with good intentions. So I ask forgiveness for my unthinking words, which might have caused you to wreak vengeance on my people for what was not their doing, but *mine, alone.*

SENATOR LOGAN. We are pleased you speak so . . . sensibly. You are . . . forgiven.

SITTING BULL. I shall tell you, then, what I want you to say to the Great Father for me. And I shall tell you everything that is in my heart. For I know the Great Spirits are looking down on me today and want me to tell you everything that is in my heart. For you are the only people now who can help us.

[*Pause.*]

My children . . . are dying. They have no warm clothes, and their food is gone. The old way is gone. No longer can they follow the buffalo and live where they wish. I have prayed to the Great Spirits to send us back the buffalo, but I have not yet seen any buffalo returning. So I know the old way is gone. I think . . . my children must learn a *new* way if they are to live. Therefore, tell the Great Father

that if he wishes us to live like white men, we will do so.

[*Stunned reaction from his Indians. He silences them with a wave of his hand.*]

For I know that if that pleases him, we will benefit. I am looking always to the benefit of my children, and so, want only to please the Great Father. . . . Therefore, tell him for me that I have never yet seen a white man starving, so he should send us food so we can live like the white man, as he wants. Tell him, also, we'd like some healthy cattle to butcher—I wish to kill three hundred head at a time. For that is the way the white man lives, and we want to please the Great Father and live the same way. Also, ask him to send us each six teams of mules, because that is the way the white men make a living, and I want my children to make as good a living. I ask for these things only because I was advised to follow your ways. I do not ask for anything that is not needed. Therefore, tell him to send to each person here a horse and buggy. And four yokes of oxen and a wagon to haul wood in, since I have never yet seen a white man dragging wood by hand. Also, hogs, male and female, and male and female sheep for my children to raise from. If I leave anything out in the way of animals that the white men have, it is a mistake, for I want every one of them! For we are great Indians, and therefore should be no less great as white men. . . . Furthermore, tell him to send us warm clothing. And glass for the windows. And toilets. And clean water. And beds, and blankets, and pillows. And fur coats, and gloves. And hats. And *pretty silk ties.* As you see, I do not ask for anything that is not needed. For the Great Father has advised us to live like white men, so clearly, this is how we should live. For it is your doing that we are here on this reservation, and it is not right for us to live in poverty. And be treated like beasts. . . . That is all I have to say.

SENATOR LOGAN. I want to say something to that man before he sits down, and I want all the Indians to listen very carefully to what I'm going to tell him. . . . Sitting Bull, this committee invited you to come here for a friendly talk. When you talked, however, you insulted them. I understand this is not the first time you have been guilty of such an offense.

SITTING BULL. Do you know who I am that you talk the way you do?

SENATOR LOGAN. I know you are Sitting Bull.

SITTING BULL. Do you really not recognize me? Do you really not know who I am?

SENATOR LOGAN. *I said, I know you are Sitting Bull*!

SITTING BULL. You know I am Sitting Bull. But do you know what *position* I hold?

SENATOR DAWES. We do not recognize any difference between you and other Indians.

SITTING BULL. Then I will tell you the difference. So you will never ever make this mistake again. I am here by the will of the Great Spirits, and by their will I am a chief. My heart is red and sweet, and I know it is sweet, for whatever I pass near tries to touch me with its tongue, as the bear tastes honey and the green leaves lick the sky. If the Great Spirits have chosen anyone to be leader of their country, know that it is not the Great Father; *it is myself*.

SENATOR DAWES. WHO IS THIS CREATURE?

SITTING BULL. I will show you.

[*He raises his hand. The Indians turn and start to leave.*]

SENATOR LOGAN. Just a minute, Sitting Bull!

[*Sitting Bull stops.*]

Let's get something straight. You said to this committee that you were chief of all the people of this country and that you were appointed chief by the Great Spirits. Well, I want to say that you were *not* appointed by the Great Spirits. Appointments are not made that way. Furthermore, I want to say that you are arrogant and stupidly proud, for you are not a great chief of this country or any other; that you have no following, no power, no control, and no right to any control

SITTING BULL. I wish to say a word about my not being a chief, having no authority, being proud—

SENATOR LOGAN. You are on an Indian reservation merely at the sufferance of the Government. You are fed by the Government, clothed by the Government, your children are educated by the Government, and all you have and are today is because of the Government. I merely say these things to notify you that you cannot insult the people of the United States of America or its committees. And I want to say to the rest of you that you must learn that you are the equals of other men and must not let this one man lead you astray. You must stand up to him and not permit him to insult people who have come all this way just to help you. . . . That is all I have to say.

SITTING BULL. I wish to say a word about my not being a chief, having no authority, being proud, and considering myself a great man in general.

SENATOR LOGAN. We do not care to talk with you any more today.

SENATOR DAWES. Next Indian.

SITTING BULL. I said, I wish to speak about my having no authority, being not a chief, and—

SENATOR LOGAN. I said, we're heard enough of you today!

[*Sitting Bull raises his hand; the Indians leave. Sitting Bull stares at Cody.*]

SITTING BULL. If a man is the chief of a great people, and has lived only for those people, and has done many great things for them, *of course he should be proud*!

[*He exits. Lights fade to black.*]

SCENE XII

[*Guitar heard: "Chisholm Trail."*
Lights up on saloon. Most of it is in shadows.
Only a poker table is well lit.
A bar is in the distance.
Swinging doors.
Various cowboys slouch about.]

JESSE JAMES [*sings*].
Walkin' down the street in ol' Dodge City,
Wherever I look things look pretty shitty.
   Coma ti yi youpy, youpy yea, youpy yea,
   Coma ti yi youpy, youpy yea.
An' the very worst thing that I can see,
Is a dead man walkin' straight toward me.
   Coma ti yi youpy, youpy yea, youpy yea,
   Coma ti yi youpy, youpy yea.
This dead man clearly ain't feelin' well,
If you ask me I think he's just found hell.
   Coma ti yi youpy, youpy yea, youpy yea,
   Coma ti yi youpy you—

[*Enter Buffalo Bill in an overcoat flecked with snow. Gloves. A warm scarf.*]

BUFFALO BILL. Where's Hickok? I'm told Hickok's here. . . . *Where's Hickok*?

BILLY THE KID. Hey, uh . . . stranger.

[*He chuckles.*
Before he can draw, Buffalo Bill gets the drop on him.]

BUFFALO BILL. Who're you?
PONCHO. He . . . is the original . . . Billy the Kid.

[*Jesse James makes a move and Buffalo Bill draws his other gun; gets the drop on him as well.*]

And *he* is the original Jesse James. The original Doc Holliday is, I'm afraid, out to lunch.

[*The Cowboys move to encircle Buffalo Bill.*]

Who're *you*?
BUFFALO BILL. Buffalo Bill.
PONCHO. Really?

[*Poncho laughs. Enter Hickok.*]

HICKOK:. Cody! My ol' buddy!

[*They embrace.*]

Oh, great balls o' fire! What a surprise! Why jus' this mornin' I was . . . was . . . [*Pause.*] *picturin'* you.
BUFFALO BILL. You were?
HICKOK. So how ya been? C'mon. Tell me.
BUFFALO BILL. Oh, I been . . . fine.
HICKOK. Great!
BUFFALO BILL. An' you?
HICKOK. Never better. *Never better!*
BUFFALO BILL. Mus' say, you've sure got some . . . famous . . . people here.

[*Slight laugh.*]

HICKOK. Well, ya know, it's . . . that kind o' place.

[*He laughs, too; slaps Cody on the back. He leads him to a table.*]

So! . . . Whatcha doin' here? Great honor. *Great honor!*
BUFFALO BILL. I hafta . . . *talk* . . . t' you.
HICKOK. Sure thing.

[*He waves the Cowboys away; they sit at the table in privacy.*]

BUFFALO BILL. I've just come from Sitting Bull's reservation.
HICKOK. Oh?

[*Slight laugh.*]

That reservation's a far piece from here.
BUFFALO BILL. I need your help! Sitting Bull is . . .

[*Pause.*]

HICKOK. What?

[*Long silence.*]

BUFFALO BILL. I'm scared . . . I dunno what's happenin' anymore . . . Things have gotten . . . *beyond* me.

[*He takes a drink.*]

I see them *everywhere.*

[*Weak smile; almost a laugh.*
Music.
Indians appear in the shadows beyond the saloon.]

In the grass. The rocks. The branches of dead trees.

[*Pause.*]

Took a drink from a river yesterday an' they were even there, beneath the water, their hands reachin' up, I dunno whether beggin', or t' . . . drag me under.

[*Pause.*]

I wiped out their food, ya see . . . Didn't *mean* to, o' course.

[*He laughs to himself.*]

I mean IT WASN'T MY FAULT! The railroad men needed food. They *hired* me t' *find* 'em food! Well. How was *I* t'know the goddam buffalo reproduced so slowly? *How was I to know that?* NO ONE KNEW THAT!

[*Pause.*
The Indians slowly disappear.]

Now, Sitting Bull is . . .

[*Long pause.*]

HICKOK. *What?*
BUFFALO BILL. The . . . hearing was a shambles. I brought these Senators, you see. To Sitting Bull's reservation. It . . . was a shambles. [*Pause.*] So we left. He . . . *insulted* them. [*Pause.*] Then I saw the letter.

[*Silence.*]

HICKOK. What letter?
BUFFALO BILL. The letter to McLaughlin. The letter ordering . . . it to be . . . done.

[*Pause.*]

So I rode back. Rode all night. Figuring, maybe . . . if I can just *warn* him . . . But the reservation soldiers stopped me and . . . made me . . . drink with them. And by the time I got there, he . . . was dead. The greatest Indian who'd ever lived. Shot. By order of the Government. Shot with a Gatling gun.

[*Pause.*]

While the . . . wonderful, gray horse I'd given him for . . . appearing in my show danced his repertory of tricks in the background. Since a gunshot was his cue to perform.

[*He laughs.*
Stops.
Long silence.]

HICKOK. Well now. In exactly what way did you imagine *I* could . . . *help* this . . . situation?
BUFFALO BILL. You have what I *need* . . . now.
HICKOK [*smiling slightly*]. Oh?
BUFFALO BILL. I'm *scared*, you see.

[*Pause.*]

Scared . . . not . . . so much of *dyin'*, but . . . dyin' *wrong.*

[*Slight laugh.*]

Dyin' . . . in the center of my arena with . . . makeup on.

[*Long pause.*]

Then I thought of you. . . . Remembered that night in the White House. Remembered thinking, "My God! Look at Hickok. Hickok *knows just who he is!*"

[*Pause.*]

"Hickok has the answer," I said . . . Hickok knows who he *is.*

[*Pause.*]

I must see Hickok again.

[*Long silence.*]

HICKOK. Well, I'm glad you came. Yes. Glad . . . to be able to . . . help.

[*Pause.*]

Funny. That night, in the White House, I remember thinking: "My God, it's *Cody* who's got the answer!"
BUFFALO BILL. . . . What?
HICKOK. Poncho!
PONCHO. *Si, señor.*
HICKOK. Bring in our . . . um . . .
PONCHO. Ah! *Si, señor! Ahorita.*

[*Exit Poncho.*]

HICKOK. Naturally, at first, you may be a bit startled. Put off. Not . . . exactly . . . what you *had in mind.* Yet! I'm sure that once you *think* about it, you'll agree *it's the only way.* Just like Jesse has. Billy. Doc Holliday. The boys.
BUFFALO BILL. *What are you talkin' about?*
HICKOK. Why, takin' what you were and raisin' it to a . . . higher level.

[*He laughs.*]

Naturally, for my services, I get a small fee. Percentage. You get 50 percent right off the top. Of course, if at any time you aren't happy, you can leave. Take your business elsewhere. That's written in. Keeps us on our toes. Mind you, this . . . *enterprise* . . . is still in its infancy. The *potential*, though . . . is unlimited. For example, think of this. The *great national good* . . . that could come from this: some of you, let's say, would concentrate strictly on theatrics.

MEANWHILE! *Others* of you would concentrate on purely humanitarian affairs. Save . . . well, not Sitting Bull, but . . . some Indian down in Florida. Another up in Michigan. Perhaps expand into Canada. Mexico. Central America. SOUTH AMERICA! My God, there must be literally *millions* of people who could benefit by your presence! Your . . *simultaneous presence!*

PONCHO. Here they are, *señor!*

[*Enter a group of men dressed as Buffalo Bill. Their faces are covered by masks of his face. They wear his florid buckskin clothes—if anything, even more elaborately designed.*]

HICKOK. Naturally, we've still got a few wrinkles to iron out. Color of hair. Color of eyes. That sort of thing. But with *you* here, exercising artistic control, why, we could go on like this *forever!*

[*Buffalo Bill, stunned by the sight, fires his guns at the duplicate Codys. They fall and immediately rise again.*
   They slowly surround him.
   He screams as he shoots.
   They disappear.
   The saloon fades to black.
   Buffalo Bill alone on stage.]

BUFFALO BILL. AND NOW TO CLOSE! AND *NOW* TO CLOSE!
VOICE. Not *yet.*

[*Pause.*]

They also killed the rest of his tribe.

[*Music.*
   Indians enter mournfully. They carry a large white sheet.
   Sound of wind.
   Buffalo Bill watches, then moves slowly away; exits.]

SCENE XIII

[*The Indians cover the center area with the huge white sheet, then lie down upon it in piles.*
   Enter Colonel Forsyth, a Lieutenant, and two reporters, their coat collars turned up for the wind. Cody is with them; he carries a satchel.]

FIRST REPORTER. Fine time of year you men picked for this thing.
COLONEL FORSYTH. They're heathens; they don't celebrate Christmas.

FIRST REPORTER. I don't mean the date, I mean the weather.
COLONEL. Uncomfortable?
FIRST REPORTED. Aren't you?
COLONEL. One gets used to it.
SECOND REPORTER. Colonel, I gather we lost twenty-nine men, thirty-three wounded. How many Indians were killed?
COLONEL. We wiped them out.
SECOND REPORTER. Yes, I know. But how many *is* that?
COLONEL. We haven't counted.
LIEUTENANT. The snow has made it difficult. It started falling right after the battle. The bodies were covered almost at once. By night they were frozen.
COLONEL. We more than made up for Custer, though, I can tell you that.
SECOND REPORTER. But Custer was killed fifteen years ago!
COLONEL. So what?
LIEUTENANT. If there are no more questions, we'll take you to—
FIRST REPORTER. I have one! Colonel Forsyth, some people are referring to your victory yesterday as a massacre. How do you feel about that?
COLONEL. One can always find someone who'll call an overwhelming victory a massacre. I suppose they'd prefer it if we'd let more of our own boys get shot!
FIRST REPORTER. Then you don't think the step you took was harsh?
COLONEL. Of course it was harsh. And I don't like it any more than you. But had we shirked our responsibility, skirmishes would have gone on for years, costing our country millions, as well as untold lives. Of course innocent people have been killed. In war they always are. And of course our hearts go out to the innocent victims of this. But war is not a game. It's tough. And demands tough decisions. In the long run I believe what happened here at this reservation yesterday will be justified.
FIRST REPORTER. Are you implying that the Indian Wars are finally over?
COLONEL. Yes, I believe they're finally over. This ludicrous buffalo religion of Sitting Bull's people was their last straw.
SECOND REPORTER. And now?
COLONEL. The difficult job of rehabilitating begins. But that's more up General Howard's line.
LIEUTENANT. Why don't we go and talk with him? He's in the temporary barracks.
COLONEL. He can tell you about our future plans.

[*They start to leave.*]

BUFFALO BILL. You said you'd—

LIEUTENANT. Ah, yes, it's that one.

[*He points to a body.*]

BUFFALO BILL. Thank you.

[*He stays. The others leave; he stares at the grave. Sitting Bull has entered, unnoticed. Buffalo Bill takes a sprig of pine from the satchel and is about to put it on the grave.*]

SITTING BULL. Wrong grave. I'm over here . . . As you see, the dead can be buried, but not so easily gotten rid of.

BUFFALO BILL. Why didn't you listen to me? I *warned* you what would happen! Why didn't you *listen?*

[*Long silence.*]

SITTING BULL. We had land. . . . You wanted it; you took it. That . . . I understand perfectly. What I cannot understand . . . is why you did all this, *and at the same time* . . . professed your love.

[*Pause.*]

BUFFALO BILL. Well . . . well, what . . . about *your* mistakes? *Hm?* For, for example: you were very unrealistic . . . about things. For . . . example: did you *really* believe the buffalo would return? *Magically* return?

SITTING BULL. It seemed no less likely than Christ's returning, and a great deal more useful. Though when I think of their reception here, I can't see why either would really want to come back.

BUFFALO BILL. Oh, God. Imagine. For awhile, I actually thought my Wild West Show would *help.* I could give you money. Food. Clothing. And also make people *understand* things . . . better.

[*He laughs to himself.*]

That was my reasoning. Or, anyway, *part. . .*

[*Pause.*]

of my reasoning.

SITTING BULL [*slight smile*]. Your show was very popular.

[*Pause.*]

BUFFALO BILL. We had . . . *fun,* though, you and I.

[*Pause.*]

Didn't we?

SITTING BULL. Oh, yes. And that's the terrible thing. We had all surrendered. We were on reservations. We could not fight, or hunt. We could do nothing. Then you came and allowed us to imitate our glory. . . . It was humiliating! For sometimes, we could almost imagine it was *real.*

BUFFALO BILL. Guess it wasn't so authentic, was it?

[*Laughs slightly to himself.*]

SITTING BULL. How could it have been? You'd have killed all your performers in one afternoon.

[*Pause.*]

BUFFALO BILL. You know what worried me most? . . . The fear that I might die, in the middle of the arena, with all my . . . makeup on. *That* . . . is what . . . worried me most.

SITTING BULL. What worried *me* most . . . was something I'd said the year before. Without thinking.

BUFFALO BILL [*softly*]. What?

SITTING BULL. I'd agreed to go onto the reservation. I was standing in front of my tribe, the soldiers leading us into the fort. And as we walked, I turned to my son, who was beside me. "Now," I said, "you will never know what it is to be an Indian, for you will never again have a gun or pony. . . ." Only later did I *realize* what I'd said. These things, the gun and the pony—they came with you. And then I thought, ah, how terrible it would be if we finally owe to the white man not only our destruction, but also our glory. . . . Farewell, Cody. You were my friend. And, indeed, you still are. . . . I never killed you . . . because I *knew it would not matter.*

[*He starts to leave.*]

BUFFALO BILL. If only I could have saved *your* life!

[*Sitting Bull stops and stares at him coldly; turns and leaves. Long pause.*]

BUFFALO BILL. Well! This is it!

[*He forces a weak laugh.*]

Naturally, I've been thinking 'bout this moment for quite some time now. As any performer would.

VOICE. And now to close!

BUFFALO BILL. NOT YET! . . . I would . . . first . . . like to . . . say a few words in defense of my country's Indian policy, which seems, in certain circles, to be meeting with considerable disapproval.

[*He smiles weakly, clears his throat, reaches into his pocket, draws out some notes, and puts on a pair of eyeglasses.*]

The—uh—State of Georgia, anxious to solidify its boundaries and acquire certain valuable mineral rights, hitherto held accidentally by the Cherokee Indians, and anxious, furthermore, to end the seemingly inevitable hostilities between its residents and these Indians on the question of land ownership, initiated, last year, the forced removal of the Cherokee nation, resettling them in a lovely and relatively unsettled area west of the Mississippi, known as the Mojave Desert. Given proper irrigation, this spacious place should soon be blooming. Reports that the Cherokees were unhappy at their removal are decidedly untrue. And though many, naturally, died while marching from Georgia to the Mojave Desert, the ones who did, I'm told, were rather ill already, and nothing short of medication could have saved them. Indeed, in all ways, our vast country is speedily being opened for settlement. The shipment of smallpox-infested blankets, sent by the Red Cross to the Mandan Indians, has, I'm please to say, worked wonders, and the Mandans are no more. Also, the Government policy of exterminating the buffalo, a policy with which I myself was intimately connected, has practically reached fruition. Almost no buffalo are now left, and soon the Indians will be hungry enough to begin farming in earnest, a step we believe necessary if they are ever to leave their barbaric ways and enter civilization. Indeed, it is for this very reason that we have begun giving rifles to the Indians as part of each treaty with them, for without armaments they could not hope to wage war with us, and the process of civilizing them would be seriously hampered in every way. Another aspect of our benevolent attitude toward these savages is shown by the Government's policy of having its official interpreters translate everything incorrectly when interpreting for the Indians, thereby angering the Indians and forcing them to learn English for themselves. Which, of course, is the first step in civilizing people. I'm reminded here of a story told me by a munitions manufacturer. It seems, by *accident*, he sent a shipment of blank bullets to the Kickapoo Indians, and . . .

[*He looks around.*]

Well, I won't tell it. It's too involved. I would just like to say that I am sick and tired of these sentimental humanitarians who take no account of the difficulties under which this Government has labored in its efforts to deal fairly with the Indian, nor of the countless lives we have lost and atrocities endured at their savage hands. I quote General Sheridan:—

[*The Indians have begun to rise from their graves; for a while they stand in silence behind Buffalo Bill, where they are joined, at intervals, by the rest of the Indian company.*]

—"I do not know how far these so-called humanitarians should be excused on account of their political ignorance; but surely it is the only excuse that can give a shadow of justification for their aiding and abetting such horrid crimes as the Indians have perpetrated on our people."

BUFFALO BILL.
The excuse that the Indian way of life is vastly different from ours, and that what seem like atrocities to us do not to them, does not hold water, I'm afraid! For the truth is, the Indian never had any real title to the soil of this country. We had that title. By *right of discovery!* And all the Indians were, were the *temporary occupants* of the land. They *had* to be vanquished by us! It was, in fact, our *moral obligation!*

For the earth was given to mankind to support the greatest number of which it is capable; and no tribe or people have a *right* to withhold from the wants of others! For example—

SITTING BULL.
[*very softly.*].
I am Sitting Bull—

[*Almost inaudible.*]
—and I am—*dying!*

BLACK HAWK.
Black Hawk *is dying.*

TECUMSEH.
Tecumseh *is dying.*

CRAZY HORSE.
Crazy Horse . . . is dying.

RED CLOUD.
Red Cloud *is dying.*

SPOTTED TAIL.
Spotted Tail . . . is dying again.

—in the case of Lone Wolf versus Hitchcock, 1902, the Supreme Court of the United States ruled that the power exists to abrogate the provisions of *any* Indian treaty if the *interests of the country demand!*

Here's another one: in the case of the Seneca Indians versus the Pennsylvania Power Authority, the courts ruled that the Seneca Treaty was invalid since perpetuity was legally a vague phrase. *Vague phrase!* Yes. Ah. Here's one, even better. In the—

No. Wait. Got it. The one I've been looking for. In the case of Sitting Bull versus Buffalo Bill, the Supreme Court ruled that the *inadvertent* slaughter of . . . buffalo by . . . I'm sorry, I'm . . . reminded here of an amusing story told me by General Custer. You remember him—one o' the great dumbass . . .

[*Pause.*]

BUFFALO BILL. Think I'd better close. I . . . just want to say that anyone who thinks we have done something wrong is *wrong!* And that I have here, in this bag, some—

[*He goes and picks up his satchel; he looks up and sees the Indians staring at him; he turns quickly away.*]

—Indian trinkets. Some . . . examples of their excellent workmanship. Moccasins. Beads. Feathered headdresses for your children.

[*He has begun to unpack these trinkets and place them, for display, on a small camp stool he has set across the front edge of the center ring.*]

SATANTA.
Satanta *is dying*.

KIOKUK.
Kiokuk *is dying*.

GERONIMO.
Geronimo . . . *is dying!*

OLD TAZA
Old Taza *is dying!*

JOHN GRASS.
John Grass is dying.

[*Long pause.*]

[*The Indians begin a soft and mournful moaning.*]

Pretty picture postcards. Tiny Navajo dolls. The money from the sale of these few trifling trinkets will go to help them help themselves. Encourage them a bit. You know, *raise their spirits* . . . Ah! Wait. No, sorry, that's a—uh—buffalo skin.

[*He shoves it back in the satchel.*]

Yes. Here it is! Look, just look . . . at this handsome replica of an . . . Indian. Made of genuine wood.

[*He puts the carved head of an Indian on the camp stool so that it overlooks all the other trinkets.*
    The lights now slowly begin to fade on him; he sits by the trinkets, trembling.]

CHIEF JOSEPH. Tell General Howard I know his heart. I am tired of fighting. Our chiefs have been killed. Looking Glass is dead. The old men are all dead. It is cold and we have no blankets. The children are freezing. My people, some of them, have fled to the hills and have no food or warm clothing. No one knows where they are—perhaps frozen. I want to have time to look for my children and see how many of them I can find. Maybe I shall find them among the dead.

[*Almost all the lights are now gone; Chief Joseph can hardly be seen; Buffalo Bill is but a shadow. Only the trinkets are clear in a pinspot of light, and that light, too, is fading.*]

Hear me, my chiefs, I am tired. My heart is sick and sad! From where the sun now stands, I will fight no more, forever.

[*And then, very slowly, even the light on the trinkets fades. And the stage is completely dark.*
    Then, suddenly, all lights blazing!
    Rodeo ring up.
    Rodeo music.
    Enter, on horseback, the Roughriders of the World. They tour the ring triumphantly, then form a line to greet Buffalo Bill, who enters on his white stallion. He tours the ring, a glassy smile on his face.
    The Roughriders exit.
    Buffalo Bill alone, on his horse. He waves his big Stetson to the unseen crowd.
    Then, Indians appear from the shadows outside the ring; they approach him slowly.
    Lights fade to black.
    Pause.
    Lights return to the way they were at the top of the show, when the audience was entering.
    The three glass cases are back in place.
    No curtain.]

ESSAY: AN APPROACH TO THE PLAY

Indians is a powerfully metadramatic play. It begins without a curtain. When the house lights dim, three glass cases are spotlit from above. The audience is reminded that it is watching an exhibit on a stage, its quality of pretense underscored. After these same lights have located Buffalo Bill in the apparent but illusory distance, he comes forward so that the audience can see that he is "dressed as in the museum case." The point is visually explicit: Buffalo Bill himself is an exhibit, an illusion in a staged museum, riding "a glorious white artificial stallion." Everything is designed to undercut whatever illusion of reality the stage may otherwise seem to achieve. A fence rises to enclose horse and rider, so that they act within an enclosure within a stage, intensifying the sense of artificiality. When "the horse shies" at the fence, the action seems dislocated: real horses shy, but artificial ones do not know surprise or fear. The whole opening sequence, before the first word is uttered, emphasizes to the audience that they are watching something constructed, something that may pretend to be real but whose "reality" will depend entirely on having the spectators accept the illusion.

When a play calls an audience's attention to its artificial qualities, it reminds them that someone made it, that a playwright is pulling the strings. With no pretense to "reality," it can take liberties with "reality"—can dramatize dreams, fantasies, and memories with just as much illusional power as it invests in "reality" itself.

During the play we learn not only that the great Buffalo Bill feels guilt but also that there is no "reality" to Buffalo Bill. There may be a William Cody, but "Buffalo Bill" is the invention of the dime novelist and scriptwriter Ned Buntline, an identity created by someone from New York City to satisfy (and justify) a nation fascinated with, and perhaps anxious over, its own power and energy as it has expanded across the continent. Buffalo Bill signifies and creates Cody's reputation as a buffalo killer and as the cause of the demise of the Indian tribes, both qualities admired by white society, as the reactions of the grand duke and the president show. The stage identity "Buffalo Bill" demonstrates the superiority of the white man over nature and native.

This is why the Grand Duke of Russia tries to be like him, "riding" a litter "carved like a horse" and shooting an Indian whom he believes to be a Comanche. It is also why, in Scene 7, the president, too, tries to imitate Buffalo Bill from the safety of his gym but will not listen to the real man's plea for the Indian. The image of the heroic white male is crucial to their version of white civilization, as is the necessity of their being blind to the fact that it is an image, not "reality." This blindness is illustrated by both the grand duke and the president, neither of whom seems to feel the falseness of their impersonation. In another context such blindness might be funny, but here, where it is the symptom as well as the basis of power, in the first case a real Indian is wrongly identified as a Comanche and killed, and in the second a committee of self-righteous senators is allowed to cut off the Indians' only avenue of appeal. Blind belief in "Buffalo Bill" leads straight to tragedy.

William Cody is caught in a classic American dilemma: he must choose whether to "be" an image that will make him a success (and therefore a hero) or a sympathetic man who gives up his image to help his friends. There are times when he vacillates and when he is dizzy and perhaps has headaches. Certainly he knows better. But at last he impersonates the image of himself which the scriptwriter has created. He reenacts all the most shameful mistakes of his life, but as if they were heroic, and he corrupts enemy and friend alike into joining him in their own self-impersonations in his "Wild West." Even when Geronimo and Sitting Bull express their enmity and opposition, these differences are domesticated by being contained within a stage. Because of this dislocation, they diminish whatever they say and perhaps humiliate themselves. They, too, become exhibits in a museum, just as the "real" Indians are to the blind senators. Geronimo, in particular, is presented as a wild beast in a parody of the standard circus presentation of big cats. He roars out his threats of sexual mutilation in defiance of the values of civilization, but Buffalo Bill, with the fearlessness of the lion tamer, walks into the cage, turns his back, and casually walks away in a bravado assertion of power. Geronimo gets to present himself as a violent but controllable threat who deserves the cage in which he is placed. He becomes a symbolic justification for the reservation system.

Cody, no less than the Indians, is self-diminished, with the difference that he is on the winning side, the side with power. He is also unlike them in buying into the myth of the white male hero, Buffalo Bill, even though he knows better. His crises of conscience show that he knows better, but gradually, in the interest of wearing his image as hero more comfortably, he stills his conscience and, in the final scene, becomes the voice of his civilization. It is his ultimate self-humiliation: at the end he fits the ideology implied by "Buffalo Bill" perfectly.

Indians is not only an indictment and a satire of those who blind themselves in the interests of success and country. Its subject is larger than this because of its high price: not just the death toll exacted of those from other societies, but the moral blindness of those who pursue an image which justifies massacre. The comfort which William Cody seeks in the image of Buffalo Bill leads to acts which disturb that comfort by causing guilt: the effect and the cause are one. In the end, the great hero Buffalo Bill willfully makes himself into a museum piece. There is, then, no "hero" in this play with whom we can sympathize, nor is there any suspense, since we all know the historical ending: the "story" is told less to unfold a tale than to present an interpretation of a story we already know. If an audience becomes engrossed in this play, it is because of its savage humor, because of its theatrical effects, and because it presents an important and difficult issue. Distanced from the main character and the story, discomforted by the unresolved moral contradictions of the characters, the audience is left having to think.

Caryl Churchill

VINEGAR TOM

About the Author   Caryl Churchill (1938–) was born in London and educated in Montreal and Oxford. She has been writing plays for the past twenty years, increasingly on radical and feminist topics, and has come to be perceived as one of England's most important and influential playwrights. *Vinegar Tom* was written in 1976 in collaboration with an all-woman theater company called Monstrous Regiment (a name taken from the title of an essay warning against females by the sixteenth-century Scots churchman John Knox, *First Blast of the Trumpet against the Monstrous Regiment of Women*).

About the Play   Although set in seventeenth-century Europe during a period of witch hunting, this play is not really about witches, but about women: there are no witches in the play—only women accused of witchcraft. The treatment of the witches may, in this view, seem merely an exaggerated manifestation of what has often passed for "normal" treatment of women in western civilization. This point is underscored by the songs which are sung between several of the scenes. In the original production, all roles were played by women, and cast members who were not currently on stage would remove their costumes and sing the songs in modern dress. Like an ancient Greek chorus, therefore, these songs comment upon or react to the action; however, the chorus here is made up not of people contemporary with the characters but of people contemporary with us in the audience, implying that the seventeenth-century actions being played out are also applicable to our own world.

Although many of the claims about the power of witches presented here will seem bizarre to modern readers, these claims are not invented but are the result of Churchill's historical research. The claims can all be found in published works well known in earlier centuries, the best known of which was the *Malleus Maleficarum*, a Latin work whose title in English would be *The Hammer of Witches*. In the play's final scene, the co-authors of the *Malleus*, two churchmen named Kramer and Sprenger, come on stage and quote passages from their work, words which provide an explanation of some aspects of the thinking that made persecution of women as witches possible.

This is in many ways a shocking play: shocking in its language, shocking in the events depicted. (Many of the most shocking examples, however, come directly from *The Hammer of Witches*.) The play shocks in order to get our attention (so invisible has the underlying misogyny of much of our culture become) and in order to dramatize a sense of outrage over this treatment of women. And yet at the center of the play is not a desire to shock but a desire to educate. In this respect and in its style, it is in the tradition of "epic theater" associated with Bertold Brecht, a resemblance which it shares with Arthur Kopit's *Indians*, also in this volume: the staged quality of the play is visually explicit, and although we may develop sympathy for the situation of particular characters, their "story" has depressingly little suspense to it. We are encouraged not to get involved in the plot but to distance ourselves from this bizarre society and to think about the issues which its portrayal poses. Thus what the play attempts to dramatize, through the treatment of a few women accused of witchcraft in one anonymous village, are the root causes of misogyny, of hostility toward women, which Churchill implies are all too much still with us, roots which are deeply embedded in the social, economic, psychological, and religious values with which we have structured our world.

CHARACTERS

ALICE, a village girl, early 20s
SUSAN, her married friend, early 20s
JOAN, Alice's mother, a poor widow, 50
MARGERY, Joan's neighbour, a farmer's wife, 40
JACK, Margery's husband, a tenant farmer, 40
BETTY, the landowner's daughter, 16
ELLEN, a cunning woman, 35
GOODY, Packer's assistant, 45

PACKER, a witchfinder, 35
MAN, a gentleman, 30
DOCTOR, a professional, 50
BELLRINGER, a local, any age
KRAMER and SPRENGER - authors of the *Malleus Maleficarum*, *The Hammer of Witches*, a book highly thought of in the seventeenth century; they appear in top hat and tails as performers in a music hall.

The play takes place in and around a small village over a period of a few weeks in the seventeenth century. The songs take place in the present.

SCENE I

Roadside.

MAN. Am I the devil?

ALICE. What, sweet?

MAN. I'm the devil. Man in black, they say, they always say, a man in black met me in the night, took me into the thicket and made me commit uncleanness unspeakable.

ALICE. I've seen men in black that's no devils unless clergy and gentlemen are devils.

MAN. Have I not got great burning eyes then?

ALICE. Bright enough eyes.

MAN. Is my body not rough and hairy?

ALICE. I don't like a man too smooth.

MAN. Am I not ice cold?

ALICE. In a ditch in November.

MAN. Didn't I lie on you so heavy I took your breath? Didn't the enormous size of me terrify you?

ALICE. It seemed a fair size like other men's.

MAN. Didn't it hurt you? Are you saying I didn't hurt you?

ALICE. You don't need be the devil, I been hurt by men. Let me go now, you're hurting my shoulder.

MAN. What it is, you didn't see my feet.

ALICE. You never took off your shoes. Take off your shoes if your feet's cloven.

MAN. If you come with me and give me body and soul, you'll never want in this world.

ALICE. Are you saying that as a man?

MAN. Am I saying it as the devil?

ALICE. If you're saying it as a man I'll go with you. There's no one round here knows me going to marry me. There's no way I'll get money. I've a child, mind, I'll not leave the child.

MAN. Has it a father?

ALICE. No, never had.

MAN. So you think that was no sin we did?

ALICE. If it was I don't care.

MAN. Don't say that.

ALICE. You'd say worse living here. Any time I'm happy someone says it's a sin.

MAN. There's some in London say there's no sin. Each man has his own religion nearly, or none at all, and there's women speak out too. They smoke and curse in the tavern and they say flesh is no sin for they are God themselves and can't sin. The men and women lie together and say that's bliss and that's heaven and that's no sin. I believe it for there's such changes.

ALICE. I'd like to go to London and hear them.

MAN. But then I believe with Calvin that few are saved and I am damned utterly. Then I think if I'm damned anyway I might as well sin to make it worthwhile. But I'm afraid to die. I'm afraid of the torture after. One of my family was burnt for a Catholic and they all changed to Protestant and one burnt for that too. I wish I was a Catholic and could confess my sins and burn them away in candles. I believe it all in turn and all at once.

ALICE. Would you take me to London? I've nothing to keep me here except my mother and I'd leave her.

MAN. You don't think I'm sent you by the devil? Sometimes I think the devil has me. And then I think there is no devil. And then I think the devil would make me think there was no devil.

Reprinted from *Churchill: Plays One*, Churchill, Caryl (1985), by permission of the publisher, Routledge, New York.

ALICE. I'll never get away from here if you don't take me.

MAN. Will you do everything I say, like a witch with the devil her master?

ALICE. I'll do like a wife with a husband her master and that's enough for man or devil.

MAN. Will you kiss my arse like the devil makes his witches?

ALICE. I'll do what gives us pleasure. Was I good just now?

MAN. In Scotland I saw a witch burnt.

ALICE. Did you? A real witch? Was she a real one?

MAN. She was really burnt for one.

ALICE. Did the spirits fly out of her like black bats? Did the devil make the sky go dark? I've heard plenty tales of witches and I've heard some called witch, there's one in the next village some say and others say not, but she's nothing to see. Did she fly at night on a stick? Did you see her flying?

MAN. I saw her burnt.

ALICE. Tell then. What did she say?

MAN. She couldn't speak, I think. They'd been questioning her. There's wrenching the head with a cord. She came to the stake in a cart and men lifted her out, and the stake held her up when she was tied. She'd been in the boots you see that break the bones.

ALICE. And wood was put round? And a fire lit just like lighting a fire? Oh, I'd have shrieked, I cry the least thing.

MAN. She did shriek.

ALICE. I long to see that. But I might hide my face. Did you hide your face?

MAN. No, I saw it.

ALICE. Did you like seeing it then?

MAN. I may have done.

ALICE. Will you take me with you, to London, to Scotland? Nothing happens here.

MAN. Take you with me?

ALICE. Please, I'd be no trouble . . .

MAN. A whore? Take a whore with me?

ALICE. I'm not that.

MAN. What are you then? What name would you put to yourself? You're not a wife or a widow. You're not a virgin. Tell me a name for what you are.

ALICE. You're not going? Stay a bit.

MAN. I've stayed too long. I'm cold. The devil's cold. Back to my warm fire, eh?

ALICE. Stay with me!

MAN. Get away, will you.

ALICE. Please.

MAN. Get away.

[*He pushes her and she falls.*]

ALICE. Go to hell then, go to the devil, you devil.

MAN. Cursing is it? I can outcurse you.

ALICE. You foul devil, you fool, bastard, damn you, you devil!

MAN. Devil take you, whore, whore, damned strumpet, succubus,[1] witch!

ALICE. But come back. I'll not curse you. Don't you curse. We were friends just now.

MAN. You should have behaved better.

ALICE. Will I see you again?

MAN. Unless I see you first.

ALICE. But will I see you? How can I find you?

MAN. You can call on me.

ALICE. How? Where? How shall I call on you?

MAN. You know how to curse. Just call on the devil.

ALICE. Don't tease me, you're not the devil, what's your name?

MAN. Lucifer, isn't it, and Beelzebub.

ALICE. No, what's your name?

MAN. Darling was my name, and sweeting, till you called me devil.

ALICE. I'll not call you devil, come back, what's your name?

MAN. You won't need to know it. You won't be seeing me.

SCENE II

Inside Jack and Margery's.

JACK. The river meadow is the one to get.

MARGERY. I thought the long field up the hill.

JACK. No, the river meadow for the cattle.

MARGERY. But Jack, for corn. Think of the long field full of wheat.

JACK. He's had a bad crop two years. That's why he can't pay the rent.

MARGERY. No, but he's got no cattle. We'd be all right.

JACK. If we took both fields.

MARGERY. Could we? Both?

JACK. The more we have the more we can afford.

MARGERY. And we'll pray God sends us sunshine.

JACK. Who's that down by the river?

---

1 **succubus:** female demon who has sexual relations with a man while he sleeps.

MARGERY. That Alice, is it, wandering about?

JACK. I'm surprised Mother Noakes can pay her rent.

MARGERY. Just a cottage isn't much.

JACK. I've been wondering if we'll see them turned out.

MARGERY. I don't know why she's let stay. If we all lived like her it wouldn't be the fine estate it is. And Alice . . .

JACK. You can't blame Alice.

MARGERY. You can blame her. You can't be surprised. She's just what I'd expect of a girl of brought up by Joan Noakes.

JACK. If we rent both fields, we'll have to hire a man to help with the harvest.

MARGERY. Hire a man?

JACK. That's not Alice.

MARGERY. It's not Miss Betty out by herself again?

JACK. I wouldn't be her father, not even to own the land.

MARGERY. That's a fine idea, hire a man.

JACK. She's coming here.

MARGERY. What we going to do?

JACK. Be respectful.

MARGERY. No, but shall we take her home? She's not meant to. She's still shut up in her room, everyone says.

JACK. I won't be sorry to see her.

MARGERY. I love to see her. She was always so soft on your lap, not like ours all hard edges. I could sit all afternoon just to smell her hair. But she's not a child, now, you can have run in and out and touch her. She's in trouble at home and we shouldn't help her do wrong.

JACK. We can't stop her, can we, if she walks in?

[*They wait and in a moment Betty does come in.*]

MARGERY. Miss Betty, how nice.

BETTY. I came to see you milking the cows.

JACK. We finished milking, miss. The cows are in.

BETTY. Is it that late?

MARGERY. You want to get home before dark.

BETTY. No, I don't. I want to be out in the dark. It's not late, it's dark in the day time. I could stay out for hours if it was summer.

JACK. If you want to come and see the farm, Miss Betty, you should ask your father to bring you one morning when he's inspecting the estate.

BETTY. I'm not let go where I like.

JACK. I've business with your father.

MARGERY. We're going to take on the river meadow for the cattle.

JACK. And the long field up the hill.

BETTY. I used to play here all day. Nothing's different. Have you still got Betty's mug?

MARGERY. That's right, she had her special mug.

BETTY. I milked the red cow right into it one day. I got milk in my eye.

JACK. She died, that red cow. But we've four new cows you've not seen.

MARGERY. Died last week. There's two or three cows died in the neighbourhood.

BETTY. I wish she hadn't.

JACK. That don't matter, losing one, we're doing well enough.

MARGERY. And you're doing well, I hear, miss.

BETTY. What?

MARGERY. I hear you're leaving us for better things.

BETTY. No.

MARGERY. I was only saying yesterday, our little Miss Betty that was and now to be a lady with her own house and . . .

BETTY. They lock me up. I said I won't marry him so they lock met up. Don't you know that?

MARGERY. I had heard something.

BETTY. I get out the window.

MARGERY. Hadn't you better have him, Betty, and be happy? Everyone hopes so. Everyone loves a wedding.

BETTY. Margery, can I stay here tonight?

MARGERY. They'd worry for you.

BETTY. Can I? Please?

JACK. There's no bed fit for you, miss.

BETTY. On my way here I climbed a tree. I could see the whole estate. I could see the other side of the river. I wanted to jump off. And fly.

MARGERY. Shall Jack walk home with you, miss, now it's getting dark?

SCENE III

Inside Joan's.

JOAN. Alice?

ALICE. No need to wake up, mum.

JOAN. You'll catch cold out all night in this weather.

ALICE. Don't wake up if it's only to moan at me.

JOAN. Who were you with?

ALICE. Did he wake up?

JOAN. No, not a sound.

ALICE. He's sleeping better. Not so much bad dreams.

JOAN. Come on, child, there's some broth left.

ALICE. I couldn't eat.

JOAN. You stay out half the night, you don't even enjoy it. You stay in with the boy. You sit by the fire with no one to talk to but old Vinegar Tomcat. I'll go out.

ALICE. You go out?

JOAN. Funny, isn't it? What would I do going out?

ALICE. I'll stay in if you like.

JOAN. Where would I go? Who wants an old woman?

ALICE. You want me to stay with you more?

JOAN. An old woman wandering about in the cold.

ALICE. Do you want some broth, mum?

JOAN. Who were you with this time? Anyone I know?

ALICE. Oh mum, I'm sick of myself.

JOAN. If we'd each got a man we'd be better off.

ALICE. You weren't better off, mum. You've told me often you're glad he's dead. Think how he used to beat you.

JOAN. We'd have more to eat, that's one thing.

Nobody Sings

I woke up in the morning,
Blood was on the sheet,
I looked at all the women
When I passed them in the street.
    Nobody sings about it
    But it happens all the time.

I met an old old woman
Who made my blood run cold.
You don't stop wanting sex, she said,
Just because you're old.
    Oh nobody sings about it,
    but it happens all the time.

I could be glad of the change of life,
But it makes me feel so strange.
If your life is being wanted
Do you want your life to change?
    Oh nobody sings about it,
    but it happens all the time.

Do you want your skin to wrinkle
And your cunt get sore and dry?
And they say it's just your hormones
If you cry and cry and cry.
    Oh nobody sings about it,
    but it happens all the time.

Nobody ever saw me,
She whispered in a rage.
They were blinded by my beauty, now
They're blinded by my age.
    Oh nobody sings about it,
    but it happens all the time.

SCENE IV

Jack and Margery's barn.

[Margery is churning.]

JACK. Hurry up with that butter, woman.

MARGERY. Butter won't come.

JACK. There's other work to do.

MARGERY. Butter won't come.

JACK. You don't churn. You sit gossiping.

MARGERY. Who would I talk to?

JACK. I heard your voice now.

MARGERY. Mother Noakes.

JACK. Always hanging about.

MARGERY. Her girl's no better.

JACK. Was her girl here? No.

MARGERY. I told her be on her way. Mother Noakes.

JACK. You tell her.

MARGERY. I told her.

JACK. Get on now with the butter and don't be always gossiping.

[Jack goes. Margery churns and sings very quietly.]

MARGERY. Come butter come, come butter come. Johnny's standing at the gate waiting for a butter cake. Come butter come, come butter come. Johnny's standing at the gate waiting for a butter cake. Come butter come, come butter come. Johnny's standing at the gate . . .

[She stops as she realises Joan Noakes has come in and is standing behind her.]

JOAN. Just passing by.

MARGERY. Again.

JOAN. I wonder could you lend me a little yeast? I've no yeast, see. I'm fresh out of yeast. I've no bread in the house and I thought, I thought . . . I'll do a little baking now and brew a little beer maybe . . . and I went to get some yeast and I've no yeast. Who'd have thought it? No yeast at all.

MARGERY. You'd be better without beer.

JOAN. I thought a little yeast as I was passing.

MARGERY. You get drunk. You should be ashamed.

JOAN. To bake a couple of little small loaves.

MARGERY. I've no yeast.

JOAN. A couple of little small loaves wouldn't take much yeast. A woman comfortable off with a fine man and a nice field and five cows and three pigs and plenty of apples that makes a good cider, bless you, Margery, many's the time . . . you'd not grudge a neighbour a little loaf? Many's the good times, eh, Margery? I've my own flour, you know, I'm not asking for flour.

MARGERY. I gave you yeast last week.

JOAN. A little small crumb of yeast and God will bless you for kindness to your poor old neighbour.

MARGERY. You're not so badly off, Joan Noakes. You're not on the parish.

JOAN. If I was I'd be fed. I should be on relief, then I'd not trouble you. There's some on relief, better off than me. I get nothing.

MARGERY. What money you get you drink.

JOAN. If you'd my troubles, Margery, you'd be glad of a drink, but as you haven't, thank God, and lend me a little yeast like a good woman.

MARGERY. I've no yeast.

JOAN. I know you, Margery.

MARGERY. What do you know?

JOAN. I know you've got yeast. My eyes are old, but I see through you. You're a cold woman and getting worse and you'll die without a friend in this parish when if you gave yeast to your good neighbours everyone would bless you . . .

MARGERY. I've no yeast.

JOAN. But you don't give and they say what a mean bitter woman and curse you.

MARGERY. There's nobody curses me. Now get out of my dairy. Dirty old woman you are, smelling of drink, come in here day after day begging, and stealing, too, I shouldn't wonder . . .

JOAN. You shouldn't say that.

MARGERY. . . . and your great ugly cat in here stealing the cream. Get out of my dairy.

JOAN. You'll be sorry you spoke to me like that. I've always been your friend, Margery, but now you'll find I'm not.

MARGERY. I've work to do. Now get out. I'm making my butter.

JOAN. Damn your butter to hell.

MARGERY. Will you get out?

JOAN. Devil take you and your man and your fields and your cows and your butter and your yeast and your beer and your bread and your cider and your cold face. . .

MARGERY. Will you go?

[*Joan goes. Margery churns.*]

MARGERY. Come butter come, come butter come. Johnny's standing at the gate waiting for a butter cake. Come butter . . . It's not coming, this butter. I'm sick of it.

[*Jack comes.*]

JACK. What's all this? You're a lazy woman, you know that? Times are bad enough. The little black calf don't look well.

MARGERY. Butter won't come. Mother Noakes said damn the butter to hell.

JACK. Lazy slut, get on with it.

MARGERY. Come butter come. Come butter come. Come butter come. Come butter come. Come butter come. Come butter come. . . Mother Noakes come begging and borrowing. She still got my big bowl and I give her some eggs in that time she was poorly. She makes out I've treated her bad. I've been a good neighbour to that woman years out of mind and no return. We'll get that bowl back off her. Jack, do you hear me? Go over Mother Noakes and get my bowl. And we'll heat a horseshoe red hot and put it in the milk to make the butter come.

SCENE V

Outside Joan's.

SUSAN. Don't always talk of men.

ALICE. He knew what he was doing.

SUSAN. You'll know what he was doing in a few months.

ALICE. No, it never happens. The cunning woman put a charm inside me.

SUSAN. Take more than a charm to do me good.

ALICE. Not again? Does he know?

SUSAN. He wants it. I know the night it was. He said, 'Let's hope a fine child comes of it.'

ALICE. And what did you say?

SUSAN. Devil take it.

ALICE. What he say to that?

SUSAN. He don't like me swearing.

ALICE. But the baby's not a year.

SUSAN. Two weeks late, so.

ALICE. But the baby's not weaned.

SUSAN. The boy wasn't weaned when I fell for the baby.

ALICE. You could go see the cunning woman.

SUSAN. What for?

ALICE. She's a good midwife.

SUSAN. I don't want a midwife. I got my mother, anyway. I don't want to think about it. Nearly died last time. I was two days.

ALICE. Go and see the cunning woman. Just go see.

SUSAN. What for?

ALICE. She could say for certain.

SUSAN. I'm sure for certain.

ALICE. She could give you a charm.

SUSAN. They do say the pain is what's sent to a woman for her sins. I complained last time after churching, and he said I must think on Eve who brought the sin into the world that got me pregnant. I must think on how woman tempts man, and how she pays God with her pain having the baby. So if we try to get round the pain, we're going against God.

ALICE. I hate my body.

SUSAN. You mustn't say that. God sent his son . . .

ALICE. Blood every month, and no way out of that but to be sick and swell up, and no way out of that but pain. No way out of all that till we're old and that's worse. I can't bear to see my mother if she changes her clothes. If I was a man I'd go to London and Scotland and never come back and take a girl under a bush and on my way.

SUSAN. You could go to the cunning woman.

ALICE. What for?

SUSAN. Charm.

ALICE. What for?

SUSAN. Love charm bring him home.

ALICE. I don't want him back.

SUSAN. Did he look wonderful, more than anyone here, that he's got you so low?

ALICE. It was dark, I wouldn't know him again.

SUSAN. Not so much how he looked as how he felt?

ALICE. I could do with it now, I can tell you. I could do with walking across that field again and finding him there just the same. I want a man I can have when I want, not if I'm lucky to meet some villain one night.

SUSAN. You always say you don't want to be married.

ALICE. I don't want to be married. Look at you. Who'd want to be you?

SUSAN. He doesn't beat me.

ALICE. He doesn't beat you.

SUSAN. What's wrong with me? Better than you.

ALICE. Three babies and what, two, three times miscarried and wonderful he doesn't beat you.

SUSAN. No one's going to marry you because they know you here. That's why you say you don't want to be married—because no one's going to ask you round here, because they know you.

[They move apart. Jack has been lingering in the background a while, and now comes up to Alice.]

JACK. It's not you I've come to see.

ALICE. Never thought it was.

JACK. You should have done then.

ALICE. Why?

JACK. You know why.

ALICE. You've come to see my mum, have you?

JACK. I've business with her, yes. That's why I came.

ALICE. She's somewhere around. I'll get her.

JACK. No hurry. Wait a bit. Never seem to talk.

ALICE. Nothing to talk about.

JACK. I'm forgetting. I brought something.

[He gives her two apples.]

ALICE. Thank you. What then?

JACK. Am I not handsome enough, is that it?

ALICE. I don't want trouble.

JACK. No one's to know.

ALICE. If I say you're not handsome enough, will you go away?

JACK. Alice, you must. I have dreams.

ALICE. You've a wife.

JACK. I'm no good to my wife. I can't do it. Not these three months. It's only when I dream of you or like now talking to you . . .

ALICE. Mum. There's someone to see you.

JACK. Alice, have some pity . . .

ALICE. Do you hear me? Mum? She'll be out to see you.

[She moves away. Joan comes.]

JOAN. What's the matter?

JACK. I've come for the bowl.

JOAN. Bowl? Bowl?

JACK. Bowl my wife gave you some eggs in, you ungrateful old hag.

JOAN. You're asking me for the bowl? You think I wouldn't give you back your bowl? You think I'm stealing your bowl? When have I ever kept anything? Have your bowl. I'll get your bowl and much good may it do you.

JACK. Then get it, damn you, and quick or you'll feel my hand.

[*She goes.*]

ALICE. Why treat her like that?

JACK. Don't speak to me. Let me get the bowl and go.

ALICE. And don't come back.

JACK. Alice, I'd be good to you. I'm not a poor man. I could give you things for your boy . . .

ALICE. Go away to hell.

[*Joan comes back.*]

JOAN. Here's your bowl, Jack, and the devil go with it. Get away home and I hope you've more trouble there than I have here.

JACK. I'll break your neck if you speak to me.

JOAN. You lift your hand to me, may it drop off.

ALICE. Go home away to hell, man.

[*Jack goes.*]

JOAN. Away to hell with him. Never liked the man. Never liked the wife.

ALICE. Don't think on them, mum. They're not worth your time. Go in by the fire, go on, go in and be warm.

[*Joan goes. Susan approaches.*]

    Nobody likes my mother. That's what it is why nobody wants me.

SUSAN. I'm sorry for what I said, Alice.

ALICE. Going to see the cunning woman then?

SUSAN. Are you going for a love charm?

ALICE. It's something to do, isn't it? Better than waiting and waiting for something to happen. If I had a charm I could make him just appear in front of me now, I'd do anything. Will you come?

[*Alice gives Susan an apple.*]

SUSAN. I'll keep you company then. Just tell her my trouble. There's no harm.

Oh Doctor

Oh, doctor, tell
me, make we well.
What's wrong with me
the way I am?
I know I'm sad.
I may be sick.
I may be bad.
Please cure me quick,
oh doctor.

SCENE VI

The landowner's house.

[*Betty tied to a chair. The doctor is about to bleed her arm.*]

BETTY. Why am I tied? Tied to be bled. Why am I bled? Because I was screaming. Why was I screaming? Because I'm bad. Why was I bad? Because I was happy. Why was I happy? Because I ran out by myself and got away from them and—Why was I screaming? Because I'm bad. Why am I bad? Because I'm tied. Why am I tied? Because I was happy. Why was I happy? Because I was screaming.

DOCTOR. Hysteria is a woman's weakness. Hysteron, Greek, the womb. Excessive blood causes an imbalance in the humours. The noxious gases that form inwardly every month rise to the brain and cause behaviour quite contrary to the patient's real feelings. After bleeding you must be purged. Tonight you shall be blistered. You will soon be well enough to be married.

Oh Doctor

Where are you taking my skin?
Where are you putting my bones?
I shut my eyes and I opened wide,
But why is my heart on the other side?
Why are you putting my brain in my cunt?
You're putting me back all back to front.

Stop looking up me with your metal eye.
Stop cutting me apart before I die.
Stop, put me back.

Stop, put me back.
Put back my body.

Who are you giving my womb?
Who are you showing my breath?
Tell me what you whisper to nurse,
Whatever I've got, you're making it worse.
I'm wide awake, but I still can't shout.
Why can't I see what you're taking out?

Stop looking up me with your metal eye.
Stop cutting me apart before I die.
Stop, put me back.
Stop, put me back.
Put back my body.

Oh, doctor, tell
me, make we well.
What's wrong with me
the way I am?
I know I'm sad
I may be sick.
I may be bad.
Please cure me quick,
oh doctor,
What's wrong with me the way I am?
What's wrong with me?

I want to see myself.
I want to see inside myself.
Give me back my head.
I'll put my heart in straight.
Let me out of bed now.
I can't wait
To see myself.
Give me back my body.
I can see myself.
Give me back my body.
I can see myself.

SCENE VII

Jack and Margery's barn.

MARGERY. Jack, Jack, come quick—Jack.
JACK. What's the matter now?
MARGERY. The calves. Have you seen the calves?

JACK. What's the woman on about?
MARGERY. The calves are shaking and they've a terrible stench, so you can't go near them and their bellies are swollen up. [Jack goes off.] There's no good running. There's nothing you can do for them. They'll die like the red cow. You don't love me. Damn this stinking life to hell. Calves stinking and shaking there. No good you going to see, Jack. Better stand and curse. Everything dying on us. Aah. What's that? Who's there? Get out, you beast, get out. [She throws her shoe.] Jack, Jack.
JACK. Hold your noise.
MARGERY. That nasty old cat of Mother Noakes. I'll kill that cat if I get it, stinking up my clean dairy, stealing my cream. Where's it gone?
JACK. Let it go.
MARGERY. What you think of those calves then? Nothing to be done is there? What can we do? Nothing. Nothing to be done. Can't do nothing. Oh, Oh.
JACK. Now what is it?
MARGERY. Jack!
JACK. What is it? Don't frighten me, woman.
MARGERY. My head, oh, my stomach. Oh, Jack, I feel ill.

[She sits on the ground.]

JACK. Get up, woman. It's no time. There's things to do.
MARGERY. Nothing.
JACK. Lie there a bit then. You'll maybe feel better. I can hardly stir myself. What have I done to deserve it? Why me? Why my calves shaking? Why my wife falling down?
MARGERY. It's passing now.
JACK. Why me?
MARGERY. That was a terrible pain. I still feel it. I'm shaking, look.
JACK. Other people sin and aren't punished so much as we are.
MARGERY. We must pray to God.
JACK. We do pray to God, and he sends afflictions.
MARGERY. It must be we deserve it somehow, but I don't know how. I do my best. I do my best, Jack, God knows, don't I, Jack? God knows I do my best.
JACK. Don't other people sin? Is it just me?
MARGERY. You're not a bad man, Jack.
JACK. I must be the worst man.
MARGERY. No, dear.

JACK. Would God send all this to a good man? Would he? It's my sins those calves shaking and stinking and swelling up their bellies in there.

MARGERY. Don't talk so.

JACK. My sins stinking and swelling up.

MARGERY. Unless it's not God.

JACK. How can I bear it?

MARGERY. If it's not God.

JACK. What?

MARGERY. If it's not God sends the trouble.

JACK. The devil?

MARGERY. One of his servants. If we're bewitched, Jack, that explains all.

JACK. If we're bewitched . . .

MARGERY. Butter not coming. Calves swelling. Me struck in the head.

JACK. Then it's not my sins. Good folk get bewitched.

MARGERY. Good folk like us.

JACK. It can happen to anyone.

MARGERY. Rich folk can have spells against them.

JACK. It's good people the witches want to hurt.

MARGERY. The devil can't bear to see us so good.

JACK. You know who it is?

MARGERY. Who?

JACK. The witch. Who it is.

MARGERY. Who?

JACK. You know who.

MARGERY. She cursed the butter to hell.

JACK. She cursed me when I got the bowl.

MARGERY. She said I'd be sorry I'd spoken to her.

JACK. She wished me trouble at home.

MARGERY. Devil take your man and your cows, she said that, and your butter. She cursed the calves see and she's made them shake. She struck me on the head and in the stomach.

JACK. I'll break her neck.

MARGERY. Be careful now, what she might do.

JACK. I'm not afraid of an old witch.

MARGERY. You should be. She could kill you.

JACK. I'll kill her first.

MARGERY. Wait, Jack. Let's meet cunning with cunning. What we must do is get the spell off.

JACK. She's not going to take it off for asking. She might for a few hard knocks.

MARGERY. No, wait, Jack. We can take the spell off and never go near her. Serve her right.

JACK. What do we do then? Burn something?

MARGERY. Burn an animal alive, don't we? Or bury it alive. That takes witchcraft off the rest.

JACK. Burn the black calf then shall we? We'll get some straw and wood and put it in the yard and the calf on top and set it on fire.

MARGERY. Will it walk?

JACK. Or I'll carry it.

MARGERY. It stinks terrible.

JACK. Stink of witchcraft it is. Burn it up.

MARGERY. We must pray to God to keep us safe from the devil. Praying's strong against witches.

JACK. We'll pray God help us and help ourselves too.

MARGERY. She'll see the fire and smell it and she'll know we're fighting back, stinking old witch, can't hurt us.

Something to Burn

What can we do, there's nothing to do,
about sickness and hunger and dying.
What can we do, there's nothing to do,
nothing but cursing and crying.
   Find something to burn.
   Let it go up in smoke.
   Burn your troubles away.

Sometimes it's witches, or what will you choose?
Sometimes it's lunatics, shut them away.
It's blacks and it's women and often it's Jews.
We'd all be quite happy if they'd go away.
   Find something to burn.
   Let it go up in smoke.
   Burn your troubles away.

SCENE VIII

Ellen's cottage.

ELLEN. Take it or leave it, my dear, it's one to me. If you want to be rid of your trouble, you'll take it. But only you know what you want.

SUSAN. It's not what I came for.

ALICE. Of course it is.

SUSAN. I wanted to know for certain.

ALICE. You know for certain.

SUSAN. I want a charm against pain.

ELLEN. I'll come as your midwife if you send for me near the time and do what I can, if that's all you want.

ALICE. She wants to be rid of it. Well, do you want it?

SUSAN. I don't want it but I don't want to be rid of it. I want to be rid of it, but not do anything to be rid of it.

ELLEN. If you won't do anything to help yourself you must stay as you are.

SUSAN. I shall pray to God.

ALICE. It's no sin. You just give yourself the drink.

SUSAN. Oh, I don't know.

ELLEN. Let her go home. She can come back. You have your charm safe, Alice? I could do more if you could come at the young man and give him a potion I'd let you have.

ALICE. If I could come at him he wouldn't need potion.

ELLEN. And you're sure you've nothing of his?

ALICE. He gave me nothing.

ELLEN. A few hairs or a drop of blood makes all the difference. It's part of him and the powers can work on it to call him.

ALICE. I'll pull a few hairs out next time I've a lover. Come on, Susan.

ELLEN. For your heartache I'll give you these herbs to boil up in water and drink at night. Give you a sound sleep and think less of him.

ALICE. Don't want to think less of him.

ELLEN. You have your sleep. There'll be other men along if not that one. Clever girl like you could think of other things.

ALICE. Like what?

ELLEN. Learn a trade.

ALICE. Nothing dangerous.

ELLEN. Where's the danger in herbs?

ALICE. Not just herbs.

ELLEN. Where's the danger in healing?

ALICE. Not just healing, is it?

ELLEN. There's powers, and you use them for healing or hurt. You use them how you like. There's no hurt if you're healing so where's the danger? You could use them. Not everyone can.

ALICE. Learn the herbs?

ELLEN. There's all kinds of wisdom. Bit by bit I'd teach you.

ALICE. I'd never thought.

ELLEN. There's no hurry. I don't want you unless it's what you want. You'll be coming by to leave a little something for me in a few days, since I have to live and wouldn't charge you. You can tell me how you've got on with your young man and what you're thinking.

ALICE. Yes, I'll be coming by. Goodnight then. What are you standing there for, Susan?

SUSAN. Maybe I'll take some potion with me. And see when I get home whether I take it.

ELLEN. Don't be afraid if it makes you sick. It's to do you good.

SCENE IX

Ellen's cottage.

BETTY. I don't know what I'm here for. I've had so much treatment already. The doctor comes every day.

ELLEN. You know what you're here for.

BETTY. The doctor says people like you don't know anything. He thinks he's cured me because I said I would get married to stop them locking me up. But I'll never do it.

ELLEN. Do you want a potion to make you love the man?

BETTY. I'd rather have one to make him hate me so he'd leave me alone. Or make him die.

ELLEN. The best I can do for you is help you sleep. I won't harm him for you, so don't ask. Get some sleep and think out what you want.

BETTY. Can I come again sometimes just to be here? I like it here.

ELLEN. Come when you like. I don't charge but you'll bring a little present.

BETTY. I'll give you anything if you can help me.

ELLEN. Come when you like.

SCENE X

Ellen's cottage.

ELLEN. I'm not saying I can't do anything. But if I can't, it's because you've left it too late.

JACK. Lift your hand to me, she said, may it drop off. Then next day it went stiff.

MARGERY. We want to be certain. I've talked to others and they've things against her too. She's cursed and scolded two or three, and one's lame and the other lost her hen. And while we were talking we thought of her great cat that's always in my dairy, stinking it up and stealing the cream. Ah what's that, I said crying out, didn't I, and that was the cat, and I was struck down with a blow inside my head. That's her familiar sent her by Satan.

JACK. I've seen a rat run out of her yard into ours and I went for it with a pitchfork and the spikes were turned aside and nearly went in my own foot by her foul magic. And that rat's another of her imps.

MARGERY. But you don't like to think it of your neighbour. Time was she was neighbourly enough. If you could tell us it was true, we could act against her more certain in our minds.

JACK. I shouted at her over the fence, I said I'll have you hanged you old strumpet, burnt and hanged, and she cursed me again.

MARGERY. We burnt a calf alive to save our calves but it was too late. If I knew for certain it was her I'd be easier.

ELLEN. I've a glass here, a cloudy glass. Look in the glass, so, and see if any face comes into it.

[She gives them a mirror.]

MARGERY. Come on, Jack, don't be afraid.

JACK. I don't like it.

MARGERY. Come on, it's good magic to find a witch.

ELLEN. Look in the glass and think on all the misfortunes you've had and see what comes.

MARGERY. Nothing yet. Do you see anything?

JACK. No.

MARGERY. Nothing still.

JACK. Don't keep talking.

MARGERY. Look.

JACK. What?

MARGERY. Did something move in the glass? My heart's beating so.

JACK. It's too dark.

MARGERY. No. Look.

JACK. I did see something.

MARGERY. It's the witch.

JACK. It's her sure enough.

MARGERY. It is, isn't it, Jack? Mother Noakes, isn't it?

JACK. It was Mother Noakes in that glass.

ELLEN. There then. You have what you came for.

MARGERY. Proves she's a witch then?

ELLEN. Not for me to say one's a witch or not a witch. I give you the glass and you see in it what you see in it.

JACK. Saw Mother Noakes.

MARGERY. Proves she's a witch.

ELLEN. Saw what you come to see. Is your mind easy?

SCENE XI

Ellen's cottage.

JACK. Want to ask you something private. It's about my . . . [He gestures, embarrassed.] It's gone. I can't do anything with it, haven't for some time. I accepted that. But now it's not even there, it's completely gone. There's a girl bewitched me. She's daughter of that witch. And I've heard how witches sometimes get a whole boxful and they move and stir by themselves like living creatures and the witch feeds them oats and hay. There was one witch told a man in my condition to climb a tree and he'd find a nest with several in it and take which he liked, and when he took the big one she said no, not that one, because that one belongs to the parish priest. I don't want a big one, I want my own back, and this witch has it.

ELLEN. You'd better go and ask her nicely for it.

JACK. Is that all you can say? Can't you force her to give it to me?

ELLEN. It's sure to come back. You ask the girl nicely, she'll give it you back. I'll give you a little potion to take.

JACK. Kill her else.

SCENE XII

Outside Jack and Margery's.

JOAN. That's a foul stink. I don't know how you can stay there. Whatever is it?

MARGERY. Do you know why you've come?

JOAN. I was passing.

MARGERY. Why were you passing?

JOAN. Can't I pass by your door now? Time was it was always open for me.

MARGERY. And what's that?

JOAN. A foul stink. Whatever are you making? I thought I'd come and see you as I was passing. I don't want any trouble between us. I thought, come and see her, make it all right.

MARGERY. You come to see me because of that. That's my piss boiling. And two feathers of your chicken burning. It's a foul stink brings a witch. If you come when I do that, proves you've a spell on me. And now I'll get it off. You know how?

JOAN. Come and see me. Make it all right.

MARGERY. Blood you, that's how.

[Margery scratches Joan's head.]

JOAN. Damn you, get away.

MARGERY. Can't hurt me now. And if that doesn't bring the spell off I'll burn your thatch.

If Everybody Worked as Hard as Me

If everybody worked as hard as me,
if our children's shirts are white,
if their language is polite
if nobody stays out late at night,
Oh, happy family.

Oh, the country's what it is because
the family's what it is because
the wife is what she is
to her man.
Oh I do all I can.
Yes, I do all I can.
I try to do what's right,
so I'll never be alone and afraid in the night.
And nobody comes knocking at my door in the night.
The horrors that are done will not be done to me.

Nobody loves a scold,
nobody loves a slut,
nobody loves you when you're old,
unless you're someone's gran.
Nobody loves you
unless you keep your mouth shut.
Nobody loves you
if you don't support your man.
Oh you can,
oh you can
have a happy family.

If everybody worked as hard as me,
sometimes you'll be bored,
you'll often be ignored,
but in your heart you'll know you are adored.
Oh, happy family.
Your dreams will all come true.
You'll make your country strong.
Oh the country's what it is because
the family's what it is because
the wife is what she is
to her man.
Oh please do all you can.
Yes, please do all you can
Oh, please don't do what's wrong,
so you'll never be alone and afraid in the night.
So nobody comes knocking at your door in the night.
So the horrors that are done will not be done to you.

Yes you can.
Yes you can.
Oh the country's what it is because

the family's what it is because
the wife is what she is
to her man.

SCENE XIII

Outside Jack and Margery's.

SUSAN. You're sure it was him? You said you wouldn't know him.
ALICE. I did when I saw him.
SUSAN. Riding? Couldn't see him close.
ALICE. Close enough to be spattered with his mud. He saw me.
SUSAN. But he didn't show he knew you.
ALICE. Pretended not to.
SUSAN. It wasn't him.
ALICE. It was him.
SUSAN. And you don't know the beautiful lady?
ALICE. I'll know her again. Scratch her eyes if I come at her.
SUSAN. What was she wearing?
ALICE. What was she wearing? How should I know? A fine rich dress made her beautiful, I suppose. Are you trying to plague me?
SUSAN. Was he in black still?
ALICE. Blue velvet jacket.
SUSAN. Blue velvet.
ALICE. Yes, damn you, I said that before. Are you stupid? [Silence.] For God's sake, now what is it? Are you crying? Shouldn't I be crying?
SUSAN. It's not your fault, Ally. I cry all the time.
ALICE. You're still weak, that's what it is. It's the blood you lost. You should rest more.
SUSAN. I don't want him to know.
ALICE. Doesn't he know?
SUSAN. He may guess but I don't dare ask. He was out all day that day and I said I'd been ill, but not why.
ALICE. It's done anyway.
SUSAN. Can't be undone.
ALICE. You're not sorry now?
SUSAN. I don't know.
ALICE. You'd be a fool to be sorry.
SUSAN. I am sorry. I'm wicked. You're wicked.

[She cries.]

ALICE. Oh, Susan, you're tired out, that's all. You're

not wicked. You'd have cried more to have it. All the extra work, another baby.

SUSAN. I like babies.

ALICE. You'll have plenty more, God, you'll have plenty. What's the use of crying?

SUSAN. You were crying for that lover.

ALICE. I'm not now. I'd sooner kill him. If I could get at him. If thoughts could get at him he'd feel it.

SUSAN. I'm so tired, Ally.

ALICE. Do you think it's true thoughts can reach someone?

SUSAN. What are you thinking of?

ALICE. Like if I had something of his, I could bring him. Or harm him.

SUSAN. Don't try that.

ALICE. But I've nothing of his. I'd have to make a puppet.

SUSAN. Don't talk so. Oh, don't, Alice, when I'm so tired.

ALICE. Does it have to be like? Is it like just if you say it's like?

SUSAN. Alice!

ALICE. If I get this wet mud, it's like clay. There should be at least a spider or some ashes of bones, but mud will do. Here's a man's shape, see, that's his head and that's arms and legs.

SUSAN. I'm going home. I'm too tired to move.

ALICE. You stay here and watch. This is the man. We know who though we don't know his name. Now here's a pin, let's prick him. Where shall I prick him? Between the legs first so he can't get on with his lady.

SUSAN. Alice, stop.

ALICE. Once in the head to drive him mad. Shall I give him one in the heart? Do I want him to die yet? Or just waste till I please.

SUSAN. Alice . . .

[Susan tries to get the mud man, it falls on the ground and breaks.]

ALICE. Now look. You've broken him up. You've killed him.

SUSAN. I haven't.

ALICE. All in pieces. Think of the poor man. Come apart.

SUSAN. I didn't. Alice, I didn't. It was you.

ALICE. If it was me, I don't care.

SUSAN. Alice, what have you done? Oh Alice, Alice.

ALICE. It's not true, stupid. It's not him.

SUSAN. How do you know?

ALICE. It's a bit of mud.

SUSAN. But you said.

ALICE. That's just words.

SUSAN. But . . .

ALICE. No. I did nothing. I never do anything. Might be better if I did. [They sit in silence.] You're crying again. Here, don't cry. [Alice holds Susan while she cries.]

SUSAN. Little clay puppet like a tiny baby not big enough to live and we crumble it away.

[Jack comes.]

JACK. Witch.

ALICE. Are you drunk?

JACK. Give it back.

ALICE. What?

JACK. Give it back.

ALICE. What now, Jack?

JACK. Give it me back. You know. You took it from me these three months. I've not been a man since. You bewitched me. You took it off me.

ALICE. Is he mad?

SUSAN. What is it?

ALICE. Susan's ill, will you leave us alone?

JACK. Everyone comes near you is ill. Give it back, come on, give it back.

ALICE. How can I?

JACK. She said speak nicely to you. I would, Alice, if you were good to me. I never wanted this. Please, sweet good Alice, give it back.

ALICE. What? How can I?

JACK. Give it me.

[He grabs her round the neck. Susan screams.]

ALICE. Damn you!

SUSAN. You'll kill her.

JACK. Give it me.

SUSAN. Let her go, she'll give it you whatever it is, you'll kill her Jack.

[Jack lets go.]

JACK. Give it me then. Come on.

SUSAN. Wait, she can't move, leave her alone.

JACK. Give it me.

[Alice puts her hand between his thighs.]

ALICE. There. It's back.

JACK. It is. It is back. Thank you, Alice. I wasn't sure you were a witch till then.

[*Jack goes.*]

SUSAN. What you doing Alice? Alice? Alice?

[*Alice turns to her.*]

ALICE. It's nothing. He's mad. Oh my neck, Susan.
   Oh, I'd laugh if it didn't hurt.
SUSAN. Don't touch me. I'll not be touched by a
   witch.

SCENE XIV

Public square.

BELLRINGER. Whereas if anyone has any complaint
   against any woman for a witch, let them go to the
   townhall and lay their complaint. For a man is in
   town that is a famous finder of witches and has had
   above thirty hanged in the country round and he
   will discover if they are or no. Whereas if anyone has
   any complaint against any woman for a witch, let
   them go . . .
MARGERY. Stopped the butter.
JACK. Killed the calves.
MARGERY. Struck me in the head.
JACK. Lamed my hand.
MARGERY. Struck me in the stomach.
JACK. Bewitched my organ.
MARGERY. When I boiled my urine she came.
JACK. Blooded her and made my hand well.
MARGERY. Burnt her thatch.
JACK. And Susan, her friend, is like possessed scream-
   ing and crying and lay two days without speaking.
MARGERY. Susan's baby turned blue and its limbs
   twisted and it died.
JACK. Boy threw stones and called them witch, and
   after he vomited pins and straw.
MARGERY. Big nasty cat she has in her bed and sends
   it to people's dairies.
JACK. A rat's her imp.
MARGERY. And the great storm last light brought a
   tree down in the lane, who made that out of a clear
   sky?
PACKER. I thank God that he has brought me again
   where I am needed. Don't be afraid any more. You
   have been in great danger but the devil can never

overcome the faithful. For God in his mercy has
called me and shown me a wonderful way of finding
out witches, which is finding the place on the body
of the witch made sensitive to pain by the devil. So
that if you prick that place with a pin no blood
comes out and the witch feels nothing at all.

[*Packer and Goody take Joan, and Goody holds her, while
Packer pulls up her skirts and pricks her legs. Joan curses
and screams throughout. Packer and Goody abuse her: a
short sharp moment of great noise and confusion.*]

GOODY. Hold still you old witch. Devil not help you
   now, no good calling him. Strong for your age,
   that's the devil's strength in her, see. Hold still, you
   stinking old strumpet.
PACKER. Hold your noise, witch, how can we tell
   what we're doing? Ah, ah, there's for you devil,
   there's blood, and there's blood, where's your spot,
   we'll find you out Satan.
JOAN. Damn you to hell, oh Christ help me! Ah, ah,
   you're hurting, let go, damn you, oh sweet God, oh
   you devils, oh devil take you.
PACKER. There, there, no blood here, Goody Haskins.
   Here's her spot. Hardly a speck here.
GOODY. How she cries the old liar, pretending it hurts
   her.
PACKER. There's one for hanging, stand aside there.
   We've others to attend to. Next please, Goody.

[*Goody takes Alice. Packer helps, and her skirts are thrown
over her head while he pricks her. She tries not to cry out.*]

GOODY. Why so much blood?
PACKER. The devil's cunning here.
GOODY. She's not crying much, she can't feel it.
PACKER. Have I the spot though? Which is the spot?
   There. There. There. No, I haven't the spot. Oh,
   it's tiring work. Set this one aside. Maybe there's
   others will speak against her and let us know more
   clearly what she is.

[*Alice is stood aside.*]

PACKER. If anyone here knows anything more of this
   woman why she might be a witch, I charge them in
   God's name to speak out, or the guilt of filthy
   witchcraft will be on you for concealing it.
SUSAN. I know something of her.
PACKER. Don't be shy then girl, speak out.
ALICE. Susan, what you doing? Don't speak against
   me.

SUSAN. Don't let her at me.
ALICE. You'll have me hanged.

[*Susan starts to shriek hysterically.*]

GOODY. Look, she's bewitched.
MARGERY. It's Alice did it to her.
ALICE. Susan, stop.
SUSAN. Alice. Alice. Alice.
PACKER. Take the witch out and the girl may be quiet.

[*Goody takes Alice off. Susan stops.*]

MARGERY. See that.
JACK. Praise God I escaped such danger.
SUSAN. She met with the devil, she told me, like a man in black she met him in the night and did uncleanness with him, and ever after she was not herself but wanted to be with the devil again. She took me to a cunning woman and they made me take a foul potion to destroy the baby in my womb and it was destroyed. And the cunning woman said she would teach Alice her wicked magic, and she'd have powers and not everyone could learn that, but Alice could because she's a witch, and the cunning woman gave her something to call the devil, and she tried to call him, and she made a puppet, and stuck pins in, and tried to make me believe that was the devil, but that was my baby girl, and next day she was sick and her face blue and limbs all twisted up and she died. And I don't want to see her.
PACKER. These cunning women are worst of all. Everyone hates witches who do harm but good witches they go to for help and come into the devil's power without knowing it. The infection will spread through the whole country if we don't stop it. Yes, all witches deserve death, and the good witch even more than the bad one. Oh God, do not let your kingdom be overrun by the devil. And you, girl, you went to this good witch, and you destroyed the child in your womb by witchcraft, which is a grievous offence. And you were there when this puppet was stuck with pins, and consented to the death of your own baby daughter?
SUSAN. No, I didn't. I didn't consent. I never wished her harm. Oh if I was angry sometimes or cursed her for crying, I never meant it. I'd take it back if I could have her back. I never meant to harm her.
PACKER. You can't take your curses back, you cursed her to death. That's two of your children you killed. And what other harm have you done? Don't look

amazed, you'll speak soon enough. We'll prick you as you pricked your babies.

SCENE XV

Public square.

[*Goody takes Susan and Packer pulls up her skirt.*]

GOODY. There's no man finds more witches than Henry Packer. He can tell by their look, he says, but of course he has more ways than that. He's read all the books and he's travelled. He says the reason there's so much witchcraft in England is England is too soft with its witches, for in Europe and Scotland they are hanged and burned and if they are not penitent they are burnt alive, but in England they are only hanged. And the ways of discovering witches are not so good here, for in other countries they have thumbscrews and racks and the bootikens which is said to be the worst pain in the world, for it fits tight over the legs from ankle to knee and is driven tighter and tighter till the legs are crushed as small as might be and the blood and marrow spout out and the bones crushed and the legs made unserviceable forever. And very few continue their lies and denials then. In England we haven't got such thorough ways, our ways are slower but they get the truth in the end when a fine skilful man like Henry Packer is onto them. He's well worth the twenty shillings a time, and I get the same, which is very good of him to insist on and well worth it though some folk complain and say, 'what, the price of a cow, just to have a witch hanged?' But I say to them think of the expense a witch is to you in the damage she does to property, such as a cow killed one or two pounds, a horse maybe four pounds, besides all the pigs and sheep at a few shillings a time, and chickens at sixpence all adds up. For two pounds and our expenses at the inn, you have all that saving, besides knowing you're free of the threat of sudden illness and death. Yes, it's interesting work being a searcher and nice to do good at the same time as earning a living. Better than staying home a widow. I'd end up like the old women you see, soft in the head and full of spite with their muttering and spells. I keep healthy keeping the country healthy. It's an honour to work with a great professional.

SCENE XVI

Ellen's cottage.

BETTY. I'm frightened to come any more. They'll say I'm a witch.

ELLEN. Are they saying I'm a witch?

BETTY. They say because I screamed that was the devil in me. And when I ran out of the house they say where was I going if not to meet other witches. And some know I come to see you.

ELLEN. Nobody's said it yet to my face.

BETTY. But the doctor says he'll save me. He says I'm not a witch, he says I'm ill. He says I'm his patient so I can't be a witch. He says he's making me better. I hope I can be better.

ELLEN. You get married, Betty, that's safest.

BETTY. But I want to be left alone. You know I do.

ELLEN. Left alone for what? To be like me? There's no doctor going to save me from being called a witch. Your best chance of being left alone is marry a rich man, because it's part of his honour to have a wife who does nothing. He has his big house and rose garden and trout stream, he just needs a fine lady to make it complete and you can be that. You can sing and sit on the lawn and change your dresses and order the dinner. That's the best you can do. What would you rather? Marry a poor man and work all day? Or go on as you're going, go on strange? That's not safe. Plenty of girls feel like you've been feeling, just for a bit. But you're not one to go on with it.

BETTY. If it's true there's witches, maybe I've been bewitched. If the witches are stopped, maybe I'll get well.

ELLEN. You'll get well, my dear, and you'll get married, and you'll tell your children about the witches.

BETTY. What's going to happen? Will you be all right?

ELLEN. You go home now. You don't want them finding you here.

[Betty goes.]

I could ask to be swum. They think the water won't keep a witch in, for Christ's baptism sake, so if a woman floats she's a witch. And if she sinks they have to let her go. I could sink. Any fool can sink. It's how to sink without drowning. It's whether they get you out. No, why should I ask to be half drowned? I've done nothing. I'll explain to them what I do. It's healing, not harm. There's no devil in it. If I keep calm and explain it, they can't hurt me.

If You Float

If you float you're a witch.
If you scream you're a witch.
If you sink, then you're dead anyway.
If you cure you're a witch
Or impure you're a witch
Whatever you do, you must pay.
Fingers are pointed, a knock at the door,
You may be a mother, a child or a whore.
If you complain you're a witch
Or you're lame you're a witch
Any marks or deviations count for more.
Got big tits you're a witch
Fall to bits you're a witch
He likes them young, concupiscent and poor.
Fingers are pointed, a knock at the door,
They're coming to get you, do you know what for?
So don't drop a stitch
My poor little bitch
If you're making a spell
Do it well
Deny it you're bad
Admit it you're mad
Say nothing at all
They'll damn you to hell.

SCENE XVII

A prison.

[Alice is tied up, sitting on the floor, Goody is eating and yawning.]

GOODY. You'd better confess, my dear, for he'll have you watched night and day and there's nothing makes a body so wretched as not sleeping. I'm tired myself. It's for your own good, you know, to save you from the devil. If we let you stay as you are, you'd be damned eternally and better a little pain now than eternal . . . [She realises Alice is nodding to sleep and picks up a drum and bangs it loudly. She gives it several bangs to keep Alice awake. Packer comes in.]

She's an obstinate young witch, this one, on her second night. She tires a body out.

PACKER. Go and sleep, Goody, I'll watch her a while.

GOODY. You're a considerate man, Mr. Packer. We earn our money.

[Goody goes.]

PACKER. I'm not a hard man. I like to have my confession so I'm easy in my mind I've done right.

ALICE. Where's my boy?

PACKER. Safe with good people.

ALICE. He wants me.

PACKER. He's safe from the devil, where you'll never come.

ALICE. I want him.

PACKER. Why won't you confess and make this shorter?

ALICE. It isn't true.

PACKER. Tell me your familiars. Tell me your imps' names. I won't let them plague you for telling. God will protect you if you repent.

ALICE. I haven't any. [Packer drums.] I want my boy.

PACKER. Then you should have stayed home at night with him and not gone out after the devil.

ALICE. I want him.

PACKER. How could a mother be a filthy witch and put her child in danger?

ALICE. I didn't.

PACKER. Night after night, it's well known.

ALICE. But what's going to happen to him? He's only got me.

PACKER. He should have a father. Who's his father? Speak up, who's his father?

ALICE. I don't know.

PACKER. You must speak.

ALICE. I don't know.

PACKER. You must confess.

[Packer drums.]

ALICE. Oh my head. Please don't. Everything's drumming.

PACKER. I'll watch. Your imps will come to see you.

ALICE. Drumming.

[Packer suddenly stops.]

PACKER. Ah. Ah. What's this? A spider. A huge black one. And it ran off when it saw a godly man. Deny if you can that spider's one of your imps.

ALICE. No.

PACKER. Then why should it come? Tell me that.

ALICE. I want my boy.

PACKER. Why? Why do you keep on about the boy? Who's his father? Is the devil his father?

ALICE. No, no, no.

PACKER. I'll have the boy to see me in the morning. If he's not the devil's child he'll speak against you. [Alice cries.] I'll watch you. I've watched plenty of witches and hanged them all. I'll get that spider too if it comes back.

SCENE XVIII

A prison.

[Goody is shaving Susan under the arm.]

GOODY. There, that's the second arm done, and no mark yet. Devil hides his marks all kinds of places. The more secret the better he likes it. Though I knew one witch had a great pink mark on her shoulder and neck so everyone could see. And a woman last week with a big lump in her breast like another whole teat where she sucked her imps, a little black one she had and a little white one and kept them in wool in a bottle. And when I squeezed it first white stuff came out like milk and then blood, for she fed those horrid creatures on milk and blood and they sucked her secret parts in the night too. Now let's see your secret parts and see what the devil does there.

[She makes Susan lie down, and pulls up her skirt to shave her. Packer comes in.]

PACKER. What devil's marks?

GOODY. No need to shave the other for she has three bigs in her privates almost an inch long like great teats where the devil sucks her and a bloody place on her side where she can't deny she cut a lump off herself so I wouldn't find it.

PACKER. Such a stinking old witch I won't look myself. Is there nothing here?

GOODY. She's clean yet but we'll shave her and see what shameful thing's hidden.

PACKER. Though a mark is a sure sign of a witch's guilt having no mark is no sign of innocence for the devil can take marks off.

JOAN. And the devil take you.

PACKER. You'll be with the devil soon enough.

JOAN. And I'll be glad to see him. I been a witch these ten years. Boys was always calling after me and one day I said to a boy, 'Boy boy you call me witch but when did I make your arse to itch.' And he ran off and I met a little grey kitling and the kitling said, 'you must go with me' and I said, 'Avoid, Satan.' And he said, 'You must give me your body and soul and you'll have all happiness.' And I did. And I gave him my blood every day, and that's my old cat Vinegar Tom. And he lamed John Peter's son that's a cripple this day, that was ten years ago. And I had two more imps sent me, crept in my bed in the night, sucked my privy parts so sore they hurt me and wouldn't leave me. And I asked them to kill Mary Johnson who crossed me and she wasted after. And everyone knows Anne that had fits and would gnash her teeth and took six strong men to hold her. That was me sent those fits to her. My little imps are like moles with four feet but no tails and a black colour. And I'd send them off and they'd come back in the night and say they did what I said. Jack is lucky I didn't bewitch him to death and Margery, but she was kind to me long ago. But I killed their cows like I killed ten cows last year. And the great storm and tempest comes when I call it and strikes down trees. But now I'm in prison my power's all gone or I'd call down thunder and twist your guts.

PACKER. Is there any reason you shouldn't be hanged?

JOAN. I'm with child.

GOODY. Who'd believe that?

SCENE XIX

Public square.

[*Joan and Ellen are hanged while Margery prays.*]

MARGERY. Dear God, thank you for saving me. Let us live safe now. I have scrubbed the dairy out. You have shown your power in destroying the wicked, and you show it in blessing the good. You have helped me in my struggle against the witches, help me in my daily struggle. Help me work harder and our good harvests will be to your glory. Bless Miss Betty's marriage and let her live happy. Bless Jack and keep him safe from evil and let him love me and give us the land, amen.

SCENE XX

Public square.

[*Joan and Ellen hanging.*]

SUSAN. Alice, how can you look? Your poor mother. You're not even crying.

ALICE. She wasn't a witch. She wouldn't know how.

SUSAN. Alice, she was.

ALICE. The cunning woman was, I think. That's why I was frightened of her.

SUSAN. I was a witch and never knew it. I killed my babies. I never meant it. I didn't know I was so wicked. I didn't know I had that mark on me. I'm so wicked. Alice, let's pray to God we won't be damned. If we're hanged, we're saved, Alice, so we mustn't be frightened. It's done to help us. Oh God, I know now I'm loathsome and a sinner and Mr. Packer has shown me how bad I am and I repent I never knew that but now I know and please forgive me and don't make me go to hell and be burnt forever—

ALICE. I'm not a witch.

SUSAN. Alice, you know you are. God, don't hear her say that.

ALICE. I'm not a witch. But I wish I was. If I could live I'd be a witch now after what they've done. I'd make wax men and melt them on a slow fire. I'd kill their animals and blast their crops and make such storms, I'd wreck their ships all over the world. I shouldn't have been frightened of Ellen, I should have learnt. Oh if I could meet with the devil now I'd give him anything if he'd give me power. There's no way for us except by the devil. If I only did have magic, I'd make them feel it.

Lament for the Witches

Where have the witches gone?
Who are the witches now?
Here we are.

All the gentle witches' spells
blast the doctors' sleeping pills.
The witches hanging in the sky
haunt the courts where lawyers lie.
Here we are.

They were gentle witches
with healing spells
They were desperate witches
with no way out but the other side of hell.

A witch's crying in the night
switches out your children's light.
All your houses safe and warm
are struck at by the witches' storm.
Here we are.

Where have the witches gone?
Who are the witches now?
Here we are.

They were gentle witches
with healing spells.
They were desperate witches
with no way out but the other side of hell.
Here we are.

Look in the mirror tonight.
Would they have hanged you then?
Ask how they're stopping you now.
Where have the witches gone?
Who are the witches now?
Ask how they're stopping you now.
Here we are.

SCENE XXI

SPRENGER. He's Kramer.

KRAMER. He's Sprenger.

KRAMER/SPRENGER. Professors of Theology

KRAMER. delegated by letters apostolic

SPRENGER. (here's a toast, non-alcoholic).

KRAMER. Inquisitors of heretical pravities

SPRENGER. we must fill those moral cavities

KRAMER. so we've written a book

SPRENGER. *Malleus Maleficarum*

KRAMER. *The Hammer of Witches.*

SPRENGER. It works like a charm

KRAMER. to discover witches

SPRENGER. and torture with no hitches.

KRAMER. Why is a greater number of witches found in the fragile feminine sex than in men?

SPRENGER. Why is a greater number of witches found in the fragile feminine sex than in men?

KRAMER. 'All wickedness is but little to the wickedness of a woman.' Ecclesiastes.

SPRENGER. Here are three reasons, first because

KRAMER. woman is more credulous and since the aim of the devil is to corrupt faith he attacks them. Second because

SPRENGER. women are more impressionable. Third because

KRAMER. women have slippery tongues and cannot conceal from other women what by their evil art they know.

SPRENGER. Women are feebler in both body and mind so it's not surprising.

KRAMER. In intellect they seem to be of a different nature from men—

SPRENGER. like children.

KRAMER. Yes.

SPRENGER. But the main reason is

KRAMER/SPRENGER. she is more carnal than a man

KRAMER. as may be seen from her many carnal abominations.

SPRENGER. She was formed from a bent rib

KRAMER. and so is an imperfect animal.

SPRENGER. Fe mina, female, that is fe faith minus without

KRAMER. so cannot keep faith.

SPRENGER. A defect of intelligence.

KRAMER. A defect of inordinate passions.

SPRENGER. They brood on vengeance.

KRAMER/SPRENGER. Wherefore it is no wonder they are witches.

KRAMER. Women have weak memories.

SPRENGER. Follow their own impulses.

KRAMER. Nearly all the kingdoms of the worlds have been overthrown by women.

SPRENGER. as Troy, etc.

KRAMER. She's a liar by nature

SPRENGER. vain

KRAMER. more bitter than death

SPRENGER. contaminating to touch

KRAMER. their carnal desires

SPRENGER. their insatiable malice

KRAMER. their hands are as bands for binding when they place their hands on a creature to bewitch it with the help of the devil.

SPRENGER. To conclude.

KRAMER. All witchcraft

SPRENGER. comes from carnal lust

KRAMER. which is in woman

KRAMER/SPRENGER. insatiable.

KRAMER. It is no wonder there are more women then men found infected with the heresy of witchcraft.

SPRENGER. And blessed be the Most High, which has so far preserved the male sex from so great a crime.

Evil Women

Evil women
Is that what you want?
Is that what you want to see?
On the movie screen
Of your own wet dream
Evil women.

If you like sex sinful, what you want is us.
You can be sucked off by a succubus.
We had this man, and afterwards he died.

Does she do what she's told or does she nag?
Are you cornered in the kitchen by a bitching hag?
Satan's lady, Satan's pride.
Satan's baby, Satan's bride,
A devil woman's not easily satisfied.

Do you ever get afraid
You don't do it right?

Does your lady demand it
Three times a night?
If we don't say you're big
Do you start to shrink?
We earn our own money
And buy our own drink.

Did you learn you were dirty boys, did you learn
Women were wicked to make you burn?

Satan's lady, Satan's pride,
Satan's baby, Satan's bride,
Witches were wicked and had to burn.

Evil women
Is that what you want?
Is that what you want to see?
In your movie dream
Do they scream and scream?
Evil women
Evil women
Women.

ESSAY: AN APPROACH TO THE PLAY

It is common for a society, or at least its leaders, to define those who oppose its version of established order with a word such as "evil" or with a modern counterpart such as "unpatriotic." Such a definition marks one's opponents as different from oneself, possibly as inhuman or subhuman, as not deserving the same treatment we give to our equals. Such definitions make it easier to persuade one's followers that these opponents are not merely opponents, but enemies, people not merely to disagree with, but to fear, to feel threatened by, even to hate. Churchill goes back to the seventeenth century for a particularly shocking example of this social practice, while presenting it with a resonance applicable to the 1990s.

In the first scene, Alice and "Man," who have just had sex, are discussing this fact and its implications, she with directness and honesty, he with deliberate obscurity. Part of this obscurity has to do with his introduction of the idea of the Devil as a power figure associated with Man and of witches as his sexual servants. Is this Man in fact the Devil? Or does he use this word playfully, perhaps also threateningly, as in some way a metaphor for his sexual power? Alice treats him like a man who is playing an unpleasant game, but she does believe in witches and can even imagine being excited by watching one killed. He then rejects her, she curses him, and he calls her a witch. The mysteriousness of man to woman seems emphasized by the ambiguity of what is meant by "Devil" in this scene, and he is still playing this game as he leaves. This first scene may also imply Alice's collusion in her own destiny: she has been taught by her society to believe in—and be fascinated by—witches. (A similar point is made by Goody at the end of Scene 15 and by Susan near the start of

Scene 20.) We also see the process by which Alice is called a witch: her curse seems to be an expression of frustration and may even express a desire to see injury done, but it is hardly black magic. It seems to be a normal angry response of the powerless against callous treatment.

Scene 2 introduces the point of view of Jack and Margery, the farmer–capitalist and his wife, perhaps the most "normal" characters in this play, and with them speculation on the question of ownership. They discuss the prospects for expanding their farm, are scandalized by what they see as the shiftlessness of Alice and her mother, and refuse a bed to Betty, a young aristocratic woman who is kept imprisoned in her house for refusing to marry the man of her family's choice. As Margery, ever judgmental, says, "We shouldn't help her do wrong." Fathers seem to own their daughters as much as Jack and Margery own their land, and ownership seems to allow these people the privilege of sitting in judgment on those without their power.

Scene 3 offers a contrast: we are given a glimpse of the world from the point of view of the poor who had been judged shiftless in the previous scene. For the first time there are only women onstage, a mother and her daughter, and, another first in the play, they act gently and caringly toward one another. Men are here represented as beating women (in the first scene, there is also reference to the woman's being physically hurt), and the advantage for a woman in being with a man is said to be, "We'd have more to eat." Men represent financial security, an idea implied in the previous scene, but here with no romantic illusions. Gender and class are interrelated: both male social power and female dependency are suggested. The song "Nobody Sings" updates these suggestions of society's impact on women and complicates them, adding to the equation a woman's sexual drive and psychic needs as well as the standards for attractiveness which guarantee that "Nobody ever saw me."

In subsequent scenes, the implications of this social system are worked out in ways which emphasize how excruciating they are. Male sexual and social power is allied to capitalist self-seeking and possessiveness in an alliance which victimizes women both physically and psychically. Packer brings this alliance to its climax of sexual humiliation with his "pricking," while the song "If You Float" emphasizes women's no-win situation. The end of Scene 13 suggests why this sexual domination might have arisen. Alice restores Jack's penis by putting her hand between his thighs. It is difficult not to read this scene figuratively: not that he has literally lost his penis, but that he cannot get an erection. Alice's power is not magical but erotic. The reality of this female erotic power is overwhelming to Jack (and perhaps to men in general). Is it this power that men resent and feel that women must be deprived of?

Near the end of the play, Kramer and Sprenger, co-authors of *The Hammer of Witches*, quote some of the misogynist assertions found in their book in the style of a modern cabaret act. The roles of the two inquisitors are played by the same actresses who had previously played the recently hanged Ellen and Joan. If we have seen modern resonances in this play's representation of a seventeenth-century fiction, we may also see a disturbing parallel between their "historically distanced" justifications and our own contemporary attitudes. There is a jarring discord in having these excerpts from a text justifying the murder of witches presented in cabaret style, and it is even more unsettling to have the misogynist cant presented by the targets of the words' abuse, women, and especially by the two actresses who had played the characters most horribly victimized in this play by these ideas. This scene becomes, therefore, the play's exclamation point: while making us laugh, it also makes us writhe. We cannot laugh off these ideas as if they have been left safely behind us in the seventeenth century; perhaps we carry remnants of these assumptions with us still. The alternation of tone, as if our play has been interrupted by conventions from a different form of entertainment, prevents us from distancing ourselves comfortably from its action.

The play's confrontational quality is repeated, although in a different key, in the closing song, "Evil Women," in which men everywhere are directly addressed, perhaps even taunted, by the female cast. The evil woman is desirable, is dreamed of, *because* she is sinful: men need evil women to feed their lust and to justify their desire to control the object of their lust. The implication is that men, therefore, create evil women, define them as evil, and yet this very definition gives women power over men and makes them frightening.

These observations may make it sound as if the play answers all the questions it poses, but it does not. For example, does the fact that all characters are played by actresses (and in this presentation of the play exclusively through women's voices, it would invert *Lysistrata*'s staging) suggest anything about how we might respond to them? What different images of women and of men does this play construct? To what degree are these differences represented as being socially rather than biologically determined? What interests are served by this particular construction of gender identities? How are these interests to be distinguished from those of our own society? Does the play seem to encourage optimism about the possibility of changing gender roles? Has the mystery of men to women with which this play opened been dissipated, or deepened, as the play progresses? One final question: Who is Vinegar Tom and why do we never see him? Is he an image of witches' power?

Martin Sherman

MESSIAH

About the Author   Martin Sherman (1938–   ) is an American playwright who now lives in London. Born in Philadelphia, he earned an MFA from Boston University in 1960 and had his first play produced in 1963. Besides being playwright-in-residence at Playwrights Horizons in New York during 1976–77, his many awards include a National Endowment of the Arts Fellowship in 1980 and a Rockefeller Fellowship in 1985. *Messiah*, his twelfth produced play, first appeared in London in 1982 and in New York in 1984.

About the Play   As Sherman's Afterpiece implies, this play is based on a historical situation, one which allows him to explore existence in a "borderland," a place where a minority group of Polish Jews are isolated by their religion and traditions from their own territorial homeland in Poland and, more crucially here, from their enemies, the Russian Cossacks. Rachel's people are without a place of their own, continually displaced and continually threatened. This particular historical situation allows the play to explore the sources from which a dislocated people can draw strength; the parallel with Sherman's own Russian parentage may have contributed to this choice of subject. The play presents the issue of alienation from one's surroundings and from conventional belief as well as the dilemma of how to deal with such alienation, problems that many in our own time also face.

In such situations, when there seems little else to hold onto, individuals are thrown back on their own resources; alternatively, they may seek to evade the problem or deny its existence. Here, the central figure Rachel tries to rely on various sources of strength: on God, on the verities of traditional Jewish teaching, on the common sense of an older husband, on the beauty of a younger man, even on the possibility of a rescue-figure, such as the Messiah. With the possible exception of her mother, each of the characters with whom she is intimate is identified with one or more of these potential sources of strength. (It is interesting, however, that the major figures in the play who are sustained by these kinds of faith are all male, and they all end up killing themselves.)

From another point of view, this is a play about the mass psychology which operates within an otherwise helpless people: the hope for a better life crystallizes for most of the characters in this play into belief in the legitimacy of Sabbatai Sevi as the long looked-for Messiah. When he fails them, it seems the end of things for believers. For us, as for Rachel, however, he may merely seem the latest, perhaps the greatest, in an apparently endless string of such failures.

CHARACTERS

RACHEL
REBECCA
TANTA ROSE
REB ELLIS
ASHER
SARAH

Neighbours, hawkers, musicians, Sarah's companions, etc.

The play is set in 1665, in Yultishk, a small village on what was once the Ukrainian border of Poland.

Note   The word 'blackout' is often used in the stage directions. It need not be taken literally. It is meant to suggest the end of a scene and some change in lighting.

Act I

Rachel is praying. Rachel is twenty-eight. She has a difficult face. Her skin is covered with spots, and she has two enormous front teeth protruding over her lips. Her movements are awkward.

RACHEL. God bless Mama. Please let Mama get well. Please keep the Cossacks away. Please let someone love me. God bless Tanta Rose. And all the Jews. And please let the Messiah come. Amen.

[Blackout].

[Lights rise on the kitchen of a small house. It is almost a hut. Rachel sits by a table, sewing. Rebecca sits in a corner. Rebecca is close to fifty: a striking woman with large, haunted eyes. A spool of lambs' wool rests in her hand; it has become tangled and knotted. Rebecca stamps on the floor. Rachel continues to sew. Rebecca stamps again. Rachel looks up; she rises and goes to Rebecca.]

RACHEL.. You're all tangled up, Mama. [She lifts the wool from Rebecca's hand and unwinds it. Rebecca stamps her foot.] Mama, don't . . . Mama, what do you want? I have to sew, Mama. If I don't sew, we don't eat. [Rebecca stamps her foot.] Yes, Mama. Your wool. [Rachel returns the wool to Rebecca in one piece. Rebecca clutches on to it.] Yes. [Rachel returns to her sewing. Rebecca looks at the wool.]

[Blackout.]

[Lights rise on Rachel praying.]

RACHEL. God bless Mama. Please let Mama get well. [Pause.] Hell! [Pause.] You heard me. [Pause.] I'm sorry. Forgive me. [Pause.] Amen.

[Blackout.]

[Lights rise on the kitchen. Rachel is sewing. Rebecca is in the corner. Tanta Rose, a middle-aged woman, is talking to Rachel.]

TANTA ROSE. Reb Ellis.
RACHEL. I don't want to hear.
TANTA ROSE. He's a nice man.
RACHEL. He's fat.

TANTA ROSE. He's rich.
RACHEL. He's old.
TANTA ROSE. He's lonely.
RACHEL. He smells funny.
TANTA ROSE. His wife died four years ago. He has no children. Everything would be yours.
RACHEL. I don't want anything.
TANTA ROSE. Suppose the Messiah comes?
RACHEL. What then? Reb Ellis becomes young and thin?
TANTA ROSE. Everyone should be married in the eyes of the Messiah.
RACHEL. Where did you hear that? Anyhow, the Messiah's not coming.
TANTA ROSE. How do you know?
RACHEL. Things have to happen. Elijah has to return. Have you seen Elijah? I haven't. The temple has to be restored. Things. I read the Torah.
TANTA ROSE. You shouldn't. That's not for women. Home is for women.
RACHEL. That's where I read it. At home.
TANTA ROSE. Rachel, I'm going to talk to you like an aunt.
RACHEL. Tanta, you *are* my aunt.
TANTA ROSE. Always a smart answer. But never the truth.
RACHEL. What's the truth?
TANTA ROSE. What's inside.
RACHEL. Oh, Tanta.
TANTA ROSE. You survive on charity.
RACHEL. I sew.
TANTA ROSE. And how much does *that* bring in? And is it good for your eyes? You should eat more carrots. You're going to need glasses. And how about your mother?
RACHEL. *She* should eat more carrots?
TANTA ROSE. She won't get better. There's . . .
RACHEL. There's what?
TANTA ROSE. A curse. [She spits.] Ach! We shouldn't talk about it. God willing, some day . . . Well, meanwhile, she needs a better home. And you're not getting younger. Twenty-eight and not married! You have no friends. You stay in this room all day and sew. You talk back to me, but with other people you're a regular sphinx. You're becoming like your mother. It's not healthy. You need a husband. Last year you turned down Reb Judah. You said he had

one leg shorter than the other. So what does that mean in a man? What's the big deal?

RACHEL. He slanted.

TANTA ROSE. And two years ago you turned down Reb Kalmeyer. He was bald.

RACHEL. Only on his head. Everywhere else was hair. His fingers.

TANTA ROSE. So who's left? Yultishk is a small town. Reb Ellis is a good man. No one else is going to ask for your hand.

RACHEL. [Looks at her hand.] Why. It's a nice hand. [She takes her scissors and makes as if to cut it off.] If that's what he wants, he can have it.

TANTA ROSE. Stop it. Rachela, you're my favourite niece.

RACHEL. I'm your only niece.

TANTA ROSE. What are you waiting for?

RACHEL. I don't know. [She smiles.] The Messiah.

TANTA ROSE. Always a joke. [Pause.] I don't know how to say this.

RACHEL. Say what?

TANTA ROSE. This.

RACHEL. What's this?

TANTA ROSE. Oh, Rachela, Rachela . . . Every man . . . every man can't be King David.

RACHEL. So?

TANTA ROSE. And every woman . . .

RACHEL. What?

TANTA ROSE. Can't be Queen Esther. [Pause.] Do you know what I mean? [Silence.]

RACHEL. Yes.

[Blackout.]

[Lights rise on Rachel praying.]

RACHEL. God bless Tanta Rose. But keep her away from me. Please. Look, I don't want to be Queen Esther. I don't want to be beautiful. Oh God. I'd settle for being plain.

[Blackout.]

[Lights rise on the kitchen. Reb Ellis and Asher sit at the table with Rachel. Rebecca is in the corner. Reb Ellis is in his fifties; he is heavy-set. Asher is twenty-four and handsome. A jug of wine sits on the table. They are drinking from wine glasses. Rachel is sewing.]

ASHER. My uncle . . .

REB ELLIS. I can speak for myself. Did you bring the plums? Where are they?

[Asher brings a bag out from under the table. Reb Ellis opens the bag and brings out plums. He hands one to Rachel.]

Try these. It's not plum season, but you wouldn't know it, they're so juicy. Rich. A good plum flavour is rich. [He devours a plum.] You keep a very clean house. The Bible says it's good to be clean. Something like that, somewhere. I forget. It says a little of everything, you know, the Bible. My nephew is going to argue. He studies the Bible all day. And Talmud. And Kabbalah. Mostly, Kabbalah, eh, Asher? Demons and dybbuks in his dreams. I don't dream of demons. I dream of fruit. Plums and apples and apricots—that's why I have the finest fruit store this side of Kiev. I'm like an artist with fruit. It's not just money to me. It's love. [He finishes his wine glass.] This is very nice wine. Good grapes. [He turns to Rebecca.] Here, Rebecca, have a glass. Give your mother a glass. No, I will.

[Reb Ellis pours another glass of wine, rises from the table and brings the glass to Rebecca.]

You don't remember me. Reb Ellis, the fruit man? [He turns back to Rachel.] I remember your mother . . . when she came back to Yultishk. We all scattered when the Cossacks came. So many were killed. But we came back. Where else to go? And one day, Rebecca returned too. So beautiful, so sad. Like a pomegranate. Holding your hand. You were a little girl, you don't remember. Four years wandering around Poland. Ach, what she must have seen. No wonder she doesn't talk. I don't think she's ill. [He turns back to Rebecca.] You just don't have anything more to say, do you?

[He tries to put the glass in her hand, but she will not let go of her wool.]

Drink. It's good.

[Frustrated, he puts the drink down by her chair. He kneels and takes out a plum.]

Well, how about a plum? I'll leave the plum—right here—for you—if you decide later, on your own, to have it.

[He puts the plum in her lap, then rises and walks back to the table.]

Your mother has beautiful eyes. Green. Greengage eyes. You don't talk much, do you? I like a quiet woman. Keeps a clean house. My nephew, Asher, I brought him because I thought he could speak for me. I get very shy. But at the same time, I can get along anywhere. I'm like that. Peasants or kings. I fit in. My nephew, Asher, keeps looking for the Messiah. In the Kabbalah, he looks, in the Kabbalah. He says the time is coming, the time is coming. I tell you something, if the Messiah comes tomorrow, it's not Asher who could talk to him. Asher can talk to books. *I'd* talk to him. We'd sit down and have a peach. Or a pear. Although if he comes tomorrow it wouldn't be a pear. The crop's not so good this year. I wouldn't give the Messiah a bad pear, believe me. Only the best. And we'd get along. *[He pours another glass of wine.]* I know human nature. That's in the Bible, too. Somewhere. So, you see, I'm quiet. I'm shy. But I get along. Peasants or kings. Messiahs. You name it. I get along. So I'm not a bad person to marry. There. That's what I want to say. You'll make a nice dinner table for me. You'll keep a clean house for me. You'll be happy. *[He rises.]* All right, Asher, you did a good job. Give her the oranges. You didn't give her the oranges.

[Blackout.]

[Lights rise on Rachel praying.]

RACHEL. God help me. Look, we're going to have to sort this out. What an exasperating man. He talks and talks and talks . . . But I don't dislike him. He spoke to Mama. You've seen for years what's happened here. People come in. They never speak to Mama. She's crazy. She's cursed. She's dead. To this whole goddamned town, she's dead. I'm sorry. I didn't mean to take your name in vain. I'm sorry. I'm sorry. Forgive me. Oh God . . . *[Pause.]* You see, the thing is that he's ugly. And I'm not sure that I care what's underneath. Now his nephew . . . His nephew is beautiful. For all I know he's an absolute idiot, but *outside*, the part with bones and tissue and flesh, *that* part—beautiful. *Him* I would marry. Oh but God, it doesn't make sense, me of all people. When all I want—all I live for—is for someone to look beneath *my* face and see

that *I'm* beautiful. Underneath the spots. Can't you take away the spots? Oh, forget it, I didn't mean to ask you again. And the teeth. I know you don't want to discuss the teeth. It's just that sometimes I forget about them. And then I pass a mirror . . . It's like lightning struck my mouth and then stayed there. The teeth! I sit here all day and try to think of some use for them. And what do I come up with? If I'm ever attacked by a lion, I can bite back. There are no lions in Yultishk. You know, if I wrote the Ten Commandments on them—five on one, five on the other—there certainly is room—and then walked out on the street, I could say *I* was the Messiah. I think and think . . . there must be a reason for them. You have reasons for everything. Don't you. *[Pause.]* So. I'm ugly. That's that. So. Who better than me to forget about Reb Ellis' fat and Reb Ellis' smell, and see the bright, blue-eyed Reb Ellis inside? But I *can't*. I can't even look at an ugly man. If the Messiah came today, and he had warts and a big belly, I would send him back. Oh God. Help me. Give me a sign. A sign. Something. A rainbow. Thunder. Locusts. Something. Do I marry him? Talk to me. Burn me a bush and talk to me. Do I marry him? *[Silence.]* He spoke to Mama. No one else has.

[Blackout.]

[A Hebraic melody pierces the darkness. Lights rise slowly. Rachel is standing in a wedding dress. She looks awkward and embarrassed. Tanta Rose and Rebecca are with her.]

TANTA ROSE. Rachela, you're a beautiful bride. *[Rachel winces.]* What? You make faces. If only your father were here to see you. May his soul rest in peace. *[Rebecca looks away.]* Rebecca, tell her. Tell her she's a beautiful bride. *[Rebecca wanders away from them.]*
RACHEL. Tanta. Just let it be. *[Rachel and Tanta go after Rebecca.]*

[A table sits in the centre of the field. Reb Ellis is at the head of the table. Rachel is at one side, with Rebecca and Tanta Rose. An old Rabbi is on the other side. They all have wine. Reb Ellis is making a toast.]

REB ELLIS. A toast! To my handsome bride. *[Rachel smiles at the word 'handsome'.]* To my friends. My family, such as it is. They're all dead, killed by the Cossacks. They can't see this happy day. There's only my nephew Asher left, and where is he? Disappeared! Ach! He's young. He's probably studying the Kabbalah somewhere. He forgot what day it was. I'll have a new family. To my new family. [*He pours another glass.*] To Rebecca, my new mother-in-law. What every man wants, a quiet mother-in-law.

[*He drinks. Rachel, despite herself, laughs. She looks at Reb Ellis with a certain affection.*]

So. [*He pours another drink.*] To the town. To the orchards. The fields. The trees that bear my beautiful fruit. To the apples, the prunes, the pears . . .

[*Asher runs in. He is in a state of ecstasy. He has letters in his hand.*]

ASHER. Uncle! He's here.
REB ELLIS. Asher. A toast. I'm making a toast.
ASHER. He's here!
REB ELLIS. Asher. Take a seat. It's my wedding day. [*To the guests.*] He forgets. He reads too much.
ASHER. *He's here!* [*Rachel rises.*]
RACHEL. *Who's* here?

[*Tanta Rose pulls Rachel down.*]

TANTA ROSE. Shh! Rachel!
ASHER. The Messiah! The Messiah is here!
REB ELLIS. Asher. Not on my wedding day. I was making a toast. . .
ASHER. Uncle, it's true. The Messiah is here. Look. Letters. I have letters. Reb Samuel, the merchant in Kiev, received them. He made copies. His messenger brought them this afternoon. I've read them and read them. Here. See. Letters. [*He opens a letter.*] This one. From Nathan of Gaza. A holy man. [*He reads from the letter.*] "Hear me, my brothers, for our Messiah has come. He was born in Izmir. His name is Sabbatai Sevi." [*He throws the letter onto the table.*] Nathan is a famous rabbi, Uncle. He doesn't make things up. Look. Letters. They tell the story of Sabbatai Sevi. Here. [*He throws another letter on the table.*] Ordained a rabbi at eighteen. Speaks aloud the sacred and forbidden name of God at twenty. In Salonica, he takes a Torah scroll as his bride. In a wedding ceremony. He *marries* the Torah! Think of that, Uncle! This *must* be the Messiah. In Jerusalem, he performs miracles and raises part of the temple. And now in Gaza, Nathan, the holy man, recognizes him as the Messiah—and he himself, Sabbatai him-

self, always silent on this subject, finally declares himself. I *am* the Messiah, he says. I *am* the Messiah! Look. Letters. Proof. [*He throws the other letters on the table.*] He leaves for Izmir again and eventually Constantinople where he's going to take the crown from the Sultan's head. And look, Uncle, news . . . [*He takes out another letter.*] News of the tribes. The ten lost tribes of Israel. They've been found. Someone saw them in Arabia, by the river Sambatyon, ready to march, ready to cross the river, ready to take vengeance on our enemies. And Uncle, the teachings always said the Messiah would come after a great catastrophe. And didn't we have a great catastrophe seventeen years ago? Right here in Poland. Our people massacred . . . What for? What *for*? To prepare for the Messiah! And now he's come. He's come in the name of our Lord. He's come as our king. And we can all leave Yultishk, we can all leave Poland, and go back, back to Jerusalem! But first—we must purge ourselves. Repent our sins. Destroy our guilt. So we can be pure in his presence. Uncle! The drums of heaven are beating. Uncle! Listen! Listen to them. Uncle! The Messiah is here! [*Asher faints.*]

[*Blackout.*]

[*Lights rise on Rachel praying.*]

RACHEL. I wanted a quiet wedding. Dear God . . . why do you play jokes on me? No one in Yultishk will ever forget my wedding. Who is this Sabbatai? I'm so confused . . . [*Pause.*] Do you know what it was like? Our wedding night? What a question! Of course you know. You saw it. You see everything. You're always there, aren't you, when people make love? No, promise me, promise me, that wasn't making love. Something else, that was something else, but not making love. I'm so smart, but I'm so dumb. I know so much and I know so little. But even if he wasn't fat, even if he didn't smell, even if he was lean and golden and beautiful, that would not have been making love. He hurt me. And hurt me. And then ignored me. And I know about my teeth, but if my teeth were *his* teeth, I still wouldn't have done that to *him*. Well. He's a man. So be it. He's a man. [*Pause.*] If you see everything, if you know everything already—then what's the point, what's the point in talking to you?

[*Blackout.*]

[*Lights rise on the kitchen of Reb Ellis' house. Fruit everywhere. Expensive furniture. Rebecca is sitting. Tanta Rose is talking to Rachel.*]

TANTA ROSE. So—Reb Yitsel's sister received a letter from Reb Jacom's brother in Prague and he said that he heard that in Salonica they're marrying all their children off—ten, eleven years old—to each other, so they can start having babies right away. All I could think of was, what a job for a matchmaker.

RACHEL. Why are they doing that?

TANTA ROSE. So there won't be any more unborn souls left.

RACHEL. So?

TANTA ROSE. So as soon as that happens, the Messiah is free to accept his crown. It says so somewhere.

RACHEL. Tanta, we don't know if this man really is the Messiah.

TANTA ROSE. So then why did Asher faint?

RACHEL. He forgot to eat.

TANTA ROSE. How do you know he's *not* the Messiah? Did God tell you? [*Silence.*]

RACHEL. I'm not talking to God.

[*Blackout.*]

[*Lights rise on Reb Ellis' kitchen. Rachel is attending to Rebecca. Asher runs in through the back door.*]

ASHER. Are there nettles?

RACHEL. Are there *what?*

ASHER. Nettles.

RACHEL. Where?

ASHER. In the house.

RACHEL. Of course not.

ASHER. I *need* nettles.

RACHEL. What for?

ASHER. To beat myself. [*Rachel laughs.*] Why are you laughing?

RACHEL. I'm not. [*She starts to laugh again.*]

ASHER. It's not funny. Sabbatai beats himself with nettles every day. And can his sins be greater than mine?

RACHEL. How old are you?

ASHER. Twenty-four.

RACHEL. And how great are your sins?

ASHER. Great! Believe me. *Great!* I have impure thoughts. [*Silence.*] You wouldn't understand. Women don't have them.

[*Asher rushes out through the door. Rachel laughs.*]

RACHEL. Mama, Mama, Mama . . .

[*Blackout.*]

[*Lights rise on Reb Ellis' kitchen. Rachel is with Rebecca. Reb Ellis comes in from the next room.*]

REB ELLIS. Have you seen my nephew? That boy is obsessed. Sabbatai this, Sabbatai that . . . And it's spreading all over town. Reb Fishel's daughter had a vision. She saw a burning moon. I think she had a fever. She's only thirteen. I sent her some oranges. And speaking of oranges, I spoke to the Rabbi. He said there's a special prayer for orange rinds. I noticed the other day you said the prayer for fruit over some orange rinds. I'm not criticizing. You said it very well. I tell all my friends, you keep a wonderful house, you know all the prayers; but orange rinds are considered to be a scent not a food, so there's a special prayer—"bore minei besamin." In the opinion of some—but not all—you can say that prayer over lemon rinds as well. But you know how rabbis are with opinions. Talk, talk, talk. They could talk you to death . . . [*He rushes back into the next room.*]

RACHEL. Oh Mama, Mama, Mama . . .

[*Blackout.*]

[*Lights rise on Reb Ellis' kitchen. Rachel is with Rebecca. Asher comes in through the back door.*]

ASHER. I'm sorry.

RACHEL. What?

ASHER. I apologize.

RACHEL. What for?

ASHER. Saying you wouldn't understand. A letter came to town yesterday all the way from Venice. And in it it says that Sabbatai says that women are equal. Equal. To us. He's removed the curse that was set upon Eve. He dances with his wife, Sarah. He takes her to the synagogue with him and lets her read from the Torah. So perhaps I was wrong. Perhaps you do have impure thoughts.

RACHEL. Perhaps.

ASHER. Then you should beat yourself with nettles too. Why should it just be the men? Half of the men in town are doing it already? Why not half the women? It's a new world . . . The problem is so many people are beating themselves with nettles that there are no nettles left. We'll have to send to Kiev.

[*Rachel laughs.*]

You're laughing again.

RACHEL. No.

[*A pause. Asher takes the comb from Rachel's hand and puts it on the table.*]

ASHER. Do you believe in him?

RACHEL. Who?

ASHER. Sabbatai. Who else? [*Rachel is silent.*] Sabbatai says we have to ask women their opinions.

RACHEL. Oh. [*Silence.*] Well. I like what he says about women. *If* he says it. They're all rumours. Stories. Don't you think we need a sign from God? [*Pause.*] I don't know. That's my answer. I don't know.

ASHER. Look.

[*He takes off his shirt, and turns around, showing her his back, which is marked and bruised and discoloured.*]

For four nights I've been purging myself. Because I *do* know. I don't need a sign.

[*He turns back. Rachel is silent. She stares at his body, which is lithe and handsome.*]

I've waited and waited. I've pored over the Kabbalah. I have no family. Only Uncle. My parents were murdered by the Cossacks. I've always known the Messiah would come. For the sake of my parents. Why do you look at me that way? Do you think I'm mad? [*Silence.*] We're supposed to ask women what they're thinking. [*Silence.*] What are you thinking?

[*Rachel takes the comb from the table and starts to comb Rebecca's hair.*]

RACHEL. I can't tell you what I'm thinking.

[*Blackout.*]

[*Lights rise on Rachel praying.*]

RACHEL. Blessed God, we have to talk. I was angry at you, I wasn't going to speak to you ever again, but we *have to talk*! I've never seen a man's body before. Reb Ellis never undresses in front of me. And when he comes into bed, it must always be dark. Well, those are *your* laws. Or at least laws made in your name—some day we have to discuss that. But with

Reb Ellis, believe me, your laws are fine. You must have made them because you knew so many women marry fat, ugly men. But suppose a woman marries an Asher? Then what an awful law! Oh Lord, do you realize a man's chest can be beautiful, not just his face? And perhaps a woman's chest too . . . To a man. My breasts . . . Did you ever think about that? My breasts may be very nice. So if that's the case why can't I wear clothes around my face and leave my breasts bare? [*Pause.*] I'm having impure thoughts. Oh, am I having impure thoughts. He asked me what I was thinking. How could I tell him? He'd run out and find me a nettle. But he is so beautiful that now I want to believe in his Messiah. And that's not right. One thing shouldn't mix itself up with the other. Why do you make everything so confusing? [*Pause.*] I'm sorry. Forgive me for the things I say. I love you. You saved me from the Cossacks. You do care. I know that. You're just quiet. Like Mama. [*Pause.*] I haven't really seen a man's body. Only *half* man's body. [*Silence.*] Only half.

[*Blackout.*]

[*Lights rise on Reb Ellis' kitchen. Reb Ellis and Rachel are at the table. Reb Ellis is drinking a glass of tea. The teapot is on the table. Rachel is sewing. Rebecca is sitting at the side.*]

REB ELLIS. It's good tea.

RACHEL. Thank you.

REB ELLIS. You make good tea.

RACHEL. Thank you.

REB ELLIS. Have you seen my nephew? I hate to go outside and look for him. It's so cold outside. I've never liked the cold. I'm afraid I'll find him buried in the snow. Reb Ginsel buried himself in the snow last week for three days. And then he went home and sold his business. And now he sits waiting for the call to Jerusalem. He'll never get to Jerusalem. He'll die from bad lungs. From burying himself in the snow. Of course it's better than hot wax. Reb Lerner poured hot wax over his body. Then he sold *his* business. Every day there's a new report, a new rumour, a new letter. Sabbatai is in Izmir. Everyone's tense. Everyone's expecting something. The day of redemption is coming. Asher says that. The day of redemption. I'm cold. It gets cold inside. Is there more tea? [*Rachel pours him another cup of tea.*] You make good tea.

RACHEL. Thank you.

REB ELLIS. You're a quiet woman. I like a quiet

woman. I can talk to you. I love tea when it burns my mouth. That's how I'll purge myself, eh? Drinking hot tea. [*Pause.*] What happens if my nephew is right? What happens if Reb Ginsel and Reb Lemer know what they're doing? What happens if Sabbatai goes to Constantinople and is crowned by the Sultan, and says, at last: my people, my people, your suffering is over, the day of redemption is here. What happens? A little more. Hot tea. [*Rachel pours him another cup.*] Thank you. You know when the Cossacks came . . . It's good tea. Good tea.

RACHEL. Thank you.

REB ELLIS. I hid in my fruit store. When the Cossacks came. I ran away from my family. My parents were old. Still. I ran away. It didn't make any sense. The Cossacks came everywhere. But I felt safe there. In my fruit store. Well, eventually they arrived. They broke down the door and marched in. I was in a corner, hunched over, in a corner. And then—I don't know what possessed me—I got up and walked to their captain and took a nectarine from a basket. A fresh, beautiful nectarine. And I handed it to him. He took it. He bit into it. It was good. And he walked out. And his men followed him. They didn't touch me. Or the store. I never understood it. [*Silence.*] I don't keep nectarines any more. [*Silence.*] All those fools outside. They bury themselves in snow. They pour hot wax on their bodies. And what do they repent? Little things. And I sit here. And I have committed the greatest crime in all of Yultishk. Even though I don't know what it is. [*Rachel goes to him and takes his hand. The gesture startles him. He holds her hand for a moment, then brushes it away.*] I'd like some more tea.

[*Blackout.*]

[*Lights rise on Rachel praying.*]

RACHEL. Help us, God. Please. Help us. It's getting out of hand. The whole town is going crazy. People are falling down. All day, all night. And foaming at the mouth. They're all screaming salvation is here. Everybody is seeing Elijah. In the market. In the synagogue. On the street. Sitting at the dinner table. Elijah. Well, I still haven't seen him. But I'm so confused. I want to believe our suffering is over. I want to believe in Sabbatai. But I need a sign. Reb Ellis is behaving strangely too. Yesterday he lay in the yard and had a huge stone put on his chest. Today he gave lemons away in his store. For free. Cyprus lemons! It's getting out of hand.

[*Blackout.*]

[*Lights rise on Reb Ellis' kitchen. Rachel is sitting at the table, sewing. Rebecca is sitting in a corner. Reb Ellis comes in from the back door. He is in a frenzy. He bends down and examines the chair Rachel is sitting in.*]

REB ELLIS. This is a nice chair. I always liked this chair. [*He rises and takes a medallion out of his pocket.*] I have a present for you. My cousin from Hamburg sent it to me. It has a drawing of Sabbatai. Look, he's riding on a dragon. And—look—above him—gold and precious stones falling from Heaven. The day of redemption. [*Pause.*] All the way from Hamburg. Even in Germany they're talking about Sabbatai. Here. It's for you. You're a good wife, you keep a clean house. [*He hands her the medallion.*] Here.

RACHEL. Thank you. [*He sits down at the table next to her.*]

REB ELLIS. My nephew tells me I'm supposed to ask you questions. Opinions. Sabbatai says women have opinions. Well, you know these Messiahs, they have some strange ideas. But this is a *real* Messiah. What do you think? You see, if he is real, I have to be free of everything. All my sins. All my material possessions. There's no way I can carry a fruit store to Jerusalem, is there? What do you think? Well. I sold the fruit store. To some goyim in the next town. Do you think I was right? I want your opinion. They say Sarah, Sabbatai's wife, influences his decisions. Reb Bisek heard rumours that she was a whore in Amsterdam. Others say she's a saint. Ach, who's to know? But she couldn't keep as good a house as you. I tell all my friends that. [*He brushes the back of her chair.*] I've always liked this chair. It's a pretty wood. So I sold the store. And all the fruit. All the fruit! Qumquats arrived yesterday, so beautiful; and today strawberries—fresh, *luscious* . . . Well, you can't take strawberries to Jerusalem. Can you? Do you think I'm right? And I sold the house. More goyim. And I'm giving away everything. Everything I own. All my possessions. That's why I want you to have this medallion. I want it to be yours. Always. You're going to have to stand up. Do you think I'm doing the right thing? [*He pulls her up. He feels her chair again.*] It's a nice chair. Belonged to my mother. [*Reb Ellis takes her chair—and his own—and walks to the back door. He opens the door. He heaves the chairs into the yard. He walks back into the kitchen.*] Can you help me with the table?

RACHEL. The table? [*Reb Ellis takes hold of the kitchen table. He motions Rachel to the other side.*]

REB ELLIS. Take that end. [*Rachel takes the other end. Together they inch towards the door, carrying the table.*] My cousin wrote from Hamburg that Sabbatai was changing all the feast days. He's changing *all* the laws. All the laws. It's a new age. What do you think? Lift it out the door. Right. [*They push the table through the door. Reb Ellis gives it a further push outside. Reb Ellis runs back into the room and starts picking up utensils, vases, pictures—anything he can lay his hands on. He runs back and forth to the door, grabbing things and heaving them out.*] They say Sabbatai sings psalms in a golden voice. He sings Castilian love songs to the Torah. Well, listen, if you're a Messiah, you can sing what you want. What do you think of that? Sometimes he seems strange this Sabbatai, don't you think?

RACHEL. No! Not the teapot!

[*Reb Ellis heaves the teapot out through the back door. He picks up dishes and plates and starts throwing them out. Rachel tries to hide whatever she's fond of.*]

REB ELLIS. I could talk to him, you know. I'm sure Sabbatai and I would get along. I would sit him down at our table—well, no longer—we'd have to stand—and I'd say, Sabbatai, tell me which day exactly is going to be the day of redemption. [*He pauses at the door. He turns and looks at Rachel. He starts to weep.*] I'm afraid. I'm afraid he'll look into my heart. Do you understand? [*He goes over to Rebecca. He looks at Rebecca's chair. He pats her on the shoulder.*] Sit, Rebecca. I'm sure the Bible says we can keep your chair. [*He walks into the next room. Asher runs in through the back door.*]

ASHER. It's a miracle. You should see the yard. He's throwing away his worldly goods. He's cleansed his soul. He sold the store. The *fruit* store. It's a miracle. [*Rachel grabs Asher's arm, then, quickly, withdraws her hand.*]

RACHEL. Stop him.

ASHER. What?

RACHEL. Please.

ASHER. What are you talking about?

RACHEL. Stop him.

ASHER. You don't believe in Sabbatai. He does. [*Reb Ellis comes out of the next room carrying handfuls of clothes. He runs past them. He heaves the clothing out through the back door. He runs back into the next room.*]

RACHEL. *Stop him*!

ASHER. Can't you recognize a miracle when it happens in front of your own eyes?

[*Reb Ellis comes out of the next room carrying sheets and bedspreads. He is all tangled up in them. He throws them out through the back door. He starts back for the next room when he notices a bag on the floor. He examines it.*]

REB ELLIS. What's this? Oh, I forgot. I was going to give you these grapefruit. Well. For the poor, eh? [*He takes a grapefruit out of the bag and examines it lovingly.*] Such beautiful grapefruit. Perhaps if we kept a few. Look how ripe they are. Just this one. For dinner. [*He puts the grapefruit back into the bag.*] No. No. [*He heaves the bag of grapefruit out through the back door.*] My soul is clean. Now my soul is clean. I've given away my life. I'll start a new one in Jerusalem. Why doesn't he tell us what day it will be? My soul is spotless. It can climb the sky. It can sit with Sabbatai in Heaven. You know, the Bible says, when the Messiah comes, man will soar up to the clouds. Says it somewhere. To the clouds. Think of that! If Sabbatai looks into my heart and sees that it's pure, he'll let me soar into the clouds.

ASHER. He's possessed. A holy spirit has entered his soul. His heart is pure now. He knows things. Things we don't know. He's in a state of grace. If he says he can fly to Jerusalem, then he can. All he ever cared about was money and fruit. And he gave it all away. That's one miracle. So why can't there be two?

RACHEL. The day of Redemption isn't here yet. Stop him!

REB ELLIS. When the Messiah comes, the angels will carry us to Jerusalem on their wings. It says so in the Bible. Somewhere. We can fly to Jerusalem. [*He goes into the next room.*]

ASHER. I'm not sure that *is* in the Bible.

RACHEL. Then tell him that. [*Reb Ellis comes out of the next room, carrying a ladder.*]

REB ELLIS. If my heart is pure, I can soar . . . [*He goes out through the back door with the ladder.*]

[*Blackout.*]

[*The lights rise on Reb Ellis' back yard. The yard is cluttered with half the contents of Reb Ellis' house. The wall of his house leads to a roof. Reb Ellis puts the ladder against the wall and starts to climb. Rachel and Asher run into the yard.*]

RACHEL. Where's he going?

ASHER. Uncle! Where are you going?

REB ELLIS [*climbing*]. To Heaven.

RACHEL. Make him come down. [*Tanta Rose arrives. She looks up at Reb Ellis. Reb Ellis reaches the roof. He pulls the ladder up with him. He stands on the roof.*]

REB ELLIS. I can fly. I can fly to Jerusalem. I will be there to greet the Messiah. He will arrive on a dragon. He will wear a white prayer shawl. He will carry a silver fan, and touch the people on the street with it. He will call out the sacred, forbidden name of God. And Elijah will ride beside him. I'll be able to see if for myself. I can fly! [*Two neighbours arrive.*]

TANTA ROSE. Reb Ellis! What are you doing?

1ST NEIGHBOUR. Come down. [*Reb Ellis looks at the sky; he hesitates.*]

REB ELLIS. I know I can fly. But I'm afraid. If I'm afraid, something is wrong. My heart isn't pure. My soul isn't saved. [*A Vagrant has arrived and is picking through the objects on the ground, carting some of them off.*]

1ST NEIGHBOUR. Reb Ellis!

2ND NEIGHBOUR. Come down! [*Reb Ellis points to something on the ground.*]

REB ELLIS. Look. Look! The grapefruit are still in the box. Asher, give out the grapefruit. And then I can fly. [*Asher hesitates, then goes to the box of grapefruit, and starts handing them out. Rachel runs back into the kitchen. Rachel prays.*]

RACHEL. Dear God in Heaven, stop him! Don't let him jump. He'll break his neck. The Bible says nothing about flying to Jerusalem. They've all gone mad. He's not a bad man, you know. All right, he talks too much; all right, he doesn't listen; all right, when the lights are off, he's not so gentle. But, still, in his way, he's kind. Don't let him jump. Make it rain. If it's wet, he'll come down. He won't want to catch cold. Make him come to his senses. This whole town will do anything, anything, in the name of the Messiah. But what kind of Messiah would let that man jump? Look, who wants the Messiah more than I do? Every day since I could speak, I've prayed for him to come. And if Sabbatai is the Messiah, I'll rejoice . . . But there has to be some kind of proof. Not rumours. Not letters from Hamburg. Not pretty medallions. *Proof.* I know how reluctant you are to give signs, but if ever we needed one . . . From *you*. Something. Something we all can see. Not some little girl waking up in the middle of the night and saying the moon is on fire. Something we *all* can see. A special rainbow. A ladder from the sky. A dead man rising. A dead man flying. [*Pause.*] A live man flying. [*Pause.*] Oh, my God.

[*Pause.*] No. No, this must be in my mind. This can't be you. You're not talking to me, are you? You're not talking to me at last? [*Pause.*] A man flying. Can I be that blind? Is this your sign? [*Pause.*] No, I'm going mad too. Like everyone else. [*Pause.*] Asher said if a miracle happens in front of my eyes, I would not see it. Have I been staring you in the face? At last? And not recognizing you? If a man can fly . . . [*Pause.*] No. Not Reb Ellis. Reb Ellis can't fly. Reb Ellis can't be a sign. [*Pause.*] Can he? [*Pause.*] Then is he here? Is the Messiah really here? Did the moon really catch fire? Are you really going to save us? Do we never have to worry about the Cossacks again? Do I never have to think about my teeth again? Is it a new world? Can it be happening? Have all my prayers come true? If a man can fly . . . [*Pause.*] *This* man? Not this man. [*Pause.*] Why do I doubt you? Oh dear God! Why do I *doubt* you? Forgive me. I'm not worthy of you. Thank you. Thank you. Let the man fly. Let *this* man fly. Let the clouds open. Let the angels carry him to Jerusalem. Let him fly! [*Rachel walks out of the back door and into the yard. She looks up to the roof.*] Reb Ellis! [*Reb Ellis looks down at her.*] Jump!

[*Blackout.*]

[*Lights rise on Rachel praying.*]

RACHEL. God bless Mama. God bless Tanta Rose. God bless Asher. God bless the soul of poor Reb Ellis. [*Pause.*] It's not your fault. [*Pause.*] What can I say? I wanted a sign.

[*Blackout.*]

[*Lights rise on Reb Ellis' kitchen. Rebecca is sitting in the corner, in the only chair. Objects are scattered on the floor. The medallion of Sabbatai lies on the floor. Rachel and Asher are standing. They are very awkward with each other.*

ASHER. Well . . . [*Silence.*]

RACHEL. Well . . . [*Silence.*]

ASHER. Well . . . [*Silence.*]

RACHEL. I'm sorry I can't give you tea.

ASHER. He gave away the teapot.

RACHEL. Yes. [*Silence.*]

ASHER. Well . . . [*Silence.*]

RACHEL. It was *my* teapot.

ASHER. Oh. [*Pause.*] I don't know if he's allowed to give away *your* worldly goods. Are yours his? It's a fine point. Ask the Rabbi. Uncle never really knew the laws. Or the Bible. He imagined things. He made them up. But with something like the Messiah, of course, you can't make things up. [*Pause.*] He wasn't ready. For Jerusalem. [*Pause.*] Why don't you come with me?

RACHEL. Come with you?

ASHER. To Constantinople. [*Rachel blushes and turns away.*] We're a family.

RACHEL. I have to sit shiva.

ASHER. You can't. He threw out the wooden benches.

RACHEL. I'll borrow.

ASHER. You have no place to live.

RACHEL. I'll find some place.

ASHER. You have nothing to do.

RACHEL. I'll sew.

ASHER. If we go to Odessa, there are boats.

RACHEL. Boats. I've never seen a boat.

ASHER. If the owners are Jewish, they'll take us for free. Holy pilgrims. In Constantinople, he will unseat the Sultan. And he'll be crowned king of the Jews. We can be there, and then we can follow him to Jerusalem.

RACHEL. Don't you ever doubt?

ASHER. No.

RACHEL. Never?

ASHER. Never.

RACHEL. Not even when Reb Ellis came crashing down?

ASHER. He wasn't ready.

RACHEL. I thought it would be a sign. I prayed to God for a sign. That Sabbatai was really the Messiah.

ASHER. I don't need a sign.

RACHEL. I do.

ASHER. Why does God have to give a sign just for you? [*Rachel turns away.*]

ASHER. I'm going. [*Rachel doesn't look at him.*] I'll send you letters.

RACHEL. Letters. More letters about the Messiah.

ASHER. You can change your mind. [*Pause.*]

RACHEL. I've never seen a boat. [*She smiles.*]

ASHER. Then come with me, Tanta.

RACHEL. Tanta? [*She looks at him in horror.*]

ASHER. We're a family. Uncle would want us to stay together.

RACHEL. [*Looks up, towards God.*] Tanta!

ASHER. You're the only family I have.

RACHEL. I have Mama. And God.

ASHER. They're both silent.

RACHEL. I need a sign.

ASHER. You're stubborn.

RACHEL. One day everything was quiet. Yultishk was like a river. Nothing—except the Cossacks—could disturb it. The next day, I'm married, and you're fainting and the whole town is going crazy, because somebody we never heard of sent some letters. We don't even know if there *is* a Sabbatai. And if there is, and if he is the Messiah, God will tell us in some way. And not by pushing Reb Ellis off the roof. [*Pause.*] I'll tell you something terrible. I don't think it had anything to do with Sabbatai. I think I really just wanted him to jump. [*Pause.*] No. If Sabbatai is the Messiah, God will find his own way to let us know. [*Pause.*] There. That's what you wanted. A woman's thoughts. [*Silence.*]

ASHER. I'm going.

RACHEL. Go. Send me letters.

ASHER. Yes. [*Silence. He goes to the door.*] Goodbye. [*He leaves. Rachel watches him. Rebecca rises and walks to the centre of the room. She sits on the floor and picks up the medallion.*]

REBECCA. [*Whispers.*] Sabbatai. [*She rises and holds the medallion.*] Sabbatai. [*Rachel turns and looks at her.*]

RACHEL. Mama!

REBECCA. Sabbatai!

RACHEL. Dear God.

REBECCA. Sabbatai! Sabbatai! [*Rachel calls out the door.*]

RACHEL. Asher! Come back! He's sent a sign!

REBECCA. Sabbatai! Sabbatai! Sabbatai! [*Rachel runs and embraces Rebecca. She holds Rebecca in her arms. Asher returns and stands in the doorway.*]

CURTAIN

Act II

Lights rise on Rachel praying.

RACHEL. Dear God, I never want to see a boat again. Up and down. Up and down. Up and down. Every-one is ill. Except Mama. Mama is calm. Yesterday I could not take the up and down anymore. I screamed, "Please God, let me die." Thank heaven —as usual—you didn't pay attention to me. We're almost there. Almost to Constantinople. But Sabbatai is some place else. He's in a castle. A fortress. A prison. There are so many stories, who knows the truth? Even on a boat, there are stories. Even on a boat, people bring out letters. Where do they find them? Floating in the sea? Well, the letters that have dried have said Sabbatai arrived in Constantinople and was arrested by the Turks and they sent him to—this castle or this fortress or this prison in a place called Gallipoli, and there he sits like a king and receives visitors, and thousands of Jews from all over the world have come to Gallipoli and the Turks are afraid to harm him because they know he's the Messiah. Dear God, after a boat trip like this, he *better* be the Messiah. Asher says I still doubt. I don't doubt. It's just that sometimes I *question*. I question everything. Except Asher's eyes. But that's a different story. It's not enough he sees my spots, it's not enough he sees my teeth, you had to make me his Tanta in the bargain. My heart goes up and down, up and down, like this boat. Life was simpler when I was just sewing, and there was no nephew, and there was no Messiah. Well. Enough of that. Your ears must burn with all our complaints. If you make the sea calm, I'd be happy. If we got to Gallipoli, I'd be happy. No matter how unhappy I am, if I'm on land, I'd be happy.

[*Blackout.*]

[*A flute. A Spanish Melody.*]

[*Lights rise on an open square in Gallipoli. People. Colour. Noise. Voices coming from all directions. A Visionary stands on a rock, talking in a frenzy. A young Singer is humming the Spanish tune to the sound of the flute. Turks are hawking wares—drawings, paintings, parchments, blankets, tents.*]

[*Rachel, Asher and Rebecca enter. They are carrying their belongings. They are exhausted. Rachel and Asher are in a state of disbelief. Rebecca is calmer. They float across the Square. It all seems a dream, an hallucination. The sounds and colours and people blend into one.*]

SINGER.

> "Meliselda
> Come . . .
> Come to me
> Meliselda . . ."

HAWKER. Paintings of the Messiah. Four hundred reals only. Just a few left. Paintings of the Messiah . . .

HAWKER. The sayings of Sabbatai. Six hundred reals for one scroll. The sayings of our Lord, Sabbatai Sevi . . .

SINGER.

> "Meliselda
> Come . . .
> Come to me
> Meliselda . . .
> Daughter of my king
> Come to my bed
> I'll touch your ruby lips
> Come to my bed
> Meliselda
> Come . . ."

VISIONARY. And Sabbatai raised his right hand and, lo, the walls of the temple sprang from the earth, and with his left hand, he summoned forth the armies of Israel, the Lost Tribes sailing in snow-white vessels toward the sun . . .

HAWKER. Sarah. Portraits of Sarah. The orphan. The wanderer. The Messiah's wife. Sarah. Beautiful. Mysterious. Only twelve reals. A special bargain.

HAWKER. Tents. For your family. Only a few tents left . . .

GUARD. Entrance to the fortress for one thousand reals . . . we guarantee a glimpse of the Messiah . . .

VISIONARY. And Sabbatai will enter Jerusalem on a celestial lion, guarded by a serpent with seven heads . . .

SINGER.

> "Meliselda
> Come . . .
> Come to me
> Meliselda . . ."

[*The Hawkers importune Asher. He looks at them but **seems** not to see. Eventually, he focusses on the Hawker selling tents. He counts his money. He refuses a tent, but takes some of his money and buys a large blanket. Then, thoroughly laden down, he continues to walk with Rachel and Rebecca, still dazed, across the square.*]

VOICES. Sabbatai . . .
  Sabbatai . . .
  Sabbatai . . .
  Meliselda . . .

[*Blackout.*]

[*Lights rise on Rachel praying. She is still in a state of shock. She looks up at God. She opens her mouth. But she cannot speak.*]

[*Blackout.*]

[*Lights rise on Rachel praying. She still cannot speak. She shakes her head.*]

RACHEL. Oh, my God.

[*Blackout.*]

[*Lights rise on Rachel praying. She has regained some composure.*]

RACHEL. So this is land. Dear God, why do you always make yesterday seem better? When I'm on the boat, I want land. When I touch the ground, I want the waves. What's wrong with me? [*Pause.*] Did you ever see so many people? Of course. *You* have. Crossing the Red Sea, leaving Egypt, all of that. But we don't get this kind of thing in Yultishk. [*Pause.*] Oh, Yultishk. [*Pause.*] Do you know where we are? A hill. I want to be in a house. No, Asher found a hill, so we can see Sabbatai when he passes. But when is he going to pass? When is he going to leave that prison? When is he getting our land back from the Sultan, and the crown of Judea? Suppose he decides to wait until Spring. I can't spend winter on a hill. [*Pause.*] Asher put up a blanket. To protect Mama and me from the wind, when we sleep. Asher sleeps outside the blanket, of course. Of course. So I don't have impure thoughts. [*Pause.*] What am I doing on this hill with this boy? [*Pause.*] Dear God, help me think *only* of Sabbatai. Sabbatai . . . [*Pause.*] Sabbatai.

[*Blackout.*]

[*Lights rise on a hillside. Rocks, leading down to a square. The large Oriental blanket is hanging, attached to the ground with rope and pegs. There is a slight wind blowing. Rebecca sits to the side, on the ground. A black shawl is draped around her shoulders. She still carries her wool. She seems to be waiting. Or, at least, listening to the wind. Rachel and Asher are seated on the ground in front of the blanket. They are reading pamphlets. There are pamphlets everywhere. Asher is in some kind of fervour.*]

RACHEL. Sabbatai . . . Sabbatai says this . . . Sabbatai says that . . . I can't keep up . . .

ASHER. [*Shows her a pamphlet.*] Look. When the Messiah comes, everything changes. [*He points to a pas-*

sage.*] See. It says so in the Zohar. There's a whole new system. All the old concepts of right and wrong are swept away. The ritual code is no longer binding. *Everything* changes. [*He gives her another pamphlet.*] See. Here. He's made new feast days. He's made a new Sabbath. He sings new psalms. He sings the song of Meliselda in the synagogue. As an allegory for the Messiah sleeping with the daughter of a king. The Torah. The daughter of God.

RACHEL. The Messiah sleeps with his wife.

ASHER. The Torah.

RACHEL. No. Sarah.

ASHER. Well—they're different kinds of wives.

RACHEL. Do you know what they say about her?

ASHER. I don't listen to gossip. [*He opens another pamphlet.*] Look at this . . .

RACHEL. They say she's a sorceress. They say she's known Satan. *Worse.* They say she's a Catholic. How could the Messiah marry a Catholic? They say she sleeps with many men. She wanders through the tents at night . . .

ASHER. *This*! [*He shakes the pamphlet at her.*] This is what you should think about. Not idle fantasies. And in the synagogue—look! [*He points to a sentence.*] In the synagogue, *everyone* can pronounce the forbidden name of God.

RACHEL. But it's forbidden.

ASHER. No longer. Nothing is forbidden. The Messiah is here. Once there's redemption, then everything is without sin. Then there is no sin. We're free. There is no more spiritual oppression. Do you understand that? It's a new world. We're free!

RACHEL. You're not going to faint again, are you?

ASHER. [*embarrassed*] No.

RACHEL. The last time you fainted you bumped your head.

ASHER. Don't make fun of me. Here. Look. I have something to show you.

[*Asher takes out a small bag and removes a piece of meat.*]

RACHEL. What is it?

ASHER. Animal fat.

RACHEL. What?

ASHER. A kidney. With fat. It's all right. It's cooked. I bought it in the square. Sabbatai says we can eat it.

RACHEL. It's not kosher.

ASHER. Sabbatai said we can eat it.

RACHEL. It says in the Talmud, your soul will be cut off if you eat animal fat . . .

ASHER. Sabbatai said we can eat it.

RACHEL. It says in the Talmud it's as bad as incest.

ASHER. Sabbatai said we can eat it. Here. See [*He hands her another pamphlet.*] It says so.

RACHEL. [*Reads the pamphlet.*] Yes. It does say so. [*Pause.*] What are you going to do?

ASHER. I'm going to eat it. [*Pause.*]

RACHEL. Oh. [*Pause.*] It doesn't look very good.

[*They both look at the meat. Silence.*]

ASHER. Sabbatai says . . .

RACHEL. Well, if he says . . .

[*Silence. Asher takes out a knife and cuts the meat in two.*]

ASHER. Here.

[*He hands Rachel a piece of meat.*]

RACHEL. What's this?

ASHER. For you.

RACHEL. I don't want it.

ASHER. It's for *you.*

RACHEL. No.

ASHER. Come on . . .

RACHEL. Take it back.

ASHER. It's for you!

RACHEL. I said I don't want it.

[*She returns the meat to him.*]

ASHER. You have to, Tanta.

RACHEL. Don't call me Tanta. [*She takes her piece back from him.*] All right. I'm not *that* much older than you. Don't call me Tanta. [*A long pause.*] Well?

ASHER. You first.

RACHEL. Me?

ASHER. Yes.

RACHEL. No. *You*

ASHER. The woman is always first.

RACHEL. Since when?

[*Silence. They stare at the meat.*]

Are you afraid? [*Pause.*] What's this I see? I don't believe it. A *doubt*?

ASHER. No. [*He looks at the meat.*] Never. [*He grabs the meat and holds it up.*] Never. There's a benediction. Sabbatai has a benediction. "Blessed are thou, oh Lord, our God, who has permitted the forbidden." [*He closes his eyes and pops the meat into his mouth. He chews.*] There. [*He swallows.*] I did it. [*Jumps about.*] I did it! See! Lightning didn't strike. Sabbatai *knows.* [*Pause.*] Well?

RACHEL. You still have a little piece left.

ASHER. It's your turn. [*Pause.*]

RACHEL. All right. Yes. Sabbatai knows. [*Pause.*] All right. [*Pause.*] "Blessed are thou, oh Lord, our God, who has permitted the forbidden." [*She stares at the meat.*] I can't.

ASHER. You must.

RACHEL. I'm afraid.

ASHER. Don't you want a new world? Don't you? [*Pause.*] Rachel?

[*Rachel stares at him.*]

RACHEL. Oh yes.

[*She puts the meat into her mouth. She pauses. She eats it. Silence.*]

ASHER. Well?

[*Silence.*]

RACHEL. Well. I suppose then . . . it's a new world.

[*Blackout.*]

[*Lights rise on Rachel praying.*]

RACHEL.. Well Lord, now there are *your* laws and *his* laws. [*Pause.*] And they're day and night. But *he* represents *you.* [*Pause.*] Doesn't he? [*Pause.*] So why are there his laws and your laws? [*Pause.*] I'm confused. [*Pause.*] I'll bet you're confused too. For once. [*Pause.*] Who do I pray to? Him? Or you? Both? Do I tell him some things—and you others? [*Pause.*] I think I'd rather talk to *him* about my teeth. He might sympathize. And my impure thoughts. [*Pause.*] He'd say they were pure. [*Pause.*] Day and night. [*Pause.*] Listen—I think the two of you have to get together and sort things out. [*Pause.*] You know, tomorrow is Tisha be'Ab. A very solemn holiday. The anniversary of the demolition of the second temple. Well—it is also *his* birthday. And he has *abolished* Tisha be'Ab. He's made it into a feast day. What do you think of *that*! [*Pause.*] He certainly has a lot more spice than Jesus, doesn't he? Oh God. He'll probably be just like Jesus. He'll die a martyr, and someone will start a whole new religion, and then they'll all go out and kill a lot of Jews. [*Pause.*] No. It's different. He *is* the Messiah. [*Pause.*] I know you. You're up to something aren't you? I can feel it. You're up to something.

[*Blackout.*]

[*Lights rise on the hillside. There is a full moon. Music and shouting—far away—in the square. Rachel is sitting with Rebecca.*]

RACHEL. Look at the moon. Mama? Look. [*Rebecca looks up, then away.*] There's a breeze. [*Silence.*] Asher's down there. Can you hear the singing? They all sound drunk. They must be dancing too. It's Sabbatai's birthday. [*Silence.*] He didn't ask me to go. Well, I don't like dancing.

[*Rachel gets up and wanders over to a rock. She sits down. She looks up at the moon. She hears a young man and woman laughing—off—in the rocks. She rises, busies herself, clears away some debris in front of the blanket, then walks behind the blanket. Silence. A Woman enters. She is startlingly beautiful. The woman, Sarah, is surrounded by a group of Men and Women paying her court. They are laughing. One of them is playing a mandolin. Another is carrying a jug of wine. Some of them have wine goblets. Sarah is restless. She pays no attention to her companions. She looks at the hillside and notices the moon. She sits on a rock. The Mandolin Player sits at her feet and continues his melody. Someone hands Sarah a wine goblet. She drinks. She looks around. She sees Rebecca on the other side of the hill. Sarah rises, as if drawn by a magnet. She walks to Rebecca. Rebecca turns and looks at her. Sarah shudders, but does not take her eyes off Rebecca.*]

SARAH. I know. I can see it in your eyes. [*Pause.*] I know who you talk to. [*She turns to her friends.*] Leave us alone.

[*Her companions start down the rocks. The Mandolin Player brings Sarah some wine. She takes the jug and his goblet. He rejoins the others as they leave.*]

Is he here now? [*She pours wine into the goblet.*] There's only one who you talk to. Isn't there? [*She smiles.*] Of course. [*She hands Rebecca the goblet.*] Here.

[*Rebecca looks at Sarah. She takes the goblet and drinks.*]

I can feel him. We used to know each other. No longer. I don't dare to talk to him now. Not in my position.

[*Sarah takes the goblet from Rebecca. She drinks. She sits next to Rebecca.*]

Do you know what he did today, my Sabbatai? He composed a new psalm. It's pretty. He likes music.

He's in a good mood. He's a creature of moods. Sometimes they're happy—exalted—and his eyes blaze with the magic of a Messiah. Sometimes they're low and melancholy and he mumbles and sleeps. My Sabbatai. Here. Have some more.

[*She hands the goblet to Rebecca and pours more wine into it.*]

I mixed it myself. From five different wines. Gifts. Look at the moon.

[*She rises and looks at the sky. Rebecca slowly drinks from the goblet.*]

Is that where he is? Behind the moon? When do you talk to him? [*She looks at Rebecca.*] I can see everything in your eyes. I know everything.

[*She takes the goblet from Rebecca and drinks. She sits.*]

There was a moon in the cemetery. When they found me. You must know the story. Everyone knows the story. They all tell the story. When they found me. I escaped from the convent. They carried me off to the convent when the Cossacks came. Oh, yes, the Cossacks. I see it in your eyes. They made me become a Catholic. That's when I started to talk to him. In the convent. The nuns knew him. Oh, yes. One night my father came to me in a dream. He was still bleeding. The Cossack knife. My dead father. He said, "You are a Jewess." I fled the convent. They found me in a cemetery. A rabbi and his wife. And I said, "I am Sarah. I am a Jewess. I shall marry the Messiah." Drink some more.

[*She fills the goblet and hands it to Rebecca. Rebecca drinks.*]

The wines come from Amsterdam, Venice, Leghorn, Hamburg and Alexandria. I know each city. I travelled for years, looking for the Messiah. When I found him, he was in Cairo. He married me at once. You know they say Sabbatai is handsome. He's not. He's rather plain. They tell stories about my travels. About men. Men and madness. Well. They don't understand convents. I didn't speak to him again, after that—the convent. And, of course, now I can't. [*Silence.*] But somebody must. I know you. You have the eyes of my father. I know what you've seen. Those things must never happen again. Life has to change. We have suffered enough. We need a Messiah. [*Pause.*] Of course I always thought the

Messiah would be golden. Riding a chariot, riding a lion, riding a dragon. I thought he would be a pillar of fire with eyes and a mouth. Not a rather plain man who gets depressed. And his stomach aches. But he's the only Messiah we have. I know. I walked across Poland, I walked across Europe, I walked across the Holy Land. Searching. He composed a psalm today, my Sabbatai. Sweet Sabbatai.

[*She takes Rebecca's hand.*]

The one you talk to. Tell him to leave us alone. Tell him to stay behind the moon. Tell him I said so. He remembers me. I am Sarah. A Jewess. Bride of the Messiah. [*She kisses Rebecca.*] Please.

[*Sarah pours some more wine. Rachel comes out from behind the blanket. She is startled to see someone with her mother. She walks to Sarah and Rebecca. She recognizes Sarah.*]

RACHEL. Are you . . . ?

[*She falls to her knees in front of Sarah. Sarah draws Rachel up. Sarah looks at Rebecca, then at Rachel.*]

SARAH. Oh, yes.

[*Sarah takes her hands and places them over Rachel's face. She moves her hands down to Rachel's mouth. Sarah closes her eyes. She presses a healing warmth into Rachel's mouth.*]

Don't be afraid.

[*Sarah pulls her hands away. She looks back at Rebecca, then turns and walks to the other side of the hill. She sits on a rock and watches the moon. Rachel sits next to her mother. Rebecca hands Rachel the goblet. Rachel is surprised at her mother's gesture. Rebecca looks at Rachel. Rachel drinks the wine. Rebecca puts her arms around Rachel. Rachel leans back against her mother. Rebecca strokes her. Rachel weeps. A mandolin. Sarah's companions return. She rises and starts off with them. She turns and looks back at Rebecca. She leaves with her friends. The Mandolin Player lingers a moment, playing a tune against the moon. Asher enters. He is drunk. He sits next to the Mandolin Player. He hums the tune. Rachel sees Asher. She rises. She walks towards him. The Mandolin Player starts down the rocks. His melody can be heard for a long time trailing off in the distance. Asher rises. He is unsteady. Rachel walks up to him. She stares at him. A long silence.*]

RACHEL. "Blessed are thou, oh Lord, our God, who has permitted that which is forbidden."

[*Rachel unbuttons her blouse. She takes Asher's face in her hands. She kisses him, passionately. Her hand explores his body. She continues to kiss him. Then she pulls away. She stares at him. Asher is silent. She continues to stare at him. Asher bends and kisses her breasts. His lips move up her body. They stop. Then he kisses her mouth.*]

ASHER. Tanta, Tanta . . .

[*The sound of the mandolin has almost disappeared. Rachel and Asher embrace and move behind the curtain. Silence. Rebecca sits staring at the moon. A wolf howls. A shadow crosses the moon. The night is darker. Rebecca rises. She walks to the centre of the hillside. She takes her roll of wool and unravels it. She spreads the wool out on the ground. In a large circle. She stands in the centre of the circle.*]

REBECCA. Where are you?

[*There is a long silence. The night gets darker. The wings of a bat can be heard flapping against a rock. Rebecca stares out into the night.*]

I remember you. I remember you. You came for my husband and my child. You rode into town with the Cossacks. You ripped my baby from my arms. You tore my baby to bits: like a piece of meat. You roasted the pieces. You took my husband . . . Oh yes, I remember you. You pointed to my husband and said to the Cossacks, that's him, that's the man who collects the taxes. I saw your face. I heard your voice. It was you who hired him. I remember you. You took my husband . . . I held my daughter. People were screaming. People were burning. I ran. I remember you. I looked behind me. I could still see my husband. I wandered. We all did. We had no homes. I had my daughter. She was young. Her face turned ugly. She saw too much. She forgot what she saw. Her face remembered. We reached a town. The Cossacks came again. We ran. I saw you—always— racing with them. I remember you. You took my husband. Everyone was fighting. You got bored. The Cossacks were gone. I went home. I hated my home. I saw your face. I heard your voice. At night I called out to you. They thought I was silent. I was calling to you. You took my husband. He was alive. That's the man who collects the taxes, you said. They took a cat. You gave them a cat. They sewed the cat up in my husband's belly. He was alive. They fastened him to a beam. The cat in his belly. Oh yes. I saw you. I called your name at night. They thought I was silent. They didn't want to hear your name. They talked to God. I talked to you. They thought I was silent. *I was never silent.*

[*Pause. She paces around in a circle. She stops.*]

And now where are you? Behind the moon? No. You've always been much closer than that. Are you waiting for your moment? Are you ready to return? No! The Messiah is here! Leave him be. Stay away. He doesn't want to see you. He doesn't want to hear you. The Messiah is here! You're starting to fade. Leave him be. I can't remember your face. I can't remember your voice. Oh my beloved. My dearest, my beautiful demon of the night. Fade away. Fade away. We are saved!

[*Blackout.*]

[*Lights rise on the hillside. Morning. Rebecca is asleep against a rock. The woollen circle remains. Rachel emerges from behind the blanket. She looks up at the sky. She is about to pray. She stops herself. She smiles. She sees the wool. She gathers it up, returns it in a pile to her mother and lays it at her feet. Asher comes out from behind the blanket. Rachel goes to him. They embrace. Rachel and Asher lie in front of the blanket, looking at the sky. Asher begins to sing.*]

ASHER.

"Meliselda
Come . . .
Come to me
Meliselda . . ."

[*Blackout.*]

[*Lights rise on Rachel praying.*]

RACHEL. God bless Asher. [*She smiles.*] Yes I know. I haven't talked to you for days. For days and days and days . . . [*She laughs.*] I start to. All the time. Then my mind drifts. Drifts . . . [*Pause.*] I'm happy. I suppose people don't pray as much when they're happy, do they? Well, you see, if you just made people happier, you'd get some rest. [*She smiles.*] Oh Lord, I love it. I love making love. I was right, Reb Ellis, that had nothing to do with making love. I'm in love with Asher making love. [*Pause.*] I don't love him as much when he talks. It's always the same thing. Sabbatai, Sabbatai. Now Reb Ellis talked in circles, but circles have some kind of dimension. I liked that. Oh, this is why I didn't want to speak to you. It's going to get confusing again. It's not going to be simple. [*Pause.*] Yes. It is. It *is* simple. [*Pause.*] Do you know what Asher said the other night? He said I was beautiful. And this is what's amazing. I

accepted it. I didn't argue. I didn't blush. I said "Thank you. I know." [*Pause.*] As if I always knew. [*Pause.*] He said, "You're beautiful, Tanta!" [*Pause.*] Ah. Tanta. [*Pause.*] Now. *This* is the problem. I'm not beautiful because I'm beautiful. After all, I'm *not* beautiful. I'm beautiful because I'm forbidden. Or was once. Do you know what I mean? Not only is he, an unmarried man, an unmarried *boy* for that matter, having sexual intercourse—but with his aunt as well. It's vague incest. Not the real thing. I'm not even an aunt by blood. Still. It counts. And I suppose I didn't help things that first night by tearing off my clothes and throwing 'forbidden' in his face. Oh God. I must have been mad. I must have been drunk. [*She smiles.*] I enjoyed it. [*Pause.*] Still. Tanta. Sabbatai says he should explore the forbidden. Bad is good. [*Pause.*] Ugly is beautiful. [*Silence.*] I don't know if I understand Sabbatai's logic. But I never understood the Kabbalah. The parts I've heard about. Still. [*Pause.*] It isn't me, is it? It's Sabbatai. [*Pause.*] Asher is sleeping with Sabbatai. [*Pause.*] Oh Lord, you know what the Bible misses? And the Talmud? And all the rabbis? And probably the Kabbalah as well? [*Pause.*] Your exquisite sense of humour.

[*Blackout.*]

[*Lights rise on the hillside. Rebecca sits at the side, looking straight ahead. Rachel is again lying in Asher's arms. Asher is singing.*]

ASHER.

"Meliselda
Come . . .
Come to me
Meliselda . . ."

RACHEL. Don't you know any other songs?
ASHER. It's Sabbatai's.
RACHEL. I know. [*Pause.*] Asher?
ASHER. What?
RACHEL. When is the day of redemption coming? When is Sabbatai going to take his crown? When do we follow him to Jerusalem?
ASHER. When he says so.
RACHEL. Isn't it taking a long time?
ASHER. Why do you always ask so many questions?
RACHEL. Don't you ever wonder? Just a little? Why is Sabbatai in a prison? It *is* a prison, Asher. He holds court like a king, but it *is* a prison. Dignitaries visit

him from all over the world. But it is a prison. Don't
you ever wonder? Why doesn't he knock the walls
down? And leave?

ASHER. He has reasons for everything. It's not for us
to understand. You mustn't question him.

RACHEL. You're a child.

ASHER. What?

RACHEL. A child. A child. [*Pause. She kisses him.*] A
child.

[*Rebecca suddenly springs up. She moves to the front of the
hillside, listening.*]

Mama, what is it?

[*In the distance, a hum. It grows louder. People can be
heard shouting. Rachel and Asher move to opposite sides of
the hill, overlooking the edge. Rebecca stands in the centre,
also at the edge, looking down. The shouting grows louder.
Rachel and Asher call to each other across the hill.*]

ASHER. Can you see anything?

RACHEL. The sun's in my eyes.

ASHER. Look . . .

RACHEL. Where?

ASHER. A procession.

RACHEL. Where?

ASHER. Can't you see?

RACHEL. A little. Turks.

ASHER. Listen! His name! They're calling his name!

RACHEL. [*startled*] Sabbatai.

ASHER. It must be him.

[*Asher runs back to the blanket, completely excited and
disorientated. He looks for something.*]

RACHEL. I see something.

ASHER. What?

RACHEL. A horse. I think it's a horse.

ASHER. Where are my things? I have to go down
there. Where's my shirt? [*Rachel turns to help him.*]
No. Keep looking. Tell me what you see.

RACHEL. Nothing. People. A blur. The wind's blowing. A horse. Yes. Definitely. A horse.

ASHER. He's left the prison. He's going to the Sultan.
[*He finds his shirt.*] You see. You ask questions. You
have no faith. He left the prison. When he wanted
to. Where are my shoes? [*Rachel turns to him.*]

RACHEL. You're in a state.

ASHER. What do you see?

RACHEL. [*turning back.*] Nothing. Just a horse.

ASHER. Is that all? A horse? That's all you see?

RACHEL. Yes. No. I think . . . Someone's on the
horse.

ASHER. It's him! My shoes!

RACHEL. I can make out an arm . . .

ASHER. He's going that way. [*He points in the direction
of the noise.*] And that way is Constantinople.

RACHEL. They're blocking my view. I only see an arm.

ASHER. He's going to Constantinople.

RACHEL. It's waving. The arm is waving!

ASHER. [*now fully dressed*] He's claiming the crown.
He's talking us back to Jerusalem. I've got to follow
him.

[*Asher, in a frenzy, runs down the side of the hill. Rachel
does not see him disappear. The noise begins to fade off into
the distance.*]

RACHEL. I saw his arm. Sabbatai's arm. I think. I'm
not sure. I guess. It's passed. Asher . . .

[*She turns and sees that Asher is gone.*]

Asher!

[*Blackout.*]

[*Lights rise on Rachel praying, almost trance-like.*]

RACHEL. God bless Sabbatai. God bless Mama. God
bless Asher. God bless Tanta Rose. God bless the
soul of Reb Ellis. God bless Papa. Papa's soul.
Thank you. Thank you for bringing the Messiah.
Forgive me for ever doubting him. Forgive me for
asking so many questions. God bless Sabbatai.
Don't let the Sultan harm him. God bless Sabbatai.
Don't let the Turks touch him. Thank you. Thank
you for leading him out of the fortress, into the
light, into our dreams. Our dreams of Jerusalem.
Thank you. God bless Sabbatai. God bless Sabbatai.
God bless the Messiah.

[*Blackout.*]

[*Lights rise on the hillside. Early morning. Rachel and
Rebecca are sitting, huddled together. It is cold.*]

RACHEL. Did you hear something? I thought I heard
something. A cry. In the distance. I wish Asher
would return. It's getting cold.

[*Rebecca springs up and walks to the edge of the hill. Rachel
goes to her.*]

What is it? It's all right, Mama. It's all right. Come on. Sit down. We have to rest. We have a long walk ahead of us.

[*Rachel leads Rebecca back. They sit.*]

I wish we could close our eyes on the hillside and then open them—and be in Jerusalem. Perhaps Sabbatai will do that. But the rest of us are going to have to walk. I know that. [*Pause.*] I wish Asher would return.

[*Rebecca springs up again.*]

Mama!

[*Rachel goes to the edge of the hillside and stands with Rebecca. They listen.*]

Yes. I did hear something. A cry. Someone's crying. Far away.

[*Asher enters. He is exhausted. And very still. His eyes are glazed. He looks at Rachel and Rebecca but doesn't speak. he sits on a rock. Rachel starts towards him.*]

Asher . . .

[*Rebecca stares at Asher. Then—suddenly—she cries out. Then she turns away.*]

What happened? [*Asher is silent.*] Asher.

[*Rachel touches his shoulder. He pushes her hand aside.*]

We've been waiting for news. For days. Tell us what happened.

[*Asher is silent. Rebecca sits, uttering low, rhythmic moans. Rachel looks at Asher, then at Rebecca, then back at Asher.*]

Now I have *two* people who won't talk. [*Silence.*] I will go mad if you don't tell me what happened.

[*Asher looks up at her.*]

ASHER. Mehemid Effendi.
RACHEL. What?
ASHER. Aziz Mehemid Effendi.
RACHEL. Who's that?
ASHER. The Keeper of the Palace Gates.
RACHEL. What are you talking about?
ASHER. I'm going to sleep.
RACHEL. You can't. Tell us what happened.

ASHER. I have to sleep.
RACHEL. What happened to Sabbatai?
ASHER. It's not important.
RACHEL. Asher, what's wrong?
ASHER. Nothing's wrong. I'm tired.
RACHEL. Did Sabbatai get the crown?
ASHER. He got something better.
RACHEL. Are we leaving for Jerusalem?
ASHER. It's not important.
RACHEL. Asher. Tell us.

[*She touches his face. He pulls her hand away.*]

ASHER. I'm so tired. All I want to do is sleep. I walked all the way to Adrianople. That's where he went. Not Constantinople. The Sultan's court is in Adrianople. We were all telling each other the name of the wrong city. Isn't that funny? The Sultan's court is in Adrianople. We had everything mixed up. He was to go to Adrianople—not Constantinople—to get his crown.
RACHEL. Did he get the crown?
ASHER. He got something better. I want to go to sleep.

[*Rachel touches him again.*]

Please. Don't put your hand on me. Please. They took him to the Sultan. The Sultan said: I hear you are the Jewish Messiah. Well, then, I've decided to lead you through the streets of Constantinople—or perhaps he said Adrianople, I don't know which—with flaming torches tied to your body until you slowly burn to death. Of course, if you *are* the Messiah, a miracle will happen. And you will not burn. Better still, make us a miracle right now. Prove to us right now that you are the Messiah. How can I, said the Messiah. Every day I wait for a sign from God to prove it to *me*. Well, then, said the Sultan, you will die. [*Pause.*]
RACHEL. He's dead. Sabbatai is dead?
ASHER. Well. There is one other choice, said the Sultan. Rather than die, you can adopt our religion. No. Sabbatai is not dead. Sabbatai is a Muslim. Sabbatai threw off his black hat. Sabbatai embraced Islam. Sabbatai went in for a crown and emerged with something better—a turban. The Messiah is not dead. The Messiah is now called Aziz Mehemid Effendi. The Messiah was given an honorary office. The Messiah was appointed Keeper of the Palace Gates. The Messiah will receive a royal pension. The Messiah is not dead. Jerusalem lives in Adrianople. Jerusalem lives in the Sultan's palace.

[Rachel gasps. She puts her arms around Asher.]

Don't touch me, harlot! [He pushes Rachel away.] You made me sin. I ate the fat of a kidney. I danced on Tisha be'Ab. I slept with my uncle's wife. I waited all my life for the Messiah. I had no family. I studied the Kabbalah. I waited. I waited for Aziz Mehemid Effendi! Keeper of the Palace Gates!

[Asher starts to weep and beat his breast. He tears his clothes. Rachel moves towards him.]

RACHEL. Asher, don't . . .

[He takes out a knife and aims it at her.]

ASHER. If you touch me, woman, I will kill you. I want to sleep. I have to sleep.

[He goes behind the blanket. Silence. Rachel stands dazed. Then she starts to laugh. She cannot stop laughing.]

[Blackout.]

[Lights rise on Rachel praying.]

RACHEL. You don't exist. I thought you should know that. You don't exist. I won't try to find excuses for you. They're finding them already for Sabbatai. They're crowding back into the square. Most are cursing him. But some have excuses. It's all part of a great design. Sabbatai is disguising himself. Every Messiah is misjudged. God has his reasons. [Pause.] There's no great design. There are no reasons. There is no God. You don't exist. [Pause.] Poor Sabbatai. Who can blame him? Burning torches? Feh! This way he gets a pension. Better this than dying like Jesus. Jesus didn't do us any favours. Dying for you. There is no you. [Pause.] Poor Sabbatai. Well. He was just a man. That's all. Just a man. Who had even heard of him a year ago? Not like you. Everyone's always heard of you. You who aren't. You who don't. You who never were. [Pause.] Poor Mehemid Effendi. He was waiting for a sign. Everybody must be waiting for a sign, then. Not just me. Well—no longer me. I've got the sign. I've received the message. I've seen the rainbow. It starts nowhere and leads nowhere. I've talked to you every day of my life. I've been talking into thin air. Into space. I've been trusting space. I've been loving space. Well—no longer. I can get along without thin air. I don't need anything to believe in. I know that I exist. That's enough. So goodbye.

[Blackout.]

[Lights rise on the hillside. Morning. Rachel is asleep in front of the blanket. Rebecca is standing in the morning light. She has a few possessions with her. She is holding her ball of wool. She takes the wool and unravels it. She makes a circle of wool on the ground around Rachel. She enters the circle. She kneels down beside Rachel. She holds her hand on Rachel's forehead. She kisses Rachel's forehead. She rises. She looks straight ahead. She walks outside the circle. She takes her long black shawl and wraps it around her body— and around her face, until only her eyes show. She stands on the edge of the hillside.]

REBECCA. Sabbatai!

[She slowly walks down the hillside and disappears. A long silence. It grows lighter. Rachel wakes up. She sees the woollen circle. She rises. She looks for Rebecca. She searches the hillside. She stops. She sits on a rock.]

RACHEL. Oh, Mama.

[She rises. She looks at the blanket. She walks to the blanket.]

RACHEL. Asher. Come on out. You've slept almost twenty-four hours. It's enough. You're a child. It's time to grow up. Asher!

[She starts to gather the wool.]

We didn't do anything wrong. Well—perhaps the kidney fat. It tasted terrible. But it wasn't wrong to sleep together. Unless it was wrong for you because you don't think I'm pretty. But that has nothing to do with the Messiah. Or laws. That's just judgement. It's no sin. Sabbatai wasn't wrong about everything. Sabbatai did some good.

[She has gathered all the wool. She looks at the blanket.]

Asher, the Messiah has come. He's inside of us. We can save ourselves. Asher. I am beautiful.

[She touches the blanket.]

Come on. You're not a child anymore. You've been asleep for too long.

[She pulls the blanket. It turns itself around. Asher is clutched against the other side of the blanket, holding his knife in his stomach. He is dead. Silence. Rachel stumbles back. She looks up at the sky. She screams.]

God damn you, God!

[She throws the wool away.]

He's a child! He doesn't know the difference! How can you be so cruel?

[She runs away from the blanket. She paces in circles. She looks up.]

Why am I talking to you? Stay away from me! You're not there! I hate you! You don't exist! Stay away!

[She runs in circles, trying to be left alone. Finally she stops.]

Why am I talking to you!

[She sits on a rock.]
[She looks around her.]
[She rises.]
[She gathers her belongings and ties them together, using the wool as string.]
[She pulls Asher's body off the blanket and takes the blanket.]
[She ties the blanket around her other belongings.]
[She starts to move away.]
[She stops.]

[She returns to Asher's body.]
[She pulls the knife out of his stomach.]
[She puts the knife in her pocket.]
[She wraps her shawl around her shoulders.]
[She holds her belongings. She looks at the hillside.]
[She starts to leave.]
[She stops.]
[She is still.]
[She looks up at the sky.]

I don't want to leave without you. But I don't want you to come with me. I don't know.

[She starts to leave.]

[She stops.]

I don't know. I don't know.

[She starts to leave.]

[She stops.]

Oh God. After all of this. I still don't know.

[She leaves.]

CURTAIN

AFTERPIECE

In the early 17th Century there was a vast Jewish population in Poland. Over three hundred thousand strong, it had become an independent, flourishing and self-governing community. Rabbinic civilization was at its height.

Poland itself led a feudal existence. The Jewish community acted as the only buffer between the wealthy noblemen and the impoverished serfs. Deprived by law of most other means of earning a livelihood, the Jews were employed as the visible representatives of the usually absent nobility. They acted as stewards, administered the land, ran the fairs, collected the taxes. They were virtually the only merchants.

The Ukraine was the southeastern borderland. The Ukrainians considered themselves Russian and hated their Polish conquerors. Some Ukrainian peasants formed themselves into marauding and blood-thirsty cavalry squads. They were known as Cossacks.

In 1648 a Cossack chief named Chmielnicki led an uprising against the Poles. After ten years of brutal fighting, peace was restored. Over one third of the Jewish population had been slaughtered, the rest impoverished.

The ravished Jewish community became obsessed with the visions of salvation. Kabbalah, the mystical interpretation of the scriptures, became a primary force. There was an all-consuming certainty that the Messiah would finally arrive.

In 1626 a son was born to a Jewish family of Spanish origin in Smyrna in Asia Minor. His name was Sabbatai Sevi. He was ordained a Sephardic rabbi at the age of eighteen . . .

ESSAY: AN APPROACH TO THE PLAY

Messiah ends as it began, with Rachel caught between hope and uncertainty; in spite of the play's many disillusionments, she says at the end, "I still don't know," refusing to deny God or the possibility of another Messiah. Her continued desire to believe, after all that has happened to her, and her continued confiding in God may seem more like habit than intelligence or self-awareness, indeed may seem like foolishness in the face of a cruelly hopeless world. Yet Rachel is fully self-aware at this moment: she knows her own foolishness, and she chooses it. Beyond knowledge and place and tradition, she finds unquenchable desire and even hope, feelings that fuel her, that provide energy for living.

The play's humor, both within Rachel's often incongruous comments to God and in the actions which surround her, underlines this essentially meaningless and yet crucial quality of hope, of endurance in spite of all. Rachel dramatizes the confusion of religion's relationship to the world and, therefore, the impossibility of steering her life by religion, and yet she does not give up her God. The Messiah's message contradicts the Jewish God of tradition; Reb Ellis, the careful merchant of fruits, throws everything away and kills himself trying to fly; Asher the beautiful kills himself when this particular Messiah is revealed as a fraud; her mother Rebecca breaks silence at the nearness of the Messiah but turns out to be a sorceress who speaks to the Devil, as had the Messiah's wife Sarah. Sarah's recognition of Rebecca near the middle of Act 2 implies their similarity, both of them have seen too much pain and evil to be so unrealistic as the men. Perhaps it is because of this that only the women survive. Sarah accepts the Messiah as a man, not a God, knowing that he is weak, and Rebecca, too, although she has given up on God and she speaks to the Devil, still wants to be saved.

Rachel derives the strength to give herself to Asher from this strange mother's loving ministrations. She is ugly because she, too, has seen too much, but at so young an age that she does not remember. The ugly Rachel knows that her ugly husband has a heart of gold and that she should love him for that, since his affection for her is based on her own essential goodness, but things are not so simple for Rachel. She cannot love him because he lacks what she also lacks, beauty. She knows that there is no sense in this, but it is so, and she does not flinch from this incongruity. She loves Asher because, though she knows he is as inexperienced and foolish as a child, he *is* beautiful. She knows that there is no sense in this either, but it, too, is so, just as Sarah loves the Messiah, though she sees through him.

Rachel "doesn't know" what to believe, but she can face her own inconsistencies because of her sense of humor. Perhaps this is the source of her self-awareness, her self-questioning, and hence her survival. Perhaps this is why she cannot deny God in spite of her recognition of His silence in the face of evil and of the many ironies he allows in her life. As with the biblical figure Job, everything dear to her is taken away; like Job, she asks God why; and like Job, she gets no answer. Yet she endures.

Perhaps this play is not about answers but about the mystery in things, about somehow keeping questions alive instead of wanting answers too much, about not jumping to believe too quickly in anything. It may be that this play encourages us to live in a perpetual suspension of belief. For in not hardening our minds into the firmness of answers, in acknowledging our questions and our feelings and our inconsistencies as Rachel does, we can remain open to possibilities of all kinds. It may be that such a suspension allows survival, even makes it possible, because it does violence to none, not even to ourselves. In such a state we do not need to suppress or deny any of our feelings, nor need we act on them unless we choose to. In this insistence on the largeness of human possibility, indeed, we might see a similarity between Sherman and another Russian, Anton Chekhov. Still, if Rachel's is the lone voice of sanity in the play, we might find ourselves asking whether we want to be sane and, if so, at what cost.

Charles Fuller

A SOLDIER'S PLAY

About the Author   Charles Fuller (1939–   ) is a Philadelphian who attended Villanova University from 1956 to 1958, served in the army until 1962, and then continued his education at La Salle University. He was co-founder and co-director of the Afro-American Arts Theatre in Philadelphia (1967–71), and his first play, *The Perfect Party*, was produced during this period, in 1968. *A Soldier's Play* was produced in 1982 by the Negro Ensemble Company, with whom Fuller had been related for years; the play won the Pulitzer Prize, the New York Drama Critics Circle Award, the Outer Circle Critics Award, and the Theatre Club Award, all in one year. Fuller rewrote the script as a screenplay for the film version, retitled *A Soldier's Story;* this film was nominated in 1984 for an Academy Award as best picture and Fuller was nominated for best screenplay.

About the Play   *A Soldier's Play* is a murder mystery. As the play begins we see a man killed, but we are unable to identify the killers; the rest of the play involves the attempt to sift the evidence and track them down. What makes the play even more interesting than a simple "whodunit," however, is its setting. The play takes place at Fort Neal, near Tynin, Louisiana, during World War II. The murdered man is Sergeant Vernon Waters, a black noncommissioned officer in charge of a group of black recruits in the racially segregated U.S. Army. The troops, black and white, are hoping for orders to go to Europe and fight against a Nazi regime dedicated to an ideology of racial purity. The international scene provides a particularly suggestive backdrop for the conflict depicted in this play.

CHARACTERS

TECH/SERGEANT VERNON C. WATERS
CAPTAIN CHARLES TAYLOR
CORPORAL BERNARD COBB
PRIVATE FIRST CLASS MELVIN PETERSON
CORPORAL ELLIS
PRIVATE LOUIS HENSON

PRIVATE JAMES WILKIE
PRIVATE TONY SMALLS
CAPTAIN RICHARD DAVENPORT
PRIVATE C. J. MEMPHIS
LIEUTENANT BYRD
CAPTAIN WILCOX

TIME: 1944

PLACE: Fort Neal, Louisiana

SCENE: The inner shell of the stage is black. On the stage, in a horseshoe-like half circle, are several platforms at varying levels.

On the left side of this horseshoe is a military office arrangement with a small desk (a nameplate on the desk reads: Captain Charles Taylor), two office-type chairs, one straight-backed, a regimental, and an American flag. A picture of F.D.R. is on the wall.

On the right side of the horseshoe, and curved toward the rear, is a barracks arrangement, with three bunk beds and footlockers set in typical military fashion. The exit to this barracks is a freestanding doorway on the far right. (This barracks should be changeable—these bunks with little movement can look like a different place.) On the edge of this barracks is a poster, semi-blown up, of Joe Louis in an army uniform, helmet, rifle, and bayonet. It reads: PVT. JOE LOUIS SAYS, "WE'RE GOING TO DO OUR PART—AND WE'LL WIN BECAUSE WE'RE ON GOD'S SIDE."

On the rear of the horseshoe, upstage center, is a bare platform, raised several feet above everything else. It can be anything we want it to be—a limbo if you will.

The entire set should resemble a courtroom. The

sets, barracks and office, will both be elevated, so that from anywhere on the horseshoe one may look down onto a space at center stage that is on the stage floor. The levels should have easy access by either stairs or ramps, and the entire set should be raked ever so slightly so that one does not perceive much difference between floor and set, and the bottom edges of the horseshoe. There must also be enough area on both sides of the horseshoe to see exits and entrances.

Lighting will play an integral part in the realization of the play. It should therefore be sharp, so that areas are clearly defined, with as little spill into other areas as possible. Lights must also be capable of suggesting mood, time, and place.

As the play opens, the stage is black. In the background, rising in volume, we hear the song "Don't Sit under the Apple Tree," sung by the Andrews Sisters. Quite suddenly, in a sharp though narrow beam of light, in limbo, Tech/Sergeant Vernon C. Waters, a well-built, light-brown-skinned man in a World War II, winter army uniform, is seen down on all fours. He is stinking drunk, trying to stand and mumbling to himself.

WATERS [*repeating*]. They'll still hate you! They still hate you . . . They still hate you!

[*Waters is laughing as suddenly someone steps into the light. (We never see this person.) He is holding a .45 caliber pistol. He lifts it swiftly and ominously toward Water's head and fires. Waters is knocked over backward. He is dead. The music has stopped and there is a strong silence onstage.*]

VOICE. Le's go!

[*The man with the gun takes a step, then stops. He points the gun at Waters again and fires a second time. There is another silence as limbo is plunged into darkness, and the barracks is just as quickly lit.*

We are in the barracks of Company B, 221st Chemical Smoke Generating Company, at Fort Neal. Five black enlisted men stand at "parade rest" with their hands above their heads and submit to a search. They are: Corporal Bernard Cobb, a man in his mid to late twenties, dressed in a T-shirt, dog tags, fatigues, and slippers. Private James Wilkie, a man in his early forties, a career soldier, is dressed in fatigues from which the stripes have been removed, with a baseball cap on, and smoking a cigar. Private Louis Henson, thin, in his late twenties or early thirties, is wearing a baseball T-shirt that reads "Fort Neal" on the front and "#4" on the back, with fatigues and boots on. PFC Melvin Peterson, a man in his late twenties, wearing glasses, looks angelic. His

shirt is open but he does not look sloppy; of all the men, his stripe is the most visible, his boots the most highly polished. Private Tony Smalls, a man in his late thirties, a career man, is as small as his name feels. All five men are being searched by Corporal Ellis, a soldier who is simply always "spit and polish." Ellis is also black, and moves from man to man, patting them down in a police-like search. Captain Charles Taylor, a young white man in his mid to late thirties, looks on, a bit disturbed. All the men's uniforms are from World War II.]

TAYLOR. I'm afraid this kind of thing can't be helped, men—you can put your arms down when Ellis finishes. [*Several men drop their arms. Ellis is searching Pvt. Henson*] We don't want anyone from Fort Neal going into Tynin looking for red-necks.

COBB. May I speak, sir? [*Taylor nods*] Why do this, Captain? They got M.P.'s surrounding us, and hell, the Colonel must know nobody colored killed the man!

TAYLOR. This is a precaution, Cobb. We can't have revenge killings, so we search for weapons.

PETERSON. Where'd they find the Sarge, sir?

TAYLOR. In the woods out by the Junction—and so we don't have any rumors. Sergeant Waters was shot twice—we don't know that he was lynched! [*Pause*] Twice. Once in the chest, and a bullet in the head. [*Ellis finishes with the last man*] You finished the footlockers?

ELLIS. Yes, sir! There aren't any weapons.

TAYLOR [*relaxes*]. I didn't think there would be. At ease, men! [*The men relax*] Tech/Sergeant Waters, in my opinion, served the 221st and this platoon in particular with distinction, and I for one shall miss the man. [*Slight pause*] But no matter what we think of the Sergeant's death, we will not allow this incident to make us forget our responsibility to this uniform. We are soldiers, and our war is with the Nazis and Japs, not the civilians in Tynin. Any enlisted man found with unauthorized weapons will be immediately subject to summary court-martial. [*Softens*] Sergeant Waters's replacement won't be assigned for several weeks. Until that time, you will all report to Sergeant Dorsey of C Company. Corporal Cobb will be barracks N.C.O.—any question?

PETERSON. Who do they think did it, sir?

TAYLOR. At this time there are no suspects.

HENSON. You know the Klan did it, sir.

TAYLOR. Were you an eyewitness, soldier?

HENSON. Who else goes around killin' Negroes in the South?—They lynched Jefferson the week I got here, sir! And that Signal Corps guy, Daniels, two months later!

TAYLOR. Henson, unless you saw it, keep your opinions to yourself! Is that clear? [*Henson nods*] And that's an order! It also applies to everybody else!

ALL [*almost simultaneously*]. Yes, sir!

TAYLOR. You men who have details this afternoon, report to the orderly room for your assignments. The rest of you are assigned to the Colonel's quarters—clean-up detail. Cobb, I want to see you in my office at 1350 hours.

COBB. Yes, sir.

TAYLOR. As of 0600 hours this morning, the town of Tynin was placed off-limits to all military personnel. [*Slight groan from the men*] The Friday night dance has also been canceled—[*All the men moan. Taylor is sympathetic*] O.K., O.K.! Some of the officers are going to the Colonel—I can't promise anything. Right now, it's canceled.

ELLIS. Tenn-hut!

[*The men snap to. The Captain salutes. Only Cobb salutes him back. The Captain starts out.*]

TAYLOR. As you were!

[*The Captain and Ellis exit the barracks. The men move to their bunks or footlockers. Wilkie goes to the rear of the bunks and looks out.*]

COBB. They still out there, Wilkie?

WILKIE. Yeah. Got the whole place surrounded.

HENSON. I don't know what the hell they thought we'd go into that town with—mops and dishrags?

WILKIE. Y'all recruits know what Colonel's clean-up detail is, don't you? Shovelin' horseshit in his stables—

COBB. Ain't no different from what we been doin'. [*He lies down and begins scratching around his groin area*]

PETERSON [*to Cobb*]. Made you the barracks Commander-in-Chief, huh? [*Cobb nods*] Don't git like ole Stone-ass—What are you doin'?

COBB. Scratchin'!

HENSON [*overlapping*]. Taylor knows the Klan did it— I hope y'all know that!

SMALLS [*sudden*]. Then why are the M.P.'s outside with rifles? Why hold us prisoner?

PETERSON. They scared we may kill a couple peckerwoods, Smalls. Calm down, man!

WILKIE [*quickly*]. Smalls, you wanna play some coon-can?

[*Smalls shakes his head no. He is quiet, staring.*]

COBB [*examining himself*]. Peterson, you know I think Eva gave me the crabs.

HENSON. Cobb, the kinda women you find, it's a wonda your nuts ain't fell off—crabs? You probably got lice, ticks, bedbugs, fleas—tapeworms–

COBB. Shut up, Henson! Pete—I ain't foolin, man! [*He starts to open his pants.*]

PETERSON. Get some powder from the PX.

WILKIE [*almost simultaneously*]. Which one of y'all feels like playin' me some cards? [*He looks at Henson*]

HENSON. Me and Peterson's goin' down the mess hall —you still goin', Pete?

PETERSON [*nods*]. Wilkie? I thought all you could do was play gofer?

HENSON [*slyly*]. Yeah, Wilkie—whose ass can you kiss, now that your number-one ass is dead?

COBB [*laughing*]. That sounds like something C.J. would sing! [*Looks at himself again*] Ain't this a bitch? [*Picks at himself*]

WILKIE [*overlapping, to Henson*]. You know what you can do for me, Henson—you too, Peterson!

PETERSON. Naughty, naughty!

[*Wilkie moves to his bunk, justifying.*]

WILKIE. I'm the one lost three stripes—and I'm the only man in here with kids, so when the man said jump, I jumped!

HENSON [*derisively*]. Don't put your wife and kids between you and Waters's ass, man!

WILKIE. I wanted my stripes back!

COBB. I'm goin' to sick call after chow.

WILKIE [*continuing*]. Y'all ain't neva' had nothin', that's why you can't understand a man like me! There was a time I was a sergeant major, you know!

[*Henson waves disdainfully at him, turning his attention to Cobb*]

HENSON. Ole V-girl slipped Cobb the crabs! How you gonna explain that to the girl back home, Corporal? How will that fine, big-thighed Moma feel, when the only ribbon you bring home from this war is the Purple Heart for crab bites? [*Henson laughs as Smalls stands suddenly*]

SMALLS. Don't any of you guys give a damn?

PETERSON. What's the matta', Smalls?

SMALLS. The man's dead! We saw him alive last night!

COBB [*quickly*]. I saw him, too. At least I know he died good and drunk!

SMALLS [*loud*]. What's the matter with y'all?

HENSON. The man got hisself lynched! We're in the

South, and we can't do a goddamn thing about it—you heard the Captain! But don't start actin' like we guilty of somethin'. [*Softens*] I just hope we get lucky enough to get shipped outta this hellhole to the war! [*To himself*] Besides, whoever did it, didn't kill much anyway.

SMALLS. He deserved better than that!

COBB. Look, everybody feels rotten, Smalls. But it won't bring the man back, so let's forget about it!

[*Peterson moves to pat Smalls on the back.*]

PETERSON. Why don't you walk it off, man?

[*Smalls moves away to his bunk. Peterson shrugs.*]

HENSON. Yeah—or go turn on a smoke machine, let the fog make you think you in London!

[*Smalls sits down on his bunk and looks at them for a moment, then lays down, his face in the pillow.*]

WILKIE [*overlapping*]. Let Cobb bring his Eva over, she'll take his mind off Waters plus give him a bonus of crabs!

[*The men laugh, but Smalls doesn't move as the lights begin slowly to fade out.*]

HENSON [*counting*]. —an' blue-balls. Clap. Syphilis. Pimples! [*Cobb throws a pillow at Henson*] Piles! Fever blisters. Cockeyes. Cooties!

[*The men are laughing as the lights go out. As they do, a rather wiry black officer wearing glasses, Captain Richard Davenport, walks across the stage from the wings, dressed sharply in an M.P. uniform, his hat cocked to the side and strapped down, the way airmen wear theirs. He is carrying a briefcase, and we are aware of a man who is very confident and self-assured. He is smiling as he faces the audience, cleaning his glasses as he begins to speak.*]

DAVENPORT. Call me Davenport—Captain, United States Army, attached to the 343rd Military Police Corps Unit, Fort Neal, Louisiana. I'm a lawyer the segregated Armed Services couldn't find a place for. My job in this war? Policing colored troops. [*Slight pause*] One morning, during mid-April 1944, a colored tech/sergeant, Vernon C. Waters, assigned to the 221st Chemical Smoke Generating Company, stationed here before transfer to Europe, was brutally shot to death in a wooded section off the New Post Road and the junction of Highway 51—just two hundred yards from the colored N.C.O. club—by a person or persons unknown. [*Pauses a little*] Naturally, the unofficial consensus was the local Ku Klux Klan, and for that reason, I was told at the time, Colonel Barton Nivens ordered the Military Police to surround the enlisted men's quarters—then instructed all his company commanders to initiate a thorough search of all personal property for unauthorized knives, guns—weapons of any kind. [*Slight pause*] You see, ninety percent of the Colonel's command—all of the enlisted men stationed here are Negroes, and the Colonel felt—and I suppose justly—that once word of the Sergeant's death spread among his troops, there might be some retaliation against the white citizens of Tynin. [*Shrugs*] What he did worked—there was no retaliation, and no racial incidents. [*Pause*] The week after the killing took place, several correspondents from the Negro press wrote lead articles about it. But the headlines faded—[*Smiles*] The NAACP got me involved in this. Rumor has it, Thurgood Marshall ordered an immediate investigation of the killing, and the army, pressured by Secretary of War Stimson, rather randomly ordered Colonel Nivens to initiate a preliminary inquiry into the Sergeant's death. Now, the Colonel didn't want to rehash the murder, but he complied with the army's order by instructing the Provost Marshal, my C.O., Major Hines, to conduct a few question-and-answer sessions among the men of Sergeant Waters's platoon and file a report. The matter was to be given the lowest priority. [*Pause*] The case was mine, five minutes later. It was four to five weeks after his death—the month of May. [*He pauses as the light builds in Captain Taylor's office. Taylor is facing Davenport, expressionless. Davenport is a bit puzzled*] Captain?

TAYLOR [*Starts back to his desk and sits on the edge of it, as Davenport starts into the office a bit cautiously*]. We'll be getting some of you as replacements, but we don't expect them until next month. Sit down, Davenport. [*Davenport sits*] You came out of Fort Benning in '43?

DAVENPORT. Yes.

TAYLOR. And they assigned a lawyer to the Military Police? I'm Infantry and I've been with the Engineers, Field Artillery, and Signal Corps—this is some army. Where'd you graduate law school?

DAVENPORT. Howard University.

TAYLOR. Your daddy a rich minister or something? [*Davenport shakes his head no*] I graduated the Point—[*Pause*] We didn't have any Negroes at the

Point. I never saw a Negro until I was twelve or
thirteen. [*Pause*] You like the army, I suppose, huh?

DAVENPORT. Captain, did you see my orders?

TAYLOR [*bristling slightly*]. I saw them right after Colonel Nivens sent them to Major Hines. I sent my
orderly to the barracks and told him to have the
men waiting for you.

DAVENPORT. Thank you.

TAYLOR. I didn't know at the time that Major Hines
was assigning a Negro, Davenport. [*Davenport
stiffens*] My preparations were made in the belief that
you'd be a white man. I think it only fair to tell you
that had I known what Hines intended I would have
requested the immediate suspension of the investigation—May I speak freely?

DAVENPORT. You haven't stopped yet, Captain.

TAYLOR. Look—how far could you get even if you
succeed? These local people aren't going to charge a
white man in this parish on the strength of an investigation conducted by a Negro!—and Nivens and
Hines know that! The Colonel doesn't give a damn
about finding the men responsible for this thing!
And they're making a fool of you—can't you see
that?—and—take off those sunglasses!

DAVENPORT. I intend to carry out my orders—and I
like these glasses—they're like MacArthur's.

TAYLOR. You go near that sheriff's office in Tynin in
your uniform—carrying a briefcase, looking and
sounding white, and charging local people—and
you'll be found just as dead as Sergeant Waters!
People around here don't respect the colored!

DAVENPORT. I know that.

TAYLOR [*annoyed*]. You know how many times I've
asked Nivens to look into this killing? Every day,
since it happened, Davenport. Major Hines didn't
tell you that!

DAVENPORT. Do you suspect someone, Captain?

TAYLOR. Don't play cat-and-mouse with me, soldier!

DAVENPORT [*calmly*]. Captain, like it or not, I'm all
you've got. I've been ordered to look into Sergeant
Waters's death, and I intend to do exactly that.

[*There is a long pause.*]

TAYLOR. Can I tell you a little story? [*Davenport nods*]
Before you were assigned here? Nivens got us
together after dinner one night, and all we did was
discuss Negroes in the officer ranks. We all commanded Negro troops, but nobody had ever come
face to face with colored officers—there were a lot
of questions that night—for example, your
quarters—had to be equal to ours, but we had

none—no mess hall for you! [*Slight pause*] Anyway,
Jed Harris was the only officer who defended it—
my own feelings were mixed. The only Negroes I've
ever known were subordinates—My father hired the
first Negro I ever saw—man named Colfax—to help
him fix the shed one summer. Nice man—worked
hard—did a good job, too. [*Remembering; smiles
thoughtfully*] But I never met a Negro with any education until I graduated the Point—hardly an officer
of equal rank. So I frankly wasn't sure how I'd
feel—until right now—and—[*Struggles*] I don't want
to offend you, but I just cannot get used to it—the
bars, the uniform—being in charge just doesn't look
right on Negroes!

DAVENPORT [*rises*]. Captain, are you through?

TAYLOR. You could ask Hines for another
assignment—this case is not for you! By the time
you overcome the obstacles to your race, this case
would be dead!

DAVENPORT [*sharply*]. I got it. And I *am* in charge! All
your orders instruct you to do is cooperate!

[*There is a moment of silence.*]

TAYLOR. I won't be made a fool of, Davenport.
[*Straightens*] Ellis! You're right, there's no need to
discuss this any further.

[*Ellis appears on the edge of the office.*]

ELLIS Yes, sir!

TAYLOR. Captain Davenport will need assistance with
the men—I can't prevent that, Davenport, but I
intend to do all I can to have this so-called investigation stopped.

DAVENPORT. Do what you like. If there's nothing
else, you'll excuse me, won't you, Captain?

TAYLOR [*sardonically*]. Glad I met you, Captain.

[*Davenport salutes and Taylor returns salute. For an instant
the two men trade cold stares, then Davenport gestures to
Ellis, and the two of them start out of the office by way of the
stage. Davenport follows Ellis out. Behind them, Taylor
stares after them as the lights in his office fade out. Davenport removes his glasses.*]

ELLIS. We heard it was you, sir—you know how the
grapevine is. Sad thing—what happened to the
Sarge.

DAVENPORT. What's on the grapevine about the
killing?

[*The two men stop as slowly, almost imperceptibly, on the*

right the barracks area is lit. In it, a small table and two chairs have been set up. Ellis shrugs.]

ELLIS. We figure the Klan. They ain't crazy about us tan yanks in this part of the country.

DAVENPORT. Is there anything on the grapevine about trouble in the town before Sergeant Waters was killed?

ELLIS. None that I know of before—after, there were rumors around the post—couple our guys from the Tank Corps wanted to drive them Shermans into Tynin—then I guess you heard that somebody said two officers did it—I figure that's why the Colonel surrounded our barracks.

DAVENPORT. Was the rumor confirmed—I didn't hear that! Did anything ever come of it?

ELLIS. Not that I know of, sir.

DAVENPORT. Thanks, Ellis—I'd better start seeing the men. [*They start into the barracks from the stage floor*] Did you set this up? [*Ellis nods*] Good— [*He sets his briefcase on the table*] Are they ready?

ELLIS. The Captain instructed everybody in the Sarge's platoon to be here, sir. He told them you'd be starting this morning.

[*Davenport smiles.*]

DAVENPORT [*to himself*]. Before he found out, huh?

ELLIS [*puzzled*]. Sir?

DAVENPORT. Nothing. Call the first man in, Corporal —and stay loose, I might need you.

ELLIS. Yes, sir! Sir, may I say something? [*Davenport nods*] It sure is good to see one of us wearin' them Captain's bars, sir.

DAVENPORT. Thank you.

[*Ellis salutes, does a sharp about-face, and starts out.*]

ELLIS [*loud*]. Private Wilkie!

WILKIE [*offstage*]. Yes, sir! [*Almost immediately, Wilkie appears in the doorway. He is dressed in proper uniform of fatigues, boots, and cap.*]

ELLIS. Cap'n wants to see you!

WILKIE. Yes indeedy! [*Moves quickly to the table, where he comes to attention and salutes*] Private James Wilkie reporting as ordered, sir.

DAVENPORT. At ease, Private. Have a seat. [*To Ellis as Wilkie sits*] That will be all, Corporal.

ELLIS. Yes, sir.

[*Ellis salutes and exits. Davenport waits until he leaves before speaking.*]

DAVENPORT. Private Wilkie, I am Captain Davenport—

WILKIE [*interjecting*]. Everybody knows that, sir. You all we got down here. [*Smiles broadly*] I was on that first detail got your quarters togetha', sir.

[*Davenport nods.*]

DAVENPORT [*coldly*]. I'm conducting an investigation into the events surrounding Sergeant Waters's death. Everything you say to me will go in my report, but that report is confidential.

WILKIE. I understand, sir.

[*Davenport removes pad and pencil from the briefcase.*]

DAVENPORT. How long did you know Sergeant Waters?

WILKIE. 'Bout a year, sir. I met him last March—March 5th—I remember the date, I had been a staff sergeant exactly two years the day after he was assigned. This company was basically a baseball team then, sir. See, most of the boys had played for the Negro League, so naturally the army put us all together. [*Chuckles at the memory*] We'd be assigned to different companies—Motor Pool—Dump Truck all week long—made us do the dirty work on the post—garbage, clean-up—but on Saturdays we were whippin' the hell out of 'em on the baseball diamond! I was hittin' .352 myself! And we had a boy, C. J. Memphis? He coulda hit a ball from Fort Neal to Berlin, Germany—or Tokyo—if he was battin' right-handed. [*Pauses, catches Davenport's impatience*] Well, the army sent Waters to manage the team. He had been in Field Artillery—Gunnery Sergeant. Had a croix de guerre from the First War, too.

DAVENPORT. What kind of man was he?

WILKIE. All spit and polish, sir.

[*At that moment, in limbo, a spotlight hits Sergeant Waters. He is dressed in a well-creased uniform, wearing a helmet liner and standing at parade-rest, facing the audience. The light around him, however, is strange—it is blue-gray like the past. The light around Davenport and Wilkie abates somewhat. Dialogue is continuous.*]

DAVENPORT. Tell me about him.

WILKIE. He took my stripes! [*Smiles*] But I was in the wrong, sir!

[*Waters stands at ease. His voice is crisp and sharp, his*

movements minimal. He is the typical hard-nosed N.C.O.— strict, soldierly.]

WATERS. Sergeant Wilkie! You are a noncommissioned officer in the army of a country at war—the penalty for being drunk on duty is severe in peacetime, so don't bring me no po-colored-folks-can't-do-nothin'-unless-they-drunk shit as an excuse! You are supposed to be an example to your men—so, I'm gonna send you to jail for ten days *and* take them goddamn stripes. Teach you a lesson—You in the army! *[Derisively]* Colored folks always runnin' off at the mouth 'bout what y'all gonna do if the white man gives you a chance—and you get it, and what do you do with it? You wind up drunk on guard duty—I don't blame the white man—why the hell should he put colored and white together in this war? You can't even be trusted to guard your own quarters—no wonder they treat us like dogs—Get outta' my sight, *Private*!

[Light fades at once on Waters.]

DAVENPORT. What about the other men?
WILKIE. Sometimes the Southern guys caught a little hell—Sarge always said he was from up North somewhere. He was a good soldier, sir. I'm from Detroit myself—born and raised there. Joe Louis started in Detroit—did you know that, sir?
DAVENPORT. What about the Southerners?
WILKIE. Sarge wasn't exactly crazy 'bout 'em—'cept for C.J. Now C.J. was from the South, but with him Sarge was different—probably because C.J. was the best ball player we had. He could sing too! *[Slight pause]* Sarge never got too close to nobody—maybe me—but he didn' mess with C.J., you know what I mean? Not like he did with everybody else.

[In limbo the spotlight illuminates C. J. Memphis, a young, handsome black man. He is in a soldier's uniform, cap on the side. He is strumming a guitar. Waters is watching him, smiling. Their light is the strange light of the past. C. J. begins to sing, his voice deep, melodious, and bluesy.]

C.J. It's a low / it's a low, low / lowdown dirty shame! Yeah, it's a low / it's a low, low / lowdown dirty shame!
WILKIE *[before C.J. finishes]*. Big Mississippi boy!

[Wilkie and C.J. simultaneously sing.]

C.J. AND WILKIE. They say we fightin' Hitler! But they won't let us in the game!

[C.J. strums and hums as Waters looks on.]

WILKIE. Worked harder and faster than everybody— wasn' a man on the team didn't like him. Sarge took to him the first time he saw him. "Wilkie," he says.
WILKIE AND WATERS *[simultaneously]*. What have we got here?
WATERS. A guitar-playin' man! Boy, you eva' heard of Blind Willie Reynolds? Son House? Henry Sims?

[C.J. nods to everything.]

C.J. You heard them play, Sarge?
WATERS. Every one of 'em. I was stationed in Mississippi couple years ago—you from down that way, ain't you?
C.J. Yes, sah!
WATERS. Well, they use ta play over at the Bandana Club outside Camp J. J. Reilly.
C.J. I played there once!
WATERS *[smiles]*. Ain't that somethin'! I'd go over there from time to time—people use ta come from everywhere! *[To Wilkie]* Place was always dark, Wilkie—smoky. Folks would be dancin'— sweatin'—guitar pickers be strummin', shoutin'—it would be wild in there sometimes. Reminded me of a place I use ta go in France durin' the First War— the women, the whiskey—place called the Café Napoleon.
C.J. You really like the blues, huh?
WATERS. No other kind of music—where'd you learn to play so good? I came by here yesterday and heard this pickin'—one of the men tol' me it was you.
C.J. My daddy taught me, Sarge.
WATERS. You play pretty good, boy. Wilkie, wasn' that good?
WILKIE. Yes indeed, Sarge.
WILKIE *[to Davenport]*. I mostly agreed with the Sarge, sir. He was a good man. Good to his men. Talked about his wife and kids all the time—*[Waters starts down from the limbo area, as the lights around C. J. fade out. Waters pulls a pipe from his pocket, lights it as he moves to the edge of the Captain's office and sits on the edge of the platform supporting it. He puffs a few times. Wilkie's talk is continuous]* Use ta write home every day. I don't see why nobody would want to kill the Sarge, sir.

[Waters smiles.]

WATERS. Wilkie? *[Wilkie rises and walks into the blue-gray light and the scene with Waters. Davenport will watch]* You know what I'ma get that boy of mine for his birthday? One of them Schwinn bikes. He'll be twelve—time flies, don't it? Let me show you something?

WILKIE [to Davenport]. He was always pullin' out snapshots, sir.

[Waters hands him a snapshot.]

WATERS. My wife let a neighbor take this a couple week ago—ain't he growin' fast?

WILKIE. He's over your wife's shoulder! [Hands it back. Waters looks at the photo]

WATERS. I hope this kid never has to be a soldier.

WILKIE. It was good enough for you.

WATERS. I couldn't do any better—and this army was the closest I figured the white man would let me get to any kind of authority. No, the army ain't for this boy. When this war's over, things are going to change, Wilkie—and I want him to be ready for it—my daughter, too! I'm sendin' bot' of 'em to some big white college—let 'em rub elbows with the whites, learn the white man's language—how he does things. Otherwise, we'll be left behind—you can see it in the army. White man runnin' rings around us.

WILKIE. A lot of us didn't get the chance or the schoolin' the white folks got.

WATERS. That ain't no excuse, Wilkie. Most niggahs just don't care—tomorrow don't mean nothin' to 'em. My daddy shoveled coal from the back of a wagon all his life. He couldn't read or write, but he saw to it we did! Not havin' ain't no excuse for not gettin'.

WILKIE. Can't get pee from a rock, Sarge.

[Waters rises abruptly.]

WATERS. You just like the rest of 'em, Wilkie—I thought bustin' you would teach you something—we got to challenge this man in his arena—use his weapons, don't you know that? We need lawyers, doctors—generals—senators! Stop thinkin' like a niggah!

WILKIE. All I said—

WATERS. Is the equipment ready for tomorrow's game?

WILKIE. Yeah.

WATERS. Good. You can go now, Wilkie. [Wilkie is stunned] That's an order!

[Wilkie turns toward Davenport. In the background, the humming of C. J. rises a bit as the light around Waters fades out.]

WILKIE. He could be two people sometimes, sir. Warm one minute—ice the next.

DAVENPORT. How did you feel about him?

WILKIE. Overall—I guess he was all right. You could always borrow a ten-spot off him if you needed it.

DAVENPORT. Did you see the Sergeant any time immediately preceding his death?

WILKIE. I don't know how much before it was, but a couple of us had been over the N.C.O. club that night and Sarge had been juicin' pretty heavy.

DAVENPORT. Did Waters drink a lot?

WILKIE. No more than most— [Pause] Could I ask you a question, sir? [Davenport nods] Is it true, when they found Sarge all his stripes and insignia were still on his uniform?

DAVENPORT. I don't recall it being mentioned in my preliminary report. Why?

WILKIE. If that's the way they found him, something's wrong, ain't it, sir? Them Klan boys don't like to see us in these uniforms. They usually take the stripes and stuff off, before they lynch us.

[Davenport is quiet, thoughtful for a moment.]

DAVENPORT. Thank you, Private—I might want to call you again, but for now you're excused.

[Wilkie rises.]

WILKIE. Yes, sir! [Sudden mood swing, hesitant] Sir?

DAVENPORT. Yes?

WILKIE. Can you do anything about allotment checks? My wife didn't get hers last month.

DAVENPORT. There's nothing I can do directly—did you see the finance officer? [Wilkie nods] Well— I'll—I'll mention it to Captain Taylor.

WILKIE. Thank you, sir. You want me to send the next man in?

[Davenport nods. Wilkie salutes, does an about-face, and exits. Davenport returns the salute, then leans back in his chair thoughtfully. In the background, the humming of C. J. rises again as the next man, PFC Melvin Peterson, enters. Dressed in fatigues, he is the model soldier. He walks quickly to the table, stands at attention, and salutes. The humming fades out as Davenport returns the salute.]

PETERSON. Private First Class Melvin Peterson reporting as ordered, sir!

DAVENPORT. Sit down, Private. [Peterson sits] Do you know why I'm here?

PETERSON. Yes, sir.

DAVENPORT. Fine. Now, everything you tell me is

confidential, so I want you to speak as freely as possible. [*Peterson nods*] Where are you from?

PETERSON. Hollywood, California—by way of Alabama, sir. I enlisted in '42—thought we'd get a chance to fight.

DAVENPORT [*ignores the comment*]. Did you know Sergeant Waters well?

PETERSON. No, sir. He was already with the company when I got assigned here. And us common G.I.'s don't mix well with N.C.O.'s.

DAVENPORT. Were you on the baseball team?

PETERSON. Yes, sir—I played shortstop.

DAVENPORT. Did you like the Sergeant?

PETERSON. No, sir.

[*Before Davenport can speak, Ellis enters.*]

ELLIS. Beg your pardon, sir. Captain Taylor would like to see you in his office at once.

DAVENPORT. Did he say why?

ELLIS. No, sir—just that you should report to him immediately.

DAVENPORT [*annoyed*]. Tell the men to stick around. When I finish with the Captain, I'll be back.

ELLIS. Yes, sir!

[*Ellis exits.*]

DAVENPORT [*to Peterson*]. Feel like walking, Private? We can continue this on the way. [*Begins to put his things in his briefcase*] Why didn't you like the Sergeant?

[*Davenport and Peterson start out as the light begins to fade in the barracks. They go through doorway, exit, and reenter the stage in full view.*]

PETERSON. It goes back to the team, sir. I got here in—baseball season had started, so it had to be June—June of last year. The team had won maybe nine—ten games in a row, there was a rumor that they would even get a chance to play the Yankees in exhibition. So when I got assigned to a team like that, sir—I mean, I felt good. Anyway, ole Stone-ass—

DAVENPORT. Stone-ass?

PETERSON. I'm the only one called him that—Sergeant Waters, sir.

[*As the two of them pass in front of the barracks area, the light begins to rise very slowly, but it is the blue-gray light of the past. The chairs and table are gone, and the room looks different.*]

DAVENPORT. Respect his rank, with me, Private.

PETERSON. I didn't mean no offense, sir. [*Slight pause*] Well, the Sergeant and that brown-nosin' Wilkie? They ran the team—and like it was a chain gang, sir. A chain gang!

[*The two men exit the stage. As they do, C.J. Memphis, Henson, Cobb, and Smalls enter in their baseball uniforms. T-shirts with "Fort Neal" stamped on the fronts, and numbers on the back, and baseball caps. They are carrying equipment—bats, gloves. C.J. is carrying his guitar. Smalls enters tossing a baseball into the air and catching it. They almost all enter at once, with the exuberance of young men. Their talk is locker-room loud, and filled with bursts of laughter.*]

HENSON. You see the look on that umpire's face when C.J. hit that home run? I thought he was gonna die on the spot, he turned so pale!

[*They move to their respective bunks.*]

SMALLS. Serves the fat bastard right! Some of them pitches he called strikes were well ova' my head!

[*C.J. strums his guitar. Cobb begins to brush off his boots.*]

COBB. C.J.? Who was that fine, river-hip thing you was talkin' to, homey?

[*C.J. shrugs and smiles.*]

HENSON. Speakin' of women, I got to write my Lady a letter. [*He begins to dig for his writing things*]

COBB. She looked mighty good to me, C.J.

SMALLS [*overlapping*]. Y'all hear Henson? Henson, you ain't had a woman since a woman had you!

[*Henson makes an obscene gesture.*]

C.J. [*overlapping Smalls*]. Now, all she did was ask me for my autograph.

COBB. Look like she was askin' you fo' mor'n that. [*To Smalls*] You see him, Smalls? Leanin' against the fence, all in the woman's face, breathin' heavy—

HENSON. If Smalls couldn't see enough to catch a ground ball right in his glove, how the hell could he see C.J. ova' by the fence?

SMALLS. That ball got caught in the sun!

HENSON. On the ground?

COBB [*at once*]. We beat 'em nine to one! Y'all be quiet, I'm askin' this man 'bout a woman he was with had tits like two helmets!

C.J. If I had'a give that gal what she asked fo'—she'da

give me somethin' I didn' want! Them V-gals git you a bad case a' clap. 'Sides, she wasn' but sixteen.

SMALLS. You shoulda introduced her to Henson—sixteen's about his speed.

[Henson makes a farting sound in retaliation.]

C.J. Aroun' home? There's a fella folks use ta call, Lil' Jimmy One Leg—on account of his thing was so big? Two years ago—ole young pretty thing laid clap on Jimmy so bad, he los' the one good leg he had! Now folks jes' call him Little!

[Laughter.]

C.J. That young thing talkin' to me ain' look so clean.

HENSON. Dirty or clean, she had them white boys lookin'.

COBB. Eyes popin' out they sockets, wasn' they? Remind me of that pitcher las' week! The one from 35th Ordnance? The one everybody claimed was so good? Afta' twelve straight hits, he looked the same way!

[Peterson enters, carrying two baseball bats.]

SMALLS. It might be funny ta y'all, but when me and Pete had duty in the Ordnance mess hall, that same white pitcher was the first one started the name-callin'—

HENSON. Forget them dudes in Ordnance—lissen to this! [Henson begins to read from a short letter] "Dear, Louis"—y'all hear that? The name is Louis—

COBB. Read the damn letter!

HENSON [makes obscene gesture]. "Dear, Louis. You and the boys keep up the good work. All of us here at home are praying for you and inspired in this great cause by you. We know the Nazis and the Japs can't be stopped unless we all work together, so tell your buddies to press forward and win this war. All our hopes for the future go with you, Louis. Love Mattie." I think I'm in love with the sepia Winston Churchill—what kinda' letter do you write a nut like this?

COBB. Send her a round of ammunition and a bayonet, *Louis!*

[Henson waves disdainfully.]

PETERSON. Y'all oughta listen to what Smalls said. Every time we beat them at baseball, they get back at us every way they can.

COBB. It's worth it to me just to wipe those superior smiles off they faces.

PETERSON. I don't know—seems like it makes it that much harder for us.

C.J. They tell me, coupla them big-time Negroes is on the verge a' gittin' all of us togetha'—colored and white—say they want one army.

PETERSON. Forget that, C.J.! White folks'll neva' integrate no army!

C.J. [strums]. If they do—I'ma be ready for 'em! [Sings] Well, I got me a bright red zoot suit / And a pair a' patent-letha' shoes / And my woman she sittin' waitin' / Fo' the day we hea' the news! Lawd, lawd, lawd, lawd, / Lawd, lawd, lawd, lawd!

[Sergeant Waters, followed by Wilkie, enters, immediately crossing to the center of the barracks, his strident voice abruptly cutting off C.J.'s singing and playing.]

WATERS. Listen up! [To C.J.] We don't need that guitar playin'-sittin'-round-the-shack music today, C.J.! [Smiles] I want all you men out of those baseball uniforms and into work clothes! You will all report to me at 1300 hours in front of the Officers Club. We've got a work detail. We're painting the lobby of the club.

[Collective groan.]

SMALLS. The officers can't paint their own club?

COBB. Hell no, Smalls! Let the great-colored-clean-up company do it! Our motto is: Anything you don't want to do, the colored troops will do for you!

HENSON [like a cheer]. Anything you don't want to do, the colored troops will do for you! [He starts to lead the others]

OTHERS. Anything you don't—

WATERS. That's enough!

[The men are instantly silent.]

HENSON. When do we get a rest? We just played nine innings of baseball, Sarge!

SMALLS. We can't go in the place, why the hell should we paint it?

COBB. Amen, brother!

[There is a moment of quiet before Waters speaks.]

WATERS. Let me tell you fancy-assed ball-playin' Negroes somethin'! The *reasons* for any orders given by a superior officer is none of y'all's business! You obey them! This country is at war, and you niggahs are soldiers—nothing' else! So baseball teams—win or lose—get no special privileges! They need to work some of you niggahs till your legs fall off! [*Intense*] And something else—from now on, when I tell you to do something, I want it done—is that clear? [*The men are quiet*] Now, Wilkie's gonna' take all them funky shirts you got on over to the laundry. I could smell you suckers before I hit the field!

PETERSON. What kinda colored man are you?

WATERS. I'm a soldier, Peterson! First, last, and always! I'm the kinda colored man that don't like lazy, shiftless, Negroes!

PETERSON. You ain't got to come in here and call us names!

WATERS. The Nazis call you schvatza! You gonna tell them they hurt your little feelings?

C.J. Don't look like to me we could do too much to them Nazis wit' paint brushes, Sarge.

[*The men laugh. The moment is gone, and though Waters is angry, his tone becomes overly solicitous, smiling.*]

WATERS. You tryin' to mock me, C.J.?

C.J. No, sah, Sarge.

WATERS. Good, because whatever an ignorant, low-class geechy like you has to say isn't worth paying attention to, is it? [*Pause*] Is it?

C.J. I reckon not, Sarge.

PETERSON. You' a creep, Waters!

WATERS. Boy, you are something—ain't been in the company a month, Wilkie, and already everybody's champion!

C.J. [*interjecting*]. Sarge was just jokin', Pete—he don't mean no harm!

PETERSON. He does! We take enough from the white boys!

WATERS. Yes, you do—and if it wasn't for you Southern niggahs, yessahin', bowin' and scrapin', scratchin' your heads, white folks wouldn't think we were all fools!

PETERSON. Where you from, England!

[*Men snicker.*]

HENSON [*at once*]. Peterson!

WATERS [*immediately*]. You got somethin' to say, Henson?

HENSON. Nothin', Sarge.

[*Henson shakes his head as Waters turns back to Peterson.*]

WATERS. Peterson, you got a real comic streak in you. Wilkie, looks like we got us a wise-ass Alabama boy here! [*He moves toward Peterson*] Yes, sir—[*He snatches Peterson in the collar*] Don't get smart, niggah!

[*Peterson yanks away.*]

PETERSON. Get your fuckin' hands off me!

[*Waters smiles, leans forward.*]

WATERS. You wanna hit ole Sergeant Waters, boy? [*Whispers*] Come on! Please! Come on, niggah!

[*Captain Taylor enters the barracks quite suddenly, unaware of what is going on.*]

HENSON. Tenn-hut!

[*All the men snap to.*]

TAYLOR. At ease! [*He moves toward Waters, feeling the tension*] What's going on here, Sergeant?

WATERS. Nothin', sir—I was going over the *Manual of Arms*. Is there something in particular you wanted, sir? Something I can do?

TAYLOR [*relaxed somewhat*]. Nothing— [*To the men*] Men, I congratulate you on the game you won today. We've only got seven more to play, and if we win them, we'll be the first team in Fort Neal history to play the Yanks in exhibition. Everyone in the regiment is counting on you. In times like these, morale is important—and winning can help a lot of things. [*Pause*] Sergeant, as far as I'm concerned, they've got the rest of the day off.

[*The men are pleased.*]

WATERS. Begging your pardon, sir, but these men need all the work they can get. They don't need time off—our fellas aren't getting time off in North Africa—besides, we've got orders to report to the Officers Club for a paint detail at 1300 hours.

TAYLOR. Who issued that order?

WATERS. Major Harris, sir.

TAYLOR. I'll speak to the Major.

WATERS. Sir, I don't think it's such a good idea to get a colored N.C.O. mixed up in the middle of you officers, sir.

TAYLOR. I said, I'd speak to him, Sergeant.

WATERS. Yes, sir!

TAYLOR. I respect the men's duty to service, but they need time off.

WATERS. Yes, sir.

[*Pause.*]

TAYLOR. You men played a great game of baseball out there today—that catch you made in center field, Memphis—how the hell'd you get up so high?

C.J. [*shrugs, smiles*]. They say I got "Bird" in mah blood, sir.

[*Taylor is startled by the statement, his smile is an uncomfortable one. Waters is standing on "eggs."*]

TAYLOR. American eagle, I hope. [*Laughs a little*]

C.J. No, sah, crow— [*Waters starts to move, but C.J. stops him by continuing. Several of the men are beginning to get uncomfortable*] Man tol' my daddy the day I was born, the shadow of a crow's wings—

TAYLOR [*cutting him off*]. Fine—men, I'll say it again —you played superbly. [*Turns to Waters*] Sergeant. [*He starts out abruptly*]

WATERS. Tenn-hut!

[*Waters salutes as the men snap to.*]

TAYLOR [*exiting*]. As you were.

[*Taylor salutes as he goes. There is an instant of quiet. The men relax a little, but their focus is C.J.*]

WATERS [*laughing*]. Ain't these geechies somethin'? How long a story was you gonna tell the man, C.J.? My God! [*The men join him, but as he turns toward Peterson, he stiffens*] Peterson! Oh, I didn't forget you, boy. [*The room quiets*] It's time to teach you a lesson!

PETERSON. Why don't you drop dead, Sarge?

WATERS. Nooo! I'ma drop you, boy! Out behind the barracks—Wilkie, you go out and make sure it's all set up.

WILKIE. You want all the N.C.O.'s?

[*Waters nods. Wilkie goes out smiling.*]

WATERS. I'm going outside and wait for you, geechy! And when you come out, I'm gonna whip your black Southern ass—let the whole company watch it, too! [*Points*] You need to learn respect, boy—how to talk to your betters. [*Starts toward the door*] Fight hard, hea'? I'ma try to bust your fuckin' head

open—the rest of you get those goddamn shirts off like I said!

[*He exits. The barracks is quiet for a moment.*]

COBB. You gonna fight him?

HENSON [*overlapping*]. I tried to warn you!

PETERSON. You ain't do nothin'!

SMALLS. He'll fight you dirty, Pete—don't do it!

[*Peterson goes to his bunk and throws his cap off angrily.*]

COBB. You don't want to do it?

PETERSON. You wanna fight in my place, Cobb? [*He sits*] Shit!

[*Slight pause. Henson pulls off his shirt.*]

C.J. I got some Farmers Dust—jes' a pinch'll make you strong as a bull—they say it comes from the city of Zar. [*Removes a pouch from his neck*] I seen a man use this stuff and pull a mule outta sinkhole by hisself!

PETERSON. Get the hell outta here with that backwater crap—can't you speak up for yourself—let that bastard treat you like a dog!

C.J.. 'Long as his han's ain't on me—he ain't done me no harm, Pete. Callin' names ain't nothing', I know what I is. [*Softens*] Sarge ain't so bad—been good to me.

PETERSON. The man despises you!

C.J.. Sarge? You wrong, Pete—plus I feel kinda sorry for him myself. Any man ain't sure where he belongs must be in a whole lotta pain.

PETERSON. Don't y'all care?

HENSON. Don't nobody like it, Pete—but when you here a little longer—I mean, what can you do? This hea's the army and Sarge got all the stripes.

[*Peterson rises, disgusted, and starts out. Smalls moves at once.*]

SMALLS. Peterson, look, if you want me to, I'll get the Captain. You don't have to go out there and get your head beat in!

PETERSON. Somebody's got to fight him.

[*He exits. There is quiet as Smalls walks back to his bunk.*]

C.J. [*singing*]. It's a low / it's a low, low / lowdown dirty shame! It's a low / it's a low, low / lowdown dirty shame! Been playin' in this hea' army / an ain't even learned the game! Lawd, lawd, lawd, lawd—

[*C.J. begins to hum as the lights slowly fade out over the barracks. As they do, the lights come up simultaneously in the Captain's office. It is empty. Peterson (in proper uniform) and Davenport enter from off-stage. They stop outside the Captain's office.*]

PETERSON. He beat me pretty bad that day, sir. The man was crazy!

DAVENPORT. Was the incident ever reported?

PETERSON. I never reported it, sir—I know I should have, but he left me alone after that. [*Shrugs*] I just played ball.

DAVENPORT. Did you see Waters the night he died?

PETERSON. No, sir—me and Smalls had guard duty.

DAVENPORT. Thank you, Private. That'll be all for now. [*Peterson comes to attention.*] By the way, did the team ever get to play the Yankees?

PETERSON. No, sir. We lost the last game to a Sanitation Company.

[*Ile salutes. Davenport returns salute. Peterson does a crisp about-face and exits. Slowly Davenport starts into the Captain's office, surprised that no one is about.*]

DAVENPORT. Captain? [*There is no response. For a moment or two, Davenport looks around. He is somewhat annoyed*] Captain?

[*He starts out. Taylor enters. He crosses the room to his desk, where he sits.*]

TAYLOR. I asked you back here because I wanted you to see the request I've sent to Colonel Nivens to have your investigation terminated. [*He picks up several sheets of paper on his desk and hands them to Davenport, who ignores them*]

DAVENPORT. What?

TAYLOR. I wanted you to see that my reasons have nothing to do with you personally—my request will not hurt your army record in any way! [*Pause*] There are other things to consider in this case!

DAVENPORT. Only the color of my skin, Captain.

TAYLOR [*sharply*]. I want the people responsible for killing one of my men found and jailed, Davenport!

DAVENPORT. So do I!

TAYLOR. Then give this up! [*Rises*] Whites down here won't see their duty—or justice. They'll see *you!* And once they do, the law—due process—it all goes! And what is the point of continuing an investigation that can't possibly get at the truth?

DAVENPORT. Captain, my orders are very specific, so unless you want charges brought against you for interfering in a criminal investigation, stay the hell out of my way and leave me and my investigation alone!

TAYLOR [*almost sneering*]. Don't take yourself too seriously, Davenport. You couldn't find an officer within five hundred miles who would convey charges to a court-martial board against me for something like that, and you know it!

DAVENPORT. Maybe not, but I'd—I'd see to it that your name, rank, and duty station got into the Negro press! Yeah, let a few colored newspapers call you a Negro-hater! Make you an embarrassment to the United States Army, Captain—like Major Albright at Fort Jefferson, and you'd never command troops again—or wear more than those captain's bars on that uniform, Mr. West Point!

TAYLOR. I'll never be more than a captain, Davenport, because I won't let them get away with dismissing things like Waters's death. I've been the commanding officer of three outfits! I raised hell in all of them, so threatening me won't change my request. Let the Negro press print that I don't like being made a fool of with phony investigations!

DAVENPORT [*studies Taylor for a moment*]. There are two white officers involved in this, Captain—aren't there?

TAYLOR. I want them in jail—out of the army! And there is no way *you* can get them charged, or court-martialed, or put away! The white officers on this post won't let you—they won't let me!

DAVENPORT. Why wasn't there any mention of them in your preliminary report? I checked my own summary on the way over here, Captain—nothing! You think I'ma let you get away with this? [*There is a long silence. Taylor walks back to his desk as Davenport watches him. Taylor sits*] Why?

TAYLOR. I couldn't prove the men in question had anything to do with it.

DAVENPORT. Why didn't you report it?

TAYLOR. I was ordered not to. [*Pause*] Nivens and Hines. The doctors took two .45 caliber bullets out of Waters—army issue. But remember what it was like that morning? If these men had thought a white officer killed Waters, there would have been a slaughter! [*Pause*] Cobb reported the incident innocently the night before—then suddenly it was all over the Fort.

DAVENPORT. Who were they, Captain? I want their names!

TAYLOR. Byrd and Wilcox. Byrd's in Ordnance—

Wilcox's with the 12th Hospital Group. I was Captain of the Guard the night Waters was killed. About 2100 hours, Cobb came into my office and told me he'd just seen Waters and two white officers fighting outside the colored N.C.O. club. I called *your* office, and when I couldn't get two M.P.'s, I started over myself to break it up. When I got there—no Waters, no officers. I checked the officers' billet and found Byrd and Wilcox in bed. Several officers verified they'd come in around 2130. I then told Cobb to go back to the barracks and forget it.

DAVENPORT. What made you do that?

TAYLOR. At the time there was no reason to believe anything was wrong! Waters wasn't found until the following morning. I told the Colonel what had happened the previous night, and about the doctor's report, and I was told, since the situation at the Fort was potentially dangerous, to keep my mouth shut until it blew over. He agreed to let me question Byrd and Wilcox, but I've asked him for a follow-up investigation every day since it happened. [*Slight pause*] When I saw you, I exploded—it was like he was laughing at me.

DAVENPORT. Then you never believed the Klan was involved?

TAYLOR. No. Now, can you see why this thing needs—someone else?

DAVENPORT. What did they tell you, Captain? Byrd and Wilcox?

TAYLOR. They're not going to let you charge those two men!

DAVENPORT [*snaps*]. Tell me what they told you!

[*Taylor is quiet for a moment. At this time, on center stage in limbo, Sergeant Waters is staggering. He is dressed as we first saw him. Behind him a blinking light reads: 221st N.C.O. Club. As he staggers toward the stairs leading to center stage, two white officers, Lieutenant Byrd, a spit-and-polish soldier in his twenties, and Captain Wilcox, a medical officer, walk on-stage. Both are in full combat gear—rifles, pistol belts, packs—and both are tired. Taylor looks out as if he can see them.*]

TAYLOR. They were coming off bivouac.

[*The two men see Waters. In the background is the faint hum of C.J.'s music.*]

TAYLOR. They saw him outside the club.

[*He rises, as Waters sees Byrd and Wilcox, and smiles.*]

WATERS. Well, if it ain't the white boys!

[*Waters straightens and begins to march in a mock circle and then down in their direction. He is mumbling, barely audibly: "One, two, three, four! Hup, hup, three, four! Hup, hup, three, four!" Byrd's speech overlaps Waters's.*]

BYRD. And it wasn't like we were looking for trouble, Captain—were we, Wilcox?

[*Wilcox shakes his head no, but he is astonished by Waters's behavior and stares at him, disbelieving.*]

WATERS. White boys! All starched and stiff! Wanted everybody to learn all that symphony shit! That's what you were saying in France—and you know, I listened to you? Am I all right now? Am I?

BYRD. Boy, you'd better straighten up and salute when you see an officer, or you'll find yourself without those stripes! [*To Wilcox as Waters nears them, smiling the "coon" smile and doing a juba*] Will you look at this niggah? [*Loud*] Come to attention, Sergeant! That's an order!

WATERS. No, sah! I ain't straightenin' up for y'all no more! I ain't doin' nothin' white folks say do, no more! [*Sudden change of mood, smiles, sings*] No more, no more / no more, no more, noooo! No more, no more / no more, no more, noooooo!

[*Byrd faces Taylor as Waters continues to sing.*]

BYRD [*overlapping*]. Sir, I thought the man was crazy.

TAYLOR. And what did you think, Wilcox?

[*Byrd moves toward Waters and Waters, still singing low, drunk and staggering, moves back and begins to circle Byrd, stalk him, shaking his head no as he sings. Wilcox watches apprehensively.*]

WILCOX [*at once*]. He did appear to be intoxicated, sir—out of his mind almost! [*He turns to Byrd*] Byrd, listen—

[*Byrd ignores him.*]

DAVENPORT [*suddenly*]. Did they see anyone else in the area?

TAYLOR. No. [*To Byrd*] I asked them what they did next.

BYRD. I told that niggah to shut up!

WATERS [*sharply*]. No! [*Change of mood*] Followin' behind y'all? Look what it's done to me!—I hate myself!

BYRD. Don't blame us, boy! God made you black, not me!

WATERS [*smiles*]. My daddy use ta say—
WILCOX. Sergeant, get hold of yourself!
WATERS [*points*]. Listen!

[*Byrd steps toward him and shoves him in the face.*]

BYRD. I gave you an order, niggah!

[*Wilcox grabs Byrd, and stops him from advancing, as Waters begins to cry.*]

WATERS. My daddy said, "Don't talk like dis'—talk like that!" "Don't live hea'—live there!" [*To them*] I've killed for you! [*To himself; incredulous*] And nothin' changed!

[*Byrd pulls free of Wilcox and charges Waters.*]

BYRD. He needs to be taught a lesson!

[*He shoves Waters onto the ground, where he begins to beat and kick the man, until he is forcibly restrained by Wilcox. Waters moans.*]

WILCOX. Let him be! You'll kill the man! He's sick—leave him alone!

[*Byrd pulls away; he is flush. Waters tries to get up.*]

WATERS. Nothin' changed—see? And I've tried everything! Everything!
BYRD. I'm gonna bust his black ass to buck private!—I should blow his coward's head off! [*Shouts*] There are good men killing for you, niggah! Gettin' their guts all blown to hell for you!

[*Wilcox pulls him away. He pulls Byrd off-stage as the light around Waters and that section of the stage begins to fade out. As it does, a trace of C.J.'s music is left on the air.*]

Waters is on his knees, groveling, as the lights go out around him.]

DAVENPORT. Did they shove Waters again?
TAYLOR. No. But Byrd's got a history of scrapes with Negroes. They told me they left Waters at 2110—and everyone in the officers' billet verifies they were both in by 2130. And neither man left—Byrd had duty the next morning, and Wilcox was scheduled at the hospital at 0500 hours—both men reported for duty.
DAVENPORT. I don't believe it.
TAYLOR. I couldn't shake their stories—
DAVENPORT. That's nothing more than officers lying to protect two of their own and you know it! I'm going to arrest and charge both of them, Captain—and you may consider yourself confined to your quarters pending my charges against *you*!
TAYLOR. What charges?
DAVENPORT. It was *your* duty to go over Nivens's head if you had to!
TAYLOR. Will you arrest Colonel Nivens too, Davenport? Because he's part of their alibi—he was there when they came in— played poker—from 2100 to 0300 hours the following morning, the Colonel—your Major Hines, "Shack" Callahan—Major Callahan, and Jed Harris—and Jed wouldn't lie for either of them!
DAVENPORT. They're all lying!
TAYLOR. Prove it, hotshot—I told you all I know, now you go out and prove it!
DAVENPORT. I will, Captain! You can bet your sweet ass on that! I will!

[*Davenport starts out as the lights begin to fade, and Taylor looks after him and shakes his head. In the background, the sound of "Don't Sit under the Apple Tree" comes up again and continues to play as the lights fade to black.*]

Act II

SCENE: As before

[*Light rises slowly over limbo. We hear a snippet of "Don't Sit under the Apple Tree" as Davenport, seated on the edge of a bunk, finishes dressing. He is putting on a shirt, tie, bars, etc., and addresses the audience as he does so.*]

DAVENPORT. During May of '44, the Allies were making final preparations for the invasion of Europe. Invasion! Even the sound of it made Negroes think we'd be in it—be swept into Europe in the waves of men and equipment—I know I felt it. [*Thoughtfully*] We hadn't seen a lot of action except in North Africa—or Sicily. But the rumor in orderly rooms that spring was, pretty soon most of us would be in combat—somebody said Ike wanted to find out if the colored boys could fight—shiiit, we'd been fighting all along—right here, in these small Southern towns— [*Intense*] I don't have the authority to arrest a white *private* without a white officer present! [*Slight pause*] Then I get a case like this? There was no way I wouldn't see this through to its end. [*Smiles*] And after my first twenty-four hours, I wasn't doing too badly. I had two prime suspects— a motive, and opportunity! [*Pause*] I went to Colonel Nivens and convinced him that word of Byrd's and Wilcox's involvement couldn't be kept secret any longer. However, before anyone in the press could accuse him of complicity—I would silence all suspicions by pursuing the investigation openly—on his orders— [*Mimics himself*] —"Yes, sir, Colonel, you can even send along a white officer—not Captain Taylor, though—I think he's a little too close to the case, sir." Colonel Nivens gave me permission to question Byrd and Wilcox, and having succeeded sooo easily, I decided to spend some time finding out more about Waters and Memphis. Somehow the real drama seemed to be there, and my curiosity wouldn't allow me to ignore it.

[*Davenport is dressed and ready to go as a spotlight in the barracks area opens on Private Henson. He is seated on a footlocker. He rises as Davenport descends to the stage. He will not enter the barracks, but will almost handle this like a courtroom interrogation. He returns Henson's salute.*]

DAVENPORT. Sit down, Private. Your name is Louis Henson, is that right?
HENSON. Yes, sir.

[*Henson sits, as Davenport paces.*]

DAVENPORT. Tell me what you know about Sergeant Waters and C.J. Memphis. [*Henson looks at him strangely*] Is there something wrong?
HENSON. No, sir—I was just surprised you knew about it.
DAVENPORT. Why?
HENSON. You're an officer.
DAVENPORT [*quickly*]. And?
HENSON [*hesitantly*]. Well—officers are up here, sir— and us enlisted men—down here. [*Slight pause*] C.J. and Waters—that was just between enlisted men, sir. But I guess ain't nothin' a secret around colored folks—not that it was a secret. [*Shrugs*] There ain't that much to tell—sir. Sarge ain't like C.J. When I got to the company in May of las' year, the first person I saw Sarge chew out was C.J.! [*He is quiet*]
DAVENPORT. Go on.

[*Henson's expression is pained.*]

HENSON. Is that an order, sir?
DAVENPORT. Does it have to be?
HENSON. I don't like tattle-talin', sir—an' I don't mean no offense, but I ain't crazy 'bout talkin' to officers—colored or white.
DAVENPORT. It's an order, Henson!

[*Henson nods.*]

HENSON. C.J. wasn' movin' fast enough for *him*. Said C.J. didn' have enough *fire-under-his-behind* out on the field.
DAVENPORT. You were on the team?
HENSON. Pitcher. [*Pause. Davenport urges with a look*] He jus' *stayed* on C.J. all the time—every little thing, it seemed like to me—then the shootin' went down, and C.J. caught all the hell.
DAVENPORT. What shooting?
HENSON. The shootin' at Williams's Golden Palace, sir—here, las' year!—way before you got here. Toward the end of baseball season. [*Davenport nods his recognition.*] The night it happened, a whole lotta gunshots went off near the barracks. I had gotten drunk over at the enlisted men's club, so when I got to the barracks I just sat down in a stupor!

[*Suddenly shots are heard in the distance and grow ever closer as the eerie blue-gray light rises in the barracks over the sleeping figures of men in their bunks. Henson is seated, staring at the ground. He looks up once as the gunshots go off, and as he does, someone—we cannot be sure who— sneaks into the barracks as the men begin to shift and awaken. This person puts something under C.J.'s bed and rushes out. Henson watches—surprised at first, rising, then disbelieving. He shakes his head, then sits back down as several men wake up. Davenport recedes to one side of the barracks, watching.*]

COBB. What the hell's goin' on? Don't they know a man needs his sleep? [*He is quickly back to sleep*]
SMALLS [*simultaneously*]. Huh? Who is it? [*Looks around, then falls back to sleep*]
DAVENPORT. Are you sure you saw someone?
HENSON. Well—I saw something, sir.
DAVENPORT. What did you do?

[*The shooting suddenly stops and the men settle down.*]

HENSON. I sat, sir—I was juiced— [*Shrugs*] The gunshots weren't any of my business—plus I wasn't sure what I had seen in the first place, then out of nowhere Sergeant Waters, he came in.

[*Waters enters the barracks suddenly, followed by Wilkie. Henson stands immediately, staggering a bit.*]

WATERS. All right, all right! Everybody up! Wake them, Wilkie!

[*Wilkie moves around the bunks, shaking the men.*]

WILKIE. Let's go! Up! Let's go, you guys!

[*Cobb shoves Wilkie's hand aside angrily as the others awaken slowly.*]

WATERS. Un-ass them bunks! Tenn-hut! [*Most of the men snap to. Smalls is the last one, and Waters moves menacingly toward him*] There's been a shooting! One of ours bucked the line at Williams's pay phone and three soldiers are dead! Two colored and one white M.P. [*Pauses*] Now, the man who bucked the line, he killed the M.P., and the white boys started shootin' everybody—that's how our two got shot. And this lowdown niggah we lookin' for got chased down here—and was almost caught, 'til somebody in these barracks started shootin' at the men chasin' him. So, we got us a vicious, murderin' piece of black trash in here somewhere—and a few people who helped him. If any of you are in this, I want you to step forward. [*No one moves*] All you baseball niggahs are innocent, huh? Wilkie, make the search. [*Peterson turns around as Wilkie begins*] Eyes front!
PETERSON. I don't want that creep in my stuff!
WATERS. You don't talk at attention!

[*Wilkie will search three bunks, top and bottom, along with footlockers. Under C.J.'s bed he will find what he is looking for.*]

WATERS. I almost hope it is some of you geechies—get rid of you Southern niggahs! [*To Wilkie*] Anything yet?
WILKIE. Nawwww
WATERS. Memphis, are you in this?
C.J. No, sah, Sarge.
WATERS. How many of you were out tonight?
SMALLS. I was over at Williams's around seven—got me some Lucky Strikes—I didn't try to call home, though.
COBB. I was there, this mornin'!
WATERS. Didn't I say *tonight*—uncle?

WILKIE. Got somethin'!

[*Wilkie is holding up a .45 caliber automatic pistol, army issue. Everyone's attention focuses on it. The men are surprised, puzzled.*]

WATERS. Where'd you find it?

[*Wilkie points to C.J., who recoils at the idea.*]

C.J. Naaaawww, man!
WATERS. C.J.? This yours?
C.J. You know it ain't mine, Sarge!
WATERS. It's still warm—how come it's under your bunk?
C.J. Anybody coulda' put it thea', Sarge!
WATERS. Who? Or maybe this .45 crawled in through an open window—looked around the whole room—passed Cobb's bunk, and decided to snuggle up under yours? Must be voodoo, right, boy? Or some of that Farmers Dust round that neck of yours, huh?
C.J. That pistol ain't mine!
WATERS. Liar!
C.J. No, Sarge—I hate guns! Make me feel bad jes' to see a gun!
WATERS. You're under arrest—Wilkie, escort this man to the stockade!

[*Peterson steps forward.*]

PETERSON. C.J. couldn't hurt a fly, Waters, you know that!
WATERS. I found a gun, soldier—now get out of the way!
PETERSON. Goddammit, Waters, you know it ain't him!
WATERS. How do I know?
HENSON. Right before you came in, I thought I saw somebody sneak in.
WATERS. You were drunk when you left the club—I saw you myself!
WILKIE. Besides, how you know it wasn't C.J.?
COBB. I was here all night. C.J. didn't go out.

[*Waters looks at them, intense.*]

WATERS. We got the right man. [*Points at C.J., impassioned*] You think he's innocent, don't you? C.J. Memphis, playin' cottonpicker singin' the blues, bowin' and scrapin'—smilin' in everybody's face—this man undermined us! You and me! The description of the man who did the shooting fits C.J.! [*To

Henson] You saw C.J. sneak in here! [*Points*] Don't be fooled—that yassah boss is hidin' something—niggahs ain't like that today! This is 1943—he shot that white boy!

[*C.J. is stunned, then suddenly the enormity of his predicament hits him and he breaks free of Wilkie and hits Waters in the chest. The blow knocks Waters down, and C.J. is immediately grabbed by the other men in the barracks. Cobb goes to Waters and helps him up slowly. The blow hurt Waters, but he forces a smile at C.J., who has suddenly gone immobile, surprised by what he has done.*]

WATERS. What did you go and do now, boy? Hit a noncommissioned officer.
COBB. Sarge, he didn't mean it!
WATERS. Shut up! [*Straightens*] Take him out, Wilkie.

[*Wilkie grabs C.J. by the arm and leads him out. C.J. goes calmly, almost passively. Waters looks at all the men quietly for a moment, then walks out without saying a word. There is a momentary silence in the barracks.*]

SMALLS. Niggah like that can't have a mother.
HENSON. I know I saw something!
PETERSON. C.J. was sleepin' when I came in! It's Waters—can't y'all see that? I've seen him before—we had 'em in Alabama! White man gives them a little ass job as a servant—close to the big house, and when the boss ain't lookin', old copycat niggahs act like they the new owner! They take to soundin' like the boss—shoutin', orderin' people aroun'—and when it comes to you and me—they sell us to continue favor. They think the high-jailers like that. Arrestin' C.J.—that'll get Waters another stripe! Next it'll be you—or you. He can't look good unless he's standin' on you! Cobb tol' him C.J. was in all evening—Waters didn't even listen! Turning somebody in [*mimics.*] "Look what I done, Captain Boss!" They let him in the army 'cause they know he'll do anything they tell him to—I've seen his kind of fool before. Someone's going to kill him.
SMALLS. I heard they killed a sergeant at Fort Robinson—recruit did it—
COBB. It'll just be our luck, Sarge'll come through the whole war without a scratch.
PETERSON. Maybe—but I'm goin' over to the stockade—tell the M.P.'s what I know—C.J. was here all evening. [*He starts dressing*]
SMALLS. I'll go with you!
COBB. Me too, I guess.

[*They all begin to dress as the light fades slowly in the barracks area. Henson rises and starts toward Davenport. In the background, C.J.'s music comes up a bit.*]

DAVENPORT. Could the person you thought you saw have stayed in the barracks—did you actually see someone go out?
HENSON. Yes, sir!
DAVENPORT. Was Wilkie the only man out of his bunk that night?
HENSON. Guess so—he came in with Sarge.
DAVENPORT. And Peterson—he did most of the talking?
HENSON. As I recall. It's been a while ago—an' I was juiced!

[*Davenport rises.*]

DAVENPORT. Ellis!

[*Ellis appears at the door.*]

ELLIS. Sir!
DAVENPORT. I want Private Wilkie and Pfc Peterson to report to me at once.
ELLIS. They're probably on work detail, sir.
DAVENPORT. Find them.
ELLIS. Yes, sir!

[*Ellis exits quickly and Davenport lapses into a quiet thoughtfulness.*]

HENSON. Is there anything else?—Sir?
DAVENPORT [*vexed*]. No! That'll be all—send in the next man.

[*Henson comes to attention and salutes. Davenport returns salute as Henson exits through the barracks. C.J.'s music plays in background. There is a silence. Davenport rises, mumbling something to himself. Cobb appears suddenly at the doorway. He watches Davenport for a moment.*]

COBB. Sir? [*Davenport faces him*] Corporal Cobb reporting as ordered, sir. [*He salutes*]
DAVENPORT. Have a seat, Corporal [*Cobb crosses the room and sits*] And let's get something straight from the beginning—I don't care whether you like officers or not—is that clear?

[*Cobb looks at him strangely.*]

COBB. Sir?

[*Pause. Davenport calms down somewhat.*]

DAVENPORT. I'm sorry—Did you know Sergeant Waters well?

COBB. As well as the next man, sir—I was already with the team when he took over. Me and C.J., we made the team the same time.

DAVENPORT. Were you close to C.J.?

COBB. Me and him were "homeys," sir! Both came from Mississippi. C.J. from Carmella—me, I'm from up 'roun' Jutlerville, what they call snake country. Plus, we both played for the Negro League before the war.

DAVENPORT. How did you feel about his arrest?

COBB. Terrible—C.J. didn't kill nobody, sir.

DAVENPORT. He struck Sergeant Waters—

COBB. Waters made him, sir! He called that boy things he had never heard of before—C.J., he was so confused he didn't know what else to do— [Pause] An' when they put him in the stockade, he jus' seemed to go to pieces. [Lowly in the background, C.J.'s music comes up] See, we both lived on farms—and even though C.J.'s daddy played music, C.J., he liked the wide-open spaces. [Shakes his head] That cell? It started closin' in on him right away. [Blue-gray light rises in limbo, where C.J. is sitting on the edge of a bunk. A shadow of bars cuts across the space. His guitar is on the bunk beside him] I went to see him, the second day he was in there. He looked pale and ashy, sir— like something dead.

[C.J. faces Cobb.]

C.J. It's hard to breathe in these little spaces, Cobb— man wasn' made for this hea'—nothin' was! I don't think I'll eva' see a' animal in a cage agin' and not feel sorry for it. [To himself] I'd rather be on the chain gang.

[Cobb looks up at him.]

COBB. Come on, homey! [He rises, moves toward C.J.]

C.J. I don't think I'm comin' outta here, Cobb—feels like I'm goin' crazy. Can't walk in hea'—can't see the sun! I tried singin', Cobb, but nothin' won't come out. I sure don't wanna die in this jail!

COBB [moving closer]. Ain't nobody gonna die, C.J.!

C.J. Yesterday I broke a guitar string—lost my Dust! I got no protection—nothin' to keep the dog from tearin' at my bones!

COBB. Stop talkin' crazy!

[C.J. is quiet for a moment. He starts forward. Slowly, in center stage, Waters emerges. He faces the audience.]

C.J. You know, he come up hea' las' night? Sergeant Waters?

[Waters smiles, pulls out his pipe, lights it.]

WATERS [calmly]. You should learn never to hit sergeants, boy—man can get in a lot of trouble doin' that kinda thing durin' wartime—they talkin' 'bout givin' you five years—they call what you did mutiny in the navy. Mutiny, boy.

C.J. That gun ain't mine!

WATERS. Oh, we know that, C.J.! [C.J. is surprised] That gun belonged to the niggah did the shootin' over at Williams's place—me and Wilkie caught him hidin' in the Motor Pool, and he confessed his head off. You're in here for striking a superior officer, boy. And I got a whole barracks full of your friends to prove it. [Smiles broadly, as C.J. shakes his head]

DAVENPORT [to Cobb, at once]. Memphis wasn't charged with the shooting?

COBB. No, sir—

WATERS. Don't feel too bad, boy. It's not your fault entirely—it has to be this way. The First War, it didn't change much for us, boy—but this one—it's gonna change a lot of things. Them Nazis ain't all crazy—a whole lot of people just can't fit into where things seem to be goin'—like you, C.J. The black race can't afford you no more. There use ta be a time when we'd see somebody like you, singin', clownin'—yas—sah—bossin'—and we wouldn't do anything. [Smiles] Folks liked that—you were good—homey kinda' niggah—they needed somebody to mistreat—call a name, they paraded you, reminded them of the old days—corn-bread bakin', greens and ham cookin'—Daddy out pickin' cotton, Grandmammy sit on the front porch smokin' a pipe. [Slight pause] Not no more. The day of the geechy is gone, boy—the only thing that can move the race is power. It's all the white respects—and people like you just make us seem like fools. And we can't let nobody go on believin' we all like you! You bring us down—make people think the whole race is unfit! [Quietly pleased] I waited a long time for you, boy, but I gotcha! And I try to git rid of you wherever I go. I put two geechies in jail at Fort Campbell, Kentucky—three at Fort Huachuca. Now I got you—one less fool for the race to be ashamed of! [Points] And I'ma git that ole boy Cobb next! [Light begins to fade around Waters]

DAVENPORT [at once]. You?

COBB. Yes, sir. [Slight pause]

DAVENPORT. Go on.

C.J. You imagin' anybody sayin' that? I know I'm not gittin' outta' hea', Cobb! [*Quiets*] You remember I tol' you 'bout a place I use ta go outside Carmella? When I was a little ole tiny thing? Place out behind O'Connell's Farm? Place would be stinkin' of plums, Cobb. Shaded—that ripe smell be weavin' through the cotton fields and clear on in ta town on a warm day. First time I had Evelyn? I had her unda' them plum trees. I wrote a song for her— [*Talks, sings*] My ginger-colored Moma—she had thighs the size of hams! [*Chuckles*] And when you spread them, Momaaaa! / [*Talks*] You let me have my jelly roll and jam! [*Pause, mood swing*] O'Connell, he had a dog—meanes' dog I *eva'* did see! An' the only way you could enjoy them plum trees was to outsmart that dog. Waters is like that ole dog, Cobb—you gotta run circles roun' ole Windy—that was his name. They say he tore a man's arm off once, and got to likin' it. So, you had to cheat that dog outta' bitin' you every time. Every time. [*Slowly the light begins to fade around C.J.*]

COBB. He didn't make sense, sir. I tried talkin' about the team—the war—ain't nothin' work—seem like he jes' got worse.

DAVENPORT. What happened to him?

[*Cobb looks at him incredulously.*]

COBB. The next day—afta' the day I saw him? C.J., he hung hisself, sir! Suicide—jes' couldn't stand it. M.P.'s found him hung from the bars.

[*Davenport is silent for a moment.*]

DAVENPORT. What happened after that?

COBB. We lost our last game—we jes' threw it—we did it for C.J.—Captain, he was mad 'cause we ain't git ta play the Yankees. Peterson was right on that one—somebody needed to protest that man!

DAVENPORT. What did Waters do?

COBB. Well, afta' we lost, the commanding officer, he broke up the team, and we all got reassigned to this Smoke Company. Waters, he started actin' funny, sir—stayed drunk—talked to hisself all the time.

DAVENPORT. Did you think you were next?

COBB. I ain't sure I eva' believed Waters said that, sir—C.J. had to be outta' his head or he wouldn'a killed hisself—Sarge, he neva' came near me afta' C.J. died.

DAVENPORT. What time did you get back the night Waters was killed?

COBB. I'd say between 2120 and 9:30.

DAVENPORT. And you didn't go out again?

COBB. No, sir—me and Henson sat and listened to the radio till Abbott and Lou Costello went off, then I played checkers with Wilkie for 'notha' hour, then everybody went to bed. What C.J. said about Waters? It ain't botha' me, sir.

[*Davenport is silent.*]

DAVENPORT. Who were the last ones in that night?

COBB. Smalls and Peterson—they had guard duty.

[*Taylor enters the barracks area and stops just inside the door when he sees Davenport isn't quite finished.*]

DAVENPORT. Thank you, Corporal.

[*Cobb rises at attention and salutes. Davenport returns salute and Cobb starts out. He nods to Taylor, who advances toward Davenport.*]

TAYLOR [*smiling*]. You surprise me, Davenport—I just left Colonel Nivens. He's given you permission to question Byrd and Wilcox? [*Davenport nods*] How'd you manage that? You threatened him with an article in the Chicago *Defender*, I suppose.

DAVENPORT. I convinced the Colonel it was in his best interests to allow it.

TAYLOR. Really? Did he tell you I would assist you?

DAVENPORT. I told him I especially didn't want you.

TAYLOR. That's precisely why he sent me—he didn't want you to think you could get your way entirely—not with him. Then neither Byrd or Wilcox would submit to it without a white officer present. That's how it is. [*There is a rather long silence*] But there's something else, Davenport. The Colonel began talking about the affidavits he and the others signed—and the discrepancies in their statements that night. [*Mimics.*] He wants me with you because he doesn't want Byrd and Wilcox giving you the wrong impression—he never elaborated on what he meant by the wrong impression. I want to be there!

DAVENPORT. So you're not on *that* side anymore—you're on *my* side now, right?

TAYLOR [*bristles*]. I want whoever killed my sergeant, Davenport!

DAVENPORT. Bullshit! Yesterday you were daring me to try! And today we're allies? Besides, you don't give that much of a damn about your men! I've been around you a full day and you haven't uttered a word that would tell me you had any more than a minor acquaintance with Waters! He managed your baseball team—was an N.C.O. in your company, and you haven't offered *any* opinion of the man as a soldier—sergeant—platoon leader! Who the hell was he?

TAYLOR. He was one of my men! On my roster—a man these bars make me responsible for! And no, I don't know a helluva lot about him—or a lot of their names or where they come from, but I'm still their commanding officer and in a little while I may have to trust them with my life! And I want them to know they can trust me with theirs—here and now! [*Pause*] I have Byrd and Wilcox in my office. [*Davenport stares at him for a long moment, then rises and starts out toward center stage*] Why didn't you tell Nivens that you'd placed me under arrest?

[*Davenport stops.*]

DAVENPORT. I didn't find it necessary.

[*They stare at one another. Taylor is noticeably strained.*]

DAVENPORT [*starts away*]. What do you know about C.J. Memphis?

[*Taylor follows.*]

TAYLOR [*shrugs*]. He was a big man as I recall—more a boy than a man, though. Played the guitar sometimes at the Officers Club—there was something embarrassing about him. Committed suicide in the stockade. Pretty good center fielder—

[*Davenport stops.*]

DAVENPORT. Did you investigate his arrest—the charges against him?

TAYLOR. He was charged with assaulting a noncommissioned officer—I questioned him—he didn't say much. He admitted he struck Waters—I started questioning several of the men in the platoon and he killed himself before I could finish—open-and-shut case.

DAVENPORT. I think Waters tricked C.J. into assaulting him.

TAYLOR. Waters wasn't that kind of a man! He admitted he might have provoked the boy—he accused him of that Golden Palace shooting—

[*Behind them, the Captain's office is lit. In two chairs facing Taylor's desk are Lieutenant Byrd and Captain Wilcox, both in dress uniform.*]

TAYLOR. Listen, Waters didn't have a fifth-grade education—he wasn't a schemer! And colored soldiers aren't devious like that.

DAVENPORT. What do you mean we aren't devious?

TAYLOR [*sharply*]. You're not as devious—! [*Davenport stares as Taylor waves disdainfully and starts into the office*] Anyway, what has that to do with this? [*He is distracted by Byrd and Wilcox before Davenport can answer. Taylor speaks as he moves to his desk*] This is *Captain* Davenport—you've both been briefed by Colonel Nivens to give the Captain your full cooperation.

[*Davenport puts on his glasses. Taylor notices and almost smiles.*]

BYRD [*to Davenport*]. They tell me you a lawyer, huh?

DAVENPORT. I am not here to answer your questions, Lieutenant. And I am Captain Davenport, is that clear?

BYRD [*to Taylor*]. Captain, is he crazy?

TAYLOR. You got your orders.

BYRD. Sir, I vigorously protest as an officer—

TAYLOR [*cuts him off*]. You answer him the way he wants you to, Byrd, or I'll have your ass in a sling so tight you won't be able to pee, soldier!

[*Byrd backs off slightly.*]

DAVENPORT. When did you last see Sergeant Waters?

BYRD. The night he was killed, but I didn't kill him—I should have blown his head off, the way he spoke to me and Captain Wilcox here.

DAVENPORT. How did he speak to you, Captain?

WILCOX. Well, he was very drunk—and he said a lot of things he shouldn't have. I told the Lieutenant here not to make the situation worse and he agreed, and we left the Sergeant on his knees, wallowing in self-pity. [*Shrugs*]

DAVENPORT. What exactly did he say?

WILCOX. Some pretty stupid things about us—I mean white people, sir.

[*Byrd reacts to the term "sir."*]

DAVENPORT. What kind of things?

BYRD [*annoyed*]. He said he wasn't going to obey no white man's orders! And that me and Wilcox here were to blame for him being black, and not able to sleep or keep his food down! And I didn't even know the man! Never even spoke to him before that night!

DAVENPORT. Anything else?

WILCOX. Well—he said he'd killed somebody.

DAVENPORT. Did he call a name—or say who?

WILCOX. Not that I recall, sir.

[Davenport looks at Byrd.]

BYRD. No— [Sudden and sharp] Look—the goddamn Negro was disrespectful! He wouldn't salute! Wouldn't come to attention! And where I come from, colored don't talk the way he spoke to us—not to white people they don't!

DAVENPORT. Is that the reason you killed him?

BYRD. I killed nobody! I said "where I come from," didn't I? You'd be dead yourself, where I come from! But I didn't kill the—the Negro!

DAVENPORT. But you hit him, didn't you?

BYRD. I knocked him down!

DAVENPORT [quickens pace]. And when you went to look at him, he was dead, wasn't he?

BYRD. He was alive when we left!

DAVENPORT. You're a liar! You beat Waters up—you went back and you shot him!

BYRD. No! [Rises.] But you better get outta my face before I kill you!

[Davenport stands firm.]

DAVENPORT. Like you killed Waters?

BYRD. No! [He almost raises a hand to Davenport.]

TAYLOR [at once]. Soldier!

BYRD. He's trying to put it on me!

TAYLOR. Answer his questions, Lieutenant.

DAVENPORT. You were both coming off bivouac, right?

WILCOX. Yes.

DAVENPORT. So you both had weapons?

BYRD. So what? We didn't fire them!

DAVENPORT. Were the weapons turned in immediately?

WILCOX. Yes, sir—Colonel Nivens took our .45's to Major Hines. It was all kept quiet because the Colonel didn't want the colored boys to know that anyone white from the Fort was involved in any way—ballistics cleared them.

DAVENPORT. We can check.

BYRD. Go ahead.

TAYLOR. I don't believe it—why wasn't I told?

WILCOX. The weapons had cleared—and the Colonel felt if he involved you further, you'd take the matter to Washington and there'd be a scandal about colored and white soldiers—as it turned out, he thinks you went to Washington anyway. [To Davenport] I'd like to say, Captain, that neither Lieutenant Byrd or myself had anything whatsoever to do with Sergeant Waters's death—I swear that as an officer and a gentleman. He was on the ground when we left him, but very much alive.

TAYLOR. Consider yourselves under arrest, gentlemen!

BYRD. On what charge?

TAYLOR. Murder! You think I believe that crap—

DAVENPORT. Let them go, Captain.

TAYLOR. You've got motive—a witness to their being at the scene—

DAVENPORT. Let them go! This is still my investigation—you two are dismissed!

[Byrd rises quickly. Wilcox follows his lead.]

WILCOX. Are we being charged, sir?

DAVENPORT. Not by me.

WILCOX. Thank you.

[Wilcox comes to attention, joined by a reluctant Byrd. They both salute. Davenport returns salute.]

BYRD. I expected more from a white man, Captain.

TAYLOR. Get out of here, before I have you cashiered out of the army, Byrd!

[Both men exit quietly, and for a moment Taylor and Davenport are quiet.]

TAYLOR. What the hell is the matter with you? You could have charged both of them—Byrd for insubordination—Wilcox, tampering with evidence.

DAVENPORT. Neither charge is murder—you think Wilcox would tell a story like that if he didn't have Hines and Nivens to back it up? [Slightly tired] They've got a report.

TAYLOR. So what do you do now?

DAVENPORT. Finish the investigation.

TAYLOR. They're lying, dammit! So is the Colonel! You were ordered to investigate and charge the people responsible—charge them! I'll back you up!

DAVENPORT. I'm not satisfied yet, Captain.

TAYLOR. I am! Dammit!—I wish they'd sent somebody else! I do—you—you're afraid! You thought you'd accuse the Klan, didn't you?—and that would be the end of it, right? Another story of midnight riders for your Negro press! And now it's officers—white men in the army. It's too much for you—what will happen when Captain Davenport comes up for promotion to major if he accuses white officers, right?

DAVENPORT. I'm not afraid of white men, Captain.

TAYLOR. Then why the hell won't you arrest them?

DAVENPORT. Because I do what the facts tell me, Captain—not you!

TAYLOR. You don't know what a fact is, Davenport!

[Ellis enters suddenly and salutes.]

ELLIS. Begging your pardon, sir.

TAYLOR. What is it, Corporal?

ELLIS. Ah—it's for Captain Davenport— [To Davenport] We found Private Wilkie, sir. We haven't located Pfc Peterson yet. Seems him and Private Smalls went out on detail together, and neither one of 'em showed up—but I got a few men from the company lookin' for 'em around the N.C.O. club and in the PX, sir.

DAVENPORT. Where's Wilkie?

ELLIS. He's waiting for you in the barracks, Captain.

[Davenport nods, and Ellis goes out after saluting. The lights come up around Wilkie, who is seated in a chair in the barracks reading a Negro newspaper. Davenport is thoughtful for a moment.]

TAYLOR. Didn't you question Wilkie and Peterson yesterday? [Davenport starts out] Davenport? [Davenport does not answer] Don't you ignore me!

DAVENPORT. Get off my back! What I do—how I do it—who I interrogate is my business, Captain! This investigation is mine! [Holds out the back of his hand, showing Taylor the color of his skin] Mine!

TAYLOR. Don't treat me with that kind of contempt— I'm not some red-neck cracker!

DAVENPORT. And I'm not your yessirin' colored boy either!

TAYLOR. I asked you a question!

DAVENPORT. I don't have to answer it!

[There is a long silence. The two men glare at one another— Taylor in another time, disturbed.]

TAYLOR. Indeed you don't—Captain.

[Pause.]

DAVENPORT. Now, Captain—what if Byrd and Wilcox are telling the truth?

TAYLOR. Neither one of us believes that.

DAVENPORT. What if they are?

TAYLOR. Then who killed the goddamn man?

DAVENPORT. I don't know yet. [Slight pause] Is there anything else?

[Taylor shakes his head no as Davenport starts toward center stage, headed toward Wilkie.]

TAYLOR. No, hotshot. Nothing.

[Davenport enters the barracks area. Wilkie quickly puts his paper aside and snaps to attention and salutes. Davenport returns salute but remains silent, going right to the desk and removing his pad and pencil. The light around the office fades out.]

DAVENPORT [snapping at Wilkie]. When did you lose your stripes? [He is standing over Wilkie]

WILKIE. Couple months before they broke up the team—right after Sergeant Waters got assigned to us, sir.

DAVENPORT. Nervous, Wilkie?

WILKIE [smiles haltingly]. I couldn't figure out why you called me back, sir? [Laughs nervously]

DAVENPORT. You lost your stripes for being drunk on duty, is that correct?

WILKIE. Yes, sir.

DAVENPORT. You said Waters busted you, didn't you?

WILKIE. He got me busted—he's the one reported me to the Captain.

DAVENPORT. How did you feel? Must have been awful— [Davenport paces] Weren't you and the Sergeant good friends? Didn't you tell me he was all right? A nice guy?

WILKIE. Yes, sir.

DAVENPORT. Would a nice guy have gotten a friend busted?

WILKIE. No, sir.

DAVENPORT. So you lied when you said he was a nice guy, right?

WILKIE. No, sir—I mean—

DAVENPORT. Speak up! Speak up! Was the Sergeant a nice guy or not?

WILKIE. No, sir.

DAVENPORT. Why not? Answer me!

WILKIE. Well, you wouldn't turn somebody in over something like that!

DAVENPORT. Not a good friend, right?

WILKIE. Right, sir—I mean, a friend would give you extra duty—I would have—or even call you a whole buncha' names—you'd expect that, sir—but damn! Three stripes? They took ten years to get in this army, sir! Ten years! I started out with the 24th Infantry—I—

DAVENPORT. Made you mad, didn't it?

WILKIE. Yeah, it made me mad—all the things I did for him!

DAVENPORT [*quickly*]. That's right! You were his assistant, weren't you? Took care of the team— [*Wilkie nods*] Ran all his errands, looked at his family snapshots [*Wilkie nods again*], policed his quarters, put the gun under C.J.'s bed—

[*Wilkie looks up suddenly.*]

WILKIE. No!

DAVENPORT [*quickly*]. It was you Henson saw, wasn't it, Wilkie?

WILKIE. No, sir!

DAVENPORT. Liar! You lied about Waters, and you're lying now! You were the only person out of the barracks that night, and the only one who knew the layout well enough to go straight to C.J.'s bunk! Not even Waters knew the place that well! Henson didn't see who it was, but he saw what the person did—he was positive about that—only you knew the barracks in the dark!

WILKIE [*pleadingly*]. It was the Sarge, Captain—he ordered me to do it—he said I'd get my stripes back—he wanted to scare that boy C.J.! Let him stew in jail! Then C.J. hit him—and he had the boy right where he wanted him— [*Confused*] But it backfired—C.J. killed hisself—Sarge didn't figure on that.

DAVENPORT. Why did he pick Memphis?

WILKIE. He despised him, Captain—he'd hide it, 'cause everybody in the company liked that boy so much. But underneath—it was a crazy hate, sir—he'd go cold when he talked about C.J. You could feel it.

[*In limbo, the blue-gray light rises on C.J. and Waters. C.J. is humming a blues song and Waters is standing smiling, smoking a pipe as he was in Act I. Waters turns away from C.J. His speech takes place over C.J.'s humming.*]

WATERS. He's the kinda boy seems innocent, Wilkie. Got everybody around the post thinking he's a strong, black buck! Hits home runs—white boys envy his strength—his speed, the power in his swing. Then this colored champion lets those same white boys call him Shine—or Sambo at the Officers Club. They laugh at his blues songs, and he just smiles—can't talk, barely read or write his own name—and don't care! He'll tell you they like him—or that colored folks ain't supposed to have but so much sense. [*Intense*] Do you know the damage one ignorant *Negro* can do? [*Remembering*] We were in France during the First War, Wilkie. We had

won decorations, but the white boys had told all the French gals we had tails. And they found this ignorant colored soldier. Paid him to tie a tail to his ass and parade around naked making monkey sounds. [*Shakes his head*] They sat him on a big, round table in the Café Napoleon, put a reed in his hand, a crown on his head, a blanket on his shoulders, and made him eat bananas in front of them Frenchies. And ohhh, the white boys danced that night— passed out leaflets with that boy's picture on them—called him Moonshine, King of the Monkeys. And when we slit his throat, you know that fool asked us what he had done wrong? [*Pause*] My daddy told me, we got to turn our backs on his kind, Wilkie. Close our ranks to the chittlins, the collard greens—the corn-bread style. We are men—soldiers, and I don't intend to have our race cheated out of its place of honor and respect in *this* war because of fools like C.J.! You watch everything he does—*everything*!

[*Light fades slowly around Waters and C.J. and as it does, C.J. stops humming.*]

WILKIE. And I watched him, sir—but Waters—he couldn't wait! He wouldn't talk about nothin' else—it was C.J. this—C.J. all the time!

DAVENPORT [*troubled*]. Why didn't he pick Peterson—they fought—

WILKIE. They fought all the time, sir—but the Sarge, he liked Peterson. [*Nods*] Peterson fought back, and Waters admired that. He promoted Pete! Imagine that—he thought Peterson would make a fine soldier!

DAVENPORT. What was Peterson's reaction—when C.J. died?

WILKIE. Like everybody else, he was sad—he put together that protest that broke up the team, but afta' that he didn' say much. And he usually runs off at the mouth. Kept to himself—or with Smalls.

[*Slight pause.*]

DAVENPORT. The night Waters was killed, what time did you get in?

WILKIE. Around nine forty-five—couple of us came from the club and listened to the radio awhile—I played some checkers, then I went to bed. Sir? I didn't mean to do what I did—it wasn't my fault—he promised me my stripes!

[*Suddenly, out of nowhere, in the near distance, is the sound* of gunfire, a bugle blaring, something like a cannon going off. The noise is continuous through scene. Davenport rises, startled.]

DAVENPORT. I'm placing you under arrest, Private!

[Ellis bursts into the room.]

ELLIS. Did you hear, sir? [Davenport, surprised, shakes his head no] Our orders! They came down from Washington, Captain! We're shippin' out! They finally gonna let us Negroes fight!

[Davenport is immediately elated, and almost forgets Wilkie as he shakes Ellis's hand.]

DAVENPORT. Axis ain't got a chance!
ELLIS. Surrrrc—we'll win this mother in six months now! Afta' what Jesse Owens did to them people? Joe Louis?

[Henson bursts in.]

HENSON. Did y'all hear it? Forty-eight hour standby alert? We goin' into combat! [Loud] Look out, Hitler, the niggahs is comin' to git your ass through the fog!
ELLIS. With real rifles—it's really O.K., you know?
HENSON. They tell me them girls in England—woooow!

[Davenport faces Wilkie as Cobb enters, yelling]

COBB. They gonna let us git in it! We may lay so much smoke the Germans may never get to see what a colored soldier looks like 'til the war's over! [To Henson] I wrote my woman jcs' the otha' day that we'd be goin' soon!
ELLIS. Go on!
HENSON [overlapping]. Man, you ain't nothin'!

[Davenport begins to move Wilkie toward Ellis.]

HENSON. If the army said we was all discharged, you'd claim you wrote that! [He quiets, watching Davenport]
COBB [quickly]. You hea' this fool, sir?
HENSON. Shhhhh!
DAVENPORT [To Ellis]. Corporal, escort Private Wilkie to the stockade.
ELLIS [surprised]. Yes, sir!

[Ellis starts Wilkie out, even though he is bewildered by it. They exit.]

HENSON. Wilkie's under arrest, sir? [Davenport nods] How come? I apologize, sir—I didn't mean that.
DAVENPORT. Do either of you know where Smalls and Peterson can be located?

[Henson shrugs.]

COBB. Your men got Smalls in the stockade, sir!
DAVENPORT. When?
COBB. I saw two colored M.P.'s takin' him through the main gate. Jes' a while ago—I was on my way ova' hea'!

[Davenport goes to the desk and picks up his things and starts out]

COBB. Tenn-hut.

[Davenport stops and salutes.]

DAVENPORT. As you were. By the way—congratulations!

[Davenport exits the barracks through the doorway.]

HENSON. Look out, Hitler!
COBB. The niggahs is coming to get yo' ass.
HENSON AND COBB. Through the fog.

[The lights in the barracks go down at once. Simultaneously, they rise in limbo, where Smalls is pacing back and forth. He is smoking a cigarette. There is a bunk, and the shadow of a screen over his cell. In the background, the sounds of celebration continue. Davenport emerges from the right, and begins to speak immediately as the noises of celebration fade.]

DAVENPORT. Why'd you go AWOL, soldier?

[Smalls faces him, unable to see Davenport at first. When he sees him, he snaps to attention and salutes.]

SMALLS. Private Anthony Smalls, sir!
DAVENPORT. At least—answer my question!
SMALLS. I didn't go AWOL, sir—I—I got drunk in Tynin and fell asleep in the bus depot—it was the only public place I could find to sleep it off.
DAVENPORT. Where'd you get drunk? Where in Tynin?
SMALLS. Jake's—Jake's and Lilly's Golden Slipper—on Melville Street—
DAVENPORT. Weren't you and Peterson supposed to be on detail? [Smalls nods] Where was Peterson? Speak up!

SMALLS. I don't know, sir!

DAVENPORT. You're lying! You just walked off your detail and Peterson did nothing?

SMALLS. No, sir—he warned me, sir— "Listen, Smalls!" he said—

DAVENPORT [cutting him off]. You trying to make a fool of me, Smalls? Huh? [Loud] Are you?

SMALLS. No, sir!

DAVENPORT. The two of you went A-W-O-L together, didn't you? [Smalls is quiet] Answer me!

SMALLS. Yes!

DAVENPORT. You left together because Peterson knew I would find out the two of you killed Waters, didn't you? [Smalls suddenly bursts into quiet tears, shaking his head] What? I can't hear you! [Smalls is sobbing] You killed Waters, didn't you? I want an answer!

SMALLS. I can't sleep—I can't sleep!

DAVENPORT. Did you kill Sergeant Waters?

SMALLS. It was Peterson, sir! [As if he can see it] I watched! It wasn't me!

[The blue-gray light builds in center stage. As it does, Sergeant Waters staggers forward and falls on his knees. He can't get up, he is so drunk. He has been beaten, and looks the way we saw him in the opening of Act I.]

SMALLS. We were changing the guard.

WATERS. Can't be trusted—no matter what we do, there are no guarantees—and your mind won't let you forget it. [Shakes his head repeatedly] No, no, no!

SMALLS [overlapping]. On our way back to the Captain's office—and Sarge, he was on the road. We just walked into him! He was ranting, and acting crazy, sir!

[Peterson emerges from the right. He is dressed in a long coat, pistol belt and pistol, rifle, helmet, his pants bloused over his boots. He sees Waters and smiles. Waters continues to babble.]

PETERSON. Smalls, look who's drunk on his ass, boy!

[He begins to circle Waters]

SMALLS [to Davenport]. I told him to forget Waters!

PETERSON. Noooo! I'm gonna' enjoy this, Smalls—big, bad Sergeant Waters down on his knees? No, sah—I'm gonna' love this! [Leans over Waters] Hey, Sarge—need some help? [Waters look up; almost smiles. He reaches for Peterson, who pushes him back

down] Tha's the kinda help I'll give yah, boy! Let me help you again—all right? [Kicks Waters] Like that, Sarge? Huh? Like that, dog?

SMALLS [shouts]. Peterson!

PETERSON. No! [Almost pleading] Smalls—some people, man—If this was a German, would you kill it? If it was Hitler—or that fuckin' Tojo? Would you kill him? [Kicks Waters again]

WATERS [mumbling throughout]. There's a trick to it, Peterson—it's the only way you can win—C.J. could never make it—he was a clown! [Grabs at Peterson] A clown in blackface! A niggah!

[Peterson steps out of reach. He is suddenly expressionless as he easily removes his pistol from his holster.]

WATERS. You got to be like them! And I was! I was—but the rules are fixed. [Whispers] Shhhh! Listen. It's C.J.— [Laughs] I made him do it, but it doesn't make any difference! They still hate you! [Looks at Peterson, who has moved closer to him] They still hate you! [Waters laughs]

PETERSON [To Smalls]. Justice, Smalls. [He raises the pistol.]

DAVENPORT [suddenly, harshly]. That isn't justice!

[Smalls almost recoils.]

PETERSON [simultaneously, continuing]. For C.J.! For everybody!

[Peterson fires the gun at Water's chest, and the shot stops everything. The celebration noise stops. Even Davenport in his way seems to hear it. Peterson fires again. There is a moment of quiet on stage. Davenport is angered and troubled.]

DAVENPORT. You call that justice?

SMALLS. No, sir.

DAVENPORT [enraged]. Then why the fuck didn't you do something?

SMALLS. I'm scared of Peterson—just scared of him!

[Peterson has been looking at Waters's body throughout. He now begins to lift Waters as best he can, and pull him off-stage. It is done with some difficulty.]

SMALLS. I tried to get him to go, sir, but he wanted to drag the Sergeant's body back into the woods—

[Light fades quickly around Peterson, as Davenport paces.]

SMALLS. Said everybody would think white people did it.

DAVENPORT [somewhat drained]. Then what happened?

SMALLS. I got sick, sir—and Peterson, when he got done, he helped me back to the barracks and told me to keep quiet. [Slight pause] I'm sorry, sir.

[There is a long pause, during which Davenport stares at Smalls with disgust, then abruptly starts out without saluting. He almost flees. Smalls rises quickly.]

SMALLS. Sir?

[Davenport turns around. Smalls comes to attention and salutes. Davenport returns salute and starts out of the cell and down toward center stage. He is thoughtful as the light fades around Smalls. Davenport removes his glasses and begins to clean them as he speaks.]

DAVENPORT. Peterson was apprehended a week later in Alabama. Colonel Nivens called it "just another black mess of cuttin', slashin', and shootin'!" He was delighted there were no white officers mixed up in it, and his report to Washington characterized the events surrounding Waters's murder as "the usual, common violence any commander faces in Negro Military units." It was the kind of "mess" that turns up on page 3 in the colored papers—the Cain and Abel story of the week—the headline we Negroes can't quite read in comfort. [Shakes head and paces] For me? Two colored soldiers are dead—two on their way to prison. Four less men to fight with— and none of their reasons—nothing anyone *said*, or *did*, would have been worth a life to men with larger hearts—men less split by the madness of race in America. [Pause] The case got little attention. The details were filed in my report and I was quickly and rather unceremoniously ordered back to my M.P. unit. [Smiles] A style of guitar pickin' and a dance called the C.J. caught on for a while in Tynin saloons during 1945. [Slight pause] In northern New Jersey, through a military foul-up, Sergeant Waters's family was informed that he had been killed in action. The Sergeant was, therefore, thought and unofficially rumored to have been the first colored casualty of the war from that county and under the circumstances was declared a hero. Nothing could be done officially, but his picture was hung on a Wall of Honor in the Dorie Miller VFW Post #978. [Pause] The men of the 221st Chemical Smoke Generating Company? The entire outfit—officers and enlisted men—was wiped out in the Ruhr Valley during a German advance. [He turns toward Taylor, who enters quietly] Captain?

TAYLOR. Davenport—I see you got your man.

DAVENPORT. I got him—what is it, Captain?

TAYLOR. Will you accept my saying, you did a splendid job?

DAVENPORT. I'll take the praise—but how did I manage it?

TAYLOR. Dammit, Davenport—I didn't come here to be made fun of—[Slight pause] The men—the regiment—we all ship out for Europe tomorrow, and [hesitates] I was wrong, Davenport—about the bars—the uniform—about Negroes being in charge. [Slight pause] I guess I'll *have* to get used to it.

DAVENPORT. Oh, you'll get used to it—you can bet your ass on that. Captain—you will get used to it.

[Lights begin to fade slowly as the music "Don't Sit under the Apple Tree" rises in the background, and the house goes to black.]

ESSAY: AN APPROACH TO THE PLAY

A Soldier's Play combines aspects of a traditional murder mystery with those of a courtroom drama. Captain Davenport, the black investigating officer assigned to learn who killed Sergeant Waters, interrogates witnesses in his attempt to discover the truth, and their testimony is presented through flashbacks. It is important to remember the "narrative" quality of these parts of the play; we are probably more familiar with the dramatic convention of the flashback as a presentation of what "really" happened, but here the flashbacks present specific characters' testimony, and we can never be sure how believable any of them are. Davenport's concern is to find out who killed Waters, but for the audience there is a second question. The play begins with Waters' murder. He is in a spotlight, his killer or killers standing invisibly in the darkness of the unlit stage. Just before the trigger is pulled, he says, "They'll still hate you! They still hate you . . . They still hate you!" Part of the mystery for us is to learn what these dying words can have meant. We want to learn who the killer is, but also who the victim is and why these would have been his dying words. As the investigation proceeds, a good deal more gets uncovered than the identity of the killer, some of it implied in the play's title. In some ways like *Oedipus the King*, the play's central question seems to shift from who committed the murder to questions of identity.

This is a soldier's play, one that keeps reminding us of the uses and abuses of power, about permitted and forbidden uses of force, concerns reinforced by the play's continual emphasis on chain of command. At the end of the play, even after confessing to Davenport his role in the murder, Smalls insists on exchanging a farewell salute with his superior officer. As a counterpoint to the institutionalized power hierarchy of military discipline, of course, the play's real focus is on power relations involving race. In the first episode in the barracks, the army's institutional racism is implied. The company's sergeant has been killed, and it is the enlisted men whose freedoms are curtailed. The army is apparently worried about possible reprisals against townspeople, and so Captain Taylor leads a detail searching the men's personal property for weapons. The town of Tynin is placed off-limits to all military personnel (a gesture that sounds racially neutral, except that all the enlisted men at the camp are black). "Why hold us prisoner," asks Smalls, as he looks out at the Military Police assigned to keep the barracks surrounded. It is a strange way for a government to treat men preparing for service in its military; men who are presumed to be innocent are confined because of skin color.

Some of the racial tensions are predictable. The white officers feel superior not just to their black subordinates but to a black officer as well. Even Captain Taylor, who seems, unlike his own superior officers, more interested in justice than in a cover-up, is disturbed that Davenport has been assigned the case. There were no blacks at West Point, and he claims never to have seen any black people with education until after his graduation, is uncomfortable with blacks in anything but a subordinate position, and assumes that Davenport was appointed as an act of bad faith to sabotage the investigation. More surprising are the racial tensions among the black soldiers, tensions which seem to express the various ways in which the men have internalized their culture's language of oppression. The focal point here is the relationship of Sergeant Waters with his men, inevitably the main subject of Davenport's investigation; Waters' relationship with all the men turns out to have been strained. He demoted Wilkie when less permanently harmful forms of discipline were apparently available and then held out the offer of restoration of rank to manipulate Wilkie into planting incriminating evidence under C.J.'s bed. After framing C.J., he taunted him into striking a blow in retaliation and so violating military code (Fuller says he had Herman Melville's *Billy Budd* in mind here), even though Waters himself had broken this code when he beat up Peterson to teach him a lesson.

Waters' greatest hostility, however, is not toward any of his men but toward himself. The first words he speaks during any of the men's testimony to Davenport, those in which he demotes Wilkie, repeat racist evaluations of blacks, and his last speech, just before Peterson shoots him, begins with the words, "You gotta be like them! And I was. . . ." He seems obsessed with white approval, both for himself and for blacks in general, but in his attempt to imitate white behavior, he has internalized the rhetoric and values of white racism as well. Thus he judges all blacks—including himself—by what he considers to be white thinking.

C.J. Memphis is the particular target onto whom he projects this self-hatred. C.J.'s rural simplicity was a continual source of embarrassment to Waters. C.J.'s belief in the magic powers of farmer's dust and in the omen of the crow flying at his birth make Waters cringe in fear that whites will judge him through C.J.'s behavior and beliefs. And yet the most accurate words spoken about Waters in the whole play belong to C.J.: "Any man ain't sure where he belongs must be in a whole lotta pain." The play presents a terrible portrait of a person in an inferior social position who wants to succeed, and of the terrible pressures which an unjust social situation can exert on individuals casually, without even intending to do so. One of the awful ironies about Waters is that he, not the whites or the blacks, really destroys himself, taking down two of his fellow black soldiers as well.

Davenport is also isolated from the others in the play, but in a different way, and this difference emphasizes Waters' qualities by contrast. Davenport is isolated because of his job and his race. He can trust no one because he must keep an open mind about who is guilty, regardless of race and rank, and because he is aware of the hostility of the white officers. Although his presence in the play makes the effects of racism palpable, he also demonstrates an alternative to Waters: that racism can be faced with dignity and without personal compromise.

Adding to the irony of Waters' self-destructiveness is the irony of the play's setting: the men are just about to go to Europe to fight (and, as we learn at the end of the play, to die) in the war against Nazi Germany. Waters, however, is engaged in a crusade to purify his race in an insane private parody of Nazi ideology. When he visits C.J. in prison he tells him: "Them Nazis ain't all crazy—a whole lot of people just can't fit into where things seem to be going—like you C.J. The black race can't afford you no more. . . . The day of the geechy is gone, boy—the only thing that can move the race is power." As a result of his vision, he undertakes a campaign of terrorism that would do a nightrider proud, and in reprisal for C.J.'s suicide, Peterson, who had seemed the most articulate defender of civil rights and human dignity among the soldiers, ends up exacting the private vengeance usually associated with a lynch mob. At the play's conclusion, even as the soldiers celebrate their orders to go overseas, the play seems to undercut its apparent resolution by broadening the question: Who are their real enemies?

August Wilson

JOE TURNER'S COME AND GONE

About the Author August Wilson (1945–   ) was born and raised in Pittsburgh, Pennsylvania, and since 1978 has lived in Minneapolis, Minnesota, where he is associated with the Playwright's Center. He left school after ninth grade and, while supporting himself with odd jobs, continued his education independently through his reading. He began publishing poetry in the 1960s and in 1968 founded the Black Horizon Theater of Pittsburgh, where he produced and directed works by other playwrights and for which he wrote his own first play, *Jitney*. Since 1984, he has perhaps been America's most successful playwright, producing a series of plays in an artistic partnership with the director Lloyd Richards, former dean of the Yale School of Drama and artistic director of the Yale Repertory Theater. In 1983 Richards accepted the then unknown Wilson as a participant in the Eugene O'Neill National Playwrights Conference (of which he also served as artistic director), and there then began a string of plays which moved from the conference's summer workshops to Yale Repertory productions and then to national tours and Broadway runs.

Joe Turner's Come and Gone (1988), set in 1911, is part of Wilson's long-term project to write a play about the African-American experience in each decade of our century. These "ensemble murals," as he has called the plays, focus on the events of a few "ordinary" people in a way that seems to widen out into an expression of larger historical significance, presenting the American experience from a perspective that has too often been silenced by our dominant cultural institutions—the commercial theater included. His first play, *Jitney*, is set in the 1970s; *Fullerton Street*, in the 1940s; *Ma Rainey's Black Bottom*, in the 1920s; *Fences*, in the 1950s; *The Piano Lesson*, in 1936; and *Two Trains Running* in the 1960s. His recent plays have been remarkably successful, many of them having won either a Pulitzer Prize or, as in the case of *Joe Turner*, the New York Drama Critics Circle Prize, and sometimes both; the play *Fences* won a Tony award in 1987.

About the Play "Joe Turner's Come and Gone" is the title of the turn-of-the-century blues song which Bynum is singing at the beginning of Act 2, Scene 2. The story of its genesis, as he and Loomis go on to explain it, is essentially the same as the story told by W.C. Handy, who said that he was influenced by having heard the song in Memphis when he was a young man. (Handy, the first person to publish his own blues compositions, began to do so in 1912, the year after the setting of the play.) Joe Turner, brother of Tennessee governor Pete Turner, used to lure black men into dice games and then, while they were preoccupied, have his henchmen arrest them, chain them together forty at a time, and take them off to seven years of enforced labor. The song is the lament of the women who learn that "Joe Turner's come and gone," taking their men with them. Loomis is presented in the play as one of Turner's victims. After his release, Loomis returned to his former home in search of his wife and daughter, found his daughter at the home of his mother-in-law, and with her set out to find his wife.

His search takes him to the Pittsburgh boarding house of Seth and Bertha Holly, which serves as the play's setting. With a dramatic tension reminiscent of the classical unities of time and place, Loomis' whole life comes to a climax—and perhaps resolution—during the play, with all the action taking place in two rooms and the adjacent yard. In the background, however, is an enormous amount of traveling: Bynum's defining vision took place on the road; Jeremy works as a road builder; Rutherford Selig, the People Finder, is continually on the road, his path intersecting with the boarding house every Saturday for business purposes; Mattie and Molly are both in transit from place to place; Martha came north with her church in search of an environment more congenial to their evangelism; Bynum is said to have been the kind of person who spent his whole life on the move until, getting older, he has settled into the boarding house for the past three years; Loomis and Zonia have been on the road for three years. The traveling is symptomatic of "the great migration," the period in the late nineteenth and especially early twentieth century when a great many African-Americans left their homes in the South to seek work in the expanding industrial economies of northern cities. The unified setting, then, serves as a point on which an entire people's movement can be concentrated.

Time is also tightly focused in the play. All the action takes place in fifteen days—from one Saturday, through a second, to a third, but events of at least the previous decade come to a climax during this brief period. In fact, a much longer time period is implied. Through Bynum, "the conjure man," "the rootworker," temporal continuities stretch back even to Africa. His shamanistic rituals and performances suggest that such a vision is necessary to heal the emotional pain which Loomis continues to suffer.

CHARACTERS

SETH HOLLY, owner of the boardinghouse
BERTHA HOLLY, his wife
BYNUM WALKER, a rootworker
RUTHERFORD SELIG, a peddler
JEREMY FURLOW, a resident
HERALD LOOMIS, a resident

ZONIA LOOMIS, his daughter
MATTIE CAMPBELL, a resident
REUBEN SCOTT, boy who lives next door
MOLLY CUNNINGHAM, a resident
MARTHA LOOMIS, Herald Loomis's wife

SETTING

August, 1911. A boardinghouse in Pittsburgh. At right is a kitchen. Two doors open off the kitchen. One leads to the outhouse and Seth's workshop. The other to Seth's and Bertha's bedroom. At left is a parlor. The front door opens into the parlor, which gives access to the stairs leading to the upstairs rooms.

There is a small outside playing area.

THE PLAY

It is August in Pittsburgh, 1911. The sun falls out of heaven like a stone. The fires of the steel mill rage with a combined sense of industry and progress. Barges loaded with coal and iron ore trudge up the river to the mill towns that dot the Monongahela and return with fresh, hard, gleaming steel. The city flexes its muscles. Men throw countless bridges across the rivers, lay roads and carve tunnels through the hills sprouting with houses.

From the deep and the near South the sons and daughters of newly freed African slaves wander into the city. Isolated, cut off from memory, having forgotten the names of the gods and only guessing at their faces, they arrive dazed and stunned, their heart kicking in their chest with a song worth singing. They arrive carrying Bibles and guitars, their pockets lined with dust and fresh hope, marked men and women seeking to scrape from the narrow, crooked cobbles and the fiery blasts of the coke furnace a way of bludgeoning and shaping the malleable parts of themselves into a new identity as free men of definite and sincere worth.

Foreigners in a strange land, they carry as part and parcel of their baggage a long line of separation and dispersement which informs their sensibilities and marks their conduct as they search for ways to reconnect, to reassemble, to give clear and luminous meaning to the song which is both a wail and a whelp of joy.

Act I

SCENE I

The lights come up on the kitchen. Bertha busies herself with breakfast preparations. Seth stands looking out the window at Bynum in the yard. Seth is in his early fifties. Born of Northern free parents, a skilled craftsman, and owner of the boardinghouse, he has a stability that none of the other characters have. Bertha is five years his junior. Married for over twenty-five years, she has learned how to negotiate around Seth's apparent orneriness.

SETH [*at the window, laughing*]. If that ain't the damndest thing I seen. Look here, Bertha.

BERTHA. I done seen Bynum out there with them pigeons before.

SETH. Naw . . . naw . . . look at this. That pigeon flopped out of Bynum's hand and he about to have a fit.

[*Bertha crosses over to the window.*]

He down there on his hands and knees behind that bush looking all over for that pigeon and it on the other side of the yard. See it over there?

BERTHA. Come on and get your breakfast and leave that man alone.

SETH. Look at him . . . he still looking. He ain't seen it yet. All that old mumbo jumbo nonsense. I don't know why I put up with it.

BERTHA. You don't say nothing when he bless the house.

SETH. I just go along with that 'cause of you. You around here sprinkling salt all over the place . . . got pennies lined up across the threshold . . . all that heebie-jeebie stuff. I just put up with that 'cause of you. I don't pay that kind of stuff no mind. And you going down there to the church and wanna come home and sprinkle salt all over the place.

BERTHA. It don't hurt none. I can't say if it help . . . but it don't hurt none.

SETH. Look at him. He done found that pigeon and now he's talking to it.

BERTHA. These biscuits be ready in a minute.

SETH. He done drew a big circle with that stick and now he's dancing around. I know he'd better not . . . [*Seth bolts from the window and rushes to the back door.*] Hey, Bynum! Don't be hopping around stepping in my vegetables.

Hey, Bynum . . . Watch where you stepping!

BERTHA. Seth, leave that man alone.

SETH [*coming back into the house*]. I don't care how much he be dancing around . . . just don't be stepping in my vegetables. Man got my garden all messed up now . . . planting them weeds out there . . . burying them pigeons and whatnot.

BERTHA. Bynum don't bother nobody. He ain't even thinking about your vegetables.

SETH. I know he ain't! That's why he out there stepping on them.

BERTHA. What Mr. Johnson say down there?

SETH. I told him if I had the tools I could go out here and find me four or five fellows and open up my own shop instead of working for Mr. Olowski. Get me four or five fellows and teach them how to make pots and pans. One man making ten pots is five men making fifty. He told me he'd think about it.

BERTHA. Well, maybe he'll come to see it your way.

SETH. He wanted me to sign over the house to him. You know what I thought of that idea.

BERTHA. He'll come to see you're right.

SETH. I'm going up and talk to Sam Green. There's more than one way to skin a cat. I'm going up and talk to him. See if he got more sense than Mr. Johnson. I can't get nowhere working for Mr. Olowski and selling Selig five or six pots on the side. I'm going up and see Sam Green. See if he loan me the money.

[*Seth crosses back to the window.*]

Now he got that cup. He done killed that pigeon and now he's putting its blood in that little cup. I believe he drink that blood.

BERTHA. Seth Holly, what is wrong with you this morning? Come on and get your breakfast so you can go to bed. You know Bynum don't be drinking no pigeon blood.

SETH. I don't know what he do.

BERTHA. Well, watch him, then. He's gonna dig a little hole and bury that pigeon. Then he's gonna pray over that blood . . . pour it on top . . . mark out his circle and come on into the house.

SETH. That's what he doing . . . he pouring that blood on top.

BERTHA. When they gonna put you back working

daytime? Told me two months ago he was gonna put you back working daytime.

SETH. That's what Mr. Olowski told me. I got to wait till he say when. He tell me what to do. I don't tell him. Drive me crazy to speculate on the man's wishes when he don't know what he want to do himself.

BERTHA. Well, I wish he go ahead and put you back working daytime. This working all hours of the night don't make no sense.

SETH. It don't make no sense for that boy to run out of here and get drunk so they lock him up either.

BERTHA. Who? Who they got locked up for being drunk?

SETH. That boy that's staying upstairs . . . Jeremy. I stopped down there on Logan Street on my way home from work and one of the fellows told me about it. Say he seen it when they arrested him.

BERTHA. I was wondering why I ain't seen him this morning.

SETH. You know I don't put up with that. I told him when he came . . .

[Bynum enters from the yard carrying some plants. He is a short, round man in his early sixties. A conjure man, or rootworker, he gives the impression of always being in control of everything. Nothing ever bothers him. He seems to be lost in a world of his own making and to swallow any adversity or interference with his grand design.]

What you doing bringing them weeds in my house? Out there stepping on my vegetables and now wanna carry them weeds in my house.

BYNUM. Morning, Seth. Morning, Sister Bertha.

SETH. Messing up my garden growing them things out there. I ought to go out there and pull up all them weeds.

BERTHA. Some gal was by here to see you this morning, Bynum. You was out there in the yard . . . I told her to come back later.

BYNUM [*To Seth*]. You look sick. What's the matter, you ain't eating right?

SETH. What if I was sick? You ain't getting near me with none of that stuff.

[Bertha sets a plate of biscuits on the table.]

BYNUM. My . . . my . . . Bertha, your biscuits getting fatter and fatter.

[Bynum takes a biscuit and begins to eat.]

Where Jeremy? I don't see him around this morn-

ing. He usually be around riffing and raffing on Saturday morning.

SETH. I know where he at. I know just where he at. They got him down there in the jail. Getting drunk and acting a fool. He down there where he belong with all that foolishness.

BYNUM. Mr. Piney's boys got him, huh? They ain't gonna do nothing but hold on to him for a little while. He's gonna be back here hungrier than a mule directly.

SETH. I don't go for all that carrying on and such. This is a respectable house. I don't have no drunkards or fools around here.

BYNUM. That boy got a lot of country in him. He ain't been up here but two weeks. It's gonna take a while before he can work that country out of him.

SETH. These niggers coming up here with that old backward country style of living. It's hard enough now without all that ignorant kind of acting. Ever since slavery got over with there ain't been nothing but foolish-acting niggers. Word get out they need men to work in the mill and put in these roads . . . and niggers drop everything and head North looking for freedom. They don't know the white fellows looking too. White fellows coming from all over the world. White fellow come over and in six months got more than what I got. But these niggers keep on coming. Walking . . . riding . . . carrying their Bibles. That boy done carried a guitar all the way from North Carolina. What he gonna find out? What he gonna do with that guitar? This the city.

[There is a knock on the door.]

Niggers coming up here from the backwoods . . . coming up here from the country carrying Bibles and guitars looking for freedom. They got a rude awakening.

[Seth goes to answer the door. Rutherford Selig enters. About Seth's age, he is a thin white man with greasy hair. A peddler, he supplies Seth with the raw materials to make pots and pans which he then peddles door to door in the mill towns along the river. He keeps a list of his customers as they move about and is known in the various communities as the People Finder. He carries squares of sheet metal under his arm.]

Ho! Forgot you was coming today. Come on in.

BYNUM. If it ain't Rutherford Selig . . . the People Finder himself.

SELIG. What say there, Bynum?

BYNUM. I say about my shiny man. You got to tell me

something. I done give you my dollar . . . I'm looking to get a report.

SELIG. I got eight here, Seth.

SETH [*Taking the sheet metal*]. What is this? What you
giving me here? What I'm gonna do with this?

SELIG. I need some dustpans. Everybody asking me
about dustpans.

SETH. Gonna cost you fifteen cents apiece. And ten
cents to put a handle on them.

SELIG. I'll give you twenty cents apiece with the handles.

SETH. Alright. But I ain't gonna give you but fifteen
cents for the sheet metal.

SELIG. It's twenty-five cents apiece for the metal.
That's what we agreed on.

SETH. This low-grade sheet metal. They ain't worth
but a dime. I'm doing you a favor giving you fifteen
cents. You know this metal ain't worth no twenty-
five cents. Don't come talking that twenty-five cent
stuff to me over no low-grade sheet metal.

SELIG. Alright, fifteen cents apiece. Just make me
some dustpans out of them.

[*Seth exits with the sheet metal out the back door.*]

BERTHA. Sit on down there, Selig. Get you a cup of
coffee and a biscuit.

BYNUM. Where you coming from this time?

SELIG. I been upriver. All along the Monongahela.
Past Rankin and all up around Little Washington.

BYNUM. Did you find anybody?

SELIG. I found Sadie Jackson up in Braddock. Her
mother's staying down there in Scotchbottom say
she hadn't heard from her and she didn't know
where she was at. I found her up in Braddock on
Enoch Street. She bought a frying pan from me.

BYNUM. You around here finding everybody how
come you ain't found my shiny man?

SELIG. The only shiny man I saw was the Nigras working on the road gang with the sweat glistening on
them.

BYNUM. Naw, you'd be able to tell this fellow. He
shine like new money.

SELIG. Well, I done told you I can't find nobody
without a name.

BERTHA. Here go one of these hot biscuits, Selig.

BYNUM. This fellow don't have no name. I call him
John 'cause it was up around Johnstown where I
seen him. I ain't even so sure he's one special fellow.
That shine could pass on to anybody. He could be
anybody shining.

SELIG. Well, what's he look like besides being shiny?
There's lots of shiny Nigras.

BYNUM. He's just a man I seen out on the road. He
ain't had no special look. Just a man walking toward
me on the road. He come up and asked me which
way the road went. I told him everything I knew
about the road, where it went and all, and he asked
me did I have anything to eat 'cause he was hungry.
Say he ain't had nothing to eat in three days. Well, I
never be out there on the road without a piece of
dried meat. Or an orange or an apple. So I give this
fellow an orange. He take and eat that orange and
told me to come and go along the road a little ways
with him, that he had something he wanted to show
me. He had a look about him made me wanna go
with him, see what he gonna show me.

We walked on a bit and it's getting kind of far
from where I met him when it come up on me all of
a sudden, we wasn't going the way he had come
from, we was going back my way. Since he said he
ain't knew nothing about the road, I asked him
about this. He say he had a voice inside him telling
him which way to go and if I come and go along
with him he was gonna show me the Secret of Life.
Quite naturally I followed him. A fellow that's
gonna show you the Secret of Life ain't to be taken
lightly. We get near this bend in the road . . .

[*Seth enters with an assortment of pots.*]

SETH. I got six here, Selig.

SELIG. Wait a minute, Seth. Bynum's telling me about
the secret of life. Go ahead, Bynum. I wanna hear
this.

[*Seth sets the pots down and exits out the back.*]

BYNUM. We get near this bend in the road and he told
me to hold out my hands. Then he rubbed them
together with his and I looked down and see they
got blood on them. Told me to take and rub it all
over me . . . say that was a way of cleaning myself.
Then we went around the bend in that road. Got
around that bend and it seem like all of a sudden we
ain't in the same place. Turn around that bend and
everything look like it was twice as big as it was. The
trees and everything bigger than life! Sparrows big
as eagles! I turned around to look at this fellow and
he had this light coming out of him. I had to cover
up my eyes to keep from being blinded. He shining
like new money with that light. He shined until all

the light seemed like it seeped out of him and then he was gone and I was by myself in this strange place where everything was bigger than life.

I wandered around there looking for that road, trying to find my way back from this big place . . . and I looked over and seen my daddy standing there. He was the same size he always was, except for his hands and his mouth. He had a great big old mouth that look like it took up his whole face and his hands were as big as hams. Look like they was too big to carry around. My daddy called me to him. Said he had been thinking about me and it grieved him to see me in the world carrying other people's songs and not having one of my own. Told me he was gonna show me how to find my song. Then he carried me further into this big place until we come to this ocean. Then he showed me something I ain't got words to tell you. But if you stand to witness it, you done seen something there. I stayed in that place awhile and my daddy taught me the meaning of this thing that I had seen and showed me how to find my song. I asked him about the shiny man and he told me he was the One Who Goes Before and Shows the Way. Said there was lots of shiny men and if I ever saw one again before I died then I would know that my song had been accepted and worked its full power in the world and I could lay down and die a happy man. A man who done left his mark on life. On the way people cling to each other out of the truth they find in themselves. Then he showed me how to get back to the road. I came out to where everything was its own size and I had my song. I had the Binding Song. I choose that song because that's what I seen most when I was traveling . . . people walking away and leaving one another. So I takes the power of my song and binds them together. [*Seth enters from the yard carrying cabbages and tomatoes.*] Been binding people ever since. That's why they call me Bynum. Just like glue I sticks people together.

SETH. Maybe they ain't supposed to be stuck some times. You ever think of that?

BYNUM. Oh, I don't do it lightly. It cost me a piece of myself every time I do. I'm a Binder of What Clings. You got to find out if they cling first. You can't bind what don't cling.

SELIG. Well, how is that the Secret of Life? I thought you said he was gonna show you the secret of life. That's what I'm waiting to find out.

BYNUM. Oh, he showed me alright. But you still got to figure it out. Can't nobody figure it out for you.

You got to come to it on your own. That's why I'm looking for the shiny man.

SELIG. Well, I'll keep my eye out for him. What you got there, Seth?

SETH. Here go some cabbage and tomatoes. I got some green beans coming in real nice. I'm gonna take and start me a grapevine out there next year. Butera says he gonna give me a piece of his vine and I'm gonna start that out there.

SELIG. How many of them pots you got?

SETH. I got six. That's six dollars minus eight on top of fifteen for the sheet metal come to a dollar twenty out the six dollars leave me four dollars and eighty cents.

SELIG [*Counting out the money*]. There's four dollars . . . and . . . eighty cents.

SETH. How many of them dustpans you want?

SELIG. As many as you can make out them sheets.

SETH. You can use that many? I get to cutting on them sheets figuring how to make them dustpans . . . ain't no telling how many I'm liable to come up with.

SELIG. I can use them and you can make me some more next time.

SETH. Alright, I'm gonna hold you to that, now.

SELIG. Thanks for the biscuit, Bertha.

BERTHA. You know you welcome anytime, Selig.

SETH. Which way you heading?

SELIG. Going down to Wheeling. All through West Virginia there. I'll be back Saturday. They putting in new roads down that way. Makes traveling easier.

SETH. That's what I hear. All up around here too. Got a fellow staying here working on that road by the Brady Street Bridge.

SELIG. Yeah, it's gonna make traveling real nice. Thanks for the cabbage, Seth. I'll see you on Saturday.

[*Selig exits*].

SETH [*To Bynum*]. Why you wanna start all that nonsense talk with that man? All that shiny man nonsense.

BYNUM. You know it ain't no nonsense. Bertha know it ain't no nonsense. I don't know if Selig know or not.

BERTHA. Seth, when you get to making them dustpans make me a coffeepot.

SETH. What's the matter with your coffee? Ain't nothing wrong with your coffee. Don't she make some good coffee, Bynum?

BYNUM. I ain't worried about the coffee. I know she makes some good biscuits.

SETH. I ain't studying no coffeepot, woman. You heard me tell the man I was gonna cut as many dustpans as them sheets will make . . . and all of a sudden you want a coffeepot.

BERTHA. Man, hush up and go on and make me that coffeepot.

[*Jeremy enters the front door. About twenty-five, he gives the impression that he has the world in his hand, that he can meet life's challenges head on. He smiles a lot. He is a proficient guitar player, though his spirit has yet to be molded into song.*]

BYNUM. I hear Mr. Piney's boys had you.

JEREMY. Fined me two dollars for nothing! Ain't done nothing.

SETH. I told you when you come on here everybody know my house. Know these is respectable quarters. I don't put up with no foolishness. Everybody know Seth Holly keep a good house. Was my daddy's house. This house been a decent house for a long time.

JEREMY. I ain't done nothing, Mr. Seth. I stopped by the Workmen's Club and got me a bottle. Me and Roper Lee from Alabama. Had us a half pint. We was fixing to cut that half in two when they came up on us. Asked us if we was working. We told them we was putting in the road over yonder and that it was our payday. They snatched hold of us to get that two dollars. Me and Roper Lee ain't even had a chance to take a drink when they grabbed us.

SETH. I don't go for all that kind of carrying on.

BERTHA. Leave the boy alone, Seth. You know the police do that. Figure there's too many people out on the street they take some of them off. You know that.

SETH. I ain't gonna have folks talking.

BERTHA. Ain't nobody talking nothing. That's all in your head. You want some grits and biscuits. Jeremy?

JEREMY. Thank you, Miss Bertha. They didn't give us a thing to eat last night. I'll take one of them big bowls if you don't mind.

[*There is a knock at the door. Seth goes to answer it. Enter Herald Loomis and his eleven-year-old daughter, Zonia. Herald Loomis is thirty-two years old. He is at times possessed. A man driven not by the hellhounds that seemingly bay at his heels, but by his search for a world that speaks to something about himself. He is unable to harmonize the forces that swirl around him, and seeks to recreate the world into one that contains his image. He wears a hat and a long wool coat.*]

LOOMIS. Me and my daughter looking for a place to stay, mister. You got a sign say you got rooms.

[*Seth stares at Loomis, sizing him up.*]

Mister, if you ain't got no rooms we can go somewhere else.

SETH. How long you plan on staying?

LOOMIS. Don't know. Two weeks or more maybe.

SETH. It's two dollars a week for the room. We serve meals twice a day. It's two dollars for room and board. Pay up in advance.

[*Loomis reaches into his pocket.*]

It's a dollar extra for the girl.

LOOMIS. The girl sleep in the same room.

SETH. Well, do she eat off the same plate? We serve meals twice a day. That's a dollar extra for food.

LOOMIS. Ain't got no extra dollar. I was planning on asking your missus if she could help out with the cooking and cleaning and whatnot.

SETH. Her helping out don't put no food on the table. I need that dollar to buy some food.

LOOMIS. I'll give you fifty cents extra. She don't eat much.

SETH. Okay . . . but fifty cents don't buy but half a portion.

BERTHA. Seth, she can help me out. Let her help me out. I can use some help.

SETH. Well, that's two dollars for the week. Pay up in advance. Saturday to Saturday. You wanna stay on then it's two more come Saturday.

[*Loomis pays Seth the money.*]

BERTHA. My name's Bertha. This my husband, Seth. You got Bynum and Jeremy over there.

LOOMIS. Ain't nobody else live here?

BERTHA. They the only ones live here now. People come and go. They the only ones here now. You want a cup of coffee and a biscuit?

LOOMIS. We done ate this morning.

BYNUM. Where you coming from, Mister . . . I didn't get your name.

LOOMIS. Name's Herald Loomis. This my daughter, Zonia.

BYNUM. Where you coming from?

LOOMIS. Come from all over. Whicheverway the road take us that's the way we go.

JEREMY. If you looking for a job, I'm working putting in that road down there by the bridge. They can't get enough mens. Always looking to take somebody on.

LOOMIS. I'm looking for a woman named Martha Loomis. That's my wife. Got married legal with the papers and all.

SETH. I don't know nobody named Loomis. I know some Marthas but I don't know no Loomis.

BYNUM. You got to see Rutherford Selig if you wanna find somebody. Selig's the People Finder. Rutherford Selig's a first-class People Finder.

JEREMY. What she look like? Maybe I seen her.

LOOMIS. She a brownskin woman. Got long pretty hair. About five feet from the ground.

JEREMY. I don't know. I might have seen her.

BYNUM. You got to see Rutherford Selig. You give him one dollar to get her name on his list . . . and after she get her name on his list Rutherford Selig will go right on out there and find her. I got him looking for somebody for me.

LOOMIS. You say he find people. How you find him?

BYNUM. You just missed him. He's gone downriver now. You got to wait till Saturday. He's gone downriver with his pots and pans. He come to see Seth on Saturdays. You got to wait till then.

SETH. Come on, I'll show you to your room.

[Seth, Loomis, and Zonia exit up the stairs.]

JEREMY. Miss Bertha, I'll take that biscuit you was gonna give that fellow, if you don't mind. Say, Mr. Bynum, they got somebody like that around here sure enough? Somebody that find people?

BYNUM. Rutherford Selig. He go around selling pots and pans and every house he come to he write down the name and address of whoever lives there. So if you looking for somebody, quite naturally you go and see him . . . 'cause he's the only one who know where everybody live at.

JEREMY. I ought to have him look for this old gal I used to know. It be nice to see her again.

BERTHA [Giving Jeremy a biscuit]. Jeremy, today's the day for you to pull them sheets off the bed and set them outside your door. I'll set you out some clean ones.

BYNUM. Mr. Piney's boys done ruined your good time last night, Jeremy . . . what you planning for tonight?

JEREMY. They got me scared to go out, Mr. Bynum. They might grab me again.

BYNUM. You ought to take your guitar and go down to Seefus. Seefus got a gambling place down there on Wylie Avenue. You ought to take your guitar and go down there. They got guitar contest down there.

JEREMY. I don't play no contest, Mr. Bynum. Had one of them white fellows cure me of that. I ain't been nowhere near a contest since.

BYNUM. White fellow beat you playing guitar?

JEREMY. Naw, he ain't beat me. I was sitting at home just fixing to sit down and eat when somebody come up to my house and got me. Told me there's a white fellow say he was gonna give a prize to the best guitar player as he could find. I take up my guitar and go down there and somebody had gone up and got Bobo Smith and brought him down there. Him and another fellow called Hooter. Old Hooter couldn't play no guitar, he do more hollering than playing, but Bobo could go at it awhile.

This fellow standing there say he the one that was gonna give the prize and me and Bobo started playing for him. Bobo play something and then I'd try to play something better than what he played. Old Hooter, he just holler and bang at the guitar. Man was the worst guitar player I ever seen. So me and Bobo played and after a while I seen where he was getting the attention of this white fellow. He'd play something and while he was playing it he be slapping on the side of the guitar, and that made it sound like he was playing more than he was. So I started doing it too. White fellow ain't knew no difference. He ain't knew as much about guitar playing as Hooter did. After we play awhile, the white fellow called us to him and said he couldn't make up his mind, say all three of us was the best guitar player and we'd have to split the prize between us. Then he give us twenty-five cents. That's eight cents apiece and a penny on the side. That cured me of playing contest to this day.

BYNUM. Seefus ain't like that. Seefus give a whole dollar and a drink of whiskey.

JEREMY. What night they be down there?

BYNUM. Be down there every night. Music don't know no certain night.

BERTHA. You go down to Seefus with them people and you liable to end up in a raid and go to jail sure enough. I don't know why Bynum tell you that.

BYNUM. That's where the music at. That's where the people at. The people down there making music and enjoying themselves. Some things is worth taking the chance going to jail about.

BERTHA. Jeremy ain't got no business going down there.

JEREMY. They got some women down there, Mr. Bynum?

BYNUM. Oh, they got women down there, sure. They

got women everywhere. Women be where the men is so they can find each other.

JEREMY. Some of them old gals come out there where we be putting in that road. Hanging around there trying to snatch somebody.

BYNUM. How come some of them ain't snatched hold of you?

JEREMY. I don't want them kind. Them desperate kind. Ain't nothing worse than a desperate woman. Tell them you gonna leave them and they get to crying and carrying on. That just make you want to get away quicker. They get to cutting up your clothes and things trying to keep you staying. Desperate women ain't nothing but trouble for a man.

[Seth enters from the stairs.]

SETH. Something ain't setting right with that fellow.

BERTHA. What's wrong with him? What he say?

SETH. I take him up there and try to talk to him and he ain't for no talking. Say he been traveling—coming over from Ohio. Say he a deacon in the church. Say he looking for Martha Pentecost. Talking about that's his wife.

BERTHA. How you know it's the same Martha? Could be talking about anybody. Lots of people named Martha.

SETH. You see that little girl? I didn't hook it up till he said it, but that little girl look just like her. Ask Bynum. [To Bynum.] Bynum. Don't that little girl look just like Martha Pentecost?

BERTHA. I still say he could be talking about anybody.

SETH. The way he described her wasn't no doubt about who he was talking about. Described her right down to her toes.

BERTHA. What did you tell him?

SETH. I ain't told him nothing. The way that fellow look I wasn't gonna tell him nothing. I don't know what he looking for her for.

BERTHA. What else he have to say?

SETH. I told you he wasn't for no talking. I told him where the outhouse was and to keep that gal off the front porch and out of my garden. He asked if you'd mind setting a hot tub for the gal and that was about the gist of it.

BERTHA. Well, I wouldn't let it worry me if I was you. Come on get your sleep.

BYNUM. He says he looking for Martha and he a deacon in the church.

SETH. That's what he say. Do he look like a deacon to you?

BERTHA. He might be, you don't know. Bynum ain't got no special say on whether he a deacon or not.

SETH. Well, if he the deacon I'd sure like to see the preacher.

BERTHA. Come on get your sleep. Jeremy, don't forget to set them sheets outside the door like I told you.

[Bertha exits into the bedroom.]

SETH. Something ain't setting right with that fellow, Bynum. He's one of them mean-looking niggers look like he done killed somebody gambling over a quarter.

BYNUM. He ain't no gambler. Gamblers wear nice shoes. This fellow got on clodhoppers. He been out there walking up and down them roads.

[Zonia enters from the stairs and looks around.]

BYNUM. You looking for the back door, sugar? There it is. You can go out there and play. It's alright.

SETH. [Showing her the door.] You can go out there and play. Just don't get in my garden. And don't go messing around in my workshed.

[Seth exits into the bedroom. There is a knock on the door.]

JEREMY. Somebody at the door.

[Jeremy goes to answer the door. Enter Mattie Campbell. She is a young woman of twenty-six whose attractiveness is hidden under the weight and concerns of a dissatisfied life. She is a woman in an honest search for love and companionship. She had suffered many defeats in her search, and though not always uncompromising, still believes in the possibility of love.]

MATTIE. I'm looking for a man named Bynum. Lady told me to come back later.

JEREMY. Sure, he here. Mr. Bynum, somebody here to see you.

BYNUM. Come to see me, huh?

MATTIE. Are you the man they call Bynum? The man folks say can fix things?

BYNUM. Depend on what need fixing. I can't make no promises. But I got a powerful song in some matters.

MATTIE. Can you fix it so my man come back to me?

BYNUM. Come on in . . . have a sit down.

MATTIE. You got to help me. I don't know what else to do.

BYNUM. Depend on how all the circumstances of the thing come together. How all the pieces fit.

MATTIE. I done everything I knowed how to do. You got to make him come back to me.

BYNUM. It ain't nothing to make somebody come back. I can fix it so he can't stand to be away from you. I got my roots and powders, I can fix it so wherever he's at this thing will come up on him and he won't be able to sleep for seeing your face. Won't be able to eat for thinking of you.

MATTIE. That's what I want. Make him come back.

BYNUM. The roots is a powerful thing. I can fix it so one day he'll walk out his front door . . . won't be thinking of nothing. He won't know what it is. All he knows is that a powerful dissatisfaction done set in his bones and can't nothing he do make him feel satisfied. He'll set his foot down on the road and the wind in the trees be talking to him and everywhere he step on the road, that road'll give back your name and something will pull him right up to your doorstep. Now, I can do that. I can take my roots and fix that easy. But maybe he ain't supposed to come back. And if he ain't supposed to come back . . . then he'll be in your bed one morning and it'll come up on him that he's in the wrong place. That he's lost outside of time from his place that he's supposed to be in. Then both of you be lost and trapped outside of life and ain't no way for you to get back into it. 'Cause you lost from yourselves and where the places come together, where you're supposed to be alive, your heart kicking in your chest with a song worth singing.

MATTIE. Make him come back to me. Make his feet say my name on the road. I don't care what happens. Make him come back.

BYNUM. What's your man's name?

MATTIE. He go by Jack Carper. He was born in Alabama then he come to West Texas and find me and we come here. Been here three years before he left. Say I had a curse prayer on me and he started walking down the road and ain't never come back. Somebody told me, say you can fix things like that.

BYNUM. He just got up one day, set his feet on the road, and walked away?

MATTIE. You got to make him come back, mister.

BYNUM. Did he say goodbye?

MATTIE. Ain't said nothing. Just started walking. I could see where he disappeared. Didn't look back. Just keep walking. Can't you fix it so he come back? I ain't got no curse prayer on me. I know I ain't.

BYNUM. What made him say you had a curse prayer on you?

MATTIE. 'Cause the babies died. Me and Jack had two babies. Two little babies that ain't lived two months before they died. He say it's because somebody cursed me not to have babies.

BYNUM. He ain't bound to you if the babies died.

Look like somebody trying to keep you from being bound up and he's gone on back to whoever it is 'cause he's already bound up to her. Ain't nothing to be done. Somebody else done got a powerful hand in it and ain't nothing to be done to break it. You got to let him go find where he's supposed to be in the world.

MATTIE. Jack done gone off and you telling me to forget about him. All my life I been looking for somebody to stop and stay with me. I done already got too many things to forget about. I take Jack Carper's hand and it feel so rough and strong. Seem like he's the strongest man in the world the way he hold me. Like he's bigger than the whole world and can't nothing bad get to me. Even when he act mean sometimes he still make everything seem okay with the world. Like there's part of it that belongs just to you. Now you telling me to forget about him?

BYNUM. Jack Carper gone off to where he belong. There's somebody searching for your doorstep right now. Ain't no need you fretting over Jack Carper. Right now he's a strong thought in your mind. But every time you catch yourself fretting over Jack Carper you push that thought away. You push it out your mind and that thought will get weaker and weaker till you wake up one morning and you won't even be able to call him up on your mind.

[Bynum gives her a small cloth packet.]

Take this and sleep with it under your pillow and it'll bring good luck to you. Draw it to you like a magnet. It won't be long before you forget all about Jack Carper.

MATTIE. How much . . . do I owe you?

BYNUM. Whatever you got there . . . that'll be alright.

[Mattie hands Bynum two quarters. She crosses to the door.]

You sleep with that under your pillow and you'll be alright.

[Mattie opens the door to exit and Jeremy crosses over to her. Bynum overhears the first part of their conversation, then exits out the back.]

JEREMY. I overheard what you told Mr. Bynum. Had me an old gal did that to me. Woke up one morning and she was gone. Just took off to parts unknown. I woke up that morning and the only thing I could do was look around for my shoes. I woke up and got out of there. Found my shoes and took off. That's the only thing I could think of to do.

MATTIE. She ain't said nothing?

JEREMY. I just looked around for my shoes and got out of there.

MATTIE. Jack ain't said nothing either. He just walked off.

JEREMY. Some mens do that. Womens too. I ain't gone off looking for her. I just let her go. Figure she had a time to come to herself. Wasn't no use of me standing in the way. Where you from?

MATTIE. Texas. I was born in Georgia but I went to Texas with my mama. She dead now. Was picking peaches and fell dead away. I come up here with Jack Carper.

JEREMY. I'm from North Carolina. Down around Raleigh where they got all that tobacco. Been up here about two weeks. I likes it fine except I still got to find me a woman. You got a nice look to you. Look like you have mens standing in your door. Is you got mens standing in your door to get a look at you?

MATTIE. I ain't got nobody since Jack left.

JEREMY. A woman like you need a man. Maybe you let me be your man. I got a nice way with the women. That's what they tell me.

MATTIE. I don't know. Maybe Jack's coming back.

JEREMY. I'll be your man till he come. A woman can't be by her lonesome. Let me be your man till he come.

MATTIE. I just can't go through life piecing myself out to different mens. I need a man who wants to stay with me.

JEREMY. I can't say what's gonna happen. Maybe I'll be the man. I don't know. You wanna go along the road a little ways with me?

MATTIE. I don't know. Seem like life say it's gonna be one thing and end up being another. I'm tired of going from man to man.

JEREMY. Life is like you got to take a chance. Everybody got to take a chance. Can't nobody say what's gonna be. Come on . . . take a chance with me and see what the year bring. Maybe you let me come and see you. Where you staying?

MATTIE. I got me a room up on Bedford. Me and Jack had a room together.

JEREMY. What's the address? I'll come by and get you tonight and we can go down to Seefus. I'm going down there and play my guitar.

MATTIE. You play guitar?

JEREMY. I play guitar like I'm born to it.

MATTIE. I live at 1727 Bedford Avenue. I'm gonna find out if you can play guitar like you say.

JEREMY. I plays it sugar, and that ain't all I do. I got a ten-pound hammer and I knows how to drive it down. Good god . . . you ought to hear my hammer ring!

MATTIE. Go on with that kind of talk, now. If you gonna come by and get me I got to get home and straighten up for you.

JEREMY. I'll be by at eight o'clock. How's eight o'clock? I'm gonna make you forget all about Jack Carper.

MATTE. Go on, now. I got to get home and fix up for you.

JEREMY. Eight o'clock, sugar.

[*The lights go down in the parlor and come up on the yard outside. Zonia is singing and playing a game.*]

ZONIA.

> I went downtown
> To get my grip
> I came back home
> Just a pullin' the skiff
>
> I went upstairs
> To make my bed
> I made a mistake
> And I bumped my head
> Just a pullin' the skiff
>
> I went downstairs
> To milk the cow
> I made a mistake
> And I milked the sow
> Just a pullin' the skiff
>
> Tomorrow, tomorrow
> Tomorrow never comes
> The marrow the marrow
> The marrow in the bone.

[*Reuben enters.*]

REUBEN. Hi.

ZONIA. Hi.

REUBEN. What's your name?

ZONIA. Zonia.

REUBEN. What kind of name is that?

ZONIA. It's what my daddy named me.

REUBEN. My name's Reuben. You staying in Mr. Seth's house?

ZONIA. Yeah.

REUBEN. That your daddy I seen you with this morning?

ZONIA. I don't know. Who you see me with?

REUBEN. I saw you with some man had on a great big old coat. And you was walking up to Mr. Seth's house. Had on a hat too.

ZONA. Yeah, that's my daddy.

REUBEN. You like Mr. Seth?

ZONIA. I ain't see him much.

REUBEN. My grandpap say he a great big old windbag. How come you living in Mr. Seth's house? Don't you have no house?

ZONIA. We going to find my mother.

REUBEN. Where she at?

ZONIA. I don't know. We got to find her. We just go all over.

REUBEN. Why you got to find her? What happened to her?

ZONIA. She ran away.

REUBEN. Why she run away?

ZONIA. I don't know. My daddy say some man named Joe Turner did something bad to him once and that made her run away.

REUBEN. Maybe she coming back and you don't have to go looking for her.

ZONIA. We ain't there no more.

REUBEN. She could have come back when you wasn't there.

ZONIA. My daddy said she ran off and left us so we going looking for her.

REUBEN. What he gonna do when he find her?

ZONIA. He didn't say. He just say he got to find her.

REUBEN. Your daddy say how long you staying in Mr. Seth's house?

ZONIA. He don't say much. But we never stay too long nowhere. He say we got to keep moving till we find her.

REUBEN. Ain't no kids hardly live around here. I had me a friend but he died. He was the best friend I ever had. Me and Eugene used to keep secrets. I still got his pigeons. He told me to let them go when he died. He say, "Reuben, promise me when I die you'll let my pigeons go." But I keep them to remember him by. I ain't never gonna let them go. Even when I get to be grown up. I'm just always gonna have Eugene's pigeons.

[Pause.]

Mr. Bynum a conjure man. My grandpap scared of him. He don't like me to come over here too much. I'm scared of him too. My grandpap told me not to let him get close enough to where he can reach out his hand and touch me.

ZONIA. He don't seem scary to me.

REUBEN. He buys pigeons from me . . . and if you get up early in the morning you can see him out in the yard doing something with them pigeons. My grandpap say he kill them. I sold him one yesterday. I don't know what he do with it. I just hope he don't spook me up.

ZONIA. Why you sell him pigeons if he's gonna spook you up?

REUBEN. I just do like Eugene do. He used to sell Mr. Bynum pigeons. That's how he got to collecting them to sell to Mr. Bynum. Sometime he give me a nickel and sometime he give me a whole dime.

[Loomis enters from the house.]

LOOMIS. Zonia!

ZONIA. Sir?

LOOMIS. What you doing?

ZONIA. Nothing.

LOOMIS. You stay around this house, you hear? I don't want you wandering off nowhere.

ZONIA. I ain't wandering off nowhere.

LOOMIS. Miss Bertha set that hot tub and you getting a good scrubbing. Get scrubbed up good. You ain't been scrubbing.

ZONIA. I been scrubbing.

LOOMIS. Look at you. You growing too fast. Your bones getting bigger everyday. I don't want you getting grown on me. Don't you get grown on me too soon. We gonna find your mamma. She around here somewhere. I can smell her. You stay on around this house now. Don't you go nowhere.

ZONIA. Yes, sir.

[Loomis exits into the house.]

REUBEN. Wow, your daddy's scary!

ZONIA. He is not! I don't know what you talking about.

REUBEN. He got them mean-looking eyes!

ZONIA. My daddy ain't got no mean-looking eyes!

REUBEN. Aw, girl, I was just messing with you. You wanna go see Eugene's pigeons? Got a great big coop out the back of my house. Come on, I'll show you.

[Reuben and Zonia exit as the lights go down.]

SCENE II

It is Saturday morning, one week later. The lights come up on the kitchen. Bertha is at the stove preparing breakfast while Seth sits at the table.

SETH. Something ain't right about that fellow. I been watching him all week. Something ain't right, I'm telling you.

BERTHA. Seth Holly, why don't you hush up about that man this morning?

SETH. I don't like the way he stare at everybody. Don't look at you natural like. He just be staring at you. Like he trying to figure out something about you. Did you see him when he come back in here?

BERTHA. That man ain't thinking about you.

SETH. He don't work nowhere. Just go out and come back. Go out and come back.

BERTHA. As long as you get your boarding money it ain't your cause about what he do. He don't bother nobody.

SETH. Just go out and come back. Going around asking everybody about Martha. Like Henry Allen seen him down at the church last night.

BERTHA. The man's allowed to go to church if he want. He say he a deacon. Ain't nothing wrong about him going to church.

SETH. I ain't talking about him going to church. I'm talking about him hanging around *outside* the church.

BERTHA. Henry Allen say that?

SETH. Say he be standing around outside the church. Like he be watching it.

BERTHA. What on earth he wanna be watching the church for, I wonder?

SETH. That's what I'm trying to figure out. Looks like he fixing to rob it.

BERTHA. Seth, now do he look like the kind that would rob the church?

SETH. I ain't saying that. I ain't saying how he look. It's how he do. Anybody liable to do anything as far as I'm concerned. I ain't never thought about how no church robbers look . . . but now that you mention it, I don't see where they look no different than how he look.

BERTHA. Herald Loomis ain't the kind of man who would rob no church.

SETH. I ain't even so sure that's his name.

BERTHA. Why the man got to lie about his name?

SETH. Anybody can tell anybody anything about what their name is. That's what you call him . . . Herald Loomis. His name is liable to be anything.

BERTHA. Well, until he tell me different that's what I'm gonna call him. You just getting yourself all worked up about the man for nothing.

SETH. Talking about Loomis: Martha's name wasn't no Loomis nothing. Martha's name is Pentecost.

BERTHA. How you so sure that's her right name? Maybe she changed it.

SETH. Martha's a good Christian woman. This fellow here look like he owe the devil a day's work and he's trying to figure out how he gonna pay him. Martha ain't had a speck of distrust about her the whole time she was living here. They moved the church out there to Rankin and I was sorry to see her go.

BERTHA. That's why he be hanging around the church. He looking for her.

SETH. If he looking for her, why don't he go inside and ask? What he doing hanging around outside the church acting sneaky like?

[*Bynum enters from the yard.*]

BYNUM. Morning, Seth. Morning, Sister Bertha.

[*Bynum continues through the kitchen and exits up the stairs.*]

BERTHA. That's who you should be asking the questions. He been out there in that yard all morning. He was out there before the sun come up. He didn't even come in for breakfast. I don't know what he's doing. He had three of them pigeons line up out there. He dance around till he get tired. He sit down awhile then get up and dance some more. He come through here a little while ago looking like he was mad at the world.

SETH. I don't pay Bynum no mind. He don't spook me up with all that stuff.

BERTHA. That's how Martha come to be living here. She come to see Bynum. She come to see him when she first left from down South.

SETH. Martha was living here before Bynum. She ain't come on here when she first left from down there. She come on here after she went back to get her little girl. That's when she come on here.

BERTHA. Well, where was Bynum? He was here when she came.

SETH. Bynum ain't come till after her. That boy Hiram was staying up there in Bynum's room.

BERTHA. Well, how long Bynum been here?

SETH. Bynum ain't been here no longer than three years. That's what I'm trying to tell you. Martha was staying up there and sewing and cleaning for Doc Goldblum when Bynum came. This the longest he ever been in one place.

BERTHA. How you know how long the man been in one place?

SETH. I know Bynum. Bynum ain't no mystery to me. I done seen a hundred niggers like him. He's one of them fellows never could stay in one place. He was wandering all around the country till he got old and settled here. The only thing different about Bynum is he bring all this heebie-geebie stuff with him.

BERTHA. I still say he was staying here when she came. That's why she came . . . to see him.

SETH. You can say what you want. I know the facts of it. She come on here four years ago all heartbroken 'cause she couldn't find her little girl. And Bynum wasn't nowhere around. She got mixed up in that old heebie-jeebie nonsense with him after he came.

BERTHA. Well, if she came on before Bynum I don't know where she stayed. 'Cause she stayed up there in Hiram's room. Hiram couldn't get along with Bynum and left out of here owing you two dollars. Now, I know you ain't forgot about that!

SETH. Sure did! You know Hiram ain't paid me that two dollars yet. So that's why he be ducking and hiding when he see me down on Logan Street. You right. Martha did come on after Bynum. I forgot that's why Hiram left.

BERTHA. Him and Bynum never could see eye to eye. They always rubbed each other the wrong way. Hiram got to thinking that Bynum was trying to put a fix on him and he moved out. Martha came to see Bynum and ended up taking Hiram's room. Now, I know what I'm talking about. She stayed on here three years till they moved the church.

SETH. She out there in Rankin now. I know where she at. I know where they moved the church to. She right out there in Rankin in that place used to be shoe store. Used to be Wolf's shoe store. They moved to a bigger place and they put that church in there. I know where she at. I know just where she at.

BERTHA. Why don't you tell the man? You see he looking for her.

SETH. I ain't gonna tell that man where that woman is! What I wanna do that for? I don't know nothing about that man. I don't know why he looking for her. He might wanna do her a harm. I ain't gonna carry that on my hands. He looking for her, he gonna have to find her for himself. I ain't gonna help him. Now, if he had come and presented himself as a gentleman—the way Martha Pentecost's husband would have done—then I would have told him. But I ain't gonna tell this old wild-eyed mean-looking nigger nothing!

BERTHA. Well, why don't you get a ride with Selig

and go up there and tell her where he is? See if she wanna see him. If that's her little girl . . . you say Martha was looking for her.

SETH. You know me, Bertha. I don't get mixed up in nobody's business.

[Bynum enters from the stairs.]

BYNUM. Morning, Seth. Morning, Bertha. Can I still get some breakfast? Mr. Loomis been down here this morning?

SETH. He done gone out and come back. He up there now. Left out of here early this morning wearing that coat. Hot as it is, the man wanna walk around wearing a big old heavy coat. He come back in here paid me for another week, sat down there waiting on Selig. Got tired of waiting and went on back upstairs.

BYNUM. Where's the little girl?

SETH. She out there in the front. Had to chase her and that Reuben off the front porch. She out there somewhere.

BYNUM. Look like if Martha was around here he would have found her by now. My guess is she ain't in the city.

SETH. She ain't! I know where she at. I know just where she at. But I ain't gonna tell him. Not the way he look.

BERTHA. Here go your coffee, Bynum.

BYNUM. He says he gonna get Selig to find her for him.

SETH. Selig can't find her. He talk all that . . . but unless he get lucky and knock on her door he can't find her. That's the only way he find anybody. He got to get lucky. But I know just where she at.

BERTHA. Here go some biscuits, Bynum.

BYNUM. What else you got over there, Sister Bertha? You got some grits and gravy over there? I could go for some of that this morning.

BERTHA [Sets a bowl on the table]. Seth, come on and help me turn this mattress over. Come on.

SETH. Something ain't right with that fellow, Bynum. I don't like the way he stare at everybody.

BYNUM. Mr. Loomis alright, Seth. He just a man got something on his mind. He just got a straightforward mind, that's all.

SETH. What's that fellow that they had around here? Moses, that's Moses Houser. Man went crazy and jumped off the Brady Street Bridge. I told you when I seen him something wasn't right about him. And I'm telling you about this fellow now.

[*There is a knock on the door. Seth goes to answer it. Enter Rutherford Selig.*]

Ho! Come on in, Selig.

BYNUM. If it ain't the People Finder himself.

SELIG. Bynum, before you start . . . I ain't seen no shiny man now.

BYNUM. Who said anything about that? I ain't said nothing about that. I just called you a first-class People Finder.

SELIG. How many dustpans you get out of that sheet metal, Seth?

SETH. You walked by them on your way in. They sitting out there on the porch. Got twenty-eight. Got four out of each sheet and made Bertha a coffeepot out the other one. They a little small but they got nice handles.

SELIG. That was twenty cents apiece, right? That's what we agreed on.

SETH. That's five dollars and sixty cents. Twenty on top of twenty-eight. How many sheets you bring me?

SELIG. I got eight out there. That's a dollar twenty makes me owe you . . .

SETH. Four dollars and forty cents.

SELIG [*Paying him*]. Go on and make me some dustpans. I can use all you can make.

[*Loomis enters from the stairs.*]

LOOMIS. I been watching for you. He say you find people.

BYNUM. Mr. Loomis here wants you to find his wife.

LOOMIS. He say you find people. Find her for me.

SELIG. Well, let see here . . . find somebody, is it?

[*Selig rummages through his pockets. He has several notebooks and he is searching for the right one.*]

Alright now . . . what's the name?

LOOMIS. Martha Loomis. She my wife. Got married legal with the paper and all.

SELIG [*Writing*]. Martha . . . Loomis. How tall is she?

LOOMIS. She five feet from the ground.

SELIG. Five feet . . . tall. Young or old?

LOOMIS. She a young woman. Got long pretty hair.

SELIG. Young . . . long . . . pretty . . . hair. Where did you last see her?

LOOMIS. Tennessee. Nearby Memphis.

SELIG. When was that?

LOOMIS. Nineteen hundred and one.

SELIG. Nineteen . . . hundred and one. I'll tell you, mister . . . you better off without them. Now you take me . . . old Rutherford Selig could tell you a thing or two about these women. I ain't met one yet I could understand. Now, you take Sally out there. That's all a man needs is a good horse. I say giddup and she go. Say whoa and she stop. I feed her some oats and she carry me wherever I want to go. Ain't had a speck of trouble out of her since I had her. Now, I been married. A long time ago down in Kentucky. I got up one morning and I saw this look on my wife's face. Like way down deep inside her she was wishing I was dead. I walked around that morning and every time I looked at her she had that look on her face. It seem like she knew I could see it on her. Every time I looked at her I got smaller and smaller. Well, I wasn't gonna stay around there and just shrink away. I walked out on the porch and closed the door behind me. When I closed the door she locked it. I went out and bought me a horse. And I ain't been without one since! Martha Loomis, huh? Well, now I'll do the best I can do. That's one dollar.

LOOMIS [*Holding out dollar suspiciously*]. How you find her?

SELIG. Well now, it ain't no easy job like you think. You can't just go out there and find them like that. There's a lot of little tricks to it. It's not an easy job keeping up with you Nigras the way you move about so. Now you take this woman you looking for . . . this Martha Loomis. She could be anywhere. Time I find her, if you don't keep your eye on her, she'll be gone off someplace else. You'll be thinking she over here and she'll be over there. But like I say there's a lot of little tricks to it.

LOOMIS. You say you find her.

SELIG. I can't promise anything but we been finders in my family for a long time. Bringers and finders. My great-granddaddy used to bring Nigras across the ocean on ships. That's wasn't no easy job either. Sometimes the winds would blow so hard you'd think the hand of God was set against the sails. But it set him well in pay and he settled in this new land and found him a wife of good Christian charity with a mind for kids and the like and well . . . here I am, Rutherford Selig. You're in good hands, mister. Me and my daddy have found plenty Nigras. My daddy, rest his soul, used to find runaway slaves for the plantation bosses. He was the best there was at it. Jonas B. Selig. Had him a reputation stretched clean across the country. After Abraham Lincoln give you all Nigras your freedom papers and with you all looking all over for each other . . . we started finding Nigras for Nigras. Of course, it don't pay as much. But the People Finding business ain't so bad.

LOOMIS [*Hands him the dollar*]. Find her. Martha Loomis. Find her for me.

SELIG. Like I say, I can't promise you anything. I'm going back upriver, and if she's around in them parts I'll find her for you. But I can't promise you anything.

LOOMIS. When you coming back?

SELIG. I'll be back on Saturday. I come and see Seth to pick up my order on Saturday.

BYNUM. You going upriver, huh? You going up around my way. I used to go all up through there. Blawknox . . . Clairton. Used to go up to Rankin and take that first righthand road. I wore many a pair of shoes out walking around that way. You'd have thought I was a missionary spreading the gospel the way I wandered all around them parts.

SELIG. Okay, Bynum. See you on Saturday.

SETH. Here, let me walk out with you. Help you with them dustpans.

[*Seth and Selig exit out the back. Bertha enters from the stairs carrying a bundle of sheets.*]

BYNUM. Herald Loomis got the People Finder looking for Martha.

BERTHA. You can call him a People Finder if you want to. I know Rutherford Selig carries people away too. He done carried a whole bunch of them away from here. Folks plan on leaving plan by Selig's timing. They wait till he get ready to go, then they hitch a ride on his wagon. Then he charge folks a dollar to tell them where he took them. Now, that's the truth of Rutherford Selig. This old People Finding business is for the birds. He ain't never found nobody he ain't took away. Herald Loomis, you just wasted your dollar.

[*Bertha exits into the bedroom.*]

LOOMIS. He say he find her. He say he find her by Saturday. I'm gonna wait till Saturday.

[*The lights fade to black.*]

SCENE III

It is Sunday morning, the next day. The lights come up on the kitchen. Seth sits talking to Bynum. The breakfast dishes have been cleared away.

SETH. They can't see that. Neither one of them can see that. Now, how much sense it take to see that? All you got to do is be able to count. One man making ten pots is five men making fifty pots. But they can't see that. Asked where I'm gonna get my five men. Hell, I can teach anybody how to make a pot. I can teach you. I can take you out there and get you started right now. Inside of two weeks you'd know how to make a pot. All you got to do is want to do it. I can get five men. I ain't worried about getting no five men.

BERTHA [*calls from the bedroom*]. Seth. Come on and get ready now. Reverend Gates ain't gonna be holding up his sermon 'cause you sitting out there talking.

SETH. Now, you take the boy, Jeremy. What he gonna do after he put in that road? He can't do nothing but go put in another one somewhere. Now, if he let me show him how to make some pots and pans . . . then he'd have something can't nobody take away from him. After a while he could get his own tools and go off somewhere and make his own pots and pans. Find him somebody to sell them to. Now, Selig can't make no pots and pans. He can sell them but he can't make them. I get me five men with some tools and we'd make him so many pots and pans he'd have to open up a store somewhere. But they can't see that. Neither Mr. Cohen nor Sam Green.

BERTHA [*Calls from the bedroom*]. Seth . . . time be wasting. Best be getting on.

SETH. I'm coming, woman! [*To Bynum.*] Want me to sign over the house to borrow five hundred dollars. I ain't that big a fool. That's all I got. Sign it over to them and then I won't have nothing.

[*Jeremy enters waving a dollar and carrying his guitar.*]

JEREMY. Look here, Mr. Bynum . . . won me another dollar last night down at Seefus! Me and that Mattie Campbell went down there again and I played contest. Ain't no guitar players down there. Wasn't even no contest. Say, Mr. Seth, I asked Mattie Campbell if she wanna come by and have Sunday dinner with us. Get some fried chicken.

SETH. It's gonna cost you twenty five cents.

JEREMY. That's alright. I got a whole dollar here. Say Mr. Seth . . . me and Mattie Campbell talked it over last night and she gonna move in with me. If that's alright with you.

SETH. Your business is your business . . . but it's

gonna cost her a dollar a week for her board. I can't be feeding nobody for free.

JEREMY. Oh, she know that, Mr. Seth. That's what I told her, say she'd have to pay for her meals.

SETH. You say you got a whole dollar there . . . turn loose that twenty-five cents.

JEREMY. Suppose she move in today, then that make seventy-five cents more, so I'll give you the whole dollar for her now till she gets here.

[Seth pockets the money and exits into the bedroom.]

BYNUM. So you and that Mattie Campbell gonna take up together?

JEREMY. I told her she don't need to be by her lonesome, Mr. Bynum. Don't make no sense for both of us to be by our lonesome. So she gonna move in with me.

BYNUM. Sometimes you got to be where you supposed to be. Sometimes you can get all mixed up in life and come to the wrong place.

JEREMY. That's just what I told her, Mr. Bynum. It don't make no sense for her to be all mixed up and lonesome. May as well come here and be with me. She a fine woman too. Got them long legs. Knows how to treat a fellow too. Treat you like you wanna be treated.

BYNUM. You just can't look at it like that. You got to look at the whole thing. Now, you take a fellow go out there, grab hold to a woman and think he got something 'cause she sweet and soft to the touch. Alright. Touching's part of life. It's in the world like everything else. Touching's nice. It feels good. But you can lay your hand upside a horse or a cat, and that feels good too. What's the difference? When you grab hold to a woman, you got something there. You got a whole world there. You got a way of life kicking up under your hand. That woman can take and make you feel like something. I ain't just talking about in the way of jumping off into bed together and rolling around with each other. Anybody can do that. When your grab hold to that woman and look at the whole thing and see what you got . . . why, she can take and make something out of you. Your mother was a woman. That's enough right there to show you what a woman is. Enough to show you what she can do. She made something out of you. Taught you converse, and all about how to take care of yourself, how to see where you at and where you going tomorrow, how to look out to see what's coming in the way of eating, and what to do with yourself when you get

lonesome. That's a mighty thing she did. But you just can't look at a woman to jump off into bed with her. That's a foolish thing to ignore a woman like that.

JEREMY. Oh, I ain't ignoring her, Mr. Bynum. It's hard to ignore a woman got legs like she got.

BYNUM. Alright. Let's try it this way. Now, you take a ship. Be out there on the water traveling about. You out there on that ship sailing to and from. And then you see some land. Just like you see a woman walking down the street. You see that land and it don't look like nothing but a line out there on the horizon. That's all it is when you first see it. A line that cross your path out there on the horizon. Now, a smart man know when he see that land, it ain't just a line setting out there. He know that if you get off the water to go take a good look . . . why, there's a whole world right there. A whole world with everything imaginable under the sun. Anything you can think of you can find on that land. Same with a woman. A woman is everything a man need. To a smart man she water and berries. And that's all a man need. That's all he need to live on. You give me some water and berries and if there ain't nothing else I can live a hundred years. See, you just like a man looking at the horizon from a ship. You just seeing a part of it. But it's a blessing when you learn to look at a woman and see in maybe just a few strands of her hair, the way her cheek curves . . . to see in that everything there is out of life to be gotten. It's a blessing to see that. You know you done right and proud by your mother to see that. But you got to learn it. My telling you ain't gonna mean nothing. You got to learn how to come to your own time and place with a woman.

JEREMY. What about your woman, Mr. Bynum? I know you done had some woman.

BYNUM. Oh, I got them in memory time. That lasts longer than any of them ever stayed with me.

JEREMY. I had me an old gal one time . . .

[There is a knock on the door. Jeremy goes to answer it. Enter Molly Cunningham. She is about twenty-six, the kind of woman that "could break in on a dollar anywhere she goes." She carries a small cardboard suitcase, and wears a colorful dress of the fashion of the day. Jeremy's heart jumps out of his chest when he sees her.]

MOLLY. You got any rooms here? I'm looking for a room.

JEREMY. Yeah . . . Mr. Seth got rooms. Sure . . . wait till I get Mr. Seth. [Calls]. Mr. Seth! Somebody here to see you! [*To Molly*]. Yeah, Mr. Seth got some rooms. Got one right next to me. This a nice place to stay, too. My name's Jeremy. What's yours?

[*Seth enters dressed in his Sunday clothes*].

SETH. Ho!

JEREMY. This here woman looking for a place to stay. She say you got any rooms.

MOLLY. Mister, you got any rooms? I seen your sign say you got rooms.

SETH. How long you plan to staying?

MOLLY. I ain't gonna be here long. I ain't looking for no home or nothing. I'd be in Cincinnati if I hadn't missed my train.

SETH. Rooms cost two dollars a week.

MOLLY. Two dollars!

SETH. That includes meals. We serve two meals a day. That's breakfast and dinner.

MOLLY. I hope it ain't on the third floor.

SETH. That's the only one I got. Third floor to the left. That's pay up in advance week to week.

MOLLY [*Going into her bosom*]. I'm gonna pay you for one week. My name's Molly. Molly Cunningham.

SETH. I'm Seth Holly. My wife's name is Bertha. She do the cooking and taking care of around here. She got sheets on the bed. Towels twenty-five cents a week extra if you ain't got none. You get breakfast and dinner. We got fried chicken on Sundays.

MOLLY. That sounds good. Here's two dollars and twenty-five cents. Look here, Mister . . . . . . ?

SETH. Holly. Seth Holly.

MOLLY. Look here, Mr. Holly. I forgot to tell you. I likes me some company from time to time. I don't like being by myself.

SETH. Your business is your business. I don't meddle in nobody's business. But this is a respectable house. I don't have no riffraff around here. And I don't have no women hauling no men up to their rooms to be making their living. As long as we understand each other then we'll be alright with each other.

MOLLY. Where's the outhouse?

SETH. Straight through the door over yonder.

MOLLY. I get my own key to the front door?

SETH. Everybody get their own key. If you come in late just don't be making no whole lot of noise and carrying on. Don't allow no fussing and fighting around here.

MOLLY. You ain't got to worry about that, mister. Which way you say that outhouse was again?

SETH. Straight through that door over yonder.

[*Molly exits out the back door. Jeremy crosses to watch her.*]

JEREMY. Mr. Bynum, you know what? I think I know what you was talking about now.

[*The lights go down on the scene.*]

SCENE IV

The lights come up on the kitchen. It is later the same evening. Mattie and all the residents of the house, except Loomis, sit around the table. They have finished eating and most of the dishes have been cleared.

MOLLY. That sure was some good chicken.

JEREMY. That's what I'm talking about. Miss Bertha, you sure can fry some chicken. I thought my mama could fry some chicken. But she can't do half as good as you.

SETH. I know it. That's why I married her. She don't know that, though. She think I married her for something else.

BERTHA. I ain't studying you, Seth. Did you get your things moved in alright, Mattie?

MATTIE. I ain't have that much. Jeremy helped me with what I did have.

BERTHA. You'll get to know your way around here. If you have any questions about anything just ask me. You and Molly both. I get along with everybody. You'll find I ain't no trouble to get along with.

MATTIE. You need some help with the dishes?

BERTHA. I got me a helper. Ain't I, Zonia? Got me a good helper.

ZONIA. Yes, ma'am.

SETH. Look at Bynum sitting over there with his belly all poked out. Ain't saying nothing. Sitting over there half asleep. Ho, Bynum!

BERTHA. If Bynum ain't saying nothing what you wanna start him up for?

SETH. Ho, Bynum!

BYNUM. What you hollering at me for? I ain't doing nothing.

SETH. Come on, we gonna Juba.

BYNUM. You know me, I'm always ready to Juba.

SETH. Well, come on, then.

[*Seth pulls out a haromnica and blows a few notes.*]

Come on there, Jeremy. Where's your guitar? Go get your guitar. Bynum say he's ready to Juba.

JEREMY. Don't need no guitar to Juba. Ain't you never Juba without a guitar?

[*Jeremy begins to drum on the table.*]

SETH. It ain't that. I ain't never Juba with one! Figured to try it and see how it worked.

BYNUM [*Drumming on the table*]. You don't need no guitar. Look at Molly sitting over there. She don't know we Juba on Sunday. We gonna show you something tonight. You and Mattie Campbell both. Ain't that right, Seth?

SETH. You said it! Come on, Bertha, leave them dishes be for a while. We gonna Juba.

BYNUM. Alright. Let's Juba down!

[*The Juba is reminiscent of the Ring Shouts of the African slaves. It is a call and response dance. Bynum sits at the table and drums. He calls the dance as others clap hands, shuffle and stomp around the table. It should be as African as possible, with the performers working themselves up into a near frenzy. The words can be improvised, but should include some mention of the Holy Ghost. In the middle of the dance Herald Loomis enters.*]

LOOMIS [*In a rage*]. Stop it! Stop!

[*They stop and turn to look at him.*]

You all sitting up here singing about the Holy Ghost. What's so holy about the Holy Ghost? You singing and singing. You think the Holy Ghost coming? You singing for the Holy Ghost to come? What he gonna do, huh? He gonna come with tongues of fire to burn up your woolly heads? You gonna tie onto the Holy Ghost and get burned up? What you got then? Why God got to be so big? Why he got to be bigger than me? How much big is there? How much big do you want?

[*Loomis starts to unzip his pants.*]

SETH. Nigger, you crazy!

LOOMIS. How much big you want?

SETH. You done plumb lost your mind!

[*Loomis begins to speak in tongues and dance around the kitchen. Seth starts after him.*]

BERTHA. Leave him alone, Seth. He ain't in his right mind.

LOOMIS [*Stops suddenly*]. You all don't know nothing about me. You don't know what I done seen. Herald Loomis done seen some things he ain't got words to tell you.

[*Loomis starts to walk out the front door and is thrown back and collapses, terror-stricken by his vision. Bynum crawls to him.*]

BYNUM. What you done seen, Herald Loomis?

LOOMIS. I done seen bones rise up out the water. Rise up and walk across the water. Bones walking on top of the water.

BYNUM. Tell me about them bones, Herald Loomis. Tell me what you seen.

LOOMIS. I come to this place . . . to this water that was bigger than the whole world. And I looked out . . . and I seen these bones rise up out the water. Rise up and begin to walk on top of it.

BYNUM. Wasn't nothing but bones and they walking on top of the water.

LOOMIS. Walking without sinking down. Walking on top of the water.

BYNUM. Just marching in a line.

LOOMIS. A whole heap of them. They come up out the water and started marching.

BYNUM. Wasn't nothing but bones and they walking on top of the water.

LOOMIS. One after the other. They just come up out the water and start to walking.

BYNUM. They walking on the water without sinking down. They just walking and walking. And then . . . what happened, Herald Loomis?

LOOMIS. They just walking across the water.

BYNUM. What happened, Herald Loomis? What happened to the bones?

LOOMIS. They just walking across the water . . . and then . . . they sunk down.

BYNUM. The bones sunk into the water. They all sunk down.

LOOMIS. All at one time! They just all fell in the water at one time.

BYNUM. Sunk down like anybody else.

LOOMIS. When they sink down they made a big splash and this here wave come up . . .

BYNUM. A big wave, Herald Loomis. A big wave washed over the land.

LOOMIS. It washed them out of the water and up on the land. Only . . . only . . .

BYNUM. Only they ain't bones no more.

LOOMIS. They got flesh on them! Just like you and me!

BYNUM. Everywhere you look the waves is washing them up on the land right on top of one another.

LOOMIS. They black. Just like you and me. Ain't no difference.

BYNUM. Then what happened, Herald Loomis?

LOOMIS. They ain't moved or nothing. They just laying there.

BYNUM. You just laying there. What you waiting on, Herald Loomis?

LOOMIS. I'm laying there . . . waiting.

BYNUM. What you waiting on, Herald Loomis?

LOOMIS. I'm waiting on the breath to get into my body.

BYNUM. The breath coming into you, Herald Loomis. What you gonna do now?

LOOMIS. The wind's blowing the breath into my body. I can feel it. I'm starting to breathe again.

BYNUM. What you gonna do, Herald Loomis?

LOOMIS. I'm gonna stand up. I got to stand up. I can't lay here no more. All the breath coming into my body and I got to stand up.

BYNUM. Everybody's standing up at the same time.

LOOMIS. The ground's starting to shake. There's a great shaking. The world's busting half in two. The sky's splitting open. I got to stand up.

[Loomis attempts to stand up.]

My legs . . . my legs won't stand up!

BYNUM. Everybody's standing and walking toward the road. What you gonna do, Herald Loomis?

LOOMIS. My legs won't stand up.

BYNUM. They shaking hands and saying goodbye to each other and walking every whichaway down the road.

LOOMIS. I got to stand up!

BYNUM. They walking around here now. Mens. Just like you and me. Come right up out the water.

LOOMIS. Got to stand up.

BYNUM. They walking, Herald Loomis. They walking around here now.

LOOMIS. I got to stand up. Get up on the road.

BYNUM. Come on, Herald Loomis.

[Loomis tries to stand up.]

LOOMIS. My legs won't stand up! my legs won't stand up!

[Loomis collapses on the floor as the lights go down to black.]

Act II

SCENE I

The lights come up on the kitchen. Bertha busies herself with breakfast preparations. Seth sits at the table.

SETH. I don't care what his problem is! He's leaving here!

BERTHA. You can't put the man out and he got that little girl. Where they gonna go then?

SETH. I don't care where he go. Let him go back where he was before he come here. I ain't asked him to come here. I knew when I first looked at him something wasn't right with him. Dragging that little girl around with him. Looking like he be sleeping in the woods somewhere. I knew all along he wasn't right.

BERTHA. A fellow get a little drunk he's liable to say or do anything. He ain't done no big harm.

SETH. I just don't have all that carrying on in my house. When he come down here I'm gonna tell him. He got to leave here. My daddy wouldn't stand for it and I ain't gonna stand for it either.

BERTHA. Well, if you put him out you have to put Bynum out too. Bynum right there with him.

SETH. If it wasn't for Bynum ain't no telling what would have happened. Bynum talked to that fellow just as nice and calmed him down. If he wasn't here ain't no telling what would have happened. Bynum ain't done nothing but talk to him and kept him calm. Man acting all crazy with that foolishness. Naw, he's leaving here.

BERTHA. What you gonna tell him? How you gonna tell him to leave?

SETH. I'm gonna tell him straight out. Keep it nice and simple. Mister, you got to leave here!

[*Molly enters from the stairs.*]

MOLLY. Morning.

BERTHA. Did you sleep alright in that bed?

MOLLY. Tired as I was I could have slept anywhere. It's a real nice room, though. This is a nice place.

SETH. I'm sorry you had to put up with all that carrying on last night.

MOLLY. It don't bother me none. I done seen that kind of stuff before.

SETH. You won't have to see it around here no more.

[*Bynum is heard singing offstage.*]

I don't put up with all that stuff. When that fellow come down here I'm gonna tell him.

BYNUM [*singing*].

> Soon my work will all be done
> Soon my work will all be done
> Soon my work will all be done
>
> I'm going to see the king.

BYNUM [*Enters*]. Morning, Seth. Morning, Sister Bertha. I see we got Molly Cunningham down here at breakfast.

SETH. Bynum, I wanna thank you for talking to that fellow last night and calming him down. If you hadn't been here ain't no telling what might have happened.

BYNUM. Mr. Loomis alright, Seth. He just got a little excited.

SETH. Well, he can get excited somewhere else 'cause he leaving here.

[*Mattie enters from the stairs.*]

BYNUM. Well, there's Mattie Campbell.

MATTIE. Good morning.

BERTHA. Sit on down there, Mattie. I got some biscuits be ready in a minute. The coffee's hot.

MATTIE. Jeremy gone already?

BYNUM. Yeah, he leave out of here early. He got to be there when the sun come up. Most working men got to be there when the sun come up. Everybody but Seth. Seth works at night. Mr. Olowski so busy in his shop he got fellows working at night.

[*Loomis enters from the stairs.*]

SETH. Mr. Loomis, now . . . I don't want no trouble.

I keeps me a respectable house here. I don't have no carrying on like what went on last night. This has been a respectable house for a long time. I'm gonna have to ask you to leave.

LOOMIS. You got my two dollars. That two dollars say we stay till Saturday.

[*Loomis and Seth glare at each other.*]

SETH. Alright. Fair enough. You stay till Saturday. But come Saturday you got to leave here.

LOOMIS [*Continues to glare at Seth. He goes to the door and calls*]. Zonia. You stay around this house, you hear? Don't you go anywhere.

[*Loomis exits out the front door.*]

SETH. I knew it when I first seen him. I knew something wasn't right with him.

BERTHA. Seth, leave the people alone to eat their breakfast. They don't want to hear that. Go on out there and make some pots and pans. That's the only time you satisfied is when you out there. Go on out there and make some pots and pans and leave them people alone.

SETH. I ain't bothering anybody. I'm just stating the facts. I told you, Bynum.

[*Bertha shoos Seth out the back door and exits into the bedroom.*]

MOLLY. I thought so. The way you talked to that man when he started all that spooky stuff. What you say you had the power to do to people? You ain't the cause of him acting like that, is you?

BYNUM. I binds them together. Sometimes I help them find each other.

MOLLY. How do you do that?

BYNUM. With a song. My daddy taught me how to do it.

MOLLY. That's what they say. Most folks be what they daddy is. I wouldn't want to be like my daddy. Nothing ever set right with him. He tried to make the world over. Carry it around with him everywhere he go. I don't want to be like that. I just take life as it come. I don't be trying to make it over.

[*Pause.*]

Your daddy used to do that too, huh? Make people stay together?

BYNUM. My daddy used to heal people. He had the Healing Song. I got the Binding Song.

MOLLY. My mama used to believe in all that stuff. If she got sick she would have gone and saw your daddy. As long as he didn't make her drink nothing. She wouldn't drink nothing nobody give her. She was always afraid somebody was gonna poison her. How your daddy heal people?

BYNUM. With a song. He healed people by singing over them. I seen him do it. He sung over this little white girl when she was sick. They made a big to-do about it. They carried the girl's bed out in the yard and had all her kinfolk standing around. The little girl laying up there in the bed. Doctors standing around can't do nothing to help her. And they had my daddy come up and sing his song. It didn't sound no different than any other song. It was just somebody singing. But the song was its own thing and it come out and took upon this little girl with its power and it healed her.

MOLLY. That's sure something else. I don't understand that kind of thing. I guess if the doctor couldn't make me well I'd try it. But otherwise I don't wanna be bothered with that kind of thing. It's too spooky.

BYNUM. Well, let me get on out here and get to work.

[Bynum gets up and heads out the back door.]

MOLLY. I ain't meant to offend you or nothing? What's your name . . . Bynum? I ain't meant to say nothing to make you feel bad now.

[Bynum exits out the back door.]

[To Mattie]. I hope he don't feel bad. He's a nice man. I don't wanna hurt nobody's feelings or nothing.

MATTIE. I got to go on up to Doc Goldblum's and finish this ironing.

MOLLY. Now, that's something I don't never wanna do. Iron no clothes. Especially somebody else's. That's what I believe killed my mama. Always ironing and working, doing somebody's else's work. Not Molly Cunningham.

MATTIE. It's the only job I got. I got to make it someway to fend for myself.

MOLLY. I thought Jeremy was your man. Ain't he working?

MATTIE. We just be keeping company till maybe Jack come back.

MOLLY. I don't trust none of these men. Jack or nobody else. These men liable to do anything. They wait just until they get one woman tied and locked up with them . . . then they look around to see if they can get another one. Molly don't pay them no mind. One's just as good as the other if you ask me. I ain't never met one that meant nobody no good. You got any babies?

MATTIE. I had two for my man, Jack Carper. But they both died.

MOLLY. That be the best. These men make all these babies, then run off and leave you to take care of them. Talking about they wanna see what's on the other side of the hill. I make sure I don't get no babies. My mama taught me how to do that.

MATTIE. Don't make me no mind. That be nice to be a mother.

MOLLY. Yeah! Well, you go on, then. Molly Cunningham ain't gonna be tied down with no babies. Had me a man one time who I thought had some love in him. Come home one day and he was packing his trunk. Told me the time come when even the best of friends must part. Say he was gonna send me a Special Delivery some old day. I watched him out the window when he carried that trunk out and down to the train station. Said if he was gonna send me a Special Delivery I wasn't gonna be there to get it. I done found out the harder you try to hold onto them, the easier it is for some gal to pull them away. Molly done learned that. That's why I don't trust nobody but the good Lord above, and I don't love nobody but my mama.

MATTIE. I got to get on. Doc Goldblum gonna be waiting.

[Mattie exits out the front door. Seth enters from his workshop with his apron, gloves, goggles, etc. He carries a bucket and crosses to the sink for water.]

SETH. Everybody gone but you, huh?

MOLLY. That little shack out there by the outhouse . . . that's where you make them pots and pans and stuff?

SETH. Yeah, that's my workshed. I go out there . . . take these hands and make something out of nothing. Take that metal and bend and twist it whatever way I want. My daddy taught me that. He used to make pots and pans. That's how I learned it.

MOLLY. I never knew nobody made no pots and pans. My uncle used to shoe horses.

[Jeremy enters at the front door.]

SETH. I thought you was working? Ain't you working today?

JEREMY. Naw, they fired me. White fellow came by told me to give him fifty cents if I wanted to keep working. Going around to all the colored making them give him fifty cents to keep hold to their jobs. Them other fellows, they was giving it to him. I kept hold to mine and they fired me.

SETH. Boy, what kind of sense that make? What kind of sense it make to get fired from a job where you making eight dollars a week and all it cost you is fifty cents. That's seven dollars and fifty cents profit! This way you ain't got nothing.

JEREMY. It didn't make no sense to me. I don't make but eight dollars. Why I got to give him fifty cents of it? He go around to all the colored and he got ten dollars extra. That's more than I make for a whole week.

SETH. I see you gonna learn the hard way. You just looking at the facts of it. See, right now, without the job, you ain't got nothing. What you gonna do when you can't keep a roof over your head? Right now, come Saturday, unless you come up with another two dollars, you gonna be out there in the streets. Down up under one of them bridges trying to put some food in your belly and wishing you had given that fellow that fifty cents.

JEREMY. Don't make me no difference. There's a big road out there. I can get my guitar and always find me another place to stay. I ain't planning on staying in one place for too long noway.

SETH. We gonna see if you feel like that come Saturday!

[*Seth exits out the back. Jeremy sees Molly.*]

JEREMY. Molly Cunningham. How you doing today, sugar?

MOLLY. You can go on back down there tomorrow and go back to work if you want. They won't even know who you is. Won't even know it's you. I had me a fellow did that one time. They just went ahead and signed him up like they never seen him before.

JEREMY. I'm tired of working anyway. I'm glad they fired me. You sure look pretty today.

MOLLY. Don't come telling me all that pretty stuff. Beauty wanna come in and sit down at your table asking to be fed. I ain't hardly got enough for me.

JEREMY. You know you pretty. Ain't no sense in you saying nothing about that. Why don't you come on and go away with me?

MOLLY. You tied up with that Mattie Campbell. Now you talking about running away with me.

JEREMY. I was just keeping her company 'cause she lonely. You ain't the lonely kind. You the kind that know what she want and how to get it. I need a woman like you to travel around with. Don't you wanna travel around and look at some places with Jeremy? With a woman like you beside him, a man can make it nice in the world.

MOLLY. Moll can make it nice by herself too. Molly don't need nobody leave her cold in hand. The world rough enough as it is.

JEREMY. We can make it better together. I got my guitar and I can play. Won me another dollar last night playing guitar. We can go around and I can play at the dances and we can just enjoy life. You can make it by yourself alright, I agrees with that. A woman like you can make it anywhere she go. But you can make it better if you got a man to protect you.

MOLLY. What places you wanna go around and look at?

JEREMY. All of them! I don't want to miss nothing. I wanna go everywhere and do everything there is to be got out of life. With a woman like you it's like having water and berries. A man got everything he need.

MOLLY. You got to be doing more than playing that guitar. A dollar a day ain't hardly what Molly got in mind.

JEREMY. I gambles real good. I got a hand for it.

MOLLY. Molly don't work. And Molly ain't up for sale.

JEREMY. Sure, baby. You ain't got to work with Jeremy.

MOLLY. There's one more thing.

JEREMY. What's that, sugar?

MOLLY. Molly ain't going South.

[*The lights go down on the scene.*]

SCENE II

The lights come up on the parlor. Seth and Bynum sit playing a game of dominoes. Bynum sings to himself.

BYNUM [*Singing*].

They tell me Joe Turner's come and gone
Ohhh Lordy

> They tell me Joe Turner's come and gone
> Ohhh Lordy
> Got my man and gone
>
> Come with forty links of chain
> Ohhh Lordy
> Come with forty links of chain
> Ohhh Lordy
> Got my man and gone

SETH. Come on and play if you gonna play.

BYNUM. I'm gonna play. Soon as I figure out what to do.

SETH. You can't figure out if you wanna play or you wanna sing.

BYNUM. Well sir, I'm gonna do a little bit of both.

[*Playing.*]

There. What you gonna do now?

[*Singing.*]

> They tell me Joe Turner's come and gone
> Ohhh Lordy
> They tell me Joe Turner's come and gone
> Ohhh Lordy

SETH. Why don't you hush up that noise.

BYNUM. That's a song the women sing down around Memphis. The women down there made up that song. I picked it up down there about fifteen years ago.

[*Loomis enters from the front door.*]

BYNUM. Evening, Mr. Loomis.

SETH. Today's Monday, Mr. Loomis. Come Saturday your time is up. We done ate already. My wife roasted up some yams. She got your plate sitting in there on the table. [*To Bynum.*] Whose play is it?

BYNUM. Ain't you keeping up with the game? I thought you was a domino player. I just played so it got to be your turn.

[*Loomis goes into the kitchen, where a plate of yams is covered and set on the table. He sits down and begins to eat with his hands.*]

SETH [*Plays*]. Twenty! Give me twenty! You didn't know I had that ace five. You was trying to play around that. You didn't know I had that lying there for you.

BYNUM. You ain't done nothing. I let you have that to get mine.

SETH. Come on and play. You ain't doing nothing but talking. I got a hundred and forty points to your eighty. You ain't doing nothing but talking. Come on and play.

BYNUM [*Singing*].

> They tell me Joe Turner's come and gone
> Ohhh Lordy
> They tell me Joe Turner's come and gone
> Ohhh Lordy
> Got my man and gone
>
> He come with fory links of chain
> Ohhh Lordy

LOOMIS. Why you singing that song? Why you singing about Joe Turner?

BYNUM. I'm just singing to entertain myself.

SETH. You trying to distract me. That's what you trying to do.

BYNUM [*Singing*].

> Come with forty links of chain
> Ohhh Lordy
> Come with forty links of chain
> Ohhh Lordy

LOOMIS. I don't like you singing that song, mister!

SETH. Now, I ain't gonna have no more disturbance around here, Herald Loomis. You start any more disturbance and you leavin' here, Saturday or no Saturday.

BYNUM. The man ain't causing no disturbance, Seth. He just say he don't like the song.

SETH. Well, we all friendly folk. All neighborly like. Don't have no squabbling around here. Don't have no disturbance. You gonna have to take that some-place else.

BYNUM. He just say he don't like the song. I done sung a whole lot of songs people don't like. I respect everybody. He here in the house too. If he don't like the song, I'll sing something else. I know lots of songs. You got "I Belong to the Band," "Don't You Leave Me Here." You got "Praying on the Old Campground," "Keep your Lamp Trimmed and Burning" . . . I know lots of songs.

[*Sings.*]

> Boys, I'll be so glad when payday come

> Captain, Captain, when payday comes
> Gonna catch that Illinois Central
> Going to Kankakee

SETH. Why don't you hush up that hollering and come on and play dominoes.

BYNUM. You ever been to Johnstown, Herald Loomis? You look like a fellow I seen around there.

LOOMIS. I don't know no place with that name.

BYNUM. That's around where I seen my shiny man. See, you looking for this woman. I'm looking for a shiny man. Seem like everybody looking for something.

SETH. I'm looking for you to come and play these dominoes. That's what I'm looking for.

BYNUM. You a farming man, Herald Loomis? You look like you done some farming.

LOOMIS. Same as everybody. I done farmed some, yeah.

BYNUM. I used to work at farming . . . picking cotton. I reckon everybody done picked some cotton.

SETH. I ain't! I ain't never picked no cotton. I was born up here in the North. My daddy was a freedman. I ain't never even seen no cotton!

BYNUM. Mr. Loomis done picked some cotton. Ain't you, Herald Loomis? You done picked a bunch of cotton.

LOOMIS. How you know so much about me? How you know what I done? How much cotton I picked?

BYNUM. I can tell from looking at you. My daddy taught me how to do that. Say when you look at a fellow, if you taught yourself to look for it, you can see his song written on him. Tell you what kind of man he is in the world. Now, I can look at you, Mr. Loomis, and see you a man who done forgot his song. Forgot how to sing it. A fellow forget that and he forget who he is. Forget how he's supposed to mark down life. Now, I used to travel all up and down this road and that . . . looking here and there. Searching. Just like you, Mr. Loomis. I didn't know what I was searching for. The only thing I knew was something was keeping me dissatisfied. Something wasn't making my heart smooth and easy. Then one day my daddy gave me a song. That song had a weight to it that was hard to handle. That song was hard to carry. I fought against it. Didn't want to accept that song. I tried to find my daddy to give him back the song. But I found out it wasn't his song. It was my song. It had come from way deep inside me. I looked long back in memory and gathered up pieces and snatches of things to make that song. I was making it up out of myself. And that song helped me on the road. Made it smooth to where my footsteps didn't bite back at me. All the time that song getting bigger and bigger. That song growing with each step of the road. It got so I used all of myself up in the making of that song. Then I was the song in search of itself. That song rattling in my throat and I'm looking for it. See, Mr. Loomis, when a man forgets his song he goes off in search of it . . . till he find out he's got it with him all the time. That's why I can tell you one of Joe Turner's niggers. 'Cause you forgot how to sing your song.

LOOMIS. You lie! How you see that? I got a mark on me? Joe Turner done marked me to where you can see it? You telling me I'm a marked man. What kind of mark you got on you?

[Bynum begins singing.]

BYNUM.

> They tell me Joe Turner's come and gone
> Ohhh Lordy
> They tell me Joe Turner's come and gone
> Ohhh Lordy
> Got my man and gone

LOOMIS. Had a whole mess of men he catched. Just go out hunting regular like you go out hunting possum. He catch you and go home to his wife and family. Ain't thought about you going home to yours. Joe Turner catched me when my little girl was just born. Wasn't nothing but a little baby sucking on her mama's titty when he catched me. Joe Turner catched me in nineteen hundred and one. Kept me seven years until nineteen hundred and eight. Kept everybody seven years. He'd go out hunting and bring back forty men at a time. And kept them seven years.

I was walking down this road in this little town outside of Memphis. Come up on these fellows gambling. I was a deacon in the Abundant Life Church. I stopped to preach to these fellows to see if maybe I could turn some of them from their sinning when Joe Turner, brother of the Governor of the great sovereign state of Tennessee, swooped down on us and grabbed everybody there. Kept us all seven years.

My wife Martha gone from me after Joe Turner catched me. Got out from under Joe Turner on his birthday. Me and forty other men put in our seven years and he let us go on his birthday. I made it back to Henry Thompson's place where me and

Martha was sharecropping and Martha's gone. She taken my little girl and left her with her mama and took off North. We been looking for her ever since. That's been going on four years now we been looking. That's the only thing I know to do. I just wanna see her face so I can get me a starting place in the world. The world got to start somewhere. That's what I been looking for. I been wandering a long time in somebody else's world. When I find my wife that be the making of my own.

BYNUM. Joe Turner tell why he caught you? You ever asked him that?

LOOMIS. I ain't never seen Joe Turner. Seen him to where I could touch him. I asked one of them fellows one time why he catch niggers. Asked him what I got he want? Why don't he keep on to himself? Why he got to catch me going down the road by my lonesome? He told me I was worthless. Worthless is something you throw away. Something you don't bother with. I ain't seen him throw me away. Wouldn't even let me stay away when I was by my lonesome. I ain't tried to catch him when he going down the road. So I must got something he want. What I got?

SETH. He just want you to do his work for him. That's all.

LOOMIS. I can look at him and see where he big and strong enough to do his own work. So it can't be that. He must want something he ain't got.

BYNUM. That ain't hard to figure out. What he wanted was your song. He wanted to have that song to be his. He thought by catching you he could learn that song. Every nigger he catch he's looking for the one he can learn that song from. Now he's got you bound up to where you can't sing your own song. Couldn't sing it them seven years 'cause you was afraid he would snatch it from under you. But you still got it. You just forgot how to sing it.

LOOMIS [To Bynum]. I know who you are. You one of them bones people.

[The lights go down to black.]

SCENE III

The lights come up on the kitchen. It is the following morning. Mattie, and Bynum, sit at the table. Bertha busies herself at the stove.

BYNUM. Good luck don't know no special time to come. You sleep with that up under your pillow and good luck can't help but come to you. Sometimes it come and go and you don't even know it's been there.

BERTHA. Bynum, why don't you leave that gal alone? She don't wanna be hearing all that. Why don't you go on and get out the way and leave her alone?

BYNUM [Getting up]. Alright, alright. But you mark what I'm saying. It'll draw it to you just like a magnet.

[Bynum exits up the stairs and Loomis enters.]

BERTHA. I got some grits here, Mr. Loomis.

[Bertha sets a bowl on the table.]

If I was you, Mattie, I wouldn't go getting all tied up with Bynum in that stuff. That kind of stuff, even if it do work for a while, it don't last. That just get people more mixed up than they is already. And I wouldn't waste my time fretting over Jeremy either. I seen it coming. I seen it when she first come here. She that kind of woman run off with the first man got a dollar to spend on her. Jeremy just young. He don't know what he getting into. That gal don't mean him no good. She's just using him to keep from being by herself. That's the worst use of a man you can have. You ought to be glad to wash him out of your hair. I done seen all kind of men. I done seen them come and go through here. Jeremy ain't had enough to him for you. You need a man who's got some understanding and who willing to work with that understanding to come to the best he can. You got your time coming. You just tries too hard and can't understand why it don't work for you. Trying to figure it out don't do nothing but give you a troubled mind. Don't no man want a woman with a troubled mind.

You get all that trouble off your mind and just when it look like you ain't never gonna find what you want . . . you look up and it's standing right there. That's how I met my Seth. You gonna look up one day and find everything you want standing right in front of you. Been twenty-seven years now since that happened to me. But life ain't no happy-go-lucky time where everything be just like you want it. You got your time coming. You watch what Bertha's saying.

[Seth enters.]

SETH. Ho!

BERTHA. What you doing come in here so late?

SETH. I was standing down there on Logan Street talking with the fellows. Henry Allen tried to sell me that old piece of horse he got.

[*He sees Loomis.*]

Today's Tuesday, Mr. Loomis.

BERTHA [*Pulling him toward the bedroom*]. Come on in here and leave that man alone to eat his breakfast.

SETH. I ain't bothering nobody. I'm just reminding him what day it is.

[*Seth and Bertha exit into the bedroom.*]

LOOMIS. That dress got a color to it.

MATTIE. Did you really see them things like you said? Them people come up out the ocean?

LOOMIS. It happened just like that, yeah.

MATTIE. I hope you find your wife. It be good for your little girl for you to find her.

LOOMIS. Got to find her for myself. Find my starting place in the world. Find me a world I can fit in.

MATTIE. I ain't never found no place for me to fit. Seem like all I do is start over. It ain't nothing to find no starting place in the world. You just start from where you find yourself.

LOOMIS. Got to find my wife. That be my starting place.

MATTIE. What if you don't find her. What you gonna do then if you don't find her?

LOOMIS. She out there somewhere. Ain't no such thing as not finding her.

MATTIE. How she got lost from you? Jack just walked away from me.

LOOMIS. Joe Turner split us up. Joe Turner turned the world upside-down. He bound me on to him for seven years.

MATTIE. I hope you find her. It be good for you to find her.

LOOMIS. I been watching you. I been watching you watch me.

MATTIE. I was just trying to figure out if you seen things like you said.

LOOMIS [*Getting up*]. Come here and let me touch you. I been watching you. You a full woman. A man needs a full woman. Come on and be with me.

MATTIE. I ain't got enough for you. You'd use me up too fast.

LOOMIS. Herald Loomis got a mind seem like you a part of it since I first seen you. It's been a long time since I seen a full woman. I can smell you from here. I know you got Herald Loomis on your mind, can't keep him apart from it. Come on and be with Herald Loomis.

[*Loomis has crossed to Mattie. He touches her awkwardly, gently, tenderly. Inside he howls like a lost wolf pup whose hunger is deep. He goes to touch her but finds he cannot.*]

I done forgot how to touch.

[*The lights fade to black*].

SCENE IV

It is early the next morning. The lights come up on Zonia and Reuben in the yard.

REUBEN. Something spookly going on around here. Last night Mr. Bynum was out in the yard singing and talking to the wind . . . and the wind it just be talking back to him. Did you hear it?

ZONIA. I heard it. I was scared to get up and look. I thought it was a storm.

REUBEN. That wasn't no storm. That was Mr. Bynum. First he say something . . . and the wind it say back to him.

ZONIA. I heard it. Was you scared? I was scared.

REUBEN. And then this morning . . . I seen Miss Mabel!

ZONIA. Who Miss Mabel?

REUBEN. Mr. Seth's mother. He got her picture hanging up in the house. She been dead.

ZONIA. How you seen her if she been dead?

REUBEN. Zonia . . . if I tell you something you promise you won't tell anybody?

ZONIA. I promise.

REUBEN. It was early this morning . . . I went out to the coop to feed the pigeons. I was down on the ground like this to open up the door to the coop . . . when all of a sudden I seen some feets in front of me. I looked up . . . and there was Miss Mabel standing there.

ZONIA. Reuben, you better stop telling that! You ain't seen nobody!

REUBEN. Naw, it's the truth. I swear! I seen her just like I see you. Look . . . you can see where she hit me with her cane.

ZONIA. Hit you? What she hit you for?

REUBEN. She says, "Didn't you promise Eugene something?" Then she hit me with her cane. She say, "Let them pigeons go." Then she hit me again. That's what made them marks.

ZONIA. Jeez man . . . get away from me. You done see a haunt!

REUBEN. Shhhh. You promised, Zonia!

ZONIA. You sure it wasn't Miss Bertha come over there and hit you with her hoe?

REUBEN. It wasn't no Miss Bertha. I told you it was Miss Mabel. She was standing right there by the coop. She had this light coming out of her and then she just melted away.

ZONIA. What she had on?

REUBEN. A white dress. Ain't even had no shoes or nothing. Just had on that white dress and them big hands . . . and that cane she hit me with.

ZONIA. How you reckon she knew about the pigeons? You reckon Eugene told her?

REUBEN. I don't know. I sure ain't asked her none. She say Eugene was waiting on them pigeons. Say he couldn't go back home till I let them go. I couldn't get the door to the coop open fast enough.

ZONIA. Maybe she an angel? From the way you say she look with that white dress. Maybe she an angel.

REUBEN. Mean as she was . . . how she gonna be an angel? She used to chase us out her yard and frown up and look evil all the time.

ZONIA. That don't mean she can't be no angel 'cause of how she looked and 'cause she wouldn't let no kids play in her yard. It go by if you got any spots on your heart and if you pray and go to church.

REUBEN. What about she hit me with her cane? An angel wouldn't hit me with her cane.

ZONIA. I don't know. She might. I still say she was an angel.

REUBEN. You reckon Eugene the one who sent old Miss Mabel?

ZONIA. Why he send her? Why he don't come himself?

REUBEN. Figured if he send her maybe that'll make me listen. 'Cause she old.

ZONIA. What you think it feel like?

REUBEN. What?

ZONIA. Being dead.

REUBEN. Like being sleep only you don't know nothing and can't move no more.

ZONIA. If Miss Mabel can come back . . . then maybe Eugene can come back too.

REUBEN. We can go down to the hideout like we used to! He could come back everyday! It be just like he ain't dead.

ZONIA. Maybe that ain't right for him to come back. Feel kinda funny to be playing games with a haunt.

REUBEN. Yeah . . . what if everybody came back? What if Miss Mabel came back just like she ain't dead? Where you and your daddy gonna sleep then?

ZONIA. Maybe they go back at night and don't need no place to sleep.

REUBEN. It still don't seem right. I'm sure gonna miss Eugene. He's the bestest friend anybody ever had.

ZONIA. My daddy say if you miss somebody too much it can kill you. Say he missed me till it liked to killed him.

REUBEN. What if your mama's already dead and all the time you looking for her?

ZONIA. Naw, she ain't dead. My daddy say he can smell her.

REUBEN. You can't smell nobody that ain't here. Maybe he smelling old Miss Bertha. Maybe Miss Bertha your mama?

ZONIA. Naw, she ain't. My mama got long pretty hair and she five feet from the ground!

REUBEN. Your daddy say when you leaving?

[Zonia doesn't respond.]

Maybe you gonna stay in Mr. Seth's house and don't go looking for your mama no more.

ZONIA. He says we got to leave on Saturday.

REUBEN. Dag! You just only been here for a little while. Don't seem like nothing ever stay the same.

ZONIA. He say he got to find her. Find him a place in the world.

REUBEN. He could find him a place in Mr. Seth's house.

ZONIA. It don't look like we never gonna find her.

REUBEN. Maybe he find her by Saturday then you don't have to go.

ZONIA. I don't know.

REUBEN. You look like a spider!

ZONIA. I ain't no spider!

REUBEN. Got them long skinny arms and legs. You look like one of them Black Widows.

ZONIA. I ain't no Black Window nothing! My name is Zonia!

REUBEN. That's what I'm gonna call you . . . Spider.

ZONIA. You can call me that, but I don't have to answer.

REUBEN. You know what? I think maybe I be your husband when I grow up.

ZONIA. How you know?

REUBEN. I ask my grandpap how you know and he say

when the moon falls into a girl's eyes that how you know.

ZONIA. Did it fall into my eyes?

REUBEN. Not that I can tell. Maybe I ain't old enough. Maybe you ain't old enough.

ZONIA. So there! I don't know why you telling me that lie!

REUBEN. That don't mean nothing 'cause I can't see it. I know it's there. Just the way you look at me sometimes look like the moon might have been in your eyes.

ZONIA. That don't mean nothing if you can't see it. You supposed to see it.

REUBEN. Shucks, I see it good enough for me. You ever let anybody kiss you?

ZONIA. Just my daddy. He kiss me on the cheek.

REUBEN. It's better on the lips. Can I kiss you on the lips?

ZONIA. I don't know. You ever kiss anybody before?

REUBEN. I had a cousin let me kiss her on the lips one time. Can I kiss you?

ZONIA. Okay.

[Reuben kisses her and lays his head against her chest.]

What are you doing?

REUBEN. Listening. Your heart singing!

ZONIA. It is not.

REUBEN. Just beating like a drum. Let's kiss again.

[They kiss again.]

Now you mine, Spider. You my girl, okay?

ZONIA. Okay.

REUBEN. When I get grown, I come looking for you.

ZONIA. Okay.

[The lights fade to black.]

SCENE V

The lights come up on the kitchen. It is Saturday. Bynum, Loomis, and Zonia sit at the table. Bertha prepares breakfast. Zonia has on a white dress.

BYNUM. With all this rain we been having he might have ran into some washed-out roads. If that wagon got stuck in the mud he's liable to be still upriver somewhere. If he's upriver than he ain't coming until tomorrow.

LOOMIS. Today's Saturday. He say he be here on Saturday.

BERTHA. Zonia, you gonna eat your breakfast this morning.

ZONIA. Yes, ma'am.

BERTHA. I don't know how you expect to get any bigger if you don't eat. I ain't never seen a child that didn't eat. You about as skinny as a bean pole.

[Pause.]

Mr. Loomis, there's a place down on Wylie. Zeke Mayweather got a house down there. You ought to see if he got any rooms.

[Loomis doesn't respond.]

Well, you're welcome to some breakfast before you move on.

[Mattie enters from the stairs.]

MATTIE. Good morning.

BERTHA. Morning, Mattie. Sit on down there and get you some breakfast.

BYNUM. Well, Mattie Campbell, you been sleeping with that up under your pillow like I told you?

BERTHA. Bynum, I done told you to leave that gal alone with all that stuff. You around here meddling in other people's lives. She don't want to hear all that. You ain't doing nothing but confusing her with that stuff.

MATTIE [To Loomis]. You all fixing to move on?

LOOMIS. Today's Saturday. I'm paid up till Saturday.

MATTIE. Where you going to?

LOOMIS. Gonna find my wife.

MATTIE. You going off to another city?

LOOMIS. We gonna see where the road take us. Ain't no telling where we wind up.

MATTIE. Eleven years is a long time. Your wife . . . she might have taken up with someone else. People do that when they get lost from each other.

LOOMIS. Zonia. Come on, we gonna find your mama.

[Loomis and Zonia cross to the door.]

MATTIE [To Zonia]. Zonia, Mattie got a ribbon here match your dress. Want Mattie to fix your hair with her ribbon?

[Zonia nods. Mattie ties the ribbon in her hair.]

There . . . it got a color just like your dress. [To Loomis.] I hope you find her. I hope you be happy.

LOOMIS. A man looking for a woman be lucky to find you. You a good woman, Mattie. Keep a good heart.

[*Loomis and Zonia exit.*]

BERTHA. I been watching that man for two weeks . . . and that's the closest I come to seeing him act civilized. I don't know what's between you all, Mattie . . . but the only thing that man needs is somebody to make him laugh. That's all you need in the world is love and laughter. That's all anybody needs. To have love in one hand and laughter in the other.

[*Bertha moves about the kitchen as though blessing it and chasing away the huge sadness that seems to envelop it. It is a dance and demonstration of her own magic, her own remedy that is centuries old and to which she is connected by the muscles of her heart and the blood's memory.*]

You hear me, Mattie? I'm talking about laughing. The kind of laugh that comes from the way deep inside. To just stand and laugh and let life flow right through you. Just laugh to let yourself know you're alive.

[*She begins to laugh. It is a near-hysterical laughter that is a celebration of life, both its pain and its blessing. Mattie and Bynum join in the laughter. Seth enters from the front door.*]

SETH. Well, I see you all having fun.

[*Seth begins to laugh with them.*]

That Loomis fellow standing up there on the corner watching the house. He standing right up there on Manila Street.

BERTHA. Don't you get started on him. The man done left out of here and that's the last I wanna hear of it. You about to drive me crazy with that man.

SETH. I just say he standing up there on the corner. Acting sneaky like he always do. He can stand up there all he want. As long as he don't come back in here.

[*There is a knock on the door. Seth goes to answer it. Enter Martha Loomis [Pentecost.] She is a young woman about twenty-eight. She is dressed as befitting a member of an Evangelist church. Rutherford Selig follows.*]

SETH. Look here, Bertha. It's Martha Pentecost. Come on in, Martha. Who that with you? Oh . . . that's Selig. Come on in, Selig.

BERTHA. Come on in, Martha. It's sure good to see you.

BYNUM. Rutherford Selig, you a sure enough first-class People Finder!

SELIG. She was right out there in Rankin. You take that first righthand road . . . right there at that church on Wooster Street. I started to go right past and something told me to stop at the church and see if they needed any dustpans.

SETH. Don't she look good, Bertha.

BERTHA. Look all nice and healthy.

MARTHA. Mr. Bynum . . . Selig told me my little girl was here.

SETH. There's some fellow around here say he your husband. Say his name is Loomis. Say you his wife.

MARTHA. Is my little girl with him?

SETH. Yeah, he got a little girl with him. I wasn't gonna tell him where you was. Not the way this fellow look. So he got Selig to find you.

MARTHA. Where they at? They upstairs?

SETH. He was standing right up there on Manila Street. I had to ask him to leave 'cause of how he was carrying on. He come in here one night—

[*The door opens and Loomis and Zonia enter. Martha and Loomis stare at each other.*]

LOOMIS. Hello, Martha.

MARTHA. Herald . . . Zonia?

LOOMIS. You ain't waited for me, Martha. I got out the place looking to see your face. Seven years I waited to see your face.

MARTHA. Herald, I been looking for you. I wasn't but two months behind you when you went to my mama's and got Zonia. I been looking for you ever since.

LOOMIS. Joe Turner let me loose and I felt all turned around inside. I just wanted to see your face to know that the world was still there. Make sure everything still in its place so I could reconnect myself together. I got there and you was gone, Martha.

MARTHA. Herald . . .

LOOMIS. Left my little girl motherless in the world.

MARTHA. I didn't leave her motherless, Herald. Reverend Tolliver wanted to move the church up North 'cause of all the trouble the colored folks was having down there. Nobody knew what was gonna happen traveling them roads. We didn't even know if we was gonna make it up here or not. I left her with my mama so she be safe. That was better than dragging her out on the road having to duck and hide from people. Wasn't no telling what was gonna happen to us. I didn't leave her motherless in the world. I been looking for you.

LOOMIS. I come up on Henry Thompson's place after seven years of living in hell, and all I'm looking to do is see your face.

MARTHA. Herald, I didn't know if you was ever coming back. They told me Joe Turner had you and my whole world split half in two. My whole life shattered. It was like I had poured it in a cracked jar and it all leaked out the bottom. When it go like that there ain't nothing you can do it back together. You talking about Henry Thompson's place like I'm still gonna be working the land by myself. How I'm gonna do that? You wasn't gone but two months and Henry Thompson kicked me off his land and I ain't had no place to go but to my mama's. I stayed and waited there for five years before I woke up one morning and decided that you was dead. Even if you weren't, you was dead to me. I wasn't gonna carry you with me no more. So I killed you in my heart. I buried you. I mourned you. And then I picked up what was left and went on to make life without you. I was a young woman with life at my beckon. I couldn't drag you behind me like a sack of cotton.

LOOMIS. I just been waiting to look on your face to say my goodbye. That goodbye got so big at times, seem like it was gonna swallow me up. Like Jonah in the whale's belly I sat up in that goodbye for three years. That goodbye kept me out on the road searching. Not looking on women in their houses. It kept me bound up to the road. All the time that goodbye swelling up in my chest till I'm about to bust. Now that I see your face I can say my goodbye and make my own world.

[*Loomis takes Zonia's hand and presents her to Martha.*]

Martha . . . here go your daughter. I tried to take care of her. See that she had something to eat. See that she was out of the elements. Whatever I know I tried to teach her. Now she need to learn from her mother whatever you got to teach her. That way she won't be no one-sided person.

[*Loomis stoops to Zonia.*]

Zonia, you go live with your mama. She a good woman. You go on with her and listen to her good. You my daughter and I love you like a daughter. I hope to see you again in the world somewhere. I'll never forget you.

ZONIA [*Throws her arms around Loomis in a panic*]. I won't get no bigger! My bones won't get no bigger! They won't! I promise! Take me with you till we keep searching and never finding. I won't get no bigger! I promise!

LOOMIS. Go on and do what I told you now.

MARTHA [*Goes to Zonia and comforts her*]. It's alright, baby. Mama's here. Mama's here. Don't worry. Don't cry.

[*Martha turns to Bynum.*]

Mr. Bynum, I don't know how to thank you. God bless you.

LOOMIS. It was you! All the time it was you that bind me up! You bound me to the road!

BYNUM. I ain't bind you, Herald Loomis. You can't bind what don't cling.

LOOMIS. Everywhere I go people wanna bind me up. Joe Turner wanna bind me up! Reverend Tolliver wanna bind me up. You wanna bind me up. Everybody wanna bind me up. Well, Joe Turner's come and gone and Herald Loomis ain't for no binding. I ain't gonna let nobody bind me up!

[*Loomis pulls out a knife.*]

BYNUM. It wasn't you, Herald Loomis. I ain't bound you. I bound the little girl to her mother. That's who I bound. You binding yourself. You bound onto your song. All you got to do is stand up and sing it, Herald Loomis. It's right there kicking at your throat. All you got to do is sing it. Then you be free.

MARTHA. Herald . . . look at yourself! Standing there with a knife in your hand. You done gone over to the devil. Come on . . . put down the knife. You got to look to Jesus. Even if you done fell away from the church you can be saved again. The Bible say, "The Lord is my shepherd I shall not want. He maketh me to lie down in green pastures. He leads me beside the still water. He restoreth my soul. He leads me in the path of righteousness for His name's sake. Even though I walk through the shadow of death—"

LOOMIS. That's just where I be walking!

MARTHA. "I shall fear no evil. For Thou art with me. Thy rod and thy staff, they comfort me."

LOOMIS. You can't tell me nothing about no valleys. I done been all across the valleys and the hills and the mountains and the oceans.

MARTHA. "Thou preparest a table for me in the presence of my enemies."

LOOMIS. And all I seen was a bunch of niggers dazed

out of their woolly heads. And Mr. Jesus Christ standing there in the middle of them, grinning.

MARTHA. "Thou anointest my head with oil, my cup runneth over."

LOOMIS. He grin that big old grin . . . and niggers wallowing at his feet.

MARTHA. "Surely goodness and mercy shall follow me all the days of my life, and I shall dwell in the house of the Lord forever."

LOOMIS. Great big old white man . . . your Mr. Jesus Christ. Standing there with a whip in one hand and tote board in another, and them niggers swimming in a sea of cotton. And he counting. He tallying up the cotton. "Well, Jeremiah . . . what's the matter, you ain't picked but two hundred pounds of cotton today? Got to put you on half rations." And Jeremiah go back and lay up there on his half rations and talk about what a nice man Mr. Jesus Christ is 'cause he give him salvation after he die. Something wrong here. Something don't fit right!

MARTHA. You got to open up your heart and have faith, Herald. This world is just a trial for the next. Jesus offers you salvation.

LOOMIS. I been wading in the water. I been walking all over the River Jordan. But what it get me, huh? I done been baptized with blood of the lamb and the fire of the Holy Ghost. But what I got, huh? I got salvation? My enemies all around me picking the flesh from my bones. I'm choking on my own blood and all you got to give me is salvation?

MARTHA. You got to be clean, Herald. You got to be washed with the blood of the lamb.

LOOMIS. Blood make you clean? You clean with blood?

MARTHA. Jesus bled for you. He's the Lamb of God who takest away the sins of the world.

LOOMIS. I don't need nobody to bleed for me! I can bleed for myself.

MARTHA. You got to be something, Herald. You just can't be alive. Life don't mean nothing unless it got a meaning.

LOOMIS. What kind of meaning you got? What kind of clean you got, woman? You want blood? Blood make you clean? You clean with blood?

[Loomis slashes himself across the chest. He rubs the blood over his face and comes to a realization.]

I'm standing! I'm standing. My legs stood up! I'm standing now!

[Having found his song, the song of self-sufficiency, fully resurrected, cleansed and given breath, free from any encumbrance other than the workings of his own heart and the bonds of the flesh, having accepted the responsibility for his own presence in the world, he is free to soar above the environs that weighed and pushed his spirit into terrifying contractions.]

Goodbye, Martha.

[Loomis turns and exits, the knife still in his hands. Mattie looks about the room and rushes out after him.]

BYNUM. Herald Loomis, you shining! You shining like new money!

[The lights go down to black.]

ESSAY: AN APPROACH TO THE PLAY

Geographical and temporal ruptures permeate the lives of all the characters at the boarding house (although that of Loomis especially), apparently a sign of the spiritual and cultural displacement which each of them needs to confront. It is a common figure of speech to speak of one's life as a journey along a road from cradle to grave. Herald Loomis finds himself, however—and presumably Wilson wants this to speak to an aspect of the African-American experience in general—on a road he did not choose. As suggested at the end of Act 1 in his vision of the bones walking on the water, Loomis is a descendant of the middle passage, of people cast on this shore against their wills. His own parents were presumably slaves, and even though it would have been nearly four decades after emancipation, he also was snatched from the path he had chosen for himself by Joe Turner. Little wonder that he finds himself, in the words of the stage direction in which Wilson introduces him, "driven . . . by his search for a world that speaks to something about himself," "unable to harmonize the forces that swirl around him," seeking "to recreate the world into one that contains his image."

If the play's focus on roads implies the need to discover or recover a sense of direction, this stage direction's metaphorical use of the musical term "harmonize" suggests another of the play's consititutive metaphors: the need to find one's own song. As is typical of literary symbolism, the exact nature of this song resists easy summary: Its meaning is contained within, and circumscribed by, its context. The play presents a great range of music, including the communal Juba which the characters perform near the end of Act 1, the guitar contest which Jeremy wins, the "Joe Turner" song that Bynum sings, the magic song that Mattie wants from Bynum that would bring her man back. None of these are like the song which each person sings uniquely and which seems to be simultaneously a performed expression of identity and of independence, of self-acceptance and of autonomy. Apparently it does not have to be literally sung: Loomis' final gesture of self-laceration and cleansing leads him to proclaims: "I'm standing! I'm standing. My legs stood up! I'm standing now!" The stage direction following this seems to provide an authorial interpretation: "Having found his song, the song of self-sufficiency, . . . he is free to soar above the environs that weighed and pushed his spirit into terrifying contractions." (This concluding scene also counters and fulfills the conclusion of Act 1, where, after Loomis and Bynum, in call-and-response fashion, proclaim the vision of the bones, Loomis is unable to stand.)

When Bynum describes his vision, in which he claims to have learned "the Secret of Life," he says that his father was grieved to see him "carrying other people's songs and not having one of his own." Bynum later tells Loomis that, if you know what to look for, you can see a fellow's song written on him, and he specifies the relationship of this song to one's authenticity or identity: "Now, I can look at you Mr. Loomis, and see you a fellow who done forgot his song. Forgot how to sing it. A fellow forget that and he forget who he is. Forget how he's supposed to mark down life." Once he finds his song, Loomis becomes what Bynum has been seeking: the Shiny Man. You will find these ideas reframed and nuanced at many other moments in the play. These suggestions are intended to point you back to the text to seek them out.

Bynum's traditional spirituality stands in counterpoint in the last scene to Martha's evangelical Christianity, and in the first scene to Seth's entrepreneurial aspirations. Selig mediates these oppositions. He finds Martha and brings her to the boarding house for the play's final encounter, and in the first scene he has separate business arrangements, with Seth to find customers for his dustpans and with Bynum to find the Shiny Man. All of the characters seem to be seeking some kind of freedom, whether it is spiritual freedom or free enterprise, a way to find an individual place in what for them is a new world.

Perhaps partly to allow this breadth of possibility, *Joe Turner*, like others of Wilson's plays, blurs the lines between the natural and the preternatural. It is never clear whether Bynum has "real" spiritual power or whether his role is to help people realize their own inner strength. What matters is his effectiveness and his affirmation of a dimension of mystery within each of us that requires respect and nurturing.

Bynum's role seems paradoxical in another way as well, one implied by his name: His is a song of binding, but one which frees. He helps things bind (at least when they already "cling"), and in bringing together what ought to be bound, he apparently liberates people from the false relationships and commitments which seem to have been imposed upon them. Bynum seems to stand as a reproach to those who would hinder a person's self-determination.

The complexity with which the play elaborates these concepts is a reminder that August Wilson began his writing career as a poet; his dramatic works display a poet's love of language. In addition to exploring questions about the meaning of freedom and its relation to binding (remember that Loomis had been "bound" to Joe Turner in a way very different from Bynum's binding), the play explores what it means to be "lost" or "found." Can a People Finder truly find someone, or can one only find oneself? The relationship of blood to rituals of spiritual power and cleansing also recur throughout the play, from the first scene with its pigeon sacrifice to the last with Martha's invocation of the blood of the lamb, to Loomis' idiosyncratic gesture of "cleansing." Traditional images of the Holy Spirit recur throughout a play that seems ultimately to affirm an alternative spirituality: The pigeon is near cousin to the dove, a traditional image of the Spirit, as is the wind which breathes life into Loomis in his vision at the end of Act 1. Reuben, in the play's next-to-last scene, tells of having heard Bynum speaking with the wind, and the characters dancing the Juba invoke the Spirit, leading to Loomis' interruption. As with the "poetic drama" of writers such as Sophocles, Shakespeare, and Ibsen (who, like Wilson, wrote poetic drama in prose), Wilson's plays need to be reread if you are to "get" the complex tonalities of his language.

Marsha Norman

GETTING OUT

About the Author   A native of Louisville, Marsha Norman (1947–   ) graduated from Agnes Scott College in 1969 and earned a master's degree from the University of Louisville in 1971 before teaching, working with disturbed children, and serving as book editor and reviewer for the *Louisville Times*. *Getting Out*, her first play, won the New Playwrights Medallion and the Outer Critics Circle Award for 1977. Norman's fifth play, *'Night Mother*, received the Susan Smith Blackburn Prize in 1982 and the Pulitzer Prize for drama in 1983; it has been made into a film. Norman continues to write plays and in 1987 published her first novel, *The Fortune Teller*.

About the Play   Based on her work at the Kentucky State Hospital, *Getting Out* portrays a main character who is always doubly "present": in her past and present selves, each played by a different actress, the two of whom are simultaneously onstage, generally on different parts of the stage. Arlene has recently been released from prison after eight years, much of it in solitary confinement. Her alter ego is Arlie, the young woman she was until very recently; it is her change in character from Arlie to Arlene which has allowed her to be granted a parole. In Arlie, we see—always on stage before us—Arlene's past, what she has changed from, and from this information we come not only to understand Arlene but also to appreciate who she is and the immense journey she has taken to get this far.

    Her journey, however, is not over. When Arlie speaks or acts, it is usually in response to a situation from her life—from Arlene's past life—similar to the one Arlene is currently facing. We are also able to see, therefore, how close her old self was to Arlene's more composed present surface, as well as to compare her present responses to those of the person she was. Her current hardships trigger Arlie's memory, reminding her of how she would have acted in the past. She is different from Arlie, but never far away from her. As Arlie, she was violent, both verbally and physically: she killed one man and thought of killing others. Her rage and frustration were so great that her way of trying to make a change and adopt Christianity was to try to kill herself. In a sense, she succeeded; Arlie died, and she became Arlene. Arlie is always present, however, on the stage and presumably within Arlene's identity. Gradually, through Arlie's words and actions, we learn that the violence she used for survival was simultaneously both necessary and self-destructive. The play presents a world in which economically deprived women are treated brutally, both on the streets and in prison, and we come to some understanding of why Arlie would be so violent and obscene in her attempts to assert herself and to find her own voice. Arlene's apartment is superficially different from Arlie's prison, but there may be even more pressure and less protection in this present life, and perhaps no more opportunity on the outside than on the inside. Arlene's world is frighteningly similar to Arlie's, but Arlene has somehow found a more controlled voice, a more mature way of dealing with it. The constant comparisons between Arlene and Arlie pose the question: in such a brutal world, what is the value of Arlene's alternative to Arlie's violence and self-destruction? If there is an answer, it is not an easy one.

CHARACTERS

ARLENE, a thin, drawn woman in her late twenties who has just served an eight-year prison term for murder.

ARLIE, Arlene at various times earlier in her life.
BENNIE, an Alabama prison guard in his fifties.
GUARD (EVANS).

GUARD (CALDWELL).

DOCTOR, a psychiatrist in a juvenile institution.

MOTHER, Arlene's mother.

SCHOOL PRINCIPAL, female.

RONNIE, a teenager in a juvenile institution.

CARL, Arlene's former pimp and partner in various crimes, in his late twenties.

WARDEN, superintendent of Pine Ridge Correctional Institute for Women.

RUBY, Arlene's upstairs neighbor, a cook in a diner, also an ex-con, in her late thirties.

PLAYWRIGHT'S NOTES

Arlie is the violent kid Arlene was until her last stretch in prison. Arlie may walk through the apartment quite freely, but no one there will acknowledge her presence. Most of her scenes take place in the prison areas.

Arlie, in a sense, is Arlene's memory of herself, called up by fears, needs and even simple word cues. The memory haunts, attacks and warns. But mainly, the memory will not go away.

Arlie's life should be as vivid as Arlene's, if not as continuous. There must be hints in both physical type and gesture that Arlie and Arlene are the same person, though seen at different times in her life. They both speak with a country twang, but Arlene is suspicious and guarded, withdrawal is always a possibility. Arlie is unpredictable and incorrigible. The change seen in Arlie during the second act represents a movement toward the adult Arlene, but the transition should never be complete. Only in the final scene are they enjoyably aware of each other.

The life in the prison "surround" needs to convince without distracting. The guards do not belong to any specific institution, but rather to all the places where Arlene has done time.

Prologue

Beginning five minutes before the houselights come down, the following announcements are broadcast over the loudspeaker. A woman's voice is preferred, a droning tone is essential.

LOUDSPEAKER VOICE. Kitchen workers, all kitchen workers report immediately to the kitchen. Kitchen workers to the kitchen. The library will not be open today. Those scheduled for book checkout should remain in morning work assignments. Kitchen workers to the kitchen. No library hours today. Library hours resume tomorrow as usual. All kitchen workers to the kitchen.

Frances Mills, you have a visitor at the front gate. All residents and staff, all residents and staff . . . . Do not, repeat, do not, walk on the front lawn today or use the picnic tables on the front lawn during your break after lunch or dinner.

Your attention please. The exercise class for Dorm A residents has been cancelled. Mrs. Fischer should be back at work in another month. She thanks you for your cards and wants all her girls to know she had an eight-pound baby girl.

Doris Creech, see Mrs. Adams at the library before lunch. Frances Mills, you have a visitor at the front gate. The Women's Associates' picnic for the beauty school class has been postponed until Friday. As picnic lunches have already been prepared, any beauty school member who so wishes, may pick up a picnic lunch and eat it at her assigned lunch table during the regular lunch period.

Frances Mills, you have a visitor at the front gate. Doris Creech to see Mrs. Adams at the library before lunch. I'm sorry, that's Frankie Hill, you have a visitor at the front gate. Repeat, Frankie Hill, not Frances Mills, you have a visitor at the front gate.

Act I

The play is set in a dingy one-room apartment in a rundown section of downtown Louisville, Kentucky. There is a twin bed and one chair. There is a sink, an apartment-size combination stove and refrigerator, and a counter with cabinets above. Dirty curtains conceal the bars on the outside of the single window. There is one closet and a door to the bathroom. The door to the apartment opens into a hall.

A catwalk stretches above the apartment and a prison cell, stage right, connects to it by stairways. An area downstage and another stage left complete the enclosure of the apartment by playing areas for the past. The apartment must seem imprisoned.

Following the prologue, lights fade to black and the warden's voice is heard on tape.

WARDEN'S VOICE. The Alabama State Parole Board hereby grants parole to Holsclaw, Arlene, subject having served eight years at Pine Ridge Correctional Institute for the second-degree murder of a cab driver in conjunction with a filling station robbery involving attempted kidnapping of attendant. Crime occurred during escape from Lakewood State Prison where subject Holsclaw was serving three years for forgery and prostitution. Extensive juvenile records from the state of Kentucky appended hereto.

[As the warden continues, light comes up on Arlene, walking around the cell, waiting to be picked up for the ride home. Arlie is visible, but just barely, down center.]

WARDEN'S VOICE. Subject now considered completely rehabilitated is returned to Kentucky under interstate parole agreement in consideration of family residence and appropriate support personnel in the area. Subject will remain under the supervision of Kentucky parole officers for a period of five years. Prospects for successful integration into community rated good. Psychological evaluation, institutional history and health records attached in Appendix C, this document.

BENNIE'S VOICE. Arlie!

[Arlene leaves the cell as light comes up on Arlie, seated down center. She tells this story rather simply. She enjoys it, but its horror is not lost on her. She may be doing some semiabsorbing activity such as painting her toenails.]

ARLIE. So, there was this little kid, see, this creepy little fucker next door. Had glasses an somethin' wrong with his foot. I don't know, seven, maybe. Anyhow, ever time his daddy went fishin', he'd bring this kid back some frogs. They built this little fence around 'em in the backyard like they was pets or somethin'. An we'd try to go over an see 'em but he'd start screamin' to his mother to come out an git rid of us. Real snotty like. So we got sick of him bein' such a goody-goody an one night me an June snuck over there an put all his dumb ol' frogs in this sack. You never heared such a fuss. [Makes croaking sounds] Slimy bastards, frogs. We was plannin' to let 'em go all over the place, but when they started jumpin' an all, we just figured they was askin' for it. So, we taken 'em out front to the porch an we throwed 'em, one at a time, into the street. [Laughs] Some of 'em hit cars goin' by but most of 'em jus' got squashed, you know, runned over? It was great, seein' how far we could throw 'em, over back of our backs an under our legs an God, it was really fun watchin' 'em fly through the air then *splat* [Claps hands] all over somebody's car window or somethin'. Then the next day, we was waitin' and this little kid comes out in his backyard lookin' for his stupid frogs and he don't see any an he gets so crazy, cryin' and everything. So me an June goes over an tells him we seen this big mess out in the street, an he goes out an sees all them frogs' legs and bodies an shit all over the everwhere, an, man, it was so funny. We 'bout killed ourselves laughin'. Then his mother come out and she wouldn't let him go out an pick up all the pieces, so he jus' had to stand there watchin' all the cars go by smush his little babies right into the street. I's gonna run out an git him a frog's head, but June yellin' at me "Arlie, git over here fore some car slips on them frog guts an crashes into you." [Pause] I never had so much fun in one day in my whole life.

[*Arlie remains seated as Arlene enters the apartment. It is late evening. Two sets of footsteps are heard coming up the stairs. Arlene opens the door and walks into the room. She stands still, surveying the littered apartment. Bennie is heard dragging a heavy trunk up the stairs. Bennie is wearing his guard uniform. He is a heavy man, but obviously used to physical work.*]

BENNIE [*From outside*]. Arlie?
ARLENE. Arlene.
BENNIE. Arlene? [*Bringing the trunk just inside the door*]
ARLENE. Leave it. I'll git it later.
BENNIE. Oh, now, let me bring it in for you. You ain't as strong as you was.
ARLENE. I ain't as mean as I was. I'm strong as ever. You go on now.

[*Beginning to walk around the room*]

ARLIE [*Irritated, as though someone is calling her*]. Lay off! [*Gets up and walks past Bennie*]
BENNIE [*Scoots the trunk into the room a little further*]. Go on where, Arlie?
ARLENE. I don't know where. How'd I know where you'd be goin'?
BENNIE. I can't go till I know you're gonna do all right.
ARLENE. Look, I'm gonna do all right. I done all right before Pine Ridge, an I done all right at Pine Ridge. An I'm gonna do all right here.
BENNIE. But you don't know nobody. I mean, nobody nice.
ARLENE. Lay off.
BENNIE. Nobody to take care of you.
ARLENE [*Picking up old newspapers and other trash from the floor*]. I kin take care of myself. I been doin' it long enough.
BENNIE. Sure you have, an you landed yourself in prison doin' it, Arlie girl.
ARLENE [*Wheels around*]. Arlie girl landed herself in prison. Arlene is out, okay?
BENNIE. Hey, now, I know we said we wasn't gonna say nuthin' about that, but I been lookin' after you for a long time. I been watchin' you eat your dinner for eight years now. I got used to it, you know!
ARLENE. Well, you kin jus' git unused to it.
BENNIE. Then why'd you ask me to drive you all the way up here?
ARLENE. I didn't, now. That was all your big ideal.
BENNIE. And what were you gonna do? Ride the bus, pick up some soldier, git yourself in another mess of trouble?

[*Arlie struts back into the apartment, speaking as if to a soldier in a bar.*]

ARLIE. Okay, who's gonna buy me a beer?
ARLENE. You oughta go by Fort Knox on your way home.
ARLIE. Fuckin' soldiers, don't care where they get theirself drunk.
ARLENE. You'd like it.
ARLIE. Well, Arlie girl, take your pick.
ARLENE. They got tanks right out on the grass to look at.
ARLIE [*Now appears to lean on a bar rail*]. You git that haircut today, honey?
BENNIE. I just didn't want you given your twenty dollars the warden gave you to the first pusher you come across.

[*Arlie laughs.*]

ARLENE. That's what you think I been waitin' for?

[*A guard appears and motions for Arlie to follow him.*]

ARLIE. Yeah! I heard ya.

[*The guard takes Arlie to the cell and slams the door.*]

BENNIE. But God almighty, I hate to think what you'd done to the first ol' bugger tried to make you in that bus station. You got grit, Arlie girl. I gotta credit you for that.
ARLIE [*From the cell, as she dumps a plate of food on the floor*]. Officer!
BENNIE. The screamin' you'd do. Wake the dead.
ARLENE. Uh huh.
BENNIE [*Proudly*]. An there ain't nobody can beat you for throwin' plates.
ARLIE. Are you gonna clean up this shit or do I have to sit here and look at it till I vomit?

[*A guard comes in to clean it up.*]

BENNIE. Listen, ever prison in Alabama's usin' plastic forks now on account of what you done.
ARLENE. You can quit talkin' just anytime now.
ARLIE. Some life you got, fatso. Bringin' me my dinner then wipin' it off the walls. [*Laughs*]
BENNIE. Some of them officers was pretty leery of you. Even the chaplain.
ARLENE. No he wasn't either.
BENNIE. Not me, though. You was just wild, that's all.

ARLENE. Animals is wild, not people. That's what he said.

ARLIE [*Mocking*]. Good behavior, good behavior. Shit.

BENNIE. Now what could that four-eyes chaplain know about wild? [*Arlene looks up sharply*] Okay. Not wild, then . . .

ARLIE. I kin git outta here anytime I want. [*Leaves the cell*]

BENNIE. But you got grit, Arlie.

ARLENE. I have said for you to call me Arlene.

BENNIE. Okay okay.

ARLENE. Huh?

BENNIE. Don't git riled. You want me to call you Arlene, then Arlene it is. Yes ma'am. Now, [*Slapping the trunk*] where do you want this? [*No response*] Arlene, I said, where do you want this trunk?

ARLENE. I don't care. [*Bennie starts to put it at the foot of the bed*] No! [*Then calmer*] I seen it there too long. [*Bennie is irritated*] Maybe over here. [*Points to a spot near the window*] I could put a cloth on it and sit an look out the . . . [*She pulls the curtains apart, sees the bars on the window*] What's these bars doin' here?

BENNIE [*Stops moving the trunk*]. I think they're to keep out burglars, you know. [*Sits on the trunk*]

ARLENE. Yeah, I know.

[*Arlie appears on the catwalk, as if stopped during a break-in.*]

ARLIE. We ain't breakin' in, cop, we're just admirin' this beautiful window.

ARLENE. I don't want them there. Pull them out.

BENNIE. You can't go tearin' up the place, Arlene. Landlord wouldn't like it.

ARLIE [*To the unseen policeman*]. Maybe I got a brick in my hand and maybe I don't.

BENNIE. Not one bit.

ARLIE. An I'm standin' on this garbage can because I like to, all right?

ARLENE [*Walking back toward Bennie*]. I ain't gonna let no landlord tell me what to do.

BENNIE. The landlord owns the building. You gotta do what he says or he'll throw you out right on your pretty little behind. [*Gives her a familiar pat*]

ARLENE [*Slaps his hand away*]. You watch your mouth. I won't have no dirty talk.

ARLIE. Just shut the fuck up, cop! Go bust a wino or somethin'. [*Returns to the cell*]

ARLENE [*Points down right*]. Here, put the trunk over here.

BENNIE [*Carrying the trunk over to the spot she has picked*]. What you got in here, anyhow? Rocks? Rocks from the rock pile?

ARLENE. That ain't funny.

BENNIE. Oh sweetie, I didn't mean nuthin' by that.

ARLENE. And I ain't your sweetie.

BENNIE. We really did have us a rock pile, you know, at the old men's prison, yes we did. And those boys, time they did nine or ten years carryin' rocks around, they was pretty mean, I'm here to tell you. And strong? God.

ARLENE. Well, what did you expect? [*Beginning to unpack the trunk*]

BENNIE. You're tellin' me. It was dumb, I kept tellin' the warden that. They coulda killed us all, easy, anytime, that outfit. Except, we did have the guns.

ARLENE. Uh-huh.

BENNIE. One old bastard sailed a throwin' rock at me one day, woulda took my eye out if I hadn't turned around just then. Still got the scar, see? [*Reaches up to the back of his head*]

ARLENE. You shoot him?

BENNIE. Nope. Somebody else did. I forget who. Hey! [*Walking over to the window*] These bars won't be so bad. Maybe you could get you some plants so's you don't even see them. Yeah, plants'd do it up just fine. Just fine.

ARLENE [*Pulls a cheaply framed picture of Jesus out of the trunk*]. Chaplain give me this.

BENNIE. He got it for free, I bet.

ARLENE. Now, look here. That chaplain was good to me, so you can shut up about him.

BENNIE [*Backing down*]. Fine. Fine.

ARLENE. Here. [*Handing him the picture*] You might as well be useful fore you go.

BENNIE. Where you want it?

ARLENE. Don't matter.

BENNIE. Course it matters. Wouldn't want me puttin' it inside the closet, would you? You gotta make decisions now, Arlene. Gotta decide things.

ARLENE. I don't care.

BENNIE [*Insisting*]. Arlene.

ARLENE [*Pointing to a prominent position on the apartment wall, center*]. There.

BENNIE. Yeah. Good place. See it first thing when you get up.

[*Arlene lights a cigarette, as Arlie retrieves a hidden lighter from the toilet in the cell.*]

ARLIE. There's ways . . . gettin' outta bars . . . [*Lights a fire in the cell, catching her blouse on fire too*]

BENNIE [*As Arlie is lighting the fire*]. This ol' nail's pretty loose. I'll find something better to hang it with . . . somewhere or other . . .

[*Arlie screams and the doctor runs toward her, getting the attention of a guard who has been goofing off on the cat-walk.*]

ARLIE. Let me outta here! There's a fuckin' fire in here!

[*The doctor arrives at the cell, pats his pockets as if looking for the keys.*]

ARLIE. Officer!
DOCTOR. Guard!

[*Guard begins his run to the cell.*]

ARLIE. It's burnin' me!
DOCTOR. Hurry!
GUARD (EVANS). I'm comin'! I'm comin'!
DOCTOR. What the hell were you—
GUARD (EVANS) [*Fumbling for the right key*]. Come on, come on.
DOCTOR [*Urgent*]. For Chrissake!

[*The guard gets the door open, they rush in. The doctor, wrestling Arlie to the ground, opens his bag.*]

DOCTOR. Lay still, dammit.

[*Arlie collapses. The doctor gives an injection.*]

DOCTOR [*Grabbing his hand*]. Ow!
GUARD (EVANS) [*Lifting Arlie up to the bed*]. Get bit, Doc?
DOCTOR. You going to let her burn this place down before you start payin' attention up there?
GUARD (EVANS) [*Walks to the toilet, feels under the rim*]. Uh-huh.
BENNIE. There, that what you had in mind?
ARLENE. Yeah, thanks.
GUARD (EVANS). She musta had them matches hid right here.
BENNIE [*Staring at the picture he's hung*]. How you think he kept his beard trimmed all nice?
ARLENE [*Preoccupied with unloading the trunk*]. Who?
BENNIE [*Pointing to the picture*]. Jesus.
DOCTOR. I'll have to report you for this, Evans.
ARLENE. I don't know.

DOCTOR. That injection should hold her. I'll check back later. [*Leaves*]
GUARD (EVANS) [*Walking over to the bed*]. Report me, my ass. We got cells don't have potties, Holsclaw. [*Begins to search her and the bed, handling her very roughly*] So where is it now? Got it up your pookie, I bet. Oh, that'd be good. Doc comin' back an me with my fingers up your . . . roll over . . . don't weigh hardly nuthin', do you, dollie?
BENNIE. Never seen him without a moustache either.
ARLENE. Huh?
BENNIE. The picture.
GUARD (EVANS). Aw now . . . [*Finding the lighter under the mattress*] That wasn't hard at all. Don't you know 'bout hide an seek, Arlie, girl? Gonna hide somethin', hide it where it's fun to find it. [*Standing up, going to the door*] Crazy fuckin' someday-we-ain't-gonna-come-save-you bitch!

[*Guard slams cell door and leaves.*]

BENNIE. Well, Arlie girl, that ol' trunk's 'bout as empty as my belly.
ARLENE. You have been talkin' 'bout your belly ever since we left this mornin'.
BENNIE. You hungry? Them hotdogs we had give out around Nashville.
ARLENE. No. Not really.
BENNIE. You gotta eat, Arlene.
ARLENE. Says who?
BENNIE [*Laughs*]. How 'bout I pick us up some chicken, give you time to clean yourself up. We'll have a nice little dinner, just the two of us.
ARLENE. I git sick if I eat this late. Besides, I'm tired.
BENNIE. You'll feel better soon's you git somethin' on your stomach. Like I always said, "Can't plow less'n you feed the mule."
ARLENE. I ain't never heard you say that.
BENNIE. There's lots you don't know about me, Arlene. You been seein' me ever day, but you ain't been payin' attention. You'll get to like me now we're out.
ARLENE. You . . . was always out.
BENNIE. Yes sir, I'm gonna like bein' retired. I kin tell already. An I can take care of you, like I been, only now—
ARLENE. You tol' me you was jus' takin' a vacation.
BENNIE. I was gonna tell you.
ARLENE. You had some time off an nothin' to do . . .
BENNIE. Figured you knew already.
ARLENE. You said you ain't never seen Kentucky like

you always wanted to. Now you tell me you done quit at the prison?

BENNIE. They wouldn't let me drive you up here if I was still on the payroll, you know. Rules, against the rules. Coulda got me in big trouble doin' that.

ARLENE. You ain't goin' back to Pine Ridge?

BENNIE. Nope.

ARLENE. An you drove me all the way up here plannin' to stay here?

BENNIE. I was thinkin' on it.

ARLENE. Well what are you gonna do?

BENNIE [*Not positive, just a possibility*]. Hardware.

ARLENE. Sell guns?

BENNIE [*Laughs*]. Nails. Always wanted to. Some little store with bins and barrels full of nails and screws. Count 'em out. Put 'em in little sacks.

ARLENE. I don't need nobody hangin' around remindin' me where I been.

BENNIE. We had us a good time drivin' up here, didn't we? You throwin' that tomato outta the car . . . hit that no litterin' sign square in the middle. [*Grabs her arm as if to feel the muscle*] Good arm you got.

ARLENE [*Pulling away sharply*]. Don't you go grabbin' me.

BENNIE. Listen, you take off them clothes and have yourself a nice hot bath. [*Heading for the bathroom*] See, I'll start the water. And me, I'll go get us some chicken. [*Coming out of the bathroom*] You like slaw or potato salad?

ARLENE. Don't matter.

BENNIE [*Asking her to decide*]. Arlene . . .

ARLENE. Slaw.

BENNIE. One big bucket of slaw comin' right up. An extra rolls. You have a nice bath, now, you hear? I'll take my time so's you don't have to hurry fixin' yourself up.

ARLENE. I ain't gonna do no fixin'.

BENNIE [*A knowing smile*]. I know how you gals are when you get in the tub. You got any bubbles?

ARLENE. What?

BENNIE. Bubbles. You know, stuff to make bubbles with. Bubble bath.

ARLENE. I thought you was goin'.

BENNIE. Right. Right. Goin' right now.

[*Bennie leaves, locking the door behind him. He has left his hat on the bed. Arlene checks the stove and refrigerator.*]

GUARD (CALDWELL) [*Opening the cell door, carrying a plastic dinner carton*]. Got your grub, girlie.

ARLIE. Get out!

GUARD (CALDWELL). Can't. Doc says you gotta take the sun today.

ARLIE. You take it! I ain't hungry.

[*The guard and Arlie begin to walk to the downstage table area.*]

GUARD (CALDWELL). You gotta eat, Arlie.

ARLIE. Says who?

GUARD (CALDWELL). Says me. Says the warden. Says the Department of Corrections. Brung you two rolls.

ARLIE. And you know what you can do with your—

GUARD (CALDWELL). Stuff'em in your bra, why don't you?

ARLIE. Ain't you got somebody to go beat up somewhere?

GUARD (CALDWELL). Gotta see you get fattened up.

ARLIE. What do you care?

[*Arlene goes into the bathroom.*]

GUARD (CALDWELL). Oh, we care all right. [*Setting the food down on the table*] Got us a two-way mirror in the shower room. [*She looks up, hostile*] And you don't know which one it is, do you? [*He forces her onto the seat*] Yes ma'am. Eat. [*Pointing to the food*] We sure do care if you go gittin' too skinny. [*Walks away but continues to watch her*] Yes ma'am. We care a hog-lickin' lot.

ARLIE [*Throws the whole carton at him*]. Sons-a-bitches!

[*Mother's knock is heard on the apartment door.*]

MOTHER'S VOICE. Arlie? Arlie girl you in there?

[*Arlene walks out of the bathroom. She stands still, looking at the door. Arlie hears the knock at the same time and slips into the apartment and over to the bed, putting the pillow between her legs and holding the yellow teddy bear Arlene has unpacked. The knocking gets louder.*]

MOTHER'S VOICE. Arlie?

ARLIE [*Pulling herself up weakly on one elbow, speaking with the voice of a very young child*]. Mama? Mama?

[*Arlene walks slowly toward the door.*]

MOTHER'S VOICE [*Now pulling the doorknob from the outside, angry that the door is locked*]. Arlie? I know you're in there.

ARLIE. I can't git up, Mama. [*Hands between her legs*] My legs is hurt.

MOTHER'S VOICE. What's takin' you so long?

ARLENE [*Smoothing out her dress*]. Yeah, I'm comin'. [*Puts Bennie's hat out of sight under the bed*] Hold on.

MOTHER'S VOICE. I brung you some stuff but I ain't gonna stand here all night.

[*Arlene opens the door and stands back. Mother looks strong but badly worn. She is wearing her cab driver's uniform and is carrying a plastic laundry basket stuffed with cleaning fluids, towels, bug spray, etc.*]

ARLENE. I didn't know if you'd come.

MOTHER. Ain't I always?

ARLENE. How are you?

[*Arlene moves as if to hug her. Mother stands still, Arlene backs off.*]

MOTHER. 'Bout the same. [*Walking into the room*]

ARLENE. I'm glad to see you.

MOTHER [*Not looking at Arlene*]. You look tired.

ARLENE. It was a long drive.

MOTHER [*Putting the laundry basket on the trunk*]. Didn't fatten you up none, I see. [*Walks around the room, looking the place over*] You always was too skinny. [*Arlene straightens her clothes again*] Shoulda beat you like your daddy said. Make you eat.

ARLIE. Nobody done this to me, Mama. [*Protesting, in pain*] No! No!

MOTHER. He weren't a mean man, though, your daddy.

ARLIE. Was . . . [*Quickly*] my bike. My bike hurt me. The seat bumped me.

MOTHER. You remember that black chewing gum he got you when you were sick?

ARLENE. I remember he beat up on you.

MOTHER. Yeah, [*Proudly*] and he was real sorry a coupla times. [*Looking in the closet*] Filthy dirty. Hey! [*Slamming the closet door. Arlene jumps at the noise*] I brung you all kinda stuff. Just like Candy not leavin' you nuthin'. [*Walking back to the basket*] Some kids I got.

ARLIE [*Curling up into a ball*]. No, Mama, don't touch it. It'll git well. It git well before.

ARLENE. Where is Candy?

MOTHER. You got her place so what do you care? I got her outta my house so whatta I care? This'll be a good place for you.

ARLENE [*Going to the window*]. Wish there was a yard, here.

MOTHER [*Beginning to empty the basket*]. Nice things, see? Bet you ain't had no colored towels where you been.

ARLENE. No.

MOTHER [*Putting some things away in cabinets*]. No place like home. Got that up on the kitchen wall now.

ARLIE. I don't want no tea, Mama.

ARLENE. Yeah?

MOTHER [*Repeating Arlene's answers*]. No . . . yeah? . . . You forgit how to talk? I ain't gonna be here all that long. Least you can talk to me while I'm here.

ARLENE. You ever git that swing you wanted?

MOTHER. Dish towels, an see here? June sent along this teapot. You drink tea, Arlie?

ARLENE. No.

MOTHER. June's havin' another baby. Don't know when to quit, that girl. Course, I ain't one to talk. [*Starting to pick up trash on the floor*]

ARLENE. Have you seen Joey?

ARLIE. I'm tellin' you the truth.

MOTHER. An Ray . . .

ARLIE [*Pleading*]. Daddy didn't do nuthin' to me.

MOTHER. Ray ain't had a day of luck in his life.

ARLIE. Ask him. He saw me fall on my bike.

MOTHER. Least bein' locked up now, he'll keep off June till the baby gits here.

ARLENE. Have you seen Joey?

MOTHER. Your daddy ain't doin' too good right now. Man's been dyin' for ten years, to hear him tell it. You'd think he'd git tired of it an jus' go ahead . . . pass on.

ARLENE [*Wanting an answer*]. Mother . . .

MOTHER. Yeah, I seen 'im. 'Bout two years ago. Got your stringy hair.

ARLENE. You got a picture?

MOTHER. You was right to give him up. Foster homes is good for some kids.

ARLIE. Where's my Joey-bear? Yellow Joey-bear? Mama?

ARLENE. How'd you see him?

MOTHER. I was down at Detention Center pickin' up Pete. [*Beginning her serious cleaning now*]

ARLENE [*Less than interested*]. How is he?

MOTHER. I could be workin' at the Detention Center I been there so much. All I gotta do's have somethin' big goin' on an I git a call to come after one of you. Can't jus' have kids, no, gotta be pickin' 'em up all over town.

ARLENE. You was just tellin' me—

MOTHER. Pete is taller, that's all.

ARLENE. You was just tellin' me how you saw Joey.

MOTHER. I'm comin' back in the cab an I seen him waitin' for the bus.

ARLENE. What'd he say?

MOTHER. Oh, I didn't stop. [*Arlene looks up quickly,*

hurt and angry] If the kid don't even know you, Arlie, he sure ain't gonna know who I am.

ARLENE. How come he couldn't stay at Shirley's?

MOTHER. 'Cause Shirley never was crazy about washin' more diapers. She's the only smart kid I got. Anyway, social worker only put him there till she could find him a foster home.

ARLENE. But I coulda seen him.

MOTHER. Thatta been trouble, him bein' in the family. Kid wouldn't have known who to listen to, Shirley or you.

ARLENE. But I'm his mother.

MOTHER. See, now you don't have to be worryin' about him. No kids, no worryin'.

ARLENE. He just had his birthday, you know.

ARLIE. Don't let Daddy come in here, Mama. Just you an me. Mama?

ARLENE. When I git workin', I'll git a nice rug for this place. He could come live here with me.

MOTHER. Fat chance.

ARLENE. I done my time.

MOTHER. You never really got attached to him anyway.

ARLENE. How do you know that?

MOTHER. Now don't you go gettin' het up. I'm telling you . . .

ARLENE. But . . .

MOTHER. Kids need rules to go by an he'll get 'em over there.

ARLIE [*Screaming*]. No Daddy! I didn't tell her nuthin'. I didn't! I didn't! [*Gets up from the bed, terrified*]

MOTHER. Here, help me with these sheets. [*Hands Arlene the sheets from the laundry basket*] Even got you a spread. Kinda goes with them curtains. [*Arlene is silent*] You ain't thanked me, Arlie girl.

ARLENE [*Going to the other side of the bed*]. They don't call me Arlie no more. It's Arlene now.

[*Arlene and Mother make up the bed. Arlie jumps up, looks around and goes over to Mother's purse. She looks through it hurriedly and pulls out the wallet. She takes some money and runs down left, where she is caught by a school principal.*]

PRINCIPAL. Arlie? You're in an awfully big hurry for such a little girl. [*Brushes at Arlie's hair*] That is you under all that hair, isn't it? [*Arlie resists this gesture*] Now, you can watch where you're going.

ARLIE. Gotta git home.

PRINCIPAL. But school isn't over for another three hours. And there's peanut butter and chili today.

ARLIE. Ain't hungry. [*Struggling free*]

[*The principal now sees Arlie's hands clenched behind her back.*]

PRINCIPAL. What do we have in our hands, Arlie?

ARLIE. Nuthin'.

PRINCIPAL. Let me see your hands, Arlie. Open up your hands.

[*Arlie brings her hands around in front, opening them, showing crumpled dollars.*]

ARLIE. It's my money. I earned it.

PRINCIPAL [*Taking the money*]. And how did we earn this money?

ARLIE. Doin' things.

PRINCIPAL. What kind of things?

ARLIE. For my daddy.

PRINCIPAL. Well, we'll see about that. You'll have to come with me.

[*Arlie resists as the principalcipal pulls her.*]

ARLIE. No.

PRINCIPAL. Your mother was right after all. She said put you in a special school. [*Quickly*] No, what she said was put you away somewhere and I said, no, she's too young, well I was wrong. I have four hundred other children to take care of here and what have I been doing? Breaking up your fights, talking to your truant officer and washing your writing off the bathroom wall. Well, I've had enough. You've made your choice. You *want* out of regular school and you're going to *get* out of regular school.

ARLIE [*Becoming more violent*]. You can't make me go nowhere, bitch!

PRINCIPAL [*Backing off in cold anger*]. I'm not making you go. You've earned it. You've worked hard for this, well, they're used to your type over there. They'll know exactly what to do with you. [*She stalks off, leaving Arlie alone*]

MOTHER [*Smoothing out the spread*]. Spread ain't new, but it don't look so bad. Think we got it right after we got you. No, I remember now. I was pregnant with you an been real sick the whole time.

[*Arlene lights a cigarette, Mother takes one, Arlene retrieves the pack quickly.*]

MOTHER. Your daddy brung me home this big bowl of chili an some jelly doughnuts. Some fare from the airport give him a big tip. Anyway, I'd been eatin' peanut brittle all day, only thing that tasted any good. Then in he come with this chili an no sooner'n I got in bed I thrown up all over everwhere. Lucky I didn't throw you up, Arlie girl. Anyhow, that's how come us to get a new spread. This one here. [*Sits on the bed*]

ARLENE. You drivin' the cab any?

MOTHER. Any? Your daddy ain't drove it at all a long time now. Six years, seven maybe.

ARLENE. You meet anybody nice?

MOTHER. Not anymore. Mostly drivin' old ladies to get their shoes. Guess it got around the nursin' homes I was reliable. [*Sounds funny to her*] You remember that time I took you drivin' with me that night after you been in a fight an that soldier bought us a beer? Shitty place, hole in the wall?

ARLENE. You made me wait in the car.

MOTHER [*Standing up*]. Think I'd take a child of mine into a dump like that?

ARLENE. You went in.

MOTHER. Weren't no harm in it. [*Walking over for the bug spray*] I didn't always look so bad, you know.

ARLENE. You was pretty.

MOTHER [*Beginning to spray the floor*]. You could look better'n you do. Do somethin' with your hair. I always thought if you'd looked better you wouldn't have got in so much trouble.

ARLENE [*Pleased and curious*]. Joey got my hair?

MOTHER. And skinny.

ARLENE. I took some beauty school at Pine Ridge.

MOTHER. Yeah, a beautician?

ARLENE. I don't guess so.

MOTHER. Said you was gonna work.

ARLENE. They got a law here. Ex-cons can't get no license.

MOTHER. Shoulda stayed in Alabama, then. Worked there.

ARLENE. They got a law there, too.

MOTHER. Then why'd they give you the trainin'?

ARLENE. I don't know.

MOTHER. Maybe they thought it'd straighten you out.

ARLENE. Yeah.

MOTHER. But you are gonna work, right?

ARLENE. Yeah. Cookin' maybe. Somethin' that pays good.

MOTHER. You? Cook? [*Laughs*]

ARLENE. I could learn it.

MOTHER. Your daddy ain't never forgive you for that bologna sandwich. [*Arlene laughs a little, finally enjoying a memory*] Oh, I wish I'd seen you spreadin' that Colgate on that bread. He'd have smelled that toothpaste if he hadn't been so sloshed. Little snotty-nosed kid tryin' to kill her daddy with a bologna sandwich. An him bein' so pleased when you brung it to him . . . [*Laughing*]

ARLENE. He beat me good.

MOTHER. Well, now, Arlie, you gotta admit you had it comin' to you. [*Wiping tears from laughing*]

ARLENE. I guess.

MOTHER. You got a broom?

ARLENE. No.

MOTHER. Well, I got one in the cab I brung just in case. I can't leave it here, but I'll sweep up fore I go. [*Walking toward the door*] You jus' rest till I git back. Won't find no work lookin' the way you do.

[*Mother leaves. Arlene finds some lipstick and a mirror in her purse, makes an attempt to look better while Mother is gone.*]

ARLIE [*Jumps up, as if talking to another kid*]. She is not skinny!

ARLENE [*Looking at herself in the mirror*]. I guess I could . . .

ARLIE. And she don't have to git them stinky permanents. Her hair just comes outta her head curly.

ARLENE. Some lipstick.

ARLIE [*Serious*]. She drives the cab to buy us stuff, 'cause we don't take no charity from nobody, 'cause we got money 'cause she earned it.

ARLENE [*Closing the mirror, dejected, afraid Mother might be right*]. But you're too skinny and you got stringy hair. [*Sitting on the floor*]

ARLIE [*More angry*]. She drives at night 'cause people needs rides at night. People goin' to see their friends that are sick, or people's cars broken down an they gotta get to work at the . . . nobody calls my mama a whore!

MOTHER [*Coming back in with the broom*]. If I'd known you were gonna sweep up with your butt, I wouldn't have got this broom. Get up! [*Sweeps at Arlene to get her to move*]

ARLIE. You're gonna take that back or I'm gonna rip out all your ugly hair and stuff it down your ugly throat.

ARLENE [*Tugging at her own hair*]. You still cut hair?

MOTHER [*Noticing some spot on the floor*]. Gonna take a razor blade to get out this paint.

ARLENE. Nail polish.

ARLIE. Wanna know what I know about your mama? She's dyin'. Somethin's eatin' up her insides piece by piece, only she don't want you to know it.

MOTHER [*Continuing to sweep*]. So, you're callin' yourself Arlene, now?

ARLENE. Yes.

MOTHER. Don't want your girlie name no more?

ARLENE. Somethin' like that.

MOTHER. They call you Arlene in prison?

ARLENE. Not at first when I was bein' hateful. Just my number then.

MOTHER. You always been hateful.

ARLENE. There was this chaplain, he called me Arlene from the first day he come to talk to me. Here, let me help you. [*She reaches for the broom*]

MOTHER. I'll do it.

ARLENE. You kin rest.

MOTHER. Since when? [*Arlene backs off*] I ain't hateful, how come I got so many hateful kids? [*Sweeping harder now*] Poor dumb-as-hell Pat, stealin' them wigs, Candy screwin' since day one, Pete cuttin' up ol' Mac down at the grocery, June sellin' dope like it was Girl Scout cookies, and you . . . thank God I can't remember it all.

ARLENE [*A very serious request*]. Maybe I could come out on Sunday for . . . you still make that pot roast?

MOTHER [*Now sweeping over by the picture of Jesus*]. That your picture?

ARLENE. That chaplain give it to me.

MOTHER. The one give you your "new name."

ARLENE. Yes.

MOTHER. It's crooked. [*Doesn't straighten it*]

ARLENE. I liked those potatoes with no skins. An that ketchup squirter we had, jus' like in a real restaurant.

MOTHER. People that run them institutions now, they jus' don't know how to teach kids right. Let 'em run around an get in more trouble. They should get you up at the crack of dawn an set you to scrubbin' the floor. That's what kids need. Trainin'. Hard work.

ARLENE [*A clear request*]. I'll probably git my Sundays off.

MOTHER. Sunday . . . is my day to clean house now.

[*Arlene gets the message, finally walks over to straighten the picture. Mother now feels a little bad about this rejection, stops sweeping for a moment.*]

MOTHER. I woulda wrote you but I didn't have nuthin' to say. An no money to send, so what's the use?

ARLENE. I made out.

MOTHER. They pay you for workin'?

ARLENE. 'Bout three dollars a month.

MOTHER. How'd you make it on three dollars a month? [*Answers her own question*] You do some favors?

ARLENE [*Sitting down in the chair under the picture, a somewhat smug look*]. You jus' can't make it by yourself.

MOTHER [*Pauses, suspicious, then contemptuous*]. You play, Arlie?

ARLENE. You don't know nuthin' about that.

MOTHER. I hear things. Girls callin' each other "mommy" an bringin' things back from the canteen for their "husbands." Makes me sick. You got family, Arlie, what you want with that playin'? Don't want nobody like that in my house.

ARLENE. You don't know what you're talkin' about.

MOTHER. I still got two kids at home. Don't want no bad example. [*Not finishing the sweeping. Has all the dirt in one place, but doesn't get it up off the floor yet*]

ARLENE. I could tell them some things.

MOTHER [*Vicious*]. Like about that cab driver.

ARLENE. Look, that was a long time ago. I wanna work, now, make somethin' of myself. I learned to knit. People'll buy nice sweaters. Make some extra money.

MOTHER. We sure could use it.

ARLENE. An then if I have money, maybe they'd let me take Joey to the fair, buy him hotdogs an talk to him. Make sure he ain't foolin' around.

MOTHER. What makes you think he'd listen to you? Alice, across the street? Her sister took care her kids while she was at Lexington. You think they pay any attention to her now? Ashamed, that's what. One of 'em told me his mother done died. Gone to see a friend and died there.

ARLENE. Be different with me and Joey.

MOTHER. He don't even know who you are, Arlie.

ARLENE [*Wearily*]. Arlene.

MOTHER. You forgot already what you was like as a kid. At Waverly, tellin' them lies about that campin' trip we took, sayin' your daddy made you watch while he an me . . . you know. I'd have killed you then if them social workers hadn't been watchin'.

ARLENE. Yeah.

MOTHER. Didn't want them thinkin' I weren't fit. Well, what do they know? Each time you'd get out of one of them places, you'd be actin' worse than ever. Go right back to that junkie, pimp, Carl, sellin' the stuff he steals, savin' his ass from the police. He follow you home this time, too?

ARLENE. He's got four more years at Bricktown.

MOTHER. Glad to hear it. Here . . . [*Handing her a bucket*] Water.

[*Arlene fills up the bucket and Mother washes several dirty spots on the walls, floor and furniture. Arlene knows better* than to try to help. The doctor walks downstage to find Arlie for their counseling session.]

DOCTOR. So you refuse to go to camp?

ARLIE. Now why'd I want to go to your fuckin' camp? Camp's for babies. You can go shit in the woods if you want to, but I ain't goin'.

DOCTOR. Oh, you're goin'.

ARLIE. Wanna bet?

MOTHER. Arlie, I'm waitin'. [For the water]

ARLIE. 'Sides, I'm waitin'.

DOCTOR. Waiting for what?

ARLIE. For Carl to come git me.

DOCTOR. And who is Carl?

ARLIE. Jus' some guy. We're goin' to Alabama.

DOCTOR. You don't go till we say you can go.

ARLIE. Carl's got a car.

DOCTOR. Does he have a driver's license to go with it?

ARLIE [Enraged, impatient]. I'm goin' now.

[Arlie stalks away, then backs up toward the doctor again. He has information she wants.]

DOCTOR. Hey!

ARLENE. June picked out a name for the baby?

MOTHER. Clara . . . or Clarence. Got it from this fancy shampoo she bought.

ARLIE. I don't feel good. I'm pregnant, you know.

DOCTOR. The test was negative.

ARLIE. Well, I should know, shouldn't I?

DOCTOR. No. You want to be pregnant, is that it?

ARLIE. I wouldn't mind. Kids need somebody to bring 'em up right.

DOCTOR. Raising children is a big responsibility, you know.

ARLIE. Yeah. I know it. I ain't dumb. Everybody always thinks I'm so dumb.

DOCTOR. You could learn if you wanted to. That's what the teachers are here for.

ARLIE. Shit.

DOCTOR. Or so they say.

ARLIE. All they teach us is about geography. Why'd I need to know about Africa. Jungles and shit.

DOCTOR. They want you to know about other parts of the world.

ARLIE. Well, I ain't goin' there so whatta I care?

DOCTOR. What's this about Cindy?

ARLIE [Hostile]. She told Mr. Dawson some lies about me.

DOCTOR. I bet.

ARLIE. She said I fuck my daddy for money.

DOCTOR. And what did you do when she said that?

ARLIE. What do you think I did? I beat the shit out of her.

DOCTOR. And that's a good way to work out your problems?

ARLIE [Proudly]. She ain't done it since.

DOCTOR. She's been in traction, since.

ARLIE. So, whatta I care? She say it again, I'll do it again. Bitch!

ARLENE [Looking down at the dirt Mother is gathering on the floor]. I ain't got a can. Just leave it.

MOTHER. And have you sweep it under the bed after I go? [Wraps the dirt in a piece of newspaper and puts it in her laundry basket]

DOCTOR [Looking at his clipboard]. You're on unit cleanup this week.

ARLIE. I done it last week!

DOCTOR. Then you should remember what to do. The session is over. [Getting up, walking away] And stand up straight! And take off that hat!

[Doctor and Arlie go offstage as Mother finds Bennie's hat.]

MOTHER. This your hat?

ARLENE. No.

MOTHER. Guess Candy left it here.

ARLENE. Candy didn't leave nuthin'.

MOTHER. Then whose is it? [Arlene doesn't answer] Do you know whose hat this is? [Arlene knows she made a mistake] I'm askin' you a question and I want an answer. [Arlene turns her back] Whose hat is this? You tell me right now, whose hat is this?

ARLENE. It's Bennie's.

MOTHER. And who's Bennie?

ARLENE. Guy drove me home from Pine Ridge. A guard.

MOTHER [Upset]. I knew it. You been screwin' a god-damn guard. [Throws the hat on the bed]

ARLENE. He jus' drove me up here, that's all.

MOTHER. Sure.

ARLENE. I git sick on the bus.

MOTHER. You expect me to believe that?

ARLENE. I'm tellin' you, he jus'—

MOTHER. No man alive gonna drive a girl five hundred miles for nuthin'.

ARLENE. He ain't never seen Kentucky.

MOTHER. It ain't Kentucky he wants to see.

ARLENE. He ain't gettin' nuthin' from me.

MOTHER. That's what you think.

ARLENE. He done some nice things for me at Pine Ridge. Gum, funny stories.

MOTHER. He'd be tellin' stories all right, tellin' his buddies where to find you.

ARLENE. He's gettin' us some dinner right now.

MOTHER. And how're you gonna pay him? Huh? Tell me that.

ARLENE. I ain't like that no more.

MOTHER. Oh you ain't. I'm your mother. I know what you'll do.

ARLENE. I tell you I ain't.

MOTHER. I knew it. Well, when you got another bastard in you, don't come cryin' to me, 'cause I done told you.

ARLENE. Don't worry.

MOTHER. An I'm gettin' myself outta here fore your boyfriend comes back.

ARLENE [*Increasing anger*]. He ain't my boyfriend.

MOTHER. I been a lotta things, but I ain't dumb, Arlene. [*"Arlene" is mocking.*]

ARLENE. I didn't say you was. [*Beginning to know how this is going to turn out*]

MOTHER. Oh no? You lied to me!

ARLENE. How?

MOTHER. You took my spread without even sayin' thank you. You're hintin' at comin' to my house for pot roast just like nuthin' ever happened, an all the time your'e hidin' a goddam guard under your bed. [*Furious*] Uh-huh.

ARLENE [*Quietly*]. Mama?

MOTHER [*Cold, fierce*]. What?

ARLENE. What kind of meat makes a pot roast?

MOTHER. A roast makes a pot roast. Buy a roast. Shoulder, chuck . . .

ARLENE. Are you comin' back?

MOTHER. You ain't got no need for me.

ARLENE. I gotta ask you to come see me?

MOTHER. I come tonight, didn't I, an nobody asked me?

ARLENE. Just forget it.

MOTHER [*Getting her things together*]. An if I hadn't told them about this apartment, you wouldn't be out at all, how 'bout that?

ARLENE. Forget it!

MOTHER. Don't you go talkin' to me that way. You remember who I am. I'm the one took you back after all you done all them years. I brung you that teapot. I scrubbed your place. You remember that when you talk to me.

ARLENE. Sure.

MOTHER. Uh-huh. [*Now goes to the bed, rips off the spread and stuffs it in her basket*] I knowed I shouldn't have come. You ain't changed a bit.

ARLENE. Same hateful brat, right?

MOTHER [*Arms full, heading for the door*]. Same hateful brat. Right.

ARLENE [*Rushing toward her*]. Mama . . .

MOTHER. Don't you touch me.

[*Mother leaves. Arlene stares out the door, stunned and hurt. Finally, she slams the door and turns back into the room.*]

ARLENE. No! Don't you touch Mama, Arlie.

[*Ronnie, a fellow juvenile offender, runs across the catwalk, waving a necklace and being chased by Arlie.*]

RONNIE. Arlie got a boyfriend, Arlie got a boyfriend. [*Throws the necklace downstage*] Whoo!

ARLIE [*Chasing him*]. Ronnie, you ugly mother, I'll smash your fuckin'—

ARLENE [*Getting more angry*]. You might steal all—

RONNIE [*Running down the stairs*]. Arlie got a boyfriend . . .

ARLIE. Gimme that necklace or I'll—

ARLENE. —or eat all Mama's precious pot roast.

RONNIE [*As they wrestle downstage*]. You'll tell the doctor on me? And get your private room back? [*Laughing*]

ARLENE [*Cold and hostile*]. No, don't touch Mama, Arlie. 'Cause you might slit Mama's throat. [*Goes into the bathroom*]

ARLIE. You wanna swallow all them dirty teeth?

RONNIE. Tell me who give it to you.

ARLIE. No, you tell me where it's at.

[*Ronnie breaks away, pushing Arlie in the opposite direction, and runs for the necklace.*]

RONNIE. It's right here. [*Drops it down his pants*] Come an git it.

ARLIE. Oh now, that was really ignorant, you stupid pig.

RONNIE [*Backing away, daring her*]. Jus' reach right in. First come, first served.

ARLIE. Now, how you gonna pee after I throw your weenie over the fence?

RONNIE. You ain't gonna do that, girl. You gonna fall in love.

[*Arlie turns vicious, pins Ronnie down, attacking. This is no longer play. He screams. The doctor appears on the catwalk.*]

DOCTOR. Arlie! [*Heads down the stairs to stop this*]

CARL'S VOICE [*From outside the apartment door*]. Arlie!

DOCTOR. Arlie!

ARLIE. Stupid, ugly—

RONNIE. Help!

[Arlie runs away and hides down left.]

DOCTOR. That's three more weeks of isolation, Arlie. [Bending down to Ronnie] You all right? Can you walk?

RONNIE [Looking back to Arlie as he gets up in great pain]. She was tryin' to kill me.

DOCTOR. Yeah. Easy now. You should've known, Ronnie.

ARLIE [Yelling at Ronnie]. You'll get yours, crybaby.

CARL'S VOICE. Arlie . . .

ARLIE. Yeah, I'm comin'!

CARL'S VOICE. Bad-lookin' dude says move your ass an open up this here door, girl.

[Arlene does not come out of the bathroom. Carl twists the door knob violently, then kicks in the door and walks in. Carl is thin and cheaply dressed. Carl's walk and manner are imitative of black pimps, but he can't quite carry it off.]

CARL. Where you at, mama?

ARLENE. Carl?

CARL. Who else? You 'spectin' Leroy Brown?

ARLENE. I'm takin' a bath!

CARL [Walking toward the bathroom]. I like my ladies clean. Matter of professional pride.

ARLENE. Don't come in here.

CARL [Mocking her tone]. Don't come in here. I seen it all before, girl.

ARLENE. I'm gittin' out. Sit down or somethin'.

CARL [Talking loud enough for her to hear him through the door]. Ain't got the time. [Opens her purse, then searches the trunk] Jus' come by to tell you it's tomorrow. We be takin' our feet to the New York street. [As though she will be pleased] No more fuckin' around with these jiveass southern turkeys. We're goin' to the big city, baby. Get you some red shades and some red shorts an' the johns be linin' up fore we hit town. Four tricks a night. How's that sound? No use wearin' out that cute ass you got. Way I hear it, only way to git busted up there's be stupid, an I ain't lived this long bein' stupid.

ARLENE [Coming out of the bathroom wearing a towel]. That's exactly how you lived your whole life—bein' stupid.

CARL. Arlie . . . [Movin in on her] be sweet, sugar.

ARLENE. Still got your curls.

CARL [Trying to hug her]. You're looking okay yourself.

ARLENE. Oh, Carl. [Noticing the damage to the door, breaking away from any closeness he might try to force]

CARL [Amused]. Bent up your door, some.

ARLENE. How come you're out?

CARL. Sweetheart, you done broke out once, been nabbed and sent to Pine Ridge and got yourself paroled since I been in. I got a right to a little free time too, ain't that right?

ARLENE. You escape?

CARL. Am I standin' here or am I standin' here? They been fuckin' with you I can tell.

ARLENE. They gonna catch you.

CARL [Going to the window]. Not where we're going. Not a chance.

ARLENE. Where you goin' they won't git you?

CARL. Remember that green hat you picked out for me down in Birmingham? Well, I ain't ever wore it yet, but I kin wear it in New York 'cause New York's where you wear whatever you feel like. One guy tol' me he saw this dude wearin' a whole ring of feathers roun' his leg, right here [Grabs his leg above the knee] an he weren't in no circus nor no Indian neither.

ARLENE. I ain't seen you since Birmingham. How come you think I wanna see you now?

[Arlie appears suddenly, confronts Carl.]

ARLIE [Pointing as if there is a trick waiting]. Carl, I ain't goin' with that dude, he's weird.

CARL. 'Cause we gotta go collect the johns' money, that's "how come."

ARLIE. I don't need you pimpin' for me.

ARLENE [Very strong]. I'm gonna work.

CARL. Work?

ARLENE. Yeah.

CARL. What's this "work"?

ARLIE. You always sendin' me to them ol' droolers . . .

CARL. You kin do two things, girl—

ARLIE. They slobberin' all over me . . .

CARL. Breakin' out an hookin'.

ARLIE. They tyin' me to the bed!

ARLENE. I mean real work.

ARLIE [Now screaming, gets further away from him]. I could git killed working for you. Some sicko, some crazy drunk . . .

[Arlie goes offstage. A guard puts her in the cell sometime before Bennie's entrance.]

CARL. You forget, we seen it all on TV in the day room, you bustin' outta Lakewood like that. Fakin' that palsy fit, then beatin' that guard half to death with his own key ring. Whoo-ee! Then that spree you went on . . . stoppin' at that fillin' station for some cash, then kidnappin' the old dude pumpin' the gas.

ARLENE. Yeah.

CARL. Then that cab driver comes outta the bathroom an tries to mess with you and you shoots him with his own piece. [*Fires an imaginary pistol*] That there's nice work, mama. [*Going over to her, putting his arms around her*]

ARLENE. That gun . . . it went off, Carl.

CARL [*Getting more determined with his affection*]. That's what guns do, doll. They go off.

BENNIE'S VOICE [*From outside*]. Arlene? Arlene?

CARL. Arlene? [*Jumping up*] Well, la-de-da.

[*Bennie opens the door, carrying the chicken dinners. He is confused, seeing Arlene wearing a towel and talking to Carl.*]

ARLENE. Bennie, this here's Carl.

CARL. You're interruptin', Jack. Me an Arlie got business.

BENNIE. She's callin' herself Arlene.

CARL. I call my ladies what I feel like, chicken man, an you call yourself "gone."

BENNIE. I don't take orders from you.

CARL. Well, you been takin' orders from somebody, or did you git that outfit at the army surplus store?

ARLENE. Bennie brung me home from Pine Ridge.

CARL [*Walking toward him*]. Oh, it's a guard now, is it? That chicken break out or what? [*Grabs the chicken*]

BENNIE. I don't know what you're doin' here, but—

CARL. What you gonna do about it, huh? Lock me up in the toilet? You an who else, Batman?

BENNIE [*Taking the chicken back, walking calmly to the counter*]. Watch your mouth, punk.

CARL [*Kicks a chair toward Bennie*]. Punk!

ARLENE [*Trying to stop this*]. I'm hungry.

BENNIE. You heard her, she's hungry.

CARL [*Vicious*]. Shut up! [*Mocking*] Ossifer.

BENNIE. Arlene, tell this guy if he knows what's good for him . . .

CARL [*Walking to the counter where Bennie has left the chicken*]. Why don't you write me a parkin' ticket? [*Shoves the chicken on the floor*] Don't fuck with me, dad. It ain't healthy.

[*Bennie pauses. A real standoff. Finally, Bennie bends down and picks up the chicken.*]

BENNIE. You ain't worth dirtyin' my hands.

[*Carl walks by him, laughing.*]

CARL. Hey, Arlie. I got some dude to see. [*For Bennie's beneift as he struts to the door*] What I need with another beat-up guard? All that blood, jus' ugly up my threads. [*Very sarcastic*] Bye y'all.

ARLENE. Bye, Carl.

[*Carl turns back quickly at the door, stopping Bennie, who was following him.*]

CARL. You really oughta shine them shoes, man. [*Vindictive laugh, slams the door in Bennie's face*]

BENNIE [*Relieved, trying to change the atmosphere*]. Well, how 'bout if we eat? You'll catch your death dressed like that.

ARLENE. Turn around then.

[*Arlene gets a shabby housecoat from the closet. She puts it on over her towel, buttons it up, then pulls the towel out from under it. This has the look of a prison ritual.*]

BENNIE [*As she is dressing*]. Your parole officer's gonna tell you to keep away from guys like that . . . for your own good, you know. Those types, just like the suckers on my tomatoes back home. Take everything right outta you. Gotta pull 'em off, Arlie, uh, Arlene.

ARLENE. Now, I'm decent now.

BENNIE. You hear what I said?

ARLENE [*Going to the bathroom for her hairbrush*]. I told him that. That's exactly what I did tell him.

BENNIE. Who was that anyhow? [*Sits down on the bed, opens up the chicken*]

ARLENE [*From the bathroom*]. Long time ago, me an Carl took a trip together.

BENNIE. When you was a kid, you mean?

ARLENE. I was at this place for kids.

BENNIE. And Carl was there?

ARLENE. No, he picked me up an we went to Alabama. There was this wreck an all. I ended up at Lakewood for forgery. It was him that done it. Got me pregnant too.

BENNIE. That was Joey's father?

ARLENE. Yeah, but he don't know that. [*Sits down*]

BENNIE. Just as well. Guy like that, don't know what they'd do.

ARLENE. Mother was here while ago. Says she's seen Joey. [*Taking a napkin from Bennie*]

BENNIE. Wish I had a kid. Life ain't, well, complete, without no kids to play ball with an take fishin'. Dorrie, though, she had them backaches an that neuralgia, day I married her to the day she died. Good woman though. No drinkin', no card playin', real sweet voice . . . what was that song she used to sing? . . . Oh, yeah . . .

ARLENE. She says Joey's a real good-lookin' kid.

BENNIE. Well, his mom ain't bad.

ARLENE. At Lakewood, they tried to git me to have an abortion.

BENNIE. They was just thinkin' of you, Arlene.

ARLENE [Matter-of-fact, no self-pity]. I told 'em I'd kill myself if they done that. I would have too.

BENNIE. But they took him away after he was born.

ARLENE. Yeah. [Bennie waits, knowing she is about to say more] An I guess I went crazy after that. Thought if I could jus' git out an find him . . .

BENNIE. I don't remember any of that on the TV.

ARLENE. No.

BENNIE. Just remember you smilin' at the cameras, yellin' how you tol' that cab driver not to touch you.

ARLENE. I never seen his cab. [Forces herself to eat]

ARLIE [In the cell, holding a pillow and singing]. Rock-a-bye baby, in the tree top, when the wind blows, the cradle will . . . [Not remembering] cradle will . . . [Now talking] What you gonna be when you grow up, pretty boy baby? You gonna be a doctor? You gonna give people medicine an take out they . . . no, don't be no doctor . . . be . . . be a preacher . . . sayin' Our Father who is in heaven . . . heaven, that's where people go when they dies, when doctors can't save 'em or somebody kills 'em fore they even git a chance to . . . no, don't be no preacher neither . . . be . . . go to school an learn good [Tone begins to change] so you kin . . . make everbody else feel so stupid all the time. Best thing you to be is stay a baby 'cause nobody beats up on babies or puts them . . . [Much more quiet] that ain't true, baby. People is mean to babies, so you stay right here with me so nobody kin git you an make you cry an they lay one finger on you [Hostile] an I'll beat the screamin' shit right out of 'em. They even blow on you an I'll kill 'em.

[Bennie and Arlene have finished their dinner. Bennie puts one carton of slaw in the refrigerator, then picks up all the paper, making a garbage bag out of one of the sacks.]

BENNIE. Ain't got a can, I guess. Jus' use this ol' sack for now.

ARLENE. I ain't never emptyin' another garbage can.

BENNIE. Yeah, I reckon you know how by now. [Yawns] You 'bout ready for bed?

ARLENE [Stands up]. I s'pose.

BENNIE [Stretches]. Little tired myself.

ARLENE [Dusting the crumbs off the bed]. Thanks for the chicken.

BENNIE. You're right welcome. You look beat. How 'bout I rub your back. [Grabs her shoulders]

ARLENE [Pulling away]. No. [Walking to the sink] You go on now.

BENNIE. Oh come on. [Wiping his hands on his pants] I ain't all that tired.

ARLENE. I'm tired.

BENNIE. Well, see then, a back rub is just what the doctor ordered.

ARLENE. No. I don't . . . [Pulling away]

[Bennie grabs her shoulders and turns her around, sits her down hard on the trunk, starts rubbing her back and neck.]

BENNIE. Muscles git real tightlike, right in here.

ARLENE. You hurtin' me.

BENNIE. Has to hurt a little or it won't do no good.

ARLENE [Jumps, he has hurt her]. Oh, stop it! [She slips away from him and out into the room. She is frightened]

BENNIE [Smiling, coming after her, toward the bed]. Be lot nicer if you was layin' down. Wouldn't hurt as much.

ARLENE. Now, I ain't gonna start yellin'. I'm jus' tellin' you to go.

BENNIE [Straightens up as though he's going to cooperate]. Okay then. I'll jus' git my hat.

[He reaches for the hat, then turns quickly, grabs her and throws her down on the bed. He starts rubbing again.]

BENNIE. Now, you just relax. Don't you go bein' scared of me.

ARLENE. You ain't gettin' nuthin' from me.

BENNIE. I don't want nuthin', honey. Jus' tryin' to help you sleep.

ARLENE [Struggling]. Don't you call me honey.

[Bennie stops rubbing, but keeps one hand on her back. He rubs her hair with his free hand.]

BENNIE. See? Don't that feel better?

ARLENE. Let me up.

BENNIE. Why, I ain't holdin' you down.

ARLENE. Then let me up.

BENNIE [Takes hands off]. Okay. Git up.

[Arlene turns over slowly, begins to lift herself up on her elbows. Bennie puts one hand on her leg.]

ARLENE. Move your hand. [She gets up, moves across the room]

BENNIE. I'd be happy to stay here with you tonight. Make sure you'll be all right. You ain't spent a night by yourself for a long time.

ARLENE. I remember how.

BENNIE. Well how you gonna git up? You got a alarm?

ARLENE. It ain't all that hard.

BENNIE [*Puts one hand in his pocket, leers a little*]. Oh yeah it is. [*Walks around her again*] Gimme a kiss. Then I'll go.

ARLENE [*Edging along the counter, seeing she's trapped*]. You stay away from me.

[*Bennie reaches for her, clamping her hands behind her, pressing up against her.*]

BENNIE. Now what's it going to hurt you to give me a little ol' kiss?

ARLENE [*Struggling*]. Git out! I said git out!

BENNIE. You don't want me to go. You're jus' beginning to git interested. Your ol' girlie temper's flarin' up. I like that in a woman.

ARLENE. Yeah, you'd love it if I'd swat you one. [*Getting away from him*]

BENNIE. I been hit by you before. I kin take anything you got.

ARLENE. I could mess you up good.

BENNIE. Now, Arlie. You ain't had a man in a long time. And the ones you had been no-count.

ARLENE. Git out!

[*She slaps him. He returns the slap.*]

BENNIE [*Moving in*]. Ain't natural goin' without it too long. Young thing like you. Git all shriveled up.

ARLENE. All right, you sunuvabitch, you asked for it!

[*She goes into a violent rage, biting and kicking him. Bennie overpowers her capably, prison-guard style.*]

BENNIE [*Amused*]. Little outta practice, ain't you?

ARLENE [*Screaming*]. I'll kill you, you creep!

[*The struggle continues, Bennie pinning her arms under his legs as he kneels over her on the bed. Arlene is terrified and in pain.*]

BENNIE. You will? You'll kill ol' Bennie . . . kill ol' Bennie like you done that cab driver?

[*A cruel reminder he employs to stun and mock her. Arlene looks as though she has been hit. Bennie, still fired up, unzips his pants.*]

ARLENE [*Passive, cold and bitter*]. This how you got your Dorrie, rapin'?

BENNIE [*Unbuttoning his shirt*]. That what you think this is, rape?

ARLENE. I oughta know.

BENNIE. Uh-huh.

ARLENE. First they unzip their pants.

[*Bennie pulls his shirttail out.*]

ARLENE. Sometimes they take off their shirt.

BENNIE. They do huh?

ARLENE. But mostly, they just pull it out and stick it in.

[*Bennie stops, finally hearing what she has been saying. He straightens up, obviously shocked. He puts his arms back in his shirt.*]

BENNIE. Don't you call me no rapist. [*Pause, then insistent*] No, I ain't no rapist, Arlie. [*Gets up, begins to tuck his shirt back in and zip up his pants*]

ARLENE. And I ain't Arlie.

[*Arlene remains on the bed as he continues dressing.*]

BENNIE. No I guess you ain't.

ARLENE [*Quietly and painfully*]. Arlie coulda killed you.

END OF ACT ONE

Prologue

These announcements are heard during the last five minutes of the intermission.

LOUDSPEAKER VOICE. Garden workers will, repeat, will, report for work this afternoon. Bring a hat and raincoat and wear boots. All raincoats will be checked at the front gate at the end of work period and returned to you after supper.

    Your attention please. A checkerboard was not returned to the recreation area after dinner last night. Anyone with information regarding the black and red checkerboard missing from the recreation area will please contact Mrs. Duvall after lunch. No checkerboards or checkers will be distributed until this board is returned.

Betty Rickey and Mary Alice Wolf report to the laundry. Doris Creech and Arlie Holsclaw report immediately to the superintendent's office. The movie this evening will be *Dirty Harry* starring Clint Eastwood. Doris Creech and Arlie Holsclaw report to the superintendent's office immediately.

The bus from St. Mary's this Sunday will arrive at 1:00 P.M. as usual. Those residents expecting visitors on that bus will gather on the front steps promptly at 1:20 and proceed with the duty officer to the visiting area after it has been confirmed that you have a visitor on the bus.

Attention all residents. Attention all residents. [*Pause*] Mrs. Helen Carson has taught needlework classes here at Pine Ridge for thirty years. She will be retiring at the end of this month and moving to Floirda where her husband has bought a trailer park. The resident council and the superintendent's staff has decided on a suitable retirement present. We want every resident to participate in this project—which is—a quilt, made from scraps of material collected from the residents and sewn together by residents and staff alike. The procedure will be as follows. A quilting room has been set up in an empty storage area just off the infirmary. Scraps of fabric will be collected as officers do evening count. Those residents who would enjoy cutting up old uniforms and bedding no longer in use should sign up for this detail with your dorm officer. If you would like to sign your name or send Mrs. Carson some special message on your square of fabric, the officers will have tubes of embroidery paint for that purpose. The backing for the quilt has been donated by the Women's Associates as well as the refreshments for the retirement party to be held after lunch on the thirtieth. Thank you very much for your attention and participation in this worthwhile tribute to someone we are all very fond of here. You may resume work at this time. Doris Creech and Arlie Holsclaw report to the superintendent's office immediately.

Act II

Lights fade. When they come up, it is the next morning. Arlene is asleep on the bed, Arlie is locked in a maximum-security cell. We do not see the officer to whom she speaks.

ARLIE. No, I don't have to shut up, neither. You already got me in seg-re-gation, what else you gonna do? I got all day to sleep, while everybody else is out bustin' ass in the laundry. [*Laughs*] Hey! I know . . . you ain't gotta go do no dorm count, I'll just tell you an you jus' sit. Huh? You 'preciate that? Ease them corns you been moanin' about . . . yeah . . . okay. Write this down. [*Pride, mixed with alternating contempt and amusement*] Startin' down by the john on the back side, we got Mary Alice. Sleeps with her pillow stuffed in her mouth. Says her mom says it'd keep her from grindin' down her teeth or somethin'. She be suckin' that pillow like she gettin' paid for it. [*Laughs*] Next, it's Betty the Frog. Got her legs all opened out like some fuckin' . . . [*Makes croaking noises*] Then it's Doris eatin' pork rinds. Thinks somebody gonna grab 'em outta her mouth if she eats 'em during the day. Doris ain't dumb. She fat, but she ain't dumb. Hey! You notice how many girls is fat here? Then it be Rhonda, snorin', Marvene, wheezin', and Suzanne, coughin'. Then Clara an Ellie be still whisperin'. Family shit, who's gettin' outta line, which girls is gittin' a new work 'signment, an who kin git extra desserts an for how much. Them's the two really run this place. My bed right next to Ellie, for sure it's got some of her shit hid in it by now. Crackers or some crap gonna leak out all over my sheets. Last time I found a fuckin' grilled cheese in my pillow. Even had two of them little warty pickles. Christ! Okay. Linda and Lucille. They be real quiet, but they ain't sleepin'. Prayin', that's them. Linda be sayin' them Hell Marys till you kin just about scream. An Lucille, she tol' me once she didn't believe in no God, jus' some stupid spirits whooshin' aroun' everwhere makin' people do stuff. Weird. Now, I'm goin' back down the other side, there's . . . [*Screams*] I'd like to see you try it! I been listenin' at you for the last three hours. Your husband's gettin' laid off an your lettuce is gettin' eat by rabbits. Crap City. *You* shut up!

Whadda I care if I wake everybody up? I want the nurse . . . I'm gittin' sick in here . . . an there's bugs in here!

[*The light comes up in the apartment. Faint morning traffic sounds are heard. Arlene does not wake up. The warden walks across the catwalk. A guard catches up with him near Arlie's cell. Bennie is stationed at the far end of the walk.*]

LOUDSPEAKER VOICE. Dorm A may now eat lunch.

GUARD (EVANS). Warden, I thought 456 . . . [*Nodding in Arlie's direction*] was leavin' here.

WARDEN. Is there some problem?

GUARD (EVANS). Oh, we can take care of her all right. We're just tired of takin' her shit, if you'll pardon the expression.

ARLENE. You ain't seen nuthin' yet, you mother.

WARDEN. Washington will decide on her transfer. Till then, you do your job.

GUARD (EVANS). She don't belong here. Rest of—

LOUDSPEAKER VOICE. Betty Rickey and Mary Alice Wolf report to the laundry.

GUARD (EVANS). Most of these girls are mostly nice people, go along with things. She needs a cage.

ARLIE [*Vicious*]. I need a knife.

WARDEN [*Very curt*]. Had it occurred to you that we could send the rest of them home and just keep her? [*Walks away*]

LOUDSPEAKER VOICE. Dorm A may now eat lunch. A Dorm to lunch.

GUARD (EVANS) [*Turning around, muttering to himself*]. Oh, that's a swell idea. Let everybody out except bitches like Holsclaw. [*She makes an obscene gesture at him, he turns back toward the catwalk*] Smartass warden, thinks he's runnin' a hotel.

BENNIE. Give you some trouble, did she?

GUARD (EVANS). I can wait.

BENNIE. For what?

GUARD (EVANS). For the day she tries gettin' out an I'm here by myself. I'll show that screechin' slut a thing or two.

BENNIE. That ain't the way, Evans.

GUARD (EVANS). The hell it ain't. Beat the livin'—

BENNIE. Outta a little thing like her? Gotta do her like all the rest. You got your shorts washed by givin' Betty Rickey Milky Ways. You git your chairs fixed givin' Frankie Hill extra time in the shower with Lucille Smith. An you git ol' Arlie girl to behave herself with a stick of gum. Gotta have her brand, though.

GUARD (EVANS). You screwin' that wildcat?

BENNIE [*Starts walk to Arlie's cell*]. Watch. [*Arlie is silent as he approaches, but is watching intently*] Now, [*To nobody in particular*] where was that piece of Juicy Fruit I had in this pocket. Gotta be here somewhere. [*Takes a piece of gum out of his pocket and drops it within Arlie's reach*] Well, [*Feigning disappointment*] I guess I already chewed it. [*Arlie reaches for the gum and gets it*] Oh, [*Looking down at her now*] how's it goin', kid?

ARLIE. Okay.

[*Arlie says nothing more, but unwraps the gum and chews it. Bennie leaves the cell area, motioning to the other guard as if to say, "See, that's how it's done." A loud siren goes by in the street below the apartment. Arlene bolts up out of bed, then turns back to it quickly, making it up in a frenzied, ritual manner. As she tucks the spread up under the pillow, the siren stops and so does she. For the first time, now, she realizes where she is and the inappropriateness of the habit she has just played out. A jackhammer noise gets louder. She walks over to the window and looks out. There is a wolf-whistle from a worker below. She shuts the window in a fury. She looks around the room as if trying to remember what she is doing there. She looks at her watch, now aware that it is late and that she has slept in her clothes.*]

ARLENE. People don't sleep in their clothes, Arlene. An people git up fore noon.

[*Arlene makes a still-disoriented attempt to pull herself together—changing shoes, combing her hair, washing her face—as prison life continues on the catwalk. The warden walks toward Arlie, stopping some distance from her but talking directly to her, as he checks files or papers.*]

WARDEN. Good afternoon, Arlie.

ARLIE. Fuck you. [*Warden walks away*] Wait! I wanna talk to you.

WARDEN. I'm listening.

ARLIE. When am I gettin' outta here?

WARDEN. That's up to you.

ARLIE. The hell it is.

WARDEN. When you can show that you can be with the other girls, you can get out.

ARLIE. How'm I supposed to prove that bein' in here?

WARDEN. And then you can have mail again and visitors.

ARLIE. You're just fuckin' with me. You ain't ever gonna let me out. I been in this ad-just-ment room four months, I think.

WARDEN. Arlie, you see the other girls in the dorm walking around, free to do whatever they want? If we felt the way you seem to think we do, everyone would be in lockup. When you get out of segregation, you can go to the records office and have your time explained to you.

ARLIE. It won't make no sense.

WARDEN. They'll go through it all very slowly . . . when you're eligible for parole, how many days of good time you have, how many industrial days you've earned, what constitutes meritorious good time . . . and how many days you're set back for your write-ups and all your time in segregation.

ARLIE. I don't even remember what I done to git this lockup.

WARDEN. Well, I do. And if you ever do it again, or anything like it again, you'll be right back in lockup where you will stay until you forget *how* to do it.

ARLIE. What was it?

WARDEN. You just remember what I said.

ARLENE. Now then . . . [*Sounds as if she has something in mind to do. Looks as though she doesn't*]

ARLIE. What was it?

WARDEN. Oh, and Arlie, the prison chaplain will be coming by to visit you today.

ARLIE. I don't want to see no chaplain!

WARDEN. Did I ask you if you wanted to see the chaplain? No, I did not. I said, the chaplain will be coming by to visit you today. [*To an unseen guard*] Mrs. Roberts, why hasn't this light bulb been replaced?

ARLIE [*Screaming*]. Get out of my hall!

[*The warden walks away. Arlene walks to the refrigerator and opens it. She picks out the carton of slaw Bennie put there last night. She walks away from the door, then turns around, remembering to close it. She looks at the slaw, as a guard comes up to Arlie's cell with a plate.*]

ARLENE. I ain't never eatin' no more scrambled eggs.

GUARD (CALDWELL). Chow time, cutie pie.

ARLIE. These eggs ain't scrambled, they's throwed up! And I want a fork!

[*Arlene realizes she has no fork, then fishes one out of the garbage sack from last night. She returns to the bed, takes a bite of slaw and gets her wallet out of her purse. She lays the bills out on the bed one at a time.*]

ARLENE. That's for coffee . . . and that's for milk and bread . . . an that's cookies . . . an cheese and crackers . . . and shampoo an soap . . . and bacon an livercheese. No, pickle loaf . . . an ketchup and some onions . . . an peanut butter an jelly . . . and shoe polish. Well, ain't no need gettin' everything all at once. Coffee, milk, ketchup, cookies, cheese, onions, jelly. Coffee, milk . . . oh, shampoo . . .

[*There is a banging on the door.*]

RUBY'S VOICE [*Yelling*]. Candy, I gotta have my five dollars back.

ARLENE [*Quickly stuffing her money back in her wallet*]. Candy ain't here!

RUBY'S VOICE. It's Ruby, upstairs. She's got five dollars I loaned her . . . Arlie? That Arlie? Candy told me her sister be . . .

[*Arlene opens the door hesitantly.*]

RUBY. It is Arlie, right?

ARLENE. It's Arlene. [*Does not extend her hand*]

RUBY. See, I got these shoes in layaway . . . [*Puts her hand back in her pocket*] she said you been . . . you just got . . . you seen my money?

ARLENE. No.

RUBY. I don't get 'em out today they go back on the shelf.

ARLENE [*Doesn't understand*]. They sell your shoes?

RUBY. Yeah. Welcome back.

ARLENE. Thank you.

RUBY. She coulda put it in my mailbox.

[*Ruby starts to leave. Arlene is closing the door when Ruby turns around.*]

RUBY. Uh . . . listen . . . if you need a phone, I got one most of the time.

ARLENE. I do have to make this call.

RUBY. Ain't got a book though . . . well, I got one but it's holdin' up my bed. [*Laughs*]

ARLENE. I got the number.

RUBY. Well, then . . .

ARLENE. Would you . . . wanna come in?

RUBY. You sure I'm not interruptin' anything?

ARLENE. I'm s'posed to call my parole officer.

RUBY. Good girl. Most of them can't talk but you call 'em anyway. [*Arlene does not laugh*] Candy go back to that creep?

ARLENE. I guess.

RUBY. I's afraid of that. [*Looking around*] Maybe an envelope with my name on it? Really cleaned out the place, didn't she?

ARLENE. Yeah. Took everything.

[*They laugh a little.*]

RUBY. Didn't have much. Didn't do nuthin' here 'cept . . . sleep.

ARLENE. Least the rent's paid till the end of the month. I'll be workin' by then.

RUBY. You ain't seen Candy in a while.

ARLENE. No. Think she was in the seventh grade when—

RUBY. She's growed up now, you know.

ARLENE. Yeah. I was thinkin' she might come by.

RUBY. Honey, she won't be comin' by. He keeps all his . . . [Starting over] his place is pretty far from here. But . . . [Stops, trying to decide what to say]

ARLENE. But what?

RUBY. But she had a lot of friends, you know. *They* might be comin' by.

ARLENE. Men, you mean.

RUBY. Yeah. [Quietly, waiting for Arlene's reaction]

ARLENE [Realizing the truth]. Mother said he was her boyfriend.

RUBY. I shouldn't have said nuthin'. I jus' didn't want you to be surprised if some john showed up, his tongue hangin' out an all. [Sits down on the bed]

ARLENE. It's okay. I shoulda known anyway. [Now suddenly angry] No, it ain't okay. Guys got their dirty fingernails all over her. Some pimp's out buyin' green pants while she . . . Goddamn her.

RUBY. Hey now, that ain't your problem. [Moves toward her, Arlene backs away]

ARLIE [Pointing]. You stick your hand in here again Doris an I'll bite it off.

RUBY. She'll figure it out soon enough.

ARLIE [Pointing to another person]. An you, you ain't my mama, so you can cut the mama crap.

ARLENE. I wasn't gonna cuss no more.

RUBY. Nuthin' in the parole rules says you can't get pissed. My first day outta Gilbertsville I done the damn craziest . . . [Arlene looks around, surprised to hear she has done time] Oh yeah, a long time ago, but . . . hell, I heaved a whole gallon of milk right out the window my first day.

ARLENE [Somewhat cheered]. It hit anybody?

RUBY. It bounced! Made me feel a helluva lot better. I said, "Ruby, if a gallon of milk can bounce back, so kin you."

ARLENE. That's really what you thought?

RUBY. Well, not exactly. I had to keep sayin' it for 'bout a year fore I finally believed it. I's moppin' this lady's floor once an she come in an heard me sayin' "gallon a milk, gallon a milk," fired me. She did. Thought I was too crazy to mop her floors.

[Ruby laughs, but is still bitter. Arlene wasn't listening. Ruby wants to change the subject now.]

RUBY. Hey! You have a good trip? Candy said you was in Arkansas.

ARLENE. Alabama. It was okay. This guard, well he used to be a guard, he just quit. He ain't never seen Kentucky, so he drove me. [Watching for Ruby's response]

RUBY. Pine Ridge?

ARLENE. Yeah.

RUBY. It's coed now, ain't it?

ARLENE. Yeah. That's dumb, you know. They put you with men so's they can git you if you're seen with 'em.

RUBY. S'posed to be more natural, I guess.

ARLENE. I guess.

RUBY. Well, I say it sucks. Still a prison. No matter how many pictures they stick up on the walls or how many dirty movies they show, you still gotta be counted five times a day. [Now beginning to worry about Arlene's silence] You don't seem like Candy said.

ARLENE. She tell you I was a killer?

RUBY. More like the meanest bitch that ever walked. I seen lots worse than you.

ARLENE. I been lots worse.

RUBY. Got to you, didn't it?

[Arlene doesn't respond, but Ruby knows she's right.]

RUBY. Well, you jus' gotta git over it. Bein' out, you gotta—

ARLENE. Don't you start in on me.

RUBY [Realizing her tone]. Right, sorry.

ARLENE. It's okay.

RUBY. Done that about a year ago. New waitress we had. Gave my little goin'-straight speech, "No booze, no men, no buyin' on credit," shit like that, she quit that very night. Stole my fuckin' raincoat on her way out. Some speech, huh? [Laughs, no longer resenting this theft]

ARLENE. You a waitress?

RUBY. I am the Queen of Grease. Make the finest french fries you ever did see.

ARLENE. You make a lot of money?

RUBY. I sure know how to. But I ain't about to go back inside for doin' it. Cookin' out's better'n eatin' in, I say.

ARLENE. You think up all these things you say?

RUBY. Know what I hate? Makin' salads—cuttin' up all the stuff 'n floppin' it in a bowl. Some day . . . some day . . . I'm gonna hear "tossed salad" an I'm gonna do jus' that. Toss out a tomato, toss out a head a lettuce, toss out a big ol' carrot. [*Miming the throwing and enjoying herself immensely*]

ARLENE [*Laughing*]. Be funny seein' all that stuff flyin' outta the kitchen.

RUBY. Hey Arlene! [*Gives her a friendly pat*] You had your lunch yet?

ARLENE [*Pulling away immediately*]. I ain't hungry.

RUBY [*Carefully*]. I got raisin toast.

ARLENE. No. [*Goes over to the sink, twists knobs as if to stop a leak*]

ARLIE. Whaddaya mean, what did she do to me? You got eyes or is they broke? You only seein' what you feel like seein'. I git ready to protect myself from a bunch of weirdos an then you look.

ARLENE. Sink's stopped up. [*Begins to work on it*]

ARLIE. You ain't seein' when they's leavin' packs of cigarettes on my bed an then thinking I owe 'em or somethin'.

RUBY. Stopped up, huh? [*Squashing a bug on the floor*]

ARLIE. You ain't lookin' when them kitchen workers lets up their mommies in line nights they know they only baked half enough brownies.

RUBY. Let me try.

ARLIE. You ain't seein' all the letters comin' in an goin' out with visitors. I'll tell you somethin'. One of them workmen buries dope for Betty Rickey in little plastic bottles under them sticker bushes at the water tower. You see that? No, you only seein' me. Well, you don't see shit.

RUBY [*A quiet attempt*]. Gotta git you some Drano if you're gonna stay here.

ARLIE. I'll tell you what she done. Doris brung me some rollers from the beauty-school class. Three fuckin' pink rollers. Them plastic ones with the little holes. I didn't ask her. She jus' done it.

RUBY. Let me give her a try.

ARLENE. I can fix my own sink.

ARLIE. I's stupid. I's thinkin' maybe she were different from all them others. Then that night everybody disappears from the john and she's wantin' to brush my hair. Sure, brush my hair. How'd I know she was gonna crack her head open on the sink. I jus' barely even touched her.

RUBY [*Walking to the bed now, digging through her purse*]. Want a Chiclet?

ARLIE. You ain't asked what she was gonna do to me. Huh? When you gonna ask that? You don't give a shit about that 'cause Doris such a good girl.

ARLENE [*Giving up*]. Don't work.

RUBY. We got a dishwasher quittin' this week if you're interested.

ARLENE. I need somethin' that pays good.

RUBY. You type?

ARLENE. No.

RUBY. Do any clerk work?

ARLENE. No.

RUBY. Any keypunch?

ARLENE. No.

RUBY. Well, then I hate to tell you, but all us old-timers already got all the good cookin' and cleanin' jobs. [*Smashes another bug, goes to the cabinet to look for the bug spray*] She even took the can of Raid! Just as well, empty anyway. [*Arlene doesn't respond*] She hit the bugs with it. [*Still no response*] Now, there's that phone call you was talkin' about.

ARLENE. Yeah.

RUBY [*Walking toward the door*]. An I'll git you that number for the dishwashin' job, just in case. [*Arlene backs off*] How 'bout cards? You play any cards? Course you do. I get sick of beatin' myself all the time at solitaire. Damn borin' bein' so good at it.

ARLENE [*Goes for her purse*]. Maybe I'll jus' walk to the corner an make my call from there.

RUBY. It's always broke.

ARLENE. What?

RUBY. The phone . . . at the corner. Only it ain't at the corner. It's inside the A & P.

ARLENE. Maybe it'll be fixed.

RUBY. Look, I ain't gonna force you to play cards with me. It's time for my programs anyway.

ARLENE. I gotta git some pickle loaf an . . . things.

RUBY. Suit yourself. I'll be there if you change your mind.

ARLENE. I have some things I gotta do here first.

RUBY [*Trying to leave on a friendly basis*]. Look, I'll charge you a dime if it'll make you feel better.

ARLENE [*Takes her seriously*]. Okay.

RUBY [*Laughs, then realizes Arlene is serious*]. Mine's the one with the little picture of Johnny Cash on the door.

[*Ruby leaves. Singing to the tune of "I'll Toe the Line," Bennie walks across the catwalk carrying a tray with cups and a pitcher of water. Arlene walks toward the closet. She is delaying going to the store, but is determined to go. She checks little things in the room, remembers to get a scarf, changes shoes, checks her wallet. Finally, as she is walking out, she stops and looks at the picture of Jesus, then moves closer, having noticed a dirty spot. She goes back into the bathroom for a tissue, wets it in her mouth, then dabs at the offending spot. She puts the tissue in her purse, then leaves the room when noted.*]

BENNIE. I keep my pants up with a piece of twine. I keep my eyes wide open all the time. Da da da da-da da da da da da. If you'll be mine, please pull the twine.

ARLIE. You can't sing for shit.

BENNIE [Starts down the stairs toward Arlie's cell]. You know what elephants got between their toes?

ARLIE. I don't care.

BENNIE. Slow natives. [Laughs]

ARLIE. That ain't funny.

GUARD (EVANS) [As Bennie opens Arlie's door]. Hey, Davis.

BENNIE. Conversation is rehabilitatin', Evans. Want some water?

ARLIE. Okay.

BENNIE. How about some Kool-Aid to go in it? [Gives her a glass of water]

ARLIE. When does the chaplain come?

BENNIE. Want some gum?

ARLIE. Is it today?

BENNIE. Kool-Aid's gone up, you know. Fifteen cents and tax. You get out, you'll learn all about that.

ARLIE. Does the chaplain come today?

BENNIE [Going back up the catwalk]. Income tax, sales tax, property tax, gas and electric, water, rent—

ARLIE. Hey!

BENNIE. Yeah, he's comin', so don't mess up.

ARLIE. I ain't.

BENNIE. What's he tell you anyway, get you so starry-eyed?

ARLIE. He jus' talks to me.

BENNIE. I talk to you.

ARLIE. Where's Frankie Hill?

BENNIE. Gone.

ARLIE. Out?

BENNIE. Pretty soon.

ARLIE. When.

BENNIE. Miss her don't you? Ain't got nobody to bullshit with. Stories you gals tell . . . whoo-ee!

ARLIE. Get to cut that grass now, Frankie, honey.

BENNIE. Huh?

ARLIE. Stupidest thing she said. [Gently] Said first thing she was gonna do when she got out—

[Arlene leaves the apartment.]

BENNIE. Get laid.

ARLIE. Shut up. First thing was gonna be going to the garage. Said it always smelled like car grease an turpur . . . somethin'.

BENNIE. Turpentine.

ARLIE. Yeah, an gasoline, wet. An she'll bend down an squirt oil in the lawnmower, red can with a long pointy spout. Then cut the grass in the backyard, up an back, up an back. They got this grass catcher on it. Says she likes scoopin' up that cut grass an spreadin' it out under the trees. Says it makes her real hungry for some lunch. [A quiet curiosity about all this]

BENNIE. I got a power mower, myself.

ARLIE. They done somethin' to her. Took out her nerves or somethin'. She . . .

BENNIE. She jus' got better, that's all.

ARLIE. Hah. Know what else? They give her a fork to eat with last week. A fork. A fuckin' fork. Now how long's it been since I had a fork to eat with?

BENNIE [Getting ready to leave the cell]. Wish I could help you with that, honey.

ARLIE [Loud]. Don't call me honey.

BENNIE [Locks the door behind him]. That's my girl.

ARLIE. I ain't your girl.

BENNIE [On his way back up the stairs]. Screechin' wild-cat.

ARLIE [Very quiet]. What time is it?

[Arlene walks back into the apartment. She is out of breath and has some trouble getting the door open. She is carrying a big sack of groceries. As she sets the bag on the counter, it breaks open, spilling cans and packages all over the floor. She just stands and looks at the mess. She takes off her scarf and sets down her purse, still looking at the spilled groceries. Finally, she bends down and picks up the package of pickle loaf. She starts to put it on the counter, then turns suddenly and throws it at the door. She stares at it as it falls.]

ARLENE. Bounce? [In disgust] Shit.

[Arlene sinks to the floor. She tears open the package of pickle loaf and eats a piece of it. She is still angry, but is completely unable to do anything about her anger.]

ARLIE. Who's out there? Is anybody out there? [Reading] Depart from evil and do good. [Yelling] Now, you pay attention out there 'cause this is right out of the Lord's mouth. [Reading] And dwell, that means live, dwell for-ever-more. [Speaking] That's like for longer than I've been in here or longer than . . . this Bible the chaplain give me's got my name right in the front of it. Hey! Somebody's s'posed to be out there watchin' me. Wanna hear some more? [Reading] For the Lord for . . . [The word is forsaketh] I can't read in here, you turn on my light, you hear me? Or let me out and I'll go read it in the TV room. Please let me out. I won't scream or nuthin'? I'll just go right to sleep, okay? Somebody! I'll go right to sleep. Okay? You won't even know I'm there. Hey! Goddammit, somebody let me out of here, I can't stand it in here anymore. Somebody! [*Her spirit finally broken*]

ARLENE [*She draws her knees up, wraps her arms around them and rests her head on her arms*]. Jus' gotta git a job an make some money an everything will be all right. You hear me, Arlene? You git yourself up an go find a job. [*Continues to sit*] An you kin start by cleanin' up this mess you made 'cause food don't belong on the floor.

[*Arlene still doesn't get up. Carl appears in the doorway of the apartment. When he sees Arlene on the floor, he goes into a fit of vicious, sadistic laughter.*]

CARL. What's happenin', mama? You havin' lunch with the bugs?

ARLENE [*Quietly*]. Fuck off.

CARL [*Threatening*]. What'd you say?

ARLENE [*Reconsidering*]. Go away.

CARL. You watch your mouth or I'll close it up for you.

[*Arlene stands up now. Carl goes to the window and looks out, as if checking for someone.*]

ARLENE. They after you, ain't they?

[*Carl sniffs, scratches at his arm. He finds a plastic bag near the bed, stuffed with brightly colored knitted things. He pulls out baby sweaters, booties and caps.*]

CARL. What the fuck is this?

ARLENE. You leave them be.

CARL. You got a baby hid here somewhere? I found its little shoes. [*Laughs, dangling them in front of him*]

ARLENE [*Chasing him*]. Them's mine.

CARL. Aw sugar, I ain't botherin nuthin'. Just lookin'. [*Pulls more out of the sack, dropping one or two booties on the floor, kicking them away*]

ARLENE [*Picking up what he's dropped*]. I ain't tellin' you again. Give me them.

CARL [*Turns around quickly, walking away with a few of the sweaters*]. How much these go for?

ARLENE. I don't know yet.

CARL. I'll jus' take care of 'em for you—a few coin for the trip. You *are* gonna have to pay your share, you know.

ARLENE. You give me them. I ain't goin' with you. [*She walks toward him*]

CARL. You ain't?

[*Mocking, Arlene walks up close to him now, taking the bag in her hands. He knocks her away and onto the bed.*]

CARL. Straighten up, girlie. [*Now kneels over her*] You done forgot how to behave yourself. [*Moves as if to threaten her, but kisses her on the forehead, then moves out into the room*]

ARLENE [*Sitting up*]. I worked hard on them things. They's nice, too, for babies and little kids.

CARL. I bet you fooled them officers good, doin' this shit. [*Throws the bag in the sink*]

ARLENE. I weren't—

CARL. I kin see that scene. They sayin' . . . [*Puts on a high southern voice*] "I'd jus' love one a them nice yella sweaters."

ARLENE. They liked them.

CARL. Those turkeys, sure they did. Where else you gonna git your free sweaters an free washin' an free step-right-up-git-your-convict-special-shoe-shine. No, don't give me no money, officer. I's jus' doin' this 'cause I likes you.

ARLENE. They give 'em for Christmas presents.

CARL [*Checks the window again, then peers into the grocery sack*]. What you got sweet, mama? [*Pulls out a box of cookies and begins to eat them*]

ARLIE. I'm sweepin', Doris, 'cause it's like a pigpen in here. So you might like it, but I don't, so if you got some mops, I'll take one of them too.

ARLENE. You caught another habit, didn't you?

CARL. You turned into a narc or what?

ARLENE. You scratchin' an sniffin' like crazy.

CARL. I see a man eatin' cookies an that's what you see too.

ARLENE. An you was laughin' at me sittin' on the floor! You got cops lookin' for you an you ain't scored yet this morning. You better get yourself back to prison where you can git all you need.

CARL. Since when Carl couldn't find it if he really wanted it?

ARLENE. An I bought them cookies for me.

CARL. An I wouldn't come no closer if I's you.

ARLENE [*Stops, then walks to the door*]. Then take the cookies an git out.

CARL [*Imitating Bennie*]. Oh, please, Miss Arlene, come go with Carl to the big city. We'll jus' have us the best time.

ARLENE. I'm gonna stay here an git a job an save up

money so's I kin git Joey. [*Opening the door*] Now, I ain't s'posed to see no ex-cons.

CARL [*Big laugh*]. You don't know nobody else. Huh, Arlie? Who you know ain't a con-vict?

ARLENE. I'll meet 'em.

CARL. And what if they don't wanna meet you? You ain't exactly a nice girl, you know. An you gotta be jivin' about that job shit. [*Throws the sack of cookies on the floor*]

ARLENE [*Retrieving the cookies*]. I kin work.

CARL. Doin' what?

ARLENE. I don't know. Cookin', cleanin', somethin' that pays good.

CARL. You got your choice, honey. You can do cookin' an cleanin' *or* you can do somethin' that pays good. You ain't gonna git rich working on your knees. You come with me an you'll have money. You stay here, you won't have shit.

ARLENE. Ruby works an she does okay.

CARL. You got any Kool-Aid? [*Looking in the cabinets, moving Arlene out of his way*] Ruby who?

ARLENE. Upstairs. She cooks. Works night an has all day to do jus' what she wants.

CARL. And what, exactly, do she do? See flicks take rides in cabs to pick up see-through shoes?

ARLENE. She watches TV, plays cards, you know.

CARL. Yeah, I know. Sounds just like the day room in the fuckin' joint.

ARLENE. She likes it.

CARL [*Exasperated*]. All right. Say you stay here an *finally* find yourself some job. [*Grabs the picture of Jesus off the wall*] This your boyfriend?

ARLENE. The chaplain give it to me.

CARL. Say it's dishwashin', okay? [*Arlene doesn't answer*] Okay?

ARLENE. Okay. [*Takes the picture, hangs it back up*]

CARL. An you git maybe seventy-five a week. Seventy-five for standin' over a sink full of greasy gray water, fishin' out blobs of bread an lettuce. People puttin' pieces of chewed-up meat in their napkins and you gotta pick it out. Eight hours a day, six days a week, to make seventy-five lousy pictures of Big Daddy George. Now, how long it'll take you to make seventy-five workin' for me?

ARLENE. A night.

[*She sits on the bed, Carl pacing in front of her.*]

CARL. Less than a night. Two hours maybe. Now, it's the same fuckin' seventy-five bills. You can either work all week for it or make it in two hours. You work two hours a night for me an how much you got in a week? [*Arlene looks puzzled by the multiplication required. He sits down beside her, even more disgusted*] Two seventy-five's is a hundred and fifty. Three hundred-and-fifties is four hundred and fifty. You stay here you git seventy-five a week. You come with me an you git four hundred and fifty a week. Now, four hundred and fifty, Arlie, is *more* than seventy-five. You stay here you gotta work eight hours a day and your hands git wrinkled and your feet swell up. [*Suddenly distracted*] There was this guy at Bricktown had webby toes like a duck. [*Back now*] You come home with me you work two hours a night an you kin sleep all mornin' an spend the day buyin' eyelashes and tryin' out perfume. Come home, have some guy openin' the door for you sayin', "Good evenin', Miss Holsclaw, nice night now ain't it?" [*Puts his arm around her*]

ARLENE. It's Joey I'm thinkin' about.

CARL. If you was a kid, would you want your mom to git so dragged out washin' dishes she don't have no time for you an no money to spend on you? You come with me, you kin send him big orange bears an Sting-Ray bikes with his name wrote on the fenders. He'll like that. Holsclaw. [*Amused*] Kinda sounds like coleslaw, don't it? Joey be tellin' all his friends 'bout his mom livin' up in New York City an bein' so rich an sendin' him stuff all the time.

ARLENE. I want to be with him.

CARL [*Now stretches out on the bed, his head in her lap*]. So, fly him up to see you. Take him on that boat they got goes roun' the island. Take him up to the Empire State Building, let him play King Kong. [*Rubs her hair, unstudied tenderness*] He be talkin' 'bout that trip his whole life.

ARLENE [*Smoothing his hair*]. I don't want to go back to prison, Carl.

CARL [*Jumps up, moves toward the refrigerator*]. There any chocolate milk? [*Distracted again*] You know they got this motel down in Mexico named after me? Carlsbad Cabins. [*Proudly*] Who said anything about goin' back to prison? [*Slams the refrigerator door, really hostile*] What do you think I'm gonna be doin'? Keepin' you out, that's what!

ARLENE [*Stands up*]. Like last time? Like you gettin' drunk? Like you lookin' for kid junkies to beat up?

CARL. God, ain't it hot in this dump. You gonna come or not? You wanna wash dishes, I could give a shit. [*Yelling*] But you comin' with me, you say it right now, lady! [*Grabs her by the arm*] Huh?

[*There is a knock on the door.*]

RUBY'S VOICE. Arlene?

CARL [*Yelling*]. She ain't here!

RUBY'S VOICE [*Alarmed*]. Arlene! You all right?

ARLENE. That's Ruby I was tellin' you about.

CARL [*Catches Arlene's arm again, very rough*]. We ain't through!

RUBY [*Opening the door*]. Hey! [*Seeing the rough treatment*] Goin' to the store. [*Very firm*] Thought maybe you forgot somethin'.

CARL [*Turns Arlene loose*]. You this cook I been hearin' about?

RUBY. I cook. So what?

CARL. Buys you nice shoes, don't it, cookin'? Why don't you hock your watch an have somethin' done to your hair? If you got a watch.

RUBY. Why don't you drop by the coffee shop. I'll spit in your eggs.

CARL. They let you bring home the half-eat chili dogs?

RUBY. You . . . you got half-eat chili dogs for brains. [*To Arlene*] I'll stop by later. [*Contemptuous look for Carl*]

ARLENE. No. Stay.

[*Carl gets the message. He goes over to the sink to get a drink of water out of the faucet, then looks down at his watch.*]

CARL. Piece a shit. [*Thumps it with his finger*] Shoulda took the dude's hat, Jack. Guy preachin' about the end of the world ain't gonna own a watch that works.

ARLENE [*Walks over to the sink, bends over Carl*]. You don't need me. I'm gittin' too old for it, anyway.

CARL. I don't discuss my business with strangers in the room. [*Heads for the door*]

ARLENE. When you leavin'?

CARL. Six. You wanna come, meet me at this bar. [*Gives her a brightly colored matchbook*] I'm havin' my wheels delivered.

ARLENE. You stealin' a car?

CARL. Take a cab. [*Gives her a dollar*] You don't come . . . well, I already laid it out for you. I ain't never lied to you, have I girl?

ARLENE. No.

CARL. Then you be there. That's all the words I got. [*Makes an unconscious move toward her*] I don't beg nobody. [*Backs off*] Be there.

[*He turns abruptly and leaves. Arlene watches him go, folding up the money in the matchbook. The door remains open.*]

ARLIE [*Reading, or trying to, from a small Testament*]. For the Lord forsaketh not his saints, but the seed of the wicked shall be cut off.

[*Ruby walks over to the counter, starts to pick up some of the groceries lying on the floor, then stops.*]

RUBY. I 'magine you'll want to be puttin' these up yourself. [*Arlene continues to stare out the door*] He do this?

ARLENE. No.

RUBY. Can't trust these sacks. I seen bag boys punchin' holes in 'em at the store.

ARLENE. Can't trust anybody. [*Finally turning around*]

RUBY. Well, you don't want to trust him, that's for sure.

ARLENE. We spent a lot of time together, me an Carl.

RUBY. He live here?

ARLENE. No, he jus' broke outta Bricktown near where I was. I got word there sayin' he'd meet me. I didn't believe it then, but he don't lie, Carl don't.

RUBY. You thinkin' of goin' with him?

ARLENE. They'll catch him. I told him but he don't listen.

RUBY. Funny ain't it, the number a men come without ears.

ARLENE. How much that dishwashin' job pay?

RUBY. I don't know. Maybe seventy-five.

ARLENE. That's what he said.

RUBY. He tell you you was gonna wear out your hands and knees grubbin' for nuthin', git old an be broke an never have a nice dress to wear? [*Sitting down*]

ARLENE. Yeah.

RUBY. He tell you nobody's gonna wanna be with you 'cause you done time?

ARLENE. Yeah.

RUBY. He tell you your kid gonna be ashamed of you an nobody's gonna believe you if you tell 'em you changed?

ARLENE. Yeah.

RUBY. Then he was right. [*Pauses*] But when you make your two nickels, you can keep both of 'em.

ARLENE [*Shattered by these words*]. Well, I can't do that.

RUBY. Can't do what?

ARLENE. Live like that. Be like bein' dead.

RUBY. You kin always call in sick . . . stay home, send out for pizza an watch your Johnny Carson on TV . . . or git a bus way out Preston Street an go bowlin'.

ARLENE [*Anger building*]. What am I gonna do? I can't git no work that will pay good 'cause I can't do nuthin'. It'll be years fore I have a nice rug for this place. I'll never even have some ol' Ford to drive around, I'll never take Joey to no fair. I won't be invited home for pot roast and I'll have to wear this fuckin' dress for the rest of my life. What kind of life is that?

RUBY. It's outside.

ARLENE. Outside? Honey I'll either be *inside* this apartment or *inside* some kitchen sweatin' over the sink. Outside's where you get to do what you want, not where you gotta do some shit job jus' so's you can eat worse than you did in prison. That ain't why I quit bein' so hateful, so I could come back and rot in some slum.

RUBY [*Word "slum" hits hard*]. Well, you can wash dishes to pay the rent on your "slum," or you can spread your legs for any shit that's got the ten dollars.

ARLENE [*Not hostile*]. I don't need you agitatin' me.

RUBY. An I don't live in no slum.

ARLENE [*Sensing Ruby's hurt*]. Well, I'm sorry . . . it's just . . . I thought . . . [*Increasingly upset*]

RUBY [*Finishing her sentence*]. . . . it was gonna be different. Well, it ain't. And the sooner you believe it, the better off you'll be.

[*A guard enters Arlie's cell.*]

ARLIE. Where's the chaplain? I got somethin' to tell him.

ARLENE. They said I's . . .

GUARD (CALDWELL). He ain't comin'.

ARLENE. . . . he tol' me if . . . I thought once Arlie . . .

ARLIE. It's Tuesday. He comes to see me on Tuesday.

GUARD (CALDWELL). Chaplain's been transferred, dollie. Gone. Bye-bye. You know.

ARLENE. He said the meek, meek, them that's quiet and good . . . the meek . . . as soon as Arlie . . .

RUBY. What, Arlene? Who said what?

ARLIE. He's not comin' back?

ARLENE. At Pine Ridge there was . . .

ARLIE. He woulda told me if he couldn't come back.

ARLENE. I was . . .

GUARD (CALDWELL). He left this for you.

ARLENE. I was . . .

GUARD (CALDWELL). Picture of Jesus, looks like.

ARLENE. . . . this chaplain . . .

RUBY [*Trying to call her back from this hysteria*]. Arlene . . .

ARLIE [*Hysterical*]. I need to talk to him.

ARLENE. This chaplain . . .

ARLIE. You tell him to come back and see me.

ARLENE. I was in lockup . . .

ARLIE [*A final, anguished plea*]. I want the chaplain!

ARLENE. I don't know . . . years . . .

RUBY. And . . .

ARLENE. This chaplain said I had . . . said Arlie was my hateful self and she was hurtin' me and God would find some way to take her away . . . and it was God's will so I could be the meek . . . the meek, them that's quiet and good an git whatever they want . . . I forgit that word . . . they git the earth.

RUBY. Inherit.

ARLENE. Yeah. And that's why I done it.

RUBY. Done what?

ARLENE. What I done. 'Cause the chaplain he said . . . I'd sit up nights waitin' for him to come talk to me.

RUBY. Arlene, what did you do? What are you talkin' about?

ARLENE. They tol' me . . . after I's out an it was all over . . . they said after the chaplain got transferred . . . I didn't know why he didn't come no more till after . . . they said it was three whole nights at first, me screamin' to God to come git Arlie an kill her. They give me this medicine an thought I's better . . . then that night it happened, the officer was in the dorm doin' count . . . an they didn't hear nuthin' but they come back out where I was an I'm standin' there tellin' em to come see, real quiet I'm tellin' 'em, but there's all this blood all over my shirt an I got this fork I'm holdin' real tight in my hand . . . [*Clenches one hand now, the other hand fumbling with the front of her dress as if she's going to show Ruby*] this fork, they said Doris stole it from the kitchen an give it to me so I'd kill myself and shut up botherin' her . . . an there's all these holes all over me where I been stabbin' myself an I'm sayin' Arlie is dead for what she done to me, Arlie is dead an it's God's will . . . I didn't scream it, I was jus' sayin' it over and over . . . Arlie is dead, Arlie is dead . . . they couldn't git that fork outta my hand till . . . I woke up in the infirmary an they said I almost died. They said they's glad I didn't. [*Smiling*] They said did I feel better now an they was real nice, bringing me chocolate puddin' . . .

RUBY. I'm sorry, Arlene.

[*Ruby reaches out for her, but Arlene pulls away sharply.*]

ARLENE. I'd be eatin' or jus' lookin' at the ceiling an git a tear in my eye, but it'd jus' dry up, you know, it didn't run out or nuthin'. An then pretty soon, I's well, an officers was sayin' they's seein' such a change in me an givin' me yarn to knit sweaters an how'd I like to have a new skirt to wear an some-times lettin' me chew gum. They said things ain't never been as clean as when I's doin' the house-keepin' at the dorm. [*So proud*] An then I got in the honor cottage an nobody was foolin' with me no more or nuthin'. An I didn't git mad like before or nuthin'. I jus' done my work an knit . . . an I don't think about it, what happened, 'cept . . . [*Now losing control*] people here keep callin' me Arlie an . . . [*Has trouble saying "Arlie"*] I didn't mean to do it, what I done . . .

RUBY. Oh, honey . . .

ARLENE. I did . . . [*This is very difficult*] I mean, Arlie was a pretty mean kid, but I did . . . [*Very quickly*] I didn't know what I . . .

[*Arlene breaks down completely, screaming, crying, falling over into Ruby's lap.*]

ARLENE [*Grieving for this lost self*]. Arlie!

[*Ruby rubs her back, her hair, waiting for the calm she knows will come.*]

RUBY [*Finally, but very quietly*]. You can still . . . [*Stops to think of how to say it*] . . . you can still love people that's gone.

[*Ruby continues to hold her tenderly, rocking as with a baby. A terrible crash is heard on the steps outside the apartment.*]

BENNIE'S VOICE. Well, chicken-pluckin', hog-kickin' shit!

RUBY. Don't you move now, it's just somebody out in the hall.

ARLENE. That's—

RUBY. It's okay Arlene. Everything's gonna be just fine. Nice and quiet now.

ARLENE. That's Bennie that guard I told you about.

RUBY. I'll get it. You stay still now. [*She walks to the door and looks out into the hall, hands on hips*] Why you dumpin' them flowers on the stairs like that? Won't git no sun at all! [*Turns back to Arlene*] Arlene, there's a man plantin' a garden out in the hall. You think we should call the police or get him a waterin' can?

[*Bennie appears in the doorway, carrying a box of dead-looking plants.*]

BENNIE. I didn't try to fall, you know.

RUBY [*Blocking the door*]. Well, when you git ready to *try*, I wanna watch!

ARLENE. I thought you's gone.

RUBY [*To Bennie*]. You got a visitin' pass?

BENNIE [*coming into the room*]. Arlie . . . [*Quickly*] Arlene. I brung you some plants. You know, plants for your window. Like we talked about, so's you don't see them bars.

RUBY [*Picking up one of the plants*]. They sure is scraggly-lookin' things. Next time, git plastic.

BENNIE. I'm sorry I dropped 'em, Arlene. We kin get 'em back together an they'll do real good. [*Setting them down on the trunk*] These ones don't take the sun. I asked just to make sure. Arlene?

RUBY. You up for seein' this petunia killer?

ARLENE. It's okay. Bennie, this is Ruby, upstairs.

BENNIE [*Bringing one flower over to show Arlene, stuffing it back into its pot*]. See? It ain't dead.

RUBY. Poor little plant. It comes from a broken home.

BENNIE [*Walks over to the window, getting the box and holding it up*]. That's gonna look real pretty. Cheerful-like.

RUBY Arlene ain't gettin' the picture yet. [*Walking to the window and holding her plant up too, posing*]. Now.

[*Arlene looks, but is not amused.*]

BENNIE [*Putting the plants back down*]. I jus' thought, after what I done last night . . . I jus' wanted to do somethin' nice.

ARLENE [*Calmer now*]. They is nice. Thanks.

RUBY. Arlene says you're a guard.

BENNIE. I was. I quit. Retired.

ARLENE. Bennie's goin' back to Alabama.

BENNIE. Well, I ain't leavin' right away. There's this guy at the motel says the bass is hittin' pretty good right now. Thought I might fish some first.

ARLENE. Then he's goin' back.

BENNIE [*To Ruby as he washes his hands*]. I'm real fond of this little girl. I ain't goin' till I'm sure she's gonna do okay. Thought I might help some.

RUBY. Arlene's had about all the help she can stand.

BENNIE. I got a car, Arlene. An money. An . . . [*Reaching into his pocket*] I brung you some gum.

ARLENE. That's real nice, too. An I 'preciate what you done, bringin' me here an all, but . . .

BENNIE. Well, look. Least you can take my number at the motel an give me a ring if you need somethin'. [*Holds out a piece of paper*] Here, I wrote it down for you. [*Arlene takes the paper*] Oh, an somethin' else, these towel things . . . [*Reaching into his pocket, pulling out a package of towelettes*] they was in the chicken last night. I thought I might be needin' em, but they give us new towels every day at that motel.

ARLENE. Okay then. I got your number.

BENNIE [*Backing up toward the door*]. Right. Right. Any ol' thing, now. Jus' any ol' thing. You even run outta gum an you call.

RUBY. Careful goin' down.

ARLENE. Bye Bennie.

BENNIE. Right. The number now. Don't lose it. You know, in case you need somethin'.

ARLENE. No.

[*Bennie leaves, Arlene gets up and picks up the matchbook Carl gave her and holds it with Bennie's piece of paper. Ruby watches a moment, sees Arlene trying to make this decision, knows that what she says now is very important.*]

RUBY. We had this waitress put her phone number in matchbooks, give 'em to guys left her nice tips. Anyway, one night this little ol' guy calls her and comes over and says he works at this museum an he don't have any money but he's got this hat belonged to Queen Victoria. An she felt real sorry for him so she screwed him for this little ol' lacy hat. Then she takes the hat back the next day to the museum thinkin' she'll git a reward or somethin' an you know what they done? [*Pause*] Give her a free membership. Tellin' her thanks so much an we're so grateful an wouldn't she like to see this mummy they got downstairs . . . an all the time jus' stallin' . . . waiting 'cause they called the police.

ARLENE. You do any time for that?

RUBY [*Admitting the story was about her*]. County jail.

ARLENE [*Quietly, looking at the matchbook*]. County jail. [*She tears up the matchbook and drops it in the sack of trash*] You got any Old Maids?

RUBY. Huh?

ARLENE. You know.

RUBY [*Surprised and pleased*]. Cards?

ARLENE [*Laughs a little*]. It's the only one I know.

RUBY. Old Maid, huh? [*Not her favorite game*]

ARLENE. I gotta put my food up first.

RUBY. 'Bout an hour?

ARLENE. I'll come up.

RUBY. Great. [*Stops by the plants on her way to the door, smiles*] These plants is real ugly.

[*Ruby exits. Arlene watches her, then turns back to the groceries still on the floor. Slowly, but with great determination, she picks up the items one at a time and puts them away in the cabinet above the counter. Arlie appears on the catwalk. There is one light on each of them.*]

ARLIE. Hey! You 'member that time we was playin' policeman an June locked me up in Mama's closet an then took off swimmin'? An I stood around with them dresses itchin' my ears an crashin' into that door tryin' to git outta there? It was dark in there. So, finally, [*Very proud*] I went around an peed in all Mama's shoes. But then she come home an tried to git in the closet only June taken the key so she said, "Who's in there?" an I said, "It's me!" and she said, "What you doin' in there?" an I started gigglin' an she started pullin' on the door an yellin', "Arlie, what you doin' in there?" [*Big laugh*]

[*Arlene has begun to smile during the story. Now they speak together, both standing as Mama did, one hand on her hip.*]

ARLIE AND ARLENE. Arlie, what you doin' in there?

ARLENE [*Still smiling and remembering, stage dark except for one light on her face*]. Aw shoot.

[*Light dims on Arlene's fond smile as Arlie laughs once more.*]

                         END OF PLAY

ESSAY: AN APPROACH TO THE PLAY

In our society, men have conventionally provided an answer to women's economic problems. In this play, however, even the best of men fail Arlene. The chaplain raises her hopes, then disappears. Bennie does her several good turns, but it is clear that he expects sexual repayment, no matter how hard he fights against this expectation, and Act 1 ends with a near-rape. In some ways it is the pimp Carl who is the most appealing male character: he is clear about his objectives; he is honest with Arlene about them; he cares about her for both sentimental and business reasons; and he is strong enough not to allow himself to be compromised by his desire for her.

Arlene's ongoing love for their child Joey may indicate that she reciprocates some of these feelings. Yet all these men are emotionally needier than women, and because they all believe that they are being helpful, they are also more blind and, therefore, more dangerous as well. All the men in this play exploit Arlene in some way. Carl exploits her sexuality for money. Bennie exploits her need for help and companionship in order to get sex and companionship for himself. Neither man is looking for an equal partner in a relationship. For both, sex is part of a business deal, something to be sold or bought, never an expression of mutual affection between two equal partners. The play seems to imply that if a woman is to keep her dignity and sense of self-esteem, she must maintain her independence.

Posed against the male-dominated world of betrayal which she has known, a world of violence and sex, of prostitution and drugs and money and prison, is Ruby's austere world in which personal dignity is the only value. Her world has little of money or physical comfort or sex, only the dignity of living independently, of keeping what little one has in a clean and orderly way, of taking control of one's life. Hers is a world stripped of grandeur and glamour and wishful thinking, one which only the maturity of experience can accept or find appealing. At the end of Act 1 Arlene repels Bennie's attempted rape with intelligence instead of violence; at the end of the play she puts her small apartment in order, accepts the boredom of an old card game, and makes peace with Arlie, her past. The overtones of this quietly enacted conclusion, given the context set up by the play as a whole, seem heroic, an act of will freely taken, its difficulties, including poverty, seen in advance and accepted. Arlie was an even more frightened version of her present self in a brutal and brutalizing world. She was not very different from Carl, an escapee from prison who still believes in prostitution and money and drugs. Norman rejects these options, but she sees the natural human impulses which lead to them. No one, not even the brutalizing men, is condemned in this compassionate play.

In making her choice, Arlene has faced the twin difficulties of class and gender, and she is indeed "getting out," but it does not come easy, and it may not be forever. The play allows no evasions and no sentimentality; Arlene continues to be misunderstood and exploited outside prison, as she was within. Norman poses tough questions that men and women equally must try to answer, but she poses them in the terms our society creates for women. For example, one obvious solution to Arlene's economic status is for her to return to prostitution, but she knows this leads to drugs, violence, and finally back to prison. Norman unflinchingly faces the problems of a unique lower-class woman and creates a compellingly powerful play.

Carlos Morton

RANCHO HOLLYWOOD

About the Author   Carlos Morton (1947–   ) was born Charles Morton in Chicago and changed his name to Carlos in the process of embracing his Latino roots. In one sense this change reversed the action of his Mexican-born grandfather, Carlos Perez, who tried to ease his assimilation into the American work force by changing his name from Perez to Morton after seeing a billboard advertising Morton salt. This gesture may also typify Morton's concern for the writing and rewriting of history, an interest he traces to his experiences working with ABC News at the 1968 Democratic National Convention in Chicago, where police violence caused him to grow increasingly disaffected with the actions of those in authority. He spent several years thereafter reexamining his identity and ended up relocating to Texas and then to southern California, areas in which he could explore his Latino heritage.

After graduating from the University of Texas at El Paso in 1975, he went on to earn a master of fine arts in theater in 1978 from the University of California at San Diego, where an earlier one-act version of *Rancho Hollywood* served as his thesis. He then worked with a variety of theatrical groups, including such well-known politically activist companies as Luis Valdez' El Teatro Campesino and the San Francisco Mime Troupe, before resuming his formal education, earning a Ph.D. from the University of Texas at Austin in 1987. He now teaches at the University of California at Riverside.

His plays have dealt with various aspects of the Latino experience. Some are based on historical events. *The Many Deaths of Danny Rosales*, for example, is a documentary piece patterned after the 1975 death while in police custody of a young man named Richard Morales near Castroville, Texas, and *The Savior* deals with the assassination of Archbishop Oscar Romero in El Salvador. Others of his plays are mythical, such as *El Jardin*, a Latino retelling of the events in the Garden of Eden. Still others, such as *El Dorado* and *Rancho Hollywood*, present a revisionist version of California history, challenging the dominant culture's traditional myth of manifest destiny.

About the Play   In 1976, the California-Pacific Theater hired Morton to write a history of San Diego county, and *El Dorado* was the result. It begins with the arrival of the Spaniards in the sixteenth century and moves up to the 1849 Gold Rush. *Rancho Hollywood*, a similarly nonchronological reinterpretation of history, may be seen as its sequel. It deals with events from 1834 to the present, but indirectly, through its central dramatic premise: that we are on the set during the filming of *Ye Olde California Days*, a stereotypical Hollywood version of California history.

Many of the play's historical references are to events from the Mexican War and its aftermath. In 1836, Texas declared its independence from Mexico, and for nearly a decade remained an independent republic. In the final days of 1845, the United States annexed Texas as the twenty-eighth state, and war with Mexico followed. This war was not universally popular. Many regarded it as a military adventure of dubious morality. (Henry David Thoreau's essay "On Civil Disobedience," for example, grew from his decision to be jailed rather than pay taxes supporting it.) The war ended in less than two years with a decisive American victory and with the ceding to the United States of an enormous area: Texas, California, and all territories between them, about a sixth of the total area of the contiguous forty-eight states. Although Article VIII of the 1848 Treaty of Guadalupe Hidalgo, which ended the war, guaranteed full citizenship rights to all Mexicans in the territories ceded to the United States, including protection of their civil and property rights, these promises were not generally respected (especially when gold was discovered in California in the year after the treaty was signed). Millions of acres of land owned by Mexican-Americans were transferred to private Anglo owners and to federal and state government authorities, and longtime residents found themselves redefined as foreigners.

CHARACTERS

GOVERNOR RIO RICO, the last Mexican Governor of California, a middle-aged mulatto or Mexican man.

DONA VICTORIA RICO, the Governor's fair-skinned "Spanish" wife.

RAMONA RICO, the Ricos' young daughter, a brown mestiza.

JEDEDIAH GOLDBANGER SMITH, a Yankee trader-trapper-goldminer-soldier-capitalist with a vision.

TONTA GERONIMA SINMUHOW, an Indian maid, maiden.

YALLER MARCUS MALCOM KUNTA KINTE, a high yaller slave, worker, invisible man.

Place: Los Angeles, California
Time: 1840s to the present

Act I

At rise the Director is assisted by his cameraman as they shoot a movie entitled "Ye Olde California Days." The principals are off stage preparing themselves for their entrance: Ramona, an ingenue, fiery Latina type; Joaquín, a young man dressed as a peon; Sinmuhow, a Native American woman; Victoria, an older matronly type, Spanish looking; and Rico, a dark debonair older Mexican male.

DIRECTOR [*To his cameraman*]. If everybody's here, let's shoot the balcony scene. [*Noises backstage, people talking.*]

CAMERAMAN. Attention everybody! Quiet on the set.

DIRECTOR. The fiery impetuous Ramona [*Enter Ramona*] is pacing nervously on her balcony waiting for her demon lover, Cisco. Stamp your feet, clap your hands, say your line! A medium shot here, camera.

RAMONA. Oh no, this cannot go on. Where is my sultry Cisco? I want him to take me away to the Rancho Grande of ecstasy!

DIRECTOR. That's good, Ronnie, but I need more of an accent. Say "dis" instead of "this" and "wan" instead of "want." And throw in a few "olés." Zoom in on a close-up on "olé."

RAMONA. Dis cun nut go on. I wan heem to take me away Olé!

DIRECTOR. Wonderful! I love it! Remember, this is nineteenth-century California, just before the Gold Rush, when all those gay caballeros and sexy señoritas were dancing fandangos until dawn. Now then, what's missing?

CAMERAMAN. You forgot the peon.

DIRECTOR. Of course, where is my sleepy peon? [*Enter Joaquín*] There you are. Oh, I love your outfit, it's so . . . I don't know . . . native. What's your name?

JOAQUIN. Joaquín.

DIRECTOR. Walking?

JOAQUIN. No, Joaquín. Like in Joaquín Valley.

DIRECTOR. Mind if I call you Jack? Up against that wall. Now squat. [*Placing a sombrero that covers up his face.*] There!

JOAQUIN. Do I have any lines?

DIRECTOR. Lines!

CAMERAMAN. No lines.

DIRECTOR. Sorry, Jack. Move your sombrero a bit from time to time so we know you're not a statue. Who's next?

CAMERAMAN. The passerby. A lady of the night.

SINMUHOW. I am Sinmuhow. [*Entering*]

DIRECTOR. Oh, you're Native American. Look everybody, a real honest to goodness Indian! We're going to have such good karma! [*He hugs her.*] Now then, this part calls for a Mexican, but I'm sure you can pass. At the very start of the scene you walk on undulating your hips like so. [*He walks across the set undulating his hips.*]

JOAQUIN. Yes, and that's my cue. I lift the brim of my sombrero, stick out my tongue, and pant.

DIRECTOR. Good. [*To Cameraman*] Couldn't we put some fruit on her head? You know, then she could do the cha-cha-cha.

CAMERAMAN. That's old hat.

DIRECTOR. All right, forget it. Who's next?

CAMERAMAN. Victoria the maid. [*Enter Victoria*]

VICTORIA. I was under the impression I was supposed to be her mother.

DIRECTOR. You are, dear, but you're also the maid. Aren't all mothers! Johnny, what is she supposed to be doing?

CAMERAMAN [*Reading script*]. It says here, "enter making a tamale."

DIRECTOR. Oh, how ethnic. Well, where's your tamale? You little hot tamale you! [*Laughing at his own joke*] Cut to a long shot.

VICTORIA [*Pulling out a fake tamale*]. Ay, que ridículo.

DIRECTOR. Great! You speak Spanish! Throw in a few words every once in a while. Doesn't matter what you say, just as long as it sounds good. Give me your line.

VICTORIA. Ay Ramona, forget that no count Cisco, he is no good for you!

DIRECTOR. More accent!

RAMONA. Ay Mamá, I lub heem, he sets my heart on fi-errrr.

DIRECTOR. What happens then?

CAMERAMAN. Her debonair, slightly-greying Spanish grandee father enters cracking his whip and drinking tequila.

DIRECTOR. Father! Father! Where's the Father?

RICO. Ay voy, I'm coming!

DIRECTOR. These people! [*To Cameraman who nods in agreement*] You'd think this was the land of manana! [*Joaquín gets up to stretch.*]

VICTORIA. He's here!

RICO. Excuse me, I was getting made up. [*He enters with an excess of white powder on his face. The Director does not really see him.*]

DIRECTOR. Let's go! We have a tight schedule! I'm going to have to be a bitch about this!

CAMERAMAN. Places! Places! [*Joaquín squats back into place*] Quiet! Quiet on the set! Ye Olde California Days, take one.

DIRECTOR. Lights! Camera! Wait. [*He runs up and places a plastic rose between Ramona's teeth*] Action! [*The Lady of the Night strolls by dancing salsa. The Peon lifts up the brim of his sombrero and starts panting, grabbing his groin.*]

RAMONA [*Stamping her feet and clapping her hands*]. Olé! O, dis can nut go on. Waer es my sultry Cisco? I wan heem to take me to El Rancho Grande of Ecstasy!

VICTORIA [*She drops her tamale as she enters*]. Ramona, forget dat no count Cisco, he es no goot for you.

RAMONA. Ay Mamá! You dropped your tamale. but I love heem, he puts my hard on fi-eerrrr.

VICTORIA. Well, put de fi-errrr out! He es un bandido, un desesperado! If your Papá finds out he weeel keeel you!

RICO [*Enter cracking his whip and drinking tequila from a bottle*]. Andale! Andale! Arriba! Arriba! [*Like Speedy González, like Trini López trilling and shouting*] Ajúa! Trllllllingg!

DIRECTOR. Cut! Cut! [*To Cameraman*] Has Central Casting gone color blind! I asked for a white Spanish grandee and they give me a dark farmworker!

VICTORIA. ¡ Qué insulto!

RICO. Por eso me tardé tanto. Me pusieron todo este polvo.

DIRECTOR. Hey, no offense fellah, but you don't look very Spanish. You're supposed to be Ramona's father, the Spanish grandee.

RICO. Sir, I don't understand, even if I am as dark as a Moor, I could still be Ramona's father.

VICTORIA. That's right. Ramona is a mestiza.

DIRECTOR. A what?

VICTORIA. A mestiza. Half and half. If I, as her mother, am fair, and the father is dark, then the child is like café con leche.

RAMONA. I've never been described that way before.

VICTORIA. Yes, but that is what the Mexican people are, a mixture of Spanish and Indian.

RICO. And Arab and Jewish and African . . .

DIRECTOR. That is very quaint, that is very informative. But this film is supposed to be about the Spanish Californios!

RICO. Mr. Director, with all due respect, I am afraid you have little conception of the Californio reality. The people of that time were Mexican, not Spanish.

RAMONA. Jed, honey, listen to these people, they're trying to tell you something.

CAMERAMAN. It says here in the script that Ramona's father is "a Spanish grandee type, representative of the early aristocratic Californios."

RICO. But did you know that many of the founding families of the City of Los Angeles were black? The last Mexican Governor of California was a mulatto. His name was Pio Pico.

RAMONA. Who told you that?

RICO. I read it in a history book. They showed photos of him.

VICTORIA. That's right. All that stuff about the Spanish is pure bunk!

RICO. Look, I'm sure if you approached this film a bit more realistically, by doing some research, you'd find I could do this part.

DIRECTOR. All right! Have you all had your little says now? If you people ever want to work in this town again, you'll play your parts exactly the way I tell you to. Or you will never work anywhere in Hollywood again! Let's go! [*He exits followed by the Cameraman*]

RICO. Oh, damn it! Now I did it!

JOAQUIN. Listen, I agree with you 100%. I'm sick and tired of playing these demeaning roles.

SINMUHOW. Me too, but I'm also sick and tired of car hopping at the Red-E-Go Drive-In.

RAMONA. I'll try and talk to him. Maybe I can cool him down a bit. [*Exits*]

VICTORIA [*To Rico*]. You did right in speaking out. Are you well versed in the California days? Oh, those must have been wonderful times, halcyon days. [*The lights fade, except for a spot on Rico and Victoria. An old waltz from the period starts to play*]

RICO. I saw an old photo of the governor's wife. She looked like you, very fair, very Spanish.

VICTORIA. They must have been very happy, before the Gringos came.

RICO [*At this point Rico and Victoria are dancing a waltz downstage. Another spotlight shines upstage to reveal Joaquín and Ramona in an embrace bidding adieu*]. Yes, but they were living on borrowed time. They had barely gained independence from Spain and secularized the missions when other problems arose.

VICTORIA. What could have possibly shattered such an idyllic dream?

RICO. The Indians, for one thing. [*As Rico says this Tonta enters and puts her head to the keyhole to eavesdrop*] They were becoming increasingly bolder, attacking settlements, running away with livestock, killing our people.

VICTORIA. That would be solved in time. We would all become one race!

RICO. Perhaps, but then there was the constant bickering between those of us in the North and those from the South. [*Rico sees Joaquín and goes for him. Exit Joaquín and Tonta. A door slams*] That young man is not to darken this door again!

VICTORIA. Don't get upset, dear, I was chaperoning them.

RICO. I don't care, he is not to set foot in this house again!

RAMONA. Why do you dislike Joaquín so much? Aside from the fact he is from the North?

RICO. I'll tell you why. He drinks, swears, reads suggestive books, shoots his pistols in the air, duels and plots insurrections. Is that enough?!

VICTORIA [*Aside to Ramona*]. Just like your father did when he was young.

RAMONA. Good God in heaven!

RICO. And there she goes, using the name of God in vain again!

RAMONA. Why don't you admit the real reason you dislike him is because he is in the forefront of steering a new and independent course for us Californios.

RICO. There she goes, using that word again— Californio!

VICTORIA. But Rico, it's just a word the young people use to describe themselves nowadays.

RICO. Not good enough to call themselves Mexicanos como sus padres.

VICTORIA. Don't you remember we used to call ourselves "Criollos" to distinguish us from the Españoles?

RICO. That was yesterday. Today we are Mexican. And we shall always remain Mexican. To call ourselves anything else is treason. I am the Governor of this territory and I refuse to hear that word in my house!

VICTORIA. You are as unbending as a mountain; no wonder all the youth are rebelling.

RAMONA. There's some other reason why Papá hates Joaquín so much. Why don't you come out with it!

RICO. Mira, mira! Don't speak to me in that tone of voice. For one thing, his people are barely gente de razón. They are but one generation removed from the savages.

RAMONA. Papá, with all due respect, you claim to dislike Joaquín because of his lower class origins, yet mother tells me your grandparents were poor shepherds of the humblest class. [*Victoria is making frantic gestures and shaking her head "no."*]

RICO. So, your aristocratic mother, descendant of the conquistadores, told you that, eh?

VICTORIA. Your father comes from good stock, dear, good sound stock.

RICO. Yes, there's no comparison between myself and that young rogue. Why, he's practically a coyote, a half breed.

RAMONA. You're calling him a coyote! What are you? What am I?

VICTORIA. Ramona, show your father more respect!

RAMONA. I see now, you dislike him because he is not "Spanish."

RICO. He's also the black sheep of the family, he is, esa bola de indios . . .

RAMONA. Well, let me tell you something, that "indio" asked me to marry him and I said "yes!"

VICTORIA. Why Ramona, how improper! You know that the parents have to be consulted before a girl receives a proposal of marriage!

RICO. You will do no such thing!

RAMONA. Yes I will!

RICO. Get me a switch! I will beat her within a very inch of her life! Listen to me, young lady, you will marry only within your own class! You will marry someone of pure Spanish blood.

RAMONA. What difference does it make! You're not Spanish, I'm not Spanish!

RICO. Yes you are. Call yourself anything else and no gentleman will ever ask for your hand in marriage. Ramona, you don't know prejudice like we do.

VICTORIA. Listen to your father, he means well.

RICO. When I married your mother in Mexico City, her relatives looked down on her because I looked like a Moor!

VICTORIA. It's true, hija, that's why we came back to California.

RICO. I don't want the same thing happening to you!

RAMONA. My God, this is so confusing! Papá, don't you see, you're being a hypocrite!

RICO [*Raising his hand to slap her. Victoria restrains him*]. Why can't you be like the little girl I once knew, who used to sit on my knee and listen to stories of why the sea is so salty, or why the full moon has the face of a rabbit.

RAMONA. I don't want to hear any more stories!

RICO. I used to tell her the reason people got dark is because they drank too much chocolate. But you're right, those days are past. Still, I have the final word in this house. You shall not see Joaquín again. I shall banish him to the farthest corners of this territory.

RAMONA. Noooooooooo! [*Ramona exits defiantly*] We shall elope!

RICO [*Trying to go after her*]. Ramona! Come back here!

VICTORIA. Let her go, give her time to cool her heels. You know, even if she marries the whitest man in California, if you can find one, their children could still be as dark as you. You never told her your grandmother was a mulatto, did you? [*Tonta reenters the scene and listens*]

RICO. Why trouble our daughter with inconsequential matters concerning my lineage!

VICTORIA. Not so inconsequential when she has to explain to her husband why the child looks like the Queen of Sheba.

RICO. Listen here, woman, don't make fun of me!

VICTORIA. Rico . . .

RICO. I never denied my origins. My grandmother may have been a mulatto but my parents were mestizos. I, in turn, have become a gente de razón, a citizen with all the rights and benefits thereof.

VICTORIA. Where else but California could you begin life as a Negro and end up as an Español?

RICO. Listen to me! I have heard of places where one drop, just one little drop of black blood automatically makes you a slave, what they call a "nigger." I may have some black blood in me, but I am no slave.

VICTORIA. No Señor, you are not a slave. [*She embraces him*]

TONTA [*Rushing in*]. Señores! Señores! The Yankee Clipper ship has been sighted in the harbor!

VICTORIA. Oh, Rico, let's go down to the wharf and get our pick of things before the others!

RICO. Now you know why we're getting into debt! But it's too late, we'll go in the morning.

VICTORIA. I have a better idea. Why don't we invite the Captain for dinner? We'll have a light supper and then maybe a small baile afterwards.

RICO [*As they walk away*]. My dear, it is precisely this ostentatious style of living wihch will be the ruin of us.

TONTA [*Aside*]. A mulatto, his grandmother. I knew it! That wooly headed old vieja was as black as Cleopatra!

DIRECTOR [*Breaking up the scene*]. I've been watching it all. I love it!

RAMONA [*By his side*]. So you see, Jed, they were real people with real problems.

CAMERAMAN. I'm concerned about the father; he's somewhat of a racist.

DIRECTOR. Exactly! Exactly!

RICO [*Re-entering*]. It's something that the Mexican

people would work out in time. Don't you see, they *talked* about it.

DIRECTOR. You know, we could do a California "West Side Story." What happens next?

RICO. The Anglos came. Some hiked in over the mountains, others sailed in on the clipper chips.

TONTA. They brought their slaves.

DIRECTOR. We could get O. J. Simpson to play the slave. Now we need a big name star for the, uh, Captain of the clipper ship. Someone with charisma, poise, good looks . . . I got it! I got it!

CAMERAMAN. Got what?

DIRECTOR. I'll play the part. [*The cameraman groans*] You play my slave. Where are we? Where are we? [*The other actors disperse, leaving the Director and Cameraman to set up the next scene.*]

CAMERAMAN. On a boat. Out in the harbor.

DIRECTOR. Oh, I love this. It's so Brechtian. What am I doing?

CAMERAMAN. You could be singing . . . a popular song of the day.

JED [*Becoming Jedediah Smith*]. "Oh Susana, oh don't you cry for me . . . for I'm bound to California with my banjo on my knee."

RUFUS [*Turning into the Slave*]. Land, Massa Jed, land!

JED. There she is, Rufus, Californee! Ain't she purty! The Spanish thought it was an island inhabited by a tribe of Amazons.

RUFUS. What's a Amazons?

JED. Warrior women, Rufus, who wore breastplates of solid gold and slew every man in their path. Their queen was named Calafia. So they named the island California. She was reputed to be a black woman.

RUFUS. Land sakes! What was a nigger woman doing out here?

JED. It was only myth, Rufus, mere fantasy. But the cursed reality is that Spanish is the language spoken here, so let's get on with our Spanish lesson. "Fina tela aquí!"

RUFUS. Fina tela aquí . . . what I say?

JED. Fine cloth here! Now, repeat after me. "Mercancías, muebles!"

RUFUS. Mercancías! Muebles! That means merchandise, furniture.

JED. Fine. Now, here's a very important phrase: "Bajas intereses de crédito."

RUFUS. Bajas intereses de crédito!

JED. Good. That means "low interest rates." Californios love buying on credit. They are all show. So put the bright colors up front and hide the drab ones in the back. And never take your eyes off of them! They'll steal you blind.

RUFUS. Just like you, eh Massa Jed?

JED [*Holding up a shoe*]. Lookee here, do you know what this is!

RUFUS. Looks like a shoe to me.

JED. This here's money, boy, money. They're called California Banknotes. Mexicans pay in rawhide, which we turn into shoes and sell it back to them.

RUFUS. Why don't they make their own shoes?

JED. Shhhh! Don't say that! They lazy, boy, they stupid. They depend almost entirely on us Yankee clipper ships.

RUFUS. Shoot! We gots the market cornered.

JED. Ya dang right!

RICO. We gonna make *us* a pile of money!

JED. *Me* a pile of money.

RUFUS. You a pile.

JED. Now then, if you're going to sell to these people you have to understand them. Let me read you a passage from a book written in 1840 by Richard Henry Dana called "Two Years Before the Mast." [*Clearing his throat and reading*] "The Californio men are generally indolent . . ."

RUFUS. What's a insolent? [*reading over his shoulder*]

JED. That's "indolent" with a "d." It means lazy. [*Reading again*] "The men are of a harmless disposition, fond of spiritous liquors, who care little for the welfare of their children. The women have but little virtue, the jealousy of their men is extreme, and the revenge deadly and almost certain." Now, what does that tell you about the Californios!

RUFUS. Whew! Don't mess wit de women folk! And, uh, some of dat dere sound what you said I is, 'specially de parts 'bout liquor and indolent.

JED [*Pulling out a flask*]. Ain't nothing wrong with having a little drink now and then. Now then, what else you want to know about greasers? I read about 'em in all these books here.

RUFUS. Why you call 'em greasers?

JED. 'Cause they got greasy hair and they eat greasy food. [*Jed combs his greasy hair*] You see, Rufus, there's very few white people in the country. The Californios are a mixture of Spanish and bloody Aztec!

RUFUS. Bloody Aztec!

JED. That's right. The bloody Aztecs used to practice human sacrifice and rip the hearts out of their victims' chests. Then they made sandwiches out of the hearts and sold them on streetcorners. That's why you have to be careful what you eat down here or you're liable to come down with Moctezuma'a revenge!

RUFUS. Must have been a white man who wrote that.

JED. So, figure them out and skin them alive! And if you make me enough money on this trip . . . I'll make you a free man!

RUFUS [*Pulling out a contract*]. You put that in writing!

JED. Hey! You're not supposed to know how to read . . . or write, you sneaky coon, you!

RUFUS. Sign! [*They shake on it. Blackout. Voices heard backstage. Spot on Tonta shown preparing herself for the next scene*]

DIRECTOR [*Voice offstage*]. What's the next scene? Where are we?

CAMERAMAN. Back at the Rancho. The gay Californios are preparing for the night's festivities. [*Voice offstage*]

TONTA. Californios didn't prepare anything. We servants did it all. [*Entering*]

DIRECTOR. Okay, Okay. Pretend you're making tortillas or something. And, uh, talk to yourself, complaining.

TONTA [*Improvising*]. Pinche gente! Puras parrandas! They have to have a fandango every night. Why they hardly pause for an earthquake and continue right on dancing when it stops! [*Tonta stops, hears voice off to the side, sees Joaquín and Ramona entering the garden, stops to listen*]

RAMONA. Joaquín! I'm so glad you're here, querido!

JOAQUIN. Your father has banished me to a military outpost in Sonoma.

RAMONA. Take me with you, I will go with you this very night!

JOAQUIN. Out of the question. It's too dangerous. Russians to the north, Yankees to the east, British pirates.

RAMONA. Well, then we'll leave the country. We'll go to Mexico or Europe. Someplace where we can be together.

JOAQUIN. I will never leave California. It is my home.

RAMONA. Well then . . . Joaquín, I thought we were going to elope tonight. I even packed my bags!

JOAQUIN. Ramona, mi amor, we must respect your father's wishes. I will work very hard and rise up through the ranks. I will repell the invaders from our land. Then he will respect me.

RAMONA. He will never respect you, Joaquín. You see, my father dislikes you because of your skin color, becasue you look like an indio.

JOAQUIN. Ramona, how can you say such a thing about your father? That's preposterous! Your father may be an old crustacean because of his politics, but a bigot he is not.

RAMONA. Joaquín, I'm speaking the truth. Listen to me, we must leave him and start our own lives. [*Tonta starts walking towards them*]

JOAQUIN. Shhh, someone is coming. I must go! Promise you'll wait for me!

RAMONA. Yes, I will, of course, but don't you see . . . my father will never have anything to do with you because you are not Spanish.

JOAQUIN. Shhh, not another word. We are all the same raza. We will work things out. We always have before. [*He starts to leave but rushes back to Ramona*] ¡Ay Ramona, no voy a poder vivir sin ti! [*He turns to go and crashes into Tonta*]

TONTA. Oye! If Don Rico sees you he'll make chorizo out of you!

JOAQUIN. I'm leaving! I'm leaving! Querida, adiós. [*Joaquín hears footsteps coming in the direction of his exit*] Who's that? One of the guests?

TONTA. By the sound of the footsteps it is Don Rico himself! He's probably loading his revolver!

RAMONA. Quick! Hide! My parents are coming! [*Joaquín makes desperate motions*] Behind the pillar, under the table, anywhere! [*Depending upon the set Joaquín can become a statue, lamp, fountain, etc.*] Tonta, cover for us, please!

TONTA. Why should I? You live in a dream world. Your life is full of intrigues and little masquerades. But who do you think get's stuck with all the mierda?

RAMONA. Tonta, ¡por favor! [*Ramona sees that Joaquín has tried to turn into a statue. She grabs him and exits opposite Rico and Victoria's entrance*]

RICO [*Entering*]. Who were you talking to?

TONTA. Nobody. You know me. I'm a little loca. Sometimes I talk to myself.

VICTORIA [*Who was not fooled*]. Tonta, be sure to prepare a room for the Captain of the Yankee clipper ship. He may stay the night.

TONTA. Shall I leave the pile of loose change in a bowl in his room as customary?

RICO. Yes, yes, of course. Show him some of that famous Californio hospitality!

VICTORIA. But I thought we were in debt!

RICO. Oh, this is just small change. Tonta, call my daughter to the living room. I want her to dance for our guests.

TONTA. Sí, Señor.

RICO. Ah, I see that my guests have arrived. [*Rico goes off into the wing and welcomes the guests in the next room*]

VICTORIA [*Taking Tonta aside*]. What did they say? [*While Victoria and Tonta are talking in private to the side, Ramona enters with Joaquín dressed in a ludicrous disguise. They kiss, he exits*]

RICO [*voice offstage*]. Welcome! Welcome all to Rancho Madera Acebo! [*Music starts playing, Rico enters on stage]* Ah, Ramona, there you are. I'm glad to see that your spirits have lifted. Come dear, dance for our guests. *[Applause is heard, shouting]*

RAMONA. Oh no, Papá, please!

RICO. Yes, you will! *[Lights out except for spot on Ramona. She dances with the audience being the guests. Taped music]*

El Borrego

Señora, su borreguito
Me quiere llevar al río
Y yo le digo que no,
Porque me muero de frío
Sale la linda
Sale la fea
Y el borreguito
Con su salea
Sale el negrito
Con su garrote
Y el borreguito
Con su salea
Tope que tope
Tope con ella
Tope que tope
Tope con él

[Somewhere towards the end, Jed and Rufus enter, interrupting the party. Lights on. All stare at Jed.]

JED. Excuse me, Señores, I didn't mean to interrupt your party.

RICO. ¡Bienvenidos! Yo soy el Gobernador Don Río Rico, para servirle.

RAMONA. My father, Don Río Rico, Governor of California, welcomes you!

RICO. ¡Mi casa es su casa!

JED. Why thank you, I think I'm going to like this casa very much.

RUFUS *[As Jed eyes Ramona]*. Massa Jed, you be careful wit dem hot tamales. Did you notice the Gubnur? He's a darky!

JED *[Motioning to Rufus]*. Damas y caballeros, I bringo you unos presentos! *[Handing Rico a six pack of beer]* Cerveza for you! Coors! Best beer in the Westo. Decado del Hispánico!

RICO. Muchas gracias.

JED. Ole! Más presentos here. Coca Cola for the little lady. And for the Señora un credit carto!

VICTORIA. ¿Para qué se usa esto?

RAMONA. What function does this serve, Señor? I will translate for my parents until they learn your language.

JED. Which should be about any minute now. Tello your padre we hablar negocio later on. You folks just go right ahead with your fiesta, pretend I'm not here . . .

RICO. Señor, ¿cuál es su misión aquí en California?

RAMONA. My father would like to know what is your mission here in California?

JED. Oh, sell a few beads, do some sightseeing . . .

RICO. Pregúntale ¿por qué no le ha fregado a su negro?

RAMONA. Why haven't you beaten your slave? *[Jed and Rufus look confused]* We hear tell that you Yankees delight in mistreating your slaves.

JED. What, me beat my nigger?! Why, el como mi sono. Aren't you boy?

RUFUS *[Aside]*. We probably is related along de way.

RICO *[Trying to speak English]*. You querer comer! *[Makes eating motion]*

RAMONA. Would you like something to eat?

RICO. Salt carne? Corn pan?

JED. No, gracias, pero I could go for a burrito or a cold margarita! Ain't you got no Taco Bells 'round here?

RICO. Tonita, prepárale una comida al señor. My Tonta, she fixe you upe. Cuánto tiempar you estar aquí?

RAMONA. My father would like to know how long you plan to stay here in California?

JED *[Looking at this wrist watch]*. What year is this? 1842? Oh, a couple of centuries, at least.

RICO. Señor, one cosa . . . muy important.

JED. Sir, I think you ready to speako el English.

RICO. Y you, señor, the Español.

JED. Claro, you hablo Español perfecto. Six weeks Berlitzo.

RICO. Ife you stay aquí por mucho tiempo . . . you deber ser ciudadano México . . . comprende? Very importante.

JED. Okay, okay. Let me tako uno siesto to thinko. After all, is this not the land of mañana?

RICO. Okay. I show you tu roomo. Tonta, el granero para el negro! *[Exit Tonta and Rufus]* My Tonta show you slave barn.

JED. Wait a minuto. You folks no have to terminar fandango so earlyo! I heard you danco until dawno!

RICO. Is all right. Party over! *[Exit Rico and Jed in fervent discourse]*

RAMONA. Buenas noches, Mamacita.

VICTORIA. ¡Qué Mamacita ni qué mi abuela! I know Joaquín was here! Drive him out of your mind.

Ramona, he's gone forever! [*Ramona stalks out. Enter Rico*] What's the matter, querido, you seem preoccupied?

RICO. It was something the Yankee said. He asked me why there were so few white people like us in the territory. And I could not help but note a tone of derision in his voice.

VICTORIA. Are you sure it wasn't your imagination?

RICO. And then I asked him if he was from New England and he said, "no, I'm from Texas."

VICTORIA. Texas!

RICO. Yes, the same Tejas they stole in 1836. The same Tejas which is now a slave state. Dios mío, time is moving by so quickly. It seems as though we conquered California only yesterday.

VICTORIA. Sí, and Mexico the day before. [*They exit. On another part of the stage Tonta is seen leading Rufus to the door of the stable*] I must tell you, the maid overhead Ramona and Joaquín talking and . . . [*Trailing off*]

TONTA. This is the barn, this is where you sleep, Mr. Nigaro.

RUFUS. My name isn't "nigaro," it's Rufus.

TONTA. Isn't that what the white man called you, "nigaro?"

RUFUS. Yes, but don't you call me that. My real name is Rufus, Rufus Smith.

TONTA. Smith, isn't that the white man's name?

RUFUS. A slave doesn't really have a choice. Your last name is what your master's name is. I've been bought and sold three times. My last name was Jefferson, but I was born with the name Washington. Come to think of it, I may be related to the father of the United States. Say, I heard them calling you "Tonta." What kind of name is that, Indian name?

TONTA. No, it's a Spanish name.

RUFUS. Are you an Indian? What kind of Indian are you?

TONTA. I am a Kemyia.

RUFUS. Keem—aaa-yaaa?

TONTA. Kemyia. People who hunt by the cliffs in the morning.

RUFUS. How come you aren't hunting in the cliffs any more?

TONTA. The white man came.

RUFUS. Oh. What does Tonta mean?

TONTA [*Ignoring the question*]. Long ago, when my people dwelt on this land, my grandfather, Chacupe-Chanush was the Chief. We lived in wickiups and gathered berries and netted fish from the sea.

RUFUS. That sounds very familiar . . .

TONTA. But then the Holy Fathers came and con-

verted us to Christianity. Are you a Catholic, or do you still believe in the mumbo jumbo?

RUFUS. No girl, I'm a Protestant.

TONTA. A Protestant! Oh, good night! [*Turning to leave and crossing herself*]

RUFUS. Say, wait a minute, stay here and talk a bit, we have a lot in common.

TONTA. Oh no, you're a Protestant! And besides that, you're a slave. I'm a free woman!

RUFUS. Now, now, now. Don't you put on no fancy airs with me. I suppose you cook and clean for them Californios from morning until night because you love them so much. You slave just like I do!

TONTA. No! Slavery is no more. Don Rico, how do you say, "abolished" it.

RUFUS. There are different kinds of slavery. Maybe you don't call it the same thing, but it doesn't make it any better. Huh, just because they made a Negro like Don Rico the governor, don't mean nothing.

TONTA. Don Rico is not a Nigero. He is Spanish.

RUFUS. Girl, you are pulling my leg. Your Don Rico is blacker than my black fanny and you're telling me he's Spanish! Oh Lord, don't make me laugh! Besides, what do you care what he is, he still treats you like a dog!

TONTA. Very well, Mr. Rufus, have it your way. Perhaps you'll stay around California and become governor yourself some day.

RUFUS. Well, maybe I will. But first I'll start by becoming the Mayor of Los Angeles.

TONTA. But for the time being, Señor Alcalde, here you sleep . . . with the mules!

RUFUS. Dang blast it! Can't get no respect! [*Getting ready his bedroll*] I'm not going to be sleeping in barns all my life, no Ma'am. Matter of fact, right after this trip, if I make Master Jed a whole pile of money, I'm going to be free. He promised! He promised.

TONTA. Don't believe a word they say, Rufus. I worked all my life for Don Rico, but I'm still just a dumb maid to him. You know what Tonta means? I'll tell you. Tonta means stupid. That's what they call us. Don't let them make a tonto out of you, Rufus! [*She exits*]

JED [*On another part of the stage, Ramona is seen standing on her balcony, dreaming of Joaquín. Jed approaches her*]. Buenas noches, Señorita.

RAMONA. Oh! Good night, Mr. Smith! [*Turning to leave*]

JED. Please, don't go inside yet! I have been trying to orient myself geographically. Could you tell me the name of the mountains to the north there?

RAMONA. Las Montañas de San Bernardino.

JED. Saint Bernard. And what's the name of the valley down there?

RAMONA. El Valle de San Fernando.

JED. Saint Ferdinand. There was an unusual amount of smog today.

RAMONA. Esmog? What is esmog?

JED. Smog is what you get when General Motors, Firestone and the oil companies buy up the Electric Trolley Car system.

RAMONA. Oh. [*Not wishing to appear unworldly*] We are very isolated from the rest of the world, Mr. Smith. We have no, uh, electric systems, yet. We do have the natural beauty of the terrain.

JED. Oh yes, I can't wait to go to Disneyland. Señorita, how far are the pyramids from here?

RAMONA. Oh, Señor, you are mistaken. We have no pyramids here in La Cuidad de La Reina de Los Angeles del Río Porciúncula.

JED. Is that the full name of this city? Is it not rather long? Why don't you just call it Los Angeles or L.A.?

RAMONA. El Lay? Sounds obscene! Los Angeles, the city of the Angels, sounds heavenly.

JED. The city of Angels . . . the Lost Angeles! My God! I see it all now!

RAMONA. What do you see?

JED. It's the City of the Lost Angels, smoldering, there in the dark, the poisoned fumes, embers burning, the maws of Hell!

RAMONA. Hell?

JED. There amidst the metallic skyscrapers, smoke! And over there, in the east side, fire!

RAMONA. I see nothing! No smoke, no fire!

JED. Jesus Christ! Can't you hear the noise, that awful droning, the machines whining, sirens howling . . . and men, the lost angels, battling each other like demi-gods!

RAMONA. Mr. Smith, are you ill? Shall I call for a physician?

JED. My mind! My mind! It's burning!

RAMONA. What shall I do? What shall I do?

JED. Water! Water! [*Ramona dumps water from a flowerpot on Jed's head*] Thank you, I needed that.

RAMONA. Are you well?

JED. Yes, yes, just a momentary burst of apocalyptic prophecy. I'll be all right. I have fits, er, visions.

RAMONA. You certainly possess a fertile imagination.

JED. I'll be okay.

RAMONA. Tell me, Mr. Smith, what vision or future do you see for yourself here in our fair city?

JED. I want to see commercial possibilities, not scenes of destruction.

RAMONA. We have need of more capital.

JED. All I want is a little piece of land. Orange County. I'll develop, but modestly, in harmony with the environment. A few condominiums, 7-11's, Dunkin Donuts . . .

RAMONA. We have a very liberal immigration policy, there being but 6,000 of us Californios, and so much land for the taking. My father, the governor, has given many land grants away quite recently.

JED. Your father, what does he think of us Yankees?

RAMONA. He likes Mexicanized Yankees the best. Many of your people have come here and adopted our ways.

JED. I'll get me a sombrero and sarape . . .

RAMONA. It takes more than that to become a Californio.

JED. I'll drink tequila, listen to mariachis. Say, what does your father think about California uniting with the United States?

RAMONA. God forbid! Don't let him hear you say that. He's a staunch Mexicano all the way. But I know that someday California will be free to decide her own destiny.

JED. You need help, you need someone to stand by your side.

RAMONA. We can handle our own affairs.

JED. No, you can't! There's too many wolves and bears around. Look at the Ruskies, why they'e already in Alaska. Next thing you know they'll be in El Salvador. You need the old Red and White and Blue beside you.

RAMONA. What can your country offer us?

JED. Uncle Sam can give you security and prosperity. Unite with us and you'll have apple pie and rock 'n roll, Mickey Mouse and the L.A.P.D.

RAMONA. We have no need of these things. We have our land and livestock, our stately churches and our merry fandangos, all of this here in Rancho Madera Acebo.

JED. Rancho Mad Era Azebo? What does that mean?

RAMONA. Literally, in English, the Ranch of the Wood Holly.

JED. Wood Holly? Woody Holly? Holly Woody. Hollywood! Hollywood! I see it all now!

RAMONA. Are you having another momentary apocalyptic fit?

JED. Hollywood and Vine! Groman's Chinese Theatre. The Brown Derby! Motion pictures! Panavision!

RAMONA. Should I get more water? Your eyes, they look like shooting stars!

JED. Stars! Stars! Movie stars! I'll make movies.

RAMONA. Un momento, por favor, slow down.

JED [*Climbing up on her balcony*]. Let me explain. [*Pull-*

ing out a photograph] See this photograph of my mother, someday we'll be able to run thousands of these together into moving pictures. We'll project them on a screen and be able to control millions of people's minds!

RAMONA. This is your mother? Where was this photograph taken?

JED. In Europe, her name was Goldie, she's dead now. I'm her only son, promised I would carry her picture around with me forever, but that's another story.

RAMONA. What are you going to do with ths invention?

JED. Make money! Become rich and powerful, I'll make porno movies. Open up a string of porno shops. Ninety-nine percent of the world's smut will come from El Lay. We'll do snuff films! After all, life is cheap in Latin America. No, just kidding! [*Down on his knees*] Ramona, marry me! Don't you see, it's in the stars!

RAMONA. Señor, please, this sort of thing is not done here. Get off your knees!

JED. You'll marry me. You will marry me.

RAMONA. No, impossible! Besides, I am promised to someone else.

JED. Who? What's his name?

RAMONA. Joaquín! And he will kill you!

JED. Is that like Joaquin Valley?

RAMONA. Get off my balcony!

JED. All right, don't get mad. But how about a good night kiss? In our country it's perfectly proper to kiss a girl on the first date. Some couples even go further. Have you ever heard of Women's Liberation?

RAMONA. Did you say emasculation? No thanks.

JED. Well then, how about a stage kiss? It's only make believe!

RAMONA [*Pushing him over the side of the balcony*]. Mañana to you, gringo! [*Ramona exits*]

JED. No, don't say mañana! It's today. Eureka! I found it! Eureka!

RICO [*Seen at another part of the stage writing at a desk*]. To the Honorable President of the Republic of Mexico. I am writing to you with a heavy heart . . .

JED [*Appearing at another writing desk*]. The conquest of California would be absolutely nothing. It would fall like a ripened fruit from its bough into the hands of the Anglo-Saxon race as the people here are incapable of defending it. [*Jed pulls out a pistol and slams it on the desk*]

RICO. The uncertainty in which we find ourselves in this territory because of the excessive introduction of armed adventurers from the United States of the North leaves us no doubt of the war we shall have with them. [*Pulls out his own pistol and loads it*]

JED [*Addressing himself to the audience*]. Therefore, I say, let us strike now and free this blessed country from Mexican tyranny.

RICO [*To the audience as well*]. The Department Treasury is exhausted. We have no standing garrison other than volunteers. Please, send money, men, and material at once. God and Liberty, Río Rico, Los Angeles, California. May 25, 1846.

JED. We'll take the capital, Monterey, and then by ship secure San Diego Bay.

RICO [*To Jed*]. By what right do you have to do this?

JED. Manifest Destiny!

RICO. Thievery!

JED. You stole it from the Indians.

RICO. You shall not have it! Do you intend to persue your insidious goal of establishing slavery in California like you did in Texas?

JED. No! California will be free! Rufus! Rufus! [*Rico and Jed are face to face*]

RUFUS [*Running in with a rifle, followed by Tonta*]. Here I is!

JED. Cover my back, boy. Make sure it's a fair fight. You stick with me and you're free, hear?

RUFUS. I hear you.

JED. August, 1846. [*To the audience*] We've met little resistance.

RICO. Mexicanos! Mexicanos! Do not fail your country now! Death to the invaders! [*Victoria and Ramona enter*]

VICTORIA. ¡Rico, estamos contigo!

RICO. Ramona, send word to Joaquín. Tell him to come quickly!

RAMONA. Papá, will you let him marry me!

RICO. Of course! He's one of us. He's a Californio. [*Ramona kisses her father, then goes to whisper a message in Tonta's ear. Exit Tonta*]

JED. Very well, shall we commence?

RICO. After you. [*The two combatants stand back to back, pistols in hand. There is a very dreamlike quality to this scene, performed to a slow minuet*]

JED [*As they pace away from each other*]. Quite obviously, my dear sir, you are incapable of governing this territory.

RICO. Excuse me, but what do you know of civilization? We founded universities in Mexico City before you landed your motley crew on the Mayflower.

JED. Yes, my dear sir, but we wrote the book on Democracy. You merely copied us, and a cheap imitation at that.

RICO. You deceived us in Texas. We welcomed you as equals and you stabbed us in the back.

JED. Remember the Alamo!

RICO. Racist!

JED. Half breed!

RICO. Gringo!

JED. Greaser! You're done fur. General Kearny, who just took all of New Mexico without a fight, is on his way to San Diego.

RICO. Wrong! Kearny was stopped at San Pasqual by my brother's California Lancers, the best horsemen in the world. Kearny's powder was wet and twenty of your men were cut down like steers. The rest are besieged and are forced to eat their mules!

JED. No! Everyone knows greasers are afraid to fight!

RICO [Shooting him down]. What do you think of Mexican cowardice now? Get back from whence you came, Yanqui!

JED. Not so fast. You may have won the battle . . . but look, look! All around you!

RICO. I see nothing. [William Tell Overture] What's that?

JED. Listen! Listen! [Confusion on the Mexican side as jets roar overhead] Up there, in the sky, it's a bird, it's a . . . Stealth Bomber! [Jets shake the set] It's the United States Air Force!

RICO. Air Force!

JED. Oh, you primitives! If only you knew the glory that awaits us! [Bombs drop. Everyone but Jed runs for cover] Surrender! Surrender! Or face total annihilation! If you stand in the way of progress, we'll drop the atom bomb, so help us God! [Aside] After all, they'se only colored people!

RICO [Dazed and confused, Rico hands over his pistol]. ¡Mi pistola!

JED. At last! She's mine, all mine! California! [While Victoria consoles Rico, Jed grabs Ramona] California!

RAMONA. No, no, no! Let me go! Let me go!

RICO. You can't have my daughter!

JED. I do believe I've taken her already! [Handing him a document] Sign, sir, sign the surrender at Cahuenga Pass, January, 1847. [Afterwhich he carries Ramona away kicking and screaming] California here I come! Right back where I started from! [He exits]

RAMONA. My name is not California! It's Ramona! [Exits]

RICO. ¡Dios mío, qué desgracia!

JOAQUIN [Rushing in]. Don Rico, Doña Victoria, the Gringos . . .

RICO. We know. We lost the war.

JOAQUIN. Where is Ramona?

VICTORIA. The Gringo took her!

JOAQUIN. Oh my God! Which way? [They point, he exits]

Act II

Place: Rancho Hollywood. Meanwhile, back at the rancho, the Californios are lamenting their fate.

RICO. I lost my daughter, I lost my state, what next?

JOAQUIN. We lost more than that, Don Rico, we lost the myth!

RICO. What myth are you talking about?

JOAQUIN. The myth of invincibility. Don't you see, the Gringos have out-conquered the conquistadores. The difference is that when the Spaniards came to Mexico they brought a statue of La Virgin de Guadalupe. The Gringos came to California and installed the dollar!

RICO. My son, what are you talking about? Have you gone crazy?

JOAQUIN. Crazy like a fox. That gives me an idea. Next time you see me I won't be dressed in sheep's clothing. Hasta la vista. [He exits]

RICO. Strange boy! Still, I should have let him marry Ramona. Oh, Victoria, what a terrible state of affairs! And I thought we could retire in a grand style and truly enjoy our old age.

VICTORIA. Don't be so despondent, we can still work, we have our health. See this mountain stream, let's look for gold.

RICO. There is no gold, it's just a myth, like the story of Calafia, the Amazon Queen . . . our ancestors imagined it.

VICTORIA. Something glitters. [She picks up a nugget] Look, I found a nugget!

RICO. It's probably fool's gold.

VICTORIA. No, bite into it, it's real! The rains have washed it down from the mountains.

RICO [Rico bites it]. You're right! Gold! We better hurry, the Gold Rush is going to start any day. [They start to pan]

JED [*Entering with Ramona, dressed as gold miners. She wears a blonde wig*]. The miners came in Forty-Nine . . .

RAMONA. The whores in Fifty-One . . .

JED. And when they got together . . .

RAMONA [*Pointing to Jed*]. They produced the native son!

JED [*Pulling out a gun*]. All right! All right! The Miner Forty-Niner and his Darlin' Clementine run the claim jumpers off their stake!

RICO [*Not recognizing them*]. I beg your pardon, Señor, but we found it first.

JED. I don't care, you are a foreigner. Only Natives can mine here.

RICO. I beg your pardon, Señor, my family has been here for over three generations.

JED. Clementine, what's he look like to you?

RAMONA. Faintly familiar . . .

JED. Well, he looks like a damn greaser to me! [*Cocking his gun*] Now, for the last time, if you want to mine here you have to pay a Foreign Miner's Tax.

RICO. But I told you, I am a Native Californio. [*Jed points the gun at him*]

JED. You still look like a greaser from Sonora or Chile to me.

RICO. Señor, I want no trouble. I will pay the tax.

JED. That'll be $300 per month.

RAMONA. $300 dollars! But we won't be able to make a profit!

JED. Exactly.

RICO. This is our claim! We won't leave without a fight!

JED [*Shooting at him*]. That's okay with me, greaser!

RAMONA [*As Rico shoots back*]. Help, help, help! It's an insurrection!

JED. Don't give it any legitimacy! Your line is "help, the bandidos are robbing us!"

RAMONA. Oh yes, "kill the Frito Bandido!"

RICO. I am not a bandido. But you are turning me into a revolucionario!

JED. Kill the terrorists!

RICO. ¡Viva Villa!

RAMONA. Wait, Jed, I know that man. . . .

JED. Don't worry, we've got 'em surrounded. We'll starve them out!

RICO. I have run out of ammunition! Estamos perdidos.

VICTORIA. Is there no one who can save us from this fate?

RAMONA. No, don't shoot! He's my . . . [*Just as Jed is about to shoot Rico we hear the strains of "Zacatecas."*]

VICTORIA. Could it be? [*Enter Joaquín dressed like Zorro.*]

JED. Who is that?

RICO. El Zorro!

RAMONA. The fox!

JOAQUIN. No, it is I, El Zorrillo!

JED. El Zorrillo? What's that mean?

RAMONA. Run! Run for your life! [*Running in the direction of her parents*] El Zorrillo means . . .

JOAQUIN [*Throwing a skunk at Jed*]. Take that . . . you stinking Gringo!

RAMONA. Skunk!

JOAQUIN [*As he exits through the audience*]. ¡El Zorrillo! ¡El Zorrillo!

JED. Oh my God!

RICO. Who was the masked man? He saved our lives! [*Up in the hills, Marcus, the soldier, has Gerónima, the Indian trapped in a cave.*]

MARCUS. You gonna have to come down sooner or later, injun.

GERONIMA. Come up and get me, white man.

MARCUS. If you give up, I promise that no harm will come to you.

GERONIMA. You will shoot me.

MARCUS. No! We're supposed to take you to a reservation in Oklahoma.

GERONIMA. Huh, so you can give me a blanket full of smallpox and tuberculosis? No thanks, I stay here among the cactus.

MARCUS. Where you hear them crazy stories, injun?

GERONIMA. From my people.

MARCUS. I can't believe that! That is sick.

GERONIMA. It is also sick the way you slaughter buffalo from passing trains, white man.

MARCUS. I'm not a white man, I am black.

GERONIMA. You a black? I knew a black.

MARCUS. Born in New England. My Daddy's name was Washington. . . .

GERONIMA. I know you! Let me see your face! [*As Marcus exposes himself Geronima fires a shot*]

MARCUS. God damn, crazy injun? What the hell you trying to do?

GERONIMA. I don't like the uniform you are wearing.

MARCUS. What's the matter with you? I'm just doing my job, I got nothing against you.

GERONIMA. Then why you try to kill me, nigger?

MARCUS. Watch you mouth, red man, or I'll make a wooden Indian out of you! Jesus!

GERONIMA. Black man, what is your name?

MARCUS. Marcus.

GERONIMA. My name is Gerónima. Let us not fight

each other. Get back on your horse and leave these hills.

MARCUS. I don't know . . .

GERONIMA. Oh, I see. Did Kemosabe promise you forty acres of OUR LAND?

MARCUS. No, yes, I mean he did, but that ain't the reason . . .

GERONIMA. Is Kemosabe going to free you like Lincoln *again*?

MARCUS. You pretty damn smart, for an injun!

GERONIMA. What is that supposed to mean? Just because I am red and did not go to Booker T. Washington University, you think I am stupid?

MARCUS. All right, look. I'm going to put down one of my rifles and just walk out of here.

GERONIMA. Thank you, we will make good use of that rifle.

MARCUS. I hope some day we can talk under more pleasant circumstances. You know, there was a time once in the Florida Everglades when the Seminoles and some runaway slaves got together and whupped old Hickory's ass. . . .

GERONIMA [*During this time Gerónima has managed to come up and over to surprise Marcus*]. Hold it, soldier!

MARCUS. Oh Lordy!

GERONIMA [*Cocking her pistol*]. One move and you go to the sacred grounds.

MARCUS. Look, I had you cornered, but I let you go. I gave you a rifle!

GERONIMA. I want to see how black you really are. Take off that uniform. Go on, strip! Black or white, soldier, you killed many of my people.

MARCUS [*Taking off his clothes*]. I had no choice, I had no job, it was the only thing I could do! [*Marcus throws his clothes in Gerónima's face and attacks her. They wrestle to the ground with Marcus on top*]

GERONIMA. Rufus!

MARCUS. Tonta! It's you! I almost killed you. What are you doing out here?

GERONIMA. I ran away to join the free tribes. Rufus, they're killing all of my people, just like the buffalo.

MARCUS. God, I'm so sorry! Did I hurt you? I'm so glad I found you again. Gerónima, I like that much better than Tonta.

GERONIMA. What are you going to do now, Marcus? Take me back to the white man? [*Fade or blackout. Meanwhile, Ramona is trying to smooth things over between Jed and her parents*]

RAMONA. Mami, Papi, I'm so glad to see you!

VICTORIA. Ramona, ¿qué estás haciendo con ese blonde wig?

RAMONA. It's the new me, Mamá. Oh, Jed, honey, come and say hello to my parents.

RICO. He almost killed us!

RAMONA. Jed's not such a bad guy once you get to know him, Papá, you'll see. Jed, *honey*, come here!

JED. Good seeing you folks again. [*Aside*] He looks like a nigra!

RAMONA [*Holding her nose*]. Oh . . . not too close . . . down wind!

JED. My apologies for this unfortunate incident. From now on let us handle matters according to the letter of the law. The war is over. Why don't we sign the Treaty of Guadalupe Hidalgo? [*Handing Rico a document to sign*]

RICO. Do you promise to honor the rights of all Mexicans in the new territories? Will you allow us the same rights accorded to the North Americans?

JED. Of course! [*Rico signs*] Now, let's apply for statehood together. Hold up your right hand. [*Everybody does so*] No, not yet, ladies! Do you swear to uphold the Constitution of the United States, so help you God?

RICO. Sí, I mean, yes.

JED. Congratulations. You are now an American citizen. [*Shaking his hand*] Now, sir, would you do the honor of marrying me to your lovely daughter?

RICO. I am afraid you have already taken her.

JED. Let's make it legitimate. For future generations.

RAMONA. You see, Mamá, he's not so bad!

VICTORIA. ¡Ay, mi hija! [*Sniffing*]

RICO [*Acting as priest*]. Do you?

JED and RAMONA. We do!

RICO [*Making the sign of the cross*]. You are! You may kiss the bride! Now, if you will excuse us, my wife and I must tend to our affairs.

JED. Not so fast, there's more documents to sign. [*Handing Rico a paper*]

RICO [*Signing it*]. What does it say? I can't read English.

JED [*Whisking it away*]. You better learn. This is the Law of 1851, under which the burden of proof is placed on the land owner to defend the title to his land.

VICTORIA [*Trying in vain to retract the paper*]. That means much time and money in court defending the rights to our land! That's not fair! What can we do?

JED. Write your congressman.

RICO. Who is he?

JED. Me.

RICO. We need someone in office who will understand the Mexicano.

RAMONA. Why don't you run, Papá? [*As Jed tries to shut her up*]

RICO. Great idea! My people will vote for me. What do I have to do?

JED. Just sign this voter registration blank.

VICTORIA. Don't sign anything without reading it first.

RICO. Don't you have any forms in Spanish?

JED. Y'all in 'Merica now, ya gotta spick good English.

RICO. Ramona, ayúdame a leer esto.

RAMONA. Sí, Papá, just sign right here. There. He's registered now, right?

JED. Right, but only if he owns property.

RICO. But you just stole my lands!

JED. Sorry, that's showbiz! [*Whisking away the old rancho sign*]

RICO. My rancho, what have you done to my rancho?

JED [*Putting up the new signs*]. Don't worry, Don Rico, Rancho Hollywood will stay in the family!

ALL. Rancho Hollywood?

JED. Yes, clever name for a housing tract or apartment complex, don't you think? . . . which it will be eventually?

RICO [*Going for Jed's throat*]. I'll kill you for this!

JED. Ah, ah, ah! I'll call the Highway Patrol! [*Enter Marcus*] Rufus, just in time. Don Rico has a problem here abiding by our laws. [*Placing Marcus between himself and Rico*]

RICO [*Being restrained by Ramona, Victoria*]. He stole my lands, my rancho!

MARCUS. Just like you stole it from the Indians.

JED. Excellent, Rufus, you are learning so well.

MARCUS. The name isn't Rufus anymore, it's Marcus.

JED. My goodness, are we moving through time that fast? [*Handing Marcus a camera*] Would you mind taking a photograph of Ramona and me kissing in front of our rancho? Fiery, impetuous Señorita and handsome Yankee soldier. Heal those old war wounds sort of thing. [*Aside to Marcus*] Did you take care of our Indian problem?

MARCUS. I sure did . . . I married her! [*Enter Gerónima*]

JED. What!

RAMONA. Tonta!

GERONIMA. The name is Gerónima.

JED [*Taking Marcus aside*]. You married a squaw, just when we were nearing the final solution! I'll have your stripes for this . . .

VICTORIA. Tonta, you're welcome to come live with us if you want.

GERONIMA. So I can be your maid? No thanks. From now on you be the maid!

JED. I'll bust you back down to buck private, you black buck you!

MARCUS. Now, you watch your mouth *Massa* Jed. I am a free man and a land owner. And me and this Kemyia woman are going way back in the hills where we can't be bothered by no white trash and raise us a whole lot of black and red children.

JED. You'll never make it alone, my boy, you'll need capital, letters of credit. Stay here, work for me.

MARCUS. I don't need a damn thing from you. All you ever done is cheat me from the day I was born.

JED. That's not true, I helped you out, I guided your way. I need you, Rufus, to help me build this country.

MARCUS. Get your Spanish boy there to do it. He'll probably work for less. [*Marcus starts to exit with Gerónima*]

JED. Rufus! Rufus, don't go! We've been through so much together. Rufus, God damn it, I'm your Daddy!

MARCUS [*Returning*]. What did you say?

JED. I said, I'm your father, boy. Your real father. Your Mama was a cook in the big house. She died when you were a baby. I took you with me on the sailing ship.

MARCUS. You've never been my father . . . and you never will! If I ever see you around me or mine again, I'll kill you! Do you hear me, motherfucker! [*He exits*]

JED. How sharper than a serpents tooth!

RAMONA. Are you all right, Jed?

JED. Well, no use crying over spilled milk. He'll be back. They both will. Now then, let's get on with the business at hand. It's the dawn of the Twentieth Century, time to usher in a new era of peace and prosperity.

RAMONA. Do you really mean it? No more war, no more killing?

JED. Oh, maybe just a little charge up San Juan Hill. . . .

RICO. The Twentieth Century already? Why, it seems as though we just settled California yesterday.

VICTORIA. And Mexico the day before.

JED. Come, come, you already said those lines. We're going to have to find you some new ones.

RAMONA. Jed's right, Mamá, we Mexican-hyphen-Americans can't be living in the past.

RICO. Mexican-hyphen-Americans now, are we?

RAMONA. Papá, I've become a child of both cultures. And my name is not Ramona anymore, it's Ronny.

RICO. Roni? Ay, Ramona, ¡cómo te has perdido!

VICTORIA. Everything is changing so fast! I wish we could go back to the old days, life was much simpler.

RICO. There was order, family, tradition.

VICTORIA. Yes, and the fiestas and ferias. . . .

JED. Wait minute! I just thought of something!

RAMONA. Jed, are you having another vision!

JED. Yes! I see how we can use the past to find our future. Why don't we have an Old Spanish Days Fiesta and celebrate your Spanish heritage!

RAMONA. Mamá, doesn't that sound like a grand idea!
[Victoria is not convinced]

JED. See those old run down adobes and missions? We'll restore them, by golly. Start a Native Sons of the Golden West club. Dress up like Spaniards and ride through downtown Santa Barbara. Name a baseball team the "Padres." Don Rico can be the Grand Marshall.

RAMONA. You can wear your charro suit, Papá.

JED. Doña Vicky can ride side saddle in her mantilla.

VICTORIA. Ramona, help me fix my hair. [Ramona does so]

RICO. I could do a few rope tricks with my lasso. You know that many things western, like rodeos and the lasso, came from the Mexican. We were the original vaqueros, what you call "buckaroos."

JED. Exactly, we'll have sangria, flamenco dancers, Taco Bells! Olé! Olé! We'll haul in tourists by the busloads. Real estate values will soar! We'll even make a movie out of it!

RAMONA. Ye Olde California Days, take two!

JED. No, we'll call it . . .RANCHO HOLLYWOOD! Ronny, I am going to make a star out of you! [As the Ricos get ready for the next scene] But where can I find an extra hand? [Jed has his camera in hand]

JOAQUIN [Entering, dressed like Cantinflas]. Didi somee bodee callee for me?

JED. Ah, hah! A wetback!

JOAQUIN. No, a wet butt. [Pointing towards his rear end]

JED. What's you name, boy?

JOAQUIN. Manual, Manual Labor.

JED. Perfect! You're just what I needed. You don't have any papers, do you?

JOAQUIN. No, Señor, that's how I got the wet butt. Me dio diarrea.

JED. Moctezuma'a revenge, eh boy?

JOAQUIN. No, Sir, Gringo's revancha!

JED. What?

JOAQUIN. Too many Big Macs.

JED. Okay. Let's get to work.

JOAQUIN. ¡Orale, el jale!

JED. If everyone's ready, let's shoot the balcony scene. [Jed assumes his old role as Director, Joaquín becomes the Cameraman]

JOAQUIN. Shut up, shut up! Get ready, get set!

VICTORIA. Wait a minute, isn't this the part we came in on?

RICO. Yes, we've been through this before. Who's going to play the male lead?

JED [Taking Rico's sombrero off his head]. I am!

RICO. But . . . you're Anglo.

JED. No problem, I'll wear brown contact lenses!

RICO. But you are white, we Californios were . . .

JED. Spanish, I can pass . . .

RICO. No, no, no! We were everything, white, black, brown . . .

RAMONA. Black!

RICO. Yes, that's what we've been trying to tell him all along. But he insists upon saying we're Spanish!

JOAQUIN [To Jed]. They are Mexican. Look how they have the nopal on their foreheads!

JED. I don't care! I've had it! Do it my way or get off the lot, now! [To Joaquín] Film this! Film this!

RAMONA. Jed, honey, just give me a couple of minutes. Papá! Your're ruining my scene! And what's all this about being black?

RICO. It's true, mi hija, I am a mulatto. My grandmother was black. Which means, you have some black blood also.

RAMONA. Me! Blonde Ronny Rico, star of the stage, screen and the Great White Way, black?

RICO. Ramona, it's nothing to be ashamed of.

VICTORIA. Your father didn't tell you sooner, dear, because we wanted to protect you.

RAMONA. If he finds out, this could be the end of my career!

JED. Well, what's it going to be?

RICO. Do I get a role?

JED. Yes, a non-speaking role!

RICO. That did it! You'll hear from my agent. ¡Vámonos, Victoria!

RAMONA. But Papá, where will you go, what will you do?

RICO. No importa, whatever is necessary. I'll go back to being a ranchero.

JED. That's ranch hand, Rico, I mean "pobre." I own the land.

RICO. I don't care, at least it's honest work.

VICTORIA. Adiós, mi hija.

RAMONA. Goodbye, Mamá. Goodbye, Papá. [She hugs her parents. They exit] My parents, they're gone!

JED. Let them go, Ronny, let them go and pick their

. . . grapes of wrath. Huh, and I could have gotten them a Coors Distributorship in Montebello. Here, take some of this, it'll make you feel better. [*Offering her a vial of white powder. To Joaquín*] Don't film this.

RAMONA. What is it?

JED. Cocaine. [*She declines. He shrugs his shoulders and snorts the entire vial*] Dynamite!

RAMONA. You don't understand how much my family means to me. You don't care.

JED. Ronny, blow them off! I'm your father now, and that camera is your mother. [*Motioning to Joaquín to film*] Yes, the audiences out there in the dark air-conditioned cinemas of America are your children.

RAMONA. What part am I playing . . . who am I?

JOAQUIN [*Reading from the script*]. It says here that you are "the fiery, impetuous Ramona Rico."

JED. Forget that! You're Ronny Rocket, Latin spitfire, the hottest thing to hit Hollywood since Carmen Miranda.

RAMONA [*Dancing and singing*]. Mamá no quiero, Mama no quiero . . . Maaaaa maaaaaa no quiero, no quiero . . .

JED. Get a close up of these beautiful Spanish tits! You've heard of "Spanish Eyes," well . . .

JOAQUIN. ¡Ahora, sí, que se está pasando!

RAMONA. Jed, what are you trying to do?

JED. Ronny, I've fallen behind schedule. The backers are breathing down my neck. I have to hit paydirt. We're going to do a sex scene soooooo torrid it'll have them panting in their Guccis.

RAMONA. What kind of sex scene?

JED. One with rising and falling action, one that reaches a climax in technicolor and panavision.

RAMONA. What's my line? Line!

JOAQUIN. ¡Chinga tu madre, güey!

RAMONA. Chinga tu maaaa . . . Jed, we can't do that on the screen!

JED. Why not? We're married.

RAMONA. You forget, we divorced last year, remember, after you had that affair with the football player?

JED. Ronny, you're too much of a conformist.

RAMONA. Jed, I thought you wanted to do art, not smut!

JED. Forget about that. Think about the Mercedes 450 SL with your own private license plate, the million dollar mansion in Beverly Hills, your name, Ronny Rocket, cast in diamonds on the marquee.

RAMONA. My name is Ramona Rico.

JED. Okay. Whatever! Now, are we going to do the scene or not?

RAMONA. I don't know, my heart isn't in it.

JED. All right, my little chile pepper, have it your way. I'll just get a Gringa to do your part.

RAMONA. Jed, how could you, after all we've been through together!

JED. There are thousands of players in this town who would just die for a part in a Jedediah Goldbanger Smith Production. I'll just put a casting call up on the board. [*Turning to leave*] Stick around, Chico, I'll be right back.

RAMONA. A Gringa, he's going to get a Gringa.

JOAQUIN. Sabes qué, ever since the talkies there have been Gringo actors in this town making their living playing Latino roles. And you know something else, there were some Latino actors like Roland Navarro who could only play white roles because they were not dark enough!

RAMONA [*Taking off her blonde wig*]. It gets rather confusing, doesn't it? No wonder I'm so screwed up. Say, don't I know you from somewhere?

JOAQUIN. You may have seen one of my movies from Mexico. I am known as Tin Can, among other things. Oye, what are you going to do now?

RAMONA. I don't know. I could play it his way, get off the lot or shoot him to death.

JOAQUIN. There is another way, Ramona, we could form our own company like the original "United Artists." [*Jed enters before she can answer*]

JED. Well, my little Taco Belle, have you decided what to do?

RAMONA. I'm going to stay here, this is where I belong.

JED. Ahhh, but it may be too late. Someone else may get the part. [*As Sinmuhow and Malcolm enter*] Here they come for the audition. Rufus! Is that you? You old sonofabitch, I knew you'd return.

MALCOLM [*Slapping his hand away*]. The name is Malcolm!

JED. Oh, right on, Malcolm. Got any experience?

MALCOLM. I have played many parts: slave, worker, soldier, invisible man.

JED. Invisible man?

MALCOLM. People, especially white people, never look at me. They pretend I am not there or else they want to forget about me.

JED. Malcolm, we're doing a film about the Old California days. We're looking for a Mexican half-breed type. You could probably pass.

MALCOLM. They aren't much better off than we are.

JED. Try this bandana on, it'll cover your Afro.

MALCOLM. Is this like when white folks used to put on black face?

JED. It's a non speaking role, Kunta, do you want it?

MALCOLM. Ain't you got no part for a black revolutionary?

JED. No, not at the moment. Maybe later on we can

work you into some kind of black action flick. You know, Shaft vs the marauding Mau Maus! Who's next?

SINMUHOW. I am Sinmuhow . . .

JED. How! A little Native American action. Come right on in, you don't even need a "reservation."

SINMUHOW. Sinmuhow, Spirit woman, woman who knows many things.

JED. Sorry, we don't need anybody like that. That part calls for a silent sexy Latina to make it with the Spanish scion, me. Have you ever done any skin flicks?

SINMUHOW. No, but I have been a slave, maid, concubine . . .

JED. Don't worry, you could do this part lying down. Try on this zarape, very authentic.

SINMUHOW. But I am a real person, my spirit is real. I cannot play a wooden Indian.

JED. Well then, let's play cowboys and Indians!

SINMUHOW. Only if we play Custer's Last Stand.

JED. Very funny! Who's next? We're Equal Opportunity Employers.

JOAQUIN. I am. Don't you remember me? I'm one of the latest in your long line of stereotypes. I am your combination sleepy peon, Frito Bandido, Zorro, Cantinflesque, vato loco, wetback.

JED. Hey, how about a little gang exploitation film set in the smoldering East Los barrio, huh? No? Well then, Kunta, how about a Bojangles movie? Let me see you dance, I know you got rhythm. [Jed dances, the rest of the players remain silent as they close in around him] Mr. Boooooooo-jangles, dance, dance, dance. Sinmuhow! How about a nice wholesome maize commercial, huh? You know: "Our ancestors scalped settlers and at the end of the day were rewarded by the golden goodness of maize." [Hopping around on one foot] Whooop! Whooop! Whooop!

MALCOLM. I have a better idea, why don't we do a "kill whitey" film.

JED. No, no, that could be labled communist propaganda. Besides, who would pay to go see it?

RAMONA. The liberals.

JED. That's right, make them feel ashamed of being white.

RAMONA. Jed, don't you see, these distortions have twisted the minds of generations of children. Is this really how you see us?

JED. You too, huh. I always knew you were one of them.

RAMONA. That's right, I am. I am black and brown and white. And I'm proud of it.

JED. Oh yeah, well let me tell you something. I'm a minority too. I'm part Jewish, just like Barry Goldwater. My grandmother Goldie, remember? We've been persecuted for over 2000 years just because they say we killed Christ, Jesus!

JOAQUIN. Ladies and gentlemen, we are gathered here today to roast a great American filmmaker over the coals.

JED. Please, please! You're all taking this much too seriously. After all, it's only make believe!

JOAQUIN. We, the assembled representatives of all the so-called minorities, although we are actually in the majority now, want to pay homage to you, Jedediah Goldbanger Smith. . . .

JED. Wait a minute, aren't you missing someone? Where's Charlie Chan? Where's our slant eyed little nip? [Assuming martial arts stance] Toyota! Datsun! Sony! Mao! Chop Suey!

JOAQUIN. Jed, thank you, from the bottom of our hearts, for the creation of such memorable stereotypes, for the advancement of collective inferiority complexes, for the maligning and desecration of our cultures and for the loss, theft, and distortion of our history.

JED. Don't forget the wops and the micks and the polacks and the frogs and the . . .

JOAQUIN. We hereby present you with this mask as a token of our esteem. [They ceremoniously hand Jed a redneck pig mask]

RAMONA. Jed, you really must change your image!

JED. My image? My image! Oh no, I couldn't accept this, really. I just want to thank all of those hardy pilgrims and pioneers for making all this possible. [Strange nightmarish music. Lights low. alone. Despite himself, he tries the mask on] I'm afraid this doesn't really fit me! Wait! Cut the scene! Cut the scene! Cut! Cuuuuuuuuuuuutttt! [Blackout. On another part of the stage, Rico and Victoria exit as though from a movie theatre, dressed in evening clothes]

VICTORIA. God, wasn't that a fantastic movie! Variety called "Rancho Hollywood the most profound statement ever made about the history of California."

RICO. I still can't believe that Joaquín, Malcolm, Jed, Ramona, all worked to make this project a success.

VICTORIA. Oh, and wasn't Ramona wonderful? I bet she gets nominated for an Oscar. Oh, how I wish we could have stayed on to work in the film.

RICO. Don't worry, I hear there might be a sequel. Well, there's the reception. Good thing we have our passes, otherwise we'd never get past security. Everybody who is anybody in Hollywood is here tonight.

VICTORIA [As they enter the central area, showing an

imaginary guard their passes]. Oh, there they are! Drinking champagne. [*We see the others partying*]

RICO. Don't be obtrusive, let them enjoy the lime-light.

SINMUHOW. The Executive Producer of Programming for CBS told me he wants to do a series based on Rancho Hollywood.

MALCOLM. Is that so? An agent for the Shuberts told me they want to stage it on Broadway.

JED. Hey, aren't you glad we buried the hatchet and got down firme! Hah! Ha!

JOAQUIN. Orale, especially since we are all equal partners in the production.

RAMONA. I was just told: Rancho Hollywood has seven Oscar nominations!

JED. Why not? It grossed twenty million in the first two weeks.

JOAQUIN. Let's drink to that! [*They all toast*]

VICTORIA [*To Rico*]. I can't believe this, I'm so proud of them.

RICO. Everything we worked for has come true.

SINMUHOW [*To Malcolm*]. You know, all of a sudden I have all this money I don't know what to do with.

MALCOLM. I put my bread back into the ghetto. I bought a controlling interest in a chain of liquor stores.

SINMUHOW. I know what you mean. I went back to the reservation and started looking into prime investment properites.

RICO. Liquor stores? Buying land on the reservations?

JED. Well, Joaquín, how is the world of art these days?

RAMONA. Oh, he's been painting some beautiful murals a la Orozco, Rivera, Siqueiros.

JED. Public art?

JOAQUIN. Not exactly, man, those pinche homeboys keep spraypainting my murals.

JED. Like I always said, the masses don't really appreciate these things.

JOAQUIN. So now I do mostly interiors, you know, the Bank of America, Hilton Inn, places like that.

RICO. Victoria, this doesn't sound right. . . .

RAMONA. Well my broker is E. F. Hutton. And E. F. Hutton says . . . [*Everybody but Rico and Victoria freeze*]

RICO. Have they forgotten everything? Wake up! ¡Despierten! [*Speaking to deaf ears*] Don't think only of your own greed and profit! You have a powerful tool at your disposal, use it!

VICTORIA. Rico, It's no use, they can't hear you.

RICO. All the social gains we made in the past . . . in danger of being swept aside. Listen to me, we, the elderly, the poor, they want to take away our social security, medicare, food stamps . . .

VICTORIA. Don't forget equal rights for women.

RICO. Affirmative action, everything! Don't turn your backs on us, please! Listen to us! Listen! [*They all come to.*]

JED. Attention! Attention, everybody! I have an announcement to make. First of all, I want to thank each and everyone of you for giving me another chance to prove to the entire world that Americans of different races, religions, and creeds can work together. That was very "white" of you! [*Everybody laughs.*]

ALL. All right! Let's here it! Orale, etc.

JED. My friends, you all know of my deep involvement with the Screen Actor's Guild, and although some have said I might make a fine governor of this golden state, I have decided to take on an even more difficult directorial responsibility because, I, for one, believe that this country has suffered long enough!

ALL. You can count on us! We're with you!

RICO. What in the devil is he talking about?

JED. Spread the word, tell everyone. We'll be needing script writers, P.R. people, make up artists, producers, everything that it takes to make a fantasy like Rancho Hollywood come true. My friends, I have decided to run for President of the United States of America! [*Silence. Everyone, except for Jed, looks at the audience. Slow fade*]

ESSAY: AN APPROACH TO THE PLAY

At the center of *Rancho Hollywood* is an examination of the power of cultural artifacts such as films and plays to construct and reconstruct history and, similarly, to construct and reconstruct roles within that history for group and individual identities. The play's different ethnic groups all have distorted stereotypical perceptions of one another, but the most destructive of these seem to be those supported by the institutions of the dominant culture. *Rancho Hollywood* is unusual in offering a double presentation of this cultural dynamic, since the dominant culture changes during the years the play covers. In the 1830s it was the culture represented by California's governor, Rio Rico (historically his name was Pio Pico), who seems preoccupied with defining himself as "Californio" rather than Mexican; as white (and culturally European) rather than black or Indian; and as associated with a leisure class rather than a working class. But the dominant culture changes almost instantaneously in the play with the arrival of the Yankee merchant Jedediah. From that time on it is Jed, along with the community which he represents, who seems to define the power relations of the ethnic groups, genders, and social classes with which he interacts.

Throughout the play, Jedediah assumes that it is his prerogative to do whatever he wants to do, including controlling others. He takes his superiority for granted and remains, even in the play's historical flashbacks, "the director." There is no evidence that Jed has ever thought critically about his social position; it just seems "natural" to him that he be in control, and not Rico or Rufus or Sinmuhow. In the play's first scene, when the actors do not behave in accordance with his stereotypes, he becomes hostile and overbearing, and the actors, despite their resentment, eventually comply with his direction. Apparently it has also come to seem "natural" to them to accept subservient roles. (The play's ending suggests that they may have become complicit in promulgating and preserving this view of social history, as well as their own ethnic stereotyping, for personal success and profit.)

However, these roles also raise difficult questions for the players. At the end of the play, when the filming is about to resume, Ramona Rico—renamed "Ronnie Rocket, Latin Spitfire" to boost box office receipts by capitalizing on stereotypes of Latina women—asks, "What part am I playing . . . who am I?" The line calls attention to a central figure of speech in the play, as does Joaquín's complaint after the first scene: "I'm sick and tired of playing these demeaning roles." Are the characters speaking about the roles they are forced to play in the film or the ones they are required to play in life? What is the relationship between film and reality? What function does the film play in limiting the range of real-life roles available to its actors and actresses? Throughout the play, characters are trying to define themselves in a world which seems to present them with predefined, spiritually limiting visions of themselves.

Rancho Hollywood is a play centrally concerned with reevaluating history, not just the events of history (although that is implied as well); it is also concerned with the process by which history is created and, within this constructed history, the roles which individuals see as open to them. The play requires us to see these events through a double lens: through the vision of American popular history, and through the words of the actor-characters who show us the perspective of people by and large silenced in this version of the "history" of the American Southwest. Cultural institutions such as films are presented as playing a central role in expressing, shaping, and sustaining the dominant culture's perceptions and values. Print culture was already doing this in the nineteenth century, for example through such books as Helen Hunt Jackson's *Ramona* and Richard Henry Dana's *Two Years before the Mast*, both mentioned in Morton's play. They helped reinforce perceptions of power and status, of morality and freedom, of one's own position in society and that of others. Film and television, which can broadcast their images much more widely and quickly and vividly, are perhaps even more insidious.

Morton's treatment of history takes a similar direction. We often think of history as different from fiction; we think of it as "fact," as "objective truth" which exists on a level of reality distinct from that of literature or theater or film. *Rancho Hollywood* reminds us, however, that history is an act of interpretation, and interpretations of necessity embody and communicate values. (A case in point occurs in the headnote before the text of this play, where our discussion concerning events from the Mexican War conveys a particular attitude toward those events.) The fact that all histories are someone's interpretation becomes an acute problem when the cultural products which embody that interpretation—the necessary presuppositions without which narrative cannot take place—make it come to seem "natural" or "true," so that it becomes accepted uncritically. Those who get the privilege of interpreting history can, whether consciously or unconsciously, reinforce a self-serving image of society. We need to ask of *any* version of history, "Who is served by this?"

In this light, it is interesting to consider whether Charles Morton could have written this play, or whether it was necessary for him to rewrite himself—and his family history—as *Carlos* Morton before undertaking the task. Even to ask such a question is to remind ourselves that in our pluralistic society, one's identity and culture are rarely a birthright. They often need to be defined, and then claimed.

Elaine Jackson

PAPER DOLLS

About the Author   Elaine Jackson (1948–   ) graduated from Wayne State University in Detroit and then worked in theater, primarily as an actress, in California and then in New York City. She performed in a wide range of plays by major European and American playwrights, an experience which helped shape her practice as a writer: she says that her primary intention in writing plays has been to create interesting roles, especially for black actresses. In her first play, *Toe Jam*, a young African-American woman tries to escape the spiritual limitations of her urban environment by dreaming of herself as a great actress and playwright. Her later plays, *Cockfight* (1978), concerning the breakup of a marriage, and *Birth Rites* (1987), set in a maternity ward, have been produced at the American Place Theater in New York, and *Paper Dolls*, published in 1986, has been widely produced by student groups. Her writing has been supported by grants from the Rockefeller Foundation and the National Endowment for the Arts. She has taught in high schools in Detroit, in California, and, currently, in New York City.

About the Play   The beauty trap awaits every woman in our culture. Women are much more likely than men to be praised and rewarded for how they look rather than for how they act or for what they accomplish; the result is that women are much more likely to have their self-esteem invested in trying to achieve and maintain that desired "look." Most of us are aware that this is a problem but seem powerless to undo what seems to be one of the most deep-rooted of our cultural values. Because of this, many women whose bodies or faces do not conform to cultural norms develop negative self-images. Many women spend large amounts of money on clothing and on cosmetics and on beauty aids and on plastic surgery to try to look "right," only to find themselves regarded—and often to regard themselves— as adornments. This double bind is even more complicated for women of color, whose beauty has often been evaluated according to criteria evolved for Caucasians; insofar as these women are praised as "beautiful," that is, as falling within the range of criteria appropriate for white women, this praise reinforces the notion that black is *not* beautiful. Even more than their white sisters, they find themselves in a no-win situation.

    Paper Dolls explores problems associated with beauty in a way that opens up still larger questions about our culture: the relationship of art (and artifice) to beauty, of art and beauty to nature, of art to the establishment of personal and gender identity. The play accomplishes this in a style that is highly complex and highly original: it uses the exaggerations of farce, burlesque, and parody to explore these serious questions, and it explores both their social implications and philosophical dimensions. The plot of the play is also unusual: it violates conventions of linear narrative, weaving events from the present with remembered experience from the women's past lives and with scenes from films in which they acted when they were younger. Staging, moreover, is often highly nonrealistic, relying on exaggerated stage props and costumes in what feels like a celebration of theatricality itself. Clearly this is not drama which strives to be a faithful reenactment of the external details of everyday experience. And yet, by stitching its scenes together with the thread of their common intellectual concerns, what the play presents is exactly that: however offbeat, a view of everyday experience.

    The winner and runner-up from a 1930 black beauty contest, ironically named the Miss Emancipation pageant, are invited to serve as honorary judges fifty years later at a similar beauty contest held in Windsor, Ontario, the Canadian border city across the river from Detroit, Michigan. Margaret-Elizabeth and Lizzie have been friends for decades; indeed, they have so much in common that they occasionally seem to be each other's double. Their names are similar, and some of their ex-husbands seem to have had the same names. But ultimately the two seem very different. Margaret-Elizabeth appears to be fixated on the past, especially on reliving the glory of her former triumph, and she seems incapable of escaping some longstanding fantasies; and yet, she is attractive for her courage and tenacity and for insisting on celebrating life in the present. Lizzie seems more practical and pragmatic; her attitude toward the present is informed by what she regards as a more realistic attitude toward the future. However, her awareness of their advancing age makes her seem—certainly to Margaret-Elizabeth—preoccupied with impending death.

CHARACTERS

MARGARET-ELIZABETH (black)
LIZZIE (black)
WOMAN ONE (black)

WOMAN TWO (white)
MAN ONE (black)
MAN TWO (white)

Act I

SCENE I

PLACE: Canadian Border (Windsor, Ontario)
TIME: 1980—spring
SCENE: Morning. Two women (Margaret-Elizabeth and Lizzie) are seated uncomfortably Downstage Left on one of several long benches. Above them, a sign reads "Canadian Customs Detaining Area." Margaret-Elizabeth is wearing a large, wide-brimmed, picture-frame hat and a low-cut, many-layered, flamboyantly flowered, chiffon whirly-gig of a dress. Lizzie is sedately dressed in a matronly, rayon print dress with Peter Pan collar and a veiled, pillbox-type hat. Both women are wearing high-heeled shoes and white gloves. They are surrounded by lots of luggage on the floor and on the adjacent benches. Some of the luggage is opened and askew.

LIZZIE [*quiet anger*]. If he so much as dares to put his infested, fat, red fingers in my personal, private belongings—I'm gonna just . . . I'm gonna just . . . *fling* everything in his puffed-up face!

MARGARET-ELIZABETH [*Quiet control*]. Shut up, Lizzie. I think we're in enough trouble because of you, without me having to sit here and listen to you pretend. When that man comes back in here all you're gonna do is burst into a flood of tears. You're not gonna do anything! You never do anything—

except *cry*. That's your solution for everything—*tears*. Occasionally, but very rarely—you LAUGH!—a nerve-racking, hysterical, nervous laugh [*Dramatically imitates laughter.*] Aaahaahahaa, Aaahaahahahaaa, Uuhahuhaaaa! . . . but, most of the time . . .

LIZZIE [*Teary*]. I am upset . . .

MARGARET-ELIZABETH. You're upset? I happen to be just an innocent traveling companion . . . I had no idea . . .

LIZZIE. . . . I am angry . . . and I'm just about to get *mad*. You know how crazy I can be when I get mad . . .

MARGARET-ELIZABETH [*Sarcastically*]. Yes, I do.

LIZZIE. It's not so much that I mind that they rummaged through my clothes—that's their job . . . but the *insult* . . . I'm gonna walk right up to him . . . you know how I walk when I get mad . . .

MARGARET-ELIZABETH [*Sarcastically*]. Yes, I do.

LIZZIE [*Sarcastically*]. Yes, I do.

LIZZIE. . . . the pure-dee *insult* . . .

MARGARET-ELIZABETH. Da punckety, punckety, punck . . . da punckety, punckety, punck . . . da punckety, punckety, punck . . .

LIZZIE. What's that? What're you mumbling?

MARGARET-ELIZABETH. That's how you walk. Da punckety, punckety, punck . . . an' it don't matter whether you mad or not . . . That's how you walk. Da punckety, punckety, punck . . .

LIZZIE. Look! Look at me! Do I look like . . .

MARGARET-ELIZABETH. I hope you don't think I'm delighted by this whole thing.

LIZZIE. Look! Look at me! Do I look like . . .

MARGARET-ELIZABETH. I'm sitting here like some kind of desperado because of you!

LIZZIE [Loudly]. Do I look like . . . a criminal?

MARGARET-ELIZABETH. Stop making so much fuss! [Whispering.] Right now we both look like criminals. It was in *your* bag. They found it in *your* bag. I'm just trying to catch my breath over the whole thing . . . [Suddenly facing Lizzie almost nose to nose.] *And* I'm looking at you! I'm looking right at you . . . for the first time in all the . . . "ho hum" years I've known you, I just don't recognize you!

LIZZIE [Drily]. Fifty years.

MARGARET-ELIZABETH. Yes? Yes? What're you saying?

LIZZIE. Fifty years! We've known each other for fifty years . . . or, at least you *told* me you were seventeen when I met you. There's been quite a bit of debate on that through the years as you know.

MARGARET-ELIZABETH. Don't you start that with me now. I'm not playing with you.

LIZZIE. Well what am I supposed to think? Joan of Arc was supposed to be seventeen . . . and you were *supposed* to be seventeen! To this day, no one has explained to *me* why you never played the role of Joan of Arc!

[Lizzie has obviously shaken Margaret Elizabeth. Margaret Elizabeth sits for some time in an emotional reverie. She begins a soft laughter that attempts to mask her vulnerability.]

MARGARET-ELIZABETH. Them people from Hollywood sure had us fooled when they told us they were going to put us in the movies! Had the nerve to tell all the people in Boley that we was playin' the leading roles! . . . and, Oh, my God! . . . [Laughing] first part! . . . they tied my head up and blackened my face . . . we went shoppin' in downtown Boley . . . 'member?

WOMAN ONE [Playing a youthful Margaret-Elizabeth; Southern accent]. Had me goin' shoppin' wid' you talkin' 'bout what color dress you was going to wear for your first appearance . . .

MARGARET-ELIZABETH. We go into all the dress shops in Boley . . . and nobody had a dress to suit me. And everytime we leave a store—we start singing that song . . . that song . . . 'bout . . . ?

LIZZIE [Drily]. Millie Biggers.

MARGARET-ELIZABETH. That's it! Millie Biggers! I'd try on every dress they had; and you'd say . . .

WOMAN ONE. "Margaret? What color you lookin' for?"

MARGARET-ELIZABETH. . . . And I'd say, "Ask Millie Biggers!" So we go skipping to the next store—asking' Millie Biggers: [Chanting.] "Oh, will you wear red, Millie Biggers?" [To Lizzie.] G'won! Say your part! [No response from Lizzie.] Oh, you done forgot that, huh? [Continuing.] And then we leave another store and you say . . .

WOMAN ONE. "What color you lookin' for, Margaret?"

MARGARET-ELIZABETH. . . . An' I say, "Ask Millie Biggers!" [Chanting.]

"Oh, will you wear blue, Millie Biggers?" [Pause.]
Don't remember nothin' 'bout it, do you, Maggie?

WOMAN ONE [Drily beginning the chant].

"You sholy would wear gray?
You sholy would wear gray?
You sholy would wear gray, Millie Biggers?"

[Looks to Margaret-Elizabeth for response. No response from Margaret-Elizabeth.]

"Well, will you wear white?
Well, will you wear white?
Well, will you wear white, Millie Biggers?"

MARGARET-ELIZABETH [Slowly and softly].

"I won't wear white,
I'd get dirty long 'fore night.
I'll wear me a cotton dress,
Dyed wid copperse and oak-bark."

WOMAN ONE. Oh! Well . . .

"Now will you wear black?
Now will you wear black?
Now will you wear black, Millie Biggers?"

MARGARET-ELIZABETH [Beginning softly, ending dramatically].

"I might wear black,
Cause it's the color o' my back;
An' it looks lak my cotton dress,
Dyed wid copperse an' oak bark."

[*Laughing.*] Oooh! Ha' mercy! Little did I know . . . that . . . *that* was *exactly* what I was gon' end up wearin'—a ol' dinky, dyed-up, cotton dress! *Every* role I played—I had the same dress on! Girl! I was one foolish somebody then!

LIZZIE. . . . come to the studio wearin' a fur coat . . .

MARGARET-ELIZABETH. . . . over my apron . . .

[*They laugh—a bittersweet laugh.*]

Did you forget about those times, Lizzie?

LIZZIE [*Quietly*]. I didn't forget, Margaret. I just don't have any reason to keep remembering.

[*Woman One exits.*]

MARGARET-ELIZABETH. At least my foolishness was under the guise of youth!

LIZZIE. That's debatable! You certainly never looked seventeen to me.

MARGARET-ELIZABETH. Don't let me start telling you how old you are, Lizzie! The last time someone told you you were sixty-seven years old—you collapsed! Your legs just folded up right under you and you fell flat on your face. So you just shut up!

LIZZIE. You didn't hear what I told the bus driver?

MARGARET-ELIZABETH. What bus driver?

LIZZIE [*Shouting*]. The bus driver! . . . that brings you over this bridge!

MARGARET-ELIZABETH [*Quietly*]. No. What did you tell the bus driver, Lizzie?

LIZZIE. I told him I was fifty-five years old and he nearly fell out of his seat.

MARGARET-ELIZABETH. No wonder! He was in shock. You're sixty-nine!

LIZZIE. That's it! That's *it*! I'm not saying another word to you! I'm not going to talk to you anymore, Margaret. [*Long, angry silence as they both stare straight ahead. Finally.*] *If* I happen to speak to you again, it's because you're the only somebody in here that I know.

MARGARET-ELIZABETH [*Incredulously*]. *What* am I doing sitting here talking to you like this? *Seven* customs agents surrounded us the moment we crossed this border . . . and I'm still trying to coax my heart to come up outta' my knees. . . !

LIZZIE. Oh, Margaret! Don't be so dramatic. *Three*! There were only three agents.

MARGARET-ELIZABETH. That's easy for you to say— you don't wear glasses.

LIZZIE. An' you don't wear them like you're supposed to. Your vanity is obnoxious, Margaret.

MARGARET-ELIZABETH. Don't argue with me! Not now, please! I can't figure out why in the *hell* you brought that stuff with you in the first goddamn place!

LIZZIE. There's no need to get nasty, Margaret. Especially since you *know* I always travel with it. Did I *ever* visit you and didn't have it with me? I never travel without baking soda—never. I don't know why you actin' like this is the first time you've ever seen me with it.

MARGARET-ELIZABETH [*Loudly*]. Why do you need so much of the goddamn stuff?

LIZZIE [*Hurt. Teary.*]. And I don't know why you shouting at me, Margaret. [*Shouting back.*] Now you just stop it!

MARGARET-ELIZABETH [*Quietly, between clenched teeth*]. Why do you need so much of the goddamn stuff?

LIZZIE. Margaret, *soda* is *very* pure . . . *very* natural! [*Rising intensity.*] Smell my feet! [*Reaches down as if to remove a shoe.*]

MARGARET-ELIZABETH. Lizzie! Lizzie!

LIZZIE. You can't smell 'em! Every day I sprinkle that stuff between my toes . . . *you cannot smell my feet*!

MARGARET-ELIZABETH. Lizzie! Lizzie!

LIZZIE. TEETH! [*Proudly baring teeth.*] SEE! SEE! [*Manic.*] UNDER MY ARMS!

MARGARET-ELIZABETH [*Commanding*]. Lizzie!

LIZZIE. CLEAN THE HOUSE WITH IT!

MARGARET-ELIZABETH. Lizzie, for Christ's sake!

LIZZIE. I EAT IT!

MARGARET-ELIZABETH. Don't you dare sit here and tell these customs agents [*Raising voice.*] this bizarre baking soda story . . . 'cause if you do they gonna . . . YOU *EAT* IT? [*Disgust.*]

LIZZIE [*Standing up, writing in anger, shaking with fury, shouting to the empty rooms*]. I WILL! I'LL TELL THEM EXACTLY WHAT I THINK ABOUT THEIR LOW INSULTS . . .

MARGARET-ELIZABETH [*Pulling Lizzie back into her seat*]. SHUT UP! They can see us! [*Sitting rigidly as her eyes search the room.*] They are looking at us *right now*!

LIZZIE [*Furtively looking around*]. Looking at us? How?

MARGARET-ELIZABETH. Through a two-way . . . two-way mirror of course. Act normal. They're watching everything we do to see if we're trying to hide and cover up anything.

LIZZIE [*Looking, trying to discover the two-way mirror*]. Really?

[*They both sit silently and rigidly self-conscious for some time. When Margaret-Elizabeth speaks, she speaks from the side of her mouth, so as not to be observed by the officials.*]

MARGARET-ELIZABETH. One thing is very clear— they don't know who we are.

LIZZIE. That's true, Margaret.

MARGARET-ELIZABETH. I think we ought to tell them who we are.

LIZZIE. Absolutely. [*Pause.*] But . . . Margaret? . . . who are we? [*Margaret-Elizabeth gives her an impossibly bitter stare.*] I mean . . . are we somebody . . . [*Groping for words and shrinking under Margaret-Elizabeth's stare.*] that . . . they're gonna . . . treat . . . nicely . . . ?

MARGARET-ELIZABETH. My dear girl, *always* let people know how important you are. Don't tell me you've forgotten who you are?

LIZZIE [*Too embarrassed to admit it*]. NOooo! [*Giggling.*] I haven't forgotten, Margaret.

MARGARET-ELIZABETH. Good. Because there's more than one way to tell people who you are.

LIZZIE [*A great mystery*]. Really?

MARGARET-ELIZABETH [*Staring straight ahead and feigning decorum. Loud whisper*]. Lizzie. Lizzie! Follow me. Do everything that I do but do it quietly and unobtrusively. Are you listening to me? Okay, follow me.

[*They delicately, in unison, remove their gloves. They cautiously rummage through their luggage with one hand as they stare straight ahead. After a short search, Margaret-Elizabeth removes a packet of papers.*]

[*Holding up papers.*] Take out your judge's notebook. [*She waits impatiently as Lizzie continues to search.*]

LIZZIE [*Finally, after searching for some time*]. What judge's notebook?

MARGARET-ELIZABETH [*Impatiently forgetting decorum. Waving the folder*]. There! In big, bold, letters! "Official Judge—MISS INTERNATIONAL SEPIA— 1980"! Christ!

LIZZIE. Margaret, if you're not going to be nice to me—don't talk to me!

MARGARET-ELIZABETH [*Looking as though she is counting to ten before she speaks*]. Okay. Okay. [*Breathing deeply.*] I'm sorry. Okay! I'm sorry. [*Holding folder in her lap like a schoolteacher. Calm restraint.*] Judge's notebook.

LIZZIE [*Removing papers*]. They call this a judge's notebook? I didn't know that.

MARGARET-ELIZABETH. It . . . really doesn't matter

what we call it, Lizzie . . . just take it out. Quietly. Quietly, Lizzie. Try not to overreact. Now open it up. [*Pause, as Lizzie rummages through papers. Still staring straight ahead.*] Tell me what you see.

LIZZIE [*Reading papers*]. Tally sheet for scores . . .

MARGARET-ELIZABETH. Umh, humm . . .

LIZZIE. List of finalists . . .

MARGARET-ELIZABETH. Quietly. Quietly, Lizzie . . .

[*They both begin leafing through the folders.*]

LIZZIE. . . . program notes . . . special events . . . contest rules . . .

MARGARET-ELIZABETH [*Dramatically*]. Look, Lizzie. Our banners.

[*She pulls out a colorful ribboned beauty contest banner that says, "Miss International Sepia—1980".*]

LIZZIE. Oooh, oooh . . . oooh . . . with a special blue ribbon that says, "Judge"—Awww . . . doesn't that make you feel important?

[*Margaret-Elizabeth stands and slips the banner on. She defiantly removes the blue "Judge" sticker.*]

MARGARET-ELIZABETH. Miss International Sepia— 1980!

LIZZIE [*Shocked*]. Oh, Margaret! Stop it!

MARGARET-ELIZABETH. Everything with a flourish, Lizzie. *Now* I feel important.

LIZZIE [*Intrigued. Beginning to smile a little*]. Margaret, how can you?

MARGARET-ELIZABETH. Just like we did fifty years ago!

LIZZIE [*Delightedly shocked*]. Oh, Margaret! How can you?

MARGARET-ELIZABETH. Like this.

[*She takes Lizzie by the shoulders and delicately gets her to stand up. Margaret-Elizabeth slips the remaining banner on Lizzie as Lizzie excitedly looks around to see who's watching.*]

LIZZIE [*Giggling like a schoolgirl*]. Oh, Margaret!

[*Margaret-Elizabeth leans over and removes the "Judge" sticker from Lizzie's banner.*]

You're sensational!

[*They sit demurely back down wearing their beauty queen banners.*]

MARGARET-ELIZABETH. We have been in Canada for about . . . [*Looking at wristwatch*] twenty-five minutes, and already they're whispering about . . . "those two front-runners for some international smuggling organization."

LIZZIE. Who? Who, Margaret? Who is that?

MARGARET-ELIZABETH. Oh, Lizzie, you make me so tired! US! They're whispering about *US.*

LIZZIE [*Giggling*]. Isn't it exciting! [*Looking around defiantly for the hidden mirrors. As if talking to the customs agents or the walls. Politely.*] Thank you. Thank you very much. I never expected a few simple bags of bicarbonate of soda would gain me such notoriety.

MARGARET-ELIZABETH. No, Lizzie. Not a few simple bags of bicarbonate of soda. PLASTIC BAGS! You had it in PLASTIC BAGS! *Ten*, balloon-size, plastic bags full of baking soda! Stuffed in your goddamn luggage! [*Shouting.*] I could kill you, woman!

[*At this point, four Customs agents (Man One and Two and Woman One and Two) enter detaining area carrying the six large plastic bags filled with white powder.*]

MAN TWO [*Dangling one bag in front of Lizzie*]. We found this in your luggage.

LIZZIE [*Quietly defiant*]. That's right.

[*There is a long pause as everyone seems to be holding their breath.*]

MAN TWO [*Clearing his throat*]. Our analysis shows that this is . . . uh . . .

MAN ONE, WOMAN ONE AND TWO. . . . bicarbonate of soda . . .

MAN TWO. Yes. Uh . . . bicarbonate of soda . . . and . . . uh . . . we are . . .

MAN ONE, WOMAN ONE AND TWO. . . . we are sorry for the inconvenience . . .

MAN TWO. Yes. We are sorry for the uh . . . inconvenience.

[*The Customs Agents deliver all the plastic bags to Margaret-Elizabeth and Lizzie. The two women line them up on the bench.*]

LIZZIE. Is that all? Is that all they're gonna say to us?

MARGARET-ELIZABETH [*Seething*]. I'm angry.

LIZZIE. I'm mad.

[*The Customs Agents, clustered Upstage, watch the two women, who are Downstage.*]

I'm mad. Margaret, I'm mad. I just don't want to walk out of here like this. Feel me! Feel my forehead! [*Takes Margaret-Elizabeth's hand and presses it to her forehead.*] I'm flushed hot! [*Breathing heavily.*] My whole back is burning with shame and anger.

MARGARET-ELIZABETH. I don't want it to end like this.

LIZZIE. If I walk out of here like this—my whole trip is gonna be in shambles.

MARGARET-ELIZABETH. I don't want it to end like *this*!

LIZZIE. Well, what do you want to do, Margaret?

MARGARET-ELIZABETH. Something. Something . . . Do you remember? . . . What was that movie? It was . . . Myra and . . . Myra and . . . they were on the train . . .

LIZZIE. AH! Wait! Wait! Don't tell me! . . . Myra and Porter . . . Porter Campbell . . . And they were on the train . . .

[*First Miniscene: Throughout the script, the two women re-create scenes from the movies they have been in. These scenes are identified as Miniscenes.*]

MARGARET-ELIZABETH [*Becoming Myra*]. And Myra says, [*English accent*] "I won't take it! I won't take it! from anyone! And you know how devastating I can be when I get mad!" [*Pause as she waits for Lizzie to join in. To Lizzie.*] G'won! Say your part.

LIZZIE. I don't want to do that part. I wanna do Myra.

MARGARET-ELIZABETH. Oh, come on, Liz. I'm just trying to remember the words.

LIZZIE. I remember her part. "I won't! I won't take it from anyone. Nobody speaks to me that way! Nobody! Eggghuggh! I'm mad! And you know how I am when I get mad!" [*To Margaret-Elizabeth*] You do the other part.

MARGARET-ELIZABETH. Lizzie, I'm just trying to . . .

LIZZIE. You always try to play the best parts.

MARGARET-ELIZABETH [*Firmly*]. Lizzie, just say your part, please.

LIZZIE [*Butterfly McQueen*]. "Miss Myra! Miss Myra! Don't hit me! I didn't do it!"

MARGARET-ELIZABETH [*As Myra*]. "Well, *somebody* did it! And by the saints—I'll make 'em pay!" [*She begins to toss clothing from the open luggage around the room.*]

LIZZIE [*In character*]. "Miss Myra! I didn't do it! Don't hit me! [*Watching items sail across the room.*] Them's yo' good clothes! Oh, Lordy! Woe is me! Woe is me!"

[*The two women are flushed with laughter and excitement as they finish the scene.*]

MARGARET-ELIZABETH [*Laughing*]. Why the hell you need so much of this goddamn stuff?

LIZZIE. I just didn't want to run out . . .

MARGARET-ELIZABETH [*Instigating*]. He put his fat, red, rusty fingers in it.

LIZZIE. He did? He did, didn't he?

MARGARET-ELIZABETH. It ain't pure no more.

LIZZIE. He sure did, didn't he?

MARGARET-ELIZABETH. I don't want it to end like this, Lizzie.

LIZZIE. Me neither.

[*They look at one another as they each pick up one of the filled plastic bags.*]

MARGARET-ELIZABETH. Ready! Aim!

MARGARET-ELIZABETH AND LIZZIE. FIRE!

[*They throw the plastic bags at the Agents. The bags burst open as they make contact. White powder begins to fly everywhere.*]

LIZZIE [*Jumping with glee*]. I got his feet! It smashed all up against his shoes! Haaahahaahaaa!

MARGARET-ELIZABETH. I think I hit his head!

[*They scream with glee as they begin a rapid-fire attack. They throw the remaining plastic bags with abandon.*]

[*Throwing another bag.*]

Oooh, my God! I hit the ceiling! Eeehahahaaaha!

[*White dust showers the room. The two women embrace and almost dance with excitement.*]

LIZZIE [*Taking aim*]. I wanna hit that little short one!

MARGARET-ELIZABETH. I wanna hit the one with the shit-grin!

LIZZIE. Which one is that?

MARGARET-ELIZABETH. The one on the end.

LIZZIE. I see him! I see him! Let's get him, girl! Get him!

[*They throw the last bags.*]

MARGARET-ELIZABETH [*Shaking hands and formally congratulating Lizzie*]. I'm very proud of you, Lizzie. This is clearly one of the finest things you've ever done.

LIZZIE [*Blushing*]. Thank you.

MARGARET ELIZABETH. You did good, Lizzie.

LIZZIE [*Proudly*]. I did, didn't I?

MARGARET-ELIZABETH. Really good. [*Embraces Lizzie.*]

[*They put on their white gloves, dust themselves off, adjust their beauty queen banners, and begin to gather up their luggage.*]

"An' then Myra walked off the train onto the beach . . ."

LIZZIE. ". . . an' Porter stood on the boardwalk . . . his eyes misted over . . . and he waved to Myra . . . [*Throws her hand up in a broad gesture of waving*] and . . . and . . . [*Begins to cough from the soda dust that Margaret is pounding from her luggage*] AND . . . [*Waving dust from her vision*] when the dust cleared . . ."

MARGARET-ELIZABETH. No, no, no! ". . . and Myra took off her shoes and left her footprints in the . . ."

[*They both pause and look dramatically around the room.*]

MARGRET-ELIZABETH AND LIZZIE. BAKING SODA!

[*They laughingly pick up their luggage and begin to walk off as the lights dim.*]

END OF SCENE I

SCENE II

TIME: Late afternoon—next day
PLACE: Luxury hotel, Windsor, Ontario
SCENE: A wide ramp, resembling a city freeway, bridges the entire upstage area from Stage Right to Stage Left. At the center of the ramp, which arches several feet from the floor, is the first-floor balcony of a luxurious, lake-front hotel in Windsor, Ontario. A large banner that reads, "Welcome—Miss International Sepia" is located at the Center of the ramp. Glass doors open out onto a European-style balcony overlooking a courtyard. Arching over the Downstage Left entrance to the ramp is a latticework trellis entwined with plastic flowers and vines.

[*Man One and Man Two, now dressed in black-and-white waiter's jackets, begin to set up small café tables and chairs Downstage. There is the heightened sound of many birds as Margaret-Elizabeth enters the hotel balcony wearing a satin dressing gown.*]

MARGARET-ELIZABETH. Shoo! Scat! Get away! [*Scattering birds from the breakfast dishes.*] Off! Off! [*Turns, calls back into the room.*] Lizzie! Look at this! Birds everywhere!

[*Margaret-Elizabeth brusquely begins to remove the breakfast trays. She spies a newspaper on the table. She picks it up and reads it.*]

It's Sunday. The only way I can ever tell it's Sunday anymore is by reading the newspapers. Seems like there was a time when you could *smell* a Sunday or *hear* a Sunday, but now you have to read about it. [*Calling in to Lizzie.*] This is a marvelous hotel! Look at that lake! [*Pause.*] We paid for this room—not the birds. So stop inviting them to dine with us.

LIZZIE [*From inside*]. I forgot.

MARGARET-ELIZABETH [*She stands, musing. Then, still talking loudly to Lizzie, who remains inside*]. You know who would have liked this hotel? William. First time I ever stayed at any hotel was with William. Did I tell you . . . ? William called me? After all these years. After all these years. And do you know what he wanted? He wanted for us to get back together! I didn't laugh in his face . . . but you know what I told him? I told him. I said, "If you can match me possession for possession—bank account for bank account—I'll consider it." Which I knew he couldn't do— 'cause . he was nothing but a wastrel . . . *but* that's what I told him . . . [*Pause.*] I think this is the best hotel I've ever stayed in. Is that possible? [*Gives a small, startled scream as she discovers a bird is still on the balcony.*] Shoo, bird! Shoo! Get away from here! [*Calling in to Lizzie again.*] It is the natural proclivity of birds to eat the food left unattended on the balcony.

LIZZIE [*From inside*]. I forgot.

MARGARET-ELIZABETH [*Sharing big secret with audience*]. She's afraid of birds. [*Laughs.*] She won't even come out here if I tell her they're still here . . . [*To Lizzie.*] If you want them to start living here with us . . .

LIZZIE [*From inside*]. I forgot!

MARGARET-ELIZABETH [*Imitating Lizzie*]. "I forgot, I forgot, I forgot." [*Spans her hands as if reprimanding Lizzie.*] Naughty. Naughty.

[*Below, the two waiters, Man One and Man Two, prepare small café tables for cocktails in the Downstage dining area.*]

[*Margaret-Elizabeth, in a childlike prank, tiptoes to the balcony doors, slowly opens them, and then shouts to Lizzie.*]

MARGARET-ELIZABETH [*Mockingly*]. There's birds out here, Lizzie!

LIZZIE [*In the process of dressing for cocktails*]. Oh, God, no! I'm afraid of birds! [*She gingerly steps out on the balcony to see if the birds have disappeared.*] Are they all gone? I like to watch them from a distance—'cause they look like all the beautiful poetry that's ever been written about them—but, up close, I can't stand to be near them . . . they frighten me. It's their fluttering . . . so erratic . . . like a desperation . . . [*She returns inside.*]

MARGARET-ELIZABETH. Did you notice when we came through the lobby? Everyone staring at us? Well, you know what they think . . .

LIZZIE [*Appearing at balcony doorway*]. And MOTHS! Birds and Moths! [*Starts to exit back into the hotel, suddenly returns.*] And CHICKENS! Chickens are like that too, you know . . . all fluttery. It seems as if they're too . . . vulnerable . . . too easily devoured by everything else. Their lives seem so tenuous. From the moment they exist they must lead desperate lives—afraid of the future because each *hour* becomes the future. [*Exits back into the hotel.*]

MARGARET-ELIZABETH. They think we're the contestants. I'm serious. Beauty *lives*! It's not something you can put on in the morning and take off at night—even after fifty years.

LIZZIE [*Still dressing as she enters the balcony*]. . . . and BUTTERFLIES! Oooh, I must not forget butterflies—I *hate* them! [*She returns to hotel room.*]

MARGARET-ELIZABETH. I still wear the same size dress I did then. We are still pretty fancy after all these years.

LIZZIE [*Entering balcony*]. Get dressed, Margaret! Please don't embarrass me by being late to everything! [*Exits back into hotel.*]

MARGARET-ELIZABETH. Very fancy. We've finally gone international. Been trying to get to the end of this story for fifty years. Fifty years is a long time. [*Disappears briefly into hotel room. Returns with a strapless, satin cocktail dress. A sinister pronouncement.*] I hate butterflies. [*Calling in to Lizzie.*] Lizzie! Did I ever tell you about how I hate butterflies? I tried to kill one once. Let's see . . . I was still living on the farm . . . so I must have been around . . . four years old. And this butterfly—this beautiful butterfly—

beautiful from a distance, but up close it was ugly . . . I tried to kill it. I picked up this wooden plank that was lying on the ground—it had a rusty nail sticking out on one end . . . I chased the butterfly all over the yard—stabbing him with that rusty nail. I remember ripping its wings a few times, but it kept flying. It kept flying like it was . . . crazy. And then it seemed to fly right at me—like it wanted to dash itself in my face—like it had the *nerve* to fight back. A little measly butterfly . . . attacking me. Boy, I threw that plank down and started running from that butterfly—screaming. [*Calling in to Lizzie.*] Nobody respects you if you're normal, Lizzie! Only the crazy things survive. [*She has begun to dress throughout this speech.*] I have an awful lot of respect for butterflies. [*Pause.*] Well . . . I don't have to worry about the important things in my life anymore. [*Pause.*] My second husband . . . [*Reflects, as if counting.*] *third* husband! I'm sorry . . . my third husband! . . . always called me Lizzie . . . can I tell you something? I actually *married* a man who called me Lizzie. Now that was my third husband . . . and I gotta tell you something else . . . my second husband called me Liza. But that wasn't as bad as my first husband. He called me Maggie! That was my first husband and my first mistake. And I done had *five* . . . [*Pauses to count*] mistakes since then. You tell me! I would *never* marry a man who calls me Maggie—and, for that matter, I ain't gon' marry nobody who calls me Lizzie no more either. And who was it that had the nerve to call me *Meg*?

LIZZIE [*Entering balcony*]. Sam! I wish you would stop dawdling and get dressed! You make me so nervous! [*Exits back into hotel.*]

MARGARET-ELIZABETH [*Still dressing*]. I believe that *was* Sam—I think so . . . yeah! Sam. Had to be Sam—let's see . . . [*Recalling*] William, Arthur . . . No! William . . . *Charlie* . . . Arthur, Sam . . . Well, anyway, it was my third husband, Arthur, who called me Lizzie. He thought he was very smart, you know. He called himself a big-time adventurer. Said he didn't like nothing commonplace—that's why he married me. Everytime I do something . . . the first thing he'd say was . . . "Lizzie, surprise me! Give me a shock! Make me gasp—once, because you've done something that I didn't already know you were going to do."

LIZZIE [*Almost completely dressed in her neat little suit, hat, and gloves*]. I wasn't going to tell you because I didn't want to hear your tongue clicking and clacking in my ear! . . . but now, I'm going to tell you—and I beg you . . . PLEASE be silent! [*Defiant pro-*

nouncement.] I gave up the house. I no longer live in the city and I do not live alone. [*Silence.*] Well, what do you have to say?

MARGARET-ELIZABETH. You . . . you . . . what can I say?

LIZZIE. Okay. There. That's it. [*She straightens her attire and approaches the ramp.*] The only thing that this *marvelous* hotel is missing is an elevator! Hurry up, Margaret. I'll meet you downstairs.

[*Lizzie goes down and is seated at a table. Lights dim briefly and back up as Margaret-Elizabeth emerges through the glass doors completely dressed in extravagant attire: a strapless cocktail dress. She slips the beauty contest ribbon on over her dress and finally places a rhinestone tiara on her head.*]

MARGARET-ELIZABETH [*From balcony, as if to herself*]. I'll tell you what! I don't ever intend to wear anymore of them dinky gray-dyed, cotton, scrubwoman, tattered, faded—RAGS! Anymore!

[*She descends the ramp as if she were the beauty contestant—flashing a brilliant smile, rhinestone tiara glittering, "Miss International Sepia" banner emblazoned across her satin dress.*]

LIZZIE [*As Margaret-Elizabeth approaches*]. You're late!

[*Man Two (Waiter) gives Margaret-Elizabeth a menu.*]

What if I were dying and you were late?

MARGARET-ELIZABETH [*Studying menu*]. Lizzie, must you be so gruesome?

LIZZIE. I don't think reality is gruesome. You do plan to die one day don't you? Or are you above that? Face it. Death could happen . . . within . . . the next ten minutes.

MARGARET-ELIZABETH. Well . . . in that case . . . I'd better hurry up and order.

LIZZIE. I've already ordered—the usual.

MARGARET-ELIZABETH. Pink Ladies? [*Loudly.*] Pink ladies be damned!

[*Lizzie self-consciously stops near the table as if she is looking for something.*]

[*To Lizzie.*] What *are* you *doing*? Pretending you don't know me?

LIZZIE. Yes.

MARGARET-ELIZABETH. Get up. Get up, Lizzie. I'm

thinking. You know what I think, Lizzie? I think . . . I don't know . . . I think we can afford to be . . .

LIZZIE. Intelligent, Margaret! Act intelligent . . . PLEASE!

MARGARET-ELIZABETH. We could very easily be standing at the pinnacle of a new epoch in our lives. Think about it. Does it seem fitting to celebrate such a potentially auspicious time with something as creatively lacking as Pink Ladies? No. No. Lizzie, while we're here for what may be an unparalleled occasion—let's do everything with a great flourish! And the first thing I say is—Pink ladies be damned!

LIZZIE. Well it took you a long time to say it, Margaret. What do you have in mind?

MARGARET-ELIZABETH [To Waiter]. An Irish coffee! [Looking excitedly at Lizzie with a gleefully devilish glint.] Don't you remember?

[Miniscene.]

[Butterfly McQueen-type characterization.] "Someone's at the door. Why don't you answer it, Beulah?"

LIZZIE. Oh! Uhm . . . uhm . . . [In half surprise, she begins to recognize the moment and assumes a similar characterization.] Uhm . . . "I cain't. I'se scared!"

[They laugh.]

Was that it? Was that it? What was it . . . ? Something about . . . ?

MARGARET-ELIZABETH. She was standing drenched and shivering in the rain . . .

LIZZIE [Laughing]. Oh, yes. And he lifted her in his arms . . .

MARGARET-ELIZABETH. Pale and near death . . .

LIZZIE. . . . and he carried her into the drawing room and placed her crumpled form on the couch in front of the fireplace . . . and then he served her . . .

MARGARET-ELIZABETH AND LIZZIE [Together].
IRISH COFFEE!

LIZZIE. Of course!

MARGARET-ELIZABETH [To Waiter]. That's it! That's what I want. I want an Irish coffee!

LIZZIE. Margaret, you're such a genius. That sounds so delightful! Do I dare?

MARGARET-ELIZABETH [Lowering her voice as if divulging a big secret]. You know what you could try, Lizzie? A hot toddy! [Suppressing her glee with a knowing look at Lizzie] It was Miss Flora. Remember! [Prodding.] Miss Flora?

LIZZIE. Oooh . . . you're right!

[Miniscene.]

"Miss Flora, sweet chile. Massa Tim say it too early fo' you to get out of bed wid' yo' sick self."

MARGARET-ELIZABETH [As Miss Flora]. "Master Tim doesn't run my life. I must get up—Courtney is waiting for me. Courtney . . . Courtney . . . Ooooh . . ."

LIZZIE. "Miss Flora has fainted! Massa Tim! Massa Tim! Miss Flora has fainted!"

MARGARET-ELIZABETH. And then . . . he fixed her . . .

MARGARET-ELIZABETH AND LIZZIE [Together]. A HOT TODDY!

LIZZIE [To Waiter]. A hot toddy, please! Thank you, Margaret, thank you! I'm so glad we're making the most of this occasion.

[Waiter exits.]

The hotel is sensational! The people have been gorgeous! Something here makes me feel like I used to feel when Charlie and I built our first house. [Pause.] Was it Charlie?

MARGARET-ELIZABETH. Arthur. It was Arthur.

LIZZIE. Something here reminds me of it. I know what it is. It's spring! It's Sunday and it's spring! You can't beat that combination. I tell you, I'm always surprised to find anyone alive after the winter is over.

MARGARET-ELIZABETH. Lizzie? Is there any subject you can discuss that doesn't involve the "Grim Reaper"? Hmmm? If there is—I wish you would find it. [Pause.] Did you see the two in the lobby when we passed through?

LIZZIE. Two who?

MARGARET-ELIZABETH. The two *ladies*.

LIZZIE. There were two ladies? Watching us? [Pause.] What are you talking about?

MARGARET-ELIZABETH. Lizzie! For Christ's sake, what are we here for? The two ladies in the lobby!

LIZZIE. Give me a clue. Help me. What's the subject?

MARGARET-ELIZABETH. Oh, my God! The first thing I'm going to do in the morning is practice increasing my lung capacity. I need more air in my lungs in order to have the strength to explain things to you. The beauty contestants in the lobby! I know . . . know [Mocking.] "What beauty contestants?" Gasping for more air, I reply, "The beauty contestants that we're here to judge." "Oh, *those* beauty contestants." You didn't see them?

[*Lizzie just stares blankly.*]

Are you with me? I'm telling you I saw two of the contestants in the lobby.

LIZZIE. I thought . . . we were still talking about . . . you know . . .

MARGARET-ELIZABETH. From now on I'll label the subjects so you won't get lost. Guess who's trying to win it again this year? [*Pause.*] Bridget and Gidget!

LIZZIE [*Shocked*]. NOooo! NOooo!

MARGARET-ELIZABETH. Yesss! Yesss!

LIZZIE. Nooo!

MARGARET-ELIZABETH. Yes! [*Pause.*] It's gonna be a doozie of a choosy this year. [*Pause.*] This is a nice hotel, isn't it? It's very nearly the finest one I've been in. Of course I'm giving it a few extra stars for all the cute waiters. Have you noticed? [*Coyly.*] *And* have you noticed how they've been staring at us?

LIZZIE. Margaret!

MARGARET-ELIZABETH. Lizzie, do you live behind a blank wall? You haven't noticed they've been staring at us? [*Adjusts the beauty contest banner across her dress.*] We could do it again, Lizzie.

LIZZIE. Hmmmm . . . what could we be talking about now?

MARGARET-ELIZABETH. I went to little Arthur's birthday party last week. [*Pause.*] My godson . . . little Arthur? He was fourteen years old last week. *And* . . . I was given the . . . privileged honor . . . of actually being invited into his room— [*Proudly*] a privilege usually reserved only for those under fifteen years old. I walked into his room— neat as a pin! And the walls—the walls were covered . . . *plastered* with posters of women. And there was not-one-picture-of-us, Lizzie—not *one*. THERE! Do you see? Do you see why we must do it again?

LIZZIE [*Completely lost*]. What's the subject?

MARGARET-ELIZABETH. US! US, Lizzie! We have to get some new posters for little Arthur's room!

LIZZIE. Oh, dear.

MARGARET-ELIZABETH. We have to do it again, Lizzie. We have to go back and set the record straight. We have to do it right. It's as simple as that. My darling Lizzie! Beauty is alive! . . . and doing quite well, thank you. I don't think it is unfounded vanity to state that after having won the official titled distinction of being the world's first . . . [*Clearing her throat as if making an announcement*] "After having won the official titled distinction of being the world's first ebony-hued beauty—Miss Emancipation of 1930—I can still do it again! And *you*, my pretty handmaiden—first runner-up to the queen . . . you could still do it again too!

LIZZIE. You got a lot of nerve! If I did it again it certainly wouldn't be as runner-up to *you*! I guarantee you that! You think you always supposed to be the queen!

MARGARET-ELIZABETH. We have to change history, Lizzie. We did it wrong the first time. We let everyone down.

LIZZIE. I don't want to do it again, Margaret. I just wanna be two old lad . . . no! Not *old* . . . two . . . *mature* ladies here on a visit as honorary judges.

MARGARET-ELIZABETH. Think of all the time we put into it. Fifty years! Do you know how many of those years I pinched my nose?

LIZZIE [*Tired*]. What's the subject?

MARGARET-ELIZABETH. It's the same subject, Lizzie. Everytime I washed my face I would leave lots of soap on my nose and let it dry while I pinched my nose . . . and, voila!—my nose would stand up straight.

LIZZIE. Margaret, you didn't.

MARGARET-ELIZABETH. Yeah. I did.

LIZZIE. Well . . . I pinched my mouth. My mother taught me how to do it. You can make your lips smaller if you tighten them over your teeth like this. [*Demonstrates.*] See. [*Talks with tightened lips.*] Do you see what that does to your lips?

MARGARET-ELIZABETH. We both used to tuck our fannies.

LIZZIE. That's right! "Tighten your fannies!"

MARGARET-ELIZABETH. . . . and straighten your hair . . .

LIZZIE. . . . had to use bleaching cream every night . . .

MARGARET-ELIZABETH. We were classics. I will not turn the title over to anyone who doesn't even have the bare standards. I'm a classic!

LIZZIE. Maybe we're antiques.

MARGARET-ELIZABETH. Oh, come on, Lizzie. There have to be standards.

LIZZIE. I agree . . . wide-set eyes, long bones . . .

MARGARET-ELIZABETH. We're gonna do it right this time, Lizzie.

LIZZIE [*Exhilarated*]. YES! YES! OOOHH, YES! [*Suddenly.*] Have you ever thought that . . . this might be . . . the last time?

MARGARET-ELIZABETH. This is the beginning, Lizzie! We're gonna put new endings on old stories!

LIZZIE. No, no. I mean . . . the last time . . . for us. [*Trying to find a way to say it delicately.*] Ten years from now we'll be seventy-seven years old . . . or [*Giggles nervously*] . . . whatever.

MARGARET-ELIZABETH. So?

LIZZIE. They only ask us to come every ten years.

MARGARET-ELIZABETH. Oh. I see. You're sounding the death knoll again.

LIZZIE. Well, you must admit that the great majority of people that were with us at the beginning are those who have passed on.

MARGARET-ELIZABETH. There must be something masochistic in my character that makes me want to be with you. You are so morbid.

LIZZIE. You can pretend to be perennial if you want to.

MARGARET-ELIZABETH. Lizzie. Lizzie. It must be fearful. *Thinking* about it all the time. I'm not afraid of dying; but *thinking* about it all the time seems far more horrible than the actual event.

LIZZIE [*Defending herself*]. I am not afraid of dying! I look forward to it. I embrace it. It'll be a great experience! I am totally prepared. The first thing I did when Sam died . . . I joined a memorial society. I wouldn't have come to this trip if I hadn't finished paying for the cemetery plot!

MARGARET-ELIZABETH. The what?

LIZZIE. The vault and the plot alone cost me fifteen hundred dollars! I promised Sam on the day we got married that I would be buried next to him.

MARGARET-ELIZABETH. Was that what you discussed on your honeymoon?

LIZZIE [*Angry*]. Laugh, Margaret! Big joke! Ahhhahahaaa!

MARGARET-ELIZABETH [*Patronizingly*]. Aahh . . . Lizzie is upset. What-is-it-Lizzie! What-are-you-upset-a-bout?

[*Silence.*]

My God, Lizzie. You're serious!

[*Silence.*]

My God, Lizzie! Are you serious?

LIZZIE [*Teary*]. It is a rather serious matter; and it happens to be all I have to be serious about. I am not going to stick my head in the sand and deny that it exists.

MARGARET-ELIZABETH. Are you telling me that you've spent . . . all these years preparing . . . to die?

LIZZIE [*Near tears*]. You see! You see how you try to make it sound stupid! Do you think you can just keel over and die without preparing for it? [*Shouting.*] HAVE YOU PAID FOR YOUR EMBALMING? Huhmmm? Two hundred dollars to be embalmed! Make me look stupid! The casket! THE CASKET? *Seven thousand dollars*! You're not prepared. A hearse! Oh! Oh, now! What about the flower car, the mortician's fee, the limousines, the . . . [*Crying.*]

MARGARET-ELIZABETH [*Stopping her, calming her*]. Oooh, poor baby. Oh, sweetheart. I'm sorry. I didn't know.

LIZZIE. You must start thinking about it, Margaret.

MARGARET-ELIZABETH. I will, dear. I will.

LIZZIE. This contest is a very brief moment in your life. When the contest is over you have to return to reality.

MARGARET-ELIZABETH. Yes, Lizzie. I'll start thinking about . . . [*Unable to say the word*] it.

LIZZIE. I'm sorry if I'm spoiling your trip . . .

[*Waiter enters with drinks.*]

MARGARET-ELIZABETH. Don't stare. But notice how the waiter looks at us.

[*They sit silently as the Waiter serves their drinks. They suppress smiles as they covertly check to see if he is looking at them. Waiter exits. They raise their glasses in a toast.*]

"To the new 'Miss International Sepia'—may she carry on the tradition!"

LIZZIE. Hear! Hear!

[*They sip.*]

MARGARET-ELIZABETH. Hmmm! Oh, this is gorgeous! The topping tastes like ice cream! I wonder if Barbie's in it this year?

LIZZIE [*Returning her drink to the table with a sour grimace*]. Ugh! This tastes like water warmed over in rusty pipes. I don't like my drink.

MARGARET-ELIZABETH. Really? Here. Taste this. [*Slides her drink to Lizzie.*]

LIZZIE [*Sipping Margaret-Elizabeth's drink*]. Yes. This is nice. You always manage to get the best. I don't like mine.

MARGARET-ELIZABETH. Let me see. [*Sips Lizzie's drink.*] That is a peculiar drink. It tastes like hot water . . .

LIZZIE. . . . warmed over in rusty pipes.

MARGARET-ELIZABETH. Yes. It does, sorta. Like . . . the beginning of tea . . . without the teabag. [*Laughing.*] With a little tea and sugar in it—it might work.

LIZZIE. Well, I don't know if I'm going to be able to drink this. I wish I had ordered your drink.

MARGARET-ELIZABETH. Why, Lizzie?

LIZZIE. Why? Why . . . ? Because I don't like this drink. That's why.

MARGARET-ELIZABETH [*Scooping all the whipped cream off her drink. Eating it like ice cream*]. No. No. I mean—*why* did you get rid of your house?

LIZZIE. Oh. Oh, that. It was the stairs, Margaret. Just too many stairs.

MARGARET-ELIZABETH. Hmmm. The whipped cream is so good. [*Pushes the sugar in front of Lizzie.*] Here. Sweeten it with a little sugar. See if that helps.

LIZZIE. That's a good idea. [*Spoons sugar into her drink. Tastes it.*]

MARGARET-ELIZABETH. Well?

LIZZIE. No. I think it's worse.

[*They sip silently for a while.*]

MARGARET-ELIZABETH. Well, I enjoyed the whipped cream, but the drink is not so tasty anymore.

LIZZIE. Makes you realize, doesn't it? All those movies . . . they made those drinks seem like the pure-dee lifeblood of goodness, didn't they?

MARGARET-ELIZABETH. You know what might work? Lemon! Ask the waiter for a slice of lemon. That ought to help it.

LIZZIE. Something! It definitely needs help! [*Signals for Waiter.*] Please. May I have a slice of lemon? [*Waiter exits. To Margaret-Elizabeth.*] What are you doing?

MARGARET-ELIZABETH. I'm putting a *little* sugar in my drink. [*Tastes it.*] Well . . . it's not exactly . . . delightful. Here, try it.

LIZZIE [*Tasting Margaret-Elizabeth's drink*]. Uhm, hum. It's better—but, you know . . . ? Cinnamon!

MARGARET-ELIZABETH. Ooh!

LIZZIE. Yes. When the waiter comes back ask him if he'll bring you a cinnamon stick.

[*Waiter appears carrying a small dish with lemon slices.*]

MARGARET-ELIZABETH. Waiter! Could you bring me a cinnamon stick? Yes. You know. A cinnamon stick.

[*He exits. Lizzie squeezes lemon into her drink.*]

LIZZIE [*Tasting*]. Oh! Oh! I'm *on* to something *now*! Taste this.

MARGARET-ELIZABETH [*Tasting Lizzie's drink*]. Needs . . . [*Suspense, as she tastes it again*] Mint!

LIZZIE. You're right! You are right, my dear Margaret! Why didn't I think of that? Oh, that's perfect! [*Calls.*] Waiter!

[*Waiter is entering with a cinnamon stick on a little dish.*]

Waiter. Could I have a little sprig of mint?

WAITER [*As he places the cinnamon on the table*]. Mint?

LIZZIE. Yes. Just a little sprig.

[*They give flirting glances to the Waiter. Waiter exits.*]

MARGARET-ELIZABETH [*Grinning contentedly*]. You do realize that we're still very fancy after all of these years, don't you, Lizzie?

LIZZIE. Now, what you do is . . . you stir the coffee with the cinnamon stick.

MARGARET-ELIZABETH. I know that, Lizzie. [*Stirs and tastes.*] It's devilish!

LIZZIE [*Grabbing a sip of Margaret-Elizabeth's drink*]. Huhmmm! It is!

MARGARET-ELIZABETH. It's downright devilish! [*Pronouncement.*] You can change *anything* until it suits your taste, Lizzie!

[*They raise their glasses in a toast.*]

LIZZIE. "To *Class*!" We had that, didn't we, Margaret? CLASS!

MARGARET-ELIZABETH. Ooh . . . we fairly reeked of it. It simply oozed from our pores!

LIZZIE [*Seriously*]. The *first* and *primary* criteria that I shall *demand* from every contestant . . . is CLASS! Margaret. How many hours did we spend? Every hair . . . carefully and immaculately in place . . .

MARGARET-ELIZABETH. Well, the wind-blown look was becoming quite popular.

LIZZIE. For you, Margaret, not for me. I don't know how you could let people see you with your hair standing all over your head.

MARGARET-ELIZABETH. But it was a carefully planned wind-blown look—every curl left askew—carefully—for effect.

LIZZIE. And . . . white gloves! Margaret, do you remember we washed our gloves out every night before we went to bed.

[*Waiter returns with mint sprig on little dish.*]

MARGARET-ELIZABETH. I think he's bashful. It's hard to find bashful men anymore.

LIZZIE. It's hard to find bashful people anymore. Everyone's so brazen.

[*They sit demurely as Waiter places dish on table.*]

LIZZIE. Thank you. Uuh . . . [*To Waiter*] could you bring me one of those cinnamon sticks too . . . [*Naughty giggle. To Margaret-Elizabeth.*] In case the mint doesn't quite do it.

[*Waiter exits trying to contain himself. Lizzie bruises the mint sprig into her drink.*]

[*Who has been looking through her contest papers.*] Well, damn-it-to-hell! They don't even list it in here! CLASS! They don't have it on here! Look! (*Reading.*) "Poise, charm, talent, intelligence . . ." But no class!

MARGARET-ELIZABETH. Well, that's the stuff that class is made of, Lizzie. That all adds up to class. How's your drink?

LIZZIE [*Sips*]. Cold.

MARGARET-ELIZABETH [*Sips her drink*]. So's mine.

LIZZIE. I wish I'd a' ordered a pink lady.

END OF SCENE II

SCENE III

SCENE: As the lights fade up, Man One, dressed in representative black tie and tails, approaches the top of the ramp and proceeds to reverse the date section on the "Welcome" banner. He flips the dates, like a calendar, over the original 1980. The year now reads 1930. Margaret-Elizabeth, in a dressing gown, rushes out through the glass doors of the hotel balcony.

MARGARET-ELIZABETH. Oh, God no! What are you trying to do to me?

[*Man One flips the date to 1940.*]

[*Shudders.*] Ooouggggh. . . . No.

[*Man One flips the date to 1950. Margaret-Elizabeth stands staunch and sullen. Man One, showing a slight impatience, flips the date to 1960.*]

Well . . . [*Smiles*] ye—ss. Yes. YES! Good year! That was definitely a good year! [*She exits.*]

[*Man One begins to descend the ramp, Stage Left.*]

MAN ONE [*Calling offstage*]. We're ready! [*He exits.*]

[*The amplified voice of Man One is heard on the loud-speaker. He now becomes the Master of Ceremonies.*]

[*Offstage.*] Ladies and Gentlemen! It is with great pleasure that I announce the new "Miss Emancipation of 1960!"

[*Man One, still dressed in tie and tails and carrying a hand-held microphone, enters the stage to the sound of loud cheering from audience. Woman Two dramatically enters through the glass doors. She is wearing a one-piece bathing suit over black leotards with a banner across the front that reads, "The Queen." She stands on the balcony waving and blowing kisses until Woman One enters the balcony. She is dressed identically, but her banner is blank. Margaret-Elizabeth dramatically enters the balcony through the glass doors and stands between the two women. Margaret-Elizabeth is wearing a one-piece bathing suit with a banner across the front that reads, "Miss Oklahoma." Her bosom is an enormously exaggerated, paddled affair that practically overflows her bathing suit. Her hair is tied up in a bouncy ponytail with a big, bright ribbon on top. Man One gestures, and she begins her descent down the ramp, Stage Left. She smiles the huge, flashing, brilliant smile of a beauty contestant. She does not stop smiling until the pageant is over. Her speech and manner revert to a childlike coyness. Margaret-Elizabeth smiles and walks regally down the ramp Stage Left as a great burst of carnival music accompanies her. Simultaneously, Woman One and Two descend the ramp, Stage Right. Their hair and manner are an imitation of Margaret-Elizabeth's. Man Two enters. He pulls a child's red wagon [slowly, almost in slow motion] in front of the Stage Left entrance to the ramp. The wagon is covered with artificial flowers like a float. As Margaret-Elizabeth passes under the flower-covered archway, Woman One and Two flank her on either side. They all stand under the arched trellis until Man Two places a bouquet of red roses in Margaret-Elizabeth's arms and a rhinestone tiara on her head. The music changes dramatically to "Caldonia" as Man Two helps Margaret-Elizabeth sit in the wagon. Once seated, she strikes a coy pose. He begins to pull the wagon around the stage in what seems to be almost suspended motion. Man One begins to sing "Mammy" [in half time] over the microphone while Margaret-Elizabeth waves, smiles, and blows kisses to the audience.*]

Lizzie enters through the glass doors and leans over the balcony. She is wearing a one-piece swimsuit over black leotards. Her banner is blank. As she speaks, the motions of the others continue, but all sound stops temporarily, as if the needle has been removed from a record.]

LIZZIE [*Calling down to Margaret-Elizabeth*]. I'm going to tell the judges about your TITS!

[*Sound resumes.*]

MAN ONE. And now—the prizes! [*His voice changes into a calm, modulated, emotionless drone—as if he were a guide on a sight-seeing tour of the city. Reading.*] "From Sarah's Sweet Shop—a special cake with the winner's name and title on it."

[*Cheers from the audience.*]

"From The Lyons Bootery—one pair of shoes of the winner's choice."

[*Cheers from the audience.*]

"From The Johnson's Jewelry Shop—a wrist-watch."

[*Cheers from the audience. His voice continues to announce the "prizes" over the loudspeaker throughout the remainder of the scene while he continues to interact, returning to his old "barker" style personality.*]

Boley is blessed! Do you hear me, ladies and gentlemen? Boley is blessed! There she is—our new and magnificent queen!

[*He sings a few more lines from "Mammy" as white lights flash intermittently and silhouette the images on the stage as if photos are being taken.*]

May I take this time to introduce our surprise judge for this year's event—all the way from Holly-Wood, California!—MR. G. W. CASTLE!

[*There is cheering from the audience as he motions for Lizzie to come forward. She stands staunch and resentful on the balcony.*]

[*Again.*] MR. G. W. CASTLE!

[*Sound stops.*]

WOMAN ONE. Where is he, Margaret?

LIZZIE. I'm certainly not going to do it, Margaret!

WOMAN TWO [*Sarcastically*]. Who's going to crown the queen?

[*Man Two disappears.*]

MARGARET-ELIZABETH [*Jumping out of the wagon—no longer the beauty contestant*]. You've been crying all these years because you were runner-up! Now I'm offering you a major part! What the hell do you want?

WOMAN ONE, TWO. I'm not going to do it, Margaret.

MARGARET-ELIZABETH [*Fuming*]. You promised. You *said* you wanted to do this. *Everybody's* waiting. What do you want . . . ? Do you want me to beg? Okay, I'll beg. "Please . . . please . . . DO IT!"

LIZZIE. You've changed everything. That's not my part.

MARGARET-ELIZABETH. I told you . . . it's gonna be different. Who knows . . . you could . . . end up . . . the queen. Help me. After all these years I would think you would be happy to finish it once and for all.

WOMAN TWO. You're not doing it right!

WOMAN ONE. You've got the whole thing wrong!

LIZZIE. You've got the wrong year . . . you've changed the entire . . .

MARGARET-ELIZABETH [*Laughing*]. Oh, come on, Lizzie! 1930! I wouldn't be caught dead in those ugly bathing suits! A little vanity! Vanity never hurt anybody. Truthfully! How do you think I got where I am? Telling the straight of things?

LIZZIE. Truthfully? You don't want anyone to know how long ago it was. [*Shouting.*] MARGARET! It's not just the year that you've randomly plucked out of a hat . . . !

MARGARET-ELIZABETH. It's my story and I can tell it any way I want to! I have kept this body in excellent condition and I intend to show it off! Now you can either cooperate—or get out of it!

LIZZIE, WOMAN ONE, TWO [*Laughing*]. You're so funny, Margaret . . . Ahaaa, ha, ha, haaa . . .

MARGARET-ELIZABETH. There are ever so many ways to tell a story, Lizzie. You can write people in or write 'em out—you're only a small part of this story. The most important thing is how it all ends.

WOMAN ONE. What about the beginning?

MARGARET-ELIZABETH [*Impatient*]. I'm here to find new endings for old stories. It's too late for new beginnings! Now anyone who doesn't want to do what we agreed . . . Make up your mind! [*Under her breath, as if to the audience.*] I can't believe this! I'm begging her to do this part!

LIZZIE. You just want someone to play runner-up to you again!

WOMAN ONE. You've got the wrong date . . .

WOMAN TWO. You've got the wrong title . . .

MARGARET-ELIZABETH. I know that. I started it all, Lizzie. Don't your forget that! *I* was the beginning!

WOMAN TWO [*Laughing uproariously*]. *I* was the beginning!

LIZZIE. Every time you want to be queen!

MARGARET-ELIZABETH. That's not true. That's not true. I want it to come to an *end*. A satisfactory ending. A good ending. A decent ending. One that I can . . . *rest* with! Now I know what I want. 1960 . . . was a good year for beauty.

WOMAN TWO. Well, if it's that flexible . . . I'll be queen!

WOMAN ONE. ME!

LIZZIE. ME!

MARGARET-ELIZABETH [*Mortified*]. You were the runner-up! I was "Miss Emancipation" and you were "Miss Emancipation Proclamation." All good things in due time, Lizzie. Each time I come I see . . . changes.

WOMAN TWO. The only thing that's changed is the title . . .

WOMAN ONE. And the bathing suits . . .

WOMAN TWO. And the people . . .

WOMAN ONE. And the time . . .

MARGARET-ELIZABETH. Thank God for that! [*Changing her approach*]. I need you, Lizzie. I need you very badly. It's a good part. I promise.

WOMAN ONE, TWO, LIZZIE. The runner-up . . .

MARGARET-ELIZABETH. Now, you see. You thought you were gonna be the runner-up. I wouldn't ask you to do that part. You've done that. I want to give you a challenge. I need you to do the most important part of all.

LIZZIE, WOMAN ONE, TWO. The queen?

MARGARET-ELIZABETH [*Sweetly*]. Nooo . . . [*Carefully.*] Mr. Castle.

LIZZIE, WOMAN ONE, TWO. MR. CASTLE! [*They all laugh hysterically.*]

LIZZIE [*Still laughing until she bursts into tears*]. I-WON'T-DO-IT!

MARGARET-ELIZABETH. You get to decide my fate.

LIZZIE [*Tearfully*]. I'm the runner-up! Now you want to take that away from me! You . . . you . . . you . . .

LIZZIE, WOMAN ONE, TWO [*Deliberately*]. . . . *black cow*!

MARGARET-ELIZABETH [*Reproachfully*]. Uh . . . Lizzie! There is no need for you to sink to such low superlatives! [*Pause.*] Don't you understand who Mr. Castle is?

LIZZIE. Yes. He's a *man*. Do I look like a *man* to you? [*Crying.*] You always want to make me look like the horse's hiney.

MARGARET-ELIZABETH. Without him there is no story, Lizzie. I have to call on you for the best part. Think about that. It's the best part in the whole story. Trust me. [*She looks at Lizzie for a few beats then nods to the announcer to continue.*]

[*Sound resumes, Woman One and Woman Two begin waving, smiling, and posing under the archway.*]

MAN ONE [*Embarrassed recovery*]. Uh . . . Ladies and gentlemen . . . Mr. Castle is a talent scout from the fabled land of Hollywood! He . . . has the power to . . . make a star. The . . .

[*Sound stops.*]

LIZZIE. I'm not going to do it, Margaret.

MARGARET-ELIZABETH. Okay, you don't want to be Mr. Castle? Then I don't want you in it! You made me waste an entire trip!

LIZZIE [*Pointing to Woman One and Two*]. What about Maggie. Make her do it. She was there. And Ginger! She knows the part! I don't wanna do it, Margaret.

WOMAN ONE. I'm not going to do it.

WOMAN TWO. I'm not going to do it, either.

MARGARET-ELIZABETH. FINE!

LIZZIE [*Crying*]. I'm the runner-up! *Not* Mr. Castle!

MARGARET-ELIZABETH. Okay! [*Holding back a smile at having won.*] You can *be* the runner-up! I'll get someone else to play his part.

LIZZIE, WOMAN ONE, TWO. You always get to play the best part!

[*Sound resumes. Margaret-Elizabeth again becomes the beauty contestant. Lizzie, Woman One, and Woman Two stand under the vine-covered trellis waving, smiling, and tossing plastic flowers to the audience.*]

MAN ONE. Ladies and gentlemen! There she is! The Queen of Boley! Miss Emancipation, 1960! And *now*—the man that can crown her Queen of the Stars. I give you—MR. G. W. CASTLE!

[*Man Two snaps on an oversized necktie and proceeds with stiff dignity down the ramp.*]

MAN TWO (MR. CASTLE) [*He speaks humbly and sincerely into the microphone*]. Citizens of Boley. The circumstances that brought me here to your beautiful little town are not as important as what I have discovered here today. I came here under the auspices of a major motion picture company to inaugurate an unprecedented event—the premiere of a major motion picture—HERE! in the all-black township of Boley, Oklahoma.

LOUDSPEAKER [*Prize announcement*]. "From the Metropolitan Movie House—two free tickets to the movie of the winner's choice."

MAN TWO (MR. CASTLE). I did not expect to be a judge today, but after witnessing and participating in today's event, I am overwhelmed by the talent that exists here.

[*Cheering from the audience.*]

[*Breaking in and quieting the cheers.*] SO . . . So overwhelmed that I am taking the liberty to offer a special prize to the winner—a SCREENTEST! . . .

[*Cheers from the audience.*]

[*Calming the audience.*] . . . for . . . FOR a new film that our studios are very excited about. A film about the life of a great saint—JOAN OF ARC! I can't help but feel that your new queen . . . the new "Miss Emancipation" . . . would make an outstanding Joan of Arc. [*He smiles benignly at Margaret-Elizabeth who is now standing under the archway between the two women. To audience.*] Our studios have gone out on a limb to dare to make a film that shows colored people as . . . as . . . PEOPLE! [*Preaching.*] Too long have you stood in the wake of sour images! That is why we were *certain* that this was the *only* place to premiere our new film. I urge you all to place your vote for humanity and the eradication of racism by attending this film. I feel that Fate brought me here for many reasons, not the least of which was to end my search for Joan of Arc.

[*The audience cheers, and he motions for Margaret-Elizabeth to come forward to the microphone. She joins him.*]

[*To Margaret-Elizabeth.*] I have been to almost every major city in America and *never* have I seen such beauty and talent as you have displayed here today. I have just one question to ask of such a talented young lady as yourself. [*To audience.*] Where did you get such pretty legs?

LOUDSPEAKER. "From Marianne's Steak and Chop House—a gift certificate for an evening's free dining."

[*Cheers from the audience.*]

MARGARET-ELIZABETH [*Giggling*]. My mama gave 'em to me.

MAN ONE (ANNOUNCER) [*Resuming microphone*]. WHAT A NIGHT! Ladies and gentlemen—our queen! Take a long, long look, for it may be the last time you get to see her in person until you see her on the SILVER SCREEN! What a night! TONIGHT! Tonight is the big night, ladies and gentlemen . . . the PREMIERE of the newly released film entitled . . . entitled . . . ? [*He looks at Mr. Castle who leans over and whispers something in his ear.*] Uh . . . Yes! Our own special premiere of the newly released film, *BLACK, WHITE, AND IN TROUBLE!* LADIES AND GENTLEMEN— Don't miss it! *Black, White, and in Trouble!*

LOUDSPEAKER. "From Ronald's Novelty Shop—a wall-sized replica of the American flag."

[*Cheering from the audience. Mr. Castle leans forward with a patronly smile and whispers something else into his ear.*]

MAN ONE (ANNOUNCER). LADIES AND GENTLEMEN! I have just been told of another new development to highlight this Night of Nights. Our queen . . . OUR QUEEN will ride through the main street of Boley on a special studio-made float tonight to officially open the world premiere of this new film. And . . . AND . . . to the first twenty-five people to attend!—FREE ADMISSION! What a night! What a night! I urge you all not to miss this exciting film.

LOUDSPEAKER. "From Lacey's Pet Shop—one full-throated singing canary."

[*A floodlight washes across the stage. Margaret-Elizabeth returns to the wagon. Man One now pulls her slowly around the stage as she waves, smiles, and tosses flowers. They are trailed by Woman One and Woman Two, who do the same. The blinding lights of photos being snapped continues intermittently. Mr. Castle begins to ascend the Stage Left ramp entrance. Margaret-Elizabeth jumps from the wagon and pursues him. The Women return to the archway.*]

MARGARET-ELIZABETH [*Calling after him*]. Mr. Castle! Mr. Castle! [*Giggles.*] The . . . the . . . premiere was nice . . . uhm . . . thank you for the honor of . . .

MAN TWO (MR. CASTLE). Aah! You're the little girlie from the beauty contest.

MARGARET-ELIZABETH. Yes. [Giggles.]

MAN TWO (MR. CASTLE). What did you say your name was?

MARGARET-ELIZABETH. Gidget. Like in *Gidget Goes to the Beach.*

MAN TWO (MR. CASTLE). Yes. Well you're very attractive. And you look a lot like Gidget . . . with your, uh . . . pony tail . . . the . . . uh . . . well . . . How'd you like it sweetheart?

MARGARET-ELIZABETH [Gushing]. Oh, it was really exciting. All those flowers . . . my friends couldn't believe . . . that I was sitting there . . . on this float —riding through the center of town. . . .

MAN TWO (MR. CASTLE). No, no. The film. How'd you like the film, girlie?

MARGARET-ELIZABETH. Well . . . I liked the part where the Black Monster starts coming up from the sewers and . . . grabbing all the people . . . I started screaming when he started ripping all the clothes off the women . . . I just wanted to leave. [Giggles.]

WOMAN ONE. You're so phony, Maggie! SMUT! Tell him it was the absolute height of smut!

WOMAN TWO. Pure SMUT!

MARGARET-ELIZABETH. . . . but I liked it. [Giggles.]

MAN TWO (MR. CASTLE). Good. Good. That's what we want. Excitement. Well, girlie, what can I do for you?

MARGARET-ELIZABETH. Uh . . . well you said . . . uh . . . the screentest . . . for Joan of Arc.

MAN TWO (MR. CASTLE). Screentest. Uhhh . . . let me see your legs, sweeetheart.

MARGARET-ELIZABETH. For Joan of Arc?

MAN TWO (MR. CASTLE). Well, now, come, come, dearie. You see, you have to understand that there's a lot of sexual implication in the fact that Joan of Arc posed as a man.

[*Margaret-Elizabeth coyly displays her legs. Lizzie, Woman One and Two do the same.*]

MAN ONE [Standing on wagon]. Oooh, Mama! Where'd you get those fine legs?

MAN TWO (MR. CASTLE). Hey, girlie, who gave you those fine legs?

MARGARET-ELIZABETH [Giggling]. I don't know. I was just born this way.

WOMAN ONE AND TWO AND LIZZIE [Giggling]. My mama gave 'em to me!

MAN TWO (MR. CASTLE). Perfect. You were born perfect. Listen, how old are you, sweetheart?

[*Woman One and Two laugh uproariously.*]

WOMAN ONE. 25!

WOMAN TWO. 28!

MARGARET-ELIZABETH. Eighteen.

MAN TWO (MR. CASTLE). Fuck. Fuck. Well, that's that. Joan of Arc was only seventeen.

LOUDSPEAKER. "From the Wilson Memorial Park Association—a free pass to the Greatest Show On Earth—The Circus."

MARGARET-ELIZABETH, WOMAN ONE, AND TWO. Oh.

MAN TWO (MR. CASTLE). That's a goddamn shame. You would have been perfect. Tell me something. Do you have a lot of fire and passion? A thought just occurred to me.

MARGARET-ELIZABETH. Passion?

[*Woman One and Two begin to breathe passionately.*]

MAN TWO (MR. CASTLE). Yeah. Our studio's been sitting on this hot story . . . love story. The lead in the movie has to have a lot of passion. The role was originally written for a male transvestite . . . but I think I can work something out. C'mere girlie, show me if you're passionate. [He begins to embrace her.]

MARGARET-ELIZABETH. Well, I don't know . . . I thought I was going to have a screentest.

MAN TWO (MR. CASTLE). You are! You are, sweetheart! It's happening right before you very eyes. Hey, look, honey. That camera is like a big, hot cock. It comes right in and fucks you. There's no fakin' it. Now that's the fuckin' truth. C'mon, sweetie, give me some passion. [He kisses her.] What's the matter, don't you like to be kissed?

MARGARET-ELIZABETH, WOMAN ONE AND TWO. NO! [Struggling.]

MARGARET-ELIZABETH. I mean . . . well . . . [He kisses her again.] Stop it!

MAN TWO (MR. CASTLE). Well, look . . . [Backing off], uh . . . as it stands now, I'm only here for a one-day promotional tour.

MAN ONE, MAN TWO (MR. CASTLE), WOMAN ONE AND TWO. I'LL BE BACK NEXT YEAR!

MAN TWO (MR. CASTLE). We'll see what we can work out then.

MARGARET-ELIZABETH. Next year? But you said . . . you announced to everyone . . .

MAN TWO (MR. CASTLE). What can I say? Joan of Arc was only seventeen . . . now that's the fuckin' truth. Look, uh . . . what did you say your name was?

[*Margaret-Elizabeth quickly fluffs her ponytail into an instant "tousled" hairdo and assumes a "girlie" pose. The Women do the same.*]

MARGARET-ELIZABETH. Bridget. Like in . . .

WOMAN TWO. *Bridget Goes to Bed.*

MAN TWO (MR. CASTLE). Oh yeah. Of course. Dead ringer. Perfect. With your . . . tousled hair and the . . . pouty lips, and the . . . uhm, uh . . . you're very beautiful!

MARGARET-ELIZABETH. Thank you.

MAN TWO (MR. CASTLE), MAN ONE, WOMAN ONE AND TWO. . . . TELL YOU WHAT I'M GONNA DO . . .

[*Man One exits.*]

MAN TWO (MR. CASTLE). I'm gonna change your image. Something . . . different. I think . . . we'll start with your name. Stand where you are and just let me look at you. [*Sizing her up*] Uhm, uhm . . . I have the power to make you the most beautiful woman in the world. Do you believe me?

MARGARET-ELIZABETH. Yes.

MAN TWO (MR. CASTLE). Good. Now! What's your name?

MARGARET-ELIZABETH. Barbie. Like in . . . *Barbie Goes to Hawaii.*

MAN TWO (MR. CASTLE). Let's see . . . Ebony . . . Jet . . . Raven . . . No, no, no. Hmmm . . . Jet . . .

MARGARET-ELIZABETH. Tammy. Like in . . . *Tammy Rides the Surf.*

MAN TWO (MR. CASTLE). JETA! JETA! . . . Johnson! You see . . . how easy it is. Already we're onto something. We've conjured up an entire new image just by changing your name. Already you're a novelty. Someone no one has ever heard of before. Jeta Johnson! Now! The next step is promotion. How shall we promote you? Something different. Let . . . me . . . see. Hmmm. Uh huh! Uh huh! [*Studying her.*] Hmmm. Did anyone ever tell you that you look a little bit Polynesian? Well you do! In profile. You look a little bit Polynesian. Uh huh. The high cheekbones . . . American Indian! Nobody could

argue with that. Okay, what have we got? Polynesian. American Indian . . . and . . . something . . . something . . . Brazilian! Yes! The forehead. Definitely a Brazilian flair to the forehead. And damn it! if your eyes don't look Turkish . . . Well, girlie, I think we're getting someplace. What d'ya think?

MARGARET-ELIZABETH. Oh, my God

[*Woman One and Two begin speaking gibberish.*]

MAN TWO (MR. CASTLE). HEY! Just for the fun of it . . . we'll throw in a little Irish. Listen, sweetheart, I've handled the best of them. I made them all what they are. What'd you think of that?

MARGARET-ELIZABETH. Well! We-lll . . . I got a little problem. I don't speak any of those languages.

MAN TWO (MR. CASTLE). No, no, no! What the hell, sweetheart! The trick is . . . silence. Don't speak. If you have to talk, use one or two syllable words.

[*Miniscene: Margaret-Elizabeth and Lizzie change into Butterfly McQueen types.*]

MARGARET-ELIZABETH. Who dat?

LIZZIE. Who dat?

WOMAN ONE, TWO, LIZZIE. Who dat what say "Who dat" when I say who dat?

MAN TWO (MR. CASTLE). Whenever you're in doubt about what to say—just smile. Got it? [*Margaret-Elizabeth smiles broadly.*] You're gonna be a winner, kid. You're gonna be imitated from coast to coast. Damn it, you're cute!

[*They have reached the Center of the ramp. Mr. Castle rushes on ahead as Margaret-Elizabeth remains at the Center of the ramp.*]

MAN TWO (MR. CASTLE) [*Calling back*]. And listen, gal . . . uh, what did we decide to call you?

MARGARET-ELIZABETH. Jet. Like in . . . jet black.

MAN TWO (MR. CASTLE). Right. Listen, Jeta, you got a year to work on it. Learn to tap dance! Smile! And don't lose your southern accent. See you next year! [*Exits.*]

[*Margaret-Elizabeth stands at the Center of the ramp looking after Mr. Castle. Lights dims. Lizzie, Woman One, and Woman Two, quietly enter stage and look at Margaret-Elizabeth in great disappointment. Margaret-Elizabeth*] *stomps her foot angrily. She repeats the angry stamping a few times until there is the hint of a rhythm. Lizzie gradually joins her and they begin a shuffling tap rhythm. Woman One and Two slowly join the "stamp dance" until they are all* angrily stomping out a tap rhythm that ends on a furious note.]

END OF ACT I

Act II

SCENE I

Hotel balcony. Morning of the following day. Margaret-Elizabeth is standing on the balcony. She is wearing a long, flowing nightgown.

MARGARET-ELIZABETH. I ought to be sitting here getting some of this sun. [*Pulls chairs to the side of the table. Sits. Props her legs up on table.*] Let the sun shine on those legs, my dear! [*Leans back.*] Oh! Oh, no, no! I can't! My back! This hurts my back! Oh, for heaven's sake! [*Gently, to herself.*] Okay. Okay. Sit up. Slowly. Slowly. Ooooaaaww . . . Old! You're gonna convince me that you're old! It *does* hurt. I know pain when I feel it. Charlie had to . . . was it Charlie? Sam! Sam had to rub my back every night. [*Firmly.*] There is nothing wrong with this back that regular exercise wouldn't cure. This is the back cure! [*Rolls over on the floor into a modified headstand. Remains there.*]

LIZZIE [*Casually entering balcony from hotel room*]. You look nasty!

MARGARET-ELIZABETH [*Coming out of the position*]. Everything looks nasty to you.

LIZZIE [*Looking out over the balcony railing*]. Margaret! People are looking up here! I bet they could see your tail!

MARGARET-ELIZABETH. Really! [*Momentarily embarrassed.*] Well, damned if I care! I paid good money to be here and if they keep looking long enough, they'll get to see everything! I plan to be myself on this trip. Before this trip is over, I plan to *free* myself—and, if that includes showing my tail—then so be it! Anybody wanna look at this well-kept, sixty-seven-year-old body, can damn well help themselves. I'd consider it a great compliment to all the years I've struggled to keep this form fit. It's like showing off your good china. I did not come here to be old! These legs . . . [*Showing her legs*] these are the legs that won the crown, Lizzie! The very same legs. They haven't changed a bit. I made sure of it.

LIZZIE. You did it again! You might as well strip butt-naked out here! I didn't know you were cuckoo! I'm going inside. [*Exits into hotel.*]

MARGARET-ELIZABETH. Ain't nobody looking up here! [*Flounces back and forth across the front of the balcony, holding her gown apart to reveal her legs.*] What good did it do you . . . saving your legs all them years? Only made *one* picture where they let my legs show . . . can't remember her name. I played . . . a native girl . . . what was her name? Uhm, uhm, uhm. Sure did, didn't I? Goodness knows, I'd almost forgotten that. [*Calling in to Lizzie.*] Darn it, Lizzie! I'd almost forgotten that movie. "Bugga Wanna, Bugga Wanna, Bugga Wanna Wanna Na."

[*Lizzie steps curiously out on balcony.*]

Those were my lines. Those were the lines I had to say when they brought me back to my tribe. "Bugga Wanna, Bugga Wanna, Bugga Wanna Wanna Na."

LIZZIE. It's too bad you remembered them, Margaret. It sort makes you want to throw up.

MARGARET-ELIZABETH. Listen, dear, you are not going to make me feel guilty about what I did. The times predicted what I had to do—but the times have changed.

LIZZIE. Margaret. Let's be honest. The odds are very much against your being available to judge the next contest.

MARGARET-ELIZABETH. They got you, Lizzie. They really sucked you in. I am truly angry about it!

LIZZIE. I know! You've told me a thousand times! Please don't start . . .

MARGARET-ELIZABETH. I'M ANGRY ABOUT THE WHOLE THING!

LIZZIE. Yes, yes! Plee-ase . . . [*Pause.*] What whole thing? What are you . . . ? Okay, Margaret, what's the subject? You've gone and changed the subject on me. I can tell.

MARGARET-ELIZABETH. I'm angry about how they made the whole process so mysterious.

LIZZIE. What! What! What's so mysterious? Am I supposed to guess or are you supposed to remain floating around on your lofty incoherence?

MARGARET-ELIZABETH. The life process, for God's sake! They took all the natural things of life and made a mess out of them! Do you realize that we spent our entire lives traumatizing over things that had been carefully worked out? Someone decided everything was too simple . . . the Grand Design just wasn't complex enough . . . so they threw a monkey wrench into the whole goddamn works. Life! Growing up! Growing old! . . . And most of all—Beauty! . . . *but*, finally, Death! Simple, natural acts . . . were just turned into . . . they took a simple little hole in the ground and dug a tunnel that leads right back to the hole. Now that's unnatural!

LIZZIE. The only unnatural thing I've done recently is to come here with you.

MARGARET-ELIZABETH. Oh, poo poo! When I was thirteen years old, my mother went around telling everyone I was nine. When I was sixteen, she told people I was twelve! I've lived my whole life never experiencing my true age. I wore ribbons in my hair until I was thirty-five years old! Mother said, "When you're young, people allow you to make mistakes. They forgive you."

LIZZIE. Well . . . we all did that, Margaret.

MARGARET-ELIZABETH. That's just what I'm talking about! If we hadn't spent so much time in awe of the natural rules of nature, we could have devoted more time to . . . to . . . putting gold trim on the overcoat!

LIZZIE [*Suspicious*]. Putting . . . gold trim . . . on-the-overcoat, Margaret? [*Sighs.*] Oh, dear! What's the subject?

MARGARET-ELIZABETH. Lizzie, you make me so tired when I talk to you—putting gold trim on the overcoat instead of always having to worry about the underwear!

LIZZIE. Hmmmm . . .

MARGARET-ELIZABETH. As it is . . . it's just a plain old overcoat because I've been so preoccupied with the underwear.

LIZZIE. Hmmmm . . .

MARGARET-ELIZABETH. I should have been about certain things—automatically . . . and with my left hand, so to speak . . . and saved my right hand for more ornate things. I mean, there's nothing wrong with being thirteen years old, for Christ's sake! [*Shouting, as if to the world.*] WELL, I'M SIXTY-SEVEN YEARS OLD, GODDAMIT!

LIZZIE. And you're more foolish now than you ever could have been at thirteen! Good God, woman!

[*The Two Men are seen preparing the stage. They set up a large artist's canvas and place a chaise lounge near Stage Right.*]

MARGARET-ELIZABETH [*Continuing to shout*]. I'm sixty-seven years old and I'm tired of pretending I'm fifty! [*To Lizzie.*] Just because I'm not a predictable, withered, white-haired, crippled . . .

LIZZIE. You dye your hair, Margaret.

MARGARET-ELIZABETH. My mother had coal-black hair until her last day . . .

LIZZIE. You dye your hair, Margaret.

MARGARET-ELIZABETH. I have to tell you something right now, Lizzie. I've bitten my tongue about it for years, but I think there's no better time than now to help you explore some of your shortcomings. I don't know of any polite way to say it, so I'm just going to be blunt . . . you're a tired, weak, snivelling, old . . . *Old* . . . 'fraidy cat! You don't have the nerve to be anything else. You're scared! You're scared because my hair is naturally black; you're scared of my flamboyance and style . . . you've always been scared of me . . . long before I won the beauty contest. Now why do you hang around? . . . in the expectation that someday I'll rub off on you!

LIZZIE. Okay, Margaret. I'm not going to argue with you. I have to learn to stop arguing with you. I get a little pain right here [*Points to her heart*]. I'd hate to be arguing with you and suddenly drop over with foam running out of my mouth. I'm not young enough to spend this much energy arguing over something that don't have any meaning—not now. And besides, you didn't win the beauty contest because you were beautiful.

MARGARET-ELIZABETH. Of course not! I carry beauty around with me! Beauty is in the eye of the beholder! I walk beautiful. I think beautiful. Therefore people perceive me as beautiful. You are as upset now as ever you were because people still think I'm only fifty years old. Admit it. You can't handle it.

LIZZIE. I'm not going to talk to you anymore. You've lost you senses.

MARGARET-ELIZABETH. Well, since we're here to have things turn out the way we want them to—you can be any age you want. Why don't you pass for forty-five. See if you can pull it off.

LIZZIE. I'm not going to talk to you anymore. [*Silence.*] If I speak to you again, it's because you happen to be all I have left to be interested in . . . so I might have to speak to you. [*Timidly.*] Margaret . . . now don't get upset. I'm not trying to spoil the trip . . . honest. I just want to . . .

MARGARET-ELIZABETH. Here we go! You're gonna be depressing. You're gonna ring the ole bell again, aren't you? Tell me something, Lizzie? When did you die? You must have died one day when I wasn't looking. I had no idea I would be traveling with a dead person.

LIZZIE. Margaret! I'm not talking about that! I'm thinking. I'm thinking . . . Have you ever thought . . . that a . . . rest home wouldn't be such a bad idea. [*Pause.*] At least we would have a lot in common with the other people there. You know, the same interests.

MARGARET-ELIZABETH. Same interests, hah! A bunch of people dying together! Before I die I'm going to demand an understanding of why I've been living!

LIZZIE. Ask me where I've living now.

MARGARET-ELIZABETH [*Annoyed*]. I don't have to ask you, Lizzie. I could take one of . . . three guesses!

LIZZIE. You're wrong, Margaret. I am now a full-time resident of the Memorial Society Rest Home. [*Silence.*] It's no sin to be living in a rest home, Margaret!

MARGARET-ELIZABETH. Did I say that?

LIZZIE. It's a very comfortable life. I eat—watch television—and, if I want to, I can even prepare my own meals.

MARGARET-ELIZABETH. That sounds nice.

LIZZIE. I don't have to stand here and defend myself to you, Margaret!

MARGARET-ELIZABETH [*Gently*]. Of course not, Lizzie. You're a sweet girl. I'm sure it took a lot of nerve to commit yourself. Well, I'm going across the finish line—my way. Growing old . . . older . . . growing older is as natural as having a regular bowel movement. I'm tired of passing.

LIZZIE [*Drily*]. I can assure you that you've made a wise decision because you would have found it progressively more difficult. [*Pause.*] The eye of the beholder! Look at yourself! Look at yourself! [*Using her hand, she mimes a mirror and presses it in front of Margaret's face.*] Your eyes have grown dim, my dear. [*Pointing into the mirror.*] You see those little things. They're called lines. Some people call them wrinkles. Frankly, after you pass the age of sixty, who's going to quibble with you over a few years one way or the other.

MARGARET-ELIZABETH [*Stares into the mirror, smiles, then laughs*]. That's what they did to me.

LIZZIE. What? Who?

MARGARET-ELIZABETH. Not who—*What*! My lines! The lines on my face. [*Speaking in the mirror to her lines.*] Such a shame! They had me spend half my life trying to get rid of these two lines. Think of it, Lizzie. All the pain and time and creams and massages, and *glue* we spent trying to erase these two big lines—and all they were there for was to help us have the proper space to laugh with. They just turned everything around. They just made a tragedy out of everything. Everyone wants to forget that we have to cross the finish line. Well, they're not going to rob me of that experience. I am going to finish with honesty.

LIZZIE. . . . the rest home. It's very nice.

MARGARET-ELIZABETH. That's terribly dishonest, Lizzie. I shall remain on the battlefield. I refuse to cloister myself away like a nun.

LIZZIE [*Sighing*]. Let's get on with it.

MARGARET-ELIZABETH. Naturally. [*Suddenly looking off into the distance.*] Ooh, look! The sailboat! Can you see it? Ooh, it's so beautiful! It doesn't look real. It looks like a painting! [*Pause.*] Everything here looks like a painting.

[*The Two Men stand under the balcony and wave. They have completed setting the stage.*]

LIZZIE. That's the cue, Margaret. Get ready.

[*Margaret-Elizabeth rushes into the room through the glass doors.*]

[*Shouting to Margaret-Elizabeth.*] Why can't I tell this story?

MARGARET-ELIZABETH [*Dressing as she sticks her head out of the door*]. Because you have the same solution for everything—TEARS! Don't you dare end up crying anymore, Lizzie.

LIZZIE [*Pouting*]. You always get to play the best part.

MARGARET-ELIZABETH [*Entering the balcony, laughing as she dresses*]. The best acting you ever did, Lizzie—you was crying. Do you remember that? It was Miss Rose's wedding. [*Acting.*] "I'm sorry I got to go and die on you now, Miss Rose. This s'posed to be the happiest day of your life. Now I got to go an' spoil yo' trip to the altar. I prayed to the Good Lord to just let me live one mo' day—I wanted to see my baby smilin' . . ."

LIZZIE. That's not it! You not doing it right. Here you go. [*Crying.*] "I'm sorry I got to go an' die on you now, Miss Rose. This s'posed to be the happiest day of your life. Now look what I done done. I had to go an' die on yo' weddin' day. I prayed to the Good Lord to just let me live long enough to see my baby smilin' as she marched to the altar. Oh, Miss Rose, forgive me."

MARGARET-ELIZABETH. Lordy, Chile! You can do that moaning and crying! I never could get that stuff straight.

LIZZIE. That's why you ain't made no more movies to this day.

MARGARET-ELIZABETH. It didn't exactly further your career either.

LIZZIE. I retired.

MARGARET-ELIZABETH. Retired! Retired! OoohAaa-hahaaa . . . Well, we ain't gon' end up crying this time, Lizzie. This time we're going to get it right.

LIZZIE. I want to tell it!

MARGARET-ELIZABETH [*Exiting into the hotel room*]. You don't know what to do with a story. You never get to the end. Tears! That's why we have to keep doing it over.

LIZZIE [*Loudly*]. You better hope that I don't die before we get to the end.

[*Woman One emerges dressed as a high-fashion model. She appears to be in her early twenties. Margaret-Elizabeth follows Woman One out onto the balcony dressed in identical garb.*]

MARGARET-ELIZABETH [*Angrily entering*]. You'd like that, wouldn't you, Lizzie? That way we'd never have to finish the story. Well I don't want any dead people in my story.

LIZZIE. Naturally.

MARGARET-ELIZABETH. Naturally.

WOMAN ONE. Naturally.

[*Woman Two, dressed in an artist's smock, approaches the easel, Downstage. She sets up her supplies and is trying to paint on the canvas that is facing Upstage. The Three Women on the balcony step out onto the Center ramp.*]

MARGARET-ELIZABETH. What strange pictures we've been given.

LIZZIE. Pictures that don't work.

WOMAN ONE. I wonder if they ever worked?

LIZZIE. They must have been real once—how else could anyone have ever thought of them?

MARGARET-ELIZABETH. Yes. Someone painted a pastoral scene once.

WOMAN ONE. It was painted by an artist who never saw the scene.

LIZZIE. He painted it from a description given to him by a traveler . . .

WOMAN ONE. . . . who had heard of it from a farmer . . .

LIZZIE. . . . who had it handed down to him as a legend by his great-great-great-grandfather . . .

WOMAN ONE. . . . who got it from the Bible . . .

MARGARET-ELIZABETH. . . . who got it from a vision . . .

LIZZIE. . . . that came from God . . .

MARGARET-ELIZABETH. . . . WHO was the only one who ever really saw it.

LIZZIE. And we keep running through the grass and flowers that the artist painted . . .

WOMAN ONE. . . . only to discover that it's really mud.

MARGARET-ELIZABETH. We ought to bring those pictures up to date.

END OF ACT II, SCENE I

SCENE II

Margaret-Elizabeth descends the ramp, Stage Left. The other two women line up behind her and follow her down the ramp. As they reach the bottom of the ramp, a doorbell chimes. Margaret-Elizabeth and Lizzie disappear. Woman One crosses toward Woman Two (The Artist.) She speaks with the breathless affectation of a "glamour girl."

WOMAN ONE. Hi. I'm answering your ad for an . . . artist's model?

[*Woman Two (The Artist) stands unanswering, staring at her.*]

[*Nervous.*] Your ad in the paper? [*Yanks out newspaper and hurriedly scrambles to page.*] Uh . . . [*Reads.*] "Wanted: Black female artist's model. Should be between the ages of twenty and fifty. Reasonable pay."

ARTIST. Oh yes! Oh! I'm . . . I'm surprised! You're not at all what I had in mind.

WOMAN ONE [*Gushing*]. Well . . . I've done some modeling before . . . most of it was . . . back home. I used to model a lot for . . . the Smutterbugs? I mean, they weren't artists . . . well, I mean they *were* artists, but not . . . you know, uh . . . painters.

They did . . . photography and I used to . . . uh, you ever hear of them?

ARTIST. Yes. Yes. Uh, NO! No. Listen, I . . . I-don't-know, you . . . uhm . . . let me look at you.

[*Woman One stands pivoting and turning like a model. She begins to strike classic poses.*]

ARTIST. My God, you're thin!

WOMAN ONE [*Proudly*]. Yes. 34-24-35. One hundred and fifteen pounds!

ARTIST. How did you let yourself get that thin? FLESH! I need FLESH! You should never have allowed yourself to get like that. Well, look, I don't know how, but I'm going to give it a try. [*Dramatically.*] When an artist is overcome with this . . . *feeling*—this . . . brilliance—any delay in the execution of it can be a death blow. I'm anxious to start. Too anxious. Take off your shoes.

WOMAN ONE [*Squealing*]. Oooh! Oooh, no! Oh, God. You're not going to believe this! I had no idea you were going to ask me to go barefoot! I didn't polish my toenails!

ARTIST [*Studying her*]. Hmm . . . hmm . . . hmm, hmm, hmm, hmm. [*Takes off her apron and hands it to Woman One.*] Here. Tie this around you.

[*Women One ties on apron. Artist stands back looking at her.*]

Nope. Nope. That's not going to work. I thought I could work it out with you . . . I . . . I don't know . . .

WOMAN ONE [*Anxious*]. What do you want me to do? I'm rather flexible. I can pose any way you want. You want to try something lying down. [*Strikes a reclining pose on the sofa.*] How's this? I mean, it's whatever you want.

ARTIST. What I want? What I want? I know exactly what I want but *you*, through no fault of you own, do not happen to be it! Now I'm trying, dear—I'm trying to fit you in. What I want to do is to paint a composite impression of The Female. More specifically, the Black Female. I want to show the myriad spectrum of the sum of her parts: The mysterious, erotic, exotic, the Earth Mother [*Afterthought.*] , the Mother. Yes, and even the negative parts: the whore, the slave, the . . . the . . .

WOMAN ONE. . . . the woman?

ARTIST. Yes, the woman. The concept is brilliant. The execution of it will be brilliant. But you—you, my dear are more than I had in mind—or is it less?

You've given me a problem. At the height of my creative surge, you've presented a problem. Why have you done this to me? *But*, I accept the challenge—and, hopefully, with my help, we will find our way there, no matter the obstacles. So! Cool your little toesies, while I think! I'm going to apologize because I know that I've lost my temper. I'm apologizing up front because I'm probably going to get worse. Please be patient enough to understand that it's not directed at you personally—even though I shall probably scream, shout, and cuss in your direction. You see, here I am at the pinnacle of freeing my creative energies to work on this inspiration and everyone knows it—and everyone wants to fuck over me! Well, you say, "Well I don't know you. I just came here in answer to your ad." Right! But *HE* knows me! AND he knows that I am at the beginning of this *moment*—so what does he do? Today of all days? He wants to fuck! Oh, God, he's such an asshole!

[*Uncomfortable silence. Finally Women One decides to speak.*]

WOMAN ONE. Uh . . . who?

ARTIST. Sweetheart, it's not your problem . . . but, do you see what I'm talking about? As an artist, you learn to foretell the weather. It's either fair or foul. Now, in fair weather, the gods are with you. Why, you have but to smile, and their gifts come pouring down on you. They share their genius with you so freely that you begin to question whether or not you're the prime mover of this exciting moment. Well, when the weather is foul, and believe me, it can conspire against you in the most unbelievable manner—your impulse is to abandon the whole thing. Allow me to bore you, please! because I have to say this out loud! You came in on my problem. You added to my problem. So therefore you have to listen to my problem. Ohhh, I'm wasting all of this time and I need to be working . . . let me look at you . . . [*She stares at her for a while.*] You know what I see? Primary colors! That's it! While we were talking?—I suddenly got a microscopic view of you and I picked up—primary colors! I know it's right. I can feel it's right! [*She stares at her again, but this time she pinches her face into a tight scowl as she throws her head back.*] Oooh! Ooooh! I just got the whole thing! Red! RED! I was standing here, talking, and I blurred my vision. I do that sometimes. I deliberately squint my eyes and view everything through my eyelashes and it gives me this blurred vision—

and I saw RED! Stay right where you are. Don't move!

[*Woman Two (The Artist) looks around distractedly as if looking for something she's not quite sure of. Margaret-Elizabeth enters carrying a long piece of red fabric with white polka dots on it. She hands it to Woman Two. She exits.*]

This is getting exciting! [*Tosses Woman One the fabric.*] Here. Try this one.

[*Woman One casually drapes it across her shoulders.*]

Anyway, I keep telling this guy, "Look, so okay, I'm freaky. I'm an artist—what do you expect." I knew a guy once that could do it just by rubbing my shoulders. Uhmm . . . uhm! I mean, there's an art to the thing! So that's where we had our big blowout, you know. So, I'm thinking—I hate to see the thing end without having communicated properly. So I write him this letter . . . [*Observes Woman One*] No, no, no, no! . . . the scarf goes on your head! [*Continuing.*] So I wrote him this letter and I . . .

[*Women One has draped the fabric very elegantly across her hair.*]

[*Looking up at her.*] Nooo, sweetheart. No, No, Like this, honey. [*Takes the scarf and ties it, Aunt Jemima–style, around Woman One's head.*] Yes! Yes. That's it. See, I'm going to concentrate on the *red*—framing your face. [*Studying her again.*] Umm hmm. [*Pause.*] Uh, unh. I need something else. Something's wrong. Some-thing's . . . wrong. Excuse me. Just ignore me. I'm blurring my vision again. [*Tosses her head back and squints her eyes, squeezing her face into a tight frown.*] Okay. Take off your makeup! You've got red tones in your makeup.

WOMAN ONE. Well . . . probably . . .

ARTIST. That's what is it—and your lipstick—too much. Wipe it off.

WOMAN ONE. Uh . . . my makeup?

ARTIST. EVERYTHING! I'm going to create . . . and I don't want any suggestions! I don't want to be subconsciously influenced.

[*Margaret-Elizabeth enters with a jar of cold cream and tissues. She hands them to The Artist and gives Woman One a look of disappointment.*]

MARGARET-ELIZABETH [*Whispering to Woman One*]. When are you gonna change this?

WOMAN ONE [*Annoyed. Whispering to Margaret-Elizabeth*]. Soon. Soon. Get out of here!

[*Margaret-Elizabeth exits. Woman Two (The Artist) smears cold cream all over Woman One's face and begins to wipe it off.*]

ARTIST. So, this letter . . . this letter I wrote him . . . I wanted him to be able to see my bare-assed psyche—you know? Well, it's no little trick to open your psyche up to someone. So I asked myself, "What's happening to you *right now*! I mean, what's really going on at this very minute?" [*Finishing the removal of the makeup.*] There. Much better. Oh, dear, I just caught sight of something. I don't like it.

WOMAN ONE. The . . . the . . . scarf? The . . . ?

ARTIST. The dress. [*Laughs.*] You look like a fashion model. Uh. Uh. Uh. Hold it! Do I have a bag of tricks today!

[*Margaret-Elizabeth and Lizzie enter carrying a bright calico blouse (yellow with large red flowers) and a large, many-colored, many-tiered, calico skirt. They hand the blouse to Woman One and remain standing nearby holding the skirt.*]

Here you are. [*Passes blouse to Woman One.*] This is going to work. [*Watches as she puts it on.*] Perfect! Now! Now we're getting someplace. Oh, wait! You're not going to believe what I just thought of.

LIZZIE [*With disgust*]. A banjo?

[*Woman Two motions, and Margaret-Elizabeth and Lizzie hand her the skirt. They remain standing side by side holding onto a small box.*]

ARTIST. Da, da, da, dum, de dum! Here, dear. Slip this on under your apron. [*Watches her.*] Yikes! I *like* it! Ummuh! Oh. Oh. And some jewelry! Uh, uh . . . [*Looking around.*]

MARGARET-ELIZABETH [*Gaily*]. Gold hoop earrings?

ARTIST [*As if Woman One had spoken*]. Hey! You're feeling it too. I know I'm on the right track when we can pick up the same feeling. Oh, damn! Earrings! Earrings!

[*Margaret-Elizabeth extends the small box to The Artist. She rummages through it.*]

Oooh, you bet your sweet life! Look-a-here! Took down the stupid drapes last week . . . [*Dramatically.*] I needed *Light*! to see by! . . . I am so brilliant today, I must have somebody working with me— Rembrandt, or Picasso, or . . . What'd I tell you! [*Holds up brass rings.*] Brass rings! Brass drapery rings!

[*Rushes over to Woman One and snaps the oversized earrings on her. She stands back admiringly.*] Uh! Uh! [*Southern accent.*] DE-VINE! CHILD! YOU LOOK DE-VINE! [*Returns to easel, begins to work.*] When I was little, the first school I ever went to was an all-girls' Catholic school—and everything in there was black and white. Black and white. Can you imagine. [*Suddenly.*] Oh, crap!

WOMAN ONE. What happened?

ARTIST. I just squinted at you again.

WOMAN ONE. What?

ARTIST. I just blurred my vision. You got some red tones in your skin. It wasn't your makeup. There's some red mixed in your skin color. How did that happen?

MARGARET-ELIZABETH. Turkish!

LIZZIE. Polynesian!

MARGARET-ELIZABETH. Brazilian

LIZZIE. American Indian!

WOMAN ONE. A little Irish . . . I think there's a little Irish on my father's side.

ARTIST. Don't worry Ginger-to-the-rescue. [*Dips her fingers into her color palate.*] By the way, I didn't get your name. I'm Ginger. [*Approaches her.*] You too?

WOMAN ONE. Me too what?

ARTIST. Your name Ginger too?

WOMAN ONE. Elizabeth.

ARTIST. Yes?

WOMAN ONE. That's my name—Elizabeth. Margaret-Elizabeth.

ARTIST. Oh, like . . . [*Regally.*] Elizabeth-the-queen! [*She begins to smear black paint onto Woman One's face.*]

WOMAN ONE. How did you know! That's it exactly! I'm Elizabeth. My sister was Victoria and my brother was James. Mother was very big on King James because of the Bible, but Daddy said the King James Version was a pile of rubbish because ole King James made up that version to suit his own perversions—which, of course, made Daddy have a little aversion to brother James . . .

ARTIST [*Finishing Woman One's face*]. Liza, honey! The gods are with us today! You look great! [*Admiring her handiwork.*] Uhm! Uhm! C'est si bon! We're on our way. Now what I want you to do is . . . just your eyes . . . not the rest of your body . . . look up.

[*Woman One rolls her eyes up. Margaret-Elizabeth and Lizzie hide their faces in shame.*]

Got it! Don't move! [*Resumes painting at canvas.*] Now, as I was saying . . . uh, what was I telling you about?

WOMAN ONE. Black and white.

ARTIST. What?

WOMAN ONE. The black-and-white colors at the girls' Catholic school.

ARTIST. No, no, before that. Ooh, about this guy—anyway, I wrote him this letter, and I asked myself, "Now what am I doing at this very moment." Well, for one thing, I was ovulating. And I thought, "Well, what does that have to do with anything?" Now you have to understand, I wanted to be very honest with myself. I'm one of those few women who can really tell when I'm ovulating—and it does all kinds of hairy things to me. So, in all honesty, I had to admit that ovulating had *everything* to do with what I was into at that very moment. I was freakin' hungry for the man! So, I did what every honest, healthy girl oughta do . . . I smeared ovulation juice all over the letter I sent to him—and POW! he came running to me like a mad dog! Listen, I have a lot of philosophies, but my through-line philosophy is that you shouldn't have any hang-ups in this world. I mean, it's like you gotta be fuckin' crazy! [*Suddenly.*] Goddamnit!

WOMAN ONE. What's the matter?

ARTIST. It's not working.

WOMAN ONE. What's not working?

ARTIST. The whole thing—it's not working. No, no, it's not you. The concept is off. There's something wrong with the concept. You look too *pretty*. It's not your fault. [*Changing her voice for humorous effect.*] Goddamnit, girl, you're just too pretty! You see, what I had in mind was . . . Ohhh! Ooohhh!

[*Margaret-Elizabeth and Lizzie exit.*]

WOMAN ONE. What'd you do?—blur your vision again?

ARTIST. Yes! Take off those clothes!

WOMAN ONE. Everything?

ARTIST. Yes. I just became a genius. I know exactly what I want.

[*She motions excitedly as Margaret-Elizabeth and Lizzie enter carrying a number of articles of clothing. The Artist examines them, tossing some away and excitedly exclaiming over others. Margaret-Elizabeth exits. Woman One, still dressed in her "Aunt Jemima" outfit, wanders Upstage to look at the painting. Lizzie angrily follows her Upstage and, using her hand as a mirror, whirls Woman One around to stare at her reflection.*]

WOMAN ONE [*Seeing her reflection*]. Eeek! Ginger! You black crow!

WOMAN TWO [*No longer The Artist*]. What the hell's wrong with you?

WOMAN ONE [*Storming over to Woman Two*]. Is that what you've done to me? Look at my face! Is that what you put on my . . . [*Rubs her hands across her face.*] Uunnggh! [*In great fury she pushes Woman Two.*] You stop it! Stop it right now! This is *my* story! [*She begins to cry loudly.*]

WOMAN TWO. I'm *doing* your story! This is the way it happened! What do you want me to do . . . change history to suit you . . . and King James!

MARGARET-ELIZABETH. If you're not going to do *my* story *my* way—then I might as well pack up and go home!

WOMAN TWO. Jesus! Get the stuff straight!

MARGARET-ELIZABETH. Look at this mess!

LIZZIE. Black Devil!

WOMAN TWO. Black Gold!

LIZZIE. Black Sambo!

WOMAN TWO. Black Jewel!

LIZZIE. Black Sheep!

WOMAN TWO. Black Rose!

LIZZIE. Snow White and Rose Red . . . and Black Tar Baby . . . and Black Dog!

MARGARET-ELIZABETH. Black Beauty!

LIZZIE [*Erupting into laughter*]. A horse! A horse! [*Changing suddenly into tears.*] A horse! A horse!

[*Margaret-Elizabeth and Woman Two go over to comfort Lizzie.*]

MARGARET-ELIZABETH. Lizzie, calm down!

WOMAN TWO. Calm down, honey.

MARGARET-ELIZABETH. You want to change the ending? Well, we have to do it the way it happened in order to get to a new ending. Now would you just calm down?

WOMAN TWO [*To Woman One*]. Put on the new clothes . . .

MARGARET-ELIZABETH. I promise you . . . the unexpected—a new ending! Trust me.

[*Lizzie calms with resistance. Margaret-Elizabeth and Woman Two begin to put the clothes on Lizzie. They have an entire suit of men's clothing including shirt, suit jacket, pants, shoes, necktie, wig, and hat. Lizzie is still challenging Margaret-Elizabeth as they help her dress. Woman One, dressed as "Aunt Jemima" stands by, arms folded in disgust and distrust—watching.*]

LIZZIE [*To Margaret-Elizabeth*]. You always want to play the best parts.

WOMAN TWO. Listen, now . . . tell the truth . . . I haven't changed anything, *really*? Right?

LIZZIE. You certainly weren't supposed to blacken my face.

MARGARET-ELIZABETH. It was the same thing! Just be patient, I'm getting to the point.

LIZZIE. I know you're gonna have me end up foolish.

MARGARET-ELIZABETH. What could be more foolish than crying? Every time we do this story, you end it by crying—and you're never satisfied. We're not going to do it that way anymore. We're gonna make it end right. Trust me. You're gonna be the hero . . .

WOMAN ONE. Heroine.

MARGARET-ELIZABETH. I mean, heroine.

LIZZIE. Huhmmmm . . .

[*Lizzie has now changed into the entire suit of men's clothes, with the exception of the short male wig.*]

WOMAN TWO [*Playing the Artist again; lifting the male wig high in the air in grandiose style*]. And now, my friend, I do crown you . . . Elizabeth-the-queen!

[*Lizzie and Woman One eye Margaret-Elizabeth suspiciously.*]

MARGARET-ELIZABETH. Trust me.

ARTIST [*She motions for Lizzie and Woman One to strike a pose as she returns to the canvas to paint*]. It won't be long now, my dear.

[*Lights dim. All Four Women merge into a Buddha-like oneness, a three-dimensional form, with arms, legs, and torsos overlapping. It could be as simple as a "stadium effect" with Margaret-Elizabeth in the forefront, Lizzie standing (sitting) behind her, Woman Two etc.—all overlapping body parts. It could be as abstract as an acrobatic stance, with arms, legs, and torsos askew in varying shapes. As the lights come back up, Woman Two (playing the Artist again) is seen arranging, touching, putting finishing touches on the Three Women.*]

ARTIST. Well, Queenie—how do you feel being party to a historic moment?

[*Margaret-Elizabeth extracts herself from the other Two Women and casually saunters around the remaining form. She studiously evaluates herself and the other Two Women, who remain locked in oneness throughout Margaret-Elizabeth's evaluation. Woman One is staring cruelly at Margaret-Elizabeth. Lizzie stares at Margaret-Elizabeth nearly in tears.*]

MARGARET-ELIZABETH [*Finally. Smiling triumphantly at Woman One and Lizzie. She begins to swagger*]. Personally, I don't think it's very original. I mean, it's been done before.

ARTIST. You're only a model, my dear. Your vision is not to be trusted.

MARGARET-ELIZABETH [*Still assessing the form, sometimes reentering the form to make a point*]. It is apparent to me that you should have spent more time studying your subject in order to render it more believable. For instance, you should have employed more care in the depiction of your subject's legs and hips. The legs and hips are crucial in determining the self-image that your subject projects. Where's the rhythm and vitality and color intensity? Where's the elegance and intelligence of your subject? My main concern centers around your lack of the use of a more subtle brushwork on the face. You see, the color *black* has within itself many colors. It is a very complex color and at the same time simple and delicate. It can be made to appear formidable and mysterious, as in a dark, unlit cave, or can appear as bright and inviting as the twinkling eyes of a child. Since black is your foreground color, you should have used the full range of its potential in its color spectrum. Your primitive application of the primary colors shows a refusal or inability to employ enlightened artistic techniques—also known as intuition. In essence, you have failed to capture your subject's *BEAUTY*!

[*Woman One and Lizzie smile in victorious anticipation.*]

[*Delighted at her own success.*] Heeey, *Now*!

LIZZIE [*Rallying*]. Bring it on down front, Margaret!

WOMAN ONE. Talk, Margaret! Talk!

LIZZIE. Go 'head, Margaret!

WOMAN ONE. Finish this mess, girl!

[*Woman Two, jolted out of Artist role, reacts with stunned silence, folding her arms in contemptuous, stubborn anger.*]

WOMAN TWO. If you want to tell the entire story by yourself, go ahead.

[*There is a long silence as Margaret-Elizabeth stands trying to bluff her way through her confusion.*]

LIZZIE. Well?

WOMAN ONE. Well?

MARGARET-ELIZABETH [*Floundering*]. . . . well, now . . . uh, don't move, don't move . . . I'm getting there . . .

LIZZIE. Finish it, Margaret. Finish it.

MARGARET-ELIZABETH. Yes . . . uh . . . you have failed to . . . to . . . uh . . . capture . . .

WOMAN ONE. Margaret? What's the matter?

MARGARET-ELIZABETH. Nothing. Nothing. Just . . . hold on. Don't be so impatient.

LIZZIE. Fifty years is a long time to be patient. [*Pause.*] Margaret . . . ?

MARGARET-ELIZABETH. Yes?

LIZZIE. You don't have an ending, do you?

MARGARET-ELIZABETH. Of course I do, I'm just . . .

WOMAN ONE. This is the same ending, Margaret.

MARGARET-ELIZABETH. Will you shut up! I'm . . . I'm working on it . . .

[*A buzzer sounds and Man One and Two rush onstage.*]

MAN ONE AND TWO. Time! Time!

[*The Two Men busily begin to remove everything from Center Stage. Lizzie and Woman One, in the throes of the gloomy reality, begin to extract themselves from their "oneness." Woman One sadly begins to remove parts of her garment. They dejectedly begin to pack up. Women Two stands impatiently waiting to see if they are going to resume the action.*]

WOMAN ONE. This is the same ending, Margaret. [*She begins to walk slowly toward the ramp.*]

LIZZIE. This is the last time, Margaret. We're not going to do it again. [*Looking down at her clothes.*] LOOK AT ME! You did it again! [*Beginning to cry.*] You turned me into a flop! A pure-dee horse's hiney, FLOP! [*She bursts into a loud wailing as she runs up the ramp.*]

WOMAN TWO [*Angrily removing her artist's smock and tossing it to the floor in disgust*]. That's it! That's the last time! [*She removes some of her supplies and stalks off Stage Right.*]

LIZZIE [*Like an angry child as she runs up the ramp*]. You *said* you were going to make me the *hero*! You did it! [*Screaming from the top of the ramp.*] You did it— you black dog!

[*Margaret-Elizabeth rushes up the ramp after the Two Women, trying to console them.*]

MARGARET-ELIZABETH [*Mounting the ramp*]. You didn't give me a chance!

WOMAN ONE. Give you a chance! You had every chance in the world!

MARGARET-ELIZABETH. There was one more thing!

WOMAN ONE. What?

LIZZIE. What?

MARGARET-ELIZABETH [*In petulant anger to mask her uncertainty*]. You didn't give me a chance!

LIZZIE. What?

WOMAN ONE. What could it have possibly have been, for God's sake!

LIZZIE. Nothing! She didn't have a thing! She's lying! Ooh, I know you, Margaret! Pretending all the time!

MARGARET-ELIZABETH. I did too!

WOMAN ONE. What?

MARGARET-ELIZABETH. You'll never know. I'm not going to tell you. You'll never know! That's the ending you picked, that's the one you'll live with.

LIZZIE [*Giving in*]. Okay, Margaret. What were we supposed to do?

MARGARET-ELIZABETH. Say! What were you supposed to say!

WOMAN ONE. Okay, Margaret. I hate to indulge you with this . . . but what were we supposed to say?

MARGARET-ELIZABETH. Fuck you! Those were going to be my last words . . . Fuck you!

WOMAN ONE. And then . . . ?

LIZZIE. And then . . . ?

MARGARET-ELIZABETH [*Caught*]. "Only if you're ovulating." Then you were supposed to say, "Only if you're ovulating." [*She stands back suspiciously eyeing her effect.*]

[*There is a long silence as Woman One and Lizzie stare in questioning disbelief.*]

WOMAN ONE [*Shaking her head in disgust*]. Have you ever considered, Margaret . . . that you might be in the last stages of senility?

LIZZIE [*Quietly, fighting back tears, holding onto Margaret-Elizabeth as if she were a child*]. Just say you didn't have an ending, Margaret. It's okay. Let's stop fighting now. Come on to the rest home. It's not bad . . . really.

END OF ACT II, SCENE II

SCENE III

Lizzie, still dressed as a man, is leaning over the hotel balcony. Margaret-Elizabeth, dressed as the beauty queen with the exaggerated bosom, begins a slow, uncertain, soft-shoe tap routine.

LOUDSPEAKER. "From Avery's Gift Shop—a fountain pen with the winner's name engraved in gold!'"

[*She struggles with the dancing until it improves. Downstage Right is a door frame that leads to a small room. The room contains a large chest of drawers with a huge mirror. The chest of drawers, with the exception of the mirror, has a long, wide strip of white fabric draped around it.*]

LIZZIE (MR. CASTLE) [*Calling to Margaret-Elizabeth*]. Jeta! Little Miss Jeta! Learn to tap dance! Smile! And don't lose your southern accent. See you next year! [*Lights fade to dim on Lizzie..*]

[*Margaret-Elizabeth begins to sing softly.*]

MARGARET-ELIZABETH [*Singing and dancing*].

> Jet-a,
> Jet-a,
> Jet-a, Jeta, Jing, Jing, Jing.

[*She continues singing and dancing until she is rather confidently and loudly performing.*]

LIZZIE [*Sighs*]. All I want to do is pick a new queen, go back home to my little room, eat, watch television . . .

[*Margaret-Elizabeth has entered the small room and is staring in the mirror atop the chest as she performs.*]

LOUDSPEAKER. "And now, ladies and gentlemen! Our five finalists!

[*The sound of festive music. Woman One and Two enter dressed in identical men's suits.*]

LIZZIE [*Excited*]. Margaret! They're starting! Hurry up! [*Calling.*] Margaret! We have to choose the new queen!

[*The Three Women (Judges) put on top hats and stand Downstage, looking up at the ramp, throughout the contest.*]

LOUDSPEAKER. Contestant Number One!

[*Man One, dressed in black, slowly and regally ascends the ramp from Stage Right. He is wearing high-heeled shoes and carrying a large, oversized painted poster. The poster is the kind used in carnivals, fairs, or amusement parks, with a cutout opening for the head and arms. Margaret-Elizabeth is still staring in the mirror. When Man One reaches the Center of the ramp, he faces the audience and pokes his head and*] arms through the cutout. Smiling, he poses and assumes the character of the cutout. The cutout is an exaggeration of Gidget.]

LIZZIE. Margaret! It's Gidget!

WOMAN TWO. Gidget?

WOMAN ONE. Gidget's in it?

WOMAN TWO. 96! I'm giving her 96 points! I want her to win, don't you?

WOMAN ONE, TWO, AND LIZZIE [As if bidding at an auction]. 96!

[Margaret-Elizabeth snaps open the top of her bathing suit. The stuffing flies, flips, and bounces all over the floor. The stuffing consists of wads of toilet tissue, foam rubber, hankies, and stockings. Man One exits to loud applause.]

LOUDSPEAKER. CONTESTANT NUMBER TWO!

[Man Two enters Stage Right. He is dressed the same as Man One and carries a large poster cutout. When he reaches the Center of the ramp, he poses and assumes the character of his poster. The cutout is an exaggeration of Tammy.]

LIZZIE. Margaret! It's Tammy!

WOMAN TWO. Do you believe that? Tammy's in it!

WOMAN ONE. Tammy?

WOMAN TWO. This is going to be a hard one.

WOMAN ONE. Okay, 97! There! I gave her a 97.

LIZZIE. What did you give her, Margaret?

WOMAN ONE, TWO, AND LIZZIE. 97!

[Margaret-Elizabeth goes to the Upstage end of the white cloth that drapes the chest of drawers and wraps it around her bosom. She pirouettes Downstage, letting the cloth completely engulf her breasts. She then tucks the ends of the cloth neatly in place. She opens a drawer in the chest and removes a pair of shoulder pads like the ones used by football players. She straps them on. She begins to remove her makeup.]

LOUDSPEAKER. CONTESTANT NUMBER THREE!

[Man One returns carrying a large poster cutout. He reaches the center of the ramp and poses as he assumes the character of his poster. The cutout is a bosomy exaggeration of Brigitte Bardot. He continues to pose and strut across the center of the ramp.]

WOMAN ONE, TWO, AND LIZZIE [Squealing]. Bridget!

[The Three Women (Judges) nearly swoon like the teenage fans of a rock idol.]

WOMAN ONE. EEEekk!

WOMAN TWO. Yee-OWWw!

LIZZIE. Oooh! OH! OH! OH! Oh, Margaret! What are we gonna do it! It's Bridget! 98! I'm giving her 98!

WOMAN ONE, TWO, AND LIZZIE. 98!

[Margaret-Elizabeth opens up another drawer and puts on a man's shirt front with tie attached. She removes a pair of men's jockey shorts and puts them on over her bathing suit.]

LIZZIE [Calling]. Margaret! [Throwing her arms up in victorious excitement.] We finally got a contest with CLASS!

[Margaret-Elizabeth begins to pick up the stuffing from the floor and pack it into the center of her jockey shorts. There should be a pocket sewn on the inside to allow her to stuff everything into it. The music continues.]

LOUDSPEAKER. CONTESTANT NUMBER FOUR!

[Man Two ascends the ramp with his poster and assumes his character. The poster is an exaggeration of Barbie.]

WOMAN TWO. Barbie!

LIZZIE. Barbie!

WOMAN ONE Barbie! [To others]. What d'ya say? I say 99!

WOMAN TWO. 99!

LIZZIE. 99!

WOMAN ONE, TWO, AND LIZZIE. 99!

[Margaret-Elizabeth opens up another drawer and removes a man's suit. She puts it on. She now looks like the other women. Man Two exits.]

WOMAN TWO. They're all winners!

WOMAN ONE. I'm going crazy! It's not fair.

LIZZIE. We've got to stop calling it a contest—it's a pageant. A pageant.

[Margaret-Elizabeth now removes a short-cropped man's wig and puts it on. As her final gesture, she picks up a top hat, places it on her head, comes through the door frame, and joins the Women.]

[To Margaret-Elizabeth.] Who did you vote for? It took you long enough! Did you see them? Who did you vote for?

MARGARET-ELIZABETH. Okay, let's go. We're gonna do the finale.

LIZZIE. Not now! The last contestant is about to appear.

MARGARET-ELIZABETH. Now.

WOMAN ONE, TWO, AND LIZZIE. Margaret!

MARGARET-ELIZABETH. Now.

WOMAN ONE AND TWO. Now?

MARGARET-ELIZABETH. Only the crazy things survive.

[*The Women stand in sullen disbelief as Margaret-Elizabeth begins a slow, rhythmic, shuffling tap dance. They are about to do the stand-up comedy routines that were popular in the early minstrel shows. After Margaret-Elizabeth establishes a beat, she begins to sing the opening strains of "Swanee River."*]

[*Dancing.*] "Way down upon the Swanee River . . ."

[*The Women stand stiff and resisting.*]

C'mon. You gotta get down on your knees, dearie.

WOMAN ONE. This is incredible.

LIZZIE. Who's gonna crown the queen?

MARGARET-ELIZABETH. We are. All in due time, Lizzie. Let's go.

[*Woman One and Two reluctantly get on their knees. Lizzie continues to stand.*]

[*Singing and dancing.*] "Way down upon the . . ." [*Commanding.*] C'mon, Lizzie. Get down on your knees!

[*Lizzie gets on her knees, and the Three Women pick up the rhythm in a swaying motion. Miniscene: Margaret-Elizabeth becomes Bubba, a stand-up comic, and Lizzie becomes Poo-Key, her straight man, in a comic minstrel routine.*]

MARGARET-ELIZABETH (BUBBA) [*Now the complete minstrel man*]. Hey, Poo-key! What 'cha doin' on yer knees? You cain't dance on yer knees.

LIZZIE (POO-KEY). Oh, yeah I can. In fact, this what they paid me to do.

MARGARET-ELIZABETH (BUBBA). Is that a fact?

LIZZIE (POO-KEY). That's a fact. [*Pause.*] But I ain't jes' dancing on my knees.

MARGARET-ELIZABETH (BUBBA). No?

LIZZIE (POO-KEY). No. I'm dancin' on a dime.

MARGARET-ELIZABETH (BUBBA). A dime? A dime, you say?

LIZZIE (POO-KEY). That's right. A dime. That's all they payin' me fo' this show.

MARGARET-ELIZABETH (BUBBA). No kiddin'? What kinda money is that?

WOMAN ONE, TWO, AND LIZZIE. SHORTCHANGE!

ALL. Aaahhahaaa!

[*The three Women stand. Everyone continues dancing and singing.*]

"Way down upon the Swanee River,
Far, far away . . ."

LIZZIE (POO-KEY). Hey, Bubba! You know, I just looked at you—and, you ugly!

MARGARET-ELIZABETH (BUBBA). Ugly? Ugly, you say!

LIZZIE (POO-KEY). Ugly, man, ugly! You got a monopoly on UGLY!

MARGARET-ELIZABETH (BUBBA). How you fix yo' mouth to say that, man?

LIZZIE (POO-KEY). My eyes said it first and then my mouth jes' followed!

ALL. Aaahhahaaa!

WOMAN ONE AND TWO. [*Chanting*].

Aww, kick it!
Aww, kick it!
Aww, get down wid' it!

ALL [*Singing and dancing*]. "Way down upon the Swanee River . . ."

MARGARET-ELIZABETH (BUBBA). Hey, Poo-key! Only a ugly can recognize another ugly.

LIZZIE (POO-KEY). Well, you got plenty of ugly around you, man. Yo' wife ugly . . .

MARGARET-ELIZABETH (BUBBA). Yeah, my wife sho' is ugly.

WOMAN TWO. Her feets is bigger dan yo' banjo.

MARGARET-ELIZABETH (BUBBA). Yeah, she gots mighty big feets.

WOMAN ONE. Her head is bigger dan Caldonia's.

MARGARET-ELIZABETH (BUBBA). Yeah, she got a mighty big head.

LIZZIE (POO-KEY). Her hair so tight that even water cain't get through it.

MARGARET-ELIZABETH (BUBBA). Aw, yeah. She got some nappy hair!

WOMAN ONE AND TWO. An' her lips!

LIZZIE (POO-KEY). Her lips so big she have trouble breathin'.

MARGARET-ELIZABETH (BUBBA). Now that's a fact!

LIZZIE (POO-KEY). So you see—you surrounded by ugly.

MARGARET-ELIZABETH (BUBBA). Yeah, but, my wife is yo' sister!

WOMAN ONE, TWO, AND LIZZIE. Oh, Sweet Georgia Brown!

ALL [*Singing and dancing*]. "Way down upon the
Swanee River . . .''

WOMAN TWO. Hey, Bubba! How come you didn't tell
nobody you had a condition?

MARGARET-ELIZABETH (BUBBA). Condition? What
condition?

WOMAN ONE, TWO, AND LIZZIE. A LIVING CON-
DITION!

ALL [*Singing*].

Caldonia!
Caldonia!
What makes yo' big head so hard! BOOM!

[*Singing.*] "Way down upon the Swanee River . . .''

MARGARET-ELIZABETH (BUBBA). Hey, Poo-Key! You
know something, man? You one *dark* Negro! You
blacker dan coal.

WOMAN ONE AND TWO. Dan coal?

LIZZIE (POO-KEY). Watch yo'self now, Bubba—
'cause me an' you the same color—an' you blacker
dan de dead of night!

WOMAN ONE AND TWO. De dead of night?

MARGARET-ELIZABETH (BUBBA). Aw, naw! We ain't
the same color 'cause you blacker dan Tar Baby.

WOMAN ONE AND TWO. Tar Baby!

LIZZIE (POO-KEY). You blacker dan chimney smoke!

WOMAN ONE AND TWO. Chimney smoke!

MARGARET-ELIZABETH (BUBBA). You blacker dan a
patent leather shoe

WOMAN ONE AND TWO. A patent leather shoe!

LIZZIE (POO-KEY). Aww, now you tryin' to hurt
me—but, I'll tell you one thing—you blacker dan
de devil!

WOMAN ONE AND TWO [*Mock horror*]. DE DEVIL!

MARGARET-ELIZABETH (BUBBA). Man, you so black,
it's hard to tell that you exist.

LIZZIE (POO-KEY). I sho' am glad ole Thomas Edison
threw some light on you, man, 'cause you damn-
near invisible yo'self.

MARGARET-ELIZABETH (BUBBA). Well, I want you to
know—that even if the lights go out—it's one
somebody always know I exist.

LIZZIE (POO-KEY). Who dat?

WOMAN ONE AND TWO. WH-OOOooo DAT!

LIZZIE (POO-KEY). Who dat what say "who dat"
when I say "who dat"?

MARGARET-ELIZABETH (BUBBA). Dat God! God
knows he put me here.

LIZZIE (POO-KEY). Say who?

MARGARET-ELIZABETH (BUBBA). I tell you what.
I'ma prove dat I'm here. You see dis here mirror
here?

[*All the Women hold the palms of their hands toward their
faces in mime gesture.*]

Dere me! [*Primps.*] Now tell me what you see.

[*No longer the minstrel men, Margaret-Elizabeth and Lizzie
revert back to character.*]

LIZZIE. Black Topsy.

MARGARET-ELIZABETH. Black Beulah.

LIZZIE. Black Mama.

MARGARET-ELIZABETH. Black Whore.

BOTH. Black Man!

[*All the Women resume the minstrel men character.*]

ALL [*Singing and dancing*].
Way down upon the Swanee River,
Far, far away . . .

LOUDSPEAKER. CONTESTANT NUMBER FIVE!

[*Woman One, Two, and Lizzie exit. Margaret-Elizabeth
moves to the Stage Left entrance of the ramp. The lights fade
on Downstage Center. Margaret-Elizabeth ascends the ramp
smiling and with great poise. When she reaches the Center
of the ramp, she begins to pose in all the masculine poses
used in the Mr. America Contest. She takes her time and
assumes each pose carefully and defiantly. She assumes all
the classic poses and delights in hyping the audience with
her show of form.*]

LOUDSPEAKER. Ladies and gentlemen! The moment
we've all been waiting for! THE NEW MISS
INTERNATIONAL SEPIA!

[*The music blares up. The Two Men rush onstage and place
the "Miss International Sepia" banner on Margaret-
Elizabeth. They place a bouquet of plastic roses in her arms
and a string of tiny Christmas tree lights around her top hat.
The lights flash on and off as she poses, waves, smiles, blows
kisses, and struts across the ramp.*]

LOUDSPEAKER. And may we take this time to introduce the first runner-up to the Queen—Miss America!

[*Lizzie enters Stage Right. She walks unenthusiastically
across the ramp and stands beside Margaret-Elizabeth. She is
carrying a large poster cutout. The poster is a composite
image. On one half of the head, we see the red and white
bandanna. On the other half of the head is a man's hat. A
gold hoop earring hangs from one ear. The chest is a large,
fat, busty affair, with the yellow-and-red flowered calico
blouse on. One arm contains many gaudy bracelets, and the
other is the sleeve of a man's suit. One leg is covered by a
short miniskirted, figure-hugging, satin skirt and a shapely*

leg fitted into a stiletto-heeled, ankle-strapped shoe. The other leg is covered by the many-tiered, calico skirt and ends with a pair of men's pants sticking out from under the skirt and a man's shoe. Lizzie sticks her head and arms through the cutouts, but she shows no excitement for the moment.]

LOUDSPEAKER. And now! The prizes! "From Mom's Eatery—One Homemade Apple Pie!"

MARGARET-ELIZABETH [*To Lizzie, as she continues to wave and smile to the audience*]. Lizzie! Smile! We did it! Aren't you happy?

LIZZIE [*Horrified*]. Look at you!

MARGARET-ELIZABETH [*Marveling*]. Look at you!

LIZZIE. *Look* at me!

MARGARET-ELIZABETH. Yes? WE WON! My darling Lizzie! WE WON!

LOUDSPEAKER. "From Avery's Five and Dime—A Brass Ring!"

LIZZIE. You always get to play the best part!

[The lights fade with Margaret-Elizabeth flowing down the ramp, smiling, waving, and tossing flowers into the audience Downstage .]

END

ESSAY: AN APPROACH TO THE PLAY

One of *Paper Dolls'* ongoing concerns is with the cultural role of art. In place of the cliché that art imitates life, this play seems to insist that art shapes life: that it intervenes in life and helps to form our perception both of our world and of our place in it. This dynamic is easiest to see, perhaps, in the play's "miniscenes," where the two women reenact moments from films in which they once performed. In them, they invariably played demeaning racial stereotypes—domestic servants or, in one case, an African who spoke gibberish—but in the miniscenes which they enact on stage and which they seem to have been playing out for years in their heads, they identify with the white heroines, the "good roles" that Lizzie laments Margaret-Elizabeth always insists on playing. In the first miniscene, the character Myra says, "I'm Mad! And you know how I am when I get mad," a line which Lizzie has already used in the play's opening moments: she has internalized Myra's rhetoric as her own, even though Myra's behavior when angry was to beat her servant, the role which Lizzie herself played in the film.

In *Paper Dolls'* second scene, the women order cocktails, apparently in an attempt to associate themselves with the glamour of the women for whom the drinks were prepared in two miniscenes. In those scenes, Margaret-Elizabeth and Lizzie played ineffectual servants who spoke absurdly stereotyped dialects, while both scenes romanticized the equally stereotypical white female invalid: the drinks are associated with the rescue of the freezing or fainted heroines by their heroes. "Miss Emancipation" and her runner-up seem enslaved by all the films' roles—both the ones which they played and in a sense continue to play in society, and those of the white women with whom they identify.

The miniscenes are perhaps the play's clearest examples of the way art shapes ideology for Margaret-Elizabeth and Lizzie, but there are other examples throughout the play—in painting and sculpture and minstrelsy and beauty pageants—of cultural forms that seem not so much to reflect the world as to shape a way of seeing the world and one's place in it. Human constructs such as "beauty" are often contrasted with "nature" (although, as the play implies, nature, too, can often be a human construct as well). For example, at the beginning of Act 2, Margaret-Elizabeth laments, "If we hadn't spent so much time in awe of the natural rules of nature, we could have devoted more time to . . . to . . . putting gold trim on the overcoat . . . instead of always having to worry about the underwear." The "natural rules of nature" with which beauty and art inevitably collide include aging and death, two more of the play's central concerns. Perhaps this helps explain the refrain that runs through Margaret-Elizabeth's dialogue, insisting on getting the ending right.

The ending of what, we are left wondering: Art or life? At the end of the baking soda scene, Margaret-Elizabeth says, "I don't want it to end like this," and her inspiration for changing the ending comes from the movies, from the play's first miniscene. Experience as shaped by art allows her to see how to change the ending of this experience in her life. We come to realize that her obsession with changing the ending refers not just to artistic closure but to changing the "plot" of her life. By contrast with Lizzie, who prepares for the end in thoroughly pragmatic fashion, paying for her casket and cemetery plot and moving into a retirement community, Margaret-Elizabeth says she is "going across the finish line—my way." Her concerns raise the question of whether we "have" a life apart from the narrative we construct for ourselves and by which we explain its significance to ourselves. She seems desperate to structure her life's story so that it has meaning, but the narrative forms and conventions which her culture has made available to her and upon which she relies are so limited and so conventional that they keep forcing her back to the celebration of her petty beauty triumphs, making it impossible for her really to change the ending.

One of the reasons for Margaret-Elizabeth's imaginative entrapment may be that for her, society's evaluation of beauty seems not to be problematical; after all, she "won," and so she refers to arbitrary cultural norms as "standards" without thinking to question how they are derived or who has the power to establish and enforce them. Margaret-Elizabeth's victory is reinforced by prizes of little inherent value—though often of great symbolic value—which are offered by local corporate sponsors and announced during the beauty contest, frequently at ironically telling moments. For example, Mr. Castle says he has just one question to ask such a talented young lady as Margaret-Elizabeth, "Where did you get such pretty legs," and the loudspeaker announces a gift certificate for dinner at Marianne's Steak and Chop House. The final prize in the play is a brass ring—the token which traditionally allows you to take another ride on the merry-go-round; the reward for playing the game well is to continue to play it. But since Margaret-Elizabeth has won, the standards by which she did so come to seem "natural" to her, and upholding them seems central to her role as judge. The play suggests, however, that it is dangerous to assign such standards to "nature," since our perceptions of nature also seems inevitably to be culturally constructed. As suggested in the conclusion of Act 2, Scene 1, we "see" in nature what art has taught us to see, the versions of nature which have been depicted by artists who themselves were taught what to see and so on *ad infinitum*. (Extending the insight to beauty pageants, we evaluate as beautiful those physical attributes which previous pageants have deemed worthy of victory.) The scene's concluding line, "we ought to bring those pictures up to date," seems to be a lead-in to the next scene, where a white woman artist imposes her preconceptions of "the black female" on a black female model who does not "naturally" fulfill those preconceptions.

Paper Dolls raises basic social and psychological questions: Who gets to judge, for example, and who gets to set the standards for judgment, and what makes us accept these standards for ourselves? Such questions may be implied in the play's first and last scenes. Baking soda, a pure and natural substance which Lizzie describes as having a wide range of applications, is judged by its appearance to be cocaine. The women who carry it seem also to be judged: they are detained, inspected, scrutinized; they feel themselves under surveillance. Their suspicion that the room has a two-way mirror may anticipate some aspects of the play's treatment of beauty competition. The mirror is a tool with which the women see their own reflections, but always aware of the imagined eyes—and standards and expectations—of others.

The play's strange final scene returns us to questions of judging. It begins as a burlesque of a conventional beauty pageant, with male actors serving as the contestants. They parade down the runway with their faces protruding through cut-outs in life-sized paper dolls of white film stars, our culture's models of conventional female beauty. The implication, perhaps, is that beauty contests do not so much evaluate the beauty of the women who are contestants as reaffirm our culture's preconceptions of what or who is beautiful. Even more strange, Margaret-Elizabeth "wins" the contest by impersonating a muscle man, a parody of a male, rather than a female, stereotype of a physically attractive body. Perhaps this implies that there is a reciprocity between the two stereotypes: the real function of female beauty is to affirm male power. What our culture seems to want, or at least what the beauty myth seems to reinforce, is the image of the compliant woman dominated by the powerful male. Perhaps beauty contests are concerned with maintaining not aesthetic standards but a distribution of power that is based on gender, and the woman who best expresses this power relationship is the one who "wins."

This last scene, with its parody of a minstrel show, also reminds us of the way our cultural institutions have helped maintain the distribution of power on the basis of race. The two women play the racially stereotyped roles and tell the racially demeaning jokes which used to be associated with that form of "entertainment." As we suggested in the brief headnote to this play, the beauty trap has an extra twist when women of color are caught in it. One of the remarkable things about *Paper Dolls* is how artfully it exposes the normally "invisible" ways in which our culture enforces and perpetuates its prejudices both against women in general and against women of color in particular.

David Henry Hwang

M. BUTTERFLY

About the Author David Henry Hwang (1957–   ) was born in the suburban Los Angeles community of San Gabriel. He entered Stanford University in 1975 intending to study law but became increasingly interested in drama and in questions of Asian-American ethnicity. These two interests combined in his first play, *F.O.B.*, which was produced in 1979 at Standford's Okada House as his dormitory's entry in a campuswide drama competition. The title's initials are a term of derision used by some Chinese-Americans to refer to newly arrived Chinese immigrants as "fresh off the boat." The play, in which an assimilated Chinese-American interacts with an "F.O.B," explores questions about Chinese identity and culture in America, as well as the temptation Chinese-Americans face to identify too closely with the dominant culture. A draft of the play was accepted for the summer Playwrights' Conference of the O'Neill Theater Center in Waterbury, Connecticut, where Hwang revised it; in the next year, 1980, the New York Shakespeare Festival Public Theater produced it. In subsequent years, this theater produced several other plays by Hwang dealing with Asian and Asian-American topics. *The Dance and the Railroad* (1981) celebrates Chinese railroad workers who organized a nineteenth-century strike to protest working conditions. *Family Devotions* is a farce dealing with three generations of a Chinese-American family. Two other plays, *The House of Sleeping Beauties* and *The Sound of a Voice*, deal with Japanese topics. Hwang's best-known play and greatest critical success, *M. Butterfly*, won the 1988 Tony award as best play on Broadway. Hwang has recently written for film and television, while continuing to write for theater.

About the Play In the May 11, 1986, issue of *The New York Times*, an article appeared with the headline, "France Jails Two in Odd Case of Espionage." It told the story of Bernard Bouriscot, a French diplomat formerly assigned to the city which is now Beijing, and Shi Peipu, a former star of the city's opera, who were found guilty of passing French state secrets to the Chinese government. What made this case of treason so interesting is that Shi was a male actor who specialized in playing female roles, and Bouriscot claimed never to have suspected that Shi was not in fact a woman, even though the two had had a twenty-year love affair. At one point Shi persuaded Bouriscot that "she" was pregnant and produced a child that Bouriscot assumed was his. It was only during the trial that Bouriscot learned the truth about his lover. As part of his explanation of how he could have been deceived, Bouriscot explained, "I thought she was very modest. I thought it was a Chinese custom."

This newspaper story was the genesis of Hwang's play, though details are much altered to suit his own ideas. He says, in fact, that he purposely chose not to learn more about the case, because he was not interested in writing a documentary. Rather, he changed the names of the principal characters to Rene Gallimard and Song Liling and made the focus of the play an exploration of the mentality that would make Gallimard's error plausible. The play's double concerns are with the West's assumption of superiority over Asia—what has come to be called "Orientalism"—and men's assumption of superiority over women, the two coming together in the western myth of the submissive Asian woman who will do whatever her man wants and who is, therefore, the "perfect" woman. "Oriental" (a word which means "Eastern" and which is not favored by Asians themselves) is literally a Eurocentric term: It presupposes that you are in Europe, from which point Asia would lie to the east. It would be meaningless to speak of Asia as the Orient if you were in Japan; from Japan, California lies to the east, and from California, the "Orient" lies to the west. In addition, the term "oriental" has connotations that suggest that Asia is exotic, mysterious, but also in need of and perhaps secretly welcoming the control of the technologically superior West.

As a counterpoint to these conventional western ideas, Hwang has woven a profound irony into the play's background, an irony suggested in its title. The background to which the title refers is the romantic love plot of Giacomo Puccini's opera, *Madame Butterfly*, which opened in Milan in 1904 and came to be one of the most popular of his works. ("M." is the French abbreviation for the word "Monsieur," but the play is always identified by saying the name of the letter, not as "Monsieur Butterfly.") Hwang reenacts relevant portions of the plot of Puccini's opera in Scenes 3, 5, and 6 of Act 1 by having Song be the actor playing the part—in a play within a play—of Cio-Cio-San, the character called Butterfly in the opera. The "actress" *seems* type cast for this stereotypical role.

CHARACTERS

RENE GALLIMARD

SONG LILING

MAN 1

MAN 2

WOMAN AT PARTY

MARC

GIRL IN MAGAZINE

COMRADE CHIN

HELGA

M. TOULON

RENEE

JUDGE

SETTING

The action of the play takes place in a Paris prison in the present, and in recall, during the decade 1960 to 1970 in Beijing, and from 1966 to the present in Paris.

Act I

SCENE I

M. Gallimard's prison cell. Paris. Present.

Lights fade up to reveal Rene Gallimard, 65, in a prison cell. He wears a comfortable bathrobe, and looks old and tired. The sparsely furnished cell contains a wooden crate upon which sits a hot plate with a kettle, and a portable tape recorder. Gallimard sits on the crate staring at the recorder, a sad smile on his face.

Upstage Song, who appears as a beautiful woman in traditional Chinese garb, dances a traditional piece from the Peking Opera, surrounded by the percussive clatter of Chinese music.

Then, slowly, lights and sound cross-fade; the Chinese opera music dissolves into a Western opera, the "Love Duet" from Puccini's *Madame Butterfly*. Song continues dancing, now to the Western accompaniment. Though her movements are the same, the difference in music now gives them a balletic quality.

Gallimard rises, and turns upstage towards the figure of Song, who dances without acknowledging him.

GALLIMARD. Butterfly, Butterfly . . .

[*He forces himself to turn away, as the image of Song fades out, and talks to us.*]

GALLIMARD. The limits of my cell are as such: four-and-a-half meters by five. There's one window against the far wall; a door, very strong, to protect me from autograph hounds. I'm responsible for the tape recorder, the hot plate, and this charming coffee table.

When I want to eat, I'm marched off to the dining room—hot, steaming slop appears on my plate. When I want to sleep, the light bulb turns itself off—the work of fairies. It's an enchanted space I occupy. The French—we know how to run a prison.

But, to be honest, I'm not treated like an ordinary prisoner. Why? Because I'm a celebrity. You see, I make people laugh.

I never dreamed this day would arrive. I've never been considered witty or clever. In fact, as a young boy, in an informal poll among my grammar school classmates, I was voted "least likely to be invited to a party." It's a title I managed to hold onto for many years. Despite some stiff competition.

But now, how the tables turn! Look at me: the life of every social function in Paris. Paris? Why be modest? My fame has spread to Amsterdam, London, New York. Listen to them! In the world's smartest parlors. I'm the one who lifts their spirits!

[With a flourish, Gallimard directs our attention to another part of the stage.]

SCENE II

A party. Present.

Lights go up on a chic-looking parlor, where a well-dressed trio, two men and one woman, make conversation. Gallimard also remains lit; he observes them from his cell.

WOMAN. And what of Gallimard?
MAN 1. Gallimard?
MAN 2. Gallimard!
GALLIMARD [To us]. You see? They're all determined to say my name, as if it were some new dance.
WOMAN. He still claims not to believe the truth.
MAN 1. What? Still? Even since the trial?
WOMAN. Yes. Isn't it mad?
MAN 2 [Laughing]. He says . . . it was dark . . . and she was very modest!

[The trio break into laughter.]

MAN 1. So—what? He never touched her with his hands?
MAN 2. Perhaps he did, and simply misidentified the equipment. A compelling case for sex education in the schools.

WOMAN. To protect the National Security—the Church can't argue with that.
MAN 1. That's impossible! How could he not know?
MAN 2. Simple ignorance.
MAN 1. For twenty years?
MAN 2. Time flies when your'e being stupid.
WOMAN. Well, I thought the French were ladies' men.
MAN 2. It seems Monsieur Gallimard was overly anxious to live up to his national reputation.
WOMAN. Well, he's not very good-looking.
MAN 1. No, he's not.
MAN 2. Certainly not.
WOMAN. Actually, I feel sorry for him.
MAN 2. A toast! To Monsieur Gallimard!
WOMAN. Yes! To Gallimard!
MAN 1. To Gallimard!
MAN 2. Vive la différence!

[They toast, laughing. Lights down on them.]

SCENE III

M. Gallimard's cell.

GALLIMARD [Smiling]. You see? They toast me. I've become patron saint of the socially inept. Can they really be so foolish? Men like that—they should be scratching at my door, begging to learn my secrets! For I, Rene Gallimard, you see, I have known, and been loved by . . . the Perfect Woman.

Alone in this cell, I sit night after night, watching our story play through my head, always searching for a new ending, one which redeems my honor, where she returns at last to my arms. And I imagine you—my ideal audience—who come to understand and even, perhaps just a little, to envy me.

[He turns on his tape recorder. Over the house speakers, we hear the opening phrases of Madame Butterfly.]

GALLIMARD. In order for you to understand what I did and why, I must introduce you to my favorite opera: Madame Butterfly. By Giacomo Puccini. First produced at La Scala, Milan, in 1904, it is now beloved throughout the Western world.

[As Gallimard describes the opera, the tape segues in and out to sections he may be describing.]

GALLIMARD. And why not? Its heroine, Cio-Cio-San, also known as Butterfly, is a feminine ideal, beautiful and brave. And its hero, the man for whom she gives up everything, is—[*He pulls out a naval officer's cap from under his crate, pops it on his head, and struts about*]—not very good-looking, not too bright, and pretty much a wimp: Benjamin Franklin Pinkerton of the U.S. Navy. As the curtain rises, he's just closed on two great bargains: one on a house, the other on a woman—call it a package deal.

Pinkerton purchased the rights to Butterfly for one hundred yen—in modern currency, equivalent to about . . . sixty-six cents. So, he's feeling pretty pleased with himself as Sharpless, the American consul, arrives to witness the marriage.

[*Marc, wearing an official cap to designate Sharpless, enters and plays the character.*]

SHARPLESS/MARC. Pinkerton!
PINKERTON/GALLIMARD. Sharpless! How's it hangin'? It's a great day, just great. Between my house, my wife, and the rickshaw ride in from town, I've saved nineteen cents just this morning.
SHARPLESS. Wonderful, I can see the inscription on your tombstone already: "I saved a dollar, here I lie." [*He looks around*] Nice house.
PINKERTON. It's artistic. Artistic, don't you think? Like the way the shoji screens slide open to reveal the wet bar and disco mirror ball? Classy, huh? Great for impressing the chicks.
SHARPLESS. "Chicks"? Pinkerton, you're going to be a married man!
PINKERTON. Well, sort of.
SHARPLESS. What do you mean?
PINKERTON. This country—Sharpless, it is okay. You got all these geisha girls running around—
SHARPLESS. I know! I live here!
PINKERTON. Then, you know the marriage laws, right? I split for one month, it's annulled!
SHARPLESS. Leave it to you to read the fine print. Who's the lucky girl?
PINKERTON. Cio-Cio-San. Her friends call her Butterfly. Sharpless, she eats out of my hand!
SHARPLESS. She's probably very hungry.
PINKERTON. Not like American girls. It's true what they say about Oriental girls. They want to be treated bad!
SHARPLESS. Oh, please!
PINKERTON. It's true!
SHARPLESS. Are you serious about this girl?
PINKERTON. I'm marrying her, aren't I?
SHARPLESS. Yes—with generous trade-in terms.
PINKERTON. When I leave, she'll know what it's like to have loved a real man. And I'll even buy her a few nylons.
SHARPLESS. You aren't planning to take her with you?
PINKERTON. Huh? Where?
SHARPLESS. Home!
PINKERTON. You mean, America? Are you crazy? Can you see her trying to buy rice in St. Louis?
SHARPLESS. So, you're not serious.

[*Pause.*]

PINKERTON/GALLIMARD [*As Pinkerton*]. Consul, I am a sailor in port. [*As Gallimard*] They then proceed to sing the famous duet, "The Whole World Over."

[*The duet plays on the speakers. Gallimard, as Pinkerton, lipsyncs his lines from the opera.*]

GALLIMARD. To give a rough translation: "The whole world over, the Yankee travels, casting his anchor wherever he wants. Life's not worth living unless he can win the hearts of the fairest maidens, then hotfoot it off the premises ASAP." [*He turns towards Marc*] In the preceding scene, I played Pinkerton, the womanizing cad, and my friend Marc from school . . . [*Marc bows grandly for our benefit*] played Sharpless, the sensitive soul of reason. In life, however, our positions were usually—no, always—reversed.

SCENE IV

Ecole Nationale. Aix-en-Provence. 1947.

GALLIMARD. No, Marc, I think I'd rather stay home.
MARC. Are you crazy?! We are going to Dad's condo in Marseille! You know what happened last time?
GALLIMARD. Of course I do.
MARC. Of course you don't! You never know. . . . They stripped, Rene!
GALLIMARD. Who stripped?
MARC. The girls!
GALLIMARD. Girls? Who said anything about girls?
MARC. Rene, we're a buncha university guys goin' up to the woods. What are we gonna do—talk philosophy?
GALLIMARD. What girls? Where do you get them?
MARC. Who cares? The point is, they come. On trucks. Packed in like sardines. The back flips open, babes hop out, we're ready to roll.
GALLIMARD. You mean, they just—?

MARC. Before you know it, every last one of them—they're stripped and splashing around my pool. There's no moon out, they can't see what's going on, their boobs are flapping, right? You close your eyes, reach out—it's grab bag, get it? Doesn't matter whose ass is between whose legs, whose teeth are sinking into who. You're just in there, going at it, eyes closed, on and on for as long as you can stand. [*Pause*] Some fun, huh?

GALLIMARD. What happens in the morning?

MARC. In the morning, you're ready to talk some philosophy. [*Beat*] So how 'bout it?

GALLIMARD. Marc, I can't . . . I'm afraid they'll say no—the girls. So I never ask.

MARC. You don't have to ask! That's the beauty—don't you see? They don't have to say yes. It's perfect for a guy like you, really.

GALLIMARD. You go ahead . . . I may come later.

MARC. Hey, Rene—it doesn't matter that you're clumsy and got zits—they're not looking!

GALLIMARD. Thank you very much.

MARC. Wimp.

[*Marc walks over to the other side of the stage, and starts waving and smiling at women in the audience.*]

GALLIMARD [*To us*]. We now return to my version of *Madame Butterfly* and the events leading to my recent conviction for treason.

[*Gallimard notices Marc making lewd gestures.*]

GALLIMARD. Marc, what are you doing?

MARC. Huh? [*Sotto voce*] Rene, there're a lotta great babes out there. They're probably lookin' at me and thinking, "What a dangerous guy."

GALLIMARD. Yes—how could they help but be impressed by your cool sophistication?

[*Gallimard pops the Sharpless cap on Marc's head, and points him offstage. Marc exits, leering.*]

SCENE V

M. Gallimard's cell.

GALLIMARD. Next, Butterfly makes her entrance. We learn her age—fifteen . . . but very mature for her years.

[*Lights come up on the area where we saw Song dancing at the top of the play. She appears there again, now dressed as Madame Butterfly, moving to the "Love Duet." Gallimard turns upstage slightly to watch, transfixed.*]

GALLIMARD. But as she glides past him, beautiful, laughing softly behind her fan, don't we who are men sigh with hope? We, who are not handsome, nor brave, nor powerful, yet somehow believe, like Pinkerton, that we deserve a Butterfly. She arrives with all her possessions in the folds of her sleeves, lays them all out, for her man to do with as he pleases. Even her life itself—she bows her head as she whispers that she's not even worth the hundred yen he paid for her. He's already given too much, when we know he's really had to give nothing at all.

[*Music and lights on Song out. Gallimard sits at his crate.*]

GALLIMARD. In real life, women who put their total worth at less than sixty-six cents are quite hard to find. The closest we come is in the pages of these magazines. [*He reaches into his crate, pulls out a stack of girlie magazines, and begins flipping through them*] Quite a necessity in prison. For three or four dollars, you get seven or eight women.

I first discovered these magazines at my uncle's house. One day, as a boy of twelve. The first time I saw them in his closet . . . all lined up—my body shook. Not with lust—no, with power. Here were women—a shelfful—who would do exactly as I wanted.

[*The "Love Duet" creeps in over the speakers. Special comes up, revealing, not Song this time, but a pinup girl in a sexy negligee, her back to us. Gallimard turns upstage and looks at her.*]

GIRL. I know you're watching me.

GALLIMARD. My throat . . . it's dry.

GIRL. I leave my blinds open every night before I go to bed.

GALLIMARD. I can't move.

GIRL. I leave my blinds open and the lights on.

GALLIMARD. I'm shaking. My skin is hot, but my penis is soft. Why?

GIRL. I stand in front of the window.

GALLIMARD. What is she going to do?

GIRL. I toss my hair, and I let my lips part . . . barely.

GALLIMARD. I shouldn't be seeing this. It's so dirty. I'm so bad.

GIRL. Then, slowly, I lift off my nightdress.

GALLIMARD. Oh, god. I can't believe it. I can't—
GIRL. I toss it to the ground.
GALLIMARD. Now, she's going to walk away. She's going to—
GIRL. I stand there, in the light, displaying myself.
GALLIMARD. No. She's—why is she naked?
GIRL. To you.
GALLIMARD. In front of a window? This is wrong. No—
GIRL. Without shame.
GALLIMARD. No, she must . . . like it.
GIRL. I like it.
GALLIMARD. She . . . she wants me to see.
GIRL. I want you to see.
GALLIMARD. I can't believe it! She's getting excited!
GIRL. I can't see you. You can do whatever you want.
GALLIMARD. I can't do a thing. Why?
GIRL. What would you like me to do . . . next?

[*Lights go down on her. Music off. Silence, as Gallimard puts away his magazines. Then he resumes talking to us.*]

GALLIMARD. Act Two begins with Butterfly staring at the ocean. Pinkerton's been called back to the U.S., and he's given his wife a detailed schedule of his plans. In the column marked "return date," he's written "when the robins nest." This failed to ignite her suspicions. Now, three years have passed without a peep from him. Which brings a response from her faithful servant, Suzuki.

[*Comrade Chin enters, playing Suzuki.*]

SUZUKI. Girl, he's a loser. What'd he ever give you? Nineteen cents and those ugly Day-Glo stockings? Look, it's finished! Kaput! Done! And you should be glad! I mean, the guy was a woofer! He tried before, you know—before he met you, he went down to geisha central and plunked down his spare change in front of the usual candidates—everyone else gagged! These are hungry prostitutes, and they were not interested, get the picture? Now, stop slathering when an American ship sails in, and let's make some bucks—I mean, yen! We are broke!

Now, what about Yamadori? Hey, hey—don't look away—the man is a prince— figuratively, and, what's even better, literally. He's rich, he's handsome, he says he'll die if you don't marry him—and he's even willing to overlook the little fact that you've been deflowered all over the place by a foreign devil. What do you mean, "But he's Japanese?"

You're Japanese! You think you've been touched by the whitey god? He was a sailor with dirty hands!

[*Suzuki stalks offstage.*]

GALLIMARD. She's also visited by Consul Sharpless, sent by Pinkerton on a minor errand.

[*Marc enters, as Sharpless.*]

SHARPLESS. I hate this job.
GALLIMARD. This Pinkerton—he doesn't show up personally to tell his wife he's abandoning her. No, he sends a government diplomat . . . at taxpayer's expense.
SHARPLESS. Butterfly? Butterfly? I have some bad— I'm going to be ill. Butterfly, I came to tell you—
GALLIMARD. Butterfly says she knows he'll return and if he doesn't she'll kill herself rather than go back to her own people. [*Beat*] This causes a lull in the conversation.
SHARPLESS. Let's put it this way . . .
GALLIMARD. Butterfly runs into the next room, and returns holding—

[*Sound cue: a baby crying. Sharpless, "seeing" this, backs away.*]

SHARPLESS. Well, good. Happy to see things going so well. I suppose I'll be going now. Ta ta. Ciao. [*He turns away. Sound cue out*] I hate this job. [*He exits*]
GALLIMARD. At that moment, Butterfly spots in the harbor an American ship—the *Abramo Lincoln!*

[*Music cue: "The Flower Duet." Song, still dressed as Butterfly, changes into a wedding kimono, moving to the music.*]

GALLIMARD. This is the moment that redeems her years of waiting. With Suzuki's help, they cover the room with flowers—

[*Chin, as Suzuki, trudges onstage and drops a lone flower without much enthusiasm.*]

GALLIMARD. —and she changes into her wedding dress to prepare for Pinkerton's arrival.

[*Suzuki helps Butterfly change. Helga enters, and helps Gallimard change into a tuxedo.*]

GALLIMARD. I married a woman older than myself— Helga.

HELGA. My father was ambassador to Australia. I grew up among criminals and kangaroos.

GALLIMARD. Hearing that brought me to the altar—

[*Helga exits.*]

GALLIMARD. —where I took a vow renouncing love. No fantasy woman would ever want me, so, yes, I would settle for a quick leap up the career ladder. Passion, I banish, and in its place—practicality!

But my vows had long since lost their charm by the time we arrived in China. The sad truth is that all men want a beautiful woman, and the uglier the man, the greater the want.

[*Suzuki makes final adjustments of Butterfly's costume, as does Gallimard of his tuxedo.*]

GALLIMARD. I married late, at age thirty-one. I was faithful to my marriage for eight years. Until the day when, as a junior-level diplomat in puritanical Peking, in a parlor at the German ambassador's house, during the "Reign of a Hundred Flowers," I first saw her . . . singing the death scene from *Madame Butterfly*.

[*Suzuki runs offstage.*]

SCENE VI

German ambassador's house. Beijing. 1960.

The upstage special area now becomes a stage. Several chairs face upstage, representing seating for some twenty guests in the parlor. A few "diplomats" —Renee, Marc, Toulon—in formal dress enter and take seats.

Gallimard also sits down, but turns towards us and continues to talk. Orchestral accompaniment on the tape is now replaced by a simple piano. Song picks up the death scene from the point where Butterfly uncovers the hara-kiri knife.

GALLIMARD. The ending is pitiful. Pinkerton, in an act of great courage, stays home and sends his American wife to pick up Butterfly's child. The truth, long deferred, has come up to her door.

[*Song, playing Butterfly, sings the lines from the opera in her own voice—which, though not classical, should be decent.*]

SONG. "Con onor muore/ chi non puo serbar/ vita con onore."

GALLIMARD [*Simultaneously*]. "Death with honor/ Is better than life/ Life with dishonor."

[*The stage is illuminated; we are now completely within an elegant diplomat's residence. Song proceeds to play out an abbreviated death scene. Everyone in the room applauds. Song, shyly, takes her bows. Others in the room rush to congratulate her. Gallimard remains with us.*]

GALLIMARD. They say in opera the voice is everything. That's probably why I'd never before enjoyed opera. Here . . . here was a Butterfly with little or no voice—but she had the grace, the delicacy . . . I believed this girl. I believed her suffering. I wanted to take her in my arms—so delicate, even I could protect her, take her home, pamper her until she smiled.

[*Over the course of the preceeding speech, Song has broken from the upstage crowd and moved directly upstage of Gallimard.*]

SONG. Excuse me. Monsieur . . . ?

[*Gallimard turns upstage, shocked.*]

GALLIMARD. Oh! Gallimard. Mademoiselle . . . ? A beautiful . . .

SONG. Song Liling.

GALLIMARD. A beautiful performance.

SONG. Oh, please.

GALLIMARD. I usually—

SONG. You make me blush. I'm no opera singer at all.

GALLIMARD. I usually don't like *Butterfly*.

SONG. I can't blame you in the least.

GALLIMARD. I mean, the story—

SONG. Ridiculous.

GALLIMARD. I like the story, but . . . what?

SONG. Oh, you like it?

GALLIMARD. I . . . what I mean is, I've always seen it played by huge women in so much bad makeup.

SONG. Bad makeup is not unique to the West.

GALLIMARD. But, who can believe them?

SONG. And you believe me?

GALLIMARD. Absolutely. You were utterly convincing. It's the first time—

SONG. Convincing? As a Japanese woman? The Japanese used hundreds of our people for medical experiments during the war, you know. But I gather such an irony is lost on you.

GALLIMARD. No! I was about to say, it's the first time I've seen the beauty of the story.

SONG. Really?

GALLIMARD. Of her death. It's a . . . a pure sacrifice. He's unworthy, but what can she do? She loves him . . . so much. It's a very beautiful story.

SONG. Well, yes, to a Westerner.

GALLIMARD. Excuse me?

SONG. It's one of your favorite fantasies, isn't it? The submissive Oriental woman and the cruel white man.

GALLIMARD. Well, I didn't quite mean . . .

SONG. Consider it this way: what would you say if a blonde homecoming queen fell in love with a short Japanese businessman? He treats her cruelly, then goes home for three years, during which time she prays to his picture and turns down marriage from a young Kennedy. Then, when she learns he has remarried, she kills herself. Now, I believe you would consider this girl to be a deranged idiot, correct? But because it's an Oriental who kills herself for a Westerner—ah!—you find it beautiful.

[Silence.]

GALLIMARD. Yes . . . well . . . I see your point . . .

SONG. I will never do Butterfly again, Monsieur Gallimard. If you wish to see some real theatre, come to the Peking Opera sometime. Expand your mind.

[Song walks offstage.]

GALLIMARD [To us]. So much for protecting her in my big Western arms.

SCENE VII

M. Gallimard's apartment. Beijing. 1960.
    Gallimard changes from his tux into a casual suit. Helga enters.

GALLIMARD. The Chinese are an incredibly arrogant people.

HELGA. They warned us about that in Paris, remember?

GALLIMARD. Even Parisians consider them arrogant. That's a switch.

HELGA. What is it that Madame Su says? "We are a very old civilization." I never know if she's talking about her country or herself.

GALLIMARD. I walk around here, all I hear every day, everywhere is how *old* this culture is. The fact that "old" may be synonymous with "senile" doesn't occur to them.

HELGA. You're not going to change them. "East is east, west is west, and . . ." whatever that guy said.

GALLIMARD. It's just that—silly. I met . . . at Ambassador Koening's tonight—you should've been there.

HELGA. Koening? Oh god, no. Did he enchant you all again with the history of Bavaria?

GALLIMARD. No. I met, I suppose, the Chinese equivalent of a diva. She's a singer in the Chinese opera.

HELGA. They have an opera, too? Do they sing in Chinese? Or maybe—in Italian?

GALLIMARD. Tonight, she did sing in Italian.

HELGA. How'd she manage that?

GALLIMARD. She must've been educated in the West before the Revolution. Her French is very good also. Anyway, she sang the death scene from *Madame Butterfly.*

HELGA. *Madame Butterfly!* Then I should have come. [*She begins humming, floating around the room as if dragging long kimono sleeves*] Did she have a nice costume? I think it's a classic piece of music.

GALLIMARD. That's what *I* thought, too. Don't let her hear you say that.

HELGA. What's wrong?

GALLIMARD. Evidently the Chinese hate it.

HELGA. She hated it, but she performed it anyway? Is she perverse?

GALLIMARD. They hate it because the white man gets the girl. Sour grapes if you ask me.

HELGA. Politics again? Why can't they just hear it as a piece of beautiful music? So, what's in their opera?

GALLIMARD. I don't know. But, whatever it is, I'm sure it must be *old.*

[Helga exits.]

SCENE VIII

Chinese opera house and the streets of Beijing. 1960.
The sound of gongs clanging fills the stage.

GALLIMARD. My wife's innocent question kept ringing in my ears. I asked around, but no one knew anything about the Chinese opera. It took four weeks, but my curiosity overcame my cowardice. This Chinese diva—this unwilling Butterfly—what did she do to make her so proud?

The room was hot, and full of smoke. Wrinkled faces, old women, teeth missing—a man with a growth on his neck, like a human toad. All smiling, pipes falling from their mouths, cracking nuts between their teeth, a live chicken pecking at my foot—all looking, screaming, gawking . . . at her.

[*The upstage area is suddenly hit with a harsh white light. It has become the stage for the Chinese opera performance. Two dancers enter, along with Song. Gallimard stands apart, watching. Song glides gracefully amidst the two dancers. Drums suddenly slam to a halt. Song strikes a pose, looking straight at Gallimard. Dancers exit. Light change. Pause, then Song walks right off the stage and straight up to Gallimard.*]

SONG. Yes. You. White man. I'm looking straight at you.

GALLIMARD. Me?

SONG. You see any other white men? It was too easy to spot you. How often does a man in my audience come in a tie?

[*Song starts to remove her costume. Underneath, she wears simple baggy clothes. They are now backstage. The show is over.*]

SONG. So, you are an adventurous imperialist?

GALLIMARD. I . . . thought it would further my education.

SONG. It took you four weeks. Why?

GALLIMARD. I've been busy.

SONG. Well, education has always been undervalued in the West, hasn't it?

GALLIMARD [*Laughing*]. I don't think it's true.

SONG. No, you wouldn't. You're a Westerner. How can you objectively judge your own values?

GALLIMARD. I think it's possible to achieve some distance.

SONG. Do you? [*Pause*] It stinks in here. Let's go.

GALLIMARD. These are the smells of your loyal fans.

SONG. I love them for being my fans, I hate the smell they leave behind. I too can distance myself from my people. [*She looks around, then whispers in his ear*] "Art for the masses" is a shitty excuse to keep artists poor. [*She pops a cigarette in her mouth*] Be a gentleman, will you? And light my cigarette.

[*Gallimard fumbles for a match.*]

GALLIMARD. I don't . . . smoke.

SONG [*Lighting her own*]. Your loss. Had you lit my cigarette, I might have blown a puff of smoke right between your eyes. Come.

[*They start to walk about the stage. It is a summer night on the Beijing streets. Sounds of the city play on the house speakers.*]

SONG. How I wish there were even a tiny cafe to sit in. With cappuccinos, and men in tuxedos and bad expatriate jazz.

GALLIMARD. If my history serves me correctly, you weren't even allowed into the clubs in Shanghai before the Revolution.

SONG. Your history serves you poorly, Monsieur Gallimard. True, there were signs reading "No dogs and Chinamen." But a woman, especially a delicate Oriental woman—we always go where we please. Could you imagine it otherwise? Clubs in China filled with pasty, big-thighed white women, while thousands of slender lotus blossoms wait just outside the door? Never. The clubs would be empty. [*Beat*] We have always held a certain fascination for you Caucasian men, have we not?

GALLIMARD. But . . . that fascination is imperialist, or so you tell me.

SONG. Do you believe everything I tell you? Yes. It is always imperialist. But sometimes . . . sometimes, it is also mutual. Oh—this is my flat.

GALLIMARD. I didn't even—

SONG. Thank you. Come another time and we will further expand your mind.

[*Song exits. Gallimard continues roaming the streets as he speak to us.*]

GALLIMARD. What was that? What did she mean, "Sometimes . . . it is mutual?" Women do not flirt with me. And I normally can't talk to them. But tonight, I held up my end of the conversation.

SCENE IX

Gallimard's bedroom. Beijing. 1960.
    Helga enters.

HELGA. You didn't tell me you'd be home late.

GALLIMARD. I didn't intend to. Something came up.

HELGA. Oh? Like what?

GALLIMARD. I went to the . . . to the Dutch ambassador's home.

HELGA. Again?

GALLIMARD. There was a reception for a visiting scholar. He's writing a six-volume treatise on the Chinese revolution. We all gathered that meant he'd have to live here long enough to actually write six volumes, and we all expressed our deepest sympathies.

HELGA. Well, I had a good night too. I went with the ladies to a martial arts demonstration. Some of those men—when they break those thick boards—[She mimes fanning herself] whoo-whoo!

[Helga exits. Lights dim.]

GALLIMARD. I lied to my wife. Why? I've never had any reason to lie before. But what reason did I have tonight? I didn't do anything wrong. That night, I had a dream. Other people, I've been told, have dreams where angels appear. Or dragons, or Sophia Loren in a towel. In my dream, Marc from school appeared.

[Marc enters, in a nightshirt and cap.]

MARC. Rene! You met a girl!

[Gallimard and Marc stumble down the Beijing streets. Night sounds over the speakers.]

GALLIMARD. It's not that amazing, thank you.

MARC. No! It's so monumental, I heard about it halfway around the world in my sleep!

GALLIMARD. I've met girls before, you know.

MARC. Name one. I've come across time and space to congratulate you. [He hands Gallimard a bottle of wine]

GALLIMARD. Marc, this is expensive.

MARC. On those rare occasions when you become a formless spirit, why not steal the best?

[Marc pops open the bottle, begins to share it with Gallimard.]

GALLIMARD. You embarrass me. She . . . there's no reason to think she likes me.

MARC. "Sometimes, it is mutual"?

GALLIMARD. Oh.

MARC. "Mutual"? "Mutual"? What does that mean?

GALLIMARD. You heard!

MARC. It means the money is in the bank, you only have to write the check!

GALLIMARD. I am a married man!

MARC. And an excellent one too. I cheated after . . . six months. Then again and again, until now—three hundred girls in twelve years.

GALLIMARD. I don't think we should hold that up as a model.

MARC. Of course not! My life—it is disgusting! Phooey! Phooey! But, you—you are the model husband.

GALLIMARD. Anyway, it's impossible. I'm a foreigner.

MARC. Ah, yes. She cannot love you, it is taboo, but something deep inside her heart . . . she cannot help herself . . . she must surrender to you. It is her destiny.

GALLIMARD. How do you imagine all this?

MARC. The same way you do. It's an old story. It's in our blood. They fear us, Rene. Their women fear us. And their men—their men hate us. And, you know something? They are all correct.

[They spot a light in a window.]

MARC. There! There, Rene!

GALLIMARD. It's her window.

MARC. Late at night—it burns. The light—it burns for you.

GALLIMARD. I won't look. It's not respectful.

MARC. We don't have to be respectful. We're foreign devils.

[Enter Song, in a sheer robe. The "One Fine Day" aria creeps in over the speakers. With her back to us, Song mimes attending to her toilette. Her robe comes loose, revealing her white shoulders.]

MARC. All your life you've waited for a beautiful girl who would lay down for you. All your life you've smiled like a saint when it's happened to every other man you know. And you see them in magazines and you see them in movies. And you wonder, what's wrong with me? Will anyone beautiful ever want me? As the years pass, your hair thins and you struggle to hold onto even your hopes. Stop struggling, Rene. The wait is over. [He exits]

GALLIMARD. Marc? Marc?

[At that moment, Song, her back still towards us, drops her robe. A second of her naked back, then a sound cue: a phone ringing, very loud. Blackout, followed in the next beat by a special up on the bedroom area, where a phone now sits. Gallimard stumbles across the stage and picks up the phone. Sound cue out. Over the course of his conversation, area lights fill in the vicinity of his bed. It is the following morning.]

GALLIMARD. Yes? Hello?

SONG [*Offstage*]. Is it very early?

GALLIMARD. Why, yes.

SONG[*Offstage*]. How early?

GALLIMARD. It's . . . it's 5:30. Why are you—?

SONG [*Offstage*]. But it's light outside. Already.

GALLIMARD. It is. The sun must be in confusion today.

[*Over the course of Song's next speech, her upstage special comes up again. She sits in a chair, legs crossed, in a robe, telephone to her ear.*]

SONG. I waited until I saw the sun. That was as much discipline as I could manage for one night. Do you forgive me?

GALLIMARD. Of course . . . for what?

SONG. Then I'll ask you quickly. Are you really interested in the opera?

GALLIMARD. Why, yes. Yes I am.

SONG. Then come again next Thursday. I am playing *The Drunken Beauty*. May I count on you?

GALLIMARD. Yes. You may.

SONG. Perfect. Well, I must be getting to bed. I'm exhausted. It's been a very long night for me.

[*Song hangs up; special on her goes off. Gallimard begins to dress for work.*]

SCENE X

Song Liling's apartment. Beijing. 1960.

GALLIMARD. I returned to the opera that next week, and the week after that . . . she keeps our meetings so short—perhaps fifteen, twenty minutes at most. So I am left each week with a thirst which is intensified. In this way, fifteen weeks have gone by. I am starting to doubt the words of my friend Marc. But no, not really. In my heart, I know she has . . . an interest in me. I suspect this is her way. She is outwardly bold and outspoken, yet her heart is shy and afraid. It is the Oriental in her at war with her Western education.

SONG [*Offstage*]. I will be out in an instant. Ask the servant for anything you want.

GALLIMARD. Tonight, I have finally been invited to enter her apartment. Though the idea is almost beyond belief, I believe she is afraid of me.

[*Gallimard looks around the room. He picks up a picture in a frame, studies it. Without his noticing, Song enters, dressed elegantly in a black gown from the twenties. She stands in the doorway looking like Anna May Wong.*]

SONG. That is my father.

GALLIMARD [*Surprised*]. Mademoiselle Song . . .

[*She glides up to him, snatches away the picture.*]

SONG. It is very good that he did not live to see the Revolution. They would, no doubt, have made him kneel on broken glass. Not that he didn't deserve such a punishment. But he is my father. I would've hated to see it happen.

GALLIMARD. I'm very honored that you've allowed me to visit your home.

[*Song curtsys.*]

SONG. Thank you. Oh! Haven't you been poured any tea?

GALLIMARD. I'm really not—

SONG [*To her offstage servant*]. Shu-Fang! Cha! Kwailah! [*To Gallimard*] I'm sorry. You want everything to be perfect—

GALLIMARD. Please.

SONG. —and before the evening even begins—

GALLIMARD. I'm really not thirsty.

SONG. —it's ruined.

GALLIMARD [*Sharply*]. Mademoiselle Song!

[*Song sits down.*]

SONG. I'm sorry.

GALLIMARD. What are you apologizing for now?

[*Pause; Song starts to giggle.*]

SONG. I don't know!

[*Gallimard laughs.*]

GALLIMARD. Exactly my point.

SONG. Oh, I am silly. Lightheaded. I promise not to apologize for anything else tonight, do you hear me?

GALLIMARD. That's a good girl.

[*Shu-Fang, a servant girl, comes out with a tea tray and starts to pour.*]

SONG [*To Shu-Fang*]. No! I'll pour myself for the gentleman!

[*Shu-Fang, staring at Gallimard, exits.*]

SONG. No, I . . . I don't even know why I invited you up.

GALLIMARD. Well, I'm glad you did.

[*Song looks around the room.*]

SONG. There is an element of danger to your presense.

GALLIMARD. Oh?

SONG. You must know.

GALLIMARD. It doesn't concern me. We both know why I'm here.

SONG. It doesn't concern me either. No . . . well perhaps . . .

GALLIMARD. What?

SONG. Perhaps I am slightly afraid of scandal.

GALLIMARD. What are we doing?

SONG. I'm entertaining you. In my parlor.

GALLIMARD. In France, that would hardly—

SONG. France. France is a country living in the modern era. Perhaps even ahead of it. China is a nation whose soul is firmly rooted two thousand years in the past. What I do, even pouring the tea for you now . . . it has . . . implications. The walls and windows say so. Even my own heart, strapped inside this Western dress . . . even it says things—things I don't care to hear.

[*Song hands Gallimard a cup of tea. Gallimard puts his hand over both the teacup and Song's hand.*]

GALLIMARD. This is a beautiful dress.

SONG. Don't.

GALLIMARD. What?

SONG. I don't even know if it looks right on me.

GALLIMARD. Believe me—

SONG. You are from France. You see so many beautiful women.

GALLIMARD. France? Since when are the European women—?

SONG. Oh! What am I trying to do, anyway?!

[*Song runs to the door, composes herself, then turns towards Gallimard.*]

SONG. Monsieur Gallimard, perhaps you should go.

GALLIMARD. But . . . why?

SONG. There's something wrong about this.

GALLIMARD. I don't see what.

SONG. I feel . . . I am not myself.

GALLIMARD. No. You're nervous.

SONG. Please. Hard as I try to be modern, to speak like a man, to hold a Western woman's strong face up to my own . . . in the end, I fail. A small, frightened heart beats too quickly and gives me away. Monsieur Gallimard, I'm a Chinese girl. I've never . . . never invited a man up to my flat before. The forwardness of my actions makes my skin burn.

GALLIMARD. What are you afraid of? Certainly not me, I hope.

SONG. I'm a modest girl.

GALLIMARD. I know. And very beautiful. [*He touches her hair*]

SONG. Please—go now. The next time you see me, I shall again be myself.

GALLIMARD. I like you the way you are right now.

SONG. You are a cad.

GALLIMARD. What do you expect? I'm a foreign devil.

[*Gallimard walks downstage. Song exits.*]

GALLIMARD [*To us*]. Did you hear the way she talked about Western women? Much differently than the first night. She does—she feels inferior to them—and to me.

SCENE XI

The French embassy. Beijing, 1960.
Gallimard moves towards a desk.

GALLIMARD. I determined to try an experiment. In *Madame Butterfly*, Cio-Cio-San fears that the Western man who catches a butterfly will pierce its heart with a needle, then leave it to perish. I began to wonder: had I, too, caught a butterfly who would writhe on a needle?

[*Marc enters, dressed as a bureaucrat, holding a stack of papers. As Gallimard speaks, Marc hands papers to him. He peruses, then signs, stamps or rejects them.*]

GALLIMARD. Over the next five weeks, I worked like a dynamo. I stopped going to the opera, I didn't phone or write her. I knew this little flower was waiting for me to call, and, as I wickedly refused to do so, I felt for the first time that rush of power—the absolute power of a man.

[*Marc continues acting as the bureaucrat, but he now speaks as himself.*]

MARC. Rene! It's me!

GALLIMARD. Marc—I hear your voice everywhere now. Even in the midst of work.

MARC. That's because I'm watching you—all the time.

GALLIMARD. You were always the most popular guy in school.

MARC. Well, there's no guarantee of failure in life like happiness in high school. Somehow I knew I'd end up in the suburbs working for Renault and you'd be in the Orient picking exotic women off the trees. And they say there's no justice.

GALLIMARD. That's why you were my friend?

MARC. I gave you a little of my life, so that now you can give me some of yours [*Pause*] Remember Isabelle?

GALLIMARD. Of course I remember! She was my first experience.

MARC. We all wanted to ball her. But she only wanted me.

GALLIMARD. I had her.

MARC. Right. You balled her.

GALLIMARD. You were the only one who ever believed me.

MARC. Well, there's a good reason for that. [*Beat*] C'mon. You must've guessed.

GALLIMARD. You told me to wait in the bushes by the cafeteria that night. The next thing I knew, she was on me. Dress up in the air.

MARC. She never wore underwear.

GALLIMARD. My arms were pinned to the dirt.

MARC. She loved the superior position. A girl ahead of her time.

GALLIMARD. I looked up, and there was this woman . . . bouncing up and down on my loins.

MARC. Screaming, right?

GALLIMARD. Screaming, and breaking off the branches all around me, and pounding my butt up and down into the dirt.

MARC. Huffing and puffing like a locomotive.

GALLIMARD. And in the middle of all this, the leaves were getting into my mouth, my legs were losing circulation, I thought, "God. So this is *it*?"

MARC. You thought that?

GALLIMARD. Well, I was worried about my legs falling off.

MARC. You didn't have a good time?

GALLIMARD. No, that's not what I—I had a great time!

MARC. You're sure?

GALLIMARD. Yeah. Really.

MARC. 'Cuz I wanted you to have a good time.

GALLIMARD. I did.

[*Pause.*]

MARC. Shit. [*Pause*] When all is said and done, she was kind of a lousy lay, wasn't she? I mean, there was a lot of energy there, but you never knew what she was doing with it. Like when she yelled "I'm coming!"—hell, it was so loud, you wanted to go "Look, it's not that big a deal."

GALLIMARD. I got scared. I thought she meant someone was actually coming. [*Pause*] But, Marc?

MARC. What?

GALLIMARD. Thanks.

MARC. Oh, don't mention it.

GALLIMARD. It was my first experience.

MARC. Yeah. You got her.

GALLIMARD. I got her.

MARC. Wait! Look at that letter again!

[*Gallimard picks up one of the papers he's been stamping and rereads it.*]

GALLIMARD [*To us*]. After six weeks, they began to arrive. The letters.

[*Upstage special on Song, as Madame Butterfly. The scene is underscored by the "Love Duet."*]

SONG. Did we fight? I do not know. Is the opera no longer of interest to you? Please come—my audiences miss the white devil in their midst.

[*Gallimard looks up from the letter, towards us.*]

GALLIMARD [*To us*]. A concession, but much too dignified. [*Beat; he discards the letter*] I skipped the opera again that week to complete a position paper on trade.

[*The bureaucrat hands him another letter.*]

SONG. Six weeks have passed since last we met. Is this your practice—to leave friends in the lurch? Sometimes I hate you, sometimes I hate myself, but always I miss you.

GALLIMARD [*to us*]. Better, but I don't like the way she calls me "friend." When a woman calls a man her "friend," she's calling him a eunuch or a homosexual. [*Beat; he discards the letter*] I was absent from the opera for the seventh week, feeling a sudden urge to clean out my files.

[*Bureaucrat hands him another letter.*]

SONG. Your rudeness is beyond belief. I don't deserve this cruelty. Don't bother to call. I'll have you turned away at the door.

GALLIMARD [*To us*]. I didn't. [*He discards the letter; bureaucrat hands him another*] And then finally, the letter that concluded my experiment.

SONG. I am out of words. I can hide behind dignity no longer. What do you want? I have already given you my shame.

[*Gallimard gives the letter back to Marc, slowly. Special on Song fades out.*]

GALLIMARD [*To us*]. Reading it, I became suddenly ashamed. Yes, my experiment had been a success. She was turning on my needle. But the victory seemed hollow.

MARC. Hollow?! Are you crazy?

GALLIMARD. Nothing, Marc. Please go away.

MARC [*Exiting, with papers*]. Haven't I taught you something?

GALLIMARD. "I have already given you my shame." I had to attend a reception that evening. On the way, I felt sick. If there is a God, surely he would punish me now. I had finally gained power over a beautiful woman, only to abuse it cruelly. There must be justice in the world. I had the strange feeling that the ax would fall this very evening.

SCENE XII

Ambassador Toulon's residence. Beijing. 1960.
    Sound cue: party noises. Light change. We are now in a spacious residence. Toulon, the French ambassador, enters and taps Gallimard on the shoulder.

TOULON. Gallimard? Can I have a word? Over here.

GALLIMARD [*To us*]. Manuel Toulon. French ambassador to China. He likes to think of us all as his children. Rather like God.

TOULON. Look, Gallimard, there's not much to say. I've liked you. From the day you walked in. You were no leader, but you were tidy and efficient.

GALLIMARD. Thank you, sir.

TOULON. Don't jump the gun. Okay, our needs in China are changing. It's embarrassing that we lost Indochina. Someone just wasn't on the ball there. I don't mean you personally, of course.

GALLIMARD. Thank you, sir.

TOULON. We're going to be doing a lot more information-gathering in the future. The nature of our work here is changing. Some people are just going to have to go. It's nothing personal.

GALLIMARD. Oh.

TOULON. Want to know a secret? Vice-Consul LeBon is being transferred.

GALLIMARD [*To us*]. My immediate superior!

TOULON. And most of his department.

GALLIMARD [*To us*]. Just as I feared! God has seen my evil heart—

TOULON. But not you.

GALLIMARD [*To us*]. —and he's taking her away just as . . . [*To Toulon*] Excuse me, sir?

TOULON. Scare you? I think I did. Cheer up, Gallimard. I want you to replace LeBon as vice-consul.

GALLIMARD. You—? Yes, well, thank you, sir.

TOULON. Anytime.

GALLIMARD. I . . . accept with great humility.

TOULON. Humility won't be part of the job. You're going to coordinate the revamped intelligence division. Want to know a secret? A year ago, you would've been out. But the past few months, I don't know how it happened, you've become this new aggressive confident . . . thing. And they also tell me you get along with the Chinese. So I think you're a lucky man, Gallimard. Congratulations.

[*They shake hands. Toulon exits. Party noises out. Gallimard stumbles across a darkened stage.*]

GALLIMARD. Vice-consul? Impossible! As I stumbled out of the party, I saw it written across the sky: There is no God. Or, no—say that there is a God. But that God . . . understands. Of course! God who creates Eve to serve Adam, who blesses Solomon with his harem but ties Jezebel to a burning bed— that God is a man. And he understands! At age thirty-nine, I was suddenly initiated into the way of the world.

SCENE XIII

Song Liling's apartment. Beijing. 1960.
Song enters, in a sheer dressing gown.

SONG. Are you crazy?

GALLIMARD. Mademoiselle Song—

SONG. To come here—at this hour? After . . . after eight weeks?

GALLIMARD. It's the most amazing—

SONG. You bang on my door? Scare my servants, scandalize the neighbors?

GALLIMARD. I've been promoted. To vice-consul.

[Pause.]

SONG. And what is that supposed to mean to me?

GALLIMARD. Are you my Butterfly?

SONG. What are you saying?

GALLIMARD. I've come tonight for an answer: are you my Butterfly?

SONG. Don't you know already?

GALLIMARD. I want you to say it.

SONG. I don't want to say it.

GALLIMARD. So, that is your answer?

SONG. You know how I feel about—

GALLIMARD. I do remember one thing.

SONG. What?

GALLIMARD. In the letter I received today.

SONG. Don't.

GALLIMARD. "I have already given you my shame."

SONG. It's enough that I even wrote it.

GALLIMARD. Well, then—

SONG. I shouldn't have it spashed across my face.

GALLIMARD. —if that's all true—

SONG. Stop!

GALLIMARD. Then what is one more short answer?

SONG. I don't want to!

GALLIMARD. Are you my Butterfly? [Silence; he crosses the room and begins to touch her hair] I want from you honesty. There should be nothing false between us. No false pride.

[Pause.]

SONG. Yes, I am. I am your Butterfly.

GALLIMARD. Then let me be honest with you. It is because of you that I was promoted tonight. You have changed my life forever. My little Butterfly, there should be no more secrets: I love you.

[He starts to kiss her roughly. She resists slightly.]

SONG. No . . . no . . . gently . . . please, I've never . . .

GALLIMARD. No?

SONG. I've tried to appear experienced, but . . . the truth is . . . no.

GALLIMARD. Are you cold?

SONG. Yes. Cold.

GALLIMARD. Then we will go very, very slowly.

[He starts to caress her; her gown begins to open.]

SONG. No . . . let me . . . keep my clothes . . .

GALLIMARD. But . . .

SONG. Please . . . it all frightens me. I'm a modest Chinese girl.

GALLIMARD. My poor little treasure.

SONG. I am your treasure. Though inexperienced, I am not . . . ignorant. They teach us things, our mothers, about pleasing a man.

GALLIMARD. Yes?

SONG. I'll do my best to make you happy. Turn off the lights.

[Gallimard gets up and heads for a lamp. Song, propped up on one elbow, tosses her hair back and smiles.]

SONG. Monsieur Gallimard?

GALLIMARD. Yes, Butterfly?

SONG. "Vieni, vieni!"

GALLIMARD. "Come, darling."

SONG. "Ah! Dolce notte!"

GALLIMARD. "Beautiful night."

SONG. "Tutto estatico d'amor ride il ciel!"

GALLIMARD. "All ecstatic with love, the heavens are filled with laughter."

[He turns off the lamp. Blackout.]

Act II

SCENE I

M. Gallimard's cell. Paris. Present.

    Lights up on Gallimard. He sits in his cell, reading from a leaflet.

GALLIMARD. This, from a contemporary critic's commentary on *Madame Butterfly*: "Pinkerton suffers from . . . being an obnoxious bounder whom every man in the audience itches to kick." Bully for us men in the audience! Then, in the same note: "Butterfly is the most irresistibly appealing of Puccini's

'Little Women.' Watching the succession of her humiliations is like watching a child under torture." [*He tosses the pamphlet over his shoulder*] I suggest that, while we men may all want to kick Pinkerton, very few of us would pass up the opportunity to *be* Pinkerton.

[*Gallimard moves out of his cell.*]

SCENE II

Gallimard and Butterfly's flat. Beijing. 1960.
We are in a simple but well-decorated parlor. Gallimard moves to sit on a sofa, while Song, dressed in a chong sam, enters and curls up at his feet.

GALLIMARD [*To us*]. We secured a flat on the outskirts of Peking. Butterfly, as I was calling her now, decorated our "home" with Western furniture and Chinese antiques. And there, on a few stolen afternoons or evenings each week, Butterfly commenced her education.

SONG. The Chinese men—they keep us down.

GALLIMARD. Even in the "New Society"?

SONG. In the "New Society," we are all kept ignorant equally. That's one of the exciting things about loving a Western man. I know you are not threatened by a woman's education.

GALLIMARD. I'm no saint, Butterfly.

SONG. But you come from a progressive society.

GALLIMARD. We're not always reminding each other how "old" we are, if that's what you mean.

SONG. Exactly. We Chinese—once, I suppose, it is true, we ruled the world. But so what? How much more exciting to be part of the society ruling the world today. Tell me—what's happening in Vietnam?

GALLIMARD. Oh, Butterfly—you want me to bring my work home?

SONG. I want to know what you know. To be impressed by my man. It's not the particulars so much as the fact that you're making decisions which change the shape of the world.

GALLIMARD. Not the world. At best, a small corner.

[*Toulon enters, and sits at a desk upstage.*]

SCENE III

French embassy. Beijing. 1961.
Gallimard moves downstage, to Toulon's desk. Song remains upstage, watching.

TOULON. And a more troublesome corner is hard to imagine.

GALLIMARD. So, the Americans plan to begin bombing?

TOULON. This is very secret, Gallimard: yes. The Americans don't have an embassy here. They're asking us to be their eyes and ears. Say Jack Kennedy signed an order to bomb North Vietnam, Laos. How would the Chinese react?

GALLIMARD. I think the Chinese will squawk—

TOULON. Uh-huh.

GALLIMARD. —but, in their hearts, they don't even like Ho Chi Minh.

[*Pause.*]

TOULON. What a bunch of jerks. Vietnam was *our* colony. Not only didn't the Americans help us fight to keep them, but now, seven years later, they've come back to grab the territory for themselves. It's very irritating.

GALLIMARD. With all due respect, sir, why should the Americans have won our war for us back in '54 if we didn't have the will to win it ourselves?

TOULON. You're kidding, aren't you?

[*Pause.*]

GALLIMARD. The Orientals simply want to be associated with whoever shows the most strength and power. You live with the Chinese, sir. Do you think they like Communism?

TOULON. I live in China. Not with the Chinese.

GALLIMARD. Well, I—

TOULON. *You* live with the Chinese.

GALLIMARD. Excuse me?

TOULON. I can't keep a secret.

GALLIMARD. What are you saying?

TOULON. Only that I'm not immune to gossip. So, you're keeping a native mistress. Don't answer. It's none of my business. [*Pause*] I'm sure she must be gorgeous.

GALLIMARD. Well . . .

TOULON. I'm impressed. You have the stamina to go out into the streets and hunt one down. Some of us have to be content with the wives of the expatriate community.

GALLIMARD. I do feel . . . fortunate.

TOULON. So, Gallimard, you've got the inside knowledge—what *do* the Chinese think?

GALLIMARD. Deep down, they miss the old days. You know, cappuccinos, men in tuxedos—

TOULON. So what do we tell the Americans about Vietnam?

GALLIMARD. Tell them there's a natural affinity between the West and the Orient.

TOULON. And that you speak from experience?

GALLIMARD. The Orientals are people too. They want the good things we can give them. If the Americans demonstrate the will to win, the Vietnamese will welcome them into a mutually beneficial union.

TOULON. I don't see how the Vietnamese can stand up to American firepower.

GALLIMARD. Orientals will always submit to a greater force.

TOULON. I'll note your opinions in my report. The Americans always love to hear how "welcome" they'll be. [*He starts to exit*]

GALLIMARD. Sir?

TOULON. Mmmm?

GALLIMARD. This . . . rumor you've heard.

TOULON. Uh-huh?

GALLIMARD. How . . . widespread do you think it is?

TOULON. It's only widespread within this embassy. Where nobody talks because everybody is guilty. We were worried about you, Gallimard. We thought you were the only one here without a secret. Now you go and find a lotus blossom . . . and top us all. [*He exits*]

GALLIMARD [*To us*]. Toulon knows! And he approves! I was learning the benefits of being a man. We form our own clubs, sit behind thick doors, smoke—and celebrate the fact that we're still boys. [*He starts to move downstage, towards Song*] So, over the—

[*Suddenly Comrade Chin enters. Gallimard backs away.*]

GALLIMARD [*To Song*]. No! Why does she have to come in?

SONG. Rene, be sensible. How can they understand the story without her? Now, don't embarrass yourself.

[*Gallimard moves down center.*]

GALLIMARD [*To us*]. Now, you will see why my story is

so amusing to so many people. Why they snicker at parties in disbelief. Please—try to understand it from my point of view. We are all prisoners of our time and place. [*He exits*]

SCENE IV

Gallimard and Butterfly's flat. Beijing. 1961.

SONG [*To us*]. 1961. The flat Monsieur Gallimard rented for us. An evening after he has gone.

CHIN. Okay, see if you can find out when the Americans plan to start bombing Vietnam. If you can find out what cities, even better.

SONG. I'll do my best, but I don't want to arouse his suspicions.

CHIN. Yeah, sure, of course. So, what else?

SONG. The Americans will increase troops in Vietnam to 170,000 soldiers with 120,000 militia and 11,000 American advisors.

CHIN [*Writing*]. Wait, wait. 120,000 militia and—

SONG. —11,000 American—

CHIN. —American advisors. [*Beat*] How do you remember so much?

SONG. I'm an actor.

CHIN. Yeah. [*Beat*] Is that how come you dress like that?

SONG. Like what, Miss Chin?

CHIN. Like that dress! You're wearing a dress. And every time I come here, you're wearing a dress. Is that because you're an actor? Or what?

SONG. It's a . . . disguise, Miss Chin.

CHIN. Actors, I think they're all weirdos. My mother tells me actors are like gamblers or prostitutes or—

SONG. It helps me in my assignment.

[*Pause.*]

CHIN. You're not gathering information in any way that violates Communist Party principles, are you?

SONG. Why would I do that?

CHIN. Just checking. Remember: when working for the Great Proletarian State, you represent our Chairman Mao in every position you take.

SONG. I'll try to imagine the Chairman taking my positions.

CHIN. We all think of him this way. Good-bye, comrade. [*She starts to exit*] Comrade?

SONG. Yes?

CHIN. Don't forget: there is no homosexuality in China!

SONG. Yes, I've heard.

CHIN. Just checking. [*She exits*]

SONG [*To us*]. What passes for a woman in modern China.

[*Gallimard sticks his head out from the wings.*]

GALLIMARD. Is she gone?

SONG. Yes, Rene. Please continue in your own fashion.

SCENE V

Beijing. 1961–63.
Gallimard moves to the couch where Song still sits. He lies down in her lap, and she strokes his forehead.

GALLIMARD [*To us*]. And so, over the years 1961, '62, '63, we settled into our routine, Butterfly and I. She would always have prepared a light snack and then, ever so delicately, and only if I agreed, she would start to pleasure me. With her hands, her mouth . . . too many ways to explain, and too sad, given my present situation. But mostly we would talk. About my life. Perhaps there is nothing more rare than to find a woman who passionately listens.

[*Song remains upstage, listening, as Helga enters and plays a scene downstage with Gallimard.*]

HELGA. Rene, I visited Dr. Bolleart this morning.

GALLIMARD. Why? Are you ill?

HELGA. No, no. You see, I wanted to ask him . . . that question we've been discussing.

GALLIMARD. And I told you, it's only a matter of time. Why did you bring a doctor into this? We just have to keep trying—like a crapshoot, actually.

HELGA. I went, I'm sorry. But listen: he says there's nothing wrong with me.

GALLIMARD. You see? Now, will you stop—?

HELGA. Rene, he says he'd like you to go in and take some tests.

GALLIMARD. Why? So he can find there's nothing wrong with both of us?

HELGA. Rene, I don't ask for much. One trip! One visit! And then, whatever you want to do about it—you decide.

GALLIMARD. You're assuming he'll find something defective!

HELGA. No! Of course not! Whatever he finds—if he finds nothing, we decide what to do about nothing! But go!

GALLIMARD. If he finds nothing, we keep trying. Just like we do now.

HELGA. But at least we'll know! [*Pause*] I'm sorry. [*She starts to exit*]

GALLIMARD. Do you really want me to see Dr. Bolleart?

HELGA. Only if you want a child, Rene. We have to face the fact that time is running out. Only if you want a child. [*She exits*]

GALLIMARD [*To Song*]. I'm a modern man, Butterfly. And yet, I don't want to go. It's the same old voodoo. I feel like God himself is laughing at me if I can't produce a child.

SONG. You men of the West—you're obsessed by your odd desire for equality. Your wife can't give you a child, and *you're* going to the doctor?

GALLIMARD. Well, you see, she's already gone.

SONG. And because this incompetent can't find the defect, you now have to subject yourself to him? It's unnatural.

GALLIMARD. Well, what is the "natural" solution?

SONG. In Imperial China, when a man found that one wife was inadequate, he turned to another—to give him his son.

GALLIMARD. What do you—? I can't . . . marry you, yet.

SONG. Please. I'm not asking you to be my husband. But I am already your wife.

GALLIMARD. Do you want to . . . have my child?

SONG. I thought you'd never ask.

GALLIMARD. But, your career . . . your—

SONG. Phooey on my career! That's your Western mind, twisting itself into strange shapes again. Of course I love my career. But what would I love most of all? To feel something inside me—day and night—something I know is yours. [*Pause*] Promise me . . . you won't go to this doctor. Who is this Western quack to set himself as judge over the man I love? I know who is a man, and who is not. [*She exits*]

GALLIMARD [*To us*]. Dr. Bolleart? Of course I didn't go. What man would?

SCENE VI

Beijing. 1963.

Party noises over the house speakers. Renee enters, wearing a revealing gown.

GALLIMARD. 1963. A party at the Austrian embassy. None of us could remember the Austrian ambassador's name, which seemed somehow appropriate. [*To Renee*] So, I tell the Americans, Diem must go. The U.S. wants to be respected by the Vietnamese, and yet they're propping up this nobody seminarian as her president. A man whose claim to fame is his sister-in-law imposing fanatic "moral order" campaigns? Oriental women—when they're good, they're very good, but when they're bad, they're Christians.

RENEE. Yeah.

GALLIMARD. And what do you do?

RENEE. I'm a student. My father exports a lot of useless stuff to the Third World.

GALLIMARD. How useless?

RENEE. You know. Squirt guns, confectioner's sugar, hula hoops . . .

GALLIMARD. I'm sure they appreciate the sugar.

RENEE. I'm here for two years to study Chinese.

GALLIMARD. Two years?

RENEE. That's what everybody says.

GALLIMARD. When did you arrive?

RENEE. Three weeks ago.

GALLIMARD. And?

RENEE. I like it. It's primitive, but . . . well, this is the place to learn Chinese, so here I am.

GALLIMARD. Why Chinese?

RENEE. I think it'll be important someday.

GALLIMARD. You do?

RENEE. Don't ask me when, but . . . that's what I think.

GALLIMARD. Well, I agree with you. One hundred percent. That's very farsighted.

RENEE. Yeah. Well of course, my father thinks I'm a complete weirdo.

GALLIMARD. He'll thank you someday.

RENEE. Like when the Chinese start buying hula hoops?

GALLIMARD. There're a billion bellies out there.

RENEE. And if they end up taking over the world—well, then I'll be lucky to know Chinese too, right?

[*Pause.*]

GALLIMARD. At this point, I don't see how the Chinese can possibly take—

RENEE. You know what I *don't* like about China?

GALLIMARD. Excuse me? No—what?

RENEE. Nothing to do at night.

GALLIMARD. You come to parties at embassies like everyone else.

RENEE. Yeah, but they get out at ten. And then what?

GALLIMARD. I'm afraid the Chinese idea of a dance hall is a dirt floor and a man with a flute.

RENEE. Are you married?

GALLIMARD. Yes. Why?

RENEE. You wanna . . . fool around?

[*Pause.*]

GALLIMARD. Sure.

RENEE. I'll wait for you outside. What's your name?

GALLIMARD. Gallimard. Rene.

RENEE. Weird. I'm Renee too. [*She exits*]

GALLIMARD [*To us*]. And so, I embarked on my first extra-extramarital affair. Renee was picture perfect. With a body like those girls in the magazines. If I put a tissue paper over my eyes, I wouldn't have been able to tell the difference. And it was exciting to be with someone who wasn't afraid to be seen completely naked. But is it possible for a woman to be *too* uninhibited, *too* willing, so as to seem almost too . . . masculine?

[*Chuck Berry blares from the house speakers, then comes down in volume as Renee enters, toweling her hair.*]

RENEE. You have a nice weenie.

GALLIMARD. What?

RENEE. Penis. You have a nice penis.

GALLIMARD. Oh. Well, thank you. That's very . . .

RENEE. What—can't take a compliment?

GALLIMARD. No, it's very . . . reassuring.

RENEE. But most girls don't come out and say it, huh?

GALLIMARD. And also . . . what did you call it?

RENEE. Oh. Most girls don't call it a "weenie," huh?

GALLIMARD. It sounds very—

RENEE. Small, I know.

GALLIMARD. I was going to say, "young."

RENEE. Yeah. Young, small, same thing. Most guys are pretty, uh, sensitive about that. Like, you know, I had a boyfriend back home in Denmark. I got mad at him once and called him a little weeniehead. He got so mad! He said at least I should call him a great big weeniehead.

GALLIMARD. I suppose I just say "penis."

RENEE. Yeah. That's pretty clinical. There's "cock," but that sound like a chicken. And "prick" is painful, and "dick" is like you're talking about someone who's not in the room.

GALLIMARD. Yes. It's a . . . bigger problem than I imagined.

RENEE. I—I think maybe it's because I really don't know what to do with them—that's why I call them "weenies."

GALLIMARD. Well, you did quite well with . . . mine.

RENEE. Thanks, but I mean really *do* with them. Like, okay, have you ever looked at one? I mean, really?

GALLIMARD. No, I suppose when it's part of you, you sort of take it for granted.

RENEE. I guess. But, like, it just hangs there. This little . . . flap of flesh. And there's so much fuss that we make about it. Like, I think the reason we fight wars is because we wear clothes. Because no one knows—between the men, I mean—who has the bigger . . . weenie. So, if I'm a guy with a small one, I'm going to build a really big building or take over a really big piece of land or write a really long book so the other men don't know, right? But, see, it never really works, that's the problem. I mean, you conquer the country, or whatever, but you're still wearing clothes, so there's no way to prove absolutely whose is bigger or smaller. And that's what we call a civilized society. The whole world run by a bunch of men with pricks the size of pins. [*She exits*]

GALLIMARD [*To us*]. This was simply not acceptable.

[*A high-pitched chime rings through the air. Song, dressed as Butterfly, appears in the upstage special. She is obviously distressed. Her body swoons as she attempts to clip the stems of flowers she's arranging in a vase.*]

GALLIMARD. But I kept up our affair, wildly, for several months. Why? I believe because of Butterfly. She knew the secret I was trying to hide. But, unlike a Western woman, she didn't confront me, threaten, even pout. I remembered the words of Puccini's *Butterfly*.

SONG. "Noi siamo gente avvezza/ alle piccole cose/ umili e silenziose."

GALLIMARD. "I come from a people/ Who are accustomed to little/ Humble and silent." I saw Pinkerton and Butterfly, and what she would say if he were unfaithful . . . nothing. She would cry, alone, into those wildly soft sleeves, once full of possessions, now empty to collect her tears. It was her tears and her silence that excited me, every time I visited Renee.

TOULON [*Offstage*]. Gallimard!

[*Toulon enters. Gallimard turns towards him. During the next section, Song, up center, begins to dance with the flowers. It is a drunken dance, where she breaks small pieces off the stems.*]

TOULON. They're killing him.

GALLIMARD. Who? I'm sorry? What?

TOULON. Bother you to come over at this late hour?

GALLIMARD. No . . . of course not.

TOULON. Not after you hear my secret. Champagne?

GALLIMARD. Um . . . thank you.

TOULON. You're surprised. There's something that you've wanted, Gallimard. No, not a promotion. Next time. Something in the world. You're not aware of this, but there's an informal gossip circle among intelligence agents. And some of ours heard from some of the Americans—

GALLIMARD. Yes?

TOULON. That the U.S. will allow the Vietnamese generals to stage a coup . . . and assassinate President Diem.

[*The chime rings again. Toulon freezes. Gallimard turns upstage and looks at Butterfly, who slowly and deliberately clips a flower off its stem. Gallimard turns back towards Toulon.*]

GALLIMARD. I think . . . that's a very wise move!

[*Toulon unfreezes.*]

TOULON. It's what you've been advocating. A toast?

GALLIMARD. Sure. I consider this a vindication.

TOULON. Not exactly. "To the test. Let's hope you pass."

[*They drink. The chime rings again. Toulon freezes. Gallimard turns upstage, and Song clips another flower.*]

GALLIMARD [*To Toulon*]. The test?

TOULON [*Unfreezing*]. It's a test of everything you've been saying. I personally think the generals probably will stop the Communists. And you'll be a hero. But if anything goes wrong, then your opinions won't be worth a pig's ear. I'm sure that won't happen. But sometimes it's easier when they don't listen to you.

GALLIMARD. They're your opinions too, aren't they?

TOULON. Personally, yes.

GALLIMARD. So we agree.

TOULON. But my opinions aren't on that report. Yours are. Cheers.

[*Toulon turns away from Gallimard and raises his glass. At that instant Song picks up the vase and hurls it to the ground. It shatters. Song sinks down amidst the shards of the vase, in a calm, childlike trance. She sings softly, as if reciting a child's nursery rhyme.*]

SONG [*Repeat as necessary*]. "The whole world over, the white man travels, setting anchor, wherever he likes. Life's not worth living, unless he finds, the finest maidens, of every land . . ."

[*Gallimard turns downstage towards us. Song continues singing.*]

GALLIMARD. I shook as I left his house. That coward! That worm! To put the burden for his decisions on my shoulders!

I started for Renee's. But no, that was all I needed. A schoolgirl who would question the role of the penis in modern society. What I wanted was revenge. A vessel to contain my humiliation. Though I hadn't seen her in several weeks, I headed for Butterfly's.

[*Gallimard enters Song's apartment.*]

SONG. Oh! Rene . . . I was dreaming!

GALLIMARD. You've been drinking?

SONG. If I can't sleep, then yes, I drink. But then, it gives me these dreams which—Rene, it's been almost three weeks since you visited me last.

GALLIMARD. I know. There's been a lot going on in the world.

SONG. Fortunately I am drunk. So I can speak freely. It's not the world, it's you and me. And an old problem. Even the softest skin becomes like leather to a man who's touched it too often. I confess I don't know how to stop it. I don't know how to become another woman.

GALLIMARD. I have a request.

SONG. Is this a solution? Or are you ready to give up the flat?

GALLIMARD. It may be a solution. But I'm sure you won't like it.

SONG. Oh well, that's very important. "Like it?" Do you think I "like" lying here alone, waiting, always waiting for your return? Please—don't worry about what I may not "like."

GALLIMARD. I want to see you . . . naked.

[*Silence.*]

SONG. I thought you understood my modesty. So you want me to—what—strip? Like a big cowboy girl? Shiny pasties on my breasts? Shall I fling my kimono over my head and yell "ya-hoo" in the process? I thought you respected my shame!

GALLIMARD. I believe you gave me your shame many years ago.

SONG. Yes—and it is just like a white devil to use it against me. I can't believe it. I thought myself so repulsed by the passive Oriental and the cruel white man. Now I see—we are always most revolted by the things hidden within us.

GALLIMARD. I just mean—

SONG. Yes?

GALLIMARD. —that it will remove the only barrier left between us.

SONG. No, Rene. Don't couch your request in sweet words. Be yourself—a cad—and know that my love is enough, that I submit—submit to the worst you can give me. [*Pause*] Well, come. Strip me. Whatever happens, know that you have willed it. Our love, in your hands. I'm helpless before my man.

[*Gallimard starts to cross the room.*]

GALLIMARD. Did I not undress her because I knew, somewhere deep down, what I would find? Perhaps. Happiness is so rare that our mind can turn somersaults to protect it.

At the time, I only knew that I was seeing Pinkerton stalking towards his Butterfly, ready to reward her love with his lecherous hands. The image sickened me, pulled me to my knees, so I was crawling towards her like a worm. By the time I reached her, Pinkerton . . . had vanished from my heart. To be replaced by something new, something unnatural, that flew in the face of all I'd learned in the world—something very close to love.

[*He grabs her around the waist; she strokes his hair.*]

GALLIMARD. Butterfly, forgive me.

SONG. Rene . . .

GALLIMARD. For everything. From the start.

SONG. I'm . . .

GALLIMARD. I want to—

SONG. I'm pregnant. [*Beat*] I'm pregnant. [*Beat*] I'm pregnant.

[*Beat.*]

GALLIMARD. I want to marry you!

SCENE VII

Gallimard and Butterfly's flat. Beijing. 1963.

Downstage, Song paces as Comrade Chin reads from her notepad. Upstage, Gallimard is still kneeling. He remains on his knees throughout the scene, watching it.

SONG. I need a baby.

CHIN [From pad]. He's been spotted going to a dorm.

SONG. I need a baby.

CHIN. At the Foreign Language Institute.

SONG. I need a baby.

CHIN. The room of a Danish girl . . . What do you mean, you need a baby?!

SONG. Tell Comrade Kang—last night, the entire mission, it could've ended.

CHIN. What do you mean?

SONG. Tell Kang—he told me to strip.

CHIN. Strip?!

SONG. Write!

CHIN. I tell you, I don't understand nothing about this case anymore. Nothing.

SONG. He told me to strip, and I took a chance. Oh, we Chinese, we know how to gamble.

CHIN [Writing]. ". . . told him to strip."

SONG. My palms were wet, I had to make a split-second decision.

CHIN. Hey! Can you slow down?!

[Pause.]

SONG. You write faster. I'm the artist here. Suddenly, it hit me—"All he wants is for her to submit. Once a woman submits, a man is always ready to become 'generous.' "

CHIN. You're just gonna end up with rough notes.

SONG. And it worked! He gave in! Now, if I can just present him with a baby. A Chinese baby with blond hair—he'll be mine for life!

CHIN. Kang will never agree! The trading of babies has to be a counterrevolutionary act!

SONG. Sometimes, a counterrevolutionary act is necessary to counter a counterrevolutionary act.

[Pause]

CHIN. Wait.

SONG. I need one . . . in seven months. Make sure it's a boy.

CHIN. This doesn't sound like something the Chairman would do. Maybe you'd better talk to Comrade Kang yourself.

SONG. Good. I will.

[Chin gets up to leave.]

SONG. Miss Chin? Why, in the Peking Opera, are women's roles played by men?

CHIN. I don't know. Maybe, a reactionary remnant of male—

SONG. No. [Beat] Because only a man knows how a woman is supposed to act.

[Chin exits. Song turns upstage, towards Gallimard.]

GALLIMARD [Calling after Chin]. Good riddance! [To Song] I could forget all that betrayal in an instant, you know. If you'd just come back and become Butterfly again.

SONG. Fat chance. You're here in prison, rotting in a cell. And I'm on a plane, winging my way back to China. Your President pardoned me of our treason, you know.

GALLIMARD. Yes, I read about that.

SONG. Must make you feel . . . lower than shit.

GALLIMARD. But don't you, even a little bit, wish you were here with me?

SONG. I'm an artist, Rene. You were my greatest . . . acting challenge. [She laughs] It doesn't matter how rotten I answer, does it? You still adore me. That's why I love you, Rene. [She points to us] So—you were telling your audience about the night I announced I was pregnant.

[Gallimard puts his arms around Song's waist. He and Song are in the positions they were in at the end of Scene VI.]

SCENE VIII

Same.

GALLIMARD. I'll divorce my wife. We'll live together here, and then later in France.

SONG. I feel so . . . ashamed.

GALLIMARD. Why?

SONG. I had begun to lose faith. And now, you shame me with your generosity.

GALLIMARD. Generosity? No, I'm proposing for very selfish reasons.

SONG. Your apologies only make me feel more ashamed. My outburst a moment ago!

GALLIMARD. Your outburst? What about my request?!

SONG. You've been very patient dealing with my . . . eccentricities. A Western man, used to women freer with their bodies—

GALLIMARD. It was sick! Don't make excuses for me.

SONG. I have to. You don't seem willing to make them for yourself.

[Pause.]

GALLIMARD. You're crazy.

SONG. I'm happy. Which often looks like crazy.

GALLIMARD. Then make me crazy. Marry me.

[Pause.]

SONG. No.

GALLIMARD. What?

SONG. Do I sound silly, a slave, if I say I'm not worthy?

GALLIMARD. Yes. In fact you do. No one has loved me like you.

SONG. Thank you. And no one ever will. I'll see to that.

GALLIMARD. So what is the problem?

SONG. Rene, we Chinese are realists. We understand rice, gold, and guns. You are a diplomat. Your career is skyrocketing. Now, what would happen if you divorced your wife to marry a Communist Chinese actress?

GALLIMARD. That's not being realistic. That's defeating yourself before you begin.

SONG. We must conserve our strength for the battles we can win.

GALLIMARD. That sounds like a fortune cookie!

SONG. Where do you think fortune cookies come from?

GALLIMARD. I don't care.

SONG. You do. So do I. And we should. That is why I say I'm not worthy. I'm worthy to love and even to be loved by you. But I am not worthy to end the career of one of the West's most promising diplomats.

GALLIMARD. It's not that great a career! I made it sound like more than it is!

SONG. Modesty will get you nowhere. Flatter yourself, and you flatter me. I'm flattered to decline your offer. [She exits]

GALLIMARD [To us]. Butterfly and I argued all night. And, in the end, I left, knowing I would never be her husband. She went away for several months—to the countryside, like a small animal. Until the night I received her call.

[A baby's cry from offstage. Song enters, carrying a child.]

SONG. He looks like you.

GALLIMARD. Oh! [Beat; he approaches the baby] Well, babies are never very attractive at birth.

SONG. Stop!

GALLIMARD. I'm sure he'll grow more beautiful with age. More like his mother.

SONG. "Chi vide mai/ a bimbo del Giappon . . ."

GALLIMARD. "What baby, I wonder, was ever born in Japan"—or China, for that matter—

SONG. ". . . occhi azzurrini?"

GALLIMARD. "With azure eyes"—they're actually sort of brown, wouldn't you say?

SONG. "E il labbro."

GALLIMARD. "And such lips!" [He kisses Song] And such lips.

SONG. "E i ricciolini d'oro schietto?"

GALLIMARD. "And such a head of golden"—if slightly patchy—"curls?"

SONG. I'm going to call him "Peepee."

GALLIMARD. Darling, could you repeat that because I'm sure a rickshaw just flew by overhead.

SONG. You heard me.

GALLIMARD. "Song Peepee"? May I suggest Michael, or Stephan, or Adolph?

SONG. You may, but I won't listen.

GALLIMARD. You can't be serious. Can you imagine the time this child will have in school?

SONG. In the West, yes.

GALLIMARD. It's worse than naming him Ping Pong or Long Dong or—

SONG. But he's never going to live in the West, is he?

[Pause.]

GALLIMARD. That wasn't my choice.

SONG. It is mine. And this is my promise to you: I will raise him, he will be our child, but he will never burden you outside of China.

GALLIMARD. Why do you make these promises? I want to be burdened! I want a scandal to cover the papers!

SONG [To us]. Prophetic.

GALLIMARD. I'm serious.

SONG. So am I. His name is as I registered it. And he will never live in the West.

[*Song exits with the child.*]

GALLIMARD [*To us*]. It is possible that her stubborness only made me want her more. That drawing back at the moment of my capitulation was the most brilliant strategy she could have chosen. It is possible. But it is also possible that by this point she could have said, could have done . . . anything, and I would have adored her still.

SCENE IX

Beijing. 1966.
    A driving rhythm of Chinese percussion fills the stage.

GALLIMARD. And then, China began to change. Mao became very old, and his cult became very strong. And, like many old men, he entered hs second childhood. So he handed over the reins of state to those with minds like his own. And children ruled the Middle Kingdom with complete caprice. The doctrine of the Cultural Revolution implied continuous anarchy. Contact between Chinese and foreigners became impossible. Our flat was confiscated. Her fame and my money now counted against us.

[*Two dancers in Mao suits and red-starred caps enter, and begin crudely mimicking revolutionary violence, in an agitprop fashion.*]

GALLIMARD. And somehow the American war went wrong too. Four hundred thousand dollars were being spent for every Viet Cong killed; so General Westmoreland's remark that the Oriental does not value life the way Americans do was oddly accurate. Why weren't the Vietnamese people giving in? Why were they content instead to die and die and die again?

[*Toulon enters.*]

TOULON. Congratulations, Gallimard.

GALLIMARD. Excuse me, sir?

TOULON. Not a promotion. That was last time. You're going home.

GALLIMARD. What?

TOULON. Don't say I didn't warn you.

GALLIMARD. I'm being transferred . . . because I was wrong about the American war?

TOULON. Of course not. We don't care about the Americans. We care about your mind. The quality of your analysis. In general, everything you've predicted here in the Orient . . . just hasn't happened.

GALLIMARD. I think that's premature.

TOULON. Don't force me to be blunt. Okay, you said China was ready to open to Western trade. The only thing they're trading out there are Western heads. And, yes, you said the Americans would succeed in Indochina. You were kidding, right?

GALLIMARD. I think the end is in sight.

TOULON. Don't be pathetic. And don't take this personally. You were wrong. It's not your fault.

GALLIMARD. But I'm going home.

TOULON. Right. Could I have the number of your mistress? [*Beat*] Joke! Joke! Eat a croissant for me.

[*Toulon exits. Song, wearing a Mao suit, is dragged in from the wings as part of the upstage dance. They "beat" her, then lampoon the acrobatics of the Chinese opera, as she is made to kneel onstage.*]

GALLIMARD [*Simultaneously*]. I don't care to recall how Butterfly and I said our hurried farewell. Perhaps it was better to end our affair before it killed her.

[*Gallimard exits. Comrade Chin walks across the stage with a banner reading: "The Actor Renounces His Decadent Profession!" She reaches the kneeling Song. Percussion stops with a thud. Dancers strike poses.*]

CHIN. Actor-oppressor, for years you have lived above the common people and looked down on their labor. While the farmer ate millet—

SONG. I ate pastries from France and sweetmeats from silver trays.

CHIN. And how did you come to live in such an exalted position?

SONG. I was a plaything for the imperialists!

CHIN. What did you do?

SONG. I shamed China by allowing myself to be corrupted by a foreigner . . .

CHIN. What does this mean? The People demand a full confession!

SONG. I engaged in the lowest perversions with China's enemies!

CHIN. What perversions? Be more clear!

SONG. I let him put it up my ass!

[Dancers look over, disgusted.]

CHIN. Aaaa-ya! How can you use such sickening language?!

SONG. My language . . . is only as foul as the crimes I committed . . .

CHIN. Yeah. That's better. So—what do you want to do now?

SONG. I want to serve the people.

[Percussion starts up, with Chinese strings.]

CHIN. What?

SONG. I want to serve the people!

[Dancers regain their revolutionary smiles, and begin a dance of victory.]

CHIN. What?!

SONG. I want to serve the people!!

[Dancers unveil a banner: "The Actor Is Rehabilitated!" Song remains kneeling before Chin, as the dancers bounce around them, then exit. Music out.]

SCENE X

A commune. Hunan Province. 1970.

CHIN. How you planning to do that?

SONG. I've already worked four years in the fields of Hunan, Comrade Chin.

CHIN. So? Farmers work all their lives. Let me see your hands.

[Song holds them out for her inspection.]

CHIN. Goddamn! Still so smooth! How long does it take to turn you actors into good anythings? Hunh. You've just spent too many years in luxury to be any good to the Revolution.

SONG. I served the Revolution.

CHIN. Serve the Revolution? Bullshit! You wore dresses! Don't tell me—I was there. I saw you! You and your white vice-consul! Stuck up there in your flat, living off the People's Treasury! Yeah, I knew what was going on! You two . . . homos! Homos!

Homos! [Pause; she composes herself] Ah! Well . . . you will serve the people, all right. But not with the Revolution's money. This time, you use your own money.

SONG. I have no money.

CHIN. Shut up! And you won't stink up China anymore with your pervert stuff. You'll pollute the place where pollution begins—the West.

SONG. What do you mean?

CHIN. Shut up! You're going to France. Without a cent in your pocket. You find your consul's house, you make him pay your expenses—

SONG. No.

CHIN. And you give us weekly reports! Useful information!

SONG. That's crazy. It's been four years.

CHIN. Either that, or back to rehabilitation center!

SONG. Comrade Chin, he's not going to support me! Not in France! He's a white man! I was just his plaything—

CHIN. Oh yuck! Again with the sickening language? Where's my stick?

SONG. You don't understand the mind of a man.

[Pause.]

CHIN. Oh no? No I don't? Then how come I'm married, huh? How come I got a man? Five, six years ago, you always tell me those kind of things, I felt very bad. But not now! Because what does the Chairman say! He tells us *I'm* now the smart one, you're now the nincompoop! *You're* the blackhead, the harebrain, the nitwit! You think you're so smart? You understand "The Mind of a Man"? Good! Then *you* go to France and be a pervert for Chairman Mao!

[Chin and Song exit in opposite directions.]

SCENE XI

Paris. 1968–70.
    Gallimard enters.

GALLIMARD. And what was waiting for me back in Paris? Well, better Chinese food than I'd eaten in China. Friends and relatives. A little accounting, regular schedule, keeping track of traffic violations in the suburbs. . . . And the indignity of students shouting the slogans of Chairman Mao at me—in French.

HELGA. Rene? Rene? [*She enters, soaking wet*] I've had a . . . a problem. [*She sneezes*]

GALLIMARD. You're wet.

HELGA. Yes, I . . . coming back from the grocer's. A group of students, waving red flags, they—

[*Gallimard fetches a towel.*]

HELGA. —they ran by, I was caught up along with them. Before I knew what was happening—

[*Gallimard gives her the towel.*]

HELGA. Thank you. The police started firing water cannons at us. I tried to shout, to tell them I was the wife of a diplomat, but—you know how it is . . . [*Pause*] Needless to say, I lost the groceries. Rene, what's happening to France?

GALLIMARD. What's—? Well, nothing, really.

HELGA. Nothing?! The storefronts are in flames, there's glass in the streets, buildings are toppling—and I'm wet!

GALLIMARD. Nothing! . . . that I care to think about.

HELGA. And is that why you stay in this room?

GALLIMARD. Yes, in fact.

HELGA. With the incense burning? You know something? I hate incense. It smells so sickly sweet.

GALLIMARD. Well, I hate the French. Who just smell—period!

HELGA. And the Chinese were better?

GALLIMARD. Please—don't start.

HELGA. When we left, this exact same thing, the riots—

GALLIMARD. No, no . . .

HELGA. Students screaming slogans, smashing down doors—

GALLIMARD. Helga—

HELGA. It was all going on in China, too. Don't you remember?!

GALLIMARD. Helga! Please! [*Pause*] You have never understood China, have you? You walk in here with these ridiculous ideas, that the West is falling apart, that China was spitting in our faces. You come in, dripping of the streets, and you leave water all over my floor. [*He grabs Helga's towel, begins mopping up the floor*]

HELGA. But it's the truth!

GALLIMARD. Helga, I want a divorce.

[*Pause; Gallimard continues, mopping the floor.*]

HELGA. I take it back. China is . . . beautiful. Incense, I like incense.

GALLIMARD. I've had a mistress.

HELGA. So?

GALLIMARD. For eight years.

HELGA. I knew you would. I knew you would the day I married you. And now what? You want to marry her?

GALLIMARD. I can't. She's in China.

HELGA. I see. You want to leave. For someone who's not here, is that right?

GALLIMARD. That's right.

HELGA. You can't live with her, but still you don't want to live with me.

GALLIMARD. That's right.

[*Pause.*]

HELGA. Shit. How terrible that I can figure that out. [*Pause*] I never thought I'd say it. But, in China, I was happy. I knew, in my own way, I knew that you were not everything you pretended to be. But the pretense—going on your arm to the embassy ball, visiting your office and the guards saying, "Good morning, good morning, Madame Gallimard"—the pretense . . . was very good indeed. [*Pause*] I hope everyone is mean to you for the rest of your life. [*She exits*]

GALLIMARD [*To us*]. Prophetic.

[*Marc enters with two drinks.*]

GALLIMARD [*To Marc*]. In China, I was different from all other men.

MARC. Sure. You were white. Here's your drink.

GALLIMARD. I felt . . . touched.

MARC. In the head? Rene, I don't want to hear about the Oriental love goddess. Okay? One night—can we just drink and throw up without a lot of conversation?

GALLIMARD. You still don't believe me, do you?

MARC. Sure I do. She was the most beautiful, et cetera, et cetera, blasé blasé.

[*Pause.*]

GALLIMARD. My life in the West has been such a disappointment.

MARC. Life in the West is like that. You'll get used to it. Look, you're driving me away. I'm leaving. Happy, now? [*He exits, then returns*] Look, I have a date tomorrow night. You wanna come? I can fix you up with—

GALLIMARD. Of course. I would love to come.

[*Pause.*]

MARC. Uh—on second thought, no. You'd better get ahold of yourself first.

[*He exits; Gallimard nurses his drink.*]

GALLIMARD [*To us*]. This is the ultimate cruelty, isn't it? That I can talk and talk and to anyone listening, it's only air—too rich a diet to be swallowed by a mundane world. Why can't anyone understand? That in China, I once loved and was loved by, very simply, the Perfect Woman.

[*Song enters, dressed as Butterfly in wedding dress.*]

GALLIMARD [*To Song*]. Not again. My imagination is hell. Am I asleep this time? Or did I drink too much?

SONG. Rene?

GALLIMARD. God, it's too painful! That you speak?

SONG. What are you talking about? Rene—touch me.

GALLIMARD. Why?

SONG. I'm real. Take my hand.

GALLIMARD. Why? So you can disappear again and leave me clutching at the air? For the entertainment of my neighbors who—?

[*Song touches Gallimard.*]

SONG. Rene?

[*Gallimard takes Song's hand. Silence.*]

GALLIMARD. Butterfly? I never doubted you'd return.

SONG. You hadn't . . . forgotten—?

GALLIMARD. Yes, actually, I've forgotten everything. My mind, you see—there wasn't enough room in this hard head—not for the world *and* for you. No,

there was only room for one. [*Beat*] Come, look. See? Your bed has been waiting, with the Klimt poster you like, and—see? The xiang lu [incense burner] you gave me?

SONG. I . . . I don't know what to say.

GALLIMARD. There's nothing to say. Not at the end of a long trip. Can I make you some tea?

SONG. But where's your wife?

GALLIMARD. She's by my side. She's by my side at last.

[*Gallimard reaches to embrace Song. Song sidesteps, dodging him.*]

GALLIMARD. Why?!

SONG [*To us*]. So I did return to Rene in Paris. Where I found—

GALLIMARD. Why do you run away? Can't we show them how we embraced that evening?

SONG. Please. I'm talking.

GALLIMARD. You have to do what I say! I'm conjuring you up in *my* mind!

SONG. Rene, I've never done what you've said. Why should it be any different in your mind? Now split—the story moves on, and I must change.

GALLIMARD. I welcomed you into my home! I didn't have to, you know! I could've left you penniless on the streets of Paris! But I took you in!

SONG. Thank you.

GALLIMARD. So . . . please . . . don't change.

SONG. You know I have to. You know I will. And anyway, what difference does it make? No matter what your eyes tell you, you can't ignore the truth. You already know too much.

[*Gallimard exits. Song turns to us.*]

SONG. The change I'm going to make requires about five minutes. So I thought you might want to take this opportunity to stretch your legs, enjoy a drink, or listen to the musicians. I'll be here, when you return, right where you left me.

[*Song goes to a mirror in front of which is a wash basin of water. She starts to remove her makeup as stagelights go to half and houselights come up.*]

Act III

SCENE I

A courthouse in Paris. 1986.

As he promised, Song has completed the bulk of his transformation, onstage by the time the houselights go down and the stagelights come up full. He removes his wig and kimono, leaving them on the floor. Underneath, he wears a well-cut suit.

SONG. So I'd done my job better than I had a right to expect. Well, give him some credit, too. He's right—I was in a fix when I arrived in Paris. I walked from the airport into town, then I located, by blind groping, the Chinatown district. Let me make one thing clear: whatever else may be said about the Chinese, they are stingy! I slept in door-ways three days until I could find a tailor who would make me this kimono on credit. As it turns out, maybe I didn't even need it. Maybe he would've been happy to see me in a simple shift and mascara. But . . . better safe than sorry.

That was 1970, when I arrived in Paris. For the next fifteen years, yes, I lived a very comfy life. Some relief, believe me, after four years on a fucking com-mune in Nowheresville, China. Rene supported the boy and me, and I did some demonstrations around the country as part of my "cultural exchange" cover. And then there was the spying.

[Song moves upstage, to a chair. Toulon enters as a judge, wearing the appropriate wig and robes. He sits near Song. It's 1986, and Song is testifying in a courtroom.]

SONG. Not much at first. Rene had lost all his high-level contacts. Comrade Chin wasn't very interested in parking-ticket statistics. But finally, at my urging, Rene got a job as a courier, handling sensitive docu-ments. He'd photograph them for me, and I'd pass them on to the Chinese embassy.

JUDGE. Did he understand the extent of his activity?

SONG. He didn't ask. He knew that I needed those documents, and that was enough.

JUDGE. But he must've known he was passing classi-fied information.

SONG. I can't say.

JUDGE. He never asked what you were going to do with them?

SONG. Nope.

[Pause.]

JUDGE. There is one thing that the court—indeed, that all of France—would like to know.

SONG. Fire away.

JUDGE. Did Monsieur Gallimard know you were a man?

SONG. Well, he never saw me completely naked. Ever.

JUDGE. But surely, he must've . . . how can I put this?

SONG. Put it however you like. I'm not shy. He must've felt around?

JUDGE. Mmmmm.

SONG. Not really. I did all the work. He just laid back. Of course we did enjoy more . . . complete union, and I suppose he *might* have wondered why I was always on my stomach, but. . . . But what you're thinking is, "Of course a wrist must've brushed . . . a hand hit . . . over twenty years!" Yeah. Well, Your Honor, it was my job to make him think I was a woman. And chew on this: it wasn't all that hard. See, my mother was a prostitute along the Bundt before the Revolution. And, uh, I think it's fair to say she learned a few things about Western men. So I borrowed her knowledge. In service to my coun-try.

JUDGE. Would you care to enlighten the court with this secret knowledge? I'm sure we're all very curious.

SONG. I'm sure you are. [Pause] Okay, Rule One is: Men always believe what they want to hear. So a girl can tell the most obnoxious lies and the guys will believe them every time— "This is my first time"— "That's the biggest I've ever seen"—or *both*, which, if you really think about it, is not possible in a single lifetime. You've maybe heard these phrases a few times in your own life, yes, Your Honor?

JUDGE. It's not my life, Monsieur Song, which is on trial today.

SONG. Okay, okay, just trying to lighten up the pro-ceedings. Tough room.

JUDGE. Go on.

SONG. Rule Two: As soon as a Western man comes into contact with the East—he's already confused.

The West has sort of an international rape mentality towards the East. Do you know rape mentality?

JUDGE. Give us your definition, please.

SONG. Basically, "Her mouth says no, but her eyes say yes."

The West thinks of itself as masculine—big guns, big industry, big money—so the East is feminine—weak, delicate, poor . . . but good at art, and full of inscrutable wisdom—the feminine mystique.

Her mouth says no, but her eyes say yes. The West believes the East, deep down, *wants* to be dominated—because a woman can't think for herself.

JUDGE. What does this have to do with my question?

SONG. You expect Oriental countries to submit to your guns, and you expect Oriental women to be submissive to your men. That's why you say they make the best wives.

JUDGE. But why would that make it possible for you to fool Monsieur Gallimard? Please—get to the point.

SONG. One, because when he finally met his fantasy woman, he wanted more than anything to believe that she was, in fact, a woman. And second, I am an Oriental. And being an Oriental, I could never be completely a man.

[*Pause.*]

JUDGE. Your armchair political theory is tenuous, Monsieur Song.

SONG. You think so? That's why you'll lose in all your dealings with the East.

JUDGE. Just answer my question: did he know you were a man?

[*Pause.*]

SONG. You know, Your Honor, I never asked.

SCENE II

Same.

Music from the "Death Scene" from *Butterfly* blares over the house speakers. It is the loudest thing we've heard in this play.

Gallimard enters, crawling towards Song's wig and kimono.

GALLIMARD. Butterfly? Butterfly?

[*Song remains a man, in the witness box, delivering a testimony we do not hear.*]

GALLIMARD [*To us*]. In my moment of greatest shame, here, in this courtroom—with that . . . person up there, telling the world. . . . What strikes me especially is how shallow he is, how glib and obsequious . . . completely . . . without substance! The type that prowls around discos with a gold medallion stinking of garlic. So little like my Butterfly.

Yet even in this moment my mind remains agile, flip-flopping like a man on a trampoline. Even now, my picture dissolves, and I see that . . . witness . . . talking to me.

[*Song suddenly stands straight up in his witness box, and looks at Gallimard.*]

SONG. Yes. You. White man.

[*Song steps out of the witness box, and moves downstage towards Gallimard. Light change.*]

GALLIMARD [*To Song*]. Who? Me?

SONG. Do you see any other white men?

GALLIMARD. Yes. There're white men all around. This is a French courtroom.

SONG. So you are an adventurous imperialist. Tell me, why did it take you so long? To come back to this place?

GALLIMARD. What place?

SONG. This theatre in China. Where we met many years ago.

GALLIMARD [*To us*]. And once again, against my will, I am transported.

[*Chinese opera music comes up on the speakers. Song begins to do opera moves, as he did the night they met.*]

SONG. Do you remember? The night you gave your heart?

GALLIMARD. It was a long time ago.

SONG. Not long enough. A night that turned your world upside down.

GALLIMARD. Perhaps.

SONG. Oh, be honest with me. What's another bit of flattery when you've already given me twenty years' worth? It's a wonder my head hasn't swollen to the size of China.

GALLIMARD. Who's to say it hasn't?

SONG. Who's to say? And what's the shame? In pride? You think I could've pulled this off if I wasn't already full of pride when we met? No, not just pride. Arrogance. It takes arrogance, really—to believe you can will, with your eyes and your lips, the destiny of another. [*He dances*] C'mon. Admit it. You still want me. Even in slacks and a button-down collar.

GALLIMARD. I don't see what the point of—

SONG. You don't? Well maybe, Rene, just maybe—I want you.

GALLIMARD. You do?

SONG. Then again, maybe I'm just playing with you. How can you tell? [*Reprising his feminine character, he sidles up to Gallimard*] "How I wish there were even a small cafe to sit in. With men in tuxedos, and cappuccinos, and bad expatriate jazz." Now you want to kiss me, don't you?

GALLIMARD [*Pulling away*]. What makes you—?

SONG. —so sure? See? I take the words from your mouth. Then I wait for you to come and retrieve them. [*He reclines on the floor*]

GALLIMARD. Why?! Why do you treat me so cruelly?

SONG. Perhaps I *was* treating you cruelly. But now—I'm being nice. Come here, my little one.

GALLIMARD. I'm not your little one!

SONG. My mistake. It's I who am *your* little one, right?

GALLIMARD. Yes, I—

SONG. So come get your little one. If you like. I may even let you strip me.

GALLIMARD. I mean, you were! Before . . . but not like this!

SONG. I was? Then perhaps I still am. If you look hard enough. [*He starts to remove his clothes*]

GALLIMARD. What—what are you doing?

SONG. Helping you to see through my act.

GALLIMARD. Stop that! I don't want to! I don't—

SONG. Oh, but you asked me to strip, remember?

GALLIMARD. What? That was years ago! And I took it back!

SONG. No. You postponed it. Postponed the inevitable. Today, the inevitable has come calling.

[*From the speakers, cacophony: Butterfly mixed in with Chinese gongs.*]

GALLIMARD. No! Stop! I don't want to see!

SONG. Then look away.

GALLIMARD. You're only in my mind! All this is in my mind! I order you! To stop!

SONG. To what? To strip? That's just what I'm—

GALLIMARD. No! Stop! I want you—!

SONG. You want me?

GALLIMARD. To stop!

SONG. You know something, Rene? Your mouth says no, but your eyes say yes. Turn them away. I dare you.

GALLIMARD. I don't have to! Every night, you say you're going to strip, but then I beg you and you stop!

SONG. I guess tonight is different.

GALLIMARD. Why? Why should that be?

SONG. Maybe I've become frustrated. Maybe I'm saying "Look at me, you fool!" Or maybe I'm just feeling . . . sexy. [*He is down to his briefs*]

GALLIMARD. Please. This is unnecessary. I know what you are.

SONG. Do you? What am I?

GALLIMARD. A—a man.

SONG. You don't really believe that.

GALLIMARD. Yes I do! I knew all the time somewhere that my happiness was temporary, my love a deception. But my mind kept the knowledge at bay. To make the wait bearable.

SONG. Monsieur Gallimard—the wait is over.

[*Song drops his briefs. He is naked. Sound cue out. Slowly, we and Song come to the realization that what we had thought to be Gallimard's sobbing is actually his laughter.*]

GALLIMARD. Oh god! What an idiot! Of course!

SONG. Rene—what?

GALLIMARD. Look at you! You're a man! [*He bursts into laughter again*]

SONG. I fail to see what's so funny!

GALLIMARD. "You fail to see—!" I mean, you never did have much of a sense of humor, did you? I just think it's ridiculously funny that I've wasted so much time on just a man!

SONG. Wait. I'm not "just a man."

GALLIMARD. No? Isn't that what you've been trying to convince me of?

SONG. Yes, but what I mean—

GALLIMARD. And now, I finally believe you, and you tell me it's not true? I think you must have some kind of identity problem.

SONG. Will you listen to me?

GALLIMARD. Why?! I've been listening to you for twenty years. Don't I deserve a vacation?

SONG. I'm not just any man!

GALLIMARD. Then, what exactly are you?

SONG. Rene, how can you ask—? Okay, what about this?

[He picks up Butterfly's robes, starts to dance around. No music.]

GALLIMARD. Yes, that's very nice. I have to admit.

[Song holds out his arm to Gallimard.]

SONG. It's the same skin you've worshiped for years. Touch it.

GALLIMARD. Yes, it does feel the same.

SONG. Now—close your eyes.

[Song covers Gallimard's eyes with one hand. With the other, Song draws Gallimard's hand up to his face. Gallimard, like a blind man, lets his hands run over Song's face.]

GALLIMARD. This skin, I remember. The curve of her face, the softness of her cheek, her hair against the back of my hand . . .

SONG. I'm your Butterfly. Under the robes, beneath everything, it was always me. Now, open your eyes and admit it—you adore me. [He removes his hand from Gallimard's eyes]

GALLIMARD. You, who knew every inch of my desires —how could you, of all people, have made such a mistake?

SONG. What?

GALLIMARD. You showed me your true self. When all I loved was the lie. A perfect lie, which you let fall to the ground—and now, it's old and soiled.

SONG. So—you never really loved me? Only when I was playing a part?

GALLIMARD. I'm a man who loved a woman created by a man. Everything else—simply falls short.

[Pause.]

SONG. What am I supposed to do now?

GALLIMARD. You were a fine spy, Monsieur Song, with an even finer accomplice. But now I believe you should go. Get out of my life!

SONG. Go where? Rene, you can't live without me. Not after twenty years.

GALLIMARD. I certainly can't live with you—not after twenty years of betrayal.

SONG. Don't be so stubborn! Where will you go?

GALLIMARD. I have a date . . . with my Butterfly.

SONG. So, throw away your pride. And come . . .

GALLIMARD. Get away from me! Tonight, I've finally learned to tell fantasy from reality. And, knowing the difference, I choose fantasy.

SONG. *I'm* your fantasy!

GALLIMARD. You? You're as real as hamburger. Now get out! I have a date with my Butterfly and I don't want your body polluting the room! [He tosses Song's suit at him] Look at these—you dress like a pimp.

SONG. Hey! These are Armani slacks and—! [He puts on his briefs and slacks] Let's just say . . . I'm disappointed in you, Rene. In the crush of your adoration, I thought you'd become something more. More like . . . a woman.

But no. Men. You're like the rest of them. It's all in the way we dress, and make up our faces, and bat our eyelashes. You really have so little imagination!

GALLIMARD. You, Monsieur Song? Accuse me of too little imagination? You, if anyone, should know—I am pure imagination. And in imagination I will remain. Now get out!

[Gallimard bodily removes Song from the stage, taking his kimono.]

SONG. Rene! I'll never put on those robes again! You'll be sorry!

GALLIMARD [To Song]. I'm already sorry! [Looking at the kimono in his hands] Exactly as sorry . . . as a Butterfly.

SCENE III

M. Gallimard's prison cell. Paris. Present.

GALLIMARD. I've played out the events of my life night after night, always searching for a new ending to my story, one where I leave this cell and return forever to my Butterfly's arms.

Tonight I realize my search is over. That I've looked all along in the wrong place. And now, to you, I will prove that my love was not in vain—by returning to the world of fantasy where I first met her.

[He picks up the kimono; dancers enter.]

GALLIMARD. There is a vision of the Orient that I have. Of slender women in chong sams and kimonos who die for the love of unworthy foreign devils. Who are born and raised to be the perfect women. Who take whatever punishment we give them, and bounce back, strengthened by love, unconditionally. It is a vision that has become my life.

[*Dancers bring the wash basin to him and help him make up his face.*]

GALLIMARD. In public, I have continued to deny that Song Liling is a man. This brings me headlines, and is a source of great embarrassment to my French colleagues, who can now be sent into a coughing fit by the mere mention of Chinese food. But alone, in my cell, I have long since faced the truth.

And the truth demands a sacrifice. For mistakes made over the course of a lifetime. My mistakes were simple and absolute—the man I loved was a cad, a bounder. He deserved nothing but a kick in the behind, and instead I gave him . . . all my love.

Yes—love. Why not admit it all? That was my undoing, wasn't it? Love warped my judgment, blinded my eyes, rearranged the very lines on my face . . . until I could look in the mirror and see nothing but . . . a woman.

[*Dancers help him put on the Butterfly wig.*]

GALLIMARD. I have a vision. Of the Orient. That, deep within its almond eyes, there are still women. Women willing to sacrifice themselves for the love of a man. Even a man whose love is completely without worth.

[*Dancers assist Gallimard in donning the kimono. They hand him a knife.*]

GALLIMARD. Death with honor is better than life . . . life wth dishonor. [*He sets himself center stage, in a seppuku position*] The love of a Butterfly can withstand many things—unfaithfulness, loss, even abandonment. But how can it face the one sin that implies all others? The devastating knowledge that, underneath it all, the object of her love was nothing more, nothing less than . . . a man. [*He sets the tip of the knife against his body*] It is 19 . And I have found her at last. In a prison on the outskirts of Paris. My name is Rene Gallimard—also known as Madame Butterfly.

[*Gallimard turns upstage and plunges the knife into his body, as music from the "Love Duet" blares over the speakers. He collapses into the arms of the dancers, who lay him reverently on the floor. The image holds for several beats. Then a tight special up on Song, who stands as a man, staring at the dead Gallimard. He smokes a cigarette; the smoke filters up through the lights. Two words leave his lips.*]

SONG. Butterfly? Butterfly?

[*Smoke rises as lights fade slowly to black.*]

END OF PLAY

ESSAY: AN APPROACH TO THE PLAY

The love affair of Song and Gallimard is played out against a background of America's war in Vietnam, formerly a colonial possession of France. In this as in other ways, the play as a whole suggests the convergence of love and power and hence the convergence of two closely related western myths: the western male belief that women—especially Asian women—welcome domination by their men, and the western colonialist assumption that people from less technologically advanced countries are better off when controlled by those who know what is best for them. The play also suggests that both of these myths cut in two directions, not just one.

M. Butterfly is a "memory play," staged nightly within the mind of the prisoner (though "tonight" with a new ending) for what Gallimard calls his ideal audience. The play quickly and cleverly dismisses what could be a distracting concern—how could he not have known his lover was a man—by staging in its second scene the cocktail party jokes at Gallimard's expense that are likely to occur to members of the audience. This is not the point, Hwang seems to be saying; rather, as Gallimard says at the start of Scene 3, he should be envied, "For I, Rene Gallimard, you see, I have known, and been loved by . . . the Perfect Woman." With its dramatic pause in staging and its capital letters in print, the sentence raises definitional questions: What is "the Perfect Woman" (especially since the role was played by a man), and who gets to set the criteria by which perfection is determined?

At its core the play examines gender roles in our society, the difference between "masculine" and "feminine," concepts which are in part culturally created and reinforced, like any of our attitudes, by our cultural artifacts and institutions. The opera *Madame Butterfly*, for example, reflects the values of its culture and, by giving such memorable and satisfying form to the love of Butterfly for Pinkerton, perpetuates and reinforces them. In addition, interwoven within the presentation of the opera's plot at the beginning of Hwang's play are two scenes that help explain the origin of Gallimard's attitudes toward masculinity. The three elements—the opera, memories of conversations with his old friend Marc, and the girlie magazines—all help explain and reinforce our culture's dominant conception of masculinity. In the dialogue with Marc in Scene 5, we see Gallimard's insecurity, his intimidation, his sense of powerlessness around women back in college; and we also see the way he has internalized Marc's evaluation of him (after all, the play presents what continues to be staged in his own head) as a "wimp." As his affair with Song progresses, he keeps conjuring Marc up to show off, to fantasize that he is receiving Marc's approval. When he stages *Madame Butterfly*, he reverses their roles, casting himself as Pinkerton, the heartless abuser of the innocent Cio-Cio-San, and Marc as Sharpless, the "wimp" who serves Pinkerton's needs despite his diplomatic stature (and possible moral reservation). In Scene VI, when the 12-year-old Rene reads the girlie magazines and fantasizes the responses of the "girl" in the photograph, he says his body shook "not with lust—no, with power. Here were women—a shelf full—who would do exactly as I wanted." The subsequent onstage dialogue with the girl— apparently a dramatization of his youthful sexual fantasy—centers on his power over her. Meanwhile, the love duet from *Madame Butterfly* plays in the background, reinforcing the continuity in gender ideology between these artifacts from such apparently different aspects of our culture.

The magazine seems to explain Gallimard's immediately preceding self-description as one of those "who are not handsome, nor brave, nor powerful, yet somehow believe, like Pinkerton, that we deserve a Butterfly." At the end of the scene, he says, "The sad truth is that all men want a beautiful woman, and the uglier the man, the greater the want." The two statements make telling assertions: a compliant and beautiful woman is something all men desire and feel somehow that they deserve. This conception makes the woman a trophy, proof of the game well played, and possession of the love of such a woman reinforces both the behavior of the lucky man and the perception of his behavior. Not to have the prize is a sign of failure, and the resulting lack of prestige undermines self-confidence. Once Gallimard feels himself to have power over Song, he is more successful at work; he is promoted because he is now perceived as "this new aggressive, confident . . . thing." When word gets around in the diplomatic grapevine that he has a Chinese mistress, Gallimard gains the admiration of all the guys—just what he has always wanted from Marc and the masculine subculture Marc represents. He is finally being a "real man" and is rewarded for it.

The young student, Renee, serves as a foil in the play, a minor character whose function is to render more visible aspects of the main characters or of the play's themes. She has a body indistinguishable from those of the women in the magazines. As with Song, Gallimard has an affair with her, and unlike Song, she is willing to be seen naked. And yet, Gallimard asks (Act 2, Scene 6), "is it possible for a woman to be *too* uninhibited, *too* willing, so as to seem almost too . . . . masculine?" The discussion of Gallimard's "weenie" follows, a scene in which Renee inverts the dynamic of the magazines. She turns the "normal" sexual gaze around and looks at, names, evaluates male body parts. She assumes what in our culture is a male prerogative, a male power, even while implying a relationship between male sexual insecurity and male aggression. As Gallimard says to the audience at the end of this brilliantly comic episode, "This was simply not acceptable." The dislocation between her appearance and behavior calls traditional gender roles into question. This provides one clue as to why Song can get away with "her" impersonation for so long: since he, by contrast with Renee, acts the way a woman is "supposed" to act, his identity is not called into question.

Thus Song can articulate the two halves of the play's power dynamics from the witness stand in Act 3, telling the judge the secret knowledge about western men passed on from his prostitute mother: men always believe what they want to hear; and the West has an international rape mentality toward the East. He enacted the role of fantasy woman so well that his lover, like any man, believed what he wanted to hear, and as an Asian, he could assume that Gallimard would never suspect his gender: he looks like one of those people who "want" to be dominated.

M. Butterfly also reminds us frequently of the roots of its own theatrical power, and this, too, is part of its subject: a man impersonates a woman; a wimp impersonates a hero; internal performances of the Puccini opera and of a scene from traditional Chinese opera comment on the main action; Song removes his stage makeup on stage and "changes" for us, a pun that connects a costume change with a gender change. The form of much of the play's action points toward the idea that the well-crafted illusion is more likely to succeed than "reality" itself, and this calls into question the meaning of reality—if you will, the "reality" of reality. A male-dominant society can get some women to think they should obey, and a technologically advanced society can sometimes persuade less advanced people to act in a subservient way, but it is *persuasion* that is of the essence, the manipulation of images and artifacts. If the woman or the less technological country learns this lesson while the "persuader" lulls himself into believing his own myth, then he himself becomes manipulatable: perpetrator becomes victim, a reversal that gives the lie to the myth of superiority.

Song uses his understanding of images to gain power over Gallimard: the stereotypical oriental "woman" gains control over the western man, and Gallimard refuses to acknowledge it. He refuses to give up the imagined love of a perfect woman, even though Song strips on stage and presents to him the fact of his biological maleness, concealed during their affair beneath the cultural forms of femininity. To preserve the myth intact, Gallimard assumes what is for him the poetically just role—and costume—of Butterfly and enacts her final, in this case metadramatic, sacrifice.

This play leaves us with many questions. If a man can play a woman so effectively, how much of our social dance is merely composed of actors playing out variants of expected social roles? Do nations behave similarly? Can individuals or nations move outside of preformed attitudes about race and gender and power to see clearly and to respect one another's uniqueness, or will our personal and political relationships always be filtered through preconceptions driven by our self-image? What would have to change for us to work through or around such cultural barriers? Is Gallimard right that "we are all prisoners of time and place," or can we hope for peace and love, at home and in the world?

Percy Mtwa, Mbongeni Ngema, and Barney Simon

WOZA ALBERT!

About the Authors Native South Africans Percy Mtwa (1953–   ), born in Wattville, Benoni, Mbongeni Ngema (1955–   ), born in Umkumbane, Durban, and Barney Simon (1934–   ), from Johannesburg, were all theater veterans before their collaboration on *Woza Albert!*, but their work involved performance or direction or production, rather than writing. Mtwa was a singer, dancer, and instrumentalist, first with his own nightclub group "Percy and the Maestros," then at the Market and the Baxter Theatres, where he met Ngema. Ngema was an actor and guitarist in the theater before writing and directing two of his own plays in Durban, then moving in 1979 to Johannesburg and his work with Mtwa. The two developed their ideas for this play at least partly while working together in a traveling production of *Mamma and the Load* through South Africa's black townships. They approached Barney Simon, who had had wide experience as a producer and director, having worked with many of South Africa's best-known playwrights, black and white, including Athol Fugard. He is best known for having helped found the Market Theatre Company in Johannesburg in 1974, where he served as artistic director, and he had already collaborated with actors in the creation of scripts on four previous occasions.

Since *Woza Albert!*, Simon has taken his directing talents to the National Theatre in London, as well as to Edinburgh and San Francisco, and he has received many directing awards. Mtwa has expanded his acting and playwriting career; the San Francisco Bay Area Critics Circle voted him its Best Play and Best Actor awards for his *Barney Simon*. He continues to work in the United States and England, as well as in South Africa. Ngema won an Obie in 1984 for his New York "Distinguished Production" of *Asinamali* and in 1987 for directing *Sarafina*.

About the Play *Woza Albert!* received the First Fringe Award at the Edinburgh Festival of 1982. The collaboration which created this play involved writing, but because all three collaborators were so strongly performance-oriented, the process also depended greatly on improvisational acting, discovering at firsthand what stage language, what gestures and acting styles, in general what visual and aural stage qualities, could best express their vision. After its successes in Johannesburg and Edinburgh, the play went on tour to Berlin, San Francisco, Seattle, and Philadelphia and was shown twice on the BBC, all in 1982.

The play makes unusual demands on its reading audience, as distinguished from its theater audience. Its spare set, minimal props and costumes, and use of pantomime all place great demands on the style and skill of the actors, talents derived largely from the players' experiences in the theaters of the townships. Much of the play's appeal derives from the extraordinary talents and versatility of Mtwa and Ngema, as well as from Simon's hand in helping to shape their unique performance skills, and these are aspects of the play which a reader must attempt to imagine. However, because they must be imagined, the reader is also given unusual freedom to use his or her imagination as director/producer. Placed as it is at the end of this volume, it can serve as a stimulating exercise for the skills developed in this course.

And exercise it is likely to be, for this play's form requires each of the actors to perform a *tour de force*. Naked above the waist, these two black actors play white as well as black roles, prime minister as well as prison inmate, in fact something approximating the full range of South African society. They not only change roles from scene to scene, but also language, moving rapidly among official "white" English, the quite different English which blacks assume when speaking to whites, the colloquial "black" English which they speak to each other, and their native Zulu. These different languages take on different tones as well, and these differences in tone are emphasized not only by acting style but also by the very spareness of costume and set. When a black actor impersonates a white prime minister or white policeman, he does not put on a full costume; rather, his black body remains exposed, but he puts on a round pink nosepiece, and sometimes a hat. Are whites just like blacks once costumes and social roles are penetrated? Is this a mockery of white pretensions to superiority? And if so, what kind of laughter does this evoke?

The circumstances of production include the fact that theaters existed in 1982 only in the white-dominated cities of South Africa; in outlying townships, in school auditoriums and community centers and churches, there were performances such as those of Mtwa and Ngema in *Mama and the Load*, but no theaters. A viable theater company requires a population willing to come to a theater on a regular basis and buy tickets at a price high enough to allow the company a profit. By 1982, however, multiracial audiences were lawful in South Africa, and a play such as this one would have been politically charged. The meaning of its Zulu title, here applied to Christ, is explained near the beginning of the last scene. What *would* happen if Christ came to the Christian country of South Africa in 1982?

(Note: At the end of the play, you will find a Glossary of Words, Places, and People, as published in the play's original 1983 edition.)

INTRODUCTION [TO THE 1983 EDITION]

Now, upon application for a permit, all theatres in South Africa can be multi-racial. These theatres are in the White cities. There are no theatres in the Black townships: performances happen in halls—churches, schools, community centres—sometimes in cavernous cinemas. There are minimal facilities—few lights, no fixed seats, no carpets. High-heels sound. Cold-drink cans roll. Babies cry. Friends call to each other. Drunks heckle. People come and go. Performers must fend for themselves— and they do—in the broad, loud, triumphantly energetic 'township' style.

Mbongeni Ngema and Percy Mtwa met on such a township tour of *Mama and the Load*, a Gibson Kente musical, Ngema as an actor, Mtwa as a singer and dancer. They both felt the need for further challenges, and in their questioning and reading came upon Jerzy Grotowski's *Towards a Poor Theatre*, and Peter Brook's *The Empty Space*. They stopped drinking and smoking and exercised their bodies, their voices, their resonators. They decided to create a piece together and hunted for a subject. One night in their touring bus, they found it. There was a heated argument on the Second Coming. What would happen to Jesus if he came back—to South Africa!

They began to read the Bible and to improvise. Finally they left *Mama and the Load* to concentrate on their piece. They approached Barney Simon, Artistic Director of the Market Theatre to collaborate with them because of his extensive experience in Black and non-racial theatre and because of the work that he had done in the creation of texts with actors.

After six weeks of intensive collaboration with Simon—writing, improvising, scouring the Gospels and the streets of Soweto and Johannesburg—the structure, text and title of *Woza Albert!* were born.

Most of the South African government's policies are the result, they say, of their Christian Nationalist principles. *Woza Albert!* is our fantasy of a Second Coming to South Africa by Morena, the Saviour.

The stage is lit by the house-lights. The set consists of two up-ended tea-chests side by side about centre stage. Further upstage an old wooden plank, about ten feet long, is suspended horizontally on old ropes. From nails in the plank hang the ragged clothes that the actors will use for their transformations. The actors wear grey track-suit bottoms and running shoes. They are bare-chested. Around each actor's neck is a piece of elastic, tied to which is half a squash ball painted pink—a clown's nose, to be placed over his own nose when he plays a white man.

SCENE I

[*The actors enter and take their positions quickly, simply. Mbongeni sits on the tea-chests at the point they meet in the middle. Percy squats between his legs. As they create their totem, the house-lights dim to blackout.*

On the first note of their music, overhead lights come on, sculpting them. They become an instrumental jazz band, using only their bodies and their mouths—double bass, saxophone, flute, drums, bongos, trumpet etc. At the climax of their performance, they transform into audience, applauding wildly.

Percy stands, disappears behind the clothes rail. Mbongeni goes on applauding. Percy reappears wearing his pink nose and a policeman's cap. He is applauding patronisingly. Mbongeni stares at him, stops applauding.]

PERCY. Hey! Beautiful audience, hey? Beautiful musician, né? Okay, now let us see how beautiful his pass-book is! [*To appalled Mbongeni*] Your pass!

MBONGENI [*playing for time*]. Excuse my boss, excuse? What?

PERCY [*smugly, to audience with his back to Mbongeni*]. Okay, I'll start again. You know you're a black man, don't you?

MBONGENI. Yes, my boss.

PERCY. And you live here in South Africa?

MBONGENI [*attempting to sidle off-stage behind Percy's back*]. Yes, my boss.

PERCY. So you know that you must always carry your pass.

MBONGENI. Yes, my boss.

PERCY. Okay, now what happens if you don't have your pass?

MBONGENI. I go to jail, my boss.

PERCY. And what happens if your pass is not in order?

MBONGENI [*nearly off-stage*]. I go to jail, my boss.

PERCY [*wheels on Mbongeni*]. H-E-E-EY! Your pass!!!

MBONGENI [*effusively*]. OOOOhhh, my pass, my con-

stable! [*Moves to Percy, holding out his pass.*] Here's my pass my lieutenant.

PERCY. Okay, now let's have a look. [*Examines the pass.*] Where do you work?

MBONGENI. I work here, my Captain.

PERCY. You work here? If you worked here your pass-book would be written 'Market Theatre, Johannesburg'. But look, it is written 'Kentucky Southern Fried'. Is this Kentucky Southern Fried? And look at the date. It tells me you haven't worked in four years. This is vagrancy, you're unemployed. [*To audience.*] Ja, this is what I call 'loafer skap!'.

MBONGENI. No, my Colonel, I am a guitarist, I've been playing music for five years, my boss.

PERCY. Hey, you lie, you fuckin' entertainer!

MBONGENI. It's true, it's true, my boss.

PERCY. Can you show me where it is written 'musician'? Hey? Where's a guitar? Where's a guitar? Where's a guitar?

MBONGENI. Ag, nee—my Brigadier, I am self-employed!

PERCY. Self-employed? [*Chuckling collusively to audience.*] Hell, but these kaffirs can lie, hey?

MBONGENI. Maar, dis die waarheid, but it is true—my General!

PERCY. You know where you should be?

MBONGENI. No, my boss.

PERCY. You should be in prison!

MBONGENI. No, my boss.

PERCY. And when you come out of prison, do you know where you should go?

MBONGENI. No, my boss.

PERCY. Back to the bush with the baboons. That's where you belong! Kom hierso! Section 29. [*To audience, pleasantly.*] Do you know about Section 29? That's a nice little law specially made for loafers like him. And I've got a nice little place waiting for him in Modder-B Prison. Kom jong! [*Pulls Mbongeni by his track-suit.*]

MBONGENI [*aside*]. Shit!

PERCY [*threatening*]. What did you say? Wat het jy gesê?

MBONGENI. Nothing—my President!

[*The policeman (Percy) chases the musician (Mbongeni) behind the clothes-rail.*]

SCENE II

[*Enter both actors with prison blankets wrapped around their shoulders. Both are singing a prison song, a prisoner's fantasy of his woman's longing for him:*]

SONG. Ha-ja-ka-rumba

Ha-ja-karumba

(*Solo*).

Bath'uyeza—uyez'uyezana?
Bath'uyeza—uyez'uyezana?
Kuthima ngizule kodwa mangicabanga
Yini s'thandwa sithando sami ye—

(*Chorus*).

Hajakarumba—hajakarumba.
Hajakarumba—hajakarumba.
[They say he is coming. Is he really coming?
I am mad when I think of it.
Come back my love, oh my love.]

[*Under the song, Mbongeni gives orders:*]

MBONGENI. Modder-B Prison . . . prisoners—line up!
Body Inspection. Hey wena cell number 16. Inspection cell number 16. Awusafuni na? Awusafunu-
kuvula vula hey wena we-neloda. Vul'inggwza
sisone. [Hey you, cell number 16. Inspection cell
number 16. Are you hiding anything? Don't you
want to show what is hidden—come on you men—
show me your arses!] Prisoners inspection!
BOTH [*doing 'Towsa' dance, revealing empty orifices and
armpits*]. Ready for body inspection, my Basie! Blankets clear, my Basie! No tobacco! No money! No
watch! My Basie! Mouth clear! Ears clear! [*Open
mouths wide.*] Hooo! Hooo! [*Pull ear-lobes.*] Haaa!
Haaa! My Basie!
PERCY. Hands up!
BOTH [*raise arms*]. Arms clear, my Basie! [*Raise legs.*]
Everything clear, my Basie! Also arse, my Basie!
MBONGENI. Inspection! [*They pull down their trousers,
display bare backsides.*] See nothing hidden, my Basie!
Prisoners! Lights out! [*Lights dim.*]
BOTH [*lying on the floor covering themselves with blankets*]. Goodnight, Basie, goodnight. Dankie Baba,
dankie. Beautiful arse, my Baba. Nothing hidden,
my Basie!

[*Lights dim on sleeping figures.*]

SCENE III

PERCY [*singing in his sleep*]. Morena walks with me all
the way / Watching over me all the day / When the
night time comes he's there with me / Watching
over, loving me.
MBONGENI [*restless, stirring from sleep*]. Hey man
uyangxola man—uyangxola man. [Hey man, you
making noise man.]

[*The singing continues.*]

MBONGENI. Hey! Hey, hey! Stop singing your bloody
hymns man, you're singing in your bladdy sleep
again! Morena! Morena hoo-hoo, there's no
Morena here!
PERCY [*dazed*]. I'm sorry. [*Silence. He begins to hum
again.*]
MBONGENI [*kicks Percy, who jumps up, is chased*]. Hayi
man—isejelela. [This is prison man.]
PERCY [*cowering*]. Morena, the saviour, is watching
over you too, my friend.
MBONGENI. Morena, the saviour, here in Modder-B
Prison? BULLSHIT!

[*Lights up bright. Work yard. Actors holding picks.*]

MBONGENI. Prisoners! Work yard!
BOTH [*working and singing a work-song*].

Siboshiwe siboshel'wa mahala
Wen'utha senzenjani
Siboshiwe siboshel'wa mahala
Wen'utha senzenjani
[They arrested us for nothing
So what can we do?]

[*Mbongeni hurts his hand, nurses it.*]

MBONGENI. It's this bladdy hard labour!
PERCY [*attempting comfort*]. Don't worry my friend.
Morena is over there, he's watching over us.
MBONGENI. Morena. Here in prison?
PERCY. He's watching over you too.
MBONGENI [*kicking at him, chasing him*]. Morena here??
BULLSHIT!!

SCENE IV

MBONGENI. Prisoners! Supper!
BOTH [*running*]. Supper! Supper! Supper!

[*Transforms to supper-time. Prisoners racing around in a
circle, carrying plates, handing them in for food. Mbongeni
bullies Percy out of the way.*]

PERCY. Thank you, soup, Baba. Thank you, Baba.

MBONGENI. Soup, Baba. Thank you soup, Baba, thank you Baba.

PERCY. Porridge, Baba. Little bit of sugar, Baba.

MBONGENI. Porridge, Baba! Porridge. A little bit of sugar, Baba. A little bit of sugar, Baba. Thank you, Baba.

PERCY. A little bit sugar, Baba. Please, little bit, Baba. Thank you, Baba. Thank you, Baba, too much sugar, Baba.

MBONGENI. Sugar . . . [*Reaches for Percy's food. Percy points to a guard, stopping Mbongeni who smiles to the guard.*] No complaints, my boss. Geen klagte nie.

PERCY. No complaints, Baba.

[*Mbongeni eats in growing disgust; Percy with relish.*]

MBONGENI [*spits on the floor*]. Ukudla kwemi godoyi lokhu [This is food for a dog]—No, a dog wouldn't even piss on this food. Ikhabishi, amazambane, ushukela, ipapa, utamatisi endishini eyodwa—ini leyo? [Cabbage, potatoes, sugar, porridge, tomatoes in one dish—what is this?]

PERCY [*eating unconcerned*]. Thank you Morena for the food that you have given me. Amen.

MBONGENI [*turns on him, furious*]. Hey uthini Amen? [What do you say Amen for?]—For this shit! Thank you Morena for this shit?

[*Percy crawls away. Mbongeni beckons him back.*]

MBONGENI. Woza la! [Come here!]

[*Percy hesitates.*]

MBONGENI [*moves threateningly; points to the ground at his feet*]. Woza *la*!

[*Percy crawls over reluctantly.*]

MBONGENI. On your knees!

[*Percy, terrified, gets down on his knees.*]

MBONGENI. Pray! Mr. Bullshit, I'm getting out of here tomorrow. Pray to your Morena, tell him thanks for me. I'll never listen to your voice again!

[*Mbongeni pushes Percy forward on to the floor. Percy goes down with a scream that becomes a siren.*]

[*Blackout.*]

SCENE V

[*The siren transforms into train sounds. Lights up. Both men are sitting back-to-back on boxes, rocking as in a train. Mbongeni is reading a newspaper, Percy a Bible. Mbangeni spits out of the window, sits again.*]

PERCY [*evangelically*]. Blessed are those that are persecuted for rightousness' sake, for theirs is the Kingdom of Heaven. Blessed are ye when men shall revile ye and persecute ye and shall send all manner of evil against ye falsely, for thy sake. Rejoice, and be exceedingly glad for great is the reward of heaven. For so persecuted they—

MBONGENI [*turns on him, hits him on the head with newspaper*]. Hey! Persecuted? Prosecuted! Voetsak! Voetsak! [*Recognises his former fellow prisoner.*] Hey, brother Bullshit! When did you come out of prison? They promised me they would keep you in for life!

PERCY. Be careful, my friend, of the anger in your heart. For Morena will return and bear witness to our lives on earth and there will be no place to hide. He will point his holy finger and there will be those who rise to heaven and those who burn in hell. Hallelujah! I hope you're not one of them!

MBONGENI. Rise to heaven? Where is heaven?

PERCY. It is the Kingdom of God.

MBONGENI. Up there? Neil Armstrong has been there.

PERCY. Neil Armstrong?

MBONGENI. Hallelujah! He's been right up to the moon and he found a desert, no god!

PERCY. My brother, I don't care what you or your friend on the moon say, because I know that he will return to his father's kingdom on earth, even as I know that his father has heard your blasphemies and forgiven you!

MBONGENI. Where does his father live? In Jerusalem?

PERCY. The Lord, our father, is everywhere.

MBONGENI. And Morena, the saviour, is coming to South Africa?

PERCY. Hallelujah!

MBONGENI. How is he coming to South Africa? By South African Airways jumbo jet? [*He transforms into a photographer photographing the audience.*] And everybody will be waiting in Johannesburg at Jan Smuts airport. Pressmen, radiomen, South African television, international television, ABC, NBC, CBS, BBC, and they will all gather around—[*He turns to Percy, who has transformed into the Prime Minister with pink nose and spectacles.*] —our honourable Prime Minister!

SCENE VI

PERCY [*moving forward ingratiatingly into spotlight*]. Thank you very much, thank you very much. My people, Morena is back and South Africa has got him! I hope that the free world will sit up and notice whose bread is buttered and where! Let them keep their boycotts, their boxers, rugby players, and tennis racketeers. Stay home Larry Holmes! Stay home John McEnroe! We have got Morena! But there is already rumours going around that this is not the real Morena, but some cheap impostor. And to those that spread such vicious rumours I can only say, 'Tough luck friends! He chose us!' [*Raises his hands in V-signs, laughs.*]

[*Blackout.*]

SCENE VII

[*Lights up on Mbongeni wearing a Cuban army cap and smoking a fat cigar.*]

PERCY [*as announcer*]. And now ladies and gentlemen, on the hotline straight from Havana—the comrade from Cuba—Fidel Castro! Sir, have you got any comments to make on the impending visit of Morena to South Africa?
MBONGENI [*laughing*]. Morena in South Africa? Who's playing the part? Ronald Reagan?

[*Blackout.*]

SCENE VIII

[*Lights up on Percy playing cool bongo on boxes.*]

MBONGENI [*dancing flashily*]. And now for you to see on Black TV—the face of Black South Africa! [*Enjoying the bongo, dancing up to the player.*] Beautiful music my brother, cool sound, man, cool! Real cool! Beautiful music, oh yeah, oh yeah. Now tell me, my brother—what would you say—if Morena —walks in—right through that door?
PERCY [*making a rude finger-sign*]. Aay, fok off man!

[*Blackout.*]

SCENE IX

[*Lights up bright on Percy, now a young street meat-vendor. The boxes are his stall. He is swatting flies with a newspaper held in one hand. His other hand holds a second newspaper as shade against the sun.*]

MBONGENI [*enters, singing, as a labourer-customer*].

[*Song.*]
Siyitshil'igusha sayigqiba
Siyitshil'igusha sayigqiba
Muhla sitsh'igusha.
Wena wendoda wawuphina
Wena wendoda wawuphina
Muhla sitsh'igusha.
[We ate and finished a big sheep the other day. Where were you when we blessed ourselves with a sheep?]

MBONGENI. Hullo, my boy.
PERCY. Hello, Baba.
MBONGENI [*not tempted by the display*]. Ehhh, what meat can you sell me today?
PERCY. I've got mutton, chicken, and nice sausages. [*Swats a fly on the sausages.*]
MBONGENI. Oh yeah . . . the chicken does not smell nice, hey? Must get some cover, some shade from the sun, hey? [*Deliberating.*] Ehhh, how much are those chops?
PERCY. It's two rand fifty, Baba.
MBONGENI. Two rand fifty? Are they mutton chops?
PERCY. Ehhh, it's mutton.
MBONGENI. No pork?
PERCY. No pork, Baba. I don't like pork.
MBONGENI. Okay my boy, give me mutton chops. Two rand fifty, hey? Where's your mother, my boy?
PERCY. She's at work.
MBONGENI. She's at work? Tell her I said 'tooka-tooka' on her nose. [*Tickles the boy's nose.*] She must visit me at the men's hostel, okay? Dube hostel, room number 126, block 'B', okay? Bye-bye, my boy. 'B', don't forget. [*About to leave, he turns astonished at sight of—invisible—TV interviewer.*]
PERCY [*awed by TV-interviewer*]. Hello, Skulu. I'm fine, thanks. And you? [*Listens.*] Morena? Here in South Africa? What shall I ask from Morena if he comes to South Africa? Baba, I want him to bring me good luck. So that the people that come will buy all this meat. And then? I want him to take me to school. Sub-A, uh huh. [*Watching the interviewer leave.*]

Thank you, Baba. Inkos'ibusise [God bless]. Yeah, Baba . . . Au! TV!

[Blackout.]

SCENE X

[Lights up, dim, on Mbongeni as Auntie Dudu, an old woman, wearing a white dust-coat as a shawl. She is searching a garbage bin (upturned box). She eats some food, chases flies, then notices the interviewer. She speaks very shyly.]

MBONGENI. Hey? My name is Auntie Dudu. No work my boy, I'm too old. Eh? [Listens.] If Morena comes to South Africa? That would be very good. Because everybody will be happy and there will be lots and lots of parties. And we'll find lots of food here— [Indicates bin.] —cabbages, tomatoes, chicken, hot-dogs, all the nice things white people eat. Huh? [Receives tip.] Oh, thank you, my boy. Thank you, Baba. Inkos'ibusise. [God bless.] God bless you. Bye bye, bye bye . . .

[A fly buzzes close. She chases it.]
[Fade.]

SCENE XI

[Lights up bright on a barber's open-air stall. Percy—the barber—is sitting on a bus, Mbongeni—the customer—between his knees. Auntie Dudu's shawl is now the barber's sheet.]

PERCY. Ehh, French cut? German cut? Cheese cut?

MBONGENI. Cheese cut.

PERCY. Cheese cut—all off!

MBONGENI [settling]. That's nice . . . How much is a cheese cut?

PERCY. Seventy-five cents.

MBONGENI. Aaay! Last week my cousin was here and it was fifty cents.

PERCY. Hey, you've got very big hair my friend. [He begins cutting hair.]

MBONGENI [squirming nervously during the—mimed—clipping, relaxing at the end of a run]. That's nice. What machine is this?

PERCY. Oh, it's number ten . . .

MBONGENI. Number ten? Ohhh.

PERCY. Though it's a very old clipper.

MBONGENI That's nice. [More cutting, more squirming.] That's nice. Where's your daughter now?

PERCY. Ohh, she's in university.

MBONGENI. University? That's nice. What standard is she doing in university?

PERCY [clipping]. Ohhh, she's doing LLLLLB. I don't know, it's some very high standard.

MBONGENI. Oh yeah, LLB.

PERCY [confirming with pleasure]. Uh huh, LLB.

MBONGENI. That's nice! I remember my school principal failed seven times LLB!

PERCY. Ohhh, I see! I understand it's a very high standard.

MBONGENI. Tell me my friend, but why don't you apply for a barbershop? Why do you work in the open air where everyone is looking?

PERCY [continuing clipping]. Aaahh, don't ask me nonsense. I had a barbershop. But the police came with the bulldozers during the Soweto riots.

MBONGENI. Ooohh, 1976?

PERCY. Uh huh. During the times of black power. Everything was upside down . . . [To the invisible interviewer as he enters.] Oh, hello, Skulu. I'm fine, thanks. And you? [Listens.] Morena? Here, in South Africa?

MBONGENI. That's nice.

PERCY [clipping, talking excitedly]. Well now, I want him to build me a barbershop in a very big shopping centre in Johannesburg city, with white tiles, mirrors all over the walls, and customers with big hair! [The clipper gets caught in Mbongeni's hair. He struggles.]

MBONGENI. EEEEeeeeiiiiii!

[Blackout.]

SCENE XII

[Lights up. Percy and Mbongeni are coal-vendors, soot-stained sacks on their heads. They are climbing on to boxes—a coal lorry—taking off.]

PERCY & MBONGENI. Hey! Firewood for sale! Coal for sale! Smokeless coal for sale! Firewood for sale! [They make the sound of the lorry's engine revving. The lorry moves off.]

PERCY. Coal for sale! Hey wena, Auntie Ma-Dlamini, phum'endlini. [Hey, you, Aunt Dlamini, come out of your house.] [He spies a young girl, gestures.] Dudlu—mayemaye, the sugar the pumpkin. [Hallo there, hi hi, you are the sugar, the pumpkin.]

MBONGENI. Red light! Hey wena! [Hey you!] Driver—awuboni irobbot? [Can't you see the red light?]

PERCY. Don't you see the red light?

MBONGENI. Awuboni la uyakhona? [Don't you see where you're going?]

PERCY. He hasn't got a licence.

[*Noise of the lorry revving. They discover the invisible interviewer below, turn to him impatiently.*]

PERCY. What? Morena here in South Africa? You're talking rubbish! [*Lorry sounds again. It jerks forward.*] Smokeless coal for sale! Firewood for sale! [*Looks back.*] Putsho putshu ikaka kwedini. You're talking shit, boy.

MBONGENI. Inkanda leyo-kwedini-iyashisa he? [Your prick is hot, boy—heh?]

[*Percy looks back contemptuously and makes a rude sign with his finger as the lorry drives off.*]

[*Fade*]

SCENE XIII

[*Lights up on Mbongeni entering as a fragile, toothless old man. He sings throughout the following action. He settles on the boxes, attempts to thread a needle. His hands tremble but he perseveres. He succeeds on the third, laborious attempt and begins to sew a button on his coat.*]

MBONGENI [*humming*].

Bamga-lo-kandaba bayimpi
Heya we-bayimpi izwelonke
Ngonyama ye zizwe
Ohlab'izitha
UNdaba bamgwazizwe lonke okazulu
Amambuka nkosi

[The soldiers of our enemies have come to attack the king
They are coming from the four corners of the world to attack the Lion
We must kill the enemies
They are attacking him from all over the world, the son of Zulu
These strangers from another place attack our King.]

[*Mbongeni becomes aware of the (invisible) interviewer. Laughs knowingly.*]

MBONGENI [*speaking*]. Eh? What would happen to Morena if he comes to South Africa? What would happen to Morena is what happened to Piet Retief! Do you know Piet Retief? The big leader of the white men long ago, the leader of the Afrikaners! Ja! He visited Dingane, the great king of the Zulus! When Piet Retief came to Dingane, Dingane was sitting in his camp with all his men. And he thought, 'Hey, these white men with their guns are wizards. They are dangerous!' But he welcomed them with a big smile. He said, he said, 'Hello. Just leave your guns outside and come inside and eat meat and drink beer.' Eeeeii! That is what will happen to Morena today! The Prime Minister will say, just leave your angels outside and the power of your father outside and come inside and enjoy the fruits of apartheid. And then, what will happen to Morena is what happened to Piet Retief when he got inside. Dingane was sitting with all his men in his camp, when Piet Retief came inside. All the Zulus were singing and dancing . . . Bamya-lo-Kandaba payimpi . . . [*Repeats snatches of the song.*] And all the time Dingane's men were singing and dancing, [*Proudly*] they were waiting for the signal from their king. And Dingane just stood up . . . He spit on the ground. He hit his beshu and he shouted, Bulalan'abatha-kathi. Kill the wizards! Kill the wizards! Kill the wizards! And Dingane's men came with all their spears. [*Mimes throat-slitting, throwing of bodies.*] Suka! That is what will happen to Morena here in South Africa. Morena here? [*Disgusted.*] Eeii! Suka!

[*Blackout.*]

SCENE XIV

[*Lights flash on, Percy, an airport announcer, is standing on a box, calling out.*]

PERCY. Attention, please! Attention, please! Now this is a great moment for South Africa! The Lord Morena has arrived! The jumbo jet from Jerusalem has landed! Now lay down your blankets, sing hosanna, hosanna, lay down your presents. Hey, you over there, move away from the tarmac! [*More urgently.*] Move away from the runway! Move away!

MBONGENI [*rushing in as a photographer*]. Hosanna! Hosanna! Son of God! 'Hosanna nyana ka thixo!' ['Son of God'.] Hey, what will you say if Morena comes to you? [*To a member of the audience.*] Smile, smile! [*He turns to Percy then back to the camera crew.*]

Sound! Rolling! Slate! Scene twenty-seven, take one. And action . . .

SCENE XV

[*Percy, wearing his pink nose and flash sunglasses, alights from the plane (box).*]

MBONGENI [*approaching him with a mimed microphone*]. Happy landings, sir.

PERCY [*flattered by this attention*]. Oh, thank you. Thank you.

MBONGENI. Well sir, you've just landed from a jumbo jet!

PERCY. Eh, yes.

MBONGENI. Any comments, sir?

PERCY. I beg your pardon?

MBONGENI [*arch interviewer*]. Would you not say that a jumbo jet is faster than a donkey, sir?

PERCY. Eh, yes.

MBONGENI. Aaahh. Now tell me, sir, where have you been all this time?

PERCY. Around and about.

MBONGENI. And how is it up there in the heavens?

PERCY. Oh, it's very cool.

MBONGENI. Cool! [*Laughs artificially loud.*] So, I'm to understand that you've been studying our slang, too!

PERCY. Right on!

[*They laugh together.*]

MBONGENI. Now tell me, sir, in the face of all boycotting moves, why did you choose South Africa for your grand return?

PERCY. I beg your pardon?

MBONGENI. I mean, uuuh, why did you come here, sir?

PERCY. To visit my Great-aunt Matilda.

MBONGENI. Excuse me, sir?

PERCY. Yes?

MBONGENI. Your name, sir?

PERCY. Patrick Alexander Smith.

MBONGENI. You mean you're not Morena, sir?

PERCY. Who?

MBONGENI. Morena.

PERCY. Morena?

MBONGENI. Are you not Morena? [*To film-makers.*] Cut!!! Morena! Where is Morena? [*Percy minces off, insulted. Stage dim, Mbongeni wanders across stage, calling disconsolately.*] Morena! Morena! Morena! M-o-o-o-r-e-e-e-n-a-a-a! . . .

[*Lights dim. Percy begins to join the call, alternating, from behind the clothes rail. He emerges calling and addressing a high and distant Morena. As he talks, the lights come up.*]

SCENE XVI

PERCY. Morena! Morena-a-a! Where are you? Come to Albert Street! Come to the Pass Office! We need you here Morena! Ja, Morena, this is the most terrible street in the whole of Johannesburg! Ja, Morena, this is the street where we Black men must come and stand and wait and wait and wait just to get a permit to work in Johannesburg! And if you're lucky enough to get the permit, what happens? You wait and wait and wait again for the white bosses to come in their cars to give you work. [*Turns back to Mbongeni.*] But I'm lucky! I've got six months special! [*Shows his pass-book.*] Qualified to work in Johannesburg for six months!

MBONGENI. How many months? Eh?

PERCY. Six months!

MBONGENI. Six months? Congratulations. [*Laughs, slaps Percy's back, shakes his hand.*] Eh! Six month special!

PERCY. Three weeks in a queue!

MBONGENI. But you're still their dog! [*Moves upstage to urinate, with his back to the audience.*]

PERCY. Aaahh, jealous! You jealous!

MBONGENI. Have you got a job? Have you got school fees for your children? Have you got money for rent? Have you got bus fare to come to the Pass Office? Oh, come on man, we've all got specials but we're still their dogs!

[*Car sounds.*]

PERCY [*leaps up*]. Hey! There's a car! A white man! [*Moves to the car at the front edge of the stage, follows it as it moves across.*] Are you looking for workers, my boss? Ya, I've got six month special, qualified to work in Johannesburg.

[*Mbongeni moves forward trying frantically to distract the driver. Car sounds continue, actors alternating.*]

MBONGENI. Boss, I've got fourteen day special. This is my last chance. This is my last chance. Take two boys, my boss, two!

PERCY. Messenger boy, tea boy, my boss. One! I make nice tea for the Madam, my boss. Bush tea, China tea, English tea! Please, Baba. Lots of experience,

Baba. Very good education, my boss. Please my boss. Standard three, very good English, Baba.

[*Mbongeni's sound of a departing car transforms into a mocking laugh.*]

MBONGENI. I told you, you're still their dog! [*Laughs, mocks.*] Standard three, bush tea, China tea—where do you get China tea in Soweto?

PERCY. Aah voetsak! I've got six months special!

MBONGENI [*shows Percy his pass-book*]. Hey, look at my picture. I look beautiful, heh?

PERCY [*laughs bitterly*]. How can you look beautiful in your pass-book?

[*Car sounds again. Mbongeni rushes forward to the stage edge, follows the car, Percy behind him.*]

MBONGENI. One! One, my boss! Everything! Sweeper, anything, everything, my boss! Give me anything. Carwash? Yeah, always smiling, my boss. Ag, have you got work for me, my boss? I'm a very good nanny. I look after small white children. I make them tomato sandwich. I take them to school, my boss. Please, my boss. Please.

[*Car leaves. Mbongeni wanders disconsolately upstage. Percy watches him.*]

PERCY [*laughing*]. Ja! Who's a dog? Don't talk like that! This is South Africa! This is Albert Street. [*Laughs.*] Nanny, nanny, tomato sandwich!

[*Car sounds again.*]

BOTH ACTORS [*confusion of requests from each*]. Six month special, my boss. Fourteen day special, Baba. This is my last chance. Hey man, this is my corner! Very strong, Baas. Ek donder die kaffers op die plaas. [*I beat up the kaffirs on the farm.*] One, my boss. Two, my boss. Anything, my boss. Have you got anything for me, Baba?

PERCY. Basie, he's a thief, this one.

MBONGENI. He can't talk Afrikaans, this one, my boss.

PERCY. He's lying, Basie. Hy lieg, my baas!

[*The third car pulls away.*]

PERCY [*confronting Mbongeni angrily*]. Hey, this is my corner, these are my cars. I've got six months special.

MBONGENI. Hey! Fuck off! I stand where I like, man.

PERCY. You've got fourteen day special. There's your corner.

MBONGENI. Hey! You don't tell me where to stand!

PERCY. You've got fourteen day special. You're not even qualified to be on Albert Street.

MBONGENI. Qualified? Qualified? Wenzani uthath'a ma shansi hey uthatha ma shansi. [*What are you trying to do? You taking chances Hey? You taking chances.*]

[*Mbongeni kicks Percy. Percy turns on him.*]

PERCY. Baas Piet! Baas Piet! I'll tell Baas Piet you got forgery.

MBONGENI [*mimes picking up stone*]. Okay, okay. Call your white boss! I've got friends too!

PERCY. Baas Piet!

MBONGENI [*beckons his friends, wildly picking up stones*]. Hey Joe! We Joe! Zwakala—sigunu mfwethu. [*To Percy.*] Angihlali eZola mina—angihlali eMdeni mina—Joe zwakala simenze njalo. [*Joe come here— It's happening. [*To Percy.*] I don't live in Zola—I'm not from Mdeni—Joe come here let's work on him.*]

[*Mbongeni quietens, struck by something in the audience.*]

PERCY [*muttering sulkily*]. These are my cars, man. I've got six month special, these are mine. This is my corner—That's the temporal corner! I'll tell Baas Piet!

MBONGENI [*now totally stunned by what he is watching*]. Heeey, heeey! Ssh man, ssh.

PERCY [*cautious*]. What?

MBONGENI [*indicating the audience*]. Morena . . .

PERCY. Aaay, fok off!

MBONGENI. It's Morena—that one there with the white shirt.

PERCY [*doubtfully*]. Morena? Ay, nonsense . . . Is it Morena?

MBONGENI. It's him—I saw him in the *Sunday Times* with Bishop Tutu. It's him!

[*He sidles forward to the edge of the stage. Percy shyly eggs him on.*]

PERCY. Hey, speak to him.

MBONGENI [*nods with the invisible Morena*]. Excuse. Are you not Morena? Yiiiii! Hosanna! Morena!

[*The actors embrace joyously. Then follow Morena, frantically showing their passes and pleading.*]

BOTH ACTORS. Morena, look at my pass-book!

PERCY. I've got six month special but I can't find work.

MBONGENI. I've been looking here two months, no work. Take us to heaven, Morena, it's terrible here.

[*Mbongeni follows Morena. Percy falls behind.*]

PERCY. Temporary or permanent is okay Morena! [*Silence as Mbongeni converses with Morena. He comes back exhilarated.*] Hey, what does he say?

MBONGENI. He says let us throw away our passes and follow him to Soweto!

PERCY. Hey! He's right! Morena! Morena!

BOTH ACTORS [*sing, exhorting the audience*].

Woza giya nansi inkonyane ye ndlovu—
Aph'amadoda sibabambe sebephelele.
Wozani madoda niyesaba na?

[Come on join this child of an elephant
Where are the men? Let us face them!
Come men, are you afraid?]

PERCY [*under the song*]. Morena says throw away your passes and follow him to Soweto.

MBONGENI. We are not pieces of paper, man! We are men!

PERCY. Ja! Let them know our faces as Morena knows our faces!

MBONGENI. Morena says no more passes!

PERCY. Ja!!

MBONGENI. We don't have numbers any more!

PERCY. Ja!

MBONGENI. Let them look at our faces to know that we are men.

PERCY. Ja! When we follow Morena we walk as one!

[*The actors throw away their passes and their song transforms into train sounds.*]

SCENE XVII

[*The actors mime standing beside each other at a train window. They wave to people outside.*]

PERCY. Hey madoda! Sanibona madoda! May God bless them! Ja, you've got a very good imagination. I really like your stories. But you must go to church sometimes—Hey, there's a train coming! [*Looks to one side.*]

[*Flurry of their faces and noises as they mime watching adjoining train pass. Then they pull their windows up. Siren. Mbongeni moves downstage. Percy stands on a box, begins Regina Mundi Song:*]

Somlandela—somlandela u Morena
Somlandela yonke indawo
Somlandela—somlandela u Morena
Lapho eyakhona somlandela.

[We shall follow—we shall follow Morena
We shall follow him everywhere
We shall follow—we shall follow Morena
Where-ever he leads—we shall follow.]

[*While the song continues.*]

MBONGENI [*joyous siren*]. Ja, madoda, hundreds of thousands will gather at the Regina Mundi Church in the heart of Soweto. And people will sing and dance. There will be bread for all. And wine for all. Our people will be left in peace, because there will be too many of us and the whole world will be watching. And people will go home to their beds. [*He joins in the song for a few phrases.*] These will be days of joy. Auntie Dudu will find chicken legs in her rubbish bin, and whole cabbages. And amadoda—our men—will be offered work at the Pass Office. The barber will be surrounded by white tiles. The young meat-seller will wear a nice new uniform and go to school, and we will all go to Morena for our blessings. [*Song subsides. Percy lies on boxes as sleeping woman. Lights dim.*] And then . . . the government will begin to take courage again . . . The police and the army will assemble from all parts of the country . . . And one night, police dogs will move in as they have done before. There will be shouts at night and bangings on the door . . .

PERCY [*banging on a box*]. Hey! Open up, it's the police! Maak die deur oop! Polisie!

MBONGENI [*ducking down by the boxes as if hiding beside a bed*]. . . . There will be sounds of police vans and the crying of women and their babies.

PERCY [*turns over on the boxes as an old woman waking in bed, starts crying and calling in Zulu*]. We Jabulani, hayi-bo-hey-hey-we-Nonoza, akenivule bo nanka amaphoyisa esesihlasele, we Thoko akenivule bo. Auw-Nkosi-Yami, ezingane ze-Black Power! [Hey, Jabulani, Hey no, hey-hey, Nonoza, open the door can't you hear the police are here. They've come to attack us. Thoko, please open the door. Oh my God, these children of Black Power!]

[*He goes to open the door. Throughout Mbongeni tries to stop him.*]

MBONGENI. Sssh Mama! Tula Mama! Mama! Mama! Leave the door! [*Mbongeni gives up, stands silent, transfixed, hiding.*] They'll start surrounding our homes at night. And some of our friends will be caught by stray bullets. There will be roadblocks at every entrance to Soweto, and Regina Mundi Church will be full of tear-gas smoke! Then life will go on as before.

[*He throws his arms up in the air in disgust, cries out.*]

SCENE XVIII

[*Lights flash on. Bright daylight. Coronation Brickyard. Mbongeni, as Zuluboy, is singing.*]

MBONGENI [*singing*].

Akuntombi lokhu kwabulala ubhuti ngesibumbu kuyamsondeza. [This is no woman. She killed my brother with a fuck and she never lets him go.]

[*He calls out towards the street.*] Hey Angelina— sweetheart! Why are you walking down the street? Come here to Coronation Brickyard! Zuluboy is waiting for you with a nice present! [*Points to his genitals, laughing*].

PERCY [*enters as Bobbejaan—Baboon—Zuluboy's fellow brickyard worker*]. Hey! Zuluboy, forget about women. Start the machine!

[*Mbongeni sings on.*]

PERCY. Hey! The white man is watching us. Boss Kom is standing by the window! Start the machine.

[*He makes machine sounds as he attempts to start it. He pulls the starter cord abortively, flies backwards across the yard.*]

MBONGENI [*laughs*]. Hey Bobbejaan! Start the machine!

PERCY. You laugh and I must do all this work! I'll tell Baas Kom. Baas Kom! Basie! Baas Kom!

MBONGENI. Ssshhhhhh! Bobbejaan! Bobbejaan . . . ssh—I want to tell you a secret.

PERCY. What secret?

MBONGENI [*whispers*]. We don't have to work so hard any more. Because Morena, the saviour, is coming here.

PERCY. Huh? Morena here? Hau! Baas Kom!

MBONGENI. Hau, no Bobbejaan! Listen—I was there on Thursday by the Jan Smuts Airport. We were delivering bricks. People were coming with taxis, bikes, trains, trucks, others on foot. There were many people, Bobbejaan. They were singing and crying and laughing and dancing and sweating and this other woman was shouting: Morena, give me bread for my baby. The other woman was shouting: Morena, my son is in detention. The other man: Morena, give me a special permit to work in Johannesburg city. The little girl, standing next to me: Morena, give me a lollipop. The big fat Zulu—the driver from Zola Hostel—Morena, give me a Chevrolet Impala! And me—I was there too—

PERCY. What did you say?

MBONGENI. Morena, come to Coronation Brickyard tomorrow morning! And he's coming here.

PERCY. To Coronation Brickyard? Morena?

MBONGENI. Hau—Bobbejaan, at the wedding, long ago—ten thousand years ago—he take a bucket of water, he make wine.

PERCY [*smugly*]. Ja, everybody knows that!

MBONGENI. He take one fish, he make fish for everybody! Fried fish!

PERCY. Hau!

MBONGENI. He take one loaf of brown bread, he make the whole bakery! Here at Coronation Brickyard, you will see wonders. He will take one brick, number one brick, and throw it up in the air. And it will fall down on our heads, a million bricks like manna from heaven!

PERCY. Hey! You're talking nonsense. Morena? Here at Coronation Bricks? Start the machine. I'll tell Baas Kom!

[*Percy goes off. Mbongeni begins rolling a cigarette, singing his Zuluboy's song. Percy, as Baas Kom with pink nose and white dust-coat, enters quietly from behind the clothes rail and creeps up on him. Mbongeni spits, just missing Percy who leaps back.*]

MBONGENI. Oh, sorry, Boss. Sorry, sorry . . . [*He runs to start the machine.*]

PERCY. Sis! Where were you brought up?

MBONGENI. Sorry boss!

PERCY. Ja Zuluboy! And what are you sitting around for?

MBONGENI. Sorry, Boss, Sorry.

PERCY. Are you waiting for Morena?

MBONGENI. No, Boss. No.

PERCY. Ja, I've been listening. I've been watching. You're waiting for Morena, Ja. Did you not listen to the Prime Minister on the radio today?

MBONGENI. I don't have a radio, Boss.

PERCY. We don't like Morena anymore. And everybody who's waiting for Morena is getting fired.

MBONGENI. Oh, very good, Boss, Me? I'm Zuluboy—ten thousand bricks in one day!

PERCY. Ja. Where's Bobbejaan?

MBONGENI [attempting to start the machine]. He's gone to the toilet.

PERCY. Call him. Call him, quickly!

MBONGENI. Hey! Bobbejaan! [He makes motor sounds as the machine kicks over but does not 'take'.] Bobbejaan!

PERCY [still as Baas Kom, with Mbongeni watching over his shoulder]. Now listen. I want two thousand bricks for Boss Koekemoer. Two thousand bricks for Baas Pretorius. Two thousand bricks for Mrs Dawson. [Mbongeni indicates his pleasure in Mrs Dawson. Percy cautions him.] Zuluboy! Six thousand bricks for Boss Van der Westhuizen. Two thousand bricks for Boss Koekemoer. Two thousand bricks for Baas Pretorius. Two thousand bricks for Mrs Dawson.

MBONGENI. Baas, sorry, I'm confused.

PERCY. What confused? What confused? You're bloody lazy, man! See to these orders and push the truck. [He indicates the truck on the side of the stage.]

MBONGENI. Hey! This truck is too heavy, Baas!

PERCY. Get other people!

MBONGENI. People have gone to lunch.

PERCY. Get Bobbejaan!

MBONGENI. Ten thousand bricks, Boss!

PERCY. Hey! Get Bobbejaan!

MBONGENI. Bobbejaan! Uyahamba laphe khaya. [They'll fire you.] Bobbejaan! [Mumbling.] Two thousand bricks Mrs Dawson . . . Hau! [Laughs with pleasure.] Mrs Dawson! Ten thousand bricks Baas van Des-des-destuizen . . . Too much! [He starts the engine. Engine 'takes'. Mbongeni shouts.] Bobbejaan!

PERCY [off-stage, as Bobbejaan]. I'm coming, man! [He enters.] Hey, hey. Where's Morena?

MBONGENI. No Morena. Hey, shovel the sand. Baas Kom is firing everybody that's waiting for Morena.

PERCY [laughing]. Ja! I've been telling you! Hey, bring down the pot. [They alternate shovel and motor sounds; as they mime shovelling. Mbongeni begins to sing and dance his Zuluboy song.] Hey, stop dancing. Stop dancing!

MBONGENI. Hey! I am boss-boy here!

[Mbongeni switches off the machine.]

PERCY. Lunch time!

MBONGENI. No Bobbejaan. First push the truck.

PERCY. Hau! Ten thousand bricks! Hau! Lunch time!

MBONGENI. Baas Kom said, push the truck! Get Bobbejaan, push the truck. PUSH!

[Percy joins him reluctantly. They start to chant while they mime pushing the heavy truck.]

BOTH [chanting].

> Woza kanye-kanye! [Come together!]
> Abelungu oswajini! [Whites are swines!]
> Basibiza ngo-damn! [They call us damns!]

> Woza kanye-kanye! [Come together!]
> Abelungu oswayini! [Whites are swines!]
> Basibiza ngo-damn! [They call us damns!]

[They finally stop, exhausted.]

PERCY [holding his back, moaning]. Oh, oh, oh, yii, yii! Lunch time! Hayi ndiva kuthi qhu. [My back is breaking.]

MBONGENI. Hayi suka unamanga. [Hey you lie.] [He squats to examine the truck.] It has gone too far. Reverse!

PERCY. Reverse?! Reverse?

[Muttering, he joins Mbongeni. They pull the truck back again, chanting.]

BOTH [chanting].

> Woza emuva! [Come reverse!]
> Phenduka ayi. [Change now.]
> Abelungu oswayini! [Whites are swines!]
> Basibiza ngo-damn! [They call us damns!]

PERCY. Hayi. [Percy goes off.]

MBONGENI. Bobbejaan, come back, it stuck in ditch.

PERCY [off-stage]. Hayi, xelel'ubaas Kom ukuba sifuna i-increase. [Tell Baas Kom we want increase.]

MBONGENI. We . . . kuyintekentekana lokhu okuwu-Bobbejaan. [Hey man, Bobbejaan is too weak.] Come back, Bobbejaan! Uyahamba laphe khaya. [They'll fire you.] Where's my cigarette? [Mimes lighting a cigarette. Talks to himself, starts praise-chant.]

PERCY [enters as Baas Kom]. And now? And now? [Mocking praise-chant.] Aaay, hakela, hakela. What the bloody hell is that? Huh? Push the truck! Come!

MBONGENI. Having rest, baas. Still smoking.

PERCY. Do you think I pay you for smoking? [Glances at the truck.] Hey, push the truck!

MBONGENI. We pushed the truck! Ten thousand bricks! Boss, there's too much work for two people. Me and Bobbejaan start the engine. Me and Bobbejaan shovel the sand. Me and Bobbejaan load the bricks. Me and Bobbejaan push the truck! Aaay suka! We need other people!

PERCY. There's no jobs!

MBONGENI. There *is* jobs!!! Ten thousand bricks! This morning there were many people at the gates standing there looking for work. And you chased them away!

PERCY. Zuluboy, you're getting cheeky, huh?

MBONGENI. I'm not getting cheeky. It's true.

PERCY. Ja! I'm cutting down your salary. I think you're getting too much. Ja! Ja!

MBONGENI. The boss can't cut salary.

PERCY. Ek gaan dit doen! [I'm going to do it.]

MBONGENI. That's not showing sympathy for another man. The cost of living is too high. There is too much inflation.

PERCY. Zuluboy! Zuluboy! You sit around waiting for Morena and then you come and tell me about the cost of living? You talk about inflation? What do you know about inflation? I've got you here, just here. One more mistake, once more cheeky, and you're fired!

MBONGENI. Okay. All right boss. Let's talk business like two people.

PERCY [bangs on the box]. He-ey! Push the truck, man!

MBONGENI [furious, bangs on the box. Percy retreats towards his office space]. Hey! You must listen nice when another man talks!

PERCY. Okay. Talk, talk. [Mbongeni advances.] No—talk over there, talk over there!

MBONGENI [backs away]. All right. Okay, okay. The people want increase. Where's the money for the people?

PERCY. Increase?

MBONGENI. Increase!

PERCY. Don't I give you free food? Free boarding and lodging?

MBONGENI. The people don't like your free food! They want money. There is too big families to support. Too many children.

PERCY. I don't give a damn about your too many children. Don't you know about family planning?

MBONGENI. Family planning? What is that?

PERCY. Don't you know that you must not have too many children? You must have two, three, and stop your fuck-fuck nonsense! Too many pic-a-ninnies! Too many black kaffir babies all over the country. [Sharing this with the audience.] Their kaffir babies cry 'Waaaaa! Waaaaa!' Just like too many piccaninny dogs!

MBONGENI [threatening]. Hey!

PERCY. Zuluboy!

MBONGENI. Whose children cry 'Waaa, waaa!'?

PERCY. Zuluboy!

MBONGENI. Whose children is piccaninny dogs?

PERCY. Bring your pass-book!

MBONGENI. Why?

PERCY. You're fired! Bring your pass-book. I'm signing you off.

MBONGENI. You can't sign me off!

PERCY. I'm calling the police! I'm calling the government buses and I'm sending you back to your homelands. Ek stuur julle na julle fokken verdomde, donrose, bliksemse plase toe! [I'm sending you to your fucking, cursed, useless farms.] You don't like my work? You don't like my food! Go back to your bladdy farms! Go starve on your bladdy farms!

MBONGENI. I must starve?

PERCY. Ja!

MBONGENI. My children must starve?

PERCY. Ja!

MBONGENI. Go on strike!!!

PERCY. Hey! Bring your pass-book!

MBONGENI [pulls out his knobkerrie from behind the box]. Here's my pass-book!

PERCY. Zuluboy!

MBONGENI [advancing]. Here's my pass-book.

PERCY [ducking behind the rack of clothes at the back of the stage]. Bobbejaan!

MBONGENI. Here's my pass-book! Stay away—hlala phansi wena ngane ka Ngema. Hlala wena ngane ka Madlokovu—hlala. Wena dlula bedlana inkunzi engena mona, hlala phansi mfana—Hlala!! Phokuhlala ba. [Stay away—sit down you son of Ngema. Sit down son of Madlokovu. Sit. You fuck and you never feel jealous. Sit down great son. Sit. So who am I—the greatest!] [Mutters to himself.] Stay away. Go on strike. My children cry 'Waa waa'. [Suddenly he sees Morena approaching. He wipes the sweat from his eyes, shakes his head in disbelief. Falls to his knees.] Hey. Hey! Morena! So you've come to Coronation Bricks! Come, Morena. Did you listen to the radio today? Everybody's waiting for you, and everybody is fired. Come, sit down here, Morena. [*Offers a box.*] Sit down. Sit down Morena. [*Calls out.*] Bobbejaan!

PERCY [*entering as Bobbejaan, angrily*]. Hau! One minute 'Bobbejaan!' One minute 'Bobbejaan!' [*He sees Morena, stops complaining and turns away shyly.*]

MBONGENI [*laughs*]. Bobbejaan, who is this? Who is this!!!

PERCY [*backs away smiling shyly*]. Hey. I don't know him. Who is it?

MBONGENI. Who is this? I win the bet. Give ten rands.

PERCY. Who is he?

MBONGENI. Give ten rands!

PERCY. Who is he?

MBONGENI. Morena!

PERCY. Hey! Morena?!

MBONGENI. He's from heaven. He has come now. He landed at Jan Smuts Airport on Thursday by the airline from Jerusalem.

PERCY. Hey Morena! [*Clapping hands.*] I saw your picture in the paper. Morena, I could not believe you're coming. I thought you're coming back by the clouds. [*He sits on the floor.*]

MBONGENI. The clouds are too hot now. It's summer. He flies air-conditioned. Excuse, Morena, this is Bobbejaan. Bobbejaan, shake hands with Morena. [*Percy stands, embarrassed, backs away.*] Shake hands with the Son of God! Shake hands, Bobbejaan! [*Percy ducks behind Zuluboy on the box. Zuluboy laughs.*] Bobbejaan is shy! We are working together here, Morena. When I say, 'Morena, come to Coronation Brickyard', I mean you must make bricks like you make bread and wine long ago. I mean you must make bricks to fall down like manna from heaven—

PERCY. Like you made fried fish!

MBONGENI. Ja! But now, I say no! Stay away! No! You must not make bricks for Coronation Brickyard! You must go on strike like me and Bobbejaan! Angithi Bobbejaan? [*Isn't it so, Bobbejaan?*] We work hard here. We sweat. Sweating for one man!

PERCY. Boss Koekemoer!

MBONGENI. Every Friday, Boss Koekemoer, seven thousand bricks—

PERCY. Boss Pretorius!

MBONGENI. Boss Pretorius ten thousand bricks!

PERCY. Van de Westhuizen!

MBONGENI. Boss Van-des-destuizen, eleven thousand bricks! Where do we stay?

PERCY. In a tin!

MBONGENI. In a tin! Like sardine fish!

PERCY. In a tin, Morena!

MBONGENI. Where do the bricks go to!? The bricks go to make a big house, six rooms, for two people. A white man and his wife! Angithi Bobbejaan? [*Isn't it so, Bobbejaan?*] Our fingers are breaking Morena! Is nie good kanjalo, man. [*That's not good like that, man.*]

PERCY. Ten thousand bricks!

MBONGENI. Ten thousand bricks! Me and Bobbejaan must push the truck. Aaay suka! Stay away! No bricks for Coronation Bricks! [*He puts out his cigarette and clears his nose—to Percy's embarrassment.*] Are you hungry, Morena? Are you hungry? I've got nice food for you. I've got a packet of chips. [*Mimes.*] It's very good, this one. There's lots of vinegar and salt—I bought them from the shop just around the corner.

PERCY. That's potatoes, Morena.

MBONGENI. I've got half-brown bread. Whole-wheat. You made this long ago, huh? I've been telling Bobbejaan, you made plenty in the wedding—He's got power, this one! [*Mimes.*] This is Coca-cola, Morena.

PERCY. It's cold drink.

MBONGENI. For quenching thirst.

PERCY. Ha, Morena, there's no Coca-cola in heaven!

MBONGENI. What do you drink up there?

[*They listen, then laugh uproariously.*]

PERCY. These two!

MBONGENI. You and your father! Skelm! [*Mischief-makers!*]

[*He mimes opening a coke bottle.*]

PERCY [*looks upstage, then calls in Baas Kom's voice, as if from off-stage*]. Bobbejaan! [*Then as Bobbejaan again.*] Baas Kom! Morena, I must go! One minute 'Bobbejaan!' One minute 'Bobbejaan!' [*Going off.*] Hey Zuluboy, I want my chips!

MBONGENI [*drinks from the mimed coke bottle, burps, offers it to Morena*]. Yabhodla ingane yenZule ukuba okungu—MSuthu ngabe kudala kuzinyele. [*There burps the son of a Zulu; if it was a Sotho he would be shitting.*] Did you hear that man who was shouting 'Bobbejaan'? That's our white boss. Boss Kom. He's not good. But don't worry . . .

PERCY [off-stage in Baas Kom's voice]. Bobbejaan!

MBONGENI. Lots of vinegar . . .

PERCY [enters as Baas Kom, stops at sight of Morena]. En nou! En nou? Who is this? Who is sitting around eating lunch with my kaffirs? That's why you're getting cheeky, hey? Ja, you sit around and have lunch with terrorists!

MBONGENI. Hau! He's not a terrorist, Baas! He's a big man from heaven!

PERCY. This man is a communist, jong! Ek het van jou nonsense gehoor. Die hele land praat van jou. [I've heard of your nonsense. The whole country is talking about you.]

MBONGENI. Excuse. He cannot understand Afrikaans.

PERCY. What? Cannot understand Afrikaans?

MBONGENI. Right.

PERCY. Cannot understand Afrikaans? Stay where you are! [Retreats to is office behind the clothes.] I'm calling the police. Fuckin' agitator!

MBONGENI. Aay suka!! Don't worry, Morena, don't worry. [He proffers the coke bottle.] He does not know who you are. He does not know who your father is.

PERCY [as Baas Kom, offstage]. Hello? Hello? Lieutenant Venter? Ja! Now listen here. There's a terrorist here who's making trouble with my kaffirs. Ek sê daar's 'n uitlander hier wat kak maak met my kaffirs. [I say there's a foreigner here who's making shit with my kaffirs.] Ja. Hello? Hello? Ag die fuckin' telephone! Bobbejaan! [As Bobbejaan.] Ja, Basie? [As Baas Kom.] Kom, kom, kom. [As Bobbejaan.] Ja, Basie? [As Baas Kom.] You see that man eating with Zuluboy? [As Bobbejaan.] Ja, Basie. [As Baas Kom.] He's a terrorist! [As Bobbejaan.] A terrorist, Basie? That's Morena! [As Baas Kom.] It's not Morena—Now listen here. Listen carefully. I'm writing down this message. You take this message to the police station and I'm going to give you a very nice present. A ten rand increase, okay? [As Bobbejaan.] Ja, thank you Basie, thank you Basie. [As Baas Kom.] Ja, go straight to the police station and don't tell Zuluboy. [As Bobbejaan.] Ja Basie, ja. [As Baas Kom.] Go to the police station and you get the ten rand increase!

MBONGENI. Did you hear that, Morena? [He listens.] What? Forgive a man seventy times seventy-seven? Aikhona Morena! This is South Africa. We fight! Bobbejaan is very dangerous. [Listens to Morena.] Okay, you win. Wait and see, Morena.

PERCY [enters as Bobbejaan, putting on his shirt]. Morena, I'm going to the shop, just around the corner.

MBONGENI. Bobbejaan, your chips are here.

PERCY. Give them to Morena.

MBONGENI. Morena is not hungry.

PERCY. Eat them yourself.

MBONGENI. I'm not hungry either. Where are you going, Bobbejaan?

PERCY. To the shop!

MBONGENI. Why, Bobbejaan?

PERCY. I'm going to buy hot-dogs for Baas Kom.

MBONGENI. Where's the money?

PERCY. I've got it here.

MBONGENI. Show it to me.

PERCY. Why?

MBONGENI. Ja. You Judas, Bobbejaan!

PERCY. What are you talking about?

MBONGENI. You betray Morena, Bobbejaan.

PERCY. Haw! Morena, do you hear that?

MBONGENI. Bobbejaan, you betray Morena, Bobbejaan! You Judas, Bobbejaan!

PERCY. I'm going to buy hot-dogs for Baas Kom!

MBONGENI. You . . . you . . . you take a message to the police. And you get ten rands increase Bobbejaan!

PERCY. Aay Morena. Morena, do you hear this?

MBONGENI. Morena, shhh. Keep quiet. This is South Africa. Ten rands increase [He reaches for the knobkerrie.]

PERCY. Baas Kom! [He runs off.]

MBONGENI. [mimes his knobkerrie being grabbed by Morena] Morena, leave it! Leave it! Morena! Morena, leave it! Morena! He has run away now. Bobbejaan, sodibana nawe wena. [Bobbejaan, you and I will meet again.] A man hits this cheek you give him the other. Aikhona, Morena! They're calling the police to arrest you now! Okay, come. Let me hide you there by the trees—Quickly—[Siren sounds. He stops.] There's one, two, three . . . there's thirteen police cars. Huh? Forgive them, they do not know what they are doing? Aikhona, Morena! They know! They know! [He sings and performs a Zulu war dance, which ends with him thrusting his knobkerrie again and again at the audience in attack.]

Qobolela njomane kandaba heya-he
soze sibajahe abelungu he ya he.

[Be ready you horses of the black warriors
Time will come when we'll chase these whites
    away.]

SCENE XIX

[The lights come up on the actors wearing military hats and pink noses. Percy has a bloody bandage under his hat.]

MBONGENI. Address! Ssshhhooo! Attention!

[*They drill in unison.*]

PERCY [*saluting*]. Reporting sir! John Vorster Squad, sir!

MBONGENI. What have you to report, Sergeant?

PERCY. Operation Coronation, sir!

MBONGENI. Meaning, Sergeant?

PERCY. We have finally captured Morena, sir!

MBONGENI. You've what? Attention! One-two-three-one-two-three-one! [*They march to each other, shake hands.*] Excellent, Sergeant! Excellent!

PERCY. Thank you, sir.

MBONGENI. And now, what's happened to your head, Sergeant?

PERCY. A mad Zulu, sir.

MBONGENI. A mad Zulu?

PERCY. Yes sir. He struck me with the branch of a tree, sir.

MBONGENI. A branch of a tree?

PERCY. They call it a knobkerrie, sir.

MBONGENI. Ah! When, Sergeant?

PERCY. During Operation Coronation, sir.

MBONGENI. You mean Morena was with a bunch of mad Zulus?

PERCY. No, sir.

MBONGENI. What does he mean, this stupid Sergeant?

PERCY. He was with one mad Zulu, sir!

MBONGENI. One mad Zulu?

PERCY. Yes, sir!

MBONGENI. And how many men did you have, Sergeant?

PERCY. Thirty, sir!

MBONGENI. And where are they now, Sergeant?

PERCY. In hospital, sir!

MBONGENI. And the mad Zulu?

PERCY. He got away, sir!

MBONGENI. God! Wat gaan aan?! [God! What's going on?!] Where is Morena now, Sergeant?

PERCY [*pointing proudly above the audience*]. He's upstairs, above us, sir. On the tenth floor of John Vorster Square Prison, sir!

MBONGENI. Aaaahhh! [*Looking up.*] And you've provided ample guard, Sergeant?

PERCY. Yes, sir. One hundred and twenty, sir!

MBONGENI [*moving forward, watching the tenth floor, mesmerised*]. Are you sure he's on the tenth floor, Sergeant?

PERCY [*following his gaze nervously*]. Yes, sir.

MBONGENI. Then what is that I see?

PERCY [*moving behind him, also mesmerised, both eyelines travelling above the audience*]. I'm sorry sir.

MBONGENI. Why are you sorry, Sergeant?

PERCY. I see two men floating, sir.

MBONGENI. Then why are you sorry, Sergeant?

PERCY. I'm afraid one of them is Morena, sir.

MBONGENI [*moving in, nose-to-nose, menacingly*]. Precisely, Sergeant! And-who-is-the-other?

PERCY. The Angel Gabriel, sir.

MBONGENI [*despairing*]. Ha! Gabriel!

PERCY. I'm sorry, sir. I never thought of air flight, sir.

MBONGENI. Eeeeiiiii! One-two-three-four-one-four! Attention! Dismissed, Sergeant!

SCENE XX

[*Lights find both actors travelling beside each other on a train.*]

MBONGENI [*laughing*]. Jaaa. And where do we go from there? After a miracle like flying men, I'm telling you the government will be real nervous. And they won't start nonsense with him for a long time. In fact, they will try very hard to please Morena. He will be taken to all the nice places in the country. Like the game reserve where he can lie down with a leopard and a lamb. [*They cuddle.*] And then—[*They mime a high-speed lift.*]—they will take him right up to the high spots of Johannesburg City—Panorama Wimpy Bar, Calton Centre, fiftieth floor! And then, on a Thursday they will take him down—[*They mime going down, pink noses on their foreheads like miners' lamps.*]—the gold mines to watch. [*They mime deafening drills.*] And then, on a Sunday the mine dancers. [*They perform a short dance routine.*] And—[*Hand to ear.*]—aah, the government gardens in Pretoria. [*Doves cooing.*] And then, they will take him on a trip to SUN CITY—[*Stage radiantly light.*]—THE LAS VEGAS OF SOUTH AFRICA, where they will build him a holy suite and President Lucas Mangope, the puppet, will offer him the key to the homeland of Bophutatswana! And then, what will happen? They will take him past the good-time girls. [*Standing on a box, Percy mimes.*] And the gambling machines. [*Percy transforms into a one-armed bandit, Mbongeni works him, wins triumphantly.*] And when television cameras turn on him, will he be smiling? Will he be joyous? No. He'll be crying. And when all the people shout—

BOTH. Speech! Morena, speech!

MBONGENI. —Morena will say, 'No.'

PERCY [*miming holding a mike*]. No, speak up.

MBONGENI. No! Morena will say, what key is this? What place is this? This place where old people weep over the graves of children? How has it happened? How has it been permitted? I've passed people with burning mouths. People buying water in a rusty piece of tin, and beside them I see people swimming in a lake that they have made from water that is here!

PERCY. Be careful, there are police spies here.

MBONGENI. What spies? Morena will say, I pass people who sit in dust and beg for work that will buy them bread. And on the other side I see people who are living in gold and glass and whose rubbish bins are loaded with food for a thousand mouths.

PERCY. Hey! That's not your business. There are security police, man.

MBONGENI. What security police? Morena will say, I see families torn apart. I see mothers without sons, children without fathers, and wives who have no men! Where are the men? Aph'amadoda madoda? [Where are the men?] And people will say, Ja, Morena, it's this bladdy apartheid. It's those puppets, u Mangope! u Matanzima! u Sebe! Together with their white Pretoria masters. They separate us from our wives, from our sons and daughters! And women will say, Morena there's no work in the homelands. There's no food. They divide us from our husbands and they pack them into hostels like men with no names, men with no lives! And Morena will say, come to me, you who are divided from your families. Let us go to the cities where your husbands work. We will find houses where you can live together and we will talk to those who you fear! What country is this? [*Spits on ground.*]

[*Percy starts to sing and march on the spot. Mbongeni joins him. They mime carrying a banner.*]

BOTH ACTORS [*sing a Zulu song and march*].

> Oyini oyini madoda
> Oyini oyini madoda
> Sibona ntoni uma sibon'u Mangope
> Siboni sell-out uma sibon'u Mangope
> Sibona ntoni uma sibon'u Gatsha
> Siboni puppet uma sibon'u Gatsha
> Khulula khulula Morena
> Khulula khulula Morena
> Sibona ntoni nang'u Matanzima
> Sibon'u mbulali nang'u Matanzima

> [What is this, what is this men
> What is this, what is this men
> What do we see when we see Mangope
> We see a sell-out when we see Mangope
> What do we see when we see Gatsha
> We see a puppet when we see Gatsha
> Help us—Help us Morena
> Help us—Help us Morena
> What do we see—there is Matanzima
> We see a killer when we see Matanzima.]

PERCY [*interrupted*]. Hey! Tear gas!

[*They struggle, continuing the song, throwing stones, sounding sirens, dogs barking.*
Lights go down as they are subdued.]

BOTH. Morena-a-a-a! Morena-a-a-a!

SCENE XXI

[*Spotlight finds Percy as Prime Minister, pink nose, spectacles.*]

PERCY. My people, as your Prime Minister I must warn you that we stand alone in the face of total onslaught. Our enemies will stop at nothing, even to the extent of sending a cheap communist magician to pose as the Morena, and undermine the security of our nation. But let me assure you that this cheap imposter is safely behind bars, from which he cannot fly. Peace and security have returned to our lovely land.

SCENE XXII

[*Lights come up on Mbongeni squatting on a box, wrapped in a prisoner's blanket.*]

MBONGENI [*knocking*]. Cell number six! Morena! [*Knocking.*] Cell number six! Morena! Bad luck, hey! I hear they got you again. They tell me you're in solitary confinement just like us. From Sun City to Robben Island! [*Laughs ruefully.*] You've made us famous, Morena. The whole world is talking about us. Hey bayasiteya labedana bamabhunu man! [Hey they are riding us these white boys.] Morena, I sit here just like you with this one light bulb and only the Bible to read! Ja! And the New Testament tells me about you, and your family, and your thoughts. But why do they give us your book to read, Morena? They must be bladdy mad, Morena. This book only proves how mad they are. Listen. [*Knocking.*] Cell number six! For people like us, to be locked here like this is just rubbish. So what do you want here? What does your father know? What does he say? Come on Morena, man! [*Knocking.*] Cell number six! You've got all the power! How can you let these things happen? How can you just sit there like that, Morena? Okay, okay, I know you don't like miracles, but these are bladdy hard times, Morena. Morena, I must tell you, now that I've gone into your book, I really like you, Morena. But I'm getting bladdy disappointed. How long must we wait for you to do something? Morena, I must tell you, I'm among those who have stopped waiting. One day we'll have to help you! Phambiti neri-hondo! [Power to the people!] Can you hear me Morena? Cell number six!! [*'Sarie Marais' being whistled off-stage. Knocking more cautiously.*] Cell number six!! Morena! Morena . . . Cell number six . . .

SCENE XXIII

[*Percy enters whistling 'Sarie Marais'. He is a soldier, pink nose, camouflage hat. Mimes carrying rifle.*]

MBONGENI [*enters similarly dressed*]. Two three! Morning Corporal!

PERCY. Morning Sergeant!

MBONGENI. How are things going, Corporal? [*He rests on a box.*]

PERCY. I'm tired, Sergeant.

MBONGENI. Oh, God. To be a guard on bladdy Robben Island!

PERCY. Ja, ever since they brought Morena out here to Robben Island everything has been upside down.

MBONGENI. All those bladdy interviews, that's what's killing us!

PERCY. I'm sick of having my photograph taken.

MBONGENI. I know. The next photographer I see, I shoot to kill!

PERCY. Daily News.

MBONGENI. Sunday Times.

PERCY. Time Life.

MBONGENI. Pravda.

PERCY. London Observer.

MBONGENI. New York Times.

PERCY. All those bladdy communists!

MBONGENI. You know, I got a letter from a woman in Sweden. She saw my photograph in her newspaper. And my wife was chasing me with a frying pan! I told her I never knew the woman, but she didn't believe me.

PERCY. I wish they had kept him in John Vorster Square or Pretoria Central.

MBONGENI. Come on, Corporal. You know what happened at John Vorster Square. Gabriel got him out of there in ten seconds flat! Only Robben Island has got the right kind of AA missiles.

PERCY. AA? What is that?

MBONGENI. Anti-Angel.

PERCY. Anti-Angel? I never heard of that!

MBONGENI. He'll never get away from Robben Island!

PERCY [*distracted, points into the audience*]. Hey! Sergeant! What's that you said? Just look over there! Just look over there!!!

MBONGENI [*moves lazily toward him singing 'Sarie Marais'*]. My Sarie Marais is so ver van my hart . . . [*Suddenly he looks into the audience, horrified.*] God! Hey! Fire! Fire!

[*They riddle the audience with machine gun fire.*]

PERCY. Call helicopter control, quick!!!

MBONGENI. Hello? Hello? Radio 1254 CB? Over. Hello? Radio 1254 . . .

SCENE XXIV

[*Lights reduce to spot-light the boxes. Actors turn their hat brims up. Mbongeni spins his hand above his head. Helicopter sounds. They are in a helicopter, looking down.*]

PERCY [*mimes radio*]. Radio 1254 CB receiving, over. What? That's impossible! Are you sure? Okay, over and out. Hey, what do you see down below?

MBONGENI [*miming binoculars*]. Oh, it's a beautiful day down below. Birds are flying, swimmers are swimming, waves are waving. Hey! Morena's walking on water to Cape Town! Ag shame! His feet must be freezing! Hey, I wish I had my camera here!

PERCY. This must be the miracle of the decade!

MBONGENI. Ag, I always forget my camera!

PERCY. Down! Down! Radio 1254 CB receiving, over. Yes, we've got him. Yeah, what? Torpedo? Oh no, have a heart! He's not even disturbing the waves! Ja, I wish you could see him, he looks amazing!

MBONGENI [*nodding frenetically into mike*]. Ja jong, ja! [Yes man, yes!]

PERCY. What? Bomb Morena? Haven't you heard what they say? You start with Morena and it's worse than an atom bomb! Over and out! Hey, this is a shit bladdy job! You pull the chain.

MBONGENI. No, you!

PERCY. No! You pull the chain!

MBONGENI. No, man!

PERCY. This man is mos' happy, why blow him up?

MBONGENI. No come on, come on. Fair deal! Eenie, meenie, minie, moe. Vang a kaffir by the toe. As hy shrik, let him go. Eenie, meenie, minie, moe! It's you!

PERCY. Okay! This is the last straw! I think I'm resigning tomorrow!

MBONGENI. Ready . . . target centre below . . . release depth charges . . . bombs . . . torpedoes . . . go!

[*They watch. The bombs fall. A moment of silence and then a terrible explosion. They separate, come together detonating each other. Light reduces to stark overhead shaft.*]

BOTH. Momeeeee! Aunti-i-i-eee! He-e-e-l-l-p!

[*Blackout.*]

SCENE XXV

[*South African television news theme is proclaimed in darkness.*]

MBONGENI. News!

[*Lights on.*]

PERCY [*in pink nose, proudly holds a cardboard TV screen shape around his face*]. Good evening. The United Nations Security Council is still waiting further information on the explosion which completely destroyed Capetown and its famous Table Mountain. [*Bland smile.*] United Nations nuclear sensors have recorded distinct signs of nuclear disturbance in the Southern African sector. Investigators have suggested a strong possibility of a mishap to a SAA Military Helicopter carrying a nuclear missile over the bay. However, Mrs Fatima Mossop, domestic servant, Sea Point, a freak survivor of the calamity, insisted that the explosion emanated from a human figure walking across the bay from the Island, supporting the superstition that the nuclear-type explo-

sion was an inevitable result of a bomb attack on Morena. The Prime Minister himself continues to deny any relationship between Morena and the agitator imprisoned on the Island. Mrs. Fatima Mossop is still under observation by the state psychiatrists. Well, that is all for tonight. Goodnight. [*Fade on fixed smile.*]

SCENE XXVI

[*The graveyard. Mbongeni in a hat and dust-coat is weeding and singing Zuluboy's song from Scene XVIII. Percy is sleeping on the boxes. Mbongeni sees him, rouses him.*]

MBONGENI. Hey! Hey! Hey! This is not a park bench. It's a tombstone. This is a cemetery, it's not Joubert Park.

PERCY [*groggy*]. I'm sorry, I should know better.

MBONGENI. You want Joubert Park? You want Joubert Park? You catch the number fifty-four bus. Or you want Zola Park? You catch a Zola taxi. Or you want to have a look at the ducks? Go to the Zoo Lake. But don't sit on my tombstones. Please.

PERCY. Okay, I'm sorry about that. Can I have a look around?

MBONGENI. Oh, well if you want to have a look around, look around, but don't sit around! The dead are having a hard enough time. These tombstones are bladdy heavy!

PERCY. Aaahh, tell me, do you keep your tombstones in alphabetical order?

MBONGENI. Yeah. What do you want?

PERCY. Where's 'L'?

MBONGENI. You want 'L'?

PERCY. Ja.

MBONGENI. Serious? Okay. Right there. That whole line is 'L'. By that big tombstone. See? Livingstone . . . Lamele . . . Lusiti . . . Lizi . . .

PERCY. Have you got any Lazarus here?

MBONGENI. Lazarus? Lazarus? Oh, Israel Lazarus! That was a very good man! You mean that one? American Half-Price Dealers? That was a very good man, I used to work for him in 1962. But he's not dead yet! Why are you looking for his grave here?

PERCY. I'm just looking for something to do.

MBONGENI. But this face I know. Are you his son?

PERCY. No, not his.

MBONGENI. Then who are you?

PERCY. Morena.

MBONGENI. You? Morena? Aaay suka! They killed him. That is his tombstone.

PERCY. Oh no, Baba. Have you forgotten? I will always come back after three days, bombs or no bombs.

MBONGENI. Hay! Morena! Aawu nkulunkulu wami! [Oh my God!]

PERCY. Ssssshhhh! Please, don't shout my name.

MBONGENI. Do you remember me?

PERCY. Who are you?

MBONGENI. Zuluboy from Coronation Brickyard!

PERCY. Hey! Zuluboy! [They embrace.] What are you doing here?

MBONGENI. I'm working here at the cemetery. I'm disguised from the police! Lazarus . . . Lazarus . . . aaaahhh! Now I understand! Morena, you're looking for people to raise!

PERCY. Ja!

MBONGENI. But why didn't you ask me?

PERCY. How would I know?

MBONGENI. I know exactly who my people want! Come, let us look at these tombstones.

[Mbongeni leads Percy in a dance around the cemetery, singing. Mbongeni stops, Percy beside him. He points to a corner of the audience.]

MBONGENI. Morena! Here's our 'L'—ALBERT LUTHULI—the Father of our Nation! Raise him Morena!

PERCY. Woza Albert! [Rise up Albert!]

[Mbongeni falls over, stunned then ecstatic.]

BOTH [singing].

Yamemeza inkosi yethu
Yathi ma thambo hlanganani
Oyawa vusa amaqhawe amnyama
Wathi kuwo

[Our Lord is calling.
He's calling for the bones of the dead to join together.
He's raising up the black heroes.
He calls to them

MBONGENI [addressing the risen but invisible Albert Luthuli]. Hey, Luthuli uyangibona mina? U Zulu boy. Ngakhula phansi kwakho e-Stanger. [Hey, Luthuli, do you remember me? I'm Zuluboy. I grew up in Stanger.]

[They dance on, repeating the song.]

BOTH [singing].

Yamemeza inkosi yethu
Yathi ma thambo hlanganani
Oyawa vusa amaqhawe amnyama
Wathi kuwo

[Our Lord is calling.
He's calling for the bones of the dead to join together.
He's raising up the black heroes.
He calls to them

[Mbongeni stops, Percy beside him.]

MBONGENI. Morena! Robert Sobukwe! He taught us Black Power! Raise him!

PERCY. Woza Robert!

MBONGENI [ecstatic]. Hau Manaliso! Manaliso!

[They dance on.]

BOTH [singing].

Yamemezo inkosi yethu
Yathi ma thambo hlanganani
Oyawa vusa amaqhawe amnyama
Wathi kuwo

[Our Lord is calling.
He's calling for the bones of the dead to join together.
He's raising up the black heroes.
He calls to them.

MBONGENI. Lilian Ngoyi! She taught our mothers about freedom. Raise her!

PERCY. Woza Lilian!

MBONGENI [spins with joy]. Woza Lilian!—Hey Lilian, uya mbona uMorena? Uvuswe uMorena. [Come Lilian—hey Lilian, do you see Morena? It's Morena who raised you.]

[They dance on.]

BOTH [singing].

Yamemeza inkosi yethu
Hathi ma thambo hlanganani
Oyawa vusa amaqhawe amnyama
Wathi kuwo

[Our Lord is calling.
He's calling for the bones of the dead to join
together.
He's raising up the black heroes.
He calls to them

MBONGENI. Steve Biko! The hero of our children!
Please Morena—Please raise him!
PERCY. Woza Steve!

MBONGENI. Steve! Steve! Uyangikhumbula ngikulan-
dela e Kingwilliams-town? [Steve, do you remember
me, following you in Kingwilliamstown?]
BOTH [dancing]. Woza Bram Fischer! . . . Woza Ruth
First! . . . Woza Griffith Mxenge . . . Woza Hector
Peterson . . . [They stop, arms raised triumphantly.]
WOZA ALBERT!!!

[Blackout.]

GLOSSARY [FROM THE 1983 EDITION]

Words

baas, basie—subservient words for boss
baba—father, a term of respect
bra—brother
hostel—all male housing compound serving the mines and industrial areas
kaffir—nigger
Morena—Sir, or Lord, term of respect
Passbook—Every black man and woman over the age of sixteen is forced by law to
carry at all times, a passbook, also known as a dompass. It contains information
about birth, family, background, employment, taxation, etc. If at any time the police
discover a person without a passbook, immediate arrest follows. The passbook is a
major symbol of oppression in South Africa.
rand—South African unit of currency, one dollar
woza—rise up

Places

Albert Street—This Johannesburg street is the location of the Pass Office that
controls the influx of black workers to and from the city. Workers often line up for
days awaiting permits to seek work. A black born outside the city becomes an illegal
immigrant if he loses his job and can be 'endorsed' out of the city back to a
homeland. Black men, legal or otherwise, wait in Albert Street for whites driving by
who are looking for labourers.

Homelands—Also known as 'Bantustans' and 'Reserves', the homelands are the
tribal areas set aside for blacks. They are run by governments set up by the South
African regime. Rather than being 'homes', they are areas of great devastation and
poverty that offer few opportunities for employment. Because young men are
recruited away by white industries and mines, homelands such as Kwazulu, the
Transkei and Bophutatswana are populated largely by women, children and old
people. Blacks employed in white areas may not bring their families with them.
Consequently they often live in all-male hostels, and are able to see their families for
only a few weeks at Christmas. Through the apartheid policy of homelands, only

13% of all South African territory is ceded to more than 20 million blacks. The rest of the land, which includes the richest agricultural and mineral areas, is reserved for five million whites.

Robben Island—Surrounded by the icy Atlantic Ocean off Cape Town, Robben Island is the high security prison where black political prisoners are confined.

Soweto—This huge black ghetto outside Johannesburg was the scene of the Childrens' Uprising in 1976, which began as a protest against poor education, became a protest against all government policies and ended in riots and the massacre of at least 467 people.

Sun City—A huge pleasure resort and gambling casino in the heart of Bophutatswana. Here top entertainers like Frank Sinatra, Liza Minelli, Olivia Newton-John, Ann-Margaret perform for enormous fees. Here gambling, barebreasted dancers, miscegenation—all illegal in South Africa—are permitted to South Africans. Sun City offers employment, but it is surrounded by terrible poverty.

People

Albert Luthuli—Born in 1898, Albert Luthuli was a Zulu chief instrumental in organizing the 1952 Defiance Campaign—a civil rights crusade in which thousands of blacks demonstrated against apartheid. The same year, Luthuli became president-general of the African National Congress. Arrested in 1956, he was released after a year, but in 1959 was banished to his small farm under the Suppression of Communism Act, which prohibited him from attending meetings, from writing for publication, and from being quoted. He was awarded the Nobel Peace Prize in 1960, published abroad his autobiography, *Let My People Go*, in 1962, and died in 1967.

Robert Sobukwe—Born in 1924, Robert Sobukwe was a militant college leader and one of the founders of the Pan Africanist Congress. He was elected its president in 1959. One of the leaders of the 1960 anti-pass laws protests, he was arrested and charged with inciting the destruction of pass books. After being sentenced to three years imprisonment, Sobukwe was released in 1963 but promptly detained through an act of parliament for an additional six years on Robben Island. This so-called "Sobukwe clause" permits indefinite detention of political prisoners after their sentences have been served. Finally released in 1969, Sobukwe was restricted by bans and confined to the Kimberley district until his death in 1978.

Bram Fischer—Born into a prominent Afrikaner family in 1908, Bram Fischer was the son of a Judge President of the Orange Free State and grandson of a Prime Minister of the Orange River Colony. He became radicalized as a law student at Oxford. After becoming a lawyer, he led the defence in a number of political trials, including the Treason Trial of 1956–1960 and the Rivonia Trial of 1963–1964. In September 1964, he was arrested and charged under the Suppression of Communism Act, but fled underground to continue his political activism. Re-arrested within a year, he was sentenced to life imprisonment, and died in 1975.

Lilian Ngoyi—Within one year of joining the Women's League of the African National Congress in 1952, Lilian Ngoyi became its president. Her eloquence as a public speaker and energy as an organizer made her a target of the government. In 1956 she was arrested and became one of those prosecuted in the massive Treason

Trial that did not end until 1960. Restricted for many years by various bans and forms of house arrest that confined her to her home and prohibited her from having visitors and from holding a job, she died in 1980.

Steve Biko—Born in 1946, Steve Biko became the first president of the All-Black South African Students' Organization in 1968. It and the Black Peoples' Convention, which Biko also helped form, were at the forefront of articulating the emerging philosophy of black consciousness. He was served with a five-year banning order in 1973. In 1975 he was arrested and held for 137 days without charge or trial. Following the Soweto riots of 1976, he was arrested and held in solitary confinement for 101 days. In 1977 he was again arrested and twenty-seven days later became the twentieth person to die in police custody over an eighteen month period. Despite numerous arrests, Biko was never convicted of a single crime.

Ruth First—Author and teacher. Born into a politically radical family in Johannesburg, she studied social science. From the mid-forties she worked with African mine strikers, and with Nelson Mandela and others of the African National Congress. She was Johannesburg editor of radical journals which were successively banned, and acting secretary of the Communist Party. Among the 156 accused and later acquitted in the Treason Trial in 1956, she was then banned and house arrested. In 1963 she was held in solitary confinement for 117 days. A leading member of the A.N.C., while running a university department in Mozambique she was killed by a letter bomb on August 17, 1982.

ESSAY: AN APPROACH TO THE PLAY

Part of the potentially revolutionary effect of *Woza Albert!* derives from its emphasis on pantomime, song, dance, and the stage business of the actors in general, including the actors' abrupt shifts from character to character, language level to language level, tone to tone. This style places the play's performance outside the kind of theater conventionally associated with the educated middle class. The bareness of the stage, which derives from the township practice, puts primary emphasis on the actors, creating not only the circumstances for the actors' *tours de force* but also the possibility of their effecting a real change of mind in its audience (as opposed to merely suggesting a mind-changing set of ideas). In conventional middle-class theater, the audience may be encouraged to feel sympathy for victims of oppression, may even by encouraged to assist people in analogous circumstances, but a far more unsettling experience would be needed for people to be willing to make fundamental changes in a system which has enabled them to be well enough off financially to go to the theater in the first place, however much pity they may feel for those victimized by this system. If real social change is a playwright's goal, the audience cannot be allowed to sit passively but must be made to feel unsettled, to become self-questioning, disturbed, motivated to change and perhaps even to destroy the status quo.

One effect of the actors' frequent shifts in role is that there is no character with whom to identify. As soon as the audience begins to do so, he is gone, replaced by the next in a parade of characters, each disturbingly true to life, all of whom together present a composite picture of South African society as a whole. One cannot identify with such a large concept—for it *is* a concept, not a person. The audience is forced to contemplate this new portrait of society as if it had never seen it clearly before, including many of the inanities which have grown so familiar that they have become invisible. Perhaps the audience will become unsettled enough to try to make a change.

The play's first five scenes introduce us to this society from the black perspective: the need for passes and (a little later) work permits, the ease with which one falls into prison, the desire of the dispossessed for a savior. The next several scenes portray this society in cross-section, so that we see its faces and hear its voices. Zulu becomes the language of humans, not sounds to ignore; ultimately, it becomes a language the audience had better learn to understand if it does not wish to become like Piet Retief, who is described in Scene 13 as being taken unaware because he did not understand that "Bulalan'abathakathi" was his death sentence.

The comedy in this play is often lighthearted and playful, but there is a pervasive irony and, on occasion, bitterness as well. To say that one tone dominates the other is probably a falsification, however; both are real and important, the positive and negative sides of the play's vision, what could be and what is, folded in upon each other in the complex texture of the present. Positive and negative are combined in other ways, too. The "objective" and omnipresent TV reporters help to make Morena into a media event, yet their callous disregard for anyone not "newsworthy" is hilariously presented in Scene 15. The prime minister's intention to use the Savior's presence as a public relations coup for the nation is also hilariously—and devastatingly—true to life. From this perspective, the official turn against Morena is merely an exaggeration of the changes in sentiment, the sloganeering and name-calling in which public officials often engage when threatened: when he inspires workers to seek higher pay, he is branded a communist terrorist agitator. This striking way of naming a Jesus-figure may seem frighteningly plausible. And if it does seem so, there could hardly be a more devastating comment on a political system. Many of the play's conceptions are wildly funny. Morena's escape from prison by flying (while the guard confesses to his superior that he "never thought of air flight"), as well as Morena's walking on water, modernize Gospel miracles. Not only is the Savior imprisoned on the tenth floor; after he flies, he is reimprisoned on an island with 120 guards and with anti-angel guns pointed at the sky. The sequence is comic, even while taking Morena's power very seriously. The sequence of exaggeration goes further and further, however, until it becomes bone-chilling. There seem to be no limits to what this society will do to protect itself. Morena becomes its demon, and South Africa's leadership will therefore destroy him in the modern way: turning machine guns, helicopter gunships, finally "depth charges . . . bombs . . . torpedoes" against the man who walks on water (although "he's not even disturbing the waves!").

Before this sequence, and counterpointed against it, is the terrible social injustice described in Scene 20, a kind of summation of the social cross-section presented in more detail during the midsection of the play. The self-destructiveness of this society's dominant group is shown after this bombing, in Scene 25, when Mrs. Fatima Mossop's interview makes it unclear whether South Africa dropped an atomic bomb on Morena to destroy what TV news, with its normal "hype" hilariously understated, calls "the miracle of the decade," or whether there is an indescribable energy within the Savior that South Africa unleashed upon itself with its attack. In any event the rulers—having made war on both religion and agitation (while, of course, denying both via TV)—have caused the destruction of Capetown.

The play's revivalist conclusion is also double-valenced: it occurs amid graves, yet proves both funny and triumphant. Conventional dramatic form, like the counterpointed pattern of the events of the play, undercuts itself. Morena raises black heroes from the dead, religious affirmation uniting with social action. Is it more—a threat to the status quo in South African society? Is the bitterness dominant at the end, or is the joy of life so affirmed that no action need be taken?

We might find it useful to ask some questions about the relations between the play and its real-world context. Why did the South African government not close this popular play down? Does the fact that it did not do so suggest that it received the play as just another criticism, perhaps as a play whose humor undercuts its threat? Does it confirm that to officials in a politically repressive regime, drama, and perhaps art in general, has no real power, and may, rather, provide a valuable outlet for the discontented, giving them the illusion of power by allowing them the appearance of freedom of expression? Or are they assuming a posture which they believe is necessary if theirs is to be perceived as a modern, open culture? Like religion, art is considered evidence of the level of a civilization. To close a play down is for this group to admit its own self-destructive qualities, to admit that its culture is self-contradictory. Perhaps one aspect of the play's genius is that its collaborators knew how to walk this line, to take advantage of and push society's limits.

We do not presume to know about cultural cause and effect in South Africa. Revolutionary events were already in motion there by 1982, and they continue to unfold. The play's role in that process is hard to determine, but it is unmistakably an expression of that process and quite possibly part of it as well.

ACKNOWLEDGMENTS

Abel, Lionel. From *Metatheatre, A New View of Dramatic Form* by Lionel Abel, copyright © Lionel Abel 1963. Reprinted by permission of the author.

Aristophanes. *Lysistrata*. From *Lysistrata* by Aristophanes, translated by Douglass Parker, Translation copyright © by William Arrowsmith. Used by permission of New American Library, a division of Penguin Books USA Inc.

Artaud, Antonin. *Antonin Artaud: Selected Writings*. Reprinted by permission of Georges Borchardt, Inc. Copyright © Éditions Gallimard, 1956, 1961, 1964, 1966, 1967, 1969, 1970, 1971, 1974. Translation copyright © 1976 by Farrar, Straus and Giroux.

Baldwin, James. *Blues for Mister Charlie*. Copyright © 1964 by James Baldwin. Copyright renewed. *Blues for Mister Charlie* published by arrangement with the James Baldwin Estate.

Beckett, Samuel. "Rough for Theatre I." From the book *The Collected Shorter Plays of Samuel Beckett* by Samuel Beckett, copyright © 1984 by Samuel Beckett. Used with the permission of Grove/Atlantic Monthly Press. To order call 800-937-5557.

Churchill, Caryl. *Vinegar Tom*. Reprinted from *Churchill: Plays One*, Churchill, Caryl (1985), by permission of the publisher, Routledge, New York.

Esslin, Martin. From *The Theatre of the Absurd* by Martin Esslin. Copyright © 1961 by Martin Esslin. Used by permission of Doubleday, a division of Bantam Doubleday Dell Publishing Group, Inc.

Euripides. *The Bacchae*. From *The Bacchae* by Euripides, Michael Cacoyannis, trans., translated by Michael Cacoyannis, Translation copyright © 1982 by Michael Cacoyannis. Used by permission of New American Library, a division of Penguin Books USA Inc.

Foucault, Michel. Reprinted from "What Is an Author?" in *Language, Counter-Memory, Practice: Selected Essays and Interviews by Michel Foucault*. Edited with an Introduction by Donald F. Bouchard. Translated from the French by Donald F. Bouchard and Sherry Simon. Copyright © 1977 by Cornell University. Used by permission of the publisher, Cornell University Press.

Frye, Northrop; *Anatomy of Criticism*. Copyright © 1957 by Princeton University Press. Renewed 1985. Reprinted by permission of Princeton University Press.

Fugard, Athol. *The Road to Mecca*. From *The Road to Mecca* by Athol Fugard, copyright 1988 by Athol Fugard.

Fuller, Charles. *A Soldier's Play* by Charles Fuller. Copyright © 1981 by Charles Fuller. Reprinted by permission of Hill and Wang, a division of Farrar, Straus & Giroux, Inc. See also the Caution at the end of these acknowledgments.

Hansberry, Lorraine. "A Raisin in the Sun." From *A Raisin in the Sun* by Lorraine Hansberry, copyright © 1958 by Robert Nemiroff, as an unpublished work. Copyright © 1959, 1966, 1984 by Robert Nemiroff. Reprinted by permission of Random House, Inc.

CAUTION: Professionals and amateurs are hereby warned that *A Raisin in the Sun*, being fully protected under the copyright Laws of the United States of America, the British Empire, including the Dominion of Canada, and all other countries of the Universal Copyright and Berne Conventions, is subject to royalty. All rights, including professional, amateur, motion picture, recitation, lecturing, public reading, radio and television broadcasting, and the rights of translation into foreign languages, are strictly reserved. Particular emphasis is laid on the question of readings, permission for which must be secured in writing. All inquiries should be addressed to the William Morris Agency, 1350 Avenue of the Americas, New York,

NY 10019, authorized agents for the Estate of Lorraine Hansberry and for Robert Nemiroff, Executor.

Hwang, David Henry. *M. Butterfly*. From *M. Butterfly* by David Henry Hwang. Copyright © 1989 by David Henry Hwang. Used by permission of New American Library, a division of Penguin Books USA Inc.

Ionesco, Eugène. "Jack, or the Submission." From the book *Four Plays* by Eugene Ionesco, copyright © 1958 by Grove Press. Used with the permission of Grove/Atlantic Monthly Press.

Jackson, Elaine. *Paper Dolls*. Copyright © 1983 by Elaine Jackson. Used by permission of the author.

Kopit, Arthur. *Indians* by Arthur Kopit. Copyright © 1969 by Arthur Kopit. Reprinted by permission of Hill and Wang, a division of Farrar, Straus & Giroux, Inc. See also the Caution at the end of these acknowledgments.

McGrath, John. From *A Good Night Out* by John McGrath, published by Methuen London and reprinted by permission of Reed Consumer Books Ltd. Copyright © 1981 John McGrath.

Meredith, George. "An Essay on Comedy." Reprinted by arrangement with Bantam Doubleday Dell Publishing Group, Inc.

Morton, Carlos. "Rancho Hollywood," by Carlos Morton is reprinted with permission from the publisher of *The Many Deaths of Danny Rosales and other plays* (Houston: Arte Publico Press–University of Houston, 1983).

Mtwa, Perry, Mbongeni Ngema, and Barney Simon. *Woza Albert!* is reprinted by permission of Methuen Drama on behalf of Reed International Books Limited of Michelin House, 81 Fulham Road, London SW3 6RB. Copyright © The Company, Market Theatre, Johannesburg 1983.

Norman, Marsha. *Getting Out*. © Copyright, 1979, by Marsha Norman. © Copyright, 1978, by Marsha Norman.

    CAUTION: Professionals and amateurs are hereby warned that *Getting Out* is subject to a royalty. It is fully protected under the copyright laws of the United States of America, and of all countries covered by the International Copyright Union (including the Dominion of Canada and the rest of the British Commonwealth), and of all countries covered by the Pan-American Copyright Convention, and of all countries with which the United States has reciprocal copyright relations. All rights, including professional, amateur, motion picture, recitation, lecturing, public reading, radio broadcasting, television, and the rights of translation into foreign languages, are strictly reserved. Particular emphasis is laid upon the question of readings, permission for which must be secured from the Author's agent in writing.

    The amateur production rights in *Getting Out* are controlled exclusively by Dramatists Play Service, Inc., 440 Park Avenue South, New York, NY 10016. No amateur performance of the play may be given without obtaining in advance the written permission of Dramatists Play Service, Inc. and paying the requisite fee.

    All inquiries concerning all other rights (other than amateur rights) should be addressed to the Author's agent, The Tantleff Office, Inc., 375 Greenwich Street, Suite 700, New York, NY 10013.

    Originally produced by Actors Theatre of Louisville, in Louisville, Kentucky.

    The West Coast premiere of *Getting Out* was produced by the Center Theatre Group of Los Angeles, Mark Taper Forum, Gordon Davidson, Artistic Director.

    Originally produced in New York by the Phoenix Theatre. Produced Off-Broadway in New York City by Lester Osterman, Lucille Lortel and Marc Howard.

O'Neill, Eugene. "The Hairy Ape." From *The Plays of Eugene O'Neill* by Eugene O'Neill, copyright © 1922 and renewed 1950 by Eugene O'Neill. Reprinted by permission of Random House, Inc.

Shakespeare, William. *The Merchant of Venice*, edited by A. D. Richardson III, revised 1960 edition, reprinted by permission of Yale University Press. Copyright, 1923, 1960, by Yale University Press.

_____*The Tragedy of Hamlet, Prince of Denmark*, edited by Tucker Brooke and Jack Randall Crawford, revised 1947 edition, reprinted by permission of Yale University Press. Copyright, 1917, 1947, by Yale University Press.

_____*The Tragedy of Othello, The Moor of Venice*, edited by Tucker Brooke and Lawrence Mason, revised 1947 edition, reprinted by permission of Yale University Press. Copyright, 1918, 1947, by Yale University Press.

Shaw, Bernard. *Pygmalion*. © Copyright: 1913, 1914, 1916, 1930, 1941 George Bernard Shaw. © Copyright: 1957 The Public Trustee as Executor of the Estate of George Bernard Shaw. Reprinted by permission of The Society of Authors on behalf of the Estate of Bernard Shaw.

Sherman, Martin. *Messiah*. Reprinted by permission of Martin Sherman and the Amber Lane Press Ltd. All rights whatsoever in this play are strictly reserved and application for performance etc., should be made before rehearsal to Casarotto Ramsay Ltd., National House, 60-66 Wardour Street, London W1V 3HP. No performance may be given unless a license has been obtained.

Sophocles. *Oedipus the King*. Translated by Robert Bagg, and reprinted by permission of The University of Massachusetts Press. Copyright © 1982 Robert Bagg.

Soyinka, Wole. "The Lion and the Jewel." Copyright © Wole Soyinka 1963. Reprinted from *Collected Plays 2* by Wole Soyinka (1974) by permission of Oxford University Press.

Walcott, Derek. *Pantomime* by Derek Walcott. Copyright © 1980 by Derek Walcott. Reprinted by permission of Farrar, Straus & Giroux, Inc. See also the Caution at the end of these acknowledgments.

Williams, Tennessee. "The Glass Menagerie." From *The Glass Menagerie* by Tennessee Williams, copyright © 1945 by Tennessee Williams and Edwina D. Williams and renewed 1973 by Tennessee Williams. Reprinted by permission of Random House, Inc.

INDEX

(Note: Italicized references indicate pages on which part or all of the indexed work is reproduced.)